THE OFFICIAL® PRICE GUIDE PAPERBACKS

FIRST EDITION

THE OFFICIAL® PRICE GUIDE
PAPERBACKS

FIRST EDITION

Jon Warren

HOUSE OF COLLECTIBLES • NEW YORK

Important Notice. All of the information, including valuations, in this book has been compiled from the most reliable sources, and every effort has been made to eliminate errors and questionable data. Nevertheless, the possibility of error, in a work of such immense scope, always exists. The publisher will not be held responsible for losses which may occur in the purchase, sale, or other transaction of items because of information contained herein. Readers who feel they have discovered errors are invited to *write* and inform us, so they may be corrected in subsequent editions. Those seeking further information on the topics covered in this book are advised to refer to the complete line of *Official Price Guides* published by the House of Collectibles.

The books in our cover photograph were provided by The American Dust Company, 47 Park Court, Staten Island, NY 10301, who buy and sell rare and desirable paperbacks, like these, in exceptional condition. Cover photo by Don Banks.

Published by: House of Collectibles
201 East 50th Street
New York, New York 10022

Distributed by Ballantine Books, a division of Random House, Inc., New York, and simultaneously in Canada by Random House of Canada Limited, Toronto.

Manufactured in the United States of America

ISBN: 0–876–37793–2

First Edition: February 1991

10 9 8 7 6 5 4 3 2

For Margaret and Elizabeth,
my luck and my inspiration.

TABLE OF CONTENTS

ACKNOWLEDGMENTS

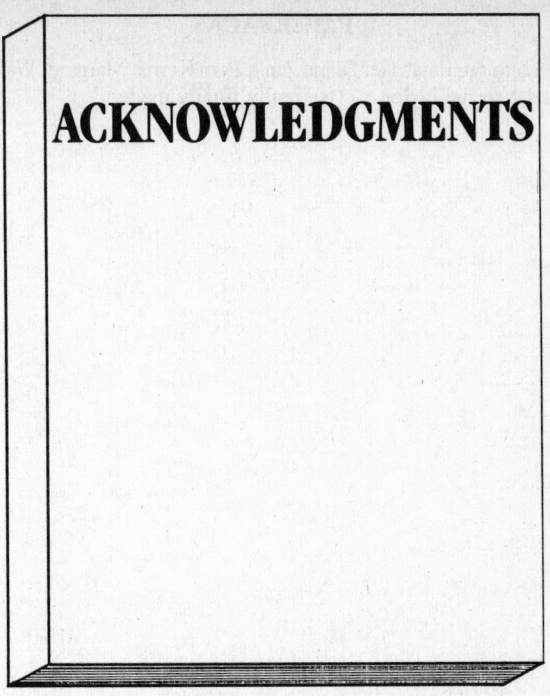

A book of this scope would be impossible if not for the help of many people. This guide is not the work of one person, but rather the result of cooperation among people who love the hobby. I take credit only for putting this together in a cohesive form—the true credit goes to everyone who took time to contribute information. Of course, in any first attempt at such a massive bibliography there are many errors. I am solely responsible for these.

My greatest appreciation is extended to my dear friends R. C. and Elwanda Holland, publishers of *Books Are Everything*, without whom this book simply would not have been possible. My use of information from their collection, their help and encouragement, proofreading, correcting, advice—I could go on and on—was crucial in producing this guide. These two are the backbone of the hobby, the keepers of the flame, and the salt of the earth. Thanks.

Another special acknowledgment goes to Dr. Robert McGeeney, Jr. for his excellent work on the publishers' histories of all of the major publishers. Thank you for your time and your talent.

Additional thanks go to the many dealers and collectors who have sent me lists and letters, including Tom Lesser (for his help with the Canadian listings), Paul Payne, Jeffrey Pressman, Wally Pattengill, Robert C. Hahn, Stan Hass, Dr. Joe L. Wheeler, John Gargiso, Moe Wadle, Lynn Munroe, Harry R. Gerdts, Thomas L. Bonn, Daniel Gobbett, and Albert Newgarden.

Special appreciation goes to Bob Overstreet, who encouraged me in this undertaking and arranged my meeting with Dorothy Harris of House of Collectibles.

A special pat-on-the-back goes out to those girls who helped type all this information into our database: Diane Zink, Pam Kerns, Margaret Warren, Maria Derrick, and Margie Taylor ... we really finally made it!

INTRODUCTION TO THE HOBBY

Collecting paperback books is not a new hobby. Indeed, collecting has been going on since the 1950s, when science fiction collectors began accumulating these new pocket-sized books by some of their favorite authors of the pulp era. In those early days, an avid reader could not avoid the colorful books that were appearing in mass numbers on the newsstands. The collecting movement took shape then, but didn't take off. Unlike comic books or baseball cards, which exploded as baby-boomer collectibles in the '70s and early '80s, paperback books lay dormant during this time. While unique or "only known" examples of rare comic books now might bring up to $75,000, and rare baseball cards like the Honus Wagner card might fetch $150,000, the rarest examples of early paperbacks (less than five known to exist) sell for less than $1,000!

In the late 1970s, during a time when comic book collectors were thinking that comic books had peaked in price, collecting paperbacks had its first euphoria. Many comic book collectors began collecting paperbacks. Prices surged. A price guide was published. Prices surged again. And yet, even with all that, the most valuable paperbacks were generally less than $100. Then the market for collectible paperbacks became sluggish again. In or around 1986, that began to change. Now, in 1990, we have a truly expansive market. Investors are being attracted to the unique opportunities available in this field. Hot new authors can appreciate in value several hundred percent in just a few *weeks*. Jim Thompson first editions in paperback have gone from $6 to $250 seemingly overnight. Dean Koontz first editions in paperback have gone from $2 to $100 very rapidly. The list goes on and on: John D. MacDonald, Charles Willeford, David Goodis, Richard Matheson. . . .

What does all this mean? What it means is this: paperbacks have arrived! Collecting paperbacks will be the hot new field of the '90s. What other area of collecting offers the collector so great a return with so little an investment? Where else can the average investor own a one-of-a-kind item for less than $1,000? Collecting comic books appeals to comic book fans, collecting ball cards appeals to sports fans, but collecting paperbacks appeals to anyone who can read! What other field has so vast an audience?

THE MARKET— WHAT IS COLLECTED

There are about as many different ways to collect paperbacks as there are paperback collectors. We have completists who want one copy of every paperback ever published, we have author collectors, cover collectors, collectors of certain publishers, digest collectors, movie tie-in collectors, TV tie-in collectors, sports tie-in collectors, artist collectors, first edition (PBO) collectors, genre collectors (such as science fiction, mystery, western, etc.), key book collectors, just plain readers, and now, since the hot growth of the last three years, we even have speculators and investors coming into the market.

Each individual collector is possessed by a different collecting bug. If you are a new collector, you may first decide to build a collection of books by a certain author, or you may like a certain publisher and wish to build a collection of that publisher's early imprints. The best motivation for pursuing any collecting goal is to pick something you *like* and collect that something with a passion. I don't recommend that a new collector be motivated by a desire to make money. By collecting an area that you like and enjoying your first reward, there will always be a pleasure in owning a collection that you built from the ground up and the pride of ownership that goes with such an accomplishment. If, as an aftereffect, your collection also rises in value, then consider it an added plus. Regardless of which direction you go, follow an old collector's adage, "Spend your time before you spend your money." This means that you should learn as much as you possibly can about your hobby before you go blindly dropping cash down some empty hole. Along the way, you should be collecting knowledge as much as you are collecting books.

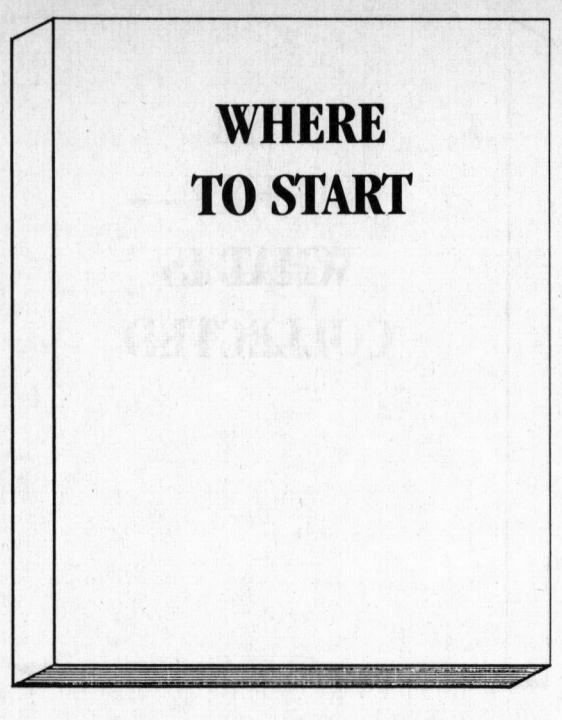

WHERE TO START

Once you have decided which way your collecting breeze is blowing, you will want to set sail in search of your first purchase. In big cities such as New York or Los Angeles, there are actually stores that specialize in vintage paperbacks (and I'm not speaking here of your common trade-two-for-one used paperback shops). If you are lucky enough to be in such a city, I would recommend that you go with haste to such a place. If you aren't that lucky, there is nothing wrong with trying your common trade-two-for-one used bookstores. I have made some great finds in such places. Bargains abound in used bookstores, but so does junk. You will see many millions of worthless used paperbacks before you stumble across a good find, like a Matheson first edition in paperback, or maybe even a Jim Thompson! Yard sales, flea markets, estate sales, etc., are all good stomping grounds if you have the time and patience. But patience is the key word. You will burn a lot of gas before you find some good vintage paperbacks. There is nothing greater than the thrill of the treasure hunt, and someday you too will walk into a paperback bonanza—hundreds or maybe even thousands of early Avons or Ace Doubles—asking the proprietor his price while holding your breath—and his answer, "A dime a piece, twelve for a dollar!" Nirvana!

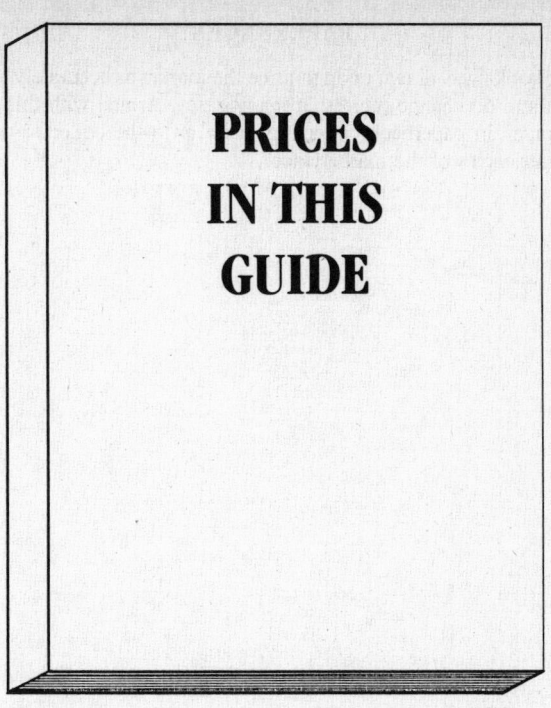

PRICES IN THIS GUIDE

Prices listed are for *first printings* and are an average of retail prices charged by established dealers.

Later printings are worth considerably less. To determine whether or not you have a first printing, consult later sections of this introduction. In many cases, later printings of paperbacks listed in this guide may have little, if any, value.

In this book, there are prices for three grades of paperbacks: *Good (G)*, *Very Good (VG)*, and *Fine (F)*. The grade of Fine has become accepted as the highest grade used by most collectors and dealers today and represents a book in almost perfect condition. Prices for books in Fine condition can vary considerably, particularly for rarities. The format of this guide allows for a 3x spread between Good and Very Good, and a 2x spread between Very Good and Fine. Using this formula, it is our opinion that a Fine condition book is worth about six times that of a Good condition one, and usually about two times that of a Very Good condition example. But remember, this is only a guideline! With rarer books, the value of a Fine copy may be three or four times that of a VG copy. Also, for paperbacks of more recent vintage, an F copy may only be worth double that of a VG, because newer paperbacks are more common in top condition than older books. Again, this price guide is a guide for the collector and not the final authority. Use the prices herein as an indicator of average prices.

There are over 120,000 prices listed in this book. Obviously, actual sales could not be found to arrive at every price shown. Dealers' price lists were reviewed, collectors and dealers were consulted, auction prices were averaged, and finally, a knowledge of values derived from our years of buying and selling paperback books was drawn upon to price the market as accurately as possible. Prices can and do change rapidly in many cases. Armed with this guide as a "crash course" in paperback collecting, it is up to the collector or dealer to learn the intricacies of the marketplace.

HOW TO USE THIS GUIDE

There are established standards within this field that are accepted by mainstream collectors. Therefore, this book is arranged alphabetically by the publisher's series name and chronologically within each listing. This is the order that long-time collectors have come to expect. Paperback publishers usually numbered their issues in a sequential order. Therefore, when *Pocket Books, Inc.* published their first book in 1939, it was numbered #1. They continued publishing using sequential catalog numbers for many years, and their listings are numbered as such. So goes it with all the publishers from *Ace Books, Inc.* through *Zenith Books*. If you are trying to find the value of a book written by John D. MacDonald, you will look it up by the publisher of the book, not by the author.

Avon Bedside Reader is listed before *Avon Books*, and *Dell Books* is listed before *Dell Ten Cent Books*. Within each series, the paperbacks are arranged by the year of issue. Usually this arrangement results in a numerically sequential sorting, for example, sorted by the publisher's catalog number found on the spine or front cover of the book. However, there are numerous exceptions. A few of these include Lancer Books, Paperback Library, and MacFadden Books. The chronological arrangement of these series results in a confusing (to the novice) arrangement of series numbers. However, as experience is gained and the collector learns the order in which these books were issued, finding the proper listings will be easier.

Additionally, it is important to identify the correct publisher's series before attempting to locate a specific listing for a paperback. For example, Berkley

Books issued numerous series including their regular series, "G-BG" series, and "Diamond" series. Avon Books issued their first series, then a "T" series, a "G" series, and others. Ace Books issued a "D" series, and an "A" series, "F" series, "G" series, "H" series, "K" series, "M" series, and "N" series. To quickly locate the correct listing in this book, one must first identify the correct series. Usually this is simply done by looking at the letter prefix on the front cover or spine of the book. Series were usually denoted by an alpha-numeral such as "D-25," "T-100," "G-5," etc. But there are exceptions to every rule: Ace Books included "G" and "S" prefixes in their "D" series, and Avon Books included a few prefixed books in their regular numbered series. Often the prefix referred to the cover price of the paperback. Normally, the lower the cover price the earlier the book. To help simplify the process of identifying the book you have: start with the publisher, then find the correct series from the listings given in this book.

For each of the most collectible paperback publishers, an Early Publisher's History precedes the listing. These histories are designed to describe the development and early history of the companies that published these collectibles. Since most of the more recently published paperbacks are not yet collectible, there was no reason to explain the latest corporate mergers. We will be updating these histories in future editions as the recently published paperbacks become collectible.

IDENTIFYING AND DATING PAPERBACKS

In most cases, identifying which paperback you have is simple. If the cover states "Avon Books" and the number "200" is found on the spine or cover, you can look under Avon Books #200 in this guide to find the information. Looking at the date on the copyright page (page after the title page) will match the date of your copy with the date listed in this guide and will help you determine whether or not you have a first printing. If your copyright page lists the book as "2nd printing," or "3rd printing," you will know that your book is a later issue and not worth the prices listed in this book. This is especially true of books published by *Pocket Books*, or *Signet Books*, as these are the most commonly misrepresented by novices. Always check the printing history of these two publishers; also, *Cardinal Books*, *Avon Books*, some *Popular Library* series, and some *Gold Medals*.

HOW TO GRADE PAPERBACK BOOKS

F (Fine). Virtually flawless. Superb. For a book to receive this grade, it may have only the slightest traces of wear noticeable upon very close inspection. Inside, the pages must be creamy, no trace of brown, and also there can be no nameplates or other writing inside the book. Outside, the spine must be solid and clean with no fading or creasing. Very tiny amounts of wear to the spine may be present. No crease of any kind is permitted. The book appears to be perfect, but upon close inspection tiny problems can be found.

AF (About Fine). A beautiful copy. Acceptable to all but the most discriminating collector. This is a sharp, almost Fine copy. It can have no major defects but may have an accumulation of several minor ones, such as a tiny color chip on the spine or extremities. Other possible flaws might include a small, penciled arrival mark on the cover on an otherwise Fine book. No creases. Pages can be slightly yellowed, but not brown.

VGF (Very Good to Fine). Closer to VG than to AF, but still a very well-preserved copy without major defects. Pages will not be brown, and no nameplate or writing can be on the endpages. Light spine wear/flaking, or minor cover wear are some of the typical problems with books in this grade. A light reading crease along the spine or very minor corner crease might be present.

VG (Very Good). The typical used paperback in average condition. A solid copy, although with wear and defects to be expected. Unusual problems should be noted. The book can have very slight browning of pages but not brittleness or flaking; it may also have a small name written on an endpage, or a small nameplate inside the book. Minor peeling of the lamination covering the book can be expected, but extreme peeling will eliminate the book from this grade. A corner crease (¼" or less) or two can be present, but numerous creases are not allowed in this grade. A light reading crease along the spine is normal for this grade. A minor spine roll is allowable; a heavy spine roll is not allowable in this grade unless noted and the book is a higher grade otherwise. General spine wear can be expected; however, unusually heavy spine wear is not allowable in this grade. The spine should be complete and solid; if not, major problems should be described, such as a split spine. In any case, a spine split should be described as to length and should eliminate the book from this grade if it is over ¾" in length. Tape anywhere on the book is not allowed in this grade. A small penmark on the cover can be present if noted, but not if large, heavy, or if affecting the eye appeal of the book. Heavy dampstains prevent the book from being VG; however, a minor dampstain on an unobtrusive part of the cover could be allowed. One small arrival date is allowable without being noted, but any other writing on the cover should be noted. Sun-fading on the spine or cover should be described and, if significant, should prevent the example from the VG grade. Insect or rodent damage is not allowable in this grade. Price stickers or peelmarks from removal of a price sticker is allowable in the VG grade only when the area affected is small and not a serious detraction from the cover art. No color touchup with colored markers is allowable in this grade.

GVG (Good to Very Good). A borderline book that is closer in condition to VG than it is to G. The accrual of several of the above mentioned defects should move an otherwise VG book to this grade. Books in this grade are similar in appearance to a VG book, but with heavier or more severe creases, flaking, etc.

G (Good). A worn, creased, flaked example. Crumpled and worn corners. Tape, water stains, writing, brittleness of pages, pieces or chips missing, heavily rolled spine, etc., are to be expected in this grade. Typically a reading copy only, with all pages complete.

NOMENCLATURE

The following terms are a selection of the most commonly used phrases by collectors and dealers in the hobby.

Anthology. A collection of works by various authors compiled by an editor.

"Black" Book. A paperback with a theme involving blacks, usually in a derogatory way. The term "Negro" or "Nigger" is usually in the title. Avon Book #314, *Nigger Heaven*, is a good example.

Cover Artist. The artist who drew or painted the cover. Artist information can be found on the inside front cover, the back cover, on the front cover itself (signed), on the copyright page, or sometimes there is no indication of the cover artist but the style is recognizable by knowledgeable collectors.

Digest. A paperback that measures approximately 5⅛" x 7¼", as opposed to the "standard" paperback sizes of 4¼" x 6½" or 4¼" x 7".

Drug Book. A paperback with a graphic cover or title related to the theme of drug abuse. A highly collectible genre.

Dust Jacket. Paperbacks were seldom issued with dust jackets, and those that were are of high collector interest. A dust jacket is a paper wrapper, often with the same artwork as on the cover of the paperback, but sometimes with new artwork.

First Paperback Printing. First appearance of this title in paperback form, preceded by a hardcover appearance. Not to be confused with PBO.

First Printing. Indicates that the book is the first printing by this publisher, although not necessarily the first edition of the title. It was common for a publisher to print a certain number of copies of a title, and when these were sold out, to do a second, third, etc., printing. Each time a new printing was done, the copyright page of the book would be amended to show this fact.

GGA. Good Girl art cover. An exceptionally graphic depiction of a beautiful female, scantily clad, and often in bondage or some other sort of precarious situation.

JD. Juvenile Delinquent story. A popular theme during the late '50s and early '60s, these titles are highly collectible today.

Lesbiana. A paperback whose main theme is involved with Lesbianism. Usually refers to titles from the '50s and early '60s, when the subject matter was considered taboo.

Movie Tie-In. A paperback that was released in conjunction with a movie. Usually these books have a photo cover or a photo section inside the book; sometimes they have both.

Original. Another term for PBO.

PBO. Paperback Original. This designates that the book is a first edition (or first book appearance of this title). Should not be confused with the term "First printing."

Pseudonym. An author writing under a penname, sometimes only used by that author and sometimes a housename used by several authors.

Rare. Almost never found for sale in any condition. Virtually impossible to find. Few copies are known to exist.

Scarce. A copy of the book is seldom offered for sale. Difficult to find in most areas of the country.

SF. Science Fiction title. This is the correct term used in the SF field, not "sci-fi."

Spine. The part of the book which is visible as it stands closed on the shelf.

TV Tie-In. A paperback which was released in conjunction with a popular television show. Usually featured a photo cover, and sometimes a photo section inside.

PUBLICATIONS OF INTEREST TO COLLECTORS

As you progress in paperback sophistication, you will begin to crave something more; to search for the fraternity of people just like you—addicted and loving it. There is an organized network of fans/collectors, and they subscribe to basically two publications: *Books Are Everything* and *Paperback Parade*. These publications are widely circulated in most well-stocked bookstores. You should be able to pick up a copy at a local bookstore specializing in used, rare, and out-of-print books. If you can't find a copy, drop me a line and I will send you a sample copy. My address is Jon Warren, P.O. Box 2512, Chattanooga, TN 37409. You can FAX me at 615-821-5316. Samples of either publication are $5 each.

MAIL-ORDER BOOKSELLERS SPECIALIZING IN PAPERBACKS

Eventually you will want to fill in those "impossible to find" titles missing from your collection. At that point you must take to the mail. There is a booming business in selling collectors' paperbacks via catalogs sent through the mail. These catalogs run the gamut from hand-scrawled, mimeographed sheets to well-produced, professionally typeset catalogs with photos. There are catalogs with fixed prices, where you simply send in an order and wait for your books, and there are mail-order auction catalogs, where you place bids and hope you are the highest bidder. There are several companies that do both. I list two here; the first one is my company, the second one is the Holland's. The Holland's have probably the top-rated catalog auction business and also sell books via a set-priced catalog. Since they were so instrumental and helpful in putting this book together, I feel more than obligated to list them here. Those dealers who might complain that they weren't listed will be offered the chance to be listed in the next edition, if they help with the revisions and corrections to that edition.

American Collectibles Exchange, P.O. Box 2512, Chattanooga, TN 37409 (615) 821-8121

Books Are Everything, P.O. Box 5068, Richmond, KY 40475 (606) 624-9176

FURTHER READING

Bonn, Thomas L. *Undercover*, 1982.
Cole, John Y. (editor). *Books in Action*, 1984.
Davis, Kenneth C. *Two-Bit Culture: The Paperbacking of America*, 1984.
O'Brien, Geoffrey. *Hardboiled America: The Lurid Years of Paperbacks*, 1981.
Schreuders, Piet. *Paperbacks, U.S.A., 1981*.

ADDITIONS AND CORRECTIONS FOR FUTURE EDITIONS

No book of this type is ever finished. It would be impossible to list every paperback ever published. We have listed, however, 41,000 of the *most* collectible paperbacks for every type of collector. Indeed, the database will continue to evolve and expand as the hobby grows and expands. Certainly many errors have slipped through the cracks. Please don't hesitate to bring them to my attention. Corrections and additions will be forthcoming in future editions. Information regarding first editions in paperback (PBO) is especially important to me, since it is reasonably certain that the phenomenal growth of the hobby will be in this area. You can participate in the evolution of paperback collecting by adding to the knowledge and submitting your input for future editions. Your help will be acknowledged and appreciated.

If you can supply an additional checklist from your personal collection, or if you have additional information regarding any of the listings, please forward the information to me. My address is: Jon Warren, P.O. Box 2512, Chattanooga, TN 37409.

PAPERBACK LISTINGS

		G	VG	F
Ace A Series. New York: Ace Books.				
A-1	Von Tessin, Brigitte - ***The Shame And The Glory*** [1966]	$ .75	$2.50	$5.00
A-3	Wolfe, Bernard - ***Limbo*** [1966] Cover by Gaughan.	$ .75	$2.50	$5.00
A-4	Tolkien, J. R. R. - ***The Fellowship Of The Ring*** [1966] Cover by Gaughan.	$1.35	$4.00	$8.00
A-5	Tolkien, J. R. R. - ***The Two Towers*** [1966] Cover by Gaughan.	$1.35	$4.00	$8.00
A-6	Tolkien, J. R. R. - ***The Return Of The King*** [1966] Cover by Gaughan.	$1.35	$4.00	$8.00
A-7	Anthology - ***World's Best Contemporary Short Stories*** [1966] PBO.	$ .75	$2.50	$5.00
A-8	Myers, John - ***Silverlock*** [1966] Cover by Gaughan.	$1.25	$3.75	$7.50
A-9	Ballard, Todhunter - ***Gold In California!*** [1966]	$ .75	$2.50	$5.00
A-10	Edited by Terry Carr & Donald Wollheim - ***World's Best Science Fiction: 1967*** [1967] PBO. Cover by Jack Gaughan.	$ .75	$2.50	$5.00
A-11	Wilkins, Harold T. - ***Flying Saucers On The Attack*** [1967]	$ .75	$2.50	$5.00
A-12	Edited by Terry Carr - ***New Worlds Of Fantasy*** [1967] Cover by Kelly Freas.	$ .65	$2.00	$4.00
A-13	Schmitz, James H. - ***The Witches Of Karres*** [1968] Cover by The Dillons.	$1.00	$3.00	$6.00
A-14	Eden, Dorothy - ***Yellow Is For Fear And Other Stories*** [1968] Cover by Lou Marchetti.	$ .75	$2.50	$5.00
A-15	Edited by T. Carr & Wollheim, Donald - ***World's Best Science Fiction: 1968*** [1968] PBO. Photo cover.	$ .65	$2.00	$4.00
A-16	Panshin, Alexei - ***Rite Of Passage*** [1968] PBO. Cover by The Dillons.	$1.00	$3.00	$6.00
A-17	Edited by Avram Davidson - ***The Best From Fantasy And SF*** [1967] Cover by Jack Gaughan.	$ .75	$2.50	$5.00
A-18	Smith, Frederick E. - ***A Killing For The Hawks*** [1967] Cover by Ed Valigursky.	$ .75	$2.50	$5.00
A-19	Anthony, Piers & Margroff, Robert E. - ***The Ring*** [1968] PBO.	$ .75	$2.50	$5.00
A-21	Griffith, Corinne - ***Eggs I Have Known*** [1968] Cookbook. Photo cover.	$ .75	$2.50	$5.00
A-22	Mattimore, Jean & Clarke - ***Cooking By The Clock*** [1968] Cookbook.	$ .75	$2.50	$5.00
A-23	Moravia, Alberto - ***The Wayward Wife*** [1968] Photo cover.	$ .65	$2.00	$4.00
A-24	Bishop, Lt. Col. William A. - ***Winged Warfare*** [1968]	$ .65	$2.00	$4.00
A-25	Burroughs, Edgar Rice - ***The Outlaw Of Torn*** [1968] Cover by Roy Krenkel.	$ .65	$2.00	$4.00
A-27	Harmon, Jim - ***The Great Radio Heroes*** [1968]	$ .65	$2.00	$4.00
A-28	Edited by Stanley M. Ulanoff - ***Ace Of Aces-Capt. Rene Fonck*** [1968] Cover by Ed Valigursky.	$ .65	$2.00	$4.00
A-29	Blish, James & Knight, Norman L. - ***A Torrent Of Faces*** [1968] Cover by Leo & Diane Dillon.	$ .75	$2.50	$5.00

Ace Books (Early Publisher's History, 1952–1959)

Ace Books entered the paperback field by offering double novels and featuring popular literature. These double novels, edited by Donald A. Wollheim, contain two stories back to back, with two covers. Even the spines bear two colors, which vary as to the combinations. Spine colors generally indicated the type of book, so buyers could glance and pick up their favorite. Usually, they used blue for science fiction, green for westerns, yellow or black for mysteries, and pink for romance. It was not until 1954 that they began offering single standard novels.

They produced books in series designated by the letters A, D, G, F, K, M, N, S,

Ace D Series, D-5

Ace D Series, D-40

Ace D Series, S-67

and T, which indicates price, and later used their publisher's code number. In addition to the work of various authors, the cover art by Norman Saunders, Frank Franzetta, Roy Krenkel, Jack Gaughan, and others make many volumes desirable.

Ace D Series. New York: A.A. Wynn/Ace Book, Inc.

		G	VG	F
D-1	Taylor, Samuel W./Vining, Keith - ***The Grinning Gismo/Too Hot For Hell*** [1952] /PBO. Covers by Norman Saunders......	$22.00	$70.00	$140.00
D-2	MacDonald, William Colt/Leithead, J. E. - ***Bad Man's Return/Bloody Hoofs*** [1952] /PBO. Covers by Saunders.	$5.00	$15.00	$30.00
D-3	Colton, Mel/Clugston, Kate - ***The Big Fix/Twist The Knife Slowly*** [1952] PBO/..........	$4.50	$14.00	$28.00
D-4	Patten, Lewis B./Tompkins, Walter A. - ***Massacre At White River/Rimrock Rider*** [1952] PBO/. Covers by Saunders.	$5.00	$15.00	$30.00
D-5	Whittington, Harry/Goldthwaite, Eaton K. - ***Drawn To Evil/ The Scarlet Spade*** [1952] PBO/. Covers by Saunders...........	$7.00	$22.50	$45.00
D-6	Vance, William E./Nye, Nelson C. - ***The Branded Lawman/ Plunder Valley*** [1952] PBO/. Cover by Saunders..................	$5.00	$15.00	$30.00
D-7	Whittington, Harry/Ransome, Stephen - ***So Dead My Love!/ I, The Executioner*** [1953] PBO/. GGA cover by Rafael DeSoto..........	$6.00	$20.00	$40.00
D-8	Echols, Alan K./West, Tom - ***Terror Rides The Range/ Gunsmoke Gold*** [1953] PBO/. Covers by Norman Saunders.	$5.00	$15.00	$30.00
D-9	King, Sherwood/Morgan, Michael - ***If I Die Before I Wake/Decoy*** [1953] /PBO. Cover by Barton.........................	$4.00	$12.50	$25.00
D-10	Scott, Leslie/Young, Gordon - ***The Brazos Firebrand/Hell On Hoofs*** [1953] PBO/. Covers by Norman Saunders/Ralph Smith.	$5.00	$15.00	$30.00
D-11	Stuart, William L./ Keene, Day - ***Dead Ahead/Mrs. Homicide*** [1953] /PBO. Cover by Norman Saunders.	$5.00	$15.00	$30.00
D-12	Stevens, Dan J./Owen, Dean - ***Wild Horse Range/The Man From Boot Hill*** [1953] /PBO. Cover by Norman Saunders. ..	$5.00	$15.00	$30.00
D-13	Drachman, Theodore S./Edgley, Leslie - ***Cry Plague!/The Judas Goat*** [1953] PBO/. First SF book in series. Cover by Marchetti.	$20.00	$60.00	$125.00
D-14	Lehman, Paul Evan/Kilrain, George - ***Vultures On Horseback/Maverick With A Star*** [1953] /PBO. Cover by Norman Saunders..........	$3.50	$10.00	$20.00
D-15	Lee, William/Helbrant, Maurice - ***Junkie/Narcotic Agent*** [1953] PBO/. William Burroughs' first book (William Lee). Cover by Al Rossi.	$32.00	$110.00	$250.00

		G	VG	F
D-16	Bourget, Paul/de Goncourt, Edmond & Jules - ***Crime d'Amour/Germinie*** [1953] First U.S. edition. Covers by Barton/Saunders.	$2.50	$7.50	$15.00
D-17	Scott, Roney/Ericson, Walter - ***Shakedown/The Darkness Within*** [1953] PBO/. Cover by Saunders.	$3.00	$9.00	$18.00
D-18	Leithead, J. Edward/Ward, Brad - ***The Lead-Slingers/The Hanging Hills*** [1953] PBO/. Cover by Saunders.	$2.50	$7.50	$15.00
D-19	Edgley, Leslie/Colton, Mel - ***Fear No More/Never Kill A Cop!*** [1953] /PBO. Covers by Barton.	$3.00	$9.00	$18.00
D-20	Echols, Allan K./Manning, Roy - ***Double-Cross Brand/The Desperado Code*** [1953] PBO/. Cover by Norman Saunders..	$2.50	$7.50	$15.00
D-21	Makris, John N./Dent, Lester - ***Nightshade/High Stakes*** [1953] PBO/. Cover by Saunders.	$3.00	$9.00	$18.00
D-22	Lomax, Bliss/Scott, Leslie - ***Mavericks Of The Plains/ Badlands Masquerader*** [1953] /PBO. Cover by Ralph Smith.	$2.50	$7.50	$15.00
D-23	Sale, Richard/Brock, Stuart - ***Passing Strange/Bring Back Her Body*** [1953] /PBO.	$3.00	$9.00	$18.00
D-24	Callahan, John/West, Tom - ***The Sidewinders/Vulture Valley*** [1953] PBO/. (Joseph Chadwick).	$2.50	$7.50	$15.00
D-25	Wodehouse, P. G. - ***The Code Of The Woosters/Quick Service*** [1953] Covers by Norman Saunders.	$2.50	$7.50	$15.00
D-26	Acton, Harold, Lee Yi-Hsie/Pettit, Charles - ***Love In A Junk And Other Exotic Tales/The Impotent General*** [1953] Covers by Norman Saunders.	$2.50	$7.50	$15.00
D-27	Fischer, Bruno/Colton, Mel - ***The Fingered Man/Double Take*** [1953] /PBO. Covers by Saunders/Paul.	$3.00	$9.00	$18.00
D-28	Evan, Paul/Vance, William E. - ***Gunsmoke Kingdom/Avenger From Nowhere*** [1953] /PBO. Cover by Saunders.	$2.50	$7.50	$15.00
D-29	Laurence, Ross/Hutton, J. F. - ***The Fast Buck/Dead Man Friday*** [1953] PBO/.	$3.00	$9.00	$18.00
D-30	Kilrain, George/Ward, Brad - ***South To Santa Fe/Johnny Sun dance*** [1953] PBO/. Cover by Norman Saunders.	$2.50	$7.50	$15.00
D-31	Van Vogt, A. E. - ***Universe Maker/The World Of Null-A*** [1953] PBO/. Covers by Orbaan/Schulz.	$2.50	$7.50	$15.00
D-32	Malone, Dorothy - ***Cookbook For Beginners*** [1953] Original title: Cookbook For Brides.	$1.50	$5.00	$10.00
D-33	Kane, Frank/Hodges, Carl G. - ***About Face/Murder By The Pack*** [1953] /PBO. Cover by Norman Saunders.	$3.00	$9.00	$18.00
D-34	Murray, Ken - ***Feud In Piney Flats/Hellions' Hole*** [1953] PBO. Covers by Norman Saunders.	$2.50	$7.50	$15.00
D-35	Loomis, Rae/Houston, Jack - ***The Marina Street Girls/Open All Night*** [1953] PBO. Cover by Victor Olson.	$2.50	$7.50	$15.00
D-36	Howard, Robert E./Brackett, Leigh - ***Conan The Conqueror/The Sword Of Rhiannon*** [1953] /PBO. Covers by Saunders/Schulz.	$7.00	$22.50	$45.00
D-37	Claire, Marvin/Oursler, Will - ***The Drowning Wire/Departure Delayed*** [1953] PBO/. Covers by Saunders/Barton.	$3.00	$9.00	$18.00
D-38	Mayo, Jim (Louis L'Amour)/Lomax, Bliss - ***Showdown At Yellow Butte/Outlaw River*** [1953] PBO/. Covers by Saunders.	$10.00	$30.00	$60.00
D-39	Gruber, Frank - ***Rebel Road/Quantrell's Raiders*** [1953] /PBO. Covers by Saunders.	$2.50	$7.50	$15.00
D-40	Irish, William/Bishop, Malden Grange - ***Waltz Into Darkness/ Scylla*** [1954] /PBO.	$8.00	$25.00	$50.00
D-41	Dewey, Thomas B./Keene, Day - ***Mourning After/Death House Doll*** [1954] /PBO. Covers by Olson/Barton.	$5.00	$15.00	$30.00

		G	VG	F
D-42	Tompkins, Walker A./Martin, Charles M. - ***One Against A Bullet Horde/Law For Tombstone*** [1954] PBO/. Covers by Saunders/Anderson.	$2.50	$7.50	$15.00
D-43	Vierick, George S. & Eldridge, Paul - ***Salome*** [1954] Cover by Geygan.	$2.50	$7.50	$15.00
D-44	Russell, Eric Frank/Anthology - ***Sentinels Of Space/The Ultimate Invader And Other Stories*** [1954] /PBO. Cover by Schulz.	$2.50	$7.50	$15.00
D-45	Edgley, Leslie/Weiss, Martin L. - ***Tracked Down/Death Hitches A Ride*** [1954] /PBO. Cover by Barton.	$3.00	$9.00	$18.00
D-46	Martin, Chuck/Manning, Roy - ***Law From Back Beyond/Vengeance Valley*** [1954] PBO/. Covers by Saunders/Leone.	$2.50	$7.50	$15.00
D-47	Barry, Joe/Powell, Richard - ***Kiss And Kill/On The Hook*** [1954] PBO/. Covers by Marchetti/Barton.	$3.00	$9.00	$18.00
D-48	Mayo, Jim (Louis L'Amour)/Ward, Brad - ***Utah Blaine/Desert Showdown*** [1954] PBO/. Cover by Saunders.	$10.00	$30.00	$60.00
D-49	Grayson, Charles/Cushman, Dan - ***Golden Temptress/Tongking!*** [1954] /PBO. Cover by De Soto.	$2.50	$7.50	$15.00
D-50	Shaw, Wilene/Grant, Ozro - ***The Mating Call/Bad'Un*** [1954] PBO.	$3.00	$9.00	$18.00
D-51	McDowell, Emmett/Treat, Lawrence - ***Switcheroo/Over The Edge*** [1954] PBO/.	$3.00	$9.00	$18.00
D-52	L'Amour, Louis/MacDonald, William Colt - ***Crossfire Trail/Boomtown Buccaneers*** [1954] PBO/.	$10.00	$30.00	$60.00
D-53	Leinster, Murray/Van Vogt, A. E. - ***Gateway To Elsewhere/The Weapon Shops Of Isher*** [1954] PBO/.	$2.50	$7.50	$15.00
S-54	Offord, Carl - ***The Naked Fear*** [1954] PBO.	$2.00	$6.00	$12.00
D-55	Turner, Robert/Stark, Michael (Lariar) - ***The Tobacco Auction Murders/Kill-Box*** [1954] PBO/.	$3.00	$9.00	$18.00
D-56	Lomax, Bliss/Hardin, Clement - ***Ambush At Coffin Canyon/Hellbent For A Hangrope*** [1954] /PBO.	$2.50	$7.50	$15.00
D-57	Fleischman, A. S./Leonard, Charles L. - ***Counterspy Express/Treachery In Trieste*** [1954] PBO/. Cover by Olson.	$3.00	$9.00	$18.00
S-58	Joesten, Joachim - ***Vice, Inc.*** [1954] PBO.	$1.50	$5.00	$10.00
D-59	Bloch, Robert/Alexander, David - ***Spiderweb/The Corpse In My Bed*** [1954] PBO/. Cover by Barton.	$12.50	$37.50	$75.00
S-60	Ward, Brad (Samuel A. Peeples) - ***The Marshall Of Medicine Bend*** [1954]	$1.50	$5.00	$10.00
D-61	De Camp, L. Sprague/Simak, Clifford D. - ***Cosmic Manhunt/Ring Around The Sun*** [1954] PBO/.	$2.50	$7.50	$15.00
D-62	Murray, Ken - ***Ken Murray's Giant Joke Book*** [1954] PBO.	$1.50	$5.00	$10.00
D-63	Davis, Frederick C./Whittington, Harry - ***Drag The Dark/You'll Die Next!*** [1954] /PBO.	$5.00	$15.00	$30.00
D-64	Lehman, Paul Evan/ Whipple, Chandler - ***Bullets Don't Bluff/Under The Mesa Rim*** [1954] PBO/.	$2.50	$7.50	$15.00
D-65	Kimbrough, Edward/Osborne, Juanita - ***Night Fire/Tornado*** [1954] /PBO. Covers by Barton/Cherry.	$2.50	$7.50	$15.00
S-66	Hubbard, L. Ron - ***Return To Tomorrow*** [1954] PBO.	$5.00	$15.00	$30.00
S-67	Bloch, Robert - ***The Will To Kill*** [1954] PBO. Cover by Rafael DeSoto.	$7.00	$22.50	$45.00
D-68	Tompkins, Walker A./Hopson, William - ***Deadwood/Bullet-Brand Empire*** [1954] PBO/. Cover by Bentley.	$2.50	$7.50	$15.00
D-69	Norton, Andre/Padgett & Moore - ***Daybreak-2250 A.D./Beyond Earth's Gates*** [1954] /PBO.	$2.50	$7.50	$15.00
S-70	Loomis, Rae - ***Luisita*** [1954] PBO. Cover by Robert Maguire.	$1.50	$5.00	$10.00

		G	VG	F
D-71	Scherf, Margaret/Ashe, Gordon - ***The Case Of The Hated Senator/Drop Dead!*** [1954] /PBO.	$2.50	$7.50	$15.00
D-72	Perry, Ralph R./Fox, Norman A. - ***Nightrider Deputy/The Devil's Saddle*** [1954] PBO/. Cover by Bentley.	$2.50	$7.50	$15.00
D-73	Anthology edited by Wollheim, Donald A. - ***Adventures In The Far Future/Tales Of Outer Space*** [1954] PBO. Cover by Mort Lawrence.	$1.50	$5.00	$10.00
S-74	Shaw, Wilene - ***Heat Lightning*** [1954]	$1.50	$5.00	$10.00
S-75	Shikes, Ralph E. - editor - ***Cartoon Annual*** [1954] PBO. Cover by Bily Snel.	$2.25	$7.00	$14.00
S-76	Zola, Emile - ***Shame*** [1954] First U.S. edition.	$1.50	$5.00	$10.00
D-77	Marlowe, Stephen/Sanders, George - ***Catch The Brass Ring/Stranger At Home*** [1954] PBO/. (/Leigh Brackett).	$2.50	$7.50	$15.00
D-78	West, Tom/Nye, Nelson - ***Lobo Legacy, The One-Shot Kid*** [1954] PBO/.	$2.50	$7.50	$15.00
D-79	Bellamy, Francis Rufus/Leinster, Murray - ***Atta/The Brain-Stealers*** [1954] /PBO	$2.50	$7.50	$15.00
S-80	Shaw, Wilene - ***The Fear And The Guilt*** [1954] PBO.	$1.50	$5.00	$10.00
D-81	Stark, Sheldon/Saxon, John A. - ***Too Many Sinners/Liability Limited*** [1954] PBO/.	$2.50	$7.50	$15.00
S-82	L'Amour, Louis - ***Kilkenny*** [1954] PBO. Cover by Bentley.	$7.00	$22.50	$45.00
S-83	Drake, Arnold - ***The Steel Noose*** [1954] PBO.	$1.50	$5.00	$10.00
D-84	Asimov, Isaac/Dee, Roger - ***The Rebellious Stars/An Earth Gone Mad*** [1954] /PBO.	$2.50	$7.50	$15.00
S-85	DeKobra, Maurice - ***The Bachelor's Widow*** [1954] First U.S. edition.	$1.50	$5.00	$10.00
D-86	Brister, Richard/Manning, Roy - ***The Shoot-Out At Sentinel Peak/Tangled Trail*** [1954] PBO/.	$2.25	$7.00	$14.00
S-87	Miller, Nolan - ***Why I Am So Beat*** [1954]	$1.50	$5.00	$10.00
D-88	Davis, Dexter - ***The 7-Day System For Gaining Self-Confidence*** [1955] PBO.	$1.25	$3.75	$7.50
D-89	Wilson, Ruth & Alexander/Marlowe, Stephen - ***Death Watch/Turn Left For Murder*** [1955] /PBO. (Milton Lesser). Cover by Barton.	$2.50	$7.50	$15.00
S-90	Williams, Robert Moore - ***The Chaos Fighters*** [1955] PBO. Author's first book.	$1.50	$5.00	$10.00
S-91	Baron, Stanley - ***End Of The Line*** [1955]	$1.50	$5.00	$10.00
D-92	Arthur, Burt/Wormser, Richard - ***The Drifter/The Longhorn Trail*** [1955]	$2.25	$7.00	$14.00
S-93	Elmo, H. T. - ***Modern Casanova's Handbook*** [1955] PBO. Bill Wenzel cover.	$3.50	$10.00	$20.00
D-94	Leinster, Murray/Van Vogt, A. E. - ***The Other Side Of Here/One Against Eternity*** [1955] PBO/.	$2.50	$7.50	$15.00
S-95	Whittington, Harry - ***The Naked Jungle*** [1955] PBO.	$3.00	$9.00	$18.00
D-96(S)	Norton, Andre - ***The Last Planet (Special Edition)*** [1955] Original title: Star Rangers.	$2.25	$7.00	$14.00
D-96	Norton, Andre/Nourse, Alan E. - ***The Last Planet/A Man Obsessed*** [1955] /PBO. Cover by Barton.	$2.25	$7.00	$14.00
S-97	Herries, Norman - ***Death Has 2 Faces*** [1955] PBO. Cover by Barton.	$1.50	$5.00	$10.00
D-98	Peeples, Samuel Anthony/Nye, Nelson - ***The Lobo Horseman/The Texas Tornado*** [1955] PBO/. Covers by Walter Popp/Norman Saunders.	$2.25	$7.00	$14.00

		G	VG	F
D-99	Brackett, Leigh/Williams, Robert Moore - ***The Galactic Breed/Conquest Of The Space Sea*** [1955] /PBO. Cover by Ed Valigursky.	$3.00	$9.00	$18.00
S-100	Nixon, Henry Lewis - ***The Caves*** [1955] PBO.	$1.50	$5.00	$10.00
D-101	Colton, Mel/Karney, Jack - ***Point Of No Escape/Knock 'Em Dead*** [1955] PBO.	$2.50	$7.50	$15.00
S-102	Glay, George Albert - ***Oath Of Seven*** [1955] PBO. Bondage/GGA cover.	$1.50	$5.00	$10.00
D-103	Dick, Philip K./Brackett, Leigh - ***Solar Lottery/The Big Jump*** [1955] PBO. Philip K. Dick's first book. Cover by Schulz.	$8.00	$25.00	$50.00
S-104	Cassill, R. V. & Protter, Eric - ***Left Bank Of Desire*** [1955] PBO. Cover by Verne Tossey.	$1.50	$5.00	$10.00
S-105	De Roo, Edward - ***The Fires Of Youth*** [1955] PBO. J.D. novel.	$3.00	$9.00	$18.00
D-106	Floren, Lee/Bonar, D.L. - ***Four Texans North/Lawman Without A Badge*** [1955] PBO. Cover by Walter Popp.	$2.00	$6.00	$12.00
S-107	Twist, Peter - ***The Gilded Hideaway*** [1955] PBO.	$1.50	$5.00	$10.00
S-108	Cody, C. S. - ***Lie Like A Lady*** [1955] PBO.	$1.50	$5.00	$10.00
D-109	Clark, Dale/Noel, Sterling - ***Mambo To Murder/I See Red*** [1955] PBO. Cover by Barton.	$2.00	$6.00	$12.00
D-110	Asimov, Isaac/Anderson, Poul - ***The 1,000-Year Plan/No World Of Their Own*** [1955] /PBO.	$2.00	$6.00	$12.00
D-110(SP)	Asimov, Isaac - ***The 1,000 Year Plan (Special Edition)*** [1955] Original title: Foundation.	$2.00	$6.00	$12.00
S-111	Kroll, Harry Harrison - ***The Smoldering Fire*** [1955] PBO.	$1.50	$5.00	$10.00
D-112	Castle, Frank/Drago, Harry Sinclair - ***Border Buccaneers/Trigger Gospel*** [1955] PBO/. Cover by Walter Popp.	$2.00	$6.00	$12.00
D-113	Swain, Dwight V./McIntosh, J.T. - ***The Transposed Man/One In 300*** [1955] PBO/. Swain's only SF novel.	$2.00	$6.00	$12.00
S-114	Adler, Edward - ***Living It Up*** [1955] PBO. Cover by Verne Tossey.	$1.50	$5.00	$10.00
D-115	Adams, Cleve F./Whittington, Harry - ***Shady Lady/One Got Away*** [1955] PBO. Covers by Barton/Schulz.	$3.50	$10.00	$20.00
S-116	Anthology ed. by Brant House - ***Words Fail Me!*** [1955] PBO. Cartoon book. Cover by Tashlin.	$2.50	$7.50	$15.00
S-117	Darien, Kim - ***Dark Rapture*** [1955] PBO.	$1.50	$5.00	$10.00
D-118	Williamson, Jack/Harness, Charles L. - ***Dome Around America/The Paradox Men*** [1955] PBO/. Cover by Richard Powers.	$2.00	$6.00	$12.00
S-119	Easton, Lawrence - ***The Driven Flesh*** [1955] PBO.	$2.00	$6.00	$12.00
D-120	Peeples, Samuel A./McGreevy, John - ***The Call Of The Gun/Bounty Man*** [1955] PBO. Cover by Walter Popp.	$2.50	$7.50	$15.00
D-121	Merwin Jr., Sam/Norton, Andre - ***3 Faces Of Time/The Stars Are Ours!*** [1955] PBO/	$2.50	$7.50	$15.00
D-121(SP)	Norton, Andre - ***The Stars Are Ours!*** [1955] Special Edition.	$1.50	$5.00	$10.00
S-122	Baker, Jr., Ledru - ***The Preying Streets*** [1955] PBO.	$1.35	$4.00	$8.00
D-123	Diamond, Frank/Brewer, Gil - ***Love Me To Death/The Squeeze*** [1955] PBO. Covers by Tossey/Barton.	$1.50	$5.00	$10.00
S-124	Loomis, Rae - ***House Of Deceit*** [1955] PBO.	$1.25	$3.75	$7.50
D-125	Asimov, Isaac - ***The Man Who Upset The Universe*** [1955]	$2.00	$6.00	$12.00
S-126	Berzen, A. H. - ***Washington Bachelor*** [1955] PBO.	$2.50	$7.50	$15.00
D-127	Payne, Robert - ***Alexander And The Camp Follower*** [1955]	$1.50	$5.00	$10.00
D-128	Hopson, William/Vance, William E. - ***High Saddle/Way Station West*** [1955] /PBO. Covers by Leone/Popp.	$1.50	$5.00	$10.00

Ace D Series, S-145

Ace D Series, D-214

Ace D Series, D-265

		G	VG	F
D-129	Keene, Day/Rosenthal, Norman C. - ***The Dangling Carrot/Silenced Witnesses*** [1955] PBO.	$2.50	$7.50	$15.00
S-130	Weissman, Sidney - ***Backlash*** [1955] PBO.	$2.25	$7.00	$14.00
D-131	Wyble, Eugene - ***The Ripening*** [1955] PBO.	$2.00	$6.00	$12.00
S-132	Anthology edited by Brant House - ***Cartoon Annual #2*** [1955] PBO. Cover by Rayon.	$2.50	$7.50	$15.00
S-133	Anthology edited by Donald Wollheim - ***Adventures On Other Planets*** [1955] PBO.	$2.25	$7.00	$14.00
D-134	Nye, Nelson/Olson, Gene - ***Tornado On Horseback/The Outsiders*** [1955] /PBO. Covers by Leone/Popp.	$2.00	$6.00	$12.00
D-135	Ozaki, Milton K./Chase, James Hadley - ***Maid For Murder/Dead Ringer*** [1955] PBO. /Cover by Barton.	$2.00	$6.00	$12.00
S-136	Cassill, R. V. - ***A Taste Of Sin*** [1955] PBO.	$1.50	$5.00	$10.00
S-137	Jackson, Ralph - ***Violent Night*** [1955] PBO. Cover by Fay.	$1.50	$5.00	$10.00
D-138	Olsen, T. V./Evan, Paul - ***Haven Of The Hunted/Gunsmoke Over Sabado*** [1956] PBO/. Cover by Walter Popp.	$2.00	$6.00	$12.00
D-139	Dickson, Gordon R./Williams, Nick Boddie - ***Alien From Arcturus/Atom Curtain*** [1956] PBO.	$2.00	$6.00	$12.00
S-140	Elmo, H. T. - ***Honeymoon Humor*** [1956] PBO. Cover by author.	$2.50	$7.50	$15.00
S-141	Crawford, Oliver - ***Blood On The Branches*** [1956] PBO.	$1.50	$5.00	$10.00
S-142	Barns, Glenn M. - ***Masquerade In Blue*** [1956] PBO.	$1.50	$5.00	$10.00
S-143	Whittington, Harry - ***A Woman On The Place*** [1956] PBO.	$3.50	$10.00	$20.00
D-144	Albert, Jay/Patterson, Rod - ***The Man From Stony Lonesome/A Killer Comes Riding*** [1956] PBO. Cover by Walter Popp.	$2.00	$6.00	$12.00
S-145	Anthology edited by Brant House - ***The Little Monsters*** [1956] PBO. Cover by David Lyons.	$4.00	$12.50	$25.00
D-146	Correy, Lee/Leinster, Murray - ***Contraband Rocket/The Forgotten Planet*** [1956] PBO/.	$2.00	$6.00	$12.00
D-146(SP)	Leinster, Murray - ***The Forgotten Planet*** [1956] Special Edition.	$2.00	$6.00	$12.00
D-147	Herries, Norman/Jones, Gregory - ***My Private Hangman/Prowl Cop*** [1956] PBO.	$1.50	$5.00	$10.00
S-148	Ward, Brad - ***The Man From Andersonville*** [1956] PBO. Cover by Leone.	$2.00	$6.00	$12.00
D-149	Clark, Dale/Macklin, Mark - ***A Run For The Money/The Thin Edge Of Mania*** [1956] PBO. Cover by Barton.	$5.50	$17.50	$35.00

		G	VG	F
D-150	Dick, Philip K./St. Clair, Margaret - ***The World Jones Made/Agent Of The Unknown*** [1956] PBO.	$1.50	$5.00	$10.00
S-151	Novak, Robert - ***Climb A Broken Ladder*** [1956] PBO.	$1.50	$5.00	$10.00
S-152	Felsen, Henry - ***Medic Mirth*** [1956] PBO. Cover by Herb Williams.	$3.50	$10.00	$20.00
S-153	Whitney, Hallam - ***The Wild Seed*** [1956] PBO.	$1.25	$3.75	$7.50
D-154	Wilson, Sloan - ***Voyage To Somewhere*** [1956]	$1.25	$3.75	$7.50
D-155	Verne, Jules - ***A Journey To The Center Of The Earth*** [1956]	$2.00	$6.00	$12.00
D-156	Floren, Lee/Lawrence, Stephen C. - ***Thruway West/The Naked Range*** [1956] PBO. Covers by Leone/Popp.	$2.00	$6.00	$12.00
D-157	Trimble, Louis/Gant, Jonathan - ***Stab In The Dark/Never Say No To A Killer*** [1956] PBO.	$1.50	$5.00	$10.00
S-158	Darien, Kim - ***Golden Girl*** [1956] PBO. Cover by Tossey.	$1.50	$5.00	$10.00
S-159	Farr, John - ***She Shark*** [1956] PBO.	$2.00	$6.00	$12.00
D-160	Carder, Michael/Kramer, Karl - ***Decision At Sundown/Action Along The Humboldt*** [1956] /PBO. Covers by Popp/Leone..	$2.25	$7.00	$14.00
S-161	Davis, Eddie - ***Gag Writer's Private Joke Book*** [1956] PBO.	$2.00	$6.00	$12.00
D-162	Sohl, Jerry/Miller, R. & Hunger, Anna - ***The Mars Monopoly/The Man Who Lived Forever*** [1956] PBO.	$1.35	$4.00	$8.00
D-163	Boltar, Russell - ***Woman's Doctor*** [1956] PBO. Cover by Tossey.	$2.00	$6.00	$12.00
D-164	Dickson, Gordon R./Norton, Andre - ***Mankind On The Run/The Crossroads Of Time*** [1956] PBO.	$3.50	$10.00	$20.00
S-165	Anthology edited by Brant House - ***Love And Hisses*** [1956]	$3.50	$10.00	$20.00
D-166	Brock, Stuart/Peeples, Samuel Anthony - ***Whispering Canyon/Terror At Tres Alamos*** [1956] /PBO. Covers by Leone/Popp.	$2.00	$6.00	$12.00
D-167	Creighton, John/Ozaki, Milton K. - ***Destroying Angel/Never Say Die*** [1956] PBO. /Cover by Tossey.	$2.00	$6.00	$12.00
S-168	Hoover, P. A. - ***Riverboat Girl*** [1956] PBO.	$1.50	$5.00	$10.00
D-169	Williamson, Jack and Gunn, James E. - ***Star Bridge*** [1956]	$1.50	$5.00	$10.00
D-170	Keene, Day/Goldman, Lawrence - ***Flight By Night/Black Fire*** [1956] PBO. Cover by Barton.	$2.50	$7.50	$15.00
S-171	Davis, Eddie - ***Campus Joke Book*** [1956] PBO. Cover by Pierce.	$2.25	$7.00	$14.00
D-172	Smith, Ben/Steelman, Robert - ***Johnny No-Name/Stages South*** [1956] PBO.	$2.00	$6.00	$12.00
D-173	Cummings, Ray/Kelleam, Joseph E. - ***The Man Who Mastered Time/Overlords From Space*** [1956] /PBO.	$2.00	$6.00	$12.00
S-174	Novak, Robert - ***B-Girl*** [1956] PBO.	$1.50	$5.00	$10.00
D-175	Anthology edited by Irving Settel - ***Best Television Humor Of The Year*** [1956] PBO. Photo cover.	$1.35	$4.00	$8.00
D-176	St. Clair, Margaret/McClary, Thomas C. - ***The Green Queen/Three Thousand Years*** [1956] PBO/.	$2.00	$6.00	$12.00
D-177	Thames, C. H./Turner, Robert - ***Violence Is Golden/The Girl In The Cop's Pocket*** [1956] PBO. Cover by Barton.	$2.00	$6.00	$12.00
D-178	Paradise, Jean - ***The Savage City*** [1956] Cover by Marchetti.	$1.25	$3.75	$7.50
S-179	Anthology edited by Brant House - ***Squelches*** [1956] PBO.	$2.50	$7.50	$15.00
D-180	Coburn, Walt/Nye, Nelson - ***One Step Ahead Of The Posse/The No-Gun Fighter*** [1956] PBO/.	$2.00	$6.00	$12.00
D-181	Conan Doyle, Adrian & Carr, John Dickson - ***The Exploits Of Sherlock Holmes*** [1956] Cover by Tossey.	$1.50	$5.00	$10.00
D-182	Zola, Emile - ***Shame/Therese Raquin*** [1956]	$1.50	$5.00	$10.00
S-183	Anthology edited by Donald A. Wollheim - ***The End Of The World*** [1956]	$1.50	$5.00	$10.00

		G	VG	F
D-184	McCague, James - ***The Big Ivy*** [1956] Cover by Walter Popp..	$1.50	$5.00	$10.00
D-185	Whittington, Harry/Homes, Geoffrey - ***The Humming Box/Build My Gallows High*** [1956] PBO/. /Cover by Barton.	$4.00	$12.50	$25.00
D-186	Hogan, Ray/Churchill, Edward - ***Ex-Marshal/Steel Horizon*** [1956] PBO/.	$2.00	$6.00	$12.00
D-187	Van Vogt, A. E. - ***The Pawns Of Null-A*** [1956] PBO.	$1.50	$5.00	$10.00
S-188	Anthology edited by Brant House - ***They Goofed!*** [1956] PBO. Cover by Wenzel.	$2.50	$7.50	$15.00
D-189	Treat, Lawrence/Marlowe, Stephen - ***Weep For A Wanton/Dead On Arrival*** [1956] PBO. Covers by Nappi/Marchetti.	$2.00	$6.00	$12.00
S-190	Nixon, Henry Lewis - ***The Golden Couch*** [1956] PBO.	$1.50	$5.00	$10.00
D-191	Slaughter, Frank G. - ***Apalachee Gold*** [1956]	$1.25	$3.75	$7.50
D-192	Manning, Roy/Callahan, John - ***Beware Of This Tenderfoot/Bad Blood At Black Range*** [1956] PBO. Covers by Walter Popp/John Leone.	$2.00	$6.00	$12.00
D-193	Tubb, E. C./Dick, Philip K. - ***The Space-Born/The Man Who Japed*** [1956] PBO. /Cover by Emsh.	$5.50	$17.50	$35.00
D-194	Plievier, Theodor - ***Moscow*** [1956]	$1.25	$3.75	$7.50
D-195	Dudley, Owen/Colby, Robert - ***The Deep End/The Quaking Widow*** [1956] PBO.	$2.00	$6.00	$12.00
D-196	Coburn, Walt/Gruber, Frank - ***The Night Branders/The Highwayman*** [1956] PBO/. Cover by Walter Popp.	$2.00	$6.00	$12.00
D-197	Byron, James/Findley, Ferguson - ***TNT For Two/Counterfeit Corpse*** [1956]	$2.00	$6.00	$12.00
S-198	Bender, Jr., William - ***Tokyo Intrigue*** [1956] PBO.	$1.50	$5.00	$10.00
D-199	Anderson, Poul/Norton, Andre - ***Planet Of No Return/Star Guard*** [1956] PBO/.	$2.00	$6.00	$12.00
D-200	Ruppelt, Edward J. - ***The Report On Unidentified Flying Objects*** [1956]	$1.00	$3.00	$6.00
D-201	Jones, Nathaniel E./Whittington, Harry - ***Saturday Mountain/Across That River*** [1956] PBO.	$3.00	$9.00	$18.00
D-202	Kaufman, Lenard - ***The Color Of Green*** [1957]	$1.35	$4.00	$8.00
D-203	Rohde, William L./Grote, William - ***Uneasy Lies The Head/Cain's Girl Friend*** [1957] PBO. Covers by Barton/Erickson.	$1.50	$5.00	$10.00
D-204	Donalds, Gordon/Durst, Paul - ***The Desperate Donigans/John Law, Keep Out!*** [1957] /PBO.	$1.50	$5.00	$10.00
D-205	Wright, Lan/Anthology ed. by Wollheim - ***Who Speaks Of Conquests?/The Earth In Peril*** [1957] PBO.	$1.50	$5.00	$10.00
D-206	Andrews, Robert Hardy - ***Great Day In The Morning*** [1957] Cover by Tossey.	$1.25	$3.75	$7.50
D-207	Grayson, Charles - ***Hollywood Doctor*** [1957]	$1.50	$5.00	$10.00
D-208	Cord, Barry/Balch, Glenn - ***The Prodigal Gun/Blind Man's Bullets*** [1957] /PBO. /Cover by Walter Popp.	$1.50	$5.00	$10.00
D-209	Jakes, John/Wallace, F. L. - ***A Night For Treason/Three Times A Victim*** [1957] /PBO. Cover by Tossey/	$2.00	$6.00	$12.00
D-210	Longstreet, Stephen - ***The Lion At Morning*** [1957]	$1.25	$3.75	$7.50
D-211	Dick, Philip K. - ***Eye In The Sky*** [1957] PBO	$5.50	$17.50	$35.00
S-212	Elmo, H. T. - ***Hollywood Humor*** [1957] PBO.	$2.00	$6.00	$12.00
D-213	Steincrohn, M.D., Peter J. - ***How To Stop Killing Yourself*** [1957]	$1.35	$4.00	$8.00
D-214	Weiss, Martin L. - ***Hate Alley*** [1957] PBO.	$4.00	$12.50	$25.00

		G	VG	F
D-215	Williams, Robert M./Russell, Eric F. - ***Doomsday Eve/Three To Conquer*** [1957] PBO/.	$1.50	$5.00	$10.00
D-216	MacDonald, William C./Cord, Barry - ***Ridin' Through/Savage Valley*** [1957] PBO/. Covers by Tossey.	$1.50	$5.00	$10.00
D-217	Lovell, B. E./McKnight, Bob - ***A Rage To Kill/Downwind*** [1957] PBO.	$1.50	$5.00	$10.00
D-218	Siemel, Sasha - ***Tigero!*** [1957] Cover by John Leone.	$1.35	$4.00	$8.00
S-219	Hoover, P. A. - ***Backwater Woman*** [1957] PBO.	$1.50	$5.00	$10.00
D-220	Jakes, John/Hogan, Ray - ***Wear A Fast Gun/The Friendless One*** [1957] /PBO. Cover by Tossey.	$1.50	$5.00	$10.00
D-221	Ashe, Gordon/Chavis, Robert - ***You've Bet Your Life/The Terror Package*** [1957] PBO. Cover by Tossey.	$1.50	$5.00	$10.00
D-222	Frison-Roche, R. - ***First On The Rope*** [1957] Cover by Tossey.	$1.25	$3.75	$7.50
D-223	Silverberg, Robert/Gunn, James E. - ***The 13th Immortal/This Fortress World*** [1957] PBO/.	$1.50	$5.00	$10.00
D-224	Steger, Shelby - ***Desire In The Ozarks*** [1957] PBO.	$1.50	$5.00	$10.00
D-225	Chaber, M. E./Giddings, Harry - ***A Lonely Walk/Loser By A Head*** [1957] /PBO. Cover by Nappi.	$1.50	$5.00	$10.00
D-226	Peeples, Samuel A./Booth, Edwin - ***Doc Colt/Showdown At Warbird*** [1957] PBO.	$1.50	$5.00	$10.00
D-227	Piper, H. Beam & McGuire/Judd, Cyril - ***Crisis In 2140/Gunner Cade*** [1957] PBO/. Cover by Barton.	$1.50	$5.00	$10.00
D-228	Howarth, David - ***We Die Alone*** [1957] Cover by Tossey.	$1.25	$3.75	$7.50
D-229	Whitney, Walter - ***Take It Out In Trade*** [1957] PBO. Cover by Tossey.	$1.35	$4.00	$8.00
D-230	Floren, Lee/Cord, Barry - ***Burn 'Em Out!/Boss Of Barbed Wire*** [1957] PBO/.	$1.50	$5.00	$10.00
D-231	Dudley, Owen/Ronns, Edward - ***Murder For Charity/Point Of Peril*** [1957] PBO/. Cover by Marchetti.	$1.50	$5.00	$10.00
D-232	Manus, Willard - ***The Fixers*** [1957] PBO.	$1.25	$3.75	$7.50
D-233	Gordon, Rex - ***First On Mars*** [1957] PBO.	$1.50	$5.00	$10.00
D-234	Scott, Jr., Robert L. - ***Look Of The Eagle*** [1957] Cover by Verne Tossey.	$1.25	$3.75	$7.50
D-235	Farr, John/Trimble, Louis - ***The Lady And The Snake/Nothing To Lose But My Life*** [1957] PBO. /Cover by Nappi.	$2.00	$6.00	$12.00
D-236	Booth, Edwin/Hogan, Ray - ***Jinx Rider/Walk A Lonely Trail*** [1957] PBO. Covers by Leone/Popp.	$1.50	$5.00	$10.00
D-237	White, James/Silverberg, Robert - ***The Secret Visitors/Master Of Life And Death*** [1957] PBO. /Cover by Emsh.	$1.50	$5.00	$10.00
D-238	Holmes, Clellon - ***Go*** [1957]	$5.00	$15.00	$30.00
D-239	Stine, G. Harry - ***Earth Satellites And The Race For Space Superiority*** [1957] PBO.	$1.00	$3.00	$6.00
D-240	Lee, Wayne C./West, Tom - ***Broken Wheel Ranch/Torture Trail*** [1957] /PBO.	$1.50	$5.00	$10.00
D-241	Tucker, Wilson/Whittington, Harry - ***The Hired Target/One Deadly Dawn*** [1957] PBO. /Cover by Nappi.	$3.00	$9.00	$18.00
D-242	Van Vogt, A. E./Long, Frank Belknap - ***Empire Of The Atom/Space Station #1*** [1957] /PBO. Cover by /Emsh.	$1.50	$5.00	$10.00
D-243	Wells, Michael - ***The Roving Eye*** [1957] PBO.	$1.35	$4.00	$8.00
D-244	Robertson, Terence - ***Night Raider Of The Atlantic*** [1957] Cover by Verne Tossey.	$1.25	$3.75	$7.50
D-245	Verne, Jules - ***Off On A Comet*** [1957] Cover by Ed Emsh.	$1.50	$5.00	$10.00
D-246	Harriman, John - ***The Magnate*** [1957] Cover by Nappi.	$1.35	$4.00	$8.00

Ace D Series, D-270

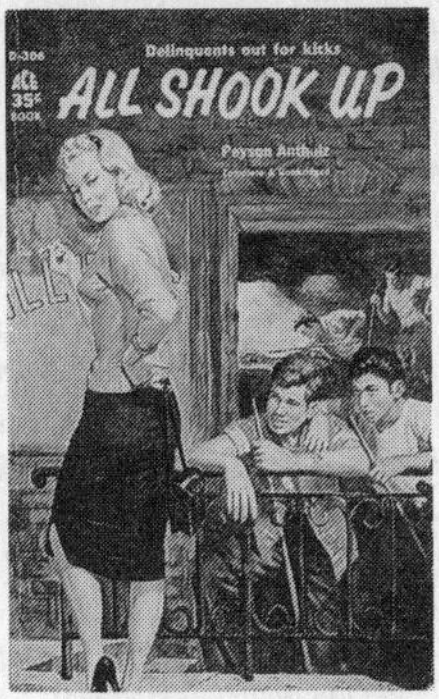

Ace D Series, D-306

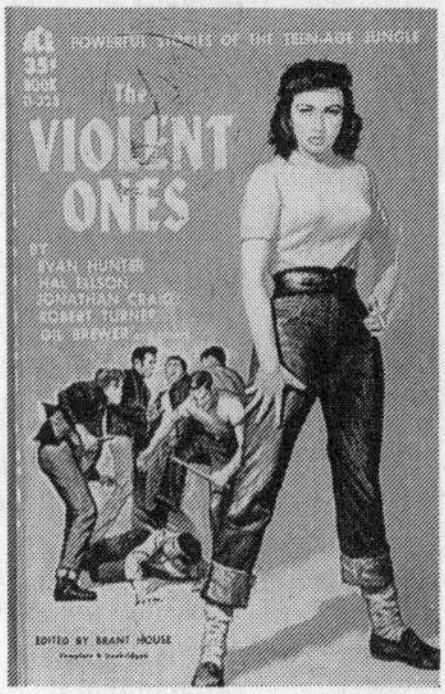

Ace D Series, D-323

		G	VG	F
D-247	Creighton, John/Lewis, Ken - ***Not So Evil As Eve/Look Out Behind You*** [1957] PBO. Cover by Barton.	$1.50	$5.00	$10.00
D-248	Hogan, Ray/Hardin, Clement - ***Longhorn Law/Cross Me In Gunsmoke*** [1957] PBO. /Cover by Walter Popp.	$1.50	$5.00	$10.00
D-249	Dick, Philip K./North, Andrew - ***The Cosmic Puppets/Sargasso Of Space*** [1957] PBO/. /Cover by Emsh.	$5.50	$17.50	$35.00
D-250	Steuer, Arthur - ***The Terrible Swift Sword*** [1957] Cover by Tossey.	$1.25	$3.75	$7.50
D-251	Cochran, Hamilton - ***Windward Passage*** [1957]	$1.25	$3.75	$7.50
D-252	Callahan, John/Patterson, Rod - ***The Rawhide Breed/Prairie Terror*** [1957] PBO.	$1.50	$5.00	$10.00
D-253	Dean, Spencer/Cassiday, Bruce - ***Marked Down For Murder/The Buried Motive*** [1957] /PBO.	$1.50	$5.00	$10.00
D-254	Spinelli, Marcos - ***The Lash Of Desire*** [1957] PBO.	$1.50	$5.00	$10.00
D-255	Anderson, Poul/Bulmer, Kenneth - ***Star Ways/City Under The Sea*** [1957] /PBO. Cover by Emsh/.	$1.50	$5.00	$10.00
S-256	Opitz, Karl Ludwig - ***The General*** [1957] Cover by Verne Tossey.	$1.35	$4.00	$8.00
D-257	Malley, Louis - ***Tiger In The Streets*** [1957] PBO. Cover by Verne Tossey.	$4.00	$12.50	$25.00
D-258	Rawicz, Slavomir - ***The Long Walk*** [1957]	$1.35	$4.00	$8.00
D-259	Avallone, Michael - ***The Case Of The Bouncing Betty/Case Of The Violent Virgin*** [1957] PBO.	$2.50	$7.50	$15.00
D-260	Hogan, Ray/Floren, Lee - ***Land Of The Strangers/The Saddle Wolves*** [1957] PBO. /Cover by Flapan.	$1.50	$5.00	$10.00
D-261	Dick, Philip K. - ***The Variable Man And Other Stories*** [1957] PBO. Cover by Emsh.	$5.00	$15.00	$30.00
S-262	Jamieson, Leland - ***Attack!*** [1957] Cover by Ed Emsh.	$1.35	$4.00	$8.00
S-263	Shaw, Wilene - ***See How They Run*** [1957] PBO.	$1.50	$5.00	$10.00
D-264	Cord, Barry/Wells, Lee E. - ***Cain Basin/Brother Outlaw*** [1958] /PBO. /Cover by Walter Popp.	$1.50	$5.00	$10.00
D-265	Bloch, Robert - ***Shooting Star/Terror In The Night*** [1958] PBO.	$12.50	$37.50	$75.00
D-266	Fontenay, Charles L./Tubb, E. C. - ***Twice Upon A Time/The Mechanical Monarch*** [1958] PBO. Cover by Emsh.	$1.50	$5.00	$10.00
D-267	Bosworth, Jim - ***Speed Demon*** [1958] PBO.	$1.25	$3.75	$7.50
D-268	Anthology edited by Brant House - ***Lincoln's Wit*** [1958] PBO.	$1.25	$3.75	$7.50

		G	VG	F
D-269	Powell, Michael - ***Death In The South Atlantic*** [1958] Movie tie-in.	$1.25	$3.75	$7.50
D-270	Clifton, Bud - ***D For Delinquent*** [1958] PBO.	$4.00	$12.50	$25.00
D-271	Howe, Cliff - ***Lovers And Libertines*** [1958] PBO.	$1.25	$3.75	$7.50
D-272	Floren, Lee/Hopson, William - ***Riders In The Night/Backlash At Cajon Pass*** [1958] /PBO. Covers by Leone/Popp.	$1.50	$5.00	$10.00
D-273	Fredericks, Ernest J./Roscoe, Mike - ***Shakedown Hotel/The Midnight Eye*** [1958] PBO. Cover by Tossey/.	$1.50	$5.00	$10.00
D-274	Maine, Charles Eric - ***World Without Men*** [1958] PBO. Cover by Ed Emsh	$3.50	$10.00	$20.00
S-275	Anthology edited by Brant House - ***Cartoon Annual #3*** [1958] PBO. Cover by Wenzel.	$2.50	$7.50	$15.00
D-276	Cord, Barry/West, Tom - ***The Gunsmoke Trail/Lead In His Fists*** [1958] /PBO	$1.50	$5.00	$10.00
D-277	Anthology/Leinster, Murray - ***Men On The Moon/City On The Moon*** [1958] PBO/. Both covers by Ed Emsh.	$1.50	$5.00	$10.00
D-278	Chidsey, Donald Barr - ***This Bright Sword*** [1958] Cover by Verne Tossey.	$1.00	$3.00	$6.00
D-279	McKnight, Bob/Bond, J. Harvey - ***Murder Mutuel/Bye-Bye Baby!*** [1958] PBO.	$1.50	$5.00	$10.00
D-280	Devereux, Col. James P. S. - ***The Story Of Wake Island*** [1958]	$1.00	$3.00	$6.00
D-281	Anthology edited by Norman Vincent Peale - ***Guideposts*** [1958]	$1.00	$3.00	$6.00
D-282	Howe, Cliff - ***Scoundrels, Fiends And Human Monsters*** [1958] PBO.	$1.25	$3.75	$7.50
D-283	Simak, Clifford D. - ***City*** [1958]	$1.50	$5.00	$10.00
D-284	Booth, Edwin/Cord, Barry - ***The Man Who Killed Tex/The Guns Of Hammer*** [1958] PBO/. Cover by Popp.	$1.50	$5.00	$10.00
D-285	Cassiday, Bruce/Linklater, Joseph - ***The Brass Shroud/Odd Woman Out*** [1958] PBO/. Covers by Barton/Tossey.	$1.50	$5.00	$10.00
D-286	Grinnell, David/Silverberg, Robert - ***Across Time/Invaders From Earth*** [1958] /PBO. /Cover by Emsh.	$1.50	$5.00	$10.00
D-287	Smith, General Holland M. - ***Coral In Brass*** [1958]	$1.25	$3.75	$7.50
D-288	Booth, Edwin/Callahan, John - ***Trail To Tomahawk/Land Beyond The Law*** [1958] PBO. /Cover by Popp.	$1.50	$5.00	$10.00
D-289	Hawkins, John & Ward/Payne, Alan - ***Violent City/This'll Slay You*** [1958] /PBO. /Cover by Barton.	$1.50	$5.00	$10.00
D-290	Hoover, P. A. - ***A Woman Called Trouble*** [1958] PBO.	$1.35	$4.00	$8.00
D-291	Gallun, Raymond Z./Knox, Calvin M. - ***People Minus X/Lest We Forget Thee, Earth*** [1958] /PBO. Cover by Ed Emsh.	$1.50	$5.00	$10.00
D-292	Mooney, Booth - ***The Insiders*** [1958] PBO. Cover by Verne Tossey.	$1.25	$3.75	$7.50
D-293	Linna, Vaino - ***The Unknown Soldier*** [1958] Cover by Verne Tossey.	$1.00	$3.00	$6.00
D-294	Coburn, Walt/Latham, John H. - ***Beyond The Wild Missouri/Bad Bunch Of The Brasada*** [1958] /PBO.	$1.50	$5.00	$10.00
D-295	Vance, Jack - ***Big Planet/Slaves Of The Klau*** [1958] /PBO. Cover by Emsh.	$2.00	$6.00	$12.00
D-296	Clagett, John - ***Run The River Gauntlet*** [1958] PBO.	$1.35	$4.00	$8.00
D-297	Kelston, Robert H./Rabe, Peter - ***Kill One, Kill Two/The Cut Of The Whip*** [1958] PBO. /Cover by Barton.	$2.50	$7.50	$15.00
D-298	Evan, Paul/Vance, William - ***Thunder Creek Range/Outlaws Welcome!*** [1958] /PBO. Covers by Tossey/Leone.	$1.50	$5.00	$10.00

		G	VG	F
D-299	Norton, Andre/Piper, H. & McGuire, J. - ***Star Born/A Planet For Texans*** [1958] /PBO.	$1.50	$5.00	$10.00
D-300	Small, J. Walter - ***The Dance Merchants*** [1958] PBO.	$1.35	$4.00	$8.00
D-301	Bond, J. Harvey/Farr, John - ***Murder Isn't Funny/The Deadly Combo*** [1958] PBO. /Cover by Barton.	$1.50	$5.00	$10.00
D-302	Druon, Maurice - ***The Iron King*** [1958]	$1.25	$3.75	$7.50
D-303	Anderson, Poul - ***War Of The Wing-Men/The Snows Of Ganymede*** [1958] PBO. Cover by Ed Emsh.	$1.50	$5.00	$10.00
D-304	Joscelyn, Archie/Smith, Ben - ***River To The Sunset/Trouble At Breakdam*** [1958] PBO/. Covers by Papp/Leone.	$1.50	$5.00	$10.00
D-305	King, Louis/Rodell, Vic - ***Cornered/Free-Lance Murder*** [1958] PBO/.	$1.50	$5.00	$10.00
D-306	Antholz, Peyson - ***All Shook Up*** [1958] PBO.	$4.00	$12.50	$25.00
D-307	Anthology edited by Brant House - ***From Eve On*** [1958] PBO. Cover by Lloyd Birmingham.	$2.50	$7.50	$15.00
D-308	Bickham, Jack M./Manning, Roy - ***Gunman's Gamble/Draw And Die!*** [1958] PBO.	$1.50	$5.00	$10.00
D-309	Wells, H. G. - ***The Island Of Dr. Moreau*** [1958]	$2.00	$6.00	$12.00
D-310	Spinelli, Marcos - ***Mocambu*** [1958] PBO.	$1.35	$4.00	$8.00
D-311	Wright, Lan/Silverberg, Robert - ***A Man Called Destiny/Step-sons Of Terra*** [1958] PBO.	$1.50	$5.00	$10.00
D-312	Ellison, Harlan - ***The Deadly Streets*** [1958] PBO.	$30.00	$100.00	$225.00
D-313	Flynn, J. M./Krasney, Samuel A. - ***The Deadly Boodle/Design For Dying*** [1958] PBO. /Cover by Barton.	$1.50	$5.00	$10.00
D-314	Ashton, Blair - ***Deeds Of Darkness*** [1958]	$1.35	$4.00	$8.00
D-315	Russell, Eric Frank - ***The Space Willies/Six Worlds Yonder*** [1958] PBO.	$2.50	$7.50	$15.00
D-316	Patterson, Rod/Cord, Barry - ***A Time For Guns/Mesquite Johnny*** [1958] PBO/. Cover by Walter Popp.	$1.50	$5.00	$10.00
D-317	Creighton, John/Travis, Gerry - ***The Wayward Blonde/The Big Bite*** [1958] PBO/.	$1.00	$3.00	$6.00
D-318	Chidsey, Donald Barr - ***Captain Crossbones*** [1958] PBO.	$1.25	$3.75	$7.50
D-319	Meissner, Hans-Otto - ***The Man With Three Faces*** [1958] Cover by Nappi	$1.25	$3.75	$7.50
D-320	McCaig, Robert/Hopson, William - ***The Range Master/The Last Shoot-Out*** [1958] PBO. Cover by Popp.	$1.50	$5.00	$10.00
D-321	Creighton, John/Trimble, Louis - ***Trial By Perjury/The Smell Of Trouble*** [1958] PBO.	$1.50	$5.00	$10.00
D-322	Williams, Robert Moore - ***The Blue Atom/The Void Beyond*** [1958] PBO.	$1.50	$5.00	$10.00
D-323	Anthology - ***The Violent Ones*** [1958] PBO. Includes Hal Ellson.	$4.00	$12.50	$25.00
D-324	Cummings, Ray - ***Brigands Of The Moon*** [1958] Cover by Ed Emsh.	$1.50	$5.00	$10.00
D-325	Werstein, Irving - ***July, 1863*** [1958]	$1.25	$3.75	$7.50
D-326	Johnen, Wilhelm - ***Battling The Bombers*** [1958] Cover by Tossey.	$1.00	$3.00	$6.00
D-327	Sutton, Jeff - ***First On The Moon*** [1958] PBO. Cover by Emsh.	$1.35	$4.00	$8.00
D-328	Constiner, Merle/West, Tom - ***The Fourth Gunman/Slick On The Draw*** [1958] PBO.	$1.50	$5.00	$10.00
D-329	McDowell, Emmett - ***Three For The Gallows/Stamped For Death*** [1958] PBO.	$1.50	$5.00	$10.00
D-330	Clifton, Bud - ***Muscle Boy*** [1958] PBO. Cover by Maguire.	$1.50	$5.00	$10.00

Ace D Series, D-343

Ace D Series, D-353

Ace D Series, D-359

		G	VG	F
D-331	Bulmer, Kenneth/Cummings, Ray - ***The Secret Of Zi/Beyond The Vanishing Point*** [1958] PBO. Cover by Ed Emsh.	$1.50	$5.00	$10.00
D-332	Smith, Ben/Welles, Kermit - ***Stranger In Sundown/Blood On Boot Hill*** [1958]	$1.50	$5.00	$10.00
D-333	Brett, Mike/Creighton, John - ***Scream Street/Stranglehold*** [1958] PBO. Cover by Barton/.	$2.00	$6.00	$12.00
D-334	Johnston, Stanley - ***Queen Of The Flat-Tops*** [1958] Photo cover.	$2.50	$7.50	$15.00
D-335	Brunner, John/Anderson, Poul - ***Threshold Of Eternity/The War Of Two Worlds*** [1959] PBO. Cover by Emsh/.	$1.50	$5.00	$10.00
D-336	Krasney, Samuel A. - ***Morals Squad*** [1959] PBO. Cover by Maguire.	$1.50	$5.00	$10.00
D-337	Gerstine, Jack - ***Play It Cool*** [1959] PBO.	$4.00	$12.50	$25.00
D-338	De Roo, Edward - ***The Fires Of Youth*** [1959]	$3.50	$10.00	$20.00
D-339	Simak, Clifford D. - ***Ring Around The Sun*** [1959]	$1.50	$5.00	$10.00
D-340	Dick, Philip K. - ***Solar Lottery*** [1959]	$1.50	$5.00	$10.00
D-341	Loomis, Rae - ***The Marina Street Girls*** [1959]	$1.35	$4.00	$8.00
D-342	Gorham, Nicholas - ***Queen's Blade*** [1959] Cover by Geygan.	$1.25	$3.75	$7.50
D-343	De Roo, Edward - ***The Young Wolves*** [1959] PBO.	$4.00	$12.50	$25.00
D-344	Landsborough, Gordon - ***Desert Fury*** [1959]	$1.25	$3.75	$7.50
D-345	North, Andrew - ***Voodoo Planet/Plague Ship*** [1959] PBO/. Cover by Ed Emsh.	$1.50	$5.00	$10.00
D-346	Hogan, Ray/Cord, Barry - ***Wanted: Alive!/Sheriff Of Big Hat*** [1959] PBO/.	$1.50	$5.00	$10.00
D-347	Whittington, Harry/Trimble, Louis - ***Play For Keeps/The Corpse Without A Country*** [1959] /PBO.	$3.00	$9.00	$18.00
D-348	Shelley, John L./Olsen, T.V. - ***The Avenging Gun/The Man From Nowhere*** [1959] PBO.	$1.50	$5.00	$10.00
D-349	Brett, Mike/Bond, J. Harvey - ***The Guilty Bystander/Kill Me With Kindness*** [1959] PBO. /Cover by Rader.	$1.50	$5.00	$10.00
D-350	Bryant, Peter - ***Red Alert*** [1959] PBO.	$1.35	$4.00	$8.00
D-351	Jorgenson, Ivar/Hamilton, Edmond - ***Starhaven/The Sun Smasher*** [1959] /PBO.	$1.50	$5.00	$10.00
G-352	Leary, Francis - ***Fire And Morning*** [1959] Cover by Geygan.	$1.25	$3.75	$7.50
D-353	Anthology edited by Donald A. Wollheim - ***The Macabre Reader*** [1959] PBO. Cover by Ed Emsh.	$3.50	$10.00	$20.00

		G	VG	F
D-354	Anthology edited by Donald A. Wollheim - ***The Hidden Planet*** [1959] PBO.	$1.50	$5.00	$10.00
D-355	Strutton, Bill & Pearson, Michael - ***The Beachhead Spies*** [1959]	$1.00	$3.00	$6.00
D-356	Durst, Paul/West, Tom - ***Kansas Guns/The Cactus Kid*** [1959] /PBO.	$1.50	$5.00	$10.00
D-357	Wallace, Floyd/Dent, Lester - ***Wired For Scandal/Lady In Peril*** [1959] PBO.	$2.00	$6.00	$12.00
D-358	Knox, Calvin M./Lesser, Milton - ***The Plot Against Earth/Recruit For Andromeda*** [1959] PBO/.	$1.50	$5.00	$10.00
D-359	Cooper, John C. - ***The Haunted Strangler*** [1959] Movie tie-in.	$3.00	$9.00	$18.00
D-360	Latham, John/Cord, Barry - ***Johnny Sixgun/War In Peaceful Valley*** [1959] PBO. Covers by R. Lance/Leone.	$1.50	$5.00	$10.00
D-361	Duff, James P./Colby, Robert - ***Dangerous To Know/Murder Mistress*** [1959] PBO.	$1.50	$5.00	$10.00
D-362	Brunner, John/Grinnell, David - ***The 100th Millennium/Edge Of Time*** [1959] PBO/. /Cover by Ed Emsh.	$1.50	$5.00	$10.00
D-363	Krasney, Samuel A. - ***The Rapist*** [1959] PBO.	$1.50	$5.00	$10.00
D-364	Chidsey, Donald Barr - ***The Pipes Are Calling*** [1959] PBO. Cover by Geygan.	$1.25	$3.75	$7.50
D-365	Eunson, Robert - ***Mig Alley*** [1959] PBO. Cover by Verne Tossey.	$1.25	$3.75	$7.50
D-366	Nourse, Alan E. & Meyer, J.A. - ***The Invaders Are Coming*** [1959] PBO. Cover by Ed Emsh.	$1.50	$5.00	$10.00
D-367	Fritch, Charles E./Trimble, Louis - ***Negative Of A Nude/Till Death Do Us Part*** [1959] PBO. Covers by Maguire/Rader.	$2.00	$6.00	$12.00
D-368	Gage, Joseph/Hogan, Ray - ***A Score To Settle/Hangman's Valley*** [1959] /PBO. /Cover by Lesser.	$1.50	$5.00	$10.00
D-369	Aldiss, Brian W./Bulmer, Kenneth - ***Vanguard From Alpha/The Changeling Worlds*** [1959] PBO. Cover by Emsh.	$1.50	$5.00	$10.00
D-370	Fredericks, Ernest Jason - ***Cry Flood!*** [1959] PBO.	$1.35	$4.00	$8.00
G-371	Plievier, Theodore - ***Berlin*** [1959]	$1.35	$4.00	$8.00
D-372	Balch, Glenn/Kirby, Dan - ***Grass Greed/Cimarron Territory*** [1959] PBO. /Cover by Verne Tossey.	$1.50	$5.00	$10.00
D-373	Warren, Doug/Karney, Jack - ***Scarlet Starlet/The Knave Of Diamonds*** [1959] PBO.	$1.50	$5.00	$10.00
D-374	Leonard, Burgess - ***The Thoroughbred And The Tramp*** [1959] PBO. Cover by Leone.	$1.35	$4.00	$8.00
D-375	Knight, Damon/Smith, George O. - ***Masters Of Evolution/Fire In The Heavens*** [1959] PBO/. Cover by Emsh.	$1.50	$5.00	$10.00
G-376	Howells, J. Harvey - ***The Big Company Look*** [1959]	$1.00	$3.00	$6.00
D-377	Sutton, Jeff - ***Bombs In Orbit*** [1959] PBO.	$1.35	$4.00	$8.00
D-378	Shaw, Wilene - ***Out For Kicks*** [1959] PBO.	$3.50	$10.00	$20.00
D-379	Flynn, J. M./Woody, William - ***Drink With The Dead/Mistress Of Horror House*** [1959]	$2.50	$7.50	$15.00
D-380	Cord, Barry/Heuman, William - ***PBO.ho Valley/My Brother The Gunman*** [1959]	$1.50	$5.00	$10.00
D-381	Sohl, Jerry/Norton, Andre - ***One Against Herculum/Secret Of The Lost Race*** [1959] PBO. Cover by Ed Emsh/.	$1.50	$5.00	$10.00
G-382	Ritchie, Cicero T. - ***The Willing Maid*** [1959] Cover art by Geygan.	$1.35	$4.00	$8.00
D-383	Clifton, Bud - ***The Murder Specialist*** [1959] PBO.	$1.50	$5.00	$10.00
D-384	Bickham, Jack M./Trimble, Louis - ***Feud Fury/Mountain Ambush*** [1959] PBO/. Cover by Tossey/.	$1.50	$5.00	$10.00

		G	VG	F
D-385	Brunner, John/Nourse, Alan E. - ***Echo In The Skull/Rocket To Limbo*** [1959] PBO/. /Cover by Emsh	$1.50	$5.00	$10.00
G-386	O'Connor, Richard - ***The Sulu Sword*** [1959] Cover art by Verne Tossey	$1.35	$4.00	$8.00
D-387	Fisher, Laine/McKnight, Bob - ***Fare Prey/The Bikini Bombshell*** [1959] PBO. Cover by Maguire.	$1.50	$5.00	$10.00
D-388	Wells, H. G. - ***When The Sleeper Wakes*** [1959] Cover by Ed Emsh.	$1.35	$4.00	$8.00
D-389	Coles, Manning - ***No Entry*** [1959]	$1.25	$3.75	$7.50
G-390	Foreman, Russell - ***Long Pig*** [1959]	$1.25	$3.75	$7.50
D-391	Brunner, John/Van Vogt, A. E. - ***The World Swappers/Seige Of The Unseen*** [1959] PBO.	$1.50	$5.00	$10.00
D-392	West, Tom/Joscelyn, Archie - ***Twisted Trail/The Man From Salt Creek*** [1959] PBO/.	$1.50	$5.00	$10.00
D-393	Creighton, John/Levey, Robert A. - ***Evil Is The Night/Dictators Die Hard*** [1959] PBO	$1.50	$5.00	$10.00
D-394	Chidsey, Donald Barr - ***The Flaming Island*** [1959] PBO.	$1.25	$3.75	$7.50
D-395	Keller, Allan - ***Thunder At Harper's Ferry*** [1959] Cover by Tossey.	$1.25	$3.75	$7.50
D-396	Loomis, Rae - ***Luisita*** [1959] Cover by Robert Maguire.	$1.50	$5.00	$10.00
D-397	Verne, Jules - ***A Journey To The Center Of The Earth*** [1959] Movie tie-in.	$1.35	$4.00	$8.00
D-398	Miller, Nolan - ***Why I Am So Beat*** [1959]	$1.35	$4.00	$8.00
D-399	Adler, Edward - ***Living It Up*** [1959] Cover by Verne Tossey.	$1.35	$4.00	$8.00
D-400	Cord, Barry/Shirreffs, Gordon D. - ***Last Chance At Devil's Canyon/Shadow Of A Gunman*** [1959] PBO.	$1.50	$5.00	$10.00
D-401	Trimble, Louis/Thomey, Tedd - ***Obit Deferred/I Want Out*** [1959] PBO.	$1.50	$5.00	$10.00
G-402	Mannix, Daniel P. - ***Kiboko*** [1959]	$1.25	$3.75	$7.50
D-403	Leinster, Murray - ***The Pirates Of Zan/The Mutant Weapon*** [1959] PBO. Cover by Emsh/.	$1.50	$5.00	$10.00
D-404	Anderson, Clifford - ***The Hollow Hero*** [1959] PBO.	$1.00	$3.00	$6.00
D-405	Gordon, Rex - ***First To The Stars*** [1959] PBO. Cover by Ed Emsh.	$1.35	$4.00	$8.00
D-406	De Roo, Edward - ***Go, Man, Go*** [1959] PBO.	$3.50	$10.00	$20.00
D-407	Silverberg, Robert/Anderson, Poul - ***The Planet Killers/We Claim These Stars!*** [1959] PBO.	$1.50	$5.00	$10.00
D-408	Booth, Edwin/Lutz, Giles A. - ***Wyoming Welcome/Law Of The Trigger*** [1959] PBO	$1.50	$5.00	$10.00
D-409	Trimble, Louis/Flynn, J. M. - ***Cargo For The Styx/Terror Tournament*** [1959] PBO/.	$1.50	$5.00	$10.00
D-410	Chidsey, Donald Barr - ***Buccaneer's Blade*** [1959] PBO.	$1.25	$3.75	$7.50
D-411	McKnight, Bob - ***Swamp Sanctuary*** [1959] PBO. Cover by Maguire.	$1.50	$5.00	$10.00
D-412	Shirreffs, Gordon D./Alman, E. A. - ***Apache Butte/Ride The Long Night*** [1960] PBO/.	$1.50	$5.00	$10.00
D-413	Ellison, Harlan - ***The Man With Nine Lives/A Touch Of Infinity*** [1960] PBO.	$6.00	$20.00	$40.00
G-414	Dumas, Alexandre - ***The Companions Of Jehu*** [1960] Cover art by Geygan	$1.25	$3.75	$7.50
D-415	Sterling, Stewart - ***Fire On Fear Street/Dead Certain*** [1960] /PBO.	$1.50	$5.00	$10.00
D-416	Kenneth, John - ***The Big Question*** [1960] PBO.	$1.00	$3.00	$6.00
D-417	De Roo, Edward - ***Rumble At The Housing Project*** [1960] PBO.	$4.00	$12.50	$25.00

		G	VG	F
D-418	West, Tom/Park, C. S. - ***Nothing But My Gun/The Quiet Ones*** [1960] PBO.	$1.50	$5.00	$10.00
D-419	McKnight, Bob/Thielen, Bernard - ***A Slice Of Death/Open Season*** [1960] PBO/. Cover by Maguire/.	$1.50	$5.00	$10.00
D-420	Williams, John A. - ***The Angry Ones*** [1960] PBO.	$1.35	$4.00	$8.00
D-421	Brunner, John/Dick, Philip K. - ***Slavers Of Space/Dr. Futurity*** [1960] PBO.	$5.00	$15.00	$30.00
D-422	Anthology edited by Boucher and McComas - ***The Best From Fantasy And Science Fiction Third Series*** [1960] Cover by Emsh.	$1.50	$5.00	$10.00
D-423	Norton, Browning - ***Tidal Wave*** [1960] PBO.	$1.25	$3.75	$7.50
D-424	McCaig, Robert/Richards, Lee - ***Wild Justice/Shoot-Out At The Way Station*** [1960] /PBO.	$1.50	$5.00	$10.00
D-425	Kruger, Paul/Creighton, John - ***Dig Her A Grave/A Half Interest In Murder*** [1960] PBO.	$1.50	$5.00	$10.00
D-426	Close, Robert S. - ***Penal Colony*** [1960]	$1.25	$3.75	$7.50
D-427	Williams, Robert Moore - ***To The End Of Time/World Of The Masterminds*** [1960] PBO.	$1.50	$5.00	$10.00
D-428	Hoover, P. A. - ***Scowtown Woman*** [1960] PBO.	$1.35	$4.00	$8.00
D-429	Runyon, Charles W. - ***The Anatomy Of Violence*** [1960] PBO.	$1.35	$4.00	$8.00
D-430	Hopson, William/Hogan, Ray - ***Born Savage/The Hasty Hangman*** [1960] PBO.	$1.50	$5.00	$10.00
D-431	Smith, George O./Van Vogt, A. E. - ***Lost In Space/Earth's Last Fortress*** [1960] /PBO. /Cover by Emsh.	$1.50	$5.00	$10.00
D-432	Broward, Donn - ***Convention Queen*** [1960] PBO.	$2.00	$6.00	$12.00
D-433	Powell, Talmage/Bradley, Jack - ***The Smasher/If Hate Could Kill*** [1960] /PBO.	$1.50	$5.00	$10.00
D-434	Verne, Jules - ***The Purchase Of The North Pole*** [1960]	$1.25	$3.75	$7.50
D-435	Ritchie, C. T. - ***Lady In Bondage*** [1960]	$1.25	$3.75	$7.50
D-436	Lutz, Giles A./West, Tom - ***The Challenger/The Phantom Pistoleer*** [1960] PBO.	$1.50	$5.00	$10.00
D-437	Norton, Andre/Wilson, Richard - ***The Sioux Spaceman/And Then The Town Took Off*** [1960] PBO.	$1.50	$5.00	$10.00
D-438	Fogg, Charles - ***The Panic Button*** [1960] PBO.	$1.00	$3.00	$6.00
D-439	Dudley, Owen/Decker, Duane - ***Run If You Can/The Devil's Punchbowl*** [1960] PBO. /Cover by Maguire.	$1.50	$5.00	$10.00
G-440	Hepburn, Andrew - ***Letter Of Marque*** [1960]	$1.00	$3.00	$6.00
D-441	Olson, Lloyd E. - ***Skip Bomber*** [1960] PBO.	$1.00	$3.00	$6.00
D-442	Patterson, Rod/Bickham, Jack M. - ***Rider Of The Rincon/Killer's Paradise*** [1960] PBO.	$1.50	$5.00	$10.00
D-443	Aldiss, Brian W./Wellman, Manley Wade - ***Bow Down To Nul/The Dark Destroyers*** [1960] PBO/.	$1.50	$5.00	$10.00
D-444	Rifkin, Shepard - ***Desire Island*** [1960] PBO.	$1.35	$4.00	$8.00
D-445	McDowell, Emmett - ***Bloodline To Murder/In At The Kill*** [1960] PBO.	$1.50	$5.00	$10.00
D-446	Moore, Edward - ***Flight 685 Is Overdue*** [1960] PBO.	$1.00	$3.00	$6.00
D-447	Flynn, J. M./McKnight, Bob - ***The Hot Chariot/Kiss The Babe Goodbye*** [1960] PBO. Cover by Maguire/.	$1.50	$5.00	$10.00
D-448	Floren, Lee/Cody, Al - ***Pistol-Whipper/Winter Range*** [1960] PBO/.	$1.50	$5.00	$10.00
D-449	Dickson, Gordon R. - ***The Genetic General/Time To Teleport*** [1960] PBO. /Cover by Emsh.	$1.50	$5.00	$10.00
D-450	West, Tom/Hogan, Ray - ***Side Me With Sixes/The Ridgerunner*** [1960] PBO.	$1.50	$5.00	$10.00

		G	VG	F
D-451	Ward, Steve/Martin, Robert - ***Odds Against Linda/A Key To The Morgue*** [1960] PBO/.	$1.50	$5.00	$10.00
D-452	Hensley, Joe L. - ***The Color Of Hate*** [1960] PBO.	$1.35	$4.00	$8.00
D-453	St. Clair, Margaret/Bulmer, Kenneth - ***The Games Of Neith/The Earth Gods Are Coming*** [1960] PBO. Cover by Ed Emsh/.	$1.50	$5.00	$10.00
G-454	Powers, Anne - ***Ride East! Ride West!*** [1960]	$1.35	$4.00	$8.00
D-455	Anthology - ***The Best From Fantasy And Science Fiction #4*** [1960] Cover by Ed Emsh.	$1.50	$5.00	$10.00
D-456	Booth, Edwin - ***Danger Trail/The Desperate Dude*** [1960] /PBO.	$1.50	$5.00	$10.00
D-457	Dick, Philip K./Brunner, John - ***Vulcan's Hammer/The Sky-nappers*** [1960] PBO.	$5.00	$15.00	$30.00
D-458	Derby, Mark - ***Womanhunt*** [1960]	$1.35	$4.00	$8.00
D-459	Olmsted, Howard J./Flynn, J. M. - ***The Hot Diary/Ring Around A Rogue*** [1960] PBO. Cover by Maguire/.	$1.50	$5.00	$10.00
D-460	MacGregor, James - ***When The Ship Sank*** [1960]	$2.00	$6.00	$12.00
D-461	Norton, Andre - ***The Time Traders*** [1960]	$1.35	$4.00	$8.00
D-462	Bickham, Jack M./Latham, John H. - ***The Useless Gun/The Long Fuse*** [1960] PBO. Cover by A. Leslie Ross/.	$1.50	$5.00	$10.00
D-463	Sterling, Stewart - ***Dying Room Only/The Body In The Bed*** [1960] PBO/.	$1.50	$5.00	$10.00
D-464	Shaw, Wilene - ***Tame The Wild Flesh*** [1960] PBO.	$1.35	$4.00	$8.00
D-465	Brunner, John/Grinnell, David - ***The Atlantic Abomination/The Martian Missile*** [1960] PBO/. Cover by Emsh/.	$1.50	$5.00	$10.00
D-466	O'Connor, Richard - ***Wild Bill Hickok*** [1960]	$1.25	$3.75	$7.50
D-467	Anderson, William C. - ***Five, Four, Three, Two, One-PFFTT*** [1960] PBO. Cover by Costanza.	$2.50	$7.50	$15.00
D-468	Russell, Eric Frank - ***Sentinels Of Space*** [1960] Cover by Schulz.	$1.50	$5.00	$10.00
D-469	McKnight, Bob/Powell, Talmage - ***Running Scared/Man-Killer*** [1960] PBO. Cover by Nappi.	$1.50	$5.00	$10.00
D-470	Olson, Gene/Smith, Ben - ***The Man Who Was Morgan/The Maverick*** [1960] PBO/.	$1.50	$5.00	$10.00
D-471	Brunner, John/Sharkey, Jack - ***Sanctuary In The Sky/The Secret Martians*** [1960] PBO. Cover by Basil Gogot/.	$1.50	$5.00	$10.00
D-472	Whittington, Harry - ***A Night For Screaming*** [1960] PBO.	$3.50	$10.00	$20.00
D-473	Taine, John - ***The Greatest Adventure*** [1960]	$1.00	$3.00	$6.00
G-474	Lovelace, Leland - ***Lost Mines And Hidden Treasure*** [1960]	$1.00	$3.00	$6.00
D-475	Ward, Brad - ***The Marshal Of Medicine Bend*** [1960]	$1.25	$3.75	$7.50
D-476	West, Tom/Booth, Edwin - ***Double-Cross Dinero/Lost Valley*** [1960] PBO/.	$1.50	$5.00	$10.00
D-477	Trimble, Louis - ***Love Me And Die/The Duchess Of Skid Row*** [1960] PBO.	$1.50	$5.00	$10.00
D-478	Sutton, Jeff - ***Spacehive*** [1960] PBO.	$1.35	$4.00	$8.00
D-479	Anderson, Poul/Tucker, Wilson - ***Earthman, Go Home!/To The Tombaugh Station*** [1960] PBO.	$1.50	$5.00	$10.00
G-480	Brick, John - ***The Strong Men*** [1960]	$1.00	$3.00	$6.00
D-481	Dinneen, Joseph F. - ***The Biggest Holdup*** [1960]	$1.00	$3.00	$6.00
D-482	Van Vogt, A. E. - ***The Weapon Shops Of Isher*** [1960]	$1.25	$3.75	$7.50
D-483	Bond, J. Harvey/Cassiday, Bruce - ***If Wishes Were Hearses/The Corpse In The Picture Window*** [1961] PBO.	$1.50	$5.00	$10.00
D-484	Cody, Al/Hogan, Ray - ***Dead Man's Spurs/Ambush At Riflestock*** [1961] PBO.	$1.50	$5.00	$10.00

		G	VG	F
D-485	Lowndes, Robert A.W./ Biggle, Jr., Lloyd - ***The Puzzle Planet/The Angry Espers*** [1961] PBO. Cover by Emsh/.	$1.50	$5.00	$10.00
D-486	DeRoo, Edward - ***The Little Caesars*** [1961] PBO.	$3.50	$10.00	$20.00
D-487	Sanders, Leonard - ***Four-Year Hitch*** [1961] PBO.	$1.00	$3.00	$6.00
D-488	Brennan, Dan - ***Third Time Down*** [1961] PBO.	$1.00	$3.00	$6.00
D-489	Arthur, Robert/Miles, John - ***Somebody's Walking Over My Grave/Dally With A Deadly Doll*** [1961] /PBO. /Cover by Bob Maguire.	$1.50	$5.00	$10.00
D-490	Anthology edited by Donald A. Wollheim - ***Adventures On Other Planets*** [1961]	$1.35	$4.00	$8.00
D-491	Leiber, Fritz - ***The Big Time/The Mind Spider And Other Stories*** [1961] PBO. /Cover by Emsh.	$3.00	$9.00	$18.00
D-492	Hopson, William/Lutz, Giles A. - ***Winter Drive/The Wild Quarry*** [1961] PBO.	$1.50	$5.00	$10.00
D-493	Anthology edited by Ellery Queen - ***The Queen's Awards*** [1961] Cover by Bob Maguire.	$1.35	$4.00	$8.00
D-494	White, Leslie Turner - ***Log Jam*** [1961]	$1.00	$3.00	$6.00
D-495	Krasney, Samuel A. - ***A Mania For Blondes*** [1961] PBO. Cover by Rader.	$2.00	$6.00	$12.00
D-496	West, Tom/Lawrence, Steven G. - ***Killer's Canyon/With Blood In Their Eyes*** [1961] PBO.	$1.50	$5.00	$10.00
D-497	Cummings, Ray/Woodcott, Keith - ***Wandl The Invader/I Speak For Earth*** [1961] PBO.	$1.50	$5.00	$10.00
D-498	Norton, Andre - ***Galactic Derelict*** [1961] Cover by Ed Emsh.	$1.35	$4.00	$8.00
D-499	Davis, Frederick C. - ***High Heel Homicide/Night Drop*** [1961] PBO/.	$1.50	$5.00	$10.00
G-500	Hendricks, George D. - ***The Bad Man Of The West*** [1961]	$1.35	$4.00	$8.00
D-501	Clifton, Bud - ***Let Him Go Hang*** [1961] PBO.	$2.50	$7.50	$15.00
D-502	Cody, Al/Lehman, Paul Evan - ***Long Night At Lodgepole/Troubled Range*** [1961] PBO/.	$1.50	$5.00	$10.00
D-503	Nichols, Fan - ***The Girl In The Death Seat*** [1961]	$1.50	$5.00	$10.00
D-504	Verne, Jules - ***Master Of The World*** [1961] Movie tie-in with Vincent Price photo cover.	$2.00	$6.00	$12.00
D-505	Trimble, Louis/Colby, Robert - ***The Surfside Caper/In A Vanishing Room*** [1961] PBO.	$1.50	$5.00	$10.00
D-506	Kroll, Harry Harrison - ***The Brazen Dream*** [1961] PBO.	$1.35	$4.00	$8.00
D-507	Brunner, John/Bulmer, Kenneth - ***Meeting At Infinity/Beyond The Silver Sky*** [1961] PBO. /Cover by Ed Emsh.	$1.50	$5.00	$10.00
D-508	Anthology edited by Donald A. Wollheim - ***More Macabre*** [1961] PBO.	$3.00	$9.00	$18.00
D-509	Norton, Andre - ***Star Hunter/The Beast Master*** [1961] PBO/.	$1.50	$5.00	$10.00
D-510	Whittington, Harry/Bickham, Jack M. - ***The Searching Rider/Hangman's Territory*** [1961] PBO.	$1.50	$5.00	$10.00
D-511	Flynn, J. M./McKnight, Bob - ***One For The Death House/Drop Dead, Please*** [1961] PBO.	$1.50	$5.00	$10.00
D-512	Chidsey, Donald Barr - ***Marooned*** [1961] PBO.	$1.25	$3.75	$7.50
D-513	Ellison, Harlan - ***The Juvies*** [1961] PBO.	$32.00	$110.00	$250.00
D-514	Shirreffs, Gordon D. - ***Hangin' Pards/Ride A Lone Trail*** [1961] PBO.	$1.50	$5.00	$10.00
D-515	Sterling, Stewart/Colby, Robert - ***Five Alarm Funeral/Kill Me A Fortune*** [1961] /PBO.	$1.50	$5.00	$10.00
D-516	Kline, Otis Adelbert - ***The Swordsman Of Mars*** [1961]	$1.35	$4.00	$8.00
D-517	Chandler, A. Bertram/Simak, Clifford - ***Bring Back Yesterday/The Trouble With Tycho*** [1961] PBO.	$1.50	$5.00	$10.00
D-518	Miller, Wade - ***Nightmare Cruise*** [1961] PBO.	$2.00	$6.00	$12.00

		G	VG	F
D-519	Glines, Jr., Carroll & Moseley, Wendell - ***Air Rescue!*** [1961] PBO. Photo cover.	$1.00	$3.00	$6.00
D-520	Shaw, Wilene - ***One Foot In Hell*** [1961] PBO.	$1.35	$4.00	$8.00
D-521	Howe, Margaret - ***The Girl In The White Cap*** [1961]	$ .65	$2.00	$4.00
D-522	Ellson, Hal - ***A Nest Of Fear*** [1961] PBO.	$1.50	$5.00	$10.00
D-523	Scotland, Jay - ***Strike The Black Flag*** [1961] PBO.	$1.00	$3.00	$6.00
D-524	Ames, Jennifer - ***Overseas Nurse*** [1961]	$ .65	$2.00	$4.00
D-525	Leinster, Murray - ***This World Is Taboo*** [1961] PBO.	$1.35	$4.00	$8.00
D-526	Darien, Kim - ***Obsession*** [1961] PBO. Cover by Elaine.	$1.25	$3.75	$7.50
D-527	Norton, Andre - ***Star Guard*** [1961]	$1.35	$4.00	$8.00
D-528	Leinster, Murray - ***The Forgotten Planet*** [1961]	$1.50	$5.00	$10.00
D-529	White, Leslie Turner - ***The Pirate And The Lady*** [1961] PBO. Cover by Chuck Smith.	$1.25	$3.75	$7.50
D-530	Williams, Robert Moore - ***The Day They H-Bombed Los Angeles*** [1961] PBO.	$1.50	$5.00	$10.00
D-531	Kline, Otis Adelbert - ***The Outlaws Of Mars*** [1961]	$1.35	$4.00	$8.00
D-532	Cabot, Isabel - ***Nurse Craig*** [1961] Cover by Koenig.	$ .65	$2.00	$4.00
D-533	Elmo, H. T. - ***Mad. Ave.*** [1961] PBO. Cover by H.T. Elmo.	$2.50	$7.50	$15.00
D-534	Norton, Andre - ***Daybreak - 2250 A.D.*** [1961]	$1.35	$4.00	$8.00
D-535	Cummings, Ray - ***The Shadow Girl*** [1962] PBO. Cover by Emsh.	$3.50	$10.00	$20.00
D-536	Gaddis, Peggy - ***The Nurse And The Pirate*** [1961]	$ .65	$2.00	$4.00
D-537	Wells, H. G. - ***The Island Of Dr. Moreau*** [1961]	$1.25	$3.75	$7.50
D-538	Asimov, Isaac - ***The 1,000 Year Plan*** [1961]	$1.35	$4.00	$8.00
D-539	Fletcher, Mary Mann - ***Psychiatric Nurse*** [1962] PBO. Cover by Nappi.	$ .65	$2.00	$4.00
D-540	Hale, Arlene - ***School Nurse*** [1962] Cover by Nappi.	$ .65	$2.00	$4.00
D-541	Nourse, Alan E. - ***Scavengers In Space*** [1962]	$1.25	$3.75	$7.50
D-542	Norton, Andre - ***The Last Planet*** [1962]	$1.35	$4.00	$8.00
D-543	Myers, Harriet Kathryn - ***Small Town Nurse*** [1962] PBO.	$ .65	$2.00	$4.00
D-544	Long, Frank Belknap - ***Space Station #1*** [1962] Cover by Emsh.	$1.35	$4.00	$8.00
D-545	Roberts, Suzanne - ***Emergency Nurse*** [1962] PBO.	$ .65	$2.00	$4.00
D-546	Norton, Andre - ***The Crossroads Of Time*** [1962]	$1.25	$3.75	$7.50
D-547	Brunner, John - ***The Super Barbarians*** [1962] PBO.	$1.35	$4.00	$8.00
D-548	Owen, Dean - ***End Of The World*** [1962] PBO. Movie tie-in.	$1.50	$5.00	$10.00
D-549	Adams, Tracy - ***Spotlight On Nurse Thorne*** [1962] PBO.	$ .65	$2.00	$4.00
D-550	Anderson, Poul - ***No World Of Their Own*** [1962]	$1.25	$3.75	$7.50
D-551	Bryant, Peter - ***Red Alert*** [1962]	$1.25	$3.75	$7.50
D-552	Libby, Patricia - ***Hollywood Nurse*** [1962] PBO.	$ .65	$2.00	$4.00
D-553	Hodgson, William Hope - ***The House On The Borderland*** [1962]	$2.50	$7.50	$15.00
D-554	Hamill, Ethel - ***Runaway Nurse*** [1962] Cover by Nappi.	$ .65	$2.00	$4.00
D-555	Williamson, Jack - ***The Trial Of Terra*** [1962] PBO. Cover by Emsh.	$1.50	$5.00	$10.00
D-556	MacLeod, Ruth - ***A Nurse For Dr. Sterling*** [1962] PBO.	$ .65	$2.00	$4.00
D-557	Stuart, Florence - ***Hope Wears White*** [1962]	$ .65	$2.00	$4.00
D-558	Roberts, Suzanne - ***Campus Nurse*** [1962] PBO.	$ .65	$2.00	$4.00
D-559	Sears, Jane L. - ***Ski Resort Nurse*** [1962] PBO.	$ .65	$2.00	$4.00
D-560	Boylan, Rowena - ***Medic In Love*** [1962] PBO.	$ .65	$2.00	$4.00
D-561	Rush, Ann - ***Nell Shannon, R.N.*** [1962] PBO.	$ .65	$2.00	$4.00
D-562	Libby, Patricia - ***Cover Girl Nurse*** [1962] PBO.	$ .65	$2.00	$4.00
D-563	Hale, Arlene - ***Leave It To Nurse Kathy*** [1962] PBO.	$ .65	$2.00	$4.00

		G	VG	F
D-564	Myers, Harriet Kathryn - ***Prodigal Nurse*** [1963] PBO.	$ .65	$2.00	$4.00
D-565	Dorien, Ray - ***The Heart Of Dr. Hilary*** [1963]	$ .65	$2.00	$4.00
D-566	Roberts, Suzanne - ***Julie Jones, Cape Canaveral Nurse*** [1963] PBO.	$ .65	$2.00	$4.00
D-567	Moore, Isabel - ***A Challenge For Nurse Melanie*** [1963] PBO.	$ .65	$2.00	$4.00
D-568	Anderson, Poul - ***Star Ways*** [1963]	$1.25	$3.75	$7.50
D-569	Hale, Arlene - ***Dude Ranch Nurse*** [1963] PBO.	$ .65	$2.00	$4.00
D-570	Foreman, L. L. - ***Spanish Grant*** [1963]	$1.25	$3.75	$7.50
D-571	McComb, Katherine - ***Princess Of White Starch*** [1963] PBO.	$ .65	$2.00	$4.00
D-572	Wynne, Frank - ***Arizona Rider*** [1963]	$1.25	$3.75	$7.50
D-573	Brock, Stuart - ***Whispering Canyon*** [1963] Cover by John Leone	$1.25	$3.75	$7.50
D-574	L'Amour, Louis - ***Kilkennny*** [1963] Cover by Bentley.	$2.50	$7.50	$15.00
D-575	Dern, Peggy - ***A Nurse Called Hope*** [1963] Cover by Bob Schinella.	$ .65	$2.00	$4.00
D-576	Dowdell, Dorothy - ***Border Nurse*** [1963]	$ .65	$2.00	$4.00
D-577	Moore, Frances Sarah - ***Legacy Of Love*** [1963] Cover by Bob Schinella.	$ .65	$2.00	$4.00
D-578	Garfield, Brian Wynne - ***The Lawbringers*** [1963]	$1.25	$3.75	$7.50
D-579	Roberts, Suzanne - ***Hootenanny Nurse*** [1963] PBO.	$ .65	$2.00	$4.00
D-580	Hale, Arlene - ***Symptoms Of Love*** [1964] PBO.	$ .65	$2.00	$4.00
D-581	Roberts, Suzanne - ***Co-Ed In White*** [1964] PBO. Cover by Schinella.	$ .65	$2.00	$4.00
D-582	Sargent, Joan - ***My Love An Altar*** [1964]	$ .65	$2.00	$4.00
D-583	Adams, Tracy - ***Hotel Nurse*** [1964] PBO.	$ .65	$2.00	$4.00
D-584	Edwards, Monica - ***Airport Nurse*** [1964] PBO.	$ .65	$2.00	$4.00
D-585	Hale, Arlene - ***Nurse Marcie's Island*** [1964] PBO.	$ .65	$2.00	$4.00
D-586	Grabendike, Barbara - ***San Francisco Nurse*** [1964] PBO.	$ .65	$2.00	$4.00
D-587	Hale, Arlene - ***Nurse Conner Comes Home*** [1964] PBO.	$ .65	$2.00	$4.00
D-588	Constiner, Merle - ***Short-Trigger Man*** [1964] PBO.	$1.25	$3.75	$7.50
D-589	McDonnell, Virginia - ***The Nurse With The Silver Skates*** [1964] PBO.	$ .65	$2.00	$4.00
D-590	Searles, Lin - ***Stampede At Hourglass*** [1964] PBO.	$1.25	$3.75	$7.50
D-591	Fitzgerald, Arlene - ***Northwest Nurse*** [1964] PBO.	$ .65	$2.00	$4.00
D-592	Nye, Nelson - ***Gunslick Mountain*** [1964]	$1.25	$3.75	$7.50
D-593	Roberts, Suzanne - ***Sisters In White*** [1964] PBO.	$ .65	$2.00	$4.00
D-594	Trimble, Louis - ***The Desperate Deputy Of Cougar Hill*** [1965] PBO.	$1.25	$3.75	$7.50
D-595	MacLeod, Ruth - ***Nurse Ann In Surgery*** [1965] PBO. Cover by Schinella	$ .65	$2.00	$4.00
D-596	Hale, Arlene - ***Nurse On The Run*** [1965] PBO.	$ .65	$2.00	$4.00
D-597	Holmes, L. P. - ***The Hardest Man In The Sierras*** [1965] PBO. Cover by Gerald McConnell.	$1.25	$3.75	$7.50
D-598	Hale, Arlene - ***Disaster Area Nurse*** [1965] PBO.	$ .65	$2.00	$4.00
D-599	Libby, Patricia - ***Winged Victory For Nurse Kerry*** [1965] PBO.	$ .65	$2.00	$4.00

Ace F Series. New York: Ace Books.

		G	VG	F
F-101	Sargent, Joan/Howe, Margaret - ***Cruise Nurse/Calling Dr. Merryman*** [1961] Cover by Maguire/.	$ .75	$2.50	$5.00
F-102	Fox, Clayton/McKnight, Bob - ***Never Forget, Never Forgive/The Flying Eye*** [1961]	$1.25	$3.75	$7.50
F-103	Whittington, Harry/Floren, Lee - ***A Trap For Sam Dodge/High Thunder*** [1961] PBO.	$2.00	$6.00	$12.00

Ace F Series, F-102

Ace M Series, M-101

Ace Numbered Series, 51708

		G	VG	F
F-104	Anderson, Poul/Bulmer, Kenneth - ***Mayday Orbit/No Man's World*** [1961]	$1.25	$3.75	$7.50
F-105	Anthology edited by Anthony Boucher - ***The Best From Fantasy And Science Fiction, 5th In Series*** [1961]	$1.00	$3.00	$6.00
F-106	Garfield, Brian/West, Tom - ***Justice At Spanish Flat/The Gun From Nowhere*** [1961] /PBO. /Cover by Jerome Podwil.	$1.25	$3.75	$7.50
F-107	Warwick, Chester/Trinian, John - ***My Pal, The Killer/Scratch A Thief*** [1961] PBO.	$1.25	$3.75	$7.50
F-108	Knight, Damon/Wallis, G. McDonald - ***The Sun Saboteurs/The Light Of Lilith*** [1961] PBO.	$1.25	$3.75	$7.50
F-109	Norton, Andre - ***Storm Over Warlock*** [1961] Cover by Ed Emsh.	$1.00	$3.00	$6.00
F-110	Hogan, Ray/Wells, Lee E. - ***Track The Man Down/Savage Range*** [1961] PBO.	$1.25	$3.75	$7.50
F-111	Martin, Robert/Flynn, J. M. - ***To Have And To Kill/The Girl From Las Vegas*** [1961] /PBO.	$1.25	$3.75	$7.50
F-112	Judson, Jeanne/Dean, Nell Marr - ***Barbara Ames, Private Secretary/Fashions For Carol*** [1961] PBO/. /Cover by Nappi.	$ .65	$2.00	$4.00
F-113	McIntosh, J. T./Fontenay, Charles L. - ***200 Years To Christmas/Rebels Of The Red Planet*** [1961] PBO.	$1.25	$3.75	$7.50
F-114	West, Wallace - ***The Bird Of Time*** [1961]	$1.00	$3.00	$6.00
F-115	Creighton, John/Flora, Fletcher - ***The Blonde Cried Murder/Killing Cousins*** [1961] PBO/.	$1.25	$3.75	$7.50
F-116	Trimble, Louis/Hardin, Clement - ***Deadman Canyon/The Lurking Gun*** [1961] /Cover by Korby.	$1.25	$3.75	$7.50
F-117	Bradley, Marion Z./Chandler, A. Bertram - ***The Door Through Space/Rendezvous On A Lost World*** [1961] PBO. /Cover by Emsh.	$1.25	$3.75	$7.50
F-118	Kamm, Ph.D., Jacob O. - ***Making Profits In The Stock Market*** [1961]	$ .75	$2.50	$5.00
F-119	Dickson, Gordon R. - ***Delusion World/Spacial Delivery*** [1961] PBO.	$1.25	$3.75	$7.50
F-120	Bickham, Jack M./Callahan, John - ***Gunmen Can't Hide/Come In Shooting*** [1961] PBO.	$1.25	$3.75	$7.50
F-121	Nielsen, Helen - ***Woman Missing/Sing Me A Murder*** [1961] PBO/.	$1.25	$3.75	$7.50

		G	VG	F
F-122	Worley, Dorothy/Stone, Patti - ***Dr. Kilbourne Come Home/Calling Nurse Linda*** [1961] /PBO. /Cover by Maguire.	$ .75	$2.50	$5.00
F-123	Silverberg, Robert/Brackett, Leigh - ***Collision Course/The Nemesis From Terra*** [1961] /PBO. /Cover by Ed Emsh.	$1.25	$3.75	$7.50
F-124	Lawrence, Steven G. - ***Slattery/Bullet Welcome For Slattery*** [1961] PBO.	$1.25	$3.75	$7.50
F-125	Flynn, J. M./Diamond, Frank - ***Deep Six/The Widow Maker*** [1961] PBO. Cover by Chuck Smith/.	$1.25	$3.75	$7.50
F-126	Booth, Edwin/Hogan, Ray - ***The Troublemaker/A Marshal For Lawless*** [1962] PBO.	$1.25	$3.75	$7.50
F-127	Laumer, Keith/Bradley, Marion Zimmer - ***Worlds Of The Imperium/Seven From The Stars*** [1962] PBO.	$1.25	$3.75	$7.50
F-128	West, Tom/Trimble, Louis - ***The Buzzard's Nest/Siege At High Meadow*** [1962] PBO.	$1.25	$3.75	$7.50
F-129	Temple, William F. - ***The Three Suns Of Amara/The Automated Goliath*** [1962] PBO.	$1.25	$3.75	$7.50
F-130	Flynn, J. M./Howard, James A. - ***The Screaming Cargo/The Bullet-Proof Martyr*** [1962] PBO/.	$1.25	$3.75	$7.50
F-131	Anthology edited by Anthony Boucher - ***The Best From Fantasy And Science Fiction Sixth Series*** [1962]	$1.00	$3.00	$6.00
F-132	Cappelli, Major Mario - ***Scramble!*** [1962] PBO. Cover by Verne Tossey.	$ .75	$2.50	$5.00
F-133	Chandler, A. Bertram/Brunner, John - ***The Rim Of Space/Secret Agent Of Terra*** [1962] /PBO. /Cover by Ed Emsh.	$1.25	$3.75	$7.50
F-134	Shirreffs, Gordon D./Patterson, Rod - ***Tumbleweed Trigger/A Shooting At Sundust*** [1962] PBO. /Cover by Ron Lesser.	$1.25	$3.75	$7.50
F-135	Brackett, Leigh - ***The Long Tomorrow*** [1962]	$1.00	$3.00	$6.00
F-136	Anthology ed. by Elyse Michaels Sommer - ***Childbirth*** [1962] PBO. Photo cover.	$ .75	$2.50	$5.00
F-137	Miller, R. Dewitt - ***Impossible Yet It Happened!*** [1962]	$ .75	$2.50	$5.00
F-138	Lawrence, Steven G. - ***Walk A Narrow Trail/A Noose For Slattery*** [1962] PBO.	$1.25	$3.75	$7.50
F-139	Anderson, Poul - ***The Makeshift Rocket/Un-Man And Other Novellas*** [1962] PBO.	$1.25	$3.75	$7.50
F-140	St. John, Leonie - ***Love With A Harvard Accent*** [1962] PBO. Cover by Johnson.	$ .65	$2.00	$4.00
F-141	Williams, Robert Moore/Woodcott, Keith - ***The Darkness Before Tomorrow/The Ladder In The Sky*** [1962] PBO.	$1.25	$3.75	$7.50
F-142	Holmes, L. P. - ***Smoky Pass/Wolf Brand*** [1962] PBO.	$1.25	$3.75	$7.50
F-143	Fox, Clayton/McKnight, Bob - ***End Of A Big Wheel/A Stone Around Her Neck*** [1962] PBO.	$1.25	$3.75	$7.50
F-144	Hardin, Clement/Wynne, Frank - ***The Badge Shooters/Massacre Basin*** [1962]	$1.25	$3.75	$7.50
F-145	Silverberg, Robert - ***Next Stop The Stars/The Seed Of Earth*** [1962] PBO.	$1.25	$3.75	$7.50
F-146	Scotland, Jay - ***Sir Scoundrel*** [1962] PBO.	$1.00	$3.00	$6.00
F-147	Norton, Andre - ***Sea Siege/Eye Of The Monster*** [1962] /PBO.	$1.25	$3.75	$7.50
F-148	Whittington, Harry/West, Tom - ***Wild Sky/Dead Man's Double Cross*** [1962]	$2.00	$6.00	$12.00
F-149	DeVet & MacLean/Williams, Robert M. - ***Cosmic Checkmate/King Of The Fourth Planet*** [1962]	$1.25	$3.75	$7.50
F-150	Nye, Nelson - ***Rafe/Hideout Mountain*** [1962] PBO.	$1.25	$3.75	$7.50
F-151	Tyre, Nedra - ***Reformatory Girls*** [1962] Cover by Johnson.	$2.50	$7.50	$15.00
F-152	Shirreffs, Gordon D. - ***Rio Desperado/Voice Of The Gun*** [1962] PBO.	$1.25	$3.75	$7.50

		G	VG	F
F-153	Bradley, Marion Zimmer - ***The Sword Of Aldones/The Planet Savers*** [1962] /Cover by Ed Emsh.	$1.25	$3.75	$7.50
F-154	Van Vogt, A. E. - ***The Wizard Of Linn*** [1962] PBO.	$1.00	$3.00	$6.00
F-155	White, Lionel - ***The Time Of Terror/A Death At Sea*** [1962]	$1.25	$3.75	$7.50
F-156	Burroughs, Edgar Rice - ***At The Earth's Core*** [1962] Cover by Roy Krenkel, Jr.	$1.35	$4.00	$8.00
F-157	Burroughs, Edgar Rice - ***The Moon Maid*** [1962] Cover by Roy Krenkel, Jr.	$1.35	$4.00	$8.00
F-158	Burroughs, Edgar Rice - ***Pellucidar*** [1962] Cover by Roy Krenkel, Jr.	$1.35	$4.00	$8.00
F-159	Burroughs, Edgar Rice - ***The Moon Men*** [1962]	$1.35	$4.00	$8.00
F-160	Hogan, Ray - ***The Shotgunner/New Gun For Kingdom City*** [1962] /Cover by Jerome Podwil.	$1.25	$3.75	$7.50
F-161	Brunner, John/Grinnell, David - ***Times Without Number/Destiny's Orbit*** [1962] PBO/.	$1.25	$3.75	$7.50
F-162	Anthology edited by Anthony Boucher - ***The Best From Fantasy and Science Fiction Seventh Series*** [1962]	$1.00	$3.00	$6.00
F-163	De Leeuw, Adele - ***Doctor Ellen*** [1962]	$ .65	$2.00	$4.00
F-164	Lawrence, Steven G. - ***Slattery's Gun Says No/Longhorns North*** [1962] PBO. /Cover by Rafael DeSoto	$1.25	$3.75	$7.50
F-165	Farmer, Philip Jose - ***Cache From Outer Space/The Celestial Blueprint*** [1962] PBO.	$2.00	$6.00	$12.00
F-166	Simenon, Georges - ***Maigret Has Scruples/Maigret And The Reluctant Witness*** [1962]	$1.25	$3.75	$7.50
F-167	Norton, Andre - ***Catseye*** [1962]	$1.00	$3.00	$6.00
F-168	Burroughs, Edgar Rice - ***Thuvia Maid Of Mars*** [1962] Cover by Roy Krenkel, Jr.	$1.35	$4.00	$8.00
F-169	Burroughs, Edgar Rice - ***Tarzan And The Lost Empire*** [1962] Cover by Frank Frazetta.	$1.35	$4.00	$8.00
F-170	Burroughs, Edgar Rice - ***The Chessmen Of Mars*** [1962] Cover by Roy Krenkel, Jr.	$1.35	$4.00	$8.00
F-171	Burroughs, Edgar Rice - ***Tanar Of Pellucidar*** [1962] Cover by Roy Krenkel, Jr.	$1.35	$4.00	$8.00
F-172	Lutz, Giles A./West, Tom - ***Gun Rich/Battling Buckaroos*** [1962]	$1.25	$3.75	$7.50
F-173	Delany, Samuel R./White, James - ***The Jewels Of Aptor/Second Ending?*** [1962] PBO. Cover by Gaughan/.	$1.50	$5.00	$10.00
F-174	Gordon, Rex - ***First Through Time*** [1962] PBO.	$1.00	$3.00	$6.00
F-175	Berckman, Evelyn - ***Lament For Four Brides*** [1962]	$1.00	$3.00	$6.00
F-176	Hogan, Ray/Stevens, Dan J. - ***The Outside Gun/Gun Trap At Bright Water*** [1963] PBO. Cover by Schinella/.	$1.25	$3.75	$7.50
F-177	Carr, Terry/Williams, Robert Moore - ***Warlord Of Kor/The Star Wasps*** [1963] PBO.	$1.25	$3.75	$7.50
F-178	Anthology edited by Donald A. Wollheim - ***More Adventures On Other Planets*** [1963] PBO. Cover by Powers.	$1.00	$3.00	$6.00
F-179	Burroughs, Edgar Rice - ***Pirates Of Venus*** [1963] Cover by Roy Krenkel, Jr.	$1.35	$4.00	$8.00
F-180	Burroughs, Edgar Rice - ***Tarzan At The Earth's Core*** [1963] Cover by Frank Frazetta.	$1.35	$4.00	$8.00
F-181	Burroughs, Edgar Rice - ***The Mastermind Of Mars*** [1963] Cover by Roy Krenkel, Jr.	$1.35	$4.00	$8.00
F-182	Burroughs, Edgar Rice - ***The Monster Men*** [1963] Cover by Frank Frazetta.	$1.35	$4.00	$8.00
F-183	Norton, Andre - ***The Defiant Agents*** [1963] Cover by Ed Emsh.	$1.00	$3.00	$6.00

		G	VG	F
F-184	Nye, Nelson - ***The Kid From Lincoln County/Death Valley Slim*** [1963]	$1.25	$3.75	$7.50
F-185	Vance, Jack - ***The Five Gold Bands/The Dragon Masters*** [1963] /PBO. /Cover by Jack Gaughan.	$1.50	$5.00	$10.00
F-186	Turner, William O./Trimble, Louis - ***The High Hander/Wild Horse Range*** [1963]	$1.25	$3.75	$7.50
F-187	Wallis, G. McDonald/Brackett, Leigh - ***Legend Of Lost Earth/Alpha Centauri Or Die!*** [1963] Cover by Powers/	$1.25	$3.75	$7.50
F-188	Nowlan, Philip Francis - ***Armageddon 2419 A.D.*** [1963] Cover by Ed Emsh.	$1.00	$3.00	$6.00
F-189	Burroughs, Edgar Rice - ***Tarzan The Invincible*** [1963] Cover by Frank Frazetta.	$1.35	$4.00	$8.00
F-190	Burroughs, Edgar Rice - ***A Fighting Man Of Mars*** [1963] Cover by Roy Krenkel, Jr.	$1.35	$4.00	$8.00
F-191	Verne, Jules - ***Journey To The Center Of The Earth*** [1963]	$ .75	$2.50	$5.00
F-192	Norton, Andre - ***Star Born*** [1963] Cover by Ed Emsh.	$ .75	$2.50	$5.00
F-193	Burroughs, Edgar Rice - ***The Son Of Tarzan*** [1963] Cover by Frank Frazetta.	$1.35	$4.00	$8.00
F-194	Burroughs, Edgar Rice - ***Tarzan Triumphant*** [1963] Cover by Roy Krenkel, Jr.	$1.35	$4.00	$8.00
F-195	Temple, William F./Silverberg, Robert - ***Battle On Venus/The Silent Invaders*** [1963] PBO. /Cover by Ed Emsh.	$1.25	$3.75	$7.50
F-196	Whittington, Harry - ***Prairie Raiders/Dry Gulch Town*** [1963] PBO. /Cover by Schinella.	$2.00	$6.00	$12.00
F-197	Norton, Andre - ***Witch World*** [1963] PBO. Cover by Jack Gaughan.	$1.00	$3.00	$6.00
F-198	Simenon, Georges - ***The Short Cases Of Inspector Maigret*** [1963]	$1.00	$3.00	$6.00
F-199	Delany, Samuel R./Woodcott, Keith - ***Captives Of The Flame/The Psionic Menace*** [1963] PBO. Cover art by Gaughan/Emsh.	$1.50	$5.00	$10.00
F-200	Wynne, Frank/West, Tom - ***The Big Snow/Triggering Texan*** [1963]	$1.25	$3.75	$7.50
F-201	MacTyre, Paul - ***Doomsday, 1999*** [1963]	$1.00	$3.00	$6.00
F-202	Berckman, Evelyn - ***The Hovering Darkness*** [1963]	$1.00	$3.00	$6.00
F-203	Burroughs, Edgar Rice - ***The Beasts Of Tarzan*** [1963] Cover by Frank Frazetta.	$1.35	$4.00	$8.00
F-204	Burroughs, Edgar Rice - ***Tarzan And The Jewels Of Opar*** [1963] Cover by Frank Frazetta.	$1.35	$4.00	$8.00
F-205	Burroughs, Edgar Rice - ***Tarzan And The City Of Gold*** [1963] Cover by Frank Frazetta.	$1.35	$4.00	$8.00
F-206	Burroughs, Edgar Rice - ***Jungle Tales Of Tarzan*** [1963] Cover by Frank Frazetta.	$1.35	$4.00	$8.00
F-207	Norton, Andre - ***The Stars Are Ours!*** [1963]	$ .75	$2.50	$5.00
F-208	Holmes, L. P. - ***Side Me At Sundown/The Buzzards Of Rocky Pass*** [1963] PBO. Cover by Bob Schinella/.	$1.25	$3.75	$7.50
F-209	Bulmer, Kenneth/Anderson, Poul - ***The Wizard Of Starship Poseidon/Let The Spacemen Beware!*** [1963] PBO. Cover by Jack Gaughan/.	$1.25	$3.75	$7.50
F-210	Bryant, Peter - ***Red Alert*** [1963]	$ .75	$2.50	$5.00
F-211	Kline, Otis Adelbert - ***Planet Of Peril*** [1963] Cover by Roy Krenkel, Jr.	$1.35	$4.00	$8.00
F-212	Burroughs, Edgar Rice - ***Tarzan And The Lion Man*** [1963] Cover by Frank Frazetta.	$1.35	$4.00	$8.00

		G	VG	F
F-213	Burroughs, Edgar Rice - ***The Land That Time Forgot*** [1963] Cover by Roy Krenkel, Jr.	$1.35	$4.00	$8.00
F-214	Burchardt, Bill/Trimble, Louis - ***The Wildcatters/The Man From Colorado*** [1963] PBO.	$1.25	$3.75	$7.50
F-215	Roberts, Jane/Brunner, John - ***The Rebellers/Listen! The Stars!*** [1963] PBO. Cover art by Jack Gaughan/Ed Emsh.	$1.25	$3.75	$7.50
F-216	Asimov, Isaac - ***The Man Who Upset The Universe*** [1963]	$1.00	$3.00	$6.00
F-217	Anthology edited by Anthony Boucher - ***The Best From Fantasy And Science Fiction 8th Series*** [1963]	$1.00	$3.00	$6.00
F-218	Churchill, Allen - ***They Never Came Back*** [1963] Cover by Scianna.	$ .75	$2.50	$5.00
F-219	Makow, Henry - ***Ask Henry*** [1963] Photo cover.	$ .75	$2.50	$5.00
F-220	Burroughs, Edgar Rice - ***The People That Time Forgot*** [1963] Cover by Roy Krenkel, Jr.	$1.35	$4.00	$8.00
F-221	Burroughs, Edgar Rice - ***Lost On Venus*** [1963] Cover by Frank Frazetta.	$1.35	$4.00	$8.00
F-222	Sutton, Jeff - ***First On The Moon*** [1963] Cover by Ed Emsh.	$1.00	$3.00	$6.00
F-223	Williams, Robert Moore/Laumer, Keith - ***Flight From Yesterday/Envoy To New Worlds*** [1963] PBO. Cover by Jack Gaughan/Ed Emsh.	$1.25	$3.75	$7.50
F-224	Nye, Nelson - ***The Seven Six-Gunners/Bancroft's Banco*** [1963]	$1.25	$3.75	$7.50
F-225	Piper, H. Beam - ***Space Viking*** [1963] PBO.	$1.00	$3.00	$6.00
F-226	Norton, Andre - ***Huon Of The Horn*** [1963] Cover by Jack Gaughan.	$1.00	$3.00	$6.00
F-227	Brunner, John - ***The Space-Time Juggler/The Astronauts Must Not Land*** [1963] PBO. Covers by Jack Gaughan.	$1.25	$3.75	$7.50
F-228	Howarth, David - ***We Die Alone*** [1963] Cover by Verne Tossey.	$ .75	$2.50	$5.00
F-229	Trimble, Louis/McKnight, Bob - ***The Dead And The Deadly/Homicide Handicap*** [1963] PBO.	$1.25	$3.75	$7.50
F-230	Hogan, Ray - ***Trail Of The Fresno Kid*** [1963]	$1.00	$3.00	$6.00
F-231	Norton, Andre - ***Star Gate*** [1963] Cover by Ed Emsh.	$ .75	$2.50	$5.00
F-232	Burroughs, Edgar Rice - ***The Land Of Hidden Men*** [1963] Cover by Roy Krenkel, Jr.	$1.35	$4.00	$8.00
F-233	Burroughs, Edgar Rice - ***Out Of Time's Abyss*** [1963] Cover by Roy Krenkel, Jr.	$1.35	$4.00	$8.00
F-234	Burroughs, Edgar Rice - ***The Eternal Savage*** [1963] Cover by Roy Krenkel, Jr.	$1.35	$4.00	$8.00
F-235	Burroughs, Edgar Rice - ***The Lost Continent*** [1963] Cover by Frank Frazetta.	$1.35	$4.00	$8.00
F-236	Norton, Andre - ***The Time Traders*** [1963]	$ .75	$2.50	$5.00
F-237	Chandler, A. Bertram - ***Beyond The Galactic Rim/The Ship From Outside*** [1963] PBO. Cover by Ed Emsh/.	$1.25	$3.75	$7.50
F-238	Payne, Stephen/Shirreffs, Gordon D. - ***Brand Him Outlaw/Quicktrigger*** [1963] Cover by Giac/.	$1.25	$3.75	$7.50
F-239	Simak, Clifford D. - ***Time And Again*** [1963] Cover by Jack Gaughan.	$1.00	$3.00	$6.00
F-240	Wells, H. G. - ***When The Sleeper Wakes*** [1963] Cover by Ed Emsh.	$1.00	$3.00	$6.00
F-241	Williamson, Jack & Gunn, James E. - ***Star Bridge*** [1963]	$ .75	$2.50	$5.00
F-242	Brunner, John - ***Castaways World/The Rites Of OHE*** [1963] PBO.	$1.25	$3.75	$7.50
F-243	Norton, Andre - ***Lord Of Thunder*** [1963] Cover by Alex Schomburg.	$ .75	$2.50	$5.00
F-244	Hogan, Ray/Booth, Edwin - ***Last Gun At Cabresto/Valley Of Violence*** [1963] PBO/.	$1.25	$3.75	$7.50

		G	VG	F
F-245	Burroughs, Edgar Rice - ***Back To The Stone Age*** [1963] Cover by Roy Krenkel, Jr. and Frank Frazetta.	$1.35	$4.00	$8.00
F-246	Von Harbou, Thea - ***Metropolis*** [1963] Cover by Jack Gaughan.	$1.00	$3.00	$6.00
F-247	Burroughs, Edgar Rice - ***Carson Of Venus*** [1963] Cover by Frank Frazetta.	$1.35	$4.00	$8.00
F-248	Cummings, Ray - ***Beyond The Stars*** [1963] Cover by Jack Gaughan.	$1.00	$3.00	$6.00
F-249	DeCamp, L. Sprague - ***The Hand Of ZEI/The Search For ZEI*** [1963] Cover by Ed Emsh	$1.25	$3.75	$7.50
F-250	Cord, Barry/West, Tom - ***The Masked Gun/Gallows Gulch*** [1963]	$1.25	$3.75	$7.50
F-251	Dick, Philip K. - ***The Game-Players Of Titan*** [1963] PBO. Cover by Jack Gaughan	$4.00	$12.50	$25.00
F-252	Clifford, John - ***The Shooting Of Storey James*** [1963]	$1.00	$3.00	$6.00
F-253	Knox, Calvin M./VanVogt, A. E. - ***One Of Our Asteroids Is Missing/The Twisted Men*** [1964] PBO. /Cover by Jack Gaughan.	$1.25	$3.75	$7.50
F-254	Heuman, William/Ketchum, Philip - ***Hardcase Halloran/The Ghost Riders*** [1964]	$1.25	$3.75	$7.50
F-255	High, Philip E. - ***The Prodigal Sun*** [1964] PBO.	$1.00	$3.00	$6.00
F-256	Burroughs, Edgar Rice - ***Land Of Terror*** [1964] Cover by Frank Frazetta.	$1.35	$4.00	$8.00
F-257	Pratt, Fletcher - ***Alien Planet*** [1964] Cover by Ed Emsh	$1.00	$3.00	$6.00
F-258	Burroughs, Edgar Rice - ***The Cave Girl*** [1964] Cover by Roy Krenkel, Jr.	$1.35	$4.00	$8.00
F-259	Kline, Otis Adelbert - ***Prince Of Peril*** [1964] Cover by Roy Krenkel, Jr.	$1.35	$4.00	$8.00
F-260	Garfield, Brian/Trimble, Louis - ***Trail Drive/Trouble At Gunsight*** [1964] /PBO.	$1.25	$3.75	$7.50
F-261	Delany, Samuel R./Williams, Robert Moore - ***The Towers Of Toron/The Lunar Eye*** [1964] PBO. Cover by Ed Emsh/.	$1.50	$5.00	$10.00
F-262	Adams, Clifton - ***Reckless Men*** [1964]	$1.00	$3.00	$6.00
F-263	Norton, Andre - ***Web Of The Witch World*** [1964] PBO. Cover by Jack Gaughan	$1.00	$3.00	$6.00
F-264	Elliott, Ben/West, Tom - ***Contract In Cartridges/Don't Cross My Line*** [1964] PBO.	$1.25	$3.75	$7.50
F-265	Vance, Jack - ***Son Of The Tree/The House Of Iszm*** [1964] PBO. Covers by Jack Gaughan.	$1.50	$5.00	$10.00
F-266	Elston, Allan Vaughan - ***Roundup On The Yellowstone*** [1964]	$1.00	$3.00	$6.00
F-267	Anthology edited by Robert P. Mills - ***The Best From Fantasy And Science Fiction Ninth Series*** [1964] Cover by Ed Emsh.	$1.00	$3.00	$6.00
F-268	Burroughs, Edgar Rice - ***Escape On Venus*** [1964] Cover by Roy Krenkel, Jr.	$1.35	$4.00	$8.00
F-269	Rosny, J. H. - ***Quest Of The Dawn Man*** [1964] Cover by Harry J. Shaare.	$1.00	$3.00	$6.00
F-270	Burroughs, Edgar Rice - ***The Mad King*** [1964] Cover by Frank Frazetta.	$1.35	$4.00	$8.00
F-271	Hamilton, Edmond - ***Outside The Universe*** [1964] PBO.	$1.00	$3.00	$6.00
F-272	Payne, Stephen/Hogan, Ray - ***No Job For A Cowboy/The Man From Barranca Negra*** [1964]	$1.25	$3.75	$7.50
F-273	Bradley, Marion Zimmer - ***The Dark Intruder & Other Stories/Falcons Of Narabedla*** [1964] PBO. Cover art by Jack Gaughan/.	$1.25	$3.75	$7.50
F-274	Piper, H. Beam - ***The Cosmic Computer*** [1964]	$1.00	$3.00	$6.00

		G	VG	F
F-275	Leinster, Murray/High, Philip E. - ***The Duplicators/No Truce With Terra*** [1964] Cover by Jack Gaughan/.	$1.25	$3.75	$7.50
F-276	Vance, William E./Wynne, Brian - ***The Wolf Slayer/Mr. Sixgun*** [1964]	$1.25	$3.75	$7.50
F-277	Brunner, John - ***To Conquer Chaos*** [1964] PBO. Cover by Ed Emsh.	$1.00	$3.00	$6.00
F-278	Leighton, Frances Spatz - ***Patty Goes To Washington*** [1964] TV tie-in with Patty Duke photo cover	$ .75	$2.50	$5.00
F-279	North, Andrew - ***Sargasso Of Space*** [1964] Cover by Ed Emsh.	$ .75	$2.50	$5.00
F-280	Burroughs, Edgar Rice - ***Savage Pellucidar*** [1964] Cover by Frank Frazetta.	$1.35	$4.00	$8.00
F-281	Benoit, Pierre - ***Atlantida*** [1964]	$ .75	$2.50	$5.00
F-282	Burroughs, Edgar Rice - ***Beyond The Farthest Star*** [1964] Cover by Frank Frazetta.	$1.35	$4.00	$8.00
F-283	Rohmer, Sax - ***The Day The World Ended*** [1964]	$2.50	$7.50	$15.00
F-284	Searles, Lin/Smith, Ben - ***Border Passage/The Homesteader*** [1964] PBO/.	$1.25	$3.75	$7.50
F-285	Leiber, Fritz/Bulmer, Kenneth - ***Ships To The Stars/The Million Year Hunt*** [1964] PBO. Cover by Jack Gaughan/Ed Emsh.	$1.35	$4.00	$8.00
F-286	Bosworth, Jim - ***The Long Way North*** [1964]	$1.00	$3.00	$6.00
F-287	Norton, Andre - ***Key Out Of Time*** [1964]	$ .75	$2.50	$5.00
F-288	Sherman, Hal - ***Fishing For Laughs*** [1964] PBO. Cover by the author. Cartoon book.	$1.50	$5.00	$10.00
F-289	Purdom, Tom/Bulmer, Kenneth - ***I Want The Stars/Demons' World*** [1964] PBO. Cover by Ed Emsh/.	$1.25	$3.75	$7.50
F-290	Olsen, D. B. - ***The Night Of The Bowstring*** [1964]	$1.00	$3.00	$6.00
F-291	North, Andrew - ***Plague Ship*** [1964]	$ .75	$2.50	$5.00
F-292	West, Tom/Shirreffs, Gordon - ***The Man At Rope's End/The Hidden Rider Of Dark Mountain*** [1964] PBO.	$1.25	$3.75	$7.50
F-293	Tubb, E. C. - ***Moon Base*** [1964] PBO.	$1.00	$3.00	$6.00
F-294	Kline, Otis Adelbert - ***The Port Of Peril*** [1964] Cover by Roy Krenkel, Jr.	$1.35	$4.00	$8.00
F-295	Van Vogt, A. E. - ***The World Of Null-A*** [1964] Cover by Ed Emsh.	$ .75	$2.50	$5.00
F-296	Arnold, Edwin L. - ***Gulliver Of Mars*** [1964] Cover by Frank Frazetta.	$1.00	$3.00	$6.00
F-297	Kuttner, Henry - ***Valley Of The Flame*** [1964] PBO. Cover by Ed Emsh.	$2.50	$7.50	$15.00
F-298	Nye, Nelson - ***Treasure Trail From Tucson/Sudden Country*** [1964] PBO.	$1.25	$3.75	$7.50
F-299	Brunner, John/Fox, Gardner F. - ***Endless Shadow/The Arsenal Of Miracles*** [1964] PBO.	$1.35	$4.00	$8.00
F-300	Garfield, Brian Wynne - ***Vultures In The Sun*** [1964]	$1.00	$3.00	$6.00
F-301	Dick, Philip K. - ***The Simulacra*** [1964] PBO. Cover by Ed Emsh.	$4.00	$12.50	$25.00
F-302	Wynne, Frank - ***Dragoon Pass*** [1964]	$1.00	$3.00	$6.00
F-303	Bradley, Marion Zimmer - ***The Bloody Sun*** [1964] PBO.	$1.25	$3.75	$7.50
F-304	Farley, Ralph Milne - ***The Radio Beasts*** [1964] PBO. Cover by Ed Emsh.	$1.25	$3.75	$7.50
F-305	Howard, Robert E. - ***Almuric*** [1964] PBO. Cover by Jack Gaughan.	$1.35	$4.00	$8.00
F-306	Moore, C.L. and Kuttner, Henry - ***Earth's Last Citadel*** [1964] PBO. Cover by Alex Schomburg.	$1.25	$3.75	$7.50

		G	VG	F
F-307	Fox, Gardner F. - ***Warrior Of Llarn*** [1964] PBO. Cover by Frank Frazetta.	$1.35	$4.00	$8.00
F-308	Norton, Andre - ***Judgment On Janus*** [1964] Cover by Alex Schomburg.	$1.00	$3.00	$6.00
F-309	Dick, Philip K. - ***Clans Of The Alphane Moon*** [1964] PBO.	$3.50	$10.00	$20.00
F-310	Norton, Andre - ***Galactic Derelict*** [1964] Cover by Ed Emsh.	$1.00	$3.00	$6.00
F-311	Anthology edited by Donald A. Wollheim - ***Swordsmen In The Sky*** [1964] PBO. Cover by Frank Frazetta.	$1.00	$3.00	$6.00
F-312	Farley, Ralph Milne - ***The Radio Planet*** [1964] PBO. Cover by John Schoenherr.	$1.25	$3.75	$7.50
F-313	Cummings, Ray - ***A Brand New World*** [1964] PBO.	$1.00	$3.00	$6.00
F-314	Schmitz, James H. - ***The Universe Against Her*** [1964] PBO.	$1.00	$3.00	$6.00
F-315	Norton, Andre - ***The Beast Master*** [1964]	$ .75	$2.50	$5.00
F-316	McCaig, Robert - ***The Burntwood Men*** [1964]	$1.00	$3.00	$6.00
F-317	White, James - ***The Escape Orbit*** [1965] PBO. Cover by Jack Gaughan.	$1.00	$3.00	$6.00
F-318	Hall, Austin - ***The Spot Of Life*** [1964] PBO.	$1.00	$3.00	$6.00
F-319	Hamilton, Edmond - ***Crashing Suns*** [1964]	$1.00	$3.00	$6.00
F-320	Woodcott, Keith - ***The Martian Sphinx*** [1965] PBO.	$1.00	$3.00	$6.00
F-321	Kline, Otis Adelbert - ***Maza Of The Moon*** [1965] Cover by Frank Frazetta.	$1.35	$4.00	$8.00
F-322	Delany, Samuel R. - ***City Of A Thousand Suns*** [1965] PBO. Cover by Jack Gaughan.	$1.50	$5.00	$10.00
F-323	Norton, Andre - ***Daybreak - 2250 A.D.*** [1965]	$ .75	$2.50	$5.00
F-324	Garfield, Brian Wynne - ***Apache Canyon*** [1965]	$1.00	$3.00	$6.00
F-325	Norton, Andre - ***Ordeal In Otherwhere*** [1965]	$ .75	$2.50	$5.00
F-326	Carter, Lin - ***The Wizard Of Lemuria*** [1965] PBO. Cover by Gray Morrow.	$1.00	$3.00	$6.00
F-327	Kuttner, Henry - ***The Dark World*** [1965] PBO. Cover by Gray Morrow.	$2.50	$7.50	$15.00
F-328	Smith, Edward E. - ***The Galaxy Primes*** [1965] PBO. Cover by Ed Valigursky.	$1.00	$3.00	$6.00
F-329	Norton, Andre - ***Storm Over Warlock*** [1965] Cover by Ed Emsh.	$ .75	$2.50	$5.00
F-330	Davidson, Avram - ***What Strange Stars And Skies*** [1965]	$ .75	$2.50	$5.00
F-331	Wilson, Gahan - ***Graveside Manner*** [1965] PBO. Cartoon book.	$2.50	$7.50	$15.00
F-332	Norton, Andre - ***Three Against The Witch World*** [1965] PBO. Cover by Jack Gaughan.	$1.00	$3.00	$6.00
F-333	De Camp, L. Sprague - ***Rogue Queen*** [1965] Cover by Gray Morrow.	$1.35	$4.00	$8.00
F-334	Levie, Rex Dean - ***The Insect Warriors*** [1965]	$1.25	$3.75	$7.50
F-335	Williams, Robert Moore - ***The Second Atlantis*** [1965] Cover by Gray Morrow.	$1.00	$3.00	$6.00
F-336	Haycox, Ernest - ***Sixgun Duo*** [1965]	$1.00	$3.00	$6.00
F-337	Dick, Philip K. - ***Dr. Bloodmoney Or How We Got Along After The Bomb*** [1965] PBO.	$3.50	$10.00	$20.00
F-338	Anthology - ***Ace Crossword Puzzle Book No. 1*** [1965]	$6.00	$20.00	$40.00
F-339	Hale, Arlene - ***Private Duty For Nurse Scott*** [1965] PBO.	$ .65	$2.00	$4.00
F-340	Shelley, John & David - ***The Relentless Rider*** [1965] PBO.	$1.00	$3.00	$6.00
F-341	Roberts, Suzanne - ***A Prize For Nurse Darci*** [1965] PBO.	$ .65	$2.00	$4.00
F-342	Piper, H. Beam - ***Lord Kalvan Of Otherwhen*** [1965]	$1.00	$3.00	$6.00
F-343	Cummings, Ray - ***The Exile Of Time*** [1965] Cover by Alex Schomburg.	$1.00	$3.00	$6.00

		G	VG	F
F-344	Kuttner, Henry - ***The Well Of The Worlds*** [1965] PBO. Cover by Alex Schomburg.	$1.50	$5.00	$10.00
F-345	Flint, Homer Eon - ***The Lord Of Death And The Queen Of Life*** [1965] PBO. Cover by Jack Gaughan.	$1.00	$3.00	$6.00
F-346	Campbell, John W. - ***The Black Star Passes*** [1965] Cover by Jerome Podwil.	$1.00	$3.00	$6.00
F-347	Wright, Lan - ***The Last Hope Of Earth*** [1965] PBO.	$1.00	$3.00	$6.00
F-348	Nye, Nelson - ***Guns Of Horse Prairie*** [1965]	$1.00	$3.00	$6.00
F-349	Roberts, Suzanne - ***Celebrity Suite Nurse*** [1965] PBO.	$ .65	$2.00	$4.00
F-350	Bradley, Marion Simmer - ***Star Of Danger*** [1965] Cover by Jack Gaughan.	$ .75	$2.50	$5.00
F-351	Trimble, Louis - ***The Holdout In The Diablos*** [1965] PBO.	$1.00	$3.00	$6.00
F-352	Hale, Arlene - ***Nurse On Leave*** [1965] PBO.	$ .65	$2.00	$4.00
F-353	Davidson, Avram - ***Rogue Dragon*** [1965] Cover by Jack Gaughan.	$1.00	$3.00	$6.00
F-354	Fox, Gardner F. - ***The Hunter Out Of Time*** [1965] Cover by Gray Morrow.	$1.25	$3.75	$7.50
F-355	Flint, Homer Eon - ***The Devolutionist And The Emancipatrix*** [1965] PBO. Cover by Jerome Podwil.	$1.00	$3.00	$6.00
F-356	Kuttner, Henry - ***The Time Axis*** [1965] Cover by Alex Schomburg.	$1.25	$3.75	$7.50
F-357	Norton, Andre - ***Year Of The Unicorn*** [1965] PBO. Cover by Jack Gaughan.	$1.00	$3.00	$6.00
F-358	Vance, William - ***The Wild Riders Of Savage Valley*** [1965] PBO.	$1.00	$3.00	$6.00
F-359	Heath, Sharon - ***Jungle Nurse*** [1965]	$ .65	$2.00	$4.00
F-360	Foreman, L. L. - ***Rawhiders Of The Brasada*** [1965] PBO.	$1.00	$3.00	$6.00
F-361	Brunner, John - ***The Day Of The Star Cities*** [1965] PBO. Cover by Jack Gaughan.	$1.00	$3.00	$6.00
F-362	Roberts, Suzanne - ***The Two Dr. Barlowes*** [1965] PBO.	$ .65	$2.00	$4.00
F-363	Cummings, Ray - ***Tama Of The Light Country*** [1965] PBO. Cover by Jerome Podwil.	$1.25	$3.75	$7.50
F-364	Campbell, John W. - ***The Mightiest Machine*** [1965] Cover by Jerome Podwil.	$1.00	$3.00	$6.00
F-365	Norton, Andre - ***Night Of Masks*** [1965] Cover by Gray Morrow.	$1.00	$3.00	$6.00
F-366	Norton, Andre - ***The Last Planet*** [1965]	$ .75	$2.50	$5.00
F-367	Farmer, Philip Jose - ***The Maker Of Universes*** [1965] PBO. Cover by Jack Gaughan.	$2.00	$6.00	$12.00
F-368	Hale, Arlene - ***Chicago Nurse*** [1965]	$ .65	$2.00	$4.00
F-369	Peeples, Samuel Anthony - ***The Lobo Horseman*** [1965]	$1.00	$3.00	$6.00
F-370	Ward, Brad - ***The Man From Andersonville*** [1965]	$1.00	$3.00	$6.00
F-371	Hale, Arlene - ***Camp Nurse*** [1965]	$ .65	$2.00	$4.00
F-372	Smith, Edward E. - ***Spacehounds Of IPC*** [1965] Cover by Ed Valigursky.	$1.00	$3.00	$6.00
F-373	Cory, Howard L. - ***The Sword Of Lankor*** [1966] PBO. Cover by Jerome Podwil.	$1.00	$3.00	$6.00
F-374	Sutton, Jeff - ***The Atom Conspiracy*** [1966] Cover by Jack Gaughan.	$1.00	$3.00	$6.00
F-375	Heinlein, Robert A. - ***The Worlds Of Robert A. Heinlein*** [1966] PBO. Cover by Jack Gaughan.	$1.00	$3.00	$6.00
F-376	Patten, Lewis B. - ***The Odds Against Circle L*** [1966] PBO.	$1.00	$3.00	$6.00
F-377	Dick, Philip K. - ***The Crack In Space*** [1966] PBO. Cover by Jerome Podwil.	$3.50	$10.00	$20.00

		G	VG	F
F-378	Fletcher, Mary Mann - ***Danger - Nurse At Work*** [1966] PBO.	$ .65	$2.00	$4.00
F-379	Herbert, Frank - ***The Green Brain*** [1966] PBO. Cover by Gerald McConnell.	$1.00	$3.00	$6.00
F-380	Hoffman, Lee - ***The Legend Of Blackjack Sam*** [1966] Cover by Gray Morrow.	$1.00	$3.00	$6.00
F-381	Heath, Sharon - ***Nurse At Shadow Manor*** [1966] PBO.	$ .65	$2.00	$4.00
F-382	Aldiss, Brian W. - ***Bow Down To Nul*** [1966]	$1.00	$3.00	$6.00
F-383	Carter, Lin - ***Thongor Of Lemuria*** [1966] PBO. Cover by Gray Morrow.	$1.00	$3.00	$6.00
F-384	Holmes, L. P. - ***The Savage Hours*** [1966] PBO.	$1.00	$3.00	$6.00
F-385	Hale, Arlene - ***Emergency For Nurse Selena*** [1966]	$ .65	$2.00	$4.00
F-386	Norton, Andre - ***The Time Traders*** [1966]	$ .75	$2.50	$5.00
F-387	Hale, Arlene - ***Mountain Nurse*** [1966]	$ .65	$2.00	$4.00
F-388	Delany, Samuel R. - ***Babel-17*** [1966] Cover by Jerome Podwil.	$2.00	$6.00	$12.00
F-389	MacDonald, William Colt - ***"Shoot Him On Sight!"*** [1966]	$1.00	$3.00	$6.00
F-390	Vance, Jack - ***The Languages Of Pao*** [1966] Cover by Gray Morrow.	$1.25	$3.75	$7.50
F-391	Norton, Andre - ***The Crossroads Of Time*** [1966]	$ .75	$2.50	$5.00
F-392	Petaja, Emil - ***Saga Of Lost Earths*** [1966] PBO. Cover by Jack Gaughan.	$1.00	$3.00	$6.00
F-393	Zelazny, Roger - ***This Immortal*** [1966] PBO. Cover by Gray Morrow.	$1.25	$3.75	$7.50
F-394	Everett, Gail - ***Journey For A Nurse*** [1966] PBO.	$ .65	$2.00	$4.00
F-395	Nye, Nelson - ***Iron Hand*** [1966] PBO.	$1.00	$3.00	$6.00
F-396	Bulmer, Kenneth - ***Worlds For The Taking*** [1966] PBO. Cover by Hoot von Zitzewitz.	$1.00	$3.00	$6.00
F-397	Roberts, Willo Davis - ***Nurse Kay's Conquest*** [1966] PBO.	$ .65	$2.00	$4.00
F-398	Russell, Eric Frank - ***Somewhere A Voice*** [1966] Cover by Kelly Freas.	$1.00	$3.00	$6.00
F-399	Fox, Gardner F. - ***Thief Of Llarn*** [1966] PBO. Cover by Gray Morrow.	$1.25	$3.75	$7.50
F-400	Kline, Otis Adelbert - ***Jan Of The Jungle*** [1966] Cover by Stephen Holland.	$1.35	$4.00	$8.00
F-401	Constiner, Merle - ***Outrage At Bearskin Forks*** [1966]	$1.00	$3.00	$6.00
F-402	Smith, Cordwainer - ***Quest Of The Three Worlds*** [1966] Cover by Gray Morrow.	$1.00	$3.00	$6.00
F-403	Zelazny, Roger - ***The Dream Master*** [1966] PBO. Cover by Kelly Freas.	$1.35	$4.00	$8.00
F-404	Adams, Clifton - ***The Brabhorn Bounty*** [1966]	$1.00	$3.00	$6.00
F-405	Roberts, Suzanne - ***Vietnam Nurse*** [1966] PBO.	$ .65	$2.00	$4.00
F-406	Cummings, Ray - ***Tama, Princess Of Mercury*** [1966] Cover by Jerome Podwil.	$1.00	$3.00	$6.00
F-407	Swann, Thomas Burnett - ***Day Of The Minotaur*** [1966] PBO. Cover by Gray Morrow.	$1.25	$3.75	$7.50
F-408	Norton, Andre - ***The Sioux Spaceman*** [1966]	$ .75	$2.50	$5.00
F-409	Searles, Lin - ***Cliff Rider*** [1966] PBO.	$1.00	$3.00	$6.00
F-410	Hale, Arlene - ***Lake Resort Nurse*** [1966] PBO.	$ .65	$2.00	$4.00
F-411	Foreman, L. L. - ***The Mustang Trail*** [1966]	$1.00	$3.00	$6.00
F-412	Farmer, Philip Jose - ***The Gates Of Creation*** [1966] PBO. Cover by Gray Morrow.	$2.00	$6.00	$12.00
F-413	Heath, Sharon - ***A Vacation For Nurse Dean*** [1966]	$ .65	$2.00	$4.00
F-414	Petaja, Emil - ***The Star Mill*** [1966] PBO. Cover by Jack Gaughan.	$1.00	$3.00	$6.00
F-415	Wynne, Brian - ***The Bravos*** [1966] PBO.	$1.00	$3.00	$6.00

		G	VG	F
F-416	Gordon, Rex - ***Utopia Minus X*** [1966] PBO.	$1.00	$3.00	$6.00
F-417	Roberts, Willo Davis - ***Once A Nurse*** [1966] PBO.	$ .65	$2.00	$4.00
F-418	Nye, Nelson - ***Single Action*** [1967] PBO.	$1.00	$3.00	$6.00
F-419	Roberts, Suzanne - ***Rangeland Nurse*** [1967]	$ .65	$2.00	$4.00
F-420	Jones, Neil R. - ***The Planet Of The Double Sun*** [1967] PBO. Cover by Gray Morrow. Professor Jameson #1.	$1.00	$3.00	$6.00
F-421	Clark, Curt - ***Anarchaos*** [1967] PBO. Cover by Lynch.	$1.25	$3.75	$7.50
F-422	Brackett, Leigh - ***The Sword Of Rhiannon*** [1967] Cover by John Schoenherr.	$1.00	$3.00	$6.00
F-423	Patten, Lewis B. - ***Giant On Horseback*** [1967]	$1.00	$3.00	$6.00
F-424	Hale, Arlene - ***Community Nurse*** [1967]	$ .65	$2.00	$4.00
F-425	Anderson, Poul - ***World Without Stars*** [1967] PBO. Cover by Kelly Freas.	$1.00	$3.00	$6.00
F-426	Dickson, Gordon R. - ***The Genetic General*** [1967]	$1.00	$3.00	$6.00
F-427	Delany, Samuel R. - ***The Einstein Intersection*** [1967] PBO. Cover by Jack Gaughan.	$2.00	$6.00	$12.00
F-428	MacDonald, William Colt - ***Mascarada Pass*** [1967]	$1.00	$3.00	$6.00
F-429	Dick, Philip K. - ***The World Jones Made*** [1967] Cover by Kelly Freas.	$1.50	$5.00	$10.00
F-430	Hale, Arlene - ***Nurse On The Beach*** [1967]	$ .65	$2.00	$4.00

Ace G Series. New York: Ace Books.

		G	VG	F
G-501	Armstrong, Charlotte - ***Incident At A Corner/The Unsuspected*** [1962]	$ .75	$2.50	$5.00
G-502	O'Connor, Richard - ***Pat Garrett*** [1963]	$ .65	$2.00	$4.00
G-503	Curtiss, Ursula - ***The Stairway/The Face Of The Tiger*** [1963] /Cover by Johnson.	$ .75	$2.50	$5.00
G-506	Disney, Doris Miles - ***Did She Fall Or Was She Pushed?/Black Mail*** [1963]	$ .75	$2.50	$5.00
G-508	Fenisong, Ruth - ***But Not Forgotten/The Schemers*** [1963]	$ .75	$2.50	$5.00
G-509	Holding, Elisabeth Saxany - ***The Virgin Huntress/The Innocent Mrs. Duff*** [1963]	$ .75	$2.50	$5.00
G-510	Armstrong, Charlotte - ***The Case Of The Weird Sisters*** [1963]	$ .65	$2.00	$4.00
G-511	Armstrong, Charlotte - ***The Chocolate Cobweb/Who's Been Sitting In My Chair?*** [1963]	$ .75	$2.50	$5.00
G-512	Holding, Elisabeth Saxany - ***The Girl Who Had To Die/Blank Wall*** [1963]	$ .75	$2.50	$5.00
G-513	Armstrong, Charlotte - ***Then Came Two Women/Catch-As-Catch-Can*** [1963]	$ .75	$2.50	$5.00
G-514	Armstrong, Charlotte - ***Something Blue*** [1963]	$ .65	$2.00	$4.00
G-515	Rawicz, Slavomir - ***The Long Walk*** [1963]	$ .65	$2.00	$4.00
G-518	Reilly, Helen - ***The Opening Door/Follow Me*** [1963]	$ .75	$2.50	$5.00
G-519	Holding, Elisabeth Saxany - ***The Old Battle Axe/The Obstinate Murderer*** [1963]	$ .75	$2.50	$5.00
G-520	Scotland, Jay - ***Arena*** [1963] PBO. Cover by Maguire.	$ .65	$2.00	$4.00
G-521	Armstrong, Charlotte - ***Mischief/The Better To Eat You*** [1963]	$ .75	$2.50	$5.00
G-522	Challis, George - ***The Firebrand*** [1963]	$ .65	$2.00	$4.00
G-523	Curtiss, Ursula - ***Hours To Kill/The Forbidden Garden*** [1963]	$ .75	$2.50	$5.00
G-524	Holding, Elisabeth Saxany - ***Who's Afraid?/Widow's Mite*** [1963] Cover by Al Brule/.	$ .75	$2.50	$5.00
G-525	Lyon, Dana - ***Spin The Web Tight/The Tentacles*** [1963]	$ .75	$2.50	$5.00
G-526	Armstrong, Charlotte - ***The Mark Of The Hand/The Dream Walker*** [1963] PBO/.	$ .75	$2.50	$5.00
G-527	Challis, George - ***The Bait And The Trap*** [1963]	$ .65	$2.00	$4.00

		G	VG	F
G-528	Reilly, Helen - ***Certain Sleep/Ding Dong Bell*** [1963] /Cover by Schinella.	$ .75	$2.50	$5.00
G-529	Disney, Doris Miles - ***Unappointed Rounds/Mrs. Meeker's Money*** [1963]	$ .75	$2.50	$5.00
G-530	Holding, Elisabeth Saxany - ***Net Of Cobwebs/The Unfinished Crime*** [1963]	$ .75	$2.50	$5.00
G-531	Reilly, Helen - ***The Canvas Dagger/Not Me, Inspector*** [1963]	$ .75	$2.50	$5.00
G-532	Scotland, Jay - ***Traitors' Legion*** [1963] PBO. Cover by Maguire.	$ .75	$2.50	$5.00
G-533	Armstrong, Charlotte - ***The Black-Eyed Stranger/The One-Faced Girl*** [1963] /PBO.	$ .75	$2.50	$5.00
G-534	Holding, Elisabeth Saxany - ***Kill Joy/Speak Of The Devil*** [1963] /Cover by Rudy Nappi.	$ .75	$2.50	$5.00
G-535	Lyon, Dana - ***The Lost One/The Frightened Child*** [1963] Cover by Bob Schinella/Rudy Nappi.	$ .75	$2.50	$5.00
G-536	Reilly, Helen - ***The Day She Died*** [1963]	$ .65	$2.00	$4.00
G-537	Ruppelt, Edward J. - ***The Report On U.F.O.'s*** [1963]	$ .50	$1.50	$3.00
G-538	Norton, Andre - ***Shadow Hawk*** [1963]	$ .65	$2.00	$4.00
G-539	Lawrence, Hilda - ***The House/Composition For Four Hands*** [1963] Cover by Bob Schinella/	$ .75	$2.50	$5.00
G-540	Armstrong, Charlotte - ***A Little Less Than Kind*** [1963]	$ .65	$2.00	$4.00
G-541	Potts, Jean - ***The Evil Wish*** [1964]	$ .65	$2.00	$4.00
G-542	Albrand, Martha - ***Meet Me Tonight*** [1964]	$ .65	$2.00	$4.00
G-543	Davis, Mildred - ***They Buried A Man/The Dark Place*** [1964]	$ .75	$2.50	$5.00
G-544	Fenisong, Ruth - ***The Wench Is Dead*** [1964]	$ .65	$2.00	$4.00
G-545	Lyon, Dana - ***The Trusting Victim*** [1964]	$ .65	$2.00	$4.00
G-546	Reilly, Helen - ***Compartment K*** [1964]	$ .65	$2.00	$4.00
G-547	Hall, Austin & Flint, Homer Eon - ***The Blind Spot*** [1964]	$ .65	$2.00	$4.00
G-548	O'Grady, Rohan - ***Let's Kill Uncle*** [1964]	$ .65	$2.00	$4.00
G-549	Curtiss, Ursula - ***The Iron Cobweb*** [1964]	$ .65	$2.00	$4.00
G-550	DuBois, Theodora - ***The Listener*** [1964]	$ .65	$2.00	$4.00
G-551	Anthology - ***World's Best Science Fiction: 1965*** [1964] PBO. Photo cover.	$1.00	$3.00	$6.00
G-552	DuBois, Theodora - ***Shannon Terror*** [1964]	$ .65	$2.00	$4.00
G-553	Avallone, Michael - ***The Thousand Coffins Affair (Man From U.N.C.L.E. #1)*** [1965] PBO. TV tie-in with photo cover.	$1.00	$3.00	$6.00
G-554	Holden, Genevieve - ***The Velvet Target*** [1965]	$ .65	$2.00	$4.00
G-555	Curtiss, Ursula - ***The Wasp*** [1965] Cover by Bob Schinella.	$ .65	$2.00	$4.00
G-557	Curtiss, Ursula - ***Out Of The Dark*** [1965]	$ .65	$2.00	$4.00
G-558	Holden, Genevieve - ***Something's Happened To Kate*** [1965]	$ .65	$2.00	$4.00
G-559	Albrand, Barbara - ***After Midnight*** [1965]	$ .65	$2.00	$4.00
G-560	Whittington, Harry - ***The Doomsday Affair (The Man From U.N.C.L.E. #2)*** [1965] PBO. TV tie-in with photo cover.	$1.25	$3.75	$7.50
G-561	Curtiss, Ursula - ***Widow's Web*** [1965]	$ .65	$2.00	$4.00
G-562	McCloy, Helen - ***The Long Body*** [1965]	$ .65	$2.00	$4.00
G-563	Albrand, Martha - ***A Day In Monte Carlo*** [1965]	$ .65	$2.00	$4.00
G-564	Oram, John - ***The Copenhagen Affair (The Man From U.N.C.L.E. #3)*** [1965] PBO. TV tie-in with photo cover.	$1.00	$3.00	$6.00
G-565	Curtiss, Ursula - ***The Deadly Climate*** [1965]	$ .65	$2.00	$4.00
G-566	Charles, Theresa - ***Lady In The Mist*** [1965]	$ .65	$2.00	$4.00
G-567	Charles, Theresa - ***The Shrouded Tower*** [1965]	$ .65	$2.00	$4.00
G-568	Marlett, Melba - ***Escape While I Can*** [1965]	$ .65	$2.00	$4.00
G-569	Howarth, David - ***We Die Alone*** [1965]	$ .65	$2.00	$4.00

		G	VG	F
G-570	Garner, Alan - ***The Weirdstone Of Brisingamen*** [1965] Cover by Jack Gaughan	$1.25	$3.75	$7.50
G-571	McDaniel, David - ***The Dagger Afair (The Man From U.N.C.L.E. #4)*** [1965] PBO. TV tie-in with photo cover	$1.00	$3.00	$6.00
G-572	Packer, Joy - ***The Man In The Mews*** [1965]	$ .65	$2.00	$4.00
G-573	West, Tom/Constiner, Merle - ***Rattlesnake Range/Top Gun From The Dakotas*** [1966] PBO.	$ .75	$2.50	$5.00
G-574	Leguin, Ursula K./Davidson, Avram - ***Rocannon's World/The Kar-Chee Reign*** [1966] PBO. Cover by McConnel/Gaughan	$ .75	$2.50	$5.00
G-575	Summerton, Margaret - ***Quin's Hide*** [1966]	$ .65	$2.00	$4.00
G-576	Davidson, Avram/Rackham, John - ***Clash Of Star Kings/Danger From Vega*** [1966] Covers by Jack Gaughan.	$ .75	$2.50	$5.00
G-577	Spellman, Roger/Hogan, Ray - ***Big Man From The Brazos/Killer's Gun*** [1966]	$ .75	$2.50	$5.00
G-578	Paradise, Mary - ***Shadow Of A Witch*** [1966]	$ .65	$2.00	$4.00
G-579	Trimble, Louis/Wells, Lee E. - ***Showdown In The Cayuse/Ride A Dim Trail*** [1966]	$ .75	$2.50	$5.00
G-580	Nunes, Claude/Reynolds, Mack - ***Inherit The Earth/Dawnman Planet*** [1966] Cover by Hanke/Gaughan	$ .75	$2.50	$5.00
G-581	Phillifent, John T. - ***The Mad Scientist Affair (The Man From U.N.C.L.E. #5)*** [1966] PBO. TV tie-in with photo cover	$1.00	$3.00	$6.00
G-582	Verne, Jules - ***Journey To The Center Of The Earth*** [1966]	$ .65	$2.00	$4.00
G-583	Garratt, Marie - ***Festival Of Darkness*** [1966]	$ .65	$2.00	$4.00
G-584	Vance, William E./Harden, Clement - ***Son Of A Desperado/The Ruthless Breed*** [1966] PBO. /Cover by Bob Schinella.	$ .75	$2.50	$5.00
G-585	Campbell, John W. - ***The Planeteers/The Ultimate Weapon*** [1966] Cover by Gaughan/McConnell.	$ .75	$2.50	$5.00
G-586	Chester, William L. - ***Hawk Of The Wilderness*** [1966] Cover by Jerome Podwil.	$1.00	$3.00	$6.00
G-587	Wynne, Frank/Hoffman, Lee - ***The Wolf Pack/Gunfight At Laramie*** [1966]	$ .75	$2.50	$5.00
G-588	Baxter, John/Carter, Lin - ***The Off-Worlders/The Star Magicians*** [1966] PBO. Covers by Freas/Gaughan.	$ .75	$2.50	$5.00
G-589	Summerton, Margaret - ***Ring Of Mischief*** [1966]	$ .65	$2.00	$4.00
G-590	McDaniel, David - ***The Vampire Affair (The Man From U.N.C.L.E. #6)*** [1966] TV tie-in with photo cover	$1.00	$3.00	$6.00
G-591	Stevens, Dan J./West, Tom - ***Stage To Durango/Hangrope Heritage*** [1966]	$ .75	$2.50	$5.00
G-592	Brunner, John/Rackham, John - ***A Planet Of Your Own/The Beasts Of Kohl*** [1966] PBO. Covers by Jack Gaughan.	$ .75	$2.50	$5.00
G-593	Paradise, Mary - ***Face Of An Angel*** [1966]	$ .65	$2.00	$4.00
G-594	Runyon, Charles W. - ***The Bloody Jungle*** [1966] PBO. Cover by Gerald McConnell.	$ .65	$2.00	$4.00
G-595	Norton, Andre - ***Quest Crosstime*** [1966] Cover by Jack Gaughan.	$ .65	$2.00	$4.00
G-596	Sullivan, Reese/Callahan, John - ***The Demanding Land/Hackett's Feud*** [1966]	$ .75	$2.50	$5.00
G-597	Disch, Thomas M./LeGuin, Ursula K. - ***Mankind Under The Leash/Planet Of Exile*** [1966] PBO. Covers by Kelly Freas/Jerome Podwil	$ .75	$2.50	$5.00
G-598	James, Barbara - ***Bright Deadly Summer*** [1966]	$ .65	$2.00	$4.00
G-599	Norton, Andre - ***Star Guard*** [1966]	$ .65	$2.00	$4.00
G-600	Leslie, Peter - ***The Radioactive Camel Affair (The Man From U.N.C.L.E. #7)*** [1966] PBO. TV tie-in with photo cover	$1.00	$3.00	$6.00

		G	VG	F
G-601	Shelley, John L./Hogan, Ray - ***The Return Of Bullet Benton/The Hellsfire Lawman*** [1966] PBO.	$ .75	$2.50	$5.00
G-602	Dick, Philip K./Cory, Howard L. - ***The Unteleported Man/The Mind Monsters*** [1966] PBO. Covers by Kelly Freas/Harry Schaare.	$2.50	$7.50	$15.00
G-603	Wilson, Carolyn - ***The Scent Of Lilacs*** [1966]	$ .65	$2.00	$4.00
G-604	Shelton, Jess - ***Daktari*** [1966] TV tie-in with photo cover.	$ .65	$2.00	$4.00
G-605	Maddock, Larry - ***The Flying Saucer Gambit (Agent Of T.E.R.R.A. #1)*** [1966] PBO. Cover by Leone.	$ .65	$2.00	$4.00
G-606	Carter, Lin/Rackham, John - ***The Man Without A Planet/Time To Live*** [1966] PBO. Covers by Peter Michael/Jack Gaughan.	$ .75	$2.50	$5.00
G-607	West, Tom/Constiner, Merle - ***Bitter Brand/Rain Of Fire*** [1966]	$ .75	$2.50	$5.00
G-609	High, Philip E./Chandler, A. Bertram - ***Reality Forbidden/Contraband From Otherspace*** [1967] PBO. Covers by Jack Gaughan/Kelly Freas.	$ .75	$2.50	$5.00
G-610	Shelley, John L./Wynne, Frank - ***The Siege At Gunhammer/The Lusty Breed*** [1967]	$ .75	$2.50	$5.00
G-611	Anthology edited by Avram Davidson - ***The Best From Fantasy And Science-Fiction*** [1967] 12th Series.	$1.00	$3.00	$6.00
G-612	Hayes, Leal - ***Harlequin House*** [1967] PBO.	$ .65	$2.00	$4.00
G-613	McDaniel, David - ***The Monster Wheel Affair (The Man From U.N.C.L.E. #8)*** [1967] PBO. TV tie-in with photo cover.	$1.00	$3.00	$6.00
G-614	Richmond, Walt & Leigh/Shaw, Jr., Fred - ***Shock Wave/Envoy To The Dog Star*** [1967] Cover by Hoot/.	$ .75	$2.50	$5.00
G-615	Hogan, Ray/Vance, William - ***Legacy Of The Slash M/Tracker*** [1967] PBO/.	$ .75	$2.50	$5.00
G-616	Bradley, Marion Zimmer - ***Souvenir Of Monique*** [1967] PBO.	$ .75	$2.50	$5.00
G-617	Leslie, Peter - ***The Diving Dames Affair (The Man From U.N.C.L.E. #9)*** [1967] TV tie-in with photo cover.	$1.00	$3.00	$6.00
G-618	Munn, H. Warner/Petaja, Emil - ***The Ship From Atlantis/The Stolen Sun*** [1967] PBO. Covers by Jack Gaughan.	$ .75	$2.50	$5.00
G-619	Payne, Stephen/Cord, Barry - ***Room To Swing A Loop/Gallows Ghost*** [1967]	$ .75	$2.50	$5.00
G-620	Maddock, Larry - ***The Golden Goddess Gambit (Agent Of T.E.R.R.A. #2)*** [1967] PBO. Cover by Leone.	$ .65	$2.00	$4.00
G-621	Kellier, Elizabeth - ***Matravers Hall*** [1967]	$ .65	$2.00	$4.00
G-622	Hardin, Clement/West, Tom - ***The Paxman Feud/Showdown At Serano*** [1967]	$ .75	$2.50	$5.00
G-623	High, Philip E./Rackham, John - ***These Savage Futurians/The Double Invaders*** [1967] PBO. Cover by Gray Morrow/.	$ .75	$2.50	$5.00
G-624	Davenport, Francine - ***The Secret Of The Bayou*** [1967]	$ .65	$2.00	$4.00
G-625	Bulmer, Kenneth - ***To Outrun Doomsday*** [1967] PBO. Cover by Kelly Freas.	$ .75	$2.50	$5.00
G-626	Le Guin, Ursula K. - ***City Of Illusions*** [1967] PBO. Cover by Jack Gaughan.	$ .75	$2.50	$5.00
G-627	Leiber, Fritz - ***The Big Time*** [1967]	$ .65	$2.00	$4.00
G-628	Adams, Clifton - ***Shorty*** [1967]	$ .65	$2.00	$4.00
G-629	Kellier, Elizabeth - ***Nurse Missing*** [1967]	$ .50	$1.50	$3.00
G-630	Norton, Andre - ***Warlock Of The Witch World*** [1967] PBO. Cover by Jack Gaughan.	$ .65	$2.00	$4.00
G-631	Jones, Neil R. - ***The Sunless World*** [1967] PBO. Cover by Gray Morrow. Professor Jameson #2.	$ .65	$2.00	$4.00
G-632	Chandler, A. Bertram/Reynolds, Mack - ***Nebula Alert/The Rival Rigelians*** [1967] PBO. Covers by Kelly Freas/Peter Michael...	$ .75	$2.50	$5.00

		G	VG	F
G-633	Lee, Wayne C./Stevens, Dan J. - ***Return To Gun Point/The Killers From Owl Creek*** [1967] PBO.	$ .75	$2.50	$5.00
G-634	Anderson, Poul - ***War Of The Wing-Men*** [1967] Cover by Ed Emsh.	$ .65	$2.00	$4.00
G-635	McNamara, Lena Brooke - ***Pilgrim's End*** [1967] PBO.	$ .65	$2.00	$4.00
G-636	Holly, J. Hunter - ***The Assassination Affair (The Man From U.N.C.L.E. #10)*** [1967] PBO. TV tie-in with photo cover.	$1.00	$3.00	$6.00
G-637	Dick, Philip K. & Nelson, Ray - ***The Ganymede Takeover*** [1967] PBO. Cover by Jack Gaughan.	$2.50	$7.50	$15.00
G-638	Booth, Edwin/Constiner, Merle - ***A Time To Shoot It Out/The Action At Redstone Creek*** [1967]	$ .75	$2.50	$5.00
G-639	Hamilton, Edmond - ***The Weapon From Beyond*** [1967] Cover by Jack Gaughan. Starwolf #1.	$ .65	$2.00	$4.00
G-640	Swann, Thomas Burnett - ***The Weirwoods*** [1967] PBO. Cover by Gray Morrow.	$1.00	$3.00	$6.00
G-641	Williamson, Jack - ***Bright New Universe*** [1967] PBO. Cover by John Schoenherr.	$ .75	$2.50	$5.00
G-642	Hollingshead, Kyle/Trimble, Louis - ***Echo Of A Texas Rifle/Standoff At Massacre Buttes*** [1967] PBO. Cover by Jerome Podwil/.	$ .75	$2.50	$5.00
G-643	Vicary, Jean - ***Saverstall*** [1967] PBO.	$ .65	$2.00	$4.00
G-644	Maddock, Larry - ***The Emerald Elephant Gambit (Agent Of T.E.R.R.A. #3)*** [1967] PBO. Cover by Sergio Leone.	$ .65	$2.00	$4.00
G-645	Strattton, Thomas - ***The Invisibility Affair (The Man From U.N.C.L.E. #11)*** [1967] TV tie-in with photo cover.	$1.00	$3.00	$6.00
G-646	Norton, Andre - ***The X Factor*** [1967] Cover by Jack Gaughan.	$ .65	$2.00	$4.00
G-647	Leinster, Murray - ***S.O.S. From Three Worlds*** [1967] PBO. Cover by Jack Gaughan.	$ .65	$2.00	$4.00
G-648	Vance, William/West, Tom - ***The Raid At Crazyhorse/Crossfire At Barbed M*** [1967]	$ .75	$2.50	$5.00
G-649	Brunner, John - ***The World Swappers*** [1967] Cover by Kelly Freas.	$ .65	$2.00	$4.00
G-650	Jones, Neil R. - ***Space War*** [1967] Cover by Gray Morrow. Professor Jameson #3.	$ .65	$2.00	$4.00
G-651	Salter, Elizabeth - ***Once Upon A Tombstone*** [1967] Cover by Schinella.	$ .65	$2.00	$4.00
G-653	Hale, Arlene - ***Doctor's Daughter*** [1967]	$ .50	$1.50	$3.00
G-654	Norton, Andre - ***Catseye*** [1967]	$ .65	$2.00	$4.00
G-655	Norton, Andre - ***Witch World*** [1967] Cover by Jack Gaughan.	$ .65	$2.00	$4.00
G-656	Jakes, John - ***When The Star Kings Die*** [1967] PBO. Cover by Jack Gaughan.	$1.00	$3.00	$6.00
G-657	Nye, Nelson - ***Rider On The Roan*** [1967] PBO. Cover by McConnell.	$ .75	$2.50	$5.00
G-658	Randall, Rona - ***Leap In The Dark*** [1967] Cover by Marchetti.	$ .65	$2.00	$4.00
G-659	Hardin, Clement/Callahan, John - ***The Oxbow Deed/Kincaid*** [1967] PBO.	$ .75	$2.50	$5.00
G-660	Van Vogt, A. E. - ***The Universe Maker*** [1967] Cover by Jack Gaughan.	$ .65	$2.00	$4.00
G-661	Vance, Jack - ***Big Planet*** [1967]	$ .65	$2.00	$4.00
G-662	Kyle, Elisabeth - ***The Second Mally Lee*** [1967] Cover by Leone.	$ .65	$2.00	$4.00
G-663	Stratton, Thomas - ***The Mind Twisters Affair (Man From U.N.C.L.E. #12)*** [1967] PBO. TV tie-in with photo cover.	$1.00	$3.00	$6.00
G-664	Brunner, John - ***Born Under Mars*** [1967] PBO. Cover by Schoenherr.	$ .65	$2.00	$4.00

		G	VG	F
G-665	Foreman, L. L. - ***The Silver Flame*** [1967] Cover by Gerald McConnel.	$ .65	$2.00	$4.00
G-666	Kellier, Elizabeth - ***Wayneston Hospital*** [1967]	$ .50	$1.50	$3.00
G-667	McDaniel, David - ***The Arsenal Out Of Time*** [1967] PBO. Cover by Kelly Freas.	$1.00	$3.00	$6.00
G-668	Wynne, Brian/Hogan, Ray - ***A Badge For A Badman/Devil's Butte*** [1967]	$ .75	$2.50	$5.00
G-669	Brackett, Leigh - ***The Coming Of The Terrans*** [1967] PBO. Cover by Gray Morrow.	$1.00	$3.00	$6.00
G-670	McDaniel, David - ***The Rainbow Affair (The Man From U.N.C.L.E. #13)*** [1967] PBO. TV tie-in with photo cover.	$1.00	$3.00	$6.00
G-671	Patten, Lewis B. - ***The Star And The Gun*** [1967] PBO. Cover by McConnell.	$ .65	$2.00	$4.00
G-672	Hale, Arlene - ***University Nurse*** [1967] PBO.	$ .50	$1.50	$3.00
G-673	Geston, Mark S. - ***Lords Of The Starship*** [1967] PBO. Cover by John Schoenherr.	$ .65	$2.00	$4.00
G-675	White, James - ***The Secret Visitors*** [1967] Cover by Bob Schinella.	$ .65	$2.00	$4.00
G-676	Buckingham, Nancy - ***Storm In The Mountains*** [1967] PBO. Cover by Bob Schinella.	$ .65	$2.00	$4.00
G-677	Knight, Damon - ***Turning On*** [1967] Cover by Gaughan.	$ .65	$2.00	$4.00
G-678	Foreman, L. L. - ***The Plundering Gun*** [1967] PBO. Cover by Gerald McConnell.	$ .65	$2.00	$4.00
G-679	Roberts, Willo Davis - ***Nurse At Mystery Villa*** [1967]	$ .50	$1.50	$3.00
G-680	Bulmer, Kenneth - ***Cycle Of Nemesis*** [1967] PBO. Cover by Kelly Freas.	$ .65	$2.00	$4.00
G-681	Jones, Neil R. - ***Twin Worlds*** [1967] PBO. Cover by Gray Morrow. Professor Jameson #4.	$ .65	$2.00	$4.00
G-682	Callahan, John/West, Tom - ***Ride For Vengeance/Bandit Brand*** [1967]	$ .75	$2.50	$5.00
G-683	Brackett, Leigh - ***The Big Jump*** [1967] Cover by Jeff Jones.	$ .65	$2.00	$4.00
G-684	James, Barbara - ***Beauty That Must Die*** [1967] Cover by Lou Marchetti.	$ .65	$2.00	$4.00
G-685	Purdum, Herbert - ***My Brother John*** [1967]	$ .65	$2.00	$4.00
G-686	Dorien, Ray - ***The Odds Against Nurse Pat*** [1967]	$ .50	$1.50	$3.00
G-687	Allen, Eric/Stevens, Dan J. - ***The Hanging At Whiskey Smith/Stranger In Rampart*** [1968] PBO. Cover by Schaare/. .	$ .75	$2.50	$5.00
G-688	Vance, Jack - ***City Of The Chasch*** [1968] PBO. Cover by Jeff Jones. Planet Of Adventures #1.	$ .65	$2.00	$4.00
G-689	Davies Frederic - ***The Cross Of Gold Affair (The Man From U.N.C.L.E. #14)*** [1968] PBO. TV tie-in with photo cover.	$1.00	$3.00	$6.00
G-690	Norton, Andre - ***The Beast Master*** [1968]	$ .65	$2.00	$4.00
G-691	Norton, Andre - ***Lord Of Thunder*** [1968] Cover by Alex Schomburg.	$ .65	$2.00	$4.00
G-692	Kline, Otis Adelbert - ***The Swordsman Of Mars*** [1968]	$1.00	$3.00	$6.00
G-693	Kline, Otis Adelbert - ***Outlaws Of Mars*** [1968]	$1.00	$3.00	$6.00
G-694	Swann, Thomas Burnett - ***The Dolphin And The Deep*** [1968] PBO. Cover by Gray Morrow.	$ .65	$2.00	$4.00
G-696	Hale, Arlene - ***Emergency Call*** [1968] PBO.	$ .50	$1.50	$3.00
G-697	Anderson, Poul - ***We Claim These Stars*** [1968] Cover by Kelly Freas.	$ .65	$2.00	$4.00
G-699	Woolrich, Cornell - ***The Bride Wore Black*** [1968]	$ .65	$2.00	$4.00
G-700	Salter, Elizabeth - ***Will To Survive*** [1968]	$ .65	$2.00	$4.00
G-701	Hamilton, Edmond - ***The Closed Worlds*** [1968] PBO. Cover by Jack Gaughan. Starwolf #2.	$1.00	$3.00	$6.00

		G	VG	F
G-702	Johnston, William - ***Miracle At San Tanco*** [1968] PBO. TV photo cover.	$ .65	$2.00	$4.00
G-703	Norton, Andre - ***Victory On Janus*** [1968] Cover by Michael Gilbert.	$ .65	$2.00	$4.00
G-705	Constiner, Merle/Cord, Barry - ***Killers' Corral/The Long Wire*** [1967]	$ .75	$2.50	$5.00
G-706	Delaney, Samuel R. - ***The Jewels Of Aptor*** [1968] Cover by Jeff Jones.	$ .65	$2.00	$4.00
G-707	Marlow, Edwina - ***The Master Of Phoenix Hall*** [1968] PBO.	$ .75	$2.50	$5.00
G-709	Brunner, John - ***Bedlam Planet*** [1968] PBO. Cover by Jeff Jones.	$ .75	$2.50	$5.00
G-712	Edited by Boucher & McComas - ***The Best From Fantasy And SF (3rd Series)*** [1968] Cover by Emsh.	$1.00	$3.00	$6.00
G-713	Edited by Boucher - ***The Best From Fantasy And SF (4th Series)*** [1968]	$1.00	$3.00	$6.00
G-714	Edited by Boucher - ***The Best From Fantasy And SF (5th Series)*** [1968]	$1.00	$3.00	$6.00
G-715	Edited by Boucher - ***The Best From Fantasy And SF (6th Series)*** [1968]	$1.00	$3.00	$6.00
G-716	Norton, Andre - ***Web Of The Witch Word*** [1968] Cover by Jack Gaughan.	$ .65	$2.00	$4.00
G-717	Norton, Andre - ***Daybreak-2250 A.D.*** [1968]	$ .65	$2.00	$4.00
G-718	Dick, Philip K. - ***Solar Lottery*** [1968] Cover by Jack Gaughan.	$1.35	$4.00	$8.00
G-719	Jones, Neil R. - ***Doomsday On Ajiat*** [1968] PBO. Cover by Gray Morrow. Professor Jameson #5	$ .75	$2.50	$5.00
G-720	Wynne, Brian - ***Brand Of The Gun*** [1968] PBO. Cover by Prezio.	$ .65	$2.00	$4.00
G-721	Jenison, Don P./Hoffman, Lee - ***The Silver Concho/Dead Man's Gold*** [1968] PBO. Covers by Prezio/Podwil.	$ .75	$2.50	$5.00
G-723	Norton, Andre - ***Star Hunter/Voodoo Planet*** [1968] Cover by Jeff Jones.	$ .75	$2.50	$5.00
G-724	Farmer, Philip Jose - ***A Private Cosmos*** [1968] PBO. Cover by Jack Gaughan.	$1.50	$5.00	$10.00
G-725	Johnston, William - ***The Littlest Rebels*** [1968] PBO. TV tie-in.	$ .75	$2.50	$5.00
G-726	Hoffman, Lee - ***The Valdez Horses*** [1968] Cover by George Gross.	$ .65	$2.00	$4.00
G-727	Ringold, Clay/Callahan, John - ***Return To Rio Fuego/Tracks Of The Hunter*** [1968]	$ .75	$2.50	$5.00
G-728	Grinnell, David - ***Across Time*** [1968] Cover by Jeff Jones.	$ .65	$2.00	$4.00
G-729	McDaniel, David - ***The Utopia Affair (The Man From U.N.C.L.E. #15)*** [1968] PBO. TV tie-in with photo cover.	$1.00	$3.00	$6.00
G-730	Nourse, Alan E. - ***Psi High And Others*** [1968] Cover by Don Ivan Punchatz.	$ .65	$2.00	$4.00
G-733	Burroughs, Edgar Rice - ***At The Earth's Core*** [1968]	$ .65	$2.00	$4.00
G-734	Burroughs, Edgar Rice - ***Pellucidar*** [1968]	$ .65	$2.00	$4.00
G-735	Burroughs, Edgar Rice - ***Tanar Of Pellucidar*** [1968] Cover by Roy Krenkel, Jr.	$ .65	$2.00	$4.00
G-736	Burroughs, Edgar Rice - ***Tarzan At The Earth's Core*** [1968]	$ .65	$2.00	$4.00
G-737	Burroughs, Edgar Rice - ***Back To The Stone Age*** [1968]	$ .65	$2.00	$4.00
G-738	Burroughs, Edgar Rice - ***Land Of Terror*** [1968]	$ .65	$2.00	$4.00
G-739	Burroughs, Edgar Rice - ***Savage Pellucidar*** [1968] Cover by Frank Frazetta.	$ .65	$2.00	$4.00
G-740	Saberhagen, Fred - ***The Broken Lands*** [1968] PBO. Cover by Powers.	$ .65	$2.00	$4.00

		G	VG	F
G-742	West, Tom/Owen, Dean - ***Write His Name In Gunsmoke/Lone Star Roundup*** [1968] PBO. Cover by Prezio/.	$ .75	$2.50	$5.00
G-743	Heath, Sharon - ***Nurse On Castle Island*** [1968]	$ .50	$1.50	$3.00
G-744	Delmonico, Andrea - ***Chateau Chaumand*** [1968] PBO.	$ .65	$2.00	$4.00
G-745	Burroughs, Edgar Rice - ***The Moon Maid*** [1968] Cover by Roy Krenkel, Jr.	$ .65	$2.00	$4.00
G-747	Hogan, Ray/Owen, Dean - ***Killer On The Warbucket/Sage Tower*** [1968] PBO. Cover by Jerome Podwil/.	$ .75	$2.50	$5.00
G-748	Burroughs, Edgar Rice - ***The Moon Men*** [1968] Cover by Ed Emsh.	$ .65	$2.00	$4.00
G-751	Davis, Mildred - ***The Dark Place*** [1968]	$ .65	$2.00	$4.00
G-752	Leslie, Peter - ***The Splintered Sunglasses Affair*** [1968] PBO. ***(The Man From U.N.C.L.E. #16.)*** TV tie-in with photo cover.	$1.00	$3.00	$6.00
G-753	Garner, Alan - ***The Moon Of Gomrath*** [1968] Cover by Jeff Jones.	$ .65	$2.00	$4.00
G-755	Constiner, Merle/Lee, Wayne C. - ***The Four Of Gila Bend/Trail Of The Skulls*** [1968]	$ .75	$2.50	$5.00
G-756	Panshin, Alexei - ***Star Well*** [1968] PBO. Cover by Kelly Freas.	$ .75	$2.50	$5.00
G-758	Swann, Thomas Burnett - ***Moondust*** [1968] PBO. Cover by Jeff Jones.	$ .75	$2.50	$5.00
G-760	Jones, X. X./Sullivan, Reese - ***Bronc/The Vengeance Ghost*** [1968] Cover by Leone/.	$ .75	$2.50	$5.00
G-761	Brunner, John - ***Catch A Falling Star*** [1968] Cover by Schoenherr.	$ .65	$2.00	$4.00
G-762	Panshin, Alexei - ***The Thurb Revolution*** [1968] PBO. Cover by Kelly Freas.	$ .75	$2.50	$5.00
G-763	Shelley, John & David - ***Hell-For-Leather Jones*** [1968] PBO.	$ .75	$2.50	$5.00
G-764	Trimble, Louis/Callahan, John - ***West To The Pecos/Jernigan*** [1968]	$ .75	$2.50	$5.00
G-766	Hamilton, Edmond - ***World Of The Starwolves*** [1968] PBO. Cover by Jack Gaughan. Starwolf #3.	$ .65	$2.00	$4.00

Ace H Series. New York: Ace Books.

		G	VG	F
H-3	Paul, Louis - ***Dara The Cypriot*** [1962]	$ .65	$2.00	$4.00
H-4	Eckerson, Olive - ***My Lord Essex*** [1966]	$ .65	$2.00	$4.00
H-5	Culp, John H. - ***Born Of The Sun*** [1966]	$ .65	$2.00	$4.00
H-6	Seward, Florence A. - ***Gold For The Caesars*** [1966]	$ .65	$2.00	$4.00
H-8	Creed, Will - ***The Sword Of Il Grande*** [1966]	$ .65	$2.00	$4.00
H-9	DuBois, Theodora - ***Captive Of Rome*** [1966] Cover by Marchetti.	$ .65	$2.00	$4.00
H-10	Plievier, Theodor - ***Berlin*** [1966]	$ .65	$2.00	$4.00
H-11	Plievier, Theodor - ***Moscow*** [1966]	$ .65	$2.00	$4.00
H-12	Wilkins, Harold - ***Strange Mysteries Of Time And Space*** [1966]	$ .65	$2.00	$4.00
H-13	Soule, Gardner - ***The Mystery Monsters*** [1966]	$ .65	$2.00	$4.00
H-14	Gaddis, Vincent - ***Invisible Horizons*** [1966]	$ .65	$2.00	$4.00
H-15	Anthology ed. by Carr & Wollheim - ***World's Best Science Fiction: 1966*** [1966] Cover by Cosimo Scianna.	$ .65	$2.00	$4.00
H-16	Holzer, Hans - ***Ghosts I've Met*** [1966] Cover by Cosimo Scianna.	$ .65	$2.00	$4.00
H-17	Vallee, Jacques - ***Anatomy Of A Phenomenon*** [1966]	$ .65	$2.00	$4.00
H-18	Sutton, Jeff - ***H-Bomb Over America*** [1966]	$ .65	$2.00	$4.00
H-19	Anthology ed. by Frederik Pohl - ***The If Reader Of Science Fiction*** [1966] Cover by Cosimo Scianna.	$ .65	$2.00	$4.00

		G	VG	F
H-20	Schwartz, Alan/Bulmer, Kenneth - ***The Wandering Tellurian/The Key To Irunium*** [1967] PBO. Covers by Podwil/Hoot.	$ .75	$2.50	$5.00
H-21	Vance, Jack/Wayman, Tony Russell - ***The Last Castle/World Of The Sleeper*** [1967] PBO. Covers by Jack Gaughan.	$1.00	$3.00	$6.00
H-22	Petaja, Emil/Purdom, Tom - ***Lord Of The Green Planet/Five Against Arlane*** [1967] PBO. Covers by Kelly Freas/Jack Gaughan.	$ .75	$2.50	$5.00
H-23	Heyer, Georgette - ***Arabella*** [1967]	$ .65	$2.00	$4.00
H-24	Fort, Charles - ***The Book Of The Damned*** [1967]	$ .75	$2.50	$5.00
H-25	Tempest, Jan - ***House Of The Pines*** [1967] Cover by Lou Marchetti.	$ .65	$2.00	$4.00
H-26	Anthology - ***The Best From Fantasy & Science Fiction (13th Series)*** [1967]	$ .75	$2.50	$5.00
H-27	Coulson, Juanita/Tubb, E. C. - ***Crisis On Cheiron/The Winds Of Gath*** [1967] PBO. Covers by Podwil/Kelly Freas.	$ .65	$2.00	$4.00
H-28	Vallee, Jacques & Janine - ***Challenge To Science*** [1967]	$ .65	$2.00	$4.00
H-29	Richmond, W. & L./Chandler, A. Bertram - ***The Lost Millennium/The Road To The Rim*** [1967] PBO. Covers by Jack Gaughan/Podwil.	$ .75	$2.50	$5.00
H-30	Simak, Clifford D. - ***City*** [1967]	$ .65	$2.00	$4.00
H-31	Eden, Dorothy - ***Sleep In The Woods*** [1967]	$ .65	$2.00	$4.00
H-32	Ellson, Hal - ***Games*** [1967] PBO. Movie tie-in.	$1.50	$5.00	$10.00
H-33	Norton, Andre - ***Moon Of Three Rings*** [1967] Cover by Jack Gaughan.	$ .65	$2.00	$4.00
H-34	Reynolds, Mack/Tubb, E. C. - ***Computer War/Death Is A Dream*** [1967] PBO.	$ .75	$2.50	$5.00
H-36	Moorcock, Michael/Petaja, Emil - ***The Wrecks Of Time/ Tramontane*** [1967] PBO. Covers by Jack Gaughan.	$ .75	$2.50	$5.00
H-37	Hunt, Charlotte - ***The Gilded Sarcophagus*** [1967]	$ .65	$2.00	$4.00
H-38	Leiber, Fritz - ***The Swords Of Lankhmar*** [1968] PBO. Cover by Jeff Jones.	$1.00	$3.00	$6.00
H-39	Dick, Philip K. - ***Eye In The Sky*** [1968] Cover by Kelly Freas.	$1.35	$4.00	$8.00
H-40	Rackham, John/Tubb, E. C. - ***Alien Sea/C.O.D. Mars*** [1968] PBO. Covers by George Ziel/Jack Gaughan.	$ .75	$2.50	$5.00
H-41	Verne, Jules - ***Into The Niger Bend*** [1968] Cover by Podwil.	$ .65	$2.00	$4.00
H-42	Simak, Clifford D. - ***Why Call Them Back From Heaven?*** [1968] Cover by Leo & Diane Dillon.	$ .65	$2.00	$4.00
H-43	Verne, Jules - ***The City In The Sahara*** [1968] Cover by Podwil.	$ .65	$2.00	$4.00
H-44	Heyer, Georgette - ***The Quiet Gentleman*** [1968] Cover by McVicker.	$ .65	$2.00	$4.00
H-45	Heyer, Georgette - ***Venetia*** [1968]	$ .65	$2.00	$4.00
H-46	Scott, Jr., Robert L. - ***Look Of The Eagle*** [1968] Cover by Verne Tossey	$ .65	$2.00	$4.00
H-47	Holzer, Hans - ***The Lively Ghosts Of Ireland*** [1968]	$ .65	$2.00	$4.00
H-48	Wobig, Ellen/Wright, Lan - ***The Youth Monopoly/The Pictures Of Pavanne*** [1968] PBO. Covers by Gaughan.	$ .75	$2.50	$5.00
H-49	Verne, Jules - ***The Begum's Fortune*** [1968] Cover by Podwil.	$ .65	$2.00	$4.00
H-51	Faucette, John/Petaja, Emil - ***Crown Of Infinity/The Prism*** [1968] PBO. Covers by Freas/Gaughan.	$ .75	$2.50	$5.00
H-52	Verne, Jules - ***Yesterday And Tomorrow*** [1968] Cover by Podwil.	$ .65	$2.00	$4.00
H-53	Whitten, Leslie H. - ***Progeny Of The Adder*** [1968]	$ .65	$2.00	$4.00
H-54	Lafferty, R. A. - ***Past Master*** [1968] PBO. Cover by Leo & Diane Dillon.	$1.35	$4.00	$8.00

		G	VG	F
H-55	Ley, Willy - ***On Earth And In The Sky*** [1968] PBO. Photo cover.	$ .65	$2.00	$4.00
H-56	Lafferty, R. A./Hill, Ernest - ***Space Chanty/Pity About Earth*** [1968] PBO. Covers by Vaughn Bode/Kelly Freas.	$1.00	$3.00	$6.00
H-57	Woolrich, Cornell - ***Rendezvous In Black*** [1968]	$ .65	$2.00	$4.00
H-58	Friedberg, Gertrude - ***The Revolving Boy*** [1968] Cover by The Dillons.	$ .65	$2.00	$4.00
H-59	High, Philip E./Trimble, Louis - ***The Time Mercenaries/Anthropol*** [1968] PBO.	$ .65	$2.00	$4.00
H-60	Verne, Jules - ***Carpathian Castle*** [1968] Cover by Podwil.	$ .65	$2.00	$4.00
H-61	Salter, Elizabeth - ***Death In A Mist*** [1968]	$ .65	$2.00	$4.00
H-62	Tucker, Wilson - ***The Lincoln Hunters*** [1968] Cover by The Dillons.	$1.35	$4.00	$8.00
H-64	Trench - ***The Flying Saucer Story*** [1968]	$ .65	$2.00	$4.00
H-65	Bulmer, Kenneth/Reynolds, Mack - ***The Key To Venudine/Mercenary From Tomorrow*** [1968] PBO. Covers by Kelly Freas/Gaughan.	$ .75	$2.50	$5.00
H-67	Verne, Jules - ***The Village In The Treetops*** [1968] Cover by Podwil.	$ .65	$2.00	$4.00
H-68	Bayless, Raymond - ***The Enigma Of The Poltergeist*** [1968] Photo cover.	$ .65	$2.00	$4.00
H-69	Randall, Rona - ***Knight's Keep*** [1968]	$ .65	$2.00	$4.00
H-70	Koontz, Dean R./Petaja, Emil - ***Star Quest/Doom Of The Green Planet*** [1968] PBO. Covers by Morrow/Podwil.	$ .75	$2.50	$5.00
H-72	Russ, Joanna - ***Picnic On Paradise*** [1968] PBO. Cover by The Dillons.	$ .75	$2.50	$5.00
H-73	Leiber, Fritz - ***Swords Against Wizardry*** [1968] PBO. Cover by Jeff Jones.	$ .75	$2.50	$5.00
H-74	Fort, Charles - ***New Lands*** [1968]	$ .65	$2.00	$4.00
H-75	Heyer, Georgette - ***Cotillion*** [1968]	$ .65	$2.00	$4.00
H-77	Tubb, E. C./Coulson, Juanita - ***Derai/The Singing Stones*** [1968] PBO. Covers by Jeff Jones/Kelly Freas.	$ .75	$2.50	$5.00
H-78	Verne, Jules - ***The Hunt For The Meteor*** [1968] Cover by Podwil.	$ .65	$2.00	$4.00
H-79	Shaw, Bob - ***The Two-Timers*** [1968] PBO. Cover by Dillons.	$ .75	$2.50	$5.00
H-81	Macklin, John - ***Passport To The Unknown*** [1968]	$ .65	$2.00	$4.00
H-83	Hurwood, Bernhardt J. - ***Vampires, Werewolves And Ghouls*** [1968] PBO.	$1.00	$3.00	$6.00
H-84	Norton, Andre - ***Sorceress Of The Witch World*** [1968] PBO. Cover by Jeff Jones.	$ .75	$2.50	$5.00
H-85	Grinnell, David & Carter, Lin/High, P.E. - ***Destination: Saturn/Invader On My Back*** [1968] /PBO. Covers by Freas/Gaughan.	$ .75	$2.50	$5.00
H-86	Compton, D. G. - ***Synthajoy*** [1968] PBO. Cover by The Dillons.	$1.35	$4.00	$8.00
H-88	Fort, Charles - ***Wild Talents*** [1968]	$1.00	$3.00	$6.00
H-89	Macklin, John - ***Dimensions Beyond The Known*** [1968] PBO. Photo cover.	$ .65	$2.00	$4.00
H-90	Leiber, Fritz - ***Swords In The Mist*** [1968] PBO. Cover by Jeff Jones.	$1.25	$3.75	$7.50
H-91	Janifer, L. & Treibich, S./Rackham, John - ***Target:Terra/The Proxima Project*** [1968] PBO.	$ .75	$2.50	$5.00
H-92	Van Vogt, A. E. - ***The Far-Out Worlds Of A.E. Van Vogt*** [1968] PBO. Cover by Jeff Jones.	$ .75	$2.50	$5.00
H-93	Ames, Delano - ***The Man In The Tricorn Hat*** [1968] Photo cover.	$ .65	$2.00	$4.00

		G	VG	F
H-94	Macklin, John - ***Dwellers In Darkness*** [1968] PBO.	$ .65	$2.00	$4.00
H-95	Simak, Clifford D./Sutton, Jeff - ***So Bright The Vision/The Man Who Saw Tomorrow*** [1968] PBO. Covers by Gray Morrow/Jack Gaughan.	$ .75	$2.50	$5.00
H-96	Jackson, Shirley - ***The Sundial*** [1968]	$ .65	$2.00	$4.00
H-97	Ames, Delano - ***The Man With Three Jaguars*** [1968] Photo cover.	$ .65	$2.00	$4.00
H-99	Nostradamus - ***Prophecies On World Events By Nostradamus*** [1968]	$ .75	$2.50	$5.00
H-100	Holzer, Hans - ***E.S.P. And You*** [1968]	$ .65	$2.00	$4.00
H-102	Smith, Edward E. - ***Subspace Explorers*** [1968] Cover by John Schoenherr.	$ .65	$2.00	$4.00
H-103	Faucette, John M./Reynolds, Mack - ***The Age Of Ruin/Code Duello*** [1968] PBO. Covers by Gary Morrow/Kelly Freas.	$ .75	$2.50	$5.00
H-104	Woolrich, Cornell - ***The Black Curtain*** [1968]	$ .65	$2.00	$4.00
H-105	Schmitz, James H. - ***The Demon Breed*** [1968] PBO.	$2.00	$6.00	$12.00
H-106	Caird, Janet - ***Perturbing Spirit*** [1968] Cover by Podwil.	$ .65	$2.00	$4.00

Ace K Series. New York: Ace Books.

		G	VG	F
K-100	Wright, Richard - ***The Long Dream*** [1959] Cover by Ron Lesser.	$ .65	$2.00	$4.00
K-101	Potter, Charles Francis - ***The Faiths Men Live By*** [1959]	$ .50	$1.50	$3.00
K-102	Byrd, Richard E. - ***Alone*** [1959]	$ .50	$1.50	$3.00
K-103	De Pereda, Prudencio - ***Fiesta*** [1959]	$ .50	$1.50	$3.00
K-104	Swanberg, W. A. - ***Sickles The Incredible*** [1959]	$ .65	$2.00	$4.00
K-105	Duggan, Alfred - ***Winter Quarters*** [1959]	$ .50	$1.50	$3.00
K-106	Churchill, Allen - ***The Improper Bohemians*** [1959] Photo cover.	$ .65	$2.00	$4.00
K-107	Cave, Hugh B. - ***The Cross On The Drum*** [1959]	$ .50	$1.50	$3.00
K-108	Robertson, Don - ***The Three Days*** [1959]	$ .50	$1.50	$3.00
K-109	Trumbo, Dalton - ***Johnny Got His Gun*** [1959]	$1.00	$3.00	$6.00
K-110	Kirst, Hans Hellmut - ***The Seventh Day*** [1959]	$ .50	$1.50	$3.00
K-111	Anthology - ***The Cracked Reader*** [1960] PBO. Cover by John Severin.	$1.50	$5.00	$10.00
K-112	Savage, Jr., Les - ***The Royal City*** [1960] Cover by G. D. Wilson.	$ .50	$1.50	$3.00
K-113	Edited by Eric Duthie - ***Tall Short Stories*** [1960] Cover by Mona Moore.	$ .65	$2.00	$4.00
K-114	Bushnell, O. A. - ***Peril In Paradise*** [1960]	$ .50	$1.50	$3.00
K-115	Hoehling, A. A. - ***They Sailed Into Oblivion*** [1960]	$ .50	$1.50	$3.00
K-116	West, Elliot - ***Man Running*** [1960] Movie tie-in.	$ .50	$1.50	$3.00
K-117	Edwards, Frank - ***Stranger Than Science*** [1960]	$ .50	$1.50	$3.00
K-118	Duggan, Alfred - ***Children Of The Wolf*** [1960] Cover by Leone.	$ .65	$2.00	$4.00
K-119	Ginsburg, Ralph - ***An Unhurried View Of Erotica*** [1960]	$1.00	$3.00	$6.00
K-121	Ruark, Robert C. - ***Grenadine Etching*** [1960]	$ .50	$1.50	$3.00
K-122	Edited by Kurt Singer - ***Spies Who Changed History*** [1960] PBO.	$ .50	$1.50	$3.00
K-123	Erno, Richard B. - ***The Hunt*** [1960]	$ .50	$1.50	$3.00
K-124	Freuchen, Peter - ***Eskimo*** [1960]	$ .50	$1.50	$3.00
K-125	Mehling, Harold - ***The Scandalous Scamps*** [1960]	$ .50	$1.50	$3.00
K-126	Dahl, Robert - ***Breakdown*** [1960]	$ .50	$1.50	$3.00
K-127	Stewart, George R. - ***Fire*** [1960]	$ .50	$1.50	$3.00
K-128	Ford, Clellan S. & Beach, Frank A. - ***Patterns Of Sexual Behavior*** [1960]	$ .50	$1.50	$3.00

		G	VG	F
K-129	Duggan, Alfred - ***Conscience Of The King*** [1960]	$ .65	$2.00	$4.00
A-130	Anthology ed. by Robert B. Douglas - ***The Hundred Stories*** [1960]	$ .65	$2.00	$4.00
K-131	Ray, Marie Beynon - ***The Importance Of Feeling Inferior*** [1960]	$ .50	$1.50	$3.00
K-132	Kane, Harnett T. - ***Spies For The Blue And Gray*** [1960]	$ .50	$1.50	$3.00
K-133	Berry, Don - ***Trask*** [1961]	$ .50	$1.50	$3.00
K-134	Fleming, Peter - ***Operation Sea Lion*** [1961]	$ .50	$1.50	$3.00
T-135	Anthology - ***More Cracked*** [1961] PBO. Cover by John Severin.	$1.50	$5.00	$10.00
K-136	MacDougall, Curtis D. - ***Hoaxes*** [1961]	$ .50	$1.50	$3.00
K-137	Bluestone, George - ***The Private World Of Cully Powers*** [1961].	$ .50	$1.50	$3.00
K-138	Stewart, George R. - ***Ordeal By Hunger*** [1961]	$ .50	$1.50	$3.00
K-139	Duggan, Alfred - ***Three's Company*** [1961]	$ .50	$1.50	$3.00
K-141	Ludwig, Emil - ***Michelangelo And Rembrandt*** [1961]	$ .65	$2.00	$4.00
K-142	Edited by Brant House - ***Crimes That Shocked America*** [1961]	$1.00	$3.00	$6.00
K-143	Gibbs, Willa - ***The Twelfth Physician*** [1961]	$ .50	$1.50	$3.00
K-144	Edwards, Frank - ***Strangest Of All*** [1962]	$ .50	$1.50	$3.00
K-145	Tashman, M.D., Harry F. - ***The Marriage Bed*** [1961]	$ .50	$1.50	$3.00
K-146	Farre, Rowena - ***Seal Morning*** [1962] Cover by Raymond Sheppard.	$ .50	$1.50	$3.00
K-147	Spinatelli, Carl J. - ***Baton Sinister*** [1962]	$ .65	$2.00	$4.00
K-148	Asbury, Herbert - ***The Chicago Underworld*** [1962]	$1.00	$3.00	$6.00
K-149	Mundy, Talbot - ***Queen Cleopatra*** [1962]	$1.25	$3.75	$7.50
K-151	Fredericks, Pierce G. - ***The Great Adventure*** [1962] Photo cover.	$ .65	$2.00	$4.00
K-152	Edited by Brant House - ***Great Trials Of Famous Lawyers*** [1962] PBO.	$ .65	$2.00	$4.00
K-153	Liswood, M.D., Rebecca - ***A Marriage Doctor Speaks Her Mind About Sex*** [1962]	$ .50	$1.50	$3.00
K-154	Stewart, George R. - ***Earth Abides*** [1962]	$ .50	$1.50	$3.00
K-155	Henry, Thomas R. - ***The Strangest Things In The World*** [1962]	$ .50	$1.50	$3.00
K-156	Fort, Charles - ***The Book Of The Damned*** [1962]	$1.00	$3.00	$6.00
K-157	Lutz, E. H. G. - ***Miracles Of Modern Surgery*** [1962]	$ .50	$1.50	$3.00
K-158	Whitney, Phyllis A. - ***Thunder Heights*** [1962] Cover by Lou Marchetti.	$ .50	$1.50	$3.00
K-159	Christophe, Robert - ***The Executioners*** [1962]	$ .50	$1.50	$3.00
K-160	Endore, Guy - ***The Werewolf Of Paris*** [1962]	$1.25	$3.75	$7.50
K-161	Collins, Frederick L. - ***The F.B.I. In Peace And War*** [1962]	$ .50	$1.50	$3.00
K-162	O'Connor, Richard - ***Gould's Millions*** [1962]	$ .50	$1.50	$3.00
K-163	Furneaux, Rupert - ***The World's Strangest Mysteries*** [1962]	$ .50	$1.50	$3.00
K-164	Whitney, Phyllis A. - ***The Trembling Hills*** [1962]	$ .50	$1.50	$3.00
K-165	Eyre, Katherine Wigmore - ***The Lute And The Glove*** [1962]	$ .50	$1.50	$3.00
K-166	Jackson, Shirley - ***The Sundial*** [1962] Cover by Powers.	$ .65	$2.00	$4.00
K-167	Andrezel, Pierre - ***The Angelic Avengers*** [1962]	$ .50	$1.50	$3.00
K-168	Miller, R. Dewitt - ***Stranger Than Life*** [1962] Cover by Scianna.	$ .50	$1.50	$3.00
K-169	Sullivan, Scott - ***The Shortest Gladdest Years*** [1962]	$ .50	$1.50	$3.00
K-170	Pugh, John J. - ***High Carnival*** [1962]	$ .50	$1.50	$3.00
K-171	Eden, Dorothy - ***Lady Of Mallow*** [1963]	$ .50	$1.50	$3.00
K-172	Bourne, Peter - ***The Golden Pagans*** [1963]	$ .50	$1.50	$3.00
K-173	Malm, Dorothea - ***To The Castle*** [1963]	$ .50	$1.50	$3.00
K-174	Heyer, Georgette - ***The Grand Sophy*** [1963]	$ .50	$1.50	$3.00
K-175	Coffman, Virginia - ***Moura*** [1963]	$ .50	$1.50	$3.00

		G	VG	F
K-176	Edited by Brant House - ***Strange Powers Of Unusual People*** [1963] PBO.	$ .65	$2.00	$4.00
K-177	Seton, Anya - ***My Theodosia*** [1963]	$ .50	$1.50	$3.00
K-178	Whitney, Phyllis A. - ***The Quicksilver Pool*** [1963]	$ .50	$1.50	$3.00
K-179	Heyer, Georgette - ***Venetia*** [1963]	$ .50	$1.50	$3.00
K-181	Summerton, Margaret - ***The Sea House*** [1963]	$ .50	$1.50	$3.00
K-182	Webster, Doris & Hopkins, Mary Alden - ***Instant Self Analysis*** [1963]	$ .50	$1.50	$3.00
K-184	Eden, Dorothy - ***Whistle For The Crows*** [1963] Cover by Schinella.	$ .50	$1.50	$3.00
K-185	Jackson, Shirley - ***Hangsaman*** [1963]	$1.25	$3.75	$7.50
K-186	Garn, Roy - ***The Magic Power Of Emotional Appeal*** [1963]	$ .50	$1.50	$3.00
K-187	Bellamann, Henry - ***Victoria Grandolet*** [1963]	$ .50	$1.50	$3.00
K-188	Byrd, Richard E. - ***Alone*** [1963]	$ .50	$1.50	$3.00
K-189	Disney, Dorothy Cameron - ***The Hangman's Tree*** [1963]	$ .50	$1.50	$3.00
K-190	Egelson, Jim & Egelson, Janet Frank - ***Parents Without Partners*** [1963]	$ .50	$1.50	$3.00
K-191	Maybury, Anne - ***The Brides Of Bellenmore*** [1963]	$ .50	$1.50	$3.00
K-192	Bishop, Sheila - ***The House With Two Faces*** [1963]	$ .50	$1.50	$3.00
K-193	Klaf, M.D., Franklin S. & Hurwood, B. J. - ***A Psychiatrist Looks At Erotica*** [1964] PBO. Cover by Scianna.	$ .50	$1.50	$3.00
K-194	Summerton, Margaret - ***Nightingale At Noon*** [1964]	$ .50	$1.50	$3.00
K-195	Schaukowitsch, Dr. Francis J. - ***How To Avoid Marriage*** [1964].	$ .50	$1.50	$3.00
K-196	Karneke, Joseph Sidney & Boesen, Victor - ***Navy Diver*** [1964]	$ .50	$1.50	$3.00
K-197	Heyer, Georgette - ***Venetia*** [1964]	$ .50	$1.50	$3.00
K-198	Bell, Josephine - ***Stranger On A Cliff*** [1964]	$ .50	$1.50	$3.00
K-199	O'Brien, Barbara - ***Operators And Things*** [1964]	$ .50	$1.50	$3.00
K-200	Whitney, J. L. H. - ***The Whisper Of Shadows*** [1964]	$ .50	$1.50	$3.00
K-201	Heyer, Georgette - ***April Lady*** [1964]	$ .50	$1.50	$3.00
K-202	Burroughs, William - ***Junkie*** [1964]	$1.50	$5.00	$10.00
K-204	Payne, Robert - ***Charlie Chaplin*** [1964] Photo cover.	$ .75	$2.50	$5.00
K-205	Willock, Ruth - ***The Night Of The Visitor*** [1964]	$ .50	$1.50	$3.00
K-206	Edwards, Frank - ***Strange World*** [1964] PBO.	$ .50	$1.50	$3.00
K-207	Smith, Lady Eleanor - ***A Dark And Splendid Passion*** [1964] Cover by Lou Marchetti.	$ .50	$1.50	$3.00
K-209	Seilaz, Aileen - ***The Veil Of Silence*** [1964] PBO.	$ .50	$1.50	$3.00
K-210	Holzer, Hans - ***Ghost Hunter*** [1964]	$ .50	$1.50	$3.00
K-211	Maybury, Anne - ***The Pavilion At Monkshood*** [1964]	$ .50	$1.50	$3.00
K-212	Bishop, Sheila - ***The Durable Fire*** [1964]	$ .50	$1.50	$3.00
K-213	Noone, Edwina - ***Dark Cypress*** [1964]	$ .50	$1.50	$3.00
K-215	O'Grady, Rohan - ***The Master Of Montrolfe Hall*** [1964]	$ .50	$1.50	$3.00
K-216	Roffman, Jan - ***The Reflection Of Evil*** [1964]	$ .50	$1.50	$3.00
K-217	Fort, Charles - ***Lo!*** [1964]	$ .50	$1.50	$3.00
K-218	Santee, Ross - ***Cowboy*** [1964] Cover by Ross Santee.	$ .50	$1.50	$3.00
K-220	Howatch, Susan - ***The Dark Shore*** [1964]	$ .50	$1.50	$3.00
K-221	Coffman, Virginia - ***The Beckoning*** [1965] PBO.	$ .50	$1.50	$3.00
K-222	Macklin, John - ***Strange Destinies*** [1965] PBO.	$ .50	$1.50	$3.00
K-223	Noone, Edwina - ***Corridor Of Whispers*** [1965] Cover by Schinella.	$ .50	$1.50	$3.00
K-224	Edited by Brant House - ***Strange Powers Of Unusual People*** [1965]	$ .50	$1.50	$3.00
K-225	Arvonen, Helen - ***The Summer Of Evil*** [1965] PBO.	$ .65	$2.00	$4.00
K-226	Heyer, Georgette - ***Sylvester Or The Wicked Uncle*** [1965]	$ .50	$1.50	$3.00

			G	VG	F
K-227	Maybury, Anne - ***Green Fire*** [1965]		$ .50	$1.50	$3.00
K-228	Winslow, Joan - ***Griffin Towers*** [1966] PBO.		$ .50	$1.50	$3.00
K-229	Miller, R. Dewitt - ***Impossible Yet It Happened!*** [1966]		$ .65	$2.00	$4.00
K-230	Eden, Dorothy - ***The Pretty Ones*** [1966]		$ .50	$1.50	$3.00
K-231	Peters, Lane - ***Promise Him Anything...*** [1966] PBO. Cover by Gray Morrow.		$ .50	$1.50	$3.00
K-234	Coffman, Virginia - ***The Devil Vicar*** [1966] PBO.		$ .50	$1.50	$3.00
K-237	Tralins, Robert - ***Beyond Human Understanding*** [1966]		$ .65	$2.00	$4.00
K-238	Maybury, Anne - ***Someone Waiting*** [1966]		$ .50	$1.50	$3.00
K-239	Eden, Dorothy - ***The Sleeping Bride*** [1966]		$ .50	$1.50	$3.00
K-240	Howatch, Susan - ***The Waiting Sands*** [1966]		$ .50	$1.50	$3.00
K-241	Steiger, Brad - ***Strange Guests*** [1966]		$ .65	$2.00	$4.00
K-242	Mitchell, Ruth C. - ***The Legend Of Susan Dane*** [1966]		$ .50	$1.50	$3.00
K-243	Eden, Dorothy - ***The Deadly Travelers*** [1966]		$ .50	$1.50	$3.00
K-244	Edited by Kurt Singer - ***The Gothic Reader*** [1966]		$ .50	$1.50	$3.00
K-245	Garratt, Marie - ***Dangerous Enchantment*** [1966] Cover by Koenig.		$ .65	$2.00	$4.00
K-246	Grant, Joan - ***Castle Cloud*** [1966]		$ .50	$1.50	$3.00
K-248	Maybury, Anne - ***Whisper In The Dark*** [1966]		$ .50	$1.50	$3.00
K-249	Eden, Dorothy - ***The Brooding Lake*** [1966] Cover by Jerome Podwil.		$ .50	$1.50	$3.00
K-250	Garrison, Dr. Webb B. - ***Strange Bonds Between Animals And Men*** [1966]		$ .65	$2.00	$4.00
K-251	Maybury, Anne - ***Shadow Of A Stranger*** [1966]		$ .50	$1.50	$3.00
K-252	Whitney, Phyllis A. - ***The Trembling Hills*** [1966]		$ .50	$1.50	$3.00
K-257	Maybury, Anne - ***I Am Gabriella!*** [1966]		$ .50	$1.50	$3.00
K-259	Hervey, Michael - ***Strange Happenings*** [1966]		$ .65	$2.00	$4.00
K-260	Rich, Joan & Leslie - ***Dating And Mating By Computer*** [1966] PBO.		$ .50	$1.50	$3.00
K-262	Randall, Rona - ***Walk Into My Parlor*** [1966]		$ .50	$1.50	$3.00
K-263	Maybury, Anne - ***The Night My Enemy*** [1966]		$ .65	$2.00	$4.00
K-264	Blackmore, Jane - ***The Dark Between The Stars*** [1966]		$ .50	$1.50	$3.00
K-265	Heyer, Georgette - ***The Reluctant Widow*** [1966]		$ .50	$1.50	$3.00
K-266	Henry, Thomas R. - ***The Strangest Things In The World*** [1966]		$ .50	$1.50	$3.00
K-267	Eden, Dorothy - ***Listen To Danger*** [1966]		$ .65	$2.00	$4.00
K-268	Steiger, Brad - ***Treasure Hunting*** [1966]		$ .50	$1.50	$3.00
K-269	Randall, Rona - ***Seven Days From Midnight*** [1966]		$ .50	$1.50	$3.00
K-270	Erskine, Margaret - ***The Silver Ladies*** [1966]		$ .50	$1.50	$3.00
K-271	Maybury, Anne - ***Falcon's Shadow*** [1966]		$ .50	$1.50	$3.00
K-272	Holzer, Hans - ***Yankee Ghosts*** [1966]		$ .65	$2.00	$4.00
K-276	Hurwood, B. J. - ***Strange Talents*** [1966]		$ .65	$2.00	$4.00
K-278	Arvonen, Helen - ***Circle Of Death*** [1967] PBO.		$ .50	$1.50	$3.00
K-279	Macklin, John - ***The Strange And Uncanny*** [1967]		$ .65	$2.00	$4.00
K-281	Erskine, Margaret - ***No. 9 Belmont Square*** [1967]		$ .50	$1.50	$3.00
K-282	Maybury, Anne - ***The Winds Of Night*** [1967]		$ .50	$1.50	$3.00
K-283	Buckingham, Nancy - ***Cloud Over Malverton*** [1967]		$ .50	$1.50	$3.00
K-284	Dickens, Monica - ***The Room Upstairs*** [1966] PBO.		$ .50	$1.50	$3.00
K-285	Randall, Rona - ***Hotel Deluxe*** [1967] Cover by Sergio Leone.		$ .50	$1.50	$3.00
K-286	Buckingham, Nancy - ***The Hour Before Moonrise*** [1967] Cover by Leone.		$ .50	$1.50	$3.00
K-288	Robb, Stewart - ***Strange Prophecies That Came True*** [1967]		$ .65	$2.00	$4.00
K-291	Steiger, Brad - ***We Have Lived Before*** [1967]		$ .65	$2.00	$4.00

		G	VG	F
K-292	Macklin, John - ***The Enigma Of The Unknown*** [1967] PBO. Photo cover.	$ .65	$2.00	$4.00
K-293	Ford, Elizabeth - ***Dangerous Holiday*** [1967] Cover by McConnell.	$ .50	$1.50	$3.00
K-294	Aiken, Joan - ***Beware Of The Bouquet*** [1967] Cover by Charles McVicker.	$ .50	$1.50	$3.00
K-295	Erskine, Margaret - ***The Woman At Belguardo*** [1967]	$ .50	$1.50	$3.00
K-297	Buckingham, Nancy - ***The Dark Summer*** [1967]	$ .50	$1.50	$3.00
K-299	Foley, Rae - ***Fear Of A Stranger*** [1967]	$ .50	$1.50	$3.00
K-300	Hervey, Michael - ***They Walk By Night*** [1967] PBO. Photo cover.	$ .65	$2.00	$4.00
K-301	Eden, Dorothy - ***The Laughing Ghost*** [1967] Cover by Jeff Jones.	$1.00	$3.00	$6.00
K-302	Buckingham, Nancy - ***The Legend Of Baverstock Manor*** [1968] PBO.	$ .65	$2.00	$4.00
K-303	Blackmore, Jane - ***Beware The Night*** [1968]	$ .50	$1.50	$3.00
K-304	Erskine, Margaret - ***The Family At Tammerton*** [1968]	$ .50	$1.50	$3.00
K-305	Macklin, John - ***Strange Encounters*** [1968] PBO.	$ .65	$2.00	$4.00
K-307	Edited by Brad Steiger - ***The Occult World Of John Pendragon*** [1968] PBO. Photo cover.	$ .65	$2.00	$4.00

Ace M Series. New York: Ace Books.

		G	VG	F
M-100	Cord, Barry/Callahan, John - ***Gun Junction/A Man Named Raglan*** [1964] PBO.	$ .75	$2.50	$5.00
M-101	Brackett, Leigh/Brackett, Leigh - ***People Of The Talisman/The Secret Of Sinharat*** [1964] PBO. Cover art by Emsh.	$1.00	$3.00	$6.00
M-102	Patterson, Rod/Hogan, Ray - ***Trouble At Hangdog Flats/Hoodoo Guns*** [1964] PBO.	$ .75	$2.50	$5.00
M-103	Saberhagen, Fred/Wright, Lan - ***The Golden People/Exile From Xanadu*** [1964] PBO/. Cover art by Emsh.	$1.00	$3.00	$6.00
M-104	West, Tom/Stevens, Dan J. - ***Sidewinder Showdown/Land Beyond The Law*** [1964] PBO.	$ .75	$2.50	$5.00
M-105	St. Clair, Margaret - ***Message From The Eocene/Three Worlds Of Futurity*** [1964] PBO. Cover art by Gaughan.	$1.00	$3.00	$6.00
M-106	Sullivan, Reese/Kelly, Tim - ***The Blind Trail/Ride Of Fury*** [1964]	$ .75	$2.50	$5.00
M-107	Chandler, A. Bertram - ***Into The Alternate Universe/The Coils Of Time*** [1964] PBO.	$1.00	$3.00	$6.00
M-108	Lee, Wayne C./Patterson, Rod - ***Warpath West/Gunfire Heritage*** [1965] PBO.	$ .75	$2.50	$5.00
M-109	Edmondson, G. C. - ***Stranger Than You Think/The Ship That Sailed The Time Stream*** [1965] PBO. Cover art by Gaughan..	$ .75	$2.50	$5.00
M-110	Constiner, Merle/West, Tom - ***Wolf On Horseback/Bushwhack Brand*** [1965]	$ .75	$2.50	$5.00
M-111	Hamilton, Edmond/Bulmer, Kenneth - ***Fugitive Of The Stars/Land Beyond The Map*** [1965] PBO. Cover art by Gaughan/.	$1.00	$3.00	$6.00
M-112	Nye, Nelson - ***Gun Feud At Tiedown/Rogue's Rendezvous*** [1965]	$ .75	$2.50	$5.00
M-113	Knight, Damon - ***Off Center/The Rithian Terror*** [1965] PBO. Cover art by Gaughan.	$1.00	$3.00	$6.00
M-114	Wynne, Frank/Payne, Stephen - ***Lynch Law Canyon/Stampede At Farway Pass*** [1965]	$ .75	$2.50	$5.00

		G	VG	F
M-115	Brunner, John - ***The Repairmen Of Cyclops/Enigma From Tantalus*** [1965] PBO. Cover arts by Gaughan/Schoenherr.	$1.00	$3.00	$6.00
M-116	Anthology edited by Robert P. Mills - ***The Best From Fantasy And Science Fiction (10th Series)*** [1965] Cover art by Jack Gaughan.	$ .75	$2.50	$5.00
M-117	Sharkey, Jack/Ronald, Bruce W. - ***Ultimatum In 2050 A.D./Our Man In Space*** [1965] PBO. Cover art by Schoenherr/Valigursky.	$1.00	$3.00	$6.00
M-118	West, Tom/Constiner, Merle - ***The Toughest Town In The Territory/Guns At Q Cross*** [1965] PBO.	$ .75	$2.50	$5.00
M-119	Verne, Jules - ***Journey To The Center Of The Earth*** [1965]	$ .75	$2.50	$5.00
M-120	Nye, Nelson/Callahan, John - ***Ambush At Yuma's Chimney/Ride The Wild Land*** [1965] PBO.	$ .75	$2.50	$5.00
M-121	Delany, Samuel R./Petaja, Emil - ***The Ballad Of Beta-2/Alpha Yes, Terra No!*** [1965] PBO. Covers by Valigursky/Gaughan.	$1.00	$3.00	$6.00
M-122	Spellman, Roger G./Vance, William - ***Tall For A Texan/Outlaw Brand*** [1965] PBO/.	$ .75	$2.50	$5.00
M-123	White, Ted/Brunner, John - ***Android Avenger/The Altar On Asconel*** [1965] PBO. Cover art by Morrow.	$1.00	$3.00	$6.00
M-124	West, Tom/Payne, Stephen - ***Battle At Rattlesnake Pass/Trail Of Vanishing Ranchers*** [1965]	$ .75	$2.50	$5.00
M-125	Vance, Jack - ***Monster In Orbit/The World Between*** [1965] PBO. Cover art by Pudwil/Gaughan.	$1.00	$3.00	$6.00
M-126	Whittington, Harry/Elliott, Ben - ***Valley Of Savage Men/Brother Badman*** [1965]	$ .75	$2.50	$5.00
M-127	Rackham, John/Saberhagen, Fred - ***We, The Venusians/The Water Of Thought*** [1965] PBO. Cover by Podwil.	$1.00	$3.00	$6.00
M-128	Wynne, Brian/Sullivan, Reese - ***The Night It Rained Bullets/Nemesis Of Circle A*** [1965]	$ .75	$2.50	$5.00
M-129	Chandler, A. Bertram - ***Empress Of Outer Space/The Alternate Martians*** [1965] PBO. Cover art by Podwil.	$1.00	$3.00	$6.00
M-130	Callahan, John/Hardin, Clement - ***Half-Injun, Half-Wildcat/Outcast Of Ute Bend*** [1965]	$ .75	$2.50	$5.00
M-131	Bulmer, Kenneth/Reynolds, Mack - ***Behold The Stars/Planetary Agent X*** [1965] PBO.	$1.00	$3.00	$6.00
M-132	Chambers, Robert W. - ***The King In Yellow*** [1965] Cover art by Jack Gaughan.	$1.00	$3.00	$6.00
M-133	Petaja, Emil/Chandler, A. Bertram - ***The Caves Of Mars/Space Mercenaries*** [1965] PBO. /Cover art by Gray Morrow.	$1.00	$3.00	$6.00
M-134	West, Tom/Searles, Lin - ***Lost Loot Of Kittycat Ranch/Saddle The Wind*** [1965]	$ .75	$2.50	$5.00
M-135	Leinster, Murray/High, Philip E. - ***Space Captain/The Mad Metropolis*** [1966] PBO. /Cover art by Gaughan.	$1.00	$3.00	$6.00
M-136	Nye, Nelson/Hogan, Ray - ***Marshal Of Pioche/Panhandle Pistolero*** [1966] PBO.	$ .75	$2.50	$5.00
M-137	Anthology - ***The Best From Fantasy And Science Fiction (11th Series)*** [1966] Cover art by Bob Schinella.	$ .75	$2.50	$5.00
M-138	Wynne, Frank/Owen, Dean - ***Call Me Hazard/The Rincon Trap*** [1966] PBO.	$ .75	$2.50	$5.00
M-139	Delany, Samuel R./Purdom, Tom - ***Empire Star/The Tree Lord Of Imeten*** [1966] PBO. Covers by Gaughan/Schoenherr.	$1.00	$3.00	$6.00
M-140	Sullivan, Reese/Cord, Barry - ***Deadly Like A .45/Last Stage To Gomorrah*** [1966]	$ .75	$2.50	$5.00
M-141	Vance, Jack - ***The Many Worlds Of Magnus Ridolph/The Brains Of Earth*** [1966] PBO. Covers by Gaughan.	$1.00	$3.00	$6.00

		G	VG	F
M-142	Heard, H.F. - ***Doppelgangers*** [1966] Cover art by Jerome Podwil.	$1.35	$4.00	$8.00
M-143	Campbell, John W. - ***Islands Of Space*** [1966] Cover art by McKeon.	$ .75	$2.50	$5.00
M-145	Kellier, Elizabeth - ***The Patient At Tonesburry Manor*** [1966].	$ .65	$2.00	$4.00
M-146	Anthology - ***Cracked Again*** [1966] PBO. Cover art by John Severin.	$1.50	$5.00	$10.00
M-147	Norton, Andre - ***The Stars Are Ours!*** [1966]	$ .65	$2.00	$4.00
M-148	Norton, Andre - ***Star Born*** [1966] Cover art by Ed Emsh.	$ .65	$2.00	$4.00
M-149	Vance, Jack - ***The Eyes Of The Overworld*** [1966] PBO. Cover art by Jack Gaughan.	$1.35	$4.00	$8.00
M-150	Norton, Andre - ***The Defiant Agents*** [1966]	$ .65	$2.00	$4.00
M-151	Norton, Andre - ***The Last Planet*** [1966]	$ .65	$2.00	$4.00
M-152	Munn, H. Warner - ***King Of The World's Edge*** [1966] PBO. Cover art by Jack Gaughan.	$1.25	$3.75	$7.50
M-153	Van Vogt, A.E. - ***The Weapon Makers*** [1966] Cover art by Gaughan.	$ .65	$2.00	$4.00
M-154	Campbell, John W. - ***Invaders From The Infinite*** [1966] Cover art by Gray Morrow	$ .75	$2.50	$5.00
M-155	Zelazny, Roger - ***Four For Tomorrow*** [1967] PBO. Cover art by Gaughan.	$ .75	$2.50	$5.00
M-156	Norton, Andre - ***Key Out Of Time*** [1966]	$ .65	$2.00	$4.00
M-157	Norton, Andre - ***Star Gate*** [1966] Cover by Ed Emsh.	$ .65	$2.00	$4.00
M-159	Lloyd, Sylvia - ***Down East Nurse*** [1966] Cover art by Koenig.	$ .50	$1.50	$3.00
M-160	Nye, Nelson - ***Trail Of Lost Skulls*** [1966]	$ .75	$2.50	$5.00
M-161	Heath, Sharon - ***Nurse At Moorcroft Manor*** [1966]	$ .50	$1.50	$3.00
M-162	Grinnell, David (Donald Wollheim) - ***Edge Of time*** [1966] Cover art by Kelly Freas.	$ .65	$2.00	$4.00
M-164	Roberts, Suzanne - ***Cross Country Nurse*** [1966]	$ .50	$1.50	$3.00
M-165	Laumer, Keith - ***Worlds Of The Imperium*** [1966]	$ .65	$2.00	$4.00

Ace N Series. New York: Ace Books.

		G	VG	F
N-1	Anthology - ***Retrospect 1964*** [1964] PBO. Photo cover. Over 1000 photos.	$1.35	$4.00	$8.00
N-2	Anthology - ***Retrospect 1965*** [1965] PBO. Over 1000 photos.	$1.00	$3.00	$6.00
N-3	Herbert, Frank - ***Dune*** [1966] Cover by John Schoenherr.	$2.50	$7.50	$15.00
N-4	Asimov, Isaac - ***Is Anyone There?*** [1966]	$1.00	$3.00	$6.00
N-5	Corson, William R. - ***The Betrayal*** [1966]	$1.00	$3.00	$6.00
N-6	Lupoff, Richard - ***E.R. Burroughs: Father Of Adventure*** [1966] Cover by Frazetta.	$1.50	$5.00	$10.00

Ace Numbered Series. New York: Ace Books.

		G	VG	F
00990	Koontz, Dean R./Putney, Susan K. - ***Time Thieves/Against Arcturus*** [1972] PBO.	$5.50	$17.50	$35.00
13973	Koontz, Dean R. - ***Dark Of The Woods/Soft Come The Dragons*** [1970] PBO. Covers by Jeff Jones/Jack Gaughan.	$5.50	$17.50	$35.00
22600	Koontz, Dean R./Bulmer, Kenneth - ***The Fall Of The Dream Machine/The Star Ventures*** [1969] PBO.	$5.50	$17.50	$35.00
23140	Koontz, Dean R./Tubb, E. C. - ***Fear That Man/Toyman*** [1969] PBO.	$5.50	$17.50	$35.00

Ace SF Specials (1st Series). New York: Ace Books.

		G	VG	F
A-13	Schmitz, James H. - ***The Witches Of Karres*** [1968].	$1.35	$4.00	$8.00
A-16	Panshin, Alexei - ***Rite Of Passage*** [1968] PBO.	$1.35	$4.00	$8.00
A-19	Anthony, Piers & Margroff, Robert E. - ***The Ring*** [1968] PBO.	$1.35	$4.00	$8.00

		G	VG	F
A-29	Blish, James & Knight, Norman L. - ***A Torrent Of Faces*** [1968]	$1.35	$4.00	$8.00
H-42	Simak, Clifford D. - ***Why Call Them Back From Heaven?*** [1968]	$1.35	$4.00	$8.00
H-54	Lafferty, R.A. - ***Past Master*** [1968] PBO	$1.35	$4.00	$8.00
H-58	Friedberg, Gertrude - ***The Revolving Boy*** [1968]	$1.35	$4.00	$8.00
H-62	Tucker, Wilson - ***The Lincoln Hunters*** [1968]	$1.35	$4.00	$8.00
H-72	Russ, Joanna - ***Picnic On Paradise*** [1968] PBO	$1.35	$4.00	$8.00
H-79	Shaw, Bob - ***The Two-Timers*** [1968] PBO	$1.35	$4.00	$8.00
H-86	Compton, D.G. - ***Synthajoy*** [1968] PBO.	$1.35	$4.00	$8.00
H-105	Schmitz, James H. - ***The Demon Breed*** [1968] PBO.	$1.50	$5.00	$10.00
00950	Goulart, Ron - ***After Things Fell Apart*** [1970] PBO	$1.35	$4.00	$8.00
02268	Russ, Joanna - ***And Chaos Died*** [1970] PBO	$1.35	$4.00	$8.00
06530	Moorcock, Michael - ***The Black Corridor*** [1969] PBO	$1.35	$4.00	$8.00
10480	Compton, D.G. - ***Chronocules*** [1970] PBO.	$1.35	$4.00	$8.00
18630	Eklund, Gordon - ***The Eclipse Of Dawn*** [1971] PBO. Cover art by Leo & Diane Dillon	$1.35	$4.00	$8.00
24590	Lafferty, R.A. - ***Fourth Mansions*** [1969] PBO.	$1.35	$4.00	$8.00
25950	Elgin, Suzette Haden - ***Furthest*** [1971] PBO. Cover art by Leo & Diane Dillon.	$1.35	$4.00	$8.00
34900	McAllister, Bruce - ***Humanity Prime*** [1971] PBO. Cover art by Davis Meltzer	$1.35	$4.00	$8.00
37425	Davidson, Avram - ***The Island Under The Earth*** [1969] PBO.	$1.35	$4.00	$8.00
37465	Zelazny, Roger - ***Isle Of The Dead*** [1969] PBO.	$1.35	$4.00	$8.00
38120	Brunner, John - ***The Jagged Orbit*** [1969] PBO.	$1.35	$4.00	$8.00
47800	Le Guin, Ursula K. - ***The Left Hand Of Darkness*** [1969] PBO if no starburst on cover	$2.50	$7.50	$15.00
52975	Conway, Gerard F. - ***The Midnight Dancers*** [1971] PBO. Cover art by Davis Meltzer.	$1.35	$4.00	$8.00
58050	Lafferty, R.A. - ***Nine Hundred Grandmothers*** [1970] PBO.	$1.35	$4.00	$8.00
62938	Shaw, Bob - ***One Million Tomorrows*** [1970] PBO. Cover art by Leo & Diane Dillon	$1.35	$4.00	$8.00
65050	Shaw, Bob - ***The Palace Of Eternity*** [1969] PBO	$1.35	$4.00	$8.00
65430	Roberts, Keith - ***Pavane*** [1969]	$1.35	$4.00	$8.00
66100	Davidson, Avram - ***The Phoenix And The Mirror*** [1970]	$1.35	$4.00	$8.00
67800	Dick, Philip K. - ***The Preserving Machine*** [1969] PBO.	$3.00	$9.00	$18.00
71435	Sladek, John T. - ***Mechasm*** [1969]	$1.35	$4.00	$8.00
76385	Compton, D.G. - ***The Silent Multitude*** [1969]	$1.35	$4.00	$8.00
78575	Compton, D.G. - ***The Steel Crocodile*** [1970] PBO	$1.35	$4.00	$8.00
82210	Brunner, John - ***The Traveller In Black*** [1971] PBO. Cover art by Leo & Diane Dillon	$1.50	$5.00	$10.00
87060	Moorcock, Michael - ***Warlord Of The Air*** [1971] PBO. Cover art by Davis Meltzer.	$1.35	$4.00	$8.00
90075	LeGuin, Ursula K. - ***A Wizard Of Earthsea*** [1970]	$1.35	$4.00	$8.00
94200	Tucker, Wilson - ***The Year Of The Quiet Sun*** [1970] PBO.	$1.35	$4.00	$8.00

Ace SF Specials (2nd Series). New York: Ace Books.

25460-1	Staton, Mary - ***From The Legend Of Biel*** [1975] PBO. Author's first book.	$1.00	$3.00	$6.00
71160-2	Chapman, D. D. & Tarzan, Deloris Lehman - ***Red Tide*** [1975] PBO.	$1.00	$3.00	$6.00
20660-3	Bradley, Marion Zimmer - ***Endless Voyage*** [1975] PBO	$1.00	$3.00	$6.00
37170-4	Lem, Stanislaw - ***The Invincible*** [1975]	$1.00	$3.00	$6.00
30420-5	Gotschalk, Felix C. - ***Growing Up In Tier 3000*** [1975] PBO. Author's first SF novel.	$1.00	$3.00	$6.00

		G	VG	F
10150-6	Richmond, Walt & Leigh - ***Challenge The Hellmaker*** [1976] PBO.	$1.00	$3.00	$6.00
46850-7	Swann, Thomas Burnett - ***Lady Of The Bees*** [1976]	$1.00	$3.00	$6.00
81900-8	Swann, Thomas Burnett - ***The Tournament Of Thorns*** [1976] PBO.	$1.00	$3.00	$6.00
66780-9	Barton, William - ***A Plague Of All Cowards*** [1976] PBO.	$1.00	$3.00	$6.00
63780-10	Shaw, Bob - ***Orbitsville*** [1977] PBO.	$1.00	$3.00	$6.00
81180-11	Yarbro, Chelsea Quinn - ***Time Of The Fourth Horseman*** [1977] Cover by David Meltzer.	$1.25	$3.75	$7.50

Ace SF Specials (3rd Series). New York: Ace Books.

		G	VG	F
88870-1	Robinson, Kim Stanley - ***The Wild Shore*** [1984] PBO. Author's first novel.	$1.00	$3.00	$6.00
30274-2	Shepard, Lucius - ***Green Eyes*** [1984] PBO. Author's first novel.	$6.00	$20.00	$40.00
56956-3	Gibson, William - ***Neuromancer*** [1984] PBO. Cover by James Warhola. Author's first novel.	$8.00	$25.00	$50.00
65065-4	Scholz, Carter & Harcourt, Glenn - ***Palimpsests*** [1984] PBO. Cover by Attilla Hejja. Authors' first novel.	$1.00	$3.00	$6.00
80557-5	Waldrop, Howard - ***Them Bones*** [1984] PBO. Cover by Marvin Mattleson. Author's first solo novel.	$1.00	$3.00	$6.00
35869-6	Swanick, Michael - ***In The Drift*** [1985] PBO. Cover by Ron Lieberman. Author's first novel.	$1.00	$3.00	$6.00
37367-7	McDevitt, Jack - ***The Hercules Text*** [1986] PBO. Cover by Earl Keleny. Author's first novel.	$1.00	$3.00	$6.00
56941-8	MacGregor, Loren J. - ***The Net*** [1987] PBO. Cover by Earl Keleny. Author's first novel.	$1.00	$3.00	$6.00
52813-9	Kadrey, Richard - ***Metrophage*** [1988] PBO. Cover by Earl Keleny. Author's first novel.	$1.00	$3.00	$6.00

Adult Books.

		G	VG	F
417	Dale - ***Chief Sexecutive*** [n.d.]	$1.50	$5.00	$10.00
1538	Smythe, R. J. - ***Switch Off*** [n.d.]	$1.50	$5.00	$10.00
1641	Lea, D. - ***His Psychic Daughter*** [n.d.]	$1.50	$5.00	$10.00

Adventure Novel Classic. New York: Novel Selections. Digest Size.

		G	VG	F
1	Buchan, John - ***The Blanket Of The Dark*** [n.d.]	$1.00	$3.00	$6.00
2	Sabatini, Rafael - ***Bardelys The Magnificent*** [n.d.]	$1.00	$3.00	$6.00
3	Titus, Harold - ***Code Of The North*** [n.d.]	$1.00	$3.00	$6.00
4	Buchan, John - ***House Of The Four Winds*** [n.d.]	$1.00	$3.00	$6.00
5	Sabatini, Rafael - ***The Queen's Messenger*** [n.d.]	$1.00	$3.00	$6.00
6	Case, Robert Ormond - ***Big Timber*** [n.d.]	$1.00	$3.00	$6.00
7	Treynor, Albert M. - ***Hands Up!*** [n.d.]	$1.00	$3.00	$6.00
9	Titus, Harold - ***Below Zero*** [n.d.]	$1.00	$3.00	$6.00
10	Hendryx, James B. - ***Connie Morgan Hits The Trail*** [n.d.]	$1.00	$3.00	$6.00
11	Young, Gordon - ***The Vengeance Of Hurricane Williams*** [n.d.]	$1.00	$3.00	$6.00
12	Sabatini, Rafael - ***The Trampling Of The Lilies*** [n.d.]	$1.00	$3.00	$6.00
13	Seltzer, Charles Alden - ***Gone North*** [n.d.]	$1.00	$3.00	$6.00
14	LeMay, Alan - ***Rivermen Die Broke*** [n.d.]	$1.00	$3.00	$6.00
15	Curwood, James Oliver - ***The Courage Of Marge O'Doone*** [n.d.]	$1.00	$3.00	$6.00
16	Parkman, Sydney - ***Out From Shanghai*** [n.d.]	$1.00	$3.00	$6.00
17	Hendryx, James - ***Death Heads North*** [n.d.]	$1.00	$3.00	$6.00
18	White, Leslie T. - ***River Of Fear*** [n.d.]	$1.00	$3.00	$6.00
19	Gill, Tom - ***The Unknown Ranger*** [n.d.]	$1.00	$3.00	$6.00

		G	VG	F
20	Foreman, L. L. - ***Flight To Glory*** [n.d.]	$1.00	$3.00	$6.00
21	Treynor, Albert M. - ***Hawk Of The Desert*** [n.d.]	$1.00	$3.00	$6.00
22	Hawkins, John & Ward - ***Secret Command*** [n.d.] Photo Cover	$1.00	$3.00	$6.00
23	Short, Luke - ***Hard Money*** [n.d.]	$1.00	$3.00	$6.00
24	Amos, Alan - ***Jungle Murder*** [n.d.]	$1.00	$3.00	$6.00
25	Kelland, Clarence Budington - ***Valley Of The Sun*** [n.d.]	$1.00	$3.00	$6.00
26	Evans, Evan - ***Montana Rides*** [n.d.]	$1.00	$3.00	$6.00
27	Gill, Tom - ***North To Danger*** [n.d.]	$1.00	$3.00	$6.00
28	Bechdolt, Frederick R. - ***Riot At Red Water*** [n.d.]	$1.00	$3.00	$6.00
29	Hawkins, John & Ward - ***Broken River*** [n.d.]	$1.00	$3.00	$6.00
30	Kelland, Clarence Budington - ***Arizona*** [n.d.]	$1.00	$3.00	$6.00
31	Adams, Eustace L. - ***Death Charter*** [n.d.]	$1.00	$3.00	$6.00
32	Evans, Evan - ***Montana Rides Again*** [n.d.]	$1.00	$3.00	$6.00
33	Drago, Harry Sinclair - ***Stagecoach Kingdom*** [n.d.]	$1.00	$3.00	$6.00
34	Koehler, Robert Portner - ***Journey To Murder*** [n.d.]	$1.00	$3.00	$6.00
35	Hawkins, John & Ward - ***Devil On His Trail*** [n.d.]	$1.00	$3.00	$6.00
36	Evans, Evan - ***The Song Of The Whip*** [n.d.]	$1.00	$3.00	$6.00
37	Gill, Tom - ***Jungle Harvest*** [n.d.]	$1.00	$3.00	$6.00
39	Titus, Harold - ***Flame In The Forest*** [n.d.]	$1.00	$3.00	$6.00
40	Parkman, Sydney - ***Ship Ashore*** [n.d.]	$1.00	$3.00	$6.00

After Hours.

105	Kosloff, Myron - ***Queen Of Evil*** [1964] PBO	$3.50	$10.00	$20.00
128	Willow, Peter - ***Pay The Devil*** [n.d.]	$3.50	$10.00	$20.00
142	DuVal, Arlene - ***Side Street*** [1966] PBO. Cover by Bill Ward.	$2.50	$7.50	$15.00
146	Spencer, Jack - ***Lady Doctor*** [1966] PBO. Cover by Bill Ward.	$2.50	$7.50	$15.00
161	Caval, Patrice - ***Out Of Action*** [1967] PBO. Cover by Ward	$2.50	$7.50	$15.00

Airmont SF Series. New York: Airmont Publishing Co.

SF-1	West, Wallace - ***The Memory Bank*** [1962] Cover by Brillhart.	$ .65	$2.00	$4.00
SF-2	Sprague de Camp, L. - ***Tower Of Zanid*** [1963]	$ .65	$2.00	$4.00
SF-3	West, Wallace - ***Lords Of Atlantis*** [1963]	$ .65	$2.00	$4.00
SF-4	Pratt, Fletcher - ***Invaders From Rigel*** [1964]	$ .65	$2.00	$4.00
SF-5	del Rey, Lester - ***Day Of The Giants*** [1964]	$ .65	$2.00	$4.00
SF-6	Coblentz, Stanton A. - ***Hidden World*** [1964]	$ .65	$2.00	$4.00
SF-7	Banister, Manly - ***Conquest Of Earth*** [1964]	$ .65	$2.00	$4.00
SF-8	Blish, James & Lowndes, Robert - ***The Duplicated Man*** [1964]	$ .65	$2.00	$4.00

Alicat Chap Books. New York: Alicat Bookshop Press. Digest Size. Cardboard covers.

12	Willeford, Charles - ***Proletarian Laughter*** [1948] PBO. Limited to 1000 copies. Author's first book	$30.00	$100.00	$225.00

All Star Books.

2	Farmer, Arthur - ***Odd Girl Out*** [1963] PBO	$2.00	$6.00	$12.00
39	Lane, Jerry - ***Sex With A Smile*** [1965] PBO.	$1.50	$5.00	$10.00
80	Flaming, I. M. - ***Snakefinger*** [1966] PBO.	$2.50	$7.50	$15.00
85	Dare, Anthony - ***The Joy Zone*** [1966] PBO. Cover by Maguire.	$1.50	$5.00	$10.00
518	Farmer, Arthur - ***The Nymph And The Satyr*** [1962] PBO. Cover by J. Healey.	$1.50	$5.00	$10.00

All-Picture Mystery. Digest Size.

NO#-1	Stokes, Manning Lee - ***The Case Of The Winking Buddha*** [1950] PBO. Story told in comic book format.	$17.00	$50.00	$100.00

		G	VG	F
NO#-2	Waller, Drake - ***It Rhymes With Lust*** [1950] PBO. Cover art and interior art by Matt Baker. Story told in comic book format.	$22.00	$70.00	$140.00

Amazing Stories Science Fiction Novel. New York: Ziff Davis Publishing. Digest Size.

		G	VG	F
NO#-1	Slesar, Henry - ***20 Million Miles To Earth*** [1957] PBO. Movie tie-in.	$22.00	$70.00	$140.00

American Red Cross. New York: Readers' League of America.

		G	VG	F
NN-1	Marsh, Ngaio - ***Death In A White Tie*** [n.d.] Special edition for free distribution. Has Pocket Books logo.	$1.25	$3.75	$7.50
NN-2	Hammett, Dashiell - ***The Thin Man*** [n.d.]	$1.50	$5.00	$10.00
NN-3	Hammett, Dashiell - ***The Maltese Falcon*** [n.d.]	$1.50	$5.00	$10.00
NN-4	Irish, William - ***Phantom Lady*** [n.d.]	$1.25	$3.75	$7.50
NN-5	Oppenheim, E. Phillips - ***The Great Impersonation*** [n.d.]	$1.25	$3.75	$7.50

American Science Fiction Magazine. Sydney, Australia: Malial Press.

		G	VG	F
NO#-1	Oliver, Chad - ***Fires Of Forever*** [n.d.] Cover by Stanley Pitt.	$2.50	$7.50	$15.00
NO#-2	Fyfe, Horace Bown - ***Moonwalk*** [n.d.] Cover by Stanley Pitt.	$2.50	$7.50	$15.00
NO#-3	St. John, Philip - ***Adventure In Time*** [n.d.] Cover by Stanley Pitt.	$2.50	$7.50	$15.00
NO#-4	Kuttner, Henry - ***Remember Tomorrow*** [n.d.] Cover by Stanley Pitt.	$3.00	$9.00	$18.00
NO#-5	Williams, Robert Moore - ***Refuge For Tonight*** [n.d.] Cover by Stanley Pitt.	$2.50	$7.50	$15.00
NO#-6	Campbell, Jr., John W. - ***The Thing From Another World*** [n.d.] Cover by Safone Jais.	$2.50	$7.50	$15.00
NO#-7	Phillips, Alexander M. - ***Death Of The Moon*** [n.d.] Cover by Stanley Pitt.	$2.50	$7.50	$15.00
NO#-8	Kuttner, Henry - ***Way Of The Gods*** [n.d.] Cover by Stanley Pitt.	$3.00	$9.00	$18.00
NO#-9	Wellman, Manly Wade - ***Men Against The Stars*** [n.d.]	$2.50	$7.50	$15.00
NO#-10	Jenkins, William Fitzgerald - ***The Soldado Ant*** [n.d.] Cover by Stanley Pitt.	$2.50	$7.50	$15.00
NO#-11	Lhin, Erik Van - ***Moon-Blind*** [n.d.]	$2.50	$7.50	$15.00
NO#-12	Harris, Clare Winger & Breur, Miles J. - ***The Dead World*** [n.d.].	$2.50	$7.50	$15.00
NO#-13	Campbell, Jr., John W. - ***Dead Knowledge*** [n.d.] Cover by Stanley Pitt.	$2.50	$7.50	$15.00
NO#-14	James, Edwin - ***Veiled Knowledge*** [n.d.]	$2.50	$7.50	$15.00
NO#-15	Carr, Robert Spencer - ***The Invaders*** [n.d.] Cover by Stanley Pitt.	$2.50	$7.50	$15.00
NO#-16	Kubilius, Walter - ***The Other Side*** [n.d.] Cover by Stanley Pitt.	$2.50	$7.50	$15.00
NO#-17	Leinster, Murray - ***The Unknown*** [n.d.] Cover by Stanley Pitt.	$2.50	$7.50	$15.00
NO#-18	O'Donnell, Lawrence - ***Clash By Night*** [n.d.] Cover by Stanley Pitt.	$2.50	$7.50	$15.00
NO#-19	Bond, Nelson - ***The Monster*** [n.d.]	$2.50	$7.50	$15.00
NO#-20	Kuttner, Henry - ***Sword Of Tomorrow*** [n.d.] Cover by Stanley Pitt.	$3.00	$9.00	$18.00
NO#-21	Livingston, Berkeley - ***The Moving Finger*** [n.d.] Cover by Stanley Pitt.	$2.50	$7.50	$15.00
NO#-22	Fairman, Paul W. - ***Nine Worlds West*** [n.d.] Cover by Stanley Pitt.	$2.50	$7.50	$15.00
NO#-23	Livingston, Berkeley - ***Meteor Of Death*** [n.d.] Cover by Stanley Pitt.	$2.50	$7.50	$15.00
NO#-24	Cox, Jr., Irving - ***Of Such As These*** [n.d.] Cover by Stanley Pitt.	$2.50	$7.50	$15.00

		G	VG	F
NO#-25	Fairman, Paul W. - ***Never Trust A Martian*** [n.d.] Cover by Stanley Pitt.	$2.50	$7.50	$15.00
NO#-26	Brackett, Leigh - ***The Ark Of Mars*** [n.d.] Cover by Stanley Pitt.	$3.00	$9.00	$18.00
NO#-27	Moore, Catherine L. - ***There Shall Be Darkness*** [n.d.] Cover by Stanley Pitt.	$2.50	$7.50	$15.00
NO#-28	Garrett, Randall - ***Derelict Of Space*** [n.d.] Cover by Stanley Pitt.	$2.50	$7.50	$15.00
NO#-29	Heinlein, Robert A. - ***The Man Who Sold The Moon*** [n.d.] Cover by Safone Jais.	$4.00	$12.50	$25.00
NO#-30	Williams, Robert Moore - ***Red Death Of Mars*** [n.d.] Cover by Stanley Pitt.	$2.50	$7.50	$15.00
NO#-31	Leinster, Murray - ***Conquest Of The Stars*** [n.d.]	$2.50	$7.50	$15.00
NO#-32	Leinster, Murray - ***The Lonely Planet*** [n.d.] Cover by Stanley Pitt.	$2.50	$7.50	$15.00
NO#-33	Campbell, Jr., John W. - ***Elimination*** [n.d.] Cover by Stanley Pitt.	$2.50	$7.50	$15.00
NO#-34	Macreigh, James - ***Danger Moon*** [n.d.]	$2.50	$7.50	$15.00
NO#-35	Blish, James - ***Common Time*** [n.d.] Cover by Stanley Pitt.	$2.50	$7.50	$15.00
NO#-36	Gallun, Raymond Z. - ***Double Identity*** [n.d.] Cover by Stanley Pitt.	$2.50	$7.50	$15.00

American Sports Library.

		G	VG	F
F-101	Anthology - ***Sport, Sport, Sport*** [1963] Photo cover.	$ .65	$2.00	$4.00
F-102	Smith, Red - ***The Best Of Red Smith*** [1963] PBO. Photo cover.	$ .65	$2.00	$4.00
F-103	Ford, Whitey & Lang, Jack - ***The Fighting Southpaw*** [1963] PBO.	$ .75	$2.50	$5.00
F-104	Berra, Yogi & Ferdenze, Til - ***Behind The Plate*** [1963] PBO.	$ .75	$2.50	$5.00
F-105	Orr, Jack - ***Baseball's Greatest Players Today*** [1963] PBO. Photo cover.	$ .75	$2.50	$5.00
F-106	Einstein, Charles - ***A Flag For San Francisco*** [1963] PBO. Photo cover.	$ .75	$2.50	$5.00
F-107	Anderson, Dave - ***Pro Football Handbook*** [1963] PBO.	$ .65	$2.00	$4.00
F-108	Anthology - ***Tom Harmon's Book Of Sports Information*** [1963] Photo cover.	$ .65	$2.00	$4.00
F-109	Cousy, Bob - ***Basketball Is My Life*** [1963] Photo cover.	$ .65	$2.00	$4.00
S-110	Rikhoff, Jim - ***The Compact Book Of Hunting*** [1964] PBO. Photo cover.	$ .65	$2.00	$4.00
S-111	Seville, Jack - ***The Compact Book Of Boating*** [1964] PBO. Photo cover.	$ .65	$2.00	$4.00
S-112	Ovington, Ray - ***The Compact Book Of Outdoor Photography*** [1964] PBO.	$ .65	$2.00	$4.00
S-113	Zwirz, Bob - ***The Compact Book Of Fresh Water Fishing*** [1964] PBO. Photo cover.	$ .65	$2.00	$4.00
S-114	Anthology - ***More Sport, Sport, Sport*** [1964]	$ .65	$2.00	$4.00
F-115	Wallop, Douglass - ***The Year The Yankees Lost The Pennant*** [1964]	$ .75	$2.50	$5.00
F-116	Mays, Willie & Harris, Jeff - ***Danger In Center Field*** [1964]	$ .75	$2.50	$5.00
F-117	Anderson, Dave - ***Major League Baseball Handbook 1964*** [1964]	$ .75	$2.50	$5.00
F-118	Anderson, Dave - ***Pro Football Handbook 1964*** [1964]	$ .65	$2.00	$4.00
F-119	Anthology - ***Pro, Pro, Pro*** [1964]	$ .65	$2.00	$4.00
F-120	Edited by Don Smith - ***The Quarterbacks*** [1964] PBO.	$ .65	$2.00	$4.00
S-121	Horsley, Fred - ***The Hot Rod Handbook*** [1964]	$ .65	$2.00	$4.00
N-122	Litsky, Frank & Tyno, Steve - ***The New York Times Sports Almanac, 1965*** [1964]	$ .65	$2.00	$4.00

Archer Book, 8

Archer Press, NN#14

Archer Press, NN#38

		G	VG	F
S-123	Edited by Ray Ovington - ***The Compact Book Of Upland Game Birds*** [1964]	$ .65	$2.00	$4.00
S-124	Edited by Ray Ovington - ***The Compact Book Of Waterfowl And Lowland Game birds*** [1964]	$ .65	$2.00	$4.00
S-125	Edited by Ray Ovington - ***The Compact Book Of Small Game And Varmints*** [1964]	$ .65	$2.00	$4.00
S-126	Edited by Ray Ovington - ***The Compact Book Of Big Game Animals*** [1965] PBO. Cover by Francis W. Davis.	$ .65	$2.00	$4.00
F-127	Anthology - ***Tom Harmon's Sports Information Book*** [1965] Photo cover.	$ .65	$2.00	$4.00

Archer Books. Cleveland, OH: Kaywin Publishers.

3	Morelli, Spike - ***Take It And Like It*** [1951] Cover by Heade.	$3.50	$10.00	$20.00
5	Storme, Michael - ***Dame In My Bed*** [1951] Cover by Heade.	$3.50	$10.00	$20.00
8	Morelli, Spike - ***You'll Never Get Me*** [n.d.] Cover by Heade.	$3.50	$10.00	$20.00
35	Vane, Roland - ***Vice Rackets Of Soho*** [1951] Classic drug/hypo cover by Heade.	$6.00	$20.00	$40.00
36	Renin, Paul - ***Flame*** [1951] Cover by Heade.	$3.50	$10.00	$20.00
50	Renin, Paul - ***Sex*** [1951]	$2.50	$7.50	$15.00
51	Vane, Roland - ***Night Haunts Of Paris*** [1951]	$1.50	$5.00	$10.00
52	Vane, Roland - ***Sinful Sisters*** [n.d.] Cover by Heade.	$3.50	$10.00	$20.00
57	Revere, Jeanette - ***Plaything Of Passion*** [1951] Cover by Heade.	$3.50	$10.00	$20.00
68	Vane, Roland - ***White Slaves Of New Orleans*** [1951] Cover by Heade.	$4.00	$12.50	$25.00
69	Vane, Roland - ***Ladies Of The Red Lamp*** [1951] Cover by Heade.	$3.50	$10.00	$20.00
70	Flammeche, Pierre - ***The Silken Lure*** [1951] Cover by Heade.	$3.50	$10.00	$20.00
71	Storme, Michael - ***Unlucky Virgin*** [1951] Cover by Thorpe.	$1.50	$5.00	$10.00
72	Della, Lew - ***Ladies Sleep Alone*** [1951]	$1.50	$5.00	$10.00
84	Storme, Michael - ***Make Mine A Harlot*** [1952] Cover by Pollack.	$3.50	$10.00	$20.00
96	Flammeche, Pierre - ***Spoiled Lives*** [1952] Cover by Heade.	$3.50	$10.00	$20.00

Archer Press, Ltd. Stoke-on-Trent, England.

NO#-1	Montesse, Ruy Du - ***Passionate Puritan*** [n.d.]	$2.50	$7.50	$15.00
NO#-2	Della, Lew - ***Be Sure It's Love*** [n.d.]	$1.50	$5.00	$10.00
NO#-3	Vincent, Slim - ***Tough Guys Fall Too*** [n.d.]	$1.50	$5.00	$10.00

		G	VG	F
NO#-4	Vincent, Slim - ***Floosie On The Run*** [n.d.]	$1.50	$5.00	$10.00
NO#-5	Vincent, Slim - ***No Tears For The Dead*** [n.d.]	$1.50	$5.00	$10.00
NO#-6	Vane, Roland - ***Woman With A Past*** [n.d.]	$1.50	$5.00	$10.00
NO#-7	Vane, Roland - ***Wanton Wife*** [1949] PBO.	$1.50	$5.00	$10.00
NO#-8	Vane, Roland - ***White Slave Racket*** [n.d.]	$1.50	$5.00	$10.00
NO#-9	Lytle, H. M. - ***The Tragedies Of The White Slaves*** [n.d.]	$1.50	$5.00	$10.00
NO#-10	Vane, Roland - ***White Slaves Of New Orleans*** [1949] Cover by Heade.	$3.50	$10.00	$20.00
NO#-11	Vane, Roland - ***Night Haunts Of Paris*** [n.d.]	$1.50	$5.00	$10.00
NO#-12	Vane, Roland - ***Ladies Of The Red Lamp*** [n.d.]	$1.50	$5.00	$10.00
NO#-13	Vane, Roland - ***Sinful Sisters*** [n.d.]	$1.50	$5.00	$10.00
NO#-14	Vane, Roland - ***Girl From Tiger Bay*** [1950] PBO. Cover by Heade.	$4.50	$14.00	$28.00
NO#-15	Vane, Roland - ***Sin-Stained*** [n.d.] Cover by Heade.	$2.50	$7.50	$15.00
NO#-16	Goodchild, George - ***The Eternal Conflict*** [n.d.] PBO. Cover by Heade.	$2.50	$7.50	$15.00
NO#-17	Ross, Gene - ***Two Smart Dames*** [1949] PBO. Cover by Pollack.	$1.50	$5.00	$10.00
NO#-18	Storme, Michael - ***Make Mine A Harlot*** [n.d.]	$1.50	$5.00	$10.00
NO#-19	Storme, Michael - ***Make Mine Beautiful*** [n.d.] Cover by Pollack.	$1.50	$5.00	$10.00
NO#-20	Renin, Paul - ***All That Glitters*** [n.d.]	$1.50	$5.00	$10.00
NO#-21	Renin, Paul - ***Heads! I Marry You*** [n.d.]	$1.50	$5.00	$10.00
NO#-22	Renin, Paul - ***Dolores*** [n.d.]	$1.50	$5.00	$10.00
NO#-23	Renin, Paul - ***Good-Time Girls*** [n.d.]	$1.50	$5.00	$10.00
NO#-24	Renin, Paul - ***Scandal*** [n.d.]	$1.50	$5.00	$10.00
NO#-25	Renin, Paul - ***Daring Diana*** [n.d.]	$1.50	$5.00	$10.00
NO#-26	Renin, Paul - ***When A Woman Loves*** [n.d.]	$1.50	$5.00	$10.00
NO#-27	Renin, Paul - ***Sex*** [n.d.]	$1.50	$5.00	$10.00
NO#-28	Renin, Paul - ***Bitter Sweets*** [n.d.]	$1.50	$5.00	$10.00
NO#-29	Renin, Paul - ***Thy Neighbour's Wife*** [n.d.]	$1.50	$5.00	$10.00
NO#-30	Renin, Paul - ***Co-Respondent*** [n.d.]	$1.50	$5.00	$10.00
NO#-31	Snow, Charles H. - ***Cardigan Cowboy*** [n.d.]	$1.50	$5.00	$10.00
NO#-32	Snow, Charles H. - ***Black Riders Of The Range*** [n.d.]	$1.50	$5.00	$10.00
NO#-33	Snow, Charles H. - ***Argonaut Gold*** [n.d.]	$1.50	$5.00	$10.00
NO#-34	Snow, Charles H. - ***Roaring Guns*** [n.d.]	$1.50	$5.00	$10.00
NO#-35	Floren, Lee - ***Puma Pistoleers*** [n.d.]	$1.50	$5.00	$10.00
NO#-36	Morelli, Spike - ***Coffin For A Cutie*** [n.d.] Cover by Heade.	$4.00	$12.50	$25.00
NO#-37	Morelli, Spike - ***You'll Never Get Me*** [n.d.]	$2.50	$7.50	$15.00
NO#-38	Morelli, Spike - ***Take It And Like It*** [n.d.]	$2.50	$7.50	$15.00
NO#-39	Flammeche, Pierre - ***When Passion Rules*** [n.d.] Cover by Heade.	$2.50	$7.50	$15.00
NO#-40	Cunningham, Louis Arthur - ***Sultry Love*** [n.d.] Cover by Heade.	$2.50	$7.50	$15.00
NO#-41	Vincent, Slim - ***Dames Are No Dice*** [n.d.] Cover by Heade.	$2.50	$7.50	$15.00
NO#-42	Vane, Roland - ***This Thing Called Sin*** [n.d.] Cover by Heade.	$2.50	$7.50	$15.00
NO#-43	Storme, Michael - ***Dame In My Bed*** [n.d.]	$2.50	$7.50	$15.00
NO#-44	Storme, Michael - ***Unlucky Virgin*** [n.d.]	$1.50	$5.00	$10.00
NO#-45	Storme, Michael - ***Make Mine A Shroud*** [n.d.]	$1.50	$5.00	$10.00
NO#-46	Storme, Michael - ***Make Mine A Virgin*** [n.d.]	$1.50	$5.00	$10.00
NO#-47	Storme, Michael - ***Make Mine Dangerous*** [n.d.]	$1.50	$5.00	$10.00
NO#-48	Storme, Michael - ***Make Mine A Corpse*** [n.d.]	$1.50	$5.00	$10.00
NO#-49	Storme, Michael - ***Sucker For A Red Head*** [n.d.]	$1.50	$5.00	$10.00
NO#-50	Storme, Michael - ***Satan Buys A Wreath*** [n.d.]	$1.50	$5.00	$10.00

		G	VG	F
NO#-51	Storme, Michael - ***Hot Dames On Cold Slabs*** [n.d.]	$2.50	$7.50	$15.00
NO#-52	Horler, Sydney - ***Virus X*** [n.d.]	$3.50	$10.00	$20.00
NO#-53	Horler, Sydney - ***The Hostage*** [n.d.]	$1.50	$5.00	$10.00
NO#-54	Horler, Sydney - ***A Bullet For The Countess*** [n.d.]	$1.50	$5.00	$10.00
NO#-55	Angelo, Tony - ***Satan's Sister*** [n.d.] Cover by Heade.	$2.50	$7.50	$15.00
NO#-56	Angelo, Tony - ***Sinner's Shroud*** [1950] PBO. Cover by Heade...	$2.50	$7.50	$15.00
NO#-57	Vane, Roland - ***Willing Sinner*** [n.d.] Cover by Heade.	$2.50	$7.50	$15.00

Armed Service Special Editions. New York: Readers' League of America.

		G	VG	F
NN-1	Kesselring, Joseph - ***Arsenic And Old Lace*** [n.d.]	$1.25	$3.75	$7.50
NN-2	Van Dine, S.S. - ***The Canary Murder Case*** [n.d.]	$1.25	$3.75	$7.50
NN-3	Bentley, E.C. - ***Trent's Last Case*** [n.d.]	$1.25	$3.75	$7.50
NN-4	Hilton, James - ***Lost Horizon*** [n.d.]	$1.25	$3.75	$7.50
NN-5	De Maupassant, Guy - ***The Great Short Stories Of De Maupassant*** [n.d.]	$1.25	$3.75	$7.50

Armed Services Editions (Early Publisher's History, 1943–1959)

During World War II, the world witnessed the unparalleled cooperation of more than seventy publishers and distributors in producing these titles. The government sponsored and helped select thirty to forty titles each month for the Armed Services Editions. Morale boosting and wholesome content, rather than cover art, concerned the editorial staff. With the exception of some of the last titles in traditional paperback format, the series used a horizontal format and dimensions of 5½" x 3⅞" or 6½" x 4½".

During their operation, they published over 1,300 classic titles from every genre and over 125 million books intended for the soldiers stationed around the world.

Armed Services Editions. New York: Editions for the Armed Services.

		G	VG	F
A-1	Ross, Leonard Q. - ***The Education Of Hyman Kaplan*** [n.d.]	$5.00	$15.00	$30.00
A-3	Nash, Ogden - ***Good Intentions*** [n.d.]	$1.35	$4.00	$8.00
A-4	Forbes, Kathryn - ***Mama's Bank Account*** [n.d.]	$1.35	$4.00	$8.00
A-5	Carse, Robert - ***There Go The Ships*** [n.d.]	$1.35	$4.00	$8.00
A-6	Feld, Rose C. - ***Sophie Halenczik, American*** [n.d.]	$1.35	$4.00	$8.00
A-7	Pratt, Theodore - ***Mr. Winkle Goes To War*** [n.d.]	$1.35	$4.00	$8.00
A-8	Dickens, Charles - ***Oliver Twist*** [n.d.]	$1.25	$3.75	$7.50
A-9	Steinbeck, John - ***Tortilla Flat*** [n.d.]	$2.00	$6.00	$12.00
A-10	Tunis, John R. - ***World Series*** [n.d.]	$1.35	$4.00	$8.00
A-11	Thurber, James - ***My World And Welcome To It*** [n.d.]	$1.35	$4.00	$8.00
A-12	Gruber, Frank - ***Peace Marshal*** [n.d.]	$1.25	$3.75	$7.50
A-13	Mencken, H.L. - ***Heathen Days*** [n.d.]	$1.35	$4.00	$8.00
A-14	Forester, C. S. - ***The Ship*** [n.d.]	$1.25	$3.75	$7.50
A-15	Saroyan, William - ***The Human Comedy*** [n.d.]	$1.25	$3.75	$7.50
A-16	De Saint-Exupery, Antoine - ***Wind, Sand, And Stars*** [n.d.]	$1.35	$4.00	$8.00
A-17	Brebner, J. B. and Nevins, Allan - ***The Making Of Modern Britain - A Short History*** [n.d.]	$1.35	$4.00	$8.00
A-18	Hitti, Philip K. - ***The Arabs*** [n.d.]	$1.25	$3.75	$7.50
A-19	Fast, Howard - ***The Unvanquished*** [n.d.]	$2.00	$6.00	$12.00
A-20	Maisel, Albert Q. - ***Miracles Of Military Medicine*** [n.d.]	$1.25	$3.75	$7.50
A-21	Agar, Herbert - ***A Time For Greatness*** [n.d.]	$1.25	$3.75	$7.50
A-22	Greene, Graham - ***The Ministry Of Fear*** [n.d.]	$1.25	$3.75	$7.50
A-23	Herzberg, Paine, Works-editors - ***Happy Landings*** [n.d.]	$1.25	$3.75	$7.50

		G	VG	F
A-24	Melville, Herman - ***Typee*** [n.d.]	$1.35	$4.00	$8.00
A-25	Holt, Rackham - ***George Washington Carver*** [n.d.]	$1.35	$4.00	$8.00
A-26	Conrad, Joseph - ***Lord Jim*** [n.d.]	$1.35	$4.00	$8.00
A-27	Sandburg, Carl - ***Storm Over The Land*** [n.d.]	$1.35	$4.00	$8.00
A-28	Allen, Hervey - ***Action At Aquila*** [n.d.]	$1.25	$3.75	$7.50
A-29	Stone, Grace Zaring - ***Reprisal*** [n.d.]	$1.35	$4.00	$8.00
A-30	Goodman, Jack - ***The Fireside Book Of Dog Stories*** [n.d.]	$1.25	$3.75	$7.50
B-31	Lane, Rose Wilder - ***Let The Hurricane Roar*** [n.d.]	$1.25	$3.75	$7.50
B-32	Herman, Fred - ***Dynamite Cargo*** [n.d.]	$1.35	$4.00	$8.00
B-33	Frost, Robert - ***Come In*** [n.d.]	$1.25	$3.75	$7.50
B-34	Wharton, Edith - ***Ethan Frome*** [n.d.]	$1.35	$4.00	$8.00
B-35	Lasswell, Mary - ***Suds In Your Eye*** [n.d.]	$1.35	$4.00	$8.00
B-36	Field, Peter - ***Fight For Powder Valley!*** [n.d.]	$1.25	$3.75	$7.50
B-37	Kimbrough, Emily, and Skinner, Cornelia - ***Our Hearts Were Young And Gay*** [n.d.]	$1.25	$3.75	$7.50
B-38	Kantor, MacKinlay - ***Gentle Annie*** [n.d.]	$1.35	$4.00	$8.00
B-39	Benchley, Robert - ***Benchley Beside Himself*** [n.d.]	$1.25	$3.75	$7.50
B-40	Sloane, William - ***To Walk The Night*** [n.d.]	$2.00	$6.00	$12.00
B-41	Gilligan, Edmund - ***The Gaunt Woman*** [n.d.]	$1.35	$4.00	$8.00
B-42	LeMay, Alan - ***Winter Range*** [n.d.]	$1.25	$3.75	$7.50
B-43	Gooden, Arthur Henry - ***Painted Buttes*** [n.d.]	$1.35	$4.00	$8.00
B-44	Taylor, Rosemary - ***Chicken Every Sunday*** [n.d.]	$1.25	$3.75	$7.50
B-45	Lowe, Q. Pardee - ***Father And Glorious Descendant*** [n.d.]	$1.35	$4.00	$8.00
B-46	Smith, H. Allen - ***Life In A Putty Knife Factory*** [n.d.]	$1.25	$3.75	$7.50
B-47	Binns, Archie - ***Lightship*** [n.d.]	$1.35	$4.00	$8.00
B-48	Spence, Hartzell - ***Get Thee Behind Me*** [n.d.]	$1.35	$4.00	$8.00
B-49	O'Hara, Mary - ***My Friend Flicka*** [n.d.]	$1.35	$4.00	$8.00
B-50	Cassidy, Henry C. - ***Moscow Dateline*** [n.d.]	$1.35	$4.00	$8.00
B-51	Macardle, Dorothy - ***The Uninvited*** [n.d.]	$1.35	$4.00	$8.00
B-52	Edmonds, Walter D. - ***Rome Haul*** [n.d.]	$1.35	$4.00	$8.00
B-53	Burt, Struthers - ***Powder River*** [n.d.]	$1.25	$3.75	$7.50
B-54	Adamic, Louis - ***The Native's Return*** [n.d.]	$1.35	$4.00	$8.00
B-55	Rawlings, Marjorie Kinnan - ***The Yearling*** [n.d.]	$1.35	$4.00	$8.00
B-56	Heym, Stefan - ***Hostages*** [n.d.]	$1.25	$3.75	$7.50
B-57	Herring, Hubert - ***Good Neighbors*** [n.d.]	$1.35	$4.00	$8.00
B-58	Denison, Merrill - ***Klondike Mike*** [n.d.]	$1.35	$4.00	$8.00
B-59	Goodrich, Marcus - ***Delilah*** [n.d.]	$1.25	$3.75	$7.50
B-60	Freuchen, Peter - ***Artic Adventure*** [n.d.]	$1.35	$4.00	$8.00
C-61	Brodrick, Alan H. - ***North Africa*** [n.d.]	$1.25	$3.75	$7.50
C-62	Richter, Conrad - ***The Sea Of Grass*** [n.d.]	$1.35	$4.00	$8.00
C-63	Robinson, James Harvey - ***The Mind In The Making*** [n.d.]	$1.25	$3.75	$7.50
C-64	Voltaire - ***Candide*** [n.d.]	$1.25	$3.75	$7.50
C-65	White, Stewart Edward - ***The Forest*** [n.d.]	$1.35	$4.00	$8.00
C-66	Nye, Nelson C. - ***Pistols For Hire*** [n.d.]	$1.35	$4.00	$8.00
C-67	Beerbohm, Max - ***Seven Men*** [n.d.]	$1.25	$3.75	$7.50
C-68	Bell, Vereen - ***Swamp Water*** [n.d.]	$1.35	$4.00	$8.00
C-69	Courtney, Charles - ***Unlocking Adventure*** [n.d.]	$1.35	$4.00	$8.00
C-70	Tarkington, Booth - ***Penrod*** [n.d.]	$1.25	$3.75	$7.50
C-71	Hudson, W. H. - ***Green Mansions*** [n.d.]	$5.50	$17.50	$35.00
C-72	Mulford, Clarence E. - ***Hopalong Cassidy Serves A Writ*** [n.d.]	$1.25	$3.75	$7.50
C-73	Lippmann, Walter - ***U.S. Foreign Policy*** [n.d.]	$1.35	$4.00	$8.00
C-74	Heyward, Du Bose - ***Star Spangled Virgin*** [n.d.]	$1.25	$3.75	$7.50

		G	VG	F
C-75	Priestley, J.B. - ***Blackout In Gretley*** [n.d.]	$1.25	$3.75	$7.50
C-76	Twain, Mark - ***The Adventures Of Tom Sawyer*** [n.d.]	$1.25	$3.75	$7.50
C-77	Benet, Stephen Vincent - ***The Short Stories Of Stephen Vincent Benet - A Selection*** [n.d.] PBO.	$3.50	$10.00	$20.00
C-78	Wason, Betty - ***Miracle In Hellas*** [n.d.]	$1.35	$4.00	$8.00
C-79	Meier, Frank - ***Fathoms Below*** [n.d.]	$1.35	$4.00	$8.00
C-80	Hill, Ernestine - ***Australian Frontier*** [n.d.]	$1.35	$4.00	$8.00
C-81	Stewart, George R. - ***Storm*** [n.d.]	$1.35	$4.00	$8.00
C-82	De Poncins, Gontran - ***Kabloona*** [n.d.]	$1.35	$4.00	$8.00
C-83	Allen, Hervey - ***The Forest And The Fort*** [n.d.]	$1.25	$3.75	$7.50
C-84	Quick, Herbert - ***The Hawkeye*** [n.d.]	$1.35	$4.00	$8.00
C-85	Thomason, Col. John W., Jr. - ***And A Few Marines*** [n.d.]	$1.25	$3.75	$7.50
C-86	Selby, John - ***Starbuck*** [n.d.]	$1.25	$3.75	$7.50
C-87	Marshall, Edison - ***Great Smith*** [n.d.]	$1.35	$4.00	$8.00
C-88	Forbes, Esther - ***Paul Revere And The World He Lived In*** [n.d.]	$1.35	$4.00	$8.00
C-89	Komroff, Manuel - ***Coronet*** [n.d.]	$1.25	$3.75	$7.50
C-90	Steinbeck, John - ***The Grapes Of Wrath*** [n.d.]	$2.50	$7.50	$15.00
D-91	Hilton, James - ***The Story Of Dr. Wassell*** [n.d.]	$1.35	$4.00	$8.00
D-92	Spalding, Charles, and Carney, Otis - ***Love At First Flight*** [n.d.].	$1.35	$4.00	$8.00
D-93	White, Stewart Edward - ***Blazed Trail Stories*** [n.d.]	$1.35	$4.00	$8.00
D-94	Tuttle, W.C. - ***Tumbling River Range*** [n.d.]	$1.35	$4.00	$8.00
D-95	Fleming, Berry - ***Colonel Effingham's Raid*** [n.d.]	$1.25	$3.75	$7.50
D-96	Albrand, Martha - ***Without Orders*** [n.d.]	$1.25	$3.75	$7.50
D-97	Cather, Willa - ***Death Comes For The Archbishop*** [n.d.]	$1.35	$4.00	$8.00
D-98	Richter, Conrad - ***The Trees*** [n.d.]	$1.25	$3.75	$7.50
D-99	Van Doren, Mark - editor (Anthology) - ***The Night Of The Summer Solstice*** [n.d.]	$1.25	$3.75	$7.50
D-100	Kelland, Clarence Budington - ***Valley Of The Sun*** [n.d.]	$1.35	$4.00	$8.00
D-101	Daly, Elizabeth - ***Evidence Of Things Seen*** [n.d.]	$2.00	$6.00	$12.00
D-102	Hergesheimer, Joseph - ***Java Head*** [n.d.]	$1.35	$4.00	$8.00
D-103	Bryan, George S. - ***Mystery Ship*** [n.d.]	$1.25	$3.75	$7.50
D-104	Seagrave, Gordon S. - ***Burma Surgeon*** [n.d.]	$1.35	$4.00	$8.00
D-105	Fosdick, Harry - ***On Being A Real Person*** [n.d.]	$1.25	$3.75	$7.50
D-106	Zinsser, Hans - ***Rats, Lice, And History*** [n.d.]	$1.35	$4.00	$8.00
D-107	Smart, Charles Allen - ***R.F.D.*** [n.d.]	$1.35	$4.00	$8.00
D-108	Mitchell, Joseph - ***McSorley's Wonderful Saloon*** [n.d.]	$1.35	$4.00	$8.00
D-109	Partridge, Bellamy - ***Country Lawyer*** [n.d.]	$1.35	$4.00	$8.00
D-110	Twain, Mark - ***The Adventures Of Huckleberry Finn*** [n.d.]	$2.50	$7.50	$15.00
D-111	Shearing, Joseph - ***Blanche Fury*** [n.d.]	$1.35	$4.00	$8.00
D-112	Rawlings, Marjorie Kinnan - ***Cross Creek*** [n.d.]	$1.35	$4.00	$8.00
D-113	Cronin, A.J. - ***The Keyes Of The Kingdom*** [n.d.]	$1.25	$3.75	$7.50
D-114	Whitaker, John T. - ***We Cannot Escape History*** [n.d.]	$1.35	$4.00	$8.00
D-115	Haines, William Wister - ***Slim*** [n.d.]	$1.25	$3.75	$7.50
D-116	Foley, Martha - editor (Anthology) - ***The Best American Short Stories Of 1942*** [n.d.]	$1.25	$3.75	$7.50
D-117	Smith, Betty A. - ***A Tree Grows In Brooklyn*** [n.d.]	$1.35	$4.00	$8.00
D-118	Douglas, Lloyd C. - ***The Robe*** [n.d.]	$1.25	$3.75	$7.50
D-119	Mason, F. Van Wyck - ***Rivers Of Glory*** [n.d.]	$1.35	$4.00	$8.00
D-120	Marquand, John P. - ***So Little Time*** [n.d.]	$1.35	$4.00	$8.00
D-123	Tuttle, W.C. - ***Ghost Trails*** [n.d.]	$1.35	$4.00	$8.00
D-128	Maugham, W. Somerset - ***The Moon And Sixpence*** [n.d.]	$1.35	$4.00	$8.00

		G	VG	F
D-131	Ratcliff, John D. - editor (Anthology) - ***Science Yearbook Of 1943*** [n.d.]	$1.25	$3.75	$7.50
E-121	Stong, Phil - ***State Fair*** [n.d.]	$1.35	$4.00	$8.00
E-122	Emerson, Ralph Waldo - ***Seven Essays*** [n.d.] PBO. First and only edition.	$5.50	$17.50	$35.00
E-124	Gooden, Arthur Henry - ***The Range Hawk*** [n.d.]	$1.25	$3.75	$7.50
E-125	Spearman, Frank - ***The Mountain Divide*** [n.d.]	$1.35	$4.00	$8.00
E-126	Damon, Bertha - ***A Sense Of Humus*** [n.d.]	$1.25	$3.75	$7.50
E-127	Pernikoff, Alexander - ***Bushido*** [n.d.]	$1.35	$4.00	$8.00
E-129	Haycox, Ernest - ***Saddle And Ride*** [n.d.]	$1.35	$4.00	$8.00
E-130	Biggers, Earl Derr - ***Seven Keyes To Baldpate*** [n.d.]	$1.35	$4.00	$8.00
E-132	Duguid, Julian - ***Green Hell*** [n.d.]	$1.35	$4.00	$8.00
E-133	Forester, C. S. - ***Ship Of The Line*** [n.d.]	$1.25	$3.75	$7.50
E-134	Stewart, George R. - ***Ordeal By Hunger*** [n.d.]	$1.25	$3.75	$7.50
E-135	Brinig, Myron - ***The Gambler Takes A Wife*** [n.d.]	$1.25	$3.75	$7.50
E-136	Grayson, Charles - ***Stories For Men*** [n.d.]	$1.25	$3.75	$7.50
E-137	Du Maurier, Daphne - ***Jamaica Inn*** [n.d.]	$1.25	$3.75	$7.50
E-138	Hilton, James - ***Random Harvest*** [n.d.]	$1.25	$3.75	$7.50
E-139	Twain, Mark - ***A Connecticut Yankee In King Arthur's Court*** [n.d.]	$2.00	$6.00	$12.00
E-140	Ferber, Edna - ***Cimarron*** [n.d.]	$1.25	$3.75	$7.50
E-141	Johnson, Osa - ***I Married Adventure*** [n.d.]	$1.35	$4.00	$8.00
E-142	Chase, Mary Ellen - ***Windswept*** [n.d.]	$1.25	$3.75	$7.50
E-143	Pierson, Louise Randall - ***Roughly Speaking*** [n.d.]	$1.35	$4.00	$8.00
E-144	Ellsberg, Commander Edward - ***Hell On Ice*** [n.d.]	$1.25	$3.75	$7.50
E-145	Flexner, James Thomas - ***Doctors On Horseback*** [n.d.]	$1.25	$3.75	$7.50
E-146	Marquand, John P. - ***The Late George Apley*** [n.d.]	$1.35	$4.00	$8.00
E-147	Crane, Stephen - ***Selected Short Stories Of Stephen Crane*** [n.d.] PBO.	$3.50	$10.00	$20.00
E-148	Lavender, David - ***One Man's West*** [n.d.]	$1.35	$4.00	$8.00
E-149	Edmonds, Walter D. - ***Drums Along The Mohawk*** [n.d.]	$1.35	$4.00	$8.00
E-150	Bellamann, Harry - ***King's Row*** [n.d.]	$1.35	$4.00	$8.00
F-151	Byrne, Donn - ***Messer Marco Polo*** [n.d.]	$1.25	$3.75	$7.50
F-152	De Saint-Exupery, Antoine - ***Night Flight*** [n.d.]	$1.25	$3.75	$7.50
F-153	Lincoln, Abraham - ***The Selected Writings Of Abraham Lincoln*** [n.d.] PBO.	$2.50	$7.50	$15.00
F-154	Vandercook, John W. - ***Black Majesty*** [n.d.]	$1.25	$3.75	$7.50
F-155	Farson, Negley - ***Going Fishing*** [n.d.]	$1.25	$3.75	$7.50
F-156	Knight, Eric - ***Lassie Come Home*** [n.d.]	$1.25	$3.75	$7.50
F-157	Forester, C. S. - ***Flying Colours*** [n.d.]	$1.25	$3.75	$7.50
F-158	Bromley, Joseph - ***Clear The Tracks!*** [n.d.]	$1.25	$3.75	$7.50
F-159	Mencken, H.L. - ***Happy Days*** [n.d.]	$1.35	$4.00	$8.00
F-160	Raine, William MacLeod - ***Border Breed*** [n.d.]	$1.25	$3.75	$7.50
F-161	Beebe, William - ***Jungle Peace*** [n.d.]	$1.25	$3.75	$7.50
F-162	Harte, Bret - ***Selected Short Stories Of Bret Harte*** [n.d.] PBO.	$5.00	$15.00	$30.00
F-163	Mulford, Clarence E. - ***The Bar 20 Rides Again*** [n.d.]	$1.35	$4.00	$8.00
F-164	Haycox, Ernest - ***The Border Trumpet*** [n.d.]	$1.35	$4.00	$8.00
F-165	Ferber, Edna - ***So Big*** [n.d.]	$1.35	$4.00	$8.00
F-166	Markham, Beryl - ***West With The Night*** [n.d.]	$1.25	$3.75	$7.50
F-167	Keith, Agnes Newton - ***Land Below The Wind*** [n.d.]	$1.25	$3.75	$7.50
F-168	Andrews, Roy Chapman - ***Under A Lucky Star*** [n.d.]	$1.35	$4.00	$8.00
F-169	Hertzler, Arthur E. - ***The Horse And Buggy Doctor*** [n.d.]	$1.25	$3.75	$7.50

		G	VG	F
F-170	Pyle, Ernie - ***Here Is Your War*** [n.d.]	$1.35	$4.00	$8.00
F-171	White, Stewart Edward - ***The Blazed Trail*** [n.d.]	$1.35	$4.00	$8.00
F-172	Lardner, Ring - ***Round Up*** [n.d.]	$1.35	$4.00	$8.00
F-173	Sandoz, Mari - ***Old Jules*** [n.d.]	$1.25	$3.75	$7.50
F-174	Twain, Mark - ***Life On The Mississippi*** [n.d.]	$1.35	$4.00	$8.00
F-175	Lamb, Charles - ***The Essays Of Charles Lamb*** [n.d.] PBO.	$2.50	$7.50	$15.00
F-176	White, E.B. and Katharine S. - ***A Subtreasury Of American Humor*** [n.d.]	$1.35	$4.00	$8.00
F-177	Guedalla, Philip - ***Wellington*** [n.d.]	$1.35	$4.00	$8.00
F-178	McFee, William - ***Casuals Of The Sea*** [n.d.]	$1.35	$4.00	$8.00
F-179	Hall, James Norman - ***Dr. Dogbody's Leg*** [n.d.]	$1.25	$3.75	$7.50
F-180	London, Jack - ***The Sea-Wolf*** [n.d.]	$2.00	$6.00	$12.00
G-181	Smith, Thorne - ***The Glorious Pool*** [n.d.]	$1.25	$3.75	$7.50
G-182	London, Jack - ***White Fang*** [n.d.]	$2.00	$6.00	$12.00
G-183	Smith, H. Allen - ***Low Man On A Totem Pole*** [n.d.]	$1.35	$4.00	$8.00
G-184	Raine, William MacLeod - ***Trail's End*** [n.d.]	$1.25	$3.75	$7.50
G-185	Cather, Willa - ***My Antonia*** [n.d.]	$1.35	$4.00	$8.00
G-186	Woollcott, Alexander - ***Long, Long Ago*** [n.d.]	$1.25	$3.75	$7.50
G-187	Knight, Eric - ***Sam Small Flies Again*** [n.d.]	$1.35	$4.00	$8.00
G-188	Stuart, Jesse - ***Taps For Private Tussie*** [n.d.]	$1.25	$3.75	$7.50
G-189	Smith, Homer W. - ***Kamongo*** [n.d.]	$1.35	$4.00	$8.00
G-190	Rhodes, Eugene Manlove - ***The Trusty Knaves*** [n.d.]	$1.35	$4.00	$8.00
G-191	Burnett, W.R. - ***Little Caesar*** [n.d.]	$2.00	$6.00	$12.00
G-192	Benchley, Robert - ***Inside Benchley*** [n.d.]	$1.35	$4.00	$8.00
G-193	Thouless, Robert H. - ***How To Think Straight*** [n.d.]	$1.25	$3.75	$7.50
G-194	Conrad, Joseph - ***The Mirror Of The Sea*** [n.d.]	$1.25	$3.75	$7.50
G-195	Short, Luke - ***Raiders Of The Rimrock*** [n.d.]	$1.25	$3.75	$7.50
G-196	Hudson, W. H. - ***A Crystal Age*** [n.d.]	$1.25	$3.75	$7.50
G-197	Leacock, Stephen - ***Laugh With Leacock*** [n.d.]	$1.25	$3.75	$7.50
G-198	Kipling, Rudyard - ***Kim*** [n.d.]	$1.25	$3.75	$7.50
G-199	Peattie, Donald Culross - ***Journey Into America*** [n.d.]	$1.35	$4.00	$8.00
G-200	Carroll, Gladys Hasty - ***As The Earth Turns*** [n.d.]	$1.35	$4.00	$8.00
G-201	Ybarra, T.R. - ***Young Man Of Caracas*** [n.d.]	$1.35	$4.00	$8.00
G-202	Kantor, MacKinlay - ***Arouse And Beware*** [n.d.]	$1.35	$4.00	$8.00
G-203	Haynes, Williams - ***This Chemical Age*** [n.d.]	$1.35	$4.00	$8.00
G-204	O'Hara, Mary - ***Thunderhead*** [n.d.]	$1.35	$4.00	$8.00
G-205	Lane, Carl D. - ***The Fleet In The Forest*** [n.d.]	$1.25	$3.75	$7.50
G-206	Foley, Martha - editor (Anthology) - ***The Best American Short Stories Of 1943*** [n.d.]	$1.25	$3.75	$7.50
G-207	Kroll, Harry Harrison - ***Rogues' Company*** [n.d.]	$1.35	$4.00	$8.00
G-208	Marquand, John P. - ***H.M. Pulham, Esq.*** [n.d.]	$1.35	$4.00	$8.00
G-209	Melville, Herman - ***Moby Dick*** [n.d.]	$1.25	$3.75	$7.50
G-210	Stewart, George R. - ***East Of The Giants*** [n.d.]	$1.35	$4.00	$8.00
H-211	St. George, Cpl. Thomas R. - ***C/O Postmaster*** [n.d.]	$1.35	$4.00	$8.00
H-212	Rhodes, Eugene Manlove - ***Beyond The Desert*** [n.d.]	$1.25	$3.75	$7.50
H-213	Forester, C. S. - ***Payment Deferred*** [n.d.]	$1.35	$4.00	$8.00
H-214	Bennett, Arnold - ***Buried Alive*** [n.d.]	$1.25	$3.75	$7.50
H-215	Benet, Stephen Vincent - ***Western Star*** [n.d.]	$1.35	$4.00	$8.00
H-216	La Farge, Oliver - ***Laughing Boy*** [n.d.]	$1.25	$3.75	$7.50
H-217	Richards, I. A. - ***The Republic Of Plato*** [n.d.]	$1.35	$4.00	$8.00
H-218	Peattie, Donald Culross - ***Forward The Nation*** [n.d.]	$1.35	$4.00	$8.00
H-219	Glick, Carl - ***Three Times I Bow*** [n.d.]	$1.35	$4.00	$8.00

		G	VG	F
H-220	Jarrett, Cora - ***Night Over Fitch's Pond*** [n.d.]	$1.35	$4.00	$8.00
H-221	London, Jack - ***The Cruise Of The Snark*** [n.d.]	$1.35	$4.00	$8.00
H-222	Cunningham, Eugene - ***Riders Of The Night*** [n.d.]	$1.25	$3.75	$7.50
H-223	MacDougall, Michael - ***Danger In The Cards*** [n.d.]	$1.25	$3.75	$7.50
H-224	Holbrook, Stewart H. - ***Burning An Empire*** [n.d.]	$1.35	$4.00	$8.00
H-225	Dempewolff, Richard - ***Animal Reveille*** [n.d.]	$1.25	$3.75	$7.50
H-226	McMeekin, Clark - ***Red Raskall*** [n.d.]	$1.25	$3.75	$7.50
H-227	Mulford, Clarence E. - ***Corson Of The JC*** [n.d.]	$1.25	$3.75	$7.50
H-228	Roberts, Kenneth - ***Captain Caution*** [n.d.]	$1.25	$3.75	$7.50
H-229	Stone, Grace Zaring - ***The Cold Journey*** [n.d.]	$1.25	$3.75	$7.50
H-230	Smith, Thorne - ***The Bishop's Jaegers*** [n.d.]	$1.35	$4.00	$8.00
H-231	Adams, Franklin P. - editor (Anthology) - ***Innocent Merriment*** [n.d.]	$1.35	$4.00	$8.00
H-232	Spearman, Frank - ***Carmen Of The Rancho*** [n.d.]	$1.25	$3.75	$7.50
H-233	Chambers, Robert W. - ***Cardigan*** [n.d.]	$1.35	$4.00	$8.00
H-234	Barrows, Marjorie, and Eaton, George - ***Box Office*** [n.d.]	$1.25	$3.75	$7.50
H-235	Riesenberg, Felix - ***The Pacific Ocean*** [n.d.]	$1.35	$4.00	$8.00
H-236	Komroff, Manuel - ***The Travels Of Marco Polo*** [n.d.]	$1.25	$3.75	$7.50
H-237	Gilligan, Edmund - ***The Ringed Horizon*** [n.d.]	$1.35	$4.00	$8.00
H-238	Nordhoff, Charles, and Hall, James N. - ***Botany Bay*** [n.d.]	$1.35	$4.00	$8.00
H-239	Lewellyn, Richard - ***How Green Was My Valley*** [n.d.]	$1.25	$3.75	$7.50
H-240	Edmonds, Walter D. - ***Chad Hanna*** [n.d.]	$1.35	$4.00	$8.00
I-241	Boyle, Kay - ***Avalanche*** [n.d.]	$1.35	$4.00	$8.00
I-242	Ayling, Keith - ***Semper Fidelis*** [n.d.]	$1.25	$3.75	$7.50
I-243	Rorick, Isabel Scott - ***Mr. And Mrs. Cugat*** [n.d.]	$1.35	$4.00	$8.00
I-244	Bradford, Roark - ***Ol' Man An' His Chillun*** [n.d.]	$1.35	$4.00	$8.00
I-245	Tuttle, W.C. - ***The Mystery Of The Red Triangle*** [n.d.]	$1.35	$4.00	$8.00
I-246	Kimbrough, Emily - ***We Followed Our Hearts To Hollywood*** [n.d.]	$1.25	$3.75	$7.50
I-247	Sears, Paul B. - ***Deserts On The March*** [n.d.]	$1.25	$3.75	$7.50
I-248	Household, Geoffrey - ***Rogue Male*** [n.d.]	$2.00	$6.00	$12.00
I-249	Haines, William Wister - ***High Tension*** [n.d.]	$1.25	$3.75	$7.50
I-250	Barton, Bruce - ***The Book Nobody Knows*** [n.d.]	$1.25	$3.75	$7.50
I-251	Drago, Harry Sinclair - ***Stagecoach Kingdom*** [n.d.]	$1.35	$4.00	$8.00
I-252	Mansfield, Katherine - ***Selected Short Stories Of Katherine Mansfield*** [n.d.] PBO.	$2.50	$7.50	$15.00
I-253	Thurber, James - ***The Middle-Aged Man On The Flying Trapeze*** [n.d.]	$1.25	$3.75	$7.50
I-254	Haycox, Ernest - ***Deep West*** [n.d.]	$1.35	$4.00	$8.00
I-255	Kelland, Clarence Budington - ***Arizona*** [n.d.]	$1.35	$4.00	$8.00
I-256	Benton, Jesse James - ***Cow By The Tail*** [n.d.]	$1.25	$3.75	$7.50
I-257	Mulford, Clarence E. - ***Hopalong Cassidy's Protege*** [n.d.]	$1.25	$3.75	$7.50
I-258	Baarslag, Karl - ***Coast Guard To The Rescue*** [n.d.]	$1.25	$3.75	$7.50
I-259	Ellsberg, Commander Edward - ***On The Bottom*** [n.d.]	$1.35	$4.00	$8.00
I-260	Maugham, W. Somerset - ***Ashenden*** [n.d.]	$1.25	$3.75	$7.50
I-261	Strachey, Lytton - ***Queen Victoria*** [n.d.]	$1.35	$4.00	$8.00
I-262	Griswold, Francis - ***Tides Of Malvern*** [n.d.]	$1.25	$3.75	$7.50
I-263	Johnston, Alexander - ***Ten...And Out!*** [n.d.]	$1.35	$4.00	$8.00
I-264	Conrad, Joseph - ***Victory*** [n.d.]	$1.35	$4.00	$8.00
I-265	Bromfield, Louis - ***Mrs. Parkington*** [n.d.]	$1.25	$3.75	$7.50
I-266	Sabatini, Rafael - ***The Sea Hawk*** [n.d.]	$1.35	$4.00	$8.00
I-267	Davis, H.L. - ***Honey In The Horn*** [n.d.]	$1.25	$3.75	$7.50

		G	VG	F
I-268	Bronte, Charlotte - ***Jane Eyre*** [n.d.]	$1.25	$3.75	$7.50
I-269	Forbes, Esther - ***Paradise*** [n.d.]	$1.35	$4.00	$8.00
I-270	Spring, Howard - ***My Son, My Son!*** [n.d.]	$1.35	$4.00	$8.00
J-271	Rhodes, Eugene Manlove - ***The Proud Sheriff*** [n.d.]	$1.25	$3.75	$7.50
J-272	Saroyan, William - ***My Name Is Aram*** [n.d.]	$1.35	$4.00	$8.00
J-273	Conrad, Joseph - ***The Shadow Line*** [n.d.]	$1.35	$4.00	$8.00
J-274	Davis, Bob - ***Tree Toad*** [n.d.]	$1.25	$3.75	$7.50
J-275	Bechdolt, Frederick R. - ***Riot At Red Water*** [n.d.]	$1.35	$4.00	$8.00
J-276	Finney, Charles J. - ***Past The End Of The Pavement*** [n.d.]	$1.35	$4.00	$8.00
J-277	Graham, Frank - ***Lou Gehrig*** [n.d.]	$2.50	$7.50	$15.00
J-278	Lardner, Ring - ***You Know Me, Al*** [n.d.]	$1.25	$3.75	$7.50
J-279	Chamberlain, George Agnew - ***The Phantom Filly*** [n.d.]	$1.35	$4.00	$8.00
J-280	Snow, Charles H. - ***Sheriff Of Yavisa*** [n.d.]	$1.35	$4.00	$8.00
J-281	Rourke, Constance - ***Davy Crockett*** [n.d.]	$1.35	$4.00	$8.00
J-282	Hughes, Richard - ***A High Wind In Jamaica*** [n.d.]	$1.25	$3.75	$7.50
J-283	Smith, Harvey - ***The Gang's All Here*** [n.d.]	$1.25	$3.75	$7.50
J-284	Smith, Thorne - ***Skin And Bones*** [n.d.]	$1.35	$4.00	$8.00
J-285	Cozzens, James Gould - ***The Last Adam*** [n.d.]	$1.35	$4.00	$8.00
J-286	Brand, Max - ***South Of Rio Grande*** [n.d.]	$1.35	$4.00	$8.00
J-287	Morehouse, Ward - ***George M. Cohan*** [n.d.]	$1.35	$4.00	$8.00
J-288	Lofts, Norah - ***The Golden Fleece*** [n.d.]	$1.25	$3.75	$7.50
J-289	Weaver, Ward - ***End Of Track*** [n.d.]	$1.25	$3.75	$7.50
J-290	Gallico, Paul - ***Selected Stories Of Paul Gallico*** [n.d.] PBO.	$2.50	$7.50	$15.00
J-291	Lincoln, Victoria - ***February Hill*** [n.d.]	$1.35	$4.00	$8.00
J-292	Tomlinson, H.M. - ***The Sea And The Jungle*** [n.d.]	$1.25	$3.75	$7.50
J-293	Cleaveland, Agnes Morley - ***No Life For A Lady*** [n.d.]	$1.25	$3.75	$7.50
J-294	Kane, Harnett T. - ***The Bayous Of Louisiana*** [n.d.]	$1.25	$3.75	$7.50
J-295	Paden, Irene D. - ***The Wake Of The Prairie Schooner*** [n.d.]	$1.25	$3.75	$7.50
J-296	Thackeray, William Makepeace - ***Vanity Fair - A Novel Without A Hero*** [n.d.]	$1.35	$4.00	$8.00
J-297	Poe, Edgar Allen - ***Selected Stories Of Edgar Allen Poe*** [n.d.] PBO thus. Original collection.	$12.50	$37.50	$75.00
J-298	Edmonds, Walter D. - ***Young Ames*** [n.d.]	$1.35	$4.00	$8.00
J-299	Asch, Sholem - ***The Apostle*** [n.d.]	$1.25	$3.75	$7.50
J-300	Fowler, Gene - ***Good Night, Sweet Prince - Life And Times Of John Barrymore*** [n.d.]	$1.25	$3.75	$7.50
J-301	Hulbert, Archer Butler - ***Forty-Niners*** [n.d.]	$1.25	$3.75	$7.50
J-302	Foreman, Carolyn Thomas - ***Indians Abroad*** [n.d.]	$1.25	$3.75	$7.50
K-1	Day, Clarence - ***This Simian World*** [n.d.]	$1.35	$4.00	$8.00
K-2	Marquis, Don - ***The Old Soak*** [n.d.]	$1.35	$4.00	$8.00
K-3	London, Jack - ***The Call Of The Wild*** [n.d.]	$2.00	$6.00	$12.00
K-4	Stern, G.B. - ***The Dark Gentleman*** [n.d.]	$1.25	$3.75	$7.50
K-5	Brand, Max - ***The Secret Of Dr. Kildare*** [n.d.]	$1.25	$3.75	$7.50
K-6	Kantor, MacKinlay - ***The Noise Of Their Wings*** [n.d.]	$1.35	$4.00	$8.00
K-7	Wilder, Walter Beebe - ***Bounty Of The Wayside*** [n.d.]	$1.25	$3.75	$7.50
K-8	Rhodes, Eugene Manlove - ***Stepsons Of Light*** [n.d.]	$1.35	$4.00	$8.00
K-9	Hemingway, Ernest - ***Selected Short Stories Of Ernest Hemingway*** [n.d.] PBO. First and only edition.	$12.50	$37.50	$75.00
K-10	Bright, Robert - ***The Life And Death of Little Jo*** [n.d.]	$1.35	$4.00	$8.00
K-11	Snow, Charles H. - ***Rebel Of Ronde Valley*** [n.d.]	$1.25	$3.75	$7.50
K-12	Beston, Henry - ***The St. Lawrence*** [n.d.]	$1.35	$4.00	$8.00
K-13	Holbrook, Stewart H. - ***Ethan Allan*** [n.d.]	$1.35	$4.00	$8.00

Armed Service Edition, L-25

Armed Service Edition, S-21

		G	VG	F
K-14	Haycox, Ernest - ***The Wild Bunch*** [n.d.]	$1.35	$4.00	$8.00
K-15	Smith, Thorne - ***The Stray Lamb*** [n.d.]	$1.25	$3.75	$7.50
K-16	Henry, O. - ***Selected Short Stories Of O. Henry*** [n.d.] PBO	$3.50	$10.00	$20.00
K-17	Berger, Meyer - ***The Eight Million*** [n.d.]	$1.35	$4.00	$8.00
K-18	Robertson, Willard - ***Moon Tide*** [n.d.]	$1.25	$3.75	$7.50
K-19	Blanco, Antonio de Fierro - ***The Journey Of The Flame*** [n.d.]	$1.35	$4.00	$8.00
K-20	Ybarra, T.R. - ***Young Man Of The World*** [n.d.]	$1.35	$4.00	$8.00
K-21	Walker, Mildred - ***Winter Wheat*** [n.d.]	$1.35	$4.00	$8.00
K-22	Canby, Henry Seidel - ***Walt Whitman*** [n.d.]	$1.25	$3.75	$7.50
K-23	James, Marquis - ***Andrew Jackson - The Border Captain*** [n.d.]	$1.35	$4.00	$8.00
K-24	Lewis, Sinclair - ***Babbitt*** [n.d.]	$1.35	$4.00	$8.00
K-25	Train, Arthur - ***Yankee Lawyer, The Autobiography Of Ephraim Tutt*** [n.d.]	$1.35	$4.00	$8.00
K-26	Asbury, Herbert - ***Sucker's Progress*** [n.d.]	$1.35	$4.00	$8.00
K-27	Douglas, Lloyd C. - ***The Robe*** [n.d.] Reprints #D-118.	$1.35	$4.00	$8.00
K-28	Smith, Betty - ***A Tree Grows In Brooklyn*** [n.d.] Reprints #D-117	$1.35	$4.00	$8.00
K-29	Gramling, Oliver - ***AP: The Story Of News*** [n.d.]	$1.25	$3.75	$7.50
K-30	Van Doren, Carl - ***Benjamin Franklin*** [n.d.]	$1.25	$3.75	$7.50
K-31	Sterne, Laurence - ***Tristram Shandy*** [n.d.]	$1.35	$4.00	$8.00
K-32	Spalding, Albert - ***Rise To Follow*** [n.d.]	$1.35	$4.00	$8.00
L-1	Benet, Rosemary and Stephen, Vincent - ***A Book Of Americans*** [n.d.]	$1.25	$3.75	$7.50
L-2	Thurber, James - ***My Life And Hard Times*** [n.d.]	$1.35	$4.00	$8.00
L-3	Lamond, Henry G. - ***Kilgour's Mare*** [n.d.]	$1.25	$3.75	$7.50
L-4	Stephens, James - ***Etched In Moonlight*** [n.d.]	$1.35	$4.00	$8.00
L-5	Heyward, Du Bose - ***Porgy*** [n.d.]	$1.25	$3.75	$7.50
L-6	Untermeyer, Louis - editor (Anthology) - ***Great Poems From Chaucer To Whitman*** [n.d.] PBO.	$2.50	$7.50	$15.00
L-7	Bromfield, Louis - ***What Became Of Anna Bolton?*** [n.d.]	$1.35	$4.00	$8.00
L-8	Evans, Evan - ***Montana Rides Again*** [n.d.]	$1.25	$3.75	$7.50
L-9	Raine, William MacLeod - ***The Sheriff's Son*** [n.d.]	$1.25	$3.75	$7.50
L-10	Leacock, Stephen - ***Happy Stories Just To Laugh At*** [n.d.]	$1.25	$3.75	$7.50
L-11	Gooden, Arthur Henry - ***Roaring River Range*** [n.d.]	$1.35	$4.00	$8.00
L-12	Eisenberg, Frances - ***There's One In Every Family*** [n.d.]	$1.35	$4.00	$8.00
L-13	Brand, Max - ***The King Bird Rides*** [n.d.]	$1.35	$4.00	$8.00
L-14	Eaton, Evelyn - ***The Sea Is So Wide*** [n.d.]	$1.25	$3.75	$7.50
L-15	Melville, Herman - ***Omoo*** [n.d.]	$1.25	$3.75	$7.50
L-16	Perry, George Sessions - ***Hackberry Cavalier*** [n.d.]	$1.25	$3.75	$7.50
L-17	Smith, Thorne - ***Turnabout*** [n.d.]	$1.35	$4.00	$8.00
L-18	Crow, Carl - ***400 Million Customers*** [n.d.]	$1.35	$4.00	$8.00

		G	VG	F
L-19	Wylie, Philip - ***Fish And Tin Fish*** [n.d.]	$1.25	$3.75	$7.50
L-20	Strachey, Lytton - ***Eminent Victorians*** [n.d.]	$1.25	$3.75	$7.50
L-21	Croy, Homer - ***Country Cured*** [n.d.]	$1.25	$3.75	$7.50
L-22	Gray, George W. - ***Science At War*** [n.d.]	$1.35	$4.00	$8.00
L-23	Allen, Hervey - ***Bedford Village*** [n.d.]	$1.35	$4.00	$8.00
L-24	Shearing, Joseph - ***The Lady And the Arsenic*** [n.d.]	$2.00	$6.00	$12.00
L-25	Stoker, Bram - ***Dracula*** [n.d.]	$8.00	$25.00	$50.00
L-26	Marquand, John P. - ***Wickford Point*** [n.d.]	$1.35	$4.00	$8.00
L-27	Graves, Robert - ***I, Claudius*** [n.d.]	$1.35	$4.00	$8.00
L-28	Mann, Thomas - ***Selected Short Stories Of Thomas Mann*** [n.d.] PBO.	$2.50	$7.50	$15.00
L-29	Stone, Irving - ***Lust For Life - The Novel Of Vincent Van Gogh*** [n.d.]	$1.35	$4.00	$8.00
L-30	Maugham, W. Somerset - ***Of Human Bondage*** [n.d.]	$1.35	$4.00	$8.00
L-31	Binns, Archie - ***The Land Is Bright*** [n.d.]	$1.35	$4.00	$8.00
L-32	Johnson, Osa - ***Four Years In Paradise*** [n.d.]	$1.25	$3.75	$7.50
M-1	Housman, A.E. - ***Selected Poems Of A. E. Housman*** [n.d.] PBO.	$3.00	$9.00	$18.00
M-2	Thurber, James, and White, E.B. - ***Is Sex Necessary?*** [n.d.]	$1.35	$4.00	$8.00
M-3	Saki (H.H. Munro) - ***Selected Short Stories Of Saki*** [n.d.] PBO.	$3.00	$9.00	$18.00
M-4	Benchley, Robert - ***20,000 Leagues Under The Sea or David Copperfield*** [n.d.]	$1.35	$4.00	$8.00
M-5	Repplier, Agnes - ***Pere Marquette*** [n.d.]	$1.25	$3.75	$7.50
M-6	Rhodes, Eugene Manlove - ***Copper Streak Trail*** [n.d.]	$1.25	$3.75	$7.50
M-7	Teale, Edwin - ***Dune Boy*** [n.d.]	$1.25	$3.75	$7.50
M-8	Stevens, James - ***Paul Bunyan*** [n.d.]	$1.25	$3.75	$7.50
M-9	Ratcliff, John D. - ***Science Year Book Of 1944*** [n.d.]	$1.25	$3.75	$7.50
M-10	Benefield, Barry - ***The Chicken-Wagon Family*** [n.d.]	$1.35	$4.00	$8.00
M-11	Wylie, Philip - ***The Big Ones Get Away*** [n.d.]	$1.25	$3.75	$7.50
M-12	McDonald, Angus - ***Old McDonald Had A Farm*** [n.d.]	$1.25	$3.75	$7.50
M-13	Haycox, Ernest - ***Action By Night*** [n.d.]	$1.35	$4.00	$8.00
M-14	Brand, Max - ***The Border Kid*** [n.d.]	$1.35	$4.00	$8.00
M-15	Coolidge, Dane - ***Fighting Men Of The West*** [n.d.]	$1.25	$3.75	$7.50
M-16	Burroughs, Edgar Rice - ***Tarzan Of The Apes*** [n.d.]	$27.50	$85.00	$200.00
M-17	Bedwell, Harry - ***The Boomer*** [n.d.]	$1.25	$3.75	$7.50
M-18	Casey, Robert J. - ***Such Interesting People*** [n.d.]	$1.25	$3.75	$7.50
M-19	Bruce, Eva - ***Call Her Rosie*** [n.d.]	$1.35	$4.00	$8.00
M-20	Beverley-Giddings, A.R. - ***Larrish Hundred*** [n.d.]	$1.35	$4.00	$8.00
M-21	Hough, Henry Beetle - ***Country Editor*** [n.d.]	$1.35	$4.00	$8.00
M-22	DeJong, David Cornel - ***With A Dutch Accent*** [n.d.]	$1.25	$3.75	$7.50
M-23	Anthology includes Thurber, Fields - ***Four Modern American Plays*** [n.d.] PBO.	$3.50	$10.00	$20.00
M-24	Schuster, M. Lincoln - editor (Anthology) - ***A Treasury Of The World's Great Letters*** [n.d.]	$1.25	$3.75	$7.50
M-25	Weston, Christine - ***Indigo*** [n.d.]	$1.35	$4.00	$8.00
M-26	Werner, M. R. - ***Barnum*** [n.d.]	$1.35	$4.00	$8.00
M-27	McMeekin, Clark - ***Show Me A Land*** [n.d.]	$1.25	$3.75	$7.50
M-28	Grayson, Captain Charles - ***New Stories For Men*** [n.d.]	$1.35	$4.00	$8.00
M-29	Collins, Wilkie - ***The Moonstone*** [n.d.]	$1.25	$3.75	$7.50
M-30	Heiden, Konrad - ***Der Fuehrer*** [n.d.]	$1.35	$4.00	$8.00
M-31	Van Wyck Mason, F. - ***Stars On The Sea*** [n.d.]	$1.35	$4.00	$8.00
M-32	MacInnes, Helen - ***While Still We Live*** [n.d.]	$1.25	$3.75	$7.50

		G	VG	F
N-1	Twain, Mark - ***The Mysterious Stranger*** [n.d.]	$2.00	$6.00	$12.00
N-2	Perelman, S. J. - ***The Dream Department*** [n.d.]	$1.35	$4.00	$8.00
N-3	Benet, Stephen Vincent - ***America: A History Of The Spirit Of America*** [n.d.]	$1.25	$3.75	$7.50
N-4	Barton, Bruce - ***The Man Nobody Knows*** [n.d.]	$1.25	$3.75	$7.50
N-5	Stephens, James - ***The Crock Of Gold*** [n.d.]	$2.50	$7.50	$15.00
N-6	Sandburg, Carl - ***Selected Poems Of Carl Sandburg*** [n.d.] PBO	$3.50	$10.00	$20.00
N-7	Thurber, James - ***Let Your Mind Alone*** [n.d.]	$1.35	$4.00	$8.00
N-8	Abbott, E. C. & Smith, Helen Huntington - ***We Pointed Them North*** [n.d.]	$1.25	$3.75	$7.50
N-9	Haycox, Ernest - ***Rim Of The Desert*** [n.d.]	$1.35	$4.00	$8.00
N-10	LeMay, Alan - ***Useless Cowboy*** [n.d.]	$1.25	$3.75	$7.50
N-11	Hughes, Dorothy B. - ***The Fallen Sparrow*** [n.d.]	$2.00	$6.00	$12.00
N-12	Hough, Donald - ***Snow Above Town*** [n.d.]	$1.25	$3.75	$7.50
N-13	Stevenson, Robert Louis - ***Kidnapped*** [n.d.]	$1.35	$4.00	$8.00
N-14	Maugham, W. Somerset - ***The Summing Up*** [n.d.]	$1.25	$3.75	$7.50
N-15	Brand, Max - ***The Iron Trail*** [n.d.]	$1.35	$4.00	$8.00
N-16	Siringo, Charles A. - ***Riata And Spurs*** [n.d.]	$1.35	$4.00	$8.00
N-17	Busch, Niven - ***Duel In The Sun*** [n.d.]	$1.35	$4.00	$8.00
N-18	Pratt, Theodore - ***Thunder Mountain*** [n.d.]	$1.35	$4.00	$8.00
N-19	Riesenberg, Lt. H.E. - ***I Dive For Treasure*** [n.d.]	$1.25	$3.75	$7.50
N-20	Iams, Jack - ***Prophet By Experience*** [n.d.]	$1.25	$3.75	$7.50
N-21	Byrne, Donn - ***Hangman's House*** [n.d.]	$1.35	$4.00	$8.00
N-22	Davis, Clyde Brion - ***The Great American Novel*** [n.d.]	$1.25	$3.75	$7.50
N-23	Robertson, Constance - ***Fire Bell In The Night*** [n.d.]	$1.25	$3.75	$7.50
N-24	Standish, Robert - ***Bonin*** [n.d.]	$1.25	$3.75	$7.50
N-25	Kasner, Edward and Newman, James - ***Mathematics And The Imagination*** [n.d.]	$1.25	$3.75	$7.50
N-26	Linklater, Eric - ***Magnus Merriman*** [n.d.]	$1.35	$4.00	$8.00
N-27	White, Leslie Turner - ***Look Away, Look Away*** [n.d.]	$1.35	$4.00	$8.00
N-28	London, Jack - ***Martin Eden*** [n.d.]	$1.35	$4.00	$8.00
N-29	Cloete, Stuart - ***The Turning Wheels*** [n.d.]	$1.35	$4.00	$8.00
N-30	Kroll, Harry Harrison and Sublette, C.M - ***Perilous Journey*** [n.d.]	$1.25	$3.75	$7.50
N-31	Dickens, Charles - ***David Copperfield*** [n.d.]	$1.35	$4.00	$8.00
N-32	Stegner, Wallace - ***The Big Rock Candy Mountain*** [n.d.]	$2.50	$7.50	$15.00
O-1	Shelley, Percy Bysshe - ***Selected Poems Of Percy Bysshe Shelley*** [n.d.] PBO.	$3.50	$10.00	$20.00
O-2	Gibran, Kahlil - ***The Prophet*** [n.d.]	$1.25	$3.75	$7.50
O-3	Mulholland, John - ***The Art Of Illusion*** [n.d.]	$1.35	$4.00	$8.00
O-4	Grayson, Harry - ***They Played The Game*** [n.d.]	$1.35	$4.00	$8.00
O-5	Hudson, W.H. - ***Tales Of The Pampas*** [n.d.]	$1.25	$3.75	$7.50
O-6	Faulkner, Edward H. - ***Plowman's Folly*** [n.d.]	$1.25	$3.75	$7.50
O-7	Gilpatric, Guy - ***Mr. Glencannon Ignores The War*** [n.d.]	$1.25	$3.75	$7.50
O-8	Kober, Arthur - ***My Dear Bella*** [n.d.]	$1.35	$4.00	$8.00
O-9	Siodmak, Curt - ***Donovan's Brain*** [n.d.]	$6.00	$20.00	$40.00
O-10	Nye, Nelson C. - ***Wild Horse Shorty*** [n.d.]	$1.25	$3.75	$7.50
O-11	Goodhue, Cornelia - ***Journey Into The Fog*** [n.d.]	$1.35	$4.00	$8.00
O-12	Forester, C. S. - ***The African Queen*** [n.d.]	$1.35	$4.00	$8.00
O-13	White, Anne Terry - ***Lost Worlds - The Romance Of Archaeology*** [n.d.]	$1.25	$3.75	$7.50
O-14	Hope, Bob - ***I Never Left Home*** [n.d.]	$1.25	$3.75	$7.50

		G	VG	F
O-15	Gann, Ernest K. - ***Island In The Sky*** [n.d.]	$1.25	$3.75	$7.50
O-16	McNichols, Charles L. - ***Crazy Weather*** [n.d.]	$1.25	$3.75	$7.50
O-17	Burnett, W.R. - ***Nobody Lives Forever*** [n.d.]	$2.00	$6.00	$12.00
O-18	Runyon, Damon - ***Runyon A La Carte*** [n.d.]	$1.35	$4.00	$8.00
O-19	Jackson, Charles - ***The Lost Weekend*** [n.d.]	$1.25	$3.75	$7.50
O-20	Russell, John - ***Selected Short Stories Of John Russell*** [n.d.] PBO.	$3.50	$10.00	$20.00
O-21	Simenon, Georges - ***On The Danger Line*** [n.d.]	$1.25	$3.75	$7.50
O-22	Burroughs, Edgar Rice - ***The Return Of Tarzan*** [n.d.]	$27.50	$85.00	$200.00
O-23	Sturgis, Robert - ***Men Like Gods*** [n.d.]	$1.35	$4.00	$8.00
O-24	Hergesheimer, Joseph - ***The Three Black Pennys*** [n.d.]	$1.25	$3.75	$7.50
O-25	Spearman, Frank - ***Selwood Of Sleepy Cat*** [n.d.]	$1.35	$4.00	$8.00
O-26	Helmericks, Constance - ***We Live In Alaska*** [n.d.]	$1.25	$3.75	$7.50
O-27	Gaither, Frances - ***The Red Cock Crows*** [n.d.]	$1.25	$3.75	$7.50
O-28	James, M.R. - ***Selected Ghost Stories*** [n.d.] PBO.	$4.00	$12.50	$25.00
O-29	Williams, Ben Ames - ***Leave Her To Heaven*** [n.d.]	$1.25	$3.75	$7.50
O-30	Kossak, Zofia - ***Blessed Are The Meek*** [n.d.]	$1.35	$4.00	$8.00
O-31	Wolfe, Thomas - ***Look Homeward Angel*** [n.d.]	$4.00	$12.50	$25.00
O-32	Cannon, Jr., Le Grand - ***Look To The Mountain*** [n.d.]	$1.25	$3.75	$7.50
P-2	Chambliss, Commander William - ***Boomerang*** [n.d.]	$1.35	$4.00	$8.00
P-3	Tunis, John R. - ***Rookie Of The Year*** [n.d.]	$1.25	$3.75	$7.50
P-4	Bemelmans, Ludwig - ***Hotel Splendide*** [n.d.]	$1.25	$3.75	$7.50
P-5	Hall, James Norman - ***Lost Island*** [n.d.]	$1.25	$3.75	$7.50
P-6	Stout, Rex - ***Not Quite Dead Enough*** [n.d.]	$2.00	$6.00	$12.00
P-7	Cuppy, Will - ***The Great Bustard And Other People*** [n.d.]	$1.35	$4.00	$8.00
P-8	Brand, Max - ***The Fighting Four*** [n.d.]	$1.35	$4.00	$8.00
P-9	Skidmore, Hubert D. - ***Valley Of The Sky*** [n.d.]	$1.25	$3.75	$7.50
P-10	Goodman, Benny and Kolodin, Irving - ***The Kingdom Of Swing*** [n.d.]	$1.25	$3.75	$7.50
P-11	Hays, H. R. - ***Lie Down In Darkness*** [n.d.]	$1.25	$3.75	$7.50
P-12	Curwood, James Oliver - ***The Valley Of Silent Men*** [n.d.]	$1.25	$3.75	$7.50
P-13	Young, Miriam - ***Mother Wore Tights*** [n.d.]	$1.25	$3.75	$7.50
P-14	Way, Frederick, Jr. - ***Pilotin' Comes Natural*** [n.d.]	$1.35	$4.00	$8.00
P-15	Gill, Tom - ***Starlight Pass*** [n.d.]	$1.35	$4.00	$8.00
P-16	Haycox, Ernset - ***Trail Town*** [n.d.]	$1.35	$4.00	$8.00
P-17	Lawrence, Hilda - ***Blood Upon The Snow*** [n.d.]	$2.00	$6.00	$12.00
P-18	Loveridge, Arthur - ***Many Happy Days I've Squandered*** [n.d.]	$1.35	$4.00	$8.00
P-19	Caldwell, Erskine - ***Stories By Erskine Caldwell*** [n.d.]	$1.25	$3.75	$7.50
P-20	Craig, Captain John D. - ***Danger Is My Business*** [n.d.]	$1.35	$4.00	$8.00
P-21	Upson, William Hazlett - ***Botts In War, Botts In Peace*** [n.d.]	$1.35	$4.00	$8.00
P-22	Cobb, Irvin S. - editor (Anthology) - ***World's Great Humorous Stories*** [n.d.]	$1.25	$3.75	$7.50
P-23	Shearing, Joseph - ***Aunt Beardie*** [n.d.]	$1.35	$4.00	$8.00
P-24	Davis, Clyde Brion - ***Rebellion Of Leo McGuire*** [n.d.]	$1.25	$3.75	$7.50
P-25	Brickell, Herschel - editor (Anthology) - ***Prize Stories Of 1943*** [n.d.]	$1.25	$3.75	$7.50
P-26	White, E.B. - ***One Man's Meat*** [n.d.]	$1.35	$4.00	$8.00
P-27	Seton, Anya - ***Dragonwyck*** [n.d.]	$1.35	$4.00	$8.00
P-28	Sandoz, Mari - ***Slogum House*** [n.d.]	$1.25	$3.75	$7.50
P-29	Beard, Charles A. - ***The Republic*** [n.d.]	$1.35	$4.00	$8.00
P-30	Pyle, Ernie - ***Brave Men*** [n.d.] PBO.	$2.50	$7.50	$15.00
P-31	Shapley, Harlow - ***A Treasury Of Science*** [n.d.]	$1.35	$4.00	$8.00

		G	VG	F
P-32	Bowen, Catherine Drinker - ***Yankee From Olympus*** [n.d.]	$1.25	$3.75	$7.50
Q-1	Skinner, Cornelia Otis - ***Excuse It, Please!*** [n.d.]	$1.25	$3.75	$7.50
Q-2	Cain, James M. - ***The Postman Always Rings Twice*** [n.d.]	$3.50	$10.00	$20.00
Q-3	Ewen, David - ***The Story Of George Gershwin*** [n.d.]	$1.25	$3.75	$7.50
Q-4	Lieber, Hugh Gray and Lillian R. - ***The Education Of T.C. Mits*** [n.d.]	$1.35	$4.00	$8.00
Q-5	Shulman, Max - ***The Feather Merchants*** [n.d.]	$1.25	$3.75	$7.50
Q-6	Heimer, Mel - ***The World Ends At Hoboken*** [n.d.]	$1.35	$4.00	$8.00
Q-7	Lasswell, Mary - ***High Time*** [n.d.]	$1.35	$4.00	$8.00
Q-8	Tunis, John R. - ***Keystone Kids*** [n.d.]	$1.35	$4.00	$8.00
Q-9	Anderson, Sherwood - ***Selected Short Stories Of Sherwood Anderson*** [n.d.] PBO	$3.50	$10.00	$20.00
Q-10	Fair, A. A. - ***Give 'Em The Ax*** [n.d.]	$2.00	$6.00	$12.00
Q-11	Halleran, E. E. - ***Prairie Guns*** [n.d.]	$1.35	$4.00	$8.00
Q-12	Naidish, Theodore - ***Watch Out For Willie Carter*** [n.d.]	$1.35	$4.00	$8.00
Q-13	Smith, Thorne - ***The Passionate Witch*** [n.d.]	$1.25	$3.75	$7.50
Q-14	Dunsany, Lord - ***Guerrilla*** [n.d.]	$3.50	$10.00	$20.00
Q-15	Walling, R.A.J. - ***The Corpse Without A Clue*** [n.d.]	$1.35	$4.00	$8.00
Q-16	Haycox, Ernest - ***Man In The Saddle*** [n.d.]	$1.35	$4.00	$8.00
Q-17	Crane, Frances - ***The Amethyst Spectacles*** [n.d.]	$1.25	$3.75	$7.50
Q-18	Forester, C. S. - ***Beat To Quarters*** [n.d.]	$1.35	$4.00	$8.00
Q-19	Grey, Zane - ***The Heritage Of The Desert*** [n.d.]	$1.25	$3.75	$7.50
Q-20	Hawkins, John and Ward - ***Devil On His Trail*** [n.d.]	$1.35	$4.00	$8.00
Q-21	Wylie, Philip - ***Salt Water Daffy*** [n.d.]	$1.35	$4.00	$8.00
Q-22	Reisner, Mary - ***The House Of Cobwebs*** [n.d.]	$1.35	$4.00	$8.00
Q-23	Haines, Donal Hamilton - ***Luck In All Weathers*** [n.d.]	$1.35	$4.00	$8.00
Q-24	Brand, Max - ***Happy Jack*** [n.d.]	$1.35	$4.00	$8.00
Q-25	Gardner, Mac - ***Mom Counted Six*** [n.d.]	$1.35	$4.00	$8.00
Q-26	Harriman, Margaret Case - ***Take Them Up Tenderly*** [n.d.]	$1.25	$3.75	$7.50
Q-27	Cronin, A. J. - ***The Green Years*** [n.d.]	$1.35	$4.00	$8.00
Q-28	Taylor, Ross McLaury - ***The Saddle And The Plow*** [n.d.]	$1.25	$3.75	$7.50
Q-29	Roberts, Kenneth - ***The Lively Lady*** [n.d.]	$1.35	$4.00	$8.00
Q-30	McMeekin, Clark - ***Reckon With The River*** [n.d.]	$1.35	$4.00	$8.00
Q-31	Maugham, W. Somerset - ***The Razor's Edge*** [n.d.]	$1.35	$4.00	$8.00
Q-32	Smith, Lillian - ***Strange Fruit*** [n.d.]	$1.35	$4.00	$8.00
Q-33	Seghers, Anna - ***The Seventh Cross*** [n.d.]	$1.25	$3.75	$7.50
Q-34	Bromfield, Louis - ***Wild Is The River*** [n.d.]	$1.25	$3.75	$7.50
Q-35	O'Neil, Eugene - ***Selected Plays Of Eugene O'Neill*** [n.d.] PBO.	$3.50	$10.00	$20.00
Q-36	Jennings, John - ***The Shadow And The Glory*** [n.d.]	$1.25	$3.75	$7.50
Q-37	Field, Rachel - ***Time Out Of Mind*** [n.d.]	$1.35	$4.00	$8.00
Q-38	Laing, Alexander - ***The Sea Witch*** [n.d.]	$1.35	$4.00	$8.00
Q-39	Williams, Ben Ames - ***The Strange Woman*** [n.d.]	$1.35	$4.00	$8.00
Q-40	Adams, Henry - ***The Education Of Henry Adams*** [n.d.]	$1.35	$4.00	$8.00
R-1	Stern, G.B. - ***The Ugly Dachshund*** [n.d.]	$1.25	$3.75	$7.50
R-2	Keats, John - ***Selected Poems Of John Keats*** [n.d.] PBO. Original collection.	$3.50	$10.00	$20.00
R-3	Nathan, Robert - ***One More Spring*** [n.d.]	$2.00	$6.00	$12.00
R-4	Parker, Dorothy - ***Selected Short Stories Of Dorothy Parker*** [n.d.] PBO.	$3.00	$9.00	$18.00
R-5	Benchley, Robert - ***After 1903—What?*** [n.d.]	$1.25	$3.75	$7.50
R-6	Roberts, William H. - ***Psychology You Can Use*** [n.d.]	$1.25	$3.75	$7.50
R-7	Corwin, Norman - ***Selected Radio Plays*** [n.d.] PBO.	$3.00	$9.00	$18.00

		G	VG	F
R-8	Stoopnagle, Colonel - ***You Wouldn't Know Me From Adam*** [n.d.]	$1.35	$4.00	$8.00
R-9	Marmur, Jacland - ***Sea Duty*** [n.d.]	$1.35	$4.00	$8.00
R-10	Fuller, Samuel Michael - ***The Dark Page*** [n.d.]	$1.25	$3.75	$7.50
R-11	Short, Luke - ***War On The Cimarron*** [n.d.]	$1.35	$4.00	$8.00
R-12	Peattie, Roderick - ***Geography In Human Destiny*** [n.d.]	$1.25	$3.75	$7.50
R-13	Garth, David - ***Bermuda Calling*** [n.d.]	$1.35	$4.00	$8.00
R-14	Dampier, Sir William Cecil - ***A Shorter History Of Science*** [n.d.]	$1.25	$3.75	$7.50
R-15	Sanders, George - ***Crime On My Hands*** [n.d.]	$5.00	$15.00	$30.00
R-16	Brogan, D.W. - ***The American Character*** [n.d.]	$1.35	$4.00	$8.00
R-17	Kimbrough, Emily and Skinner, Cornelia - ***Our Hearts Were Young And Gay*** [n.d.] Reprints #B-37.	$1.35	$4.00	$8.00
R-18	LeMay, Alan - ***Winter Range*** [n.d.] Reprints #B-42.	$1.25	$3.75	$7.50
R-19	Gilligan, Edmund - ***The Gaunt Woman*** [n.d.] Reprints #B-41.	$1.35	$4.00	$8.00
R-20	Gooden, Arthur Henry - ***Painted Buttes*** [n.d.] Reprints #B-43.	$1.25	$3.75	$7.50
R-21	Porter, Katherine Anne - ***Selected Short Stories Of Katherine Anne Porter*** [n.d.] PBO.	$2.50	$7.50	$15.00
R-22	Sharp, Margery - ***Cluny Brown*** [n.d.]	$1.25	$3.75	$7.50
R-23	Taylor, Deems - ***Of Men And Music*** [n.d.]	$1.35	$4.00	$8.00
R-24	Brand, Max - ***The Long Chance*** [n.d.]	$1.35	$4.00	$8.00
R-25	Morley, Christopher - ***Kitty Foyle*** [n.d.]	$1.35	$4.00	$8.00
R-26	Cohn, David L. - ***Combustion On Wheels*** [n.d.]	$1.35	$4.00	$8.00
R-27	Graham, Gwethalyn - ***Earth And High Heaven*** [n.d.]	$1.35	$4.00	$8.00
R-28	Best, Herbert - ***Young'un*** [n.d.]	$1.25	$3.75	$7.50
R-29	Dowdey, Clifford - ***Gamble's Hundred*** [n.d.]	$1.35	$4.00	$8.00
R-30	Undset, Sigrid - ***The Bridal Wreath*** [n.d.]	$1.35	$4.00	$8.00
R-31	Cerf, Bennett - ***Try And Stop Me*** [n.d.]	$1.35	$4.00	$8.00
R-32	Sabatini, Rafael - ***Captain Blood*** [n.d.]	$1.25	$3.75	$7.50
R-33	Derleth, August - ***Sleep No More*** [n.d.]	$10.00	$30.00	$60.00
R-34	Heym, Stefan - ***Of Smiling Peace*** [n.d.]	$1.25	$3.75	$7.50
R-35	Welles, Sumner - ***The Time For Decision*** [n.d.]	$1.35	$4.00	$8.00
R-36	Costain, Thomas B. - ***For My Great Folly*** [n.d.]	$1.25	$3.75	$7.50
R-37	Douglas, Lloyd C. - ***Disputed Passage*** [n.d.]	$1.35	$4.00	$8.00
R-38	Woodward, W. E. - ***The Way Our People Lived*** [n.d.]	$1.25	$3.75	$7.50
R-39	Buckmaster, Henrietta - ***Deep River*** [n.d.]	$1.35	$4.00	$8.00
R-40	Adams, Samuel Hopkins - ***Canal Town*** [n.d.]	$1.35	$4.00	$8.00
S-1	Aiken, Major William - editor (Anthology) - ***A Wartime Whitman*** [n.d.]	$1.25	$3.75	$7.50
S-2	Saroyan, William - ***Dear Baby*** [n.d.]	$1.35	$4.00	$8.00
S-3	Bemelmans, Ludwig - ***I Love You, I Love You, I Love You*** [n.d.]	$1.35	$4.00	$8.00
S-4	Cozzens, James Gould - ***Castaway*** [n.d.]	$1.35	$4.00	$8.00
S-5	Thurber, James - ***My World - And Welcome To It*** [n.d.] Reprints #A-11.	$1.25	$3.75	$7.50
S-6	Gruber, Frank - ***Peace Marshall*** [n.d.] Reprints #A-12.	$1.35	$4.00	$8.00
S-7	Sale, Richard - ***Not Too Narrow...Not Too Deep*** [n.d.]	$2.00	$6.00	$12.00
S-8	Wylie, Philip - ***Selected Short Stories Of Philip Wylie*** [n.d.] PBO.	$2.00	$6.00	$12.00
S-9	Twain, Mark - ***Selected Short Stories Of Mark Twain*** [n.d.] PBO. Original collection.	$6.00	$20.00	$40.00
S-10	Baker, Dorothy - ***Young Man With A Horn*** [n.d.]	$1.25	$3.75	$7.50
S-11	Sullivan, Frank - ***A Pearl In Every Oyster*** [n.d.]	$1.25	$3.75	$7.50

		G	VG	F
S-12	Hatch, Eric - ***Unexpected Uncle*** [n.d.]	$1.25	$3.75	$7.50
S-13	Beer, Thomas - ***The Mauve Decade*** [n.d.]	$1.35	$4.00	$8.00
S-14	Eaton, Evelyn - ***In What Torn Ship*** [n.d.]	$1.25	$3.75	$7.50
S-15	Laing, Alexander - ***Clipper Ship Men*** [n.d.]	$1.35	$4.00	$8.00
S-16	Perdue, Virginia - ***Alarum And Excursion*** [n.d.]	$1.35	$4.00	$8.00
S-17	Hough, Donald - ***Captain Retread*** [n.d.]	$1.35	$4.00	$8.00
S-18	Raine, William MacLeod - ***Guns Of The Frontier*** [n.d.]	$1.35	$4.00	$8.00
S-19	Brown, Joe E. - ***Your Kids And Mine*** [n.d.]	$1.35	$4.00	$8.00
S-20	Irish, William - ***After-Dinner Story*** [n.d.]	$5.00	$15.00	$30.00
S-21	Gardner, Erle Stanley - ***The Case Of The Black-Eyed Blonde*** [n.d.]	$2.00	$6.00	$12.00
S-22	Smith, H. Allen - ***Lost In The Horse Latitudes*** [n.d.]	$1.25	$3.75	$7.50
S-23	Brand, Max - ***Hunted Riders*** [n.d.]	$1.35	$4.00	$8.00
S-24	Clark, Walter Van Tilburg - ***The Ox-Bow Incident*** [n.d.]	$1.25	$3.75	$7.50
S-25	Lieb, Frederick G. - ***The St. Louis Cardinals*** [n.d.]	$2.50	$7.50	$15.00
S-26	Blackwood, Algernon - ***Selected Short Stories Of Algernon Blackwood*** [n.d.] PBO. First and only edition.	$10.00	$30.00	$60.00
S-27	Peattie, Donald Culross - ***An Almanac For Moderns*** [n.d.]	$1.35	$4.00	$8.00
S-28	Smith, Thorne - ***The Night Life Of The Gods*** [n.d.]	$1.35	$4.00	$8.00
S-29	Snow, Edgar - ***People On Our Side*** [n.d.]	$1.25	$3.75	$7.50
S-30	Hatcher, Harlan - ***The Great Lakes*** [n.d.]	$1.35	$4.00	$8.00
S-31	Bromfield, Louis - ***The Farm*** [n.d.]	$1.25	$3.75	$7.50
S-32	Bayliss, Marguerite F. - ***The Bolinvars*** [n.d.]	$1.35	$4.00	$8.00
S-33	Rawlings, Marjorie Kinnan - ***The Yearling*** [n.d.] Reprints #B-55.	$1.25	$3.75	$7.50
S-34	Denison, Merrill - ***Klondike Mike*** [n.d.] Reprints #B-58.	$1.25	$3.75	$7.50
S-35	Thackeray, William Makepeace - ***Henry Esmond*** [n.d.]	$1.35	$4.00	$8.00
S-36	Pennel, Joseph Stanley - ***The History Of Rome Hanks*** [n.d.]	$1.35	$4.00	$8.00
S-37	Hackett, Francis - ***Henry The Eighth*** [n.d.]	$1.35	$4.00	$8.00
S-38	Roberts, Kenneth - ***Arundel*** [n.d.]	$1.25	$3.75	$7.50
S-39	Goudge, Elizabeth - ***Green Dolphin Street*** [n.d.]	$1.25	$3.75	$7.50
S-40	Stafford, Jean - ***Boston Adventure*** [n.d.]	$1.25	$3.75	$7.50
T-1	Skinner, Cornelia Otis - ***Dithers And Jitters*** [n.d.]	$1.35	$4.00	$8.00
T-2	Wells, H. G. - ***The Time Machine*** [n.d.]	$5.50	$17.50	$35.00
T-3	Papashvily, George and Waite, Helen - ***Anything Can Happen*** [n.d.]	$1.25	$3.75	$7.50
T-4	Ewen, David - ***Men Of Popular Music*** [n.d.]	$1.35	$4.00	$8.00
T-5	Steinbeck, John - ***Cannery Row*** [n.d.]	$2.00	$6.00	$12.00
T-6	Fuller, Timothy - ***This Is Murder, Mr. Jones*** [n.d.]	$2.00	$6.00	$12.00
T-7	Levant, Oscar - ***A Smattering Of Ignorance*** [n.d.]	$1.25	$3.75	$7.50
T-8	Untermeyer, Louis - editor (Anthology) - ***The Fireside Book Of Verse*** [n.d.] PBO.	$2.50	$7.50	$15.00
T-9	Stone, Ezra, and Melick, Weldon - ***Coming, Major!*** [n.d.]	$1.35	$4.00	$8.00
T-10	Nordhoff, Charles, and Hall, James N. - ***Men Against The Sea*** [n.d.]	$1.25	$3.75	$7.50
T-11	Tetlow, Henry - ***We Farm For A Hobby And Make It Pay*** [n.d.]	$1.25	$3.75	$7.50
T-12	Sharp, Margery - ***The Stone Of Chastity*** [n.d.]	$2.50	$7.50	$15.00
T-13	Benchley, Robert - ***Benchley Beside Himself*** [n.d.] Reprints #B-39.	$1.35	$4.00	$8.00
T-14	Kantor, MacKinlay - ***Gentle Annie*** [n.d.] Reprints #B-38.	$1.25	$3.75	$7.50
T-15	Coates, Robert M. - ***The Outlaw Years*** [n.d.]	$1.25	$3.75	$7.50
T-16	Seltzer, Charles Alden - ***Range Boss*** [n.d.]	$1.35	$4.00	$8.00

		G	VG	F
T-17	Quentin, Patrick - ***Puzzle For Puppets*** [n.d.]	$2.00	$6.00	$12.00
T-18	James, Henry - ***Daisy Miller And Other Stories*** [n.d.] PBO.	$3.50	$10.00	$20.00
T-19	Taylor, Rosemary - ***Ridin' The Rainbow*** [n.d.]	$1.35	$4.00	$8.00
T-20	Cunningham, Eugene - ***Pistol Passport*** [n.d.]	$1.35	$4.00	$8.00
T-21	Brand, Max - ***Riders Of The Plains*** [n.d.]	$1.35	$4.00	$8.00
T-22	Rame, David - ***Tunnel From Calais*** [n.d.]	$1.25	$3.75	$7.50
T-23	Sloane, William - ***The Edge Of Running Water*** [n.d.]	$4.00	$12.50	$25.00
T-24	Graham, Frank - ***The New York Yankees*** [n.d.]	$2.50	$7.50	$15.00
T-25	Mantle, Burns - editor (Anthology) - ***The Best Plays Of 1943–1944*** [n.d.]	$1.35	$4.00	$8.00
T-26	Fast, Howard - ***Freedom Road*** [n.d.]	$1.25	$3.75	$7.50
T-27	Burman, Ben Lucien - ***Blow For A Landing*** [n.d.]	$1.25	$3.75	$7.50
T-28	Anthology includes Foster, Nafziger - ***Wolf Law And Three Other Stories Of The West*** [n.d.] PBO.	$3.00	$9.00	$18.00
T-29	Forbes, Esther - ***The General's Lady*** [n.d.]	$1.25	$3.75	$7.50
T-30	Carmer, Carl - ***Genesee Fever*** [n.d.]	$1.35	$4.00	$8.00
T-31	Karig, Commander Walter - ***Battle Report - Pearl Harbor To Coral Sea*** [n.d.]	$1.25	$3.75	$7.50
T-32	Bromfield, Louis - ***The World We Live In*** [n.d.]	$1.25	$3.75	$7.50
T-33	Cronin, A.J. - ***The Citadel*** [n.d.]	$1.35	$4.00	$8.00
T-34	Wolfe, Maritta M. - ***Whistle Stop*** [n.d.]	$1.25	$3.75	$7.50
T-35	Fuller, Iola - ***The Loon Feather*** [n.d.]	$1.35	$4.00	$8.00
T-36	Du Maurier, Daphne - ***Rebecca*** [n.d.]	$1.25	$3.75	$7.50
T-37	Goodrich, Marcus - ***Delilah*** [n.d.] Reprints #B-59.	$1.25	$3.75	$7.50
T-38	Freuchen, Peter - ***Arctic Adventure*** [n.d.] Reprints #B-60.	$1.25	$3.75	$7.50
T-39	Winsor, Kathleen - ***Forever Amber*** [n.d.]	$1.35	$4.00	$8.00
T-40	Landon, Margaret - ***Anna And The King Of Siam*** [n.d.]	$1.25	$3.75	$7.50
655	Nathan, Robert - ***Portrait Of Jennie*** [n.d.]	$1.35	$4.00	$8.00
656	Lowther, George - ***Adventures Of Superman*** [n.d.]	$35.00	$125.00	$300.00
657	Shulman, Max - ***Barefoot Boy With Cheek*** [n.d.]	$1.35	$4.00	$8.00
658	Tennyson, Lord Alfred - ***The Charge Of The Light Brigade And Other Poems*** [n.d.] PBO thus (first edition of this collection).	$3.00	$9.00	$18.00
659	Dunninger, Joseph - ***What's On Your Mind?*** [n.d.]	$1.35	$4.00	$8.00
660	Beston, Henry - ***The Outermost House*** [n.d.]	$1.25	$3.75	$7.50
661	Peattie, Roderick - ***Look To The Frontiers*** [n.d.]	$1.25	$3.75	$7.50
662	Sousa III, John Philip - ***My Family Right Or Wrong*** [n.d.]	$1.35	$4.00	$8.00
663	Halliday, Brett - ***Murder And The Married Virgin*** [n.d.]	$2.00	$6.00	$12.00
664	Perry, George S., and Leighton, Isabel - ***Where Away*** [n.d.]	$1.35	$4.00	$8.00
665	Priestley, J.B. - ***The Old Dark House*** [n.d.]	$2.00	$6.00	$12.00
666	Caspary, Vera - ***Laura*** [n.d.]	$2.00	$6.00	$12.00
667	Hemingway, Ernest - ***To Have And Have Not*** [n.d.]	$1.35	$4.00	$8.00
668	Beer, Thomas - ***Mrs. Egg And Other Barbarians*** [n.d.]	$1.25	$3.75	$7.50
669	De Maupassant, Guy - ***Mademoiselle Fifi And Other Stories*** [n.d.] PBO.	$2.50	$7.50	$15.00
670	Short, Luke - ***Gunman's Chance*** [n.d.]	$1.25	$3.75	$7.50
671	Smith, Thorne - ***The Glorious Pool*** [n.d.] Reprints #G-181.	$1.35	$4.00	$8.00
672	London, Jack - ***White Fang*** [n.d.] Reprints #G-182.	$2.00	$6.00	$12.00
673	Smith, H. Allen - ***Low Man On A Totem Pole*** [n.d.] Reprints #G-183.	$1.25	$3.75	$7.50
674	Raine, William MacLeod - ***Trail's End*** [n.d.] Reprints #G-184.	$1.25	$3.75	$7.50
675	Disney, Dorothy Cameron - ***The 17th Letter*** [n.d.]	$2.00	$6.00	$12.00

		G	VG	F
676	Miller, Paul Eduard - editor (Anthology) - ***Esquire's Jazz Book 1944*** [n.d.]	$1.25	$3.75	$7.50
677	Edmonds, Walter D. - ***Selected Short Stories Of Walter D. Edmonds*** [n.d.] PBO.	$3.50	$10.00	$20.00
678	Grey, Zane - ***Western Union*** [n.d.]	$1.35	$4.00	$8.00
679	Forester, C. S. - ***The Captain From Connecticut*** [n.d.]	$1.35	$4.00	$8.00
680	Queen, Ellery - ***Calamity Town*** [n.d.]	$2.00	$6.00	$12.00
681	Arnold, Elliott - ***Tomorrow Will Sing*** [n.d.]	$1.25	$3.75	$7.50
682	Stokley, James - ***Science Remakes Our World*** [n.d.]	$1.25	$3.75	$7.50
683	Haycox, Ernest - ***Bugles In The Afternoon*** [n.d.]	$1.35	$4.00	$8.00
684	O'Neill, John J. - ***Prodigal Genius - The Life Of Nikola Tesla*** [n.d.]	$1.35	$4.00	$8.00
685	Laing, Alexander - editor (Anthology) - ***The Cadaver Of Gideon Wyck*** [n.d.]	$1.35	$4.00	$8.00
686	Targ, William - editor (Anthology) - ***Western Story Omnibus*** [n.d.]	$1.35	$4.00	$8.00
687	Dinesen, Isak - ***Seven Gothic Tales*** [n.d.]	$1.35	$4.00	$8.00
688	Glasgow, Ellen - ***Barren Ground*** [n.d.]	$1.35	$4.00	$8.00
689	Marshall, Edison - ***Great Smith*** [n.d.] Reprints #C-87.	$1.25	$3.75	$7.50
690	Steinbeck, John - ***The Grapes Of Wrath*** [n.d.] Reprints #C-90.	$2.00	$6.00	$12.00
691	Dickens, Charles - ***The Posthumous Papers Of The Pickwick Club*** [n.d.]	$1.35	$4.00	$8.00
692	Rigby, Elizabeth and Douglas - ***Lock, Stock and Barrel - The Story Of Collecting*** [n.d.] A history of collectors and collecting.	$1.35	$4.00	$8.00
693	Stone, Irving - ***Immortal Wife*** [n.d.]	$1.25	$3.75	$7.50
694	Flavin, Martin - ***Journey In The Dark*** [n.d.]	$1.35	$4.00	$8.00
695	McKenney, Ruth - ***The McKenneys Carry On*** [n.d.]	$1.35	$4.00	$8.00
696	White, E.B. - ***Quo Vadimus Or The Case For The Bicycle*** [n.d.]	$1.25	$3.75	$7.50
697	Kober, Arthur - ***Thunder Over The Bronx*** [n.d.]	$1.25	$3.75	$7.50
698	Wells, H. G. - ***The Island Of Dr. Moreau*** [n.d.]	$5.00	$15.00	$30.00
699	Benson, Sally - ***Meet Me In St. Louis*** [n.d.]	$1.35	$4.00	$8.00
700	Van De Water, Frederic F. - ***A Home In The Country*** [n.d.]	$1.25	$3.75	$7.50
701	Franken, Rose - ***Another Claudia*** [n.d.]	$1.25	$3.75	$7.50
702	Wilson, Earl - ***I Am Gazing Into My 8-Ball*** [n.d.]	$1.25	$3.75	$7.50
703	Steinbeck, John - ***The Pastures Of Heaven*** [n.d.]	$2.00	$6.00	$12.00
704	Longfellow, Henry Wadsworth - ***Paul Revere's Ride And Other Poems*** [n.d.] PBO. First and only edition.	$8.00	$25.00	$50.00
705	Thurber, James - ***The Middle-Aged Man On The Flying Trapeze*** [n.d.] Reprints #I-253.	$1.35	$4.00	$8.00
706	Haycock, Ernest - ***Deep West*** [n.d.]	$1.25	$3.75	$7.50
707	Kelland, Clarence Budington - ***Arizona*** [n.d.] Reprints #I-255.	$1.35	$4.00	$8.00
708	Benton, Jesse James - ***Cow By The Tail*** [n.d.] Reprints #I-256.	$1.35	$4.00	$8.00
709	Forester, C. S. - ***To The Indies*** [n.d.]	$1.35	$4.00	$8.00
710	Benefield, Barry - ***Eddie And The Archangel Mike*** [n.d.]	$1.35	$4.00	$8.00
711	Eberhart, Mignon G. - ***Wings Of Fear*** [n.d.]	$2.00	$6.00	$12.00
712	MacDonald, William Colt - ***The Three Mesquiteers*** [n.d.]	$1.35	$4.00	$8.00
713	Fisher, Vardis - ***The Golden Rooms*** [n.d.]	$1.25	$3.75	$7.50
714	Terhune, Albert Payson - ***Lad: A Dog*** [n.d.]	$1.25	$3.75	$7.50
715	Brand, Max - ***Gunman's Gold*** [n.d.]	$1.35	$4.00	$8.00
716	Blair, Walter - ***Tall Tale America-A Legendary History Of Our Humorous Heroes*** [n.d.]	$1.25	$3.75	$7.50

Armed Service Edition, 719

Armed Service Edition, 760

		G	VG	F
717	Compilation - ***Webster's New Handy Dictionary Vol. I*** [n.d.]	$1.35	$4.00	$8.00
718	Compilation - ***Webster's New Handy Dictionary Vol. II*** [n.d.]	$1.25	$3.75	$7.50
719	Baker, Sgt. George - ***The Sad Sack*** [n.d.]	$4.00	$12.50	$25.00
720	Gilligan, Edmund - ***Voyage Of The Golden Hind*** [n.d.]	$1.25	$3.75	$7.50
721	Hudson, W. H. - ***The Purple Land*** [n.d.]	$3.50	$10.00	$20.00
722	Grey, Zane - ***Sunset Pass*** [n.d.]	$1.25	$3.75	$7.50
723	Wallis, J. H. - ***The Woman In The Window*** [n.d.]	$1.25	$3.75	$7.50
724	Rawlings, Marjorie Kinnan - ***South Moon Under*** [n.d.]	$1.35	$4.00	$8.00
725	Nordhoff, Charles & Hall, James Norman - ***Pitcairn's Island*** [n.d.]	$1.25	$3.75	$7.50
726	Ramsey, Jr., Frederick & Smith, Charles - ***Jazzmen*** [n.d.]	$1.35	$4.00	$8.00
727	Marsh, Ngaio - ***Death And The Dancing Footman*** [n.d.]	$2.00	$6.00	$12.00
728	Gallico, Paul - ***Farewell To Sport*** [n.d.]	$1.25	$3.75	$7.50
729	Howells, William - ***Mankind So Far*** [n.d.]	$1.35	$4.00	$8.00
730	Lovecraft, H.P. - ***The Dunwich Horror And Other Weird Tales*** [n.d.] PBO thus (first edition of this collection).	$12.50	$37.50	$75.00
731	Thomason, Col. John W., Jr. - ***And A Few Marines*** [n.d.] Reprints #C-85.	$1.25	$3.75	$7.50
732	Selby, John - ***Starbuck*** [n.d.] Reprints #C-86.	$1.35	$4.00	$8.00
733	Maltz, Albert - ***The Cross And The Arrow*** [n.d.]	$1.25	$3.75	$7.50
734	Karig, Walter - ***Lower Than Angels*** [n.d.]	$1.25	$3.75	$7.50
735	Johnson, Gerald W. - ***A Little Night Music*** [n.d.]	$1.25	$3.75	$7.50
736	Wordsworth, William - ***My Heart Leaps Up And Other Poems*** [n.d.] PBO.	$3.50	$10.00	$20.00
737	Nathan, Robert - ***The Enchanted Voyage*** [n.d.]	$1.35	$4.00	$8.00
738	Eckstein, Gustav - ***Lives*** [n.d.]	$1.25	$3.75	$7.50
739	Anthology of artworks by servicemen - ***Soldier Art*** [n.d.] Many full-color plates.	$1.35	$4.00	$8.00
740	Brandt, Sgt. Frank - editor (Anthology) - ***Cartoons For Fighters*** [n.d.]	$1.25	$3.75	$7.50
741	O'Hara, John - ***Pipe Night*** [n.d.]	$1.35	$4.00	$8.00
742	Thompson, Morton - ***Joe, The Wounded Tennis Player*** [n.d.]	$1.25	$3.75	$7.50
743	Bell, Vereen - ***Brag Dog And Other Stories*** [n.d.]	$1.35	$4.00	$8.00
744	Fuller, Timothy - ***Harvard Has A Homicide*** [n.d.]	$2.00	$6.00	$12.00
745	Wells, H. G. - ***The War Of The Worlds*** [n.d.]	$5.00	$15.00	$30.00
746	Wallace, Francis - ***Kid Galahad*** [n.d.]	$1.25	$3.75	$7.50
747	Lockridge, Frances and Richard - ***Death On The Aisle*** [n.d.]	$2.00	$6.00	$12.00
748	Haycox, Ernest - ***Starlight Rider*** [n.d.]	$1.25	$3.75	$7.50
749	Wechsburg, Joseph - ***Looking For A Bluebird*** [n.d.]	$1.25	$3.75	$7.50
750	Steinbeck, John - ***Cup Of Gold*** [n.d.]	$2.00	$6.00	$12.00
751	Chandler, Raymond - ***The Big Sleep*** [n.d.]	$4.00	$12.50	$25.00

		G	VG	F
752	Gooden, Arthur Henry - ***The Valley Of Dry Bones*** [n.d.]	$1.35	$4.00	$8.00
753	Cunningham, Eugene - ***Diamond River Man*** [n.d.]	$1.35	$4.00	$8.00
754	Gallico, Paul - ***Adventures Of Hiram Holliday*** [n.d.]	$1.35	$4.00	$8.00
755	Thurber, James - ***Let Your Mind Alone*** [n.d.] Reprints #N-7.	$1.25	$3.75	$7.50
756	Abbott, E. C. & Smith, Helena Huntington - ***We Pointed Them North*** [n.d.] Reprints #N-8.	$1.35	$4.00	$8.00
757	Berger, Meyer - ***The Eight Million*** [n.d.] Reprints #K-17.	$1.25	$3.75	$7.50
758	Robertson, Willard - ***Moon Tide*** [n.d.] Reprints #K-18.	$1.35	$4.00	$8.00
759	Mulford, Clarence E. - ***Buck Peters, Ranchman*** [n.d.]	$1.25	$3.75	$7.50
760	Marsh, Ngaio - ***Died In The Wool*** [n.d.]	$2.00	$6.00	$12.00
761	Upson, William Hazlett - ***Keep 'Em Crawling*** [n.d.]	$1.35	$4.00	$8.00
762	Truax, Rhoda - ***Joseph Lister - Father Of Modern Surgery*** [n.d.]	$1.25	$3.75	$7.50
763	Carmer, Carl - ***Listen For A Lonesome Drum*** [n.d.]	$1.35	$4.00	$8.00
764	Prokosch, Frederic - ***The Asiatics*** [n.d.]	$1.25	$3.75	$7.50
765	McFee, William - editor (Anthology) - ***World's Great Tales Of The Sea*** [n.d.]	$1.25	$3.75	$7.50
766	Cain, James M. - ***Double Indemnity And Two Other Stories*** [n.d.]	$5.00	$15.00	$30.00
767	Poe, Edgar Allan - ***Selected Stories Of Edgar Allan Poe*** [n.d.] Reprints #J-297.	$5.00	$15.00	$30.00
768	Edmonds, Walter D. - ***Young Ames*** [n.d.] Reprints #J-298.	$1.35	$4.00	$8.00
769	Day, Clarence - ***Life With Father And Mother*** [n.d.]	$1.35	$4.00	$8.00
770	Eaton, Evelyn - ***Quietly My Captain Waits*** [n.d.]	$1.35	$4.00	$8.00
771	Lewis, Lloyd - ***Myths After Lincoln*** [n.d.]	$1.25	$3.75	$7.50
772	Woolf, Virginia - ***The Years*** [n.d.]	$1.35	$4.00	$8.00
773	Fowler, Gene - ***Timber Line - A Story Of Bonfils And Tammen*** [n.d.]	$1.35	$4.00	$8.00
774	Wylie, Philip - ***Night Unto Night*** [n.d.]	$1.25	$3.75	$7.50
775	March, William - ***Some Like Them Short*** [n.d.]	$1.35	$4.00	$8.00
776	Brooke, Rupert - ***The Collected Poems Of Rupert Brooke*** [n.d.].	$1.25	$3.75	$7.50
777	Eckstein, Gustav - ***Canary - The History Of A Family Of Birds*** [n.d.]	$1.25	$3.75	$7.50
778	Maxim, Hiram Percy - ***A Genius In The Family*** [n.d.]	$1.35	$4.00	$8.00
779	Watkin, Lawrence Edward - ***On Borrowed Time*** [n.d.]	$1.25	$3.75	$7.50
780	Lomax, Bliss - ***Horsethief Creek*** [n.d.]	$1.35	$4.00	$8.00
781	Graham, Frank - ***Lou Gehrig*** [n.d.] Reprints #J-277	$2.50	$7.50	$15.00
782	Lardner, Ring - ***You Know Me, Al*** [n.d.] Reprints #J-278.	$1.35	$4.00	$8.00
783	Chamberlain, George Agnew - ***The Phantom Filly*** [n.d.] Reprints #J-279.	$1.35	$4.00	$8.00
784	Snow, Charles H. - ***Sheriff Of Yavisa*** [n.d.] Reprints #J-280.	$1.25	$3.75	$7.50
785	Hughes, Dorothy B. - ***The So Blue Marble*** [n.d.]	$2.00	$6.00	$12.00
786	Kendrick, Baynard - ***Blind Man's Bluff*** [n.d.]	$2.00	$6.00	$12.00
787	Fast, Howard - ***Patrick Henry And The Frigate's Keel*** [n.d.]	$1.35	$4.00	$8.00
788	McKenna, Edward L. - ***The Bruiser*** [n.d.]	$1.25	$3.75	$7.50
789	Lockridge, Frances and Richard - ***Payoff For The Banker*** [n.d.].	$2.00	$6.00	$12.00
790	Sears, Paul B. - ***This Is Our World*** [n.d.]	$1.35	$4.00	$8.00
791	Haycox, Ernest - ***Trail Smoke*** [n.d.]	$1.35	$4.00	$8.00
792	Wescott, Glenway - ***Apartment In Athens*** [n.d.]	$1.35	$4.00	$8.00
793	Pratt, Theodore - ***The Barefoot Mailman*** [n.d.]	$1.35	$4.00	$8.00
794	Steinbeck, John - ***The Long Valley*** [n.d.]	$2.00	$6.00	$12.00
795	Haggard, H. Rider - ***King Solomon's Mines*** [n.d.]	$1.50	$5.00	$10.00
796	Train, Arthur - ***Mr. Tutt Finds A Way*** [n.d.]	$2.00	$6.00	$12.00

		G	VG	F
797	Grey, Zane - ***Forlorn River*** [n.d.]	$1.35	$4.00	$8.00
798	Shriber, Ione Sandberg - ***Pattern For Murder*** [n.d.]	$2.00	$6.00	$12.00
799	O'Hara, John - ***Butterfield 8*** [n.d.]	$1.35	$4.00	$8.00
800	Nathan, Robert - ***The Bishop's Wife And Two Other Novels*** [n.d.] PBO.	$3.00	$9.00	$18.00
801	Balmer, Edwin, and Wylie, Philip - ***When Worlds Collide*** [n.d.]	$5.00	$15.00	$30.00
802	Dinesen, Isak - ***Winter's Tales*** [n.d.]	$1.25	$3.75	$7.50
803	Anthology including Coburn, Foster - ***Five Western Stories*** [n.d.] PBO. First and only edition.	$4.00	$12.50	$25.00
804	Forester, C. S. - ***Commodore Hornblower*** [n.d.]	$1.25	$3.75	$7.50
805	Baume, Eric - ***Yankee Woman*** [n.d.]	$1.35	$4.00	$8.00
806	Carmer, Carl - ***The Hudson*** [n.d.]	$1.35	$4.00	$8.00
807	Barrett, Monte - ***Sun In Their Eyes*** [n.d.]	$1.25	$3.75	$7.50
808	De Kruif, Paul - ***Men Against Death*** [n.d.]	$1.35	$4.00	$8.00
809	Jaffe, Bernard - ***Men Of Science In America*** [n.d.]	$1.25	$3.75	$7.50
810	Prochnow, Herbert V. - ***Great Stories From Great Lives*** [n.d.]	$1.25	$3.75	$7.50
811	Bromfield, Louis - ***Mrs. Parkington*** [n.d.] Reprints #I-265.	$1.35	$4.00	$8.00
812	Sabatini, Rafael - ***The Sea Hawk*** [n.d.] Reprints #I-266.	$1.25	$3.75	$7.50
813	Kantor, MacKinlay - ***Author's Choice*** [n.d.]	$1.35	$4.00	$8.00
814	Costain, Thomas B. - ***Ride With Me*** [n.d.]	$1.25	$3.75	$7.50
815	Van Druten, John - ***The Voice Of The Turtle*** [n.d.]	$1.35	$4.00	$8.00
816	Davis, Richard Harding - ***In the Fog*** [n.d.]	$1.35	$4.00	$8.00
817	O'Hara, John - ***Pal Joey*** [n.d.]	$1.25	$3.75	$7.50
818	Sayre, Joel - ***Rackety Rax*** [n.d.]	$1.35	$4.00	$8.00
819	Anthology selected from *The New Yorker* - ***The New Yorker's Baedeker*** [n.d.] PBO.	$2.50	$7.50	$15.00
820	Masefield, John - ***Selected Poems Of John Masefield*** [n.d.] PBO.	$3.00	$9.00	$18.00
821	Shattuck, Richard - ***The Half-Haunted Saloon*** [n.d.]	$1.35	$4.00	$8.00
822	Mauldin, Bill - ***Up Front*** [n.d.]	$1.25	$3.75	$7.50
823	Cather, Willa - ***O Pioneers!*** [n.d.]	$1.25	$3.75	$7.50
824	Mills, John - ***Electronics Today And Tomorrow*** [n.d.]	$1.35	$4.00	$8.00
825	Faulkner, William - ***A Rose For Emily And Other Stories*** [n.d.] PBO. First and only edition.	$22.00	$70.00	$140.00
826	Mead, Margaret - ***Coming Of Age In Samoa*** [n.d.]	$1.25	$3.75	$7.50
827	Crane, Frances - ***The Indigo Necklace*** [n.d.]	$2.00	$6.00	$12.00
828	Hughes, Dorothy B. - ***The Delicate Ape*** [n.d.]	$2.00	$6.00	$12.00
829	Forester, C.S. - ***Payment Deferred*** [n.d.] Reprints #H-213	$2.00	$6.00	$12.00
830	Bennett, Arnold - ***Buried Alive - A Tale Of These Days*** [n.d.] Reprints #H-214	$1.35	$4.00	$8.00
831	Powers, Tom - ***Virgin With Butterflies*** [n.d.]	$1.25	$3.75	$7.50
832	Stix, Thomas L. - editor (Anthology) - ***The Sporting Gesture*** [n.d.]	$1.35	$4.00	$8.00
833	Seltzer, Charles Alden - ***Square Deal Sanderson*** [n.d.]	$1.25	$3.75	$7.50
834	Mulford, Clarence E. - ***Bar 20 Days*** [n.d.]	$1.25	$3.75	$7.50
835	Wolfert, Ira - ***American Guerrilla In The Phillipines*** [n.d.]	$1.35	$4.00	$8.00
836	Franken, Rose - ***Claudia And David*** [n.d.]	$1.25	$3.75	$7.50
837	Haycox, Ernest - ***Sundown Jim*** [n.d.]	$1.35	$4.00	$8.00
838	Chandler, Raymond - ***The Lady In The Lake*** [n.d.]	$3.50	$10.00	$20.00
839	Hamilton, Harry - ***River Song*** [n.d.]	$1.35	$4.00	$8.00
840	Street, James - ***The Biscuit Eater And Other Stories*** [n.d.] PBO.	$4.00	$12.50	$25.00
841	Marshall, Edison - ***The Upstart*** [n.d.]	$1.25	$3.75	$7.50
842	Grey, Zane - ***Twin Sombreros*** [n.d.]	$1.35	$4.00	$8.00

Armed Service Edition, 885

Armed Service Edition, 984

		G	VG	F
843	Irwin, Margaret - ***Young Bess*** [n.d.]	$1.25	$3.75	$7.50
844	Tarkington, Booth - ***Little Orvie*** [n.d.]	$1.35	$4.00	$8.00
845	Bromfield, Louis - ***Pleasant Valley*** [n.d.]	$1.25	$3.75	$7.50
846	Graham, Frank - ***McGraw Of The Giants*** [n.d.]	$1.35	$4.00	$8.00
847	Temple, Ralph - ***Cuckoo Time*** [n.d.]	$1.25	$3.75	$7.50
848	Burnett, Whit - editor (Anthology) - ***Time To Be Young*** [n.d.]	$1.25	$3.75	$7.50
849	Allen, Hervey - ***Bedford Village*** [n.d.] Reprints #L-23.	$1.35	$4.00	$8.00
850	Shearing, Joseph - ***The Lady And The Arsenic*** [n.d.] Reprints #L-24.	$2.00	$6.00	$12.00
851	Stoker, Bram - ***Dracula*** [n.d.] Reprints #L-25.	$6.00	$20.00	$40.00
852	Marquand, John P. - ***Wickford Point*** [n.d.] Reprints #L-26.	$1.35	$4.00	$8.00
853	Langley, Adria Locke - ***A Lion Is In The Streets*** [n.d.]	$1.25	$3.75	$7.50
854	Shellabarger, Samuel - ***Captain From Castile*** [n.d.]	$1.25	$3.75	$7.50
855	Benet, Rosemary & Stephen Vincent - ***A Book Of Americans*** [n.d.] Reprints #L-1.	$1.35	$4.00	$8.00
856	Thurber, James - ***My Life And Hard Times*** [n.d.] Reprints #L-2.	$1.35	$4.00	$8.00
857	Millay, Edna St. Vincent - ***Lyrics And Sonnets*** [n.d.] PBO.	$3.50	$10.00	$20.00
858	Delavan, Maude Smith - ***The Rumelhearts Of Rampler Avenue*** [n.d.]	$1.25	$3.75	$7.50
859	Richter, Conrad - ***Tacey Cromwell*** [n.d.]	$1.35	$4.00	$8.00
860	Zweig, Stefan - ***The Royal Game*** [n.d.]	$1.25	$3.75	$7.50
861	Nordhoff, Charles - ***The Pearl Lagoon*** [n.d.]	$1.35	$4.00	$8.00
862	Fitzgerald, F. Scott - ***The Great Gatsby*** [n.d.]	$1.35	$4.00	$8.00
863	Hawthorne, Nathaniel - ***The Gray Champion And Other Tales*** [n.d.] PBO.	$3.50	$10.00	$20.00
864	Maurois, André - ***Ariel - The Life Of Shelley*** [n.d.]	$1.35	$4.00	$8.00
865	Benchley, Robert - ***My Ten Years In A Quandary And How They Grew*** [n.d.]	$1.25	$3.75	$7.50
866	Caldwell, Erskine - ***Tragic Ground*** [n.d.]	$1.35	$4.00	$8.00
867	Haycox, Ernest - ***Rim Of The Desert*** [n.d.] Reprints #N-9.	$1.35	$4.00	$8.00
868	LeMay, Alan - ***Useless Cowboy*** [n.d.] Reprints #N-10.	$1.25	$3.75	$7.50
869	Hughes, Dorothy B. - ***The Fallen Sparrow*** [n.d.] Reprints #N-11.	$2.00	$6.00	$12.00
870	Hough, Donald - ***Snow Above Town*** [n.d.]	$1.25	$3.75	$7.50
871	Collier, John - ***Green Thoughts And Other Strange Tales*** [n.d.] PBO. First and only edition.	$12.50	$37.50	$75.00
872	Perelman, S.J. - ***Crazy Like A Fox*** [n.d.]	$1.35	$4.00	$8.00
873	Greene, Graham - ***The Confidential Agent*** [n.d.]	$1.35	$4.00	$8.00
874	Short, Luke - ***Ramrod*** [n.d.]	$1.25	$3.75	$7.50
875	Edmonds, Walter D. - ***Mostly Canallers*** [n.d.]	$1.25	$3.75	$7.50
876	Iams, Jack - ***The Countess To Boot*** [n.d.]	$1.35	$4.00	$8.00

		G	VG	F
877	Brand, Max - ***Danger Trail*** [n.d.]	$1.25	$3.75	$7.50
878	Irish, William - ***Deadline At Dawn*** [n.d.]	$5.00	$15.00	$30.00
879	Weaver, John D. - ***Wind Before Rain*** [n.d.]	$1.35	$4.00	$8.00
880	Thoreau, Henry D. - ***Walden Or Life In The Woods*** [n.d.]	$1.35	$4.00	$8.00
881	Haggard, H. Rider - ***She*** [n.d.]	$1.50	$5.00	$10.00
882	Marsh, Ngaio - ***Colour Scheme*** [n.d.]	$2.00	$6.00	$12.00
883	Grey, Zane - ***Desert Gold*** [n.d.]	$1.25	$3.75	$7.50
884	Wilson, Harry Leon - ***Ruggles Of Red Gap*** [n.d.]	$1.25	$3.75	$7.50
885	Stevenson, Robert Louis - ***The Strange Case Of Dr. Jekyll And Mr. Hyde*** [n.d.] PBO thus. Original collection.	$12.50	$37.50	$75.00
886	Gilligan, Edmund - ***White Sails Crowding*** [n.d.]	$1.25	$3.75	$7.50
887	Wister, Owen - ***The Virginian*** [n.d.]	$1.25	$3.75	$7.50
888	Stuart, Jesse - ***Head O'W-Hollow*** [n.d.]	$1.35	$4.00	$8.00
889	Kains, M. G. - ***Five Acres And Independence*** [n.d.]	$1.35	$4.00	$8.00
890	Sayers, Dorothy L. - ***Busman's Honeymoon*** [n.d.]	$2.00	$6.00	$12.00
891	Cronin, A.J. - ***Hatter's Castle*** [n.d.]	$1.25	$3.75	$7.50
892	Botkin, B.A. - editor (Anthology) - ***The Sky's The Limit*** [n.d.] PBO. Foreword by Carl Sandburg.	$2.50	$7.50	$15.00
893	Bodmer, Frederick - ***The Loom Of Language*** [n.d.]	$1.35	$4.00	$8.00
894	Leach, Margaret - ***Reveille In Washington*** [n.d.]	$1.35	$4.00	$8.00
895	Lowell, Juliet - ***Dear Sir And Dumb-Belles Letters*** [n.d.]	$1.25	$3.75	$7.50
896	Goodman, Jack - ***How To Do Practically Anything*** [n.d.]	$1.35	$4.00	$8.00
897	Digges, Jeremiah - ***Bowleg Bill*** [n.d.]	$1.25	$3.75	$7.50
898	Perry, George Sessions - ***Walls Rise Up*** [n.d.]	$1.25	$3.75	$7.50
899	Lawson, Robert - ***Mr. Wilmer*** [n.d.]	$1.35	$4.00	$8.00
900	Beauchamp, D.D. - ***The Full Life And Other Stories*** [n.d.] PBO. First and only edition.	$4.00	$12.50	$25.00
901	Lindsay, Vachel - ***The Daniel Jazz And Other Poems*** [n.d.] PBO.	$2.50	$7.50	$15.00
902	Weaver, John - ***My Bitter Half And Other Stories*** [n.d.] PBO.	$2.50	$7.50	$15.00
903	Bernstein, Walter - ***Keep Your Head Down*** [n.d.]	$1.35	$4.00	$8.00
904	Sokoloff, Boris, M.D. - ***The Story Of Penicillin*** [n.d.]	$1.35	$4.00	$8.00
905	Hall, James Norman - ***Lost Island*** [n.d.] Reprints #P-5.	$1.35	$4.00	$8.00
906	Stout, Rex - ***Not Quite Dead Enough*** [n.d.] Reprints #P-6.	$2.00	$6.00	$12.00
907	Cuppy, Will - ***The Great Bustard And Other People*** [n.d.] Reprints #P-7.	$1.25	$3.75	$7.50
908	Brand, Max - ***The Fighting Four*** [n.d.] Reprints #P-8.	$1.25	$3.75	$7.50
909	Shelley, Mary - ***Frankenstein*** [n.d.]	$6.00	$20.00	$40.00
910	Fontaine, Robert - ***The Happy Time*** [n.d.]	$1.25	$3.75	$7.50
911	Lewis, Sinclair - ***Mantrap*** [n.d.]	$1.35	$4.00	$8.00
912	Connell, Richard - ***Ironies*** [n.d.]	$1.35	$4.00	$8.00
913	Marsh, Irving T. - editor (Anthology) - ***Best Sport Stories Of 1944*** [n.d.]	$1.35	$4.00	$8.00
914	Rice, Craig - ***The Lucky Stiff*** [n.d.]	$2.00	$6.00	$12.00
915	Gardner, Erle Stanley - ***The Case Of The Golddigger's Purse*** [n.d.]	$2.00	$6.00	$12.00
916	Haycox, Ernest - ***Canyon Passage*** [n.d.]	$1.25	$3.75	$7.50
917	Seltzer, Charles Alden - ***The Trail Horde*** [n.d.]	$1.25	$3.75	$7.50
918	Mulford, Clarence E. - ***Tex*** [n.d.]	$1.35	$4.00	$8.00
919	Maxwell, William - ***The Folded Leaf*** [n.d.]	$1.35	$4.00	$8.00
920	Goffin, Robert - ***Jazz*** [n.d.]	$1.25	$3.75	$7.50
921	Hecht, Ben - ***Concerning A Woman Of Sin And Other Stories*** [n.d.] PBO.	$3.50	$10.00	$20.00

		G	VG	F
922	Smith, Thorne - ***Rain In The Doorway*** [n.d.]	$1.25	$3.75	$7.50
923	Shearing, Joseph - ***Aunt Beardie*** [n.d.] Reprints #P-23.	$1.35	$4.00	$8.00
924	Davis, Clyde Brion - ***Rebellion Of Leo McGuire*** [n.d.] Reprints #P-24.	$1.35	$4.00	$8.00
925	Homer, translation by T.E. Shaw - ***The Odyssey*** [n.d.]	$1.25	$3.75	$7.50
926	Huxley, Aldous - ***The Gioconda Smile And Other Stories*** [n.d.] PBO.	$3.50	$10.00	$20.00
927	Paul, Elliott - ***The Last Time I Saw Paris*** [n.d.]	$1.35	$4.00	$8.00
928	Walpole, Hugh - ***Fortitude*** [n.d.]	$1.25	$3.75	$7.50
929	Stewart, George R. - ***Names On The Land*** [n.d.]	$1.35	$4.00	$8.00
930	Ehrlich, Leonard - ***God's Angry Men*** [n.d.]	$1.35	$4.00	$8.00
931	Adams, Samuel Hopkins - ***A. Woollcott - His Life And His World*** [n.d.]	$1.25	$3.75	$7.50
932	MacLennan, Hugh - ***Two Solitudes*** [n.d.]	$1.25	$3.75	$7.50
933	Anthology, introduction by Peter Arno - ***The Bedside Tales*** [n.d.]	$1.25	$3.75	$7.50
934	Anthology from Yank Magazine - ***The Best From Yank*** [n.d.]	$1.35	$4.00	$8.00
935	Krasna, Norman - ***Dear Ruth*** [n.d.]	$1.25	$3.75	$7.50
936	Madden, Joe - ***Set 'Em Up*** [n.d.]	$1.35	$4.00	$8.00
937	King, Rufus - ***The Deadly Dove*** [n.d.]	$2.00	$6.00	$12.00
938	Hart, Francis Russell - ***Admirals Of The Caribbean*** [n.d.]	$1.35	$4.00	$8.00
939	Browning, Elizabeth Barrett and Robert - ***Love Poems*** [n.d.] PBO.	$3.00	$9.00	$18.00
940	Machen, Arthur - ***The Great God Pan And Other Weird Stories*** [n.d.] PBO.	$7.00	$22.50	$45.00
941	Brown, Harry - ***Artie Greengroin, PFC*** [n.d.]	$1.25	$3.75	$7.50
942	Marshall, Bruce - ***The World, The Flesh And Father Smith*** [n.d.]	$1.35	$4.00	$8.00
943	Caspary, Vera - ***Bedelia*** [n.d.]	$1.25	$3.75	$7.50
944	Henry, O. - ***The Ransom Of Red Chief And Other Stories*** [n.d.] PBO.	$5.00	$15.00	$30.00
945	Caldwell, Erskine - ***God's Little Acre*** [n.d.]	$1.35	$4.00	$8.00
946	Gunn, James - ***Deadlier Than The Male*** [n.d.]	$2.00	$6.00	$12.00
947	Mann, E.B. - ***Comanche Kid*** [n.d.]	$1.25	$3.75	$7.50
948	Derrickson, Marione E. - editor (Anthology) - ***Laugh It Off*** [n.d.]	$1.25	$3.75	$7.50
949	Seltzer, Charles Alden - ***The Boss Of The Lazy Y*** [n.d.]	$1.35	$4.00	$8.00
950	Lockridge, Frances and Richard - ***Killing The Goose*** [n.d.]	$2.00	$6.00	$12.00
951	Halleran, E.E. - ***Prairie Guns*** [n.d.] Reprints #Q-11.	$1.35	$4.00	$8.00
952	Naidish, Theodore - ***Watch Out For Willie Carter*** [n.d.] Reprints #Q-12.	$1.35	$4.00	$8.00
953	Smith, Thorne - ***The Passionate Witch*** [n.d.]	$1.25	$3.75	$7.50
954	Dunsany, Lord - ***Guerilla*** [n.d.] Reprints #Q-14.	$3.50	$10.00	$20.00
955	Anthology selected from *The New Yorker* - ***The New Yorker Profiles*** [n.d.] PBO.	$2.50	$7.50	$15.00
956	MacDonald, William Colt - ***Cartridge Carnival*** [n.d.]	$1.35	$4.00	$8.00
957	Kirkbride, Ronald - ***Winds, Blow Gently*** [n.d.]	$1.25	$3.75	$7.50
958	Wells, H.G. - ***The Food Of The Gods*** [n.d.]	$5.00	$15.00	$30.00
959	Ferber, Edna - ***Great Son*** [n.d.]	$1.25	$3.75	$7.50
960	Zim, Herbert S. - ***Rockets And Jets*** [n.d.]	$1.25	$3.75	$7.50
961	Stong, Phil - ***Marta Of Muscovy*** [n.d.]	$1.25	$3.75	$7.50
962	Ratcliff, John D. - editor (Anthology) - ***Science Yearbook Of 1945*** [n.d.]	$1.25	$3.75	$7.50

		G	VG	F
963	Graham, Frank - ***The Brooklyn Dodgers*** [n.d.]	$4.00	$12.50	$25.00
964	Ripley, Dillon - ***Trail Of The Money Bird*** [n.d.]	$1.35	$4.00	$8.00
965	Graffis, Herb - editor (Anthology) - ***Esquire's First Sports Reader*** [n.d.]	$1.35	$4.00	$8.00
966	Hilton, James - ***So Well Remembered*** [n.d.]	$1.25	$3.75	$7.50
967	Gaver, Jack & Stanley, Dave - ***There's Laughter In The Air!*** [n.d.]	$1.25	$3.75	$7.50
968	Shaw, Lau - ***Rickshaw Boy*** [n.d.]	$1.25	$3.75	$7.50
969	Lewis, Sinclair - ***Cass Timberlane*** [n.d.]	$1.35	$4.00	$8.00
970	Thurber, James - ***The Thurber Carnival*** [n.d.]	$1.25	$3.75	$7.50
971	Maugham, W. Somerset - ***The Razor's Edge*** [n.d.] Reprints #Q-31.	$1.25	$3.75	$7.50
972	Smith, Lillian - ***Strange Fruit*** [n.d.] Reprints #Q-32.	$1.35	$4.00	$8.00
973	Cloete, Stuart - ***Against These Three*** [n.d.]	$1.25	$3.75	$7.50
974	Clark, Walter Van Tilburg - ***The City Of Trembling Leaves*** [n.d.]	$1.25	$3.75	$7.50
975	Lewis, Herbert Clyde - ***Gentleman Overboard*** [n.d.]	$1.25	$3.75	$7.50
976	Leacock, Stephen - ***My Remarkable Uncle And Other Sketches*** [n.d.]	$1.35	$4.00	$8.00
977	Corey, Paul - ***Buy An Acre*** [n.d.]	$1.35	$4.00	$8.00
978	Macauley, C.B.F. - ***The Helicopters Are Coming*** [n.d.]	$1.25	$3.75	$7.50
979	O'Hara, John - ***The Doctor's Son And Other Stories*** [n.d.]	$1.25	$3.75	$7.50
980	Trumbull, Robert - ***Silversides*** [n.d.]	$1.35	$4.00	$8.00
981	Nash, Ogden - ***I'm A Stranger Here Myself*** [n.d.]	$1.25	$3.75	$7.50
982	Brand, Max - ***Silvertip's Search*** [n.d.]	$1.25	$3.75	$7.50
983	Bayer, Oliver Weld - ***An Eye For An Eye*** [n.d.]	$1.25	$3.75	$7.50
984	Chesterton, G.K. - ***The Man Who Was Thursday*** [n.d.]	$4.00	$12.50	$25.00
985	Robertson, Archie - ***Slow Train To Yesterday*** [n.d.]	$1.25	$3.75	$7.50
986	Crump, Irving - ***Our United States Secret Service*** [n.d.]	$1.25	$3.75	$7.50
987	Seltzer, Charles Alden - ***Beau Rand*** [n.d.]	$1.25	$3.75	$7.50
988	Powell, Richard - ***Lay That Pistol Down*** [n.d.]	$2.00	$6.00	$12.00
989	Raine, William MacLeod - ***Who Wants To Live Forever?*** [n.d.]	$1.35	$4.00	$8.00
990	Clarke, Donald Henderson - ***Louis Beretti*** [n.d.]	$1.25	$3.75	$7.50
991	Dickson, Carter - ***The Curse Of The Bronze Lamp*** [n.d.]	$2.50	$7.50	$15.00
992	Wright, Sewell Peaslee - editor (Anthology) - ***Chicago Murders*** [n.d.]	$1.35	$4.00	$8.00
993	Frank, Stanley - editor (Anthology) - ***Sports Extra*** [n.d.]	$1.35	$4.00	$8.00
994	Erskine, John - ***The Private Life Of Helen Of Troy*** [n.d.]	$1.25	$3.75	$7.50
995	Crane, Frances - ***The Amethyst Spectacles*** [n.d.] Reprints #Q-17.	$1.35	$4.00	$8.00
996	Forester, C.S. - ***Beat To Quarters*** [n.d.] Reprints #Q-18.	$1.35	$4.00	$8.00
997	Grey, Zane - ***The Heritage Of The Desert*** [n.d.] Reprints #Q-19.	$1.25	$3.75	$7.50
998	Hawkins, John and Ward - ***Devil On His Trail*** [n.d.] Reprints #Q-20.	$1.35	$4.00	$8.00
999	Burman, Ben Lucien - ***Rooster Crows For A Day*** [n.d.]	$1.35	$4.00	$8.00
1000	Miller, Paul Eduard, editor (Anthology) - ***Esquire's 1945 Jazz Book*** [n.d.]	$1.35	$4.00	$8.00
1001	McMeekin, Clark - ***Black Moon*** [n.d.]	$1.35	$4.00	$8.00
1002	Huff, Darrell and Frances - ***Twenty Careers Of Tomorrow*** [n.d.]	$1.35	$4.00	$8.00
1003	Pinchon, Edgcumb - ***Dan Sickles*** [n.d.]	$1.25	$3.75	$7.50
1004	Partridge, Bellamy - ***January Thaw*** [n.d.]	$1.25	$3.75	$7.50
1005	Shaw, George Bernard - ***Arms And The Man And Two Other Plays*** [n.d.] PBO.	$2.50	$7.50	$15.00
1006	Sabatini, Rafael - ***The Birth Of Mischief*** [n.d.]	$1.25	$3.75	$7.50

		G	VG	F
1007	Bell, Thomas - ***All Brides Are Beautiful*** [n.d.]	$1.35	$4.00	$8.00
1008	Harrison, George Russell - ***Atoms In Action*** [n.d.]	$1.25	$3.75	$7.50
1009	Cronin, A. J. - ***The Green Years*** [n.d.] Reprints #Q-27	$1.35	$4.00	$8.00
1010	Taylor, Ross McLaury - ***The Saddle And The Plow*** [n.d.] Reprints #Q-28.	$1.35	$4.00	$8.00
1011	London, Jack - ***Best Short Stories Of Jack London*** [n.d.]	$3.00	$9.00	$18.00
1012	Tucker, Sophie - ***Some Of These Days*** [n.d.]	$1.25	$3.75	$7.50
1013	Wolfe, Thomas - ***Of Time And The River*** [n.d.]	$4.00	$12.50	$25.00
1014	Roberts, Kenneth - ***Northwest Passage*** [n.d.]	$1.25	$3.75	$7.50
1015	Housman, A.E. - ***Selected Poems Of A.E. Housman*** [n.d.] Reprints #M-1.	$1.35	$4.00	$8.00
1016	Thurber, James and White, E.B. - ***Is Sex Necessary?*** [n.d.] Reprints #M-2.	$1.35	$4.00	$8.00
1017	Russell, Fred - ***I'll Try Anthing Twice*** [n.d.]	$1.35	$4.00	$8.00
1018	Andrews, John Paul - ***Your Personal Plane*** [n.d.]	$1.35	$4.00	$8.00
1019	Perelman, S.J., and Reynolds, Q.J. - ***Parlor, Bedlam, And Bath*** [n.d.]	$1.25	$3.75	$7.50
1020	Bell, Thomas - ***Till I Come Back To You*** [n.d.]	$1.25	$3.75	$7.50
1021	Tuttle, W.C. - ***The Wolf Pack Of Lobo Butte*** [n.d.]	$1.35	$4.00	$8.00
1022	Lomax, Bliss - ***Rusty Guns*** [n.d.]	$1.35	$4.00	$8.00
1023	Thomson, Virgil - ***The State Of Music*** [n.d.]	$1.35	$4.00	$8.00
1024	Van Doren, Mark - ***Liberal Education*** [n.d.]	$1.25	$3.75	$7.50
1025	Kelland, Clarence Budington - ***Dreamland*** [n.d.]	$1.25	$3.75	$7.50
1026	Bonnamy, Francis - ***The King Is Dead On Queen Street*** [n.d.]	$2.00	$6.00	$12.00
1027	Miers, Earl Schenck - ***Big Ben*** [n.d.]	$1.35	$4.00	$8.00
1028	Stribling, T.S. - ***Red Sand*** [n.d.]	$1.35	$4.00	$8.00
1029	Price, George - ***Is It Anyone We Know?*** [n.d.]	$1.25	$3.75	$7.50
1030	Seltzer, Charles Alden - ***Drag Harlan*** [n.d.]	$1.25	$3.75	$7.50
1031	Blake, Nicholas - ***The Corpse In The Snowman*** [n.d.]	$2.00	$6.00	$12.00
1032	Lurton, Douglas E. - ***Make The Most Of Your Life*** [n.d.]	$1.25	$3.75	$7.50
1033	Forbes, Esther - ***O Genteel Lady!*** [n.d.]	$1.35	$4.00	$8.00
1034	McCloy, Helen - ***Panic*** [n.d.]	$1.35	$4.00	$8.00
1035	Segre, Alfredo - ***Mahogany*** [n.d.]	$1.35	$4.00	$8.00
1036	Cunningham, Eugene - ***Buckaroo*** [n.d.]	$1.25	$3.75	$7.50
1037	Ward, Arch - ***Frank Leahy And The Fighting Irish*** [n.d.]	$1.35	$4.00	$8.00
1038	Coles, Manning - ***They Tell No Tales*** [n.d.]	$1.25	$3.75	$7.50
1039	Gardner, Erle Stanley - ***The Case Of The Half-Wakened Wife*** [n.d.]	$2.00	$6.00	$12.00
1040	Embree, John F. - ***The Japanese Nation*** [n.d.]	$1.35	$4.00	$8.00
1041	Jackson, Charles - ***The Lost Weekend*** [n.d.] Reprints #O-19.	$1.35	$4.00	$8.00
1042	Russell, John - ***Selected Short Stories Of John Russell*** [n.d.] Reprints #O-20.	$1.35	$4.00	$8.00
1043	Fitzgerald, F. Scott - ***The Diamond As Big As The Ritz And Other Stories*** [n.d.] PBO	$6.00	$20.00	$40.00
1044	Manchester, Harland - ***New World of Machines*** [n.d.]	$1.25	$3.75	$7.50
1045	Stewart, George R. - ***Storm*** [n.d.] Reprints #C-81.	$1.25	$3.75	$7.50
1046	De Poncins, Gontran - ***Kabloona*** [n.d.] Reprints #C-82	$1.35	$4.00	$8.00
1047	Pinckney, Josephine - ***Three O'Clock Dinner*** [n.d.]	$1.25	$3.75	$7.50
1048	Armstrong, Margaret - ***Trelawny*** [n.d.]	$1.35	$4.00	$8.00
1049	Hobart, Alice Tisdale - ***Oil For The Lamps Of China*** [n.d.]	$1.25	$3.75	$7.50
1050	Cerf, Bennett - editor (Anthology) - ***Modern American Short Stories*** [n.d.]	$1.35	$4.00	$8.00
1051	Steinman, D.B. - ***The Builders Of The Bridge*** [n.d.]	$1.35	$4.00	$8.00

Armed Service Edition, 1074

Armed Service Edition, 1075

		G	VG	F
1052	Willison, George F. - ***Saints And Strangers*** [n.d.]	$1.35	$4.00	$8.00
1053	Ullman, James Ramsey - ***The White Tower*** [n.d.]	$1.35	$4.00	$8.00
1054	Cronin, A.J. - ***The Stars Look Down*** [n.d.]	$1.25	$3.75	$7.50
1055	Gilligan, Edmund - ***Hunter's Moon And Other Stories*** [n.d.] PBO.	$3.50	$10.00	$20.00
1056	Herrick, Robert - ***Love Poems*** [n.d.] PBO.	$2.50	$7.50	$15.00
1057	Skinner, Cornelia Otis - ***Excuse It, Please!*** [n.d.] Reprints #Q-1..	$1.35	$4.00	$8.00
1058	Cain, James M. - ***The Postman Always Rings Twice*** [n.d.] Reprints #Q-2.	$2.50	$7.50	$15.00
1059	Ewen, David - ***The Story Of George Gershwin*** [n.d.] Reprints #Q-3.	$1.35	$4.00	$8.00
1060	Lieber, Hugh Gray and Lillian R. - ***The Education Of T.C. Mills*** [n.d.] Reprints #Q-4.	$1.25	$3.75	$7.50
1061	Carrighar, Sally - ***One Day On Beetle Rock*** [n.d.]	$1.35	$4.00	$8.00
1062	Kalashnikoff, Nicholas - ***Jumper*** [n.d.]	$1.35	$4.00	$8.00
1063	Dietz, David - ***Atomic Energy in the Coming Era*** [n.d.]	$1.25	$3.75	$7.50
1064	Brooks, George S. - ***Block That Bride And Other Stories*** [n.d.] PBO.	$2.50	$7.50	$15.00
1065	Curwood, James Oliver - ***Kazan*** [n.d.]	$1.35	$4.00	$8.00
1066	Anthology selected from *The New Yorker* - ***The New Yorker Reporter At Large*** [n.d.] PBO.	$2.50	$7.50	$15.00
1067	Perry, George Sessions - ***Hold Autumn In Your Hand*** [n.d.]	$1.35	$4.00	$8.00
1068	Floherty, John J. - ***Inside The F.B.I.*** [n.d.]	$1.35	$4.00	$8.00
1069	Dickson, Carter - ***The Department of Queer Complaints*** [n.d.] ...	$3.50	$10.00	$20.00
1070	Caruso, Dorothy - ***Enrico Caruso*** [n.d.]	$1.35	$4.00	$8.00
1071	Seltzer, Charles Alden - ***The Vengeance Of Jefferson Gawne*** [n.d.]	$1.35	$4.00	$8.00
1072	Mulford, Clarence E. - ***The Man From Bar-20*** [n.d.]	$1.25	$3.75	$7.50
1073	Hendryx, James B. - ***Gold And Guns On Halfaday Creek*** [n.d.] .	$1.35	$4.00	$8.00
1074	Rice, Craig - ***The Sunday Pigeon Murders*** [n.d.]	$2.00	$6.00	$12.00
1075	Footner, Hulbert - ***The Murder That Had Everything*** [n.d.]	$2.00	$6.00	$12.00
1076	Linscott, R.N. - editor (Anthology) - ***Comic Relief*** [n.d.]	$1.35	$4.00	$8.00
1077	Rich, Louise Dickinson - ***We Took To The Woods*** [n.d.]	$1.25	$3.75	$7.50
1078	Teilhet, Darwin L. - ***My True Love*** [n.d.]	$1.25	$3.75	$7.50
1079	Fenton, Carroll Lane & Mildred Adams - ***The Story Of The Great Geologists*** [n.d.]	$1.25	$3.75	$7.50
1080	Tolstoy, Count Leo - ***Tales By Tolstoy*** [n.d.] PBO.	$2.50	$7.50	$15.00
1081	Campbell, William G., and Bedford, James - ***You And Your Future Job*** [n.d.]	$1.25	$3.75	$7.50
1082	Costain, Thomas B. - ***The Black Rose*** [n.d.]	$1.25	$3.75	$7.50
1083	Tulley, Walt - ***Baseball Recorder*** [n.d.]	$1.35	$4.00	$8.00

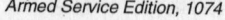

		G	VG	F
1084	Marquand, John P. - ***Repent In Haste*** [n.d.]	$1.25	$3.75	$7.50
1085	Lariar, Lawrence - editor (Anthology) - ***Best Cartoons Of The Year, 1945*** [n.d.]	$2.50	$7.50	$15.00
1086	Clouston, J. Storer - ***The Lunatic At Large*** [n.d.]	$1.35	$4.00	$8.00
1087	Gamow, George - ***Biography Of The Earth*** [n.d.]	$1.25	$3.75	$7.50
1088	Huggins, Roy - ***The Double Take*** [n.d.]	$2.00	$6.00	$12.00
1089	Haystead, Ladd - ***If The Prospect Pleases*** [n.d.]	$1.25	$3.75	$7.50
1090	Dowst, Robert S. - ***Straight, Place, And Show*** [n.d.]	$1.25	$3.75	$7.50
1091	Wells, H.G. - ***The War Of The Worlds*** [n.d.] Reprints #745.	$4.00	$12.50	$25.00
1092	Wallace, Francis - ***Kid Galahad*** [n.d.] Reprints #746.	$1.35	$4.00	$8.00
1093	Lockridge, Frances and Richard - ***Death On The Aisle*** [n.d.] Reprints #747.	$2.00	$6.00	$12.00
1094	Haycox, Ernest - ***Starlight Rider*** [n.d.] Reprints #748.	$1.35	$4.00	$8.00
1095	Greenberg, David B. & Schindall, Henry - ***A Small Store And Independence*** [n.d.]	$1.25	$3.75	$7.50
1096	Burman, Ben Lucien - ***Steamboat Round The Bend*** [n.d.]	$1.25	$3.75	$7.50
1097	Kendrick, Baynard - ***Out Of Control*** [n.d.]	$2.00	$6.00	$12.00
1098	Treat, Lawrence - ***V As In Victim*** [n.d.]	$2.00	$6.00	$12.00
1099	Conrad, Joseph - ***Typhoon And The End Of The Tether*** [n.d.]	$1.35	$4.00	$8.00
1100	MacDonald, Betty - ***The Egg And I*** [n.d.]	$1.25	$3.75	$7.50
1101	Seltzer, Charles Alden - ***The Ranchman*** [n.d.]	$1.35	$4.00	$8.00
1102	Butcher, Capt. Harry C. - ***My Three Years With Eisenhower*** [n.d.]	$1.35	$4.00	$8.00
1103	Taylor, Deems - ***The Well-Tempered Listener*** [n.d.]	$1.35	$4.00	$8.00
1104	Bruff, Nancy - ***The Manatee*** [n.d.]	$1.25	$3.75	$7.50
1105	Wharton, John F. - ***The Theory And Practice Of Earning A Living*** [n.d.]	$1.25	$3.75	$7.50
1106	Rice, Craig - ***The Big Midget Murders*** [n.d.]	$1.35	$4.00	$8.00
1107	Grey, Zane - ***The Border Legion*** [n.d.]	$1.35	$4.00	$8.00
1108	Burns, Walter Noble - ***The Saga Of Billy The Kid*** [n.d.]	$2.00	$6.00	$12.00
1109	Welch, Douglass - ***Mr. Digby*** [n.d.]	$1.35	$4.00	$8.00
1110	Gill, Richard C. - ***White Water And Black Magic*** [n.d.]	$1.25	$3.75	$7.50
1111	Ferber, Edna - ***Saratoga Trunk*** [n.d.]	$1.35	$4.00	$8.00
1112	Dunlap, Orrin E., Jr. - ***Radio's 100 Men Of Science*** [n.d.]	$1.25	$3.75	$7.50
1113	Simonov, Konstantine - ***Days And Nights*** [n.d.]	$1.25	$3.75	$7.50
1114	Benet, Stephen Vincent - ***John Brown's Body*** [n.d.]	$1.35	$4.00	$8.00
1115	Isherwood, Christopher - ***Prater Violet*** [n.d.]	$1.25	$3.75	$7.50
1116	Sansone, Sgt. Leonard - ***The Wolf*** [n.d.] PBO.	$2.50	$7.50	$15.00
1117	Dixon, H. Vernor - ***Come In Like A Yankee And Other Stories*** [n.d.] PBO.	$5.00	$15.00	$30.00
1118	Miller, Margery - ***Joe Louis: American*** [n.d.]	$1.35	$4.00	$8.00
1119	Shulman, Max - ***The Zebra Derby*** [n.d.]	$1.25	$3.75	$7.50
1120	Lamond, Henry G. - ***Dingo*** [n.d.]	$1.25	$3.75	$7.50
1121	Stephens, James - ***The Crock Of Gold*** [n.d.] Reprints #N-5.	$2.50	$7.50	$15.00
1122	Sandburg, Carl - ***Selected Poems Of Carl Sandburg*** [n.d.] Reprints #N-6.	$1.35	$4.00	$8.00
1123	Knight, Kathleen Moore - ***Port of Seven Strangers*** [n.d.]	$1.35	$4.00	$8.00
1124	Johnson, Martin - ***Safari*** [n.d.]	$1.25	$3.75	$7.50
1125	Stone, Grace Zaring - ***The Bitter Tea Of General Yen*** [n.d.]	$1.35	$4.00	$8.00
1126	Crow, Carl - ***The Great American Customer*** [n.d.]	$1.35	$4.00	$8.00
1127	Benefield, Barry - ***Valient Is The Word For Carrie*** [n.d.]	$1.25	$3.75	$7.50
1128	Carmichael, John P. and others - ***My Greatest Day In Baseball*** [n.d.]	$2.00	$6.00	$12.00

		G	VG	F
1129	Raine, William MacLeod - ***Courage Stout*** [n.d.]	$1.25	$3.75	$7.50
1130	Barber, Willetta Ann and Schabelitz, R.F - ***The Noose Is Drawn*** [n.d.]	$1.35	$4.00	$8.00
1131	Gardner, Erle Stanley - ***The Case Of The Black-Eyed Blonde*** [n.d.] Reprints #S-21.	$2.00	$6.00	$12.00
1132	Smith, H. Allen - ***Lost In The Horse Latitudes*** [n.d.] Reprints #S-22.	$1.35	$4.00	$8.00
1133	Brand, Max - ***Hunted Riders*** [n.d.] Reprints #S-23.	$1.35	$4.00	$8.00
1134	Clark, Walter Van Tilburg - ***The Ox-Bow Incident*** [n.d.] Reprints #S-24.	$1.25	$3.75	$7.50
1135	Parkhill, Forbes - ***Troopers West*** [n.d.]	$1.35	$4.00	$8.00
1136	Coxe, George Harmon - ***Woman At Bay*** [n.d.]	$1.35	$4.00	$8.00
1137	Fitzgerald, Ed - editor (Anthology) - ***Tales For Males*** [n.d.]	$1.35	$4.00	$8.00
1138	Standish, Robert - ***The Small General*** [n.d.]	$1.25	$3.75	$7.50
1139	Sanderson, Ivan T. - ***Caribbean Treasure*** [n.d.]	$1.35	$4.00	$8.00
1140	Carlisle, Norman V., and Latham, Frank - ***Miracles Ahead*** [n.d.]	$1.25	$3.75	$7.50
1141	Mulford, Clarence E. - ***The Bar-20 Three*** [n.d.]	$1.35	$4.00	$8.00
1142	Van Doren, Mark - ***Shakespeare*** [n.d.]	$1.25	$3.75	$7.50
1143	Steiner, Lee R. - ***Where Do People Take Their Troubles?*** [n.d.]	$1.25	$3.75	$7.50
1144	James, Marquis - ***The Cherokee Strip*** [n.d.]	$1.35	$4.00	$8.00
1145	Stead and Blake - editors (Anthology) - ***Modern Women In Love*** [n.d.]	$1.35	$4.00	$8.00
1146	Steele, Wilbur Daniel - ***That Girl From Memphis*** [n.d.]	$1.35	$4.00	$8.00
1147	O'Hara, John - ***Pal Joey*** [n.d.] Reprints #817.	$1.35	$4.00	$8.00
1148	Sayre, Joel - ***Rackety Rax*** [n.d.] Reprints #818.	$1.35	$4.00	$8.00
1149	Papashvily, George and Helen - ***Anything Can Happen*** [n.d.] Reprints #T-3.	$1.25	$3.75	$7.50
1150	Ewen, David - ***Men Of Popular Music*** [n.d.] Reprints #T-4.	$1.25	$3.75	$7.50
1151	Nash, Ogden - ***Many Long Years Ago*** [n.d.]	$1.35	$4.00	$8.00
1152	Stone, Grace Zaring - ***Winter Meeting*** [n.d.]	$1.25	$3.75	$7.50
1153	Musselman, M.M. - ***Wheels In His Head*** [n.d.]	$1.35	$4.00	$8.00
1154	Field, Peter - ***The End Of The Trail*** [n.d.]	$1.25	$3.75	$7.50
1155	Scherf, Margaret - ***The Owl In The Cellar*** [n.d.]	$1.25	$3.75	$7.50
1156	Anthology from *The New Yorker* - ***The Dark Ship And Other Selections*** [n.d.] PBO.	$2.50	$7.50	$15.00
1157	Fisher, Clyde - ***The Story Of The Moon*** [n.d.]	$1.35	$4.00	$8.00
1158	Kent, W.H.B. - ***The Tenderfoot*** [n.d.]	$1.35	$4.00	$8.00
1159	Maloney, Russell - ***It's Still Maloney*** [n.d.]	$1.25	$3.75	$7.50
1160	Andrews, Roy Chapman - ***Meet Your Ancestors*** [n.d.]	$1.25	$3.75	$7.50
1161	Burnett, W.R. - ***Tomorrow's Another Day*** [n.d.]	$2.00	$6.00	$12.00
1162	Lockridge, Frances and Richard - ***Murder Within Murder*** [n.d.]	$2.00	$6.00	$12.00
1163	Gill, Tom - ***Starlight Pass*** [n.d.] Reprints #P-15.	$1.25	$3.75	$7.50
1164	Haycox, Ernest - ***Trail Town*** [n.d.] Reprints #P-16.	$1.35	$4.00	$8.00
1165	Household, Geoffrey - ***The Salvation Of Pisco Gabar And Other Stories*** [n.d.]	$1.25	$3.75	$7.50
1166	Wentworth, Patricia - ***She Came Back*** [n.d.]	$2.00	$6.00	$12.00
1167	Landis, Walter S. - ***Your Servant The Molecule*** [n.d.]	$1.25	$3.75	$7.50
1168	Ellsberg, Commander Edward - ***Treasure Below*** [n.d.]	$1.35	$4.00	$8.00
1169	Sloane, William - ***The Edge Of Running Water*** [n.d.] Reprints #T-23.	$3.50	$10.00	$20.00
1170	Graham, Frank - ***The New York Yankees*** [n.d.] Reprints #T-24.	$2.00	$6.00	$12.00
1171	Hart, Harold - editor (Anthology) - ***Top Stuff*** [n.d.]	$1.35	$4.00	$8.00

		G	VG	F
1172	Stockton, J. Roy - ***The Gashouse Gang*** [n.d.]	$2.50	$7.50	$15.00
1173	Irish, William - ***I Wouldn't Be In Your Shoes*** [n.d.]	$4.00	$12.50	$25.00
1174	Rainier, Peter W. - ***Green Fire*** [n.d.]	$1.35	$4.00	$8.00
1175	Zevin, B.D. - editor (Anthology) - ***Cobb's Cavalcade*** [n.d.]	$1.35	$4.00	$8.00
1176	Du Maurier, Daphne - ***The King's General*** [n.d.]	$1.25	$3.75	$7.50
1177	Remarque, Erich Maria - ***Arch Of Triumph*** [n.d.]	$1.35	$4.00	$8.00
1178	Goodman, Jack - editor (Anthology) - ***While You Were Gone*** [n.d.]	$1.35	$4.00	$8.00
1179	Pyle, Ernie - ***Last Chapter*** [n.d.]	$1.35	$4.00	$8.00
1180	McNulty, John - ***Third Avenue, New York*** [n.d.]	$1.25	$3.75	$7.50
1181	Field, Peter - ***Ravaged Range*** [n.d.]	$1.25	$3.75	$7.50
1182	Vidal, Gore - ***Williwaw*** [n.d.]	$1.35	$4.00	$8.00
1183	Ermine, Will - ***Outlaw On Horseback*** [n.d.]	$1.35	$4.00	$8.00
1184	Short, Luke - ***Coroner Creek*** [n.d.]	$1.25	$3.75	$7.50
1185	Macardle, Dorothy - ***The Unforeseen*** [n.d.]	$2.00	$6.00	$12.00
1186	Cores, Lucy - ***Let's Kill George*** [n.d.]	$1.35	$4.00	$8.00
1187	Forester, C. S. - ***Lord Hornblower*** [n.d.]	$1.35	$4.00	$8.00
1188	Campbell, Alice - ***With Bated Breath*** [n.d.]	$1.35	$4.00	$8.00
1189	Fowler, Gene - ***A Solo In Tom-Toms*** [n.d.]	$1.25	$3.75	$7.50
1190	Anthology from *Saturday Evening Post* - ***The Saturday Evening Post Stories 1942–1945*** [n.d.]	$1.35	$4.00	$8.00
1191	Casey, Lee - editor (Anthology) - ***Denver Murders*** [n.d.]	$2.00	$6.00	$12.00
1192	Bishop, Curtis - ***By Way Of Wyoming*** [n.d.]	$1.35	$4.00	$8.00
1193	Sullivan, Frank - ***A Rock In Every Snowball*** [n.d.]	$1.35	$4.00	$8.00
1194	Stagge, Jonathan - ***Death's Old Sweet Song*** [n.d.]	$1.25	$3.75	$7.50
1195	Beach, Rex - ***The World In His Arms*** [n.d.]	$1.25	$3.75	$7.50
1196	Raine, William MacLeod - ***Clattering Hoofs*** [n.d.]	$1.25	$3.75	$7.50
1197	Brown, Warren - ***The Chicago Cubs*** [n.d.]	$1.25	$3.75	$7.50
1198	Corbett, Jim - ***Man-Eaters Of Kumaon*** [n.d.]	$1.35	$4.00	$8.00
1199	Vestal, Stanley - ***Jim Bridger, Mountain Man*** [n.d.]	$1.35	$4.00	$8.00
1200	Gann, Ernest K. - ***Blaze Of Noon*** [n.d.]	$1.35	$4.00	$8.00
1201	Warren, Robert Penn - ***All The King's Men*** [n.d.]	$2.00	$6.00	$12.00
1202	Gibbs, Willa - ***Tell Your Sons*** [n.d.]	$1.35	$4.00	$8.00
1203	Heggen, Thomas - ***Mister Roberts*** [n.d.]	$1.35	$4.00	$8.00
1204	Sampson, Arthur - ***Football Coach*** [n.d.]	$1.25	$3.75	$7.50
1205	Sale, Richard - ***Benefit Performance*** [n.d.]	$1.35	$4.00	$8.00
1206	Halleran, E. E. - ***Double Cross Trail*** [n.d.]	$1.25	$3.75	$7.50
1207	Wilson, Earl - ***Pikes Peek Or Bust*** [n.d.]	$1.35	$4.00	$8.00
1208	MacDonald, William Colt - ***Thunderbird Trail*** [n.d.]	$1.25	$3.75	$7.50
1209	Caspary, Vera - ***Stranger Than Truth*** [n.d.]	$2.00	$6.00	$12.00
1210	Tabori, George - ***Companions Of The Left Hand*** [n.d.]	$1.35	$4.00	$8.00
1211	O'Hara, Mary - ***Green Grass Of Wyoming*** [n.d.]	$1.35	$4.00	$8.00
1212	Stanwell-Fletcher, Theodora C. - ***Driftwood Valley*** [n.d.]	$1.35	$4.00	$8.00
1213	Steele, Wilbur Daniel - ***The Best Stories Of Wilbur Daniel Steele*** [n.d.]	$1.25	$3.75	$7.50
1214	Ellsberg, Commander Edward - ***Under The Red Sea Sun*** [n.d.]	$1.25	$3.75	$7.50
1215	Fearing, Kenneth - ***The Big Clock*** [n.d.]	$1.25	$3.75	$7.50
1216	Brand, Max - ***Mountain Riders*** [n.d.]	$1.25	$3.75	$7.50
1217	Frank, Pat - ***Mr. Adam*** [n.d.]	$1.35	$4.00	$8.00
1218	Gardner, Erle Stanley - ***The Case Of The Borrowed Brunette*** [n.d.]	$2.00	$6.00	$12.00
1219	La Farge, Christopher - ***The Sudden Guest*** [n.d.]	$1.35	$4.00	$8.00
1220	Freuchen, Peter - ***White Man*** [n.d.]	$1.25	$3.75	$7.50

		G	VG	F
1221	Daniels, Jonathan - ***Frontier On The Potomac*** [n.d.]	$1.25	$3.75	$7.50
1222	Stout, Rex - ***The Silent Speaker*** [n.d.]	$2.00	$6.00	$12.00
1223	Margolies, Joseph A. - editor (Anthology) - ***Strange And Fantastic Stories*** [n.d.]	$2.50	$7.50	$15.00
1224	Shepard, Odell and Willard - ***Holdfast Gaines*** [n.d.]	$1.35	$4.00	$8.00
1225	Marquand, John P. - ***B.F.'s Daughter*** [n.d.]	$1.25	$3.75	$7.50
1226	Jennings, John - ***The Salem Frigate*** [n.d.]	$1.35	$4.00	$8.00
1227	Martin, Ralph G. - ***Boy From Nebraska*** [n.d.]	$1.35	$4.00	$8.00
1228	Stern, David - ***Francis*** [n.d.]	$1.35	$4.00	$8.00
1229	George, Willis - ***Surreptitious Entry*** [n.d.]	$1.25	$3.75	$7.50
1230	Hendryx, James B. - ***Courage Of The North*** [n.d.]	$1.25	$3.75	$7.50
1231	Lockridge, Frances and Richard - ***Death Of A Tall Man*** [n.d.]	$2.00	$6.00	$12.00
1232	Steinbeck, John - ***The Wayward Bus*** [n.d.]	$2.00	$6.00	$12.00
1233	Kantor, MacKinlay - ***But Look, The Morn*** [n.d.]	$1.35	$4.00	$8.00
1234	Mason, Van Wyck - ***Saigon Singer*** [n.d.]	$1.25	$3.75	$7.50
1235	Gipson, Fred - ***Fabulous Empire*** [n.d.]	$1.25	$3.75	$7.50
1236	Waters, Frank - ***The Colorado*** [n.d.]	$1.35	$4.00	$8.00
1237	Ainsworth, Ed - ***Eagles Fly West*** [n.d.]	$1.35	$4.00	$8.00
1238	Fletcher, Inglis - ***Toil Of The Brave*** [n.d.]	$1.35	$4.00	$8.00
1239	Savage, Les, Jr. - ***Treasure Of The Brasada*** [n.d.]	$1.25	$3.75	$7.50
1240	West, Tom - ***Six Gun Showdown*** [n.d.]	$1.35	$4.00	$8.00
1241	Reilly, Helen - ***The Silver Leopard*** [n.d.]	$2.00	$6.00	$12.00
1242	Whiteman, Luther - ***The Face Of The Clam*** [n.d.]	$1.35	$4.00	$8.00
1243	Haines, William Wister - ***Command Decision*** [n.d.]	$1.25	$3.75	$7.50
1244	Gooden, Arthur Henry - ***The Shadowed Trail*** [n.d.]	$1.35	$4.00	$8.00
1245	Evans, Bergen - ***The Natural History Of Nonsense*** [n.d.]	$1.25	$3.75	$7.50
1246	Dickson, Carter - ***My Late Wives*** [n.d.]	$1.35	$4.00	$8.00
1247	Walker, Mildred - ***The Quarry*** [n.d.]	$1.25	$3.75	$7.50
1248	Michener, James A. - ***Tales Of The South Pacific*** [n.d.]	$1.35	$4.00	$8.00
1249	Cahill, Holger - ***Look South To The Polar Star*** [n.d.]	$1.35	$4.00	$8.00
1250	Sevareid, Eric - ***Not So Wild A Dream*** [n.d.]	$1.25	$3.75	$7.50
1251	Nye, Nelson C. - ***The Barber Of Tubac*** [n.d.]	$1.25	$3.75	$7.50
1252	Faralla, Dana - ***The Magnificent Barb*** [n.d.]	$1.35	$4.00	$8.00
1253	Feldkamp, Fred - editor (Anthology) - ***Mixture For Men*** [n.d.]	$1.25	$3.75	$7.50
1254	Overholser, Wayne D. - ***Buckaroo's Code*** [n.d.]	$1.35	$4.00	$8.00
1255	McGerr, Pat - ***Pick Your Victim*** [n.d.]	$2.00	$6.00	$12.00
1256	Blankfort, Michael - ***The Widow-Makers*** [n.d.]	$1.25	$3.75	$7.50
1257	Evans, Evan - ***The Border Bandit*** [n.d.]	$1.35	$4.00	$8.00
1258	Beymer, William Gilmore - ***The Middle Of Midnight*** [n.d.]	$1.25	$3.75	$7.50
1259	Davis, Clyde Brion - ***Jeremy Bell*** [n.d.]	$1.35	$4.00	$8.00
1260	Lieb, Frederick G. - ***The Detroit Tigers*** [n.d.]	$2.50	$7.50	$15.00
1261	Roark, Garland - ***Wake Of The Red Witch*** [n.d.]	$1.25	$3.75	$7.50
1262	Wellman, Paul I. - ***The Walls Of Jericho*** [n.d.]	$1.35	$4.00	$8.00
1263	Brand, Max - ***Valley Of Vanishing Men*** [n.d.]	$1.25	$3.75	$7.50
1264	Field, Peter - ***Gambler's Gold*** [n.d.]	$1.25	$3.75	$7.50
1265	Wouk, Herman - ***Aurora Dawn*** [n.d.]	$1.25	$3.75	$7.50
1266	Merrick, Gordon - ***The Strumpet Wind*** [n.d.]	$1.35	$4.00	$8.00
1267	Haycox, Ernest - ***Long Storm*** [n.d.]	$1.35	$4.00	$8.00
1268	Hobson, Laura Z. - ***Gentleman's Agreement*** [n.d.]	$1.25	$3.75	$7.50
1269	Marsh, Ngaio - ***Final Curtain*** [n.d.]	$2.00	$6.00	$12.00
1270	Lawrence, Hilda - ***Death Of A Doll*** [n.d.]	$2.00	$6.00	$12.00
1271	Lieb, Frederick G. - ***The Boston Red Sox*** [n.d.]	$2.50	$7.50	$15.00

		G	VG	F
1272	Manus, Max - ***Nine Lives Before Thirty*** [n.d.]	$1.35	$4.00	$8.00
1273	Arnold, Elliott - ***Blood Brother*** [n.d.]	$1.35	$4.00	$8.00
1274	Cohn, David L. - ***This Is The Story*** [n.d.]	$1.25	$3.75	$7.50
1275	Bishop, Curtis - ***Shadow Range*** [n.d.]	$1.25	$3.75	$7.50
1276	Thorne, Anthony - ***So Long At The Fair*** [n.d.]	$1.25	$3.75	$7.50
1277	Layton, Mark - ***Silver Spurs*** [n.d.]	$1.25	$3.75	$7.50
1278	Herron, Edward A. - ***Alaska: Land Of Tomorrow*** [n.d.]	$1.35	$4.00	$8.00
1279	Coles, Manning - ***With Intent To Deceive*** [n.d.]	$1.35	$4.00	$8.00
1280	Carr, John Dickson - ***The Sleeping Sphinx*** [n.d.]	$2.00	$6.00	$12.00
1281	Standish, Robert - ***Mr. On Loong*** [n.d.]	$1.25	$3.75	$7.50
1282	Eyssen, Marguerite - ***Go-Devil*** [n.d.]	$1.25	$3.75	$7.50
1283	Graham, Shirley - ***There Was Once A Slave...*** [n.d.]	$1.25	$3.75	$7.50
1284	Grafton, C. W. - ***My Name Is Christopher Nagel*** [n.d.]	$1.35	$4.00	$8.00
1285	Myers, John Myers - ***The Wild Yazoo*** [n.d.]	$1.35	$4.00	$8.00
1286	Wells, Evelyn - ***Jed Blaine's Woman*** [n.d.]	$1.35	$4.00	$8.00
1287	Rich, Harold - ***Within The Ropes*** [n.d.]	$1.25	$3.75	$7.50
1289	Dodge, David - ***How Green Was My Father*** [n.d.]	$1.25	$3.75	$7.50
1290	Ermine, Will - ***The Drifting Kid*** [n.d.]	$1.25	$3.75	$7.50
1291	Quentin, Patrick - ***Puzzle For Pilgrims*** [n.d.]	$2.00	$6.00	$12.00
1292	Roos, Kelley - ***Ghost Of A Chance*** [n.d.]	$2.00	$6.00	$12.00
1293	Lockridge, Frances and Richard - ***Think Of Death*** [n.d.]	$2.00	$6.00	$12.00
1294	Grey, Zane - ***Valley Of Wild Horses*** [n.d.]	$1.25	$3.75	$7.50
1295	Freedman, Benedict and Nancy - ***Mrs. Mike*** [n.d.]	$1.25	$3.75	$7.50
1296	Ewing, Annemarie - ***Little Gate*** [n.d.]	$1.25	$3.75	$7.50
1297	Guthrie, Jr., A. B. - ***The Big Sky*** [n.d.]	$1.35	$4.00	$8.00
1298	Bond, Raymond T. - editor (Anthology) - ***Famous Stories Of Code And Cipher*** [n.d.]	$1.25	$3.75	$7.50
1299	Bosworth, Allan R. - ***Hang And Rattle*** [n.d.]	$1.35	$4.00	$8.00
1300	Field, Peter - ***Trail From Needle Rock*** [n.d.]	$1.35	$4.00	$8.00
1301	Milburn, George - ***Flannigan's Folly*** [n.d.]	$1.35	$4.00	$8.00
1302	Gardner, Erle Stanley - ***The Case Of The Fan-Dancer's Horse*** [n.d.]	$2.00	$6.00	$12.00
1303	Bellamy, Francis Rufus - ***Blood Money*** [n.d.]	$2.00	$6.00	$12.00
1304	MacDonald, William Colt - ***Master Of The Mesa*** [n.d.]	$1.25	$3.75	$7.50
1305	Loveridge, Arthur - ***Tomorrow's A Holiday*** [n.d.]	$1.35	$4.00	$8.00
1306	Jennings, John - ***Boston: Cradle Of Liberty*** [n.d.]	$1.25	$3.75	$7.50
1307	Leigh, Michael - ***Comrade Forest*** [n.d.]	$1.35	$4.00	$8.00
1308	McLaughlin, Robert - ***The Side Of The Angels*** [n.d.]	$1.35	$4.00	$8.00
1309	Krause, Herbert - ***The Thresher*** [n.d.]	$1.35	$4.00	$8.00
1310	Jones, Idwal - ***Vermilion*** [n.d.]	$1.35	$4.00	$8.00
1311	Brand, Max - ***The False Rider*** [n.d.]	$1.25	$3.75	$7.50
1312	Knight, Kathleen Moore - ***The Blue Horse Of Taxco*** [n.d.]	$1.25	$3.75	$7.50
1313	Rice, Craig - editor (Anthology) - ***Los Angeles Murders*** [n.d.]	$2.50	$7.50	$15.00
1314	Merrick, Elliott - ***Passing By*** [n.d.]	$1.35	$4.00	$8.00
1315	Phenix, Richard - ***On My Way Home*** [n.d.]	$1.35	$4.00	$8.00
1316	Feller, Bob - ***Strikeout Story*** [n.d.]	$2.00	$6.00	$12.00
1317	Schulberg, Budd - ***The Harder They Fall*** [n.d.]	$1.35	$4.00	$8.00
1318	Gillham, Charles E. - ***Raw North*** [n.d.]	$1.35	$4.00	$8.00
1319	Scott, Natalie Anderson - ***The Story Of Mrs. Murphy*** [n.d.]	$1.25	$3.75	$7.50
1320	Costain, Thomas B. - ***The Moneyman*** [n.d.]	$1.25	$3.75	$7.50
1321	Shellabarger, Samuel - ***Prince Of Foxes*** [n.d.]	$1.35	$4.00	$8.00
1322	Pyle, Ernie - ***Home Country*** [n.d.]	$1.35	$4.00	$8.00

		G	VG	F
Army Romances. Digest Size.				
NN-#1	- - ***Anthology Of 11*** [1945] PBO.	$2.50	$7.50	$15.00
V2-1	***Anthology*** - - [1946] Cover by Warren King. Illus. by Warren King.	$2.50	$7.50	$15.00
Arrow Mystery. New York: Arrow Publishers. Digest Size.				
5	Burke, Richard - ***Murder On High Heels*** [1943] Cover by Otto Muhlfeld.	$2.50	$7.50	$15.00
6	Ashbrook, Harriette - ***Murder On Friday*** [1943] Cover by Robert Paulsen.	$2.50	$7.50	$15.00
7	Gilbert, Anthony - ***Death Takes A Redhead*** [1944] Cover by Robert Paulsen.	$2.50	$7.50	$15.00
8	Baker, Asa - ***The Kissed Corpse*** [1944] Cover by Robert Paulsen.	$2.50	$7.50	$15.00
9	Long, Manning - ***Invitation To Murder*** [1944] Cover by Robert Paulsen.	$2.50	$7.50	$15.00
10	Corne, M. E. - ***Death Hides A Mask*** [1944] Cover by Robert Paulsen.	$2.50	$7.50	$15.00
11	Kummer, Frederic Arnold - ***Design For Murder*** [1944] Cover by Robert Paulsen.	$2.50	$7.50	$15.00
Arrow Publications. Toronto: Arrow Publishing Company				
100	Eldridge, Paul - ***Men And Women*** [1949]	$2.50	$7.50	$15.00
101	Freund, Philip - ***Easter Island*** [1949]	$5.50	$17.50	$35.00
102	Joyce, Claire - ***Charm Is Every Woman's Business*** [1949] PBO.	$2.50	$7.50	$15.00
103	Wilcox, Wendell - ***Everything Is Quite All Right*** [1949] PBO.	$2.50	$7.50	$15.00
105	Falk, Norma - Insane [1949] PBO.	$2.50	$7.50	$15.00
106	Aistrop, Jack - ***Backstage With Joe*** [1949]	$2.50	$7.50	$15.00
107	Miller, Helen Topping - ***The White Pelican*** [1949] PBO.	$2.50	$7.50	$15.00
108	Eldridge, Paul - ***Sextet*** [1949]	$3.50	$10.00	$20.00
109	Hobrecht, Earnest - ***Tokyo Romance*** [1950] PBO.	$4.00	$12.50	$25.00
110	Wyman, Justus E. - ***Hallelujah Brother*** [1950] PBO.	$2.50	$7.50	$15.00
115	Kelley, Thomas P. - ***Bad Men Of Canada*** [1950]	$2.50	$7.50	$15.00
116	Strong, Phil - ***Seconds To Go*** [1950] PBO.	$2.50	$7.50	$15.00
117	Fleming, Jack C. - ***No Tears For Goldie*** [1950] PBO.	$2.50	$7.50	$15.00
118	Poe, Edgar Allan - ***The Murders In The Rue Morgue/The Mystery Of Marie Roget*** [1950]	$6.00	$20.00	$40.00
119	Anthology - ***Four Great Classics*** [1950] PBO.	$4.00	$12.50	$25.00
Artful. New York: Artful Publications. Digest Size.				
1	Anthology - ***Honeymoon Romance*** [1950] PBO. Story told in full color illustration à la Dell Told In Pictures series. Cover and interior art by Matt Baker.	$12.50	$37.50	$75.00
2	Anthology - ***Confessions Of Love*** [1950] PBO. Story told in full color illustration à la Dell Told In Pictures series.	$12.50	$37.50	$75.00
Astro Books. New York: Astro Distributing Corp.				
1	Clayford, James - ***Part-Time Virgin*** [n.d.] Cover by Rodewald.	$3.50	$10.00	$20.00
2	Clayford, James - ***Week-End Girl*** [n.d.] Cover by Rodewald.	$3.50	$10.00	$20.00
4	Author Unknown - ***Any Man's Girl*** [n.d.]	$2.50	$7.50	$15.00
5	Author Unknown - ***Divorce Bait*** [n.d.]	$2.50	$7.50	$15.00
8	Bull, Lois - ***Virgin By Day*** [n.d.]	$2.50	$7.50	$15.00
9	Owen, Ethel - ***Unwilling Bride*** [n.d.]	$2.50	$7.50	$15.00
10	Owen, Ethel - ***Confessions Of A Goodtime Girl*** [n.d.] Photo cover.	$2.50	$7.50	$15.00

Atlas Mystery (Margood), NN

Atlas Mystery, 5

Atlas Mystery NN

		G	VG	F
11	Ahern, Helen - ***Confessions Of A Party Wife*** [n.d.] Cover by Rodewald.	$3.50	$10.00	$20.00
12	Herzog, Dorothy - ***Shakedown Dame*** [n.d.] Photo cover.	$2.50	$7.50	$15.00
14	Gaddis, Peggy - ***Shameless Virgin*** [1948] aka "One More Woman"	$2.50	$7.50	$15.00
15	Clayford, James - ***Illicit Wife*** [n.d.]	$2.50	$7.50	$15.00
16	Clayford, James - ***Wedding Night Confession*** [n.d.]	$2.50	$7.50	$15.00
17	Clayford, James - ***Careless Virgin*** [n.d.] Cover by Rodewald.	$3.50	$10.00	$20.00
18	Clayford, James - ***Strange Mistress*** [n.d.]	$3.50	$10.00	$20.00
31	Sherman, Joan - ***Overnight Girl*** [n.d.]	$3.50	$10.00	$20.00

Atlas Mystery. New York: Bard Publishing Corp. Digest Size.

NO#-1	McVeigh, Sue - ***The Corpse And The Three Ex-Husbands*** [1944] Cover by Peter Driben.	$3.50	$10.00	$20.00
NO#-2	Johns, Veronica Parker - ***The Singing Widow*** [1945]	$3.50	$10.00	$20.00

Atlas Mystery. New York: Cornell Publishing Corp. Digest Size.

NO#-1	Treat, Lawrence - ***H As In Hangman*** [1944] Cover by Cardwell Higgins.	$3.00	$9.00	$18.00
NO#-2	Steel, Kurt - ***Murder Goes To College*** [1944]	$3.50	$10.00	$20.00

Atlas Mystery. New York: Euclid Publishing Co. Digest Size.

NO#-1	Johns, Veronica Parker - ***Hush, Gabriel!*** [1944]	$3.00	$9.00	$18.00
NO#-2	Peterson, Herman - ***Murder RFD*** [1944]	$3.50	$10.00	$20.00

Atlas Mystery. New York: Gem Publications, Inc. Digest Size.

NO#-1	Long, Max - ***Death Goes Native*** [1944]	$3.00	$9.00	$18.00
NO#-2	Wells, Carolyn - ***Murder Will In*** [1944] Cover by Peter Driben.	$3.50	$10.00	$20.00

Atlas Mystery. New York: Hercules Publishing Corp. Digest Size.

NO#-1	Treat, Lawrence - ***D As In Dead*** [1943] Cover art by Cardwell Higgins.	$3.50	$10.00	$20.00
NO#-2	Rawlings, Frank - ***The Lisping Man*** [1944]	$3.00	$9.00	$18.00

Atlas Mystery. New York: London Publishing Corp. Digest Size.

NO#-1	Shore, Julian - ***Rattle His Bones*** [1944] Cover by Cardwell Higgins.	$3.50	$10.00	$20.00

Atlas Mystery. New York: Margood Publishing Corp. Digest Size.

NO#-1	Darby, J.N. - ***Murder In The House With The Blue Eyes*** [1944]	$3.50	$10.00	$20.00

		G	VG	F
Atlas Mystery. New York: Mohawk Publishing Corp. Digest Size.				
NO#-1	Anderson, W. W. - ***Kill One, Kill Two*** [1944]	$3.50	$10.00	$20.00
Atlas Mystery. New York: Select Publications, Inc. Digest Size.				
NO#-1	Crosby, Lee - ***Midsummer Night's Murder*** [1945] Cover by Peter Driben.	$3.00	$9.00	$18.00
NO#-2	Montgomery, Ione - ***The Golden Dress*** [1944] Cover by Cardwell Higgins.	$3.00	$9.00	$18.00
NO#-3	Johns, Veronica Parker - ***Shady Doings*** [1944]	$3.50	$10.00	$20.00
Atlas Mystery. New York: Sphere Publications, Inc. Digest Size.				
NO#-1	Nolan, Jeannette Covert - ***Final Appearance*** [1944] Cover by Hoffman.	$3.00	$9.00	$18.00
Atlas Mystery. New York: Vital Publishing Corp. Digest Size.				
1	Carter, Nick - ***Rendezvous With Dead Men*** [n.d.]	$3.50	$10.00	$20.00
2	Gibson, Walter B. - ***A Blonde For Murder*** [1948] PBO.	$6.00	$20.00	$40.00
3	Carter, Nick - ***The Yellow Disc Murder Case*** [n.d.]	$3.50	$10.00	$20.00
4	Hopkins, Tom J. - ***A Western Thriller Book: Open Land Renegades*** [1948]	$1.50	$5.00	$10.00
5	Gibson, Walter B. - ***Looks That Kill!*** [1948] PBO.	$6.00	$20.00	$40.00
Atlas Mystery. New York: Zenith Publishing Corp. Digest Size.				
NO#-1	Spatz, H. Donald - ***Murder With Long Hair*** [1944]	$3.50	$10.00	$20.00
NO#-2	Mersereau, John - ***The Corpse Comes Ashore*** [1945]	$3.00	$9.00	$18.00
Atomic Books. Digest Size.				
NN-1	Garrett, Pat F. - ***Billy The Kid, The Outlaw*** [1946] PBO.	$2.50	$7.50	$15.00
NN-2	Buel, J.W. - ***"Wild Bill" Hickok, Gunfighter*** [1946] PBO.	$2.50	$7.50	$15.00
NN-3	Unknown - ***Jesse James, King Of Robbers*** [1946] PBO.	$2.50	$7.50	$15.00
NN-4	LeBlanc, Maurice - ***The Case Of The Golden Blonde*** [1946] PBO.	$5.00	$15.00	$30.00
Avon Annual. New York: Avon Book Company. Digest Size.				
NO#-1	Anthology - ***18 Great Stories Of Today*** [1944] PBO.	$4.00	$12.50	$25.00
NO#-2	Anthology - ***1945*** [1945] PBO.	$4.00	$12.50	$25.00
NO#-3	Anthology - ***1946*** [1946] PBO.	$4.00	$12.50	$25.00
NO#-4	Anthology - ***1947*** [1947] PBO.	$4.00	$12.50	$25.00
Avon Bard Series. New York: Avon Book Company.				
T-01	Fitzgerald, Edward - translator - ***The Rubaiyat Of Omar Khayyam*** [1960]	$1.00	$3.00	$6.00
T-02	Stekel, Wilheim - ***The Meaning And Psychology Of Dreams*** [1960]	$ .75	$2.50	$5.00
T-03	Stephenson, J.L. - ***Anyone Can Have A Great Vocabulary*** [1960]	$ .75	$2.50	$5.00
T-04	Maugham, W. Somerset - ***Favorite Stories*** [1960]	$1.00	$3.00	$6.00
T-05	Anderson, Marian - ***My Lord, What A Morning*** [1960] Photo cover.	$ .75	$2.50	$5.00
T-06	Wendt, Gerald - ***You And The Atom*** [1960]	$ .75	$2.50	$5.00
T-07	Keller, Hellen - ***My Religion*** [1960] Photo cover.	$1.00	$3.00	$6.00
T-08	Housman, A.E. - ***A Shropshire Lad*** [1960]	$ .75	$2.50	$5.00
T-09	Beckhard, Arthur - ***Albert Einstein*** [1960]	$1.00	$3.00	$6.00
G-10	Evans, Edwin - ***Tchaikovsky*** [1960]	$ .75	$2.50	$5.00
G-11	Browning, Elizabeth Barrett - ***Sonnets From The Portuguese*** [1960]	$ .75	$2.50	$5.00

Avon Bedside Novel, 6

Avon, NN#6

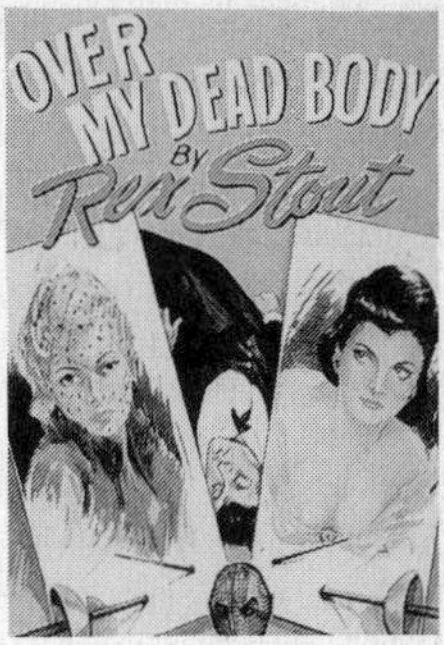

Avon, 62

		G	VG	F
G-12	Douglas, William O. - ***America Challenged*** [1960] Photo cover..	$1.00	$3.00	$6.00
G-13	Anthology - ***Bertrand Russell Speaks His Mind*** [1960] Photo cover.	$1.00	$3.00	$6.00

Avon Bedside Novel. New York: Avon Books, Inc. Digest Size.

1	Woodford, Jack - ***The Rites Of Love*** [1950]	$4.00	$12.50	$25.00
2	Woodford, Jack - ***The Hard-Boiled Virgin*** [1951]	$4.00	$12.50	$25.00
3	Brock, Lilyan - ***Queer Patterns*** [1951]	$5.50	$17.50	$35.00
4	Dekobra, Maurice - ***Bedroom Eyes*** [1951] Cover by Peter Driben.	$6.00	$20.00	$40.00
5	Woodford, Jack - ***Male And Female*** [1951]	$4.00	$12.50	$25.00
6	Woodford, Jack - ***The Passionate Princess*** [1951]	$4.00	$12.50	$25.00
7	Clarke, Donald Henderson - ***Millie*** [1952]	$4.00	$12.50	$25.00

Avon Book (An). New York: Avon Book Company. Digest Size.

NN	Campbell, E. Simms - ***Cuties*** [1945] PBO. All cartoons.	$12.50	$37.50	$75.00

Avon Book Dividend. New York: Avon Book Company. Digest Size.

1	Woodford, Jack - ***The Abortive Hussy*** [1950] Cover by Strick. ...	$4.00	$12.50	$25.00
2	Hanley, Jack - ***Star Lust*** [1951]	$4.00	$12.50	$25.00
3	Bodenheim, Maxwell - ***New York Madness*** [1951]	$4.00	$12.50	$25.00
4	Woodford, Jack - ***Grounds For Divorce*** [1949]	$4.00	$12.50	$25.00
5	Holland, Marty - ***Her Private Passions*** [1949] Photo cover.	$4.00	$12.50	$25.00
6	Woodford, Jack - ***Teach Me To Love*** [1949]	$5.00	$15.00	$30.00
7	Anthology - ***Tropical Passions*** [1949]	$4.50	$14.00	$28.00

Avon Books (Early Publisher's History, 1941–1959)

Using a marketing strategy with brightly colored covers and "spicy" themes, Avon offered the first real competition of Pocket Books. John Myers, a pulp publisher, began the company for the American News Agency to distribute. Flashy covers reminiscent of the type on pulp literature and interior illustrations offer the collectors of paperback art many possibilities. Gradually, Avon moved away from the lurid covers to a more traditional cover art. Many of the early titles, mysteries, and science fiction books are collectible. Later series included the T/AT, G, and others.

Avon Publishing Company published two additional paperback lines. Avon Fantasy Novels published two very collectible fantasy/science fiction books, and Avon

Bard published nonfiction, biography, and literary works. The following digest-sized series represent the scope of Avon's contribution and are all collectible: Avon Annual, Avon Bedside Novels, Avon Book Dividend, Avon Detective Mysteries, Avon Fantasy Reader, Avon Love Book Monthly, Avon Monthly Novel, Avon Modern Short Story Monthly, Avon Murder of the Month and Avon Murder Mystery Monthly, Avon Romance Novel Monthly, Avon Science Fiction and Fantasy Reader, Avon Science Fiction Reader, Avon Specials, Avon Western Reader, Avon Western Novel Monthly, and Avon Unnumbered.

Avon Books. New York: Avon Publishing Co.

		G	VG	F
NO#-1	Lewis, Sinclair - ***Elmer Gantry*** [1941]	$20.00	$60.00	$125.00
NO#-2	Khayyam, Omar - ***Rubaiyat Of Omar Khayyam*** [1941] Rendered into English by Edward Fitzgerald. With drawings by Edmund J. Sullivan.	$12.50	$37.50	$75.00
NO#-3	Christie, Agatha - ***The Big Four*** [1941]	$17.00	$50.00	$100.00
NO#-4	Hilton, James - ***Ill Wind*** [1941]	$15.00	$45.00	$90.00
NO#-5	Rhode, John - ***Dr. Priestley Investigates*** [1941]	$15.00	$45.00	$90.00
NO#-6	Anthology ed. by Wilkie Collins - ***The Haunted Hotel And 25 Other Ghost Stories*** [1941]	$17.00	$50.00	$100.00
NO#-7	Dickson, Carter - ***The Plague Court Murders*** [1941] Cover by Robert Cole.	$17.00	$50.00	$100.00
NO#-8	Walling, R. A. J. - ***The Corpse In The Green Pyjamas*** [1941]	$17.00	$50.00	$100.00
NO#-9	Crofts, Freeman Wills - ***Willful And Premeditated*** [1941]	$15.00	$45.00	$90.00
NO#-10	Freeman, R. Austin - ***Dr. Thorndyke's Discovery*** [1941]	$17.00	$50.00	$100.00
NO#-11	Hecht, Ben - ***Count Bruga*** [1941]	$15.00	$45.00	$90.00
NO#-12	Faulkner, William - ***Mosquitoes*** [1941]	$17.00	$50.00	$100.00
NO#-13	Gregory, Jackson - ***Mystery At Spanish Hacienda*** [1942]	$15.00	$45.00	$90.00
NO#-14	Thayer, Tiffany - ***Call Her Savage*** [1942]	$15.00	$45.00	$90.00
NO#-15	Anthology - ***The Avon Book Of Modern Short Stories*** [1942] Cover by W. L. White.	$12.50	$37.50	$75.00
NO#-16	Walling, R.A.J. - ***Murder At Midnight*** [1942]	$15.00	$45.00	$90.00
NO#-17	Biggers, Earl Derr - ***The Agony Column*** [1942] Cover by Claude Blaiklock.	$5.50	$17.50	$35.00
NO#-18	Homes, Geoffrey - ***The Man Who Murdered Himself*** [1942] Cover by Gil Tompkins.	$5.50	$17.50	$35.00
NO#-19	Saroyan, William - ***48 Saroyan Stories*** [1942]	$3.50	$10.00	$20.00
NO#-20	Stout, Rex - ***The League Of Frightened Men*** [1942] Cover by I.N. Steinberg.	$6.00	$20.00	$40.00
NO#-21	Anthology ed. by John Rhode - ***The Avon Book Of Modern Crime Stories*** [1942] Cover by I.N. Steinberg.	$4.00	$12.50	$25.00
NO#-22	Brush, Katherine - ***Red-Headed Woman*** [1942] Cover by I. N. Steinberg.	$5.50	$17.50	$35.00
NO#-23	Sayers, Dorothy L. - ***Suspicious Characters*** [1943] Cover by Leo Manso.	$3.50	$10.00	$20.00
NO#-24	Maugham, W. Somerset - ***Ashenden Or The British Agent*** [1943]	$3.50	$10.00	$20.00
NO#-25	Fowler, Gene - ***Trumpet In The Dust*** [1943] Cover by I.N. Steinberg.	$4.00	$12.50	$25.00
NO#-26	Merritt, A. - ***Seven Footprints To Satan*** [1943]	$8.00	$25.00	$50.00
NO#-27	Stolberg, Charles - editor - ***The Avon Book Of Puzzles*** [1943]	$32.00	$110.00	$250.00
NO#-28	Coward, Neol - ***Tonight At 8:30*** [1943] Cover by I.N. Steinberg.	$3.50	$10.00	$20.00
NO#-29	Allingham, Margery - ***The Sabotage Murder Mystery*** [1943] Cover by William Forrest.	$5.00	$15.00	$30.00

		G	VG	F
NO#-30	Babcock, Dwight V. - ***The Gorgeous Ghoul Murder Case*** [1943]	$5.50	$17.50	$35.00
NO#-31	O'Hara, John - ***Doctor's Son And Other Stories*** [1943] Cover by William Forrest.	$4.00	$12.50	$25.00
NO#-32	Daves, Delmar - ***Stage Door Canteen*** [1943] PBO. Movie tie-in with photos.	$4.00	$12.50	$25.00
NO#-33	Carr, John Dickson - ***Corpse In The Waxworks*** [1943]	$6.00	$20.00	$40.00
NO#-34	Charteris, Leslie - ***The Saint Goes On*** [1943]	$5.00	$15.00	$30.00
NO#-35	Rhode, John - ***Poison For One*** [1943]	$5.50	$17.50	$35.00
NO#-37	Beeding, Francis - ***Coffin For One*** [1943]	$5.50	$17.50	$35.00
NO#-38	Chandler, Raymond - ***The Big Sleep*** [1943] Cover by Paul Stahr.	$17.00	$50.00	$100.00
NO#-39	Hilton, James - ***Rage In Heaven*** [1943] Cover by A. Gonzales.	$3.50	$10.00	$20.00
NO#-40	Sayers, Dorothy - ***In The Teeth Of The Evidence*** [1943]	$5.50	$17.50	$35.00
NO#-41	Maugham, W. Somerset - ***The Narrow Corner*** [1944] Cover by A. Gonzales.	$3.50	$10.00	$20.00
42	Hilton, James - ***The Passionate Year*** [1944]	$3.50	$10.00	$20.00
43	Merritt, A. - ***Burn Witch, Burn!*** [1944]	$6.00	$20.00	$40.00
44	Charteris, Leslie - ***The Saint In New York*** [1944]	$5.00	$15.00	$30.00
45	Lord Vansittart - ***Roots Of The Trouble And The Black Record Of Germany*** [1944]	$3.50	$10.00	$20.00
46	Christie, Agatha - ***Death On The Nile*** [1944]	$5.00	$15.00	$30.00
47	Fowler, Gene - ***Shoe The Wild Mare*** [1944]	$4.00	$12.50	$25.00
48	Spellman, Archbishop Francis J. - ***The Road To Victory*** [1944] Cover by A. Gonzales.	$3.50	$10.00	$20.00
49	Cheyney, Peter - ***The London Spy Murders*** [1944]	$4.00	$12.50	$25.00
50	Maugham, W. Somerset - ***Cakes And Ale*** [1944]	$3.50	$10.00	$20.00
51	Ferber, Edna - ***Nobody's In Town*** [1944] Cover by A. Gonzales.	$3.50	$10.00	$20.00
52	Bromfield, Louis - ***The Man Who Had Everything*** [1944]	$4.00	$12.50	$25.00
53	Tuttle, W.C. - ***The Mystery Of The Red Triangle*** [1944] Cover by Paul Stahr.	$4.00	$12.50	$25.00
54	Browne, Lewis - ***See What I Mean?*** [1944] Cover by Paul Stahr.	$3.50	$10.00	$20.00
55	Tarkington, Booth - ***Presenting Lily Mars*** [1944]	$4.00	$12.50	$25.00
56	Maugham, W. Somerset - ***Theatre*** [1944] Cover by A. Gonzales.	$3.50	$10.00	$20.00
57	Wolfe, Thomas - ***The Hills Beyond*** [1944]	$3.50	$10.00	$20.00
58	Hart, Moss - ***Winged Victory*** [1944]	$3.50	$10.00	$20.00
59	Wilder, Thornton - ***Heaven's My Destination*** [1945]	$3.50	$10.00	$20.00
60	Cain, James M. - ***Double Indemnity*** [1945]	$7.00	$22.50	$45.00
61	Christie, Agatha - ***Murder In Three Acts*** [1945]	$5.00	$15.00	$30.00
62	Stout, Rex - ***Over My Dead Body*** [1945]	$5.00	$15.00	$30.00
63	Chandler, Raymond - ***Five Murderers*** [1944]	$15.00	$45.00	$90.00
64	Baum, Vicki - ***Back Stage*** [1945] PBO. Cover by Paul Stahr.	$3.50	$10.00	$20.00
65	Hershfield, Harry - ***Now I'll Tell One - Harry Hershfield's Book Of Jokes*** [1945] Cover by A. Gonzales.	$5.50	$17.50	$35.00
66	Burnett, W.R. - ***Little Caesar*** [1945] Cover by Paul Stahr. Same cover as comic book Famous Gangsters #3	$8.00	$25.00	$50.00
67	Spellman, Archbishop Francis J. - ***Action This Day*** [1945] Cover by Carl Bower.	$3.00	$9.00	$18.00
68	Babcock, Dwight V. - ***A Homocide For Hannah*** [1945] Cover by Paul Stahr.	$5.00	$15.00	$30.00
69	Smith, Thorne - ***The Stray Lamb*** [1945] Cover by A. Gonzales.	$5.00	$15.00	$30.00
70	Christie, Agatha - ***Poirot Loses A Client*** [1945]	$5.00	$15.00	$30.00

		G	VG	F
71	Charteris, Leslie - ***The Saint Intervenes*** [1945] Cover by Paul Stahr.	$4.00	$12.50	$25.00
72	Anthology - ***The Avon Story Teller*** [1945] PBO. Includes Chandler, Cain, et al.	$4.00	$12.50	$25.00
73	Chase, Mary Ellen - ***A Goodly Heritage*** [1945]	$3.00	$9.00	$18.00
74	Lewis, Sinclair - ***The Ghost Patrol And Other Stories*** [1946]	$4.50	$14.00	$28.00
75	Christie, Agatha - ***The Mysterious Affair At Styles*** [1945] Cover by A. Gonzales.	$4.00	$12.50	$25.00
76	Dietz, David - ***Atomic Energy In The Coming Era*** [1945]	$3.00	$9.00	$18.00
77	Steinbeck, John - ***The Long Valley*** [1945] Cover by LaCarrada.	$3.50	$10.00	$20.00
78	Coward, Noel - ***To Step Aside*** [1946]	$3.50	$10.00	$20.00
79	Hilton, James - ***Catherine Herself*** [1946] PBO.	$3.50	$10.00	$20.00
80	Cheyney, Peter - ***You Can't Keep The Change*** [1946]	$3.50	$10.00	$20.00
81	Delmar, Vina - ***Bad Girl*** [1944]	$3.50	$10.00	$20.00
82	Stout, Rex - ***The Red Box*** [1946]	$5.50	$17.50	$35.00
83	Rinehart, Mary Roberts - ***Sight Unseen And The Confession*** [1946] Cover by Renaldo Epworth.	$4.00	$12.50	$25.00
84	Sabatini, Rafael - ***Mistress Wilding*** [1946] Cover by Merson Winter.	$3.00	$9.00	$18.00
85	Christie, Agatha - ***The Regatta Mystery And Other Stories*** [1946]	$5.00	$15.00	$30.00
86	Anthology - ***Avon Mystery Storyteller*** [1946] PBO. Includes Christie, Irish, Carr.	$5.50	$17.50	$35.00
87	DeMaupassant, Guy - ***The Private Affairs Of Bel Ami*** [1946] Movie tie-in	$3.00	$9.00	$18.00
88	Chandler, Raymond - ***Five Sinister Characters*** [1946]	$15.00	$45.00	$90.00
89	Christie, Agatha - ***Death In The Air*** [1946] Cover by Robert Cole.	$4.00	$12.50	$25.00
90	Anthology - ***Avon Ghost Reader*** [1946] PBO. Includes Lovecraft, Merritt, Stoker.	$4.50	$14.00	$28.00
91	Gruber, Frank - ***The French Key Mystery*** [1946] Cover by Robert Cole	$4.00	$12.50	$25.00
92	Delmar, Vina - ***Loose Ladies*** [1946]	$3.00	$9.00	$18.00
93	Cheyney, Peter - ***The Dark Street Murders*** [1946]	$3.50	$10.00	$20.00
94	O'Hara, John - ***Butterfield 8*** [1946]	$2.50	$7.50	$15.00
95	Stout, Rex - ***Black Orchids*** [1946]	$3.50	$10.00	$20.00
96	Woolrich, Cornell - ***The Black Angel*** [1946]	$5.50	$17.50	$35.00
97	Brown, Beth - ***Wedding Ring*** [1946]	$2.50	$7.50	$15.00
98	Lawrence, D. H. - ***The Virgin And The Gypsy*** [1946] Cover by Paul Stahr.	$2.00	$6.00	$12.00
99	Cain, James M. - ***The Embezzler*** [1946]	$2.50	$7.50	$15.00
100	Christie, Agatha - ***The Secret Adversary*** [1946] Cover by Carl Bower.	$2.25	$7.00	$14.00
101	Metzelthin, Mme. Pearl V. - ***Improved Cookbook And Complete Guide To Pressure Cooking*** [1947] PBO.	$4.00	$12.50	$25.00
102	Runyon, Damon - ***Three Wise Guys*** [1946] Cover by Endris. Collection of 9 stories	$2.00	$6.00	$12.00
103	Stout, Rex - ***Where There's A Will*** [1946]	$2.50	$7.50	$15.00
104	Irish, William - ***If I Should Die Before I Wake*** [1946] Collection of 6 stories.	$3.50	$10.00	$20.00
105	Clarke, Donald Henderson - ***Lady Ann*** [1946]	$2.00	$6.00	$12.00
106	Woolrich, Cornell - ***The Black Path Of Fear*** [1946]	$3.50	$10.00	$20.00
107	Delmar, Vina - ***The Marriage Racket*** [1946] Cover by Don Milsop.	$2.00	$6.00	$12.00

Avon, 117

Avon, 136

Avon, 178

		G	VG	F
108	Heard, H. F. - ***A Taste For Honey*** [1946]	$3.00	$9.00	$18.00
109	Anthology - ***Avon Bedside Companion*** [1946] Cover by Killam.	$2.00	$6.00	$12.00
110	Williams, Herbert - editor (Anthology) - ***Terror At Night*** [1947] PBO. Cover by George Mayers.	$10.00	$30.00	$60.00
111	Saltus, Edgar - ***The Imperial Orgy*** [1947] Cover by George Mayers	$2.00	$6.00	$12.00
112	Wallace, Edgar - ***The Squealer*** [1946]	$2.00	$6.00	$12.00
113	Louys, Pierre - ***Aphrodite*** [1946]	$2.00	$6.00	$12.00
114	Cheyney, Peter - ***Sinister Errand*** [1946] Cover by William Stanke.	$2.50	$7.50	$15.00
115	Maugham, W. Somerset - ***The Avon Book Of W. Somerset Maugham*** [1946]	$2.00	$6.00	$12.00
116	Clarke, Donald Henderson - ***Kelly*** [1946] Cover by Don Milsop.	$2.00	$6.00	$12.00
117	Merritt, A. - ***Creep, Shadow, Creep*** [1947]	$8.00	$25.00	$50.00
118	Charteris, Leslie - ***The Saint In Action*** [1947] Cover by Robert Hilbert.	$2.50	$7.50	$15.00
119	Taylor, Richard - ***The Better Taylors*** [1947] PBO. Cartoon book.	$6.00	$20.00	$40.00
120	Clarke, Donald Henderson - ***Alabam'*** [1947]	$2.00	$6.00	$12.00
121	Delmar, Vina - ***Kept Woman*** [1947]	$2.00	$6.00	$12.00
122	Freeman, R. Austin - ***The Unconscious Witness*** [1947]	$5.00	$15.00	$30.00
123	Cheyney, Peter - ***The Case Of The Dark Hero*** [1947]	$4.00	$12.50	$25.00
124	Christie, Agatha - ***A Holiday For Murder*** [1947]	$4.00	$12.50	$25.00
125	Wallace, Edgar - ***The Door With Seven Locks*** [1947]	$4.00	$12.50	$25.00
126	Crofts, Freeman Wills - ***Cold-Blooded Murder*** [1947]	$4.00	$12.50	$25.00
127	Anthology - ***Eastern Shame Girl And Other Stories*** [1947] Cover by George Mayers.	$4.50	$14.00	$28.00
128	Anthology - ***Ten Nights Of Love*** [1947] PBO.	$2.25	$7.00	$14.00
129	Maugham, W. Somerset - ***The Gentleman In The Parlour*** [1947]	$2.00	$6.00	$12.00
130	Charteris, Leslie - ***The Saint Goes West*** [1947] Cover by Harley Wood.	$2.50	$7.50	$15.00
131	Lockridge, Frances & Richard - ***Death Takes A Bow*** [1947]	$2.50	$7.50	$15.00
132	Steinbeck, John - ***14 Great Short Stories From The Long Valley*** [1947]	$2.50	$7.50	$15.00
133	Meyers, Harold - ***Naughty 90's Joke Book and Dyspeptic's Guide To The Grave*** [1947]	$3.00	$9.00	$18.00

		G	VG	F
134	Caldwell, Erskine - ***Georgia Boy And Other Stories*** [1947] Reprints Avon Modern Short Story Monthly 30. Cover by Mayan.	$1.50	$5.00	$10.00
135	Louys, Pierre - ***The Woman And The Puppet*** [1947]	$1.50	$5.00	$10.00
136	Lovecraft, H. P. - ***The Lurking Fear And Other Stories*** [1947] PBO. Cover by A.R. Tilburne.	$10.00	$30.00	$60.00
137	Cain, James M. - ***Double Indemnity*** [1947] Cover by T. Varaday.	$4.00	$12.50	$25.00
138	Woodford, Jack - ***The Hard-Boiled Virgin*** [1947] Cover by Barye Phillips.	$2.00	$6.00	$12.00
139	Maugham, W. Somerset - ***Liza Of Lambeth*** [1947]	$2.00	$6.00	$12.00
140	Chase, Ilka - ***In Bed We Cry*** [1947]	$1.50	$5.00	$10.00
141	Cain, James M. - ***Career In C Major*** [1947]	$3.50	$10.00	$20.00
142	Lockridge, Frances & Richard - ***Killing The Goose*** [1947] Cover by Barry Stephens.	$3.00	$9.00	$18.00
143	Coxe, George Harmon - ***Flash Casey... Detective*** [1948] Cover by Perlowen. Collection of 4 stories.	$4.00	$12.50	$25.00
144	O'Hara, John - ***Hope Of Heaven*** [1948]	$2.00	$6.00	$12.00
145	Delmar, Vina - ***The Restless Passion*** [1947]	$2.00	$6.00	$12.00
146	Woodford, Jack - ***The Abortive Hussy*** [1947] Cover by Strick.	$2.00	$6.00	$12.00
147	Charteris, Leslie - ***The Avenging Saint*** [1948] Photo Cover.	$2.25	$7.00	$14.00
148	Revised and Edited by William Fielding - ***Love, Health And Marriage*** [1948]	$3.50	$10.00	$20.00
149	Clarke, Donald Henderson - ***John Bartel, Jr.*** [1948] Cover by Strick.	$2.00	$6.00	$12.00
150	Zola, Emile - ***A Love Episode*** [1948] First U.S. edition. Cover by John Alan Maxwell.	$2.00	$6.00	$12.00
151	Caldwell, Erskine - ***Where The Girls Were Different And Other Stories*** [1948] Cover by Perlowen.	$1.50	$5.00	$10.00
152	Bodenheim, Maxwell - ***Georgie May*** [1948]	$2.00	$6.00	$12.00
153	Williams, Ben Ames - ***Valley Vixen*** [1948] Cover by Carl Stricker.	$2.00	$6.00	$12.00
154	Brush, Katharine - ***When She Was Bad*** [1948] Photo Cover.	$2.00	$6.00	$12.00
155	Pettit, Charles - ***The Unfaithful Lady*** [1948] Cover by George Mayers.	$3.50	$10.00	$20.00
156	Lomax, Bliss - ***Pardners Of The Badlands*** [1948] Cover by Paul Freedberg.	$2.50	$7.50	$15.00
157	Farrell, James T. - ***Yesterday's Love And Eleven Other Stories*** [1948] PBO. Cover by M. Bouldin.	$2.00	$6.00	$12.00
158	Hershfield, Harry - ***Now I'll Tell One—Harry Hershfield's Book Of Jokes*** [1948]	$4.50	$14.00	$28.00
159	Keene, Day - ***This Is Murder, Mr. Herbert And Other Stories*** [1948] PBO	$7.00	$22.50	$45.00
160	Schnitzler, Arthur - ***Casanova's Homecoming*** [1948] Cover by J. Biernacki.	$1.50	$5.00	$10.00
161	Cain, James M. - ***Love's Lovely Counterfeit*** [1948] Reprints Murder Mystery Monthly 44.	$2.50	$7.50	$15.00
162	Kinnaird, Clark - ***The Avon Book Of Complete Crosswords And Cryptograms*** [1948]	$32.00	$110.00	$250.00
163	Murger, Henri - ***Love In The Latin Quarter*** [1948]	$2.25	$7.00	$14.00
164	Christie, Agatha - ***The Moving Finger*** [1948] Photo cover.	$4.00	$12.50	$25.00
165	Sharp, Margery - ***The Stone Of Chastity*** [1948]	$4.00	$12.50	$25.00
166	Louys, Pierre - ***Psyche*** [1948] Cover by John Alan Maxwell	$2.00	$6.00	$12.00
167	Zola, Emile - ***Piping Hot*** [1948] Cover by Ann Cantor.	$2.50	$7.50	$15.00

Avon, 186

Avon, 189

Avon, 204

		G	VG	F
168	Bodenheim, Maxwell - ***Virtuous Girl*** [1948] Cover by Phillips and Troeger.	$2.50	$7.50	$15.00
169	Shulman, Irving - ***The Amboy Dukes*** [1948] Cover by Ann Cantor.	$2.25	$7.00	$14.00
170	Leithead, J. Edward - ***Bronc Buckeroo*** [1948] PBO. Cover by Edward Moore.	$2.50	$7.50	$15.00
171	DeBibiena, Jean-Galli - ***Amorous Philandre*** [1948] Cover by Barry Stephens.	$2.00	$6.00	$12.00
172	Philippe, Charles-Louis - ***Bubu Of Montparnasse*** [1948]	$2.00	$6.00	$12.00
173	Wallace, Edgar - ***On The Spot*** [1948] Cover by Monroe Reisman.	$3.50	$10.00	$20.00
174	Cain, James M. - ***Sinful Woman*** [1948] Cover by Phillips and Troeger.	$5.00	$15.00	$30.00
175	De Maupassant, Guy - ***A Woman's Heart*** [1948] Cover by Ann Cantor.	$2.00	$6.00	$12.00
176	Sayers, Dorothy L. - ***Whose Body?*** [1948] Cover by Ann Cantor.	$4.00	$12.50	$25.00
177	Caldwell, Erskine - ***Midsummer Passion*** [1948] Cover by Ann Cantor.	$1.50	$5.00	$10.00
178	Cain, Paul - ***Fast One*** [1948]	$7.00	$22.50	$45.00
179	Lustgarten, Edgar - ***Blondie Iscariot*** [1948]	$5.00	$15.00	$30.00
180	Gilpatric, Guy - ***French Summer*** [1948]	$1.50	$5.00	$10.00
181	Holland, Marty - ***Her Private Passions*** [1948] Cover by Ann Cantor.	$2.00	$6.00	$12.00
182	Anthology - ***The New Avon Bedside Companion*** [1949] PBO.	$1.50	$5.00	$10.00
183	Dortort, David - ***Burial Of The Fruit*** [1948] Cover by Ann Cantor.	$2.00	$6.00	$12.00
184	Anthology ed. by Donald A. Wollheim - ***The Girl With The Hungry Eyes And Other Stories*** [1949] PBO. Cover by Ann Cantor.	$10.00	$30.00	$60.00
185	Algren, Nelson - ***Never Come Morning*** [1948] Cover by Ann Cantor.	$2.00	$6.00	$12.00
186	Stuart, William L. - ***Night Cry*** [1949] Cover by Ann Cantor.	$3.50	$10.00	$20.00
187	Delmar, Vina - ***The Love Trap*** [1949] Cover by Ann Cantor.	$2.50	$7.50	$15.00
188	Maugham, W. Somerset - ***Fools And Their Folly*** [1949] Cover by Barton.	$2.00	$6.00	$12.00
189	Rohmer, Sax - ***The Daughter Of Fu Manchu*** [1949] Cover by Ann Cantor.	$10.00	$30.00	$60.00

Avon, 214

Avon, 219

Avon, 264

		G	VG	F
190	Greene, Ward - ***The Life And Loves Of A Modern Mr. Bluebeard*** [1949] Cover by Ann Cantor.	$3.50	$10.00	$20.00
191	Bodenheim, Maxwell - ***Replenishing Jessica*** [1949] Cover by Phillips and Troeger	$2.50	$7.50	$15.00
192	Brush, Katherine - ***Young Man Of Manhattan*** [1949] Cover by Ann Cantor	$2.00	$6.00	$12.00
193	Clarke, Donald Henderson - ***Impatient Virgin*** [1949] Cover by Ann Cantor	$2.00	$6.00	$12.00
194	Anthology - ***The Avon Book Of New Stories Of The Great Wild West*** [1949] PBO	$3.00	$9.00	$18.00
195	Lewis, C. S. - ***Out Of The Silent Planet*** [1949] Cover by Ann Cantor.	$5.50	$17.50	$35.00
196	Breuer, Bessie - ***Memory Of Love*** [1949] Cover by Ann Cantor.	$2.50	$7.50	$15.00
197	Pettit, Charles - ***The Son Of The Grand Eunich*** [1949] Cover by Ann Cantor.	$3.00	$9.00	$18.00
198	De Maupassant, Guy - ***Yvette And Other Stories*** [1949] Cover by Barry Stephens	$2.25	$7.00	$14.00
199	De Alarcon, Pedro - ***The Miller And The Mayor's Wife*** [1949] Cover by Ann Cantor.	$2.50	$7.50	$15.00
200	Gould, Lawrence - ***Your Most Intimate Problems*** [1949] PBO	$2.50	$7.50	$15.00
201	Zinberg, Len - ***Strange Desires*** [1949] Cover by Ann Cantor.	$2.50	$7.50	$15.00
202	Adams, Joey - ***From Gags To Riches*** [1949] Cover by Cugat.	$3.00	$9.00	$18.00
203	Maugham, W. Somerset - ***Quartet*** [1949] Cover by Harry Barton	$1.50	$5.00	$10.00
204	Walpole, Hugh - ***Portrait Of A Man With Red Hair*** [1949] Cover by Ed Paulsen.	$6.00	$20.00	$40.00
205	Fast, Howard - ***The Last Frontier*** [1949]	$2.50	$7.50	$15.00
206	De La Morliere, Jacques-Rochette - ***The Palace Of Pleasure*** [1949] Cover by Ann Cantor.	$2.00	$6.00	$12.00
207	Rothman, Nathan - ***Virgie, Goodbye*** [1949] Photo cover.	$1.50	$5.00	$10.00
208	Du Soe, Robert C. - ***The Devil Thumbs A Ride*** [1949] Cover by Ann Cantor.	$3.50	$10.00	$20.00
209	Delmar, Vina - ***New Orleans Lady*** [1949] Cover by Ann Cantor.	$2.00	$6.00	$12.00
210	Miller, Helen Topping - ***Wicked Sister*** [1949]	$2.25	$7.00	$14.00
211	Bloch, Robert - ***The Scarf Of Passion*** [1949]	$8.00	$25.00	$50.00
212	Burnett, W. R. - ***Iron Man*** [1949]	$3.00	$9.00	$18.00
213	Clarke, Donald Henderson - ***Nina*** [1949]	$1.50	$5.00	$10.00
214	Merritt, A. - ***The Fox Woman And Other Stories*** [1949]	$10.00	$30.00	$60.00

		G	VG	F
215	Williams, Ben Ames - ***All The Brothers Were Valiant*** [1949]	$1.50	$5.00	$10.00
216	Wylie, Philip - ***Gladiator*** [1949]	$2.50	$7.50	$15.00
217	Hahn, Emily - ***Miss Jill From Shanghai*** [1950] Cover by Dale Randall.	$2.50	$7.50	$15.00
218	Drake, Alfred - ***Anyone Can Win At Gin Rummy And Canasta*** [1950]	$1.50	$5.00	$10.00
219	Chandler, Raymond - ***Finger Man*** [1950]	$10.00	$30.00	$60.00
220	Irish, William - ***I Married A Dead Man*** [1950]	$8.00	$25.00	$50.00
221	Lewisohn, Ludwig - ***Don Juan*** [1950]	$2.00	$6.00	$12.00
222	Algren, Nelson - ***The Neon Wilderness*** [1950]	$4.00	$12.50	$25.00
223	Hilton, James - ***Three Loves Had Margaret*** [1950]	$2.00	$6.00	$12.00
224	Dryer, Bernard Victor - ***Port Afrique*** [1950]	$2.00	$6.00	$12.00
225	Stephenson, J. L. - ***Anyone Can Have A Great Vocabulary*** [1950]	$1.35	$4.00	$8.00
226	Weidman, Jerome - ***I Can Get It For You Wholesale!*** [1950]	$1.50	$5.00	$10.00
227	Bassler, Dr. Anthony - ***Just What The Doctor Ordered*** [1949] PBO. Cover by Richter	$2.00	$6.00	$12.00
228	Gilbert & Sullivan - ***Gilbert And Sullivan Operas*** [1950] PBO	$1.35	$4.00	$8.00
229	Anthology - ***All About Girls*** [1950] Cover by Dale Randall.	$3.00	$9.00	$18.00
230	Anthology edited by Harold Meyers - ***The Big Fights*** [1950] PBO. Photo Cover.	$3.00	$9.00	$18.00
231	O'Hara, John - ***Butterfield 8*** [1950]	$2.00	$6.00	$12.00
232	Clarke, Donald Henderson - ***Alabam'*** [1950]	$2.00	$6.00	$12.00
233	Maugham, Robin - ***The Servant*** [1949] Cover by Bert Lannon.	$1.50	$5.00	$10.00
234	Thayer, Tiffany - ***The Old Goat*** [1950]	$2.00	$6.00	$12.00
235	Merritt, A. - ***Seven Footprints To Satan*** [1950]	$6.00	$20.00	$40.00
236	Zola, Emile - ***Venus Of The Counting House*** [1950] Cover by Earle Bergey.	$2.50	$7.50	$15.00
237	Clarke, Donald Henderson - ***Tawny*** [1950]	$2.00	$6.00	$12.00
238	Lawrence, D. H. - ***The First Lady Chatterley*** [1950]	$2.00	$6.00	$12.00
239	Brush, Katharine - ***Bad Girl From Maine*** [1950]	$2.50	$7.50	$15.00
240	Willingham, Calder - ***End As A Man*** [1950]	$1.50	$5.00	$10.00
241	Weidman, Jerome - ***What's In It For Me?*** [1950]	$2.00	$6.00	$12.00
242	Lockridge, Frances & Richard - ***The Case Of The Untidy Murder*** [1950]	$2.50	$7.50	$15.00
243	Paul, Elliot - ***Mysterious Mickey Finn*** [1950]	$3.00	$9.00	$18.00
244	Shulman, Irving - ***Cry Tough!*** [1950]	$2.00	$6.00	$12.00
245	Christie, Agatha - ***The Big Four*** [1950]	$4.00	$12.50	$25.00
246	Housman, A. E. - ***A Shropshire Lad*** [1950]	$3.50	$10.00	$20.00
247	Aswell, James - ***The Midsummer Fires*** [1950]	$2.00	$6.00	$12.00
248	Lawrence, D. H. - ***Love Among The Haystacks*** [1950]	$2.00	$6.00	$12.00
249	Davies, Valentine - ***It Happens Every Spring*** [1950]	$1.50	$5.00	$10.00
250	Briffault, Robert - ***Carlotta*** [1950]	$4.50	$14.00	$28.00
251	Browning, Elizabeth Barrett - ***Sonnets From The Portuguese*** [1950]	$2.00	$6.00	$12.00
252	Farrell, James T. - ***A Hell Of A Good Time And Other Stories*** [1950] Cover by George Mayers.	$2.00	$6.00	$12.00
253	Clarke, Donald Henderson - ***Confidential*** [1950]	$2.00	$6.00	$12.00
254	Miller, Helen Topping - ***Flame Vine*** [1950]	$3.00	$9.00	$18.00
255	Anthology - ***Tropical Passions*** [1950]	$2.00	$6.00	$12.00
256	Stout, Rex - ***The Case Of The Black Orchids*** [1950]	$3.50	$10.00	$20.00
257	Louys, Pierre - ***Aphrodite*** [1950]	$3.00	$9.00	$18.00
258	O'Hara, John - ***Hope Of Heaven*** [1950]	$2.50	$7.50	$15.00

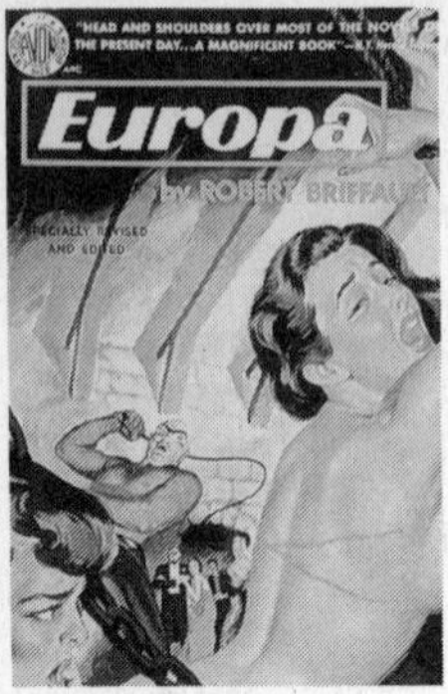

Avon, 272-B

Avon, 280

Avon, 282

		G	VG	F
259	Zola, Emile - ***For A Night Of Love*** [1950]	$2.50	$7.50	$15.00
260	Farrell, James T. - ***Yesterday's Love And Eleven Other Stories*** [1950]	$2.00	$6.00	$12.00
261	Metzelthin, Pearl V. - ***The Avon Improved Cook Book*** [1950]	$2.50	$7.50	$15.00
262	Omar Khayyam - ***The Rubaiyat Of Omar Khayam*** [1950] Translated by Edward Fitzgerald.	$2.00	$6.00	$12.00
263	Asbury, Herbert - ***The Gangs Of New York*** [1950]	$3.00	$9.00	$18.00
264	Nebel, Frederick - ***Six Deadly Dames*** [1950]	$8.00	$25.00	$50.00
265	Baum, Vicki - ***Mortgage On Life*** [1950]	$2.00	$6.00	$12.00
266	Greene, Ward - ***Death In The Deep South*** [1950]	$6.00	$20.00	$40.00
267	Nye, Nelson - ***A Bullet For Billy The Kid*** [1950] Cover by James Bama (his first PB cover)	$3.00	$9.00	$18.00
268	Cain, Paul - ***Seven Slayers*** [1950]	$7.00	$22.50	$45.00
269	Young, I. S. - ***Jadie Greenway*** [1950]	$5.00	$15.00	$30.00
270	Clarke, Donald Henderson - ***The Chastity Of Gloria Boyd*** [1950]	$2.00	$6.00	$12.00
271	Zola, Emile - ***Nana's Mother*** [1950]	$2.00	$6.00	$12.00
272-B	Briffault, Robert - ***Europa*** [1950] Bondage cover variation.	$7.00	$22.50	$45.00
272	Briffault, Robert - ***Europa*** [1950] Map cover variation.	$4.00	$12.50	$25.00
273	Rice, Elmer - ***Imperial City*** [1950]	$2.00	$6.00	$12.00
274	Treat, Lawrence - ***T As In Trapped*** [1950]	$2.50	$7.50	$15.00
275	Pratt, Theodore - ***My Bride In The Storm*** [1950]	$2.00	$6.00	$12.00
276	Harvin, Emily - ***Madwoman?*** [1950]	$3.50	$10.00	$20.00
277	Lewis, C.S. - ***Perelandra*** [1950]	$5.50	$17.50	$35.00
278	Terrall, Robert - ***A Killer Is Loose Among Us*** [1950]	$2.50	$7.50	$15.00
279	Weidman, Jerome - ***The Price Is Right*** [1950]	$2.00	$6.00	$12.00
280	Woodford, Jack - ***Dangerous Love*** [1950]	$2.50	$7.50	$15.00
281	Coblentz, Stanton A. - ***Into Plutonium Depths*** [1950] PBO.	$8.00	$25.00	$50.00
282	Huggins, Roy - ***Lovely Lady, Pity Me*** [1951]	$3.00	$9.00	$18.00
283	Gordon, Russell - ***She Posed For Death*** [1950]	$3.00	$9.00	$18.00
284	Terrall, Robert - ***Madam Is Dead*** [1951]	$3.50	$10.00	$20.00
285	Farley, Ralph M. - ***An Earthman On Venus*** [1951]	$12.50	$37.50	$75.00
286	Delmar, Vina - ***Kept Woman*** [1951]	$2.00	$6.00	$12.00
287	Frey, Richard L. - ***How To Play Samba Canasta*** [1951] PBO.	$1.35	$4.00	$8.00
288	Emery, Guy - ***Front For Murder*** [1951]	$1.50	$5.00	$10.00
289	Lariar, Lawrence - ***Friday For Death*** [1951]	$1.50	$5.00	$10.00

Avon, 297

Avon Home Gardener, One-Shot

Avon Monthly Novel, 7

		G	VG	F
290	Farrell, James T. - ***Gas-House McGinty*** [1951]	$1.50	$5.00	$10.00
291	Thayer, Tiffany - ***Call Her Savage*** [1951]	$2.50	$7.50	$15.00
292	Weiner, Willard - ***Four Boys, A Girl And A Gun*** [1951]	$2.50	$7.50	$15.00
293	O'Hara, John - ***Hellbox*** [1951]	$2.00	$6.00	$12.00
294	Daudet, Alphonse - ***Sappho*** [1951]	$2.50	$7.50	$15.00
295	Adams, John Paul - editor - ***Avon Book Of Puzzles For Everybody*** [1951] PBO.	$27.50	$85.00	$200.00
296	Lawrence, D. H. - ***A Modern Lover And Other Stories*** [1951]	$2.00	$6.00	$12.00
297	Woodford, Jack - ***Untamed Darling*** [1951]	$3.50	$10.00	$20.00
298	Swados, Felice - ***House Of Fury*** [1951]	$6.00	$20.00	$40.00
299	Friend, Oscar J. - ***The Round-Up*** [1951]	$2.00	$6.00	$12.00
300	Shulman, Irving - ***The Amboy Dukes*** [1951] Cover by Ann Cantor.	$2.00	$6.00	$12.00
301	Hilton, James - ***We Are Not Alone*** [1950]	$1.50	$5.00	$10.00
302	Carco, Francis - ***Perversity*** [1951] Photo cover.	$2.00	$6.00	$12.00
303	Sylvester, Robert - ***Dream Street*** [1951] Cover by Barye Phillips.	$2.00	$6.00	$12.00
304	Woolf, James - ***Song Without Sermon*** [1951]	$2.00	$6.00	$12.00
305	Stuart, Lyle - ***God Wears A Bow Tie*** [1950]	$5.00	$15.00	$30.00
306	Thomason, Jr., John W. - ***Gone To Texas*** [1950]	$2.00	$6.00	$12.00
307	Anthology - ***Big League Baseball*** [1950] PBO. Photos throughout.	$5.50	$17.50	$35.00
308	France, Hector - ***Musk, Hashish And Blood*** [1951] PBO.	$6.00	$20.00	$40.00
309	Caldwell, Erskine - ***Midsummer Passion*** [1951] Cover by Ann Cantor.	$2.00	$6.00	$12.00
310	Philippe, Charles Louis - ***Bubu Of Montparnasse*** [1951] Cover by Victor Durba.	$2.00	$6.00	$12.00
311	Anthology - ***The Saturday Evening Post Western Stories*** [1951]	$2.00	$6.00	$12.00
312	Christie, Agatha - ***The Mysterious Affair At Styles*** [1951] Cover by Barye Phillips.	$3.00	$9.00	$18.00
313	Feuchtwanger, Lion - ***The Ugly Duchess*** [1951]	$2.50	$7.50	$15.00
314	Van Vechten, Carl - ***Nigger Heaven*** [1951]	$10.00	$30.00	$60.00
315	Merritt, A. - ***The Metal Monster*** [1951]	$5.50	$17.50	$35.00
316	Christie, Agatha - ***Murder In Three Acts*** [1951]	$3.50	$10.00	$20.00
317	Christie, Agatha - ***Death On The Nile*** [1951]	$5.00	$15.00	$30.00
318-A	Lowell, Juliet - ***Dear Sir:*** [1951] Illus. by Carl Rose. Variation with clothes.	$5.00	$15.00	$30.00

		G	VG	F
318-B	Lowell, Juliet - ***Dear Sir:*** [1951] Illus. by Carl Rose. Variation without clothes.	$1.50	$5.00	$10.00
319	Sobol, Louis - ***Along The Broadway Beat*** [1951] PBO.	$5.50	$17.50	$35.00
320	Babcock, Dwight V. - ***The Gorgeous Ghoul Murder Case*** [1951]	$5.00	$15.00	$30.00
321	Charteris, Leslie - ***The Saint In New York*** [1951]	$2.50	$7.50	$15.00
322	Weidman, Jerome - ***Slipping Beauty & Other Stories*** [1951]	$2.50	$7.50	$15.00
323	Endore, Guy - ***The Furies In Her Body*** [1951]	$2.50	$7.50	$15.00
324	Merritt, A. - ***The Ship Of Ishtar*** [1951]	$5.50	$17.50	$35.00
325	Hilton, James - ***Ill Wind*** [1951]	$2.00	$6.00	$12.00
326	Dortort, David - ***Burial Of The Fruit*** [1951]	$2.25	$7.00	$14.00
327	Thayer, Tiffany - ***One Man Show*** [1951]	$2.25	$7.00	$14.00
328	Sayers, Dorothy L. - ***Strong Poison*** [1951]	$2.50	$7.50	$15.00
329	Burnett, W. R. - ***Little Caesar*** [1951]	$2.50	$7.50	$15.00
330	Horan, James D. - ***Desperate Men*** [1951] The True Story Of Jesse James And Gang.	$2.50	$7.50	$15.00
331	Maugham, W. Somerset - ***Trio*** [1951]	$1.50	$5.00	$10.00
332	Babcock, Dwight V. - ***A Homicide For Hannah*** [1951]	$2.50	$7.50	$15.00
333	Maugham, Robin - ***Line On Ginger*** [1951]	$3.00	$9.00	$18.00
334	Tillery, Carlyle - ***Red Bone Woman*** [1951]	$3.00	$9.00	$18.00
335	Sayers, Dorothy L. - ***In The Teeth Of The Evidence*** [1951]	$3.00	$9.00	$18.00
336	Clarke, Donald Henderson - ***The Housekeeper's Daughter*** [1951]	$2.50	$7.50	$15.00
337	Biggers, Earl Derr - ***The Agony Column*** [1951]	$2.50	$7.50	$15.00
338	Anthology - ***Hollywood Bedside Reader*** [1951] PBO.	$2.00	$6.00	$12.00
339	Kennerley, Juba - ***The Terror Of The Leopard Men*** [1951]	$5.00	$15.00	$30.00
340	Caldwell, Erskine - ***Midsummer Passion*** [1951]	$2.00	$6.00	$12.00
341	Charteris, Leslie - ***The Saint Sees It Through*** [1951]	$2.00	$6.00	$12.00
342	Lacey, Ed - ***The Woman Aroused*** [1951]	$4.50	$14.00	$28.00
343	MacDonald, William Colt - ***Six-Gun Melody*** [1951]	$2.00	$6.00	$12.00
344	Biggers, Earl Derr - ***The Chinese Parrot*** [1951]	$5.50	$17.50	$35.00
345	Allen, Jane - ***I Lost My Girlish Laughter*** [1951]	$2.50	$7.50	$15.00
346	Nichols, Fan - ***Possess Me Not*** [1951]	$3.50	$10.00	$20.00
347	Charteris, Leslie - ***The Saint At The Thieves' Picnic*** [1951]	$2.00	$6.00	$12.00
348	Cain, James M. - ***Jealous Woman*** [1951]	$2.25	$7.00	$14.00
349	Cheyney, Peter - ***Mistress Murder*** [1951]	$2.50	$7.50	$15.00
350	Biggers, Earl Derr - ***Charlie Chan Carries On*** [1951] Cover by Ray Johnson.	$5.50	$17.50	$35.00
351	Clarke, Donald Henderson - ***Millie's Daughter*** [1951] Photo cover.	$2.00	$6.00	$12.00
352	Bodenheim, Maxwell - ***Ninth Avenue*** [1951]	$1.50	$5.00	$10.00
353	Christie, Agatha - ***Poirot Loses A Client*** [1951]	$3.00	$9.00	$18.00
354	Endore, Guy - ***The Werewolf Of Paris*** [1951]	$5.00	$15.00	$30.00
355	Chase, James Hadley - ***No Orchids For Miss Blandish*** [1951]	$5.50	$17.50	$35.00
356	Weidman, Jerome - ***I Can Get It For You Wholesale*** [1951] Movie tie-in with photo cover, front and back.	$2.00	$6.00	$12.00
357	Anthology - ***All About Girls*** [1951] Cover by Bill Wenzel.	$3.50	$10.00	$20.00
358	Louys, Pierre - ***Woman And The Puppet*** [1951]	$2.00	$6.00	$12.00
359	Meyers, Harold - ***Can Can Americana*** [1951] PBO.	$2.50	$7.50	$15.00
360	Wylie, Philip - ***As They Reveled*** [1951]	$2.25	$7.00	$14.00
362	Hueston, Ethel - ***Calamity Jane Of Deadwood Gulch*** [1951] Cover by Ray Johnson	$4.00	$12.50	$25.00
363	Lockridge, Frances & Richard - ***Murder Is Served*** [1951]	$2.50	$7.50	$15.00

		G	VG	F
364	Maugham, W. Somerset - ***The Point Of Honour*** [1951]	$2.00	$6.00	$12.00
365	Clarke, Donald Henderson - ***Impatient Virgin*** [1951] Photo cover.	$2.00	$6.00	$12.00
366	Hatlo, Jimmy - ***They'll Do It Every Time*** [1951] PBO. Cover by Hatlo. Cartoon book.	$2.50	$7.50	$15.00
367	Halleran, E. E. - ***Outlaw Guns*** [1951]	$2.00	$6.00	$12.00
368	O'Hara, John - ***All The Girls He Wanted*** [1951]	$2.50	$7.50	$15.00
369	Lockridge, Frances & Richard - ***The Dishonest Murderer*** [1951]	$2.50	$7.50	$15.00
370	Merritt, A. - ***The Moon Pool*** [1951]	$6.00	$20.00	$40.00
371	Christie, Agatha - ***The Regatta Mystery*** [1951]	$2.25	$7.00	$14.00
372	Shulman, Irving - ***Cry Tough!*** [1951]	$2.00	$6.00	$12.00
373	Payne, Robert - ***The Blue Negro And Other Stories*** [1951] PBO.	$5.00	$15.00	$30.00
374	Bower, B. M. - ***Gun Fight At Horsethief Range*** [1951]	$2.00	$6.00	$12.00
375	Wylie, Philip - ***Babes And Sucklings*** [1951]	$2.00	$6.00	$12.00
376	McKay, Claude - ***Home To Harlem*** [1951]	$5.50	$17.50	$35.00
377	Kaye, Philip B. - ***Taffy*** [1951]	$5.00	$15.00	$30.00
378	Cody, Al - ***The Marshall Of Deer Creek*** [1951]	$2.00	$6.00	$12.00
379	Christie, Agatha - ***Death In The Air*** [1951] Cover by Robert Hilbert.	$2.50	$7.50	$15.00
380	Wahl, Loren - ***If This Be Sin*** [1951]	$2.50	$7.50	$15.00
381	Hilton, James - ***Nothing So Strange*** [1951]	$1.50	$5.00	$10.00
382	Mende, Robert - ***Tough Kid From Brooklyn*** [1951]	$2.00	$6.00	$12.00
383	Munro, W. Carroll - ***The Untamed Wife Of Louis Scott*** [1951]	$2.50	$7.50	$15.00
384	Clarke, Donald Henderson - ***Louis Beretti*** [1951]	$2.50	$7.50	$15.00
385	Brand, Christianna - ***Cat And Mouse*** [1951]	$2.00	$6.00	$12.00
387	Brandel, Marc - ***Maniac Rendezvous*** [1951]	$4.50	$14.00	$28.00
389	Anthology edited by Barthold Fles - ***The Saturday Evening Post Fantasy Stories*** [1951] PBO. Cover by William Randall.	$2.50	$7.50	$15.00
390	Wylie, Philip - ***The Savage Gentleman*** [1951]	$3.00	$9.00	$18.00
391	Anderson, Oliver - ***Maidens In The Midden*** [1951] Cover by John Mackey.	$1.50	$5.00	$10.00
392	Merritt, A. - ***Burn Witch Burn*** [1951] Cover by William Forrest.	$3.50	$10.00	$20.00
393	Brandel, Marc - ***The Moron*** [1951]	$2.50	$7.50	$15.00
394	Clarke, Donald Henderson - ***Murderer's Holiday*** [1951]	$2.50	$7.50	$15.00
395	Ford, Terence - ***The Drunk, The Damned And The Bedevilled*** [1952]	$2.50	$7.50	$15.00
396	Weston, George - ***His First Million Women*** [1952]	$4.00	$12.50	$25.00
397	Clarke, Donald Henderson - ***Nina*** [1952]	$2.00	$6.00	$12.00
398	Schiller, Cicely - ***Element Of Shame*** [1952] Photo cover.	$2.00	$6.00	$12.00
399	Smith, Robert Paul - ***Plus Blood In Their Veins*** [1952]	$2.50	$7.50	$15.00
400	Henderson, George Wylie - ***Jule: Alabama Boy In Harlem*** [1952]	$3.50	$10.00	$20.00
401	Carco, Francis - ***Perversity*** [1952] Photo cover.	$2.00	$6.00	$12.00
402	Woodford, Jack - ***Dangerous Love*** [1952]	$3.00	$9.00	$18.00
403	Woodford, Jack - ***Untamed Darling*** [1952]	$3.00	$9.00	$18.00
404	Klein, Ernst - ***The Blackmailer*** [1952]	$2.00	$6.00	$12.00
405	Monash, Paul - ***How Brave We Live*** [1952]	$1.50	$5.00	$10.00
406	Longstreet, Stephen - ***Two Beds For Roxane*** [1952]	$2.00	$6.00	$12.00
407	Niles, Blair - ***Strange Brother*** [1952]	$2.50	$7.50	$15.00
408	Clarke, Donald Henderson - ***Tawny*** [1952]	$2.00	$6.00	$12.00
410	Christie, Agatha - ***The Secret Adversary*** [1952]	$1.50	$5.00	$10.00

	G	VG	F
411 Dunn, M.D., Bob - ***Hospital Happy*** [1952] PBO. Cartoon book.	$2.50	$7.50	$15.00
412 Houston, Jack - ***Waiting For Willy*** [1952] Cover by George Erickson.	$2.50	$7.50	$15.00
413 Merritt, A. - ***Dwellers In The Mirage*** [1952]	$5.50	$17.50	$35.00
414 Hopson, William - ***The Gringo Bandit*** [1952]	$2.00	$6.00	$12.00
415 France, Hector - ***Musk, Hashish And Blood*** [1952]	$5.00	$15.00	$30.00
416 Uchard, Mario - ***The Frenchman In Mohammed's Harem*** [1952]	$2.25	$7.00	$14.00
417 Hanley, Jack - ***Star Lust*** [1952]	$2.50	$7.50	$15.00
418 Thayer, Tiffany - ***Call Her Savage*** [1952]	$2.50	$7.50	$15.00
419 Algren, Nelson - ***Never Come Morning*** [1952] Cover by Ann Cantor.	$2.00	$6.00	$12.00
420 Charteris, Leslie - ***The Saint Goes West*** [1952] Cover by Harley Wood.	$2.00	$6.00	$12.00
421 Cain, James M. - ***Love's Lovely Counterfeit*** [1952] Cover by Kampen.	$2.00	$6.00	$12.00
422 O'Hara, John - ***Butterfield 8*** [1952]	$1.50	$5.00	$10.00
423 Lawrence, D. H. - ***Love Among The Haystack And Other Stories*** [1952]	$2.00	$6.00	$12.00
424 Algren, Nelson - ***The Neon Wilderness*** [1952]	$3.50	$10.00	$20.00
425 Queen, Ellery - ***The Tragedy Of X*** [1952]	$1.50	$5.00	$10.00
426 Cody, Al - ***Guns Blaze At Sundown*** [1952]	$1.50	$5.00	$10.00
427 Bodenheim, Maxwell - ***Georgie May*** [1952] Photo cover.	$1.50	$5.00	$10.00
428 Maugham, Robin - ***The Servant*** [1952]	$1.50	$5.00	$10.00
429 Weidman, Jerome - ***The Price Is Right*** [1952]	$1.50	$5.00	$10.00
430 Swados, Felice - ***House Of Fury*** [1952]	$4.00	$12.50	$25.00
431 Clarke, Donald Henderson - ***That Mrs. Renney*** [1952]	$2.00	$6.00	$12.00
432 Charteris, Leslie - ***Saint Overboard*** [1952]	$2.00	$6.00	$12.00
433 Kaufman, Lenard - ***Juvenile Delinquents*** [1952]	$2.50	$7.50	$15.00
434 Lockridge, Frances & Richard - ***Murder Comes First*** [1952] Cover by Leone.	$2.50	$7.50	$15.00
AT-435 Huxley, Aldous - ***After Many A Summer Dies The Swan*** [1952]	$2.50	$7.50	$15.00
A-436 Chase, James Hadley - ***Too Dangerous To Be Free*** [1952]	$2.50	$7.50	$15.00
437 Conrad, Harold - ***The Battle At Apache Pass*** [1952] PBO. Movie tie-in and photo cover.	$3.00	$9.00	$18.00
438 Clarke, Donald Henderson - ***Confidential*** [1952]	$1.50	$5.00	$10.00
A-439 Taylor, Phoebe Atwood - ***Diplomatic Corpse*** [1952]	$2.00	$6.00	$12.00
440 Charteris, Leslie - ***The Saint At The Thieves' Picnic*** [1952]	$2.00	$6.00	$12.00
441 Loos, Anita - ***A Mouse Is Born*** [1952]	$1.50	$5.00	$10.00
442 Weidman, Jerome - ***Slipping Beauty*** [1952]	$1.50	$5.00	$10.00
443 Christie, Agatha - ***A Holiday For Murder*** [1952]	$1.50	$5.00	$10.00
444 Wiener, Willard - ***Four Boys, A Girl And A Gun*** [1952]	$1.50	$5.00	$10.00
AT-445 Willingham, Calder - ***End As A Man*** [1952]	$1.50	$5.00	$10.00
446 Harte, Bret - ***Outcasts Of Poker Flat*** [1952] PBO. Movie tie-in and photo cover.	$2.50	$7.50	$15.00
AT-447 Wallenstein, Marcel - ***Red Canvas*** [1952]	$2.00	$6.00	$12.00
448 Isherwood, Christopher - ***The Last Of Mr. Norris*** [1952]	$1.50	$5.00	$10.00
449 Lawrence, D. H. - ***The Virgin And The Gypsy*** [1952] Cover by Victor Olson.	$2.00	$6.00	$12.00
450 Queen, Ellery - ***Tragedy Of Y*** [1952]	$1.50	$5.00	$10.00
451 Thomason, Jr., John W. - ***Gone To Texas*** [1952]	$2.50	$7.50	$15.00
452 Tillery, Carlyle - ***Red Bone Woman*** [1952]	$2.00	$6.00	$12.00

		G	VG	F
453	Flowers, Don - ***Glamor Girls*** [1952] PBO. Cover by Flowers. Cartoon book.	$3.00	$9.00	$18.00
454	Hogan, Robert J. - ***The Challenge Of Smoke Wade*** [1952]	$2.00	$6.00	$12.00
455	Cain, James M. - ***The Root Of His Evil*** [1952]	$2.50	$7.50	$15.00
456	Clarke, Donald Henderson - ***The Chastity Of Gloria Boyd*** [1952]	$1.50	$5.00	$10.00
457	Hunt, Howard - ***Bimini Run*** [1952] Cover by Erickson.	$2.00	$6.00	$12.00
458	Smith, Robert Paul - ***Because Of My Love*** [1952] Cover by Victor Olson.	$2.00	$6.00	$12.00
459	De Maupassant, Guy - ***Mademoiselle Fifi*** [1952] Cover by Erickson.	$2.00	$6.00	$12.00
460	Cody, Al - ***Outlaw Justice At Hangman's Coulee*** [1952]	$2.00	$6.00	$12.00
461	Shallit, Joseph - ***Lady, Don't Die On My Doorstep*** [1952]	$3.00	$9.00	$18.00
462	Lomax, Bliss - ***Pardners Of The Badlands*** [1952] Cover by Paul Freedberg.	$2.50	$7.50	$15.00
463	Charteris, Leslie - ***The Saint In Action*** [1952] Cover by Robert Hilbert.	$2.00	$6.00	$12.00
464	Maugham, Robin - ***The Rough And The Smooth*** [1952]	$2.00	$6.00	$12.00
465	Queen, Ellery - ***The Tragedy Of Z*** [1952]	$2.00	$6.00	$12.00
466	Farrell, James T. - ***Gas-House McGinty*** [1952] Cover by Erickson.	$1.50	$5.00	$10.00
467	La Due, Russell - ***Hell-Bent With Jake*** [1952] Cover by Victor Olson.	$2.00	$6.00	$12.00
468	Farrell, James T. - ***A Hell Of A Good Time*** [1952]	$2.00	$6.00	$12.00
469	Hogan, Robert J. - ***Roaring Guns At Apache Landing*** [1952]	$2.00	$6.00	$12.00
470	Benney, Mark - ***Low Company*** [1952]	$1.50	$5.00	$10.00
471	Lockridge, Frances & Richard - ***Mr. & Mrs. North Meet Murder*** [1952]	$2.00	$6.00	$12.00
472	Clarke, Donald Henderson - ***The Headstrong Young Man*** [1952] Cover by Victor Olson.	$2.00	$6.00	$12.00
473	Charteris, Leslie - ***Saint's Getaway*** [1952]	$2.00	$6.00	$12.00
474	Hopkins, Tom J. - ***Outlaw Ambush On The Drumfire Trail*** [1952]	$2.00	$6.00	$12.00
475	Farrell, James T. - ***Yesterday's Love*** [1952] Cover by Rudy Nappi.	$2.00	$6.00	$12.00
476	Carr, John Dickson - ***The Bride Of Newgate*** [1952]	$2.50	$7.50	$15.00
477	Charteris, Leslie - ***The Saint Meets The Tiger*** [1952]	$2.00	$6.00	$12.00
478	Nye, Nelson - ***A Bullet For Billy The Kid*** [1952] Cover by James Bama.	$2.00	$6.00	$12.00
479	Cain, James M. - ***Jealous Woman*** [1952]	$1.50	$5.00	$10.00
480	Clarke, Donald Henderson - ***Millie*** [1952]	$1.50	$5.00	$10.00
481	Wakeman, Frederic - ***The Hucksters*** [1952]	$1.50	$5.00	$10.00
482	Anthology - ***Avon Bedside Companion*** [1952] PBO.	$1.50	$5.00	$10.00
483	Clarke, Donald Henderson - ***A Lady Named Lou*** [1952] Cover by Victor Olson.	$2.00	$6.00	$12.00
484	Lockridge, Frances & Richard - ***Murder In A Hurry*** [1952]	$2.00	$6.00	$12.00
485	Chase, James Hadley - ***12 Chinks And A Woman*** [1952]	$4.00	$12.50	$25.00
486	Leithead, J. Edward - ***The Bronc Buckaroo*** [1952]	$2.00	$6.00	$12.00
487	Jasper, Bob - ***Feud At Sundown*** [1952]	$2.00	$6.00	$12.00
488	Queen, Ellery - ***Drury Lane's Last Case*** [1952]	$2.50	$7.50	$15.00
489	Charteris, Leslie - ***The Saint Meets His Match*** [1952]	$2.00	$6.00	$12.00
490	Shallit, Joseph - ***Yell Bloody Murder*** [1952]	$2.00	$6.00	$12.00
491	MacDonald, William Colt - ***Mesquiteer Mavericks*** [1952]	$2.00	$6.00	$12.00

		G	VG	F
492	Houston, Jack - ***Waiting For Willy*** [1952] Cover by George Erickson.	$2.00	$6.00	$12.00
493	Niles, Blair - ***Strange Brother*** [1952]	$2.00	$6.00	$12.00
494	Bloch, Robert - ***The Scarf*** [1952]	$3.00	$9.00	$18.00
495	Claussen, W. Edmunds - ***Rebel's Roundup*** [1952]	$2.00	$6.00	$12.00
496	Cain, Paul - ***Fast One*** [1952]	$2.50	$7.50	$15.00
497	Cook, Whitfield - ***A Night With Mr. Primrose*** [1952] Cover by Barye Phillips.	$2.00	$6.00	$12.00
498	MacDonald, William Colt - ***Six-Gun Melody*** [1952]	$2.00	$6.00	$12.00
499	Campbell, E. Simms - ***Chorus Of Cuties*** [1952] PBO. Cover by Campbell. Cartoon book.	$3.00	$9.00	$18.00
500	Raine, William MacLeod - ***Colorado*** [1952]	$2.00	$6.00	$12.00
501	Munro, W. Carroll - ***The Untamed Wife Of Louis Scott*** [1953]	$2.50	$7.50	$15.00
502	Lockridge, Frances & Richard - ***Mr. and Mrs. North And A Pinch Of Poison*** [1952]	$2.00	$6.00	$12.00
503	Clarke, Donald Henderson - ***The Housekeeper's Daughter*** [1953]	$2.00	$6.00	$12.00
504	Hubler, Richard G. - ***The Chase*** [1953]	$2.00	$6.00	$12.00
505	Bower, B. M. - ***Gun Fight At Horse Thief Range*** [1953]	$2.00	$6.00	$12.00
506	Brandon, Michael - ***Nonce*** [1953]	$2.50	$7.50	$15.00
507	Halleran, E. E. - ***Straw Boss*** [1953]	$2.00	$6.00	$12.00
508	O'Brien, Eugene - ***He Swung And He Missed*** [1953]	$2.50	$7.50	$15.00
509	Queen, Ellery - ***The Four Of Hearts*** [1953]	$2.00	$6.00	$12.00
510	Atiyah, Edward - ***The Thin Line*** [1953]	$1.50	$5.00	$10.00
511	Cody, Al - ***The Marshall Of Deer Creek*** [1953]	$2.00	$6.00	$12.00
512	Ham, Jr., Roswell G. - ***The Gifted*** [1953]	$1.50	$5.00	$10.00
513	Guild, Leo - ***Bachelor's Joke Book*** [1953] PBO. Cover by Carl Rose.	$2.50	$7.50	$15.00
514	MacDonald, William Colt - ***The Vanishing Gun-Slinger*** [1953]	$2.00	$6.00	$12.00
515	Lockridge, Frances & Richard - ***Murder Out Of Turn*** [1953]	$2.00	$6.00	$12.00
516	Hopson, William - ***Gringo Bandit*** [1953]	$2.00	$6.00	$12.00
517	Wheeler, Elmer - ***The Fat Boy's Book*** [1953]	$2.50	$7.50	$15.00
518	Charteris, Leslie - ***The Avenging Saint*** [1953]	$1.50	$5.00	$10.00
519	Ketcham, Hank - ***Dennis The Menace*** [1953] PBO. Cover by Ketchum. Cartoon book.	$2.50	$7.50	$15.00
520	Schiddel, Edmund - ***Scratch The Surface*** [1953] Cover by Nappi.	$1.50	$5.00	$10.00
521	Ellison, Jerome - ***The Prisoner Ate A Hearty Breakfast*** [1953]	$2.00	$6.00	$12.00
522	Halleran, E. E. - ***Outlaw Guns*** [1953]	$1.50	$5.00	$10.00
523	Queen, Ellery - ***The American Gun Mystery*** [1953]	$1.50	$5.00	$10.00
524	Hatlo, Jimmy - ***The New Jimmy Hatlo Book*** [1953] PBO. Cover by Hatlo. Cartoon book.	$2.50	$7.50	$15.00
525	Cody, Al - ***Guns Blaze At Sundown*** [1953]	$1.50	$5.00	$10.00
526	Charteris, Leslie - ***Call For The Saint*** [1953]	$1.50	$5.00	$10.00
527	Anthology - ***All About Girls*** [1953] PBO.	$2.50	$7.50	$15.00
528	Shallit, Joseph - ***Kiss The Killer*** [1953]	$1.50	$5.00	$10.00
529	Wells, Lee E. - ***Gunshot Empire*** [1953]	$1.50	$5.00	$10.00
530	Clarke, Donald Henderson - ***Impatient Virgin*** [1953] Photo cover.	$1.50	$5.00	$10.00
531	Arnaud, Georges - ***Wages Of Fear*** [1953]	$1.50	$5.00	$10.00
532	Gooden, Arthur Henry - ***Trouble In The Saddle*** [1953]	$1.50	$5.00	$10.00
533	Charteris, Leslie - ***Follow The Saint*** [1953] Cover by Rudy Nappi.	$1.50	$5.00	$10.00

		G	VG	F
534	Smith, Robert Paul - ***Time And The Place*** [1953]	$1.50	$5.00	$10.00
535	Lockridge, Frances & Richard - ***Dead As A Dinosaur*** [1953]	$2.00	$6.00	$12.00
536	MacDonald, William Colt - ***Three-Notch Cameron*** [1953]	$1.50	$5.00	$10.00
537	Conrad, Barnaby - ***The Innocent Villa*** [1953]	$1.50	$5.00	$10.00
A-538	Joesten, Joachim - ***Dope, Inc.*** [1953] PBO. Photo cover.	$4.00	$12.50	$25.00
539	Kinkaid, Matt - ***Hardcase*** [1953] Cover by Meese.	$1.50	$5.00	$10.00
540	Lehman, Paul Evan - ***Pistols On The Pecos*** [1953] PBO.	$2.00	$6.00	$12.00
541	Dortort, David - ***Burial Of The Fruit*** [1953]	$1.50	$5.00	$10.00
A-542	Carter, Max - ***Call Me Killer!*** [1953] PBO.	$2.00	$6.00	$12.00
543	Clarke, Donald Henderson - ***Millie's Daughter*** [1953] Photo cover.	$1.50	$5.00	$10.00
544	Charteris, Leslie - ***The Saint And The Last Hero*** [1953]	$1.50	$5.00	$10.00
545	Smith, Robert Paul - ***Circle Of Desire*** [1953]	$1.50	$5.00	$10.00
546	Eagle, John - ***The Hoodlums*** [1953] PBO. Cover by Kirk Wilson.	$2.50	$7.50	$15.00
547	White, Daniel - ***Southern Daughter*** [1953] PBO.	$2.50	$7.50	$15.00
548	Van Vogt, A. E. - ***Away And Beyond*** [1953]	$2.00	$6.00	$12.00
A-549	Anthology - ***Tales Of Love And Fury*** [1953] PBO.	$2.50	$7.50	$15.00
550	Hogan, Robert J. - ***Renegade Guns*** [1953]	$1.50	$5.00	$10.00
551	Malley, Louis - ***Stool Pigeon*** [1953] PBO. Cover by Meese.	$2.50	$7.50	$15.00
552	Paterson, Neil - ***Man On The Tightrope*** [1953]	$1.50	$5.00	$10.00
553	January, Steve - ***Rusty Desmond*** [1954] PBO.	$2.50	$7.50	$15.00
554	Hitt, Orrie - ***I'll Call Every Monday*** [1954]	$2.00	$6.00	$12.00
555	Carco, Francis - ***Rue Pigalle*** [1954]	$1.50	$5.00	$10.00
556	Cochran, Jeff - ***Guns Of Circle 8*** [1954] PBO.	$2.00	$6.00	$12.00
557	Flowers, Don - ***Glamor Girls*** [1954] Cover by the author.	$2.50	$7.50	$15.00
558	Shallit, Joseph - ***The Case Of The Billion Dollar Body*** [1954]	$2.00	$6.00	$12.00
559	Anthology edited by Charles Preston - ***A Cartoon Guide To The Kinsey Report*** [1954] PBO. Cartoon book.	$1.50	$5.00	$10.00
560	Brown, Wenzell - ***Gang Girl*** [1954] PBO.	$2.50	$7.50	$15.00
561	Lacy, Ed - ***Enter Without Desire*** [1954] Cover by Robert Schulz.	$2.00	$6.00	$12.00
562	Gooden, Arthur Henry - ***Call Of The Range*** [1954]	$1.50	$5.00	$10.00
563	Creasey, John - ***The Creepers*** [1954] Cover by Al Rossi.	$1.50	$5.00	$10.00
564	Dewey, Thomas B. - ***Every Bet's A Sure Thing*** [1954]	$1.50	$5.00	$10.00
565	Rourke, Thomas - ***Thunder Below*** [1954]	$2.00	$6.00	$12.00
566	Lacy, Ed - ***Go For The Body*** [1954] PBO.	$2.50	$7.50	$15.00
567	Anthology - ***Ship Ahoy*** [1954] PBO. Cartoon book.	$2.00	$6.00	$12.00
568	Anonymous - ***I Worked For Lucky Luciano*** [1954] PBO. Photo cover.	$2.50	$7.50	$15.00
569	Heuman, William - ***Gunhand From Texas*** [1954] PBO.	$1.50	$5.00	$10.00
570	Shaw, Floyd - ***Devil's Daughter*** [1954] Cover by Michael.	$2.00	$6.00	$12.00
571	Wylie, Philip - ***As They Reveled*** [1954] Cover by Barye Phillips.	$2.00	$6.00	$12.00
572	Kane, Henry - ***Laughter Came Screaming*** [1954] PBO.	$1.50	$5.00	$10.00
573	Wells, Lee E. - ***The Long Noose*** [1954]	$1.50	$5.00	$10.00
574	Sanford, John - ***Make My Bed In Hell*** [1954]	$1.50	$5.00	$10.00
575	Clarke, Donald Henderson - ***Louis Beretti*** [1954] Cover by Al Rossi.	$1.50	$5.00	$10.00
576	Brattes, Leo - ***Forbidden*** [1954] PBO.	$1.50	$5.00	$10.00
577	Henderson, George Wylie - ***Jule: Alabama Boy In Harlem*** [1954]	$2.50	$7.50	$15.00
578	Shepherd, Joan - ***Girl On The Left Bank*** [1954] Cover by Cardiff.	$2.00	$6.00	$12.00

		G	VG	F
579	MacDonald, William Colt - ***Rebel Ranger*** [1954] Cover by Kirk Wilson.	$1.50	$5.00	$10.00
580	Hanley, Jack - ***The Guy From Coney Island*** [1954] PBO.	$2.00	$6.00	$12.00
581	Cain, James M. - ***Love's Lovely Counterfeit*** [1954]	$1.50	$5.00	$10.00
582	Weiss, Joe - ***How Rough Can It Get?*** [1954]	$1.50	$5.00	$10.00
583	Lockridge, Frances & Richard - ***Death Has A Small Voice*** [1954]	$1.50	$5.00	$10.00
584	Noel, Sterling - ***Few Die Well*** [1954]	$1.50	$5.00	$10.00
585	Richter, Mischa - ***Keeping Women In Line*** [1954] PBO. Cartoon book.	$3.00	$9.00	$18.00
586	MacDonald, William Colt - ***The Riddle Of Ramrod Ridge*** [1954] PBO.	$1.50	$5.00	$10.00
587	Lawrence, D.H. - ***The Virgin And The Gypsy*** [1954]	$1.50	$5.00	$10.00
588	Charteris, Leslie - ***Saint Errant*** [1954]	$1.50	$5.00	$10.00
589	Schiddel, Edmund - ***The Other Side Of The Night*** [1954] PBO.	$2.00	$6.00	$12.00
590	Creasy, John - ***The Figure In The Dusk*** [1954]	$1.50	$5.00	$10.00
591	Harper, Daniel - ***The Wrong Turn*** [1954]	$1.50	$5.00	$10.00
592	MacDonald, William Colt - ***The Phantom Pass*** [1954] Cover by Leone.	$1.50	$5.00	$10.00
593	Clarke, Donald Henderson - ***Nina*** [1954]	$1.50	$5.00	$10.00
594	Proctor, Maurice - ***The Pennycross Murders*** [1954]	$1.50	$5.00	$10.00
595	Monash, Paul - ***How Brave We Live*** [1954]	$1.50	$5.00	$10.00
596	Peeples, Samuel Anthony - ***Gun Feud At Stampede Valley*** [1954] PBO.	$1.50	$5.00	$10.00
597	Stuart, William L. - ***Night Cry*** [1954]	$3.50	$10.00	$20.00
598	Anthology - ***More All About Girls*** [1954] PBO. Cover by Wenzel. Cartoon book.	$3.50	$10.00	$20.00
599	Cain, James M. - ***Sinful Woman*** [1954]	$2.00	$6.00	$12.00
600	Ketcham, Hank - ***More Dennis The Menace*** [1954] PBO. Cover by Ketchum. Cartoon book.	$2.50	$7.50	$15.00
601	McCoy, John Pleasant - ***Love For A Stranger*** [1954] PBO.	$2.00	$6.00	$12.00
602	Kane, Henry - ***My Business Is Murder*** [1954] PBO.	$2.00	$6.00	$12.00
603	Anthology - ***Avon Bedside Companion*** [1954]	$1.50	$5.00	$10.00
604	Hynd, Alan - ***The Case Of The Burning Bride*** [1954]	$1.50	$5.00	$10.00
605	Tiger, John - ***Death Hits The Jackpot*** [1954] PBO.	$1.50	$5.00	$10.00
606	Brister, Richard - ***The Kansan*** [1954]	$1.50	$5.00	$10.00
607	Philippe, Charles-Louis - ***Bubu Of Montparnasse*** [1954]	$2.00	$6.00	$12.00
608	Lockridges, Frances & Richard - ***Curtain For A Jester*** [1954]	$1.50	$5.00	$10.00
609	Anthology - ***French Postcards*** [1954] PBO. Cartoon book.	$1.50	$5.00	$10.00
610	Charteris, Leslie - ***The Saint Steps In*** [1954]	$1.50	$5.00	$10.00
611	Charteris, Leslie - ***The Saint In Europe*** [1954]	$1.50	$5.00	$10.00
612	Hatlo, Jimmy - ***The New Jimmy Hatlo Book*** [1954] Cover by author.	$2.00	$6.00	$12.00
613	Schiddel, Edmund - ***Break-Up*** [1954]	$1.50	$5.00	$10.00
614	Thomey, Tedd - ***And Dream Of Evil*** [1954]	$1.50	$5.00	$10.00
615	Clarke, Donald Henderson - ***Tawny*** [1954]	$1.50	$5.00	$10.00
616	Christie, Agatha - ***A Holiday For Murder*** [1954]	$1.50	$5.00	$10.00
617	Anthology - ***Battle Of The Sexes*** [1955] PBO. Cartoon book.	$4.00	$12.50	$25.00
618	Kane, Henry - ***Trinity In Violence*** [1955] PBO.	$2.00	$6.00	$12.00
619	Charteris, Leslie - ***The Saint Sees It Through*** [1955]	$1.50	$5.00	$10.00
620	Wells, Lee E. - ***Death In The Desert*** [1955]	$1.50	$5.00	$10.00
621	Carr, John Dickson - ***It Walks By Night*** [1954]	$2.00	$6.00	$12.00
622	Monash, Paul - ***Hellbound*** [1955] PBO. Cover by Hulings.	$1.50	$5.00	$10.00

		G	VG	F
623	Jay, Charlotte - ***Beat Not The Bones*** [1955]	$2.00	$6.00	$12.00
624	Sharp, Margery - ***The Stone Of Chastity*** [1955]	$2.00	$6.00	$12.00
625	Heard, H. F. - ***A Taste For Murder*** [1955]	$2.00	$6.00	$12.00
626	Dewey, Thomas B. - ***The Case Of The Murdered Model*** [1955].	$2.00	$6.00	$12.00
627	Anthology edited by Harold Meyers - ***Caveman Cartoons*** [1955] PBO. Cartoon book.	$2.50	$7.50	$15.00
628	Bierce, Ambrose - ***The Monk And The Hangman's Daughter*** [1955] PBO.	$2.50	$7.50	$15.00
629	Charteris, Leslie - ***The Saint And Mr. Teal*** [1955]	$1.50	$5.00	$10.00
630	Anthology - ***20 Great Ghost Stories*** [1955]	$4.00	$12.50	$25.00
631	Clarke, Donald Henderson - ***Murderer's Holiday*** [1955]	$1.50	$5.00	$10.00
632	Thomey, Tedd - ***Jet Pilot*** [1955] PBO.	$1.50	$5.00	$10.00
633	Anthology edited by Harold Meyers - ***Klever Kid Kartoons*** [1955] PBO. Cartoon book.	$3.50	$10.00	$20.00
634	West, Nathaniel - ***Miss Lonelyhearts*** [1955]	$2.00	$6.00	$12.00
635	Charteris, Leslie - ***The Saint Goes West*** [1955]	$1.50	$5.00	$10.00
636	Christie, Agatha - ***The Moving Finger*** [1955] Photo cover.	$1.50	$5.00	$10.00
637	Meyers, Harold - editor - ***Animals Are Funnier Than People*** [1955] PBO.	$2.00	$6.00	$12.00
638	Anthology - ***Tropical Passions*** [1955]	$1.50	$5.00	$10.00
639	Hatlo, Jimmy - ***Cartoons By Jimmy Hatlo*** [1955] PBO. Cover by Hatlo. Cartoon book.	$2.50	$7.50	$15.00
640	Montagu, Ewen - ***The Man Who Never Was*** [1955]	$1.50	$5.00	$10.00
641	Creasey, John - ***The Case Of The Acid Throwers*** [1955]	$1.50	$5.00	$10.00
642	Lehman, Paul Evan - ***The Fighting Texan*** [1955] PBO.	$1.50	$5.00	$10.00
643	Meyers, Harold - editor - ***South Sea Cartoons*** [1955] PBO. Cover by Bill Ward. Cartoon book.	$2.50	$7.50	$15.00
644	Anthology - ***Stories For Tonight*** [1955] PBO. Includes Steinbeck.	$2.00	$6.00	$12.00
645	Adams, John Paul - editor - ***Puzzles For Everybody*** [1955]	$22.00	$70.00	$140.00
646	Kane, Henry - ***Case Of The Murdered Madam*** [1955]	$1.50	$5.00	$10.00
647	Baxter, John - ***Unfaithful*** [1955] PBO.	$1.50	$5.00	$10.00
648	Christie, Agatha - ***Murder In Three Acts*** [1955]	$1.50	$5.00	$10.00
649	Anthology - ***Nudist Cartoons, Stories & Jokes*** [1955]	$3.00	$9.00	$18.00
650	Clarke, Donald Henderson - ***Confidential*** [1955]	$1.50	$5.00	$10.00
651	Waer, Jack - ***Murder In Las Vegas*** [1955] PBO.	$1.50	$5.00	$10.00
652	Hatlo, Jimmy - ***Hatlo's Inferno*** [1955] PBO. Cover by Hatlo. Cartoon book.	$3.50	$10.00	$20.00
653	Charteris, Leslie - ***The Saint Goes On*** [1955]	$1.50	$5.00	$10.00
654	Martin, Chuck - ***Bloody Kansas*** [1955] PBO.	$1.50	$5.00	$10.00
655	Andreyev, Leonid - ***Seven Who Were Hanged*** [1955]	$1.50	$5.00	$10.00
656	Clarke, Donald Henderson - ***Impatient Virgin*** [1955]	$1.50	$5.00	$10.00
657	Koenig, H. P. - ***The Doctor's Woman*** [1955]	$1.50	$5.00	$10.00
658	Christie, Agatha - ***Death In The Air*** [1955]	$1.50	$5.00	$10.00
659	Ernenwein, Leslie - ***Hell-Town In Texas*** [1955]	$1.50	$5.00	$10.00
660	Keene, Day - ***Wake Up To Murder*** [1955]	$1.50	$5.00	$10.00
661	O'Hara, John - ***Stories Of Venial Sin*** [1955]	$1.50	$5.00	$10.00
662	Meyers, Harold - ***Teen-Age Cartoons And Jokes*** [1955] PBO. Cartoon book.	$3.50	$10.00	$20.00
663	Charteris, Leslie - ***The Saint And The Ace Of Knaves*** [1955]	$1.50	$5.00	$10.00
664	Greene, Ward - ***Desire In The Deep South*** [1955]	$2.00	$6.00	$12.00
665	Ketcham, Hank - ***Dennis The Menace*** [1955]	$1.50	$5.00	$10.00
666	Lockridge, Frances & Richard - ***A Key To Death*** [1955]	$1.50	$5.00	$10.00

		G	VG	F
667	Fowler, Kenneth - ***The Range Bum*** [1955] PBO.	$1.50	$5.00	$10.00
668	Louys, Pierre - ***Woman And The Puppet*** [1955]	$1.50	$5.00	$10.00
669	De La Fouchardiere, Georges - ***Sensualite*** [1955]	$1.50	$5.00	$10.00
670	Jay, Charlotte - ***The Fugitive Eye*** [1955]	$1.50	$5.00	$10.00
671	Clarke, Donald Henderson - ***A Lady Named Lou*** [1955]	$1.50	$5.00	$10.00
672	Kane, Henry - ***Too French And Too Deadly*** [1955] PBO.	$2.00	$6.00	$12.00
673	Anthology - ***Henry Morgan's Jokebook*** [1955] PBO. Cover by Ernest Marquez.	$3.00	$9.00	$18.00
674	Hogan, Robert J. - ***The Challenge Of Smoke Wade*** [1955]	$1.50	$5.00	$10.00
675	Birkenfeld, Gunther - ***Room In Berlin*** [1955] Cover by Hooks.	$1.50	$5.00	$10.00
676	Clad, Noel - ***White Barrier*** [1955] PBO.	$2.00	$6.00	$12.00
677	Freyer, Frederic - ***The Case Of The Black Black Hearse*** [1955].	$1.50	$5.00	$10.00
678	MacDonald, William Colt - ***Fighting Kid From Eldorado*** [1955]	$1.50	$5.00	$10.00
679	O'Hara, John - ***Hellbox*** [1955]	$1.50	$5.00	$10.00
680	Charteris, Leslie - ***The Happy Highwayman*** [1955]	$1.50	$5.00	$10.00
681	Anthology - ***Showgirl Cartoons And Photographs*** [1955] PBO. Cartoon book.	$3.50	$10.00	$20.00
682	Mathers, E. Powys - ***Chinese Love Tales*** [1955]	$4.00	$12.50	$25.00
683	Anthology - ***Coming, Aphrodite! And Other Stories*** [1955] PBO. Photo Cover. Includes Steinbeck.	$2.50	$7.50	$15.00
684	Keene, Day - ***The Passion Murders*** [1955]	$1.50	$5.00	$10.00
685	Sterling, Stewart - ***Alibi Baby*** [1955] PBO.	$1.50	$5.00	$10.00
686	Cassill, R. V. - ***The Hungering Shame*** [1956] PBO.	$1.50	$5.00	$10.00
687	Hopson, William - ***Vegas, Gunman Marshal*** [1956] Cover by Kenyon.	$1.50	$5.00	$10.00
688	Ronns, Edward - ***The Art Studio Murders*** [1956]	$1.50	$5.00	$10.00
689	MacDonald, William Colt - ***Riders Of The Whistling Skull*** [1956]	$1.50	$5.00	$10.00
690	Christie, Agatha - ***The Big Four*** [1956]	$2.00	$6.00	$12.00
691	Daudet, Alphonse - ***Sappho*** [1956]	$1.50	$5.00	$10.00
692	James, M. E. Clifton - ***The Counterfeit General Montgomery*** [1956] Photo cover.	$1.50	$5.00	$10.00
693	Flora, Fletcher - ***The Hot-Shot*** [1956] PBO.	$2.00	$6.00	$12.00
694	Charteris, Leslie - ***The Saint—Wanted For Murder*** [1956]	$1.50	$5.00	$10.00
695	Maugham, Robin - ***The Jungle Of Love*** [1956]	$1.50	$5.00	$10.00
696	Procter, Maurice - ***Murder Somewhere In This City*** [1956]	$1.50	$5.00	$10.00
697	De Balzac, Honore - ***The Girl With The Golden Eyes*** [1956] Photo cover.	$1.50	$5.00	$10.00
698	Anthology edited by Harold Meyers - ***Smoking-Room Joke Book*** [1956]	$4.00	$12.50	$25.00
699	Cheyney, Peter - ***Counterspy Murders*** [1956]	$1.50	$5.00	$10.00
700	Whitney, Joseph - ***Mirror Of Your Mind*** [1956] PBO.	$1.35	$4.00	$8.00
701	Dinneen, Joseph F. - ***The Anatomy Of A Crime*** [1956]	$1.50	$5.00	$10.00
702	LeFanu, Joseph Sheridan - ***The Room In The Dragon Inn*** [1956]	$1.50	$5.00	$10.00
703	Kane, Henry - ***Armchair In Hell*** [1956]	$1.50	$5.00	$10.00
704	Cody, Al - ***Whiplash War*** [1956] PBO.	$1.50	$5.00	$10.00
705	Keene, Day - ***Hunt The Killer*** [1956]	$1.50	$5.00	$10.00
706	Hermann, Walter - ***Operation Intrigue*** [1956]	$1.35	$4.00	$8.00
707	Hatlo, Jimmy - ***Hatlo Cartoons - 1956*** [1956] PBO. Cover by Hatlo. Cartoon book.	$2.50	$7.50	$15.00
708	Charteris, Leslie - ***Arrest The Saint*** [1956]	$1.35	$4.00	$8.00
709	Hopson, William - ***Montana Gunslinger*** [1956]	$1.50	$5.00	$10.00

		G	VG	F
710	Cassill, R.V. - ***The Wound Of Love*** [1956]	$1.50	$5.00	$10.00
711	Wylie, Philip - ***Experiment In Crime*** [1956]	$1.35	$4.00	$8.00
712	Cheyney, Peter - ***The Man Nobody Saw*** [1956] Cover by Kinstler.	$1.50	$5.00	$10.00
713	Davis, Jada M. - ***The Outraged Sect*** [1956]	$1.50	$5.00	$10.00
714	Stout, Rex - ***The Case Of The Black Orchids*** [1956]	$1.35	$4.00	$8.00
715	Lehman, Paul Evan - ***The Vengeance Trail*** [1956]	$1.50	$5.00	$10.00
716	Christie, Agatha - ***Poirot Investigates*** [1956]	$1.35	$4.00	$8.00
717	Weiss, Joe - ***How Rough Can It Get?*** [1956] Cover by Marchetti.	$1.35	$4.00	$8.00
718	Charteris, Leslie - ***Enter The Saint*** [1956]	$1.35	$4.00	$8.00
719	Noel, Sterling - ***Few Die Well*** [1956]	$1.50	$5.00	$10.00
720	Creasey, John - ***Give A Man A Gun*** [1956]	$1.35	$4.00	$8.00
721	Wilson, Ethel - ***Lilly's Story*** [1956]	$1.35	$4.00	$8.00
722	Brown, Wenzell - ***Gang Girl*** [1956]	$2.00	$6.00	$12.00
723	Hopson, William - ***Yucca City Outlaw*** [1956] Jack Davis illustrations.	$3.00	$9.00	$18.00
724	Cody, Al - ***Empty Saddles*** [1956] Cover by Kenyon. Illustrated by Jack Davis.	$3.00	$9.00	$18.00
725	Hollis, Jim - ***The Case Of The Bludgeoned Teacher*** [1956]	$1.50	$5.00	$10.00
726	Queen, Ellery - ***The Tragedy Of Z*** [1956] Cover by Marchetti.	$1.35	$4.00	$8.00
727	Wylie, Philip - ***The Smuggled Atom Bomb*** [1956]	$1.50	$5.00	$10.00
728	Schiddel, Edmund - ***Safari To Dishonor*** [1956]	$1.35	$4.00	$8.00
729	Conrad, Harold - ***Battle At Apache Pass*** [1956] Cover by Everett Raymond Kinstler. Movie tie-in.	$1.50	$5.00	$10.00
730	Roeburt, John - ***The Case Of The Hypnotized Virgin*** [1956] Photo cover.	$1.50	$5.00	$10.00
731	Middleton, Ted - ***Operation Tokyo*** [1956] PBO. Cover by Everett Raymond Kinstler.	$1.50	$5.00	$10.00
732	Brister, Richard - ***The Kansan*** [1956] Cover by Walter Popp.	$1.35	$4.00	$8.00
733	Kane, Henry - ***Who Killed Sweet Sue?*** [1956] PBO.	$2.00	$6.00	$12.00
734	Cheyney, Peter - ***The Case Of The Dark Hero*** [1956]	$1.35	$4.00	$8.00
735	Eagle, John - ***The Hoodlums*** [1956] Cover by Kirk Wilson.	$1.50	$5.00	$10.00
736	Jay, Charlotte - ***The Yellow Turban*** [1956] Cover by Sussman.	$1.35	$4.00	$8.00
737	Thomey, Tedd - ***And Dream Of Evil*** [1956]	$2.00	$6.00	$12.00
738	Stout, Rex - ***Invitation To Murder*** [1956] Cover by Marchetti.	$1.35	$4.00	$8.00
739	Joscelyn, Archie - ***Hired Gun*** [1956]	$1.35	$4.00	$8.00
740	Shaw, Floyd - ***Park Avenue Girl*** [1956] Cover by Michael.	$1.35	$4.00	$8.00
741	Lehman, Paul Evan - ***Outlaw Loot*** [1956]	$1.35	$4.00	$8.00
742	Walsh, Paul E. - ***KKK*** [1956] PBO.	$3.00	$9.00	$18.00
743	Russell, William - ***Love Affair*** [1956]	$1.35	$4.00	$8.00
744	Charteris, Leslie - ***The Saint And The Sizzling Saboteur*** [1956]	$1.35	$4.00	$8.00
745	Kane, Henry - ***Martinis And Murder*** [1956]	$1.50	$5.00	$10.00
746	Lariar, Lawrence - ***The Girl With The Frightened Eyes*** [1956]	$1.50	$5.00	$10.00
747	Clarke, Donald Henderson - ***Tawny*** [1956]	$1.35	$4.00	$8.00
748	McCulley, Johnston - ***Gunsight Showdown*** [1956]	$1.35	$4.00	$8.00
749	Coburn, Walt - ***Violent Maverick*** [1956]	$1.35	$4.00	$8.00
750	White, Daniel - ***Southern Daughter*** [1956]	$1.50	$5.00	$10.00
751	Kane, Henry - ***Murder Of The Park Ave. Playgirl*** [1956]	$1.35	$4.00	$8.00
752	Innes, Michael - ***Death By Moonlight*** [1956]	$1.35	$4.00	$8.00
753	Matthiessen, Peter - ***The Passionate Seekers*** [1956]	$1.35	$4.00	$8.00
754	Wells, Lee E. - ***The Long Noose*** [1956]	$1.35	$4.00	$8.00
755	Nin, Anais - ***A Spy In The House Of Love*** [1956]	$1.50	$5.00	$10.00

		G	VG	F
756	Charteris, Leslie - ***The Brighter Buccaneer*** [1956]	$1.35	$4.00	$8.00
757	Simenon, Georges - ***Inspector Maigret And The Dead Girl*** [1956] Raymond Everett Kinstler cover art	$1.35	$4.00	$8.00
758	Nye, Nelson - ***Arizona Dead-Shot*** [1956]	$1.35	$4.00	$8.00
759	Lehman, Paul Evan - ***Fighting Buckaroo*** [1956]	$1.35	$4.00	$8.00
760	Gallico, Paul - ***Love Of 7 Dolls*** [1956]	$1.50	$5.00	$10.00
761	Kane, Henry - ***Death On The Double*** [1957] PBO.	$2.00	$6.00	$12.00
762	Sterling, Stewart - ***The Hotel Murders*** [1957]	$1.35	$4.00	$8.00
763	Carey, Michael - ***Vice-Squad Cop*** [1957] PBO. Cover by Nappi.	$2.00	$6.00	$12.00
764	Cheyney, Peter - ***The Dark Street Murders*** [1957]	$1.50	$5.00	$10.00
765	MacDoanld, William Colt - ***California Gunman*** [1957]	$1.35	$4.00	$8.00
766	Lockridge, Frances & Richard - ***Mr. & Mrs. North & The Poisoned Playboy*** [1957]	$1.35	$4.00	$8.00
767	Walsh, Paul E. - ***The Murder Room*** [1957]	$1.35	$4.00	$8.00
768	Cain, James M. - ***Sinful Woman*** [1957]	$1.50	$5.00	$10.00
769	MacDonald, William Colt - ***The Phantom Pass*** [1957] Cover by John Leone	$1.35	$4.00	$8.00
770	Arthur, Burt - ***Outlaw Fury*** [1957]	$1.35	$4.00	$8.00
771	Charteris, Leslie - ***The Saint On The Spanish Main*** [1957]	$1.35	$4.00	$8.00
772	Roeburt, John - ***Murder In Manhattan*** [1957]	$1.35	$4.00	$8.00
773	Friedman, Stuart - ***The Woman And The Prowler*** [1957] PBO.	$1.50	$5.00	$10.00
774	Skullin, George - ***Gunfight At The O.K. Corral*** [1957] PBO. Movie photo cover and tie-in.	$2.50	$7.50	$15.00
775	Anthology - ***The Tall T*** [1957] PBO. Includes Elmore Leonard. Movie photo cover. Movie tie-in with photos thru-out.	$3.50	$10.00	$20.00
776	Cheyney, Peter - ***Sinister Murders*** [1957] Cover by Art Sussman.	$1.35	$4.00	$8.00
777	McCary, Reed - ***Kiss And Kill*** [1957]	$1.35	$4.00	$8.00
778	Anthology - ***Tales Of Midsummer Passion*** [1956] PBO. Cover by David Stone.	$2.50	$7.50	$15.00
779	McCulley, Johnston - ***Gunsmoke Vengeance!*** [1957] Cover by Everett Raymond Kinstler.	$1.35	$4.00	$8.00
780	Turner, Robert - ***The Lonely Man*** [1957] Movie photo cover. Movie tie-in with photos thru-out.	$1.50	$5.00	$10.00
781	Mulholland, P.H. - ***Calypso Murders*** [1957] PBO.	$1.50	$5.00	$10.00
782	Peeples, Samuel Anthony - ***Gun Feud In Stampede Valley*** [1957]	$1.35	$4.00	$8.00
783	Dolinsky, Meyer - ***Hot Rod Gang Rumble*** [1957] PBO. Photos front and back cover. Movie photos thru-out. Movie tie-in.	$3.00	$9.00	$18.00
784	Waer, Jack - ***Murder In Las Vegas*** [1957] Photo cover.	$1.35	$4.00	$8.00
785	Arthur, Burt - ***Gunplay At The X Bar X*** [1957]	$1.35	$4.00	$8.00
786	Atiyah, Edward - ***Murder, My Love*** [1957]	$1.35	$4.00	$8.00
787	Dewey, Thomas B. - ***The Case Of The Murdered Model*** [1957].	$1.35	$4.00	$8.00
788	Joscelyn, Archie - ***Six-Gun Sawbones*** [1957] Cover by S. Wisnom.	$1.35	$4.00	$8.00
789	Hatlo, Jimmy - ***More They'll Do It Every Time*** [1957] PBO. Cover by Hatlo. Cartoon Book.	$2.50	$7.50	$15.00
790	Kane, Henry - ***My Business Is Murder*** [1957] Cover by Robert Maguire.	$2.00	$6.00	$12.00
791	Joscelyn, Archie - ***Texas Revenge*** [1957]	$1.35	$4.00	$8.00
792	Levey, Robert A. - ***Murder In Lima*** [1957] PBO. Cover by Art Sussman.	$1.35	$4.00	$8.00
793	Christie, Agatha - ***The Moving Finger*** [1957]	$1.35	$4.00	$8.00
794	Procter, Maurice - ***The Ripper Murders*** [1957]	$2.50	$7.50	$15.00

		G	VG	F
795	McCulley, Johnston - ***Blood On The Saddle*** [1957]	$1.35	$4.00	$8.00
796	Kane, Henry - ***Mask For Murder*** [1956]	$1.35	$4.00	$8.00
797	Cheyney, Peter - ***Cocktails And The Killer*** [1957]	$1.35	$4.00	$8.00
798	Joscelyn, Archie - ***Outlaw*** [1958] PBO.	$1.50	$5.00	$10.00
799	MacDonald, William Colt - ***Powdersmoke Range*** [1958]	$1.35	$4.00	$8.00
800	Lockridge, Frances & Richard - ***Case Of The Murdered Redhead*** [1958]	$1.35	$4.00	$8.00
801	Stuart, William L. - ***Night Cry*** [1958]	$1.50	$5.00	$10.00
802	Walsh, Paul - ***Murder In Baracoa*** [1958] PBO. Cover by Rudy Nappi.	$1.50	$5.00	$10.00
803	Charteris, Leslie - ***Featuring The Saint*** [1958]	$1.35	$4.00	$8.00
804	Arnaud, Georges - ***Flesh And Fire*** [1958] Cover by Victor Kalin.	$1.35	$4.00	$8.00
805	Lehman, Paul Evan - ***The Tough Texan*** [1958] PBO.	$1.50	$5.00	$10.00
806	Lehman, Paul Evan - ***Bandit In Black*** [1958] PBO.	$1.50	$5.00	$10.00
807	Roeburt, John - ***Wine, Women And Murder*** [1958]	$1.35	$4.00	$8.00
808	Heard, H.F. - ***A Taste For Murder*** [1958]	$1.35	$4.00	$8.00
809	Carey, Michael - ***The Vice Net*** [1958] PBO.	$1.50	$5.00	$10.00
810	Cody, Al - ***Montana Helltown*** [1958]	$1.35	$4.00	$8.00
811	Flora, Fletcher - ***Let Me Kill You, Sweetheart!*** [1958] PBO.	$1.50	$5.00	$10.00
812	Cody, Al - ***Bloody Wyoming*** [1958]	$1.35	$4.00	$8.00
813	Joscelyn, Archie - ***Fighting Kid From Texas*** [1958] PBO.	$1.50	$5.00	$10.00
814	Keene, Day - ***It's A Sin To Kill*** [1958]	$1.50	$5.00	$10.00
815	Lief, Max & Pichard, Georges - ***Bachelor's Guide To The Opposite Sex*** [1958]	$2.50	$7.50	$15.00
816	Lehman, Paul Evan - ***Thunderbolt Range*** [1958] Cover by Walker.	$1.35	$4.00	$8.00
817	Koenig, H.P. - ***The Doctor's Woman*** [1958]	$1.35	$4.00	$8.00
818	Charteris, Leslie - ***Alias The Saint*** [1958]	$1.35	$4.00	$8.00
819	Joscelyn, Archie - ***Cheyenne Kid*** [1958]	$1.35	$4.00	$8.00
820	Hogan, Robert J. - ***Stampede Canyon*** [1958]	$1.35	$4.00	$8.00
821	Coburn, Walt - ***Guns Blaze On Spiderweb Range*** [1958] Cover by Kinstler.	$1.35	$4.00	$8.00
822	Martin, Chuck - ***Montana Dead-Shot*** [1958]	$1.35	$4.00	$8.00
823	Fearing, Kenneth - ***Cry Killer!*** [1958]	$1.35	$4.00	$8.00
824	Hopson, William - ***Notched Guns*** [1958]	$1.35	$4.00	$8.00
825	Lehman, Paul Evan - ***Gun-Whipped!*** [1958] PBO.	$1.50	$5.00	$10.00
826	Hatlo, Jimmy - ***Another New Jimmy Hatlo Book*** [1958] PBO. Cover by Hatlo. Cartoon book.	$2.50	$7.50	$15.00
827	Charteris, Leslie - ***The Saint On Guard*** [1958] Cover by Victor Kalin.	$1.35	$4.00	$8.00
828	Martin, Chuck - ***Tall In The Saddle*** [1958] PBO. Cover by Abbett.	$1.50	$5.00	$10.00
829	Grinstead, J.E. - ***Hell Range In Texas*** [1958] Cover by Tom Ryan.	$1.35	$4.00	$8.00
830	Brewer, Gil - ***The Bitch*** [1958] PBO.	$2.00	$6.00	$12.00
831	Lehman, Paul Evan - ***Renegade Marshal*** [1958] Cover by Abbett.	$1.35	$4.00	$8.00
832	Cody, Al - ***Disaster Trail*** [1958] Cover by Len Goldberg.	$1.35	$4.00	$8.00
833	Brister, Richard - ***The Wolf Streak*** [1958] PBO. Cover by Mel Crair.	$1.50	$5.00	$10.00
834	Charteris, Leslie - ***Concerning The Saint*** [1958]	$1.35	$4.00	$8.00
835	Sterling, Stewart - ***Too Hot To Kill*** [1958] Cover by Darcy.	$1.35	$4.00	$8.00
836	Baxter, John - ***Unfaithful*** [1958]	$1.35	$4.00	$8.00

		G	VG	F
837	Hopson, William - ***Long Ride To Abilene*** [1958] Cover by Len Goldberg.	$1.35	$4.00	$8.00
838	Westland, Lynn - ***The Dead Ride Hard*** [1958]	$1.35	$4.00	$8.00
839	Flora, Fletcher - ***Leave Her To Hell!*** [1958] PBO.	$1.50	$5.00	$10.00
840	Anthology - ***Battle Of The Sexes*** [1958] Cartoon book.	$3.50	$10.00	$20.00
841	Martin, Chuck - ***Day Of Vengeance*** [1959] Cover by Schaare.	$1.35	$4.00	$8.00
842	Cody, Al - ***Wyoming Ambush*** [1959]	$1.35	$4.00	$8.00
843	Lehman, Paul Evan - ***Gunsmoke At Buffalo Basin*** [1959] Cover by Everett Raymond Kinstler.	$1.50	$5.00	$10.00
844	Floren, Lee - ***Deadly Draw*** [1959]	$1.35	$4.00	$8.00
845	Lehman, Paul Evan - ***The Man From The Badlands*** [1959]	$1.35	$4.00	$8.00
846	Rogers, Milton - ***Born Reckless*** [1959] PBO. Movie photo cover. Movie tie-in with Mamie Van Doren.	$2.25	$7.00	$14.00
847	Matthews, John D. - ***My Name Is Violence*** [1959] PBO.	$2.00	$6.00	$12.00
848	Charteris, Leslie - ***The Saint Cleans Up*** [1959]	$1.35	$4.00	$8.00
849	Lomax, Bliss - ***It Happened At Thunder River*** [1959]	$1.35	$4.00	$8.00
850	Lehman, Paul Evan - ***The Manhunter*** [1959]	$1.35	$4.00	$8.00
851	Anthology - ***Ship Ahoy*** [1959] Cartoon book.	$2.00	$6.00	$12.00
852	Coburn, Walt - ***Fast Gun*** [1959]	$1.35	$4.00	$8.00
853	Anthology - ***French Postcards*** [1959] Cartoon book.	$1.35	$4.00	$8.00
854	Colby, Robert - ***Make Mine Vengeance*** [1959]	$1.35	$4.00	$8.00
855	Heuman, William - ***Then Came Mulvane*** [1959]	$1.35	$4.00	$8.00
856	McCulley, Johnston - ***Bullet Law*** [1959]	$1.35	$4.00	$8.00
857	Hatlo, Jimmy - ***The Newest Jimmy Hatlo Cartoon Book*** [1959] PBO. Cover by Hatlo.	$2.50	$7.50	$15.00
858	Coburn, Walt - ***Branded*** [1959] PBO.	$1.50	$5.00	$10.00
859	Anthology - ***More All About Girls*** [1959] Cover by Bill Wenzel. Cartoon book.	$2.50	$7.50	$15.00
860	Meyers, Harold - ***Caveman Cartoons*** [1959]	$2.50	$7.50	$15.00
861	Cord, Barry - ***Six Bullets Left*** [1959]	$1.35	$4.00	$8.00
862	Shirreffs, Gordon D. - ***Renegade Lawman*** [1959]	$1.35	$4.00	$8.00
863	Martin, Chuck - ***Bloody Kansas*** [1959]	$1.35	$4.00	$8.00
864	Daniels, Norman - ***The Deadly Game*** [1959] PBO. Cover by Bob Abbett.	$1.50	$5.00	$10.00
865	MacDonald, William Colt - ***Fighting Kid From Eldorado*** [1959]	$1.35	$4.00	$8.00
866	Brewer, Gil - ***Angel*** [1959] PBO.	$2.50	$7.50	$15.00
868	Daniels, Norman - ***Lady For Sale*** [1959]	$1.35	$4.00	$8.00
869	Anthology - ***Another All About Girls Book*** [1960] PBO. Cover by Don Flowers.	$2.50	$7.50	$15.00
871	Fowler, Kenneth - ***The Range Bum*** [1960]	$1.35	$4.00	$8.00
872	Nye, Nelson - ***Long Run*** [1960] Cover by Abbett.	$1.35	$4.00	$8.00
873	Ernenwein, Leslie - ***Hell-Town In Texas*** [1960]	$1.35	$4.00	$8.00
874	Reed, Mark - ***Sinners Wild*** [1960] PBO. Cover by Victor Kalin.	$2.00	$6.00	$12.00
876	Daniels, Norman - ***Some Die Running*** [1960] PBO. Cover by Milo.	$1.50	$5.00	$10.00
877	Walker, Mort & Browne, Dik - ***Trixie*** [1960]	$1.35	$4.00	$8.00
878	Owen, Dean - ***Guns To The Sunset*** [1960]	$1.35	$4.00	$8.00

Avon Detective Mysteries. New York: Avon Books. Digest Size.

		G	VG	F
1	Anthology - ***Includes Woolrich, Starrett, Christie*** [1947] PBO.	$4.50	$14.00	$28.00
2	Williams, Herbert - editor - ***Includes Dickson, Eberhart, and others*** [1947] PBO.	$4.50	$14.00	$28.00
3	Anthology - ***Includes Rohmer, Fredric Brown*** [1947] PBO.	$5.00	$15.00	$30.00

Avon F Series. New York: Avon Publishing Co.

		G	VG	F
100	Wallach, Ira - ***The Absence Of A Cello*** [1962] Cover by Victor Kalin.	$ .65	$2.00	$4.00
101	Halsey, Margaret - ***This Demi-Paradise*** [1961] Cover by Bob Abbett.	$ .65	$2.00	$4.00
104	Wodehouse, P.G. - ***Cocktail Time*** [1961]	$ .65	$2.00	$4.00
107	Blish, James - ***A Life For The Stars*** [1961]	$ .65	$2.00	$4.00
109	Loos, Anita - ***Gentlemen Prefer Blondes*** [1961]	$ .75	$2.50	$5.00
112	Noel, Sterling - ***Empire Of Evil*** [1961] PBO. Cover by Victor Kalin.	$ .75	$2.50	$5.00
113	Burlingame, Roger - ***Scientists Behind The Inventors*** [1962]	$ .65	$2.00	$4.00
115	Author Unknown - ***The Little Friar*** [1962]	$ .65	$2.00	$4.00
116	Arthur, Burt - ***Nevada*** [1962]	$ .65	$2.00	$4.00
118	Piper, H. Beam - ***Little Fuzzy*** [1962] PBO. Cover by Victor Kalin.	$3.50	$10.00	$20.00
119	Loomis, Noel - ***Ferguson's Ferry*** [1962] PBO.	$ .65	$2.00	$4.00
120	Halleran, E.E. - ***Boot Hill Silver*** [1962]	$ .65	$2.00	$4.00
121	Slesar, Henry - ***Alfred Hitchcock Introduces A Crime For Mothers And Others*** [1962] PBO.	$1.50	$5.00	$10.00
122	Blish, James - ***The Star Dwellers*** [1962]	$ .65	$2.00	$4.00
123	Scotland, Jay (John Jakes) - ***The Veils Of Salome*** [1962] PBO.	$1.50	$5.00	$10.00
125	De Ford, Miriam Allen - ***The Overbury Affair*** [1962]	$ .65	$2.00	$4.00
126	Ketchum, Philip - ***Traitor Guns*** [1962]	$ .65	$2.00	$4.00
128	Patten, Lewis B. - ***The Scaffold At Hangman's Creek*** [1962] PBO.	$1.00	$3.00	$6.00
132	Hogan, Ray - ***Rebel In Yankee Blue*** [1962]	$ .65	$2.00	$4.00
133	Brand, Max - ***Young Doctor Kildare*** [1962]	$ .65	$2.00	$4.00
136	Author Unknown - ***Not So Dumb Animals*** [1962]	$1.35	$4.00	$8.00
137	Foreman, L.L. - ***Longrider*** [1962] Cover by George Gross.	$ .65	$2.00	$4.00
139	Stark, James - ***The Greek Virgin*** [1962] PBO. Cover by Victor Kalin.	$ .65	$2.00	$4.00
140	Giberson, Dorothy - ***The Echoing Wave*** [1962]	$ .65	$2.00	$4.00
142	Maltz, Maxwell - ***The Miracle Of Doctor MacLennon*** [1962] PBO.	$ .65	$2.00	$4.00
146	Whittington, Harry - ***69 Babylon Park*** [1962] PBO. Cover by Johnson.	$2.00	$6.00	$12.00
147	Anthology - ***Incurably Sick*** [1962] PBO. Cartoon book.	$2.50	$7.50	$15.00
149	Wormser, Richard - ***Three-Cornered War*** [1962] PBO.	$ .75	$2.50	$5.00
152	Garrison, Joan - ***Nurse Greer*** [1962]	$ .65	$2.00	$4.00
154	Anthology edited by Nelson Nye - ***They Won Their Spurs*** [1962]	$ .65	$2.00	$4.00
156	Flynn, Jay - ***The Five Faces Of Murder*** [1962] PBO. Cover by Maguire.	$1.00	$3.00	$6.00
161	Hopson, William - ***Straight From Boothill*** [1962]	$ .65	$2.00	$4.00
162	Chadwick, Joseph - ***No Land Is Free*** [1962]	$ .65	$2.00	$4.00
163	Cord, Barry - ***The Gun-Shy Kid*** [1962] Cover by Carl Hantman.	$ .65	$2.00	$4.00
164	Craig, Georgia - ***Reach For Tomorrow*** [1962] Cover by Matt Engel.	$ .65	$2.00	$4.00
165	Kane, Henry - ***Death Of A Hooker*** [1962]	$1.50	$5.00	$10.00
168	Way, Isabel Stewart - ***Nurse In Love*** [1962] PBO.	$ .65	$2.00	$4.00
171	Columbo, Pat - ***Throw Back The Little Ones*** [1963] PBO.	$ .75	$2.50	$5.00
172	Humpries, Adelaide - ***New England Nurse*** [1962] Cover by Maguire.	$ .75	$2.50	$5.00
175	Neubauer, William - ***Prison Nurse*** [1963] Cover by Maguire.	$ .75	$2.50	$5.00

No.	Title	G	VG	F
176	Carey, Michael - ***Vice-Squad Cop*** [1963]	$ .65	$2.00	$4.00
179	Sears, Jane L. - ***Las Vegas Nurse*** [1962] PBO.	$ .65	$2.00	$4.00
183	Putnam, Nina Wilcox - ***A Career For Lynn*** [1963] Cover by Maguire.	$ .75	$2.50	$5.00
185	Shirreffs, Gordon D. - ***Slaughter At Broken Bow*** [1963] PBO. Cover by George Gross.	$1.00	$3.00	$6.00
187	Arthur, Burt and Budd - ***Requiem For A Gun*** [1963] PBO. Cover by James Bama.	$1.00	$3.00	$6.00
190	Adams, Tracy - ***Washington Nurse*** [1963] PBO.	$ .65	$2.00	$4.00
192	Stout, Rex - ***Where There's A Will*** [1963]	$1.00	$3.00	$6.00
194	Gaddis, Peggy - ***The Girl Next Door*** [1963]	$ .65	$2.00	$4.00
204	Wayne, Joseph - ***Land Of Promises*** [1963]	$ .65	$2.00	$4.00
206	Noyes, Stanley - ***Rodeo Clown*** [1964]	$ .65	$2.00	$4.00
207	Way, Isabel Stewart - ***Dr. Jenny Of Timberland*** [1964] PBO.	$ .75	$2.50	$5.00
211	Maugham, Robin - ***The Servant*** [1964] Movie Tie-in. Movie photo cover.	$ .75	$2.50	$5.00
214	Shirreffs, Gordon - ***Too Tough To Die*** [1964]	$ .65	$2.00	$4.00
216	Fitzgerald, Arlene J. - ***Harbor Nurse*** [1964] PBO.	$ .65	$2.00	$4.00
217	Patten, Lewis B. - ***Ride For Vengeance*** [1964] PBO.	$ .75	$2.50	$5.00
218	Floren, Lee - ***The Tall Texan*** [1964]	$ .65	$2.00	$4.00
220	Wayne, Joseph - ***Deadman Junction*** [1964] PBO.	$ .75	$2.50	$5.00
221	Shirreffs, Gordon - ***Last Man Alive*** [1964] PBO.	$ .75	$2.50	$5.00
222	Brister, Richard - ***Renegade Brand*** [1964]	$ .65	$2.00	$4.00
223	Owen, Dean - ***The Latchy Gun*** [1964]	$ .65	$2.00	$4.00
229	Arthur, Burt and Budd - ***Action At Truxton*** [1965] PBO. Cover by Ronnie Lesser.	$ .75	$2.50	$5.00
234	Adams, Clifton - ***The Dangerous Days Of Kiowa Jones*** [1965]	$ .65	$2.00	$4.00
235	Brister, Richard - ***Law Killer*** [1965]	$ .65	$2.00	$4.00
236	Peeples, Samuel A. - ***Gun Feud At Stampede Valley*** [1965]	$ .65	$2.00	$4.00
237	Arthur, Burt - ***The Gunslinger*** [1965]	$ .65	$2.00	$4.00
238	Lawrence, Steven C. - ***Gun Fury*** [1965]	$ .65	$2.00	$4.00
239	Arthur, Burt - ***Gunsmoke In Nevada*** [1965]	$ .65	$2.00	$4.00
240	Ketchum, Philip - ***Apache Dawn*** [1965]	$ .65	$2.00	$4.00
241	Wayne, Joseph - ***The Bad Man*** [1965] Cover by James Beecham.	$ .75	$2.50	$5.00
242	MacDonald, William Colt - ***Action At Arcanum*** [1965]	$ .65	$2.00	$4.00
244	Lawrence, Steven C. - ***The Iron Marshall*** [1965]	$ .65	$2.00	$4.00

Avon Fantasy Novel. New York: Avon Books, Inc.

No.	Title	G	VG	F
1	Cummings, Ray - ***Princess Of The Atom*** [1950]	$5.00	$15.00	$30.00
2	Williamson, Jack - ***The Green Girl*** [1950] PBO.	$12.50	$37.50	$75.00

Avon Fantasy Reader. New York: Avon Books. Digest Size.

No.	Title	G	VG	F
1	Wollheim, Donald - editor - ***Includes The Power Planet by Murray Leinster*** [1947] Also Merritt, Wells, Derleth, et al.	$3.50	$10.00	$20.00
2	Wollheim, Donald - editor - ***Includes The City Of The Living Dead by Fletcher Pratt*** [1947] Also R.E. Howard, Wright, Endore, et al.	$3.50	$10.00	$20.00
3	Wollheim, Donald - editor - ***Includes Merritt, Moore, Lovecraft, et al*** [1947]	$3.50	$10.00	$20.00
4	Wollheim, Donald - editor - ***Includes The Arrhenius Horror by P. Schuyler Miller*** [1947] Also Bradbury, Van Vogt, Dunsany, et al.	$3.00	$9.00	$18.00

		G	VG	F
5	Wollheim, Donald - editor - ***Includes Scarlet Dream by C. L. Moore*** [1947] Also Bloch, Owen, Harvey, et al.	$3.50	$10.00	$20.00
6	Wollheim, Donald - editor - ***Includes The Crawling Horror by Thorp McClusky*** [1948] Also Lovecraft, Williamson, Merritt, et al.	$3.50	$10.00	$20.00
7	Wollheim, Donald - editor - ***Includes The Curse Of A Thousand Kisses by Sax Rohmer*** [1948] Also Merritt, Moore, et al.	$3.00	$9.00	$18.00
8	Wollheim, Donald - editor - ***Includes Queen Of The Black Coast by Robert E. Howard*** [1948] Also Blackwood, Lovecraft, Bradbury, et al.	$3.50	$10.00	$20.00
9	Wollheim, Donald - editor - ***Includes The Flower-Women by Clarke Ashton Smith*** [1949] Also Miller, Kleiber, Kline, et al.	$3.50	$10.00	$20.00
10	Wollheim, Donald - editor - ***Includes A Witch Shall Be Born by Robert E. Howard*** [1949] Also Lovecraft, Morgan, James, et al.	$3.50	$10.00	$20.00
11	Wollheim, Donald - editor - ***Includes Glamour by Seabury Quinn*** [1949] Also Bond, Bradbury, Stribling, et al.	$3.00	$9.00	$18.00
12	Wollheim, Donald - editor - ***Includes The Blonde Goddess Of Bal-Sagoth by Robert E. Howard*** [1950] Also Rohmer, Breuer, Smith, et al.	$3.50	$10.00	$20.00
13	Wollheim, Donald - editor - ***The Love Slave And The Scientists by Frank Belknap Long*** [1950] Also Cummings, Wetjen, Derleth, et al.	$3.50	$10.00	$20.00
14	Wollheim, Donald - editor - ***Temptress Of The Tower Of Torture And Sin by R.E. Howard*** [1950] Also Bradbury, Dwyer, Keller, et al.	$3.00	$9.00	$18.00
15	Wollheim, Donald - editor - ***A Man, A Maid, And Saturn's Temptation by Stanley Weinbaum*** [1951] Also Miller, Morgan, Breuer, et al.	$4.00	$12.50	$25.00
16	Wollheim, Donald - editor - ***Includes The Black Kiss by Robert Bloch*** [1951] Also Wandrei, Long, La Spina, et al.	$4.00	$12.50	$25.00
17	Wollheim, Donald - editor - ***Includes The Sapphire Siren by Nichtzin Dvalhis*** [1951] Also Bradbury, Lovecraft, Boucher, et al. Cover by Harry Barton.	$4.00	$12.50	$25.00
18	Wollheim, Donald - editor - ***Includes The Witch From Hell's Kitchen by Robert E. Howard*** [1952] Also Dale Clark, Heard, Blackwood, et al.	$4.00	$12.50	$25.00

Avon G Series. New York: Avon Publishing Co.

		G	VG	F
1001	Feuchtwanger, Lion - ***Jew Suss*** [1951] Cover and illos by Raymond Everett Kinstler.	$3.50	$10.00	$20.00
1002	Anthology - ***The Avon All-American Fiction Reader*** [1951] Includes James Cain.	$4.00	$12.50	$25.00
1003	Anthology - ***The Collected Works Of Pierre Louys*** [1951]	$1.50	$5.00	$10.00
1004	Anthology - ***Giant Mystery Reader*** [1951] PBO. Includes J. D. Carr, Christie, Hammett & Bradbury.	$4.00	$12.50	$25.00
G-1005	Willingham, Calder - ***Geraldine Bradshaw*** [1951]	$1.50	$5.00	$10.00
G-1006	Anthology edited by Ernest Hemingway - ***Men At War*** [1951] Photo cover.	$1.50	$5.00	$10.00
G-1007	Dictionary - ***Avon Webster English Dictionary*** [1951]	$5.50	$17.50	$35.00
G-1008	Pen, John - ***Temptation*** [1951]	$2.50	$7.50	$15.00
G-1009	Shulman, Irving - ***The Big Brokers*** [1951]	$ .75	$2.50	$5.00
G-1010	Thomas, Jr., Lowell - ***Out Of This World To Forbidden Tibet*** [1951]	$ .75	$2.50	$5.00

		G	VG	F
G-1011	O'Neal, Cothburn - ***Master Of The World*** [1951]	$ .75	$2.50	$5.00
G-1012	Steig, Henry - ***Send Me Down*** [1951]	$ .75	$2.50	$5.00
G-1013	Zola, Emile - ***The Human Beast*** [1951]	$1.00	$3.00	$6.00
G-1014	Celine, Louis-Ferdinand - ***Journey To The End Of The Night*** [1951]	$ .75	$2.50	$5.00
G-1015	Preedy, George - ***Queen's Caprice*** [1951]	$ .75	$2.50	$5.00
G-1016	Phillips, William & Rahr, Philip - editor - ***Avon Book Of Modern Writing #2*** [1951]	$ .65	$2.00	$4.00
G-1017	Weidman, Jerome - ***The Third Angel*** [1951] Cover by Hulings	$ .75	$2.50	$5.00
G-1018	Anthology - ***The Collected Works Of Pierre Louys*** [1951]	$ .75	$2.50	$5.00
G-1019	Pen, John - ***Temptation*** [1951]	$ .75	$2.50	$5.00
G-1020	Huxley, Aldous - ***Point Counter Point*** [1955]	$ .75	$2.50	$5.00
G-1021	Lawrence, D. H. - ***Women In Love*** [1951]	$ .75	$2.50	$5.00
G-1022	Celine, Louis-Ferdinand - ***Death On The Installment Plan*** [1955]	$ .65	$2.00	$4.00
G-1023	Shulman, Irving - ***The Big Brokers*** [1955]	$ .65	$2.00	$4.00
G-1024	Dostoyevsky, Fyodor - ***Crime And Punishment*** [1956] Cover by Lynd Ward.	$1.00	$3.00	$6.00
G-1025	Lawrence, D. H. - ***Aaron's Rod*** [1956]	$ .75	$2.50	$5.00
G-1026	Weidman, Jerome - ***Your Daughter Iris*** [1956]	$ .65	$2.00	$4.00
G-1027	Huxley, Aldous - ***Those Barren Leaves*** [1957]	$ .75	$2.50	$5.00
G-1028	Lawrence, D. H. - ***The Rainbow*** [1957]	$ .75	$2.50	$5.00
G-1029	Pennell, Joseph - ***Dishonored Flesh: The History Of Rome Hanks*** [1957]	$ .65	$2.00	$4.00
G-1030	O'Neal, Cothburn - ***Conquests Of Tamerlane*** [1957]	$ .65	$2.00	$4.00
G-1031	Huxley, Aldous - ***Point Counter Point*** [1957]	$ .75	$2.50	$5.00
G-1032	Weidman, Jerome - ***The Third Angel*** [1957]	$ .75	$2.50	$5.00
G-1033	Pen, John - ***Temptation*** [1957]	$ .65	$2.00	$4.00
G-1034	Agee, James - ***A Death In The Family*** [1959]	$ .65	$2.00	$4.00
G-1035	Kerouac, Jack - ***Maggie Cassidy*** [1959] PBO.	$3.00	$9.00	$18.00
G-1036	Pasternak, Boris - ***The Last Summer*** [1959] Cover by V. Konashevich	$ .65	$2.00	$4.00
G-1037	Graves, Robert - ***They Hanged My Saintly Billy*** [1959]	$1.50	$5.00	$10.00
G-1038	Lawrence, D. H. - ***The Rainbow*** [1959]	$ .75	$2.50	$5.00
G-1039	Lawrence, D. H. - ***Aaron's Rod*** [1959]	$ .75	$2.50	$5.00
G-1040	Anthology edited by George Reavey - ***14 Great Short Stories By Soviet Authors*** [1959] PBO. Cover by Victor Kalin	$1.00	$3.00	$6.00
G-1041	Gerson, Noel B. - ***Daughter Of Eve*** [1959]	$1.00	$3.00	$6.00
G-1042	Tarkington, Booth - ***The Magnificent Ambersons*** [1959]	$ .75	$2.50	$5.00
G-1043	Hersey, John - ***A Bell For Adano*** [1959] Cover by Avati	$1.00	$3.00	$6.00
G-1045	Ferber, Edna - ***So Big*** [1959]	$ .65	$2.00	$4.00
G-1046	Pearson, William - ***A Fever In The Blood*** [1959] Cover by Gregori.	$ .65	$2.00	$4.00
G-1047	West, Mae - ***Goodness Had Nothing To Do With It*** [1959] Mae West photo cover	$ .75	$2.50	$5.00
G-1048	Coulter, Stephen - ***Damned Shall Be Desire*** [1959]	$ .65	$2.00	$4.00
G-1049	Weidman, Jerome - ***The Third Angel*** [1959] Cover by Avati	$1.00	$3.00	$6.00
G-1050	Lansing, A. - ***Endurance*** [1959]	$ .65	$2.00	$4.00
G-1051	Glasgow, Ellen - ***In This Our Life*** [1959]	$ .65	$2.00	$4.00
S-1053A	Fadiman, Clifton - ***Any Number Can Play*** [1959]	$ .65	$2.00	$4.00
G-1054	Keyes, Frances Parkinson - ***Station Wagon In Spain*** [1959]	$ .65	$2.00	$4.00
G-1055	Chidsey, Donald Barr - ***Captain Adam*** [1959]	$ .75	$2.50	$5.00
G-1059	Huxley, Aldous - ***Those Barren Leaves*** [1959]	$ .75	$2.50	$5.00

		G	VG	F
G-1060	Hearst, Considine & Conniff - ***Khrushchev And The Russian Challenge*** [1959] Photo cover.	$ .75	$2.50	$5.00
G-1063	Burns, James MacGregor - ***John Kennedy: A Political Profile*** [1959] Photo cover.	$ .65	$2.00	$4.00
G-1064	Sanders, George - ***Memoirs Of A Professional Cad*** [1960] Cover by Norkin.	$ .65	$2.00	$4.00
G-1065	Guttmacher, M.D., Alan F. - ***Babies By Choice Or By Chance*** [1961] Cover by Hampshire.	$ .65	$2.00	$4.00
G-1066	Mesta, Perle (as told to Robert Cahn) - ***Perle*** [1961]	$ .65	$2.00	$4.00
G-1067	Robinson, Anthony - ***A Departure From The Rules*** [1960]	$ .65	$2.00	$4.00
G-1068	Dempsey, Jack - ***Dempsey*** [1960] Photo cover.	$1.25	$3.75	$7.50
G-1070	Flavin, Martin - ***Journey In The Dark*** [1960]	$ .65	$2.00	$4.00
G-1071	Orwell, George - ***A Clergyman's Daughter*** [1960] Cover by Leibman.	$ .75	$2.50	$5.00
G-1072	Gallup, Dr. George & Hill, Evan - ***The Secrets Of Long Life*** [1960]	$ .65	$2.00	$4.00
G-1073	Treece, Henry - ***The Master Of Badger's Hall*** [1960] Cover by James Meese.	$ .75	$2.50	$5.00
G-1077	Livingston, Belle - ***Belle Out Of Order*** [1960] Cover by Gregori.	$ .65	$2.00	$4.00
G-1078	Le Comte, Edward - ***He And She*** [1960] Cover by McGinnis.	$1.00	$3.00	$6.00
G-1079	Chidsey, Donald Barr - ***The Iron Cavalier*** [1960]	$ .65	$2.00	$4.00
G-1081	Keyes, Frances Parkinson - ***Fielding's Folly*** [1960] Cover by Meese.	$ .65	$2.00	$4.00
G-1082	Ham, Jr., Roswell G. - ***A Peak In Darien*** [1960] Cover by McGinnis.	$1.00	$3.00	$6.00
G-1087	Wright, Richard - ***Eight Men*** [1960]	$ .65	$2.00	$4.00
G-1088	Miller, Caroline - ***Lamb In His Bosom*** [1960]	$ .65	$2.00	$4.00
G-1091	Christian, Paula - ***Love Is Where You Find It*** [1961]	$ .65	$2.00	$4.00
G-1092	Herbert, Frank - ***21st Century Sub*** [1961] Cover by Art Sussman.	$ .65	$2.00	$4.00
G-1094	Wilson, Margaret - ***The Able McLaughlins*** [1961]	$ .65	$2.00	$4.00
G-1096	Simak, Clifford - ***The Worlds Of Clifford Simak*** [1962] Cover by Richard Powers.	$1.00	$3.00	$6.00
G-1099	D'Allard, Hunter (W. T. Ballard) - ***The Long Sword*** [1962] PBO. Cover by James Meese.	$1.00	$3.00	$6.00
G-1100	Gallagher, Richard F. - ***Women Without Morals*** [1962] PBO.	$ .75	$2.50	$5.00
G-1101	Bennett, Adrian - ***My Lovely Adele*** [1962]	$ .65	$2.00	$4.00
G-1109	Johnson, Josephine - ***Now In November*** [1962]	$ .65	$2.00	$4.00
G-1110	Abby, Alain - ***Libido Beach*** [1962] PBO. Cover by Binger.	$1.50	$5.00	$10.00
G-1111	Clausen, C. - ***I Love You Honey, But*** [1962]	$ .65	$2.00	$4.00
G-1116	Mead, Shepherd - ***Four Window Girl!*** [1962]	$ .75	$2.50	$5.00
G-1119	Jessel, George - ***Elegy In Manhattan*** [1962]	$ .65	$2.00	$4.00
G-1120	Leinster, Murray - ***Talents Incorporated*** [1962] PBO.	$1.25	$3.75	$7.50
G-1121	Siegel, Benjamin - ***A Kind Of Justice*** [1962]	$ .65	$2.00	$4.00
G-1122	Poole, Ernest - ***His Family*** [1962]	$ .65	$2.00	$4.00
G-1124	Anthology - ***Other Worlds Of Simak*** [1962] Cover by Powers.	$1.25	$3.75	$7.50
G-1125	Fox, Gardner, F. - ***Tom Blood, Highwayman*** [1962] PBO.	$1.50	$5.00	$10.00
G-1127	Anderson, Paul - ***Three Hearts And Three Lions*** [1962]	$2.00	$6.00	$12.00
G-1129	Mead, Shepherd - ***The Big Ball Of Wax*** [1962]	$ .75	$2.50	$5.00
G-1132	Taylor, Robert Lewis - ***Adrift In A Boneyard*** [1962]	$1.00	$3.00	$6.00
G-1134	Kirk, Russell - ***Old House Of Fear*** [1962]	$1.25	$3.75	$7.50
G-1137	Cox, Wally - ***My Life As A Small Boy*** [1962] PBO	$ .75	$2.50	$5.00

		G	VG	F
G-1138	Harwood, Ronald - ***George Washington September, Sir!*** [1962] Cover by Dillons.	$ .65	$2.00	$4.00
G-1143	MacLean, Katherine - ***The Diploids*** [1962] PBO.	$1.50	$5.00	$10.00
G-1144	Coughlan, Robert - ***The Private World Of William Faulkner*** [1962]	$ .75	$2.50	$5.00
G-1146	Farrell, Henry - ***What Ever Happened To Baby Jane?*** [1962] Movie tie-in and photo cover.	$1.35	$4.00	$8.00
G-1147	Purdy, James - ***The Nephew*** [1963] Cover by Powers.	$ .65	$2.00	$4.00
G-1148	Tiempo, E.K. - ***Cry Slaughter!*** [1963]	$ .65	$2.00	$4.00
G-1149	Farrington, Robert - ***Balboa*** [1963] PBO. Cover by Meese.	$ .75	$2.50	$5.00
G-1152	Singer, Isaac B. - ***Spinoza Of Market Street*** [1963]	$ .65	$2.00	$4.00
G-1153	Howe, Helen - ***The Whole Heart*** [1963] Cover by Hoyle.	$ .65	$2.00	$4.00
G-1154	Smith, George O. - ***Space Plague*** [1963]	$ .75	$2.50	$5.00
G-1155	Simms, John - ***Gibral-Taric*** [1963] PBO.	$ .75	$2.50	$5.00
G-1156	Lyon, Peter - ***The U. N. In Action*** [1963]	$ .65	$2.00	$4.00
G-1157	Farrell, Henry - ***Death On the 6th Day*** [1963]	$ .65	$2.00	$4.00
G-1159	Anthology edited by Anthony Boucher - ***The Quintessence Of Ellery Queen*** [1963]	$1.35	$4.00	$8.00
G-1164	Ketchum, Philip - ***Woman In Armor*** [1963] PBO. Cover by Barye Phillips.	$ .75	$2.50	$5.00
G-1165	Unknown - ***The Iron Ring*** [1963]	$ .65	$2.00	$4.00
G-1166	Aylesworth, John - ***Fee, Fei, Fo, Fum*** [1963] PBO.	$1.00	$3.00	$6.00
G-1167	Maddox, Gaynor - ***Slim Down, Shape Up Diets For Teen-Agers*** [1963] PBO. Photo cover.	$ .65	$2.00	$4.00
G-1168	Clement, Hal - ***From Outer Space*** [1963]	$ .75	$2.50	$5.00
G-1169	Sakol, Jeanne - ***What About Teen-Age Marriage?*** [1963] Photo cover.	$ .65	$2.00	$4.00
G-1170	Raven, Simon - ***Doctors Wear Scarlet*** [1963]	$ .65	$2.00	$4.00
G-1171	Singer, Isaac B. - ***Satan In Goray*** [1963] Cover by Dillons.	$ .75	$2.50	$5.00
G-1173	Dietrich, Marlene - ***Marlene Dietrich's ABC*** [1963]	$ .75	$2.50	$5.00
G-1175	Kendrick, Baynard - ***Hot Red Money*** [1963]	$ .75	$2.50	$5.00
G-1177	Van Gulik, Robert - ***The Chinese Bell Murders*** [1963]	$ .65	$2.00	$4.00
G-1178	Anthology edited by Charles M. Collins - ***Fright*** [1963] PBO. Includes Lovecraft.	$1.25	$3.75	$7.50
G-1179	Christopher, John - ***The White Voyage*** [1963]	$ .75	$2.50	$5.00
G-1180	Peters, Ellis - ***Death And The Joyful Woman*** [1963]	$ .75	$2.50	$5.00
G-1181	Wyden, Peter - ***Suburbia's Coddled Kids*** [1963] Photo cover.	$ .65	$2.00	$4.00
G-1183	Fish, Robert - ***The Fugitive*** [1963]	$ .75	$2.50	$5.00
G-1184	Sayers, Dorothy L. - ***The Unpleasantness At The Bellona Club*** [1963]	$ .65	$2.00	$4.00
G-1185	Henderson, Zenna - ***Pilgrimage: The Book Of The People*** [1963]	$1.35	$4.00	$8.00
G-1186	Lawrence, R. T. - ***The Journal Of Kitty Adair*** [1963] PBO. Cover by Victor Kalin.	$ .65	$2.00	$4.00
G-1189	Farrell, H. - ***The Hostage*** [1963]	$ .65	$2.00	$4.00
G-1191	Wormser, Richard - ***Pan Satyrus*** [1963] PBO. Cover by Powers.	$1.00	$3.00	$6.00
G-1192	Merritt, A. - ***Seven Footprints To Satan*** [1963]	$1.35	$4.00	$8.00
G-1193	Head, Matthew - ***The Devil In The Bush*** [1963] Cover by Roy La Grone.	$1.25	$3.75	$7.50
G-1195	Van Gulik, Robert - ***The Chinese Lake Murders*** [1963] Cover by Joseph Lombardero.	$ .75	$2.50	$5.00
G-1197	Haggard, William - ***The Unquiet Sleep*** [1963] Cover by Victor Kalin.	$ .75	$2.50	$5.00
G-1199	Aylesworth, John B. - ***Fee Fei Fo Fum*** [1963]	$1.00	$3.00	$6.00

		G	VG	F
G-1203	Fay, Jerry - ***The Clampetts Of Beverly Hills*** [1964] PBO. TV tie-in with photo cover.	$2.50	$7.50	$15.00
G-1211	Heinlein, Robert - ***Podkayne Of Mars*** [1963] Cover by Lehr.	$1.25	$3.75	$7.50
G-1214	MacKenzie, Donald - ***I, Spy*** [1963] Photo cover.	$ .75	$2.50	$5.00
G-1218	Webb, Jack - ***One For My Dame*** [1964]	$1.00	$3.00	$6.00
G-1219	Van Gulik, Robert - ***The Chinese Mail Murders*** [1964]	$ .75	$2.50	$5.00
G-1220	Piper, H. Beam - ***The Other Human Race*** [1964] PBO	$2.00	$6.00	$12.00
G-1221	Vance, Louis Joseph - ***The Lone Wolf*** [1964] Cover by Saul Lambert.	$ .65	$2.00	$4.00
G-1222	Johnson, Nora - ***The World Of Henry Orient*** [1964]	$ .65	$2.00	$4.00
G-1224	Maugham, W. Somerset - ***Ashenden: The British Agent*** [1964]	$ .65	$2.00	$4.00
G-1227	Lewis, Irwin - ***The Day They Invaded New York*** [1964] PBO.	$1.00	$3.00	$6.00
G-1229	Head, Matthew - ***The Smell Of Money*** [1964]	$ .75	$2.50	$5.00
G-1230	Ellis, George - ***The Richer They Are...*** [1964] PBO	$ .75	$2.50	$5.00
G-1231	Holly, J. Hunter - ***The Time Twisters*** [1964] PBO.	$1.00	$3.00	$6.00
G-1233	Masur, Harold Q. - ***Tall, Dark And Deadly*** [1964]	$ .75	$2.50	$5.00
G-1235	Vance, Louis Joseph - ***The False Faces*** [1964]	$ .65	$2.00	$4.00
G-1237	Cooper, Morton - ***The Munsters*** [1964] PBO. TV tie-in with photo cover.	$3.00	$9.00	$18.00
G-1239	Waugh, Hillary - ***Born Victim*** [1964]	$ .65	$2.00	$4.00
G-1240	Hirschberg, Cornelius - ***Florentine Finish*** [1964]	$ .65	$2.00	$4.00
G-1241	Fish, Robert L. - ***Isle Of The Snakes*** [1964]	$ .65	$2.00	$4.00
G-1242	Arthur, Burt - ***Freedom Run*** [1964]	$ .65	$2.00	$4.00
G-1243	Kauffmann, Lane - ***The Perfectionist*** [1964]	$ .65	$2.00	$4.00
G-1246	Fenwick, Elizabeth - ***The Make Believe Man*** [1964] Photo cover.	$ .65	$2.00	$4.00
G-1247	Innes, Michael - ***The Man From The Sea*** [1964]	$ .65	$2.00	$4.00
G-1248	Asimov, Isaac - ***Second Foundation*** [1964]	$ .65	$2.00	$4.00
G-1249	Cleeve, Brian - ***Death Of A Painted Lady*** [1964]	$ .65	$2.00	$4.00
G-1251	Sentner, David - ***How The F.B.I. Gets Its Man*** [1965] PBO	$ .75	$2.50	$5.00
G-1252	Head, Matthew - ***The Accomplice*** [1965]	$ .75	$2.50	$5.00
G-1254	Anthology - ***Boris Karloff's Favorite Horror Stories*** [1965] PBO.	$1.50	$5.00	$10.00
G-1255	Williams, Charles - ***Dead Calm*** [1965] Cover by Bill Johnson.	$ .65	$2.00	$4.00
G-1256	MacDonald, Philip - ***Murder Gone Mad*** [1965]	$ .65	$2.00	$4.00
G-1257	MacDonald, Philip - ***The Rasp*** [1965]	$ .65	$2.00	$4.00
G-1259	Masur, Harold Q. - ***Make A Killing*** [1965]	$ .65	$2.00	$4.00
G-1260	Stevenson, D. E. - ***Bel Lamington*** [1965] Cover by Lorraine Fox.	$ .65	$2.00	$4.00
G-1261	Head, Matthew - ***Congo Venus*** [1965] Cover by Hans Zander.	$ .65	$2.00	$4.00
G-1262	Kirk, Russell - ***Old House Of Fear*** [1965]	$ .75	$2.50	$5.00
G-1264	MacDonald, Philip - ***The Rynox Murder*** [1965]	$ .65	$2.00	$4.00
G-1266	Fish, Robert L. - ***The Shrunken Head*** [1965] Cover by Barbara Koontz.	$1.00	$3.00	$6.00
G-1268	Blish, James - ***The Star Dwellers*** [1965]	$ .75	$2.50	$5.00
G-1269	Molloy, Paul - ***A Pennant For The Kremlin*** [1965]	$ .65	$2.00	$4.00
G-1273	Innes, Michael - ***One Man Show*** [1965]	$ .65	$2.00	$4.00
G-1274	Burlingame, Roger - ***Scientists Behind The Inventors*** [1965] Photo cover.	$ .65	$2.00	$4.00
G-1276	Pentecost, Hugh - ***The Tarnished Angel*** [1965] Cover by Pucci.	$ .65	$2.00	$4.00
G-1277	Webb, Jack - ***Make My Bed Soon*** [1965] Cover by Ronnie Lesser.	$ .75	$2.50	$5.00

		G	VG	F
G-1278	Anthology edited by William F. Nolan - ***Man Against Tomorrow*** [1965] PBO.	$1.00	$3.00	$6.00
G-1280	Blish, James - ***A Life For The Stars*** [1965]	$ .75	$2.50	$5.00
G-1281	Jay, Charlotte - ***Beat Not The Bones*** [1965] Cover by Ronnie Lesser.	$ .75	$2.50	$5.00
G-1282	Weber, Rubin - ***The Grave-Maker's House*** [1965] Cover by Don Crowley	$ .75	$2.50	$5.00
G-1283	McGerr, Patricia - ***Is There A Traitor In The House?*** [1965] Cover by Ronnie Lesser.	$ .65	$2.00	$4.00
G-1285	Stout, Rex - ***Where There's A Will*** [1965]	$1.00	$3.00	$6.00
G-1286	Forbes, Stanton - ***Grieve For The Past*** [1965] Cover by Hector Garrido.	$ .75	$2.50	$5.00
G-1288	Waugh, Hillary - ***Death And Circumstance*** [1966] Cover by Ronnie Lesser.	$ .75	$2.50	$5.00
G-1289	Marlowe, Hugh - ***Passage By Night*** [1966]	$ .65	$2.00	$4.00
G-1290	Creasey, John - ***Blood Red*** [1966] Cover by Bob Abbett.	$ .75	$2.50	$5.00
G-1291	Creasey, John - ***Deaf, Dumb And Blonde*** [1966] Cover by Bob Abbett.	$ .75	$2.50	$5.00
G-1292	Lathen, E. - ***Accounting For Murder*** [1965]	$ .75	$2.50	$5.00
G-1294	Lutz, Giles - ***The Golden Land*** [1966]	$ .65	$2.00	$4.00
G-1295	Meynell, L. - ***Virgin Luck*** [1966]	$ .65	$2.00	$4.00
G-1296	Creasey, John - ***If Anything Happens To Hester*** [1966] Cover by Bob Abbett	$ .65	$2.00	$4.00
G-1297	Creasey, John - ***The Double Frame*** [1966] Cover by Bob Abbett.	$ .65	$2.00	$4.00
G-1298	Field, Della - ***Vietnam Nurse*** [1966] PBO. Cover by Mort Rosenberg.	$ .65	$2.00	$4.00
G-1299	Rios, Tere - ***The Fifteenth Pelican*** [1966]	$ .65	$2.00	$4.00
G-1300	MacDonald, William Colt - ***Stir Up The Dust*** [1966]	$ .65	$2.00	$4.00
G-1301	Tucker, Wilson - ***Wild Talent*** [1966] Photo cover.	$1.35	$4.00	$8.00
G-1302	Chase, James Hadley - ***No Orchids For Miss Blandish*** [1966] Photo cover.	$1.35	$4.00	$8.00
G-1304	Creasey, John - ***The Baron And The Chinese Puzzle*** [1967] Cover by Bob Abbett	$1.00	$3.00	$6.00
G-1306	Leinster, Murray - ***The Wailing Asteroid*** [1966] Cover by Paul Lehr.	$1.00	$3.00	$6.00
G-1307	Avallone, Michael - ***The Man From Avon*** [1967] PBO. Cover by Stan Borack.	$1.25	$3.75	$7.50
G-1308	Kenyon, Larry - ***Challenge At Le Mans*** [1967] PBO. Cover by Don Stivers.	$ .65	$2.00	$4.00
G-1309	Olsen, Theodore V. - ***The Stalking Moon*** [1967] Cover by James Beecham. Movie tie-in.	$1.25	$3.75	$7.50
G-1310	Leinster, Murray - ***Miners In The Sky*** [1967] PBO. Cover by Paul Lehr.	$1.00	$3.00	$6.00
G-1311	Jones, Philip - ***The Month Of The Pearl*** [1966] Cover by Hector Garrido.	$ .65	$2.00	$4.00
G-1312	Alter, Robert Edmond - ***The Red Fathom*** [1967] PBO. Cover by Bill Johnson.	$ .65	$2.00	$4.00
G-1313	Duerrenmatt, Friedrich - ***The Pledge*** [1967] Cover by Milton Charles.	$ .65	$2.00	$4.00
G-1315	Lewis, Irwin - ***The Day New York Trembled*** [1967] PBO.	$1.00	$3.00	$6.00
G-1316	Kenyon, Larry - ***Countdown At Monaco*** [1967]	$ .65	$2.00	$4.00
G-1318	Leinster, Murray - ***Space Gypsies*** [1967] PBO. Cover by Paul Lehr.	$1.00	$3.00	$6.00

		G	VG	F
G-1319	Fitzgerald, Arlene J. - ***Volunteer Nurse*** [1967] PBO. Cover by Mort Rosenfeld.	$ .65	$2.00	$4.00
G-1321	Kenyon, Larry - ***Revenge At Indy*** [1967]	$ .65	$2.00	$4.00
G-1322	Whitaker, David - ***Doctor Who In An Exciting Adventure With The Daleks*** [1967] TV tie-in with BBC and photo cover.	$1.50	$5.00	$10.00
G-1324	Kenyon, Larry - ***The Devil's Ring*** [1967] PBO. Cover by Don Stivers.	$1.00	$3.00	$6.00
G-1325	Coburn, Walt - ***La Jornada*** [1967] Cover by James Beecham.	$1.00	$3.00	$6.00
G-1334	Heckelmann, Charles N. - ***The Glory Riders*** [1967] PBO. Cover by James Beecham.	$1.00	$3.00	$6.00
G-1335	Shirreffs, Gordon D. - ***Five Graves To Boot Hill*** [1968] PBO. Cover by Thomas Beecham.	$1.00	$3.00	$6.00
G-1337	Halleran, E. E. - ***Boot Hill Silver*** [1968] Cover by James Beecham.	$ .75	$2.50	$5.00

Avon H Series. New York: Avon Book Company.

		G	VG	F
100	Lutz, Giles A. - ***The Honyocker*** [1960]	$ .65	$2.00	$4.00
101	Davidson, Lionel - ***Night Of Wenceslas*** [1960] Cover art by Bill Johnson.	$ .75	$2.50	$5.00
102	Dutourd, Jean - ***A Dog's Head*** [1960] Cover art by Bob Abbett.	$1.00	$3.00	$6.00
103	Pentecost, Hugh - ***The Cannibal Who Overate*** [1960]	$ .65	$2.00	$4.00
107	Blish, James - ***Life For the Stars*** [1960]	$ .75	$2.50	$5.00
108	Carr, John Dickson - ***It Walks By Night*** [1960] Cover art by Paul Bacon Studio.	$1.25	$3.75	$7.50

Avon Home Gardener. New York: Avon Book Company. Digest Size.

		G	VG	F
NO#	Halliday, Dean - ***Collection*** [1952] PBO. One shot. Color illos. on every page.	$4.00	$12.50	$25.00

Avon If You Were Born Series. New York: Avon Readers Guild, Inc.

		G	VG	F
NN-1	Anthology - ***If You Were Born In January*** [1952] Similar to Dell Ten Cent editions in size and format. 10 cent cover price.	$2.50	$7.50	$15.00
NN-2	Anthology - ***If You Were Born In February*** [1952]	$2.50	$7.50	$15.00
NN-3	Anthology - ***If You Were Born In March*** [1952]	$2.50	$7.50	$15.00
NN-4	Anthology - ***If You Were Born In April*** [1952]	$2.50	$7.50	$15.00
NN-5	Anthology - ***If You Were Born In May*** [1952]	$2.50	$7.50	$15.00
NN-6	Anthology - ***If You Were Born In June*** [1952]	$2.50	$7.50	$15.00
NN-7	Anthology - ***If You Were Born In July*** [1952]	$2.50	$7.50	$15.00
NN-8	Anthology - ***If You Were Born In August*** [1952]	$2.50	$7.50	$15.00
NN-9	Anthology - ***If You Were Born In September*** [1952]	$2.50	$7.50	$15.00
NN-10	Anthology - ***If You Were Born In October*** [1952]	$2.50	$7.50	$15.00
NN-11	Anthology - ***If You Were Born In November*** [1952]	$2.50	$7.50	$15.00
NN-12	Anthology - ***If You Were Born In December*** [1952]	$2.50	$7.50	$15.00

Avon Love Book Monthly. New York: Avon Book Company. Digest Size.

		G	VG	F
1	Holland, Marty - ***Blonde Baggage*** [1949]	$6.00	$20.00	$40.00
2	Winslow, Thyra Samter - ***Chorus Girl*** [1949]	$5.50	$17.50	$35.00

Avon Modern Short Story Monthly. New York: Avon Books. Digest Size.

		G	VG	F
1	Maugham, W. Somerset - ***Cosmopolitans: Twenty-Nine Short Stories*** [1943]	$1.25	$3.75	$7.50
2	O'Hara, John - ***Files On Parade: Thirty Five Short Stories*** [1954]	$1.00	$3.00	$6.00
3	Coward, Noel - ***To Step Aside—Seven Long Short Stories*** [1943]	$1.00	$3.00	$6.00

		G	VG	F
4	Saroyan, William - ***From Inhale & Exhale: Thirty-One Selected Stories*** [1943]	$1.00	$3.00	$6.00
5	Hilton, James - ***Ill Wind: Nine Stories With A Single Thread*** [1943]	$1.00	$3.00	$6.00
6	Lewis, Sinclair - ***Selected Short Storeis*** [1943]	$1.00	$3.00	$6.00
7	Anthology - ***14 Great Stories by 14 Great Authors*** [1943]	$1.00	$3.00	$6.00
8	Maugham, W. Somerset - ***First Person Singular*** [1943]	$1.00	$3.00	$6.00
9	Steinbeck, John - ***13 Great Short Stories From The Long Valley*** [1943] PBO.	$2.50	$7.50	$15.00
10	Farrell, James T. - ***Fifteen Selected Stories*** [1943]	$1.00	$3.00	$6.00
11	Hecht, Ben - ***11 Selected Great Stories*** [1943]	$1.00	$3.00	$6.00
12	Saroyan, William - ***34 More Great Stories*** [1943]	$1.00	$3.00	$6.00
13	Bromfield, Louis - ***Three Short Novels From Here Today And Gone Tomorrow*** [1944]	$1.00	$3.00	$6.00
14	Caldwell, Erskine - ***22 Great Modern Short Stories From Jackpot*** [1944]	$1.00	$3.00	$6.00
15	Anthology - ***Thirteen Great Modern Stories*** [1944] PBO.	$1.00	$3.00	$6.00
16	Hurst, Fannie - ***8 Long Short Storries From "We Are Ten"*** [1944]	$1.00	$3.00	$6.00
17	Wolfe, Thomas - ***Stories*** [1944]	$1.25	$3.75	$7.50
18	Maugham, W. Somerset - ***Ah King And Other Romance Stories Of The Tropics*** [1944]	$1.00	$3.00	$6.00
19	Ferber, Edna - ***They Brought Their Woman: Sophisticated Short Stories*** [1949]	$1.00	$3.00	$6.00
20	Anthology - ***Twelve Great Modern Stories*** [1944] PBO.	$1.50	$5.00	$10.00
21	Farrell, James T. - ***Twelve Great Stories*** [1945]	$1.00	$3.00	$6.00
22	Cain, James M. - ***Career In C Major And Other Stories*** [1945]	$3.00	$9.00	$18.00
23	Buck, Pearl S. - ***The First Wife And Other Stories*** [1945]	$1.00	$3.00	$6.00
24	Bromfield, Louis - ***Five Long Short Stories From "It Takes All Kinds"*** [1945]	$1.00	$3.00	$6.00
25	Anthology - ***Ten Great Stories*** [1945] PBO.	$1.50	$5.00	$10.00
26	Hecht, Ben - ***Stories From 1001 Afternoons In New York*** [1945]	$1.00	$3.00	$6.00
27	Runyon, Damon - ***Ten Hilarious Stories*** [1945]	$1.00	$3.00	$6.00
28	Anthology - ***Twelve Great Stories*** [1946] includes Hammett, Steinbeck.	$1.25	$3.75	$7.50
29	O'Hara, John - ***Hope Of Heaven And Other Stories*** [1946]	$1.00	$3.00	$6.00
30	Caldwell, Erskine - ***Georgia Boy And Other Stories*** [1946]	$1.00	$3.00	$6.00
31	Anthology - ***Twelve Great Stories*** [1946] includes Steinbeck, Christie	$1.25	$3.75	$7.50
32	Shaw, Irwin - ***Welcome To The City And Other Stories*** [1946]	$1.00	$3.00	$6.00
33	Anthology - ***Famous Short Stories*** [1946]	$1.00	$3.00	$6.00
34	Bromfield, Louis - ***Great Stories*** [1946]	$1.00	$3.00	$6.00
35	Maugham, W. Somerset - ***The Trembling Of A Leaf*** [1946]	$1.50	$5.00	$10.00
36	Sabatini, Rafael - ***Stories Of Love And Adventure*** [1947] Cover art by Emerson Winter.	$1.50	$5.00	$10.00
37	Hecht, Ben - ***Concerning A Woman Of Sin And Other Stories*** [1947] Cover art by Doyle.	$1.50	$5.00	$10.00
38	Maugham, W. Somerset - ***Stories Of Love And Intrigue From The Mixture As Before*** [1947]	$1.50	$5.00	$10.00
39	O'Hara, John - ***Stories From "Pipe Night"*** [1947]	$1.50	$5.00	$10.00
40	Feuchtwanger, Lion - ***Great Short Stories*** [1947]	$1.50	$5.00	$10.00
41	Farrell, James T. - ***A Hell Of A Good Time*** [1947]	$1.50	$5.00	$10.00
42	Anthology - ***Famous Movieland Love Stories*** [1947]	$2.00	$6.00	$12.00

		G	VG	F
43	Maugham, W. Somerset - ***East Of Suez: Great Stories Of The Tropics*** [1948]	$1.50	$5.00	$10.00
44	Anthology - ***Tropical Love Tales*** [1948]	$1.50	$5.00	$10.00
45	O'Hara, John - ***Hellbox*** [1949]	$2.50	$7.50	$15.00
46	Lawrence, D.H. - ***Love Among The Haystacks*** [1949]	$2.00	$6.00	$12.00
48	Brush, Katherine - ***Night Club*** [1949]	$2.50	$7.50	$15.00
49	Lawrence, D.H. - ***A Modern Lover And Other Stories*** [1949]	$2.00	$6.00	$12.00
50	O'Hara, John - ***All The Girls He Wanted*** [1949]	$2.50	$7.50	$15.00

Avon Monthly Novel. New York: Avon Books. Digest Size.

		G	VG	F
1	Cain, James M. - ***Sinful Woman*** [1947] PBO. Cover by Barye Phillips.	$20.00	$60.00	$125.00
2	Holland, Marty - ***Her Private Passions*** [1947]	$4.00	$12.50	$25.00
3	Clarke, Donald Henderson - ***The Regenerate Lover*** [1948]	$5.00	$15.00	$30.00
4	Chase, James Hadley - ***The Villain And The Virgin*** [1948]	$5.00	$15.00	$30.00
5	Wilson, Dana - ***Uneasy Virtue*** [1948]	$4.00	$12.50	$25.00
6	Zinberg, Len - ***Strange Desires*** [1948] Photo cover.	$4.50	$14.00	$28.00
7	Chase, James Hadley - ***12 Chinks And A Woman*** [1948] Photo cover.	$6.00	$20.00	$40.00
8	Rothman, Nathan - ***Virgie, Goodbye*** [1948]	$4.00	$12.50	$25.00
9	Bloch, Robert - ***The Scarf Of Passion*** [1948] Photo cover.	$8.00	$25.00	$50.00
10	Martin, George Victor - ***The Lady Said Yes*** [1949] Photo cover.	$4.00	$12.50	$25.00
11	Lobaugh, Elma K. - ***The Devil Is Loneliness*** [1949] Photo cover.	$4.00	$12.50	$25.00
12	Brush, Katharine - ***Little Sins*** [1949]	$5.00	$15.00	$30.00
13	Briffault, Robert - ***Carlotta*** [1949]	$6.00	$20.00	$40.00
14	Hanline, M. A. - ***The Man Who Drove Girls Wild*** [1949]	$5.00	$15.00	$30.00
15	Holland, Marty - ***The Darling Of Paris*** [1949] PBO. Photo cover.	$4.00	$12.50	$25.00
16	Clarke, Donald Henderson - ***Millie's Daughter*** [1949]	$4.00	$12.50	$25.00
17	Cain, James M. - ***Jealous Woman*** [1949]	$5.50	$17.50	$35.00
18	Chase, James Hadley - ***I'll Get You For This*** [1950]	$5.00	$15.00	$30.00
19	Collison, Wilson - ***One Night With Nancy*** [1951]	$6.00	$20.00	$40.00
20	Woodford, Jack - ***Ecstasy Girl*** [1951]	$5.50	$17.50	$35.00
21	Hanley, Jack - ***Tomcat In Tights*** [1951]	$7.00	$22.50	$45.00

Avon Murder Mystery Monthly. New York: Avon Books. Digest Size.

		G	VG	F
1	Merritt, A. - ***Seven Footprints To Satan*** [1942] (Murder Of The Month).	$4.00	$12.50	$25.00
2	Paul, Elliot - ***Mysterious Mickey Finn*** [1942] Cover by W. L. White. (Murder Of The Month).	$3.50	$10.00	$20.00
3	Wallace, Edgar - ***Silinski Master Criminal*** [1942] Cover by Gil Tompkins. (Murder Of The Month).	$3.50	$10.00	$20.00
4	Gruber, Frank - ***The French Key Mystery*** [1942] Cover by Gil Tompkins and Harold Black. (Murder Of The Month).	$3.00	$9.00	$18.00
5	Merritt, A. - ***Burn Witch Burn!*** [1942] Cover by William Forrest.	$2.50	$7.50	$15.00
6	Cain, James M. - ***The Postman Always Rings Twice*** [1942] Cover by William Forrest.	$7.00	$22.50	$45.00
7	Chandler, Raymond - ***The Big Sleep*** [1942]	$20.00	$60.00	$125.00
8	Simenon, Georges - ***Maigret Abroad*** [1942] Cover by William Forrest.	$3.00	$9.00	$18.00
9	Stout, Rex - ***The Red Box*** [1942] Cover by William Forrest.	$5.00	$15.00	$30.00

Avon Murder Mystery Monthly, 19

Avon Murder Mystery Monthly, 28

Avon Murder Mystery Monthly, 46

		G	VG	F
10	Babcock, Dwight V. - ***Homocide For Hannah*** [1943] Cover by William Forrest.	$3.50	$10.00	$20.00
11	Merritt, A. - ***Creep Shadow Creep*** [1943]	$2.50	$7.50	$15.00
12	Gruber, Frank - ***Hungry Dog Murders*** [1943] Cover by William Forrest.	$5.00	$15.00	$30.00
13	Roos, Kelly - ***If The Shroud Fits*** [1943] Cover by William Forrest.	$3.50	$10.00	$20.00
14	Sayers, Dorothy L. - ***Whose Body?*** [1943] Cover by Gaspano and Ricco.	$4.00	$12.50	$25.00
15	Cheyney, Peter - ***Premeditated Murder*** [1943] Original title: "A Trap For Bellamy"	$4.00	$12.50	$25.00
16	Cain, James M. - ***Double Indemnity*** [1943] PBO. Cover by William Forrest.	$15.00	$45.00	$90.00
17	Allingham, Margery - ***Who Killed Chloe?*** [1943]	$3.00	$9.00	$18.00
18	Merritt, A. - ***The Moon Pool*** [1943]	$2.50	$7.50	$15.00
19	Chandler, Raymond - ***5 Murderers*** [1944] PBO.	$22.00	$70.00	$140.00
20	Cain, James M. - ***The Embezzler*** [1944] PBO. Cover by Jack Deckter.	$12.50	$37.50	$75.00
21	Cheyney, Peter - ***The Counter Spy Murders*** [1943] Same cover as Avon Detective Mystery #1.	$3.50	$10.00	$20.00
22	Charteris, Leslie - ***The Ace Of Knaves*** [1943]	$4.00	$12.50	$25.00
23	Gruber, Frank - ***Simon Lash, Private Detective*** [1944]	$5.50	$17.50	$35.00
24	Merritt, A. - ***Dwellers In The Mirage*** [1944]	$2.50	$7.50	$15.00
25	Abbot, Anthony (Fulton Oursler) - ***About The Murder Of The Startled Lady*** [1944]	$5.50	$17.50	$35.00
26	Christie, Agatha - ***The Mysterious Affair At Styles*** [1944] Cover by A. Gonzales.	$4.00	$12.50	$25.00
27	Woolrich, Cornell - ***The Black Angel*** [1944]	$12.50	$37.50	$75.00
28	Chandler, Raymond - ***Five Sinister Characters*** [1945] PBO. Cover by Paul Stahr.	$25.00	$75.00	$180.00
29	Merritt, A. - ***The Face In The Abyss*** [1945] Cover by Paul Stahr.	$2.50	$7.50	$15.00
30	Cheyney, Peter - ***Farewell To The Admiral*** [1945] Cover by A. Gonzales.	$3.00	$9.00	$18.00
31	Irish, William - ***If I Should Die Before I Wake*** [1945] PBO. Cover by A. Gonzales.	$17.00	$50.00	$100.00
32	Charteris, Leslie - ***The Saint Vs. Scotland Yard*** [1945] Cover by Paul Stahr. Same cover as #39.	$3.50	$10.00	$20.00

		G	VG	F
33	Burnett, W.R. - ***Nobody Lives Forever*** [1945]	$3.50	$10.00	$20.00
34	Merritt, A. - ***The Ship of Ishtar*** [1945] Cover by Paul Stahr.	$2.50	$7.50	$15.00
35	Allingham, Margery - ***Flowers For The Judge*** [1945]	$3.00	$9.00	$18.00
36	Babcock, Dwight V. - ***They Never Say When!*** [1945]	$3.50	$10.00	$20.00
37	Footner, Hulbert - ***Orchids To Murder*** [1945]	$4.00	$12.50	$25.00
38	Babcock, Dwight V. - ***Hannah Says Foul Play!*** [1945]	$3.00	$9.00	$18.00
39	Coxe, George Harmon - ***Flash Casey - Detective*** [1946] PBO. Same cover as #32.	$6.00	$20.00	$40.00
40	Burnett, W. R. - ***High Sierra*** [1946]	$4.50	$14.00	$28.00
41	Merritt, A. - ***The Metal Monster*** [1946] PBO.	$2.50	$7.50	$15.00
42	Irish, William - ***Borrowed Crime*** [1946] PBO.	$17.00	$50.00	$100.00
43	Chandler, Raymond - ***The Finger Man*** [1946] PBO.	$20.00	$60.00	$125.00
44	Cain, James M. - ***Love's Lovely Counterfeit*** [1947] Cover by Don Milsop.	$10.00	$30.00	$60.00
45	Wallace, Edgar - ***On The Spot*** [1946] Cover by Renaldo Epworth.	$7.00	$22.50	$45.00
46	Whitfield, Raoul - ***The Green Ice Murders*** [1947]	$12.50	$37.50	$75.00
47	Clark, Dale - ***The Blonde, The Gangster, And The Private Eye*** [1947] Cover by Ann Cantor.	$15.00	$45.00	$90.00
48	Long, Julius - ***Murder In Her Big Blue Eyes*** [1950] Cover by Ann Cantor. Original title: *Keep The Coffins Coming.*	$15.00	$45.00	$90.00
49	Ronns, Edward - ***Lady, The Guy is Dead*** [1950] Same cover as Avon comic book Saint #10. Original title: *No Place To Live.*	$15.00	$45.00	$90.00

Avon Romance Novel Monthly. New York: Avon Book Company. Digest Size.

1	Ayers, Ruby M. - ***The Little Sinner*** [n.d.] Digest size.	$5.00	$15.00	$30.00
2	Moore, Frances S. - ***Love Should Be Laughter*** [n.d.] Digest size.	$5.00	$15.00	$30.00
3	Dern, Peggy - ***Help Yourself To Love*** [n.d.] Digest size.	$5.00	$15.00	$30.00

Avon S Series. New York: Avon Book Company.

S-101	Anthology - ***The Art Of Keeping Fit*** [1964] Cover by Robert Osborn.	$ .65	$2.00	$4.00
S-102	Barber, Rowland - ***The Night They Raided Minsky's*** [1964] Cover by Gregori.	$1.25	$3.75	$7.50
S-106	Romulo, Carlos P. - ***I Walked With Heroes*** [1964]	$ .65	$2.00	$4.00
S-107	Lytton, David - ***The Goddam White Man*** [1964] Cover by Dillons.	$2.00	$6.00	$12.00
S-113	Keyes, Frances Parkinson - ***The Safe Bridge*** [1964]	$ .65	$2.00	$4.00
S-117	Wormser, Richard - ***Battalion Of Saints*** [1964]	$ .65	$2.00	$4.00
S-119	Price, Reynolds - ***A Long And Happy Life*** [1964]	$ .65	$2.00	$4.00
S-126	Wright, Richard - ***Lawd Today*** [1964]	$1.35	$4.00	$8.00
S-127	Anthology edited by Isaac Asimov - ***The Hugo Winners*** [1964] Cover by Powers. Includes Robert Bloch.	$1.25	$3.75	$7.50
S-128	Dennis, Patrick - ***Genius*** [1964]	$ .65	$2.00	$4.00
S-129	Gregory, Dick - ***From The Back Of The Bus*** [1964] Photo cover.	$ .75	$2.50	$5.00
S-130	Derleth, August - ***Concord Rebel: A Life Of Thoreau*** [1964]	$ .65	$2.00	$4.00
S-132	Robbins, Harold - ***Never Leave Me*** [1964] Cover by McGinnis...	$ .65	$2.00	$4.00
S-133	Agee, James - ***A Death In The Family*** [1964]	$ .65	$2.00	$4.00
S-135	Brinton, Henry - ***Purple-6*** [1964]	$ .65	$2.00	$4.00
S-137	Maloney, Ralph - ***The 24-Hour Drink Book*** [1964] Photo cover.	$ .65	$2.00	$4.00
S-139	Van Vogt, A. E. - ***The Violent Man*** [1964] Cover by Robert Jones.	$ .65	$2.00	$4.00

		G	VG	F
S-145	Gehman, Richard - ***That Kid: The Story Of Jerry Lewis*** [1964] PBO. Photo cover.	$ .75	$2.50	$5.00
S-148	Mooney, Booth - ***The Lyndon Johnson Story*** [1964] Photo cover.	$ .65	$2.00	$4.00
S-152	Ferber, Edna - ***American Beauty*** [1964]	$ .65	$2.00	$4.00
S-153	Feiffer, Jules - ***Harry, The Rat With Women*** [1964] Cover by Saul Lambert.	$ .65	$2.00	$4.00
S-157	Dolim, Mary N. - ***The Ruling Family*** [1964]	$ .65	$2.00	$4.00
S-161	Hughes, Dorothy B. - ***The Expendable Man*** [1964]	$ .65	$2.00	$4.00
S-163	North, Sterling - ***Rascal*** [1964]	$ .65	$2.00	$4.00
S-168	Benjamin, Philip - ***Quick, Before It Melts*** [1964] Movie tie-in.	$ .65	$2.00	$4.00
S-170	Griffin, Gwyn - ***A Significant Experience*** [1964]	$ .65	$2.00	$4.00
S-171	Maxfield, Henry X. - ***Legacy Of A Spy*** [1964]	$ .65	$2.00	$4.00
S-174	Murphy, Robert - ***The Pond*** [1964]	$ .65	$2.00	$4.00
S-176	John Q. - ***The Bunnies*** [1965] PBO.	$ .65	$2.00	$4.00
S-180	MacDonald, Betty - ***The Egg And I*** [1965]	$ .65	$2.00	$4.00
S-181	North, Sterling - ***So Dear To My Heart*** [1965]	$ .65	$2.00	$4.00
S-183	Jenkins, Geoffrey - ***A Twist Of Sand*** [1965]	$ .65	$2.00	$4.00
S-185	Miller, Arthur - ***Focus*** [1965] Cover by Ronnie Lesser	$ .65	$2.00	$4.00
S-186	Saunders, Marshall - ***Beautiful Joe*** [1965]	$ .65	$2.00	$4.00
S-187	Pyle, Howard - ***Men Of Iron*** [1965] PBO.	$ .65	$2.00	$4.00
S-188	King, Alan - ***Anybody Who Owns His Own Home Deserves It*** [1965] Photo cover.	$ .65	$2.00	$4.00
S-194	Tripp, Miles - ***Kilo 40*** [1965] Cover by Stan Borack.	$ .65	$2.00	$4.00
S-195	King, Alan - ***Help! I'm A Prisoner In A Chinese Bakery*** [1965] Photo cover.	$ .65	$2.00	$4.00
S-196	Jenkins, Geoffrey - ***The River Of Diamonds*** [1965] Cover by Borack.	$ .65	$2.00	$4.00
S-197	Jackson, Shirley - ***The Lottery*** [1965] Cover by Walter Brooks.	$1.00	$3.00	$6.00
S-200	Carrighar, Sally - ***Wild Voice Of The North*** [1965]	$ .65	$2.00	$4.00
S-201	Bowen, Jeffrey - ***The Guarded Palace*** [1965] PBO. Cover by Bob Abbett.	$ .65	$2.00	$4.00
S-203	Duncan, Thomas - ***Virgo Descending*** [1965]	$ .65	$2.00	$4.00
S-204	Canning, Victor - ***The Scorpio Letters*** [1965] Cover by Hector Garrido.	$ .65	$2.00	$4.00
S-205	Fleming, Peter - ***The Sixth Column*** [1965]	$ .65	$2.00	$4.00
S-206	Queen, Ellery - ***The Tragedy Of X*** [1965] Cover by Mort Engel.	$ .65	$2.00	$4.00
S-207	Queen, Ellery - ***The Tragedy Of Y*** [1965] Cover by Mort Engel.	$ .65	$2.00	$4.00
S-208	Knowler, John - ***The Trap*** [1965]	$ .65	$2.00	$4.00
S-210	Blish, James - ***They Shall Have Stars*** [1965]	$ .65	$2.00	$4.00
S-211	Queen, Ellery - ***The Tragedy Of Z*** [1965] Cover by Mort Engel.	$ .65	$2.00	$4.00
S-212	Masterson, Whit - ***The Dark Fantastic*** [1965] Cover by Bob Abbett.	$ .65	$2.00	$4.00
S-213	Sandberg, Sara - ***Mama Made Minks*** [1965]	$ .65	$2.00	$4.00
S-217	Gallagher, Thomas - ***Oona O'*** [1965]	$ .65	$2.00	$4.00
S-218	Blish, James - ***Earthman, Come Home*** [1965]	$1.00	$3.00	$6.00
S-220	Schoonover, Lawrence - ***Prisoner Of Tordesillas*** [1965]	$ .65	$2.00	$4.00
S-221	Blish, James - ***The Triumph Of Time*** [1965]	$ .65	$2.00	$4.00
S-224	Asimov, Isaac - ***Foundation*** [1965]	$ .65	$2.00	$4.00
S-225	Price, Reynolds - ***The Names And Faces Of Heroes*** [1965] Cover by Ben Wohlberg	$ .65	$2.00	$4.00
S-229	Merritt, A. - ***The Ship Of Ishtar*** [1965] Cover by Douglas Rosa.	$1.25	$3.75	$7.50

		G	VG	F
S-230	Christopher, John - ***The Possessors*** [1965] Cover by Don Crowley.	$1.00	$3.00	$6.00
S-231	Merritt, A. - ***The Metal Monster*** [1965]	$1.25	$3.75	$7.50
S-232	Powell, Dawn - ***A Cage For Lovers*** [1965] Cover by Robert McGinnis.	$ .75	$2.50	$5.00
S-233	Heyman, Evan Lee - ***Dead Heat On A Merry-Go-Round*** [1966] PBO. Movie tie-in with James Coburn.	$ .65	$2.00	$4.00
S-234	Asimov, Isaac - ***Foundation And Empire*** [1966]	$ .65	$2.00	$4.00
S-236	O'Rourke, Frank - ***The Professionals*** [1966]	$ .65	$2.00	$4.00
S-237	Asimov, Isaac - ***Second Foundation*** [1966]	$ .65	$2.00	$4.00
S-240	Mahan, Patte Wheat - ***Doctor, You've Got To Be Kidding!*** [1966] Movie tie-in with Sandra Dee and George Hamilton photo cover.	$ .65	$2.00	$4.00
S-242	Jenkins, Geoffrey - ***A Grue Of Ice*** [1966] Cover by Stanley Borack.	$ .65	$2.00	$4.00
S-243	Henderson, Zenna - ***Pilgrimage: The Book Of The People*** [1966]	$1.00	$3.00	$6.00
S-246	Coulter, Stephen - ***Threshold*** [1966] Cover by Paul Lehr.	$ .65	$2.00	$4.00
S-250	Bronstein, Mrs. Yetta - ***The President I Almost Was*** [1966] Cover by Sandy Kossin.	$ .65	$2.00	$4.00
S-251	Wilkinson, G. K. - ***Monkey, Go Home!*** [1966]	$ .65	$2.00	$4.00
S-255	Clement, Hal - ***Needle*** [1966] Cover by Hector Garrido.	$ .65	$2.00	$4.00
S-263	Fleischman, Sid - ***Bullwhip Griffin*** [1967] Movie tie-in with photo cover.	$ .65	$2.00	$4.00
S-269	Deal, Borden - ***A Long Way To Go*** [1967]	$ .65	$2.00	$4.00
S-270	Simak, Clifford D. - ***Ring Around The Sun*** [1967] Photo cover.	$ .65	$2.00	$4.00
S-271	Merritt, A. - ***The Dwellers In The Mirage*** [1967] Cover by Douglas Rosa.	$1.25	$3.75	$7.50
S-274	Stokes, Manning Lee - ***Grand Prix*** [1967] PBO. Movie tie-in.	$ .65	$2.00	$4.00
S-275	Fremlin, Celia - ***The Trouble Makers*** [1967] Cover by Mort Rosenfeld.	$ .65	$2.00	$4.00
S-277	Anthology edited by Charles M. Collins - ***A Feast Of Blood*** [1967] PBO. Photo cover.	$1.25	$3.75	$7.50
S-280	Merritt, A. - ***Seven Footprints To Satan*** [1967] Cover by Douglas Rosa.	$1.25	$3.75	$7.50
S-281	Lyall, Gavin - ***Shooting Script*** [1967] Cover by Milton Charles.	$ .65	$2.00	$4.00
S-284	Williams, A. - ***The Long Run South*** [1967]	$ .65	$2.00	$4.00
S-285	Adams, Joey - ***The Borscht Belt*** [1967] Cover by Rowland B. Wilson.	$ .65	$2.00	$4.00
S-288	Christopher, John - ***No Blade Of Grass*** [1967] Cover by Hector Garrido.	$ .65	$2.00	$4.00
S-290	Herbert, Frank - ***The Dragon In The Sea*** [1967]	$ .65	$2.00	$4.00
S-291	Wolfert, Ira - ***American Guerrilla In The Philippines*** [1967] Cover by Carl Cassler.	$ .65	$2.00	$4.00
S-294	Murphy, Robert - ***The Golden Eagle*** [1967] Cover by John Schoenherr.	$ .65	$2.00	$4.00
S-297	Wilk, Max - ***The Beard*** [1967] Cover by Larry Ratzkin.	$ .65	$2.00	$4.00
S-298	Guin, Wyman - ***Living Way Out*** [1967] PBO. Cover by Ron Walotsky.	$2.00	$6.00	$12.00
S-302	Thomas, Ross - ***The Cold War Swap*** [1967] Photo cover.	$ .65	$2.00	$4.00
S-303	Mundy, Talbot - ***Tros*** [1967] Cover by Douglas Rosa. Tros Of Samothrace #1.	$1.25	$3.75	$7.50
S-304	Burke, J. - ***Privilege*** [1967] Movie tie-in.	$ .65	$2.00	$4.00
S-308	Ball, John - ***Rescue Mission*** [1967] Cover by Dean Ellis.	$ .65	$2.00	$4.00

		G	VG	F
S-309	Mundy, Talbot - ***Helma*** [1967] Cover by Douglas Rosa. Tros Of Samothrace #2.	$1.25	$3.75	$7.50
S-312	Mishima, Yukio - ***After The Banquet*** [1967] Photo cover.	$ .65	$2.00	$4.00
S-313	Blish, James - ***Vor*** [1967] Cover by Don Crowley.	$ .65	$2.00	$4.00
S-316	Mundy, Talbot - ***Liafail*** [1967] Cover by Douglas Rosa. Tros Of Samothrace #3.	$1.25	$3.75	$7.50
S-318	Mundy, Talbot - ***Helene*** [1967] Cover by Douglas Rosa. Tros Of Samothrace #4.	$1.25	$3.75	$7.50
S-319	Herbert, Frank - ***The Heaven Makers*** [1968] PBO. Cover by John Schoenherr.	$1.00	$3.00	$6.00
S-320	Innes, Hammond - ***The Angry Mountain*** [1968]	$ .65	$2.00	$4.00
S-323	Brunner, John - ***Now Then*** [1968] Cover by Hector Garrido.	$ .65	$2.00	$4.00
S-324	Innes, Hammond - ***The Blue Ice*** [1968]	$ .65	$2.00	$4.00
S-325	Alter, Robert Edmond - ***Thieves Like Us*** [1968] PBO. Cover by Hector Garrido.	$ .75	$2.50	$5.00
S-327	Cairo, Jon - ***Posh*** [1968] PBO. Photo cover.	$ .65	$2.00	$4.00
S-328	Henderson, Zenna - ***The People: No Different Flesh*** [1968]	$1.00	$3.00	$6.00
S-329	Silverberg, Robert - ***Master Of Life And Death*** [1968] Cover by Hector Garrido.	$ .75	$2.50	$5.00
S-331	Cochran, Russ - ***Be Prepared!*** [1968] Cover by Robert Osborn.	$ .65	$2.00	$4.00
S-332	Kirk, Russell - ***Old House Of Fear*** [1968] Cover by Hector Garrido.	$ .75	$2.50	$5.00
S-333	Innes, Hammond - ***The Killer Mine*** [1968]	$ .65	$2.00	$4.00
S-335	Heinlein, Robert A. - ***Podkayne Of Mars*** [1968]	$ .75	$2.50	$5.00
S-336	Sturgeon, Bradbury & Oliver - ***3 To The Highest Power*** [1968] PBO.	$1.00	$3.00	$6.00
S-337	Blish, James - ***Jack Of Eagles*** [1968]	$ .65	$2.00	$4.00
S-339	Innes, Hammond - ***Gale Warning*** [1968]	$ .65	$2.00	$4.00
S-341	Maxfield, Henry S. - ***The Double Man*** [1968] Movie tie-in with Yul Brynner.	$ .75	$2.50	$5.00
S-345	Anthology - ***Weird Shadows*** [1968]	$ .65	$2.00	$4.00
S-347	McIntosh, J. T. - ***Snow White And The Giants*** [1968] PBO. Cover by Carl Cassler.	$1.35	$4.00	$8.00
S-349	Sohl, Jerry - ***Costigan's Needle*** [1968] Cover by Don Crowley.	$ .65	$2.00	$4.00
S-351	Moorcock, Michael - ***The Final Programme*** [1968] PBO.	$ .65	$2.00	$4.00
S-354	Heyman, Evan Lee - ***The Thomas Crown Affair*** [1968] PBO. Movie tie-in with Steve McQueen photo cover.	$ .65	$2.00	$4.00
S-355	Pohl, Frederick - editor - ***The Expert Dreamers*** [1968] Cover by Don Crowley.	$ .65	$2.00	$4.00
S-357	Olsen, Theodore V. - ***The Stalking Moon*** [1968] Movie tie-in. Gregory Peck photo cover.	$1.35	$4.00	$8.00
S-361	Giles, Raymond - ***Night Of The Vampire*** [1969] PBO. Cover by Hector Garrido.	$1.00	$3.00	$6.00
S-363	Jakes, John - ***Brak The Barbarian*** [1968] PBO. Cover by Frank Frazetta.	$1.35	$4.00	$8.00
S-365	Silverberg, Robert - ***Invaders From Earth*** [1968] Cover by Don Crowley	$ .65	$2.00	$4.00
S-367	Thomas, Ross - ***Cast A Yellow Shadow*** [1968]	$ .65	$2.00	$4.00
S-368	Hoffe, Arthur - ***Something Evil*** [1968] PBO. Cover by Bob Foster.	$ .65	$2.00	$4.00
S-369	Romano, Deane Louis - ***The Town That Took A Trip*** [1968] PBO. Photo cover.	$ .75	$2.50	$5.00
S-370	Stout, Rex - ***Where There's A Will*** [1968]	$ .65	$2.00	$4.00
S-371	Victor, Charles - ***The Whole Sky Burned*** [1968] PBO.	$1.00	$3.00	$6.00

		G	VG	F
S-372	Silverberg, Robert - ***The Time Hoppers*** [1968] Cover by Don Punchatz.	$ .65	$2.00	$4.00
S-375	Cameron, Lou - ***The Dragon's Spine*** [1969] PBO. Cover by Douglas Rosa.	$1.00	$3.00	$6.00
S-376	Lanning, George - ***The Pedestal*** [1969] Cover by Hector Garrido.	$ .65	$2.00	$4.00
S-377	Neill, Robert - ***Witch Bane*** [1969]	$ .65	$2.00	$4.00
S-378	Moore, C. L. - ***Doomsday Morning*** [1969] Cover by Douglas Rosa.	$ .65	$2.00	$4.00
S-379	Whittington, Harry - ***Burden's Mission*** [1968] PBO. Cover by Victor Prezio.	$1.50	$5.00	$10.00
S-380	Alter, Robert Edmond - ***Path To Savagery*** [1969] PBO. Cover by Edward Soyka.	$ .65	$2.00	$4.00
S-382	Lytle, Andrew - ***A Name For Evil*** [1969]	$ .65	$2.00	$4.00
S-383	Steen, Marguerite - ***The Unquiet Spirit*** [1969] Cover by Edward Soyka.	$ .65	$2.00	$4.00
S-384	Anthology - ***The Avon Fantasy Reader*** [1969] PBO. Cover by Gray Morrow.	$1.50	$5.00	$10.00
S-385	Anthology - ***The 2nd Avon Fantasy Reader*** [1969] PBO. Cover by Gray Morrow.	$1.50	$5.00	$10.00
S-386	Drake, Stan - ***The Heart Of Juliet Jones*** [1969] PBO. All comic strips.	$1.25	$3.75	$7.50
S-387	Saunders & Ernst - ***Mary Worth*** [1969] PBO. Cover by Dick Smith. All comic strips.	$1.25	$3.75	$7.50
S-389	Anthology edited by Douglas Hill - ***The Devil His Due*** [1969] Cover by Hector Garrido.	$1.25	$3.75	$7.50
S-392	Matheson, Richard - ***A Stir Of Echos*** [1969]	$ .75	$2.50	$5.00
S-394	Frazee, Steve - ***Flight 409*** [1969] PBO.	$ .65	$2.00	$4.00
S-398	Shaw, Bob - ***Shadow Of Heaven*** [1969] PBO.	$1.00	$3.00	$6.00
S-399	Mason, Douglas R. - ***Ring Of Violence*** [1969] PBO.	$1.00	$3.00	$6.00
S-400	Seymour, Henry - ***Infernal Idol*** [1969]	$ .65	$2.00	$4.00
S-401	McCloy, Helen - ***Mister Splitfoot*** [1969]	$ .65	$2.00	$4.00
S-406	Shaw, Bob - ***Night Walk*** [1969]	$1.35	$4.00	$8.00
S-409	Anthology edited by Robert Tralins - ***The Hidden Spectre*** [1970] PBO. Photo cover.	$ .65	$2.00	$4.00
S-410	Anthology - ***The Man In The Cannibal Pot*** [1970] Cartoon book by Gahan Wilson.	$2.00	$6.00	$12.00
S-411	Silverberg, Robert - ***Hawksbill Station*** [1970]	$ .65	$2.00	$4.00
S-412	Anderson, Poul - ***Three Hearts And Three Lions*** [1970] Cover by Jeff Jones.	$1.00	$3.00	$6.00
S-415	Blish, James - ***Vor*** [1970]	$ .65	$2.00	$4.00
S-417	Hoffman, Lee - ***Always The Black Knight*** [1970] PBO. Cover by Paul Lehr.	$ .65	$2.00	$4.00

Avon SF And Fantasy Reader. New York: Avon Book Company. Digest Size.

		G	VG	F
VOL 1 #1	Anthology - ***Includes John Jakes*** [1953] PBO. Cover by Leo Manso.	$2.50	$7.50	$15.00
VOL 1 #2	Anthology - ***Includes John Jakes and Jack Vance*** [1953] PBO. Cover by Leo Manso.	$2.50	$7.50	$15.00

Avon Science Fiction Reader. New York: Avon Novels, Inc. Digest Size.

		G	VG	F
1	Anthology - ***"The War Of The Sexes" by Edmond Hamilton*** [1951] Includes stories by Leinster, Merritt, Williamson, et al.	$3.00	$9.00	$18.00
2	Anthology - ***Includes Wandrei, Cummings, Dunsany, et al*** [1952]	$3.00	$9.00	$18.00

		G	VG	F
3	Anthology - ***Includes "The Robot Empire" by Frank Belknap Long*** [1952] Also stories by Bok, Counselman, et al.	$3.00	$9.00	$18.00

Avon Specials. New York: Avon Book Company. Digest Size.

		G	VG	F
NO#-1	Guild, Leo - ***Seduction*** [1951]	$4.00	$12.50	$25.00
NO#-2	Clarke, Donald Henderson - ***A Lady Named Lou*** [1951]	$4.00	$12.50	$25.00
NO#-3	Woodford, Jack - ***Peeping Tom*** [1951]	$6.00	$20.00	$40.00
NO#-4	Wilstach, John - ***Night Club Girl*** [1951]	$5.00	$15.00	$30.00
NO#-5	Woodford, Jack - ***Three Gorgeous Hussies*** [1951]	$5.50	$17.50	$35.00
NO#-6	Woodford, Jack - ***Free Lovers*** [1951]	$5.00	$15.00	$30.00
NO#-7	Bloch, Robert - ***Scarf Of Passion*** [1951] Photo cover.	$8.00	$25.00	$50.00
NO#-8	O'Hara, John - ***Stories Of Venial Sin*** [1951]	$5.00	$15.00	$30.00

Avon T Series. New York: Avon Book Company.

		G	VG	F
AT-51	Delmar, Vina - ***Bad Girl*** [1953]	$1.25	$3.75	$7.50
AT-52	Dowd, Harrison - ***The Night Air*** [1953]	$1.00	$3.00	$6.00
AT-53	Sylvester, Robert - ***The Second Oldest Profession*** [1953]	$1.25	$3.75	$7.50
AT-54	Plaidy, Jean - ***Madame Serpent*** [1953]	$1.25	$3.75	$7.50
AT-55	Lindsay, Philip - ***The Rake's Progress*** [1953]	$1.00	$3.00	$6.00
AT-57	Stong, Phil - ***Jessamy John*** [1953]	$1.00	$3.00	$6.00
AT-58	Weirauch, Anna Elisabet - ***The Scorpion*** [1953]	$1.00	$3.00	$6.00
AT-59	Lauritzen, Jonreed - ***Rose And The Flame*** [1953]	$1.25	$3.75	$7.50
AT-60	Henri, Florette - ***Kings Mountain*** [1953]	$1.00	$3.00	$6.00
AT-61	Anthology edited by Phillips & Rahv - ***Stories In The Modern Manner*** [1953] PBO. Includes Charles Jackson.	$1.35	$4.00	$8.00
AT-62	Stover, Herbert E. - ***Powder Mission*** [1953] Cover by James Meese.	$1.25	$3.75	$7.50
AT-63	Weidman, Jerome - ***The Hand Of The Hunter*** [1953]	$1.00	$3.00	$6.00
AT-64	Busbee, Jr., James - ***Son Of Egypt*** [1953]	$1.00	$3.00	$6.00
AT-65	Wittels, M.D., Fritz - ***Sex Habits Of American Women*** [1953]	$ .75	$2.50	$5.00
AT-66	Anthology edited by Phillips & Rahv - ***The Avon Book Of Modern Writing*** [1953] PBO.	$1.00	$3.00	$6.00
AT-67	Sanderson, Douglas - ***Dark Passions Subdue*** [1953]	$1.00	$3.00	$6.00
AT-68	Graves, Robert - ***I, Claudius*** [1953]	$1.35	$4.00	$8.00
AT-69	Sartre, Jean-Paul - ***Intimacy And Other Stories*** [1953]	$1.25	$3.75	$7.50
AT-70	Hardy, W. G. - ***Turn Back The River*** [1953]	$1.00	$3.00	$6.00
T-71	Huneker, James - ***Painted Veils*** [1954]	$1.00	$3.00	$6.00
T-72	Baldwin, Bates - ***Tide Of Empire*** [1954]	$1.00	$3.00	$6.00
T-73	Busbee, Jr., James - ***Yankee Mariner*** [1954] Cover by Meese.	$1.00	$3.00	$6.00
T-74	Robbins, Harold - ***Never Leave Me*** [1953]	$1.25	$3.75	$7.50
T-75	Huxley, Aldous - ***After Many A Summer Dies The Swan*** [1954]	$1.00	$3.00	$6.00
T-76	Lauritzen, Jonreed - ***Blade Of Conquest*** [1954] Cover by Meese.	$1.00	$3.00	$6.00
T-77	Anthology From Partison Review - ***More Stories In The Modern Manner*** [1954] PBO.	$1.25	$3.75	$7.50
T-78	Baxter, John - ***A Foreign Affair*** [1954] PBO.	$1.00	$3.00	$6.00
T-79	Jones, Nard - ***The Scarlet Petticoat*** [1954] Cover by Fullington.	$1.00	$3.00	$6.00
T-80	Bond, Nelson - ***No Time Like The Future*** [1954] PBO. Cover by Powers.	$1.35	$4.00	$8.00
T-81	Chidsey, Donald Barr - ***Captain Adam*** [1954] Cover by Cardiff.	$1.00	$3.00	$6.00
T-82	Weidman, Jerome - ***I'll Never Go There Anymore*** [1954]	$1.00	$3.00	$6.00
T-83	Phillips, Thomas Hal - ***The Bitterweed Path*** [1954] Cover by Gilbert Fullington.	$1.00	$3.00	$6.00
T-84	Mitchell, Francis - ***Naked Acre*** [1954]	$1.00	$3.00	$6.00

		G	VG	F
T-85	Thomason, Jr., John W. - ***Gone To Texas*** [1954] Cover by Everett Raymond Kinstler.	$1.25	$3.75	$7.50
T-86	Wright, Richard - ***Savage Holiday*** [1954] PBO. Cover by Hulings.	$1.35	$4.00	$8.00
T-87	Robles, Emmanuel - ***Dawn On Our Darkness*** [1954] Cover by Hy Rubin.	$1.00	$3.00	$6.00
T-88	Martin, Hansford - ***Send Them Summer*** [1954]	$1.00	$3.00	$6.00
T-89	Lindsay, Philip - ***Merry Mistress*** [1954] Cover by Maguire.	$1.35	$4.00	$8.00
T-90	Prokosch, Frederic - ***Nine Days To Mukalla*** [1954]	$1.00	$3.00	$6.00
T-91	Green, Julian - ***The Dark Journey*** [1954]	$1.00	$3.00	$6.00
T-92	Meyers, Harold - ***Belly Laughs Annual*** [1955] PBO. Cartoon book.	$2.50	$7.50	$15.00
T-93	Zinberg, Len - ***What D'Ya Know For Sure?*** [1955]	$1.00	$3.00	$6.00
T-94	Mirbeau, Octave - ***Diary Of A Chambermaid*** [1955]	$1.00	$3.00	$6.00
T-95	Anthology edited by Harold Meyers - ***Honeymoon Guide*** [1955] PBO. 10 pages cartoons by Bill Ward.	$2.00	$6.00	$12.00
T-96	Chidsey, Donald Barr - ***Lord Of The Isles*** [1955] Cover by Darcy.	$ .75	$2.50	$5.00
T-97	Weidman, Jerome - ***I Can Get It For You Wholesale!*** [1955]	$ .75	$2.50	$5.00
T-98	Bracco, Edgar Jean - ***Chattels Of Eldorado*** [1955] Cover by Kinstler.	$1.00	$3.00	$6.00
T-99	Mende, Robert - ***Tough Kid From Brooklyn*** [1955]	$ .75	$2.50	$5.00
T-100	Dobbin, John - ***Flesh And The Sea*** [1955]	$1.00	$3.00	$6.00
T-101	Appel, Benjamin - ***Life And Death Of A Tough Guy*** [1955] PBO. Cover by Paul Stone Martin.	$1.25	$3.75	$7.50
T-102	DeBalzac, Honore - ***Droll Stories*** [1955]	$1.25	$3.75	$7.50
T-103	Weidman, Jerome - ***What's In It For Me?*** [1955]	$ .75	$2.50	$5.00
T-104	Evans, John - ***Love In The Shadows*** [1955]	$1.00	$3.00	$6.00
T-105	Kaufman, Lenard - ***Juvenile Delinquents*** [1955]	$1.35	$4.00	$8.00
T-106	H.R.H. - ***Confessions Of A Princess*** [1955]	$1.00	$3.00	$6.00
T-107	O'Hara, John - ***Butterfield 8*** [1955]	$ .75	$2.50	$5.00
T-108	Algren, Nelson - ***Never Come Morning*** [1955]	$ .75	$2.50	$5.00
T-109	Anthology - ***Various Temptations*** [1955] Includes Steinbeck.	$1.00	$3.00	$6.00
T-110	Lindsay, Philip - ***Royal Scandal*** [1955] Cover by Kinstler.	$1.00	$3.00	$6.00
T-111	Kersh, Gerald - ***Dishonor*** [1955]	$1.00	$3.00	$6.00
T-112	Lindsay, Philip - ***An Artist In Love*** [1956] Cover by Kinstler.	$1.00	$3.00	$6.00
T-113	Anthology - ***Stories Of Scarlet Women*** [1956] PBO. Photo cover.	$1.35	$4.00	$8.00
T-114	Lawrence, D.H. - ***The First Lady Chatterley*** [1956]	$ .75	$2.50	$5.00
T-115	Merritt, A. - ***Seven Footprints To Satan*** [1956]	$1.00	$3.00	$6.00
T-116	Lauritzen, Jonreed - ***Suzanne, Savage Vixen*** [1956]	$1.00	$3.00	$6.00
T-117	Melville, Herman - ***Typee: A Peep At Polynesian Life*** [1956] Cover by Paul Gauguin.	$1.00	$3.00	$6.00
T-118	Guild, Leo - ***The Loves Of Liberace*** [1956] PBO. Photo cover, photos throughout.	$1.50	$5.00	$10.00
T-119	Maugham, William Somerset - ***Ashenden Or The British Agent*** [1956] Cover by Kinstler. Reprints Avon 24.	$ .75	$2.50	$5.00
T-120	Chekhov, Anton - ***The Kiss And The Duel*** [1956]	$1.00	$3.00	$6.00
T-121	Orwell, George - ***Down And Out In Paris And London*** [1956]	$1.00	$3.00	$6.00
T-122	Lindsay, Philip - ***To Love By Candlelight*** [1956]	$1.00	$3.00	$6.00
T-123	Adams, John Paul - ***Girls- For Men Only*** [1956]	$1.35	$4.00	$8.00
T-124	Shulman, Irving - ***Cry Tough!*** [1956]	$ .75	$2.50	$5.00
T-125	Algren, Nelson - ***The Neon Wilderness*** [1956]	$1.25	$3.75	$7.50

		G	VG	F
T-126	Gray, Harriet - ***Gold For The Gay Masters*** [1956] PBO.	$1.35	$4.00	$8.00
T-127	Lewis, C. S. - ***Out Of The Silent Planet*** [1956] Cover by Kinstler.	$1.00	$3.00	$6.00
T-128	Kenyon, F. W. - ***Emma: My Lord Admiral's Mistress*** [1956]	$1.00	$3.00	$6.00
T-129	Zola, Emile - ***The Gin Palace*** [1956]	$1.00	$3.00	$6.00
T-130	Waters, Harold and Aubrey Wisberg - ***The Savage Soldiers*** [1956]	$1.00	$3.00	$6.00
T-131	Weidman, Jerome - ***Slipping Beauty*** [1956]	$ .75	$2.50	$5.00
T-132	Mitchell, Francis - ***Naked Acre*** [1956]	$1.00	$3.00	$6.00
T-133	Tolstoy, Leo - ***Polikushka And Two Hussars*** [1956]	$1.00	$3.00	$6.00
T-134	Chidsey, Donald Barr - ***Captain Adam*** [1956]	$ .75	$2.50	$5.00
T-135	Merritt, A. - ***The Moon Pool*** [1956] Cover By Sussman.	$1.00	$3.00	$6.00
T-136	Lindsay, Philip - ***Sir Naked Blade*** [1956]	$1.00	$3.00	$6.00
T-137	Crane, Stephen - ***The Bride Comes To Yellow Sky*** [1956] PBO.	$1.50	$5.00	$10.00
T-138	Shulman, Irving - ***The Amboy Dukes*** [1956]	$ .75	$2.50	$5.00
T-139	Ham, Jr., Roswell G. - ***The Gifted Sinners*** [1956]	$1.00	$3.00	$6.00
T-140	DeBalzac, Honore - ***Temptation In Paris*** [1956]	$1.00	$3.00	$6.00
T-141	Queen, Ellery - ***The Tragedy Of X*** [1956]	$ .75	$2.50	$5.00
T-142	Dryer, Bernard - ***Murder In Port Afrique*** [1956] Movie tie-in and photo cover.	$1.25	$3.75	$7.50
T-143	Dortort, David - ***Burial Of The Fruit*** [1956] Cover by Ann Cantor.	$ .75	$2.50	$5.00
T-144	Orwell, George - ***Coming Up For Air*** [1956] Cover by Marchetti.	$1.00	$3.00	$6.00
T-145	Mirbeau, Octave - ***Diary Of A Chambermaid*** [1956]	$1.00	$3.00	$6.00
T-146	Herbert, Frank - ***21st Century Sub*** [1956] Cover by Sussman.	$ .75	$2.50	$5.00
T-147	Wagoner, David - ***Money, Money, Money*** [1956] Photo cover	$ .75	$2.50	$5.00
T-148	Verne, Jules - ***Around The World In 80 Days*** [1956] Photo cover. Movie tie-in.	$1.00	$3.00	$6.00
T-149	Christie, Agatha - ***Death On The Nile*** [1956]	$1.25	$3.75	$7.50
T-150	Bevan, A.J. - ***Zarak*** [1956] Movie tie-in. Photo cover	$2.00	$6.00	$12.00
T-151	Dolan, Mary - ***Hannibal: Scourge Of Imperial Rome*** [1956]	$ .65	$2.00	$4.00
T-152	Merritt, A. - ***The Ship Of Ishtar*** [1956] Cover by Powers.	$1.00	$3.00	$6.00
T-153	Weidman, Jerome - ***I'll Never Go There Anymore*** [1956]	$1.00	$3.00	$6.00
T-154	Gorky, Maxim - ***26 Men And A Girl And Other Stories*** [1957]	$1.00	$3.00	$6.00
T-155	Wylie, Philip - ***Gladiator*** [1957]	$ .75	$2.50	$5.00
T-156	Gray, Harriet - ***Bride Of Violence*** [1957]	$1.00	$3.00	$6.00
T-157	Lewis, C.S. - ***Perelandra*** [1957] Cover by Sussman.	$1.00	$3.00	$6.00
T-158	Smith, Robert Paul - ***A Man Can Love Twice*** [1957] Photo cover.	$1.00	$3.00	$6.00
T-159	Noel, Sterling - ***Intrigue In Paris*** [1957] Photo cover.	$ .75	$2.50	$5.00
T-160	Huxley, Aldous - ***After The Fireworks*** [1957]	$1.00	$3.00	$6.00
T-161	Merritt, A. - ***Face In The Abyss*** [1957] Cover by Art Sussman.	$1.00	$3.00	$6.00
T-162	Appel, Benjamin - ***Teen-age Mobster*** [1957]	$1.35	$4.00	$8.00
T-163	Lawrence, D.H. - ***Love Among The Haystacks*** [1957]	$ .75	$2.50	$5.00
T-164	Jones, Nard - ***Scarlet Petticoat*** [1957] Cover by Gilbert Fullington.	$1.00	$3.00	$6.00
T-165	Divine, David - ***Boy On A Dolphin*** [1957] PBO. Movie tie-in. Photos cover and throughout.	$2.00	$6.00	$12.00
T-166	Nezelof, N.P. - ***Josephine, The Great Lover*** [1957]	$1.00	$3.00	$6.00
T-167	Christie, Agatha - ***7 Dials Mystery*** [1957] Cover by Sussman.	$ .75	$2.50	$5.00
T-168	Tucker, Wilson - ***Tomorrow Plus X*** [1957] Cover by Powers.	$1.00	$3.00	$6.00

		G	VG	F
T-169	Roeburt, John - ***The Unholy Wife*** [1957] Movie tie-in. Diana Dors photo cover.	$1.50	$5.00	$10.00
T-170	Shallit, Joseph - ***Juvenile Hoods*** [1957]	$1.50	$5.00	$10.00
T-171	Batchelor, Paula - ***The Duke's Temptation*** [1957] Cover by Everett Raymond Kinstler.	$1.00	$3.00	$6.00
T-172	Merritt, A. - ***The Metal Monster*** [1957] Cover by Richard Powers.	$1.00	$3.00	$6.00
T-173	Cassil, R.V. - ***Naked Morning*** [1957] PBO. Cover by Hulings.	$1.00	$3.00	$6.00
T-174	Weiner, Willard - ***The Young Killers*** [1957] Cover by Sussman.	$1.50	$5.00	$10.00
T-175	Clement, Hal - ***From Outer Space*** [1957]	$1.00	$3.00	$6.00
T-176	Christie, Agatha - ***A Holiday For Murder*** [1957]	$1.00	$3.00	$6.00
T-177	Aherne, Owen - ***Man On Fire*** [1957] Bing Crosby photo cover. Movie photos throughout.	$1.00	$3.00	$6.00
T-178	Hilton, Joseph - ***Beyond Mombasa*** [1957] Movie tie-in. Photo cover.	$1.00	$3.00	$6.00
T-179	Tiempo, E.K. - ***Cry Slaughter!*** [1957] PBO.	$1.00	$3.00	$6.00
T-180	Smith, George O. - ***Space Plague*** [1957] Cover by Powers.	$1.25	$3.75	$7.50
T-181	Ronns, Edward - ***Pick Up Alley*** [1957] PBO. Movie tie-in. Photo cover.	$2.00	$6.00	$12.00
T-182	Aherne, Owen - ***An Affair To Remember*** [1957] PBO. Movie tie-in. Photo cover and thoughout.	$1.25	$3.75	$7.50
T-183	O'Hara, John - ***Butterfield 8*** [1957]	$ .75	$2.50	$5.00
T-184	Queen, Ellery - ***Drury Lane's Last Case*** [1957] Cover by Sussman.	$1.00	$3.00	$6.00
T-185	Algren, Nelson - ***The Jungle*** [1957]	$1.00	$3.00	$6.00
T-186	Sohl, Jerry - ***The Time Dissolver*** [1957] PBO. Cover by Powers.	$1.00	$3.00	$6.00
T-187	Whittington, Harry - ***Temptations Of Valerie*** [1957] PBO. Movie tie-in. Photo cover.	$1.50	$5.00	$10.00
T-188	Wellard, James - ***Action Of The Tiger*** [1957] Movie tie-in. Photos throughout.	$1.00	$3.00	$6.00
T-189	Sanford, John - ***Make My Bed In Hell*** [1957]	$1.00	$3.00	$6.00
T-190	Hugo, Victor - ***Hunchback Of Notre Dame*** [1957] PBO. Movie tie-in. Photos cover and throughout.	$2.50	$7.50	$15.00
T-191	Landon, Joseph - ***Bomber Crew*** [1957]	$1.00	$3.00	$6.00
T-192	Christie, Agatha - ***Poirot Loses A Client*** [1957]	$ .75	$2.50	$5.00
T-193	Blish, James - ***Year 2018*** [1957] First U.S. edition.	$1.00	$3.00	$6.00
T-194	Golightly, Bonnie - ***The Wild One*** [1957]	$1.35	$4.00	$8.00
T-195	Bosquet, Jean - ***The Flesh Agents*** [1957]	$1.00	$3.00	$6.00
T-196	Whittington, Harry - ***Man In The Shadow*** [1957] PBO. Movie tie-in. Photos cover and throughout..	$2.50	$7.50	$15.00
T-197	Goethals, Thomas - ***Panzer Ghost Division*** [1957]	$1.00	$3.00	$6.00
T-198	Arthur, Burt - ***Ride Out For Revenge*** [1957]	$ .75	$2.50	$5.00
T-199	Charteris, Leslie - ***The Saint Vs. Scotland Yard*** [1957]	$ .75	$2.50	$5.00
T-200	Colette - ***Diary Of A 16 Year Old French Girl*** [1957]	$1.00	$3.00	$6.00
T-201	Mills, Mervyn - ***The Long Haul*** [1957] Movie tie-in. Photos cover and throughout.	$1.35	$4.00	$8.00
T-202	Leinster, Murray - ***Planet Explorer*** [1957]	$1.00	$3.00	$6.00
T-203	Tomkinson, Constance - ***Les Girls*** [1957] Cover by George Ziel.	$1.00	$3.00	$6.00
T-204	Christie, Agatha - ***Mysterious Affair At Styles*** [1957] Cover by David Stone.	$ .75	$2.50	$5.00
T-205	McIntyre, Captain Donald - ***U-Boat Killer*** [1957]	$1.00	$3.00	$6.00
T-206	Martin, Hansford - ***Soldier's Weekend*** [1957] Cover by Victor Kalin.	$1.00	$3.00	$6.00
T-207	Weidman, Jerome - ***The Price Is Right*** [1957]	$ .75	$2.50	$5.00

Avon T Series, T-219

Avon T Series, T-262

Avon T Series, T-287

		G	VG	F
T-208	Merritt, A. - ***Seven Footprints To Satan*** [1957]	$1.35	$4.00	$8.00
T-209	Parise, Goffredo - ***Don Gastone And The Women*** [1957]	$ .75	$2.50	$5.00
T-210	Christie, Agatha - ***The Secret Adversary*** [1957] Cover by Victor Kalin.	$ .75	$2.50	$5.00
T-211	Lewis, C.S. - ***The Tortured Planet*** [1957]	$1.00	$3.00	$6.00
T-212	Cheyney, Peter - ***Case Of The Dark Wanton*** [1958] Cover by Sussman.	$1.00	$3.00	$6.00
T-213	Lengyel, Olga - ***I Survived Hitler's Ovens*** [1958] Photo cover.	$1.25	$3.75	$7.50
T-214	Coleman, Lonnie - ***Hot Spell*** [1958] PBO. Movie tie-in. Photos cover and throughout.	$1.25	$3.75	$7.50
T-215	Landsborough, Gordon - ***Tobruk Commando*** [1958] Photo cover.	$1.00	$3.00	$6.00
T-216	Stout, Rex - ***Case Of The Red Box*** [1958]	$1.00	$3.00	$6.00
T-217	Kaufman, Lenard - ***Juvenile Delinquents*** [1958]	$1.25	$3.75	$7.50
T-218	Lawrence, D.H. - ***A Modern Lover*** [1958]	$ .75	$2.50	$5.00
T-219	Counsel, Firth - ***Juvenile Jungle*** [1958] PBO. Movie tie-in and photo cover.	$1.35	$4.00	$8.00
T-220	Christie, Agatha - ***The Regatta Mystery And Other Stories*** [1958]	$1.00	$3.00	$6.00
T-221	Shiras, Wilmar H. - ***Children Of The Atom*** [1958] Cover by Powers.	$1.00	$3.00	$6.00
T-222	Fitzgibbon, Constantine - ***Officer's Plot To Kill Hitler*** [1958] Photo cover.	$ .75	$2.50	$5.00
T-223	Algren, Nelson - ***Never Come Morning*** [1958]	$ .75	$2.50	$5.00
T-224	Williams, Wirt - ***Passiontide*** [1958]	$ .75	$2.50	$5.00
T-225	Blish, James - ***Earthman, Come Home*** [1958]	$1.00	$3.00	$6.00
T-226	Reynolds, Quentin - ***Raid At Dieppe*** [1958]	$1.00	$3.00	$6.00
T-227	Anthology edited by Harold Meyers - ***Belly Laughs Annual*** [1958] Cartoon and joke book.	$2.00	$6.00	$12.00
T-228	Ronns, Edward - ***The Lady Takes A Flyer*** [1958] PBO. Movie tie-in and photo cover.	$1.35	$4.00	$8.00
T-229	Cooper, Morton - ***Young And Wild*** [1958] Movie tie-in. Cover by Victor Kalin.	$2.00	$6.00	$12.00
T-230	Hilton, Joseph - ***Cry Baby Killer*** [1958] PBO. Movie tie-in and photo cover.	$2.00	$6.00	$12.00
T-231	Chapman, Maristan - ***Rogue's March*** [1958]	$ .75	$2.50	$5.00

		G	VG	F
T-232	Asimov, Isaac - ***2nd Foundation: Galactic Empire*** [1958] Cover by Powers	$1.35	$4.00	$8.00
T-233	Clarke, Donald Henderson - ***Impatient Virgin*** [1958] Photo cover.	$ .75	$2.50	$5.00
T-234	Charteris, Leslie - ***The Saint In Miami*** [1958] Cover by David Stone.	$ .75	$2.50	$5.00
T-235	Brown, Wenzell - ***Gang Girl*** [1958]	$1.35	$4.00	$8.00
T-236	Woodward, David - ***The Secret Raiders*** [1958]	$ .75	$2.50	$5.00
T-237	Golightly, Bonnie - ***The High Cost Of Loving*** [1958] Movie tie-in.	$1.25	$3.75	$7.50
T-238	Blish, James - ***Vor*** [1958] PBO.	$1.00	$3.00	$6.00
T-239	Gunther, John - ***D-Day*** [1958] Photo cover.	$ .75	$2.50	$5.00
T-240	Weidman, Jerome - ***I Can Get It For You Wholesale*** [1958]	$ .75	$2.50	$5.00
T-241	Whittington, Harry - ***Teenage Jungle*** [1958]	$2.50	$7.50	$15.00
T-242	Queen, Ellery - ***The Four Of Hearts*** [1958]	$ .75	$2.50	$5.00
T-243	Christie, Agatha - ***Murder In 3 Acts*** [1958]	$ .75	$2.50	$5.00
T-244	Clark, Gordon - ***The Naked Sin*** [1958] PBO. Cover by Hulings.	$1.25	$3.75	$7.50
T-245	Christie, Agatha - ***The Tuesday Club Murders*** [1958] Cover by Stone.	$ .75	$2.50	$5.00
T-246	Hashimoto, Mochitsura - ***Sunk!*** [1958] Photo cover.	$1.00	$3.00	$6.00
T-247	Cooper, Morton - ***Delinquent!*** [1958] PBO.	$1.50	$5.00	$10.00
T-248	Bracco, Edgar Jean - ***Chattels Of Eldorado*** [1958] Cover by Rudy Nappi.	$1.00	$3.00	$6.00
T-249	McIntosh, J.T. - ***Worlds Apart*** [1958] Cover by Powers.	$1.00	$3.00	$6.00
T-250	Charteris, Leslie - ***The Saint In England*** [1958]	$ .75	$2.50	$5.00
T-251	Haase, John - ***The Young Who Sin*** [1958] PBO.	$1.50	$5.00	$10.00
T-252	Van Vogt, A.E. - ***The Mind Cage*** [1958]	$1.00	$3.00	$6.00
T-253	Lacy, Ed - ***Breathe No More, My Lady*** [1958] PBO.	$1.35	$4.00	$8.00
T-254	Marsh, Ngaio - ***Death Of A Fool*** [1958]	$1.00	$3.00	$6.00
T-255	Rourke, Thomas - ***Of All My Sins*** [1958]	$1.00	$3.00	$6.00
T-256	Thomey, Tedd - ***Jet Ace*** [1958] PBO.	$1.00	$3.00	$6.00
T-257	Cooper, Morton - ***High School Confidential*** [1958] PBO. Movie tie-in	$2.00	$6.00	$12.00
T-258	Lee, Gypsy Rose - ***The G-String Murders*** [1958]	$1.00	$3.00	$6.00
T-259	Hachiya, Michihiko - ***Hiroshima Diary*** [1958]	$1.00	$3.00	$6.00
T-260	Huneker, James - ***Painted Veils*** [1958]	$1.00	$3.00	$6.00
T-261	Heinlein, Robert A. - ***Waldo: Genius In Orbit*** [1958]	$1.00	$3.00	$6.00
T-262	Ronns, Edward - ***Gang Rumble*** [1958] PBO.	$2.00	$6.00	$12.00
T-263	Evans, John - ***Love In The Shadows*** [1958]	$1.00	$3.00	$6.00
T-264	Kane, Henry - ***Trinity In Violence*** [1958]	$1.00	$3.00	$6.00
T-265	Burgan, John - ***Cry Attack!*** [1958] Cover by Victor Kalin	$ .75	$2.50	$5.00
T-266	Gilbert, Elliott - ***Vice Trap*** [1958] PBO. Cover by Shaare.	$ .75	$2.50	$5.00
T-267	Hastings, Roderic - ***Naked Tide*** [1958] PBO. Cover by Shaare.	$1.00	$3.00	$6.00
T-268	Blish, James - ***ESPer*** [1958]	$1.00	$3.00	$6.00
T-269	Colette - ***Mitsou*** [1958] Movie tie-in. Cover by Hulings.	$1.25	$3.75	$7.50
T-270	Noel, Sterling - ***Run For Your Life*** [1958] PBO.	$1.25	$3.75	$7.50
T-271	Robinson, Ed - ***Raw Wind In Eden*** [1958] Movie tie-in.	$1.25	$3.75	$7.50
T-272	Anonymous - ***I Am A Marked Woman*** [1958] Photo cover.	$1.00	$3.00	$6.00
T-273	Phillips, Thomas Hal - ***The Bitterweed Path*** [1958]	$1.00	$3.00	$6.00
T-274	Cody, Al - ***West Of The Law*** [1958]	$ .75	$2.50	$5.00
T-275	Kuttner, Henry - ***Destination: Infinity*** [1958] Cover by Powers	$1.00	$3.00	$6.00
T-276	Kane, Henry - ***Fistful Of Death*** [1958] PBO.	$1.35	$4.00	$8.00
T-277	Frame, Bart - ***Sinful*** [1958]	$1.00	$3.00	$6.00

		G	VG	F
T-278	Vandercook, John - ***Out For A Killing*** [1958]	$1.00	$3.00	$6.00
T-279	Blish, James - ***The Triumph Of Time*** [1958] PBO. Cover by Powers.	$1.25	$3.75	$7.50
T-280	Wager, Walter - ***Death Hits The Jackpot*** [1958]	$1.00	$3.00	$6.00
T-281	Cassill, R.V. - ***Lustful Summer*** [1958]	$ .75	$2.50	$5.00
T-282	Anthology edited by Harold Meyers - ***The Honeymoon Guide*** [1958] Cover by Bill Ward. Cartoon book.	$1.50	$5.00	$10.00
T-283	Carrier, Warren - ***A Hell Of A Murder*** [1958] Cover by Victor Kalin.	$1.00	$3.00	$6.00
T-284	Lovecraft, H.P. - ***Cry Horror!*** [1958] Cover by Richard Powers.	$1.50	$5.00	$10.00
T-285	Cain, James M. - ***Shameless*** [1958]	$1.35	$4.00	$8.00
T-286	Lindsay, Philip - ***The Merry Mistress*** [1958]	$1.00	$3.00	$6.00
T-287	Asimov, Isaac - ***The Death Dealers*** [1958] PBO. Author's first work in the mystery genre.	$4.00	$12.50	$25.00
T-288	Lacy, Ed - ***Shakedown For Murder*** [1958] PBO.	$1.35	$4.00	$8.00
T-289	Anthology edited by Groff Conklin - ***Br-r-r-!*** [1959] PBO.	$1.35	$4.00	$8.00
T-290	Noel, Sterling - ***Prelude To Murder*** [1959] PBO. Cover by Maguire.	$1.25	$3.75	$7.50
T-291	Kane, Henry - ***Death Is The Last Lover*** [1959]	$1.00	$3.00	$6.00
T-292	Queen, Ellery - ***The American Gun Mystery*** [1959]	$ .75	$2.50	$5.00
T-293	Cassill, R.V. - ***The Buccaneer*** [1959] PBO. Movie tie-in.	$1.00	$3.00	$6.00
T-294	Houston, Jack - ***Waiting For Willy*** [1959]	$ .75	$2.50	$5.00
T-295	Foreman, Robert L. - ***Hot Half Hour*** [1959] Photo cover.	$1.00	$3.00	$6.00
T-296	Stout, Rex - ***Over My Dead Body*** [1959]	$1.00	$3.00	$6.00
T-297	Moore, C.L. - ***Doomsday Morning*** [1959]	$1.00	$3.00	$6.00
T-298	Schiddel, Edmund - ***Break-up*** [1959]	$ .75	$2.50	$5.00
T-299	Whittington, Harry - ***Halfway To Hell*** [1959] PBO.	$2.50	$7.50	$15.00
T-300	Clarke, Donald Henderson - ***Confidential*** [1959]	$ .75	$2.50	$5.00
T-301	Colette - ***Claudine*** [1959]	$ .75	$2.50	$5.00
T-302	Kerouac, Jack - ***The Subterraneans*** [1959] "Beat" novel.	$2.00	$6.00	$12.00
T-303	Shulman, Irving - ***Cry Tough!*** [1959] Cover by Darcy.	$ .75	$2.50	$5.00
T-304	Sturgeon, Theodore - ***Aliens 4*** [1959] PBO.	$1.25	$3.75	$7.50
T-305	Chidsey, Donald Barr - ***The Naked Sword*** [1959] PBO. Cover by Shaare.	$1.00	$3.00	$6.00
T-306	Cotton, Will - ***The Night Was Made For Murder*** [1959] PBO.	$1.25	$3.75	$7.50
T-307	Marlowe, Dan - ***Doorway To Death*** [1959] PBO.	$1.25	$3.75	$7.50
T-308	Koenig, H.P. - ***And Sin No More*** [1959] PBO.	$1.25	$3.75	$7.50
T-309	Sanderson, Douglas - ***Mark It For Murder*** [1959]	$1.00	$3.00	$6.00
T-310	Golightly, Bonnie - ***Beat Girl*** [1959] PBO.	$2.00	$6.00	$12.00
T-311	Cooper, Morton - ***Anything For Kicks*** [1959] PBO.	$2.00	$6.00	$12.00
T-312	Shirreffs, Gordon D. - ***The Lonely Gun*** [1959]	$1.00	$3.00	$6.00
T-313	Omura, Kimiko - ***Diary Of A Geisha Girl*** [1959] PBO.	$1.00	$3.00	$6.00
T-314	Cheyney, Peter - ***Undressed To Kill*** [1959] Cover by Darcy.	$1.00	$3.00	$6.00
T-315	Wells, Lee E. - ***Death In The Desert*** [1959]	$1.00	$3.00	$6.00
T-316	Cooper, Morton - ***Ginny*** [1959]	$1.00	$3.00	$6.00
T-317	Charteris, Leslie - ***The Saint In New York*** [1959]	$ .75	$2.50	$5.00
T-318	Chidsey, Donald Barr - ***Lord Of The Isles*** [1959] Cover by Darcy.	$ .75	$2.50	$5.00
T-319	Disney, Doris Miles - ***Too Innocent To Kill*** [1959] Cover by Darcy.	$ .75	$2.50	$5.00
T-320	Sterling, Stewart - ***The Blonde In Suite 14*** [1959] Cover by Mort Engel.	$1.00	$3.00	$6.00
T-321	Roeburt, John - ***They Who Sin*** [1959] PBO.	$1.00	$3.00	$6.00

Avon T Series, T-328

Avon T Series, T-354

Avon Western Novel Monthly, 1

		G	VG	F
T-322	Ketchum, Philip - ***Hard Man*** [1959] PBO.	$1.00	$3.00	$6.00
T-323	Nabokov, Vladimir - ***Pnin*** [1959]	$ .75	$2.50	$5.00
T-324	Algren, Nelson - ***The Jungle*** [1959] Cover by Darcy.	$ .75	$2.50	$5.00
T-325	Treece, Henry - ***The Savage Warriors*** [1959]	$ .75	$2.50	$5.00
T-326	Robbins, Harold - ***Never Leave Me*** [1959] Cover by Darcy.	$ .75	$2.50	$5.00
T-327	Wells, Lee E. - ***Gun For Sale*** [1959]	$ .75	$2.50	$5.00
T-328	Himes, Chester - ***The Real Cool Killers*** [1959] PBO.	$2.50	$7.50	$15.00
T-329	Himmel, Richard - ***The Shame*** [1959]	$1.00	$3.00	$6.00
T-330	Marlowe, Stephen - ***Blonde Bait*** [1959] PBO. Cover by Darcy.	$1.25	$3.75	$7.50
T-331	Patten, Lewis B. - ***Savage Star*** [1959]	$ .75	$2.50	$5.00
T-332	Weiss, Joe - ***How Rough Can It Get?*** [1959] Cover by Milo.	$ .75	$2.50	$5.00
T-333	Vaughan, Carter A. - ***The Devil's Bride*** [1959]	$1.00	$3.00	$6.00
T-334	Shulman, Irving - ***The Amboy Dukes*** [1959] Cover by Darcy.	$ .75	$2.50	$5.00
T-335	Brewer, Gil - ***Sugar*** [1959] PBO.	$1.35	$4.00	$8.00
T-336	Frame, Burt - ***The Strange Co-ed*** [1959] Cover by Darcy.	$1.00	$3.00	$6.00
T-337	Queen, Ellery - ***The Tragedy Of Y*** [1959] Cover by Gross.	$ .75	$2.50	$5.00
T-338	Djebar, Assia - ***Nadia*** [1959]	$ .75	$2.50	$5.00
T-339	Patten, Lewis B. - ***The Man Who Rode Alone*** [1959]	$1.00	$3.00	$6.00
T-340	Kerouac, Jack - ***The Subterraneans*** [1959]	$1.35	$4.00	$8.00
T-341	Fox, Gardner F. - ***Iron Lover*** [1959] PBO. Cover by Darcy.	$1.25	$3.75	$7.50
T-342	Monash, Paul - ***The Unholy Lovers*** [1959]	$1.25	$3.75	$7.50
T-343	Frazer, Andrew - ***Find Eileen Hardin Alive!*** [1959]	$1.00	$3.00	$6.00
T-344	Schorer, Mark - ***Three Loves Had She*** [1959]	$ .75	$2.50	$5.00
T-345	Leinster, Murray - ***Monsters And Such*** [1959] PBO. Cover by Victor Kalin.	$1.50	$5.00	$10.00
T-346	Guild, Leo - ***Bachelor's Joke Book*** [1959]	$1.35	$4.00	$8.00
T-347	Whittington, Harry - ***Strange Bargain*** [1959] PBO.	$2.50	$7.50	$15.00
T-348	Owen, Dean - ***This Range Is Mine*** [1959]	$ .75	$2.50	$5.00
T-349	Marlowe, Dan - ***Killer With A Key*** [1959] PBO. Cover by Kalin.	$1.25	$3.75	$7.50
T-350	McCoy, John Pleasant - ***Love For A Stranger*** [1959] Photo cover.	$1.00	$3.00	$6.00
T-351	Innes, Michael - ***Murder Is An Art*** [1959]	$ .75	$2.50	$5.00
T-352	Shirreffs, Gordon D. - ***Fort Suicide*** [1959]	$ .75	$2.50	$5.00
T-353	MacDonald, William Colt - ***The Town That God Forgot*** [1959]	$ .75	$2.50	$5.00

		G	VG	F
T-354	Woolrich, Cornell - ***Beyond The Night*** [1959] PBO.	$5.00	$15.00	$30.00
T-355	Kastle, Herbert D. - ***Bachelor Summer*** [1959] PBO. Photo cover.	$1.00	$3.00	$6.00
T-356	Savage, James - ***Girl In A Jam*** [1959] PBO.	$1.00	$3.00	$6.00
T-357	Himes, Chester - ***The Crazy Kill*** [1959] PBO.	$2.50	$7.50	$15.00
T-358	Keogh, Theodora - ***The Mistress*** [1959]	$1.00	$3.00	$6.00
T-359	January, Steve - ***Rusty Desmond*** [1959]	$1.25	$3.75	$7.50
T-360	Noel, Sterling - ***We Who Survived...The Fifth Ice Age*** [1959] PBO.	$1.35	$4.00	$8.00
T-361	White, Lionel - ***Run, Killer, Run!*** [1959]	$1.00	$3.00	$6.00
T-362	Lyndon and Sangster - ***The Man Who Could Cheat Death*** [1959] PBO. Movie tie-in. Photo cover.	$2.00	$6.00	$12.00
T-363	Treece, Henry - ***The Pagan Queen*** [1959] Cover by Darcy.	$1.25	$3.75	$7.50
T-364	Fontaine, Robert - ***Young Awakening*** [1959] PBO.	$1.00	$3.00	$6.00
T-365	Cheyney, Peter - ***The Terrible Night*** [1959]	$ .75	$2.50	$5.00
T-366	Creasey, John - ***The Figure In The Dusk*** [1959]	$ .75	$2.50	$5.00
T-367	Anthology - ***Avon Bedside Companion*** [1959] Cover by Darcy	$ .75	$2.50	$5.00
T-368	Loomis, Noel M. - ***Cheyenne War Cry*** [1959]	$1.00	$3.00	$6.00
T-369	MacDonald, William Colt - ***Ambush At Scorpion Valley*** [1959]	$ .75	$2.50	$5.00
T-370	Daniels, Norman - ***The Captive*** [1959] PBO. Cover by Abbett.	$1.00	$3.00	$6.00
T-371	Christopher, John - ***Planet In Peril*** [1959] Cover by Emsh.	$1.00	$3.00	$6.00
T-372	Demaris, Ovid - ***The Long Night*** [1959] PBO. Cover by Darcy.	$1.35	$4.00	$8.00
T-373	Brister, Richard - ***Law Killer*** [1959] PBO.	$1.35	$4.00	$8.00
T-374	Stout, Rex - ***Where There's A Will*** [1959] Cover by Darcy.	$1.25	$3.75	$7.50
T-375	Scotland, Jay (John Jakes) - ***I, Barbarian*** [1959] PBO.	$1.50	$5.00	$10.00
T-376	Jay, Charlotte - ***Beat Not The Bones*** [1959]	$ .75	$2.50	$5.00
T-377	Flynn, Jay - ***McHugh*** [1959] PBO. First book in series.	$1.25	$3.75	$7.50
T-378	Wells, Lee E. - ***The Naked Land*** [1959] PBO.	$1.00	$3.00	$6.00
T-379	Clebert, Jean-Paul - ***The Block House*** [1960]	$1.00	$3.00	$6.00
T-380	Fox, Gardner F. - ***The Bastard Of Orleans*** [1960] PBO.	$1.35	$4.00	$8.00
T-381	Queen, Ellery - ***Drury Lane's Last Case*** [1960] Cover by Sussman.	$ .75	$2.50	$5.00
T-382	Loomis, Noel M. - ***Short Cut To Red River*** [1960]	$ .75	$2.50	$5.00
T-383	Drachman, Theodore S. - ***Addicted To Murder*** [1960]	$ .75	$2.50	$5.00
T-384	Himes, Chester - ***The Big Gold Dream*** [1960]	$2.50	$7.50	$15.00
T-385	Anthology - ***Various Temptations*** [1960]	$ .75	$2.50	$5.00
T-386	Heuman, William - ***Mulvane's War*** [1960] PBO. Cover by Mort Engel.	$1.00	$3.00	$6.00
T-387	Kempton, Edward - ***Swamp Tease*** [1960] PBO. Cover by Darcy.	$1.25	$3.75	$7.50
T-388	Anderson, Poul - ***The Golden Slave*** [1960] PBO. Cover by Darcy.	$2.00	$6.00	$12.00
T-389	Leinster, Murray - ***Twists In Time*** [1960] PBO. Cover by Powers.	$1.35	$4.00	$8.00
T-390	Kerouac, Jack - ***The Subterraneans*** [1960] Movie tie-in.	$1.35	$4.00	$8.00
T-391	Carr, John Dickson - ***The Bride Of Newgate*** [1960] Cover by Kalin.	$1.25	$3.75	$7.50
T-392	Marlowe, Dan - ***Doom Service*** [1960] PBO.	$1.00	$3.00	$6.00
T-393	Cassill, R.V. - ***Naked Morning*** [1960]	$ .75	$2.50	$5.00
T-394	Malley, Louis - ***Shakedown Strip*** [1960]	$1.00	$3.00	$6.00
T-396	MacDonald, William Colt - ***Rebel Ranger*** [1960]	$ .75	$2.50	$5.00
T-397	Robertiello, Richard D., M.D. - ***Voyage From Lesbos*** [1960]	$ .75	$2.50	$5.00
T-398	Block, Eugene B. - ***Great Train Robberies Of The West*** [1960]	$1.00	$3.00	$6.00
T-399	Lawrence, Steve C. - ***The Iron Marshal*** [1960]	$ .75	$2.50	$5.00

		G	VG	F
T-400	Treece, Henry - ***The Invaders*** [1960] Cover by Geygan.	$1.00	$3.00	$6.00
T-401	Christie, Agatha - ***Death On The Nile*** [1960]	$1.00	$3.00	$6.00
T-402	Lehman, Paul Evan - ***West Of The Wolverine*** [1960]	$1.00	$3.00	$6.00
T-403	Whittington, Harry - ***Rebel Woman*** [1960]	$2.50	$7.50	$15.00
T-404	Howard, Leigh - ***Chance Meeting*** [1960] Movie tie-in and photo cover.	$1.00	$3.00	$6.00
T-405	Cooper, Morton - ***Stop-Over*** [1960]	$1.00	$3.00	$6.00
T-406	Flynn, Jay - ***It's Murder McHugh*** [1960] PBO. Second book in series.	$1.25	$3.75	$7.50
T-407	Goeney, William M. - ***Power Play*** [1960]	$1.00	$3.00	$6.00
T-408	Woolrich, Cornell - ***The Doom Stone*** [1960] PBO.	$5.00	$15.00	$30.00
T-410	Lewis, C.S. - ***Out Of The Silent Planet*** [1960] Cover by Art Sussman.	$1.00	$3.00	$6.00
T-411	Hogan, Ray - ***The Shotgunner*** [1960]	$ .75	$2.50	$5.00
T-412	Maugham, W. Somerset - ***Favorite Stories*** [1960] Photo cover.	$ .75	$2.50	$5.00
T-413	Thomas, Paul - ***Cargo = Trouble*** [1960] PBO.	$1.00	$3.00	$6.00
T-414	Lauritzen, Jonreed - ***Suzanne, Savage Vixen*** [1960]	$ .75	$2.50	$5.00
T-415	Nemerov, Howard - ***The Homecoming Game*** [1960]	$ .75	$2.50	$5.00
T-416	Mazo, Earl - ***Richard Nixon*** [1960] Photo cover.	$ .75	$2.50	$5.00
T-417	Morrison, Ray - ***Reformatory Girls*** [1960] PBO. Cover by Darcy.	$2.50	$7.50	$15.00
T-418	Ketchum, Philip - ***The Buzzard Guns*** [1960]	$ .75	$2.50	$5.00
T-419	Frazer, Andrew - ***The Fall Of Marty Moon*** [1960]	$ .75	$2.50	$5.00
T-420	Maugham, W. Somerset - ***Ashenden Or The British Agent*** [1960] Cover by Kossim.	$ .75	$2.50	$5.00
T-421	MacDonald, William Colt - ***Roaring Lead*** [1960]	$ .75	$2.50	$5.00
T-422	Lockridge, Richard and Frances - ***Death Has A Small Voice*** [1960] Cover by Mort Engel.	$ .75	$2.50	$5.00
T-423	Daniels, Max - ***Passport To Terror*** [1960] PBO. Cover by Darcy.	$1.00	$3.00	$6.00
T-424	Gordon, Richard - ***Doctor In Love*** [1960] Cover by Abbett.	$ .75	$2.50	$5.00
T-425	Weidman, Jerome - ***What's In It For Me?*** [1960] Cover by Victor Kalin.	$ .75	$2.50	$5.00
T-426	Sanderson, Douglas - ***Catch A Fallen Starlet*** [1960] PBO. Cover by Harry Bennett.	$1.00	$3.00	$6.00
T-427	Hilton, James - ***We Are Not Alone*** [1960]	$ .75	$2.50	$5.00
T-428	MacDonald, William Colt - ***The Sunrise Guns*** [1960]	$ .75	$2.50	$5.00
T-429	Kerouac, Jack - ***Tristessa*** [1960] PBO. Cover by Elliott.	$3.50	$10.00	$20.00
T-430	Colby, Robert - ***Run For The Money*** [1960] PBO.	$1.00	$3.00	$6.00
T-431	Cody, Al - ***Bitter Creek*** [1960]	$ .75	$2.50	$5.00
T-432	Chidsey, Donald Barr - ***Fancy-Man*** [1960] PBO.	$1.00	$3.00	$6.00
T-433	Heuman, William - ***Gunhand From Texas*** [1960]	$ .75	$2.50	$5.00
T-434	Himes,,Chester - ***All Shot Up*** [1960] PBO.	$2.50	$7.50	$15.00
T-436	Lengyel, Olga - ***Hitler's Ovens*** [1960] Photo cover.	$1.00	$3.00	$6.00
T-437	Thurber, James - ***The Beast In Me And Other Animals*** [1960]	$1.25	$3.75	$7.50
T-438	Cuneo, Ernest - ***Life With Fiorello*** [1960] Cover by Gregori.	$ .75	$2.50	$5.00
T-439	Sturgeon, Theodore - ***Beyond*** [1960] PBO. Cover by Sussman.	$1.00	$3.00	$6.00
T-440	Zolotow, Maurice - ***Oh Careless Love*** [1960] Cover by McGinnis.	$1.00	$3.00	$6.00
T-441	Cassill, R.V. - ***My Sister's Keeper*** [1960] PBO. Cover by Elliott.	$ .75	$2.50	$5.00
T-442	Palmer, Bruce - ***The Shattered Affair*** [1960]	$ .75	$2.50	$5.00
T-443	MacDonald, William Colt - ***Spanish Pesos*** [1960]	$ .75	$2.50	$5.00
T-444	Flynn, Jay - ***A Body For McHugh*** [1960] PBO.	$1.25	$3.75	$7.50

		G	VG	F
T-446	Frazee, Steve - ***The Alamo*** [1960] Movie tie-in. John Wayne photo cover.	$1.35	$4.00	$8.00
T-448	Torres, Tereska - ***The Golden Cage*** [1960] Photo cover.	$1.35	$4.00	$8.00
T-449	Jackson, Shirley - ***The Lottery*** [1960]	$1.00	$3.00	$6.00
T-450	Whittington, Harry - ***Die Lover*** [1960]	$2.50	$7.50	$15.00
T-451	Patten, Lewis B. - ***Savage Town*** [1960] PBO.	$1.00	$3.00	$6.00
T-452	Marlowe, Dan - ***The Fatal Frails*** [1960] PBO.	$1.00	$3.00	$6.00
T-453	Hogan, Ray - ***Guns Against The Sun*** [1960] PBO. Cover by Carl Hantman.	$1.00	$3.00	$6.00
T-454	Haase, John - ***The Young Who Sin*** [1960] Cover by Meese.	$1.00	$3.00	$6.00
T-455	Boulle, Pierre - ***Face Of A Hero*** [1960]	$ .75	$2.50	$5.00
T-456	Des Ligneris, Francoise - ***Fort Frederick*** [1960]	$1.50	$5.00	$10.00
T-457	Wells, Lee E. - ***Tarnished Star*** [1960] PBO. Cover by Carl Hantman.	$1.00	$3.00	$6.00
T-458	Frazee, Steve - ***A Day To Die*** [1960] PBO.	$1.00	$3.00	$6.00
T-459	Keene, Day - ***The Brimstone Bed*** [1960] PBO.	$1.25	$3.75	$7.50
T-460	Kane, Henry - ***Martinis And Murder*** [1960]	$1.00	$3.00	$6.00
T-462	Demaris, Ovid - ***The Gold-Plated Sewer*** [1960] PBO.	$1.25	$3.75	$7.50
T-463	Christopher, John - ***A Scent Of White Poppies*** [1960]	$1.25	$3.75	$7.50
T-464	Donovan, John - ***Eichmann, Man Of Slaughter*** [1960] PBO. Photo cover.	$ .75	$2.50	$5.00
T-465	Purdy, James - ***Malcolm*** [1960]	$1.00	$3.00	$6.00
T-466	Flynn, Jay - ***Viva McHugh!*** [1960] PBO.	$1.25	$3.75	$7.50
T-467	Ketchum, Philip - ***Apache Dawn*** [1960] PBO.	$1.00	$3.00	$6.00
T-469	Trimble, Louis - ***Girl On A Slay Ride*** [1960] PBO. Cover by Kalin.	$1.00	$3.00	$6.00
T-470	Brewer, Gil - ***Nude On Thin Ice*** [1960] PBO.	$1.35	$4.00	$8.00
T-471	Erikson, Nancy Watson - ***Splinters Of Fear*** [1960] Photo cover.	$1.00	$3.00	$6.00
T-472	Anderson, Poul - ***Rogue Sword*** [1960] PBO.	$1.50	$5.00	$10.00
T-474	Golightly, Bonnie - ***A Breath Of Scandal*** [1960] PBO. Movie tie-in and photo cover.	$1.25	$3.75	$7.50
T-475	Maltz, Maxwell, M.D. - ***The Magic Scapel*** [1960] PBO.	$ .75	$2.50	$5.00
T-477	Noel, Sterling - ***Intrigue In Paris*** [1960] Photo cover.	$1.00	$3.00	$6.00
T-478	Ernenwein, Leslie - ***Warrior Basin*** [1960]	$ .75	$2.50	$5.00
T-479	Daniels, Norman - ***Lover, Let Me Live!*** [1960] PBO. Cover by Darcy.	$1.00	$3.00	$6.00
T-480	Schoonover, Lawrence - ***The Prisoner Of Tordesillas*** [1960]	$ .75	$2.50	$5.00
T-482	Des Ligneris, Francoise - ***Psyche 59*** [1960]	$1.00	$3.00	$6.00
T-483	Leinster, Murray - ***The Wailing Asteroid*** [1960] PBO. Cover by Powers.	$1.25	$3.75	$7.50
T-484	Anthology - ***Puzzle It Out!*** [1960] PBO. Puzzle book.	$5.50	$17.50	$35.00
T-485	Slesar, Henry - ***Clean Crimes And Neat Murders*** [1960] PBO.	$1.50	$5.00	$10.00
T-487	Collier, Jim - ***Cheers!*** [1960]	$ .75	$2.50	$5.00
T-488	Anthology edited by Ira U. Cobleigh - ***Guide To Success In The Stock Market*** [1961]	$ .75	$2.50	$5.00
T-489	Mandel, George - ***Beatville, U.S.A.*** [1961] PBO. Beatnik cartoon book.	$1.35	$4.00	$8.00
T-490	Gordon, Richard - ***Doctor In Clover*** [1961] Cover by Abbett.	$ .75	$2.50	$5.00
T-491	Marlowe, Dan - ***Shake A Crooked Town*** [1961]	$1.00	$3.00	$6.00
T-492	Thompson, Thomas - ***Bitter Water*** [1961]	$ .75	$2.50	$5.00
T-493	Allingham, Margery - ***Flowers For The Judge*** [1961] Photo cover.	$ .75	$2.50	$5.00
T-494	Nye, Nelson - ***Trouble On The Tonto Rim*** [1961]	$ .75	$2.50	$5.00

		G	VG	F
T-495	Martin, Kay - ***Suburban Wife*** [1961] PBO.	$1.00	$3.00	$6.00
T-496	Sanders, Jacquin - ***Look To Your Geese*** [1961]	$ .75	$2.50	$5.00
T-497	Williams, Lawrence - ***The Fiery Furnace*** [1961]	$ .75	$2.50	$5.00
T-498	Fox, Gardner F. - ***Ivan The Terrible*** [1961] PBO.	$1.35	$4.00	$8.00
T-499	Ballard, Todhunter (W. T. Ballard) - ***The Long Trail Back*** [1961]	$1.25	$3.75	$7.50
T-500	Flynn, Jay - ***The Action Man*** [1961] PBO. Cover by Abbett.	$1.25	$3.75	$7.50
T-501	Hatlo, Jimmy - ***Office Hi-Jinks*** [1961] PBO. Cover by Hatlo. Cartoon book.	$2.50	$7.50	$15.00
T-502	Orrmont, Arthur - ***Little Mistress*** [1961] PBO. Photo cover.	$1.00	$3.00	$6.00
T-503	Ishlon, Deborah - ***Girl Singer*** [1961]	$ .75	$2.50	$5.00
T-504	Karp, David - ***Enter, Sleeping*** [1961] Cover by Gregori.	$1.35	$4.00	$8.00
T-505	Monsey, Derek - ***It's Ugly Head*** [1961] Cover by Liebman.	$ .75	$2.50	$5.00
T-506	Giffen, Warren - ***Hell Hath No Fury*** [1961] PBO.	$1.00	$3.00	$6.00
T-507	Thomason, John W., Jr. - ***Gone To Texas*** [1961]	$ .75	$2.50	$5.00
T-510	Murray, Kathryn - ***My Husband, Arthur Murray*** [1961] Photos throughout.	$ .75	$2.50	$5.00
T-511	O'Hara, John - ***The Doctor's Son*** [1961]	$ .75	$2.50	$5.00
T-512	Anthology edited by Donald Honig - ***Blue And Gray*** [1961] PBO. Cover by Hampshire.	$1.00	$3.00	$6.00
T-513	Ruth, Mrs. Babe - ***The Babe And I*** [1961] Babe Ruth photo cover.	$2.00	$6.00	$12.00
T-515	Shirreffs, Gordon D. - ***The Proud Gun*** [1961]	$ .75	$2.50	$5.00
T-516	Queen, Ellery - ***The Tragedy Of Z*** [1961]	$ .75	$2.50	$5.00
T-518	Charteris, Leslie - ***The Avenging Saint*** [1961]	$ .75	$2.50	$5.00
T-520	Borden, Lee - ***The Devil's Whisper*** [1961]	$1.00	$3.00	$6.00
T-521	Castle, Frank - ***Nero*** [1961] PBO.	$1.00	$3.00	$6.00
T-524	Maine, Charles Eric - ***He Owned The World*** [1961]	$1.00	$3.00	$6.00
T-525	Wesley, Elizabeth - ***Nurse Judy*** [1961]	$ .75	$2.50	$5.00
T-526	Christie, Agatha - ***The Big Four*** [1961]	$1.00	$3.00	$6.00
T-527	Kennaway, James - ***Tunes Of Glory*** [1961] Movie tie-in. Photo cover.	$1.00	$3.00	$6.00
T-528	Koningsberger, Hans - ***An American Romance*** [1961] Cover by Mcginnis.	$1.00	$3.00	$6.00
T-530	Allingham, Margery - ***The Tiger In The Smoke*** [1961] Photo cover.	$ .75	$2.50	$5.00
T-531	Heyman, Evan Lee - ***Survive!*** [1961] PBO.	$1.00	$3.00	$6.00
T-532	Gregor, Manfred - ***The Bridge*** [1961] Movie tie-in. Photo cover.	$1.00	$3.00	$6.00
T-533	Hopson, William - ***Apache Kill*** [1961]	$ .75	$2.50	$5.00
T-534	Anthology edited by Maynard C. Nichols - ***Avon Crossword Puzzler*** [1961]	$4.00	$12.50	$25.00
T-535	Cooper, Morton - ***The Love Survey*** [1961] PBO.	$1.00	$3.00	$6.00
T-536	Patten, Lewis B. - ***Renegade Gun*** [1961]	$ .75	$2.50	$5.00
T-538	Lacy, Ed. - ***Bugged For Murder*** [1961] PBO.	$1.35	$4.00	$8.00
T-539	White, Lionel - ***The Snatchers*** [1961]	$ .75	$2.50	$5.00
T-541	Parsons, E. M. - ***The Dark Of Summer*** [1961] PBO. Cover by Johnson.	$1.00	$3.00	$6.00
T-542	Hogan, Robert J. - ***Wanted: Smoke Wade*** [1961]	$ .75	$2.50	$5.00
T-543	Gaddis, Peggy - ***Settlement Nurse*** [1961]	$ .75	$2.50	$5.00
T-548	Brister, Richard - ***The Wolf Streak*** [1961]	$ .75	$2.50	$5.00
T-549	Appell, George C. - ***Posse*** [1961]	$ .75	$2.50	$5.00
T-553	Hopson, William - ***Hangtree Range*** [1961]	$ .75	$2.50	$5.00
T-556	Brister, Richard - ***The Shoot-out At Sentinel Peak*** [1961]	$ .75	$2.50	$5.00

		G	VG	F
T-588	Charteris, Leslie - ***Saint Errant*** [n.d.]	$ .75	$2.50	$5.00
T-610	Charteris, Leslie - ***The Saint Steps In*** [n.d.]	$ .75	$2.50	$5.00
T-611	Charteris, Leslie - ***The Saint In Europe*** [n.d.]	$ .75	$2.50	$5.00
T-619	Charteris, Leslie - ***The Saint Sees It Through*** [n.d.]	$ .75	$2.50	$5.00
T-629	Charteris, Leslie - ***The Saint And Mr. Teal*** [n.d.]	$ .75	$2.50	$5.00
T-634	West, Nathaniel - ***Miss Lonelyhearts*** [n.d.]	$ .75	$2.50	$5.00
T-658	Christie, Agatha - ***Death In The Air*** [n.d.]	$ .75	$2.50	$5.00
T-690	Christie, Agatha - ***The Big Four*** [n.d.]	$ .75	$2.50	$5.00
T-694	Charteris, Leslie - ***The Saint—Wanted For Murder*** [n.d.]	$ .75	$2.50	$5.00
T-708	Charteris, Leslie - ***Arrest The Saint*** [n.d.]	$ .75	$2.50	$5.00
T-716	Christie, Agatha - ***Poirot Investigates*** [n.d.]	$ .75	$2.50	$5.00
T-771	Charteris, Leslie - ***The Saint On The Spanish Main*** [n.d.]	$ .75	$2.50	$5.00
T-793	Christie, Agatha - ***The Case Of The Moving Finger*** [n.d.]	$ .75	$2.50	$5.00

Avon Western Novel Monthly. New York: Avon Books. Digest Size.

1	Nye, Nelson - ***The Gun-Wolf Of Tubac*** [1949]	$4.00	$12.50	$25.00
2	Hopson, William - ***Cattle War Buckaroo*** [1950]	$4.00	$12.50	$25.00
3	Hopson, William - ***Arizona Roundup*** [1950]	$4.00	$12.50	$25.00

Avon Western Reader. New York: Avon Book Company. Digest Size.

2	Anthology - ***Includes six new short stories*** [1947] PBO.	$3.50	$10.00	$20.00

Badger "Out Of This World" Series. London: Badger Books.

1	Anthology - ***Includes A Place Of Madness by A. J. Merak*** [1954] Cover by R. Theobald.	$3.50	$10.00	$20.00
2	Anthology - ***Includes Time To Die by Randall Conway*** [1955] Cover by R. Turner	$3.50	$10.00	$20.00

Badger Science Fiction Series. London: Badger Books.

11	Manning, P. L. - ***The Destroyers*** [1959]	$2.50	$7.50	$15.00
13	LaSalle, Victor - ***Twilight Zone*** [1959]	$2.50	$7.50	$15.00
14	Kenton, L. P. - ***Destination Moon*** [1959]	$2.50	$7.50	$15.00
15	Fanthorpe, R. L. - ***Alien From The Stars*** [1959]	$2.50	$7.50	$15.00
17	Fanthorpe, R. L. - ***Hyper Space*** [1959]	$2.50	$7.50	$15.00
18	Roberts, Lionel - ***Dawn Of The Mutants*** [1959]	$2.50	$7.50	$15.00
23	Roberts, Lionel - ***Time Echo*** [1959] PBO. Cover by Eddie Jones.	$2.50	$7.50	$15.00
29	Merwin, Jr., Sam - ***Three Facts Of Time*** [1959]	$2.50	$7.50	$15.00
31	Adams, John - ***When The Gods Came*** [1959]	$2.50	$7.50	$15.00
32	Powers, J. L. - ***Black Abyss*** [1959]	$2.50	$7.50	$15.00
40	Brett, Leo - ***Exit Humanity*** [1960] PBO.	$2.50	$7.50	$15.00
58	Muller, John E. - ***The Mind Makers*** [1960]	$2.50	$7.50	$15.00
62	Muller, John E. - ***The Venus Venture*** [1960]	$2.50	$7.50	$15.00
64	Norwood, Victor - ***Night Of The Black Horror*** [1960] Cover by Fox.	$2.50	$7.50	$15.00
67	Muller, John E. - ***Uranium 235*** [1960]	$2.50	$7.50	$15.00
69	Muller, John E. - ***Orbit One*** [1960]	$2.50	$7.50	$15.00
73	Muller, John E. - ***The Day The World Died*** [1960]	$2.50	$7.50	$15.00
76	Muller, John E. - ***In The Beginning*** [1960] Cover by Fox.	$2.50	$7.50	$15.00
85	Zeigfreid, Karl - ***The World That Never Was*** [1960]	$2.50	$7.50	$15.00
97	Muller, John E. - ***Special Mission*** [1960] Cover by Fox.	$2.50	$7.50	$15.00
99	Barton, Erle - ***The Planet Seekers*** [1960] Cover by Fox.	$2.50	$7.50	$15.00
104	Muller, John E. - ***Dark Continuum*** [1960]	$2.50	$7.50	$15.00
108	Fanthorpe, R. L. - ***Neuron World*** [1960]	$2.50	$7.50	$15.00
118	Fanthorpe, R. L. - ***The Watching World*** [1960]	$2.50	$7.50	$15.00

Badger Supernatural Series. London: Badger Books.

		G	VG	F
1	Anthology - ***Includes The Cloak Of Darkness by Max Chartair*** [1954] Cover by R. Theobald.	$3.50	$10.00	$20.00
2	Anthology - ***Includes The Incredulist by John Raymond*** [1954] Cover by R. Theobald.	$3.50	$10.00	$20.00
3	Anthology - ***Includes Something From The Sea by Ray Cosmic*** [1954] Cover by G. Facey	$3.50	$10.00	$20.00
4	Anthology - ***Includes House Of Unreason by H. J. Merak*** [1954] Cover by G. Facey	$3.50	$10.00	$20.00
5	Anthology - ***Includes My Name Is Satan by A. J. Merak*** [1955] Cover by G. Facey	$3.50	$10.00	$20.00
6	Anthology - ***Includes Voice of The Drum by Randall Conway*** [1955] Cover by R. Turner	$3.50	$10.00	$20.00
7	Anthology - ***Includes Moonbeast by A. J. Merak*** [1955] Cover by G. Facey	$3.50	$10.00	$20.00
8	Anthology - ***Includes The Golden Scarab by Ray Cosmic*** [1955]	$3.50	$10.00	$20.00
9	Anthology - ***Includes The Devil's Dictionary by Edward Richards*** [1957] Cover by R. Theobald.	$3.50	$10.00	$20.00
10	Anthology - ***Includes Nightmare by Randall Conway*** [1957] Cover by J. Pollack	$3.50	$10.00	$20.00
11	Anthology - ***Includes The Night Creatures by Michael Hamilton*** [1957] Cover by H. Fox	$2.50	$7.50	$15.00
12	Anthology - ***Includes Resurgam by R. L. Fanthorpe*** [1957] Cover by H. Fox.	$2.50	$7.50	$15.00
13	Anthology - ***Includes The Secret Of The Snows by R. L. Fanthorpe*** [1957] Cover by R. Theobald.	$2.50	$7.50	$15.00
14	Anthology - ***Includes Flight Of The Valkyries by R. L. Fanthorpe*** [1958] Cover by R. Theobald.	$2.50	$7.50	$15.00
15	Anthology - ***Includes Watchers Of The Forest by R. L. Fanthorpe*** [1958] Cover by H. Fox.	$2.50	$7.50	$15.00
16	Anthology - ***Includes Guardians Of The Tomb by Lionel Roberts*** [1958] Cover by H. Fox.	$2.50	$7.50	$15.00
17	Anthology - ***Includes Call Of The Werwolf by R. L. Fanthorpe*** [1958] Cover by R. Theobald.	$2.50	$7.50	$15.00
18	Anthology - ***Includes The Chalice Of Circe by A. J. Merak*** [1958] Cover by R. Theobald.	$2.50	$7.50	$15.00
19	Anthology - ***Includes The Golden Warrior by Lionel Roberts*** [1958] Cover by R. Theobald.	$2.50	$7.50	$15.00
20	Anthology - ***Includes The Death Note by R. L. Fanthorpe*** [1958] Cover by R. Theobald.	$2.50	$7.50	$15.00
21	Anthology - ***The Haunted Pool by Trebor Thorpe*** [1958] Cover by R. Theobald.	$2.50	$7.50	$15.00
22	Anthology - ***Out Of The Shadows by R. L. Fanthorpe*** [1959] Cover by R. Theobald.	$2.50	$7.50	$15.00
23	Anthology - ***Includes Mermaid Reef*** [1959] Cover by R. Theobald.	$2.50	$7.50	$15.00
24	Anthology - ***Includes The Druid by Leo Brett*** [1959] Cover by R. Theobald	$2.50	$7.50	$15.00
25	Anthology - ***Includes The Guide And The God by R. L. Fanthorpe*** [1959] Cover by R. Theobald	$2.50	$7.50	$15.00
26	Anthology - ***Includes The Dark Possessed by Michael Hamilton*** [1959] Cover by R. Theobald.	$2.50	$7.50	$15.00
27	Anthology - ***Includes The Ghost Rider by R. L. Fanthorpe*** [1959] Cover by R. Theobald.	$2.50	$7.50	$15.00
28	Anthology - ***Includes The Creatures In The Depths by J. J. Hansby*** [1959] Cover by R. Theobald	$2.50	$7.50	$15.00
29	Merak, A. J. - ***Dark Conflict*** [1959]	$2.50	$7.50	$15.00
30	Anthology - ***Includes The Crawling Fiend by Bron Fane*** [1960] Cover by E. Jones.	$2.50	$7.50	$15.00

		G	VG	F
31	Anthology - ***Includes The Sorcerers Of Bast by A. J. Merak*** [1960] Cover by Caesar.	$2.50	$7.50	$15.00
32	Thorpe, Trebor - ***Five Faces Of Fear*** [1960]	$2.50	$7.50	$15.00
33	Anthology - ***Includes The Man Who Couldn't Die*** [1960] Cover by Jacobson.	$2.50	$7.50	$15.00
34	Anthology - ***Includes A Place Of Madness by A. J. Merak*** [1960] Cover by H. Fox.	$2.50	$7.50	$15.00
35	Fanthorpe, R. L. - ***Out Of The Darkness*** [1960]	$2.50	$7.50	$15.00
36	Anthology - ***Includes Face Of Evil by R. L. Fanthorpe*** [1960] Cover by Barton.	$2.50	$7.50	$15.00
37	Anthology - ***Includes Bardell's Wild Talent by Trebor Thorpe*** [1960] Cover by Rainey.	$2.50	$7.50	$15.00
38	Anthology - ***Includes Black Marsh Hill by Trebor Thorpe*** [1961] Cover by H. Fox.	$2.50	$7.50	$15.00
39	Anthology - ***Includes Land Of The Living Dead by Leo Brett*** [1961] Cover by Rainey.	$2.50	$7.50	$15.00
40	Roberts, Lionel - ***The Last Valkyrie*** [1961]	$2.50	$7.50	$15.00
41	Anthology - ***Includes The Green Sarcophagus by Bron Fane*** [1961] Cover by H. Fox.	$2.50	$7.50	$15.00
42	Muller, John E. - ***The Unpossessed*** [1961]	$2.50	$7.50	$15.00
43	Anthology - ***Includes Face In The Dark*** [1961] Cover by Rainey.	$2.50	$7.50	$15.00
44	Brett, Leo - ***Black Infinity*** [1961]	$2.50	$7.50	$15.00
45	Anthology - ***Includes Something About Spiders by A. J. Merak*** [1961] Cover by Rainey.	$2.50	$7.50	$15.00
46	Roberts, Lionel - ***Flame Goddess*** [1961]	$2.50	$7.50	$15.00
47	Anthology - ***Includes Devil From The Depths*** [1961] Cover by Rainey.	$2.50	$7.50	$15.00
48	Torro, Pel - ***The Phantom Ones*** [1961]	$2.50	$7.50	$15.00
49	Anthology - ***Includes The Centurion's Vengeance by R. L. Fanthorpe*** [1961] Cover by H. Fox.	$2.50	$7.50	$15.00
50	Fanthorpe, R. L. - ***The Golden Chalice*** [1961]	$2.50	$7.50	$15.00
51	Fanthorpe, R. L. - ***Includes The Grip Of Fear*** [1961]	$2.50	$7.50	$15.00
52	Muller, John E. - ***Return Of Zeus*** [1962]	$2.50	$7.50	$15.00
53	Anthology - ***Includes Chariot Of Apollo by R. L. Fanthorpe*** [1962] Cover by H. Fox.	$2.50	$7.50	$15.00
54	Brett, Leo - ***Nightmare*** [1962]	$2.50	$7.50	$15.00
55	Anthology - ***Includes Storm God's Fury*** [1962] Cover by H. Fox.	$2.50	$7.50	$15.00
56	Muller, John E. - ***The Eye Of Karnak*** [1962]	$2.50	$7.50	$15.00
57	Anthology - ***Includes Hell Has Wings by R. L. Fanthorpe*** [1962] Cover by H. Fox.	$2.50	$7.50	$15.00
58	Brett, Leo - ***Face In The Night*** [1962] Cover by H. Fox.	$2.50	$7.50	$15.00
59	Fanthorpe, R. L. - ***Includes Graveyard Of The Damned*** [1962] Cover by H. Fox.	$2.50	$7.50	$15.00
60	Muller, John E. - ***Vengeance Of Siva*** [1962] Cover by H. Fox.	$2.50	$7.50	$15.00
61	Fanthorpe, R. L. - ***Includes The Darker Drink*** [1962] Cover by H. Fox.	$2.50	$7.50	$15.00
62	Brett, Leo - ***The Immortals*** [1962]	$2.50	$7.50	$15.00
63	Anthology - ***Includes The Lonely Shadows*** [1962] Cover by H. Fox.	$2.50	$7.50	$15.00
64	Zeigfreid, Karl - ***Gods Of Darkness*** [1962]	$2.50	$7.50	$15.00
65	Anthology - ***Includes Curse Of The Totem*** [1962] Cover by Rainey.	$2.50	$7.50	$15.00
66	Torro, Pel - ***Legion Of The Lost*** [1962]	$2.50	$7.50	$15.00
67	Anthology - ***Includes The Frozen Tomb*** [1962] Cover by Rainey.	$2.50	$7.50	$15.00
68	Brett, Leo - ***They Never Come Back*** [1963]	$2.50	$7.50	$15.00
69	Anthology - ***Includes Goddess Of Night*** [1963] Cover by H. Fox.	$2.50	$7.50	$15.00

		G	VG	F
70	Torro, Pel - ***The Strange Ones*** [1963]	$2.50	$7.50	$15.00
71	Anthology - ***Includes Twilight Ancestor*** [1963] Cover by H. Fox.	$2.50	$7.50	$15.00
72	Brett, Leo - ***The Forbidden*** [1963]	$2.50	$7.50	$15.00
73	Anthology - ***Includes Sands Of Eternity*** [1963] Cover by H. Fox.	$2.50	$7.50	$15.00
74	Brett, Leo - ***From Realms Beyond*** [1963]	$2.50	$7.50	$15.00
75	Anthology - ***Includes Phantom Crusader by Leo Brett*** [1963] Cover by H. Fox.	$2.50	$7.50	$15.00
76	Torro, Pel - ***The Timeless Ones*** [1963]	$2.50	$7.50	$15.00
77	Anthology - ***Includes Moon Wolf by R. L. Fanthorpe*** [1963] Cover by H. Fox.	$2.50	$7.50	$15.00
78	Barton, Lee - ***The Unseen*** [1963]	$2.50	$7.50	$15.00
79	Anthology - ***Includes In The Midst Of Night by Peter Laynham*** [1963] Cover by H. Fox.	$2.50	$7.50	$15.00
80	Fane, Bron - ***Softly By Moonlight*** [1963]	$2.50	$7.50	$15.00
81	Anthology - ***Includes The Thing From Sheol by Bron Fane*** [1963] Cover by H. Fox.	$2.50	$7.50	$15.00
82	Torro, Pel - ***The Face Of Fear*** [1963]	$2.50	$7.50	$15.00
83	Anthology - ***Includes Roman Twilight by Olaf Trent*** [1963] Cover by H. Fox.	$2.50	$7.50	$15.00
84	Fane, Bron - ***Unknown Destiny*** [1964] Cover by H. Fox.	$2.50	$7.50	$15.00
85	Anthology - ***Includes The Sword And The Statue by Trebor Thorpe*** [1964] Cover by H. Fox.	$2.50	$7.50	$15.00
86	Thanet, Neil - ***Beyond The Veil*** [1964] Cover by H. Fox.	$2.50	$7.50	$15.00
87	Anthology - ***Includes The Warlock by Bron Fane*** [1964] Cover by H. Fox.	$2.50	$7.50	$15.00
88	Thanet, Neil - ***The Man Who Came Back*** [1964] Cover by H. Fox.	$2.50	$7.50	$15.00
89	Anthology - ***Includes The Shrouded Abbot by R. L. Fanthorpe*** [1964] Cover by H. Fox.	$2.50	$7.50	$15.00
90	Fane, Bron - ***The Macabre Ones*** [1964] Cover by H. Fox.	$2.50	$7.50	$15.00
91	Anthology - ***Includes The Hand From Gehenna by Phil Nobel*** [1964] Cover by H. Fox.	$2.50	$7.50	$15.00
92	Bell, Thornton - ***Chaos*** [1964]	$2.50	$7.50	$15.00
93	Anthology - ***Includes Time Out Of Mind by Lee Barton*** [1964] Cover by H. Fox.	$2.50	$7.50	$15.00
94	Muller, John E. - ***The Exorcists*** [1965]	$2.50	$7.50	$15.00
95	Anthology - ***Includes Bitter Reflection by R. L. Fanthorpe*** [1965] Cover by H. Fox.	$2.50	$7.50	$15.00
96	Fanthorpe, R. L. - ***The Triple Man*** [1965]	$2.50	$7.50	$15.00
97	Anthology - ***Includes The Call Of The Wild by R. L. Fanthorpe*** [1965] Cover by H. Fox.	$2.50	$7.50	$15.00
98	Muller, John E. - ***Spectre Of Darkness*** [1965] Cover by H. Fox.	$2.50	$7.50	$15.00
99	Anthology - ***Includes Vision Of The Damned by R. L. Fanthorpe*** [1965] Cover by H. Fox.	$2.50	$7.50	$15.00
100	Muller, John E. - ***Out Of The Night*** [1965]	$2.50	$7.50	$15.00
101	Anthology - ***Includes The Sealed Sarcophagus by R. L. Fanthorpe*** [1965] Cover by H. Fox.	$2.50	$7.50	$15.00
102	Fanthorpe, R. L. - ***The Unconfined*** [1966]	$2.50	$7.50	$15.00
103	Anthology - ***Includes Repeat Programme by Bron Fane*** [1966] Cover by H. Fox.	$2.50	$7.50	$15.00
104	Barton, Lee - ***The Shadow Man*** [1966]	$2.50	$7.50	$15.00
105	Anthology - ***Includes Curse Of The Kahn by R. L. Fanthorpe*** [1966] Cover by H. Fox.	$2.50	$7.50	$15.00
106	Crawford, John - ***Dark Legion*** [1966] Cover by H. Fox.	$2.50	$7.50	$15.00
107	Anthology - ***Includes Body And Soul by Randall Conway*** [1967] Cover by H. Fox.	$2.50	$7.50	$15.00
109	Anthology - ***Includes The Thing In The Mist*** [1967] PBO. Cover by Fox.	$2.50	$7.50	$15.00

Ballantine Books (Early Publisher's History, 1953–1959)

Ian Ballantine, formerly of American Penguin and founder of Bantam Books, established this paperback firm. He founded this publishing house with the hope of releasing the paperback books at the same time as the hardcover. Several early Ballantine Books titles bear two publishers' names on the covers, as they worked with Houghton Mifflin and others. Desirable cover art includes the work of Richard Powers, who did many of the science fiction covers, Robert Maguire, and others. Volumes of great interest consist of numbers 10 and F558 in dust jacket, plus many of the science fiction, western, and humor titles.

Ballantine Books published a collectible series of books within the Ballantine Books imprint. The Ballantine Adult Fantasy Series brought forth new authors and also reprinted neglected known authors. The words Ballantine Adult Fantasy Series on the cover identifies the series and a unicorn logo appears on most volumes.

Del Rey, Ballantine Ladder Editions, Ballantine Special Student Editions, and Ballantine Bal-Hi Books comprise the other imprints of Ballantine Books, Inc.

Ballantine Books. New York: Ballantine Books, Inc.

		G	VG	F
1	Hawley, Cameron - ***Executive Suite*** [1952]	$2.50	$7.50	$15.00
2	Ellson, Hal - ***The Golden Spike*** [1952] PBO. Cover by Maguire.	$3.00	$9.00	$18.00
3	Baron, Stanley - ***All My Enemies*** [1952] PBO. Photo cover.	$1.35	$4.00	$8.00
4	Short, Luke - ***Saddle By Starlight*** [1952] PBO. Cover by Norman Saunders.	$1.35	$4.00	$8.00
5	Park, Ruth - ***The Witch's Thorn*** [1952] PBO.	$1.35	$4.00	$8.00
6	Danoen, Emile - ***Tides Of Time*** [1952]	$1.25	$3.75	$7.50
7	Bonham, Frank - ***Blood On The Land*** [1952] PBO. Cover by Norman Saunders.	$1.35	$4.00	$8.00
8	Capp, Al - ***The World Of Li'l Abner*** [1953] PBO. Cover by Author. Cartoon strip reprint book. Foreword by Charles Chaplin. Original introduction by John Steinbeck.	$4.00	$12.50	$25.00
9	Gilman, LaSelle - ***The Red Gate*** [1952] PBO.	$1.35	$4.00	$8.00
10-DJ	O'Rourke, Frank - ***Concannon*** [1952] PBO. In dust jacket. Book cover by Saunders, DJ cover by Maguire.	$25.00	$75.00	$180.00
10	O'Rourke, Frank - ***Concannon*** [1952] PBO. Book cover by Saunders.	$1.50	$5.00	$10.00
11	Fisher, Clay - ***War Bonnet*** [1952] PBO.	$1.35	$4.00	$8.00
12	Spackman, W. M. - ***Heyday*** [1953] PBO.	$1.25	$3.75	$7.50
13	Schaefer, Jack - ***First Blood*** [1953] PBO. Cover by Verne Tossey.	$2.00	$6.00	$12.00
14	Martin, John Bartow - ***Why Did They Kill?*** [1953] PBO. True crime stories with photo cover.	$1.50	$5.00	$10.00
15	Moore, Lucia W. - ***The Wheel And The Hearth*** [1953] PBO. Cover by Verne Tossey.	$1.35	$4.00	$8.00
16	Anthology edited by Frederick Pohl - ***Star Science Fiction Stories #1*** [1953] PBO. Cover by Powers.	$2.00	$6.00	$12.00
17	Ruesch, Hans - ***The Racer*** [1953] PBO. Cover by Geygan.	$1.25	$3.75	$7.50
18	Markey, Gene - ***Kingdom Of The Spur*** [1953] PBO. Cover by Verne Tossey.	$1.35	$4.00	$8.00
19	Anthology by Joseph Greene & E. Abell - ***Stories Of Sudden Truth*** [1953] PBO.	$1.35	$4.00	$8.00
20	Wilson, Edmund - ***I Thought Of Daisy*** [1953] PBO.	$1.25	$3.75	$7.50
21	Pohl, Frederick & Kornbluth, C. M. - ***The Space Merchants*** [1953] PBO. Cover by Powers.	$2.50	$7.50	$15.00
22	Schaefer, Jack - ***The Big Range*** [1953] PBO. Cover by Verne Tossey.	$1.50	$5.00	$10.00
23	Majdalany, Fred - ***Patrol*** [1953] PBO. Cover by Singer.	$1.25	$3.75	$7.50

Ballantine, 27

Ballantine, 28

		G	VG	F
24	Poole, Richard - ***Desert Passage*** [1953] PBO. Cover by Verne Tossey.	$1.35	$4.00	$8.00
25	Pratt, Fletcher - ***The Undying Fire*** [1953] PBO. Cover by Powers.	$2.00	$6.00	$12.00
26	Manchester, William - ***The City Of Anger*** [1953]	$1.25	$3.75	$7.50
27	Ellson, Hal - ***Summer Street*** [1953] PBO. Cover by Maguire.	$2.50	$7.50	$15.00
28	Kersh, Gerald - ***The Secret Masters*** [1953] Cover by Powers.	$3.50	$10.00	$20.00
29	Johnson, Dorothy M. - ***Indian Country*** [1953] PBO.	$1.35	$4.00	$8.00
30	Kuttner, Henry - ***Ahead Of Time*** [1953] PBO. Cover by Powers.	$2.50	$7.50	$15.00
31	Routsong, Alma - ***A Gradual Joy*** [1953] PBO.	$1.25	$3.75	$7.50
32	Chamberlain, Elinor - ***The Far Command*** [1953] PBO. Cover by Verne Tossey.	$1.25	$3.75	$7.50
33	Clarke, Arthur C. - ***Childhood's End*** [1953] PBO.	$2.25	$7.00	$14.00
34	Anthology edited By Martha Foley - ***The Best American Short Stories: 1953*** [1953] PBO.	$1.50	$5.00	$10.00
35	O'Rourke, Frank - ***Gun Hand*** [1953] PBO.	$1.35	$4.00	$8.00
36	Jackson, Charles - ***Earthly Creatures*** [1953] PBO. Cover by Maguire.	$2.00	$6.00	$12.00
37	Onn, Chin Kee - ***Silent Army*** [1953] PBO.	$1.35	$4.00	$8.00
38	Moore, Ward - ***Bring The Jubilee*** [1953] Cover by Powers.	$2.00	$6.00	$12.00
39	Anthology edited by Rolfe Humphries - ***New Poems By American Poets*** [1953] PBO.	$1.25	$3.75	$7.50
40	Fisher, Clay - ***Yellow Hair*** [1953] PBO.	$1.35	$4.00	$8.00
41	Bradbury, Ray - ***Fahrenheit 451*** [1953] PBO. Cover by Joe Mugnaini.	$5.50	$17.50	$35.00
42	Rooke, Daphne - ***Ratoons*** [1953] PBO.	$1.25	$3.75	$7.50
43	Short, Luke - ***Silver Rock*** [1953] PBO. Cover by Verne Tossey.	$1.35	$4.00	$8.00
44	Bellah, James Warner - ***The Valiant Virginians*** [1953] PBO.	$1.35	$4.00	$8.00
45	Schaefer, Jack - ***The Canyon*** [1953] PBO. Cover by Verne Tossey.	$1.50	$5.00	$10.00
46	Sturgeon, Theodore - ***More Than Human*** [1953] PBO. Cover by Powers.	$2.50	$7.50	$15.00
47	Thompson, Thomas - ***King Of Abilene*** [1953]	$1.35	$4.00	$8.00
48	Ives, Burl - ***The Burl Ives Song Book*** [1953] PBO. Photo cover.	$2.50	$7.50	$15.00
49	O'Rourke, Frank - ***Ride West*** [1953] PBO.	$1.35	$4.00	$8.00
50	Wyndham, John - ***Out Of The Deeps*** [1953] First U.S. edition.	$2.00	$6.00	$12.00
51	Leighton, Lee - ***Law Man*** [1953] PBO. Cover by Schulz.	$1.35	$4.00	$8.00
52	Clarke, Arthur C. - ***Expedition To Earth*** [1953] PBO. Cover by Powers.	$2.00	$6.00	$12.00
53	McHugh, Vincent - ***Edge Of The World*** [1953] PBO.	$1.35	$4.00	$8.00

Ballantine, 41

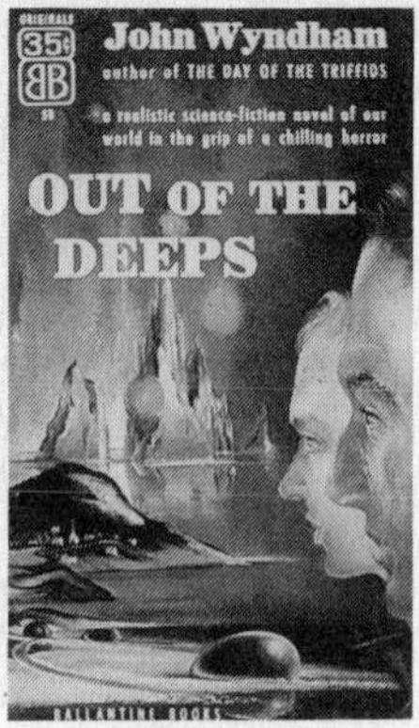

Ballantine, 50

		G	VG	F
54	Leonard, Elmore - ***The Bounty Hunters*** [1953] PBO. Author's first book.	$10.00	$30.00	$60.00
55	Anthology edited by Frederik Pohl - ***Star Science Fiction Stories #2*** [1953] PBO.	$2.00	$6.00	$12.00
56	Duncan, David - ***Dark Dominion*** [1953] PBO. Cover by Powers.	$2.00	$6.00	$12.00
57	Hardin, Dave - ***Brandon's Empire*** [1953] PBO.	$1.35	$4.00	$8.00
58	Siodmak, Curt - ***Riders To The Stars*** [1953] PBO. Cover by Powers. Movie tie-in.	$1.50	$5.00	$10.00
59	Fisher, Clay - ***The Tall Men*** [1953]	$1.35	$4.00	$8.00
60	Poole, Richard - ***The Peacemaker*** [1953] PBO. Cover by Schulz.	$1.35	$4.00	$8.00
61	Pohl, Frederick & Kornbluth, C. M. - ***Search The Sky*** [1954] PBO. Cover by Powers.	$1.50	$5.00	$10.00
62	Cleeve, Brian Talbot - ***The Night Winds*** [1954]	$1.25	$3.75	$7.50
63	Anthology - ***New Short Novels*** [1954] PBO.	$1.35	$4.00	$8.00
64	Bonham, Frank - ***Night Raid*** [1954] PBO.	$1.35	$4.00	$8.00
65	Hunter, John - ***West Of Justice*** [1954] PBO. Cover by Schulz.	$1.35	$4.00	$8.00
66	Livingston, Harold E. - ***The Coasts Of The Earth*** [1954] PBO.	$1.25	$3.75	$7.50
67	Bryan, III, Joe - ***Aircraft Carrier*** [1954] PBO.	$1.25	$3.75	$7.50
68	Clarke, Arthur C. - ***Prelude To Space*** [1954] Cover by Powers.	$2.00	$6.00	$12.00
69	O'Rourke, Frank - ***Thunder In The Sun*** [1954] PBO. Cover by Verne Tossey.	$1.35	$4.00	$8.00
70	Fox, Norman A. - ***Broken Wagon*** [1954]	$1.35	$4.00	$8.00
71	Crane, Robert - ***Hero's Walk*** [1954] PBO.	$2.25	$7.00	$14.00
72	Anthology edited by Llewellyn Miller - ***Prize Articles 1954*** [1954] PBO. Includes Ray Bradbury.	$2.50	$7.50	$15.00
73	Sheckley, Robert - ***Untouched By Human Hands*** [1954] PBO. Cover by Jack Coggins.	$2.00	$6.00	$12.00
74	Thompson, Thomas - ***Trouble Rider*** [1954]	$1.35	$4.00	$8.00
75	Anthology edited by Elizabeth Abell - ***American Accent*** [1954] PBO. Includes Isaac Asimov.	$1.25	$3.75	$7.50
76	Chamberlain, William - ***Trumpets Of Company K*** [1954] PBO. Cover by W. Kumme.	$1.25	$3.75	$7.50
F-77	Martin, John Bartlow - ***Break Down The Walls*** [1954] PBO. Photo cover.	$1.35	$4.00	$8.00
78	Harris, Eleanor - ***The Real Story Of Lucille Ball*** [1954] PBO. Cover by Hy Rubin. Eight pages of photos.	$2.50	$7.50	$15.00
80	Anderson, Poul - ***Brain Wave*** [1954] PBO. Cover by Powers.	$2.00	$6.00	$12.00
82	O'Rourke, Frank - ***High Vengeance*** [1954] PBO.	$1.35	$4.00	$8.00

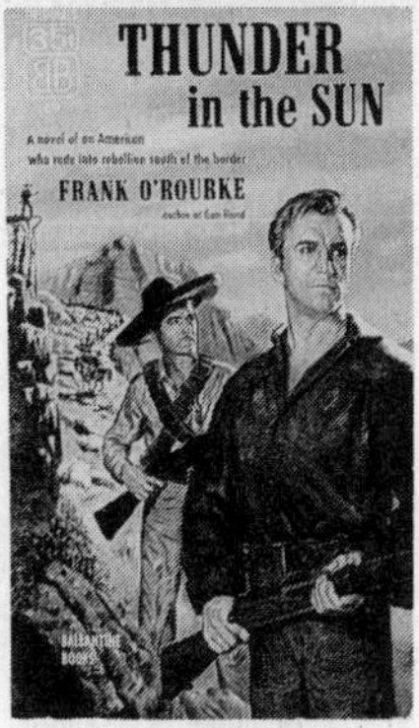

Ballantine, 69

Ballantine, 78

		G	VG	F
84	Thompson, Thomas - ***They Brought Their Guns*** [1954] PBO.	$1.35	$4.00	$8.00
85	Bonham, Frank - ***The Feud At Spanish Ford*** [1954] PBO. Cover by Schulz.	$1.35	$4.00	$8.00
86	Kornbluth, C. M. - ***The Explorers*** [1954] PBO.	$2.00	$6.00	$12.00
87	Logan, Ford - ***Fire In The Desert*** [1954] PBO.	$1.25	$3.75	$7.50
88	Neumann, Alfred - ***Strange Conquest*** [1954] PBO.	$1.25	$3.75	$7.50
89	Anthology edited by Frederick Pohl - ***Star Short Novels*** [1954] PBO.	$2.00	$6.00	$12.00
90	Anthology - ***Security And The Middle East*** [1954]	$1.25	$3.75	$7.50
91	Oliver, Chad - ***Shadows In The Sun*** [1954] PBO.	$2.00	$6.00	$12.00
92	Fanger, Horst - ***A Life For A Life*** [1954] First U.S. edition. Cover by Maguire.	$1.35	$4.00	$8.00
93	Kurtzman, Harvey - ***The Mad Reader*** [1954] PBO. Cover by Jack Davis.	$3.50	$10.00	$20.00
94	Vidal, Gore - ***Messiah*** [1954] Cover by Powers.	$2.00	$6.00	$12.00
95	Cargoe, Richard - ***Brave Harvest*** [1954] PBO. Cover by Verne Tossey.	$1.35	$4.00	$8.00
96	Anthology edited by Frederik Pohl - ***Star Science Fiction Stories #3*** [1954] PBO. Cover by Powers.	$2.00	$6.00	$12.00
97	Clarke, Arthur C. - ***Earthlight*** [1955] PBO. Cover by Powers.	$2.00	$6.00	$12.00
98	O'Rourke, Frank - ***Violence At Sundown*** [1955]	$1.35	$4.00	$8.00
99	Tenn, William - ***Of All Possible Worlds*** [1955] PBO. Cover by Richard Powers.	$2.00	$6.00	$12.00
100	Colwell, Miriam - ***Young*** [1955] PBO.	$1.25	$3.75	$7.50
101	Brickhill, Paul - ***The Dam Busters*** [1955] Cover by Schulz.	$1.25	$3.75	$7.50
102	Duncan, David - ***Beyond Eden*** [1955] PBO. Cover by Powers.	$2.00	$6.00	$12.00
103	Ellson, Hal - ***Rock*** [1955] PBO.	$2.50	$7.50	$15.00
104	Wyndham, John - ***Re-Birth*** [1955] PBO. Cover by Powers.	$2.50	$7.50	$15.00
105	Arnold, Arnold - ***How To Play With Your Child*** [1955] Photo cover.	$1.25	$3.75	$7.50
106	Kurtzman, Harvey - ***Mad Strikes Back!*** [1955] Cover by Jack Davis.	$3.00	$9.00	$18.00
107	Pohl, Frederick and Kornbluth, C. M. - ***Gladiator-At-Law*** [1955] PBO. Cover by Richard Powers.	$2.00	$6.00	$12.00
108	Shaw, Sam - ***Marilyn Monroe As The Girl*** [1955] PBO. Movie tie-in with Monroe photo cover.	$10.00	$30.00	$60.00
109	Boucher, Anthony - ***Far And Away*** [1955] PBO. Cover art by Powers.	$2.00	$6.00	$12.00
110	Reeder, Colonel Red - ***The MacKenzie Raid*** [1955] PBO. Cover by Orbaan.	$1.25	$3.75	$7.50

Ballantine, 103

Ballantine, 124

		G	VG	F
111	O'Rourke, Frank - ***Car Deal!*** [1955] PBO.	$1.25	$3.75	$7.50
112	Beresford-Howe, Constance - ***My Lady Greensleeves*** [1955] PBO.	$1.25	$3.75	$7.50
113	Oliver, Chad - ***Another Kind*** [1955] PBO. Cover art by Powers.	$2.00	$6.00	$12.00
114	Stern, Daniel - ***The Guests Of Fame*** [1955] PBO.	$1.35	$4.00	$8.00
115	Anthology edited by Charles Preston - ***The Power Of Negative Thinking*** [1955] PBO.	$1.25	$3.75	$7.50
116	Harvey, Frank - ***Jet*** [1955] PBO.	$1.25	$3.75	$7.50
117	Wilson, Richard - ***The Girls From Planet 5*** [1955] PBO. Cover art by Powers.	$2.50	$7.50	$15.00
118	Anthology - ***Great Dog Stories*** [1955] PBO. Photo cover.	$1.50	$5.00	$10.00
119	Sturgeon, Theodore - ***Caviar*** [1955] PBO. Cover art by Powers.	$2.00	$6.00	$12.00
120	Busch, Harald - ***U-Boats At War*** [1955]	$1.25	$3.75	$7.50
121	Brooker, Clark - ***Lone Gun*** [1955] PBO. Cover by Mel Crair.	$1.35	$4.00	$8.00
122	Kuttner, Henry & Moore, C. L. - ***No Boundaries*** [1955] PBO. Cover by Powers	$2.00	$6.00	$12.00
123	Pohl, Frederik & Kornbluth, C. M. - ***A Town Is Drowning*** [1955] PBO. Cover by Ed Emsh.	$3.00	$9.00	$18.00
124	Kurtzman, Harvey - ***Inside Mad*** [1955] PBO.	$3.00	$9.00	$18.00
125	Loomis, Noel - ***North To Texas*** [1955] PBO. Cover by Orbaan.	$1.35	$4.00	$8.00
126	Sheckley, Robert - ***Citizen in Space*** [1955] PBO. Cover by Powers.	$2.00	$6.00	$12.00
127	Mead, Shepherd - ***How To Succeed In Business Without Really Trying*** [1955]	$1.25	$3.75	$7.50
128	Kelton, Elmer - ***Hot Iron*** [1956] PBO. Cover by Mel Crair.	$1.35	$4.00	$8.00
129	Ellson, Hal - ***Tell Them Nothing*** [1956]	$2.50	$7.50	$15.00
130	Pohl, Frederik - ***Alternating Currents*** [1956] PBO. Cover by Powers.	$2.00	$6.00	$12.00
F-131	Reynolds, Jack - ***A Woman Of Bangkok*** [1956] PBO. Cover by Maguire.	$1.35	$4.00	$8.00
132	Price, Roger - ***In One Head And Out The Other*** [1956]	$1.25	$3.75	$7.50
F-133	Anthology edited by Martha Foley - ***Best American Short Stories 1955*** [1956]	$1.35	$4.00	$8.00
134	Blair, Jr., Clay - ***Beyond Courage*** [1956]	$1.25	$3.75	$7.50
135	Clarke, Arthur C. - ***Reach For Tomorrow*** [1956] PBO. Cover by Powers	$2.00	$6.00	$12.00
136	Schaefer, Jack - ***The Pioneers*** [1956]	$1.50	$5.00	$10.00
137	Stacy, Donald - ***The God Of Channel 1*** [1956] PBO.	$2.00	$6.00	$12.00
138	Edwards, Frank - ***My First 10,000,000 Sponsors*** [1956] PBO. Photo cover.	$1.25	$3.75	$7.50
F-139	Bradbury, Ray - ***The October Country*** [1956] Includes 15 stories originally published in the author's first book, *Dark Carnival*.	$6.00	$20.00	$40.00

Ballantine, 129

Ballantine, 180

		G	VG	F
140	Anthology - ***New Short Novels 2*** [1956] PBO. Cover by Powers.	$1.35	$4.00	$8.00
141	Averbuch, Bernard/Noble, John W. - ***Never Plead Guilty*** [1956] Photo cover.	$1.35	$4.00	$8.00
142	Halleran, E. E. - ***Devil's Canyon*** [1956] PBO. Cover by Mel Crair.	$1.35	$4.00	$8.00
143	Dempsey, David - ***Flood*** [1956]	$1.25	$3.75	$7.50
144	Kornbluth, C. M./Pohl, Frederik - ***Presidential Year*** [1956] PBO.	$2.50	$7.50	$15.00
145	Scott, Col. Robert L. - ***God Is My Co-Pilot*** [1956] Cover by John T. McCoy.	$1.25	$3.75	$7.50
146	Ives, Burl - ***Sea Songs Of Sailing, Whaling And Fishing*** [1956] PBO. Photo cover.	$2.00	$6.00	$12.00
147	Mead, Harold - ***The Bright Phoenix*** [1956] PBO. Cover by Powers.	$2.00	$6.00	$12.00
148	Leighton, Lee - ***Beyond The Pass*** [1956] PBO.	$1.35	$4.00	$8.00
149	O'Rourke, Frank - ***Hard Men*** [1956]	$1.35	$4.00	$8.00
F-150	Swiggett, Howard - ***The Power And The Prize*** [1956] Movie tie-in.	$1.35	$4.00	$8.00
151	Del Rey, Lester - ***Nerves*** [1956] PBO. Cover by Powers.	$2.00	$6.00	$12.00
152	Price, Roger - ***I'm For Me First*** [1956]	$1.25	$3.75	$7.50
153	Halleran, E. E. - ***Blazing Border*** [1956]	$1.35	$4.00	$8.00
155	Kelly, Fred C. - ***The Wright Brothers*** [1956] Cover by John T. McCoy	$1.25	$3.75	$7.50
157	Karr, David - ***Fight For Control*** [1956] PBO. Photo cover.	$1.25	$3.75	$7.50
158	Ketchum, Phil - ***The Night Of The Coyotes*** [1956]	$1.35	$4.00	$8.00
159	Tenn, William - ***The Human Angle*** [1956] PBO. Cover by Powers.	$2.00	$6.00	$12.00
160	Anthology edited by Gore Vidal - ***Best Television Plays*** [1956] PBO. Photo cover.	$1.35	$4.00	$8.00
161	Grombach, John V. - ***Olympic Cavalcade Of Sports*** [1956] PBO.	$1.50	$5.00	$10.00
F-162	Tute, Warrren - ***The Cruiser*** [1956]	$1.25	$3.75	$7.50
163	Silverstein, Shel - ***Grab Your Socks*** [1956] PBO. Cover by Silverstein. Cartoon book.	$2.50	$7.50	$15.00
164	De Vries, Marvin - ***Frontier*** [1956] PBO.	$1.35	$4.00	$8.00
165	Ewing, Frederick R. (Theodore Sturgeon) - ***I, Libertine*** [1956] PBO. Cover by Kelly Freas	$5.50	$17.50	$35.00
166	Roberts, R. M. - ***Scout*** [1956] PBO. Cover by Mel Crair.	$1.35	$4.00	$8.00
167	Vance, Jack - ***To Live Forever*** [1956] PBO. Cover by Powers.	$3.50	$10.00	$20.00
168	Zieser, Benno - ***The Road To Stalingrad*** [1956] Photo cover.	$1.25	$3.75	$7.50

Ballantine, 301-K

Ballantine U Series, U-2106

		G	VG	F
F-169	Russell, Lord (Of Liverpool) - ***The Scourge Of The Swastika*** [1956]	$1.25	$3.75	$7.50
170	Halleran, E. E. - ***Wagon Captain*** [1956]	$1.35	$4.00	$8.00
171	Cliff, Shir - ***The Wild Reader*** [1956]	$2.50	$7.50	$15.00
172	Capp, Al - ***The World Of Li'l Abner*** [1956]	$3.00	$9.00	$18.00
173	Lasly, Lt. Col. Walt - ***Turn The Tigers Loose*** [1956] PBO.	$1.25	$3.75	$7.50
174	Mead, Shepherd - ***The Big Ball Of Wax*** [1956]	$2.00	$6.00	$12.00
175	McDonald, N. C. - ***Fish The Strong Waters*** [1956] PBO. Cover by Kelly Freas	$1.25	$3.75	$7.50
176	Giles, Hascal - ***Kansas Trail*** [1956]	$1.35	$4.00	$8.00
177	Kearney, Paul W. - ***I Drive The Turnpikes... And Survive*** [1956] PBO. Photo cover.	$1.25	$3.75	$7.50
178	Gaines, William M. - ***Utterly Mad*** [1956] Cover by Jack Davis.	$3.00	$9.00	$18.00
179	Sturgeon, Theodore - ***E Pluribus Unicorn*** [1956]	$2.00	$6.00	$12.00
180	Bast William - ***James Dean*** [1956] PBO. Biographical, photo cover.	$5.00	$15.00	$30.00
181	Savage, Jr., Les - ***Hangtown*** [1956] PBO. Cover by Mel Crair.	$1.35	$4.00	$8.00
182	Wyndham, John - ***Tales Of Gooseflesh And Laughter*** [1956] PBO. Cover by Powers.	$2.00	$6.00	$12.00
183	Bekker, C. D. - ***Defeat At Sea*** [1956] Photo cover.	$1.25	$3.75	$7.50
184	Frank, Wolfgang/Rogge, Capt. Bernhard - ***German Raider Atlantis*** [1956] Photo cover.	$1.25	$3.75	$7.50
185	Appell, George - ***Shadow On The Border*** [1957] PBO. Cover by Mel Crair.	$1.35	$4.00	$8.00
186	Clarke, Arthur C. - ***Tales From The White Hart*** [1957] PBO. Cover by Powers	$2.00	$6.00	$12.00
187	Kelton, Elmer - ***Buffalo Wagons*** [1956] PBO.	$1.35	$4.00	$8.00
188	Whitman, Sidney E. - ***Cavalry Raid*** [1956] Cover by Tony Kokinos.	$1.25	$3.75	$7.50
189	Mulvihill, William - ***Fire Mission*** [1957] PBO.	$1.25	$3.75	$7.50
190	Merriam, Robert E. - ***The Battle Of The Bulge*** [1957] Photo cover.	$1.25	$3.75	$7.50
191	Flair, Terrance - ***Halfway To Heaven*** [1957] PBO. Cover by John T. McCoy.	$1.25	$3.75	$7.50
192	Pohl, Frederik - ***Slave Ship*** [1957] PBO.	$2.00	$6.00	$12.00
F-193	Galland, Adolf - ***The First And The Last*** [1957]	$1.25	$3.75	$7.50
194	Dillon, Jack - ***The Spotted Horse*** [1957] PBO.	$1.35	$4.00	$8.00
F-195	Johnson, Capt. J. E. - ***Wing Leader*** [1957]	$1.25	$3.75	$7.50
196	Rhoads, Gerda - ***The Lonely Women*** [1957] Photo cover.	$1.25	$3.75	$7.50
197	Blish, James - ***The Frozen Year*** [1957] PBO. Cover by Powers.	$2.00	$6.00	$12.00

		G	VG	F
198	Brooker, Clark - ***Fight At Sun Mountain*** [1957] PBO. Cover by Mel Crair.	$1.35	$4.00	$8.00
199	Pohl, Frederik - ***Edge Of The City*** [1957] PBO. Movie tie-in with Sidney Poitier and John Cassavettes. Photo cover.	$2.00	$6.00	$12.00
200	Clement, Hal - ***Cycle Of Fire*** [1957] PBO.	$1.50	$5.00	$10.00
F-201	Okumiya & Horikoshi - ***Zero*** [1957]	$1.25	$3.75	$7.50
202	Brown, Dee - ***Yellowhorse*** [1957] Cover by Mel Crair.	$1.35	$4.00	$8.00
203	Flender, Harold - ***Paris Blues*** [1957] PBO. Photo cover.	$1.35	$4.00	$8.00
F-204	Anthology edited by Martha Foley - ***The Best American Short Stories 1956*** [1957] Cover by Bates.	$1.35	$4.00	$8.00
205	Halleran, E. E. - ***The Hostile Hills*** [1957] PBO. Cover by Mel Crair.	$1.35	$4.00	$8.00
206	Pohl, Frederik - ***The Case Against Tomorrow*** [1957] PBO. Cover by Powers	$2.00	$6.00	$12.00
207	Schaeffer, Heinz - ***U-Boat 977*** [1957] Photo cover.	$1.25	$3.75	$7.50
208	Robertson, Frank C. - ***Lawman's Pay*** [1957] PBO. Cover by Mel Crair	$1.35	$4.00	$8.00
209	Foley, Charles - ***Commando Extraordinary*** [1957] Photo cover.	$1.25	$3.75	$7.50
210	Farmer, Philip Jose - ***The Green Odyssey*** [1957] PBO. Cover by Powers	$5.50	$17.50	$35.00
211	O'Rourke, Frank - ***Legend In The Dust*** [1957] PBO.	$1.35	$4.00	$8.00
212	O'Rourke, Frank - ***Gun Hand*** [1957]	$1.35	$4.00	$8.00
213	O'Rourke, Frank - ***Violence At Sundown*** [1957]	$1.35	$4.00	$8.00
214	O'Rourke, Frank - ***High Vengeance*** [1957]	$1.35	$4.00	$8.00
215	Anthology - ***Sometime, Never*** [1957] PBO. Cover by Powers.	$2.00	$6.00	$12.00
216	Stiles, Bert - ***Serenade To The Big Bird*** [1957] Photo cover	$1.25	$3.75	$7.50
217	Scott, General Robert L. - ***Between The Elephant's Eyes*** [1957] Cover by Kuhn	$1.25	$3.75	$7.50
218	Maine, Charles Eric - ***High Vacuum*** [1957] PBO. Cover by Powers.	$1.50	$5.00	$10.00
219	Halleran, E. E. - ***Spanish Ridge*** [1957] PBO. Cover by Mel Crair.	$1.35	$4.00	$8.00
220	Martin, John Bartlow - ***The Deep South Says "Never"*** [1957] PBO. Photo cover.	$2.25	$7.00	$14.00
221	Castle, John - ***The Password Is Courage*** [1957]	$1.25	$3.75	$7.50
222	Ryan, Cornelius - ***One Minute To Ditch!*** [1957] Photo cover.	$1.25	$3.75	$7.50
223	Anonymous - ***A Woman In Berlin*** [1957]	$1.25	$3.75	$7.50
F-224	Fushida, Mitsuo & Okumiya, Masatake - ***Midway*** [1957]	$1.25	$3.75	$7.50
F-225	Guderian, Heinz - ***Panzer Leader*** [1957]	$1.25	$3.75	$7.50
226	Anthology - ***New Poems By American Poets #2*** [1957]	$1.25	$3.75	$7.50
227	Woodward, C. Vann - ***The Battle For Leyte Gulf*** [1957]	$1.25	$3.75	$7.50
228	Bryan III, Joe - ***Aircraft Carrier*** [1957] Photo cover	$1.25	$3.75	$7.50
229	Hiken, Nat - ***Sergeant Bilko*** [1957] PBO. TV tie-in with photo cover.	$2.50	$7.50	$15.00
230	Duncan, David - ***Occam's Razor*** [1957] PBO. Cover by Powers.	$2.00	$6.00	$12.00
F-231	Thompson, R. W. - ***The 85 Days*** [1957] PBO. Photo cover.	$1.25	$3.75	$7.50
232	Robertson, Frank C. - ***Disaster Valley*** [1957] PBO. Cover by Mel Crair	$1.35	$4.00	$8.00
233	Keats, John - ***The Crack In The Picture Window*** [1957]	$1.50	$5.00	$10.00
F-234	Hechler, Ken - ***The Bridge At Remagen*** [1957] Photo cover	$1.25	$3.75	$7.50
235	Settel, Irving - ***Best TV Humor Of 1957*** [1957]	$1.50	$5.00	$10.00
236	Ward, Don - ***Gunsmoke*** [1957] PBO. TV tie-in with James Arness photo cover.	$2.50	$7.50	$15.00
237	Wilson, Richard - ***Those Idiots From Earth*** [1957] PBO. Cover by Powers	$2.00	$6.00	$12.00
238	Anthology edited by Florence Britton - ***Best Television Plays 1957*** [1957] PBO. Cover by Bunce.	$1.50	$5.00	$10.00
239	Anthology edited by Don Congdon - ***The Wild Sweet Wine*** [1957] PBO. Includes Ray Bradbury.	$2.00	$6.00	$12.00
240	Evens, Owen - ***Chain Link*** [1957] PBO. Cover by Mel Crair.	$1.25	$3.75	$7.50

		G	VG	F
241	Johnson, Dorothy M. - ***Indian Country*** [1957]	$1.25	$3.75	$7.50
242	Anthology edited by Harvey Kurtzman - ***The Humbug Digest*** [1957] Cover by Jack Davis.	$3.50	$10.00	$20.00
243	Budrys, Algis - ***Man Of Earth*** [1957] PBO. Cover by Powers.	$2.00	$6.00	$12.00
244	Kuwahara, Yasuo & Allred, Gordon T. - ***Kamikaze*** [1957] Photo cover.	$1.25	$3.75	$7.50
245	Brickhill, Paul - ***The Dam Busters*** [1957]	$1.25	$3.75	$7.50
246	Del Rey, Lester - ***Robots And Changelings*** [1957] PBO. Cover by Powers.	$2.00	$6.00	$12.00
247	Kelton, Elmer - ***Barbed Wire*** [1957] PBO. Cover by Mel Crair.	$1.35	$4.00	$8.00
F-248	Sakai, Saburo - ***Samurai*** [1957] Photo cover.	$1.25	$3.75	$7.50
249	Clarke, Arthur C. - ***Earthlight*** [1957]	$1.35	$4.00	$8.00
250	Maund, Alfred - ***The Big Boxcar*** [1957] PBO. Cover by S. Wisnom.	$1.35	$4.00	$8.00
251	Grove, Fred - ***Sun Dance*** [1957]	$1.25	$3.75	$7.50
F-252	Majdalany, Fred - ***The Battle Of Cassino*** [1957]	$1.25	$3.75	$7.50
253	Majdalany, Fred - ***Patrol*** [1957]	$1.25	$3.75	$7.50
254	Bonham, Frank - ***Blood On The Land*** [1957]	$1.25	$3.75	$7.50
255	Leighton, Lee - ***Tomahawk*** [1957] PBO. Cover by Mel Crair.	$1.35	$4.00	$8.00
256	Blish, James - ***A Case Of Conscience*** [1958] PBO. Cover by Powers.	$2.00	$6.00	$12.00
257	Anthology edited by Groff Conklin - ***The Graveyard Reader*** [1958] PBO. Cover by Powers.	$3.00	$9.00	$18.00
F-258	Frank, Wolfgang - ***The Sea Wolves*** [1957] Photo cover.	$1.25	$3.75	$7.50
259	Foreman, L. L. - ***The Return Of The Texan*** [1958] PBO.	$1.35	$4.00	$8.00
260	Cooper, Edmund - ***Deadly Image*** [1958] PBO. Cover by Powers.	$2.00	$6.00	$12.00
F-261	Clostermann, Pierre - ***The Big Show*** [1958] Photo cover.	$1.25	$3.75	$7.50
F-262	Burt, Harry Kendal & Leasor, Thomas J. - ***The One That Got Away*** [1958] Photo cover.	$1.25	$3.75	$7.50
263	Anthology - ***The Mad Reader*** [1958]	$1.35	$4.00	$8.00
264	Anthology - ***Mad Strikes Back*** [1958]	$1.35	$4.00	$8.00
265	Gaines, William M. - ***Inside Mad*** [1958]	$1.35	$4.00	$8.00
266	Gaines, William M. - ***Utterly Mad*** [1958]	$1.35	$4.00	$8.00
267-K	Gaines, William M. - ***The Brothers Mad*** [1958] PBO.	$2.50	$7.50	$15.00
268	Kersh, Gerald - ***On An Odd Note*** [1958] PBO. Cover by Powers.	$2.25	$7.00	$14.00
269-K	Bonham, Frank - ***Hardrock*** [1958] PBO. Cover by Mel Crair.	$1.35	$4.00	$8.00
272-K	Anthology edited by Frederik Pohl - ***Star Science Fiction Stories #4*** [1958] PBO. Cover by Powers.	$2.00	$6.00	$12.00
F-273-K	Dornberger, Walter - ***V-2: The Nazi Rocket*** [1958]	$1.25	$3.75	$7.50
274-K	Johnson, Dorothy M. - ***The Hanging Tree*** [1958] PBO.	$1.35	$4.00	$8.00
275-K	Mannix, Daniel P. - ***Those About To Die*** [1958] PBO.	$1.35	$4.00	$8.00
F-276-K	Rudel, Hans Ulrich - ***Stuka Pilot*** [1958] PBO.	$1.25	$3.75	$7.50
F-277-K	di Donato, Pietro - ***This Woman*** [1958] PBO.	$1.25	$3.75	$7.50
278-K	Wynne, Barry - ***Count 5 And Die*** [1958] Photo cover.	$1.25	$3.75	$7.50
279-K	Cooper, Edmund - ***Tomorrow's Gift*** [1958] PBO. Cover by Powers.	$2.00	$6.00	$12.00
F-280-K	Greenwald, Dr. Harold - ***The Call Girl*** [1958]	$1.25	$3.75	$7.50
281-K	Cushman, Dan - ***The Old Copper Collar*** [1958]	$1.25	$3.75	$7.50
282-K	Merriman, Chad & Leighton, Lee - ***Colorado Gold*** [1958] PBO. Cover by Mel Crair.	$1.35	$4.00	$8.00
283-K	Howarth, David - ***Sledge Patrol*** [1958] Photo cover.	$1.25	$3.75	$7.50
284-K	Bowen, John - ***After The Rain*** [1958] PBO. Cover art by Blanchard.	$2.00	$6.00	$12.00
285-K	Whitman, S. E. - ***Rebel Ranger*** [1958]	$1.35	$4.00	$8.00
286-K	Brower, Millicent - ***Ingenue*** [1958] Photo cover.	$1.25	$3.75	$7.50
287-K	Mead, Shepherd - ***How To Succeed With Women Without Really Trying*** [1959] PBO. Cover by Claude. Serialized in *Playboy* magazine.	$1.25	$3.75	$7.50

		G	VG	F
288-K	Stern, Richard Martin - ***The Bright Road To Fear*** [1959] PBO...	$1.50	$5.00	$10.00
289-K	Merriman, Chad - ***The Avengers*** [1959]........	$1.35	$4.00	$8.00
290-K	Maine, Charles Eric - ***The Tide Went Out*** [1959] PBO. Cover by Powers........	$2.00	$6.00	$12.00
F-291-K	Thompson, R. W. - ***Battle For The Rhine*** [1959] Photo cover.....	$1.25	$3.75	$7.50
292-K	Sharpe, Dr. William - ***Brain Surgeon*** [1959] Photo cover........	$1.25	$3.75	$7.50
293-K	Smith, Caesar - ***Heat Wave*** [1959] Movie tie-in, photo cover.......	$1.35	$4.00	$8.00
294-K	Steelman, Robert - ***Apache Wells*** [1959]........	$1.25	$3.75	$7.50
F-295-K	Ives, Burl - ***The Burl Ives Song Book*** [1959]........	$1.35	$4.00	$8.00
296-K	Hurtzman, Harvey - ***The Mad Reader*** [1959]........	$1.25	$3.75	$7.50
297-K	Kurtzman, Harvey - ***Mad Strikes Back*** [1959]........	$1.25	$3.75	$7.50
298	Anthology - ***Sgt. Bilko Joke Book*** [1959] PBO. TV tie-in with photo cover.	$2.25	$7.00	$14.00
299-K	Wyndham, John - ***The Midwich Cuckoos*** [1959]	$1.35	$4.00	$8.00
300-K	Loomis, Edward - ***End Of A War*** [1959]........	$1.25	$3.75	$7.50
301-K	Matheson, Richard - ***Ride The Nightmare*** [1959] PBO. Photo cover........	$15.00	$45.00	$90.00
302-K	Mannix, Daniel P. - ***The Beast*** [1959]........	$1.25	$3.75	$7.50
303-K	Kornbluth, C. M. - ***The Marching Morons And Other Famous Science Fiction Stories*** [1959] PBO. Photo cover........	$2.00	$6.00	$12.00
304-K	Kelton, Elmer - ***Shadow Of A Star*** [1959]........	$1.25	$3.75	$7.50
305-K	Anthology edited by Don Congdon - ***Sensual Love*** [1959] PBO..	$1.25	$3.75	$7.50
306-K	Scott, General Robert L. - ***Tiger In The Sky*** [1959] PBO. Photo cover........	$1.25	$3.75	$7.50
F-307-K	Babington-Smith, Constance - ***Air Spy*** [1959] Photo cover.........	$1.25	$3.75	$7.50
308-K	Anthology edited by Frederik Pohl - ***Star Science Fiction Stories #5*** [1959] PBO.	$2.00	$6.00	$12.00
309-K	Everett, Wade - ***Fort Starke*** [1959]........	$1.25	$3.75	$7.50
310-K	Nielsen, Helen - ***False Witness*** [1959] Photo cover........	$1.25	$3.75	$7.50
311-K	Fry, Monroe - ***Sex, Vice And Business*** [1959] PBO.	$1.25	$3.75	$7.50
312-K	McDonald, N. C. - ***Witch Doctor*** [1959]........	$1.25	$3.75	$7.50
F-313-K	Cowles, Virginia - ***Who Dares, Wins*** [1959] Photo cover........	$1.25	$3.75	$7.50
314-K	Scott, General Robert L. - ***God Is My Co-Pilot*** [1959]........	$1.25	$3.75	$7.50
315-K	Merriman, Chad - ***Bunch Quitter*** [1959]........	$1.25	$3.75	$7.50
316-K	Smith, George O. - ***The Fourth "R"*** [1959] PBO. Cover by Powers........	$1.50	$5.00	$10.00
317-K	Kuwahara & Allred - ***Kamikaze*** [1959]........	$1.25	$3.75	$7.50
F-318-K	Feldt, Commander E. A. - ***The Coast Watchers*** [1959]........	$1.25	$3.75	$7.50
319	Ellson, Hal - ***Stairway To Nowhere*** [1959]........	$1.35	$4.00	$8.00
320	Davis, Helen Miles - ***The Chemical Elements*** [1959]........	$1.25	$3.75	$7.50
F-322-K	Caidin, Martin - ***Boing 707*** [1959] PBO. Photo cover........	$1.25	$3.75	$7.50
F-323-K	Johnson & Caidin - ***Thunderbolt*** [1959]........	$1.25	$3.75	$7.50
324-K	Grove, Fred - ***No Bugles, No Glory*** [1959] PBO. Cover by E. Means........	$1.25	$3.75	$7.50
325-K	Pohl, Frederik - ***Tomorrow Times Seven*** [1959] PBO. Cover by Powers........	$1.50	$5.00	$10.00
326-K	Anthology edited by Basil Davenport - ***Deals With The Devil*** [1959] Cover by Powers........	$2.00	$6.00	$12.00
327-K	Cooper, Edmund - ***Seed Of Light*** [1959] PBO.	$1.50	$5.00	$10.00
328-K	Whitman, S. E. - ***Black Rock Valley*** [1959] PBO.	$1.35	$4.00	$8.00
329-K	Harvey, Frank - ***Air Force!*** [1959]........	$1.25	$3.75	$7.50
331-K	Stern, Richard Martin - ***Suspense*** [1959] PBO. Photo cover........	$1.50	$5.00	$10.00
F-332-K	Pitt, Barrie - ***Zeebrugge*** [1959]........	$1.25	$3.75	$7.50
F-333-K	Anthology edited by Harold Greenwald - ***Great Cases In Psychoanalysis*** [1959] PBO.	$1.25	$3.75	$7.50
334-K	Steelman, Robert - ***Winter Of The Sioux*** [1959]........	$1.25	$3.75	$7.50
335-K	Pohl, Frederik & Kornbluth, C. M. - ***Wolfbane*** [1959] PBO. Cover by Powers........	$1.50	$5.00	$10.00
F-336-K	Thorwald, Jurgen - ***Defeat In The East*** [1959]........	$1.25	$3.75	$7.50
337-K	Jackson, Shirley - ***Life Among The Savages*** [1959]........	$1.35	$4.00	$8.00

		G	VG	F
338-K	Kurtzman, Harvey - ***Jungle Book*** [1959] PBO. Cover by Jack Davis.	$3.50	$10.00	$20.00
F-339-K	Gazel, Stefan - ***To Live And Kill*** [1959] Photo cover.	$1.25	$3.75	$7.50
340-K	Wiseman, Bernard - ***Cartoon Countdown*** [1959] PBO. Cover by Wiseman. Cartoon book.	$4.00	$12.50	$25.00
341-K	Wyndham, John and Parkes, Lucas - ***The Outward Urge*** [1959] Cover by Lehr. First U.S. edition.	$1.50	$5.00	$10.00
342-K	Jackson, Shirley - ***Raising Demons*** [1959]	$1.35	$4.00	$8.00
343-K	Merriman, Chad - ***Stampede*** [1959]	$1.25	$3.75	$7.50
344-K	Everett, Wade - ***First Command*** [1959]	$1.25	$3.75	$7.50
345-K	Appel, Benjamin - ***The Funhouse*** [1959] PBO. Cover by Ben Shahn.	$1.50	$5.00	$10.00
S-346-K	Eberhard, Dr. & Kronhausen, Phyllis - ***Pornography And The Law*** [1959] PBO.	$1.25	$3.75	$7.50
347-K	Chaplin, J. P. - ***Rumor, Fear And The Madness Of Crowds*** [1959] PBO.	$1.35	$4.00	$8.00
348-K	Mannix, Jule - ***Eagle In The Bathtub*** [1959]	$1.35	$4.00	$8.00
F-349-K	Sims, Edward H. - ***American Aces*** [1959] Photo cover.	$1.25	$3.75	$7.50
350K	Capp, Al with intro. by John Steinbeck - ***The World Of Li'l Abner*** [1953] PBO. Movie tie-in with photo cover.	$3.50	$10.00	$20.00
S-351-K	Brinley, Capt. Bertrand R. - ***Rocket Manual For Amateurs*** [1960] PBO.	$1.35	$4.00	$8.00
352-K	Bellah, James Warner - ***Blood River*** [1959] PBO.	$1.35	$4.00	$8.00
353-K	Anthology edited by Frederik Pohl - ***Star Science Fiction Stories #6*** [1959] PBO. Cover by Powers.	$2.00	$6.00	$12.00
354-K	Mannix, Daniel P. - ***The Hell Fire Club*** [1959] PBO.	$1.35	$4.00	$8.00
355-K	Mannix, Daniel P. - ***Those About To Die*** [1959]	$1.25	$3.75	$7.50
F-356-K	MacDonald, Betty - ***The Plague And I*** [1959]	$1.25	$3.75	$7.50
357-K	Bonham, Frank - ***The Feud At Spanish Ford*** [1959] Cover by Mel Crair.	$1.25	$3.75	$7.50
F-358-K	Russell, Lord - ***The Scourge Of The Swastika*** [1959]	$1.25	$3.75	$7.50
F-359-K	Caidin, Martin - ***The Night Hamburg Died*** [1959]	$1.25	$3.75	$7.50
360-K	Maine, Charles Eric - ***Fire Past The Future*** [1959] PBO.	$1.50	$5.00	$10.00
361-K	Mason, Ernst - ***Tiberius*** [1960] PBO.	$3.50	$10.00	$20.00
364-K	Ward, Don (Adaptation) - ***Gunsmoke*** [1960] TV tie-in with photo cover.	$1.50	$5.00	$10.00
365-K	Oliver, Chad - ***Unearthly Neighbors*** [1960] PBO.	$1.50	$5.00	$10.00
366-K	Shelley, John L. - ***Cavalry Sergeant*** [1960] PBO.	$1.25	$3.75	$7.50
S-367-K	Taylor, G. Rattray - ***Sex In History*** [1960]	$1.25	$3.75	$7.50
F-368-K	Divine, David - ***The Nine Days Of Dunkirk*** [1960] Photo cover.	$1.25	$3.75	$7.50
370-K	Zacherley - editor - ***Zacherleys Midnight Snacks*** [1960] PBO. Cover by Powers	$2.50	$7.50	$15.00
371-K	Patterson, Robert - ***Gold Is The Color of Blood*** [1960] PBO. Photo cover.	$1.25	$3.75	$7.50
372-K	Anthology edited by Alexander Klein - ***Grand Deception*** [1960].	$1.25	$3.75	$7.50
373-K	Bonham, Frank - ***Night Raid*** [1960]	$1.25	$3.75	$7.50
F-374-K	Seagrave, M.D., Gordon S. - ***The Life Of A Burma Surgeon*** [1960]	$1.25	$3.75	$7.50
F-375-K	Mansfield, Harold - ***How Wide We Stray*** [1960]	$1.25	$3.75	$7.50
S-376-K	Martin, John Bartlow - ***Break Down The Walls*** [1960]	$1.50	$5.00	$10.00
377-K	Sarban - ***The Sound Of His Horn*** [1960] PBO.	$3.00	$9.00	$18.00
F-378-K	di Donato, Pietro - ***This Woman*** [1960]	$1.25	$3.75	$7.50
379-K	Nochl, Johannes - ***The Black Death*** [1960] PBO.	$1.35	$4.00	$8.00
380-K	Anthology edited by Basil Davenport - ***Horror Stories From Tales To Be Told In The Dark*** [1960]	$2.50	$7.50	$15.00
381-K	Phol, Frederik & Kornbluth, C. M. - ***The Space Merchants*** [1960]	$1.25	$3.75	$7.50
382-K	Bradbury, Ray - ***Fahrenheit 451*** [1960] Cover by Joe Mugnaini.	$1.25	$3.75	$7.50
F-384-K	Schroter, Heinz - ***Stalingrad*** [1960]	$1.25	$3.75	$7.50
F-386-K	Grombach, John V. - ***The Olympics 1960*** [1960]	$1.25	$3.75	$7.50

		G	VG	F
F-387-K	Mowat, Farley - ***Grey Seas Under*** [1960] Cover by Ed Valigursky.	$1.25	$3.75	$7.50
388-K	Budrys, Algis - ***The Unexpected Dimension*** [1960] PBO. Cover by Blanchard.	$1.50	$5.00	$10.00
S-389-K	Kronhausen, Drs. Phyliss & Eberhard - ***Sex Histories Of American College Men*** [1960]	$1.25	$3.75	$7.50
F-390-K	Wolff, Leon - ***In Flanders Fields*** [1960]	$1.25	$3.75	$7.50
391-K	Farmer, Philip Jose - ***Strange Relations*** [1960] PBO. Cover by Blanchard.	$2.50	$7.50	$15.00
392-K	Spears, John R. - ***The American Slave Trade*** [1960]	$1.25	$3.75	$7.50
393-K	Anderson, Pohl - ***Brain Wave*** [1960] Cover by Powers.	$1.50	$5.00	$10.00
394-K	Harrison, C. William - ***Outlaw Of The Natchez Trace*** [1960] PBO. Cover by G. D. Wilson.	$1.35	$4.00	$8.00
395-K	Frank, Wolfgang & Rogge, Capt. Bernhard - ***Under Ten Flags*** [1960]	$1.25	$3.75	$7.50
396-K	Halleran, E. E. - ***Shadow Of The Big Horn*** [1960] PBO.	$1.35	$4.00	$8.00
397-K	Pohl, Frederik - ***The Man Who Ate The World*** [1960] PBO.	$1.50	$5.00	$10.00
398-K	Clarke, Arthur C. - ***Childhood's End*** [1960]	$1.25	$3.75	$7.50
F-399-K	Anthology edited by Greenwald & Krich - ***The Prostitute In Literature*** [1960] PBO.	$1.25	$3.75	$7.50
401-K	Anthology edited by Basil Davenport - ***Invisible Men*** [1960] PBO.	$2.00	$6.00	$12.00
402-K	Johnson, Dorothy - ***The Hanging Tree*** [1960]	$1.25	$3.75	$7.50
F-403-K	Turner, E. S. - ***The Shocking History Of Advertising*** [1960]	$1.25	$3.75	$7.50
F-404-K	Sakai, Saburo - ***Samurai*** [1960]	$1.25	$3.75	$7.50
405-K	Ahlswede, A. - ***Day Of The Hunter*** [1960] PBO. Cover by Doug Rosa.	$1.35	$4.00	$8.00
406-K	Livingston, Harold - ***The Climacticon*** [1960] PBO. Cover by Powers.	$1.50	$5.00	$10.00
407-K	Tenn, William - ***Of All Possible Worlds*** [1960] Cover by Blanchard.	$1.25	$3.75	$7.50
408-K	Klein, Alexander - editor - ***The Fabulous Rogues*** [1960]	$1.25	$3.75	$7.50
F-409-K	Frischauer, Willi - ***The Rise And Fall Of Herman Goering*** [1960]	$1.25	$3.75	$7.50
410-K	Robertson, Terence - ***The Hurricane*** [1960] PBO.	$1.35	$4.00	$8.00
F-411-K	King, Jr., Martin Luther - ***Stride Toward Freedom*** [1960]	$1.25	$3.75	$7.50
S-412-K	Simonov, Konstantine - ***Days And Nights*** [1960] Cover by Blanchard.	$1.25	$3.75	$7.50
413-K	Leighton, Lee - ***Fight For The Valley*** [1960]	$1.25	$3.75	$7.50
S-414-K	Wells, H. G. - ***Best Stories Of H. G. Wells*** [1960]	$1.50	$5.00	$10.00
F-415-K	Turner, E. S. - ***A History Of Courting*** [1960]	$1.25	$3.75	$7.50
S-416-K	Moorehead, Alan - ***Gallipoli*** [1960]	$1.25	$3.75	$7.50
417-K	Anthology edited by Zacherley - ***Zacherley's Vulture Stew*** [1960] PBO. Cover by Powers.	$2.50	$7.50	$15.00
418-K	Castle, John - ***The Password Is Courage*** [1960]	$1.25	$3.75	$7.50
F-419-K	Galland, Adolf - ***The First And The Last*** [1960] Photo cover.	$1.25	$3.75	$7.50
F-420-K	Mills, C. Wright - ***The Causes Of World War Three*** [1960]	$1.25	$3.75	$7.50
421-K	O'Rourke, Frank - ***Legion In The Dust*** [1960]	$1.25	$3.75	$7.50
422-K	Anderson, Poul - ***Guardians Of Time*** [1960] PBO. Cover by Powers.	$1.50	$5.00	$10.00
423-K	Wyndham, John - ***Re-Birth*** [1960] Cover by Powers.	$1.25	$3.75	$7.50
F-424-K	Clarke, Comer - ***Eichmann*** [1960] PBO.	$1.35	$4.00	$8.00
F-425-K	Caidin, Martin - ***A Torch To The Enemy*** [1960] PBO. Cover by Valigursky.	$1.35	$4.00	$8.00
427-K	Anthology edited by Alexander Klein - ***The Magnificent Scoundrels*** [1960] PBO.	$1.35	$4.00	$8.00
F-428-K	Greenwald, Dr. Harold - ***The Call Girl*** [1960] Movie tie-in.	$1.25	$3.75	$7.50
429-K	Everett, Wade - ***Last Scout*** [1960]	$1.25	$3.75	$7.50
F-430-K	Bowles, Chester - ***The Coming Political Breakthrough*** [1960] Photo cover.	$1.25	$3.75	$7.50

		G	VG	F
431-K	Sarban - ***The Doll Maker*** [1960]	$2.50	$7.50	$15.00
F-432-K	Marais & Miranda - ***Folk Song Jamboree*** [1960] PBO.	$2.25	$7.00	$14.00
F-433-K	Lampe, David - ***The Danish Resistance*** [1960]	$1.25	$3.75	$7.50
434-K	Wilson, Richard - ***30-Day Wonder*** [1960] PBO. Cover by Powers.	$1.50	$5.00	$10.00
F-435-K	Bloom, Murray Teigh - ***Money Of Their Own*** [1960]	$1.25	$3.75	$7.50
437-K	Sheckley, Robert - ***Untouched By Human Hands*** [1960]	$1.25	$3.75	$7.50
438-K	Merriman, Chad - ***Night Killer*** [1960] PBO.	$1.35	$4.00	$8.00
439-K	Pohl, Frederik - ***Drunkard's Walk*** [1960] PBO. Cover by Puspurica.	$1.50	$5.00	$10.00
441-K	Laski, Marghanita - ***The Victorian Chaise Longue*** [1960]	$1.25	$3.75	$7.50
F-443-K	Chaplin, J. P. - ***The Unconscious*** [1960]	$1.25	$3.75	$7.50
F-444-K	Isaksson, Ulla - ***The Virgin Spring*** [1960] PBO. Movie tie-in with Ingmar Bergman and photo cover.	$1.35	$4.00	$8.00
445	Anthology edited by Shirley Moore - ***Science Projects Handbook*** [1960]	$1.35	$4.00	$8.00
F-446-K	Gardner, Martin - ***Fads And Fallacies In The Name Of Science*** [1960] Includes a chapter on L. Ron Hubbard's Dianetics.	$1.50	$5.00	$10.00
F-447-K	Bryant, Rear Admiral Ben - ***Submarine Commander*** [1960]	$1.25	$3.75	$7.50
448-K	Ahlswede, Ann - ***Hunting Wolf*** [1960]	$1.25	$3.75	$7.50
449-K	Wyndham, John - ***Trouble With Lichen*** [1960] PBO. Cover by Powers.	$1.50	$5.00	$10.00
F-450-K	Mathison, Richard - ***The Shocking History Of Drugs*** [1960]	$1.25	$3.75	$7.50
451-K	Hough, Richard - ***The Fleet That Had To Die*** [1960]	$1.25	$3.75	$7.50
452-K	Mannix, Daniel P. - ***Those About To Die*** [1960]	$1.25	$3.75	$7.50
453-K	Wyndham, John - ***Village Of The Damned*** [1960] aka *The Midwich Cuckoos*. Movie tie-in, movie photo cover.	$2.00	$6.00	$12.00
F-454-K	Mills, C. Wright - ***Listen, Yankee*** [1960]	$1.25	$3.75	$7.50
455-K	Shelley, John L. - ***The Rimlanders*** [1960]	$1.25	$3.75	$7.50
F-456-K	Orrmont, Arthur - ***Love Cults And Faith Healers*** [1960] PBO.	$1.35	$4.00	$8.00
458-K	Sturgeon, Theodore - ***Some Of Your Blood*** [1961] PBO.	$5.00	$15.00	$30.00
F-459-K	Rudel, Hans Ulrich - ***Stuka Pilot*** [1960]	$1.25	$3.75	$7.50
460-K	Reeder, Col. Red - ***The MacKenzie Raid*** [1960] TV tie-in. Cover by Orbaan.	$1.25	$3.75	$7.50
462-K	Sturgeon, Theodore - ***More Than Human*** [1960]	$1.25	$3.75	$7.50
F-463-K	di Donato, Pietro - ***Three Circles Of Light*** [1960]	$1.25	$3.75	$7.50
464-K	Roberts, R. M. - ***Smoke Wagon Road*** [1960]	$1.25	$3.75	$7.50
465-K	Blish, James - ***So Close To Home*** [1961] PBO.	$1.50	$5.00	$10.00
466-K	Anthology edited by Whit & Hallie Burnett - ***Things With Claws*** [1961] PBO. Cover by Powers.	$2.50	$7.50	$15.00
S-467	Caidin, Martin - ***Zero*** [1961]	$1.25	$3.75	$7.50
F-468-K	Crisp, Major Robert - ***Brazen Chariots*** [1961] Photo cover.	$1.25	$3.75	$7.50
F-469-K	Turner, E. S. - ***The Astonishing History Of The Medical Profession*** [1961]	$1.25	$3.75	$7.50
471-K	Halleran, E. E. - ***Warbonnet Creek*** [1961]	$1.25	$3.75	$7.50
472-K	Clarke, Arthur C. - ***Expedition To Earth*** [1961] Cover by Powers.	$1.25	$3.75	$7.50
S-473-K	Anthology - ***The Best American Short Stories: 1960*** [1961]	$1.25	$3.75	$7.50
F-474-K	Russell, Lord - ***The Scourge Of The Swastika*** [1961]	$1.25	$3.75	$7.50
476-K	Pohl, Frederik - ***Turn Left At Thursday*** [1961] PBO.	$2.50	$7.50	$15.00
477-K	Scott, Col. Robert L. - ***God Is My Co-Pilot*** [1961] Cover by John T. McCoy, Jr..	$1.25	$3.75	$7.50
478-K	Klein, Alexander - editor - ***Rebels, Rogues And Rascals*** [1961] PBO.	$1.35	$4.00	$8.00
479-K	Amis, Kingsley - ***New Maps Of Hell*** [1960] Cover by Powers.	$1.25	$3.75	$7.50
480-K	Cross, John Keir - ***Stories From The Other Passenger*** [1961] PBO. Cover art by Powers.	$2.00	$6.00	$12.00
481-K	O'Rourke, Frank - ***Gunlaw Hill*** [1961] PBO.	$1.35	$4.00	$8.00

		G	VG	F
483-K	Anderson, Poul - ***Strangers From Earth*** [1961] PBO. Cover by Powers.	$1.50	$5.00	$10.00
484-K	Vidal, Gore - ***Messiah*** [1961]	$1.25	$3.75	$7.50
486-K	Schaefer, Jack - ***The Canyon*** [1961]	$1.25	$3.75	$7.50
F-487-K	Sartre, Jean-Paul - ***Sartre On Cuba*** [1961] PBO.	$1.25	$3.75	$7.50
488	Gurney, G. - ***Five Down And Glory*** [1961]	$1.25	$3.75	$7.50
496-K	O'Rourke, Frank - ***Bandoleer Crossing*** [1961]	$1.25	$3.75	$7.50
497-K	Kuttner, Henry - ***Bypass To Otherness*** [1961] PBO.	$2.00	$6.00	$12.00
498-K	Sarban - ***Ringstones*** [1961] First U.S. edition.	$3.50	$10.00	$20.00
505-K	Everett, Wade - ***Big Man, Big Mountain*** [1961]	$1.25	$3.75	$7.50
506-K	Sturgeon, Theodore - ***Not Without Sorcery*** [1961]	$1.25	$3.75	$7.50
507-K	Farmer, Philip Jose - ***The Lovers*** [1961] PBO. Cover by Powers.	$3.00	$9.00	$18.00
508-K	Lieber, Jr., Fritz - ***Tales From Night's Black Agents*** [1961]	$2.50	$7.50	$15.00
S-509-K	Taylor, Telford - ***Grand Inquest*** [1961]	$1.25	$3.75	$7.50
510-K	Donner, Frank J. - ***The Un-Americans*** [1961]	$1.25	$3.75	$7.50
511-K	Van Vogt, A. E. - ***Slan*** [1961]	$1.25	$3.75	$7.50
512-K	Clarke, Comer - ***England Under Hitler*** [1961] Photo cover.	$1.25	$3.75	$7.50
513-K	Hough, Richard - ***Admirals In Collision*** [1961]	$1.25	$3.75	$7.50
F-514	Johnson, Robert S. & Caidin, Martin - ***Thunderbolt*** [1961]	$1.25	$3.75	$7.50
F-515-K	Walker, Bill - ***The Case Of Barbara Graham*** [1961] Photo cover.	$1.25	$3.75	$7.50
S-517-K	Fellini, Federico - ***La Dolce Vita*** [1961] Movie tie-in with photo cover.	$1.35	$4.00	$8.00
518-K	Booth, Edwin - ***Outlaw Town*** [1961] Cover by Chuck Smith.	$1.25	$3.75	$7.50
519-K	Clingerman, Mildred - ***A Cupful Of Space*** [1961] PBO. Cover by Powers	$1.50	$5.00	$10.00
520K	Fearing, Kenneth - ***The Hospital*** [1961] Cover by Powers.	$1.25	$3.75	$7.50
521-K	Anthology - ***Star Science Fiction Stories #1*** [1961]	$1.00	$3.00	$6.00
522-K	Anthology edited by Don Congdon - ***Tales Of Love And Horror*** [1961] PBO. Cover by Powers. Includes Matheson, et al.	$3.00	$9.00	$18.00
523	Forden, L. - ***Glory Gamblers*** [1961]	$1.25	$3.75	$7.50
526-K	Leonard, Elmore - ***Hombre*** [1961] PBO.	$3.50	$10.00	$20.00
527	Moore, Ward - ***Greener Than You Think*** [1961]	$1.25	$3.75	$7.50
F-528	Clarke, Arthur C. - ***The Challenge Of The Space Ship*** [1961]	$1.25	$3.75	$7.50
S-529	MacDonald, Charles B. - ***Company Commander*** [1961]	$1.25	$3.75	$7.50
S-530	Liebling, A. J. - ***The Press*** [1961] PBO.	$1.25	$3.75	$7.50
531	Wakefield, H. Russell - ***Stories From The Clock Strikes 12*** [1961] Cover by Powers.	$1.25	$3.75	$7.50
F-533	Tilsley, Frank - ***Mutiny*** [1961] PBO.	$1.25	$3.75	$7.50
534	Kelton, Elmer - ***Donovan*** [1961]	$1.25	$3.75	$7.50
535	Kelton, Elmer - ***Buffalo Wagons*** [1961]	$1.25	$3.75	$7.50
X-536	Unwin, Rayner - ***The Defeat Of John Hawkins*** [1961]	$1.25	$3.75	$7.50
538	Anthology - ***Science Projects Handbook*** [1961] Photo cover.	$1.25	$3.75	$7.50
539	Clarke, Arthur C. - ***Tales From The White Hart*** [1961] Cover by Powers.	$1.25	$3.75	$7.50
540	Russell, Ray - ***Sardonicus*** [1961] PBO. Cover by Powers. Movie tie-in.	$2.50	$7.50	$15.00
S-541	Anthology edited by Will & Martin Lieberson - ***College Parodies*** [1961] PBO.	$1.35	$4.00	$8.00
542	Derleth, August - ***Tales From Not Long For This World*** [1961]	$1.35	$4.00	$8.00
F-543	King-Hall, Stephen - ***Moment Of No Return*** [1961] First U.S. edition. (Not early Stephen King).	$1.25	$3.75	$7.50
544	Merriman, Chad - ***Ride West For War*** [1961] PBO.	$1.35	$4.00	$8.00
545	Wyndham, John - ***Out Of The Deeps*** [1961]	$1.25	$3.75	$7.50
546	Wyndham, John - ***The Infinite Moment*** [1961] PBO. Covers by Powers.	$1.50	$5.00	$10.00
S-547-K	Turner, E. S. - ***The Court Of St. James's*** [1961]	$1.25	$3.75	$7.50
550	Anthology edited by Gore Vidal - ***Best Television Plays*** [1961] Photo cover.	$1.25	$3.75	$7.50

		G	VG	F
551	Flender, Harold - ***Paris Blues*** [1961] Movie tie-in and photo cover with Paul Newman and Sidney Poitier.	$1.35	$4.00	$8.00
552	Del Rey, Lester - ***And Some Were Human*** [1961]	$1.25	$3.75	$7.50
554	Everett, Wade - ***Temporary Duty*** [1961] Cover by Chuck Smith.	$1.25	$3.75	$7.50
F-555	Aldiss, Brian - ***The Primal Urge*** [1961] PBO. Cover by Powers.	$1.50	$5.00	$10.00
556	Anthology - ***Zacherley's Midnight Snacks*** [1961] Cover by Powers.	$1.35	$4.00	$8.00
X-557	Vidal, Gore - ***The Judgement Of Paris*** [1961] Cover by Powers.	$1.25	$3.75	$7.50
F-558	Mead, Shepherd - ***How To Succeed In Business Without Really Trying*** [1961]	$1.00	$3.00	$6.00
F-559	Deutscher, Isaac - ***The Great Contest*** [1961]	$1.25	$3.75	$7.50
560	Grove, Fred - ***Comanche Captives*** [1961] PBO.	$1.25	$3.75	$7.50
F-561	Leiber, Fritz - ***The Silver Eggheads*** [1961] PBO. Cover by Powers.	$1.50	$5.00	$10.00
F-562	Sturgeon, Theodore - ***Caviar*** [1961]	$1.25	$3.75	$7.50
563	Anthology edited by Michael/Don Congdon - ***Alone By Night*** [1961] PBO.	$2.00	$6.00	$12.00
F-564	Melman, Seymour - ***The Peace Race*** [1961]	$1.25	$3.75	$7.50
F-565	Crisp, Major Robert - ***The Gods Were Neutral*** [1961] Photo cover.	$1.25	$3.75	$7.50
F-567	Anthology - ***The Nonconformers*** [1961]	$1.25	$3.75	$7.50
569	Adams, Clifton - ***Day Of The Gun*** [1961]	$1.25	$3.75	$7.50
F-570	Pohl, Frederik & Kornbluth, C. M. - ***Gladiator-At-Law*** [1961]	$1.25	$3.75	$7.50
F-571	Gillon, Diana and Meir - ***The Unsleep*** [1962] Cover by Powers. First U.S. edition.	$2.50	$7.50	$15.00
574	Anthology - ***Zacherly's Vulture Stew*** [1961] Cover by Powers.	$1.35	$4.00	$8.00
F-575	Hives, Frank & Lumley, Gascoine - ***Ju-Ju And Justice In Nigeria*** [1962] PBO.	$1.25	$3.75	$7.50
F-576	Mead, Shepherd - ***How To Succeed With Women Without Really Trying*** [1962] Cover by Claude.	$1.00	$3.00	$6.00
577	Leiber, Fritz - ***Shadows With Eyes*** [1962] PBO.	$2.50	$7.50	$15.00
578	Leighton, Lee - ***Gut Shot*** [1962] PBO.	$1.25	$3.75	$7.50
579	Anderson, Poul - ***After Doomsday*** [1962] PBO. Cover by Brillhart.	$1.50	$5.00	$10.00
F-580	Bradbury, Ray - ***The October Country*** [1962] Cover by Joe Mugnaini.	$1.35	$4.00	$8.00
F-581	Goldston, Robert - ***Satan's Disciples*** [1962] PBO. Cover by Jack Thurston.	$2.00	$6.00	$12.00
X-582	Liebling, A. J. - ***The Jollity Building*** [1962]	$1.25	$3.75	$7.50
F-583	Caidin, Martin - ***The Night Hamburg Died*** [1962]	$1.25	$3.75	$7.50
585	Ketchum, Phil - ***Harsh Reckoning*** [1962] PBO. Cover by Jack Thurston.	$1.25	$3.75	$7.50
S-586	Vadim, Roger - ***Les Liaisons Dangereuses*** [1962] PBO. Movie tie-in with photo cover.	$1.35	$4.00	$8.00
587	Brennan, Joseph Payne - ***Nine Horrors And A Dream*** [1962] Cover by Powers.	$1.25	$3.75	$7.50
F-588	Farmer, Philip Jose - ***The Alley God*** [1962] PBO. Cover by Powers.	$2.00	$6.00	$12.00
F-589	Rubin, Theodore Isaac - ***In The Life*** [1962]	$1.25	$3.75	$7.50
590	Anthology - ***Mad Strikes Back!*** [1962]	$1.25	$3.75	$7.50
F-591	Trevor, Elleston - ***Squadron Airborne*** [1962] PBO.	$1.25	$3.75	$7.50
F-592	Monsarrat, Nicholas - ***Three Corvettes*** [1962] Cover by Valiqursky.	$1.25	$3.75	$7.50
594	Kelton, Elmer - ***Bitter Trail*** [1962]	$1.25	$3.75	$7.50
F-595	White, James - ***Hospital Station*** [1962] PBO.	$1.35	$4.00	$8.00
F-596	Tilsley, Frank - ***H.M.S. Defiant*** [1962] Movie tie-in with photo cover.	$1.25	$3.75	$7.50
597	Pohl, Frederik - ***The Man Who Ate The World*** [1962]	$1.25	$3.75	$7.50
S-600	Yokota, Yutaka - ***The Kaiten Weapon*** [1962]	$1.00	$3.00	$6.00
S-601	Bayer, Sanford - ***Each Man Kills*** [1962] PBO.	$1.25	$3.75	$7.50

		G	VG	F
F-602	Wells, Barry - ***The Day The Earth Caught Fire*** [1962] PBO. Movie tie-in.	$1.50	$5.00	$10.00
F-603	Horowitz, David - ***Student*** [1962]	$1.00	$3.00	$6.00
604	Everett, Wade - ***Killer*** [1962]	$1.25	$3.75	$7.50
F-605	Tegner, Bruce - ***Bruce Tegner Method Of Self-Defense*** [1962] Photo cover.	$1.00	$3.00	$6.00
F-606	Fearing, Kenneth - ***The Big Clock*** [1962]	$1.00	$3.00	$6.00
F-609	Sellings, Arthur - ***Telepath*** [1962] PBO. Cover by Powers.	$1.50	$5.00	$10.00
610	Johnson, Dorothy - ***Indian Country*** [1962]	$1.00	$3.00	$6.00
612	Anthology - ***Star Science Fiction Stories #2*** [1962]	$1.00	$3.00	$6.00
F-613	Greenwald, Harold - ***The Call Girl*** [1962]	$1.00	$3.00	$6.00
F-614	Innes, Hammond - ***Gale Warning*** [1962]	$1.00	$3.00	$6.00
F-615	Innes, Hammond - ***The Blue Ice*** [1962]	$1.00	$3.00	$6.00
617	Booth, Edwin - ***Sidewinder*** [1962] PBO.	$1.25	$3.75	$7.50
F-619	Kuttner, Henry - ***Return To Otherness*** [1962] PBO.	$2.50	$7.50	$15.00
F-621	Durrell, Gerald M. - ***The Overloaded Ark*** [1962] Cover by Sabine Baur.	$1.25	$3.75	$7.50
S-622	Weinberg, Meyer - ***TV In America*** [1962]	$1.25	$3.75	$7.50
F-624	Paul, Elliot - ***Hugger-Mugger In The Louvre*** [1962]	$1.00	$3.00	$6.00
F-626	Miller, Jr., Walter M. - ***Conditionally Human*** [1962] PBO. Cover by Powers	$1.00	$3.00	$6.00
629	Lovecraft, H. P. & Derleth, August - ***The Survivor And Others*** [1962] Cover by Powers.	$1.35	$4.00	$8.00
635	Halleran, E. E. - ***Crimson Desert*** [1962] PBO.	$1.25	$3.75	$7.50
F-636	Gardner, Dick - ***The Impossible*** [1962] PBO.	$1.35	$4.00	$8.00
F-637	Moffett, Cleveland - ***The Reign Of Terror*** [1962] Cover by Erickson.	$1.00	$3.00	$6.00
F-638	Kornbluth, C. M./Pohl, Frederik - ***The Wonder Effect*** [1962] PBO.	$1.50	$5.00	$10.00
F-639	Clifton, Mark - ***Eight Keys To Eden*** [1962]	$1.00	$3.00	$6.00
640	Merriman, Chad - ***Rogue River*** [1962]	$1.00	$3.00	$6.00
F-641	Anthology edited by Charles Beaumont - ***The Fiend In You*** [1962] PBO. Includes stories by Matheson, Beaumont, Bloch et al.	$3.00	$9.00	$18.00
F-642	Innes, Hammond - ***The Angry Mountain*** [1962]	$1.00	$3.00	$6.00
F-643	Rubin, Theodore Isaac - ***Jordi/Lisa And David*** [1962] Movie tie-in with photo cover.	$1.00	$3.00	$6.00
F-646	Coles, Manning - ***Concrete Crime*** [1962]	$1.00	$3.00	$6.00
F-647	Blish, James - ***The Night Shapes*** [1962] PBO. Cover by Powers.	$2.50	$7.50	$15.00
F-648	Sheckley, Robert - ***Citizen In Space*** [1962] Cover by Powers.	$1.00	$3.00	$6.00
649	Capps, Benjamin - ***Hanging At Comanche Wells*** [1962] PBO.	$1.25	$3.75	$7.50
S-650	Paul, Eugene - ***The Hungry Eye*** [1962] Photo cover.	$1.00	$3.00	$6.00
F-651	Fearing, Kenneth - ***Dagger Of The Mind*** [1962] Cover by Lehr.	$1.00	$3.00	$6.00
F-652	Schroter, Heinz - ***Stalingrad*** [1962]	$1.00	$3.00	$6.00
X-655	Waskow, Arthur I. & Newman, Stanley L. - ***America In Hiding*** [1962] PBO.	$1.00	$3.00	$6.00
F-656	Brickhill, Paul - ***The Dam Busters*** [1962]	$1.00	$3.00	$6.00
F-657	Anthology - ***Sometime, Never*** [1962] Three tales by William Golding, John Wyndham, and Mervyn Peake.	$1.25	$3.75	$7.50
F-658	Wilson, Richard - ***Time Out For Tomorrow*** [1962] PBO. Cover by Powers	$1.50	$5.00	$10.00
659	Everett, Wade - ***The Big Drive*** [1962]	$1.00	$3.00	$6.00
F-660	Cook, Will - ***The Crossing*** [1962]	$1.00	$3.00	$6.00
F-661	Innes, Hammond - ***The Killer Mine*** [1962]	$1.00	$3.00	$6.00
S-663	Maugham, W. Somerset - ***Stories Of The East*** [1962]	$1.25	$3.75	$7.50
F-664	Anthology edited by Shirley Moore - ***Science Projects Handbook*** [1962]	$1.00	$3.00	$6.00
F-665	Keats, John - ***The Crack In The Picture Window*** [1962]	$1.00	$3.00	$6.00
672	Leighton, Lee - ***Tomahawk*** [1962]	$1.00	$3.00	$6.00

		G	VG	F
F-675	Anthology - ***Star Science Fiction Stories #3*** [1962] Cover by Powers.	$1.00	$3.00	$6.00
F-676	Bradbury, Ray - ***Fahrenheit 451*** [1962]	$1.00	$3.00	$6.00
677	Leighton, Lee - ***Beyond The Pass*** [1962]	$1.00	$3.00	$6.00
F-678	Busch, Harald - ***U-Boats At War*** [1962]	$1.00	$3.00	$6.00
F-679	Duerrenmatt, Friedrich - ***Traps*** [1962]	$1.00	$3.00	$6.00
F-680	Anthology edited by Calvin Beck - ***The Frankenstein Reader*** [1962] PBO. Cover by Powers	$2.50	$7.50	$15.00
S-681	Kipling, Rudyard - ***Famous Tales Of India*** [1962]	$1.25	$3.75	$7.50
682	Halleran, E. E. - ***The Hostile Hills*** [1962] Cover by Mel Crair.	$1.00	$3.00	$6.00
F-683	Kronhausen, Dr.'s E. & P. - ***Pornography And The Law*** [1962]	$1.00	$3.00	$6.00
F-684	Foley, Charles - ***Commando Extra Ordinary*** [1962]	$1.00	$3.00	$6.00
F-685	Pohl, Frederik - ***The Abominable Earthman*** [1963] PBO. Cover by Powers	$1.50	$5.00	$10.00
F-687	Wells, H. G. - ***The First Men In The Moon*** [1963]	$1.25	$3.75	$7.50
X-688	Shute, Nevil - ***The Legacy*** [1962]	$1.00	$3.00	$6.00
X-689	Shute, Nevil - ***Most Secret*** [1962]	$1.00	$3.00	$6.00
F-690	Bentley, E. C. - ***Trent's Last Case*** [1962]	$1.25	$3.75	$7.50
691	Harvey, Frank - ***Jet*** [1962]	$1.00	$3.00	$6.00
692	Bryan, III, J. - ***Aircraft Carrier*** [1962]	$1.00	$3.00	$6.00
693	Kuwahara, Yasuo & Allred, Gordon T. - ***Kamikaze*** [1962]	$1.00	$3.00	$6.00
694	Scott, Col. Robert L. - ***God Is My Co-Pilot*** [1962]	$1.00	$3.00	$6.00
S-695	Anthology - ***Best American Short Stories 1962*** [1962]	$1.00	$3.00	$6.00
F-696	Innes, Hammond - ***The Naked Land*** [1962]	$1.00	$3.00	$6.00
F-697	Merriam, Robert - ***The Battle Of The Bulge*** [1962]	$1.00	$3.00	$6.00
F-698	Clarke, Arthur C. - ***Earthlight*** [1962]	$1.00	$3.00	$6.00
699	O'Rourke, Frank - ***Violence At Sundown*** [1962]	$1.00	$3.00	$6.00
DF-700	Mills, C. Wright - ***Power, Politics And People*** [1962] Photo cover.	$1.00	$3.00	$6.00
F-701	Burroughs, Edgar Rice - ***A Princess Of Mars*** [1963] Cover by Abbett. Martian Series #1	$1.25	$3.75	$7.50
F-702	Burroughs, Edgar Rice - ***The Gods Of Mars*** [1963] Cover by Abbett. Martian Series #2	$1.25	$3.75	$7.50
F-703	Brown, Rosel George - ***A Handful Of Time*** [1963] PBO. Cover art by Powers.	$1.50	$5.00	$10.00
F-704	Rubin, Theodore Isaac - ***Sweet Daddy*** [1963]	$1.00	$3.00	$6.00
F-706	Bell, Josephine - ***Bones In The Barrow*** [1963]	$1.00	$3.00	$6.00
F-707	Stern, Richard Martin - ***The Bright Road To Fear*** [1963]	$1.00	$3.00	$6.00
F-708	Kornbluth, C. M. - ***The Explorers*** [1963]	$1.00	$3.00	$6.00
F-709	White, James - ***Star Surgeon*** [1963] PBO.	$1.25	$3.75	$7.50
F-711	Burroughs, Edgar Rice - ***The Warlord Of Mars*** [1963] Cover by Ed Abbett. Martian Series #3.	$1.25	$3.75	$7.50
F-712	Riccio, Vincent & Slocum, Bill - ***All The Way Down*** [1963] Photo cover.	$1.00	$3.00	$6.00
F-713	Styles, Showell - ***The Sea Lord*** [1963]	$1.00	$3.00	$6.00
X-720	Shute, Nevil - ***No Highway*** [1963]	$1.00	$3.00	$6.00
F-721	Keogh, Theodora - ***The Double Door*** [1963]	$1.00	$3.00	$6.00
F-722	Patrick, Quentin - ***The Grindle Nightmare*** [1963]	$1.25	$3.75	$7.50
F-723	Sims, Edward H. - ***American Aces*** [1963]	$1.00	$3.00	$6.00
F-724	Kuttner, Henry - ***Mutant*** [1963]	$1.25	$3.75	$7.50
F-725	Wells, H. G. - ***The Food Of The Gods*** [1963]	$1.00	$3.00	$6.00
X-726	Stacton, David - ***A Dancer In Darkness*** [1963]	$1.00	$3.00	$6.00
F-727	Bell, Josephine - ***Fall Over Cliff*** [1963] Cover by Lehr.	$1.00	$3.00	$6.00
F-728	Burroughs, Edgar Rice - ***Swords Of Mars*** [1963] Cover by Bob Abbett. Martian Series #8	$1.25	$3.75	$7.50
Y-729	Kelton, Elmer - ***Barbed Wire*** [1963] Cover by Mel Crair.	$1.00	$3.00	$6.00
F-730	Anthology - ***Star Short Novels*** [1963]	$1.00	$3.00	$6.00
X-732	Standish, Robert - ***Elephant Walk*** [1963]	$1.00	$3.00	$6.00
X-733	Haggard, H. Rider - ***King Solomon's Mines*** [1963]	$1.25	$3.75	$7.50
F-734	Innnes, Hammond - ***Campbell's Kingdom*** [1963]	$1.00	$3.00	$6.00

		G	VG	F
Y-735	Kelton, Elmer - ***Horsehead Crossing*** [1963] PBO	$1.35	$4.00	$8.00
F-738	Pohl, Frederik & Kornbluth, C. M. - ***Search The Sky*** [1963] Cover by Powers	$1.00	$3.00	$6.00
F-739	Burroughs, Edgar Rice - ***Synthetic Men Of Mars*** [1963] Cover by Bob Abbett. Martian Series #9	$1.25	$3.75	$7.50
F-741	Quentin, Patrick - ***A Puzzle For Fools*** [1963] Cover by Lehr.	$1.00	$3.00	$6.00
S-742	Anthology - ***Best Stories Of H. G. Wells*** [1963]	$1.00	$3.00	$6.00
X-743	Haggard, H. Rider - ***Allan Quatermain*** [1963]	$1.25	$3.75	$7.50
F-745	Burroughs, Edgar Rice - ***Tarzan Of The Apes*** [1963] Tarzan Series #1	$1.25	$3.75	$7.50
F-746	Burroughs, Edgar Rice - ***The Return Of Tarzan*** [1963] Tarzan Series #2	$1.25	$3.75	$7.50
F-747	Burroughs, Edgar Rice - ***The Beasts Of Tarzan*** [1963] Tarzan Series #3	$1.25	$3.75	$7.50
F-748	Burroughs, Edgar Rice - ***The Son Of Tarzan*** [1963] Tarzan Series #4	$1.25	$3.75	$7.50
F-749	Burroughs, Edgar Rice - ***Tarzan And The Jewels Of Opar*** [1963] Tarzan Series #5.	$1.25	$3.75	$7.50
F-750	Burroughs, Edgar Rice - ***Jungle Tales Of Tarzan*** [1963] Tarzan Series #6	$1.25	$3.75	$7.50
F-751	Burroughs, Edgar Rice - ***Tarzan The Untamed*** [1963] Tarzan Series #7	$1.25	$3.75	$7.50
F-752	Burroughs, Edgar Rice - ***Tarzan The Terrible*** [1963] Tarzan Series #8	$1.25	$3.75	$7.50
F-753	Burroughs, Edgar Rice - ***Tarzan And The Golden Lion*** [1963] Tarzan Series #9.	$1.25	$3.75	$7.50
F-754	Burroughs, Edgar Rice - ***Tarzan And The Ant-Men*** [1963] Tarzan Series #10.	$1.25	$3.75	$7.50
F-755	Trevor, Elleston - ***The Pillars Of Midnight*** [1963] Cover by James Bama.	$1.00	$3.00	$6.00
F-756	Keogh, Theodora - ***Street Music*** [1963] Cover by Jo Polseno.	$1.00	$3.00	$6.00
X-757	Shute, Nevil - ***Pastoral*** [1963]	$1.00	$3.00	$6.00
Y-759	Halleran, E. E. - ***Devil's Canyon*** [1963] Cover by Thurston	$1.00	$3.00	$6.00
F-760	Kornbluth, C. M. - ***The Marching Morons*** [1963]	$1.00	$3.00	$6.00
F-761	Wells, H. G. - ***The Island Of Dr. Moreau*** [1963]	$1.25	$3.75	$7.50
F-762	Burroughs, Edgar Rice - ***Llana Of Gathol*** [1963] Martian Series #10	$1.00	$3.00	$6.00
F-764	Johnson, Robert S. & Caidin, Martin - ***Thunderbolt*** [1963] Cover by Valigursky	$1.00	$3.00	$6.00
F-765	Mannix, Daniel P. - ***Those About To Die*** [1963]	$ .75	$2.50	$5.00
F-766	Mannix, Daniel P. - ***The Hell Fire Club*** [1963]	$ .75	$2.50	$5.00
F-767	Bell, Josephine - ***Death In Retirement*** [1963]	$ .75	$2.50	$5.00
F-768	Innes, Hammond - ***Trapped*** [1963]	$ .75	$2.50	$5.00
F-770	Burroughs, Edgar Rice - ***Thuvia, Maid Of Mars*** [1963] Cover by Bob Abbett. Martian Series #4	$1.25	$3.75	$7.50
F-772	Burroughs, Edgar Rice - ***Tarzan, Lord Of The Jungle*** [1963] Tarzan Series #11.	$1.25	$3.75	$7.50
F-773	Monsarrat, Nicholas - ***H.M.S. Marlborough Will Enter Harbor*** [1963] Cover by Ed Valigursky.	$ .75	$2.50	$5.00
X-774	Anthology - ***The Burl Ives Song Book*** [1963] Photo cover.	$1.00	$3.00	$6.00
Y-775	Kelton, Elmer - ***Shadow Of A Star*** [1963]	$ .75	$2.50	$5.00
F-776	Burroughs, Edgar Rice - ***The Chessmen Of Mars*** [1963] Cover by Bob Abbett. Martian Series #5	$1.25	$3.75	$7.50
F-777	Burroughs, Edgar Rice - ***Tarzan And The Lost Empire*** [1963] Cover by Dick Powers. Tarzan Series #12.	$1.25	$3.75	$7.50
F-778	Quentin, Patrick - ***A Puzzle For Fiends*** [1963]	$ .75	$2.50	$5.00

Ballantine Adult Fantasy. New York: Ballantine Books, Inc.

01602	Pratt, Fletcher - ***The Blue Star*** [1969]	$2.00	$6.00	$12.00
01628	Dunsany, Lord - ***The King Of Elfland's Daughter*** [1969]	$2.25	$7.00	$14.00

		G	VG	F
01652	Morris, William - ***The Wood Beyond The World*** [1969]	$2.00	$6.00	$12.00
01678	Cabell, James Branch - ***The Silver Stallion*** [1969] Cover art by Bob Pepper.	$2.00	$6.00	$12.00
01711	MacDonald, George - ***Lilith*** [1969]	$2.00	$6.00	$12.00
01730	Anthology edited by Lin Carter - ***The Young Magicians*** [1969] PBO. Cover by Sheryl Slavitt.	$2.00	$6.00	$12.00
01731	Anthology edited by Lin Carter - ***Dragons, Elves, And Heroes*** [1969] PBO. Cover by Sheryl Slavitt.	$2.25	$7.00	$14.00
01763	Cabell, James Branch - ***Figures Of Earth*** [1969] Cover art by Bob Pepper.	$2.00	$6.00	$12.00
01795	Bok, Hannes - ***The Sorcerer's Ship*** [1969] Cover art by Ray Crue.	$2.00	$6.00	$12.00
01814	Pratt, Fletcher/de Camp, L. Sprague - ***Land Of Unreason*** [1970] Cover by Donna Violetti.	$2.00	$6.00	$12.00
01855	Cabell, James Branch - ***The High Place*** [1970] First U.S. edition. Cover by Frank C. Pape.	$2.25	$7.00	$14.00
01879	Dunsany, Lord - ***At The Edge Of The World*** [1970] Cover by Ray Cruz.	$2.25	$7.00	$14.00
01880	Mirrlees, Hope - ***Lud-In-The-Mist*** [1970] Cover art by Gervasio Gellardo.	$2.00	$6.00	$12.00
01902	MacDonald, George - ***Phantastes*** [1970] Cover art by Gervasio Gellardo.	$2.00	$6.00	$12.00
01923	Lovecraft, H. P. - ***The Dream-Quest Of Unknown Kadath*** [1970] Cover by Gervasio Gallardo.	$2.00	$6.00	$12.00
01938	Smith, Clark Ashton - ***Zothique*** [1970] Cover by George Barr.	$2.25	$7.00	$14.00
01958	Meredith, George - ***The Shaving Of Shagpat*** [1970] Cover art by Ray Cruz.	$2.00	$6.00	$12.00
01959	Walton, Evangeline - ***The Island Of The Mighty*** [1970] Cover art by Bob Pepper.	$2.00	$6.00	$12.00
01981	Kurtz, Katherine - ***Deryni Rising*** [1970] Cover art by Bob Pepper.	$2.00	$6.00	$12.00
01982	Morris, William - ***The Well At The World's End: Vol. I*** [1970] Cover art by Gervasio Gallardo.	$2.00	$6.00	$12.00
02015	Morris, William - ***The Well At The World's End: Vol. II*** [1970] Cover art by Gervasio Gallardo.	$2.25	$7.00	$14.00
02045	Anthology edited by Lin Carter - ***Golden Cities, Far*** [1970] PBO. Cover by Ralph Iwamoto & Kathleen Zimmerman.	$2.25	$7.00	$14.00
02067	Cabell, James Branch - ***Something About Eve*** [1971] Cover art by Bob Pepper.	$2.00	$6.00	$12.00
02093	Bok, Hannes - ***Beyond The Golden Stair*** [1970] Cover art by Gervasio Gallardo.	$2.00	$6.00	$12.00
02094	Norman, John - ***Assassin Of Gor*** [1970] PBO. Cover art by Gino d'Achille.	$2.25	$7.00	$14.00
02107	Anderson, Poul - ***The Broken Sword*** [1971] Cover art by George Barr.	$2.00	$6.00	$12.00
02145	Hodgson, William Hope - ***The Boats Of The Glen Carrig*** [1971] PBO. Cover art by Robert LoGrippo.	$2.00	$6.00	$12.00
02146	Lovecraft, H. P. - ***The Doom That Came To Sarnath*** [1971] Cover art by Gervasio Gallardo.	$2.00	$6.00	$12.00
02147	Lovecraft, H. P. - ***Fungi From Yuggoth*** [1971] Cover art by Gervasio Gallardo.	$2.25	$7.00	$14.00
02178	Chant, Joy - ***Red Moon And Black Mountain*** [1971] Cover art by Bob Pepper.	$2.00	$6.00	$12.00
02206	Smith, Clark Ashton - ***Hyperborea*** [1971] Cover by Bill Martin.	$2.00	$6.00	$12.00
02244	Dunsany, Lord - ***Don Rodriguez: Chronicles Of Shadow Valley*** [1971]	$2.00	$6.00	$12.00
02279	Beckford, William - ***Vathek*** [1971] Cover art by Ray Cruz.	$2.25	$7.00	$14.00
02305	Chesterton, G.K. - ***The Man Who Was Thursday*** [1971] Cover art by Gervasio Gallardo.	$8.00	$25.00	$50.00

		G	VG	F
02332	Walton, Evangeline - ***The Children Of Llyr*** [1971] PBO. Cover art by David Johnston.	$2.00	$6.00	$12.00
02364	Cabell, James Branch - ***The Cream Of The Jest*** [1971] Cover art by Brian Froud.	$2.00	$6.00	$12.00
02365	Anthology edited by Lin Carter - ***New Worlds For Old*** [1971] Cover art by David Johnson.	$2.25	$7.00	$14.00
02394	Anthology edited by Lin Carter - ***The Spawn Of Cthulhu*** [1971] Cover art by Gallardo.	$2.25	$7.00	$14.00
02420	Cooper, Edmond & Green, Roger Lancelyn - ***Double Phoenix*** [1971] Cover art by Gallardo.	$2.00	$6.00	$12.00
02421	Morris, William - ***The Water Of The Wondrous Isles*** [1971] Cover art by Gallardo.	$2.00	$6.00	$12.00
02446	Crawford, F. Marion - ***Khaled*** [1971] Cover art by Gervasio Gallardo.	$2.00	$6.00	$12.00
02467	Haggard, H. Rider & Lang, Andrew - ***The World's Desire*** [1972] Cover art by Vincent di Fate.	$2.25	$7.00	$14.00
02501	Smith, Clark Ashton - ***Xiccarph*** [1972] Cover art by Gallardo.	$2.25	$7.00	$14.00
02502	Hyne, C. J. Cutliffe - ***The Lost Continent*** [1972] Cover art by Dean Ellis.	$2.25	$7.00	$14.00
02545	Cabell, James Branch - ***Domnei*** [1972] Cover art by Brian Froude.	$2.00	$6.00	$12.00
02546	Anthology edited by Lin Carter - ***Discoveries In Fantasy*** [1972] Cover art by Peter le Vasseur.	$2.00	$6.00	$12.00
02574	Bramah, Ernest - ***Kai Lung's Golden Hours*** [1972] Cover art by Ian Miller.	$2.00	$6.00	$12.00
02598	Kurtz, Katherine - ***Deryni Checkmate*** [1972] Cover art by Bob Pepper.	$2.00	$6.00	$12.00
02599	Dunsany, Lord - ***Beyond The Fields We Know*** [1972] Cover art by Gervasio Gallardo.	$2.25	$7.00	$14.00
02643	Machen, Arthur - ***The Three Imposters*** [1972] Cover art by Bob Logrippo.	$2.25	$7.00	$14.00
02669	Hodgson, William Hope - ***The Night Land: Vol. I*** [1972] Cover art by Robert Logrippo.	$2.25	$7.00	$14.00
02670	Hodgson, William Hope - ***The Night Land: Vol. II*** [1972] Cover art by Robert Logrippo.	$2.25	$7.00	$14.00
02773	Walton, Evangeline - ***The Song Of Rhiannon*** [1972] Cover art by David Johnston.	$2.00	$6.00	$12.00
02789	Anthology edited by Lin Carter - ***Great Short Novels Of Adult Fantasy (Vol. I)*** [1972] Cover art by Gervasio Gallardo.	$2.00	$6.00	$12.00
02874	MacDonald, George - ***Evenor*** [1972] Cover art by Gervasio Gallardo.	$2.25	$7.00	$14.00
03057	Ariosto, Ludovico - ***Orlando Furioso-Vol. I: The Ring Of Angelica*** [1973] Cover art by David Johnston.	$2.00	$6.00	$12.00
03085	Dunsany, Lord - ***The Charwoman's Shadow*** [1973] Cover art by Gallardo.	$2.25	$7.00	$14.00
03162	Anthology edited by Lin Carter - ***Great Short Novels Of Adult Fantasy: Vol. II*** [1973] Cover art by Gallardo.	$2.00	$6.00	$12.00
03261	Morris, William - ***The Sundering Flood*** [1973] Cover art by Gallardo.	$2.25	$7.00	$14.00
03309	Carter, Lin - ***Imaginary Worlds*** [1973] Cover art by Gallardo.	$2.25	$7.00	$14.00
03353	Smith, Clark Ashton - ***Poseidonis*** [1973] Cover art by Gallardo.	$2.25	$7.00	$14.00
23416	Laubenthal, Sanders Anne - ***Excalibur*** [1973] Cover art by Gervasio Gallardo.	$2.25	$7.00	$14.00
23485	Kurtz, Katherine - ***High Deryni*** [1973] Cover art by Alan Mardon.	$2.25	$7.00	$14.00
23518	Peake, Mervyn - ***Titus Groan*** [1974] Cover art by Bob Pepper.	$2.25	$7.00	$14.00
23519	Peake, Mervyn - ***Gormenghast*** [1973] Cover art by Bob Pepper.	$2.25	$7.00	$14.00
23520	Peake, Mervyn - ***Titus Alone*** [1973]	$2.25	$7.00	$14.00
23562	Anderson, Poul - ***Hrolf Kraki's Saga*** [1973] Cover art by Allan Mardon.	$2.00	$6.00	$12.00

		G	VG	F
23660	Haggard, H. Rider - ***The People Of The Mist*** [1973] Cover art by Dean Ellis.	$2.00	$6.00	$12.00
23787	Bramah, Ernest - ***Kai Lung Unrolls His Mat*** [1974] Cover art by Ian Miller.	$2.25	$7.00	$14.00
23886	Dunsany, Lord - ***Over The Hills And Far Away*** [1974] Cover art by Gervasio Gallardo.	$2.00	$6.00	$12.00
24010	Munn, H. Warner - ***Merlin's Ring*** [1969]	$2.00	$6.00	$12.00

Ballantine Miscellany.

		G	VG	F
3055	Koontz, Dean R. - ***A Werewolf Among Us*** [1973] PBO.	$5.50	$17.50	$35.00
24810	Matheson, Richard - ***Bid Time Return*** [1970]	$8.00	$25.00	$50.00
25115	De Camp, L. Sprague - ***Lovecraft A Biography*** [1976] Abridged by the author.	$1.50	$5.00	$10.00
28900	Matheson, Richard - ***Somewhere In Time*** [1980] Movie tie-in with photo cover.	$4.00	$12.50	$25.00

Ballantine Special Book Club Edition. New York: Ballantine Books, Inc.

		G	VG	F
NO#	Chandler, Raymond - ***Farewell, My Lovely*** [1975] Robert Mitchum photo cover. Movie tie-in.	$1.00	$3.00	$6.00

Ballantine U Series. New York: Ballantine Books, Inc.

		G	VG	F
U-1021	Whittington, Harry - ***Hangrope Town*** [1964] PBO. Cover by Herb Mott.	$1.50	$5.00	$10.00
U-2001	Burroughs, Edgar Rice - ***Tarzan Of The Apes*** [1963] Cover by Powers. Tarzan Series #1.	$ .40	$1.25	$2.50
U-2002	Burroughs, Edgar Rice - ***The Return Of Tarzan*** [1963] Cover by Powers. Tarzan Series #2.	$ .40	$1.25	$2.50
U-2003	Burroughs, Edgar Rice - ***The Beasts Of Tarzan*** [1963] Cover by Powers. Tarzan Series #3.	$ .40	$1.25	$2.50
U-2004	Burroughs, Edgar Rice - ***The Son Of Tarzan*** [1963] Cover by Powers. Tarzan Series #4.	$ .40	$1.25	$2.50
U-2005	Burroughs, Edgar Rice - ***Tarzan And The Jewels Of Opar*** [1963] Cover by Powers. Tarzan Series #5.	$ .40	$1.25	$2.50
U-2006	Burroughs, Edgar Rice - ***Jungle Tales Of Tarzan*** [1963] Cover by Powers. Tarzan Series #6.	$ .40	$1.25	$2.50
U-2007	Burroughs, Edgar Rice - ***Tarzan The Untamed*** [1963] Cover by Powers. Tarzan Series #7.	$ .40	$1.25	$2.50
U-2008	Burroughs, Edgar Rice - ***Tarzan The Terrible*** [1963] Cover by Powers. Tarzan Series #8.	$ .40	$1.25	$2.50
U-2009	Burroughs, Edgar Rice - ***Tarzan And The Golden Lion*** [1963] Cover by Powers. Tarzan Series #9.	$ .40	$1.25	$2.50
U-2010	Burroughs, Edgar Rice - ***Tarzan And The Ant Men*** [1963] Cover by Powers. Tarzan Series #10.	$ .40	$1.25	$2.50
U-2011	Burroughs, Edgar Rice - ***Tarzan, Lord Of The Jungle*** [1963] Tarzan Series #11.	$ .40	$1.25	$2.50
U-2012	Burroughs, Edgar Rice - ***Tarzan And The Lost Empire*** [1963] Tarzan Series #12.	$ .40	$1.25	$2.50
U-2013	Burroughs, Edgar Rice - ***Tarzan At The Earth's Core*** [1964] Cover by Powers. Tarzan Series #13.	$ .40	$1.25	$2.50
U-2014	Burroughs, Edgar Rice - ***Tarzan The Invincible*** [1964] Cover by Dick Powers. Tarzan Series #14.	$ .40	$1.25	$2.50
U-2015	Burroughs, Edgar Rice - ***Tarzan Triumphant*** [1964] Cover by Dick Powers. Tarzan Series #15.	$ .40	$1.25	$2.50
U-2016	Burroughs, Edgar Rice - ***Tarzan And The City Of Gold*** [1964] Cover by Dick Powers. Tarzan Series #16.	$ .40	$1.25	$2.50
U-2017	Burroughs, Edgar Rice - ***Tarzan And The Lion Man*** [1964] Cover by Dick Powers. Tarzan Series #17.	$ .40	$1.25	$2.50
U-2018	Burroughs, Edgar Rice - ***Tarzan And The Leopard Men*** [1964] Cover by Dick Powers. Tarzan Series #18.	$ .40	$1.25	$2.50

		G	VG	F
U-2019	Burroughs, Edgar Rice - ***Tarzan's Quest*** [1964] Cover by Dick Powers. Tarzan Series #19.	$ .40	$1.25	$2.50
U-2020	Burroughs, Edgar Rice - ***Tarzan And The Forbidden City*** [1964] Cover by Dick Powers. Tarzan Series #20.	$ .40	$1.25	$2.50
U-2021	Burroughs, Edgar Rice - ***Tarzan The Magnificent*** [1964] Cover by Dick Powers. Tarzan Series #21.	$ .40	$1.25	$2.50
U-2022	Burroughs, Edgar Rice - ***Tarzan And "The Foreign Legion"*** [1964] Cover by Dick Powers. Tarzan Series #22.	$ .40	$1.25	$2.50
U-2023	Burroughs, Edgar Rice - ***Tarzan And The Madman*** [1965] Tarzan Series #23.	$ .40	$1.25	$2.50
U-2024	Burroughs, Edgar Rice - ***Tarzan And The Castaways*** [1965] Tarzan Series #24.	$ .40	$1.25	$2.50
U-2031	Burroughs, Edgar Rice - ***A Princess Of Mars*** [1964] Cover by Bob Abbett. Martian Series #1.	$ .40	$1.25	$2.50
U-2032	Burroughs, Edgar Rice - ***The Gods Of Mars*** [1964] Cover by Bob Abbett. Martian Series #2.	$ .40	$1.25	$2.50
U-2033	Burroughs, Edgar Rice - ***The Warlord Of Mars*** [1964] Cover by Bob Abbett. Martian Series #3.	$ .40	$1.25	$2.50
U-2034	Burroughs, Edgar Rice - ***Thuvia, Maid Of Mars*** [1964] Martian Series #4.	$ .40	$1.25	$2.50
U-2035	Burroughs, Edgar Rice - ***Chessmen Of Mars*** [1964] Martian Series #5.	$ .40	$1.25	$2.50
U-2036	Burroughs, Edgar Rice - ***The Master Mind Of Mars*** [1963] Martian Series #6.	$ .40	$1.25	$2.50
U-2037	Burroughs, Edgar Rice - ***A Fighting Man Of Mars*** [1964] Cover by Bob Abbett. Martian Series #7.	$ .40	$1.25	$2.50
U-2038	Burroughs, Edgar Rice - ***Swords Of Mars*** [1964] Martian Series #8.	$ .40	$1.25	$2.50
U-2039	Burroughs, Edgar Rice - ***Synthetic Men Of Mars*** [1964] Cover by Bob Abbett. Martian Series. #9.	$ .40	$1.25	$2.50
U-2040	Burroughs, Edgar Rice - ***Llana Of Gathol*** [1964] Martian Series #10.	$ .40	$1.25	$2.50
U-2041	Burroughs, Edgar Rice - ***John Carter Of Mars*** [1965] Martian Series #11.	$ .40	$1.25	$2.50
U-2045	Burroughs, Edgar Rice - ***The War Chief*** [1964]	$2.00	$6.00	$12.00
U-2046	Burroughs, Edgar Rice - ***Apache Devil*** [1964]	$2.00	$6.00	$12.00
U-2048	Burroughs, Edgar Rice - ***The Lad And The Lion*** [1964] PBO. Cover by A. Bartram.	$2.50	$7.50	$15.00
U-2101	Anthology - ***The Mad Reader*** [1964]	$ .40	$1.25	$2.50
U-2102	Anthology - ***Mad Strikes Back*** [1964]	$ .40	$1.25	$2.50
U-2103	Anthology - ***Inside Mad*** [1964]	$ .40	$1.25	$2.50
U-2104	Anthology - ***Utterly Mad*** [1964] Cover by Jack Davis.	$ .40	$1.25	$2.50
U-2105	Anthology - ***The Brothers Mad*** [1964]	$ .40	$1.25	$2.50
U-2106	Anthology - ***Tales From The Crypt*** [1964] PBO. Cover by Frazetta. E.C. Comic reprints.	$2.50	$7.50	$15.00
U-2107	Anthology - ***The Vault Of Horror*** [1965] PBO. E.C. Comic reprints.	$2.50	$7.50	$15.00
U-2110	Clarke, Arthur C. - ***Reach For Tomorrow*** [1965] Cover by Powers.	$ .40	$1.25	$2.50
U-2111	Clarke, Arthur C. - ***Childhood's End*** [1965]	$ .40	$1.25	$2.50
U-2112	Clarke, Arthur C. - ***Expedition To Earth*** [1965] Cover by Powers.	$ .40	$1.25	$2.50
U-2113	Clarke, Arthur C. - ***Tales From The White Hart*** [1965] Cover by Powers.	$ .40	$1.25	$2.50
U-2120	Keogh, Theodora - ***The Tattooed Heart*** [1965]	$ .40	$1.25	$2.50
U-2121	Keogh, Theodora - ***The Fascinator*** [1965]	$ .40	$1.25	$2.50
U-2125	Blackstock, Charity - ***Dewey Death*** [1965] Cover by Schulz.	$ .40	$1.25	$2.50
U-2126	Blackstock, Charity - ***The Foggy, Foggy Dew*** [1965]	$ .40	$1.25	$2.50
U-2127	Blackstock, Lee Charity - ***The Shadow Of Murder*** [1965]	$ .40	$1.25	$2.50
U-2128	Blackstock, Charity - ***The Bitter Conquest*** [1965]	$ .40	$1.25	$2.50

		G	VG	F
U-2129	Blackstock, Charity - ***Mr. Christopoulos*** [1965]	$ .40	$1.25	$2.50
U-2130	Freeling, Nicolas - ***Death In Amsterdam*** [1965]	$ .40	$1.25	$2.50
U-2131	Freeling, Nicolas - ***Because Of The Cats*** [1965]	$ .40	$1.25	$2.50
U-2133	Freeling, Nicolas - ***Double Barrel*** [1965]	$ .40	$1.25	$2.50
U-2136	Guttmacher, M.D., Alan F. - ***The Complete Book Of Birth Control*** [1965]	$ .40	$1.25	$2.50
U-2138	Bradbury, Ray - ***Fahrenheit 451*** [1965]	$ .40	$1.25	$2.50
U-2139	Bradbury, Ray - ***The October Country*** [1965]	$ .40	$1.25	$2.50
U-2140	Anthology - ***Tales Of The Incredible*** [1965] PBO. Cover by Frazetta. Reprints classic E.C. horror stories from the comic books. First book publication of these stories.	$2.50	$7.50	$15.00
U-2141	Bradbury, Ray - ***The Autumn People*** [1965] PBO. Cover by Frazetta. Adapted from the E.C. comic books.	$2.50	$7.50	$15.00
U-2142	Bradbury, Ray - ***Tomorrow Midnight*** [1966] PBO. Cover by Frank Frazetta. Reprints the classic Bradbury comic book adaptations published by E.C. comics in the 1950s. First book publication.	$2.50	$7.50	$15.00
U-2155	Bell, Josephine - ***Double Doom*** [1965] Cover by Lehr.	$ .40	$1.25	$2.50
U-2156	Bell, Josephine - ***Easy Prey*** [1965] Cover by Lehr.	$ .40	$1.25	$2.50
U-2157	Bell, Josephine - ***Room For A Body*** [1965]	$ .40	$1.25	$2.50
U-2158	Bell, Josephine - ***Death At The Medical Board*** [1964] PBO.	$ .50	$1.50	$3.00
U-2159	Tey, Josephine - ***Murder On The Merry-Go-Round*** [1965] PBO.	$ .50	$1.50	$3.00
U-2166	Anthology edited by Greenwald, Harold - ***Great Cases In Psychoanalysis*** [1965]	$ .40	$1.25	$2.50
U-2169	Vance, Jack - ***The Blue World*** [1966] PBO. Cover by Jeff Jones.	$1.35	$4.00	$8.00
U-2170	Smith, Caesar - ***Heat Wave*** [1966] Cover by Lehr.	$ .40	$1.25	$2.50
U-2171	Anthology edited by Frederik Pohl - ***Star Of Stars*** [1960] Reprints the Doubleday hardcover edition.	$ .40	$1.25	$2.50
U-2172	Pohl, Frederik/Williamson, Jack - ***The Reefs Of Space*** [1964] PBO.	$ .40	$1.25	$2.50
U-2173	Pohl, Frederik & Kornbluth, C. M. - ***The Space Merchants*** [1964]	$ .40	$1.25	$2.50
U-2174	Pohl, Frederik - ***A Plague Of Pythons*** [1965] PBO.	$ .40	$1.25	$2.50
U-2175	Pohl, Frederik - ***The Case Against Tomorrow*** [1965] Cover by Powers.	$ .40	$1.25	$2.50
U-2176	Pohl, Frederik/Williamson, Jack - ***Starchild*** [1965] PBO.	$ .50	$1.50	$3.00
U-2177	Pohl, Frederik - ***Slave Ship*** [1965]	$ .40	$1.25	$2.50
U-2178	Pohl, Frederik - ***Digits & Dastards*** [1966] PBO.	$ .50	$1.50	$3.00
U-2190	Tenn, William - ***The Human Angle*** [1964] Cover by Powers.	$ .40	$1.25	$2.50
U-2191	Dick, Philip K. - ***Martian Time-Slip*** [1964] PBO. Cover by Brillhart.	$3.00	$9.00	$18.00
U-2192	Farmer, Philip Jose - ***Inside Outside*** [1964] Cover by Bob Abbett.	$1.50	$5.00	$10.00
U-2193	Farmer, Philip Jose - ***Dare*** [1965] PBO. Cover by Abbett.	$1.50	$5.00	$10.00
U-2200	Anthology - ***The Harry Hershfield Joke Book*** [1965]	$ .40	$1.25	$2.50
U-2202	Frank, Wolfgang - ***The Sea Wolves*** [1965]	$ .40	$1.25	$2.50
U-2203	Bixby, Jerome - ***Space By The Tale*** [1964] PBO. Cover by Brillhart.	$ .40	$1.25	$2.50
U-2209	Blair, Jr., Clay - ***Beyond Courage*** [1964] Cover by Mel Crair.	$ .40	$1.25	$2.50
U-2210	Bekker, C. D. - ***Defeat At Sea*** [1965] Cover by Valigursky.	$ .40	$1.25	$2.50
U-2212	Miller, Jr., Walter M. - ***The View From The Stars*** [1965] PBO. Cover by Dick Powers	$ .40	$1.25	$2.50
U-2213	Conquest, Robert - ***A World Of Difference*** [1964] PBO.	$ .40	$1.25	$2.50
U-2214	Vance, Jack - ***Future Tense*** [1964] PBO.	$ .50	$1.50	$3.00
U-2215	Clement, Hal - ***Close To Critical*** [1964] PBO. Cover by Lehr.	$ .40	$1.25	$2.50
U-2216	Leiber, Fritz - ***A Pail Of Air*** [1964] PBO. Cover by Powers.	$ .40	$1.25	$2.50
U-2217	Hubbard, P. M. - ***Flush As May*** [1964] Cover by Lehr.	$ .40	$1.25	$2.50
U-2218	Parkinson, C. Northcote - ***Parkinson's Law*** [1964]	$ .40	$1.25	$2.50

		G	VG	F
U-2219	Brunner, John - ***The Whole Man*** [1964] PBO.	$ .50	$1.50	$3.00
U-2220	Anthology edited by Joseph W. Ferman - ***No Limits*** [1964] PBO.	$ .50	$1.50	$3.00
U-2222	Wellman, Manly Wade - ***Who Fears The Devil?*** [1964]	$ .50	$1.50	$3.00
U-2223	Trevor, Elleston - ***Squadron Airborne*** [1964]	$ .40	$1.25	$2.50
U-2224	White, James - ***Deadly Litter*** [1964] PBO.	$ .40	$1.25	$2.50
U-2225	Mannix, Dan - ***Memoirs Of A Sword Swallower*** [1964]	$ .40	$1.25	$2.50
U-2226	Rougvie, Cameron - ***Medal From Pamplona*** [1964]	$ .40	$1.25	$2.50
U-2230	Duerrenmatt, Friedrich - ***Traps*** [1964]	$ .40	$1.25	$2.50
U-2231	Sturgeon, Theodore - ***More Than Human*** [1964]	$ .40	$1.25	$2.50
U-2232	Wells, H. G. - ***First Men In The Moon*** [1964] Movie tie-in with photo cover.	$ .50	$1.50	$3.00
U-2233	Green, Joseph L. - ***The Loafers Of Refuge*** [1965] PBO.	$ .50	$1.50	$3.00
U-2234	Canaway, W. H. - ***A Boy Ten Feet Tall*** [1965] Movie tie-in.	$ .50	$1.50	$3.00
U-2235	Clement, Hal - ***Natives Of Space*** [1965] PBO. Cover by Powers.	$ .50	$1.50	$3.00
U-2236	Del Rey, Lester - ***Mortals And Monsters*** [1965] PBO.	$ .50	$1.50	$3.00
U-2239	McKimmey, James - ***Blue Mascara Tears*** [1965] PBO. Cover by McGinnis.	$ .50	$1.50	$3.00
U-2240	Moyes, Patricia - ***Down Among The Dead Men*** [1965]	$ .40	$1.25	$2.50
U-2241	Moyes, Patricia - ***Death On The Agenda*** [1965]	$ .40	$1.25	$2.50
U-2243	Moyes, Patricia - ***Murder À La Mode*** [1965]	$ .40	$1.25	$2.50
U-2244	Moyes, Patricia - ***Falling Star*** [1965]	$ .40	$1.25	$2.50
U-2247	Sturgeon, Theodore - ***E Pluribus Unicorn*** [1965] Cover by Powers.	$ .40	$1.25	$2.50
U-2248	Bowen, John - ***After The Rain*** [1965]	$ .40	$1.25	$2.50
U-2249	Capp, Al - ***The World Of Li'L Abner*** [1965] Cover by Author.	$ .65	$2.00	$4.00
U-2250	Rougvie, Cameron - ***Tangier Assignment*** [1965] PBO.	$ .40	$1.25	$2.50
U-2251	Blish, James - ***A Case Of Conscience*** [1965] Cover by Hoot.	$ .40	$1.25	$2.50
U-2252	Turner, William O. - ***Five Days To Salt Lake*** [1966] PBO.	$ .40	$1.25	$2.50
U-2253	Sturgeon, Theodore - ***Some Of Your Blood*** [1966]	$ .50	$1.50	$3.00
U-2254	Leiber, Fritz - ***The Night Of The Wolf*** [1966] PBO. Cover by Powers.	$ .65	$2.00	$4.00
U-2256	Halleran, E. E. - ***Red River Country*** [1966] PBO.	$ .40	$1.25	$2.50
U-2260	Everett, Wade - ***Vengeance*** [1966] PBO. Cover by Lesser.	$ .40	$1.25	$2.50
U-2271	Binder, Otto & Tennis, Craig - ***Dracula*** [1966] PBO. Illustrated in comic book form by Alden McWilliams.	$2.50	$7.50	$15.00
U-2285	White, James - ***The Watch Below*** [1966] PBO. Photo cover.	$ .40	$1.25	$2.50
U-2301	Leighton, Lee - ***Big Ugly*** [1966] PBO.	$ .40	$1.25	$2.50
U-2327	Connell, Edwin - ***I Had To Kill Her*** [1966]	$ .40	$1.25	$2.50
U-2328	Niven, Larry - ***World Of Ptavvs*** [1966] PBO. Author's first book.	$3.50	$10.00	$20.00
U-2329	Brunner, John - ***The Long Result*** [1966] Cover by Hoot. First U.S. edition.	$ .50	$1.50	$3.00
U-2330	Silverberg, Robert - ***Needle In A Timestack*** [1966] PBO. Cover by Powers.	$ .50	$1.50	$3.00
U-2331	Anthology edited by James Blish - ***New Dreams This Morning*** [1966] PBO. Cover by Dick Powers.	$ .50	$1.50	$3.00
U-2333	Hoffman, Lee - ***Bred To Kill*** [1967] PBO. Cover by Carl Hantman.	$ .40	$1.25	$2.50
U-2334	Ketchum, Philip - ***The Man From Granite*** [1967] PBO.	$ .40	$1.25	$2.50
U-2335	Ketchum, Philip - ***Wyoming*** [1967] PBO.	$ .40	$1.25	$2.50
U-2341	Huttner, Henry - ***Ahead Of Time*** [1967] Cover by Powers.	$ .40	$1.25	$2.50
U-2342	Anderson, Poul - ***Brain Wave*** [1967]	$ .40	$1.25	$2.50
U-2343	Pohl, Frederik & Kornbluth, C. M. - ***Gladiator-At-Law*** [1967] Cover by Powers.	$ .40	$1.25	$2.50
U-2344	Del Rey, Lester - ***Nerves*** [1967] Cover by Powers.	$ .40	$1.25	$2.50
U-2345	Farmer, Philip Jose - ***The Green Odyssey*** [1967] Cover by Powers.	$ .40	$1.25	$2.50
U-2346	Vance, Jack - ***To Live Forever*** [1966]	$ .40	$1.25	$2.50

		G	VG	F
U-2350	Ingram, Hunter - ***Contested Valley*** [1968] PBO. Cover by Carl Hantman.	$ .40	$1.25	$2.50
U-2822	Anthology edited by Groff Conklin - ***The Graveyard Reader*** [1965] Second printing.	$ .50	$1.50	$3.00
U-5030	Burgess, Anthony - ***The Wanting Seed*** [1964]	$ .40	$1.25	$2.50
U-5050	Sheckley, Robert - ***The 10th Victim*** [1967]	$ .40	$1.25	$2.50
U-5063	Saberhagen, Fred - ***Berserker*** [1967] PBO.	$ .40	$1.25	$2.50
U-5064	Brunner, John - ***Out Of My Mind*** [1967] PBO.	$ .50	$1.50	$3.00
U-6010	Leiber, Fritz - ***The Wanderer*** [1964] PBO.	$ .50	$1.50	$3.00
U-6018	Pangborn, Edgar - ***Davy*** [1964]	$ .50	$1.50	$3.00
U-6035	Brunner, John - ***The Squares Of The City*** [1965] PBO.	$ .50	$1.50	$3.00
U-6039	Burroughs, Edgar Rice - ***The Mucker*** [1966]	$ .65	$2.00	$4.00
U-6071	Norman, John - ***Tarnsman Of Gor*** [1966] PBO.	$1.00	$3.00	$6.00
U-6072	Norman, John - ***Outlaw Of Gor*** [1967] PBO.	$1.00	$3.00	$6.00
U-6085	Burroughs, John Coleman - ***Treasure Of The Black Falcon*** [1967] PBO.	$ .50	$1.50	$3.00
U-6092	Maine, Charles Eric - ***B. E. A. S. T.*** [1967] PBO. First U.S. edition.	$ .50	$1.50	$3.00
U-6097	Silverberg, Robert - ***Thorns*** [1967] PBO.	$ .40	$1.25	$2.50
U-6100	Meyers, Roy - ***Dolphin Boy*** [1967] PBO.	$1.50	$5.00	$10.00
U-6107	Anthony, Piers - ***Chthon*** [1967] PBO.	$ .50	$1.50	$3.00
U-6108	McCaffrey, Anne - ***Restoree*** [1967] PBO.	$1.50	$5.00	$10.00
U-6121	Silverberg, Robert - ***The Masks Of Time*** [1968] PBO.	$ .50	$1.50	$3.00
U-6124	McCaffrey, Anne - ***Dragonflight*** [1968] PBO.	$1.35	$4.00	$8.00
U-6125	Leiber, Fritz - ***Tarzan And The Valley Of Gold*** [1966] PBO. Adapted from the motion picture by Banner Productions. Authorized.	$2.50	$7.50	$15.00
U-6131	Tenn, William - ***Of Men And Monsters*** [1968] PBO.	$ .50	$1.50	$3.00
U-6132	Tenn, William - ***The Square Root Of Man*** [1968] PBO.	$ .50	$1.50	$3.00
U-6133	Tenn, William - ***The Wooden Star*** [1968] PBO.	$ .50	$1.50	$3.00
U-6134	Tenn, William - ***The Seven Sexes*** [1968] PBO.	$ .50	$1.50	$3.00
U-6135	Tenn, William - ***The Human Angle*** [1968] Third printing.	$ .40	$1.25	$2.50
U-6136	Tenn, William - ***Of All Possible Worlds*** [1968] Third printing.	$ .40	$1.25	$2.50
U-7038	Tolkien, J. R. R. - ***The Tolkien Reader*** [1966] PBO.	$1.50	$5.00	$10.00
U-7039	Tolkien, J. R. R. - ***The Hobbit*** [1965]	$1.50	$5.00	$10.00
U-7061	Eddison, E. R. - ***The Worm Ouroboros*** [1967]	$ .40	$1.25	$2.50
U-7083	Moskowitz, Sam - ***Seekers Of Tomorrow*** [1967] Biographical sketches of the top science fiction writers with an author reference index.	$ .50	$1.50	$3.00

Banner Books. New York: Banner Books, Inc.

		G	VG	F
B40-101	Owen, Dean - ***Gundown In Quintana*** [1967] PBO.	$1.25	$3.75	$7.50
B40-102	West, Kingsley - ***Ride West To Pueblo*** [1967]	$1.25	$3.75	$7.50
B40-103	West, Kingsley - ***Apache Lance*** [1967] PBO.	$1.25	$3.75	$7.50
B40-104	Bonner, Michael - ***The Iron Noose*** [1967]	$1.25	$3.75	$7.50
B40-105	Bonner, Parker - ***Superstition Range*** [1967]	$1.25	$3.75	$7.50
B40-106	Owen, Dean - ***Guns Of Spring*** [1967] PBO.	$1.35	$4.00	$8.00
B40-107	Bouma, J. L. - ***Outlaw Frenzy*** [1967] PBO.	$1.35	$4.00	$8.00
B40-108	Bonner, Parker - ***Plunder Canyon*** [1967]	$1.25	$3.75	$7.50
B50-101	Charbonneau, Louis - ***Way Out*** [1967] PBO.	$1.35	$4.00	$8.00
B50-102	Brewer, Gil - ***The Tease*** [1967] PBO.	$2.00	$6.00	$12.00
B50-103	Brewer, Jordan - ***Get Dumm!*** [1967] PBO.	$1.35	$4.00	$8.00
B50-104	Cox, William R. - ***Way To Go, Doll Baby!*** [1967]	$1.35	$4.00	$8.00
B50-105	Karp, David - ***The Girl On Crown Street*** [1967]	$1.50	$5.00	$10.00
B50-106	Sheldon, Walt - ***The House Of Happy Mayhem*** [1967] PBO.	$1.35	$4.00	$8.00
B50-107	Karp, David - ***Platoon*** [1967]	$1.50	$5.00	$10.00
B50-108	Brewer, Gil - ***Sin For Me*** [1967] PBO.	$2.00	$6.00	$12.00
B50-109	Hale, Arlene - ***Stay With Me, Love*** [1967]	$1.25	$3.75	$7.50
B50-110	Karp, David - ***The Big Feeling*** [1967] PBO.	$2.50	$7.50	$15.00
B50-111	Karp, David - ***Hardman*** [1967]	$1.50	$5.00	$10.00

		G	VG	F
B50-112	Cleri, Mario - ***Six Graves To Munich*** [1967] PBO.	$1.35	$4.00	$8 00
B50-113	Karp, David - ***The Brotherhood Of Velvet*** [1967]	$1.50	$5.00	$10.00
B50-114	Morton, Patricia - ***Province Of Darkness*** [1967] PBO.	$1.35	$4.00	$8.00
B50-115	Bonner, Parker - ***Plunder Canyon*** [1967]	$1.25	$3.75	$7.50
B50-116	Wyler, Richard - ***Incident At Butler's Station*** [1967]	$1.25	$3.75	$7.50
B50-117	Luther, Ray (Arthur Sellings) - ***Intermind*** [1967] PBO.	$1.35	$4.00	$8.00
B50-121	Hale, Arlene - ***Bend Of The River*** [1967]	$1.25	$3.75	$7.50
B60-101	Harris, John - ***The Old Trade Of Killing*** [1967]	$1.25	$3.75	$7.50
B60-102	Black, Gavin - ***A Dragon For Christmas*** [1967]	$1.35	$4.00	$8.00
B60-103	Dembo, Samuel - ***Kalihari Kill*** [1967]	$1.25	$3.75	$7.50
B60-104	Ross, Sam - ***Day Of The Shark*** [1967] PBO.	$1.35	$4.00	$8.00
B60-105	Milton, Henry A. - ***The President Is Missing!*** [1967] PBO.	$1.35	$4.00	$8.00
B60-106	Whittington, Harry - ***Doomsday Mission*** [1967] PBO.	$3.50	$10.00	$20.00
B60-107	Jarrett, Kay - ***Sex Is A Private Affair*** [1967]	$1.35	$4.00	$8.00
B60-108	Saber, W. J. - ***The Devious Defector*** [1967] PBO.	$1.35	$4.00	$8.00
B60-109	Ford, Hilary - ***Bella On The Roof*** [1967] PBO.	$1.35	$4.00	$8.00
B60-110	Shaw, Bob - ***Night Walk*** [1967] PBO. Cover art by Frazetta.	$2.50	$7.50	$15.00
B60-111	Goodis, David - ***Somebody's Done For*** [1967] PBO.	$12.50	$37.50	$75.00
B60-112	Ross, Clarissa - ***Face In The Pond*** [1967]	$1.25	$3.75	$7.50

Banner Mysteries. Digest Size.

1	Rice, Craig - ***The Sunday Pigeon Murders*** [1945] Cover art by Mac Raboy	$6.00	$20.00	$40.00
2	Patrick, Quentin - ***Death Goes To School*** [1945] Cover art by Mac Raboy	$10.00	$30.00	$60.00

Bantam A Series. New York: Bantam Books, Inc.

A-1	Miller, John A. - ***Men And Volts At War*** [n.d.]	$1.25	$3.75	$7.50
A-3	Beasley, Norman - ***Main Street Merchant*** [n.d.]	$1.25	$3.75	$7.50
A-5	McCormick, Charles P. - ***The Power Of People*** [n.d.]	$1.25	$3.75	$7.50

Bantam Books, Los Angeles, Western Printing and Lithographing Co. (Early Publisher's History, 1939–1959)

Do not confuse this publisher with Bantam Books Inc., with whom they have no connection. In 1942, Western Printing and Lithographing Co., Racine, Wisconsin, would work with George Delacorte to produce Dell Books. Rare and valuable collectibles seem understatements about this series of twenty-eight titles. Originally, Bantam Books, Los Angeles, sold in vending machines with a cover price of 10¢. Some of the volumes have three cover variations to include illustrations and color changes. Every title with the Bantam Books, Los Angeles, imprint attracts the attention of collectors.

Bantam Books. Los Angeles: Bantam Publications.

		G	VG	F
1	Queen, Ellery - ***The Spanish Cape Mystery*** [n.d.]	$20.00	$60.00	$125.00
1-A(P)	Stout, Rex - ***The Red Threads*** [n.d.] Pictorial cover.	$35.00	$125.00	$300.00
1-A	Stout, Rex - ***The Red Threads*** [n.d.]	$17.00	$50.00	$100.00
2	Carnegie, Dale - ***Little Known Facts About Well Known People*** [n.d.]	$13.50	$40.00	$80.00
3	Fishbein, M.D., Morris - ***Your Questions On Health*** [1940] PBO.	$15.00	$45.00	$90.00
4	Author not listed - ***Everybody's Dream Book*** [1940]	$17.00	$50.00	$100.00
5	Currie, S., M.A., D.Sc. - ***How To Make Friends Easily*** [1940] PBO.	$17.00	$50.00	$100.00

		G	VG	F
6	Gregory, Jerome - editor - ***Everybody's Book Of Jokes And Wisecracks*** [1940] PBO.	$20.00	$60.00	$125.00
7	Based on the famous radio series - ***The Voice Of Experience*** [1940] PBO.	$17.00	$50.00	$100.00
8	Brown, Henry C. - editor - ***Favorite Poems*** [1940] PBO.	$15.00	$45.00	$90.00
9	Engle, William - ***Enter The G-Men*** [1940] PBO.	$20.00	$60.00	$125.00
10	Anthology - ***1000 Facts Worth Knowing*** [n.d.]	$17.00	$50.00	$100.00
11	Martin, Libby - ***How To Win And Hold A Husband*** [n.d.]	$15.00	$45.00	$90.00
12	Packer, Eleanor - editor - ***The World's Great Love Affairs*** [1940] PBO.	$17.00	$50.00	$100.00
13	Lewis, Ellen - editor - ***Children's Favorite Stories*** [1940] PBO.	$20.00	$60.00	$125.00
14	Striker, Fran - ***The Lone Ranger And The Secret Of Thunder Mountain*** [n.d.]	$27.50	$85.00	$200.00
15	Wilcox, Ella Wheeler - ***Poems Of Passion*** [1940] PBO.	$17.00	$50.00	$100.00
16	Anthology - ***Grimm's Fairy Tales*** [n.d.]	$22.00	$70.00	$140.00
17	Packer, Eleanor - ***Private Lives Of The Movie Stars*** [1940] PBO.	$22.00	$70.00	$140.00
18	MacIsaac, Fred - ***Love On The Run*** [n.d.]	$20.00	$60.00	$125.00
19	Beach, Rex - ***The Tower Of Flame/Jaragu Of The Lost Islands*** [1940] PBO.	$20.00	$60.00	$125.00
20	Van Loon, Hendrik Willem - ***The Story Of Rabelais And Voltaire*** [n.d.]	$17.00	$50.00	$100.00
21-P	Grant, Maxwell - ***The Shadow And The Voice Of Murder*** [1940] PBO. Pictorial cover.	$50.00	$175.00	$400.00
21	Grant, Maxwell - ***The Shadow And The Voice Of Murder*** [1940] PBO. First book publication of "The Voice Of Death" from Shadow Magazine.	$30.00	$100.00	$225.00
22-P	Hutton, Brett - ***The Green Death And Other Stories*** [1940] Pictorial cover.	$40.00	$140.00	$350.00
22	Hutton, Brett - ***The Green Death And Other Stories*** [1940]	$22.00	$70.00	$140.00
23	Burroughs, Edgar Rice - ***Tarzan In The Forbidden City*** [n.d.] Authorized abridged edition.	$30.00	$100.00	$225.00
23-P	Burroughs, Edgar Rice - ***Tarzan In The Forbidden City*** [n.d.] Authorized abridged edition. Pictorial cover.	$50.00	$175.00	$400.00
24	Packer, Eleanor - editor - ***Humorous Anecdotes And Funny Stories*** [1940] PBO.	$17.00	$50.00	$100.00
24-P	Packer, Eleanor - editor - ***Humorous Anecdotes And Funny Stories*** [1943] PBO. Pictorial cover.	$35.00	$125.00	$300.00
25-P	Chidsey, Donald Barr - ***Nobody Heard The Shot*** [1941] Pictorial cover.	$35.00	$125.00	$300.00
25	Chidsey, Donald Barr - ***Nobody Heard The Shot*** [1941]	$17.00	$50.00	$100.00
26-P	Christie, Agatha - ***The Blue Geranium And Other Tuesday Club Murders*** [n.d.] Pictorial cover.	$40.00	$140.00	$350.00
26	Christie, Agatha - ***The Blue Geranium And Other Tuesday Club Murders*** [n.d.]	$22.00	$70.00	$140.00
27	Wylie, Philip - ***Danger Mansion/A Resourceful Lady*** [n.d.]	$20.00	$60.00	$125.00
27-P	Wylie, Philip - ***Danger Mansion/A Resourceful Lady*** [n.d.] Pictorial cover.	$35.00	$125.00	$300.00
28	Eberhart, Mignon G. - ***Strangers In Flight*** [1940] PBO.	$20.00	$60.00	$125.00
28-P	Eberhart, Mignon G. - ***Strangers In Flight*** [1940] PBO. Pictorial cover.	$35.00	$125.00	$300.00

Bantam Books (Early Publisher's History, 1945–1959)

After leaving Penguin Books in America, Ian Ballantine founded Bantam Books. Early titles reprinted the work of top American writers such as John Steinbeck, F. Scott Fitzgerald, and Zane Grey. In the coming years, Bantam branched out in mysteries, westerns, and other popular fiction. Covers for these books changed a number of times, but always featured a rooster logo. Bantam books display dust jackets, wrap-around covers, and movie tie-in photo covers. The most valuable books in this series are the dust-jacketed editions of Bantam Books, Superior Reprints, Infantry Journal Book, and Infantry Journal-Penguin Books. Other imprints include Bantam Classics, Bantam Biographies, Bantam Special Edition, Bantam Unnumbered, and Pennant Books.

Bantam Books. New York: Bantam Books, Inc.

		G	VG	F
1	Twain, Mark - ***Life On The Mississippi*** [1945] Cover by H. Lawrence Hoffman.	$1.50	$5.00	$10.00
2	Gruber, Frank - ***The Gift Horse*** [1945]	$1.25	$3.75	$7.50
3	Grey, Zane - ***Nevada*** [1945] Cover by Triggs.	$1.50	$5.00	$10.00
4	Daly, Elizabeth - ***Evidence Of Things Seen*** [1945]	$1.25	$3.75	$7.50
5	Sabatini, Rafael - ***Scaramouche*** [1945] Cover by Cirlin.	$1.00	$3.00	$6.00
6	Dean, Robert George - ***A Murder By Marriage*** [1945] Cover by Cal Diehl.	$1.25	$3.75	$7.50
7	Steinbeck, John - ***The Grapes Of Wrath*** [1945] Cover by Brat..	$2.00	$6.00	$12.00
8(DJ)	Fitzgerald, F. Scott - ***The Great Gatsby*** [1945] Dust-jacketed edition. DJ cover by Skemp.	$12.50	$37.50	$75.00
8	Fitzgerald, F. Scott - ***The Great Gatsby*** [1945] Cover by Cirlin.	$1.00	$3.00	$6.00
9	Household, Geoffrey - ***Rogue Male*** [1945]	$1.25	$3.75	$7.50
9(DJ)	Household, Geoffrey - ***Rogue Male*** [1945] Dust-jacketed edition.	$10.00	$30.00	$60.00
10	Rawlings, Marjorie Kinnan - ***South Moon Under*** [1945] Cover by Palacios.	$1.00	$3.00	$6.00
11	Rorick, Isabel Scott - ***Mr. And Mrs. Cugat*** [1945] Cover by Floyd A Hardy.	$1.00	$3.00	$6.00
12	Homes, Geoffrey - ***Then There Were Three*** [1945] Cover by Clement.	$1.25	$3.75	$7.50
13	Paul, Elliot - ***The Last Time I Saw Paris*** [1945] Cover by Maurice Utrillo.	$1.00	$3.00	$6.00
14	Exupery, Antoine de Saint - ***Wind, Sand And Stars*** [1945] Cover by Cal Diehl.	$1.00	$3.00	$6.00
15	Benson, Sally - ***Meet Me In St. Louis*** [1945] Cover by Cirlin.	$1.00	$3.00	$6.00
16	Ford, Leslie - ***The Town Cried Murder*** [1945] Cover by Jonas..	$1.25	$3.75	$7.50
17	Tarkington, Booth - ***Seventeen*** [1945] Cover by Hoffman.	$1.00	$3.00	$6.00
18	Schulberg, Budd - ***What Makes Sammy Run?*** [1945] Photo cover.	$1.00	$3.00	$6.00
19(DJ)	Nathan, Robert - ***One More Spring*** [1945] Dust-jacketed edition. DJ has photo cover.	$4.50	$14.00	$28.00
19	Nathan, Robert - ***One More Spring*** [1945] Photo cover.	$1.00	$3.00	$6.00
20	Hobart, Alice Tisdale - ***Oil For The Lamps Of China*** [1945] Cover by Palacios.	$1.00	$3.00	$6.00
21	Thurber, James - ***Men, Women And Dogs*** [1946] Cartoon Book.	$1.25	$3.75	$7.50
22(DJ)	Lewis, Sinclair - ***Babbitt*** [1946] Dust-jacketed edition. DJ cover by B. Barton.	$4.50	$14.00	$28.00
22	Lewis, Sinclair - ***Babbitt*** [1946] Cover by Cirlin.	$1.25	$3.75	$7.50
23	Collins, Mary - ***The Fog Comes*** [1946] Cover by Cal Diehl.	$1.25	$3.75	$7.50
24	Benefield, Harry - ***Valiant Is The Word For Carrie*** [1946] Cover by Palacios.	$1.00	$3.00	$6.00
24(DJ)	Benefield, Harry - ***Valiant Is The Word For Carrie*** [1946] Cover by Paul Koloda. In dust-jacket.	$4.50	$14.00	$28.00
25	Haycox, Ernest - ***Bugles In The Afternoon*** [1946]	$1.00	$3.00	$6.00
26	Holding, Elizabeth Sax - ***Net Of Cobwebs*** [1946]	$1.25	$3.75	$7.50
26(DJ)	Holding, Elizabeth Sax - ***Net Of Cobwebs*** [1946] In dust-jacket.	$7.00	$22.50	$45.00
27	Allen, Frederick Lewis - ***Only Yesterday*** [1946]	$1.00	$3.00	$6.00
28	Bromfield, Louis - ***Night In Bombay*** [1946] Cover by Palacios.	$1.00	$3.00	$6.00
29	Hilton, James - ***Was It Murder*** [1946]	$1.25	$3.75	$7.50

		G	VG	F
30	Fast, Howard - ***Citizen Tom Paine*** [1946] Cover by Charles Andres.	$1.00	$3.00	$6.00
31	Buchan, John - ***The Three Hostages*** [1946] Cover by Bill English.	$1.00	$3.00	$6.00
32	Fowler, Gene - ***The Great Mouthpiece*** [1946] Photo cover.	$1.25	$3.75	$7.50
33	Hope, Anthony - ***The Prisoner Of Zenda*** [1946] Cover by Cirlin.	$1.00	$3.00	$6.00
34	Allan, Francis - ***First Come, First Kill*** [1946] Cover by Arnold.	$1.25	$3.75	$7.50
35	Kober, Arthur - ***My Dear Bella*** [1946] Cover by Hoffman.	$1.00	$3.00	$6.00
36	Dawson, Peter - ***Trail Boss*** [1946]	$1.00	$3.00	$6.00
37	Addams, Charles - ***Drawn And Quartered*** [1946] Cover by Charles Addams. Cartoon Book.	$2.50	$7.50	$15.00
38	Avery, A. A. - ***Anything For A Quiet Life*** [1946] Cover by Bill English.	$1.00	$3.00	$6.00
39	Woollcott, Alexander - ***Long, Long Ago*** [1946] Cover by Cotton.	$1.00	$3.00	$6.00
40	Forester, C. S. - ***The Captain From Connecticut*** [1946] Cover by Cal Diehl.	$1.00	$3.00	$6.00
41	Westscott, Edward Noyes - ***David Harum*** [1946] Cover by Cirlin.	$1.00	$3.00	$6.00
42	Ford, Leslie - ***Road To Folly*** [1946] Photo cover.	$1.25	$3.75	$7.50
43	Yeats-Brown, Francis - ***The Lives Of A Bengal Lancer*** [1946] Cover by Cal Diehl.	$1.00	$3.00	$6.00
44(DJ)	Stone, Grace Zaring - ***The Cold Journey*** [1946]	$12.50	$37.50	$75.00
44	Stone, Grace Zaring - ***The Cold Journey*** [1946] Cover by Charles Andres.	$1.00	$3.00	$6.00
45	Hersey, John - ***A Bell For Adano*** [1946] Cover by Cal Diehl.	$1.00	$3.00	$6.00
46	Eberhart, Mignon G. - ***Escape The Night*** [1946] Photo cover.	$1.25	$3.75	$7.50
47	James, Will - ***Home Ranch*** [1946] Cover by Will James.	$1.00	$3.00	$6.00
48	Bulosan, Carlos - ***The Laughter Of My Father*** [1946] Cover by Alexander.	$1.00	$3.00	$6.00
49	Crane, Frances - ***The Amethyst Spectacles*** [1946] Photo cover.	$1.25	$3.75	$7.50
50	Gruber, Frank - ***The Buffalo Box*** [1946] Photo cover.	$1.25	$3.75	$7.50
51	Gilbert, Anthony - ***Death In The Blackout*** [1946]	$1.25	$3.75	$7.50
52	Homes, Geoffrey - ***No Hands On The Clock*** [1946] Photo cover.	$1.25	$3.75	$7.50
53	Daly, Elizabeth - ***Nothing Can Rescue Me*** [1946] Photo cover.	$1.25	$3.75	$7.50
54	Massie, Chris - ***The Love Letters*** [1946]	$1.00	$3.00	$6.00
55	Train, Arthur - ***Tutt And Mr. Tutt*** [1946]	$1.50	$5.00	$10.00
56	Knibbs, Henry Herbert - ***The Tonto Kid*** [1946] Cover by Charles Andres.	$1.00	$3.00	$6.00
57	Cerf, Bennett - ***Anything For A Laugh*** [1946] PBO. Cover by O'Connor Barrett.	$1.00	$3.00	$6.00
58	Kipling, Rudyard - ***Captains Courageous*** [1946] Cover by Cal Diehl.	$1.00	$3.00	$6.00
59	Seton, Ernest Thompson - ***Wild Animals I Have Known*** [1946] Cover by Willig.	$1.35	$4.00	$8.00
60	Dine, S. S. Van - ***The Kennel Murder Case*** [1946] Photo cover.	$1.50	$5.00	$10.00
61	Anthology - ***The Bantam Concise Dictionary*** [1946] PBO.	$1.35	$4.00	$8.00
62	Collins, Mary - ***Dead Center*** [1946] Photo cover.	$1.25	$3.75	$7.50
63	Hudson, W. H. - ***Green Mansions*** [1946]	$1.50	$5.00	$10.00
64	Jenkins, Elizabeth - ***Harriet*** [1946]	$1.00	$3.00	$6.00
65	Douglas, Norman - ***South Wind*** [1946] Cover by Steinberg.	$1.00	$3.00	$6.00
66	Hope, Edward - ***She Loves Me Not*** [1946] Cover by Alexander.	$1.00	$3.00	$6.00
67	Tully, Jim - ***The Bruiser*** [1946] Cover by Charles Andres.	$1.00	$3.00	$6.00
68	Field, Peter - ***Guns From Powder Valley*** [1946]	$1.00	$3.00	$6.00
69	Wescott, Glenway - ***The Grandmothers*** [1946] Cover by Cal Diehl.	$2.50	$7.50	$15.00
70	Powell, Richard - ***Lay That Pistol Down*** [1946]	$1.25	$3.75	$7.50

		G	VG	F
71	Buchan, John - ***Mountain Meadow*** [1946]	$1.00	$3.00	$6.00
72	Wallis, Ruth Sawtell - ***No Bones About It*** [1946] Cover by Hoffman.	$1.25	$3.75	$7.50
73	Grey, Zane - ***The Last Of The Plainsmen*** [1946]	$1.35	$4.00	$8.00
74	Evans, John - ***Halo In Blood*** [1946]	$1.50	$5.00	$10.00
75(DJ)	Steinbeck, John - ***Cannery Row*** [1947] Cover by Kohs.	$22.00	$70.00	$140.00
75	Steinbeck, John - ***Cannery Row*** [1947] Cover by Kohs.	$1.35	$4.00	$8.00
76	Coles, Manning - ***Drink To Yesterday*** [1947]	$1.25	$3.75	$7.50
77	Cunningham, Eugene - ***Pistol Passport*** [1947]	$1.25	$3.75	$7.50
78	Daly, Elizabeth - ***Deadly Nightshade*** [1947] Photo cover.	$1.25	$3.75	$7.50
79	Smith, Betty - ***A Tree Grows In Brooklyn*** [1947]	$1.00	$3.00	$6.00
80	Ford, Leslie - ***False To Any Man*** [1947] Photo cover.	$1.25	$3.75	$7.50
81	Fraser, Phyllis & Young, Edith - ***Puzzles, Quizzes and Games*** [1947] PBO.	$1.25	$3.75	$7.50
82	Short, Luke - ***Ride The Man Down*** [1947]	$1.00	$3.00	$6.00
83	Mauldin, Bill - ***Up Front*** [1947] Cover by Bill Mauldin.	$1.00	$3.00	$6.00
84	Marshall, Bruce - ***The World, The Flesh And Father Smith*** [1947]	$1.00	$3.00	$6.00
85	Gilbert, Anthony - ***Death At The Door*** [1947] Cover by Kohs.	$1.25	$3.75	$7.50
86	Bosworth, Allan R. - ***Border Roundup*** [1947] Cover by Charles Andres.	$1.00	$3.00	$6.00
87	Wescott, Glenway - ***Apartment In Athens*** [1947] Cover by Kohs.	$1.00	$3.00	$6.00
88	Foster, Bennett - ***Trigger Kid*** [1947]	$1.00	$3.00	$6.00
89	Homes, Geoffrey - ***Finders Keepers*** [1947] Photo cover.	$1.25	$3.75	$7.50
90	Macardle, Dorothy - ***The Uninvited*** [1947] Photo cover.	$1.50	$5.00	$10.00
91	Disney, Dorothy Cameron - ***The 17th Letter*** [1947]	$1.25	$3.75	$7.50
92	Thurber, James - ***My Life And Hard Times*** [1947] Cover by James Thurber.	$1.00	$3.00	$6.00
93	Fearing, Kenneth - ***Dagger Of The Mind*** [1947] Cover by Galdone.	$1.25	$3.75	$7.50
94	Dawson, Peter - ***The Crimson Horseshoe*** [1947]	$1.00	$3.00	$6.00
95	Spinelli, Marcos - ***Assignment Without Glory*** [1947]	$1.00	$3.00	$6.00
96	Dine, S. S. Van - ***The Scarab Murder Case*** [1947]	$1.50	$5.00	$10.00
97	Bell, Vereen - ***Swamp Water*** [1947] Cover by Galdone.	$1.00	$3.00	$6.00
98	Carleton, Marjorie - ***Cry Wolf*** [1947] Cover by Galdone.	$1.00	$3.00	$6.00
99	Coolidge, Dane - ***Comanche Chaser*** [1947] Cover by Charles Andres.	$1.00	$3.00	$6.00
100	Lindsay, Norman - ***The Cautious Amorist*** [1947] Cover by Van Kaufman.	$1.00	$3.00	$6.00
101	Carr, John Dickson - ***The Problem Of The Green Capsule*** [1947] Photo cover.	$2.00	$6.00	$12.00
102	Kent, W. H. B. - ***Range Rider*** [1947]	$1.00	$3.00	$6.00
103	Martin, George Victor - ***The Bells Of St. Mary's*** [1947] Photo cover. Movie tie-in.	$1.25	$3.75	$7.50
104	Field, Peter - ***Powder Valley Pay-Off*** [1947]	$1.00	$3.00	$6.00
105	Skinner, Cornelia & Kimbrough, Emily - ***Our Hearts Were Young And Gay*** [1947] Cover by Alajalov.	$1.00	$3.00	$6.00
106	Seabrook, William - ***Asylum*** [1947] Cover by Charles Andres.	$1.00	$3.00	$6.00
107	Padgett, Lewis - ***Murder In Brass*** [1947] Cover by Dreany.	$2.50	$7.50	$15.00
108	Bishop, Curtis - ***Quick Draw*** [1947] Cover by Joel King.	$1.00	$3.00	$6.00
109	Wallis, Ruth Sawtell - ***Blood From A Stone*** [1947] Cover by Cappello.	$1.25	$3.75	$7.50
110	Greig, Maysie - ***Romance For Sale*** [1947]	$1.00	$3.00	$6.00
111	Traver, Robert - ***Trouble Shooter*** [1947] Cover by Joel King.	$1.00	$3.00	$6.00
112	Short, Luke - ***Hardcase*** [1947] Cover by Van Swearingen.	$1.00	$3.00	$6.00
113	Cunningham, Eugene - ***Riders Of The Night*** [1947] Cover by James Anthony Kelly.	$1.00	$3.00	$6.00
114	Ford, Leslie - ***Old Lover's Ghost*** [1947] Cover by Kohs.	$1.25	$3.75	$7.50
115	Lees, Hannah - ***Women Will Be Doctors*** [1947]	$1.00	$3.00	$6.00

		G	VG	F
116	Anthology edited by Ben Hibbs - ***Great Stories From The Saturday Evening Post*** [1947] PBO. Cover by Stevan Dohanos.	$1.00	$3.00	$6.00
117	Homes, Geoffrey - ***Stiffs Don't Vote*** [1947] Cover by Hy Ruben.	$1.25	$3.75	$7.50
118	Coles, Manning - ***A Toast To Tomorrow*** [1947]	$1.25	$3.75	$7.50
119	Bosworth, Allan R. - ***Double Deal*** [1947]	$1.25	$3.75	$7.50
120	King, Rufus - ***Secret Beyond The Door*** [1947] Cover by David Attie. Movie tie-in.	$1.25	$3.75	$7.50
121	Hatch, Eric - ***My Man Godfrey*** [1947]	$1.00	$3.00	$6.00
122	Seifert, Elizabeth - ***A Certain Doctor French*** [1947] Cover by Norbert J. Lannon.	$1.00	$3.00	$6.00
123	Kolb, Sylvia & John - ***A Treasury Of Folk Songs*** [1948] PBO. Cover by Van Kaufman.	$1.50	$5.00	$10.00
124	Sherman, Richard - ***To Mary With Love*** [1947] Cover by Bert Lannon.	$1.00	$3.00	$6.00
125	Lincoln, Victoria - ***February Hill*** [1947] Cover by Van Kaufman.	$1.00	$3.00	$6.00
126	Sumner, Cid Ricketts - ***Quality*** [1947] Cover by Bernard D'Andrea.	$1.00	$3.00	$6.00
127	Anthology edited by Sewell P. Wright - ***Chicago Murders*** [1947] Cover by Hy Rubin.	$1.25	$3.75	$7.50
128	Heckelmann, Charles N. - ***Six-Gun Outcast*** [1947]	$1.00	$3.00	$6.00
129	Taylor, Grant - ***"Whip" Ryder's Way*** [1947] Cover by Joel King.	$1.00	$3.00	$6.00
130	Crane, Frances - ***The Cinnamon Murder*** [1947] Cover by Denver Gillen.	$1.25	$3.75	$7.50
131	Steinbeck, John - ***The Pearl*** [1947] Movie tie-in. Eight pages of photos.	$1.35	$4.00	$8.00
132	Goldthwaite, Eaton K. - ***Date With Death*** [1947] Cover by Bert Lannon.	$1.25	$3.75	$7.50
133	Wallace, Francis - ***Kid Galahad*** [1947] Cover by Charles Andres.	$1.00	$3.00	$6.00
134	Lemay, Alan - ***Hell For Breakfast*** [1947] Cover by James Anthony Kelly.	$1.00	$3.00	$6.00
135	Forbes, Kathryn - ***Mama's Bank Account*** [1947] Movie tie-in with photo cover.	$1.00	$3.00	$6.00
136	Maugham, W. Somerset - ***Up At The Villa*** [1947] Cover by Charles Andres.	$1.00	$3.00	$6.00
137	Eberhart, Mignon G. - ***Wings Of Fear*** [1948] Photo cover.	$1.25	$3.75	$7.50
138	Gilbert, Anthony - ***Murder Cheats The Bride*** [1948]	$1.25	$3.75	$7.50
139	Short, Luke - ***Station West*** [1948] Movie photo cover. Movie tie-in with Dick Powell.	$1.00	$3.00	$6.00
140	Short, Luke - ***Coroner Creek*** [1948] Cover by Joel King.	$1.00	$3.00	$6.00
141	Chevallier, Gabriel - ***The Scandals Of Clochemerle*** [1948] Cover by Van Kaufman.	$1.00	$3.00	$6.00
142	Stevenson, Robert Louis - ***Treasure Island*** [1948] Cover by Milton Wolsky.	$1.00	$3.00	$6.00
143(DJ)	Munro, H. H. - ***The She-Wolf And Other Stories*** [1945] Superior Reprint in Bantam DJ.	$10.00	$30.00	$60.00
144(DJ)	Gruber, Frank - ***The Mighty Blockhead*** [1946] Superior reprint in a Bantam dust jacket.	$17.00	$50.00	$100.00
145(DJ)	Lardner, Ring - ***The Love Nest And Other Stories*** [1945] Superior Reprint in a Bantam DJ.	$17.00	$50.00	$100.00
146(DJ)	MacDonald, Philip - ***The Rynox Murder Mystery*** [1945] Superior Reprint in a Bantam DJ.	$17.00	$50.00	$100.00
147	Collins, Mary - ***Only The Good*** [1945] Cover by B. Barton.	$1.00	$3.00	$6.00
148(DJ)	Dean, Robert George - ***On Ice*** [1945] Superior Reprint in a Bantam DJ.	$17.00	$50.00	$100.00
149(DJ)	Steeves, Harrison R. - ***Good Night, Sheriff*** [1945] Superior Reprint in a Bantam DJ.	$17.00	$50.00	$100.00

		G	VG	F
150(DJ)	O'Flaherty, Liam - ***The Informer*** [1945] Bantam dust jacket on Superior Reprint.	$17.00	$50.00	$100.00
151(DJ)	Gruber, Frank - ***The Navy Colt*** [1945] Superior Reprint in a Bantam DJ.	$17.00	$50.00	$100.00
152	Freedman, Nancy & Benedict - ***Mrs. Mike*** [1948] Cover by Bert Lannon.	$1.00	$3.00	$6.00
154	Anthology edited by Ernestine Taggard - ***Twenty Grand Short Stories*** [1947]	$1.00	$3.00	$6.00
155(DJ)	Stewart, George R. - ***Storm*** [1945] Penguin Special S238 in a Bantam DJ. Cover by Denver Gillen.	$6.00	$20.00	$40.00
156(DJ)	Chambliss, William C. - ***Boomerang! And Baby Fights Back*** [1945] Bantam dust jacket on Infantry Journal J101.	$6.00	$20.00	$40.00
158	Ferguson, Margaret - ***The Sign Of The Ram*** [1948] Movie tie-in with photo cover.	$1.25	$3.75	$7.50
200	Anthology edited by Arnold Hano - ***Western Triggers*** [1948] PBO. Cover by Van Swearingen.	$1.00	$3.00	$6.00
201	Field, Peter - ***Trail South From Powder Valley*** [1948] Cover by Bob Doares.	$1.00	$3.00	$6.00
202	Kent, W. H. B. - ***The Tenderfoot*** [1948] Cover by Bob Doares.	$1.00	$3.00	$6.00
203	Kelland, Clarence Budington - ***Sugarfoot!*** [1948] Cover by Bob Doares.	$1.00	$3.00	$6.00
204	Short, Luke - ***Blood On The Moon*** [1948] Cover by Joel King.	$1.00	$3.00	$6.00
205	Chase, Borden - ***Red River*** [1948] Cover by James Dwyer. Movie tie-in with John Wayne photo on back cover.	$1.00	$3.00	$6.00
206	Heckelmann, Charles - ***Deputy Marshal*** [1948] Cover by Saunders.	$1.00	$3.00	$6.00
207	Blackburn, Thomas W. - ***Short Grass*** [1948] Cover by Saunders.	$1.00	$3.00	$6.00
208	Hopkins, Tom J. - ***Dead Man's Range*** [1948] Cover by Bob Doares.	$1.00	$3.00	$6.00
209	Short, Luke - ***Hard Money*** [1949] Cover by Saunders.	$1.00	$3.00	$6.00
210	Field, Peter - ***The Land Grabber*** [1949] Cover by Charles La Salle.	$1.00	$3.00	$6.00
211	Evans, Evan - ***The Rescue Of Broken Arrow*** [1949] Cover by Bob Doares.	$1.00	$3.00	$6.00
212	Gruber, Frank - ***Fighting Man*** [1949] Cover by Robert Stanley.	$1.00	$3.00	$6.00
213	Pearce, Dick - ***Hell Or High Water*** [1949] Cover by Milton Wolsky.	$1.00	$3.00	$6.00
214	Hankins, R. M. - ***Rio Grande Kid*** [1949] Cover by Saunders.	$1.00	$3.00	$6.00
227	Ernst, Morris L. & Loth, David - ***American Sexual Behavior And The Kinsey Report*** [1948]	$ .75	$2.50	$5.00
250	Dawson, Peter - ***The Stagline Feud*** [1948] Cover by Cliff Young.	$1.00	$3.00	$6.00
251	Perkins, Kenneth - ***Relentless*** [1948] Cover by Cliff Young.	$1.00	$3.00	$6.00
252	Foster, Bennett - ***Barbed Wire*** [1948] Cover by A. Leslie Ross.	$1.00	$3.00	$6.00
252(DJ)	Foster, Bennett - ***Barbed Wire*** [1948] Dust-jacketed edition.	$22.00	$70.00	$140.00
253	LeMay, Alan - ***Wild Justice*** [1948] Cover by Bill Wirts.	$1.00	$3.00	$6.00
254	Evans, Evan - ***The Border Bandit*** [1948] Cover by Saunders.	$1.00	$3.00	$6.00
255	Foster, Bennent - ***Badlands*** [1948] Cover by Saunders.	$1.00	$3.00	$6.00
256	Anthology edited by Arnold Hano - ***Western Roundup*** [1948] PBO. Cover by Cliff Young.	$1.25	$3.75	$7.50
257	Kelland, Clarence Budington - ***Arizona*** [1948] Cover by Bob Doares.	$1.00	$3.00	$6.00
258	Short, Luke - ***Raiders Of The Rimrock*** [1949] Cover by Stanley.	$1.00	$3.00	$6.00
259	Hankins, R. M. - ***The Man From Wyoming*** [1949] Cover by Stanley.	$1.00	$3.00	$6.00
260	Foster, Bennett - ***Pay-Off At Ladron*** [1949] Cover by Bob Doares.	$1.00	$3.00	$6.00
261	Haycox, Ernest - ***The Wild Bunch*** [1949] Cover by Saunders.	$1.00	$3.00	$6.00

Bantam Book, 302

Bantam Book, 407

Bantam Book, 505

		G	VG	F
262	Paul, Elliot - ***A Ghost Town On The Yellowstone*** [1949] Cover by C. C. Beall.	$1.00	$3.00	$6.00
300	Dine, S. S. Van - ***The Kidnap Murder Case*** [1948] Cover by Casimer Norwaish.	$1.50	$5.00	$10.00
301	Lanham, Edwin - ***Headlined For Murder*** [1948] Cover by Gilbert Darling.	$1.25	$3.75	$7.50
302	Brown, Fredric - ***The Fabulous Clipjoint*** [1948] Cover by Ed Grant.	$6.00	$20.00	$40.00
303	Ford, Leslie - ***Siren In The Night*** [1948] Cover by Robert G. Harris.	$1.25	$3.75	$7.50
304	Carr, John Dickson - ***The Problem Of The Wire Cage*** [1948] Cover by Gilbert Fullington.	$2.00	$6.00	$12.00
305	Lockridge, Frances and Richard - ***Hanged For A Sheep*** [1948] Cover by Gilbert Fullington.	$1.25	$3.75	$7.50
306	Padgett, Lewis - ***The Day He Died*** [1948] Cover by Gilbert Fullington.	$1.50	$5.00	$10.00
307	Carson, Robert - ***The Bride Saw Red*** [1948] Cover by Bert Lannon.	$1.25	$3.75	$7.50
308	Stout, Rex - ***The Silent Speaker*** [1948] Cover by Hy Rubin.	$2.00	$6.00	$12.00
309	Homes, Geoffrey - ***The Case Of The Mexican Knife*** [1948]	$1.25	$3.75	$7.50
310	Rolfe, Edwin & Fuller, Lester - ***Murder In The Glass Room*** [1948] Cover by Al Werner.	$1.25	$3.75	$7.50
311	Mason, Van Wyck - ***Saigon Singer*** [1948] Cover by C. C. Beall.	$1.25	$3.75	$7.50
312	Crane, Frances - ***The Indigo Necklace Murders*** [1948] Cover by Jules Karl.	$1.25	$3.75	$7.50
313	Canning, Victor - ***The Chasm*** [1949] Cover by Geoffrey Biggs.	$1.25	$3.75	$7.50
313(DJ)	Canning, Victor - ***The Chasm*** [1949] Dust-jacketed edition.	$15.00	$45.00	$90.00
314	Rinehart, Mary Roberts - ***The Yellow Room*** [1949] Cover by Bernard Barton.	$1.25	$3.75	$7.50
315(DJ)	Greene, Graham - ***Brighton Rock*** [1949] Dust-jacketed edition.	$17.00	$50.00	$100.00
315	Greene, Graham - ***Brighton Rock*** [1949] Cover by William Wirts.	$1.25	$3.75	$7.50
317	Gilbert, Anthony - ***Murder Is Cheap*** [1949] Cover by Stanley.	$1.25	$3.75	$7.50
320	Shriber, Ione Sandberg - ***As Long As I Live*** [1949] Cover by Herman Bischoff.	$1.00	$3.00	$6.00
350	Anderson, Edward - ***Your Red Wagon*** [1948] Movie tie-In.	$1.35	$4.00	$8.00
350(DJ)	Anderson, Edward - ***Your Red Wagon*** [1948] Dust-jacketed edition. Movie tie-in.	$20.00	$60.00	$125.00
351	Finnegan, Robert - ***The Lying Ladies*** [1948] Cover by William Wirts.	$1.25	$3.75	$7.50

		G	VG	F
352	Fletcher, H. L. V. - ***Miss Agatha Doubles For Death*** [1948] Cover by Norman Mingo.	$1.25	$3.75	$7.50
353	Daly, Elizabeth - ***The Book Of The Dead*** [1948] Cover by Ed Grant.	$1.25	$3.75	$7.50
354	Anthology edited by Joseph H. Jackson - ***San Francisco Murders*** [1948] Cover by Bob Doares.	$1.25	$3.75	$7.50
355	Greene, Graham - ***The Man Within*** [1948] Cover by Jules Karl.	$1.25	$3.75	$7.50
355(DJ)	Greene, Graham - ***The Man Within*** [1948] In dust-jacket.	$15.00	$45.00	$90.00
356	Ullman, Allan & Fletcher, Lucille - ***Sorry, Wrong Number*** [1948] Cover by Gilbert Darling. Movie tie-in.	$1.25	$3.75	$7.50
357	Shapiro, Lionel - ***The Sealed Verdict*** [1948] Cover by J. Karl. Movie tie-in with Ray Milland.	$1.25	$3.75	$7.50
358	Murray, Max - ***The Voice Of The Corpse*** [1948] Cover by Gilbert Fullington.	$1.25	$3.75	$7.50
359	Ford, Leslie - ***All For The Love Of A Lady*** [1949] Cover by Schucker.	$1.00	$3.00	$6.00
360	Lustgarten, Edgar - ***One More Unfortunate*** [1949] Cover by Safran.	$1.25	$3.75	$7.50
360(DJ)	Lustgarten, Edgar - ***One More Unfortunate*** [1949] Cover by Bern Safran. In dust-jacket.	$17.00	$50.00	$100.00
361	Brown, Fredric - ***The Dead Ringer*** [1949]	$5.50	$17.50	$35.00
362	Dine, S. S. Van - ***The Dragon Murder Case*** [1949] Cover by A. Freudeman.	$1.50	$5.00	$10.00
363	Finnegan, Robert - ***Many A Monster*** [1949] Cover by Bernard Barton.	$1.25	$3.75	$7.50
364	Innes, Hammond - ***Fire In The Snow*** [1949] Cover by Bob Doares.	$1.25	$3.75	$7.50
365	Carr, John Dickson - ***The Man Who Could Not Shudder*** [1949] Cover by Gilbert Fullington.	$2.00	$6.00	$12.00
366	Doyle, Arthur Conan - ***Sherlock Holmes: The Hound Of The Baskervilles*** [1949] Cover by William Shoyer.	$2.00	$6.00	$12.00
400	Vance, Ethel - ***Winter Meeting*** [1948] Photo cover. Movie tie-in with Bette Davis.	$1.25	$3.75	$7.50
401	Cockrell, Marian - ***Yesterday's Madness*** [1948] Cover by Bert Lannon.	$1.00	$3.00	$6.00
402	Steinbeck, John - ***The Red Pony*** [1948] Movie tie-in with Myrna Loy & Robert Mitchum photo cover.	$2.50	$7.50	$15.00
403	Axelrod, George - ***Beggar's Choice*** [1948] Cover by Van Kaufman.	$1.00	$3.00	$6.00
404	Hersey, John - ***Hiroshima*** [1948] Cover by Geoffrey Biggs.	$1.00	$3.00	$6.00
405	Wakeman, Frederic - ***The Hucksters*** [1948] Cover by Bernard D'Andrea.	$1.00	$3.00	$6.00
406	Goodin, Peggy - ***Mickey*** [1948] Movie tie-in.	$1.00	$3.00	$6.00
407	Goodis, David - ***Behold This Woman*** [1948] Cover by Shoyer.	$8.00	$25.00	$50.00
408	Hancock, Lucy Agnes - ***Doctor Kim*** [1948] Cover by David Attie.	$ .75	$2.50	$5.00
409	Smith, H. Allen - ***Low Man On A Totem Pole*** [1948]	$1.00	$3.00	$6.00
410	Smith, George Malcolm - ***The Grass Is Always Greener*** [1948] Cover by Casey Jones.	$1.00	$3.00	$6.00
411	Baldwin, Faith - ***Hotel Hostess*** [1948]	$1.00	$3.00	$6.00
412	Dunlap, Katharine - ***Encore For Love*** [1948] Cover by Bert Lannon.	$ .75	$2.50	$5.00
413	Croy, Homer - ***Family Honeymoon*** [1949] Cover by Gilbert Darling. Movie tie-in with Fred MacMurray.	$1.35	$4.00	$8.00
414	Hatch, Eric - ***Spendthrift*** [1948]	$1.00	$3.00	$6.00
415	Teilhet, Darwin L. - ***Something Wonderful To Happen*** [1948] Cover by Leon Gregori.	$1.00	$3.00	$6.00
416	Pratt, Theodore - ***Miss Dilly Says No*** [1948] Cover by Casey Jones.	$1.00	$3.00	$6.00
417	Tina, Dorothy Les - ***Confession*** [1948] Cover by Shoyer.	$1.00	$3.00	$6.00

		G	VG	F
418	Wees, Frances Shelley - ***Someone Called Maggie Lane*** [1948] Cover by Bert Lannon.	$1.00	$3.00	$6.00
419	Maresca, James V. - ***My Flag Is Down*** [1949] Cover by Casey Jones.	$1.00	$3.00	$6.00
420	Corliss, Allene - ***Illusion*** [1949] Cover by Bert Lannon.	$1.00	$3.00	$6.00
421	Bradley, David - ***No Place To Hide*** [1949] Cover by Jules Karl.	$1.00	$3.00	$6.00
421(DJ)	Bradley, David - ***No Place To Hide*** [1949] Dust-jacketed edition.	$5.50	$17.50	$35.00
422	Humphries, Adelaide - ***Office Nurse*** [1949]	$ .75	$2.50	$5.00
423	Maugham, W. Somerset - ***Stranger In Paris*** [1949] Cover by Tom Lovell	$1.35	$4.00	$8.00
425	Modell, Merriam - ***My Sister, My Bride*** [1949] Cover by Denver Gillen	$1.00	$3.00	$6.00
426	Ross, Lillian Bos - ***The Stranger*** [1949] Cover by Bernard Barton.	$1.00	$3.00	$6.00
427	Berg, Louis - ***Prison Nurse*** [1949] Cover by Shoyer.	$1.00	$3.00	$6.00
450	Dunn, Elizabeth - ***Moonlit Voyage*** [1948] Cover by David Attie.	$1.00	$3.00	$6.00
451	Shipman, Natalie - ***Love Is The Winner*** [1948]	$ .75	$2.50	$5.00
452	Thorne, Anthony - ***Cabbage Holiday*** [1948] Cover by Stahl.	$1.00	$3.00	$6.00
453	Hatch, Eric - ***Five Nights*** [1948]	$1.00	$3.00	$6.00
454	Connell, Vivian - ***The Chinese Room*** [1948] Cover by Ben Stahl.	$1.25	$3.75	$7.50
455	Baldwin, Faith - ***Love Is A Surprise!*** [1948] Cover by Bert Lannon.	$1.00	$3.00	$6.00
456	Gould, R. E. - ***Yankee Storekeeper*** [1948] Cover by Casey Jones.	$1.00	$3.00	$6.00
458	Seifert, Elizabeth - ***Dr. Woodward's Ambition*** [1948] Cover by Bert Lannon.	$1.00	$3.00	$6.00
459	Winwar, Frances - ***Joan Of Arc*** [1948] Movie photo cover. Movie tie-in with Ingrid Bergman.	$1.35	$4.00	$8.00
460	Graham, Gwethalyn - ***Earth And High Heaven*** [1948] Cover by Mal Thompson.	$1.00	$3.00	$6.00
461	Mauldin, Bill - ***Back Home*** [1948] Cover by Bill Mauldin.	$1.25	$3.75	$7.50
462	Bromfield, Louis - ***What Became Of Anna Bolton?*** [1948] Cover by Shoyer.	$1.00	$3.00	$6.00
462(DJ)	Bromfield, Louis - ***What Became Of Anna Bolton?*** [1948] Dust-jacketed edition.	$5.00	$15.00	$30.00
463	Hedden, Worth Tuttle - ***The Other Room*** [1948] Cover by Avati.	$1.00	$3.00	$6.00
464	Marshall, Marguerite Mooers - ***Nurse Into Woman*** [1948] Cover by David Attie.	$ .75	$2.50	$5.00
465	Robinson, Mabel Louise - ***Bitter Forfeit*** [1948] Cover by Remie Hamon.	$1.00	$3.00	$6.00
466	Lardner, Ring W. - ***The Big Town*** [1949] Cover by Van Kaufman.	$1.00	$3.00	$6.00
467	Hemingway, Ernest - ***A Farewell To Arms*** [1948] Cover by C. C. Beall.	$1.50	$5.00	$10.00
469	Faure, Raoul C. - ***Lady Godiva And Master Tom*** [1949] Cover by Van Kaufman.	$1.25	$3.75	$7.50
470	Roberts, Edith - ***The Men In Her Life*** [1949] Cover by Remie Hamon.	$1.00	$3.00	$6.00
471	Baldwin, Faith - ***Marry For Money*** [1949] Cover by Remie Hamon.	$1.00	$3.00	$6.00
473	Pratt, Theodore - ***Danger Trail*** [1949] Cover by Ed Paulsen.	$1.00	$3.00	$6.00
474	Chanslor, Roy - ***Hazard*** [1949] Cover by Shoyer.	$1.00	$3.00	$6.00
476	Hatch, Eric - ***Road Show*** [1949] Cover by Fritz Willis.	$1.00	$3.00	$6.00
477	Pedrick, Jean - ***The Fascination*** [1949] Cover by Bob Skemp.	$1.00	$3.00	$6.00
500	Carmichael, J. P. - ***My Greatest Day In Baseball*** [1948] Cover by Hy Rubin.	$2.50	$7.50	$15.00

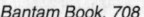

Bantam Book, 708

Bantam Book, 712

Bantam Book, 748

		G	VG	F
501	Feller, Bob - ***Bob Feller's Strikeout Story*** [1948] Photo cover...	$3.00	$9.00	$18.00
502	Anthology edited by Bennett Cerf - ***The Unexpected!*** [1948] PBO. Cover by Ed Grant.	$1.50	$5.00	$10.00
503	Greene, Joseph & Abell, Elizabeth - ***Ed. - First Love*** [1948] PBO. Cover by Al Brule.	$1.00	$3.00	$6.00
504	Anthology edited by Ed Fitzgerald - ***Kick-Off!*** [1948] PBO. Cover by Jules Karl.	$1.25	$3.75	$7.50
505	Meany, Tom - ***Babe Ruth*** [1948] Cover by Griffith Foxley. Eight pages of photos.	$3.50	$10.00	$20.00
506	DiMaggio, Joe - ***Lucky To Be A Yankee*** [1949] DiMaggio painted cover by Hy Rubin. Eight pages of photos.	$3.50	$10.00	$20.00
507	Schacht, Al - ***Clowning Through Baseball*** [1949] Cover by Hy Rubin.	$1.25	$3.75	$7.50
550	Berle, Milton - ***Out Of My Trunk*** [1948] Cover by Denver Gillen.	$1.25	$3.75	$7.50
551	Parker, Dan - ***The ABC Of Horse Racing*** [1948] Cover by Bob Kuhn.	$1.25	$3.75	$7.50
552	Stockton, J. Roy - ***The Gashouse Gang*** [1948] Cover by Jules Karl.	$3.00	$9.00	$18.00
553	Heth, Edward Harris - ***The Big Bet*** [1948] Cover by Bob Doares.	$1.00	$3.00	$6.00
554	Millhauser, Bertram & Dix, Beulah Marie - ***Hot Leather*** [1948] Cover by Charles Andres.	$1.25	$3.75	$7.50
555	Anthology edited by Ben Hibbs - ***Great Stories From The Saturday Evening Post*** [1948] PBO. Cover by Stevan Dohanos.	$1.25	$3.75	$7.50
556	Anthology edited by Ed Fitzgerald - ***The Story Of The Brooklyn Dodgers*** [1949] PBO. Cover by Hy Rubin. Eight pages of photos.	$3.50	$10.00	$20.00
557	Fleischer, Nat - ***Jack Dempsey*** [1949] Cover by Bob Doares. Eight pages of photos.	$2.00	$6.00	$12.00
700	Kelleam, Joseph E. - ***Blackjack*** [1949] Cover by C. C. Beall.	$1.25	$3.75	$7.50
701	Homes, Geoffrey - ***Dead As A Dummy*** [1949]	$1.25	$3.75	$7.50
702	Short, Luke - ***The Rustlers*** [1949] Cover by Bob Doares.	$1.00	$3.00	$6.00
703	Short, Luke - ***Hands Off!*** [1949] Cover by Bob Stanley.	$1.00	$3.00	$6.00
704	Doyle, Sir Arthur Conan - ***Memoirs Of Sherlock Holmes*** [1949]	$1.35	$4.00	$8.00
705	Lewis, Sinclair - ***Kingsblood Royal*** [1949] Cover by James Avati..	$1.00	$3.00	$6.00
706	Moore, Isabel - ***The Other Woman*** [1949]	$1.00	$3.00	$6.00
707	Schulberg, Budd - ***The Harder They Fall*** [1949] Cover by R. Skemp.	$1.00	$3.00	$6.00
708	Edmonds, Walter D. - ***The Captive Women*** [1949] Cover by Denver Gillen.	$1.00	$3.00	$6.00

		G	VG	F
709	Lee, Edna - ***The Web Of Days*** [1949] Cover by Gillen.	$1.00	$3.00	$6.00
710	Dratler, Jay - ***The Pitfall*** [1949] Cover by Peter Paul.	$1.00	$3.00	$6.00
711	Corliss, Allene - ***Summer Lightning*** [1949] Cover by Ken Riley.	$1.00	$3.00	$6.00
712	Forester, C. S. - ***The African Queen*** [1949] Cover by Ken Riley.	$1.35	$4.00	$8.00
713	Daly, Elizabeth - ***Murder Listens In*** [1949]	$1.25	$3.75	$7.50
714	Roberts, Richard Emery - ***The Gilded Rooster*** [1949] Cover by Skemp.	$1.00	$3.00	$6.00
715	Goodman, Murray & Lewin, Leonard - ***My Greatest Day In Football*** [1949] Cover by Saunders.	$1.35	$4.00	$8.00
716(DJ)	Kamal, Ahmad - ***High Pressure*** [1949] Dust-jacketed edition.	$27.50	$85.00	$200.00
716	Kamal, Ahmad - ***High Pressure*** [1949] Cover by Skemp.	$1.35	$4.00	$8.00
717	Hemingway, Ernest - ***The Sun Also Rises*** [1949] Cover by Ken Riley.	$2.00	$6.00	$12.00
718	Collins, Mary - ***Death Warmed Over*** [1949] Cover by Gilbert Fullington.	$1.25	$3.75	$7.50
720	O'Rourke, Frank - ***Action At Three Peaks*** [1949]	$1.00	$3.00	$6.00
721	Martin, Pete - ***Hollywood Without Makeup*** [1949] Ava Gardner photo cover.	$1.25	$3.75	$7.50
722	Stout, Rex - ***Too Many Women*** [1949] Cover by Hy Rubin.	$1.50	$5.00	$10.00
723	Weston, Christine - ***The Dark Wood*** [1949] Cover by Ed Paulsen.	$1.00	$3.00	$6.00
724	Henning, William E. - ***The Heller*** [1949] Cover by Ed Paulsen.	$1.25	$3.75	$7.50
725	Foster, Bennett - ***Blackleg Range*** [1949] Cover by Bob Doares.	$1.00	$3.00	$6.00
726	Kelland, Clarence Budington - ***Desert Law*** [1949] Cover by Norman Saunders.	$1.00	$3.00	$6.00
727	Summers, Hollis - ***City Limit*** [1949] Cover by Denver Gillen.	$1.00	$3.00	$6.00
728	Belbenoit, Rene - ***I Escaped From Devils Island*** [1949] Photo cover.	$1.25	$3.75	$7.50
729	Davenport, Guinn - ***Belvedere*** [1949] Cover by Casey Jones.	$1.00	$3.00	$6.00
730	Cheyney, Peter - ***Dark Interlude*** [1949] Cover by C. C. Beall.	$1.25	$3.75	$7.50
731	Field, Peter - ***Sheriff's Revenge*** [1949] Cover by Norman Saunders.	$1.00	$3.00	$6.00
732	Warren, Charles Marquis - ***Valley Of The Shadow*** [1949] Cover by Gillen.	$1.00	$3.00	$6.00
733	Doyle, Sir Arthur Conan - ***The Valley Of Fear*** [1950]	$1.35	$4.00	$8.00
734	Canning, Victor - ***Panthers' Moon*** [1949] Cover by Harry Schaare. Movie tie-in.	$1.35	$4.00	$8.00
735	Brown, Fredric - ***A Plot For Murder*** [1949] Photo cover.	$5.00	$15.00	$30.00
736	Gellhorn, Martha - ***The Wine Of Astonishment*** [1949] Cover by Avati.	$1.00	$3.00	$6.00
737	Moon, Bucklin - ***The Darker Brother*** [1949]	$1.35	$4.00	$8.00
738	Fearing, Kenneth - ***The Big Clock*** [1949] Movie tie-in.	$1.25	$3.75	$7.50
739	Eberhart, Mignon G. - ***The White Dress*** [1949]	$1.25	$3.75	$7.50
740	Ernenwein, Leslie - ***Bullet Breed*** [1949] Cover by Norman Saunders.	$1.00	$3.00	$6.00
741	Innes, Hammond - ***Gale Warning*** [1949] Cover by R. Skemp.	$1.25	$3.75	$7.50
742	Anthology edited by Greene & Abell - ***Husbands And Lovers*** [1949] Cover by Ben Stahl.	$1.25	$3.75	$7.50
743	Lay, Jr., Beirne & Bartlett, Sy - ***Twelve O'Clock High*** [1949] Cover by Hy Rubin. Movie tie-in with Gregory Peck.	$1.00	$3.00	$6.00
744	Rich, Helen - ***The Spring Begins*** [1949]	$1.00	$3.00	$6.00
745	Dumas, Alexandre - ***Camille*** [1949] Cover by James Avati.	$1.00	$3.00	$6.00
746	Lanham, Edwin - ***Politics Is Murder*** [1949]	$1.25	$3.75	$7.50
747	Short, Luke - ***Bull-Whip*** [1949]	$1.00	$3.00	$6.00
748	Short, Luke - ***And The Wind Blows Free*** [1950]	$1.00	$3.00	$6.00
749	Ronald, James - ***The Angry Woman*** [1950]	$1.00	$3.00	$6.00
750	Bezzerides, A. I. - ***Thieves' Market*** [1950]	$1.00	$3.00	$6.00

Bantam Book, 751

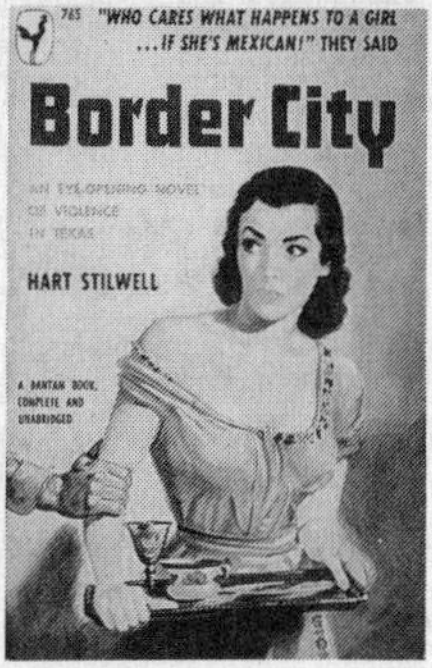

Bantam Book, 765

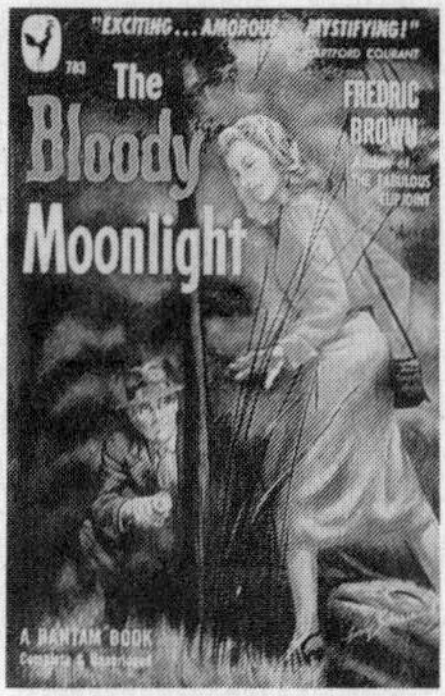

Bantam Book, 783

		G	VG	F
751	Anthology edited by Judith Merril - ***Shot In The Dark*** [1950] PBO. Cover by H. E. Bischoff.	$5.00	$15.00	$30.00
752	Steinbeck, John - ***The Wayward Bus*** [1950] Cover by Ben Stahl.	$2.50	$7.50	$15.00
753	Kantor, Mac Kinlay - ***Midnight Lace*** [1950] Cover by Ben Stahl.	$1.25	$3.75	$7.50
754	Davidson, David - ***The Hour Of Truth*** [1950] Cover by R. Skemp.	$1.00	$3.00	$6.00
755	Chute, Berne - ***Wayward Angel*** [1950] Cover by Harry Schaare.	$1.00	$3.00	$6.00
756	Dine, S. S. Van - ***The Smell Of Murder*** [1950]	$1.50	$5.00	$10.00
757	Hankins, R. M. - ***Ace-In-The-Hole Haggarty*** [1950]	$1.00	$3.00	$6.00
758	Speare, Dorothy - ***Desperate Choice*** [1950] Cover by James Avati.	$1.00	$3.00	$6.00
759	Richter, Conrad - ***Tacey Cromwell*** [1950]	$1.00	$3.00	$6.00
A-760	Caldwell, Taylor - ***This Side Of Innocence*** [1950]	$1.50	$5.00	$10.00
761	Disney, Dorothy Cameron - ***Explosion*** [1950]	$1.25	$3.75	$7.50
762	Foster, Bennett - ***Seven Slash Range*** [1950] Cover by Bob Doares.	$1.00	$3.00	$6.00
763	Meany, Tom - ***Baseball's Greatest Teams*** [1950] Cover by Hy Rubin.	$2.50	$7.50	$15.00
764	Thompson, Thomas - ***Range Drifter*** [1950]	$1.00	$3.00	$6.00
765	Stilwell, Hart - ***Border City*** [1950]	$1.00	$3.00	$6.00
766	Lofts, Norah - ***Jassy*** [1950] Cover by Avati.	$1.25	$3.75	$7.50
767	Brinig, Myron - ***No Marriage In Paradise*** [1950]	$1.00	$3.00	$6.00
768	Gilbert, Anthony - ***Death Lifts The Latch*** [1950]	$1.25	$3.75	$7.50
769	Trimble, Louis - ***Valley Of Violence*** [1950]	$1.00	$3.00	$6.00
770	Mason, Sara Elizabeth - ***The Whip*** [1950]	$1.00	$3.00	$6.00
A-771	Williams, Ben Ames - ***Leave Her To Heaven*** [1950] Cover by Harry Schaare.	$1.25	$3.75	$7.50
772	Forester, C. S. - ***Flying Colours*** [1950]	$1.00	$3.00	$6.00
773	Taylor, Rosemary - ***Come Clean, My Love*** [1950] Cover by Bob Fink.	$1.00	$3.00	$6.00
774	Elwood, Muriel - ***Heritage Of The River*** [1950]	$1.00	$3.00	$6.00
775	Field, Peter - ***Hell's Corner*** [1950] Cover by A. Leslie Ross.	$1.00	$3.00	$6.00
776	Warren, Charles Marquis - ***Only The Valiant*** [1950]	$1.00	$3.00	$6.00
777	Busch, Niven - ***The Furies*** [1950] Cover by Fink. Movie tie-in with Barbara Stanwyck.	$1.00	$3.00	$6.00
778	Marsh, Ronald - ***Irene*** [1950]	$1.00	$3.00	$6.00
779	Homes, Geoffrey - ***The Case Of The Unhappy Angels*** [1950]	$1.25	$3.75	$7.50

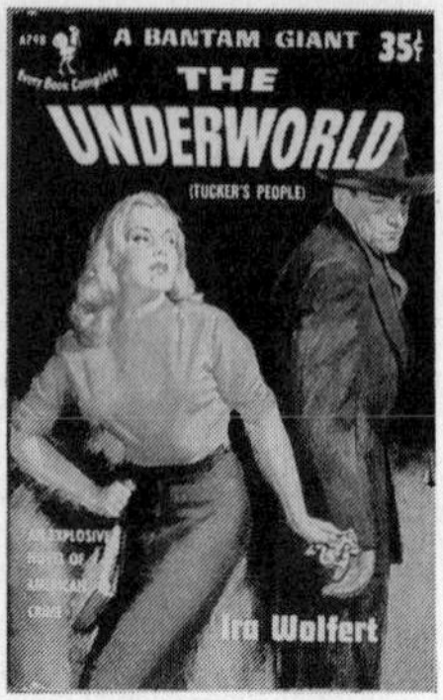

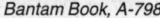

Bantam Book, A-798

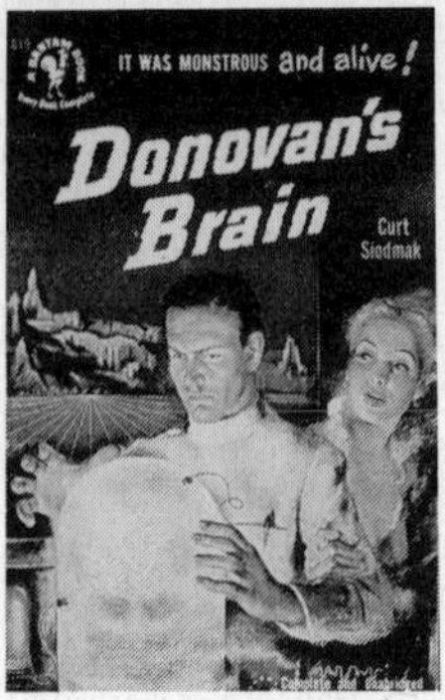

Bantam Book, 819

Bantam Book, 972

		G	VG	F
780	Krasner, William - ***Walk The Dark Streets*** [1950] Cover by Bischoff.	$2.00	$6.00	$12.00
781	Worthington, Marjorie - ***The Enchanted Heart*** [1950] Cover by Skemp.	$1.25	$3.75	$7.50
782	Cronin, A. J. - ***The Keys Of The Kingdom*** [1950]	$1.00	$3.00	$6.00
783	Brown, Fredric - ***The Bloody Moonlight*** [1950] Cover by Harry Schaare.	$5.50	$17.50	$35.00
784	Evans, Evan - ***Gunman's Legacy*** [1950] Cover by Stanley.	$1.00	$3.00	$6.00
785	Maier, William - ***Pleasure Island*** [1950]	$1.00	$3.00	$6.00
786	Anthology edited by Milton Crane - ***Sins Of New York*** [1950] Cover by C. C. Beall.	$1.35	$4.00	$8.00
787	Collins, Mary - ***The Sister Of Cain*** [1950]	$1.25	$3.75	$7.50
788	Haycox, Ernest - ***Long Storm*** [1950] Cover by Zuckerberg.	$1.00	$3.00	$6.00
789	Ertz, Susan - ***Mary Hallam*** [1950]	$1.00	$3.00	$6.00
790	Collins, Norman - ***The Blazing Land*** [1950]	$1.00	$3.00	$6.00
791	Short, Luke - ***The Feud At Single Shot*** [1950]	$1.00	$3.00	$6.00
792	Short, Luke - ***War On The Cimarron*** [1950]	$1.00	$3.00	$6.00
793	Carr, John Dickson - ***Til Death Do Us Part*** [1950]	$1.50	$5.00	$10.00
794	Morrison, Ray - ***Angels Camp*** [1950] Cover by Gillen.	$1.25	$3.75	$7.50
795	McDonell, Gordon - ***My Sister, Goodnight*** [1950]	$1.00	$3.00	$6.00
796	Standish, Robert - ***Lord And Master*** [1950]	$1.00	$3.00	$6.00
797	Greene, Graham - ***The 3rd Man*** [1950] Movie tie-in with photo cover.	$1.25	$3.75	$7.50
A-798	Wolfert, Ira - ***The Underworld*** [1950]	$2.00	$6.00	$12.00
799	O'Rourke, Frank - ***Thunder On The Buckhorn*** [1950] Cover by Saunders.	$1.00	$3.00	$6.00
800	Evans, John - ***Halo For Satan*** [1950]	$1.50	$5.00	$10.00
801	Davidson, David - ***The Steeper Cliff*** [1950]	$1.00	$3.00	$6.00
802	Stewart, George R. - ***Fire*** [1950] Cover by Hy Rubin.	$1.00	$3.00	$6.00
803	Jepson, Selwyn - ***Killer By Proxy*** [1950]	$1.25	$3.75	$7.50
A-804	Edmonds, Walter D. - ***Drums Along The Mohawk*** [1950]	$1.00	$3.00	$6.00
A-805	Marquand, John P. - ***H. M. Pulham, Esquire*** [1950]	$1.00	$3.00	$6.00
A-806	Seeley, Mabel - ***Woman Of Property*** [1950]	$1.00	$3.00	$6.00
A-807	Burns, John Horne - ***The Gallery*** [1950]	$1.00	$3.00	$6.00
808	Foster, Bennett - ***The Owl Hoot Trail*** [1950]	$1.00	$3.00	$6.00
809	Kantor, Mac Kinlay - ***Wicked Water*** [1950]	$1.00	$3.00	$6.00
810	Maugham, W. Somerset - ***The Moon And Sixpence*** [1950]	$1.00	$3.00	$6.00
811	Daly, Elizabeth - ***Any Shape Or Form*** [1950]	$1.25	$3.75	$7.50
812	Creekmore, Hubert - ***Cotton Country*** [1950]	$1.00	$3.00	$6.00
813	Fox, Paul - ***Sailor Town*** [1950] Cover by R. Skemp.	$1.00	$3.00	$6.00

		G	VG	F
A-814	Robbins, Harold - ***Never Love A Stranger*** [1950]	$1.35	$4.00	$8.00
A-815	Langley, Adria Locke - ***The Lion In The Streets*** [1950]	$1.25	$3.75	$7.50
816	Forester, C. S. - ***Payment Deferred*** [1950]	$1.25	$3.75	$7.50
817	Flannagan, Roy - ***The Whipping*** [1950] Cover by Schaare.	$2.00	$6.00	$12.00
A-818	Costain, Thomas B. - ***The Black Rose*** [1950] Cover by Robert Maguire.	$1.25	$3.75	$7.50
819	Siodmak, Curt - ***Donovan's Brain*** [1950]	$4.00	$12.50	$25.00
820	Bates, H. E. - ***The Purple Plain*** [1950]	$1.25	$3.75	$7.50
821	McCullers, Carson - ***Reflections In A Golden Eye*** [1950]	$1.35	$4.00	$8.00
822	McCullers, Carson - ***The Member Of The Wedding*** [1950]	$1.35	$4.00	$8.00
823	Holmes, L. P. - ***Range Pirate*** [1950]	$1.00	$3.00	$6.00
824	Stout, Rex - ***And Be A Villain*** [1950]	$2.00	$6.00	$12.00
825	Benet, James - ***A Private Killing*** [1950]	$1.25	$3.75	$7.50
826	Burnett, W. R. - ***High Sierra*** [1950] Cover by Harry Schaare.	$1.25	$3.75	$7.50
827	Laird, Charlton - ***Thunder On The River*** [1950]	$1.00	$3.00	$6.00
828	Wolfert, Ira - ***American Guerrilla In The Philippines*** [1950] Photo cover.	$1.00	$3.00	$6.00
829	Frank, Pat - ***An Affair Of State*** [1950] Cover by Denver Gillen.	$1.00	$3.00	$6.00
830	White, Max - ***Anna Becker*** [1950]	$1.00	$3.00	$6.00
831	Brown, Fredric - ***The Screaming Mimi*** [1950]	$6.00	$20.00	$40.00
832	Powers, Paul S. - ***Six-Gun Doctor*** [1950]	$1.00	$3.00	$6.00
833	Schaefer, Jack - ***Shane*** [1950]	$2.50	$7.50	$15.00
834	Canning, Victor - ***The Golden Salamander*** [1950]	$1.25	$3.75	$7.50
835	Brown, Fredric - ***What Mad Universe*** [1950] Cover by Herman Bischoff.	$3.50	$10.00	$20.00
836	Boyd, James - ***Long Hunt*** [1950]	$1.00	$3.00	$6.00
837	Spinelli, Marcos - ***The Green Flames*** [1950] Cover by Mayan.	$1.00	$3.00	$6.00
838	Davis, Clyde Brion - ***The Rebellion Leo McGuire*** [1950]	$1.00	$3.00	$6.00
839	Orsborne, Capt. Dod - ***Mission: Danger*** [1950] Cover by R. Skemp.	$1.00	$3.00	$6.00
840	Espy, Willard R. - ***Bold New Program*** [1950]	$1.00	$3.00	$6.00
841	Foster, Bennett - ***Rider Of The Rifle Rock*** [1950]	$1.00	$3.00	$6.00
842	Williams, Eric - ***The Wooden Horse*** [1951] Cover by Skemp. Movie tie-in.	$1.00	$3.00	$6.00
843	Lattimore, Owen - ***Ordeal By Slander*** [1950]	$1.00	$3.00	$6.00
844	Taylor, Ross McLaury - ***Brazos*** [1950] Cover by Haskell.	$1.00	$3.00	$6.00
845	Gerstell, Richard - ***How To Survive An Atomic Bomb*** [1950]	$1.00	$3.00	$6.00
846	Roosevelt, Eleanor - ***This Is My Story*** [1950]	$1.00	$3.00	$6.00
A-847	Williams, Ben Ames - ***The Strange Woman*** [1950]	$1.00	$3.00	$6.00
848	Lee, Edna - ***The Queen Bee*** [1950]	$1.25	$3.75	$7.50
849	Eberhart, Mignon G. - ***Another Woman's House*** [1950]	$1.25	$3.75	$7.50
850	Paul, Elliot - ***Mayhem In B Flat*** [1950] Cover by Skemp.	$1.00	$3.00	$6.00
851	Gilbert, Anthony - ***The Innocent Bottle*** [1950]	$1.25	$3.75	$7.50
852	Maugham, W. Somerset - ***Catalina*** [1951]	$1.25	$3.75	$7.50
853	Short, Luke - ***Ambush*** [1950]	$1.00	$3.00	$6.00
854	Short, Luke - ***Fiddlefoot*** [1950] Cover by Mayan.	$1.00	$3.00	$6.00
855	Mauldin, Bill - ***A Sort Of A Saga*** [1950] Cover by Bill Mauldin.	$1.00	$3.00	$6.00
856	Teilhet, Hildegarde Tolman - ***The Rim Of Terror*** [1950]	$1.25	$3.75	$7.50
857	Strauss, Theodore - ***The Haters*** [1950]	$1.35	$4.00	$8.00
858	Hahn, Emily - ***With Naked Foot*** [1951]	$1.35	$4.00	$8.00
859	Rostand, Edmund - ***Cyrano De Bergerac*** [1950]	$1.00	$3.00	$6.00
A-860	Shellabarger, Samuel - ***Captain From Castile*** [1950] Cover by Hy Rubin.	$1.00	$3.00	$6.00
861	Lustgarten, Edgar - ***Verdict In Dispute*** [1951] Cover by Mayan.	$1.25	$3.75	$7.50
862	Marchal, Lucie - ***The Mesh*** [1951]	$1.00	$3.00	$6.00
863	Disney, Dorothy Cameron - ***The Hangman's Tree*** [1951] Cover by Harry Schaare.	$1.25	$3.75	$7.50
864	Thompson, Thomas - ***Broken Valley*** [1951]	$1.00	$3.00	$6.00
865	Fosburgh, Hugh - ***The Hunter*** [1951]	$1.00	$3.00	$6.00

		G	VG	F
A-866	Wilder, Robert - ***Bright Feather*** [1950] Cover by Mayan.	$1.00	$3.00	$6.00
A-867	Fitzgerald, F. Scott - ***Tender Is The Night*** [1950]	$1.00	$3.00	$6.00
A-868	Steinbeck, John - ***The Grapes Of Wrath*** [1951]	$1.35	$4.00	$8.00
A-869	Bromfield, Louis - ***Night In Bombay*** [1950]	$1.00	$3.00	$6.00
870	Williams, Ben Ames - ***Evered*** [1950]	$1.00	$3.00	$6.00
A-871	Every, Dale Van - ***Bridal Journey*** [1951] Cover by Mayan.	$1.00	$3.00	$6.00
872	Terrot, Charles - ***The Passionate Pilgrim*** [1951]	$1.00	$3.00	$6.00
873	Foster, Bennett - ***Cow Thief Trail*** [1951]	$1.00	$3.00	$6.00
874	Crane, Frances - ***Murder On The Purple Water*** [1951] Cover by Denver Gillen.	$1.25	$3.75	$7.50
875	Dixon, H. Vernor - ***Something For Nothing*** [1951] Cover by Mayan.	$1.00	$3.00	$6.00
876	Brown, Fredric - ***Compliments Of A Fiend*** [1951] Cover by Robert Skemp.	$5.50	$17.50	$35.00
877	Collins, Mary - ***Dog Eat Dog*** [1951]	$1.25	$3.75	$7.50
878	Parker, Robert - ***Ticket To Oblivion*** [1951]	$1.00	$3.00	$6.00
879	Packard, Reynolds - ***Low-Down*** [1951]	$1.00	$3.00	$6.00
880	Gaines, Diana - ***Tasker Martin*** [1951] Cover by Mayan.	$1.00	$3.00	$6.00
881	Marquand, John P. - ***Repent In Haste*** [1951]	$1.25	$3.75	$7.50
882	Evans, Evan - ***Lone Hand*** [1951] Cover by Mayan.	$1.00	$3.00	$6.00
A-883	Hemingway, Ernest - ***For Whom The Bell Tolls*** [1951] Cover by Mayan.	$1.35	$4.00	$8.00
A-884	Michener, James A. - ***The Fires Of Spring*** [1951] Cover by Zuckerberg.	$1.25	$3.75	$7.50
885	Eberhart, Mignon G. - ***House Of Storm*** [1951]	$1.25	$3.75	$7.50
886	Bradbury, Ray - ***The Martian Chronicles*** [1951]	$3.50	$10.00	$20.00
887	Dolson, Hildegarde - ***The Husband Who Ran Away*** [1951]	$1.00	$3.00	$6.00
888	Burnett, W. R. - ***Nobody Lives Forever*** [1951]	$1.35	$4.00	$8.00
889	Strauss, Theodore - ***Dark Hunger*** [1951]	$1.00	$3.00	$6.00
890	Innes, Hammond - ***Run By Night*** [1951] Cover by Shoyer.	$1.25	$3.75	$7.50
891	Fergusson, Harvey - ***Wolf Song*** [1951] Cover by Mayan.	$1.00	$3.00	$6.00
892	Trimble, Louis - ***Gunsmoke Justice*** [1951]	$1.00	$3.00	$6.00
A-893	Lewis, Sinclair - ***Cass Timberlane*** [1951] Cover by Zuckerberg.	$1.00	$3.00	$6.00
894	Krepps, Robert W. - ***The Courts Of The Lion*** [1951] Cover by Mayan.	$1.00	$3.00	$6.00
895	Walsh, Thomas - ***Nightmare In Manhattan*** [1951]	$1.25	$3.75	$7.50
896	Carr, John Dickson - ***He Who Whispers*** [1951]	$2.00	$6.00	$12.00
897	Boutell, Anita - ***Death Has A Past*** [1951]	$1.25	$3.75	$7.50
898	Holmes, L. P. - ***Black Sage*** [1951]	$1.00	$3.00	$6.00
899	Steinbeck, John - ***The Pastures Of Heaven*** [1951]	$1.35	$4.00	$8.00
900	Kantor, Mac Kinlay - ***Arouse And Beware*** [1951]	$1.00	$3.00	$6.00
901	Cerf, Bennett - ***Shake Well Before Using*** [1951] Cover by Carl Rose.	$1.00	$3.00	$6.00
A-902	Kendrick, Baynard - ***The Flames Of Time*** [1951]	$1.00	$3.00	$6.00
A-903	Schoonover, Lawrence - ***The Burnished Blade*** [1951] Cover by Mayan.	$1.00	$3.00	$6.00
A-904	Fowler, Gene - ***The Great Mouthpiece*** [1951]	$1.00	$3.00	$6.00
905	Highsmith, Patricia - ***Strangers On A Train*** [1951] Cover by Zuckerberg.	$1.25	$3.75	$7.50
906	Gulick, Bill - ***Bend Of The Snake*** [1951]	$1.00	$3.00	$6.00
907	Tree, Gregory - ***The Case Against Myself*** [1951] Cover by Geygan.	$1.00	$3.00	$6.00
908	Hall, Oakley - ***So Many Doors*** [1951]	$1.00	$3.00	$6.00
909	Maugham, W. Somerset - ***The Narrow Corner*** [1951]	$1.00	$3.00	$6.00
A-910	Bromfield, Louis - ***Wild Is The River*** [1951]	$1.00	$3.00	$6.00
911	Short, Luke - ***Vengeance Valley*** [1951] Cover by Mayan.	$1.00	$3.00	$6.00
A-912	Forester, C. S. - ***Captain Horatio Hornblower*** [1951] Cover by Hy Rubin. Movie tie-in.	$1.00	$3.00	$6.00
913	Anthology - ***Saturday Review Reader*** [1951]	$1.00	$3.00	$6.00
A-914	Anthology - ***Stories For Here And Now*** [1951] PBO.	$1.25	$3.75	$7.50

		G	VG	F
915	Macardle, Dorothy - ***The Unforseen*** [1951] Cover by H. E. Bischoff.	$2.00	$6.00	$12.00
916	O'Rourke, Frank - ***Blackwater*** [1951]	$1.00	$3.00	$6.00
917	Forester, C. S. - ***To The Indies*** [1951] Cover by Geygan.	$1.00	$3.00	$6.00
A-918	Arnold, Elliott - ***Blood Brother*** [1951] Cover by Mayan.	$1.00	$3.00	$6.00
A-919	Marquand, John P. - ***B.F.'s Daughter*** [1951] Cover by Zuckerberg.	$1.00	$3.00	$6.00
920	Patterson, Haywood & Conrad, Earl - ***Scottsboro Boy*** [1951] Cover by Joseph Hirsch.	$1.35	$4.00	$8.00
921	Radin, Edward D. - ***12 Against Crime*** [1951] Photo cover.	$1.50	$5.00	$10.00
922	Comfort, Will Levington - ***Apache*** [1952]	$1.00	$3.00	$6.00
923	Felsen, Henry Gregor - ***Hot Rod*** [1951]	$1.00	$3.00	$6.00
924	Stuart, Matt - ***Saddle-Man*** [1951]	$1.00	$3.00	$6.00
925	Stout, Rex - ***Trouble In Triplicate*** [1951]	$2.00	$6.00	$12.00
926	Moll, Elick - ***Night Without Sleep*** [1951]	$1.00	$3.00	$6.00
927	Davis, Dorothy Salisbury - ***The Judas Cat*** [1951]	$1.25	$3.75	$7.50
A-928	Wilder, Robert - ***Flamingo Road*** [1951]	$1.00	$3.00	$6.00
929	Bosworth, Allan R. - ***Steel To The Sunset*** [1951] Cover by Saunders.	$1.00	$3.00	$6.00
A-930	Cronin, A. J. - ***The Citadel*** [1951]	$1.00	$3.00	$6.00
931	Long, Margaret - ***Louisville Saturday*** [1951] Cover by R. Skemp.	$1.00	$3.00	$6.00
932	Shapiro, Lionel - ***Torch For A Long Journey*** [1951]	$1.00	$3.00	$6.00
A-933	Cannon, Jr., Le Grand - ***Look To The Mountain*** [1951]	$1.00	$3.00	$6.00
934	Spicer, Bart - ***Blues For The Prince*** [1951]	$1.25	$3.75	$7.50
F-935	O'Hara, John - ***A Rage To Live*** [1951] Cover by Stahl.	$1.00	$3.00	$6.00
936	Seldes, Gilbert - ***Previews Of Entertainment*** [1951] PBO.	$1.00	$3.00	$6.00
937	Kendrick, Baynard - ***Bright Victory*** [1951] Cover by Hy Rubin. Movie tie-in.	$1.00	$3.00	$6.00
A-938	Taylor, Robert Lewis - ***W.C. Fields: His Follies & Fortunes*** [1951] Cover by Hy Rubin. Sixteen pages of photos.	$1.50	$5.00	$10.00
A-939	Warren, Robert Penn - ***All The King's Men*** [1951]	$1.50	$5.00	$10.00
940	Dobie, J. Frank - ***Apache Gold & YaQui Silver*** [1951]	$1.00	$3.00	$6.00
941	Thompson, Thomas - ***Sundown Riders*** [1951]	$1.00	$3.00	$6.00
942	Burnett, W. R. - ***Romelle*** [1951]	$1.00	$3.00	$6.00
943	Brown, Fredric - ***Here Comes A Candle*** [1951] Cover by Mayan.	$5.00	$15.00	$30.00
A-944	Anthology edited by Ray Bradbury - ***Timeless Stories For Today And Tomorrow*** [1952] PBO. Steinbeck, Kafka, Bradbury, et al.	$1.25	$3.75	$7.50
945	Ellson, Hal - ***Tomboy*** [1951]	$2.00	$6.00	$12.00
946	Henry, Will - ***No Survivors*** [1951] Cover by Mayan.	$1.00	$3.00	$6.00
947	Blunden, Godfrey - ***A Room On The Route*** [1951]	$1.25	$3.75	$7.50
948	Canning, Victor - ***A Forest Of Eyes*** [1951]	$1.25	$3.75	$7.50
949	Maugham, W. Somerset - ***Woman Of The World*** [1951] Cover by Ben Stahl.	$1.00	$3.00	$6.00
A-950	Crane, Milton - ***Fifty Great Short Stories*** [1951]	$1.00	$3.00	$6.00
A-951	Costain, Thomas B. - ***For My Great Folly*** [1951]	$1.00	$3.00	$6.00
952	Miller, Arthur - ***Death Of A Salesman*** [1951]	$1.00	$3.00	$6.00
953	Steinbeck, John - ***Burning Bright*** [1951] Cover by Ben Stahl.	$1.35	$4.00	$8.00
A-954	Finlay, Lucile - ***Grant Of Land*** [1951]	$1.00	$3.00	$6.00
A-955	Robbins, Harold - ***The Dream Merchants*** [1952]	$1.25	$3.75	$7.50
A-956	Caldwell, Taylor - ***The Earth Is The Lord's*** [1951] Cover by Mayan.	$1.25	$3.75	$7.50
957	Bromfield, Louis - ***Colorado*** [1951]	$1.00	$3.00	$6.00
958	Blackburn, Thomas W. - ***Raton Pass*** [1951]	$1.00	$3.00	$6.00
959	O'Malley, Frank - ***The Best Go First*** [1951]	$1.00	$3.00	$6.00
960	Carey, Ernestine & Gilbreth, Jr., Frank - ***Cheaper By The Dozen*** [1951]	$1.25	$3.75	$7.50
961	Fergusson, Harvey - ***What A Man Wants*** [1951]	$1.00	$3.00	$6.00

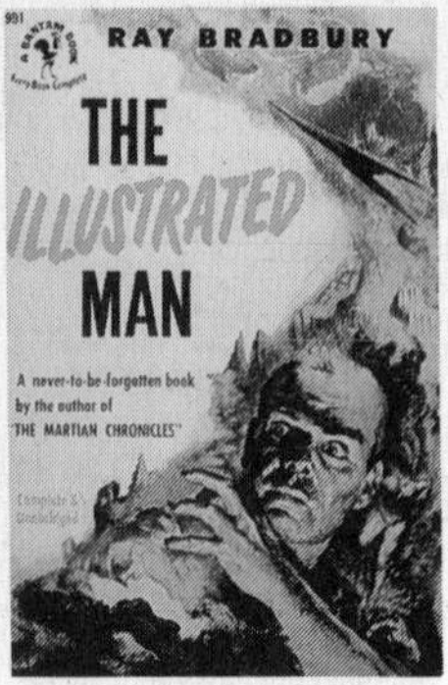

Bantam Book, 991

Bantam Book, 1029

Bantam Book, 1176

		G	VG	F
962	Richter, Conrad - ***The Trees*** [1951] Cover by Maquire.	$1.00	$3.00	$6.00
963	Anthology ed. by Richard Crossman - ***The God That Failed*** [1951] Photo cover.	$1.00	$3.00	$6.00
A-964	Whitman, Howard - ***Terror In The Streets*** [1951] Cover by Maguire.	$1.25	$3.75	$7.50
A-965	Kantor, Mackinlay - ***Signal Thirty-Two*** [1951] Cover by Hooks.	$1.00	$3.00	$6.00
966	Evans, Evan - ***Sawdust And Sixguns*** [1952]	$1.00	$3.00	$6.00
967	Echard, Margaret - ***A Man Without Friends*** [1952] Cover by George Gross	$1.00	$3.00	$6.00
968	Spain, John - ***Dig Me A Grave*** [1951] Cover by Geygan.	$1.25	$3.75	$7.50
969	Crawford, Marion - ***The Little Princesses*** [1952]	$1.00	$3.00	$6.00
970	Ross, Fred - ***Jackson Mahaffey*** [1952]	$1.00	$3.00	$6.00
971	Greene, Graham - ***The Confidential Agent*** [1951] Cover by Hooks.	$1.00	$3.00	$6.00
972	Faulkner, John - ***Dollar Cotton*** [1951] Cover by Schaare.	$1.00	$3.00	$6.00
A-973	Shellabarger, Samuel - ***The Prince Of Foxes*** [1952]	$1.00	$3.00	$6.00
974	Dawson, Peter - ***The Outlaw Of Longbow*** [1952]	$1.00	$3.00	$6.00
975	Spicer, Bart - ***The Golden Door*** [1952]	$1.00	$3.00	$6.00
976	Krasner, William - ***The Gambler*** [1952] Cover by Schaare.	$1.00	$3.00	$6.00
977	Mortimer, John - ***The Silver Hook*** [1952]	$1.00	$3.00	$6.00
978	Hanlin, Tom - ***Mima*** [1952]	$1.00	$3.00	$6.00
A-979	Anthology - ***Model Railroading*** [1952]	$1.35	$4.00	$8.00
A-980	Ernest, Haycox - ***Bugles In The Afternoon*** [1952]	$1.00	$3.00	$6.00
A-981	Every, Dale Van - ***The Shining Mountains*** [1951] Cover by Hooks.	$1.00	$3.00	$6.00
982	Moyzisch, L. C. - ***Operation Cicero*** [1952] Cover by Hooks.	$1.00	$3.00	$6.00
A-983	Wilder, Robert - ***God Has A Long Face*** [1952]	$1.00	$3.00	$6.00
A-984	Costain, Thomas B. - ***Ride With Me*** [1952] Cover by Schaare.	$1.00	$3.00	$6.00
A-985	Waters, Ethel - ***His Eye Is On The Sparrow*** [1952]	$1.25	$3.75	$7.50
A-986	Lake, Stuart N. - ***Wyatt Earp, Frontier Marshal*** [1952]	$1.35	$4.00	$8.00
A-987	Marquand, John Phillips - ***Point Of No Return*** [1952]	$1.00	$3.00	$6.00
988	Holmes, L. P. - ***Dead Man's Saddle*** [1952]	$1.00	$3.00	$6.00
989	Blake, Forrester - ***Johnny Christmas*** [1952]	$1.25	$3.75	$7.50
990	Brown, Fredric - ***Night Of The Jabberwock*** [1952] Cover by Skemp.	$5.50	$17.50	$35.00
991	Bradbury, Ray - ***The Illustrated Man*** [1952] Cover by Binger...	$3.00	$9.00	$18.00
992	Henderson, J. Y. - ***Circus Doctor*** [1952]	$1.25	$3.75	$7.50
993	Forester, C. S. - ***The Gun*** [1952] Cover by Harry Schaare.	$1.00	$3.00	$6.00
A-994	Schoonover, Lawrence - ***The Gentle Infidel*** [1952]	$1.00	$3.00	$6.00

		G	VG	F
A-995	West, Jessamyn - ***The Witch Diggers*** [1951]	$1.25	$3.75	$7.50
996	Carr, John Dickson - ***The Sleeping Sphinx*** [1952]	$2.00	$6.00	$12.00
997	Radin, Edward D. - ***12 Against The Law*** [1952] Cover by Mitchell Hooks.	$1.35	$4.00	$8.00
998	Burnett, W. R. - ***Tomorrow's Another Day*** [1952]	$1.25	$3.75	$7.50
A-999	Michener, James A. - ***Return To Paradise*** [1952] Cover by Stahl.	$1.00	$3.00	$6.00
A-1000	Michener, James A. - ***The Voice Of Asia*** [1951]	$1.00	$3.00	$6.00
1001	Bennett, Dwight - ***Stormy Range*** [1952]	$1.00	$3.00	$6.00
A-1002	Elwood, Muriel - ***Web Of Destiny*** [1952]	$1.00	$3.00	$6.00
A-1003	Mason, Richard - ***Far From Home*** [1952] Cover by Maquire.	$1.00	$3.00	$6.00
1004	Halleran, E. E. - ***High Prairie*** [1952]	$1.00	$3.00	$6.00
1005	O'Rourke, Frank - ***Warbonnet Law*** [1952]	$1.00	$3.00	$6.00
1006	Mannix, Daniel P. - ***Step Right Up!*** [1952] Cover by Harry Schaare.	$1.00	$3.00	$6.00
1007	Cozzens, James Gould - ***Castaway*** [1952]	$1.00	$3.00	$6.00
A-1008	Kantor, MacKinlay - ***Long Remember*** [1952] Cover by Mayan.	$1.00	$3.00	$6.00
A-1009	Carr, John Dickson - ***The Devil In Velvet*** [1952] Cover by Harry Schaare.	$2.50	$7.50	$15.00
1010	Cerf, Bennett - ***Laughter Incorporated*** [1952] Cover by Carl Rose.	$ .75	$2.50	$5.00
1011	Forester, C. S. - ***Rifleman Dodd*** [1952] Cover by Maguire.	$1.00	$3.00	$6.00
1012	Paul, Elliot - ***Murder On The Left Bank*** [1952] Cover by Hooks.	$1.25	$3.75	$7.50
1013	Davis, Dorothy Salisbury - ***The Clay Hand*** [1952]	$1.25	$3.75	$7.50
1014	Benson, Ben - ***Alibi At Dusk*** [1952] Cover by Al Rossi	$1.25	$3.75	$7.50
A-1016	Swanson, Neil H. - ***The Judas Tree*** [1952]	$1.25	$3.75	$7.50
A-1017	Birney, Hoffman - ***Ann Carmeny*** [1952] Cover by Schaare.	$1.00	$3.00	$6.00
1018	Stuart, Matt - ***Gun Law At Vermillion*** [1952] Cover by Mayan.	$1.00	$3.00	$6.00
1019	Household, Geoffrey - ***A Rough Shoot*** [1953] Cover by Binger.	$1.25	$3.75	$7.50
1020	Zola, Emile - ***Theresa*** [1952] Cover by Maguire.	$1.25	$3.75	$7.50
F-1021	Davis, Kenneth S. - ***Eisenhower: Soldier Of Democracy*** [1952]	$1.00	$3.00	$6.00
A-1022	Sabatini, Rafael - ***Scaramouche*** [1952] Cover by Schaare.	$1.00	$3.00	$6.00
1023	Faulkner, John - ***Men Working*** [1952] Cover by Harry Schaare.	$1.25	$3.75	$7.50
1024	Innes, Hammond - ***The Survivors*** [1952] Cover by Mitchell Hooks.	$1.00	$3.00	$6.00
1025	Summers, Richard - ***Dark Madonna*** [1952] Cover by Erickson.	$1.00	$3.00	$6.00
1026	Treat, Lawrence - ***Big Shot*** [1952]	$1.25	$3.75	$7.50
A-1027	Costain, Thomas B. - ***High Towers*** [1952] Cover by Hooks.	$1.00	$3.00	$6.00
A-1028	Wilder, Robert - ***Written On The Wind*** [1952] Cover by Schaare.	$1.00	$3.00	$6.00
1029	Hitrec, Joseph - ***Angel Of Gaiety*** [1952] Cover by Mayan.	$1.00	$3.00	$6.00
1030	Hardin, Peter - ***The Frightened Dove*** [1952]	$1.25	$3.75	$7.50
1031	Roe, Vingie - ***West Of Abilene*** [1952]	$1.00	$3.00	$6.00
1032	Stout, Rex - ***The Second Confession*** [1952]	$2.00	$6.00	$12.00
A-1033	Gunther, John - ***Inside U.S.A. (Vol. I)*** [1952]	$1.00	$3.00	$6.00
A-1034	Gunther, John - ***Inside U.S.A. (Vol. II)*** [1952]	$1.00	$3.00	$6.00
A-1035	Wilson, Mitchell - ***Live With Lightning*** [1952]	$1.00	$3.00	$6.00
A-1036	O'Meara, Walter - ***The Grand Portage*** [1952] Cover by Schaare.	$1.00	$3.00	$6.00
A-1037	Anthology - ***Harper's Magazine Reader*** [1952]	$1.00	$3.00	$6.00
1038	Kantor, MacKinlay - ***Don't Touch Me*** [1952]	$1.00	$3.00	$6.00
1039	Mauriac, Francois - ***The Desert Of Love*** [1952] Cover by Robert Maguire.	$1.00	$3.00	$6.00
1040	Brown, Fredric - ***Death Has Many Doors*** [1952] Cover by Barye Phillips.	$5.50	$17.50	$35.00
F-1041	Swanson, Neil H. - ***The Silent Drum*** [1952]	$1.00	$3.00	$6.00
F-1042	Cronin, A. J. - ***The Stars Look Down*** [1953]	$1.00	$3.00	$6.00
A-1043	Coolidge, Dane - ***Fighting Men Of The West*** [1952] Cover by Mayan.	$1.00	$3.00	$6.00

		G	VG	F
A-1044	Chevallier, Gabriel - ***The Affairs Of Flavie*** [1952]	$1.00	$3.00	$6.00
1045	Lessing, Doris - ***The Grass Is Singing*** [1952] Cover by Martin.	$1.00	$3.00	$6.00
1046	O'Hara, John - ***The Farmers Hotel*** [1952] Cover by Mitchell Hooks.	$1.00	$3.00	$6.00
1047	BourJaily, Vance - ***The End Of My Life*** [1952] Cover by Mayan.	$1.00	$3.00	$6.00
1048	Holmes, L. P. - ***Summer Range*** [1952]	$1.00	$3.00	$6.00
1049	Spicer, Bart - ***Black Sheep, Run*** [1952] Cover by Al Rossi.	$1.00	$3.00	$6.00
1050	Cronin, A. J. - ***Grand Canary*** [1952] Cover by Hooks.	$1.00	$3.00	$6.00
A-1051	Schulberg, Budd - ***The Disenchanted*** [1952] Cover by Harry Schaare.	$1.00	$3.00	$6.00
A-1052	Weenolsen, Hebe - ***The Last Englishman*** [1952] Cover by Harry Schaare.	$1.00	$3.00	$6.00
A-1053	Zolotow, Maurice - ***No People Like Show People*** [1952]	$1.00	$3.00	$6.00
1054	Masson, Rene - ***Cage Of Darkness*** [1952] Cover by William Gropper.	$1.00	$3.00	$6.00
1055	Phillips, James Atlee - ***Pagoda*** [1952]	$1.00	$3.00	$6.00
1056	Wormser, Richard - ***The Lonesome Quarter*** [1952] Cover by Harry Schaare.	$1.00	$3.00	$6.00
1057	Carder, Michael - ***Cimarron Crossing*** [1952] Cover by Mayan..	$1.00	$3.00	$6.00
1058	Innes, Hammond - ***The Angry Mountain*** [1952] Cover by Hooks.	$1.25	$3.75	$7.50
1059	Symons, Julian - ***The 31st Of February*** [1953]	$1.25	$3.75	$7.50
A-1060	Cronin, A. J. - ***The Keys Of The Kingdom*** [1952]	$1.00	$3.00	$6.00
1061	Kelland, Clarence Buddington - ***Arizona*** [1952]	$1.00	$3.00	$6.00
1062	Knibbs, H. H. - ***The Tonto Kid*** [1952]	$1.00	$3.00	$6.00
1063	Short, Luke - ***Ride The Man Down*** [1952]	$1.00	$3.00	$6.00
1064	Dawson, Peter - ***Trail Boss*** [1952]	$1.00	$3.00	$6.00
1065	Steinbeck, John - ***Cannery Row*** [1952]	$1.35	$4.00	$8.00
1066	Steinbeck, John - ***The Pastures Of Heaven*** [1952]	$1.35	$4.00	$8.00
1067	Grey, Zane - ***Nevada*** [1952]	$1.00	$3.00	$6.00
1068	Warren, Charles Marquis - ***Valley Of The Shadow*** [1952] Cover by Hooks.	$1.00	$3.00	$6.00
A-1069	Allen, Frederick Lewis - ***Only Yesterday*** [1952]	$1.00	$3.00	$6.00
1070	Benson, Ben - ***Beware The Pale Horse*** [1953] Cover by Al Rossi.	$1.00	$3.00	$6.00
A-1071	Huxley, Aldous - ***Brave New World*** [1952] Cover by Binger.	$2.00	$6.00	$12.00
A-1072	Masters, John - ***Nightrunners Of Bengal*** [1952] Cover by Maguire.	$1.00	$3.00	$6.00
A-1073	Hine, Al - ***An Unfound Door*** [1952] Cover by Hooks.	$1.00	$3.00	$6.00
1074	Berenstain, Janice & Stanley - ***Berenstains' Baby Book*** [1952] Cover by Berenstain.	$1.00	$3.00	$6.00
1075	Short, Luke - ***Play A Lone Hand*** [1952] Cover by Mayan.	$1.00	$3.00	$6.00
1076	Barbette, Jay - ***Final Copy*** [1952] Cover by Al Rossi.	$1.00	$3.00	$6.00
1077	Brown, Fredric - ***Space On My Hands*** [1952] Cover by Binger.	$2.50	$7.50	$15.00
1078	Frank, Pat - ***Hold Back The Night*** [1952]	$1.00	$3.00	$6.00
1079	Heard, Gerald - ***Is Another World Watching?*** [1953]	$2.00	$6.00	$12.00
1080	Forester, C. S. - ***Single - Handed*** [1953] Cover by Maguire.	$1.00	$3.00	$6.00
1081	Giles, Henry - ***Harbin's Ridge*** [1953] Cover by Mayan.	$1.00	$3.00	$6.00
1082	Thompson, Thomas - ***Gunman Brand*** [1952] Cover by Matt Clark.	$1.00	$3.00	$6.00
1083	Davis, Dorothy Salisbury - ***A Gentle Murderer*** [1953] Cover by Barye Phillips.	$1.25	$3.75	$7.50
A-1084	March, William - ***The Looking Glass*** [1953] Cover by Harry Schaare.	$1.00	$3.00	$6.00
A-1085	Standish, Robert - ***Storm Centre*** [1953] Cover by Hooks.	$1.00	$3.00	$6.00
A-1086	Rainier, Peter W. - ***Green Fire*** [1953]	$1.00	$3.00	$6.00
F-1087	Marquand, John P. - ***So Little Time*** [1953]	$1.00	$3.00	$6.00
A-1088	Goodrich, Marcus - ***Delilah*** [1953] Cover by Hooks.	$1.25	$3.75	$7.50
A-1089	Dobie, J. Frank - ***Coronado's Children*** [1953]	$1.00	$3.00	$6.00

		G	VG	F
A-1090	Every, Dale Van - ***The Captive Witch*** [1953] Cover by Schaare.	$1.25	$3.75	$7.50
A-1091	McCullers, Carson - ***The Heart Is A Lonely Hunter*** [1953] Cover by Hooks.	$1.35	$4.00	$8.00
1092	Dressler, David - ***Parole Chief*** [1953] Cover by Maguire.	$1.25	$3.75	$7.50
1093	West, Nathanael - ***The Day Of The Locust*** [1953]	$1.25	$3.75	$7.50
1094	Gulick, Bill - ***A Drum Calls West*** [1953]	$1.00	$3.00	$6.00
1095	Stuart, Matt - ***The Smoky Trail*** [1953]	$1.00	$3.00	$6.00
1096	Ehrlich, Max - ***Spin The Glass Web*** [1953]	$1.25	$3.75	$7.50
A-1097	Ware, Harlan - ***Come, Fill The Cup*** [1953]	$1.00	$3.00	$6.00
A-1098	Miller, Lee G. - ***The Story Of Ernie Pyle*** [1953] Cover by Schaare.	$1.00	$3.00	$6.00
A-1099	Edmonds, Walter D. - ***Rome Haul*** [1953]	$1.00	$3.00	$6.00
A-1100	Raddall, Thomas H. - ***Roger Sudden*** [1953] Cover by Mayan.	$1.00	$3.00	$6.00
1101	Cameron, Owen - ***The Mountains Have No Shadow*** [1953]	$1.00	$3.00	$6.00
1102	Evans, Evan - ***Strange Courage*** [1953]	$1.00	$3.00	$6.00
1103	Holmes, L. P. - ***Black Sage*** [1953]	$1.00	$3.00	$6.00
1104	Short, Luke - ***Ambush*** [1953]	$1.00	$3.00	$6.00
1105	Short, Luke - ***Fiddlefoot*** [1953]	$1.00	$3.00	$6.00
A-1106	Collier, John - ***Fancies and Goodnights*** [1953] Cover by Binger.	$2.50	$7.50	$15.00
A-1107	Adams, Samuel Hopkins - ***Sunrise To Sunset*** [1953] Cover by Schaare.	$1.00	$3.00	$6.00
1108	Fante, John - ***Full Of Life*** [1953]	$1.00	$3.00	$6.00
1109	Coleman, Lonnie - ***Clara*** [1953]	$1.00	$3.00	$6.00
1110	Pease, Howard - ***Road Kid*** [1953]	$1.00	$3.00	$6.00
1111	Taylor, Ross McLaury - ***Brazos*** [1953]	$1.00	$3.00	$6.00
1112	Foster, Bennett - ***Bad Lands*** [1953]	$1.00	$3.00	$6.00
1113	Dawson, Peter - ***The Crimson Horseshoe*** [1953]	$1.00	$3.00	$6.00
1115	Haycox, Ernest - ***The Wild Bunch*** [1953]	$1.00	$3.00	$6.00
1116	Foster, Bennett - ***Trigger Kid*** [1953]	$1.00	$3.00	$6.00
1117	Hopson, William - ***The Last Apaches*** [1953]	$1.00	$3.00	$6.00
1118	Anthology - ***Saturday Review Reader No. 2*** [1953]	$1.00	$3.00	$6.00
1119	Carr, John Dickson - ***Below Suspicion*** [1953]	$2.00	$6.00	$12.00
1120	Trimble, Louis - ***Gaptown Law*** [1953]	$1.00	$3.00	$6.00
A-1121	Schoonover, Lawrence L. - ***The Golden Exile*** [1953] Cover by Schaare.	$1.25	$3.75	$7.50
A-1123	Laird, Emma - ***Of Former Love*** [1953]	$1.00	$3.00	$6.00
1124	Burnett, W. R. - ***Little Men, Big World*** [1953]	$1.00	$3.00	$6.00
1125	Innes, Hammond - ***Air Bridge*** [1953] Cover by Al Rossi.	$1.00	$3.00	$6.00
1126	Spicer, Bart - ***The Long Green*** [1953] Cover by Hooks.	$1.00	$3.00	$6.00
1127	Lamb, Harold - ***Genghis Khan*** [1953] Cover by Binger.	$1.00	$3.00	$6.00
1128	O'Farrell, William - ***Thin Edge Of Violence*** [1953] Cover by Rossi.	$1.00	$3.00	$6.00
F-1130	Gordon, Caroline - ***Green Centuries*** [1953] Cover by R. Skemp.	$1.00	$3.00	$6.00
A-1131	Shellabarger, Samuel - ***The King's Cavalier*** [1953]	$1.00	$3.00	$6.00
1132	Loomis, Noel M. - ***Rim Of The Caprock*** [1953]	$1.00	$3.00	$6.00
1133	Brown, Fredric - ***The Far Cry*** [1953]	$5.50	$17.50	$35.00
1134	Brown, Fredric - ***The Fabulous Clipjoint*** [1953]	$2.50	$7.50	$15.00
1135	Conrad, Earl - ***Rock Bottom*** [1953]	$1.00	$3.00	$6.00
A-1136	Tucker, Lael - ***Lament For Four Virgins*** [1953]	$1.00	$3.00	$6.00
A-1137	Lofts, Norah - ***The Lute Player*** [1953]	$1.00	$3.00	$6.00
A-1138	O'Dell, Scott - ***Hill Of The Hawk*** [1953]	$1.00	$3.00	$6.00
A-1139	Caldwell, Taylor - ***Melissa*** [1953]	$1.00	$3.00	$6.00
1140	Ullman, Allan & Fletcher, Lucille - ***Night Man*** [1953]	$1.00	$3.00	$6.00
1141	Bennett, Dwight - ***Lost Wolf River*** [1953]	$1.00	$3.00	$6.00
1142	Huxley, Aldous - ***Antic Hay*** [1953] Cover by Binger.	$1.35	$4.00	$8.00
1143	Buchan, John - ***Mountain Meadow*** [1953]	$1.00	$3.00	$6.00
A-1144	Every, Dale Van - ***Westward The River*** [1953] Cover by Schaare.	$1.00	$3.00	$6.00

		G	VG	F
A-1145	Monaghan, Jay - ***The Great Rascal*** [1953]	$1.00	$3.00	$6.00
A-1146	Burns, John Horne - ***The Gallery*** [1953]	$1.00	$3.00	$6.00
1147	Burns, John Horne - ***A Cry Of Children*** [1953] Cover by Binger.	$1.00	$3.00	$6.00
1148	Morgan, Claire - ***The Price Of Salt*** [1953]	$1.00	$3.00	$6.00
1149	O'Rourke, Frank - ***Gold Under Skull Peak*** [1953] Cover by Crair.	$1.00	$3.00	$6.00
1150	Walsh, Thomas - ***The Night Watch*** [1953] Cover by Hooks.	$1.00	$3.00	$6.00
A-1151	Forbes, Esther - ***Paradise*** [1953]	$1.00	$3.00	$6.00
F-1152	Anthology - ***Model Railroading*** [1953]	$1.25	$3.75	$7.50
1153	Standish, Robert - ***A Worthy Man*** [1953]	$1.00	$3.00	$6.00
1154	Kuttner, Henry - ***Man Drowning*** [1953] Cover by Mitchell Hooks.	$2.50	$7.50	$15.00
1156	McCullers, Carson - ***Reflections In A Golden Eye*** [1953]	$1.35	$4.00	$8.00
A-1157	Mahler, Helen A. - ***Empress Of Byzantium*** [1953] Cover by Schaare.	$1.00	$3.00	$6.00
A-1158	Anthology edited by Rogers Terrill - ***The Argosy Book Of Adventure Stories*** [1953]	$1.25	$3.75	$7.50
A-1159	Swanson, Neil H. - ***The Forbidden Ground*** [1953]	$1.00	$3.00	$6.00
A-1160	Nogales, Manuel & Charteris, Leslie - ***Juan Belmonte: Killer Of Bulls*** [1953] Cover by Schaare.	$1.00	$3.00	$6.00
1161	Hostovsky, Egon - ***Missing*** [1953]	$1.00	$3.00	$6.00
A-1162	Wilder, Robert - ***And Ride A Tiger*** [1953] Cover by Hooks.	$1.00	$3.00	$6.00
1164	Blackburn, Thomas W. - ***Short Grass*** [1953]	$ .75	$2.50	$5.00
F-1165	Mandel, George - ***Flee The Angry Strangers*** [1953] Cover by Schaare.	$1.00	$3.00	$6.00
1166	Cerf, Bennett - ***Laughter, Incorporated*** [1953]	$ .75	$2.50	$5.00
1167	Allen, John Houghton - ***Southwest*** [1953] Cover by Binger.	$1.00	$3.00	$6.00
1168	Henry, Will - ***No Survivors*** [1953]	$1.00	$3.00	$6.00
1169	Brincourt, Andre - ***The Paradise Below The Stairs*** [1953]	$1.00	$3.00	$6.00
1170	Forester, C. S. - ***The General*** [1953] Cover by Barye Phillips.	$1.00	$3.00	$6.00
F-1171	Myers, Bernard - ***50 Great Artists*** [1953] PBO. Photo cover.	$1.00	$3.00	$6.00
A-1172	Wilder, Robert - ***Bright Feather*** [1953]	$1.00	$3.00	$6.00
1173	Stout, Rex - ***In The Best Families*** [1953]	$1.35	$4.00	$8.00
A-1174	Wilson, Mitchell - ***My Brother, My Enemy*** [1953] Cover by Hooks.	$1.00	$3.00	$6.00
1175	Kantor, MacKinlay - ***Warwhoop*** [1953]	$1.00	$3.00	$6.00
1176	Brown, Fredric - ***We All Killed Grandma*** [1953] Cover by Binger.	$6.00	$20.00	$40.00
1177	Canning, Victor - ***Bird Of Prey*** [1953]	$1.25	$3.75	$7.50
1178	Schoonover, Lawrence - ***The Quick Brown Fox*** [1953] Cover by Schaare.	$1.00	$3.00	$6.00
1179	Webb, Jon Edgar - ***Four Steps To The Wall*** [1953] Cover by Gross.	$1.00	$3.00	$6.00
1180	Hopson, William - ***Gunfighters Pay*** [1953]	$ .75	$2.50	$5.00
A-1181	Wilder, Robert - ***Wait For Tomorrow*** [1953]	$ .75	$2.50	$5.00
A-1182	Walz, Jay & Audrey - ***The Bizarre Sisters*** [1953] Cover by Schaare.	$ .75	$2.50	$5.00
A-1183	Bowen, Robert O. - ***The Weight Of The Cross*** [1953] Cover by Hooks.	$ .75	$2.50	$5.00
1184	Steinbeck, John - ***Cup Of Gold*** [1953] Cover by Mayan.	$1.00	$3.00	$6.00
A-1185	DeMille, Agnes - ***Dance To The Piper*** [1953]	$ .75	$2.50	$5.00
F-1186	Costain, Thomas B. - ***The Moneyman*** [1953]	$ .75	$2.50	$5.00
1187	Masters, John - ***The Deceivers*** [1953]	$ .75	$2.50	$5.00
1188	Hansen, Robert P. - ***Dead Pigeon*** [1953] Cover by Binger.	$1.00	$3.00	$6.00
1189	Daniels, John S. - ***Gunflame*** [1953]	$ .75	$2.50	$5.00
A-1190	Lea, Tom - ***The Wonderful Country*** [1953] Cover by Hooks.	$ .75	$2.50	$5.00
1191	Cochran, Louis - ***Son Of Haman*** [1953]	$ .75	$2.50	$5.00
A-1192	Hedden, Worth Tuttle - ***The Other Room*** [1953]	$ .75	$2.50	$5.00
A-1193	Murray, Chalmers S. - ***Here Come Joe Mungin*** [1954]	$ .75	$2.50	$5.00

		G	VG	F
1194	Fante, John - ***Ask The Dust*** [1954] Cover by Schaare.	$ .75	$2.50	$5.00
1195	Cameron, Owen - ***Catch A Tiger*** [1954]	$ .75	$2.50	$5.00
A-1196	Forester, C. S. - ***The Ship*** [1954]	$ .75	$2.50	$5.00
1197	Bagby, George - ***Dead On Arrival*** [1954] Cover by George Gross.	$1.00	$3.00	$6.00
1198	Gruber, Frank - ***Broken Lance*** [1954]	$ .75	$2.50	$5.00
F-1200	Marquand, John P. - ***Melville Goodwin, U.S.A.*** [1954]	$ .75	$2.50	$5.00
A-1201	Anthology edited by Seymour Krim - ***Manhattan*** [1954] PBO	$ .75	$2.50	$5.00
F-1203	Purdy, Ken W. - ***The Kings Of The Road*** [1954]	$ .75	$2.50	$5.00
A-1204	Busch, Niven - ***The Hate Merchant*** [1954] Cover by Schaare.	$1.00	$3.00	$6.00
A-1205	Garside, E. B. - ***The Man From Brazil*** [1954]	$1.00	$3.00	$6.00
1206	Dawson, Peter - ***Royal Gorge*** [1954]	$ .75	$2.50	$5.00
1207	Carr, John Dickson - ***The Burning Court*** [1954] Cover by Binger.	$1.35	$4.00	$8.00
1208	Richter, Conrad - ***The Sea Of Grass*** [1954] Cover by Schaare.	$ .75	$2.50	$5.00
A-1209	Rawlings, Marjorie Kinnan - ***Gal Young Un*** [1954]	$1.00	$3.00	$6.00
A-1210	Patman, Wright - ***Our American Government*** [1954]	$ .75	$2.50	$5.00
A-1211	Spicer, Bart - ***The Wild Ohio*** [1954]	$ .75	$2.50	$5.00
A-1212	Dobie, J. Frank - ***The Mustangs*** [1954]	$ .75	$2.50	$5.00
A-1213	Schulberg, Budd - ***Some Faces In The Crowd*** [1954] Cover by Binger.	$ .75	$2.50	$5.00
A-1214	Ross, Sam - ***Someday, Boy*** [1954] Cover by Schaare.	$ .75	$2.50	$5.00
1215	Brown, Fredric - ***The Deep End*** [1954] Cover by Binger.	$2.50	$7.50	$15.00
1216	Brown, Fredric - ***The Dead Ringer*** [1954] Cover by Binger.	$2.50	$7.50	$15.00
A-1217	Greene, Graham - ***The Power And The Glory*** [1954] Cover by Gross.	$ .75	$2.50	$5.00
1219	Hersey, John - ***Hiroshima*** [1954]	$ .75	$2.50	$5.00
A-1220	Dudley, Ernest - ***Picaroon*** [1954] Cover by Hooks.	$ .75	$2.50	$5.00
A-1221	Sheldon, Walt - ***Troubling Of A Star*** [1954]	$ .75	$2.50	$5.00
1225	Bell, Vereen - ***Swamp Water*** [1954] Cover by George Gross.	$ .75	$2.50	$5.00
1226	Bagby, George - ***Blood Will Tell*** [1954] Cover by R. Skemp.	$ .75	$2.50	$5.00
A-1227	Kolb, Sylvia & John - ***A Treasury Of Folk Songs*** [1954]	$1.00	$3.00	$6.00
A-1228	Fitzgerald, F. Scott - ***The Great Gatsby*** [1954]	$ .75	$2.50	$5.00
A-1229	Anthology edited by Richard Crossman - ***The God That Failed*** [1954]	$ .75	$2.50	$5.00
A-1230	Rostand, Edmond - ***Cyrano de Bergerac*** [1954]	$ .75	$2.50	$5.00
A-1231	Cerf, Bennett - ***Good For A Laugh*** [1954]	$ .75	$2.50	$5.00
1232	McNulty, John - ***A Man Gets Around*** [1954] Cover by George Gross.	$ .75	$2.50	$5.00
1233	Huxley, Aldous - ***Eyeless In Gaza*** [1954] Cover by Binger.	$1.35	$4.00	$8.00
A-1234	Lamb, Harold - ***Suleiman The Magnificent*** [1954] Cover by Schaare.	$ .75	$2.50	$5.00
A-1235	McCullers, Carson - ***Seven*** [1954]	$2.00	$6.00	$12.00
A-1236	Clayton, John Bell - ***Wait, Son, October Is Near*** [1954] Cover by Binger.	$ .75	$2.50	$5.00
1237	Kantor, MacKinlay - ***The Daughter Of Bugle Ann*** [1954] Cover by George Gross.	$ .75	$2.50	$5.00
1238	Kantor, MacKinlay - ***Wicked Water*** [1954]	$ .75	$2.50	$5.00
1239	Pearce, Dick - ***The Restless Border*** [1954] Cover by Crair.	$ .75	$2.50	$5.00
A-1240	Hemingway, Ernest - ***A Farewell To Arms*** [1954] Cover by Binger.	$1.00	$3.00	$6.00
A-1241	Bradbury, Ray - ***The Golden Apples Of The Sun*** [1954] Cover by Binger.	$2.00	$6.00	$12.00
A-1242	Anthology - ***Saturday Review Reader #3*** [1954]	$ .75	$2.50	$5.00
1243	Small, Sidney Herschel - ***Sword And Candle*** [1954] Cover by Gross.	$ .75	$2.50	$5.00
A-1244	Zola, Emile - ***Restless House*** [1954]	$ .75	$2.50	$5.00
A-1245	Young, Jefferson - ***A Good Man*** [1954] Cover by Mitchell Hooks.	$ .75	$2.50	$5.00
A-1246	Corle, Edwin - ***Billy The Kid*** [1954] Cover by George Gross.	$1.00	$3.00	$6.00

		G	VG	F
1247	Doyle, William & O'Dell, Scott - ***Man Alone*** [1954] Cover by Binger.	$ .75	$2.50	$5.00
A-1249	Hemingway, Ernest - ***The Sun Also Rises*** [1954] Cover by Binger.	$1.35	$4.00	$8.00
A-1250	Every, Dale Van - ***The Trembling Earth*** [1954] Cover by Crair.	$1.00	$3.00	$6.00
1251	Padgett, Lewis - ***Line To Tomorrow*** [1954] PBO. Cover by Hooks.	$2.50	$7.50	$15.00
1252	Stout, Rex - ***Murder By The Book*** [1954] Cover by Crair.	$2.00	$6.00	$12.00
1253	Brown, Fredric - ***What Mad Universe*** [1954] Cover by Binger.	$1.35	$4.00	$8.00
A-1254	Edmonds, Walter D. - ***The Boyds Of Black River*** [1954] Cover by Schaare.	$ .75	$2.50	$5.00
1255	Williamson, Thames - ***The Woods Colt*** [1954] Cover by George Gross.	$ .75	$2.50	$5.00
A-1257	Stanley, Bennett - ***Sea Struck*** [1954] Cover by Binger.	$ .75	$2.50	$5.00
A-1258	Wilder, Robert - ***Autumn Thunder*** [1954]	$ .75	$2.50	$5.00
A-1260	Huxley, Aldous - ***Crome Yellow*** [1954]	$1.35	$4.00	$8.00
1261	Bradbury, Ray - ***The Martian Chronicles*** [1954]	$1.35	$4.00	$8.00
A-1262	Vonnegut, Jr., Kurt - ***Utopia 14*** [1954]	$3.50	$10.00	$20.00
1262	Vonnegut, Jr., Kurt - ***Utopia 14*** [1954] Cover by Binger.	$3.50	$10.00	$20.00
1264	Richter, Conrad - ***The Light In The Forest*** [1954] Cover by Gross.	$ .75	$2.50	$5.00
1266	Steinbeck, John - ***Cannery Row*** [1954]	$1.00	$3.00	$6.00
F-1267	Steinbeck, John - ***East Of Eden*** [1954]	$1.00	$3.00	$6.00
A-1268	Connell, Vivian - ***The Chinese Room*** [1954] Cover by Ben Stahl.	$ .75	$2.50	$5.00
1269	Michener, James A. - ***The Bridges At Toko-Ri*** [1954]	$ .75	$2.50	$5.00
1271	Benson, Ben - ***The Venus Death*** [1954] Cover by Hooks.	$1.00	$3.00	$6.00
1272	McNichols, Charles L. - ***Crazy Weather*** [1954] Cover by E. Means.	$ .75	$2.50	$5.00
1273	The Gordons - ***Case File - FBI*** [1954]	$1.00	$3.00	$6.00
F-1274	Anthology edited by Arnold Gingrich - ***Best Of The Bedside Esquire*** [1954]	$1.00	$3.00	$6.00
A-1275	Komroff, Manuel - ***In The Years Of Our Lord*** [1954]	$ .75	$2.50	$5.00
A-1276	Boles, Paul Darcy - ***The Streak*** [1954]	$ .75	$2.50	$5.00
1277	Dawson, Peter - ***The Stagline Feud*** [1954]	$ .75	$2.50	$5.00
1278	Sohl, Jerry - ***Costigan's Needle*** [1954]	$2.00	$6.00	$12.00
F-1279	Uris, Leon - ***Battle Cry*** [1954]	$1.35	$4.00	$8.00
A-1281	Viertel, Peter - ***White Hunter, Black Heart*** [1954] Cover by Binger.	$ .75	$2.50	$5.00
1282	Bradbury, Ray - ***The Illustrated Man*** [1954] Cover by Binger.	$1.35	$4.00	$8.00
1283	Fox, Paul - ***Sailor Town*** [1954]	$1.00	$3.00	$6.00
F-1284	Shellabarger, Samuel - ***Lord Vanity*** [1954] Cover by Hooks.	$ .75	$2.50	$5.00
1285	Brown, Fredric - ***The Lights In The Sky Are Stars*** [1954] Cover by Mitchell Hooks.	$2.50	$7.50	$15.00
1286	Ellington, Richard - ***Shakedown*** [1954] Cover by Binger.	$1.00	$3.00	$6.00
1287	Gruber, Frank - ***Bitter Sage*** [1955] Cover by George Gross.	$ .75	$2.50	$5.00
1288	Lindsay, Norman - ***The Cautious Amorist*** [1955] Cover by Whitney Darrow, Jr.	$ .75	$2.50	$5.00
A-1289	Harris, John - ***The Undaunted*** [1955]	$ .75	$2.50	$5.00
A-1290	Zola, Emile - ***The Kill*** [1955] Cover by Barye Phillips.	$ .75	$2.50	$5.00
A-1291	Lamb, Harold - ***Tamerlane*** [1955]	$ .75	$2.50	$5.00
A-1292	Capek, Karel - ***War With The Newts*** [1955]	$2.00	$6.00	$12.00
1293	Short, Luke - ***And The Wind Blows Free*** [1955]	$ .75	$2.50	$5.00
1294	Matheson, Richard - ***Third From The Sun*** [1955] Cover by Binger.	$5.00	$15.00	$30.00
1295	MacDonald, John Ross - ***The Name Is Archer*** [1955] PBO. Cover by Hooks. Author's only first edition in paperbacks.	$6.00	$20.00	$40.00
A-1296	Engel, Louis - ***How To Buy Stocks*** [1955]	$ .50	$1.50	$3.00
1297	Schaefer, Jack - ***Shane*** [1955]	$ .75	$2.50	$5.00

		G	VG	F
1298	Grey, Zane - ***Nevada*** [1955] Cover by E. Means.	$ .75	$2.50	$5.00
F-1299	Anthology - ***The Thorndike Barnhart Handy Dictionary*** [1955]	$ .75	$2.50	$5.00
A-1300	Robbins, Harold - ***Never Love A Stranger*** [1955]	$ .75	$2.50	$5.00
F-1301	Steinbeck, John - ***The Grapes Of Wrath*** [1955]	$ .75	$2.50	$5.00
F-1302	Anthology edited by Milton Crane - ***Fifty Great Short Stories*** [1955]	$ .75	$2.50	$5.00
A-1303	Anthology - ***Twenty Grand Short Stories*** [1955]	$ .75	$2.50	$5.00
A-1304	Eyster, Warren - ***Far From The Customary Skies*** [1955] Cover by Hooks.	$ .75	$2.50	$5.00
A-1305	Forester, C. S. - ***Mr. Midshipman Hornblower*** [1955]	$ .75	$2.50	$5.00
A-1306	Greene, Graham - ***The End Of The Affair*** [1955]	$ .75	$2.50	$5.00
A-1307	Linford, Dee - ***Man Without A Star*** [1955] Cover by George Gross.	$ .75	$2.50	$5.00
1308	Bagby, George - ***Drop Dead*** [1955]	$1.00	$3.00	$6.00
1309	Weisinger, Mort - ***1001 Valuable Things You Can Get Free*** [1955] PBO.	$ .50	$1.50	$3.00
1310	Anthology edited by Healy & McComas - ***More Adventures In Time And Space*** [1955]	$1.25	$3.75	$7.50
1311	Burke, Jack - ***The Natural Way To Better Golf*** [1955]	$1.25	$3.75	$7.50
1312	Brown, Fredric - ***The Screaming Mimi*** [1955] Cover by Binger.	$2.50	$7.50	$15.00
1313	Jones, Evan - ***High Gear*** [1955]	$ .50	$1.50	$3.00
A-1314	Forester, C. S. - ***To The Indies*** [1955] Cover by Geygan.	$ .50	$1.50	$3.00
1315	Alexander, David - ***Murder Points A Finger*** [1955] Cover by Hooks.	$1.00	$3.00	$6.00
1316	Greene, Graham - ***This Gun For Hire*** [1955]	$ .75	$2.50	$5.00
1317	Kornbluth, Cyril M. - ***The Syndic*** [1955]	$1.00	$3.00	$6.00
A-1318	Michener, James A. - ***Sayonara*** [1955]	$ .50	$1.50	$3.00
A-1319	Roberts, Dorothy James - ***The Enchanted Cup*** [1955] Cover by Barye Phillips.	$ .50	$1.50	$3.00
A-1320	Liebman, Joshua Loth - ***Peace Of Mind*** [1955]	$ .50	$1.50	$3.00
F-1321	Cronin, A. J. - ***Beyond This Place*** [1955]	$ .50	$1.50	$3.00
A-1322	Miller, Arthur - ***Death Of A Salesman*** [1955] Cover by Joseph Hirsch.	$ .50	$1.50	$3.00
1323	Benson, Ben - ***Target In Taffeta*** [1955] Cover by Barye Phillips.	$ .50	$1.50	$3.00
A-1324	Steinbeck, John - ***To A God Unknown*** [1955] Cover by Philippe Haisman.	$1.25	$3.75	$7.50
1325	Carr, John Dickson - ***The Nine Wrong Answers*** [1955]	$1.25	$3.75	$7.50
1326	Stout, Rex - ***Prisoner's Base*** [1955] Cover by Barye Phillips.	$1.25	$3.75	$7.50
1327	Ambler, Eric - ***The Schirmer Inheritance*** [1955] Cover by George Gross.	$ .75	$2.50	$5.00
1328	Edited by Everett F. Bleiler & T. E. Dikty - ***Frontiers In Space*** [1955]	$1.25	$3.75	$7.50
A-1329	Steinbeck, John - ***Of Mice And Men*** [1955] Cover by Philippe Haisman.	$2.00	$6.00	$12.00
1330	Breger, Dave - ***But That's Unprintable*** [1955] Cartoon Book.	$ .50	$1.50	$3.00
A-1331	Burnett, W. R. - ***Captain Lightfoot*** [1955] Cover by Hooks.	$ .75	$2.50	$5.00
A-1332	Brandel, Marc - ***The Time Of The Fire*** [1955]	$ .75	$2.50	$5.00
1333	Greene, Graham - ***Orient Express*** [1955] Cover by Gross.	$ .50	$1.50	$3.00
1334	Hix, Elsie - ***Strange As It Seems*** [1955]	$ .75	$2.50	$5.00
A-1335	Masters, John - ***The Lotus And The Wind*** [1955] Cover by Barye Phillips.	$ .75	$2.50	$5.00
A-1336	Giles, Janice Holt - ***The Kentuckians*** [1955]	$1.00	$3.00	$6.00
F-1337	Gibson, William - ***The Cobweb*** [1955] Part photo cover.	$ .75	$2.50	$5.00
F-1338	Warren, Robert Penn - ***All The King's Men*** [1955]	$1.00	$3.00	$6.00
A-1339	Maugham, W. Somerset - ***The Moon And Sixpence*** [1955]	$ .75	$2.50	$5.00
A-1340	Karig, Captain Walt - ***Don't Tread On Me*** [1955]	$ .75	$2.50	$5.00
A-1342	Cerf, Bennett - ***Laughter, Incorporated*** [1955]	$ .50	$1.50	$3.00
1343	Tucker, Wilson - ***Man From Tomorrow*** [1955]	$1.35	$4.00	$8.00

		G	VG	F
1344	O'Rourke, Frank - ***High Dive*** [1955]	$ .75	$2.50	$5.00
1345	Webber, Gordon - ***The Far Shore*** [1955]	$ .75	$2.50	$5.00
1346	Short, Luke - editor - ***Cattle, Guns & Men*** [1955] PBO. Cover by Gross. Includes Elmore Leonard.	$ .75	$2.50	$5.00
1347	Gruber, Frank - ***Johnny Vengeance*** [1955]	$ .75	$2.50	$5.00
1348	The Gordons - ***FBI Story*** [1955]	$ .75	$2.50	$5.00
1349	Barbette, Jay - ***Death's Long Shadow*** [1955] Cover by Mitchell Hooks.	$ .75	$2.50	$5.00
F-1350	Michener, James A. - ***The Fires Of Spring*** [1955]	$ .75	$2.50	$5.00
1351	Kantor, MacKinlay - ***God And My Country*** [1955]	$ .75	$2.50	$5.00
1352	Anthology edited by Groff Conklin - ***Science-Fiction Thinking Machines*** [1955] Cover by Powers.	$1.35	$4.00	$8.00
A-1353	Lamb, Harold - ***Alexander Of Macedon*** [1955]	$ .75	$2.50	$5.00
A-1355	Fosburgh, Hugh - ***View From The Air*** [1955]	$ .75	$2.50	$5.00
1356	Short, Luke - ***Station West*** [1955]	$ .75	$2.50	$5.00
A-1357	O'Flaherty, Liam - ***The Informer*** [1955]	$ .75	$2.50	$5.00
A-1358	Steiner, Paul - ***Women And Children First*** [1955]	$ .75	$2.50	$5.00
1359	Benson, Ben - ***The Girl In The Cage*** [1955]	$ .75	$2.50	$5.00
1360	MacDonald, John Ross - ***Find A Victim*** [1955] Cover by Mitchell Hooks.	$1.35	$4.00	$8.00
1361	Dawson, Peter - ***The Big Outfit*** [1955]	$ .75	$2.50	$5.00
1362	Russell, Eric Frank - ***Deep Space*** [1955] Cover by Mel Hunter.	$1.35	$4.00	$8.00
1363	Anthology edited by Peter Dawson - ***The Killers*** [1955]	$1.25	$3.75	$7.50
1364	Nickels, Marione R., editor - ***Honey, I'm Home*** [1955] Cartoon book.	$ .75	$2.50	$5.00
F-1365	Henderson, Dr. John - ***The Complete Book Of First Aid*** [1955]	$ .75	$2.50	$5.00
F-1366	Schoonover, Lawrence - ***The Spider King*** [1955]	$ .75	$2.50	$5.00
F-1367	Anthology - ***New Campus Writing*** [1955]	$1.35	$4.00	$8.00
A-1368	Phillips, John - ***The Second Happiest Day*** [1955]	$ .75	$2.50	$5.00
A-1369	Huxley, Aldous - ***Brave New World*** [1955]	$ .75	$2.50	$5.00
A-1370	Gerson, Noel B. - ***Port Royal*** [1955]	$ .75	$2.50	$5.00
1371	Axlerod, George - ***The Seven Year Itch*** [1955] Marilyn Monroe photo cover. Movie tie-in.	$4.00	$12.50	$25.00
1372	Martin, Robert - ***Tears For The Bride*** [1955]	$ .75	$2.50	$5.00
1373	Short, Luke - ***Hardcase*** [1955]	$ .75	$2.50	$5.00
A-1374	Jessup, M. K. - ***The Case For The U.F.O.*** [1955]	$ .75	$2.50	$5.00
A-1375	Brown, Croswell - ***They Went Wrong*** [1955]	$ .75	$2.50	$5.00
1376	Fisher, Steve - ***Giveaway*** [1955] Cover by Hill.	$1.00	$3.00	$6.00
1377	Chevallier, Gabrielle - ***Scandals Of Clochmerle*** [1955]	$ .75	$2.50	$5.00
A-1378	Pinto, Mario Lo - ***The Art Of Italian Cooking*** [1955]	$ .75	$2.50	$5.00
F-1379	Arnold, Elliott - ***The Time Of The Gringo*** [1955]	$ .75	$2.50	$5.00
1381	Masters, John - ***Bhowani Junction*** [1955] Cover by Hooks. Movie tie-in.	$ .75	$2.50	$5.00
A-1382	Lamb, Harold - ***Genghis Khan The Conqueror*** [1955] Cover by Binger.	$ .75	$2.50	$5.00
1383	Ullman, James Ramsey - ***The Sands Of Karakorum*** [1955] Cover by Hooks.	$ .75	$2.50	$5.00
1384	Holmes, L. P. - ***Delta Deputy*** [1955]	$ .75	$2.50	$5.00
1385	Halleran, E. E. - ***Winter Ambush*** [1955]	$ .75	$2.50	$5.00
1386	Stout, Rex - ***The Black Mountain*** [1955]	$1.00	$3.00	$6.00
1387	Stout, Rex - ***The Golden Spiders*** [1955]	$1.00	$3.00	$6.00
1388	Stout, Rex - ***Three Men Out*** [1955]	$1.00	$3.00	$6.00
1389	Anthology ed. by Henry Boltinoff - ***The Howls Of Ivy*** [1955] PBO. Cartoon Book.	$ .75	$2.50	$5.00
1390	L'Amour, Louis - ***Guns Of The Timberlands*** [1955]	$2.50	$7.50	$15.00
A-1391	Hunter, J. A. - ***Hunter*** [1955]	$ .65	$2.00	$4.00
A-1392	Anthology edited by William Manners - ***The Do-It-Yourself Gadget Hunter's Guide*** [1955] Photo cover.	$ .65	$2.00	$4.00
F-1393	Lund, Robert - ***The Alaskan*** [1955] Cover by Hooks.	$ .75	$2.50	$5.00
1394	Stout, Rex - ***Trouble In Triplicate*** [1955]	$1.00	$3.00	$6.00

		G	VG	F
1395	Stout, Rex - ***Too Many Women*** [1955]	$1.00	$3.00	$6.00
1396	Dawson, Peter - ***Dead Man Pass*** [1955]	$ .65	$2.00	$4.00
1397	Martin, Robert - ***The Widow And The Web*** [1955] Cover by Hooks.	$ .65	$2.00	$4.00
1398	McConnaughey, Susanne - ***Pagan In Paradise*** [1955]	$ .65	$2.00	$4.00
A-1399	Maugham, W. Somerset - ***Stranger In Paris*** [1955]	$ .65	$2.00	$4.00
1400	Tucker, Wilson - ***Time: X*** [1955]	$1.35	$4.00	$8.00
A-1401	Anthology edited by Luke Short - ***Frontier: 150 Years Of The West*** [1955] PBO. Cover by Bates.	$1.35	$4.00	$8.00
A-1402	Horan, James D. - ***King's Rebel*** [1955] Cover by Hooks.	$ .65	$2.00	$4.00
A-1403	Starrett, Vincent - ***Best Loved Books Of The Twentieth Century*** [1955] PBO.	$ .65	$2.00	$4.00
1404	Key, Ted - ***Hazel*** [1955] Cover by Ted Key. Cartoon Book.	$1.25	$3.75	$7.50
A-1405	Bonner, Paul Hyde - ***Hotel Tallyrand*** [1955] Cover by Barye Phillips.	$ .65	$2.00	$4.00
1406	Steinbeck, John - ***The Red Pony*** [1955]	$ .65	$2.00	$4.00
1407	Thompson, Thomas - ***The Steel Web*** [1956]	$ .65	$2.00	$4.00
1408	Alexander, David - ***Terror On Broadway*** [1956]	$ .65	$2.00	$4.00
1409	Spicer, Bart - ***The Taming Of Carney Wilde*** [1956]	$ .65	$2.00	$4.00
A-1410	Krepps, Robert W. - ***The Courts Of The Lion*** [1956] Cover by Barye Phillips.	$ .65	$2.00	$4.00
A-1411	Henry, Will - ***Who Rides With Wyatt*** [1956] Cover by Bates.	$ .75	$2.50	$5.00
A-1412	Steinbeck, John - ***Sweet Thursday*** [1956] Cover by Barye Phillips.	$ .65	$2.00	$4.00
A-1413	Lindner, Robert - ***The Fifty-Minute Hour*** [1956]	$ .65	$2.00	$4.00
A-1414	Byrne, Bendran - ***Three Weeks To A Better Memory*** [1956]	$ .65	$2.00	$4.00
F-1415	Dodson, Kenneth - ***Away All Boats*** [1956]	$ .65	$2.00	$4.00
F-1416	Masters, John - ***Coromandel!*** [1956]	$ .65	$2.00	$4.00
F-1417	Short, Luke - ***Three Complete Western Novels*** [1956]	$ .65	$2.00	$4.00
A-1418	Jenkins, Dorothy H. - ***The Complete Book Of Roses*** [1956] PBO. Sixteen color photos of roses.	$ .75	$2.50	$5.00
1419	Stuart, Matthew - ***Deep Hills*** [1956]	$ .65	$2.00	$4.00
1420	Wilmer, Dale - ***Dead Fall*** [1956]	$ .65	$2.00	$4.00
1421	Benson, Ben - ***The Burning Fuse*** [1956]	$ .65	$2.00	$4.00
1422	O'Hara, John - ***Hope Of Heaven*** [1956] Cover by Barye Phillips.	$ .65	$2.00	$4.00
1423	Brown, Fredric - ***Star Shine*** [1956]	$ .75	$2.50	$5.00
A-1424	Greene, Graham - ***The Heart Of The Matter*** [1956]	$ .65	$2.00	$4.00
A-1425	Frankland, Edward - ***The Long Swords*** [1956]	$ .65	$2.00	$4.00
A-1426	Roberts, Richard Emery - ***Last Frontier*** [1956]	$ .65	$2.00	$4.00
A-1427	Waldo, Myra - ***The Round-The-World Cookbook*** [1956]	$ .75	$2.50	$5.00
F-1428	Bishop, Jim - ***The Day Lincoln Was Shot*** [1956]	$ .65	$2.00	$4.00
F-1429	Cronin, A. J. - ***The Citadel*** [1956]	$ .65	$2.00	$4.00
F-1430	Anthology - ***Model Railroading*** [1956]	$ .75	$2.50	$5.00
F-1431	Robbins, Harold - ***The Dream Merchants*** [1956]	$ .65	$2.00	$4.00
1432	Lees, Hannah - ***Woman Doctor*** [1956]	$ .50	$1.50	$3.00
1433	Hancock, L. A. - ***Graduate Nurse*** [1956]	$ .50	$1.50	$3.00
1434	Marshall, M. M. - ***Ward Nurse*** [1956]	$ .50	$1.50	$3.00
1435	McCaig, Robert - ***Haywire Town*** [1956]	$ .65	$2.00	$4.00
1436	Brown, Fredric - ***His Name Was Death*** [1956] Cover by Hooks.	$2.50	$7.50	$15.00
1437	Felsen, Henry Gregor - ***Street Rod*** [1956]	$ .65	$2.00	$4.00
1438	Heath, William - ***Violent Saturday*** [1956]	$ .65	$2.00	$4.00
A-1439	Burman, Ben Lucien - ***The Four Lives Of Mundy Tolliver*** [1956]	$ .65	$2.00	$4.00
F-1441	Anthology - ***Golden Argosy*** [1956]	$ .65	$2.00	$4.00
F-1442	Edited by William Oliver Stevens - ***The Inspirational Reader*** [1956]	$ .65	$2.00	$4.00
A-1443	Stuart, W. J. - ***Forbidden Planet*** [1956] Movie tie-in.	$4.00	$12.50	$25.00
F-1444	Costain, Thomas B. - ***For My Great Folly*** [1956]	$ .65	$2.00	$4.00

		G	VG	F
F-1445	Twain, Mark - ***Life On The Mississippi*** [1956]	$ .50	$1.50	$3.00
1446	Short, Luke - ***High Vermillion*** [1956]	$ .65	$2.00	$4.00
1447	Carr, John Dickson - ***The Third Bullet*** [1956]	$ .65	$2.00	$4.00
1448	Black, Thomas - ***Million Dollar Murder*** [1956] Cover by Hooks.	$ .65	$2.00	$4.00
A-1450	Wallace, Lew - ***Ben Hur*** [1956]	$ .75	$2.50	$5.00
1451	Trimble, Louis - ***Crossfire*** [1956]	$ .65	$2.00	$4.00
A-1452	Edited by Charles Neider - ***Man Against Nature*** [1956]	$ .65	$2.00	$4.00
F-1453	Marquand, John P. - ***Sincerely, Willis Wade*** [1956]	$ .65	$2.00	$4.00
F-1454	Marquand, John P. - ***Point Of No Return*** [1956]	$ .65	$2.00	$4.00
1455	The Gordons - ***The Case Of The Talking Bug*** [1956]	$ .75	$2.50	$5.00
F-1456	Schoonover, Lawrence - ***The Burnished Blade*** [1956]	$ .65	$2.00	$4.00
1457	Inge, William - ***Picnic*** [1956] Photo cover. Movie tie-in.	$ .75	$2.50	$5.00
A-1458	Rostand, Edmond - ***Cyrano de Bergerac*** [1956]	$ .65	$2.00	$4.00
F-1459	Shapiro, Lionel - ***The Sixth Of June*** [1956]	$ .65	$2.00	$4.00
1460	Keller, Reamer - ***Why The Long Puss?*** [1956] PBO. Cover by Reamer Keller. Cartoon Book.	$ .75	$2.50	$5.00
1461	Hopson, William - ***Cry Viva!*** [1956]	$ .65	$2.00	$4.00
A-1462	Jackson, Felix - ***So Help Me God*** [1956]	$ .65	$2.00	$4.00
A-1463	Schulberg, Budd - ***The Harder They Fall*** [1956]	$ .65	$2.00	$4.00
A-1464	Cardoza, Peter - ***A Wonderful World For Children*** [1956]	$ .65	$2.00	$4.00
A-1465	Ullman, James Ramsey - ***Tiger Of The Snows*** [1956]	$ .65	$2.00	$4.00
1466	Short, Luke - ***Rimrock*** [1956]	$ .65	$2.00	$4.00
1467	Prescott, John - ***The Renegade*** [1956]	$ .65	$2.00	$4.00
1468	Benson, Ben - ***The Silver Cobweb*** [1956]	$ .65	$2.00	$4.00
1469	Hansen, Robert P. - ***Trouble Comes Double*** [1956]	$ .65	$2.00	$4.00
A-1470	Maine, Charles Eric - ***Timeliner*** [1956]	$ .65	$2.00	$4.00
1471	Maresca, James - ***My Flag Is Down*** [1956]	$ .65	$2.00	$4.00
A-1472	Carr, John Dickson - ***Captain Cut-Throat*** [1956]	$ .75	$2.50	$5.00
F-1473	Wilder, Robert - ***The Wine Of Youth*** [1956]	$ .65	$2.00	$4.00
F-1474	Cronin, A. J. - ***The Keys Of The Kingdom*** [1956]	$ .65	$2.00	$4.00
1475	The Gordons - ***Campaign Train*** [1956]	$ .75	$2.50	$5.00
1476	Herber, William E. - ***Some Die Slow*** [1956] Cover by Hooks.	$ .75	$2.50	$5.00
1477	Key, Ted - ***Here's Hazel*** [1956] Cover by Ted Key. Cartoon Book.	$1.00	$3.00	$6.00
A-1478	Steinbeck, John - ***The Pastures Of Heaven*** [1956]	$ .65	$2.00	$4.00
1479	Hahn, Emily - ***With Naked Foot*** [1956] Cover by Barye Phillips.	$ .65	$2.00	$4.00
A-1480	Greene, Graham - ***The Ship Wrecked*** [1956]	$ .65	$2.00	$4.00
A-1481	Henry, Will - ***The Raiders*** [1956]	$ .65	$2.00	$4.00
A-1482	Henry, Will - ***The Fourth Horseman*** [1956]	$ .65	$2.00	$4.00
A-1483	Henry, Will - ***Pillars Of The Sky*** [1956]	$ .65	$2.00	$4.00
A-1484	O'Hara, John - ***Great Short Stories Of John O'Hara*** [1956] Cover by Barye Phillips.	$ .65	$2.00	$4.00
1485	Short, Luke - ***Vengeance Valley*** [1956]	$ .65	$2.00	$4.00
1486	L'Amour, Louis - ***The Burning Hills*** [1956]	$2.50	$7.50	$15.00
1487	Masterson, Whit - ***A Cry In The Night*** [1956]	$ .65	$2.00	$4.00
1488	Gruber, Frank - ***The Limping Goose*** [1956] Cover by Barye Phillips.	$ .65	$2.00	$4.00
1489	Maugham, W. Somerset - ***Up At The Villa*** [1956] Cover by Hooks.	$ .65	$2.00	$4.00
A-1490	Huxley, Aldous - ***The Genuis And The Goddess*** [1956]	$ .75	$2.50	$5.00
A-1491	O'Connor, Richard - ***Guns Of Chickamauga*** [1956]	$ .65	$2.00	$4.00
A-1492	Kornbluth, C. M. - ***Not This August*** [1956]	$1.50	$5.00	$10.00
A-1493	Loewenstein, Prince Leopold - ***Analyze Yourself*** [1956]	$ .50	$1.50	$3.00
F-1494	Santee, Ross - ***Lost Pony Tracks*** [1956] Photo cover.	$ .65	$2.00	$4.00
F-1495	Santee, Ross - ***Apache Land*** [1956]	$ .65	$2.00	$4.00
1496	Humphries, Adelaide - ***Nurse Landon's Challenge*** [1956]	$ .50	$1.50	$3.00
S-1497	Tolstoy, Leo - ***War And Peace*** [1956] Cover by John Groth.	$ .65	$2.00	$4.00
1498	McElfresh, Adeline - ***Doctor Jane*** [1956]	$ .50	$1.50	$3.00

		G	VG	F
A-1499	Waldo, Myra - ***Dining Out In Any Language*** [1956] PBO. Cover by Muni.	$ .75	$2.50	$5.00
F-1500	Arnold, Elliott - ***Blood Brother*** [1956]	$ .65	$2.00	$4.00
1501	Farrell, Cliff - ***Follow The New Grass*** [1956]	$ .65	$2.00	$4.00
1503	Carr, John Dickson - ***The Problem Of The Wire Cage*** [1956]	$ .75	$2.50	$5.00
1504	Carr, John Dickson - ***The Man Who Could Not Shudder*** [1956]	$ .75	$2.50	$5.00
1505	Carr, John Dickson - ***The Problem Of The Green Capsule*** [1956]	$ .75	$2.50	$5.00
1506	Werry, Richard R. - ***Hammer Me Home*** [1956] Cover by Barye Phillips.	$ .65	$2.00	$4.00
1507	Miller, R. Dewitt - ***Reincarnation - The Whole Startling Story*** [1956]	$ .65	$2.00	$4.00
A-1508	Van de Water, Frederic F. - ***The Green Cockade*** [1956]	$ .65	$2.00	$4.00
A-1509	Kipling, Rudyard - ***Captains Courageous*** [1956]	$ .65	$2.00	$4.00
F-1510	Schulberg, Budd - ***Waterfront*** [1956] Movie tie-in.	$ .75	$2.50	$5.00
1511	Frank, Pat - ***Hold Back The Night*** [1956]	$ .65	$2.00	$4.00
1513	Forbes, Kathryn - ***Mama's Bank Account*** [1956] TV & movie tie-in.	$ .65	$2.00	$4.00
1514	Holmes, L. P. - ***Somewhere They Die*** [1956]	$ .65	$2.00	$4.00
1515	Loomis, Noel M. - ***The Buscadero*** [1956]	$ .65	$2.00	$4.00
1516	Innes, Hammond - ***Campbell's Kingdom*** [1956]	$ .65	$2.00	$4.00
1517	Burton, Carl D. - ***Satan's Rock*** [1956] Cover by Hooks.	$ .75	$2.50	$5.00
1518	Inge, William - ***Bus Stop*** [1956] Movie tie-in with Marilyn Monroe photo cover.	$3.50	$10.00	$20.00
A-1519	Bradbury, Ray - ***The Circus Of Dr. Lao*** [1956] PBO. Cover by D. Swartz.	$2.50	$7.50	$15.00
F-1520	Dumas, Alexandre - ***The Count Of Monte Cristo*** [1956]	$ .65	$2.00	$4.00
1523	Edited by Jerome Beatty, Jr. - ***Sex Rears Its Lovely Head*** [1956] PBO. Cover by Burr Shafer. Cartoon Book.	$ .75	$2.50	$5.00
A-1525	Grierson, Edward - ***The Royalist*** [1956] Cover by Hooks.	$ .65	$2.00	$4.00
F-1526	Hugo, Victor - ***The Hunchback Of Notre Dame*** [1956] Cover by Barye Phillips.	$1.00	$3.00	$6.00
1527	Gruber, Frank - ***Bitter Sage*** [1956] Cover by George Gross. Movie tie-in.	$ .65	$2.00	$4.00
A-1528	Miller, Harry - ***Puppy And Dog Care*** [1956] Photo cover.	$ .65	$2.00	$4.00
1529	Hersey, John - ***Hiroshima*** [1956]	$ .65	$2.00	$4.00
1531	Short, Luke - ***Sunset Graze*** [1956]	$ .65	$2.00	$4.00
1532	Short, Luke - ***Gunman's Chance*** [1956] Cover by William George.	$ .65	$2.00	$4.00
1533	Short, Luke - ***Coroner Creek*** [1956] Cover by William George.	$ .65	$2.00	$4.00
1534	Alexander, David - ***Paint The Town Black*** [1956]	$ .65	$2.00	$4.00
1535	Roberts, Lee - ***The Pale Door*** [1956]	$ .65	$2.00	$4.00
F-1536	Cronin, A. J. - ***The Green Years*** [1956] Cover by Mitchell Hooks.	$ .65	$2.00	$4.00
F-1537	Cronin, A. J. - ***Shannon's Way*** [1956]	$ .65	$2.00	$4.00
1538	Felsen, Henry Gregor - ***Rag Top*** [1956] Cover by Hooks.	$ .65	$2.00	$4.00
1539	Lord, Walter - ***A Night To Remember*** [1956]	$ .65	$2.00	$4.00
A-1540	Wilder, Robert - ***Written On The Wind*** [1956]	$ .65	$2.00	$4.00
1541	Smith, H. Allen - ***The Age Of The Tail*** [1956]	$ .65	$2.00	$4.00
1542	Millar, Margaret - ***Beasts In View*** [1956] Cover by Hooks.	$ .75	$2.50	$5.00
1543	Masterson, Whit - ***Dead, She Was Beautiful*** [1956] Cover by Barye Phillips.	$ .75	$2.50	$5.00
1544	Steinbeck, John - ***The Pearl*** [1956]	$ .65	$2.00	$4.00
A-1545	Lamb, Harold - ***Omar Khayyam*** [1956] Cover by Barye Phillips.	$ .65	$2.00	$4.00
A-1546	Brown, Fredric - ***Martians, Go Home*** [1956]	$1.50	$5.00	$10.00
1547	Burnett, W. R. - ***Adobe Walls*** [1956]	$ .65	$2.00	$4.00
1549	O'Rourke, Frank - ***Latigo*** [1956]	$ .65	$2.00	$4.00

		G	VG	F
A-1550	Burnett, Whit & Hallie - ***19 Tales Of Terror*** [1957] PBO. Cover by Tom Hill.	$2.00	$6.00	$12.00
1551	Sumner, Nick - ***The Boss Of Broken Spur*** [1956]	$ .65	$2.00	$4.00
1552	Benson, Ben - ***Broken Shield*** [1957] Cover by Barye Phillips.	$ .65	$2.00	$4.00
A-1553	Frank, Pat - ***Forbidden Area*** [1957] Cover by Barye Phillips.	$ .65	$2.00	$4.00
F-1554	O'Hara, John - ***Ten North Frederick*** [1957] Cover by Hooks.	$ .65	$2.00	$4.00
A-1555	Steinbeck, John - ***The Wayward Bus*** [1957]	$ .75	$2.50	$5.00
F-1556	Edited by Robert Penn Warren - ***New Southern Harvest*** [1957]	$ .65	$2.00	$4.00
1557	Williams, Jay - ***The Siege*** [1957] Cover by Barye Phillips.	$ .65	$2.00	$4.00
F-1558	Black, Lucy & Johnson, Jr., Pyke - ***Cartoon Treasury*** [1957]	$ .75	$2.50	$5.00
1559	Nash, N. Richard - ***The Rainmaker*** [1957] Movie tie-in. Movie photo cover.	$ .75	$2.50	$5.00
A-1560	Huxley, Aldous - ***Antic Hay*** [1957] Cover by Barye Phillips.	$ .65	$2.00	$4.00
1561	Ellson, Hal - ***Tomboy*** [1957] Cover by Mitch Hooks.	$ .65	$2.00	$4.00
1562	MacDonald, Zillah K. - ***Nurse Fairchild's Decision*** [1957]	$ .50	$1.50	$3.00
1564	Short, Luke - ***Dead Freight For Piute*** [1957]	$ .65	$2.00	$4.00
1565	Brown, Fredric - ***The Wench Is Dead*** [1957] Cover by Mitchell Hooks.	$5.50	$17.50	$35.00
1566	Brown, Fredric - ***The Fabulous Clipjoint*** [1957]	$1.50	$5.00	$10.00
1567	Brown, Fredric - ***Death Has Many Doors*** [1957] Cover by Barye Phillips.	$1.50	$5.00	$10.00
F-1568	Waugh, Alec - ***Island In The Sun*** [1957]	$ .65	$2.00	$4.00
A-1569	Wolford, Nelson & Shirley - ***Dragoon*** [1957] Cover by Hooks.	$ .65	$2.00	$4.00
A-1570	Anderson, Thomas - ***Your Own Beloved Sons*** [1957]	$ .65	$2.00	$4.00
A-1571	Matheson, Richard - ***The Shores Of Space*** [1957] PBO.	$5.50	$17.50	$35.00
F-1572	Lewis, Sinclair - ***Cass Timberlane*** [1957]	$ .65	$2.00	$4.00
1574	Fante, John - ***Full Of Life*** [1957]	$ .65	$2.00	$4.00
1575	Marshall, M. M. - ***Nurse With Wings*** [1957]	$ .50	$1.50	$3.00
1576	Miller, Frank - ***Tejas Country*** [1957] Cover by Bill George.	$ .65	$2.00	$4.00
1577	Martin, Robert - ***The Tough Die Hard*** [1957]	$ .65	$2.00	$4.00
A-1578	Matthiessen, Peter - ***The Year Of The Tempest*** [1957]	$ .65	$2.00	$4.00
F-1579	Boyd, James - ***Bitter Creek*** [1957]	$ .65	$2.00	$4.00
F-1580	Gilbert, Edwin - ***Native Stone*** [1957] Cover by Hooks.	$ .65	$2.00	$4.00
S-1581	Farmer, Fannie - ***The Boston Cooking School Cook Book*** [1957]	$2.50	$7.50	$15.00
A-1582	Piersall, Jim & Hirshberg, Al - ***Fear Strikes Out*** [1957] Photo cover. Movie tie-in.	$ .75	$2.50	$5.00
F-1583	O'Hara, John - ***A Rage To Live*** [1957]	$ .65	$2.00	$4.00
1584	Heuman, William - ***Captain McRae*** [1957] Cover by Barye Phillips.	$ .65	$2.00	$4.00
1585	Seifert, Elizabeth - ***Dr. Woodward's Ambition*** [1957]	$ .50	$1.50	$3.00
A-1586	Tarkington, Booth - ***Seventeen*** [1957]	$ .50	$1.50	$3.00
A-1587	Forester, C. S. - ***The Good Shepherd*** [1957]	$ .65	$2.00	$4.00
1588	Short, Luke - ***The Feud At Single Shot*** [1957]	$ .65	$2.00	$4.00
1589	Herber, William E. - ***Live Bait For Murder*** [1957] Cover by Hooks.	$ .65	$2.00	$4.00
1590	Fosburgh, Hugh - ***The Sound Of White Water*** [1957]	$ .65	$2.00	$4.00
F-1591	Millar, George - ***A Crossbowman's Story*** [1957]	$ .65	$2.00	$4.00
1592	West, Ruth - ***Stop Dieting! Start Losing!*** [1957]	$ .50	$1.50	$3.00
A-1593	Robinson, Frank M. - ***The Power*** [1957]	$ .65	$2.00	$4.00
1594	O'Hara, John - ***The Farmer's Hotel*** [1957]	$ .65	$2.00	$4.00
1595	Martin, George Victor - ***The Bells Of St. Mary's*** [1957]	$ .50	$1.50	$3.00
1596	Ward, Brad - ***The Baron Of Boot Hill*** [1957]	$ .65	$2.00	$4.00
F-1597	Conrad, Joseph - ***Lord Jim*** [1957]	$ .65	$2.00	$4.00
A-1598	Gruber, Frank - ***The Big Land*** [1957] Cover by Muni. Movie tie-in.	$ .75	$2.50	$5.00
F-1599	Heinrich, Willi - ***The Cross Of Iron*** [1957]	$ .65	$2.00	$4.00
A-1600	Ballard, Willis T. - ***The Package Deal*** [1957]	$ .65	$2.00	$4.00
1601	Alexander, David - ***Shoot A Sitting Duck*** [1957]	$ .65	$2.00	$4.00

		G	VG	F
1602	Gault, William Campbell - ***Square In The Middle*** [1957] Cover by Kokinos.	$ .65	$2.00	$4.00
A-1603	Laird, Charlton - ***West Of The River*** [1957]	$ .65	$2.00	$4.00
F-1604	Maugham, A. M. - ***Harry Of Monmouth*** [1957]	$ .65	$2.00	$4.00
1606	Weisinger, Mort - ***1001 Things You Can Get Free #2*** [1957] Cover by Roy Doty	$ .50	$1.50	$3.00
1607	Wesley, Elizabeth - ***Nora Meade, M.D.*** [1957]	$ .50	$1.50	$3.00
A-1608	Savage, Thomas - ***The Pass*** [1957]	$ .65	$2.00	$4.00
S-1609	Kipling, Rudyard - ***A Treasury Of Short Stories*** [1957]	$ .75	$2.50	$5.00
1610	Forester, C. S. - ***The Gun*** [1957] Cover by William George. Movie tie-in.	$ .75	$2.50	$5.00
A-1611	Forester, C. S. - ***Randall And The River Of Time*** [1957]	$ .50	$1.50	$3.00
1612	Cheshire, Giff - ***Starlight Basin*** [1957] Cover by William George.	$ .50	$1.50	$3.00
1613	MacDonald, Ross - ***The Barbarous Coast*** [1957]	$2.00	$6.00	$12.00
1614	Judson, Jeanne - ***Visiting Nurse*** [1957]	$ .50	$1.50	$3.00
A-1615	Brown, Fredric & Reynolds, Mack - editors - ***Science Fiction Carnival*** [1957]	$3.00	$9.00	$18.00
F-1616	Anthology - ***Amy Vanderbilt's Everyday Etiquette*** [1957]	$ .50	$1.50	$3.00
A-1617	Schulberg, Budd - ***What Makes Sammy Run?*** [1957]	$ .50	$1.50	$3.00
1618	Loring, Emile - ***For All Your Life*** [1957]	$ .50	$1.50	$3.00
A-1619	Forester, C. S. - ***The Ship*** [1957]	$ .50	$1.50	$3.00
F-1620	Allen, Frederick Lewis - ***Only Yesterday*** [1957]	$ .50	$1.50	$3.00
A-1621	Connell, Vivian - ***The Chinese Room*** [1957]	$ .50	$1.50	$3.00
F-1622	Huxley, Aldous - ***Eyeless In Gaza*** [1957]	$ .50	$1.50	$3.00
1623	Keller, Reamer - ***Mating Manual*** [1957]	$ .50	$1.50	$3.00
F-1624	Cronin, A. J. - ***A Thing Of Beauty*** [1957]	$ .50	$1.50	$3.00
A-1625	Kantor, MacKinley - ***Arouse And Beware*** [1957]	$ .50	$1.50	$3.00
A-1626	Fowler, Gene - ***Beau James*** [1957] Cover by Hooks. Movie tie-in with Bob Hope.	$ .65	$2.00	$4.00
A-1627	Haycox, Ernest - ***Long Storm*** [1957]	$ .50	$1.50	$3.00
1628	Haycox, Ernest - ***The Wild Bunch*** [1957]	$ .50	$1.50	$3.00
A-1630	Moore, Pamela - ***Chocolates For Breakfast*** [1957] Photo cover.	$ .50	$1.50	$3.00
A-1631	Stout, Rex - ***Triple Jeopardy*** [1957]	$ .65	$2.00	$4.00
A-1632	Stout, Rex - ***Before Midnight*** [1957]	$ .65	$2.00	$4.00
A-1633	Stout, Rex - ***Three Witnesses*** [1957] Cover by Muni.	$ .65	$2.00	$4.00
A-1634	Baron, Alexander - ***The Golden Princess*** [1957] Cover by Zuckerberg.	$ .50	$1.50	$3.00
A-1635	Schulberg, Budd - ***A Face In The Crowd*** [1957] Movie tie-in.	$ .50	$1.50	$3.00
A-1636	Hilton, James - ***Goodbye, Mr. Chips*** [1957] Cover by Hooks.	$ .50	$1.50	$3.00
F-1637	Wilder, Robert - ***God Has A Long Face*** [1957] Cover by Hooks.	$ .50	$1.50	$3.00
1638	Gault, William Campbell - ***Day Of The Ram*** [1957] Cover by Hooks.	$ .50	$1.50	$3.00
1639	Carder, Michael - ***Return Of The Outlaw*** [1957]	$ .50	$1.50	$3.00
1640	O'Hara, John - ***A Family Party*** [1957] Cover by Schwartz.	$ .50	$1.50	$3.00
A-1641	Michener, James A. - ***Sayonara*** [1957]	$ .50	$1.50	$3.00
1642	Dawson, Peter - ***Man On The Buckskin*** [1957]	$ .50	$1.50	$3.00
F-1643	Laing, Alexander - ***Jonathan Eagle*** [1957] Cover by Zuckerberg.	$ .50	$1.50	$3.00
1645	Marshall, M. M. - ***Her Soul To Keep*** [1957]	$ .50	$1.50	$3.00
A-1646	Asimov, Isaac - ***Pebble In The Sky*** [1957]	$ .65	$2.00	$4.00
F-1647	Cohn, Art - ***The Joker Is Wild*** [1957]	$ .50	$1.50	$3.00
F-1648	Edmonds, Walter D. - ***Drums Along The Mohawk*** [1957]	$ .50	$1.50	$3.00
F-1649	Edited by Nolan Miller - ***New Campus Writing II*** [1957]	$1.35	$4.00	$8.00
A-1650	Michener, James A. - ***The Bridge At Andau*** [1957] Photo cover.	$ .65	$2.00	$4.00
A-1651	Engel, Louis - ***How To Buy Stocks*** [1957]	$ .50	$1.50	$3.00
1652	Short, Luke - ***Raiders Of The Rimrock*** [1957] Cover by Abbett.	$ .65	$2.00	$4.00

		G	VG	F
A-1653	Axelrod, George - ***Will Success Spoil Rock Hunter?*** [1957] Photo cover. Movie tie-in. Sixteen pages of photos of Jayne Mansfield.	$1.50	$5.00	$10.00
1654	Prescott, John - ***Wagon Train*** [1957]	$1.25	$3.75	$7.50
1655	Alexander, David - ***Die, Little Goose*** [1957] Cover by Mitchell Hooks.	$ .65	$2.00	$4.00
A-1656	Sheldon, Walt - ***The Man Who Paid His Way*** [1957]	$ .65	$2.00	$4.00
A-1657	Edwards, Samuel - ***The Scimitar*** [1957] Cover by Barye Phillips.	$ .50	$1.50	$3.00
A-1658	Anthology - ***100 Stories Of Business Success*** [1957]	$ .50	$1.50	$3.00
F-1659	O'Connor, Edwin - ***The Last Hurrah*** [1957] Movie tie-in.	$ .65	$2.00	$4.00
F-1660	Williams, Ben Ames - ***The Strange Woman*** [1957]	$ .50	$1.50	$3.00
F-1661	Downey, Fairfax - ***Indian-Fighting Army*** [1957] Photo cover.	$ .50	$1.50	$3.00
F-1662	Vestal, Stanley - ***The Old Santa Fe Trail*** [1957] Photo cover.	$ .50	$1.50	$3.00
S-1663	Anthology - ***Model Railroading*** [1957]	$ .50	$1.50	$3.00
A-1664	Wilder, Robert - ***Flamingo Road*** [1957] Cover by Zuckerberg.	$ .50	$1.50	$3.00
F-1665	Henderson, Dr. John - ***A Parents' Guide To Children's Illnesses*** [1957]	$ .40	$1.25	$2.50
1666	Gruber, Frank - ***Bugles West*** [1957]	$ .50	$1.50	$3.00
1667	Judson, Jeanne - ***Carol Trent, Air Stewardess*** [1957]	$ .40	$1.25	$2.50
1668	Short, Luke - ***The Whip*** [1957]	$ .50	$1.50	$3.00
A-1669	Greene, Graham - ***The Quiet American*** [1957]	$ .50	$1.50	$3.00
A-1670	Earl, Lawrence - ***The Frozen Jungle*** [1957] Cover by Barye Phillips.	$ .50	$1.50	$3.00
A-1671	Ambler, Eric - ***State Of Siege*** [1957]	$ .50	$1.50	$3.00
A-1672	Sheckley, Robert - ***Pilgrimage To Earth*** [1957] PBO.	$1.25	$3.75	$7.50
F-1673	Schoonover, Lawrence - ***The Queen's Cross*** [1957] Cover by Hooks.	$ .50	$1.50	$3.00
F-1674	Michener, James A. - ***Return To Paradise*** [1957]	$ .50	$1.50	$3.00
F-1675	Marquand, John P. - ***H.M. Pulham, ESQ.*** [1957]	$ .40	$1.25	$2.50
A-1676	Seton, Ernest Thompson - ***Wild Animals I Have Known*** [1957]	$ .50	$1.50	$3.00
A-1677	Boulle, Pierre - ***The Bridge Over The River Kwai*** [1957] Movie tie-in.	$ .65	$2.00	$4.00
F-1678	Hugo, Victor - ***The Hunchback Of Notre Dame*** [1957]	$ .65	$2.00	$4.00
1679	O'Hara, John - ***Pal Joey*** [1957]	$ .50	$1.50	$3.00
1680	Edited by Luke Short - ***Colt's Law*** [1957]	$ .50	$1.50	$3.00
1681	L'Amour, Louis - ***Silver Canyon*** [1957]	$2.50	$7.50	$15.00
1682	Carr, John Dickson - ***Patrick Butler For The Defense*** [1957] Cover by Kossim.	$ .50	$1.50	$3.00
1683	Carr, John Dickson - ***Til Death Do Us Part*** [1957] Cover by Kossim.	$ .65	$2.00	$4.00
1684	Carr, John Dickson - ***He Who Whispers*** [1957] Cover by Kossim.	$ .65	$2.00	$4.00
A-1685	Newson, Ed - ***Wagons To Tucson*** [1957]	$ .50	$1.50	$3.00
F-1687	Vestal, Stanley - ***Dodge City: Queen Of Cowtowns*** [1957]	$ .65	$2.00	$4.00
F-1688	Anthology - ***The Art Of Mixing Drinks*** [1957]	$ .40	$1.25	$2.50
A-1689	Heyward, DuBose - ***Porgy*** [1957]	$ .50	$1.50	$3.00
A-1690	Marquand, John P. - ***Stop Over Tokyo*** [1957] Cover by Kossim.	$ .50	$1.50	$3.00
A-1691	Marquand, John P. - ***Thank You, Mr. Moto*** [1957] Cover by Kossim.	$ .50	$1.50	$3.00
S-1692	Myers, Bernard - ***50 Great Artists*** [1957]	$ .50	$1.50	$3.00
A-1693	Wertenbaker, Lael Tucker - ***Death Of A Man*** [1957] Photo cover.	$ .50	$1.50	$3.00
1694	Hatch, Eric - ***My Man Godfrey*** [1957] Cover by Hooks.	$ .40	$1.25	$2.50
1695	Dawson, Peter - ***Trail Boss*** [1957]	$ .50	$1.50	$3.00
1696	Stuart, Matt - ***Gun Smoke Showdown*** [1957]	$ .50	$1.50	$3.00
1697	Anthology - ***The Secret World Of Roy Williams*** [1957] PBO. Cover by Roy Williams. Cartoon book.	$1.35	$4.00	$8.00
A-1698	Benson, Ben - ***The Ninth Hour*** [1957]	$ .50	$1.50	$3.00
A-1699	Masterson, Whit - ***Touch Of Evil*** [1957]	$ .50	$1.50	$3.00

		G	VG	F
A-1700	Salter, James - ***The Hunters*** [1957]	$ .50	$1.50	$3.00
A-1701	Brown, Fredric - ***Rogue In Space*** [1957]	$2.50	$7.50	$15.00
F-1702	Caldwell, Taylor - ***The Earth Is The Lord's*** [1957]	$ .50	$1.50	$3.00
F-1703	Collier, John - ***Fancies And Goodnights*** [1957]	$ .65	$2.00	$4.00
A-1704	West, Nathanael - ***The Day Of The Locust*** [1957]	$ .50	$1.50	$3.00
F-1705	Michener, James A. - ***The Fires Of Spring*** [1957] Cover by Barye Phillips.	$ .50	$1.50	$3.00
A-1706	Weeks, William Rawle - ***Knock And Wait A While*** [1957]	$ .50	$1.50	$3.00
F-1707	Myrer, Anton - ***The Big War*** [1958] Movie tie-in.	$ .65	$2.00	$4.00
A-1708	Henning, William E. - ***The Heller*** [1957]	$ .50	$1.50	$3.00
1709	Evans, Evan - ***Outlaw's Code*** [1958] Cover by Abbett.	$ .50	$1.50	$3.00
1710	Short, Luke - ***Ambush*** [1958]	$ .50	$1.50	$3.00
1711	Howe, Margaret - ***Special Nurse*** [1958]	$ .40	$1.25	$2.50
1712	Brown, Fredric - ***The Lenient Beast*** [1958]	$5.00	$15.00	$30.00
A-1713	L'Amour, Louis - ***Sitka*** [1958]	$2.50	$7.50	$15.00
F-1714	Masters, John - ***Bugles And A Tiger*** [1958]	$ .50	$1.50	$3.00
F-1715	Lord, Walter - ***Day Of Infamy*** [1958] Photo cover.	$ .50	$1.50	$3.00
A-1717	Grey, Zane - ***Nevada*** [1958]	$ .50	$1.50	$3.00
A-1718	Grey, Zane - ***The Last Of The Plainsmen*** [1958]	$ .50	$1.50	$3.00
A-1719	Cronin, A. J. - ***The Spanish Gardener*** [1958]	$ .40	$1.25	$2.50
F-1720	Shellabarger, Samuel - ***Tolbecken*** [1958]	$ .50	$1.50	$3.00
A-1721	Wolff, Maritta - ***The Big Nickelodeon*** [1958]	$ .50	$1.50	$3.00
F-1722	Auchincloss, Louis - ***The Great World And Timothy Colt*** [1958]	$ .50	$1.50	$3.00
F-1723	Mercer, Charles - ***Rachel Cade*** [1958]	$ .50	$1.50	$3.00
A-1724	Marshall, Rosamond - ***Captain Ironhand*** [1958]	$ .50	$1.50	$3.00
1725	Chase, Borden - ***Red River*** [1958]	$ .50	$1.50	$3.00
1726	Gruber, Frank - ***Tales Of Wells Fargo*** [1958] PBO. TV tie-in.	$2.00	$6.00	$12.00
1727	Evans, John - ***Halo In Brass*** [1958]	$ .50	$1.50	$3.00
1728	Evans, John - ***Halo In Blood*** [1958]	$ .50	$1.50	$3.00
1729	Evans, John - ***Halo For Satan*** [1958]	$ .50	$1.50	$3.00
A-1730	Resko, John - ***Reprieve*** [1958]	$ .50	$1.50	$3.00
A-1731	Asimov, Isaac - ***The Naked Sun*** [1958]	$ .50	$1.50	$3.00
A-1732	Cerf, Bennett - ***The Life Of The Party*** [1958] Photo cover.	$ .50	$1.50	$3.00
S-1734	Beyle De Stendhal, Marie-Henri - ***The Red And The Black*** [1958] Cover by Hooks.	$ .50	$1.50	$3.00
F-1735	Dostoevsky, Fyodor - ***Crime And Punishment*** [1958]	$ .75	$2.50	$5.00
1736	Alexander, David - ***The Murder Of Whistler's Brother*** [1957] Cover by Hooks.	$ .75	$2.50	$5.00
1737	Richter, Conrad - ***The Light In The Forest*** [1958]	$ .50	$1.50	$3.00
F-1738	Rogers, Garet - ***Lancet*** [1958]	$ .50	$1.50	$3.00
A-1739	Astrachan, Sam - ***An End To Dying*** [1958]	$ .50	$1.50	$3.00
F-1740	Bissell, Richard - ***Say, Darling*** [1958]	$ .50	$1.50	$3.00
1741	Gruber, Frank - ***Peace Marshal*** [1958]	$ .75	$2.50	$5.00
1742	Gruber, Frank - ***Lonesome River*** [1958] Cover by Dwyer.	$ .50	$1.50	$3.00
1743	Gruber, Frank - ***Fighting Man*** [1958]	$ .50	$1.50	$3.00
F-1744	Wyckmason, F. Van - ***Our Valiant Few*** [1958] Cover by Barye Phillips.	$ .50	$1.50	$3.00
A-1746	Baker, Samm Sinclair - ***Miracle Gardening*** [1958]	$ .40	$1.25	$2.50
F-1747	Watson, Lillian Eichler - ***The Bantam Book Of Correct Letterwriting*** [1958]	$ .40	$1.25	$2.50
A-1748	Yeats-Brown, Francis - ***The Lives Of A Bengal Lancer*** [1958] Cover by Kossim.	$ .50	$1.50	$3.00
F-1749	Gipson, Fred - ***Cowhand: The Story Of A Working Cowboy*** [1958]	$ .50	$1.50	$3.00
1751	Judson, Jeanne - ***Nancy Ross, Private Secretary*** [1958]	$ .40	$1.25	$2.50
A-1752	Robbins, Harold - ***Never Love A Stranger*** [1958]	$ .50	$1.50	$3.00
A-1753	Steinbeck, John - ***The Short Reign Of Pippin IV*** [1958]	$1.50	$5.00	$10.00
F-1754	Ferber, Edna - ***Cimarron*** [1958]	$ .50	$1.50	$3.00
1755	Short, Luke - ***Fiddlefoot*** [1958]	$ .50	$1.50	$3.00

		G	VG	F
1756	Maresca, James - ***Mr. Taxicab*** [1958]	$ .50	$1.50	$3.00
1757	Brown, Fredric - ***The Screaming Mimi*** [1958] Cover by Binger. Movie tie-in.	$1.35	$4.00	$8.00
1758	Gilbert, Anthony - ***Riddle Of A Lady*** [1958] Photo cover.	$ .50	$1.50	$3.00
A-1759	Beaumont, Charles - ***Yonder*** [1958] PBO.	$2.50	$7.50	$15.00
A-1760	Anthony, Joseph - ***The Invisible Curtain*** [1958]	$ .50	$1.50	$3.00
A-1761	McCullers, Carson - ***The Member Of The Wedding*** [1958]	$ .50	$1.50	$3.00
F-1762	McCullers, Carson - ***The Heart Is A Lonely Hunter*** [1958]	$ .50	$1.50	$3.00
A-1763	McCullers, Carson - ***Reflections In A Golden Eye*** [1958]	$ .50	$1.50	$3.00
F-1764	McCullers, Carson - ***Ballad Of The Sad Cafe*** [1958]	$ .50	$1.50	$3.00
A-1765	Bergaust, Erik & Beller, William - ***Satellite!*** [1958]	$ .50	$1.50	$3.00
A-1766	Castle, Jeffery Lloyd - ***Satellite E One*** [1958] Cover by Lehr.	$ .50	$1.50	$3.00
F-1767	Gilbert, Edwin - ***Silver Spoon*** [1958]	$ .50	$1.50	$3.00
A-1768	Bezzerides, A. I. - ***Thieves' Market*** [1958]	$ .50	$1.50	$3.00
1769	Daniels, John S. - ***The Land Grabbers*** [1958]	$ .50	$1.50	$3.00
A-1770	Arnold, Elliott - ***Rescue*** [1958]	$ .50	$1.50	$3.00
1771	Fletcher, & Ullman - ***Sorry, Wrong Number*** [1958] Photo cover.	$ .50	$1.50	$3.00
A-1772	Ambler, Eric - ***Epitaph For A Spy*** [1958]	$ .50	$1.50	$3.00
A-1773	Greene, Graham - ***Confidential Agent*** [1958]	$ .50	$1.50	$3.00
A-1774	Pierce, Glenn - ***The Tyrant Of Bagdad*** [1958] Cover by Kossim.	$ .50	$1.50	$3.00
F-1775	Anthology - ***The Art Of Barbecue And Outdoor Cooking*** [1958]	$ .40	$1.25	$2.50
1776	McElfresh, Adeline - ***Calling Doctor Jane*** [1958]	$ .40	$1.25	$2.50
F-1777	Douglas, Norman - ***South Wind*** [1958]	$ .50	$1.50	$3.00
F-1778	Dobie, J. Frank - ***The Mustangs*** [1958]	$ .50	$1.50	$3.00
A-1779	Mason, Richard - ***The Wind Cannot Read*** [1958]	$ .50	$1.50	$3.00
1780	Kanin, Fay & Michael - ***Teacher's Pet*** [1958] PBO. Movie tie-in.	$ .65	$2.00	$4.00
A-1781	Marquand, John P. - ***Life At Happy Knoll*** [1958]	$ .50	$1.50	$3.00
1782	The Gordons - ***The Big Frame*** [1958]	$ .50	$1.50	$3.00
F-1783	Kelley, Wellborne - ***Alabama Empire*** [1958]	$ .50	$1.50	$3.00
A-1784	West, Ruth - ***The Teen-Age Diet Book*** [1958]	$ .40	$1.25	$2.50
A-1785	Reynolds, Quentin - ***They Fought For The Sky*** [1958]	$ .50	$1.50	$3.00
A-1786	Tenn, William - ***Time In Advance*** [1958] PBO.	$1.25	$3.75	$7.50
1787	Loring, Emile - ***What Then Is Love*** [1958]	$ .50	$1.50	$3.00
F-1788	Morse, Jim - ***Folk Songs Of The Caribbean*** [1958] PBO.	$1.25	$3.75	$7.50
F-1789	Wilder, Thornton - ***Three Plays*** [1958]	$ .50	$1.50	$3.00
A-1790	Cardozo, Peter - ***A Wonderful World For Children II*** [1958]	$ .50	$1.50	$3.00
F-1791	Shulman, Max - ***Rally Round The Flag, Boys!*** [1958]	$ .50	$1.50	$3.00
A-1792	Richter, Conrad - ***The Lady*** [1958]	$ .50	$1.50	$3.00
A-1793	Huxley, Aldous - ***Ape And Essence*** [1958]	$ .50	$1.50	$3.00
1794	Porter, William - ***The Lawbringers*** [1958]	$ .50	$1.50	$3.00
A-1795	Stout, Rex - ***Might As Well Be Dead*** [1958] Cover by Muni.	$ .50	$1.50	$3.00
A-1796	Stout, Rex - ***3 For The Chair*** [1958] Cover by Muni.	$ .50	$1.50	$3.00
A-1797	Stout, Rex - ***The Silent Speaker*** [1958]	$ .50	$1.50	$3.00
A-1798	Blackburn, Thomas W. - ***Sierra Baron*** [1958]	$ .50	$1.50	$3.00
1799	Rush, Ann - ***Eve Cameron, M.D.*** [1958]	$ .40	$1.25	$2.50
A-1800	Burgess, Alan - ***The Inn Of The Sixth Happiness*** [1958] Photo cover. Movie tie-in.	$ .50	$1.50	$3.00
A-1801	Pei, Dr. Mario A. - ***Getting Along In French*** [1958]	$ .40	$1.25	$2.50
A-1802	Pei, Dr. Mario A. - ***Getting Along In Italian*** [1958]	$ .40	$1.25	$2.50
F-1803	Melville, Herman - ***Typee*** [1958]	$ .50	$1.50	$3.00
F-1804	Brantome - ***Tales Of Fair And Gallant Ladies*** [1958]	$ .50	$1.50	$3.00
F-1805	Masters, John - ***Far, Far The Mountain Peak*** [1958]	$ .50	$1.50	$3.00
1806	Kohner, Frederick - ***Gidget*** [1958]	$ .50	$1.50	$3.00
F-1807	Bassing, Eileen - ***Home Before Dark*** [1958] Movie tie-in.	$ .50	$1.50	$3.00
A-1808	Blake, Forrester - ***Wilderness Passage*** [1958]	$ .50	$1.50	$3.00
A-1809	Blake, Forrester - ***Johnny Christmas*** [1958]	$ .50	$1.50	$3.00

		G	VG	F
1810	Marquand, John P. - ***Think Fast, Mr. Moto*** [1958] Cover by Kossim.	$ .50	$1.50	$3.00
A-1811	Forester, C. S. - ***Lieutenant Hornblower*** [1958]	$ .50	$1.50	$3.00
A1812	Brown, Fredric - ***Honeymoon In Hell*** [1958] PBO.	$2.50	$7.50	$15.00
1813	Key, Ted - ***If You Like Hazel*** [1958] Cover by Ted Key. Cartoon book.	$1.25	$3.75	$7.50
F-1814	Leterman, Elmer G. - ***The New Art Of Selling*** [1958]	$ .40	$1.25	$2.50
A-1815	Forester, C. S. - ***Mr. Midshipman Hornblower*** [1958]	$ .50	$1.50	$3.00
A-1816	Forester, C. S. - ***Beat To Quarters*** [1958]	$ .50	$1.50	$3.00
F-1817	Powell, Richard - ***The Philadelphian*** [1958]	$ .50	$1.50	$3.00
F-1818	Mercer, Charles - ***The Drummond Tradition*** [1958]	$ .50	$1.50	$3.00
A-1819	Burnett, W. R. - ***Underdog*** [1958]	$ .50	$1.50	$3.00
1820	Carse, Robert - ***Great Circle*** [1958]	$ .50	$1.50	$3.00
1821	Short, Luke - ***Play A Lone Hand*** [1958]	$ .50	$1.50	$3.00
1822	Holmes, L. P. - ***The Plunderers*** [1958]	$ .50	$1.50	$3.00
1823	Krasner, William - ***The Stag Party*** [1958]	$ .50	$1.50	$3.00
A-1824	Derby, Mark - ***Echo Of A Bomb*** [1958]	$ .50	$1.50	$3.00
A-1825	Gunn, James - ***Station In Space*** [1958]	$ .50	$1.50	$3.00
A-1826	Leckie, Robert - ***Helmet For My Pillow*** [1958]	$ .50	$1.50	$3.00
A-1827	Garvin, Fernande Silve - ***The Art Of French Cooking*** [1958]	$ .40	$1.25	$2.50
A-1828	Walker, David - ***Harry Black*** [1958] Cover by Zuckerberg. Movie tie-in.	$ .65	$2.00	$4.00
A-1831	Morgan, Claire - ***The Price Of Salt*** [1958]	$ .50	$1.50	$3.00
F-1832	Serling, Rod - ***Patterns*** [1958] Photo cover. Movie tie-in with 14 pages photos.	$1.50	$5.00	$10.00
F-1833	Cheever, John - ***The Wapshot Chronicle*** [1958]	$ .50	$1.50	$3.00
A-1834	Goldman, William - ***The Temple Of Gold*** [1958]	$ .50	$1.50	$3.00
A-1835	Trevor, Elleston - ***The Killing Ground*** [1958]	$ .50	$1.50	$3.00
A-1836	Keveson, Peter - ***Tubie's Monument*** [1958]	$ .50	$1.50	$3.00
1837	Evans, Evan - ***Outlaw Valley*** [1958]	$ .50	$1.50	$3.00
1838	Homer, Dale - ***The Trail From Texas*** [1958]	$ .50	$1.50	$3.00
1839	MacDonald, Ross - ***Blue City*** [1958]	$ .50	$1.50	$3.00
1840	Walsh, Thomas - ***The Dark Window*** [1958]	$ .50	$1.50	$3.00
1841	Hamill, Ethel - ***A Nurse For Galleon Key*** [1958]	$ .40	$1.25	$2.50
A-1842	Druten, John Van - ***Bell, Book And Candle*** [1958] Photo cover. Movie tie-in.	$ .50	$1.50	$3.00
S-1843	Ferber, Edna - ***One Basket*** [1958]	$ .50	$1.50	$3.00
F-1844	Michener, James A. & Day, A. Grove - ***Rascals In Paradise*** [1958] Cover by Hooks.	$ .50	$1.50	$3.00
A-1845	Deiss, Jay - ***The Blue Chips*** [1958]	$ .50	$1.50	$3.00
F-1846	de Hartog, Jan - ***The Spiral Road*** [1958]	$ .50	$1.50	$3.00
A-1847	Carr, John Dickson - ***Fire, Burn*** [1958]	$ .50	$1.50	$3.00
A-1848	Long, Margaret - ***Louisville, Saturday*** [1958]	$ .50	$1.50	$3.00
A-1849	Carr, John Dickson - ***The Sleeping Sphinx*** [1958]	$ .50	$1.50	$3.00
A-1850	Richter, Conrad - ***The Fields*** [1958]	$ .50	$1.50	$3.00
F-1851	Richter, Conrad - ***The Town*** [1958]	$ .50	$1.50	$3.00
A-1852	Richter, Conrad - ***The Trees*** [1958]	$ .50	$1.50	$3.00
1853	L'Amour, Louis - ***Radigan*** [1958] PBO.	$2.50	$7.50	$15.00
F-1854	Anthology - ***1000 Ways To Make $1000*** [1958]	$ .40	$1.25	$2.50
1855	Henry, Will - ***The North Star*** [1958]	$ .50	$1.50	$3.00
1856	Dawson, Peter - ***The Outlaw Of Longbow*** [1958]	$ .50	$1.50	$3.00
A-1857	Forster, Logan A. - ***Proud Land*** [1958] Cover by William George.	$ .50	$1.50	$3.00
1858	Reilly, Helen - ***The Canvas Dagger*** [1959] Photo cover.	$ .50	$1.50	$3.00
A-1859	Ehrlich, Max - ***First Train To Babylon*** [1959]	$ .50	$1.50	$3.00
A-1860	Ehrlich, Max - ***The Big Eye*** [1959] Cover by Hooks	$ .50	$1.50	$3.00
1861	Smith, H. Allen - ***Write Me A Poem, Baby*** [1959] Cover by Goodman.	$ .50	$1.50	$3.00
F-1862	Roscoe, Theodore - ***Pigboats*** [1959]	$ .50	$1.50	$3.00
A-1864	de la Roche, Mazo - ***Jaina*** [1959]	$ .50	$1.50	$3.00

		G	VG	F
1865	Edited by Luke Short - ***Rawhide And Bob-Wire*** [1958] PBO.	$1.25	$3.75	$7.50
1866	Short, Luke - ***Summer Of The Smoke*** [1959]	$ .50	$1.50	$3.00
A-1867	Wilder, Robert - ***A Stranger In My Arms*** [1959] Cover by Zuckerberg. Movie tie-in.	$ .65	$2.00	$4.00
A-1868	Tabori, George - ***The Journey*** [1959] Cover by Barye Phillips. Movie tie-in with Yul Brynner and Deborah Kerr.	$ .65	$2.00	$4.00
F-1869	Kovacs, Ernie - ***Zoomar*** [1959] Cover by Dedini.	$ .50	$1.50	$3.00
F-1870	Giovannitti, Len - ***The Prisoners Of Combine D*** [1959]	$ .50	$1.50	$3.00
A-1871	Burnett, W. R. - ***Little Caesar*** [1959]	$ .50	$1.50	$3.00
F-1872	Haycox, Ernest - ***The Earthbreakers*** [1959]	$ .50	$1.50	$3.00
1873	Holmes, L. P. - ***Modoc The Last Sundown*** [1959]	$ .50	$1.50	$3.00
1875	Simenon, Georges - ***No Vacation For Maigret*** [1959]	$ .50	$1.50	$3.00
1876	Pinchot, Ann - ***Rival To My Heart*** [1959]	$ .50	$1.50	$3.00
F-1877	Schever, Steven H. - ***TV Movie Almanac And Ratings, 1958–1959*** [1959]	$ .50	$1.50	$3.00
F-1878	Hudson, W. H. - ***Green Mansions*** [1959]	$ .50	$1.50	$3.00
S-1879	Caldwell, Taylor - ***The Sound Of Thunder*** [1959]	$ .50	$1.50	$3.00
A-1880	Hayes, Alfred - ***My Face For The World To See*** [1959]	$ .50	$1.50	$3.00
1883	Creasey, John - ***Death Of A Postman*** [1959]	$ .50	$1.50	$3.00
1884	Creasey, John - ***The Gelignite Gang*** [1959] Cover by Barye Phillips.	$ .50	$1.50	$3.00
A-1885	Bradbury, Ray - ***The Martian Chronicles*** [1959]	$ .65	$2.00	$4.00
F-1886	Spicer, Bart - ***The Tall Captains*** [1959]	$ .50	$1.50	$3.00
A-1888	O'Conner, Richard - ***Bat Masterson*** [1958] TV tie-in.	$1.25	$3.75	$7.50
A-1890	Schulberg, Budd - ***Across The Everglades*** [1958] Movie tie-in with Burl Ives.	$1.00	$3.00	$6.00
A-1891	Benson, Sally - ***Meet Me In St. Louis*** [1959]	$ .40	$1.25	$2.50
A-1892	Felsen, Henry Gregor - ***Hot Rod*** [1959]	$ .40	$1.25	$2.50
1893	Brackett, Leigh - ***Rio Bravo*** [1959] PBO. Cover by Barye Phillips. Movie tie-in with John Wayne.	$5.50	$17.50	$35.00
A-1894	Skinner, Cornelia Otis & Kimbrough, E. - ***Our Hearts Were Young And Gay*** [1959]	$ .40	$1.25	$2.50
F-1895	Steinbeck, John - ***East Of Eden*** [1959]	$ .50	$1.50	$3.00
F-1896	Bullock, Alan - ***Hitler, A Study In Tyranny*** [1959]	$ .50	$1.50	$3.00
A-1897	Bissell, Betty - ***The Betty Bissell Book Of Home Cleaning*** [1959]	$ .40	$1.25	$2.50
A-1898	Hall, Oakley - ***So Many Doors*** [1959]	$ .50	$1.50	$3.00
A-1899	Campbell, George - ***Cry For Happy*** [1959] Cover by Alex Ross.	$ .50	$1.50	$3.00
F-1900	Smith, Betty - ***Maggie Now*** [1959]	$ .50	$1.50	$3.00
A-1901	Haines, William Wister - ***The Hon. Rocky Slade*** [1959] Cover by Alex Ross.	$ .50	$1.50	$3.00
F-1902	Haines, William Wister - ***Slim*** [1959]	$ .50	$1.50	$3.00
F-1903	Wallace, Lew - ***Ben Hur*** [1959]	$ .50	$1.50	$3.00
A-1904	Freedman, Benedict & Nancy - ***Mrs. Mike*** [1959]	$ .50	$1.50	$3.00
1905	L'Amour, Louis - ***The First Fast Draw*** [1959] PBO.	$2.50	$7.50	$15.00
1907	Roberts, Virginia - ***Nurse Howard's Assignment*** [1959]	$ .40	$1.25	$2.50
A-1908	Anders, Curt - ***The Price Of Courage*** [1959]	$ .50	$1.50	$3.00
1909	Benson, Ben - ***The Black Mirror*** [1958]	$ .50	$1.50	$3.00
1910	Benson, Ben - ***The Running Man*** [1959] Cover by Barye Phillips.	$ .50	$1.50	$3.00
1911	Loring, Emilie - ***I Take This Man*** [1959]	$ .50	$1.50	$3.00
F-1912	Ferber, Edna - ***Ice Palace*** [1959]	$ .50	$1.50	$3.00
F-1913	Heinrich, Willis - ***Crack Of Doom*** [1959]	$ .50	$1.50	$3.00
A-1914	Vail, Amanda - ***Love Me Little*** [1959]	$ .50	$1.50	$3.00
F-1915	Wellman, Paul - ***Ride The Red Earth*** [1959]	$ .50	$1.50	$3.00
1916	Short, Luke - ***And The Wind Blows Free*** [1959]	$ .50	$1.50	$3.00
A-1917	Beaumont, Charles - ***The Hunger And Other Stories*** [1959] Cover by Heinrich Kley.	$2.50	$7.50	$15.00
A-1919	Gibbons, Floyd - ***The Red Knight Of Germany*** [1959]	$ .50	$1.50	$3.00

		G	VG	F
F-1920	Garrett, James - ***... And Save Them For Pallbearers*** [1959]	$ .50	$1.50	$3.00
A-1921	Delman, David - ***The Hard Sell*** [1959]	$ .50	$1.50	$3.00
A-1922	Bradbury, Ray - ***Dandelion Wine*** [1959] Photo cover.	$ .50	$1.50	$3.00
A-1923	Marchal, Lucie - ***The Mesh*** [1959]	$ .50	$1.50	$3.00
A-1924	West, Ruth - ***The Teen-Age Diet Book*** [1959]	$ .40	$1.25	$2.50
1925	Roberts, Wayne - ***Silent River*** [1959]	$ .50	$1.50	$3.00
1926	Harrison, C. William - ***Barbed Wire Kingdom*** [1959]	$ .50	$1.50	$3.00
1927	Gault, Bill - ***The Convertible Hearse*** [1959]	$ .50	$1.50	$3.00
1929	McElfresh, Adeline - ***Young Doctor Randall*** [1959]	$ .40	$1.25	$2.50
A-1930	Maugham, W. Somerset - ***Theatre*** [1959]	$ .50	$1.50	$3.00
A-1931	Maugham, W. Somerset - ***The Narrow Corner*** [1959]	$ .50	$1.50	$3.00
F-1932	Shulberg, Bud - ***The Disenchanted*** [1959]	$ .50	$1.50	$3.00
A-1933	L'Amour, Louis - ***The Daybreakers*** [1960] PBO.	$2.50	$7.50	$15.00
1934	Gruber, Frank - ***Outlaw*** [1959]	$ .50	$1.50	$3.00
A-1935	Henry, Will - ***Reckoning At Yankee Flat*** [1959]	$ .50	$1.50	$3.00
1936	Myers, Beth - ***The Doctor Is A Lady*** [1959]	$ .40	$1.25	$2.50
A-1937	Williams, Jay - ***The Witches*** [1959]	$ .50	$1.50	$3.00
1938	Loring, Emilie - ***My Dearest Love*** [1959]	$ .50	$1.50	$3.00
A-1939	Shulman, Max - ***Barefoot Boy With Cheek*** [1959] Cover by Muni.	$ .50	$1.50	$3.00
A-1940	Shulman, Max - ***The Feather Merchants*** [1959]	$ .50	$1.50	$3.00
A-1941	Edwards, Samuel - ***The Naked Maja*** [1959]	$ .50	$1.50	$3.00
A-1942	Coen, Franklin - ***Night Of The Quarter Moon*** [1959] PBO. Movie tie-in.	$1.00	$3.00	$6.00
A-1943	Pei, Mario & Vaquero, Eloy - ***Getting Along In Spanish*** [1959]	$ .40	$1.25	$2.50
A-1944	Pei, Mario & Politzer, Robert - ***Getting Along In German*** [1959]	$ .40	$1.25	$2.50
1945	Lord, Walter - ***A Night To Remember*** [1959]	$ .50	$1.50	$3.00
F-1946	Dryer, Bernard - ***The Image Makers*** [1959]	$ .50	$1.50	$3.00
F-1947	Cronin, A. J. - ***The Northern Light*** [1959]	$ .50	$1.50	$3.00
1948	Hayes, Joseph - ***The Hours After Midnight*** [1959]	$ .50	$1.50	$3.00
1949	Smith, Ben - ***Gunfighter's Return*** [1959]	$ .50	$1.50	$3.00
1951	McElfresh, Adeline - ***Hill Country Nurse*** [1959]	$ .40	$1.25	$2.50
A-1952	Sohl, Jerry - ***Point Ultimate*** [1959] Cover by Kossim.	$ .50	$1.50	$3.00
A-1953	Goren, Charles H. - ***Goren Presents The Italian Bridge System*** [1959]	$ .40	$1.25	$2.50
A-1954	Alpert, Hollis - ***The Summer Lovers*** [1959]	$ .50	$1.50	$3.00
F-1955	Bourjaily, Vance - ***The Violated*** [1959]	$ .50	$1.50	$3.00
F-1956	Lea, Tom - ***The Wonderful Country*** [1959]	$ .50	$1.50	$3.00
A-1957	Herlihy, James Leo & Noble, William - ***Blue Denim*** [1959]	$ .50	$1.50	$3.00
A-1958	Williams, Jay - ***Solomon And Sheba*** [1959] Cover by Zuckerberg. Movie tie-in.	$ .75	$2.50	$5.00
A-1959	Short, Luke - ***Hard Money*** [1959]	$ .50	$1.50	$3.00
A-1961	Stout, Rex - ***If Death Ever Slept*** [1959]	$1.00	$3.00	$6.00
1962	Wesley, Elizabeth - ***Doctor Barbara*** [1959]	$ .40	$1.25	$2.50
F-1963	O'Hara, John - ***A Rage To Live*** [1959]	$ .50	$1.50	$3.00
A-1964	Haines, William Wister - ***Command Decision*** [1959]	$ .50	$1.50	$3.00
1965	Zugsmith, Albert - ***The Beat Generation*** [1959] Cover by Barye Phillips. Movie tie-in.	$2.00	$6.00	$12.00
A-1966	Chayefsky, Paddy - ***Middle Of The Night*** [1959] Cover by Barye Phillips. Movie tie-in.	$ .50	$1.50	$3.00
F-1968	Mergendahl, Charles - ***The Bramble Bush*** [1959] Cover by Barye Phillips. Movie tie-in.	$ .50	$1.50	$3.00
F-1969	Herber, William - ***Tomorrow To Live*** [1959]	$ .50	$1.50	$3.00
A-1970	Yaffe, James - ***Nothing But The Night*** [1959] Photo cover.	$ .50	$1.50	$3.00
A-1971	Sohl, Jerry - ***The Transcendent Man*** [1959] Cover by Abbett.	$ .50	$1.50	$3.00
F-1972	Anthology - ***Hoof Trails And Wagon Tracks*** [1959]	$ .50	$1.50	$3.00
1973	Burnett, W. R. - ***Bitter Ground*** [1959] Cover by Kossim.	$ .50	$1.50	$3.00
1974	Benson, Ben - ***The Blonde In Black*** [1959] Cover by Barye Phillips.	$ .50	$1.50	$3.00

		G	VG	F
1975	Roberts, Virginia - ***Nurse On Location*** [1959]	$ .40	$1.25	$2.50
F-1976	Waters, Ethel & Samuels, Charles - ***His Eye Is On The Sparrow*** [1959]	$ .50	$1.50	$3.00
1977	L'Amour, Louis - ***Taggart*** [1959] PBO.	$2.50	$7.50	$15.00
A-1978	Asimov, Isaac - ***Earth Is Room Enough*** [1959]	$ .50	$1.50	$3.00
A-1979	Millar, Margaret - ***An Air That Kills*** [1959]	$ .50	$1.50	$3.00
F-1980	Hall, Oakley - ***Warlock*** [1959] Movie tie-in.	$ .50	$1.50	$3.00
A-1981	Davis, Mac - ***Sports Shorts*** [1959]	$ .50	$1.50	$3.00
A-1982	Wibberley, Leonard - ***The Mouse That Roared*** [1959]	$ .50	$1.50	$3.00
A-1983	Wolfe, Winifred - ***Ask Any Girl*** [1959] Photo cover.	$ .50	$1.50	$3.00
1984	Dawson, Peter - ***The Savages*** [1959]	$ .50	$1.50	$3.00
H-1985	Fast, Howard - ***Spartacus*** [1959] Cover by Tom Van Sant. Movie tie-in with 16 pages of drawings by Tom Van Sant.	$ .75	$2.50	$5.00
A-1986	Kozol, Jonathan - ***The Fume Of Poppies*** [1959] Photo cover.	$ .50	$1.50	$3.00
F-1987	Livingston, Harold - ***The Detroiters*** [1959] Cover by Zuckerberg.	$ .50	$1.50	$3.00
F-1988	Every, Dale Van - ***The Voyagers*** [1959] Cover by Zuckerberg.	$ .50	$1.50	$3.00
A-1989	Short, Luke - ***War On The Cimarron*** [1959]	$ .50	$1.50	$3.00
1990	Brown, Fredric - ***One For The Road*** [1959] Cover by Barye Phillips.	$3.50	$10.00	$20.00
A-1991	Sheckley, Robert - ***Immortality, Inc.*** [1959]	$1.00	$3.00	$6.00
A-1992	Worley, Dorothy - ***Dr. John's Decision*** [1959]	$ .40	$1.25	$2.50
S-1994	Edited by Angel Flores - ***Spanish Stories: A Bantam Dual-Language Book*** [1960]	$ .40	$1.25	$2.50
S-1995	Uris, Leon - ***Exodus*** [1959]	$ .50	$1.50	$3.00
F-1996	Uris, Leon - ***Battle Cry*** [1959]	$ .50	$1.50	$3.00
A-1998	Gruber, Frank - ***Town Tamer*** [1959]	$ .50	$1.50	$3.00
A-1999	Dawson, Peter - ***The Crimson Horseshoe*** [1959]	$ .50	$1.50	$3.00
2000	Dickson, Carter - ***Fear Is The Same*** [1959] Cover by Barye Phillips.	$2.50	$7.50	$15.00
A-2016	Stout, Rex - ***And Four To Go*** [1959]	$ .50	$1.50	$3.00
A-2020	Wagoner, David - ***Rock*** [1959]	$ .50	$1.50	$3.00
A-2069	Bradbury, Ray - ***A Medicine For Melancholy*** [1960]	$5.00	$15.00	$30.00
A-2103	Shulman, Irving - ***Platinum High School*** [1960]	$ .50	$1.50	$3.00
A-2135	Brown, Fredric - ***Knock Three-One-Two*** [1960]	$5.00	$15.00	$30.00
A-2156	Stout, Rex - ***Plot It Yourself*** [1960]	$1.00	$3.00	$6.00
N-2173	Bradbury, Ray - ***Pillar Of Fire And Other Plays*** [1975]	$1.00	$3.00	$6.00
A-2219	Gunn, James - ***The Joy Makers*** [1961] PBO. (SF).	$ .50	$1.50	$3.00
F-2255	Fitzgibbon, Constantine - ***When The Kissing Had To Stop*** [1960]	$ .50	$1.50	$3.00
A-2320	Christie, Agatha - ***Poirot Investigates*** [1961]	$ .50	$1.50	$3.00
J2323	Brackett, Leigh - ***13 West Street*** [1962]	$2.00	$6.00	$12.00
J-2578	Brown, Fredric - ***The Lights In The Sky Are Stars*** [1963]	$1.35	$4.00	$8.00
HZ-2850	Shepherd, Billy - ***The True Story Of The Beatles*** [1964] PBO. Photo covers and illustrations.	$2.50	$7.50	$15.00
E2854	Robeson, Kenneth - ***The Thousand-Headed Man*** [1964] Doc Savage #2.	$1.25	$3.75	$7.50
E-3017	Robeson, Kenneth - ***The Lost Oasis*** [1965] PBO. Doc Savage #6.	$1.25	$3.75	$7.50
E-3047	Robeson, Kenneth - ***The Phantom City*** [1966] PBO. Doc Savage #10.	$1.25	$3.75	$7.50
E-3202	Robeson, Kenneth - ***Land Of Always-Night*** [1966] PBO. Doc Savage #13.	$1.25	$3.75	$7.50
F3459	Blish, James - ***Star Trek*** [1967] TV tie-in.	$2.50	$7.50	$15.00
Y-5869	Bode, Vaughn - ***Deadbone Erotica*** [1971] PBO. Cover and illus by Vaughn Bode.	$8.00	$25.00	$50.00
Q-6352	Robeson, Kenneth - ***The Man Of Bronze*** [1964] Doc Savage #1 reprint.	$ .40	$1.25	$2.50
S-6977	Koontz, Dean R. - ***The Flesh In The Furnace*** [1972] PBO.	$5.50	$17.50	$35.00
N-7190	Koontz, Dean R. - ***Demon Seed*** [1973] PBO.	$5.50	$17.50	$35.00

		G	VG	F
S-7492	Robeson, Kenneth - ***The Seven Agate Devils*** [1973] PBO. Doc Savage #73. Reprints Doc Savage Magazine from May 1936.	$1.25	$3.75	$7.50
11345	Ellison, Harlan - ***City On The Edge Of Forever*** [1977] Star Trek Fotonovel #1	$4.00	$12.50	$25.00
11346	Peeples, Samuel A. - ***Where No Man Has Gone Before*** [1977] Star Trek Fotonovel #2.	$2.50	$7.50	$15.00
11347	Gerrold, David - ***The Trouble With Tribbles*** [1977] Star Trek Fotonovel #3	$2.50	$7.50	$15.00
11348	Hamner, Robert - ***A Taste Of Armegeddon*** [1978] Star Trek Fotonovel #4	$2.50	$7.50	$15.00
11349	Coon, Gene L. - ***Metamorphosis*** [1978] Star Trek Fotonovel #5.	$2.50	$7.50	$15.00
11350	Aroeste, Jean Lissette - ***All Our Yesterdays*** [1978] Star Trek Fotonovel #6	$2.50	$7.50	$15.00
12012	Sturgeon, Theodore - ***Amok Time*** [1978] Star Trek Fotonovel #12.	$3.50	$10.00	$20.00
12017	Bixby, Jerome - ***Day Of The Dove*** [1978] Star Trek Fotonovel #10.	$2.50	$7.50	$15.00
12021	Coon, Gene L. - ***The Devil In The Dark*** [1978] Star Trek Fotonovel #9	$2.50	$7.50	$15.00
12022	Harmon, David P. and Coon, Gene L. - ***A Piece Of The Action*** [1978] Star Trek Fotonovel #8.	$2.50	$7.50	$15.00
12028	Harmon, David P. - ***The Deadly Years*** [1978] Star Trek Fotonovel #11	$2.50	$7.50	$15.00
12041	Crawford, Oliver - ***The Galileo 7*** [1978] Star Trek Fotonovel #7.	$2.50	$7.50	$15.00
12787-X	Robeson, Kenneth - ***The Red Spider*** [1979] PBO. Doc Savage #95.	$1.25	$3.75	$7.50

Bard Books. New York: Bard Publishing. Digest Size.

NN-1	Wheelock, Dorothy - ***Dead Giveaway*** [1944]	$3.50	$10.00	$20.00

Barker Dragon Books. London: Arthur Barker Ltd.

1	Anderson, Oliver - ***Grit And Polish*** [n.d.]	$1.25	$3.75	$7.50
2	Burton, Sir Richard - ***Tales From The Thousand And One Nights*** [n.d.]	$1.35	$4.00	$8.00
3	Goodwin, R.B. - ***Hong Kong Escape*** [n.d.]	$1.25	$3.75	$7.50
4	Langley, Noel - ***The Cabbage Patch*** [n.d.]	$1.25	$3.75	$7.50
5	Sandstrom, Flora - ***The Dancing Giant*** [n.d.]	$1.25	$3.75	$7.50
6	Spillane, Mickey - ***One Lonely Night*** [n.d.]	$2.50	$7.50	$15.00
7	Cohen, Octavus Roy - ***My Love Wears Black*** [n.d.]	$1.35	$4.00	$8.00
8	Johnston, J. - ***Patrol Of The Dead*** [n.d.]	$1.35	$4.00	$8.00
9	Phillips, Conrad - ***The Barber's Wife*** [n.d.]	$1.25	$3.75	$7.50
10	Halliday, Brett - ***Murder Is My Business*** [n.d.]	$1.35	$4.00	$8.00
11	Birmingham, F., editor - ***The Girls From Esquire*** [n.d.]	$1.25	$3.75	$7.50
12	Dodge, David - ***How Lost Was My Weekend*** [n.d.]	$1.35	$4.00	$8.00
13	Anderson, Oliver - ***Painless Extractions*** [n.d.]	$1.25	$3.75	$7.50
14	Chegaray, Jacques - ***Going My Way*** [n.d.]	$1.25	$3.75	$7.50
15	Gainham, Sarah - ***Time Right Deadly*** [1957]	$1.25	$3.75	$7.50
16	Halliday, Brett - ***When Dorinda Dances*** [n.d.]	$1.35	$4.00	$8.00
17	King, Robin - ***No Paradise*** [n.d.]	$1.25	$3.75	$7.50
18	Spillane, Mickey - ***The Big Kill*** [n.d.]	$2.50	$7.50	$15.00

Bart House. New York: Bartholomew House, Inc.

NO#-1	Bailey, Seth - ***The Hand In The Cobbler's Safe*** [1944] PBO.	$5.50	$17.50	$35.00
NO#-2	Hatch, Eric - ***The Delinquent Ghost*** [1944]	$2.50	$7.50	$15.00
3	Gilman, William - ***The Spy Trap*** [1944] PBO.	$2.50	$7.50	$15.00
4	Lovecraft, H. P. - ***The Weird Shadow Over Innsmouth*** [1944] PBO.	$12.50	$37.50	$75.00

Bart House, 4

Bart House, 29

Bart House, 102

		G	VG	F
5	Blassingame, Wyatt - ***John Smith Hears Death Walking*** [1944] PBO.	$3.50	$10.00	$20.00
6	McClary, Thomas Calvert - ***Rebirth*** [1944] PBO. SF.	$4.00	$12.50	$25.00
7	Burke, Noel - ***The Shivering Bough*** [1944]	$2.00	$6.00	$12.00
8	Birkley, Dolan - ***The Blue Geranium*** [1944]	$2.00	$6.00	$12.00
9	Maxon, P. B. - ***The Waltz Of Death*** [1944]	$2.00	$6.00	$12.00
10	Markham, Virgil - ***The Devil Drives*** [1944]	$2.00	$6.00	$12.00
11	Mario, Queena - ***Murder Meets Mephisto*** [1945]	$2.00	$6.00	$12.00
12	Lovecraft, H. P. - ***The Dunwich Horror*** [1945] PBO.	$12.50	$37.50	$75.00
13	Long, Amelia Reynolds - ***4 Feet In The Grave*** [1945]	$2.00	$6.00	$12.00
14	Levinrew, Will - ***The Wheelchair Corpse*** [1945]	$2.00	$6.00	$12.00
15	Starr, Jimmy - ***Three Short Biers*** [1945]	$2.00	$6.00	$12.00
16	Thayer, Lee - ***Murder Is Out*** [1945]	$2.00	$6.00	$12.00
17	McDougald, Roman - ***The Deaths Of Lora Karen*** [1945]	$2.00	$6.00	$12.00
18	Comstock, Harriet T. - ***Terry*** [1945]	$1.50	$5.00	$10.00
19	Nash, Anne - ***Said With Flowers*** [1945]	$2.00	$6.00	$12.00
20	Norris, Kathleen - ***Motionless Shadows*** [1945]	$2.00	$6.00	$12.00
21	Buck, Pearl S. - ***The Promise*** [1946]	$1.50	$5.00	$10.00
22	Lorac, E. C. R. - ***Checkmate To Murder*** [1946]	$2.00	$6.00	$12.00
23	Pierson, Louise Randall - ***Roughly Speaking*** [1946] Photo cover. Movie tie-in.	$2.50	$7.50	$15.00
24	Beyer, William - ***Murder Secretary*** [1946]	$2.00	$6.00	$12.00
25	Hecht, Ben - ***Hollywood Mystery*** [1946]	$2.00	$6.00	$12.00
26	Long, Manning - ***Bury The Hatchet*** [1946]	$2.00	$6.00	$12.00
27	Trimble, Louis - ***Design For Dying*** [1946]	$2.00	$6.00	$12.00
28	Baum, Vicki - ***Grand Hotel*** [1946]	$1.50	$5.00	$10.00
29	Grey, Robin - ***Puzzle In Porcelain*** [1946]	$2.00	$6.00	$12.00
30	Sabatini, Rafael - ***The Lion's Skin*** [1946]	$1.50	$5.00	$10.00
31	Bailey, Temple - ***The Blue Cloak*** [1946]	$2.00	$6.00	$12.00
32	Hale, Christopher - ***Hangman's Tie*** [1946]	$2.00	$6.00	$12.00
33	Levant, Oscar - ***A Smattering Of Ignorance*** [1946] Movie tie-in and photo cover.	$1.50	$5.00	$10.00
34	Smith, Ann T. - ***Death In The Cards*** [1946]	$2.00	$6.00	$12.00
35	Olsen, D. B. - ***The Clue In The Clay*** [1946]	$2.00	$6.00	$12.00
36	Lewis, Lange - ***Murder Among Friends*** [1946] Photo cover.	$2.00	$6.00	$12.00
39	Ford, Hershfield & Laurie - ***Can You Top This?*** [1946] Photo cover.	$1.50	$5.00	$10.00
101	Christy, Helen - ***Mr. Ace*** [1946] PBO. Photo cover. Movie tie-in.	$4.00	$12.50	$25.00

Beacon, B-108

Beacon, B-109

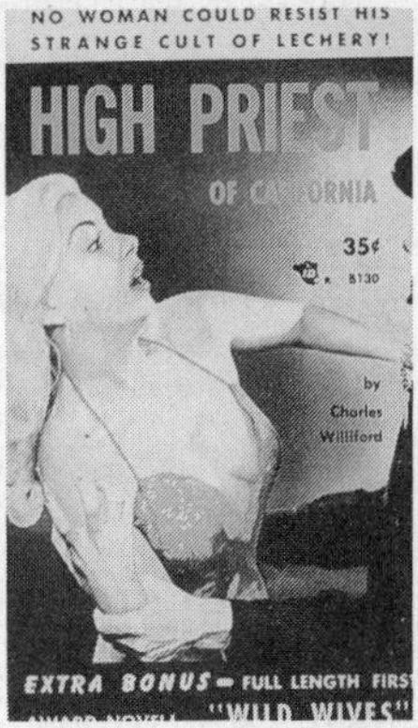

Beacon, B-130

		G	VG	F
102	Hershfield, Harry - ***The Sin Of Harold Diddlebock*** [1946] Photo cover. Movie tie-in. Ghost-written by Walter B. Gibson.	$7.00	$22.50	$45.00
103	Ogilvie, Elizabeth - ***Honeymoon*** [1946]	$4.00	$12.50	$25.00

Bartholomew House. New York: Bartholomew House, Inc. Digest Size.

NN-1	Anthology - ***Great Western Heroes*** [1957] Edited by Rafer Brent	$2.50	$7.50	$15.00
NN-2	Anthology - ***True Stories Of Love And Passion*** [1956] Photo cover	$4.00	$12.50	$25.00
NN-3	Anthology - ***$20,000 Worth Of Prize True Stories*** [1958] Photo cover	$4.00	$12.50	$25.00
NN-4	Anthology - ***The Intimate Side Of Love*** [1958] Photo cover	$4.00	$12.50	$25.00
NN-5	Lieferant, Henry - editor - ***The Defendant In The Case*** [1946] PBO	$6.00	$20.00	$40.00

Beacon Books (Early Publisher's History, 1954–1959)

Beacon offers many esoteric titles. The covers frequently display good girl art. Titles of interest include those by Charles Willeford, Talbut Mundy, and John Jakes. As a part of their imprint, Beacon Books continued the Galaxy Novel series. They produced ten very desirable novels and one anthology (#249) in conjunction with the editors of *Galaxy* magazine. The books lack the traditional B prior to their number. They include numbers 236, 242, 249, 256, 263, 270, 277, 284, 291, 298, 305, and 312.

The publisher also offered the following collectible imprints: Uni-books, Universal Giant, Universal Romance, and Royal Giant Editions.

Beacon Books. New York: Universal Publishing.

		G	VG	F
B-101	Hitt, Orrie - ***She Got What She Wanted*** [1954]	$3.00	$9.00	$18.00
B-102	Nichols, Fan - ***Pawn*** [1950]	$2.50	$7.50	$15.00
B-103	Malloy, Fred - ***Rooming House*** [1954]	$2.50	$7.50	$15.00
B-104	Hitt, Orrie - ***Shabby Street*** [1954] PBO	$2.50	$7.50	$15.00
B-105	Mundy, Talbot - ***King Of The Khyber Rifles*** [1954]	$4.00	$12.50	$25.00
B-106	Habe, Hans - ***Walk In Darkness*** [1954]	$3.00	$9.00	$18.00
B-107	Rebel, Adam - ***Stable Boy*** [1954]	$3.00	$9.00	$18.00
B-108	De Bekker, Jay - ***Gutter Gang*** [1954]	$4.00	$12.50	$25.00
B-109	Willeford, Charles - ***Pick-Up*** [1955] PBO	$20.00	$60.00	$125.00

		G	VG	F
B-110	de Bekker, Jay - ***Keyhole Peeper*** [1955] PBO.	$2.50	$7.50	$15.00
B-111	Kane, Frank - ***Liz*** [1955] PBO	$2.00	$6.00	$12.00
B-112	Pritchard, J. T. - ***Lady Cop*** [1954]	$2.50	$7.50	$15.00
B-113	Anthology - ***Highlights From Yank*** [1954]	$3.50	$10.00	$20.00
B-114	Nichols, Fan - ***Scandalous Lady*** [1951]	$2.00	$6.00	$12.00
B-115	Jakes, John - ***Gonzaga's Woman*** [1954]	$4.00	$12.50	$25.00
B-116	Taylor, Valerie - ***Hired Girl*** [1954]	$2.00	$6.00	$12.00
B-117	Williams, Idabel - ***The Hussy*** [1954]	$2.00	$6.00	$12.00
B-118	Winston, Daoma - ***The Woman He Wanted*** [1954]	$2.00	$6.00	$12.00
B-119	Lucas, Curtis - ***Forbidden Fruit*** [1954]	$2.50	$7.50	$15.00
B-120	Nixon, Henry Lewis - ***Confessions Of A Psychiatrist*** [1954]	$2.00	$6.00	$12.00
B-121	Pritchard, Janet - ***Warped Women*** [1956]	$2.50	$7.50	$15.00
B-122	Nichols, Fan - ***Dolly*** [1956] Photo cover.	$2.00	$6.00	$12.00
B-123	Woodford, Jack & Thompson, John B. - ***Passion In The Pines*** [1956] Cover by Bernard Safran.	$3.00	$9.00	$18.00
B-124	Woodford, Jack & Thompson, John B. - ***Honey*** [1956]	$2.50	$7.50	$15.00
B-125	Woodford, Jack & Thompson, John B. - ***Swamp Hoyden*** [1956]	$2.50	$7.50	$15.00
B-126	Hitt, Orrie - ***Unfaithful Wives*** [1956] PBO.	$2.00	$6.00	$12.00
B-127	Woodford, Jack & Thompson, John B. - ***Savage Eve*** [1956]	$2.00	$6.00	$12.00
B-128	Boltin, William - ***Witch On Wheels*** [1956] Photo cover.	$2.00	$6.00	$12.00
B-129	Thompson, John - ***Bayou Girl*** [1956]	$2.50	$7.50	$15.00
B-130	Williford, Charles - ***High Priest Of California/Wild Wives*** [1956] PBO.	$20.00	$60.00	$125.00
B-131	Weatherall, Ernie - ***Rock 'N Roll Gal*** [1957] PBO. Cover by Owen Kampen.	$7.00	$22.50	$45.00
B-132	Hitt, Orrie - ***The Sucker*** [1957] PBO. Cover by Warren King...	$2.00	$6.00	$12.00
B-133	Barr, Cecil - ***French Model*** [1957] Photo cover.	$2.00	$6.00	$12.00
B-134	Jones, George - ***Twisted*** [1957] PBO. Cover by George Gross.	$2.00	$6.00	$12.00
B-135	Emery, Carol - ***Queer Affair*** [1957] PBO.	$2.50	$7.50	$15.00
B-136	Williams, Lon - ***Shack Baby*** [1957] PBO.	$2.50	$7.50	$15.00
B-137	Hitt, Orrie - ***Nudist Camp*** [1957] PBO. Cover by Bernard Safran.	$2.50	$7.50	$15.00
BB-138	Woodford, Jack & Thompson, John B. - ***Hitch-Hike Hussy*** [1957] Cover by Saul Levine.	$2.00	$6.00	$12.00
BB-139	Hitt, Orrie - ***Pushover*** [1957] PBO. Cover by Geygan.	$2.00	$6.00	$12.00
B-140	Woodford, Jack & Thompson, John B. - ***Sugar Doll*** [1957]	$2.00	$6.00	$12.00
BB-141	Weiss, Joe - ***Love Peddler*** [1957] Cover by Owen Kampen.	$2.50	$7.50	$15.00
BB-142	Hitt, Orrie - ***The Promoter*** [1957] PBO.	$2.00	$6.00	$12.00
BB-143	Williams, Wright - ***Shock Treatment*** [1957] PBO. Photo cover.	$2.50	$7.50	$15.00
BB-144	Thompson, John B. - ***Girls Of The French Quarter*** [1957]	$2.00	$6.00	$12.00
BB-145	Weiss, Joe - ***Passion Blues*** [1957] Photo cover.	$2.50	$7.50	$15.00
BB-146	Hitt, Orrie - ***Ladies Man*** [1957] PBO. Photo cover.	$2.00	$6.00	$12.00
BB-147	Habe, Hans - ***Footloose Fraulein*** [1957]	$2.50	$7.50	$15.00
B-148	Weiss, Joe - ***Lovely Fraud*** [1957]	$2.50	$7.50	$15.00
B-149	Williams, Lon - ***Call Her Wanton*** [1957] PBO.	$2.50	$7.50	$15.00
B-150	Weatherall, Ernie - ***Blonde Trap*** [1957] Photo cover.	$2.00	$6.00	$12.00
BB-151	Hitt, Orrie - ***Dolls And Dues*** [1957] PBO.	$2.00	$6.00	$12.00
B-152	Anonymous - ***Adam And Two Eves*** [1957]	$2.50	$7.50	$15.00
B-153	Hitt, Orrie - ***Trailer Tramp*** [1957] PBO.	$2.50	$7.50	$15.00
B-154	Thompson, John B. - ***Sinful Virgin*** [1957]	$2.50	$7.50	$15.00
B-155	Weiss, Joe - ***Gang Girl*** [1957] PBO.	$3.50	$10.00	$20.00
B-156	Scott, Les - ***Twilight Women*** [1957]	$2.50	$7.50	$15.00
B-157	Von Stroheim, Eric - ***Paprika*** [1957]	$2.50	$7.50	$15.00
B-158	Hitt, Orrie - ***Teaser*** [1957] Photo cover.	$2.00	$6.00	$12.00
B-159	Hitt, Orrie - ***Ellie's Shack*** [1958] PBO.	$2.50	$7.50	$15.00
B-160	Willeford, Charles - ***Honey Gal*** [1958] PBO.	$25.00	$75.00	$180.00
B-161	Pruett, Herbert - ***Back Of Town*** [1958] PBO.	$2.00	$6.00	$12.00
B-162	Williams, Lon - ***Hill Hoyden*** [1958] PBO.	$2.50	$7.50	$15.00

Beacon, B-175

Beacon, B-179

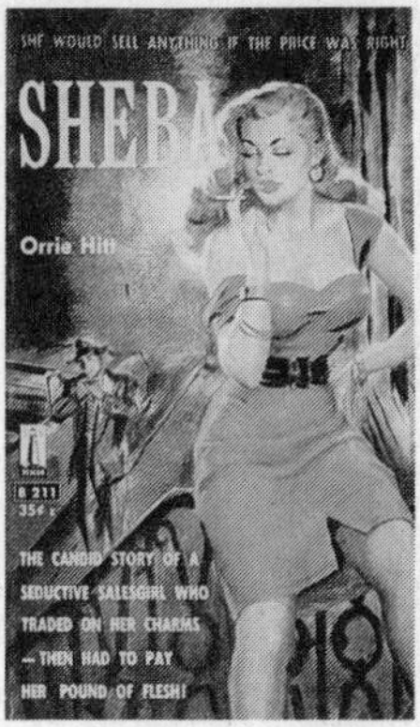

Beacon, B-211

		G	VG	F
B-163	Ames, H. P. - ***Hell Bent*** [1958]	$2.50	$7.50	$15.00
B-164	Hitt, Orrie - ***Suburban Wife*** [1958] PBO. Photo cover.	$2.00	$6.00	$12.00
B-165	de Bekker, Jay - ***Gutter Gang*** [1958] Cover by Walter Popp.	$2.50	$7.50	$15.00
B-166	Arthur, William - ***The Private Pleasures Of Mary Linton*** [1958]	$2.00	$6.00	$12.00
BB-167	Williams, Wright - ***Play For Pay*** [1958] Photo cover.	$2.00	$6.00	$12.00
B-168	Hitt, Orrie - ***Summer Hotel*** [1958] PBO.	$2.00	$6.00	$12.00
B-169	Hitt, Orrie - ***Wild Oats*** [1958] PBO.	$2.50	$7.50	$15.00
B-170	Williams, Wright - ***Side Street*** [1958] Photo cover.	$2.00	$6.00	$12.00
B-171	Malloy, Fred - ***Wild Hunger*** [1958]	$2.50	$7.50	$15.00
B-172	Winston, Daoma - ***The Woman He Wanted*** [1958]	$2.50	$7.50	$15.00
B-173	Lucas, Curtis - ***Forbidden Fruit*** [1958]	$3.00	$9.00	$18.00
B-174	Hitt, Orrie - ***Affairs Of A Beauty Queen*** [1958] PBO. Photo cover.	$2.00	$6.00	$12.00
B-175	Willeford, Charles - ***Lust Is A Woman*** [1958] PBO. Cover by Micarelli.	$22.00	$70.00	$140.00
B-176	Hitt, Orrie - ***Call South 3300: Ask For Molly!*** [1958] PBO.	$2.00	$6.00	$12.00
B-177	Williams, Lon - ***Hill Hellion!*** [1958] PBO.	$2.00	$6.00	$12.00
B-178	Wood, Clement & Goddard, Gloria - ***Fair Game*** [1958]	$2.00	$6.00	$12.00
B-179	Scott, Les - ***The Girl In The Black Chemise*** [1958] Cover by Owen Kampen.	$2.00	$6.00	$12.00
B-180	Hitt, Orrie - ***Burlesque Queen*** [1958] PBO	$2.50	$7.50	$15.00
B-181	Smith, Frank - ***Back Alley*** [1958] Cover by Geygan.	$2.00	$6.00	$12.00
B-182	West, Token - ***Fast Girl*** [1958] Cover by Micarelli.	$2.00	$6.00	$12.00
B-183	Moore, Hal R. - ***The Naked And The Fair*** [1958] PBO. Cover by Micarelli.	$2.00	$6.00	$12.00
B-184	Nixon, Henry Lewis - ***Confessions Of A Psychiatrist*** [1958]	$2.00	$6.00	$12.00
B-185	Malloy, Fred - ***Rooming House*** [1958]	$2.00	$6.00	$12.00
B-186	Hitt, Orrie - ***Trapped*** [1958] Photo cover.	$2.00	$6.00	$12.00
B-187	Gooch, Mary S. - ***The Lusting Breed*** [1958] PBO.	$2.00	$6.00	$12.00
B-188	Hye, Celia - ***I Made My Bed*** [1958] PBO. Photo cover.	$2.00	$6.00	$12.00
B-189	Wood, Clement - ***Studio Affair*** [1958] Cover art by Micarelli.	$2.00	$6.00	$12.00
B-190	Hastings, March - ***Three Women*** [1958] PBO.	$2.50	$7.50	$15.00
B-191	Hitt, Orrie - ***Girl's Dormitory*** [1958] PBO. Cover by Micarelli.	$2.50	$7.50	$15.00
B-192	Priest, J. C. - ***Forbidden*** [1958]	$2.00	$6.00	$12.00
B-193	Winston, Daoma - ***The Other Stranger*** [1958] Cover by Saul Levine.	$2.00	$6.00	$12.00
B-194	Hitt, Orrie - ***Shabby Street*** [1958] Cover by Walter Popp.	$2.00	$6.00	$12.00
B-195	Hitt, Orrie - ***She Got What She Wanted*** [1958] Cover by Al Rossi.	$2.00	$6.00	$12.00

Beacon, B-222

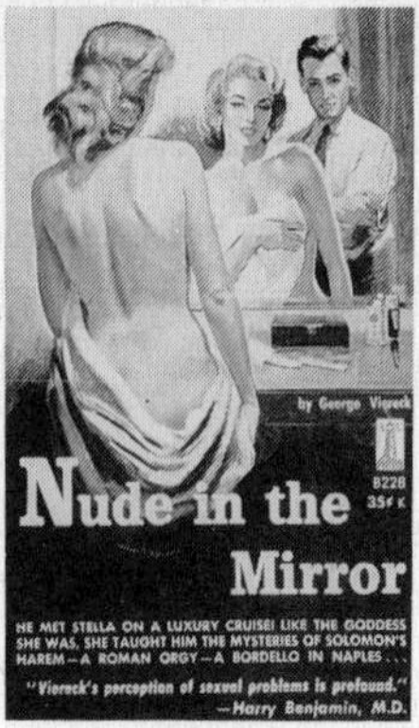

Beacon, B-228

Beacon, 291

		G	VG	F
B-196	Ross, Colin - ***The Mistress*** [1958]	$2.00	$6.00	$12.00
B-197	Hitt, Orrie - ***Woman Hunt*** [1958] PBO. Cover by George Gross.	$2.00	$6.00	$12.00
B-198	Hastings, March - ***Shame*** [1958] PBO.	$2.50	$7.50	$15.00
B-199	Anthology - ***Combat*** [1958]	$3.00	$9.00	$18.00
B-200	Willeford, Charles - ***Pick-Up*** [1955]	$12.50	$37.50	$75.00
B-201	de Bekker, Jay - ***Keyhole Peeper*** [1958]	$2.00	$6.00	$12.00
B-202	Kramer, George - ***School For Girls*** [1958]	$2.50	$7.50	$15.00
B-203	Hitt, Orrie - ***Hot Cargo*** [1958] PBO.	$2.50	$7.50	$15.00
B-204	Fox, James - ***Surabaya*** [1958] PBO.	$2.50	$7.50	$15.00
B-205	Taylor, Duncan - ***Red Curtain*** [1959] PBO. Photo cover.	$2.00	$6.00	$12.00
B-206	Hitt, Orrie - ***The Cheat*** [1958] PBO. Photo cover.	$2.00	$6.00	$12.00
B-207	Hastings, March - ***Circle Of Sin*** [1958] PBO.	$2.00	$6.00	$12.00
B-208	Thompson, John B. - ***Spawn Of The Bayou*** [1958] PBO.	$2.50	$7.50	$15.00
B-209	Hitt, Orrie - ***Rotten To The Core*** [1958] PBO.	$2.50	$7.50	$15.00
B-210	Wagner, Geoffrey - ***The Dispossessed*** [1959] Cover by Walter Popp.	$2.00	$6.00	$12.00
B-211	Hitt, Orrie - ***Sheba*** [1959] PBO.	$2.50	$7.50	$15.00
B-212	Hitt, Orrie - ***Nudist Camp*** [1959]	$2.50	$7.50	$15.00
B-213	Thompson, John B. & Woodford, Jack - ***Hitch-Hike Hussy*** [1959]	$2.00	$6.00	$12.00
B-214	Williams, Lon - ***Adulteress*** [1959] PBO. Cover by Darcy.	$2.00	$6.00	$12.00
B-215	Wagner, Geoffrey - ***Passionate Land*** [1959]	$2.00	$6.00	$12.00
B-216	Gray, Eunice - ***Steffi*** [1959] Cover by Micarelli.	$2.00	$6.00	$12.00
B-217	Drake, H. B. - ***Slave Ship*** [1959]	$2.50	$7.50	$15.00
B-218	Malloy, Fred - ***Strumpet's Seed*** [1959]	$2.00	$6.00	$12.00
B-219	Thompson, John B. - ***Tabasco*** [1959] PBO.	$2.50	$7.50	$15.00
B-220	Nichols, Fan - ***Scandalous Lady*** [1959] Photo cover.	$2.00	$6.00	$12.00
B-221	Williams, Idabel - ***The Hussy*** [1959]	$2.00	$6.00	$12.00
B-222	Hitt, Orrie - ***The Widow*** [1959] PBO.	$2.50	$7.50	$15.00
B-223	Salem, Randy - ***Chris*** [1959] PBO.	$2.50	$7.50	$15.00
B-224	Thompson, John B. - ***Half-Caste*** [1959] PBO. Cover by Barton.	$2.50	$7.50	$15.00
B-225	Kinsey, Chet - ***Kate*** [1959] PBO.	$2.00	$6.00	$12.00
B-226	Travis, Ben - ***The Strange Ones*** [1959] PBO. Cover by Darcy.	$2.50	$7.50	$15.00
B-227	Hitt, Orrie - ***Add Flesh To The Fire*** [1959] PBO.	$2.50	$7.50	$15.00
B-228	Viereck, George - ***Nude In The Mirror*** [1959]	$6.00	$20.00	$40.00
B-229	Walsh, Ruth M. - ***Alcoholic Woman*** [1959]	$2.00	$6.00	$12.00
B-230	Smith, Artemis - ***Odd Girl*** [1959]	$2.00	$6.00	$12.00

		G	VG	F
B-231	Lewis, Roswell - ***Tap Softly On My Bedroom Door*** [1959] PBO.	$2.00	$6.00	$12.00
B-232	Hitt, Orrie - ***Private Club*** [1959] PBO.	$2.00	$6.00	$12.00
B-233	Fox, Richard - ***Turncoat*** [1959] PBO.	$2.50	$7.50	$15.00
B-234	Lester, Lewis - ***Night Of Shame*** [1959] PBO.	$2.50	$7.50	$15.00
B-235	Malloy, Fred - ***Lita*** [1959] PBO.	$2.00	$6.00	$12.00
236	Stapledon, Olaf - ***Odd John*** [1959] Cover by Robert Stanley.	$7.00	$22.50	$45.00
B-237	Britain, Sloane M. - ***The Needle*** [1959] PBO.	$8.00	$25.00	$50.00
B-238	Hitt, Orrie - ***Carnival Girl*** [1959] PBO. Photo cover.	$2.50	$7.50	$15.00
B-239	Hitt, Orrie - ***The Peeper*** [1959] PBO.	$3.00	$9.00	$18.00
B-240	Thompson, John B. - ***Temple Of Lust*** [1959] PBO.	$2.50	$7.50	$15.00
B-241	Seeley, E. S. - ***Street Walker*** [1959] PBO. Cover by Barton.	$2.50	$7.50	$15.00
242	Jones, Raymond F. - ***The Deviates*** [1959] Cover by Robert Stanley.	$5.50	$17.50	$35.00
B-243	Clark, Dorine - ***Hell Cat*** [1959] PBO.	$2.50	$7.50	$15.00
B-244	Morro, Don - ***The Virgin*** [1959]	$2.00	$6.00	$12.00
B-245	Castro, Joe - ***The Young Hoods*** [1959] PBO. Cover by E. Uppwall.	$3.50	$10.00	$20.00
B-246	Stone, Scott - ***The Divorcees*** [1959]	$2.00	$6.00	$12.00
B-247	Devlin, Barry - ***Too Many Women*** [1959]	$2.00	$6.00	$12.00
B-248	Stone, Scott - ***Margo*** [1959]	$2.00	$6.00	$12.00
249	Anthology - ***31 Short Short Stories From Collier's*** [1959] PBO.	$2.50	$7.50	$15.00
B-250	Hitt, Orrie - ***Too Hot To Handle*** [1959] PBO.	$2.00	$6.00	$12.00
B-251	Dean, Ralph - ***One Kind Of Woman*** [1959] PBO.	$2.50	$7.50	$15.00
B-252	Devlin, Barry - ***Cheating Wives*** [1959] Photo cover.	$2.00	$6.00	$12.00
B-253	Thompson, John Burton - ***Nude In The Sand*** [1959] PBO.	$2.50	$7.50	$15.00
B-254	Hitt, Orrie - ***Sin Doll*** [1959] PBO. Cover by Milo.	$2.00	$6.00	$12.00
B-255	Devlin, Barry - ***Make Sure I Win*** [1959]	$2.00	$6.00	$12.00
256	Smith, George O. - ***Troubled Star*** [1959] Cover by Ed Emsh.	$5.50	$17.50	$35.00
B-257	Reed, Kathie - ***Shack Woman*** [1959] Cover by George Gross.	$2.50	$7.50	$15.00
B-258	Kelly, Jack - ***Wild Blonde*** [1959] PBO.	$2.50	$7.50	$15.00
B-259	Addams, Kay - ***Queer Patterns*** [1959] PBO.	$3.00	$9.00	$18.00
B-260	Williams, David - ***Basement Gang*** [1959] PBO. Photo "JD" cover.	$4.00	$12.50	$25.00
B-261	Hitt, Orrie - ***Tawny*** [1959] PBO.	$2.50	$7.50	$15.00
B-262	Foster, Joseph - ***Danielle*** [1959] PBO. Cover by Milo.	$2.50	$7.50	$15.00
263	Garrett, Randall - ***Pagan Passions*** [1959] PBO. Cover by Robert Stanley.	$6.00	$20.00	$40.00
B-264	Norday, Michael - ***Strange Thirsts*** [1959]	$2.50	$7.50	$15.00
B-265	Thompson, John Burton - ***Hot Blood*** [1959] PBO. Cover by Milo.	$2.50	$7.50	$15.00
B-266	Anton, Cal - ***Strip-Tease Girl*** [1959] PBO.	$2.50	$7.50	$15.00
B-267	Hitt, Orrie - ***Ex-Virgin*** [1959] PBO.	$2.50	$7.50	$15.00
B-268	Smith, Artemis - ***The Third Sex*** [1959] PBO.	$2.50	$7.50	$15.00
B-269	Priest, J. C. - ***Private School*** [1959] PBO.	$2.50	$7.50	$15.00
270	Anderson, Poul - ***Virgin Planet*** [1960] Cover by Robert Stanley.	$7.00	$22.50	$45.00
B-271	Nixon, Henry Louis - ***Naked Desire*** [1959] PBO.	$2.50	$7.50	$15.00
B-272	Winston, Daoma - ***Golden Tramp*** [1959] PBO.	$2.50	$7.50	$15.00
B-273	Tryon, Mark - ***Of G-Strings And Strippers*** [1959]	$2.00	$6.00	$12.00
B-274	Hitt, Orrie - ***Suburban Sin*** [1959] PBO.	$2.00	$6.00	$12.00
B-275	Morell, Lee - ***Mimi*** [1959] PBO.	$2.00	$6.00	$12.00
B-276	Stokes, Manning - ***Triangle Of Sin*** [1959] PBO. Cover by Milo.	$2.00	$6.00	$12.00
277	Farmer, Philip Jose - ***Flesh*** [1960] PBO. Cover by Gerald McConnel.	$10.00	$30.00	$60.00
B-278	Seeley, E. S. - ***Sorority Sin*** [1959] PBO. Cover by Rodewald.	$2.50	$7.50	$15.00
B-279	Lucas, Rick - ***Convention Girl*** [1959]	$2.50	$7.50	$15.00
B-280	Norday, Michael - ***Warped*** [1959] Cover art by Micarelli.	$2.50	$7.50	$15.00

		G	VG	F
B-281	Sydney, Gale - ***Strange Circle*** [1959] PBO.	$2.50	$7.50	$15.00
B-282	Kent, Justin - ***Mavis*** [1960]	$2.00	$6.00	$12.00
B-283	Devlin, Barry - ***Night Of The Lash*** [1959] Cover by Barton.	$2.50	$7.50	$15.00
284	Merwin Jr., Sam - ***The Sex War*** [1960] Cover by Gerald McConnel.	$7.00	$22.50	$45.00
B-285	Stone, Thomas - ***Ex-Mistress*** [1960] PBO.	$2.00	$6.00	$12.00
B-286	Savage, Kim - ***Helena's House*** [1960] Cover by Barton.	$2.00	$6.00	$12.00
B-287	Albert, Simms - ***Pound Of Flesh*** [1960] PBO.	$2.50	$7.50	$15.00
B-288	Hitt, Orrie - ***Wayward Girl*** [1960] PBO.	$2.50	$7.50	$15.00
B-289	Addams, Kay - ***Warped Desire*** [1960] PBO.	$2.00	$6.00	$12.00
B-290	Barry, Winchell - ***Scarlet City*** [1960] PBO.	$2.50	$7.50	$15.00
291	Farmer, Philip Jose - ***A Woman A Day*** [1960] PBO. Cover by Gerald McConnel.	$12.50	$37.50	$75.00
B-292	Woodford, Jack & Thompson, John Burton - ***Male Virgin*** [1960] PBO.	$2.00	$6.00	$12.00
B-293	Pritchard, Janet - ***Station Wagon Wives*** [1960] PBO.	$2.00	$6.00	$12.00
B-294	Hitt, Orrie - ***The Torrid Teens*** [1960] PBO.	$3.00	$9.00	$18.00
B-295	Devlin, Barry - ***Song Of The Whip*** [1960] Cover by Bob Maguire.	$2.50	$7.50	$15.00
B-296	Hanley, Jack - ***Very Private Secretary*** [1960] PBO.	$2.00	$6.00	$12.00
B-297	Semple, Gordon - ***Summer Resort Women*** [1960] PBO.	$2.00	$6.00	$12.00
298	Van Vogt, A. E. - ***The Mating Cry*** [1960] Cover by Gerald McConnel.	$10.00	$30.00	$60.00
B-299	Wall, Evans - ***Ask For Therese*** [1960] PBO.	$2.00	$6.00	$12.00
B-300	Dean, Ralph - ***Lingerie LTD.*** [1960] PBO.	$2.00	$6.00	$12.00
B-301	Thompson, John Burton - ***One More For The Road*** [1960] PBO. Cover by Micarelli.	$2.00	$6.00	$12.00
B-302	Gaddis, Peggy - ***Doctor Prescott's Secret*** [1960]	$2.00	$6.00	$12.00
B-303	Lucas, Rick - ***Restless Women*** [1960] PBO.	$2.00	$6.00	$12.00
B-304	Hitt, Orrie - ***From Door To Door*** [1960] PBO.	$2.00	$6.00	$12.00
305	Aldiss, Brian - ***The Male Response*** [1961] PBO. Cover by Robert Stanley.	$7.00	$22.50	$45.00
B-306	Rifkin, Leo & Norman, Tony - ***Gutter Girl*** [1960] PBO.	$2.00	$6.00	$12.00
B-307	Carter, Ralph - ***Pleasure Alley*** [1960]	$2.00	$6.00	$12.00
B-308	Addams, Kay - ***Lucy*** [1960] PBO. Cover by Darcy.	$2.00	$6.00	$12.00
B-309	Lucas, Rick - ***Huckster's Women*** [1960]	$2.00	$6.00	$12.00
B-310	Malloy, Fred - ***Infidelity*** [1960] PBO.	$2.00	$6.00	$12.00
B-311	Clark, Dorene - ***Different*** [1960] PBO.	$2.50	$7.50	$15.00
312	Judd, Cyril - ***Sin In Space*** [1961] Cover by Robert Stanley.	$7.00	$22.50	$45.00
B-313	De Mexico, N. R. - ***Private Chauffeur*** [1960] PBO. Cover by Paul Rader.	$2.50	$7.50	$15.00
B-314	Hitt, Orrie - ***Motel Girls*** [1960] PBO.	$2.00	$6.00	$12.00
B-315	Stone, Scott - ***She Learned The Hard Way*** [1960] Cover by Faragasso.	$2.00	$6.00	$12.00
B-316	Morell, Lee - ***Nurses' Quarters*** [1960] PBO.	$2.00	$6.00	$12.00
B-317	Duperrault, Doug - ***Trailer Camp Woman*** [1960]	$1.50	$5.00	$10.00
B-318	Lester, Lewis - ***Philanderer's Women*** [1960] Cover by Milo.	$1.50	$5.00	$10.00
B-320	Swanson, Gregory - ***The Hayloft*** [1960] PBO.	$2.50	$7.50	$15.00
B-321	Stonebraker, Florence - ***Lust For Love*** [1960] PBO.	$2.00	$6.00	$12.00
B-322	Branch, Florenz - ***Intimate Physician*** [1960] PBO.	$2.00	$6.00	$12.00
B-323	Smith, Ben - ***Wanton*** [1960] PBO.	$2.00	$6.00	$12.00
B-324	McKnight, Evans - ***She Made Her Bed*** [1960] PBO.	$2.00	$6.00	$12.00
B-325	Hitt, Orrie - ***Tell Them Anything*** [1960] PBO.	$2.00	$6.00	$12.00
B-327	De Forest, Barry - ***Play Girl*** [1960] PBO.	$2.00	$6.00	$12.00
B-328	De Mexico, N. R. - ***Marijuana Girl*** [1960]	$7.00	$22.50	$45.00
B-329	Thompson, John Burton - ***The Eager Ones*** [1960] PBO.	$2.00	$6.00	$12.00
B-330	Revelle, G. G. - ***Alcoholic Wife*** [1960] PBO.	$2.00	$6.00	$12.00
B-331	Wall, Evans - ***Wedding Night*** [1960] PBO. Cover by Darcy.	$2.00	$6.00	$12.00
B-332	Hitt, Orrie - ***Call Me Bad*** [1960] PBO. Cover by Frace.	$2.00	$6.00	$12.00
B-334	Day, Max - ***The Resort*** [1960] PBO.	$2.00	$6.00	$12.00

		G	VG	F
B-335	Grant, Richard - ***Office Wife*** [1960] PBO.	$2.00	$6.00	$12.00
B-336	Hitt, Orrie - ***Untamed Lust*** [1960] PBO.	$2.00	$6.00	$12.00
B-337	Whittington, Harry - ***Prime Sucker*** [1960] PBO. Cover by Barton.	$2.00	$6.00	$12.00
B-338	Hitt, Orrie - ***Never Cheat Alone*** [1960] PBO. Cover by Milo.	$2.00	$6.00	$12.00
B-339	Pritchard, Janet - ***One Hot Night*** [1960] PBO.	$2.00	$6.00	$12.00
B-341	Carter, Jesse Lee - ***Tami*** [1960]	$1.50	$5.00	$10.00
B-342	Hitt, Orrie - ***The Lady Is A Lush*** [1960] PBO.	$2.00	$6.00	$12.00
B-343	Tryon, Mark - ***The Twisted Loves Of Nym O'Sullivan*** [1960] PBO.	$2.50	$7.50	$15.00
B-344	Manning, Bruce - ***Off Limits*** [1960] PBO.	$2.00	$6.00	$12.00
B-345	Harding, Matt - ***Young Widow*** [1960] PBO. Cover by Al Rossi.	$2.00	$6.00	$12.00
B-346	Day, Max - ***Girl On The Beach*** [1960] PBO.	$2.00	$6.00	$12.00
B-348	Salem, Randy - ***Man Among Women*** [1960] PBO.	$2.00	$6.00	$12.00
B-349	Stone, Thomas - ***Tramp Girl*** [1960] PBO.	$2.00	$6.00	$12.00
B-350	Harrison, Whit - ***Strip The Town Naked*** [1960] PBO.	$4.00	$12.50	$25.00
B-351	Pruett, Herbert Q. - ***Scandal High*** [1960] PBO. Cover by Faragasso.	$2.00	$6.00	$12.00
B-352	Semple, Gordon - ***Waterfront Blonde*** [1960] PBO. Cover by Frace.	$2.00	$6.00	$12.00
B-353	Lutz, Giles A. - ***Stranger In My Bed*** [1960] PBO.	$2.00	$6.00	$12.00
B-355	Manning, Bruce - ***Cafe Society Sinner*** [1960] PBO. Cover by Al Rossi.	$2.00	$6.00	$12.00
B-356	Hitt, Orrie - ***Sexurbia County*** [1960] PBO. Cover by Robert Maguire.	$2.00	$6.00	$12.00
B-357	West, Ben - ***Loves Of A Girl Wrestler*** [1960]	$3.00	$9.00	$18.00
B-358	Addams, Kay - ***Three Strange Women*** [1960] PBO.	$2.50	$7.50	$15.00
B-359	West, Ben - ***Girl Artist*** [1960] PBO.	$2.50	$7.50	$15.00
B-360	Harding, Matt - ***Man Trap*** [1960] PBO. Cover by Barton.	$2.00	$6.00	$12.00
B-362	Burgess, Charles - ***The Other Woman*** [1960] PBO.	$2.00	$6.00	$12.00
B-363	Bligh, Norman - ***The Sisters*** [1960] PBO.	$2.00	$6.00	$12.00
B-364	Sherman, Joan - ***Suzy*** [1960] PBO.	$2.00	$6.00	$12.00
B-365	Harding, Matt - ***All Woman*** [1960]	$2.00	$6.00	$12.00
B-366	Foster, Gerald - ***Irene's Room*** [1960] PBO.	$2.00	$6.00	$12.00
B-367	Sherman, Joan - ***Wild Fruit*** [1960] PBO. Cover by Milo.	$2.00	$6.00	$12.00
B-369	Gooch, Mary Shomette - ***Cheating Woman*** [1960] PBO. Cover by Al Rossi.	$2.00	$6.00	$12.00
B-370	Hitt, Orrie - ***The Sucker*** [1960] Cover by Warren King.	$1.50	$5.00	$10.00
371	Woodford, Jack - ***Honey*** [1961]	$1.50	$5.00	$10.00
B-372	Weiss, Joe - ***Gang Girl*** [1961]	$2.00	$6.00	$12.00
B-373	Jones, George - ***Twisted*** [1961] Cover by George Gross.	$1.50	$5.00	$10.00
B-374	Harding, Matt - ***They Couldn't Say No*** [1961] PBO. Cover by Faragasso.	$2.00	$6.00	$12.00
B-376	Clay, Manning - ***Wild Body*** [1961] PBO.	$2.00	$6.00	$12.00
B-377	Emery, Carol - ***Queer Affair*** [1961]	$2.00	$6.00	$12.00
B-378	Hitt, Orrie - ***Unfaithful Wives*** [1961]	$1.50	$5.00	$10.00
B-379	Weatherall, Ernie - ***Rock N' Roll Gal*** [1961] Cover by Kampen.	$5.00	$15.00	$30.00
B-380	Hitt, Orrie - ***Pushover*** [1961]	$1.50	$5.00	$10.00
B-381	Woodford, Jack & Thompson, John B. - ***Savage Eve*** [1961]	$1.50	$5.00	$10.00
B-383	Thompson, John B. - ***Girls Of The French Quarter*** [1961]	$1.50	$5.00	$10.00
B-384	Kirby, Mark - ***Harling College*** [1961] PBO.	$2.00	$6.00	$12.00
B-385	Vaneer, William - ***Lust In Paradise*** [1961] PBO.	$2.00	$6.00	$12.00
B-386	Chadwick, Joseph - ***Man Chase*** [1961] PBO.	$2.00	$6.00	$12.00
B-387	Lord, Sheldon - ***Pads Are For Passion*** [1961] PBO.	$2.00	$6.00	$12.00
B-388	Stonebraker, Florence - ***Kept Sisters*** [1961] PBO.	$2.00	$6.00	$12.00
B-390	Martin, Della - ***Twilight Girl*** [1961] PBO.	$2.00	$6.00	$12.00
B-391	Williams, Wright - ***Side Street*** [1961]	$1.50	$5.00	$10.00

		G	VG	F
B-392	Harrison, Whit - ***Any Woman He Wanted*** [1961] PBO. Cover by Micarelli.	$4.00	$12.50	$25.00
B-393	Evens, Hodge - ***Sherry*** [1961] PBO.	$2.00	$6.00	$12.00
B-394	Stonebraker, Florence - ***Summer Widow*** [1961] PBO. Cover by Al Rossi.	$2.00	$6.00	$12.00
B-395	Hitt, Orrie - ***Ladies' Man*** [1961]	$1.50	$5.00	$10.00
B-397	Thompson, John B. - ***Sinful Virgin*** [1961]	$1.50	$5.00	$10.00
B-398	Stone, Tom - ***Reckless*** [1961] PBO.	$2.00	$6.00	$12.00
B-399	Edd, Karl - ***Teen Tramp*** [1961] PBO.	$2.50	$7.50	$15.00
B-400	Harding, Matt - ***The Mattress Game*** [1961] PBO.	$2.00	$6.00	$12.00
B-401	Hitt, Orrie - ***I Prowl By Night*** [1961] PBO.	$2.00	$6.00	$12.00
B-402	Carruthers, Margaret - ***His Best Friend's Wife*** [1961] PBO.	$2.00	$6.00	$12.00
B-403	Balmer, Jon - ***Lusting Women*** [1961] PBO.	$2.00	$6.00	$12.00
B-404	Lorraine, Louis - ***The Cheating Game*** [1961] PBO.	$2.00	$6.00	$12.00
B-405	Boyd, T. S. - ***Kitty*** [1961] PBO.	$2.00	$6.00	$12.00
B-406	James, Al - ***The Running Girls*** [1961] PBO.	$2.00	$6.00	$12.00
B-407	Hale, Laura - ***Sensual Woman*** [1961] PBO.	$2.00	$6.00	$12.00
B-408	Munroe, Val - ***After Hours*** [1961] PBO.	$2.00	$6.00	$12.00
B-409F	Stokes, Manning - ***Girl On A Couch*** [1961] PBO. Cover by Al Rossi.	$2.00	$6.00	$12.00
B-410	Gordon, Joseph - ***Passion Island*** [1961] PBO.	$2.00	$6.00	$12.00
B-411	Carr, Jay - ***Love Fever*** [1961] PBO.	$2.00	$6.00	$12.00
B-412	Deas, Garrett W. - ***Hell Is A Woman*** [1961] PBO. Cover by Jack Thurston.	$2.00	$6.00	$12.00
B-413F	Layne, James - ***Lend Me Your Wife*** [1961] PBO.	$2.00	$6.00	$12.00
B-414F	McCoy, Dean - ***The Development*** [1961] PBO. Cover by Barton.	$2.00	$6.00	$12.00
B-415Y	Hitt, Orrie - ***Dirt Farm*** [1961] PBO.	$2.00	$6.00	$12.00
B-416Y	Harrison, Whit - ***A Woman Possessed*** [1961] PBO. Cover by Robert Maguire.	$4.00	$12.50	$25.00
B-417Y	McCollum, R. R. - ***One Of Those Cruises*** [1961] PBO.	$2.00	$6.00	$12.00
B-418F	Merrick, Clyde - ***Sex Pack*** [1961] PBO.	$2.50	$7.50	$15.00
B-419B	Gilbert, Elliott - ***Too Much Woman*** [1961] PBO.	$2.00	$6.00	$12.00
B-420B	Low, Glenn - ***Reckless Virgin*** [1961] PBO.	$2.00	$6.00	$12.00
B-421Y	West, Mark - ***Office Affair*** [1961] PBO.	$2.00	$6.00	$12.00
B-422	Hitt, Orrie - ***Summer Of Sin*** [1961] PBO.	$2.00	$6.00	$12.00
B-423Y	Elliott, Ben - ***Weekend Wife*** [1961] PBO.	$2.00	$6.00	$12.00
B-424F	Huish, Leonard - ***The Window*** [1961] PBO.	$2.00	$6.00	$12.00
B-425F	Richard, Louis - ***The Sex Pulse*** [1961] PBO. Cover by Ray Johnson.	$2.00	$6.00	$12.00
B-426F	Lorraine, Louis - ***Commuter Widow*** [1961] PBO.	$2.00	$6.00	$12.00
B-427B	Evens, Hodge - ***The Lash Of Lust*** [1961] PBO.	$2.50	$7.50	$15.00
B-428B	Demaris, Oscar J. - ***Chips' Girls*** [1961] PBO.	$2.50	$7.50	$15.00
B-429Y	Hitt, Orrie - ***Four Women*** [1961] PBO.	$2.00	$6.00	$12.00
B-430F	Somervill, J. W. - ***Tomorrow's Call Girls*** [1961] PBO.	$2.00	$6.00	$12.00
B-431Y	Carr, Jay - ***Weekend*** [1961] PBO. Cover by Darcy.	$2.00	$6.00	$12.00
B-432	Turner, Robert - ***Cheater*** [1961] PBO.	$2.00	$6.00	$12.00
B-433Y	Harding, Matt - ***Fly Girl*** [1961] PBO. Cover by Darcy.	$2.00	$6.00	$12.00
B-434F	Hitt, Orrie - ***The Love Season*** [1961] PBO.	$2.00	$6.00	$12.00
B-435Y	McCoy, Dean - ***Double Up*** [1961]	$1.50	$5.00	$10.00
B-436Y	Hale, Laura - ***Lessons In Lust*** [1961] PBO.	$2.00	$6.00	$12.00
B-437Y	Donovan, Curt - ***The Lusting Hours*** [1961] PBO.	$2.00	$6.00	$12.00
B-438Y	Low, Glenn - ***The Barn*** [1961] PBO.	$2.00	$6.00	$12.00
B-439F	Napier, Dominique - ***House Party*** [1961] PBO.	$2.00	$6.00	$12.00
B-440F	Matthews, Clayton - ***Discontented Wives*** [1961] PBO.	$2.00	$6.00	$12.00
B-441Y	Balmer, Jon - ***Squeeze Play*** [1961] PBO. Cover by Barton.	$2.00	$6.00	$12.00
B-442F	Savage, George - ***Runaway Wife*** [1961] PBO.	$2.00	$6.00	$12.00
B-443Y	Evens, Hodge - ***Two Faces Of Passion*** [1961] PBO. Cover by Ray Johnson.	$2.00	$6.00	$12.00
B-444Y	Addams, Kay - ***The Strangest Sin*** [1961] PBO.	$2.50	$7.50	$15.00

		G	VG	F
B-445F	Carson, Dave - ***Sex III*** [1961] PBO.	$2.50	$7.50	$15.00
B-446F	Lord, Sheldon - ***Community Of Women*** [1961] PBO.	$2.00	$6.00	$12.00
B-447Y	Harding, Matt - ***The Office Game*** [1961] PBO.	$2.00	$6.00	$12.00
B-448F	Hitt, Orrie - ***Frigid Wife*** [1961] PBO.	$2.00	$6.00	$12.00
B-449F	Dorian, Elaine - ***Love Now, Pay Later*** [1961] PBO.	$2.00	$6.00	$12.00
B-450F	Beck, Charles - ***The Wife Traders*** [1961] PBO.	$2.00	$6.00	$12.00
B-451Y	Hitt, Orrie - ***Virgins No More*** [1961] PBO.	$2.00	$6.00	$12.00
B-452F	Layne, Jim - ***Party Wives*** [1961] PBO.	$2.00	$6.00	$12.00
B-453F	Webster, Sam - ***Stolen Woman*** [1961] PBO. Cover by Darcy.	$2.00	$6.00	$12.00
B-454F	Viletti, Marco - ***Cry Rape*** [1961] PBO. Cover by Darcy.	$2.00	$6.00	$12.00
B-455F	Carr, Jay - ***The Motel*** [1961] PBO. Cover by Ray Johnson.	$2.00	$6.00	$12.00
B-456F	Lord, Sheldon - ***April North*** [1961] PBO. Cover by Al Rossi.	$2.00	$6.00	$12.00
B-457F	Adlon, Arthur - ***By Love Depraved*** [1961] PBO. Cover by Darcy.	$2.00	$6.00	$12.00
B-458F	Lorraine, Louis - ***Blonde Dynamite*** [1961] PBO.	$2.00	$6.00	$12.00
B-459F	Gregory, Paul - ***Naked Lens*** [1961] PBO.	$2.00	$6.00	$12.00
B-460F	McCoy, Dean - ***Sexbound*** [1961]	$1.50	$5.00	$10.00
B-461F	Williams, Sandra - ***A Woman's Need*** [1962] PBO.	$2.00	$6.00	$12.00
B-462F	Hitt, Orrie - ***Love Thief*** [1962] PBO.	$2.00	$6.00	$12.00
B-463F	Dorian, Elaine - ***Suburbia: Jungle Of Sex*** [1962] PBO. Cover by Ray Johnson.	$2.00	$6.00	$12.00
B-464F	Turner, Robert - ***Woman Chaser*** [1962] PBO.	$2.00	$6.00	$12.00
B-465F	Hitt, Orrie - ***Dial "M" For Man*** [1962] PBO. Cover by Brule.	$2.00	$6.00	$12.00
B-466F	West, Mark - ***His Boss' Wife*** [1962] PBO. Cover by Al Rossi.	$2.00	$6.00	$12.00
B-467F	Furlough, John - ***Half Girl, Half Woman*** [1962] PBO. Cover by Micarelli.	$2.00	$6.00	$12.00
B-468F	West, Mark - ***Object Of Lust*** [1962] PBO. Cover by Darcy.	$2.00	$6.00	$12.00
B-469F	Lord, Sheldon - ***Husband Chaser*** [1962] PBO.	$2.00	$6.00	$12.00
B-470F	Munroe, Val - ***Lisette*** [1962] PBO. Cover by Darcy.	$2.00	$6.00	$12.00
B-471F	Holmes, Rick - ***Man Crazy*** [1962] PBO.	$2.00	$6.00	$12.00
B-472F	Adeon, Arthur - ***Neglected Wives*** [1962]	$2.00	$6.00	$12.00
B-473K	Collins, A. J. - ***The Wild Wants*** [1962] PBO. Cover by Darcy.	$2.00	$6.00	$12.00
B-474F	Barry, Ken - ***The Golden Girls*** [1962] PBO.	$2.00	$6.00	$12.00
B-475F	Richard, Louis - ***Secret Lusts*** [1962]	$1.50	$5.00	$10.00
B-476	Lorraine, Louis - ***Wives And Lovers*** [1962] PBO.	$2.00	$6.00	$12.00
B-477F	Beck, Charles - ***The Bed At The Top*** [1962] PBO. Cover by Barton.	$2.00	$6.00	$12.00
B-478F	Gibbs, Carlton - ***Troubled Town*** [1962] PBO.	$2.00	$6.00	$12.00
B-479F	Dorian, Elaine - ***Second-Time Woman*** [1962] PBO.	$2.00	$6.00	$12.00
B-480F	Harding, Matt - ***Men On Her Mind*** [1962] PBO.	$2.00	$6.00	$12.00
B-481F	Gibbs, Carlton - ***Behind Respectable Doors*** [1962] PBO.	$2.00	$6.00	$12.00
B-482F	Hale, Laura - ***The Zipper Girls*** [1962] PBO.	$2.00	$6.00	$12.00
B-483F	Ammons, Pat - ***Faithful To None*** [1962] PBO. Cover by Darcy.	$2.00	$6.00	$12.00
B-484F	Layne, Jim - ***The Six-Weekers*** [1962] PBO. Cover by Darcy.	$2.00	$6.00	$12.00
B-485	Harrison, Timothy - ***Hot Summer*** [1962] PBO.	$2.00	$6.00	$12.00
B-486F	Sorrell, Phillip - ***Doctors' Women*** [1962] PBO. Cover by Darcy.	$2.00	$6.00	$12.00
B-487F	Christopher, Ben - ***Strange Embrace*** [1962] PBO.	$2.50	$7.50	$15.00
B-488F	Barry, Ken - ***Executive Boudoir*** [1962] PBO.	$2.00	$6.00	$12.00
B-489F	Moran, Allan - ***The Wife Spoilers*** [1962] PBO.	$2.00	$6.00	$12.00
B-490F	Layne, Jim - ***Company Woman*** [1962] PBO.	$2.00	$6.00	$12.00
B-491F	Lord, Sheldon - ***The Third Way*** [1962] PBO.	$2.50	$7.50	$15.00
B-492F	Adlon, Arthur - ***The Odd Kind*** [1962] PBO. Cover by Milo.	$2.50	$7.50	$15.00
B-493F	March, Kim - ***Bachelor Nurse*** [1962] PBO.	$2.00	$6.00	$12.00
B-494F	Savage, George - ***Suburban High School*** [1962] PBO.	$2.00	$6.00	$12.00
B-495F	Lorraine, Louis - ***The Split-Level Game*** [1962] PBO. Cover by Darcy.	$2.00	$6.00	$12.00
B-496F	Furlough, John - ***Cult-Priest's Daughter*** [1962] PBO. Cover by Darcy.	$2.00	$6.00	$12.00

		G	VG	F
B-497F	Roberts, Herb - ***Motel Mismates*** [1962] PBO. Cover by Jack Thurston.	$2.00	$6.00	$12.00
B-498F	Gregory, Paul - ***The Office Couch*** [1962] PBO.	$2.00	$6.00	$12.00
B-499F	Dorian, Elaine - ***The Infidelity Game*** [1962] PBO.	$2.00	$6.00	$12.00
B-500F	Hart, Brad - ***The Thrill Makers*** [1962] PBO.	$2.00	$6.00	$12.00
B-501F	Vincent, Gabrielle - ***Woman Alone*** [1962] PBO. Cover by Barton.	$2.00	$6.00	$12.00
B-502	Gold, R. C. - ***Bedroom Beat*** [1962] PBO.	$2.00	$6.00	$12.00
B-503F	Taylor, R. W. - ***She Devil*** [1962] PBO.	$2.00	$6.00	$12.00
B-504F	Donovan, Curt - ***Witch With Blue Eyes*** [1962] PBO. Cover by Darcy.	$2.00	$6.00	$12.00
B-505	James, Terry - ***The Professor's Wife*** [1962] PBO.	$2.00	$6.00	$12.00
B-506F	Brill, Lee - ***The Skin-Tight Sheath*** [1962] PBO.	$2.00	$6.00	$12.00
B-507F	Winters, Dee - ***Offshore Resort*** [1962] PBO.	$2.00	$6.00	$12.00
B-508F	Carter, Alex - ***High School Jungle*** [1962] PBO.	$2.00	$6.00	$12.00
B-509	Carr, Jay - ***Unnatural Wife*** [1962]	$1.35	$4.00	$8.00
B-510F	Trainer, Russell - ***The Warden's Wife*** [1962] PBO.	$1.50	$5.00	$10.00
B-511F	Napier, Dominique - ***Never Love A Man*** [1962] PBO. Cover by Darcy.	$2.00	$6.00	$12.00
B-512F	Dorian, Elaine - ***Suburban Affair*** [1962] PBO.	$1.50	$5.00	$10.00
B-513F	Adler, Toni - ***A Woman's Woman*** [1962] PBO.	$2.00	$6.00	$12.00
B-514F	Layne, Jim - ***Lust In Orbit*** [1962] PBO. Cover by Darcy.	$1.50	$5.00	$10.00
B-515F	Carr, Jay - ***Episode In A Town*** [1962] PBO.	$1.50	$5.00	$10.00
B-516F	Adlon, Arthur - ***Shared Lover*** [1962] PBO.	$1.50	$5.00	$10.00
B-517	Gregory, Paul - ***Like A Tigress At Bay*** [1962] PBO.	$1.50	$5.00	$10.00
B-518F	Winters, Dee - ***Weekend Arrangements*** [1962] PBO.	$1.50	$5.00	$10.00
B-519	Ellson, Hal - ***That Glover Woman*** [1962] PBO.	$2.50	$7.50	$15.00
B-520F	Lorraine, Louis - ***That Summer In Rome*** [1962]	$1.50	$5.00	$10.00
B-521F	Savage, George - ***The Deal Makers*** [1962] PBO.	$1.50	$5.00	$10.00
B-522F	Matthews, Clayton - ***Sex Dancer*** [1962] PBO.	$1.50	$5.00	$10.00
B-523F	Clubb, Stacey - ***Trap Of Lesbos*** [1962] PBO.	$1.50	$5.00	$10.00
B-524F	Gregory, Paul - ***The Casting Couch*** [1962] PBO.	$1.50	$5.00	$10.00
B-525F	Cassidy, George - ***Bait*** [1962] PBO.	$1.50	$5.00	$10.00
B-526	Turner, Robert - ***Strange Sisters*** [1962]	$1.50	$5.00	$10.00
B-527	Hale, Laura - ***The Marriage Bed*** [1962]	$1.50	$5.00	$10.00
B-528F	Loren, Francis - ***Nest Of Summer Widows*** [1962] PBO.	$1.50	$5.00	$10.00
B-529F	Woodward, L. T. (Robert Silverberg) - ***The Deceivers*** [1962] PBO.	$1.50	$5.00	$10.00
B-530F	O'Bannon, Brian - ***Bedrooms On Wheels*** [1962] PBO.	$1.50	$5.00	$10.00
B-531	Gibbs, Carlton - ***Neighbors and Lovers*** [1962] PBO.	$1.50	$5.00	$10.00
B-532F	Adlon, Arthur - ***The Set*** [1962] PBO.	$1.50	$5.00	$10.00
B-533F	Temple, Dan - ***The Love Goddess*** [1962] PBO.	$1.50	$5.00	$10.00
B-534F	Reeves, Abbot J. - ***Rage To Rape*** [1962] PBO.	$1.50	$5.00	$10.00
B-535F	Dorian, Elaine - ***The Sex Cure*** [1962] PBO.	$1.50	$5.00	$10.00
B-536F	Barry, Ken - ***The Love Itch*** [1962] PBO. Cover by Brule.	$1.50	$5.00	$10.00
B-537F	Gibbs, Carlton - ***Girl In A Cage*** [1962] PBO. Cover by Robert Maguire.	$2.00	$6.00	$12.00
B-538F	Layne, Jim - ***Borrowed Lover*** [1962] PBO.	$1.50	$5.00	$10.00
B-539F	Joyce, Carlton - ***Campus Scandal*** [1962] PBO.	$1.50	$5.00	$10.00
B-540F	Roberts, Herb - ***Love-Hungry Women*** [1962] PBO.	$1.50	$5.00	$10.00
B-541	Adlon, Arthur - ***The One Between*** [1962] PBO.	$1.50	$5.00	$10.00
B-542F	Rabe, Peter - ***His Neighbor's Wife*** [1962] PBO.	$1.50	$5.00	$10.00
B-543F	Furlough, John - ***Yesterday's Virgin*** [1962] PBO.	$1.50	$5.00	$10.00
B-544F	Pruett, Herbert O. - ***Her Mother's Lover*** [1962] PBO. Cover by Milo.	$1.50	$5.00	$10.00
B-545	Anonymous - ***Motel Marriage*** [1962]	$1.35	$4.00	$8.00
B-546F	Adlon, Arthur - ***Strange Nurse*** [1962] PBO.	$1.35	$4.00	$8.00
B-547F	Day, Max - ***Bachelor In Suburbia*** [1962] PBO. Cover by Bob Schinella.	$1.35	$4.00	$8.00

		G	VG	F
B-548F	Dorian, Elaine - ***Double Trouble*** [1962] PBO. Cover by Darcy.	$1.35	$4.00	$8.00
B-549F	Harding, Matt - ***Motel Trap*** [1962] PBO.	$1.35	$4.00	$8.00
B-550F	McCoy, Dean - ***No Empty Bed For Her*** [1962] PBO.	$1.35	$4.00	$8.00
B-551F	Villanova, Richard - ***Her Woman*** [1962] PBO.	$1.35	$4.00	$8.00
B-552F	Lord, Sheldon - ***Older Woman*** [1962] PBO.	$1.35	$4.00	$8.00
B-553F	James, Terry - ***Woman's Doctor*** [1962] PBO.	$1.35	$4.00	$8.00
B-554F	Thomas, Lee - ***A Woman's Game*** [1962] PBO.	$1.35	$4.00	$8.00
B-555F	Loren, Francis - ***Sun, Sex And Frenzy*** [1962] PBO. Cover by Al Rossi.	$1.35	$4.00	$8.00
B-556F	Harland, Tom - ***The Lustful Three*** [1962] PBO.	$1.35	$4.00	$8.00
B-557	Gregory, Paul - ***The Price Was Perversity*** [1962] PBO.	$1.35	$4.00	$8.00
B-558	Swiven, Jason - ***Pampered Women*** [1962] PBO.	$1.35	$4.00	$8.00
B-559F	Carver, John - ***The Sex Twist*** [1962] PBO.	$1.35	$4.00	$8.00
B-560F	Dorian, Elaine - ***The Country Club Set*** [1962] PBO. Cover by Milo.	$1.35	$4.00	$8.00
B-561F	Adlon, Arthur - ***Adam's Women*** [1962] PBO.	$1.35	$4.00	$8.00
B-562F	Roberts, Herb - ***Bedrooms Are Not For Sleeping*** [1962] PBO.	$1.35	$4.00	$8.00
B-563F	McCoy, Dean - ***Anything To Win*** [1962] PBO. Cover by Jerry Podwil.	$1.35	$4.00	$8.00
B-564F	Adlon, Arthur - ***Strange Seduction*** [1962] PBO.	$1.35	$4.00	$8.00
B-565F	Richard, Louis - ***And Sex Is The Payoff*** [1962] PBO.	$1.35	$4.00	$8.00
B-566	Gold, R. C. - ***For Lydia*** [1962]	$1.35	$4.00	$8.00
B-567F	Lorraine, Louis - ***The Empty Bed*** [1963] PBO. Cover by Al Rossi.	$1.35	$4.00	$8.00
B-568F	Carter, Alex - ***Change Partners*** [1963] PBO.	$1.35	$4.00	$8.00
B-569F	Hart, Brad - ***Bella Vista's Wives*** [1963] PBO.	$1.35	$4.00	$8.00
B-570F	Maxwell, J. Malcolm - ***From Other Women*** [1963] PBO.	$1.35	$4.00	$8.00
B-571F	Layne, Jim - ***The Party Game*** [1963] PBO.	$1.35	$4.00	$8.00
B-572F	Harding, Matt - ***The Near-Nudes*** [1963] PBO.	$1.50	$5.00	$10.00
B-573F	Gregory, David - ***Man-Minded*** [1963] PBO. Cover by Victor Olson.	$1.35	$4.00	$8.00
B-574F	Lord, Sheldon - ***Fever In The Sun*** [1963] PBO. Cover by Al Rossi.	$1.35	$4.00	$8.00
B-575F	Carr, Jay - ***The She-Wolves*** [1963] PBO.	$1.50	$5.00	$10.00
B-576F	St. John, Burton - ***Twin Taboos*** [1963] PBO.	$2.00	$6.00	$12.00
B-577F	Shubin, Seymour - ***Floating Bedroom*** [1963] PBO.	$1.35	$4.00	$8.00
B-578F	Hilton, Hilary - ***The Shadowy Sex*** [1963] PBO.	$1.50	$5.00	$10.00
B-579F	White, Jr., William M. - ***Summer Swap*** [1963] PBO. Cover by Al Rossi.	$1.35	$4.00	$8.00
B-580	McCoy, Dean - ***Beach Binge*** [1963] PBO.	$1.35	$4.00	$8.00
B-581F	Richards, Lee - ***The Sexecutives*** [1963] PBO.	$1.35	$4.00	$8.00
B-582F	Geis, Richard E. - ***The Saturday Night Party*** [1963] PBO. Cover by Brule.	$2.50	$7.50	$15.00
B-583F	Loren, Francis - ***Bachelor Girl*** [1963] PBO. Cover by Maguire.	$2.00	$6.00	$12.00
B-584F	Maxwell, J. Malcolm - ***The Other Side Of Love*** [1963] PBO.	$2.00	$6.00	$12.00
B-585F	St. John, Burton - ***Smoldering Women*** [1963] PBO.	$1.35	$4.00	$8.00
B-586	Simon, George - ***The Third Lust*** [1963] PBO.	$1.35	$4.00	$8.00
B-587F	Layne, Jim - ***Girl In The Motel*** [1963] PBO.	$1.35	$4.00	$8.00
B-588F	Shubin, Seymour - ***Wellville, U.S.A.*** [1963] PBO.	$1.35	$4.00	$8.00
B-589F	Roberts, Herb - ***Love In The Shadows*** [1963] PBO.	$1.35	$4.00	$8.00
B-590F	Gibbs, Carlton - ***That Kind Of Widow*** [1963] PBO. Cover by Harry Barton.	$1.35	$4.00	$8.00
B-591	Carter, Alex - ***Boy-Lover*** [1963] PBO. Cover by Micarelli.	$1.35	$4.00	$8.00
B-592F	St. John, Burton - ***Maureen*** [1963] PBO.	$1.35	$4.00	$8.00
B-593F	Albert, Jay - ***Stranger In Her Bed*** [1963] PBO.	$1.35	$4.00	$8.00
B-594	Brill, Lee - ***Country Club Confidential*** [1963] PBO.	$1.35	$4.00	$8.00
B-595	Trainer, Russell - ***Lonesome Widow*** [1963] PBO.	$1.35	$4.00	$8.00
B-596F	Blake, Alfred - ***Faithful For Eight Hours*** [1963] PBO.	$1.35	$4.00	$8.00

		G	VG	F
B-597F	Barry, Ken - ***The Bigamist*** [1963] PBO. Cover by Darcy.	$1.35	$4.00	$8.00
B-598F	McCoy, Dean - ***The Friendship Club*** [1963] PBO.	$1.35	$4.00	$8.00
B-599F	Fields, Vin - ***The Schemers*** [1963] PBO.	$1.35	$4.00	$8.00
B-600	Rogers, Joel Townsley - ***Never Leave My Bed*** [1963] Cover by Darcy.	$1.35	$4.00	$8.00
B-601F	Thomas, Lee - ***The Dean's Wife*** [1963] PBO.	$1.35	$4.00	$8.00
B-602F	Adlon, Arthur - ***She Who Strays*** [1963] PBO. Cover by Darcy.	$1.35	$4.00	$8.00
B-603F	Lord, Sheldon - ***The Bedroom Route*** [1963] PBO. Cover by Barton.	$1.35	$4.00	$8.00
B-604F	Furlough, John - ***The Love Camp*** [1963] PBO.	$1.35	$4.00	$8.00
B-605F	Carr, Jay - ***Motel Wives*** [1963] PBO.	$1.35	$4.00	$8.00
B-606F	Thomas, Lee - ***A Woman's Wants*** [1963] PBO.	$1.35	$4.00	$8.00
B-607F	Woodford, Jack - ***Illegitimate*** [1963] PBO.	$1.35	$4.00	$8.00
B-608F	Johns, Colin - ***7 Days To Love*** [1963] PBO. Cover by Victor Olson.	$1.35	$4.00	$8.00
B-609F	Parrish, Jud - ***Trina*** [1963] PBO.	$1.35	$4.00	$8.00
B-610F	Roberts, Herb - ***The Narrow Line*** [1963] PBO.	$2.00	$6.00	$12.00
B-611F	Avallone, Michael - ***Lust At Leisure*** [1963] PBO. Cover by Darcy.	$1.50	$5.00	$10.00
B-612F	Adlon, Arthur - ***The Wife Sharers*** [1963] PBO.	$1.35	$4.00	$8.00
B-613F	Dare, Will - ***Paid Lover*** [1963] PBO. Cover by Darcy.	$1.35	$4.00	$8.00
B-614F	Lorraine, Louis - ***Season Of Sin*** [1963] PBO.	$1.35	$4.00	$8.00
B-615F	Malaponte, Marco - ***Her High-School Lover*** [1963] PBO.	$1.35	$4.00	$8.00
B-616F	Harland, Tom - ***The Torrid Widow*** [1963] PBO. Cover by Darcy.	$1.35	$4.00	$8.00
B-617F	Woodford, Jack - ***Possessed*** [1963] PBO.	$1.50	$5.00	$10.00
B-618F	Pruett, Herbert O. - ***Lost Virgin*** [1963] PBO.	$1.35	$4.00	$8.00
B-619F	Villanova, Richard - ***The Other Kind*** [1963] PBO. Cover by Darcy.	$2.00	$6.00	$12.00
B-620	Holmes, Rick - ***New Widow*** [1963] PBO.	$1.35	$4.00	$8.00
B-621F	Maxwell, J. Malcolm - ***The Twisted Path*** [1963] PBO. Cover by Barton.	$2.00	$6.00	$12.00
B-622F	Layne, Jim - ***The Swap Set*** [1963] PBO.	$1.35	$4.00	$8.00
B-623F	Black, Brian - ***Jeanne*** [1963] PBO.	$1.35	$4.00	$8.00
B-624F	Simon, George - ***Love Tutor*** [1963] PBO.	$1.35	$4.00	$8.00
B-625F	Blake, Andrew - ***Sex-Swinger*** [1963] PBO.	$1.35	$4.00	$8.00
B-626F	Avallone, Michael - ***The Doctor's Wife*** [1963] PBO.	$1.35	$4.00	$8.00
B-627	Thomas, Lee - ***Mask Of Lesbos*** [1963] PBO. Cover by Darcy.	$2.00	$6.00	$12.00
B-628F	Richards, Lee - ***The Eager Beavers*** [1963] PBO.	$1.35	$4.00	$8.00
B-629F	Carter, Alex - ***The Free Lovers*** [1963] PBO.	$1.35	$4.00	$8.00
B-630	Donovan, Curt - ***The Wife Game*** [1963] PBO. Cover by Barton.	$1.35	$4.00	$8.00
B-631F	James, Neal - ***Her Shacktown Lover*** [1963] PBO.	$1.35	$4.00	$8.00
B-632F	Carr, Jay - ***The Love Seekers*** [1963] PBO.	$1.35	$4.00	$8.00
B-633F	Anders, Burt - ***The Perfumed World*** [1963] PBO.	$1.35	$4.00	$8.00
B-634F	McCoy, Dean - ***The Night It Happened*** [1963] PBO. Cover by Darcy.	$1.35	$4.00	$8.00
B-635F	Hilton, Hilary - ***Sing A Song Of Sex*** [1963] PBO. Cover by Darcy.	$1.35	$4.00	$8.00
B-636F	Lord, Sheldon - ***A Special Kind Of Love*** [1963] PBO.	$1.35	$4.00	$8.00
B-637F	Woodford, Jack - ***Cravings*** [1963] PBO.	$1.50	$5.00	$10.00
B-638F	Black, Brian - ***The Strangest Marriage*** [1963] PBO.	$1.35	$4.00	$8.00
B-639F	Malaponte, Marco - ***New Man In The House*** [1963] PBO.	$1.35	$4.00	$8.00
B-640F	Roberts, Herb - ***These Women*** [1963] PBO.	$1.35	$4.00	$8.00
B-641X	Adlon, Arthur - ***Lesbos Is For Lonnie*** [1963] PBO.	$2.00	$6.00	$12.00
B-642F	Harding, Matt - ***That Wild Summer*** [1963] PBO.	$1.35	$4.00	$8.00
B-643F	Hitt, Orrie - ***Too Hot To Handle*** [1963]	$1.35	$4.00	$8.00
B-644F	Foran, Tom - ***The Twisted Ones*** [1963] PBO.	$2.00	$6.00	$12.00
B-645F	Layne, Jim - ***Her Young Lover*** [1963] PBO. Cover by Barton.	$1.35	$4.00	$8.00

		G	VG	F
B-646	North, Kevin - ***A Bunch Of Women*** [1963] PBO. Cover by Maguire.	$1.50	$5.00	$10.00
B-647F	Carver, John - ***The Shame Of Jenny*** [1963] PBO.	$1.35	$4.00	$8.00
B-648X	McCoy, Dean - ***The Husband Hunters*** [1963] PBO.	$1.35	$4.00	$8.00
B-649F	Smith, Artemis - ***The Third Sex*** [1963]	$1.50	$5.00	$10.00
B-650F	Hitt, Orrie - ***Suburban Sin*** [1963]	$1.35	$4.00	$8.00
B-651X	Wollfe, Charles X. - ***High-School Scandal*** [1963] PBO.	$1.35	$4.00	$8.00
B-652F	O'Bannon, Brian - ***Instant Love*** [1963] PBO. Cover by Barton.	$1.35	$4.00	$8.00
B-653F	Vail, Tom - ***The Marriage Club*** [1963] PBO. Cover by Darcy.	$1.35	$4.00	$8.00
B-654X	Clubb, Stacey - ***The Middle Sex*** [1963] PBO.	$1.35	$4.00	$8.00
B-655F	Hitt, Orrie - ***Sin Doll*** [1963]	$1.35	$4.00	$8.00
B-656F	Dare, Will - ***Web Of Women*** [1963] PBO.	$1.35	$4.00	$8.00
B-657F	Dean, Ralph - ***One Kind Of Woman*** [1963]	$1.35	$4.00	$8.00
B-658X	MacLeod, Kevin - ***What Color Is Love?*** [1963] PBO. Cover by Darcy.	$1.50	$5.00	$10.00
B-659X	Lord, Sheldon - ***The Sisterhood*** [1963] PBO.	$1.35	$4.00	$8.00
B-660F	Black, Brian - ***The Passionate Professor*** [1963] PBO. Cover by Barton.	$1.35	$4.00	$8.00
B-661F	James, Neal - ***Cheaters' Paradise*** [1963] PBO.	$1.35	$4.00	$8.00
B-662F	Norday, Michael - ***Strange Thirsts*** [1963]	$1.35	$4.00	$8.00
B-663X	Addams, Kay - ***Queer Patterns*** [1963] Photo cover.	$1.35	$4.00	$8,00
B-664F	Blake, Andrew - ***Love Hostess*** [1963] PBO. Cover by App.	$1.35	$4.00	$8.00
B-665X	Woodford, Jack - ***The College Crowd*** [1963] PBO.	$1.35	$4.00	$8.00
B-666X	Johns, Colin - ***Rendezvous In Lesbos*** [1963] PBO.	$1.50	$5.00	$10.00
B-667X	Adlon, Arthur - ***The Hot Kiss Of Youth*** [1963] PBO. Cover by Bob Maguire.	$1.50	$5.00	$10.00
B-668	Hitt, Orrie - ***Ex-Virgin*** [1963]	$1.35	$4.00	$8.00
B-669X	MacLeod, Kevin - ***The Sweet Pain*** [1963] PBO.	$1.35	$4.00	$8.00
B-670F	Harland, Tom - ***Love Camp On Wheels*** [1963] PBO.	$1.35	$4.00	$8.00
B-671X	Gordon, Anthony - ***Doctor Of Lesbos*** [1963] PBO. Photo cover.	$1.50	$5.00	$10.00
B-672X	Wolffe, Charles X. - ***The Education Of Lydia*** [1963] PBO.	$1.50	$5.00	$10.00
B-673	Hilton, Hilary - ***The Love Trap*** [1963] PBO. Cover by Barton.	$1.35	$4.00	$8.00
B-674X	Lord, Sheldon - ***Marta*** [1963] PBO.	$1.35	$4.00	$8.00
B-675	Carr, Jay - ***Vacation Girls*** [1963]	$1.35	$4.00	$8.00
B-676X	Johnson, Kay - ***Color Blind*** [1963] PBO.	$1.50	$5.00	$10.00
B-677X	James, Neal - ***Her Student Lover*** [1963] PBO.	$1.35	$4.00	$8.00
B-678X	Richard, Louis - ***Artist's Woman*** [1963] PBO.	$1.35	$4.00	$8.00
B-679F	Avallone, Michael - ***And Sex Walks In*** [1963] PBO.	$1.35	$4.00	$8.00
B-680	Lord, Sheldon - ***The Rivals*** [1963]	$1.35	$4.00	$8.00
B-681X	Gibbs, Carlton - ***The Night Lovers*** [1963] PBO.	$1.35	$4.00	$8.00
B-682X	Holland, Kel - ***The Strange Young Wife*** [1963] PBO.	$1.35	$4.00	$8.00
B-683X	Storm, Christopher - ***The Young Duke*** [1963] PBO.	$1.35	$4.00	$8.00
B-684F	Thomas, Lee - ***Mazie*** [1963] PBO.	$1.35	$4.00	$8.00
B-685	Norday, Michael - ***Warped*** [1963]	$1.35	$4.00	$8.00
B-686X	Savage, George - ***Toni*** [1963] PBO. Photo cover.	$1.35	$4.00	$8.00
B-687X	Herbert, Anne - ***Summer Camp*** [1963] PBO.	$1.35	$4.00	$8.00
B-688X	Simon, George - ***Scrambled Sex*** [1963] PBO.	$1.35	$4.00	$8.00
B-689X	Kelly, Gerald R. - ***Teach Me To Love!*** [1963] PBO.	$1.35	$4.00	$8.00
B-690X	Lang, Oran A. - ***The Sex Kitten And The Scientist*** [1963] PBO.	$1.35	$4.00	$8.00
B-691X	McGuire, Shelagh - ***A Room At Polly's Place*** [1964] PBO. Cover by Darcy.	$1.35	$4.00	$8.00
B-692X	Black, Brian - ***Eve Without Adam*** [1963]	$1.35	$4.00	$8.00
B-693X	McCoy, Dean - ***Commuting Wife*** [1964] PBO.	$1.35	$4.00	$8.00
B-694X	Clubb, Stacey - ***Left Of Sex*** [1964] PBO.	$1.35	$4.00	$8.00
B-695X	Kent, Justin - ***Mavis*** [1964]	$1.25	$3.75	$7.50
B-696X	Roberts, Herb - ***The Silken Trap*** [1964]	$1.25	$3.75	$7.50
B-697X	Layne, Jim - ***The Fire In A Woman*** [1964] PBO.	$1.35	$4.00	$8.00

		G	VG	F
B-698X	Stuart, Clay - ***His Brother's Wife*** [1964] PBO. Cover by Al Rossi.	$1.35	$4.00	$8.00
B-699X	O'Rourke, Jay - ***The Summer Lovers*** [1964] PBO. Photo cover.	$1.35	$4.00	$8.00
B-700X	Adlon, Arthur - ***Private Nurse*** [1964]	$1.25	$3.75	$7.50
B-701X	Vail, Tom - ***This Too Is Love*** [1964] PBO. Cover by Ray App.	$1.35	$4.00	$8.00
B-702X	Morgan, Jason - ***The Scandal Set*** [1964] PBO.	$1.35	$4.00	$8.00
B-703X	Carter, Alex - ***Nice Girls Finish Last*** [1964] PBO.	$1.35	$4.00	$8.00
B-704X	Lord, Sheldon - ***Sex Is A Woman*** [1964] PBO.	$1.35	$4.00	$8.00
B-705	Savage, Kim - ***Helena's House*** [1964]	$1.25	$3.75	$7.50
B-706X	Richards, Lee - ***The Punks*** [1964] PBO.	$2.00	$6.00	$12.00
B-707X	Adlon, Arthur - ***Experiment In Love*** [1964] PBO. Photo cover.	$2.50	$7.50	$15.00
B-708X	Anonymous - ***Sherri*** [1964]	$1.35	$4.00	$8.00
B-709X	Carr, Jay - ***Cindy*** [1964] PBO. Photo cover.	$1.35	$4.00	$8.00
B-710	James, Neal - ***Teasing Woman*** [1964]	$1.25	$3.75	$7.50
B-711X	Carter, Alex - ***Traded Wives*** [1964] PBO.	$1.35	$4.00	$8.00
B-712X	St. John, Burton - ***One Touch Of Satin*** [1964]	$1.25	$3.75	$7.50
B-713X	Rico, Don - ***The Unmarried Ones*** [1964] PBO.	$1.35	$4.00	$8.00
B-714X	Holland, Kel - ***The Tempted*** [1964] PBO.	$1.35	$4.00	$8.00
B-715X	Carson, Dave - ***Sex III*** [1964]	$1.25	$3.75	$7.50
B-716X	Black, Brian - ***Summer Affair*** [1964] PBO.	$1.35	$4.00	$8.00
B-717X	Naylor, Anthony - ***Girl In Trouble*** [1964] PBO. Photo cover. Movie tie-in.	$1.35	$4.00	$8.00
B-718X	McCoy, Dean - ***Wife Lender*** [1964] PBO. Cover by Victor Olson.	$1.35	$4.00	$8.00
B-719X	Parrish, Jud - ***Women On Wheels*** [1964] PBO.	$1.35	$4.00	$8.00
B-720X	Thompson, J. B. - ***The Couch Cure*** [1964] PBO.	$1.35	$4.00	$8.00
B-721X	Furlough, John - ***Tarnished*** [1964] PBO.	$1.35	$4.00	$8.00
B-722X	Collyer, Nell - ***No Wedding Ring For Them*** [1964] PBO.	$1.35	$4.00	$8.00
B-723X	Lord, Sheldon - ***Sidney's Wife*** [1964] PBO. Photo cover.	$1.35	$4.00	$8.00
B-724X	Gibbs, Carlton - ***Split-Level Love*** [1964] PBO.	$1.25	$3.75	$7.50
B-725X	Lord, Sheldon - ***Community Of Women*** [1964]	$1.25	$3.75	$7.50
B-726X	Locke, Douglas - ***Customer's Woman*** [1964] PBO.	$1.35	$4.00	$8.00
B-727X	Bartell, Dan - ***Strange Lovers*** [1964] PBO.	$1.35	$4.00	$8.00
B-728X	Fanchon, Lisa - ***Migrant Girl*** [1964] PBO.	$1.35	$4.00	$8.00
B-729X	Savage, George - ***The Affairs Of Laura*** [1964] PBO. Cover by Maguire.	$1.50	$5.00	$10.00
B-730X	Carver, John - ***The Scuba Set*** [1964] PBO.	$1.35	$4.00	$8.00
B-731X	Williams, A. P. - ***Tutor From Lesbos*** [1964] PBO.	$1.35	$4.00	$8.00
B-732	Harland, Tom - ***This Breed Of Woman*** [1964] PBO.	$1.35	$4.00	$8.00
B-733X	Daniels, Mark - ***Wake Up With A Stranger*** [1964] PBO.	$1.35	$4.00	$8.00
B-734X	Morgan, Jason - ***The Bored Young Wives*** [1964] PBO.	$1.35	$4.00	$8.00
B-735X	Hitt, Orrie - ***Summer Of Sin*** [1964]	$1.25	$3.75	$7.50
B-736	Addams, Kay - ***Three Strange Women*** [1964]	$1.25	$3.75	$7.50
B-737X	Hitt, Orrie - ***Sexurbia County*** [1964]	$1.25	$3.75	$7.50
B-738X	Devlin, Barry - ***Make Sure I Win*** [1964] Cover by Bob Maguire.	$1.35	$4.00	$8.00
B-739X	Sherman, Joan - ***Suzy*** [1964]	$1.25	$3.75	$7.50
B-740X	Devlin, Barry - ***Cheating Wives*** [1964]	$1.25	$3.75	$7.50
B-741X	Edmund, Matty - ***Anatomy Of A Heel*** [1964] PBO.	$1.35	$4.00	$8.00
B-742X	O'Bannon, Brian - ***Any Number Can Love*** [1964] PBO. Photo cover.	$1.35	$4.00	$8.00
B-743X	MacLane, Kirby - ***For Women Only*** [1964] PBO. Cover by Victor Olson.	$1.35	$4.00	$8.00
B-744X	Franchon, Lisa - ***Girls Wanted*** [1964] PBO. Photo cover.	$1.35	$4.00	$8.00
B-745X	Black, Brian - ***Nina*** [1964] PBO. Cover by Barton.	$1.35	$4.00	$8.00
B-746X	Thompson, John Burton - ***What Makes Sherry Love?*** [1964] PBO.	$1.35	$4.00	$8.00

		G	VG	F
B-747X	Hunter, Wayne - ***Love Me Quick*** [1964] PBO.	$1.35	$4.00	$8.00
B-748X	Preston, Lillian - ***Sex Habits Of Single Women*** [1964] PBO.	$1.35	$4.00	$8.00
B-749X	Clubb, Stacey - ***The Hot Blood Of Youth*** [1964] PBO.	$1.35	$4.00	$8.00
B-750X	Roberts, Herb - ***Strange Wife*** [1964] PBO.	$1.35	$4.00	$8.00
B-751X	McCoy, Dean - ***The Love Pool*** [1964] PBO.	$1.35	$4.00	$8.00
B-752X	Adlon, Arthur - ***Teen-Age Stray*** [1964] PBO.	$1.35	$4.00	$8.00
B-753X	Layne, Jim - ***That Lambert Girl*** [1964] PBO.	$1.35	$4.00	$8.00
B-754X	Storm, Christopher - ***The Sex Rebels*** [1964] Cover by Al Rossi.	$1.25	$3.75	$7.50
B-755X	Priest, James Clark - ***Private School*** [1964]	$1.25	$3.75	$7.50
B-756	McEvilley, Tom - ***Partygoing*** [1964]	$1.25	$3.75	$7.50
B-757X	Lord, Sheldon - ***The Sex Shuffle*** [1964] PBO.	$1.35	$4.00	$8.00
B-758X	Thompson, Joan Burton - ***Shayne*** [1964] PBO.	$1.35	$4.00	$8.00
B-759	Black, Brian - ***The Jet Sex*** [1964]	$1.25	$3.75	$7.50
B-760X	Kirby, Mark - ***Harling College*** [1964]	$1.25	$3.75	$7.50
B-761X	Carter, Alex - ***Sex Around The Clock*** [1964] Cover by Robert Maguire.	$1.35	$4.00	$8.00
B-762X	Preston, Lillian - ***Part-Time Call Girl*** [1964]	$1.25	$3.75	$7.50
B-763X	O'Bannon, Brian - ***Ordeal By Sex*** [1964]	$1.25	$3.75	$7.50
B-764X	Lang, Oren A. - ***Shopping Center Sex*** [1964] PBO.	$1.35	$4.00	$8.00
B-765X	Johnson, Kay - ***Her Raging Needs*** [1964] PBO.	$1.35	$4.00	$8.00
B-766X	Simon, George - ***Girls Without Men*** [1964] PBO.	$1.35	$4.00	$8.00
B-767X	Wolffe, Charles X. - ***Resort Girls*** [1964] PBO. Cover by Robert Schulz.	$1.35	$4.00	$8.00
B-768X	West, Mark - ***His Boss's Wife*** [1964] Cover by Victor Olson.	$1.25	$3.75	$7.50
B-769	Carver, John - ***Campus Nymphs*** [1964] Cover by Al Rossi.	$1.25	$3.75	$7.50
B-770X	Savage, George - ***Suburban High School*** [1964] Cover by Al Rossi.	$1.25	$3.75	$7.50
B-771X	Pruett, Herbert O. - ***The Abnormal Ones*** [1964] PBO.	$1.35	$4.00	$8.00
B-772	Black, Brian - ***After Office Hours*** [1964]	$1.25	$3.75	$7.50
B-773X	Fickling, G. G. - ***Mother, Daughter And Lover*** [1964] PBO.	$1.35	$4.00	$8.00
B-774X	McCoy, Dean - ***House-Boy Lover*** [1964] PBO.	$1.35	$4.00	$8.00
B-775X	Lorraine, Louis - ***Wives And Lovers*** [1964]	$1.25	$3.75	$7.50
B-776	Sarver, Steve - ***Weekend Women*** [1964]	$1.25	$3.75	$7.50
B-777X	Wolffe, Charles X. - ***Model's Daughter*** [1964] PBO. Cover by Darcy.	$1.35	$4.00	$8.00
B-778	Morgan, Jason - ***The Swimming-Pool Set*** [1964]	$1.25	$3.75	$7.50
B-779X	Grefe, William - ***Racing Fever*** [1964] PBO. Photo cover.	$1.35	$4.00	$8.00
B-780X	Sorrell, Philip - ***Doctor's Women*** [1964] Cover by Maguire.	$1.35	$4.00	$8.00
B-781X	Burke, Fern - ***Women Who Cheat*** [1964]	$1.25	$3.75	$7.50
B-782	Donner, James - ***That Motel Weekend*** [1964]	$1.25	$3.75	$7.50
B-783X	Gordon, Anthony - ***The Sex Ladder*** [1964] PBO.	$1.35	$4.00	$8.00
B-784X	McNeill, George - ***The Tease*** [1964] PBO.	$1.35	$4.00	$8.00
B-785	Layne, Jim - ***Company Woman*** [1964]	$1.25	$3.75	$7.50
B-786X	Stevens, Toni - ***Carla*** [1964]	$1.25	$3.75	$7.50
B-787	Adlon, Arthur - ***The Seduction Of Denby Martin*** [1964] PBO.	$1.35	$4.00	$8.00
B-788X	Harland, Tom - ***S As In Sex*** [1964] PBO. Photo cover.	$1.35	$4.00	$8.00
B-789X	Burke, Fern - ***Young Wife*** [1964] PBO. Cover by Al Rossi.	$1.35	$4.00	$8.00
B-790X	Lord, Sheldon - ***The Third Way*** [1964] Cover by Miller.	$1.25	$3.75	$7.50
B-791X	Salem, Randy - ***Baby Face*** [1964] PBO.	$1.35	$4.00	$8.00
B-792	St. John, Burton - ***Virgin In Bluejeans*** [1964]	$1.25	$3.75	$7.50
B-793X	Gibbs, Carlton - ***Neighbors And Lovers*** [1964] Cover by Miller.	$1.25	$3.75	$7.50
B-794X	Cross, Dr. Harold H. U. - ***The Cross Report On Perversion*** [1964] PBO. Photo cover.	$1.35	$4.00	$8.00
B-795X	Adlon, Arthur - ***The Odd Kind*** [1964] Cover by Darcy.	$1.25	$3.75	$7.50
B-796X	Black, Brian - ***Undercover Sex*** [1965] PBO.	$1.35	$4.00	$8.00
B-797X	Adlon, Arthur - ***The Female Animal*** [1965] PBO. Cover by Barton.	$1.35	$4.00	$8.00
B-798X	Preston, Lillian - ***Lust For Youth*** [1965] PBO.	$1.35	$4.00	$8.00

		G	VG	F
B-799	Salem, Randy - ***Sex In The Shadows*** [1965] PBO. Cover by Al Rossi.	$1.35	$4.00	$8.00
B-800X	Sand, Eric - ***The Seduction*** [1965]	$1.25	$3.75	$7.50
B-801X	Lord, Sheldon - ***April North*** [1965] Cover by Al Rossi.	$1.25	$3.75	$7.50
B-802X	Held, Bette - ***The Invitation*** [1965] PBO.	$1.35	$4.00	$8.00
B-803X	McCoy, Dean - ***Free-Loving Wives*** [1965] PBO.	$1.35	$4.00	$8.00
B-804	Simon, George - ***Sex Off Limits*** [1965]	$1.25	$3.75	$7.50
B-805X	Jones, Webb - ***Sex Starved*** [1965]	$1.25	$3.75	$7.50
B-806X	Stern, Meredith - ***Sex Nest*** [1965] PBO. Cover by Darcy.	$1.35	$4.00	$8.00
B-807X	Blaine, Jud - ***The Wife Exchange*** [1965] PBO.	$1.35	$4.00	$8.00
B-808X	Beck, Charles - ***The Wife Traders*** [1965]	$1.25	$3.75	$7.50
B-809X	Preston, Lillian - ***The Exhibitionist*** [1965] PBO.	$1.35	$4.00	$8.00
B-810X	Thompson, John Burton - ***Lakeside Love Nest*** [1965] PBO.	$1.35	$4.00	$8.00
B-811X	Black, Brian - ***The Unfaithful*** [1965] PBO.	$1.35	$4.00	$8.00
B-812X	Layne, Jim - ***Sex Lane*** [1965] PBO.	$1.35	$4.00	$8.00
B-813X	Sarver, Steve - ***Thrill Crazy*** [1965]	$1.25	$3.75	$7.50
B-814X	Lorraine, Louis - ***Commuter Widow*** [1965]	$1.25	$3.75	$7.50
B-815X	Winters, Dee - ***Weekend Arrangements*** [1965]	$1.25	$3.75	$7.50
B-816X	Layne, James - ***Lend Me Your Wife*** [1965]	$1.25	$3.75	$7.50
B-817X	Low, Glenn - ***Reckless Virgin*** [1965]	$1.25	$3.75	$7.50
B-818	Carr, Jay - ***The Motel*** [1965]	$1.25	$3.75	$7.50
B-819X	Seeley, E. S. - ***Sorority Sin*** [1965]	$1.25	$3.75	$7.50
B-820X	Vincent, Jay - ***Girls' School*** [1965] PBO. Cover by Al Rossi.	$1.35	$4.00	$8.00
B-821X	Savage, George - ***The Co-Eds*** [1965] Cover by Al Rossi.	$1.25	$3.75	$7.50
B-822X	McCoy, Dean - ***Sexbound*** [1965]	$1.25	$3.75	$7.50
B-823X	Hamilton, William - ***Lover-Driver*** [1965] PBO.	$1.35	$4.00	$8.00
B-824X	Fickling, G. G. - ***Sex Pit*** [1965]	$1.35	$4.00	$8.00
B-825X	Thompson, John B. - ***The Lash*** [1965]	$1.25	$3.75	$7.50
B-826X	Furlough, John - ***The Loves Of Lucy*** [1965] PBO. Photo cover.	$1.35	$4.00	$8.00
B-827X	Clubb, Stacey - ***Young Lust*** [1965] PBO. Cover by Milo.	$1.35	$4.00	$8.00
B-828X	Burke, Fern - ***Wrong-Way Love*** [1965] PBO.	$1.35	$4.00	$8.00
B-829X	McCoy, Dean - ***Cheating Wife*** [1965] Photo cover.	$1.25	$3.75	$7.50
B-830X	Adlon, Arthur - ***Girl Trap*** [1965] PBO.	$1.35	$4.00	$8.00
B-831X	Donner, James - ***The Sex Mob*** [1965] PBO. Photo cover.	$1.35	$4.00	$8.00
B-832	Andrew, Din - ***Big Orvie*** [1965] PBO.	$1.35	$4.00	$8.00
B-833	Roberts, Herbert - ***The "In" Group*** [1965]	$1.25	$3.75	$7.50
B-834X	Black, Brian - ***The Bed Sharers*** [1965] Cover by Prezio.	$1.25	$3.75	$7.50
B-835X	Carter, Alex - ***Call-Girl Wives*** [1965] PBO.	$1.35	$4.00	$8.00
B-836	Hitt, Orrie - ***Dirt Farm*** [1965]	$1.25	$3.75	$7.50
B-837X	Nixon, Henry Lewis - ***Confessions Of A Psychiatrist*** [1965]	$1.25	$3.75	$7.50
B-838X	Hastings, March - ***Abnormal Wife*** [1965] PBO.	$1.35	$4.00	$8.00
B-839X	Sarver, Steve - ***The Hot Ones*** [1965]	$1.25	$3.75	$7.50
B-840X	Hitt, Orrie - ***Nudist Camp*** [1965]	$1.25	$3.75	$7.50
B-841X	Cardinal, Mark - ***A Night With Lana*** [1965] PBO.	$1.35	$4.00	$8.00
B-842X	Thompson, John B. - ***Bayou Girl*** [1965]	$1.25	$3.75	$7.50
B-843X	Fanchon, Lisa - ***Key Club*** [1965] PBO. Cover by Barton.	$1.35	$4.00	$8.00
B-844X	Bartell, Dan - ***The One-Nighter*** [1965] PBO. Photo cover.	$1.35	$4.00	$8.00
B-845X	Harding, Matt - ***Career Sexpots*** [1965] PBO.	$1.35	$4.00	$8.00
B-846X	Thompson, John B. - ***Sinful Virgin*** [1965]	$1.25	$3.75	$7.50
B-847X	Hitt, Orrie - ***Unfaithful Wives*** [1965]	$1.25	$3.75	$7.50
B-848X	Munroe, Val - ***Sex Fever*** [1965]	$1.25	$3.75	$7.50
B-849X	McCoy, Dean - ***The Married Kind*** [1965] PBO.	$1.35	$4.00	$8.00
B-850X	Carver, John - ***Undress Rehearsal*** [1965] PBO.	$1.35	$4.00	$8.00
B-851X	Weatherwall, Ernie - ***Blonde Trap*** [1965] Photo cover.	$1.25	$3.75	$7.50
B-852	Storm, Christopher - ***Campus Motel*** [1965]	$1.25	$3.75	$7.50
B-853	Clubb, Stacey - ***The Oddballs*** [1965] PBO.	$1.25	$3.75	$7.50
B-854X	Black, Brian - ***The Secrets*** [1965] PBO.	$1.25	$3.75	$7.50
B-855X	Gregory, Paul - ***Naked Lens*** [1965]	$1.25	$3.75	$7.50
B-856X	Blaine, Jud - ***Anatomy Of Seduction*** [1965] PBO.	$1.35	$4.00	$8.00

		G	VG	F
B-857X	Harding, Matt - ***Morgan's Girls*** [1965] PBO. Cover by Barton.	$1.35	$4.00	$8.00
B-858	Harland, Tom - ***Insatiable*** [1965] PBO.	$1.35	$4.00	$8.00
B-859X	Carter, Alex - ***High School Jungle*** [1965]	$1.35	$4.00	$8.00
B-860	Black, Brian - ***Lollipops And Lovers*** [1965]	$1.25	$3.75	$7.50
B-861X	Adlon, Arthur - ***The Great Husband Swap*** [1965] PBO.	$1.25	$3.75	$7.50
B-862X	Lorraine, Louis - ***Blonde Dynamite*** [1965]	$1.25	$3.75	$7.50
B-863X	Thompson, John Burton - ***The Eager Ones*** [1965]	$1.25	$3.75	$7.50
B-864	Winters, Dee - ***The Swingers*** [1965]	$1.25	$3.75	$7.50
B-865X	Adlon, Arthur - ***Bedroom Windows*** [1965]	$1.25	$3.75	$7.50
B-866X	Brill, Lee - ***The Bedroom Game*** [1965] PBO. Cover by Barton.	$1.35	$4.00	$8.00
B-867X	Lord, Sheldon - ***Older Woman*** [1965]	$1.25	$3.75	$7.50
B-868X	Geis, Richard E. - ***Young Tiger*** [1965] PBO.	$1.35	$4.00	$8.00
B-869X	Burke, Fern - ***The Beach Set*** [1965] PBO.	$1.35	$4.00	$8.00
B-870X	Lorraine, Louis - ***That Summer In Rome*** [1965]	$1.25	$3.75	$7.50
B-871	James, Terry - ***The Professor's Wife*** [1965]	$1.25	$3.75	$7.50
B-872X	Naylor, Anthony - ***The Sex Kitten Grows Up*** [1965] PBO.	$1.35	$4.00	$8.00
B-873X	McCoy, Dean - ***My Lover, My Neighbor*** [1965] PBO.	$1.35	$4.00	$8.00
B-874X	Yardley, Steve - ***The Club*** [1965] PBO.	$1.35	$4.00	$8.00
B-875X	Matthews, Clayton - ***Discontented Wives*** [1965]	$1.25	$3.75	$7.50
B-876	Carter, Alex - ***The Affair*** [1965]	$1.25	$3.75	$7.50
B-877X	Black, Brian - ***The Husband Trader*** [1965] PBO.	$1.35	$4.00	$8.00
B-878	Wallace, Wolf - ***The Watcher*** [1965] PBO.	$1.35	$4.00	$8.00
B-879X	Thompson, John B. - ***Nude In The Sand*** [1965]	$1.35	$4.00	$8.00
B-880X	Harding, Matt - ***The Sex Bums*** [1965] PBO.	$1.35	$4.00	$8.00
B-881	Layne, Jim - ***Woman Patient*** [1965]	$1.25	$3.75	$7.50
B-882	Jones, George - ***Twisted*** [1965]	$1.25	$3.75	$7.50
B-883X	Thompson, John B. - ***Male Virgin*** [1965]	$1.25	$3.75	$7.50
B-884X	Nathan, Rick - ***She Liked Them Young*** [1965]	$1.25	$3.75	$7.50
B-885X	Chambord, Mimi - ***Virgin At The Window*** [1965] PBO.	$1.35	$4.00	$8.00
B-886	Garcon, Morgana - ***Summer Heat*** [1965]	$1.25	$3.75	$7.50
B-887X	McCoy, Dean - ***Beach Binge*** [1965]	$1.25	$3.75	$7.50
B-888	Lorraine, Louis - ***The Split-Level Game*** [1965]	$1.25	$3.75	$7.50
B-889	Sarver, Steve - ***The Arrangers*** [1965]	$1.25	$3.75	$7.50
B-890	Gibbs, Carlton - ***Suburbia After Dark*** [1965]	$1.25	$3.75	$7.50
B-891X	Huish, Leonard - ***The Window*** [1965]	$1.25	$3.75	$7.50
B-892X	Balt, Jon - ***The Weekend Group*** [1965]	$1.25	$3.75	$7.50
B-893	Brill, Lee - ***The Skin-Tight Sheath*** [1965]	$1.25	$3.75	$7.50
B-894X	Hudson, Jan - ***The Lovemakers*** [1965] PBO.	$1.50	$5.00	$10.00
B-895X	Adlon, Arthur - ***Neglected Wives*** [1965]	$1.25	$3.75	$7.50
B-896	Hilton, Hilary - ***Old Enough*** [1965]	$1.25	$3.75	$7.50
B-897X	Layne, Jim - ***Party Wives*** [1965]	$1.25	$3.75	$7.50
B-898	Hitt, Orrie - ***Rotten To The Core*** [1965]	$1.25	$3.75	$7.50
B-899X	Travis, Ben - ***The Strange Ones*** [1965]	$1.25	$3.75	$7.50
B-900X	Swiven, Jason - ***Pampered Women*** [1965]	$1.25	$3.75	$7.50
B-901X	Beck, Charles - ***The Bed At The Top*** [1965]	$1.25	$3.75	$7.50
B-902X	Gibbs, Carlton - ***Behind Respectable Doors*** [1965]	$1.25	$3.75	$7.50
B-903X	Low, Glenn - ***The Barn*** [1965]	$1.25	$3.75	$7.50
B-904X	O'Shea, Sean - ***Whisper*** [1965]	$1.25	$3.75	$7.50
B-905X	Carter, Alex - ***Velvet Jackpot*** [1965]	$1.25	$3.75	$7.50
B-906X	McCoy, Dean - ***Group Sex*** [1965] PBO.	$1.35	$4.00	$8.00
B-907X	Black, Brian - ***Vacation Affairs*** [1965]	$1.25	$3.75	$7.50
B-908X	Orth, Richard - ***The Pad Upstairs*** [1966] PBO.	$1.35	$4.00	$8.00
B-909X	Blaine, Jud - ***The Fling*** [1966]	$1.25	$3.75	$7.50
B-910X	Roberts, Herbert - ***Early Fruit*** [1966] PBO. Cover by George Gross.	$1.35	$4.00	$8.00
B-911X	Carver, John - ***The Fair Young Wives*** [1966] PBO.	$1.35	$4.00	$8.00
B-912X	Black, Brian - ***The Teacher*** [1966]	$1.25	$3.75	$7.50
B-913X	Monte, Jill - ***Thrill Clinic*** [1966] PBO. Cover by Al Rossi.	$1.35	$4.00	$8.00
B-914X	Hitt, Orrie - ***Women's Ward*** [1966] PBO. Cover by Al Rossi.	$1.35	$4.00	$8.00

		G	VG	F
B-915X	Lorraine, Louis - ***The Empty Bed*** [1966]	$1.25	$3.75	$7.50
B-916X	Donovan, Curt - ***The Smoothie*** [1966] PBO.	$1.35	$4.00	$8.00
B-917X	Tierney, Tom - ***The Photograph*** [1966] PBO. Photo cover.	$1.35	$4.00	$8.00
B-918X	Black, Brian - ***High Fever*** [1966]	$1.25	$3.75	$7.50
B-919X	Carter, Alex - ***Boy-Lover*** [1966]	$1.25	$3.75	$7.50
B-920X	Pruett, Herbert O. - ***Whose Wife Tonight?*** [1966]	$1.25	$3.75	$7.50
B-921X	Carver, John - ***That Motorcycle Boy*** [1966] PBO.	$1.35	$4.00	$8.00
B-922X	Bligh, Norman - ***The Sisters*** [1966]	$1.25	$3.75	$7.50
B-923X	Brill, Lee - ***Country Club Confidential*** [1966]	$1.25	$3.75	$7.50
B-924X	Camp, Lon - ***The Experiment*** [1966] PBO.	$3.00	$9.00	$18.00
B-925X	Carter, Alex - ***The Games She Played*** [1966] PBO. Cover by George Gross.	$1.35	$4.00	$8.00
B-926X	Sarver, Steve - ***The Part-Timers*** [1966] PBO.	$1.35	$4.00	$8.00
B-927X	Carr, Jay - ***Episode In A Town*** [1966]	$1.25	$3.75	$7.50
B-928X	Lee, Eric - ***Amoralwife*** [1966] PBO. Photo cover.	$1.35	$4.00	$8.00
B-929X	Furlough, John - ***Yesterday's Virgin*** [1966]	$1.25	$3.75	$7.50
B-930X	Vincent, Jay - ***The Hostesses*** [1966] PBO.	$1.35	$4.00	$8.00
B-931X	Elliott, Ben - ***Weekend Wife*** [1966]	$1.25	$3.75	$7.50
B-932X	McCoy, Dean - ***The Friendship Club*** [1966]	$1.25	$3.75	$7.50
B-933X	Carr, Jay - ***Unnatural Wife*** [1966] Cover by Darcy.	$1.25	$3.75	$7.50
B-934X	Day, Max - ***Bachelor In Suburbia*** [1966]	$1.25	$3.75	$7.50
B-935X	Gregory, David - ***Man-Minded*** [1966] Cover by Victor Olson.	$1.25	$3.75	$7.50
B-936X	Burke, Fern - ***The Jebson Kids*** [1966] PBO.	$1.35	$4.00	$8.00
B-937X	Hara, Gil - ***Love As You Are*** [1966] PBO. Cover by Barton.	$1.35	$4.00	$8.00
B-938X	McCoy, Dean - ***The Unattached*** [1966] PBO.	$1.35	$4.00	$8.00
B-939X	Adlon, Arthur - ***Strange Nurse*** [1966]	$1.25	$3.75	$7.50
B-940X	Lorraine, Louis - ***The Cheating Game*** [1966]	$1.25	$3.75	$7.50
B-941X	West, Mark - ***Object Of Lust*** [1966] Cover by Darcy.	$1.25	$3.75	$7.50
B-942X	Vincent, Gabrielle - ***Woman Alone*** [1966] Cover by Barton.	$1.25	$3.75	$7.50
B-943X	Simon, George - ***The Third Lust*** [1966]	$1.25	$3.75	$7.50
B-944X	Black, Brian - ***The Sorority*** [1966] PBO.	$1.35	$4.00	$8.00
B-945X	Adlon, Arthur - ***The Place*** [1966] PBO.	$1.35	$4.00	$8.00
B-946X	Carver, John - ***Weekend Partners*** [1966] PBO.	$1.35	$4.00	$8.00
B-947X	Merrick, Clyde - ***Sex Pack*** [1966]	$1.25	$3.75	$7.50
B-948X	Wallace, Wolf - ***The Hive*** [1966] PBO.	$1.35	$4.00	$8.00
B-949X	Gibbs, Carlton - ***Weekday Widows*** [1966] PBO.	$1.35	$4.00	$8.00
B-950X	Munroe, Val - ***Second-Year Intern*** [1966] PBO.	$1.35	$4.00	$8.00
B-951X	Christy, Mame - ***Campus Affair*** [1966] PBO. Cover by Victor Olson.	$1.35	$4.00	$8.00
B-952X	Black, Brian - ***The Overnighters*** [1966] PBO.	$1.35	$4.00	$8.00
B-953X	Nathan, Rick - ***The Love Pill*** [1966]	$3.00	$9.00	$18.00
B-954X	Brill, Lee - ***The Neighbors*** [1966] PBO.	$1.35	$4.00	$8.00
B-955X	Savage, George - ***Runaway Wife*** [1966]	$1.25	$3.75	$7.50
B-956X	Furlough, John - ***Pot Of Honey*** [1966]	$1.25	$3.75	$7.50
B-957X	Sarver, Steve - ***Julie*** [1966] PBO. Photo cover.	$1.25	$3.75	$7.50
B-958X	Clay, Paul - ***The Housewarming*** [1966] PBO.	$1.35	$4.00	$8.00
B-959X	Black, Brian - ***Summer Affair*** [1966]	$1.25	$3.75	$7.50
B-960X	Wallace, Wolf - ***That Swedish Girl*** [1966] PBO. Photo cover.	$1.35	$4.00	$8.00
B-962X	Harrison, Timothy - ***Hot Summer*** [1966] Photo cover.	$1.25	$3.75	$7.50
B-963X	Carruthers, Margaret - ***His Best Friend's Wife*** [1966]	$1.25	$3.75	$7.50
B-964X	Blaine, Jud - ***The Awakening*** [1966]	$1.25	$3.75	$7.50
B-965X	Winters, Dee - ***You May Hate Lonnie Browning*** [1966] PBO.	$1.35	$4.00	$8.00
B-966X	Roberts, Herbert - ***Mardi*** [1966] PBO.	$1.35	$4.00	$8.00
B-967X	McCoy, Dean - ***The Night It Happened*** [1966]	$1.25	$3.75	$7.50
B-968X	Hiner, Phil - ***Whose Man?*** [1966] PBO.	$1.35	$4.00	$8.00
B-969X	Morgan, Jason - ***The Bored Young Wives*** [1966]	$1.25	$3.75	$7.50
B-970X	Black, Brian - ***Off-Campus Apartment*** [1966] PBO.	$1.35	$4.00	$8.00
B-971X	Lord, Sheldon - ***Sidney's Wife*** [1966]	$1.25	$3.75	$7.50
B-973X	Johnson, Kay - ***The Corrupted*** [1966] PBO.	$1.35	$4.00	$8.00
B-974X	Stuart, Clay - ***His Brother's Wife*** [1966]	$1.25	$3.75	$7.50

		G	VG	F
B-975X	Villanova, Richard - ***A Game For Grown-Ups*** [1966]	$1.25	$3.75	$7.50
B-976X	Demaris, Ovid - ***Chip's Girls*** [1966]	$1.25	$3.75	$7.50
B-977X	Allison, Leslie - ***The Spoiler*** [1966] PBO. Cover by George Gross.	$1.35	$4.00	$8.00
B-978	McCoy, Dean - ***Love Hunters*** [1966] PBO. Cover by George Gross.	$1.35	$4.00	$8.00
B-979X	Malaponte, Marco - ***New Man In The House*** [1966]	$1.25	$3.75	$7.50
B-980X	Locklear, Edmond - ***Route 301, South*** [1966] PBO.	$1.35	$4.00	$8.00
B-981	Wollfe, Charles X. - ***High-School Scandal*** [1966]	$1.25	$3.75	$7.50
B-982X	Bargi, Lorraine - ***Secret Affair*** [1966] PBO. Photo cover.	$1.35	$4.00	$8.00
B-983X	Richards, Lee - ***The Punks*** [1966]	$1.35	$4.00	$8.00
B-984X	Stokes, Manning - ***Girl On A Couch*** [1966]	$1.25	$3.75	$7.50
B-985X	Black, Brian - ***The Love Test*** [1966] PBO.	$1.35	$4.00	$8.00
B-986X	Daniels, Mark - ***The Drug*** [1966] PBO.	$1.35	$4.00	$8.00
B-988X	Layne, Jim - ***Her Young Lover*** [1966]	$1.25	$3.75	$7.50
B-989X	Black, Brian - ***The Strangest Marriage*** [1966]	$1.25	$3.75	$7.50
B-990X	Herbert, Anne - ***Summer Camp*** [1966]	$1.25	$3.75	$7.50
B-991X	Munroe, Val - ***The Naked View*** [1966] PBO.	$1.35	$4.00	$8.00
B-992X	Gibbs, Carlton - ***Love Jungle*** [1966] PBO.	$1.35	$4.00	$8.00
B-993X	Napier, Dominique - ***House Party*** [1966]	$1.25	$3.75	$7.50
B-994X	Hara, Gil - ***The Love Clinic*** [1966] PBO.	$1.35	$4.00	$8.00
B-995X	Clubb, Stacey - ***Girl High*** [1966] PBO. Photo cover.	$1.35	$4.00	$8.00
B-996X	Lord, Sheldon - ***The Rivals*** [1966]	$1.25	$3.75	$7.50
B-998X	Savage, George - ***Toni*** [1966]	$1.25	$3.75	$7.50
B-999X	Carver, John - ***The Shame Of Jenny*** [1966]	$1.25	$3.75	$7.50
B-1014X	Adlon, Arthur - ***The Hot Kiss Of Youth*** [1967] Cover by Maguire.	$1.35	$4.00	$8.00
B-1060SK	Willeford, Charles - ***Pick-Up*** [1967]	$6.00	$20.00	$40.00
B-1081S	Willeford, Charles - ***Lust Is A Woman*** [1967] Reprints Beacon B-175.	$22.00	$70.00	$140.00

Beacon Double. New York: Universal Publishing.

		G	VG	F
DB-106-N	Sarver, Steve/Balt, Jon - ***The Arrangers/The Weekend Group*** [1965] PBO.	$2.50	$7.50	$15.00
DB-111	Black, Brian/Monte, Jill - ***The Teacher/Thrill Clinic*** [1965]	$2.50	$7.50	$15.00
DB-113	Swiven, Jason/Hitt, Orrie - ***Pampered Women/Rotten To The Core*** [1965] Cover art by Maguire.	$2.50	$7.50	$15.00

Beacon Envoy. New York: Universal Publishing.

		G	VG	F
101	Graves, Robert - ***King Jesus*** [1961]	$2.00	$6.00	$12.00
E-102	Williams, David - ***Horns Of Ecstasy*** [1961] PBO.	$1.50	$5.00	$10.00
103	Boland, John - ***The League Of Gentlemen*** [1961] Movie tie-in.	$1.50	$5.00	$10.00
104-F	Smythe, Joseph Hilton - ***The Sex Probers*** [1961] PBO.	$1.50	$5.00	$10.00
E-105-F	Wade, Carlson - ***The Troubled Sex*** [1961] PBO.	$1.50	$5.00	$10.00
E-106-F	Cook, Will - ***Ambush At Antlers Spring*** [1962] PBO.	$1.50	$5.00	$10.00
E-107-F	Whipple, Chandler - ***Lt. John F. Kennedy - Expendable!*** [1962] PBO.	$1.50	$5.00	$10.00
E-108	Chanslor, Roy - ***Passion Makers*** [1962] PBO.	$1.50	$5.00	$10.00
E-109	Anthology - ***The Little Encyclopedia Of Home Designs*** [1962]	$2.50	$7.50	$15.00

Beagle Books. New York: Beagle Books, Inc.

		G	VG	F
94-001	Rendell, Ruth - ***From Doon With Death*** [1970]	$ .65	$2.00	$4.00
95-002	Rendall, Ruth - ***To Fear A Painted Devil*** [1970]	$ .65	$2.00	$4.00
95-003	Rendell, Ruth - ***Wolf To The Slaughter*** [1970]	$ .65	$2.00	$4.00
95-004	Rendall, Ruth - ***The Secret House Of Death*** [1970]	$ .65	$2.00	$4.00
95-011	Clapperton, Richard - ***No News On Monday*** [1970]	$ .50	$1.50	$3.00
95-012	Deere, Alan C. - ***Nine Lives*** [1970]	$ .50	$1.50	$3.00
95-018	Asquith, Lady Cynthia - editor - ***The Second Ghost Book*** [1970]	$1.25	$3.75	$7.50
95-029	Rendall, Ruth - ***Vanity Dies Hard*** [1970]	$ .65	$2.00	$4.00
95-032	Lovecraft, H. P. - ***The Tomb*** [1970]	$1.25	$3.75	$7.50

		G	VG	F
95-041	Lovecraft, H. P. - ***At The Mountains Of Madness*** [1971]	$1.25	$3.75	$7.50
95-042	Lovecraft, H. P. - ***The Lurking Fear And Other Stories*** [1971]	$1.25	$3.75	$7.50
95-044	Anthology - ***Special Wonder*** [1971] Edited by J. Francis McComas.	$ .75	$2.50	$5.00
95-045	Hunt, Kyle (John Creasey) - ***Wicked As The Devil*** [1971]	$ .75	$2.50	$5.00
95-053	Cheyney, Peter - ***Dark Duet*** [1971]	$ .65	$2.00	$4.00
95-057	McComas, J. Francis - editor - ***Special Wonder*** [1971]	$ .75	$2.50	$5.00
95-058	Lovecraft, H. P./Derleth, August - ***The Lurker At The Threshold*** [1971]	$1.25	$3.75	$7.50
95-064	Symons, Julian - ***The Broken Penny*** [1971]	$ .65	$2.00	$4.00
95-068	Lovecraft, H.P. w/Derleth, August - ***The Shuttered Room And Other Tales Of Horror*** [1971]	$1.25	$3.75	$7.50
95-069	McComas, J. Francis - editor - ***Crimes And Misfortunes*** [1971]	$ .65	$2.00	$4.00
95-070	Wellen, Edward - ***Hijack*** [1971] PBO.	$ .65	$2.00	$4.00
94-071	Hall, Angus - ***The Scars Of Dracula*** [1971]	$1.25	$3.75	$7.50
95-092	Symons, Julian - ***The Paper Chase*** [1971]	$ .50	$1.50	$3.00
95-093	Symons, Julian - ***The Gigantic Shadow*** [1971]	$ .50	$1.50	$3.00
95-094	Rickman, Robert - editor - ***The Fontana Book Of Great Ghost Stories*** [1971]	$1.25	$3.75	$7.50
94-095	Hughes, William - ***Lust For A Vampire*** [1971]	$1.25	$3.75	$7.50
95-107	Derleth, August - ***The Mask Of Cthulhu*** [1971] Cover art by Vincent DiFate.	$1.25	$3.75	$7.50
95-108	Derleth, August - ***The Trail Of Cthulhu*** [1971] Cover art by Vincent DiFate.	$1.25	$3.75	$7.50
95-109	Asquith, Lady Cynthia - editor - ***The Third Ghost Book*** [1970]	$1.25	$3.75	$7.50
95-111	Goulart, Ron - ***Death Cell*** [1971] PBO. Cover art by Vincent DiFate.	$ .75	$2.50	$5.00
95-123	Lovecraft, H.P. - ***The Case Of Charles Dexter Ward*** [1971] Cover art by Vincent DiFate.	$1.25	$3.75	$7.50
95-124	Anthology - ***Tales Of The Cthulhu Mythos*** [1971] Includes H.P. Lovecraft & others. Cover art by Vincent DiFate.	$1.25	$3.75	$7.50
95-125	Woodman, Michael - ***The Medusa Kiss*** [1971]	$ .50	$1.50	$3.00
95-126	Harrington, Joseph - ***The Last Known Address*** [1971]	$ .50	$1.50	$3.00
95-138	Hickman, Robert - editor - ***The Second Fontana Book Of Great Ghost Stories*** [1971]	$1.25	$3.75	$7.50
95-140	Symons, Julian - ***Bland Beginning*** [1971]	$ .50	$1.50	$3.00
95-141	Woodman, Michael - ***Bullion*** [1971]	$ .50	$1.50	$3.00
95-142	Bernard, Christine - editor - ***The Fontana Book Of Great Horror Stories*** [1971]	$1.25	$3.75	$7.50
95-143	Lupoff, Richard - ***Sacred Locomotive Flies*** [1971] PBO. Cover art by Valla.	$ .75	$2.50	$5.00
94-145	Deming, Richard - ***What's The Matter With Helen?*** [1971] PBO.	$ .65	$2.00	$4.00
95-155	Asquith, Lady Cynthia - editor - ***The Ghost Book*** [1971]	$1.25	$3.75	$7.50
95-156	Hickman, Robert - editor - ***The Third Fontana Book Of Great Ghost Stories*** [1971]	$1.25	$3.75	$7.50
95-158	Brunner, John - ***The Gaudy Shadows*** [1971]	$1.00	$3.00	$6.00
95-159	Anthology - ***The Horror In The Museum*** [1971] Includes H.P. Lovecraft & others. Cover art by Vincent DiFate.	$1.25	$3.75	$7.50
95-160	Bernard, Christine - editor - ***The Second Fontana Book Of Great Horror Stories*** [1971]	$1.25	$3.75	$7.50
95-174	Turner, James - editor - ***The Fourth Ghost Book*** [1971]	$1.25	$3.75	$7.50
95-185	Bernard, Christine - editor - ***The Fourth Fontana Book Of Great Horror Stories*** [1971]	$1.25	$3.75	$7.50
95-186	Rickman, Robert - editor - ***The Fourth Fontana Book Of Great Ghost Stories*** [1971]	$1.25	$3.75	$7.50
95-197	Harrington, Joseph - ***Blind Spot*** [1972]	$ .50	$1.50	$3.00
95-199	Danby, Mary - editor - ***The Fifth Fontana Book Of Great Horror Stories*** [1972]	$1.25	$3.75	$7.50

		G	VG	F
95-210	Goulart, Ron - ***Plunder*** [1972] PBO. Cover art by Vincent DiFate.	$ .65	$2.00	$4.00
95124	Derleth, August - editor - ***Tales Of The Cthulhu Mythos Volume 2*** [1971] Includes H. P. Lovecraft et al.	$1.25	$3.75	$7.50

Beaver Publications. Toronto: Beaver Publishing Co.

NN-1	Hamilton, Leslie - ***Rendezvous In Vienna*** [1941] PBO.	$5.50	$17.50	$35.00
NN-2	McCaughey, Banks & Hamilton - editors - ***Modern Shorts*** [1941] PBO.	$5.50	$17.50	$35.00
NN-3	Hamilton, Leslie - ***Cherchez La Femme (Find The Woman)*** [1941] PBO.	$5.50	$17.50	$35.00

Bedside/Bedtime Books.

814	Masters, Lou - ***Sin Cruise*** [1959] PBO. Cover by Maguire.	$1.50	$5.00	$10.00

Bee-Line.

118	Savage, Hardley - ***Jetman Meets The Mad Madam*** [1966] PBO.	$4.00	$12.50	$25.00
133	— ***Forever Ember*** [n.d.]	$2.50	$7.50	$15.00
145	— ***The Girl From B.U.S.T.*** [n.d.]	$2.50	$7.50	$15.00
177	— ***The Great Sex Race*** [n.d.]	$2.50	$7.50	$15.00
182	— ***The Naked Trap*** [n.d.]	$2.50	$7.50	$15.00
187	— ***King's Woman*** [n.d.]	$2.50	$7.50	$15.00
194	Carnelle, Inge - ***Joy Ride*** [1967] PBO. Cover by Maguire.	$2.50	$7.50	$15.00
208	— ***The Hijacked Harlot*** [n.d.]	$2.50	$7.50	$15.00
216	Carnelle, Inge - ***Sexplosion*** [1967] PBO.	$2.50	$7.50	$15.00
221	Palmer, M. Earle - ***Southern Exposure*** [1967] PBO.	$2.50	$7.50	$15.00
222	— ***The Sex Goddess*** [n.d.]	$2.50	$7.50	$15.00
307N	— ***The S.E.X. Machine*** [n.d.]	$2.50	$7.50	$15.00
313N	— ***Revolt*** [n.d.]	$2.50	$7.50	$15.00
427Z	Coxe, M. - ***The Oversexed Astronauts*** [n.d.]	$2.50	$7.50	$15.00
OB-514	Reynolds, J. - ***Stranger Than Paradise*** [n.d.]	$2.50	$7.50	$15.00
OB-562Z	— ***Taste Of Evil*** [n.d.]	$2.50	$7.50	$15.00
OB-569Z	— ***The Story Of "F"*** [n.d.]	$2.50	$7.50	$15.00
OB-585K	— ***Unnatural Urges*** [n.d.]	$2.50	$7.50	$15.00
603K	Kanto, Peter - ***Rosy Cheeks*** [n.d.]	$2.50	$7.50	$15.00
617K	— ***Fruit Of The Loins*** [n.d.]	$2.50	$7.50	$15.00
655T	— ***The Ghost Came Twice*** [n.d.]	$2.50	$7.50	$15.00
677T	— ***Operation: Sextrip*** [n.d.]	$2.50	$7.50	$15.00
713T	— ***The Great 24 Hour Thing*** [n.d.]	$2.50	$7.50	$15.00
764T	— ***Pleasure Us*** [n.d.]	$2.50	$7.50	$15.00
765T	— ***The Balling Machine*** [n.d.]	$2.50	$7.50	$15.00
OB-1017	— ***The Coming Of Cormac*** [n.d.]	$2.50	$7.50	$15.00
OB-1023T	Bennett - ***Cosmic Rape*** [n.d.]	$2.50	$7.50	$15.00
OB-1032T	— ***Manlib!*** [n.d.]	$2.50	$7.50	$15.00
OB-1054T	— ***The Flesh Hunters*** [n.d.]	$2.50	$7.50	$15.00
OB-1061R	— ***Who Put The Devil In Miss Jones?*** [n.d.]	$2.50	$7.50	$15.00
OB-1063T	— ***Pleasure Planet*** [n.d.]	$2.50	$7.50	$15.00
OB-1082	— ***The Sexorcist*** [n.d.]	$2.50	$7.50	$15.00
OB-1166R	Giles, B. - ***The Pleasure Principal*** [n.d.]	$2.50	$7.50	$15.00
CC-3001R	— ***Sex Trek*** [n.d.]	$2.50	$7.50	$15.00
BL-5255	— ***The Spy With The Versatile Tool*** [n.d.]	$2.50	$7.50	$15.00

Bell Novels. Toronto: Bell Publishing. Digest Size.

NN-1	Yates, Peter - ***The Dress Circle Murders*** [1945]	$4.00	$12.50	$25.00
NN-2	Leinster, Murray - ***The Blonde And The Outlaw*** [1945]	$6.00	$20.00	$40.00

Belmont Books (Early Publisher's History, 1960–1965)

Belmont published a diversity of collectible popular literature. Often, the artists incorporated the lettering with the artwork to form a unique approach to cover art. Collectible items include biographies, mysteries, horror, esoteric, juvenile delinquency, comic, and science fiction. They issued a number of western and science fiction double novels. Books by Robert Bloch, biographies of Marilyn Monroe and Brigitte Bardot, plus titles from the Shadow series, highlight this publisher. In 1971, Belmont joined with Tower Books of the World Publishing Company to form Belmont-Tower, as Midwood Books did in 1964.

Belmont Books. New York: Belmont Productions, Inc.

		G	VG	F
201	Maurois, Andre - ***Temptress*** [1960]	$1.25	$3.75	$7.50
202	Alleg, Henri - ***The Question*** [1960]	$1.25	$3.75	$7.50
203	Bingham, Carson (Bruce Cassiday) - ***Payola Woman*** [1960] PBO.	$1.25	$3.75	$7.50
204	Jakes, John - ***Johnny Havoc*** [1960]	$1.50	$5.00	$10.00
205	Murtagh, Judge John M. & Harris, Sara - ***Who Live In Shadow*** [1960]	$1.25	$3.75	$7.50
206	Douglas, Bill - ***Bloody Precinct*** [1960] PBO.	$1.25	$3.75	$7.50
207	Mackey, Joe - ***The Cruel City*** [1960] PBO.	$1.25	$3.75	$7.50
208	Maurel, Micheline - ***The Slave*** [1960]	$1.25	$3.75	$7.50
209	Peters, Bryan - ***Hong Kong Kill*** [1960]	$1.25	$3.75	$7.50
210	Campbell, Jean - ***The Oldest Profession*** [1960]	$1.00	$3.00	$6.00
211	Mari, Isa - ***Cage Of Passion*** [1960]	$1.35	$4.00	$8.00
212	Karmel, Alex - ***Something Wild*** [1960]	$1.35	$4.00	$8.00
213	Murray, A.A. - ***The Blanket*** [1960]	$1.25	$3.75	$7.50
214	Friedman, Stuart - ***Come-On Girl*** [1960] PBO.	$1.25	$3.75	$7.50
215	Shepherd, John (W.T. Ballard) - ***Lights, Camera, Murder*** [1960]	$1.35	$4.00	$8.00
216	Sollers, Philippe - ***Concha*** [1960] Cover art by Maguire.	$1.25	$3.75	$7.50
217	Knight, Adam - ***Sugar Shannon*** [1960]	$1.25	$3.75	$7.50
218	Anthology - ***Sex-Clusive*** [1960] PBO. Edited by Jack Heller. Cover art by Bill Wenzel.	$2.00	$6.00	$12.00
219	Gronowicz, Antoni - ***Hitler's Woman*** [1961]	$1.25	$3.75	$7.50
220	Lacy, Ed - ***South Pacific Affair*** [1961]	$1.35	$4.00	$8.00
221	Deming, Richard - ***Vice-Cop*** [1961] PBO. Cover art by Rader.	$1.25	$3.75	$7.50
222	Russell, William - ***A Wind Is Rising*** [1961]	$1.25	$3.75	$7.50
223	Harris, Sara - ***Skid Row U.S.A.*** [1961]	$1.25	$3.75	$7.50
224	Kapelner, Alan - ***Lonely Boy Blues*** [1961]	$1.25	$3.75	$7.50
225	Mosley, Leonard - ***Foxhole In Cairo*** [1961]	$1.35	$4.00	$8.00
226	Marie, Ann & Burgess, Michael - ***Neither Sin Nor Shame*** [1961] PBO.	$1.25	$3.75	$7.50
227	Fox, Gardner F. - ***The Borgia Blade*** [1961] Cover art by Bob Maguire.	$1.50	$5.00	$10.00
228	Winston, Carl - ***The Ladies' Man*** [1961] PBO.	$1.35	$4.00	$8.00
229	Smith, Stanley E. - ***Ten Against The Third Reich*** [1961]	$1.25	$3.75	$7.50
230	Anthology - ***Creeps By Night*** [1961] Edited by Dashiell Hammett. Cover art by Maguire.	$2.50	$7.50	$15.00
231	Bodenheim, Maxwell - ***My Life And Loves In Greenwich Village*** [1961]	$1.25	$3.75	$7.50
232	Shaw, Irwin - ***The Day The War Ends*** [1961]	$1.25	$3.75	$7.50
233	Bloch, Robert - ***Nightmares*** [1961] PBO.	$3.50	$10.00	$20.00
234	Stonebraker, Florence - ***Love Doctor*** [1961] Cover art by Maguire.	$ .75	$2.50	$5.00
235	Drago, Harry Sinclair - ***A Gun For Cantrell*** [1961]	$1.25	$3.75	$7.50
236	Block, Lawrence - ***Markham*** [1961] PBO.	$1.35	$4.00	$8.00

		G	VG	F
237	Tregaskis, Richard - ***Stronger Than Fear*** [1961] Cover art by Maguire.	$1.25	$3.75	$7.50
238	Smith, Stanley E. - ***13 Against The Rising Sun*** [1961]	$1.25	$3.75	$7.50
239	Anthology - ***The Red Brain*** [1961] PBO. Edited by Dashiell Hammett.	$2.50	$7.50	$15.00
240	Flint, John B. - ***Lover Boy*** [1961]	$1.25	$3.75	$7.50
241	Drago, Harry Sinclair - ***The Trial Of Johnny Dice*** [1961]	$1.25	$3.75	$7.50
242	Cargoe, Richard - ***The Back Of The Tiger*** [1961]	$1.25	$3.75	$7.50
243	Malley, Louis - ***The Love Mill*** [1961] PBO.	$1.25	$3.75	$7.50
244	Gaddis, Peggy - ***Nurse Durand's Affair*** [1961]	$ .75	$2.50	$5.00
91-245	Haskell, Frank - ***Hotel Doctor*** [1961]	$ .75	$2.50	$5.00
246	Long, Frank - ***The Horror Expert*** [1961] PBO. Cover art by Schulz.	$2.00	$6.00	$12.00
91-247	Anthology - ***More Sex-Clusive*** [1961] Edited by Jack Heller	$2.00	$6.00	$12.00
91-248	Shepherd, John (W.T. Ballard) - ***The Demise Of A Louse*** [1962] Cover art by Al Brule.	$1.35	$4.00	$8.00
91-249	Haskell, Frank - ***Young Dr. Masters*** [1962]	$ .75	$2.50	$5.00
91-250	Meyer, Jerome S. - ***The New Twist In Crossword Puzzles*** [1962]	$2.00	$6.00	$12.00
91-251	Nye, Nelson - ***Gun-Hunt For The Sundance Kid*** [1962]	$1.00	$3.00	$6.00
91-252	Fickling, G.G. - ***Naughty But Dead*** [1962]	$1.25	$3.75	$7.50
91-253	Cooper, Morton - ***The Private Life Of A Strip-Tease Artist*** [1962]	$1.25	$3.75	$7.50
91-254	Saunders, David - ***M Squad*** [1962] PBO. TV tie-in.	$1.50	$5.00	$10.00
91-255	Hearn, J. Van - ***Don't Betray Me*** [1962]	$1.25	$3.75	$7.50
91-257	Dispaldo, A.R. - ***I Am Teresa*** [1962]	$1.25	$3.75	$7.50
91-258	Seltzer, Charles Alden - ***Gun-Law For Lavercombe*** [1962]	$1.25	$3.75	$7.50
90-259	Kane, Henry - ***Kisses Of Death*** [1962] PBO.	$1.35	$4.00	$8.00
91-260	Gaddis, Peggy - ***Women Of The Evening*** [1962]	$1.25	$3.75	$7.50
90-261	Jakes, John - ***Johnny Havoc Meets Zelda*** [1962]	$1.50	$5.00	$10.00
90-262	Eliat, Helene - ***Arena Of Love*** [1962]	$1.00	$3.00	$6.00
90-263	McDonnell, Virginia, R.N. - ***Doctors And Nurses*** [1962] PBO. Cover art by Robert Maguire	$1.00	$3.00	$6.00
91-264	Seltzer, Charles Alden - ***The Stranger From Neutral Strip*** [1962]	$1.25	$3.75	$7.50
90-265	Brown, Wenzell - ***Jailbait Jungle*** [1962]	$2.00	$6.00	$12.00
90-266	Roeburt, John - ***Triple Cross*** [1962] Cover art by Robert Maguire.	$1.25	$3.75	$7.50
91-267	Rand, Matt - ***Gun-Hell At Big Bend*** [1962]	$1.25	$3.75	$7.50
90-268	Turner, John - ***By-Line, Mona Knox*** [1962] PBO. Cover art by Maguire.	$1.25	$3.75	$7.50
90-269	Whittington, Harry - ***Hot As Fire, Cold As Ice*** [1962]	$3.00	$9.00	$18.00
90-270	Stonebraker, Florence - ***Young Doctor Elliot*** [1962] Cover art by Maguire.	$ .75	$2.50	$5.00
90-271	Turner, John - ***Love Secret*** [1962]	$1.00	$3.00	$6.00
90-272	Didelot, Francis - ***The Seventh Juror*** [1962]	$1.25	$3.75	$7.50
90-273	Rand, Matt - ***It Happened In A Town Named Lawless*** [1962]	$1.25	$3.75	$7.50
90-274	Martin, Kay - ***Nymph In Suburbia*** [1963] PBO.	$1.25	$3.75	$7.50
90-275	Bloch, Robert - ***Horror - 7*** [1963] PBO. Cover art by Maguire.	$3.50	$10.00	$20.00
90-276	Avallone, Michael - ***The Bedroom Bolero*** [1963]	$1.35	$4.00	$8.00
90-277	Long, Frank Belknap - ***It Was The Day Of The Robot*** [1963]	$2.50	$7.50	$15.00
90-278	Gaddis, Peggy - ***Young Nurse Desmond*** [1963]	$ .75	$2.50	$5.00
90-279	Rand, Matt - ***Seven Seconds To Sundown*** [1963]	$1.25	$3.75	$7.50
90-280	Hall, Babette - ***The Professor And The Co-Ed*** [1963]	$1.00	$3.00	$6.00
90-281	Fickling, G.G. - ***The Case Of The Radioactive Redhead*** [1963] Cover art by Maguire.	$1.35	$4.00	$8.00
90-282	Bergman, Lee - ***Walk Softly, Walk Deadly*** [1963] PBO.	$1.25	$3.75	$7.50
90-283	Anonymous - ***My Profession Is Sin*** [1963]	$1.25	$3.75	$7.50
90-284	Rand, Matt - ***Shoot-Out At Split Rock*** [1963]	$1.25	$3.75	$7.50
90-285	Brennan, Alice - ***Nurse Keane's Affair*** [1963]	$ .75	$2.50	$5.00

Belmont, L-508

Belmont, L92-527

Belmont, 92-618

		G	VG	F
90-286	Willeford, Charles - ***The Machine In Ward Eleven*** [1963] PBO. Cover art by Maguire.	$5.00	$15.00	$30.00
90-287	Campbell, Ciff - ***Rider Of The Yellow Dust*** [1963]	$1.25	$3.75	$7.50
90-288	Unknown - ***My Son The Teenager: A Cartoon Satire*** [1963] PBO.	$1.35	$4.00	$8.00
90-289	Jakes, John - ***Johnny Havoc And the Doll Who Had "It"*** [1963]	$1.35	$4.00	$8.00
90-290	Fox, Edward S. - ***Thus A Boy Becomes A Man*** [1964]	$1.25	$3.75	$7.50
90-291	Rand, Matt - ***The Sheriff Of Hangman's Gulch*** [1964]	$1.25	$3.75	$7.50
90-292	Brossard, Chandler - ***Episode With Erika*** [1963]	$1.25	$3.75	$7.50
90-293	Avallone, Michael - ***There Is Something About A Dame*** [1963] PBO.	$1.35	$4.00	$8.00
90-294	Shelley, Sidney - ***Francine*** [1963]	$1.25	$3.75	$7.50
90-295	Seltzer, Charles Alden - ***West Of Apache Pass*** [1963]	$1.25	$3.75	$7.50
90-296	McAlmon, Robert - ***There Was A Rustle Of Black Silk Stockings*** [1963]	$1.25	$3.75	$7.50
90-297	Avallone, Michael - ***Tales Of The Frightened*** [1963] PBO.	$2.00	$6.00	$12.00
90-298	Gibson, Walter B. - ***Return Of The Shadow*** [1963] PBO.	$2.50	$7.50	$15.00
90-299	Seltzer, Charles Alden - ***"Slow" Burgess*** [1963] Cover art by A. Leslie Ross.	$1.25	$3.75	$7.50
90-300	Lawrence, William - ***After Hours*** [1963]	$1.25	$3.75	$7.50
90-301	Robertson, Frank C. - ***Feud At Blue Canyon*** [1963]	$1.25	$3.75	$7.50
90-302	Kane, Henry - ***Nobody Loves A Loser*** [1963]	$1.25	$3.75	$7.50
90-303	Ronald, James - ***Murder In The Family*** [1963]	$1.25	$3.75	$7.50
90-304	Piper, Anson - ***Black Creek Buckaroo*** [1963]	$1.25	$3.75	$7.50
90-305	Anthology - ***A Guide For The Broad-Minded*** [1963] Edited by Jack Heller. Cover by Bill Wentzel.	$2.00	$6.00	$12.00
90-306	Hershman, Morris - ***Guilty Witness*** [1963]	$1.25	$3.75	$7.50
90-307	Seltzer, Charles Alden - ***Double Cross Ranch*** [1964]	$1.25	$3.75	$7.50
90-308	Field, Peter - ***Trail South From Powder Valley*** [1964]	$1.25	$3.75	$7.50
90-309	Benet, Robert Ames - ***Snake River Ambush*** [1964]	$1.25	$3.75	$7.50
90-310	Seltzer, Charles Alden - ***Sure Shot*** [1964]	$1.25	$3.75	$7.50
90-311	Dean, Nell Marr - ***The Trials Of Dr. Carol*** [1964]	$1.00	$3.00	$6.00
90-312	Seltzer, Charles Alden - ***Ferguson's Trail*** [1964]	$1.25	$3.75	$7.50
90-313	Strong, Zachary - ***Brett Randal, Gambler*** [1964]	$1.25	$3.75	$7.50
90-314	Robertson, Frank C. - ***Outlaw Ranch*** [1964]	$1.25	$3.75	$7.50
90-315	Nye, Nelson - ***Quick-Fire Hombre*** [1964]	$1.25	$3.75	$7.50
90-316	Ellson, Hal - ***Nightmare Street*** [1964] PBO.	$2.50	$7.50	$15.00
90-317	Nye, Nelson - ***Strawberry Roan*** [1964]	$1.25	$3.75	$7.50
90-318	Avallone, Michael - ***Lust Is No Lady*** [1964] PBO.	$1.35	$4.00	$8.00

		G	VG	F
90-319	Arthur, Burt - ***Sheriff Of Lonesome*** [1964]	$1.25	$3.75	$7.50
90-320	Robertson, Frank C. - ***The Trouble Grabber*** [1964]	$1.25	$3.75	$7.50
90-321	Arthur, Burt - ***Gunsmoke Over Utah*** [1964]	$1.25	$3.75	$7.50
90-322	Brennan, Alice - ***The Romances Of Young Dr. Masters*** [1964].	$1.00	$3.00	$6.00
90-323	Nye, Nelson - ***Desert Of The Damned*** [1965] Cover art by Gross.	$1.25	$3.75	$7.50
L-501	Kubly, Herbert - ***Varieties Of Love*** [1960]	$1.00	$3.00	$6.00
L-502	Wiegand, William - ***The Incorrigibles*** [1960] Cover art by Ross.	$1.00	$3.00	$6.00
L-503	Glover, Dr. Leland E. - ***Sex Life Of The Modern Adult*** [1960].	$1.00	$3.00	$6.00
L-504	Carpozi, George, Jr. - ***The Brigitte Bardot Story*** [1961] PBO.	$4.00	$12.50	$25.00
L-505	Jackson, Charles - ***The Cheat*** [1961]	$1.35	$4.00	$8.00
L-506	Collection - ***The Secret Agent's Badge Of Courage*** [1961]	$1.00	$3.00	$6.00
L-507	Mullady & Kofoed - ***Meet The Mob*** [1961]	$1.00	$3.00	$6.00
L-508	Carpori, George, Jr. - ***Marilyn Monroe: "Her Own Story"*** [1961] PBO.	$8.00	$25.00	$50.00
L-509	Smith, Stan - ***The Battle Of Leyte Gulf*** [1961]	$1.00	$3.00	$6.00
L-510	Dos Passos, John - ***Most Likely To Succeed*** [1961]	$1.00	$3.00	$6.00
L-511	Maugham, W. Somerset - ***The Traitor*** [1961]	$1.00	$3.00	$6.00
L-512	Lawrence, D.H. - ***The Shadow In The Rose Garden*** [1961]	$1.00	$3.00	$6.00
L-513	Cobleigh, Dr. Ira V. - ***How To Get Rich Buying Stocks*** [1961].	$1.00	$3.00	$6.00
L-514	Gehman, Richard - ***Sinatra And His Rat Pack*** [1961]	$1.25	$3.75	$7.50
L-515	Doenitz, Grand Admiral Karl - ***Memoirs*** [1961]	$1.00	$3.00	$6.00
L-516	Huxley, Aldous - ***The Embassador*** [1961]	$1.00	$3.00	$6.00
L-517	Kordel, Dr. Lelord - ***Eat Your Troubles Away*** [1961]	$1.00	$3.00	$6.00
L-518	Washburn, Charles - ***Come Into My Parlor*** [1961]	$1.00	$3.00	$6.00
L-519	Salisbury, Harrison E. - ***Khrushchev's "Mein Kampf"*** [1961]	$1.00	$3.00	$6.00
L-520	Fisher, Graham & McNair-Wilson, Michael - ***Black-Shirt*** [1961] PBO.	$1.00	$3.00	$6.00
L-521	Golightly, Bonnie - ***The Integration Of Maybelle Brown*** [1961]	$1.00	$3.00	$6.00
L-522	Horwitz, Julius - ***Behind Every Door*** [1961]	$1.00	$3.00	$6.00
L-523	Glover, Dr. Leland E. - ***Sex-Life Of The Modern Teen-Ager*** [1961]	$1.00	$3.00	$6.00
L-524	Frischauer, Willi - ***Berlin Betrayal*** [1961]	$1.00	$3.00	$6.00
L-525	Kiki - ***The Education Of A French Model*** [1962]	$1.00	$3.00	$6.00
L92-526	Frischauer, Willi - ***Himmler*** [1962]	$1.00	$3.00	$6.00
L92-527	Bloch, Robert - ***Yours Truly, Jack The Ripper*** [1962] PBO.	$7.00	$22.50	$45.00
L92-528	Oleck, Major Howard - ***Heroic Battles Of World War II*** [1962]	$1.00	$3.00	$6.00
L92-529	Caprio, Frank S., M.D. - ***A Psychiatrist Talks About Sex*** [1962]	$1.00	$3.00	$6.00
L92-530	Bloch, Robert - ***More Nightmares*** [1962]	$3.50	$10.00	$20.00
L92-531	Heise, Jack - ***The Amazing Hypno-Diet*** [1962]	$1.00	$3.00	$6.00
L92-532	Dunham, Donald - ***Zone Of Violence*** [1962] Cover art by Maguire.	$1.00	$3.00	$6.00
L92-533	Kordel, Dr. Lelord - ***Eat Your Way To Happiness*** [1962]	$1.00	$3.00	$6.00
L92-534	Bove, Charles F., M.D. - ***Diary Of A French Doctor*** [1962]	$1.00	$3.00	$6.00
L92-535	Anthology - ***Twisted*** [1962] edited by Groff Conklin	$2.00	$6.00	$12.00
L92-536	Roeburt, John - ***Get Me Giesler*** [1962] Cover art by Jerome Podwil	$1.00	$3.00	$6.00
L92-537	Bloch, Robert - ***Terror*** [1962] PBO. Cover by Podwil.	$3.50	$10.00	$20.00
L94-538	Levin, Meyer - ***Citizens*** [1962]	$1.00	$3.00	$6.00
L92-539	Camper, Mrs. Shirley - ***How To Get Along With Your Child*** [1962]	$1.00	$3.00	$6.00
L92-540	Wachtel, Curt S., M.D. - ***Private Casebook Of An M.D.*** [1962].	$ .75	$2.50	$5.00
L92-541	Anthology - ***The Weird Ones*** [1962]	$2.00	$6.00	$12.00
L92-542	Ries, Estelle H. - ***The Lonely Sex*** [1962]	$1.00	$3.00	$6.00
L92-543	Wachtel, Curt S., M.D. - ***A Doctor's Personal Files*** [1962]	$ .75	$2.50	$5.00
L92-544	Barron, Mike "Pitcher" - ***A Professional Gambler Tells*** [1962].	$1.00	$3.00	$6.00
L92-545	Brown, Beth - ***For Men Only*** [1962]	$1.25	$3.75	$7.50
L92-546	Perles, Alfred - ***My Friend, Henry Miller*** [1962]	$1.25	$3.75	$7.50
L92-547	Anthology - ***The X Report*** [1962] Articles from *Sexology* mags.	$1.25	$3.75	$7.50

		G	VG	F
L92-548	English & Foster - ***Fathers Are Parents Too*** [1962]	$1.25	$3.75	$7.50
L92-549	Wood, H. Curtis, M.D. - ***Calories, Vitamins And Common Sense*** [1962]	$1.00	$3.00	$6.00
L92-550	Gaddis, Peggy - ***Lulie*** [1962] Cover art by Nappi.	$1.25	$3.75	$7.50
L92-551	Matthews, John D. - ***My Name Is Violence*** [1962]	$1.25	$3.75	$7.50
L92-552	Klein, Dr. Leo - ***Normal And Abnormal Sex-Ways*** [1962]	$1.00	$3.00	$6.00
L92-553	Grant, E. Stanley, M.B.A. - ***How To Get Rich With Security*** [1962]	$1.00	$3.00	$6.00
L92-554	Brown, Beth - ***The Profession Of Marie Simone*** [1962]	$1.25	$3.75	$7.50
L92-555	Halper, Albert - ***Union Square*** [1962]	$1.25	$3.75	$7.50
L92-556	Carpozi, George, Jr. - ***Vince Edwards*** [1962] PBO.	$1.35	$4.00	$8.00
L92-557	Anthology - ***Rare Science Fiction*** [1962] edited by Ivan Howard.	$1.50	$5.00	$10.00
L92-558	Oleck, Maj. Howard - ***Eye-Witness World War II Battles*** [1963] PBO.	$1.00	$3.00	$6.00
L92-559	"Constella" - ***Your Happiness Is In The Stars*** [1963] PBO.	$1.00	$3.00	$6.00
L92-560	Roeburt, John - ***Sex-Life And The Criminal Law*** [1963] PBO.	$1.00	$3.00	$6.00
L92-561	Goodwin, Laurel - ***How To Be Lovelier*** [1963]	$1.00	$3.00	$6.00
L92-562	Anonymous - ***I Am Desire*** [1963] PBO.	$1.00	$3.00	$6.00
L92-563	Popenoe, Dr. Paul - ***Sex, Love, And Marriage*** [1963]	$1.00	$3.00	$6.00
L92-564	Anthology - ***6 And The Silent Scream*** [1963] PBO. Edited by Ivan Howard. Cover art by Maguire.	$2.00	$6.00	$12.00
L92-565	Patrick, John - ***The Main Attraction*** [1963]	$1.35	$4.00	$8.00
L92-566	Thurber, James - ***In A Word*** [1963]	$1.50	$5.00	$10.00
L92-567	Anthology - ***Novelets Of Science Fiction*** [1963] edited by Ivan Howard.	$1.50	$5.00	$10.00
L92-568	Anthology - ***Erotica Exotica*** [1963] PBO. Edited by Jay Garon & Morgan Wilson.	$1.00	$3.00	$6.00
L92-569	Long, Frank Belknap - ***The Hounds Of Tindalos*** [1963]	$2.50	$7.50	$15.00
L92-570	Avallone, Michael - ***Shock Corridor*** [1963] PBO. Movie tie-in.	$1.35	$4.00	$8.00
L92-571	Anthology - ***Escape To Earth*** [1963] edited by Ivan Howard. Cover art by Emsh.	$1.35	$4.00	$8.00
L92-572	Chandler, Noel - ***Satan In High-Heels*** [1963] PBO.	$1.35	$4.00	$8.00
L92-573	Casanova, Jacques - ***Casanova Confidential*** [1963]	$1.00	$3.00	$6.00
L92-574	Kandel & Safran - ***Nudeniks*** [1963]	$1.35	$4.00	$8.00
L92-575	Anthology - ***Way Out*** [1963] edited by Ivan Howard.	$1.50	$5.00	$10.00
L92-576	Gaddis, Peggy - ***The Wild Girls*** [1963] Cover art by Powers.	$1.25	$3.75	$7.50
L92-577	Halper, Albert - ***Only An Inch From Glory*** [1963]	$1.25	$3.75	$7.50
L92-578	Camisso, Giovanni - ***Loves Of The Orient*** [1964] Cover art by Victor Kalin.	$1.25	$3.75	$7.50
L92-579	Long, Frank Belknap - ***The Dark Beasts*** [1963]	$2.50	$7.50	$15.00
L92-580	Austin, Alex - ***The Greatest Lover In The World*** [1964] Cover art by Victor Kalin.	$1.25	$3.75	$7.50
L92-581	Masoch, Leopold Sacher - ***Bed Of An Empress*** [1963] Cover art by Victor Kalin.	$1.25	$3.75	$7.50
L92-582	Anthology - ***Things*** [1964] PBO. Edited by Ivan Howard.	$2.00	$6.00	$12.00
L92-583	Colette - ***Claudine In Paris*** [1964]	$1.00	$3.00	$6.00
L92-584	Simak, Clifford D. - ***Worlds Without End*** [1964] PBO.	$1.35	$4.00	$8.00
L92-585	Frame, Bart - ***Andrea Holland*** [1964]	$1.00	$3.00	$6.00
L92-586	Gruber, Frank - ***Swing Low, Swing Dead*** [1964]	$1.25	$3.75	$7.50
L92-587	Casanova, Jacques - ***The Lusts Of Casanova*** [1964]	$1.00	$3.00	$6.00
L92-588	Jones, Raymond F. - ***The Non-Statistical Man*** [1964] PBO.	$1.35	$4.00	$8.00
L92-589	Baker, Denys Val - ***Bizarre Loves*** [1964] PBO.	$1.25	$3.75	$7.50
L92-590	Coleman, Mitchell - ***Born To Be Bad*** [1964]	$1.25	$3.75	$7.50
L92-591	Silverberg, Robert - ***Godling Go Home!*** [1964]	$1.35	$4.00	$8.00
L92-592	Gruber, Frank - ***The French Key*** [1964]	$1.35	$4.00	$8.00
L92-593	Moray, Helga - ***Not For A Day*** [1964]	$1.25	$3.75	$7.50
L92-594	Derleth, Auguth - ***Mr. George And Other Odd Persons*** [1964] Cover art by Ralph Brillhart.	$2.50	$7.50	$15.00
L92-595	Anthology - ***My Strangest Case*** [1964] edited by Kurt Singer.	$1.00	$3.00	$6.00

Belmont, 92-624

Berkley, G-46

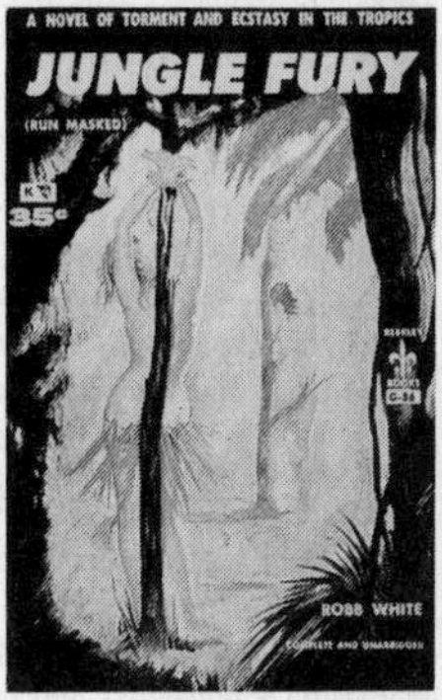

Berkley, G-56

		G	VG	F
L92-596	Fuller, Samuel - ***The Naked Kiss*** [1964] PBO.	$1.00	$3.00	$6.00
L92-597	Laflin, Jack - ***The Spy Who Loved America*** [1964] PBO.	$1.25	$3.75	$7.50
L92-598	Hope, Fielding - ***Marie Arnaud, Spy*** [1964]	$1.25	$3.75	$7.50
L92-599	Dane, Mark - ***Felicia*** [1964] PBO.	$1.25	$3.75	$7.50
L92-600	Long, Frank Belknap - ***Odd Science Fiction*** [1964]	$1.35	$4.00	$8.00
92-601	Clay, Matthew - ***French Alley*** [1964]	$1.00	$3.00	$6.00
92-602	Grant, Maxwell - ***The Shadow Strikes*** [1964] PBO.	$2.50	$7.50	$15.00
92-603	Dick, Philip K. - ***The Penultimate Truth*** [1964] PBO.	$3.50	$10.00	$20.00
92-604	Elsner, Don Von - ***Pour A Swindle Through A Loophole*** [1964]	$1.25	$3.75	$7.50
92-605	Gaddis, Peggy - ***The Lust Seekers*** [1964]	$1.25	$3.75	$7.50
92-606	Anthology - ***Masters Of Science Fiction*** [1964] PBO.	$1.35	$4.00	$8.00
92-607	Gruber, Frank - ***The Corpse Moved Upstairs*** [1964]	$1.35	$4.00	$8.00
92-608	Gaddis, Peggy - ***Private Secretary*** [1964]	$1.00	$3.00	$6.00
92-609	Fickling, G.G. - ***The Crazy Mixed-Up Nude*** [1964] PBO.	$1.25	$3.75	$7.50
92-610	Bombal, Maria-Luisa - ***House Of Mist*** [1964]	$1.00	$3.00	$6.00
92-611	Neville, Kris - ***The Unearth People*** [1964] PBO.	$1.35	$4.00	$8.00
92-612	Blish, James/Silverberg, Robert - ***Giants In The Earth/We, The Marauders*** [1964] PBO.	$1.35	$4.00	$8.00
92-613	Laflan, Jack - ***A Silent Kind Of War*** [1965] PBO.	$1.25	$3.75	$7.50
92-614	Moray, Helga - ***Love The Hour*** [1965]	$1.00	$3.00	$6.00
92-615	Grant, Maxwell - ***Shadow Beware*** [1965] PBO.	$2.50	$7.50	$15.00
92-616	Thompson, Arthur - ***The Starved*** [1965]	$1.00	$3.00	$6.00
92-617	Lovecraft, H.P. - ***The Case Of Charles Dexter Ward*** [1965] PBO.	$2.50	$7.50	$15.00
92-618	Dick, Philip K. - ***Time Out Of Joint*** [1965]	$3.50	$10.00	$20.00
92-619	Lawrence, William - ***End Of Innocence*** [1965]	$1.00	$3.00	$6.00
92-620	Smith, Stan - ***Resist!*** [1965] y	$1.00	$3.00	$6.00
92-621	Lesser, Milton - ***Secret Of The Black Planet*** [1965]	$1.35	$4.00	$8.00
92-622	Anthology - ***The Unearthly*** [1965] PBO. Edited by Kurt Singer.	$1.35	$4.00	$8.00
92-623	Kane, Henry - ***Dirty Gertie*** [1965]	$1.35	$4.00	$8.00
92-624	Grant, Maxwell - ***Cry Shadow!*** [1965]	$2.50	$7.50	$15.00
92-625	Leinster, Murray - ***Space Platform*** [1965]	$1.35	$4.00	$8.00
92-626	Smith, Stan - ***Dive, Dive!*** [1965] PBO.	$1.00	$3.00	$6.00
92-627	Binder, Eando - ***Anton York, Immortal*** [1965] PBO.	$1.25	$3.75	$7.50
92-628	Gaddis, Peggy - ***Office Love Affair*** [1965]	$ .75	$2.50	$5.00
92-629	Crosby, Lee - ***Doors To Death*** [1965] PBO.	$1.25	$3.75	$7.50
92-630	Mann, E.B. - ***Gunslick-By Request!/Luck Rides With The Fastest Gun*** [1965]	$1.25	$3.75	$7.50
B50-631	Laflan, Jack - ***The Spy In White Gloves*** [1965] PBO.	$1.25	$3.75	$7.50

		G	VG	F
B50-632	Leinster, Murray - ***Space Tug*** [1965] Cover art by Jack Gaughan.	$1.35	$4.00	$8.00
B50-633	Anthology - ***Basil Rathbone Selects Strange Tales*** [1965] PBO. Edited by Lyle Kenyon Engel. Cover art by Elliot.	$1.50	$5.00	$10.00
92-634	Gaddis, Peggy - ***Love Is Enough*** [1965]	$ .75	$2.50	$5.00
92-635	McCarthy, Delphina - ***Beyond The Clouds*** [1965]	$1.00	$3.00	$6.00
92-636	Stuart, Sidney (Michael Avallone) - ***Young Dillinger*** [1965]	$1.25	$3.75	$7.50
B50-637	Gaddis, Peggy - ***Peacock Hill*** [1965]	$ .75	$2.50	$5.00
B50-638	Garrison, Joan - ***The Loving Heart*** [1965]	$ .75	$2.50	$5.00
B50-639	Wallace, C.H. - ***Crashland In The Congo*** [1965] PBO.	$1.00	$3.00	$6.00
B50-640	Christian, Paula - ***Amanda*** [1965]	$1.35	$4.00	$8.00
B50-641	Reisner, Mary - ***Shadows On The Wall*** [1965]	$1.00	$3.00	$6.00
B50-642	Sarac, Roger (Roger Caras) - ***The Throwbacks*** [1965] PBO.	$1.35	$4.00	$8.00
B50-643	Schmitz, James H. - ***A Tale Of Two Clocks*** [1965]	$1.25	$3.75	$7.50
B50-644	Crosby, Lee - ***Bridge House*** [1965]	$1.00	$3.00	$6.00
B50-645	Didelot, Francis - ***The Many Ways Of Death*** [1965]	$1.00	$3.00	$6.00
B50-646	Anthology - ***Now And Beyond*** [1965] PBO.	$1.50	$5.00	$10.00
B50-647	Grant, Maxwell - ***The Shadow's Revenge*** [1965] PBO.	$2.50	$7.50	$15.00
B50-648	Gaddis, Peggy - ***Temptation*** [1965]	$1.00	$3.00	$6.00
B50-649	Gaddis, Peggy - ***The Persistent Suitor*** [1965]	$ .75	$2.50	$5.00
B50-650	Blocklinger, Betty - ***Escape From Love*** [1965]	$ .75	$2.50	$5.00
B50-651	Tralins, Robert - ***Squaresville Jag*** [1965]	$1.35	$4.00	$8.00
B50-652	Gaddis, Peggy - ***Painted Lips*** [1965]	$ .75	$2.50	$5.00
B50-653	Gaddis, Peggy - ***The Joyous Hills*** [1965]	$ .75	$2.50	$5.00
B50-654	Garrison, Joan - ***Snatch A Dream*** [1965]	$1.00	$3.00	$6.00
B50-655	Mann, E.B. - ***Shootin' Melody*** [1965]	$1.00	$3.00	$6.00
B50-657	Hamilton, Edmond - ***Doomstar*** [1966] PBO.	$1.35	$4.00	$8.00
B50-658	Nelson, Marguerite - ***Wait For The Day*** [1966]	$1.00	$3.00	$6.00
B50-659	Gaddis, Peggy - ***Beloved Intruder*** [1966]	$1.00	$3.00	$6.00
B50-660	McElfresh, Adeline - ***Homecoming*** [1966]	$ .75	$2.50	$5.00
B50-661	Gaddis, Peggy - ***Where Love Is*** [1966]	$ .75	$2.50	$5.00
B50-662	Bond, Evelyn - ***House Of Distant Voices*** [1966]	$1.00	$3.00	$6.00
B50-663	Long, Frank Belknap - ***This Strange Tomarrow*** [1966]	$1.50	$5.00	$10.00
B50-664	Wallace, C.H. - ***Tail Wind To Danger*** [1966] PBO.	$1.00	$3.00	$6.00
B50-665	Gaddis, Peggy - ***Come Into My Heart*** [1966]	$ .75	$2.50	$5.00
B50-666	Bowman, Jeanne - ***Ready To Love*** [1966]	$ .75	$2.50	$5.00
B50-667	St. John, Genevieve - ***The Dark Watch*** [1966]	$1.00	$3.00	$6.00
B50-669	St. John, Genevieve - ***The Shadow On Spanish Swamp*** [1966]	$1.00	$3.00	$6.00
B50-670	Mann, E.B. - ***Buzzards Of Apache Gap/Return Of The Gun Club*** [1966]	$1.25	$3.75	$7.50
B50-671	Gaddis, Peggy - ***A Little Love*** [1966]	$ .75	$2.50	$5.00
B50-672	Bangert, Ethel - ***Clover Hill*** [1966]	$ .75	$2.50	$5.00
B50-673	Gaddis, Peggy - ***Rehearsal For A Wedding*** [1966]	$ .75	$2.50	$5.00
B50-674	McElfresh, Adeline - ***Shattered Halo*** [1966]	$1.00	$3.00	$6.00
B50-675	Noone, Edwina - ***The Victorian Crown*** [1966] Cover art by Jack Gaughan.	$1.25	$3.75	$7.50
B50-676	Leinster, Murray - ***Get Off My World!*** [1966] PBO. Cover by Gaughan.	$1.35	$4.00	$8.00
B50-677	Dean, Nell Marr - ***A Time For Strength*** [1966]	$ .75	$2.50	$5.00
B50-678	Gaddis, Peggy - ***Robin*** [1966]	$ .75	$2.50	$5.00
B50-679	Roberts, Irene - ***Golden Rain*** [1966]	$ .75	$2.50	$5.00
B50-680	Reynolds, Mack - ***Of Godlike Power*** [1966]	$1.25	$3.75	$7.50
B50-681	Wetherell, June - ***The House On Cabra*** [1966] PBO.	$1.00	$3.00	$6.00
B50-682	del Rey, Lester - ***The Scheme Of Things*** [1966] PBO.	$1.25	$3.75	$7.50
B50-683	Grant, Maxwell - ***Mark Of The Shadow*** [1966] PBO.	$2.50	$7.50	$15.00
B50-684	Gaddis, Peggy - ***Wedding Song*** [1966]	$ .75	$2.50	$5.00
B50-685	Garrison, Joan - ***The Questing Heart*** [1966]	$ .75	$2.50	$5.00
B50-686	Noone, Edwina (Michael Avallone) - ***The Second Secret*** [1966]	$1.00	$3.00	$6.00
B50-687	Gaddis, Peggy - ***Unfaithful*** [1966]	$ .75	$2.50	$5.00
B50-688	Mann, E.B. - ***Rustler's Roundup*** [1966]	$1.00	$3.00	$6.00

		G	VG	F
B50-689	Blocklinger, Betty - ***Love's Legacy*** [1966]	$ .75	$2.50	$5.00
B50-690	Garrison, Joan - ***The Walks Of Dreams*** [1966]	$1.00	$3.00	$6.00
B50-691	Laflin, Jack - ***The Spy Who Didn't*** [1966]	$1.25	$3.75	$7.50
B50-692	Tralins, Robert - ***The Cosmozoids*** [1966] PBO.	$1.35	$4.00	$8.00
B50-693	Meisner, Mary - ***Black Hazard*** [1966]	$1.00	$3.00	$6.00
B50-694	Robertson, Frank C. - ***Wild Riding Runt*** [1966]	$1.00	$3.00	$6.00
B50-695	Siegel, Jerry - ***High Camp Superheroes*** [1966] PBO.	$2.00	$6.00	$12.00
B50-696	Robertson, Frank C. - ***Freewater Range*** [1966]	$1.00	$3.00	$6.00
B50-697	Seltzer, Charles Alden - ***The Defiant One*** [1966]	$1.25	$3.75	$7.50
B50-698	Gaddis, Peggy - ***Shadows On The Moon*** [1966]	$ .75	$2.50	$5.00
B50-699	Smith, George Henry - ***The Four Day Weekend*** [1966] PBO.	$1.25	$3.75	$7.50
B50-700	St. John, Genevieve - ***Death In The Desert*** [1966]	$ .75	$2.50	$5.00
B50-701	Gaddis, Peggy - ***The Sins Of Jamie Lanham*** [1966]	$ .75	$2.50	$5.00
B50-702	Seltzer, Charles Alden - ***Gunslammer*** [1966]	$1.00	$3.00	$6.00
B50-703	Gaddis, Peggy - ***A Guest In Paradise*** [1966]	$ .75	$2.50	$5.00
B50-704	Tralins, Bob - ***The Miss From S.I.S.*** [1966] PBO.	$1.35	$4.00	$8.00
B50-705	Olmstead, Lorena Ann - ***To Love A Stranger*** [1966]	$ .75	$2.50	$5.00
B50-706	McElfresh, Adeline - ***Charlotte Wade*** [1966]	$ .75	$2.50	$5.00
B50-707	O'Shea, Sean - ***What A Way To Go!*** [1966]	$1.25	$3.75	$7.50
B50-708	Jones, Raymond F. - ***The Alien*** [1966]	$1.25	$3.75	$7.50
B50-709	Grant, Maxwell - ***Shadow - Go Mad!*** [1966] PBO.	$2.50	$7.50	$15.00
B50-710	Floren, Lee - ***Shadow Of My Gun*** [1966]	$1.00	$3.00	$6.00
B50-711	Gaddis, Peggy - ***Intruders In Eden*** [1966]	$ .75	$2.50	$5.00
B50-712	Unknown - ***Vultures Of Paradise Valley*** [1966]	$1.00	$3.00	$6.00
B50-713	Lehman, Paul Evan - ***Outlaws Of Lost River*** [1966]	$1.00	$3.00	$6.00
B50-714	Bond, Evelyn - ***Heritage Of Fear*** [1966]	$ .75	$2.50	$5.00
B50-715	Mann, E.B. - ***Killer's Range*** [1966]	$1.00	$3.00	$6.00
B50-716	Gaddis, Peggy - ***Lulie*** [1966] Cover art by Nappi.	$ .75	$2.50	$5.00
B50-717	Farmer, Philip Jose - ***The Gate Of Time*** [1966] PBO.	$2.50	$7.50	$15.00
B50-718	Tralins, Bob - ***The Chic Chick Spy*** [1966] PBO.	$1.35	$4.00	$8.00
B50-720	Hopson, William - ***Desert Rampage*** [1966]	$1.00	$3.00	$6.00
B50-721	Anonymous - ***I Am Desire*** [1966]	$1.00	$3.00	$6.00
B50-722	Wallace, C.H. - ***Highflight To Hell*** [1966]	$1.25	$3.75	$7.50
B50-724	Seltzer, Charles Alden - ***The Law Of The Gun*** [1966]	$1.00	$3.00	$6.00
B50-725	Grant, Maxwell - ***The Night Of The Shadow*** [1966] PBO.	$2.50	$7.50	$15.00
B50-726	Long, Frank Belknap - ***Lest Earth Be Conquered*** [1966]	$1.35	$4.00	$8.00
B50-727	Steiger, Brad - ***World Of The Weird*** [1966]	$1.35	$4.00	$8.00
B50-728	Nye, Nelson - ***Shotgun Law*** [1966]	$1.00	$3.00	$6.00
B50-729	Oleck, Major Howard - ***Heroic Battles*** [1966]	$1.00	$3.00	$6.00
B50-730	Neville, Kris - ***The Mutants*** [1966] PBO.	$1.35	$4.00	$8.00
B50-731	Rico, Don - ***Lorelei*** [1966] PBO.	$1.00	$3.00	$6.00
B50-732	Shepard, Jane - ***Coolman*** [1966] PBO.	$1.35	$4.00	$8.00
B50-733	Laflin, Jack - ***The Reluctant Spy*** [1966] PBO.	$1.35	$4.00	$8.00
B50-734	Wallace, C.H. - ***E.T.A. For Death*** [1966]	$1.00	$3.00	$6.00
B50-735	Hurwood, Bernhardt J. - ***Monsters And Nightmares*** [1967] PBO.	$1.50	$5.00	$10.00
B50-736	Avallone, Michael - ***Tales Of The Frightened*** [1967]	$1.50	$5.00	$10.00
B50-737	Grant, Maxwell - ***The Shadow: Destination Moon*** [1966] PBO.	$2.50	$7.50	$15.00
B50-738	Flora, Fletcher - ***Skulldoggery*** [1967]	$1.00	$3.00	$6.00
B50-739	Spinrad, Norman - ***Agent Of Chaos*** [1967] PBO.	$1.35	$4.00	$8.00
B50-741	Harwick, Richard - ***Hawk*** [1967]	$1.25	$3.75	$7.50
B50-742	Reisner, Mary - ***The Hunted*** [1967]	$1.00	$3.00	$6.00
B50-743	Calin, Harold - ***Search And Kill*** [1967]	$1.00	$3.00	$6.00
B50-744	Oleck, Major Howard - ***Eyewitness World War II Battles*** [1967]	$1.00	$3.00	$6.00
B50-745	Tralins, Bob - ***The Ring-A-Ding UFOs*** [1967] PBO.	$1.25	$3.75	$7.50
B50-747	St. John, Genevieve - ***The Sinister Voice*** [1967] PBO.	$1.00	$3.00	$6.00
B50-748	Hershman, Morris - ***Target For Terror*** [1967]	$1.00	$3.00	$6.00
B50-749	Knight, Doris - ***Nurse On Terror Island*** [1967] PBO.	$ .75	$2.50	$5.00
B50-750	Winfield, Dick - ***How To Make Out On Campus*** [1967] PBO.	$1.00	$3.00	$6.00

		G	VG	F
B50-751	White, Ted - ***The Jewels Of Elsewhen*** [1967] PBO.	$1.35	$4.00	$8.00
B50-753	Moore, Emma - ***Shallow Runs The River*** [1967] PBO.	$1.00	$3.00	$6.00
B50-754	Mann, E.B. - ***Masked Outlaw/The Gun*** [1967]	$1.25	$3.75	$7.50
B50-755	Martin, Kay - ***Nymph In Suburbia*** [1967]	$1.00	$3.00	$6.00
B50-756	Seltzer, Charles Alden - ***War On Wishbone Range*** [1967]	$1.00	$3.00	$6.00
B50-757	Long, Frank Belknap - ***Journey Into Darkness*** [1967]	$1.50	$5.00	$10.00
B50-758	Kane, Henry - ***The Perfecrt Crime*** [1967]	$1.35	$4.00	$8.00
B50-759	Carter, Lin/Neville, Kris - ***The Flame Of Iridar/Peril Of The Starmen*** [1967] PBO.	$1.35	$4.00	$8.00
B50-760	O'Shea, Sean - ***Operation Boudoir*** [1967]	$1.25	$3.75	$7.50
B50-761	Stanton, L. Lerome - ***Flying Saucers: Hoax Or Reality?*** [1967]	$1.00	$3.00	$6.00
B50-762	Jakes, John - ***Making It Big*** [1967]	$1.25	$3.75	$7.50
B50-764	Janifer, Laurence - ***The Final Fear*** [1967] PBO.	$1.35	$4.00	$8.00
B50-765	Richards, Monty - ***Surgeon At Sea*** [1967] PBO.	$ .75	$2.50	$5.00
B50-766	Seltzer, Charles Alden - ***Hellfire*** [1967]	$1.00	$3.00	$6.00
B50-767	Unknown - ***Last Hope Ranch*** [1967]	$1.00	$3.00	$6.00
B50-768	Coffman, Virginia - ***A Few Fiends To Tea*** [1967]	$3.00	$9.00	$18.00
B50-769	O'Shea, Sean - ***Win With Sin*** [1967]	$1.25	$3.75	$7.50
B50-770	Anthology - ***Novelets Of Science Fiction*** [1967] edited by Ivan Howard.	$1.25	$3.75	$7.50
B50-771	Conklin, Groff - editor - ***Twisted*** [1967]	$1.35	$4.00	$8.00
B50-772	Coburn, Walt/Arthur, Burt - ***Bordertown/Showdown*** [1967]	$1.00	$3.00	$6.00
B50-773	Lehman, Paul Evan - ***Bullets Don't Bluff*** [1967]	$1.25	$3.75	$7.50
B50-774	Gaddis, Peggy - ***The Wild Girls*** [1967]	$1.00	$3.00	$6.00
B50-775	Lehman, Paul Evan - ***West Of The Wolverine*** [1967]	$1.25	$3.75	$7.50
B50-776	Joscelyn, Archie - ***Gunfighter*** [1967]	$1.25	$3.75	$7.50
B50-777	Joscelyn, Archie - ***Lone Tree Renegade*** [1968]	$1.25	$3.75	$7.50
B50-778	Cameron, Lou - ***Iron Men With Wooden Wings*** [1968]	$1.25	$3.75	$7.50
B50-779	Ellison, Harlan/Hoffman, Lee - ***Doomsman/Telepower*** [1967] PBO.	$2.50	$7.50	$15.00
B50-780	Hennesey, Hal - ***Free Fall Into Hell*** [1967]	$1.00	$3.00	$6.00
B50-781	Anthology - ***Time Untamed*** [1967] PBO. Edited by Robert Bloch.	$1.35	$4.00	$8.00
B50-782	O'Shea, Sean - ***The Nymph Island Affair*** [1967] PBO.	$1.25	$3.75	$7.50
B50-784	Coburn, Walt/Mann, E.B. - ***El Hombre/Rustler's Warning*** [1967]	$1.25	$3.75	$7.50
B50-785	Winfield, Dick - ***How To Make Out Off Campus*** [1967] PBO.	$1.00	$3.00	$6.00
B50-786	Hall, Babette - ***The Professor And The Co-Ed*** [1967]	$ .75	$2.50	$5.00
B50-787	Bloch, Robert - ***The Living Demons*** [1967] PBO.	$4.00	$12.50	$25.00
B50-788	Neville, Kris/Arnam, Dave Van - ***Special Delivery/Star Gladiator*** [1967]	$1.25	$3.75	$7.50
B50-789	Seltzer, Charles Alden - ***The Range Boss*** [1967]	$1.00	$3.00	$6.00
B50-790	Richards, Monty - ***Surgeon In Peril*** [1967]	$ .75	$2.50	$5.00
B50-791	Simak, Clifford D. - ***Worlds Without End*** [1967]	$1.25	$3.75	$7.50
B50-792	Mann, E.B./Arthur, Burt - ***Claim Jumpers/Dead Man's Gulch*** [1967]	$1.25	$3.75	$7.50
B50-793	Winston, Daoma - ***Pity My Love*** [1967]	$ .75	$2.50	$5.00
B50-794	Coburn, Walt/Mann, E.B. - ***Montana Man/The Gunners*** [1967]	$1.25	$3.75	$7.50
B50-795	Reynolds, Mack - ***After Some Tomorrow*** [1967]	$1.35	$4.00	$8.00
B50-796	Seltzer, Charles Alden - ***Brannon*** [1967]	$1.00	$3.00	$6.00
B50-797	Kelley, Leo F. - ***The Counterfeits*** [1967]	$1.35	$4.00	$8.00
B50-798	O'Shea, Sean - ***Invasion Of The Nymphomaniacs*** [1967] PBO.	$1.25	$3.75	$7.50
B50-799	Morton, Patricia - ***Destiny's Child*** [1967]	$1.00	$3.00	$6.00
B50-800	Stonebraker, Florence - ***Pawn Of Love*** [1967]	$1.00	$3.00	$6.00
B50-801	Seltzer, Charles Alden - ***Revenge Ambush*** [1967] Cover art by Prezio.	$1.25	$3.75	$7.50
B50-802	Lehman, Paul Evan - ***Cowhand Justice*** [1967]	$1.25	$3.75	$7.50
B50-803	Tidyman, Ernest - ***The Anzio Death Trap*** [1967]	$1.00	$3.00	$6.00
B50-804	Carter, Lin - ***Tower At The Edge Of Time*** [1967]	$1.35	$4.00	$8.00
B50-805	Mann, E.B. - ***Troubled Range*** [1967]	$1.00	$3.00	$6.00

		G	VG	F
B50-806	Peterson, Laura/Little, Paula - ***Promise Of The Heart/Love Conquers All*** [1967]	$1.00	$3.00	$6.00
B50-807	Reisner, Mary - ***Bride Of Death*** [1968] PBO.	$1.00	$3.00	$6.00
B50-808	Lehman, Paul Evan - ***Helltown*** [1968]	$1.00	$3.00	$6.00
B50-809	Carter, Lin/Long, Frank Belknap - ***The Theif Of Thoth/And Others Shall Be Born*** [1968]	$1.50	$5.00	$10.00
B50-810	Lanifer, Laurence M. - ***Impossible?*** [1968] PBO.	$1.50	$5.00	$10.00
B50-811	Lanifer, Laurence M. - ***A Piece Of Martin Cann*** [1968] PBO.	$1.50	$5.00	$10.00
B50-812	Coburn, Walt/Mann, E.B. - ***Reckless!/Men Of Blood*** [1968] PBO.	$1.25	$3.75	$7.50
B50-813	Blish, James/Silverberg, Robert - ***Giants In The Earth/We, The Marauders*** [1968]	$1.25	$3.75	$7.50
B50-814	Seltzer, Charles Alden - ***The Loner*** [1968]	$1.00	$3.00	$6.00
B50-815	Gaddis, Peggy - ***Private Secretary*** [1968]	$ .75	$2.50	$5.00
B50-816	Grinstead, J.G. - ***Maverick Guns*** [1968]	$1.00	$3.00	$6.00
B50-817	Hale, Arlene - ***Private Nurse*** [1968] PBO.	$ .75	$2.50	$5.00
B50-818	Martin, Chuck - ***Gunsmoke And Guts*** [1968]	$1.00	$3.00	$6.00
B50-819	Elliott, Bruce - ***Asylum Earth*** [1968] PBO.	$1.35	$4.00	$8.00
B50-820	Jones, Raymond F. - ***The Non-Statistical Man*** [1968]	$1.25	$3.75	$7.50
B50-821	Fitzgerald, Arlene - ***Double Duty Nurse*** [1968]	$ .75	$2.50	$5.00
B50-822	Seltzer, Charles Alden - ***Desert Rider*** [1968]	$1.00	$3.00	$6.00
B50-823	Grinstead, J.E. - ***The Lightning Kid*** [1968]	$1.00	$3.00	$6.00
B50-824	Lehman, Paul Evan - ***Blood On The Range*** [1968]	$1.00	$3.00	$6.00
B50-826	Reynolds, Mack - ***Earth Unaware*** [1968] Cover art by Jeff Jones.	$1.25	$3.75	$7.50
B50-827	Seltzer, Charles Alden - ***Night Of Vengeance*** [1968]	$1.00	$3.00	$6.00
B50-828	Cody, Al - ***Bloody Wyoming*** [1968]	$1.00	$3.00	$6.00
B50-829	Seltzer, Charles Alden - ***Double Cross Ranch*** [1968]	$1.00	$3.00	$6.00
B50-830	Nye, Nelson - ***Quick-Fire Hombre*** [1968]	$1.00	$3.00	$6.00
B50-831	Robertson, Frank C. - ***Outlaw Ranch*** [1968]	$1.00	$3.00	$6.00
B50-832	St. John, Genevieve - ***The Secret Of Dresden Farm*** [1968]	$ .75	$2.50	$5.00
B50-833	Brossard, Chandler - ***Episode With Erika*** [1968]	$1.00	$3.00	$6.00
B50-834	O'Shea, Sean - ***The Topless Kitties*** [1968]	$1.25	$3.75	$7.50
B50-836	Lehman, Paul Evan - ***Hell's Trail*** [1968]	$1.00	$3.00	$6.00
B50-837	Grinstead, J.E. - ***Raging Guns*** [1968]	$1.00	$3.00	$6.00
B50-838	Daniels, Dorothy - ***Blue Devil Suite*** [1968]	$ .75	$2.50	$5.00
B50-839	Anthology - ***Basil Rathbone Selects Strange Tales*** [1968] edited by Lyle Kenyon Engel. Cover art by Elliot.	$1.35	$4.00	$8.00
B50-840	Cogswell, Theodore - ***The Third Eye*** [1968] PBO. Cover art by Ralph Brillhart.	$1.35	$4.00	$8.00
B50-841	Grinstead, J.E. - ***Phantom Rustlers*** [1968]	$1.00	$3.00	$6.00
B50-843	Neville, Kris - ***The Unearth People*** [1968]	$1.25	$3.75	$7.50
B50-846	Leinster, Murray - ***Space Tug*** [1968]	$1.25	$3.75	$7.50
B50-847	Winston, Daomi - ***The Long And Living Shadow*** [1968]	$1.00	$3.00	$6.00
B50-849	Jorgensen, Ivar (Paul Fairman) - ***Whom The Gods Would Slay*** [1968] PBO. Cover art by Jeff Jones.	$1.35	$4.00	$8.00
B50-851	Seltzer, Charles Alden - ***Gold Rock Ambush*** [1968]	$1.00	$3.00	$6.00
B50-852	Binder, Eando - ***Lords of Creation*** [1969] Cover art by Jeff Jones.	$1.25	$3.75	$7.50
B50-853	Carter, Lin - ***Giant Of World's End*** [1969] PBO. Cover art by Jeff Jones.	$1.35	$4.00	$8.00
B50-855	Arthur, Burt - ***Gunsmoke Over Utah*** [1969]	$1.00	$3.00	$6.00
B50-858	Hopson, William - ***Desert Maverick*** [1969]	$1.00	$3.00	$6.00
B50-859	Arhtur, Burt - ***Killer's Crossing*** [1969]	$1.00	$3.00	$6.00
91-900	Seltzer, Charles Alden - ***Boss Of The Lazy Y*** [1969]	$1.00	$3.00	$6.00
B45-901	Arthur, Burt - ***Trouble At Moon Pass*** [1969]	$1.00	$3.00	$6.00
B45-902	Knight, Doris - ***Nurse By Night*** [1969]	$ .75	$2.50	$5.00
B45-903	Floren, Lee - ***Senora Stage*** [1969]	$1.00	$3.00	$6.00
B45-904	Seltzer, Charles Alden - ***Kingdom In The Cactus*** [1969]	$1.00	$3.00	$6.00
B45-905	Gruber, Frank - ***Town Tamer*** [1969]	$1.00	$3.00	$6.00

		G	VG	F
B45-906	Robertson, Frank C. - ***The Powder Burner*** [1966]	$1.00	$3.00	$6.00
B45-907	Arthur, Burt - ***Lead Hungry Lobos*** [1969]	$1.00	$3.00	$6.00

Belmont B60 Series.

		G	VG	F
B60-069	Ellison, Harlan - ***From The Land Of Fear*** [1967] PBO. Cover by Leo & Diane Dillon	$5.50	$17.50	$35.00
B60-080	Bloch, Robert - ***Ladies' Day/This Crowded Earth*** [1968] PBO.	$5.50	$17.50	$35.00

Belmont B75 Series.

		G	VG	F
B75-202	Woodward, L.T., M.D. (Robert Silverberg) - ***I Am A Nymphomaniac*** [1965] PBO	$1.25	$3.75	$7.50
B75-203	Christian, Paula - ***This Side Of Love/Edge Of Twilight*** [1966]	$1.25	$3.75	$7.50
B75-204	Fils, Crebillon - ***My Bachelor's Life*** [1966]	$ .75	$2.50	$5.00
B75-205	Aretino, Pietro - ***Sisters, Wives And Courtesans*** [1966]	$ .75	$2.50	$5.00
B75-206	Royal, D. - ***She Couldn't Say No*** [1967] PBO	$ .75	$2.50	$5.00
B75-207	Royal, D. - ***The Compulsive Male*** [1967]	$ .75	$2.50	$5.00
B75-208	Cross, Dr. Harold H.U. - ***The Lust Market*** [1967]	$ .75	$2.50	$5.00
B75-209	Traube, Ruy - ***The Seduction Art*** [1968]	$ .75	$2.50	$5.00
B75-210	Royal, D. - ***The Sex Revolutionary*** [1968]	$ .75	$2.50	$5.00
B75-211	O'Toole, Rex - ***Cheating & Infidelity American Style*** [1968]	$ .75	$2.50	$5.00
B75-212	Ward, L.T., M.D. (Robert Silverberg) - ***I Am A Nymphomaniac*** [1967]	$1.25	$3.75	$7.50
B75-213	Fils, Crebillion - ***My Bachelor's Life*** [1968]	$ .75	$2.50	$5.00
B75-214	Anthology - ***In Other Beds*** [1968] edited by Chandler Brossard.	$ .75	$2.50	$5.00
B75-217	Sacher-Masoch, Leopold - ***Bed Of An Empress*** [1968] Cover art by Victor Kalin.	$ .75	$2.50	$5.00
B75-218	Binder, Otto O. - ***Flying Saucers Are Watching Us*** [1968]	$ .75	$2.50	$5.00
B75-219	Royal, D. - ***Swing High Sweet Pussycat*** [1968]	$ .75	$2.50	$5.00
B75-220	Sacher-Masoch, Leopold - ***Venis In Furs*** [1968]	$ .75	$2.50	$5.00
B75-221	Archer, Jules - ***Cool Kids With Hot Ideas*** [1968]	$ .75	$2.50	$5.00
B75-222	Anthology - ***The X Report*** [1968] Selections from *Sexology* magazine	$ .75	$2.50	$5.00
B75-223	Casanova, Jacques - ***The Lusts Of Casanova*** [1968]	$ .75	$2.50	$5.00
B75-224	Tully, Geri - ***Don't Be A Wife - Be A Mistress!*** [1968]	$ .75	$2.50	$5.00
B75-228	Wilde, D. Gunther - ***The Erotic Adventures*** [1968]	$ .75	$2.50	$5.00

Berkley Books (Early Publisher's History, 1954–1959)

Charles Byrne and Frederick Klein left Avon to found Berkley Books, Inc. Robert Maguire provides excellent cover art for many of the Berkley titles, as well as good girl art by other artists. Esoteric novels with fine cover art provide the bulk of the desirable titles from this publisher. A number of mysteries, science fiction, and humor books round out the offerings from Berkley Books.

Prior to publishing Berkley Books, they published *Chic* magazine and *News* magazine in paperback format. Other lines include Berkley Medallion, Berkley Diamond, and Berkley Giants or G/BG series.

Berkley Books. New York: Berkley Books, Inc.

		G	VG	F
101	Edited by William Hodapp - ***The Pleasures Of The Jazz Age*** [1955]	$1.25	$3.75	$7.50
102	Donisthorpe, G. Sheila - ***Loveliest Of Friends*** [1955] Photo cover	$1.25	$3.75	$7.50
103	Cozzens, James Gould - ***S. S. San Pedro*** [1955]	$1.25	$3.75	$7.50
104	Waters, Frank - ***Fever Pitch*** [1955]	$1.25	$3.75	$7.50
105	Eichler, Alfred - ***Death Of An Ad Man*** [1955] Photo cover.	$1.25	$3.75	$7.50
106	Burke, J. W. & Grace, Edward - ***3 Day Pass-To Kill*** [1955] PBO.	$1.50	$5.00	$10.00
107	Hopson, William - ***Border Raider*** [1955] Photo cover.	$1.25	$3.75	$7.50

		G	VG	F
108	McCoy, Horace - ***They Shoot Horses, Don't They*** [1955]	$1.35	$4.00	$8.00
109	Smith, Robert Paul - ***So It Doesn't Whistle*** [1955] Photo cover.	$1.25	$3.75	$7.50
110	De Pereda, Prudencio - ***All The Girls We Loved*** [1955]	$1.25	$3.75	$7.50
111	Mirbeau, Octave - ***Torture Garden*** [1955]	$3.00	$9.00	$18.00
112	Roth, Holly - ***Mask Of Glass*** [1955]	$1.00	$3.00	$6.00
313	Lomax, Bliss - ***Saddle Hawks*** [1955]	$1.25	$3.75	$7.50
314	Evans, John - ***Andrew's Harvest*** [1955]	$1.25	$3.75	$7.50
315	Roueche, Berton - ***Eleven Blue Men*** [1955]	$1.00	$3.00	$6.00
316	Prather, Richard S. - ***Pattern For Panic*** [1955] Photo cover.	$1.25	$3.75	$7.50
317	Bryant, Arthur Herbert - ***Roadside Motel*** [1955] Photo cover.	$1.00	$3.00	$6.00
318	Tracy, Don - ***White Hell*** [1955]	$1.25	$3.75	$7.50
319	Preston, John Hyde - ***Portrait Of A Woman*** [1955]	$1.00	$3.00	$6.00
320	Seltzer, Nadine - ***Sweetie Pie*** [1955] Cartoon book.	$1.35	$4.00	$8.00
321	Nye, Nelson - ***Gunfighter Breed*** [1955] Cover by Cherry.	$1.25	$3.75	$7.50
322	Simenon - ***Danger At Sea*** [1955] Photo cover.	$1.25	$3.75	$7.50
323	Newhouse, Edward - ***The Temptation Of Roger Heriott*** [1955] Photo cover.	$1.00	$3.00	$6.00
324	Hopson, William - ***Cowpoke Justice*** [1955]	$1.25	$3.75	$7.50
325	Preston, Charles - ***Oh, Doctor!*** [1955]	$1.35	$4.00	$8.00
326	Snyder, Leonard - ***The Velvet Whip*** [1955]	$1.25	$3.75	$7.50
327	Wilhelm, Gale - ***We Too Are Drifting*** [1955] Photo cover.	$1.35	$4.00	$8.00
328	McCoy, Horace - ***I Should Have Stayed Home*** [1955]	$1.50	$5.00	$10.00
329	Price, George - ***Whose In Charge Here?*** [1955] PBO. Cover by George Price. Cartoon book.	$1.35	$4.00	$8.00
330	Nye, Nelson C. - ***Cartridge - Case Law*** [1955]	$1.25	$3.75	$7.50
331	Clarke, Donald Henderson - ***Joe And Jennie*** [1955] Photo cover.	$1.25	$3.75	$7.50
332	Lehman, Paul Evan - ***The Twisted Trail*** [1955]	$1.25	$3.75	$7.50
333	Bryant, Matt - ***Cue For Murder*** [1955] Photo cover.	$1.25	$3.75	$7.50
334	Van Doren Stern, Philip - ***Manhunt*** [1955]	$1.25	$3.75	$7.50
335	Cody, Al - ***Powder Burns*** [1955] Photo cover.	$1.25	$3.75	$7.50
336	Parker, Gladys - ***Mopsy*** [1955] PBO. Cover by Gladys Parker.	$1.35	$4.00	$8.00
337	Carco, Francis - ***Only A Woman*** [1955] Cover by Rudy Nappi.	$1.25	$3.75	$7.50
338	Taylor, Samuel W. - ***The Man With My Face*** [1955] Photo cover.	$1.25	$3.75	$7.50
339	Schiddel, Edmund - ***The Girl With The Golden Yo-Yo*** [1955] PBO. Photo cover.	$1.25	$3.75	$7.50
340	Simenon, Georges - ***Danger Ashore*** [1955] Photo cover.	$1.25	$3.75	$7.50
341	Hopson, William - ***Outlaw Of Hidden Valley*** [1955] Cover by Nick Eggenhofer.	$1.25	$3.75	$7.50
342	Du Gard, Roger Martin - ***The Postman*** [1955]	$1.00	$3.00	$6.00
343	Nye, Nelson C. - ***Gunshot Trail*** [1955]	$1.25	$3.75	$7.50
344	Van Vogt, A.E. - ***Mission To The Stars*** [1955] Cover by Richard Powers.	$1.25	$3.75	$7.50
345	Hunt, Howard - ***Cruel Is The Night*** [1955] Photo cover.	$1.25	$3.75	$7.50
346	Preston, Charles - editor - ***The $64,000,000 Answer*** [1955] PBO. Cartoon book.	$1.35	$4.00	$8.00
347	Hopson, William - ***Tombstone Stage*** [1955] Cover by Nick Eggenhofer.	$1.25	$3.75	$7.50
348	Curran, Dale - ***Dupree Blues*** [1955] Photo cover.	$1.00	$3.00	$6.00
349	McFeatters, Dale - ***Strictly Business*** [1955] PBO. Cartoon book.	$1.35	$4.00	$8.00
350	Nye, Nelson C. - ***Saddle Bow Slim*** [1956] Cover by Harry Rosenbaum.	$1.25	$3.75	$7.50
351	Simenon, Georges - ***The Magician*** [1956] Photo cover.	$1.25	$3.75	$7.50
353	Cody, Al - ***Forbidden River*** [1956]	$1.25	$3.75	$7.50
354	Symons, Julian - ***The Narrowing Circle*** [1956]	$1.25	$3.75	$7.50
356	Lehman, Paul Evan - ***Outlaws Of Lost River*** [1956]	$1.25	$3.75	$7.50
358	De Meyer, John - ***Bailey's Daughters*** [1956] Photo cover.	$1.00	$3.00	$6.00
359	Donisthorpe, G. Sheila - ***Loveliest Of Friends*** [1956] Photo cover.	$1.00	$3.00	$6.00

		G	VG	F
360	Seltzer, Nadine - ***Sweetie Pie*** [1956] Cover by Nadine Seltzer. Cartoon book.	$1.25	$3.75	$7.50
361	Kennedy, Burt - ***Seven Men From Now*** [1956] Movie photo cover. Movie tie-in with Randolph Scott and Lee Marvin.	$1.25	$3.75	$7.50
362	Prather, Richard S. - ***Pattern For Panic*** [1956] Cover by Robert Maguire.	$1.50	$5.00	$10.00
363	Nye, Nelson C. - ***Ranger's Revenge*** [1956]	$1.25	$3.75	$7.50
364	Lehman, Paul Evan - ***Pistol Law*** [1956] Cover by Vic Donahue.	$1.25	$3.75	$7.50
365	Preston, Charles - editor - ***No Money Down - 36 Months To Pay!*** [1956] PBO.	$1.35	$4.00	$8.00
366	Hopson, William - ***Ramrod Vengeance*** [1956]	$1.25	$3.75	$7.50
367	Wilhelm, Gale - ***We Too Are Drifting*** [1956] Photo cover.	$1.35	$4.00	$8.00
368	Ernenwein, Leslie - ***Kinkaid Of Red Butte*** [1956] Cover by Mel Crair.	$1.25	$3.75	$7.50
369	Carco, Francis - ***Only A Woman*** [1957]	$1.00	$3.00	$6.00
370	Lehman, Paul Evan - ***Texas Vengeance*** [1957]	$1.25	$3.75	$7.50
371	Philippe, Charles-Louis - ***Bubu Of Montparnasse*** [1957]	$1.00	$3.00	$6.00
372	Lehman, Paul Evan - ***Rustlers Of The Rio Grande*** [1957]	$1.25	$3.75	$7.50
373	O'Farrell, William - ***The Devil His Due*** [1957]	$1.00	$3.00	$6.00
374	Cody, Al - ***Red Man's Range*** [1957] PBO. Cover by Newquist.	$1.25	$3.75	$7.50
375	Carrier, Warren - ***The Lost And The Damned*** [1957]	$1.25	$3.75	$7.50
376	Adams, John Paul - ***We Dare You To Solve This!*** [1957] PBO. Puzzle book.	$1.35	$4.00	$8.00
377	Canning, Victor - ***Twist Of The Knife*** [1957]	$1.25	$3.75	$7.50
378	Cody, Al - ***Brand Of Iron*** [1957]	$1.25	$3.75	$7.50
379	Simenon, Georges - ***The Burial Of Monsieur Bouvet*** [1957] Cover by Rudy Nappi.	$1.25	$3.75	$7.50
380	Wells, H. G. - ***The Time Machine*** [1957]	$1.25	$3.75	$7.50
381	Seltzer, Nadine - ***More Sweetie Pie*** [1957] PBO. Cover by Nadine Seltzer. Cartoon book.	$1.35	$4.00	$8.00
382	Osann, Kate - ***Tizzy*** [1957]	$1.35	$4.00	$8.00
383	Neher, Fred - ***Will - Yum*** [1957] PBO. Cover by Fred Neher. Cartoon book.	$1.35	$4.00	$8.00
384	Moore, Mary Furlong - ***The Baby Sitter's Guide*** [1957] Photo cover.	$1.00	$3.00	$6.00
385	Neher, Fred - ***Hi - Teens*** [1957] PBO. Cover by Fred Neher. Cartoon book.	$1.35	$4.00	$8.00
386	Key, Ted - ***Phyllis*** [1959] Cover by Shanks.	$1.35	$4.00	$8.00

Berkley Diamond Series. New York: Berkley Books, Inc.

		G	VG	F
D-2001	Hunt, Howard - ***Cruel Is The Night*** [1959] Cover art by Maguire.	$1.35	$4.00	$8.00
D-2002	Floren, Lee - ***Guns Along The Arrowhead*** [1959]	$1.25	$3.75	$7.50
D-2003	Keene, Day - ***The Big Kiss-Off*** [1959] Cover by Darcy.	$1.35	$4.00	$8.00
D-2004	Whittington, Harry - ***Shack Road Girl*** [1959]	$2.00	$6.00	$12.00
D-2005	Peters, Fritz - ***Descent To Darkness*** [1959] Cover art by Maguire.	$1.35	$4.00	$8.00
D-2006	Nye, Nelson - ***Wildcats Of Tonto Basin*** [1959]	$1.25	$3.75	$7.50
D-2007	Ozaki, Milton - ***Dressed To Kill*** [1959] Cover art by Darcy.	$1.25	$3.75	$7.50
D-2008	Nichols, Fan - ***Hideaway*** [1959]	$1.25	$3.75	$7.50
D-2009	Floren, Lee - ***Rifle Law*** [1959]	$1.25	$3.75	$7.50
D-2010	Norman, Earl - ***Kill Me In Shimbashi*** [1959] PBO. Cover art by Maguire.	$1.35	$4.00	$8.00
D-2011	Martin, Charles M. - ***Vengeance Trail*** [1959]	$1.25	$3.75	$7.50
D-2012	Crockett, Vivian - ***Messalina*** [1959] Cover art by Maguire.	$1.35	$4.00	$8.00
D-2013	Coburn, Walt - ***Drift Fence*** [1959]	$1.25	$3.75	$7.50
D-2014	Hopson, William - ***Twin Mavericks*** [1959]	$1.25	$3.75	$7.50
D-2015	Craig, Jonathan - ***Renegade Cop*** [1959] Cover by Milo.	$1.25	$3.75	$7.50
D-2016	Ozaki, Milton - ***Murder Doll*** [1959]	$1.25	$3.75	$7.50
D-2017	Floren, Lee - ***Guns Along The Pecos*** [1959]	$1.25	$3.75	$7.50

		G	VG	F
D-2018	Nye, Nelson C. - ***The Desert Desperados*** [1959] Cover by Prezio.	$1.25	$3.75	$7.50
D-2019	Whittington, Harry - ***Married To Murder*** [1959] Cover art by Copeland.	$2.00	$6.00	$12.00
D-2020	Keene, Day - ***Naked Fury*** [1959] Cover art by Milo.	$1.35	$4.00	$8.00
D-2022	Gorham, Charles - ***Martha Crane*** [1959] Cover by Rudy Nappi.	$1.25	$3.75	$7.50
D-2023	Marlowe, Stephen - ***Model For Murder*** [1959]	$1.25	$3.75	$7.50
D-2024	Keene, Day - ***Sleep With The Devil*** [1959]	$1.35	$4.00	$8.00
D-2026	Carco, Francis - ***Only A Woman*** [1960]	$1.25	$3.75	$7.50
D-2027	Harper, E.M. - ***The Assassin*** [1960] PBO. Cover art by Copeland.	$1.25	$3.75	$7.50
D-2028	Wade, David - ***Walk The Evil Street*** [1960] Cover art by Nappi.	$1.25	$3.75	$7.50
D-2030	Cody, Al - ***Outpost Trail*** [1960]	$1.25	$3.75	$7.50
D-2031	Carco, Francis - ***Street Of The Lost*** [1960]	$1.25	$3.75	$7.50
D-2032	Woolfolk, William - ***The Naked Hunter*** [1960]	$1.25	$3.75	$7.50
D-2034	Anthology - ***Nude Croquet*** [1960] Cover art by Maguire.	$1.35	$4.00	$8.00
D-2035	Lake, Barry - ***Three For The Money*** [1960] Cover art by Maguire.	$1.35	$4.00	$8.00
D-2036	Wolfson, P.J. - ***Hell Cop*** [1960] Cover art by Darcy.	$1.25	$3.75	$7.50
D-2037	Ard, William - ***You'll Get Yours*** [1960] Cover art by Maguire.	$1.35	$4.00	$8.00
D-2038	Ozaki, Milton - ***The Deadly Pick-Up*** [1960] Cover art by Nappi.	$1.25	$3.75	$7.50
D-2040	Stern, Philip Van Doren - ***Evil Is My Love*** [1960] Cover art by Darcy.	$1.25	$3.75	$7.50
D-2041	Ronns, Edward - ***Say It With Murder*** [1960] Cover art by Nappi.	$1.25	$3.75	$7.50
D-2042	Carlova, John - ***Song Of Penang*** [1960] PBO. Cover art by Nappi.	$1.25	$3.75	$7.50
D-2043	Whittington, Harry - ***Slay Ride For A Lady*** [1960] Cover art by Darcy.	$2.00	$6.00	$12.00

Berkley Letter Prefix Series. New York: Berkley Books, Inc.

		G	VG	F
G-1	Jackson, Charles - ***The Lost Weekend*** [1955]	$1.25	$3.75	$7.50
G-2	Lawton & Archer - ***Sexual Conduct Of The Teen-Ager*** [1955].	$1.00	$3.00	$6.00
G-3	Edited by Groff Conklin - ***Possible Worlds Of Science Fiction*** [1955]	$1.25	$3.75	$7.50
G-4	Smith, William Gardner - ***South Street*** [1955] Cover by Rudy Nappi.	$1.25	$3.75	$7.50
G-5	Flaubert, Gustave - ***Salambo*** [1955] Cover by Rudy Nappi.	$1.50	$5.00	$10.00
G-6	Himes, Chester B. - ***If He Hollers Let Him Go*** [1955] Photo cover.	$1.35	$4.00	$8.00
G-7	Michelfelder, William - ***A Seed Upon The Wind*** [1955]	$1.25	$3.75	$7.50
G-8	Ryan, Don - ***The Devil's Brigadier*** [1955] Photo cover.	$1.25	$3.75	$7.50
G-9	Harris, Weegee & Mel - ***Naked Hollywood*** [1955] Photo cover.	$3.50	$10.00	$20.00
G-10	Thomason, Jr., John W. - ***Lone Star Preacher*** [1955] Cover by Harry Schaare.	$1.25	$3.75	$7.50
G-11	Fredericks, Diana - ***Diana*** [1955] Photo cover.	$1.25	$3.75	$7.50
G-12	Hodapp, William - editor - ***Crazy Mixed - Up Kids*** [1955] PBO.	$1.50	$5.00	$10.00
G-13	Bodin, Paul - ***The Sign Of Eros*** [1955] Photo cover.	$1.00	$3.00	$6.00
G-14	Crockett, Vivian - ***Messalina*** [1955] Cover by Rudy Nappi.	$1.35	$4.00	$8.00
G-15	Garside, E. B. - ***A Lust To Live*** [1956] Cover by David Attie.	$1.25	$3.75	$7.50
G-16	White, Robb - ***Jungle Fury*** [1956]	$2.50	$7.50	$15.00
G-17	Lawrence, D. H. - ***The Thorn In The Flesh*** [1956] PBO. Photo cover. Edited by Phillips & Rahv.	$1.25	$3.75	$7.50
BG-18	Anthology - ***The Berkley Book Of Modern Writing No. 3*** [1956]	$1.00	$3.00	$6.00
G-19	Bester, Alfred - ***The Rat Race*** [1956] Cover by Sardis.	$1.00	$3.00	$6.00
G-20	Calet, Henri - ***Paris, My Love*** [1956] Cover by William Rose.	$1.00	$3.00	$6.00
G-21	Smith, Wallace - ***Bessie Cotter*** [1956] Photo cover.	$1.00	$3.00	$6.00
G-22	Lenormand, H. - ***R. - Renee*** [1956] Photo cover.	$1.00	$3.00	$6.00
G-23	Hardy, Ronald - ***The Place Of Jackals*** [1956]	$1.25	$3.75	$7.50
G-24	Tallman, Robert - ***Adios, O'Shaughnessy*** [1956]	$1.35	$4.00	$8.00

		G	VG	F
G-25	Morris, Donald R. - ***A Girl In Every Port*** [1956] Cover by L. R. Summers.	$1.25	$3.75	$7.50
G-26	Chaze, Elliott - ***Love On The Rocks*** [1956] Photo cover.	$1.00	$3.00	$6.00
G-27	Heppenstall, Rayner - ***The Blaze Of Noon*** [1956] Photo cover...	$1.25	$3.75	$7.50
G-28	Calet, Henri - ***Young Man Of Paris*** [1956] Cover by Victor Kalin.	$1.25	$3.75	$7.50
G-29	Wolfe, Bernard & Rosenthal, Raymond - ***Hypnotism Comes Of Age*** [1956]	$1.00	$3.00	$6.00
G-30	Sartre, Jean - ***Paul - Intimacy*** [1956] Cover by Nappi.	$1.25	$3.75	$7.50
G-31	Edited by Groff Conklin. - ***Science Fiction Omnibus*** [1956] Cover by Powers.	$1.25	$3.75	$7.50
G-32	Scott, Paul - ***Six Days In Marapore*** [1956]	$1.25	$3.75	$7.50
G-33	Carco, Francis - ***Perversity*** [1956] Cover by Barton.	$1.35	$4.00	$8.00
G-34	Clarke, Donald Henderson - ***Alabam*** [1956]	$1.25	$3.75	$7.50
BG-35	Warren, Robert Penn - ***Night Rider*** [1956]	$1.35	$4.00	$8.00
G-36	Bromfield, Louis - ***The Strange Case Of Miss Annie Spragg*** [1956]	$1.25	$3.75	$7.50
G-37	Rothman, Nathan - ***Virgie, Goodbye*** [1956] Photo cover.	$1.00	$3.00	$6.00
G-38	Reid, P. R. - ***Escape From Colditz*** [1956]	$1.00	$3.00	$6.00
G-39	Mirbeau, Octave - ***Torture Garden*** [1956]	$2.50	$7.50	$15.00
G-40	Edited by T. A. Dardis - ***Daughters Of Eve*** [1956] PBO. Cover by Maguire.	$2.00	$6.00	$12.00
G-41	Edited by John W. Campbell, Jr. - ***The Astounding SF Anthology*** [1957] PBO. Cover by Powers.	$1.25	$3.75	$7.50
G-42	Carr, John Dickson - ***To Wake The Dead*** [1957]	$1.50	$5.00	$10.00
G-43	Lawrence, D. H. - ***The Captain's Doll*** [1957] Cover by Maguire.	$2.00	$6.00	$12.00
G-44	Mark, Edwina - ***My Sister, My Beloved*** [1957] Photo cover.	$1.50	$5.00	$10.00
G-45	Schiddel, Edmund - ***Scratch The Surface*** [1957]	$1.00	$3.00	$6.00
G-46	Louys, Pierre - ***Aphrodite*** [1957] Cover by Bob Maguire.	$2.00	$6.00	$12.00
G-47	Anthology - ***Astounding Tales Of Space & Time*** [1957] Cover by Powers.	$1.25	$3.75	$7.50
G-48	Carr, John Dickson - ***The Eight Of Swords*** [1957] Cover by Maguire.	$2.00	$6.00	$12.00
G-49	Weidman, Jerome - ***A Dime A Throw And Other Stories*** [1957] PBO.	$1.35	$4.00	$8.00
G-50	Fredericks, Diana - ***Diana*** [1957] Photo cover.	$1.00	$3.00	$6.00
G-51	Keats, Charles - ***The Body Of Love*** [1957] PBO. Cover by Robert Maguire.	$1.50	$5.00	$10.00
G-52	Lawrence, D. H. - ***The Virgin And The Gypsy*** [1957] Cover by Maguire.	$2.00	$6.00	$12.00
G-53	Edited by Groff Conklin - ***Big Book Of Science Fiction*** [1957] Cover by Powers.	$1.25	$3.75	$7.50
G-54	Bodin, Paul - ***The Sign Of Eros*** [1957] Photo cover.	$1.00	$3.00	$6.00
G-55	Schiddel, Edmund - ***Love In A Hot Climate*** [1957] PBO.	$1.25	$3.75	$7.50
G-56	White, Robb - ***Jungle Fury*** [1957]	$2.25	$7.00	$14.00
G-57	Wahl, Loren - ***Take Me As I Am*** [1957] Cover by Rudy Nappi.	$1.25	$3.75	$7.50
G-58	Abzug, Martin - ***How Cheap Can You Get?*** [1957]	$1.00	$3.00	$6.00
G-59	Lawrence, D. H. - ***The Woman Who Rode Away*** [1957] Cover by Maguire.	$4.00	$12.50	$25.00
G-60	Carr, John Dickson - ***The Case Of The Constant Suicides*** [1957] Cover by Maguire.	$2.00	$6.00	$12.00
G-61	Evans, John - ***Andrews' Harvest*** [1957]	$1.50	$5.00	$10.00
G-62	Anthology - ***The Most Dangerous Game*** [1957] Cover by Mel Crair.	$1.35	$4.00	$8.00
G-63	Edited by Groff Conklin - ***A Treasury Of Science Fiction*** [1957] Cover by Powers.	$1.25	$3.75	$7.50
G-64	Woodward, David - ***The Tirpitz*** [1957] Photo cover.	$1.00	$3.00	$6.00
G-65	Michelfelder, William - ***A Seed Upon The Wind*** [1957]	$1.25	$3.75	$7.50

Berkley, BG-73

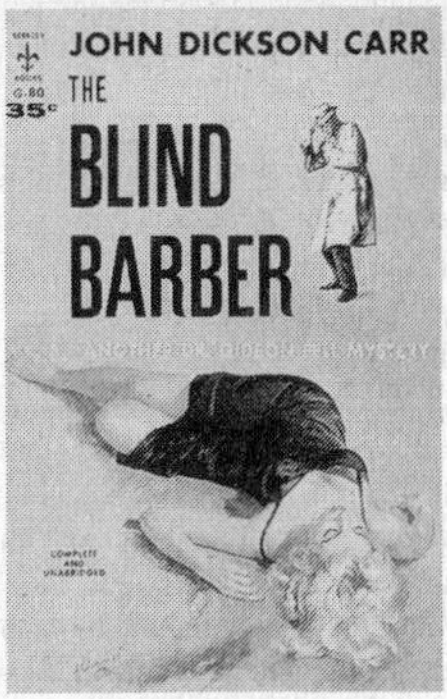

Berkley, G-80

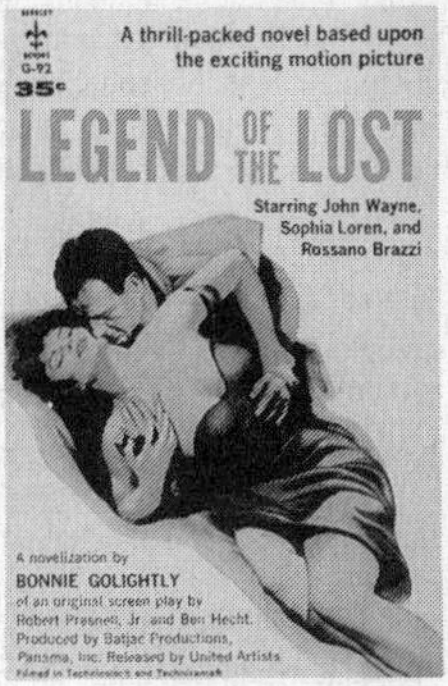

Berkley, G-92

		G	VG	F
BG-66	Huxley, Aldous - ***Time Must Have A Stop*** [1957] Cover by Maguire.	$2.00	$6.00	$12.00
G-67	Pinto, Oreste - ***Spy Catcher*** [1957]	$1.00	$3.00	$6.00
G-68	Anthology - ***This Is My Body*** [1957] PBO. Cover by Maguire...	$1.50	$5.00	$10.00
G-69	Soldati, Mario - ***Affair In Capri*** [1957] Cover by Copeland.	$1.35	$4.00	$8.00
BG-70	Trevor-Roper, H. R. - ***The Last Days Of Hitler*** [1957] Hitler photo cover.	$1.25	$3.75	$7.50
G-71	Simak, Clifford D. - ***Strangers In The Universe*** [1957] Cover by Powers.	$1.25	$3.75	$7.50
G-72	Carr, John Dickson - ***Poison In Jest*** [1957] Cover by Maguire.	$2.00	$6.00	$12.00
BG-73	Flaubert, Gustave - ***Salambo*** [1957] Cover by Maguire.	$5.50	$17.50	$35.00
G-74	Olivia - ***Olivia*** [1957] Cover by Maguire.	$2.25	$7.00	$14.00
G-75	Hynd, Alan - ***The Case Of The Lady Who Took A Bath And Other Stories*** [1957]	$1.25	$3.75	$7.50
G-76	Clarke, Donald H. - ***The Chastity Of Gloria Boyd*** [1957] Cover by Maguire.	$1.50	$5.00	$10.00
G-77	Edited by August Derleth - ***Beachheads In Space*** [1957] Cover by Powers.	$1.25	$3.75	$7.50
G-78	Gordon, Ian - ***Harlem Is My Heaven*** [1957]	$1.50	$5.00	$10.00
G-79	Nye, Nelson C. - ***Gun - Quick*** [1957]	$1.25	$3.75	$7.50
G-80	Carr, John Dickson - ***The Blind Barber*** [1957] Kimmel cover.	$1.50	$5.00	$10.00
G-81	Carco, Francis - ***Depravity*** [1957]	$1.35	$4.00	$8.00
BG-82	Pope, Dudley - ***Graf Spee*** [1957] Photo cover. Movie tie-in.	$1.00	$3.00	$6.00
G-83	Gorham, Charles - ***Martha Crane*** [1957]	$1.35	$4.00	$8.00
G-84	Bagby, George - ***The Corpse With Sticky Fingers*** [1957]	$1.25	$3.75	$7.50
G-85	Wolfson, P. J. - ***Three Of A Kind*** [1957]	$1.25	$3.75	$7.50
G-86	Anthology - ***Juvenile Jungle*** [1957] PBO.	$2.00	$6.00	$12.00
G-87	Hopson, William - ***Gunthrower*** [1957]	$1.25	$3.75	$7.50
G-88	Craig, Margaret Maze - ***Trish*** [1957]	$1.25	$3.75	$7.50
G-89	Masin, Herman L. - ***Great Sports Stories*** [1957]	$1.25	$3.75	$7.50
BG-90	Allen, Col. Robert S. - ***Drive To Victory*** [1957]	$1.00	$3.00	$6.00
G-91	Carr, John Dickson - ***The Four False Weapons*** [1957] Cover by Maguire.	$2.00	$6.00	$12.00
G-92	Golightly, Bonnie - ***Legend Of The Lost*** [1957] PBO. Movie tie-in.	$2.00	$6.00	$12.00
G-93	Bodin, Paul - ***All Women's Flesh*** [1957]	$1.35	$4.00	$8.00
G-94	Williams, Eric - ***The Tunnel Escape*** [1957] Photo cover.	$1.25	$3.75	$7.50
G-95	Hales, Carol - ***Such Is My Beloved*** [1958] Photo cover.	$1.35	$4.00	$8.00
BG-96	Young, Desmond - ***Rommel, The Desert Fox*** [1958] PBO. Photo cover.	$1.25	$3.75	$7.50
G-97	Anthology - ***Nude Croquet*** [1958] PBO. Cover by Maguire.	$2.00	$6.00	$12.00

		G	VG	F
G-98	Prather, Richard S. - ***Pattern For Panic*** [1958] Cover by Rader.	$1.50	$5.00	$10.00
G-99	Nye, Nelson C. - ***G Stands For Gun*** [1958]	$1.25	$3.75	$7.50
BG-100	Wylie, Philip - ***Finnley Wren*** [1958] Photo cover.	$1.00	$3.00	$6.00
G-101	Carr, John Dickson - ***Death Watch*** [1958] Cover by Maguire.	$2.00	$6.00	$12.00
BG-102	Plievier, Theodor - ***Stalingrad*** [1958] Photo cover.	$1.00	$3.00	$6.00
G-103	Fuller, Blair - ***Forbid Me Not*** [1958]	$1.35	$4.00	$8.00
G-104	Anthology - ***Beyond Time And Space*** [1958]	$1.25	$3.75	$7.50
G-105	Sartre, Jean - ***Paul - Intimacy*** [1958]	$1.25	$3.75	$7.50
G-106	Cozzens, James Gould - ***S. S. San Pedro*** [1958]	$1.00	$3.00	$6.00
G-107	Reid, P. R. - ***Escape From Colditz*** [1958] Movie photo cover. Movie tie-in.	$1.00	$3.00	$6.00
BG-108	Spectorsky, A. C. - ***The Exurbanites*** [1958] Cover by Robert Osborn.	$1.00	$3.00	$6.00
G-109	Craig, Margaret Maze - ***Marsha*** [1958] Cover by Dave Attie.	$1.25	$3.75	$7.50
BG-110	Kogon, Eugen - ***The Theory And Practice Of Hell*** [1958] Photo cover.	$1.00	$3.00	$6.00
G-111	Wilhelm, Gale - ***The Strange Path*** [1958] Cover by Maguire.	$3.00	$9.00	$18.00
G-112	Smith, Wallace - ***Bessie Cotter*** [1958]	$1.25	$3.75	$7.50
G-113	Arfelli, Dante - ***The Girl Of The Roman Night*** [1958]	$1.25	$3.75	$7.50
G-114	Garve, Andrew - ***The End Of The Track*** [1958]	$1.00	$3.00	$6.00
G-115	Busch, Fritz Otto - ***Holocaust At Sea: The Drama Of The Scharnhorst*** [1958]	$1.00	$3.00	$6.00
G-116	Derleth, August - editor - ***The Outer Reaches*** [1958]	$1.25	$3.75	$7.50
G-117	Carr, John Dickson - ***The Mad Hatter Mystery*** [1958] Cover by Kimmel.	$2.00	$6.00	$12.00
G-118	Nye, Nelson - ***Guns Of Arizona*** [1958]	$1.25	$3.75	$7.50
G-119	Cheever, John - ***The Enormous Radio*** [1958]	$2.50	$7.50	$15.00
G-120	Farrere, Claude - ***Black Opium*** [1958] Classic cover by Maguire.	$12.50	$37.50	$75.00
BG-121	Edited by Seymour Freiden & W. Richardson - ***The Fatal Decisions*** [1958]	$1.00	$3.00	$6.00
G-122	Marric, J. J. - ***Gideon Of Scotland Yard*** [1958] Movie tie-in.	$1.25	$3.75	$7.50
G-123	Lowell, Juliet - ***To Whom It May Concern*** [1958] Cover by Carl Rose.	$1.00	$3.00	$6.00
G-124	Clarke, Donald Henderson - ***Joe And Jennie*** [1958]	$1.25	$3.75	$7.50
G-125	Smith, Robert Paul - ***So It Doesn't Whistle*** [1958] Cover by Maguire.	$1.50	$5.00	$10.00
G-126	Crane, Clarkson - ***Naomi Martin*** [1958] Cover by Copeland.	$1.35	$4.00	$8.00
S-127	Edited by Ernest Hemingway - ***Men At War*** [1958]	$1.50	$5.00	$10.00
BG-128	McPartland, John - ***Sex In Our Changing World*** [1958]	$1.00	$3.00	$6.00
G-129	Carr, John Dickson - ***Hag's Nook*** [1958] Cover by Maguire.	$2.00	$6.00	$12.00
G-130	Anderson, Edward - ***Thieves Like Us*** [1958] Photo cover.	$1.50	$5.00	$10.00
G-131	Anthology - ***Strange Ports Of Call*** [1958]	$1.25	$3.75	$7.50
G-132	Weston, Carolyn - ***Tormented*** [1958]	$1.00	$3.00	$6.00
G-133	Simenon, Georges - ***Tropic Moon*** [1958]	$1.25	$3.75	$7.50
G-134	McCoy, Horace - ***I Should Have Stayed Home*** [1958]	$1.35	$4.00	$8.00
BG-135	Hart, B. H. Liddell - ***The German Generals Talk*** [1958] Photo cover.	$1.00	$3.00	$6.00
G-136	Bracco, Edgar Jean - ***China Doll*** [1958] PBO. Cover by Kimmel. Movie tie-in.	$2.00	$6.00	$12.00
G-137	Symons, Julian - ***The 31st Of February*** [1958] Cover by Maguire.	$1.50	$5.00	$10.00
G-138	Nye, Nelson - ***Gunfighter Brand*** [1958]	$1.25	$3.75	$7.50
G-139	Himes, Chester B. - ***If He Hollers Let Him Go*** [1958] Cover by Nappi.	$1.35	$4.00	$8.00
G-140	Carco, Francis - ***Infamy*** [1958]	$1.35	$4.00	$8.00
G-141	Mark, Edwina - ***My Sister, My Beloved*** [1958]	$1.35	$4.00	$8.00
G-142	Wolff, Leon - ***Low Level Mission*** [1958] Photo cover.	$1.00	$3.00	$6.00
G-143	Carr, John Dickson - ***The Corpse In The Waxworks*** [1958] Cover by Maguire.	$2.00	$6.00	$12.00

Berkley, G-152

Berkley, G-161

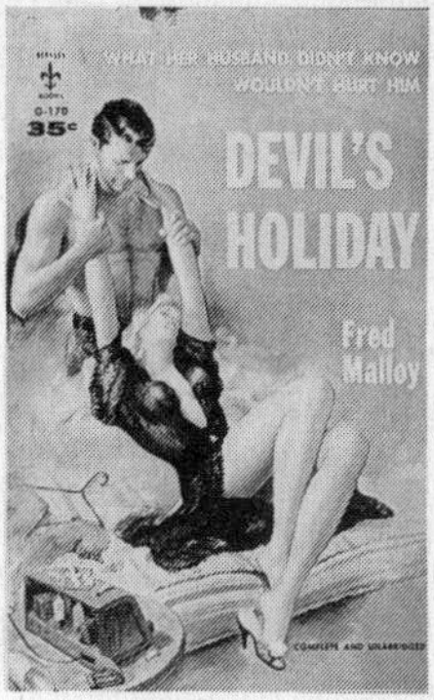

Berkley, G-170

		G	VG	F
G-144	Eliot, Alexander - ***Proud Youth*** [1958] Cover by Harry Schaare.	$1.00	$3.00	$6.00
G-145	Simenon, Georges - ***The Man Who Watched The Trains Go By*** [1958]	$2.50	$7.50	$15.00
G-146	Greene, Graham - ***The Man Within*** [1958]	$1.25	$3.75	$7.50
G-147	De Meyer, John - ***Bailey's Daughters*** [1958] Photo cover.	$1.00	$3.00	$6.00
G-148	Russell, Eric Frank - ***Men, Martians & Machines*** [1958] Cover by Powers.	$1.25	$3.75	$7.50
BG-149	Maugham, W. Somerset - ***Ah King*** [1958] Cover by Maguire.	$1.35	$4.00	$8.00
BG-150	Lawrence, D. H. - ***The First Lady Chatterly*** [1958]	$1.25	$3.75	$7.50
G-151	Harris, William Howard - ***The Golden Jungle*** [1958]	$1.25	$3.75	$7.50
G-152	Appel, Benjamin - ***Hell's Kitchen*** [1958]	$2.50	$7.50	$15.00
G-153	Isherwood, Christopher - ***The Last Of Mr. Norris*** [1958] Cover by Maguire.	$1.50	$5.00	$10.00
G-154	Nye, Nelson C. - ***Gunshot Trail*** [1958]	$1.25	$3.75	$7.50
G-155	Carco, Francis - ***Perversity*** [1958] PBO. Cover by Barton.	$2.50	$7.50	$15.00
G-156	Nabokov, Vladimir - ***Laughter In The Dark*** [1958] Cover by Maguire.	$1.50	$5.00	$10.00
G-157	Carr, John Dickson - ***The Crooked Hinge*** [1958] Cover by Kimmel.	$2.00	$6.00	$12.00
G-160	Wood, Clement - ***Desire*** [1958] Photo cover.	$1.00	$3.00	$6.00
G-161	Alth, Max - ***The Wicked And The Warped*** [1958]	$2.00	$6.00	$12.00
G-162	Martin, George Victor - ***The Evil That Men Do*** [1958]	$1.35	$4.00	$8.00
G-163	Edited by August Derleth - ***Worlds Of Tomorrow*** [1958] PBO. Cover by Powers.	$1.25	$3.75	$7.50
G-164	Burke, J. W. & Grace, Edward - ***Three Day Pass To Hell*** [1958]	$1.25	$3.75	$7.50
G-165	Procter, Maurice - ***The Pub Crawler*** [1958] Cover by Maguire..	$1.35	$4.00	$8.00
G-167	Carlova, John - ***Adam And Evil*** [1958] PBO.	$1.35	$4.00	$8.00
G-169	Moore, Dan Tyler - ***The Terrible Game*** [1958]	$1.25	$3.75	$7.50
G-170	Malloy, Fred - ***Devil's Holiday*** [1958]	$1.25	$3.75	$7.50
G-171J	Hanley, Jack - ***Stag Stripper*** [1958] Photo cover.	$1.25	$3.75	$7.50
G-172	Donisthorpe, G. Sheila - ***Loveliest Of Friends*** [1958] Photo cover.	$1.35	$4.00	$8.00
G-174	Carco, Francis - ***Only A Woman*** [1958]	$1.25	$3.75	$7.50
G-175	Olivia - ***Olivia*** [1958] Cover by Maguire.	$3.00	$9.00	$18.00
G-176	Author Unknown - ***Mystery On Graveyard Head*** [1958]	$1.25	$3.75	$7.50
G-179	Schiller, Cicely - ***No Bed Of Her Own*** [1958] Cover by Maguire.	$1.50	$5.00	$10.00
G-180	Bracco, Edgar Jean - ***Boots And Saddles*** [1958] PBO. TV tie-in.	$1.25	$3.75	$7.50

Berkley, G-240

Berkley, G-243

Berkley, G-260

		G	VG	F
G-181	Wolfson, P. J. - ***Is My Flesh Of Brass?*** [1958]	$1.35	$4.00	$8.00
G-182	Tracy, Don - ***Too Many Girls*** [1958]	$1.25	$3.75	$7.50
G-183	Rothman, Nathan - ***Virgie, Goodbye*** [1958] Photo cover.	$1.00	$3.00	$6.00
G-184	Quintavalle, Uberto Paolo - ***The Shameless Ones*** [1958] Cover by Copeland.	$1.50	$5.00	$10.00
G-186	Clark, Dorene - ***Scarlet Angel*** [1958] Photo cover.	$1.00	$3.00	$6.00
G-188	Roueche, Berton - ***The Incurable Wound*** [1958]	$ .75	$2.50	$5.00
G-189	Anthology - ***Time To Come*** [1958]	$1.25	$3.75	$7.50
G-190	Durrenmatt, Friedrich - ***The Judge And His Hangman*** [1958] Cover by Schaare.	$1.25	$3.75	$7.50
G-192	Norman, Earl - ***Kill Me In Tokyo*** [1958] PBO. Cover by Maguire.	$2.25	$7.00	$14.00
G-194	Du Gard, Roger Martin - ***The Postman*** [1958] Cover by Nappi.	$1.25	$3.75	$7.50
G-196	Marshe, Richard - ***Passion In Panama*** [1959]	$1.35	$4.00	$8.00
BG-197	Heinz, W. C. - ***The Professional*** [1959]	$1.00	$3.00	$6.00
G-198	Grisman, Arnold - ***Early To Rise*** [1959] Cover by Maguire.	$1.50	$5.00	$10.00
G-199	Gorham, Charles - ***Make Me An Offer*** [1959]	$1.00	$3.00	$6.00
G-201	Colt, Clem - ***Smoke - Wagon Kid*** [1959]	$1.25	$3.75	$7.50
BG-202	Pattinson, James - ***Last In Convoy*** [1959] Photo cover.	$1.00	$3.00	$6.00
G-203	Anthology - ***Love Around The World*** [1959] PBO. Cover by Maguire.	$1.50	$5.00	$10.00
G-204	Heppenstall, Rayner - ***The Blaze Of Noon*** [1959]	$1.25	$3.75	$7.50
G-206	Tryon, Mark - ***The Sinning Lens*** [1959] Photo cover.	$1.00	$3.00	$6.00
G-208	Mallette, Gertrude E. - ***Mystery In Blue*** [1958]	$1.25	$3.75	$7.50
BG-211	Pope, Dudley - ***73 North - The Defeat Of Hitler's Navy*** [1959] Photo cover.	$1.00	$3.00	$6.00
BG-212	Fall, Thomas - ***Prettiest Girl In Town*** [1959] Cover by Copeland.	$1.35	$4.00	$8.00
BG-213	Maugham, W. Somerset - ***First Person Singular*** [1959] Cover by Maguire.	$1.35	$4.00	$8.00
G-214	Dickson, Carter - ***The Bowstring Murders*** [1959] Cover by Maguire.	$2.00	$6.00	$12.00
G-215	Van Vogt, A. E. - ***Away And Beyond*** [1959] Cover by Powers.	$1.25	$3.75	$7.50
G-216	Bodin, Paul - ***The Sign Of Eros*** [1959] Photo cover.	$1.00	$3.00	$6.00
G-217	Chaze, Elliott - ***Love On The Rocks*** [1959] Photo cover.	$1.00	$3.00	$6.00
G-218	Henderson, George Wylie - ***Jule*** [1959]	$1.25	$3.75	$7.50
G-220	Tryon, Mark - ***The Fire That Burns*** [1959]	$1.25	$3.75	$7.50
G-222	Edited by Page Cooper - ***The Big Book Of Horse Stories*** [1959]	$1.00	$3.00	$6.00
G-224	Knoke, Heinz - ***I Flew For The Führer*** [1959] Photo cover.	$1.35	$4.00	$8.00

		G	VG	F
G-225	Zinberg, Len - ***What D'ya Know For Sure*** [1959] Cover by Maguire.	$1.35	$4.00	$8.00
G-226	Bodin, Paul - ***All Women's Flesh*** [1959]	$1.25	$3.75	$7.50
G-227	Stone, Scott - ***Blaze*** [1959]	$1.00	$3.00	$6.00
G-228	Lucas, Rick - ***Dreamboat*** [1959] Photo cover.	$1.00	$3.00	$6.00
G-229	Ford, Terance - ***Easy Living*** [1959]	$1.00	$3.00	$6.00
BG-231	Packer, Reynolds - ***Dateline: Paris*** [1959] Cover by Maguire.	$1.35	$4.00	$8.00
G-232	Gunn, James - ***Deadlier Than The Male*** [1959]	$1.35	$4.00	$8.00
G-233	Edited by Everett F. Bleiler & T. E. Dikty - ***Imagination Unlimited*** [1959] Cover by Powers.	$1.25	$3.75	$7.50
G-234	Nye, Nelson C. - ***Guns Of Horse Prairie*** [1959]	$1.25	$3.75	$7.50
G-235	Robertson, Terence - ***Channel Dash*** [1959]	$1.00	$3.00	$6.00
G-236	Marshe, Richard - ***A Woman Called Desire*** [1959] Photo cover.	$1.25	$3.75	$7.50
G-237	West, Token - ***Showroom Girls*** [1959]	$1.35	$4.00	$8.00
BG-238	Munro, W. Carroll - ***The Lessons Of Love*** [1959]	$1.00	$3.00	$6.00
BG-239	Williams, Eric - ***The Wooden Horse*** [1959] Photo cover.	$1.25	$3.75	$7.50
G-240	Swados, Felice - ***House Of Fury*** [1959] Cover by Maguire.	$6.00	$20.00	$40.00
G-241	Prather, Richard S. - ***Pattern For Panic*** [1959] Cover by Paul Rader.	$1.35	$4.00	$8.00
G-242	Arthur, Burt - ***Duel On The Range*** [1959]	$1.25	$3.75	$7.50
G-243	Nichols, Fan - ***Count Me In*** [1959]	$1.25	$3.75	$7.50
G-244	Albert, Sim - ***Vice Girl*** [1959] Photo cover.	$1.00	$3.00	$6.00
G-245	Mark, Edwina - ***The Odd Ones*** [1959] Cover by Rudy Nappi.	$2.00	$6.00	$12.00
G-246	Waldron, T. J. & Gleeson, James - ***The Frogmen*** [1959]	$1.00	$3.00	$6.00
G-248	Wolfson, P. J. - ***Three Of A Kind*** [1959]	$1.25	$3.75	$7.50
G-249	Edited by August Derleth - ***The Other Side Of The Moon*** [1959]	$1.25	$3.75	$7.50
G-250	Whittington, Harry - ***Native Girl*** [1959]	$3.00	$9.00	$18.00
G-253	Nichols, Fan - ***Devil Take Her*** [1959]	$1.35	$4.00	$8.00
G-256	Massie, Chris - ***The Incredible Truth*** [1959]	$1.25	$3.75	$7.50
G-258	Keene, Day - ***Wake Up To Murder*** [1959] Cover by Maguire.	$2.00	$6.00	$12.00
G-259	Gordon, Ian - ***Harlem Is My Heaven*** [1959]	$1.35	$4.00	$8.00
G-260	Westley, Kirk - ***Shanty Boat Girl*** [1959]	$1.25	$3.75	$7.50
G-261	Hanley, Jack - ***Strip Street*** [1959] Photo cover.	$1.25	$3.75	$7.50
BG-264	Donleavy, J. P. - ***The Ginger Man*** [1959] Cover by Powers.	$1.25	$3.75	$7.50
G-265	Tey, Josephine - ***The Daughter Of Time*** [1959] Photo cover.	$1.25	$3.75	$7.50
G-267	Dickson, Carter - ***The Plague Court Murders*** [1959]	$1.50	$5.00	$10.00
G-268	Maugham, W. Somerset - ***Cosmopolitans*** [1959] Cover by Maguire.	$1.35	$4.00	$8.00
G-272	Dooley, M.D., Thomas A. - ***The Edge Of Tomorrow*** [1959] Photo cover.	$1.25	$3.75	$7.50
G-273	Sire, Glen and Jane - ***Something Foolish, Something Gay*** [1959]	$1.00	$3.00	$6.00
G-274	Hahn, Emily - ***Francie Comes Home*** [1959]	$1.00	$3.00	$6.00
G-275	Leighton, Margaret - ***Comanche Of The Seventh*** [1959]	$1.25	$3.75	$7.50
G-277	de Montherlant, Henry - ***Desert Love*** [1959] Cover by Ginnis.	$1.35	$4.00	$8.00
G-279	Lebherz, Richard - ***The Alters Of The Heart*** [1959] Photo cover.	$1.00	$3.00	$6.00
G-280	Sturgeon, Theodore - ***A Touch Of Strange*** [1959]	$1.25	$3.75	$7.50
G-281	Carr, John Dickson - ***Death Turns The Tables*** [1959] Cover by Victor Kaun.	$1.25	$3.75	$7.50
G-285	McIlvaine, Jane - ***Blue Ribbon Romance*** [1959] Cover by Maguire.	$1.25	$3.75	$7.50
G-286	Turngren, Annette - ***The Mystery Of Hidden Village*** [1959]	$1.25	$3.75	$7.50
G-287	Carr, John Dickson - ***The Emperor's Snuff Box*** [1959]	$1.50	$5.00	$10.00
G-289	Anderson, Poul - ***The Enemy Stars*** [1959]	$1.25	$3.75	$7.50
G-290	Lawrence, D. H. - ***The Thorn In The Flesh*** [1959] Photo cover.	$1.00	$3.00	$6.00
G-291	Bracco, Edgar Jean - ***Flight*** [1959] PBO. TV tie-in.	$1.00	$3.00	$6.00

Berkley, G-406

Broadway Novel Monthly, 2

Cameo Books, 309

		G	VG	F
G-293	Weber, Lenora Mattingly - ***Meet The Malones*** [1959] Cover by Harry Bennett	$ .75	$2.50	$5.00
G-295	MacDonald, Zillah K. - ***Roxanne, Company Nurse*** [1959]	$ .65	$2.00	$4.00
G-299	Cavanna, Betty - ***Passport To Romance*** [1959]	$ .65	$2.00	$4.00
G-300	Coles, Manning - ***The Mystery Of The Stolen Plans*** [1959] Cover by Victor Kalin.	$1.25	$3.75	$7.50
G-401	Carr, John Dickson - ***The Lost Gallows*** [1960]	$1.50	$5.00	$10.00
G-402	Robertson, Terence - ***The Ship With Two Captains*** [1960]	$1.25	$3.75	$7.50
BG-404	Edited by Herbert Haufrecht - ***Folksing*** [1960] Cover by Kelly Freas. Songbook.	$1.50	$5.00	$10.00
G-406	Cleary, Beverly - ***Leave It To Beaver*** [1960] PBO. Photo cover. TV tie-in.	$2.50	$7.50	$15.00
G-407	Tey, Josephine - ***A Shilling For Candles*** [1960] Photo cover.	$1.25	$3.75	$7.50
BG-408	Scott, Jr., Robert Lee - ***Flying Tiger: Chennault Of China*** [1960] Photo cover.	$1.00	$3.00	$6.00
G-409	Southern, Jerry - ***Flash And Filigree*** [1960] Photo cover.	$1.35	$4.00	$8.00
G-410	Leinster, Murray - ***The Aliens*** [1960] PBO. Cover by Powers.	$1.25	$3.75	$7.50
G-411	Carleton, Marjorie - ***One Night Of Terror*** [1960] Cover by Harry Bennett.	$1.00	$3.00	$6.00
G-412	Carr, John Dickson - ***Castle Skull*** [1960]	$1.50	$5.00	$10.00
BG-414	Huxley, Aldous - ***Time Must Have A Stop*** [1960] Photo cover.	$1.35	$4.00	$8.00
G-415	Tey, Josephine - ***Miss Pym Disposes*** [1960] Photo cover.	$1.25	$3.75	$7.50
BG-417	Koestler, Arthur - ***Thieves In The Night*** [1960]	$1.25	$3.75	$7.50
G-418	Marric, J. J. - ***Gideon's Staff*** [1960] Cover by Victor Kalin.	$1.00	$3.00	$6.00
BG-421	Gallagher, Thomas - ***Fire At Sea*** [1960] Photo cover. 4 pages of photos.	$1.25	$3.75	$7.50
G-422	Tey, Josephine - ***To Love And Be Wise*** [1960]	$1.25	$3.75	$7.50
S-426	Edited by Ernest Hemingway - ***Men At War*** [1960]	$1.25	$3.75	$7.50
BG-427	Leonard, George - ***Shoulder The Sky*** [1960] Cover by Harry Bennett.	$1.00	$3.00	$6.00
G-430	Sellers, Naomi John - ***Cross My Heart*** [1960]	$ .75	$2.50	$5.00
G-432	Howe, Margaret - ***Nurse Jenny*** [1960]	$ .65	$2.00	$4.00
G-433	Turner, William O. - ***War Country*** [1960]	$1.00	$3.00	$6.00
G-434	Tey, Josephine - ***Brat Farrar*** [1960] Photo cover.	$1.25	$3.75	$7.50
BG-436	Ennis, John - ***The Great Bombay Explosion*** [1960] Photo cover. 4 pages of photos.	$1.25	$3.75	$7.50
G-437	Crouzat, Henri - ***Island At The End Of The World*** [1960] Cover by Rudy Nappi.	$1.25	$3.75	$7.50
G-438	Marsh, Ngaio - ***Singing In The Shrouds*** [1960] Photo cover.	$1.25	$3.75	$7.50
BG-439	O'Donnell, Eugene - ***The Night Cometh*** [1960] Cover by Richard Powers.	$1.00	$3.00	$6.00

		G	VG	F
G-441	Welch, Maud McCurdy - ***Nurse Carol*** [1960]	$ .65	$2.00	$4.00
G-442	Koestler, Arthur - ***Arrival And Departure*** [1960]	$ .75	$2.50	$5.00
G-443	Karney, Jack - ***Layoff For Murder*** [1960] PBO.	$1.25	$3.75	$7.50
G-445	Wells, H. G. - ***The Time Machine*** [1960] Cover by Richard Powers. Movie tie-in.	$1.25	$3.75	$7.50
G-446	Green, Henry - ***Back*** [1960]	$1.00	$3.00	$6.00
G-450	Deming, Richard - ***Edge Of The Law*** [1960] PBO. Cover by James Meese.	$1.25	$3.75	$7.50
G-451	Marsh, Ngaio - ***Scales Of Justice*** [1960] Photo cover.	$1.25	$3.75	$7.50
G-452	Lehman, Paul Evan - ***Only The Brave*** [1960]	$1.00	$3.00	$6.00
G-453	Weber, Lenora Mattingly - ***Leave It To Beany*** [1960]	$1.00	$3.00	$6.00
G-454	Adams, John Paul - ***We Dare You To Solve This*** [1960] Puzzle book.	$1.35	$4.00	$8.00
G-455	Judd, Frances K. - ***The Mansion Of Secrets*** [1960]	$1.25	$3.75	$7.50
G-458	Judd, Frances K. - ***The Sacred Feather*** [1960]	$1.00	$3.00	$6.00
BG-459	Benzaquin, Paul - ***Holocaust!*** [1960] Photo cover. 4 pages of photos.	$1.25	$3.75	$7.50
G-460	Martin, Kay - ***On Easy Terms*** [1960] PBO. Cover by Copeland.	$1.35	$4.00	$8.00
G-461	Leinster, Murray - ***Men Into Space*** [1960] PBO. TV tie-in.	$1.35	$4.00	$8.00
G-462	Lambert, Gavin - ***The Slide Area*** [1960] Cover by Richard Powers.	$1.00	$3.00	$6.00
G-463	MacKenzie, Donald - ***Dangerous Silence*** [1960]	$1.00	$3.00	$6.00
G-464	MacDonald, William Colt - ***The Gun Branders*** [1960]	$1.00	$3.00	$6.00
G-466	Hadley, Arthur T. - ***The Joy Wagon*** [1960]	$1.00	$3.00	$6.00
G-467	Jacobs, Bruce - ***Heroes Of The Army*** [1960] Cover by Richard Powers.	$1.00	$3.00	$6.00
S-468	Kogon, Eugen - ***The Theory And Practice Of Hell*** [1960]	$ .75	$2.50	$5.00
G-469	Adams, Clifton - ***The Legend Of Lonnie Hall*** [1960]	$1.00	$3.00	$6.00
G-470	Hudson, Nick - ***The Very Wicked*** [1960]	$1.00	$3.00	$6.00
G-471	Edited by Groff Conklin - ***Possible Worlds Of Science Fiction*** [1960] Cover by Richard Powers.	$1.00	$3.00	$6.00
BG-472	Green, Henry - ***Caught*** [1960] Photo cover.	$1.00	$3.00	$6.00
G-473	Bok, Curtis - ***Star Wormwood*** [1960] Cover by Richard Powers.	$1.00	$3.00	$6.00
G-474	Carco, Francis - ***Frenzy*** [1960]	$1.00	$3.00	$6.00
G-475	Tanizaki, Junichiro - ***Some Prefer Neetles*** [1960] Cover by Harry Schaare	$1.00	$3.00	$6.00
G-477	Edited by John Norment - ***Monkeyshines!*** [1960] PBO. Cartoon book.	$1.50	$5.00	$10.00
BG-478	Sartre, Jean Paul - ***Intimacy*** [1960] Cover by Hill.	$1.00	$3.00	$6.00
G-479	Worley, Dorothy - ***Dr. Michael's Challenge*** [1960]	$ .65	$2.00	$4.00
G-480	Richards, Robert - ***I Can Lick Seven*** [1960]	$1.00	$3.00	$6.00
G-482	Naughton, Edmund - ***McCabe*** [1960]	$1.00	$3.00	$6.00
G-483	Prosser, W. H. - ***Nine To Five*** [1960]	$ .75	$2.50	$5.00
G-484	Chaland, Paul - ***The Witch Of Modane*** [1960] Photo cover.	$1.00	$3.00	$6.00
S-485	Trevor-Roper, H. R. - ***The Last Days Of Hitler*** [1960] Photo cover.	$ .75	$2.50	$5.00
G-487	Albrand, Martha - ***The Linden Affair*** [1960]	$1.25	$3.75	$7.50
G-488	Edited by John Norment - ***Fast Laughs*** [1960] PBO. Cartoon book.	$1.50	$5.00	$10.00
BG-489	Waterhouse, Keith - ***Billy Liar*** [1961]	$1.25	$3.75	$7.50
G-490	Gregor, Paul - ***Jump Into The Sun*** [1961]	$1.00	$3.00	$6.00
BG-491	Tuleja, Thaddeus V. - ***Climax At Midway*** [1961]	$ .75	$2.50	$5.00
G-492	Potts, Jean - ***Death Of A Stray Cat*** [1961] Photo cover.	$1.25	$3.75	$7.50
G-493	Smith, Ben - ***Renegade Rider*** [1961]	$1.00	$3.00	$6.00
G-494	Corey, Frank - ***By Blood Alone*** [1961] PBO.	$1.25	$3.75	$7.50
G-495	Hoyle, Fred - ***Ossian's Ride*** [1961] Cover by Richard Powers.	$1.00	$3.00	$6.00
G-496	Allingham, Margery - ***Traitor's Purse*** [1961] Photo cover.	$1.25	$3.75	$7.50

		G	VG	F
G-497	Cleary, Beverly - ***Here's Beaver!*** [1961] PBO. Photo cover. TV tie-in.	$2.50	$7.50	$15.00
BG-498	Osaragi, Jiro - ***Homecoming*** [1961]	$ .75	$2.50	$5.00
BG-500	Southern, Terry - ***The Magic Christian*** [1961] Cover by Richard Powers.	$1.35	$4.00	$8.00
G-501	Superveille, Anne-Marie - ***The Night Lover*** [1961] Cover by Barye Phillips.	$1.00	$3.00	$6.00
G-502	Norman, Earl - ***Kill Me In Yoshiwara*** [1961] PBO. Cover by Barye Phillips.	$1.35	$4.00	$8.00
G-503	De Vilallonga, Jose Luis - ***The Man Of Blood*** [1961]	$1.00	$3.00	$6.00
S-504	Ward, Brad - ***The Missourian*** [1961] Cover by Harry Schaare.	$1.00	$3.00	$6.00
G-505	Potts, Jean - ***Go, Lovely Rose*** [1961] Photo cover.	$1.25	$3.75	$7.50
G-507	Blish, James - ***Titan's Daughter*** [1961] Cover by Barye Phillips.	$1.00	$3.00	$6.00
BG-508	Marsh, Ngaio - ***Spinsters In Jeopardy*** [1961] Photo cover.	$1.25	$3.75	$7.50
G-509	Brewer, Gil - ***A Taste For Sin*** [1961] Cover by Harry Schaare.	$1.35	$4.00	$8.00
G-510	Ketchum, Philip - ***The Stalkers*** [1961] PBO. Cover by Carl Hantman.	$1.25	$3.75	$7.50
BG-511	Tey, Josephine - ***The Franchise Affair*** [1961] Photo cover.	$1.25	$3.75	$7.50
BG-512	Russell, Lord - ***The Knights Of Bushido*** [1961]	$1.00	$3.00	$6.00
G-513	Roberts, Virginia - ***Terry Randolph: Registered Nurse*** [1961]	$ .65	$2.00	$4.00
G-514	Marric, J. J. - ***Gideon's Risk*** [1961] Cover by Victor Kalin.	$ .75	$2.50	$5.00
G-515	Ryder, Sabin - ***Dr. Stephanie's Decision*** [1961]	$ .65	$2.00	$4.00
BG-517	Orwell, George - ***The Road To Wigan Pier*** [1961]	$1.25	$3.75	$7.50
G-518	Kerr, Geoffrey - ***Under The Influence*** [1961] Cover by Richard Powers.	$ .75	$2.50	$5.00
BG-519	Cary, Joyce - ***Mister Johnson*** [1961] Cover by Hill.	$ .75	$2.50	$5.00
G-520	Fisher, Lawrence - ***Death By The Day*** [1961]	$1.00	$3.00	$6.00
BG-521	Marsh, Ngaio - ***Final Curtain*** [1961] Photo cover.	$1.25	$3.75	$7.50
BG-522	Young, Desmond - ***Rommel, The Desert Fox*** [1961] Photo cover.	$1.00	$3.00	$6.00
G-523	Fotre, Vincent - ***The Trailmakers*** [1961] PBO. Cover by Robert Abbett.	$1.00	$3.00	$6.00
G-525	Flaubert, Gustave - ***Salambo*** [1961] Cover by James Hill.	$1.35	$4.00	$8.00
G-528	Norman, Earl - ***Kill Me In Tokyo*** [1961]	$1.50	$5.00	$10.00
BG-529	Marsh, Ngaio - ***Died In The Wool*** [1961] Photo cover.	$1.25	$3.75	$7.50
G-530	Potts, Jean - ***The Man With The Cane*** [1961] Photo cover.	$1.25	$3.75	$7.50
G-532	Wayne, Joseph - ***Pistol Johnny*** [1961]	$1.00	$3.00	$6.00
BG-534	Marsh, Ngaio - ***Colour Scheme*** [1961] Photo cover.	$1.25	$3.75	$7.50
BG-535	Orwell, George - ***Down And Out In Paris And London*** [1961]	$1.00	$3.00	$6.00
G-536	deCamp, L. Sprague & Miller, P. Schuyler - ***Genus Homo*** [1961] Cover by Richard Powers.	$1.25	$3.75	$7.50
S-538	Anthology - ***Banned*** [1961] PBO.	$2.00	$6.00	$12.00
G-539	Craig, Georgia - ***Perry Kimbro, R.N.*** [1961]	$ .65	$2.00	$4.00
G-540	Marsh, Ngaio - ***Death Of A Peer*** [1961] Photo cover.	$1.25	$3.75	$7.50
G-541	Rabe, Peter - ***Anatomy Of A Killer*** [1961] Photo cover.	$2.00	$6.00	$12.00
G-543	Carr, Harriett H. - ***Confidential Secretary*** [1961]	$ .65	$2.00	$4.00
G-544	Lacy, Ed - ***The Freeloaders*** [1961]	$1.25	$3.75	$7.50
BG-545	Viscardi, Jr., Henry - ***Give Us The Tools*** [1961]	$ .75	$2.50	$5.00
G-547	Stolz, Mary - ***Hospital Zone*** [1961]	$ .65	$2.00	$4.00
G-549	Leinster, Murray - ***Creatures Of The Abyss*** [1961] PBO. Cover by Richard Powers.	$1.35	$4.00	$8.00
G-550	Norman, Earl - ***Kill Me In Shinjuku*** [1961] PBO.	$1.50	$5.00	$10.00
G-551	Thomason, Jr., John W. - ***Texas Rebel*** [1961]	$1.00	$3.00	$6.00
G-552	Creasey, John - ***Hit And Run*** [1961] Cover by Victor Kalin.	$1.00	$3.00	$6.00
BG-553	Nabokov, Vladimir - ***Laughter In The Dark*** [1961]	$ .75	$2.50	$5.00
G-554	Koh, Taiwon - ***Divided Family*** [1961]	$ .75	$2.50	$5.00
G-556	Jacobs, Bruce - ***Korea's Heroes*** [1961] Cover by Richard Powers.	$1.00	$3.00	$6.00

		G	VG	F
G-557	Cleary, Beverly - ***Beaver And Wally*** [1961] PBO. Photo cover. TV tie-in.	$2.50	$7.50	$15.00
G-560	Gaddis, Peggy - ***Palm Beach Nurse*** [1961]	$ .65	$2.00	$4.00
G-561	Wesley, Elizabeth - ***Summer Stock Romance*** [1961] Cover by Harry Bennett.	$ .65	$2.00	$4.00
G-562	Hogan, Ray - ***Rebel Raid*** [1961]	$1.00	$3.00	$6.00
F-563	Stapledon, Olaf - ***The Star Maker*** [1961] PBO.	$1.50	$5.00	$10.00
F-564	Marsh, Ngaio - ***Death And The Dancing Footman*** [1961] Photo cover.	$1.25	$3.75	$7.50
G-565	Craig, Margaret Maze - ***Now That I'm Sixteen*** [1961]	$ .75	$2.50	$5.00
G-567	Seltzer, Nadine - ***Sweetie Pie*** [1961] Cartoon book.	$1.35	$4.00	$8.00
G-568	Thomey, Tedd - ***The Sadist*** [1961]	$1.25	$3.75	$7.50
Y-572	Farrere, Claude - ***Black Opium*** [1961] Cover by Robert Maguire.	$6.00	$20.00	$40.00
X-573	Edited by Oscar Brand - ***Folksongs For Fun*** [1961] PBO. Cover by Will Elder.	$1.50	$5.00	$10.00
G-574	Creasey, John - ***Doorway Of Death*** [1961]	$1.00	$3.00	$6.00
G-576	Gaddis, Peggy - ***Hurricane Nurse*** [1961] PBO. Cover by Harry Bennett.	$ .65	$2.00	$4.00
G-577	Clinton, Jeff - ***The Fighting Buckaroo*** [1961] PBO.	$1.00	$3.00	$6.00
Y-581	Potts, Jean - ***Home Is The Prisoner*** [1961]	$1.25	$3.75	$7.50
Y-582	Gantz, Kenneth F. - ***Not In Solitude*** [1961] Cover by Richard Powers.	$ .75	$2.50	$5.00
G-583	Holloway, Teresa - ***Lynn Daly: Newspaper Girl*** [1961] Cover by Miller.	$ .65	$2.00	$4.00
G-584	Patten, Lewis B. - ***Outlaw Canyon*** [1961]	$1.00	$3.00	$6.00
G-586	Reid, P. R. - ***Escape From Colditz*** [1961] Photo cover.	$ .75	$2.50	$5.00
F-594	Tey, Josephine - ***The Singing Sands*** [1961] Photo cover.	$1.25	$3.75	$7.50
F-595	Tey, Josephine - ***A Shilling For Candles*** [1961] Photo cover.	$1.00	$3.00	$6.00
F-596	Tey, Josephine - ***Miss Pym Disposes*** [1961]	$1.25	$3.75	$7.50
F-597	Tey, Josephine - ***To Love And Be Wise*** [1961]	$1.25	$3.75	$7.50
Y-599	Martin, George Victor - ***The Evil That Men Do*** [1962]	$1.00	$3.00	$6.00
F-600	Ballard, J. G. - ***The Wind From Nowhere*** [1962] PBO. Cover by Richard Powers.	$3.00	$9.00	$18.00
G-601	Young, Carter Travis - ***The Wild Breed*** [1962]	$1.00	$3.00	$6.00
F-602	Marsh, Ngaio - ***Death At The Bar*** [1962] Photo cover.	$1.25	$3.75	$7.50
Y-603	Anthology - ***The Berkley Book Of Crossword Puzzles*** [1962] PBO. Puzzle book.	$2.00	$6.00	$12.00
G-604	Craig, Georgia - ***Piney Woods Nurse*** [1962]	$ .65	$2.00	$4.00
S-605	Barnett, Correlli - ***The Desert Generals*** [1962]	$ .75	$2.50	$5.00
F-606	Levy, Alan - ***Wanted: Nazi Criminals At Large*** [1962] PBO. Photo cover.	$1.00	$3.00	$6.00
F-607	Ballard, J. G. - ***The Voices Of Time*** [1962] PBO. Cover by Richard Powers.	$2.50	$7.50	$15.00
G-608	Gilmore, Cecile - ***Never Another Love*** [1962]	$ .65	$2.00	$4.00
F-610	Marsh, Ngaio - ***A Wreath For Rivera*** [1962] Photo cover.	$1.25	$3.75	$7.50
G-612	Harris, Kathleen - ***Camp Nurse*** [1962]	$ .65	$2.00	$4.00
F-613	Tey, Josephine - ***Brat Farrar*** [1962]	$1.25	$3.75	$7.50
Y-615	de Bollene, Anne - ***Voyage To Eros*** [1962]	$ .75	$2.50	$5.00
F-616	Knight, Damon - ***Far Out*** [1962] Cover by Richard Powers.	$1.25	$3.75	$7.50
G-618	MacDonald, William Colt - ***Trouble Shooter*** [1962] PBO.	$1.00	$3.00	$6.00
G-620	Stolz, Mary - ***Student Nurse*** [1962] Cover by Harry Bennett.	$ .65	$2.00	$4.00
F-621	Leiber, Fritz - ***Conjure Wife*** [1962] Movie tie-in as *Burn Witch Burn*.	$3.50	$10.00	$20.00
G-622	Shann, Renee - ***Ring For The Nurse*** [1962]	$ .65	$2.00	$4.00
F-624	Schwartz, Harry - editor - ***The Many Faces Of Communism*** [1962] PBO. Cover by Richard Powers.	$ .75	$2.50	$5.00
Y-625	Parturier, Francoise - ***The Five Day Lover*** [1962]	$ .75	$2.50	$5.00
F-627	Anthology - ***Daughters Of Eve*** [1962]	$1.00	$3.00	$6.00

		G	VG	F
Y-628	Creasey, John - ***Death Of An Assassin*** [1962] Cover by Victor Kalin.	$1.00	$3.00	$6.00
F-629	Daly, Elizabeth - ***Murders In Volumn 2*** [1962] Photo cover.	$1.25	$3.75	$7.50
F-630	Marsh, Ngaio - ***A Man Lay Dead*** [1962] Photo cover.	$1.25	$3.75	$7.50
G-631	Wolford, Colby - ***Blow-Up At Three Springs*** [1962]	$1.00	$3.00	$6.00
F-633	Unknown - ***Brothers Of The Sword*** [1962]	$1.00	$3.00	$6.00
F-634	Ayme, Marcel - ***The Walker-Through-Walls*** [1962]	$1.00	$3.00	$6.00
G-636	Randall, Rona - ***Lab Nurse*** [1962]	$ .65	$2.00	$4.00
S-637	Anthology - ***Banned #2*** [1962] PBO.	$2.00	$6.00	$12.00
G-638	Ford, Marcia - ***Nurse Craig*** [1962]	$ .65	$2.00	$4.00
F-639	Davidson, Avram - ***Or All The Seas With Oysters*** [1962] PBO. Cover by Richard Powers.	$2.00	$6.00	$12.00
F-640	Marsh, Ngaio - ***Death In Ecstasy*** [1962] Photo cover.	$1.25	$3.75	$7.50
X-642	Donleavy, J. P. - ***The Ginger Man*** [1962]	$1.35	$4.00	$8.00
F-644	Daly, Elizabeth - ***Evidence Of Things Seen*** [1962]	$1.25	$3.75	$7.50
F-645	Roueche, Berton - ***Eleven Blue Men*** [1962]	$ .75	$2.50	$5.00
F-647	Knight, Damon - ***Analogue Men*** [1962] Cover by Richard Powers.	$1.25	$3.75	$7.50
F-648	Marsh, Ngaio & Jellett, Dr. Henry - ***The Nursing-Home Murders*** [1962] Photo cover.	$1.25	$3.75	$7.50
Y-649	Creasey, John - ***Murder Tips The Scales*** [1962] Cover by Victor Kalin.	$1.00	$3.00	$6.00
Y-650	Massart, Philippe - ***Venus In Mink*** [1962]	$ .75	$2.50	$5.00
Y-651	Carco, Francis - ***Only A Woman*** [1962]	$1.00	$3.00	$6.00
G-652	Patten, Lewis B. - ***Flame In The West*** [1962]	$1.00	$3.00	$6.00
G-653	Lindsay, Rachel - ***Lesley Forrest: M.D.*** [1962]	$ .65	$2.00	$4.00
F-655	Ballard, J. G. - ***The Drowned World*** [1962] PBO.	$2.50	$7.50	$15.00
F-656	Daly, Elizabeth - ***The Book Of The Dead*** [1962]	$1.25	$3.75	$7.50
F-657	Tey, Josephine - ***The Man In The Queue*** [1962] Photo cover.	$1.25	$3.75	$7.50
Y-658	Chaze, Elliott - ***One For The Money*** [1962] Cover by Copeland.	$1.00	$3.00	$6.00
Y-659	Gilmore, Cecile - ***Hold Me Fast*** [1962] Cover by Miller.	$ .75	$2.50	$5.00
Y-660	Clinton, Jeff - ***Range Killer*** [1962]	$1.00	$3.00	$6.00
Y-661	Ives, Ruth - ***Surgical Nurse*** [1962] PBO.	$ .65	$2.00	$4.00
Y-662	Gallico, Paul - ***The Hurricane Story*** [1962]	$ .75	$2.50	$5.00
F-665	Marsh, Ngaio - ***Vintage Murder*** [1962] Photo cover.	$1.25	$3.75	$7.50
F-666	Anthology - ***Ghosts And Things*** [1962] PBO.	$1.35	$4.00	$8.00
F-667	Ballard, J. G. - ***Billenium*** [1962] PBO. Cover by Richard Powers.	$2.50	$7.50	$15.00
Y-668	MacLeod, Ruth - ***Dr. Grayson's Crisis*** [1962] PBO.	$ .65	$2.00	$4.00
Y-670	Newton, D. B. - ***On The Dodge*** [1962]	$1.00	$3.00	$6.00
Y-671	Massart, Philippe - ***The Love Expert*** [1962]	$ .75	$2.50	$5.00
F-672	Edited by Stewart Beach - ***This Week's Stories Of Mystery & Suspense*** [1962]	$1.00	$3.00	$6.00
F-673	Daly, Elizabeth - ***Arrow Pointing Nowhere*** [1962] Photo cover.	$1.25	$3.75	$7.50
Y-674	Patrick, Leal - ***Border Town Nurse*** [1962] PBO.	$ .65	$2.00	$4.00
Y-675	Lec, Jean - ***The Passionate Minx*** [1962]	$ .75	$2.50	$5.00
Y-676	Norman, Earl - ***Kill Me In Atami*** [1962] PBO. Cover by Barye Phillips.	$1.50	$5.00	$10.00
Y-677	Clinton, Jeff - ***Wildcat's Rampage*** [1962]	$1.00	$3.00	$6.00
Y-678	Gilmore, Cecile - ***The Man In The Moonlight*** [1962]	$1.00	$3.00	$6.00
F-679	Leiber, Fritz - ***Gather, Darkness!*** [1962] Cover by Richard Powers.	$2.50	$7.50	$15.00
Y-680	Moore, Mary F. - ***The Baby Sitter's Guide*** [1962]	$ .75	$2.50	$5.00
Y-682	Dirksen, Joan - ***I'll Find My Love*** [1962]	$ .65	$2.00	$4.00
Y-683	McIlvaine, Jane S. - ***Blue Ribbon Romance*** [1962]	$ .65	$2.00	$4.00
G-684	Neher, Fred - ***Will-Yum*** [1962] Cover by Author. Cartoon book.	$1.35	$4.00	$8.00
Y-685	Hill, Marjorie Yourd - ***Look For The Stars*** [1962]	$ .75	$2.50	$5.00
Y-686	Cadell, Elizabeth - ***I Love A Lass*** [1962]	$ .65	$2.00	$4.00

		G	VG	F
Y-688	Butters, Dorothy Gilman - ***Heart's Design*** [1963] Cover by Harry Bennett.	$ .65	$2.00	$4.00
Y-689	Cadell, Elizabeth - ***The Singing Heart*** [1963]	$ .65	$2.00	$4.00
Y-691	Sellers, Naomi John - ***Cross My Heart*** [1963]	$ .65	$2.00	$4.00
F-692	Marsh, Ngaio - ***Death In A White Tie*** [1963] Photo cover.	$1.25	$3.75	$7.50
F-694	Leinster, Murray - ***Operation Terror*** [1963] PBO. Cover by Richard Powers.	$1.35	$4.00	$8.00
Y-695	Creasey, John - ***The Killing Strike*** [1962] Cover by Victor Kalin.	$1.00	$3.00	$6.00
Y-696	Castle, Frank - ***Guns To Sonora*** [1962] PBO. Cover by Jerome Podwil.	$1.00	$3.00	$6.00
Y-699	Brennan, Alice - ***Visiting Nurse*** [1963] PBO.	$ .65	$2.00	$4.00
F-700	Daly, Elizabeth - ***The Book Of The Lion*** [1963] Photo cover.	$1.25	$3.75	$7.50
Y-701	Shelley, John L. - ***The Dying Breed*** [1963]	$1.00	$3.00	$6.00
Y-702	Creasey, John - ***Murder, London-New York*** [1962] Cover by Victor Kalin.	$1.00	$3.00	$6.00
F-703	Marsh, Ngaio - ***Enter A Murderer*** [1962] Photo cover.	$1.25	$3.75	$7.50
F-704	Van Vogt, A. E. - ***Mission To The Stars*** [1962] Cover by Richard Powers.	$1.00	$3.00	$6.00
Y-705	Allison, Clyde - ***Have Nude, Will Travel*** [1962] PBO. Cover by Victor Kalin.	$2.50	$7.50	$15.00
Y-706	Patten, Lewis B. - ***Vengeance Rider*** [1962] PBO.	$1.00	$3.00	$6.00
Y-707	Ives, Ruth - ***Navy Nurse*** [1963] PBO. Cover by Kane.	$ .65	$2.00	$4.00
Y-709	Emery, Anne - ***Married On Wednesday*** [1963] Cover by Harry Bennett.	$ .65	$2.00	$4.00
F-712	Anthology edited by H. L. Gold - ***Beyond*** [1963] PBO. Cover by Richard Powers.	$1.35	$4.00	$8.00
Y-713	Roth, Holly - ***The Mask Of Glass*** [1963] Photo cover.	$ .75	$2.50	$5.00
F-714	Marquand, John P. - ***Thank You, Mr. Moto*** [1963]	$1.25	$3.75	$7.50
S-715	Tey, Josephine - ***The Daughter Of Time*** [1963]	$1.00	$3.00	$6.00
Y-716	Cavanna, Betty - ***The Boy Next Door*** [1963]	$ .65	$2.00	$4.00
Y-718	Adams, Clifton - ***Hogan's Way*** [1963]	$ .75	$2.50	$5.00
Y-719	Gaddis, Peggy - ***Young Doctor Talbot*** [1963]	$ .65	$2.00	$4.00
Y-721	Williams, Jeanne - ***To Buy A Dream*** [1963]	$ .75	$2.50	$5.00
Y-723	MacDonald, Zillah K. - ***Marcia, Private Secretary*** [1963]	$ .65	$2.00	$4.00
F-724	Daly, Elizabeth - ***Somewhere In The House*** [1963] Photo cover.	$1.25	$3.75	$7.50
F-725	Marquand, John P. - ***Think Fast, Mr. Moto*** [1963] Cover by Barye Phillips.	$1.25	$3.75	$7.50
F-726	Marsh, Ngaio - ***Artists In Crime*** [1963] Photo cover.	$1.25	$3.75	$7.50
727	Weil, Jerry - ***All Sorts Of Love*** [1963]	$ .65	$2.00	$4.00
Y-729	Booth, Edwin - ***Hardcase Hotel*** [1963]	$1.00	$3.00	$6.00
F-730	Canning, Victor - ***The House Of The Seven Flies*** [1963]	$1.25	$3.75	$7.50
Y-731	Allen, Elizabeth - ***The In-Between*** [1963]	$ .75	$2.50	$5.00
Y-732	Dorian, Edith - ***The Twisted Shadow*** [1963]	$ .75	$2.50	$5.00
F-733	Edited by Kingsley Amis & Robert Conquest - ***Spectrum*** [1963] Cover by Richard Powers.	$1.25	$3.75	$7.50
F-734	Marsh, Ngaio - ***Overture To Death*** [1963] Photo cover.	$1.25	$3.75	$7.50
F-735	Marric, J. J. - ***Gideon's March*** [1963]	$1.00	$3.00	$6.00
Y-736	De Jong, Dola - ***By Marvelous Agreement*** [1963]	$ .75	$2.50	$5.00
F-737	Marquand, John P. - ***Mr. Moto Is So Sorry*** [1963] Cover by Barye Phillips.	$1.25	$3.75	$7.50
Y-739	Cheshire, Giff - ***Edge Of The Desert*** [1963]	$1.00	$3.00	$6.00
Y-740	Newell, Hope - ***A Cap For Mary Ellis*** [1963]	$ .65	$2.00	$4.00
Y-741	Lawrence, Mildred - ***The Questing Heart*** [1963]	$ .65	$2.00	$4.00
N-742	Edited by Philip Rahv - ***Eight Great American Short Novels*** [1963]	$1.00	$3.00	$6.00
F-743	Anderson, Poul - ***Shield*** [1963] PBO. Cover by Richard Powers.	$1.35	$4.00	$8.00
F-744	Marquand, John P. - ***Last Laugh, Mr. Moto*** [1963]	$1.25	$3.75	$7.50

		G	VG	F
F-745	Daly, Elizabeth - ***Nothing Can Rescue Me*** [1963] Photo cover..	$1.25	$3.75	$7.50
F-746	Canning, Victor - ***The Man From The "Turkish Slave"*** [1963].	$1.25	$3.75	$7.50
X-747	Craciunas, Silviu - ***The Lost Footsteps*** [1963]	$1.00	$3.00	$6.00
F-748	Marsh, Ngaio - ***Death Of A Fool*** [1963]	$1.25	$3.75	$7.50
Y-749	Newton, D. B. - ***Guns Of Warbonnet*** [1963]	$1.00	$3.00	$6.00
Y-752	Vincent, Claire - ***Emergency Room Nurse*** [1963] PBO.	$ .65	$2.00	$4.00
Y-753	Walden, Amelia Elizabeth - ***My Sister Mike*** [1963] Cover by Harry Bennett.	$ .65	$2.00	$4.00
Y-754	Hartwell, Nancy - ***Blue Ribbon Winner*** [1963]	$ .65	$2.00	$4.00
N-755	Edited by Philip Rahv - ***Seven Great British Short Novels*** [1963]	$ .75	$2.50	$5.00
F-756	Marquand, John P. - ***Your Turn, Mr. Moto*** [1963]	$1.25	$3.75	$7.50
F-757	Creasey, John - ***Death Of A Racehorse*** [1963] Cover by Victor Kalin.	$1.25	$3.75	$7.50
F-758	Canning, Victor - ***The Golden Salamander*** [1963] Cover by Barye Phillips.	$1.25	$3.75	$7.50
F-759	Daly, Elizabeth - ***Deadly Nightshade*** [1963] Photo cover.	$1.25	$3.75	$7.50
F-760	Knight, Damon - ***In Deep*** [1963] PBO. Cover by Richard Powers.	$1.35	$4.00	$8.00
Y-762	Appell, George C. - ***The Savage Breed*** [1963]	$1.00	$3.00	$6.00
Y-763	Walden, Amelia Elizabeth - ***A Boy To Remember*** [1963]	$ .75	$2.50	$5.00
Y-764	Cavanna, Betty - ***The Scarlet Sail*** [1963]	$ .65	$2.00	$4.00
Y-765	Turngren, Annette - ***Mystery Walks The Campus*** [1963]	$1.00	$3.00	$6.00
Y-770	Weber, Lenora M. - ***Beany Malone*** [1963]	$ .75	$2.50	$5.00
Y-772	Weber, Lenora M. - ***Leave It To Beany*** [1963]	$1.50	$5.00	$10.00
Y-775	Craig, Margaret Maze - ***Now That I'm Sixteen*** [1963]	$ .65	$2.00	$4.00
F-776	Marquand, John P. - ***The Last Of Mr. Moto*** [1963] Cover by Barye Phillips.	$1.25	$3.75	$7.50
F-777	Marsh, Ngaio - ***Hand In Glove*** [1963] Photo cover.	$1.25	$3.75	$7.50
F-778	Canning, Victor - ***Panther's Moon*** [1963]	$1.25	$3.75	$7.50
F-779	Daly, Elizabeth - ***Death And Letters*** [1963] Photo cover.	$1.25	$3.75	$7.50
F-780	Laumer, Keith - ***A Trace Of Memory*** [1963] PBO. Cover by Richard Powers.	$1.35	$4.00	$8.00
Y-781	Ives, Ruth - ***Congo Nurse*** [1963] PBO.	$ .65	$2.00	$4.00
Y-782	Patten, Lewis B. - ***The Ruthless Range*** [1963] PBO.	$1.00	$3.00	$6.00
Y-784	du Jardin, Rosamond - ***Marcy Catches Up*** [1963]	$ .65	$2.00	$4.00
Y-785	Walden, Amelia Elizabeth - ***Waverly*** [1963] Cover by Harry Bennett	$ .65	$2.00	$4.00
Y-788	McKown, Robin - ***Foreign Service Girl*** [1963]	$ .65	$2.00	$4.00
Y-792	Edited by Page Cooper - ***The Big Book Of Horse Stories*** [1963]	$ .75	$2.50	$5.00
F-798	Doyle, Sir Arthur Conan - ***A Study In Scarlet/The Sign Of Four*** [1963] Cover by William Teason.	$1.25	$3.75	$7.50
F-799	Budrys, Algis - ***Budrys' Inferno*** [1963] PBO. Cover by Richard Powers.	$2.50	$7.50	$15.00
F-800	Marsh, Ngaio - ***Night At The Vulcan*** [1963] Photo cover.	$1.25	$3.75	$7.50
F-801	Daly, Elizabeth - ***The Wrong Way Down*** [1963] Photo cover.	$1.25	$3.75	$7.50
F-802	Canning, Victor - ***The Chasm*** [1963]	$1.25	$3.75	$7.50
Y-803	Clinton, Jeff - ***Wildcat Against The House*** [1963] PBO. Cover by George Gross.	$1.25	$3.75	$7.50
X-808	Conan Doyle, Sir Arthur - ***The Adventures Of Sherlock Holmes*** [1963] Cover by William Teason.	$1.25	$3.75	$7.50
F-809	Creasey, John - ***Give A Man A Gun*** [1963] Cover by Victor Kalin.	$1.00	$3.00	$6.00
F-810	Canning, Victor - ***Bird Of Prey*** [1963]	$1.25	$3.75	$7.50
F-811	Daly, Elizabeth - ***Night Walk*** [1963] Photo cover.	$1.25	$3.75	$7.50
F-812	Van Vogt, A. E. - ***Away And Beyond*** [1963] Cover by Richard Powers.	$1.00	$3.00	$6.00
Y-817	Emery, Anne - ***Dinny Gordon: Freshman*** [1963]	$ .65	$2.00	$4.00
Y-818	Cavanna, Betty - ***Passport To Romance*** [1963]	$ .65	$2.00	$4.00

		G	VG	F
X-819	Doyle, Sir Arthur Conan - ***The Memoirs Of Sherlock Holmes*** [1963] Cover by William Teason.	$1.25	$3.75	$7.50
F-820	Innes, Michael - ***The Crabtree Affair*** [1963] Cover by William Teason.	$1.25	$3.75	$7.50
F-821	Innes, Michael - ***The Long Farewell*** [1963] Cover by William Teason.	$1.25	$3.75	$7.50
F-823	Ballard, J. G. - ***Passport To Eternity*** [1963] PBO. Cover by Richard Powers.	$2.50	$7.50	$15.00
Y-827	Walden, Amelia - ***Where Is My Heart?*** [1963] Cover by Harry Bennett.	$ .65	$2.00	$4.00
Y-828	Emery, Anne - ***Dinny Gordon: Sophomore*** [1963]	$ .65	$2.00	$4.00
X-829	McCarthy, Mary - ***Memories Of A Catholic Girlhood*** [1963]	$ .65	$2.00	$4.00
830	Doyle, Sir Arthur Conan - ***The Return Of Sherlock Holmes*** [1963] Cover by William Teason.	$1.25	$3.75	$7.50
F-831	Upfield, Arthur W. - ***Death Of A Lake*** [1963]	$1.35	$4.00	$8.00
F-832	Upfield, Arthur W. - ***The Bushman Who Came Back*** [1963] Cover by Barye Phillips.	$1.35	$4.00	$8.00
F-833	Innes, Michael - ***A Night Of Errors*** [1963]	$1.25	$3.75	$7.50
F-835	Simak, Clifford D. - ***Strangers In The Universe*** [1963]	$1.00	$3.00	$6.00
Y-838	Lawrence, Mildred - ***Along Comes Spring*** [1963]	$ .65	$2.00	$4.00
Y-839	Ogilvie, Elisabeth - ***Becky's Island*** [1963]	$ .65	$2.00	$4.00
Y-841	Craig, Margaret Maze - ***Trish*** [1963]	$ .65	$2.00	$4.00
Y-845	Weber, Lenora - ***Beany And The Beckoning Road*** [1963]	$ .75	$2.50	$5.00
F-846	Monat, Pawel & Dille, John - ***Spy In The U.S.*** [1963]	$1.00	$3.00	$6.00
F-847	Dickson, Carter - ***The White Priory Murders*** [1963]	$1.25	$3.75	$7.50
F-848	Dickson, Carter - ***The Red Widow Murders*** [1963]	$1.25	$3.75	$7.50
F-849	Innes, Michael - ***Death On A Quiet Day*** [1963] Photo cover.	$1.25	$3.75	$7.50
F-850	Upfield, Arthur W. - ***Murder Must Wait*** [1963]	$1.35	$4.00	$8.00
F-851	Edited by Groff Conklin - ***Science Fiction Omnibus*** [1963] Cover by Richard Powers.	$1.00	$3.00	$6.00
Y-852	Dean, Dudley - ***Cross Of Rope*** [1963] PBO.	$1.00	$3.00	$6.00
Y-855	Emery, Anne - ***Vagabond Summer*** [1963]	$ .65	$2.00	$4.00
Y-856	Tunis, John R. - ***Schoolboy Johnson*** [1963] Cover by Robert Abbett.	$ .65	$2.00	$4.00
F-858	Doyle, Sir Arthur Conan - ***The Hound Of The Baskervilles*** [1963]	$1.25	$3.75	$7.50
F-859	Upfield, Arthur W. - ***Venom House*** [1963] Cover by Barye Phillips.	$1.35	$4.00	$8.00
F-860	Innes, Michael - ***The Case Of The Journeying boy*** [1963] Photo cover.	$1.25	$3.75	$7.50
F-861	Dickson, Carter - ***The Peacock Feather Murders*** [1963]	$1.25	$3.75	$7.50
F-862	Wilhelm, Kate - ***The Mile-Long Spaceship*** [1963] PBO. Cover by Powers.	$1.35	$4.00	$8.00
C-866	Emery, Anne - ***County Fair*** [1963]	$ .65	$2.00	$4.00
R-867	Wellman, Paul I. - ***Death On The Desert*** [1963]	$1.00	$3.00	$6.00
G-868	Jaffee, Al - ***Tall Tales*** [1963] Cover by Al Jaffee. Cartoon book.	$1.35	$4.00	$8.00
F-870	Dickson, Carter - ***The Crossbow Murder*** [1963]	$1.25	$3.75	$7.50
F-872	Coles, Manning - ***Drink To Yesterday*** [1963]	$1.25	$3.75	$7.50
F-873	Coles, Manning - ***A Toast To Tomorrow*** [1963] Photo cover.	$1.25	$3.75	$7.50
F-874	Canning, Victor - ***A Forest Of Eyes*** [1964] Cover by Barye Phillips.	$1.25	$3.75	$7.50
F-875	Edited by John W. Campbell - ***The Astounding Science Fiction Anthology*** [1964] Cover by Richard Powers.	$1.00	$3.00	$6.00
C-878	Tunis, John R. - ***Silence Over Dunkerque*** [1963]	$ .75	$2.50	$5.00
F-879	Dickson, Carter - ***Death In Five Boxes*** [1964]	$1.25	$3.75	$7.50
F-880	Coles, Manning - ***The Fifth Man*** [1964] Photo cover.	$1.25	$3.75	$7.50
F-881	Canning, Victor - ***Burden Of Proof*** [1964]	$1.25	$3.75	$7.50
F-882	Daly, Elizabeth - ***Unexpected Night*** [1964] Photo cover.	$1.25	$3.75	$7.50

		G	VG	F
F-883	Edited by John Carnell - ***Lambda I, And Other Stories*** [1964] PBO. Cover by Richard Powers.	$1.35	$4.00	$8.00
Y-884	Newton, D. B. - ***The Savage Hills*** [1964]	$1.00	$3.00	$6.00
X-885	Himes, Chester - ***If He Hollers Let Him Go*** [1964]	$1.00	$3.00	$6.00
S-888	Kogon, Eugen - ***The Theory And Practice Of Hell*** [1964] Photo cover.	$ .75	$2.50	$5.00
F-889	Canning, Victor - ***A Handful Of Silver*** [1964]	$1.25	$3.75	$7.50
F-890	Doyle, Sir Arthur Conan - ***The Valley Of Fear*** [1964] Cover by William Teason.	$1.25	$3.75	$7.50
F-891	Innes, Michael - ***The Weight Of The Evidence*** [1964]	$1.25	$3.75	$7.50
F-892	Coles, Manning - ***The Basle Express*** [1964] Cover by S. Neil Fujita.	$1.25	$3.75	$7.50
F-893	Van Vogt, A. E. - ***Destination: Universe!*** [1964] Cover by Richard Powers.	$1.00	$3.00	$6.00
X-894	Bridge, Ann - ***The Light Hearted Quest*** [1964]	$ .65	$2.00	$4.00
X-895	Bridge, Ann - ***The Portuguese Escape*** [1964]	$ .65	$2.00	$4.00
Y-896	Ward, Brad - ***The Missourian*** [1964]	$1.00	$3.00	$6.00
F-899	Coles, Manning - ***They Tell No Tales*** [1964] Photo cover.	$1.25	$3.75	$7.50
F-900	Marric, J. J. - ***Gideon's Ride*** [1964]	$1.25	$3.75	$7.50
F-901	Daly, Elizabeth - ***Any Shape Or Form*** [1964] Photo cover.	$1.25	$3.75	$7.50
F-902	Dickson, Carter - ***The Punch And Judy Murders*** [1964]	$1.25	$3.75	$7.50
X-903	Bridge, Ann - ***The Numbered Account*** [1964] Cover by Harry Bennett.	$ .65	$2.00	$4.00
X-904	Young, Desmond - ***Rommel, The Desert Fox*** [1964] Photo cover.	$1.00	$3.00	$6.00
F-905	Vance, Jack - ***The Star King*** [1964] PBO. Cover by Richard Powers.	$2.00	$6.00	$12.00
Y-906	Wells, Lee E. - ***Treachery Pass*** [1964]	$1.00	$3.00	$6.00
C-907	Emery, Anne - ***First Love, True Love*** [1964]	$ .65	$2.00	$4.00
C-908	du Jardin, Rosamond - ***Senior Prom*** [1964]	$ .65	$2.00	$4.00
C-909	Wells, H. G. - ***The Island Of Dr. Moreau*** [1964] Cover by Paul Lehr.	$1.25	$3.75	$7.50
F-912	Doyle, Sir Arthur Conan - ***His Last Bow*** [1964] Cover by William Teason.	$1.25	$3.75	$7.50
F-913	Upfield, Arthur W. - ***The New Shoe*** [1964] Cover by Barye Phillips.	$1.35	$4.00	$8.00
F-914	Canning, Victor - ***A Delivery Of Furies*** [1964]	$1.25	$3.75	$7.50
F-915	Innes, Michael - ***Silence Observed*** [1964]	$1.25	$3.75	$7.50
F-916	Upfield, Arthur W. - ***The Will Of The Tribe*** [1964]	$1.35	$4.00	$8.00
X-917	Bridge, Ann - ***Peking Picnic*** [1964]	$ .65	$2.00	$4.00
F-918	Leinster, Murray - ***The Other Side Of Nowhere*** [1964] PBO. Cover by Richard Powers.	$1.35	$4.00	$8.00
Y-919	Patten, Lewis B. - ***The Killer From Yuma*** [1964] PBO.	$1.00	$3.00	$6.00
C-920	Du Jardin, Rosamond - ***Showboat Summer*** [1964]	$ .65	$2.00	$4.00
C-922	Wells, H. G. - ***The War Of The Worlds*** [1964]	$1.00	$3.00	$6.00
X-923	Durrell, Gerald - ***The Drunken Forests*** [1964] Photo cover.	$ .75	$2.50	$5.00
X-924	Bridge, Ann - ***Illyran Spring*** [1964] Cover by Harry Bennett.	$ .65	$2.00	$4.00
F-925	Innes, Michael - ***The Daffodil Affair*** [1964]	$1.25	$3.75	$7.50
F-926	Coles, Manning - ***Not Negotiable*** [1964]	$1.25	$3.75	$7.50
F-927	Upfield, Arthur W. - ***Sinister Stones*** [1964]	$1.35	$4.00	$8.00
F-928	Ballard, J. G. - ***Terminal Beach*** [1964] PBO. Cover by Richard Powers.	$2.50	$7.50	$15.00
F-929	Carr, John Dickson - ***Death Turns The Tables*** [1964] Cover by Muni.	$1.25	$3.75	$7.50
Y-930	Ketchum, Philip - ***The Stalkers*** [1964]	$1.00	$3.00	$6.00
Y-931	West, Kingsley - ***A Time For Vengeance*** [1964] Cover by Tom Ryan.	$1.00	$3.00	$6.00
C-932	Emery, Anne - ***A Dream To Touch*** [1964] Cover by Harry Bennett.	$ .65	$2.00	$4.00
C-933	Edited by Page Cooper - ***Famous Dog Stories*** [1964]	$ .75	$2.50	$5.00

		G	VG	F
X-940	Orwell, George - ***The Road To Wigan Pier*** [1964]	$ .75	$2.50	$5.00
X-945	Wylie, Philip - ***Finnley Wren*** [1964]	$1.00	$3.00	$6.00
X-946	Doyle, Sir Arthur Conan - ***The Case Book Of Sherlock Holmes*** [1964] Cover by William Teason.	$1.25	$3.75	$7.50
F-947	Innes, Michael - ***Appleby On Ararat*** [1964]	$1.25	$3.75	$7.50
F-948	Dickson, Carter - ***The Unicorn Murders*** [1964]	$1.25	$3.75	$7.50
F-949	Marsh, Ngaio - ***Singing In The Shrouds*** [1964]	$1.25	$3.75	$7.50
F-950	Edited by Kingsley Amis & Robert Conquest - ***Spectrum II*** [1964] Cover by Paul Lehr.	$1.25	$3.75	$7.50
F-951	Edited by John W. Campbell - ***Astounding Tales Of Space And Time*** [1964] Cover by Paul Lehr.	$1.00	$3.00	$6.00
Y-952	Clinton, Jeff - ***Wildcat's Revenge*** [1964]	$1.00	$3.00	$6.00
X-957	Sharp, Margery - ***Cluny Brown*** [1964] Natalie Wood photo cover. Movie tie-in with Natalie Wood.	$ .75	$2.50	$5.00
F-958	Innes, Michael - ***Hare Sitting Up*** [1964]	$1.25	$3.75	$7.50
F-959	Daly, Elizabeth - ***The Book Of The Crime*** [1964] Photo cover.	$1.25	$3.75	$7.50
F-961	Ballard, J. G. - ***The Burning World*** [1964] PBO.	$2.50	$7.50	$15.00
F-962	Newton, D. B. - ***Bullets On The Wind*** [1964]	$1.00	$3.00	$6.00
Y-963	Wayne, Joseph - ***Pistol Johnny*** [1964]	$1.00	$3.00	$6.00
C-964	du Jardin, Rosamond - ***The Real Thing*** [1964]	$ .75	$2.50	$5.00
C-966	Emery, Anne - ***First Orchid For Pat*** [1964] Cover by Harry Bennett.	$ .65	$2.00	$4.00
X-968	Edited by Berton Roueche - ***Curiousities Of Medicine*** [1964]	$ .75	$2.50	$5.00
F-970	Blake, Nicholas - ***The Smiler With The Knife*** [1964]	$1.25	$3.75	$7.50
F-971	Blake, Nicholas - ***The Beast Must Die*** [1964]	$1.25	$3.75	$7.50
F-972	Dickson, Carter - ***The Reader Is Warned*** [1964]	$1.25	$3.75	$7.50
F-973	Marric, J. J. - ***Gideon's Day*** [1964] Cover by Victor Kalin.	$1.25	$3.75	$7.50
F-974	Kapp, Colin - ***Transfinite Man*** [1964] PBO.	$1.35	$4.00	$8.00
F-975	Edited by Groff Conklin - ***The Big Book Of Science Fiction*** [1964]	$1.00	$3.00	$6.00
F-977	Tunis, John R. - ***The Kid From Tomkinsville*** [1964] Cover by Vic Donahue.	$ .75	$2.50	$5.00
F-978	du Jardin, Rosamond - ***Double Wedding*** [1964]	$ .65	$2.00	$4.00
X-981	Manning, Frederic - ***Her Privates We*** [1964]	$ .65	$2.00	$4.00
F-983	Innes, Michael - ***A Comedy Of Terrors*** [1964] Photo cover.	$1.25	$3.75	$7.50
F-984	Coles, Manning - ***With Intent To Deceive*** [1964] Photo cover.	$1.25	$3.75	$7.50
F-985	Blake, Nicholas - ***Head Of A Traveler*** [1964] Photo cover.	$1.25	$3.75	$7.50
F-986	Marsh, Ngaio - ***Scales Of Justice*** [1964]	$1.25	$3.75	$7.50
F-987	Moudy, Walter - ***No Man On Earth*** [1964] PBO. Cover by Richard Powers.	$1.35	$4.00	$8.00
Y-988	Wells, Lee E. - ***Brand Of Evil*** [1964] PBO.	$1.00	$3.00	$6.00
Y-989	Ward, Brad - ***Frontier Street*** [1964]	$1.00	$3.00	$6.00
C-990	Bonham, Frank - ***War Beneath The Sea*** [1964]	$1.00	$3.00	$6.00
991	Dickson, Carter - ***Seeing Is Believing*** [1964]	$1.25	$3.75	$7.50
C-992	Emery, Anne - ***First Love Farewell*** [1964]	$ .65	$2.00	$4.00
C-993	Bunn, Martin - ***Gus Wilson's Model Garage*** [1964]	$ .65	$2.00	$4.00
C-997	Emery, Anne - ***Married On Wednesday*** [1964]	$ .65	$2.00	$4.00
X-998	Bridge, Ann - ***The Dangerous Islands*** [1964] Cover by Harry Bennett.	$ .65	$2.00	$4.00
F-1000	Hunter, Alan - ***Gently In The Sun*** [1964] Cover by Muni.	$ .65	$2.00	$4.00
F-1001	Hunter, Alan - ***Gently Floating*** [1964] Cover by Muni.	$ .65	$2.00	$4.00
F-1003	Vance, Jack - ***The Killing Machine*** [1964] PBO.	$2.00	$6.00	$12.00
Y-1004	Newton, D. B. - ***Fury At Three Forks*** [1964] PBO.	$1.00	$3.00	$6.00
X-1005	Wallant, Edward Lewis - ***The Human Season*** [1964]	$ .75	$2.50	$5.00
Y-1006	MacDonald, William Colt - ***Wildcat Range*** [1964] Cover by Jerome Podwil.	$1.00	$3.00	$6.00
C-1007	Reeder, Colonel Red - ***West Point Plebe*** [1964]	$ .65	$2.00	$4.00
X-1011	Kawabata, Yasunari - ***Snow Country*** [1964]	$1.00	$3.00	$6.00
X-1012	Tanizaki, Junichiro - ***Some Prefer Nettles*** [1964]	$ .75	$2.50	$5.00
X-1013	Mishima, Yukio - ***The Sound Of Waves*** [1964]	$ .75	$2.50	$5.00

		G	VG	F
F-1014	Sharp, Margery - ***Miss Bianca*** [1964] Cover by Garth Williams.	$ .75	$2.50	$5.00
F-1015	Roueche, Berton - ***The Incurable Wound*** [1964]	$ .65	$2.00	$4.00
S-1017	Plievier, Theodor - ***Stalingrad*** [1964]	$ .75	$2.50	$5.00
F-1019	Dickson, Carter - ***And So To Murder*** [1964]	$1.25	$3.75	$7.50
F-1020	Upfield, Arthur W. - ***Winds Of Evil*** [1964]	$1.25	$3.75	$7.50
F-1021	Hunter, Alan - ***Gently Go Man*** [1964] Cover by Muni.	$ .65	$2.00	$4.00
F-1022	Leinster, Murray - ***Invaders Of Space*** [1964] PBO.	$1.35	$4.00	$8.00
C-1024	Tunis, John R. - ***Young Razzle*** [1964]	$ .75	$2.50	$5.00
C-1025	Emery, Anne - ***Hickory Hill*** [1964] Cover by Harry Bennett.	$ .65	$2.00	$4.00
F-1027	Carr, John Dickson - ***The Emperor's Snuff Box*** [1964] Cover by Muni.	$1.25	$3.75	$7.50
F-1028	Clinton, Jeff - ***Fighting Buckaroo*** [1964]	$1.00	$3.00	$6.00
F-1029	Cooke, Kenneth - ***Man On A Raft*** [1965]	$1.00	$3.00	$6.00
F-1030	Innes, Michael - ***The Secret Vanguard*** [1964] Photo cover.	$1.25	$3.75	$7.50
F-1031	Blake, Nicholas - ***The Corpse In The Snowman*** [1964]	$1.25	$3.75	$7.50
F-1032	Kornbluth, C. M. - ***The Syndic*** [1965]	$1.25	$3.75	$7.50
F-1038	Canning, Victor - ***Black Flamingo*** [1965] Cover by Barye Phillips.	$1.25	$3.75	$7.50
F-1040	Hunter, Alan - ***Gently To The Summit*** [1965]	$ .65	$2.00	$4.00
F-1041	Marsh, Ngaio - ***Spinsters In Jeopardy*** [1964]	$1.25	$3.75	$7.50
Y-1042	Castle, Frank - ***King Of The Frontier*** [1965] PBO.	$1.00	$3.00	$6.00
C-1043	O'Connor, Patrick - ***The Black Tiger*** [1965]	$ .75	$2.50	$5.00
F-1047	Anthology - ***A Treasury Of Science Fiction*** [1965]	$1.00	$3.00	$6.00
N-1048	Warren, Robert Penn - ***Night Rider*** [1965]	$1.00	$3.00	$6.00
X-1049	Bridge, Ann - ***A Place To Stand*** [1965]	$ .65	$2.00	$4.00
F-1050	McCutchan, Philip - ***Gibraltar Road*** [1965]	$ .75	$2.50	$5.00
F-1051	McCutchan, Philip - ***Redcap*** [1965]	$ .75	$2.50	$5.00
F-1052	Creasey, John - ***The Blind Spot*** [1965]	$1.00	$3.00	$6.00
F-1053	Edited by Groff Conklin - ***Science Fiction Adventures In Dimension*** [1965]	$1.00	$3.00	$6.00
F-1057	Woodward, David - ***The Tirpitz*** [1965]	$ .75	$2.50	$5.00
F-1058	Sturgeon, Theodore - ***A Touch Of Strange*** [1965]	$1.25	$3.75	$7.50
X-1061	Sartre, Jean-Paul - ***Intimacy*** [1965]	$ .75	$2.50	$5.00
C-1063	Wells, H. G. - ***The Time Machine*** [1965]	$1.00	$3.00	$6.00
C-1065	Tunis, John R. - ***Schoolboy Johnson*** [1965] Cover by Robert Abbett.	$ .75	$2.50	$5.00
S-1066	Fuchs, Daniel - ***Summer In Williamsburg*** [1965]	$ .65	$2.00	$4.00
F-1067	Shearing, Joseph - ***Moss Rose*** [1965] Cover by Harry Bennett.	$1.00	$3.00	$6.00
X-1068	Shearing, Joseph - ***The Crime Of Laura Sarelle*** [1965] Cover by Harry Bennett.	$1.00	$3.00	$6.00
F-1069	McCutchan, Philip - ***Bluebolt One*** [1965]	$1.00	$3.00	$6.00
F-1070	Creasey, John - ***Murder On The Line*** [1965] Covr by Victor Kalin.	$1.00	$3.00	$6.00
F-1071	Ray, Jean - ***Ghouls In My Grave*** [1965] PBO. Cover by Paul Lehr.	$1.35	$4.00	$8.00
C-1073	Felsen, Henry Gregor - ***Davey Logan, Interne*** [1965]	$ .65	$2.00	$4.00
F-1074	Reid, P. R. - ***Escape From Colditz*** [1965]	$ .65	$2.00	$4.00
C-1076	du Jardin, Rosamond - ***Double Date*** [1965]	$ .65	$2.00	$4.00
C-1078	Anthology - ***The Most Dangerous Game*** [1965] Cover by Mel Crair.	$ .65	$2.00	$4.00
C-1079	Waldron, T. J. & Gleeson, James - ***The Frogmen*** [1965]	$ .65	$2.00	$4.00
S-1081	Fuchs, Daniel - ***Homage To Blenholt*** [1965] Photo cover.	$ .75	$2.50	$5.00
X-1082	Kawabata, Yasunari - ***Thousand Cranes*** [1965]	$ .75	$2.50	$5.00
F-1084	Creasey, John - ***Death In Cold Print*** [1965] Cover by Victor Kalin.	$1.00	$3.00	$6.00
F-1085	Canning, Victor - ***The Limbo Line*** [1965]	$1.25	$3.75	$7.50
F-1086	Laumer, Keith - ***A Plague Of Demons*** [1965] PBO. Cover by Richard Powers.	$2.00	$6.00	$12.00
F-1088	Russell, Eric Frank - ***Men, Martians And Machines*** [1965] Cover by Paul Lehr.	$ .75	$2.50	$5.00

		G	VG	F
S-1091	Fuchs, Daniel - ***Low Company*** [1965]	$ .75	$2.50	$5.00
S-1093	Tanizaki, Junichiro - ***Seven Japanese Tales*** [1965]	$1.00	$3.00	$6.00
X-1094	Shearing, Joseph - ***The Spectral Bride*** [1965] Cover by Harry Bennett.	$1.00	$3.00	$6.00
F-1095	Creasey, John - ***The Beauty Queen Killer*** [1965] Cover by Victor Kalin.	$1.00	$3.00	$6.00
F-1096	Edited by Groff Conklin - ***Science-Fiction Adventures In Mutation*** [1965]	$ .75	$2.50	$5.00
F-1098	Cavanna, Betty - ***Diane's New Love*** [1965]	$ .65	$2.00	$4.00
F-1100	Tey, Josephine - ***The Man In The Queue*** [1965] Photo cover.	$1.00	$3.00	$6.00
N-1102	Donleavy, J. P. - ***The Ginger Man*** [1965]	$1.00	$3.00	$6.00
S-1103	Algren, Nelson - ***The Neon Wilderness*** [1965]	$1.00	$3.00	$6.00
S-1104	Abe, Kobo - ***The Woman In The Dunes*** [1965] Movie tie-in.	$ .75	$2.50	$5.00
X-1105	Shearing, Joseph - ***The Spider In The Cup*** [1965] Cover by Harry Bennett.	$1.00	$3.00	$6.00
X-1108	Edited by Kingsley Amis & Robert Conquest - ***Spectrum 3*** [1965] Cover by Paul Lehr.	$1.25	$3.75	$7.50
F-1110	Cavanna, Betty - ***Tou Jours Diane*** [1965]	$ .65	$2.00	$4.00
F-1112	Anderson, Poul - ***The Enemy Stars*** [1965]	$1.00	$3.00	$6.00
F-1114	Weber, Lenora Mattingly - ***Beany Malone*** [1965]	$ .65	$2.00	$4.00
F-1115	Weber, Lenora Mattingly - ***Meet The Malones*** [1965]	$ .75	$2.50	$5.00
F-1116	Weber, Lanora Mattingly - ***Leave It To Beany*** [1965] Cover by Harry Bennett.	$ .65	$2.00	$4.00
F-1117	Cavanna, Betty - ***Passport To Romance*** [1965]	$ .65	$2.00	$4.00
F-1118	Walden, Amelia Elizabeth - ***My Sister Mike*** [1965]	$ .65	$2.00	$4.00
F-1121	Emery, Anne - ***Dinny Gordon: Freshman*** [1965] Cover by Harry Bennett.	$ .65	$2.00	$4.00
F-1122	Gault, William Campbell - ***Drag Strip*** [1965]	$ .65	$2.00	$4.00
S-1123	Powell, Anthony - ***A Question Of Upbringing*** [1965] Cover art by Weller. #1 in "Music of Time" series.	$1.35	$4.00	$8.00
S-1124	Powell, Anthony - ***A Buyer's Market*** [1965] Cover art by Weller. #2 in "Music of Time" series.	$1.35	$4.00	$8.00
S-1126	Powell, Anthony - ***The Acceptance World*** [1965] Cover art by Weller. #3 in "Music of Time" series.	$1.35	$4.00	$8.00
F-1127	McCutchan, Philip - ***Warmaster*** [1965]	$1.00	$3.00	$6.00
F-1128	Stapleton, Olaf - ***Odd John*** [1965] Cover art by Richard Powers.	$1.25	$3.75	$7.50
F-1129	Laumer, Keith - ***The Other Side Of Time*** [1965] PBO. Cover by Jerome Podwil.	$1.35	$4.00	$8.00
F-1130	Carr, John Dickson - ***The Lost Gallows*** [1965] Cover art by Muni.	$1.00	$3.00	$6.00
C-1131	Patten, Lewis B. - ***Flame In The West*** [1965]	$1.00	$3.00	$6.00
F-1132	Bonham, Frank - ***Burma Rifles*** [1965]	$1.00	$3.00	$6.00
S-1133	Collette - ***Claudine At School*** [1965]	$ .65	$2.00	$4.00
S-1134	Donohue, H.E.F. - ***Conversations With Nelson Algren*** [1965]	$ .75	$2.50	$5.00
F-1136	Knight, Damon - ***A For Anything*** [1965] Cover art by Paul Lehr.	$1.25	$3.75	$7.50
F-1138	Tunis, John R. - ***World Series*** [1965]	$ .65	$2.00	$4.00
F-1139	Leinster, Murray - ***The Aliens*** [1965] Cover art by Hoot.	$1.25	$3.75	$7.50
F-1140	Marsh, Ngaio & Jellett, Dr. H. - ***The Nursing-Home Murders*** [1965]	$1.00	$3.00	$6.00
X-1141	Colette - ***Claudine In Paris*** [1965]	$ .65	$2.00	$4.00
S-1142	Powell, Anthony - ***At Lady Molly's*** [1965] Cover art by Weller. #4 in "Music of Time" series.	$1.35	$4.00	$8.00
X-1143	Colette - ***Claudine Married*** [1965]	$ .65	$2.00	$4.00
X-1144	Sharp, Margery - ***The Stone Of Chasity*** [1965]	$1.00	$3.00	$6.00
F-1146	Davidson, Avram - ***Rork!*** [1965] PBO. Cover art by Hoot.	$1.35	$4.00	$8.00
F-1147	Dickson, Gordon - ***Mission To Universe*** [1965] PBO.	$1.35	$4.00	$8.00
F-1153	Tunis, John R. - ***Silence Over Dunkerque*** [1968] Cover art by Robert Abbett.	$ .65	$2.00	$4.00

		G	VG	F
F-1154	Gallico, Paul - ***The Hurricane Story*** [1965]	$ .65	$2.00	$4.00
F-1155	Anthology - ***The Boy's Book Of Great Detective Stories*** [1965] Edited by Howard Haycraft.	$ .65	$2.00	$4.00
S-1156	Powell, Anthony - ***Casanova's Chinese Restaurant*** [1965] Cover art by Weller. #5 in "Music of Time" series.	$1.35	$4.00	$8.00
X-1157	Colette - ***Claudine Annie*** [1965]	$ .65	$2.00	$4.00
F-1158	Innes, Michael - ***Seven Suspects*** [1965] Photo cover.	$1.00	$3.00	$6.00
X-1159	Shearing, Joseph - ***To Bed At Noon*** [1965] PBO. Cover art by Harry Bennett.	$1.00	$3.00	$6.00
F-1160	Knight, Damon - ***Mind Switch*** [1965] PBO. Cover art by Hoot.	$1.35	$4.00	$8.00
F-1162	Doyle, Sir Arthur Conan - ***The Lost World*** [1966]	$1.00	$3.00	$6.00
F-1163	Blish, James - ***Titans' Daughter*** [1966] Cover art by Hoot.	$1.00	$3.00	$6.00
X-1164	Pinto, Oreste - ***Spy Catcher*** [1966]	$ .75	$2.50	$5.00
S-1165	Powell, Anthony - ***The Kindly Ones*** [1966] Cover art by Weller. #6 in "Music of Time" series.	$1.35	$4.00	$8.00
F-1167	Creasey, John - ***Death Of A Postman*** [1966] Cover art by Victor Kalin.	$1.00	$3.00	$6.00
S-1168	Godard, Jean-Luc - ***The Married Woman*** [1965] Photo cover. Movie tie-in with hundreds of photos.	$1.00	$3.00	$6.00
F-1169	Thomas, Theodore L. & Wilhelm, Kate - ***The Clone*** [1965] PBO. Cover art by Hoot.	$1.50	$5.00	$10.00
F-1170	Disch, Thomas M. - ***The Genocides*** [1965] PBO.	$1.50	$5.00	$10.00
S-1171	Powell, Anthony - ***The Valley Of Bones*** [1966] Cover art by Weller. #7 in "Music of Time" series.	$1.35	$4.00	$8.00
C-1172	Newton, D. B. - ***On The Dodge*** [1966]	$ .75	$2.50	$5.00
F-1173	Cavanna, Betty - ***The Boy Next Door*** [1966]	$ .65	$2.00	$4.00
X-1174	Colette - ***Cheri*** [1966] Cover art by James Bama.	$ .65	$2.00	$4.00
F-1176	Creasy, John - ***Night Of The Watchman*** [1966] Cover art by Victor Kalin.	$ .75	$2.50	$5.00
F-1177	Roberts, Keith - ***The Furies*** [1966] PBO. Cover art by Paul Lehr.	$1.35	$4.00	$8.00
C-1178	West, Kingsley - ***Arroyo Hondo*** [1966]	$ .75	$2.50	$5.00
F-1179	Nelson, Marg - ***Mystery At Little Squaw River*** [1966]	$ .75	$2.50	$5.00
S-1180	Flaubert, Gustave - ***Salambo*** [1966]	$1.35	$4.00	$8.00
S-1182	Golding, William - ***Pincher Martin*** [1966]	$ .65	$2.00	$4.00
F-1183	McCutchan, Philip - ***The Man From Moscow*** [1966]	$ .75	$2.50	$5.00
X-1184	Shearing, Joseph - ***The Abode Of Love*** [1966] Cover art by Harry Bennett.	$ .75	$2.50	$5.00
F-1185	Laumer, Keith - ***The Time Bender*** [1966] PBO. Cover by Richard Powers.	$1.50	$5.00	$10.00
F-1186	Harrison, Harry - ***Bill, The Galactic Hero*** [1966]	$1.25	$3.75	$7.50
F-1188	Marsh, Ngaio - ***Vintage Murder*** [1966]	$1.00	$3.00	$6.00
C-1189	Clinton, Jeff - ***Wildcat's Rampage*** [1966]	$ .75	$2.50	$5.00
S-1191	Richards, Frank - ***Old Soldiers Never Die*** [1965]	$ .65	$2.00	$4.00
X-1192	Sharp, Margery - ***The Eye Of Love*** [1966]	$ .65	$2.00	$4.00
F-1193	Marric, J. J. - ***Gideon's Vote*** [1965] Cover art by Victor Kalin.	$ .75	$2.50	$5.00
F-1195	Vogt, A.E. Van - ***The Players of Null-A*** [1966]	$1.00	$3.00	$6.00
C-1196	Adams, Clifton - ***The Hottest Fourth Of July In The History Of Hangtree County*** [1965]	$1.00	$3.00	$6.00
F-1198	Weber, Lenora Mattingly - ***Happy Birthday, Dear Benny*** [1965] Cover art by Harry Bennett.	$ .65	$2.00	$4.00
F-1202	Creasey, John - ***Policeman's Dread*** [1966] Cover art by Victor Kalin.	$1.00	$3.00	$6.00
F-1203	Doyle, Sir Arthur Conan - ***The Poison Belt*** [1966] Cover art by Victor Kalin.	$1.00	$3.00	$6.00
F-1204	Ballard, J. G. - ***The Impossible Man*** [1966] PBO. Cover art by Richard Powers.	$2.50	$7.50	$15.00
X-1205	Innes, Michael - ***The Paper Thunderbolt*** [1966]	$1.00	$3.00	$6.00
F-1206	Gault, William Campbell - ***Thunder Road*** [1966]	$1.00	$3.00	$6.00
C-1207	Castle, Frank - ***Guns To Sonora*** [1966]	$ .75	$2.50	$5.00

		G	VG	F
F-1208	Marsh, Ngaio - ***A Man Lay Dead*** [1966]	$1.00	$3.00	$6.00
S-1211	McCarthy, Mary - ***Memories Of A Catholic Girlhood*** [1966]	$ .65	$2.00	$4.00
F-1221	Cavanna, Betty - ***Love, Laurie*** [1966]	$ .65	$2.00	$4.00
F-1222	Cavanna, Betty - ***6 On Easy Street*** [1966] Cover art by Harry Bennett	$1.00	$3.00	$6.00
F-1226	Dirksen, Joan - ***I'll Find My Love*** [1966] Cover art by David Attie.	$ .65	$2.00	$4.00
F-1229	Walden, Amelia Elizabeth - ***A Boy To Remember*** [1966]	$ .65	$2.00	$4.00
F-1230	Walden, Amelia Elizabeth - ***Waverly*** [1966]	$ .65	$2.00	$4.00
F-1231	Turngren, Annette - ***The Mystery Of Hidden Village*** [1966]	$ .65	$2.00	$4.00
S-1235	Taylor, A.J.P. - ***A History Of The First World War*** [1966] Photo cover	$ .75	$2.50	$5.00
N-1236	Burton, Sir Richard & Arbuthnot, F. F. - ***The Kama Sutra Of Vatsyayana*** [1966] Translation. Photo cover.	$ .65	$2.00	$4.00
F-1238	Braun, M. G. - ***Apostles Of Violence*** [1966]	$ .75	$2.50	$5.00
F-1239	Braun, M. G. - ***Operation Atlantis*** [1966]	$ .75	$2.50	$5.00
X-1240	Laumer, Keith - ***Galactic Diplomat*** [1966] Cover art by Richard Powers.	$1.00	$3.00	$6.00
F-1241	Patten, Lewis, B. - ***Prodigal Gunfighter*** [1966]	$ .75	$2.50	$5.00
F-1242	Cavanna, Betty - ***Accent On April*** [1970] Cover art by Harry Bennett	$ .65	$2.00	$4.00
F-1243	Ballard, J. G. - ***The Voices Of Time*** [1966] Cover by Richard Powers.	$1.00	$3.00	$6.00
X-1244	Bridge, Ann - ***Emergency In The Pyrenees*** [1966]	$ .65	$2.00	$4.00
F-1245	Creasey, John - ***The Scene Of The Crime*** [1966] Cover art by Victor Kalin	$1.00	$3.00	$6.00
F-1246	Marric, J. J. - ***Gideon's Lot*** [1966] Cover art by Victor Kalin	$1.00	$3.00	$6.00
F-1247	Braun, M. G. - ***That Girl From Istanbul*** [1966]	$1.00	$3.00	$6.00
F-1248	Farmer, Philip Jose - ***Night Of Light*** [1966] PBO. Cover art by Paul Lehr.	$2.00	$6.00	$12.00
F-1249	Herbert, Frank - ***Destination: Void*** [1966] PBO. Cover by Hoot.	$1.50	$5.00	$10.00
F-1250	Clinton, Jeff - ***Wildcat Takes His Medicine*** [1966]	$ .75	$2.50	$5.00
S-1254	Orwell, George - ***Down And Out In Paris And London*** [1966].	$ .65	$2.00	$4.00
F-1255	Wells, H. G. - ***The War Of The Worlds*** [1966]	$ .75	$2.50	$5.00
F-1256	Wells, H. G. - ***The Invisible Man*** [1966]	$ .75	$2.50	$5.00
S-1257	Roueche, Berton - ***Eleven Blue Men*** [1966]	$ .65	$2.00	$4.00
S-1258	Nabokov, Vladimir - ***Lolita*** [1966]	$ .75	$2.50	$5.00
S-1259	Roueche, Berton - ***A Man Named Hoffman*** [1966]	$ .65	$2.00	$4.00
X-1260	McCoy, J. J. - ***How To Live With A Dog*** [1966]	$ .65	$2.00	$4.00
F-1261	Himes, Chester - ***The Crazy Kill*** [1966] Cover art by Harry Bennett	$1.00	$3.00	$6.00
F-1262	Himes, Chester - ***The Real Cool Killers*** [1966] Cover by Harry Bennett	$1.00	$3.00	$6.00
F-1263	Leinster, Murray - ***Checkpoint Lambda*** [1966] PBO. Cover art by Richard Powers.	$1.35	$4.00	$8.00
F-1264	Turner, William O. - ***Ride The Vengeance Trail*** [1966]	$ .75	$2.50	$5.00
F-1265	O'Connor, Patrick - ***Mexican Road Race*** [1966]	$ .65	$2.00	$4.00
F-1266	Ballard, J. G. - ***The Drowned World*** [1966]	$1.00	$3.00	$6.00
F-1269	McCutchan, Philip - ***The Dead Line*** [1966] Cover art by Robert McGinnis	$ .75	$2.50	$5.00
F-1270	Himes, Chester - ***The Big Gold Dream*** [1966]	$1.00	$3.00	$6.00
F-1271	Dickson, Carter - ***Nine—And Death Makes Ten*** [1966] Cover art by Muni	$1.00	$3.00	$6.00
S-1272	Anthology - ***Spectrum 4*** [1966] Anthology edited by Amis & Conquest.	$1.25	$3.75	$7.50
F-1273	Laumer, Keith - ***Catastrophe Planet*** [1966] PBO.	$2.00	$6.00	$12.00
F-1274	Elston, Allan Vaughan - ***The Lawless Border*** [1966]	$ .75	$2.50	$5.00
F-1275	Cavanna, Betty - ***A Time For Tenderness*** [1966]	$ .65	$2.00	$4.00

		G	VG	F
F-1276	Fader, Daniel N. & Shaevitz, Morton H. - ***Hooked On Books*** [1966] PBO. Photo cover.	$1.25	$3.75	$7.50
N-1277	Edited by Solomon, David - ***LSD: The Consciouness-Expanding Drug*** [1966]	$1.00	$3.00	$6.00
S-1278	Frieden, Seymour & Richardson, William - ***The Fatal Decisions*** [1966] Photo cover.	$ .75	$2.50	$5.00
F-1280	Creasey, John - ***Hang The Little Man*** [1966] Cover art by Victor Kalin.	$1.00	$3.00	$6.00
F-1282	Dickson, Carter - ***Seeing Is Believing*** [1966]	$1.00	$3.00	$6.00
F-1283	Herbert, Frank - ***The Eyes Of Heisenberg*** [1966] PBO.	$1.25	$3.75	$7.50
F-1284	Anderson, Paul - ***Trader To The Stars*** [1966]	$1.00	$3.00	$6.00
F-1285	Newton, D. B. - ***The Manhunters*** [1966]	$1.00	$3.00	$6.00
F-1287	Braun, M. G. - ***Operation Jealousy*** [1966]	$1.00	$3.00	$6.00
F-1290	Dickson, Carter - ***The Gilded Man*** [1966]	$1.00	$3.00	$6.00
F-1291	Edited by Knight, Damon - ***Orbit I*** [1966] PBO. Cover by Richard Powers.	$1.35	$4.00	$8.00
F-1292	Vogt, Van A.E. - ***Rogue Ship*** [1966]	$1.00	$3.00	$6.00
F-1293	Whitman, S. E. - ***Change Of Command*** [1966]	$ .75	$2.50	$5.00
F-1294	Booth, Edwin - ***Trouble At Tragedy Springs*** [1966]	$ .75	$2.50	$5.00
F-1295	Weber, Lenora Mattingly - ***Beany Has A Secret Life*** [1966]	$ .65	$2.00	$4.00
F-1297	O'Connor, Patrick - ***The Black Tiger*** [1966]	$ .65	$2.00	$4.00
F-1299	Bonham, Frank - ***War Beneath The Sea*** [1966]	$ .75	$2.50	$5.00
S-1300	Roueche, Berton - ***The Incurable Wound*** [1966]	$ .50	$1.50	$3.00
F-1309	Creasey, John - ***Look Three Ways At Murder*** [1966] Cover art by Victor Kalin	$ .75	$2.50	$5.00
F-1310	Dickson, Carter - ***She Died A Lady*** [1966]	$1.00	$3.00	$6.00
S-1311	Edited by Conklin, Groff - ***Science Fiction Oddities*** [1966]	$1.00	$3.00	$6.00
X-1312	Simak, Clifford D. - ***All Flesh Is Grass*** [1966] Photo cover.	$1.25	$3.75	$7.50
F-1313	Clinton, Jeff - ***Wanted: Wildcat O'Shea*** [1966] PBO.	$ .75	$2.50	$5.00
F-1314	Wells, Lee E. - ***The Devil's Range*** [1966]	$ .75	$2.50	$5.00
S-1315	Household, Geoffrey - ***The Spanish Cave*** [1966]	$1.00	$3.00	$6.00
F-1316	Hale, Nancy - ***A New England Girlhood*** [1966] Cover art by Harry Bennett.	$ .65	$2.00	$4.00
F-1319	Edited by Schwartz, Harry - ***The Many Faces Of Communism*** [1966]	$ .65	$2.00	$4.00
N-1320	White, T. H. - ***The Once And Future King*** [1966] Movie tie-in.	$ .75	$2.50	$5.00
F-1323	Cavanna, Betty - ***A Date For Diane*** [1966]	$ .50	$1.50	$3.00
F-1324	Sire, Glen & Jane - ***Something Foolish, Something Gay*** [1966] Cover art by Kelly Freas.	$ .65	$2.00	$4.00
F-1328	Harkins, Philip - ***The Day Of The Drag Race*** [1966]	$ .50	$1.50	$3.00
F-1330	Wehen, Joy Deweese - ***The Golden Hill Mystery*** [1966]	$ .75	$2.50	$5.00
F-1331	Cleary, Beverly - ***Leave It To Beaver*** [1966] Photo cover. TV tie-in.	$1.25	$3.75	$7.50
F-1332	Cleary, Beverly - ***Here's Beaver*** [1966] TV tie-in.	$1.25	$3.75	$7.50
F-1333	Cleary, Beverly - ***Beaver And Wally*** [1966] TV tie-in.	$1.25	$3.75	$7.50
X-1338	Fish, Robert L. - ***The Diamond Bubble*** [1966] Photo cover.	$ .75	$2.50	$5.00
X-1339	Dickson, Carter - ***He Wouldn't Kill Patience*** [1966] Cover art by Muni.	$1.00	$3.00	$6.00
X-1340	Laumer, Keith - ***The Monitors*** [1966] PBO. Cover art by Richard Powers.	$2.00	$6.00	$12.00
X-1341	Davidson, Avram - ***The Enemy Of My Enemy*** [1966] PBO. Cover art by Richard Powers.	$1.50	$5.00	$10.00
F-1342	Cort, Van - ***Journey Of The Gun*** [1966] PBO.	$1.00	$3.00	$6.00
F-1343	McCaig, Robert J. - ***The Gotherson Spread*** [1966]	$ .75	$2.50	$5.00
F-1344	Walden, Amelia Elizabeth - ***Daystar*** [1966]	$ .65	$2.00	$4.00
S-1346	Foley, Charles - ***Commando Extrodinary*** [1967] Photo cover.	$ .65	$2.00	$4.00
X-1347	Dickson, Carter - ***The Curse Of The Bronze Lamp*** [1967]	$ .75	$2.50	$5.00
X-1348	Fish, Robert L. - ***Brazilian Sleigh Ride*** [1967]	$ .65	$2.00	$4.00
X-1349	Disch, Thomas M. - ***Echo Round His Bones*** [1967] PBO.	$2.00	$6.00	$12.00

		G	VG	F
X-1350	Sellings, Arthur - ***The Quy Effect*** [1967] PBO. Cover art by Richard Powers.	$1.00	$3.00	$6.00
F-1351	Newton, D. B. - ***Hideout Valley*** [1966]	$ .75	$2.50	$5.00
F-1352	Wells, Lee E. - ***Nine Must Die*** [1967]	$ .75	$2.50	$5.00
F-1353	Walden, Amelia Elizabeth - ***I Found My Love*** [1967] Photo cover.	$ .65	$2.00	$4.00
S-1354	Fuller, John G. - ***Incident At Exeter*** [1967]	$ .65	$2.00	$4.00
F-1359	Anthology - ***The Boy's Second Book Of Great Detective Stories*** [1967] Edited by Howard Haycraft.	$ .75	$2.50	$5.00
F-1361	Wells, H. G. - ***The Time Machine*** [1967]	$ .65	$2.00	$4.00
F-1362	Weber, Lenora Mattingly - ***Don't Call Me Katie Rose*** [1967]	$ .50	$1.50	$3.00
F-1363	Wells, H. G. - ***The Island Of Dr. Moreau*** [1967]	$ .65	$2.00	$4.00
X-1369	Creasey, John - ***Murder, London-Australia*** [1967] Cover art by Victor Kalin.	$1.00	$3.00	$6.00
X-1370	Francis, Dick - ***Odds Against*** [1967]	$1.00	$3.00	$6.00
X-1372	Dick, Philip K. - ***Counter-Clock World*** [1967] PBO. Cover art by Hoot.	$1.35	$4.00	$8.00
F-1373	Ellston, Allan Vaughan - ***Montana Passage*** [1967]	$1.35	$4.00	$8.00
F-1374	Gaulden, Ray - ***Glory Gulch*** [1967]	$3.50	$10.00	$20.00
S-1376	Veeck, Bill & Linn, Ed - ***The Hustler's Handbook*** [1967]	$ .75	$2.50	$5.00
X-1377	McCutchan, Philip - ***Moscow Coach*** [1967]	$ .75	$2.50	$5.00
X-1379	Sellings, Arthur - ***The Uncensored Man*** [1967] PBO. Cover art by Hoot.	$ .75	$2.50	$5.00
X-1380	Ballard, J. G. - ***The Crystal World*** [1967]	$ .75	$2.50	$5.00
F-1381	Newton, D. B. - ***The Tabbart Brand*** [1967]	$ .75	$2.50	$5.00
F-1382	Clinton, Jeff - ***Wildcat On The Loose*** [1967]	$ .75	$2.50	$5.00
F-1385	Turngren, Annette - ***Mystery Walks The Campus*** [1967]	$ .75	$2.50	$5.00
F-1386	Harkins, Philip - ***Young Skin Diver*** [1967]	$ .75	$2.50	$5.00
S-1388	Bridge, Ann - ***Enchanter's Nightshade*** [1967]	$ .75	$2.50	$5.00
X-1389	Mark, Ted - ***The Square Root Of Sex*** [1967] PBO. Cover by Stanley Borack.	$ .65	$2.00	$4.00
X-1390	Zetterling, Mai - ***Night Games*** [1967] Photo cover. Movie tie-in.	$ .65	$2.00	$4.00
X-1391	Armstrong, Charlotte - ***The Unsuspected*** [1967]	$ .75	$2.50	$5.00
X-1392	Orvis, Kenneth - ***Night Without Darkness*** [1967]	$1.00	$3.00	$6.00
X-1393	Biggle, Lloyd, Jr. - ***The Fury Out Of Time*** [1967]	$1.00	$3.00	$6.00
X-1394	Raphael, Rick - ***Code Three*** [1967] Cover by Jerome Podwil.	$ .65	$2.00	$4.00
F-1395	Hunter, John - ***The Man From Yuma*** [1967]	$ .75	$2.50	$5.00
F-1396	Patten, Lewis B. - ***The Arrogant Guns*** [1967]	$ .75	$2.50	$5.00
F-1397	Cavanna, Betty - ***Almost Like Sisters*** [1967]	$ .50	$1.50	$3.00
F-1398	Wells, H. G. - ***The First Men In The Moon*** [1967]	$ .50	$1.50	$3.00
S-1400	Bridge, Ann - ***Four-Part Setting*** [1967] Cover by Harry Bennett.	$ .50	$1.50	$3.00
X-1401	Gardner, Alan - ***Six Day Week*** [1967]	$ .50	$1.50	$3.00
X-1403	Vogt, A.E. Van & Hull, E. Mayne - ***The Winged Man*** [1967] Cover art by Hoot.	$ .75	$2.50	$5.00
S-1404	Capek, Karel - ***War With The Newts*** [1967] Cover art by Jerome Podwil.	$ .75	$2.50	$5.00
F-1405	Booth, Edwin - ***Triple Cross Trail*** [1967] PBO.	$ .75	$2.50	$5.00
F-1406	Thompson, Gene - ***Ambush In Abilene*** [1967]	$ .75	$2.50	$5.00
X-1407	Wells, H. G. - ***The Food Of The Gods*** [1967]	$ .50	$1.50	$3.00
X-1408	Sternberg, Jacques - ***Sexualis '95*** [1967] Photo cover.	$ .65	$2.00	$4.00
F-1409	Lewiton, Mina - ***The Divided Heart*** [1967] Cover art by Jerome Podwil.	$ .50	$1.50	$3.00
F-1410	Garforth, John - ***"The Floating Game"*** [1967] PBO. Photo cover. TV tie-in. Avengers #1.	$1.25	$3.75	$7.50
F-1411	Garforth, John - ***"The Laugh Was On Lazarus"*** [1967] PBO. Photo cover. TV tie-in. Avengers #2.	$1.25	$3.75	$7.50
S-1413	Bridge, Ann - ***Frontier Passage*** [1967] Cover by Harry Bennett.	$ .50	$1.50	$3.00

		G	VG	F
X-1414	Anthology - ***Horror Times Ten*** [1967] Anthology edited by Alden H. Norton.	$1.00	$3.00	$6.00
X-1415	Innes, Michael - ***The Bloody Wood*** [1967]	$ .75	$2.50	$5.00
X-1416	Harrison, Harry - ***Make Room! Make Room!*** [1967]	$1.00	$3.00	$6.00
X-1417	Anderson, Poul - ***The Trouble Twisters*** [1967] Cover art by Richard Powers.	$1.00	$3.00	$6.00
F-1418	Booth, Edwin - ***Shoot-Out At Twin Buttes*** [1967]	$ .75	$2.50	$5.00
F-1419	Martin, Gil - ***Trail Of The Damned*** [1967]	$ .75	$2.50	$5.00
F-1420	Walden, Amelia Elizabeth - ***How Bright The Dawn*** [1967] Cover art by Jerome Podwil.	$ .50	$1.50	$3.00
S-1421	Bridge, Ann - ***The Ginger Griffin*** [1967]	$ .50	$1.50	$3.00
S-1422	Crawford, Stanley - ***Gascoyne*** [1967]	$ .50	$1.50	$3.00
X-1424	Pike, Robert L. - ***Police Blotter*** [1967] Cover art by Victor Kalin.	$ .65	$2.00	$4.00
S-1426	Anthology - ***Tomorrow, The Stars*** [1967] Anthology edited by Robert A. Heinlein.	$ .75	$2.50	$5.00
X-1427	Laumer, Keith - ***Retief's War*** [1967] Cover art by Richard Powers.	$ .75	$2.50	$5.00
F-1428	Young, Carter Travis - ***The Savage Plain*** [1967]	$ .75	$2.50	$5.00
F-1429	Stark, Joshua - ***The Lockhart Breed*** [1967]	$ .75	$2.50	$5.00
F-1431	Garforth, John - ***The Passing Of Gloria Mundy*** [1967] PBO. Photo cover. TV tie-in. Avengers #3	$1.25	$3.75	$7.50
F-1432	Bennett, Dwight - ***The Oregon Rifles*** [1967]	$ .75	$2.50	$5.00
S-1433	Anonymous, M. D. - ***The Healers*** [1967]	$ .65	$2.00	$4.00
N-1434	Waltari, Mika - ***The Roman*** [1967]	$ .65	$2.00	$4.00
S-1435	Raven, Simon - ***Doctors Wear Scarlet*** [1967] Photo cover.	$ .65	$2.00	$4.00
X-1436	Pike, Robert L. - ***The Quarry*** [1967] Cover art by Victor Kalin.	$ .75	$2.50	$5.00
S-1437	Anthology - ***The Pseudo-People*** [1967] Edited by William F. Nolan. Cover art by Hoot.	$1.00	$3.00	$6.00
X-1438	Coleman, James Nelson - ***Seeker From The Stars*** [1967] PBO. Cover art by Richard Powers	$1.25	$3.75	$7.50
F-1439	Turner, William D. - ***Blood Dance*** [1967]	$ .75	$2.50	$5.00
X-1440	Wells, H. G. - ***In The Days Of The Comet*** [1967]	$ .50	$1.50	$3.00
X-1441	Marsh, Ngaio - ***Killer Dolphin*** [1967]	$ .75	$2.50	$5.00
S-1444	Raven, Simon - ***Brother Cain*** [1967]	$ .75	$2.50	$5.00
F-1445	Garforth, John - ***Heil Harris!*** [1967] PBO. Photo cover. TV tie-in. Avengers #4.	$1.25	$3.75	$7.50
X-1446	Creasey, John - ***The Case Of The Innocent Victims*** [1967] Cover art by Victor Kalin.	$ .75	$2.50	$5.00
X-1447	Laumer, Keith - ***Galactic Odyssey*** [1967] PBO. Cover art by Richard Powers.	$2.00	$6.00	$12.00
S-1448	Anthology - ***Orbit II*** [1967] Edited by Damon Knight. Cover art by Paul Lehr.	$1.25	$3.75	$7.50
F-1449	Bennett, Dwight - ***Rebel Trail*** [1967]	$ .75	$2.50	$5.00
F-1450	Patten, Lewis B. - ***Ambush Creek*** [1967]	$ .75	$2.50	$5.00
X-1451	Anthology - ***Spectrum 2*** [1967] Edited by Amis & Conquest.	$ .75	$2.50	$5.00
X-1453	Bark, Conrad Voss - ***The Shepherd File*** [1967] Photo cover.	$ .65	$2.00	$4.00
X-1454	Vance, Jack - ***The Palace Of Love*** [1967] PBO.	$2.00	$6.00	$12.00
X-1455	Jones, D. F. - ***Colossus*** [1967]	$1.00	$3.00	$6.00
F-1456	Martin, Gil - ***McCord*** [1967]	$ .75	$2.50	$5.00
F-1457	Gaulden, Ray - ***The Lawless Land*** [1967]	$ .75	$2.50	$5.00
X-1462	Hitchens, Dolores - ***Postscript To Nightmare*** [1967]	$1.00	$3.00	$6.00
S-1463	Simak, Clifford D. - ***The Werewolf Principle*** [1968] Cover art by Richard Powers.	$1.00	$3.00	$6.00
S-1464	Denis, Armand - ***Taboo*** [1968] Photo cover.	$ .75	$2.50	$5.00
S-1465	Hodder, Williams - ***The Higher They Fly*** [1967]	$ .50	$1.50	$3.00
X-1467	Dickson, Carter - ***My Late Wives*** [1967] Cover art by Muni.	$ .75	$2.50	$5.00
X-1468	Creasey, John - ***Murder, London-South Africa*** [1967] Cover art by Victor Kalin.	$ .75	$2.50	$5.00
X-1469	Cooper, Edmund - ***All Fools Day*** [1967]	$ .75	$2.50	$5.00

		G	VG	F
X-1470	Platt, Charles - ***Garbage World*** [1967] PBO.	$1.50	$5.00	$10.00
F-1471	Bennett, Dwight - ***Crooked River Canyon*** [1967]	$ .75	$2.50	$5.00
F-1472	Lott, Milton - ***Backtrack*** [1967]	$ .75	$2.50	$5.00
S-1477	Bridge, Ann - ***The Episode At Toledo*** [1967]	$ .50	$1.50	$3.00
X-1479	Dickson, Carter - ***The Skeleton In The Clock*** [1967] Cover art by Muni.	$ .75	$2.50	$5.00
F-1480	Cavanna, Betty - ***Angel On Skis*** [1967] Photo cover.	$ .50	$1.50	$3.00
F-1481	Cavanna, Betty - ***Fancy Free*** [1967]	$ .50	$1.50	$3.00
N-1485	Plievier, Theodor - ***Stalingrad*** [1967]	$ .65	$2.00	$4.00
N-1487	Falk, Stanley L. - ***Decision At Leyte*** [1967] Photo cover.	$ .65	$2.00	$4.00
X-1490	Anthology - ***Astounding S-F Anthology*** [1967] edited by J. W. Campbell, Jr. Cover art by Paul Lehr.	$ .75	$2.50	$5.00
X-1491	Daventry, Leonard - ***A Man Of Double Deed*** [1967] Cover by Richard Powers.	$ .75	$2.50	$5.00
F-1492	Booth, Edwin - ***No Spurs For Johnny Loop*** [1967]	$ .75	$2.50	$5.00
F-1493	Elston, Allan Vaughan - ***Montana Manhunt*** [1967]	$ .75	$2.50	$5.00
F-1495	Clarke, Arthur C. - ***Dolphin Island*** [1968]	$ .50	$1.50	$3.00
X-1496	Mark, Ted - ***I Was A Teeny-Bopper For The CIA*** [1967] PBO.	$1.00	$3.00	$6.00
X-1497	Anthology - ***Masters Of Horror*** [1967]	$1.00	$3.00	$6.00
S-1498	Marsh, Ngaio - ***Final Curtain*** [1967]	$ .75	$2.50	$5.00
S-1499	Jenkins, Geoffrey - ***Hunter Killer*** [1968] Cover art by Foster.	$ .75	$2.50	$5.00
S-1500	Reeman, Douglas - ***Dive In The Sun*** [1968]	$ .50	$1.50	$3.00
X-1502	Dickson, Carter - ***A Graveyard To Let*** [1968] Cover art by Muri.	$ .75	$2.50	$5.00
X-1503	Brown, Rosel George - ***Galactic Sibyl Sue Blue*** [1968] Cover art by Hoot.	$1.00	$3.00	$6.00
F-1504	Wells, Lee E. - ***Incident At Warbow*** [1968]	$ .75	$2.50	$5.00
F-1505	Clinton, Jeff - ***Watch Out For Wildcat*** [1968] PBO.	$ .75	$2.50	$5.00
X-1506	Hoyle, Fred - ***Ossian's Ride*** [1968]	$ .75	$2.50	$5.00
F-1507	Kantor, MacKinlay - ***The Voice Of Bugle Ann*** [1968]	$ .50	$1.50	$3.00
S-1508	Fader & McNeil - ***Hooked On Books: Program & Proof*** [1968]	$ .75	$2.50	$5.00
S-1509	Burton, Sir Richard - ***The Erotic Traveler*** [1968]	$ .65	$2.00	$4.00
X-1510	Mark, Ted - ***Back Home At The O.R.G.Y.*** [1968] PBO.	$1.00	$3.00	$6.00
X-1511	Fish, Robert L. - ***Always Kill A Stranger*** [1968]	$ .75	$2.50	$5.00
X-1513	Anthology - ***The Best Stories From New Worlds*** [1968] edited by Michael Moorcock. Cover by Paul Lehr.	$ .75	$2.50	$5.00
X-1514	Laumer, Keith - ***Greylorn*** [1968] PBO.	$2.00	$6.00	$12.00
S-1517	Cramer, Polly - ***Polly's Homemaking Pointers*** [1968] Photo cover.	$ .50	$1.50	$3.00
F-1519	Gault, William Campbell - ***Speedway Challenge*** [1968]	$ .65	$2.00	$4.00
S-1523	Meyerhoff, Arthur E. - ***The Strategy Of Persuasion*** [1968]	$ .50	$1.50	$3.00
N-1524	Fitzgibbon, Constantine - ***20 July*** [1968] 4 pages of photos.	$ .50	$1.50	$3.00
X-1526	McCutchan, Philip - ***Skyprobe*** [1968]	$ .65	$2.00	$4.00
X-1527	Dewey, Thomas B. - ***Death And Taxes*** [1968]	$1.00	$3.00	$6.00
X-1528	Lafferty, R. A. - ***The Reefs Of Earth*** [1968] PBO. Cover art by Richard Powers.	$1.00	$3.00	$6.00
S-1529	Anthology - ***Best Science Fiction: 1967*** [1968] Edited by Brian W. Aldiss.	$1.00	$3.00	$6.00
F-1532	Queen, Ellery - ***The Brown Fox Mystery*** [1968]	$ .75	$2.50	$5.00
F-1533	Queen, Ellery - ***The Blue Herring Mystery*** [1968]	$ .75	$2.50	$5.00
F-1534	Queen, Ellery - ***The White Elephant Mystery*** [1968]	$ .75	$2.50	$5.00
S-1535	Orwell, George - ***The Road To Wigan Pier*** [1968]	$ .50	$1.50	$3.00
F-1537	Anthology - ***The Most Dangerous Game*** [1968] Cover art by Mel Crair.	$ .50	$1.50	$3.00
X-1542	Francis, Dick - ***For Kicks*** [1968]	$1.35	$4.00	$8.00
X-1543	Vogt, A. E. Van - ***Slan*** [1968]	$ .75	$2.50	$5.00
X-1544	Laumer, Keith & Brown, R. G. - ***Earthblood*** [1968]	$1.00	$3.00	$6.00
F-1545	Cavanna, Betty - ***Mystery At Love's Creek*** [1968] Cover art by Harry Bennett.	$ .50	$1.50	$3.00

		G	VG	F
X-1547	Laumer, Keith - ***"The Afrit Affair"*** [1968] PBO. Photo cover. TV tie-in. Avengers #5.	$1.25	$3.75	$7.50
N-1548	Alliluyev, Anna & Sergel - ***The Alliluyev Memoirs*** [1968] Photo cover. 8 pages of photos	$ .75	$2.50	$5.00
N-1550	Valensin, Georges, Dr. - ***The French Art Of Sexual Love*** [1968]	$ .50	$1.50	$3.00
N-1555	Kantor, MacKinlay - ***Long Remember*** [1968]	$ .50	$1.50	$3.00
X-1558	Anthology - ***Lie Ten Nights Awake*** [1968] edited by Herbert Van Thai	$1.00	$3.00	$6.00
S-1560	Heinlein, Robert A. - ***Starship Troopers*** [1968] Cover art by Paul Lehr.	$1.00	$3.00	$6.00
S-1561	Anthology - ***Elsewhere And Elsewhere*** [1968] PBO. edited by Groff Conklin.	$1.00	$3.00	$6.00
S-1564	Mark, Ted - ***Come Be My O.R.G.Y.*** [1968] PBO. Cover by Stanley Borack.	$1.00	$3.00	$6.00
X-1565	Laumer, Keith - ***"The Drowned Queen"*** [1968] PBO. Photo cover. TV tie-in. Avengers #6.	$1.25	$3.75	$7.50
X-1566	Francis, Dick - ***Flying Finish*** [1968]	$1.35	$4.00	$8.00
S-1567	Anthology - ***Science Fiction: Author's Choice 1*** [1968] edited by Harry Harrison.	$1.00	$3.00	$6.00
N-1571	Heinlein, Robert A. - ***Stranger In A Strange Land*** [1968]	$1.00	$3.00	$6.00
N-1572	Donleavy, J. P. - ***The Ginger Man*** [1968]	$ .75	$2.50	$5.00
X-1573	Carr, John Dickson - ***Death Turns The Tables*** [1968] Photo cover.	$ .75	$2.50	$5.00
X-1575	Doyle, Sir Arthur Conan - ***A Study In Scarlet & The Sign Of Four*** [1968] Cover art by William Teason.	$ .75	$2.50	$5.00
X-1576	Doyle, Sir Arthur Conan - ***His Last Bow*** [1968] Cover by Teason.	$ .75	$2.50	$5.00
F-1577	Cavanna, Betty - ***The Scarlet Sail*** [1968] Cover by Bennett.	$ .50	$1.50	$3.00
N-1580	Nabokov, Vladimir - ***Pale Fire*** [1968]	$ .65	$2.00	$4.00
X-1581	Sellers, Naomi Sellers - ***Cross My Heart*** [1968]	$ .50	$1.50	$3.00
F-1582	Emery, Anne - ***Married On Wednesday*** [1968] Cover by Harry Bennett	$ .50	$1.50	$3.00
N-1584	Accoce, Pierre & Quet, Pierre - ***A Man Called Lucy*** [1968] Four pages of photos	$ .65	$2.00	$4.00
X-1585	James, Leigh - ***The Chameleon File*** [1968]	$ .50	$1.50	$3.00
X-1586	Watson, Colin - ***Lonelyheart 4122*** [1968]	$ .50	$1.50	$3.00
X-1588	Laumer, Keith & Dickson, Gordon - ***Planet Run*** [1968] Cover by Lehr.	$ .75	$2.50	$5.00
X-1589	Smiak, Clifford D. - ***Strangers In The Universe*** [1968]	$ .75	$2.50	$5.00
S-1590	Freedman, Benedict & Nancy - ***Mrs. Mike*** [1968]	$ .50	$1.50	$3.00
X-1592	Laumer, Keith - ***"The Gold Bomb"*** [1968] PBO. Photo cover. TV tie-in. Avengers #7.	$1.25	$3.75	$7.50
X-1593	Hitchens, Delores - ***Sleep With Strangers*** [1968]	$ .75	$2.50	$5.00
X-1594	Pickering, R. E. - ***The Uncommitted Man*** [1968]	$ .75	$2.50	$5.00
S-1595	Anthology - ***Spectrum 5*** [1968] edited by Kingsley Amis & Robert Conquest. Cover by Lehr.	$ .75	$2.50	$5.00
X-1596	Laumer, Keith - ***Assignment in Nowhere*** [1968] Cover by Powers.	$1.50	$5.00	$10.00
N-1599	Nabokov, Vladimir - ***Lolita*** [1968]	$ .65	$2.00	$4.00
N-1601	Heinlein, Robert A. - ***The Moon Is A Harsh Mistress*** [1968]	$1.00	$3.00	$6.00
S-1602	Garrett, Eileen J. - ***Telepathy*** [1968]	$ .75	$2.50	$5.00
X-1605	Mair, George B. - ***Miss Turquoise*** [1968] Photo cover	$ .50	$1.50	$3.00
X-1606	Creasy, John - ***The Dissemblers*** [1968]	$ .65	$2.00	$4.00
X-1607	Cooper, Edmund - ***A Far Sunset*** [1968] Cover by Powers.	$ .65	$2.00	$4.00
S-1608	Knight, Damon - ***Editor - Orbit 3*** [1968]	$ .75	$2.50	$5.00
N-1610	Tapsell, R. F. - ***The Year Of The Horsetails*** [1968]	$ .65	$2.00	$4.00
X-1613	Creasey, John - ***The Depths*** [1968]	$ .65	$2.00	$4.00
X-1614	Mair, George B. - ***The Girl From Peking*** [1968]	$ .65	$2.00	$4.00

		G	VG	F
S-1615	Herbert, Frank - ***The Santaroga Barrier*** [1968] PBO. Cover by Lehr.	$ .75	$2.50	$5.00
X-1616	Wallace, Ian - ***Croyd*** [1968]	$ .50	$1.50	$3.00
S-1619	Toms, Bernard - ***The Strange Affair*** [1968] Movie tie-in.	$ .75	$2.50	$5.00
S-1623	Mark, Ted - ***The Square Root Of Sex*** [1968]	$ .50	$1.50	$3.00
S-1624	Harburg, E. Y. and Saidy, Fred - ***Finian's Rainbow*** [1968] Movie tie-in with Fred Astaire. Four pages of photos.	$ .75	$2.50	$5.00
S-1625	Mark, Ted - ***The Pussycat Transplant*** [1968] PBO. Cover by Borack.	$1.00	$3.00	$6.00
S-1626	Doyle, Sir Arthur Conan - ***The Edge Of The Unknown*** [1968] Photo cover.	$ .75	$2.50	$5.00
X-1627	Creasey, John - ***The Inferno*** [1968]	$ .75	$2.50	$5.00
X-1629	Mair, George B. - ***Live, Love And Cry*** [1968] Photo cover.	$ .65	$2.00	$4.00
X-1630	Harness, Charles L. - ***The Ring Of Ritornel*** [1968] PBO. Cover art by Lehr.	$1.35	$4.00	$8.00
F-1632	Daniels, Norman - ***The Kono Diamond*** [1969] PBO. Photo cover.	$ .75	$2.50	$5.00
X-1633	Conklin, Groff - editor - ***Possible Worlds Of Science Fiction*** [1968]	$ .75	$2.50	$5.00
S-1636	Garrett, Eileen J. - ***The Sense And Nonsense Of Prophecy*** [1968] Photo cover.	$ .50	$1.50	$3.00
X-1637	Daniels, Norman - ***"The Magnetic Man"*** [1968] PBO. Photo cover. TV tie-in. Avengers #8.	$1.25	$3.75	$7.50
X-1638	Mair, George B. - ***Kisses From Satan*** [1968]	$ .75	$2.50	$5.00
X-1639	Creasey, John - ***The Terror*** [1968]	$ .75	$2.50	$5.00
X-1640	Harrison, Harry - ***The Technicolor Time Machine*** [1968] Cover by Kossin.	$1.00	$3.00	$6.00
X-1641	Laumer, Keith - ***It's A Mad, Mad, Mad Galaxy*** [1968] PBO. Cover by Powers.	$1.50	$5.00	$10.00
X-1644	Gaulden, Ray - ***5 Card Stud*** [1968] Movie tie-in with Robert Mitchum and Dean Martin. Cover by Peter Caras.	$ .75	$2.50	$5.00
N-1646	Grant, Joan - ***Winged Pharaoh*** [1968]	$ .50	$1.50	$3.00
X-1647	Blake, Nichols - ***End Of Chapter*** [1968]	$ .75	$2.50	$5.00
X-1648	Harness, Charles L. - ***The Rose*** [1969] PBO.	$1.00	$3.00	$6.00
S-1653	Fast, Julius - ***The Beatles - The Real Story*** [1969] 16 pages of photos.	$3.00	$9.00	$18.00
S-1654	Leasor, James - ***The Yang Meridian*** [1968]	$ .50	$1.50	$3.00
X-1657	Hitchens, Dolores - ***Sleep With Slander*** [1969]	$ .65	$2.00	$4.00
X-1658	Daniels, Norman - ***Moon Express*** [1968] PBO. Photo cover. TV tie-in. Avengers #9.	$1.25	$3.75	$7.50
X-1659	Laumer, Keith - ***Nine By Laumer*** [1969] Cover by Richard Powers.	$ .75	$2.50	$5.00
X-1660	Coleman, James Nelson - ***The Null-Frequency Impulser*** [1969] PBO.	$ .65	$2.00	$4.00
S-1663	Kawabata, Yasunari - ***Snow Country*** [1968]	$ .65	$2.00	$4.00
S-1665	Dewey, Thomas B. - ***The King Killers*** [1968] Photo cover.	$1.00	$3.00	$6.00
X-1666	Garforth, John - ***The Floating Game*** [1968] Photo cover. TV tie-in. Avengers #1.	$ .75	$2.50	$5.00
X-1667	Garforth, John - ***"The Laugh Was On Lazarus"*** [1968] Photo cover. TV tie-in. Avengers #2.	$ .75	$2.50	$5.00
X-1668	Garforth, John - ***"The Passing Of Gloria Munday"*** [1968] Photo cover. TV tie-in. Avengers #3.	$ .75	$2.50	$5.00
X-1669	Garforth, John - ***"Heil Harris!"*** [1968] Photo cover. TV tie-in. Avengers #4.	$ .75	$2.50	$5.00
S-1671	Simak, Clifford D. - ***The Goblin Reservation*** [1968] Cover art by Powers.	$ .75	$2.50	$5.00
X-1673	Hitchens, Delores - ***The Watcher*** [1968]	$ .75	$2.50	$5.00
X-1674	Anthology - ***Hauntings And Horrors: Ten Grisly Tales*** [1968] Edited by Alden H. Norton.	$1.00	$3.00	$6.00
S-1675	Boyd, John - ***The Last Starship From Earth*** [1968]	$ .75	$2.50	$5.00

		G	VG	F
X-1676	Anthology - ***The Best SF Stories From New Worlds #2*** [1968] Edited by Michael Moorcock.	$1.00	$3.00	$6.00
X-1680	Anthology - ***Astounding Tales Of Space And Time*** [1968] edited by John W. Campbell, Jr. Cover by Paul Lehr.	$ .50	$1.50	$3.00
X-1681	Grierson, Edward - ***A Crime Of One's Own*** [1968]	$ .75	$2.50	$5.00
N-1682	Inglis, Brian - ***The Case For Unorthodox Medicine*** [1968]	$ .65	$2.00	$4.00
S-1683	Mark, Ted - ***The Nude For Hire*** [1968]	$ .65	$2.00	$4.00
S-1684	MacKenzie, Donald - ***Salute From A Dead Man*** [1969] Cover art by Peter Caras.	$ .75	$2.50	$5.00
X-1685	Fish, Robert L. - ***The Bridge That Went Nowhere*** [1969]	$ .50	$1.50	$3.00
N-1686	Ellison, Harlan - editor - ***Dangerous Visions #1*** [1969]	$3.50	$10.00	$20.00
X-1687	Alban, Antony - ***Catharsis Central*** [1969] PBO. Cover by Paul Lehr.	$1.00	$3.00	$6.00
D-1691	Valensin, Georges Dr. - ***Sex From A To Z*** [1969]	$ .50	$1.50	$3.00
X-1692	Petaja, Emil - ***The Nets Of Space*** [1969] PBO. Cover art by Paul Lehr.	$1.25	$3.75	$7.50
X-1693	Mair, George B. - ***Black Champagne*** [1969]	$ .75	$2.50	$5.00
X-1694	MacKenzie, Donald - ***The Quiet Killer*** [1969]	$ .75	$2.50	$5.00
X-1695	McCutchan, Philip - ***The Screaming Dead Balloons*** [1969]	$ .75	$2.50	$5.00
X-1696	Cooper, Edmund - ***News From Elsewhere*** [1969] Cover art by Kelly Freas.	$1.00	$3.00	$6.00
S-1698	Marsh, Ngaio - ***Death And The Dancing Footman*** [1969] Photo cover.	$ .75	$2.50	$5.00
N-1700	Chapman, M.D., A. H. - ***Put-Offs And Come-Ons*** [1969]	$ .50	$1.50	$3.00
X-1701	Watson, Colin - ***Coffin Scarcely Used*** [1969]	$ .75	$2.50	$5.00
X-1703	Saxon, Peter - ***The Killing Bone*** [1969] PBO. Cover art by Jeff Jones.	$1.35	$4.00	$8.00
N-1704	Ellison, Harlan - editor - ***Dangerous Visions #2*** [1969]	$3.50	$10.00	$20.00
X-1705	Dick, Philip K. - ***Galactic Pot-Healer*** [1969] PBO.	$4.00	$12.50	$25.00
X-1706	Knight, Damon - ***Three Novels*** [1969]	$ .75	$2.50	$5.00
S-1708	Christian, Tina Chad - ***Baby Love*** [1969] PBO. Movie tie-in.	$ .65	$2.00	$4.00
S-1709	Carr, John Dickson - ***Most Secret*** [1969] Photo cover.	$ .75	$2.50	$5.00
X-1713	Saxon, Peter - ***Dark Ways To Death*** [1969] PBO. Cover art by Jeff Jones.	$1.35	$4.00	$8.00
N-1714	Ellison, Harlan - editor - ***Dangerous Visions #3*** [1969]	$3.50	$10.00	$20.00
S-1715	Dickson, Gordon R. - ***Spacepaw*** [1969] Cover art by Paul Lehr.	$ .75	$2.50	$5.00
X-1716	Siodmak, Curt - ***Donovan's Brain*** [1969]	$ .75	$2.50	$5.00
F-1717	Ashford, Jeffrey - ***Grand Prix Monaco*** [1969] Cover art by Sharpe.	$ .50	$1.50	$3.00
X-1719	London, Jack & Fish, Robert L. - ***The Assassination Bureau Ltd.*** [1969] Movie tie-in.	$ .65	$2.00	$4.00
X-1723	Curtis, Wade (Jerry Pournelle) - ***Red Heroin*** [1969] PBO.	$2.00	$6.00	$12.00
S-1724	Anthology - ***Orbit 4*** [1969] edited by Damon Knight. Cover art by Paul Lehr.	$1.00	$3.00	$6.00
X-1725	Harrison, Harry - ***Captive Universe*** [1969] Cover art by Paul Lehr.	$ .75	$2.50	$5.00
S-1726	Woodhouse, Martin - ***Bush Baby*** [1969] Cover art by Peter Caras.	$ .75	$2.50	$5.00
X-1727	Saxon, Peter - ***The Haunting Of Alan Mais*** [1969] PBO. Cover art by Jeff Jones.	$1.35	$4.00	$8.00
X-1728	Booth, Edwin - ***Stranger In Buffalo Springs*** [1969] Cover art by Jim Sharpe.	$ .75	$2.50	$5.00
X-1730	McCutchan, Philip - ***Gibraltar Road*** [1969]	$ .65	$2.00	$4.00
X-1731	McCutchan, Philip - ***Redcap*** [1969] Cover art by Peter Caras.	$ .65	$2.00	$4.00
X-1732	McCutchan, Philip - ***Bluebolt One*** [1969]	$ .65	$2.00	$4.00
X-1733	Arrighi, Mel - ***Freak-Out*** [1969]	$ .75	$2.50	$5.00
X-1734	Hogan, Robert J. - ***The Bat Staffel*** [1969] Cover by James Steranko. G8 #1.	$1.25	$3.75	$7.50
X-1735B	Scott, R.T.M. - ***The Wheel Of Death*** [1969] PBO. The Spider #2. No #; given free with purchase of the Spider #1.	$1.25	$3.75	$7.50

		G	VG	F
X-1735A	Scott, R.T.M. - ***The Spider Strikes!*** [1969] PBO. The Spider #1.	$1.25	$3.75	$7.50
S-1736	Mark, Ted - ***Here's Your O.R.G.Y.!*** [1971] Cover by Stanley Borack.	$1.00	$3.00	$6.00
N-1737	Kent, Alexander - ***To Glory We Steer*** [1969]	$ .50	$1.50	$3.00
X-1738	Innes, Michael - ***Death By Water*** [1969]	$ .75	$2.50	$5.00
X-1739	James, Leigh - ***The Capitol Hill Affair*** [1969] Cover art by Peter Caras.	$ .50	$1.50	$3.00
X-1741	Page, Norvell W. - ***Flame Winds*** [1969] PBO. Cover art by Jeff Jones.	$1.50	$5.00	$10.00
S-1742	Anthology - ***Best Science Fiction: 1968*** [1968] Edited by Brian W. Aldiss.	$ .75	$2.50	$5.00
X-1743	Garnett, Dav - ***Mirror In The Sky*** [1969] PBO. Cover art by Richard Powers.	$ .75	$2.50	$5.00
X-1746	Hogan, Robert L. - ***Purple Aces*** [1969] PBO. Cover by James Steranko. G8 #2.	$1.25	$3.75	$7.50
X-1747	York, Andrew - ***The Predator*** [1969]	$ .75	$2.50	$5.00
X-1749	Moorcock, Michael - ***The Ice Schooner*** [1969] PBO. Cover by Kossin.	$1.25	$3.75	$7.50
X-1750	Vinge, Vernor - ***Grimm's World*** [1969] PBO. Cover art by Paul Lehr.	$1.25	$3.75	$7.50
X-1751	Williamson, Jack - ***Darker Than You Think*** [1969] Cover art by Jeff Jones.	$ .75	$2.50	$5.00
S-1753	Mark, Ted - ***I Was A Teeny-Booper For The CIA*** [1969] Cover by Stanley Borack.	$1.00	$3.00	$6.00
Z-1756	Heinlein, Robert A. - ***Stranger In A Strange Land*** [1969]	$ .65	$2.00	$4.00
S-1758	Anthology - ***The New Roget's Thesaurus In Dictionary Form*** [1969] edited by Norman Lewis.	$ .65	$2.00	$4.00
N-1760	Killen, John - ***A History Of The Luftwaffe*** [1969] Photo cover. 8 pages of photos.	$ .75	$2.50	$5.00
X-1764	Hogan, Robert J. - ***Ace Of The White Death*** [1969] PBO. Cover art by James Steranko. G8 #3.	$1.25	$3.75	$7.50
X-1765	Mather, Berkley - ***A Spy For A Spy*** [1969] Cover art by Peter Caras.	$ .75	$2.50	$5.00
S-1767	Wallace, Ian - ***Dr. Orpheus*** [1969] Cover art by Paul Lehr	$ .75	$2.50	$5.00
X-1768	Cooper, Edmund - ***Five To Twelve*** [1969] Cover art by Jeff Jones.	$1.35	$4.00	$8.00
X-1769	Page, Norvell W. - ***Sons Of The Bear-God*** [1969] PBO. cover art by Jeff Jones.	$1.35	$4.00	$8.00
N-1772	Chapman, M.D., A. H. - ***The Strategy Of Sex*** [1969]	$ .50	$1.50	$3.00
X-1775	Sangster, Jimmy - ***Foreign Exchange*** [1969]	$ .65	$2.00	$4.00
X-1776	Watson, Colin - ***Hopjoy Was Here*** [1969] Photo cover.	$1.00	$3.00	$6.00
X-1777	Carter, Lin - ***Thongor And The Wizard Of Lemuria*** [1969] Cover art by Jeff Jones.	$1.35	$4.00	$8.00
S-1778	Anthology - ***Orbit 5*** [1969] edited by Damon Knight. Cover art by Paul Lehr.	$1.00	$3.00	$6.00
X-1779	Wells, Robert - ***The Parasaurians*** [1969]	$ .75	$2.50	$5.00
X-1782	Stockbridge, Grant - ***Wings Of The Black Death*** [1969] PBO. Cover art by Peter Caras. The Spider #3.	$1.25	$3.75	$7.50
S-1786	White, Stewart Edward & Harwood - ***Across The Unknown*** [1969]	$ .50	$1.50	$3.00
S-1788	Francis, Dick - ***Nerve*** [1969]	$1.35	$4.00	$8.00
S-1789	Sangster, Jimmy - ***Touchfeather*** [1969]	$ .65	$2.00	$4.00
S-1791	Heinlein, Robert A. - ***Podkayne Of Mars*** [1970]	$1.25	$3.75	$7.50
X-1792	Gaulden, Ray - ***Rage At Red Butte*** [1971]	$1.25	$3.75	$7.50
X-1795	Stockbridge, Grant - ***City Of Flaming Shadows*** [1970] PBO. Cover art by Peter Caras. The Spider #4.	$1.25	$3.75	$7.50
S-1797	Meade, Richard - ***The Danube Runs Red*** [1970] Cover art by Peter Caras.	$ .65	$2.00	$4.00
X-1798	Innes, Michael - ***Picture Of Guilt*** [1970]	$ .50	$1.50	$3.00

		G	VG	F
X-1799	Carter, Lin - ***Thongor And The Dragon City*** [1970] Cover art by Jeff Jones.	$1.35	$4.00	$8.00
X-1800	Laumer, Keith - ***Retief And The Warlords*** [1970] Cover by Richard Powers.	$1.00	$3.00	$6.00
X-1801	Sellings, Arthur - ***The Power Of X*** [1970] PBO. Cover by Paul Lehr.	$1.25	$3.75	$7.50
S-1802	Vogt, A. E. Van - ***The World Of Null-A*** [1970]	$ .50	$1.50	$3.00
S-1807	Francis, Dick - ***Forfeit*** [1970]	$1.35	$4.00	$8.00
X-1808	Saxon, Peter - ***The Vampires Of Finistere*** [1970] PBO. Cover art by Jeff Jones.	$1.35	$4.00	$8.00
N-1809	Heinlein, Robert A. - ***Glory Road*** [1970]	$ .65	$2.00	$4.00
S-1810	Laumer, Keith - ***The Long Twilight*** [1970] Cover art by Paul Lehr.	$ .65	$2.00	$4.00
S-1811	Hubbard, L. Ron - ***Fear And The Ultimate Adventure*** [1970] PBO. Cover by Paul Lehr.	$1.50	$5.00	$10.00
S-1816	Marsh, Ngaio - ***Clutch Of Constables*** [1970] Photo cover.	$ .75	$2.50	$5.00
S-1817	Fish, Robert L. - ***The Xavier Affair*** [1970]	$ .65	$2.00	$4.00
N-1819	Anthology - ***Apeman, Spaceman*** [1970] edited by Leon E. Slover & Harry Harrison. Cover art by Paul Lehr.	$1.00	$3.00	$6.00
S-1820	Moorcock, Michael - ***The Twilight Man*** [1970] PBO.	$1.25	$3.75	$7.50
X-1821	Stark, Joshua - ***Keno*** [1970]	$ .65	$2.00	$4.00
X-1826	Doyle, Sir Arthur Conan - ***The Lost World*** [1970]	$ .50	$1.50	$3.00
X-1827	Doyle, Sir Arthur Conan - ***The Poison Belt*** [1969]	$ .50	$1.50	$3.00
S-1828	Anthology - ***Horror Stories #3*** [1970] edited by Herbert Van Thal.	$1.00	$3.00	$6.00
S-1829	Laumer, Keith - ***Retief: Ambassador To Space*** [1969]	$ .65	$2.00	$4.00
N-1830	Sturgeon, Theodore - ***A Touch Of Strange*** [1970]	$ .65	$2.00	$4.00
N-1831	Kent, Alexander - ***Form Line Of Battle!*** [1970]	$ .50	$1.50	$3.00
Z-1832	Waltari, Mika - ***The Roman*** [1970]	$ .50	$1.50	$3.00
Z-1833	Glass, Justine - ***They Foresaw The Future*** [1970]	$ .50	$1.50	$3.00
S-1834	Mather, Berkely - ***The Gold Of Malabar*** [1970] Cover art by Peter Caras.	$ .65	$2.00	$4.00
S-1835	Armstrong, Charlotte - ***The Case Of The Weird Sisters*** [1970]	$ .65	$2.00	$4.00
X-1836	Reagon, Thomas B. - ***The Caper*** [1970]	$ .65	$2.00	$4.00
S-1837	Anthology - ***SF: Author's Choice 2*** [1970] PBO. Edited by Harry Harrison.	$1.25	$3.75	$7.50
S-1840	Jones, Dennis Feltham - ***Colossus*** [1970] Cover art by Mont Kunstler.	$ .65	$2.00	$4.00
S-1841	Edgley, Leslie - ***A Dirty Business*** [1970] Photo cover.	$ .65	$2.00	$4.00
S-1843	Garner, William - ***The Us Or Them War*** [1970]	$ .65	$2.00	$4.00
S-1844	Armstrong, Charlotte - ***The Better To Eat You*** [1970]	$ .75	$2.50	$5.00
S-1845	Fish, Robert L. - ***The Fugitive*** [1970]	$ .75	$2.50	$5.00
S-1846	Zelazny, Roger - ***Damnation Alley*** [1970] Cover art by Paul Lehr.	$1.00	$3.00	$6.00
N-1847	Herbert, Frank - ***Dune Messiah*** [1970]	$1.00	$3.00	$6.00
S-1848	Anthology - ***Orbit 6*** [1970] edited by Damon Knight. Cover art by Paul Lehr.	$1.00	$3.00	$6.00
S-1850	Blackburn, John - ***Children Of The Night*** [1970]	$ .65	$2.00	$4.00
N-1855	Greer, Rebecca - ***Why Isn't A Nice Girl Like You Married?*** [1970]	$ .50	$1.50	$3.00
S-1856	Lathen, Emma - ***When In Greece*** [1970]	$ .50	$1.50	$3.00
S-1857	Harrison, Harry - ***Prime Number*** [1970] PBO. Cover art by Paul Lehr.	$1.35	$4.00	$8.00
X-1861	Carter, Lin - ***Thongor Fights The Pirates Of Tarakus*** [1970] PBO. Cover art by Jeff Jones.	$1.35	$4.00	$8.00
X-1862	Anderson, Paul - ***Shield*** [1970]	$ .75	$2.50	$5.00
S-1864	Herbert, Frank - ***Destinatin: Void*** [1971]	$ .75	$2.50	$5.00
S-1865	Herbert, Frank - ***The Eyes Of Heisenberg*** [1970] Cover art by Paul Lehr.	$ .75	$2.50	$5.00
Z-1866	Rosebury, Theodor - ***Life On Man*** [1970]	$ .50	$1.50	$3.00

		G	VG	F
S-1868	Mark, Ted - ***The Nude Who Did*** [1970]	$ .65	$2.00	$4.00
S-1869	Arden, William - ***A Dark Power*** [1970]	$ .50	$1.50	$3.00
S-1870	Moorcock, Michael - ***The Singing Citadel*** [1970] Cover art by G. Burwen.	$ .75	$2.50	$5.00
S-1871	Laumer, Keith - ***Time Trap*** [1970] Cover art by Richard Powers.	$ .75	$2.50	$5.00
S-1872	Collins, Michael - ***The Planets Of Death*** [1970]	$ .50	$1.50	$3.00
S-1873	Tey, Josephine - ***The Man In The Queue*** [1970]	$ .50	$1.50	$3.00
N-1875	Graham, Winston - ***Rose Poldark*** [1970] Cover art by Mort Kunstler.	$ .50	$1.50	$3.00
Z-1877	Waltari, Mika - ***The Egyptian*** [1970]	$ .50	$1.50	$3.00
S-1879	Simak, Clifford D. - ***Out Of Their Minds*** [1970] Cover art by Herbert Norton Rogoff.	$ .75	$2.50	$5.00
S-1880	Harrison, Harry - ***The Daleth Effect*** [1970] Cover art by Kelly Freas.	$ .75	$2.50	$5.00
S-1882	Crawford, Robert - ***The Shroud Society*** [1970]	$ .50	$1.50	$3.00
S-1883	York, Andrew - ***The Deviator*** [1970] Cover art by Peter Caras.	$ .65	$2.00	$4.00
X-1884	Wells, Lee E. - ***The Tall Texan*** [1970]	$ .65	$2.00	$4.00
N-1886	Roueche, Berton - ***What's Left*** [1970]	$ .50	$1.50	$3.00
N-1887	Graham, Winston - ***Demelza*** [1970] Cover art by Mort Kunstler.	$ .50	$1.50	$3.00
S-1890	Carr, John Dickson - ***The Problem Of The Green Capsule*** [1970] Photo cover.	$ .65	$2.00	$4.00
S-1891	Arden, William - ***Deal In Violence*** [1970]	$ .65	$2.00	$4.00
S-1892	Rathbone, Julian - ***With My Knives I Know I'm Good*** [1970]	$ .50	$1.50	$3.00
S-1893	DeCamp, L. Sprague - ***The Wheels Of It*** [1970] Cover art by Paul Lehr.	$ .65	$2.00	$4.00
S-1894	Smith, Cordwainer - ***You Will Never Be The Same*** [1970]	$1.25	$3.75	$7.50
S-1895	Laumer, Keith - ***The World Shuffler*** [1970] Cover art by Richard Powers.	$ .75	$2.50	$5.00
X-1897	Patten, Lewis B. - ***The Killer From Yuma*** [1970]	$ .50	$1.50	$3.00
N-1899	Kawabata, Yasunari - ***Thousand Cranes*** [1970]	$ .50	$1.50	$3.00
S-1900	Anthology - ***Orbit 7*** [1970] edited by Damon Knight. Cover art by Paul Lehr.	$1.00	$3.00	$6.00
N-1903	Graham, Winston - ***Jeremy Poldark*** [1970] Cover art by Mort Kunstler.	$ .50	$1.50	$3.00
Z-1905	Martin, Jay - ***Digging The Love Goddess*** [1970] PBO. Cover by Robert McGinnis.	$ .75	$2.50	$5.00
S-1906	Masur, Harold Q. - ***The Big Money*** [1970]	$ .65	$2.00	$4.00
S-1907	Anthology - ***The Problem Of The Wire Cage*** [1970] Photo cover.	$ .65	$2.00	$4.00
S-1908	Heinlein, Robert A. - ***Orphans Of The Sky*** [1970]	$ .75	$2.50	$5.00
S-1909	Herbert, Frank - ***Whipping Star*** [1970]	$ .75	$2.50	$5.00
S-1910	Van Thal, Herbert - editor - ***Horror Stories #4*** [1970]	$ .75	$2.50	$5.00
X-1911	Elston, Allan Vaughan - ***The Big Pasture*** [1970]	$ .75	$2.50	$5.00
S-1912	Van Vogt, A. E. - ***Destination: Universe*** [1970]	$ .65	$2.00	$4.00
S-1913	Marsh, Ngaio - ***A Man Lay Dead*** [1970]	$ .65	$2.00	$4.00
S-1914	Clarke, Arthur C. - ***Dolphin Island*** [1970]	$ .50	$1.50	$3.00
Z-1915	Fast, Julius - ***The New Sexual Fulfillment*** [1972] PBO. Photo cover.	$ .50	$1.50	$3.00
N-1917	Carr, Donald E. - ***The Breath Of Life*** [1970]	$ .50	$1.50	$3.00
N-1918	Graham, Winston - ***The Last Gamble*** [1970] Cover art by Mort Kunstler.	$ .50	$1.50	$3.00
S-1920	Lyall, Gavin - ***Venus With Pistol*** [1970]	$ .65	$2.00	$4.00
S-1921	Masur, Harold Q. - ***Tall, Dark And Deadly*** [1970]	$ .65	$2.00	$4.00
S-1922	Blish, James - ***The Star Dwellers*** [1970]	$ .65	$2.00	$4.00
S-1923	Anthology - ***Twenty Years Of The Magazine Of Fantasy And Science Fiction*** [1970] Cover by Mel Hunter.	$ .65	$2.00	$4.00
S-1924	Wallace, Ian - ***Deathstar Voyage*** [1970]	$ .65	$2.00	$4.00

		G	VG	F
S-1925	Anthology - ***Horror Stories #5*** [1970] Edited by Herbert Van Thal. Cover art by Valla.	$1.00	$3.00	$6.00
X-1926	West, Kingsley - ***A Time For Vengeance*** [1970]	$ .75	$2.50	$5.00
S-1927	Tey, Josephine - ***The Daughter Of Time*** [1970] Photo cover.	$ .50	$1.50	$3.00
X-1928	Eyerly, Jeanette - ***The Girl Inside*** [1970]	$ .50	$1.50	$3.00
S-1930	Vogt, A. E. Van - ***Slan*** [1972]	$ .50	$1.50	$3.00
S-1933	Armstrong, Charlotte - ***The Chocolate Cobweb*** [1970] Cover art by Harry Bennett.	$ .50	$1.50	$3.00
S-1940	Herron, Shaun - ***Miro*** [1970]	$ .50	$1.50	$3.00
S-1942	Anthology - ***The 3rd Fontana Book Of Great Horror Stories*** [1971] edited by Christine Bernard.	$1.00	$3.00	$6.00
S-1943	Anthology - ***Best Sf Stories From New Worlds #4*** [1971] edited by Michael Morrcock. Cover art by Paul Lehr.	$1.00	$3.00	$6.00
S-1944	Anthology - ***Warlocks And Warriors*** [1971] edited by L. Sprague de Camp.	$1.00	$3.00	$6.00
S-1946	Vogt, A. E. Van & Hull, E. Mayne - ***The Winged Man*** [1971]	$ .65	$2.00	$4.00
Z-1949	Cherio - ***You And Your Hand*** [1971]	$ .50	$1.50	$3.00
S-1952	Morris, John - ***Fever Grass*** [1971]	$ .50	$1.50	$3.00
S-1953	Blackburn, John - ***Bury Him Darkly*** [1971]	$ .65	$2.00	$4.00
N-1954	Furst, Jeffrey - ***Arranged - Edgar Cayce's Story Of Jesus*** [1971]	$1.00	$3.00	$6.00
S-1955	Moorcock, Michael - ***The Time Dweller*** [1971] Cover art by Paul Lehr.	$ .65	$2.00	$4.00
S-1956	Garnett, Dav - ***The Starseekers*** [1971] PBO. Cover by Paul Lehr.	$ .65	$2.00	$4.00
S-1957	Dickson, Gordon - ***Hour Of The Horde*** [1971]	$ .65	$2.00	$4.00
S-1962	Tey, Josephine - ***The Franchise Affair*** [1971] Photo cover.	$ .65	$2.00	$4.00
S-1969	Crawford, Robert - ***Pay As You Die*** [1971]	$ .65	$2.00	$4.00
S-1970	Anthology - ***Orbit 8*** [1971] edited by Damon Knight. Cover art by Paul Lehr.	$1.00	$3.00	$6.00
S-1971	Moorcock, Michael - ***The Knight Of The Swords*** [1971] PBO. Cover art by David McCall Johnson.	$1.25	$3.75	$7.50
S-1973	Vogt, A. E. Van - ***Mission To The Stars*** [1971] Cover art by Hinge.	$ .65	$2.00	$4.00
N-1974	Tanizaki, Junichiro - ***Diary Of A Mad Old Man*** [1971]	$ .50	$1.50	$3.00
X-1976	Leiber, Fritz - ***Gather, Darkness!*** [1971]	$ .65	$2.00	$4.00
S-1979	Carr, John Dickson - ***Till Death Do Us Part*** [1971] Photo cover.	$ .65	$2.00	$4.00
S-1980	Ballard, J. G. - ***Vermillion Sands*** [1971] PBO. Cover art by Richard Powers.	$2.50	$7.50	$15.00
Z-1981	Heinlein, Robert A. - ***Farmham's Freehold*** [1971]	$ .65	$2.00	$4.00
S-1985	Armstrong, Charlotte - ***Mischief*** [1971] Cover art by Harry Bennett	$ .65	$2.00	$4.00
N-1992	Callison, Brian - ***A Flock Of Ships*** [1971]	$ .50	$1.50	$3.00
N-1994	Ostrow, Joanna - ***... In The Highlands Since Time Immemorial*** [1971]	$ .50	$1.50	$3.00
S-1996	Curtis, Wade (Jerry E. Pournelle) - ***Red Dragon*** [1971] PBO.	$1.35	$4.00	$8.00
S-1997	Cooper, Edmund - ***Sea-Horse In The Sky*** [1971]	$ .65	$2.00	$4.00
S-1998	Laumer, Keith - ***The House In November*** [1971] Cover by Richard Powers.	$ .65	$2.00	$4.00
S-1999	Moorcock, Michael - ***The Queen Of The Swords*** [1971] PBO. Cover by David McCall Johnson.	$1.25	$3.75	$7.50
X-2000	Turner, William O. - ***Gunpoint*** [1971]	$ .65	$2.00	$4.00
X-2002	Hogan, Robert L. - ***Bombs From The Murder Wolves*** [1971] PBO. G8 #4.	$1.25	$3.75	$7.50
S-2003	Anthology - ***Best SF Stories From New Worlds 5*** [1969] edited by Michael Moorcock.	$1.00	$3.00	$6.00
X-2004	Hogan, Robert L. - ***Vultures Of The White Death*** [1971] G8 #5.	$1.25	$3.75	$7.50
Z-2007	K, Mr. and Mrs. (Anonymous) - ***The Couple*** [1971]	$ .50	$1.50	$3.00

		G	VG	F
N-2009	Arleo, Joseph - ***The Grand Street Collector*** [1971]	$ .50	$1.50	$3.00
S-2015	Harrison, Hary - ***The Stainless Steel Rat*** [1971]	$ .65	$2.00	$4.00
S-2016	Wells, Robert - ***Candle In The Sun*** [1971]	$ .50	$1.50	$3.00
X-2017	Turner, William O. - ***Mayberly's Kill*** [1971]	$ .65	$2.00	$4.00
S-2019	Sanborn, Robin - ***The Book Of Sier*** [1971] PBO.	$ .65	$2.00	$4.00
X-2023	Hogan, Robert J. - ***Flight From The Grave*** [1971] G8 #6.	$1.25	$3.75	$7.50
S-2025	Laumer, Keith - ***The Star Treasure*** [1971]	$ .65	$2.00	$4.00
X-2026	Booth, Edwin - ***The Prodigal Gun*** [1971]	$ .50	$1.50	$3.00
S-2029	Doyle, Sir Arthur Conan - ***The Adventures Of Sherlock Holmes*** [1971]	$ .50	$1.50	$3.00
S-2041	Matheson, Richard - ***I Am Legend*** [1971] Movie tie-in.	$1.25	$3.75	$7.50
S-2042	Meade, Richard - ***The Lost Fraulein*** [1971]	$ .50	$1.50	$3.00
X-2043	Hogan, Robert J. - ***Fangs Of The Sky Leopard*** [1971] G8 #7.	$1.25	$3.75	$7.50
S-2044	Disch, Thomas - ***One Hundred And Two H-Bombs*** [1971] PBO. Cover art by Paul Lehr.	$1.50	$5.00	$10.00
S-2045	Sturgeon, Theodore - ***Sturgeon Is Alive And Well*** [1971]	$ .65	$2.00	$4.00
X-2046	Elston, Allan Vaughan - ***Paradise Prairie*** [1971]	$ .50	$1.50	$3.00
N-2047	Marsh, Ngaio - ***Killer Dolphin*** [1971]	$ .65	$2.00	$4.00
Z-2050	Ellison, Jerome - ***A Serious Call To An American (R)evolution*** [1971]	$ .50	$1.50	$3.00
S-2053	Creasey, John - ***A Part For A Policeman*** [1971]	$ .50	$1.50	$3.00
N-2054	Tey, Josephine - ***To Love And Be Wise*** [1971] Photo cover.	$ .65	$2.00	$4.00
S-2057	Farmer, Philip Jose - ***To Your Scattered Bodies Go*** [1971]	$1.50	$5.00	$10.00
X-2058	Hogan, Robert J. - ***The Mark Of The Vulture*** [1971] PBO. G8 #8.	$1.25	$3.75	$7.50
N-2059	Mishima, Yukio - ***The Sound Of Waves*** [1971]	$ .50	$1.50	$3.00
N-2063	Frederics, MacDowell - ***Emergency Procedure*** [1971]	$ .50	$1.50	$3.00
S-2068	Cooper, Edmund - ***Kronk*** [1971]	$ .75	$2.50	$5.00
S-2069	Kelley, Leo P. - ***The Coins Of Murph*** [1971] PBO.	$ .65	$2.00	$4.00
S-2070	Moorcock, Michael - ***The King Of The Swords*** [1971] PBO. Cover art by David McCall Johnson.	$1.25	$3.75	$7.50
X-2071	Wells, Lee E. - ***Brand Of Evil*** [1971]	$ .50	$1.50	$3.00
N-2072	Marsh, Ngaio - ***Enter A Murderer*** [1971]	$ .50	$1.50	$3.00
N-2073	Heinlein, Robert A. - ***Podkayne Of Mars*** [1971] Cover art by Paul Lehr.	$ .65	$2.00	$4.00
N-2074	Anthology - ***New Worlds Quarterly #1*** [1971] PBO. Edited by Michael Moorcock.	$1.00	$3.00	$6.00
Z-2076	Longstreet, Stephen - ***Nell Kimball: Her Life As An American Madam*** [1971]	$ .50	$1.50	$3.00
Z-2078	Rival, Paul - ***The Six Wives Of Henry VIII*** [1971]	$ .50	$1.50	$3.00
Z-2085	Heinlein, Robert A. - ***I Will Fear No Evil*** [1971]	$ .65	$2.00	$4.00
S-2086	Reed, Kit - ***Armed Camps*** [1971] Cover art by Richard Powers.	$ .65	$2.00	$4.00
S-2088	Purdom, Tom - ***Reduction In Arms*** [1971] PBO.	$1.00	$3.00	$6.00
X-2089	Bickham, Jack - ***Fletcher*** [1971]	$ .50	$1.50	$3.00
S-2101	Stainslaw, Lem - ***Solaris*** [1970]	$ .50	$1.50	$3.00
N-2102	Moorcock, Michael - editor - ***New World Quarterly #2*** [1970] PBO.	$1.00	$3.00	$6.00
S-2103	Simak, Clifford D. - ***Destiny Doll*** [1972]	$ .65	$2.00	$4.00
X-2104	Elston, Allan Vaughan - ***The Seven Silver Mountains*** [1972]	$ .50	$1.50	$3.00
X-2106	Wells, H. G. - ***The Time Machine*** [1971]	$ .50	$1.50	$3.00
N-2117	Anthology - ***The Year 2000*** [1972] edited by Harry Harrison. Cover art by Richard Powers.	$ .65	$2.00	$4.00

Berkley Numbered Series. New York: Berkley Publishing.

		G	VG	F
04202	Matheson, Richard - ***What Dreams May Come*** [1979] PBO.	$8.00	$25.00	$50.00

Best Detective Novel. New York: Select Pubs, Inc. Digest Size.

		G	VG	F
1	Bennett, Dorothy - ***Come And Be Killed*** [1942] PBO. Cover art by Peter Driben.	$4.00	$12.50	$25.00
2	Ronns, Edward - ***$1,000,000 In Corpses*** [1942]	$3.50	$10.00	$20.00

Best Detective Selection. New York: Select Publications, Inc. Digest Size.

		G	VG	F
3	Jaffe, Michael - ***Death Goes To A Party*** [1942] PBO. Cover by Cardwell Higgins.	$3.50	$10.00	$20.00
4	Bagby, George - ***The Bloody Wig Murders*** [1942]	$3.50	$10.00	$20.00
5	Patrick, Keats - ***The Pool Of Death*** [1942]	$3.50	$10.00	$20.00
6	Treat, Lawrence - ***Wail For The Corpses*** [1943] Cover art by George Dunsford Klein.	$3.50	$10.00	$20.00
7	Ronns, Edward - ***The Corpse Hangs High*** [1943] Cover art by George Dunsford Klein.	$3.50	$10.00	$20.00
8	Long, Manning - ***Modeled In Murder*** [1943]	$3.50	$10.00	$20.00
9	Ballard, W.T. - ***Say Yes To Murder*** [1943] Cover art by Peter Driben.	$3.50	$10.00	$20.00
10	Petersen, Herman - ***Murder R.F.D.*** [1943] Cover by Peter Driben.	$3.50	$10.00	$20.00

Best Seller Classics. New York: Award Books, Inc. Leatherette Covers.

		G	VG	F
CL-450	London, Jack - ***The Call Of The Wild*** [n.d.]	$ .50	$1.50	$3.00
CL-451	Wells, H.G. - ***The Invisible Man*** [n.d.]	$ .50	$1.50	$3.00
CL-452	Poe, Edgar Allan - ***Tales Of Mystery*** [n.d.]	$ .50	$1.50	$3.00
CL-454	Stevenson, Robert Louis - ***Treasure Island*** [n.d.]	$ .50	$1.50	$3.00
CL-455	Doyle, Sir Arthur Conan - ***Adventures Of Sherlock Holmes*** [n.d.]	$ .50	$1.50	$3.00
CL-456	Kipling, Rudyard - ***Captains Courageous*** [n.d.]	$ .50	$1.50	$3.00
CL-601	Carroll, Lewis - ***Alice In Wonderland*** [n.d.]	$ .50	$1.50	$3.00
CL-602	Sewell, Anna - ***Black Beauty*** [n.d.]	$ .50	$1.50	$3.00
CL-603	Anthology - ***Arabian Nights*** [n.d.]	$ .50	$1.50	$3.00
CL-604	Kipling, Rudyard - ***The Jungle Book*** [n.d.]	$ .50	$1.50	$3.00
CL-605	Baum, L. Frank - ***The Wizard Of Oz*** [n.d.]	$ .50	$1.50	$3.00
CL-606	Hawthorne, Nathaniel - ***The Scarlet Letter*** [n.d.]	$ .50	$1.50	$3.00

Bestseller Mystery. New York: Lawrence E. Spivak. Digest Size.

		G	VG	F
NO#(B-1)	Queen, Ellery - ***Adventures Of Ellery Queen*** [n.d.]	$1.25	$3.75	$7.50
NO#(B-2)	Nathan, Robert - ***One More Spring*** [n.d.]	$1.00	$3.00	$6.00
B-3	Queen, Ellery - ***More Adventures Of Ellery Queen*** [n.d.]	$ .75	$2.50	$5.00
B-4	Pitkin, Walter B. - ***Life Begins At Forty*** [n.d.] Abridged.	$1.00	$3.00	$6.00
B-5	Kirkland, Jack (Erskine Caldwell) - ***Tobacco Road*** [n.d.]	$1.00	$3.00	$6.00
B-6	Bromfield, Louis - ***24 Hours*** [n.d.]	$1.00	$3.00	$6.00
B-7	Hart, Frances Noyes - ***The Bellamy Trail*** [n.d.] Abridged.	$ .75	$2.50	$5.00
B-8	Queen, Ellery - ***The Devil To Pay*** [n.d.]	$1.00	$3.00	$6.00
B-9	Christie, Agatha - ***The Mysterious Mr. Quin*** [n.d.] Abridged.	$ .75	$2.50	$5.00
B-10	Gardner, Erle Stanley - ***The Case Of The Curious Bride*** [n.d.] Abridged.	$ .75	$2.50	$5.00
B-11	Queen, Ellery - ***The Spanish Cape Mystery*** [n.d.] Abridged.	$1.00	$3.00	$6.00
B-12	Marquand, John P. - ***Thank You, Mr. Moto*** [n.d.] Abridged.	$1.00	$3.00	$6.00
B-13	Sayers, Dorothy L. - ***Lord Peter Views The Body*** [n.d.] Unabridged.	$ .75	$2.50	$5.00
B-14	Queen, Ellery - ***The Greek Coffin Mystery*** [n.d.]	$ .75	$2.50	$5.00
B-15	Wilde Percival - ***Inquest*** [n.d.]	$1.00	$3.00	$6.00
B-16	Armstrong, Margaret - ***Murder In Stained Glass*** [n.d.] Abridged.	$1.00	$3.00	$6.00
B-17	Queen, Ellery - ***The Egyptian Cross Mystery*** [n.d.] Abridged.	$ .75	$2.50	$5.00
B-18	Christie, Agatha - ***Dead Man's Mirror*** [n.d.]	$ .75	$2.50	$5.00
B-19	Gardner, Erle Stanley - ***The Case Of The Sleepwalker's Niece*** [n.d.] Abridged.	$1.00	$3.00	$6.00
B-20	Sayers, Dorothy L. - ***In The Teeth Of The Evidence*** [n.d.]	$1.00	$3.00	$6.00
B-21	Christie, Agatha - ***Murder In 3 Acts*** [n.d.] Abridged.	$ .75	$2.50	$5.00
B-22	Gardner, Erle Stanley - ***The D.A. Holds The Candle*** [n.d.]	$1.00	$3.00	$6.00
B-23	Marsh, Ngaio - ***Death In Ecstasy*** [n.d.]	$ .75	$2.50	$5.00
B-24	Simenon, Georges - ***A Face For A Clue*** [n.d.] Unabridged.	$ .75	$2.50	$5.00
B-25	Christie, Agatha - ***Partners In Crime*** [n.d.] Abridged.	$1.00	$3.00	$6.00

		G	VG	F
B-27	Mason, Van Wyck - ***The Cairo Garter Murders*** [n.d.] Abridged.	$1.00	$3.00	$6.00
B-28	Queen, Ellery - ***The Tragedy Of Y*** [n.d.] Cover art by Salter. Abridged.	$1.00	$3.00	$6.00
B-29	Gardner, Erle Stanley - ***Murder Up My Sleeve*** [n.d.]	$ .75	$2.50	$5.00
B-30	Armstrong, Margaret - ***The Man With No Face*** [n.d.] Abridged.	$1.00	$3.00	$6.00
B-31	Stout, Rex - ***Some Buried Caesar*** [n.d.]	$1.00	$3.00	$6.00
B-32	Christie, Agatha - ***The Seven Dials Mystery*** [n.d.] Abridged.	$ .75	$2.50	$5.00
B-33	Allingham, Margery - ***Black Plumes*** [n.d.] Abridged.	$ .75	$2.50	$5.00
B-34	Dickson, Carter - ***The Department Of Queer Complaints*** [1943] Unabridged.	$1.50	$5.00	$10.00
B-35	Gardner, Erle Stanley - ***This Is Murder*** [n.d.] Cover art by Salter. Abridged.	$1.00	$3.00	$6.00
B-36	Christie, Agatha - ***The Regatta Mystery And Other Stories*** [1944] Unabridged.	$1.00	$3.00	$6.00
B-37	Seeley, Mabel - ***The Whispering Cup*** [n.d.]	$1.00	$3.00	$6.00
B-38	Sayers, Dorothy L. - ***Hangman's Holiday*** [n.d.]	$ .75	$2.50	$5.00
B-39	Christie, Agatha - ***The Boomerang Clue*** [n.d.] Abridged.	$1.00	$3.00	$6.00
B-40	Hammett, Dashiell - ***$106,000 Blood Money*** [1943] PBO.	$12.50	$37.50	$75.00
B-41	Simenon, Georges - ***The Flemish Shop*** [n.d.]	$ .75	$2.50	$5.00
B-42	Lee, Gypsy Rose (Ghosted By Craig Rice) - ***The G-String Murders*** [n.d.]	$1.00	$3.00	$6.00
B-43	Christie, Agatha - ***Poirot Investigates*** [n.d.] Cover art by Salter. Unabridged.	$1.00	$3.00	$6.00
B-44	Stout, Rex - ***Where There Is A Will*** [1943] Unabridged.	$ .75	$2.50	$5.00
B-45	Dickson, Carter - ***Death In Five Boxes*** [n.d.]	$1.00	$3.00	$6.00
B-46	Lees, Hannah & Bachmann, Lawrence - ***Death In The Doll's House*** [n.d.] Unabridged.	$ .75	$2.50	$5.00
B-47	Carr, John Dickson - ***The Three Coffins*** [1944] Abridged.	$1.00	$3.00	$6.00
B-48	Christie, Agatha - ***The Secret Adversary*** [n.d.] Abridged.	$ .75	$2.50	$5.00
B-49	Eberhart, Mignon G. - ***The Dark Garden*** [n.d.]	$1.00	$3.00	$6.00
B-50	Hammett, Dashiell - ***The Adventures Of Sam Spade*** [1944] PBO.	$12.50	$37.50	$75.00
B-51	Allingham, Margery - ***Police At The Funeral*** [n.d.]	$ .75	$2.50	$5.00
B-52	Christie, Agatha - ***The Man In The Brown Suit*** [n.d.] Abridged.	$ .75	$2.50	$5.00
B-53	Disney, Dorothy C. & Perry, George S. - ***Thirty Days Hath September*** [n.d.] Abridged.	$ .75	$2.50	$5.00
B-54	Christie, Agatha - ***Sad Cypress*** [n.d.] Abridged.	$ .75	$2.50	$5.00
B-55	Eberhart, Mignon - ***The Pattern*** [n.d.]	$1.00	$3.00	$6.00
B-56	Allingham, Margery - ***Kingdom Of Death*** [n.d.] Abridged.	$1.00	$3.00	$6.00
B-57	Mason, Van Wyck - ***Washington Legation Murders*** [n.d.]	$ .75	$2.50	$5.00
B-58	Christie, Agatha - ***Appointment For Death*** [n.d.]	$ .75	$2.50	$5.00
B-59	Queen, Ellery - ***The Case Book Of Ellery Queen*** [n.d.]	$1.00	$3.00	$6.00
B-60	Eberhart Mignon G. - ***The Hangman's Whip*** [n.d.]	$ .75	$2.50	$5.00
B-61	Christie, Agatha - ***Murder At Hazelmoor*** [n.d.] Abridged.	$ .75	$2.50	$5.00
B-62	Hammett, Dashiell - ***The Continental OP*** [1945] PBO.	$12.50	$37.50	$75.00
B-63	Mason, F. Van Wyck - ***The Budapest Parade Murders*** [n.d.] Abridged.	$1.00	$3.00	$6.00
B-64	Marsh, Ngaio - ***Artists In Crime*** [n.d.] Abridged.	$ .75	$2.50	$5.00
B-65	Disney, Doris M. - ***A Compound For Death*** [n.d.]	$ .75	$2.50	$5.00
B-66	Olsen, D.B. - ***Alarm Of The Black Cat*** [n.d.]	$ .75	$2.50	$5.00
B-67	Fearing, Kenneth - ***Dagger Of The Mind*** [n.d.] Unabridged.	$ .75	$2.50	$5.00
B-68	Marsh, Ngaio - ***Vintage Murder*** [n.d.]	$ .75	$2.50	$5.00
B-69	Simenon, Georges - ***Patience Of Maigret*** [n.d.]	$1.00	$3.00	$6.00
B-70	Daly, Elizabeth - ***Deadly Nightshade*** [n.d.] Abridged.	$ .75	$2.50	$5.00
B-71	Wallace, Edgar - ***The Crimson Circle*** [n.d.] Unabridged.	$ .75	$2.50	$5.00
B-72	Hopkins, Jr., Stanley - ***Parchment Key*** [n.d.]	$1.00	$3.00	$6.00
B-73	Knight, Clifford - ***Affair Of The Crimson Gull*** [n.d.]	$ .75	$2.50	$5.00

		G	VG	F
B-74	Caspary, Vera - ***Laura*** [n.d.] Unabridged.	$ .75	$2.50	$5.00
B-75	Wentworth, Patricia - ***Miss Silver Deals With Death*** [n.d.] Abridged.	$1.00	$3.00	$6.00
B-76	Branson, H. C. - ***The Pricking Thumb*** [n.d.] Unabridged.	$1.00	$3.00	$6.00
B-77	White, Ethel Lina - ***While She Sleeps*** [n.d.] Unabridged.	$1.00	$3.00	$6.00
B-78	Carr, John Dickson - ***Death-Watch*** [n.d.] Cover art by Salter. Abridged.	$1.00	$3.00	$6.00
B-79	Christie, Agatha - ***Mr. Parker Pyne, Detective*** [n.d.]	$ .75	$2.50	$5.00
B-80	Seeley, Mabel - ***The Chuckling Fingers*** [n.d.] Abridged.	$ .75	$2.50	$5.00
B-81	Hammett, Dashiell - ***Hammett Homicides*** [1946] PBO.	$12.50	$37.50	$75.00
B-82	Fischer, Bruno - ***Quoth The Raven*** [n.d.]	$ .75	$2.50	$5.00
B-83	Warren, James - ***She Fell Among Actors*** [n.d.]	$ .75	$2.50	$5.00
B-84	Martin, A.E. - ***Sinners Never Die*** [n.d.]	$ .75	$2.50	$5.00
B-85	Little, Constance & Gwenyth - ***The Black Honeymoon*** [n.d.]	$ .75	$2.50	$5.00
B-86	Christie, Agatha - ***Murder In The Calais Coach*** [n.d.]	$1.00	$3.00	$6.00
B-87	Bagby, George - ***The Corpse With The Purple Thighs*** [n.d.] Unabridged.	$1.00	$3.00	$6.00
B-88	Kelsey, Vera - ***Whisper Murder*** [n.d.]	$ .75	$2.50	$5.00
B-89	Chambers, Dana - ***The Blonde Died First*** [n.d.]	$1.00	$3.00	$6.00
B-90	Irish, William - ***Deadline At Dawn*** [n.d.]	$1.25	$3.75	$7.50
B-91	Vickers, Roy - ***The Department Of Dead Ends*** [n.d.]	$1.00	$3.00	$6.00
B-92	Siller, Van - ***One Alone*** [n.d.]	$1.00	$3.00	$6.00
B-93	Daly, Elizabeth - ***The Book Of The Dead*** [1947] Cover art by George Salter. Unabridged.	$1.00	$3.00	$6.00
B-94	Henry, O. - ***Cops And Robbers*** [n.d.]	$1.00	$3.00	$6.00
B-95	Rinehart, Mary Roberts - ***The Yellow Room*** [n.d.] Abridged.	$1.00	$3.00	$6.00
B-96	Dent, Lester - ***Dead At The Take-Off*** [n.d.] Abridged.	$ .75	$2.50	$5.00
B-97	Venning, Michael - ***The Man Who Slept All Day*** [1947] Abridged.	$1.00	$3.00	$6.00
B-98	Sanders, George (Leigh Brackett) - ***Stranger At Home*** [1947] Abridged.	$1.25	$3.75	$7.50
B-99	Olsen, D.B. - ***Cats Don't Need Coffins*** [n.d.]	$1.00	$3.00	$6.00
B-100	Vickers, Roy - ***The Hawk*** [n.d.] Cover art by George Salter. Abridged.	$1.00	$3.00	$6.00
B-101	Dent, Lester - ***Lady To Kill*** [n.d.] Cover art by George Salter. Unabridged.	$ .75	$2.50	$5.00
B-102	McDermid, Finlay - ***Kiss The Blonde Goodbye*** [1948] Cover art by George Salter. Abridged.	$ .75	$2.50	$5.00
B-103	Chambers, Dana - ***Rope For An Ape*** [n.d.] Abridged.	$1.00	$3.00	$6.00
B-104	Edgley, Leslie - ***Fear No More*** [n.d.]	$1.00	$3.00	$6.00
B-105	Walker, Gertrude - ***So Deadly Fair*** [n.d.] Cover art by George Salter. Abridged.	$ .75	$2.50	$5.00
B-106	Fischer, Bruno - ***The Bleeding Scissors*** [n.d.] Unabridged.	$ .75	$2.50	$5.00
B-107	Strange, John Stephen - ***Make My Bed Soon*** [n.d.] Unabridged.	$ .75	$2.50	$5.00
B-108	Hunt, Harrison - ***Murder Picks The Jury*** [n.d.]	$1.00	$3.00	$6.00
B-109	Edgley, Leslie - ***The Angry Heart*** [n.d.] Abridged.	$1.00	$3.00	$6.00
B-110	Oursler, Will - ***Bullets For A Blonde*** [1949] Abridged.	$ .75	$2.50	$5.00
B-111	Disney, Doris Miles - ***Death For My Beloved*** [n.d.]	$1.00	$3.00	$6.00
B-112	Daly, Elizabeth - ***The Book Of The Lion*** [1949] Unabridged.	$1.00	$3.00	$6.00
B-113	Bagby, George - ***In Cold Blood*** [1949] Abridged.	$1.00	$3.00	$6.00
B-114	Knight, Kathleen Moore - ***The Blue Horse Of Taxco*** [n.d.] Abridged.	$ .75	$2.50	$5.00
B-115	Dent, Lester - ***Lady Afraid*** [1949] Cover art by George Salter. Abridged.	$ .75	$2.50	$5.00
B-116	Nelson, Hugh Lawrence - ***Fountain Of Death*** [n.d.]	$1.00	$3.00	$6.00
B-117	Lawrence, Hilda - ***Death Has Four Hands*** [n.d.]	$ .75	$2.50	$5.00
B-118	Long, Manning - ***Short Shrift*** [n.d.]	$1.00	$3.00	$6.00
B-119	Clark, Philip - ***The Dark River*** [n.d.]	$ .75	$2.50	$5.00
B-120	Olsen, D.B. - ***Devious Design*** [n.d.]	$ .75	$2.50	$5.00
B-121	Goodis, David - ***Nightfall*** [n.d.]	$2.50	$7.50	$15.00

		G	VG	F
B-122	Lawrence, Hilda - ***The Bleeding House*** [n.d.]	$1.00	$3.00	$6.00
B-123	Knight, Kathleen Moore - ***Bait For Murder*** [n.d.]	$1.00	$3.00	$6.00
B-124	Marquand, John P. - ***Think Fast, Mr. Moto*** [n.d.]	$1.00	$3.00	$6.00
B-125	Powell, Richard - ***Shark River*** [n.d.]	$ .75	$2.50	$5.00
B-126	Scherf, Margaret - ***For The Love Of Murder*** [n.d.]	$1.00	$3.00	$6.00
B-127	Spicer, Bart - ***The Dark Light*** [n.d.] Unabridged.	$ .75	$2.50	$5.00
B-128	Palmer, Stuart - ***The Monkey Murder*** [n.d.]	$1.00	$3.00	$6.00
B-129	Lorac, E.C.R. - ***Place For A Poisoner*** [n.d.]	$ .75	$2.50	$5.00
B-130	Fischer, Bruno - ***Kill To Fit*** [n.d.] Unabridged.	$1.00	$3.00	$6.00
B-131	Dickenson, Fred - ***Kill 'Em With Kindness*** [n.d.]	$1.00	$3.00	$6.00
B-132	Stein, Aaron Marc - ***Days Of Misfortune*** [n.d.] Unabridged.	$1.00	$3.00	$6.00
B-133	Chambers, Dana - ***Too Like The Dead*** [n.d.] Unabridged.	$ .75	$2.50	$5.00
B-134	Debrett, Hal - ***A Lonely Way To Die*** [n.d.]	$1.00	$3.00	$6.00
B-135	Rutledge, Nancy - ***Murder For Millions*** [n.d.] Cover art by George Salter. Abridged.	$1.00	$3.00	$6.00
B-136	Leslie, Jean - ***Blood On My Shoe*** [n.d.] Cover art by George Salter. Unabridged.	$1.00	$3.00	$6.00
B-137	Gilbert, Michael - ***He Didn't Mind Danger*** [n.d.] Abridged.	$ .75	$2.50	$5.00
B-138	Black, Thomas B. - ***The White Bird Murders*** [n.d.] Abridged.	$1.00	$3.00	$6.00
B-139	Knight, Clifford - ***Death Of A Big Shot*** [n.d.] Cover art by George Salter. Unabridged.	$1.00	$3.00	$6.00
B-140	Blochman, Lawrence G. - ***Rather Cool For Mayhem*** [n.d.]	$1.00	$3.00	$6.00
B-141	Leonard, Charles L. - ***Sinister Shelter*** [n.d.] Unabridged.	$ .75	$2.50	$5.00
B-142	Dolph, Jack - ***Hot Tip*** [n.d.]	$ .75	$2.50	$5.00
B-143	Fuller, Samuel Michael - ***Murder Makes A Deadline*** [n.d.]	$1.00	$3.00	$6.00
B-144	Sherwood, John - ***Mr. Blessington's Imperialist Plot*** [n.d.] Cover art by George Salter. Abridged.	$1.00	$3.00	$6.00
B-147	Bonnamy, Francis - ***The Man In The Mist*** [n.d.] Abridged.	$1.00	$3.00	$6.00
B-149	O'Farrell, William - ***These Arrows Point To Death*** [n.d.] Unabridged.	$ .75	$2.50	$5.00
B-150	Sheridan, Juanita - ***The Kahuna Killer*** [n.d.] Abridged.	$1.00	$3.00	$6.00
B-151	Black, Thomas B. - ***The 3-13 Murders*** [n.d.]	$1.00	$3.00	$6.00
B-152	McCloy, Helen - ***Alias Basil Willing*** [n.d.]	$1.00	$3.00	$6.00
B-153	The Gordons - ***F.B.I. Story*** [n.d.] Unabridged.	$1.00	$3.00	$6.00
B-154	Siller, Van - ***Fatal Lover*** [n.d.]	$1.00	$3.00	$6.00
B-155	Sheridan, Juanita - ***The Mamo Murders*** [n.d.]	$1.00	$3.00	$6.00
B-156	Foley, Rae - ***Don't Kill My Love*** [n.d.]	$ .75	$2.50	$5.00
B-157	Treat, Lawrence - ***F As In Flight*** [n.d.]	$1.00	$3.00	$6.00
B-158	Stein, Aaron Marc - ***Mask For Murder*** [n.d.]	$1.00	$3.00	$6.00
B-159	Scherf, Margaret - ***Divine And Deadly*** [n.d.]	$1.00	$3.00	$6.00
B-160	Findley, Ferguson - ***Dead Ringer*** [n.d.]	$1.00	$3.00	$6.00
B-161	Strange, John Stephen - ***The Fair And The Dead*** [n.d.] Abridged.	$1.00	$3.00	$6.00
B-162	Barns, Glenn M. - ***Murder Is A Gamble*** [n.d.] Cover art by George Salter. Unabridged.	$ .75	$2.50	$5.00
B-163	Bloomfield, Robert - ***Lust For Vengeance*** [n.d.]	$ .75	$2.50	$5.00
B-164	Stagge, Jonathan - ***Death, My Darling Daughters*** [n.d.]	$ .75	$2.50	$5.00
B-165	White, Leslie T. - ***Vice Squad*** [n.d.]	$ .75	$2.50	$5.00
B-166	McCloy, Helen - ***Dance Of Death*** [n.d.] Unabridged.	$1.00	$3.00	$6.00
B-167	Holding, Elizabeth Sanxay - ***The Virgin Huntress*** [n.d.]	$ .75	$2.50	$5.00
B-168	Fenisong, Ruth - ***Dead Yesterday*** [n.d.] Unabridged.	$ .75	$2.50	$5.00
B-169	Lanham, Edwin - ***One Murder Too Many*** [n.d.] Unabridged.	$ .75	$2.50	$5.00
B-170	The Gordons - ***Make Haste To Live*** [n.d.] Unabridged. Photo covers. Movie tie-in.	$1.00	$3.00	$6.00
B-171	Edgley, Leslie - ***One Blonde Died*** [n.d.]	$1.00	$3.00	$6.00
B-172	Holden, Genevieve - ***Killer Loose!*** [n.d.]	$ .75	$2.50	$5.00
B-173	Stone, Hampton - ***The Corpse Who Had Too Many Friends*** [1954] Unabridged.	$1.00	$3.00	$6.00
B-174	Godey, John - ***This Year's Death*** [n.d.] Unabridged.	$ .75	$2.50	$5.00
B-175	Barns, Glenn M. - ***Lawyers Don't Hang*** [n.d.]	$ .75	$2.50	$5.00

		G	VG	F
B-176	Lewis, Lange - ***The Passionate Victims*** [n.d.]	$ .75	$2.50	$5.00
B-177	Hitchens, Delores - ***Terror Lurks In Darkness*** [n.d.]	$ .75	$2.50	$5.00
B-178	Treat, Lawrence - ***V As In Victim*** [n.d.]	$1.00	$3.00	$6.00
B-179	O'Farrell, William - ***Lovely In Death*** [n.d.] Cover art by George Salter. Abridged.	$ .75	$2.50	$5.00
B-180	Godey, John - ***Killer At His Back*** [n.d.] Abridged.	$ .75	$2.50	$5.00
B-181	Heberden, M.V. - ***You'll Fry Tomorrow*** [n.d.] Unabridged.	$1.00	$3.00	$6.00
B-182	Lanham, Edwin - ***The Case Of The Missing Corpse*** [n.d.] Abridged.	$1.00	$3.00	$6.00
B-183	Estes, Carroll Cox - ***Embrace Of Death*** [n.d.] Unabridged.	$1.00	$3.00	$6.00
B-185	Fenisong, Ruth - ***Too Lovely To Live*** [n.d.] Unabridged.	$1.00	$3.00	$6.00
B-186	Sted, Richard - ***They All Bleed Red*** [n.d.] Unabridged.	$ .75	$2.50	$5.00
B-187	Crispin, Edmund - ***Buried For Pleasure*** [n.d.]	$1.00	$3.00	$6.00
B-188	Godey, John - ***The Blonde Betrayer*** [n.d.] Unabridged.	$ .75	$2.50	$5.00
B-189	Palmer, Stuart - ***Trap For A Redhead*** [n.d.]	$ .75	$2.50	$5.00
B-190	Treat, Lawrence - ***Trial And Terror*** [n.d.] Abridged.	$1.00	$3.00	$6.00
B-191	Daly, Elizabeth - ***Shroud For A Lady*** [n.d.]	$1.00	$3.00	$6.00
B-192	Davis, Frederick - ***Another Morgue Heard From*** [n.d.]	$1.00	$3.00	$6.00
B-193	Blake, Nicholas - ***Catch And Kill*** [n.d.] Abridged.	$ .75	$2.50	$5.00
B-194	Yudkoff, Alvin - ***Network of Fear*** [n.d.] Abridged.	$ .75	$2.50	$5.00
B-195	MacDonald, Philip - ***No Time For Terror*** [n.d.] Abridged.	$ .75	$2.50	$5.00
B-196	Franklin, Max - ***Murder Muscles In*** [n.d.] Abridged.	$1.00	$3.00	$6.00
B-197	Kelland, Clarence Budington - ***Murder Makes An Entrance*** [n.d.] Abridged.	$1.00	$3.00	$6.00
B-198	Woolrich, Cornell - ***Black Alibi*** [n.d.] Abridged.	$1.50	$5.00	$10.00
B-200	Bagby, George - ***A Dirty Way To Die*** [n.d.] Abridged.	$1.00	$3.00	$6.00
B-202	Chaber, M.E. - ***Take One For Murder*** [n.d.] Unabridged.	$1.00	$3.00	$6.00
B-203	McCloy, Helen - ***The Long Body*** [n.d.] Unabridged.	$1.00	$3.00	$6.00
B-204	Fisher, Steve - ***I Wake Up Screaming*** [n.d.] Unabridged.	$ .75	$2.50	$5.00
B-205	Borgenicht, Miriam - ***Don't Look Back*** [n.d.] Abridged.	$ .75	$2.50	$5.00
B-206	Woolrich, Cornell - ***The Black Angel*** [n.d.] Abridged.	$1.50	$5.00	$10.00
B-207	Household, Geoggrey - ***Hang The Man High*** [n.d.] Abridged.	$1.00	$3.00	$6.00
B-209	Graham, Winston - ***Bridge To Vengeance*** [n.d.] Abridged.	$ .75	$2.50	$5.00
210	Woolrich, Cornell - ***The Black Path Of Fear*** [1958] *Bestseller Mystery Magazine*.	$ .75	$2.50	$5.00

Big Green Detective. New York: Green Publishing. Digest Size.

2	Nyland, Gentry - ***Hot Bullets For Love*** [n.d.]	$2.50	$7.50	$15.00
3	Pemberhiller, Guy - ***Run Corpse Run*** [n.d.]	$2.50	$7.50	$15.00
4	Lord, Garland - ***Murder With Love*** [n.d.]	$2.50	$7.50	$15.00
5	Giles, Guy Elwyn - ***Target For Murder*** [n.d.]	$2.50	$7.50	$15.00

Black Cat Detective. New York: Crestwood Publications, Inc. Digest Size.

1	Giles, Guy Elwyn - ***3 Died Variously*** [1943]	$2.00	$6.00	$12.00
2	Veiller, Bayard - ***Bait For A Tiger*** [1943] Cover by Hoffman.	$1.50	$5.00	$10.00
3	Polsky, Thomas - ***Curtains For The Judge*** [1943]	$1.50	$5.00	$10.00
4	Spain, John - ***Dig Me A Grave*** [1943] States #3 on the cover, but is actually #4.	$1.50	$5.00	$10.00
5	Propper, Milton - ***The Case Of The Cheating Bride*** [1943]	$1.50	$5.00	$10.00
6	Lilly, Jean - ***Death Thumbs A Ride*** [1943] Cover art by Hoffman.	$2.00	$6.00	$12.00
7	Blake, Nicholas - ***The Beast Must Die*** [1943] Cover by Hoffman.	$2.00	$6.00	$12.00
8	Dalton, Moray - ***The Body In The Road*** [1944]	$1.50	$5.00	$10.00
9	Billany, Dan - ***It Takes A Thief*** [1944]	$1.50	$5.00	$10.00
10	Cardwell, Ann - ***Crazy To Kill*** [1944]	$1.50	$5.00	$10.00
11	Dale, William - ***John Doe-Murderer*** [1944]	$1.50	$5.00	$10.00
12	Wales, Kirk - ***6 Were To Die*** [1944]	$1.50	$5.00	$10.00
13	Jerome, Owen Fox - ***Murder As Usual*** [1944]	$1.50	$5.00	$10.00
14	Holding, Elisabeth Sanxay - ***Dark Power*** [1945]	$1.50	$5.00	$10.00

		G	VG	F
15	Mace, Merlda - ***Headlong For Murder*** [1945]	$1.50	$5.00	$10.00
16	Verner, Gerald - ***The Crooked Circle*** [1945]	$1.50	$5.00	$10.00
17	Mace, Merlda - ***Motto For Murder*** [1945]	$1.50	$5.00	$10.00
18	Trimble, Louis - ***Murder Trouble*** [1945]	$1.50	$5.00	$10.00
19	Merwin, Jr., Sam - ***Murder In Miniatures*** [1945]	$2.00	$6.00	$12.00
20	Brown, Gerald - ***Murder In Plain Sight*** [1946]	$1.50	$5.00	$10.00
21	Gaines, A. - ***The Voodoo Goat*** [1946]	$1.50	$5.00	$10.00
22	Cameron, Donald Clough - ***And So He Had To Die*** [1946]	$1.50	$5.00	$10.00
23	Goldman, Raymond Leslie - ***Judge Robinson Murdered!*** [1946]	$1.50	$5.00	$10.00
24	Knox, Timothy - ***Death In The State House*** [1945]	$1.50	$5.00	$10.00
25	LaRoche, K. Alison - ***Dear Dead Professor*** [1946]	$1.50	$5.00	$10.00
26	Fenwick, E.P. - ***Murder In Haste*** [1946]	$1.50	$5.00	$10.00
27	Fast, Julius - ***The Bright Face Of Danger*** [1946]	$1.50	$5.00	$10.00
28	Mace, Merlda - ***Blondes Don't Cry*** [1946]	$1.50	$5.00	$10.00

Black Cat Western. New York: Crestwood Publications, Inc. Digest Size.

29	Robertson, Frank C. - ***The Outlaw Of Antler*** [1946]	$1.25	$3.75	$7.50
30	Westland, Lynn - ***Prairie Pioneers*** [1946]	$1.25	$3.75	$7.50
31	Joscelyn, Archie - ***Blue River Riders*** [1946]	$1.25	$3.75	$7.50
32	Grinstead, J. E. - ***The Flying Y Brand*** [1946]	$1.25	$3.75	$7.50
33	Arthur, Bert - ***Gunsmoke In Paradise*** [1946]	$1.25	$3.75	$7.50
34	Westland, Lynn - ***The Silver Cayuse*** [1946]	$1.25	$3.75	$7.50
35	Riley, Tex - ***Bullet Justice*** [1946]	$1.25	$3.75	$7.50
36	Ermine, Will - ***Trail Trouble*** [1946]	$1.25	$3.75	$7.50
37	Gunn, Tom - ***Painted Post Range*** [1946]	$1.25	$3.75	$7.50
38	Westland, Lynn - ***Saddle River Spread*** [1946]	$1.25	$3.75	$7.50
39	Knight, Kim - ***Nighthawk's Gold*** [1946]	$1.25	$3.75	$7.50
40	Joscelyn, Archie - ***The Faceless Riders*** [1946]	$1.25	$3.75	$7.50
41	Joscelyn, Archie - ***Smoke In The West*** [1946]	$1.25	$3.75	$7.50
42	Floren, Lee - ***Gunslammer*** [1946]	$1.25	$3.75	$7.50
43	Rubel, James L. - ***Renegade Guns*** [1946]	$1.25	$3.75	$7.50
44	Floren, Lee - ***Mad River Guns*** [1946]	$1.25	$3.75	$7.50
45	Joscelyn, Archie - ***Outcast Law*** [1946]	$1.25	$3.75	$7.50
46	Montana, Zed - ***Six Gun Pay-Off!*** [1946]	$1.25	$3.75	$7.50

Black Knight Mysteries. New York: Ideal Dist. Co.

15	Koehler, Robert Portner - ***Corpse In The Wind*** [1946] Digest size.	$2.00	$6.00	$12.00
16	Tracy, Don - ***Last Year's Snow*** [1946] Digest size.	$2.00	$6.00	$12.00
17	Lane, Jeremy - ***Death To Drumbeat*** [1946] Digest size.	$2.00	$6.00	$12.00
18	Goldman, R.L. - ***Murder Behind The Mike*** [1946] Digest size.	$2.00	$6.00	$12.00
19	Bonney, Joseph L. - ***Death By Dynamite*** [1947] Digest size.	$2.00	$6.00	$12.00
22	Cameron, Donald Clough - ***Murder's Coming*** [1947] Digest size.	$2.00	$6.00	$12.00
24	Bardon, Minna - ***Murder For Fun XXX Real*** [1947] Digest size.	$2.00	$6.00	$12.00
25	Glidden, M. W. - ***Come Dwell With Death*** [1944]	$2.50	$7.50	$15.00
26	Corne, M.E. - ***Death Is No Lady*** [1945] Paperback size.	$2.50	$7.50	$15.00
27	Michel, M. Scott - ***The Psychiatric Murders*** [1945] Paperback size.	$2.50	$7.50	$15.00
28	Ullman, Albert E. - ***The Kidnappers*** [1947] Paperback size.	$2.50	$7.50	$15.00
29	Stokes, Manning Lee - ***Green For A Grave*** [1947] Paperback size.	$2.50	$7.50	$15.00
30	Bowen, Robert Sidney - ***Make Mine Murder*** [1947]	$2.50	$7.50	$15.00
31	Simmons, Addison - ***Dead Weight*** [1947] Paperback size.	$2.50	$7.50	$15.00
32	Lane, Jeremy - ***Kill Him Tonight*** [1948] Paperback size.	$2.50	$7.50	$15.00
33	Stirling, Peter - ***Stop Press - Murder!*** [1948] Paperback size.	$2.50	$7.50	$15.00
34	Kootz - ***Puzzle In Petticoats*** [1948] Paperback size.	$2.50	$7.50	$15.00

		G	VG	F
Bleak House Mystery. New York: Parsee Publications.				
12	Jeffers, Albert - ***Design For Dying*** [1947] Digest size.	$2.50	$7.50	$15.00
14	Barton, Minna - ***The Case Of The Blood-Stained Dime*** [1945] Paperback size.	$3.00	$9.00	$18.00
15	Langer, Joan - ***The Case Of The Missing Corpse*** [1947] Paperback size.	$3.00	$9.00	$18.00
16	Wood, Clement - ***The Corpse In The Guest Room*** [1947] Paperback size.	$3.00	$9.00	$18.00
17	Spewack, Samuel - ***The Skyscraper Murders*** [1948] Paperback size.	$3.00	$9.00	$18.00
18	Lane, Jeremy - ***Murder Menagerie*** [1948] Came out in both digest and paperback size.	$3.00	$9.00	$18.00
19	Laing, Patrick - ***If I Should Murder*** [1948] Paperback size.	$3.00	$9.00	$18.00
20	Dale, William - ***The Terror Of The Handless Corpse*** [1948] Paperback size.	$3.00	$9.00	$18.00
21	Koehler, Robert Portner - ***Here Come The Dead*** [1948] Paperback size.	$3.00	$9.00	$18.00
22	Cameron, Don - ***White For A Shroud*** [1948] Paperback size.	$3.00	$9.00	$18.00
Bob Hope. Digest Size.				
NN-1	Hope, Bob - ***They Got Me Covered*** [1941] PBO. Photos throughout.	$1.50	$5.00	$10.00
Bobley Books. New York: Harry W. Bobley, Robert Edwards. Digest Size.				
B-3	Anthology - ***Bestread Short Stories*** [1946] PBO. Edited by Max Levin.	$1.50	$5.00	$10.00
B-4	Anthology - ***Bestread Short Stories*** [1946] PBO. Edited by Max Levin.	$1.50	$5.00	$10.00
Bonded Books. New York: Bonded Books, Inc. Digest Size.				
NN	Charteris, Leslie - ***Lady On A Train*** [1945] PBO. Movie tie-in with Deanna Durbin.	$8.00	$25.00	$50.00
1	Charteris, Leslie - ***The Saint Meets The Tiger*** [1945] Cover art by Fritz Willis.	$3.50	$10.00	$20.00
2	Charteris, Leslie - ***Featuring The Saint*** [1945]	$3.50	$10.00	$20.00
3	Charteris, Leslie - ***The Saint's Getaway*** [1945] Cover art by Fritz Willis.	$3.50	$10.00	$20.00
4	Edited by Leslie Charteris - ***The Saint's Choice Of English Crime (Vol I)*** [1945]	$3.50	$10.00	$20.00
5	Charteris, Leslie - ***Alias The Saint*** [1945]	$3.50	$10.00	$20.00
6	Charteris, Leslie - editor - ***The Saint's Choice of American Crime (Vol. II)*** [1945]	$3.50	$10.00	$20.00
7	Charteris, Leslie - ***Paging The Saint*** [1945]	$3.50	$10.00	$20.00
8	Anthology edited by Leslie Charteris - ***The Saint's Choice Of True Crime Stories (Vol. 3)*** [1945] PBO.	$4.00	$12.50	$25.00
9	Anthology edited by Leslie Charteris - ***The Saint's Choice Of Humorous Crime Stories (Vol. 4)*** [1945] PBO.	$4.00	$12.50	$25.00
10-B	Friend, Oscar J. - ***Guns Of Powder River*** [1945]	$3.50	$10.00	$20.00
10-A	Jameson, Malcolm - ***Atomic Bomb*** [1945]	$3.50	$10.00	$20.00
10	Cain, Paul - ***Fast One*** [1943]	$12.50	$37.50	$75.00
11	Charteris, Leslie - editor - ***The Saint's Choice Of Impossible Crime (Vol. 5)*** [1945] PBO.	$4.00	$12.50	$25.00
12	Rice, Craig - editor - ***The Craig Rice Mystery Digest*** [1945] PBO.	$4.00	$12.50	$25.00
13	Rice, Craig - ***Eight Faces At Three*** [1945]	$3.50	$10.00	$20.00
14	Charteris, Leslie - ***The Saint Meets His Match*** [1945]	$3.50	$10.00	$20.00
15	Sanders, George - ***Crime On My Hands*** [1945]	$4.00	$12.50	$25.00
16	Paul, Elliot - ***I'll Hate Myself In The Morning*** [1945]	$3.50	$10.00	$20.00

		G	VG	F

Bonded Movie-Mystery. Digest Size.

		G	VG	F
1	- - ***The Stranger*** [1946] PBO. Movie tie-in with Orson Welles, Loretta Young and Edward G. Robinson.	$4.00	$12.50	$25.00
2	Rice, Craig - ***Home Sweet Homicide*** [1946] PBO. Movie tie-in with Randolph Scott.	$4.00	$12.50	$25.00

Bonded Mystery. Hollywood: Anson Bond Publications. Inc. Digest Size.

		G	VG	F
1	Hogarth, Emnett - ***The Goose Is Cooked*** [1946] Digest size.	$3.50	$10.00	$20.00
2	Wood, Sally - ***Murder Of A Novelist*** [1946] Digest size.	$3.00	$9.00	$18.00
3	Lauferty, Lilian - ***The Hungry House*** [1946] Digest size.	$3.00	$9.00	$18.00
4	Booth, Charles G. - ***Murder Strikes Thrice*** [1946] PBO. Digest size.	$3.00	$9.00	$18.00
5	Branson, Henry C. - ***I'll Eat You Last*** [1946] Paperback size.	$2.50	$7.50	$15.00
6	Storme, Peter - ***The Thing In The Brook*** [1946] Paperback size.	$2.50	$7.50	$15.00
7	Knight, Kathleen Moore - ***Death Blew Out The Match*** [1946] Paperback size.	$2.50	$7.50	$15.00
8	Bailey, H.C. - ***Twittering Bird Mystery*** [1946] Paperback size.	$2.50	$7.50	$15.00
9	Fenisong, Rugh - ***Murder Needs A Name*** [1946] Paperback size.	$2.50	$7.50	$15.00
10	Treat, Lawrence - ***B As In Banshee*** [1946] Paperback size.	$2.50	$7.50	$15.00
11	Hughes, Dorothy B. - ***Johnnie*** [1946] Paperback size.	$2.50	$7.50	$15.00
12	Allingham, Margery - ***Kingdom Of Death*** [1946] Cover art by Hill. Paperback size.	$2.50	$7.50	$15.00
13	MacDonald, Philip (Anthony Lawless) - ***Harbour*** [1946] Paperback size.	$2.50	$7.50	$15.00
14	Holding, Elisabeth Saxany - ***Who's Afraid?*** [1946] Paperback size.	$2.50	$7.50	$15.00

Book Co. Of America.

		G	VG	F
NO#-1	Gershenson, Alvin H. - ***The Bench Is Warped*** [1964] Photo cover.	$1.25	$3.75	$7.50
002	Hebert, Bob - ***Secrets Of Handicapping*** [1964] Photo cover.	$1.25	$3.75	$7.50
NO#-2	Wills, Maury - ***It Pays To Steal*** [1964] Photo cover. Four pages of photos.	$2.00	$6.00	$12.00
NO#-3	Gershenson, Alvin H. - ***Kennedy And Big Business*** [1964].	$1.25	$3.75	$7.50
005	McPhaul, John J. - ***Chicago City Of Sin*** [n.d.] Photo cover.	$1.35	$4.00	$8.00
006	Casriel, M.D., Daniel - ***The Story Of Synanon*** [1963]	$2.50	$7.50	$15.00
007	Beaman, J. Frank - ***The Dotmakers*** [1965] Cover art by Sorcone.	$1.25	$3.75	$7.50
008	Nuetzel, Charles - ***Whodunit? Hollywood Style*** [1965] Photo cover.	$2.50	$7.50	$15.00
009	Mayfair, Franklin - ***Over My Dead Body*** [1965]	$1.25	$3.75	$7.50
010	Stroup, William - ***The Mark Of Pak San Ri*** [1965]	$1.25	$3.75	$7.50
011	Konraad, William - ***Someone You May Know*** [1965] Photo cover.	$1.25	$3.75	$7.50
012	Olivetti, Woodrow - ***Telephone A-Go-Go Hollywood West*** [1965]	$1.25	$3.75	$7.50
013	Mendelsohn, Jr., Felix - ***Club Tycoon Sends Man To Moon*** [1965]	$1.35	$4.00	$8.00
014	Van Vogt, A.E. & Hull, E. Mayne - ***Planets For Sale*** [1965] Cover art by Nuetzell.	$1.50	$5.00	$10.00
015	Anthology - ***If This Goes On*** [1965] edited by Charles Nuetzel. Cover art by Nuetzell.	$2.00	$6.00	$12.00
016	Adlai, Sadik - ***King Tarick*** [1965] PBO.	$1.50	$5.00	$10.00
017	Mendelsohn, Jr., Felix - ***Barney Crome*** [1965]	$1.35	$4.00	$8.00

Books, Inc.

		G	VG	F
102	Garrigus, Fred - ***Giant Quiz Book*** [1939] PBO.	$3.50	$10.00	$20.00

Boudoir.

		G	VG	F
1027	Jason, Jerry (George H. Smith) - ***Sexodus!*** [1963] PBO.	$2.50	$7.50	$15.00

		G	VG	F
Brandon House. North Hollywood: Brandon House Inc.				
615	Adams, Gerald Drayson - ***Rawhide Killer*** [1963] PBO. Cover by Wil Hulsey.	$1.50	$5.00	$10.00
711	Trelos, Tony - ***Cindy Baby*** [1964] PBO.	$1.25	$3.75	$7.50
1009	Lee, T. F. - ***In A Bedroom Darkly*** [1966] PBO. Cartoons.	$2.00	$6.00	$12.00
6134	Farmer, Philip Jose - ***Love Song*** [1970] PBO.	$50.00	$175.00	$400.00
Brentwood Books.				
1007	Brent, Lynton Wright - ***The Sex Demon Of Jangal*** [n.d.]	$2.00	$6.00	$12.00
Broadway Novel Monthly. New York: Diverssey Publications. Digest Size.				
1	Weigall, Arthur - ***Infidelity*** [1950]	$4.00	$12.50	$25.00
2	Dekobra, Maurice - ***Venus On Wheels*** [1950]	$4.00	$12.50	$25.00
3	Gropper, Milton Herbert - ***Ladies Of The Evening*** [1950]	$4.00	$12.50	$25.00
4	Prince, Don - ***Tom's Temptations*** [1950]	$4.50	$14.00	$28.00
5	Trent, Timothy - ***Night Boat*** [1950]	$4.00	$12.50	$25.00
6	Gropper, M.H. - ***Three Loose Ladies*** [1950]	$4.00	$12.50	$25.00
7	Graham, Carroll & Garrett - ***Fleshpots Of Malibu*** [1950]	$4.00	$12.50	$25.00
8	Collison, Wilson - ***Blonde Baby*** [1950]	$4.50	$14.00	$28.00
9	Woodford, Jack - ***Dangerous Love*** [1950]	$4.50	$14.00	$28.00
10	Woodford, Jack - ***Untamed Darling*** [1950]	$4.50	$14.00	$28.00
Bronze Books. New York: Designs Publishing Corp. Digest Size.				
1	Roberts, Luke - ***Harlem Model*** [1952] PBO. Photo cover.	$22.00	$70.00	$140.00
2	Carter, Jesse Lee - ***Hot Chocolate*** [1952] PBO. Photo cover.	$22.00	$70.00	$140.00
Brussel, J. Digest Size.				
NN	Leroux, Gaston - ***Murder In The Bedroom*** [1945] PBO.	$2.50	$7.50	$15.00
Bull's-Eye. Toronto: Duchess Printing. Digest Size.				
1	Jacobs, T.C.H. - ***Silent Terror*** [1944]	$3.50	$10.00	$20.00
2	Goyne, Richard - ***Death By Desire*** [1944]	$3.50	$10.00	$20.00
Cameo Books. New York: Detective House, Inc. Digest Size.				
300	Stonebraker, Stone - ***No Man Of Her Own*** [1951] PBO. Cover art by Gross.	$3.50	$10.00	$20.00
301	Harvey, Gene - ***The Loves Of Alice Brandt*** [1951] PBO.	$3.50	$10.00	$20.00
302	Arnold, William - ***Night Of Ecstasy*** [1951] Cover art by Gross.	$3.50	$10.00	$20.00
303	Bligh, Norman - ***Conquest Of Margie*** [1951] Cover art by Gross.	$3.50	$10.00	$20.00
304	Stonebraker, Florence - ***Naughty Blonde*** [1951] PBO. Cover art by Nappi.	$3.50	$10.00	$20.00
305	Harvey, Gene - ***Pick-Up At Midnight*** [1951] PBO.	$3.50	$10.00	$20.00
306	Quandt, Albert L. - ***Passion C.O.D.*** [1951] PBO. Cover art by George Gross.	$3.50	$10.00	$20.00
307	Welles, Kermit - ***Sin Preferred*** [1951] PBO. Cover by Rudy Nappi.	$3.50	$10.00	$20.00
308	Hatter, Amos - ***Secret Affair*** [1951] PBO.	$3.50	$10.00	$20.00
309	Harvey, Gene - ***A Girl Called Joy*** [1951] PBO. Cover art by Gross.	$3.50	$10.00	$20.00
310	Welles, Kermit - ***Pleasure Bound*** [1952] PBO.	$3.50	$10.00	$20.00
311	Jordan, Gail - ***The Affairs Of A Country Girl*** [1952] PBO.	$3.50	$10.00	$20.00
312	Hatter, Amos - ***Crossroads Of Desire*** [1952]	$3.00	$9.00	$18.00
313	Bligh, Norman - ***Three-Time Sinner*** [1952]	$3.00	$9.00	$18.00
314	Arnold, William - ***The Big Tease*** [1952] PBO.	$3.50	$10.00	$20.00
315	Stonebraker, Florence - ***Passion's Harvest*** [1952] Cover art by George Gross.	$3.50	$10.00	$20.00
316	Bligh, Norman - ***Soft Shoulders*** [1952]	$3.50	$10.00	$20.00
317	Gaddis, Peggy - ***Woman Of Fire*** [1952]	$3.50	$10.00	$20.00
318	Hatter, Amos - ***Island Ecstasy*** [1952]	$3.00	$9.00	$18.00
319	Douglas, Ralph - ***Beach Party*** [1952] PBO.	$3.50	$10.00	$20.00

Cameo Books, 318

Cameo Books, 327

Carnival Books, 902

		G	VG	F
320	Hatter, Amos - ***Girl Of The Midway*** [1952] PBO. Cover art by Nappi.	$3.50	$10.00	$20.00
321	Spencer, Frederic - ***Tight Skirt*** [1952] PBO. Cover art by Belarski.	$4.00	$12.50	$25.00
322	Reynolds, Robert E. - ***Loose Women*** [1952] PBO.	$3.50	$10.00	$20.00
323	Dixon, Lewis - ***Wild Girl*** [1952] PBO. Cover art by Rudolph Belarski.	$4.00	$12.50	$25.00
324	Erskine, Sylvia - ***Young Nurse*** [1952]	$3.00	$9.00	$18.00
325	Gaddis, Peggy - ***Mountain Bride*** [1952] PBO. Cover by George Gross.	$3.50	$10.00	$20.00
326	Tucker, Joan - ***At Ruby's Place*** [1952] PBO. Cover by Paul Kresse.	$3.50	$10.00	$20.00
327	Spencer, Frederic - ***Cleo*** [1952]	$3.00	$9.00	$18.00
328	Jordan, Gail - ***The Affairs Of A Country Girl*** [1952] Cover art by George Gross.	$3.50	$10.00	$20.00
329	Reynolds, Robert E. - ***Backwoods Bride*** [1953] PBO. Cover by Gross.	$3.50	$10.00	$20.00
330	Manning, Jane - ***Reefer Girl*** [1953] PBO. Cover by Nappi.	$3.50	$10.00	$20.00
331	Haskell, Frank - ***House Of Lost Women*** [1953] PBO.	$3.50	$10.00	$20.00
332	Erskine, Sylvia - ***Nurse's Quarters*** [1953] Cover art by Belarski.	$3.00	$9.00	$18.00
333	Gill, Elisabeth - ***Young Sinner*** [1953] PBO.	$3.00	$9.00	$18.00
334	Harvey, Gene - ***Office Sinner*** [1953] Cover art by Ray Pease.	$3.50	$10.00	$20.00
335	Dixon, Lewis - ***Wild Girl*** [1952] Cover art by Belarski.	$3.00	$9.00	$18.00
336	Harvey, Gene - ***Doctor's Nurse*** [1952]	$3.00	$9.00	$18.00
338	Welles, Kermit - ***Shanty Boat Girl*** [1952]	$3.50	$10.00	$20.00
339	Cooper, Morton - ***French Maid*** [1954] PBO. Cover art by Tauss.	$3.50	$10.00	$20.00
340	Erskine, Sylvia - ***Young Nurse*** [1954]	$3.00	$9.00	$18.00
341	Jordan, Gail - ***Country Girl*** [1954] Cover by George Gross.	$3.50	$10.00	$20.00
342	Tucker, Joan - ***Shanty Girl*** [1954] Cover art by Belarski.	$3.00	$9.00	$18.00
343	Clay, Matthew - ***Slum Doctor*** [1954] Cover art by Robert Schulz.	$3.00	$9.00	$18.00
345	Reynolds, Robert E. - ***Lost Women*** [1954]	$3.00	$9.00	$18.00
348	Haskell, Frank - ***Boarding House*** [1954] Cover by George Gross.	$3.00	$9.00	$18.00
354	Tucker, Joan - ***Shanty Girl*** [1954] Cover art by Belarski.	$3.00	$9.00	$18.00
355	Arnold, William - ***Runaway Girl*** [1954]	$3.00	$9.00	$18.00
359	Nickerson, Ralph - ***Boy-Chaser*** [1954]	$3.00	$9.00	$18.00
360	Manning, Tom - ***Hotel Waitress*** [1954] Cover art by Gross.	$3.00	$9.00	$18.00
361	Westley, Kirk - ***Shanty Boat Girl*** [1954]	$3.00	$9.00	$18.00
362	Gaddis, Peggy - ***Mountain Bride*** [1954] Cover art by Gross.	$3.00	$9.00	$18.00
365	Haskell, Frank - ***Boarding House*** [1954]	$3.00	$9.00	$18.00

		G	VG	F
368	Marin, Arthur - ***Blonde Hellcat*** [1954] Cover by Ray Pease.	$3.00	$9.00	$18.00
369	Dickson, Lewis - ***Wild Girl*** [1954] Cover art by Belarski.	$3.00	$9.00	$18.00

Candid Books. New York: Crestwood Pub. Co., Inc. Digest Size.

		G	VG	F
20	Sloan, Gladys - ***Love For Sale*** [1949] Cover art by Wenzel.	$3.50	$10.00	$20.00
21	Harvey, Gene - ***Wild Weekend*** [1949] Cover art by Wenzel.	$3.50	$10.00	$20.00
22	Harlow, James - ***Notorious Woman*** [1949] Cover art by Wenzel.	$3.50	$10.00	$20.00
23	Stonebraker, Florence - ***Lessons In Love*** [1949] Cover art by Wenzel.	$3.50	$10.00	$20.00
24	Williams, Wright - ***Hired Husband*** [1949] Cover art by Wenzel.	$3.50	$10.00	$20.00
25	Strong, Charles S. - ***Disorderly Conduct*** [1949] Cover art by Wenzel.	$3.50	$10.00	$20.00
26	Brown, Beth - ***For Men Only*** [1949] Cover art by Wenzel.	$3.50	$10.00	$20.00

Candid Reader.

		G	VG	F
901	- - ***The Sin Funnel*** [n.d.]	$2.50	$7.50	$15.00
909	- - ***The N.U.D.E. Caper*** [n.d.]	$2.50	$7.50	$15.00
930	- - ***The Desert Damsels*** [n.d.]	$2.50	$7.50	$15.00
940	- - ***Sin Seance*** [n.d.]	$2.50	$7.50	$15.00
981	Stanley, M. - ***God's Little Orgy*** [n.d.]	$2.00	$6.00	$12.00
1030	Pygaster, Cal. I. - ***Zero Gravity Swap*** [1970] PBO.	$2.50	$7.50	$15.00

Cardinal Books (Early Publisher's History, 1951–1959)

Pocket Books, Inc., established Cardinal Books to market more expensive titles than the 25¢ Pocket Book editions. Pricing for Cardinal Books began at 35¢. A bright red cardinal and gold spine adorned each book. Throughout the Cardinal books you will find a large number of nonfiction titles. They produced one very collectible title with a dust jacket, Nelson Algren's *The Man with the Golden Arm.* Other books of interest from Cardinal include a Marilyn Monroe exposé, westerns by Zane Grey, and movie-related titles.

Cardinal C Series. New York: Pocket Books, Inc.

		G	VG	F
C-1	Shakespeare, William - ***Four Great Historical Plays*** [1951]	$ .65	$2.00	$4.00
C-2	Bellamann, Henry - ***King's Row*** [n.d.]	$ .50	$1.50	$3.00
C-3	Fisher, Vardis - ***In Tragic Life*** [n.d.]	$ .50	$1.50	$3.00
C-4	Mason, F. Van Wyck - ***Cutlass Empire*** [n.d.]	$ .50	$1.50	$3.00
C-5	Merriam-Webster - ***The Merriam-Webster Pocket Dictionary*** [n.d.]	$ .50	$1.50	$3.00
C-6	du Maurier - ***Hungry Hill*** [n.d.]	$ .40	$1.25	$2.50
C-7	Pratt, Fletcher - ***A Short History Of The Civil War*** [n.d.]	$ .50	$1.50	$3.00
C-9	Edited by Ernest Sutherland Bates - ***The Pocket Bible*** [1951] Cover by Charles Skages.	$ .50	$1.50	$3.00
C-13	Roget - ***Roget's Pocket Thesaurus*** [n.d.]	$ .40	$1.25	$2.50
C-17	Translated by Sir Richard Burton - ***Tales From The Arabian Nights*** [1951] Cover by Al Schmidt.	$ .50	$1.50	$3.00
C-20	Atlas - ***The Rand McNally Pocket World Atlas*** [n.d.]	$ .50	$1.50	$3.00
C-21	Yerby, Frank - ***Pride's Castle*** [1951] Cover by Carl Mueller.	$ .40	$1.25	$2.50
C-22	Jennings, John - ***The Pepper Tree*** [1951] Cover by Al Schmidt...	$ .40	$1.25	$2.50
C-27	St. Augustine - ***Confessions Of St. Augustine*** [n.d.]	$ .50	$1.50	$3.00
C-28	Wechsler, Herman J. - ***Lives Of Famous French Painters*** [1952] PBO.	$ .50	$1.50	$3.00
C-30	Guthrie, Jr., A.B. - ***The Way West*** [n.d.]	$ .50	$1.50	$3.00
C-31(DJ)	Algren, Nelson - ***The Man With The Golden Arm*** [1951] Dust-jacketed edition. Cardinal DJ over Pocketbook #757.	$10.00	$30.00	$60.00
C-31	Algren, Nelson - ***The Man With The Golden Arm*** [1951]	$ .40	$1.25	$2.50

		G	VG	F
C-34	Nordhoff, Charles & Hall, James Norman - ***Mutiny On The Bounty*** [1952] Cover by Al Schmidt.	$ .40	$1.25	$2.50
C-38	Presnell, Jr., Robert - ***The Witching Pool*** [n.d.]	$ .40	$1.25	$2.50
C-39	Lund, Robert - ***Hour Of Glory*** [1952] Cover by Tom Dunn.	$ .40	$1.25	$2.50
C-40	Wylie, Philip - ***The Disappearance*** [n.d.]	$ .50	$1.50	$3.00
C-41	Tebbel, John - ***The Conqueror*** [1952] Cover by Ernest Chiriaka.	$ .50	$1.50	$3.00
C-43	Thane, Elswyth - ***Dawn's Early Light*** [1952] Cover by Ernest Chiriaka.	$ .40	$1.25	$2.50
C-48	Stevenson, Robert Louis - ***The Great Short Stories Of Robert Louis Stevenson*** [1952] PBO as an original collection.	$ .40	$1.25	$2.50
C-49	Bristow, Gwen - ***Jubilee Trail*** [1952] Cover by Tom Dunn.	$ .50	$1.50	$3.00
C-50	Edited by Oscard Williams - ***Immortal Poems Of The English Language*** [1952]	$ .40	$1.25	$2.50
C-52	Guthrie, Jr., A.B. - ***The Big Sky*** [n.d.]	$ .40	$1.25	$2.50
C-53	Du Maurier, Daphne - ***Rebecca*** [1952] Cover by Tom Dunn.	$ .40	$1.25	$2.50
C-55	Edited by Henry W. Simon - ***The Complete Sonnets, Songs, And Poems Of Shakespeare*** [n.d.]	$ .40	$1.25	$2.50
C-56	Karig, Walter - ***Caroline Hicks*** [1952] Cover by Tom Dunn.	$ .40	$1.25	$2.50
C-58	Ullman, James Ramsey - ***River Of The Sun*** [1951] Cover by Walter Baumhofer.	$ .40	$1.25	$2.50
C-59	Flaubert, Gustave - ***Madame Bovary*** [1952] Cover by Carl Mueller.	$ .50	$1.50	$3.00
C-61	Anthology - ***Questions And Answers From The Book Of Knowledge*** [1952] Photo cover.	$ .40	$1.25	$2.50
C-62	Translated by Robert Graves - ***The Golden Ass Of Apuleius*** [1952] Cover art by Frank Lieberman.	$ .40	$1.25	$2.50
C-63	Maugham, W. Somerset - ***Of Human Bondage*** [1952]	$ .50	$1.50	$3.00
C-67	Werfel, Frank - ***The Song Of Bernadette*** [1952]	$ .50	$1.50	$3.00
C-68	Du Maurier, Daphne - ***The Parasites*** [1952]	$ .50	$1.50	$3.00
C-69	Spellman, Francis Cardinal - ***The Foundling*** [1952]	$ .40	$1.25	$2.50
C-70	Hilton, James - ***Morning Journey*** [1952] Cover art by Stanley Zuckerberg.	$ .40	$1.25	$2.50
C-72	Dos Passos, John - ***The 42nd Parallel*** [1952]	$ .50	$1.50	$3.00
C-77	Wilson, Donald Powell - ***My Six Convicts*** [1953]	$ .50	$1.50	$3.00
C-80	Anthology - ***Discovery No. 1*** [1954] PBO.	$ .50	$1.50	$3.00
C-81	Crabb, Alfred Leland - ***Dinner At Belmont*** [1952] Cover art by Barye Phillips.	$ .50	$1.50	$3.00
C-84	Brooks, Richard - ***The Producer*** [1953] Cover art by Ray Johnson.	$ .40	$1.25	$2.50
C-90	Anthology edited by N.H. & S.K. Mager - ***The Pocket Household Encyclopedia*** [1953] PBO. Photo cover.	$ .40	$1.25	$2.50
C-91	Robbins, Harold - ***A Stone For Danny Fisher*** [1953] Cover art by Tom Dunn.	$ .40	$1.25	$2.50
C-92	White, Leslie Turner - ***Look Away, Look Away*** [1953]	$ .50	$1.50	$3.00
C-96	Wellman, Paul I. - ***The Iron Mistress*** [1953] Cover art by Ray Johnson.	$ .50	$1.50	$3.00
C-97	Haycox, Ernest - ***The Earthbreakers*** [1953] Cover art by Ray Johnson.	$ .40	$1.25	$2.50
C-98	Longstreet, Stephen - ***The Pedlocks*** [1953] Cover art by Stanley Zuckerberg.	$ .50	$1.50	$3.00
C-99	DuMaurier, Daphne - ***The King's General*** [1953]	$ .50	$1.50	$3.00
C-100	Williams, George - ***Flesh And The Dream*** [1953] Cover art by Tom Dunn.	$ .40	$1.25	$2.50
C-103	Thane, Elswyth - ***Yankee Stranger*** [1953] Cover art by Stanley Borack.	$ .40	$1.25	$2.50
C-108	Buck, Pearl S. - ***Come, My Beloved*** [1954]	$ .50	$1.50	$3.00
C-110	Lipsky, Eleazar - ***Lincoln McKeever*** [1953]	$ .40	$1.25	$2.50
C-111	Buck, Pearl S. - ***The Good Earth*** [1953]	$ .50	$1.50	$3.00
C-115	Anthology edited by Vance Bourjaily - ***Discovery No. 2*** [1953] PBO.	$ .40	$1.25	$2.50

		G	VG	F
C-116	McNeilly, Mildred Masterson - ***Matthew Steel*** [1953] Cover art by George Erickson.	$ .40	$1.25	$2.50
C-117	Davidson, Louis B. & Doherty, Eddie - ***Captain Marooner*** [1953] Cover art by Ray Johnson.	$ .40	$1.25	$2.50
C-119	Fisher, Vardis - ***We Are Betrayed*** [1953] Cover art by Tom Dunn.	$ .40	$1.25	$2.50
C-120	Ferber, Edna - ***Giant*** [1953] Cover art by Stanley Borack.	$ .40	$1.25	$2.50
C-123	Davis, Burke - ***Yorktown*** [1953] Cover art by Tom Dunn.	$ .40	$1.25	$2.50
C-125	Curtis, Carol - ***Carol Curtis' Complete Book Of Knitting And Crocheting*** [1953] PBO.	$ .50	$1.50	$3.00
C-126	Gardner, Erle Stanley - ***The Court Of Last Resort*** [1954] Cover art by Charles Skaggs.	$ .50	$1.50	$3.00
C-127	Tracy, Don - ***Crimson Is The Eastern Shore*** [1954] Cover art by James Meese.	$ .40	$1.25	$2.50
C-128	Ehrlich, Leonard - ***God's Angry Man*** [1954] Cover art by Tom Dunn.	$ .40	$1.25	$2.50
C-130	Bourjaily, Vance - editor - Discovery No. 3 [1954] PBO.	$ .50	$1.50	$3.00
C-133	Tayor, Robert Lewis - ***Winston Churchill*** [1954]	$ .40	$1.25	$2.50
C-135	Clarke, Arthur C. - ***The Exploration Of Space*** [1954] Photo cover. Twelve pages of photos.	$ .50	$1.50	$3.00
C-137	Jennings, John - ***The Strange Brigade*** [1954] Cover art by Rudy Nappi.	$ .40	$1.25	$2.50
C-138	Bromfield, Louis - ***Pleasant Valley*** [1954] Photo cover.	$ .40	$1.25	$2.50
C-140	Andersen, U.S. - ***The Smoldering Sea*** [1954] Cover art by Tom Dunn.	$ .50	$1.50	$3.00
C-141	Wellman, Paul I. - ***Jubal Troop*** [1954] Cover by Clark Hulings.	$ .40	$1.25	$2.50
C-143	Anthology edited by Vance Bourjaily - ***Discovery No. 4*** [1954] PBO.	$ .40	$1.25	$2.50
C-144	Wallop, Douglass - ***Night Light*** [1954] Cover by Tom Dunn.	$ .40	$1.25	$2.50
C-146	Crosby, Bing - ***Call Me Lucky*** [1954] Photo cover. Four pages of photos.	$ .40	$1.25	$2.50
C-149	Lindop, Audrey Erskine - ***The Bandit And The Priest*** [1954] Cover art by Tom Dunn.	$ .50	$1.50	$3.00
C-150	Jastrow, Joseph - ***Freud: His Dream And Sex Theories*** [1954] Cover by Charles Skaggs.	$ .50	$1.50	$3.00
C-151	Payne, Robert - ***The Chieftain*** [1954]	$ .50	$1.50	$3.00
C-152	Anthology edited by Franklin Watts - ***The Pocket Book Magazine*** [1954] PBO.	$ .40	$1.25	$2.50
C-155	Anthology edited by Christopher Cross - ***A Minute Of Prayer*** [1954]	$ .50	$1.50	$3.00
C-159	Anthology edited by Vance Bourjaily - ***Discovery No. 5*** [1955] PBO.	$ .50	$1.50	$3.00
C-161	Maugham, W. Somerset - ***The Razor's Edge*** [1954] Cover art by Tom Dunn.	$ .40	$1.25	$2.50
C-162	Wicker, Tom - ***The Kingpin*** [1954] Cover by Tom Dunn.	$ .50	$1.50	$3.00
C-163	Cousteau, Captain J.Y. - ***The Silent World*** [1954] Photo cover. Fourty-eight pages of photos, sixteen in color.	$ .50	$1.50	$3.00
C-165	Mason, F. Van Wyck - ***Golden Admiral*** [1954]	$ .50	$1.50	$3.00
C-173	Oursler, Will - ***N.Y., N.Y.*** [1954] Cover by John McClelland.	$ .40	$1.25	$2.50
C-175	Yerby, Frank - ***The Vixens*** [1955]	$ .40	$1.25	$2.50
C-178	White, Leslie Turner - ***Sir Rogue*** [1955] Cover art by Clark Hulings.	$ .50	$1.50	$3.00
C-180	Hammett, Catherine T. - ***Your Own Book Of Campcraft*** [1955]	$ .40	$1.25	$2.50
C-181	Anthology - ***The Pocket Cook Book*** [1955]	$ .40	$1.25	$2.50
C-182	Fuller, Roger - ***Sign Of The Pagan*** [1955] Cover art by Clark Hulings.	$ .40	$1.25	$2.50
C-183	Anthology edited by E.B. White - ***A Subtreasury Of American Humor*** [1955] Cover art by Philip Grushkin.	$ .40	$1.25	$2.50
C-184	Best, Herbert - ***Diane*** [1955] Cover art by Barye Phillips.	$ .40	$1.25	$2.50

		G	VG	F
C-187	Hunter, Evan - ***The Blackboard Jungle*** [1955] Cover art by Clark Hulings.	$1.00	$3.00	$6.00
C-189	Tracy, Don - ***Roanoke Renegade*** [1955] Cover art by Clark Hulings.	$ .40	$1.25	$2.50
C-192	Manfred, Frederick F. - ***Lord Grizzly*** [1955] Cover art by Clark Hulings.	$ .50	$1.50	$3.00
C-195	Asbury, Herbert - ***The French Quarter*** [1955] Cover art by Clark Hulings.	$ .50	$1.50	$3.00
C-200	Watts, Franklin - editor - The Pocket Magazine No. 3 [1955] PBO.	$ .50	$1.50	$3.00
C-203	Lott, Milton - ***The Last Hunt*** [1955]	$ .40	$1.25	$2.50
C-204	Haycox, Ernest - ***The Adventurers*** [1955] Cover art by Charles Binger.	$ .40	$1.25	$2.50
C-205	Hope, Bob - ***Have Tux, Will Travel*** [1955] Photo cover.	$ .50	$1.50	$3.00
C-207	Goodwin, Harold Leland - ***The Science Book Of Space Travel*** [1955] Cover art by Mel Hunter.	$ .40	$1.25	$2.50
C-209	Wister, Owen - ***The Virginian*** [1956] Cover art by James Meese.	$ .50	$1.50	$3.00
C-210	Graziano, Rocky - ***Somebody Up There Likes Me*** [1956] Cover art by Tom Dunn.	$ .75	$2.50	$5.00
C-211	Mason, F. Van Wyck - ***Blue Hurricane*** [1956] Cover by Clark Hulings.	$ .40	$1.25	$2.50
C-214	Lofts, Norah - ***Bless This House*** [1956] Cover art by Charles Binger.	$ .50	$1.50	$3.00
C-215	Griffith, Maxwell - ***The Gadget Maker*** [1956] Cover art by James Meese.	$ .40	$1.25	$2.50
C-216	DuMaurier, Daphne - ***Mary Anne*** [1956]	$ .50	$1.50	$3.00
C-223	Morgan, Al - ***The Great Man*** [1956] Cover by James Meese.	$ .50	$1.50	$3.00
C-224	Davenport, Marcia - ***My Brother's Keeper*** [1956] Cover art by Tom Dunn.	$ .50	$1.50	$3.00
C-226	Michener, James - ***Tales Of The South Pacific*** [1956]	$ .40	$1.25	$2.50
C-227	Castle, Marian - ***Roxana*** [1956]	$ .40	$1.25	$2.50
C-228	Tracy, Don - ***Carolina Corsair*** [1956]	$ .40	$1.25	$2.50
C-230	Wilson, Sloan - ***The Man In The Gray Flannel Suit*** [1956] Photo cover.	$ .50	$1.50	$3.00
C-231	Grey, Zane - ***The U.P. Trail*** [1956]	$ .50	$1.50	$3.00
C-232	Mager, Sylvia K. - ***A Complete Guide To Home Sewing*** [1956] Cover art by Ernest Chiriaka.	$ .40	$1.25	$2.50
C-234	Viertel, Joseph - ***The Last Temptation*** [1956] Cover art by Tom Dunn.	$ .50	$1.50	$3.00
C-236	Hunter, Evan - ***Quartet In "H"*** [1956] Cover art by Tom Dunn.	$1.00	$3.00	$6.00
C-239	Grey, Zane - ***The Border Legion*** [1956]	$ .40	$1.25	$2.50
C-240	Douglas, Lloyd C. - ***Forgive Us Our Trespasses*** [1957]	$ .50	$1.50	$3.00
C-248	Martin, Pete - ***Will Acting Spoil Marilyn Monroe?*** [1957] Photo cover. Forty-three pages of photos.	$6.00	$20.00	$40.00
C-249	Yerby, Frank - ***Captain Rebel*** [1957]	$ .50	$1.50	$3.00
C-252	Caldwell, Taylor - ***Dynasty Of Death*** [1957] Cover art by Tony Kokinos.	$ .40	$1.25	$2.50
C-253	Fisher, Vardis - ***Pemmican*** [1957] Cover art by Daniel Schwartz.	$ .40	$1.25	$2.50
C-261	Maugham, W. Somerset - ***The Painted Veil*** [1957] Photo cover. Movie tie-in.	$ .40	$1.25	$2.50
C-263	Waltari, Mika - ***The Dark Angel*** [1957] Cover art by Charles Binger.	$ .50	$1.50	$3.00
C-267	Guthrie, Jr., A.B. - ***These Thousand Hills*** [1957] Cover art by Jerry Allison.	$ .50	$1.50	$3.00
C-268	Gardner, Erle Stanley - ***The Case Of The Sun Bather's Diary*** [1958] Cover by Mitchell Hooks.	$ .50	$1.50	$3.00
C-270	Collection - ***The Pocket Book Of Erskine Caldwell Stories*** [1957] Cover art by Clark Hulings.	$ .40	$1.25	$2.50

		G	VG	F
C-273	Maugham, W. Somerset - ***The Magician*** [1957] Cover art by Clark Hulings.	$ .40	$1.25	$2.50
C-276	DuMaurier, Daphne - ***The Scapegoat*** [1958] Cover art by Tom Dunn.	$ .40	$1.25	$2.50
C-285	Gardner, Erle Stanley - ***The Case Of The Lazy Lover*** [1958]	$ .40	$1.25	$2.50
C-286	Murtaugh, Judge John & Harris, Sara - ***Cast The First Stone*** [1958] Photo cover.	$ .50	$1.50	$3.00
C-288	Packard, Vance - ***The Hidden Persuaders*** [1958]	$ .40	$1.25	$2.50
C-291	Gardner, Erle Stanley - ***The D.A. Calls A Turn*** [1958]	$ .50	$1.50	$3.00
C-292	Gardner, Erle Stanley - ***The D.A. Breaks A Seal*** [1958]	$ .50	$1.50	$3.00
C-293	Gardner, Erle Stanley - ***The D.A. Takes A Chance*** [1958]	$ .50	$1.50	$3.00
C-297	Gardner, Erle Stanley - ***The Case Of The Nervous Accomplice*** [1958]	$ .50	$1.50	$3.00
C-298	McPartland, John - ***No Down Payment*** [1957] Photo cover. Movie tie-in.	$ .50	$1.50	$3.00
C-300	Tracy, Don - ***Cherokee*** [1958] Cover art by Tom Dunn.	$ .40	$1.25	$2.50
C-301	Manfred, Frederick - ***Riders Of Judgment*** [1958]	$ .50	$1.50	$3.00
C-309	Gardner, Erle Stanley - ***The Case Of The Sulky Girl*** [1958] Cover art by Mark Dawson.	$ .40	$1.25	$2.50
C-310	Yerby, Frank - ***Fairoaks*** [1958]	$ .50	$1.50	$3.00
C-311	Caldwell, Taylor - ***The Final Hour*** [1958] Cover art by Clark Hulings.	$ .50	$1.50	$3.00
C-313	Hawley, Cameron - ***Cash McCall*** [1958] Cover art by Tom Dunn.	$ .40	$1.25	$2.50
C-315	Brown, Joe David - ***Kings Go Forth*** [1958] Photo cover. Movie tie-in.	$ .50	$1.50	$3.00
C-317	Frank, Ann - ***Anne Frank: The Diary Of A Young Girl*** [1958]	$ .50	$1.50	$3.00
C-318	Christie, Agatha - ***"Murder She Said"*** [1961] Movie tie-in.	$ .50	$1.50	$3.00
C-321	Tracy, Don - ***On The Midnight Tide*** [1958] Cover art by Clark Hulings.	$ .40	$1.25	$2.50
C-323	Gardner, Erle Stanley - ***The Case of The Demure Defendant*** [1959]	$ .40	$1.25	$2.50
C-324	Gardner, Erle Stanley - ***The Case Of The Curious Bride*** [1959]	$ .40	$1.25	$2.50
C-326	DuMaurier, Daphne - ***Jamaica Inn*** [1959]	$ .50	$1.50	$3.00
C-328	Wallop, Douglass - ***The Year The Yankees Lost The Pennant*** [1959] Movie photo cover. Movie tie-in.	$ .40	$1.25	$2.50
C-330	Linkletter, Art - ***Kids Say The Darndest Things!*** [1959]	$ .40	$1.25	$2.50
C-331	Anthology - ***The Pocket Book Of Esquire Cartoons*** [1959] Cover art by E. Simms Campbell. Cartoon book.	$ .50	$1.50	$3.00
C-337	Gardner, Erle Stanley - ***The Case Of The Gilded Lily*** [1959] Cover art by John Fernie.	$ .40	$1.25	$2.50
C-338	Ross, Walter - ***The Immortal*** [1959]	$ .50	$1.50	$3.00
C-341	Gardner, Erle Stanley - ***The Case Of The Lucky Loser*** [1959] Cover art by Darrell Green.	$ .50	$1.50	$3.00
C-343	Queen, Ellery - ***The Finishing Stroke*** [1959] Cover art by Jerry Allison.	$ .50	$1.50	$3.00
C-350	Buchwald, Art - ***A Gift From The Boys*** [1959] Cover by Bayre Phillips.	$ .40	$1.25	$2.50
C-352	Yerby, Frank - ***The Serpent And The Staff*** [1959]	$ .40	$1.25	$2.50
C-356	Van Buren, Abigail - ***Dear Abby*** [1959]	$ .50	$1.50	$3.00
C-363	Lawrence, D. H. - ***Lady Chatterley's Lover*** [1959]	$ .50	$1.50	$3.00
C-365	Mason, F. Van Wyck - ***Return Of The Eagles*** [1959] PBO. Cover art by Darrel Greene.	$ .40	$1.25	$2.50
C-366	DuMaurier, Daphne - ***Frenchman's Creek*** [1959]	$ .50	$1.50	$3.00
C-368	Brand, Max - ***Lucky Larribee*** [1959] Cover art by Jack Hines.	$ .50	$1.50	$3.00
C-369	Gary, Romain - ***Lady L.*** [1959] Cover art by Charles.	$ .50	$1.50	$3.00
C-371	Cloete, Stuart - ***Gazella*** [1959] Cover by Charles.	$ .40	$1.25	$2.50
C-375	Chandler, Raymond - ***Playback*** [1960] Cover art by Bill Rose.	$2.50	$7.50	$15.00
C-377	Gardner, Erle Stanley - ***The Case Of The Screaming Woman*** [1959] Cover art by Charles. TV tie-in.	$ .50	$1.50	$3.00

		G	VG	F
C-379	Gardner, Erle Stanley - ***The Case Of The Perjured Parrot*** [1959] Cover art by Ric Grasso. TV tie-in.	$ .50	$1.50	$3.00
C-380	Gardner, Erle Stanley - ***The Case Of The Borrowed Brunette*** [1959] Cover art by Charles. TV tie-in.	$ .50	$1.50	$3.00
C-383	Lindsay, Norman - ***Age Of Consent*** [1959] Cover art by Barye Phillips.	$ .50	$1.50	$3.00
C-384	Linkletter, Art - ***People Are Funny*** [1960]	$ .50	$1.50	$3.00
C-385	Grey, Zane - ***Raiders Of Spanish Peaks*** [1960] Cover art by Jerry Allison.	$ .50	$1.50	$3.00
C-386	Christie, Agatha - ***Ordeal By Innocence*** [1960] Cover by Wayne Blickenstaff.	$ .50	$1.50	$3.00
C-389	Albert, Marvin H. - ***All The Young Men*** [1960] PBO. Movie tie-in.	$ .50	$1.50	$3.00
C-391	Ullman, James Ramsey - ***Third Man On The Mountain*** [1959] Movie tie-in.	$ .50	$1.50	$3.00
C-401	Kanin, Garson - ***The Rat Race*** [1960] PBO. Photo cover. Movie tie-in.	$ .50	$1.50	$3.00
C-404	Levin, Meyer - ***Eva*** [1960]	$ .50	$1.50	$3.00
C-405	Mason, F. Van Wyck - ***The Multimillion-Dollar Murders*** [1960] Cover art by Bob Abbett.	$ .50	$1.50	$3.00
C-406	Morgan, Al - ***One Star General*** [1960] Cover by Jerry Allison.	$ .40	$1.25	$2.50
C-409	Sher, Jack - ***Love In A Goldfish Bowl*** [1961] PBO. Photo cover. Movie tie-in.	$ .50	$1.50	$3.00
C-410	Buck, Pearl S. - ***Command The Morning*** [1960]	$ .50	$1.50	$3.00
C-411	Flynn, Errol - ***Showdown*** [1960] Cover art by Jerry Allison.	$ .40	$1.25	$2.50
C-412	Johnson, George Clayton & Russell, Jack - ***Ocean's Eleven*** [1960]	$ .50	$1.50	$3.00
C-414	DuMaurier, Daphne - ***The Breaking Point*** [1960]	$ .50	$1.50	$3.00
C-417	Grey, Zane - ***Knights Of The Range*** [1960]	$ .50	$1.50	$3.00
C-421	Christie, Agatha - ***Funerals Are Fatal*** [1961]	$ .50	$1.50	$3.00
C-424	Cloete, Stuart - ***The Fiercest Heart*** [1961] Photo cover. Movie tie-in.	$ .40	$1.25	$2.50
C-429	Buck, Pearl S. - ***Satan Never Sleeps*** [1962] Movie photo covers. Movie tie-in.	$ .50	$1.50	$3.00
C-430	Gray, Zane - ***The Rainbow Trail*** [1961]	$ .50	$1.50	$3.00
C-437	Milner, Michael - ***Hatari!*** [1962] PBO. Movie tie-in with John Wayne. Eight pages of photos.	$ .50	$1.50	$3.00
C-439	Brean, Herbert - ***How To Stop Smoking*** [1962]	$ .50	$1.50	$3.00
C-440	Grey, Zane - ***Code Of The West*** [1963] Cover art by Maguire.	$ .40	$1.25	$2.50
C-442	Nugent, Elliot - ***Of Cheat And Charmer*** [1962] Cover by Barye Phillips.	$ .40	$1.25	$2.50
C-457	Nordhoff, Charles & Hall, James - ***Pitcairn's Island*** [1962]	$ .50	$1.50	$3.00
C-458	Nordhoff, Charles & Hall, James - ***Men Against The Sea*** [1962]	$ .40	$1.25	$2.50

Cardinal GC Series. New York: Pocket Books, Inc.

		G	VG	F
GC6	Mason, F. Van Wyck - ***Stars On The Sea*** [1953] Cover art by Ray Johnson.	$ .40	$1.25	$2.50
GC8	Street, James - ***Oh, Promised Land*** [1953] Cover art by Ray Johnson.	$ .50	$1.50	$3.00
GC9	Mason, F. Van Wyck - ***Eagle In The Sky*** [1953] Cover art by Ray Johnson.	$ .40	$1.25	$2.50
GC10	Monsarrat, Nicholas - ***The Cruel Sea*** [1953]	$ .50	$1.50	$3.00
GC14	Griffin, John H. - ***The Devil Rides Outside*** [1954] Cover art by Tom Dunn.	$ .40	$1.25	$2.50
GC17	Mason, F. Van Wyck - ***Proud New Flags*** [1954] Cover art by James Meese.	$ .50	$1.50	$3.00
GC20	Wellman, Paul I. - ***The Female*** [1954] Cover art by Stanley Meltzoff.	$ .40	$1.25	$2.50
GC25	Geismar, Maxwell - editor - The Whitman Reader [1954] Cover by Leo Manso.	$ .50	$1.50	$3.00

		G	VG	F
GC27	Edited by Dr. Robert E. Rothenberg - ***Understanding Surgery*** [1954]	$ .40	$1.25	$2.50
GC31	Waltari, Mika - ***The Egyptian*** [1955] Cover art by Charles Binger.	$ .40	$1.25	$2.50
GC34	Waltari, Mika - ***The Adventurer*** [1956] Cover art by Charles Binger.	$ .40	$1.25	$2.50
GC35	Buck, Pearl S. - ***My Several Worlds*** [1956] Cover art by Charles Binger.	$ .40	$1.25	$2.50
GC36	Asch, Sholem - ***The Nazarene*** [1956] Cover art by Clark Hulings.	$ .50	$1.50	$3.00
GC37	Bernstein, Morey - ***The Search For Bridey Murphy*** [1956]	$ .50	$1.50	$3.00
GC38	Asch, Sholem - ***The Apostle*** [1956] Cover art by James Meese.	$ .40	$1.25	$2.50
GC40	Spock, Dr. Benjamin - ***Baby And Child Care*** [1956]	$ .40	$1.25	$2.50
GC45	Whitehead, Don - ***The FBI Story*** [1958]	$ .50	$1.50	$3.00
GC48	Catton, Bruce - ***A Stillness At Appomattox*** [1958] Cover art by Isa Barnett.	$ .50	$1.50	$3.00
GC49	Asch, Sholem - ***The Prophet*** [1958] Cover art by James Meese.	$ .50	$1.50	$3.00
GC53	Douglas, Lloyd C. - ***The Robe*** [1958] Cover art by Tom Dunn.	$ .50	$1.50	$3.00
GC54	Hulme, Kathryn - ***The Nun's Story*** [1958]	$ .50	$1.50	$3.00
GC56	Hunter, Evan - ***Strangers When We Meet*** [1959]	$ .65	$2.00	$4.00
GC59	Douglas, Lloyd C. - ***The Big Fisherman*** [1959] Cover art by James Meese.	$ .40	$1.25	$2.50
GC61	Gary, Romain - ***The Roots Of Heaven*** [1958] Photo cover. Movie tie-in.	$ .40	$1.25	$2.50
GC62	Wylie, Philip - ***Generation Of Vipers*** [1958]	$ .40	$1.25	$2.50
GC66	Mayer, Martin - ***Madison Avenue, U.S.A.*** [1959]	$ .50	$1.50	$3.00
GC69	Payne-Gaposchkin, Cecilia - ***Stars In The Making*** [1959] Cover by Richard Powers.	$ .40	$1.25	$2.50
GC70	Haggard, M.D., Howard W. - ***Devils, Drugs, And Doctors*** [1959] Photo cover.	$ .40	$1.25	$2.50
GC72	Savage, Mildred - ***Parrish*** [1959]	$ .40	$1.25	$2.50
GC75	Wallace, Lew - ***Ben-Hur*** [1959] Photo cover. Movie tie-in.	$ .50	$1.50	$3.00
GC79	Weidman, Jerome - ***The Enemy Camp*** [1960] Cover by James Meese.	$ .50	$1.50	$3.00
GC80	Mannix, Edward - ***An End To Fury*** [1960] Cover art by Bob Maguire.	$ .50	$1.50	$3.00
GC81	Fisher, Vardis - ***Tale Of Valor*** [1960] Cover art by Bill George.	$ .50	$1.50	$3.00
GC84	Green, Gerald - ***The Last Angry Man*** [1960]	$ .40	$1.25	$2.50
GC85	Wylie, Philip - ***Opus 21*** [1960]	$ .50	$1.50	$3.00
GC91	Wellman, Paul I. - ***Jubal Troop*** [1960]	$ .50	$1.50	$3.00
GC92	Linkletter, Art - ***The Secret World Of Kids*** [1960]	$ .50	$1.50	$3.00
GC93	Wylie, Philip - ***An Essay On Morals*** [1960]	$ .40	$1.25	$2.50
GC94	Hunter, Evan - ***A Matter Of Conviction*** [1960] Photo cover. Movie tie-in.	$ .65	$2.00	$4.00
GC96	Clark, Dick - ***Your Happiest Years*** [1961] Photo cover.	$ .40	$1.25	$2.50
GC98	Basso, Hamilton - ***The Light Infantry Ball*** [1960]	$ .50	$1.50	$3.00
GC103	Paar, Jack - ***I Kid You Not*** [1960] Photo cover. Twelve pages of photos.	$ .40	$1.25	$2.50
GC109	Yerby, Frank - ***Gillian*** [1961]	$ .50	$1.50	$3.00
GC110	Whitehead, Don - ***Journey Into Crime*** [1961]	$ .40	$1.25	$2.50
GC114	Goudge, Elizabeth - ***The Dean's Watch*** [1961]	$ .50	$1.50	$3.00
GC125	Yerby, Frank - ***A Woman Called Fancy*** [1962]	$ .40	$1.25	$2.50
GC130	Robbins, Harold - ***79 Park Avenue*** [1964]	$ .40	$1.25	$2.50
GC139	Black, Hillel - ***Buy Now, Pay Later*** [1962]	$ .40	$1.25	$2.50
GC141	Yerby, Frank - ***The Garfield Honor*** [1962]	$ .40	$1.25	$2.50
GC146	Monsarrat, Nicholas - ***The White Rajah*** [1962] Cover by Hill.	$ .40	$1.25	$2.50
GC148	Paar, Jack - ***My Saber Is Bent*** [1962] Photo cover. Sixteen pages of photos.	$ .40	$1.25	$2.50
GC150	Yerby, Frank - ***Captain Rebel*** [1962]	$ .50	$1.50	$3.00
GC154	Westcott, Jan - ***The Border Lord*** [1962]	$ .50	$1.50	$3.00

Carnival Books, 916

Carnival Books, 931

Century Books, 32

		G	VG	F
GC164	Buck, Pearl S. - ***A Bridge For Passing*** [1963]	$ .40	$1.25	$2.50
GC165	Priestley, J.B. - ***Saturn Over The Water*** [1963]	$ .40	$1.25	$2.50
GC167	Du Maurier, Daphne - ***Gerald: A Portrait*** [1963] Cover art by Harry Bennett	$ .40	$1.25	$2.50
GC169	Edited by Henry Anatole Grunwald - ***Salinger*** [1963]	$ .50	$1.50	$3.00
GC179	Erskine, Rosalind - ***The Passion-Flower Hotel*** [1963]	$ .50	$1.50	$3.00
GC203	Schiddel, Edmund - ***Scandal's Child*** [1963]	$ .50	$1.50	$3.00
GC221	Undset, Sigrid - ***The Snake Pit*** [1963] Cover by Charles	$ .50	$1.50	$3.00

Carnival Books. New York: Hanro Corp. Digest Size.

901	Harmon, Robert W. - ***A Body To Own*** [1953]	$3.50	$10.00	$20.00
902	Caldwell, John - ***Midnight Sinners*** [1953]	$3.50	$10.00	$20.00
903	Gordon, William E. - ***Lovers Bewitched*** [1952]	$3.50	$10.00	$20.00
904	Wright, Watkins E. - ***Borrowed Ecstasy*** [1953]	$3.50	$10.00	$20.00
905	Gaddis, Peggy - ***Strangers In The Dark*** [1953] Cover art by George Gross.	$3.50	$10.00	$20.00
906	Erskine, Sylvia - ***A Lover For Anne*** [1953] PBO. Cover by George Gross.	$3.50	$10.00	$20.00
907	Underwood, John - ***Tempting Tigress*** [1953]	$3.50	$10.00	$20.00
908	Gordon, William E. - ***Girl - Hungry*** [1953] Cover by Rudy Nappi	$3.50	$10.00	$20.00
909	Tucker, Joan - ***The Girl From Mimi's*** [1953]	$3.50	$10.00	$20.00
910	Quandt, Albert L. - ***Pick-Up!*** [1953] Cover by Rafael de Soto.	$3.50	$10.00	$20.00
911	Coleman, Mitchell - ***Affairs Of A Ward Nurse*** [1953] Cover by Ray Pense	$3.00	$9.00	$18.00
912	Spencer, Frederic - ***Wild Party*** [1953]	$3.50	$10.00	$20.00
913	Coleman, MItchell - ***Affairs Of A Career Girl*** [1953] Cover art by George Gross.	$3.50	$10.00	$20.00
914	Blair, Raymond - ***Girl Of The Slums*** [1953]	$3.00	$9.00	$18.00
915	Gaddis, Peggy - ***Lost To Desire*** [1953]	$3.50	$10.00	$20.00
916	Gaddis, Peggy - ***Passion's Harvest*** [1953] Cover art by George Gross.	$3.50	$10.00	$20.00
917	Charlson, David - ***Frenchie*** [1953]	$3.00	$9.00	$18.00
918	Harrison, Whit (Harry Whittington) - ***Rapture Alley*** [1953] PBO. Cover art by Rudolph Belarski	$4.00	$12.50	$25.00
920	Harvey, Gene - ***Hotel Waitress*** [1953] Cover art by George Gross.	$3.50	$10.00	$20.00
922	Saber, Robert O. - ***City Of Sin*** [1953] PBO. Cover art by George Gross.	$3.50	$10.00	$20.00
923	Whitney, Hallam - ***Sinners Club*** [1953] Cover art by Rudolph Belarski.	$4.00	$12.50	$25.00
925	Welles, Kermit - ***Reckless!*** [1953]	$3.00	$9.00	$18.00

		G	VG	F
926	Haskell, Frank - ***Hotel Doctor*** [1954] PBO.	$3.00	$9.00	$18.00
929	Erskine, Sylvia - ***Farm Hussy*** [1954]	$3.50	$10.00	$20.00
931	Whitney, Hallam (Harry Whittington) - ***Backwoods Shack*** [1953] PBO.	$4.00	$12.50	$25.00
933	Manning, Jane - ***City Hotel*** [1953]	$3.00	$9.00	$18.00
934	Gaddis, Peggy - ***Farmer's Wife*** [1953]	$3.00	$9.00	$18.00
937	Nickerson, Kate - ***Boy-Chaser*** [1953]	$3.00	$9.00	$18.00
938	Erskine, Sylvia - ***Farm Hussy*** [1954]	$3.00	$9.00	$18.00
948	Blair, Raymond - ***Big City Hellcat*** [1954]	$3.00	$9.00	$18.00
949	Westley, Kirk - ***Man - Chaser*** [1954]	$3.00	$9.00	$18.00
950	Harrison, Whit (Harry Whittington) - ***Rapture Alley*** [1953] Cover by Rudolph Belarski.	$3.50	$10.00	$20.00
951	Nickerson, Kate - ***Boy Hungry*** [1953]	$3.00	$9.00	$18.00
955	Wright, Watkins E. - ***Young Passion*** [1953]	$3.00	$9.00	$18.00
956	Hatter, Amos - ***Big - Town Hellcat*** [1953]	$3.00	$9.00	$18.00

Castle Publications. Toronto: Baxter Publishing Co.

NN-1	Fitkin, Ed - ***Come On Teeder*** [1950] PBO.	$2.50	$7.50	$15.00
NN-2	Fitkin, Ed - ***Footloose In Hockey*** [1950]	$2.50	$7.50	$15.00
NN-3	Fitkin, Ed - ***Maurice Richard*** [1950]	$2.50	$7.50	$15.00
NN-4	Fitkin, Ed - ***Max Bentley*** [1950]	$2.50	$7.50	$15.00
NN-5	Fitkin, Ed - ***On The Hockey Beat*** [1950]	$2.50	$7.50	$15.00
NN-6	Fitkin, Ed - ***Turk Broda Of The Leafs*** [1950]	$2.50	$7.50	$15.00
NN-7	Fitkin, Ed - ***Detroit's Big Three*** [n.d.]	$2.50	$7.50	$15.00

Catechetical Guild.

GFR-137	Breig, Joseph A. - ***Meditations For The Family Rosary*** [1953] Same size and format as Dell 10 Cent.	$1.25	$3.75	$7.50

Cavalcade Books. New York: Delta Libraries, Inc. Digest Size.

NN	DeMexico, N.R. - ***Madman On A Drum*** [1944] PBO.	$3.00	$9.00	$18.00
1	Livingston, Ruth - ***Men Are Molehills*** [1946] PBO.	$3.00	$9.00	$18.00
2	Livingston, Armstrong - ***Magic For Murder*** [1947]	$3.00	$9.00	$18.00

Centaur Press – Time Lost Series.

NN-1	Friel, Arthur O. - ***The Pathless Trail*** [1969] Cover art by Jeff Jones.	$1.25	$3.75	$7.50
NN-2	Howard, Robert E. - ***The Moon Of Skulls*** [1969] Cover art by Jeff Jones.	$1.25	$3.75	$7.50
NN-3	Dunn, J. Allan - ***The Treasure Of Atlantis*** [1969] Cover art by Robert Bruce Acheson.	$1.00	$3.00	$6.00
NN-4	Howard, Robert E. - ***The Hand Of Kane*** [1970] Cover art by Jeff Jones.	$1.25	$3.75	$7.50
NN-5	Howard, Robert E. - ***Solomon Kane*** [1971] Cover art by Jeff Jones.	$1.25	$3.75	$7.50
NN-6	Friel, Arthur O. - ***Tiger River*** [1971] Cover art by Jeff Jones.	$1.25	$3.75	$7.50
NN-7	Bennet, Robert Ames - ***The Bowl Of Baal*** [1972]	$1.00	$3.00	$6.00
NN-8	Anthology including R. E. Howard - ***Swordsmen And Supermen*** [1972] PBO. Cover art by Virgil Finlay.	$1.25	$3.75	$7.50
NN-9	Bill, Alfred H. - ***The Wolf In The Garden*** [1972] Cover art by Virgil Finlay.	$1.25	$3.75	$7.50
NN-10	Mundy, Talbot - ***Caesar Dies*** [1973] Cover art by Frank Brunner.	$1.00	$3.00	$6.00
NN-11	Vivian, E. Charles - ***City Of Wonder*** [1973] Cover art by David Ireland.	$1.00	$3.00	$6.00
NN-12	Howden Smith, Arthur D. - ***Grey Maiden*** [1973] Cover by David Ireland.	$1.00	$3.00	$6.00
NN-13	Garth, Will - ***Dr. Cyclops*** [1976] Cover art by David Ireland.	$1.00	$3.00	$6.00
NN-14	Munn, H. Warner - ***The Werewolf Of Ponkert And The Werewolf's Daughter*** [1976]	$1.00	$3.00	$6.00

Century Books, 66

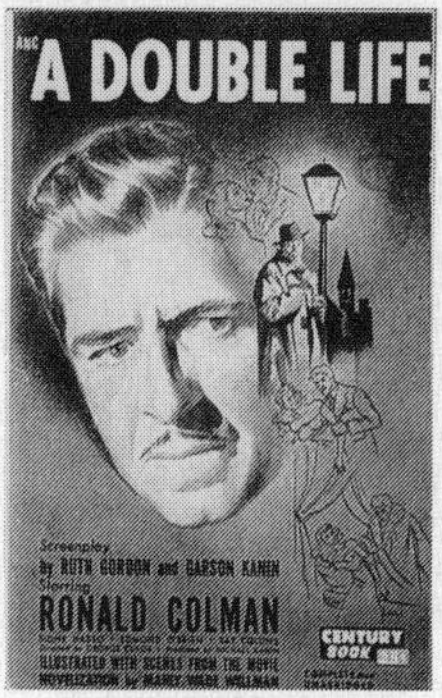

Century Books, 68

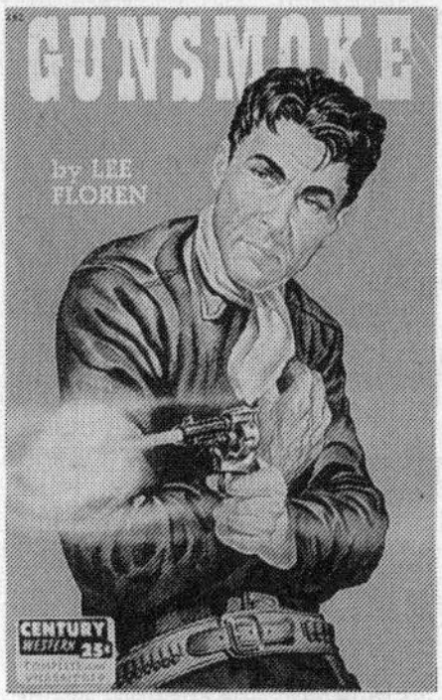

Century Books, 78

Century Books. Adult.

		G	VG	F
001	Van Doren, Mamie - ***My Naughty, Naughty Life*** [1964] PBO. Photo cover. 32 pages of photos.	$2.50	$7.50	$15.00

Century Books. Chicago: Century Publications. Digest Size.

		G	VG	F
10	Homes, Geoffrey - ***The Man Who Murdered Himself*** [1945]	$2.00	$6.00	$12.00
11	Field, Peter - ***Outlaws Three*** [1945]	$1.50	$5.00	$10.00
12	Benjamin, Edla - ***Murder Without Make-up*** [1944] Digest size...	$2.00	$6.00	$12.00
13	Bagby, George - ***Here Comes The Corpse*** [1945]	$2.00	$6.00	$12.00
14	King, Rufus - ***Diagnosis: Murder*** [1945]	$2.00	$6.00	$12.00
15	Tuttle, William C. - ***Ghost Trails*** [1945]	$1.50	$5.00	$10.00
16	MacDonald, William Colt - ***Renegade Roundup*** [1945]	$1.50	$5.00	$10.00
17	O'Hanlon, James - ***As Good As Murdered*** [1945]	$2.00	$6.00	$12.00
18	Wylie, Philip/Philips, Judson - ***Stab In The Back/Bottom Deal*** [1945]	$2.00	$6.00	$12.00
19	Eberhart, Mignon G. - ***Fair Warning*** [1945]	$2.00	$6.00	$12.00
20	Cunningham, Eugene - ***Gun Bulldogger*** [1945]	$1.50	$5.00	$10.00
21	Mason, Van Wyck - ***The Sulu Sea Murders*** [1945]	$2.00	$6.00	$12.00
22	Trace, John - ***Trigger Vengeance*** [1945]	$1.50	$5.00	$10.00
23	Knight, Kathleen Moore - ***Death Came Dancing*** [1945]	$2.00	$6.00	$12.00
24	Coolidge, Dane - ***The Trail Of Gold*** [1945] Cover art by G. Hukkaia.	$1.50	$5.00	$10.00
25	Popkin, Zelda - ***Time Off For Murder*** [1945]	$2.00	$6.00	$12.00
26	Holland, Marty - ***Fallen Angel*** [1945] Movie tie-in.	$2.50	$7.50	$15.00
27	Strange, John F. - ***Picture Of The Victim*** [1945]	$2.00	$6.00	$12.00
28	Stout, Rex - ***Bad For Business*** [1945]	$5.50	$17.50	$35.00
29	Reilly, Helen - ***All Concerned Notified*** [1945]	$2.00	$6.00	$12.00
30	Nebel, Frederick & Pentecost, Hugh - ***Weekend To Kill/Secret Corridors*** [1945]	$2.00	$6.00	$12.00
31	Ross, Leonard Q. - ***The Dark Corner*** [1945] Cover art by Malcolm Smith. Movie tie-in with Lucille Ball.	$4.00	$12.50	$25.00
32	Mason, Van Wyck - ***The Shanghai Bund Murders*** [1945] Cover art by Malcolm Smith.	$3.50	$10.00	$20.00
33	Wylie, Philip - ***Corpses At Indian Stones*** [1945]	$2.00	$6.00	$12.00
35	Eberhart, Mignon G. - ***The Glass Slipper*** [1945] Cover art by Malcolm Smith. Paperback size.	$2.50	$7.50	$15.00
37	Bogart, William - ***Singapore*** [1945] Movie tie-in with Ava Gardner.	$4.00	$12.50	$25.00
50	Short, Luke - ***Dead Freight For Piute*** [1945]	$1.50	$5.00	$10.00
51	Foster, Bennett - ***Dust Of The Trail*** [1945]	$1.50	$5.00	$10.00
52	Bechdolt, Frederick R. - ***Danger On The Border*** [1945]	$1.50	$5.00	$10.00

Century Books, 79

Century Books, 103

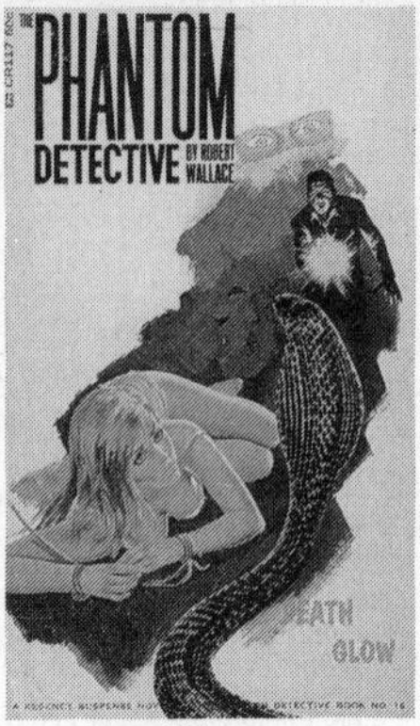

Corinth, CR-117

		G	VG	F
53	Gill, Tom - ***Death Rides The Mesa*** [1945]	$1.50	$5.00	$10.00
54	Lomax, Bliss - ***The Leather Burners*** [1945]	$1.50	$5.00	$10.00
55	Foreman, L.L. - ***Don Desperado*** [1945]	$1.50	$5.00	$10.00
56	MacDonald, William Colt - ***The Phantom Pass*** [1945]	$1.50	$5.00	$10.00
57	Drago, Harry Sinclair - ***Buckskin Empire*** [1945]	$1.50	$5.00	$10.00
58	Lomax, Bliss - ***Gringo Gunfire*** [1945]	$1.50	$5.00	$10.00
59	Lomax, Bliss - ***Secret Of The Wasteland*** [1945] Cover art by Malcolm Smith.	$1.50	$5.00	$10.00
NN-60	Gruber, Frank - ***Peace Marshall*** [1945] Cover art by Malcolm Smith. Digest Size.	$1.50	$5.00	$10.00
61	MacDonald, William Colt - ***Roaring Lead*** [1945] Paperback size.	$2.00	$6.00	$12.00
NN-62	Lomax, Bliss - ***Colt Comrades*** [1945] Digest size.	$1.50	$5.00	$10.00
NN-63	Merwin, Jr., Sam - ***Body And Soul*** [1945] Movie tie-in. Digest size.	$4.00	$12.50	$25.00
64	Gruber, Frank - ***Outlaw*** [1945] Cover art by Malcolm Smith.	$1.50	$5.00	$10.00
65	MacDonald, William Colt - ***California Caballero*** [1945]	$1.50	$5.00	$10.00
66	Ross, Leonard Q. - ***Sleep My Love*** [1946] PBO. Paperback size. Movie tie-in. 2 pages of photos	$4.00	$12.50	$25.00
67	Lindsay, Perry (Peggy Gaddis) - ***No Nice Girl*** [1946] Paperback size.	$2.50	$7.50	$15.00
68	Wellman, Manly Wade - ***A Double Life*** [1947] PBO. Paperback size. Movie tie-in. 20 pages of photos.	$6.00	$20.00	$40.00
69	MacDonald, William Colt - ***California Caballero*** [1945]	$1.50	$5.00	$10.00
NN-70	Mason, Van Wyck - ***The Cairo Garter Murders*** [1945] Paperback size.	$2.50	$7.50	$15.00
71	Joscelyn, Archie - ***Sign Of The Gun*** [1945]	$1.50	$5.00	$10.00
72	Gruber, Frank - ***Gunsight*** [1947]	$1.50	$5.00	$10.00
73	Hickley, H.B. - ***Saddles West!*** [1947] Paperback size.	$2.00	$6.00	$12.00
74	Hopson, William - ***Notched Guns*** [1947]	$1.50	$5.00	$10.00
75	Saxon, John - ***The Scarlet Sin*** [1947] Cover by Malcolm Smith. Paperback size.	$2.50	$7.50	$15.00
76	MacDonald, William Colt - ***Powdersmoke Range*** [1947] Cover art by Malcolm Smith.	$1.50	$5.00	$10.00
77	Lindsay, Perry (Peggy Gaddis) - ***Blonde Trouble*** [1947] Cover by Malcolm Smith. Paperback size.	$2.50	$7.50	$15.00
78	Floren, Lee - ***Gunsmoke*** [1947] Cover art by Malcolm Smith. Paperback size.	$2.00	$6.00	$12.00
79	Arthur, William - ***Love Business*** [1948] Cover by Malcolm Smith. Paperback size.	$2.50	$7.50	$15.00

		G	VG	F
80	Semple, Gordon - ***Cue For Passion*** [1948] Cover by Malcolm Smith. Paperback size.	$2.50	$7.50	$15.00
81	Bechdolt, Frederick R. - ***Drygulch Canyon*** [1946]	$1.50	$5.00	$10.00
82	Grinstead, J.E. - ***Ranger Justice*** [1947] Paperback size.	$2.00	$6.00	$12.00
83	Gay, Carmen - ***Ripe For Love*** [1947] Paperback size.	$2.50	$7.50	$15.00
84	Arthur, Phyllis - ***Marriage Is For Two*** [1947] Cover by Malcolm Smith. Paperback size.	$2.50	$7.50	$15.00
85	Lindsay, Perry - ***Unashamed*** [1947] Cover by Malcolm Smith. Paperback size.	$2.50	$7.50	$15.00
86	Semple, Gordon - ***Bad Company*** [1947] Paperback size.	$2.50	$7.50	$15.00
87	Stone, Thomas - ***One More Lover*** [1947] Paperback size.	$2.50	$7.50	$15.00
88	Hopson, William - ***Hell's Horseman*** [1947] Cover art by Malcolm Smith. Paperback size.	$2.00	$6.00	$12.00
89	Saxon, John - ***Common Passion*** [1947] Paperback size.	$2.50	$7.50	$15.00
90	Baker, Carlotta - ***Too Loose*** [1947] Cover art by Malcolm Smith. Paperback size.	$2.50	$7.50	$15.00
91	Carter, Ralph - ***Scandalous*** [1970] Cover art by Malcolm Smith. Paperback size.	$2.50	$7.50	$15.00
92	Carder, Leigh - ***Outlaw Justice*** [1947] Cover art by Malcolm Smith. Paperback size.	$2.00	$6.00	$12.00
93	Branch, Florenz - ***The Fleshpots*** [1947] Paperback size.	$2.50	$7.50	$15.00
94	Semple, Gordon - ***Passion's Way*** [1947] Paperback size.	$2.50	$7.50	$15.00
95	Shepard, Craig - ***Teaser*** [1947] Cover by Malcolm Smith. Paperback size.	$2.50	$7.50	$15.00
96-PB	Brewster, Elliot - ***Body For Sale*** [1947] Paperback size.	$2.50	$7.50	$15.00
96-DG	Holland, Marty - ***Fallen Angel*** [1947]	$2.00	$6.00	$12.00
97	Bennett, Hall - ***Call It Love*** [1947] Paperback size.	$2.50	$7.50	$15.00
98	Carter, Ralph - ***Quick Passion*** [1947] Paperback size.	$2.50	$7.50	$15.00
99	Semple, Gordon - ***Naughty And Nice*** [1947] Cover art by Malcolm Smith. Paperback size.	$2.50	$7.50	$15.00
100	Latimer, Jonathan - ***Dark Memory*** [1947] Paperback size.	$2.50	$7.50	$15.00
101	Chambers, W.C. - ***Bright Star Of Danger*** [1947]	$2.00	$6.00	$12.00
102	Bechdolt, Frederick R. - ***Hot Gold*** [1946]	$2.00	$6.00	$12.00
103	Allen, Jane & Livingston, Mae - ***Without Reservations*** [1947] PBO. Cover art by Malcolm Smith. Movie tie-in.	$4.00	$12.50	$25.00
104	Sherman, Harold M. - ***The Green Man*** [1946] PBO.	$17.00	$50.00	$100.00
105	Bennett, Hall - ***Man-Handled*** [1947] Paperback size.	$2.50	$7.50	$15.00
106	Arthur, William - ***Marriage Later*** [1947] Paperback size.	$2.50	$7.50	$15.00
107	Gilmore, Cecile - ***Inherited Husband*** [1948] Cover art by Malcolm Smith. Paperback size.	$2.50	$7.50	$15.00
108	Saxon, John - ***Kept Woman*** [1947] Paperback size.	$2.50	$7.50	$15.00
109	Semple, Gordon - ***Passion's Lesson*** [1948] Paperback size.	$2.50	$7.50	$15.00
110	Stone, Thomas - ***Three Times Sin*** [1948] Cover art by Malcolm Smith. Paperback size.	$2.50	$7.50	$15.00
111	Arthur, William - ***Sinner Take All*** [1948] Paperback size.	$2.50	$7.50	$15.00
112	Carter, Ralph - ***Profane*** [1948] Paperback size.	$2.50	$7.50	$15.00
113	Semple, Gordon - ***Sinful Lady*** [1948] Paperback size.	$2.50	$7.50	$15.00
114	Branch, Florenz - ***Passion's Program*** [1948] Paperback size.	$2.50	$7.50	$15.00
115	Arthur, William - ***Two Time Lover*** [1948] Cover by Malcolm Smith. Paperback size.	$2.50	$7.50	$15.00
116	Phillips, Rog - ***Time Trap*** [1949] PBO. Cover by Malcolm Smith. Paperback size.	$8.00	$25.00	$50.00
117	Stone, Thomas - ***Red For Passion*** [1949] Cover art by Harold MacCauley. Paperback size.	$2.50	$7.50	$15.00
118	Hopson, William - ***Desperado*** [1949] Cover art by Malcolm Smith. Paperback size.	$2.00	$6.00	$12.00
119	Jordan, Gail - ***Love Slave*** [1949] Paperback size.	$2.50	$7.50	$15.00
120	Arthur, William - ***Forbidden Sin*** [1949] Paperback size.	$2.50	$7.50	$15.00
121	Thornton, Charles - ***Voluptuous*** [1949] Paperback size.	$2.50	$7.50	$15.00
122	Carter, Ralph - ***Passion's Sin*** [1950] Paperback size.	$2.50	$7.50	$15.00

		G	VG	F
123	Branch, Florenz - ***Past Folly*** [1950] Paperback size.	$2.50	$7.50	$15.00
124	Phillips, Rog - ***Worlds Within*** [1950] PBO. Cover by Malcolm Smith. Paperback size.	$5.00	$15.00	$30.00
125	Craigie, Hamilton - ***Trigger Trails*** [1950] Paperback size.	$2.00	$6.00	$12.00
126	Brewster, Elliot - ***Street Girl*** [1950] Paperback size.	$2.50	$7.50	$15.00
127	DeForest, Barry - ***Charming Sinner*** [1950] Paperback size.	$2.50	$7.50	$15.00
128	Arthur, Burt - ***Bullet Trail*** [1950] Cover art by Malcolm Smith. Paperback size.	$2.00	$6.00	$12.00
129	Hopson, William - ***Tombstone Stage*** [1950] Cover art by Malcolm Smith. Paperback size.	$2.00	$6.00	$12.00
130	Arthur, William - ***Sinful Love*** [1950] Paperback size.	$2.50	$7.50	$15.00
131	McCulley, Johnson - ***Reckless Range*** [1950] Cover art by Malcolm Smith. Paperback size.	$2.00	$6.00	$12.00
132	Cole, Jackson - ***Six-Gun Stampede*** [1950] Cover art by Malcolm Smith. Paperback size.	$2.00	$6.00	$12.00
133	Jones, H. Bedford - ***California Trail*** [1950] Cvoer art by Malcolm Smith. Paperback size.	$2.00	$6.00	$12.00
134	Joscelyn, Archie - ***Renegade Range*** [1950] Cover art by Malcolm Smith. Paperback size.	$2.00	$6.00	$12.00
135	Echols, Allan K. - ***Saddle Wolves*** [1950] PBO. Cover by Malcolm Smith. Paperback size.	$2.00	$6.00	$12.00
136	Latimer, Jonathan - ***Headed For A Hearse*** [1950] Cover art by Duur. Paperback size.	$1.50	$5.00	$10.00

Challenge Book.

		G	VG	F
209	Sherman, Jory - ***The Summer Man*** [1967] PBO.	$1.25	$3.75	$7.50

Chariot Books.

		G	VG	F
CB-101	Wright, Donald M. - ***Convention Girl*** [n.d.]	$1.25	$3.75	$7.50
CB-102	Dumont, Mel - ***Mr. Madame*** [1959]	$1.25	$3.75	$7.50
CB-103	Little, Chuck - ***The Naked Lovers*** [1959] PBO.	$1.25	$3.75	$7.50
CB-104	Coss, Rollin - ***The Private Life Of Eleanor*** [1959]	$1.25	$3.75	$7.50
CB-105	Noderheim, Boris - ***Sex On Tap*** [1959] PBO.	$1.25	$3.75	$7.50
CB-106	O'Hara, Noel - ***The Last Virgin*** [1959]	$1.25	$3.75	$7.50
CB-109	Klein, Ph.D., Leo - ***You Are Not Alone*** [1959]	$1.25	$3.75	$7.50
CB-111	Damon, Ray - ***Broadway Bait*** [1959] PBO.	$1.25	$3.75	$7.50
112	Sardoux, Victor - ***Queen Of Sheba*** [1959] PBO.	$1.25	$3.75	$7.50
CB-112	Sardoux, Victor - ***Queen Of Sheba*** [1959] PBO.	$1.50	$5.00	$10.00
CB-113	Gareth, Max - ***Carnival Girl*** [1959]	$1.25	$3.75	$7.50
CB-114	Bernard, Ronald - ***The Deadly Passion*** [1959]	$1.25	$3.75	$7.50
CB-115	Devlin, Robert - ***Bed Bait*** [1959]	$1.25	$3.75	$7.50
CB-116	Adlon, Arthur (Wade, Carlson) - ***Blue Denim Doll*** [1959]	$1.25	$3.75	$7.50
CB-117	Chessman, Robert - ***Boulevard Girl*** [1959]	$1.25	$3.75	$7.50
CB-119	O'Hara, Noel - ***A Time To Love*** [1959]	$1.25	$3.75	$7.50
CB-120	Adlon, Arthur (Wade, Carlson) - ***Bad Girl Abroad*** [1959]	$1.25	$3.75	$7.50
CB-121	Damon, Ray - ***Jessica*** [1960] PBO.	$1.25	$3.75	$7.50
CB-122	Chessman, Robert - ***Driven Desire*** [1960]	$1.25	$3.75	$7.50
CB-123	Long, Frank - ***Woman From Another Planet*** [1960] PBO. Cover by Basil Gogot.	$1.25	$3.75	$7.50
CB-124	Podolsky, Dr. - ***Your Sex Problems in Marriage*** [1960]	$1.25	$3.75	$7.50
CB-125	Devlin, Robert - ***Lover Girl*** [1960]	$1.25	$3.75	$7.50
CB-126	Chessman, Robert - ***Hideaway Love*** [1960] PBO.	$1.25	$3.75	$7.50
CB-127	Adlon, Arthur (Wade, Carlson) - ***Crazy Street U.S.A.*** [1960]	$1.25	$3.75	$7.50
128	Wells, H. G. - ***The Invisible Man*** [n.d.]	$1.25	$3.75	$7.50
CB-128	Wells, H. G. - ***The Invisible Man*** [1960]	$2.50	$7.50	$15.00
CB-129	Wentworth, Rick - ***Untamed*** [1960]	$1.25	$3.75	$7.50
CB-130	Roland - ***Dangerous Affairs*** [1960]	$1.25	$3.75	$7.50
CB-131	Lindsey, Hyman - ***Backstage Girl*** [1960]	$1.25	$3.75	$7.50
CB-132	Chessman, Robert - ***The Park Jungle*** [1960]	$1.25	$3.75	$7.50
CB-133	Wade, Carlson - ***Jamestown Mistress*** [1960] PBO.	$1.25	$3.75	$7.50

		G	VG	F
CB-134	Adlon, Arthur (Carlson Wade) - ***The Prince Of Poisoners*** [1960] PBO. Cover by Basil Gogot.	$1.50	$5.00	$10.00
CB-135	Brandon, Phil - ***Virgie*** [1960]	$1.25	$3.75	$7.50
CB-136	Tandy - ***The Wild Party*** [1960]	$1.25	$3.75	$7.50
CB-137	Vernon - ***Continental Tramp*** [1960]	$1.25	$3.75	$7.50
CB-138	Sprague, W. H. - ***Sex Behavior Of The American Secretary*** [1960]	$1.25	$3.75	$7.50
CB-139	Roskolenko, Harry - ***Black Is A Man*** [1960] PBO.	$1.25	$3.75	$7.50
CB-140	Devlin, Robert - ***Parlor Girl*** [1960]	$1.25	$3.75	$7.50
CB-141	Sardoux, Victorien - ***The King's Lust*** [1960] PBO.	$1.25	$3.75	$7.50
CB-142	Wade, Carlson - ***Butchers In Waiting*** [1960] Photo cover.	$1.25	$3.75	$7.50
CB-143	Challon, David - ***Man Mad*** [1960]	$1.25	$3.75	$7.50
CB-144	Adlon, Arthur (Wade, Carlson) - ***Lady Darton's Sin*** [1960]	$1.25	$3.75	$7.50
CB-145	Richards, Lee - ***The Mercenary Lover*** [1960]	$1.25	$3.75	$7.50
CB-146	Ravelle - ***The Crest Inn Rape*** [1960]	$1.25	$3.75	$7.50
CB-147	Thorne - ***Prize Girl*** [1960]	$1.25	$3.75	$7.50
CB-148	Demetre, Margaret K. - ***Creole Desire*** [1960] PBO. Photo cover.	$1.25	$3.75	$7.50
CB-149	MacDonald, Wilson - ***Passion Slave*** [1960] PBO.	$1.25	$3.75	$7.50
CB-150	Barr, Tyrone C. - ***The Last 14*** [1960] PBO.	$2.50	$7.50	$15.00
CB-151	Lorenz, Frederick - ***Dungaree Sin*** [1960] PBO. Photo cover.	$1.25	$3.75	$7.50
CB-153	Hitt, Orrie - ***Tramp Wife*** [1960]	$1.25	$3.75	$7.50
CB-154	Adlon, Arthur (Wade, Carlson) - ***Driven Virgin*** [1960]	$1.25	$3.75	$7.50
CB-156	Devlin, Robert - ***Bitch On Wheels*** [1960] Photo cover.	$1.25	$3.75	$7.50
CB-157	Adlon, Arthur (Wade, Carlson) - ***The Sex Peddler*** [1960]	$1.25	$3.75	$7.50
CB-159	Adlon, Arthur (Wade, Carlson) - ***Video Virgin*** [1960] Photo cover.	$1.25	$3.75	$7.50
CB-161	Wright, Donald - ***Wild Model*** [1960] Photo cover.	$1.25	$3.75	$7.50
CB-164	Seeley, Jr., E. S. - ***One Hell Of A Dame*** [1960]	$1.25	$3.75	$7.50
CB-166	Simpson, Lew (Adams, Norman) - ***Twisted Lust*** [1961]	$1.25	$3.75	$7.50
CB-167	Hitt, Orrie - ***Party Doll*** [1961] Photo cover.	$1.25	$3.75	$7.50
CB-168	Davis, C. E. - ***Loril Was A Tramp*** [1961] PBO. Photo cover.	$1.25	$3.75	$7.50
CB-170	Stemmer, Arch - ***Hot Bed Hotel*** [1961]	$1.25	$3.75	$7.50
CB-171	Adlon, Arthur (Wade, Carlson) - ***Passion Nurse*** [1961] PBO.	$1.25	$3.75	$7.50
CB-172	Damon, Ray - ***Sinful Wife*** [1961]	$1.25	$3.75	$7.50
CB-174	Seeley, Jr., E. S. - ***Pillow Girl*** [1961] PBO.	$1.25	$3.75	$7.50
CB-175	Clark, V. S. - ***Company Girl*** [1961]	$1.25	$3.75	$7.50
CB-178	Anderson, Ben - ***Wild Oats*** [1961]	$1.25	$3.75	$7.50
CB-179	Adlon, Arthur (Wade, Carlson) - ***Key Club Girl*** [1961]	$1.25	$3.75	$7.50
CB-180	Thompson, John B. - ***Texas Tramp*** [1961]	$1.25	$3.75	$7.50
CB-181	Gesson, Matt - ***The Affairs Of Cleo*** [1961]	$1.25	$3.75	$7.50
CB-182	Coss, Rollin - ***The Private Life Of Eleanor*** [1961]	$1.25	$3.75	$7.50
CB-184	Sprague, W. H., Ph.D. - ***Sex Behavior Of The American Secretary*** [1961]	$1.25	$3.75	$7.50
CB-185	Gareth, Max - ***Carnival Girl*** [1960] PBO.	$1.25	$3.75	$7.50
CB-186	Thompson, John B. - ***Gay Wanton*** [1960]	$1.25	$3.75	$7.50
CB-187	Hitt, Orrie - ***Man's Nurse*** [1960]	$1.25	$3.75	$7.50
CB-189	Dumont, Mel - ***Vicky*** [1960]	$1.25	$3.75	$7.50
CB-190	Simon, George - ***Wild Bride*** [1960]	$1.25	$3.75	$7.50
CB-194	Seeley, Jr., E. S. - ***Suburban Sexpot*** [1960]	$1.25	$3.75	$7.50
CB-197	Craig, D. W. - ***Swamp Girl*** [1961] PBO.	$1.25	$3.75	$7.50
CB-198	Oliver, A. E. - ***Arlette*** [1961]	$1.25	$3.75	$7.50
CB-199	Seeley, Jr., E. S. - ***Lens Girl*** [1962] PBO. Photo cover.	$1.25	$3.75	$7.50
CB-206	Adlon, Arthur (Wade, Carlson) - ***Virgin Nurse*** [1962]	$1.25	$3.75	$7.50
CB-208	Anderson, Ben - ***Love For Hire*** [1962]	$1.25	$3.75	$7.50
CB-210	Adlon, Arthur (Wade, Carlson) - ***The Sex Peddler*** [1962]	$1.25	$3.75	$7.50
CB-211	Craig, D. W. - ***Man Hunger*** [1962]	$1.25	$3.75	$7.50
CB-212	Hitt, Orrie - ***Torrid Cheat*** [1962] Photo cover.	$1.25	$3.75	$7.50
CB-213	Oliver, A. E. - ***Tonite!*** [1962] PBO.	$1.25	$3.75	$7.50
CB-215	Simon, George - ***Bare Skin*** [1962] Photo cover.	$1.25	$3.75	$7.50

		G	VG	F
CB-216	Anderton, Ben - ***Naked Nurse*** [1962] PBO.	$1.25	$3.75	$7.50
CB-217	Roget, Alexis - ***Man Bait*** [1962] Photo cover.	$1.25	$3.75	$7.50
CB-218	Cally, John - ***Campus Tramp*** [1962] PBO. Photo cover.	$1.25	$3.75	$7.50
CB-220	Powers, S. R. - ***Willing Flesh*** [1962] Photo cover.	$1.25	$3.75	$7.50
CB-221	Mulash, Stan - ***Sex Couch*** [1962]	$1.25	$3.75	$7.50
CB-222	Simon, George (Wade, Carlson) - ***The Sheer Affair*** [1962]	$1.25	$3.75	$7.50
6C-630	Elgun, Max - ***"Nylon" Jungle*** [1963] PBO.	$1.25	$3.75	$7.50
635	Hill - ***Her Own Kind*** [1963]	$1.25	$3.75	$7.50
636	Elgun - ***Lesbo Nurse*** [1963]	$1.25	$3.75	$7.50
6C-637	Nurabin, M. S. - ***Gina*** [1963]	$1.25	$3.75	$7.50
638	Simms - ***Lesbo On The Make*** [1963]	$1.25	$3.75	$7.50
7C-907	Woodley, Dennis R. - ***Blacklace Girls*** [1963]	$1.25	$3.75	$7.50
CB-1601	Craig, D. W. - ***Love For Sale*** [1962]	$1.25	$3.75	$7.50
CB-1602	Adlon, Arthur (Wade, Carlson) - ***Cold Wife*** [1961] PBO.	$1.25	$3.75	$7.50
CB-1605	Cally, John - ***Torrid Tramp*** [1962]	$1.25	$3.75	$7.50
CB-1606	Powers, Jeffrey - ***Heat Wave*** [1961] PBO.	$1.25	$3.75	$7.50
CB-1607	Adlon, Arthur (Wade, Carlson) - ***Female Fire*** [1962] PBO. Photo cover.	$1.25	$3.75	$7.50
CB-1609	Simon, George - ***Sin Gym*** [1962] Photo cover.	$1.25	$3.75	$7.50
CB-1610	Hitt, Orrie - ***Twin Beds*** [1962] Photo cover.	$1.25	$3.75	$7.50
CB-1616	March, Sheldon - ***Hungry Thighs*** [1962] Photo cover.	$1.25	$3.75	$7.50
CB-1619	Hitt, Orrie - ***Passion Street*** [1962]	$1.25	$3.75	$7.50
CB-1620	Hitt, Orrie - ***Bad Wife*** [1962] PBO.	$1.25	$3.75	$7.50
CB-1622	P, Laverne - ***I Am A Lesbian*** [1962] PBO. Photo cover.	$1.25	$3.75	$7.50
CB-1625	Craig, D. N. - ***Kis Like A Nymph*** [1962] Photo cover.	$1.25	$3.75	$7.50
CB-1627	Craig, D. W. - ***Insatiable Desire*** [1962]	$1.25	$3.75	$7.50

Charles Boni Paper Books. New York: Charles Boni Books.

		G	VG	F
NN-1	Wilder, Thornton - ***The Bridge Of San Luis Rey*** [1929] May. Trial format. Cover by Rockwell Kent.	$1.50	$5.00	$10.00
NN-2	Ohta, Takashi and Sperry, Margaret - ***The Golden Wind*** [1929] Sept. 25. Cover by Rockwell Kent.	$1.50	$5.00	$10.00
NN-3	Goldsmith, Margaret - ***Frederick The Great*** [1929] Oct. 25. Cover by Rockwell Kent.	$1.50	$5.00	$10.00
NN-4	Strong, L. A. G. - ***Dewer Rides*** [1929] Nov. 25. Cover by Rockwell Kent.	$1.50	$5.00	$10.00
NN-5	Chase, Stuart - ***Prosperity: Fact Or Myth*** [1929] Dec. 26. Cover by Rockwell Kent.	$1.50	$5.00	$10.00
NN-6	Reitz, Deneys - ***Commando*** [1930] Jan. 25. Cover by Rockwell Kent.	$1.50	$5.00	$10.00
NN-7	Harris, Frank - ***My Reminiscences As A Cowboy*** [1930] Feb. 25. Cover by Rockwell Kent.	$1.50	$5.00	$10.00
NN-8	Prutz, Leo - ***The Master Of The Day Of Judgement*** [1930] Mar. 25. Cover by Rockwell Kent.	$1.50	$5.00	$10.00
NN-9	Anthology - ***Prize Poems, 1913–1929*** [1930] Apr. 25. Cover by Rockwell Kent.	$1.50	$5.00	$10.00
NN-10	Figgis, Darrell - ***The Return Of The Hero*** [1930] May 25. Cover by Rockwell Kent.	$1.50	$5.00	$10.00
NN-11	Reznikoff, Charles - ***By The Waters Of Manhattan*** [1930] June 25. Cover by Rockwell Kent.	$1.50	$5.00	$10.00
NN-12	Weeks, William E. - ***All In The Racket*** [1930] July 25. Cover by Rockwell Kent.	$1.50	$5.00	$10.00
NN-13	Bell, Margaret - ***Margaret Fuller*** [1930] Aug. 25. Cover by Rockwell Kent.	$1.50	$5.00	$10.00
NN-14	Cournos, John - ***Wandering Women*** [1930] Sept. 25. Cover by Rockwell Kent.	$1.50	$5.00	$10.00

Chartered Books. New York: Bond-Charteris Pubs./Saint Ent. Digest Size.

		G	VG	F
17	Charteris, Leslie - editor - ***The Saint's Choice Of Hollywood Crime Stories*** [1946] PBO.	$3.50	$10.00	$20.00

		G	VG	F
18	Gunn, James - ***Deadlier Than The Male*** [1946]	$3.00	$9.00	$18.00
21	Cain, Paul - ***Seven Slayers*** [1946] PBO.	$17.00	$50.00	$100.00
22	Kline, Otis Adelbert - ***The Man Who Limped*** [1946] PBO.	$17.00	$50.00	$100.00
25	Gruber, Frank - ***The Last Doorbell*** [1946]	$3.00	$9.00	$18.00
26	Charteris, Leslie - ***The Brighter Buccaneer*** [1944]	$3.00	$9.00	$18.00
27	Anthology edited by Leslie Charteris - ***The Saint's Choice Of Radio Thrillers*** [1946] PBO.	$3.50	$10.00	$20.00
28	Langham, James R. - ***A Pocketful Of Clues*** [1946]	$3.00	$9.00	$18.00

Checkerbooks. New York: Checkerbooks, Inc.

		G	VG	F
1	Boylan, Jr., Edward J. - ***Terry And The Pirates in "The Jewels Of Jade"*** [1949] PBO. Cover by Bill Wenzel.	$6.00	$20.00	$40.00
2	Bliss, Tip - ***The Broadway Butterfly Murders*** [1949] Cover by Leon H. Liederman.	$4.00	$12.50	$25.00
3	Bowen, Robert Sidney - ***Make Mine Murder*** [1949] Cover art by Leon H. Leiderman.	$3.50	$10.00	$20.00
4	Martin, Charles M. - ***Lost River Buckaroo*** [1949] Cover by Leon H. Liederman.	$3.50	$10.00	$20.00
5	Anthology - ***Horror And Homicide*** [1949] Cover art by Bob Schwartz.	$4.00	$12.50	$25.00
6	Bodenheim, Maxwell - ***Duke Herring*** [1949] Cover art by Bill Wenzel.	$3.50	$10.00	$20.00
7	Sabatini, Rafael - ***Master-At-Arms*** [1949] Cover by Leon H. Liederman.	$3.00	$9.00	$18.00
8	Bernstein, Abraham - ***Taxi*** [1949] Cover by Bob Ritter.	$3.50	$10.00	$20.00
9	Hecht, Ben - ***The Florentine Dagger*** [1949] Cover by Bob Ritter.	$3.00	$9.00	$18.00
10	Janson, Hank - ***Lady, Mind That Corpse*** [1949] Cover art by Heade.	$6.00	$20.00	$40.00
11	Bannett, Dorothy and Fifi - ***The Practical Party Guide And Cookbook*** [1949] PBO. Cover by Shirley Unger.	$5.00	$15.00	$30.00
12	Complied by Patricia Fulford - ***Over 100 Best Cartoons*** [1949] PBO. Cover art by Bob Ritter.	$5.00	$15.00	$30.00

Chesterfield. Digest Size.

		G	VG	F
NO#-1	Contreras, Charles - ***How To Fascinate Men*** [n.d.]	$2.50	$7.50	$15.00

Chicago Paperback House. Chicago: Chicago Paperback House, Inc.

		G	VG	F
A-100	Bell, Steve - ***Doctors Are Lovers Too*** [1962] PBO. Cover art by Robert Bonfils.	$1.25	$3.75	$7.50
A-101	Cloutier, Helen - ***Murder, Absolutely Murder*** [1962] PBO. Cover art by Robert Bonfils.	$1.35	$4.00	$8.00
A-102	Athens, Christopher - ***The Big Squeeze*** [1962] PBO.	$1.25	$3.75	$7.50
A-103	Potter, J.L. - ***Room At The Bottom*** [1962] PBO.	$1.25	$3.75	$7.50
A-104	Potter, J.L. - ***Or Murder For Free*** [1962] PBO. Cover art by Cloutier.	$1.25	$3.75	$7.50
A-105	Vining, Keith - ***Keep Running*** [1962] PBO.	$1.25	$3.75	$7.50
A-106	Hansen, Zora - ***Power's Pool*** [1962] PBO. Cover art by Cloutier.	$1.25	$3.75	$7.50
A-107	Taylor, Frank - ***House Of The Hunter*** [1962] PBO. Cover art by Cloutier.	$1.35	$4.00	$8.00
A-108	Kemper, Jr., William E. - ***Another Man's Hell*** [1962] PBO. Cover art by Cloutier.	$1.35	$4.00	$8.00
A-109	Potter, J.L. - ***Kill, Sweet Charity-Kill*** [1962] PBO. Cover art by Cloutier.	$1.25	$3.75	$7.50
A-110	Smith, Pauline C. - ***Nothing But Blood*** [1962] PBO. Cover art by Nystrom.	$1.25	$3.75	$7.50
A-111	Collins, A.J. - ***Wail Of The Lonely Wench*** [1962] PBO. Cover art by Nystrom.	$1.25	$3.75	$7.50
B-100	Levin, Beatrice - ***Eyewitness To Exodus*** [1962] PBO. Cover art by Robert Bonfils.	$1.25	$3.75	$7.50

		G	VG	F
B-110	Marino, Vic - ***The Paths Are Three*** [1962] PBO.	$1.25	$3.75	$7.50
B-120	Willeford, Charles - ***Cockfighter*** [1962] PBO. Cover art by Cloutier.	$20.00	$60.00	$125.00
B-130	Woodford, Jack - ***Home Away From Home*** [1962] PBO. Cover art by Cloutier.	$1.25	$3.75	$7.50
B-140	Glenn, R. Traviers - ***Postmark Of America*** [1962] PBO. Cover art by Kugach.	$1.25	$3.75	$7.50
B-150	Brennan, Dan - ***The Velvet Rut*** [1962] PBO. Cover art by Cloutier.	$1.25	$3.75	$7.50

Columbia Broadcasting System.

NN	Hollister, Paul & Stusky, Robert - editors - ***From D-Day Through Victory In Europe*** [1945] PBO. Photos throughout.	$2.00	$6.00	$12.00

Comet Books. New York: Pocket Books, Inc. Digest Size.

1	Sperry, Armstrong - ***Wagons Westward*** [1948]	$1.25	$3.75	$7.50
2	Scholz, Jackson - ***Batter Up*** [1948]	$1.25	$3.75	$7.50
3	Lambert, Janet - ***Star-Spangled Summer*** [1948]	$1.25	$3.75	$7.50
4	Hinkle, Thomas C. - ***Tawny*** [1948] First printing is paperback size.	$1.50	$5.00	$10.00
5	Thurston, Howard - ***300 Tricks You Can Do*** [1948]	$1.25	$3.75	$7.50
6	Bugbee, Emma - ***Peggy Covers The News*** [1948]	$1.25	$3.75	$7.50
7	Gregg, Alan - ***Winged Mystery*** [1948]	$1.25	$3.75	$7.50
8	Compiled by Gertrude Crampton - ***Your Own Joke Book*** [1948]	$1.25	$3.75	$7.50
9	Boylston, Helen Dore - ***Sue Barton, Student Nurse*** [1948]	$1.00	$3.00	$6.00
10	Pease, Howard - ***The Tattooed Man*** [1948]	$1.25	$3.75	$7.50
11	Brier, Howard M. - ***Skycruiser*** [1948]	$1.25	$3.75	$7.50
12	Household, Geoffrey - ***The Spanish Cave*** [1948]	$1.35	$4.00	$8.00
13	Queen, Jr., Ellery - ***The Green Turtle Mystery*** [1948] Cover art by Richard Powers.	$1.50	$5.00	$10.00
14	Hinkle, Thomas C. - ***Silver: The Story Of A Wild Horse*** [1948] Cover by Richard Powers.	$1.25	$3.75	$7.50
15	Russell, Alice Dyar - ***Strangers In The Desert*** [1948] Cover by Richard Powers.	$1.25	$3.75	$7.50
16	Haines, Donald Hamilton - ***The Southpaw*** [1948]	$1.25	$3.75	$7.50
17	Garreau, Garth - ***Bat Boy Of The Giants*** [1949]	$1.25	$3.75	$7.50
18	Kjelgaard, Jim - ***Big Red*** [1949]	$1.25	$3.75	$7.50
19	Seaman, Augusta Huiell - ***The Mystery Of The Empty Room*** [1949] Cover art by Richard Powers.	$1.25	$3.75	$7.50
20	Mongomery, Rutherford - ***Husky: Co-Pilot Of The Pilgrim*** [1949]	$1.25	$3.75	$7.50
21	Brown, Roderick L. Haig - ***Starbuck Valley Winter*** [1949] Cover art by Shilstone.	$1.25	$3.75	$7.50
22	Davis, Lavinia R. - ***Hobby Horse Hill*** [1949] Cover art by R.M. Powers.	$1.00	$3.00	$6.00
23	Crampton, Gertrude - ***Your Own Party Book*** [1949]	$1.25	$3.75	$7.50
24	Montgomery, Rutherford - ***Gray Wolf*** [1949]	$1.25	$3.75	$7.50
25	Scholz, Jackson - ***Fighting Coach*** [1949] Cover art by Richard Powers.	$1.25	$3.75	$7.50
26	Montgomery, Rutherford - ***Midnight*** [1949]	$1.25	$3.75	$7.50
27	Kjelgaard, Jim - ***Forest Patrol*** [1949]	$1.25	$3.75	$7.50
28	Norton, Andre - ***Scarface*** [1949]	$3.50	$10.00	$20.00
29	Harkins, Philip - ***Lightning On Ice*** [1949]	$1.25	$3.75	$7.50
30	Davis, Julia - ***No Other White Men*** [1949]	$1.25	$3.75	$7.50
31	Balch, Glen - ***Indian Paint*** [1949]	$1.25	$3.75	$7.50
32	Cavanna, Betty - ***Puppy Stakes*** [1949]	$1.25	$3.75	$7.50
33	Pease, Howard - ***Long Wharf*** [1949]	$1.25	$3.75	$7.50
34	Leeming, Joseph - ***Fun With Puzzles*** [1949]	$1.35	$4.00	$8.00

		G	VG	F
Confession Stories. Toronto: Pocket Library Of Best Sellers. Digest Size.				
102	Richard, Leona S. - ***Legion Of Lost Souls*** [1948] Photo cover.....	$6.00	$20.00	$40.00
Continental Books. New York: Continental Books, Inc. Digest Size.				
NN-1	Rinehart, Mary Roberts - ***The Street Of Seven Stars*** [n.d.] Cover by Carroll Snell........	$1.50	$5.00	$10.00
Corgi Books. London: Transworld Publishers.				
SC-758	Brown, Fredric - ***The Lenient Beast*** [1959]........	$3.50	$10.00	$20.00

Corinth Regency Suspense Novels (Early Publisher's History, 1960–1965)

Every Corinth Regency book contains reprints from the pulp magazines. Even the cover art resembles the shocking covers from the pulp magazine era. They published forty-nine books from five series. The five series include The Phantom Detective, Operator #5, Doctor Death, Secret Agent X, and Dusty Ayers. All of the Corinth Regency titles are collectible.

		G	VG	F
Corinth Suspense Novels. San Diego, CA: Corinth Publications.				
CR-101	Wallace, Robert - ***The Phantom Detective-Book No. 1/The Vampire Murders*** [1965] PBO. Cover art by Robert Bonfils. ..	$2.50	$7.50	$15.00
CR-102	Wallace, Robert - ***The Phantom Detective-Book No. 2/The Dancing Doll Murders*** [1965] PBO. Cover art by Robert Bonfils........	$2.50	$7.50	$15.00
CR-103	Wallace, Robert - ***The Phantom Detective-Book No. 3/The Beast-King Murders*** [1965] PBO. Cover art by Robert Bonfils........	$2.50	$7.50	$15.00
CR-104	Wallace, Robert - ***The Phantom Detective-Book No. 4/Tycoon Of Crime*** [1965] PBO. Cover art by Robert Bonfils.	$2.50	$7.50	$15.00
CR-105	Wallace, Robert - ***The Phantom Detective-Book No. 5/The Broadway Murders*** [1965] PBO. Cover art by Robert Bonfils.	$2.50	$7.50	$15.00
CR-106	Wallace, Robert - ***The Phantom Detective-Book No. 6/The Daggers Of Kali*** [1965] PBO. Cover art by Robert Bonfils.	$2.50	$7.50	$15.00
CR-107	Wallace, Robert - ***The Phantom Detective-Book No. 7/Murder Under The Big Top*** [1965] PBO. Cover art by Robert Bonfils........	$2.50	$7.50	$15.00
CR-108	Wallace, Robert - ***The Phantom Detective-Book No. 8/The Trail To Death*** [1965] PBO. Cover art by Robert Bonfils........	$2.50	$7.50	$15.00
CR-109	Wallace, Robert - ***The Phantom Detective-Book No.9/Yellow Shadows Of Death*** [1965] PBO. Cover art by Robert Bonfils..	$2.50	$7.50	$15.00
CR-110	Wallace, Robert - ***The Phantom Detective-Book No. 10/Murder Trail*** [1965] PBO. Cover art by Robert Bonfils........	$2.50	$7.50	$15.00
CR-111	Wallace, Robert - ***The Phantom Detective-Book No. 11/The Green Glare Murders*** [1966] PBO. Cover art by Robert Bonfils........	$2.50	$7.50	$15.00
CR-112	Wallace, Robert - ***The Phantom Detective-Book No. 12/Fangs Of Murder*** [1966] PBO. Cover art by Robert Bonfils........	$2.50	$7.50	$15.00
CR-113	Wallace, Robert - ***The Phantom Detective-Book No. 13/The Curio Murders*** [1966] PBO. Cover art by Robert Bonfils........	$2.50	$7.50	$15.00
CR-114	Wallace, Robert - ***The Phantom Detective-Book No. 14/Murder Stalks A Billion*** [1966] PBO. Cover art by Robert Bonfils.......	$2.50	$7.50	$15.00
CR-115	Wallace, Robert - ***The Phantom Detective-Book No. 15/Murder Money*** [1966] PBO. Cover art by Robert Bonfils........	$2.50	$7.50	$15.00
CR-116	Steele, Curtis - ***Operator #5-Book No. 1/Legions Of The Death Master*** [1966] PBO. Cover art by Robert Bonfils.	$3.00	$9.00	$18.00
CR-117	Wallace, Robert - ***The Phantom Detective-Book No. 16/Death Glow*** [1966] PBO. Cover art by Robert Bonfils.	$2.50	$7.50	$15.00

Corinth, CR-121

Corinth, CR-147

Crest Book, 150

		G	VG	F
CR-118	Zorro - ***Doctor Death-Book No. 1/12 Must Die*** [1966] PBO. Cover art by Robert Bonfils.	$4.00	$12.50	$25.00
CR-119	Wallace, Robert - ***The Phantom Detective-Book No. 17/Stones Of Satan*** [1966] PBO. Cover art by Robert Bonfils.	$2.50	$7.50	$15.00
CR-120	Steele, Curtis - ***Operator #5-Book No. 2/The Army Of The Dead*** [1966] PBO. Cover art by Robert Bonfils.	$3.00	$9.00	$18.00
CR-121	Zorro - ***Doctor Death-Book No. 2/The Gray Creatures*** [1966] PBO. Cover art by Robert Bonfils.	$4.00	$12.50	$25.00
CR-122	House, Brant - ***Secret Agent "X"-Book No. 1/The Torture Trust*** [1966] PBO. Cover art by Robert Bonfils.	$3.00	$9.00	$18.00
CR-123	Wallace, Robert - ***The Phantom Detective-Book No. 18/The Melody Murders*** [1966] PBO. Cover art by Robert Bonfils.	$2.50	$7.50	$15.00
CR-124	Steele, Curtis - ***Operator #5-Book No. 3/The Invisible Empire*** [1966] PBO. Cover art by Robert Bonfils.	$3.00	$9.00	$18.00
CR-125	Zorro - ***Doctor Death-Book No. 3/The Shriveling Murders*** [1966] PBO. Cover art by Robert Bonfils.	$4.00	$12.50	$25.00
CR-126	House, Brant - ***Secret Agent "X"-Book No. 2/Servants Of The Skull*** [1966] PBO. Cover art by Robert Bonfils.	$3.00	$9.00	$18.00
CR-127	Wallace, Robert - ***The Phantom Detective-Book No. 19/The Uniformed Killers*** [1966] PBO. Cover art by Robert Bonfils.	$2.50	$7.50	$15.00
CR-128	Steele, Curtis - ***Operator #5-Book No. 4/Master Of Broken Men*** [1966] PBO. Cover art by Robert Bonfils.	$3.00	$9.00	$18.00
CR-129	Hanlon, Jon - editor - ***Doctor Death-Book No. 4/Doctor Death And Other Terror Tales*** [1966] PBO. Cover art by Robert Bonfils.	$4.00	$12.50	$25.00
CR-130	House, Brant - ***Secret Agent "X"-Book No. 3/Curse Of The Mandarin's Fan*** [1966] PBO. Cover art by Robert Bonfils.	$3.00	$9.00	$18.00
CR-131	Wallace, Robert - ***The Phantom Detective-Book No. 20/The Forty Thieves*** [1966] PBO. Cover art by Robert Bonfils.	$2.50	$7.50	$15.00
CR-132	Steele, Curtis - ***Operator #5-Book No. 5/Hosts Of The Flaming Death*** [1966] PBO. Cover art by Robert Bonfils.	$3.00	$9.00	$18.00
CR-133	Bowen, Robert Sidney - ***Dusty Ayres-Book No. 1/Black Lightning*** [1966] PBO. Cover art by Robert Bonfils.	$2.50	$7.50	$15.00
CR-134	House, Brant - ***Secret Agent "X"-Book No. 4/City Of The Living Dead*** [1966] PBO. Cover art by Robert Bonfils.	$3.00	$9.00	$18.00
CR-135	Wallace, Robert - ***The Phantom Detective-Book No. 21/Death Under Contract*** [1966] PBO. Cover art by Robert Bonfils.	$2.50	$7.50	$15.00
CR-136	Steele, Curtis - ***Operator #5-Book No. 6/Blood Reign Of The Dictator*** [1966] PBO. Cover art by Robert Bonfils.	$3.00	$9.00	$18.00

		G	VG	F
CR-137	Bowen, Robert Sidney - ***Dusty Ayres-Book No.2/Crimson Doom*** [1966] PBO. Cover art by Robert Bonfils.	$2.50	$7.50	$15.00
CR-138	House, Brant - ***Secret Agent "X"-Book No. 5/The Death-Torch Terror*** [1966] PBO. Cover art by Robert Bonfils.	$3.00	$9.00	$18.00
CR-139	Wallace, Robert - ***The Phantom Detective-Book No. 22/The Corpse Parade*** [1966] PBO. Cover art by Robert Bonfils.	$2.50	$7.50	$15.00
CR-140	Steele, Curtis - ***Operator #5-Book No. 7/March Of The Flame Marauders*** [1966] PBO. Cover art by Robert Bonfils.	$3.00	$9.00	$18.00
CR-141	Bowen, Robert Sidney - ***Dusty Ayres-Book No. 3/Purple Tornado*** [1966] PBO. Cover art by Robert Bonfils.	$2.50	$7.50	$15.00
CR-142	House, Brant - ***Secret Agent "X"-Book No. 6/Octopus Of Crime*** [1966] PBO. Cover art by Robert Bonfils.	$2.50	$7.50	$15.00
CR-143	Hanlon, Jon - editor - ***Terror Tales-Book #1/The House Of Living Death & Other Terror*** [1966] PBO. Cover art by Robert Bonfils.	$5.00	$15.00	$30.00
CR-144	Steele, Curtis - ***Operator #5-Book No. 8/Invasion Of The Yellow Warlords*** [1966] PBO. Cover art by Robert Bonfils.	$3.00	$9.00	$18.00
CR-145	Bowen, Robert Sidney - ***Dusty Ayres-Book No. 4/The Telsa Raiders*** [1966] PBO. Cover art by Rober Bonfils.	$2.50	$7.50	$15.00
CR-146	House, Brant - ***Secret Agent "X"-Book No. 7/The Sinister Scourge*** [1966] PBO. Cover art by Robert Bonfils.	$3.00	$9.00	$18.00
CR-147	Hanlon, Jon - editor - ***Terror Tales-Book # 2/Death's Loving Arms & Other Terror Tales*** [1966] PBO. Cover art by Robert Bonfils.	$5.00	$15.00	$30.00
CR-148	Bowen, Robert Sidney - ***Dusty Ayres-Book No. 5/Black Invaders Vs. The Battle Birds*** [1966] PBO. Cover art by Robert Bonfils.	$2.50	$7.50	$15.00

Cosmic Publications.

NN	Patterson, Bruce - ***Best Cartoons Of Bruce Patterson*** [1953] PBO. Cover by Bruce Patterson. All cartoons.	$1.50	$5.00	$10.00

Crawford Digest. Los Angeles: Crawford Publishing House. Digest Size.

NO#	Anthology - ***The Garden Of Fear And Other Stories Of The Bizarre*** [1945] PBO. Includes Howard, Lovecraft, et al. Three states: blue cover, green cover, yellow cover. Price is for blue cover, other covers worth double price listed.	$3.50	$10.00	$20.00

Crescent Private Editions. Digest Size.

2	Bennent, Hall - ***Playful Wife*** [1951] Photo cover.	$2.50	$7.50	$15.00

Crest Books (Early Publisher's History, 1955–1960)

Roscoe and Wilford Fawcett, who in the 1920s began as magazine publishers, founded Gold Medal Books in 1949 and then in 1955 established this imprint. This line of paperbacks brought forth a cultural grab bag from Fawcett. Some of the notable volumes include cartoon and humor, a number of juvenile delinquency novels and anthologies, and *Psycho* by Robert Bloch. The imprint continued as Fawcett Crest or Fawcett.

Fawcett Publications also published Red Seal Books, Gold Medal Books, and Premier Books. They established Premier Books as a line of nonfiction and literary titles.

Crest Books. New York: Fawcett Publications.

		G	VG	F
114	Anthology by editors of *True* - ***Best Cartoons From True*** [1955] PBO. Cover by Vip.	$1.25	$3.75	$7.50
115	Gruber, Frank - ***Run Thief Run*** [1955] Cover art by Lu Kimmel.	$1.35	$4.00	$8.00

		G	VG	F
116	Drago, Harry Sinclair - ***Top Hand With A Gun*** [1955]	$1.25	$3.75	$7.50
117	Meynier, Gil - ***Stranger At The Door*** [1955] Cover art by Mitcell Hooks.	$1.35	$4.00	$8.00
118	Anthology - ***Captain Billy's Whiz Bang*** [1955] PBO.	$1.50	$5.00	$10.00
119	Greenhood, David - ***Love In Dishevelment*** [1955] Cover art by James Meese.	$1.25	$3.75	$7.50
120	Ermine, Will - ***Avenger From Texas*** [1955]	$1.25	$3.75	$7.50
121	Hahn, Emily - ***Affair*** [1955] Cover art by James Meese.	$1.25	$3.75	$7.50
122	Val Baker, Denys - ***A Journey With Love*** [1956] Cover art by Barye Phillips.	$1.00	$3.00	$6.00
123	Nye, Nelson - ***Riders By Night*** [1956] Cover art by Lu Kimmel.	$1.25	$3.75	$7.50
S-124	Cohen, Octavus Roy - ***The Golden Hussy*** [1956]	$1.25	$3.75	$7.50
125	Farren, Julian - ***So Sweet, So Cruel*** [1956] Cover art by Charles Binger.	$1.25	$3.75	$7.50
126	Stokes, Donald - ***Captive In The Night*** [1956] Cover art by James Meese.	$1.35	$4.00	$8.00
127	Kiki - ***The Education Of A French Model*** [1956] Cover art by Barye Phillips.	$1.00	$3.00	$6.00
128	Fox, Norman A. - ***The Thundering Trail*** [1956] Cover art by George Gross.	$1.25	$3.75	$7.50
S-129	Engstrand, Stuart - ***Son Of The Giant*** [1956]	$1.25	$3.75	$7.50
130	Young, I.S. - ***Jadie*** [1956] Cover art by James Meese.	$1.25	$3.75	$7.50
131	Dresser, Davis - ***Gun Smoke On The Mesa*** [1956]	$1.25	$3.75	$7.50
132	Prather, Richard S. - ***Lie Down, Killer*** [1956] Cover art by James Meese.	$1.35	$4.00	$8.00
S-133	Estey, Norbert - ***All My Sins*** [1956] Cover art by Charles Binger.	$1.25	$3.75	$7.50
134	MacDonald, William Colt - ***Destination, Danger*** [1956]	$1.25	$3.75	$7.50
135	Powell, Dawn - ***A Man's Affair*** [1956]	$1.25	$3.75	$7.50
136	Fast, Julius - ***Down Through The Night*** [1956] Cover art by Barye Phillips.	$1.25	$3.75	$7.50
137	Fox, Norman, A. - ***War On The Range*** [1956]	$1.25	$3.75	$7.50
138	Hutchins, Maude - ***The Memoirs Of Maisie*** [1956] Cover art by Maxwell.	$1.00	$3.00	$6.00
139	Marsten, Richard (Ed McBain) - ***So Nude, So Dead*** [1956] Cover art by Mitchell Hooks.	$1.35	$4.00	$8.00
S-140	DeVries, Robert - ***Of Sin And The Flesh*** [1956]	$1.25	$3.75	$7.50
141	Lockridge, Norman & Partch, Virgil - ***Sex Without Tears*** [1956]	$1.00	$3.00	$6.00
142	Prather, Richard S. - ***Dagger Of Flesh*** [1956] Cover by James Meese.	$1.35	$4.00	$8.00
S-143	Van Pelt, Dr. S.J. - ***Hypnotism And The Power Within*** [1956]	$1.00	$3.00	$6.00
S-144	Fereva, Anton - ***Come Desire Me*** [1956] Cover art by Barye Phillips.	$1.00	$3.00	$6.00
S-145	Sherman, Harold - ***You Live After Death*** [1956]	$1.25	$3.75	$7.50
146	Shirreffs, Gordon D. - ***Code Of The Gun*** [1956] PBO. Cover art by Roy Lance.	$1.25	$3.75	$7.50
147	Brewer, Gil - ***And The Girl Screamed*** [1956]	$1.50	$5.00	$10.00
S-148	Eldridge, Paul & Viereck, George S. - ***My First Two Thousand Years*** [1956]	$1.35	$4.00	$8.00
149	MacDonald, William Colt - ***The Comanche Scalp*** [1956]	$1.25	$3.75	$7.50
150	McIntosh, J.T. - ***The Rule Of The Pagbeasts*** [1956] Cover art by Docktor.	$2.00	$6.00	$12.00
151	Whittington, Harry - ***Saturday Night Town*** [1956]	$2.50	$7.50	$15.00
152	Allen, T.D. - ***Ambush At Buffalo Wallow*** [1956]	$1.25	$3.75	$7.50
153	Barrett, Michael - ***The Golden Lure*** [1956] Cover art by Harry Schaare.	$1.25	$3.75	$7.50
154	Dean, Dudley - ***Six-Gun Vengeance*** [1956]	$1.25	$3.75	$7.50
155	Partch, Virgil - ***Crazy Cartoons*** [1956]	$1.35	$4.00	$8.00
S-156	Hoffman, William - ***The Trumpet Unblown*** [1956]	$1.00	$3.00	$6.00
D-157	Algren, Nelson - ***A Walk On The Wild Side*** [1956]	$1.35	$4.00	$8.00

Crest Book, S-178

Crest Book, S-308

Crest Book, 357

		G	VG	F
158	Huffaker, Clair - ***Badge For A Gunfighter*** [1956]	$1.25	$3.75	$7.50
159	Preston, Charles - ***Office Laughs*** [1956]	$1.35	$4.00	$8.00
D-160	Grubb, Davis - ***A Dream Of Kings*** [1956]	$1.00	$3.00	$6.00
161	Constiner, Merle - ***Last Stand At Anvil Pass*** [1957] PBO.	$1.35	$4.00	$8.00
162	Scott, J.M. - ***Seawife*** [1957] Movie photo cover. Movie tie-in with Richard Burton & Joan Collins.	$1.35	$4.00	$8.00
S-163	DeMare, George - ***The Empire And Martin Brill*** [1957]	$1.00	$3.00	$6.00
164	Gordon, Stewart - ***Gunswift*** [1957]	$1.25	$3.75	$7.50
165	Fischer, Markoosha - ***The Right To Love*** [1957]	$1.00	$3.00	$6.00
166	Fox, Gardner F. - ***The Conquering Prince*** [1957] PBO. Cover art by Charles Binger	$1.50	$5.00	$10.00
167	Huffaker, Clair - ***Badman*** [1957] Movie tie-in.	$1.35	$4.00	$8.00
S-168	Sheen, Fulton J. - ***Way To Happiness*** [1957]	$ .75	$2.50	$5.00
169	Verissimo, Erico - ***Evil In The Night*** [1957] Cover by Barye Phillips.	$1.25	$3.75	$7.50
170	Lutz, Giles A. - ***Fury Trail*** [1957]	$1.25	$3.75	$7.50
S-171	Otway, Howard - ***Stranger In Paradise*** [1957]	$1.25	$3.75	$7.50
172	Waugh, Hillary - ***Case Of The Brunette Bombshell*** [1957] Cover art by Robert Abbett.	$1.25	$3.75	$7.50
173	Brewer, Gil - ***Little Tramp*** [1957] PBO. Cover art by Barye Phillips.	$1.50	$5.00	$10.00
174	Patten, Lewis B. - ***Valley Of Violent Men*** [1957] PBO.	$1.25	$3.75	$7.50
S-175	Lord, James - ***The Loving And The Lost*** [1957]	$1.25	$3.75	$7.50
D-176	Fielding, Henry - ***Tom Jones*** [1957]	$1.00	$3.00	$6.00
177	Dean, Dudley - ***Border Renegade*** [1957]	$1.25	$3.75	$7.50
S-178	Marsten, Richard - ***The Spiked Heel*** [1957]	$1.35	$4.00	$8.00
179	Wilder, Robert - ***Walk With Evil*** [1957] PBO. Cover by Charles Binger.	$1.25	$3.75	$7.50
D-180	Frey, Richard - ***According To Hoyle*** [1957]	$ .75	$2.50	$5.00
181	Lutz, Giles A. - ***Gun The Man Down*** [1957]	$1.25	$3.75	$7.50
S-182	Forrest, Williams - ***Seed Of Violence*** [1957] PBO. Cover art by Barye Phillips.	$1.35	$4.00	$8.00
183	Catanzard, Angela - ***The Home Book Of Italian Cooking*** [1957] Cook book.	$ .75	$2.50	$5.00
S-184	Hamilton, Edmond - ***City At World's End*** [1957] Cover art by Richard Powers.	$1.35	$4.00	$8.00
185	Donalds, Gordon - ***Top Gun*** [1957]	$1.00	$3.00	$6.00
T-186	Duchess of Windsor - ***The Heart Has Its Reasons*** [1957]	$ .75	$2.50	$5.00
187	Taylor, Valerie - ***Whisper Their Love*** [1957] PBO. Photo cover.	$2.50	$7.50	$15.00
S-188	Richter, Hans Werner - ***Beyond Defeat*** [1957]	$1.00	$3.00	$6.00

		G	VG	F
189	Shannon, Steve - ***The Hell-Fire Kid*** [1957]	$1.25	$3.75	$7.50
S-190	Cohen, Lester - ***Sweepings*** [1957] Cover art by Barye Phillips	$1.00	$3.00	$6.00
191	Armstrong, Charlotte - ***A Dram Of Poison*** [1957]	$1.35	$4.00	$8.00
192	Yarnell, Duane - ***Mantrap*** [1957] PBO. Photo cover	$1.25	$3.75	$7.50
193	Huffaker, Clair - ***Rider From Thunder Mountain*** [1957] PBO	$1.25	$3.75	$7.50
194	Clayton, John Bell - ***And Come Back A Man*** [1957] Cover art by James Meese.	$1.00	$3.00	$6.00
195	Baynes, Jack - ***Meet Morocco Jones*** [1957] PBO.	$1.25	$3.75	$7.50
196	Freeman, James - ***The New Crest Crossword Puzzle Book*** [1957]	$4.00	$12.50	$25.00
S-197	Anthology edited by T. E. Dikty - ***5 Tales From Tomorrow*** [1957] PBO. Cover by Richard Powers.	$1.50	$5.00	$10.00
198	Poole, Richard - ***West Of Devil's Canyon*** [1958] PBO.	$1.25	$3.75	$7.50
D-199	Mathers, Edward Powys - ***Eastern Love*** [1958] Cover art by Docktor.	$1.00	$3.00	$6.00
S-200	Farrell, James T. - ***Gas-House McGinty*** [1958] Cover art by Barye Phillips.	$1.25	$3.75	$7.50
S-201	Johnson, Annabel - ***The Hungry Years*** [1958]	$1.00	$3.00	$6.00
T-202	Onstott, Kyle - ***Mandingo*** [1961] Cover art by Stanley Zuckerberg.	$1.25	$3.75	$7.50
S-203	Hahn, Emily - ***House In Shanghai*** [1958]	$1.25	$3.75	$7.50
S-204	Andors, Lisa & Abbott, Anita - ***The Home Book Of French Cooking*** [1958] Photo cover. Cook book.	$1.00	$3.00	$6.00
205	Frazee, Steve - ***High Hell*** [1958] Movie tie-in	$1.35	$4.00	$8.00
206	Brackeen, Steve - ***Baby Moll*** [1958] PBO. Cover art by Barye Phillips.	$1.35	$4.00	$8.00
S-207	Habe, Hans - ***Off Limits*** [1958] Cover art by Barye Phillips.	$1.25	$3.75	$7.50
S-208	Sancton, Thomas - ***The Magnificent Rascal*** [1958] Cover art by Mitchell Hooks.	$1.25	$3.75	$7.50
S-209	Mantley, John - ***The 27th Day*** [1958]	$1.35	$4.00	$8.00
210	Faherty, Robert - ***Swamp Babe*** [1958] Cover art by James Meese.	$1.35	$4.00	$8.00
211	Callahan, John - ***Texas Fury*** [1958] Cover art by A. Leslie Ross.	$1.25	$3.75	$7.50
S-212	Coppel, Alfred - ***Night Of Fire And Snow*** [1958]	$1.25	$3.75	$7.50
213	Roeburt, John - ***Did You Kill Mona Leeds?*** [1958] Cover art by Darcy.	$1.25	$3.75	$7.50
S-214	Weinrauch, Anna Elizabet - ***Of Love Forbidden*** [1958] Photo cover.	$1.35	$4.00	$8.00
S-215	Remarque, Erich Maria - ***All Quiet On The Western Front*** [1958]	$1.00	$3.00	$6.00
S-216	Verne, Jules - ***From The Earth To The Moon & A Trip Around It*** [1958]	$1.35	$4.00	$8.00
S-217	Hassel, Sven - ***The Legend Of The Damned*** [1958] Cover art by Stanley Zuckerberg	$1.00	$3.00	$6.00
S-218	Manson, John - ***A Fool There Was*** [1958]	$1.25	$3.75	$7.50
219	Lieferaut, Henry & Sylvia - ***Dr. Anders' Dilemma*** [1958]	$ .75	$2.50	$5.00
S-220	De Balzac, Honore - ***Best Of Balzac*** [1958] Cover art by Ralph Barton. Movie tie-in with Brigitte Bardot	$1.35	$4.00	$8.00
S-221	McKenna, George - ***Yanqui's Woman*** [1958] PBO. Cover art by James Meese.	$1.25	$3.75	$7.50
222	Huffaker, Clair - ***Posse From Hell*** [1958] PBO.	$1.25	$3.75	$7.50
S-223	Nathan, Simon - editor - ***How You Can Take Better Photos*** [1958] PBO. 16 pages of photos.	$ .75	$2.50	$5.00
224	Baynes, Jack - ***Hand Of The Mafia*** [1958] PBO. Cover art by Barye Phillips	$1.35	$4.00	$8.00
225	Cross, James - ***Root Of Evil*** [1958] Cover art by Barye Phillips.	$1.25	$3.75	$7.50
S-226	Gernsback, Hugo - ***Ralph 124C 41+*** [1958]	$2.50	$7.50	$15.00
S-227	Erskine, Dorothy and Dennis, Patrick - ***The Pink Hotel*** [1958] Cover by Mitchell Hooks.	$1.25	$3.75	$7.50

		G	VG	F
D-228	Swiggett, Howard - ***The Durable Fire*** [1958] Photo cover.	$1.00	$3.00	$6.00
229	Brewer, Gil - ***Wild*** [1958] PBO.	$2.50	$7.50	$15.00
230	Wormser, Richard - ***The Widow Wore Red*** [1958]	$1.25	$3.75	$7.50
S-231	Van Royen, Astrid - ***Awake Monique*** [1958]	$1.00	$3.00	$6.00
D-232	Keyes, Frances Parkinson - ***Blue Camellia*** [1958]	$1.00	$3.00	$6.00
S-233	Traver, Robert - ***Small Town D.A.*** [1958] Cover art by James Meese.	$1.25	$3.75	$7.50
234	Baynes, Jack - ***The Peeping Tom Murders*** [1958] PBO. Cover by Barye Phillips.	$1.35	$4.00	$8.00
235	Nye, Nelson - ***The Red Sombrero*** [1958]	$1.25	$3.75	$7.50
S-236	Forest, Williams - ***Stigma For Valor*** [1958]	$1.00	$3.00	$6.00
S-237	Bachmann, Lawrence - ***Ten Seconds To Hell*** [1958] Movie photo cover. Movie tie-in with Jeff Chandler & Jack Palance.	$1.35	$4.00	$8.00
238	Brewer, Gil - ***The Vengeful Virgin*** [1958] PBO.	$2.50	$7.50	$15.00
239	*True* Magazine - editors - ***Cartoon Laffs From True*** [1958] PBO. Cartoon book.	$1.35	$4.00	$8.00
S-240	Wylie, Philip - ***The Best Of Crunch And Des*** [1958] Cover art by Barye Phillips.	$1.25	$3.75	$7.50
S-241	Lurton, Douglas - ***The Power Of Positive Living*** [1958]	$ .75	$2.50	$5.00
242	Cook, Will - ***The Wind River Kid*** [1958]	$1.25	$3.75	$7.50
S-243	Torres, Tereska - ***The Dangerous Games*** [1958]	$1.50	$5.00	$10.00
S-244	Le May, Alan - ***The Unforgiven*** [1959]	$1.25	$3.75	$7.50
S-245	Anthology edited by Marguiles & Friend - ***Race To The Stars*** [1958]	$1.35	$4.00	$8.00
246	Roeburt, John - ***The Long Nightmare*** [1958]	$1.25	$3.75	$7.50
247	Armstrong, Charlotte - ***Mask Of Evil*** [1958] Cover art by Barye Phillips.	$1.25	$3.75	$7.50
248	Gault, William Campbell - ***End Of A Call Girl*** [1958] PBO.	$1.25	$3.75	$7.50
D-249	Remarque, Erich Maria - ***The Black Obelisk*** [1958] Cover art by Stanley Zuckerberg.	$1.00	$3.00	$6.00
S-250	Ayme, Marcel - ***The Grand Seduction*** [1958]	$1.00	$3.00	$6.00
S-251	Seifert, Elizabeth - ***The Doctor's Husband*** [1958]	$ .75	$2.50	$5.00
S-252	Withers, E.L. - ***The House On The Beach*** [1958] Cover art by Richard Powers.	$1.00	$3.00	$6.00
253	Yarnell, Duane - ***Murder Bait*** [1958] PBO. Photo cover.	$1.25	$3.75	$7.50
S-254	Anthology edited by Leo Marguiles - ***Bad Girls*** [1958]	$1.25	$3.75	$7.50
255	Prather, Richard S. - ***Lie Down, Killer*** [1958] Cover art by Darcy.	$1.00	$3.00	$6.00
D-256	Barnard, Charles N. - editor - ***A Treasury Of True*** [1958] Photo cover.	$1.00	$3.00	$6.00
S-257	Gotshall, Jack - ***Pappy's Women*** [1958] Cover art by Barye Phillips.	$1.00	$3.00	$6.00
S-258	Anthology edited by T. E. Dikty - ***6 From Worlds Beyond*** [1958]	$1.25	$3.75	$7.50
S-259	Edwards, Samuel - ***Devil's Prize*** [1958] PBO. Cover art by James Meese.	$1.35	$4.00	$8.00
260	Gault, William Campbell - ***Night Lady*** [1958] PBO.	$1.35	$4.00	$8.00
261	Frazee, Steve - ***Gold At Kansas Gulch*** [1958]	$1.25	$3.75	$7.50
D-262	Meyer, Jerome S. - ***Fun With Mathematics*** [1958]	$ .75	$2.50	$5.00
S-263	Kerr, Jean - ***Please Don't Eat The Daisies*** [1959] Cover by Blanchard.	$ .75	$2.50	$5.00
D-264	Cushman, Dan - ***The Silver Mountain*** [1958]	$1.25	$3.75	$7.50
S-265	Treece, Henry - ***The Great Captains*** [1959] Cover art by Kossin.	$1.00	$3.00	$6.00
266	Bellus, Jean - ***Clementine Cherie*** [1959] Cover art by Jean Bellus. Cartoon book.	$1.00	$3.00	$6.00
S-267	Christian, Paula - ***Edge Of Twilight*** [1959] PBO. Photo cover.	$2.50	$7.50	$15.00
268	Sparkia, Roy B. - ***The Vanishing Vixen*** [1959] PBO. Cover art by Barye Phillips.	$1.25	$3.75	$7.50
S-269	Ross, Floyd H. & Hills, Tynette - ***The Great Religions*** [1959]	$ .75	$2.50	$5.00

		G	VG	F
S-270	Habe, Hans - ***The Devil's Agent*** [1959]	$1.25	$3.75	$7.50
D-271	Kastle, Herbert D. - ***7 Keys To Koptic Court*** [1959]	$1.00	$3.00	$6.00
S-272	Anthology edited by Leo Margulies - ***Young And Deadly*** [1959] PBO.	$2.50	$7.50	$15.00
S-273	Christopher, John - ***The Caves Of Night*** [1959] Cover art by Barye Phillips.	$1.35	$4.00	$8.00
274	Patten, Lewis B. - ***Fighting Rawhide*** [1959]	$1.25	$3.75	$7.50
S-275	Giles, Ray - ***How To Retire And Enjoy It*** [1959] Cover art by Muni.	$ .75	$2.50	$5.00
D-276	Maugham, W. Somerset - ***The World's Ten Greatest Novels*** [1959]	$1.00	$3.00	$6.00
277	Prather, Richard S. - ***Dagger Of Flesh*** [1959]	$1.00	$3.00	$6.00
D-278	Hoffman, William - ***Days In The Yellow Leaf*** [1959]	$1.00	$3.00	$6.00
S-279	Reiner, Carl - ***Enter Laughing*** [1959]	$1.25	$3.75	$7.50
S-280	Camerer, David M. - ***The Damned Wear Wings*** [1959]	$1.00	$3.00	$6.00
281	Gault, William Campbell - ***The Wayward Widow*** [1959] PBO.	$1.35	$4.00	$8.00
S-282	Anthology edited by Leo Margulies - ***3 From Out There*** [1959] PBO. Cover art by Richard Powers.	$1.50	$5.00	$10.00
S-283	Sheen, Fulton J. - ***Way To Inner Peace*** [1959] Photo cover.	$ .75	$2.50	$5.00
S-284	Allen, Edward Frank - ***How To Write And Speak Effective English*** [1959]	$ .75	$2.50	$5.00
D-285	Gorham, Charles - ***Wine Of Life*** [1959]	$1.00	$3.00	$6.00
286	Keene, Day - ***Dead Dolls Don't Talk*** [1959] PBO. Photo cover.	$2.00	$6.00	$12.00
287	Eimerl, Sarel - ***The Cautious Bachelor*** [1959] Cover art by Mitchell Hooks.	$1.00	$3.00	$6.00
S-288	Maxfield, Henry S. - ***Legacy Of A Spy*** [1959] Cover art by Robert McGinnis.	$1.00	$3.00	$6.00
S-289	Pratt, Theodore - ***Handsome's Seven Women*** [1959] PBO. Cover art by Barye Phillips.	$1.00	$3.00	$6.00
S-290	Taylor, Valerie - ***The Girls In 3-B*** [1959]	$2.00	$6.00	$12.00
S-291	Murphy, Dennis - ***The Sergeant*** [1959]	$1.00	$3.00	$6.00
292	Waugh, Hillary - ***The Eighth Mrs. Bluebeard*** [1959]	$1.25	$3.75	$7.50
D-293	Keyes, Frances Parkinson - ***Steamboat Gothic*** [1959]	$ .75	$2.50	$5.00
294	Schafer, Kermit - ***Pardon My Blooper*** [1959] Humorous bloopers and cartoons. Cover by Bernard Thompson.	$1.00	$3.00	$6.00
S-295	MacDonald, John D. - ***The Executioners*** [1959] Photo cover.	$2.50	$7.50	$15.00
296	Marlowe, Stephen - ***Passport To Peril*** [1959] PBO. Photo cover.	$1.35	$4.00	$8.00
297	Lieferant, Sylvia & Henry - ***Doctor's Temptation*** [1959] Cover by Barye Phillips.	$ .75	$2.50	$5.00
S-298	Ketcham, Hank - ***In This Corner . . . Dennis The Menace*** [1959] Cartoon book.	$1.25	$3.75	$7.50
S-299	Miller, Warren - ***The Way We Live Now*** [1959] Cover art by Robert McGinnis.	$1.00	$3.00	$6.00
D-300	MacInnes, Helen - ***North From Rome*** [1959]	$ .75	$2.50	$5.00
S-301	Conner, Rearden - ***Shake Hands With The Devil*** [1959] Photo cover. Movie tie-in with James Cagney.	$1.35	$4.00	$8.00
S-302	Mergendahl, Charles - ***The Girl Cage*** [1959] Cover art by Charles.	$1.25	$3.75	$7.50
303	Charbonneau, Louis - ***Night Of Violence*** [1959]	$1.25	$3.75	$7.50
304	Fox, Gardner F. - ***Creole Woman*** [1959] PBO.	$2.00	$6.00	$12.00
D-305	Mittelholzer, Edgar - ***The Old Blood*** [1959]	$1.25	$3.75	$7.50
S-306	Derby, Mark - ***Sun In The Hunter's Eyes*** [1959]	$1.00	$3.00	$6.00
S-307	Holmes, John Clellon - ***The Horn*** [1959] Cover art by Mitchell Hooks.	$1.25	$3.75	$7.50
S-308	Matheson, Richard - ***A Stir Of Echoes*** [1959]	$4.00	$12.50	$25.00
309	Gault, William Campbell - ***Sweet Wild Wench*** [1959] PBO.	$1.50	$5.00	$10.00
310	Brewer, Gil - ***The Red Scarf*** [1959] PBO. Cover art by Robert McGinnis.	$2.50	$7.50	$15.00
311	Partch, Virgil - ***Crazy Cartoons*** [1959]	$1.35	$4.00	$8.00
D-312	Dibner, Martin - ***Showcase*** [1959] Cover art by Mitchell Hooks.	$1.00	$3.00	$6.00

		G	VG	F
S-313	Israel, Charles E. - ***The Mark*** [1959]	$1.00	$3.00	$6.00
D-314	Keyes, Frances Parkinson - ***Joy Street*** [1959]	$1.00	$3.00	$6.00
315	Frazee, Steve - ***Rendezvous*** [1959]	$1.25	$3.75	$7.50
316	Brackeen, Steve - ***Danger In My Blood*** [1959] PBO. Cover art by Barye Phillips.	$1.25	$3.75	$7.50
S-317	Keats, John - ***The Insolent Chariots*** [1959] Cover art by Robert Osborn.	$ .75	$2.50	$5.00
S-318	Clark, Lemon - ***The Enjoyment Of Love In Marriage*** [1959]	$ .75	$2.50	$5.00
D-319	Davis, Christopher - ***Lost Summer*** [1959]	$1.00	$3.00	$6.00
S-320	Auchincloss, Louis - ***Venus In Sparta*** [1959]	$1.00	$3.00	$6.00
S-321	Salisbury, Harrison E. - ***The Shook-Up Generation*** [1959] Photo cover.	$1.35	$4.00	$8.00
S-322	Black, Ian Stuart - ***The Passionate City*** [1959] Cover art by Robert McGinnis.	$1.25	$3.75	$7.50
323	Dewey, Thomas B. - ***You've Got Him Cold*** [1959]	$1.35	$4.00	$8.00
S-324	McGovern, Ann - ***Treasure Book Of Fairy Tales*** [1959]	$1.50	$5.00	$10.00
325	Baynes, Jack - ***Morocco Jones In The Case Of The Golden Angel*** [1959] PBO. Cover art by Barye Phillips.	$1.35	$4.00	$8.00
T-326	Cozzens, James Gould - ***By Love Possessed*** [1959]	$1.25	$3.75	$7.50
S-327	Malo, Vincent Gaspard - ***Murder On The Mistral*** [1959]	$1.25	$3.75	$7.50
S-328	Guerard, Albert J. - ***The Bystander*** [1959]	$1.00	$3.00	$6.00
S-329	Hamilton, Edmond - ***The Star Of Life*** [1959] Cover art by Richard Powers.	$1.50	$5.00	$10.00
D-330	Fielding, Henry - ***Tom Jones*** [1959]	$ .75	$2.50	$5.00
S-331	Anthology edited by Lester Grady - ***Drink And Be Merry*** [1959] Cover by Vip. Cartoon book.	$1.00	$3.00	$6.00
S-332	Bennett, Margot - ***Someone From The Past*** [1959]	$1.00	$3.00	$6.00
D-333	Keyes, Frances Parkinson - ***Victorine*** [1959]	$ .75	$2.50	$5.00
334	Hunt, Kyle - ***Kill My Love*** [1959] Cover art by Robert McGinnis.	$1.25	$3.75	$7.50
S-335	Edmondson, Paul - ***The Little Revolution*** [1959] Cover art by Mitchell Hooks.	$1.00	$3.00	$6.00
S-336	Evans, Lesley - ***Strange Are The Ways Of Love*** [1959] PBO. Cover art by Barye Phillips.	$1.00	$3.00	$6.00
S-337	Remarque, Erich Maria - ***All Quiet On The Western Front*** [1959]	$ .75	$2.50	$5.00
D-338	Nabokov, Vladimir - ***Lolita*** [1959]	$1.00	$3.00	$6.00
339	Dorien, Ray - ***Lyn Darling, M.D.*** [1959]	$ .65	$2.00	$4.00
340	Martin, John Bartlow - ***Jimmy Hoffa's Hot*** [1959] PBO. Photo cover.	$1.25	$3.75	$7.50
S-341	Webb, Jack - ***The Badge*** [1959] Photo cover.	$1.25	$3.75	$7.50
S-342	Charbonneau, Louis - ***No Place On Earth*** [1959] Cover by Paul Lehr.	$1.50	$5.00	$10.00
S-343	De Mare, George - ***The Ruling Passion*** [1959]	$1.00	$3.00	$6.00
344	Baynes, Jack - ***Meet Morocco Jones*** [1959]	$1.25	$3.75	$7.50
S-345	Allen, Johannes - ***Young Love*** [1960] Photo cover.	$ .75	$2.50	$5.00
346	Yarnell, Duane - ***Mantrap*** [1960] Photo cover.	$1.00	$3.00	$6.00
S-347	Plagemann, Bentz - ***The Steel Cocoon*** [1960]	$1.00	$3.00	$6.00
S-348	Forrest, Williams - ***Trail Of Tears*** [1960]	$1.25	$3.75	$7.50
349	Conroy, Albert - ***Devil In Dungarees*** [1960] PBO. Cover art by Barye Phillips.	$2.00	$6.00	$12.00
D-351	Stewart, Mary - ***Nine Coaches Waiting*** [1960]	$1.00	$3.00	$6.00
S-352	Harris, Sara - ***They Sell Sex*** [1960] PBO.	$1.00	$3.00	$6.00
S-353	Vail, Amanda - ***The Bright Young Things*** [1959]	$ .75	$2.50	$5.00
354	Causey, James O. - ***Frenzy*** [1960] PBO.	$1.35	$4.00	$8.00
357	Whittington, Harry - ***Trouble Rides Tall*** [1960]	$2.50	$7.50	$15.00
S-359	MacDonald, John D. - ***Please Write For Details*** [1960] Cover art by Mitchell Hooks.	$1.50	$5.00	$10.00
360	Dewey, Thomas B. - ***The Chased And The Unchaste*** [1960]	$1.35	$4.00	$8.00

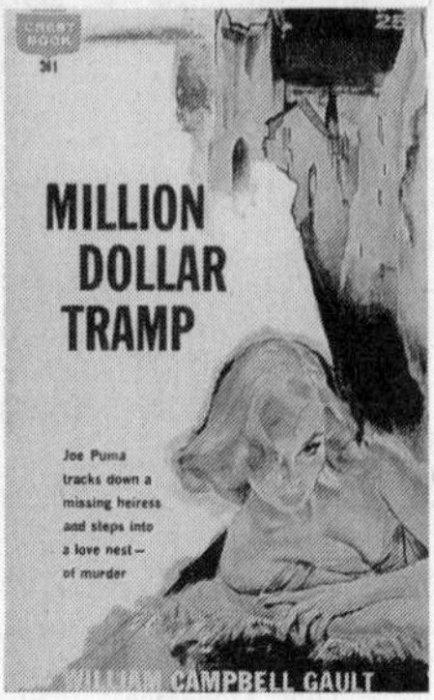

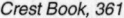

Crest Book, 361

Crest Book, S-413

Croydon, 12

		G	VG	F
361	Gault, William Campbell - ***Million Dollar Tramp*** [1960] PBO. Cover art by Charles.	$1.35	$4.00	$8.00
S-362	Anthology edited by Leo Margulies - ***Get Out Of My Sky*** [1960] PBO. Cover art by Richard Powers.	$1.50	$5.00	$10.00
S-364	Habe, Hans - ***Off Limits*** [1960] Cover art by Barye Phillips.	$1.00	$3.00	$6.00
D-365	Lederer, William J. & Burdick, Eugene - ***The Ugly American*** [1960]	$ .75	$2.50	$5.00
366	Cross, James - ***The Dark Road*** [1960]	$1.00	$3.00	$6.00
S-367	Gutwillig, Robert - ***The Fugitives*** [1960]	$1.00	$3.00	$6.00
368	Neider, Charles - ***The Authentic Death Of Hendry Jones*** [1960] Movie tie-in.	$1.25	$3.75	$7.50
369	Guild, Leo - ***What Are The Odds?*** [1960] PBO. Cover art by Earl Willis. TV Tie-in.	$1.00	$3.00	$6.00
D-372	Vatsek, Joan - ***This Fiery Night*** [1960]	$1.00	$3.00	$6.00
S-373	Gorham, Charles - ***Carlotta McBride*** [1960]	$1.00	$3.00	$6.00
S-374	Linkletter, Monte - ***The Life And Loves Of Cricket Smith*** [1960]	$ .75	$2.50	$5.00
375	Rank, Mary O. - ***A Dream Of Falling*** [1960]	$1.00	$3.00	$6.00
378	Ketcham, Hank - ***Teacher's Threat*** [1960]	$1.25	$3.75	$7.50
D-379	Gwaltney, Francis Irby - ***The Violators*** [1960]	$1.00	$3.00	$6.00
S-380	McLaughlin, Robert - ***The Notion Of Sin*** [1960]	$1.00	$3.00	$6.00
S-381	Cushman, Dan - ***The Con Man*** [1960] Cover by Barye Phillips.	$1.00	$3.00	$6.00
382	Armstrong, Charlotte - ***The Girl With A Secret*** [1960]	$1.25	$3.75	$7.50
383	Armstrong, Charlotte - ***A Dram Of Poison*** [1960]	$1.25	$3.75	$7.50
S-385	Bloch, Robert - ***Psycho*** [1961] Movie photo cover. Movie tie-in with Tony Perkins & Janet Leigh.	$4.00	$12.50	$25.00
S-386	Miller, Warren - ***The Cool World*** [1960]	$1.50	$5.00	$10.00
S-387	Seifert, Elizabeth - ***The Story Of Andrea Fields, Woman And Doctor*** [1960]	$ .75	$2.50	$5.00
S-388	Blake, Nicholas - ***A Penknife In My Heart*** [1960]	$1.25	$3.75	$7.50
D-389	Hill, Napoleon - ***Think And Grow Rich*** [1960]	$ .65	$2.00	$4.00
390	*True* Magazine - editor - ***Best Cartoons*** [1960] Cover by Vip. Cartoon book.	$1.25	$3.75	$7.50
S-393	Hawkins, Ward - ***Kings Will Be Tyrants*** [1960] Cover art by Mitchell Hooks.	$1.00	$3.00	$6.00
394	Partch, Virgil Franklin - ***Vip Tosses A Party*** [1960] Cover by Vip. Cartoon book.	$1.00	$3.00	$6.00
S-395	Baum, L. Frank - ***The Wizard Of Oz*** [1960] Cover art by W. W. Denslow.	$2.00	$6.00	$12.00

		G	VG	F
S-396	Wilder, Robert - ***A Handful Of Men*** [1960] PBO. Cover art by James Meese.	$1.25	$3.75	$7.50
398	Huffaker, Claire - ***Seven Ways From Sundown*** [1960] PBO. Movie tie-in with Audie Murphy.	$1.25	$3.75	$7.50
S-400	MacDonald, John D. - ***The Crossroads*** [1960] Cover art by Robert McGinnis.	$1.50	$5.00	$10.00
S-401	Delmar, Vina - ***The Breeze From Camelot*** [1960] PBO.	$1.00	$3.00	$6.00
402	Ketcham, Hank - ***Dennis The Menace Rides Again*** [1960]	$1.25	$3.75	$7.50
403	Rigsby, Howard - ***Clash Of Shadows*** [1960]	$1.00	$3.00	$6.00
D-404	Coppel, Alfred - ***Night Of Fire And Snow*** [1960]	$1.00	$3.00	$6.00
405	Erskine, Dorothy & Dennis, Patrick - ***The Pink Hotel*** [1960] Cover art by Mitchell Hooks.	$1.00	$3.00	$6.00
S-407	Rochefort, Christiane - ***Warrior's Rest*** [1960]	$1.00	$3.00	$6.00
408	Buell, John - ***The Pyx*** [1960] Cover art by Barye Phillips.	$1.00	$3.00	$6.00
D-409	Kruger, Judith - ***My Fight For Sanity*** [1960]	$ .75	$2.50	$5.00
D-412	Nabokov, Vladimia - ***Invitation To A Beheading*** [1960]	$ .75	$2.50	$5.00
S-413	Lee, Marjorie - ***The Lion House*** [1960] Cover art by Robert McGinnis.	$1.00	$3.00	$6.00
S-414	Berle, Milton & Roeburt, John - ***Earthquake*** [1960]	$ .75	$2.50	$5.00
415	Roberts, Lee - ***If The Shoe Fits*** [1960] Cover art by Robert McGinnis.	$1.25	$3.75	$7.50
D-416	Williams, Thomas - ***Town Burning*** [1960] Cover art by Barye Phillips.	$1.00	$3.00	$6.00
D-417	Wellard, James - ***The Affair In Arcady*** [1960]	$1.00	$3.00	$6.00
419	Anthology edited by Leo Margulies - ***Back Alley Jungle*** [1960] PBO. Cover art by James Meese.	$2.50	$7.50	$15.00
S-420	Cleary, Jon - ***Back Of Sunset*** [1960]	$1.00	$3.00	$6.00
S-421	Huffaker, Clair - ***Flaming Lance*** [1960] Movie tie-in with Elvis Presley.	$2.00	$6.00	$12.00
D-422	Onstott, Kyle & Horner, Lance - ***The Tattooed Rood*** [1960] Cover art by Stanley Zuckerburg.	$1.00	$3.00	$6.00
S-424	Hilton, Joseph - ***That French Girl*** [1961]	$1.00	$3.00	$6.00
D-425	Eldridge, Paul & Viereck, George S. - ***My First Two Thousand Years*** [1961]	$1.25	$3.75	$7.50
D-426	Frey, Richard L. - ***How To Win At Contract Bridge In 10 Easy Lessons*** [1961]	$ .65	$2.00	$4.00
D-427	Angus, Douglas - ***The Ivy Trap*** [1961] Cover art by Charles.	$1.00	$3.00	$6.00
D-428	Kelley, William - ***Gemini*** [1961] Cover art by Stanley Zuckerburg.	$1.00	$3.00	$6.00
S-429	Anthology edited by Robert Deindorfer - ***True Spy Stories*** [1961] PBO.	$1.25	$3.75	$7.50
S-430	Raspail, Jean - ***Welcome Honorable Visitors*** [1961] Cover art by Mitchell Hooks.	$1.00	$3.00	$6.00
S-431	Conroy, Albert - ***The Looters*** [1961] PBO.	$1.25	$3.75	$7.50
D-434	Shelton, Jess - ***Brood Of Fury*** [1961] Cover art by Stanley Zuckerberg.	$1.00	$3.00	$6.00
D-435	Leslie, Warren - ***Love Or Whatever It Is*** [1961] Cover art by Robert McGinnis.	$ .75	$2.50	$5.00
S-436	Brickhill, Paul - ***The Great Escape*** [1961]	$1.00	$3.00	$6.00
D-437	Meyer, Jerome S. - ***1001 Selections From The Big Fun Book*** [1961] Puzzle & quiz book.	$1.25	$3.75	$7.50
D-438	Jarvis, M.D., D.C. - ***Folk Medicine*** [1961]	$1.25	$3.75	$7.50
D-440	Sire, Glen - ***The Death Makers*** [1961]	$1.00	$3.00	$6.00
D-441	Vale, Eugene - ***The 13th Apostle*** [1961] Cover art by Stanley Zuckerberg.	$1.00	$3.00	$6.00
S-442	Torres, Tereska - ***The Dangerous Games*** [1961]	$1.00	$3.00	$6.00
S-443	O'Neal, Cothburn - ***The Gods Of Our Time*** [1961]	$ .75	$2.50	$5.00
S-444	Anthology edited by Ashley Halsey, Jr. - ***You Be The Judge*** [1961] Cartoon & joke book.	$1.25	$3.75	$7.50
D-445	Charell, Lissa - ***The Happy Medium*** [1961]	$1.00	$3.00	$6.00

		G	VG	F
D-446	Stewart, Mary - ***My Brother Michael*** [1961]	$1.00	$3.00	$6.00
S-447	Haase, John - ***Road Show*** [1961] Cover art by Barye Phillips.	$1.00	$3.00	$6.00
S-448	Benchley, Nathaniel - ***Sail A Crooked Ship*** [1961]	$1.00	$3.00	$6.00
S-450	Ketcham, Hank - ***Dennis The Menace, A.M. Ambassador Of Michief*** [1961]	$1.25	$3.75	$7.50
S-451	Condon, Richard - ***Some Angry Angel*** [1961]	$1.25	$3.75	$7.50
S-452	Marsh, Ngaio - ***False Scent*** [1961] Cover art by Robert McGinnis.	$1.25	$3.75	$7.50
D-453	Cooper, Jr., Clarence L. - ***The Scene*** [1961]	$1.00	$3.00	$6.00
D-455	Frank, Gerold - ***Zsa Zsa Gabor*** [1961] Photo cover. 16 pages of photos.	$1.35	$4.00	$8.00
D-459	Ross, Martin J. - ***Handbook Of Everyday Law*** [1961]	$ .65	$2.00	$4.00
D-461	Remarque, Erich Maria - ***All Quiet On The Western Front*** [1961]	$ .65	$2.00	$4.00
R-462	Jaffe, Rona - ***Away From Home*** [1961]	$1.00	$3.00	$6.00
S-464	MacDonald, John D. - ***The End Of The Night*** [1961] Cover art by Barye Phillips.	$1.50	$5.00	$10.00
S-465	Ketcham, Hank - ***Wanted: Dennis The Menace*** [1961]	$1.25	$3.75	$7.50
S-466	Shaw, Howard - ***The Crime Of Giovanni Venturi*** [1961] Cover art by Ron Wing.	$1.00	$3.00	$6.00
S-467	Ketcham, Hank - ***Dennis The Menace Rides Again*** [1961]	$1.25	$3.75	$7.50
D-468	Holt, Victoria - ***Mistress Of Mellyn*** [1961] Movie tie-in.	$ .75	$2.50	$5.00
S-471	Williams, Charles - ***Aground*** [1961]	$1.25	$3.75	$7.50
D-474	Sheen, Fulton J. - ***Way To Inner Peace*** [1961] Photo cover.	$ .65	$2.00	$4.00
S-479	Whittington, Harry - ***Vengeance Is The Spur*** [1961]	$1.50	$5.00	$10.00
D-480	Considine, Bob - editor - ***True War Stories*** [1961] PBO.	$1.00	$3.00	$6.00
S-481	Pratt, Theodore - ***Handsome's Seven Women*** [1961] Cover by Barye Phillips.	$1.00	$3.00	$6.00
M-482	Fedoroff, Alexander - ***The Side Of The Angels*** [1961]	$ .65	$2.00	$4.00
S-484	Canning, Victor - ***The Burning Eye*** [1961]	$1.25	$3.75	$7.50
S-485	Maloney, Ralph - ***Daily Bread*** [1961] Cover art by Robert McGinnis.	$ .65	$2.00	$4.00
D-486	Traver, Robert - ***Small Town U.S.A.*** [1961] Cover art by James Meese.	$ .75	$2.50	$5.00
D-489	McDougall, Colin - ***Execution*** [1961]	$1.00	$3.00	$6.00
T-490	West, Anthony - ***The Trend Is Up*** [1961]	$ .75	$2.50	$5.00
S-491	Kastle, Herbert D. - ***Countdown To Murder*** [1961] PBO.	$1.25	$3.75	$7.50
492	Fields, Alonzo - ***My 21 Years In The White House*** [1916] Photo cover.	$ .65	$2.00	$4.00
S-493	Ketcham, Hank - ***Baby Sitter's Guide By Dennis The Menace*** [1961]	$1.25	$3.75	$7.50
S-494	Hamilton, Edmond - ***City At World's End*** [1961] Cover art by Richard Powers.	$1.00	$3.00	$6.00
S-495	Christian, Paula - ***Edge Of Twilight*** [1961] Photo cover.	$1.25	$3.75	$7.50
D-497	Olivier, Stefan - ***I Swear and Vow*** [1961] Cover art by Stanley Zuckerberg.	$1.00	$3.00	$6.00
S-499	McGivern, William P. - ***Seven Lies South*** [1962] Cover art by Harry Bennett.	$1.25	$3.75	$7.50
D-500	Graham, Winston - ***Marnie*** [1962] Movie tie-in.	$1.00	$3.00	$6.00
S-501	Ketcham, Hank - ***Dennis The Menace Vs. Everybody*** [1962]	$1.25	$3.75	$7.50
D-508	Stewart, Mary - ***Thunder On The Right*** [1962]	$ .75	$2.50	$5.00
R-509	Carson, Robert - ***My Hero*** [1962]	$ .75	$2.50	$5.00
S-511	Dorien, Ray - ***Call Dr. Margaret*** [1962]	$ .65	$2.00	$4.00
S-512	Ketcham, Hank - ***In This Corner . . . Dennis The Menace*** [1962]	$1.25	$3.75	$7.50
S-514	Kerr, Jean - ***The Snake Has All The Lines*** [1962]	$ .65	$2.00	$4.00
D-515	Remarque, Erich Maria - ***Heaven Has No Favorites*** [1962]	$ .65	$2.00	$4.00
S-518	Blaisdell, Anne - ***Nightmare*** [1962]	$1.00	$3.00	$6.00
S-520	MacDonald, John D. - ***Cape Fear*** [1962] Movie tie-in with Gregory Peck & Robert Mitchum/	$2.50	$7.50	$15.00

		G	VG	F
A-522	Smirer, William - ***The Rise And Fall Of The Third Reich*** [1962]	$ .65	$2.00	$4.00
D-523	Donovan, Robert J. - ***PT 109*** [1962]	$ .65	$2.00	$4.00
S-524	Bennett, Jay - ***Murder Money*** [1962] Cover art by Harry Bennett.	$ .75	$2.50	$5.00
M-525	Keyes, Frances Parkinson - ***Came A Cavalier*** [1962]	$ .65	$2.00	$4.00
R-528	Keyes, Frances Parkinson - ***Blue Camellia*** [1962]	$ .65	$2.00	$4.00
D-531	Wyndham, John - ***The Day Of The Triffids*** [1962] Movie tie-in.	$1.50	$5.00	$10.00
D-532	Stern, Richard Martin - ***These Unlucky Deeds*** [1962] Cover art by Harry Bennett.	$ .65	$2.00	$4.00
D-535	Anthology edited by Charles Kennedy - ***American Ballads*** [1962]	$1.00	$3.00	$6.00
D-537	Jarvis, M.D., D.C. - ***Arthritis And Folk Medicine*** [1962]	$1.00	$3.00	$6.00
R-538	Updike, John - ***Rabbit, Run*** [1962]	$ .50	$1.50	$3.00
D-541	Cooley, Donald G. - ***Eat And Get Slim*** [1961]	$ .50	$1.50	$3.00
D-545	Lederer, William J. - ***A Nation Of Sheep*** [1962]	$ .50	$1.50	$3.00
R-546	Burdick, Eugene - ***The Blue Of Capricorn*** [1962]	$ .50	$1.50	$3.00
D-547	Simak, Clifford D. - ***Time Is The Simplest Thing*** [1962] Cover art by Richard Powers.	$ .75	$2.50	$5.00
S-548	Anthology - ***New Faces On The Barroom Floor*** [1962] Cover by Vip. Cartoon book.	$1.00	$3.00	$6.00
D-550	Stewart, Mary - ***Nine Coaches Waiting*** [1962]	$ .50	$1.50	$3.00
M-553	Keyes, Frances Parkinson - ***The Chess Players*** [1962]	$ .50	$1.50	$3.00
D-555	Ruark, Robert - ***The Old Man And The Boy*** [1962] Photo cover.	$ .65	$2.00	$4.00
D-557	Anthology edited by David Alexander - ***Tales For A Rainy Night*** [1962]	$ .65	$2.00	$4.00
561	Ketchum, Hank - ***Happy Half-Pint*** [1962]	$1.25	$3.75	$7.50
D-563	Stewart, Mary - ***Wildfire At Midnight*** [1962]	$ .65	$2.00	$4.00
570	Poitrine, Belle - ***Little Me*** [1962] Contains over 150 photos.	$1.25	$3.75	$7.50
S-572	Rose, Alexander - ***Whose Got The Action?*** [1962] Photo cover. Movie tie-in with Dean Martin & Lana Turner.	$1.25	$3.75	$7.50
S-573	Schulz, Charles M. - ***Hey, Peanuts!*** [1962] Cover art by Schulz. Cartoon book.	$1.25	$3.75	$7.50
R-575	Ryan, Cornelius - ***The Longest Day*** [1962] Movie tie-in. Photos inside.	$1.00	$3.00	$6.00
D-576	Golden, Harry - ***Carl Sandburg*** [1962]	$ .65	$2.00	$4.00
D-578	Grubb, Davis - ***The Watchman*** [1962]	$ .65	$2.00	$4.00
D-579	Hanser, Richard - ***True Tales Of Hitler's Reich*** [1962] PBO. Photo cover.	$ .75	$2.50	$5.00
R-582	Keyes, Frances Parkinson - ***Victorine*** [1962]	$ .65	$2.00	$4.00
586	Vercors - ***Sylva*** [1963]	$2.50	$7.50	$15.00
D-587	Gorham, Charles - ***McCaffery*** [1963] Cover art by Stanley Zuckerberg.	$ .65	$2.00	$4.00
S-588	Kerr, Jean - ***Please Don't Eat The Daisies*** [1962]	$ .50	$1.50	$3.00
S-589	Taylor, Valerie - ***The Girls In 3-B*** [1962]	$1.00	$3.00	$6.00
R-590	Stewart, Mary - ***The Ivy Tree*** [1963]	$ .50	$1.50	$3.00
T-593	Hemingway, Leicester - ***My Brother, Ernest Hemingway*** [1963] Photo cover. 8 pages of photos.	$1.25	$3.75	$7.50
S-595	Cunningham, E.V. - ***Phyllis*** [1963]	$ .65	$2.00	$4.00
K-596	Rochefort, Christiane - ***Warrior's Rest*** [1963] Photo cover. Movie tie-in with Brigitte Bardot.	$1.25	$3.75	$7.50
D-597	Anthology - ***5 Tales From Tomorrow*** [1963]	$ .65	$2.00	$4.00
T-600	Keyes, Frances Parkinson - ***The Royal Box*** [1963]	$ .50	$1.50	$3.00
R-604	Rosten, Leo - ***Captain Newman, M.D.*** [1963] Movie tie-in with Tony Curtis & Gregory Peck.	$1.00	$3.00	$6.00
605	Updike, John - ***Pigeon Feathers*** [1963]	$ .65	$2.00	$4.00
D-609	Stewart, Mary - ***Thunder On The Right*** [1963]	$ .65	$2.00	$4.00
D-612	Christopher, John - ***The Long Winter*** [1963]	$ .65	$2.00	$4.00
K-616	Lemay, Alan - ***The Unforgiven*** [1963]	$1.00	$3.00	$6.00
R-617	Frey, Richard L. - ***According To Hoyle*** [1963]	$ .50	$1.50	$3.00

		G	VG	F
R-618	Holt, Victoria - ***Kirkland Revels*** [1963]	$ .50	$1.50	$3.00
620	Waldo, M. - ***The Home Book Of Barbecue Cooking*** [1963] Cook book.	$ .65	$2.00	$4.00
D-622	Sire, Glen - ***The Deathmakers*** [1963]	$ .50	$1.50	$3.00
R-627	Golden, Harry - ***You're Entitle'*** [1963]	$ .50	$1.50	$3.00
D-629	Holt, Victoria - ***Mistress Of Mellyn*** [1963]	$ .50	$1.50	$3.00
T-631	MacInnes, Helen - ***Decision At Delphi*** [1963]	$ .50	$1.50	$3.00
S-640	Drago, Harry Sinclair - ***Top Hand With A Gun*** [1963]	$ .50	$1.50	$3.00
S-643	Donalds, Gordon - ***Top Gun*** [1963]	$ .50	$1.50	$3.00

Crime Case Book Magazine. Digest Size.

1	Abbington, John (Walter B. Gibson) - ***John Christie And His House Of Death*** [1954] PBO.	$5.50	$17.50	$35.00
2	Gibson, Walter - ***The Castle Of Horrors*** [1954] PBO.	$5.50	$17.50	$35.00
3	Raymond, P.L. (Walter Gibson) - ***The Coronation Murders*** [1954] PBO.	$5.50	$17.50	$35.00

Crime Novel Selection. New York: Red Circle Magazines, Inc. Digest Size.

1	Steel, Kurt - ***Strangler's Holiday*** [1942] Cover art by Norman Saunders.	$3.50	$10.00	$20.00
2	Steel, Kurt - ***The Traveling Corpses*** [1942] Cover art by Peter Driben.	$3.50	$10.00	$20.00
3	Bosworth, Allan R. - ***The Submarine Signaled...Murder!*** [1942]	$3.00	$9.00	$18.00
4	Steel, Kurt - ***Murder For What?*** [1943] Cover art by George Dunsford Klein.	$3.00	$9.00	$18.00
5	Spatz, H. Donald - ***3 Girls And A Killer*** [1943] Cover by Peter Driben.	$3.50	$10.00	$20.00
NN-6	Lariar, Lawrence - ***Death Is The Host*** [1943] Listed as #6 inside book.	$3.50	$10.00	$20.00

Crimes Of Love And Passion. New York: Louellen Publishing Co. Digest Size.

1	Anthology - ***The Secret Lover Of Madeleine Smith*** [n.d.] edited by Paul Renin.	$4.00	$12.50	$25.00
2	Anthology - ***The Crimes Of Belle Gunness*** [n.d.] edited by Paul Renin.	$4.00	$12.50	$25.00
3	Anthology - ***Dorothy Jordan, The Siren Of Old Drury*** [n.d.] edited by Paul Renin.	$4.00	$12.50	$25.00
4	Anthology - ***Bela Kiss*** [n.d.] edited by Paul Renin.	$4.00	$12.50	$25.00

Crow Books. Toronto: Alval Pub. Of Canada, Ltd.

21	Jefferson, Lara - ***Sister Of The Damned*** [1949]	$6.00	$20.00	$40.00
22	Dexter, Daryl X. - ***Red Moon Of Desire*** [1949]	$6.00	$20.00	$40.00
23	Clayford, James (Peggy Gaddis) - ***Careless Virgin*** [1949]	$6.00	$20.00	$40.00
24	Sherman, Joan (Peggy Gaddis) - ***Overnight Girl*** [1949]	$6.00	$20.00	$40.00
25	Gaddis, Peggy - ***Reckless Maiden*** [1949]	$6.00	$20.00	$40.00
26	Clayford, James (Peggy Gaddis) - ***Week-End Girl*** [1949]	$6.00	$20.00	$40.00
27	Clayford, James (Peggy Gaddis) - ***Impatient Temptress*** [1949]	$6.00	$20.00	$40.00
28	Ahern, Helen - ***Party-Wife*** [1949]	$6.00	$20.00	$40.00
29	Gordon, Luther - ***Wedding Night Confession*** [1949]	$6.00	$20.00	$40.00
30	Bellamy, Harmon - ***Frenchy*** [1949]	$6.00	$20.00	$40.00
31	Clayford, James (Peggy Gaddis) - ***Good Girl-By Day*** [1949]	$6.00	$20.00	$40.00
32	Clayford, James (Peggy Gaddis) - ***Illicit Honeymoon*** [1949]	$6.00	$20.00	$40.00
33	Bellamy, Harmon - ***Pick-Up*** [1949]	$6.00	$20.00	$40.00
34	Gordon, Luther - ***Night Of Passion*** [1949]	$6.00	$20.00	$40.00
35	Langdale, Roy - ***Hot Number*** [1949]	$6.00	$20.00	$40.00
36	Caldwell, John - ***Midnight Sinners*** [1949]	$6.00	$20.00	$40.00
37	Gordon, Luther - ***Desirable*** [1950]	$6.00	$20.00	$40.00
38	Bellamy, Harmon - ***Paid In Full*** [1950]	$6.00	$20.00	$40.00
39	Bligh, Norman - ***Lady In A Hurry*** [1950]	$6.00	$20.00	$40.00
40	Clayford, James (Peggy Gaddis) - ***Side Show Girl*** [1950]	$6.00	$20.00	$40.00

Croydon, 17

Croydon, 18

Dell Book, 1

		G	VG	F
41	Clayford, James (Peggy Gaddis) - ***Lady In Waiting*** [1950]	$6.00	$20.00	$40.00
42	Bligh, Norman - ***Too Many Sweethearts*** [1950]	$6.00	$20.00	$40.00
43	Langdale, Roy - ***Easy Come-Easy Go*** [1950]	$6.00	$20.00	$40.00
44	Bellamy, Harmon - ***Lovely To Look At*** [1950]	$6.00	$20.00	$40.00

Croydon Series. New York: Croydon Publishing/Star Publications.

		G	VG	F
NN-1	Mannon, M.M. - ***Here Lies Blood*** [1945] Cover art by L.B. Cole.	$2.00	$6.00	$12.00
NN-2	Mechem, Philip - ***Murders I've Seen*** [1945] Cover art by L.B. Cole.	$2.00	$6.00	$12.00
NN-3	Van Deusen, Delia - ***Many A Murder*** [1945] Cover art by L.B. Cole.	$2.00	$6.00	$12.00
NN-4	Long, Manning - ***Vicious Circle*** [1945] Cover art by L.B. Cole.	$2.00	$6.00	$12.00
NN-5	Hurley, Gene - ***Have You Seen This Man?*** [1945] Cover art by L.B. Cole.	$2.00	$6.00	$12.00
NN-6	Scott, Dennis - ***Murder Makes A Villain*** [1945] Cover art by L.B. Cole.	$2.00	$6.00	$12.00
NN-7	Coffin, Carlyn - ***Dogwatch*** [1946] Cover art by Dan Barry.	$2.00	$6.00	$12.00
8K	Govan, Christine Noble - ***Murder On The Mountain*** [1945] Cover art by L.B. Cole.	$2.00	$6.00	$12.00
9K	Burke, Richard - ***The Dead Take No Bows*** [1946] Cover art by L.B. Cole.	$2.00	$6.00	$12.00
NN-10	Barrett, Monte - ***Murder At Belle Camille*** [1947] Cover art by L.B. Cole.	$2.00	$6.00	$12.00
11	Williams, Wright - ***Cheaters At Love*** [1946] Cover art by L.B. Cole.	$2.50	$7.50	$15.00
12	Jerome, E.D. - ***Love Hungry*** [1949] Cover art by L.B. Cole.	$2.50	$7.50	$15.00
13	Watkins, Glen - ***Reckless Virgin*** [1949] Cover art by L.B. Cole. Paperback size.	$2.50	$7.50	$15.00
14	Carter, Ralph - ***Shadows Of Lust*** [1949] Cover art by L.B. Cole. Paperback size.	$2.50	$7.50	$15.00
15	Williams, Wright - ***Fool For Love*** [1950] Cover by L. B. Cole. Paperback size.	$2.50	$7.50	$15.00
16	Semple, Gordon - ***Sinner*** [1949] Cover art by L.B. Cole. Paperback size.	$2.50	$7.50	$15.00
17	Williams, Wright - ***Street Of Sin*** [1951] PBO. Cover by Bernard Safran.	$2.00	$6.00	$12.00
18	Semple, Gordon - ***Slave Of Desire*** [1951] PBO. Cover by Bernard Safran.	$2.00	$6.00	$12.00
19	Jordan, Gail (Peggy Gaddis) - ***Restless Wife*** [1952] Cover art by Lamanna.	$1.50	$5.00	$10.00
20	Watkins, Glenn - ***The Shame Of Vanna Gilbert*** [1952]	$1.50	$5.00	$10.00

		G	VG	F
21	Semple Gordon - ***Shameless Sue*** [1952] PBO. Cover art by Lou Marchetti.	$1.50	$5.00	$10.00
22	Himmel, Richard - ***Strange Desires*** [1952] Cover art by Lou Marchetti.	$1.50	$5.00	$10.00
23	Jordan, Gail (Peggy Gaddis) - ***Sins Of A Private Secretary*** [1952] PBO. Cover art by Lou Marchetti.	$1.50	$5.00	$10.00
24	Stonebraker, Florence - ***Love-Hungry Doctor*** [1952] PBO. Cover art by Lou Marchetti.	$1.35	$4.00	$8.00
25	Duperrault, Doug - ***Spotlight On Sin*** [1952] PBO. Cover art by Lou Marchetti.	$1.50	$5.00	$10.00
26	Sherman, Joan - ***Immoral Models*** [1952] PBO. Cover by Lou Marchetti.	$1.50	$5.00	$10.00
27	Semple, Gordon - ***Career Of Sin*** [1952]	$1.50	$5.00	$10.00
28	Kingsland, Delmar - ***Mountain Sinner*** [1953] PBO. Cover art by Bernard Safran.	$1.50	$5.00	$10.00
30	Stonebraker, Florence - ***Intimate Affairs Of A French Nurse*** [1953] PBO. Cover art by Lou Marchetti.	$1.35	$4.00	$8.00
31	David, William - ***Army Mistress*** [1953] PBO. Cover art by Lou Marchetti.	$2.00	$6.00	$12.00
32	Sherman, Joan - ***Two Timing Wife*** [1953] PBO. Cover art by Bernard Safran.	$1.50	$5.00	$10.00
34	Duperrault, Doug - ***Gang Mistress*** [1953] PBO. Cover art by Safran.	$3.50	$10.00	$20.00
35	Whittington, Harry - ***Vengeful Sinner*** [1953] PBO. Cover art by Lou Marchetti.	$4.00	$12.50	$25.00
36	Semple, Gordon - ***Blonde Temptress*** [1953] PBO.	$2.00	$6.00	$12.00
37	Stonebaker, Florence - ***Strange Passions*** [1953] Cover art by Safran.	$1.50	$5.00	$10.00
39	Frame, Bart - ***Indiscretions Of A French Model*** [1953] PBO. Cover art by B. Safran.	$3.50	$10.00	$20.00
40	Bennett, Alan - ***Cellar Club Girl*** [1953] Cover art by Lou Marchetti.	$2.00	$6.00	$12.00
41	Marcelle, Denise - ***Secrets Of Paris Nights*** [1953] PBO. Cover art by Bernard Safran.	$2.00	$6.00	$12.00
42	Vaneer, William - ***Scandals At A Nudist Colony*** [1953]	$2.00	$6.00	$12.00
43	Gaddis, Peggy - ***Love-Hungry Boss*** [1953] PBO. Cover art by Bernard Safran.	$2.00	$6.00	$12.00
44	Albert, Sim - ***Confessions Of A B-Girl*** [1953] PBO. Cover art by Lou Marchetti.	$2.00	$6.00	$12.00
46	Stonebraker, Florence - ***Girl Crazy Professor*** [1953] PBO. Cover by Bernard Safran.	$1.50	$5.00	$10.00
47	Craig, Jonathan - ***Red-Headed Sinners*** [1953] PBO.	$1.50	$5.00	$10.00
48	Frame, Bart - ***Co-Ed Sinners*** [1953] PBO. Cover by Bernard Safran.	$1.50	$5.00	$10.00
50	Duperrault, Doug - ***Soldier's Sinner*** [1953]	$1.50	$5.00	$10.00
51	Gaddis, Peggy - ***Love-Starved Woman*** [1953]	$1.50	$5.00	$10.00
53	Semple, Gordon - ***Warped Desires*** [1953] Cover by Bernard Safran.	$1.50	$5.00	$10.00
54	Calvet, Jean - ***Scandalous French Doctor*** [1954] PBO.	$1.50	$5.00	$10.00
55	Stonebraker, Florence - ***Shameless Play-Girl*** [1954] PBO. Cover art by Lou Marchetti.	$1.50	$5.00	$10.00
56	Albert, Sim - ***Confessions Of A Pick-Up Girl*** [1954] PBO. Cover art by Bernard Safran.	$1.50	$5.00	$10.00
57	Semple, Gordon - ***Love-Crazy Millionaire*** [1954] PBO. Cover art by Bernard Safran.	$1.50	$5.00	$10.00
58	Vaneer, William - ***Back-Road Motel*** [1954] PBO. Cover art by Bernard Safran.	$1.50	$5.00	$10.00
59	Frame, Bart - ***Scandals At A Country Club*** [1954] PBO. Cover art by Bernard Safran.	$1.50	$5.00	$10.00
60	Williams, Wright - ***Forbidden Passions*** [1954]	$2.00	$6.00	$12.00

		G	VG	F
61	Semple, Gordon - ***Sinner*** [1954] Cover by Rudy Nappi.	$2.00	$6.00	$12.00
62	Whittington, Harry - ***Nightclub Sinner*** [1954] Cover art by Bernard Safran.	$4.00	$12.50	$25.00
63	Semple, Gordon - ***Man-Crazy Hussy*** [1954] Cover art by Bernard Safran.	$2.00	$6.00	$12.00
65	Semple, Gordon - ***Indiscretions Of A TV Sinner*** [1954] PBO.	$2.00	$6.00	$12.00
67	Gaddis, Peggy - ***House Of Sinners*** [1954]	$1.50	$5.00	$10.00
68	Foster, Gerald - ***Lady Of Many Sins*** [1954]	$2.00	$6.00	$12.00
69	Gaddis, Peggy - ***Scandalous Nurse*** [1954]	$1.50	$5.00	$10.00
70	Stonebraker, Florence - ***Confessions Of A Ladies' Chauffeur*** [1970] PBO. Cover by Bernard Safran.	$1.50	$5.00	$10.00
71	Davids, William - ***Bad Girls' Club*** [1954] Cover art by Lou Marchetti.	$2.50	$7.50	$15.00
72	Kingsland, Delmar - ***Hoyden Of The Mountains*** [1954]	$2.00	$6.00	$12.00
74	Semple, Gordon - ***Playboy's Nurse*** [1970] PBO.	$1.50	$5.00	$10.00
75	Himmel, Richard - ***Strange Desires*** [1954] Cover art by Lou Marchetti.	$1.50	$5.00	$10.00
76	Semple, Gordon - ***Career Of Sin*** [1954]	$1.50	$5.00	$10.00
77	Albert, Sim - ***French Sinner*** [1954] PBO.	$1.50	$5.00	$10.00
78	Frame, Bart - ***Stag-Party Girl*** [1954] PBO. Cover art by Bernard Safran.	$2.00	$6.00	$12.00
82	Gaddis, Peggy - ***Thrill-Hungry Girl*** [1954] PBO. Cover art by Bernard Safran.	$2.00	$6.00	$12.00
85	Frame, Bart - ***Indiscretions Of A French Model*** [1954]	$1.50	$5.00	$10.00
86	Sherman, Joan - ***Soldier's Girl*** [1954]	$1.50	$5.00	$10.00
88	Frame, Bart - ***Georgia Girl In Harlem*** [1954] PBO.	$2.50	$7.50	$15.00
90	Gaddis, Peggy - ***Man-Crazy Nurse*** [1954] PBO.	$1.50	$5.00	$10.00
91	Semple, Gordon - ***Waterfront Hotel*** [1954]	$1.50	$5.00	$10.00
93	Albert, Sim - ***Confessions Of A B-Girl*** [1955]	$1.50	$5.00	$10.00
95	Stonebraker, Florence - ***Wild Co-Ed*** [1955] PBO. Cover by Bernard Safran.	$1.50	$5.00	$10.00
96	Marcelle, Denise - ***French Pick-Up*** [1955]	$1.50	$5.00	$10.00
97	Gaddis, Peggy - ***Man-Hungry Widow*** [1954]	$1.50	$5.00	$10.00
101-R	Carter, Ralph - ***She Lived In Sin*** [1954] Cover art by Lou Marchetti.	$2.00	$6.00	$12.00
102-R	Stone, Thomas - ***Shameful Love*** [1954] Cover art by Gazzola.	$2.00	$6.00	$12.00
103	Semple, Gordon - ***Sinner*** [1954] Cover by Rudy Nappi.	$2.00	$6.00	$12.00
104	Williams, Wright - ***Life Of Lust*** [1954]	$1.50	$5.00	$10.00
105	Carter, Ralph - ***Sin Island*** [1954] Cover art by Gazzola.	$1.50	$5.00	$10.00
106	Jackquin, Lee - ***Immoral Woman*** [1954]	$1.50	$5.00	$10.00
107	Sherman, Joan (Peggy Gaddis) - ***Intimate Affairs Of A Sinful Model*** [1954]	$1.50	$5.00	$10.00
108	Duperrault, Doug - ***Sins Of An Aspiring Actress*** [1954]	$1.50	$5.00	$10.00
109	Jordan, Gail - ***Back-Country Wench*** [1954]	$1.50	$5.00	$10.00
110	Semple, Gordon - ***Scandalous Career Girl*** [1954] Cover art by Lou Marchetti.	$1.50	$5.00	$10.00

Curtis Books. London: Curtis Warren Ltd.

NO#-1	Kinley, George - ***Ferry Rocket*** [1954]	$2.50	$7.50	$15.00

Curtis Books. New York: Curtis Publications.

7147	Bloch, Robert - ***It's All In Your Mind*** [1971] PBO.	$5.50	$17.50	$35.00
7156	Koontz, Dean R. - ***The Crimson Witch*** [1971] PBO.	$5.50	$17.50	$35.00

Dagger House/Red Dagger. New York: Dagger House Pub., Inc. Digest Size.

20	Brucker, Margaretta - ***Murder At Lover's Lake*** [1946] (Dagger House).	$2.50	$7.50	$15.00
21	Holt, Allison - ***Death For A Hussy*** [1946] (Red Dagger).	$2.50	$7.50	$15.00
22	Ketchum, Philip - ***Good Night For Murder*** [1946] (Dagger House).	$2.50	$7.50	$15.00

		G	VG	F
23	Ketchum, Philip - ***Kill At Dusk*** [1946] (Red Dagger).	$2.50	$7.50	$15.00
24	Mortimer, Peter - ***If A Body Kill A Body*** [1946] (Dagger House).	$2.50	$7.50	$15.00
25	Laing, Patrick - ***Murder From The Mind*** [1947] (Red Dagger).	$2.50	$7.50	$15.00
26	Trimble, Louis - ***You Can't Kill A Corpse*** [1947] Cover art by Levine. (Dagger House).	$2.50	$7.50	$15.00
27	Roeburt, John - ***There Are Dead Men In Manhattan*** [1947] (Red Dagger).	$2.50	$7.50	$15.00
28	Broocks, Schuyler - ***Murder Makes A Marriage*** [1947] (Dagger House).	$2.50	$7.50	$15.00
29	Holley, Helen - ***Blood On The Beach*** [1947] (Red Dagger).	$2.50	$7.50	$15.00

DAW Books (Early Publisher's History, 1972–1977)

Founded by Donald A. Wollheim, an established writer and editor, this publishing house uses his initials as its name. DAW Books became the first exclusive science fiction, fantasy, and horror paperback publisher to print fifty or more titles and survive for over a decade without diversifying. Economical prices and distinctive yellow spines drew attention to the early DAW Books. In 1984, they diversified the spine colors and altered their logo. Kelly Freas, Jack Gaughan, George Barr, and others provided cover art for this line of books. Each book received the logo and logo number. All DAW first editions receive a collector's number on the cover, except for the Cap Kennedy Series and John Norman's nonfantasy books.

DAW Books. New York: DAW Books, Inc.

		G	VG	F
1	Norton, Andre - ***Spell Of The Witch World*** [1972] PBO. Cover by Gaughan.	$ .75	$2.50	$5.00
2	Green, Joseph - ***The Mind Behind The Eye*** [1972] Cover by Josh Kirby.	$1.00	$3.00	$6.00
3	Ball, Brian N. - ***The Probability Man*** [1972] PBO. Cover by Kelly Freas.	$ .75	$2.50	$5.00
4	Van Vogt, A. E. - ***The Book Of Van Vogt*** [1972] PBO. Cover by Karel Thole.	$1.00	$3.00	$6.00
5	Wollheim, Donald A. - editor - ***The 1972 Annual World's Best SF*** [1972] PBO.	$ .75	$2.50	$5.00
6	Geston, Mark S. - ***The Day Star*** [1972] PBO. Cover by George Barr.	$ .75	$2.50	$5.00
7	Stableford, Brian M. - ***To Challenge Chaos*** [1972] PBO. Cover by Kelly Freas.	$1.00	$3.00	$6.00
8	Sutton, Jeff - ***The Mindblocked Man*** [1972] PBO. Cover by Jack Gaughan.	$1.00	$3.00	$6.00
9	Dickson, Gordon R. - ***Tactics Of Mistake*** [1972] Cover by Kelly Freas.	$ .75	$2.50	$5.00
10	Elgin, Suzette Haden - ***At The Seventh Level*** [1972] PBO. Cover by George Barr.	$ .75	$2.50	$5.00
11	Klein, Gerard - ***The Day Before Tomorrow*** [1972] Cover by Josh Kirby.	$1.00	$3.00	$6.00
12	Koontz, Dean R. - ***A Darkness In My Soul*** [1972] PBO. Cover by Jack Gaughan.	$4.00	$12.50	$25.00
13	Davis, Richard - editor - ***The Year's Best Horror Stories Vol. I*** [1972] Cover by Karel Thole.	$1.25	$3.75	$7.50
14	Dick, Philip K. - ***We Can Build You*** [1972] PBO. Cover by John Schoenherr.	$3.50	$10.00	$20.00
15	Biggle, Jr., Lloyd - ***The World Menders*** [1972] Cover by Kelly Freas.	$1.00	$3.00	$6.00
16	Phillifent, John T. - ***Genius Unlimited*** [1972] PBO.	$1.00	$3.00	$6.00
17	Edmondson, G. C. - ***Blue Face*** [1972] Cover by Karel Thole.	$ .75	$2.50	$5.00

		G	VG	F
18	Tubb, E. C. - ***Century Of The Manikin*** [1972] PBO. Cover by Gaughan.	$ .75	$2.50	$5.00
19	Ball, Brian N. - ***The Regiments Of Night*** [1972] PBO. Cover by Kelly Freas.	$1.00	$3.00	$6.00
20	Hubbard, L. Ron - ***Ole Doc Methuselah*** [1972] Cover by Josh Kirby.	$2.50	$7.50	$15.00
21	Laumer, Keith - ***Dinosaur Beach*** [1972] Cover by Kelly Freas.	$ .75	$2.50	$5.00
22	Friedell, Egon - ***The Return Of The Time Machine*** [1972] Cover by Karel Thole.	$1.00	$3.00	$6.00
23	Brunner, John - ***The Stardroppers*** [1972] Cover by Jack Gaughan.	$ .75	$2.50	$5.00
24	Trimble, Louis - ***The City Machine*** [1972] PBO. Cover by Kelly Freas.	$1.00	$3.00	$6.00
25	Jakes, John - ***Mention My Name In Atlantis*** [1972] PBO. Cover by H. J. Bluck.	$ .75	$2.50	$5.00
26	Brunner, John - ***Entry To Elsewhen*** [1972]	$1.00	$3.00	$6.00
27	Swann, Thomas Burnett - ***Green Phoenix*** [1972] PBO. Cover by George Barr.	$ .75	$2.50	$5.00
28	Dickson, Gordon R. - ***SleepwalkerWorld*** [1972] Cover by Kelly Freas.	$ .75	$2.50	$5.00
29	Aldiss, Brian W. - ***The Book Of Brian Aldiss*** [1972] PBO. Cover by Karel Thole.	$1.00	$3.00	$6.00
30	Carter, Lin - ***Under The Green Star*** [1972] PBO. Cover by Tim Kirk.	$ .75	$2.50	$5.00
31	Coney, Michael G. - ***Mirror Image*** [1972] PBO. Cover by Kelly Freas.	$1.00	$3.00	$6.00
32	Stableford, Brian M. - ***The Halcyon Drift*** [1972] PBO. Cover by Jack Gaughan. Star-Pilot Grainger #1.	$ .75	$2.50	$5.00
33	Akers, Alan Burt (Bulmer, Kenneth) - ***Transit To Scorpio*** [1972] PBO. Cover by Tim Kirk. Dray Prescot #1.	$1.00	$3.00	$6.00
34	Trimble, Louis - ***The Wandering Variables*** [1972] PBO.	$ .75	$2.50	$5.00
35	Barbet, Pierre - ***Baphomet's Meteor*** [1972] Cover by Karel Thole.	$1.00	$3.00	$6.00
36	Bradley, Marion Zimmer - ***Darkover Landfall*** [1972] PBO. Cover by Jack Gaughan. Darkover novel.	$1.00	$3.00	$6.00
37	Goulart, Ron - ***A Talent For The Invisible*** [1973] PBO. Cover by Jack Gaughan.	$1.00	$3.00	$6.00
38	Schmitz, James H. - ***The Lion Game*** [1973] PBO. Kelly Freas cover.	$1.00	$3.00	$6.00
39	Herbert, Frank - ***The Book Of Frank Herbert*** [1973] PBO. Cover by Jack Gaughan.	$ .75	$2.50	$5.00
40	Ball, Brian N. - ***Planet Probability*** [1973] PBO. Cover by Kelly Freas.	$ .75	$2.50	$5.00
41	Saberhagen, Fred - ***Changeling Earth*** [1973] PBO. Cover by Tim Kirk.	$ .75	$2.50	$5.00
42	Pournelle, Jerry - ***A Spaceship For The King*** [1973] PBO. Cover by Kelly Freas.	$1.00	$3.00	$6.00
43	Bayley, Barrington J. - ***Collision Course*** [1973] PBO. Cover by Chris Foss.	$ .75	$2.50	$5.00
44	Dick, Philip K. - ***The Book Of Philip K. Dick*** [1973] PBO.	$3.50	$10.00	$20.00
45	Norton, Andre - ***Garan The Eternal*** [1973] Cover by Jack Gaughan.	$ .75	$2.50	$5.00
46	Phillifent, John T. - ***King Of Argent*** [1973] PBO. Cover by Kelly Freas.	$ .75	$2.50	$5.00
47	Gordon, Stuart - ***Time Story*** [1973] Cover by Josh Kirby.	$ .75	$2.50	$5.00
48	Farmer, Philip Jose - ***The Other Log Of Phileas Fogg*** [1973] PBO. Cover by Jack Gaughan.	$2.00	$6.00	$12.00
49	Akers, Alan Burt (Bulmer, Kenneth) - ***The Suns Of Scorpio*** [1973] PBO. Dray Prescot #2.	$1.00	$3.00	$6.00

		G	VG	F
50	Lafferty, R. A. - ***Strange Doings*** [1973] Cover by Jack Gaughan.	$1.00	$3.00	$6.00
51	Van Herck, Paul - ***Where Were You Last Pluterday?*** [1973] Cover by Karel Thole.	$1.00	$3.00	$6.00
52	Biggle, Jr., Lloyd - ***The Light That Never Was*** [1973] Cover by Kelly Freas.	$1.00	$3.00	$6.00
53	Wollheim, Donald A. - editor - ***The 1973 Annual World's Best SF*** [1973] Cover by Jack Gaughan.	$ .75	$2.50	$5.00
54	Tubb, E. C. - ***Mayenne*** [1973] PBO. Cover by Kelly Freas. Dumarest #9.	$ .75	$2.50	$5.00
55	Dickson, Gordon R. - ***The Book Of Gordon R. Dickson*** [1973] Cover by Karel Thole.	$ .75	$2.50	$5.00
56	Coney, Michael G. - ***Friends Come In Boxes*** [1973] PBO. Cover by John Holmes.	$ .75	$2.50	$5.00
57	Clement, Hal - ***Ocean On Top*** [1973] PBO. Cover by Jack Gaughan.	$1.00	$3.00	$6.00
58	Lundwall, Sam J. - ***Bernhard The Conqueror*** [1973] PBO. Cover by Tim Kirk.	$ .75	$2.50	$5.00
59	Stableford, Brian M. - ***Rhapsody In Black*** [1973] PBO. Cover by Kelly Freas. Star-Pilot Grainger #2.	$ .75	$2.50	$5.00
60	Goulart, Ron - ***What's Become Of Screwloose? And Other Inquiries*** [1973] Cover by Josh Kirby.	$1.00	$3.00	$6.00
61	Brunner, John - ***The Wrong End Of Time*** [1973] Cover by Chris Foss.	$ .75	$2.50	$5.00
62	Carter, Lin - ***When The Green Star Calls*** [1973] PBO. Cover by Luis Dominguez.	$ .75	$2.50	$5.00
63	Farmer, Philip Jose - ***The Book Of Philip Jose Farmer*** [1973] PBO. Cover by Jack Gaughan.	$1.50	$5.00	$10.00
64	Snyder, Guy - ***Testament XXI*** [1973] PBO. Cover by Kelly Freas.	$ .75	$2.50	$5.00
65	Akers, Alan Burt (Bulmer, Kenneth) - ***Warrior Of Scorpio*** [1973] PBO. Cover by Tim Kirk. Dray Prescot #3.	$ .75	$2.50	$5.00
66	Anvil, Christopher (Crosby, Harry C.) - ***Pandora's Planet*** [1973] Cover by Kelly Freas.	$1.00	$3.00	$6.00
67	Walker, David - ***The Lord's Pink Ocean*** [1973] Cover by Josh Kirby.	$1.00	$3.00	$6.00
68	Klein, Gerard - ***Starmasters' Gambit*** [1973] Cover by Kelly Freas.	$1.00	$3.00	$6.00
69	Dickson, Gordon R. - ***The Pritcher Mass*** [1973] Cover by Kelly Freas.	$1.00	$3.00	$6.00
70	Coney, Michael G. - ***The Hero Of Downways*** [1973] PBO. Cover by Josh Kirby.	$1.00	$3.00	$6.00
71	Bradley, Marion Zimmer - ***Hunters Of The Red Moon*** [1973] PBO. Cover by George Barr.	$1.00	$3.00	$6.00
72	Brunner, John - ***From This Day Forward*** [1973]	$ .75	$2.50	$5.00
73	Gunn, James - ***Breaking Point*** [1973] Cover by Michael Gilbert.	$ .75	$2.50	$5.00
74	Tubb, E. C. - ***Jondelle*** [1973] PBO. Cover by Kelly Freas. Dumarest #10.	$ .75	$2.50	$5.00
75	Norton, Andre - ***The Crystal Gryphon*** [1973] Cover by Jack Gaughan.	$ .75	$2.50	$5.00
76	Gordon, Stuart - ***One-Eye*** [1973] PBO. Cover by Tim Kirk.	$ .75	$2.50	$5.00
77	Wylie, Philip - ***The End Of The Dream*** [1973] Cover by Podium II.	$1.00	$3.00	$6.00
78	Rackham, John (Phillifent, John T.) - ***Beanstalk*** [1973] PBO. Cover by Kelly Freas.	$ .75	$2.50	$5.00
79	Franke, Herbert W. - ***The Orchid Cage*** [1973] Cover by Vincent Difate.	$ .75	$2.50	$5.00
80	Goulart, Ron - ***The Tin Angel*** [1973] PBO. Cover by Jack Gaughan.	$ .75	$2.50	$5.00

		G	VG	F
81	Akers, Alan Burt (Bulmer, Kenneth) - ***Swordships Of Scorpio*** [1973] PBO. Cover by Tim Kirk. Dray Prescot #4.	$ .75	$2.50	$5.00
82	Schmitz, James H. - ***The Telzey Toy*** [1973] PBO. Cover by Kelly Freas.	$ .75	$2.50	$5.00
83	Barbet, Pierre - ***Games Psyborgs Play*** [1973] Cover by George Barr.	$1.00	$3.00	$6.00
84	Ball, Brian N. - ***Singularity Station*** [1973] PBO. Cover by Chris Foss.	$1.00	$3.00	$6.00
85	Brunner, John - ***Polymath*** [1974] Cover by Vincent Difate.	$1.00	$3.00	$6.00
86	Trimble, Louis - ***The Bodelan Way*** [1974] PBO. Cover by Kelly Freas.	$1.00	$3.00	$6.00
87	Lieber, Fritz - ***The Book Of Fritz Leiber*** [1974] PBO. Cover by Jack Gaughan.	$ .75	$2.50	$5.00
88	Shea, Michael - ***A Quest For Simbilis*** [1974] PBO. Cover by George Barr.	$1.00	$3.00	$6.00
89	Blish, James - ***Midsummer Century*** [1974] Cover by Josh Kirby.	$1.00	$3.00	$6.00
90	Conway, Gerard F. - ***Mindship*** [1974] Cover by Kelly Freas.	$ .75	$2.50	$5.00
91	Lumley, Brian - ***The Burrowers Beneath*** [1974] PBO. Cover by Tim Kirk.	$ .75	$2.50	$5.00
92	Stableford, Brian M. - ***Promised Land*** [1974] PBO. Cover by Kelly Freas. Star-Pilot Grainger #3.	$1.00	$3.00	$6.00
93	Klein, Gerard - ***The Overlords Of War*** [1974] Cover by Karel Thole.	$1.00	$3.00	$6.00
94	Swann, Thomas Burnett - ***How Are The Mighty Fallen*** [1974] PBO. Cover by George Barr.	$1.00	$3.00	$6.00
95	Lory, Robert - ***Identity Seven*** [1974] PBO. Cover by Kelly Freas.	$1.00	$3.00	$6.00
96	Norman, John - ***Hunters Of Gor*** [1974] PBO. Cover by Gino D'Achille. Gor #7.	$1.00	$3.00	$6.00
97	Akers, Alan Burt (Bulmer, Kenneth) - ***Prince Of Scorpio*** [1974] PBO. Dray Brescot #5.	$ .75	$2.50	$5.00
98	Chilson, Robert - ***As The Curtain Falls*** [1974] PBO. Cover by Hans Ulrich and Ute Oster-Walder.	$ .75	$2.50	$5.00
99	Sheckley, Robert - ***Can You Feel Anything When I Do This?*** [1974] Cover by Hans Arnold.	$1.00	$3.00	$6.00
100	Farmer, Philip Jose - ***Hadon Of Ancient Opar*** [1974] PBO. Cover by Ron Krenkel.	$2.00	$6.00	$12.00
101	Wollheim, Donald A. - editor - ***The 1974 Annual World's Best SF*** [1974] PBO. Cover by Jack Gaughan.	$ .75	$2.50	$5.00
102	Compton, D. G. - ***The Unsleeping Eye*** [1974] PBO. Cover by Karel Thole.	$ .75	$2.50	$5.00
103	Snyder III, Cecil - ***The Hawks Of Arcturus*** [1974] PBO. Cover by Kelly Freas.	$1.00	$3.00	$6.00
104	Dickinson, Peter - ***The Weathermonger*** [1974] Cover by George Barr.	$ .75	$2.50	$5.00
105	Bayley, Barrington J. - ***The Fall Of Chronopolis*** [1974] PBO.	$1.00	$3.00	$6.00
106	Biggle, Jr., Lloyd - ***The Metallic Muse*** [1974] Cover by George Barr.	$1.00	$3.00	$6.00
107	Goulart, Ron - ***Flux*** [1974] PBO. Cover by Jack Gaughan.	$ .75	$2.50	$5.00
108	Eklund, Gordon - ***All Times Possible*** [1974] PBO. Cover by Charles Gross.	$1.00	$3.00	$6.00
109	Davis, Richard - editor - ***The Year's Best Horror Stories #2*** [1974] Cover by Hans Arnold.	$1.25	$3.75	$7.50
110	Carter, Lin - ***By The Light Of The Green Star*** [1974] PBO. Cover by Roy Krenkel.	$1.00	$3.00	$6.00
111	Stableford, Brian M. - ***The Paradise Game*** [1974] PBO. Cover by Kelly Freas. Star-Pilot Grainger #4.	$1.00	$3.00	$6.00
112	Brunner, John - ***Give Warning To The World*** [1974] Cover by Jack Gaughan.	$ .75	$2.50	$5.00

		G	VG	F
113	Akers, Alan Burt (Bulmer, Kenneth) - ***Manhounds Of Antares*** [1974] PBO. Dray Prescot #6.	$ .75	$2.50	$5.00
114	Van Vogt, A. E. - ***The Man With A Thousand Names*** [1974] PBO. Cover by Vincent Difate.	$1.00	$3.00	$6.00
115	Tubb, E. C. - ***Zenya*** [1974] PBO. Cover by Kelly Freas. Dumarest #11.	$1.00	$3.00	$6.00
116	Dickson, Gordon R. - ***The Star Road*** [1974] Cover by Eddie Jones.	$1.00	$3.00	$6.00
117	Zelasny, Roger - ***To Die In Italbar*** [1974] Cover by Carl Lundgren.	$1.00	$3.00	$6.00
118	Anthony, Piers - ***Triple Detente*** [1974] PBO. Cover by Jack Gaughan.	$1.00	$3.00	$6.00
119	Bradley, Marion Zimmer - ***The Spell Sword*** [1974] PBO. Cover by George Barr. Darkover novel.	$1.00	$3.00	$6.00
120	Coney, Michael G. - ***Monitor Found In Orbit*** [1974] PBO. Cover by Kelly Freas.	$1.00	$3.00	$6.00
121	Norton, Andre - ***Here Abide Monsters*** [1974] Cover by Jack Gaughan.	$ .75	$2.50	$5.00
122	Gordon, Stuart - ***Two-Eyes*** [1974] PBO. Cover by Peter Manesis.	$1.00	$3.00	$6.00
123	Franke, Herbert W. - ***The Mind Net*** [1974] Cover by Kelly Freas.	$ .75	$2.50	$5.00
124	Fast, Howard - ***A Touch Of Infinity*** [1974] Cover by Charles Gross.	$ .75	$2.50	$5.00
125	Carter, Lin - ***The Warrior Of World's End*** [1974] PBO. Cover by Vincent Difate. Gondwane Epic #1.	$1.00	$3.00	$6.00
126	Strugatski, Arkadi and Boris - ***Hard To Be A God*** [1974] Cover by Kelly Freas.	$1.00	$3.00	$6.00
127	Wallace, Ian - ***A Voyage To Dari*** [1974] PBO. Cover by Peter Manesis.	$1.00	$3.00	$6.00
128	Barrett, Jr., Neal - ***Stress Pattern*** [1974] PBO. Cover by Josh Kirby.	$1.00	$3.00	$6.00
129	Akers, Alan Burt (Bulmer, Kenneth) - ***Arena Of Antares*** [1974] PBO. Cover by Jack Gaughan. Dray Prescot #7.	$ .75	$2.50	$5.00
130	Stapleford, Brian M. - ***The Fenris Device*** [1974] PBO. Cover by Kelly Freas. Star-Pilot Grainger #5.	$1.00	$3.00	$6.00
131	Green, Joseph - ***Conscience Interplanetary*** [1974] Cover by Kelly Freas.	$ .75	$2.50	$5.00
132	Goulart, Ron - ***Spacehawk, Inc.*** [1974] PBO. Cover by Hans Arnold.	$ .75	$2.50	$5.00
133	Brunner, John - ***The Stone That Never Came Down*** [1975] Cover by Kelly Freas.	$1.00	$3.00	$6.00
134	Klein, Gerard - ***The Mote In Time's Eye*** [1975] Cover by Josh Kirby.	$1.00	$3.00	$6.00
135	Foster, M. A. - ***The Warriors Of Dawn*** [1975] PBO. Cover by Kelly Freas.	$ .75	$2.50	$5.00
136	Saberhagen, Fred - ***The Book Of Saberhagen*** [1975] PBO. Cover by Jack Gaughan.	$ .75	$2.50	$5.00
137	Dickson, Gordon R. - ***The R-Master*** [1975] Cover by Jack Gaughan.	$1.00	$3.00	$6.00
138	Carter, Lin - ***As The Green Star Rises*** [1975] PBO. Cover by Krenkel. Green Star #4.	$1.00	$3.00	$6.00
139	Chandler, A. Bertram - ***The Big Black Mark*** [1975] PBO. Cover by Kelly Freas.	$ .75	$2.50	$5.00
140	Swann, Thomas Burnett - ***The Not-World*** [1975] PBO. Cover by George Barr.	$1.00	$3.00	$6.00
141	Norman, John - ***Marauders Of Gor*** [1975] PBO. Cover by Kelly Freas. Gor #8.	$ .75	$2.50	$5.00
142	Lundwall, Sam J. - ***2018 A.D. Or The King Kong Blues*** [1975] Cover by Josh Kirby.	$1.00	$3.00	$6.00

		G	VG	F
143	Tubb, E. C. - ***Eloise*** [1975] PBO. Cover by George Barr. Dumarest #12.	$1.00	$3.00	$6.00
144	Coney, Michael G. - ***The Jaws That Bite, The Claws That Catch*** [1975] PBO. Cover by Kelly Freas.	$ .75	$2.50	$5.00
145	Akers, Alan Burt (Bulmer, Kenneth) - ***Fliers Of Antares*** [1975] PBO. Dray Prescot #8.	$ .75	$2.50	$5.00
146	Dick, Philip K. - ***Flow My Tears, The Policeman Said*** [1975] Cover by Hans Ulrich & Ute Osterwalder.	$1.50	$5.00	$10.00
147	Saberhagen, Fred - ***Berserker's Planet*** [1975] PBO.	$ .75	$2.50	$5.00
148	Wollheim, Donald A. - editor - ***The 1975 Annual World's Best SF*** [1975] PBO. Cover by Jack Gaughan.	$ .75	$2.50	$5.00
149	Stableford, Brian M. - ***Swan Song*** [1975] PBO. Cover by Kelly Freas.	$1.00	$3.00	$6.00
150	Carter, Lin - ***The Enchantress Of World's End*** [1975] PBO. Cover by Michael Whelan. Gondwane Epic #2.	$ .75	$2.50	$5.00
151	Lumley, Brian - ***The Transition Of Titus Crow*** [1975] PBO. Cover by Michael Whelan.	$ .75	$2.50	$5.00
152	Norton, Andre - ***Merlin's Mirror*** [1975] PBO. Cover by Jack Gaughan.	$1.00	$3.00	$6.00
153	Anderson, Poul - ***The Book Of Poul Anderson*** [1975] Cover by Jack Gaughan.	$1.00	$3.00	$6.00
154	Lee, Tanith - ***The Birthgrave*** [1975] PBO. Cover by George Barr. The author's first paperback and second novel.	$ .75	$2.50	$5.00
155	Davis, Richard - editor - ***The Year's Best Horror Stories #3*** [1975] PBO. Cover by Michael Whelan.	$1.25	$3.75	$7.50
156	Barbet, Pierre - ***The Enchanted Planet*** [1975] Cover by Michael Whelan.	$ .75	$2.50	$5.00
157	Kurland, Michael - ***The Whenabouts Of Burr*** [1975] PBO. Cover by Kelly Freas.	$ .75	$2.50	$5.00
158	Cowper, Richard - ***The Twilight of Briareus*** [1975] Cover by Kelly Freas.	$ .75	$2.50	$5.00
159	Akers, Alan Burt (Bulmer, Kenneth) - ***Bladesman Of Antares*** [1975] PBO. Cover by Jack Gaughan. Dray Prescot #9.	$ .75	$2.50	$5.00
160	Bradley, Marion Zimmer - ***The Heritage Of Hastur*** [1975] PBO.	$1.00	$3.00	$6.00
161	Chilson, Robert - ***The Star-Crowned Kings*** [1975] PBO. Cover by Kelly Freas.	$ .75	$2.50	$5.00
162	Brunner, John - ***Total Eclipse*** [1975] Cover by Christopher Foss.	$1.00	$3.00	$6.00
163	Tubb, E. C. - ***Eye Of The Zodiac*** [1975] PBO. Cover by George Barr. Dumarest #13.	$ .75	$2.50	$5.00
164	Leiber, Fritz - ***The Second Book Of Fritz Leiber*** [1975] PBO. Cover by Jack Gaughan.	$1.00	$3.00	$6.00
165	Norton, Andre - ***The Book Of Andre Norton*** [1975]	$ .75	$2.50	$5.00
166	Carter, Lin - editor - ***The Year's Best Fantasy Stories: 1*** [1975] PBO. Cover by George Barr.	$ .75	$2.50	$5.00
167	Defontenay, C. I. - ***Star*** [1975] Cover by George Barr.	$ .75	$2.50	$5.00
168	Anvil, Christoper (Crosby, Jr., Harry) - ***Warlord's World*** [1975] PBO. Cover by Kelly Freas.	$1.00	$3.00	$6.00
169	Norman, John - ***Time Slave*** [1975] PBO. Cover by Gin D'Achille.	$ .75	$2.50	$5.00
170	Coney, Michael G. - ***Rax*** [1975] PBO. Cover by Josh Kirby.	$ .75	$2.50	$5.00
171	Gordon, Stuart - ***Three-Eyes*** [1975] PBO. Cover by Michael Whelan.	$ .75	$2.50	$5.00
172	Dickson, Gordon R. - ***Soldier Ask Not*** [1975]	$1.00	$3.00	$6.00
173	Akers, Alan Burt (Bulmer, Kenneth) - ***Avenger Of Antares*** [1975] PBO. Cover by Jack Gaughan. Dray Prescot #10.	$1.00	$3.00	$6.00
174	Dickinson, Peter - ***The Green Gene*** [1975]	$ .75	$2.50	$5.00
175	Goulart, Ron - ***When The Waker Sleeps*** [1975] PBO. Cover by Michael Whelan.	$ .75	$2.50	$5.00
176	Kern, Gregory - ***Beyond The Galactic Lens*** [1975]	$ .75	$2.50	$5.00

		G	VG	F
177	Brunner, John - ***The Book Of John Brunner*** [1976] Cover by Jack Gaughan.	$1.00	$3.00	$6.00
178	Moorcock, Michael - ***The Land Leviathan*** [1976] Cover by Michael Whelan.	$ .75	$2.50	$5.00
179	Vinge, Vernor - ***The Whitling*** [1976] PBO. Cover by George Barr.	$ .75	$2.50	$5.00
180	Carter, Lin - ***In The Green Star's Glow*** [1976] PBO. Cover by Michael Whelan. Green Star #5.	$1.00	$3.00	$6.00
181	Dickson, Gordon R. - ***Dorsai!*** [1976]	$ .75	$2.50	$5.00
182	Swann, Thomas Burnett - ***The Minikins Of Yam*** [1976] PBO. Cover by George Barr.	$ .75	$2.50	$5.00
183	Kurland, Michael - ***Tomorrow Knight*** [1976] PBO. Cover by Douglas Beekman.	$ .75	$2.50	$5.00
184	Lee, Tanith - ***Don't Bite The Sun*** [1976] PBO. Cover by Brian Froud.	$1.00	$3.00	$6.00
185	Norman, John - ***Tribesmen Of Gor*** [1976] Cover by Gino D'Achille.	$ .75	$2.50	$5.00
186	Rohmer, Sax - ***The Wrath Of Fu Manchu*** [1976] Cover by Jack Gaughan.	$2.50	$7.50	$15.00
187	Farmer, P. J. & Rosny, J. H. - ***Ironcastle*** [1976] PBO. Illustrated by Roy Krenkel.	$1.00	$3.00	$6.00
188	Cherryh, C. J. - ***Gate Of Ivrel*** [1976] PBO. Cover by Michael Whelan.	$1.00	$3.00	$6.00
189	Akers, Alan Burt (Bulmer, Kenneth) - ***Armada Of Antares*** [1976] PBO. Cover by Michael Whelan. Dray Prescot #11.	$ .75	$2.50	$5.00
190	Dickson, Gordon R. - ***Ancient My Enemy*** [1976]	$1.00	$3.00	$6.00
191	Bradley, Marion Zimmer - ***The Shattered Chain*** [1976] PBO. Cover by George Barr. Darkover novel.	$1.00	$3.00	$6.00
192	Wollheim, Donald A. - editor - ***The 1976 Annual World's Best SF*** [1976] PBO. Cover by Jack Gaughan.	$ .75	$2.50	$5.00
193	Lee, Tanigh - ***The Storm Lord*** [1976] PBO. Cover by Gino D'Achille.	$ .75	$2.50	$5.00
194	Stableford, Brian M. - ***The Mind-Riders*** [1976] PBO. Cover by Vincent Difate.	$ .75	$2.50	$5.00
195	Barrett, Jr., Neal - ***Aldair In Albion*** [1976] PBO. Cover by Josh Kirby.	$ .75	$2.50	$5.00
196	Norton, Andre - ***Perilous Dreams*** [1976] PBO. Cover by George Barr.	$ .75	$2.50	$5.00
197	Farmer, Philip Jose - ***Flight To Opar*** [1976] PBO. Cover by Roy Krenkel.	$2.00	$6.00	$12.00
198	Tubb, E. C. - ***Jack Of Swords*** [1976] PBO. Cover by Thomas Barber, Jr. Dumarest #14.	$ .75	$2.50	$5.00
199	Barbet, Pierre - ***The Napoleons Of Eridanus*** [1976] Cover by Karel Thole.	$1.00	$3.00	$6.00
200	Wollheim, Donald A. - editor - ***The DAW Science Fiction Reader*** [1976] PBO.	$1.00	$3.00	$6.00
201	Edson, J. T. - ***Bunduki*** [1976] Cover by Michael Whelan.	$1.00	$3.00	$6.00
202	Landis, Arthur H. - ***A World Called Camelot*** [1976] PBO. Cover by Thomas Barber, Jr.	$ .75	$2.50	$5.00
203	Brunner, John - ***Quicksand*** [1976] Cover by Paul Lehr.	$ .75	$2.50	$5.00
204	Akers, Alan Burt (Kenneth Bulmer) - ***The Tides Of Kregen*** [1976] PBO. Cover by Michael Whelan.	$1.00	$3.00	$6.00
205	Carter, Lin - editor - ***The Year's Best Fantasy Stories: 2*** [1976] PBO. Cover by George Barr.	$1.00	$3.00	$6.00
206	Van Vogt, A. E. - ***Earth Factor X*** [1976] Cover by Deane Cate.	$1.00	$3.00	$6.00
207	Goulart, Ron - ***A Whiff Of Madness*** [1976] PBO. Cover by Josh Kirby.	$ .75	$2.50	$5.00
208	Brunner, John - ***Interstellar Empire*** [1976] PBO. Cover by Paul Lehr.	$1.00	$3.00	$6.00

		G	VG	F
209	Chester, William L. - ***Kioga Of The Wilderness*** [1976] PBO. Cover by John Hamberger.	$ .75	$2.50	$5.00
210	Carter, Lin - ***The Immortal Of World's End*** [1976] PBO. Cover by Michael Whelan.	$1.00	$3.00	$6.00
211	Stableford, Brian M. - ***The Florians*** [1976] PBO. Cover by Michael Whelan.	$1.00	$3.00	$6.00
212	Cherryh, C. J. - ***Brothers Of Earth*** [1976] Cover by Alan Atkinson.	$1.00	$3.00	$6.00
213	Berglund, Edward P. - editor - ***The Disciples Of Cthulhu*** [1976] PBO. Cover by Karel Thole.	$ .75	$2.50	$5.00
214	Moorcock, Michael - ***Elric Of Melnibone*** [1976] Cover by Michael Whelan.	$1.00	$3.00	$6.00
215	Smith, George H. - ***The Second War Of The Worlds*** [1976] PBO. Cover by Jac Gaughan.	$ .75	$2.50	$5.00
216	Wallace, Ian - ***The World Asunder*** [1976] PBO. Cover by Jack Gaughan.	$ .75	$2.50	$5.00
217	Page, Gerald W. - editor - ***The Year's Best Horror Stories*** [1976] PBO. Cover by Michael Whelan.	$1.25	$3.75	$7.50
218	Strugatski, Arkadi & Boris - ***The Final Circle Of Paradise*** [1976] Cover by Laurence Kresek.	$1.00	$3.00	$6.00
219	Tubb, E. C. - ***Spectrum Of A Forgotten Sun*** [1976] PBO. Cover by Ray Feibush.	$ .75	$2.50	$5.00
220	Moorcock, Michael - ***The Sailor On The Seas Of Fate*** [1976] PBO. Cover by Michael Whelan.	$1.00	$3.00	$6.00
221	Akers, Alan Burt (Kenneth Bulmer) - ***Renegade Of Kregen*** [1976] PBO. Cover by Michael Whelan.	$ .75	$2.50	$5.00
222	Swann, Thomas Burnett - ***The Gods Abide*** [1976] PBO. Cover by Georg Barr.	$1.00	$3.00	$6.00
223	Lake, David J. - ***Walkers On The Sky*** [1976] PBO. Cover by Richard Hescox.	$ .75	$2.50	$5.00
224	Van Vogt, A. E. - ***Supermind*** [1977] PBO. Cover by Vincent Difate.	$1.00	$3.00	$6.00
225	Moorcock, Michael - ***The Jewel In The Skull*** [1977] Cover by Richard Clifton-Dey.	$ .75	$2.50	$5.00
226	Lee, Tanith - ***Drinking Sapphire Wine*** [1977] PBO. Cover by Don Maitz.	$ .75	$2.50	$5.00
227	Dickson, Gordon R. - ***Naked To The Stars*** [1977]	$1.00	$3.00	$6.00
228	Chester, William L. - ***One Against A Wilderness*** [1977] PBO. Cover by Richard Hescox.	$ .75	$2.50	$5.00
229	Moorcock, Michael - ***Legions From The End Of Time*** [1977] Cover by Bob Pepper.	$1.00	$3.00	$6.00
230	Stableford, Brian M. - ***Critical Threshold*** [1977] PBO. Cover by Douglas Beckman.	$1.00	$3.00	$6.00
231	Goulart, Ron - ***The Panchronicon Plot*** [1977] PBO. Cover by Josh Kirby.	$ .75	$2.50	$5.00
232	Norman, John - ***Slave Girl Of Gor*** [1977] Cover by Gino D'Achille.	$ .75	$2.50	$5.00
233	Moorcock, Michael - ***The Weird Of The White Wolf*** [1977] PBO. Cover by Michael Whelan.	$1.00	$3.00	$6.00
234	Chandler, A. Bertram - ***Star Courier*** [1977] PBO. Cover by Ray Feibush.	$1.00	$3.00	$6.00
235	Clayton, Jo - ***Diadem From The Stars*** [1977] PBO. Cover by Michael Whelan.	$ .75	$2.50	$5.00
236	Foster, M. A. - ***The Game Players Of Zan*** [1977] PBO.	$1.00	$3.00	$6.00
237	Akers, Alan Burt (Kenneth Bulmer) - ***Kroziar Of Kregen*** [1977] PBO.	$1.00	$3.00	$6.00
238	Moorcock, Michael - ***The Mad God's Amulet*** [1977] Cover by Richard Clifton-Dey.	$ .75	$2.50	$5.00
239	Lake, David J. - ***The Right Hand Of Dextra*** [1977] PBO. Cover by George Barr.	$ .75	$2.50	$5.00

		G	VG	F
240	Wollheim, Donald A. - editor - ***The 1977 Annual World's Best SF*** [1977] PBO. Cover by Jack Gaughan.	$ .75	$2.50	$5.00
241	Piserchia, Doris - ***Earthchild*** [1977] PBO. Cover by Michael Whelan.	$ .75	$2.50	$5.00
242	Tubb, E. C. - ***Haven Of Darkness*** [1977] PBO. Cover by Don Maitz.	$1.00	$3.00	$6.00
243	Carter, Lin - ***The Barbarian Of World's End*** [1977] PBO. Cover by John Bierley.	$ .75	$2.50	$5.00
244	Anthology - ***The Best Of John Jakes*** [1977] PBO. Cover by Jack Gaughan.	$ .75	$2.50	$5.00
245	Moorcock, Michael - ***The Vanishing Tower*** [1977] Cover by Michael Whelan.	$1.00	$3.00	$6.00
246	Bishop, Michael - ***Beneath The Shattered Moons*** [1977] Cover by H. R. Van Dongen.	$ .75	$2.50	$5.00
247	Lake, David J. - ***The Wildings Of Westron*** [1977] PBO. Cover by George Barr.	$ .75	$2.50	$5.00
248	Stableford, Brian M. - ***The Realms Of Tartarus*** [1977] PBO. Cover by Ron Walోticy.	$ .75	$2.50	$5.00
249	Moorcock, Michael - ***The Sword Of The Dawn*** [1977] Cover by Richard Clifton-Dey.	$1.00	$3.00	$6.00
250	Page, Gerald W. - editor - ***The Year's Best Horror Stories*** [1977] PBO. Cover by Michael Whelen.	$ .75	$2.50	$5.00
251	Lee, Tanith - ***Volkhavaar*** [1977] PBO.	$1.00	$3.00	$6.00
252	Cherryh, C. J. - ***Hunter Of Worlds*** [1977]	$1.00	$3.00	$6.00
253	Dowdell, Del - ***Warlord Of Ghandor*** [1977] PBO. Cover by Don Maitz.	$1.00	$3.00	$6.00
254	Moorcock, Michael - ***The Bane Of The Black Sword*** [1977] Cover by Michael Whelan.	$1.00	$3.00	$6.00
255	Bayley, Barrington J. - ***The Grand Wheel*** [1977] PBO. Cover by Don Maitz.	$ .75	$2.50	$5.00
256	Bradley, Marion Zimmer - ***The Forbidden Tower*** [1977] PBO. Cover by Richard Hescox.	$ .75	$2.50	$5.00
257	Moorcock, Michael - ***The Runestaff*** [1977] Cover by Richard Clifton-Dey.	$1.00	$3.00	$6.00
258	Geston, Mark S. - ***The Siege Of Wonder*** [1977] Cover by H. R. Van Dongen.	$ .75	$2.50	$5.00
259	Barrett, Jr., Neal - ***Aldar, Master Of Ships*** [1977] PBO. Cover by Josh Kirby.	$1.00	$3.00	$6.00
260	Manning, Norvil - ***Dream Chariots*** [1977] PBO. Cover by Richard Clifton-Dey.	$ .75	$2.50	$5.00
261	Brunner, John - ***The Productions Of Time*** [1977] Cover by Don Maitz.	$1.00	$3.00	$6.00
262	Scott, Jody - ***Passing For Human*** [1977] PBO. Cover by Bob Pepper.	$ .75	$2.50	$5.00
263	Moorcock, Michael - ***Wildeblood's Empire*** [1977] Cover by Michael Whelan.	$ .75	$2.50	$5.00
264	Moorcock, Michael - ***Stormbringer*** [1977] Cover by Michael Whelan.	$1.00	$3.00	$6.00
265	Strugatski, Arkadi & Boris - ***Monday Begins On Saturday*** [1977] Cover by Bob Pepper.	$ .75	$2.50	$5.00
266	Dickson, Gordon, R. - ***None But Man*** [1977] Cover by Don Maitz.	$1.00	$3.00	$6.00
267	Carter, Lin - editor - ***The Year's Best Fantasy Stories: 3*** [1977] PBO. Cover by Josh Kirby.	$1.00	$3.00	$6.00
268	Wollheim, Donald, A. - editor - ***The Best From The Rest Of The World*** [1977] Cover by Jack Gaughan.	$ .75	$2.50	$5.00
269	Akers, Alan Burt (Kenneth Bulmer) - ***Secret Scorpio*** [1977] PBO. Cover by Josh Kirby.	$ .75	$2.50	$5.00
270	Swann, Thomas Burnett - ***Cry Silver Bells*** [1977] PBO. Cover by George Barr.	$ .75	$2.50	$5.00

		G	VG	F
271	Tubb, E. C. - ***Prison Of Night*** [1977] PBO. Cover by Don Maitz.	$1.00	$3.00	$6.00
272	Lee, Tanith - ***Vazkor, Son Of Vazkor*** [1978] PBO. Cover by Gino D'Chille.	$ .75	$2.50	$5.00
273	Chandler, A. Bertram - ***The Way Back*** [1978] PBO. Cover by John Berkey.	$1.00	$3.00	$6.00
274	Dickson, Gordon R. - ***Necromancer*** [1978]	$1.00	$3.00	$6.00
275	Clayton, Jo - ***Lamarchos*** [1978] PBO.	$ .75	$2.50	$5.00
276	Lee, Tanith - ***Quest For The White Witch*** [1978] PBO. Cover by Gino D'Chille.	$ .75	$2.50	$5.00
277	Moorcock, Michael - ***The Messiah At The End Of Time*** [1978] PBO.	$ .75	$2.50	$5.00
278	Leiber, Fritz - ***A Specter Is Haunting Texas*** [1978] Cover by H. R. Van Dongen.	$1.00	$3.00	$6.00
279	Lake, David J. - ***The Gods Of Xuma*** [1978] PBO.	$1.00	$3.00	$6.00
280	Norman, John - ***Beasts Of Gor*** [1978] PBO. Cover by Gino D'Achille.	$ .75	$2.50	$5.00
281	Norvil, Manning - ***Whetted Bronze*** [1978] PBO.	$ .75	$2.50	$5.00
282	Moorcock, Michael - ***Dying For Tomorrow*** [1978] Cover by Michael Whelan.	$1.00	$3.00	$6.00
283	Goulart, Ron - ***Calling Dr. Patchwork*** [1978] PBO. Cover by Josh Kirby.	$ .75	$2.50	$5.00
284	Cherryh, C. J. - ***Well Of Shivan*** [1978] PBO.	$ .75	$2.50	$5.00
285	Akers, Alan Burt (Kenneth Bulmer) - ***Strange Scorpio*** [1978] PBO. Cover by Josh Kirby.	$1.00	$3.00	$6.00
286	Sturgeon, Theodore - ***A Touch Of Strange*** [1978] Cover by Hans Arnold.	$ .75	$2.50	$5.00
287	Barbet, Pierre - ***The Joan-Of-Arc Replay*** [1978] Cover by Karel Thole.	$1.00	$3.00	$6.00
288	Wollheim, Donald A. - editor - ***The 1978 Annual World's Best SF*** [1978] PBO. Cover by Jack Gaughan.	$1.00	$3.00	$6.00
289	Stableford, Brian M. - ***The City Of The Sun*** [1978] PBO. Cover by Don Maitz.	$ .75	$2.50	$5.00
290	Chester, William L. - ***Kioga Of The Unknown Land*** [1978] PBO. Cover by Richard Hescox.	$ .75	$2.50	$5.00
291	Moorcock, Michael - ***The Warlord Of The Air*** [1978] Cover by Gino D'Achille.	$1.00	$3.00	$6.00
292	Bradley, Marion Zimmer - ***Storm Queen!*** [1978] Cover by Michael Whelan.	$1.00	$3.00	$6.00
293	Carter, Lin - ***The Wizard Of Zao*** [1978] PBO.	$ .75	$2.50	$5.00
294	Bayley, Barrington J. - ***Star Winds*** [1978] PBO. Cover by David Bergen.	$1.00	$3.00	$6.00
295	Chandler, A. Bertram - ***To Keep The Ship*** [1978] PBO. Cover by H. R. Van Dongen.	$1.00	$3.00	$6.00
296	Dibell, Ansen - ***Pursuit Of The Screamer*** [1978] PBO.	$ .75	$2.50	$5.00
297	Page, Gerald W. - editor - ***The Year's Best Horror Stories*** [1978] PBO. Cover by Michael Whelan.	$1.25	$3.75	$7.50
298	Smith, George H. - ***The Island Snatchers*** [1978] PBO. Cover by Josh Kirby.	$1.00	$3.00	$6.00
299	Tubb, E. C. - ***Incident On Ath*** [1978] PBO. Cover by David Bergen.	$1.00	$3.00	$6.00
300	Cherryh, C. J. - ***The Faded Sun: Kesrith*** [1978]	$ .75	$2.50	$5.00
301	Akers, Alan Burt (Kenneth Bulmer) - ***Captive Scorpio*** [1978] PBO. Cover by Josh Kirby.	$1.00	$3.00	$6.00
302	Silas, A. E. - ***The Panorama Egg*** [1978] PBO.	$ .75	$2.50	$5.00
303	Dickson, Gordon R. - ***Hour Of The Horde*** [1978]	$1.00	$3.00	$6.00
304	Norton, Andre - ***Yurth Burden*** [1978] PBO. Cover by Jack Gaughan.	$1.00	$3.00	$6.00
305	Vance, Jack - ***Star King*** [1978]	$1.00	$3.00	$6.00
306	Clayton, Jo - ***Irsud*** [1978] PBO. Cover by Eric Ladd.	$1.00	$3.00	$6.00

		G	VG	F
307	Moorcock, Michael - ***The Rituals Of Infinity*** [1978] Cover by Michael Mariano.	$1.00	$3.00	$6.00
308	Wallace, Ian (John Pritchard) - ***Z-Sting*** [1978] PBO.	$1.00	$3.00	$6.00
309	Vance, Jack - ***The Killing Machine*** [1978]	$1.00	$3.00	$6.00
310	Carter, Lin - ***The Pirate Of World's End*** [1978] PBO.	$ .75	$2.50	$5.00
311	Goulart, Ron - ***The Wicked Cyborg*** [1978] PBO. Cover by Josh Kirby.	$ .75	$2.50	$5.00
312	Vance, Jack - ***Wyst: Alastor 1716*** [1978] PBO. Cover by Eric Ladd.	$1.00	$3.00	$6.00
313	Lee, Tanith - ***Night's Master*** [1978] PBO. Cover by George Barr.	$ .75	$2.50	$5.00
314	Walker, Hugh - ***War-Gamers' World*** [1978] Cover by Michael Mariano.	$1.00	$3.00	$6.00
315	Landis, Arthur H. - ***Camelot In Orbit*** [1978] PBO. Cover by Don Maitz.	$1.00	$3.00	$6.00
316	Van Vogt, A. E. - ***Pendulum*** [1978] Cover by Penalva.	$ .75	$2.50	$5.00
317	Akers, Alan Burt (Kenneth Bulmer) - ***Golden Scorpio*** [1978] PBO. Cover by Josh Kirby.	$1.00	$3.00	$6.00
318	Lin, Carter - editor - ***The Year's Best Fantasy Stories: 4*** [1978] PBO. Cover by Esteban Maroto.	$ .75	$2.50	$5.00
319	Tubb, E. C. - ***The Quillian Sector*** [1978] PBO. Cover by H. R. Van Dongen.	$ .75	$2.50	$5.00
320	Bradley, Marion Zimmer & Zimmer, Paul - ***The Survivors*** [1979] PBO. Cover by Enrich.	$1.00	$3.00	$6.00
321	Moorcock, Michael - ***City Of The Beast*** [1979]	$1.00	$3.00	$6.00
322	Stableford, Brian M. - ***Balance Of Power*** [1979] PBO.	$ .75	$2.50	$5.00
323	Walker, Hugh - ***Army Of Darkness*** [1979] Cover by Jad.	$ .75	$2.50	$5.00
324	Lee, Tanith - ***Death's Master*** [1979] PBO. Cover by David Schleinkofer.	$1.00	$3.00	$6.00
325	Vance, Jack - ***The Palace Of Love*** [1979]	$1.00	$3.00	$6.00
326	Moorcock, Michael - ***Lord Of The Spiders*** [1954] Cover by Richard Hescox.	$1.00	$3.00	$6.00
327	Chandler, A. Bertram - ***The Far Traveler*** [1979] PBO. Cover by Don Maitz.	$1.00	$3.00	$6.00
328	Norman, John - ***Explorers Of Gor*** [1979] PBO. Cover by Gino D'Achille.	$ .75	$2.50	$5.00
329	Asimov, Isaac & Greenberg, Martin - editors - ***Isaac Asimov Presents The Great SF Stories #1*** [1979] Cover by Jack Gaughan.	$1.00	$3.00	$6.00
330	Moorcock, Michael - ***Masters Of The Pit*** [1979] Cover by Richard Hescox.	$ .75	$2.50	$5.00
331	Goulart, Ron - ***Hello, Lemuria, Hello*** [1979] PBO.	$ .75	$2.50	$5.00
332	Walker, Hugh - ***Messengers Of Darkness*** [1979] PBO.	$ .75	$2.50	$5.00
333	Cherryh, C. J. - ***The Faded Sun: Shon'Jir*** [1979] Cover by Gino D'Achille.	$1.00	$3.00	$6.00
334	Page, Gerald & Reinhardt, Hank - editors - ***Heroic Fantasy*** [1979] PBO. Cover by Jad.	$ .75	$2.50	$5.00
335	Akers, Alan Burt (Kenneth Bulmer) - ***A Life For Kregen*** [1979] PBO. Cover by Richard Hescox.	$ .75	$2.50	$5.00
336	Vance, Jack - ***Space Opera*** [1979] Cover by Don Maitz.	$1.00	$3.00	$6.00
337	Wollheim, Donald A. - editor - ***The 1979 Annual World's Best SF*** [1979] PBO.	$1.00	$3.00	$6.00
338	Piserchia, Doris - ***Spaceling*** [1979]	$ .75	$2.50	$5.00
339	Vance, Jack - ***City Of The Chasch*** [1979] Cover by H. R. Van Dongen.	$ .75	$2.50	$5.00
340	Petaja, Emil - ***Saga Of Lost Earths*** [1979] PBO. Cover by Penalva.	$ .75	$2.50	$5.00
341	Cherryh, C. J. - ***Fires Of Azeroth*** [1979]	$ .75	$2.50	$5.00
342	Vance, Jack - ***Servants Of The Wankh*** [1979] Cover by H. R. Van Dongen.	$ .75	$2.50	$5.00

		G	VG	F
343	Jeter, K. W. - ***Morlock Night*** [1979] PBO. Cover by Josh Kirby.	$1.50	$5.00	$10.00
344	Clayton, Jo - ***Maeve*** [1979] PBO. Cover by Richard Hescox........	$1.00	$3.00	$6.00
345	Wallace, Ian - ***Heller's Leap*** [1979]	$1.00	$3.00	$6.00
346	Page, Gerald W. - editor - ***The Year's Best Horror Stories*** [1979] PBO. Cover by Michael Whelan..	$ .75	$2.50	$5.00
347	Vance, Jack - ***The Dirdir*** [1979] Cover by H. A. Van Dongen.....	$ .75	$2.50	$5.00
348	Tubb, E. C. - ***Web Of Sand*** [1979] PBO. Cover by Don Maitz....	$1.00	$3.00	$6.00
349	Lee, Tanith - ***Electric Forest*** [1979] Cover by Don Maitz............	$1.00	$3.00	$6.00
350	Asimov, Isaac & Greenberg, Martin - editors - ***Isaac Asimov Presents The Great SF Stories #2*** [1979] PBO. Cover by Jack Gaughan..	$1.00	$3.00	$6.00
351	Vance, Jack - ***The Pnume*** [1979] Cover by H. R. Van Dongen...	$1.00	$3.00	$6.00
352	Akers, Alan Burt (Kenneth Bulmer) - ***A Sword For Kregen*** [1979] PBO..	$1.00	$3.00	$6.00
353	Norton, Andre - ***Quag Keep*** [1979] Cover by Jack Gaughan.......	$1.00	$3.00	$6.00
354	Cherryh, C. J. - ***Hestia*** [1979] PBO. Cover by Don Maitz...........	$ .75	$2.50	$5.00
355	Moorcock, Michael - ***The Time Dweller*** [1979] Cover by Pujolar..	$ .75	$2.50	$5.00
356	Petaja, Emil - ***The Stolen Sun*** [1979]..	$1.00	$3.00	$6.00
357	Foster, M. A. - ***The Day Of The Klesh*** [1979]	$ .75	$2.50	$5.00
358	Stableford, Brian M. - ***The Paradox Of The Sets*** [1979]	$1.00	$3.00	$6.00
359	Llewellyn, Edward - ***The Douglas Convolution*** [1979] PBO. Cover by Don Maitz..	$1.00	$3.00	$6.00
360	Chandler, A. Bertram - ***The Broken Cycle*** [1979] PBO. Cover by Richard Hescox.	$1.00	$3.00	$6.00
361	Vance, Jack - ***The Face*** [1979] PBO. Cover by Gino D'Achille..	$ .75	$2.50	$5.00
362	Carter, Lin - ***Journey To The Underground World*** [1979] PBO. Cover by Josh Kirby..	$ .75	$2.50	$5.00
363	Tubb, E. C. - ***Iduna's Universe*** [1979] PBO. Cover by Michael Mariano..	$ .75	$2.50	$5.00
364	Salmonson, Jessica - editor - ***Amazons!*** [1979]	$1.00	$3.00	$6.00
365	Vance, Jack - ***Emphyrio*** [1979]	$1.00	$3.00	$6.00
366	Prescot, Dray (Kenneth Bulmer) - ***A Fortune For Kregen*** [1979] PBO. Cover by Richard Hescox.	$ .75	$2.50	$5.00
367	Purtill, Richard - ***The Golden Gryphon Feather*** [1979] PBO. Cover by George Barr.	$1.00	$3.00	$6.00
368	Huntley, Tim - ***One On Me*** [1980] PBO. Cover by H. R. Van Dongen..	$ .75	$2.50	$5.00
369	Brunner, John - ***The Avengers Of Carrig*** [1980] Cover by Gin D'Achille..	$1.00	$3.00	$6.00
370	Carter, Lin - editor - ***The Year's Best Fantasy Stories: 5*** [1980] PBO. Cover by Penalva..	$ .75	$2.50	$5.00
371	Llewellyn, Edward - ***The Bright Companion*** [1980] PBO. Cover by Don Maitz..	$ .75	$2.50	$5.00
372	Cherryh, C. J. - ***The Faded Sun: Kutath*** [1980]........................	$ .75	$2.50	$5.00
373	Bradley, Marion Zimmer & Others - ***The Keeper's Price*** [1980] PBO. Cover by Don Maitz..	$1.00	$3.00	$6.00
374	Vance, Jack - ***The Five Gold Bands*** [1980]................................	$ .75	$2.50	$5.00
375	Bayley, Barrington J. - ***The Garments Of Caean*** [1980] Cover by H. R. Van Dongen..	$1.00	$3.00	$6.00
376	Norman, John - ***Fighting Slave Of Gor*** [1980]............................	$1.00	$3.00	$6.00
377	Asimov & Greenberg - editors - ***Isaac Asimov Presents The Great SF Stories: 3*** [1980]	$ .75	$2.50	$5.00
378	Van Vogt, A. E. & Hull, E. Mayne - ***The Winged Man*** [1980] Cover by Douglas Beekman..	$ .75	$2.50	$5.00
379	Barrett, Jr., Neal - ***Aldair, Across The Misty Sea*** [1980] PBO. Cover by Josh Kirby..	$1.00	$3.00	$6.00
380	Lee, Tanith - ***Sabella*** [1980] PBO. Cover by George Smith.	$ .75	$2.50	$5.00
381	Vance, Jack - ***The Many Worlds Of Magnus Ridolph*** [1980] Cover by David Russell..	$1.00	$3.00	$6.00

		G	VG	F
382	Prescot, Dray - ***A Victory For Kregen*** [1980]	$ .75	$2.50	$5.00
383	Tubb, E. C. - ***The Terra Data*** [1980] PBO. Cover by Michael Mariano.	$ .75	$2.50	$5.00
384	Wollheim, Donald A. - editor - ***The 1980 Annual World's Best SF*** [1980]	$ .75	$2.50	$5.00
385	Van Vogt, A. E. - ***Rogue Ship*** [1980] Cover by Greg Theakston.	$1.00	$3.00	$6.00
386	Tall, Stephen (Compton N. Crook) - ***The People Beyond The Wall*** [1980] PBO. Cover by Gino D'Achille.	$ .75	$2.50	$5.00
387	Henneberg, N. C. - ***The Green Gods*** [1980] Cover by Don Maitz.	$1.00	$3.00	$6.00
388	Bradley, Marion Zimmer - ***Two To Conquer*** [1980] PBO. Cover by John Pound.	$1.00	$3.00	$6.00
389	Vance, Jack - ***The Languages Of Pao*** [1980]	$1.00	$3.00	$6.00
390	Norvil, Manning - ***Crown Of the Sword God*** [1980] PBO. Cover by Richard Hescox.	$ .75	$2.50	$5.00
391	Carter, Lin - ***Zanthodon*** [1980]	$ .75	$2.50	$5.00
392	Piserchia, Doris - ***The Spinner*** [1980] PBO. Cover by H. R. Van Dongen.	$1.00	$3.00	$6.00
393	Wagner, Karl Edward - ***The Year's Best Horror Stories*** [1980] PBO. Cover by Michael Whelan.	$1.25	$3.75	$7.50
394	Clayton, Jo - ***Star Hunters*** [1980] PBO. Cover by Michael Mariano.	$ .75	$2.50	$5.00
395	Stasheff, Christopher - ***A Wizard In Bedlam*** [1980]	$ .75	$2.50	$5.00
396	Cherryh, C. J. - ***Serpent's Reach*** [1980]	$1.00	$3.00	$6.00
397	Prescot, Dray (Kenneth Bulmer) - ***Beasts Of Antares*** [1980] PBO. Cover by Richard Hescox.	$ .75	$2.50	$5.00
398	Carter, Lin - ***Lost Worlds*** [1980]	$ .75	$2.50	$5.00
399	Goulart, Ron - ***Hail Hibbler*** [1980]	$1.00	$3.00	$6.00
400	Norton, Andre - ***Lore Of The Witch World*** [1980]	$ .75	$2.50	$5.00
401	Lee, Tanith - ***Kill The Dead*** [1980]	$1.00	$3.00	$6.00
402	Vance, Jack - ***Nopalgarth*** [1980] PBO. Cover by Gino D'Achille.	$ .75	$2.50	$5.00
403	Chandler, A. Bertram - ***Star Loot*** [1980] PBO. Cover by Attila Hejja.	$ .75	$2.50	$5.00
404	Foster, M. A. - ***Waves*** [1980]	$ .75	$2.50	$5.00
405	Asimov & Greenberg - editors - ***Isaac Asimov Presents The Great SF Stories: 4*** [1980]	$1.00	$3.00	$6.00
406	Stableford, Brian M. - ***Optiman*** [1980] PBO. Cover by Michael Mariano.	$1.00	$3.00	$6.00
407	Moorcock, Michael - ***The Golden Barge*** [1980] Cover by John Pound.	$ .75	$2.50	$5.00
408	Lee, Tanith - ***Day By Night*** [1980] PBO. Cover by Don Maitz.	$1.00	$3.00	$6.00
409	Piserchia, Doris - ***The Fluger*** [1980] PBO. Cover by H. R. Van Dongen.	$ .75	$2.50	$5.00
410	Carter, Lin - editor - ***The Year's Best Fantasy Stories: 6*** [1980] PBO. Cover by Josh Kirby.	$1.00	$3.00	$6.00
411	Tubb, E. C. - ***World Of Promise*** [1980] PBO. Cover by Ken. W. Kelly.	$ .75	$2.50	$5.00
412	Wallace, Ian - ***The Lucifer Comet*** [1980] PBO. Cover by Gino D'Achille.	$1.00	$3.00	$6.00
413	Prescot, Dray (Kenneth Bulmer) - ***Rebel Of Antares*** [1980] PBO. Cover by Ken W. Kelly.	$1.00	$3.00	$6.00
414	Barbet, Pierre - ***Cosmic Crusaders*** [1980]	$ .75	$2.50	$5.00
415	Purtill, Richard - ***The Stolen Goddess*** [1980]	$1.00	$3.00	$6.00
416	Vance, Jack - ***The Book Of Dreams*** [1981] PBO. Cover by Ken W. Kelly.	$ .75	$2.50	$5.00
417	Vance, Jack - ***Dust Of Far Suns*** [1980]	$1.00	$3.00	$6.00
418	Vance, Jack - ***Trullion: Alastor 2262*** [1981] Cover by David B. Mattingly.	$ .75	$2.50	$5.00

		G	VG	F
419	Vance, Jack - ***Marune: Alastor 933*** [1981] Cover by David B. Mattingly.	$1.00	$3.00	$6.00
420	Cherryh, C. J. - ***Downbelow Station*** [1981]	$ .75	$2.50	$5.00
421	Nolane, Richard D. - editor - ***Terra SF*** [1981]	$ .75	$2.50	$5.00
422	Brunner, John - ***To Conquer Chaos*** [1981]	$1.00	$3.00	$6.00
423	Carter, Lin - ***Hurok Of The Stone Age*** [1981]	$1.00	$3.00	$6.00
424	Norman, John - ***Rogue Of Gor*** [1981]	$ .75	$2.50	$5.00
425	Dibell, Ansen - ***Circle, Crescent, Star*** [1981] PBO. Cover by Ken W. Kelly.	$1.00	$3.00	$6.00
426	Anthology - ***Isaac Asimov Presents The Great SF Stories #5*** [1981] PBO.	$ .75	$2.50	$5.00
427	Johnson, James B. - ***Daystar And Shadow*** [1981] PBO. Cover by Ken Kelly	$1.00	$3.00	$6.00
428	Stableford, Brian M. - ***The Castaways Of Tanagar*** [1981]	$1.00	$3.00	$6.00
429	Lee, Tanith - ***Lycanthia*** [1981]	$1.00	$3.00	$6.00
430	Mendelson, Drew - ***Pilgrimage*** [1981] PBO. Cover by John Pound.	$1.00	$3.00	$6.00
431	Tubb, E. C. - ***Necta Of Heaven*** [1981] PBO. Cover by Ken W. Kelly.	$ .75	$2.50	$5.00
432	Wollheim, Donald - editor - ***The 1981 Annual World's Best SF*** [1981] PBO. Cover by Michael Mariano.	$ .75	$2.50	$5.00
433	Cherryh, C. J. - ***Sunfall*** [1981] PBO. Cover by Michael Whelen.	$1.00	$3.00	$6.00
434	Piserchia, Doris - ***Doomtime*** [1981] PBO. Cover by H. R. Van Dongen.	$1.00	$3.00	$6.00
435	DeVet, Charles V. & MacLean, Katherine - ***Second Game*** [1981] PBO. Cover by Michael Mariano.	$1.00	$3.00	$6.00
436	Selby, Curt - ***Blood Country*** [1981] PBO. Cover by Ken Kelly.	$1.00	$3.00	$6.00
437	Landis, Arthur H. - ***The Magick Of Camelot*** [1981] PBO. Cover by Richard Hescox.	$ .75	$2.50	$5.00
438	Dick, Philip K. - ***Flow My Tears, The Policeman Said*** [1981] Cover by Oliviero Berni.	$1.00	$3.00	$6.00
439	Goulart, Ron - ***The Robot In The Closet*** [1981]	$1.00	$3.00	$6.00
440	Norton, Andre - ***Horn Crown*** [1981]	$ .75	$2.50	$5.00
441	Stateham, B. R. - ***Banners Of The Sa'Yen*** [1981] PBO. Cover by Ken Kelly	$1.00	$3.00	$6.00
442	Farmer, Philip Jose - ***Hadon Of Ancient Opar*** [1981]	$ .75	$2.50	$5.00
443	Brunner, John - ***The Repairmen Of Cyclops*** [1981] Cover by H. R. Van Dongen.	$1.00	$3.00	$6.00
444	Cherryh, C. J. - ***Wave Without A Shore*** [1981]	$ .75	$2.50	$5.00
445	Wagner, Karl Edward - editor - ***The Year's Best Horror Stories*** [1981] PBO. Cover by Michael Whelan.	$ .75	$2.50	$5.00
446	Akers, Alan Burt (Kenneth Bulmer) - ***Legions Of Antares*** [1981] PBO. Cover by Ken W. Kelly.	$ .75	$2.50	$5.00
447	Phillifent, John T. - ***King Of Argent*** [1981]	$ .75	$2.50	$5.00
448	Lee, Tanith - ***Delusion's Master*** [1981]	$ .75	$2.50	$5.00
449	Chandler, A. Bertram - ***The Anarch Lords*** [1981] PBO. Cover by David B. Mattingly.	$ .75	$2.50	$5.00
450	Dick, Philip K. - ***Now Wait For Last Year*** [1981]	$ .75	$2.50	$5.00
451	Carter, Lin - ***Darya Of The Bronze Age*** [1981]	$ .75	$2.50	$5.00
452	Bradley, Marion Zimmer - ***Sharra's Exile*** [1981] PBO. Cover by Mannah Shapero.	$ .75	$2.50	$5.00
453	Vance, Jack - ***Showboat World*** [1981] Cover by David B. Mattingly.	$1.00	$3.00	$6.00
454	Saha, Arthur W. - editor - ***The Year's Best Fantasy Stories: 7*** [1981] PBO. Cover by Michael Whelan.	$ .75	$2.50	$5.00
455	Tubb, E. C. - ***The Terridae*** [1981] PBO. Cover by Richard Hescox.	$1.00	$3.00	$6.00
456	Norman, John - ***Guardsman Of Gor*** [1981]	$ .75	$2.50	$5.00
457	Clayton, Jo - ***The Nowhere Hunt*** [1981]	$1.00	$3.00	$6.00

		G	VG	F
458	Piserchia, Doris - ***Earth In Twilight*** [1981] PBO. Cover by Wayne D. Barlowe.	$1.00	$3.00	$6.00
459	Saunders, Charles R. - ***Imaro*** [1981]	$1.00	$3.00	$6.00
460	Foster, M. A. - ***The Morphodite*** [1981]	$1.00	$3.00	$6.00
461	Asimov & Greenberg - editors - ***Isaac Asimov Presents The Great SF: 6*** [1981]	$1.00	$3.00	$6.00
462	Prescot, Dray (Kenneth Bulmer) - ***Allies Of Antares*** [1981] PBO. Cover by Clyde Cradwell.	$1.00	$3.00	$6.00
463	Lee, Tanith - ***The Birthgrave*** [1981]	$1.00	$3.00	$6.00
464	Cherryh, C. J. - ***The Pride Of Chanur*** [1981]	$ .75	$2.50	$5.00
465	Van Vogt, A. E. - ***The Silkie*** [1981]	$1.00	$3.00	$6.00
466	Barrett, Jr., Neal - ***Aldair: The Legion Of Beasts*** [1981]	$ .75	$2.50	$5.00
467	Goulart, Ron - ***Upside Downside*** [1982] PBO. Cover by Josh Kirby.	$1.00	$3.00	$6.00
468	Wallace, Ian - ***The Rape Of The Sun*** [1982]	$1.00	$3.00	$6.00
469	Shwartz, Susan - editor - ***Hecate's Cauldron*** [1982]	$ .75	$2.50	$5.00
470	Green, Sharon - ***The Warrior Within*** [1982] PBO. Cover by Ken W. Kelly.	$1.00	$3.00	$6.00
471	Simak, Clifford D. - ***The Werewolf Principle*** [1982] Cover by Frank Kelly Freas.	$ .75	$2.50	$5.00
472	Norman, John - ***Savages Of Gor*** [1982]	$ .75	$2.50	$5.00
473	Vance, Jack - ***The Gray Prince*** [1981] Cover by David B. Mattingly.	$1.00	$3.00	$6.00
474	Bayley, Barrington J. - ***The Pillars Of Eternity*** [1981]	$1.00	$3.00	$6.00
475	Farmer, Philip Jose - ***Flight To Opar*** [1981]	$ .75	$2.50	$5.00
476	Lee, Tanith - ***The Silver Metal Lover*** [1982] Cover by Don Maitz.	$1.00	$3.00	$6.00
477	Bradley, Marion Zimmer - ***Sword Of Chaos*** [1982] PBO. Cover by Kannah M. G. Shapero.	$ .75	$2.50	$5.00
478	Van Vogt, A. E. - ***The Darkness On Diamondia*** [1982]	$ .75	$2.50	$5.00
479	Tubb, E. C. - ***The Coming Event*** [1982]	$1.00	$3.00	$6.00
480	Wollheim, Donald A. - editor - ***The 1982 Annual World's Best SF*** [1982]	$1.00	$3.00	$6.00
481	Clayton, Jo - ***Moongather*** [1982] PBO. Cover by Ken Kelly.	$ .75	$2.50	$5.00
482	Simak, Clifford D. - ***The Goblin Reservation*** [1982]	$1.00	$3.00	$6.00
483	Carter, Liz - ***Eric Of Zanthodon*** [1982]	$1.00	$3.00	$6.00
484	Green, Sharon - ***The Crystals Of Mida*** [1982] PBO. Cover by Ken W. Kelly.	$1.00	$3.00	$6.00
492	Stableford, Brian - ***Journey To The Center*** [1982] PBO.	$ .75	$2.50	$5.00
493	Wagner, Karl Edward - editor - ***The Year's Best Horror Stories: Series X*** [1982] PBO. Cover by Michael Whelan.	$1.00	$3.00	$6.00
496	Bradley, Marion Zimmer - ***Hawkmistress!*** [1982] PBO. Cover by Hannah M. G. Shapero.	$1.00	$3.00	$6.00
498	Brunner, John - ***Manshape*** [1982] PBO. Cover by David B. Mattingly.	$1.00	$3.00	$6.00
500	Cherryh, C. J. - ***Port Eternity*** [1982] PBO. Cover by Ken W. Kelly.	$ .75	$2.50	$5.00
501	Saha, Arthur, W. - editor - ***The Year's Best Fantasy Stories: 8*** [1982] PBO. Cover by Oliviero Berni.	$1.00	$3.00	$6.00
503	Moorcock, Michael - ***The Steel Tsar*** [1982] PBO. Cover by Walter Velez.	$ .75	$2.50	$5.00
510	Tubb, E. C. - ***Earth Is Heaven*** [1982] PBO. Cover by Michael Mariano.	$ .75	$2.50	$5.00
512	Green, Sharon - ***The Warrior Enchained*** [1983] PBO. Cover by Ken W. Kelly.	$ .75	$2.50	$5.00
515	Piserchia, Doris - ***The Deadly Sky*** [1983] PBO. Cover by Kelly Freas.	$1.00	$3.00	$6.00
516	Clayton, Jo - ***Moonscatter*** [1983] PBO. Cover by Ken Kelly.	$ .75	$2.50	$5.00
521	Cherryh, C. J. - ***The Dreamstone*** [1983] PBO. Cover by David A. Cherry.	$1.00	$3.00	$6.00

		G	VG	F
523	Dick, Philip K. - ***The Three Stigmata Of Palmer Eldritch*** [1983] Cover by Bob Pepper.	$1.00	$3.00	$6.00
525	Bradley, Marion Zimmer - ***Greyhaven*** [1983] PBO. Cover by Victoria Poyser.	$1.00	$3.00	$6.00
526	Akers, Alan Burt (Kenneth Bulmer) - ***Fires Of Scorpio*** [1983] PBO. Cover by Richard Hescox.	$1.00	$3.00	$6.00
527	Vance, Jack - ***The Blue World*** [1983] Cover by David B. Mattingly.	$ .75	$2.50	$5.00
529	Clayton, Jo - ***Ghosthunt*** [1983] PBO. Cover by Ken W. Kelly.	$ .75	$2.50	$5.00
531	Simak, Clifford D. - ***Cemetery World*** [1983] Cover by Kelly Freas.	$1.00	$3.00	$6.00
534	Tubb, E. C. - ***Melome*** [1983] PBO. Cover by Vincent DiFate.	$1.00	$3.00	$6.00
536	Zahn, Timothy - ***The Blackcollar*** [1983] PBO. Cover by Vincent DiFate.	$ .75	$2.50	$5.00
538	Chandler, A. Bertram - ***Matilda's Stepchildren*** [1983] Cover by Ken W. Kelly.	$ .75	$2.50	$5.00
539	Kern, Gregory (E. C. Tubb) - ***The Galactiad*** [1983] PBO. Cover by Wayne Douglas Barlowe.	$ .75	$2.50	$5.00
542	Bulmer, Kenneth - ***The Diamond Contessa*** [1983] PBO. Cover by Ken W. Kelly.	$ .75	$2.50	$5.00
544	Bradley, Marion Zimmer - ***Thendara House*** [1983] PBO. Cover by Hannah M. G. Shapero.	$1.00	$3.00	$6.00
550	Saha, Arthur W. - editor - ***The Year's Best Fantasy Stories: 9*** [1983] PBO. Cover by San Julian.	$1.00	$3.00	$6.00
553	Wagner, Karl Edward - editor - ***The Year's Best Horror Stories: Series XI*** [1983] PBO. Cover by Michael Whelan.	$ .75	$2.50	$5.00
556	Lorrah, Jean & Lichtenberg, Jacqueline - ***Channel's Destiny*** [1983] Cover by Don Maitz.	$ .75	$2.50	$5.00
560	Green, Sharon - ***The Warrior Rearmed*** [1984] PBO. Cover by Ken W. Kelly.	$1.00	$3.00	$6.00
561	Correy, Lee - ***Manna*** [1984] Cover by Vincent DiFate.	$ .75	$2.50	$5.00
565	Tubb, E. C. - ***Angado*** [1984] PBO. Cover by Ken W. Kelly.	$1.00	$3.00	$6.00
574	Clough, B. W. - ***The Crystal Crown*** [1984] PBO. Cover by Ken W. Kelly.	$ .75	$2.50	$5.00
578	Bradley, Marion Zimmer - editor - ***Sword And Sorceress*** [1984] PBO. Cover by Victoria Poyser.	$ .75	$2.50	$5.00
579	Elgin, Suzette Haden - ***Star-Anchored, Star-Angered*** [1984] Cover by Kelly Freas.	$1.00	$3.00	$6.00
583	Chandler, A. Bertram - ***The Last Amazon*** [1984] PBO. Cover by Richard Hescox.	$1.00	$3.00	$6.00
585	Pohl, Frederik - ***Demon In The Skull*** [1984] Cover by Don Maitz.	$1.00	$3.00	$6.00
588	Kapp, Colin - ***Star-Search*** [1984] Cover by Vincent Difate.	$1.00	$3.00	$6.00
595	Shea, Michael - ***The Color Out Of Time*** [1984] PBO. Cover by Ken W. Kelly.	$1.00	$3.00	$6.00
597	Saha, Arthur W. - editor - ***The Year's Best Fantasy Stories: 10*** [1984] PBO. Cover by Jim Burns.	$ .75	$2.50	$5.00
600	Bradley, Marion Zimmer - ***City Of Sorcery*** [1984] PBO. Cover by James Gurney.	$ .75	$2.50	$5.00
603	Wagner, Karl Edward - editor - ***The Year's Best Horror Stories: Series XII*** [1984] PBO. Cover by Sagrelles.	$ .75	$2.50	$5.00

Death House. Digest Size.

NO#-1	Braithwaite, Eaton K. - ***Death Springs The Trap*** [1944]	$3.50	$10.00	$20.00
NO#-2	Schley, Sturges Mason - ***Vengeance Pulls The Trigger*** [1944]	$3.50	$10.00	$20.00
3	Avery, Robert - ***Murder On The Downbeat*** [1944] Cover by Hoffman.	$3.50	$10.00	$20.00
4	Braithwaite, Eaton K. - ***The Case Of The Nameless Corpse*** [1944] Cover art by Hoffman.	$3.50	$10.00	$20.00
5	Bonnamy, Francis - ***Dead Reckoning*** [1945]	$3.50	$10.00	$20.00

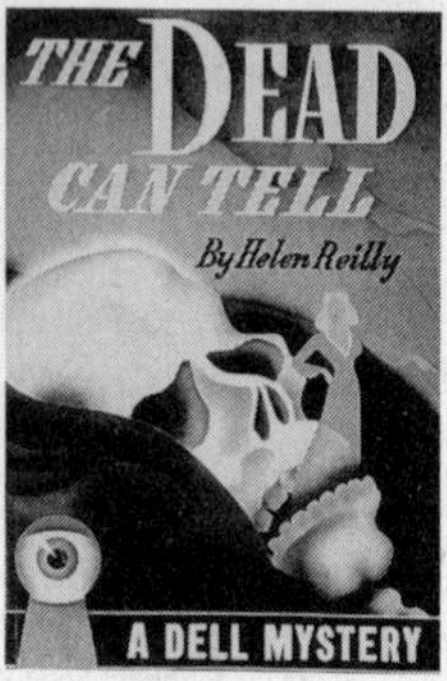

Dell Book, 17

Dell Book, 38

Dell Book, 50

		G	VG	F
6	Bosworth, Allan R. - ***Full Crash Dive*** [1945]	$3.50	$10.00	$20.00

Dell Books (Early Publisher's History, 1942–1959)

A keyhole on the cover and a map on the back describe most of the early Dell books. Western Printing and Lithographing Co., Racine, WI, who published the Bantam Los Angeles, and George Delacorte, Jr., who began publishing pulps, comics, and magazines in 1922, jointly published Dell Books. Dell published 577 titles with map back covers beginning with Dell #5, but they phased out the practice. Bright colors on the cover, lamination, and airbrushed covers by Robert Stanley, Gerald Gregg, and others drew attention to these books. They gave one title a dust jacket in the Dell D series, D144. Dell Books presented a strong set of mysteries, along with other literature.

Dell Publishing Company also published a number of other series. The Dell 10 Cent Books consist of thirty-six collectible titles of sixty-four pages each. Dell First Editions series published originals, Dell F series focused on literary works, and Dell Laurel Editions published classical works. Other series of interest include the Dell Unnumbered Books and Dell Told In Pictures.

Dell Books. New York: Dell Publishing Co.

		G	VG	F
1	Ketchum, Philip - ***Death In The Library*** [1943] Cover by William Strohmer.	$12.50	$37.50	$75.00
2	Wentworth, Patricia - ***Dead Or Alive*** [1943] Cover by William Strohmer.	$6.00	$20.00	$40.00
3	Jones, Jennifer - ***Murder-On-Hudson*** [1943] Cover by George A. Frederiksen.	$5.50	$17.50	$35.00
4	Queen, Ellery - ***The American Gun Mystery*** [1943] Cover by Gerald Gregg.	$5.00	$15.00	$30.00
5	Coxe, George Harmon - ***Four Frightened Women*** [1943] Cover by Gerald Gregg. The first Dell Mapback.	$5.50	$17.50	$35.00
6	Ford, Leslie - ***Ill Met By Moonlight*** [1943] Cover by Gerald Gregg.	$5.50	$17.50	$35.00
7	Blochman, Lawrence G. - ***See You At The Morgue*** [1943] Cover by Gerald Gregg.	$5.50	$17.50	$35.00
8	Christie, Agatha - ***The Tuesday Club Murders*** [1943] Cover by George A. Frederiksen.	$5.50	$17.50	$35.00
9	Stout, Rex - ***Double For Death*** [1943] Cover by George A. Frederiksen.	$6.00	$20.00	$40.00

		G	VG	F
10	Vance, Louis Joseph - ***The Lone Wolf*** [1943] Cover by Gerald Gregg.	$5.50	$17.50	$35.00
11	Ransome, Stephen - ***Hearses Don't Hurry*** [1943] Cover by Gerald Gregg.	$5.00	$15.00	$30.00
12	Baldwin, Faith - ***Wife Vs. Secretary*** [1943] Cover by William Strohmer.	$3.50	$10.00	$20.00
13	Popkin, Zelda - ***Death Wears A White Gardenia*** [1943] Cover by Gerald Gregg.	$5.00	$15.00	$30.00
14	Homes, Geoffrey - ***The Doctor Died At Dusk*** [1943] Cover by William Strohmer.	$5.00	$15.00	$30.00
15	Disney, Dorothy Cameron - ***The Golden Swan Murder*** [1943] Cover by Gerald Gregg.	$5.00	$15.00	$30.00
16	Dickson, Carter - ***The Unicorn Murders*** [1943] Cover by Gerald Gregg.	$5.50	$17.50	$35.00
17	Reilly, Helen - ***The Dead Can Tell*** [1943] Cover by Gerald Gregg.	$5.00	$15.00	$30.00
18	Palmer, Stuart - ***The Puzzle Of The Silver Persian*** [1943] Cover by Gerald Gregg.	$5.00	$15.00	$30.00
19	Bonnell, James Francis - ***Death Over Sunday*** [1943] Cover by Gerald Gregg.	$5.00	$15.00	$30.00
20	Adams, Samuel Hopkins - ***Tambay Gold*** [1943] Cover by Gerald Gregg.	$5.00	$15.00	$30.00
21	Leske, Gottfried - ***I Was A Nazi Flier*** [1943] Cover by Gerald Gregg.	$7.00	$22.50	$45.00
22	King, Rufus - ***Holiday Homicide*** [1943] Cover by Gerald Gregg.	$4.00	$12.50	$25.00
23	Halliday, Brett - ***The Private Practice Of Michael Shayne*** [1943] Cover by William Strohmer.	$4.00	$12.50	$25.00
24	Leroux, Gaston - ***The Phantom Of The Opera*** [1943] Cover by Gerald Gregg.	$5.50	$17.50	$35.00
25	Eberhart, Mignon G. - ***Speak No Evil*** [1944] Cover by Gerald Gregg.	$4.00	$12.50	$25.00
26	Trumbull, Robert - ***The Raft*** [1944] Cover by George A. Frederiksen.	$4.00	$12.50	$25.00
27	Coxe, George Harmon - ***The Camera Clue*** [1944] Cover by Gerald Gregg.	$4.00	$12.50	$25.00
28	Stout, Rex - ***The Mountain Cat Murders*** [1944] Cover by Gerald Gregg.	$4.50	$14.00	$28.00
29	Polsky, Thomas - ***Curtains For The Copper*** [1944] Cover by Gerald Gregg.	$4.00	$12.50	$25.00
30	Brennan, Frederick Hazlitt - ***Memo To A Firing Squad*** [1944] Cover by Gerald Gregg.	$5.00	$15.00	$30.00
31	Hughes, Dorothy B. - ***The Fallen Sparrow*** [1944] Cover by George A. Frederiksen.	$4.00	$12.50	$25.00
32	MacCormac, John - ***This Time For Keeps*** [1944] Cover by Gerald Gregg.	$4.00	$12.50	$25.00
33	McCloy, Helen - ***Dance Of Death*** [1944] Cover by Gerald Gregg.	$4.00	$12.50	$25.00
34	Scott, Mary Semple - ***Crime Hound*** [1944] Cover by Gerald Gregg.	$4.00	$12.50	$25.00
35	Olsen, D. B. - ***The Cat Saw Murder*** [1944] Cover by Gerald Gregg.	$4.00	$12.50	$25.00
36	Frome, David - ***The Hammersmith Murders*** [1944] Cover by Gerald Gregg.	$4.00	$12.50	$25.00
37	Johnston, Stanley - ***Queen Of The Flat-Tops*** [1944] Cover by George A. Frederiksen. Seven pages of photos.	$4.00	$12.50	$25.00
38	Anthology edited by Cavanah & Weir - ***Liberty Laughs*** [1944] Cover by Gerald Gregg. Cartoon and joke book.	$8.00	$25.00	$50.00
39	King, Rufus - ***Murder Challenges Valcour In The Lesser Antilles Case*** [1944] Cover by Gerald Gregg.	$4.00	$12.50	$25.00

		G	VG	F
40	Rinehart, Mary Roberts - ***The Case Of Janice Brice*** [1944] Cover by Gerald Gregg.	$4.00	$12.50	$25.00
41	Homes, Geoffrey - ***The Man Who Didn't Exist*** [1944] Cover by George A. Frederiksen.	$4.00	$12.50	$25.00
42	Hunt, Peter - ***Murders At Scandal House*** [1944] Cover by Gerald Gregg.	$4.00	$12.50	$25.00
43	Blochman, Lawrence G. - ***Midnight Sailing*** [1944] Cover by Gerald Gregg.	$4.00	$12.50	$25.00
44	Heard, H. F. - ***Reply Paid*** [1944] Cover by Gerald Gregg.	$4.00	$12.50	$25.00
45	Stout, Rex - ***Too Many Cooks*** [1944] Cover by Gerald Gregg.	$5.00	$15.00	$30.00
46	Christie, Agatha - ***The Boomerang Clue*** [1944] Cover by Gerald Gregg	$4.00	$12.50	$25.00
47	Biggers, Earl Derr - ***Keeper Of The Keys*** [1944] Cover by Gerald Gregg.	$4.50	$14.00	$28.00
48	Hughes, Dorothy B. - ***The Cross-Eyed Bear Murders*** [1944] Cover by Gerald Gregg.	$4.00	$12.50	$25.00
49	Wallace, Edgar - ***The Feathered Serpent*** [1944] Cover by Gerald Gregg.	$4.00	$12.50	$25.00
50	Kendrick, Baynard H. - ***The Iron Spiders Murders*** [1944] Cover by Gerald Gregg and Byron Gere.	$4.00	$12.50	$25.00
51	Gaines, Audrey - ***While The Wind Howled*** [1944] Cover by George A. Frederiksen.	$4.00	$12.50	$25.00
52	Yates, George Worthing - ***The Body That Wasn't Uncle*** [1944] Cover by Gerald Gregg.	$4.00	$12.50	$25.00
53	Hammett, Dashiell - ***Blood Money*** [1944] Cover by Gerald Gregg.	$12.50	$37.50	$75.00
54	Fuller, Timothy - ***Harvard Has A Homicide*** [1944] Cover by Gerald Gregg.	$4.00	$12.50	$25.00
55	Petersen, Herman - ***The D. A.'s Daughter*** [1944] Cover by George A. Frederiksen.	$4.00	$12.50	$25.00
56	Roos, Kelley - ***The Frightened Stiff*** [1944] Cover by Gerald Gregg.	$4.00	$12.50	$25.00
57	Rinehart, Mary Roberts - ***The Window At The White Cat*** [1944] Cover by Gerald Gregg.	$4.00	$12.50	$25.00
58	Coxe, George Harmon - ***Murder For The Asking*** [1944] Cover by Gerald Gregg.	$4.00	$12.50	$25.00
59	Fair, A. A. - ***Turn On The Heat*** [1944] Cover by Gerald Gregg.	$4.00	$12.50	$25.00
60	Christie, Agatha - ***Thirteen At Dinner*** [1944] Cover by Gerald Gregg.	$4.00	$12.50	$25.00
61	Ford, Leslie - ***The Clue Of The Judas Tree*** [1944] Cover by Gerald Gregg.	$4.00	$12.50	$25.00
62	Disney, Dorothy Cameron - ***The Strawstack Murders*** [1944] Cover by Gerald Gregg.	$4.00	$12.50	$25.00
63	Reilly, Helen - ***Mourned On Sunday*** [1944] Cover by Gerald Gregg.	$4.00	$12.50	$25.00
64	Halliday, Brett - ***Blood On The Black Market*** [1944] Cover by Ben Hallam.	$4.00	$12.50	$25.00
65	Dickson, Carter - ***Scotland Yard: The Department Of Queer Complaints*** [1944] Cover by Gerald Gregg.	$10.00	$30.00	$60.00
66	Wells, Anna Mary - ***A Talent For Murder*** [1944] Cover by Gerald Gregg.	$3.50	$10.00	$20.00
67	Van de Water, Frederic F. - ***Hidden Ways*** [1944] Cover by Gerald Gregg.	$3.50	$10.00	$20.00
68	Lewis, Lange - ***Juliet Dies Twice*** [1944] Cover by Gerald Gregg.	$3.50	$10.00	$20.00
69	Rawson, Clayton - ***Death From A Top Hat*** [1945] Cover by Gerald Gregg.	$3.50	$10.00	$20.00
70	Stout, Rex - ***The Red Bull*** [1945] Cover by Gerald Gregg.	$4.00	$12.50	$25.00

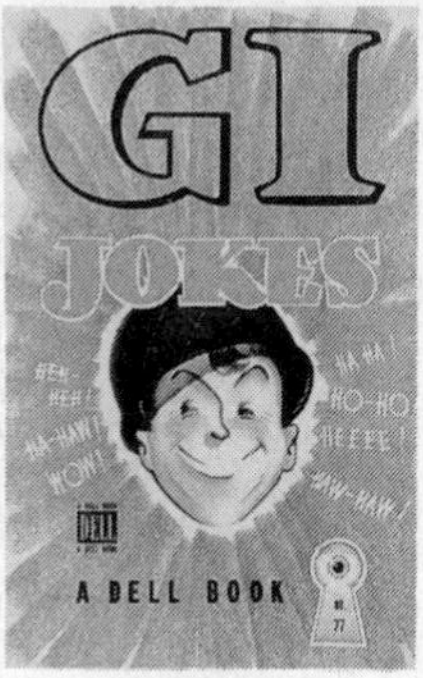

Dell Book, 77

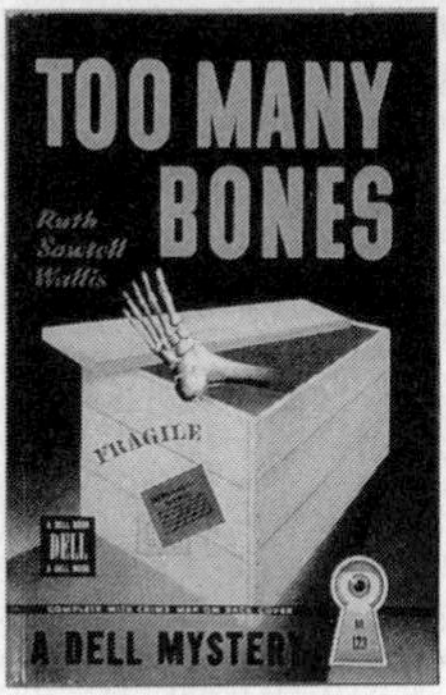

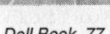

Dell Book, 123

Dell Book, 135

		G	VG	F
71	Popkin, Zelda - ***Murder In The Mist*** [1945] Cover by Gerald Gregg	$3.50	$10.00	$20.00
72	McCloy, Helen - ***The Man In The Moonlight*** [1945] Cover by Gerald Gregg.	$3.50	$10.00	$20.00
73	Baldwin, Faith - ***Week-End Marriage*** [1945] Cover by Gerald Gregg	$3.50	$10.00	$20.00
74	Footner, Hulbert - ***The Murder That Had Everything*** [1945] Cover by Gerald Gregg.	$3.50	$10.00	$20.00
75	Knight, Clifford - ***The Affair Of The Scarlet Crab*** [1945] Cover by Gerald Gregg.	$3.50	$10.00	$20.00
76	Disney, Dorothy Cameron - ***Death In The Back Seat*** [1945] Cover by Ben Hallam.	$3.50	$10.00	$20.00
77	Anthology edited by Lou Nielsen - ***G. I. Jokes*** [1945] Cover by William Strohmer.	$12.50	$37.50	$75.00
78	Halliday, Brett - ***Murder Wears A Mummer's Mask*** [1945] Cover by Gerald Gregg.	$3.50	$10.00	$20.00
79	Fischer, Bruno - ***The Hornets' Nest*** [1945] Cover by Gerald Gregg	$3.50	$10.00	$20.00
80	Lees, Hannah - ***Prescription For Murder*** [1945] Cover by Gerald Gregg.	$3.50	$10.00	$20.00
81	Coxe, George Harmon - ***The Glass Triangle*** [1945]	$3.50	$10.00	$20.00
82	Polsky, Thomas - ***Curtains For The Editor*** [1945] Cover by Gerald Gregg.	$3.50	$10.00	$20.00
83	Eberhart, Mignon G. - ***With This Ring*** [1945]	$3.50	$10.00	$20.00
84	Fair, A. A. - ***Gold Comes In Bricks*** [1945] Cover by Gerald Gregg	$3.50	$10.00	$20.00
85	Wylie, Philip - ***The Savage Gentleman*** [1945]	$4.00	$12.50	$25.00
86	Homes, Geoffrey - ***The Man Who Murdered Goliath*** [1945] Cover by Gerald Gregg.	$3.50	$10.00	$20.00
87	Cores, Lucy - ***Painted For The Kill*** [1945] Cover by Gerald Gregg	$3.50	$10.00	$20.00
88	Abbot, Anthony - ***The Creeps*** [1945]	$3.50	$10.00	$20.00
89	Anthology edited by Cavanah & Weir - ***Dell Book of Jokes*** [1945] PBO. Cover by Gerald Gregg.	$12.50	$37.50	$75.00
90	Hammett, Dashiell - ***A Man Called Spade And Other Stories*** [1945]	$10.00	$30.00	$60.00
91	Carr, John Dickson - ***The Case Of The Constant Suicides*** [1945]	$4.00	$12.50	$25.00
92	Anthology edited by Alfred Hitchcock - ***Suspense Stories*** [1945] PBO.	$3.50	$10.00	$20.00

		G	VG	F
93	Abbey, Kieran - ***Beyond The Dark*** [1945]	$3.50	$10.00	$20.00
94	Popkin, Zelda - ***No Crime For A Lady*** [1945]	$3.50	$10.00	$20.00
95	Kendrick, Baynard - ***The Last Express*** [1945] Cover by Gerald Gregg	$3.50	$10.00	$20.00
96	Offord, Lenore Glen - ***Skeleton Key*** [1945]	$3.50	$10.00	$20.00
97	Wire, Harold Channing - ***Trail Boss Of Indian Beef*** [1946]	$3.00	$9.00	$18.00
98	Taylor, Phoebe Atwood - ***Spring Harrowing*** [1946] Cover by Gerald Gregg.	$3.50	$10.00	$20.00
99	Prouty, Olive Higgins - ***Now, Voyager*** [1946]	$3.00	$9.00	$18.00
100	Hughes, Dorothy B. - ***The So Blue Marble*** [1946]	$3.50	$10.00	$20.00
101	Coxe, George Harmon - ***Murder With Pictures*** [1946]	$3.00	$9.00	$18.00
102	Roden, H. W. - ***You Only Hang Once*** [1946]	$3.00	$9.00	$18.00
103	Holding, Elisabeth Saxany - ***Murder Is A Kill-Joy*** [1946] Cover by Gerald Gregg.	$3.00	$9.00	$18.00
104	Adams, Cleve F. - ***The Crooking Finger*** [1946] Cover by Gerald Gregg	$3.00	$9.00	$18.00
105	Christie, Agatha - ***Appointment With Death*** [1946] Cover by Gerald Gregg.	$3.00	$9.00	$18.00
106	Roos, Kelley - ***Made Up To Kill*** [1946]	$3.00	$9.00	$18.00
107	McCloy, Helen - ***The Deadly Truth*** [1946]	$3.00	$9.00	$18.00
108	Dickson, Carter - ***Death In Five Boxes*** [1946]	$4.00	$12.50	$25.00
109	Fair, A. A. - ***Spill The Jackpot*** [1946]	$3.00	$9.00	$18.00
110	Millar, Margaret - ***Wall Of Eyes*** [1946] Cover by Gerald Gregg	$2.50	$7.50	$15.00
111	Farjeon, Jefferson - ***Greenmask*** [1946] Cover by Gerald Gregg	$2.50	$7.50	$15.00
112	Halliday, Brett - ***Michael Shayne's Long Chance*** [1946] Cover by Gerald Gregg.	$3.00	$9.00	$18.00
113	Kendrick, Baynard - ***The Whistling Hangman*** [1946]	$2.50	$7.50	$15.00
114	Reilly, Helen - ***Three Women In Black*** [1946]	$2.50	$7.50	$15.00
115	Stout, Rex - ***The Broken Vase*** [1946] Cover by Gerald Gregg..	$3.00	$9.00	$18.00
116	Baldwin, Faith - ***Honor Bound*** [1946] Cover by Gerald Gregg.	$2.00	$6.00	$12.00
117	Lambert, Alice Elinor - ***Women Are Like That*** [1946]	$2.00	$6.00	$12.00
118	Lea, Fanny Heaslip - ***Half Angel*** [1946]	$2.00	$6.00	$12.00
119	Larrimore, Lida - ***Robin Hill*** [1946]	$2.00	$6.00	$12.00
120	Haycox, Ernest - ***Man In The Saddle*** [1946]	$2.50	$7.50	$15.00
121	Rawson, Clayton - ***The Footprints On The Ceiling*** [1946]	$2.50	$7.50	$15.00
122	Lees, Hannah and Bachmann, Lawrence - ***Death In The Doll's House*** [1946]	$3.00	$9.00	$18.00
123	Wallis, Ruth Sawtell - ***Too Many Bones*** [1946] Cover by Gerald Gregg	$2.50	$7.50	$15.00
124	Rinehart, Mary Roberts - ***The Man In Lower Ten*** [1946]	$2.50	$7.50	$15.00
125	Karlova, Irina - ***Dreadful Hollow*** [1946]	$2.50	$7.50	$15.00
126	Wells, Anna Mary - ***Murderer's Choice*** [1946]	$2.50	$7.50	$15.00
127	Petersen, Herman - ***Old Bones*** [1946]	$2.50	$7.50	$15.00
128	Halliday, Brett - ***Murder And The Married Virgin*** [1946]	$3.00	$9.00	$18.00
129	Hammett, Dashiell - ***The Continental Op*** [1946]	$7.00	$22.50	$45.00
130	Adams, Samuel Hopkins - ***The Harvey Girls*** [1946]	$2.00	$6.00	$12.00
131	Rinehart, Mary Roberts - ***The Red Lamp*** [1946]	$2.50	$7.50	$15.00
132	Randau, Carl and Zugsmith, Leane - ***The Visitor*** [1946]	$2.00	$6.00	$12.00
133	Holloway, Elizabeth Hughes - ***Cobweb House*** [1946]	$2.50	$7.50	$15.00
134	Blochman, Lawrence G. - ***Wives To Burn*** [1947]	$2.00	$6.00	$12.00
135	Lewis, Lange - ***Meat For Murder*** [1947]	$2.50	$7.50	$15.00
136	Eberhart, Mignon G. - ***Wolf In Man's Clothing*** [1947]	$2.50	$7.50	$15.00
137	Disney, Dorothy Cameron - ***Crimson Friday*** [1947]	$2.50	$7.50	$15.00
138	Baldwin, Faith - ***Men Are Such Fools!*** [1947]	$2.00	$6.00	$12.00
139	Iams, Jack - ***Love—And The Countess To Boot*** [1947]	$2.00	$6.00	$12.00
140	Wylie, Philip - ***Footprint Of Cinderella*** [1947]	$2.00	$6.00	$12.00
141	Thurman, Harriett - ***The Swift Hour*** [1947]	$2.00	$6.00	$12.00
142	Tilton, Alice - ***Cold Steal*** [1947] Cover by Gerald Gregg.	$2.50	$7.50	$15.00

Dell Book, 143

Dell Book, 181

Dell Book, 221

		G	VG	F
143	Anthology selected by Alfred Hitchcock - ***Bar The Doors!*** [1946] PBO. Cover by Gerald Gregg.	$3.00	$9.00	$18.00
144	Marshall, Edison - ***The White Brigand*** [1947]	$2.00	$6.00	$12.00
145	Christie, Agatha - ***Murder In Mesopotamia*** [1947]	$2.50	$7.50	$15.00
146	Stout, Rex - ***Alphabet Hicks*** [1947]	$3.00	$9.00	$18.00
147	Coxe, George Harmon - ***The Lady Is Afraid*** [1947]	$2.50	$7.50	$15.00
148	Reilly, Helen - ***Name Your Poison*** [1947]	$2.50	$7.50	$15.00
149	Hughes, Dorothy B. - ***The Blackbirder*** [1947]	$2.50	$7.50	$15.00
150	Hale, Christopher - ***Midsummer Nightmare*** [1947]	$2.50	$7.50	$15.00
151	McCloy, Helen - ***Who's Calling?*** [1947]	$2.50	$7.50	$15.00
152	Anthology edited by Ted Shane - ***Jokes, Gags, And Wisecracks*** [1947] Cartoon and joke book.	$12.50	$37.50	$75.00
153	Anthology edited by Gene Autry - ***Western Stories*** [1947] PBO.	$2.50	$7.50	$15.00
154	Hammett, Dashiell - ***The Return Of The Continental Op*** [1947]	$7.00	$22.50	$45.00
155	Roos, Kelley - ***Sailor, Take Warning!*** [1947]	$2.50	$7.50	$15.00
156	Blochman, Lawrence G. - ***Blow-Down*** [1947]	$2.50	$7.50	$15.00
157	Millar, Margaret - ***Fire Will Freeze*** [1947]	$2.50	$7.50	$15.00
158	Head, Matthew - ***The Devil In The Bush*** [1947]	$3.00	$9.00	$18.00
159	Yates, George Worthing - ***If A Body*** [1947]	$2.50	$7.50	$15.00
160	Fair, A. A. - ***Double Or Quits*** [1947] Cover by Gerald Gregg.	$2.50	$7.50	$15.00
161	Eberhart, Mignon G. - ***The Man Next Door*** [1947]	$2.50	$7.50	$15.00
162	Kendrick, Baynard - ***Odor Of Violets*** [1947]	$2.50	$7.50	$15.00
163	Baldwin, Faith - ***Self-Made Woman*** [1947]	$1.50	$5.00	$10.00
164	Tilton, Alice - ***The Left Leg*** [1947]	$2.50	$7.50	$15.00
165	Newsom, John D. - ***Wiped Out!*** [1947]	$2.00	$6.00	$12.00
166	Rinehart, Mary Roberts - ***The Wall*** [1947]	$2.50	$7.50	$15.00
167	Prouty, Olive Higgins - ***White Fawn*** [1947]	$2.00	$6.00	$12.00
168	Halliday, Brett - ***The Corpse Came Calling*** [1947] Cover by Gerald Gregg.	$2.50	$7.50	$15.00
169	Coxe, George Harmon - ***Murdock's Acid Test*** [1947]	$2.50	$7.50	$15.00
170	Greig, Maysie - ***Reluctant Millionaire*** [1947]	$1.50	$5.00	$10.00
171	Taylor, Phoebe Atwood - ***Octagon House*** [1947]	$2.50	$7.50	$15.00
172	Christie, Agatha - ***Sad Cypress*** [1947]	$2.50	$7.50	$15.00
173	Talbot, Hake - ***Rim Of The Pit*** [1947]	$2.50	$7.50	$15.00
174	Hull, E. M. - ***The Sheik*** [1947]	$1.50	$5.00	$10.00
175	Dickson, Carter - ***And So To Murder*** [1947]	$2.50	$7.50	$15.00
176	Rawson, Clayton - ***The Headless Lady*** [1947]	$3.00	$9.00	$18.00
177	Stout, Rex - ***The Hand In The Glove*** [1947]	$3.00	$9.00	$18.00
178	Bailey, Temple - ***The Pink Camellia*** [1947]	$1.50	$5.00	$10.00

		G	VG	F
179	Raine, William MacLeod - ***Trail's End*** [1947]	$2.00	$6.00	$12.00
180	Grafton, C.W. - ***The Rat Began To Gnaw The Rope*** [1947]	$2.50	$7.50	$15.00
181	Little, Constance and Gwenyth - ***Great Black Kanba*** [1947]	$2.50	$7.50	$15.00
182	Coxe, George Harmon - ***No Time To Kill*** [1947]	$2.50	$7.50	$15.00
183	Peattie, Louise Redfield - ***American Acres*** [1947]	$1.50	$5.00	$10.00
184	Halliday, Brett - ***Murder Is My Business*** [1947]	$2.50	$7.50	$15.00
185	Roden, H. W. - ***Too Busy To Die*** [1947]	$2.50	$7.50	$15.00
186	Treynor, Blair - ***She Ate Her Cake*** [1947]	$2.00	$6.00	$12.00
187	Christie, Agatha - ***N Or M?*** [1947]	$2.50	$7.50	$15.00
188	Marshall, Edison - ***The Splendid Quest*** [1947]	$1.50	$5.00	$10.00
189	Renault, Mary - ***Kind Are Her Answers*** [1947]	$1.50	$5.00	$10.00
190	Popkin, Zelda - ***Dead Man's Gift*** [1947]	$2.50	$7.50	$15.00
191	Burt, Katharine Newlin - ***Lady In The Tower*** [1947]	$2.00	$6.00	$12.00
192	Raine, Norman Reilly - ***Tugboat Annie*** [1947]	$2.00	$6.00	$12.00
193	Goldthwaite, Eaton K. - ***Scarecrow*** [1947]	$2.50	$7.50	$15.00
194	Holding, Elisabeth Saxany - ***The Innocent Mrs. Duff*** [1947]	$2.50	$7.50	$15.00
195	Flynn, Errol - ***Beam Ends*** [1947]	$1.50	$5.00	$10.00
196	Baldwin, Faith - ***Rich Girl, Poor Girl*** [1947]	$1.50	$5.00	$10.00
197	Butler, Gerald - ***Kiss The Blood Off My Hands*** [1947]	$2.50	$7.50	$15.00
198	Offord, Lenore Glen - ***The Glass Mask*** [1947]	$2.50	$7.50	$15.00
199	Christie, Agatha - ***The Secret Of Chimneys*** [1947]	$2.50	$7.50	$15.00
200	Reilly, Helen - ***The Opening Door*** [1947]	$2.50	$7.50	$15.00
201	Wells, H. G. - ***The First Men In The Moon*** [1947] Cover by Earl Sherwan	$3.50	$10.00	$20.00
202	Coxe, George Harmon - ***Mrs. Murdock Takes A Case*** [1947]	$2.50	$7.50	$15.00
203	Rinehart, Mary Roberts - ***The State Versus Elinor Norton*** [1947]	$2.50	$7.50	$15.00
204	Burke, Richard - ***The Frightened Pigeon*** [1947]	$2.50	$7.50	$15.00
205	Rafferty and O'Neill - editors - ***The Dell Book Of Crossword Puzzles*** [1947] PBO.	$35.00	$125.00	$300.00
206	Anthology selected by Alfred Hitchcock - ***Hold Your Breath*** [1948] PBO. Cover by Earl Sherwan	$3.00	$9.00	$18.00
207	Mason, Sara Elizabeth - ***The Crimson Feather*** [1948]	$2.50	$7.50	$15.00
208	Woolrich, Cornell - ***The Black Curtain*** [1948] Cover by George A. Frederikson.	$3.50	$10.00	$20.00
209	Millar, Margaret - ***The Iron Gates*** [1948]	$2.00	$6.00	$12.00
210	Hughes, Dorothy B. - ***Ride The Pink Horse*** [1948]	$2.00	$6.00	$12.00
211	Fair, A. A. - ***Owls Don't Blink*** [1948]	$2.00	$6.00	$12.00
212	McCloy, Helen - ***Cue For Murder*** [1948]	$2.00	$6.00	$12.00
213	Eberhart, Mignon G. - ***Unidentified Woman*** [1948]	$2.00	$6.00	$12.00
214	Lewis, Lange - ***The Birthday Murder*** [1948]	$2.00	$6.00	$12.00
215	Thompson, Sydney - ***Dr. Parrish, Resident*** [1948]	$1.35	$4.00	$8.00
216	Foldes, Yolanda - ***Golden Earrings*** [1948]	$1.35	$4.00	$8.00
217	Anthology edited by Gene Autry - ***Gun Smoke Yarns*** [1948] PBO.	$1.50	$5.00	$10.00
218	Treat, Lawrence - ***"H" As In Hunted*** [1948]	$2.00	$6.00	$12.00
219	Head, Matthew - ***The Smell Of Money*** [1948]	$2.00	$6.00	$12.00
220	Lambert, Alice Eleanor - ***Hospital Nocturne*** [1948]	$1.35	$4.00	$8.00
221	Goodis, David - ***Dark Passage*** [1948]	$8.00	$25.00	$50.00
222	Halliday, Brett - ***Marked For Murder*** [1948]	$2.00	$6.00	$12.00
223	Hammett, Dashiell - ***Hammett Homicides*** [1948] Cover by Gerald Gregg.	$7.00	$22.50	$45.00
224	Adams, Dr. Clifford R. & Packard, Vance - ***How To Pick A Mate*** [1948]	$1.35	$4.00	$8.00
225	Coxe, George Harmon - ***Silent Are The Dead*** [1948]	$2.00	$6.00	$12.00
226	Christie, Agatha - ***The Murder At The Vicarage*** [1948]	$2.00	$6.00	$12.00
227	Haycox, Ernest - ***Trail Town*** [1948]	$1.50	$5.00	$10.00
228	Reilly, Helen - ***Murder On Angler's Island*** [1948]	$2.00	$6.00	$12.00
229	Lockridge, Frances and Richard - ***Murder Within Murder*** [1948]	$2.00	$6.00	$12.00

Dell Book, 246

Dell Book, 414

Dell First Edition, 2-E

		G	VG	F
230	Kendrick, Baynard - ***Blind Man's Bluff*** [1948]	$2.00	$6.00	$12.00
231	Kane, Henry - ***A Halo For Nobody*** [1948]	$2.00	$6.00	$12.00
232	Grafton, C. W. - ***The Rope Began To Hang The Butcher*** [1948]	$2.00	$6.00	$12.00
233	Marshall, Edison - ***The Upstart*** [1948]	$1.35	$4.00	$8.00
234	Shann, Renee - ***Student Nurse*** [1948] Cover by Gerald Gregg	$1.35	$4.00	$8.00
235	Stout, Rex - ***Red Threads*** [1948]	$3.00	$9.00	$18.00
236	Baldwin, Faith - ***Skyscraper*** [1948]	$1.35	$4.00	$8.00
237	MacKinnon, Allan - ***House Of Darkness*** [1948]	$2.00	$6.00	$12.00
238	Raine, William Macleod - ***Gunsight Pass*** [1948]	$1.50	$5.00	$10.00
239	Greig, Maysie - ***Candidate For Love*** [1948] Cover by Gerald Gregg	$1.35	$4.00	$8.00
240	Coxe, George Harmon - ***The Charred Witness*** [1948]	$2.00	$6.00	$12.00
241	Rinehart, Mary Roberts & Hopwood, Avery - ***The Bat*** [1948]	$2.00	$6.00	$12.00
242	Butler, Gerald - ***The Unafraid*** [1948] Movie tie-in with Burt Lancaster and Joan Fontaine. Photo cover.	$2.50	$7.50	$15.00
243	Fair, A. A. - ***Owls Don't Blink*** [1948]	$2.00	$6.00	$12.00
244	Steel, Kurt - ***Judas, Incorporated*** [1948]	$2.00	$6.00	$12.00
245	Bailey, Temple - ***Wallflowers*** [1948]	$1.35	$4.00	$8.00
246	Mulford, Clarence E. - ***Bar-20 Days*** [1948]	$1.50	$5.00	$10.00
247	Roden, H. W. - ***One Angel Less*** [1948]	$2.00	$6.00	$12.00
248	Wickware, Francis Sill - ***Dangerous Ground*** [1948]	$1.50	$5.00	$10.00
249	Larrimore, Lida - ***Stars Still Shine*** [1948]	$1.35	$4.00	$8.00
250	Hilton, Francis W. - ***Skyline Riders*** [1948]	$1.50	$5.00	$10.00
251	Taylor, Phoebe Atwood - ***Banbury Bog*** [1948]	$2.00	$6.00	$12.00
252	Sale, Richard - ***Benefit Performance*** [1948]	$1.50	$5.00	$10.00
253	Savage, Jr., Les - ***Treasure Of The Brasada*** [1948]	$1.50	$5.00	$10.00
254	Fair, A. A. - ***Bats Fly At Dusk*** [1948]	$1.50	$5.00	$10.00
255	Baldwin, Faith - ***Enchanted Oasis*** [1948] Cover by F. Ken-wood Giles.	$1.35	$4.00	$8.00
256	Dekobra, Maurice - ***The Madonna Of The Sleeping Cars*** [1948]	$1.50	$5.00	$10.00
257	Christie, Agatha - ***Murder In Retrospect*** [1948]	$2.00	$6.00	$12.00
258	Rawson, Clayton - ***No Coffin For The Corpse*** [1948]	$2.00	$6.00	$12.00
259	Boyd, Eunice Mays - ***Murder Wears Mukluks*** [1948]	$2.00	$6.00	$12.00
260	Burke, Richard - ***Chinese Red*** [1948]	$2.50	$7.50	$15.00
261	McCloy, Helen - ***Do Not Disturb*** [1948]	$2.00	$6.00	$12.00
262	Hitchcock, Alfred - ***Rope*** [1948] PBO. Movie photo cover, movie tie-in with James Stewart.	$5.00	$15.00	$30.00
263	Wilson, Mitchell - ***The Panic-Stricken*** [1948]	$2.00	$6.00	$12.00

		G	VG	F
264	Anthology edited by Alfred Hitchcock - ***Fear And Trembling*** [1948]	$3.00	$9.00	$18.00
265	Meier, Frank - ***Men Under The Sea*** [1948]	$2.50	$7.50	$15.00
266	Roos, Kelley - ***Ghost Of A Chance*** [1948]	$2.00	$6.00	$12.00
267	Stout, Rex - ***Not Quite Dead Enough*** [1948] Cover by Gerald Gregg	$2.50	$7.50	$15.00
268	Halliday, Brett - ***Blood On Biscayne Bay*** [1948]	$2.00	$6.00	$12.00
269	Wells, H. G. - ***The Invisible Man*** [1949] Cover by Gerald Gregg	$3.50	$10.00	$20.00
270	Dodge, David - ***It Ain't Hay*** [1949] Cover by Gerald Gregg	$5.00	$15.00	$30.00
271	Lomax, Bliss - ***Gunsmoke And Trail Dust*** [1949]	$1.50	$5.00	$10.00
272	Eby, Lois and Fleming, John - ***The Velvet Fleece*** [1949]	$2.00	$6.00	$12.00
273	Kendrick, Baynard - ***Death Knell*** [1949]	$2.00	$6.00	$12.00
274	Iams, Jack - ***The Body Missed The Boat*** [1949]	$2.00	$6.00	$12.00
275	Sterling, Stewart - ***Where There's Smoke*** [1949]	$2.00	$6.00	$12.00
276	Coxe, George Harmon - ***Murder For Two*** [1949]	$2.00	$6.00	$12.00
277	Parrott, Ursula - ***Ex-Wife*** [1949]	$1.35	$4.00	$8.00
278	Rafferty and O'Neill - editors - ***Second Dell Book Of Cross-word Puzzles*** [1949] PBO.	$50.00	$175.00	$400.00
279	Hull, E. M. - ***Sons Of The Sheik*** [1949] Cover by F. Kenwood Giles.	$1.50	$5.00	$10.00
280	Halliday, Brett - ***Counterfeit Wife*** [1949]	$2.00	$6.00	$12.00
281	Allen, Hervey - ***Anthony Adverse In Italy*** [1949]	$1.35	$4.00	$8.00
282	Anthology edited by William M. Raine - ***Western Stories*** [1949]	$1.50	$5.00	$10.00
283	Allen, Hervey - ***Anthony Adverse In Africa*** [1949]	$1.35	$4.00	$8.00
284	Ermine, Will - ***Outlaw On Horseback*** [1949]	$1.50	$5.00	$10.00
285	Allen, Hervey - ***Anthony Adverse In America*** [1949]	$1.35	$4.00	$8.00
286	Summersby, Kay - ***Eisenhower Was My Boss*** [1949] Cover by Alexander T. Kozloff.	$1.35	$4.00	$8.00
287	Reilly, Helen - ***The Silver Leopard*** [1949]	$2.50	$7.50	$15.00
288	Baldwin, Faith - ***The Heart Remembers*** [1949]	$1.35	$4.00	$8.00
289	Irving, Alexander - ***Bitter Ending*** [1949]	$1.35	$4.00	$8.00
290	Cooper, Courtney Ryley - ***The Pioneers*** [1949]	$1.35	$4.00	$8.00
291	North, Sterling - ***So Dear To My Heart*** [1949] Movie tie-in.	$1.35	$4.00	$8.00
292	Smith, Robert - ***Hits, Runs, And Errors*** [1949]	$1.35	$4.00	$8.00
293	Christie, Agatha - ***Cards On The Table*** [1949]	$2.00	$6.00	$12.00
294	Kyne, Peter B. - ***Jim The Conqueror*** [1949]	$1.35	$4.00	$8.00
295	McCloy, Helen - ***The Goblin Market*** [1949]	$2.00	$6.00	$12.00
296	Alcott, Louisa Mae & Webb, Jean Francis - ***Little Women*** [1949] Movie photo cover and tie-in.	$3.50	$10.00	$20.00
297	Rinehart, Mary Roberts - ***The Great Mistake*** [1949]	$2.00	$6.00	$12.00
298	Renault, Mary - ***Promise Of Love*** [1949]	$1.35	$4.00	$8.00
299	Stout, Rex - ***Bad For Business*** [1949]	$4.00	$12.50	$25.00
300	Tompkins, Walker A. - ***The Paintin' Pistoleer*** [1949] PBO. Cover by William George Jacobson.	$3.00	$9.00	$18.00
301	Treat, Lawrence - ***"Q" As In Quicksand*** [1949]	$2.00	$6.00	$12.00
302	Lees, Hannah - ***The Dark Device*** [1949] Cover by Gerald Gregg	$2.00	$6.00	$12.00
303	Odlum, Jerome - ***The Mirabilis Diamond*** [1949] Cover by Gerald Gregg.	$2.00	$6.00	$12.00
304	Douglas, Lloyd C. - ***Doctor Hudson's Secret Journal*** [1949] Cover by F. Kenwood Giles	$1.35	$4.00	$8.00
305	Anthology edited by Orson Welles - ***Invasion From Mars*** [1949] PBO. Cover by Malcolm Smith.	$3.50	$10.00	$20.00
306	O'Farrell, William - ***Brandy For A Hero*** [1949]	$1.50	$5.00	$10.00
307	McGerr, Pat - ***Pick Your Victim*** [1949]	$2.00	$6.00	$12.00
308	Hammett, Dashiell - ***Dead Yellow Women*** [1949]	$10.00	$30.00	$60.00
309	Greig, Maysie - ***Satin Straps*** [1949]	$1.35	$4.00	$8.00
310	Tompkins, Walker A. - ***West Of Texas Law*** [1949] PBO.	$1.50	$5.00	$10.00

		G	VG	F
311	Blochman, Lawrence G. - ***Bengal Fire*** [1949]	$1.50	$5.00	$10.00
312	Gilligan, Edmund - ***The Gaunt Woman*** [1949]	$1.35	$4.00	$8.00
313	Cunningham, A. B. - ***Death Of A Bullionaire*** [1949]	$1.50	$5.00	$10.00
314	Sterling, Stewart - ***Dead Wrong*** [1949]	$2.00	$6.00	$12.00
315	Fair, A. A. - ***Cats Prowl At Night*** [1949]	$2.00	$6.00	$12.00
316	Kane, Henry - ***Armchair In Hell*** [1949]	$2.00	$6.00	$12.00
317	Haycox, Ernest - ***Alder Gulch*** [1949]	$1.50	$5.00	$10.00
318	Baldwin, Faith - ***Alimony*** [1949]	$1.35	$4.00	$8.00
319	Christie, Agatha - ***The Man In The Brown Suit*** [1949]	$1.50	$5.00	$10.00
320	Burroughs, Edgar Rice - ***Cave Girl*** [1949] Cover by Jean Des Vignes.	$5.00	$15.00	$30.00
321	Coxe, George Harmon - ***Assignment in Guiana*** [1949]	$1.50	$5.00	$10.00
322	Lockridge, Frances and Richard - ***Death Of A Tall Man*** [1949]	$2.00	$6.00	$12.00
323	Halliday, Brett - ***Murder And The Married Virgin*** [1949]	$1.50	$5.00	$10.00
324	Halliday, Brett - ***The Corpse Came Calling*** [1949]	$1.50	$5.00	$10.00
325	Halliday, Brett - ***Michael Shayne's Long Chance*** [1949]	$1.50	$5.00	$10.00
326	Halliday, Brett - ***Murder Is My Business*** [1949]	$1.50	$5.00	$10.00
327	Monsarrat, Nicholas - ***Leave Cancelled*** [1949]	$1.50	$5.00	$10.00
328	Anthology - ***Cream Of The Crop*** [1949] Photo cover. Cartoon and joke book	$1.35	$4.00	$8.00
329	Brand, Max - ***Young Dr. Kildare*** [1949]	$1.35	$4.00	$8.00
330	Kane, Henry - ***Report For A Corpse*** [1949]	$1.50	$5.00	$10.00
331	Yordan, Philip - ***Anna Lucasta*** [1949] PBO. Movie tie-in and movie photo cover.	$1.35	$4.00	$8.00
332	Anthology edited by W. A. Swanberg - ***Fact Detective Mysteries*** [1949] PBO.	$2.00	$6.00	$12.00
333	Mann, E. B. - ***Stampede*** [1949]	$1.50	$5.00	$10.00
334	Boucher, Anthony - ***The Case Of The Seven Sneezes*** [1949]	$1.50	$5.00	$10.00
335	Kelland, Clarence Budington - ***Double Treasure*** [1949]	$1.50	$5.00	$10.00
336	Ayres, Ruby M. - ***Afterglow*** [1949]	$1.50	$5.00	$10.00
337	Brock, Stuart - ***Just Around The Coroner*** [1949]	$1.50	$5.00	$10.00
338	Fox, James M. - ***The Lady Regrets*** [1949]	$1.50	$5.00	$10.00
339	Haggard, H. Rider; retold by Don Ward - ***She*** [1949] Cover by Marchetti.	$3.50	$10.00	$20.00
340	Schick, M.D., Bela & Rosenson, M.D., W. - ***The Care Of Your Child*** [1949] Photo cover	$1.25	$3.75	$7.50
341	Marshall, Edison - ***The Upstart*** [1949]	$1.35	$4.00	$8.00
342	Hull, E. M. - ***Sons Of The Sheik*** [1949]	$1.35	$4.00	$8.00
343	Tucker, Wilson - ***The Chinese Doll*** [1949] Author's first book.	$3.50	$10.00	$20.00
344	Block, Libbie - ***Bedeviled*** [1949]	$1.50	$5.00	$10.00
345	Roden, H. W. - ***Wake For A Lady*** [1949]	$1.50	$5.00	$10.00
346	Head, Matthew - ***The Accomplice*** [1949]	$1.50	$5.00	$10.00
347	Haycox, Ernest - ***Trail Town*** [1949]	$1.35	$4.00	$8.00
348	Kane, Henry - ***A Halo For Nobody*** [1949]	$1.50	$5.00	$10.00
349	Roden, H. W. - ***Too Busy To Die*** [1949]	$1.50	$5.00	$10.00
350	Dodge, David - ***It Ain't Hay*** [1949]	$4.00	$12.50	$25.00
351	Flynn, Errol - ***Showdown*** [1949]	$1.35	$4.00	$8.00
352	Dawson, Peter - ***Gunsmoke Graze*** [1949]	$1.35	$4.00	$8.00
353	Marshall, Edison - ***Yankee Pasha*** [1949] Cover by Robert Stanley	$1.35	$4.00	$8.00
354	Ford, Leslie - ***The Philadelphia Murder Story*** [1949]	$1.35	$4.00	$8.00
355	McCloy, Helen - ***The One That Got Away*** [1949]	$1.50	$5.00	$10.00
356	Lees, Hannah and Bachman, Lawrence - ***Death In The Doll's House*** [1949] Photo cover. Movie tie-in with Ann Southern.	$2.50	$7.50	$15.00
357	Wodehouse, P. G. - ***Leave It To PSmith*** [1949] Cover by Coconos	$1.35	$4.00	$8.00
358	Steinbeck, John - ***To A God Unknown*** [1949]	$3.00	$9.00	$18.00
359	Raine, William MacLeod - ***Trail's End*** [1949]	$1.35	$4.00	$8.00
360	Savage, Juanita - ***Don Lorenzo's Bride*** [1949]	$1.35	$4.00	$8.00

		G	VG	F
361	Rinehart, Mary Roberts - ***Haunted Lady*** [1949]	$1.50	$5.00	$10.00
362	Fox, Norman A. - ***Silent In The Saddle*** [1950] Cover by Bob Meyers.	$1.35	$4.00	$8.00
363	Millar, Kenneth - ***Blue City*** [1950]	$4.00	$12.50	$25.00
364	Marshall, Edison - ***Forlorn Island*** [1950]	$1.35	$4.00	$8.00
365	Cunningham, A. B. - ***The Death Of A Worldly Woman*** [1950]	$1.35	$4.00	$8.00
366	Lucas, Cary - ***Unfinished Business*** [1950]	$1.50	$5.00	$10.00
367	Anthology edited by Alfred Hitchcock - ***Suspense Stories*** [1950] PBO.	$3.00	$9.00	$18.00
368	Baldwin, Faith - ***The Moon's Our Home*** [1950]	$1.25	$3.75	$7.50
369	McCloy, Helen - ***Panic*** [1950]	$1.35	$4.00	$8.00
370	Dickson, Carter - ***He Wouldn't Kill Patience*** [1950] Cover by Griffith Foxley.	$2.00	$6.00	$12.00
371	Coates, Robert M. - ***Wisteria Cottage*** [1950]	$1.50	$5.00	$10.00
372	Overholser, Wayne D. - ***Buckaroo's Code*** [1950] Cover by Bob Meyers.	$1.35	$4.00	$8.00
373	Taber, Gladys - ***The Heart Has April Too*** [1950]	$1.25	$3.75	$7.50
374	Kersh, Gerald - ***Night And The City*** [1950] Photo cover. Movie tie-in with Richard Widmark.	$3.50	$10.00	$20.00
375	Hamilton, Donald - ***Date With Darkness*** [1950] Cover by Robert Stanley.	$2.50	$7.50	$15.00
376	Kendrick, Baynard - ***Out Of Control*** [1950] Photo cover.	$1.50	$5.00	$10.00
377	Coxe, George Harmon - ***Alias The Dead*** [1950]	$1.50	$5.00	$10.00
378	Ermine, Will - ***Last Of The Longhorns*** [1950] Cover by Robert Stanley.	$1.35	$4.00	$8.00
379	Hammett, Dashiell - ***Nightmare Town*** [1950] Cover by Robert Stanley.	$5.00	$15.00	$30.00
380	Douglas, Lloyd C. - ***Invitation To Live*** [1950] Cover by Robert Stanley.	$1.25	$3.75	$7.50
381	Banning, Margaret Culkin - ***The Clever Sister*** [1950]	$1.35	$4.00	$8.00
382	Marshall, Rosamond - ***Celeste...The Gold Coast Virgin*** [1950].	$1.50	$5.00	$10.00
383	Raine, William MacLeod - ***Rutledge Trails The Ace Of Spades*** [1950] Cover by Robert Stanley.	$1.35	$4.00	$8.00
384	Iams, Jack - ***Girl Meets Body*** [1950]	$1.35	$4.00	$8.00
385	Halliday, Brett - ***Blood On The Stars*** [1950]	$1.50	$5.00	$10.00
386	Halliday, Brett - ***The Uncomplaining Corpses*** [1950]	$1.50	$5.00	$10.00
387	Halliday, Brett - ***Tickets For Death*** [1950]	$1.50	$5.00	$10.00
388	Halliday, Brett - ***Murder Wears A Mummer's Mask*** [1950] Cover by Robert Stanley.	$1.50	$5.00	$10.00
389	Fair, A. A. - ***Give 'Em The Ax*** [1950]	$1.50	$5.00	$10.00
390	Head, Matthew - ***The Cabinda Affair*** [1950]	$1.50	$5.00	$10.00
391	Christie, Agatha - ***Murder At Hazlemoor*** [1950]	$1.50	$5.00	$10.00
392	Powers, Tom - ***Virgin With Butterflies*** [1950]	$1.35	$4.00	$8.00
393	Wodehouse, P. G. - ***The Code Of The Woosters*** [1950] Cover by Van Kaufman.	$1.35	$4.00	$8.00
394	Renault, Mary - ***Return To Night*** [1950]	$1.25	$3.75	$7.50
395	Ford, Leslie - ***The Devil's Stronghold*** [1950] Cover by Robert Stanley.	$1.50	$5.00	$10.00
396	Albrand, Martha - ***After Midnight*** [1950]	$1.50	$5.00	$10.00
397	Reilly, Helen - ***The Farmhouse*** [1950] Cover by Reynold Brown.	$1.50	$5.00	$10.00
398	Roos, Kelley - ***Murder In Any Language*** [1950]	$1.50	$5.00	$10.00
399	Knibbs, Henry Herbert - ***The Ridin' Kid From Powder River*** [1950] Cover by Robert Stanley.	$1.35	$4.00	$8.00
400	Lait, Jack and Mortimer, Lee - ***New York: Confidential!*** [1950]	$1.25	$3.75	$7.50
401	Heberden, M. V. - ***They Can't All Be Guilty*** [1950]	$1.50	$5.00	$10.00
402	Hull. E. M. - ***The Captive Of The Sahara*** [1950] Cover by Harry Bennett.	$1.35	$4.00	$8.00

		G	VG	F
403	Rinehart, Mary Roberts - ***The Man In Lower 10*** [1950] Cover by Robert Stanley.	$1.50	$5.00	$10.00
404	Rinehart, Mary Roberts - ***The Case Of Jennie Brice*** [1950] Cover by Bill Fleming.	$1.50	$5.00	$10.00
405	Dodge, David - ***The Long Escape*** [1950] Cover by Robert Stanley	$2.00	$6.00	$12.00
406	Fox, Norman A. - ***Cactus Cavalier*** [1950] Cover by Robert Stanley	$1.35	$4.00	$8.00
407	Steinbeck, John - ***To A God Unknown*** [1950]	$2.50	$7.50	$15.00
408	Millar, Kenneth - ***Blue City*** [1950]	$2.50	$7.50	$15.00
409	Parrott, Ursula - ***Strangers May Kiss*** [1950]	$1.25	$3.75	$7.50
410	Cunningham, A. B. - ***The Affair At The Boat Landing*** [1950].	$1.50	$5.00	$10.00
411	Hammett, Dashiell - ***A Man Called Spade And Other Stories*** [1950] Cover by Robert Stanley.	$5.00	$15.00	$30.00
412	McGerr, Pat - ***The Seven Deadly Sisters*** [1950] Cover by Paul C. Burns.	$1.50	$5.00	$10.00
413	Adams, Frank R. - ***Arizona Feud*** [1950] Cover by Robert Stanley	$1.35	$4.00	$8.00
414	Anthology edited by Allan Bernard - ***Cleopatra's Nights*** [1950] PBO. Cover by Ray Johnson.	$2.50	$7.50	$15.00
415	Kummer, Frederic Arnold - ***Ladies In Hades*** [1950]	$3.00	$9.00	$18.00
416	Bezzerides, A. I. - ***They Drive By Night*** [1950] Cover by Robert Stanley.	$1.35	$4.00	$8.00
417	Reasoner, Harry - ***Tell Me About Women*** [1950]	$1.25	$3.75	$7.50
418	Lomax, Bliss - ***Gunsmoke And Trail Dust*** [1950] Cover by Bob Meyers.	$1.35	$4.00	$8.00
419	Dolph, Jack - ***Murder Is Mutual*** [1950]	$1.50	$5.00	$10.00
420	Sterling, Stewart - ***Dead Sure*** [1950] Cover by James Bama.	$2.00	$6.00	$12.00
421	Hammett, Dashiell - ***Dead Yellow Women*** [1950]	$6.00	$20.00	$40.00
422	Marshall, Edison - ***Yankee Pasha*** [1950] Cover by Robert Stanley	$1.35	$4.00	$8.00
423	Coxe, George Harmon - ***Murder In Havana*** [1950]	$1.35	$4.00	$8.00
424	Raine, William MacLeod - ***The Bandit Trail*** [1950] Cover by Robert Stanley	$1.25	$3.75	$7.50
425	Paul, Louis - ***Breakdown*** [1950]	$1.35	$4.00	$8.00
426	Halliday, Brett - ***A Taste For Violence*** [1950]	$1.25	$3.75	$7.50
427	Halliday, Brett - ***Dead Man's Diary And Dinner At Dupre's*** [1950] Cover by Robert Stanley.	$1.35	$4.00	$8.00
428	Halliday, Brett - ***Call For Michael Shayne*** [1950] Cover by Robert Stanley	$1.25	$3.75	$7.50
429	Halliday, Brett - ***The Private Practice Of Michael Shayne*** [1950] Cover by Robert Stanley.	$1.25	$3.75	$7.50
430	McCloy, Helen - ***She Walks Alone*** [1950] Cover by Bill Fleming.	$1.35	$4.00	$8.00
431	Marshall, Edison - ***Benjamin Blake: Son Of Fury*** [1950]	$1.00	$3.00	$6.00
432	Rogers, Phillips - ***Stag Night*** [1950]	$1.00	$3.00	$6.00
433	Haggard, H. Rider - ***King Solomon's Mines*** [1950] PBO. Movie tie-in and photo cover.	$4.00	$12.50	$25.00
434	Rafferty, Kathleen - editor - ***Dell Crossword Dictionary*** [1950]	$2.50	$7.50	$15.00
435	Kroll, Harry Harrison - ***Their Ancient Grudge*** [1950] Cover by Victor Kalin.	$1.35	$4.00	$8.00
436	Webb, Mary - ***Gone To Earth*** [1950]	$1.25	$3.75	$7.50
437	Sinclair, Bertrand W. - ***Gunpowder Lightning*** [1950] Cover by Robert Stanley.	$1.35	$4.00	$8.00
438	Strange, John Stephen - ***All Men Are Liars*** [1950]	$1.25	$3.75	$7.50
439	Westcott, Jan - ***The Border Lord*** [1950]	$1.25	$3.75	$7.50
440	Lait, Jack and Mortimer, Lee - ***New York: Confidential!*** [1950]	$1.00	$3.00	$6.00
441	Coxe, George Harmon - ***Murder With Pictures*** [1950] Cover by Robert Stanley.	$1.35	$4.00	$8.00

		G	VG	F
442	Goldthwaite, Eaton K. - ***Root Of Evil*** [1950] Cover by Robert Stanley	$1.35	$4.00	$8.00
443	Keyes, Frances Parkinson - ***Dinner At Antoine's*** [1950]	$1.00	$3.00	$6.00
444	Kaufman, Lenard - ***Tender Mercy*** [1950] Cover by Bill Fleming	$1.25	$3.75	$7.50
445	Baldwin, Faith - ***The High Road*** [1950]	$1.00	$3.00	$6.00
446	Greig, Maysie - ***Yours Ever*** [1950]	$1.00	$3.00	$6.00
447	Ford, Leslie - ***The Woman In Black*** [1950]	$1.50	$5.00	$10.00
448	Tompkins, Walker A. - ***Flaming Canyon*** [1950] Cover by Robert Stanley	$1.35	$4.00	$8.00
449	Tompkins, Walker A. - ***West Of Texas Law*** [1950]	$1.35	$4.00	$8.00
450	Haycox, Ernest - ***Alder Gulch*** [1950] Cover by Bob Meyers	$1.50	$5.00	$10.00
451	Hilton, Francis W. - ***The Long Rope*** [1950] Cover by Robert Stanley	$1.35	$4.00	$8.00
452	Hammett, Dashiell - ***A Man Called Spade*** [1950] Cover by Robert Stanley	$5.00	$15.00	$30.00
453	Coxe, George Harmon - ***The Camera Clue*** [1950]	$1.50	$5.00	$10.00
454	Christie, Agatha - ***Murder On The Links*** [1950] Cover by Al Brule	$2.00	$6.00	$12.00
455	Kane, Henry - ***Hang By Your Neck*** [1950] Cover by Victor Kalin	$2.00	$6.00	$12.00
456	Gill, Tom - ***Gentleman Of The Jungle*** [1950] Cover by Robert Stanley.	$1.35	$4.00	$8.00
457	Iams, Jack - ***Death Draws The Line*** [1950] Cover by Harry Barton	$2.00	$6.00	$12.00
458	Halliday, Brett - ***A Taste For Violence*** [1950] Cover by Robert Stanley.	$1.50	$5.00	$10.00
459	Halliday, Brett - ***Blood On Biscayne Bay*** [1950]	$1.35	$4.00	$8.00
460	Fair, A. A. - ***Give 'Em The Ax*** [1950]	$1.35	$4.00	$8.00
461	Rice, Craig - ***Innocent Bystander*** [1950] Cover by Bill Fleming	$2.00	$6.00	$12.00
462	Miller, Helen Topping - ***Desperate Angel*** [1950]	$1.35	$4.00	$8.00
463	Fox, James M. - ***The Inconvenient Bride*** [1950] Cover by Robert Stanley	$1.50	$5.00	$10.00
464	Stone, Hampton - ***The Corpse In The Corner Saloon*** [1950] Cover by Robert Stanley.	$1.50	$5.00	$10.00
465	Cunningham, A. B. - ***Death Haunts The Dark Lane*** [1950] Cover by Robert Stanley.	$1.50	$5.00	$10.00
466	Bower, B. M. - ***Pirates Of The Range*** [1950] Cover by Robert Stanley.	$1.35	$4.00	$8.00
467	Kyne, Peter B. - ***Money To Burn*** [1950] Cover by David Attie	$1.35	$4.00	$8.00
468	Marshall, Edison - ***Jungle Hunting Thrills*** [1950] Cover by Robert Stanley	$1.35	$4.00	$8.00
469	Wodehouse, P. G. - ***Uncle Dynamite*** [1950]	$1.35	$4.00	$8.00
470	Chute, Verne - ***Flight Of An Angel*** [1950]	$1.25	$3.75	$7.50
471	Summers, Richard - ***Vigilante*** [1950] Cover by Robert Stanley.	$1.25	$3.75	$7.50
472	Fair, A. A. - ***Crows Can't Count*** [1950] Cover by Robert Stanley	$1.35	$4.00	$8.00
473	Hamilton, Donald - ***The Steel Mirror*** [1950] Cover by Robert Stanley	$1.50	$5.00	$10.00
474	Janney, Russell - ***The Miracle Of The Bells*** [1951] Cover by Richard Munsell	$1.25	$3.75	$7.50
475	Baldwin, Faith - ***Manhattan Nights*** [1951] Cover by Robert Stanley	$1.00	$3.00	$6.00
476	Offord, Lenore Glen - ***My True Love Lies*** [1951] Cover by Frank Vaughn.	$1.00	$3.00	$6.00
477	Held, Jr., John - ***Crosstown*** [1951]	$1.25	$3.75	$7.50
478	Dodge, David - ***Plunder Of The Sun*** [1951] Cover by Robert Stanley	$2.00	$6.00	$12.00

		G	VG	F
479	Emerick, Lucille - ***The Web Of Evil*** [1951] Cover by Robert Stanley.	$1.50	$5.00	$10.00
480	Fox, Norman A. - ***The Thirsty Land*** [1951] Cover by Robert Stanley.	$1.35	$4.00	$8.00
481	Dickson, Carter - ***The Skeleton In The Clock*** [1951] Cover by Robert Stanley.	$1.50	$5.00	$10.00
482	Knight, Ruth Adams - ***Women Must Weep*** [1951]	$1.25	$3.75	$7.50
483	Green, Alan - ***What A Body!*** [1951] Cover by Gilbert Darling.	$2.50	$7.50	$15.00
484	Moray, Helga - ***Untamed*** [1951] Cover by Barye Phillips.	$1.35	$4.00	$8.00
485	Murray, Max - ***The Queen And The Corpse*** [1951] Cover by Robert Stanley.	$1.35	$4.00	$8.00
486	Hammett, Dashiell - ***Blood Money*** [1951] Cover by Robert Stanley.	$5.00	$15.00	$30.00
487	Marshall, Edison - ***Castle In The Swamp*** [1951]	$1.25	$3.75	$7.50
488	Blochman, Lawrence G. - ***Bombay Mail*** [1951] Cover by Robert Stanley.	$1.35	$4.00	$8.00
489	Eskelund, Karl - ***My Chinese Wife*** [1951] Cover by George de Lara.	$1.25	$3.75	$7.50
490	Dawson, Peter - ***The Stirrup Boss*** [1951] Cover by Robert Stanley.	$1.35	$4.00	$8.00
491	Christie, Agatha - ***The Labors Of Hercules*** [1951]	$1.50	$5.00	$10.00
492	Baker, Jr., Charles H. - ***Blood Of The Lamb*** [1951] Cover by Victor Kalin.	$1.25	$3.75	$7.50
493	Ames, Delano - ***She Shall Have Murder*** [1951] Cover by Robert Stanley.	$1.35	$4.00	$8.00
494	Rinehart, Mary Roberts - ***Miss Pinkerton*** [1951] Cover by Barye Phillips.	$1.35	$4.00	$8.00
495	Stout, Rex - ***Double For Death*** [1951] Cover by Robert Stanley.	$1.25	$3.75	$7.50
496	Greig, Maysie - ***Whispers In The Sun*** [1951] Cover by Robert Stanley.	$1.00	$3.00	$6.00
497	Millar, Kenneth - ***The Three Roads*** [1951] Cover by Robert Stanley.	$1.50	$5.00	$10.00
498	Reilly, Helen - ***Staircase 4*** [1951] Cover by Barye Phillips.	$1.35	$4.00	$8.00
499	Overholser, Wayne D. - ***West Of The Rimrock*** [1951]	$1.25	$3.75	$7.50
500	Ibanez, V. Blasco - ***Blood And Sand*** [1951]	$1.00	$3.00	$6.00
501	Surdez, Georges - ***The Demon Caravan*** [1951] Cover by Robert Stanley.	$1.25	$3.75	$7.50
502	Coxe, George Harmon - ***The Groom Lay Dead*** [1951] Cover by Robert Stanley.	$1.35	$4.00	$8.00
503	Halliday, Brett - ***Marked For Murder*** [1951] Cover by Robert Stanley.	$1.35	$4.00	$8.00
504	Jackson, Charles - ***The Sunnier Side*** [1951] Cover by George Mayers.	$1.35	$4.00	$8.00
505	Ford, Leslie - ***Murder With Southern Hospitality*** [1951] Cover by Robert Stanley.	$1.35	$4.00	$8.00
506	Rinehart, Mary Roberts - ***The Window At The White Cat*** [1951]	$1.25	$3.75	$7.50
507	Stern, David - ***Francis*** [1951] Cover by Richard Hook. Movie mention.	$2.00	$6.00	$12.00
508	MacLean, Robinson - ***The Baited Blonde*** [1951] Cover by Robert Stanley.	$1.35	$4.00	$8.00
509	Hilton, Francis W. - ***Blazing Trails*** [1951] Cover by Robert Stanley.	$1.25	$3.75	$7.50
510	Hallas, Richard - ***You Play The Black And The Red Comes Up*** [1951] Cover by Victor Kalin.	$3.00	$9.00	$18.00
511	Butler, Gerald - ***Slippery Hitch*** [1951] Cover by Robert Stanley.	$1.25	$3.75	$7.50
512	Cuthbert, Clifton - ***The Robbed Heart*** [1951] Cover by Robert Stanley.	$1.00	$3.00	$6.00

		G	VG	F
513	Sterling, Stewart - ***Alarm In The Night*** [1951]	$1.25	$3.75	$7.50
514	Iams, Jack - ***Do Not Murder Before Christmas*** [1951]	$1.50	$5.00	$10.00
515	Mannes, Marya - ***Message From A Stranger*** [1951] Cover by Robert Stanley	$1.35	$4.00	$8.00
516	Shute, Nevil - ***No Highway*** [1951] Photo cover and movie tie-in with James Stewart.	$1.25	$3.75	$7.50
517	Lomax, Bliss - ***Sagebrush Bandit*** [1951] Cover by Robert Stanley	$1.25	$3.75	$7.50
518	Powell, Richard - ***Shell Game*** [1951] Cover by Robert Stanley.	$1.25	$3.75	$7.50
519	McCloy, Helen - ***Through A Glass, Darkly*** [1951] Cover by Robert Stanley	$1.35	$4.00	$8.00
520	Nelson, Hugh Lawrence - ***Dead Giveaway*** [1951] Cover by Robert Stanley	$1.35	$4.00	$8.00
521	Williams, Isabel - ***Hell Cat*** [1951] Cover by Barye Phillips	$1.50	$5.00	$10.00
522	Coxe, George Harmon - ***The Glass Triangle*** [1951] Cover by Robert Stanley	$1.35	$4.00	$8.00
523	Anthology from "Zane Grey's Western Mag" - ***Zane Grey Western Award Stories*** [1951] PBO. Cover by Robert Stanley.	$2.50	$7.50	$15.00
524	Baum, Vicki - ***Once In Vienna*** [1951]	$1.00	$3.00	$6.00
525	West, Mae - ***Diamond Lil*** [1951] Cover by James Meese	$1.25	$3.75	$7.50
526	Fox, James M. - ***The Gentle Hangman*** [1951] Cover by Robert Stanley.	$1.35	$4.00	$8.00
527	West, Ward - ***Trouble Valley*** [1951] Cover by Robert Stanley.	$1.25	$3.75	$7.50
528	Franken, Rose - ***Young Claudia*** [1951]	$1.00	$3.00	$6.00
529	Christie, Agatha - ***Sad Cypress*** [1951] Cover by Robert Stanley.	$1.25	$3.75	$7.50
530	Marshall, Edison - ***Love Stories Of India*** [1951]	$1.00	$3.00	$6.00
531	Bird, Brandon - ***Death In Four Colors*** [1951] Cover by S. B. Jones.	$1.25	$3.75	$7.50
532	Baldwin, Faith - ***The Incredible Year*** [1951] Cover by S. B. Jones.	$1.00	$3.00	$6.00
533	Halliday, Brett - ***This Is It, Michael Shayne*** [1951] Cover by Robert Stanley	$1.25	$3.75	$7.50
534	Lait, Jack and Mortimer, Lee - ***New York: Confidential!*** [1951] Cover by Robert Stanley.	$1.00	$3.00	$6.00
535	Kane, Henry - ***Edge Of Panic*** [1951] Cover by Victor Kalin.	$1.25	$3.75	$7.50
536	Burroughs, Edgar Rice - ***Tarzan And The Lost Empire*** [1951] Cover by Robert Stanley.	$4.00	$12.50	$25.00
537	Carr, John Dickson - ***Hag's Nook*** [1951] Cover by Robert Stanley	$1.50	$5.00	$10.00
538	Hammett, Dashiell - ***The Creeping Siamese*** [1951] Cover by Robert Stanley	$5.00	$15.00	$30.00
539	Fox, Norman A. - ***Shadow On The Range*** [1951] Cover by Robert Stanley	$1.25	$3.75	$7.50
540	Stout, Rex - ***Too Many Cooks*** [1951]	$1.35	$4.00	$8.00
541	Rinehart, Mary Roberts - ***Episode Of The Wandering Knife*** [1951]	$1.25	$3.75	$7.50
542	Fair, A. A. - ***Fools Die On Friday*** [1951] Cover by Robert Stanley	$1.25	$3.75	$7.50
543	Dickson, Carter - ***A Graveyard To Let*** [1951]	$1.25	$3.75	$7.50
544	Albrand, Martha - ***Wait For The Dawn*** [1951] Cover by Rafael de Soto.	$1.00	$3.00	$6.00
545	Elston, Allan Vaughan - ***The Sheriff Of San Miguel*** [1951] Cover by Robert Stanley.	$1.00	$3.00	$6.00
546	Eberhart, Mignon G. - ***Hunt With The Hounds*** [1951] Cover by George Mayers.	$1.00	$3.00	$6.00
547	Ford, Leslie - ***Date With Death*** [1951] Cover by Rafael de Soto.	$1.25	$3.75	$7.50

		G	VG	F
548	Steele, Wilbur Daniel - ***That Girl From Memphis*** [1951] Cover by Rafael de Soto.	$1.25	$3.75	$7.50
549	Coxe, George Harmon - ***The Jade Venus*** [1951] Cover by Robert Stanley	$1.25	$3.75	$7.50
550	Christie, Agatha - ***Mr. Parker Pyne, Detective*** [1951] Cover by Rafael de Soto.	$1.25	$3.75	$7.50
551	Tompkins, Walker A. - ***Manhunt West*** [1951] Cover by Robert Stanley.	$1.25	$3.75	$7.50
552	Ames, Delano - ***Murder Begins At Home*** [1951] Cover by Robert Stanley	$1.25	$3.75	$7.50
553	McCulley, Johnston - ***The Mark Of Zorro*** [1951] Cover by Robert Stanley	$4.00	$12.50	$25.00
554	Klempner, John - ***Letter To Five Wives*** [1951]	$1.00	$3.00	$6.00
555	O'Farrell, William - ***Causeway To The Past*** [1951] Cover by Robert Stanley	$1.00	$3.00	$6.00
556	Overholser, Wayne D. - ***Draw Or Drag*** [1951] Cover by Robert Stanley.	$1.00	$3.00	$6.00
557	Boone, Jack - ***Backwoods Woman*** [1951] Cover by Victor Kalin.	$1.25	$3.75	$7.50
558	Millar, Margaret - ***Do Evil In Return*** [1951] Cover by Bill Fleming.	$1.25	$3.75	$7.50
559	Dawson, Peter - ***Renegade Canyon*** [1951] Cover by Robert Stanley	$1.00	$3.00	$6.00
560	Murray, Max - ***The Neat Little Corpse*** [1951] Cover by Robert Stanley.	$1.25	$3.75	$7.50
561	Keyes, Frances Parkinson - ***Crescent Carnival*** [1952] Cover by George Mayers.	$1.00	$3.00	$6.00
562	Short, Luke - ***Raw Land*** [1952] PBO. Cover by Robert Stanley.	$1.25	$3.75	$7.50
563	Barnes, Margaret Campbell - ***The King's Choice*** [1952]	$1.00	$3.00	$6.00
564	Carr, John Dickson - ***Death-Watch*** [1952] Cover by George Mayers	$1.35	$4.00	$8.00
565	Dodge, David - ***The Red Tassel*** [1952] Cover by Robert Stanley	$1.50	$5.00	$10.00
566	Fontaine, Robert - ***The Happy Time*** [1952] Cover by Sheilah Beckett.	$1.00	$3.00	$6.00
567	Royer, Louis-Charles - ***The Harem*** [1952] Cover by Robert Stanley	$2.50	$7.50	$15.00
568	Parker, Robert - ***Passport To Peril*** [1952] Cover by Robert Stanley	$1.25	$3.75	$7.50
569	Fox, Norman A. - ***Stormy In The West*** [1952] Cover by Robert Stanley.	$1.25	$3.75	$7.50
570	Christie, Agatha - ***The Mysterious Mr. Quin*** [1952] Cover by Robert Jonas	$1.35	$4.00	$8.00
571	Garve, Andrew - ***No Mask For Murder*** [1952] Cover by Robert Stanley.	$1.25	$3.75	$7.50
572	Gowen, Emmett - ***Dark Moon Of March*** [1952] Cover by Victor Kalin.	$1.25	$3.75	$7.50
573	Fox, James M. - ***The Wheel Is Fixed*** [1952] Cover by Willard Downs	$1.25	$3.75	$7.50
574	Baldwin, Faith - ***For Richer, For Poorer*** [1952] Cover by John Fernie	$1.00	$3.00	$6.00
575	Cushman, Dan - ***Montana, Here I Be!*** [1952] Cover by Robert Stanley.	$1.00	$3.00	$6.00
576	Reilly, Helen - ***Murder At Arroways*** [1952] Cover by Eddie Chan.	$1.25	$3.75	$7.50
577	Hamilton, Donald - ***Murder Twice Told*** [1952] Cover by Robert Stanley.	$1.25	$3.75	$7.50
578	Halliday, Brett - ***Framed In Blood*** [1952] Cover by Robert Stanley	$1.25	$3.75	$7.50

		G	VG	F
579	Ames, Delano - ***Nobody Wore Black*** [1952] Cover by Robert Stanley	$1.25	$3.75	$7.50
580	Kane, Henry - ***Until You Are Dead*** [1952] Cover by Victor Kalin	$1.25	$3.75	$7.50
581	Lomax, Bliss - ***The Last Buckaroo*** [1952] Cover by Robert Stanley	$1.00	$3.00	$6.00
582	Bell, Vereen - ***Trial By Marriage*** [1952]	$1.00	$3.00	$6.00
583	Sterling, Stewart - ***Dead Of Night*** [1952] Cover by Willard Downs.	$1.25	$3.75	$7.50
584	Wilkinson, Burke - ***Proceed At Will*** [1952] Cover by Robert Stanley	$1.00	$3.00	$6.00
585	Rinehart, Mary Roberts - ***The Circular Staircase*** [1952] Cover by Robert Stanley.	$1.25	$3.75	$7.50
586	Coxe, George Harmon - ***Dangerous Legacy*** [1952] Cover by Willard Downs.	$1.25	$3.75	$7.50
587	Hendryx, James B. - ***The Stampeders*** [1952] Cover by Robert Stanley	$1.00	$3.00	$6.00
588	Meredith, Anne - ***The Unknown Path*** [1952]	$1.00	$3.00	$6.00
589	Kroll, Harry Harrison - ***The Cabin In The Cotton*** [1952] Cover by Saul Levine.	$1.35	$4.00	$8.00
590	Halliday, Brett - ***Counterfeit Wife*** [1952] Cover by Robert Stanley	$1.25	$3.75	$7.50
591	Boucher, Anthony - ***Rocket To The Morgue*** [1952] Cover by Robert Stanley	$1.50	$5.00	$10.00
592	Ermine, Will - ***Rustlers' Bend*** [1952] Cover by Robert Stanley	$1.25	$3.75	$7.50
593	Presnell, Frank G. - ***Too Hot To Handle*** [1952] Cover by Robert Stanley	$1.00	$3.00	$6.00
594	Fuller, Timothy - ***Keep Cool, Mr. Jones*** [1952] Cover by Robert Stanley.	$1.25	$3.75	$7.50
595	Haden, Allen - ***My Enemy, My Wife*** [1952] Cover by Mike Ludlow.	$1.00	$3.00	$6.00
596	Cannan, Joanna - ***The Taste Of Murder*** [1952] Cover by Willard Downs.	$1.25	$3.75	$7.50
597	Lay, Margaret Rebecca - ***Georgia Girl*** [1952] Cover by Gross.	$1.50	$5.00	$10.00
598	Haycox, Ernest - ***Return Of A Fighter*** [1952] Cover by Robert Stanley.	$1.00	$3.00	$6.00
599	McGivern, William P. - ***Heaven Ran Last*** [1952] Cover by James Meese.	$1.25	$3.75	$7.50
600	de Camp, L. Sprague - ***Rogue Queen*** [1952] Cover by Mike Ludlow.	$5.00	$15.00	$30.00
601	Palmer, Stuart - ***Before It's Too Late*** [1952] Cover by Willard Downs.	$1.25	$3.75	$7.50
602	Hood, Margaret Page - ***Tequila*** [1952] Cover by James Meese.	$1.00	$3.00	$6.00
603	Fair, A. A. - ***Bedrooms Have Windows*** [1952]	$1.25	$3.75	$7.50
604	Sherry, Edna - ***Sudden Fear*** [1952] Cover by James Meese	$1.00	$3.00	$6.00
605	Head, Matthew - ***Congo Venus*** [1952] Cover by Robert Stanley	$1.00	$3.00	$6.00
606	Short, Luke - ***Savage Range*** [1952] Cover by Robert Stanley.	$1.00	$3.00	$6.00
607	Anthology - ***Funny Side Up*** [1952] PBO. Cover by Jaro Fabry. Cartoon and joke book	$1.25	$3.75	$7.50
608	Zola, Emile - ***The Human Beast*** [1952]	$1.35	$4.00	$8.00
609	Lodwick, John - ***Brother Death*** [1952] Cover by Mike Ludlow	$1.00	$3.00	$6.00
610	Walker, Mildred - ***Dr. Norton's Wife*** [1952] Cover by Al Brule	$ .65	$2.00	$4.00
611	Bolles, Blair - ***How To Get Rich In Washington*** [1952] Cover by Jerry Cummins	$ .50	$1.50	$3.00
612	McGerr, Pat - ***Follow As The Night*** [1952] Cover by Phil Marini	$1.00	$3.00	$6.00

		G	VG	F
613	Raine, William MacLeod - ***Saddlebum*** [1952] Cover by Robert Stanley.	$1.00	$3.00	$6.00
614	de Steiguer, Walter - ***Jewels For A Shroud*** [1952] Cover by Ray Pease.	$1.25	$3.75	$7.50
615	Coleman, Lonnie - ***The Sea Is A Woman*** [1952] Cover by James Meese.	$ .75	$2.50	$5.00
616	Halleran, E. E. - ***No Range Is Free*** [1952] Cover by Robert Stanley.	$ .75	$2.50	$5.00
617	Halliday, Brett - ***Dividend On Death*** [1952] Cover by Robert Stanley.	$ .75	$2.50	$5.00
618	Haycox, Ernest - ***Man In The Saddle*** [1952] Cover by Stanley Borack.	$ .75	$2.50	$5.00
619	Fair, A. A. - ***Spill The Jackpot*** [1952]	$ .75	$2.50	$5.00
620	Fair, A. A. - ***Turn On The Heat*** [1952]	$ .75	$2.50	$5.00
621	Reilly, Helen - ***Lament For The Bride*** [1952] Cover by Phil Marini.	$1.00	$3.00	$6.00
622	Yore, Clem - ***Age Of Consent*** [1952] Cover by Robert Stanley.	$ .75	$2.50	$5.00
623	Fox, James M. - ***Fatal In Furs*** [1952] Cover by James Meese.	$1.00	$3.00	$6.00
624	Overholser, Wayne D. - ***Steel To The South*** [1952] Cover by Robert Stanley.	$ .75	$2.50	$5.00
625	Graham, Carroll - ***Border Town*** [1952] Cover by Mike Ludlow.	$ .75	$2.50	$5.00
626	Stout, Rex - ***Three Doors To Death*** [1952] Cover by Rafael Desoto.	$1.25	$3.75	$7.50
627	Wylie, Philip and Balmer, Edwin - ***When Worlds Collide*** [1952] Cover by Robert Stanley.	$2.50	$7.50	$15.00
628	Eberhart, Mignon G. - ***Speak No Evil*** [1952] Cover by Walter Brooks.	$1.00	$3.00	$6.00
629	Raine, William MacLeod - ***Gunsight Pass*** [1952] Cover by Robert Stanley.	$ .75	$2.50	$5.00
630	Moray, Helga - ***Untamed*** [1952]	$ .75	$2.50	$5.00
631	Iams, Jack - ***What Rhymes With Murder?*** [1952] Cover by James Meese.	$1.00	$3.00	$6.00
632	Tompkins, Walker A. - ***Border Ambush*** [1952] Cover by Griffith Foxley.	$ .75	$2.50	$5.00
633	Christie, Agatha - ***Three Blind Mice And Other Stories*** [1952] Cover by Mike Ludlow.	$1.25	$3.75	$7.50
634	Bax, Roger - ***Two If By Sea*** [1952] Cover by Frank McCarthy.	$1.00	$3.00	$6.00
635	Carr, John Dickson - ***To Wake The Dead*** [1952] Cover by Denver Gillen.	$1.25	$3.75	$7.50
636	Austin, Frank - ***Triggerman*** [1952]	$ .75	$2.50	$5.00
637	Wire, Harold Channing - ***Indian Beef*** [1952] Cover by Robert Stanley.	$ .75	$2.50	$5.00
638	Blochman, Lawrence G. - ***See You At The Morgue*** [1952] Cover by Mike Ludlow.	$ .75	$2.50	$5.00
639	Murray, Max - ***Good Luck To The Corpse*** [1952] Cover by James Meese.	$ .75	$2.50	$5.00
640	King-Hall, Magdalen - ***The Life And Death Of The Wicked Lady Skelton*** [1952] Cover by Herman Bischoff.	$1.00	$3.00	$6.00
641	Herrington, Lee - ***Carry My Coffin Slowly*** [1952] Cover by Phil Marini.	$1.00	$3.00	$6.00
642	Fox, Norman A. - ***Tall Man Riding*** [1952] Cover by Moe Gollub.	$ .75	$2.50	$5.00
643	Elston, Allan Vaughan - ***Deadline At Durango*** [1952] Cover by Stanley Borack.	$ .75	$2.50	$5.00
644	Coxe, George Harmon - ***The Fifth Key*** [1952] Cover by James Meese.	$ .75	$2.50	$5.00
645	Yates, George Worthing - ***The Body That Wasn't Uncle*** [1952]	$ .75	$2.50	$5.00

		G	VG	F
646	Presnell, Frank G. - ***No Mourners Present*** [1953] Cover by Robert Stanley	$ .75	$2.50	$5.00
647	Short, Luke - ***King Colt*** [1953] PBO. Cover by Stanley Borack.	$ .75	$2.50	$5.00
648	Prouty, Olive Higgins - ***Fabia*** [1953]	$ .75	$2.50	$5.00
649	Nielsen, Helen - ***The Kind Man*** [1953] Cover by Griffith Foxley	$ .75	$2.50	$5.00
650	Dickson, Carter - ***Night At The Mocking Widow*** [1953] Cover by Bob Hilbert.	$1.35	$4.00	$8.00
651	Albrand, Martha - ***Desperate Moment*** [1953] Cover by Len Oehmen.	$ .75	$2.50	$5.00
652	Rinehart, Mary Roberts - ***The Bat*** [1953] Cover by Walter Brooks.	$ .75	$2.50	$5.00
653	Ermine, Will - ***Outlaw On Horseback*** [1953] Cover by Robert Stanley.	$ .75	$2.50	$5.00
654	Anthology edited by Kathleen Rafferty - ***Dell Crossword Puzzles*** [1953]	$12.50	$37.50	$75.00
655	Garve, Andrew - ***No Tears For Hilda*** [1953] Cover by Phil Marini.	$1.00	$3.00	$6.00
656	Cushman, Dan - ***Badlands Justice*** [1953] Cover by Robert Stanley.	$1.00	$3.00	$6.00
657	Aldridge, James - ***The Hunter*** [1953] Cover by Dale Nichols	$1.00	$3.00	$6.00
658	Dodge, David - ***To Catch A Thief*** [1953] Cover by Mike Ludlow.	$1.00	$3.00	$6.00
659	Hitchens, Delores - ***Stairway To An Empty Room*** [1953] Cover by James Meese.	$1.00	$3.00	$6.00
660	Drago, Harry Sinclair - ***Buckskin Empire*** [1953] Cover by Robert Stanley.	$1.00	$3.00	$6.00
661	Field, Hope - ***Stormy Present*** [1953] Cover by Griffith Foxley.	$ .75	$2.50	$5.00
662	Stanley, Fay Grissom - ***Murder Leaves A Ring*** [1953] Cover by James Meese.	$1.00	$3.00	$6.00
663	Appleby, John - ***The Arms Of Venus*** [1953] Cover by Carl Bobertz.	$ .75	$2.50	$5.00
664	Christie, Agatha - ***The Boomerang Clue*** [1953] Cover by Texidor.	$1.00	$3.00	$6.00
665	Kane, Frank - ***Dead Weight*** [1953] Cover by Bill George.	$1.00	$3.00	$6.00
666	Lomax, Bliss - ***The Law Busters*** [1953] Cover by Robert Stanley.	$ .75	$2.50	$5.00
667	Anthology - ***Four Fallen Women*** [1953] Cover by Morton Roberts.	$1.00	$3.00	$6.00
668	Halliday, Brett - ***Bodies Are Where You Find Them*** [1953] Cover by Robert Stanley. Includes Michael Shayne bibliography by Brett Halliday.	$1.35	$4.00	$8.00
669	Eberhart, Mignon G. - ***Never Look Back*** [1953]	$1.00	$3.00	$6.00
670	Cody, C. S. - ***The Witching Night*** [1953]	$1.00	$3.00	$6.00
671	Day, Jr., John I. and Barber, Rowland - ***1953 Racing Almanac*** [1953]	$ .75	$2.50	$5.00
672	Gault, William Campbell - ***Don't Cry For Me*** [1953] Cover by James Meese.	$1.25	$3.75	$7.50
673	Savage, Jr., Les - ***Treasure Of The Brasada*** [1953] Cover by Stanley Borack.	$1.00	$3.00	$6.00
674	Stout, Rex - ***The Broken Vase*** [1953] Cover by Carl Bobertz.	$1.25	$3.75	$7.50
675	Brean, Herbert - ***Hardly A Man Is Now Alive*** [1953] Cover by Tommy Shoemaker.	$1.00	$3.00	$6.00
676	Milburn, George - ***All Over Town*** [1953] Cover by George Garland.	$1.00	$3.00	$6.00
677	Callahan, John - ***Texas Fury*** [1953] Cover by Robert Stanley	$1.00	$3.00	$6.00
678	Coxe, George Harmon - ***Fashioned For Murder*** [1953] Cover by Fred Scotwood.	$1.25	$3.75	$7.50
679	Hopley, George - ***Night Has 1000 Eyes*** [1953]	$6.00	$20.00	$40.00

		G	VG	F
680	Simak, Clifford D. - ***First He Died*** [1953]	$2.50	$7.50	$15.00
681	Wilde, Oscar - ***The Picture Of Dorian Gray*** [1953] Cover by Griffith Foxley.	$1.50	$5.00	$10.00
682	Deming, Richard - ***The Gallows In My Garden*** [1953] Cover by Bob Hilbert.	$1.35	$4.00	$8.00
683	Christie, Agatha - ***An Overdose Of Death*** [1953] Cover by Carl Bobertz.	$1.35	$4.00	$8.00
684	Ermine, Will - ***The Silver Star*** [1953] Cover by Robert Stanley.	$1.00	$3.00	$6.00
685	Fox, James M. - ***The Scarlet Slippers*** [1953]	$1.00	$3.00	$6.00
686	Blankfort, Michael - ***The Juggler*** [1953] Cover by Michael. Movie tie-in with Kirk Douglas.	$1.50	$5.00	$10.00
687	Roos, Kelley - ***The Frightened Stiff*** [1953] Cover by Len Oehmen.	$1.00	$3.00	$6.00
688	Rhodes, Eugene Manlove - ***The Proud Sheriff*** [1953] Cover by Robert Stanley.	$1.25	$3.75	$7.50
689	Ford, Leslie - ***The Bahamas Murder Case*** [1953] Cover by Mike Ludlow.	$1.25	$3.75	$7.50
690	Dickson, Carter - ***Behind The Crimson Blind*** [1953] Cover by Gail Phillips.	$1.35	$4.00	$8.00
691	Fair, A. A. - ***Bats Fly At Dusk*** [1953] Cover by Robert Stanley.	$1.00	$3.00	$6.00
692	Keyes, Frances Parkinson - ***The River Road*** [1953] Cover by Griffith Foxley.	$1.00	$3.00	$6.00
693	Sterling, Stewart - ***Nightmare At Noon*** [1953] Cover by Bob Hilbert.	$1.35	$4.00	$8.00
694	Fox, Norman A. - ***Roughshod*** [1953] Cover by George Gross.	$1.00	$3.00	$6.00
695	Turney, Catherine - ***The Other One*** [1953] Cover by Bob Hilbert.	$1.00	$3.00	$6.00
696	Van Vogt, A. E. - ***Slan*** [1953]	$2.00	$6.00	$12.00
697	Wiegand, William - ***At Last, Mr. Tolliver*** [1953] Cover by Powers.	$1.00	$3.00	$6.00
698	Ragsdale, Clyde B. - ***The Big Fist*** [1953] Cover by Carl Bobertz.	$1.00	$3.00	$6.00
699	Overholser, Wayne D. - ***Buckaroo's Code*** [1953] Cover by Robert Stanley	$1.00	$3.00	$6.00
700	Polsky, Thomas - ***Curtains For The Copper*** [1953]	$1.00	$3.00	$6.00
701	Green, Alan - ***They Died Laughing*** [1953] Cover by Powers.	$1.00	$3.00	$6.00
702	Short, Luke - ***Bounty Guns*** [1953] PBO. Cover by Stanley Borack.	$1.25	$3.75	$7.50
703	Lamott, Kenneth - ***The Stockade*** [1953] Cover by Griffith Foxley	$1.00	$3.00	$6.00
704	Bentley, E. C. - ***The Chill*** [1953] Cover by Carl Bobertz.	$1.25	$3.75	$7.50
705	Pope, Edith - ***Brutally With Love*** [1953] Cover by Lou Glanzman.	$ .75	$2.50	$5.00
706	Carr, John Dickson - ***The Mad Hatter Mystery*** [1953] Cover by Denver Gillen.	$2.00	$6.00	$12.00
707	Elston, Allan Vaughan - ***Gold Brick Range*** [1953] Cover by Gross.	$1.00	$3.00	$6.00
708	Faulkner, William - ***Mosquitoes*** [1953] Cover by Lou Glanzman.	$2.00	$6.00	$12.00
709	Reilly, Helen - ***Three Women In Black*** [1953] Cover by Griffith Foxley.	$1.00	$3.00	$6.00
710	Quentin, Patrick - ***The Follower*** [1953] Cover by George Geygan.	$1.00	$3.00	$6.00
711	Raine, William MacLeod - ***Challenge To Danger*** [1953] Cover by Robert Stanley.	$1.00	$3.00	$6.00
712	Malamud, Bernard - ***The Natural*** [1953] Cover by Bill George.	$ .75	$2.50	$5.00
713	McMullen, Mary - ***Strangle Hold*** [1953]	$1.00	$3.00	$6.00

		G	VG	F
714	Conrad, Barnaby - ***Matador*** [1953] Cover by Stanley Borack.	$1.00	$3.00	$6.00
715	Palmer, Stuart - ***Four Lost Ladies*** [1953] Cover by Griffith Foxley	$1.25	$3.75	$7.50
716	Dawson, Peter - ***Gunsmoke Graze*** [1953] Cover by Robert Stanley	$1.00	$3.00	$6.00
717	Gallico, Paul - ***Trial By Terror*** [1953] Cover by Walter Brooks.	$1.00	$3.00	$6.00
718	Fair, A. A. - ***Double Or Quits*** [1953] Cover by Fred Scotwood.	$1.00	$3.00	$6.00
719	Fox, James M. - ***The Iron Virgin*** [1953] Cover by Carl Bobertz.	$1.25	$3.75	$7.50
720	Cushman, Dan - ***The Ripper From Rawhide*** [1953] Cover by Robert Stanley	$1.00	$3.00	$6.00
721	Pratt, Theodore - ***Mercy Island*** [1953]	$1.00	$3.00	$6.00
722	Iams, Jack - ***A Shot Of Murder*** [1953]	$1.35	$4.00	$8.00
723	Halliday, Brett - ***When Dorinda Dances*** [1953] Cover by Robert Stanley.	$1.00	$3.00	$6.00
724	Lomax, Bliss - ***Guns Along The Yellowstone*** [1953] Cover by Stanley Borack.	$1.00	$3.00	$6.00
725	Merton, Thomas - ***Seeds Of Contemplation*** [1953]	$1.00	$3.00	$6.00
726	Butler, Gerald - ***Blow Hot, Blow Cold*** [1953] Cover by Griffith Foxley.	$1.00	$3.00	$6.00
727	Gordon, Ian - ***The Burden Of Guilt*** [1953] Cover by Stanley Borack.	$1.00	$3.00	$6.00
728	Falcaro, Joe and Goodman, Murray - ***The Dell Bowling Handbook*** [1953] Photo cover.	$ .75	$2.50	$5.00
729	Overholser, Wayne D. - ***Fabulous Gunman*** [1953] Cover by Bob Stanley.	$1.00	$3.00	$6.00
730	Millar, Margaret - ***Vanish In An Instant*** [1953] Cover by Griffith Foxley.	$1.25	$3.75	$7.50
731	Garnier, Christine - ***Fetish*** [1953] Cover by Griffith Foxley.	$2.00	$6.00	$12.00
732	Reilly, Helen - ***The Double Man*** [1953] Cover by Denver Gillen.	$1.00	$3.00	$6.00
733	Barker, Richard - editor - ***The Fatal Caress*** [1953] Cover by Griffith Foxley.	$1.00	$3.00	$6.00
734	Coxe, George Harmon - ***The Lady Is Afraid*** [1953] Cover by Frank Cazzorelli	$1.00	$3.00	$6.00
735	Kane, Henry - ***A Corpse For Christmas*** [1953] Cover by Griffith Foxley.	$1.35	$4.00	$8.00
736	Gerson, Noel B. - ***The Cumberland Rifles*** [1953] Cover by Carl Mueller.	$1.00	$3.00	$6.00
737	Fox, Norman A. - ***Ghostly Hoofbeats*** [1953] Cover by George Gross.	$1.00	$3.00	$6.00
738	Thompson, Jim - ***Nothing More Than Murder*** [1953] Cover by George Geygan.	$6.00	$20.00	$40.00
739	Proctor, Maurice - ***Hurry The Darkness*** [1953]	$1.00	$3.00	$6.00
740	Blochman, Lawrence G. - ***Blow-Down*** [1953] Cover by Griffith Foxley.	$1.00	$3.00	$6.00
741	Conant, Paul - ***Dr. Gatskill's Blue Shoes*** [1953] Cover by Carl Bobertz.	$ .75	$2.50	$5.00
742	Elston, Allan Vaughan - ***Colorado Showdown*** [1953] Cover by Robert Stanley.	$1.00	$3.00	$6.00
743	Halliday, Brett - ***Mum's The Word For Murder*** [1953] Cover by Bill George.	$1.00	$3.00	$6.00
744	Gilbert, Michael - ***Death Has Deep Roots*** [1953] Cover by E. Harper Johnson.	$1.25	$3.75	$7.50
745	Coxe, George Harmon - ***Venturous Lady*** [1953] Cover by Griffith Foxley.	$1.00	$3.00	$6.00
746	Gault, William Campbell - ***The Bloody Bokhara*** [1953] Cover by Griffith Foxley.	$1.00	$3.00	$6.00

		G	VG	F
747	Nielson, Helen - ***Dead On The Level*** [1953] Cover by Carl Bobertz.	$1.00	$3.00	$6.00
748	Haycox, Ernest - ***Trail Town*** [1954] Cover by Robert Stanley.	$1.00	$3.00	$6.00
749	Kane, Frank - ***Bare Trap*** [1954] Cover by Carl Bobertz.	$1.25	$3.75	$7.50
750	Holt, Felix - ***The Gabriel Horn*** [1954]	$1.00	$3.00	$6.00
751	Appleby, John - ***Barbary Hoard*** [1954] Cover by Griffith Foxley	$1.25	$3.75	$7.50
752	Fischer, Bruno - ***The Spider Lily*** [1954] Cover by Griffith Foxley	$1.25	$3.75	$7.50
753	Christie, Agatha - ***Murder After Hours*** [1954] Cover by Griffith Foxley	$1.25	$3.75	$7.50
754	Anthology edited by Bill Yates - ***Laughing On The Inside*** [1954] PBO. Cover by Mischa Richter. Cartoon and joke book	$1.25	$3.75	$7.50
755	Halleran, E. E. - ***Smoky Range*** [1954] Cover by Griffith Foxley	$1.00	$3.00	$6.00
756	Siodmak, Curt - ***Whomsoever I Shall Kiss*** [1954]	$1.50	$5.00	$10.00
757	Coxe, George Harmon - ***The Hollow Needle*** [1954]	$1.25	$3.75	$7.50
758	Brean, Herbert - ***The Clock Strikes 13*** [1954] Cover by Griffith Foxley.	$1.25	$3.75	$7.50
759	Quentin, Patrick - ***Black Widow*** [1954] Cover by Bill George.	$1.25	$3.75	$7.50
760	Judd, Cyril - ***Outpost Mars*** [1954] Cover by Richard Powers.	$2.00	$6.00	$12.00
761	Lewin, M.D., S.A. & Gilmore, Ph.D., John - ***Sex After 40*** [1954]	$ .75	$2.50	$5.00
762	Treynor, Blair - ***Silver Doll*** [1954] Cover by Stanley Borack.	$1.25	$3.75	$7.50
763	Ellin, Stanley - ***The Key To Nicholas Street*** [1954] Cover by Verne Tossey.	$1.25	$3.75	$7.50
764	Tompkins, Walker A. - ***Prairie Marshal*** [1954]	$1.00	$3.00	$6.00
765	Garve, Andrew - ***By-Line For Murder*** [1954] Cover by Robert Stanley.	$1.25	$3.75	$7.50
766	Wilson, John H. - ***Nell Gwyn: Royal Mistress*** [1954]	$ .75	$2.50	$5.00
767	Eberhart, Mignon G. - ***Dead Men's Plans*** [1954] Cover by Powers.	$1.25	$3.75	$7.50
768	Halliday, Brett - ***What Really Happened*** [1954] Cover by Robert Stanley	$1.25	$3.75	$7.50
769	Short, Luke - ***Brand Of Empire*** [1954] PBO. Cover by Stanley Borack.	$1.25	$3.75	$7.50
770	Christie, Agatha - ***Thirteen At Dinner*** [1954] Cover by Griffith Foxley.	$1.25	$3.75	$7.50
771	Waugh, Evelyn - ***The Loved One*** [1954]	$ .75	$2.50	$5.00
772	Fair, A. A. - ***Top Of The Heap*** [1954] Cover by Griffith Foxley	$1.00	$3.00	$6.00
773	Root, Pat - ***Evil Became Them*** [1954] Cover by Griffith Foxley	$1.00	$3.00	$6.00
774	Snead, Sam - ***Sam Snead's Natural Golf*** [1954]	$ .75	$2.50	$5.00
775	Carr, John Dickson - ***The Corpse In The Wax Works*** [1954] Cover by Richard Powers	$1.50	$5.00	$10.00
776	Cunningham, Eugene - ***Gun Bulldogger*** [1954] Cover by Robert Stanley.	$1.00	$3.00	$6.00
777	Allingham, Margery - ***The Tiger In The Smoke*** [1954]	$1.00	$3.00	$6.00
778	Fair, A. A. - ***Crows Can't Count*** [1954] Cover by Arthur Sussman.	$1.00	$3.00	$6.00
779	Hitchens, Dolores - ***Widows Won't Wait*** [1954] Cover by Griffith Foxley	$1.00	$3.00	$6.00
780	Young, Gordon - ***Tall In The Saddle*** [1954] Cover by Robert Stanley	$1.00	$3.00	$6.00
781	Carr, Robert Spencer - ***Beyond Infinity*** [1954] Cover by Richard Powers.	$1.50	$5.00	$10.00
782	Rinehart, Mary Roberts - ***The Red Lamp*** [1954] Cover by Griffith Foxley.	$1.00	$3.00	$6.00

		G	VG	F
783	Fox, Norman A. - ***Long Lightning*** [1954] Cover by Norton Stewart.	$1.00	$3.00	$6.00
784	Olsen, D. B. - ***Dead Babes In The Wood*** [1954] Cover by Griffith Foxley.	$1.00	$3.00	$6.00
785	Kane, Frank - ***Bullet Proof*** [1954] Cover by Robert Stanley.	$1.00	$3.00	$6.00
786	Darrow, Jr., Whitney - ***Hold It, Florence*** [1954] PBO. Cover by author. Cartoon book.	$ .75	$2.50	$5.00
787	Clewes, Harold - ***The Long Memory*** [1954] Cover by Frank Cazzorelli.	$1.00	$3.00	$6.00
788	Ford, Leslie - ***Murder Is The Pay-Off*** [1954] Cover by Carl Bobertz.	$1.00	$3.00	$6.00
789	Drago, Harry Sinclair - ***Stagecoach Kingdom*** [1954]	$1.00	$3.00	$6.00
790	Stone, Hampton - ***The Corpse That Refused To Stay Dead*** [1954]	$1.25	$3.75	$7.50
791	Tucker, Wilson - ***The Long Loud Silence*** [1954] Cover by Richard Powers.	$2.00	$6.00	$12.00
792	Kiely, Benedict - ***The Evil Men Do*** [1954]	$1.25	$3.75	$7.50
793	Raine, William MacLeod - ***The Bandit Trail*** [1954] Cover by Robert Stanley.	$1.00	$3.00	$6.00
794	Martin, Robert - ***Sleep, My Love*** [1954] Cover by Griffith Foxley	$1.00	$3.00	$6.00
795	Gault, William Campbell - ***The Canvas Coffin*** [1954]	$1.25	$3.75	$7.50
796	Overholser, Wayne D. - ***West Of The Rimrock*** [1954] Cover by Robert Stanley.	$1.00	$3.00	$6.00
797	Anthology edited by Allan Bernard - ***The Harlot Killer*** [1954] "Jack the Ripper" stories. Cover by Bill George.	$2.50	$7.50	$15.00
798	Hill, Janet McKenzie & Larkin, Sally - ***Cooking For Two*** [1954]	$1.35	$4.00	$8.00
799	Coxe, George Harmon - ***Inland Passage*** [1954] Cover by Carl Bobertz.	$1.00	$3.00	$6.00
800	James, Henry - ***The Turn Of The Screw And Daisy Miller*** [1954] Cover by Walter Brooks.	$1.00	$3.00	$6.00
801	Lomax, Bliss - ***Riders Of The Buffalo Grass*** [1954] Cover by Robert Stanley.	$1.00	$3.00	$6.00
802	Seabrook, William - ***Asylum*** [1954] Cover by Richard Powers.	$1.00	$3.00	$6.00
803	Halliday, Brett - ***One Night With Nora*** [1954] Cover by Robert Stanley.	$1.00	$3.00	$6.00
804	Nye, Nelson - ***Wide Loop*** [1954] Cover by Robert Stanley	$1.00	$3.00	$6.00
805	Christie, Agatha - ***Murder In Mesopotamia*** [1954] Cover by Griffith Foxley.	$1.00	$3.00	$6.00
806	Nielsen, Helen - ***Obit Delayed*** [1954] Cover by John McDermott.	$1.00	$3.00	$6.00
807	Waugh, Evelyn - ***Vile Bodies*** [1954] Cover by Sheilah Beckett.	$1.00	$3.00	$6.00
808	Fenisong, Ruth - ***Deadlock*** [1954] Cover by John McDermott.	$1.00	$3.00	$6.00
809	Fair, A. A. - ***Some Women Won't Wait*** [1955] Cover by Griffith Foxley.	$1.00	$3.00	$6.00
810	Elston, Allan Vaughan - ***Roundup On The Picketwire*** [1955] Cover by Robert Stanley.	$1.00	$3.00	$6.00
811	Eberhart, Mignon G. - ***The Unknown Quantity*** [1955] Cover by Stanley Borack.	$1.25	$3.75	$7.50
812	Wellard, James - ***Deep Is The Night*** [1955] Cover by Erickson.	$1.00	$3.00	$6.00
813	Bingham, John - ***My Name Is Michael Sibley*** [1955] Cover by William Rose.	$1.00	$3.00	$6.00
814	Rinehart, Mary Roberts - ***Haunted Lady*** [1955] Cover by Bill George.	$1.00	$3.00	$6.00
815	Overholser, Wayne D. - ***Valley Of Guns*** [1955] Cover by Robert Stanley.	$1.00	$3.00	$6.00
816	Sterling, Stewart - ***Five Alarm Funeral*** [1955]	$1.00	$3.00	$6.00

		G	VG	F
817	Fischer, Bruno - ***The Pigskin Bag*** [1955] Cover by Bill George.	$1.00	$3.00	$6.00
818	Shearing, Joseph - ***The Golden Violet*** [1955]	$1.00	$3.00	$6.00
819	Chesterton, G. K. - ***The Amazing Adventures Of Father Brown*** [1955] Cover by Denver Gillen.	$1.35	$4.00	$8.00
820	Thurber, James and White, E. B. - ***Is Sex Necessary?*** [1955] Cover by James Thurber.	$ .75	$2.50	$5.00
821	Raine, William MacLeod - ***Riders Of Buck River*** [1955] Cover by Robert Stanley.	$1.00	$3.00	$6.00
822	Kane, Frank - ***Poisons Unknown*** [1955] Cover by William George.	$1.25	$3.75	$7.50
823	Davis, Dorothy Salisbury - ***A Town Of Masks*** [1955] Cover by William George.	$1.00	$3.00	$6.00
824	McCarthy, Mary - ***The Company She Keeps*** [1955] Cover by Maguire.	$1.25	$3.75	$7.50
825	Foreman, L. L. - ***Gunfire Men*** [1955]	$1.00	$3.00	$6.00
826	Short, Luke - ***Savage Range*** [1955] Cover by Robert Stanley.	$1.00	$3.00	$6.00
827	Garve, Andrew - ***Murder Through The Looking Glass*** [1955] Cover by William George.	$1.00	$3.00	$6.00
828	Colt, Clem - ***Strawberry Roan*** [1955]	$1.00	$3.00	$6.00
829	Halliday, Brett - ***Before I Wake*** [1955] Cover by Shulz.	$1.00	$3.00	$6.00
830	Christie, Agatha - ***There Is A Tide*** [1955] Cover by William Rose.	$1.00	$3.00	$6.00
831	Fox, Norman A. - ***The Rawhide Years*** [1955]	$1.00	$3.00	$6.00
832	Dawson, Peter - ***The Stirrup Boss*** [1955]	$1.00	$3.00	$6.00
833	Blochman, Lawrence G. - ***Recipe For Homicide*** [1955]	$1.00	$3.00	$6.00
834	Wilson, William E. - ***The Strangers*** [1955]	$1.00	$3.00	$6.00
835	Gault, William Campbell - ***Blood On The Boards*** [1955] Cover by Don Neiser.	$1.25	$3.75	$7.50
836	Fair, A. A. - ***Gold Comes In Bricks*** [1955] Cover by William George.	$1.00	$3.00	$6.00
837	Nielsen, Helen - ***Detour To Death*** [1955] Cover by Robert Stanley.	$1.00	$3.00	$6.00
838	Coxe, George Harmon - ***The Frightened Fiancee*** [1955] Cover by William Rose.	$1.00	$3.00	$6.00
839	Meany, Tom - ***Baseball's Greatest Players*** [1955] Photo cover.	$3.00	$9.00	$18.00
840	Martin, A. E. - ***The Bridal Bed Murders*** [1955] Cover by William Rose.	$1.00	$3.00	$6.00
841	Berckman, Evelyn - ***The Evil Of Time*** [1955] Cover by William Rose.	$1.00	$3.00	$6.00
842	Halliday, Brett - ***The Corpse Came Calling*** [1955] Cover by Robert Schulz.	$1.00	$3.00	$6.00
843	Partch, Virgil Franklin - ***Man The Beast And The Wild, Wild Women*** [1955] Cover by author. Cartoon book.	$ .75	$2.50	$5.00
844	Turner, William O. - ***The Proud Diggers*** [1955] Cover by Robert Stanley.	$1.00	$3.00	$6.00
845	Fox, James M. - ***Death Commits Bigamy*** [1955] Cover by Mike Privatello.	$1.00	$3.00	$6.00
846	Overholser, Wayne D. - ***Tough Hand*** [1955] Cover by Robert Schulz.	$1.00	$3.00	$6.00
847	March, William - ***The Bad Seed*** [1955] Cover by Lawrence S. Kamp.	$1.00	$3.00	$6.00
848	Bagby, George - ***Give The Little Corpse A Great Big Hand*** [1955] Cover by Victor Kalin.	$1.25	$3.75	$7.50
849	Roan, Tom - ***Wyoming Gun*** [1955] Cover by Robert Stanley.	$1.00	$3.00	$6.00
850	Roth, Holly - ***The Shocking Secret*** [1955] Cover by William Rose.	$1.00	$3.00	$6.00
851	Quentin, Patrick - ***Run To Death*** [1955] Cover by William George.	$1.00	$3.00	$6.00

		G	VG	F
852	St. Laurent, Cecil - ***The Affairs Of Caroline Cherie*** [1955] Cover by Freeman Elliot.	$ .75	$2.50	$5.00
853	Hughes, Dorothy B. - ***The Body On The Bench*** [1955] Cover by William George.	$1.00	$3.00	$6.00
854	Scott, J. M. - ***Heather Mary*** [1955] Cover by Raymond Pease.	$1.00	$3.00	$6.00
855	Christie, Agatha - ***The Witness For The Prosecution*** [1955] Cover by William George.	$1.00	$3.00	$6.00
856	Sloane, William - ***To Walk The Night*** [1955] Cover by William Rose.	$1.25	$3.75	$7.50
857	Bird, Brandon - ***Dead And Gone*** [1955] Cover by William George.	$1.00	$3.00	$6.00
858	Bosworth, Allan R. - ***Bury Me Not*** [1955] Cover by Tom Ryan.	$1.00	$3.00	$6.00
859	Carr, John Dickson - ***The Crooked Hinge*** [1955] Cover by William George.	$1.35	$4.00	$8.00
860	DuBois, Theodora - ***Seeing Red*** [1956] Cover by William George.	$1.00	$3.00	$6.00
861	Elston, Allan Vaughan - ***Saddle Up For Sunlight*** [1956] Cover by Robert Stanley.	$1.00	$3.00	$6.00
862	Anthology edited by Harold "Red" Grange - ***My Favorite Football Stories*** [1956] Photo cover.	$1.00	$3.00	$6.00
863	Leonard, Elmore - ***The Law At Randado*** [1956] Cover by George Gross.	$5.50	$17.50	$35.00
864	Fox, Norman A. - ***The Thirsty Land*** [1956] Cover by Robert Stanley.	$1.00	$3.00	$6.00
865	Halliday, Brett - ***Death Has Three Lives*** [1956] Cover by William George.	$1.00	$3.00	$6.00
866	Halliday, Brett - ***Michael Shayne's Long Chance*** [1956] Cover by Robert Stanley.	$1.00	$3.00	$6.00
867	Halliday, Brett - ***She Woke To Darkness*** [1956] Cover by Robert Schulz.	$1.00	$3.00	$6.00
868	Gault, Bill - ***Run, Killer, Run*** [1956] Cover by Stanley Borack.	$1.25	$3.75	$7.50
869	Short, Luke - ***Bounty Guns*** [1956] Cover by Stanley Borack.	$1.00	$3.00	$6.00
870	Gilbert, Michael - ***The Danger Within*** [1956] Cover by Robert Stanley.	$1.00	$3.00	$6.00
871	Christie, Agatha - ***Murder In Retrospect*** [1956] Cover by William George.	$1.00	$3.00	$6.00
872	Lichty, George - ***Grin And Bear It*** [1956] Cartoon book.	$1.35	$4.00	$8.00
873	Bingham, John - ***The Tender Poisoner*** [1956] Cover by William George.	$1.25	$3.75	$7.50
874	Masur, Harold Q. - ***The Big Money*** [1956] Cover by Seymour Chwast.	$1.00	$3.00	$6.00
875	Overholser, Wayne D. - ***The Violent Land*** [1956] Cover by William George.	$1.00	$3.00	$6.00
876	Hendryx, James B. - ***The Long Chase*** [1956] Cover by Stanley Borack.	$1.00	$3.00	$6.00
877	Eberhart, Mignon G. - ***Man Missing*** [1956] Cover by Bill George.	$1.00	$3.00	$6.00
878	Brown, Will C. - ***The Border Jumpers*** [1956] Cover by Robert Stanley.	$1.00	$3.00	$6.00
879	Tompkins, Walker A. - ***Gold On The Hoof*** [1956]	$1.00	$3.00	$6.00
880	Hood, Margaret Page - ***The Silent Women*** [1956] Cover by William George.	$1.00	$3.00	$6.00
881	Brand, Christianna - ***Fog Of Doubt*** [1956]	$1.00	$3.00	$6.00
882	Reese, John - ***The High Passes*** [1956]	$1.00	$3.00	$6.00
883	Stone, Hampton - ***The Murder That Wouldn't Stay Solved*** [1956] Cover by William Rose.	$1.25	$3.75	$7.50
884	McCaig, Robert - ***Danger West!*** [1956]	$1.00	$3.00	$6.00

		G	VG	F
885	Disney, Doris Miles - ***Straw Man*** [1956] Cover by William George.	$1.00	$3.00	$6.00
886	Kane, Frank - ***Grave Danger*** [1956] Cover by Victor Kalin.	$1.00	$3.00	$6.00
887	Welty, Eudora - ***The Ponder Heart*** [1956] Cover by Joe Krush.	$ .75	$2.50	$5.00
888	Christie, Agatha - ***The Murder At The Vicarage*** [1956] Cover by Milton Glaser.	$1.00	$3.00	$6.00
889	Raine, William MacLeod - ***Trail's End*** [1956] Cover by Robert Stanley.	$1.00	$3.00	$6.00
890	Quentin, Patrick - ***My Son, The Murderer*** [1956] Cover by Walter Brooks.	$1.00	$3.00	$6.00
891	Halliday, Brett - ***Blood On The Stars*** [1956] Cover by Robert Stanley.	$1.00	$3.00	$6.00
892	Appell, George C. - ***Quick On The Shoot*** [1956]	$1.00	$3.00	$6.00
893	Dean, Spencer - ***The Frightened Fingers*** [1956] Cover by William George.	$1.00	$3.00	$6.00
894	Browne, Howard - ***Thin Air*** [1956] Cover by William George.	$1.00	$3.00	$6.00
895	Short, Luke - ***Raw Land*** [1956] Cover by Robert Stanley.	$1.00	$3.00	$6.00
896	Cameron, Owen - ***The Butcher's Wife*** [1956] Cover by William Rose.	$1.00	$3.00	$6.00
897	Loomis, Noel M. - ***The Twilighters*** [1956] Cover by George Gross.	$1.00	$3.00	$6.00
898	Williams, Charles - ***Gulf Coast Girl*** [1956] Cover by McGuire.	$1.35	$4.00	$8.00
899	Fair, A. A. - ***Cats Prowl At Night*** [1956] Photo cover.	$1.00	$3.00	$6.00
900	Nielsen, Helen - ***The Woman On The Roof*** [1956] Cover by William George.	$1.00	$3.00	$6.00
901	Kane, Frank - ***Red Hot Ice*** [1956] Cover by Victor Kalin.	$1.25	$3.75	$7.50
902	Coxe, George Harmon - ***Eye Witness*** [1956] Photo cover.	$1.00	$3.00	$6.00
903	Overholser, Wayne D. - ***Draw Or Drag*** [1956] Cover by George Gross.	$1.00	$3.00	$6.00
904	Bagby, George - ***The Body In The Basket*** [1956] Cover by Art Sussman.	$1.00	$3.00	$6.00
905	Halliday, Brett - ***In A Deadly Vein*** [1956] Cover by Robert Stanley.	$1.00	$3.00	$6.00
906	Wells, Lee - ***Day Of The Outlaw*** [1956] Cover by Robert Stanley.	$1.00	$3.00	$6.00
907	Fox, Norman A. - ***Shadow On The Range*** [1956] Cover by George Gross.	$1.00	$3.00	$6.00
908	Ford, Leslie - ***Washington Whispers Murder*** [1956] Cover by William Rose.	$1.00	$3.00	$6.00
909	Spicer, Bart - ***The Day Of The Dead*** [1956] Cover by Arthur Sussman.	$1.00	$3.00	$6.00
910	Fischer, Bruno - ***The Restless Hands*** [1956]	$1.00	$3.00	$6.00
911	Vanway, Ed La - ***Lazy H Feud*** [1956] Cover by Robert Stanley.	$1.00	$3.00	$6.00
912	Christie, Agatha - ***Cards On The Table*** [1956] Cover by Milton Glaser.	$1.00	$3.00	$6.00
913	Catlin, Ralph - ***Good-By To Gunsmoke*** [1956] Cover by Robert Stanley.	$1.00	$3.00	$6.00
914	Halliday, Brett - ***Stranger In Town*** [1956] Cover by Robert Stanley.	$1.00	$3.00	$6.00
915	Powell, Richard - ***Masterpiece Of Murder*** [1956] Cover by Arthur Sussman.	$1.00	$3.00	$6.00
916	Ermine, Will - ***Last Of The Longhorns*** [1956] Cover by Robert Stanley.	$1.00	$3.00	$6.00
917	Reilly, Helen - ***The Opening Door*** [1956] Cover by Victor Kalin.	$1.00	$3.00	$6.00
918	Kane, Frank - ***Green Light For Death*** [1956] Cover by Victor Kalin.	$1.35	$4.00	$8.00
919	Drago, Harry Sinclair - ***Their Guns Were Fast*** [1956]	$1.00	$3.00	$6.00

		G	VG	F
920	Millar, Margaret - ***The Lively Corpse*** [1956] Cover by Victor Kalin.	$1.00	$3.00	$6.00
921	Saint-Laurent, Cecil - ***The Cautious Maiden*** [1957]	$1.00	$3.00	$6.00
922	Hardin, Peter - ***The Hidden Grave*** [1957] Cover by Denver Gillen.	$1.00	$3.00	$6.00
923	Whitman, S. E. - ***Scout Commander*** [1957] Cover by Nick Eggenhofer.	$ .75	$2.50	$5.00
924	Overholser, Wayne D. - ***Cast A Long Shadow*** [1957]	$1.00	$3.00	$6.00
925	Chamberlain, Anne - ***The Tall Dark Man*** [1957] Cover by Victor Kalin.	$1.00	$3.00	$6.00
926	Gault, Bill - ***Murder In The Raw*** [1957] Cover by Victor Kalin.	$1.00	$3.00	$6.00
927	Fox, Norman A. - ***Stormy In The West*** [1957] Cover by George Gross.	$1.00	$3.00	$6.00
928	Sloane, William - ***The Unquiet Corpse*** [1957] Cover by Harry Schaare.	$1.00	$3.00	$6.00
929	Disney, Doris Miles - ***Dead Stop*** [1957] Cover by William Rose.	$1.00	$3.00	$6.00
930	Keene, James - ***The Texas Pistol*** [1957] Cover by Robert Stanley.	$1.25	$3.75	$7.50
931	Coxe, George Harmon - ***Never Bet Your Life*** [1957]	$1.00	$3.00	$6.00
932	Ermine, Will - ***Rustlers' Bend*** [1957] Cover by Robert Stanley.	$1.00	$3.00	$6.00
933	Sherry, Edna - ***Murder At Nightfall*** [1957] Cover by Victor Kalin.	$1.00	$3.00	$6.00
934	Halliday, Brett - ***A Taste For Violence*** [1957] Cover by Robert Stanley.	$1.00	$3.00	$6.00
935	Cunningham, Eugene - ***Border Guns*** [1957] Cover by Robert Stanley.	$1.00	$3.00	$6.00
936	Berckman, Evelyn - ***Worse Than Murder*** [1957] Cover by Arthur Sussman.	$1.25	$3.75	$7.50
937	Christie, Agatha - ***Murder At Hazelmoor*** [1957] Cover by Milton Glaser.	$1.00	$3.00	$6.00
938	Dawson, Peter - ***Renegade Canyon*** [1957]	$1.00	$3.00	$6.00
939	Fair, A. A. - ***Fools Die On Friday*** [1957] Cover by Victor Kalin.	$1.00	$3.00	$6.00
940	Leonard, Elmore - ***Escape From Five Shadows*** [1957] Cover by Harper Johnson.	$5.50	$17.50	$35.00
941	Bingham, John - ***Murder Is A Witch*** [1957] Cover by Powers.	$1.00	$3.00	$6.00
942	Lomax, Bliss - ***Sagebrush Bandit*** [1957] Cover by George Gross.	$1.00	$3.00	$6.00
943	Stone, Hampton - ***The Man Who Had Too Much To Lose*** [1957] Cover by Al Brule.	$1.00	$3.00	$6.00
944	Masur, Harold Q. - ***Bury Me Deep*** [1957] Cover by Victor Kalin.	$1.00	$3.00	$6.00
945	Haycox, Ernest - ***Alder Gulch*** [1957] Cover by George Gross.	$1.35	$4.00	$8.00
946	Halliday, Brett - ***The Blonde Cried Murder*** [1957] PBO.	$1.25	$3.75	$7.50
947	Turner, William O. - ***The Settler*** [1957]	$1.00	$3.00	$6.00
948	Overholser, Wayne D. - ***Steel To The South*** [1957]	$1.00	$3.00	$6.00
949	Bagby, George - ***Dead Storage*** [1957] Cover by Al Brule.	$1.00	$3.00	$6.00
950	Fox, Norman A. - ***Night Passage*** [1957] Cover by Victor Kalin. Movie tie-in.	$1.00	$3.00	$6.00
951	Shepherd, Eric - ***Murder In A Nunnery*** [1957] Cover by Richard Powers.	$1.00	$3.00	$6.00
952	Haycox, Ernest - ***Man In The Saddle*** [1957]	$1.00	$3.00	$6.00
953	Moseley, Dana - ***Dead Of Summer*** [1957] Cover by Al Brule.	$ .75	$2.50	$5.00
954	Raine, William MacLeod - ***To Ride The River With*** [1957] Cover by Sam Bates.	$1.00	$3.00	$6.00
955	Eberhart, Mignon G. - ***Postmark Murder*** [1957]	$ .75	$2.50	$5.00
956	Cunningham, Eugene - ***Riding Gun*** [1957]	$1.00	$3.00	$6.00

		G	VG	F
957	Halliday, Brett - ***This Is It, Michael Shayne*** [1957]	$1.00	$3.00	$6.00
958	Halliday, Brett - ***Framed In Blood*** [1957]	$1.00	$3.00	$6.00
959	Keene, James - ***The Brass And The Blue*** [1957]	$1.00	$3.00	$6.00
960	Halliday, Brett - ***Murder And The Married Virgin*** [1957]	$1.00	$3.00	$6.00
961	Christie, Agatha - ***Mr. Parker Pyne, Detective*** [1957]	$1.00	$3.00	$6.00
962	Short, Luke - ***King Colt*** [1957]	$1.00	$3.00	$6.00
963	Short, Luke - ***Savage Range*** [1957] Cover by Sam Bates.	$1.00	$3.00	$6.00
964	Simenon, Georges - ***Inspector Maigret And The Burglar's Wife*** [1957]	$1.25	$3.75	$7.50
965	Halliday, Brett - ***Murder Is My Business*** [1958]	$1.00	$3.00	$6.00
966	O'Rourke, Frank - ***The Diamond Hitch*** [1958]	$1.00	$3.00	$6.00
967	Lomax, Bliss - ***Secret Of The Wastelands*** [1958] Cover by George Gross.	$1.00	$3.00	$6.00
968	Roos, Kelley - ***The Blonde Died Dancing*** [1958] Cover by Victor Kalin.	$1.00	$3.00	$6.00
969	Fox, Norman A. - ***Stranger From Arizona*** [1958]	$1.00	$3.00	$6.00
970	Coxe, George Harmon - ***Focus On Murder*** [1958] Photo cover.	$1.00	$3.00	$6.00
971	Nielsen, Helen - ***Seven Days Before Dying*** [1958] Cover by R. Del Rossi.	$1.00	$3.00	$6.00
972	Overholser, Wayne D. - ***Gunlock*** [1958] Cover by Robert Stanley.	$1.00	$3.00	$6.00
973	Kane, Frank - ***The Fatal Foursome*** [1958] Cover by Victor Kalin.	$1.00	$3.00	$6.00
974	Olson, Gene - ***Stampede At Blue Springs*** [1958] Cover by Robert Stanley	$1.00	$3.00	$6.00
975	Haycox, Ernest - ***Return Of A Fighter*** [1958] Cover by Gerald McConnell.	$1.00	$3.00	$6.00
976	Anthology edited by Juliet Lowell - ***Dear Doctor*** [1958] Cover by Howard Baer. Cartoon and joke book.	$ .75	$2.50	$5.00
977	Boileau, Pierre & Narcejac, Thomas - ***Vertigo*** [1958] Cover by Maguire. Movie tie-in.	$2.50	$7.50	$15.00
978	Halliday, Brett - ***Weep For A Blonde*** [1958] Photo cover.	$1.00	$3.00	$6.00
979	Sumner, Nick - ***Bullet Brand*** [1958]	$1.00	$3.00	$6.00
980	Fox, Norman A. - ***Tall Man Riding*** [1958]	$1.00	$3.00	$6.00
981	Halliday, Brett - ***The Uncomplaining Corpses*** [1958]	$1.00	$3.00	$6.00
982	Potts, Jean - ***The Diehard*** [1958] Cover by Powers.	$1.00	$3.00	$6.00
983	Cameron, Owen - ***The Demon Stirs*** [1958]	$1.00	$3.00	$6.00
984	Coxe, George Harmon - ***Man On A Rope*** [1958] Cover by Schaare.	$1.00	$3.00	$6.00
985	Creasey, John - ***So Young, So Cold, So Fair*** [1958]	$1.00	$3.00	$6.00
986	Brown, Will C. - ***Man Of The West*** [1958] Cover by George Gross. Movie tie-in.	$1.25	$3.75	$7.50
987	Halliday, Brett - ***Heads You Lose*** [1958] Cover by Robert Stanley.	$1.00	$3.00	$6.00
988	Halliday, Brett - ***Shoot The Works*** [1958] Cover by Robert Stanley.	$1.00	$3.00	$6.00
989	Halliday, Brett - ***Tickets For Death*** [1958] Cover by Robert Stanley.	$1.00	$3.00	$6.00
990	Partch, Virgil Franklin - ***Here We Go Again And Bottle Fatigue*** [1958] Cover by Vip. Cartoon book.	$1.25	$3.75	$7.50
991	Ard, William - ***Deadly Beloved*** [1958] Cover by Victor Kalin.	$1.35	$4.00	$8.00
992	Monig, Christopher - ***Don't Count The Corpses*** [1958] Cover by Robert McGinnis.	$1.00	$3.00	$6.00
993	Overholser, Wayne D. - ***Desperate Man*** [1958]	$1.00	$3.00	$6.00
994	Appleby, John - ***Grounds For Murder*** [1958]	$1.00	$3.00	$6.00
995	Hardy, William - ***Lady Killer*** [1958] Cover by Victor Kalin.	$1.00	$3.00	$6.00
996	Olesker, Harry - ***Now, Will You Try For Murder?*** [1959] Cover by McGinnis.	$1.00	$3.00	$6.00
997	Bagby, George - ***Cop Killer*** [1959] Cover by James Hill.	$1.00	$3.00	$6.00

		G	VG	F
998	Berenstain, Stanley and Janice - ***Lover Boy*** [1959]	$1.25	$3.75	$7.50
999	Malcolm-Smith, George - ***The Trouble With Fidelity*** [1959] Cover by William Teodecki.	$1.00	$3.00	$6.00
1000	Keene, James - ***Justice, My Brother!*** [1959] Cover by Robert Abbett	$1.00	$3.00	$6.00
1001	Lowell, Juliet - ***Dear Hollywood*** [1959] Cover by Bill Yates.	$1.25	$3.75	$7.50
1002	Fox, Norman A. - ***The Badlands Beyond*** [1959] Cover by Robert Stanley	$1.00	$3.00	$6.00
1003	Roberts, Lee - ***Once A Widow*** [1959] Cover by Robert McGinnis	$1.00	$3.00	$6.00
1004	Sherry, Edna - ***She Asked For Murder*** [1959] Cover by Robert McGinnis.	$1.00	$3.00	$6.00
1005	Lomax, Bliss - ***Stranger With A Gun*** [1959]	$1.00	$3.00	$6.00
1006	Hougron, Jean - ***Trapped*** [1959] Cover by Bob Schulz.	$1.00	$3.00	$6.00
1007	Keith, Carlton - ***A Gem Of A Murder*** [1959] Cover by Harry Schaare.	$1.00	$3.00	$6.00
1008	Overholser, Wayne D. - ***The Lone Deputy*** [1959] Cover by Robert Stanley	$1.00	$3.00	$6.00
1009	Olson, Gene - ***Last Night At Black Hammer*** [1960] Cover by John Leone.	$1.00	$3.00	$6.00
1010	Lomax, Bliss - ***Last Call For A Gunfighter*** [1960] Cover by John Leone.	$1.00	$3.00	$6.00
1012	Gault, Bill - ***Death Out Of Focus*** [1960] Cover by Robert McGinnis	$1.00	$3.00	$6.00
1013	Bohle, Edgar - ***The Man Who Disappeared*** [1960] Cover by William Rose.	$1.00	$3.00	$6.00
1014	Fox, Norman A. - ***Roughshod*** [1960]	$1.00	$3.00	$6.00
1019	Lowell, Juliet - ***Dear Justice*** [1960] Cover by Bill Yates	$1.25	$3.75	$7.50
1020	Fox, Norman A. - ***Rope The Wind*** [1960] Cover by John Leone	$1.00	$3.00	$6.00

Dell D Series. New York: Dell Publishing Co.

		G	VG	F
D-101	Lait, Jack and Mortimer, Lee - ***Chicago Confidential*** [1952] Cover by Robert Stanley.	$ .65	$2.00	$4.00
D-102	Marshall, Edison - ***Great Smith*** [1952] Cover by Robert Stanley	$1.00	$3.00	$6.00
D-103	Marshall, Edison - ***Gypsy Sixpence*** [1952] Cover by Barye Phillips.	$1.00	$3.00	$6.00
D-104	Smith, Betty - ***Tomorrow Will Be Better*** [1952]	$ .65	$2.00	$4.00
D-105	Graham, Alice Walworth - ***The Natchez Woman*** [1952] Cover by Barye Phillips.	$1.25	$3.75	$7.50
D-106	Maugham, W. Somerset - ***Mrs. Craddock*** [1952]	$1.00	$3.00	$6.00
D-107	Barker, Shirley - ***Rivers Parting*** [1952] Cover by George Mayers.	$1.00	$3.00	$6.00
D-108	Lait, Jack and Mortimer, Lee - ***Washington Confidential*** [1952] Cover by Mike Ludlow.	$ .65	$2.00	$4.00
D-109	Shute, Nevil - ***The Chequer Board*** [1952]	$ .75	$2.50	$5.00
D-110	Allen, Hervey - ***The Forest And The Fort*** [1952] Cover by Carl Mueller.	$1.25	$3.75	$7.50
D-111	Courtier, Sidney Hobson - ***Gold For My Fair Lady*** [1952] Cover by Griffith Foxley.	$1.00	$3.00	$6.00
D-112	Anthology - ***Three Hundred Pillsbury Prize Recipes*** [1952]	$1.00	$3.00	$6.00
D-113	Swanson, Neil H. - ***The Phantom Emperor*** [1952] Cover by Carl Mueller.	$1.25	$3.75	$7.50
D-114(DJ)	Hatch, Richard Warren - ***Go Down To Glory*** [1952] In dust-jacket.	$32.00	$110.00	$250.00
D-114	Hatch, Richard Warren - ***Go Down To Glory*** [1952]	$1.00	$3.00	$6.00
D-115	Howe, Helen - ***The Circle Of The Day*** [1952]	$ .75	$2.50	$5.00
D-116	Sandoz, Mari - ***Slogum House*** [1952]	$ .75	$2.50	$5.00

D-117	Hemingway, Ernest - ***Across The River And Into The Trees*** [1953] Cover by Griffith Foxley.	$1.50	$5.00	$10.00
D-118	Mezzrow, Milton and Wolfe, Bernard - ***Really The Blues*** [1953] Cover by Walter Brooks.	$1.35	$4.00	$8.00
D-119	Marshall, Edison - ***Castle In The Swamp*** [1953]	$1.00	$3.00	$6.00
D-120	Jonas, Carl - ***Snowslide*** [1953] Cover by Griffith Foxley.	$1.25	$3.75	$7.50
D-121	Saint-Laurent, Cecil - ***Caroline Cherie*** [1953]	$1.00	$3.00	$6.00
D-122	Marshall, Edison - ***The Infinite Woman*** [1953]	$1.00	$3.00	$6.00
D-123	Shute, Nevil - ***The Legacy*** [1953] Cover by Carl Mueller.	$1.00	$3.00	$6.00
D-124	Jonas, Carl - ***Jefferson Selleck*** [1953] Cover by Stanley Borack.	$1.00	$3.00	$6.00
D-125	Cochran, Hamilton - ***Captain Ebony*** [1953] Cover by Carl Mueller.	$1.25	$3.75	$7.50
D-126	Rinehart, Mary Roberts - ***The Swimming Pool*** [1953] Cover by Carl Bobertz.	$1.00	$3.00	$6.00
D-127	Branch, Houston and Waters, Frank - ***Diamond Head*** [1953] Cover by George Garland.	$1.25	$3.75	$7.50
D-128	Allen, Hervey - ***Bedford Village*** [1953] Cover by Carl Mueller.	$1.00	$3.00	$6.00
D-129	O'Connor, Jack - ***Boom Town*** [1953] Cover by Stanley Borack.	$1.00	$3.00	$6.00
D-130	Shute, Nevil - ***Round The Bend*** [1953] Cover by George Garland.	$1.00	$3.00	$6.00
D-131	Glay, George Albert - ***Gina*** [1953] Cover by Victor Kalin.	$1.00	$3.00	$6.00
D-132	Bankhead, Tallulah - ***Tallulah*** [1953] Photo cover.	$1.25	$3.75	$7.50
D-133	Saint-Laurent, Cecil - ***Caroline Coquette*** [1954]	$ .75	$2.50	$5.00
D-134	Carhart, Arthur H. - ***Fresh Water Fishing*** [1954] 16 pages of color photos.	$1.00	$3.00	$6.00
D-135	Hougron, Jean - ***Reap The Whirlwind*** [1954] Cover by Griffith Foxley.	$1.25	$3.75	$7.50
D-136	Williams, Jay - ***The Rogue From Padua*** [1954] Cover by Phil Marini.	$1.00	$3.00	$6.00
D-137	Brossard, Chandler - ***The Bold Saboteurs*** [1954]	$ .75	$2.50	$5.00
D-138	Coker, Elizabeth Boatwright - ***Daughter Of Strangers*** [1954] Cover by Freeman Elliot.	$1.00	$3.00	$6.00
D-139	Marshall, Edison - ***The Viking*** [1954] Cover by Griffith Foxley.	$1.00	$3.00	$6.00
D-140	Fitzgerald, F. Scott - ***This Side Of Paradise*** [1954]	$ .75	$2.50	$5.00
D-141	Sheen, Fulton J. - ***Three To Get Married*** [1954] Photo cover.	$ .65	$2.00	$4.00
D-142	Van Loon, Hendrik - ***The Story Of America*** [1954]	$ .65	$2.00	$4.00
D-143	Kent, Simon - ***The Doctor Of Bean Street*** [1954]	$ .65	$2.00	$4.00
D-144	Cochran, Hamilton - ***Rogue's Holiday*** [1954] Cover by Bill George.	$1.00	$3.00	$6.00
D-145	Crockett, Lucy Herndon - ***The Magnificent Bastards*** [1955] Cover by Ray Pease	$1.00	$3.00	$6.00
D-146	Alvarez, Dr. Walter C. - ***How To Help Your Doctor Help You*** [1955] Cover by Richard Powers.	$ .65	$2.00	$4.00
D-147	White, Steward Edward - ***The Long Rifle*** [1955] Cover by Nick Eggenhoffer.	$1.25	$3.75	$7.50
D-148	Burns, Eugene - ***Fresh And Salt Water Spinning*** [1955]	$1.00	$3.00	$6.00
D-149	Grubb, Davis - ***The Night Of The Hunter*** [1955]	$1.00	$3.00	$6.00
D-150	Campbell, Jr., John W. - ***Who Goes There?*** [1955] Cover by Richard Powers.	$3.50	$10.00	$20.00
D-151	Mittelholzer, Edgar - ***Sylvia*** [1955] Cover by Robert Maguire.	$1.35	$4.00	$8.00
D-152	Rhodes, Eugene Manlove - ***Sunset Land*** [1955] Cover by Robert Stanley.	$1.25	$3.75	$7.50
D-153	Cary, Joyce - ***Herself Surprised*** [1955]	$ .65	$2.00	$4.00
D-154	Rinehart, Mary Roberts - ***The Frightened Wife And Other Murder Stories*** [1955]	$1.25	$3.75	$7.50
D-155	Brown, Pete - ***Guns And Hunting*** [1955]	$1.00	$3.00	$6.00
D-156	Krepps, Robert W. - ***Tell It On The Drums*** [1955] Cover by Robert Stanley.	$1.35	$4.00	$8.00
D-157	Marshall, Edison - ***Caravan To Xanadu*** [1955]	$1.00	$3.00	$6.00
D-158	Weston, Christine - ***Indigo*** [1955]	$1.25	$3.75	$7.50

		G	VG	F
D-159	Van Doren Stern, Philip - ***The Man Who Killed Lincoln*** [1955] ..	$1.00	$3.00	$6.00
D-160	Mankiewicz, Don M. - ***Trial*** [1956] Cover by Richard Powers.	$1.00	$3.00	$6.00
D-161	Rice, Grantland - ***The Tumult And The Shouting*** [1956] Cover by Willard Mullin.	$ .75	$2.50	$5.00
D-162	Fallada, Hans - ***The Drinker*** [1956] Cover by William George.	$ .75	$2.50	$5.00
D-163	Waugh, Evelyn - ***Brideshead Revisited*** [1956]	$1.00	$3.00	$6.00
D-164	Puzo, Mario - ***The Dark Arena*** [1956] Cover by Mitchell Hooks.	$ .75	$2.50	$5.00
D-165	Rinehart, Mary Roberts - ***The Wall*** [1956]	$1.25	$3.75	$7.50
D-166	Sagan, Francoise - ***Bonjour Tristesse*** [1956] Photo cover.	$ .65	$2.00	$4.00
D-167	Wilde, Oscar - ***The Picture Of Dorian Gray*** [1956]	$1.25	$3.75	$7.50
D-168	Faulkner, William - ***Mosquitoes*** [1956]	$1.35	$4.00	$8.00
D-169	Shulenberger, Arvid - ***Roads From The Fort*** [1956] Cover by Mitchell Hooks.	$1.00	$3.00	$6.00
D-170	Halevy, Julian - ***The Young Lovers*** [1956]	$ .75	$2.50	$5.00
D-171	Lindbergh, Anne Morrow - ***The Steep Ascent*** [1956] Cover by Walter Brooks.	$ .75	$2.50	$5.00
D-172	Allen, Steve - ***Fourteen For Tonight*** [1956]	$ .75	$2.50	$5.00
D-173	Marshall, Edison - ***Benjamin Blake*** [1956] Cover by Harry Schaare.	$ .75	$2.50	$5.00
D-174	Brennan, Louis A. - ***An Affair Of Dishonor*** [1956]	$ .65	$2.00	$4.00
D-175	Shute, Nevil - ***The Far Country*** [1956] Cover by Nevil Shute..	$ .65	$2.00	$4.00
D-176	Maugham, W. Somerset - ***Mrs. Craddock*** [1956]	$ .65	$2.00	$4.00
D-177	Cunningham, John - ***Warhorse*** [1956] Cover by Mitchell Hooks..	$1.25	$3.75	$7.50
D-178	Schneider, John G. - ***The Golden Kazoo*** [1956] Cover by Walter Brooks.	$ .65	$2.00	$4.00
D-179	Rinehart, Mary Roberts - ***The Yellow Room*** [1956]	$ .75	$2.50	$5.00
D-181	James, Henry - ***The Turn Of The Screw And Daisy Miller*** [1956] Cover by Walter Brooks.	$1.00	$3.00	$6.00
D-182	Lindbergh, Anne Morrow - ***Listen! The Wind*** [1956]	$ .75	$2.50	$5.00
D-183	Endore, Guy - ***Nightmare*** [1956]	$1.50	$5.00	$10.00
D-184	McCarthy, Mary - ***The Company She Keeps*** [1956]	$ .65	$2.00	$4.00
D-185	Coleman, Lonnie - ***Ship's Company*** [1957] Cover by Harry Schaare.	$ .65	$2.00	$4.00
D-186	Woolrich, Cornell - ***The Bride Wore Black*** [1957]	$1.00	$3.00	$6.00
D-187	Rice, Craig - ***Trial By Fury*** [1957]	$1.25	$3.75	$7.50
D-188	Caspary, Vera - ***Laura*** [1957]	$1.00	$3.00	$6.00
D-189	Merton, Thomas - ***No Man Is An Island*** [1957] Cover by Enrico Arno.	$ .75	$2.50	$5.00
D-190	Hougron, Jean - ***Blaze Of The Sun*** [1957] Cover by Victor Kalin.	$ .75	$2.50	$5.00
D-191	Dinesen, Isak - ***Winter's Tales*** [1957]	$ .75	$2.50	$5.00
D-192	Quentin, Patrick - ***A Puzzle For Fools*** [1957]	$1.00	$3.00	$6.00
D-193	Garnett, David - ***Aspects Of Love*** [1957] Cover by Reynold Ruffins.	$ .75	$2.50	$5.00
D-194	MacDonald, Philip - ***Warrant For X*** [1957]	$1.00	$3.00	$6.00
D-195	Chevallier, Gabriel - ***The Wicked Village*** [1957] Cover by Sheilah Beckett.	$ .75	$2.50	$5.00
D-196	Latimer, Jonathan - ***Headed For A Hearse*** [1957]	$1.00	$3.00	$6.00
D-197	Rinehart, Mary Roberts - ***The Circular Staircase*** [1957]	$1.00	$3.00	$6.00
D-198	Phillips, Thomas Hal - ***The Loved And The Unloved*** [1957] Cover by Milton Glaser.	$ .75	$2.50	$5.00
D-199	Danielsson, Bengt - ***Love In The South Seas*** [1957] Photo cover. Eight pages of photos.	$ .75	$2.50	$5.00
D-200	Rafferty, Kathleen - ***Dell Crossword Puzzle Dictionary*** [1957].	$1.00	$3.00	$6.00
D-201	Ambler, Eric - ***A Coffin For Dimitrios*** [1957]	$1.00	$3.00	$6.00
D-202	Holt, Felix - ***Mountain Boy*** [1957] Cover by Owen Kampen....	$1.00	$3.00	$6.00
D-203	Rogers, Joel Townsley - ***The Red Right Hand*** [1957]	$1.00	$3.00	$6.00
D-204	McCulley, Johnston - ***The Mark Of Zorro*** [1957] Cover by Victor Kalin. TV tie-in.	$2.50	$7.50	$15.00

		G	VG	F
D-205	Moore, Brian - ***The Lonely Passion Of Judith Hearne*** [1958] Cover by Walter Brooks	$ .65	$2.00	$4.00
D-206	Sagan, Francoise - ***A Certain Smile*** [1958] Photo cover.	$ .65	$2.00	$4.00
D-207	Irish, William - ***Phantom Lady*** [1958]	$1.25	$3.75	$7.50
D-208	Merton, Thomas - ***Seeds Of Contemplation*** [1958]	$ .65	$2.00	$4.00
D-209	Cobb, Humphrey - ***Paths Of Glory*** [1958] Movie tie-in with Kirk Douglas	$ .75	$2.50	$5.00
D-210	Fair, A. A. - ***Owls Don't Blink*** [1958] Photo cover.	$ .75	$2.50	$5.00
D-211	Fair, A. A. - ***Spill The Jackpot*** [1958]	$ .75	$2.50	$5.00
D-212	Fair, A. A. - ***Bedrooms Have Windows*** [1958] Photo cover.	$ .75	$2.50	$5.00
D-213	Fair, A. A. - ***Give 'Em The Ax*** [1958]	$ .75	$2.50	$5.00
D-214	McCarthy, Mary - ***A Charmed Life*** [1958] Cover by Reynold Ruffins	$ .65	$2.00	$4.00
D-215	Iles, Frances - ***Before The Fact*** [1958]	$ .65	$2.00	$4.00
D-216	White, Stewart Edward - ***The Long Rifle*** [1958]	$1.00	$3.00	$6.00
D-217	Christie, Agatha - ***Sad Cypress*** [1958]	$1.00	$3.00	$6.00
D-218	Christie, Agatha - ***Witness For The Prosecution*** [1958]	$1.00	$3.00	$6.00
D-219	Rowans, Virginia - ***House Party*** [1958]	$ .65	$2.00	$4.00
D-220	Rinehart, Mary Roberts - ***The Door*** [1958]	$ .75	$2.50	$5.00
D-221	Brean, Herbert - ***Dead Sure*** [1958]	$ .75	$2.50	$5.00
D-222	Waugh, Evelyn - ***The Loved One*** [1958] Cover by Sheilah Beckett.	$ .75	$2.50	$5.00
D-223	Stout, Rex - ***Fer-De-Lance*** [1958]	$1.00	$3.00	$6.00
D-224	Einstein, Charles - ***No Time At All*** [1958] TV tie-in.	$1.35	$4.00	$8.00
D-225	Hughes, Dorothy B. - ***Ride The Pink Horse*** [1958]	$1.00	$3.00	$6.00
D-226	Kane, Frank - ***A Real Gone Guy*** [1958] Cover by Victor Kalin	$1.00	$3.00	$6.00
D-227	Blake, Nicholas - ***The Beast Must Die*** [1958]	$1.00	$3.00	$6.00
D-228	McCloy, Helen - ***Two-Thirds Of A Ghost*** [1958] Cover by Milton Glaser.	$1.00	$3.00	$6.00
D-229	Housepian, Marjorie - ***A Houseful Of Love*** [1958]	$ .75	$2.50	$5.00
D-230	Chesterton, G. K. - ***The Amazing Adventures Of Father Brown*** [1958] Cover by Denver Gillen.	$1.25	$3.75	$7.50
D-231	Hitchcock, Alfred - editor (anthology) - ***Twelve Stories They Wouldn't Let Me Do On TV*** [1958]	$1.25	$3.75	$7.50
D-232	Masur, Harold Q. - ***Tall, Dark And Deadly*** [1958]	$1.00	$3.00	$6.00
D-233	Hart, Frances Noyes - ***The Bellamy Trial*** [1958]	$1.00	$3.00	$6.00
D-234	Allingham, Margery - ***Death Of A Ghost*** [1958]	$1.00	$3.00	$6.00
D-235	Christie, Agatha - ***Dead Man's Mirror*** [1958]	$1.00	$3.00	$6.00
D-236	Christie, Agatha - ***Appointment With Death*** [1958]	$1.00	$3.00	$6.00
D-237	Burnett, Hallie - ***The Brain Pickers*** [1958]	$1.00	$3.00	$6.00
D-238	Ambler, Eric - ***Background To Danger*** [1958]	$1.00	$3.00	$6.00
D-239	Baum, Vicki - ***Grand Hotel*** [1958] Cover by Richard Powers	$ .75	$2.50	$5.00
D-240	Mergendahl, Charles - ***Rage Of Desire*** [1958]	$ .75	$2.50	$5.00
D-241	Lee, C.Y. - ***The Flower Drum Song*** [1958] Movie tie-in.	$ .75	$2.50	$5.00
D-242	Rinehart, Mary Roberts - ***Miss Pinkerton*** [1958] Cover by Victor Kalin.	$1.00	$3.00	$6.00
D-243	Murphy, John D. - editor (anthology) - ***Secrets Of Successful Selling*** [1958]	$ .65	$2.00	$4.00
D-244	Hillary, Richard - ***Falling Through Space*** [1958] Cover by Jack Hearne	$ .75	$2.50	$5.00
D-245	Simmons, Herbert - ***Corner Boy*** [1958]	$ .75	$2.50	$5.00
D-246	Pangborn, Edgar - ***A Mirror For Observers*** [1958] Cover by Richard Powers	$ .65	$2.00	$4.00
D-247	MacDonald, Philip - ***The Mystery Of The Dead Police*** [1958]	$1.00	$3.00	$6.00
D-248	Halliday, Brett - ***The Private Practice Of Michael Shayne*** [1958] Cover by Robert McGinnis.	$1.00	$3.00	$6.00
D-249	Christie, Agatha - ***The Man In The Brown Suit*** [1958]	$1.00	$3.00	$6.00
D-250	Masur, Hal - ***Suddenly A Corpse*** [1958] Cover by Victor Kalin	$1.00	$3.00	$6.00

		G	VG	F
D-251	Rinehart, Mary Roberts - ***The Great Mistake*** [1958] Cover by Victor Kalin.	$1.00	$3.00	$6.00
D-252	Stout, Rex - ***The Mountain Cat Murders*** [1958]	$1.00	$3.00	$6.00
D-253	Fair, A. A. - ***Turn On The Heat*** [1958] Cover by Robert Abbett.	$1.00	$3.00	$6.00
D-254	Saint-Laurent, Cecil - ***The Secrets Of Caroline Cherie*** [1959] Cover by Freeman Elliot.	$ .75	$2.50	$5.00
D-255	Tey, Josephine - ***The Man In The Queue*** [1959] Cover by William Teason.	$1.00	$3.00	$6.00
D-256	Merton, Thomas - ***The Living Bread*** [1959] Cover by Richard Powers.	$ .75	$2.50	$5.00
D-257	Cuppy, Will - ***The Decline And Fall Of Practically Everybody*** [1959]	$ .75	$2.50	$5.00
D-258	Pirro, Ugo - ***The Camp Followers*** [1959]	$ .75	$2.50	$5.00
D-259	Eberhart, Mignon G. - ***Another Man's Murder*** [1959] Cover by Al Brule.	$1.00	$3.00	$6.00
D-260	Shann, Renee - ***Student Nurse*** [1959]	$ .65	$2.00	$4.00
D-261	Quentin, Patrick - ***The Man In The Net*** [1959] Cover by Victor Kalin. Movie tie-in.	$1.00	$3.00	$6.00
D-262	Christie, Agatha - ***The Secret Of Chimneys*** [1959] Cover by William Teason.	$1.00	$3.00	$6.00
D-263	Hersey, John - ***Into The Valley*** [1959]	$ .75	$2.50	$5.00
D-264	Kane, Frank - ***Slay Ride*** [1959] Cover by Victor Kane.	$1.00	$3.00	$6.00
D-265	Kades, Hans - ***The Doctor's Secret*** [1959] Cover by James Hill.	$ .65	$2.00	$4.00
D-266	Miller, Diane Disney - ***The Story Of Walt Disney*** [1959] Eight pages of photos.	$1.50	$5.00	$10.00
D-267	Jennings, John - ***The Golden Eagle*** [1959] Cover by Rafael DeSoto.	$ .65	$2.00	$4.00
D-268	Berckman, Evelyn - ***The Strange Bedfellow*** [1959] Cover by James Hill.	$ .65	$2.00	$4.00
D-269	Halliday, Brett - ***Call For Michael Shayne*** [1959] Cover by Robert McGinnis.	$1.00	$3.00	$6.00
D-270	Sterling, Thomas - ***Murder In Venice*** [1959] Cover by James Hill.	$1.00	$3.00	$6.00
D-271	Coxe, George Harmon - ***Murder On Their Minds*** [1959] Cover by Harry Schaare.	$1.00	$3.00	$6.00
D-272	Mole, William - ***Shadow Of A Killer*** [1959] Cover by James Hill.	$1.00	$3.00	$6.00
D-273	Miller, Arthur - ***Focus*** [1959]	$ .65	$2.00	$4.00
D-274	Finney, Jack - ***The Third Level*** [1959] Cover by Richard Powers.	$1.25	$3.75	$7.50
D-275	Garve, Andrew - ***A Hole In The Ground*** [1959] Cover by William Teason.	$ .65	$2.00	$4.00
D-276	Rinehart, Mary Roberts - ***The Man In Lower Ten*** [1959] Cover by Paul Muni.	$1.00	$3.00	$6.00
D-277	Sagan, Francoise - ***Those Without Shadows*** [1959] Cover by Mitchell Hooks.	$ .65	$2.00	$4.00
D-278	Stone, Hampton - ***The Girl Who Kept Knocking Them Dead*** [1959] Cover by Robert McGinnis.	$1.00	$3.00	$6.00
D-279	Simenon, Georges - ***In Case Of Emergency*** [1959] Photo cover. Movie tie-in with Brigitte Bardot. Eight pages of photos.	$1.00	$3.00	$6.00
D-280	Kane, Frank - ***Trigger Mortis*** [1959] Cover by Victor Kalin.	$1.00	$3.00	$6.00
D-281	Hitchcock, Alfred - editor (anthology) - ***Thirteen More Stories They Wouldn't Let Me Do On TV*** [1959] Photo cover.	$1.25	$3.75	$7.50
D-282	Highsmith, Patricia - ***The Talented Mr. Ripley*** [1959]	$ .65	$2.00	$4.00
D-283	Halliday, Brett - ***Murder And The Wanton Bride*** [1959] PBO. Cover by Robert McGinnis.	$1.00	$3.00	$6.00
D-284	Krepps, Robert W. - ***Earthshaker*** [1959]	$ .75	$2.50	$5.00
D-285	Lee, C.Y. - ***Lover's Point*** [1959] Cover by James Hill.	$ .65	$2.00	$4.00
D-286	Davis, Dorothy Salisbury - ***A Gentle Murderer*** [1959]	$1.00	$3.00	$6.00
D-287	Hall, Calvin S. - ***The Meaning Of Dreams*** [1959]	$ .65	$2.00	$4.00

		G	VG	F
D-288	Christie, Agatha - ***Murder On The Links*** [1959]	$1.00	$3.00	$6.00
D-289	Short, Luke - ***Brand Of Empire*** [1959] Cover by Robert McGinnis.	$ .65	$2.00	$4.00
D-290	Haycox, Ernest - ***Trail Town*** [1959] Cover by John Leone.	$ .65	$2.00	$4.00
D-291	Halliday, Brett - ***Marked For Murder*** [1959] Cover by Robert McGinnis.	$1.00	$3.00	$6.00
D-292	Halliday, Brett - ***Dead Man's Diary And A Taste For Cognac*** [1959] Cover by Robert McGinnis.	$1.25	$3.75	$7.50
D-293	Halliday, Brett - ***Dividend On Death*** [1959] Cover by Robert McGinnis.	$1.00	$3.00	$6.00
D-294	Hecht, Ben - ***The Sensualists*** [1959] Cover by Freeman Eliott.	$ .65	$2.00	$4.00
D-295	Croy, Homer - ***Jesse James Was My Neighbor*** [1959]	$1.00	$3.00	$6.00
D-296	Symons, Julian - ***The Color Of Murder*** [1959] Cover by Robert Maguire.	$1.00	$3.00	$6.00
D-297	Wagner, Geoffrey - ***Sophie*** [1959] Cover by Freeman Eliott.	$ .65	$2.00	$4.00
D-298	Masur, Hal - ***Murder On Broadway*** [1959] Cover by Victor Kalin.	$1.00	$3.00	$6.00
D-299	Lustgarten, Edgar - ***One More Unfortunate*** [1959]	$1.00	$3.00	$6.00
D-300	Mark, David - ***Long Shot*** [1959]	$ .65	$2.00	$4.00
D-301	Blackstock, Lee - ***The Woman In The Woods*** [1959] Cover by James Hill.	$ .75	$2.50	$5.00
D-302	Doyle, Sir Arthur Conan - ***The Hound Of The Baskervilles*** [1959]	$1.00	$3.00	$6.00
D-303	Thorp, Duncan - ***Only Akiko*** [1959] Cover by Mitchell Hooks.	$ .65	$2.00	$4.00
D-304	Dodge, David - ***Angel's Ransom*** [1959] Cover by Robert McGinnis.	$1.00	$3.00	$6.00
D-305	Christie, Agatha - ***The Labors Of Hercules*** [1959] Cover by William Teason.	$1.00	$3.00	$6.00
D-306	Rice, Craig and McBain, Ed - ***The April Robin Murders*** [1959] Cover by Robert McGinnis.	$1.25	$3.75	$7.50
D-307	Lee, Gypsy Rose - ***Gypsy*** [1959] Photo cover.	$ .65	$2.00	$4.00
D-308	Renault, Mary - ***Kind Are Her Answers*** [1959]	$ .65	$2.00	$4.00
D-309	Fair, A. A. - ***Top Of The Heap*** [1959] Cover by Robert McGinnis.	$ .75	$2.50	$5.00
D-310	Sabatier, Robert - ***Boulevard*** [1959]	$ .65	$2.00	$4.00
D-311	Ellin, Stanley - ***The Eighth Circle*** [1959] Cover by Robert McGinnis.	$ .75	$2.50	$5.00
D-312	Boone, Pat - ***'Twixt Twelve And Twenty*** [1959] Photo cover.	$ .65	$2.00	$4.00
D-313	Merton, Thomas - ***The Silent Life*** [1959] Cover by Richard Powers.	$ .65	$2.00	$4.00
D-314	Halliday, Brett - ***Fit To Kill*** [1959] Cover by Robert McGinnis.	$ .75	$2.50	$5.00
D-315	Land, Myrick - ***The Search*** [1959] Cover by Mitchell Hooks.	$ .65	$2.00	$4.00
D-316	Rinehart, Mary Roberts - ***The Confession And Sight Unseen*** [1959] Cover by Victor Kalin.	$ .75	$2.50	$5.00
D-317	Baldwin, Faith - ***The Heart Remembers*** [1959]	$ .65	$2.00	$4.00
D-318	Smith, Shelley - ***The Shrew Is Dead*** [1959] Cover by Robert McGinnis.	$ .75	$2.50	$5.00
D-319	Del Castillo, Michel - ***Child Of Our Time*** [1959] Cover by Richard Powers.	$ .65	$2.00	$4.00
D-320	Derby, Mark - ***The Sunlit Ambush*** [1959] Cover by Tommy Shoemaker.	$ .65	$2.00	$4.00
D-321	Milne, A. A. - ***The Red House Mystery*** [1959] Cover by William Teason.	$ .75	$2.50	$5.00
D-322	Quentin, Patrick - ***The Man With Two Wives*** [1959]	$ .75	$2.50	$5.00
D-323	Carr, John Dickson - ***The Three Coffins*** [1960]	$ .75	$2.50	$5.00
D-324	Connell, Jr., Evan S. - ***Mrs. Bridge*** [1960] Cover by William Teason.	$ .65	$2.00	$4.00
D-325	Ellin, Stanley - ***Quiet Horror*** [1960]	$1.00	$3.00	$6.00

		G	VG	F
D-326	Christie, Agatha - ***The Mysterious Mr. Quin*** [1960] Cover by William Teason.	$ .75	$2.50	$5.00
D-327	Halliday, Brett - ***Bodies Are Where You Find Them*** [1960] Cover by Robert McGinnis.	$ .75	$2.50	$5.00
D-328	MacKenzie, Donald - ***Moment Of Danger*** [1960] Cover by Robert McGinnis.	$ .75	$2.50	$5.00
D-329	Masur, Hal - ***You Can't Live Forever*** [1960] Cover by Robert McGinnis.	$ .75	$2.50	$5.00
D-330	Rinehart, Mary Roberts - ***The Bat*** [1960] Cover by Victor Kalin.	$ .75	$2.50	$5.00
D-331	Shayne, Mike - editor (anthology) - ***Mike Shayne Selects Ten Cases Of Murder In Miami*** [1959] Cover by Robert McGinnis.	$1.00	$3.00	$6.00
D-332	Millar, Margaret - ***The Iron Gates*** [1960] Cover by William Teason.	$ .65	$2.00	$4.00
D-333	Kane, Frank - ***Bare Trap*** [1960] Cover by Harry Bennett.	$1.00	$3.00	$6.00
D-334	Kane, Frank - ***Poisons Unknown*** [1960] Cover by Harry Bennett.	$1.00	$3.00	$6.00
D-335	Kane, Frank - ***Grave Danger*** [1960] Cover by Harry Bennett.	$1.00	$3.00	$6.00
D-336	Trail, Armitage - ***Scarface*** [1960] Cover by Victor Kalin.	$ .65	$2.00	$4.00
D-337	Williams, Charles - ***Gulf Coast Girl*** [1960] Cover by Robert McGinnis.	$ .75	$2.50	$5.00
D-338	Waugh, Hillary - ***The Girl Who Cried Wolf*** [1960] Cover by Robert McGinnis.	$ .75	$2.50	$5.00
D-339	Blake, Nicholas - ***Death And Daisy Bland*** [1960] Cover by Armand Seguso.	$ .75	$2.50	$5.00
D-340	Christie, Agatha - ***The Boomerang Clue*** [1960]	$ .75	$2.50	$5.00
D-341	Roth, Arthur J. - ***A Terrible Beauty*** [1960] Cover by George Gross. Movie tie-in with Robert Mitchum.	$ .65	$2.00	$4.00
D-342	Halliday, Brett - ***Blood On Biscayne Bay*** [1960] Cover by Robert McGinnis.	$ .75	$2.50	$5.00
D-343	Ambler, Eric - ***Journey Into Fear*** [1960] Cover by William Teason.	$ .75	$2.50	$5.00
D-344	Seifert, Elizabeth - ***Home-Town Doctor*** [1960] Cover by Tommy Shoemaker.	$ .50	$1.50	$3.00
D-345	Berckman, Evelyn - ***House Of Terror*** [1960] Cover by Tommy Shoemaker.	$1.00	$3.00	$6.00
D-346	Coxe, George Harmon - ***One Minute Past Eight*** [1960]	$ .75	$2.50	$5.00
D-347	Arquette, Cliff - ***Charley Weaver's Letters From Mama*** [1960] Photo cover. TV tie-in.	$1.25	$3.75	$7.50
D-348	Fair, A. A. - ***Bats Fly At Dusk*** [1960] Cover by Robert McGinnis.	$ .75	$2.50	$5.00
D-349	Fisher, Richard - ***The Very First Time*** [1960] Cover by Mitchell Hooks.	$ .65	$2.00	$4.00
D-350	Short, Luke - ***Bounty Guns*** [1960] Cover by John Leone.	$ .75	$2.50	$5.00
D-351	Bingham, John - ***Murder Off The Record*** [1960] Cover by Robert Maguire.	$1.00	$3.00	$6.00
D-352	Rinehart, Mary Roberts - ***The After House*** [1960]	$ .75	$2.50	$5.00
D-353	Whitehill, Joseph - ***The Way Up*** [1960] Cover by Tom Miller.	$ .65	$2.00	$4.00
D-354	Christie, Agatha - ***The Mousetrap*** [1960]	$ .75	$2.50	$5.00
D-355	Halliday, Brett - ***Target: Mike Shayne*** [1960] Cover by Robert McGinnis.	$ .75	$2.50	$5.00
D-356	Caspary, Vera - ***Bedelia*** [1960]	$ .75	$2.50	$5.00
D-357	Wallach, Ira - ***Muscle Beach*** [1960] Cover by Dick McCabe.	$ .65	$2.00	$4.00
D-358	Halliday, Brett - ***Counterfeit Wife*** [1960] Cover by Robert McGinnis.	$ .75	$2.50	$5.00
D-359	Halliday, Brett - ***When Dorinda Dances*** [1960] Cover by Robert McGinnis.	$ .75	$2.50	$5.00
D-360	Hardy, William M. - ***The Case Of The Missing Coed*** [1960] Cover by Ted Coconos.	$ .75	$2.50	$5.00

		G	VG	F
D-361	Fair, A. A. - ***Double Or Quits*** [1960] Cover by Robert McGinnis.	$ .75	$2.50	$5.00
D-362	Alexander, David - ***Dead, Man, Dead*** [1960] Cover by Robert Maguire.	$ .75	$2.50	$5.00
D-363	Stone, Philip Alston - ***No Place To Run*** [1960] Cover by Harry Bennett.	$ .65	$2.00	$4.00
D-364	Ard, William - ***Wanted: Danny Fontaine*** [1960]	$1.00	$3.00	$6.00
D-365	Hood, Margaret Page - ***The Murders On Fox Island*** [1960]	$ .75	$2.50	$5.00
D-366	Rinehart, Mary Roberts - ***The Case Of Jennie Brice*** [1960] Cover by Victor Kalin.	$ .75	$2.50	$5.00
D-367	Maule, Harry E. - editor (anthology) - ***Rawhiders And Renegades*** [1960] Cover by John Kulor.	$1.00	$3.00	$6.00
D-368	Stewart, Donald - ***Strange Bondage*** [1960] Cover by Robert Maguire.	$1.00	$3.00	$6.00
D-369	Barry, Jerome - ***Murder Is No Accident*** [1960] Cover by Ted Coconos.	$ .75	$2.50	$5.00
D-370	Christie, Agatha - ***An Overdose Of Death*** [1960]	$ .75	$2.50	$5.00
D-372	Fair, A. A. - ***Some Women Won't Wait*** [1960] Cover by Robert McGinnis.	$ .75	$2.50	$5.00
D-373	Fair, A. A. - ***Crows Can't Count*** [1960]	$ .75	$2.50	$5.00
D-374	Halliday, Brett - ***Date With A Dead Man*** [1960] PBO. Cover by Robert McGinnis.	$ .75	$2.50	$5.00
D-375	Pentecost, Hugh - ***The Obituary Club*** [1960] Cover by Robert Maguire.	$ .75	$2.50	$5.00
D-376	Olesker, Harry - ***Exit Dying*** [1960] Cover by Robert McGinnis.	$ .75	$2.50	$5.00
D-377	Finney, Jack - ***Assault On A Queen*** [1960] Cover by Jack Mitchell.	$1.25	$3.75	$7.50
D-378	Lowell, Juliet - ***Dear Mr. Congressman*** [1960] Cover by William F. Brown.	$ .65	$2.00	$4.00
D-379	Halliday, Brett - ***Murder Takes No Holiday*** [1961] PBO. Cover by Robert McGinnis. TV tie-in.	$ .75	$2.50	$5.00
D-380	Lambert, Alice Elinor - ***Hospital Nocturne*** [1960] Cover by Tommy Shoemaker.	$ .50	$1.50	$3.00
D-381	Halliday, Brett - ***What Really Happened*** [1960] Cover by Robert McGinnis.	$ .75	$2.50	$5.00
D-382	Fox, Norman A. - ***Ghostly Hoofbeats*** [1960]	$ .75	$2.50	$5.00
D-383	Masur, Hal Q. - ***So Rich, So Lovely, And So Dead*** [1961] Cover by Robert McGinnis.	$ .75	$2.50	$5.00
D-384	Christie, Agatha - ***Murder In Retrospect*** [1961] Cover by William Teason.	$ .75	$2.50	$5.00
D-385	Chute, B. J. - ***Greenwillow*** [1960]	$ .65	$2.00	$4.00
D-386	Roos, Kelley - ***Requiem For A Blonde*** [1960] Cover by Robert McGinnis.	$ .75	$2.50	$5.00
D-387	Halliday, Brett - ***One Night With Nora*** [1960]	$ .75	$2.50	$5.00
D-388	Vexin, Noel - ***Murder In Montmartre*** [1960]	$ .75	$2.50	$5.00
D-390	Christie, Agatha - ***Murder After Hours*** [1960]	$ .75	$2.50	$5.00
D-391	Halliday, Brett - ***Die Like A Dog*** [1960] Cover by Robert McGinnis.	$ .75	$2.50	$5.00
D-392	Bagby, George - ***Dead Wrong*** [1960] Cover by Robert McGinnis.	$ .75	$2.50	$5.00
D-393	Erdman, Loula Grace - ***Three At The Wedding*** [1960] Cover by Tommy Shoemaker.	$ .65	$2.00	$4.00
D-394	Quentin, Patrick - ***Suspicious Circumstances*** [1960]	$ .75	$2.50	$5.00
D-395	Lowell, Juliet - ***Dear Doctor*** [1960]	$ .65	$2.00	$4.00
D-396	Lipsky, Eleazar - ***The Kiss Of Death*** [1961]	$ .75	$2.50	$5.00
D-397	Lariar, Lawrence - editor (anthology) - ***Teensville USA*** [1961] Cartoon book.	$1.25	$3.75	$7.50
D-398	Eberhart, Mignon G. - ***The Promise Of Murder*** [1961]	$ .75	$2.50	$5.00
D-399	Baldwin, Faith - ***You Can't Escape*** [1961]	$ .50	$1.50	$3.00

		G	VG	F
D-400	Overholser, Wayne D. - ***Hearn's Valley*** [1961] Cover by Robert Stanley.	$ .65	$2.00	$4.00
D-401	Halliday, Brett - ***The Corpse Came Calling*** [1961]	$ .75	$2.50	$5.00
D-402	Baldwin, Faith - ***Private Duty*** [1961]	$ .50	$1.50	$3.00
D-403	Christie, Agatha - ***There Is A Tide*** [1961]	$ .75	$2.50	$5.00
D-404	Christie, Agatha - ***Thirteen At Dinner*** [1961] Cover by William Teason.	$ .75	$2.50	$5.00
D-405	Christie, Agatha - ***Murder In Mesopotamia*** [1961]	$ .75	$2.50	$5.00
D-406	Fair, A. A. - ***Gold Comes In Bricks*** [1961] Cover by Robert McGinnis.	$ .75	$2.50	$5.00
D-407	Cotler, Gordon - ***The Bottletop Affair*** [1961]	$ .65	$2.00	$4.00
D-408	Kuby, Erich - ***Rosemarie*** [1960]	$ .65	$2.00	$4.00
D-409	Fox, Norman A. - ***Reckoning At Rimbow*** [1961]	$ .65	$2.00	$4.00
D-410	Williams, Charles - ***The Sailcloth Shroud*** [1961]	$ .65	$2.00	$4.00
D-411	Rinehart, Mary Roberts - ***The Window At The White Cat*** [1961] Cover by Victor Kalin.	$ .75	$2.50	$5.00
D-412	Seifert, Elizabeth - ***Doctor On Trial*** [1961] Cover by Victor Kalin.	$ .50	$1.50	$3.00
D-413	Hall, Bennie C. - ***Redheaded Nurse*** [1961] Cover by Gilbert Riswold.	$ .50	$1.50	$3.00
D-415	Baldwin, Faith - ***Innocent Bystander*** [1961] Cover by Victor Kalin.	$ .75	$2.50	$5.00
D-416	Halliday, Brett - ***Michael Shayne's Long Chance*** [1961]	$ .75	$2.50	$5.00
D-417	Manceron, Genevieve - ***The Deadlier Sex*** [1961] Photo cover.	$ .65	$2.00	$4.00
D-418	James, Walter S. - ***Dust Devil*** [1961] Cover by Robert Stanley.	$ .65	$2.00	$4.00
D-419	Humphries, Adelaide - ***Nurse Barclay's Dilemma*** [1961] Cover by Robert Abbett.	$ .50	$1.50	$3.00
D-420	Stokes, Manning Lee - ***The Grave's In The Meadow*** [1961] Cover by Robert Abbett.	$1.00	$3.00	$6.00
D-421	Coxe, George Harmon - ***The Impetuous Mistress*** [1961]	$ .75	$2.50	$5.00
D-422	Fremlin, Celia - ***The Hours Before Dawn*** [1961]	$ .65	$2.00	$4.00
D-423	Halliday, Brett - ***Death Has Three Lives*** [1961] Cover by Robert McGinnis.	$ .75	$2.50	$5.00
D-424	Halliday, Brett - ***Dolls Are Deadly*** [1961] PBO. Cover by Robert McGinnis. TV tie-in.	$ .75	$2.50	$5.00
D-425	Halliday, Brett - ***Stranger In Town*** [1961] Cover by Robert McGinnis. TV tie-in.	$ .75	$2.50	$5.00
D-427	Berenstain, Stanley and Janice - ***Have A Baby, My Wife Just Had A Cigar*** [1961] Cartoon book.	$ .65	$2.00	$4.00
D-428	Seifert, Elizabeth - ***When Doctors Marry*** [1961] Cover by Tom Miller.	$ .50	$1.50	$3.00
D-429	La Vanway, Ed - ***Brand Rider*** [1961]	$ .65	$2.00	$4.00
D-430	Meyer, Lewis - ***Preposterous Papa*** [1961]	$ .65	$2.00	$4.00
D-431	Fair, A. A. - ***Cats Prowl At Night*** [1961]	$ .75	$2.50	$5.00
D-432	Fox, Norman A. - ***The Hard Pursued*** [1961]	$ .65	$2.00	$4.00
D-433	Rinehart, Mary Roberts - ***Episode Of The Wandering Knife*** [1961] Cover by Victor Kalin.	$ .75	$2.50	$5.00
D-434	Tevis, Walter - ***The Hustler*** [1961] Cover by Clark Hulings. Movie tie in with Paul Newman.	$1.35	$4.00	$8.00
D-436	Seifert, Elizabeth - ***Doctor At The Crossroads*** [1961]	$ .50	$1.50	$3.00
D-437	Halliday, Brett - ***The Homicidal Virgin*** [1961] Cover by Robert McGinnis. TV tie-in.	$ .75	$2.50	$5.00
D-442	Overholser, Wayne D. - ***The Judas Gun*** [1961] Cover by Ronnie Lesser.	$ .65	$2.00	$4.00
D-443	Seifert, Elizabeth - ***The Doctor's Bride*** [1961] Cover by Tom Miller.	$ .50	$1.50	$3.00
D-444	Compiled by Kathleen Rafferty - ***Sixth Book Of Dell Crossword Puzzles*** [1961] PBO.	$1.50	$5.00	$10.00
D-446	Halliday, Brett - ***She Woke To Darkness*** [1962] Cover by Robert McGinnis.	$ .75	$2.50	$5.00

		G	VG	F
D-447	Berenstain, Stanley and Janice - ***Call Me Mrs.*** [1961] Cartoon book.	$ .65	$2.00	$4.00
D-451	Kane, Frank - ***Bullet Proof*** [1961] Cover by Harry Bennett.	$ .75	$2.50	$5.00
D-457	Short, Luke - ***Raw Land*** [1962]	$ .65	$2.00	$4.00
D-463	Halliday, Brett - ***A Taste For Violence*** [1962] Cover by Robert McGinnis.	$ .75	$2.50	$5.00

Dell F Series. New York: Dell Publishing Co.

		G	VG	F
F-50	Duncan, Thomas W. - ***Gus The Great*** [1953] Cover by Morton Roberts.	$1.25	$3.75	$7.50
F-51	Adams, Samuel Hopkins - ***Canal Town*** [1953]	$1.25	$3.75	$7.50
F-52	Roark, Garland - ***Wake Of The Red Witch*** [1953] Cover by George Geygan.	$1.25	$3.75	$7.50
F-53	Tolstoy, Leo - ***War And Peace*** [1955] Cover by Richard Powers.	$1.25	$3.75	$7.50
F-55	Dostoyevsky, Fyodor - ***The Brothers Karamazov*** [1956]	$ .75	$2.50	$5.00
F-56	Sugrue, Thomas - ***The Story Of Edgar Cayce*** [1956]	$ .75	$2.50	$5.00
F-57	Becker, Belle & Linscott, Robert N. - ***Bedside Book Of Famous French Stories*** [1956]	$ .75	$2.50	$5.00
F-58	Lockridge, Jr., Ross - ***Raintree County*** [1957] Cover by Victor Kalin. Movie tie-in.	$ .75	$2.50	$5.00
F-59	Papini, Giivanni - ***Life Of Christ*** [1957]	$ .75	$2.50	$5.00
F-60	Burdick, Eugene - ***The Ninth Wave*** [1957] Cover by Richard Powers.	$ .75	$2.50	$5.00
F-61	Metalious, Grace - ***Peyton Place*** [1957]	$1.00	$3.00	$6.00
F-62	Keeley, Joseph C. - ***How To Take Better Pictures*** [1957] Photo cover.	$ .75	$2.50	$5.00
F-63	Lewis, Sinclair - ***Dodsworth*** [1957]	$ .75	$2.50	$5.00
F-64	Arden, Leon - ***The Savage Place*** [1958]	$ .75	$2.50	$5.00
F-65	Keller, James - ***Make Each Day Count*** [1958] Cover by Jeannette Cissman.	$ .75	$2.50	$5.00
F-66	Klaas, Joe - ***Maybe I'm Dead*** [1958] Cover by Daniel Schwartz.	$ .75	$2.50	$5.00
F-67	Marshall, Edison - ***The Viking*** [1958] Cover by George Gross. Movie tie-in.	$1.00	$3.00	$6.00
F-68	Waugh, Evelyn - ***Brideshead Revisited*** [1957]	$ .75	$2.50	$5.00
F-69	Delmar, Vina - ***Beloved*** [1958] Cover by Victor Kalin.	$ .75	$2.50	$5.00
F-70	Dickens, Charles - ***David Copperfield*** [1958]	$1.25	$3.75	$7.50
F-71	Ellis, William Donohue - ***The Bounty Lands*** [1958] Cover by Warren Baumgartner.	$ .75	$2.50	$5.00
F-72	Marshall, Edison - ***The Upstart*** [1959] Cover by Harry Schaare.	$ .75	$2.50	$5.00
F-73	Ott, Wolfgang - ***Sharks And Little Fish*** [1959]	$ .75	$2.50	$5.00
F-74	Waugh, Evelyn - ***A Handful Of Dust/Decline And Fall*** [1959]	$ .75	$2.50	$5.00
F-75	Traver, Robert - ***Anatomy Of A Murder*** [1959]	$1.00	$3.00	$6.00
F-76	Sinclair, Harold - ***The Horse Soldiers*** [1959] Movie tie-in with John Wayne.	$ .75	$2.50	$5.00
F-77	Sandburg, Carl - ***The Fiery Trail*** [1959]	$ .75	$2.50	$5.00
F-78	Werfel, Franz - ***Embezzled Heaven*** [1959] Cover by Victor Kalin. Movie Tie-in.	$ .75	$2.50	$5.00
F-79	Wallace, Lew - ***Ben-Hur*** [1959]	$ .75	$2.50	$5.00
F-80	Hobart, Alice Tisdale - ***This Earth Is Mine*** [1959]	$ .75	$2.50	$5.00
F-81	Appel, Benjamin - ***The Raw Edge*** [1959] Photo cover.	$ .75	$2.50	$5.00
F-82	Warren, Robert Penn - ***The Circus In The Attic And Other Stories*** [1959]	$ .75	$2.50	$5.00
F-83	Baum, Vicki - ***Theme For Ballet*** [1959]	$ .75	$2.50	$5.00
F-84	Feldman & Gartenberg - editors - ***The Beat Generation And The Angry Young Men*** [1959]	$2.00	$6.00	$12.00
F-85	White, Stewart Edward - ***Ranchero*** [1959]	$ .75	$2.50	$5.00
F-86	Roosevelt, Eleanor - ***On My Own*** [1959]	$ .75	$2.50	$5.00
F-87	Marshall, Edison - ***Yankee Pasha*** [1959]	$ .75	$2.50	$5.00

		G	VG	F
F-88	Boyington, Col. Gregory "Pappy" - ***Baa Baa Black Sheep*** [1959] Photo cover.	$ .75	$2.50	$5.00
F-89	Thomas, Lowell - editor (anthology) - ***Great True Adventures*** [1959]	$ .75	$2.50	$5.00
F-90	Farris, John - ***Harrison High*** [1959] Cover by Maguire.	$1.00	$3.00	$6.00
F-91	Metalious, Grace - ***Return To Peyton Place*** [1960]	$1.00	$3.00	$6.00
F-92	Astor, Mary - ***Mary Astor, My Story*** [1960] Photo cover.	$ .75	$2.50	$5.00
F-93	White, Robin - ***Elephant Hill*** [1960] Cover by Tom Dunn.	$ .75	$2.50	$5.00
F-94	Beaumont, Charles - ***The Intruder*** [1960] Cover by Al Brule.	$ .75	$2.50	$5.00
F-95	Crockett, Lucy Herndon - ***The Magnificent Bastards*** [1959]	$ .75	$2.50	$5.00
F-97	Mittelholzer, Edgar - ***Savage Destiny*** [1960]	$ .75	$2.50	$5.00
F-98	Marshall, Edison - ***Gypsy Sixpence*** [1960] Cover by Robert McGinnis.	$ .75	$2.50	$5.00
F-99	Morros, Boris - ***My Ten Years As A Counterspy*** [1959]	$ .75	$2.50	$5.00
F-100	Sheen, D.D. and Fulton J. - ***Three To Get Married*** [1959]	$ .75	$2.50	$5.00
F-101	Busch, Niven - ***California Street*** [1960]	$ .75	$2.50	$5.00
F-102	Moscow, Alvin - ***Collision Course*** [1960]	$ .75	$2.50	$5.00
F-103	Oleck, Jack - ***Messalina*** [1960]	$1.35	$4.00	$8.00
F-104	Knowles, John - ***A Separate Peace*** [1961]	$ .75	$2.50	$5.00
F-105	Allen, Hervey - ***Toward The Morning*** [1960]	$ .75	$2.50	$5.00
F-106	Trapp, Maria Augusta - ***The Story Of The Trapp Family Singers*** [1960]	$ .75	$2.50	$5.00
F-107	Groninger, William - ***The Run From The Mountain*** [1960] Cover by Harry Schaare.	$ .75	$2.50	$5.00
F-108	Campanella, Roy - ***It's Good To Be Alive*** [1960]	$ .75	$2.50	$5.00
F-109	Leggett, John - ***Wilder Stone*** [1961] Cover by Leon Gregori.	$ .75	$2.50	$5.00
F-110	Havoc, June - ***Early Havoc*** [1960] Photo cover.	$ .75	$2.50	$5.00
F-111	Keller, Helen - ***The Story Of My Life*** [1961] Photo cover.	$ .75	$2.50	$5.00
F-112	Marx, Groucho - ***Groucho And Me*** [1960] Photo cover.	$1.00	$3.00	$6.00
F-113	Coker, Elizabeth Boatwright - ***La Belle*** [1960] Cover by Mitchell Hooks.	$ .75	$2.50	$5.00
F-114	Halevy, Julian - ***The Young Lovers*** [1960]	$ .75	$2.50	$5.00
F-115	Miller, Arthur - ***The Misfits*** [1961] Movie tie-in with Marilyn Monroe and Clark Gable photo cover. Eight pages of photos.	$3.50	$10.00	$20.00
F-116	Merton, Thomas - ***The Secular Journal Of Thomas Merton*** [1960]	$ .75	$2.50	$5.00
F-117	Killilea, Marie - ***Karen*** [1960]	$ .75	$2.50	$5.00
F-118	Merrill, Judith - editor - ***The Year's Best SF: 5th Annual Edition*** [1961] Cover by Richard Powers.	$1.00	$3.00	$6.00
F-119	Godden, Rumer - ***The Greengage Summer*** [1961]	$ .75	$2.50	$5.00
F-120	Osborn, Alex - ***Your Creative Power*** [1961]	$ .75	$2.50	$5.00
F-121	Searls, Hank - ***The Crowded Sky*** [1960] Cover by Tom Miller.	$ .75	$2.50	$5.00
F-122	Guareschi, Giovanni - ***Don Camillo's Dilemma*** [1960] Cover by Edgar Blakeney.	$ .75	$2.50	$5.00
F-123	Brunini, John Gilland - ***Whereon To Stand: What Catholics Believe And Why*** [1961]	$ .75	$2.50	$5.00
F-124	Searls, Hank - ***The Big X*** [1960] Cover by William Teason.	$ .75	$2.50	$5.00
F-125	Anthology edited by Alfred Hitchcock - ***Fourteen Of My Favorites In Suspense*** [1960] Photo cover.	$ .75	$2.50	$5.00
F-127	Marshall, Peter - ***Mr. Jones, Meet The Master*** [1961]	$ .75	$2.50	$5.00
F-128	Dahl, Roald - ***Kiss Kiss*** [1961]	$ .75	$2.50	$5.00
F-129	Dowdey, Clifford - ***Gamble's Hundred*** [1961] Cover by Mitchell Hooks.	$ .75	$2.50	$5.00
F-130	Anthology edited by Alfred Hitchcock - ***Alfred Hitchcock Presents: More Of My Favorites In Suspense*** [1961] Photo cover.	$1.00	$3.00	$6.00
F-131	Francis, Arlene - ***That Certain Something*** [1961] Photo cover.	$ .75	$2.50	$5.00
F-132	Merton, Thomas - ***Thoughts In Solitude*** [1961]	$ .75	$2.50	$5.00
F-133	Chesterton, G. K. - ***Ten Adventures Of Father Brown*** [1961]	$ .75	$2.50	$5.00
F-135	Weeks, Jack - ***The Grey Affair*** [1961] PBO. Cover by Victor Kalin.	$ .75	$2.50	$5.00

		G	VG	F
F-136	Kern, Seymour - ***The Golden Scalpel*** [1961] Cover by Bob Abbett.	$ .75	$2.50	$5.00
F-137	Caidin, Martin - ***Thunderbirds!*** [1961]	$ .75	$2.50	$5.00
F-138	Mauriac, Francois - ***Flesh And Blood*** [1961] Cover by William Teason.	$ .75	$2.50	$5.00
F-139	Dahl, Roald - ***Someone Like You*** [1961] Cover by Victor Kalin.	$ .75	$2.50	$5.00
F-140	Goldman, William - ***Soldier In The Rain*** [1961] Cover by Casey Jones.	$ .75	$2.50	$5.00
F-141	Wilson, John Harold - ***The Private Life Of Mr. Pepys*** [1961]	$ .75	$2.50	$5.00
F-142	Merton, Thomas - ***Seeds Of Contemplation*** [1960]	$ .75	$2.50	$5.00
F-143	Caspary, Vera - ***Evvie*** [1961]	$ .75	$2.50	$5.00
F-144	Buchwald, Art - ***Don't Forget To Write*** [1961]	$ .75	$2.50	$5.00
F-145	Smythe, David Mynders - ***Golden Venus*** [1961] Cover by Freeman Elliot.	$ .75	$2.50	$5.00
F-147	Moore, Brian - ***The Luck Of Ginger Coffey*** [1962]	$ .75	$2.50	$5.00
F-148	Terasaki, Gwen - ***Bridge To The Sun*** [1961] Cover by Ted Coconis. Movie tie-in.	$ .75	$2.50	$5.00
F-150	Rowans, Virginia - ***Love And Mrs. Sargent*** [1962]	$ .75	$2.50	$5.00
F-151	Mitchell, Robert M. & Klein, Ted - ***Nine Months To Go*** [1962]	$ .75	$2.50	$5.00
F-152	Reynolds, Quentin - ***Minister Of Death*** [1961] Photo cover. Eight pages of photos.	$ .75	$2.50	$5.00
F-153	Brosnan, Jim - ***The Long Season*** [1961] Cover by Leon Gregori.	$ .75	$2.50	$5.00
F-154	Darvas, Nicolas - ***How I Made $2,000,000 In The Stock Market*** [1961] Photo cover.	$ .75	$2.50	$5.00
F-155	Merton, Thomas - ***The Living Bread*** [1961]	$ .75	$2.50	$5.00
F-156	Merton, Thomas - ***No Man Is An Island*** [1961]	$ .75	$2.50	$5.00
F-158	Forester, C. S. - ***The Nightmare*** [1961] Cover by Tony Kokinos.	$ .75	$2.50	$5.00
F-159	McManus, Virginia - ***Not For Love*** [1961]	$ .75	$2.50	$5.00
F-162	Lyle, Judge John H. - ***The Dry And Lawless Years*** [1961] Cover by Victor Kalin.	$ .75	$2.50	$5.00
F-163	Caspary, Vera - ***Laura*** [1961] Cover by Forte.	$ .75	$2.50	$5.00
F-164	Gregor, Manfred - ***Town Without Pity*** [1961] Cover by Tom Miller. Movie tie-in.	$ .75	$2.50	$5.00
F-165	Moore, Brian - ***The Lonely Passion Of Judith Hearne*** [1962]	$ .75	$2.50	$5.00
F-166	Anthology edited by Alfred Hitchcock - ***Bar The Doors*** [1962] Photo cover.	$ .75	$2.50	$5.00
F-167	Straight, Michael - ***Carrington*** [1961]	$ .75	$2.50	$5.00
F-169	Doyle, Sir Arthur Conan - ***Great Stories Of Sherlock Holmes*** [1962]	$ .75	$2.50	$5.00
F-170	Troy, Una - ***The Graces Of Ballykeen*** [1961] Cover by Clark Hulings.	$ .75	$2.50	$5.00
F-171	Boltar, Russell - ***The Operation*** [1962]	$ .75	$2.50	$5.00
F-172	Sheen, Fulton, J. - ***Go To Heaven*** [1961]	$ .75	$2.50	$5.00
F-174	Krepps, Robert W. - ***Diamond Fever*** [1961] Cover by Bob Abbett.	$ .75	$2.50	$5.00
F-175	Lee, C. Y. - ***The Flower Drum Song*** [1961] Cover by Victor Kalin. Movie tie-in.	$ .75	$2.50	$5.00
F-176	Westlake, Donald E. - ***The Smashers*** [1962]	$ .75	$2.50	$5.00
F-178	West, Morris L. - ***The Crooked Road*** [1962] Cover by Bob Abbett.	$ .75	$2.50	$5.00
F-179	Di Donato, Pietro - ***Immigrant Saint*** [1962]	$ .75	$2.50	$5.00
F-180	March, William - ***The Bad Seed*** [1961]	$ .75	$2.50	$5.00
F-181	Gerson, Noel B. - ***That Egyptian Woman*** [1962] Cover by Bob Abbett.	$ .75	$2.50	$5.00
F-182	Kessel, Joseph - ***The Man With The Miraculous Hands*** [1962] Cover by William Teason.	$ .75	$2.50	$5.00
F-183	Cuppy, Will - ***How To Get From January To December*** [1962] Cover by Robert J. Lee.	$ .75	$2.50	$5.00

Dell First Edition, 12

Dell First Edition, B-182

Dell First Edition, B-199

		G	VG	F
F-184	MacDonald, Philip - ***Warrant For X*** [1962] Cover by Robert McGinnis	$ .75	$2.50	$5.00
F-187	McGerr, Patricia - ***Martha, Martha*** [1962]	$ .75	$2.50	$5.00
F-188	Hardy, William M. - ***Wolfpack*** [1962]	$ .75	$2.50	$5.00
F-190	Sneider, Vern - ***The King From Ashtabula*** [1962]	$ .75	$2.50	$5.00
F-193	Brodkey, Harold - ***First Love And Other Sorrows*** [1962] Photo cover	$ .75	$2.50	$5.00
F-194	Tregaskis, Richard - ***John F. Kennedy: War Hero*** [1962]	$ .75	$2.50	$5.00
F-206	Hitchcock, Alfred - editor (anthology) - ***Twelve Stories They Wouldn't Let Me Do On TV*** [1961]	$ .75	$2.50	$5.00
F-207	Hitchcock, Alfred - editor (anthology) - ***Thirteen More Stories They Wouldn't Let Me Do On TV*** [1961]	$ .75	$2.50	$5.00

Dell First Editions. New York: Dell Publishing Co.

		G	VG	F
1-E	Grove, Walt - ***Down*** [1953] PBO. Cover by C. E. Monroe, Jr.	$1.35	$4.00	$8.00
2-E	Brown, Fredric - ***Madball*** [1953] PBO. Cover painting by Griffith Foxley	$8.00	$25.00	$50.00
D-3	Anthology edited by A. M. Krich - ***Women*** [1953] PBO. Cover by Walter Brooks	$1.25	$3.75	$7.50
4	Albee, George Sumner - ***Girl On The Beach*** [1953] PBO. Cover by Carl Bobertz	$1.25	$3.75	$7.50
5	Einstein, Charles - ***The Bloody Spur*** [1953] PBO. Cover by Phil Marini.	$1.35	$4.00	$8.00
6	Warren, Paul - ***Next Time Is For Life*** [1953] PBO. Cover by Robert Schulz	$1.25	$3.75	$7.50
7	Short, Luke - ***Bold Rider*** [1953] PBO. Cover by Bill Reusswig	$1.25	$3.75	$7.50
8	Fuller, William - ***Back Country*** [1954] PBO. Cover by Stanley Borack.	$1.25	$3.75	$7.50
D-9	Anthology edited by Groff Conklin - ***Six Great Short Novels Of Science Fiction*** [1954] PBO. Cover by Richard Powers	$1.35	$4.00	$8.00
F-10	Anthology edited by A. M. Krich - ***The Ribald Reader: 2000 Years Of Lusty Love And Laughter*** [1954] PBO. Cover by Sheilah Beckett.	$1.25	$3.75	$7.50
11	Foreman, L. L. - ***Arrow In The Dust*** [1954] PBO. Cover by Robert Stanley.	$1.25	$3.75	$7.50
12	MacDonald, John D. - ***Area Of Suspicion*** [1954] PBO. Cover by Stanley Borack	$7.00	$22.50	$45.00
13	Vicker, Angus - ***Fever Heat*** [1954] PBO. Cover by Carl Bobertz	$1.25	$3.75	$7.50
14	Flynn, T. T. - ***The Man From Laramie*** [1954] PBO. Cover by Stanley Borack	$1.25	$3.75	$7.50

		G	VG	F
D-15	Anthology edited by A. M. Krich - ***Men*** [1954] PBO. Cover by Walter Brooks.	$1.25	$3.75	$7.50
F-16	Warren, Robert P. & Erskine, Albert - editors - ***Short Story Masterpieces*** [1954] PBO. Cover by Walter Brooks.	$1.35	$4.00	$8.00
17	Kyle, Robert - ***The Crooked City*** [1954] PBO. Cover by Verne Tossey.	$1.25	$3.75	$7.50
18	Hamilton, Donald - ***Smoky Valley*** [1954] PBO. Cover by Verne Tossey.	$1.25	$3.75	$7.50
19	Fenton, Charles - ***Conduct Unbecoming*** [1954] PBO. Cover by Jerry Powell.	$1.00	$3.00	$6.00
D-20	Weeks, Jack - ***I Detest All My Sins*** [1954] PBO. Cover by Jack McDermott.	$1.00	$3.00	$6.00
21	Cole, William & McKee, Douglas - editors - ***French Cartoons*** [1954] PBO. Cover by Andre Francois.	$1.00	$3.00	$6.00
22	Thompson, Jim - ***The Nothing Man*** [1954] PBO. Cover by Stanley Borack.	$15.00	$45.00	$90.00
23	Savage, Jr., Les - ***Teresa*** [1954] PBO. Cover by Bill George.	$1.25	$3.75	$7.50
24	Peters, Matthew - ***The Joys She Chose*** [1954] PBO. Cover by Stanley Borack.	$1.25	$3.75	$7.50
25	Corbin, Glenn - ***Trouble On Big Cat*** [1954] PBO. Cover by Stanley Borack.	$1.25	$3.75	$7.50
26	Phillips, James Atlee - ***The Deadly Mermaid*** [1954] PBO. Cover by Bill George.	$1.25	$3.75	$7.50
27	Hamilton, Donald - ***Night Walker*** [1954] PBO. Cover by Carl Bobertz.	$1.35	$4.00	$8.00
28	Fuller, William - ***Goat Island*** [1954] PBO. Cover by George Gross.	$1.25	$3.75	$7.50
29	Falstein, Louis - ***Sole Survivor*** [1954] PBO. Cover by Jack McDermott.	$1.25	$3.75	$7.50
30	Forester, C. S. - ***Plain Murder*** [1954] PBO. Cover by Bill George.	$1.25	$3.75	$7.50
31	Short, Luke - ***The Man On The Blue*** [1954] PBO. Cover by Stanley Borack.	$1.25	$3.75	$7.50
32	Crossen, Kendell Foster - ***Year Of Consent*** [1954] PBO. Cover by Robert Stanley.	$1.25	$3.75	$7.50
33	Flynn, T. T. - ***Two Faces West*** [1954] PBO. Cover by Verne Tossey.	$1.25	$3.75	$7.50
34	Cort, David - ***The Calm Man*** [1954] PBO. Cover by George Erikson.	$1.25	$3.75	$7.50
F-35	Anthology edited by Edward Parone - ***Six Great Modern Short Novels*** [1954] PBO. Cover by Walter Brooks.	$1.00	$3.00	$6.00
36	Kyle, Robert - ***The Golden Urge*** [1954] PBO. Cover by Barye Phillips.	$1.25	$3.75	$7.50
37	Savage, Jr., Les - ***Last Of The Breed*** [1954] PBO. Cover by Stanley Borack.	$1.25	$3.75	$7.50
38	Anthology edited by McCauley & Elfrieda - ***The Book Of Prayers: Compiled For Protestant Worship*** [1954] PBO.	$1.00	$3.00	$6.00
39	Anthology edited by Bill Yates - ***Too Funny For Words: A Book For People Who Can't Read*** [1954] PBO. Cartoon book.	$1.00	$3.00	$6.00
D-40	Hart, Constance - ***The Handbook Of Beauty*** [1955] PBO. Photo cover.	$ .75	$2.50	$5.00
41	O'Rourke, Frank - ***Dakota Rifle*** [1955] PBO. Cover by Stanley Borack.	$ .50	$1.50	$3.00
42	Finney, Jack - ***The Body Snatchers*** [1955] PBO. Cover by Jack McDermott.	$3.50	$10.00	$20.00
43	Goodman, Roger B. and Lewin, David - ***New Ways To Greater Word Power*** [1955] PBO. Cover by Walter Brooks.	$ .75	$2.50	$5.00
44	Smith, Lillian - ***Now Is The Time*** [1955] PBO. Cover by Walter Brooks.	$1.00	$3.00	$6.00

		G	VG	F
45	Anthology edited by Daniel Talbot - ***City Of Love*** [1955] PBO. Cover by David Shaw.	$1.00	$3.00	$6.00
46	Hamilton, Donald - ***Line Of Fire*** [1955] PBO. Cover by Raymond Pease.	$1.25	$3.75	$7.50
47	Einstein, Charles - ***The Only Game In Town*** [1955] PBO. Cover by Fletcher Martin.	$1.35	$4.00	$8.00
F-48	Anthology edited by W. W. Goodpasture - ***The Complete Book Of Gardening*** [1955] PBO.	$ .75	$2.50	$5.00
49	Thompson, C. Hall - ***A Gun For Billy Reo*** [1955] PBO. Cover by Stanley Borack.	$1.25	$3.75	$7.50
50	Berenstain, Stanley and Janice - ***Marital Blitz*** [1955] PBO. Cover by Stanley & Janice Berenstain. Cover book.	$1.25	$3.75	$7.50
51	Kyle, Robert - ***Nice Guys Finish Last*** [1955] PBO. Cover by Harry Schaare.	$1.25	$3.75	$7.50
52	Wellman, Manly Wade - ***Fort Sun Dance*** [1955] PBO. Cover by Verne Tossey.	$2.50	$7.50	$15.00
D-53	Fleck, Henrietta and Munves, Elizabeth - ***Everybody's Book Of Modern Diet And Nutrition*** [1955] PBO.	$ .75	$2.50	$5.00
FE-54	Gasser, N.A., Henry - ***How To Draw And Paint*** [1955] PBO. Cover by author.	$ .75	$2.50	$5.00
55	Williams, Richard L. & Myers, David - ***What, When, Where And How To Drink*** [1955] PBO. Cover by Richard Powers.	$ .75	$2.50	$5.00
D-56	Forbes, Gordon - ***Too Near The Sun*** [1955] PBO. Cover by Robert Maguire.	$1.35	$4.00	$8.00
57	Foreman, L. L. - ***Woman Of The Avalon*** [1955] PBO. Cover by Stanley Borack.	$1.25	$3.75	$7.50
58	Gordon, Ian - ***After Innocence*** [1955] PBO. Cover by Robert Maguire.	$1.35	$4.00	$8.00
59	O'Rourke, Frank - ***The Big Fifty*** [1955] PBO. Cover by George Gross.	$1.25	$3.75	$7.50
60	Anthology edited by Rafferty & Moore - ***Dell Crossword Puzzles*** [1955] PBO.	$4.00	$12.50	$25.00
61	Humphreys, John R. - ***The Dirty Shame*** [1955] PBO. Cover by Eugene DiScala.	$1.25	$3.75	$7.50
62	MacDonald, John D. - ***A Bullet For Cinderella*** [1955] PBO. Cover by George Gross.	$7.00	$22.50	$45.00
63	Scott, William R. - ***Hunger Mountain*** [1955] PBO. Cover by Louis Marchetti.	$1.25	$3.75	$7.50
64	Anthology edited by Cole & McKee - ***More French Cartoons*** [1955] PBO. Cover by Andre Francois. Cartoon book.	$1.00	$3.00	$6.00
65	Savage, Jr., Les - ***Return To Warbow*** [1955] PBO. Cover by Frank McCarthy.	$1.25	$3.75	$7.50
66	Kyle, Robert - ***A Tiger In The Night*** [1955] PBO. Cover by George Gross.	$1.25	$3.75	$7.50
67	Cushman, Dan - ***The Fastest Gun*** [1955] PBO. Cover by George Gross.	$1.25	$3.75	$7.50
68	Short, Luke - ***Bought With A Gun*** [1955] PBO. Cover by Stanley Borack.	$1.25	$3.75	$7.50
FE-69	Anthology edited by Warren & Erskine - ***Six Centuries Of Great Poetry*** [1955] PBO. Cover by Jerome Kuhl.	$1.35	$4.00	$8.00
70	Short, Luke - ***Marauders' Moon*** [1955] PBO. Cover by Stanley Borack.	$1.25	$3.75	$7.50
71	Rice, John Andrew - ***Local Color*** [1955] PBO. Cover by Arthur Shilstone.	$1.00	$3.00	$6.00
D-72	McClintock, Marshall - ***How To Build And Operate A Model Railroad*** [1955] PBO. Sixteen pages of photos.	$1.00	$3.00	$6.00
73	Daniels, Harold R. - ***In His Blood*** [1955] PBO. Cover by Stanley Borack.	$1.25	$3.75	$7.50
74	Appell, George C. - ***Queen's Own*** [1955] PBO. Cover by George Gross.	$1.25	$3.75	$7.50

		G	VG	F
FE-75	De Motte, Warren - ***The Long Playing Record Guide*** [1955] PBO.	$1.00	$3.00	$6.00
76	Einstein, Charles - ***Wiretap!*** [1955] PBO. Cover by Robert Schulz.	$1.35	$4.00	$8.00
77	Anthology selected by Michael Shayne - ***Dangerous Dames*** [1955] PBO. Cover by Robert Stanley.	$1.50	$5.00	$10.00
78	Hatlo, Jimmy - ***Little Iodine*** [1955] PBO. Cover by Jimmy Hatlo. Cartoon book.	$6.00	$20.00	$40.00
79	Anthology edited by Louis G. Cowan - ***The $64,000 Question Official Quiz Book*** [1955] PBO. TV tie-in.	$ .75	$2.50	$5.00
D-80	Collection edited by Gilbert Millstein - ***Short Stories, Short Plays And Songs By Noel Coward*** [1955] PBO.	$1.00	$3.00	$6.00
D-81	Grove, Walt - ***Down*** [1955] Cover by C. E. Monroe, Jr.	$ .65	$2.00	$4.00
82	Rifkin, Shepard - ***Texas, Blood Red*** [1956] PBO. Cover by George Gross.	$1.25	$3.75	$7.50
83	Samuels, Charles and Louise - ***Night Fell On Georgia*** [1956] PBO. Cover by Richard Powers.	$1.25	$3.75	$7.50
FE-84	Anthology - ***The New Hammond-Dell World Atlas*** [1956] PBO.	$ .75	$2.50	$5.00
85	MacDonald, John D. - ***April Evil*** [1956] PBO. Cover by Robert Maguire.	$7.00	$22.50	$45.00
D-86	Einstein, Charles - ***While The City Sleeps*** [1956] Cover by Mitchell Hooks. Movie tie-in.	$1.25	$3.75	$7.50
87	Lomax, Bliss - ***The Loner*** [1956] PBO. Cover by Tom Ryan.	$1.25	$3.75	$7.50
88	Bryan, Michael - ***Intent To Kill*** [1956] PBO. Cover by Richard Powers.	$1.25	$3.75	$7.50
89	O' Rourke, Frank - ***Battle Royal*** [1956] PBO. Cover by George Gross.	$1.25	$3.75	$7.50
D-90	Roueche, Berton - ***The Last Enemy*** [1956] PBO. Cover by Mitchell Hooks.	$1.00	$3.00	$6.00
91	Hamilton, Donald - ***Mad River*** [1956] PBO. Cover by George Gross.	$1.25	$3.75	$7.50
92	Jessup, Richard - ***Night Boat To Paris*** [1956] PBO. Cover by George Ziel.	$1.25	$3.75	$7.50
93	Anthology edited by Bill Yates - ***Forever Funny*** [1956] PBO. Cartoon book.	$1.00	$3.00	$6.00
94	Halper, Albert - ***Atlantic Avenue*** [1956] PBO. Cover by Arthur Shilstone.	$ .75	$2.50	$5.00
95	Carse, Robert - ***The Devil's Spawn*** [1956] PBO. Cover by Mitchell Hooks.	$1.35	$4.00	$8.00
96	Roberts, MacLennan - ***The Great Locomotive Chase*** [1956] PBO. Cover by William George. Movie tie-in.	$1.50	$5.00	$10.00
97	Anthology edited by Charles Preston - ***Juvenile Delinquency*** [1956] PBO. Cover by Irwin Caplan. Cartoon book.	$1.25	$3.75	$7.50
FE-98	Hunter, Sam - ***Modern French Painting 1855-1956*** [1956] PBO. Cover by Georges Seurat.	$ .75	$2.50	$5.00
D-99	Anthology edited by Daniel Talbot - ***Thirteen Great Stories*** [1956] PBO. Cover by Mitchell Hooks.	$1.00	$3.00	$6.00
FE-100	Anthology edited by Edward Parone - ***Six Great Modern Plays*** [1956] PBO. Cover by Walter Brooks.	$ .75	$2.50	$5.00
103	Flynn, I. I. - ***The Angry Man*** [1956] PBO. Cover by George Gross.	$1.25	$3.75	$7.50
104	O'Rourke, Frank - ***The Last Chance*** [1956] PBO. Cover by John McDermott.	$1.00	$3.00	$6.00
105	Fuller, William - ***The Pace That Kills*** [1956] PBO. Cover by Mitchell Hooks.	$1.25	$3.75	$7.50
106	Dietrich, Robert (Howard Hunt) - ***Be My Victim*** [1956] PBO. Cover by Arthur Sussman.	$1.25	$3.75	$7.50
107	Chidsey, Donald Barr - ***Singapore Passage*** [1956]. PBO. Cover by Mitchell Hooks.	$1.00	$3.00	$6.00
108	O'Rourke, Frank - ***Segundo*** [1956] PBO. Cover by Sam Bates.	$1.00	$3.00	$6.00

		G	VG	F
109	Jessup, Richard - ***Cry Passion*** [1956] PBO. Cover by Victor Kalin.	$1.00	$3.00	$6.00
A-110	Anthology - ***Riders West -*** [1956] PBO.	$1.00	$3.00	$6.00
A-111	Gordon, Ian - ***The Big Success*** [1956] PBO. Cover by Richard Powers.	$ .75	$2.50	$5.00
A-112	Daniels, Harold R. - ***The Girl in 304*** [1956] PBO. Cover by Walter Brooks.	$1.00	$3.00	$6.00
A-113	MacDonald, John D. - ***Murder in The Wind*** [1956] PBO. Cover by George Gross.	$7.00	$22.50	$45.00
A-114	Williams, Charles - ***The Big Bite*** [1956] PBO. Cover by Arthur Sussman.	$1.50	$5.00	$10.00
A-115	Athanas, Verne - ***Maverick*** [1956] PBO. Cover by Sam Bates.	$1.00	$3.00	$6.00
A-116	West, Morris - ***Kundu*** PBO. Cover by Victor Kalin.	$1.00	$3.00	$6.00
A-117	Kane, Frank - ***Johnny Liddell's Morgue*** [1956] PBO. Cover by Robert Stanley.	$1.35	$4.00	$8.00
A-118	Kinkaid, Matt - ***The Race of Giants*** [1956] PBO.	$1.00	$3.00	$6.00
A-119	Norman, James - ***Cimarron Trace*** [1956] PBO. Cover by George Gross.	$1.00	$3.00	$6.00
A-120	O'Farrell, William - ***Wetback*** [1956] PBO. Cover by Mitchell Hooks.	$1.25	$3.75	$7.50
A-121	Einstein, Charles - ***The Last Laugh*** [1956] PBO. Cover by John Fernie.	$1.35	$4.00	$8.00
A-122	Short, Luke - ***The Branded Men*** [1956] PBO. Cover by Sam Bates.	$1.00	$3.00	$6.00
A-123	Hamilton, Donald - ***Assignment: Murder*** [1956] PBO. Cover by Victor Kalin.	$1.25	$3.75	$7.50
A-124	Steur, Arthur - ***Rebel Gun*** [1956] PBO.	$1.00	$3.00	$6.00
A-125	Marge - ***This is Little Lulu*** [1956] PBO. Cover by Marge.	$8.00	$25.00	$50.00
A-126	Kane, Frank - ***Key Witness*** [1956] PBO. Cover by Victor Kalin.	$1.25	$3.75	$7.50
A-127	Foreman, L. L. - ***Lone Hand*** [1956] PBO. Cover by Sam Bates.	$1.00	$3.00	$6.00
A-128	Sturgeon, Theodore - ***The King And Four Queens*** [1956] PBO. Cover by Sam Bates. Movie tie-in with Clark Gable.	$6.00	$20.00	$40.00
A-129	Anthology edited by Charles Preston - ***Bottoms Up!*** [1957] PBO.	$1.00	$3.00	$6.00
A-130	MacDonald, John D. - ***Death Trap*** [1956] PBO. Cover by Victor Kalin.	$6.00	$20.00	$40.00
A-131	O'Rourke, Frank - ***The Bravados*** [1957] PBO.	$1.00	$3.00	$6.00
A-132	Thompson, C. Hall - ***Under The Badge*** [1957} PBO.	$1.25	$3.75	$7.50
A-133	Fuller, William - ***The Girl in The Frame*** [1957] PBO. Cover by Victor Kalin.	$1.25	$3.75	$7.50
A-134	Short, Luke - ***Bold Rider*** [1957] PBO.	$1.00	$3.00	$6.00
A-135	Frazee, Steve - ***Desert Guns*** [1957] PBO. Cover by Harry Schaare.	$1.00	$3.00	$6.00
A-136	Locke, Robert Donald - ***A Taste Of Brass*** [1957] PBO. Cover by Al Brule.	$1.00	$3.00	$6.00
A-137	Savage, John - ***A Shady Place To Die*** [1957] PBO.	$1.00	$3.00	$6.00
A-138	Wayne, Joseph - ***Showdown At Stony Crest*** [1957] PBO. Cover by Harry Schaare.	$1.00	$3.00	$6.00
A-139	Jack Finney - ***The House Of Numbers*** [1957] PBO. Cover by Daniel Schwartz.	$2.50	$7.50	$15.00
A-140	Cushman, Dan - ***Tall Wyoming*** [1957] PBO. Cover by Victor Kalin.	$1.00	$3.00	$6.00
A-141	Dietrich, Robert (Howard Hunt) - ***Murder On The Rocks*** [1956] PBO. Cover by Arthur Sussman.	$1.25	$3.75	$7.50
A-142	Kane, Frank - ***The Living End*** [1957] PBO. Cover by Victor Kalin.	$1.25	$3.75	$7.50
A-143	Ferber, Richard - ***The Outcast*** [1957] PBO.	$1.00	$3.00	$6.00
A-144	Kane, Henry - ***Death For Sale*** [1957] PBO. Cover by Victor Kalin.	$1.25	$3.75	$7.50
A-145	Bryan, Michael - ***Murder in Majorca*** [1957] PBO.	$1.00	$3.00	$6.00

		G	VG	F
A-146	Fray, Al - ***The Dice Spelled Murder*** [1957] PBO.	$1.25	$3.75	$7.50
A-147	Cheshire, Giff - ***Year Of The Gun*** [1957] PBO. Cover by Victor Kalin.	$1.00	$3.00	$6.00
A-148	Dawson, Peter - ***Treachery At Rock Point*** [1957] PBO. Cover by Victor Kalin.	$1.00	$3.00	$6.00
A-149	Brennan, Louis A. - ***Death At Flood Tide*** [1958] PBO. Cover by Victor Kalin.	$ .75	$2.50	$5.00
A-150	Bonham, Frank - ***Tough Country*** [1958]	$1.00	$3.00	$6.00
A-151	Short, Luke - ***The Man On The Blue*** [1958]	$1.00	$3.00	$6.00
A-152	MacDonald, John D. - ***The Price of Murder*** [1957] Cover by Victor Kalin.	$7.00	$22.50	$45.00
A-153	Fuller, William - ***Brad Dolan's Blonde Cargo*** [1957] PBO. Cover by Victor Kalin.	$1.25	$3.75	$7.50
A-154	Short, Luke - ***Bought With A Gun*** [1958] Cover by Stanley Borack.	$1.00	$3.00	$6.00
A-155	Kyle, Robert - ***Blackmail, Inc.*** [1958] Cover by Victor Kalin	$1.25	$3.75	$7.50
A-156	Wormser, Richard - ***The Body Looks Familiar*** [1958] PBO.	$1.25	$3.75	$7.50
A-157	O'Rourke, Frank - ***The Bravados*** [1958] Cover by Sam Bates. Movie tie-in	$1.00	$3.00	$6.00
A-158	Fuller, William - ***Brad Dolan's Miami Manhunt*** [1958] PBO.	$1.25	$3.75	$7.50
A-159	McKimmey, James - ***The Perfect Victim*** [1958] PBO. Cover by Abbett.	$1.25	$3.75	$7.50
A-160	Kruger, Paul - ***A Bullet For A Blonde*** [1958] PBO.	$1.25	$3.75	$7.50
A-161	Fray, Al - ***Come Back For More*** [1958] PBO.	$1.00	$3.00	$6.00
A-162	Ferber, Richard - ***The Hostiles*** [1958] PBO.	$1.00	$3.00	$6.00
A-163	Stokes, Manning Lee - ***Under Cover Of Night*** [1958] PBO. Cover by Darcy	$1.25	$3.75	$7.50
A-164	Williams, Charles - ***Talk Of The Town*** [1958]	$1.35	$4.00	$8.00
A-165	Williams, Charles - ***All The Way*** [1958] PBO. Cover by Darcy...	$1.35	$4.00	$8.00
A-166	Flynn, T. T. - ***The Man From Nowhere*** [1958]	$1.25	$3.75	$7.50
A-167	Fray, Al - ***Built For Trouble*** [1958] PBO. Cover by Robert McGinnis.	$1.25	$3.75	$7.50
A-168	Ehrlich, Jack - ***Revenge*** [1958] PBO. Cover by Robert McGinnis.	$1.35	$4.00	$8.00
A-169	East, Michael - ***The Concubine*** [1958] PBO. Cover by Robert McGinnis.	$1.00	$3.00	$6.00
A-170	Daniels, Harold - ***The Snatch*** [1958] PBO. Cover by Mitchell Hooks.	$1.00	$3.00	$6.00
A-171	Blackburn, Tom W. - ***Buckskin Man*** [1958] PBO. Cover by Victor Kalin.	$1.00	$3.00	$6.00
A-172	Evarts, Hal G. - ***The Long Rope*** [1958] PBO. Cover by Robert McGinnis.	$1.00	$3.00	$6.00
A-173	Kaz - ***Nellie The Nurse*** [1958]	$1.50	$5.00	$10.00
A-174	Ferber, Richard - ***The Raiders*** [1959] PBO. Cover by Robert Stanley.	$1.00	$3.00	$6.00
A-175	Dietrich, Robert (Howard Hunt) - ***The House On Q Street*** [1959] PBO. Cover by Robert McGinnis.	$1.25	$3.75	$7.50
A-176	Huggins, Roy - ***Seventy-Seven Sunset Strip*** [1959] PBO. Cover by Robert McGinnis. TV tie-in.	$1.50	$5.00	$10.00
A-177	Bonham, Frank - ***Sound Of Gunfire*** [1959] PBO. Cover by Robert McGinnis.	$1.00	$3.00	$6.00
A-178	Anthology ed. by Bill Yates - ***The Other Woman*** [1959] PBO.	$1.00	$3.00	$6.00
A-179	Williams, Mary McGee & Kane, Irene - ***On Becoming A Woman*** [1959] PBO. Illus. by Gregori.	$1.00	$3.00	$6.00
A-180	Einstein, Charles & Silliphant, S. - ***The Naked City*** [1959] TV tie-in.	$1.25	$3.75	$7.50
A-181	Watkin, Lawrence Edward - ***Darby O'Gill And The Little People*** [1959] PBO. Movie tie-in with photo cover.	$2.00	$6.00	$12.00
A-182	Duncan, Peter - ***Sweet Cheat*** [1959] PBO. Cover by Darcy.	$1.00	$3.00	$6.00

		G	VG	F
A-183	Brown, Will C. - ***Laredo Road*** [1959] PBO. Cover by Robert Stanley	$1.00	$3.00	$6.00
A-184	Leonard, Elmore - ***Last Stand At Saber River*** [1959]	$5.50	$17.50	$35.00
A-185	McKimmey, James - ***Winner Take All*** [1959] PBO. Cover by Darcy	$1.25	$3.75	$7.50
A-186	Bonham, Frank - ***Last Stage West*** [1959] PBO. Cover by George Gross.	$1.00	$3.00	$6.00
A-187	McElfresh, Adeline - ***Kay Manion, M.D.*** [1959] PBO. Cover by Victor Kalin.	$ .50	$1.50	$3.00
A-188	McCoy, Horace - ***Corruption City*** [1959]	$2.00	$6.00	$12.00
A-189	Fuller, William - ***Tight Squeeze*** [1959] PBO. Cover by Victor Kalin	$1.25	$3.75	$7.50
A-190	Keene, James - ***McCracken in Command*** [1959] PBO. Cover by John Leone	$1.00	$3.00	$6.00
A-191	Parsons, E. M. - ***Texas Heller*** [1959] PBO. Cover by Robert Stanley	$1.00	$3.00	$6.00
A-192	Kyle, Robert - ***Model For Murder*** [1959] PBO. Cover by Robert McGinnis.	$1.25	$3.75	$7.50
A-193	Markson, David - ***Epitaph For A Tramp*** [1959] PBO. Cover by Robert McGinnis.	$1.25	$3.75	$7.50
A-194	Jessup, Richard - ***The Deadly Duo*** [1959] PBO. Cover by Freeman Elliot	$1.25	$3.75	$7.50
A-197	Dietrich, Robert (Howard Hunt) - ***End Of A Stripper*** [1960] PBO. Cover by Freeman Elliot.	$1.50	$5.00	$10.00
A-198	Ferber, Richard - ***Doctor With A Gun*** [1960] PBO. Cover by John Leone	$1.00	$3.00	$6.00
A-199	Adams, Clifton - ***Killer In Town*** [1960]	$1.00	$3.00	$6.00
A-200	Benson, O. G. - ***Cain's Woman*** [1960] PBO. Cover by Darcy	$1.00	$3.00	$6.00
A-201	Wayne, Joseph - ***The Gun And The Law*** [1960]	$1.00	$3.00	$6.00
A-202	Cushman, Dan - ***The Half-Caste*** [1960] PBO. Cover by Robert McGinnis	$1.25	$3.75	$7.50
A-205	Keene, James - ***Gunman's Harvest*** [1960]	$1.00	$3.00	$6.00
A-206	McElfresh, Adeline - ***Wings For Nurse Bennett*** [1960] PBO. Cover by Tommy Shoemaker.	$ .50	$1.50	$3.00
A-207	Evarts, Hal G. - ***The Blazing Land*** [1960] PBO. Cover by Bob Stanley	$1.00	$3.00	$6.00
A-209	Kaz - ***Nellie's Bedfellows*** [1960] PBO. Cover by Kaz.	$1.50	$5.00	$10.00
B-101	Anthology edited by Dr. W. W. Bauer - ***The Official American Medical Association Book Of Health*** [1957]	$ .50	$1.50	$3.00
B-102	Anthology edited by Leonard Engel - ***New Worlds Of Modern Science*** [1956] PBO. Cover by Seymour Chwast.	$ .50	$1.50	$3.00
B-103	Anthology edited by Judith Merril - ***SF: The Year's Greatest Science-Fiction And Fantasy*** [1956] PBO. Cover by Richard Powers	$1.35	$4.00	$8.00
B-104	Haber, Ph.D., Heinz - ***The Walt Disney Story Of Our Friend The Atom*** [1956] PBO. Cover by Richard Powers.	$2.00	$6.00	$12.00
B-105	Ilton, Paul & Roberts, MacLennan - ***Moses And The Ten Commandments*** [1956] PBO. Cover by Mitchell Hooks.	$1.25	$3.75	$7.50
B-106	Anthology edited by Leon McCauley - ***A Treasury Of Faith*** [1957]	$ .50	$1.50	$3.00
B-107	Anthology edited by Don Congdon - ***Stories For The Dead Of Night*** [1957] PBO. Cover by Jeanette Cissman.	$2.00	$6.00	$12.00
B-108	Brennan, Louis A. - ***More Than Flesh*** [1957]	$1.25	$3.75	$7.50
B-109	Carse, Robert - ***The Fabulous Buccaneer*** [1957]	$1.00	$3.00	$6.00
B-110	Anthology edited by Judith Merril - ***SF: The Year's Greatest Science-Fiction and Fantasy #2*** [1957] PBO. Second Annual Volume. Cover by Richard Powers	$1.35	$4.00	$8.00
B-111	Boltar, Russell - ***By Appointment Only*** [1957]	$ .75	$2.50	$5.00
B-112	MacDonald, John D. - ***A Man Of Affairs*** [1957] PBO. Cover by Victor Kalin.	$6.00	$20.00	$40.00

		G	VG	F
B-113	Beater, Jack and Roberts, MacLennan - ***Sea Avenger*** [1957] PBO. Cover by Harry Schaare.	$1.00	$3.00	$6.00
B-114	Williams, Charles - ***Girl Out Back*** [1958] PBO. Cover by Darcy.	$1.35	$4.00	$8.00
B-115	Hamilton, Donald - ***The Big Country*** [1958] PBO.	$1.25	$3.75	$7.50
B-116	Daniels, Harold R. - ***The Accused*** [1958] PBO. Cover by Stone.	$1.25	$3.75	$7.50
B-117	MacDonald, John D. - ***The Deceivers*** [1958] PBO. Cover by Mitchell Hooks.	$6.00	$20.00	$40.00
B-118	Jessup, Richard - ***Lowdown*** [1958] PBO.	$1.00	$3.00	$6.00
B-119	Anthology edited by Judith Merril - ***SF: The Year's Greatest Science-Fiction And Fantasy #3*** [1958] PBO. Cover by Richard Powers.	$1.35	$4.00	$8.00
B-120	Sturgeon, Theodore - ***The Cosmic Rape*** [1958] PBO. Cover by Richard Powers.	$6.00	$20.00	$40.00
B-121	MacDonald, John D. - ***Soft Touch*** [1958] PBO. Cover by Victor Kalin.	$7.00	$22.50	$45.00
B-122	Hall, Warner - ***Untamed*** [1958] PBO. Cover by Ray Olivere.	$1.00	$3.00	$6.00
B-123	Kane, Frank - ***Syndicate Girl*** [1958] PBO. Cover by Robert McGinnis.	$1.25	$3.75	$7.50
B-124	Boltar, Russell - ***The Two Lives Of Dr. Stratton*** [1959]	$ .50	$1.50	$3.00
B-125	Kane, Frank - ***The Lineup*** [1959] PBO. Cover by Victor Kalin.	$1.25	$3.75	$7.50
B-126	Shiflet, Kenneth E. - ***The Valiant Strain*** [1959] PBO.	$1.00	$3.00	$6.00
B-127	MacDonald, John D. - ***Deadly Welcome*** [1959] PBO. Cover by Robert McGinnis.	$7.00	$22.50	$45.00
B-128	Johnson, Grady - ***The Five Pennies*** [1959] PBO. Cover by Victor Kalin. Movie tie-in.	$1.00	$3.00	$6.00
B-129	Anthology edited by Judith Merril - ***SF: The Year's Greatest Science-Fiction And Fantasy #4*** [1959] PBO. Cover by Richard Powers.	$1.35	$4.00	$8.00
B-130	Short, Luke - ***Marauders' Moon*** [1959]	$1.00	$3.00	$6.00
B-131	Albee, George Sumner - ***Girl On The Beach*** [1959]	$ .75	$2.50	$5.00
B-132	Kingery, Don - ***Paula*** [1959]	$ .75	$2.50	$5.00
B-133	Thomas, Bob - ***The Flesh Merchants*** [1959] PBO. Cover by Robert McGinnis.	$1.00	$3.00	$6.00
B-134	MacDonald, John D. - ***On The Make*** [1959]	$2.50	$7.50	$15.00
B-135	O'Brien, Thomas L. - ***The Witch Finder*** [1959] PBO. Cover by Mitchell Hooks.	$1.35	$4.00	$8.00
B-136	Grove, Walt - ***The Joy Boys*** [1959] PBO. Cover by Mitchell Hooks.	$1.25	$3.75	$7.50
B-137	Kane, Frank - ***Juke Box King*** [1959] PBO. Cover by Freeman Eliot.	$1.35	$4.00	$8.00
B-138	Vonnegut, Jr., Kurt - ***The Sirens Of Titan*** [1959] PBO. Cover by Richard Powers.	$6.00	$20.00	$40.00
B-139	Bristow, Bob - ***Sin Street*** [1959]	$1.00	$3.00	$6.00
B-140	Thompson, C. Hall - ***Montana!*** [1959] PBO. Cover by Victor Kalin.	$1.00	$3.00	$6.00
B-141	Anthology edited by John D. MacDonald - ***The Lethal Sex*** [1959] PBO. Cover by Bob McGinnis.	$4.50	$14.00	$28.00
B-142	- ***Poker According To Maverick*** [1959] PBO. TV photo cover and tie-in.	$2.50	$7.50	$15.00
B-143	Berenstain, Stanley and Janice - ***Marital Blitz*** [1959] Cover by Berenstains.	$1.00	$3.00	$6.00
B-144	Fuller, William - ***The Pace That Kills*** [1960]	$1.25	$3.75	$7.50
B-145	Ard, William - ***When She Was Bad*** [1960] PBO. Cover by Bob McGinnis.	$1.50	$5.00	$10.00
B-146	MacDonald, John D. - ***April Evil*** [1960] Cover by Robert McGinnis.	$2.50	$7.50	$15.00
B-147	Sheridan, Jack - ***Fire In The Flesh*** [1960] PBO. Cover by Mitchell Hooks.	$1.25	$3.75	$7.50

		G	VG	F
B-148	Chapin, Victor (Adaptation) - ***Career*** [1959] PBO. Photo cover and movie tie-in.	$1.00	$3.00	$6.00
B-149	Anthology edited by K. Rafferty & R. Moore - ***Dell Crossword Puzzles*** [1960]	$2.50	$7.50	$15.00
B-150	Kane, Frank - ***A Short Bier*** [1960] PBO. Cover by Harry Bennett.	$1.25	$3.75	$7.50
B-151	Brennan, Louis A. - ***The Long Knife*** [1960] PBO. Cover by Robert McGinnis.	$1.00	$3.00	$6.00
B-152	Roos, Kelley - ***The Scent Of Mystery*** [1959] PBO. Movie tie-in.	$1.00	$3.00	$6.00
B-153	Dolan, Brad - ***Local Talent*** [1960] Cover by Mitchell Hooks.	$ .75	$2.50	$5.00
B-154	Ehrlich, Jack - ***Parole*** [1960] PBO. Cover by Robert Abbett.	$1.35	$4.00	$8.00
B-155	Kane, Henry - ***Peter Gunn*** [1960] PBO. Photo cover & TV tie-in.	$1.50	$5.00	$10.00
B-156	Loomis, Noel - ***Have Gun, Will Travel*** [1960] PBO. Cover by Robert Stanley. TV tie-in.	$2.50	$7.50	$15.00
B-157	McKimmey, James - ***Cornered!*** [1960] PBO. Cover by Harry Schaare.	$1.25	$3.75	$7.50
B-158	Liston, Jack - ***Man Bait*** [1960] PBO. Cover by Maguire.	$1.00	$3.00	$6.00
B-159	Kane, Frank - ***Time To Prey*** [1960] PBO. Cover by Harry Bennett.	$1.25	$3.75	$7.50
B-160	Haedrich, Marcel - ***Crack In The Mirror*** [1960] PBO. 1st U.S. printing. Cover by Tom Miller. Movie tie-in.	$1.00	$3.00	$6.00
B-161	Marcus, Jerry - ***Just Married*** [1960]	$1.00	$3.00	$6.00
B-162	Dietrich, Robert (Howard Hunt) - ***Mistress To Murder*** [1960] PBO. Cover by McGinnis.	$1.25	$3.75	$7.50
B-163	Dietrich, Robert (Howard Hunt) - ***Murder On Her Mind*** [1960] PBO. Cover by McGinnis.	$1.25	$3.75	$7.50
B-164	Kingery, Don - ***Good Time Girl*** [1960] PBO. Cover by McGinnis.	$1.00	$3.00	$6.00
B-165	Conroy, Albert - ***Mr. Lucky*** [1960] PBO. Cover by Mort Engle.	$1.25	$3.75	$7.50
B-166	Berenstain, Stanley and Janice - ***Bedside Lover Boy*** [1960] PBO. Cover by author.	$1.25	$3.75	$7.50
B-167	MacDonald, John D. - ***Murder In The Wind*** [1960] Cover by Bob Abbett.	$2.50	$7.50	$15.00
B-168	McElfresh, Adeline - ***Ann Kenyon: Surgeon*** [1960] PBO. Cover by Bob Abbett.	$ .50	$1.50	$3.00
B-169	McKimmey, James - ***Twenty Four Hours To Kill*** [1961] PBO. Cover by Robert McGinnis.	$1.25	$3.75	$7.50
B-170	Hamilton, Donald - ***The Man From Santa Clara*** [1960]	$1.00	$3.00	$6.00
B-171	Howard, Mark - ***A Time For Passion*** [1960] PBO. Cover by Mitchell Hooks.	$1.00	$3.00	$6.00
B-172	Richmond, Roe - ***The Deputy*** [1960] PBO. TV tie-in. Cover by John Leone.	$1.00	$3.00	$6.00
B-173	Kane, Frank - ***Key Witness*** [1960] Movie tie-in. Cover by Darrel Greene.	$1.00	$3.00	$6.00
B-174	Kane, Frank - ***Due Or Die*** [1960] PBO. Cover by Harry Bennett.	$1.25	$3.75	$7.50
B-175	Wiseman, B. - ***Boatniks*** [1961]	$1.00	$3.00	$6.00
B-176	Ferber, Richard - ***Bitter Valley*** [1961] PBO. Cover by Carl Hantman.	$1.00	$3.00	$6.00
B-177	McElfresh, Adeline - ***Night Call*** [1961] PBO. Cover by Bob Abbett.	$ .75	$2.50	$5.00
B-178	Kyle, Robert - ***Kill Now, Pay Later*** [1960] PBO. Cover by McGinnis.	$1.25	$3.75	$7.50
B-179	Stowe, Elizabeth - ***RX For Love*** [1960] PBO. Cover by Victor Kalin.	$ .50	$1.50	$3.00
B-180	Wohl, Burton - ***A Cold Wind In August*** [1960] PBO. Cover by Bob Abbett.	$1.00	$3.00	$6.00
B-181	O'Rourke, Frank - ***The Great Bank Robbery*** [1961] PBO. Cover by Carl Hantman.	$1.25	$3.75	$7.50

		G	VG	F
B-182	Dietrich, Robert (Howard Hunt) - ***Steve Bentley's Calypso Caper*** [1961] PBO. Cover by Tom Miller.	$1.50	$5.00	$10.00
B-183	Manners, Margaret - ***Love Of Life*** [1961] PBO. Cover by Tom Miller. TV tie-in.	$1.00	$3.00	$6.00
B-184	Anthology edited by Cole & Mckee - ***Touche*** [1961] PBO. Cover by Herve.	$1.00	$3.00	$6.00
B-185	McElfresh, Adeline - ***Kay Manion, M. D.*** [1960]	$ .50	$1.50	$3.00
B-186	Sheers, James C. - ***The Counterfeit Courier*** [1961] PBO. Cover by Bob Abbett.	$ .75	$2.50	$5.00
B-187	Kane, Frank - ***Dead Rite*** [1962] PBO. Cover by Harry Bennett.	$1.25	$3.75	$7.50
B-188	Carroll, Robert - ***Champagne At Dawn*** [1961] PBO. Cover by Bob Abbett.	$1.00	$3.00	$6.00
B-189	Markson, David - ***Epitaph For A Dead Beat*** [1961]	$1.25	$3.75	$7.50
B-190	Kaz (Lawrence Katzman) - ***Calling Nurse Nellie!*** [1961] PBO. Cover by Kaz.	$1.50	$5.00	$10.00
B-191	Cox, William R. - ***Death Comes Early*** [1961] PBO. Cover by McGinnis.	$1.25	$3.75	$7.50
B-192	McKimmey, James - ***The Wrong Ones*** [1961] PBO. Cover by McGinnis.	$1.25	$3.75	$7.50
B-193	Bristow, Bob - ***Marked!*** [1961] PBO. Cover by McGinnis.	$1.25	$3.75	$7.50
B-194	Brown, Will C. - ***Think Fast, Ranger!*** [1961] PBO. Cover by Ronnie Lesser.	$1.00	$3.00	$6.00
B-195	Matheson, Richard - ***Shock!*** [1961] PBO. Cover by Richard Powers.	$3.50	$10.00	$20.00
B-197	Kane, Frank - ***Frank Kane's Stacked Deck*** [1961] PBO. Cover by McGinnis.	$1.25	$3.75	$7.50
B-198	Kane, Henry - ***My Darlin' Evangeline*** [1961] PBO. Cover by Barye Phillips.	$1.25	$3.75	$7.50
B-199	Barbera, Joe & Hanna, Bill - ***Yogi Bear Goes To College*** [1961] PBO. TV tie-in.	$4.00	$12.50	$25.00
B-200	Williams, Mary McGee & Kane, Irene - ***On Becoming A Woman*** [1960]	$ .50	$1.50	$3.00
B-201	McElfresh, Adeline - ***Hospital Hill*** [1961]	$ .50	$1.50	$3.00
B-202	Fradon, Dana - ***Breaking The Laugh Barrier*** [1961] PBO.	$1.00	$3.00	$6.00
B-203	Dietrich, Robert (Howard Hunt) - ***Angel Eyes*** [1961] PBO. Cover by McGinnis.	$1.25	$3.75	$7.50
B-204	Finney, Jack - ***The Body Snatchers*** [1961] Cover by Richard Powers.	$1.50	$5.00	$10.00
B-206	Garis, Roger - ***Never Take Candy From A Stranger*** [1961]	$1.00	$3.00	$6.00
B-207	Dewey, Thomas B. - ***The Golden Hooligan*** [1961] PBO. Cover by Barye Phillips. Drug Book.	$1.35	$4.00	$8.00
B-209	Flynn, T. T. - ***Riding High*** [1961]	$ .75	$2.50	$5.00
B-210	Terrell, Gilbert - ***Willa*** [1961]	$ .75	$2.50	$5.00
B-211	McKimmey, James - ***The Long Ride*** [1961] PBO. Cover by Bob Abbett.	$1.00	$3.00	$6.00
B-213	Kaz - ***Nellie's New Frontier*** [1961] PBO. Cover by Kaz.	$1.50	$5.00	$10.00
B-214	Carse, Robert - ***Morgan The Pirate*** [1961] PBO. Cover by George Gross. Movie tie-in.	$1.50	$5.00	$10.00
B-215	Dewey, Tomas B. - ***Go, Honey Lou*** [1962] PBO. Cover by Victor Kalin.	$1.35	$4.00	$8.00
B-216	Wormser, Richard - ***Thief Of Baghdad*** [1961] PBO. Cover by George Gross. Movie tie-in.	$1.35	$4.00	$8.00
B-218	Conroy, Al - ***Clayburn*** [1961] PBO. Cover by George Gross.	$ .75	$2.50	$5.00
B-220	Ehrlich, Jack - ***Slow Burn*** [1961] PBO. Cover by Bob Abbett.	$1.25	$3.75	$7.50
B-225	Prescott, John B. - ***Treasure Of The Black Hills*** [1961] PBO. Cover by George Gross.	$ .75	$2.50	$5.00
B-226	Kane, Frank - ***The Mourning After*** [1961] PBO. Cover by Harry Bennett.	$1.25	$3.75	$7.50
B-227	Ehrlich, Jack - ***Cry, Baby*** [1962] PBO. Cover by Bob Abbett.	$1.25	$3.75	$7.50

		G	VG	F
B-230	McKimmey, James - ***Squeeze Play*** [1962] PBO. Cover by Bob Abbett.	$1.25	$3.75	$7.50
B-232	Rome, Anthony - ***My Kind Of Game*** [1962] PBO. Cover by Victor Kalin.	$ .75	$2.50	$5.00
C-101	Anthology edited by Stephen Becker - ***The American Heritage Reader*** [1956] PBO. Cover by Irwin Glusker.	$ .65	$2.00	$4.00
C-102	Harman, Carter - ***A Popular History Of Music*** [1956] PBO. Cover by Jerome Kuhl.	$ .65	$2.00	$4.00
C-103	Anthology edited by Jan Ehrenwald, M.D. - ***From Medicine Man To Freud*** [1956]	$ .65	$2.00	$4.00
C-104	Anthology edited by A. M. Krich - ***The Second Ribald Reader*** [1956] PBO.	$1.25	$3.75	$7.50
C-105	Anthology edited by Robert Terrall - ***Great Scenes From Great Novels*** [1956]	$ .65	$2.00	$4.00
C-106	Hart, Constance - ***The Handbook Of Beauty*** [1958]	$ .50	$1.50	$3.00
C-107	Anthology edited by Don Congdon - ***Combat: European Theater: World War II*** [1958] PBO. Cover by Robert Schulz.	$1.00	$3.00	$6.00
C-108	Anthology edited by Don Congdon - ***Combat: Pacific Theater: World War II*** [1958]	$1.00	$3.00	$6.00
C-109	Rafferty, Kathleen - ***Dell Crossword Dictionary*** [1960]	$1.00	$3.00	$6.00
C-110	Krich, A.M. - editor (anthology) - ***Women*** [1960]	$ .65	$2.00	$4.00
C-111	Anthology edited by Groff Conklin - ***Six Great Short Science Fiction Novels*** [1960] PBO. Cover by Richard Powers.	$1.35	$4.00	$8.00
C-112	Mergendahl, Charles - ***Call After Six*** [1961] PBO. Cover by Bob McGinnis.	$1.25	$3.75	$7.50
C-113	Krich, A.M. - editor (anthology) - ***Men*** [1960]	$ .65	$2.00	$4.00
C-115	Robbins, Harold - ***Stiletto*** [1960] PBO. Cover by Abbett. Robbins' only paperback original.	$3.50	$10.00	$20.00
C-117	Boltar, Russell - ***By Appointment Only*** [1961]	$ .65	$2.00	$4.00
C-120	Wohl, Burton - ***A Cold Wind In August*** [1961] Cover by Bob Abbett.	$ .65	$2.00	$4.00
C-121	Caspary, Vera - ***Bachelor In Paradise*** [1961] PBO. Cover by Bob McGinnis. Movie tie-in.	$1.00	$3.00	$6.00
C-127	Kane, Frank - ***The Conspirators*** [1962] PBO. Cover by Mort Engle.	$1.25	$3.75	$7.50
K-101	Albert, Marvin H. - ***Come September*** [1961] Movie tie-in with Rock Hudson & photo cover.	$1.00	$3.00	$6.00
K-102	East, Michael - ***The Naked Country*** [1961]	$ .65	$2.00	$4.00
K-103	Cassill, R. V. - ***Night School*** [1961] PBO. Cover by Robert McGinnis.	$ .65	$2.00	$4.00
K-104	Hume, Doris - ***The Sin Of Susan Slade*** [1961] PBO. Cover by Robert McGinnis. Movie tie-in.	$1.00	$3.00	$6.00
K-105	Roeburt, John - ***Sing Out Sweet Homicide*** [1961] PBO. Cover by Mort Engle. TV tie-in.	$1.25	$3.75	$7.50
K-106	Cooper, Saul - ***My Geisha*** [1961] PBO. Cover by Robert McGinnis. Movie tie-in.	$1.25	$3.75	$7.50
K-107	Wenner, Sim - ***Daisy*** [1961] PBO. Photo cover.	$ .65	$2.00	$4.00
K-108	Pendleton, Chris - ***Too Soon Tomorrow*** [1961] PBO. Cover by Mike Ludlow.	$ .65	$2.00	$4.00
K-109	Anthology edited by Leo Marguiles - ***Mike Shayne's Torrid Twelve*** [1961] PBO. Cover by Robert McGinnis.	$1.35	$4.00	$8.00
K-110	McElfresh, Adeline - ***Jeff Banton, M.D.*** [1962] PBO. Cover by Tom Miller.	$ .50	$1.50	$3.00
K-111	Tetlair, Richard (Richard Jessup) - ***Target For Tonight*** [1962] PBO. Cover by Bob Abbett.	$1.00	$3.00	$6.00
K-112	Castle, Frank - ***Hawaiian Eye*** [1962] PBO. Cover by Harry Bennett. TV tie-in.	$1.35	$4.00	$8.00
K-113	Carroll, Robert - ***Cruise To The Sun*** [1962] PBO. Cover by Terpning.	$ .65	$2.00	$4.00
K-115	McElfresh, Adeline - ***Jill Nolan, R. N.*** [1962]	$ .50	$1.50	$3.00

		G	VG	F
K-116	MacDonald, John D. - ***Soft Touch*** [1962] Cover by McGinnis	$2.50	$7.50	$15.00
K-117	Terrell, Gilbert - ***Missy*** [1962] PBO. Cover by Mort Engel.	$ .65	$2.00	$4.00
M-101	Advisory Board of Aurora Plastics Corp. - ***The Complete Book Of Plastic Model Kits*** [1961]	$3.50	$10.00	$20.00
M-102	Shakespeare, Henry - ***Secrets Of Successful Fishing*** [1962]	$ .75	$2.50	$5.00
R-102	Allingham, Margery - ***Ten Were Missing*** [1961] Cover art by Victor Kalin.	$1.00	$3.00	$6.00
R-103	Rinehart, Mary Roberts - ***The Red Lamp*** [1961] Cover art by Victor Kalin.	$1.00	$3.00	$6.00
R-104	Holton, Leonard - ***The Saint Maker*** [1961] Cover art by Bob Abbett.	$ .65	$2.00	$4.00
R-105	Fair, A.A. - ***Fools Die On Friday*** [1961] Cover art by McGinnis.	$1.00	$3.00	$6.00
R-106	Christie, Agatha - ***Murder At The Vicarage*** [1961] Cover art by William Teason.	$1.00	$3.00	$6.00
R-107	Rinehart, Mary Roberts - ***The State VS Elinor Norton*** [1961] Cover art by Victor Kalin.	$1.00	$3.00	$6.00
R-108	Hely, Elizabeth - ***I'll Be Judge, I'll Be Jury*** [1962] Cover art by Victor Kalin.	$ .65	$2.00	$4.00
R-109	Christie, Agatha - ***Mr. Parker Pyne, Detective*** [1962] Cover art by William Teason.	$1.00	$3.00	$6.00
R-110	Christie, Agatha - ***Murder At Hazelmoor*** [1962] Cover art by William Teason.	$1.00	$3.00	$6.00
R-111	Christie, Agatha - ***Cards On The Table*** [1962] Cover art by William Teason.	$1.00	$3.00	$6.00
R-112	Bingham, John - ***Murder Plan Six*** [1962] Cover art by O.J. Watson.	$1.25	$3.75	$7.50
R-114	McCann, Edson (F. Pohl/Lester Del Ray) - ***Preferred Risk*** [1962] Cover art by Richard Powers.	$2.00	$6.00	$12.00
R-118	Rinehart, Mary Roberts - ***Haunted Lady*** [1962]	$1.00	$3.00	$6.00
R-120	Potts, Jean - ***Lightning Strikes Twice*** [1962] Cover art by William Teason.	$ .65	$2.00	$4.00
R-123	Brand, Max - ***Calling Dr. Kildare*** [1961] Cover art by Tom Miller.	$ .50	$1.50	$3.00
R-125	Brand, Max (Frederick Faust) - ***Dr. Kildare's Trial*** [1962] Cover art by Tom Miller.	$ .65	$2.00	$4.00
R-129	Partch, Virgil Franklin - ***Man The Beast And The Wild, Wild Women*** [1962]	$ .75	$2.50	$5.00
R-137	Cotler, Gordon - ***The Horizontal Lieutenant*** [1962] Cover art by Lee Gregori.	$ .65	$2.00	$4.00

Dell Laurel LB Series. New York: Dell Publishing Co.

		G	VG	F
LB-110	Goodman, Roger B. & Lewin, David - ***New Ways To Greater Word Power*** [1960]	$ .50	$1.50	$3.00
LB-111	Marshack, Alexander - ***The World In Space*** [1958] PBO.	$ .50	$1.50	$3.00
LB-112	Shakespeare, William - ***Hamlet Prince Of Denmark*** [1958]	$ .65	$2.00	$4.00
LB-113	Shakespeare, William - ***The Taming Of The Shrew*** [1958]	$ .65	$2.00	$4.00
LB-114	Shakespeare, William - ***Romeo And Juliet*** [1958]	$ .65	$2.00	$4.00
LB-115	Shakespeare, William - ***Richard III*** [1958]	$ .65	$2.00	$4.00
LB-116	Andersen, Jr., Frank W. - ***Great Flying Stories*** [1958]	$ .65	$2.00	$4.00
LB-117	Haber, Heinz - ***The Walt Disney Story Of Our Friend The Atom*** [1958] Cover by Richard Powers.	$ .65	$2.00	$4.00
LB-118	Shakespeare, William - ***The Merchant Of Venice*** [1958]	$ .65	$2.00	$4.00
LB-119	Shakespeare, William - ***Julius Caesar*** [1958]	$ .65	$2.00	$4.00
LB-120	Poe, Edgar Allan - ***Poe*** [1959] edited by Richard Wilbur.	$ .65	$2.00	$4.00
LB-121	Whitman, Walt - ***Whitman*** [1959] edited by Leslie A. Fiedler.	$ .65	$2.00	$4.00
LB-122	Coleridge, Samuel Taylor - ***Coleridge*** [1959] Edited by G. Robert Strange.	$ .65	$2.00	$4.00
LB-123	Wordsworth, William - ***Wordsworth*** [1959] Edited by David Ferry.	$ .65	$2.00	$4.00

		G	VG	F
LB-124	Shakespeare, William - ***Macbeth*** [1959]	$ .65	$2.00	$4.00
LB-125	Shakespeare, William - ***Twelfth Night Or, What You Will*** [1959]	$ .65	$2.00	$4.00
LB-126	Bennett, George - editor (anthology) - ***Great Tales Of Action And Adventure*** [1959] Cover by Richard Powers.	$ .65	$2.00	$4.00
LB-127	Villiers, Captain A. - editor (anthology) - ***Great Sea Stories*** [1959] Cover by Richard Powers.	$ .65	$2.00	$4.00
LB-128	Kipling, Rudyard - ***Kim*** [1959]	$ .65	$2.00	$4.00
LB-129	Shakespeare, William - ***Othello The Moor Of Venice*** [1959]	$ .65	$2.00	$4.00
LB-130	Shakespeare, William - ***As You Like It*** [1959]	$ .65	$2.00	$4.00
LB-131	Keats, John - ***Keats*** [1959] edited by Richard Wilbur. Cover by Richard Powers.	$ .65	$2.00	$4.00
LB-132	Longfellow, Henry Wadsworth - ***Longfellow*** [1959] edited by Richard Wilbur. Cover by Richard Powers.	$ .65	$2.00	$4.00
LB-133	Shakespeare, William - ***The Winter's Tale*** [1959] Cover by Jerome Kuhl.	$ .65	$2.00	$4.00
LB-134	Shakespeare, William - ***The First Part Of King Henry The Fourth*** [1959] Cover by Jerome Kuhl	$ .65	$2.00	$4.00
LB-135	Stevenson, Robert Louis - ***Kidnapped*** [1960] Cover by Richard Powers.	$ .65	$2.00	$4.00
LB-136	Blake, William - ***Blake*** [1960] edited by Richard Wilbur. Cover by Richard Powers.	$ .65	$2.00	$4.00
LB-137	Shakespeare, William - ***A Midsummer Night's Dream*** [1960] Cover by Jerome Kuhl	$ .65	$2.00	$4.00
LB-138	Dickinson, Emily - ***Emily Dickinson*** [1960] edited by Richard Wilbur. Cover by Richard Powers.	$ .65	$2.00	$4.00
LB-139	Shakespeare, William - ***Much Ado About Nothing*** [1960] Cover by Jerome Kuhl	$ .65	$2.00	$4.00
LB-140	Wyss, Johann - ***The Swiss Family Robinson*** [1960] Cover by Richard Powers.	$ .65	$2.00	$4.00
LB-141	Shakespeare, William - ***King Lear*** [1960] Cover by Jerome Kuhl	$ .65	$2.00	$4.00
LB-144	Shakespeare, William - ***The Sonnets*** [1960] Cover by Jerome Kuhl	$ .65	$2.00	$4.00
LB-145	Wilde, Oscar - ***The Picture Of Dorian Gray*** [1960] Cover by Walter Brooks.	$ .65	$2.00	$4.00
LB-146	Waugh, Evelyn - ***The Loved One*** [1960] Cover by Sheilah Beckett.	$ .65	$2.00	$4.00
LB-147	Browning, Robert - ***Browning*** [1960] edited by Richard Wilbur.	$ .65	$2.00	$4.00
LB-148	Whittier, John Greenleaf - ***Whittier*** [1960] edited by Richard Wilbur.	$ .65	$2.00	$4.00
LB-149	Shakespeare, William - ***The Tempest*** [1961]	$ .65	$2.00	$4.00
LB-150	Shakespeare, William - ***King Richard The Second*** [1961]	$ .65	$2.00	$4.00
LB-151	Marvell, Andrew - ***Marvell*** [1961]	$ .65	$2.00	$4.00
LB-152	Jonson, Ben - ***Ben Jonson*** [1961]	$ .65	$2.00	$4.00
LB-153	Shakespeare, William - ***All's Well That Ends Well*** [1961]	$ .65	$2.00	$4.00
LB-154	Shakespeare, William - ***Antony And Cleopatra*** [1961]	$ .65	$2.00	$4.00
LB-155	Eliot, George - ***Silas Marner*** [1961]	$ .65	$2.00	$4.00
LB-156	Shelley, Percy Bysshe - ***Shelley*** [1962] edited by Richard Wilbur. Cover by Richard Powers.	$ .65	$2.00	$4.00
LB-157	Dryden, John - ***Dryden*** [1962]	$ .65	$2.00	$4.00
LB-158	Shakespeare, William - ***Henry V*** [1962]	$ .65	$2.00	$4.00
LB-159	Shakespeare, William - ***Measure For Measure*** [1962]	$ .65	$2.00	$4.00

Dell Reprint Series. New York: Dell Publishing Co.

1174	Hull, E. M. - ***The Sheik*** [1951]	$1.00	$3.00	$6.00
1333	Mann, E. B. - ***Stampede*** [1950]	$1.00	$3.00	$6.00
1339	Haggard, H. Rider - ***She*** [1950]	$1.25	$3.75	$7.50
1341	Marshall, Edison - ***The Upstart*** [1950]	$1.00	$3.00	$6.00
1348	Kane, Henry - ***A Halo For Nobody*** [1950]	$1.00	$3.00	$6.00

		G	VG	F
1366	Lucas, Cary - ***Unfinished Business*** [1950]	$1.00	$3.00	$6.00
1367	Hitchcock, Alfred - editor (anthology) - ***Suspense Stories*** [1950]	$1.25	$3.75	$7.50
1385	Halliday, Brett - ***Blood On The Stars*** [1950]	$1.25	$3.75	$7.50
1386	Halliday, Brett - ***The Uncomplaining Corpses*** [1950]	$1.00	$3.00	$6.00
1387	Halliday, Brett - ***Tickets For Death*** [1950]	$1.00	$3.00	$6.00
1388	Halliday, Brett - ***Murder Wears A Mummer's Mask*** [1950]	$1.00	$3.00	$6.00
1399	Knibbs, Henry Herbert - ***The Ridin' Kid From Powder River*** [1950]	$1.00	$3.00	$6.00
1402	Hull, E. M. - ***The Captive Of The Sahara*** [1951]	$1.00	$3.00	$6.00
1407	Steinbeck, John - ***To A God Unknown*** [1951]	$1.25	$3.75	$7.50
1422	Marshall, Edison - ***Yankee Pasha*** [1951]	$1.00	$3.00	$6.00
1434	Rafferty, Kathleen - ***Dell Crossword Puzzle Dictionary*** [1951]	$1.50	$5.00	$10.00
1440	Lait, Jack and Mortimer, Lee - ***New York: Confidential*** [1950]	$1.00	$3.00	$6.00
1492	Baker, Jr., Charles H. - ***Blood Of The Lamb*** [1950]	$1.00	$3.00	$6.00
1499	Overholser, Wayne D. - ***West Of The Rimrock*** [1951]	$1.00	$3.00	$6.00
1533	Halliday, Brett - ***This Is It, Michael Shayne*** [1951]	$1.00	$3.00	$6.00
1534	Lait, Jack and Mortimer, Lee - ***New York: Confidential!*** [1951]	$1.00	$3.00	$6.00
1542	Fair, A. A. - ***Fools Die On Friday*** [1951]	$1.00	$3.00	$6.00
1590	Halliday, Brett - ***Counterfeit Wife*** [1952]	$1.00	$3.00	$6.00

Dell Ten Cent Books. New York: Dell Publishing Co.

		G	VG	F
1	Short, Luke - ***Trumpets West!*** [1951] PBO. Cover by H. W. Scott.	$3.00	$9.00	$18.00
2	Maugham, W. Somerset - ***Rain*** [1951] Cover by Victor Kalin.	$2.50	$7.50	$15.00
3	Adams, Samuel Hopkins - ***Night Bus*** [1951] Cover by Sandor Klein.	$2.50	$7.50	$15.00
4	Rinehart, Mary Roberts - ***Locked Doors*** [1951] Cover by Barye Phillips.	$3.50	$10.00	$20.00
5	Baldwin, Faith - ***The Bride From Broadway*** [1951] Cover by Wesley Snyder.	$2.50	$7.50	$15.00
6	Edmonds, Walter D. - ***The Wedding Journey*** [1951] Cover by George Mayers.	$2.50	$7.50	$15.00
7	Eberhart, Mignon G. - ***Deadly Is The Diamond*** [1951] Cover by Bill Fleming.	$3.50	$10.00	$20.00
8	Buck, Pearl - ***Journey For Life*** [1951] Cover by Robert Stanley.	$2.50	$7.50	$15.00
9	Delmar, Vina - ***Strangers In Love*** [1951] Cover by Robert Stanley.	$2.50	$7.50	$15.00
10	Ferber, Edna - ***Trees Die At The Top*** [1951] Cover by George Mayers.	$2.50	$7.50	$15.00
11	Irish, William - ***Marihuana*** [1951] PBO. Cover by Bill Fleming.	$25.00	$75.00	$180.00
12	Fox, Norman A. - ***The Longhorn Legion*** [1951] Cover by Robert Stanley.	$3.00	$9.00	$18.00
13	Marquand, John P. - ***Sun, Sea, And Sand*** [1951] Cover by S. B. Jones.	$2.50	$7.50	$15.00
14	Hurst, Fannie - ***The Name Is Mary*** [1951] Cover by John Allan Maxwell.	$2.50	$7.50	$15.00
15	Halliday, Brett - ***A Taste For Cognac*** [1951] Cover by Robert Stanley.	$4.00	$12.50	$25.00
16	Maugham, W. Somerset - ***The Beachcomber*** [1951] Cover by Rafael De Soto.	$2.50	$7.50	$15.00
17	Stegner, Wallace - ***Remembering Laughter*** [1951] Cover by Isabel Dawson.	$4.00	$12.50	$25.00
18	Brush, Katharine - ***Free Woman*** [1951] Cover by Barye Phillips.	$2.50	$7.50	$15.00
19	Blochman, Lawrence G. - ***Death Walks In Marble Halls*** [1951] Cover by Maurice Thomas.	$3.50	$10.00	$20.00
20	Blackburn, Tom W. - ***Broken Arrow Range*** [1951] PBO. Cover by Robert Stanley.	$3.00	$9.00	$18.00
21	Stout, Rex - ***Door To Death*** [1951] Cover by Robert Stanley.	$4.00	$12.50	$25.00
22	Rinehart, Mary Roberts - ***Alibi For Isabel*** [1951] Cover by Robert Stanley.	$3.50	$10.00	$20.00

Dell Unnumbered Series, NN-2

Diversey Novel, 2

Galaxy Novel, 29

		G	VG	F
23	Queen, Ellery - ***The Lamp Of God*** [1951] Cover by George Mayers.	$3.50	$10.00	$20.00
24	O'Hara, John - ***Pal Joey*** [1951] Cover by Victor Kalin.	$2.50	$7.50	$15.00
25	Hersey, John - ***South Of Cancer*** [1951] Cover by Nelson Davis.	$2.50	$7.50	$15.00
26	Irish, William - ***You'll Never See Me Again*** [1951] PBO. Cover by Robert Stanley.	$20.00	$60.00	$125.00
27	Gallico, Paul - ***Thief Is An Ugly Word*** [1951] Cover by Barye Phillips.	$2.50	$7.50	$15.00
28	Roos, Kelley - ***Beauty Marks The Spot*** [1951] Cover by Rafael De Soto.	$3.50	$10.00	$20.00
29	Household, Geoffrey - ***Delilah Of The Back Stairs*** [1951] Cover by John Fernie.	$2.50	$7.50	$15.00
30	Baldwin, Faith - ***Wife Vs. Secretary*** [1951] Cover by Maurice Thomas.	$2.50	$7.50	$15.00
31	Pentecost, Hugh - ***Chinese Nightmare*** [1951] Cover by Rafael De Soto.	$4.00	$12.50	$25.00
32	Kendrick, Baynard - ***The Murderer Who Wanted More*** [1951] Cover by Rafael De Soto.	$4.00	$12.50	$25.00
33	Brown, Fredric - ***The Case Of The Dancing Sandwiches*** [1951] PBO. Cover by Robert Stanley.	$25.00	$75.00	$180.00
34	McCloy, Helen - ***Better Off Dead*** [1951] PBO. Cover by Robert Stanley.	$4.00	$12.50	$25.00
35	Stowe, Perry - ***Superstition Farm*** [1951] Cover by Robert Stanley.	$5.50	$17.50	$35.00
36	Heinlein, Robert A. - ***Universe*** [1951] PBO. Cover by Robert Stanley.	$12.50	$37.50	$75.00

Dell Told in Pictures. New York: Dell Publishing Co.

		G	VG	F
1	No Author - ***Twice Loved*** [1950] Story told in comic book form, in color. Photo cover.	$8.00	$25.00	$50.00
2	Coxe, George Harmon - ***Four Frightened Women*** [1950] Story told in comic book form, in color, by Robert Stanley.	$15.00	$45.00	$90.00

Dell Unnumbered Series. New York: Dell Publishing Co.

		G	VG	F
NN-1	Young, Chic - ***Blondie And Dagwood In Footlight Folly*** [1947] PBO. Paperback size.	$12.50	$37.50	$75.00
NN-2	Gould, Chester - ***Dick Tracy And The Woo-Woo Sisters*** [1947] PBO. Paperback size.	$12.50	$37.50	$75.00
NN-3	Mulford, Clarence - ***Hopalong Cassidy*** [1947] Photo cover. Movie tie-in. Digest size.	$6.00	$20.00	$40.00

		G	VG	F
NN-4	No Author - ***Jungle Belles*** [1947] PBO. All photos. Oversized digest.	$15.00	$45.00	$90.00

Del Rey Books. New York: Ballantine Books, Inc.

		G	VG	F
1	Foster, Alan Dean - ***Orphan Star*** [1977] PBO	$1.25	$3.00	$7.50
2	Gerrold, David and Niven, Larry - ***The Flying Sorcerers*** [1977] PBO	$ .75	$2.50	$5.00
3	Heinlein, Robert A. - ***Tunnel In The Sky*** [1977]	$ .75	$2.50	$5.00
4	McCaffrey, Anne - ***Restoree*** [1977] PBO	$ .75	$2.50	$5.00
5	Herbert, Frank - ***The Heaven Makers*** [1977]	$ .75	$2.50	$5.00
6	Dickson, Gordon R. - ***Mission To Universe*** [1977]	$ .75	$2.50	$5.00
7	Anderson, Poul - ***The Broken Sword*** [1977] PBO	$ .75	$2.50	$5.00
8	Daley, Brian - ***The Doomfarers of Coramonde*** [1977] PBO	$ .75	$2.50	$5.00
9	Brunner, John - editor - ***The Best Of Philip K. Dick*** [1977] PBO	$ .75	$2.50	$5.00
10	White, James - ***Monsters And Medics*** [1977] PBO	$ .75	$2.50	$5.00
11	de Camp, L. Sprague - ***The Tritonian Ring*** [1977]	$ .75	$2.50	$5.00
12	Silverberg, Robert - ***Son Of Man*** [1977] PBO	$ .75	$2.50	$5.00
13	Pohl, Frederick - ***Gateway*** [1978] PBO	$ .75	$2.50	$5.00
14	Foster, Alan Dean - ***Star Trek Log Ten*** [1978] PBO	$ .75	$2.50	$5.00
15	Del Rey, Lester - ***Outpost Of Jupiter*** [1978]	$ .75	$2.50	$5.00
16	Tiptree, Jr., James - ***Star Songs Of An Old Primate*** [1978] PBO.	$ .75	$2.50	$5.00
17	Clement, Hal - ***Mission Of Gravity*** [1978]	$ .75	$2.50	$5.00
18	Eddison, E.R. - ***Mistress Of Mistresses*** [1978]	$ .75	$2.50	$5.00
19	McKillip, Patricia A. - ***The Riddle Master Of Hed*** [1978]	$ .75	$2.50	$5.00
20	Chalker, Jack L. - ***The Web Of The Chozen*** [1978] PBO	$ .75	$2.50	$5.00
21	McCaffrey, Anne - ***To Ride Pegasus*** [1978]	$ .75	$2.50	$5.00
22	Heinlein, Robert A. - ***Between Planets*** [1978]	$ .75	$2.50	$5.00
23	Clement, Hal - ***Star Light*** [1978]	$ .75	$2.50	$5.00
24	Haggard, H. Rider - ***When The World Shook*** [1978]	$ .75	$2.50	$5.00

Derby Books. Toronto: Derby Publishing Co.

		G	VG	F
1	Carter, Ralph - ***Profane*** [1949] Cover by Rickard.	$3.50	$10.00	$20.00
2	Arthur, William - ***Sinner Take All*** [1949]	$3.50	$10.00	$20.00
3	Anet, Claude - ***Passion Or Kingdom*** [1949]	$3.50	$10.00	$20.00
4	Lindsay, Perry (Peggy Gaddis) - ***Burning Desire*** [1949] Cover art by Rickard.	$3.50	$10.00	$20.00
5	Norcross, Robert - ***French Wench*** [1949]	$3.50	$10.00	$20.00
6	Lederer, Joe - ***The Long Night*** [1949] Cover art by Rickard.	$3.50	$10.00	$20.00
7	Arthur, William - ***Men To Burn*** [1950]	$3.50	$10.00	$20.00
8	Thornton, Charles - ***Bedroom For Three*** [1950]	$3.50	$10.00	$20.00
9	Way, Wayne - ***The Body Betrays*** [1950] Cover art by Rickard.	$3.50	$10.00	$20.00
10	Jordan, Gail (Peggy Gaddis) - ***Lush Lady*** [1950] Cover art by Rickard.	$3.50	$10.00	$20.00
11	Semple, Gordon - ***Highway Jane*** [1950]	$3.50	$10.00	$20.00
12	Branch, Florenz - ***Borrowed Husband*** [1950]	$3.50	$10.00	$20.00

Detective Novel Classic. New York: Novel Selections. Digest Size.

		G	VG	F
NN	Wells, Caroline - ***Murder In The Bookshop*** [1942]	$1.50	$5.00	$10.00
2	Fletcher, J.S. - ***The Pedigreed Murder Case*** [1942]	$1.25	$3.75	$7.50
3	Hogarth, Emmett - ***Death By Remote Control*** [1942]	$1.25	$3.75	$7.50
4	Wentworth, Patricia - ***The Case Is Closed*** [1942]	$1.25	$3.75	$7.50
5	Wells, Caroline - ***The Radio Studio Murder*** [1942]	$1.25	$3.75	$7.50
6	Kummer, Frederic Arnold - ***The Scarecrow Murders*** [1942]	$1.25	$3.75	$7.50
7	Donavan, John - ***The Case Of The Rusted Room*** [1942]	$1.25	$3.75	$7.50
8	Nolan, Jeannette Covert - ***Murder Will Out*** [1942]	$1.25	$3.75	$7.50
9	Mason, Van Wyck - ***Hong Kong Air Base Murders*** [1942]	$1.25	$3.75	$7.50
10	Kummer, Frederic Arnold - ***The Clue Of The Twisted Face*** [1942]	$1.25	$3.75	$7.50
11	Punshon, E.R. - ***The Bathtub Murder Case*** [1942]	$1.25	$3.75	$7.50
12	Armstrong, Margaret - ***The Blue Santo Murder Mystery*** [1942]	$1.25	$3.75	$7.50

		G	VG	F
13	Wilde, Percival - ***Design For Murder*** [1942]	$1.25	$3.75	$7.50
14	Wynne, Anthony - ***Murder In The Morning*** [1942]	$1.25	$3.75	$7.50
15	Cunningham, A.B. - ***The Strange Death Of Manny Square*** [1942]	$1.25	$3.75	$7.50
16	Forrest, Norman - ***Death Took A Greek God*** [1942]	$1.25	$3.75	$7.50
17	Dean, Gregory - ***Murder On Stilts*** [1943]	$1.25	$3.75	$7.50
18	Palmer, Stuart - ***The Penguin Pool Murder*** [1943]	$1.25	$3.75	$7.50
19	Allan, Dennis - ***The Case Of The Headless Corpse*** [1943]	$1.25	$3.75	$7.50
20	Cunningham, A.B. - ***Death At "The Bottoms"*** [1943]	$1.25	$3.75	$7.50
21	Halliday, Brett - ***Tickets For Death*** [1943]	$1.35	$4.00	$8.00
22	Chambers, Whitman - ***Murder For A Wanton*** [1943]	$1.25	$3.75	$7.50
23	Reilly, Helen - ***Murder In The Mews*** [1943]	$1.25	$3.75	$7.50
24	Wallace, Francis - ***Little Hercules*** [1943]	$1.25	$3.75	$7.50
25	Cunningham, A.B. - ***The Bancock Murder Case*** [1943]	$1.25	$3.75	$7.50
26	Halliday, Brett - ***The Uncomplaining Corpses*** [1943]	$1.35	$4.00	$8.00
27	Koehler, Robert Portner - ***Steps To Murder*** [1943]	$1.25	$3.75	$7.50
28	Chambers, Whitman - ***Dead Men Leave No Fingerprints*** [1943]	$1.25	$3.75	$7.50
29	Saxby, Charles & Molnar, Louis - ***Death Over Hollywood*** [1943]	$1.25	$3.75	$7.50
30	Cunningham, A.B. - ***The Affair At The Boat Landing*** [1943]	$1.25	$3.75	$7.50
31	Halliday, Brett - ***Bodies Are Where You Find Them*** [1943]	$1.35	$4.00	$8.00
32	Carr, John Dickson - ***The Eight Of Swords*** [1943]	$1.50	$5.00	$10.00
33	King, Rufus - ***Murder By Latitude*** [1943]	$1.25	$3.75	$7.50
34	Hale, Christopher - ***Exit Screaming*** [1943]	$1.25	$3.75	$7.50
35	Spain, John - ***Death Is Like That*** [1943]	$1.25	$3.75	$7.50
36	Christian, Kit - ***Death And Bitters*** [1943]	$1.25	$3.75	$7.50
37	Cunningham, A.B. - ***The Great Yant Mystery*** [1943]	$1.25	$3.75	$7.50
38	King, Rufus - ***A Murderer In This House*** [1943]	$1.25	$3.75	$7.50
39	Hale, Christopher - ***Dead Of Winter*** [1943]	$1.25	$3.75	$7.50
40	Carr, John Dickson - ***The Four False Weapons*** [1943]	$1.50	$5.00	$10.00
41	Colter, Eli - ***The Gull Cove Murders*** [1943]	$1.25	$3.75	$7.50
42	Cunningham, A.B. - ***The Cane-Patch Mystery*** [1943]	$1.25	$3.75	$7.50
43	Olsen, D. B. - ***The Cat Wears A Noose*** [1946]	$1.25	$3.75	$7.50
44	Spain, John - ***The Evil Star*** [1943]	$1.25	$3.75	$7.50
45	Sterling, Stewart - ***Down Among The Dead Men*** [1943]	$1.25	$3.75	$7.50
46	Cunningham, A.B. - ***Death Visits The Apple Hole*** [1943]	$1.25	$3.75	$7.50
47	McCully, Walbridge - ***Blood On Nassau's Moon*** [1946]	$1.25	$3.75	$7.50
48	Heberden, M.V. - ***Murder Makes A Racket*** [1946]	$1.25	$3.75	$7.50
49	Nolan, Jeannette Covert - ***I Can't Die Here*** [1946]	$1.25	$3.75	$7.50
51	Hale, Christopher - ***Rumor Hath It*** [1946] Photo cover.	$1.25	$3.75	$7.50
52	Cunningham, A.B. - ***Murder Before Midnight*** [1946]	$1.25	$3.75	$7.50
53	McCully, Walbridge - ***Doctors Beware!*** [1946]	$1.25	$3.75	$7.50
54	Ferrars, E.X. - ***Neck In A Noose*** [1946]	$1.25	$3.75	$7.50

Diamond Library. New York: Diamond Library, Inc. Digest Size.

		G	VG	F
NN-1	Pratt, Theodore - ***Murder Goes Fishing*** [1945] PBO. Cover by Clyde Prettyman.	$5.50	$17.50	$35.00
NN-2	- - ***Murder By Mandate*** [1945]	$5.00	$15.00	$30.00

Diversey Love Book Monthly. New York: Diversey Publications. Digest Size.

		G	VG	F
1	Dekobra, Maurice - ***Bedroom Eyes*** [1948] Cover art by Peter Driben.	$7.00	$22.50	$45.00
2	Collison, Wilson - ***One Night With Nancy*** [1948]	$7.00	$22.50	$45.00

Diversey Novels. New York: Diversey Publications. Digest Size.

		G	VG	F
1	Bull, Lois - ***Broadway Virgin*** [1949]	$5.00	$15.00	$30.00
2	Bodenheim, Maxwell - ***Naked On Roller Skates*** [1949]	$17.00	$50.00	$100.00
3	Marion, Frances - ***The Passions Of Linda Lane*** [1949] Photo cover.	$5.00	$15.00	$30.00
4	Holland, Marty - ***Fast Woman*** [1949]	$5.00	$15.00	$30.00

		G	VG	F
5	Wilstach, John - ***Love For Sale*** [1949]	$5.00	$15.00	$30.00
6	Reltid, Edward - ***The Amorous Interne*** [1949]	$5.00	$15.00	$30.00

Diversey Romance Novel. New York: Diversey Publications. Digest Size.

		G	VG	F
1	Swados, Felice - ***Reform School Girl*** [1948]	$50.00	$175.00	$400.00

Dollar Double Books.

		G	VG	F
950	Smith, George H./Hastings, March - ***Lash Of Desire/Pillow Tramp*** [1962] Cover art by Bonfils.	$1.50	$5.00	$10.00
951	Britain, Sloan/Rubel, J.L. - ***Strumpets' Jungle/Any Man's Playmate*** [1962] Cover art by Bonfils.	$1.50	$5.00	$10.00
952	Lane, Wanda/Glaser, Alfred B. - ***The Sporting Parlor/Platinum Blonde*** [1962] Cover art by Bonfils.	$1.50	$5.00	$10.00
953	Hastings, March/Jackson, Warner - ***Design For Debauchery/My Mother, The Madam*** [1962] Cover art by Bonfils.	$1.50	$5.00	$10.00
954	Bell, Steve/Hastings, March - ***Honey At Her Lips/Third Sex Syndrome*** [1962] Cover art by Bonfils.	$1.50	$5.00	$10.00
955	Laird, Andrew/Geis, Richard E. - ***Every Bed Is Narrow/The Beatniks*** [1962] Cover art by Bonfils.	$1.50	$5.00	$10.00
956	Dean, Nancy/Hastings, March - ***Oh, Sweet And Gentle Harlot/The Sherwood Scandal!*** [1962]	$1.50	$5.00	$10.00
957	Toward, Howard/Hastings, March - ***All Cats Are Grey/Rage Of Desire*** [1962] Cover art by Bonfils.	$1.50	$5.00	$10.00

Domino Mysteries. Toronto: Duchess Printing. Digest Size.

		G	VG	F
1	Verner, Gerald - ***The "Q" Squad*** [1944]	$4.00	$12.50	$25.00
2	Gask, Arthur - ***The Gentleman Of Crime*** [1945]	$4.00	$12.50	$25.00

Dorene Publishing. New York: Dorene Publishing Co. Digest Size.

		G	VG	F
1	Anthology edited by Arnold Shaw - ***30 Tales Of Romance And Adventure*** [1945]	$2.00	$6.00	$12.00

Double Action Detective Novel. New York: Close-up, Inc. Digest Size.

		G	VG	F
1	Hiller, Guy Pember - ***Run Corpse Run*** [1943] PBO.	$4.00	$12.50	$25.00
2	Nyland, Gentry - ***Hot Bullets For Love*** [1943]	$4.50	$14.00	$28.00
3	Corne, M.E. - ***Jealousy Pulls The Trigger*** [1943]	$4.00	$12.50	$25.00

Double-Action Pocketbook. New York: Columbia Publications. Digest Size.

		G	VG	F
NO#	Loomis, Noel - ***City Of Glass*** [1955] PBO. Cover by Ed Emsh.	$2.50	$7.50	$15.00

Duchess/Superior
8@A-H-2 = . Toronto: Superior Publishers, Ltd.

		G	VG	F
VOL 1 #1	Anthology - ***Cartoon Parade*** [1945] PBO. All cartoons and jokes.	$5.00	$15.00	$30.00
NN-1	Anthology - ***Marijuana Murder*** [n.d.] PBO.	$4.00	$12.50	$25.00
NN-2	Anthology - ***Daylight Murder Mystery*** [n.d.] PBO.	$4.00	$12.50	$25.00
NN-3	Anthology - ***Lips Of Death*** [n.d.] PBO.	$4.00	$12.50	$25.00
NN-4	Anthology - ***Lurking Shadow of Death***[n.d.] PBO.	$4.00	$12.50	$25.00
NN-5	Anthology - ***Killers On The Loose*** [n.d.] PBO.	$4.00	$12.50	$25.00
NN-6	Anthology - ***The Jam Session Slayer***[n.d.] PBO.	$4.00	$12.50	$25.00
NN-7	Todd, Robert Henry & Steele, Lloyd C. - ***True Mysteries And Murders*** [1945] PBO.	$4.00	$12.50	$25.00

Eagle Books.

		G	VG	F
1	Lowell, Juliet - ***Dear Sir*** [1944] PBO.	$3.50	$10.00	$20.00
NO#-2	Marshall, Rosamond - ***Kitty*** [1945]	$2.00	$6.00	$12.00
E-3	Marshall, Rosamond - ***Duchess Hotspur*** [1947]	$1.25	$3.75	$7.50

Ecstasy Books.

		G	VG	F
1	Hamilton, Trudy - ***A Body To Own*** [1949] PBO.	$4.00	$12.50	$25.00

		G	VG	F
2	Lindsay, Perry - ***Paula Has A Price!*** [1950] PBO. Cover art by Rodewald.	$4.00	$12.50	$25.00
3	Bligh, Norman - ***Harlot In Her Heart*** [1950] PBO. Cover art by Rodewald.	$4.00	$12.50	$25.00
4	Clayford, James (Peggy Gaddis) - ***The Private Life Of A Street Girl!*** [1950] PBO. Cover by George Gross.	$4.00	$12.50	$25.00
5	Bligh, Norman - ***Intimate Confessions Of An Artist's Model*** [1950] PBO.	$4.00	$12.50	$25.00
6	Stonebraker, Florence - ***Reno Tramp*** [1950] PBO.	$4.00	$12.50	$25.00
NN7	Duperrault, Doug - ***Confessions Of A Dime-A-Dance Queen*** [1950] PBO. Cover by George Gross.	$4.00	$12.50	$25.00
NN-8	Gaddis, Peggy - ***Virgin Or Harlot?*** [1950] PBO.	$4.00	$12.50	$25.00
NN-9	Bligh, Norman - ***Bed-Time Angel*** [1951] PBO.	$4.00	$12.50	$25.00
NN-10	Gordon, Luthor - ***Never Say No!*** [1951]	$4.00	$12.50	$25.00
NN-11	Gordon, Luther - ***Free And Easy*** [1951]	$4.00	$12.50	$25.00
12	Scott, Anthony (Brett Halliday) - ***Web Of Sin*** [1951]	$5.00	$15.00	$30.00
14	Deane, Elizabeth - ***Doris - Broadway Virgin*** [1951]	$4.00	$12.50	$25.00
15	Clayford, James (Gaddis, Peggy) - ***Wanton By Night*** [1951]	$4.00	$12.50	$25.00
16	Lyons, Gwen - ***They Call Her "Easy"*** [1951] PBO.	$4.00	$12.50	$25.00
17	Wade, David - ***Come Night - Come Desire*** [1951] PBO.	$4.00	$12.50	$25.00

Eerie Series. Digest Size.

		G	VG	F
1	Crossen, Ken - ***The Case Of The Curious Heel*** [1944]	$3.50	$10.00	$20.00
2	Crowell, Will - ***Murder In Mocking Valley*** [1942]	$4.00	$12.50	$25.00
3	Thompson, Donald - ***The Corpse Wore No Shoes*** [1945]	$4.00	$12.50	$25.00
4	Barlay, Bennett - ***Satan Comes Across*** [1945] PBO.	$4.00	$12.50	$25.00
5	Eichler, Alfred - ***Murder In The Radio Department*** [1944]	$4.00	$12.50	$25.00
6	Anthology - ***The Omnibus Of Pleasure*** [1944] Edited by Walter S. Keating.	$2.50	$7.50	$15.00
7	Clift, Denison - ***The Spy In The Room*** [1944]	$3.50	$10.00	$20.00
8	Gould, Stephen - ***Homicide Johnny*** [1944] States #7 Metro Publications.	$3.50	$10.00	$20.00
9	Douglas, Dayle - ***Haunted Harbor*** [1945] PBO. States Metro Publications.	$3.50	$10.00	$20.00
10	Anthology - ***Adventures Of The Great Crime Busters*** [1945]	$4.00	$12.50	$25.00

Ember Library Book. San Diego: Greenleaf Classics, Inc.

		G	VG	F
EL301	Allison, Clyde - ***Our Man From Sadisto*** [1965] Agent 0008.	$4.00	$12.50	$25.00
EL302	Elliott, Don (Robert Silverberg) - ***The Shame Protector*** [1965] PBO. Cover art by Robert Bonfils.	$1.35	$4.00	$8.00
EL303	Hudson, Dean - ***Nightmare Clinic*** [1965]	$1.50	$5.00	$10.00
EL304	Calvano, Tony - ***Night Train To Sodom*** [1965] PBO.	$1.25	$3.75	$7.50
EL305	Allison, Clyde - ***Our Girl From Mephisto*** [1965] PBO. 0008.	$4.00	$12.50	$25.00
EL307	Holliday, Don - ***Chain Gang*** [1965] PBO.	$1.25	$3.75	$7.50
EL309	Allison, Clyde - ***Nautipuss*** [1965] PBO.	$3.50	$10.00	$20.00
EL310	Elliott, Don (Ronbert Silverberg) - ***Naked She Died*** [1965] PBO.	$1.35	$4.00	$8.00
EL312	Hudson, Dean - ***Sinner Come Home*** [1965] PBO.	$1.25	$3.75	$7.50
EL320	Dexter, John - ***Hay Ride To Hell*** [1966] PBO.	$1.25	$3.75	$7.50
EL321	Allison, Clyde - ***Gamefinger*** [1966] PBO. Agent 0008.	$4.00	$12.50	$25.00
EL322	Williams, J.X. - ***The Sin Collector*** [1966] PBO.	$1.25	$3.75	$7.50
EL323	Dexter, John - ***Garden Of Shame*** [1966] PBO.	$1.25	$3.75	$7.50
EL324	Bellmore, Don - ***Campus Cheat*** [1966] PBO.	$1.25	$3.75	$7.50
EL325	Allison, Clyde - ***Sadisto Royale*** [1966] PBO. Agent 0008.	$4.00	$12.50	$25.00
EL326	Shaw, Andrew - ***Willing Intern*** [1966] PBO.	$1.25	$3.75	$7.50
EL327	Dexter, John - ***The Shame Tigers*** [1966] PBO.	$1.25	$3.75	$7.50
EL328	Williams, J.X. - ***Boudoir Nymph*** [1966] PBO.	$1.25	$3.75	$7.50
EL329	Allison, Clyde - ***For Your Sighs Only*** [1966] PBO. Agent 0008.	$4.00	$12.50	$25.00
EL330	Holliday, Don - ***Drifter's Delight*** [1966] PBO.	$1.25	$3.75	$7.50
EL333	Allison, Clyde - ***The Lost Bomb*** [1966] PBO. Agent 0008.	$4.00	$12.50	$25.00
EL335	Dexter, John - ***Nylon Passport*** [1966] PBO.	$1.25	$3.75	$7.50

		G	VG	F
EL339	Dexter, John - ***Flee The Night*** [1966] PBO. Cover by Robert Bonfils.	$1.25	$3.75	$7.50
EL340	Williams, J.X. - ***John Henry's Prison*** [1966] PBO.	$1.25	$3.75	$7.50
EL341	Shaw, Andrew - ***Bad Town*** [1966] PBO.	$1.25	$3.75	$7.50
EL342	Hudson, Dean - ***Honeysuckle Rose*** [1966] PBO.	$1.25	$3.75	$7.50
EL343	Dexter, John - ***Househop*** [1966] PBO.	$1.25	$3.75	$7.50
EL345	Dexter, John - ***The Secret-Sharer*** [1966] PBO.	$1.25	$3.75	$7.50
EL347	Aldrich, Curt - ***The Bikini Bride*** [1966]	$1.25	$3.75	$7.50
EL349	Hudson, Dean - ***Randy*** [1966] PBO.	$1.25	$3.75	$7.50
EL354	Dexter, John - ***Playboy's Lament*** [1966] PBO.	$1.25	$3.75	$7.50
EL355	Marshall, Alan - ***Travelin' Tramp*** [1966] PBO.	$1.25	$3.75	$7.50
EL356	Shaw, Andrew - ***A Plague Of Passions*** [1966] PBO.	$2.50	$7.50	$15.00
EL359	Cross, Gene - ***The Tigerlilly Affair*** [1967]	$2.50	$7.50	$15.00
EL361	Cross, Gene - ***The Nitty-Gritty Affair*** [1967] PBO.	$2.50	$7.50	$15.00
EL364	Hudson, Dean - ***House Of 7 Shames*** [1967] PBO.	$1.50	$5.00	$10.00
EL365	Allison, Clyde - ***The Ice Maiden*** [1967] PBO. Agent 0008.	$4.00	$12.50	$25.00
EL368	Cross, Gene - ***The Wild Mare Affair*** [1967] PBO.	$1.50	$5.00	$10.00
EL370	Aldrich, Curt - ***Spurs And All*** [1967] PBO.	$1.25	$3.75	$7.50
EL372	Hudson, Dean - ***The Bodyguard*** [1967] PBO.	$1.25	$3.75	$7.50
EL380	Williams, J.X. - ***The Worried Wantons*** [1967] PBO.	$1.25	$3.75	$7.50
EL384	Jordan, Kenneth - ***Rough Trade*** [1967] PBO.	$1.25	$3.75	$7.50
EL392	Williams, J.X. - ***The Flesh Outlaws*** [1967] PBO.	$1.25	$3.75	$7.50

Epic.

103	Smith, George H. - ***1976 - The Year Of Terror*** [n.d.]	$2.50	$7.50	$15.00
110	Smith, George - ***Scourge Of The Blood Cult*** [1961] PBO.	$3.50	$10.00	$20.00
144	Camra, R. - ***Assault*** [n.d.]	$1.50	$5.00	$10.00

Essex House (Early Publisher's History, 1968–1973)

Essex House existed as a pornographic publishing house of interest to collectors. They published original titles from twenty different authors, who they encouraged to experiment. Forty-two titles appeared prior to ceasing operation in 1970. Volumes of note include a number of science fiction titles, especially three books by Philip José Farmer. Afterwords by Norman Spinrad, Theodore Sturgeon, Philip José Farmer, and Harlan Ellison add to the value of a number of the books. The outrageous covers add a distinctive touch to Essex House Books.

Parliament News, Inc., the parent publisher, presented a number of other lines to include: Cameo Library Novels, Barclay House Books, Branson House Books, and Brandon House Library Editions.

Essex House. North Hollywood, CA.

		G	VG	F
0101	Perkins, Michael - ***Blue Movie*** [1968] PBO. Photo cover.	$8.00	$25.00	$50.00
0102	Meltzer, David - ***The Agency*** [1968] PBO.	$10.00	$30.00	$60.00
0103	Dalls, Paul V. - ***Binding With Briars*** [1968] PBO. Photo cover...	$8.00	$25.00	$50.00
0104	Meltzer, David - ***The Agent*** [1968] PBO.	$10.00	$30.00	$60.00
0105	MacPherson, Michael - ***Abducted*** [1968] PBO.	$8.00	$25.00	$50.00
0106	Doyle, Kirby - ***Happiness Bastard*** [1968] PBO.	$8.00	$25.00	$50.00
0107	Meltzer, David - ***How Many Blocks In The Pile?*** [1968] PBO.	$10.00	$30.00	$60.00
0108	Farmer, Philip Jose - ***The Image Of The Beast*** [1966] PBO.	$22.00	$70.00	$140.00
0109	Perkins, Michael - ***Evil Companions*** [1968] PBO.	$8.00	$25.00	$50.00
0110	Porter, Gil - ***Coupled*** [1968]	$8.00	$25.00	$50.00
0111	Meltzer, David - ***Orf*** [1968] PBO.	$10.00	$30.00	$60.00
0112	Stine, Hank - ***Season Of The Witch*** [1968] PBO. Photo cover.	$12.50	$37.50	$75.00
0113	Geis, Richard E. - ***Ravished*** [1968] PBO.	$8.00	$25.00	$50.00
0114	Perkins, Michael - ***Queen Of Heat*** [1968] PBO. Photo cover.	$10.00	$30.00	$60.00

		G	VG	F
0115	Bukowski, Charles - ***Notes Of A Dirty Old Man*** [1969] PBO. Cover art by Larry Gaynor.	$12.50	$37.50	$75.00
0116	Meltzer, David - ***The Martyr*** [1969] PBO.	$10.00	$30.00	$60.00
0117	Meltzer, David - ***Lovely*** [1969]	$10.00	$30.00	$60.00
0118	Perkins, Michael - ***The Tour*** [1969] PBO.	$10.00	$30.00	$60.00
0119	Toledano, Henry - ***The Bitter Seed*** [1969] PBO.	$8.00	$25.00	$50.00
0120	McNaughton, Jr., Charles - ***Mind Blower*** [1969] PBO.	$8.00	$25.00	$50.00
0121	Farmer, Philip Jose - ***A Feast Unknown*** [1966] PBO	$22.00	$70.00	$140.00
0122	Meltzer, David - ***Healer*** [1969] PBO.	$10.00	$30.00	$60.00
0123	Perkins, Michael - ***Whacking Off*** [1969] PBO.	$8.00	$25.00	$50.00
0124	Gallion, Jane - ***Biker*** [1969]	$10.00	$30.00	$60.00
0125	Perkins, Michael - ***Terminus*** [1969] PBO.	$10.00	$30.00	$60.00
0126	Dedeaux, P.N. - ***Tender Buns*** [1969] PBO.	$8.00	$25.00	$50.00
0127	Marlowe, Alan S. - ***Over Easy*** [1969] PBO.	$8.00	$25.00	$50.00
0128	Gallion, Jane - ***Stoned*** [1969] PBO.	$10.00	$30.00	$60.00
0129	Meltzer, David - ***Out*** [1969] PBO.	$10.00	$30.00	$60.00
0130	Anderson, Jerry - ***Trans*** [1969]	$10.00	$30.00	$60.00
0131	Lamont, Gil - ***Roach*** [1969] PBO.	$10.00	$30.00	$60.00
0132	Perkins, Michael - ***Estelle*** [1969] PBO.	$8.00	$25.00	$50.00
0133	Ramirez, Alice Louise - ***The Geek*** [1969] PBO.	$10.00	$30.00	$60.00
0134	Meltzer, David - ***Glue Factory*** [1969] PBO.	$10.00	$30.00	$60.00
0135	Dedeaux, P.N. - ***The Nothing Things*** [1969] PBO.	$8.00	$25.00	$50.00
0136	Geis, Richard E. - ***Raw Meat*** [1969] PBO.	$10.00	$30.00	$60.00
0137	Toledano, Henry - ***A Sort Of Justice*** [1969] PBO.	$8.00	$25.00	$50.00
0138	Bradbrook, Gary - ***Get It On*** [1969] PBO.	$8.00	$25.00	$50.00
0139	Farmer, Philip Jose - ***Blown*** [1967] PBO.	$32.00	$110.00	$250.00
0140	Perkins, Michael - ***Down Here*** [1969] PBO.	$15.00	$45.00	$90.00
0141	Stein, Hank - ***Thrill City*** [1969]	$15.00	$45.00	$90.00
0142	Luck, Barry - ***Gropie*** [1969]	$15.00	$45.00	$90.00

Eton Books. New York: Eton Books, Inc.

ET-51	Wittels, M.D., Fritz - ***The Sex Habits Of American Women*** [1952]	$ .75	$2.50	$5.00
101	Anthology - ***United States Book Of Baby And Child Care*** [1951] PBO. Photo cover.	$ .75	$2.50	$5.00
102	Wittels, M.D., Fritz - ***The Sex Habits Of American Women*** [1951] PBO.	$ .75	$2.50	$5.00
103	Everett, Millard Spencer - ***The Hygiene Of Marriage*** [1951]	$ .75	$2.50	$5.00
ET-104	Pomeranz, M.D., Herman - ***Control High Blood Pressure And Live Longer*** [1952] PBO.	$ .75	$2.50	$5.00
ET-105	Stekel, M.D., Wilhelm - ***How To Understand Your Dreams*** [1952]	$ .75	$2.50	$5.00
E-106	Wertham, M.D., Fredric - ***The Show Of Violence*** [1951]	$1.00	$3.00	$6.00
ET-108	Stevens, Edmund - ***This Is Russia Un-Censored!*** [1951]	$ .75	$2.50	$5.00
E-109	Fielding, William J. - ***Self-Mastery Through Psycho-Analysis*** [1952]	$ .75	$2.50	$5.00
E-110	Noel, Sterling - ***I Killed Stalin*** [1952]	$2.00	$6.00	$12.00
E-111	Lacy, Ed - ***Sin In Their Blood*** [1952] PBO.	$2.50	$7.50	$15.00
E-112	Chase, James Hadley - ***Kiss My Fist!*** [1952] PBO.	$2.50	$7.50	$15.00
E-113	Echols, Allan K. - ***The Renegade Hills*** [1952] PBO.	$2.00	$6.00	$12.00
E-114	Weidman, Jerome - ***Give Me Your Love*** [1952] PBO.	$2.00	$6.00	$12.00
E-115	Cheyney, Peter - ***I'll Bring Her Back*** [1952]	$2.50	$7.50	$15.00
E-116	Chase, James Hadley - ***The Marijuana Mob*** [1952]	$10.00	$30.00	$60.00
E-117	Arthur, Eric - ***Invitation To Dishonor*** [1952] PBO. Cover art by Victor Olson.	$2.50	$7.50	$15.00
E-118	Miller, Tevis - ***Gun-Play In Killer Canyon*** [1952] PBO.	$2.00	$6.00	$12.00
E-119	Noel, Sterling - ***I Killed Stalin*** [1952]	$5.00	$15.00	$30.00
E-120	Martin, George Victor - ***Mark It With A Stone*** [1952] Cover by Victor Olson.	$2.50	$7.50	$15.00
E-121	Brock, Lilyan - ***Queer Patterns*** [1952] Cover art by Nappi.	$4.00	$12.50	$25.00

		G	VG	F
E-122	Harper, Daniel - ***Paris Escort*** [1953] PBO.	$2.50	$7.50	$15.00
E-123	Lacy, Ed - ***Strip For Violence*** [1953] PBO.	$2.50	$7.50	$15.00
E-124	Wallenstein, Marcel - ***Tuck's Girl*** [1953] PBO.	$2.00	$6.00	$12.00
E-125	Craig, Paul - ***Gunfighter*** [1953] PBO. Cover art by Nappi.	$2.00	$6.00	$12.00
E-127	MacDonald, William Colt - ***Stir Up The Dust*** [1953]	$2.00	$6.00	$12.00
E-128	Lehman, Paul Evan - ***Stagecoach To Hellfire Pass*** [1953] PBO.	$2.00	$6.00	$12.00
E-129	Anthology - ***Wit From Overseas*** [1953] PBO. Edited by Roy H. Hoopes, Jr. Cartoon and joke book.	$3.00	$9.00	$18.00
E-131	Echols, Allen K. - ***Vengeance Valley*** [1953] PBO.	$2.00	$6.00	$12.00
E-132	Holden, Larry - ***Hide-out*** [1953] PBO.	$2.50	$7.50	$15.00

Eugenics.

100	Stopes, Dr. Marie C. - ***Married Love*** [n.d.]	$ .65	$2.00	$4.00
101	Rossiter, M.D., Frederick M. - ***The Torch Of Life*** [1952]	$ .65	$2.00	$4.00
102	Chideckel, M.D., Maurice - ***The Single, The Engaged And The Married*** [1952]	$ .65	$2.00	$4.00
103	Robinson, M.D., William J. - ***Medical Sex Dictionary*** [1952]	$ .65	$2.00	$4.00

Europa.

1101	Jantzen, Fritz - ***Berlin Bed*** [1963] PBO.	$4.00	$12.50	$25.00
1102	Romer, Art - ***Sin On The Continent*** [1963] PBO.	$4.00	$12.50	$25.00
1103	Lord, H. T. - ***Sin Safari*** [1963] PBO.	$4.00	$12.50	$25.00
1104	Leech, Jack - ***Satan's Daughters*** [1963] PBO.	$4.00	$12.50	$25.00
1105	Dessiers, Frederick - ***Sexual Interlude*** [1963] PBO.	$4.00	$12.50	$25.00

Evening Reader.

1234	Williams, J. X. - ***Devil's Degradation*** [n.d.]	$1.50	$5.00	$10.00

Exotic Books. Digest Size.

1	Gordon, Luthor - ***Pay For My Kiss!*** [1949] PBO. Cover art by Rodewald.	$4.00	$12.50	$25.00
2	Gordon, Luthor - ***Any Man's Girl*** [1949] PBO. Cover art by Rodewald.	$4.00	$12.50	$25.00
3	Clayford, James (Peggy Gaddis) - ***Divorce Bait*** [1949]	$4.00	$12.50	$25.00
4	Woodford, Jack - ***Her First Sin*** [1949] PBO.	$4.00	$12.50	$25.00
NO#-5	Lindsay, Perry - ***Buy My Love!*** [1950] PBO. Cover art by Rodewald.	$4.00	$12.50	$25.00
NO#-6	Harvey, Gene - ***Passion's Slave*** [1950] PBO. Cover art by George Gross.	$4.00	$12.50	$25.00
NO#-7	Bligh, Norman - ***Once There Was A Virgin*** [1950] PBO. Cover art by George Gross.	$4.00	$12.50	$25.00
NO#-8	Stonebraker, Florence - ***Three Men And A Mistress*** [1950]	$4.00	$12.50	$25.00
NO#-9	Sherman, Joan - ***Suzy Needs A Man*** [1950] PBO. Cover art by George Gross.	$4.00	$12.50	$25.00
NO#-10	Harvey, Gene - ***Thrill Girl!*** [1950]	$4.00	$12.50	$25.00
NO#-11	Sherman, Joan - ***Men Call Her "Tramp"*** [1950] PBO.	$4.00	$12.50	$25.00
NO#-12	Sherman, Joan - ***Bodies On Fire*** [1951] PBO.	$4.00	$12.50	$25.00
14	Clayford, James (Peggy Gaddis) - ***Tonight For Sure*** [1951] PBO. Cover art by George Gross.	$4.00	$12.50	$25.00
15	Clayford, James (Peggy Gaddis) - ***Man Crazy*** [1951]	$4.00	$12.50	$25.00
16	Stone, Tom - ***Bad As The Rest*** [1951] PBO.	$4.00	$12.50	$25.00
17	Scott, Anthony (Brett Halliday) - ***Ten Toes Up*** [1951] PBO.	$5.00	$15.00	$30.00
18	Reed, Mark (Norman Daniels) - ***Give Me Ecstasy*** [1951] PBO.	$4.00	$12.50	$25.00
19	Balmer, Jon - ***Fever Hot!*** [1951]	$4.00	$12.50	$25.00
20	Hale, Laura - ***Lovers Don't Sleep*** [1951] PBO.	$4.00	$12.50	$25.00

F. E. Howard Digests. Toronto: F. E. Howard Publications.

NN-1	Edgar, Keith - ***I Hate You To Death*** [1944] PBO.	$3.50	$10.00	$20.00
NN-2	Anthology - ***True Mysteries And Murders*** [1944]	$3.50	$10.00	$20.00
NN-3	Edgar, Keith - ***Honduras Double Cross*** [1944] PBO.	$3.50	$10.00	$20.00

		G	VG	F
NN-4	Edgar, Keith - ***The Incendiary Blonde*** [1944]	$3.50	$10.00	$20.00

F. J. Low. New York: F. J. Low Company, Inc. Digest Size.

		G	VG	F
NN	Mann, Arthur - ***The Jackie Robinson Story*** [1950] PBO. Photo covers. Movie tie-in.	$22.00	$70.00	$140.00

Falcon Books. New York: Falcon Books, Inc. Digest Size.

		G	VG	F
21	Scott, Anthony - ***Season For Sin*** [1952]	$5.00	$15.00	$30.00
22	Reed, Mark - ***The Scarlet Bride*** [1952]	$6.00	$20.00	$40.00
23	Bottari, George - ***Mabel And Men*** [1952] PBO.	$4.00	$12.50	$25.00
24	Evens, Hodge - ***Three For Passion*** [1952] PBO.	$4.00	$12.50	$25.00
25	Daly, Hamlin - ***Case Of The Cancelled Redhead*** [1952] PBO.	$4.50	$14.00	$28.00
26	Reed, Mark - ***Lay Down And Die!*** [1952] PBO.	$4.00	$12.50	$25.00
27	Dann, Norma (Norman Daniels) - ***Lida Lynn*** [1952] PBO.	$4.00	$12.50	$25.00
28	Weiss, Joe - ***Girls Out Of Hell*** [1952] PBO. Cover by Gross.	$4.50	$14.00	$28.00
29	Daniels, Norman A. - ***Mistress On A Deathbed*** [1952] PBO. Cover by Gross.	$4.00	$12.50	$25.00
30	Prather, Richard S. - ***Dagger Of Flesh!*** [1952] PBO. Cover by Rudy Nappi.	$5.00	$15.00	$30.00
31	Roan, Tom - ***Slave Girl*** [1952]	$4.50	$14.00	$28.00
32	Reed, Mark - ***Sins Of The Flesh*** [1952] PBO. Cover by Gross.	$4.00	$12.50	$25.00
33	Evans, Hodge - ***Yellow-Head*** [n.d.]	$4.50	$14.00	$28.00
34	Dann, Norma (Norman Daniels) - ***Shack Girl!*** [n.d.]	$4.00	$12.50	$25.00
35	Wade, David - ***Raise The Devil!*** [1952] PBO.	$4.00	$12.50	$25.00
36	Craig, Jonathan - ***Junkie*** [1952] PBO.	$6.00	$20.00	$40.00
37	Hale, Laura - ***Woman Hunter*** [1952] PBO.	$4.00	$12.50	$25.00
38	Daniels, Norman - ***Sweet Savage*** [1952] PBO.	$4.00	$12.50	$25.00
39	Kinsey, Chet - ***Joy Street*** [n.d.]	$4.00	$12.50	$25.00
40	Evans, Hodge - ***Whip-Hand!*** [n.d.]	$4.00	$12.50	$25.00
41	Hunter, Evan - ***The Evil Sleep!*** [1952] PBO.	$4.00	$12.50	$25.00
42	Walton, Bryce - ***The Long Night*** [1952] PBO.	$4.00	$12.50	$25.00
43	Reed, Mark - ***House Of A Thousand Desires*** [1953] PBO.	$4.00	$12.50	$25.00
44	Beckman, Jr., Charles - ***Honky Tonk Girl*** [1953] PBO.	$4.00	$12.50	$25.00

Famous Mystery. Toronto: Howard Publications. Digest Size.

		G	VG	F
1	Fleming, Ethel - ***Murder Takes A Honeymoon*** [1944]	$3.50	$10.00	$20.00
2	Barry, Joe - ***The Pay-Off*** [1944]	$3.00	$9.00	$18.00

Fantasy Books. London: Fantasy Books, Inc.

		G	VG	F
400	Long, Frank Belknap - ***John Carstairs—Space Detective*** [n.d.]	$3.00	$9.00	$18.00
401	Friend, Oscar J. - ***The Kid From Mars*** [n.d.]	$2.50	$7.50	$15.00
402	Coblentz, Stanton A. - ***The Sunken World*** [n.d.]	$2.50	$7.50	$15.00
403	Wollheim, Donald A. - ***Flight Into Space*** [n.d.]	$2.50	$7.50	$15.00
404	Leinster, Murray - ***The Last Space Ship*** [n.d.]	$2.50	$7.50	$15.00
405	Tweed, Thomas F. - ***Gabriel Over The White House*** [n.d.]	$2.50	$7.50	$15.00
406	Gernsback, Hugo - ***Ralph 124C 41+*** [n.d.]	$3.00	$9.00	$18.00
407	Russell, Eric Frank - ***Sinister Barrier*** [n.d.]	$2.50	$7.50	$15.00
408	Campbell, Jr., John W. - ***The Thing*** [n.d.]	$4.00	$12.50	$25.00
409	Hubbard, L. Ron - ***Typewriter In The Sky*** [n.d.]	$6.00	$20.00	$40.00
410	Walsh, John - ***Vanguard To Neptune*** [n.d.]	$2.50	$7.50	$15.00
411	Dubois, Theodora - ***Solution T-25*** [n.d.]	$2.50	$7.50	$15.00

Fantasy Classics.

		G	VG	F
1	Machen, Arthur - ***The Terror*** [1974]	$1.50	$5.00	$10.00
2	Housman, Clemence - ***Werewolf*** [1974]	$1.50	$5.00	$10.00
3	Leath, Robert Neal - ***The Obsidian Ape*** [1974]	$1.50	$5.00	$10.00
4	Blackwood, Algernon - ***Ancient Sorceries*** [1974]	$1.50	$5.00	$10.00

		G	VG	F
Fantasy Reader.				
1	Liebscher, Walt - ***Alien Carnival*** [1974] Cover art by Robert Kline.	$1.50	$5.00	$10.00
2	Evans, E. Everett - ***Food For Demons*** [1974] Cover art by John Pound.	$1.50	$5.00	$10.00
3	Machen, Arthur - ***The Great God Pan*** [1974]	$2.50	$7.50	$15.00
4	Chambers, Robert W. - ***The Maker Of Moons*** [1974]	$1.50	$5.00	$10.00
5	Burroughs, Edgar Rice - ***The Man Eater*** [1974] Cover art by Robert Kline.	$4.00	$12.50	$25.00
6	Machen, Arthur & Chambers, Robert W. - ***Kings Of Horror*** [1974] PBO. Cover art by Greg Bear.	$2.50	$7.50	$15.00
7	Kinross, Albert - ***The Fearsome Island*** [1974] Cover art by John Pound.	$1.50	$5.00	$10.00
Federal Books. Toronto: Federal Publishing Co.				
FP1	Lane, Tex - ***Marjorie*** [n.d.]	$5.50	$17.50	$35.00
FP2	Brown, Beth - ***Room Girl*** [n.d.]	$5.50	$17.50	$35.00
FP3	Kane, Frank E. - ***Varities Of Life*** [n.d.]	$5.50	$17.50	$35.00
FP4	Kane, Frank E. - ***Jetsam Journey*** [n.d.]	$5.50	$17.50	$35.00
Femack. New York: The Femack Co. Digest Size.				
NN-1	Lariar, Lawrence - ***He Died Laughing*** [1945]	$3.50	$10.00	$20.00
NN-2	Livingston, Armstrong - ***Murder Is Easy!*** [1945]	$3.00	$9.00	$18.00
Fiesta Books. New York: Rio Publishing. Digest Size.				
1	Anton, Cal - ***The Private Life Of A Strip-Tease Girl*** [1952] PBO. Photo cover.	$3.00	$9.00	$18.00
2	Wall, Evans - ***Ask For Therese*** [1952] Photo cover.	$3.00	$9.00	$18.00
3	Wall, Evans - ***Love Fetish*** [1952]	$3.00	$9.00	$18.00
4	Baroni, Nick - ***The Lady Was A Tramp*** [1952] Photo cover.	$3.00	$9.00	$18.00
5	McKnight, Evans - ***Television Tramp*** [1952] PBO. Cover art by Geygan.	$3.00	$9.00	$18.00
6	Smith, Ben - ***Unwanted Wife*** [1952] Cover art by Warren King.	$3.00	$9.00	$18.00
Fighting Western Novel (A). Digest Size.				
1	McCulley, Johnston - ***The Cougar Kid*** [n.d.] Cover art by Charles Wood.	$1.25	$3.75	$7.50
3	Shappiro, Herbert - ***Two-Gun Texan*** [n.d.] Cover art by Charles Wood.	$1.00	$3.00	$6.00
5	Bardwell, Denver - ***Coyote Hunter*** [n.d.]	$1.00	$3.00	$6.00
6	Seltzer, Charles Alden - ***Silverspurs*** [n.d.]	$1.00	$3.00	$6.00
7	James, Dan - ***Stranger At Storm Ranch*** [n.d.] Cover art by Charles Wood.	$1.00	$3.00	$6.00
12	McCulley, Johnson - ***Ghost Bullet Range*** [n.d.]	$1.00	$3.00	$6.00
13	Young, Gordon - ***Red Clark At The Showdown*** [n.d.] Cover art by Charles Wood.	$1.00	$3.00	$6.00
14	Grinstead, J.E. - ***Law Of The Trail*** [n.d.] Cover art by Charles Wood.	$1.00	$3.00	$6.00
15	Ernenwein, Leslie - ***Kincaid Of Red Butte*** [n.d.] Cover art by A. Leslie Ross.	$1.00	$3.00	$6.00
16	Manning, Roy - ***Trigger Trail*** [n.d.] Cover art by Charles Wood.	$1.00	$3.00	$6.00
18	Manning, Roy - ***Vengeance Valley*** [n.d.] Cover by Charles Wood.	$1.00	$3.00	$6.00
22	Lehman, Paul Evan - ***The Cougar Of Canyon Caballo*** [n.d.]	$1.00	$3.00	$6.00
29	Haley, Glen - ***Rustler's Odds*** [n.d.]	$1.00	$3.00	$6.00
30	Young, Gordon - ***Tall In The Saddle*** [n.d.]	$1.00	$3.00	$6.00
33	Piper, Anson - ***Black Creek Buckaroo*** [n.d.] Cover art by Charles Wood.	$1.00	$3.00	$6.00
34	Phillips, Ernie - ***Rustlers Of Table Butte*** [n.d.] Cover art by Charles Wood.	$1.00	$3.00	$6.00

		G	VG	F
35	Roan, Tom - ***The Rio Kid*** [n.d.]	$1.00	$3.00	$6.00
36	Snow, Charles H. - ***The Cowboy From Alamos*** [n.d.] Cover art by Charles Wood.	$1.00	$3.00	$6.00
37	Hilton, Francis W. - ***Phantom Rustlers*** [n.d.] Cover art by Earl Elton.	$1.00	$3.00	$6.00
38	Nye, Nelson C. - ***Wild Horse Shorty*** [n.d.] Cover by Charles Wood.	$1.00	$3.00	$6.00
40	Westland, Lynn - ***Return To The Range*** [n.d.] Cover art by Charles Wood.	$1.00	$3.00	$6.00
42	Roan, Tom - ***Gun Lord Of Silver River*** [n.d.]	$1.00	$3.00	$6.00

Fingerprint Mystery. Digest Size.

		G	VG	F
NN-1	Bowen, Joseph - ***The Man Without A Head*** [n.d.]	$2.50	$7.50	$15.00
NN-2	Hultman, Helen Joan - ***Murder Rings Twice*** [n.d.]	$2.50	$7.50	$15.00

First Niter.

		G	VG	F
101	Polk, Richard - ***Strange Hungers*** [1963] PBO.	$2.50	$7.50	$15.00
102	Kosloff, Myron - ***Running Wild*** [1963] PBO.	$2.00	$6.00	$12.00

Five Star Mystery. New York: Green Publishing Co. Digest Size.

		G	VG	F
1	Yates, Peter - ***The Dress Circle Murders*** [1945] PBO.	$2.50	$7.50	$15.00
2	Crossen, Ken - ***Murder Out Of Mind*** [1945] PBO.	$2.50	$7.50	$15.00
3	Elliot, Bruce - ***You'll Die Laughing*** [n.d.]	$2.50	$7.50	$15.00
4	Yates, Peter - ***Death Comes To Dinner*** [n.d.]	$2.50	$7.50	$15.00
5	Foster, Richard - ***The Invisible Man Murders*** [1945] PBO.	$2.50	$7.50	$15.00
6	Brown, Wenzell - ***Murder Seeks An Agent*** [n.d.]	$2.50	$7.50	$15.00
7	Yates, Peter - ***Death In The Hands Of Talent*** [1945] PBO.	$2.50	$7.50	$15.00
41	Wolffe, Katherine - ***Death's Long Shadow*** [n.d.] PBO.	$2.50	$7.50	$15.00
42	Creed, Will - ***Death Wears A Green Hat*** [1946] PBO.	$2.50	$7.50	$15.00
43	Csida, Joseph - ***Crime Is Of The Essence*** [n.d.] PBO.	$2.50	$7.50	$15.00
44	Stapleton, Douglas & Carey, Helen A. - ***The Corpse Is Indignant*** [n.d.]	$2.50	$7.50	$15.00
45	Allen, Leslie - ***Murder In The Rough*** [n.d.] PBO.	$2.50	$7.50	$15.00
46	Fischer, Bruno - ***Kill To Fit*** [1946] PBO.	$2.50	$7.50	$15.00
47	Creed, Will - ***Death Comes Grinning*** [1946] PBO.	$2.50	$7.50	$15.00
48	Kane, Frank - ***Johnny On A Slay Ride*** [n.d.]	$3.50	$10.00	$20.00

Flagship Books.

		G	VG	F
701	Kelly, K.P. - ***The Plot*** [1967] PBO.	$1.00	$3.00	$6.00
702	Olemy, P.T. - ***Pink Dolphin*** [1967] PBO.	$1.25	$3.75	$7.50
703	Gilford, C.B. - ***Dead Man Out*** [1967] PBO.	$1.00	$3.00	$6.00
704	Henry, Vera - ***Portrait In Fear*** [1967]	$1.00	$3.00	$6.00
705	Dencs, Gyela - ***The Sex-Conscious And The Love-Shy*** [1967]	$ .65	$2.00	$4.00
706	Prescott, Allen - ***Corinthian Class*** [1967]	$ .75	$2.50	$5.00
707	Campbell, Maury - ***A Present For Harry*** [1967] PBO.	$1.00	$3.00	$6.00
708	Manson, Will - ***A Man Called Black*** [1967] PBO.	$1.00	$3.00	$6.00
709	Olemy, P.T. - ***The Transgressors*** [1967]	$1.00	$3.00	$6.00
710	Post, Carl - ***Turn Your Back On Heaven*** [1967]	$ .75	$2.50	$5.00
711	Kovalsky, J.R. - ***The Runner Is Red*** [1967] PBO.	$1.00	$3.00	$6.00
712	d'Allesandro, Countess Elena - ***So Long Remembered*** [1967] PBO.	$ .65	$2.00	$4.00
713	Campbell, Dr. Giraud W. - ***How To Control Arthritis*** [1967]	$ .65	$2.00	$4.00
714	Freedman, Cole - ***In Praise Of Love*** [1967]	$ .65	$2.00	$4.00
715	Carpenter, Elmer J. - ***Moonspin*** [1967] PBO.	$1.25	$3.75	$7.50
716	Manson, Will - ***The Mathematician*** [1967] PBO.	$ .65	$2.00	$4.00
717	Brand, Oscar - ***Bawdy Songs & Backroom Ballads*** [1967] Cover art by Irving Sloane. Song book.	$1.25	$3.75	$7.50
718	Carpenter, Elmer J. - ***To Serve And Cry*** [1967] PBO.	$ .75	$2.50	$5.00
719	Day, Will B. - ***Bravo 9*** [1967] PBO. Cover art by Adolph Le Moutt.	$1.00	$3.00	$6.00

		G	VG	F
720	Keller, Drew - ***The Spare Room*** [1967]	$1.00	$3.00	$6.00
721	France, Jay - ***The Desperate Sex*** [1967] PBO.	$ .75	$2.50	$5.00
722	Hornsby, J. Thomas - ***Valley Of The Moon Goddess*** [1967] PBO.	$1.25	$3.75	$7.50
723	Manson, Will - ***A Deadly Game*** [1967] PBO.	$1.00	$3.00	$6.00
724	Fenton, Pat - ***This Little Angel Went To Hell*** [1967] PBO. Photo cover.	$1.00	$3.00	$6.00
725	Brown, Kenneth R. - ***A Tiger In Haight-Ashbury*** [1967] PBO.	$ .75	$2.50	$5.00
726	Perkins, Faith - ***Come My Love*** [1967]	$ .65	$2.00	$4.00
727	Kovalsky, J.R. - ***The Early Days Of August*** [1967] PBO.	$ .75	$2.50	$5.00
728	Pope, Leo - ***Malachi Breen Times 2*** [1967] PBO.	$ .75	$2.50	$5.00
729	Parkes, Patrick B. - ***To Hell - Or Connaught*** [1967] PBO.	$ .75	$2.50	$5.00
730	Gibson, William C. - ***Therapeutic Self-Hypnosis*** [1967]	$ .65	$2.00	$4.00
731	Manson, Will - ***The Chinese Conundrum*** [1967] PBO.	$1.00	$3.00	$6.00
732	LeRoy, Howard - ***The Jay*** [1967]	$ .75	$2.50	$5.00
733	Cummins, Walter - ***A Stranger To The Deed*** [1967] PBO.	$ .75	$2.50	$5.00
734	Churchill, David B. - ***The Jade Madelaine*** [1967]	$ .75	$2.50	$5.00
735	Day, Will B. - ***The Man From M.O.D.*** [1967] PBO.	$1.25	$3.75	$7.50
736	Rader, M.D., J. Paul - ***An Anatomy Of The Mind*** [1967] PBO.	$1.00	$3.00	$6.00
837	Barbanell, Maurice - ***He Walks In Two Worlds*** [1968]	$1.00	$3.00	$6.00
838	Cummings, Walter - ***Into Temptation*** [1968]	$1.00	$3.00	$6.00
839	Manson, Will - ***The Dangerous Ones*** [1968] PBO.	$1.00	$3.00	$6.00
840	Olemy, P.T. - ***The Clones*** [1968] PBO.	$1.25	$3.75	$7.50
841	Tchakmankian, Pascal - ***Death Of A Child*** [1968]	$1.00	$3.00	$6.00
842	LeRoy, Howard - ***The Keeper*** [1968] PBO.	$1.00	$3.00	$6.00
843	Kasper, Ray Charles - ***Love Spy, Love*** [1968] PBO. Cover by Chitouras.	$1.00	$3.00	$6.00
844	Prescott, Allen - ***Salads, Sandwiches & Hors d'Oeuvres*** [1968]	$ .75	$2.50	$5.00
846	Brennan, Dan - ***Lay-Over Town*** [1968] PBO. Cover art by Guzzi.	$1.00	$3.00	$6.00
847	Cearley, J.B. - ***A Touch Of Murder*** [1968] PBO.	$1.00	$3.00	$6.00
848	Saunders, Carole - ***The Now Girls*** [1968]	$ .75	$2.50	$5.00
849	Garten, John G. - ***Ride The Rainbow*** [1968]	$ .75	$2.50	$5.00
850	Brennan, Dan - ***The Manipulator*** [1968] PBO. Photo cover.	$1.00	$3.00	$6.00
851	De Cyr - ***Vendetta*** [1968] PBO. Cover art by Chitouras.	$ .75	$2.50	$5.00
852	Manson, Will - ***The Duke*** [1968] PBO. Cover art by Guzzi.	$1.00	$3.00	$6.00
853	Myers, John - ***The Miracle Within You*** [1968]	$ .75	$2.50	$5.00
854	Leikam, William C. - ***Run For The Waves*** [1968]	$ .75	$2.50	$5.00
855	Kanto, Peter - ***A Small Slice Of War*** [1968] PBO.	$1.00	$3.00	$6.00
856	Forbes, J.D. - ***Murder ... In Full View*** [1968] PBO.	$1.00	$3.00	$6.00
857	Maidment, William - ***The Adulteress*** [1968]	$ .75	$2.50	$5.00
858	Avereen, Jack - ***Cynthia*** [1968]	$ .75	$2.50	$5.00
859	Manring, Eric Hammond - ***The Spur Of Fear*** [1968] PBO.	$1.00	$3.00	$6.00
860	Manson, Will - ***A Very Black Deed*** [1968]	$1.00	$3.00	$6.00
861	Maidment, William - ***The Last Free Man*** [1968] PBO.	$1.00	$3.00	$6.00
863	Thompson, Sharon L. - ***Reaper Of Wild Oats*** [1968] PBO. Photo cover.	$1.00	$3.00	$6.00
864	Cummings, M.A. - ***Exile And Other Tales Of Fantasy*** [1968] PBO.	$1.25	$3.75	$7.50

Fotonovels. Los Angeles: Fotonovel Publications.

		G	VG	F
001	Photo story - ***Heaven Can Wait*** [1979] PBO. Movie tie-in. Color photos.	$1.50	$5.00	$10.00
002	Photo story - ***Ice Castles*** [1978] PBO. Movie tie-in. Color photos.	$1.50	$5.00	$10.00
003	Photo story - ***Invasion Of The Body Snatchers*** [1979] PBO. Movie tie-in. Color photos.	$2.50	$7.50	$15.00
004	Photo story - ***The Champ*** [1979] PBO. Movie tie-in. Color photos.	$1.50	$5.00	$10.00
005	Photo story - ***Hair*** [1979] PBO. Movie tie-in. Color photos.	$1.50	$5.00	$10.00

		G	VG	F
006	Photo story - ***Love At First Bite*** [1979] PBO. Movie tie-in. Color photos.	$2.00	$6.00	$12.00
007	Photo story - ***J. R. R. Tolkien's The Lord Of The Rings*** [1979] PBO. Movie tie-in. Color photos.	$2.50	$7.50	$15.00
008	Photo story - ***Nightwing*** [1979] PBO. Movie tie-in. Color photos.	$1.50	$5.00	$10.00
009	Photo story - ***Revenge Of The Pink Panther*** [1979] PBO. Movie tie-in. Color photos.	$1.50	$5.00	$10.00
010	Photo story - ***The Best Of Rocky And The Complete Rocky II*** [1979] PBO. Movie tie-in. Color photos.	$1.50	$5.00	$10.00
013	Photo story - ***Grease*** [1979] Movie tie-in. Photo cover and interiors.	$1.50	$5.00	$10.00
014	Photo story - ***Buck Rogers In The 25th Century*** [1979] PBO. Movie tie-in. Color photos.	$2.50	$7.50	$15.00
016	Photo story - ***Americathon 1998*** [1979] PBO. Movie tie-in. Color photos.	$1.50	$5.00	$10.00

Freeway Press. New York: The Freeway Press.

FP-2041	Steele, Curtis - ***The Masked Invasion (Operator 5 Number 1)*** [1974]	$1.50	$5.00	$10.00

Futura Books. London: Futura Books, Ltd.

NO#-1	Tremlett, George - ***The John Lennon Story*** [1976] PBO. 16 pages of photos.	$1.50	$5.00	$10.00

Galaxy Books (Early Publisher's History, 1950–1959)

Galaxy Publishing Corporation began *Galaxy* magazine and a line of science fiction novels in September 1950. The format of the novels changed from digests to paperbacks in 1958. They issued thirty-five books, of which the first thirty-one are digest sized.

Beacon Books continued the series from 1959 until they ceased publishing novels edited by Galaxy in July 1961. They produced ten novels and one anthology (#249), which all lack the traditional B prior to their logo number. Beacon's adult themes were added. Listed with the other Beacon books, their numbers are 236, 242, 249, 256, 263, 270, 277, 284, 291, 298, 305, and 312.

In 1963, they began another series, Magabooks, consisting of three digest-sized, double novels. This series was the first to specialize in publishing science fiction paperbacks for over a decade. Changing formats and publishers make these three connected series unique.

Galaxy Science Fiction Novel. New York: World Editions Inc./Galaxy Pub. Corp.

		G	VG	F
1	Russell, Eric Frank - ***Sinister Barrier*** [1950] Digest size.	$2.50	$7.50	$15.00
2	Williamson, Jack - ***The Legion Of Space*** [1950] Digest size. Cover by Calle.	$2.50	$7.50	$15.00
3	Clarke, Arthur C. - ***Prelude To Space*** [1951] PBO. Digest size. Cover by Bunch.	$2.50	$7.50	$15.00
4	Wright, S. Fowler - ***The Amphibians*** [1950] Digest size.	$2.50	$7.50	$15.00
5	Wright, S. Fowler - ***The World Below*** [1950] Digest size.	$2.50	$7.50	$15.00
6	Jones, Raymond F. - ***The Alien*** [1951] PBO. Digest size.	$2.50	$7.50	$15.00
7	Simak, Clifford D. - ***Empire*** [1951] PBO. Digest size.	$2.50	$7.50	$15.00
8	Stapledon, Olaf - ***Odd John*** [1951] Digest size. Cover by Ed Emsh.	$3.00	$9.00	$18.00
9	Temple, William F. - ***Four Sided Triangle*** [1951] Digest size. Cover by Samson Pollen.	$2.50	$7.50	$15.00
10	Franklin, Jay - ***Rat Race*** [1951] Digest size.	$2.50	$7.50	$15.00

Galaxy Novel, 35

Gold Medal, 103

Gold Medal, 126

		G	VG	F
11	Tucker, Wilson - ***The City In The Sea*** [1952] Digest size. Cover by Ed Emsh.	$3.00	$9.00	$18.00
12	Merwin, Jr., Sam - ***The House Of Many Worlds*** [1952] Digest size. Cover by Emsh.	$3.00	$9.00	$18.00
13	Taine, John - ***Seeds Of Life*** [1952] Digest size.	$2.50	$7.50	$15.00
14	Asimov, Isaac - ***Pebble In The Sky*** [1953] Digest size.	$2.50	$7.50	$15.00
15	Mitchell, J. Leslie - ***Three Go Back*** [1953] Digest size.	$2.50	$7.50	$15.00
16	Blish, James - ***The Warriors Of Day*** [1953] PBO. Digest size. Cover by Calle.	$2.50	$7.50	$15.00
17	Padgett, Lewis - ***Well Of The Worlds*** [1953] PBO. Digest size.	$3.00	$9.00	$18.00
18	Hamilton, Edmond - ***City At World's End*** [1953] Digest size. Cover by Ed Emsh.	$3.00	$9.00	$18.00
19	Blish, James - ***Jack Of Eagles*** [1953] Digest size. Cover by Ed Emsh.	$3.50	$10.00	$20.00
20	Leinster, Murray - ***The Black Galaxy*** [1954] Digest size. Cover by Ed Emsh.	$2.50	$7.50	$15.00
21	Williamson, Jack - ***The Humanoids*** [1954] Digest size. Cover by Ed Emsh.	$2.50	$7.50	$15.00
22	Merwin, Jr., Sam - ***Killer To Come*** [1954] Digest size.	$3.00	$9.00	$18.00
23	Reed, David V. - ***Murder In Space*** [1954] Digest size.	$2.50	$7.50	$15.00
24	DeCamp, L. Sprague - ***Lest Darkness Fall*** [1956] Digest size.	$2.50	$7.50	$15.00
25	Leinster, Murray - ***The Last Spaceship*** [1955] Digest size. Cover by Ed Emsh.	$2.50	$7.50	$15.00
26	Padgett, Lewis - ***Chessboard Planet*** [1956] Digest size.	$3.00	$9.00	$18.00
27	Jameson, Malcolm - ***Tarnished Utopia*** [1956] PBO. Digest size.	$2.50	$7.50	$15.00
28	Leiber, Fritz - ***Destiny Times Three*** [1957] PBO. Digest size.	$4.00	$12.50	$25.00
29	Hubbard, L. Ron - ***Fear*** [1957] Digest size.	$5.50	$17.50	$35.00
30	Pratt, Fletcher - ***Double Jeopardy*** [1957] Digest size. Cover by Wallace Wood.	$3.00	$9.00	$18.00
31	Moore, C. L. - ***Shambleau*** [1957] Digest size. Cover by Wallace Wood.	$4.00	$12.50	$25.00
32	Wallace, F.L. - ***Address: Centauri*** [1958] Paperback size. Cover by Wallace Wood.	$3.50	$10.00	$20.00
33	Clement, Hal - ***Mission Of Gravity*** [1958] Paperback size. Cover by Wallace Wood.	$3.50	$10.00	$20.00
34	Wellman, Manly Wade - ***Twice In Time*** [1958] Paperback size. Cover by Wallace Wood.	$3.50	$10.00	$20.00
35	Clifton, Mark and Riley, Frank - ***The Forever Machine*** [1958] Paperback size. Cover by Wallace Wood.	$3.50	$10.00	$20.00

Gem Books. New York: Croydon Publishing Co. Digest Size.

		G	VG	F
101	Carter, Ralph - ***She Lived In Sin*** [1952] Cover art by Lou Marchetti.	$2.50	$7.50	$15.00
102	Stone, Thomas - ***Shameful Love*** [1952] Cover by Gazzola.	$2.50	$7.50	$15.00

Gnome Press. New York: Gnome Press Pubs.

		G	VG	F
NO#	Bond, Nelson - ***The Thirty-First Of February*** [1952] First edition, second printing. Printed for distribution to U.S. military personnel.	$5.00	$15.00	$30.00

Gold Medal Books (Early Publisher's History, 1949–1959)

Yellow spines and a gold medal on the front identify early Gold Medal Books. Roscoe and Wilford Fawcett, publishers of magazines in the 1920s, founded this line of books. Fawcett Publications intended to print first editions by a wide variety of authors. In doing so, they brought forth authors like Richard Himmel, Richard Prather, Vin Packer, John Flagg, Theodore Pratt, Bruno Fischer, Sax Rohmer, and John D. MacDonald, to name a few. Lamination and colorful artwork by Mitchell Hooks and others grace their covers.

Related imprints include Red Seal Books, Crest Books, and Premier Books.

Gold Medal Books. Greenwich, CT: Fawcett Publishing.

		G	VG	F
NO#-99	Anthology from *True* magazine - ***The Best From True*** [1949] PBO. Photo cover.	$3.50	$10.00	$20.00
NO#-100	Anthology from *Today's Woman* magazine - ***Marriage And Sex*** [1949]	$1.50	$5.00	$10.00
101	Hynd, Alan - ***We Are The Public Enemies*** [1949] PBO.	$2.50	$7.50	$15.00
102	Anthology from *True* magazine - ***Man Story*** [1950] PBO.	$1.50	$5.00	$10.00
103	Flagg, John - ***The Persian Cat*** [1950] PBO. Cover by Downes.	$2.50	$7.50	$15.00
104	Himmel, Richard - ***I'll Find You*** [1950] PBO. Cover by Stanley Meltzoff.	$2.00	$6.00	$12.00
105	Rohmer, Sax - ***Nude In Mink*** [1950] PBO.	$4.00	$12.50	$25.00
106	Burnett, W.R. - ***Stretch Dawson*** [1950] PBO.	$2.00	$6.00	$12.00
107	Keyhoe, Donald - ***The Flying Saucers Are Real*** [1950] PBO. Cover by Frank Tinsley.	$1.25	$3.75	$7.50
108	Miller, Wade - ***Devil May Care*** [1950] PBO.	$2.00	$6.00	$12.00
109	Colter, Lillian - ***Awakening Of Jenny*** [1950] PBO. Cover by Barye Phillips.	$2.00	$6.00	$12.00
110	Ronns, Edward - ***Million Dollar Murder*** [1950] PBO.	$2.00	$6.00	$12.00
111	Savage, Jr., Les - ***The Wild Horse*** [1950] PBO.	$1.50	$5.00	$10.00
112	Gruenberg, Sidonie - ***Your Child And You*** [1950] PBO. Photo Cover.	$1.35	$4.00	$8.00
113	Hunt, Howard - ***The Violent Ones*** [1950] PBO. Cover by Barye Phillips.	$2.00	$6.00	$12.00
114	Rubel, James L. - ***No Business For A Lady*** [1950] PBO.	$2.00	$6.00	$12.00
115	Rohde, William L. - ***Help Wanted - For Murder*** [1950] PBO. Cover by Barye Phillips.	$2.00	$6.00	$12.00
116	Stanford, Don - ***The Slaughtered Lovelies*** [1950] PBO.	$2.00	$6.00	$12.00
117	Ronns, Edward - ***State Department Murders*** [1950] PBO. Cover by Barye Phillips.	$2.00	$6.00	$12.00
118	Mitchell, Will - ***The Goldfish Murders*** [1950] PBO.	$2.00	$6.00	$12.00
119	Pratt, Theodore - ***The Tormented*** [1950] PBO. Cover by Barye Phillips.	$1.50	$5.00	$10.00
120	Grove, Walt - ***The Man Who Said No*** [1950] PBO.	$2.00	$6.00	$12.00
121	Adams, Clifton - ***The Desperado*** [1950] PBO.	$1.50	$5.00	$10.00
122	Kantor, MacKinlay - ***One Wild Oat*** [1950] PBO. Cover by Downes.	$2.00	$6.00	$12.00

Gold Medal, 129

Gold Medal, 136

Gold Medal, 169

		G	VG	F
123	Fischer, Bruno - ***House Of Flesh*** [1950] PBO.	$2.50	$7.50	$15.00
124	MacDonald, John D. - ***The Brass Cupcake*** [1950] PBO. Author's first novel. Cover by Barye Phillips.	$20.00	$60.00	$125.00
125	Schweitzer, Gertrude - ***The Obsessed*** [1950] PBO.	$1.50	$5.00	$10.00
126	Jenkins, Will F. - ***Dallas*** [1950] PBO. Movie tie-in with Gary Cooper.	$4.00	$12.50	$25.00
127	Prather, Richard S. - ***Case Of The Vanishing Beauty*** [1950] PBO. First Shell Scott novel.	$3.50	$10.00	$20.00
128	Runbeck, Margaret Lee - ***Three Secrets*** [1950] PBO. Movie tie-in.	$2.50	$7.50	$15.00
129	Millard, Joseph - ***Mansion Of Evil*** [1950] PBO. Interior in color comic book format.	$25.00	$75.00	$180.00
130	Connell, Vivian - ***A Man Of Parts*** [1950] PBO.	$1.50	$5.00	$10.00
131	Heuman, William - ***Guns At Broken Bow*** [1950] PBO.	$1.50	$5.00	$10.00
132	Torres, Tereska - ***Women's Barracks*** [1950] PBO. Cover by Barye Phillips.	$3.00	$9.00	$18.00
133	Ronns, Edward - ***Catspaw Ordeal*** [1950] PBO. Cover by Downes.	$2.00	$6.00	$12.00
134	Grove, Walt - ***Hell-Bent For Danger*** [1950] PBO.	$2.00	$6.00	$12.00
135	Shane, Ted - ***Bar Guide*** [1950] PBO. Contains cartoons by VIP.	$1.50	$5.00	$10.00
136	Woolrich, Cornell - ***Savage Bride*** [1950] PBO. Cover by Barye Phillips.	$7.00	$22.50	$45.00
137	Stewart, Logan - ***War Bonnet Pass*** [1950] PBO.	$1.50	$5.00	$10.00
138	Cohen, Octavus Roy - ***The Corpse That Walked*** [1951] PBO.	$2.00	$6.00	$12.00
139	Miller, Wade - ***Stolen Woman*** [1950] PBO. Cover by Barye Phillips.	$2.00	$6.00	$12.00
140	Ernenwein, Leslie - ***Gunfighter's Return*** [1950] PBO.	$1.50	$5.00	$10.00
141	Williams, Charles - ***Hill Girl*** [1951] PBO. Cover by Barye Phillips.	$2.50	$7.50	$15.00
142	Cushman, Dan - ***Jewel Of The Java Sea*** [1951] PBO.	$2.50	$7.50	$15.00
143	Himmel, Richard - ***The Chinese Keyhole*** [1951] PBO. Cover by Barye Phillips.	$2.00	$6.00	$12.00
144	Sabin, Mark - ***Winchester Cut*** [1951] PBO.	$1.50	$5.00	$10.00
145	Rohde, William L. - ***High Red For Dead*** [1951] PBO.	$2.00	$6.00	$12.00
146	Heuman, William - ***Roll The Wagons*** [1951] PBO. Cover by Stan Getti.	$1.50	$5.00	$10.00
147	Prather, Richard S. - ***Bodies In Bedlam*** [1951] PBO. Cover by Barye Phillips.	$2.00	$6.00	$12.00
148	Fischer, Bruno - ***The Lady Kills*** [1951] PBO.	$2.50	$7.50	$15.00

		G	VG	F
149	Chadwick, Joseph - ***Gunsmoke Reckoning*** [1951] PBO. Cover by A. Leslie Ross.	$2.00	$6.00	$12.00
150	Kieran, James - ***Come Murder Me*** [1951] PBO. Cover by Barye Phillips.	$2.00	$6.00	$12.00
151	Flagg, John - ***Death And The Naked Lady*** [1951] PBO. Cover by Downes.	$2.50	$7.50	$15.00
152	Miller, Wade - ***The Killer*** [1951] PBO. Cover by C.C. Beall.	$2.00	$6.00	$12.00
153	Pratt, Theodore - ***Cocotte*** [1951] PBO.	$1.50	$5.00	$10.00
154	Rosen, Victor - ***A Gun In His Hand*** [1951] PBO. Cover by Barye Phillips.	$1.50	$5.00	$10.00
155	Bellah, James Warner - ***The Apache*** [1951] PBO. Cover by Barye Phillips.	$1.50	$5.00	$10.00
156	Ernenwein, Leslie - ***The Texas Gun*** [1951] PBO. Cover by A. Leslie Ross.	$1.50	$5.00	$10.00
157	Hatten, Homer - ***Westport Landing*** [1951] PBO.	$1.50	$5.00	$10.00
158	Cushman, Dan - ***Naked Ebony*** [1951] PBO. Cover by Barye Phillips.	$2.50	$7.50	$15.00
159	Short, Luke - ***Barren Land Murders*** [1951] PBO.	$2.00	$6.00	$12.00
160	Anthology - ***Catnips At Love And Marriage*** [1951] PBO. Photo covers and interior. Book of cat photos.	$1.50	$5.00	$10.00
161	Jenkins, Will F. - ***Son Of The Flying Y*** [1951] PBO. Cover by A. Leslie Ross.	$4.00	$12.50	$25.00
162	Stanford, Don - ***Bargain In Blood*** [1951] PBO.	$2.00	$6.00	$12.00
163	Williams, Charles - ***Big City Girl*** [1951] PBO. Cover by Barye Phillips.	$2.50	$7.50	$15.00
164	MacDonald, John D. - ***Murder For The Bride*** [1951] PBO. Cover by Barye Phillips.	$12.50	$37.50	$75.00
165	Prather, Richard S. - ***Everybody Had A Gun*** [1951] PBO.	$2.00	$6.00	$12.00
166	Ronns, Edward - ***I Can't Stop Running*** [1951] PBO. Cover by Barye Phillips.	$2.00	$6.00	$12.00
167	Hunt, Howard - ***The Judas Hour*** [1951] PBO.	$2.00	$6.00	$12.00
168	Adams, Clifton - ***A Noose For The Desperado*** [1951] PBO.	$1.50	$5.00	$10.00
169	Brewer, Gil - ***Satan Is A Woman*** [1951] PBO. Cover by Barye Phillips.	$3.00	$9.00	$18.00
170	Martin, Aylwin Lee - ***Death On A Ferris Wheel*** [1951] PBO. Cover by Barye Phillips.	$2.00	$6.00	$12.00
171	Anonymous - ***I, Mobster*** [1951] PBO.	$2.00	$6.00	$12.00
172	Cohen, Octavus Roy - ***Lost Lady*** [1951] PBO.	$2.00	$6.00	$12.00
173	Miller, Wade - ***The Tiger's Wife*** [1951] PBO.	$2.00	$6.00	$12.00
174	Chadwick, Joseph - ***Rider From Nowhere*** [1951] PBO.	$1.50	$5.00	$10.00
175	Blayne, Sebastian - ***Gay Ghastly Holiday*** [1951] PBO. Cover by Barye Phillips.	$2.00	$6.00	$12.00
176	Hatch, Eric - ***Crockett's Woman*** [1951] PBO.	$2.00	$6.00	$12.00
177	Mockridge, Norton and Prall, Robert H. - ***This Is Costello*** [1951] PBO. Photo cover.	$2.00	$6.00	$12.00
178	Faulkner, John - ***Cabin Road*** [1951] PBO. Cover by Barye Phillips.	$2.50	$7.50	$15.00
179	Himmel, Richard - ***I Have Gloria Kirby*** [1951] PBO.	$2.00	$6.00	$12.00
180	Boswell, Charles and Thompson, Lewis - ***The Girl In The Stateroom*** [1951] PBO. Cover by Barye Phillips. Classic murder trial #1	$2.50	$7.50	$15.00
181	Fleischman, A. S. - ***Shanghai Flame*** [1951] PBO. Cover by Barye Phillips.	$2.50	$7.50	$15.00
182	Stewart, Logan - ***They Died Healthy*** [1951] PBO.	$1.50	$5.00	$10.00
183	Baker, Jr., Ledru - ***And Be My Love*** [1951] PBO. Cover by Barye Phillips.	$1.50	$5.00	$10.00
184	Sheridan, Jack - ***Thunderclap*** [1951] PBO.	$1.50	$5.00	$10.00
185	Bennett, Harry - ***We Never Called Him Henry*** [1951] PBO. Biography of Henry Ford.	$1.50	$5.00	$10.00

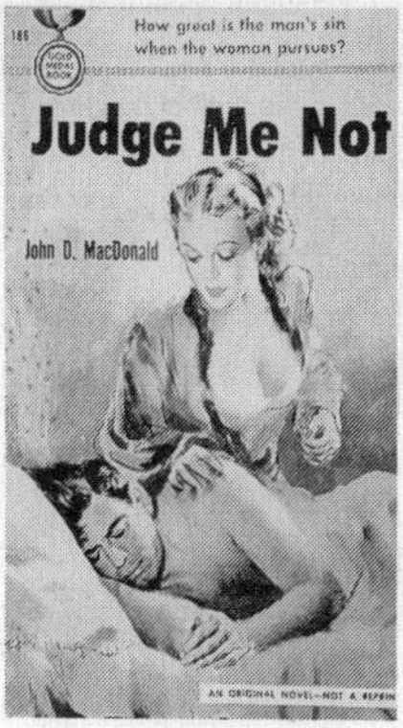

Gold Medal, 186

Gold Medal, 189

Gold Medal, 206

		G	VG	F
186	MacDonald, John D. - ***Judge Me Not*** [1951] PBO. Cover by Barye Phillips.	$12.50	$37.50	$75.00
187	Heuman, William - ***Hunt The Man Down*** [1951] PBO.	$1.50	$5.00	$10.00
188	Connolly, Paul - ***Get Out Of Town*** [1951] PBO.	$2.00	$6.00	$12.00
189	Goodis, David - ***Cassidy's Girl*** [1951] PBO. Cover by Kampen.	$17.00	$50.00	$100.00
190	Whittington, Harry - ***Fires That Destroy*** [1951] PBO.	$5.50	$17.50	$35.00
191	Margolius, Sidney - ***It's Your Money-Come And Get It*** [1951] PBO. Cover by Axel.	$1.50	$5.00	$10.00
192	Thomas, Kenneth - ***The Devil's Mistress*** [1951] PBO. Cover by Barye Phillips.	$2.50	$7.50	$15.00
193	Stewart, Logan - ***The Trail*** [1951] PBO.	$1.50	$5.00	$10.00
194	Ronns, Edward - ***The Decoy*** [1951] PBO. Cover by Barye Phillips.	$2.50	$7.50	$15.00
195	St. Clare, Dexter - ***Saratoga Mantrap*** [1951] PBO.	$2.00	$6.00	$12.00
196	Brewer, Gil - ***So Rich, So Dead*** [1951] PBO. Cover by Barye Phillips.	$3.00	$9.00	$18.00
197	Flagg, John - ***The Lady And The Cheetah*** [1951] PBO. Cover by Barye Phillips.	$2.50	$7.50	$15.00
198	Dixon, H. Vernor - ***To Hell Together*** [1951] PBO. Cover by Barye Phillips.	$2.00	$6.00	$12.00
199	Rohmer, Sax - ***Sumuru*** [1951] PBO. Cover by Barye Phillips.	$5.50	$17.50	$35.00
200	MacDonald, John D. - ***Weep For Me*** [1951] PBO. Cover by Kampen.	$10.00	$30.00	$60.00
201	Miles, Yukon - ***Stampede*** [1951] PBO. Cover by A. Leslie Ross.	$1.50	$5.00	$10.00
202	Fielding, William H. - ***The Unpossessed*** [1951] PBO. Cover by Kampen.	$1.50	$5.00	$10.00
203	Prather, Richard S. - ***Find This Woman*** [1951] PBO.	$2.00	$6.00	$12.00
204	Gonzales, John - ***Death For Mr. Big*** [1951] PBO.	$1.50	$5.00	$10.00
G-205	Pratt, Theodore - ***Handsome*** [1951] PBO.	$1.50	$5.00	$10.00
206	Keene, Day - ***To Kiss, Or Kill*** [1951] PBO. Cover by Barye Phillips.	$2.50	$7.50	$15.00
G-207	Williams, Charles - ***River Girl*** [1951] PBO. Cover by Barye Phillips.	$2.50	$7.50	$15.00
208	Abbott, A.C. - ***Wild Blood*** [1951] PBO.	$2.00	$6.00	$12.00
209	Fischer, Bruno - ***Fools Walk In*** [1951] PBO. Cover by Barye Phillips.	$2.00	$6.00	$12.00
210	Cullen, Carter - ***Don't Get Caught*** [1951] PBO. Cover by Kampen.	$2.00	$6.00	$12.00

Gold Medal, 208

Gold Medal, 226

Gold Medal, 283

		G	VG	F
211	Brewer, Gil - ***13 French Street*** [1951] PBO. Cover by Dom Lupo.	$3.00	$9.00	$18.00
G-212	Dixon, H. Vernor - ***Deep Is The Pit*** [1952] PBO. Cover by Barye Phillips.	$1.50	$5.00	$10.00
213	Hatch, Eric - ***The Golden Woman*** [1952] PBO. Cover by Barye Phillips.	$2.00	$6.00	$12.00
214	Martin, Aylwin Lee - ***Fear Comes Calling*** [1952] PBO. Cover by Carl Bobertz.	$2.00	$6.00	$12.00
215	Hatten, Homer - ***Conquest*** [1952] PBO.	$1.50	$5.00	$10.00
216	Heuman, William - ***Red Runs The River*** [1952] PBO. Cover by Barye Phillips.	$1.50	$5.00	$10.00
217	Ronns, Edward - ***Passage To Terror*** [1952] PBO. Cover by C.C. Beall.	$2.50	$7.50	$15.00
218	Mooney, Booth - ***Here Is My Body*** [1952] PBO.	$2.00	$6.00	$12.00
219	Fisher, Steve - ***The Sheltering Night*** [1952] PBO.	$2.50	$7.50	$15.00
220	Ernenwein, Leslie - ***Give A Man A Gun*** [1952] PBO.	$1.50	$5.00	$10.00
221	Steele, Jaclen - ***The Forbidden Room*** [1952] PBO. Cover by Barye Phillips.	$1.35	$4.00	$8.00
222	Packer, Vin - ***Spring Fire*** [1952] PBO. Cover by Barye Phillips.	$2.50	$7.50	$15.00
223	Fleischman, A.S. - ***Look Behind You Lady*** [1952] PBO.	$2.00	$6.00	$12.00
224	Connolly, Paul - ***Tears Are For Angels*** [1952] PBO. Cover by Barye Phillips.	$2.00	$6.00	$12.00
225	Keene, Day - ***Home Is The Sailor*** [1952] PBO.	$3.00	$9.00	$18.00
226	Goodis, David - ***Of Tender Sin*** [1952] PBO.	$17.00	$50.00	$100.00
227	Merwin, Jr., Sam - ***The Creeping Shadow*** [1952] PBO. Cover by Carl Bobertz.	$3.00	$9.00	$18.00
228	Adams, Fay - ***Appointment In Paris*** [1952] PBO.	$1.50	$5.00	$10.00
229	Roberts, Lee - ***Little Sister*** [1952] PBO. Photo Cover.	$1.50	$5.00	$10.00
230	Adams, Clifton - ***The Colonel's Lady*** [1952] PBO. Cover by A. Leslie Ross.	$2.00	$6.00	$12.00
231	Conroy, Albert - ***The Road's End*** [1952] PBO. Cover by Barye Phillips.	$1.50	$5.00	$10.00
232	Rodin, Arnold - ***Woman Soldier*** [1952] PBO. Cover by Barye Phillips.	$2.00	$6.00	$12.00
233	Prather, Richard S. - ***Way Of A Wanton*** [1952] PBO.	$2.00	$6.00	$12.00
234	Himmel, Richard - ***The Sharp Edge*** [1952] PBO. Cover by Barye Phillips.	$2.00	$6.00	$12.00
235	Blood, Matthew - ***The Avenger*** [1952] PBO. Cover by Barye Phillips.	$2.50	$7.50	$15.00

		G	VG	F
236	Chase, Borden - ***Lone Star*** [1952] PBO. Cover by Barye Phillips.	$1.50	$5.00	$10.00
237	Glendinning, Richard - ***Terror In The Sun*** [1952] PBO. Cover by Barye Phillips.	$2.00	$6.00	$12.00
238	Faulkner, John - ***Uncle Good's Girls*** [1952] PBO. Cover by Barye Phillips.	$2.00	$6.00	$12.00
239	Ronns, Edward - ***Don't Cry, Beloved*** [1952] PBO. Cover by Barye Phillips.	$2.00	$6.00	$12.00
240	MacDonald, John D. - ***The Damned*** [1952] PBO.	$10.00	$30.00	$60.00
241	Cushman, Dan - ***Savage Interlude*** [1952] PBO.	$3.50	$10.00	$20.00
242	Hayward, Richard - ***Trapped*** [1952] PBO.	$2.00	$6.00	$12.00
243	Stewart, Logan - ***The Secret Rider*** [1952] PBO.	$1.50	$5.00	$10.00
244	Baker, Jr., Ledru - ***The Cheaters*** [1952] PBO.	$2.00	$6.00	$12.00
245	Chadwick, Joseph - ***Double Cross*** [1952] PBO.	$1.50	$5.00	$10.00
246	Green, Chalmers - ***The Scarlet Venus*** [1952] PBO.	$2.50	$7.50	$15.00
247	Dent, Lester - ***Cry At Dusk*** [1952] PBO. Cover by Barye Phillips.	$3.00	$9.00	$18.00
248	Axelrod, George - ***Blackmailer*** [1952] PBO.	$2.00	$6.00	$12.00
249	Anthology edited by Clyde Carley - ***Cartoon Laffs From True*** [1952] PBO. Cover by Vip. Cartoon book.	$1.50	$5.00	$10.00
250	Packer, Vin - ***Dark Intruder*** [1952] PBO. Cover by Amos Sewell.	$2.00	$6.00	$12.00
251	Nichols, Fan - ***The Caged*** [1952] PBO.	$1.50	$5.00	$10.00
252	Clements, Calvin - ***Satan Takes The Helm*** [1952] PBO. Cover by Barye Phillips.	$2.00	$6.00	$12.00
253	Martin, Aylwin Lee - ***The Crimson Frame*** [1952] PBO. Cover by Barye Phillips.	$2.00	$6.00	$12.00
254	Keene, Day - ***About Doctor Ferrel*** [1952] PBO. Cover by Barye Phillips..	$2.50	$7.50	$15.00
255	Sutter, Larabie - ***The White Squaw*** [1952] PBO.	$2.00	$6.00	$12.00
256	Goodis, David - ***Street Of The Lost*** [1952] PBO. Cover by Barye Phillips.	$17.00	$50.00	$100.00
257	Miller, Wade - ***Branded Woman*** [1952] PBO. Cover by John Floherty, Jr.	$2.00	$6.00	$12.00
258	Aarons, Edward S. - ***Escape To Love*** [1952] PBO.	$2.00	$6.00	$12.00
259	Ballard, W. T. - ***Walk In Fear*** [1952] PBO. Cover by C.C. Beall.	$3.00	$9.00	$18.00
260	Viereck, George Sylvester - ***Men Into Beasts*** [1952] PBO.	$2.50	$7.50	$15.00
261	Chadwick, Joseph - ***Devil's Legacy*** [1952] PBO. Cover by A. Leslie Ross.	$1.50	$5.00	$10.00
262	Glendinning, Richard - ***Who Evil Thinks*** [1952] PBO.	$2.00	$6.00	$12.00
263	McPartland, John - ***Love Me Now*** [1952] PBO. Cover by Barye Phillips.	$2.50	$7.50	$15.00
264	Zane, Lehi - ***Brenda*** [1952] PBO.	$1.50	$5.00	$10.00
265	Prather, Richard S. - ***Darling, It's Death*** [1952] PBO.	$2.00	$6.00	$12.00
266	Appel, Benjamin - ***Plunder*** [1952] PBO. Cover by Barye Phillips.	$2.00	$6.00	$12.00
267	Heuman, William - ***Secret Of Death Valley*** [1952] PBO. Cover by A. Leslie Ross.	$1.50	$5.00	$10.00
268	Hunt, Howard - ***Whisper Her Name*** [1952] PBO.	$2.00	$6.00	$12.00
269	Ames, Robert - ***The Devil Drives*** [1952] PBO. Cover by Barye Phillips.	$2.00	$6.00	$12.00
270	Fischer, Bruno - ***The Fast Buck*** [1952] PBO. Cover by Barye Phillips.	$2.00	$6.00	$12.00
271	Merriman, Chad - ***Blood On The Sun*** [1952] PBO.	$1.50	$5.00	$10.00
272	Fielding, William H. - ***Take Me As I Am*** [1952] PBO.	$1.50	$5.00	$10.00
273	Rosmanith, Olga - ***Unholy Flame*** [1952] PBO.	$1.50	$5.00	$10.00
274	Himmel, Richard - ***Beyond Desire*** [1952] PBO. Cover by Walter Baumhofer.	$2.00	$6.00	$12.00
275	Castle, Frank - ***Move Along, Stranger*** [1952] PBO.	$2.00	$6.00	$12.00

Gold Medal, 292

Gold Medal, 328

Gold Medal, 354

		G	VG	F
276	Wainer, Cord - ***Mountain Girl*** [1952] PBO. Cover by Barye Phillips.	$2.00	$6.00	$12.00
277	Brewer, Gil - ***Flight To Darkness*** [1952] PBO. Cover by Barye Phillips.	$3.00	$9.00	$18.00
278	Hilton, Joseph - ***That French Girl*** [1952] PBO.	$1.50	$5.00	$10.00
279	Miller, Wade - ***The Big Guy*** [1953] PBO. Cover by Floherty, Jr.	$2.00	$6.00	$12.00
280	Aarons, Edward S. - ***The Sinners*** [1953] PBO. Photo cover.	$2.00	$6.00	$12.00
281	O'Quinn, Allen - ***Swamp Brat*** [1953] PBO. Cover by Barye Phillips.	$3.50	$10.00	$20.00
282	Flagg, John - ***Woman Of Cairo*** [1953] PBO.	$2.50	$7.50	$15.00
283	Rohmer, Sax - ***The Fire Goddess*** [1952] PBO.	$5.50	$17.50	$35.00
284	Chadwick, Joseph - ***Whip Hand*** [1953] PBO.	$1.50	$5.00	$10.00
285	Dixon, H. Vernor - ***Too Rich To Die*** [1953] PBO.	$2.00	$6.00	$12.00
286	Williams, Charles - ***Hell Hath No Fury*** [1953] PBO. Cover by Barye Phillips.	$2.50	$7.50	$15.00
287	Heuman, William - ***On To Santa Fe*** [1953] PBO	$1.50	$5.00	$10.00
288	Caldwell, Taylor - ***Maggie - Her Marriage*** [1953] PBO.	$2.50	$7.50	$15.00
289	Conroy, Albert (Marvin H. Albert) - ***The Chiselers*** [1953] PBO.	$2.00	$6.00	$12.00
290	Cushman, Dan - ***Jungle She*** [1953] PBO.	$2.50	$7.50	$15.00
291	Adams, Clifton - ***Whom Gods Destroy*** [1953] PBO.	$1.50	$5.00	$10.00
292	Brown, Wenzell - ***Run, Chico, Run*** [1953] PBO. Cover by Barye Phillips.	$4.00	$12.50	$25.00
293	Ernenwein, Leslie - ***Mystery Raider*** [1953] PBO.	$1.50	$5.00	$10.00
294	Samuels, Charles - ***The Girl In The Red Velvet Swing*** [1953] PBO. Classic murder trial #2.	$2.50	$7.50	$15.00
295	Fleischman, A. S. - ***Danger In Paradise*** [1953] PBO. Cover by Barye Phillips.	$2.00	$6.00	$12.00
296	Chaze, Elliott - ***Black Wings Has My Angel*** [1953] PBO.	$2.00	$6.00	$12.00
297	Hunt, Howard - ***Lovers Are Losers*** [1953] PBO. Cover by Barye Phillips.	$2.00	$6.00	$12.00
298	MacDonald, John D. - ***Dead Low Tide*** [1953] PBO. Cover by Barye Phillips.	$8.00	$25.00	$50.00
299	Westwood, Perry - ***Six-Gun Code*** [1953] PBO.	$1.50	$5.00	$10.00
300	Fox, Gardner F. - ***The Borgia Blade*** [1953] PBO.	$3.00	$9.00	$18.00
301	Osborne, O. O. - ***Leave Her To God*** [1953] PBO. Cover by Barye Phillips.	$1.50	$5.00	$10.00
302	Meservey, Russ - ***Masquerade Into Madness*** [1953] PBO.	$2.00	$6.00	$12.00

		G	VG	F
303	Clements, Calvin - ***Barge Girl*** [1953] PBO. Cover by Barye Phillips.	$2.00	$6.00	$12.00
304	White, Lionel - ***The Snatchers*** [1953] PBO. Cover by John Floherty, Jr.	$2.50	$7.50	$15.00
305	Merriman, Chad - ***Ridge Runner*** [1953] PBO.	$1.50	$5.00	$10.00
306	Cook, Fred J. - ***The Girl In The Death Cell*** [1953] PBO. Classic murder trial #3.	$2.50	$7.50	$15.00
307	Siegel, Benjamin - ***Witch Of Salem*** [1953] PBO. Cover by Amos Sewell.	$3.00	$9.00	$18.00
308	Content, Nikki (Fan Nichols) - ***Hideaway*** [1953] PBO. Cover by Barye Phillips.	$2.00	$6.00	$12.00
309	Vail, John - ***Sword In His Hand*** [1953] PBO.	$2.00	$6.00	$12.00
310	Heuman, William - ***Keelboats North*** [1953] PBO.	$2.00	$6.00	$12.00
311	Kay, Cameron - ***Thieves Fall Out*** [1953] PBO. Cover by Barye Phillips.	$2.00	$6.00	$12.00
S-312	Anthology - ***Gold Medal Treasury of American Verse*** [1953] PBO. Cover by John Floherty, Jr.	$1.50	$5.00	$10.00
313	Stewart, Logan - ***War Bonnet Pass*** [1953]	$1.50	$5.00	$10.00
314	Chadwick, Joseph - ***Gunsmoke Reckoning*** [1953]	$1.50	$5.00	$10.00
315	Shelly, Paul - ***Saturday's Harvest*** [1953] PBO. Cover by Barye Phillips.	$1.50	$5.00	$10.00
316	Dixon, H. Vernor - ***Up A Winding Stair*** [1953] PBO.	$1.50	$5.00	$10.00
317	Cooper, Morton - ***Come Feed On Me*** [1953] PBO.	$1.50	$5.00	$10.00
318	Dean, Dudley - ***Ambush At Rincon*** [1953] PBO.	$1.50	$5.00	$10.00
319	Fagan, Norbert - ***The Crooked Mile*** [1953] PBO.	$2.00	$6.00	$12.00
320	Myers, Virginia - ***Escape From Morales*** [1953] PBO.	$1.50	$5.00	$10.00
321	Rohmer, Sax - ***Nude In Mink*** [1953]	$5.50	$17.50	$35.00
322	Heuman, William - ***Guns At Broken Bow*** [1953]	$1.35	$4.00	$8.00
323	MacDonald, John D. - ***The Neon Jungle*** [1953] PBO.	$3.00	$9.00	$18.00
324	Packer, Vin - ***Look Back To Love*** [1953]	$1.35	$4.00	$8.00
325	Blayne, Sebastian - ***Terror In The Night*** [1953] PBO.	$1.50	$5.00	$10.00
326	Rodin, Arnold - ***Moment Of Truth*** [1953]	$1.50	$5.00	$10.00
327	Stewart, Logan - ***Savage Stronghold*** [1953]	$1.50	$5.00	$10.00
328	Fox, Gardner F. - ***Madame Buccaneer*** [1953] PBO. Cover by Barye Phillips.	$3.00	$9.00	$18.00
329	Ernenwein, Leslie - ***Gunfighter's Return*** [1953]	$1.35	$4.00	$8.00
330	Heuman, William - ***Roll The Wagons*** [1953] Cover by Stan Getti.	$1.35	$4.00	$8.00
331	Miller, Wade - ***South Of The Sun*** [1953] PBO.	$2.00	$6.00	$12.00
332	Cushman, Dan - ***Timberjack*** [1953] PBO. Cover by Barye Phillips.	$2.00	$6.00	$12.00
333	Adams, Fay - ***To Love, To Hate*** [1953] PBO.	$1.50	$5.00	$10.00
334	Boswell, Charles & Thompson, Lewis - ***The Girl In Lover's Lane*** [1953] PBO. Classic murder trial #4.	$2.50	$7.50	$15.00
335	Gant, Matthew - ***Valley Of Angry Men*** [1953] PBO.	$1.50	$5.00	$10.00
336	McPartland, John - ***Tokyo Doll*** [1953] PBO. Cover by Barye Phillips.	$4.00	$12.50	$25.00
337	Shane, Ted - ***Bar Guide*** [1953] Cover by Vip.	$1.35	$4.00	$8.00
338	Chadwick, Joseph - ***Rider From Nowhere*** [1953]	$1.35	$4.00	$8.00
S-339	Pratt, Theodore - ***Escape To Eden*** [1953] PBO. Cover by Herman Bischoff.	$2.00	$6.00	$12.00
340	Williams, Charles - ***Nothing In Her Way*** [1953] PBO.	$2.50	$7.50	$15.00
341	Prather, Richard S. - ***Ride A High Horse*** [1953] PBO. Cover by Barye Phillips.	$2.00	$6.00	$12.00
342	Anonymous - ***Belle Bradley—Her Story*** [1953] PBO.	$1.50	$5.00	$10.00
343	Fischer, Bruno - ***Run For Your Life*** [1953] PBO. Cover by Barye Phillips.	$2.00	$6.00	$12.00
344	Henry, Alan - ***Wagon Train Woman*** [1953]	$2.50	$7.50	$15.00
345	Brewer, Gil - ***Hell's Our Destination*** [1953] PBO. Cover by Meese.	$3.00	$9.00	$18.00

		G	VG	F
346	Jenkins, Will F. - ***Son Of The Flying 'Y'*** [1953] Cover by A. Leslie Ross.	$2.00	$6.00	$12.00
347	L'Amour, Louis - ***Hondo*** [1953] PBO.	$12.50	$37.50	$75.00
348	Goodis, David - ***The Moon In The Gutter*** [1953] PBO. Cover by Victor Olson.	$17.00	$50.00	$100.00
349	Davis, Gordon - ***I Came To Kill*** [1953] PBO. Cover by Meese..	$2.00	$6.00	$12.00
350	Rigsby, Howard - ***Rage In Texas*** [1953] PBO. Cover by Barye Phillips.	$1.50	$5.00	$10.00
351	Bishop, Jim & Hoffmann, M.D., Richard H. - ***The Girl In Poison Cottage*** [1953] PBO. Cover by Barye Phillips. Classic murder trial #5.	$2.50	$7.50	$15.00
352	Hatten, Homer - ***Eagle On His Wrist*** [1953] PBO.	$1.50	$5.00	$10.00
353	McMillen, V. A. - ***The Fall Of Suzanne Swift*** [1953] PBO.	$1.50	$5.00	$10.00
354	McPartland, John - ***Big Red's Daughter*** [1953] PBO.	$2.50	$7.50	$15.00
355	Monahan, John - ***Big Stan*** [1953] Cover by Barye Phillips.	$2.00	$6.00	$12.00
356	Sheridan, Jack - ***Paradise Motel*** [1953] PBO. Cover by Meltzoff.	$1.50	$5.00	$10.00
357	Newton, D. B. - ***Guns Along The Wickiup*** [1953] PBO.	$1.50	$5.00	$10.00
358	Gotshall, Jack - ***PappyAnd The Promised Land*** [1953]	$2.00	$6.00	$12.00
359	Samuels, Charles & Louise - ***The Girl In The House Of Hate*** [1953] PBO. Cover by Barye Phillips. Classic murder trial #6.	$2.50	$7.50	$15.00
360	Fox, Gardner F. - ***One Sword For Love*** [1953] PBO. Cover by Geygan.	$3.00	$9.00	$18.00
361	Ernenwein, Leslie - ***Rampage*** [1953] PBO.	$1.50	$5.00	$10.00
362	Aarons, Edward S. - ***Come Back, My Love*** [1953] PBO. Cover by Barye Phillips.	$2.00	$6.00	$12.00
363	Packer, Vin - ***Come Destroy Me*** [1954] PBO	$2.00	$6.00	$12.00
364	Loth, David - ***Gold Brick Cassie*** [1954] PBO.	$2.00	$6.00	$12.00
365	Connell, Vivian - ***Monte Carlo Mission*** [1954] PBO.	$1.50	$5.00	$10.00
366	Whittington, Harry - ***The Woman Is Mine*** [1954] PBO. Cover by James Meese.	$4.00	$12.50	$25.00
367	Stewart, Logan - ***Rails West*** [1954] PBO.	$1.50	$5.00	$10.00
368	Fleischman, A. S. - ***Malay, Woman*** [1954] PBO.	$2.50	$7.50	$15.00
369	Pratt, Theodore - ***Seminole*** [1954] PBO. Cover by John Floherty, Jr.	$4.00	$12.50	$25.00
370	Dixon, H. Vernor - ***A Lover For Cindy*** [1954] PBO.	$1.50	$5.00	$10.00
371	Williams, Charles - ***Go Home, Stranger*** [1954] PBO.	$2.50	$7.50	$15.00
372	Keene, Day - ***Notorious*** [1954] PBO.	$2.50	$7.50	$15.00
373	Himmel, Richard - ***Two Deaths Must Die*** [1954] PBO.	$2.00	$6.00	$12.00
374	Chadwick, Joseph - ***Come Out Shooting*** [1954] PBO.	$1.50	$5.00	$10.00
375	Rigsby, Howard - ***As A Man Falls*** [1954] PBO.	$1.50	$5.00	$10.00
376	Brady, Matt - ***Take Your Last Look*** [1954] PBO.	$1.50	$5.00	$10.00
377	Stewart, Sidney - ***The Range Grabbers*** [1954] PBO	$1.50	$5.00	$10.00
378	Schoenfeld, Howard - ***Let Them Eat Bullets*** [1954] PBO. Cover by Barye Phillips.	$2.00	$6.00	$12.00
379	Torres, Tereska - ***Women's Barracks*** [1954]	$1.50	$5.00	$10.00
380	Brewer, Gil - ***A Killer Is Loose*** [1954] PBO. Cover by Lu Kimmel.	$3.00	$9.00	$18.00
381	Merriman, Chad - ***Fury On The Plains*** [1954] PBO. Cover by A. Leslie Ross.	$1.50	$5.00	$10.00
382	Fagan, Norbert - ***One Against The Odds*** [1954] PBO. Cover by Ray Johnson.	$1.50	$5.00	$10.00
383	Lieberson, Will - ***Cartoon Fun From True*** [1954] Cover by Vip.	$1.50	$5.00	$10.00
384	Boswell, Charles & Thompson, Lewis - ***The Girl With The Scarlet Brand*** [1954] PBO. Classic murder trial #7.	$2.50	$7.50	$15.00
385	Appel, Benjamin - ***Sweet Money Girl*** [1954] PBO. Cover by Barye Phillips.	$1.50	$5.00	$10.00

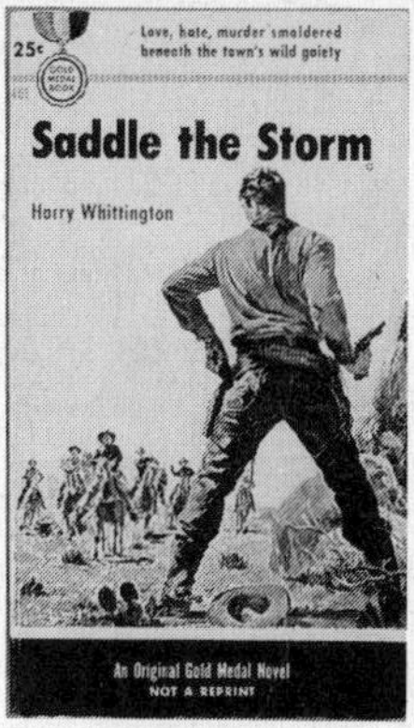

Gold Medal, 401

Gold Star, IL7-45

Gold Star, IL7-54

		G	VG	F
386	MacRoss, Ross - ***The Beautiful And Dead*** [1954] PBO. Cover by James Meese.	$2.00	$6.00	$12.00
387	Gehman, Richard - ***Driven*** [1954] PBO. Cover by Arthur Sarnoff.	$2.00	$6.00	$12.00
388	Jones, Nard - ***I'll Take What's Mine*** [1954] PBO. Cover by Saul Tepper.	$2.00	$6.00	$12.00
389	Glendinning, Richard - ***Retreat Into Night*** [1954] PBO. Cover by Barye Phillips.	$2.00	$6.00	$12.00
390	Chadwick, Joseph - ***Renegade Gun*** [1954] PBO. Cover by Dom Lupo.	$1.50	$5.00	$10.00
391	Flagg, John - ***Dear, Deadly Beloved*** [1954] PBO. Cover by Barye Phillips.	$2.00	$6.00	$12.00
392	Cushman, Dan - ***The Fabulous Finn*** [1954] PBO. Cover by Lu Kimmel.	$2.00	$6.00	$12.00
393	McPartland, John - ***The Face Of Evil*** [1954] PBO.	$2.50	$7.50	$15.00
394	Fox, Gardner F. - ***The Gentleman Rogue*** [1954] PBO. Cover by Walter Baumhofer.	$3.00	$9.00	$18.00
395	Mason, Raymond - ***And Two Shall Meet*** [1954] PBO. Cover by James Meese.	$1.50	$5.00	$10.00
396	Vail, John - ***The Dark Throne*** [1954] PBO. Cover by Meese.	$2.00	$6.00	$12.00
397	Patrick, Quentin - ***The Girl On The Gallows*** [1954] PBO. Cover by Barye Phillips. Classic murder trial #8.	$2.50	$7.50	$15.00
398	Packer, Vin - ***Spring Fire*** [1954]	$1.50	$5.00	$10.00
399	O'Quinn, Allen - ***A Woman For Henry*** [1954] PBO. Cover by Barye Phillips.	$1.50	$5.00	$10.00
400	Rigsby, Howard - ***Lucinda*** [1954] PBO. Cover by George Mayer.	$1.50	$5.00	$10.00
401	Whittington, Harry - ***Saddle The Storm*** [1954] PBO. Cover by Lu Kimmel.	$3.00	$9.00	$18.00
402	Mara, Bernard - ***French For Murder*** [1954] PBO. Cover by Clark Hulings	$2.50	$7.50	$15.00
S403	Brothers, William P. - ***Portrait Of Lisa*** [1954] PBO. Cover by Ray Johnson.	$1.50	$5.00	$10.00
404	Millard, Joseph - ***The Wickedest Man*** [1954] PBO. Cover by Lu Kimmel.	$2.00	$6.00	$12.00
405	Keene, Day - ***There Was A Crooked Man*** [1954] PBO. Cover by Ray Johnson.	$2.50	$7.50	$15.00
406	McPartland, John - ***Affair In Tokyo*** [1954] PBO. Cover by Clark Hulings.	$4.00	$12.50	$25.00

		G	VG	F
407	Douglas, Dean - ***Man Divided*** [1954] PBO. Cover by Barye Phillips.	$1.50	$5.00	$10.00
408	Rohmer, Sax - ***Return Of Sumuru*** [1954] PBO. Cover by James Meese.	$5.50	$17.50	$35.00
409	Brewer, Gil - ***Some Must Die*** [1954] PBO. Cover by Ray Johnson.	$3.00	$9.00	$18.00
410	Faulkner, John - ***Uncle Good's Girls*** [1954] Cover by Barye Phillips.	$1.50	$5.00	$10.00
411	Savage, Jr., Les - ***Black Horse Canyon*** [1954] Cover by Frank McCarthy. Movie tie-in.	$1.50	$5.00	$10.00
412	Clements, Calvin - ***Hell Ship To Kuma*** [1954] PBO. Cover by James Meese.	$2.50	$7.50	$15.00
413	Prather, Richard S. - ***Always Leave 'em Dying*** [1954] PBO. Cover by Barye Phillips.	$2.00	$6.00	$12.00
414	Heuman, William - ***Ride For Texas*** [1954]	$1.50	$5.00	$10.00
415	Marston, Richard - ***Runaway Black*** [1954] Cover by Kimmel.	$4.00	$12.50	$25.00
416	Hatton, Homer - ***Jezebel In Crinoline*** [1954] PBO. Cover by Barye Phillips.	$2.00	$6.00	$12.00
417	Matheson, Richard - ***I Am Legend*** [1954] PBO. Cover by Stan Meltzoff.	$22.00	$70.00	$140.00
418	Brewer, Gil - ***13 French Street*** [1954] Cover by Dom Lupo.	$1.50	$5.00	$10.00
419	Kieran, James - ***Come Murder Me*** [1954] Cover by Barye Phillips.	$1.50	$5.00	$10.00
420	MacDonald, John D. - ***All These Condemned*** [1954] PBO. Cover by James Meese.	$7.00	$22.50	$45.00
421	Pratt, Theodore - ***Smash-Up*** [1954] PBO. Cover by Jack Floherty, Jr.	$1.50	$5.00	$10.00
422	Adams, Clifton - ***Two-Gun Law*** [1954]	$1.50	$5.00	$10.00
423	Blood, Matthew - ***Death Is A Lovely Dame*** [1954] PBO. Cover by Barye Phillips.	$2.00	$6.00	$12.00
424	Aarons, Edward S. - ***Girl On The Run*** [1954]	$2.00	$6.00	$12.00
425	Prather, Richard S. - ***Case Of The Vanishing Beauty*** [1954] Cover by Barye Phillips.	$1.50	$5.00	$10.00
426	Packer, Vin - ***Whisper His Sin*** [1954]	$1.50	$5.00	$10.00
427	White, Milton - ***Cry Down The Lonely Night*** [1954] PBO. Cover by Barye Phillips.	$2.00	$6.00	$12.00
428	Goodis, David - ***Street Of No Return*** [1954] PBO. Cover by Barye Phillips.	$17.00	$50.00	$100.00
429	Heuman, William - ***The Range Buster*** [1954] PBO.	$1.50	$5.00	$10.00
430	Fielding, William H. - ***Beautiful Humbug*** [1954]	$1.50	$5.00	$10.00
431	Cook, Fred J. - ***The Girl On The Lonely Beach*** [1954] PBO. Photo cover. Classic murder trial #9.	$2.50	$7.50	$15.00
432	Pratt, Theodore - ***Handsome*** [1954]	$1.35	$4.00	$8.00
433	Morgan, Nancy - ***Somebody Loves Me*** [1954] PBO. Cover by Erickson.	$1.50	$5.00	$10.00
434	Williams, Charles - ***A Touch Of Death*** [1954] PBO. Cover by Saul Tepper.	$2.50	$7.50	$15.00
435	Ames, Robert - ***The Dangerous One*** [1954] PBO. Cover by James Meese.	$2.00	$6.00	$12.00
436	Dean, Dudley - ***The Man From Riondo*** [1954] PBO. Cover by Frank McCarthy.	$1.50	$5.00	$10.00
437	Fischer, Bruno - ***So Wicked My Love*** [1954] PBO. Cover by Barye Phillips.	$2.00	$6.00	$12.00
438	Fox, Gardner F. - ***Woman Of Kali*** [1954] PBO. Cover by Herman Bischoff.	$3.00	$9.00	$18.00
439	Faulkner, John - ***Cabin Road*** [1954] Cover by Barye Phillips.	$1.35	$4.00	$8.00
S440	Jessup, Richard - ***The Cunning And The Haunted*** [1954] PBO. Cover by Ray Johnson.	$2.00	$6.00	$12.00
441	Vail, John - ***Sow The Wild Wind*** [1954] PBO. Cover by Clark Hulings.	$2.00	$6.00	$12.00

		G	VG	F
442	Chadwick, Joseph - ***Rebel Raider*** [1954] PBO. Cover by A. Leslie Ross.	$1.50	$5.00	$10.00
443	Stratton, Ted - ***Wild Breed*** [1954] PBO. Cover by Barye Phillips.	$1.50	$5.00	$10.00
444	Glendinning, Richard - ***Mission To Murder*** [1954] PBO. Cover by Barye Phillips.	$2.00	$6.00	$12.00
445	Partch, Virgil Franklin - ***Funny Cartoons By Vip*** [1954] PBO. Cover by Vip. Cartoon book.	$1.50	$5.00	$10.00
446	Williams, Charles - ***Hill Girl*** [1954] Cover by Barye Phillips.	$1.35	$4.00	$8.00
447	Cox, William R. - ***Make My Coffin Strong*** [1954] PBO. Cover by Barye Phillips.	$2.00	$6.00	$12.00
448	Brewer, Gil - ***77 Rue Paradis*** [1954] PBO. Cover by Meese.	$3.00	$9.00	$18.00
449	Daniels, Frank - ***The Mating Cry*** [1954] PBO. Cover by Barye Phillips.	$2.00	$6.00	$12.00
450	Morningside, Mee - editor - ***Strange But True*** [1954] PBO. Cover by Ballantine.	$1.50	$5.00	$10.00
451	Niall, Michael - ***Bad Day At Black Rock*** [1954] PBO. Cover by Barye Phillips. Movie tie-in.	$2.50	$7.50	$15.00
452	Fowler, Kenneth - ***Outcast Of Murder Mesa*** [1954] PBO. Cover by Frank McCarthy.	$1.50	$5.00	$10.00
S453	Morgan, Nancy - ***City Of Women*** [1955] Cover by Barye Phillips.	$2.00	$6.00	$12.00
S454	Dixon, H. Vernor - ***The Hunger And The Hate*** [1955] PBO. Cover by Meese.	$2.00	$6.00	$12.00
455	Faulkner, John - ***The Sin Shouter Of Cabin Road*** [1955] PBO. Cover by Barye Phillips.	$2.00	$6.00	$12.00
456	Dodge, Steve - ***Shanghai Incident*** [1955] PBO. Cover by Lu Kimmel.	$2.50	$7.50	$15.00
457	Frazee, Steve - ***Many Rivers To Cross*** [1955] PBO. Cover by Meese.	$2.50	$7.50	$15.00
458	Heimer, Mel - ***The Girl In Murder Flat*** [1955] PBO. Photo cover. Classic murder trial #10.	$2.50	$7.50	$15.00
459	Johnson, Ryerson - ***Lady In Dread*** [1955] PBO. Cover by Barye Phillips.	$2.00	$6.00	$12.00
460	Himmel, Richard - ***I'll Find You*** [1955] Cover by Stanley Meltzoff.	$1.35	$4.00	$8.00
461	Taylor, Robert W. - ***The Glitter And The Greed*** [1955] PBO. Cover by Maguire.	$2.00	$6.00	$12.00
462	Preston, Charles - editor - ***Funny Business*** [1955] PBO. Cover by Taber. Cartoon book.	$1.50	$5.00	$10.00
463	O'Quinn, Allen - ***Strangers In My Bed*** [1955] PBO.	$2.00	$6.00	$12.00
464	Ernenwein, Leslie - ***Bullet Barricade*** [1955] PBO. Cover by Frank McCarthy.	$1.50	$5.00	$10.00
465	Cooley, Donald G. - ***A New Way To Eat And Get Slim*** [1955] PBO.	$1.50	$5.00	$10.00
466	Samuels, Charles - ***Death Was The Bridegroom*** [1955] PBO. Cover by Barye Phillips. Classic murder trial #11.	$2.50	$7.50	$15.00
467	Williams, Charles - ***River Girl*** [1955] Cover by Barye Phillips.	$1.35	$4.00	$8.00
468	Mason, Raymond - ***Forever Is Today*** [1955] PBO. Cover by James Meese.	$1.50	$5.00	$10.00
469	Miller, Wade - ***Mad Baxter*** [1955] PBO. Cover by Lu Kimmel.	$2.00	$6.00	$12.00
470	White, Lionel - ***The Big Caper*** [1955] PBO. Cover by Barye Phillips.	$2.00	$6.00	$12.00
471	Dean, Dudley - ***Song Of The Gun*** [1955] PBO. Cover by A. Leslie Ross.	$1.50	$5.00	$10.00
472	Mara, Bernard - ***A Bullet For My Lady*** [1955] PBO. Cover by Meese.	$2.00	$6.00	$12.00
473	Hynd, Alan - ***Violence In The Night*** [1955] PBO. Cover by Clark Huling.	$2.00	$6.00	$12.00

		G	VG	F
474	Pratt, Theodore - ***The Tormented*** [1955] Cover by Barye Phillips.	$1.35	$4.00	$8.00
475	Hilton, Joseph - ***Angels In The Gutter*** [1955] PBO. Photo cover.	$2.50	$7.50	$15.00
476	Vail, John - ***Blonde Savage*** [1955] PBO. Cover by Barye Phillips.	$2.00	$6.00	$12.00
477	Douglas, Malcolm - ***Prey By Night*** [1955] PBO. Cover by James Meese.	$2.00	$6.00	$12.00
478	L'Amour, Louis - ***Heller With A Gun*** [1955] PBO. Cover by Walter Baumhofer.	$7.00	$22.50	$45.00
479	Hayward, Richard - ***The Soft Arms Of Death*** [1955] PBO. Cover by James Meese.	$2.00	$6.00	$12.00
480	Boswell, Charles & Thompson, Lewis - ***The Girls In Nightmare House*** [1955] PBO. Cover by Clark Hulings.	$2.50	$7.50	$15.00
481	MacDonald, John D. - ***The Damned*** [1955]	$2.50	$7.50	$15.00
482	MacDonald, John D. - ***The Brass Cupcake*** [1955] Cover by Barye Phillips.	$2.50	$7.50	$15.00
483	Adams, Clifton - ***Death's Sweet Song*** [1955] PBO. Cover by Barye Phillips.	$2.00	$6.00	$12.00
484	Fox, Gardner F. - ***Rebel Wench*** [1955] PBO. Cover by Walter Baumhofer.	$3.00	$9.00	$18.00
485	Loomis, Noel M. - ***West To The Sun*** [1955]	$1.50	$5.00	$10.00
486	Foster, John - ***Dark Heritage*** [1955] PBO. Cover by James Meese.	$2.00	$6.00	$12.00
487	de La Torre, Lillian - ***The Truth About Belle Gunness*** [1955] PBO. Cover by Barye Phillips.	$2.00	$6.00	$12.00
488	Himmel, Richard - ***Cry Of The Flesh*** [1955] PBO. Cover by Jack Floherty, Jr.	$2.00	$6.00	$12.00
489	Prather, Richard S. - ***Find This Woman*** [1955]	$1.35	$4.00	$8.00
490	Wills, Thomas - ***Mine To Avenge*** [1955] PBO. Cover by Jack Floherty, Jr.	$2.50	$7.50	$15.00
491	Aarons, Edward S. - ***Assignment To Disaster*** [1955] PBO.	$2.00	$6.00	$12.00
492	Hatten, Homer - ***Plunder Range*** [1955]	$1.50	$5.00	$10.00
493	Chadwick, Joseph - ***The Golden Frame*** [1955] PBO. Cover by Meese.	$1.50	$5.00	$10.00
494	Keene, Day - ***Who Has Wilma Lathrop?*** [1955] PBO. Cover by Barye Phillips.	$2.50	$7.50	$15.00
495	Richards, Lee - ***Hell Strip*** [1955] PBO. Cover by Lu Kimmel.	$2.00	$6.00	$12.00
496	Prather, Richard S. - ***Bodies In Bedlam*** [1955] Cover by Barye Phillips.	$1.35	$4.00	$8.00
497	Prather, Richard S. - ***Way Of A Wanton*** [1955]	$1.35	$4.00	$8.00
498	Brennan, Frederick Hazlitt - ***One Of Our H Bombs Is Missing*** [1955] PBO. Cover by Stan Meltzoff.	$2.50	$7.50	$15.00
499	Fleischman, A. S. - ***Blood Alley*** [1955] PBO. Cover by Barye Phillips. Movie tie-in with John Wayne.	$2.50	$7.50	$15.00
500	Connolly, Paul - ***So Fair, So Evil*** [1955] PBO.	$1.50	$5.00	$10.00
501	Hopson, William - ***Trouble Rides Tall*** [1955] PBO. Cover by Frank McCarthy.	$1.50	$5.00	$10.00
502	McGuire, Atha - ***Homicide Hussy*** [1955] PBO. Cover by James Meese.	$2.00	$6.00	$12.00
503	Guinn, William - ***Death Lies Deep*** [1955] PBO. Cover by Lu Kimmel.	$2.00	$6.00	$12.00
504	Prather, Richard S. - ***Everybody Had A Gun*** [1955]	$1.35	$4.00	$8.00
505	Prather, Richard S. - ***Darling, It's Death*** [1955]	$1.25	$3.75	$7.50
506	Rabe, Peter - ***Stop This Man!*** [1955] PBO. Cover by Kimmel.	$3.50	$10.00	$20.00
507	Marsten, Richard - ***Murder In The Navy*** [1955] PBO. Cover by Clark Hulings.	$3.00	$9.00	$18.00
508	Prather, Richard S. - ***Strip For Murder*** [1955] PBO.	$2.00	$6.00	$12.00
509	Aldrich, Ann - ***We Walk Alone*** [1955] PBO. Cover by Jack Floherty, Jr.	$3.50	$10.00	$20.00

Ace Book, D-15
$32–$110–$250

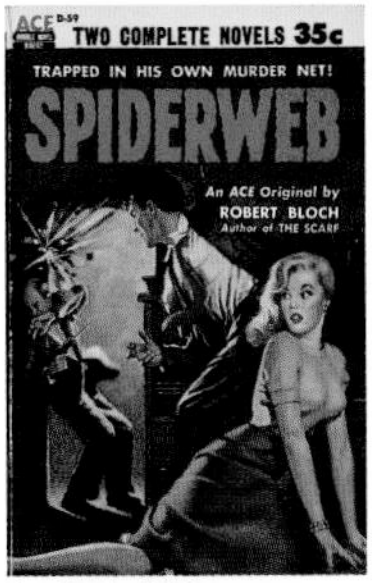

Ace Book, D-59
$12.50–$37.50–$75

Ace Book, S-82
$7–$22.50–$45

Ace Book, D-513
$32–$110–$250

All-Picture (No #),
"Case of the Winking Buddha"
$17–$50–$100

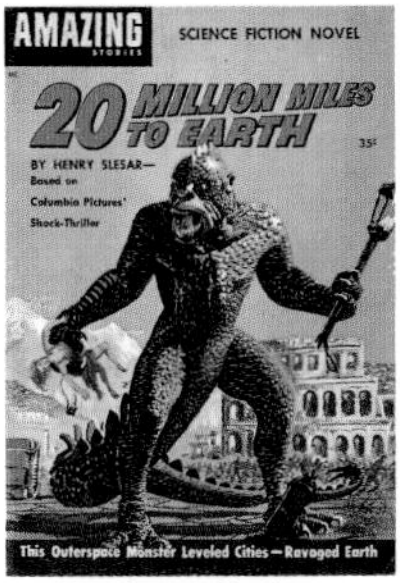

Amazing Stories (No #)
$22–$70–$140

Armed Service Edition, M-16
$27.50–$85–$200

Armed Service Edition, O-22
$27.50–$85–$200

Archer Book, 35
$6–$20–$40

Arrow, 118
$6–$20–$40

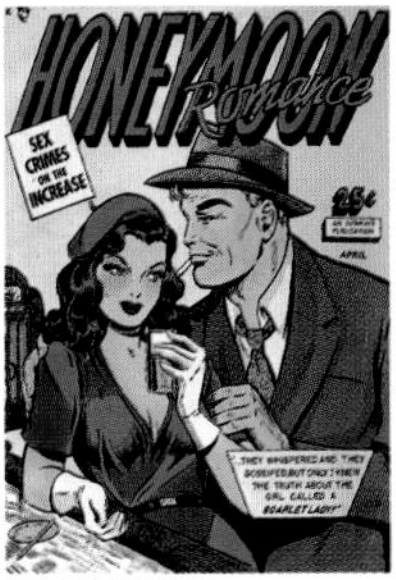

Artful Publications
$12.50–$37.50–$75

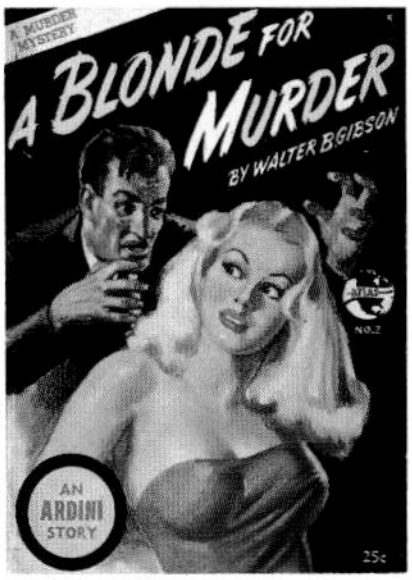

Atlas Digest, #2
$6–$20–$40

An Avon Book Digest
$12.50–$37.50–$75

Avon Book, 38
$17–$50–$100

Avon Book, 220
$8–$25–$50

Avon Book, 281
$8–$25–$50

Avon Book, 295
$27.50–$85–$200

Avon Fantasy Novel, 2
$12.50–$37.50–$75

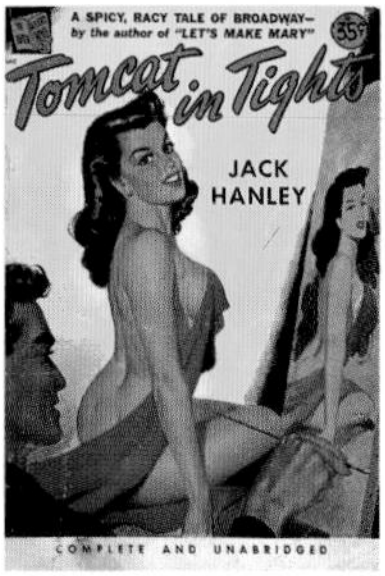

Avon Monthly Novel, 21
$7–$22.50–$45

Avon Murder Mystery, 47
$15–$45–$90

Avon Murder Mystery, 49
$15–$45–$90

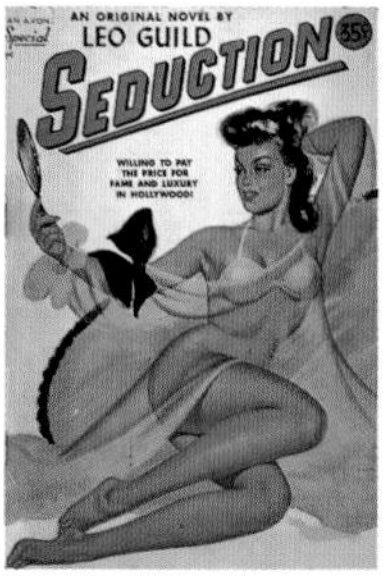

Avon Special (No #)
$8–$25–$50

Ballantine Book, 8
$4–$12.50–$25

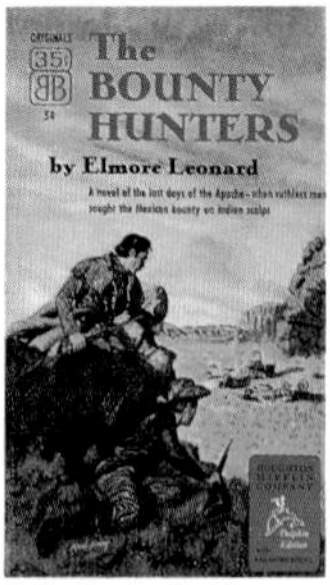

Ballantine Book, 54
$10–$30–$60

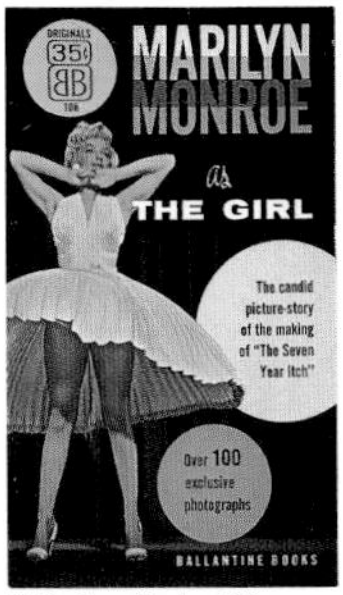

Ballantine Book, 108
$10-$30-$60

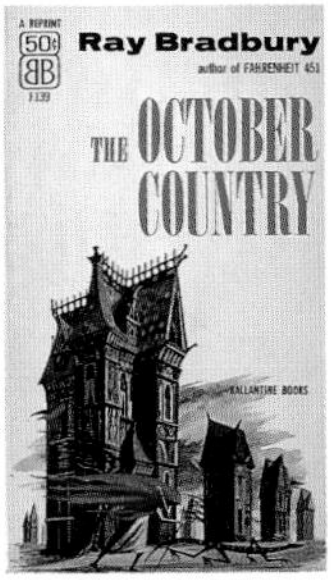

Ballantine Book, F-139
$6-$20-$40

Ballantine Book, 165
$5.50-$17.50-$35

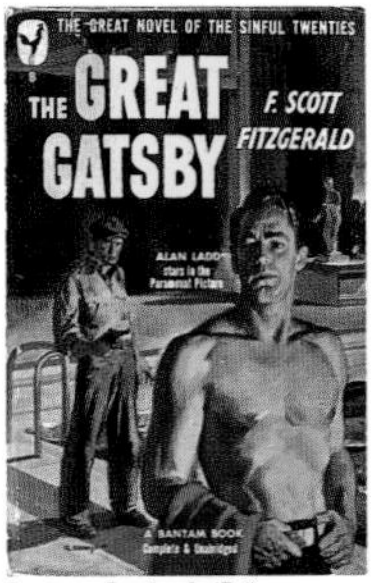

Bantam Book, 8 (DJ)
$12.50-$37.50-$75

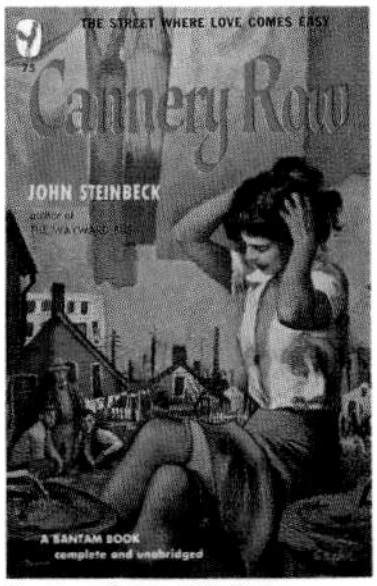

Bantam Book, 75 (DJ)
$22-$70-$140

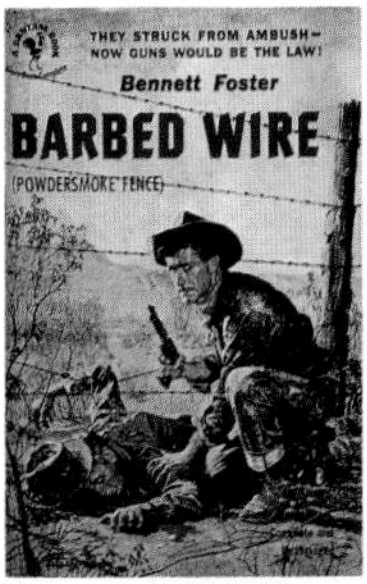

Bantam Book, 252 (DJ)
$22-$70-$140

Bantam Book, 361
$5.50-$17.50-$35

Beacon Book, 130
$20-$60-$125

Beacon Book, 160
$25-$75-$180

Beacon Book, 237
$8-$25-$50

Beacon Book, 298
$10-$30-$60

Beacon Book, 328
$7-$22.50-$45

Berkley, G-120
$12.50–$37.50–$75

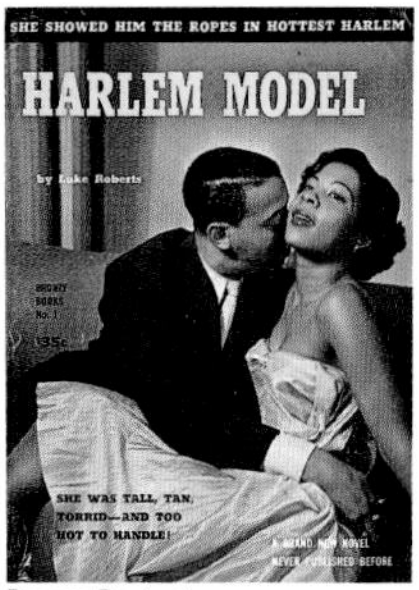

Bronze Book, 1
$22–$70–$140

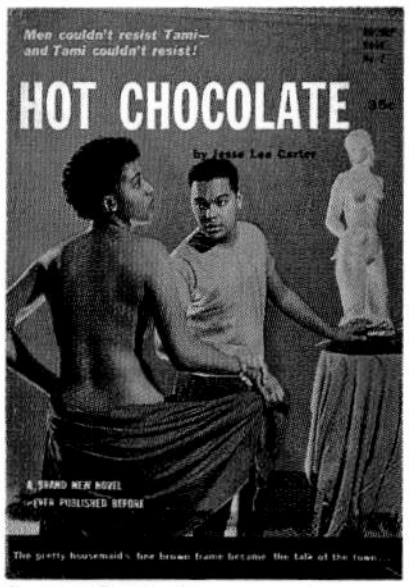

Bronze Book, 2
$22–$70–$140

Cardinal, C-31 (DJ)
$10–$30–$60

Cardinal, C-248
$6–$20–$40

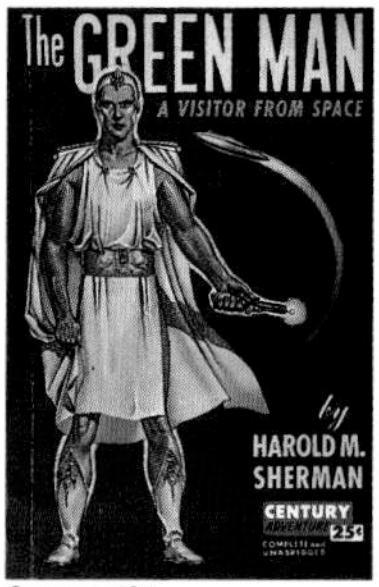

Century, 104
$17–$50–$100

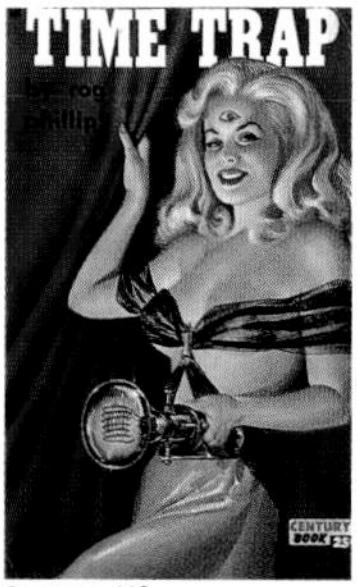

Century, 116
$8–$25–$50

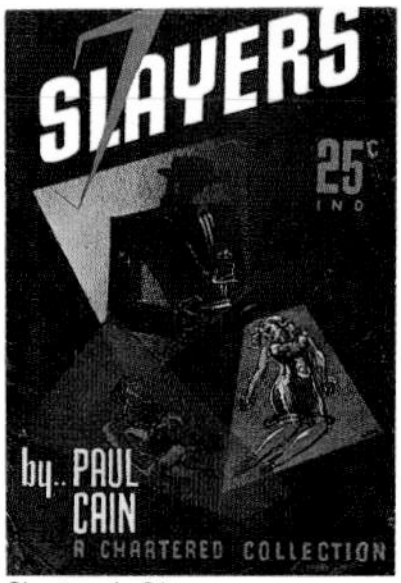

Chartered, 21
$17–$50–$100

Chartered, 22
$17–$50–$100

Crow Book, 36
$6–$20–$40

Dell Book, 89
$12.50–$37.50–$75

Dell Book, 278
$50–$175–$400

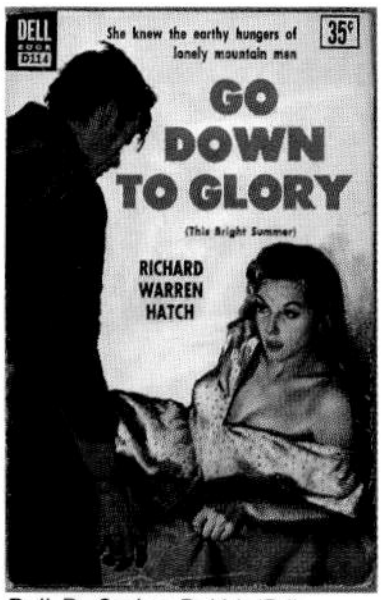

Dell D, Series D-114 (DJ)
$32-$110-$250

Dell (No #) (Jungle Bells)
$15-$45-$90

Dell Ten Cent, 33
$25-$75-$180

Dell Ten Cent, 36
$12.50-$37.50-$75

Diversey Romance Novel, 1
$50-$175-$400

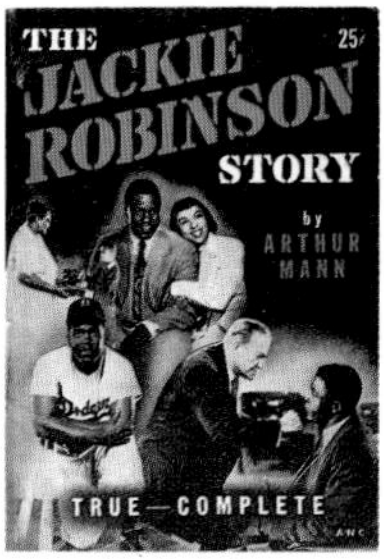

F. J. Low (Jackie Robinson)
$22-$70-$140

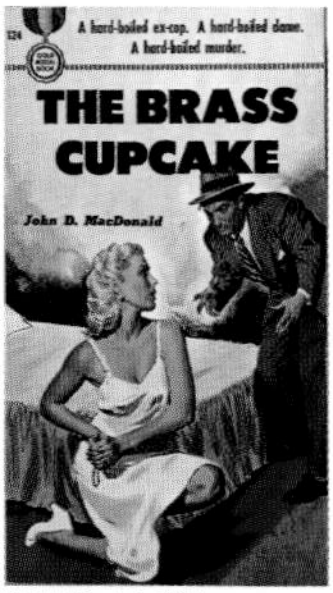

Gold Medal, 124
$20-$60-$125

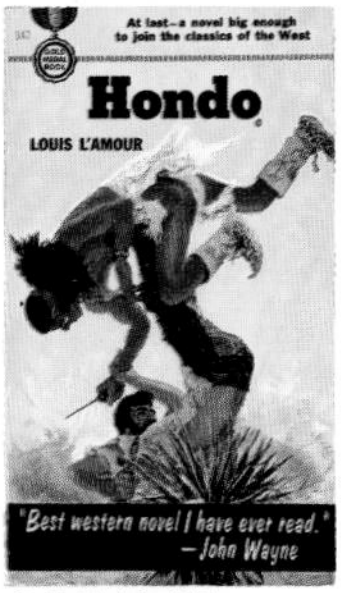

Gold Medal, 347
$12.50-$37.50-$75

Gold Medal, S1153
$15-$45-$90

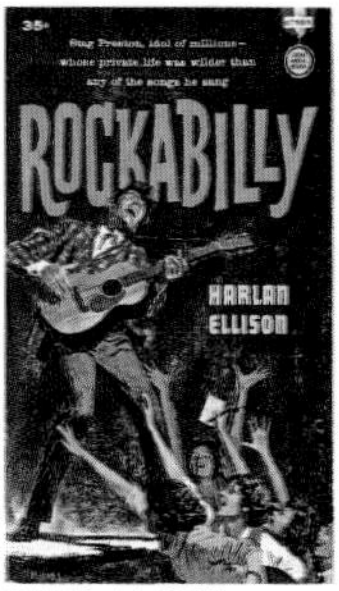

Gold Medal, S1161
$25-$75-$180

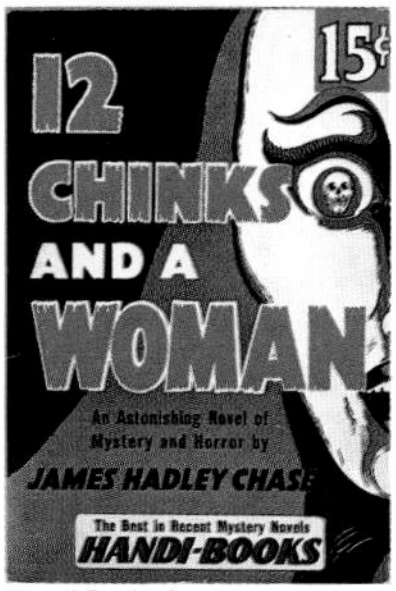

Handi-Book, 3
$10-$30-$60

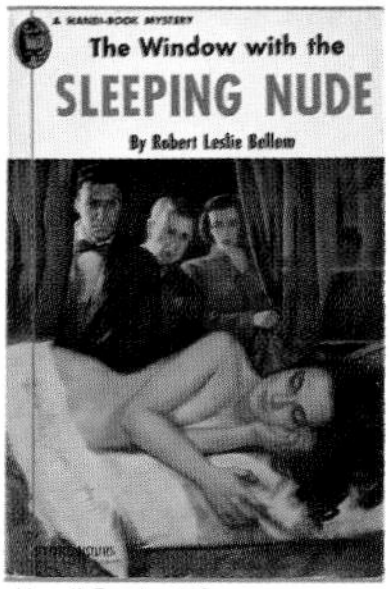

Handi-Book, 118
$12.50-$37.50-$75

Handi-Book, 138
$8-$25-$50

Handy Library, 1
$17-$50-$100

Harlequin, 177
$22-$70-$140

Harlequin, 218
$25-$75-$180

Harlequin, 311
$22-$70-$140

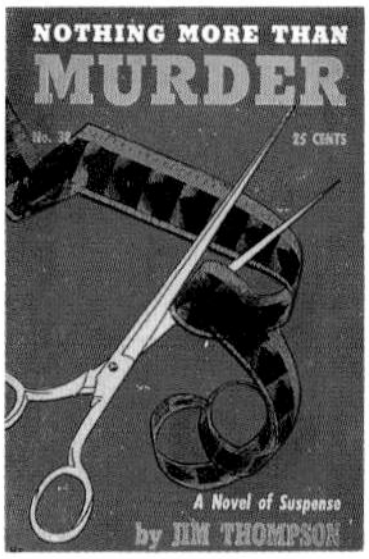

Hillman, 38
$20-$60-$125

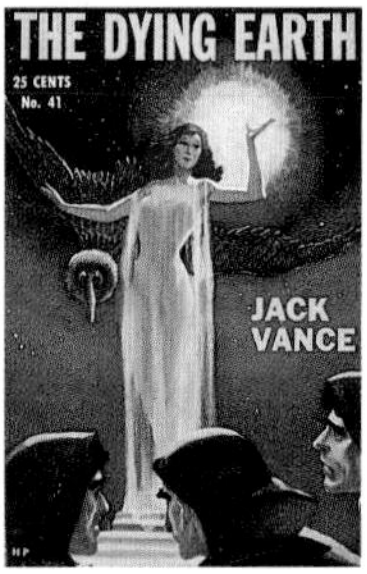

Hillman, 41
$32-$110-$250

Lancer, 75-342
$32-$110-$250

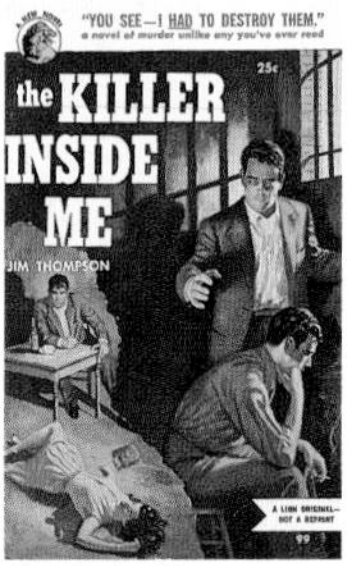

Lion Book, 99
$30-$100-$225

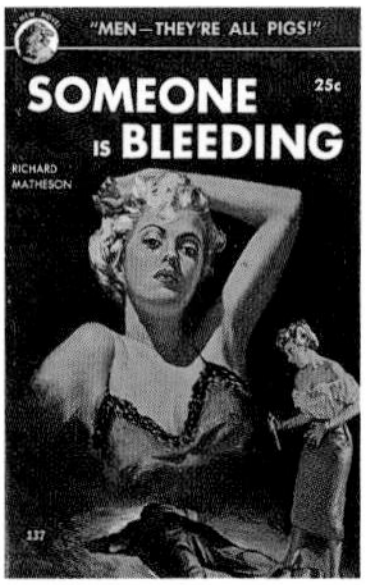

Lion Book, 137
$32-$110-$250

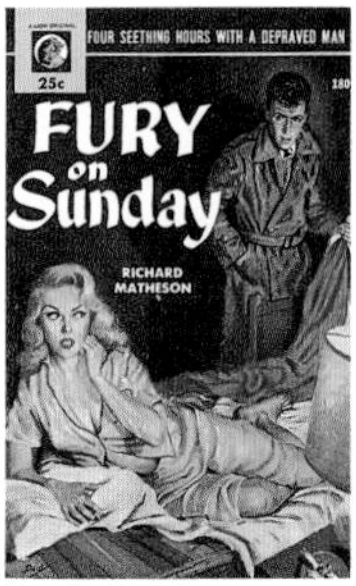

Lion Book, 180
$32-$110-$250

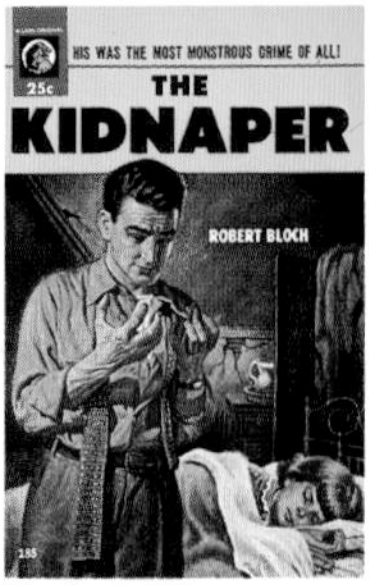

Lion Book, 185
$25-$75-$180

Lion Book, 186
$22-$70-$140

Newsstand, 54
$35-$125-$300

Newsstand, 112
$5.50-$17.50-$35

Newsstand, 122
$20-$60-$120

Novel Library, 45
$8-$25-$50

Penguin, 538 (DJ)
$12.50-$37.50-$75

Penguin, 586 (DJ)
$12.50-$37.50-$75

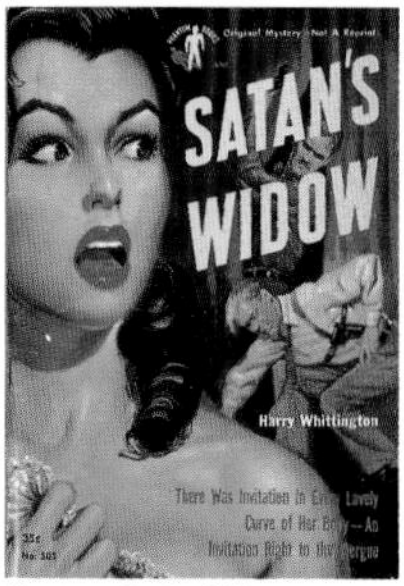

Phantom Book, 505
$5.50-$17.50-$35

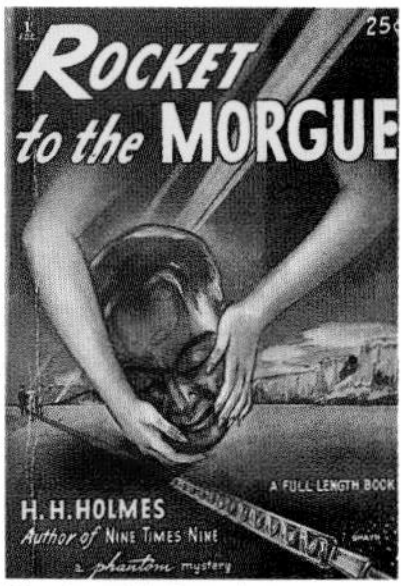

Phantom Mystery, 1
$12.50-$37.50-$75

Pike Book, 203
$8-$25-$50

Pinnacle (No #)
$3.50-$10-$20

Pocket Book (No #),
the rarest paperback
$80-$250-$600

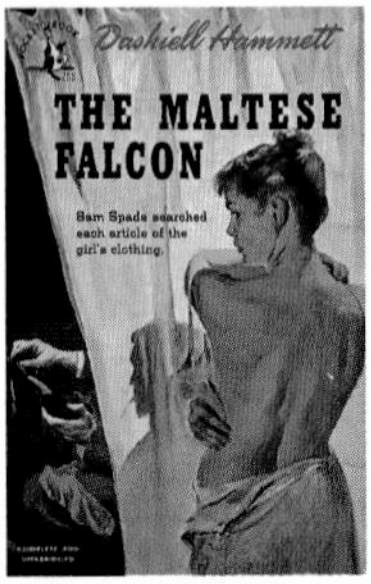

Pocket Book, 268 (DJ)
$22–$70–$140

Popular Library, 211
$17–$50–$100

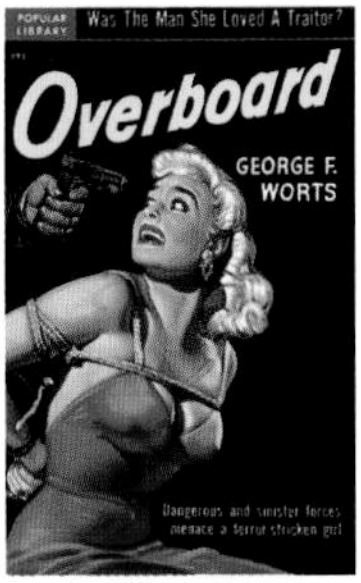

Popular Library, 292
$17–$50–$100

Pyramid, G-352
$32–$110–$250

Quick Reader, 140
$4–$12.50–$25

Reed Nightstand, 3003
$27.50–$85–$200

Studio Pocket, 4
$35–$125–$300

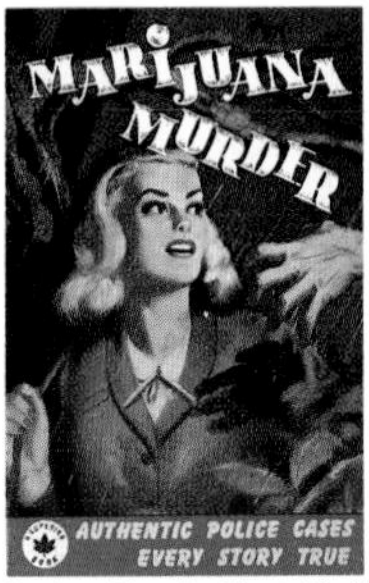

Duchess/Superior Digest (No #)
$4–$12.50–$25

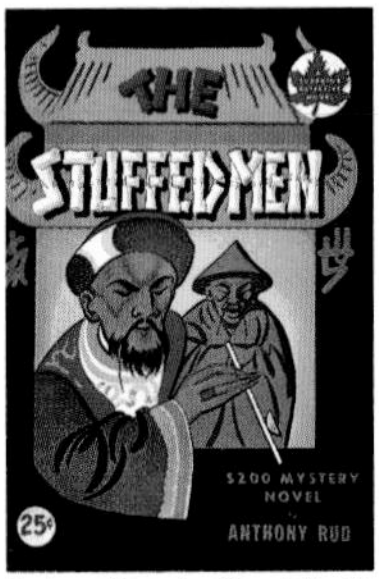

Duchess/Superior Digest (No #)
$4–$12.50–$25

Uni-Book, 49
$5.50–$17.50–$35

Whitman, 556
$50–$175–$400

Yogi Mystery (No #)
$35–$125–$300

		G	VG	F
510	Packer, Vin - ***The Thrill Kids*** [1955] PBO. Cover by Meese.	$3.50	$10.00	$20.00
511	Dean, Dudley - ***The Broken Spur*** [1955]	$1.50	$5.00	$10.00
512	Jones, Nard - ***Ride The Dark Storm*** [1955] PBO. Cover by Robert Maguire.	$1.50	$5.00	$10.00
513	Miller, Wade - ***Stolen Woman*** [1955] Cover by Barye Phillips.	$1.25	$3.75	$7.50
514	Fleischman, A. S. - ***Shanghai Flame*** [1955]	$1.25	$3.75	$7.50
515	Jessup, Richard - ***A Rage To Die*** [1955]	$1.25	$3.75	$7.50
516	L'Amour, Louis - ***To Tame A Land*** [1955] PBO.	$6.00	$20.00	$40.00
517	Jones, Jack - ***Journey Into Death*** [1955] PBO. Cover by Maguire.	$2.00	$6.00	$12.00
518	Ames, Robert - ***Awake And Die*** [1955] PBO. Cover by Hulings.	$2.00	$6.00	$12.00
519	Albert, Marvin H. - ***Lie Down With Lions*** [1955] PBO. Cover by James Meese.	$2.00	$6.00	$12.00
520	Rabe, Peter - ***Benny Muscles In*** [1955] PBO. Cover by Lu Kimmel.	$3.00	$9.00	$18.00
521	Miller, Wade - ***The Killer*** [1955] Cover by C. C. Beall	$1.25	$3.75	$7.50
S-522	Brown, Wenzell - ***Run, Chico, Run*** [1955] Cover by Barye Phillips.	$1.35	$4.00	$8.00
523	Marlowe, Stephen - ***The Second Longest Night*** [1955] PBO. Cover by Ernest Chiriaka	$2.00	$6.00	$12.00
524	Chelton, John - ***My Deadly Angel*** [1955] PBO. Cover by Ernest Chiriaka	$2.00	$6.00	$12.00
525	Caldwell, Taylor - ***Your Sins And Mine*** [1955] PBO. Photo cover.	$2.50	$7.50	$15.00
526	Patten, Lewis B. - ***Gunsmoke Empire*** [1955]	$1.50	$5.00	$10.00
527	Brister, Richard - ***Renegade Brand*** [1955] PBO. Cover by Bob Stanley.	$1.50	$5.00	$10.00
528	Rabe, Peter - ***A Shroud For Jesso*** [1955] PBO. Cover by Lu Kimmel.	$3.00	$9.00	$18.00
529	Ronns, Edward - ***The Decoy*** [1955] Cover by Barye Phillips.	$1.35	$4.00	$8.00
530	Goodis, David - ***The Wounded And The Slain*** [1955] PBO. Cover by Ernest Chiriaka	$17.00	$50.00	$100.00
531	Craig, Jonathan - ***The Dead Darling*** [1955] PBO. Cover by Barye Phillips.	$2.00	$6.00	$12.00
532	Clark, George - ***The Neighbor's Kids*** [1955] PBO. Cover by George Clark. Cartoon book.	$1.50	$5.00	$10.00
533	Adams, Clifton - ***Gambling Man*** [1955] PBO. Cover by Frank McCarthy	$2.00	$6.00	$12.00
534	Newton, D. B. - ***The Outlaw Breed*** [1955]	$1.50	$5.00	$10.00
535	Cushman, Dan - ***Port Orient*** [1955] PBO. Cover by Kimmel.	$2.00	$6.00	$12.00
536	Pratt, Theodore - ***Cocotte*** [1955]	$1.25	$3.75	$7.50
537	Fischer, Bruno - ***House Of Flesh*** [1955] Cover by C. C. Beall.	$1.25	$3.75	$7.50
538	Cooper, Morton - ***The Flesh-And Mr. Rawlie*** [1955] PBO. Cover by Barye Phillips	$2.00	$6.00	$12.00
540	Preston, Charles - ***Zowie! Girl Meets Boy*** [1955] PBO. Cartoon book	$2.00	$6.00	$12.00
541	Hatten, Homer - ***Horsemen From Hell*** [1955] PBO. Cover by Frank McCarthy.	$2.00	$6.00	$12.00
542	Rigsby, Howard - ***The Lone Gun*** [1955] PBO. Cover by Bob Schulz.	$1.50	$5.00	$10.00
543	Himmel, Richard - ***The Chinese Keyhole*** [1955] Cover by Barye Phillips.	$1.25	$3.75	$7.50
544	Goodis, David - ***Cassidy's Girl*** [1955] Cover by Kampen.	$5.50	$17.50	$35.00
545	Grove, Walt - ***Hell-Bent For Danger*** [1955]	$1.25	$3.75	$7.50
546	Thomey, Tedd - ***Killer In White*** [1956] PBO. Cover by James Meese.	$2.00	$6.00	$12.00
547	Rabe, Peter - ***A House In Naples*** [1956] Cover by Lu Kimmel.	$1.25	$3.75	$7.50
548	Lutz, Giles A. - ***To Hell And Texas*** [1956] PBO. Cover by Frank McCarthy.	$1.50	$5.00	$10.00

		G	VG	F
549	Fox, Gardner F. - ***Queen Of Sheba*** [1956] PBO. Cover by Jack Floherty, Jr.	$4.00	$12.50	$25.00
550	O'Connor, Richard - ***Down To Eternity*** [1956] PBO. Cover by Charles Binger	$1.50	$5.00	$10.00
551	Prather, Richard S. - ***Too Many Crooks*** [1956] Cover by Barye Phillips.	$1.25	$3.75	$7.50
552	Viereck, George Sylvester - ***Men Into Beasts*** [1956]	$1.25	$3.75	$7.50
553	Albert, Marvin H. - ***The Law And Jack Wade*** [1956] PBO. Cover by Robert Schulz.	$1.50	$5.00	$10.00
554	Castle, Frank - ***The Violent Hours*** [1956] PBO. Cover by Lu Kimmel.	$2.00	$6.00	$12.00
555	Rohmer, Sax - ***Sinister Madonna*** [1956] PBO. Cover by Charles Binger	$5.50	$17.50	$35.00
556	Vail, John - ***Hold Back The Sun*** [1956]	$1.50	$5.00	$10.00
557	Baird, Jack - ***Hot, Sweet And Blue*** [1956] PBO. Cover by Mitchell Hooks.	$1.50	$5.00	$10.00
558	Hayward, Richard - ***Trapped*** [1956]	$1.25	$3.75	$7.50
559	Rodin, Arnold - ***Woman Soldier*** [1956] Cover by Barye Phillips.	$1.25	$3.75	$7.50
560	Harrison, C. William - ***The Guns Of Fort Petticoat*** [1956] PBO. Cover by Frank McCarthy.	$2.50	$7.50	$15.00
561	Kingery, Don - ***Death Must Wait*** [1956] PBO. Cover by Charles Binger	$2.00	$6.00	$12.00
562	Mara, Bernard - ***This Gun For Gloria*** [1956] PBO.	$2.50	$7.50	$15.00
563	Sparkia, Roy Benard - ***Build My Gallows High*** [1956] PBO. Cover by Hooks.	$2.00	$6.00	$12.00
S-564	Dixon, H. Vernor - ***Cry Blood*** [1956]	$1.25	$3.75	$7.50
565	Roberts, Lee - ***Little Sister*** [1956] Photo cover.	$1.25	$3.75	$7.50
566	Himmel, Richard - ***I Have Gloria Kirby*** [1956]	$1.25	$3.75	$7.50
567	Lutz, Giles A. - ***The Golden Bawd*** [1956] PBO. Cover by Lu Kimmel.	$1.50	$5.00	$10.00
568	Aarons, Edward S. - ***Assignment-Treason*** [1956] PBO. Cover by Barye Phillips.	$2.00	$6.00	$12.00
569	Hopson, William - ***Gunfire At Salt Fork*** [1956] PBO.	$1.50	$5.00	$10.00
570	Spafford, Robert - ***My Mistress, Death*** [1956] Cover by Charles Binger	$2.00	$6.00	$12.00
571	McPartland, John - ***I'll See You In Hell*** [1956] PBO. Cover by Barye Phillips.	$3.50	$10.00	$20.00
572	Fleischman, A. S. - ***Look Behind You, Lady*** [1956]	$1.25	$3.75	$7.50
573	Patten, Lewis B. - ***Rope Law*** [1956]	$1.50	$5.00	$10.00
574	McPartland, John - ***Danger For Breakfast*** [1956] PBO. Cover by Barye Phillips.	$3.50	$10.00	$20.00
575	Marlowe, Stephen - ***Mecca For Murder*** [1956] PBO. Cover by James Meese.	$2.00	$6.00	$12.00
576	Marr, Reed - ***Catch A Falling Star*** [1956] PBO. Cover by Lloyd Baker	$1.50	$5.00	$10.00
S-577	Matheson, Richard - ***The Shrinking Man*** [1956] PBO. Cover by Mitchell Hooks	$20.00	$60.00	$125.00
578	Packer, Vin - ***Dark Intruder*** [1956]	$1.25	$3.75	$7.50
579	Conroy, Albert - ***The Road's End*** [1956] Cover by Barye Phillips	$1.25	$3.75	$7.50
580	Shirreffs, Gordon - ***Rio Bravo*** [1956] PBO. Cover by Frank McCarthy	$1.50	$5.00	$10.00
581	Packer, Vin - ***The Young And Violent*** [1956] PBO. Cover by James Meese.	$2.50	$7.50	$15.00
582	Craig, Jonathan - ***Morgue For Venus*** [1956] PBO. Cover by Barye Phillips.	$2.00	$6.00	$12.00
S-583	Benson, Ben & Tawney, Howard D. - ***Hypnosis And You*** [1956]	$1.35	$4.00	$8.00
584	Dean, Dudley - ***The Diehards*** [1956]	$1.50	$5.00	$10.00

		G	VG	F
585	O'Quinn, Allen - ***Swamp Brat*** [1956] Cover by Barye Phillips.	$1.25	$3.75	$7.50
586	Schoenfeld, Howard - ***Let Them Eat Bullets*** [1956]	$1.25	$3.75	$7.50
S-587	Loomis, Noel M. - ***Johnny Concho*** [1956] Movie tie-in.	$2.00	$6.00	$12.00
S-588	Cooper, Morton - ***The Innocent And Willing*** [1956]	$1.50	$5.00	$10.00
589	Mason, Raymond - ***Love After Five*** [1956] PBO. Cover by Charles Binger.	$1.25	$3.75	$7.50
S-590	Millard, Joseph - ***Edgar Cayce—Mystery Man Of Miracles*** [1956]	$2.00	$6.00	$12.00
591	Fischer, Bruno - ***Knee-Deep In Death*** [1956] PBO. Cover by Lu Kimmel.	$2.00	$6.00	$12.00
592	Prather, Richard S. - ***The Wailing Frail*** [1956] PBO. Cover by Barye Phillips.	$2.00	$6.00	$12.00
593	Adams, Clifton - ***Law Of The Trigger*** [1956] PBO. Cover by Roy Lance.	$2.00	$6.00	$12.00
594	Rabe, Peter - ***Kill The Boss Good-Bye*** [1956] PBO. Cover by Barye Phillips.	$2.50	$7.50	$15.00
595	Whittington, Harry - ***Brute In Brass*** [1956] PBO. Cover by Mitchell Hooks.	$3.50	$10.00	$20.00
596	McPartland, John - ***The Wild Party*** [1956] PBO. Cover by James Meese.	$3.50	$10.00	$20.00
S-597	Forrest, Williams - ***The Woman With Claws*** [1956] PBO. Cover by Bob Peake.	$2.00	$6.00	$12.00
598	Prather, Richard S. - ***Always Leave 'em Dying*** [1956]	$1.25	$3.75	$7.50
599	Wainer, Cord - ***Mountain Girl*** [1956]	$1.25	$3.75	$7.50
600	Fischer, Bruno - ***Fools Walk In*** [1956]	$1.25	$3.75	$7.50
601	Dean, Dudley - ***Tough Hombre*** [1956] PBO. Cover by Frank McCarthy.	$1.50	$5.00	$10.00
602	Patten, Lewis B. - ***White Warrior*** [1956] Cover by Frank McCarthy.	$1.50	$5.00	$10.00
603	Keene, Day - ***Bring Him Back Dead*** [1956] PBO. Cover by Barye Phillips.	$2.50	$7.50	$15.00
604	Ward, Jonas - ***The Name's Buchanan*** [1956]	$1.50	$5.00	$10.00
605	Castle, Frank - ***Dead And Kicking*** [1956] PBO. Cover by Mitchell Hooks.	$2.00	$6.00	$12.00
606	White, Lionel - ***Operation-Murder*** [1956] PBO. Cover by James Meese.	$2.00	$6.00	$12.00
S-607	Wiliams, Charles - ***The Diamond Bikini*** [1956] PBO. Cover by Casey Jones.	$2.50	$7.50	$15.00
608	Conroy, Albert - ***The Chiselers*** [1956]	$1.25	$3.75	$7.50
609	Fox, Gardner F. - ***The Borgia Blade*** [1956]	$1.25	$3.75	$7.50
610	Cullen, Carter - ***Don't Get Caught*** [1956] Cover by Kampen.	$1.25	$3.75	$7.50
611	Whittington, Harry - ***Desire In The Dust*** [1956] PBO. Cover by Barye Phillips.	$3.50	$10.00	$20.00
612	Rabe, Peter - ***Dig My Grave Deep*** [1956] PBO. Cover by Lu Kimmel.	$3.00	$9.00	$18.00
613	Frazee, Steve - ***He Rode Alone*** [1956] PBO.	$1.50	$5.00	$10.00
614	Douglas, Malcolm - ***The Deadly Dames*** [1956] Cover by Bob Peake.	$1.50	$5.00	$10.00
615	Praskins, Leonard & Slater, Barney - ***Three Violent People*** [1956] Movie tie-in.	$2.00	$6.00	$12.00
S-616	Dixon, H. Vernor - ***Killer In Silk*** [1956] PBO. Cover by Mitchell Hooks.	$1.50	$5.00	$10.00
617	Keene, Day - ***About Doctor Ferrel*** [1956] Cover by Barye Phillips.	$1.25	$3.75	$7.50
S-618	Pratt, Theodore - ***Handsome*** [1956]	$1.25	$3.75	$7.50
619	Durst, Paul - ***Prairie Reckoning*** [1956] PBO.	$1.25	$3.75	$7.50
620	Ernenwein, Leslie - ***High Gun*** [1956] PBO. Cover by Frank McCarthy.	$1.50	$5.00	$10.00
621	Aarons, Edward S. - ***Assignment-Suicide*** [1956] PBO.	$2.00	$6.00	$12.00

		G	VG	F
622	Keene, Day - ***Murder On The Side*** [1956] PBO. Cover by Barye Phillips.	$2.50	$7.50	$15.00
623	Goodis, David - ***Down There*** [1956] PBO. Cover by Mitchell Hooks.	$17.00	$50.00	$100.00
S-624	Packer, Vin - ***Dark Don't Catch Me*** [1956] PBO. Cover by James Meese.	$2.50	$7.50	$15.00
625	Williams, Charles - ***Go Home, Stranger*** [1956]	$1.25	$3.75	$7.50
626	Goodis, David - ***Of Tender Sin*** [1956]	$5.50	$17.50	$35.00
627	Marlowe, Stephen - ***Trouble Is My Name*** [1957] PBO. Cover by Kimmel.	$2.00	$6.00	$12.00
628	Flagg, John - ***Murder In Monaco*** [1957] PBO. Cover by Robert Peak.	$2.00	$6.00	$12.00
629	Cullen, Carter - ***The Deadly Chase*** [1957] PBO. Cover by Mitchell Hooks.	$2.00	$6.00	$12.00
630	Sutter, Larabie - ***The White Squaw*** [1957]	$1.50	$5.00	$10.00
631	Heuman, William - ***Violence Valley*** [1957] PBO. Cover by Frank McCarthy.	$1.50	$5.00	$10.00
S-632	Deal, Borden - ***Search For Surrender*** [1957] PBO. Cover by Barye Phillips.	$1.50	$5.00	$10.00
633	Faulkner, John - ***The Sin Shouter Of Cabin Road*** [1957]	$1.25	$3.75	$7.50
634	Ronns, Edward - ***State Department Murders*** [1957] Cover by Barye Phillips.	$1.25	$3.75	$7.50
635	Pratt, Theodore - ***Seminole*** [1957] Cover by John Floherty, Jr.	$1.25	$3.75	$7.50
636	Castle, Frank - ***Vengeance Under Law*** [1957]	$1.50	$5.00	$10.00
637	Frazee, Steve - ***Running Target*** [1957] PBO. Cover by Hooks.	$1.50	$5.00	$10.00
638	Reed-Marr, P. J. - ***Women Without Men*** [1957] PBO. Cover by Barye Phillips.	$2.50	$7.50	$15.00
639	Shirreffs, Gordon D. - ***Bugles On The Prairie*** [1957] PBO. Cover by Frank McCarthy.	$1.50	$5.00	$10.00
640	Brown, Wenzell - ***The Wicked Streets*** [1957] PBO. Cover by Barye Phillips.	$4.00	$12.50	$25.00
S-641	Pratt, Theodore - ***The Golden Sorrow*** [1957]	$1.50	$5.00	$10.00
S-642	Appel, Benjamin - ***Sweet Money Girl*** [1957]	$1.50	$5.00	$10.00
643	Matheson, Richard - ***I am Legend*** [1957] Cover by Stanley Meltzoff.	$5.00	$15.00	$30.00
644	Demaris, Ovid - ***Ride The Gold Mare*** [1957] PBO. Cover by Barye Phillips.	$2.50	$7.50	$15.00
645	Craig, Jonathan - ***Case Of The Cold Coquette*** [1957] PBO. Cover by George Mayers.	$2.00	$6.00	$12.00
646	Rigsby, Howard - ***The Reluctant Gun*** [1957]	$1.50	$5.00	$10.00
647	Jessup, Richard - ***Cheyenne Saturday*** [1957] PBO. Cover by Kimmel.	$1.50	$5.00	$10.00
648	Fox, Gardner F. - ***Terror Over London*** [1957] PBO. Cover by Hooks.	$4.00	$12.50	$25.00
S-649	Grove, Walt - ***The Wings Of Eagles*** [1957] Movie tie-in.	$2.50	$7.50	$15.00
650	Cohen, Octavus Roy - ***The Corpse That Walked*** [1957]	$1.25	$3.75	$7.50
651	Williams, Charles - ***Big City Girl*** [1957]	$1.25	$3.75	$7.50
652	Goodis, David - ***Street Of The Lost*** [1957] Cover by Barye Phillips.	$5.50	$17.50	$35.00
S-653	Bannon, Ann - ***Odd Girl Out*** [1957] PBO. Cover by Barye Phillips.	$3.50	$10.00	$20.00
654	Douglas, Malcolm - ***Pure Sweet Hell*** [1957] Cover by Barye Phillips.	$1.25	$3.75	$7.50
655	Dean, Dudley - ***Gun In The Valley*** [1957]	$1.50	$5.00	$10.00
656	Hearne, L. A. - ***Westward The Drums*** [1957]	$1.50	$5.00	$10.00
657	Rabe, Peter - ***The Out Is Death*** [1957] PBO. Cover by Mitchell Hooks.	$2.50	$7.50	$15.00
658	Marlowe, Stephen - ***Murder Is My Dish*** [1957] PBO. Cover by Kimmel.	$2.00	$6.00	$12.00
659	Richards, Lee - ***Hell Strip*** [1957] Cover by Lu Kimmel.	$2.00	$6.00	$12.00

		G	VG	F
S-660	Jessup, Richard - ***The Young Don't Cry*** [1957] Cover by Ray Johnson.	$1.25	$3.75	$7.50
S-661	Loomis, Noel - ***The Maricopa Trail*** [1957] PBO. Cover by Frank McCarthy.	$1.50	$5.00	$10.00
662	Ward, Jonas - ***Buchanan Says No*** [1957] PBO. Cover by Lu Kimmel.	$1.50	$5.00	$10.00
663	White, Lionel - ***Death Takes The Bus*** [1957] PBO. Cover by Hooks.	$2.00	$6.00	$12.00
664	Heller, Mike - ***So I'm A Heel*** [1957] PBO. Cover by Barye Phillips.	$2.00	$6.00	$12.00
665	Prather, Richard S. - ***Three's A Shroud*** [1957] PBO. Cover by Roy Lance.	$2.00	$6.00	$12.00
666	Aarons, Edward S. - ***Assignment-Stella Marni*** [1957] PBO. Cover by Robert Abbett.	$2.00	$6.00	$12.00
667	Lawrence, Steven C. - ***Saddle Justice*** [1957]	$1.50	$5.00	$10.00
668	Scott, Tarn - ***Don't Let Her Die*** [1957] PBO. Cover by Hooks.	$2.00	$6.00	$12.00
669	Craig, Jonathan - ***So Young, So Wicked*** [1957] PBO. Cover by William Rose.	$2.00	$6.00	$12.00
670	Rabe, Peter - ***Agreement To Kill*** [1957] PBO. Cover by Barye Phillips.	$2.50	$7.50	$15.00
671	Richards, Lee - ***Lusty Conquest*** [1957]	$1.50	$5.00	$10.00
672	Jessup, Richard - ***Long Ride West*** [1957]	$1.50	$5.00	$10.00
S-673	Torres, Toreska - ***Women's Barracks*** [1957] Cover by Barye Phillips.	$1.35	$4.00	$8.00
674	Adams, Clifton - ***Outlaw's Son*** [1957]	$1.50	$5.00	$10.00
675	Kantor, MacKinlay - ***One Wild Oat*** [1957]	$1.25	$3.75	$7.50
676	Conroy, Albert - ***Nice Guys Finish Dead*** [1957] PBO. Cover by Mitchell Hooks.	$2.00	$6.00	$12.00
677	Prather, Richard S. - ***Have Gat-Will Travel*** [1957] PBO. Cover by Barye Phillips.	$2.00	$6.00	$12.00
678	Rabe, Peter - ***It's My Funeral*** [1957] PBO. Cover by John Floherty, Jr.	$2.50	$7.50	$15.00
679	Castle, Frank - ***Gun Talk At Yuma*** [1957]	$1.50	$5.00	$10.00
680	Demaris, Ovid - ***The Hoods Take Over*** [1957] PBO. Cover by Barye Phillips.	$2.00	$6.00	$12.00
681	Heuman, William - ***Heller From Texas*** [1957] PBO. Cover by Lu Kimmel.	$1.50	$5.00	$10.00
682	Miller, Wade - ***The Tiger's Wife*** [1957]	$1.25	$3.75	$7.50
683	Adams, Clifton - ***A Noose For The Desperado*** [1957]	$1.50	$5.00	$10.00
S-684	Rohmer, Sax - ***Re-enter Fu Manchu*** [1957] PBO. Cover by Barye Phillips.	$5.00	$15.00	$30.00
685	Howard, Vechel - ***Sundown At Crazy Horse*** [1957]	$1.50	$5.00	$10.00
686	L'Amour, Louis - ***Last Stand At Papago Wells*** [1957] PBO. Cover by Frank McCarthy.	$7.00	$22.50	$45.00
687	White, Lionel - ***Hostage For A Hood*** [1957] PBO.	$2.00	$6.00	$12.00
S-688	Jackson, Joseph Henry & Offord, Lenore - ***The Girl In The Belfry*** [1957] PBO. Cover by Powers. Classic murder trial #12.	$2.50	$7.50	$15.00
689	Packer, Vin - ***3 Day Terror*** [1957] PBO. Cover by Louis Glanzman.	$2.00	$6.00	$12.00
690	Hatch, Eric - ***Crockett's Woman*** [1957]	$1.25	$3.75	$7.50
691	Goodis, David - ***Fire In The Flesh*** [1957] PBO. Cover by Barye Phillips.	$17.00	$50.00	$100.00
692	Loomis, Noel & Peil, Paul Leslie - ***Hang The Men High*** [1957]	$1.50	$5.00	$10.00
693	Marlowe, Stephen - ***Killers Are My Meat*** [1957] PBO. Cover by Gerry Powell.	$2.00	$6.00	$12.00
694	Fischer, Bruno - ***Murder In The Raw*** [1957] PBO.	$2.00	$6.00	$12.00
695	Castle, Frank - ***Lovely And Lethal*** [1957] PBO. Photo cover.	$2.00	$6.00	$12.00

		G	VG	F
696	Albert, Marvin H. - ***Apache Rising*** [1957] PBO. Cover by Frank McCarthy.	$1.50	$5.00	$10.00
697	Williams, Charles - ***Hill Girl*** [1957]	$1.25	$3.75	$7.50
698	Causey, James O. - ***The Baby Doll Murders*** [1957] PBO. Cover by Barye Phillips.	$2.50	$7.50	$15.00
699	Jessup, Richard - ***Comanche Vengeange*** [1957] PBO.	$1.50	$5.00	$10.00
700	L'Amour, Louis - ***The Tall Stranger*** [1957] PBO. Movie tie-in.	$8.00	$25.00	$50.00
701	Grantland, Keith - ***Run From The Hunter*** [1957] PBO.	$4.00	$12.50	$25.00
702	Craig, Jonathan - ***The Case Of The Beautiful Body*** [1957] PBO. Cover by Stanley Zuckerberg.	$2.00	$6.00	$12.00
703	Avalione, Mike - ***The Voodoo Murders*** [1957] PBO. Cover by Hooks.	$2.00	$6.00	$12.00
S-704	Mockridge, Norton & Prall, Robert - ***This Is Costello On The Spot*** [1957] Photo cover.	$1.25	$3.75	$7.50
705	Heuman, William - ***Stagecoach West*** [1957] PBO.	$1.50	$5.00	$10.00
706	Patten, Lewis B. - ***Massacre at San Pablo*** [1957] PBO. Cover by A. Leslie Ross.	$1.50	$5.00	$10.00
707	Aarons, Edward S. - ***Assignment-Budapest*** [1957] PBO.	$2.00	$6.00	$12.00
708	Brewer, Gil - ***The Brat*** [1957] PBO. Cover by Barye Phillips.	$2.50	$7.50	$15.00
709	Castle, Frank - ***Murder In Red*** [1957] PBO.	$2.00	$6.00	$12.00
710	Rabe, Peter - ***Journey Into Terror*** [1957] PBO. Cover by Hooks.	$2.50	$7.50	$15.00
711	Connell, Vivian - ***A Man Of Parts*** [1957] Cover by Meese.	$1.25	$3.75	$7.50
712	Prather, Richard S. - ***The Wailing Frail*** [1957]	$1.25	$3.75	$7.50
713	Fowler, Kenneth - ***Summons To Silverhorn*** [1957] PBO	$1.50	$5.00	$10.00
714	Shirreffs, Gordon D. - ***Ambush On The Mesa*** [1957]	$1.50	$5.00	$10.00
715	Ozaki, Milton K. - ***Case Of The Deadly Kiss*** [1957] PBO.	$2.00	$6.00	$12.00
716	Craig, Jonathan - ***Come Night, Come Evil*** [1957] PBO. Cover by Rader.	$2.00	$6.00	$12.00
717	Himes, Chester - ***For Love Of Imabelle*** [1957] PBO. Cover by Hooks.	$3.50	$10.00	$20.00
718	Avalone, Mike - ***The Crazy Mixed-Up Corpse*** [1957] PBO. Cover by John Floherty, Jr.	$2.00	$6.00	$12.00
719	Woolrich, Cornell - ***Savage Bride*** [1957] Cover by Barye Phillips.	$2.50	$7.50	$15.00
720	Short, Luke - ***Barren Land Showdown*** [1957]	$1.25	$3.75	$7.50
721	Rohde, William L. - ***Murder On The Line*** [1957]	$1.25	$3.75	$7.50
722	Chadwick, Joseph - ***A Town To Tame*** [1958] PBO. Cover by Harry Schaare.	$1.50	$5.00	$10.00
723	Patten, Lewis B. - ***Five Rode West*** [1958] PBO.	$1.50	$5.00	$10.00
724	MacDonald, John D. - ***The Damned*** [1958]	$2.50	$7.50	$15.00
S-725	Forrest, Williams - ***The Great Debauch*** [1958] PBO. Cover by Barye Phillips.	$1.50	$5.00	$10.00
S-726	Margulies, Leo - editor - ***Three Times Infinity*** [1958] PBO.	$2.00	$6.00	$12.00
S-727	Aldrich, Ann - ***We, Too, Must Love*** [1958] PBO. Cover by John Floherty, Jr.	$4.00	$12.50	$25.00
728	L'Amour, Louis - ***Heller With A Gun*** [1958]	$2.50	$7.50	$15.00
729	Faulkner, John - ***Uncle Good's Girls*** [1958] Cover by Barye Phillips.	$1.25	$3.75	$7.50
730	Faulkner, John - ***Cabin Road*** [1958] Cover by Barye Phillips.	$1.25	$3.75	$7.50
S-731	Packer, Vin - ***5:45 To Suburbia*** [1958] PBO.	$1.50	$5.00	$10.00
732	McPartland, John - ***Ripe Fruit*** [1958] PBO. Cover by Ernest Chiriaka.	$2.50	$7.50	$15.00
733	Huffaker, Clair - ***Guns Of Rio Conchos*** [1958] PBO.	$1.50	$5.00	$10.00
S-734	Brown, Wenzell - ***Teen-age Terror*** [1958] PBO. Cover by Meese.	$4.00	$12.50	$25.00
S-735	Himmel, Richard - ***The Rich And The Damned*** [1958] PBO. Cover by Darcy.	$2.00	$6.00	$12.00
736	Huffaker, Clair - ***Cowboy*** [1958] PBO. Movie photo cover. Movie tie-in.	$2.50	$7.50	$15.00

		G	VG	F
737	MacDonald, John D. - ***Dead Low Tide*** [1958]	$2.50	$7.50	$15.00
738	Hunt, Howard - ***The Violent Ones*** [1958]	$1.25	$3.75	$7.50
739	Anonymous - ***I, Mobster*** [1958]	$1.25	$3.75	$7.50
740	Whittington, Harry - ***Web Of Murder*** [1958] PBO.	$3.50	$10.00	$20.00
741	Lutz, Giles A. - ***Outcast Gun*** [1958] PBO.	$1.50	$5.00	$10.00
742	Ward, Jonas - ***One-Man Massacre*** [1958] PBO. Cover by Kimmel.	$1.50	$5.00	$10.00
743	Cannon, Curt - ***I Like 'Em Tough*** [1958] PBO. Cover by Gerry Powell.	$2.00	$6.00	$12.00
744	Borden, Lee - ***The Secret Of Sylvia*** [1958] PBO.	$1.50	$5.00	$10.00
745	Prather, Richard S. - ***Take A Murder, Darling*** [1958] PBO. Cover by Barye Phillips.	$2.00	$6.00	$12.00
S-746	Williams, Charles - ***River Girl*** [1958] Cover by Barye Phillips...	$1.25	$3.75	$7.50
747	Quarry, Nick - ***The Hoods Come Calling*** [1958] PBO. Cover by Barye Phillips.	$2.50	$7.50	$15.00
748	Cook, Will - ***Badman's Holiday*** [1958] PBO. Cover by Robert Schulz.	$1.50	$5.00	$10.00
749	Aarons, Edward S. - ***Assignment-Angelina*** [1958] PBO. Cover by Gerry Powell.	$2.00	$6.00	$12.00
750	Demaris, Ovid - ***The Lusting Drive*** [1958] PBO.	$2.00	$6.00	$12.00
S-751	Leinster, Murray - ***War With The Gizmos*** [1958] PBO. Cover by Richard Powers.	$3.00	$9.00	$18.00
752	Castle, Frank - ***Dakota Boomtown*** [1958] PBO.	$1.50	$5.00	$10.00
753	Fischer, Bruno - ***So Wicked My Love*** [1958] Photo cover.	$1.25	$3.75	$7.50
754	Schweitzer, Gertrude - ***The Obsessed*** [1958] Cover by Barye Phillips.	$1.25	$3.75	$7.50
755	Fischer, Bruno - ***The Lady Kills*** [1958]	$1.25	$3.75	$7.50
756	Albert, Marvin H. - ***The Law And Jake Wade*** [1958] Movie photo cover. Movie tie-in.	$1.35	$4.00	$8.00
S-757	Rohmer, Sax - ***Sumuru*** [1958] Cover by Barye Phillips.	$1.50	$5.00	$10.00
758	Miller, Wade - ***Devil May Care*** [1958]	$1.25	$3.75	$7.50
759	Telfair, Richard - ***Wyoming Jones*** [1958] PBO.	$1.50	$5.00	$10.00
760	Albert, Marvin H. - ***The Bounty Killer*** [1958] PBO.	$1.50	$5.00	$10.00
761	Flora, Fletcher - ***Park Avenue Tramp*** [1958] PBO. Photo cover.	$1.50	$5.00	$10.00
S-762	Cox, William - ***The Tycoon And The Tigress*** [1958] PBO. Cover by Barye Phillips.	$1.50	$5.00	$10.00
763	Rabe, Peter - ***Stop This Man!*** [1958] Cover by Darcy.	$1.35	$4.00	$8.00
S-764	Osborne, O. O. - ***The Rise And Fall Of Dr. Carey*** [1958] PBO.	$1.35	$4.00	$8.00
765	Rubel, James L. - ***No Business For A Lady*** [1958]	$1.25	$3.75	$7.50
766	Ronns, Edward - ***Catspaw, Ordeal*** [1958]	$1.25	$3.75	$7.50
767	MacDonald John D. - ***Murder For The Bride*** [1958]	$2.50	$7.50	$15.00
D-768	Potter, Charles Francis - ***The Lost Years Of Jesus Revealed*** [1958] PBO.	$1.50	$5.00	$10.00
769	Marlowe, Stephen - ***Violence Is My Business*** [1958] PBO. Cover by Barye Phillips.	$2.00	$6.00	$12.00
770	Prather, Richard S. - ***The Scrambled Yeggs*** [1958]	$1.50	$5.00	$10.00
771	Jessup, Richard - ***Texas Outlaw*** [1958] PBO.	$1.50	$5.00	$10.00
772	Ketchum, Philip - ***Feud At Forked River*** [1958] PBO.	$1.50	$5.00	$10.00
S-773	Rabe, Peter - ***Mission For Vengeance*** [1958] PBO. Cover by Darcy.	$2.50	$7.50	$15.00
S-774	Aldrich, Ann - ***We Walk Alone*** [1958]	$2.50	$7.50	$15.00
775	White, Lionel - ***Coffin For A Hood*** [1958] PBO. Cover by Darcy.	$2.50	$7.50	$15.00
776	Douglas, Malcolm - ***Murder Comes Calling*** [1958] PBO.	$2.00	$6.00	$12.00
S-777	MacDonald John D. - ***Clemmie*** [1958] PBO. Cover by Barye Phillips.	$5.50	$17.50	$35.00
778	Patten, Lewis B. - ***Home Is The Outlaw*** [1958]	$1.50	$5.00	$10.00
779	Peil, Paul Leslie - ***Tucson*** [1958] PBO. Movie tie-in.	$1.50	$5.00	$10.00
780	Conroy, Albert - ***The Mob Says Murder*** [1958] PBO.	$2.00	$6.00	$12.00
781	Mooney, Booth - ***Here Is My Body*** [1958]	$1.50	$5.00	$10.00

		G	VG	F
782	MacDonald John D. - ***Judge Me Not*** [1958] Photo cover.	$2.50	$7.50	$15.00
S-783	Fischer, Bruno - ***The Fast Buck*** [1958] Cover by James Meese.	$1.25	$3.75	$7.50
784	Craig, Jonathan - ***Case Of The Petticoat Murder*** [1958] PBO.	$2.00	$6.00	$12.00
785	Cushman, Dan - ***The Forbidden Land*** [1958] PBO. Cover by Barye Phillips.	$2.00	$6.00	$12.00
786	White, Lionel - ***Too Young To Die*** [1958] PBO.	$2.00	$6.00	$12.00
787	Flagg, John - ***Death's Lovely Mask*** [1958] PBO. Photo cover.	$2.00	$6.00	$12.00
788	Lawrence, Steven C. - ***Brand Of A Texan*** [1958] PBO. Cover by Darcy.	$1.50	$5.00	$10.00
789	Howard, Vechel - ***Tall In The West*** [1958] PBO. Cover by Robert Abbett.	$1.50	$5.00	$10.00
S-790	MacDonald John D. - ***The Neon Jungle*** [1958]	$2.50	$7.50	$15.00
S-791	Miller, Wade - ***Branded Woman*** [1958] Cover by John Floherty, Jr.	$1.25	$3.75	$7.50
792	MacDonald, John D. - ***The Brass Cupcake*** [1958] Cover by Barye Phillips.	$1.50	$5.00	$10.00
S-793	Packer, Vin - ***Spring Fire*** [1958] Cover by Barye Phillips.	$1.25	$3.75	$7.50
794	Owen, Mark - ***Trouble At Borrasca Rim*** [1958] PBO.	$1.50	$5.00	$10.00
795	Ozaki, Milton K. - ***Case Of The Cop's Wife*** [1958] PBO. Cover by Darcy.	$2.00	$6.00	$12.00
S-796	Race, Philip - ***Self-Made Widow*** [1958]	$1.50	$5.00	$10.00
797	Packer, Vin - ***The Evil Friendship*** [1958] PBO. Photo cover.	$2.50	$7.50	$15.00
798	Cook, Will - ***Guns Of North Texas*** [1958] PBO.	$1.50	$5.00	$10.00
799	Aarons, Edward S. - ***Assignment-Madeleine*** [1958] PBO.	$2.00	$6.00	$12.00
800	Himmel, Richard - ***Two Deaths Must Die*** [1958]	$1.25	$3.75	$7.50
S-801	Grove, Walt - ***The Man Who Said No*** [1958]	$1.25	$3.75	$7.50
S-802	Thomas, Kenneth - ***The Devil's Mistress*** [1958] Movie tie-in. Brigitte Bardot photo cover.	$1.35	$4.00	$8.00
803	Ward, Jonas - ***Buchanan Gets Mad*** [1958] PBO.	$1.50	$5.00	$10.00
804	Lutz, Giles A. - ***Relentless Gun*** [1958] PBO.	$1.50	$5.00	$10.00
805	Duhart, William H. - ***The Deadly Pay-Off*** [1958] PBO. Cover by Milton Charles.	$2.00	$6.00	$12.00
806	Conroy, Albert - ***Murder In Room 13*** [1958] PBO.	$2.00	$6.00	$12.00
807	MacNeil, Neil - ***Death Takes An Option*** [1958] PBO. Cover by Gerry Powell.	$2.50	$7.50	$15.00
808	Albert, Marvin H. - ***Party Girl*** [1958] PBO. Movie photo cover. Movie tie-in.	$2.00	$6.00	$12.00
S-809	Appel, Benjamin - ***Plunder*** [1958]	$1.25	$3.75	$7.50
810	Miller, Wade - ***The Killer*** [1958]	$1.25	$3.75	$7.50
811	Brady, Matt - ***Take Your Last Look*** [1958] Photo cover.	$1.25	$3.75	$7.50
S-812	Cooper, Morton - ***The Ungilded Lily*** [1958] PBO, Cover by Milton Charles.	$1.50	$5.00	$10.00
813	Marlowe, Stephen - ***Terror Is My Trade*** [1958] PBO. Cover by Gerry Powell.	$2.00	$6.00	$12.00
814	Cannon, Curt - ***I'm Cannon-For Hire*** [1958] PBO. Cover by Milton Charles.	$2.00	$6.00	$12.00
815	Patten, Lewis B. - ***Showdown At War Cloud*** [1958] PBO.	$1.50	$5.00	$10.00
816	Castle, Frank - ***Fort Desperation*** [1958] PBO.	$1.50	$5.00	$10.00
S-817	Prather, Richard S. - ***Slab Happy*** [1958] PBO.	$2.00	$6.00	$12.00
818	Prather, Richard S. - ***Everybody Had A Gun*** [1958] Cover by Barye Phillips.	$1.25	$3.75	$7.50
819	Prather, Richard S. - ***Bodies In Bedlam*** [1958] Cover by Barye Phillips.	$1.25	$3.75	$7.50
820	Prather, Richard S. - ***The Case Of The Vanishing Beauty*** [1958]	$1.25	$3.75	$7.50
821	Prather, Richard S. - ***Find This Woman*** [1958] Cover by Barye Phillips.	$1.25	$3.75	$7.50
822	Williams, Charles - ***Man On The Run*** [1958] PBO.	$2.50	$7.50	$15.00
823	Keene, Day - ***Passage To Samoa*** [1958] PBO.	$2.50	$7.50	$15.00
824	Quarry, Nick - ***Trail Of A Tramp*** [1958] PBO.	$2.00	$6.00	$12.00

		G	VG	F
S-825	Rabe, Peter - ***Blood On The Desert*** [1958] PBO. Cover by Richard Powers.	$2.50	$7.50	$15.00
826	Albert, Marvin H. - ***Renegade Posse*** [1958]	$1.50	$5.00	$10.00
827	Telfair, Richard - ***Day Of The Gun*** [1958] PBO.	$1.50	$5.00	$10.00
S-828	Cushman, Dan - ***Naked Ebony*** [1958] Cover by Barye Phillips.	$1.25	$3.75	$7.50
S-829	Colter, Lillian - ***The Awakening Of Jenny*** [1958]	$1.25	$3.75	$7.50
830	Prather, Richard S. - ***Way Of A Wanton*** [1958]	$1.25	$3.75	$7.50
831	Whittington, Harry - ***Fires That Destroy*** [1958] Photo cover.	$1.50	$5.00	$10.00
S-832	Leinster, Murray - ***The Monster From Earth's End*** [1959] PBO. Cover by Muni.	$3.00	$9.00	$18.00
D-833	Bannon, Ann - ***I Am A Woman*** [1959] PBO. Photo cover.	$3.50	$10.00	$20.00
834	Aarons, Edward S. - ***Assignment-Carlotta Cortez*** [1959] PBO. Cover by Barye.	$2.00	$6.00	$12.00
835	Colby, Robert - ***The Captain Must Die*** [1959] PBO. Cover by Wexler.	$2.00	$6.00	$12.00
S-836	Frazee, Steve - ***Smoke In The Valley*** [1959] PBO.	$1.50	$5.00	$10.00
837	Cook, Will - ***Outcast Of Cripple Creek*** [1959] PBO.	$1.50	$5.00	$10.00
838	Prather, Richard S. - ***Darling, It's Death*** [1959] Cover by Barye Phillips.	$1.00	$3.00	$6.00
D-839	Morgan, Nancy - ***City Of Women*** [1959]	$1.50	$5.00	$10.00
S-840	Cushman, Dan - ***Jewel Of The Java Sea*** [1959] Cover by Barye Phillips.	$1.25	$3.75	$7.50
841	Baker, Jr., Ledru - ***... And Be My Love*** [1959] Cover by Barye Phillips.	$1.25	$3.75	$7.50
842	Heuman, William - ***Wagon Train West*** [1959] PBO.	$1.50	$5.00	$10.00
843	Hogan, Ray - ***Outlaw Marshal*** [1959] PBO.	$1.50	$5.00	$10.00
S-844	MacNeil, Neil - ***Third On A Seesaw*** [1959] PBO. Cover by Gerry Powell.	$2.50	$7.50	$15.00
S-845	Miller, Wade - ***Kitten With A Whip*** [1959] PBO. Photo cover.	$2.50	$7.50	$15.00
846	Albert, Marvin H. - ***That Jane From Maine*** [1959] PBO. Movie photo cover. Movie tie-in with Doris Day	$2.50	$7.50	$15.00
847	Telfair, Richard - ***The Bloody Medallion*** [1959] PBO.	$1.25	$3.75	$7.50
848	Prather, Richard S. - ***Strip For Murder*** [1959]	$1.25	$3.75	$7.50
849	Prather, Richard S. - ***Always Leave 'Em Dying*** [1959]	$1.00	$3.00	$6.00
850	Prather, Richard S. - ***Too Many Crooks*** [1959] Cover by Barye Phillips.	$1.00	$3.00	$6.00
851	Prather, Richard S. - ***The Wailing Frail*** [1959]	$1.00	$3.00	$6.00
D-852	Cassill, R. V. - ***Tempest*** [1959] PBO. Movie photo cover. Movie tie-in.	$1.50	$5.00	$10.00
S-853	Foster, Richard - ***The Rest Must Die*** [1959] PBO. Cover by Richard Powers.	$2.00	$6.00	$12.00
854	Howard, Vechel - ***Murder With Love*** [1959] PBO.	$1.50	$5.00	$10.00
855	Colby, Robert - ***Secret Of The Second Door*** [1959] PBO. Cover by Charles.	$1.35	$4.00	$8.00
856	Albert, Marvin H. - ***The Reformed Gun*** [1959] PBO.	$1.35	$4.00	$8.00
857	Chadwick, Joseph - ***Savage Breed*** [1959] PBO.	$1.35	$4.00	$8.00
858	Brewer, Gil - ***13 French Street*** [1959] Photo cover.	$1.00	$3.00	$6.00
S-859	Himmel, Richard - ***Beyond Desire*** [1959]	$1.25	$3.75	$7.50
860	Prather, Richard S. - ***Have Gat-Will Travel*** [1959]	$1.25	$3.75	$7.50
S-861	Packer, Vin - ***The Twisted Ones*** [1959] PBO. Cover by Robert Abbett.	$2.50	$7.50	$15.00
862	Whittington, Harry - ***A Ticket To Hell*** [1959] PBO. Photo cover.	$3.50	$10.00	$20.00
863	Aarons, Edward S. - ***Assignment-Helene*** [1959] PBO.	$1.50	$5.00	$10.00
864	Rabe, Peter - ***Bring Me Another Corpse*** [1959] PBO. Photo cover.	$2.50	$7.50	$15.00
865	Loomis, Noel M. - ***Above The Palo Duro*** [1959]	$1.50	$5.00	$10.00
866	Patten, Lewis B. - ***The Ruthless Men*** [1959] PBO.	$1.50	$5.00	$10.00
867	Pratt, Theodore - ***Smash-Up*** [1959] Cover by John Floherty, Jr.	$1.25	$3.75	$7.50

		G	VG	F
868	Rohmer, Sax - ***Return Of Sumuru*** [1959] Cover by James Meese.	$1.50	$5.00	$10.00
S-869	Hunt, Howard - ***The Judas Hour*** [1959] Cover by Charles.	$1.25	$3.75	$7.50
870	Schoenfeld, Howard - ***Let Them Eat Bullets*** [1959] Cover by Barye Phillips.	$1.25	$3.75	$7.50
871	O'Quinn, Allen - ***Strangers In My Bed*** [1959] Cover by Barye Phillips.	$1.25	$3.75	$7.50
872	Craig, Jonathan - ***Case Of The Nervous Nude*** [1959] PBO.	$1.50	$5.00	$10.00
873	Matcha, Jack - ***Prowler In The Night*** [1959] PBO.	$1.50	$5.00	$10.00
874	Keene, Day - ***Take A Step To Murder*** [1959] PBO. Cover by Robert Abbett.	$2.50	$7.50	$15.00
875	May, Daniel - ***Armande*** [1959] Cover by Barye Phillips.	$1.35	$4.00	$8.00
876	Shirreffs, Gordon D. - ***The Brave Rifles*** [1959]	$1.35	$4.00	$8.00
877	Lutz, Giles A. - ***The Homing Bullet*** [1959]	$1.35	$4.00	$8.00
878	Howard, Vechel - ***Murder On Her Mind*** [1959] PBO.	$1.50	$5.00	$10.00
879	Ozaki, Milton K. - ***Wake Up And Scream*** [1959] PBO.	$1.50	$5.00	$10.00
880	Marlowe, Stephen - ***Homicide Is My Game*** [1959] PBO.	$1.50	$5.00	$10.00
881	McPartland, John - ***The Kingdom Of Johnny Cool*** [1959] PBO. Photo cover.	$1.50	$5.00	$10.00
882	Dean, Dudley - ***Lawless Guns*** [1959] PBO.	$1.35	$4.00	$8.00
883	Telfair, Richard - ***Wyoming Jones For Hire*** [1959] PBO.	$1.35	$4.00	$8.00
884	MacDonald, John D. - ***Weep For Me*** [1959] Cover by Barye Phillips.	$2.00	$6.00	$12.00
885	Daniels, Frank - ***The Mating Cry*** [1959]	$1.35	$4.00	$8.00
886	Fischer, Bruno - ***House Of Flesh*** [1959] Cover by Barye Phillips.	$1.00	$3.00	$6.00
S-887	Prather, Richard S. - ***Over Her Dear Body*** [1959] PBO. Cover by Barye Phillips.	$1.50	$5.00	$10.00
888	Race, Philip - ***Killer Take All*** [1959] PBO.	$1.50	$5.00	$10.00
889	Whittington, Harry - ***Backwoods Tramp*** [1959] PBO. Cover by Barye Phillips.	$3.50	$10.00	$20.00
890	Telfair, Richard - ***The Corpse That Talked*** [1959] PBO	$1.50	$5.00	$10.00
891	Schulman, Arnold - ***A Hole In The Head*** [1959] PBO. Movie photo cover. Movie tie-in with Frank Sinatra.	$1.35	$4.00	$8.00
892	Hogan, Ray - ***Marshal Without A Badge*** [1959] PBO. Cover by Lesser.	$1.35	$4.00	$8.00
893	L'Amour, Louis - ***To Tame A Land*** [1959]	$2.50	$7.50	$15.00
894	MacDonald, John D. - ***All These Condemned*** [1959] Photo cover.	$2.50	$7.50	$15.00
895	Aarons, Edward S. - ***Assignment-To Disaster*** [1959] Cover by Charles.	$1.00	$3.00	$6.00
896	Prather, Richard S. - ***Three's A Shroud*** [1959]	$1.00	$3.00	$6.00
897	Brown, Wenzell - ***Cry Kill*** [1959] PBO. Cover by James Meese.	$2.50	$7.50	$15.00
898	MacNeil, Neil - ***2 Guns For Hire*** [1959] PBO.	$2.00	$6.00	$12.00
899	Foster, Richard - ***Bier For A Chaser*** [1959] PBO. Cover by Barye Phillips.	$2.00	$6.00	$12.00
900	Tomerlin, John - ***Return To Vikki*** [1959] PBO. Photo cover.	$1.35	$4.00	$8.00
901	Fischer, Bruno - ***The Lustful Ape*** [1959]	$1.50	$5.00	$10.00
902	Albert, Marvin H. - ***Rider From Wind River*** [1959] PBO.	$1.35	$4.00	$8.00
S-903	Packer, Vin - ***The Thrill Kids*** [1959]	$2.00	$6.00	$12.00
904	Anthology - ***Cartoon Fun*** [1959] Cover by VIP. Cartoon book.	$1.00	$3.00	$6.00
905	L'Amour, Louis - ***Hondo*** [1959]	$2.50	$7.50	$15.00
906	Aarons, Edward S. - ***Assignment-Stella Marni*** [1959] Cover by Robert Abbett.	$1.00	$3.00	$6.00
S-907	MacDonald, John D. - ***The Beach Girls*** [1959] PBO.	$5.50	$17.50	$35.00
S-908	Williams, Charles - ***Uncle Sagamore And His Girls*** [1959] PBO.	$2.50	$7.50	$15.00
909	McPartland, John - ***The Last Night*** [1959] PBO.	$2.50	$7.50	$15.00

		G	VG	F
S-910	Demaris, Ovid - ***The Slasher*** [1959] PBO. Cover by Barye Phillips.	$2.00	$6.00	$12.00
S-911	Aarons, Edward S. - ***Assignment-Lili Lamaris*** [1959] PBO. Cover by Barye Phillips.	$1.50	$5.00	$10.00
912	Savage, Jr., Les & Dean, Dudley - ***Gun Shy*** [1959] PBO. Cover by A. Leslie Ross.	$1.35	$4.00	$8.00
S-913	Hilton, Joseph - ***Angels In The Gutter*** [1959] Photo cover.	$1.25	$3.75	$7.50
914	Marlowe, Stephen - ***Trouble Is My Name*** [1959] Cover by Kimmel.	$1.00	$3.00	$6.00
915	Rabe, Peter - ***It's My Funeral*** [1959] Cover by Floherty, Jr.	$1.25	$3.75	$7.50
916	Ernenwein, Leslie - ***Bullet Barricade*** [1959]	$1.00	$3.00	$6.00
S-917	Brown, Wenzell - ***Teen-Age Mafia*** [1959] PBO. Cover by Barye Phillips.	$4.00	$12.50	$25.00
918	Albert, Marvin H. - ***Pillow Talk*** [1959] PBO. Movie photo cover. Movie tie-in with Rock Hudson and Doris Day.	$2.50	$7.50	$15.00
S-919	Bannon, Ann - ***Women In The Shadows*** [1959] PBO. Photo cover.	$3.50	$10.00	$20.00
920	Patten, Lewis B. - ***Top Man With A Gun*** [1959] PBO.	$1.35	$4.00	$8.00
921	Cassill, R. V. - ***The Wife Next Door*** [1959] PBO.	$1.35	$4.00	$8.00
S-922	Dixon, H. Vernor - ***To Hell Together*** [1959] Cover by Barye Phillips.	$1.00	$3.00	$6.00
923	Aarons, Edward S. - ***Assignment-Suicide*** [1959]	$1.00	$3.00	$6.00
924	Blood, Matthew - ***The Avenger*** [1959]	$1.00	$3.00	$6.00
925	Dean, Dudley - ***Song Of The Gun*** [1959]	$1.25	$3.75	$7.50
D-926	Marlowe, Stephen & Prather, Richard S. - ***Double In Trouble*** [1959] PBO. Cover by Barye Phillips.	$1.50	$5.00	$10.00
927	Faulkner, John - ***Ain't Gonna Rain No More*** [1959] PBO. Cover by Hooks.	$1.50	$5.00	$10.00
928	Fischer, Bruno - ***Second-Hand Nude*** [1959] PBO.	$1.50	$5.00	$10.00
S-929	Rohmer, Sax - ***Emperor Fu Manchu*** [1959] PBO. Cover by Abbett.	$4.00	$12.50	$25.00
930	Craig, Jonathan - ***Case Of The Village Tramp*** [1959] PBO.	$1.50	$5.00	$10.00
931	Keene, Day - ***Too Hot To Hold*** [1959] PBO.	$2.50	$7.50	$15.00
932	Telfair, Richard - ***The Secret Of Apache Canyon*** [1959]	$1.35	$4.00	$8.00
933	Pratt, Theodore - ***The Tormented*** [1959]	$1.00	$3.00	$6.00
934	Roberts, Lee - ***Little Sister*** [1959] Photo cover.	$1.00	$3.00	$6.00
935	Frazee, Steve - ***Many Rivers To Cross*** [1959]	$1.00	$3.00	$6.00
936	Miller, Wade - ***The Big Guy*** [1959] Cover by Barye Phillips.	$1.00	$3.00	$6.00
S-937	Leinster, Murray - ***Four From Planet 5*** [1959] PBO. Cover by Lehr.	$2.00	$6.00	$12.00
938	Quarry, Nick - ***The Girl With No Place To Hide*** [1959] PBO.	$1.50	$5.00	$10.00
939	Rabe, Peter - ***Time Enough To Die*** [1959] PBO. Photo cover.	$2.50	$7.50	$15.00
940	Colby, Robert - ***The Deadly Desire*** [1959] PBO.	$1.50	$5.00	$10.00
S-941	Packer, Vin - ***The Young And Violent*** [1959] Cover by Meese.	$1.25	$3.75	$7.50
942	Fox, Gardner F. - ***Witness This Woman*** [1959] PBO. Cover by Barye Phillips.	$3.00	$9.00	$18.00
943	Howard, Vechel - ***Stage To Painted Creek*** [1959]	$1.35	$4.00	$8.00
944	Heuman, William - ***The Range Buster*** [1959] Cover by Frank McCarthy.	$1.00	$3.00	$6.00
945	Miller, Wade - ***The Tiger's Wife*** [1959] Cover by Hulings.	$1.00	$3.00	$6.00
S-946	Sheridan, Jack - ***Thunderclap*** [1959]	$1.00	$3.00	$6.00
947	Marlowe, Stephen - ***Danger Is My Line*** [1959] PBO.	$1.50	$5.00	$10.00
948	Garrity - ***Kiss Off The Dead*** [1960] PBO. Cover by Abbett.	$2.00	$6.00	$12.00
949	White, Lionel - ***Lament For A Virgin*** [1960] PBO. Photo cover.	$2.00	$6.00	$12.00
950	Brewer, Gil - ***Backwoods Teaser*** [1960] PBO. Cover by Robert McGinns.	$2.50	$7.50	$15.00
951	Ward, Jonas - ***Buchanan's Revenge*** [1960] PBO.	$1.35	$4.00	$8.00
952	Tessitore, John - ***Nero's Mistress*** [1960] PBO. Movie tie-in with Brigitte Bardot.	$1.50	$5.00	$10.00

		G	VG	F
S-953	Idell, Albert - ***This Woman*** [1960] Cover by Barye Phillips.	$1.25	$3.75	$7.50
954	Craig, Jonathan - ***So Young, So Wicked*** [1960] Cover by Barye Phillips.	$1.00	$3.00	$6.00
955	L'Amour, Louis - ***Heller With A Gun*** [1960] Movie photo cover. Movie tie-in with Sophia Loren.	$3.50	$10.00	$20.00
S-956	Brown, Wenzell - ***Teen-Age Terror*** [1960]	$1.50	$5.00	$10.00
957	Hamilton, Donald - ***Death Of A Citizen*** [1960] PBO.	$2.00	$6.00	$12.00
958	Fleischman, A. S. - ***Yellowleg*** [1960] PBO.	$1.50	$5.00	$10.00
959	Whittington, Harry - ***Heat Of Night*** [1960] PBO.	$3.50	$10.00	$20.00
960	Demaris, Ovid - ***The Extortioners*** [1960] PBO.	$1.50	$5.00	$10.00
S-961	MacDonald, John D. - ***Slam The Big Door*** [1960] PBO.	$5.50	$17.50	$35.00
S-962	MacDonald, John D. - ***The Damned*** [1960] Cover by Barye Phillips.	$2.00	$6.00	$12.00
963	MacDonald, John D. - ***Dead Low Tide*** [1960]	$2.00	$6.00	$12.00
964	MacNeil, Neil - ***Hot Dam*** [1960] PBO.	$2.50	$7.50	$15.00
S-965	Bannon, Ann - ***Odd Girl Out*** [1960] Cover by Barye Phillips.	$1.50	$5.00	$10.00
S-966	Packer, Vin - ***5:45 To Suburbia*** [1960]	$1.25	$3.75	$7.50
967	Rabe, Peter - ***My Lovely Executioner*** [1960] PBO. Photo cover.	$2.50	$7.50	$15.00
968	Roberts, Lee - ***Death Of A Ladies' Man*** [1960] PBO.	$2.00	$6.00	$12.00
969	Preston, Charles - editor - ***Thimk*** [1960] PBO. Cartoon book.	$1.50	$5.00	$10.00
970	Castle, Frank - ***Blood Moon*** [1960] PBO.	$1.35	$4.00	$8.00
971	Aarons, Edward S. - ***Assignment-Budapest*** [1960] Cover by Barye Phillips.	$1.00	$3.00	$6.00
972	Douglas, Malcolm - ***Pure Sweet Hell*** [1960] Cover by Barye Phillips.	$1.00	$3.00	$6.00
D-973	Gehman, Richard - ***Driven*** [1960]	$1.25	$3.75	$7.50
974	Fowler, Kenneth - ***Outcast Of Murder Mesa*** [1960]	$1.00	$3.00	$6.00
S-975	Keene, Day & Pruyn, Leonard - ***World Without Women*** [1960] PBO. Cover by McGinnis.	$3.50	$10.00	$20.00
S-976	Packer, Vin - ***The Girl On The Best Seller List*** [1960] PBO. Cover by McGinnis.	$2.00	$6.00	$12.00
S-977	Bannon, Ann - ***Journey To A Woman*** [1960] PBO. Photo cover.	$3.50	$10.00	$20.00
978	Cook, Will - ***The Wranglers*** [1960] PBO.	$1.35	$4.00	$8.00
979	Aarons, Edward S. - ***Assignment-Zoraya*** [1960] PBO. Cover by Milton Charles.	$1.50	$5.00	$10.00
980	Boyd, Frank - ***Johnny Staccato*** [1960] PBO.	$2.00	$6.00	$12.00
981	Ozaki, Milton K. - ***Inquest*** [1960] PBO. Cover by Barye Phillips.	$1.50	$5.00	$10.00
S-982	Krim, Seymour - editor - ***The Beats*** [1960] PBO. Photo cover.	$2.50	$7.50	$15.00
983	MacDonald, John D. - ***Murder For The Bride*** [1960]	$2.50	$7.50	$15.00
984	Chadwick, Joseph - ***Rebel Raider*** [1960] Cover by A. Leslie Ross.	$1.00	$3.00	$6.00
985	Castle, Frank - ***Lovely And Lethal*** [1960]	$1.00	$3.00	$6.00
986	Marlowe, Stephen - ***Death Is My Comrade*** [1960] PBO. Cover by Charles.	$1.50	$5.00	$10.00
987	Brewer, Gil - ***The Three-Way Split*** [1960] PBO.	$2.50	$7.50	$15.00
988	Bonham, Frank - ***One For Sleep*** [1960] PBO.	$1.35	$4.00	$8.00
S-989	Coppel, Alfred - ***Dark December*** [1960] PBO.	$2.50	$7.50	$15.00
S-990	Prather, Richard S. - ***Dance With The Dead*** [1960] PBO. Cover by Barye Phillips.	$1.50	$5.00	$10.00
992	Heuman, William - ***Ride For Texas*** [1960]	$1.35	$4.00	$8.00
994	Becker, Stephen - ***Shanghai Incident*** [1960] Cover by McGinnis.	$1.00	$3.00	$6.00
995	Foster, Richard - ***Too Late For Mourning*** [1960] PBO. Cover by Abbett.	$2.00	$6.00	$12.00
996	Rabe, Peter - ***Murder Me For Nickels*** [1960] PBO.	$2.50	$7.50	$15.00
S-997	Anthology - ***Thirteen Great Stories Of Science-Fiction*** [1960] PBO. Cover by Powers.	$2.00	$6.00	$12.00
998	White, Lionel - ***Steal Big*** [1960] PBO. Cover by Abbett.	$2.00	$6.00	$12.00

		G	VG	F
999	Telfair, Richard - ***Sundance*** [1960] PBO.	$2.00	$6.00	$12.00
S-1000	Trinian, John - ***North Beach Girl*** [1960] PBO.	$2.00	$6.00	$12.00
1001	Miller, Wade - ***South Of The Sun*** [1960] Cover by Barye Phillips.	$1.00	$3.00	$6.00
S-1002	Chessman, Caryl - ***The Kid Was A Killer*** [1960] PBO.	$2.50	$7.50	$15.00
1003	Marlowe, Stephen - ***The Second Longest Night*** [1960] Cover by Ernest Chiriaka.	$1.00	$3.00	$6.00
S-1005	Shulman, Irving - ***College Confidential*** [1960] PBO. Movie photo cover. Movie tie-in.	$2.50	$7.50	$15.00
1006	Telfair, Richard - ***Scream Bloody Murder*** [1960] PBO.	$2.00	$6.00	$12.00
1007	Demaris, Ovid - ***The Enforcer*** [1960] PBO. Cover by Darcy.	$1.50	$5.00	$10.00
S-1008	Gifford, Lee - ***Pieces Of The Game*** [1960] PBO.	$1.50	$5.00	$10.00
D-1009	Anthology edited by Ann Aldrich - ***Carol In A Thousand Cities*** [1960] PBO. Photo cover.	$3.50	$10.00	$20.00
1010	Olsen, T. V. - ***McGivern*** [1960]	$1.50	$5.00	$10.00
1011	Fischer, Bruno - ***Murder In The Raw*** [1960]	$1.00	$3.00	$6.00
S-1012	Williams, Charles - ***Hell Hath No Fury*** [1960]	$1.00	$3.00	$6.00
S-1013	Brown, Wenzel - ***The Murder Kick*** [1960] PBO.	$3.00	$9.00	$18.00
1014	Dean, Dudley - ***Lila My lovely*** [1960] PBO. Photo cover.	$1.35	$4.00	$8.00
S-1015	MacDonald, John D. - ***The Only Girl In The Game*** [1960] PBO.	$5.00	$15.00	$30.00
1016	Olsen, T. V. - ***High Lawless*** [1960] PBO.	$1.35	$4.00	$8.00
1017	Cooper, Saul - ***It Started In Naples*** [1960] PBO. Photo cover. Movie tie-in.	$1.35	$4.00	$8.00
1018	Marlowe, Stephen - ***Peril Is My Pay*** [1960] PBO.	$1.50	$5.00	$10.00
1019	Wainer, Cord - ***Mountain Girl*** [1960] Cover by Barye Phillips.	$1.00	$3.00	$6.00
1020	White, Lionel - ***Hostage For A Hood*** [1960] Cover by Meese.	$1.00	$3.00	$6.00
1021	Ward, Jonas - ***The Name's Buchanan*** [1960]	$1.00	$3.00	$6.00
S-1022	Prather, Richard S. - ***Find This Woman*** [1960] Cover by Barye Phillips.	$1.00	$3.00	$6.00
1023	Aarons, Edward S. - ***Hell To Eternity*** [1960] PBO. Movie tie-in. Cover by Barye Phillips.	$1.50	$5.00	$10.00
1024	Avallone, Mike - ***Meanwhile Back At The Morgue*** [1960] PBO. Photo cover.	$1.50	$5.00	$10.00
1025	Hamilton, Donald - ***The Wrecking Crew*** [1960] PBO.	$1.50	$5.00	$10.00
1026	Ward, Jonas - ***Buchanan On The Prod*** [1960] PBO.	$1.35	$4.00	$8.00
1027	Miller, Wade - ***Sinner Take All*** [1960] PBO.	$1.50	$5.00	$10.00
S-1028	Pratt, Theodore - ***Seminole*** [1960]	$1.00	$3.00	$6.00
S-1029	Prather, Richard S. - ***Strip For Murder*** [1962] Cover by Barye Phillips.	$1.00	$3.00	$6.00
1030	Frazee, Steve - ***He Rode Alone*** [1960]	$1.00	$3.00	$6.00
1031	Faulkner, John - ***Uncle Good's Week-End Party*** [1960] PBO. Cover by Barye Phillips.	$2.00	$6.00	$12.00
S-1032	Prather, Richard S. - ***Way Of A Wanton*** [1960]	$1.00	$3.00	$6.00
1033	Quarry, Nick - ***No Chance In Hell*** [1960] PBO. Cover by Abbett.	$1.50	$5.00	$10.00
1034	Reed-Marr, P. J. - ***Hot Saturday*** [1960] PBO.	$1.50	$5.00	$10.00
S-1036	Aarons, Edward S. - ***Assignment: Mara Tirana*** [1960] PBO.	$1.50	$5.00	$10.00
1037	Heatter, Basil - ***The Trouble With Love*** [1960]	$1.35	$4.00	$8.00
1038	Anthology - ***Vip's All New Bar Guide*** [1960] PBO. Cover by Vip. Cartoon book.	$1.35	$4.00	$8.00
S-1039	Prather, Richard S. - ***Darling, It's Death*** [1960]	$1.00	$3.00	$6.00
S-1040	Prather, Richard S. - ***Always Leave 'Em Dying*** [1960]	$1.00	$3.00	$6.00
1041	L'Amour, Louis - ***The Tall Stranger*** [1960]	$2.50	$7.50	$15.00
S-1042	Brown, Wenzell - ***Run, Chico Run*** [1960]	$1.50	$5.00	$10.00
1043	Colby, Robert - ***The Star Trap*** [1960] PBO.	$1.50	$5.00	$10.00
1044	Whittington, Harry - ***Hell Can Wait*** [1960] PBO.	$3.50	$10.00	$20.00
1045	Evarts, Hal G. - ***The Turncoat*** [1960] PBO.	$1.50	$5.00	$10.00
S-1046	Prather, Richard - editor - ***The Comfortable Coffin*** [1960] PBO. Cover by Barye Phillips.	$2.00	$6.00	$12.00

		G	VG	F
S-1047	Cameron, Lou - ***Angel's Flight*** [1960] PBO. Cover by Hooks.	$1.50	$5.00	$10.00
1048	Jessup, Richard - ***Sabadilla*** [1960] PBO.	$1.50	$5.00	$10.00
S-1049	Prather, Richard S. - ***Have Gat-Will Travel*** [1962] Cover by Barye Phillips.	$1.00	$3.00	$6.00
1050	Whittington, Harry - ***Desire In The Dust*** [1960] Cover by Barye Phillips. Movie tie-in.	$1.50	$5.00	$10.00
S-1051	Prather, Richard S. - ***The Wailing Frail*** [1962] Cover by Barye Phillips.	$1.00	$3.00	$6.00
S-1052	MacDonald John D. - ***The Brass Cupcake*** [1960]	$2.00	$6.00	$12.00
1053	Quarry, Nick - ***Til It Hurts*** [1960] PBO. Cover by Barye Phillips.	$1.50	$5.00	$10.00
1054	Fischer, Bruno - ***The Girl Between*** [1960] PBO.	$1.50	$5.00	$10.00
1055	MacNeil, Neil - ***The Death Ride*** [1960] PBO.	$2.50	$7.50	$15.00
1056	Halleran, E. E. - ***The Dark Raiders*** [1960] PBO.	$1.35	$4.00	$8.00
S-1057	Budrys, Algis - ***Rogue Moon*** [1960] PBO. Cover by Powers.	$2.00	$6.00	$12.00
1058	Whittington, Harry - ***Connolly's Woman*** [1960] PBO.	$3.50	$10.00	$20.00
S-1059	Prather, Richard S. - ***Too Many Crooks*** [1960] Cover by Barye Phillips.	$1.00	$3.00	$6.00
S-1061	MacDonald, John D. - ***The Neon Jungle*** [1960]	$2.00	$6.00	$12.00
1062	Grantland, Keith - ***Run From The Hunter*** [1960] Cover by Barye Phillips.	$1.35	$4.00	$8.00
1063	Wormser, Richard - ***The Late Mrs. Five*** [1960] PBO.	$1.50	$5.00	$10.00
S-1064	Gonzales, John - ***End Of A J.D.*** [1960] PBO. Cover by Hooks.	$3.00	$9.00	$18.00
S-1065	Craig, Jonathan - ***Case Of The Laughing Virgin*** [1960] PBO. Cover by George Gross.	$1.50	$5.00	$10.00
S-1066	Bannon, Ann - ***The Marriage*** [1960] PBO.	$3.50	$10.00	$20.00
1067	Olsen, T. V. - ***Gunswift*** [1960] PBO.	$1.35	$4.00	$8.00
S-1068	Longstreet, Stephen - ***Wild Harvest*** [1960] PBO. Cover by McGinnis.	$1.50	$5.00	$10.00
1069	MacDonald, John D. - ***Judge Me Not*** [1960]	$2.00	$6.00	$12.00
1071	Shirreffs, Gordon D. - ***Ambush On The Mesa*** [1960]	$1.00	$3.00	$6.00
S-1072	Prather, Richard S. - ***Shell Scott's Seven Slaughters*** [1961] PBO.	$2.00	$6.00	$12.00
S-1073	Aarons, Edward S. - ***Assignment-Lowlands*** [1961] PBO. Cover by Rader.	$1.50	$5.00	$10.00
S-1074	Packer, Vin - ***The Damnation Of Adam Blessing*** [1961] PBO. Cover by McGinnis.	$1.50	$5.00	$10.00
S-1075	Braly, Malcolm - ***Felony Tank*** [1961] PBO.	$1.35	$4.00	$8.00
S-1076	MacDonald, John D. - ***Where Is Janice Gantry?*** [1961] PBO.	$4.50	$14.00	$28.00
S-1077	Telfair, Richard - ***The Slavers*** [1961] PBO. Cover by Barye Phillips.	$1.35	$4.00	$8.00
S-1078	Marlowe, Stephen - ***Murder Is My Dish*** [1961] Cover by Kimmel.	$1.00	$3.00	$6.00
S-1079	Conroy, Albert - ***Nice Guys Finish Dead*** [1961]	$1.00	$3.00	$6.00
S-1080	Short, Luke - ***Barren Land Showdown*** [1961]	$1.00	$3.00	$6.00
S-1081	Ernenwein, Leslie - ***High Gun*** [1961]	$1.00	$3.00	$6.00
S-1082	Hamilton, Donald - ***The Removers*** [1961] PBO. Cover by Barye Phillips.	$1.50	$5.00	$10.00
S-1083	Goodis, David - ***Night Squad*** [1961] PBO.	$10.00	$30.00	$60.00
S-1084	Cook, Will - ***Badman's Holiday*** [1961]	$1.50	$5.00	$10.00
S-1085	Block, Lawrence - ***Mona*** [1961] PBO. Author's first book.	$4.00	$12.50	$25.00
S-1086	Young, Carter Travis - ***Shadow Of A Gun*** [1961] PBO.	$1.35	$4.00	$8.00
S-1087	Sanders, W. Franklin - ***Whip Hand*** [1961] PBO. Cover by Abbett.	$1.35	$4.00	$8.00
S-1088	Demaris, Ovid - ***The Hoods Take Over*** [1961] Cover by Barye Phillips.	$1.00	$3.00	$6.00
S-1090	McPartland, John - ***Ripe Fruit*** [1961]	$1.25	$3.75	$7.50
S-1091	Aarons, Edward S. - ***Assignment-Burma Girl*** [1961] PBO.	$1.35	$4.00	$8.00
S-1092	Prather, Richard S. - ***Pattern For Panic*** [1961] Cover by Barye Phillips.	$1.50	$5.00	$10.00

		G	VG	F
S-1093	Wagner, Geoffrey - ***Season Of Assassins*** [1961] PBO. Cover by Abbett.	$1.50	$5.00	$10.00
S-1094	Telfair, Richard - ***Good Luck, Sucker*** [1961]	$1.25	$3.75	$7.50
S-1095	Alter, Robert Edmond - ***Swamp Sister*** [1961] PBO. Cover by Hooks.	$1.50	$5.00	$10.00
S-1097	Ward, Jonas - ***One-Man Massacre*** [1961] Cover by Kimmel.	$1.00	$3.00	$6.00
S-1098	Marlowe, Stephen - ***Killers Are My Meat*** [1961] Cover by Gerry Powell.	$1.00	$3.00	$6.00
S-1100	Gonzales, John - ***Death For Mr. Big*** [1961] Cover by Barye Phillips.	$1.00	$3.00	$6.00
S-1101	Krepps, Robert W. - ***The Big Gamble*** [1961] PBO. Cover by Barye Phillips. Movie tie-in.	$1.35	$4.00	$8.00
S-1102	Cassill, R. V. - ***Nurses' Quarters*** [1961] PBO. Cover by Barye Phillips.	$ .75	$2.50	$5.00
S-1103	Davis, Gordon - ***House Dick*** [1961] PBO. Cover by McGinnis.	$1.35	$4.00	$8.00
S-1104	Trinian, John - ***The Savage Breast*** [1961] PBO. Cover by Barye Phillips.	$1.50	$5.00	$10.00
S-1105	Jessup, Richard - ***Chuka*** [1961] PBO.	$1.50	$5.00	$10.00
S-1106	Miller, Sigmund - ***The Snow Leopard*** [1961] PBO.	$1.35	$4.00	$8.00
S-1108	Goodis, David - ***Street Of No Return*** [1961] Cover by Barye Phillips.	$5.50	$17.50	$35.00
S-1109	Flora, Fletcher - ***Park Avenue Tramp*** [1961] Photo cover.	$1.00	$3.00	$6.00
S-1110	Fischer, Bruno - ***So Wicked My Love*** [1961] Photo cover.	$1.00	$3.00	$6.00
S-1112	MacDonald, John D. - ***Area Of Suspicion*** [1961] Cover by Barye Phillips.	$2.00	$6.00	$12.00
S-1113	Daniels, Norman - ***Suddenly By Shotgun*** [1961] PBO.	$1.35	$4.00	$8.00
S-1114	Cameron, Lou - ***The Big Red Ball*** [1961] PBO.	$1.35	$4.00	$8.00
S-1115	Morheim & Kaufman - ***Isolation Booth*** [1961] PBO. Cover by Hooks.	$1.25	$3.75	$7.50
S-1116	Marlowe, Stephen - ***Man Hunt Is My Mission*** [1961] PBO.	$1.35	$4.00	$8.00
S-1117	Olsen, T. V. - ***Ramrod Rider*** [1961] PBO.	$1.35	$4.00	$8.00
S-1118	Aarons, Edward S. - ***Assignment-Angelina*** [1961] Cover by Powell.	$1.00	$3.00	$6.00
S-1121	Howard, Vechel - ***The Last Sunset*** [1961] Movie photo cover. Movie tie-in with Rock Hudson.	$1.25	$3.75	$7.50
S-1122	Vicker, Angus - ***Fever Heat*** [1961]	$1.00	$3.00	$6.00
S-1123	Whittington, Harry - ***Desert Stake-Out*** [1961] PBO.	$3.50	$10.00	$20.00
S-1124	Judd, Harrison - ***Shadow Of A Doubt*** [1961] PBO. Photo cover.	$1.35	$4.00	$8.00
D-1125	Bishop, Leonard - ***Make My Bed In Hell*** [1961] PBO. Cover by Zuckerberg.	$1.35	$4.00	$8.00
S-1126	Heatter, Basil - ***Any Man's Girl*** [1961]	$1.35	$4.00	$8.00
S-1127	Duncan, Peter - ***The Telltale Tart*** [1961] PBO. Cover by Hooks.	$1.35	$4.00	$8.00
S-1128	Miller, Wade - ***Stolen Woman*** [1961]	$1.00	$3.00	$6.00
S-1129	Prather, Richard S. - ***Take A Murder, Darling*** [1961] Cover by Barye Phillips.	$1.00	$3.00	$6.00
S-1130	Goodis, David - ***Cassidy's Girl*** [1961] Cover by Barye Phillips.	$4.00	$12.50	$25.00
S-1132	Brown, Fredric - ***Madball*** [1961] Cover by Hooks.	$3.00	$9.00	$18.00
S-1133	Wormer, Richard - ***Drive East On 66*** [1961] PBO.	$1.35	$4.00	$8.00
S-1134	Whittington, Harry - ***God's Back Was Turned*** [1961] PBO. Cover by Meese.	$3.50	$10.00	$20.00
S-1135	Flagg, John - ***The Paradise Gun*** [1961] PBO. Photo cover.	$1.35	$4.00	$8.00
S-1136	Demaris, Ovid - ***"Candyleg"*** [1961] PBO.	$1.35	$4.00	$8.00
S-1139	Prather, Richard S. - ***The Scrambled Yeggs*** [1961]	$1.00	$3.00	$6.00
S-1140	Packer, Vin - ***Three Day Terror*** [1961]	$1.00	$3.00	$6.00
S-1142	Hasty, John Eugene - ***Angel With Dirty Wings*** [1961] PBO.	$1.35	$4.00	$8.00
S-1143	Pratt, Theodore - ***Tropical Disturbance*** [1961] PBO. Cover by McGinnis.	$1.35	$4.00	$8.00
S-1144	Prather, Richard S. - ***Dig That Crazy Grave*** [1961] PBO. Cover by Barye Phillips.	$1.50	$5.00	$10.00

		G	VG	F
1145	Burnett, W. R. - ***Round The Clock At Volari's*** [1961] PBO.	$2.00	$6.00	$12.00
S-1146	Packer, Vin - ***Something In The Shadows*** [1961] PBO. Cover by The Dillons.	$1.50	$5.00	$10.00
S-1148	Lutz, Giles A. - ***To Hell-And Texas*** [1961]	$1.00	$3.00	$6.00
S-1150	Quarry, Nick - ***Some Die Hard*** [1961] PBO. Cover by Johnson.	$1.35	$4.00	$8.00
S-1151	Calef, Noel - ***Frantic*** [1961]	$1.25	$3.75	$7.50
S-1153	Vonnegut, Jr., Kurt - ***Canary In A Cat House*** [1961] PBO. Author's first book. Cover by The Dillons.	$15.00	$45.00	$90.00
S-1154	Michaels, Dale - ***The Warring Breed*** [1961] PBO. Cover by Bill Johnson.	$1.35	$4.00	$8.00
S-1156	Woolrich, Cornell - ***Savage Bride*** [1961] Cover by Barye Phillips.	$1.35	$4.00	$8.00
S-1157	Prather, Richard S. - ***Dagger Of Flesh*** [1962]	$1.00	$3.00	$6.00
S-1160	Brown, Wenzell - ***Girls On The Rampage*** [1961] PBO.	$3.50	$10.00	$20.00
S-1161	Ellison, Harlan - ***Rockabilly*** [1961] PBO. Cover by Hooks.	$25.00	$75.00	$180.00
S-1162	Block, Lawrence - ***Death Pulls A Doublecross*** [1961] PBO. Photo cover.	$2.50	$7.50	$15.00
S-1163	Anthology edited by Harry Kurtzman - ***Help!*** [1961] PBO. Photo cover.	$2.50	$7.50	$15.00
S-1164	Aarons, Edward S. - ***The Defenders*** [1961] PBO. TV tie-in.	$1.50	$5.00	$10.00
S-1166	Prather, Richard S. - ***Lie Down Killer*** [1961] Cover by Barye Phillips.	$1.00	$3.00	$6.00
S-1167	Albert, Marvin H. - ***Apache Rising*** [1961]	$1.00	$3.00	$6.00
S-1168	Olsen, T. V. - ***Brand Of The Star*** [1961] PBO.	$1.35	$4.00	$8.00
D-1169	Krepps, Robert - ***El Cid*** [1961] PBO. Movie tie-in.	$1.35	$4.00	$8.00
S-1170	Garrity - ***Cry Me A Killer*** [1961] PBO. Cover by Hooks.	$1.50	$5.00	$10.00
S-1171	Torres, Tereska - ***Women's Barracks*** [1961] Cover by Barye Phillips.	$1.00	$3.00	$6.00
S-1172	Jessup, Richard - ***Wolf Cop*** [1961] PBO. Cover by Bill Johnson.	$1.25	$3.75	$7.50
S-1173	Marshall, Joseph R. - ***Carla*** [1961] PBO.	$1.25	$3.75	$7.50
D-1174	Osborne, O. O. - ***The Rise And Fall Of Dr. Carey*** [1961]	$ .75	$2.50	$5.00
S-1175	O'Farrell, William - ***Gypsy, Go Home*** [1961] PBO. Cover by Barye Phillips.	$1.50	$5.00	$10.00
D-1176	Hassel, Sven - ***Wheels Of Terror*** [1961]	$1.35	$4.00	$8.00
S-1177	MacDonald, John D. - ***One Monday We Killed Them All*** [1961] PBO. Cover by Bill Johnson.	$6.00	$20.00	$40.00
S-1178	Bonham, Frank - ***The Skin Game*** [1961]	$1.35	$4.00	$8.00
S-1179	Daniels, Norman - ***Jennifer James, R.N.*** [1961] PBO. Cover by Mitchell Hooks.	$ .75	$2.50	$5.00
S-1180	Heuman, William - ***Heller From Texas*** [1961] Cover by Kimmel.	$1.00	$3.00	$6.00
S-1181	Kantor, MacKinlay - ***One Wild Oat*** [1961] Cover by Barye Phillips.	$1.00	$3.00	$6.00
S-1182	MacNeil, Neil - ***Mexican Slay Ride*** [1962] PBO. Cover by Hooks.	$2.00	$6.00	$12.00
S-1183	Cameron, Lou - ***The Sky Divers*** [1962]	$1.25	$3.75	$7.50
S-1184	Marlowe, Dan J. - ***The Name Of The Game Is Death*** [1962] PBO. Cover by Barye Phillips.	$1.35	$4.00	$8.00
S-1185	Anthology edited by Ashley Halsey - ***The Perfect Squelch*** [1962] PBO. Cartoon and joke book.	$1.25	$3.75	$7.50
S-1186	Costigan, Lee - ***The New Breed*** [1962] PBO. Cover by Barye Phillips. TV tie-in.	$1.35	$4.00	$8.00
D-1187	Boswell & Thompson - ***The Girl In Lover's Lane*** [1962] Photo cover.	$1.25	$3.75	$7.50
D-1188	Samuels, Charles & Louise - ***The Girl In The House Of Hate*** [1962] Photo cover.	$1.25	$3.75	$7.50
S-1189	Aarons, Edward S. - ***Assignment-Madeleine*** [1962]	$1.00	$3.00	$6.00
1190	Whittington, Harry - ***A Haven For The Damned*** [1962]	$1.50	$5.00	$10.00

		G	VG	F
S-1191	Vonnegut, Jr., Kurt - ***Mother Night*** [1962] PBO. Cover by The Dillons.	$10.00	$30.00	$60.00
S-1192	Bloch, Robert - ***The Couch*** [1962] PBO. Photo cover. Movie tie-in.	$6.00	$20.00	$40.00
S-1193	Albert, Marvin H. - ***Lover Come Back*** [1962] Movie photo cover. Movie tie-in with Rock Hudson & Doris Day.	$1.50	$5.00	$10.00
S-1194	Hamilton, Donald - ***The Silencers*** [1962] PBO.	$1.35	$4.00	$8.00
S-1196	Aldrich, Ann - ***We Walk Alone*** [1962]	$1.35	$4.00	$8.00
S-1197	Shulman, Irving - ***The Notorious Landlady*** [1962] PBO. Photo cover. Movie tie-in.	$1.25	$3.75	$7.50
S-1198	MacDonald, John D. - ***A Key To The Suite*** [1962] PBO.	$4.00	$12.50	$25.00
S-1200	Williams, Charles - ***The Long Saturday Night*** [1962] PBO.	$2.00	$6.00	$12.00
S-1201	Wormser, Richard - ***Perfect Pigeon*** [1962] PBO.	$1.35	$4.00	$8.00
D-1202	Thomas, Kenneth - ***The Devil's Mistress*** [1962] Photo cover.	$1.35	$4.00	$8.00
D-1203	Matheson, Richard - ***The Shrinking Man*** [1962] Cover by Mitchell Hooks. Movie tie-in.	$2.50	$7.50	$15.00
D-1204	Anthology edited by Frank J. McGowan, M.D. - ***Because You Are A Woman*** [1962] PBO. Photo cover.	$1.35	$4.00	$8.00
S-1205	Longstreet, Stephen - ***Living High*** [1962] PBO. Cover by Harry Bennett.	$1.35	$4.00	$8.00
S-1206	Barrett, Michael - ***Escape From Zahrain*** [1962]	$1.35	$4.00	$8.00
S-1207	Cunningham, John - ***Wait Till Dark*** [1962] PBO. Photo cover.	$1.50	$5.00	$10.00
1208	Prather, Richard S. - ***Kill The Clown*** [1962] PBO. Cover by Hooks.	$1.50	$5.00	$10.00
S-1209	Anthology - ***Cartoon Fun*** [1962] Cover by V.I.P. Cartoon book.	$1.00	$3.00	$6.00
S-1211	Krepps, Robert W. - ***Boys' Night Out*** [1962] PBO. Photo cover. Movie tie-in.	$1.25	$3.75	$7.50
S-1212	Beech, Webb - ***No French Leave*** [1962] PBO.	$1.25	$3.75	$7.50
S-1213	Tessitore, John - ***That Touch Of Mink*** [1962]	$1.35	$4.00	$8.00
S-1214	Marlowe, Stephen - ***Jeopardy Is My Job*** [1962] PBO.	$1.35	$4.00	$8.00
S-1215	Anonymous, told to Margaret Witte Moore - ***Abortion-Murder Of Mercy?*** [1962] PBO.	$1.25	$3.75	$7.50
S-1218	Bellah, James Warner - ***Reveille*** [1962] PBO.	$1.35	$4.00	$8.00
D-1220	Clark, Ford - ***The Open Square*** [1962] PBO.	$1.35	$4.00	$8.00
S-1221	Miller, Wade - ***The Girl From Midnight*** [1962] PBO. Cover by Abbett.	$1.50	$5.00	$10.00
S-1223	Partch, Virgil Franklin - ***Crazy Cartoons*** [1962] Cover by V.I.P. Cartoon book.	$1.00	$3.00	$6.00
S-1225	Kurtzman, Harvey - ***Second Helping!*** [1962] PBO. Photo cover.	$2.50	$7.50	$15.00
R-1227	Martin, Ralph G. & Harrity, Richard - ***World War II*** [1962] PBO. Contains hundreds of photos.	$1.50	$5.00	$10.00
S-1228	Gonzales, John - ***Someone's Sleeping In My Bed*** [1962] PBO. Cover by Barye Phillips.	$1.50	$5.00	$10.00
S-1229	Lutz, Giles A. - ***Relentless Gun*** [1962] Photo cover.	$1.00	$3.00	$6.00
K-1230	Johnson, Hope - ***Creative Hairdo Ideas*** [1962] PBO. Photo cover.	$1.35	$4.00	$8.00
S-1231	Bloch, Robert - ***Atoms And Evil*** [1962] PBO.	$2.00	$6.00	$12.00
K-1232	Fox, William Price - ***Southern Fried*** [1962] PBO. Cover by Jack Davis.	$3.50	$10.00	$20.00
S-1233	Evarts, Hal G. - ***Massacre Creek*** [1962]	$1.35	$4.00	$8.00
D-1234	Marks, Jason & Phillips, Howard - ***Two Souls, One Body*** [1962] PBO. Cover by Harry Bennett.	$1.50	$5.00	$10.00
S-1235	Prather, Richard S. - ***Everybody Had A Gun*** [1962] Cover by Barye Phillips.	$1.00	$3.00	$6.00
S-1236	Patten, Lewis B. - ***Five Rode West*** [1962]	$1.00	$3.00	$6.00
S-1237	Aarons, Edward S. - ***Assignment-Karachi*** [1962] PBO.	$1.35	$4.00	$8.00
S-1238	Heatter, Basil - ***The Mutilators*** [1962] PBO.	$1.35	$4.00	$8.00
S-1239	Olsen, T. V. - ***Savage Sierra*** [1962] PBO.	$1.25	$3.75	$7.50

		G	VG	F
S-1240	Lynch, Dan - ***Four-Time Loser*** [1962] PBO. Cover by Barye Phillips.	$2.50	$7.50	$15.00
S-1241	Packer, Vin - ***Intimate Victims*** [1962] PBO.	$1.50	$5.00	$10.00
S-1242	Prather, Richard S. - ***Bodies In Bedlam*** [1962] Cover by Barye Phillips.	$ .75	$2.50	$5.00
K-1243	Anthology edited by Groff Conklin - ***13 Great Stories Of Sf*** [1962] Cover by Powers.	$1.00	$3.00	$6.00
K-1245	Wormser, Richard - ***The Last Days Of Sodom And Gomorrah*** [1962] Cover by Stanley Zuckerberg. Movie tie-in.	$2.50	$7.50	$15.00
S-1246	Hamilton, Donald - ***Murderers' Row*** [1962] PBO.	$1.35	$4.00	$8.00
K-1247	Bishop, Leonard - ***The Desire Years*** [1962] PBO.	$2.00	$6.00	$12.00
S-1248	Mason, Raymond - ***Someone And Felicia Warwick*** [1962] PBO. Cover by McGinnis.	$1.35	$4.00	$8.00
S-1249	Prather, Richard S. - ***Case Of The Vanishing Beauty*** [1962] Cover by Barye Phillips.	$ .75	$2.50	$5.00
S-1250	Telfair, Richard - ***Day Of The Gun*** [1962].	$ .75	$2.50	$5.00
K-1251	Prather, Richard S. - ***Dance With The Dead*** [1962] Cover by Barye Phillips.	$ .75	$2.50	$5.00
S-1252	Pratt, Theodore - ***Without Consent*** [1962] PBO. Cover by Harry Bennett.	$1.35	$4.00	$8.00
S-1253	Krepps, Robert W. - ***Taras Bulba*** [1962] PBO. Cover by McCarthy. Movie tie-in.	$1.35	$4.00	$8.00
S-1254	Anthology edited by Cole & McKee - ***You Damn Men Are All Alike*** [1962] PBO. Cartoon book.	$1.25	$3.75	$7.50
S-1255	Brackeen, Steve - ***Delfina*** [1962] PBO. Photo cover.	$1.25	$3.75	$7.50
S-1256	Cameron, Lou - ***The Enemy Quarter*** [1962] PBO. Cover by Zuckerberg.	$1.25	$3.75	$7.50
S-1258	Brewer, Gil - ***The Brat*** [1962] Cover by Barye Phillips.	$ .75	$2.50	$5.00
S-1259	MacDonald, John D. - ***The Girl, The Gold Watch And Everything*** [1962] PBO.	$4.00	$12.50	$25.00
S-1260	Fox, Gardner F. - ***One Wife's Ways*** [1962] PBO. Cover by McGinnis.	$2.00	$6.00	$12.00
K-1261	Pritchie, Neil - ***The Savage Kick*** [1962] PBO. Cover by Zuckerberg.	$1.50	$5.00	$10.00
S-1262	Rabe, Peter - ***The Box*** [1962] PBO. Cover by Barye Phillips.	$2.00	$6.00	$12.00
S-1263	Johnson, George - ***The Real Jack Paar*** [1962] PBO. Photo cover.	$1.25	$3.75	$7.50
K-1264	Prather, Richard S. - ***Slab Happy*** [1962]	$ .75	$2.50	$5.00
S-1265	Hopson, William - ***Gunfire At Salt Fork*** [1962].	$ .75	$2.50	$5.00
1266	Aldrich, Ann - ***We Too Must Love*** [1962]	$1.35	$4.00	$8.00
S-1267	Gardner, Gerald - ***Miss Caroline*** [1963] PBO. Cover by Frank Johnson. Cartoon book.	$1.35	$4.00	$8.00
S-1268	Runyon, Charles - ***The Death Cycle*** [1963] PBO.	$1.35	$4.00	$8.00
S-1269	Hasty, John Eugene - ***Some Mischief Still*** [1963] PBO. Cover by Harry Bennett.	$1.35	$4.00	$8.00
S-1270	Aarons, Edward S. - ***Assignment-Sorrento Siren*** [1963] PBO. Cover by McGinnis.	$1.35	$4.00	$8.00
S-1271	Wormser, Richard - ***A Nice Girl Like You...*** [1963] PBO. Cover by Bill Johnson.	$1.50	$5.00	$10.00
S-1273	Jessup, Richard - ***Texas Outlaw*** [1963] Cover by Abbett.	$ .75	$2.50	$5.00
S-1275	Anthology compiled from *True* magazine - ***Strange But True*** [1963]	$1.00	$3.00	$6.00
K-1276	Tevis, Walter - ***The Man Who Fell To Earth*** [1963] PBO. Cover by The Dillons.	$4.00	$12.50	$25.00
K-1277	Prather, Richard S. - ***The Peddler*** [1963] Cover by Harry Bennett.	$1.50	$5.00	$10.00
S-1278	Daniels, Norman - ***County Hospital*** [1963] PBO. Cover by Zuckerberg.	$1.00	$3.00	$6.00
K-1280	Prather, Richard S. - ***Pattern For Panic*** [1963] Cover by Barye Phillips.	$ .75	$2.50	$5.00

		G	VG	F
S-1281	Howard, Vechel - ***Tall In The West*** [1963] Cover by Abbett.	$ .75	$2.50	$5.00
K-1282	Prather, Richard S. - ***Too Many Crooks*** [1963] Cover by Barye Phillips.	$ .75	$2.50	$5.00
K-1284	Kaylin, Walter - ***Another Time, Another Woman*** [1963] PBO. Cover by Bennett.	$1.35	$4.00	$8.00
K-1285	Marlowe, Stephen - ***Francesca*** [1963] PBO. Cover by McGinnis.	$1.35	$4.00	$8.00
K-1286	Cameron, Lou - ***The Black Camp*** [1963] PBO.	$1.25	$3.75	$7.50
K-1287	Prather, Richard S. - ***Shell Scott's 7 Slaughters*** [1963]	$ .75	$2.50	$5.00
D-1288	Prather, Richard S. & Marlowe, Stephen - ***Double In Trouble*** [1963] Cover by Barye Phillips.	$ .75	$2.50	$5.00
K-1289	Williams, Charles - ***Nothing In Her Way*** [1963] Cover by Robert McGinnis.	$1.35	$4.00	$8.00
K-1290	Packer, Vin - ***Spring Fire*** [1963] Photo cover.	$1.35	$4.00	$8.00
K-1291	MacDonald, John D. - ***I Could Go On Singing*** [1963] PBO. Movie photo cover. Movie tie-in with Judy Garland.	$10.00	$30.00	$60.00
K-1293	Gonzales, John - ***Follow That Hearse!*** [1963] PBO.	$1.35	$4.00	$8.00
K-1294	Packer, Vin - ***Alone At Night*** [1963] PBO. Cover by Harry Bennett.	$1.50	$5.00	$10.00
D-1296	Anthology - ***1963 Official Baseball Almanac*** [1963] PBO. Photo cover.	$1.35	$4.00	$8.00
K-1298	Prather, Richard S. - ***Dig That Crazy Grave*** [1963] Cover by Barye Phillips.	$ .75	$2.50	$5.00
K-1301	Edwards, Herb - ***Island Of Love*** [1963]	$ .75	$2.50	$5.00
K-1302	MacDonald, John D. - ***The Drowner*** [1963] PBO. Cover by Zuckerberg.	$3.50	$10.00	$20.00
K-1304	Aarons, Edward S. - ***Assignment-Manchurian Doll*** [1963] PBO.	$1.25	$3.75	$7.50
S-1305	Rifkin, Shepard - ***King Fisher's Road*** [1963]	$1.00	$3.00	$6.00
K-1306	Reed-Marr P.J. - ***Women Without Men*** [1963]	$ .75	$2.50	$5.00
K-1307	Aarons, Edward S. - ***Assignment-Mara Tirana*** [1963]	$ .75	$2.50	$5.00
K-1308	Borden, Lee - ***The Secret Of Sylvia*** [1963]	$ .75	$2.50	$5.00
S-1309	Lawrence, Steven C. - ***Brand Of A Texan*** [1963] Cover by Darcy.	$ .75	$2.50	$5.00
K-1310	Heatter, Basil - ***Virgin Cay*** [1963] PBO.	$1.00	$3.00	$6.00
K-1311	Braly, Malcolm - ***Shake Him Till He Rattles*** [1963] PBO. Cover by Harry Bennett.	$1.35	$4.00	$8.00
K-1312	St. Clair, Dexter - ***The Lady's Not For Living*** [1963] PBO.	$1.25	$3.75	$7.50
S-1314	Lutz, Giles A. - ***Halfway To Hell*** [1963]	$1.25	$3.75	$7.50
S-1315	Thomey, Tedd - ***Killer In White*** [1963]	$ .75	$2.50	$5.00
S-1317	Patten, Lewis B. - ***Top Man With A Gun*** [1963]	$ .65	$2.00	$4.00
K-1319	Waller, Leslie - ***"K"*** [1963] PBO.	$ .75	$2.50	$5.00
K-1320	Runyon, Charles - ***Color Him Dead*** [1963] PBO.	$1.35	$4.00	$8.00
K-1321	Atlee, Philip - ***The Green Wound*** [1963] PBO. Cover by Bennett.	$1.25	$3.75	$7.50
S-1322	Anthology - ***My Son, The Doctor*** [1963] PBO. Cover by Gill Fox. Cartoon book.	$1.25	$3.75	$7.50
K-1323	Kruger, Paul - ***Message From Marise*** [1963] PBO. Cover by Zuckerberg.	$1.00	$3.00	$6.00
K-1324	Anthology edited by Leo Margulies - ***Three Times Infinity*** [1963]	$ .75	$2.50	$5.00
K-1325	Cannon, Curt - ***I'm Cannon-For Hire*** [1963] Cover by Milton Charles.	$ .75	$2.50	$5.00
S-1330	Mac Leod, Robert - ***The Appaloosa*** [1963] PBO.	$1.25	$3.75	$7.50
S-1331	Schafer, Kermit - ***Super Bloopers*** [1963] PBO. Cover by Howard Schneider.	$1.25	$3.75	$7.50
K-1333	Hamilton, Donald - ***The Ambushers*** [1963] PBO.	$1.35	$4.00	$8.00
K-1334	Hamilton, Donald - ***Death Of A Citizen*** [1963]	$ .65	$2.00	$4.00
K-1335	Hamilton, Donald - ***The Wrecking Crew*** [1963]	$ .65	$2.00	$4.00
K-1336	Hamilton, Donald - ***The Removers*** [1963]	$ .65	$2.00	$4.00

		G	VG	F
K-1337	Rabe, Peter - ***A House In Naples*** [1963] Cover by Lu Kimmel.	$ .65	$2.00	$4.00
K-1338	Kyle, Robert - ***The Golden Urge*** [1963]	$ .75	$2.50	$5.00
S-1341	Tessitore, John - ***For Love Or Money*** [1963] PBO. Movie photo cover. Movie tie-in with Kirk Douglas.	$1.50	$5.00	$10.00
S-1342	Randall, Clay - ***The Oceola Kid*** [1963] PBO. Cover by Bill Johnson.	$1.35	$4.00	$8.00
K-1343	McPartland, John - ***The Kingdom Of Johnny Cool*** [1963] Photo cover. Movie tie-in.	$1.00	$3.00	$6.00
K-1344	Williams, Charles - ***Go Home, Stranger*** [1964] Cover by Barye Phillips.	$1.00	$3.00	$6.00
S-1345	Albert, Marvin H. - ***The Bounty Hunter*** [1963]	$1.00	$3.00	$6.00
K-1347	Cameron, Lou - ***The Bastard's Name Is War*** [1963] PBO.	$1.35	$4.00	$8.00
K-1348	Davis, Gordon - ***Counterfeit Kill*** [1963] PBO.	$1.25	$3.75	$7.50
K-1349	Kaufman, Robert & Barry, Peter - ***The Right People*** [1963]	$1.25	$3.75	$7.50
K-1350	Wormser, Richard - ***McLintock*** [1963] PBO. Photo cover. Movie tie-in with John Wayne.	$1.35	$4.00	$8.00
S-1351	Savage, Les & Dean, Dudley - ***Gun Shy*** [1963]	$1.25	$3.75	$7.50
D-1352	Ballard, P.D. - ***Age Of The Junkman*** [1963] PBO. Cover by McGinnis.	$2.00	$6.00	$12.00
K-1353	Williams, Charles - ***A Touch Of Death*** [1963]	$ .75	$2.50	$5.00
K-1355	Miller, Wade - ***Mad Baxter*** [1963]	$ .65	$2.00	$4.00
S-1357	Randall, Clay - ***Hardcase For Hire*** [1963] PBO.	$ .75	$2.50	$5.00
K-1358	Stone, Peter - ***Charade*** [1963] PBO. Movie tie-in.	$1.25	$3.75	$7.50
D-1359	Storer, Doug - ***Amazing But True Animals*** [1963] PBO. Photo cover. Photos throughout.	$1.25	$3.75	$7.50
K-1360	Brett, Michael - ***Diecast*** [1963] PBO.	$1.00	$3.00	$6.00
K-1361	Lewis, Claude - ***Adam Clayton Powell*** [1963] PBO. Photo cover.	$1.00	$3.00	$6.00
K-1364	Fleischman, A.S. - ***Look Behind You, Lady*** [1963]	$ .65	$2.00	$4.00
D-1366	Anthology edited by Groff Conklin - ***12 Great Classics Of SF*** [1963] PBO.	$1.50	$5.00	$10.00
K-1367	Fleischman, A.S. - ***The Venetian Blonde*** [1963] PBO.	$1.35	$4.00	$8.00
K-1368	Hassel, Sven - ***Comrades Of War*** [1963]	$1.25	$3.75	$7.50
S-1369	Rigsby, Howard - ***The Lone Gun*** [1963] Cover by Robert Schulz.	$ .65	$2.00	$4.00
K-1370	Aarons, Edward S. - ***Assignment-Helene*** [1963] Cover by Barye Phillips.	$ .65	$2.00	$4.00
S-1371	Frazee, Steve - ***Many Rivers To Cross*** [1963]	$ .65	$2.00	$4.00
K-1372	Aarons, Edward S. - ***Assignment-Lili Lamaris*** [1963] Cover by Barye Phillips.	$ .65	$2.00	$4.00
K-1373	Aarons, Edward S. - ***Assignment-Carlotta Cortez*** [1963]	$ .65	$2.00	$4.00
K-1376	Prather, Richard S. - ***Joker In The Deck*** [1964] PBO. Cover by Barye Phillips.	$1.50	$5.00	$10.00
K-1377	Thomas, Bob - ***Dead Ringer*** [1964] PBO. Bette Davis photo cover. Movie tie-in with Bette Davis.	$1.50	$5.00	$10.00
S-1378	Scott, William R. - ***Gun Slingers Can't Quit*** [1964] PBO.	$1.25	$3.75	$7.50
K-1379	Anthology edited by Leo Guild - ***Strictly Personal*** [1964] PBO. Cover by Charles Rodrigues.	$1.00	$3.00	$6.00
K-1380	Davis, Gordon - ***Ring Around Rosy*** [1964] PBO. Cover by McGinnis.	$1.00	$3.00	$6.00
K-1381	Prather, Richard S. - ***Strip For Murder*** [1964] Cover by Barye Phillips.	$ .75	$2.50	$5.00
K-1382	Prather, Richard S. - ***Way Of A Wanton*** [1964]	$ .75	$2.50	$5.00
K-1383	Prather, Richard S. - ***Find This Woman*** [1964] Cover by Barye Phillips.	$ .75	$2.50	$5.00
K-1384	Longbaugh, Harry - ***No Way To Treat A Lady*** [1964] PBO.	$1.25	$3.75	$7.50
D-1385	Whittington, Harry - ***The Fall Of The Roman Empire*** [1964] PBO. Movie cover. Movie tie-in Sophia Loren.	$3.50	$10.00	$20.00
K-1386	Hamilton, Donald - ***The Shadowers*** [1964] PBO.	$1.35	$4.00	$8.00
S-1387	Albert, Marvin H. - ***Posse At High Pass*** [1964] PBO.	$1.25	$3.75	$7.50

		G	VG	F
K-1388	Cort, Van - ***Mail Order Bride*** [1964] PBO. Photo cover. Movie tie-in with Buddy Ebsen.	$1.50	$5.00	$10.00
D-1389	MacDonald, John D. - ***The Only Girl In The Game*** [1964] Cover by Robert McGinnis.	$1.35	$4.00	$8.00
K-1391	Hamilton, Donald - ***Murderer's Row*** [1964]	$ .65	$2.00	$4.00
K-1392	Hamilton, Donald - ***The Silencers*** [1964]	$ .65	$2.00	$4.00
S-1393	Lewellen, T.C. - ***The Ruthless Gun*** [1964]	$ .65	$2.00	$4.00
K-1394	MacDonald, John D. - ***Judge Me Not*** [1964] Cover by Barye Phillips.	$1.00	$3.00	$6.00
K-1396	Craig, Jonathan - ***The Case Of The Silent Stranger*** [1964]	$1.25	$3.75	$7.50
K-1397	Leinster, Murray - ***Four From Planet 5*** [1964] Cover by Lehr.	$1.00	$3.00	$6.00
K-1398	Aarons, Edward S. - ***Assignment-The Girl In The Gondola*** [1964] PBO. Cover by McGinnis.	$1.35	$4.00	$8.00
K-1399	Roberts, Lee - ***Little Sister*** [1964]	$ .65	$2.00	$4.00
D-1400	Anthology - ***The 1964 Official Baseball Almanac*** [1964] PBO. Photos.	$1.25	$3.75	$7.50
K-1403	Rabe, Peter - ***Stop This Man!*** [1964]	$1.00	$3.00	$6.00
K-1405	MacDonald, John D. - ***The Deep Blue Good-By*** [1964] PBO. Cover by Ronnie Lesser. First Travis McGee.	$5.00	$15.00	$30.00
K-1406	MacDonald, John D. - ***Nightmare In Pink*** [1964] PBO. Cover by Ronnie Lesser.	$4.00	$12.50	$25.00
D-1408	Considine, Bob - ***General Douglas MacArthur*** [1964] PBO. Photo cover. Photos throughout.	$1.25	$3.75	$7.50
K-1410	Albert, Marvin H. - ***Pillow Talk*** [1964] Photo cover. Movie tie-in with Rock Hudson and Doris Day.	$ .75	$2.50	$5.00
D-1411	Bannon, Ann - ***Odd Girl Out*** [1964] Cover by Barye Phillips.	$1.00	$3.00	$6.00
K-1412	Partch, Virgil Franklin - ***Funny Cartoons*** [1964] Cover by Vip. Cartoon book.	$ .75	$2.50	$5.00
K-1413	Marlowe, Stephen - ***Violence Is My Business*** [1964] Cover by Barye Phillips.	$ .75	$2.50	$5.00
S-1414	Cushman, Dan - ***North Fork To Hell*** [1964] PBO.	$1.25	$3.75	$7.50
K-1417	MacDonald, John D. - ***A Purple Place For Dying*** [1964] PBO. Cover by Ronnie Lesser.	$4.00	$12.50	$25.00
K-1418	Bannister, Pat - ***Seven Votes For Death*** [1964] PBO. Photo cover.	$1.25	$3.75	$7.50
K-1420	Marlowe, Stephen - ***Drum Beat-Berlin*** [1964] PBO. Cover by Zuckerberg.	$1.35	$4.00	$8.00
D-1421	MacDonald, John D. - ***Clemmie*** [1964] Cover by Barye Phillips.	$1.25	$3.75	$7.50
K-1422	Prather, Richard S. - ***The Wailing Frail*** [1964]	$ .65	$2.00	$4.00
K-1423	Aarons, Edward S. - ***Assignment-Burma Girl*** [1964]	$ .65	$2.00	$4.00
K-1426	Rabe, Peter - ***Journey Into Terror*** [1964] Cover by Hooks.	$ .65	$2.00	$4.00
K-1427	Wormser, Richard - ***Bedtime Story*** [1964] PBO. Photo cover. Movie tie-in.	$1.25	$3.75	$7.50
D-1428	Anthology edited by Damon Knight - ***Tomorrow X 4*** [1964] PBO.	$1.35	$4.00	$8.00
S-1429	Foreman, L.L. - ***Gringo*** [1964]	$1.25	$3.75	$7.50
1430	L'Amour, Louis - ***The Tall Stranger*** [1964]	$1.50	$5.00	$10.00
K-1431	Beech, Webb - ***Article 92*** [1964] PBO. Cover by Victor Kalin.	$1.00	$3.00	$6.00
K-1433	Hine, Al - ***The Unsinkable Molly Brown*** [1964] PBO. Movie cover. Movie tie-in with Debbie Reynolds.	$1.00	$3.00	$6.00
D-1434	Bannon, Ann - ***Women In The Shadows*** [1964]	$1.25	$3.75	$7.50
K-1435	Riley, Nord - ***The Armored Dove*** [1964] PBO	$1.00	$3.00	$6.00
S-1436	Olsen, T.V. - ***Gunswift*** [1964]	$ .65	$2.00	$4.00
K-1437	Prather, Richard S. - ***Lie Down, Killer*** [1964] Cover by Barye Phillips.	$ .65	$2.00	$4.00
K-1438	Thompson, Jim - ***Pop. 1280*** [1964] PBO. Cover by McGinnis.	$12.50	$37.50	$75.00
K-1441	Marlowe, Dan J. - ***Never Live Twice*** [1964] PBO.	$1.00	$3.00	$6.00
K-1442	Aarons, Edward S. - ***Assignment-Ankara*** [1964]	$1.25	$3.75	$7.50
D-1443	Glover, Dr. Leland E. - ***How Do You Feel About Sex?*** [1964]	$1.00	$3.00	$6.00

		G	VG	F
D-1444	Anthology edited by Groff Conkin - ***13 Great Stories Of SF*** [1964] Cover by Powers.	$ .75	$2.50	$5.00
K-1445	Prather, Richard S. - ***Case Of The Vanishing Beauty*** [1964] Cover by Barye Phillips.	$ .65	$2.00	$4.00
K-1446	Einstein, Charles - ***The Day New York Went Dry*** [1964] PBO.	$2.50	$7.50	$15.00
S-1447	Olsen, T.V. - ***A Man Called Brazos*** [1964] PBO.	$1.00	$3.00	$6.00
K-1449	Trinian, John - ***Scandal On The Sand*** [1964] PBO. Cover by McGinnis.	$1.25	$3.75	$7.50
K-1450	Torres, Tereska - ***Women's Barracks*** [1964] Cover by Barye Phillips.	$ .65	$2.00	$4.00
K-1451	MacDonald, John D. - ***One Monday We Killed Them All*** [1964] Cover by Bill Johnson.	$1.25	$3.75	$7.50
K-1452	Hamilton, Donald - ***The Ravagers*** [1964] PBO.	$1.35	$4.00	$8.00
K-1455	Aarons, Edward S. - ***Hell To Eternity*** [1964] Cover by Barye Phillips.	$ .65	$2.00	$4.00
K-1456	Aarons, Edward S. - ***Assignment-Zoraya*** [1964] Cover by Milton Charles.	$ .65	$2.00	$4.00
1457	Leisy, J. - ***Hootenanny Tonight*** [1964]	$1.50	$5.00	$10.00
K-1458	Rohmer, Sax - ***Re-Enter Fu Manchu*** [1964] Cover by Barye Phillips.	$1.00	$3.00	$6.00
S-1459	Huffaker, Clair - ***Guns Of Rio Conchos*** [1964] Movie poster cover. Movie tie-in.	$1.00	$3.00	$6.00
S-1460	Chamberlain, William - ***Last Ride To Los Lobos*** [1964]	$1.25	$3.75	$7.50
K-1461	MacDonald, John D. - ***The Damned*** [1964] Cover by Barye Phillips.	$1.00	$3.00	$6.00
K-1462	Prather, Richard S. - ***The Cockeyed Corpse*** [1964] PBO. Cover by Barye Phillips.	$1.35	$4.00	$8.00
K-1464	MacDonald, John D. - ***The Quick Red Fox*** [1964] PBO. Cover by Ronnie Lesser.	$4.00	$12.50	$25.00
K-1465	Krepps, Robert W. - ***Send Me No Flowers*** [1964] PBO. Movie photo cover. Movie tie-in with Rock Hudson and Doris Day.	$1.25	$3.75	$7.50
K-1466	Brewer, Gil - ***Wild*** [1964]	$1.00	$3.00	$6.00
K-1468	Telfair, Richard - ***Wyoming Jones*** [1964]	$ .65	$2.00	$4.00
K-1470	Forrest, Williams - ***The Huntress*** [1964] PBO.	$1.00	$3.00	$6.00
K-1472	Hamilton, Donald - ***Night Walker*** [1964] Cover by Harry Bennett.	$1.00	$3.00	$6.00
L-1474	Budrys, Algis - ***Rogue Moon*** [1964] Cover by Powers.	$ .65	$2.00	$4.00
K-1476	Shirreffs, Gordon - ***Judas Gun*** [1964]	$ .65	$2.00	$4.00
K-1477	Smythe, Reginald - ***Meet Andy Capp*** [1964] PBO. Cover by Reginald Smythe. Cartoon book.	$1.00	$3.00	$6.00
K-1478	Patten, Lewis B. - ***Home Is The Outlaw*** [1964]	$1.00	$3.00	$6.00
D-1479	Idell, Albert - ***This Woman*** [1984] Cover by Barye Phillips.	$1.00	$3.00	$6.00
K-1480	Hamilton, Donald - ***Line Of Fire*** [1964]	$1.00	$3.00	$6.00
K-1481	Aarons, Edward S. - ***Assignment-Madeleine*** [1964]	$1.00	$3.00	$6.00
K-1482	Randall, Clay - ***Lawman*** [1964] PBO.	$1.00	$3.00	$6.00
K-1484	MacNeil, Neil - ***2 Guns For Hire*** [1964]	$ .65	$2.00	$4.00
K-1485	Kurtzman, Harvey - ***Help!*** [1964] Photo cover.	$ .75	$2.50	$5.00
D-1486	Ballard P.D. - ***End Of A Millionaire*** [1964] PBO. Cover by Harry Bennett.	$2.00	$6.00	$12.00
K-1487	Rabe, Peter - ***Mission For Vengeance*** [1964]	$1.25	$3.75	$7.50
K-1488	Gotlieb, Phyllis - ***Sunburst*** [1964] PBO.	$1.35	$4.00	$8.00
K-1489	Atlee, Phillip - ***The Silken Baroness Contract*** [1964] PBO. Cover by McGinnis.	$1.35	$4.00	$8.00
K-1490	Miller, Wade - ***Kitten With A Whip*** [1964] Ann-Margret photo cover. Movie tie-in with Ann-Margret.	$1.25	$3.75	$7.50
K-1491	Hamilton, Donald - ***Assassins Have Starry Eyes*** [1964]	$1.00	$3.00	$6.00
K-1492	L'Amour, Louis - ***Hondo*** [1964]	$1.25	$3.75	$7.50
K-1493	Cameron, Lou - ***The Green Fields Of Hell*** [1964] PBO.	$1.00	$3.00	$6.00
L-1494	Kastle, Herbert D. - ***The Reassembled Man*** [1964] PBO. Cover by Frazetta	$1.50	$5.00	$10.00

		G	VG	F
K-1497	Aarons, Edward S. - ***Assignment-Sulu Sea*** [1964] PBO.	$1.35	$4.00	$8.00
S-1498	Vip - ***Cartoon Fun*** [1964] Cartoon book.	$1.00	$3.00	$6.00
K-1500	Hamilton, Donald - ***Mad River*** [1964]	$1.00	$3.00	$6.00
K-1501	L'Amour, Louis - ***To Tame A Land*** [1964]	$1.50	$5.00	$10.00
K-1502	Thompson, Jim - ***Texas By The Tail*** [1965] PBO. Cover by Barye Phillips.	$12.50	$37.50	$75.00
K-1503	Williams, Mona - ***The Company Girls*** [1965]	$1.00	$3.00	$6.00
L-1504	Keene, Day & Pruyn, Leonard - ***World Without Women*** [1965]	$ .75	$2.50	$5.00
K-1505	Aarons, Edward S. - ***Assignment-Karachi*** [1965]	$ .65	$2.00	$4.00
D-1506	Kurtzman, Harvey - ***Fun And Games*** [1965] PBO. Photo cover.	$2.50	$7.50	$15.00
K-1508	Marlowe, Stephen - ***Drum Beat-Dominque*** [1965] PBO.	$1.35	$4.00	$8.00
K-1509	Anthology - ***Sex And The Man Who Used To Be Single*** [1965] PBO. Cover by Rodrigues. Cartoon book.	$1.25	$3.75	$7.50
K-1510	Castle, Frank - ***Dakota Boomtown*** [1965]	$1.00	$3.00	$6.00
K-1511	Cameron, Lou - ***None But The Brave*** [1965] PBO. Movie photo cover. Movie tie-in Frank Sinatra.	$1.25	$3.75	$7.50
K-1512	Shirreffs, Gordon D. - ***Now He Is Legend*** [1965] PBO.	$1.25	$3.75	$7.50
K-1513	MacDonald, John D. - ***The Girl, The Gold Watch and Everything*** [1965] Photo cover.	$ .75	$2.50	$5.00
D-1514	Herndon, Booton - ***The Humor Of JFK*** [1964] PBO. JFK photo cover. Photos throughout.	$1.00	$3.00	$6.00
K-1515	Aarons, Edward S. - ***Assignment-Stella Marni*** [1965]	$ .65	$2.00	$4.00
R-1516	Anthology edited by Bill Wise - ***1965 Official Baseball Almanac*** [1965] PBO. Mickey Mantle photo cover.	$1.00	$3.00	$6.00
D-1518	Pratt, Theodore - ***Handsome*** [1965]	$ .65	$2.00	$4.00
K-1519	Fink, Harry Julian - ***Major Dundee*** [1965] PBO. Photo cover. Movie tie-in.	$1.00	$3.00	$6.00
K-1520	Rubel, James L. - ***No Business For A Lady*** [1965]	$ .65	$2.00	$4.00
K-1521	Riley, Nord - ***The Bedroom Derby*** [1965]	$1.00	$3.00	$6.00
K-1522	Thompson, Jim - ***The Killer Inside Me*** [1965]	$5.00	$15.00	$30.00
K-1523	Anthology - ***Harvey Kurtzman's Second Help!-ing*** [1965]	$1.25	$3.75	$7.50
K-1524	Marlowe, Dan J. - ***Death Deep Down*** [1965] PBO.	$1.00	$3.00	$6.00
K-1525	Aarons, Edward S. - ***Assignment-Budapest*** [1965] Cover by Barye Phillips.	$ .65	$2.00	$4.00
K-1526	Evarts, Hal G. - ***The Branded Man*** [1965] PBO.	$1.00	$3.00	$6.00
D-1528	MacDonald, John D. - ***Area Of Suspicion*** [1965] Cover by Barye Phillips.	$1.25	$3.75	$7.50
K-1529	Ballinger, Bill S. - ***Not I, Said The Vixen*** [1965] PBO. Cover by Bill Johnson.	$1.25	$3.75	$7.50
K-1531	Davis, Gordon - ***Where Murder Waits*** [1965] PBO.	$1.00	$3.00	$6.00
K-1532	Clark, Ford - ***The Wicked Walk On Every Side*** [1965] PBO.	$1.50	$5.00	$10.00
K-1533	Schafer, Kermit - ***Prize Bloopers*** [1965] PBO. Cover by Howard Schneider.	$1.00	$3.00	$6.00
K-1534	Aarons, Edward S. - ***Assignment-To Disaster*** [1965]	$1.00	$3.00	$6.00
K-1535	Aarons, Edward S. - ***Assignment-Angelina*** [1965] Cover by Gerry Powell.	$1.00	$3.00	$6.00
K-1536	Heuman, William - ***Heller From Texas*** [1965] Cover by Kimmel.	$ .65	$2.00	$4.00
K-1538	Lutz, Giles A. - ***Relentless Gun*** [1965] Photo cover.	$1.00	$3.00	$6.00
K-1539	Aarons, Edward S. - ***Assignment-Suicide*** [1965]	$1.00	$3.00	$6.00
K-1540	Rabe, Peter - ***Girl In A Big Brass Bed*** [1965] PBO. Photo cover.	$2.00	$6.00	$12.00
D-1543	MacDonald, John D. - ***Murder In The Wind*** [1965]	$1.25	$3.75	$7.50
D-1544	Anthology edited by Bernhardt J. Hurwood - ***Monsters Galore*** [1965] PBO. Cover by Harry Bennett.	$2.50	$7.50	$15.00
1545	Taylor, Valerie - ***The Girls In 3-B*** [1965]	$1.25	$3.75	$7.50
K-1546	Sheldon, Walt - ***The Blue Kimono Kill*** [1965] PBO.	$1.35	$4.00	$8.00
K-1547	MacDonald, John D. - ***All These Condemned*** [1965] Photo cover.	$1.35	$4.00	$8.00
D-1548	Beech, Webb - ***Make War In Madness*** [1965] PBO.	$1.25	$3.75	$7.50

		G	VG	F
D-1549	Anthology edited by Groff Conklin - ***5 Unearthly Visions*** [1965] PBO.	$1.35	$4.00	$8.00
R-1550	MacGowan, Norman - ***My Years With Churchill*** [1965] Photo cover. Sixteen pages of photos.	$1.00	$3.00	$6.00
K-1551	Hamilton, Donald - ***Texas Fever*** [1965]	$1.00	$3.00	$6.00
D-1552	MacDonald, John D. - ***A Man Of Affairs*** [1965]	$1.25	$3.75	$7.50
D-1554	Hobson, Burton - ***What You Should Know About Coins & Coin Collecting*** [1965] Photo cover.	$1.00	$3.00	$6.00
D-1555	Aldrich, Ann - ***We, Too, Must Love*** [1965] Photo cover.	$1.25	$3.75	$7.50
K-1556	Aarons, Edward S. - ***Assignment-Sorrento Siren*** [1965]	$ .65	$2.00	$4.00
D-1558	Prather, Richard S. - ***Pattern For Panic*** [1965] Cover by Barye Phillips.	$ .65	$2.00	$4.00
K-1559	Aarons, Edward S. - ***Assignment-Manchurian Doll*** [1965]	$ .65	$2.00	$4.00
D-1561	Sohl, Jerry - ***Night Slaves*** [1965] PBO. Cover by Lehr.	$2.00	$6.00	$12.00
D-1562	Lueddecke, W.J. - ***Morituri*** [1965] PBO. Cover by Bill Johnson.	$1.00	$3.00	$6.00
D-1563	MacDonald, John D. - ***The Deceivers*** [1965]	$1.25	$3.75	$7.50
R-1564	Martin, Ralph G. - ***World War II*** [1965] PBO. Photo cover.	$1.00	$3.00	$6.00
R-1565	Martin, Ralph G. & Harrity, Richard - ***World War II*** [1965] Photo cover	$1.00	$3.00	$6.00
K-1566	MacDonald, John D. - ***The Brass Cupcake*** [1965]	$1.25	$3.75	$7.50
K-1567	Patten, Lewis, B. - ***Five Rode West*** [1965]	$ .65	$2.00	$4.00
K-1568	Olsen, T.V. - ***Canyon Of The Gun*** [1965] PBO.	$1.00	$3.00	$6.00
K-1569	Marko, Zekial - ***Once A Thief*** [1965] Photo cover. Movie tie-in.	$1.00	$3.00	$6.00
K-1570	Aarons, Edward S. - ***Assignment-Mara Tirana*** [1965]	$ .65	$2.00	$4.00
D-1572	Biography by Richard Gehman - ***Bogart*** [1965] PBO. Photo cover.	$1.00	$3.00	$6.00
D-1573	MacDonald, John D. - ***Bright Orange For The Shroud*** [1965] PBO. Cover by Ronnie Lesser.	$3.50	$10.00	$20.00
K-1577	Barrett, Michael - ***The Reward*** [1965] PBO. Movie cover. Movie tie-in.	$1.25	$3.75	$7.50
D-1579	MacDonald, John D. - ***April Evil*** [1965] Cover by Bill Johnson.	$1.25	$3.75	$7.50
D-1580	MacDonald, John D. - ***Judge Me Not*** [1965] Cover by Barye Phillips.	$1.25	$3.75	$7.50
D-1582	Hamblett, Charles & Deverson, Jane - ***Generation X*** [1965] Photo cover	$1.50	$5.00	$10.00
D-1583	Aarons, Edward S. - ***Assignment-The Cairo Dancers*** [1965] PBO.	$1.35	$4.00	$8.00
D-1584	- - ***Poor H. Allen Smith's Almanac*** [1965] PBO. Cover by Huehnergarth.	$1.50	$5.00	$10.00
K-1585	Telfair, Richard - ***Day Of The Gun*** [1965]	$ .65	$2.00	$4.00
D-1586	Beaumont, Charles - ***The Magic Man*** [1965] PBO. Photo cover.	$3.50	$10.00	$20.00
D-1587	MacDonald, John D. - ***On The Run*** [1965] Cover by McGinnis.	$1.25	$3.75	$7.50
D-1588	MacDonald, John D. - ***Death Trap*** [1965] Cover by Bill Johnson.	$1.25	$3.75	$7.50
D-1590	MacDonald, John D. - ***The Beach Girls*** [1965] Cover by Milton Charles.	$1.25	$3.75	$7.50
D-1591	Kastle, Herbert - ***Hot Prowl*** [1965]	$1.00	$3.00	$6.00
D-1592	Prather, Richard S. - ***Darling, It's Death*** [1965] Cover by Barye.	$ .65	$2.00	$4.00
D-1593	Packer, Vin - ***Spring Fire*** [1965]	$ .65	$2.00	$4.00
1594	Anthology from *True* magazine - ***Man To Man Answers*** [1965]	$1.00	$3.00	$6.00
K-1597	Olsen, T.V. - ***Ramrod Rider*** [1965]	$ .65	$2.00	$4.00
D-1599	MacDonald, John D. - ***The Drowner*** [1965] Cover by Zuckerberg.	$1.25	$3.75	$7.50
D-1602	Hamilton, Donald - ***The Shadowers*** [1965]	$ .65	$2.00	$4.00
K-1603	Whittington, Harry - ***Desert Stake-Out*** [1965]	$1.50	$5.00	$10.00

		G	VG	F
S-1605	Shayne, Ted - ***Cockeyed Crosswords*** [1965]	$1.50	$5.00	$10.00
D-1606	MacDonald, John D. - ***Slam The Big Door*** [1965] Cover by Charles.	$1.25	$3.75	$7.50
D-1607	Prather, Richard S. - ***Way Of A Wanton*** [1965]	$1.35	$4.00	$8.00
D-1608	Hamilton, Donald - ***The Devastators*** [1965] PBO.	$1.35	$4.00	$8.00
D-1609	MacDonald, John D. - ***The Price Of Murder*** [1965]	$1.25	$3.75	$7.50
D-1611	Alter, Robert Edmond - ***Carny Kill*** [1966] PBO.	$2.00	$6.00	$12.00
D-1612	Aarons, Edward S. - ***Assignment-Burma Girl*** [1966]	$ .65	$2.00	$4.00
D-1613	Aarons, Edward S. - ***Assignment-Madeleine*** [1966]	$ .65	$2.00	$4.00
D-1614	Linden, Millicent - ***Tension In Repose*** [1966] PBO.	$1.00	$3.00	$6.00
K-1615	Lutz, Giles A. - ***Outcast Gun*** [1966]	$ .65	$2.00	$4.00
D-1616	Coppel, Alec - ***Moment To Moment*** [1966] PBO. Photo cover. Movie tie-in.	$1.00	$3.00	$6.00
D-1617	Hamilton, Donald - ***The Steel Mirror*** [1966]	$ .65	$2.00	$4.00
D-1618	Hamilton, Donald - ***The Ambushers*** [1966]	$ .65	$2.00	$4.00
D-1621	MacDonald, John D. - ***Soft Touch*** [1966]	$1.25	$3.75	$7.50
K-1624	Chadwick, Joseph - ***A Town To Tame*** [1966] Cover by Harry Schaare.	$ .65	$2.00	$4.00
K-1625	Vip - ***Crazy Cartoons*** [1966] Cartoon Book.	$1.00	$3.00	$6.00
D-1626	Sturgeon, Theodore - ***The Rare Breed*** [1966] PBO. Cover by Carl Hantman. Movie tie-in.	$5.50	$17.50	$35.00
D-1628	Anthology edited by Groff Conklin - ***Another Part Of The Galaxy*** [1966] PBO.	$1.35	$4.00	$8.00
D-1629	Prather, Richard S. - ***The Peddler*** [1966] Cover by Harry Bennett.	$ .65	$2.00	$4.00
D-1630	Aarons, Edward S. - ***Assignment-Ankara*** [1966]	$ .65	$2.00	$4.00
D-1631	Aarons, Edward S. - ***Assignment-Zoraya*** [1966]	$ .65	$2.00	$4.00
D-1632	Atlee, Philip - ***The Death Bird Contract*** [1966] PBO. Cover by Thurston.	$1.35	$4.00	$8.00
D-1633	MacDonald, John D. - ***The End Of The Night*** [1966]	$1.25	$3.75	$7.50
D-1634	Atlee, Philip - ***The Paper Pistol Contract*** [1966] PBO. Cover by Thurston.	$1.35	$4.00	$8.00
D-1635	MacDonald, John D. - ***A Bullet For Cinderella*** [1966] Photo cover.	$1.25	$3.75	$7.50
D-1640	Aarons, Edward S. - ***Assignment-School For Spies*** [1966] PBO.	$1.35	$4.00	$8.00
D-1641	Hamilton, Donald - ***The Silencers*** [1966]	$ .65	$2.00	$4.00
1643	Lawrence, Steven C. - ***The Texan Comes Riding*** [1966]	$1.00	$3.00	$6.00
D-1646	Hamilton, Donald - ***The Wrecking Crew*** [1966]	$ .65	$2.00	$4.00
D-1647	Brewer, Gil - ***The Hungry One*** [1966] PBO. Cover by Barye Phillips.	$2.00	$6.00	$12.00
R-1649	MacDonald, John D. - ***Please Write For Details*** [1966]	$1.25	$3.75	$7.50
D-1653	Aarons, Edward S. - ***Assignment-Budapest*** [1966] Cover by Barye Phillips.	$ .65	$2.00	$4.00
D-1654	Aarons, Edward S. - ***Assignment-Sulu Sea*** [1966]	$ .65	$2.00	$4.00
D-1656	Aarons, Edward S. - ***Assignment-Treason*** [1966]	$ .65	$2.00	$4.00
K-1657	Lawrence, Steven C. - ***Brand Of A Texan*** [1966] Cover by Darcy.	$ .65	$2.00	$4.00
D-1658	MacNeil, Neil - ***The Death Ride*** [1966]	$1.00	$3.00	$6.00
D-1659	MacDonald, John D. - ***Deadly Welcome*** [1966]	$1.25	$3.75	$7.50
D-1660	Aarons, Edward S. - ***Assignment-Helene*** [1966]	$ .65	$2.00	$4.00
D-1661	Aarons, Edward S. - ***Assignment-The Girl In The Gondola*** [1966] Cover by McGinnis.	$ .65	$2.00	$4.00
D-1664	Cameron, Lou - ***The Dirty War Of Sergeant Slade*** [1966]	$1.00	$3.00	$6.00
D-1665	Telfair, Richard - ***The Bloody Medallion*** [1966] Cover by Bill Johnson.	$ .65	$2.00	$4.00
K-1666	Albert, Marvin H. - ***Duel At Diablo*** [1966]	$1.25	$3.75	$7.50
K-1667	Krepps, Robert W. - ***Stagecoach*** [1966] Movie tie-in with Ann-Margret.	$1.25	$3.75	$7.50
D-1669	Anthology - ***12 Great Classics Of Science Fiction*** [1966]	$1.00	$3.00	$6.00

		G	VG	F
D-1670	Brossard, Chandler - ***A Man For All Women*** [1966] PBO. Cover by McGinnis.	$1.25	$3.75	$7.50
R-1671	Ryan, J.M. - ***Brooks Wilson LTD*** [1966] PBO. Cover by McGinnis.	$1.25	$3.75	$7.50
D-1672J	Aarons, Edward S. - ***Assignment-Suicide*** [1966]	$ .65	$2.00	$4.00
D-1673	Hamilton, Donald - ***The Ravagers*** [1966]	$ .65	$2.00	$4.00
D-1674	MacDonald, John D. - ***Darker Than Amber*** [1966] PBO. Cover by Ronnie Lasser.	$3.50	$10.00	$20.00
D-1676	Dewey, Thomas B. - ***A Season For Violence*** [1966]	$1.25	$3.75	$7.50
K-1677	Randall, Clay - ***Amos Flagg Rides Out*** [1966] PBO.	$1.00	$3.00	$6.00
D-1681	Prather, Richard S. - ***Joker In The Deck*** [1966] Cover by Barye Phillips.	$ .65	$2.00	$4.00
D-1682	MacDonald, John D. - ***Nightmare In Pink*** [1966] Cover by Ronnie Lesser.	$1.25	$3.75	$7.50
T-1684	MacDonald, John D. - ***A Flash Of Green*** [1966]	$1.25	$3.75	$7.50
D-1686	Marlowe, Stephen - ***Drum Beat-Madrid*** [1966] PBO.	$1.25	$3.75	$7.50
D-1687	Hamilton, Donald - ***Murderers Row*** [1966] Movie tie-in.	$ .75	$2.50	$5.00
K-1689	Ward, Jonas - ***Buchanan Says No*** [1966]	$ .65	$2.00	$4.00
D-1690	MacDonald, John D. - ***End Of The Tiger*** [1966] PBO. Photo cover.	$3.50	$10.00	$20.00
D-1693	Anthology edited by Herbert Van Thal - ***The Pan Book Of Horror Stories*** [1966]	$2.00	$6.00	$12.00
D-1694	Atlee, Philip - ***The Irish Beauty Contract*** [1966] PBO.	$1.35	$4.00	$8.00
D-1695	Aarons, Edward S. - ***Assignment-Cong Hai Kill*** [1966] PBO.	$1.35	$4.00	$8.00
D-1697	Hamilton, Donald - ***Death Of A Citizen*** [1966]	$ .65	$2.00	$4.00
D-1699	MacDonald, John D. - ***The Neon Jungle*** [1966]	$1.25	$3.75	$7.50
D-1702	Atlee, Philip - ***The Silken Baroness Contract*** [1966] Cover by McGinnis.	$ .65	$2.00	$4.00
D-1704	Lacour, Jose-Andre - ***Venice In October*** [1966] Cover by Harry Bennett.	$1.00	$3.00	$6.00
K-1705	Adams, Clifton - ***The Moonlight War*** [1966]	$1.00	$3.00	$6.00
D-1706	Craig, Jonathan - ***Case Of The Brazen Beauty*** [1966] PBO. Cover by McGinnis.	$1.35	$4.00	$8.00
K-1708	Anthology, editors of *True* magazine - ***The True Album Of Cartoons*** [1966] Cover by V.I.P. Cartoon book.	$1.35	$4.00	$8.00
D-1709	Hurd, Florence - ***Secret Of Canfield House*** [1966] PBO.	$1.25	$3.75	$7.50
K-1711	Smythe - ***Andy Capp Sounds Off*** [1966] PBO. Cover by Smythe. Cartoon book.	$1.25	$3.75	$7.50
D-1714	Rabe, Peter - ***The Spy Who Was 3 Feet Tall*** [1966] PBO.	$1.50	$5.00	$10.00
K-1715	Hopson, William - ***Gunfire At Salt Fork*** [1966]	$1.00	$3.00	$6.00
D-1716	Cashman, John - ***The LSD Story*** [1966] PBO.	$1.00	$3.00	$6.00
D-1718	Prather, Richard S. - ***Bodies In Bedlam*** [1966] Cover by Barye Phillips.	$ .65	$2.00	$4.00
D-1719	Keel, John A. - ***The Fickle Finger Of Fate*** [1966] PBO. Cover by Jaffee.	$3.50	$10.00	$20.00
D-1722	Block, Lawrence - ***The Thief Who Couldn't Sleep*** [1966] PBO.	$3.50	$10.00	$20.00
D-1723	Fox, William Price - ***Southern Fried*** [1966] Cover by Jack Davis.	$1.50	$5.00	$10.00
K-1725	Olsen, T.V. - ***Brand Of The Star*** [1966]	$ .65	$2.00	$4.00
D-1726	Aarons, Edward S. - ***Assignment-Lowlands*** [1966] Cover by Rader.	$ .65	$2.00	$4.00
D-1727	Bloch, Robert - ***The Scarf*** [1966]	$1.50	$5.00	$10.00
K-1732	Friend, Ed - ***Alvarez Kelly*** [1966] PBO. Movie cover. Movie tie-in.	$1.25	$3.75	$7.50
1734	Marlowe, Dan - ***Four For The Money*** [1966]	$ .65	$2.00	$4.00
1735	MacDonald, John D. - ***Dead Low Tide*** [1966]	$1.25	$3.75	$7.50
D-1736	Hamilton, Donald - ***The Betrayers*** [1966]	$ .65	$2.00	$4.00
D-1737	Aarons, Edward S. - ***Passage To Terror*** [1966]	$ .65	$2.00	$4.00
K-1738	Olsen, T.V. - ***The Hard Men*** [1966]	$1.00	$3.00	$6.00
D-1739	MacDonald, John D. - ***Cry Hard, Cry Fast*** [1966]	$1.25	$3.75	$7.50

		G	VG	F
D-1741	Lane, Kendall - ***Gambit*** [1966] PBO. Movie cover. Movie tie-in with S. MacLaine & M. Caine.	$1.00	$3.00	$6.00
D-1742	L'Amour, Louis - ***The Tall Stranger*** [1966]	$1.00	$3.00	$6.00
R-1744	Brossard, Chandler - ***The Insane World Of Adolph Hitler*** [1966] PBO. Photo cover.	$1.25	$3.75	$7.50
K-1746	Robinson, Jerry - ***True Classroom Flubs And Fluffs*** [1966] PBO. Cover by Jerry Robinson.	$1.00	$3.00	$6.00
D-1747	Block, Lawrence - ***The Cancelled Czech*** [1966] PBO.	$2.50	$7.50	$15.00
D-1748	MacDonald, John D. - ***All These Condemned*** [1966] Photo cover.	$1.25	$3.75	$7.50
D-1749	MacDonald, John D. - ***The Brass Cupcake*** [1966]	$1.25	$3.75	$7.50
D-1750	MacDonald, John D. - ***One Fearful Yellow Eye*** [1966] PBO. Cover by Ronnie Lesser.	$3.50	$10.00	$20.00
D-1751	MacLeod, Robert - ***The Californo*** [1966] PBO.	$1.00	$3.00	$6.00
D-1752	Anthology edited by Groff Conklin - ***Seven Come Infinity*** [1966] PBO.	$1.25	$3.75	$7.50
D-1753	Aarons, Edward S. - ***Assignment-Palermo*** [1966] PBO.	$1.25	$3.75	$7.50
R-1754	Anthology edited by Chandler Brossard - ***Love Me, Love Me!*** [1966] PBO.	$1.00	$3.00	$6.00
D-1755	Aarons, Edward S. - ***Decoy*** [1966]	$ .65	$2.00	$4.00
D-1756	Aarons, Edward S. - ***Come Back My Love*** [1966]	$ .65	$2.00	$4.00
1758	MacDonald, John D. - ***A Deadly Shade Of Gold*** [1966]	$1.25	$3.75	$7.50
D-1761	MacDonald, John D. - ***You Live Once*** [1966]	$1.25	$3.75	$7.50
D-1762	Aarons, Edward S. - ***Don't Cry Beloved*** [1966]	$ .65	$2.00	$4.00
D-1768	MacDonald, John D. - ***The Deep Blue Good-By*** [1966]	$1.25	$3.75	$7.50
R-1769	Boros, Julius - ***How To Win At Weekend Golf*** [1966] Photo cover.	$1.00	$3.00	$6.00
D-1770	Atlee, Philip - ***The Star Ruby Contract*** [1967] PBO.	$1.25	$3.75	$7.50
D-1771	Randall, Clay - ***Amos Flagg-Bushwhacked*** [1967]	$1.00	$3.00	$6.00
D-1772	Aarons, Edward S. - ***Girl On The Run*** [1967]	$ .65	$2.00	$4.00
D-1773	Cushman, Dan - ***The Long Riders*** [1967]	$1.00	$3.00	$6.00
D-1775	Reiner, Carl - ***Enter Laughing*** [1967] Photo cover. Movie tie-in.	$1.25	$3.75	$7.50
D-1777	L'Amour, Louis - ***Hondo*** [1967]	$1.25	$3.75	$7.50
D-1778	Aarons, Edward S. - ***Assignment-Manchurian Doll*** [1967]	$ .65	$2.00	$4.00
1779	Anthology - ***Woman's Day Cookbook Favorite Recipes*** [1967].	$1.25	$3.75	$7.50
D-1780	Atlee, Philip - ***The Green Wound Contract*** [1967]	$ .65	$2.00	$4.00
D-1781	Anthology edited by Chuck Alverson - ***Wonder Wart-Hog, Captain Crud & Other Super Stuff*** [1967] PBO. Cover by Vaughn Bode.	$3.50	$10.00	$20.00
D-1782	MacDonald, John D. - ***One Monday We Killed Them All*** [1967] Cover by Bill Johnson.	$1.25	$3.75	$7.50
D-1783	Chamberlain, William - ***China Strike*** [1967] PBO.	$1.00	$3.00	$6.00
D-1785	MacDonald, John D. - ***The Empty Trap*** [1967]	$1.25	$3.75	$7.50
D-1786	MacLeod, Robert - ***The Muleskinner*** [1967] PBO.	$1.00	$3.00	$6.00
R-1788	Nichlaus, Jack - ***The Best Way To Better Golf*** [1967] PBO. Photo cover.	$1.00	$3.00	$6.00
D-1789	Hart, Johnny - ***Hey! B.C.*** [1967] Cover by Johnny Hart. Cartoon book.	$1.00	$3.00	$6.00
D-1790	Shirreffs, Gordon D. - ***Southwest Drifter*** [1967] PBO.	$1.00	$3.00	$6.00
D-1791	Marlowe, Dan J. - ***Route Of The Red Gold*** [1967] PBO.	$1.25	$3.75	$7.50
D-1793	Thompson, Jim - ***South Of Heaven*** [1967] PBO. Photo cover.	$10.00	$30.00	$60.00
D-1794	Cassill, R.V. - ***The Wife Next Door*** [1967]	$ .65	$2.00	$4.00
D-1796	Marlowe, Stephen - ***Drum Beat-Erica*** [1967] PBO. Cover by McGinnis.	$1.35	$4.00	$8.00
D-1797	Aarons, Edward S. - ***Assignment-Karachi*** [1967]	$ .65	$2.00	$4.00
D-1803	Stark, Richard - ***The Rare Coin Score*** [1967] PBO. Cover by McGinnis.	$2.50	$7.50	$15.00
R-1805	Nicholas, William - ***The Bobby Kennedy Nobody Knows*** [1967] PBO. Photo cover.	$1.00	$3.00	$6.00

		G	VG	F
D-1806	Frazee, Steve - ***Many Rivers To Cross*** [1967]	$ .65	$2.00	$4.00
D-1807	Huffaker, Clair - ***The War Wagon*** [1967] Movie tie-in with John Wayne.	$1.25	$3.75	$7.50
R-1809	MacDonald, John D. - ***Area Of Suspicion*** [1967] Cover by Barye Phillips.	$1.25	$3.75	$7.50
D-1810	Bergson, Leo & McMahon, Robert - ***The Widow Master*** [1967] PBO.	$1.00	$3.00	$6.00
D-1816	Archer, Frank - ***The Turguoise Spike*** [1967] PBO.	$1.25	$3.75	$7.50
T-1817	Thoms, Wayne - ***What's New In Hot-Rodding*** [1967] PBO. Photo cover.	$1.00	$3.00	$6.00
D-1818	Prather, Richard S. - ***Dance With The Dead*** [1967] Cover by Barye Phillips.	$ .65	$2.00	$4.00
D-1821	Anthology edited by Donald Hamilton - ***Iron Men And Silver Stars*** [1967] PBO. Cover by Stan Galli.	$1.25	$3.75	$7.50
K-1822	Anthology - ***Cartoon Laffs From True*** [1967] Cover by VIP. Cartoon book.	$ .65	$2.00	$4.00
D-1823	Aarons, Edward S. - ***Assignment: Black Viking*** [1967] PBO.	$1.25	$3.75	$7.50
D-1826	MacDonald, John D. - ***A Purple Place For Dying*** [1967] Cover by Ronnie Lesser.	$1.25	$3.75	$7.50
D-1828	Thornburg, Newton - ***Gentlemen Born*** [1967]	$1.00	$3.00	$6.00
K-1829	Anthology compiled by Kermit Schafer - ***Super Bloopers*** [1967] Cover by Howard Schneider.	$ .65	$2.00	$4.00
D-1830	Rabe, Peter - ***Code Name Gadget*** [1967] PBO. Cover by Bennett.	$1.50	$5.00	$10.00
R-1831	Millard, Joseph - ***Edgar Cayce, Man Of Miracles*** [1967]	$1.00	$3.00	$6.00
D-1833	Einstein, Charles - ***Woman Times Seven*** [1967] PBO. Movie tie-in with Shirley Maclaine.	$1.25	$3.75	$7.50
D-1835	Albert, Marvin H. - ***The Reformed Gun*** [1967]	$1.00	$3.00	$6.00
T-1837	MacLean, Alistair - ***H.M.S. Ulysses*** [1967] Cover by Bill Johnson.	$1.00	$3.00	$6.00
D-1838	Smythe - ***Andy Capp Strikes Back*** [1967] PBO. Cartoon cover by Smythe. Cartoon book.	$1.25	$3.75	$7.50
D-1839	Ernenwein, Leslie - ***Bullet Barricade*** [1967]	$ .65	$2.00	$4.00
D-1842	VIP - ***New Faces On The Barroom Floor*** [1961] Cartoons.	$1.00	$3.00	$6.00
D-1843	Forrester, Larry - ***A Girl Called Fathom*** [1967] Photo cover. Movie tie-in with Raquel Welch.	$1.25	$3.75	$7.50
D-1845	Smythe - ***What Next, Andy Capp*** [1967] Cover by Smythe. Cartoon book.	$1.00	$3.00	$6.00
D-1846	Meade, Richard - ***Rough Night In Jericho*** [1967] PBO. Movie tie-in.	$1.00	$3.00	$6.00
D-1848	MacDonald, John D. - ***One Fearful Yellow Eye*** [1967]	$1.25	$3.75	$7.50
D-1849	Aarons, Edward S. - ***Assignment-Moon Girl*** [1967] PBO.	$1.35	$4.00	$8.00
D-1850	Castle, Frank - ***Dakota Boomtown*** [1967]	$ .65	$2.00	$4.00
D-1852	Budrys, Algis - ***The Amsirs And The Iron Thorn*** [1967] PBO. Cover by Frazetta.	$2.00	$6.00	$12.00
D-1853	Smythe - ***Meet Andy Capp*** [1967] Cartoon cover by Smythe. Cartoon book.	$1.00	$3.00	$6.00
D-1854	Krepps, Robert - ***Hour Of The Gun*** [1967] PBO. Movie tie-in.	$1.25	$3.75	$7.50
D-1855	Smythe - ***Andy Capp Sounds Off*** [1967] Cartoon cover by Smythe. Cartoon book.	$ .65	$2.00	$4.00
D-1856	Stark, Richard - ***Point Blank!*** [1967] Cover by McGinnis. Movie tie-in with Lee Marvin.	$1.50	$5.00	$10.00
D-1857	Hanley, Gerald - ***The Last Safari*** [1968] Movie tie-in with Stewart Granger.	$1.00	$3.00	$6.00
D-1858	Pearce, Donn - ***Cool Hand Luke*** [1968] Photo cover. Movie tie-in with Paul Newman.	$2.50	$7.50	$15.00
D-1859	Smythe - ***Andy Capp-Man Of The Hour*** [1968] Cartoon cover. Cartoon book.	$1.00	$3.00	$6.00
D-1860	Hamilton, Donald - ***The Ambushers*** [1967] Movie tie-in.	$ .65	$2.00	$4.00

		G	VG	F
D-1861	Stark, Richard - ***The Green Eagle Score*** [1967] PBO. Cover by McGinnis.	$2.50	$7.50	$15.00
D-1865	Evarts, Hal G. - ***The Branded Man*** [1967]	$ .65	$2.00	$4.00
D-1868	Anthology - ***5 Unearthly Visions*** [1967]	$ .65	$2.00	$4.00
D-1869	Block, Lawrence - ***Tanner's Twelve Swingers*** [1967] PBO.	$3.50	$10.00	$20.00
D-1870	Hamilton, Donald - ***Line Of Fire*** [1967]	$ .65	$2.00	$4.00
D-1871	Hamilton, Donald - ***Mad River*** [1967]	$ .65	$2.00	$4.00
D-1873	Runyon, Charles - ***The Black Moth*** [1967] PBO.	$1.00	$3.00	$6.00
D-1876	Taylor, Valerie - ***Stranger On Lesbos*** [1967]	$1.00	$3.00	$6.00
D-1877	Dillon, Jack - ***A Great Day For Dying*** [1968] PBO.	$1.25	$3.75	$7.50
D-1878	Hamilton, Donald - ***Night Walker*** [1968] Cover by Harry Bennett.	$1.00	$3.00	$6.00
D-1882	Smythe - ***Hurray For Andy Capp!*** [1968] PBO. Cover by Smythe. Cartoon book.	$1.00	$3.00	$6.00
D-1883	Baum, L. Frank - ***The Wizard Of Oz*** [1968] Cover by W.W. Denslow.	$1.25	$3.75	$7.50
D-1884	Hamilton, Donald - ***The Menacers*** [1968]	$1.00	$3.00	$6.00
D-1885	MacDonald, John D. - ***The Price Of Murder*** [1968]	$1.25	$3.75	$7.50
R-1887	Kersh, Gerald - ***Nightshade & Damnations*** [1968] PBO. Cover by Dillons.	$3.50	$10.00	$20.00
D-1888	Author Unknown - ***True Cartoon Treasury*** [1968]	$1.00	$3.00	$6.00
D-1890	Burnett, W.R. - ***The Cool Man*** [1968] PBO.	$2.00	$6.00	$12.00
D-1893	MacDonald, John D. - ***Pale Gray For Guilt*** [1968] PBO. Cover by Ronnie Lesser.	$3.50	$10.00	$20.00
D-1894	MacDonald, John D. - ***Soft Touch*** [1968]	$1.25	$3.75	$7.50
D-1896	Block, Lawrence - ***Two For Tanner*** [1968] PBO. Cover by McGinnis.	$2.00	$6.00	$12.00
D-1897	Heuman, William - ***Heller From Texas*** [1968] Cover by Kimmel.	$1.00	$3.00	$6.00
D-1900	Hamilton, Donald - ***Texas Fever*** [1968]	$1.00	$3.00	$6.00
D-1901	Atlee, Philip - ***The Rockabye Contract*** [1968] PBO.	$1.25	$3.75	$7.50
1902	Zolar - ***It's All In The Stars*** [1968]	$1.00	$3.00	$6.00
R-1903	MacDonald, John D. - ***The Deceivers*** [1968]	$1.25	$3.75	$7.50
D-1904	Hart, Johnny - ***Hurray For B.C.*** [1968]	$1.00	$3.00	$6.00
D-1905	Goldman, William - ***No Way To Treat A Lady*** [1968] Movie tie-in.	$1.00	$3.00	$6.00
D-1909	Marlowe, Stephen - ***Drum Beat-Marianne*** [1968] PBO.	$1.25	$3.75	$7.50
1910	Simmons, H. - ***So You Think You Know Baseball*** [1968]	$1.00	$3.00	$6.00
D-1911	Friend, Ed - ***The Scalphunters*** [1968] PBO. Movie tie-in with Burt Lancaster.	$1.00	$3.00	$6.00
D-1913	Pritchett, Ariadne - ***Mill Reef Hall*** [1968] PBO. Cover by Harry Bennett.	$1.00	$3.00	$6.00
R-1915	MacDonald, John D. - ***Bright Orange For The Shroud*** [1968]	$1.25	$3.75	$7.50
T-1916	MacLean, Alistair - ***Fear Is The Key*** [1968]	$1.00	$3.00	$6.00
D-1917	Prather, Richard S. - ***Have Gat-Will Travel*** [1968] Cover by Barye Phillips.	$ .65	$2.00	$4.00
R-1918	Maine, Clarles Eric - ***Survival Margin*** [1968] PBO.	$1.00	$3.00	$6.00
R-1919	Nicklaus, Jack - ***The Best Way To Better Golf #2*** [1968] PBO. Photo cover.	$1.00	$3.00	$6.00
D-1920	Aarons, Edward S. - ***Assignment-Mara Tirana*** [1968]	$ .65	$2.00	$4.00
D-1921	Fitzpatrick, Thomas K. - ***The Blood Circus*** [1968] PBO. Cover by Bill Johnson.	$1.50	$5.00	$10.00
R-1924	Anthology edited by Groff Conklin - ***Seven Trips Through Time And Space*** [1968] PBO.	$1.50	$5.00	$10.00
D-1926	Ward, Jonas - ***Buchanan's Gun*** [1968]	$1.00	$3.00	$6.00
D-1927	Ward, Jonas - ***The Name's Buchanan*** [1968]	$1.00	$3.00	$6.00
D-1928	Ward, Jonas - ***Buchanan Gets Mad*** [1968]	$1.00	$3.00	$6.00
D-1929	Smythe - ***In Your Eye, Andy Capp*** [1968] PBO. Cover by Smythe. Cartoon book.	$1.00	$3.00	$6.00
1930	Pottor - ***The Lost Years Of Jesus Revealed*** [1968]	$ .65	$2.00	$4.00

		G	VG	F
T-1931	MacLean, Alistair - ***The Secret Ways*** [1968] Cover by Bill Johnson.	$ .75	$2.50	$5.00
D-1933	Thornburg, Newton - ***Knockover*** [1968] PBO.	$1.00	$3.00	$6.00
D-1934	MacDonald, John D. - ***A Bullet For Cinderella*** [1968]	$1.25	$3.75	$7.50
R-1936	Crawford, William - ***Gresham's War*** [1968] PBO.	$1.00	$3.00	$6.00
D-1937	Ward, Jonas - ***Buchanan's Revenge*** [1968]	$ .65	$2.00	$4.00
D-1938	Ward, Jonas - ***Buchanan On The Prod*** [1968]	$ .65	$2.00	$4.00
1939	Ryan, T. - ***Tumbleweeds*** [1968]	$2.50	$7.50	$15.00
D-1940	Block, Lawrence - ***Tanner's Tiger*** [1968] PBO. Cover by McGinnis.	$2.00	$6.00	$12.00
R-1943	MacDonald, John D. - ***One Fearful Yellow Eye*** [1968]	$1.25	$3.75	$7.50
D-1944	Aarons, Edward S. - ***Assignment-Suicide*** [1968]	$ .65	$2.00	$4.00
D-1945	MacDonald, John D. - ***The Quick Red Fox*** [1968]	$1.25	$3.75	$7.50
D-1947	Hamilton, Donald - ***The Silencers*** [1968]	$ .65	$2.00	$4.00
D-1948	MacDonald, John D. - ***Judge Me Not*** [1968] Cover by Barye Phillips.	$1.25	$3.75	$7.50
D-1949	Stark, Richard - ***The Black Ice Score*** [1968] PBO. Cover by McGinnis.	$2.50	$7.50	$15.00
D-1950	Aarons, Edwards - ***Assignment: Madeline*** [1968]	$ .65	$2.00	$4.00
D-1951	Hart, Johnny - ***What's New B.C.*** [1968] Cartoon cover. Cartoon book.	$1.00	$3.00	$6.00
D-1952	Ward, Jonas - ***Buchanan Says No*** [1968]	$ .65	$2.00	$4.00
D-1953	Ward, Jonas - ***One-Man Massacre*** [1968]	$ .65	$2.00	$4.00
R-1954	MacDonald, John D. - ***Murder In The Wind*** [1968]	$1.25	$3.75	$7.50
T-1955	Panger, Daniel - ***Ol'Prophet Nat*** [1968]	$1.25	$3.75	$7.50
D-1956	Godey, John - ***A Thrill A Minute With Jack Albany*** [1968] Cover by Jack Davis.	$ .75	$2.50	$5.00
R-1957	MacDonald, John D. - ***Darker Than Amber*** [1968]	$1.25	$3.75	$7.50
D-1958	Aarons, Edward S. - ***Assignment-Treason*** [1968]	$ .65	$2.00	$4.00
D-1959	Barns, Glenn M. - ***Only The Losers Win*** [1968] PBO.	$1.00	$3.00	$6.00
D-1960	Ward, Jonas - ***One-Man Massacre*** [1968]	$ .65	$2.00	$4.00
D-1961	Whittington, Harry - ***Desert Stake-Out*** [1968]	$1.50	$5.00	$10.00
D-1962	Keane, Bil - ***I Need A Hug*** [1968] PBO. Cover by Keane. Cartoon book.	$1.00	$3.00	$6.00
T-1964	Dury, David - ***Before I Wake*** [1968] PBO. Photo cover.	$1.00	$3.00	$6.00
D-1965	Cook, L.H. Longley - ***Fun With Brain Puzzlers*** [1968]	$1.00	$3.00	$6.00
D-1967	Aarons, Edward S. - ***Assignment-Sulu Sea*** [1968]	$ .65	$2.00	$4.00
R-1970	MacDonald, John D. - ***Pale Gray For Guilt*** [1968] PBO. Cover by Ronnie Lesser.	$3.50	$10.00	$20.00
D-1971	Franklin, Keith - ***Murder At Shirttail Flats*** [1968] PBO.	$1.00	$3.00	$6.00
D-1976	Atlee, Philip - ***The Irish Beauty Contract*** [1968]	$ .65	$2.00	$4.00
D-1977	Atlee, Philip - ***The Skeleton Coast Contract*** [1968] PBO.	$1.25	$3.75	$7.50
T-1978	Horner, Lance - ***Rogue Roman*** [1968] Cover by Frazetta.	$1.00	$3.00	$6.00
D-1981	Smythe - ***Take A Bow, Andy Capp*** [1968] PBO. Cartoon cover by Smythe. Cartoon book.	$1.00	$3.00	$6.00
D-1983	Aarons, Edward S. - ***Assignment-The Cairo Dancers*** [1968]	$ .65	$2.00	$4.00
D-1987	Taylor, Theodore - ***The Body Trade*** [1968] PBO.	$1.00	$3.00	$6.00
R-1988	Hamilton, Donald - ***The Betrayers*** [1968]	$ .65	$2.00	$4.00
T-1990	Heinz, W.C. - ***The Surgeon*** [1968]	$ .65	$2.00	$4.00
D-1991	Schafer, Kermit - ***Blooper Parade*** [1968] PBO. Cover by Schneider.	$1.00	$3.00	$6.00
T-1992	MacDonald, John D. - ***A Flash Of Green*** [1968]	$2.00	$6.00	$12.00
R-1993	MacDonald, John D. - ***Ballroom Of The Skies*** [1968]	$2.00	$6.00	$12.00
R-1994	MacDonald, John D. - ***Wine Of The Dreamers*** [1968]	$1.25	$3.75	$7.50
D-1997	Stark, Richard - ***The Split*** [1968] Cover by McGinnis.	$1.25	$3.75	$7.50
R-1998	Pritchett, Ariadne - ***Karamour*** [1968] PBO. Cover by Harry Bennett.	$1.00	$3.00	$6.00
A-2000	Aarons, Edward S. - ***Assignment-Nuclear Nude*** [1968] PBO.	$1.00	$3.00	$6.00
R-2001	Christopher, John - ***The Long Winter*** [1968]	$ .50	$1.50	$3.00
T-2003	Gabree, John - ***The World Of Rock*** [1968] PBO.	$1.00	$3.00	$6.00

		G	VG	F
T-2004	Dine, S.S. Van - ***The "Canary" Murder Case*** [1968] Cover by McDaniel.	$ .50	$1.50	$3.00
R-2005	MacDonald, John D. - ***The Crossroads*** [1968]	$ .50	$1.50	$3.00
R-2008	Block, Lawrence - ***Here Comes A Hero*** [1968] PBO. Cover by McGinnis.	$2.00	$6.00	$12.00
D-2009	Smythe - ***Hats Off, Andy Capp*** [1968] Cartoon cover. Cartoon book.	$ .50	$1.50	$3.00
R-2013	Cameron, Lou - ***File On A Missing Redhead*** [1968] PBO.	$1.00	$3.00	$6.00
R-2020	Hamilton, Donald - ***The Wrecking Crew*** [1968]	$ .50	$1.50	$3.00
R-2021	Hamilton, Donald - ***The Devastators*** [1968]	$ .50	$1.50	$3.00
T-2023	MacDonald, John D. - ***The Girl In The Plain Brown Wrapper*** [1968] PBO.	$3.50	$10.00	$20.00
R-2024	Aarons, Edward S. - ***Assignment-Moon Girl*** [1968]	$ .50	$1.50	$3.00
R-2025	MacDonald, John D. - ***The Deep Blue Good-By*** [1968]	$1.25	$3.75	$7.50
T-2026	MacDonald, John D. - ***A Deadly Shade Of Gold*** [1968]	$1.25	$3.75	$7.50
2033	- - ***Cool Hand Luke*** [1968]	$ .50	$1.50	$3.00
R-2035	Rifkin, Shepard - ***Lady Fingers*** [1968]	$ .50	$1.50	$3.00
R-2037	Stark, Richard - ***The Sour Lemon Score*** [1969] PBO. Cover by McGinnis.	$2.00	$6.00	$12.00
R-2038	MacDonald, John D. - ***You Live Once*** [1969]	$1.25	$3.75	$7.50
2041	Kastle, Herbert D. - ***The Reassembled Man*** [1969]	$ .65	$2.00	$4.00
R-2044	Anthology Edited By Terry Carr - ***The Others*** [1969] PBO.	$1.25	$3.75	$7.50
M-2048	Horner, Lance - ***The Street Of The Sun*** [1969]	$1.25	$3.75	$7.50
R-2050	Marlowe, Dan J. - ***One Endless Hour*** [1969]	$1.00	$3.00	$6.00
R-2051	Hamilton, Donald - ***Murder Twice Told*** [1969]	$ .50	$1.50	$3.00
R-2052	MacDonald, John D. - ***The Damned*** [1969]	$1.25	$3.75	$7.50
T-2053	MacDonald, John D. - ***Contrary Pleasure*** [1969]	$1.25	$3.75	$7.50
R-2055	McDonald, John D. - ***The Executioners*** [1969]	$1.25	$3.75	$7.50
R-2056	Aarons, Edward S. - ***Assignment-Ankara*** [1969]	$ .50	$1.50	$3.00
R-2057	Hamilton, Donald - ***The Removers*** [1969]	$ .50	$1.50	$3.00
R-2060	MacDonald, John D. - ***The Quick Red Fox*** [1969]	$1.25	$3.75	$7.50
D-2061	Anthology - ***True Cartoon Parade*** [1969] PBO. Cover by Frank Ridgeway. Cartoon book.	$1.00	$3.00	$6.00
R-2062	MacDonald, John D. - ***A Purple Place For Dying*** [1969]	$1.25	$3.75	$7.50
R-2067	Block, Lawrence - ***The Specialists*** [1969] PBO.	$1.50	$5.00	$10.00
R-2072	Hamilton, Donald - ***The Ravagers*** [1969]	$ .50	$1.50	$3.00
T-2073	Hamilton, Donald - ***The Interlopers*** [1969]	$ .50	$1.50	$3.00
R-2074	MacDonald, John D. - ***Nightmare In Pink*** [1969]	$1.25	$3.75	$7.50
T-2075	MacDonald, John D. - ***Clemmie*** [1969]	$1.25	$3.75	$7.50
D-2076	Smythe - ***You're Some Hero, Andy Capp*** [1969] Cartoon cover. Cartoon book.	$ .50	$1.50	$3.00
R-2079	Leonard, Elmore - ***The Big Bounce*** [1969] PBO. Movie tie-in...	$4.00	$12.50	$25.00
D-2080	Smythe - ***Andy Capp Strikes Back*** [1969] Cartoon cover.	$ .50	$1.50	$3.00
T-2081	Anthology - ***Beyond Tomorrow*** [1969]	$1.00	$3.00	$6.00
R-2085	Hamilton, Donald - ***The Shadowers*** [1969]	$ .65	$2.00	$4.00
R-2087	Atlee, Philip - ***The Ill Wind Contract*** [1969] PBO.	$1.00	$3.00	$6.00
R-2088	Aarons, Edward S. - ***Assignment-Carlotta Cortez*** [1969]	$ .50	$1.50	$3.00
R-2097	MacDonald, John D. - ***Border Town Girl*** [1969] Cover by McGinnis.	$2.00	$6.00	$12.00
T-2100	Anthology edited by Bill Adler - ***The McCarthy Wit*** [1969] PBO. Photo cover.	$1.00	$3.00	$6.00
2105	Grubb, Davis - ***Twelve Tales Of Suspense And The Supernatural*** [1969]	$ .65	$2.00	$4.00

Gold Star Books.

		G	VG	F
IL7-11	Janson, Hank - ***Kill Her With Passion*** [1963] Cover art by Harry Barton.	$2.50	$7.50	$15.00
IL7-12	Janson, Hank - ***Lover*** [1963] Cover art by Maguire.	$2.50	$7.50	$15.00
IL7-13	Janson, Hank - ***Brazen Seductress*** [1963] Cover art by Maguire..	$2.50	$7.50	$15.00
IL7-14	Janson, Hank - ***A Nice Way To Die*** [1963] Cover art by Rader. ..	$2.50	$7.50	$15.00

		G	VG	F
IL7-15	Janson, Hank - ***It's Bedtime, Baby!*** [1964] Cover art by Harry Barton.	$2.50	$7.50	$15.00
IL7-16	Janson, Hank - ***Hell's Angels*** [1964] Cover art by Maguire.	$2.50	$7.50	$15.00
IL7-17	Janson, Hank - ***Hot House*** [1964] Cover art by Harry Barton.	$2.50	$7.50	$15.00
IL7-18	Janson, Hank - ***Passionate Playmates*** [1964] Cover art by Maguire.	$2.50	$7.50	$15.00
IL7-19	Young, Donald Jordon - ***Demented*** [1964] PBO. Cover art by Maguire.	$1.35	$4.00	$8.00
IL7-20	Janson, Hank - ***Her Weapon Is Passion*** [1964]	$2.50	$7.50	$15.00
IL7-21	Thurman, Steve - ***Sanitarium Of Tears*** [1964] PBO. Cover by Barton.	$2.50	$7.50	$15.00
IL7-22	Janson, Hank - ***Cold Dead Coed*** [1964] Cover by Barton.	$2.50	$7.50	$15.00
IL7-23	Szedenik, Alex M. - ***Psycho-Sexual Problems*** [1964] PBO.	$1.25	$3.75	$7.50
IL7-24	Bradley, Matthew - ***Lay Down Dead*** [1964] PBO. Photo cover.	$1.25	$3.75	$7.50
IL7-25	Krone, Jr., Chester W. - editor - ***Shocking Tales Of Perversion*** [1964] PBO.	$1.25	$3.75	$7.50
IL7-26	Frame, Marurite - ***All The Gay Girls*** [1964] PBO. Cover by Barton.	$2.50	$7.50	$15.00
IL7-27	Werner, George - ***One Helluva Blow*** [1964] PBO. Cover by Barton.	$1.25	$3.75	$7.50
IL7-28	Janson, Hank - ***Fanny*** [1964] Cover by Barton.	$2.50	$7.50	$15.00
IL7-29	Bradley, Matthew - ***Adultery In Suburbia*** [1964] PBO. Cover by Barton.	$1.25	$3.75	$7.50
IL7-30	Stuart, Matt - ***The Hackamore Feud*** [1964] PBO.	$1.25	$3.75	$7.50
IL7-31	Taylor, R. W. - ***Whiplash*** [1964] PBO. Cover by Barton.	$2.50	$7.50	$15.00
IL7-32	Janson, Hank - ***Expectant Nymph*** [1964] Cover by Maguire.	$2.50	$7.50	$15.00
IL7-33	LeBlanc, Edward T. - editor - ***Buffalo Bill's Leap For Life*** [1964] PBO.	$1.00	$3.00	$6.00
IL7-34	LeBlanc, Edward T. - editor - ***Buffalo Bull's Spy Shadower*** [1964] PBO.	$1.00	$3.00	$6.00
IL7-35	O'Neill, Scott - ***Campus Call Girl*** [1964] PBO.	$1.25	$3.75	$7.50
IL7-36	Szedenik, Alex M. - ***Anatomy Of A Psycho*** [1964] PBO. Photo cover.	$1.25	$3.75	$7.50
IL7-37	LeBlanc, Edward T. - editor - ***Running The Gauntlet*** [1964] PBO.	$1.25	$3.75	$7.50
IL7-38	LeBlanc, Edward T. - editor - ***Green Corn Dance*** [1964] PBO.	$1.25	$3.75	$7.50
IL7-39	Gilbert, Angela - ***Love Is For Everybody*** [1964] PBO. Cover by Barton.	$2.50	$7.50	$15.00
IL7-40	Fairly, James B. - ***Sex And The Coed*** [1964] PBO. Photo cover.	$1.25	$3.75	$7.50
IL7-41	Owen, Dean - ***Girl Possessed*** [1964] PBO. Cover by Barton.	$2.50	$7.50	$15.00
IL7-42	Werper, Barton - ***Tarzan And The Silver Globe*** [1964] PBO. Unauthorized. (#1).	$4.00	$12.50	$25.00
IL7-43	LeBlanc, Edward T. - editor - ***Buffalo Bill's Raid Of Death*** [1964] PBO.	$1.00	$3.00	$6.00
IL7-44	LeBlanc, Edward T. - editor - ***Buffalo Bill's Feather-Weight*** [1964] PBO.	$1.00	$3.00	$6.00
IL7-45	Pfieffer, Orville - editor - ***Puzzle Lovers Dictionary*** [1964] PBO.	$1.00	$3.00	$6.00
IL7-46	LeBlanc, Edward T. - editor - ***Young Wild West's Prairie Pioneers*** [1964] PBO.	$1.00	$3.00	$6.00
IL7-47	LeBlanc, Edward T. - editor - ***The Renegade Rustlers*** [1964] PBO.	$1.00	$3.00	$6.00
IL7-48	Janson, Hank - ***The Exotic Seductress*** [1964] Cover by Barton.	$2.50	$7.50	$15.00
IL7-49	Werper, Barton - ***Tarzan And The Cave City*** [1964] PBO. Unauthorized. (#2).	$4.00	$12.50	$25.00
IL7-50	O'Neill, Scott - ***Sex And The Starlets*** [1964] PBO. Photo cover.	$1.25	$3.75	$7.50
IL7-51	Edmund, Matty - ***Vicki*** [1964] PBO. Cover by Barton.	$2.50	$7.50	$15.00
IL7-52	LeBLanc, Edward T. - editor - ***Buffalo Bill's Tomahawk Duel*** [1964] PBO.	$1.00	$3.00	$6.00
IL7-53	Leblanc, Edward T. - editor - ***Buffalo Bill's Double*** [1964] PBO.	$1.00	$3.00	$6.00

Gold Star, IL7-60

Graphic, 31

Graphic, 58

		G	VG	F
IL7-54	Werper, Barton - ***Tarzan And The Snake People*** [1964] PBO. Unauthorized. (#3).	$4.00	$12.50	$25.00
IL7-55	O'Neill, Scott - ***Sex And The Jet Set*** [1964] PBO. Photo cover.	$1.25	$3.75	$7.50
IL7-56	Mason, Margot - ***What Makes You Tick? Volume I*** [1964] PBO.	$1.25	$3.75	$7.50
IL7-57	Janson, Hank - ***The Sexy Vixen*** [1964] Cover by Barton.	$2.50	$7.50	$15.00
IL7-58	LeBlanc, Edward T. - editor - ***Wild West And The Salted Mines*** [1965] PBO.	$1.00	$3.00	$6.00
IL7-59	LeBlanc, Edward T. - editor - ***Wild West's Whirlwind Riders*** [1965] PBO.	$1.00	$3.00	$6.00
IL7-60	Werper, Barton - ***Tarzan And The Abominable Snowmen*** [1965] PBO. Unauthorized. (#4).	$4.00	$12.50	$25.00
IL7-61	O'Neill, Scott - ***Sex And The Divorcee*** [1965] PBO. Photo cover.	$1.25	$3.75	$7.50
IL7-62	Mason, Margot - ***What Makes You Tick? Volume II*** [1965] PBO.	$1.25	$3.75	$7.50
IL7-63	Janson, Hank - ***The Affairs Of Paula*** [1965] Cover art by Harry Barton.	$2.50	$7.50	$15.00
IL7-64	Trott, Helen - ***Part-Time Call Girl*** [1965] PBO. Cover art by Harry Barton.	$2.50	$7.50	$15.00
IL7-65	Werper, Barton - ***Tarzan And The Winged Invaders*** [1975] PBO. Unauthorized. (#5). Cover art by Jack Endeweldt.	$4.00	$12.50	$25.00
IL7-66	O'Neill, Scott - ***Sex In The Service*** [1965] PBO. Photo cover.	$1.25	$3.75	$7.50
IL7-67	Howard, Peter - ***Sex And The Oriental*** [1965] PBO. Photo cover.	$1.25	$3.75	$7.50
IL7-68	Janson, Hank - ***A Nympho Named Sylvia*** [1965]	$2.50	$7.50	$15.00
IL7-69	Mason, Margot - ***What Makes You Tick? Volume III*** [1965] PBO.	$1.00	$3.00	$6.00
IL7-70	Janson, Hank - ***Becky*** [1965] PBO. Cover art by Maguire.	$2.50	$7.50	$15.00
IL7-71	O'Neill, Scott - ***Sex And The Alcoholic*** [1965] PBO. Photo cover.	$1.25	$3.75	$7.50
IL7-72	Mason, Margot - ***What Makes You Tick? Volume IV*** [1965] PBO.	$1.00	$3.00	$6.00
IL7-73	Dale, Sherry - ***Twilight Girls*** [1965] PBO. Cover art by Harry Schaare.	$2.50	$7.50	$15.00
IL7-74	Edited by Edward T. LeBlanc - ***Buffalo Bill's Fair Square Deal*** [1965] PBO.	$1.00	$3.00	$6.00
IL7-75	James, Jerry - ***Nympho Nurse*** [1965] PBO.	$2.00	$6.00	$12.00
IL7-76	James, Jerry - ***Woman-Hating Surgeon*** [1965] PBO.	$1.25	$3.75	$7.50

		G	VG	F
Golden Willow. Digest Size.				
51	Green, Shoshone - ***Rampage In The Rockies*** [1946]	$1.50	$5.00	$10.00
52	Fischer, Bruno - ***So Much Blood*** [1946]	$2.50	$7.50	$15.00
53	Nielsen, Virginia - ***Try To Forget Me*** [1946]	$1.50	$5.00	$10.00
54	Bosworth, Allan R. - ***Steel To The Sunset*** [1946]	$1.50	$5.00	$10.00
55	Hinckley, Julian - ***Murder By Schedule*** [1946]	$2.50	$7.50	$15.00
56	Eberhard, Florence - ***It's Love I'm After*** [1946]	$1.50	$5.00	$10.00

Graphic Books (Early Publisher's History, 1948–1959)

Sam Tankel and Zane Bouregy founded Graphic Books. Exceptional covers occur on many of these books, as Tankel and Bouregy co-wrote a book on two-color printing. Robert Maguire provided cover art for a few of the Graphic titles. Their line featured mysteries, westerns, and historical novels. The most noteworthy books are mysteries by William Irish, Day Keene, S. S. Van Dine, and Harry Whittington.

Graphic Publishing Company also presented the Graphic Giants or G series.

		G	VG	F
Graphic Books. New York: Graphic Publishing Co.				
11	Wade, Bob & Bill Miller - ***Murder Queen High*** [1949]	$1.25	$3.75	$7.50
12	Waugh, Hillary - ***If I Live To Dine*** [1949]	$1.25	$3.75	$7.50
13	Whelton, Paul - ***Flash-Hold For Murder*** [1949]	$1.25	$3.75	$7.50
14	Fox, James M. - ***Death Commits Bigamy*** [1949]	$1.25	$3.75	$7.50
15	Mulford, Clarence E. - ***Tex*** [1949]	$1.25	$3.75	$7.50
16	Irish, William - ***Deadline At Dawn*** [1949]	$3.00	$9.00	$18.00
17	Whelton, Paul - ***Call The Lady Indiscreet*** [1949]	$1.25	$3.75	$7.50
18	Ballard, W.T. - ***Dealing Out Death*** [1950]	$2.00	$6.00	$12.00
19	Whelton, Paul - ***Lures Of Death*** [1950]	$1.25	$3.75	$7.50
20	Irish, William - ***Dilemma Of The Dead Lady*** [1950]	$3.00	$9.00	$18.00
21	Marcus, Arthur A. - ***The Widow Gay*** [1950]	$1.25	$3.75	$7.50
22	Roeburt, John - ***Tough Cop*** [1950]	$1.25	$3.75	$7.50
23	Mulford, Clarence E. - ***The Man From Bar-20*** [1950]	$1.25	$3.75	$7.50
24	Whelton, Paul - ***Uninvited Corpse*** [1950]	$1.25	$3.75	$7.50
25	MacDonald, William Colt - ***The Singing Scorpion*** [1950]	$1.25	$3.75	$7.50
26	Ballard, W.T. - ***Murder Can't Stop*** [1950]	$2.00	$6.00	$12.00
27	Roeburt, John - ***Corpse On The Town*** [1950] PBO.	$1.25	$3.75	$7.50
28	Mulford, Clarence E. - ***Tex*** [1950]	$1.25	$3.75	$7.50
29	Wilmer, Dale - ***Memo For Murder*** [1951] PBO.	$1.35	$4.00	$8.00
30	Runyon, Damon - ***Runyon First And Last*** [1951]	$1.25	$3.75	$7.50
31	Irish, William - ***Deadly Night Call*** [1951]	$3.00	$9.00	$18.00
32	Rohmer, Sax - ***Hangover House*** [1951]	$3.00	$9.00	$18.00
33	Ozaki, Milton K. - ***The Dummy Murder Case*** [1951] PBO.	$1.50	$5.00	$10.00
34	Lehman, Paul E. - ***Texas Men*** [1951] PBO.	$1.35	$4.00	$8.00
35	Marcus, Arthur A. - ***Walk The Bloody Boulevard*** [1951] PBO.	$1.50	$5.00	$10.00
36	Whittington, Harry - ***Call Me Killer*** [1951] PBO.	$3.50	$10.00	$20.00
37	Whelton, Paul - ***Pardon My Blood*** [1951]	$1.25	$3.75	$7.50
38	Roeburt, John - ***Tough Cop*** [1951]	$1.25	$3.75	$7.50
39	Lehman, Paul Evan - ***Vultures Of Paradise Valley*** [1951] PBO.	$1.35	$4.00	$8.00
40	Stokes, Manning Lee - ***The Crooked Circle*** [1951] PBO.	$1.50	$5.00	$10.00
41	Whittington, Harry - ***Murder Is My Mistress*** [1951] PBO.	$3.50	$10.00	$20.00
42	Roeburt, John - ***There Are Dead Men In Manhattan*** [1951]	$1.25	$3.75	$7.50
43	Keene, Day - ***If The Coffin Fits*** [1952] PBO.	$2.50	$7.50	$15.00
44	Ernenwein, Leslie - ***Gun Hawk*** [1952] PBO.	$1.35	$4.00	$8.00
45	Martin, Aylwin Lee - ***Death For A Hussy*** [1952] PBO.	$1.50	$5.00	$10.00
46	Whittington, Harry - ***Mourn The Hangman*** [1952] PBO.	$3.50	$10.00	$20.00
47	Lehman, Paul Evan - ***Faces In The Dust*** [1952] PBO.	$1.35	$4.00	$8.00
48	Knight, David (Richard S. Prather) - ***Pattern For Murder*** [1952] PBO.	$2.50	$7.50	$15.00

Graphic, 87

Handi Book, NN #1

Handi Book, 8

		G	VG	F
49	Whelton, Paul - ***In Comes Death*** [1952]	$1.25	$3.75	$7.50
50	MacDonald, William Colt - ***The Singing Scorpion*** [1952]	$1.25	$3.75	$7.50
51	Keene, Day - ***Framed In Guilt*** [1952]	$2.50	$7.50	$15.00
52	Shorten and Fagaly - ***There Oughta Be A Law!*** [1952] PBO. Cover art by Al Fagaly. Cartoon book.	$2.50	$7.50	$15.00
53	Mulford, Clarence E. - ***Tex*** [1952]	$1.00	$3.00	$6.00
54	Wade, Bob & Miller, Bill - ***Murder-Queen High-*** [1952]	$1.00	$3.00	$6.00
55	Powell, Richard - ***A Shot In The Dark*** [1952]	$1.25	$3.75	$7.50
56	Lehman, Paul Evan - ***Texas Men*** [1952]	$1.25	$3.75	$7.50
57	Ozaki, Milton K. - ***The Deadly Pick-Up*** [1953] PBO.	$1.50	$5.00	$10.00
58	Keene, Day - ***Strange Witness*** [1953] PBO.	$2.50	$7.50	$15.00
59	Ronns, Edward - ***Dark Destiny*** [1953] PBO.	$1.50	$5.00	$10.00
60	Richards, William (Day Keene) - ***Dead Man's Tide*** [1953] PBO.	$2.50	$7.50	$15.00
61	Fagaly & Shorten - ***There Oughta Be A Law!*** [1953] Cover art by Al Fagaly. Cartoon book.	$2.50	$7.50	$15.00
62	Ernenwein, Leslie - ***Gun Hawk*** [1953]	$1.00	$3.00	$6.00
63	Roeburt, John - ***Tough Cop*** [1953]	$1.00	$3.00	$6.00
64	Marcus, Arthur A. - ***Walk The Bloody Boulevard*** [1953]	$1.00	$3.00	$6.00
65	Ballard, W.T. - ***Murder Can't Stop*** [1953]	$1.25	$3.75	$7.50
66	Lehman, Paul Evan - ***Vultures Of Paradise Valley*** [1953]	$1.00	$3.00	$6.00
67	Marcus, Arthur A. - ***Post-Mark Homicide*** [1953]	$1.00	$3.00	$6.00
68	Ronns, Edward - ***The Net*** [1953] PBO.	$1.50	$5.00	$10.00
69	Runyon, Damon - ***Runyon First And Last*** [1953]	$1.00	$3.00	$6.00
70	Reach, James - ***Late Last Night*** [1954]	$1.00	$3.00	$6.00
71	Whelton, Paul - ***Pardon My Blood*** [1954]	$1.00	$3.00	$6.00
72	Ballard, W.T. - ***Dealing Out Death*** [1954] Cover art by Walter Popp.	$1.25	$3.75	$7.50
73	Dewey, Thomas B. - ***Handle With Fear*** [1954] Cover art by Walter Popp.	$1.50	$5.00	$10.00
74	Martin, Chuck - ***Two-Gun Fury*** [1954] PBO. Cover art by John Leone.	$1.35	$4.00	$8.00
75	Keene, Day - ***The Big Kiss-Off*** [1954] PBO. Cover art by Clyde Ross.	$2.50	$7.50	$15.00
76	Ronns, Edward - ***Say It With Murder*** [1954] PBO. Cover art by Lou Marchetti.	$1.50	$5.00	$10.00
77	Holmes, L.P. - ***Gunman's Greed*** [1954] Cover art by John Leone.	$1.00	$3.00	$6.00
78	Rohmer, Sax - ***Hangover House*** [1954]	$1.50	$5.00	$10.00
79	Ozaki, Milton - ***Dressed To Kill*** [1954] PBO. Cover art by Walter Popp.	$1.50	$5.00	$10.00
80	Colter, Eli - ***Blood On The Range*** [1954]	$1.00	$3.00	$6.00
81	Irish, William - ***Deadly Night Call*** [1954]	$1.25	$3.75	$7.50

		G	VG	F
82	Lockridge, Richard & Frances - ***Stand Up And Die*** [1954] Cover art by Saul Levine.	$1.25	$3.75	$7.50
83	Gardner, Curtiss T. - ***The Fatal Cast*** [1954] Cover art by Clyde Ross.	$1.25	$3.75	$7.50
84	Bergquist, Lillian & Moore, Irving - ***Your Shot, Darling*** [1954] Cover art by Walter Popp.	$1.35	$4.00	$8.00
85	Fagaly & Shorten - ***More There Oughta Be A Law*** [1954] PBO. Cover art by Al Fagaly. Cartoon book.	$1.50	$5.00	$10.00
86	Martin, Chuck - ***Texas Pride*** [1954] PBO.	$1.35	$4.00	$8.00
87	Keene, Day - ***Homicidal Lady*** [1954] PBO.	$2.50	$7.50	$15.00
88	Pendleton, Ford - ***Outlaw Justice*** [1954] PBO. Cover art by John Leone.	$1.35	$4.00	$8.00
90	Saber, Robert O. - ***Too Young To Die*** [1954] PBO. Cover art by Walter Popp.	$1.50	$5.00	$10.00
91	Mulford, Clarence E. - ***Tex*** [1954]	$1.00	$3.00	$6.00
92	Ozaki, Milton K. - ***The Deadly Pick-Up*** [1954]	$1.25	$3.75	$7.50
93	Powell, Richard - ***Say It With Bullets*** [1954] Cover art by Walter Popp.	$1.25	$3.75	$7.50
94	Marlowe, Stephen - ***Model For Murder*** [1955] PBO. Cover art by Walter Popp.	$1.50	$5.00	$10.00
95	Welton, Paul - ***Call The Lady Indiscreet*** [1954]	$1.25	$3.75	$7.50
96	Thurman, Steve - ***Gun Lightning!*** [1955] PBO.	$1.35	$4.00	$8.00
97	Baker, Samm Sinclair - ***One Touch Of Blood*** [1955] PBO. Cover art by Clyde Ross.	$1.50	$5.00	$10.00
98	Stokes, Manning Lee - ***Too Many Murderers*** [1955] Cover art by Clyde Ross.	$1.25	$3.75	$7.50
99	Saber, Robert O. - ***Sucker Bait*** [1955] PBO.	$1.50	$5.00	$10.00
100	Lehman, Paul E. - ***Faces In The Dust*** [1955]	$1.25	$3.75	$7.50
101	Johnson, Victor H. - ***Cry Torment*** [1955] PBO.	$1.25	$3.75	$7.50
102	Marble, M.S. - ***Die By Night*** [1955] Cover art by Walter Popp.	$1.25	$3.75	$7.50
103	Gargoe, Richard - ***Girl In The Red Dress*** [1955] PBO.	$2.00	$6.00	$12.00
104	Malcolm-Smith, George - ***Mugs, Molls And Dr. Harvey*** [1955] Cover art by Carl Rose.	$1.50	$5.00	$10.00
105	Grew, William - ***Murder Has Many Faces*** [1955] PBO.	$1.50	$5.00	$10.00
106	Jones, George E. - ***Trap*** [1955] PBO.	$1.50	$5.00	$10.00
107	Anthology by Mik - ***The Adventures Of Ferd'Nand*** [1955] PBO. Cover art by Mik. Cartoon book.	$2.50	$7.50	$15.00
108	Irish, William - ***The Phantom Lady*** [1955]	$2.00	$6.00	$12.00
109	Fagaly & Shorten - ***More There Oughta Be A Law!*** [1955] Cover art by Al Fagaly. Cartoon book.	$1.50	$5.00	$10.00
110	Roeburt, John - ***The Hollow Man*** [1955] Cover art by Saul Levine.	$1.25	$3.75	$7.50
111	Saber, Robert O. - ***A Dame Called Murder*** [1955] PBO. Cover art by Walter Popp.	$1.50	$5.00	$10.00
112	Ernenwein, Leslie - ***Gun Hawk*** [1955]	$1.00	$3.00	$6.00
113	McCloy, Helen - ***Unfinished Crime*** [1955]	$1.25	$3.75	$7.50
114	Ronns, Edward - ***They All Ran Away*** [1955] PBO.	$1.50	$5.00	$10.00
115	Marcus, A.A. - ***Make Way For Murder*** [1955] PBO. Cover art by Barye Phillips.	$1.50	$5.00	$10.00
116	Pendleton, Ford - ***Hell Rider*** [1955] PBO. Cover art by George Gross.	$1.35	$4.00	$8.00
117	Stokes, Manning - ***Murder Can't Wait*** [1955] PBO. Cover art by Saul Levine.	$1.50	$5.00	$10.00
118	Fray, Al - ***And Kill Once More*** [1955] PBO. Cover art by Saul Levine.	$1.50	$5.00	$10.00
119	Gruber, Frank - ***Mood For Murder*** [1956] Photo cover.	$1.25	$3.75	$7.50
120	Ernenwein, Leslie - ***Texas Guns*** [1956] PBO. Cover art by Leo Summers.	$1.35	$4.00	$8.00
121	Roeburt, John - ***Tough Cop*** [1956]	$1.00	$3.00	$6.00

		G	VG	F
122	Vance, William - ***Homicide Lost*** [1956] PBO. Cover art by Barye Phillips.	$1.50	$5.00	$10.00
123	Saber, Robert O. - ***A Time For Murder*** [1956] PBO. Cover art by Walter Popp.	$1.50	$5.00	$10.00
124	Shelley, John L. - ***Gunpoint!*** [1956] PBO. Cover art by Saul Levine.	$1.35	$4.00	$8.00
125	Cohen, Octavus Roy - ***The Intruder*** [1956] Cover art by Saul Levine.	$1.25	$3.75	$7.50
126	Kelston, Robert - ***Murder's End*** [1956] PBO. Cover art by Robert Maguire.	$2.00	$6.00	$12.00
127	Wade, Harrison - ***So Lovely To Kill*** [1956] PBO. Cover art by Barye Phillips.	$1.50	$5.00	$10.00
128	Martin, Chuck - ***Two-Gun Fury*** [1956]	$1.00	$3.00	$6.00
129	Ward, Brad - ***Six-Gun Heritage*** [1956] Cover art by George Gross.	$1.25	$3.75	$7.50
130	Reach, James - ***Late Last Night*** [1956]	$1.00	$3.00	$6.00
131	Evans, Dean - ***This Kill Is Mine*** [1956] Cover art by Oliver Brabbins.	$1.25	$3.75	$7.50
132	Norton, Browning & Landolf, Charles A. - ***I Prefer Murder*** [1956] PBO. Cover art by Saul Levine.	$1.50	$5.00	$10.00
133	Pendleton, Ford - ***Gunmaster*** [1956] PBO. Cover art by Roy Lance.	$1.35	$4.00	$8.00
134	Duff, James - ***Who Dies There?*** [1956] PBO. Cover art by Walter Popp.	$1.50	$5.00	$10.00
135	Baker, Samm Sinclair - ***Murder - Very Dry*** [1956] PBO. Cover art by Oliver Brabbins.	$1.50	$5.00	$10.00
136	Brock, Stuart - ***Killer's Choice*** [1956] PBO. Cover art by Oliver Brabbins.	$1.50	$5.00	$10.00
137	Colter, Eli - ***Blood On The Range*** [1956]	$1.35	$4.00	$8.00
138	Farris, John - ***The Corpse Next Door*** [1956] PBO. Cover art by Oliver Brabbins.	$2.50	$7.50	$15.00
139	Duff, James - ***Some Die Young*** [1956] PBO. Cover art by Roy Lance.	$1.50	$5.00	$10.00
140	Saunders, Mack - ***Gun Trail*** [1956] PBO. Cover art by George Gross.	$1.35	$4.00	$8.00
141	Ozaki, Milton - ***Dressed To Kill*** [1956] Cover art by Walter Popp.	$1.25	$3.75	$7.50
142	Duke, Will - ***Fair Prey*** [1956] PBO. Cover art by Oliver Brabbins.	$1.35	$4.00	$8.00
143	Gregory, Dan - ***Three Must Die!*** [1956] PBO. Cover art by Roy Lance.	$1.50	$5.00	$10.00
144	Holmes, L.P. - ***Gunman's Creed*** [1956] Cover art by John Leone.	$1.00	$3.00	$6.00
145	Cassiday, Bruce - ***While Murder Waits*** [1957] PBO. Photo cover.	$1.50	$5.00	$10.00
146	Thompson, Gene - ***Six-Guns Wild*** [1957] PBO. Cover art by George Gross.	$1.35	$4.00	$8.00
147	Causey, James O. - ***Killer Take All!*** [1957] PBO. Cover art by Roy Lance.	$1.50	$5.00	$10.00
148	Powell, Richard - ***Say It With Bullets*** [1956] Cover art by Walter Popp.	$1.25	$3.75	$7.50
149	Lupton, Leonard - ***Murder Without Tears*** [1957] PBO. Cover art by Roy Lance.	$1.50	$5.00	$10.00
150	Saber, Robert O. - ***Too Young To Die*** [1957] Cover art by Walter Popp.	$1.25	$3.75	$7.50
151	Patten, Lewis B. - ***Gun Proud*** [1957] PBO. Cover art by Robert Stanley.	$1.35	$4.00	$8.00
152	Braham, Hal - ***Call Me Deadly*** [1957] PBO. Cover art by Walter Popp.	$1.50	$5.00	$10.00
153	Thurman, Steve - ***Gun Lightning!*** [1957]	$1.00	$3.00	$6.00

		G	VG	F
154	Pendleton, Ford - ***Outlaw Justice*** [1957] Cover art by John Leone.	$1.00	$3.00	$6.00
155	Pendleton, Ford - ***Gun Chance*** [1957] PBO. Cover art by George Gross.	$1.35	$4.00	$8.00
156	Saber, Robert O. - ***Sucker Bait*** [1957]	$1.00	$3.00	$6.00
157	Pendleton, Ford - ***Hell Rider*** [1957] Cover art by George Gross.	$1.00	$3.00	$6.00

Graphic Giant Series. Hasbrook Heights, NJ: Graphic Publishing Co.

		G	VG	F
G-101	Westcott, Jan - ***Captain For Elizabeth*** [1952] Cover art by Barye Phillips.	$1.25	$3.75	$7.50
G-201	Westcott, Jan - ***Captain For Elizabeth*** [1953]	$1.25	$3.75	$7.50
G-202	Heckelmann, Charles N. - ***River Queen*** [1953]	$1.25	$3.75	$7.50
G-203	Anthology edited by Craig Rice - ***45 Murderers*** [1954] A collection of true crime stories.	$1.50	$5.00	$10.00
G-204	Steincrohn, Peter J., M.D. - ***How To Live With Your Heart*** [1954]	$1.00	$3.00	$6.00
G-205	Peacock, Max - ***King's Rogue*** [1954] Cover art by Saul Levine.	$1.25	$3.75	$7.50
G-206	Koestler, Arthur - ***The Gladiators*** [1954]	$1.25	$3.75	$7.50
G-207	Edited by William McFee - ***Great Sea Stories*** [1954]	$1.35	$4.00	$8.00
G-208	Pei, Mario - ***Swords For Charlemagne*** [1955] Cover art by Maguire.	$1.25	$3.75	$7.50
G-209	Clou, John - ***The Golden Blade*** [1955] Cover art by Robert Maquire.	$1.25	$3.75	$7.50
G-210	Thompson, Ben - ***Gunman's Spawn*** [1955] PBO. Cover art by Robert Stanley.	$1.25	$3.75	$7.50
G-211	Westcott, Jan - ***Captain For Elizabeth*** [1955]	$1.25	$3.75	$7.50
G-212	O'Hara, Donn - ***Rogue Royal*** [1956] PBO. Cover art by Robert Maguire.	$1.25	$3.75	$7.50
G-213	Koestler, Arthur - ***The Gladiators*** [1956]	$1.25	$3.75	$7.50
G-214	Chidsey, Donald Barr - ***Captain Bashful*** [1956]	$1.25	$3.75	$7.50
G-215	Grey, Harry - ***Call Me Duke*** [1956] Cover art by Samson Pollen.	$1.25	$3.75	$7.50
G-216	Erskine, John - ***The Private Life Of Helen Of Troy*** [1956]	$1.25	$3.75	$7.50
G-217	Edited by Laurette Pizer - ***Eve's Daughters*** [1957] PBO.	$1.35	$4.00	$8.00
G-218	Prescott, John - ***Guns Of Hell Valley*** [1957] PBO. Cover art by Roy Lance.	$1.35	$4.00	$8.00
G-219	Pei, Mario - ***Swords For Charlemagne*** [1957] Cover art by Robert Maguire.	$1.25	$3.75	$7.50
G-220	Clou, John - ***The Golden Blade*** [1957] Cover art by Robert Maguire.	$1.25	$3.75	$7.50
G-221	Heckelmann, Charles N. - ***River Queen*** [1957] Cover art by Harry Barton.	$1.25	$3.75	$7.50
G-222	O'Hara, Donn - ***The Fair And The Bold*** [1957] PBO. Cover art by Barye Phillips.	$1.25	$3.75	$7.50
G-223	Thompson, Ben - ***Gunman's Spawn*** [1957] Cover art by Robert Stanley.	$1.25	$3.75	$7.50

Green Dragon Books. New York: William H. Wise. Digest Size.

		G	VG	F
NO#	Smith, Laurence Dwight - ***The Corpse With The Listening Ear*** [1944] Digest size. Cover by Hoffman.	$2.00	$6.00	$12.00
1	Secrist, Kelliher - ***Murder Makes By-Lines*** [1944] Cover by Hoffman. Digest size.	$2.00	$6.00	$12.00
2	Daniels, Norman A. - ***The Mausoleum Key*** [1944] Cover by Hoffman. Digest size.	$2.00	$6.00	$12.00
3	Dell, Amen - ***Johnny On The Spot*** [1944] Digest size. Cover by Hoffman.	$2.00	$6.00	$12.00
4	Avery, Robert - ***A Murder A Day!*** [1944] Digest size.	$2.00	$6.00	$12.00
5	Litvinoff, Ivy - ***The Moscow Mystery*** [1944] Digest size.	$2.00	$6.00	$12.00
6	Goldman, R. L. - ***The Snatch*** [1944] Digest size. Cover by Hoffman.	$2.00	$6.00	$12.00

		G	VG	F
8	Ashbrook, H. - ***A Most Immoral Murder*** [1944] Cover by Hoffman. Digest size.	$2.00	$6.00	$12.00
9	Dall, Jack - ***Murder Moves On*** [1944] Cover by Hoffman. Digest size.	$2.00	$6.00	$12.00
10	Goldman, R. L. - ***Death Plays Solitaire*** [1944] Cover by Hoffman. Digest size.	$2.00	$6.00	$12.00
11	Childerness, George - ***Too Many Murderers*** [1944] Digest size.	$2.00	$6.00	$12.00
12	Cameron, Donald Clough - ***Grave Without Grass*** [1944] Digest size.	$2.00	$6.00	$12.00
13	Perowne, Barry - ***Ten Words Of Poison*** [1945] Cover by Hoffman. Digest Size.	$2.00	$6.00	$12.00
14	Benton, John L. - ***Talent For Murder*** [1945] Cover by Hoffman. Digest size.	$2.00	$6.00	$12.00
16	Bonney, Joseph L. - ***Murder Without Clues*** [1945] Digest size.	$2.00	$6.00	$12.00
17	Fleming, Robert - ***... And Death Drove On*** [1945] Digest size.	$2.00	$6.00	$12.00
18	Ashbrook, H. - ***Murder Comes Back*** [1945] Cover by Hoffman. Digest size.	$2.00	$6.00	$12.00
19	Muir, Denis - ***Death Defies The Doctor*** [1945] Digest size.	$2.00	$6.00	$12.00
20	Cameron, Donald Clough - ***Death At Her Elbow*** [1945] Digest size.	$2.00	$6.00	$12.00
21	Leitfred, Robert H. - ***The Man Who Was Murdered Twice*** [1945] Digest size.	$2.00	$6.00	$12.00
23	Reed, David V. - ***I Thought I'd Die*** [1945] Digest size.	$2.50	$7.50	$15.00
24	Ervin, Mari - ***If I Die - It's Murder*** [1945] Digest size.	$2.00	$6.00	$12.00
25	Secrist, Kelliher - ***She Screamed Blue Murder*** [1945] Paperback size.	$2.50	$7.50	$15.00
26	Laing, Patrick - ***Stone Dead*** [1945] Paperback size.	$2.50	$7.50	$15.00
27	Abbot, Anthony - ***About The Murder Of The Night Club Lady*** [1945] Paperback size.	$2.50	$7.50	$15.00
28	Hawkins, Dean - ***Headsman's Holiday*** [1946] Paperback size.	$2.50	$7.50	$15.00
29	Blizard, Marie - ***The Late Lamented Lady*** [1946] Paperback size.	$2.50	$7.50	$15.00
30	Merwin, Jr., Sam - ***A Matter Of Policy*** [1946] Paperback size.	$3.00	$9.00	$18.00
31	Long, Amelia Reynolds - ***Murder By Magic*** [1946] Paperback size.	$2.50	$7.50	$15.00
32	Blizard, Marie - ***The Men In Her Death*** [1946] Paperback size.	$2.50	$7.50	$15.00
33	Smith, Lawrence Dwight - ***Death Is Thy Neighbor*** [1946] Paperback size.	$2.50	$7.50	$15.00

Green Publishing. New York: Green Publishing Co. Digest Size.

		G	VG	F
1	Francis, William - ***Rough On Rats*** [1945]	$1.50	$5.00	$10.00
2	Landon, Herman - ***The Back-Seat Murder*** [1945]	$1.50	$5.00	$10.00
3	DeWitt, Jack - ***Murder On Shark Island*** [1945]	$1.50	$5.00	$10.00
4	Francis, William - ***Bury Me Not*** [1945]	$1.50	$5.00	$10.00
5	Rowe, Anne - ***The Little Dog Barked*** [1944]	$1.50	$5.00	$10.00
6	Marshall, Sidney - ***Some Like It Hot*** [1945]	$1.50	$5.00	$10.00
7	Gollomb, Joseph - ***Eleven True Crimes*** [1945] PBO.	$2.00	$6.00	$12.00
8	Greene, Josiah E. - ***The Laughing Loon*** [1945]	$1.50	$5.00	$10.00
9	Landon, Herman - ***The Owl's Warning*** [1945]	$1.50	$5.00	$10.00
10	Saxby, Charles - ***Death In The Sun*** [1945]	$1.50	$5.00	$10.00
11	Eberhardt, Walter E. - ***A Dagger In The Dark*** [1945]	$1.50	$5.00	$10.00
12	Francis, William - ***Kill Or Cure*** [1945]	$1.50	$5.00	$10.00
13	Scott, R.T.M. - ***Murder Stalks The Mayor*** [1945]	$1.50	$5.00	$10.00
14	Cohen, Octavus Roy - ***The Backstage Mystery*** [1945]	$1.50	$5.00	$10.00

Greenleaf Classic.

		G	VG	F
GC-101	Kenton, Maxwell - ***Candy*** [1965]	$1.00	$3.00	$6.00
GC-107	Miller, Henry - ***The Rosy Crucifixion*** [1965]	$1.25	$3.75	$7.50
GC-202	Haas, Ben - ***KKK*** [1965]	$1.00	$3.00	$6.00

		G	VG	F
GC-205	Wood, Jr., Edward D. - ***Orgy Of The Dead*** [1966] PBO. Movie tie-in with photos throughout.	$17.00	$50.00	$100.00
GC-206	Nuetzel, Charles - ***Queen Of Blood*** [1966] PBO. Movie tie-in with photos throughout.	$15.00	$45.00	$90.00
GC-209	Banis, Victor J. - ***The Why Not*** [1966] PBO.	$1.00	$3.00	$6.00
GC-210	Miller, Henry - ***Tropic Of Cancer/Tropic Of Capricorn*** [1966] PBO.	$1.25	$3.75	$7.50
GC-212	Lockwood, Tom - ***Sons Of A Beach*** [1966] PBO.	$1.25	$3.75	$7.50
GC-214	Hudson, Jan (George H. Smith) - ***Hell's Angels*** [1966] PBO.	$2.50	$7.50	$15.00
GC-217	Van Heller, Marcus - ***The House Of Borgia*** [1966]	$1.25	$3.75	$7.50
GC-218	Kalnen, Ray - ***The Love Box*** [1967] PBO.	$3.50	$10.00	$20.00
GC-219	Credit, Richard W. - ***Apple Pie*** [1967] PBO.	$1.00	$3.00	$6.00
GC-220	Hudson, Jan (George H. Smith) - ***Those Sexy Saucer People*** [1967] PBO.	$1.00	$3.00	$6.00
GC-221	Rogers, Mick - ***Freakout On Sunset Strip*** [1967] PBO.	$1.00	$3.00	$6.00
GC-224	Shuffler, Jack C. - ***The Charmer*** [1967]	$1.00	$3.00	$6.00
GC-228	Jones, Henry - ***The Enormous Bed*** [1967] PBO.	$1.00	$3.00	$6.00
GC-229	De La Bretonne, Restif - ***Pleasures And Follies*** [1967]	$1.25	$3.75	$7.50
GC-233	Cantab, A. - ***Two Flappers In Paris*** [1967]	$1.25	$3.75	$7.50
GC-236	Daimler, Harriet - ***Darling*** [1967] PBO.	$1.25	$3.75	$7.50
GC-237	Desmond, Robert - ***The Libertine*** [1967] PBO.	$1.25	$3.75	$7.50
GC-238	Desmond, Robert - ***Heaven, Hell And The Whore*** [1967] PBO.	$1.25	$3.75	$7.50
GC-240	Harrack, Tim - ***Melting*** [1967] PBO.	$1.25	$3.75	$7.50
GC-251	Baron, Willie - ***Play This Love With Me*** [1967] PBO.	$1.25	$3.75	$7.50
GC-257	Daimler, Harriet - ***Innocence*** [1967] PBO.	$1.00	$3.00	$6.00
GC-258	Archer, Jack/Herbert, Lord George - ***Flossie/A Night In A Moorish Harem*** [1967]	$1.00	$3.00	$6.00
GC-259	De Las Lunas, Carmencita - ***Thongs*** [1967] PBO.	$1.00	$3.00	$6.00
GC-260	Lengel, Frances - ***The Carnal Days Of Helen Seferis*** [1967]	$1.25	$3.75	$7.50
GC-264	Anonymous - ***Maudie*** [1967] PBO.	$1.00	$3.00	$6.00
GC-266	Homer & Associates - ***A Bedside Odyssey*** [1967] PBO.	$1.00	$3.00	$6.00
GC-274	Daimler, Harriet & Crannach, Henry - ***The Pleasure Theives*** [1968] PBO.	$1.00	$3.00	$6.00
GC-275	Nakoff, Yuri - ***Desire And Molly's Mishap*** [1968] PBO.	$1.00	$3.00	$6.00
GC-280	? - ***The Story Of Juliette (Vol. I)*** [1968]	$1.00	$3.00	$6.00
GC-281	? - ***The Story Of Juliette (Vol. II)*** [1968]	$1.25	$3.75	$7.50
GC-283	Vicarion, Count Palmiro - ***Lust*** [1968]	$1.25	$3.75	$7.50
GC-284	Amory, R. - ***Listen, The Loon Sings*** [1968]	$1.25	$3.75	$7.50
GC-285	Del Piombo, Akbar - ***The Double-Bellied Companion*** [1968] PBO.	$1.25	$3.75	$7.50
GC-287	? - ***The Seduction Of Suzy*** [1968]	$1.00	$3.00	$6.00
GC-289	Van Heller, Marcus - ***The Head Humper*** [1968]	$1.00	$3.00	$6.00
GC-290	Dikes, Mickey - ***Sarabande For A Bitch*** [1968] PBO.	$1.25	$3.75	$7.50
GC-292	Anthology - ***Only A Boy & Others*** [1968]	$1.00	$3.00	$6.00
GC-297	Anonymous - ***The Way Of A Man With A Maid*** [1968] PBO.	$1.25	$3.75	$7.50
GC-298	Van Heller, Marcus - ***Cruel Lips*** [1968] PBO.	$1.25	$3.75	$7.50
GC-303	Walker, L.H. - ***The Lascivious Abbot*** [1967] PBO.	$1.00	$3.00	$6.00
GC-304	? - ***Pursuit Of Happiness*** [1968]	$1.00	$3.00	$6.00
GC-309	Anthology told by students - ***True Love: Its First Practice*** [1968] PBO.	$1.00	$3.00	$6.00
GC-315	Angelique, Pierre - ***A Tale Of Satisfied Desire*** [1968] PBO.	$1.00	$3.00	$6.00
GC-316	Anonymous - ***The Old Man Young Again*** [1968]	$1.00	$3.00	$6.00
GC-317	Arnoldson, P. - ***Fleshly Inheritance*** [1968]	$1.25	$3.75	$7.50
GC-318	Graham, Whidden - ***Crimson Hairs*** [1968] PBO.	$1.25	$3.75	$7.50
GC-319	Wagner, Geoffrey - ***Axel*** [1968] PBO.	$1.50	$5.00	$10.00
GC-322	Anonymous - ***Adventures Of Nemesis Hunt*** [1968] PBO.	$1.00	$3.00	$6.00
GC-323	Greene, Bob - ***Sex Rebel: Black*** [1968] PBO.	$1.25	$3.75	$7.50
GC-326	? - ***Little Janie Horner*** [1968]	$1.25	$3.75	$7.50
GC-331	Newton, Orville - ***Cruise To The End Of Love*** [1968] PBO.	$1.25	$3.75	$7.50
GC-332	Kem, Arnold - ***The Misfortunes Of Mary*** [1968] PBO.	$1.25	$3.75	$7.50

		G	VG	F
GC-333	Kleft, B. Van - ***The Voluptuous Experiment*** [1968] PBO.	$1.00	$3.00	$6.00
GC-334	Cocteau, Jean/Angelique, Pierre - ***The White Paper/The Naked Beast At Heaven's Gate*** [1968] PBO.	$1.00	$3.00	$6.00
GC-336	Anonymous/Anonymous - ***The Blue Cinema/The Memoirs Of A Singer*** [1968] PBO.	$1.25	$3.75	$7.50
GC-337	Anonymous/Anonymous - ***The Good Samaritan/My Romance Of The Alcove*** [1968] PBO.	$1.25	$3.75	$7.50
GC-340	Linder, D. Barry - ***Somebody Is Watching You*** [1968] PBO.	$1.00	$3.00	$6.00
GC-341	Fredericks, David - ***Degenerate Empress*** [1968] PBO.	$1.25	$3.75	$7.50
GC-344	? - ***The Voice Of Erotica*** [1968]	$1.25	$3.75	$7.50
GC-345	Laird, Andrew - ***The Diary Of Kathleen O'Day*** [1968] PBO.	$1.25	$3.75	$7.50
GC-348	Trevor, Jay - ***Run Into The Sea*** [1968] PBO.	$1.00	$3.00	$6.00
GC-352	Hughes, Peter Tuesday - ***The Other Party*** [1968] PBO.	$1.25	$3.75	$7.50
GC-353	Baxter, Shane V. - ***Mission: Sinpossible*** [1968] PBO.	$1.00	$3.00	$6.00
GC-354	? - ***The Constant Virgin*** [1968]	$1.00	$3.00	$6.00
GC-356	? - ***The Epic*** [1968]	$1.00	$3.00	$6.00
GC-357	Gray, Sebastion - ***Tropic Of Taurus*** [1968]	$1.00	$3.00	$6.00
GC-361	? - ***The Pleasure Web*** [1968]	$1.00	$3.00	$6.00
GC-363	Nolan, Lewis - ***Nature's Way*** [1968]	$1.00	$3.00	$6.00
GC-364	George, Carter - ***Shameri La*** [1968]	$1.25	$3.75	$7.50
GC-365	? - ***The Odor Of Sin*** [1968]	$1.25	$3.75	$7.50
GC-373	Wilson, Ben - ***The Bet-Set Orgies*** [1969]	$1.25	$3.75	$7.50
GC-375	Roxbury, Kyle - ***The Golden Girl Of Hockeinbeck*** [1969]	$1.00	$3.00	$6.00
GC-376	Fanchon, Lisa - ***The Plundered Virgin*** [1969]	$1.25	$3.75	$7.50
GC-377	Linder, D. Barry - ***Silver Bells And Cockle Shells*** [1969]	$1.50	$5.00	$10.00
GC-378	Jorgen, Peter - ***Nut-Cracker Sweet*** [1969]	$1.25	$3.75	$7.50
GC-379	Johns, Ian - ***Charlotte*** [1969]	$1.00	$3.00	$6.00
GC-381	Gray, Sebastian - ***Partygirl*** [1969]	$1.00	$3.00	$6.00
GC-382	Adams, Cleveland - ***Letters From Three Maids*** [1969]	$1.00	$3.00	$6.00
GC-383	? - ***The Olympians*** [1969]	$1.00	$3.00	$6.00
GC-385	De Granamour, A. - ***The Mandarin Orgies*** [1969]	$1.00	$3.00	$6.00
GC-386	Linder, D. Barry - ***Turned On*** [1969]	$1.50	$5.00	$10.00
GC-387	Savage, Steve - ***The Daemon Lover*** [1969]	$1.50	$5.00	$10.00
GC-388	? - ***Flesh Scavenger*** [1969]	$1.00	$3.00	$6.00
GC-389	? - ***The Devil's Breath*** [1969]	$1.35	$4.00	$8.00
GC-393	Linder, D. Barry - ***Libido/23*** [1969]	$1.00	$3.00	$6.00
GC-407	? - ***Sally In Black Bondage*** [1969]	$1.00	$3.00	$6.00
GC-408	Regret, Winston - ***Orinoco Captive*** [1969]	$1.00	$3.00	$6.00
PC-1006	Del Piombo, Akbar - ***Skirts*** [1971] PBO.	$1.35	$4.00	$8.00
PC-1068	Power, C. - ***Spell Of Madness*** [1971]	$1.00	$3.00	$6.00

Griffin Books. New York: Griffin Books, Inc. Digest Size.

NO#-1	Saxon, John - ***Love On Call*** [n.d.]	$4.00	$12.50	$25.00
NO#-2	Sturdy, Carl - ***Confessions Of A Hat Check Girl*** [n.d.]	$4.00	$12.50	$25.00
NO#-3	McClellan, William - ***Hotel Love*** [n.d.]	$4.00	$12.50	$25.00
NO#-4	Stone, Thomas - ***Stolen Love*** [n.d.]	$4.00	$12.50	$25.00
NO#-5	Sturdy, Carl - ***Easy Virtue*** [n.d.]	$4.00	$12.50	$25.00
NO#-6	Sloan, Gladys - ***Wronged Virgin*** [n.d.]	$4.00	$12.50	$25.00
NO#-7	Brewster, Eliot - ***Office Playgirl*** [n.d.]	$4.00	$12.50	$25.00
NO#-8	Branca, Florenz - ***Love Siren*** [n.d.] Cover by Rodewald.	$4.00	$12.50	$25.00

Grove Press Black Cat Books. New York: Grove Press, Inc.

BC-135	Kerouac, Jack - ***Satori In Paris*** [1966] PBO.	$2.00	$6.00	$12.00

Guinn Company.

NN	Stafford, Muriel - ***X Marks The Dot*** [1943] PBO.	$1.50	$5.00	$10.00

Gunfire Western Novel. Digest Size.

6	Tuttle, W.C. - ***The Morgan Trail*** [n.d.]	$1.25	$3.75	$7.50
7	Mulford, Clarence E. - ***The Deputy Sheriff*** [n.d.]	$1.25	$3.75	$7.50

		G	VG	F
9	Robertson, Frank C. - ***Vigilante War In Buena Vista*** [n.d.]	$1.25	$3.75	$7.50
10	Bardwell, Denver - ***Prairie Fire*** [n.d.]	$1.25	$3.75	$7.50
11	MacDonald, William Colt - ***Rebel Ranger*** [n.d.]	$1.25	$3.75	$7.50
12	Robertson, Frank C. - ***Cowman's Jack-Pot*** [n.d.]	$1.25	$3.75	$7.50
13	Moore, Amos - ***Devlin's Day Off*** [n.d.] Cover art by Charles Wood.	$1.25	$3.75	$7.50
14	MacDonald, William Colt - ***Six-Gun Melody*** [n.d.] Cover art by Charles Wood.	$1.25	$3.75	$7.50
15	Robertson, Frank C. - ***Getley's Gold*** [n.d.] Cover art by Saunders.	$1.25	$3.75	$7.50
16	Gooden, Arthur Henry - ***Smoke Tree Range*** [n.d.]	$1.25	$3.75	$7.50
17	MacDonald, William Colt - ***Thunderbird Trail*** [n.d.]	$1.25	$3.75	$7.50
18	Knight, Kim - ***Dangerous Dust*** [n.d.] Cover by Charles Wood.	$1.25	$3.75	$7.50
19	MacDonald, William Colt - ***The Vanishing Gunslinger*** [n.d.]	$1.25	$3.75	$7.50
20	Robertson, Frank C. - ***Grizzly Meadows*** [n.d.]	$1.25	$3.75	$7.50
21	Lomas, Bliss - ***The Phantom Corral*** [n.d.]	$1.25	$3.75	$7.50
22	MacDonald, William Colt - ***The Three Mesquiteers*** [n.d.]	$1.25	$3.75	$7.50
23	Newland, N.M. - ***Dunn Of The Double D*** [n.d.] Cover art by Charles Wood.	$1.25	$3.75	$7.50
24	Hoffman, W.D. - ***The Range Rebellion*** [n.d.]	$1.25	$3.75	$7.50
25	Rider, Brett - ***Boss Of The OK*** [n.d.] Cover art by Charles Wood.	$1.25	$3.75	$7.50
26	MacDonald, William Colt - ***Master Of The Mesa*** [n.d.] Cover by Charles Wood.	$1.25	$3.75	$7.50
27	Gunn, Tom - ***Painted Post Law*** [n.d.] Cover art by Charles Wood.	$1.25	$3.75	$7.50
28	Halleran, E.E. - ***Outlaw Guns*** [n.d.]	$1.25	$3.75	$7.50
30	Hardy, Stuart - ***The Miracle At Gopher Creek*** [n.d.]	$1.25	$3.75	$7.50
32	Drago, Harry Sinclair - ***Desert Water*** [n.d.]	$1.25	$3.75	$7.50
33	Robertson, Frank C. - ***Rope Crazy*** [n.d.]	$1.25	$3.75	$7.50
34	Sims, John - ***Outlaw Of Hidden Valley*** [n.d.]	$1.25	$3.75	$7.50
35	West, Tom - ***Botched Brand*** [n.d.] Cover art by Charles Wood.	$1.25	$3.75	$7.50
36	Grinstead, J.E. - ***Feud At Silver Bend*** [n.d.]	$1.25	$3.75	$7.50
37	Hardy, Stuart - ***The Man From Nowhere*** [n.d.]	$1.25	$3.75	$7.50
41	Floren, Lee - ***Milk River Range*** [n.d.]	$1.25	$3.75	$7.50
42	Snow, Charles H. - ***Guns Along The Border*** [n.d.]	$1.25	$3.75	$7.50
43	Floren, Lee - ***The Long S*** [n.d.]	$1.25	$3.75	$7.50
45	Lee, Ranger - ***Rebel On The Range*** [n.d.]	$1.25	$3.75	$7.50
46	Robertson, Frank C. - ***The Pride Of Pine Creek*** [n.d.]	$1.25	$3.75	$7.50
48	Roan, Tom - ***Montana Outlaw*** [n.d.]	$1.25	$3.75	$7.50
49	McCulley, Johnston - ***Range Lawyer*** [n.d.] Cover by Charles Wood.	$1.25	$3.75	$7.50
50	Hopson, William - ***Silver Gulch*** [n.d.] Cover art by Charles Wood.	$1.25	$3.75	$7.50
51	Floren, Lee - ***Smugglers' Range*** [n.d.] PBO.	$1.25	$3.75	$7.50
53	Thomas, Lee - ***Dusty Boots*** [n.d.]	$1.25	$3.75	$7.50

Handi-Books (Early Publisher's History, 1941–1959)

Stapled rather than glued bindings differentiate Handi-Books from most of their competitors. They offered a strong line of mysteries and westerns. They interspersed three very collectible science fiction novels and a few esoteric novels throughout the line. The quality of the covers remains high, with fine, colorful, and attractive artwork.

Quinn Publishing Company, Inc., offered a number of other lines, including a short four-volume series entitled Handi-Books Western. Also, Quinn published two science digests of anthologies from material in *If* magazine.

Handi-Books. Kingston, NY: Quinn Publishing Co.

		G	VG	F
NO#-1	Philips, Judson - ***Odds On The Hot Seat*** [1941]	$6.00	$20.00	$40.00
NO#-2	Adams, Cleve F. - ***Decoy*** [1942]	$4.00	$12.50	$25.00
NO#-3	Chase, James Hadley - ***12 Chinks And A Woman*** [1942]	$10.00	$30.00	$60.00
NO#-4	Roscoe, Theodore - ***7 Men*** [1942] PBO.	$4.00	$12.50	$25.00
NO#-5	Polsky, Thomas - ***Curtains For The Copper*** [1942]	$4.00	$12.50	$25.00
NO#-6	Fleming, Robert - ***A Bullet In His Cap*** [1942]	$4.00	$12.50	$25.00
NO#-7	Adams, Cleve F. - ***The Black Door*** [1942]	$4.00	$12.50	$25.00
8	Ronald, James - ***She Got What She Asked For*** [1942] Cover art by J. L. Quinn.	$4.00	$12.50	$25.00
9	Long, Manning - ***Vicious Circle*** [1942]	$4.00	$12.50	$25.00
10	Archer, Robert - ***The Case Of The Vanishing Women*** [1943] Cover art by J. L. Quinn.	$4.00	$12.50	$25.00
11	Offord, Lenore Glen - ***The 9 Dark Hours*** [1943] Cover art by J. L. Quinn.	$4.00	$12.50	$25.00
12	Merwin, Jr., Sam - ***The Big Frame*** [1943]	$4.00	$12.50	$25.00
13	Sale, Richard - ***Lazarus #7*** [1943]	$10.00	$30.00	$60.00
14	Woolrich, Cornell - ***Black Alibi*** [1943]	$6.00	$20.00	$40.00
15	Hallidays, Brett - ***The Case Of The Walking Corpse*** [1943] Cover art by Colitzer.	$5.50	$17.50	$35.00
16	Philips, Judson - ***The 14th Trump*** [1943]	$4.00	$12.50	$25.00
17	Wilson, Mitchell - ***Footsteps Behind Her*** [1943]	$4.00	$12.50	$25.00
18	Cheyney, Peter - ***The Unscrupulous Mr. Callaghan*** [1943]	$4.00	$12.50	$25.00
19	Sale, Richard - ***Passing Strange*** [1943]	$5.50	$17.50	$35.00
20	Purtell, Joseph - ***To A Blindfold Lady*** [1943]	$4.00	$12.50	$25.00
21	Phillips, James Atlee - ***The Case Of The Shivering Chorus Girls*** [1943]	$3.50	$10.00	$20.00
22	Chambers, Dana - ***The Blonde Died First*** [1944]	$3.50	$10.00	$20.00
23	Sterling, Stewart - ***Five Alarm Funeral*** [1944]	$3.50	$10.00	$20.00
24	Philips, Judson - ***Murder In Marble*** [1944]	$3.50	$10.00	$20.00
25	Jackson, Giles - ***The Court Of Shadows*** [1944]	$3.50	$10.00	$20.00
26	Sanders, Daphne (Craig Rice) - ***To Catch A Thief*** [1944]	$4.00	$12.50	$25.00
27	Fisher, Steve - ***I Wake Up Screaming*** [1944]	$3.50	$10.00	$20.00
28	Chambers, Dana - ***The Frightened Man*** [1944]	$3.50	$10.00	$20.00
29	Gilbert, Anthony - ***The Woman In Red*** [1944]	$3.50	$10.00	$20.00
30	Michel, M. Scott - ***The X-Ray Murders*** [1944]	$3.50	$10.00	$20.00
31	Powell, Richard - ***The Case Of The Curious Chair*** [1944]	$3.50	$10.00	$20.00
32	Brackett, Leigh - ***No Good From A Corpse*** [1944]	$8.00	$25.00	$50.00
33	Adams, Cleve - ***Up Jumped The Devil*** [1944]	$3.50	$10.00	$20.00
34	Chambers, Dana - ***The Last Secret*** [1945]	$5.00	$15.00	$30.00
35	Wellard, James Howard - ***The Snake In The Grass*** [1945]	$3.50	$10.00	$20.00
36	Eisinger, Jo - ***The Walls Came Tumbling Down*** [1945]	$3.50	$10.00	$20.00
37	Addis, Hugh - ***The Dark Voyage*** [1945]	$3.50	$10.00	$20.00
38	Lariar, Lawrence - ***The Man With The Lumpy Nose*** [1945]	$3.50	$10.00	$20.00
39	Presnell, F. G. - ***Send Another Coffin*** [1945]	$3.50	$10.00	$20.00
40	Davis, Norbert - ***Dead Little Rich Girl*** [1945]	$4.00	$12.50	$25.00
41	Hawkins, John and Ward - ***If I Kill Him*** [1945]	$3.50	$10.00	$20.00
42	Barry, Joe - ***The Fall Guy*** [1945]	$3.50	$10.00	$20.00
43	Meyrick, Gordon - ***The Body On The Pavement*** [1945]	$3.50	$10.00	$20.00
44	Merwin, Jr., Sam - ***Knife In My Back*** [1945]	$4.00	$12.50	$25.00
45	Dow, John - ***The Blonde Is Dead*** [1945]	$3.50	$10.00	$20.00
46	Roeburt, John - ***The Case Of The Tearless Widow*** [1946]	$3.50	$10.00	$20.00
47	Michel, M. Scott - ***Sweet Murder*** [1946]	$3.50	$10.00	$20.00
48	Goldthwaite, Eaton K. - ***The Body Next Door*** [1946]	$3.50	$10.00	$20.00
49	Doherty, Ed - ***The Corpse Who Wouldn't Die*** [1946]	$3.50	$10.00	$20.00
50	Brandon, William - ***The Dangerous Dead*** [1946]	$3.50	$10.00	$20.00
51	Chambers, Dana - ***Darling, This Is Death*** [1946]	$3.50	$10.00	$20.00
52	Barry, Joe - ***The Triple Cross*** [1946]	$3.50	$10.00	$20.00
53	Quentin, Patrick - ***Puzzle For Players*** [1946]	$3.50	$10.00	$20.00
54	Davis, Norbert - ***Oh, Murderer Mine*** [1946] PBO.	$4.00	$12.50	$25.00

Handi Book, 110

Handi Book, 120

Handi Book, 131

		G	VG	F
55	Rutledge, Nancy - ***Blood On The Cat*** [1946]	$3.50	$10.00	$20.00
56	Rogers, Joel Townsley - ***Lady With The Dice*** [1946] PBO.	$4.00	$12.50	$25.00
57	Chambers, Dana - ***Death Against Venus*** [1946] Cover art by Clark.	$3.50	$10.00	$20.00
58	Jerome, Owen Fox - ***The Corpse Awaits*** [1947] Cover by J. L. Quinn.	$3.50	$10.00	$20.00
59	Logan, Carolynne and Malcolm - ***One Of These Seven*** [1947]	$3.50	$10.00	$20.00
60	Bryson, Leigh - ***The Gloved Hand*** [1947] PBO.	$4.00	$12.50	$25.00
61	Michel, M. Scott - ***The Black Key*** [1947]	$3.50	$10.00	$20.00
62	Jenkins, Will F. - ***The Murder Of The U.S.A.*** [1947]	$8.00	$25.00	$50.00
63	Barry, Joe - ***The Clean-Up*** [1947]	$3.50	$10.00	$20.00
64	Burke, Richard - ***The Fourth Star*** [1947]	$3.50	$10.00	$20.00
65	Miller, Wade (Bob Wade and Bill Miller) - ***Guilty Bystander*** [1947]	$3.50	$10.00	$20.00
68	Ring, Adam - ***Killers Play Rough*** [1947]	$3.50	$10.00	$20.00
69	Ernenwein, Leslie - ***Bullet Breed*** [1947]	$3.00	$9.00	$18.00
70	Stark, Michael - ***Run For Your Life*** [1948]	$3.50	$10.00	$20.00
71	Friend, Oscar J. - ***The Range Maverick*** [1948]	$3.00	$9.00	$18.00
72	Kane, Frank - ***Death About Face*** [1948]	$3.50	$10.00	$20.00
73	Lehman, Paul Evan - ***Only The Brave*** [1948]	$3.00	$9.00	$18.00
74	Evans, John - ***If You Have Tears*** [1948]	$3.50	$10.00	$20.00
75	Ernenwein, Leslie - ***Boss Of Panamint*** [1948]	$3.00	$9.00	$18.00
76	Currier, Jay L. - ***Cargo Of Fear*** [1948]	$3.50	$10.00	$20.00
77	Lehman, Paul Evan - ***Calamity Range*** [1948]	$3.00	$9.00	$18.00
78	Wilson, Lee - ***This Deadly Dark*** [1948]	$3.50	$10.00	$20.00
79	Friend, Oscar J. - ***Gun Harvest*** [1948]	$3.00	$9.00	$18.00
80	Van Dycke, Tom and Kerner, Ben - ***Not With My Neck*** [1948]	$3.50	$10.00	$20.00
81	Cody, Al - ***Empty Saddles*** [1948]	$3.00	$9.00	$18.00
82	Jackson, Giles - ***Witch's Moon*** [1949]	$3.50	$10.00	$20.00
83	Ernewein, Leslie - ***The Faro Kid*** [1949]	$3.00	$9.00	$18.00
84	Lee, Carolina - ***Yaller Gal*** [1949]	$3.00	$9.00	$18.00
85	Graham, Lewis - ***The Great I Am*** [1949]	$2.50	$7.50	$15.00
86	Cameron, Don - ***Dig Another Grave*** [1949]	$3.50	$10.00	$20.00
87	Lehman, Paul Evan - ***Idaho*** [1949]	$3.00	$9.00	$18.00
88	Waugh, Hillary - ***Hope To Die*** [1949]	$3.50	$10.00	$20.00
89	Joscelyn, Archie - ***The Kind Of Thunder Valley*** [1949]	$3.00	$9.00	$18.00
90	Gaddis, Peggy - ***Love To Burn*** [1949]	$2.50	$7.50	$15.00
91	Sherman, Joan - ***Lulie*** [1949]	$2.50	$7.50	$15.00
92	Lariar, Lawrence - ***The Girl With The Frightened Eyes*** [1949]	$3.50	$10.00	$20.00
93	Ernenwein, Leslie - ***Rebel Yell*** [1949]	$3.00	$9.00	$18.00
94	Boswell, Charles - ***They All Died Young*** [1949] PBO.	$4.00	$12.50	$25.00

Handi Book, 139

Harlequin, 20

Harlequin, 25

		G	VG	F
95	Colter, Eli - ***The Outcast Of Lazy S*** [1949]	$3.00	$9.00	$18.00
96	Saber, Robert O. - ***The Black Dark Murders*** [1949] PBO.	$4.00	$12.50	$25.00
97	Herbert, F. Hugh - ***A Lover Would Be Nice*** [1949]	$2.50	$7.50	$15.00
98	Van Wyck, Mason - ***Spider House*** [1949]	$3.50	$10.00	$20.00
99	Lehman, Paul Evan - ***The Cold Trail*** [1949] PBO.	$3.50	$10.00	$20.00
100	Ozaki, Milton K. - ***Too Many Women*** [1950]	$3.50	$10.00	$20.00
101	Friend, Oscar J. - ***The Range Doctor*** [1950]	$3.00	$9.00	$18.00
102	Lee, Carolina - ***Satan's Gal*** [1950] PBO.	$4.00	$12.50	$25.00
103	Grinstead, J. E. - ***Maverick Guns*** [1950]	$3.00	$9.00	$18.00
104	Pruitt, Alan - ***The Restless Corpse*** [1950]	$3.50	$10.00	$20.00
105	Fox, Norman A. - ***The Rider From Yonder*** [1950]	$3.00	$9.00	$18.00
106	Barry, Joe - ***Three For The Money*** [1950] PBO.	$4.00	$12.50	$25.00
107	Lehman, Paul Evan - ***The Siren Of Silver Valley*** [1950] PBO.	$3.50	$10.00	$20.00
108	Saber, Robert O. - ***The Affair Of The Frigid Blonde*** [1950] PBO.	$4.00	$12.50	$25.00
109	Joscelyn, Archie - ***Shannahan's Feud*** [1950] PBO.	$3.50	$10.00	$20.00
110	Fairman, Paul W. - ***The Glass Ladder*** [1950] PBO. Cover art by Privitello.	$5.00	$15.00	$30.00
111	Ernenwein, Leslie - ***Renegade Ramrod*** [1950] PBO.	$3.50	$10.00	$20.00
112	Adams, Cleve F. - ***No Wings On A Cop*** [1950] PBO. Cover art by Privitello.	$4.00	$12.50	$25.00
113	Friend, Oscar J. - ***Barricade*** [1950] PBO.	$3.50	$10.00	$20.00
114	Edgley, Leslie - ***False Face*** [1950]	$3.50	$10.00	$20.00
115	Grinstead, J. E. - ***Range King*** [1950]	$3.00	$9.00	$18.00
116	Ozaki, Milton K. - ***A Fiend In Need*** [1950]	$3.50	$10.00	$20.00
117	Holt, Tex - ***Thunder Of Hoofs*** [1950]	$3.00	$9.00	$18.00
118	Bellem, Robert Leslie - ***The Window With The Sleeping Nude*** [1950] PBO. Only two books by this "Black Mask" writer. This book is his second.	$12.50	$37.50	$75.00
119	Lehman, Paul Evan - ***Vengeance Valley*** [1950] PBO.	$3.50	$10.00	$20.00
120	Whittington, Harry - ***Slay Ride For A Lady*** [1950] PBO.	$12.50	$37.50	$75.00
121	Austin, Brett - ***Rawhide Summons*** [1950]	$3.00	$9.00	$18.00
122	Ronns, Edward (Edward S. Aarons) - ***Dark Memory*** [1950] PBO. Cover art by Privitello.	$4.00	$12.50	$25.00
123	Grinstead, J. E. - ***When Texans Ride*** [1950]	$3.00	$9.00	$18.00
124	Saber, Robert O. - ***The Scented Flesh*** [1951] PBO. Cover art by Privitello.	$4.00	$12.50	$25.00
125	Pearce, Dick - ***Valley Of The Tyrant*** [1951] PBO.	$3.50	$10.00	$20.00
126	Lee, Carolina - ***Yaller Gal*** [1951]	$2.50	$7.50	$15.00
127	Ernenwein, Leslie - ***The Faro Kid*** [1951]	$2.50	$7.50	$15.00
128	Blochmann, Lawrence G. - ***Pursuit*** [1951] PBO.	$4.00	$12.50	$25.00

		G	VG	F
129	Fairman, Paul W. - ***The Heiress Of Copper Butte*** [1951] PBO.	$4.00	$12.50	$25.00
130	Saber, Robert O. - ***The Dove*** [1951] PBO.	$4.00	$12.50	$25.00
131	Whittington, Harry - ***The Lady Was A Tramp*** [1951] PBO.	$6.00	$20.00	$40.00
132	Westland, Lynn - ***Trail Rider*** [1951]	$2.50	$7.50	$15.00
133	Clay, Weston - ***Boot Hill*** [1951]	$2.50	$7.50	$15.00
134	Levinson, Saul - ***Murder Is Dangerous*** [1951] Cover by Norman Saunders.	$2.50	$7.50	$15.00
135	Pruitt, Alan - ***Typed For A Corpse*** [1951] PBO. Cover by Norman Saunders.	$2.50	$7.50	$15.00
136	Holt, Tex - ***Dark Canyon*** [1951] Cover by Norman Saunders.	$2.50	$7.50	$15.00
137	Hopson, William - ***Yucca City Outlaw*** [1951] Cover by Norman Saunders.	$2.50	$7.50	$15.00
138	Whittington, Harry - ***The Brass Monkey*** [1951] PBO.	$8.00	$25.00	$50.00
139	Brannon, William T. - ***The Lady Killers*** [1951] PBO.	$3.50	$10.00	$20.00

Handi-Book Western. Kingston, NY: Quinn Publishing Co.

		G	VG	F
1	Lehman, Paul Evan - ***The Cow Kingdom*** [1946]	$5.00	$15.00	$30.00
2	Ernenwein, Leslie - ***Rio Renegade*** [1946]	$5.00	$15.00	$30.00
3	Friend, Oscar J. - ***The Long Noose*** [1947]	$5.00	$15.00	$30.00
4	Lehman, Paul Evan - ***West Of The Wolverine*** [1947]	$5.00	$15.00	$30.00

Handy Books. Toronto: Adam Publishing Co. Digest size.

		G	VG	F
1	Kelley, Thomas P. - ***The Face That Launched A Thousand Ships*** [1941]	$17.00	$50.00	$100.00
2	Smith, Major E. Cecil - ***Red Ally*** [1941]	$22.00	$70.00	$140.00

Hangman's House Mystery. New York: Journal of Living Publishing Corp. Digest Size.

		G	VG	F
1	Nonweiler, Arville - ***Murder On The Pike*** [1946] Digest size.	$2.00	$6.00	$12.00
2	Kootz - ***Puzzle In Paint*** [1946] Digest size.	$2.00	$6.00	$12.00
3	Childerness, George - ***Murder In False Face*** [1946] Digest size.	$2.00	$6.00	$12.00
4	Jenkins, Will F. - ***The Man Who Feared*** [1946] Digest size.	$4.00	$12.50	$25.00
5	McKenzie, A.R. - ***Death Gets A Head*** [1946] Digest size.	$2.00	$6.00	$12.00
6	Owen, Hans C. - ***Fit To Kill*** [1946] Digest size.	$2.00	$6.00	$12.00
7	Brown, Gerald - ***Murder On Beacon Hill*** [1946] Digest size.	$2.00	$6.00	$12.00
8	Holman, Hugh - ***Death Like Thunder*** [1946] Digest size.	$2.00	$6.00	$12.00
9	Vinton, Aldin - ***The Corpse In The Cab*** [1943] Digest size.	$2.00	$6.00	$12.00
10	Hultman, Helen Joan - ***Murder In Odd Sizes*** [1946] Digest size.	$2.00	$6.00	$12.00
11	Koehler, Robert Portner - ***Murder Wore Green*** [1942] Digest size.	$2.00	$6.00	$12.00
13	Ronns, Edward (Edward S. Arrons) - ***The Cowl Of Doom*** [1946] Paperback size.	$2.50	$7.50	$15.00
14	Leitfred, Robert H. - ***The Corpse That Spoke*** [1946] Paperback size.	$2.50	$7.50	$15.00
15	Gregory, F.L. - ***The Cipher Of Death*** [1946] Paperback size.	$2.50	$7.50	$15.00
16	Mullen, Clarence - ***Therby Hangs A Corpse*** [1946] Paperback size.	$2.50	$7.50	$15.00
17	Koehler, Robert Portner - ***The Road House Murders*** [1946] Paperback size.	$2.50	$7.50	$15.00
18	Manners, David X. - ***Memory Of A Scream*** [1946] Paperback size.	$2.50	$7.50	$15.00
19	Abrahams, Robert D. - ***Death In 1-2-3*** [1946] Paperback size.	$2.50	$7.50	$15.00
20	Hirsch, Lee - ***Murder Steals The Show*** [1946] Paperback size.	$2.50	$7.50	$15.00
21	Shannon, Carl - ***Lady That's My Skull*** [1946] Paperback size.	$2.50	$7.50	$15.00

Hanro. Digest size.

		G	VG	F
1	Stone, Thomas - ***Careless Hussy*** [1945]	$2.50	$7.50	$15.00
2	Lindsay, Perry - ***Shady Lady*** [1945]	$2.50	$7.50	$15.00
3	Williams, Wright - ***Illegal Wife*** [1945]	$2.50	$7.50	$15.00
4	Bennett, Hall - ***Confessions Of A Part-Time Bride*** [1945]	$2.50	$7.50	$15.00

Harborough. London: Harbrough Publishing Co. Digest size.

		G	VG	F
NO#-1	Elliott, William J. - ***Lost Souls In Bohemia*** [n.d.] Cover by Heade.	$6.00	$20.00	$40.00
NO#-2	Elliott, William J. - ***The Demon Of Desire*** [n.d.]	$5.50	$17.50	$35.00
NO#-3	Elliott, William J. - ***Shipwreck Passion*** [1950] PBO. Cover by Heade.	$8.00	$25.00	$50.00
NO#-4	Elliott, William J. - ***And Worms Have Eaten Them*** [n.d.]	$5.50	$17.50	$35.00
NO#-5	Renin, Paul - ***Virtue*** [n.d.] Cover by Heade.	$3.50	$10.00	$20.00
NO#-6	Renin, Paul - ***Love*** [n.d.] Cover by Heade.	$3.50	$10.00	$20.00
NO#-7	Renin, Paul - ***A Fortnight's Folly*** [n.d.] Cover by Heade.	$3.50	$10.00	$20.00
NO#-8	Renin, Paul - ***Men, Women, Love*** [n.d.] Cover by Heade.	$3.50	$10.00	$20.00
NO#-9	Renin, Paul - ***The Brute*** [n.d.]	$5.50	$17.50	$35.00
NO#-10	Renin, Paul - ***The Sin Called Love*** [n.d.]	$3.50	$10.00	$20.00
NO#-11	Renin, Paul - ***Eve's Daughter*** [n.d.]	$4.00	$12.50	$25.00
NO#-12	Renin, Paul - ***Heads! I Marry You*** [n.d.]	$4.00	$12.50	$25.00
NO#-13	Renin, Paul - ***Divorce*** [n.d.]	$3.50	$10.00	$20.00
NO#-14	Renin, Paul - ***Scandal*** [n.d.]	$3.50	$10.00	$20.00
NO#-15	Renin, Paul - ***A Night Out*** [n.d.]	$3.50	$10.00	$20.00
NO#-16	Renin, Paul - ***Can A Man Forgive?*** [n.d.]	$3.50	$10.00	$20.00
NO#-17	Renin, Paul - ***All That Glitters*** [n.d.]	$3.50	$10.00	$20.00
NO#-18	Renin, Paul - ***Daring Diana*** [n.d.]	$3.50	$10.00	$20.00
NO#-19	Renin, Paul - ***She Who Hesitates*** [n.d.]	$3.50	$10.00	$20.00
NO#-20	Renin, Paul - ***Secret Lovers*** [n.d.]	$3.50	$10.00	$20.00
NO#-21	Renin, Paul - ***When A Woman Loves*** [n.d.]	$3.50	$10.00	$20.00
NO#-22	Renin, Paul - ***Sex*** [n.d.]	$2.50	$7.50	$15.00
NO#-23	Renin, Paul - ***Broken Vows*** [n.d.]	$3.50	$10.00	$20.00
NO#-24	Renin, Paul - ***Foolish Women*** [n.d.]	$3.50	$10.00	$20.00
NO#-25	Renin, Paul - ***The Kiss Of Shame*** [n.d.]	$3.50	$10.00	$20.00
NO#-26	Renin, Paul - ***Sacrifice*** [n.d.]	$3.50	$10.00	$20.00
NO#-27	Renin, Paul - ***Those Without Shame*** [n.d.]	$3.50	$10.00	$20.00
NO#-28	Renin, Paul - ***When Men Betray*** [n.d.]	$3.50	$10.00	$20.00
NO#-29	Renin, Paul - ***Dolores*** [n.d.]	$3.50	$10.00	$20.00
NO#-30	Renin, Paul - ***Good Time Girls*** [n.d.]	$3.50	$10.00	$20.00
NO#-31	Renin, Paul - ***Thy Neighbour's Wife*** [n.d.]	$3.50	$10.00	$20.00
NO#-32	Renin, Paul - ***Love*** [n.d.]	$3.50	$10.00	$20.00
NO#-33	Renin, Paul - ***Midnight*** [n.d.]	$3.50	$10.00	$20.00
NO#-34	Renin, Paul - ***The Lady Of Leicester Square*** [n.d.]	$3.50	$10.00	$20.00
NO#-35	Renin, Paul - ***Compromised*** [n.d.]	$3.50	$10.00	$20.00
NO#-36	Renin, Paul - ***Outrage*** [n.d.]	$3.50	$10.00	$20.00
NO#-37	Renin, Paul - ***Beyond Convention*** [n.d.]	$3.50	$10.00	$20.00
NO#-38	Renin, Paul - ***Enticed*** [n.d.]	$3.50	$10.00	$20.00
NO#-39	Renin, Paul - ***Bright Young Things*** [n.d.]	$3.50	$10.00	$20.00
NO#-40	Renin, Paul - ***Atonement*** [n.d.]	$3.50	$10.00	$20.00
NO#-41	Renin, Paul - ***Afterwards*** [n.d.]	$3.50	$10.00	$20.00
NO#-42	Renin, Paul - ***Bitter Sweets*** [n.d.]	$3.50	$10.00	$20.00
NO#-43	Renin, Paul - ***Co-Respondent*** [n.d.]	$3.50	$10.00	$20.00
NO#-44	Renin, Paul - ***Pampered Passion*** [n.d.]	$3.50	$10.00	$20.00
NO#-45	Renin, Paul - ***White Woman*** [n.d.]	$3.50	$10.00	$20.00
NO#-46	Renin, Paul - ***Unfaithful*** [n.d.]	$3.50	$10.00	$20.00
NO#-47	Renin, Paul - ***Unforgivable Sin*** [n.d.]	$3.50	$10.00	$20.00
NO#-48	Renin, Paul - ***The Other Woman*** [n.d.]	$3.50	$10.00	$20.00
NO#-49	Renin, Paul - ***Pleasure's Price*** [1949] PBO. Cover by Heade	$4.00	$12.50	$25.00
NO#-50	Renin, Paul - ***A Double Life*** [n.d.] Cover by Heade.	$3.50	$10.00	$20.00
NO#-51	Renin, Paul - ***Flame*** [n.d.] PBO. Cover by Heade.	$4.00	$12.50	$25.00
NO#-52	Renin, Paul - ***Gilded Women*** [n.d.]	$3.50	$10.00	$20.00
NO#-53	Renin, Paul - ***One Night In Paris*** [n.d.]	$3.50	$10.00	$20.00
NO#-54	Royer, Louis Charles - ***Where They Breed*** [n.d.]	$2.50	$7.50	$15.00

Harlequin, 33

Harlequin, 51

Harlequin, 108

Harlequin Books (Early Publisher's History, 1949–1959)

One thinks of Harlequin Books upon hearing the words "Romance paperback." They published more romance titles than any North American publisher, but in the early years, they published a variety of books. Richard H. G. Bonneycastle founded this Canadian publishing dynasty. The first 768 titles represent the full spectrum of genres. They published science fiction, literature, sports, mystery, westerns, cookbooks, nonfiction, adventures, and even esoteric titles. Fragile covers or those damaged in the binding occur frequently. Colorful and vivid art covers these early volumes. The most desirable titles come from the first 768 books, with the exception of some of the romance titles. Highly sought titles include all the science fiction and fantasy titles plus many of the mystery and esoteric titles.

In addition to a number of Romance lines, Harlequin Books, Ltd., published Laser Books.

		G	VG	F
Harlequin Books. Toronto: Harlequin Books, Inc.				
1	Bruff, Nancy - ***The Manatee*** [1949]	$12.50	$37.50	$75.00
2	Wees, Frances Shelly - ***Lost House*** [1949]	$10.00	$30.00	$60.00
3	Hunt, Howard - ***Maelstrom*** [1949]	$5.00	$15.00	$30.00
4	Bryant, Arthur Herbert - ***Double Image*** [1949]	$5.00	$15.00	$30.00
5	Nichols, Margaret - ***Close To My Heart*** [1949]	$5.00	$15.00	$30.00
6	Snow, Charles H. - ***Wolf Of The Mesas*** [1949]	$5.00	$15.00	$30.00
7	Cooke, Ronald J. - ***The House On Craig Street*** [1949] PBO. Cover by Rickard.	$5.50	$17.50	$35.00
8	Wees, Frances Shelly - ***Honeymoon Mountain*** [1949]	$5.00	$15.00	$30.00
9	Fuller, Samuel Michael - ***The Dark Page*** [1949]	$5.00	$15.00	$30.00
10	Long, Manning - ***Here's Blood In Your Eye*** [1949]	$5.00	$15.00	$30.00
11	King-Hall, Magdalen - ***The Wicked Lady Skelton*** [1949]	$5.50	$17.50	$35.00
12	Terrall, Robert - ***A Killer Is Loose Among Us*** [1949] Cover by Rickard.	$5.50	$17.50	$35.00
13	McCord, Joseph - ***His Wife The Doctor*** [1949]	$4.00	$12.50	$25.00
14	Snow, Charles H. - ***Six-Guns Of Sandoval*** [1949]	$5.00	$15.00	$30.00
15	Powers, Tom - ***Virgin With Butterflies*** [1949]	$4.00	$12.50	$25.00
16	Lindsay, Perry - ***No Nice Girl*** [1949]	$4.00	$12.50	$25.00
17	Petersen, Herman - ***The D.A.'s Daughter*** [1949]	$4.00	$12.50	$25.00
18	Snow, Charles H. - ***Rebel Of Ronde Valley*** [1949]	$4.00	$12.50	$25.00
19	Glay, George Albert - ***Gina*** [1949] Cover by Rickard.	$3.00	$9.00	$18.00
20	Miller, Helen Topping - ***Flame Vine*** [1949]	$5.00	$15.00	$30.00

		G	VG	F
21	Snow, Charles H. - ***Renegade Ranger*** [1949]	$3.50	$10.00	$20.00
22	Cardwell, Ann - ***Crazy To Kill*** [1949]	$4.00	$12.50	$25.00
23	Kandel, Aben - ***City For Conquest*** [1949]	$3.50	$10.00	$20.00
24	Gunn, Tom - ***Painted Post Outlaws*** [1949]	$3.50	$10.00	$20.00
25	Mace, Merlda - ***Blondes Don't Cry*** [1949] Cover by Rickard.	$4.00	$12.50	$25.00
26	Jordan, Gail - ***Gambling On Love*** [1950]	$3.50	$10.00	$20.00
27	Handley, Alan - ***Kiss Your Elbow*** [1950]	$4.00	$12.50	$25.00
28	Mooney, Martin - ***One Year With Grace*** [1950] Cover by Rickard.	$3.50	$10.00	$20.00
29	Nye, Nelson C. - ***Gunfighter Breed*** [1950]	$3.50	$10.00	$20.00
30	Nichols, Margaret - ***Portrait Of Love*** [1950] Cover by Cy Heal	$3.00	$9.00	$18.00
31	Kenyon, Theda - ***The Golden Feather*** [1950]	$4.00	$12.50	$25.00
32	Hecht, Ben - ***Hollywood Mystery!*** [1950]	$4.00	$12.50	$25.00
33	Miller, Helen Topping - ***Candle In The Morning*** [1950] Cover by Cy Heal.	$4.00	$12.50	$25.00
34	Rabl, S. S. - ***Mobtown Clipper*** [1950]	$3.50	$10.00	$20.00
35	Campbell, Patricia - ***Lush Valley*** [1950]	$3.00	$9.00	$18.00
36	Malina, Fred - ***Murder Over Broadway*** [1950]	$4.00	$12.50	$25.00
37	Frisbie, R. D. - ***Amaru*** [1950]	$3.50	$10.00	$20.00
38	Snow, Charles H. - ***Sheriff Of Yavisa*** [1950]	$3.50	$10.00	$20.00
39	Truesdell, June - ***Be Still My Love*** [1950]	$3.00	$9.00	$18.00
40	Reed, Blair - ***Pass Key To Murder*** [1950]	$4.00	$12.50	$25.00
41	Canning, Victor - ***Panthers' Moon*** [1950]	$4.50	$14.00	$28.00
42	Michel, M. Scott - ***House In Harlem*** [1950]	$4.00	$12.50	$25.00
43	Barry, Joe - ***The Clean-Up*** [1950]	$4.00	$12.50	$25.00
44	Hughes, Dorothy B. - ***The So Blue Marble*** [1950]	$4.00	$12.50	$25.00
45	Kersh, Gerald - ***Night And The City*** [1950]	$5.50	$17.50	$35.00
46	Gilmore, Cecile - ***Fair Stranger*** [1950] Cover by Cy Heal.	$3.00	$9.00	$18.00
47	Sturdy, Carl - ***Registered Nurse*** [1950]	$2.50	$7.50	$15.00
48	Weston, Garnett - ***Poldrate Street*** [1950] Cover by Ralph.	$3.00	$9.00	$18.00
49	Evans, John - ***Weep Not Fair Lady*** [1950]	$4.00	$12.50	$25.00
50	McCord, Joseph - ***One Way Street*** [1950]	$3.50	$10.00	$20.00
51	Cookbook - ***The Pocket Purity Cook Book*** [1950] PBO. Photo cover.	$20.00	$60.00	$125.00
52	Cookbook - ***Livre de Cuisine Purity Petit Format*** [1950]	$25.00	$75.00	$180.00
53	White, William Chapman - ***The Pale Blonde Of Sands Street*** [1950] Cover by Rickard.	$5.50	$17.50	$35.00
54	Holding, Elizabeth Saxany - ***Speak Of The Devil*** [1950]	$4.00	$12.50	$25.00
55	Healy, Eugene - ***Mr. Sandeman Loses His Life*** [1950]	$3.50	$10.00	$20.00
56	Cooke, Ronald J. - ***The Mayor Of Cote St. Paul*** [1950] PBO.	$3.50	$10.00	$20.00
57	Bogart, William - ***Murder Man*** [1950]	$4.00	$12.50	$25.00
58	Halleran, E. E. - ***Outposts Of Vengeance*** [1950]	$3.00	$9.00	$18.00
59	Sale, Richard - ***Cardinal Rock*** [1950]	$4.00	$12.50	$25.00
60	Holding, Elisabeth Saxany - ***Lady Killer*** [1950]	$4.00	$12.50	$25.00
61	Halleran, E.E. - ***Shadow Of The Badlands*** [1950]	$3.50	$10.00	$20.00
62	Merwin, Jr., Sam - ***Message From A Corpse*** [1950]	$4.00	$12.50	$25.00
63	Brandon, William - ***The Dangerous Dead*** [1950]	$4.00	$12.50	$25.00
64	Michel, M. Scott - ***Sinister Warning*** [1950]	$4.00	$12.50	$25.00
65	Clamp, H. M. E. - ***Bridewell Beauty*** [1950]	$3.00	$9.00	$18.00
66	Moore, Amos - ***Royce Of The Royal Mounted*** [1950] Cover by Glover.	$3.50	$10.00	$20.00
67	Tracy, Don - ***Criss Cross*** [1950]	$4.00	$12.50	$25.00
68	Bogart, William G. - ***The Queen City Murder Case*** [1950] Cover by Rickard.	$4.00	$12.50	$25.00
69	Schofield, William G. - ***Payoff In Black*** [1950]	$4.00	$12.50	$25.00
70	Merwin, Jr., Sam - ***Knife In My Back*** [1950]	$4.00	$12.50	$25.00
71	Anthology - ***Bouquet Knitter's Guide*** [1950] Photos throughout.	$5.00	$15.00	$30.00
72	Brown, Joy - ***Night Of Terror*** [1950]	$4.00	$12.50	$25.00
73	Joscelyn, Archie - ***The King Of Thunder Valley*** [1950]	$3.00	$9.00	$18.00
74	Mason, Van Wyck - ***Spider House*** [1950]	$4.00	$12.50	$25.00

		G	VG	F
75	Grinstead, J. E. - ***Maverick Guns*** [1950] Cover by Rickard.	$3.00	$9.00	$18.00
76	Long, Amelia Reynolds - ***The Corpse Came Back*** [1950] Cover by Glover.	$4.00	$12.50	$25.00
77	Jerome, Owen Fox - ***A Night At Club Bagdad*** [1950]	$4.00	$12.50	$25.00
78	MacMillan, Don - ***Rink Rat*** [1950] Cover by Ralph.	$3.00	$9.00	$18.00
79	Sale, Richard - ***Lazarus #7*** [1950] Photo cover.	$17.00	$50.00	$100.00
80	Laurenson, R. M. - ***Case Of The Six Bullets*** [1950]	$3.00	$9.00	$18.00
81	Lehman, Paul Evan - ***Idaho*** [1950] Cover by Glover.	$3.00	$9.00	$18.00
82	Lehman, Paul Evan - ***The Cold Trail*** [1950]	$3.00	$9.00	$18.00
83	Barry, Joe - ***The Fall Guy*** [1950] Cover by Glover.	$4.00	$12.50	$25.00
84	Barry, Joe - ***The Triple Cross*** [1950]	$4.00	$12.50	$25.00
85	Rhoades, Knight - ***She Died On The Stairway*** [1950]	$4.00	$12.50	$25.00
86	Jerome, Owen Fox - ***Double Life*** [1950]	$4.00	$12.50	$25.00
87	Merwin, Jr., Sam - ***Murder In Miniatures*** [1950]	$4.00	$12.50	$25.00
88	Ernenwein, Leslie - ***Renegade Ramrod*** [1950]	$3.00	$9.00	$18.00
89	Ernenwein, Leslie - ***The Faro Kid*** [1950]	$3.00	$9.00	$18.00
90	Marcus, Arthur A. - ***The Widow Gay*** [1950]	$4.00	$12.50	$25.00
91	Shannon, Carl - ***Lady, That's My Skull*** [1951]	$4.00	$12.50	$25.00
92	Cameron, Doug - ***Dig Another Grave*** [1951]	$4.00	$12.50	$25.00
93	Cody, Al - ***Empty Saddles*** [1951]	$3.00	$9.00	$18.00
94	Friend, Oscar J. - ***The Range Doctor*** [1951]	$3.00	$9.00	$18.00
95	Chase, James Hadley - ***You're Lonely When You're Dead*** [1951]	$5.50	$17.50	$35.00
96	Fox, Norman A. - ***The Rider From Yonder*** [1951] Cover by Glover.	$3.00	$9.00	$18.00
97	Findley, Ferguson - ***My Old Man's Badge*** [1951] Cover by Glover.	$4.00	$12.50	$25.00
98	Roeburt, John - ***Jigger Moran*** [1951]	$3.50	$10.00	$20.00
99	Wade, Bob & Miller, Bill - ***Murder-Queen High*** [1951] Cover by Glover.	$3.50	$10.00	$20.00
100	Cole, Jackson - ***Black Rider*** [1951]	$3.00	$9.00	$18.00
101	Barry, Joe - ***Three For The Money*** [1951]	$3.50	$10.00	$20.00
102	Moore, Brian - ***Wreath For A Redhead*** [1951]	$4.00	$12.50	$25.00
103	Hall, O. M. - ***Wanton City*** [1951]	$3.50	$10.00	$20.00
104	Roeburt, John - ***Tough Cop*** [1951]	$3.50	$10.00	$20.00
105	Lehman, Paul Evan - ***Vengeance Valley*** [1951]	$3.00	$9.00	$18.00
106	Bellem, Robert Leslie - ***The Window With The Sleeping Nude*** [1951]	$10.00	$30.00	$60.00
107	Mulford, Clarence E. - ***The Man From Bar-20*** [1951]	$3.00	$9.00	$18.00
108	Chase, James Hadley - ***No Orchids For Miss Blandish*** [1951]	$8.00	$25.00	$50.00
109	Roeburt, John - ***Corpse On The Town*** [1951]	$3.50	$10.00	$20.00
110	Hopson, William - ***Tombstone Stage*** [1951]	$3.00	$9.00	$18.00
111	Chase, James Hadley - ***The Flesh Of The Orchid*** [1951]	$4.00	$12.50	$25.00
112	Glay, George Albert - ***Gina*** [1951] Photo cover.	$2.50	$7.50	$15.00
113	Plaidy, Jean - ***Beyond The Blue Mountains*** [1951]	$2.50	$7.50	$15.00
114	Bogart, William G. - ***Johnny Saxon*** [1951] Cover by Harmon.	$4.00	$12.50	$25.00
115	Roeburt, John - ***Manhatten Underworld*** [1951]	$3.50	$10.00	$20.00
116	Creasey, John - ***Kill The Toff*** [1951] Cover by Shane.	$3.50	$10.00	$20.00
117	Moore, Brian - ***The Executioners*** [1951] PBO.	$12.50	$37.50	$75.00
118	Lehman, Paul Evan - ***Range Justice*** [1951] Cover by Derrett.	$3.00	$9.00	$18.00
119	Grinstead, J. E. - ***When Texans Ride*** [1951]	$3.00	$9.00	$18.00
120	Whittington, Harry - ***Slay Ride For A Lady*** [1951]	$6.00	$20.00	$40.00
121	Stark, Michael - ***Run For Your Life*** [1951] Cover by Harmon.	$3.50	$10.00	$20.00
122	Merwin, Jr., Sam - ***A Matter Of Policy*** [1951]	$3.50	$10.00	$20.00
123	Echols, Allan K. - ***Saddle Wolves*** [1951] Cover by Derrett.	$3.00	$9.00	$18.00
124	Chase, James Hadley - ***The Dead Stay Dumb*** [1951]	$4.00	$12.50	$25.00
125	Weston, Garnett - ***The Hidden Portal*** [1951] Cover by Glover.	$3.50	$10.00	$20.00
126	Kane, Frank - ***Death About Face*** [1951] Cover by Shane.	$4.00	$12.50	$25.00
127	Ronns, Edward - ***Dark Memory*** [1951] Cover by Glover.	$3.50	$10.00	$20.00
128	Lehman, Paul Evan - ***Law Of The '45*** [1951]	$3.00	$9.00	$18.00

Harlequin, 130

Harlequin, 160

Harlequin, 187

		G	VG	F
129	Findley, Ferguson - ***Hire This Killer*** [1951]	$3.50	$10.00	$20.00
130	Chase, James Hadley - ***Figure It Out For Yourself*** [1951] Cover by Harman.	$4.00	$12.50	$25.00
131	Mulford, Clarence E. - ***Tex*** [1951]	$2.50	$7.50	$15.00
132	Edgley, Leslie - ***False Face*** [1951]	$3.00	$9.00	$18.00
133	Scott, Bradford - ***Frontier Doctor*** [1951] Cover by Harman.	$2.50	$7.50	$15.00
134	Henderson, George C. - ***The Killers*** [1951]	$3.00	$9.00	$18.00
135	Chase, James Hadley - ***Lay Her Among The Lilies*** [1951]	$4.00	$12.50	$25.00
136	Clay, Weston - ***Boot Hill*** [1951] Cover by Harmon.	$2.50	$7.50	$15.00
137	Joseph, Robert - ***Berlin At Midnight*** [1951] Cover by Harmon.	$2.50	$7.50	$15.00
138	Prole, Lozania - ***Emma Hart*** [1951] Cover by Harmon.	$2.50	$7.50	$15.00
139	Fairman, Paul W. - ***The Glass Ladder*** [1951]	$3.00	$9.00	$18.00
140	Whittington, Harry - ***The Lady Was A Tramp*** [1951] Cover by Harmon.	$3.00	$9.00	$18.00
141	Raddall, Thomas H. - ***Roger Sudden*** [1951] Cover by Harmon.	$2.50	$7.50	$15.00
142	Stone, Thomas - ***Doctor By Day*** [1951] Cover by Derrett.	$2.00	$6.00	$12.00
143	Ernenwein, Leslie - ***Rebel Yell*** [1951]	$2.50	$7.50	$15.00
144	Kandel, Aben - ***City For Conquest*** [1951] Cover by Harmon.	$3.00	$9.00	$18.00
145	Ernenwein, Leslie - ***Rio Renegade*** [1951]	$2.50	$7.50	$15.00
146	Westland, Lynn - ***Trail Rider*** [1951] Cover by Derrett.	$2.50	$7.50	$15.00
147	Bogard, Dale - ***Pardon My Body*** [1951]	$3.00	$9.00	$18.00
148	Westland, Lynn - ***Wagon Train Westward*** [1952] Cover by Wes.	$2.50	$7.50	$15.00
149	Stegner, Wallace - ***Remembering Laughter*** [1952]	$5.50	$17.50	$35.00
150	Von Stroheim, Eric - ***Paprika*** [1952] Photo cover.	$2.50	$7.50	$15.00
151	Graham, Lewis - ***The Great I Am*** [1952] Cover by Derrett.	$2.00	$6.00	$12.00
152	Williams, Ben Ames - ***Great Oaks*** [1952]	$2.00	$6.00	$12.00
153	Cody, Al - ***Outlaw Valley*** [1952]	$2.50	$7.50	$15.00
154	Hirsch, Richard - ***Rasputin And Crimes That Shook The World*** [1952]	$5.00	$15.00	$30.00
155	Holt, Tex - ***Canyon Of The Damned*** [1952] PBO. Cover by Derrett.	$3.50	$10.00	$20.00
156	Hendryx, James B. - ***Blood Of The North*** [1952]	$2.50	$7.50	$15.00
157	Walz, Jay and Audrey - ***The Bizarre Sisters*** [1952] Cover by Derrett.	$3.00	$9.00	$18.00
158	Hopson, William - ***Yucca City Outlaw*** [1952] Cover by Norman Saunders.	$2.50	$7.50	$15.00
159	Offord, Lenore Glen - ***The Smiling Tiger*** [1952]	$2.50	$7.50	$15.00
160	Chase, James Hadley - ***Twelve Chinks And A Woman*** [1952] Cover by Wes.	$20.00	$60.00	$125.00

Harlequin, 199

Harlequin, 295

Harlequin, 318

		G	VG	F
161	Ryberg, Dr. Percy E. - ***Health, Sex And Birth Control*** [1952]	$2.00	$6.00	$12.00
162	Curwood, James Oliver - ***The River's End*** [1952] Cover by Wes.	$2.50	$7.50	$15.00
163	Carew, Dan - ***Guntown*** [1952] PBO.	$3.00	$9.00	$18.00
164	Westcott, Jan - ***Captain For Elizabeth*** [1952] Cover by Derrett.	$2.50	$7.50	$15.00
165	Moss, W. Stanley - ***Rats With Baby Faces*** [1952]	$4.00	$12.50	$25.00
166	Ragsdale, Clyde B. - ***The Big Fist*** [1952] Cover by Derrett.	$3.00	$9.00	$18.00
167	Keene, Day - ***Love Me And Die*** [1952]	$4.00	$12.50	$25.00
168	Keene, Day - ***Hunt The Killer*** [1952]	$4.00	$12.50	$25.00
169	Barnes, Margaret Campbell - ***Lady Of Cleves*** [1952] Cover by Derrett.	$3.50	$10.00	$20.00
170	Eaton, Evelyn - ***The Sea Is So Wide*** [1952]	$3.00	$9.00	$18.00
171	Ernenwein, Leslie - ***Savage Justice*** [1952]	$2.50	$7.50	$15.00
172	Lehman, Paul Evan - ***Gun Law*** [1952]	$2.50	$7.50	$15.00
173	de Lange, Anneke - ***Anna*** [1952]	$2.50	$7.50	$15.00
174	Leitfred, Robert H. - ***Murder Is My Racket*** [1952]	$3.00	$9.00	$18.00
175	Arnold, Elliot - ***The Commandos*** [1952]	$2.00	$6.00	$12.00
176	Curwood, James Oliver - ***Valley Of Silent Men*** [1952]	$2.50	$7.50	$15.00
177	Van Vogt, A. E. - ***The House That Stood Still*** [1952]	$22.00	$70.00	$140.00
178	Plaidy, Jean - ***The Goldsmith's Wife*** [1952] Cover by Derrett.	$3.00	$9.00	$18.00
179	Plaidy, Jean - ***Madame Serpent*** [1952]	$3.00	$9.00	$18.00
180	Keene, Day - ***If The Coffin Fits*** [1952]	$4.00	$12.50	$25.00
181	King-Hall, Magdalen - ***The Wicked Lady Skelton*** [1952]	$3.00	$9.00	$18.00
182	Hodges, Carl G. - ***Crime On My Hands*** [1952]	$3.50	$10.00	$20.00
183	Johnson, Katrina - ***Evening Street*** [1952]	$3.00	$9.00	$18.00
184	Taylor, Angeline - ***Black Jade*** [1952] PBO.	$4.00	$12.50	$25.00
185	Keene, Day - ***Naked Fury*** [1952]	$4.00	$12.50	$25.00
186	LeBourdais, D. M. - ***Why Be A Sucker?*** [1952] Photo cover.	$2.50	$7.50	$15.00
187	Corrigan, Mark - ***Shanghai Jezebel*** [1952] Cover by Derrett.	$4.00	$12.50	$25.00
188	Glay, George Albert - ***Beggars Might Ride*** [1952]	$3.50	$10.00	$20.00
189	Raddall, Thomas H. - ***The Nymph And The Lamp*** [1952]	$3.50	$10.00	$20.00
190	Drake, H. B. - ***Slave Ship*** [1952]	$4.00	$12.50	$25.00
191	Berg, M.D., Louis - ***Prison Doctor*** [1952] PBO. Cover by Derrett.	$2.50	$7.50	$15.00
192	Elroy, Edwina - ***Swamp Willow*** [1952]	$3.00	$9.00	$18.00
193	Challis, George - ***The Firebrand*** [1952] Cover by Friede.	$2.50	$7.50	$15.00
194	Shott, Abel - ***Triggerman*** [1952]	$2.50	$7.50	$15.00
195	Smith, Harvey - ***Nine To Five*** [1952]	$2.50	$7.50	$15.00
196	Raddall, Thomas H. - ***His Majesty's Yankees*** [1952]	$2.50	$7.50	$15.00
197	Chase, James Hadley - ***Strictly For Cash*** [1952]	$4.00	$12.50	$25.00

		G	VG	F
198	Heckelmann, Charles N. - ***The Rawhider*** [1952] Cover by Derrett.	$2.50	$7.50	$15.00
199	Chase, James Hadley - ***The Double Shuffle*** [1952]	$4.00	$12.50	$25.00
200	Marshall, Edison - ***Doctor Of Lonesome River*** [1952]	$2.00	$6.00	$12.00
201	Hardy, W. G. - ***The Unfulfilled*** [1952] Cover by Derrett	$2.50	$7.50	$15.00
202	Fairman, Paul W. - ***Copper Town*** [1952]	$2.50	$7.50	$15.00
203	Plaidy, Jean - ***Daughter Of Satan*** [1952] Cover by Derrett.	$3.00	$9.00	$18.00
204	Ernenwein, Leslie - ***Gun Hawk*** [1953]	$2.50	$7.50	$15.00
205	Weinbaum, Stanley G. - ***The Black Flame*** [1953]	$25.00	$75.00	$180.00
206	Chase, James Hadley - ***You Never Know With Women*** [1953] Cover by Derrett.	$4.00	$12.50	$25.00
207	Symons, Harry - ***Three Ships West*** [1953] Cover by Derrett.	$2.50	$7.50	$15.00
208	Borodin, George - ***Pillar Of Fire*** [1953]	$2.50	$7.50	$15.00
209	Stanley, Edward - ***The Rock Cried Out*** [1953]	$2.50	$7.50	$15.00
210	Mitchell, Joseph - ***McSorley's Wonderful Saloon*** [1953]	$2.00	$6.00	$12.00
211	Lindsay, Norman - ***The Cautious Amorist*** [1953] Cover by Derrett.	$2.00	$6.00	$12.00
212	Westland, Lynn - ***Shooting Valley*** [1953] PBO.	$2.50	$7.50	$15.00
213	Doyle, Richard J. - ***The Royal Story*** [1953] PBO.	$2.00	$6.00	$12.00
214	Von Stroheim, Erich - ***Paprika*** [1953]	$2.50	$7.50	$15.00
215	Hardy, W. G. - ***Turn Back The River*** [1953] PBO.	$2.50	$7.50	$15.00
216	McArthur, A. & Long, H. Kingsley - ***No Mean City*** [1953]	$2.50	$7.50	$15.00
217	Sabatini, Rafael - ***The Sea Hawk*** [1953] Cover by Derrett.	$3.00	$9.00	$18.00
218	Fearn, John Russell - ***The Golden Amazon*** [1953] Cover by Paul Anna Soik.	$25.00	$75.00	$180.00
219	Randall, Rona - ***Girls In White*** [1953] PBO.	$1.35	$4.00	$8.00
220	Garth, Will - ***Masked Rider*** [1953] Cover by Hewetson.	$3.00	$9.00	$18.00
221	Oppenheim, E. Phillips - ***The Great Impersonation*** [1953] Cover by Rickard.	$2.50	$7.50	$15.00
222	Goodchild, George - ***Mad Mike*** [1953] Cover by Derrett.	$3.00	$9.00	$18.00
223	Wren, P. C. - ***The Wages Of Virtue*** [1953]	$2.50	$7.50	$15.00
224	Brown, Beth - ***Lady Hobo*** [1953] PBO.	$4.00	$12.50	$25.00
225	Lindsay, Phillip - ***Sir Rusty Sword*** [1953]	$3.00	$9.00	$18.00
226	Billings, Buck - ***The Owl Hoot Trail*** [1953]	$2.50	$7.50	$15.00
227	Le Butt, Paul - ***We Too Can Die*** [1953] PBO.	$3.00	$9.00	$18.00
228	Jones, H. Bedford - ***Drums Of Dambala*** [1953] PBO.	$4.50	$14.00	$28.00
229	Keene, Day - ***Framed In Guilt*** [1953]	$4.00	$12.50	$25.00
230	Singer, Kurt - ***Women Spies*** [1953]	$2.50	$7.50	$15.00
231	Robb, John - ***Legionnaire*** [1953]	$2.50	$7.50	$15.00
232	Jones, H. Bedford - ***Malay Gold*** [1953]	$3.00	$9.00	$18.00
233	Cocking, Ronald - ***Die With Me Lady*** [1953]	$3.50	$10.00	$20.00
234	Diespecker, Dick - ***Rebound*** [1953] PBO.	$3.50	$10.00	$20.00
235	Hancock, Lucy Agnes - ***General Duty Nurse*** [1953]	$1.35	$4.00	$8.00
236	Hopson, William - ***Gunthrower*** [1953]	$2.50	$7.50	$15.00
237	Key, Alexander - ***Island Of Escape*** [1953]	$3.00	$9.00	$18.00
238	Doyle, Sir Arthur Conan - ***The Lost World*** [1953]	$25.00	$75.00	$180.00
239	Marshall, Edison - ***Mission Of Revenge*** [1953] Cover by Hewetson.	$2.50	$7.50	$15.00
240	Harrison, Whit - ***Violent Night*** [1953]	$5.00	$15.00	$30.00
241	Beach, Rex - ***Son Of The Gods*** [1953]	$2.50	$7.50	$15.00
242	Christie, Agatha - ***The Murder On The Links*** [1953] Cover by Dyke.	$4.00	$12.50	$25.00
243	Anderson, Oliver - ***School For Love*** [1953]	$3.50	$10.00	$20.00
244	Joscelyn, Archie - ***Hostage*** [1953] PBO.	$3.50	$10.00	$20.00
245	Chase, James Hadley - ***The Soft Touch*** [1953]	$4.00	$12.50	$25.00
246	Smith, Arnold - ***The Law's Outlaw*** [1953] Cover by Dyke.	$2.50	$7.50	$15.00
247	Williams, Ben Ames - ***Dark Surgery*** [1953]	$1.50	$5.00	$10.00
248	Westland, Lynn - ***Legion Of The Lawless*** [1953]	$2.50	$7.50	$15.00
249	George, Peter - ***Come Blonde, Came Murder*** [1953]	$4.00	$12.50	$25.00
250	Findley, Ferguson - ***The Man In The Middle*** [1953]	$2.50	$7.50	$15.00

		G	VG	F
251	Allen, T. D. - ***Doctor In Buckskin*** [1953]	$1.35	$4.00	$8.00
252	Lebedeff, Ivan - ***Legion Of Dishonor*** [1953]	$1.50	$5.00	$10.00
253	Keene, Day - ***Wake Up To Murder*** [1953]	$3.50	$10.00	$20.00
254	Cord, Barry - ***Mesquite Johnny*** [1953]	$2.50	$7.50	$15.00
255	Marshall, Raymond - ***Lady - Here's Your Wreath*** [1953]	$4.00	$12.50	$25.00
256	Adams, F. Cleve - ***No Wings On A Cop*** [1953] Cover by Dyke.	$2.50	$7.50	$15.00
257	Rennie, George Murdoch - ***One Man Front*** [1953]	$1.50	$5.00	$10.00
258	Berg, M.D., Louis - ***World Behind Bars*** [1953] PBO.	$1.50	$5.00	$10.00
259	Scott, Bradford - ***Silver City*** [1953]	$1.50	$5.00	$10.00
260	McCulley, Johnson - ***The Outlaw Trail*** [1953] PBO.	$1.50	$5.00	$10.00
261	Osler, E. B. - ***Light In The Wilderness*** [1953] PBO. Cover by Rickard.	$1.50	$5.00	$10.00
262	Montrose, David - ***The Body On Mount Royal*** [1953] PBO.	$1.50	$5.00	$10.00
263	Joscelyn, Archie - ***Texas Showdown*** [1953] PBO. Cover by Ikeno.	$1.50	$5.00	$10.00
264	Hancock, Lucy Agnes - ***Community Nurse*** [1953]	$1.35	$4.00	$8.00
265	Marshall, Raymond - ***The Paw In The Bottle*** [1954]	$4.00	$12.50	$25.00
266	Maugham, W. Somerset - ***Catalina*** [1954] Cover by Dyke.	$2.00	$6.00	$12.00
267	Chase, James Hadley - ***I'll Bury My Dead*** [1954]	$4.00	$12.50	$25.00
268	Plaidy, Jean - ***The Unholy Woman*** [1954]	$2.50	$7.50	$15.00
269	Plaidy, Jean - ***Queen Jezebel*** [1954]	$3.00	$9.00	$18.00
270	Lehman, Paul Evan - ***Fighting Buckaroo*** [1954] PBO.	$2.50	$7.50	$15.00
271	Wallace, Clair - ***Mind Your Manners*** [1954]	$1.50	$5.00	$10.00
272	Prole, Lozania - ***The Fabulous Nell Gwynne*** [1954]	$1.50	$5.00	$10.00
273	Herbert, A. P. - ***Holy Deadlock*** [1954] Cover by Dyke.	$1.50	$5.00	$10.00
274	Cody, Al - ***Lost Valley*** [1954]	$1.50	$5.00	$10.00
275	Hopson, William - ***Hell's Horseman*** [1954]	$1.50	$5.00	$10.00
276	Timms, E. V. - ***Conflict*** [1954]	$1.50	$5.00	$10.00
277	Corrigan, Mark - ***Lady Of China Street*** [1954]	$2.00	$6.00	$12.00
278	Challis, George - ***The Bait And The Trap*** [1954] Cover by Dyke.	$2.00	$6.00	$12.00
279	Hodges, Carl G. - ***Crime On My Hands*** [1954]	$3.00	$9.00	$18.00
280	Lindsay, Philip - ***The Nut Brown Maid*** [1954] Cover by Paul Anna Soik.	$2.50	$7.50	$15.00
281	Leinster, Murray - ***Outlaw Deputy*** [1954]	$5.50	$17.50	$35.00
282	Liggett, Walter W. - ***Frozen Frontier*** [1954]	$1.50	$5.00	$10.00
283	McLeod, Ken - ***A Body For A Blonde*** [1954] PBO. Cover by Paul Anna Soik.	$4.00	$12.50	$25.00
284	Hancock, Lucy Agnes - ***Calling Nurse Blair*** [1954]	$1.35	$4.00	$8.00
285	Cody, Al - ***Texas Outlaw*** [1954] PBO. Cover by Nasmith.	$1.50	$5.00	$10.00
286	Peacock, Max - ***Colonel Blood*** [1954]	$2.00	$6.00	$12.00
287	Glay, George Albert - ***Gina*** [1954] Cover by Paul Anna Soik.	$1.50	$5.00	$10.00
288	Sinclair, Gordon - ***Bright Path To Adventure*** [1954]	$1.50	$5.00	$10.00
289	Kelley, Thomas P. - ***The Black Donnellys*** [1954] PBO. Photo cover.	$2.00	$6.00	$12.00
290	Timms, E. V. - ***The Violent Years*** [1954] Cover by Soik.	$2.25	$7.00	$14.00
291	Andrews, Roy Chapman - ***Heart Of Asia*** [1954]	$1.50	$5.00	$10.00
292	Hancock, Lucy Agnes - ***Nurse Barlow*** [1954]	$1.35	$4.00	$8.00
293	Webster, M. Coates - ***Mona*** [1954]	$1.50	$5.00	$10.00
294	Randall, Rona - ***Girls In White*** [1954]	$1.35	$4.00	$8.00
295	Wees, Frances Shelley - ***Lost House*** [1954] Cover by Rickard.	$4.00	$12.50	$25.00
296	Baume, Eric - ***Half-Caste*** [1954]	$2.50	$7.50	$15.00
297	McCary, Reed - ***The Vice Merchants*** [1954]	$2.00	$6.00	$12.00
298	Raddall, Thomas H. - ***Pride's Fancy*** [1954]	$1.50	$5.00	$10.00
299	McGrath, Lieut. Tom - ***Copper*** [1954]	$1.50	$5.00	$10.00
300	Marshall, Raymond - ***Mallory*** [1954]	$3.50	$10.00	$20.00
301	Rush, Phillip - ***Mary Read, Buccaneer*** [1954]	$1.50	$5.00	$10.00
302	Hancock, Lucy Agnes - ***The Nurse*** [1954]	$1.25	$3.75	$7.50
303	Fletcher, Verne - ***Captain Gentleman*** [1954] Cover by Paul Anna Soik.	$1.50	$5.00	$10.00

Harlequin, 320

Hillman, 11

Hillman, 20

		G	VG	F
304	Hopson, William - ***High Saddle*** [1954] PBO.	$2.00	$6.00	$12.00
305	Saber, Robert O. - ***Out Of The Night*** [1954] PBO. Cover by Glover.	$4.00	$12.50	$25.00
306	Fabian, Robert - ***Fabian Of The Yard*** [1954]	$2.50	$7.50	$15.00
307	Horler, Sidney - ***The Cage*** [1954]	$4.00	$12.50	$25.00
308	Allan, Bette - ***Doctor Paul*** [1954]	$1.25	$3.75	$7.50
309	Hopson, William - ***Notched Guns*** [1954]	$1.50	$5.00	$10.00
310	Marshall, Raymond - ***Why Pick On Me?*** [1954]	$4.00	$12.50	$25.00
311	Goodis, David - ***Convicted*** [1954]	$22.00	$70.00	$140.00
312	Burtis, Thomas - ***The Seeker*** [1954]	$2.00	$6.00	$12.00
313	Hancock, Lucy Agnes - ***Hospital Nurse*** [1954]	$1.25	$3.75	$7.50
314	Bull, Lois - ***Forbidden*** [1954] PBO.	$1.35	$4.00	$8.00
315	Burtis, Thomas - ***The Black Eagle*** [1954]	$1.50	$5.00	$10.00
316	Chase, James Hadley - ***This Way For A Shroud*** [1954] Cover by Paul Anna Soik.	$4.00	$12.50	$25.00
317	Marshall, Raymond - ***Blondes' Requiem*** [1954]	$4.00	$12.50	$25.00
318	Constantin-Weyer, M. - ***The Half-Breed*** [1954] PBO. Cover by Soik.	$3.50	$10.00	$20.00
319	Walker, Dorothy Pierce - ***Woman Doctor*** [1954]	$1.25	$3.75	$7.50
320	Fearn, John Russell - ***The Deathless Amazon*** [1955] Cover by Paul Anna Soik.	$25.00	$75.00	$180.00
321	Fabian, Robert - ***London After Dark*** [1955]	$3.50	$10.00	$20.00
322	Horler, Sidney - ***The Webb*** [1955]	$3.50	$10.00	$20.00
323	Chase, James Hadley - ***Tiger By The Tail*** [1955] PBO. Cover by Paul Anna Soik.	$4.50	$14.00	$28.00
324	Hancock, Lucy Agnes - ***West End Nurse*** [1955] PBO. Cover by Paul Anna Soik.	$1.25	$3.75	$7.50
325	Cody, Al - ***Satan's Range*** [1955] PBO.	$2.00	$6.00	$12.00
326	Seifert, Elizabeth - ***Girl Intern*** [1955] Cover by Rickard.	$1.25	$3.75	$7.50
327	O'Donnell, Bernard - ***The World's Worst Women*** [1955] PBO.	$4.00	$12.50	$25.00
328	Stringer, Arthur - ***The Wife Traders*** [1955] Cover by Paul Anna Soik.	$3.50	$10.00	$20.00
329	Russell, Victor - ***People Of The Night*** [1955] PBO. Cover by Paul Anna Soik.	$3.50	$10.00	$20.00
330	Timms, E. V. - ***Convict Town*** [1955] PBO. Cover by Paul Anna Soik.	$4.00	$12.50	$25.00
331	Timms, E. V. - ***Woman In Chains*** [1955] PBO. Cover by Paul Anna Soik.	$4.00	$12.50	$25.00
332	Hancock, Lucy Agnes - ***Staff Nurse*** [1955]	$1.25	$3.75	$7.50
333	Hancock, Lucy Agnes - ***Resident Nurse*** [1955]	$1.25	$3.75	$7.50

		G	VG	F
334	Wallace, Edgar - ***The Square Emerald*** [1955] Cover by Paul Anna Soik.	$3.50	$10.00	$20.00
335	Ullman, Albert E. - ***Hoodlum Alley*** [1955] PBO. Cover by Paul Anna Soik.	$5.00	$15.00	$30.00
336	Fleming, Joan - ***The Good And The Bad*** [1955] Cover by Paul Anna Soik.	$3.50	$10.00	$20.00
337	Christie, Agatha - ***The Man In The Brown Suit*** [1955] Cover by Dyke.	$3.50	$10.00	$20.00
338	Hancock, Lucy Agnes - ***District Nurse*** [1955] PBO. Cover by Paul Anna Soik.	$1.25	$3.75	$7.50
339	Hancock, Lucy Agnes - ***Nurses Are People*** [1955] PBO. Cover by Paul Anna Soik.	$1.25	$3.75	$7.50
340	Marshall, Raymond - ***The Pick-Up*** [1955]	$4.00	$12.50	$25.00
341	Marshall, Raymond - ***Ruthless*** [1955]	$4.00	$12.50	$25.00
342	Ford, Marcia - ***Nancy Craig, R.N.*** [1955] Cover by Paul Anna Soik.	$1.25	$3.75	$7.50
343	Cody, Al - ***Gun Thunder Valley*** [1955] PBO.	$1.50	$5.00	$10.00
344	Hancock, Lucy Agnes - ***Village Doctor*** [1955] PBO. Cover by Paul Anna Soik.	$1.25	$3.75	$7.50
345	Cody, Al - ***The Gunman*** [1955] PBO.	$1.50	$5.00	$10.00
346	Hancock, Lucy Agnes - ***Doctor Bill*** [1955] PBO.	$1.25	$3.75	$7.50
347	Hancock, Lucy Agnes - ***Pat Whitney, R.N.*** [1955] PBO.	$1.25	$3.75	$7.50
348	Hamilton, Kay - ***The Doctor On Elm Street*** [1956] PBO.	$1.25	$3.75	$7.50
349	Wallace, Edgar - ***The Four Just Men*** [1956]	$2.00	$6.00	$12.00
350	Coburn, Walt - ***The Renegade*** [1956]	$1.50	$5.00	$10.00
351	Thompson, Sidney - ***Dr. Parrish, Resident*** [1956]	$1.25	$3.75	$7.50
352	Wallace, Edgar - ***The India-Rubber Men*** [1956] Cover by Paul Anna Soik.	$1.50	$5.00	$10.00
353	Lehman, Paul Evan - ***Gun Law*** [1956]	$1.50	$5.00	$10.00
354	Cheyney, Peter - ***Dark Bahama*** [1956]	$2.50	$7.50	$15.00
355	Ernenwein, Leslie - ***Savage Justice*** [1956]	$1.50	$5.00	$10.00
356	Hancock, Lucy Agnes - ***Nurse's Aide*** [1956]	$1.25	$3.75	$7.50
357	Hamilton, Kay - ***Young Doctor Glenn*** [1956]	$1.25	$3.75	$7.50
358	Lehman, Paul Evan - ***Redrock Gold*** [1956]	$1.50	$5.00	$10.00
359	Christie, Agatha - ***The Secret Adversary*** [1956] Cover by Paul Anna Soik.	$3.00	$9.00	$18.00
360	Hopson, William - ***Yucca City Outlaw*** [1956]	$2.00	$6.00	$12.00
361	Wallace, Edgar - ***The Clue Of The Silver Key*** [1956] Cover by Norm Eastman.	$2.00	$6.00	$12.00
362	Dern, Peggy - ***Nora Was A Nurse*** [1956]	$1.25	$3.75	$7.50
363	Hamilton, Kay - ***Doctor Alice's Daughter*** [1956]	$1.25	$3.75	$7.50
364	Seifert, Elizabeth - ***Surgeon In Charge*** [1956]	$1.25	$3.75	$7.50
365	Walker, Dorothy Pierce - ***Doctors Are Different*** [1956] PBO. Cover by Norm Eastman.	$1.25	$3.75	$7.50
366	Whittington, Harry - ***The Brass Monkey*** [1956]	$6.00	$20.00	$40.00
367	Orvis, Kenneth - ***Hickory House*** [1956]	$1.50	$5.00	$10.00
368	Gaddis, Peggy - ***Meredith Blake, M.D.*** [1956] PBO. Cover by Paul Anna Soik.	$1.25	$3.75	$7.50
369	Seifert, Elizabeth - ***Three Doctors*** [1956]	$1.25	$3.75	$7.50
370	Tickell, Jerrard - ***Appointment With Venus*** [1956]	$2.00	$6.00	$12.00
371	Ernenwein, Leslie - ***Renegade Ramrod*** [1956]	$1.50	$5.00	$10.00
372	Hancock, Lucy Agnes - ***Meet The Warrens*** [1956]	$1.25	$3.75	$7.50
373	Prole, Lozania - ***To-Night, Josephine!*** [1956] Cover by Norm Eastman.	$1.50	$5.00	$10.00
374	Joscelyn, Archie - ***Valley Of The Sun*** [1956]	$1.50	$5.00	$10.00
375	Seifert, Elizabeth - ***Miss Doctor*** [1956] PBO. Cover by Norm Eastman.	$1.25	$3.75	$7.50
376	Worley, Dorothy - ***Blake Hospital*** [1957]	$1.25	$3.75	$7.50
377	Christie, Agatha - ***The Secret Of Chimneys*** [1957]	$3.00	$9.00	$18.00
378	Wallace, Edgar - ***The Ringer*** [1957]	$2.00	$6.00	$12.00

		G	VG	F
379	Seifert, Elizabeth - ***The Doctor Takes A Wife*** [1957] PBO. Cover by Norm Eastman.	$1.25	$3.75	$7.50
380	Curwood, James Oliver - ***The River's End*** [1957]	$2.00	$6.00	$12.00
381	Wright, Watkins E. - ***Doctor Joel*** [1957] PBO. Cover by Norm Eastman.	$1.25	$3.75	$7.50
382	Marshall, Raymond - ***Never Trust A Woman*** [1957]	$4.00	$12.50	$25.00
383	Curwood, James Oliver - ***The Valley Of Silent Men*** [1957]	$2.25	$7.00	$14.00
384	Dern, Peggy - ***Nurse Ellen*** [1957] PBO.	$1.25	$3.75	$7.50
385	Chase, James Hadley - ***Eve*** [1957]	$3.50	$10.00	$20.00
386	Ernenwein, Leslie - ***The Faro Kid*** [1957]	$1.50	$5.00	$10.00
387	Wallace, Edgar - ***White Face*** [1957] Cover by Norm Eastman.	$2.00	$6.00	$12.00
388	Dern, Peggy - ***Doctor Scott*** [1957]	$1.25	$3.75	$7.50
389	Martin, Chuck - ***Circle F Cowboy*** [1957]	$1.50	$5.00	$10.00
390	Phillips, Bluebell S. - ***Adopted Derelicts*** [1957]	$2.00	$6.00	$12.00
391	Young, W. J. & McCrea, E. R. - ***How To Get More From Your Car*** [1957]	$2.00	$6.00	$12.00
392	Seifert, Elizabeth - ***Doctor Of Mercy*** [1957] PBO. Cover by Norm Eastman.	$1.25	$3.75	$7.50
393	Canning, Victor - ***A Forest Of Eyes*** [1957] Cover by Norm Eastman.	$2.50	$7.50	$15.00
394	Gaddis, Peggy - ***Lady Doctor*** [1957]	$1.25	$3.75	$7.50
395	Wallace, Edgar - ***The Angel Of Terror*** [1957]	$2.00	$6.00	$12.00
396	Watson, Will - ***Double Cross Ranch*** [1957]	$1.50	$5.00	$10.00
397	Hancock, Lucy Agnes - ***The Shorn Lamb*** [1957]	$1.25	$3.75	$7.50
398	Hamilton, Wade - ***Sagebrush*** [1957] PBO. Cover by Norm Eastman.	$1.50	$5.00	$10.00
399	Moore, Amos - ***Royce Of The Royal Mounted*** [1957]	$1.50	$5.00	$10.00
400	Horler, Sydney - ***The Cage*** [1957]	$2.50	$7.50	$15.00
401	Seifert, Elizabeth - ***The Doctor Disagrees*** [1957] PBO.	$1.25	$3.75	$7.50
402	O'Rourke, Frank - ***The Football Gravy Train*** [1957] Cover by Norm Eastman.	$2.50	$7.50	$15.00
403	Goodchild, George - ***Next Of Kin*** [1957]	$1.50	$5.00	$10.00
404	Lehman, Paul Evan - ***Law In The Saddle*** [1957]	$1.50	$5.00	$10.00
405	Gaddis, Peggy - ***City Nurse*** [1957] PBO. Cover by Norm Eastman.	$1.25	$3.75	$7.50
406	Curwood, James Oliver - ***The Flaming Forest*** [1957] Cover by Norm Eastman.	$2.00	$6.00	$12.00
407	Vinton, Anne - ***The Hospital In Buwambo*** [1957]	$1.25	$3.75	$7.50
408	MacMillan, Don - ***Rink Rat*** [1957]	$2.00	$6.00	$12.00
409	Burchell, Mary - ***Hospital Corridors*** [1958]	$1.25	$3.75	$7.50
410	Horler, Sidney - ***Dark Journey*** [1958]	$3.00	$9.00	$18.00
411	Grinstead, J. E. - ***Range King*** [1958]	$1.50	$5.00	$10.00
412	Trench, Caroline - ***Nurse Trenton*** [1958] Cover by Norm Eastman.	$1.25	$3.75	$7.50
413	Chase, James Hadley - ***I'll Get You For This*** [1958]	$3.50	$10.00	$20.00
414	Stoddard, Charles - ***Devil's Portage*** [1958] PBO. Cover by Paul Anna Soik.	$3.50	$10.00	$20.00
415	Brown, Dr. Alan & Robertson, Dr. E. C. - ***The Normal Child*** [1958] Photo cover.	$1.25	$3.75	$7.50
416	Allen, Barbara - ***Doctor Lucy*** [1958]	$1.25	$3.75	$7.50
417	Grinstead, J. E. - ***Maverick Guns*** [1958]	$1.50	$5.00	$10.00
418	Wallace, Edgar - ***The Feathered Serpent*** [1958] Cover by Norm Eastman.	$2.00	$6.00	$12.00
419	Trench, Caroline - ***In And Out Of Love*** [1958]	$1.25	$3.75	$7.50
420	Wallace, Edgar - ***The Squeaker*** [1958] Cover by Paul Anna Soik.	$2.00	$6.00	$12.00
421	Fearn, John Russell - ***The Golden Amazon's Triumph*** [1958] Cover by Norm Eastman.	$25.00	$75.00	$180.00
422	Burchell, Mary - ***Then Come Kiss Me*** [1958]	$1.25	$3.75	$7.50
423	Arbor, Jane - ***Nurse Greve*** [1958] Cover by Paul Anna Soik.	$1.25	$3.75	$7.50

		G	VG	F
424	O'Rourke, Frank - ***Flashing Spikes*** [1958]	$1.50	$5.00	$10.00
425	Horler, Sidney - ***The Return Of Nighthawk*** [1958]	$3.50	$10.00	$20.00
426	Anthology edited by Kurt Singer - ***The World's Greatest Spy Stories*** [1958] Cover by Paul Anna Soik.	$2.50	$7.50	$15.00
427	Norway, Kate - ***Nurse Brookes*** [1958]	$1.25	$3.75	$7.50
428	Wallace, Edgar - ***The Strange Countess*** [1958] Cover by Norm Eastman.	$2.00	$6.00	$12.00
429	Curwood, James Oliver - ***Steele Of The Royal Mounted*** [1958]	$2.00	$6.00	$12.00
430	Stuart, Alex - ***Ship's Nurse*** [1958]	$1.25	$3.75	$7.50
431	MacLeod, Jean S. - ***The Silent Valley*** [1958]	$1.50	$5.00	$10.00
432	Stokes, Manning Lee - ***The Lady Lost Her Head*** [1958] PBO.	$4.00	$12.50	$25.00
433	Hoy, Elizabeth - ***Because Of Doctor Danville*** [1958]	$1.25	$3.75	$7.50
434	MacLeod, Jean S. - ***Dear Doctor Everett*** [1958]	$1.25	$3.75	$7.50
435	Kelley, Thomas P. - ***Canada's Greatest Crimes*** [1958]	$2.50	$7.50	$15.00
436	Stuart, Alex - ***Garrison Hospital*** [1958] Cover by Paul Anna Soik.	$1.25	$3.75	$7.50
437	Tyre, Robert - ***Saddlebag Surgeon*** [1958] Cover by Norm Eastman.	$1.25	$3.75	$7.50
438	Stuart, Alex - ***That Wonderful Feeling*** [1958] Cover by Paul Anna Soik.	$1.35	$4.00	$8.00
439	Vinton, Anne - ***Hospital In Sudan*** [1958]	$1.25	$3.75	$7.50
440	Walker, Joan - ***Pardon My Parka*** [1958] Cover by Norm Eastman.	$1.35	$4.00	$8.00
441	Christie, Agatha - ***The Murder On The Links*** [1958]	$3.00	$9.00	$18.00
442	Watson, Ken - ***Curling With Ken Watson*** [1958] PBO. Photo cover. 32 pages of photos.	$2.50	$7.50	$15.00
443	Gilzean, Elizabeth - ***Nurse On Call*** [1958]	$1.25	$3.75	$7.50
444	Wallace, Edgar - ***Double Dan*** [1958]	$2.00	$6.00	$12.00
445	Dern, Peggy - ***Nurse In The Tropics*** [1958]	$1.25	$3.75	$7.50
446	Moore, Marjorie - ***Borne On The Wind*** [1958]	$1.35	$4.00	$8.00
447	Wallace, Edgar - ***The Crimson Circle*** [1959] Cover by Paul Anna Soik.	$2.00	$6.00	$12.00
448	Cadell, Elizabeth - ***Bridal Array*** [1959]	$1.35	$4.00	$8.00
449	Hoy, Elizabeth - ***Come Back, My Dream*** [1959]	$1.35	$4.00	$8.00
450	Rasky, Frank - ***Gay Canadian Rogues*** [1959] Cover by Norm Eastman.	$2.50	$7.50	$15.00
451	MacLeod, Jean S. - ***Air Ambulance*** [1959] Cover by Paul Anna Soik.	$1.25	$3.75	$7.50
452	Anthology - ***Crescent Dream Book And Fortune Teller*** [1959]	$2.50	$7.50	$15.00
453	Allison, Carlyle - ***The Corner Cupboard*** [1959] PBO. Photo cover.	$1.50	$5.00	$10.00
454	Arbor, Jane - ***Such Frail Armor*** [1959]	$1.35	$4.00	$8.00
455	Gowland, J. S. - ***Smoke Over Sikanaska*** [1959] Cover by Norm Eastman.	$1.50	$5.00	$10.00
456	Wallace, Edgar - ***The Yellow Snake*** [1959] Cover by Norm Eastman.	$2.00	$6.00	$12.00
457	Percival, Lloyd - ***Physical Fitness For All The Family*** [1959] PBO.	$1.50	$5.00	$10.00
458	Gilzean, Elizabeth - ***Next Patient, Doctor Anne*** [1959]	$1.25	$3.75	$7.50
459	Moore, Marjorie - ***Second Love*** [1959]	$1.25	$3.75	$7.50
460	Mason, A. E. W. - ***At The Villa Rose*** [1959]	$1.35	$4.00	$8.00
461	Burchell, Mary - ***For Ever And Ever*** [1959]	$1.35	$4.00	$8.00
462	Gilzean, Elizabeth - ***Love From A Surgeon*** [1959] Cover by Paul Anna Soik.	$1.25	$3.75	$7.50
463	Norway, Kate - ***The Morning Star*** [1959]	$1.35	$4.00	$8.00
464	Stuart, Alex - ***The Captain's Table*** [1959]	$1.50	$5.00	$10.00
465	Singer, Kurt - editor - ***My Greatest Crime Story*** [1959]	$2.50	$7.50	$15.00
466	Wallace, Edgar - ***The Traitor's Gate*** [1959] Cover by Norm Eastman.	$2.00	$6.00	$12.00
467	Trench, Caroline - ***Nurse To The Island*** [1959]	$1.25	$3.75	$7.50

		G	VG	F
468	Burchell, Mary - ***Surgeon Of Distinction*** [1959] Cover by Paul Anna Soik.	$1.25	$3.75	$7.50
469	Seale, Sara - ***Maggy*** [1959]	$1.35	$4.00	$8.00
470	Schofield, William G. - ***The Cat In The Convoy*** [1959] Cover by Norm Eastman.	$1.50	$5.00	$10.00
471	Gaddis, Peggy - ***Nurse Hilary*** [1959] PBO. Cover by Paul Anna Soik.	$1.25	$3.75	$7.50
472	Hoy, Elizabeth - ***Young Doctor Kirkdene*** [1959] Cover by Paul Anna Soik.	$1.25	$3.75	$7.50
473	Cadell, Elizabeth - ***The Cuckoo In Spring*** [1959]	$1.35	$4.00	$8.00
474	Arbor, Jane - ***Towards The Dawn*** [1959]	$1.35	$4.00	$8.00
475	Wallace, Edgar - ***The Mind Of Mr. J. G. Reeder*** [1959]	$2.00	$6.00	$12.00
476	Dingwell, Joyce - ***Nurse Jess*** [1959]	$1.25	$3.75	$7.50
477	Vinton, Anne - ***Hospital Blue*** [1959] Cover by Paul Anne Soik.	$1.25	$3.75	$7.50
478	Burchell, Mary - ***Dear Trustee*** [1959]	$1.35	$4.00	$8.00
479	Adkins, Cleo - ***The Case Of The Ebony Queen*** [1959]	$1.50	$5.00	$10.00
480	Allan, Tony - ***Grey Cup Cavalcade*** [1959]	$1.50	$5.00	$10.00
481	Stuart, Alex - ***Bachelor Of Medicine*** [1959] Cover by Harman.	$1.35	$4.00	$8.00
482	Arbor, Jane - ***Folly Of The Heart*** [1959]	$1.25	$3.75	$7.50
483	Hoy, Elizabeth - ***My Heart Has Wings*** [1959]	$1.25	$3.75	$7.50
484	Wallace, Edgar - ***The Northing Tramp*** [1959]	$2.00	$6.00	$12.00
485	Houghton, Elizabeth - ***Island Hospital*** [1959]	$1.25	$3.75	$7.50
486	Trench, Caroline - ***Nurse Caril's New Post*** [1959] Cover by Paul Anna Soik.	$1.25	$3.75	$7.50
487	Farnes, Eleanor - ***The Happy Enterprise*** [1959]	$1.35	$4.00	$8.00
488	Horler, Sydney - ***The Man Who Died Twice*** [1959] Cover by Harman.	$3.50	$10.00	$20.00
489	Arbor, Jane - ***Consulting Surgeon*** [1959] Cover by Paul Anna Soik.	$1.25	$3.75	$7.50
490	Gilzean, Elizabeth - ***Nurse MacLean Goes West*** [1959]	$1.25	$3.75	$7.50
491	Hoy, Elizabeth - ***Nurse Tennant*** [1959] Cover by Harmon.	$1.25	$3.75	$7.50
492	Moore, Marjorie - ***Follow A Dream*** [1959]	$1.25	$3.75	$7.50
493	Wallace, Edgar - ***The Man At The Carleton*** [1959]	$2.00	$6.00	$12.00
494	Burchell, Mary - ***Love Is My Reason*** [1959]	$1.25	$3.75	$7.50
495	Ford, Norrey - ***Nurse With A Dream*** [1959]	$1.25	$3.75	$7.50
496	Hancock, Lucy Agnes - ***Nurse In White*** [1959]	$1.25	$3.75	$7.50
497	Hoy, Elizabeth - ***Doctor Garth*** [1959] Cover by Paul Anna Soik.	$1.25	$3.75	$7.50
498	Arbor, Jane - ***The Eternal Circle*** [1959]	$1.25	$3.75	$7.50
499	Norway, Kate - ***People Like Us*** [1959]	$1.35	$4.00	$8.00
500	Moore, Marjorie - ***Unsteady Flame*** [1959]	$1.35	$4.00	$8.00
501	Hoy, Elizabeth - ***Do Something Dangerous*** [1959]	$1.35	$4.00	$8.00
522	Phillips, Alan - ***The Living Legend*** [1960] Cover by Harman.	$2.00	$6.00	$12.00
550	Wallace, Clair - ***Canadian Etiquette Dictionary*** [1961]	$3.50	$10.00	$20.00
602	Walker, Joan - ***Repent At Leisure*** [1961]	$1.35	$4.00	$8.00
622	Allan, Tony - ***Football Flashbacks*** [1961]	$2.00	$6.00	$12.00
635	Watson, Ken - ***Curling Today With Ken Watson*** [1961] PBO. Photo cover.	$2.00	$6.00	$12.00
694	Allan, Tony - ***Football Today And Yesteryear*** [1961]	$2.00	$6.00	$12.00
695	Kelley, Thomas P. - ***Vengeance Of The Black Donnellys*** [1961] PBO. Cover by Bern Smith.	$2.00	$6.00	$12.00
706	Allen, Ralph - ***Peace River Country*** [1962] Cover by Smith.	$2.00	$6.00	$12.00

Hart Book. Digest Size.

		G	VG	F
K-1	Worts, George F. - ***The House Of Creeping Horror*** [n.d.]	$3.50	$10.00	$20.00
K-2	Chase, Borden - ***The Diamonds Of Death*** [n.d.]	$3.50	$10.00	$20.00

Headline. Los Angeles: World News, Inc.

		G	VG	F
102	Kane, Sid - ***Naked Obsession*** [1960] PBO.	$1.50	$5.00	$10.00
103	Louis, Jacques - ***Devil's Cult*** [1960] PBO. Photo cover.	$1.50	$5.00	$10.00
104	Kane, Sid - ***Jill*** [1960] PBO.	$1.50	$5.00	$10.00

		G	VG	F
105	Sellers, Connie - ***Red Rape!*** [1960] PBO.	$2.50	$7.50	$15.00
106	Winski, Norman - ***Six In Hell!*** [1960] PBO.	$1.50	$5.00	$10.00
107	Kane, Sid - ***Hot Tequila*** [1960] PBO.	$1.50	$5.00	$10.00
108	Lewis, Jack - ***Blood Money*** [1960] PBO.	$2.00	$6.00	$12.00

Heart Volume.

		G	VG	F
101	Bodine, Eric - ***Soho Sin Girl*** [n.d.] PBO. Photo cover.	$1.25	$3.75	$7.50
102	Raye, Alan - ***Sin-Sob Sister*** [n.d.] PBO. Photo cover.	$1.25	$3.75	$7.50
105	Warren, Roy - ***Space Sex*** [n.d.] PBO.	$3.50	$10.00	$20.00

Hecker H-O.

		G	VG	F
NN	Dixon, Peter - ***Bobby Benson And The Lost Herd*** [1936] PBO. Cover by Glen Thomas.	$2.50	$7.50	$15.00

Hillman Books (Early Publisher's History, 1943–1959)

A strong set of westerns and a variety of popular literature summarize the contribution of Hillman Books. Books of note include movie tie-in, an Elvis Presley biography, and a volume by Jim Thompson. Hillman #41, *The Dying Earth* by Jack Vance, his first published book, remains one of the most collectible paperbacks. Covers provide a selection of pulp and other styles to include artwork by Robert Maguire.

Hillman Periodicals, Inc., published a number of other series in digest format. These digest series consist of the following lines: Adventure Novel Classics, Detective Novel Classics, Fighting Western Novels, Gunfire Western Novels, Hillman Detective Novel, Western Action Novels, Western Novel Classics, and Western Novel of the Month.

Hillman Books. New York: Hillman Periodicals, Inc.

		G	VG	F
1	Hanley, Jack - ***Let's Make Mary*** [1948]	$1.50	$5.00	$10.00
2	Tuttle, W.C. - ***Tumbling River Range*** [1948] Cover art by Charles Wood.	$2.00	$6.00	$12.00
3	Edited by Joseph Monet - ***Casanova's Memoirs*** [1948]	$1.25	$3.75	$7.50
4	Raine, William MacLeod - ***Ironheart*** [1948] Cover art by Charles Wood.	$2.00	$6.00	$12.00
5	Tuttle, W.C. - ***Bluffer's Luck*** [1948] Cover art by Charles Wood.	$2.00	$6.00	$12.00
6	Raine, William MacLeod - ***Riders Of Buck River*** [1948] Cover art by Charles Wood.	$2.00	$6.00	$12.00
7	Taylor, E.B. - ***Sex And Marriage Problems*** [1948] PBO. Photo cover.	$1.25	$3.75	$7.50
8	Kravchenko, Victor - ***I Chose Freedom*** [1948]	$1.25	$3.75	$7.50
9	Gooden, Arthur Henry - ***Guns On The High Mesa*** [1948] Cover art by Charles Wood.	$2.00	$6.00	$12.00
10	MacVeigh, Sue - ***Murder Under Construction*** [1948]	$2.00	$6.00	$12.00
11	Raine, William MacLeod - ***Steve Yeager—A Rip-Roaring Cowpuncher*** [1948] Cover art by Charles Wood.	$2.00	$6.00	$12.00
12	De Balzac, Honore - ***Ten Droll Tales*** [1949] Photo cover.	$2.25	$7.00	$14.00
13	Repp, Ed Earl - ***Hell In The Saddle*** [1949] Cover art by Charles Wood.	$2.00	$6.00	$12.00
14	DeGourmont, Remy - ***The Physiology Of Love*** [1949]	$1.25	$3.75	$7.50
15	Hamilton, Bruce - ***Hanging Judge*** [1949] Photo cover.	$1.00	$3.00	$6.00
16	Kelland, Clarence Budington - ***Gold*** [1949] Cover art by Charles Wood.	$2.00	$6.00	$12.00
17	Repp, Ed Earl - ***Gunhawk*** [1949] Cover art by Charles Wood.	$2.00	$6.00	$12.00
18	Irwin, Theodore D. - ***Collusion*** [1949] Photo cover.	$1.50	$5.00	$10.00
19	MacDonald, William Colt - ***The Red Rider Of Smoky Range*** [1949]	$2.00	$6.00	$12.00

		G	VG	F
20	Burnett, W.R. - ***Dark Hazard*** [1949] Photo cover.	$4.00	$12.50	$25.00
21	Anthony, John J. - ***Marriage, Sex And Family Problems*** [1949] Photo cover.	$1.25	$3.75	$7.50
22	Gooden, Arthur Henry - ***The Shadowed Trail*** [1949]	$2.00	$6.00	$12.00
23	Torrey, Roger - ***42 Days For Murder*** [1949] Photo cover.	$2.25	$7.00	$14.00
24	Raine, William MacLeod - ***The Trail Of Danger*** [1949] Cover art by Charles Wood.	$2.00	$6.00	$12.00
25	MacDonald, William Colt - ***The Deputy Of Carabina*** [1949]	$2.00	$6.00	$12.00
26	Tuttle, W.C. - ***Straws In The Wind*** [1949] Cover art by Charles Wood.	$2.00	$6.00	$12.00
27	Anthology - ***Dead On Arrival*** [1949] PBO. Photo cover.	$2.50	$7.50	$15.00
28	Tuttle, W.C. - ***The Redhead From Sun Dog*** [1949]	$2.00	$6.00	$12.00
29	Raine, William MacLeod - ***Big-Town Round-Up*** [1949] Cover art by Charles Wood.	$2.00	$6.00	$12.00
30	Hopkins, Tom J. - ***Buzzard Tracks*** [1949] Cover art by Charles Wood.	$2.00	$6.00	$12.00
31	Macdonald, William Colt - ***Wheels In The Dust*** [1949] Cover art by Charles Wood.	$2.00	$6.00	$12.00
32	Coolidge, Dane - ***Bear Paw*** [1949] Cover art by Earl Elton.	$2.00	$6.00	$12.00
33	Lomax, Bliss - ***Rusty Guns*** [1949] Cover art by Charles Wood.	$2.00	$6.00	$12.00
34	McDonald, William Colt - ***King Of Crazy River*** [1949] Cover by Charles Wood.	$2.00	$6.00	$12.00
35	Roan, Tom - ***Smoke River*** [1949] Cover by Charles Wood.	$2.00	$6.00	$12.00
36	Raine, William MacLeod - ***King Of The Bush*** [1949]	$2.00	$6.00	$12.00
37	Tuttle, W.C. - ***Hashknife Of Stormy River*** [1949] Cover by Charles Wood.	$2.00	$6.00	$12.00
38	Thompson, Jim - ***Nothing More Than Murder*** [1949]	$20.00	$60.00	$125.00
39	Wodehouse, P.G. - ***Meet Mr. Mulliner*** [1949] Cover by Roy Houlihan.	$4.00	$12.50	$25.00
40	Tuttle, W.C. - ***Trouble At The JHC*** [1949] Cover by A. Leslie Ross.	$2.00	$6.00	$12.00
41	Vance, Jack - ***The Dying Earth*** [1947] PBO, author's first book.	$32.00	$110.00	$250.00
42	Raine, William MacLeod - ***Roaring River*** [1950] Cover by Charles Wood.	$2.00	$6.00	$12.00
43	White, Stewart Edward - ***Arizona Nights*** [1950] Cover by A. Leslie Ross.	$2.00	$6.00	$12.00
44	Rhodes, Eugene Manlove - ***The Trusty Knaves*** [1950] Cover art by A. Leslie Ross.	$2.00	$6.00	$12.00
45	Foote, Alexander - ***Story Of A Russian Spy*** [1950]	$1.50	$5.00	$10.00
46	Rhodes, Eugene Manlove - ***Copper Streak Trail*** [1950]	$2.00	$6.00	$12.00
47	Hopkins, Tom J. - ***Scattergun Ranch*** [1950] Cover art by Charles Wood.	$2.00	$6.00	$12.00
48	Streeter, Edward - ***Father Of The Bride*** [1950] Movie tie-in. Movie photo cover.	$3.50	$10.00	$20.00
100	Simenon, Georges - ***The Witnesses*** [1957] Cover art by Robert Maguire.	$2.50	$7.50	$15.00
101	Raine, William MacLeod - ***Texas Man*** [1957] Cover art by Tom Ryan.	$1.50	$5.00	$10.00
102	MacDonald, William Colt - ***Lightning Swift*** [1957]	$1.50	$5.00	$10.00
103	Turner, Russell - ***The Short Night*** [1957] PBO.	$2.00	$6.00	$12.00
104	Heuman, William - ***Rimrock Town*** [1950]	$1.50	$5.00	$10.00
105	Simenon, Georges - ***The Watchmaker*** [1957] Cover art by Jerry Waldman.	$1.50	$5.00	$10.00
106	Ellis, Ph.D., Albert - ***Sex Without Guilt*** [1959] Photo cover.	$1.25	$3.75	$7.50
107	Payne, Robert - ***The Tormentors*** [1959] Cover art by Paul Rader.	$1.50	$5.00	$10.00
108	Sonnichsen, C.L. - ***Roy Bean: Law West Of The Pecos*** [1959]	$2.50	$7.50	$15.00
109	Nye, Nelson C. - ***Horses, Women And Guns*** [1959] PBO. Cover art by Harry Schaare.	$1.50	$5.00	$10.00

Hillman, 130

Lancer, 70-073

Lancer, 71-301

		G	VG	F
110	Austin, Alex - ***The Greatest Lover In The World*** [1959] Cover art by Leon Gregori.	$1.35	$4.00	$8.00
111	Brothers, Bill - ***Morocco Episode*** [1959] PBO. Cover art by Robert Maguire.	$2.50	$7.50	$15.00
112	White, John - ***The Sins Of Skid Row*** [1959]	$1.50	$5.00	$10.00
113	Smith, Stan - ***Soldiers' Women*** [1959] PBO. Photo cover.	$2.00	$6.00	$12.00
114	Heath, William L. - ***Temptation In A Southern Town*** [1959]	$1.50	$5.00	$10.00
115	Myers, John Myers - ***Dead Warrior*** [1959] Cover art by Tom Ryan.	$2.50	$7.50	$15.00
116	Meregendahl, Charles - ***A Strange Innocence*** [1959]	$1.50	$5.00	$10.00
117	Clippinger, Frances - ***Cassandra*** [1959]	$1.35	$4.00	$8.00
118	Cooper, Saul - ***The Jayhawkers*** [1959] PBO. Movie tie-in.	$1.50	$5.00	$10.00
119	Ellson, Hal - ***A Killer's Kiss*** [1959] PBO.	$3.00	$9.00	$18.00
120	Hanley, Jack - ***Let's Make Mary*** [1959]	$1.25	$3.75	$7.50
121	Mark, Edwina - ***The Sinful One*** [1959] PBO. Photo cover.	$1.35	$4.00	$8.00
122	Martin, Chuck - ***Sixgun Helltown*** [1959]	$1.50	$5.00	$10.00
123	Steward, Davenport - ***Savage Conqueror*** [1959] Cover art by Kinstler.	$1.35	$4.00	$8.00
124	Turner, Calvin - ***The Sinful Love*** [1959] PBO.	$1.25	$3.75	$7.50
125	Lariar, Lawrence - ***Death Is Confidential*** [1959]	$1.50	$5.00	$10.00
126	Fast, Julius - ***And Then Murder*** [1959]	$1.50	$5.00	$10.00
127	Cord, Barry - ***Maverick Gun*** [1959]	$1.50	$5.00	$10.00
128	DeGoncourt, Edmond - ***Elisa*** [1959] Cover by Milo.	$1.35	$4.00	$8.00
129	Ackworth, Robert C. - ***The Moments Between*** [1959] PBO. Cover art by Darcy.	$1.35	$4.00	$8.00
130	Edited by James Gregory - ***The Elvis Presley Story*** [1960] PBO. 32 pages of photos.	$8.00	$25.00	$50.00
131	Brennan, Alice - ***An Acre Of Love*** [1960] PBO.	$1.25	$3.75	$7.50
132	Nye, Nelson C. - ***The Last Bullet*** [1960] PBO.	$1.50	$5.00	$10.00
133	Cooper, Saul - ***Dillinger*** [1960] PBO. Cover art by Everett Raymond Kinstler.	$1.35	$4.00	$8.00
134	Anthony, Evelyn - ***Warriors Mistress*** [1960] Cover art by Darcy.	$1.35	$4.00	$8.00
135	Golightly, Bonnie - ***The Intimate Ones*** [1960] PBO. Cover art by Darcy.	$1.35	$4.00	$8.00
136	Stout, Rex - ***To Kill Again*** [1960]	$2.50	$7.50	$15.00
137	Ketchum, Philip - ***Gunsmoke Territory*** [1960] PBO.	$1.50	$5.00	$10.00
138	Martin, Kay - ***The Whispered Sex*** [1960] PBO. Cover art by Darcy.	$1.25	$3.75	$7.50
139	Owen, Dean - ***A Killer's Bargain*** [1960] PBO.	$1.50	$5.00	$10.00

		G	VG	F
140	Matthews, Kevin (Gardner F. Fox) - ***The Devil Sword*** [1960] PBO. Cover art by Darcy.	$2.50	$7.50	$15.00
141	Anthology edited by Ed Lowe - ***Sextasy*** [1960] PBO. Cartoon book.	$3.00	$9.00	$18.00
142	Roy, Claude - ***The Agony Of Love*** [1960] Cover art by Milo.	$1.25	$3.75	$7.50
143	Anthology edited by Brett Halliday - ***You Killed Elizabeth*** [1960]	$2.50	$7.50	$15.00
144	Patten, Lewis B. - ***The Angry Horseman*** [1960] PBO.	$1.35	$4.00	$8.00
145	Fox, James M. - ***A Lover's Blade*** [1960] PBO.	$1.50	$5.00	$10.00
146	Lacy, Ed - ***A Deadly Affair*** [1960] PBO.	$2.00	$6.00	$12.00
147	Cody, Al - ***Shield For A Killer*** [1960] PBO.	$1.50	$5.00	$10.00
148	DeStefani, Livia - ***The Forbidden*** [1960] Cover by Milo.	$1.35	$4.00	$8.00
149	Van Der Meersch, Maxence - ***The Strange Diagnosis*** [1960]	$1.25	$3.75	$7.50
150	Lehman, Paul Evan - ***Smoke Of The Texan*** [1960] PBO.	$1.50	$5.00	$10.00
151	Roeburt, John - ***Ruby MacLain*** [1960] PBO.	$1.50	$5.00	$10.00
153	Wadleigh, John W. - ***The Bitter Passion*** [1960]	$1.35	$4.00	$8.00
154	Fox, Gardner F. - ***Scandal In Suburbia*** [1960] PBO. Cover art by Milo.	$2.00	$6.00	$12.00
155	Floren, Lee - ***The Outlaw Breed*** [1960]	$1.50	$5.00	$10.00
156	Cantwell, John - ***The Awakening*** [1960]	$1.35	$4.00	$8.00
157	Purvis, Melvin H. - ***The Violent Years*** [1960] Photo cover.	$1.50	$5.00	$10.00
158	Martin, Kay - ***A Taste Of Passion*** [1960] PBO.	$2.00	$6.00	$12.00
159	Lomax, Bliss - ***The Lawless Guns*** [1960]	$1.50	$5.00	$10.00
160	McGovern, James - ***Love Among The Damned*** [1960]	$1.50	$5.00	$10.00
161	Lancaster, Evelyn - ***The Final Face Of Eve*** [1960] Photo cover.	$2.00	$6.00	$12.00
162	Golightly, Bonnie - ***The Shades Of Evil*** [1960]	$1.35	$4.00	$8.00
163	Carlisle, Robin - ***Blood And Roses*** [1960] PBO. Movie tie-in.	$1.50	$5.00	$10.00
164	Nye, Nelson C. - ***Gunfight At The O.K. Corral*** [1960]	$2.00	$6.00	$12.00
165	Simmons, K.W. - ***Kriegie: Prisoner Of War*** [1960]	$1.50	$5.00	$10.00
166	Patten, Lewis B. - ***Hangman's Country*** [1960]	$1.35	$4.00	$8.00
167	Bazin, Herve - ***An End To Passion*** [1960]	$1.35	$4.00	$8.00
169	Sinclair, Upton - ***Theirs Be The Guilt*** [1960]	$1.25	$3.75	$7.50
170	Kurst, Otto - ***Auschwitz*** [1960] Photo cover.	$1.35	$4.00	$8.00
171	Koten, Bernard - ***The Low Calory Cookbook*** [1960]	$1.50	$5.00	$10.00
172	Iverson, Andrina - ***The Gifts Of Love*** [1960]	$1.25	$3.75	$7.50
173	Hamill, Ethel - ***Candy Frost, Emergency Nurse*** [1960]	$1.00	$3.00	$6.00
174	Mitgang, Herbert - ***The Return*** [1960]	$1.35	$4.00	$8.00
175	Mason, Raymond - ***Bedeviled*** [1960] PBO.	$1.50	$5.00	$10.00
176	Chadwick, Joseph - ***Edge Of The Badlands*** [1960] PBO.	$1.50	$5.00	$10.00
177	Caprio, M.D., Frank S. - ***Sex And Love*** [1960]	$1.00	$3.00	$6.00
178	Owen, Dean - ***Rebel Ramrod*** [1960] PBO. Cover art by Tom Ryan.	$1.50	$5.00	$10.00
179	Race, Phillip - ***Johnny Come Deadly*** [1960] PBO. Cover art by Darcy.	$2.00	$6.00	$12.00
180	Smith, Lillian - ***The Journey*** [1960]	$1.35	$4.00	$8.00
181	Forton, Jean - ***Isabelle*** [1960]	$1.25	$3.75	$7.50
182	Wilson, Mitchell - ***None So Blind*** [1960]	$1.25	$3.75	$7.50
183	Turner, William O. - ***The Long Rope*** [1961] Cover art by Ron Lesser.	$1.35	$4.00	$8.00
184	Gosling, John & Warner, Douglas - ***City Of Vice*** [1961] Photo cover.	$1.35	$4.00	$8.00
186	Wells, Michael - ***The Captives*** [1961] PBO.	$1.35	$4.00	$8.00
187	Steiner, Paul - editor - ***Sex After Six*** [n.d.] PBO.	$1.25	$3.75	$7.50
188	Anthology - ***How To Buy Real Estate*** [1961]	$1.35	$4.00	$8.00
189	Lehman, Paul Evan - ***Colt '60*** [1961]	$1.35	$4.00	$8.00
190	Martin, Kay - ***Payment In Sin*** [1961] PBO.	$1.35	$4.00	$8.00
191	Gibbs, Willa - ***The Dedicated*** [1961]	$1.25	$3.75	$7.50
192	Anthology edited by Ed Lowe - ***More Sextasy*** [1961] Cartoon book.	$2.50	$7.50	$15.00
194	Stern, Bill - ***The Taste Of Ashes*** [1961] Photo cover.	$1.35	$4.00	$8.00

		G	VG	F
195	duMilieu, Pierre - ***The Bachelor's Guide To Women*** [1961] PBO. Cover art by Mort Drucker	$1.50	$5.00	$10.00
196	Davis, Roger - ***Always Love A Stranger*** [1961]	$1.35	$4.00	$8.00
F-199	Churchill, Allen - ***The Year The World Went Mad*** [1961]	$1.00	$3.00	$6.00
200	Cord, Barry - ***Slade*** [1961] Cover art by Korby	$1.35	$4.00	$8.00
201	Froscher, Wingate - ***The Comforts Of The Damned*** [1961]	$1.25	$3.75	$7.50
203	Farrington, Fielden - ***Street Of Brass*** [1961] PBO	$1.35	$4.00	$8.00
204	Hamill, Ethel - ***The Golden Image*** [1961]	$1.35	$4.00	$8.00
205	Mathews, Kevin (Gardner F. Fox) - ***Cardboard Lover*** [1961] PBO	$2.00	$6.00	$12.00

Hillman Detective Novel.

1	Carr, John Dickson - ***The Arabian Nights Murder*** [1943]	$8.00	$25.00	$50.00

Holloway House Books.

101	Linze, Dewey W. - ***The Trial Of Adolf Eichmann*** [1961] PBO. Cover art by Bill Edwards	$1.00	$3.00	$6.00
102	Singer, Kurt - ***Hemingway: Life & Death Of A Giant*** [1961] PBO. Cover art by Chet Collom.	$1.35	$4.00	$8.00
103	Memoirs - ***The Many Loves Of Casanova (Vol. I)*** [1961] PBO. Cover art by Bill Edwards	$1.00	$3.00	$6.00
104	Memoirs - ***The Many Loves Of Casanova (Vol. II)*** [1961] PBO. Cover art by Bill Edwards	$1.00	$3.00	$6.00
105	Guild, Leo - ***Hollywood Screwballs*** [1961]	$1.00	$3.00	$6.00
106	Anthology - ***The Best Of Adam*** [1962] PBO. Photo cover.	$1.35	$4.00	$8.00
107	Goodman, Mike - ***How To Win At Cards, Dice, Races, Roulette*** [1962] Cover art by Monte Rogers	$1.00	$3.00	$6.00
108	Payton, Barbara - ***I Am Not Ashamed*** [1962] Autobiography. 16 pages of photos. Photo cover.	$1.00	$3.00	$6.00
109	Hegeler, Inge & Sten - ***An Adult View Of Love And Sex*** [1962].	$1.00	$3.00	$6.00
110	Mansfield, Jayne & Hargitay, Mickey - ***Jane Mansfield's Wild, Wild World*** [1962] PBO. 32 pages of photos. Photo cover	$1.00	$3.00	$6.00
113	Yankowski & Wolfe - ***The Tortured Sex*** [1964]	$1.00	$3.00	$6.00
114	Yankowski - ***Yankowski Report On Premarital Sex*** [1964]	$1.00	$3.00	$6.00
115	Backus, Jim - ***Only When I Laugh*** [1964]	$1.00	$3.00	$6.00
116	Gillette, Paul J. - ***Satyricon*** [1965]	$1.00	$3.00	$6.00
117	Bruno, Mike & Weiss, David B. - ***Prostitution, U.S.A.*** [1965] PBO. Photo cover.	$1.00	$3.00	$6.00
118	Gillette, P.J. - ***An Uncensored History Of Pornography*** [1965] PBO	$1.00	$3.00	$6.00
119	Gage, Leona - ***My Name Is Leona Gage (Miss U.S.A.)*** [1965]	$1.00	$3.00	$6.00
120	Thompson, Fresco & Rice, Cy - ***Inside The Dodgers*** [1965]	$1.35	$4.00	$8.00
121	Emmett, Jeri - ***Point Your Tail In The Right Direction*** [1965]	$1.00	$3.00	$6.00
122	Washington, Kipp - ***Some Like It Dark*** [1965] PBO. Photo cover	$1.00	$3.00	$6.00
123	? - ***The Complete Marquis de Sade (Vol. I)*** [1965]	$1.00	$3.00	$6.00
124	? - ***The Complete Marquis de Sade (Vol. II)*** [1965]	$1.00	$3.00	$6.00
125	Olender, Terrys T. - ***My Life In Crime*** [1966]	$1.00	$3.00	$6.00
126	Wolfe, H.K. - ***The Role Of Dominant Females*** [1966]	$1.00	$3.00	$6.00
127	Rice, Cy - ***Get Me Gladys!*** [1966]	$1.00	$3.00	$6.00
128	Wolff, Hermann K. - ***Compulsive Desire*** [1966]	$1.00	$3.00	$6.00
129	Anthology edited by Thomas H. Schulz - ***Adam's Best Fiction*** [1966] PBO. Cover art by Harry Wysocki.	$1.35	$4.00	$8.00
130	Gillette, P.J. - ***Unconventional Sex Behavior*** [1966]	$1.00	$3.00	$6.00
131	? - ***The Ribald Russian Classics*** [1966]	$1.00	$3.00	$6.00
132	? - ***Adam's Swinging Party Humor*** [1966]	$1.00	$3.00	$6.00
133	? - ***Memoirs Of Dolly Morton*** [1966]	$1.00	$3.00	$6.00
134	? - ***Grushenka: Three Times A Woman*** [1966]	$1.00	$3.00	$6.00
135	de Sade, Marquis - ***Francon Duclos*** [1966]	$1.00	$3.00	$6.00
136	Rice, Cy - ***Children In Danger: The Molesters*** [1966]	$1.00	$3.00	$6.00

		G	VG	F
137	Forberg, F.K. - ***De Figuris Veneris*** [1966]	$1.00	$3.00	$6.00
138	Devereaux, Capt. C. - ***Venus In India*** [1966]	$1.00	$3.00	$6.00
139	Slim, Iceberg - ***Pimp: The Story Of My Life*** [1966]	$1.00	$3.00	$6.00
140	Gillette, P.J. - ***The Lopinson Case*** [1966]	$1.00	$3.00	$6.00
141	Curti, Carlo - ***Skouras: King Of Fox Studios*** [1966] PBO. Cover by Weller.	$1.00	$3.00	$6.00
142	Gillette, P.J. - ***The Art And Science Of Lovemaking*** [1966]	$1.00	$3.00	$6.00
143	Ling, Su - ***The 9 Holes Of Jade*** [1967]	$1.00	$3.00	$6.00
144	Unknown - ***The Harem Omnibus*** [1967]	$1.00	$3.00	$6.00
145	Apollinaire - ***Debauched Hospodar, Etc.*** [1967]	$1.00	$3.00	$6.00
146	? - ***Pauline: Memoirs Of A Singer*** [1967]	$1.00	$3.00	$6.00
147	? - ***Memoirs Of A Russian Princess*** [1967]	$1.00	$3.00	$6.00
148	? - ***Father Silas And Flesh And Bone*** [1967]	$1.00	$3.00	$6.00
149	McGuire, Don - ***1600 Floogle Street*** [1967]	$1.00	$3.00	$6.00
150	de Coy, Robert - ***The Nigger Bible*** [1967]	$2.50	$7.50	$15.00
151	Slim, Iceberg - ***Trick Baby*** [1967]	$1.00	$3.00	$6.00
152	Benuto, Rita - ***Mistress Of Cuba*** [1967]	$1.00	$3.00	$6.00
153	Kaye, H.R. - ***A Place In Hell*** [1967]	$1.00	$3.00	$6.00
154	Slatzer, Robert F. - ***The Hellcats*** [1967]	$2.50	$7.50	$15.00
155	Quirk, Lawrence - ***Robert Francis Kennedy*** [1967]	$1.00	$3.00	$6.00
156	The Rogets - ***A Swinger's Guide For The Single Girl*** [1967]	$1.00	$3.00	$6.00
157	Diderot, Denis - ***The Nun*** [1967]	$1.00	$3.00	$6.00
158	Panos, Mike - ***Honey Man*** [1967]	$1.00	$3.00	$6.00
159	Holtman, Jerry - ***Freak Show Man*** [1967]	$1.00	$3.00	$6.00
160	Lomax, Louis - ***To Kill A Black Man*** [1967]	$1.00	$3.00	$6.00
161	Davis, Hurk - ***Legion Of Outcasts*** [1968]	$1.00	$3.00	$6.00
162	Stanton, Elaine - ***Divorcee A Go-Go*** [1968] PBO. Photo cover.	$1.00	$3.00	$6.00
163	Mitsuko, Iolana - ***Honolulu Madam*** [1968]	$1.00	$3.00	$6.00
164	Miyoshi, Tami - ***The Cherry Dance*** [1968]	$1.00	$3.00	$6.00
165	McGuire, Don - ***The Day Television Died*** [1968]	$1.00	$3.00	$6.00
166	de Coy, Robert - ***The Big Black Fire*** [1968]	$1.00	$3.00	$6.00
177	Flohr, Scott - ***A Memory Without Pain*** [1968] Photo cover.	$1.00	$3.00	$6.00

International Humor Publishing.

1	Mirbeau, Octave - ***Diary Of A Chambermaid*** [1945] Movie tie-in.	$1.50	$5.00	$10.00

Intimate Edition.

720	Royce, Lloyd - ***"H" Is For Hell*** [1963] PBO.	$1.50	$5.00	$10.00

Intimate Novel. New York: Designs Pub. Corp. Digest Size.

1	Gaillard, Paul - ***Wayward Bride*** [1950] Photo cover.	$2.50	$7.50	$15.00
2	Barr, Cecil - ***French Model*** [1950] Photo cover.	$2.00	$6.00	$12.00
3	Foster, Gerald - ***Cheap Hotel*** [1950]	$2.00	$6.00	$12.00
4	Semple, Gordon - ***Plaything*** [1950] Photo cover.	$2.00	$6.00	$12.00
5	Cole, Jerry - ***Secrets Of A Society Doctor*** [1950]	$2.00	$6.00	$12.00
6	Anthony, Jed - ***Divorce Racket Girls*** [1951] Photo cover.	$2.00	$6.00	$12.00
7	Norcross, Robert - ***Greenwich Village Girl*** [1951] Photo cover.	$2.00	$6.00	$12.00
8	Lawrence, Ann - ***Gin Wedding*** [1951] Photo cover.	$2.00	$6.00	$12.00
9	Brewster, Elliot - ***Temptress*** [1951] Photo cover.	$2.00	$6.00	$12.00
10	Thornton, Charles - ***Dangerous Trade*** [1951] Photo cover.	$2.00	$6.00	$12.00
11	Lindsay, Perry (Peggis Gaddis) - ***Swamp Girl*** [1951]	$2.50	$7.50	$15.00
12	de Forest, Barry - ***Seventh Wife*** [1951] Photo cover.	$2.00	$6.00	$12.00
13	Stonebraker, Florence - ***Local Talent*** [1952] PBO.	$2.50	$7.50	$15.00
14	Manning, Bruce - ***Off Limits*** [1952] PBO. Cover art by Warren King.	$2.50	$7.50	$15.00
15	de Mexico, N.R. - ***Private Chauffeur*** [1952] PBO.	$3.00	$9.00	$18.00
16	Stonebraker, Florence - ***Lust For Love*** [1952] PBO. Cover art by Owen Kampen.	$2.50	$7.50	$15.00

		G	VG	F
17	West, Ben - ***The Sins Of Janet Benson-Showgirl*** [1952] PBO. Photo cover.	$2.00	$6.00	$12.00
18	Hanley, Jack - ***Hot Lips*** [1952] PBO. Cover art by Warren King.	$3.00	$9.00	$18.00
19	Bennett, Hall - ***Mail-Order Passion*** [1952] PBO. Cover art by George Gross.	$3.00	$9.00	$18.00
20	Carter, Ralph - ***Pleasure Alley*** [1952] PBO. Cover art by Geygan.	$3.00	$9.00	$18.00
21	Stone, Thomas - ***Dr. Randolph's Women*** [1952] PBO. Photo cover.	$2.00	$6.00	$12.00
22	Grant, Richard - ***Office Wife*** [1952] Photo cover.	$2.00	$6.00	$12.00
23	Stone, Thomas - ***Ex-Mistress*** [1952] PBO. Photo cover.	$2.00	$6.00	$12.00
24	Branch, Florenz - ***The Whipping Room*** [1952] PBO.	$3.50	$10.00	$20.00
25	Manning, Bruce - ***Triangle Of Sin*** [1952] PBO.	$2.50	$7.50	$15.00
26	Hanley, Jack - ***Very Private Secretary*** [1952] PBO.	$2.50	$7.50	$15.00
27	Stone, Thomas - ***Tramp Girl*** [1952] Cover art by Warren King.	$3.00	$9.00	$18.00
28	Wall, Evans - ***Black Country Woman*** [1952]	$3.50	$10.00	$20.00
29	Way, Wayne - ***Shameless Wife*** [1953] PBO. Photo cover.	$2.00	$6.00	$12.00
30	Hanley, Jack - ***Tent-Show Bride*** [1953] PBO. Photo cover.	$2.00	$6.00	$12.00
31	Nixon, Henry Louis - ***Naked Desire*** [1953] PBO.	$2.50	$7.50	$15.00
32	Williams, David - ***Basement Gang*** [1953] PBO. Photo cover.	$4.50	$14.00	$28.00
33	Barry, Winchell - ***Scarlet City*** [1953] PBO. Photo cover.	$2.00	$6.00	$12.00
34	Reed, Kathie - ***Shack Woman*** [1953] PBO.	$3.50	$10.00	$20.00
35	Stone, Thomas - ***Private Practice*** [1953] PBO. Photo cover.	$2.00	$6.00	$12.00
36	Semple, Gordon - ***Waterfront Blonde*** [1953] PBO. Cover by Warren King.	$3.00	$9.00	$18.00
37	Hanley, Jack - ***New York Model*** [1953] PBO. Cover art by Walter Popp.	$2.50	$7.50	$15.00
38	Brown, Beth - ***Lily Of New Orleans*** [1953] Cover art by Walter Popp.	$2.50	$7.50	$15.00
39	Branch, Florenz - ***Dr. Breyton's Wife*** [1953] PBO.	$2.50	$7.50	$15.00
40	Semple, Gordon - ***Crusher's Girl*** [1953] PBO.	$3.00	$9.00	$18.00
41	Reed, Kathie - ***Forbidden Desire*** [1953] PBO.	$3.50	$10.00	$20.00
42	Reed, Kathie - ***Village Girl*** [1953] PBO. Cover art by E. Uppwall.	$3.50	$10.00	$20.00
43	Wall, Evans - ***The Marriage Rite*** [1953]	$2.50	$7.50	$15.00
44	Harvey, Gene - ***Miami Widow*** [1953] PBO.	$2.50	$7.50	$15.00
45	Albert, Simms - ***Pound Of Flesh*** [1953] PBO. Cover art by Owen Kampen.	$3.00	$9.00	$18.00
46	Duperrault, Doug - ***Trailer-Camp Girl*** [1953] PBO.	$3.50	$10.00	$20.00
47	Stone, Thomas - ***Red-Headed Nurse*** [1953] PBO. Photo cover.	$2.00	$6.00	$12.00
48	Manning, Bruce - ***Cafe Society Sinner*** [1953] PBO. Photo cover.	$2.00	$6.00	$12.00
49	Sydney, Gale - ***Strange Circle*** [1953] PBO.	$2.50	$7.50	$15.00
51	Nixon, Henry Lewis - ***Ship's Doctor*** [1954] PBO. Cover art by Walter Popp.	$2.50	$7.50	$15.00
52	Clark, Dorine B. - ***Gutter Star*** [1954] PBO. Cover art by Uppwall.	$3.00	$9.00	$18.00
53	Booth, Roy - ***Girl Stowaway*** [1954] Cover art by B. Safran.	$3.50	$10.00	$20.00
54	Clark, Dorine B. - ***Bachelor Girl*** [1954] PBO.	$2.50	$7.50	$15.00
55	Nixon, Henry Lewis - ***Secrets Of A Doctor's Bride*** [1954] PBO. Photo cover.	$2.50	$7.50	$15.00
56	Moore, Hal R. - ***Odd Girl*** [1954] PBO. Photo cover.	$2.00	$6.00	$12.00

Invincible Mystery. Melbourne, Australia: Invincible Mystery Press.

NN-1	Starr, Jimmy - ***The Corpse Came C.O.D.*** [n.d.]	$4.00	$12.50	$25.00
NN-2	Starr, Jimmy - ***Three Short Biers*** [n.d.]	$4.00	$12.50	$25.00
NN-3	Starr, Jimmy - ***The Lady Lost Her Head*** [n.d.]	$4.00	$12.50	$25.00
NN-4	Starr, Jimmy - ***Just Around The Coroner*** [n.d.]	$4.00	$12.50	$25.00
NN-5	Kane, Frank - ***Green Light For Death*** [n.d.]	$4.00	$12.50	$25.00

		G	VG	F

Jacket Library.

		G	VG	F
NN	Rostand, Edmund - ***The Art Of Love (Cyrano de Bergerac)*** [1933]	$4.00	$12.50	$25.00
NN-1	Stevenson, Robert Louis - ***Treasure Island*** [1932]	$4.00	$12.50	$25.00
NN-2	Anthology - ***The New Testament*** [1932]	$5.00	$15.00	$30.00
NN-3	Hudson, W. H. - ***Green Mansions*** [1932]	$4.00	$12.50	$25.00
NN-4	Butler, Samuel - ***The Way Of All Flesh*** [1932]	$4.00	$12.50	$25.00
NN-5	Shakespeare, William - ***The Merchant Of Venice*** [1932]	$4.00	$12.50	$25.00
NN-6	Emerson, Ralph Waldo - ***Emerson's Essays*** [1932]	$4.00	$12.50	$25.00
NN-7	de Balzac, Honore - ***Pere Goriot*** [1932]	$4.00	$12.50	$25.00
NN-8	Carroll, Lewis - ***Alice's Adventures In Wonderland, and others*** [1932]	$4.00	$12.50	$25.00
NN-9	Clemens, Samuel L. - ***The Adventures of Tom Sawyer*** [1932]	$4.00	$12.50	$25.00
NN-10	Doyle, Arthur Conan - ***Tales of Sherlock Holmes*** [1932]	$4.00	$12.50	$25.00
NN-11	Hardy, Thomas - ***Under The Greenwood Tree*** [1932]	$4.00	$12.50	$25.00
NN-12	Palgrave, Francis Turner - editor - ***The Golden Treasury*** [1932]	$4.00	$12.50	$25.00
NN-13	Rostand, Edmund - ***The Art Of Love (Cyrano de Bergerac)*** [1933]	$4.00	$12.50	$25.00
NN-14	Rostand, Edmund - ***Other People's Money*** [1932]	$4.00	$12.50	$25.00

Jade Book.

		G	VG	F
211	O'Neill, Scott - ***Martian Sexpot*** [1963]	$2.50	$7.50	$15.00
212	Howard, Vince - ***Countdown For Lisa*** [1963]	$1.50	$5.00	$10.00

Joe Moss Mystery. Digest size.

		G	VG	F
NN	Sideman, Abner - ***Murder On Both Sides*** [1945] PBO.	$2.50	$7.50	$15.00

Jonathan Press Mystery. Digest Size.

		G	VG	F
J1	Queen, Ellery - ***The Chinese Orange Mystery*** [n.d.]	$1.35	$4.00	$8.00
J2	Stout, Rex - ***Too Many Cooks*** [n.d.]	$1.25	$3.75	$7.50
J3	Marsh, Ngaio - ***A Man Lay Dead*** [1943] Abridged. Cover by George Salter.	$1.00	$3.00	$6.00
J4	Dickson, Carter - ***The Bowstring Murders*** [n.d.] Abridged. Cover by George Salter.	$1.25	$3.75	$7.50
J5	Queen, Ellery - ***The French Powder Mystery*** [n.d.] Abridged. Cover by George Salter.	$1.25	$3.75	$7.50
J6	Stout, Rex - ***Over My Dead Body*** [n.d.] Abridged. Cover by George Salter.	$1.25	$3.75	$7.50
J7	Christie, Agatha - ***Murder For Christmas*** [n.d.] Abridged. Cover by George Salter.	$1.00	$3.00	$6.00
J8	Simenon, Georges - ***Maigret Sits It Out*** [n.d.] Unabridged. Cover by George Salter.	$1.00	$3.00	$6.00
J9	Stout, Rex - ***The Broken Vase*** [n.d.]	$1.25	$3.75	$7.50
J10	Christie, Agatha - ***Death In The Air*** [n.d.]	$1.00	$3.00	$6.00
J11	Dickson, Carter - ***The Red Widow Murders*** [n.d.] Abridged. Cover by George Salter.	$1.25	$3.75	$7.50
J12	Queen, Ellery - ***The Roman Hat Mystery*** [n.d.] Abridged. Cover by George Salter.	$1.25	$3.75	$7.50
J13	Christie, Agatha - ***N Or M?*** [n.d.]	$1.00	$3.00	$6.00
J14	Dickson, Carter - ***The White Priory Murders*** [n.d.] Abridged. Cover by George Salter.	$1.25	$3.75	$7.50
J15	Stout, Rex - ***Cordially Invited To Meet Death*** [n.d.]	$1.25	$3.75	$7.50
J16	Christie, Agatha - ***Murder In Retrospect*** [n.d.] Abridged. Cover by George Salter.	$1.00	$3.00	$6.00
J17	Hammett, Dashiell - ***The Return Of The Continental Op*** [1945] PBO. Cover by George Salter.	$17.00	$50.00	$100.00
J18	Simenon, Georges - ***Maigret Returns*** [n.d.]	$1.25	$3.75	$7.50
J19	Dickson, Carter - ***The Plague Court Murders*** [n.d.]	$1.25	$3.75	$7.50
J20	Sale, Richard - ***Passing Strange*** [n.d.] Unabridged. Cover by George Salter.	$1.00	$3.00	$6.00

		G	VG	F
J21	Daly, Elizabeth - ***Arrow Pointing Nowhere*** [n.d.] Abridged.	$1.00	$3.00	$6.00
J22	Wilde, Percival - ***Design For Murder*** [n.d.]	$1.00	$3.00	$6.00
J23	Woolrich, Cornell - ***Black Alibi*** [n.d.] Abridged. Cover by George Salter.	$2.50	$7.50	$15.00
J24	Sale, Richard - ***Lazarus 7*** [n.d.] Unabridged. Cover by George Salter.	$2.50	$7.50	$15.00
J25	Carr, John Dickson - ***It Walks By Night*** [n.d.]	$1.25	$3.75	$7.50
J26	Palmer, Stuart - ***The Riddles Of Hildegarde Withers*** [n.d.]	$1.00	$3.00	$6.00
J27	Stout, Rex - ***Not Quite Dead Enough*** [n.d.]	$1.25	$3.75	$7.50
J28	Venning, Michael - ***Jethro Hammer*** [n.d.]	$1.00	$3.00	$6.00
J29	Hammett, Dashiell - ***Dead Yellow Women*** [1947] PBO. Cover by George Salter.	$17.00	$50.00	$100.00
J30	Coxe, George Harmon - ***The Glass Triangle*** [n.d.] Abridged. Cover by George Salter.	$1.00	$3.00	$6.00
J31	Irish, William - ***And So To Death*** [n.d.]	$2.50	$7.50	$15.00
J32	Allingham, Margery - ***Dancers In Mourning*** [n.d.] Abridged. Cover by George Salter.	$1.00	$3.00	$6.00
J33	Stout, Rex - ***The League Of Frightened Men*** [n.d.]	$1.25	$3.75	$7.50
J34	Chambers, Dana - ***Dear, Dead Women*** [n.d.] Abridged. Cover by George Salter.	$1.00	$3.00	$6.00
J35	Homes, Geoffrey - ***Build My Gallows High*** [n.d.]	$1.00	$3.00	$6.00
J36	Hammett, Dashiell - ***The Big Knock-Over*** [n.d.]	$8.00	$25.00	$50.00
J37	Black, Thomas B. - ***The Pinball Murders*** [n.d.]	$1.00	$3.00	$6.00
J38	Chambers, Dana - ***The Frightened Man*** [n.d.]	$1.00	$3.00	$6.00
J39	Coles, Manning - ***With Intent To Deceive*** [n.d.] Abridged. Cover by George Salter.	$1.00	$3.00	$6.00
J40	Hammett, Dashiell - ***The Continental Op*** [n.d.]	$8.00	$25.00	$50.00
J41	Black, Thomas B. - ***The 3-13 Murders*** [n.d.]	$1.00	$3.00	$6.00
J42	Shallit, Joseph - ***The Billion Dollar Body*** [n.d.] Abridged. Cover by George Salter.	$1.00	$3.00	$6.00
J43	Chambers, Dana - ***Darling, This Is Death*** [n.d.]	$1.00	$3.00	$6.00
J44	Gordon, Russell - ***Dead Level*** [n.d.]	$1.00	$3.00	$6.00
J45	Fischer, Bruno - ***The Spider Lily*** [n.d.] Abridged. Cover by George Salter.	$1.00	$3.00	$6.00
J46	Chambers, Dana - ***The Last Secret*** [n.d.]	$1.00	$3.00	$6.00
J47	Warren, Charles Marquis - ***Deadhead*** [n.d.]	$1.00	$3.00	$6.00
J48	Hammett, Dashiell - ***The Creeping Siamese*** [1948] PBO. Cover by George Salter.	$17.00	$50.00	$100.00
J49	Marquand, John P. - ***Mr. Moto Is So Sorry*** [n.d.]	$1.00	$3.00	$6.00
J50	Chambers, Dana - ***Death Against Venus*** [n.d.]	$1.00	$3.00	$6.00
J51	Woolrich, Cornell - ***The Black Angel*** [n.d.]	$2.50	$7.50	$15.00
J52	Marquand, John P. - ***No Hero*** [n.d.] Unabridged. Cover by George Salter.	$1.00	$3.00	$6.00
J53	Roos, Kelley - ***Dangerous Blondes*** [n.d.]	$1.00	$3.00	$6.00
J54	Marquand, John P. - ***Ming Yellow*** [n.d.] Unabridged. Cover by George Salter.	$1.00	$3.00	$6.00
J55	Chambers, Dana - ***Blood On The Blonde*** [n.d.] Unabridged. Photo cover.	$1.00	$3.00	$6.00
J56	Kane, Frank - ***Dead Weight*** [n.d.]	$1.25	$3.75	$7.50
J57	Coles, Manning - ***Dangerous By Nature*** [n.d.]	$1.00	$3.00	$6.00
J58	Chambers, Dana - ***The Blonde Died First*** [n.d.] Unabridged. Cover by George Salter.	$1.00	$3.00	$6.00
J59	Hammett, Dashiell - ***Woman In The Dark*** [n.d.]	$8.00	$25.00	$50.00
J60	Innes, Hammond - ***The Blue Ice*** [n.d.]	$1.00	$3.00	$6.00
J61	Woolrich, Cornell - ***The Black Path Of Fear*** [n.d.] Unabridged. Photo cover.	$2.50	$7.50	$15.00
J62	Coles, Manning - ***Now Or Never*** [n.d.]	$1.00	$3.00	$6.00
J63	Chambers, Dana - ***Rope For An Ape*** [n.d.]	$1.00	$3.00	$6.00
J64	Kane, Frank - ***Bullet Proof*** [n.d.]	$1.00	$3.00	$6.00

		G	VG	F
J65	Latimer, Jonathan - ***The Fifth Grave*** [n.d.] Abridged. Cover by George Salter.	$1.00	$3.00	$6.00
J66	Gruber, Frank - ***Die Like A Dog*** [n.d.] Unabridged. Cover by George Salter.	$1.25	$3.75	$7.50
J67	Bagby, George - ***Scared To Death*** [n.d.]	$1.00	$3.00	$6.00
J68	Coles, Manning - ***Operation Manhunt*** [n.d.]	$1.00	$3.00	$6.00
J69	Latimer, Jonathan - ***Murder In The Madhouse*** [n.d.] Abridged. Photo cover.	$1.00	$3.00	$6.00
J70	Hughes, Dorothy B. - ***Kiss For A Killer*** [n.d.] Unabridged. Cover by George Salter.	$1.00	$3.00	$6.00
J71	Bagby, George - ***A Body For The Bride*** [n.d.] Abridged. Cover by George Salter.	$1.00	$3.00	$6.00
J72	Gruber, Frank - ***Too Touch To Die*** [n.d.] Unabridged. Cover by George Salter.	$1.25	$3.75	$7.50
J73	Bagby, George - ***Dead Drunk*** [n.d.] Unabridged. Cover by George Salter.	$1.00	$3.00	$6.00
J74	Coles, Manning - ***All That Glitters*** [n.d.]	$1.00	$3.00	$6.00
J75	Goldsmith, Gene - ***Layout For A Corpse*** [n.d.]	$1.00	$3.00	$6.00
J76	Gruber, Frank - ***Fall-Guy For A Killer*** [n.d.]	$1.25	$3.75	$7.50
J77	Latimer, Jonathan - ***Some Dames Are Deadly*** [n.d.] Unabridged. Cover by George Salter.	$1.00	$3.00	$6.00
J78	Calin, Hal Jason - ***Payoff In Blood*** [n.d.] Unabridged. Cover by George Salter.	$1.00	$3.00	$6.00
J79	Chambers, Whitman - ***Deadly Lure*** [n.d.]	$1.00	$3.00	$6.00
J80	Wilmot, Robert Patrick - ***Death Rides A Painted Horse*** [n.d.] Abridged. Cover by George Salter.	$1.00	$3.00	$6.00
J84	Latimer, Jonathan - ***Headed For A Hearse*** [n.d.] Abridged. Cover by Ed Emsh.	$1.00	$3.00	$6.00
J85	Gruber, Frank - ***The Long Arm Of Murder*** [n.d.] Unabridged.Cover by George Salter.	$1.25	$3.75	$7.50
J86	Franklin, Max - ***Hell Street*** [n.d.] Abridged. Cover by Dick Shelton.	$1.00	$3.00	$6.00
J89	Gruber, Frank - ***Once Over Deadly*** [n.d.] Abridged. Cover by George Salter.	$1.25	$3.75	$7.50
J90	Coles, Manning - ***The Man In The Green Hat*** [n.d.] Abridged. Cover by Ed Emsh.	$1.00	$3.00	$6.00
J91	Deming, Richard - ***Hand-Picked To Die*** [n.d.] Abridged. Cover by Schulz.	$1.00	$3.00	$6.00
J93	Coles, Manning - ***The Basle Express*** [n.d.] Abridged. Cover by Ed Emsh.	$1.00	$3.00	$6.00
J94	Barns, Glenn M. - ***Murder Is Insane*** [n.d.] Abridged. Photo cover.	$1.00	$3.00	$6.00
J95	Dodge, David - ***The Long Escape*** [n.d.] Unabridged. Cover by Waldman.	$1.25	$3.75	$7.50
J96	Fox, James M. - ***Rites For A Killer*** [n.d.] Unabridged. Photo cover.	$1.00	$3.00	$6.00

Kanrom Books. New York: Kanrom Inc.

K-102	Kandel, Howard & Safran, Don - ***Stoned Like A Statue*** [1963] Introduction by Dean Martin. Cartoons.	$ .65	$2.00	$4.00

Kirby Books. New York: Kirby Publishing. Digest size.

NN-1	Anthology - ***Candid Tales*** [1950] PBO. All color comics illustrations.	$17.00	$50.00	$100.00
NN-2	Anthology - ***Bold Stories*** [1950] PBO. All color comics illustrations.	$17.00	$50.00	$100.00

Knickerbocker. New York: Knickerbocker Publications. Digest size.

NO#-1	Jordan, Gail (Peggy Gaddis) - ***Professional Glamor Girl*** [1946]	$1.50	$5.00	$10.00
NO#-2	Brewster, Eliot - ***Plenty Of Love*** [1946]	$2.00	$6.00	$12.00

		G	VG	F
NO#-3	Keller, H.A. - ***Her Day Of Sin*** [1946] Cover art by Bill Fow.	$1.50	$5.00	$10.00
NO#-4	Carter, Ralph - ***A Little Sin*** [1946]	$2.00	$6.00	$12.00
NO#-5	Sloan, Gladys - ***Confessions Of A Studio Model*** [1949] Cover art by Cravath.	$2.00	$6.00	$12.00
NO#-6	Branch, Florenz - ***Unwilling Virgin*** [1946] Cover art by Cravath.	$1.50	$5.00	$10.00
NO#-7	Lindsay, Perry (Peggy Gaddis) - ***Shameless Woman*** [1946]	$1.50	$5.00	$10.00
NO#-8	Stone, Thomas - ***Two-Time Girl*** [1946]	$2.00	$6.00	$12.00
NO#-9	Norcross, Robert - ***Love At A Price*** [1946]	$2.00	$6.00	$12.00
NO#-10	Watkins, Glen - ***The Hard-Boiled Blonde*** [1946]	$1.50	$5.00	$10.00
NO#-11	Branch, Florenz - ***Pick-Up Girl*** [1946]	$1.50	$5.00	$10.00
NO#-12	Jordan, Gail (Peggy Gaddis) - ***The Wanton Blonde*** [1946]	$2.00	$6.00	$12.00
NO#-13	Carter, Ralph - ***Torrid Love*** [1946]	$2.00	$6.00	$12.00
NO#-14	Jordan, Gail (Peggy Gaddis) - ***Once A Sinner*** [1946]	$2.00	$6.00	$12.00
NO#-15	Saxon, John - ***A Touch Of Passion*** [1946]	$1.50	$5.00	$10.00
NO#-16	Branch, Florenz - ***Unfaithful*** [1946] Cover art by Cravath.	$1.50	$5.00	$10.00
NO#-17	Jordan, Gail (Peggy Gaddis) - ***Part Time Passion*** [1946]	$2.00	$6.00	$12.00
NO#-18	Gay, Carmen - ***Illicit Passion*** [1946]	$2.00	$6.00	$12.00
NO#-19	Brewster, Eliot - ***Past Sin*** [1946]	$2.00	$6.00	$12.00
NO#-20	Jordan, Gail (Peggy Gaddis) - ***Desirous*** [1946]	$1.50	$5.00	$10.00
NO#-21	Jordan, Gail (Peggy Gaddis) - ***The Lost Virgin*** [1946]	$1.50	$5.00	$10.00
NO#-22	Jordan, Gail (Peggy Gaddis) - ***Made For Love*** [1946]	$2.00	$6.00	$12.00
NO#-23	Jordan, Gail (Peggy Gaddis) - ***Palm Beach Apartment*** [1946]	$1.50	$5.00	$10.00
NO#-24	Lindsay, Perry (Peggy Gaddis) - ***The Passionate Widow*** [1946]	$1.50	$5.00	$10.00
NO#-25	Keller, H.A. - ***Her Sacred Sin*** [1946]	$2.00	$6.00	$12.00
NO#-26	Carter, Ralph - ***Blonde Venus*** [1946]	$2.00	$6.00	$12.00
NO#-27	Sloan, Gladys - ***The Sinful Sisters*** [1946]	$2.00	$6.00	$12.00
NO#-28	Branch, Florenz - ***Pleasure After Hours*** [1946]	$2.00	$6.00	$12.00
NO#-29	Stone, Thomas - ***Careless Caresses*** [1946]	$1.50	$5.00	$10.00
NO#-30	Stone, Thomas - ***A Talent For Love*** [1946]	$1.50	$5.00	$10.00
NO#-31	Watkins, Glen - ***Over-Time Love*** [1946]	$2.00	$6.00	$12.00
NO#-32	Watkins, Glen - ***Tavern Girl*** [1946]	$1.50	$5.00	$10.00
NO#-33	Saxon, John - ***Forgotten Passion*** [1946]	$1.50	$5.00	$10.00
NO#-34	Arthur, William - ***Marriage Later*** [1946]	$1.50	$5.00	$10.00
NO#-35	Arthur, William - ***Convention Girl*** [1946]	$2.00	$6.00	$12.00
NO#-36	Baker, Carlotta - ***The Fallen Woman*** [1946]	$2.00	$6.00	$12.00
NO#-37	Baker, Carlotta - ***Wayward Girl*** [1946]	$1.50	$5.00	$10.00
NO#-38	Gates, H.L. - ***Born To Sin*** [1946]	$2.00	$6.00	$12.00
NO#-39	Jacquin, Lee - ***Studio Lovers*** [1946]	$2.00	$6.00	$12.00
NO#-40	Jacquin, Lee - ***The Wife And The Wolf*** [1946]	$1.50	$5.00	$10.00
NO#-41	James, Griffith - ***Dangerous Loves*** [1946]	$1.50	$5.00	$10.00
NO#-42	Strong, Charles S. - ***Immoral Woman*** [1946]	$2.00	$6.00	$12.00
NO#-43	Strong, Charles S. - ***Love For Sale*** [1946]	$2.00	$6.00	$12.00
NO#-44	Williams, Wright - ***Bar-Fly Wives*** [1946]	$1.50	$5.00	$10.00
NO#-45	Williams, Wright - ***Beautiful Body*** [1946]	$1.50	$5.00	$10.00
NO#-46	Williams, Wright - ***Carnival Girl*** [1946]	$2.00	$6.00	$12.00
NO#-47	Williams, Wright - ***Excess Wife*** [1946]	$1.50	$5.00	$10.00
NO#-48	Williams, Wright - ***Loose Ladies*** [1946] Cover art by R. Failla.	$2.00	$6.00	$12.00
NO#-49	Long, Amelia Reynolds - ***Death Has A Will*** [1946] Cover art by Ancona.	$1.50	$5.00	$10.00
NO#-50	Brooks, William Allan - editor - ***The Playboy's Handbook*** [1946] PBO.	$2.00	$6.00	$12.00
NO#-51	Jordan, Gail (Peggy Gaddis) - ***Love On The Run*** [1946]	$1.50	$5.00	$10.00

Kozy Books.

136	Lewis, Pete - ***Father Of The Amazons*** [1961]	$3.50	$10.00	$20.00

Lancer Books. New York: Lancer Books, Inc.

Lancer 70 Series.

70-001	Blatty, William - ***Which Way To Mecca, Jack?*** [1962]	$1.25	$3.75	$7.50

		G	VG	F
70-002	Gold, Herbert - ***Therefore Be Bold*** [1962]	$1.25	$3.75	$7.50
70-003	Bromfield, Louis - ***What Became Of Anna Bolton*** [1962]	$1.25	$3.75	$7.50
70-004	Willingham, Calder - ***Natural Child*** [1962] Photo cover.	$1.00	$3.00	$6.00
70-005	Carr, William H. A. - ***What Is Jack Parr Really Like?*** [1962] PBO. Photocover. TV tie-in.	$1.25	$3.75	$7.50
70-006	Johnston, Willian - ***Ben Casey*** [1962] PBO. Photo cover. TV tie-in.	$1.25	$3.75	$7.50
70-007	Daniels, Norman - ***Dr. Kildare's Secret Romance*** [1962] PBO. Photo cover. TV tie-in.	$1.25	$3.75	$7.50
70-008	Brewer, Gil - ***Memory Of Passion*** [1962] PBO.	$2.50	$7.50	$15.00
70-009	Lucas, Bob - ***Naked In Hollywood*** [1962]	$1.25	$3.75	$7.50
70-010	Dietrich, Robert (E. Howard Hunt) - ***My Body*** [1962] PBO. Cover art by Ronnie Lesser.	$1.25	$3.75	$7.50
70-011	Daniels, Norman - ***A Rage For Justice*** [1962] PBO. TV tie-in.	$1.25	$3.75	$7.50
70-012	Meade, Richard - ***Two Surgeons*** [1962] PBO. Cover by Harry Schaare.	$1.00	$3.00	$6.00
70-013	Craig, Jonathan - ***Frenzy*** [1962]	$1.35	$4.00	$8.00
70-015	Sudak, Eunice - ***White Slave Ship*** [1962] PBO. Movie tie-in.	$1.50	$5.00	$10.00
70-016	Allen, Eric - ***Lone Gun*** [1962]	$1.25	$3.75	$7.50
70-029	O'Farrell, William - ***The Golden Key*** [1962] PBO.	$1.25	$3.75	$7.50
70-030	Creasey, John - ***The Creepers*** [1962]	$1.25	$3.75	$7.50
70-031	Cassiday, Bruce - ***Dr. Reade's Decision*** [1962] PBO.	$1.00	$3.00	$6.00
70-032	Daniels, Norman - ***Dr. Kildare's Finest Hour*** [1963] PBO. Photo cover. TV tie-in.	$1.25	$3.75	$7.50
70-033	Cody, Al - ***Empty Saddles*** [1963]	$1.25	$3.75	$7.50
70-034	Poe, Edgar Allan - ***The Raven*** [1963] PBO. Eunice Sudak adaptation. Movie tie-in. Photo cover.	$2.50	$7.50	$15.00
70-035	Daniels, Norman - ***Sam Benedict Casts The First Stone*** [1963] PBO. Cover art by Hector Garrido. TV tie-in.	$1.25	$3.75	$7.50
70-036	Ernenwein, Leslie - ***Trigger Justice*** [1963]	$1.25	$3.75	$7.50
70-037	Elkin, Sam - ***The Strength Of His Hands*** [1963] PBO. Photo cover. Movie tie-in.	$1.25	$3.75	$7.50
70-038	Marsh, Rebecca - ***Nurse Annette*** [1963]	$1.00	$3.00	$6.00
70-039	Craig, Georgia - ***Society Nurse*** [1963]	$1.00	$3.00	$6.00
70-040	Calin, Harold - ***The Young Racers*** [1963] PBO. Movie tie-in.	$1.25	$3.75	$7.50
70-041	Boal, Sam - ***The Man From The Diner's Club*** [1963] PBO. Photo cover. Movie tie-in.	$1.25	$3.75	$7.50
70-042	Calin, Harold - ***Combat*** [1963] PBO. Photo cover. TV tie-in.	$1.25	$3.75	$7.50
70-043	Johnston, William - ***Dr. Kildare: The Heart Has An Answer*** [1963] PBO. Photo cover. TV tie-in.	$1.25	$3.75	$7.50
70-044	Hopson, William - ***Border Raider*** [1963] Cover art by Armand Weston.	$1.25	$3.75	$7.50
70-045	Daniels, Norman - ***Ben Casey: The Fire Within*** [1963] PBO. Photo cover. TV tie-in.	$1.25	$3.75	$7.50
70-046	Paul, Art - ***You Are Invited To Our Orgy*** [1963] PBO. Cartoon Book.	$1.35	$4.00	$8.00
70-047	Hopson, William - ***Tombstone Stage*** [1963]	$1.25	$3.75	$7.50
70-048	Kane, Henry - ***Never Give A Millionaire An Even Break*** [1963] PBO.	$1.35	$4.00	$8.00
70-049	Johnston, William - ***Dr. Kildare: The Facts Of Love*** [1963] PBO. Photo cover. TV tie-in.	$1.25	$3.75	$7.50
70-050	Hilton, Joseph - ***President's Agent*** [1963] PBO. Cover art by James Bama.	$1.25	$3.75	$7.50
70-051	Hopson, William - ***High Saddle*** [1963]	$1.25	$3.75	$7.50
70-052	Adapted by Eunice Sudak - ***X*** [1963] PBO. Photo cover. Movie tie-in.	$2.00	$6.00	$12.00
70-053	Dern, Peggy (Peggy Gaddis) - ***Orchids For A Nurse*** [1968]	$1.00	$3.00	$6.00
70-054	Coburn, Walt - ***Violent Maverick*** [1963]	$1.25	$3.75	$7.50
70-055	Hirschfeld, Burt - ***General Hospital*** [1963] PBO. TV tie-in.	$1.25	$3.75	$7.50

		G	VG	F
70-056	Coburn, Walt - ***Ramrod Sons of Gunfighters*** [1963] Cover art by Armand Weston.	$1.25	$3.75	$7.50
70-058	Hopson, William - ***The Gringo Bandit*** [1963]	$1.25	$3.75	$7.50
70-059	Milner, Michael - ***Wives And Lovers*** [1963] Photo cover. Movie tie-in with Van Johnson.	$1.25	$3.75	$7.50
70-060	Calin, Harold - ***Combat: Men, Not Heroes*** [1963] TV tie-in.	$1.25	$3.75	$7.50
70-061	Floren, Lee - ***Renegade Gambler*** [1963]	$1.25	$3.75	$7.50
70-062	Calin, Harold - ***Kings Of The Sun*** [1963] PBO. Photo cover. Movie tie-in with Yul Brynner.	$1.25	$3.75	$7.50
70-063	Coburn, Walt - ***Gun Grudge*** [1963]	$1.25	$3.75	$7.50
70-064	Coburn, Walt - ***Law Rides The Range*** [1963]	$1.25	$3.75	$7.50
70-065	Coburn, Walt - ***Feud Valley*** [1964] PBO.	$1.25	$3.75	$7.50
70-067	Lee, Elsie - ***Comedy Of Terrors*** [1964] PBO. Photo cover. Movie tie-in.	$2.50	$7.50	$15.00
70-069	Hopson, William - ***Gunthrower*** [1964]	$1.25	$3.75	$7.50
70-070	Hopson, William - ***Outlaw Of Hidden Valley*** [1964]	$1.25	$3.75	$7.50
70-072	Floren, Lee - ***Montana Maverick*** [1964]	$1.25	$3.75	$7.50
70-073	Lee, Elsie - ***Muscle Beach Party*** [1964] PBO. Photo cover. Movie tie-in.	$3.00	$9.00	$18.00
70-074	Heckelmann, Charles N. - ***Guns Of Arizona*** [1964]	$1.25	$3.75	$7.50
70-078	Bennett, Dwight - ***Cherokee Outlet*** [1964]	$1.25	$3.75	$7.50
70-079	Hopson, William - ***Ramrod Vengeance*** [1964]	$1.25	$3.75	$7.50
70-080	Stuart, Florence - ***The New Nurse*** [1965]	$1.00	$3.00	$6.00
70-081	Rico, Don - ***The Last Of The Breed*** [1965] PBO.	$1.25	$3.75	$7.50
70-082	Floren, Lee - ***Gunslammer*** [1965]	$1.25	$3.75	$7.50
70-084	Patten, Lewis B. - ***Deputy From Furnace Creek*** [1966] PBO.	$1.25	$3.75	$7.50

Lancer 71 Series.

		G	VG	F
71-301	Ellson, Hal - ***The Knife*** [1961] PBO. Cover art by P. Max. The first Lancer.	$3.50	$10.00	$20.00
71-302	Gordon, James - ***The Lust Of Private Cooper*** [1961]	$1.25	$3.75	$7.50
71-303	Poe, Edgar Allan - ***The Pit And The Pendulum*** [1961] PBO. Lee Sheridan adaptation. Movie tie-in.	$2.50	$7.50	$15.00
71-304	Kane, Henry - ***Dead In Bed*** [1961] PBO. Cover by Oscar Leibman.	$1.50	$5.00	$10.00
71-306	Welch, Maude McCurdy - ***Country Nurse*** [1962]	$1.00	$3.00	$6.00
71-307	Burnett, W. R. - ***Dark Hazard*** [1962]	$1.35	$4.00	$8.00
71-308	Ackworth, Robert C. - ***Dr. Kildare*** [1962] PBO. Photo cover. TV tie-in.	$1.25	$3.75	$7.50
71-309	James, Stuart - ***Too Late Blues*** [1962] PBO. Photo cover. Movie tie-in.	$1.25	$3.75	$7.50
71-311	Dietrich, Robert - ***Curtains For A Lover*** [1962] PBO. Cover by Ron Lesser.	$1.25	$3.75	$7.50
71-312	Lee, Elsie - ***The Blood Red Oscar*** [1962]	$2.00	$6.00	$12.00
71-313	Danne, Max Hallan - ***Premature Burial*** [1962] PBO. Movie tie-in with Ray Milland.	$2.00	$6.00	$12.00
71-315	Whittington, Harry - ***Love Cult*** [1962]	$4.00	$12.50	$25.00
71-316	Daniels, Norman - ***The Detectives*** [1962] PBO. Photo cover. TV tie-in.	$1.25	$3.75	$7.50
71-317	Craig, Jonathan - ***Red-Headed Sinners*** [1962]	$1.35	$4.00	$8.00
71-319	Sheridan, Michael - ***Hitler!*** [1962] PBO. Movie tie-in with Richard Basehart.	$1.25	$3.75	$7.50
71-320	Smith, Stan - ***Escape From Hell*** [1962] PBO.	$1.25	$3.75	$7.50
71-321	Halleran, E. E. - ***Gringo Gun*** [1962]	$1.25	$3.75	$7.50
71-322	Anthology edited by Art Paul - ***Vive La Femme*** [1962] PBO. Cover art by De Carlo. Cartoon book.	$1.25	$3.75	$7.50
71-324	Gogol, Nicolai - ***Taras Bulba*** [1962] PBO.	$1.25	$3.75	$7.50
71-325	Sudak, Eunice - ***Tales Of Terror*** [1962] PBO. Edgar Allen Poe retold. Movie tie-in.	$2.50	$7.50	$15.00
71-326	Brennan, Alice - ***Nurses Dormitory*** [1962] PBO.	$1.00	$3.00	$6.00

Lancer 72 Series.

		G	VG	F
601	Dos Passos, John - ***Number One*** [1961]	$1.00	$3.00	$6.00
602	Sinclair, Jo - ***Wasteland*** [1961]	$1.00	$3.00	$6.00
603	Montagu, Ashley - ***The Natural Superiority Of Women*** [1961] Cover art by Art Magee.	$1.00	$3.00	$6.00
604	Gallico, Paul - ***The Foolish Immortals*** [1961]	$1.00	$3.00	$6.00
605	Maugham, W. Somerset - ***Catalina*** [1961] Cover art by Oscar Liebman.	$1.00	$3.00	$6.00
606	Bodenheim, Maxwell - ***Georgia May*** [1961]	$1.00	$3.00	$6.00
609	Keyes, Frances Parkinson - ***The Career Of David Noble*** [1961]	$1.00	$3.00	$6.00
72-101	Eby, Lois - ***Nurse On Nightmare Island*** [1966] PBO. Cover art by Marchetti.	$ .75	$2.50	$5.00
72-102	Warren, John T. - ***Age Of The Wife Swappers*** [1966] PBO.	$1.25	$3.75	$7.50
72-103	Asimov, Isaac - ***The Stars Like Dust*** [1966] Cover art by Kelly Freas.	$1.35	$4.00	$8.00
72-104	Asimov, Isaac - ***The Currents Of Space*** [1966] Cover art by Kelly Freas.	$1.35	$4.00	$8.00
72-105	Milton, Joseph - ***The Man Who Bombed The World*** [1966] PBO.	$1.25	$3.75	$7.50
72-106	Long, Frank Belknap - ***So Dark A Heritage*** [1966]	$1.35	$4.00	$8.00
72-107	Asimov, Isaac - ***The End Of Eternity*** [1966] Cover art by Kelly Freas.	$1.35	$4.00	$8.00
72-108	Asimov, Isaac - ***The Naked Sun*** [1966] Cover art by Kelly Freas.	$1.35	$4.00	$8.00
72-109	Calin, Anne - ***A Multitude Of Shadows*** [1966] PBO.	$1.25	$3.75	$7.50
72-110	St. Michaels, Donella - ***The Prisoner*** [1966] PBO.	$1.25	$3.75	$7.50
72-111	Lee, Stan - ***The Fantastic Four*** [1966] PBO. Cover art by Jack Kirby.	$1.35	$4.00	$8.00
72-112	Lee, Stane - ***The Amazing Spiderman*** [1966] PBO. Cover art by Steve Ditko.	$1.35	$4.00	$8.00
72-113	Wells, Lee - ***Spanish Range*** [1966] Cover art by Bob Stanley.	$1.25	$3.75	$7.50
72-114	Randolph, Boris - ***Quick Crosswords*** [1966]	$2.50	$7.50	$15.00
72-115	Kane, Henry - ***Dead In Bed*** [1966]	$1.35	$4.00	$8.00
72-116	Kane, Henry - ***Never Give A Millionaire An Even Break*** [1966]	$1.35	$4.00	$8.00
72-117	Stuart, Matt - ***Edge Of The Desert*** [1966]	$1.25	$3.75	$7.50
72-118	Bradbury, Edward P. (Michael Moorcock) - ***Warriors Of Mars*** [1966] Cover art by Gray Morrow	$1.35	$4.00	$8.00
72-119	Ayling, Kaye - ***The Impulsive Heart*** [1966] PBO. Cover art by Leone.	$1.00	$3.00	$6.00
72-121	Holden, Joanne - ***Nurse At The Castle*** [1966]	$ .75	$2.50	$5.00
72-122	Bradbury, Edward P. (Michael Moorcock) - ***Blades Of Mars*** [1966] Cover art by Gray Morrow	$1.35	$4.00	$8.00
72-123	Sherman, Robert - ***Picture Mommy Dead*** [1966] PBO.	$1.25	$3.75	$7.50
72-124	Anthology - ***The Incredible Hulk*** [1966] PBO.	$1.35	$4.00	$8.00
72-125	Anthology - ***The Mighty Thor*** [1966] PBO.	$1.35	$4.00	$8.00
72-127	Bradbury, Edward P. (Michael Moorcock) - ***Barbarians Of Mars*** [1966] Cover art by Gray Morrow	$1.35	$4.00	$8.00
72-128	White, Lionel - ***The House Next Door*** [1966] PBO. Cover art by Peter Baum.	$1.25	$3.75	$7.50
72-129	Williamson, Jack - ***The Humanoids*** [1966] Cover art by Emsh.	$1.35	$4.00	$8.00
72-130	Buck, Frank - ***Wild Cargo*** [1966] Cover art by Gray Morrow.	$1.25	$3.75	$7.50
72-131	Whitney, Phillis - ***Ever After*** [1966]	$1.00	$3.00	$6.00
72-132	Gordon, James - ***Collision*** [1966]	$1.25	$3.75	$7.50
72-133	Dorien, Ray - ***New Nurse At Noonday*** [1966] Cover art by Weston.	$ .75	$2.50	$5.00
72-135	DeRosso, H. A. - ***.44*** [1966]	$1.25	$3.75	$7.50
72-136	Blanco, L. W. - ***Spykill*** [1966]	$1.25	$3.75	$7.50
72-138	Fairman, Paul W. - ***The Heiress Of Copper Butte*** [1966]	$1.25	$3.75	$7.50
72-145	Anthology edited by Damon Knight - ***First Flight*** [1966] Cover art by Emsh.	$1.25	$3.75	$7.50

		G	VG	F
72-146	Weinbaum, Stanley G. - ***A Martian Odyssey*** [1966] Cover art by Robert Schultz.	$1.35	$4.00	$8.00
72-148	Stone, Patti - ***Nina Grant Pediatric Nurse*** [1966]	$ .75	$2.50	$5.00
72-149	Russell, Eric Frank - ***Dreadful Sanctuary*** [1967] Cover art by Kelly Freas.	$1.35	$4.00	$8.00
72-155	Harris, John Beynon (John Wyndham) - ***The Secret People*** [1967] Cover art by Frank Frazetta.	$1.35	$4.00	$8.00
72-156	Silverberg, Robert - ***Recalled To Life*** [1967]	$1.35	$4.00	$8.00
72-157	Ostrow, Albert A. - ***Time Fillers*** [1967]	$1.25	$3.75	$7.50
72-159	Nourse, Alan E. - ***Trouble On Titan*** [1967] Cover art by Edward Valigursky.	$1.25	$3.75	$7.50
72-162	Lacy, Ed - ***Double Trouble*** [1867] Cover art by Weston.	$1.25	$3.75	$7.50
72-164	? - ***Flaming Feud*** [1967]	$1.25	$3.75	$7.50
72-165	Williams, Rose - ***Nurse In Jeopardy*** [1967] Cover art by Lou Marchetti.	$ .75	$2.50	$5.00
72-166	West, Tom - ***Spectre Spread*** [1967]	$1.25	$3.75	$7.50
72-168	Anthology - ***Boris Randolph's Quick Crosswords #2*** [1967] PBO.	$2.50	$7.50	$15.00
72-169	Anthology - ***The Fantastic Four Return*** [1967] PBO. Cover art by Jack Kirby.	$1.35	$4.00	$8.00
72-170	Anthology - ***Here Comes...Daredevil*** [1967] PBO.	$1.35	$4.00	$8.00
72-173	Ketchum, Philip - ***The Man Who Tamed Dodge*** [1967] PBO.	$1.25	$3.75	$7.50
72-174	Ketchum, Philip - ***The Man Who Turned Outlaw*** [1967] PBO.	$1.25	$3.75	$7.50
72-175	Drago, Harry Sinclair - ***Montana Road*** [1967]	$1.25	$3.75	$7.50
72-176	Ketchum, Philip - ***The Man Who Sold Leadville*** [1967] PBO.	$1.25	$3.75	$7.50
72-179	Dana, Rose - ***Network Nurse*** [1968]	$ .75	$2.50	$5.00
72-212	Hitt, Orrie - ***The Passion Hunters*** [1964] PBO. Cover art by Domino.	$1.00	$3.00	$6.00
72-608	Mozes, M.D., Eugene B. - ***Plain Facts About Sex*** [1961]	$ .75	$2.50	$5.00
72-610	Clarke, Arthur C. - ***Master Of Space*** [1961] Cover art by Oscar Liebman.	$1.35	$4.00	$8.00
72-611	Aronowitz & Hamill - ***Ernest Hemingway: The Life & Death Of A Man*** [1961]	$1.25	$3.75	$7.50
72-612	Meyer, Jerome S. - ***The Book Of Amazing Facts*** [1961]	$1.25	$3.75	$7.50
72-613	Anthology edited by Robert Stein - ***Lancer Singalong Song Book*** [1961]	$1.25	$3.75	$7.50
72-614	Haggard, H. Rider - ***She*** [1961]	$1.35	$4.00	$8.00
72-617	Williams, Ben Ames - ***The Strumpet Sea*** [1961]	$1.25	$3.75	$7.50
72-619	Farrow, E. Pickworth - ***Psychoanalyse Yourself*** [1961]	$ .75	$2.50	$5.00
72-620	Zolar - ***Dream Book*** [1961]	$1.00	$3.00	$6.00
72-621	Carr, William H. A. - ***JFK, An Informal Biography*** [1962] PBO. Cover art by Oscar Liebman.	$1.00	$3.00	$6.00
72-622	Pyle, Ernie - ***Here Is Your War*** [1962]	$1.25	$3.75	$7.50
72-623	Louys, Pierre - ***Aphrodite*** [1962] Cover art by Dillon.	$1.25	$3.75	$7.50
72-625	Anthology edited by John A. Williams - ***The Angry Black*** [1962]	$1.25	$3.75	$7.50
72-627	Anthology edited by Chandler Brossard - ***Desire In The Suburbs*** [1962] PBO.	$1.25	$3.75	$7.50
72-628	Keene, Day/Ozaki, Milton K. - ***Joy House/City Of Sin*** [1962]	$2.00	$6.00	$12.00
72-630	Sabatini, Rafael - ***The Black Swan*** [1962]	$1.25	$3.75	$7.50
72-631	Duperrault, Doug/Whittington, Harry - ***Spotlight On Sin/Backwoods Shack*** [1962]	$3.50	$10.00	$20.00
72-632	Shute, Nevil - ***Landfall*** [1962]	$1.25	$3.75	$7.50
72-633	Keene, Day/Keene, Day - ***Who Has Wilma Lathrop?/Murder On The Side*** [1962] PBO.	$3.00	$9.00	$18.00
72-634	Ross, Colin/Harper, Daniel - ***Season Of Love/The Wrong Turn*** [1962] PBO.	$1.50	$5.00	$10.00
72-635	Brossard, Chandler - ***The Bold Saboteurs*** [1962]	$1.25	$3.75	$7.50
72-637	Stonebraker, Florence/Gordon, Luther - ***Shanty-Town Tease/Shamed*** [1962]	$1.50	$5.00	$10.00

Lancer, 72-670

Lancer, 72-732

Lancer, 75-165

		G	VG	F
72-638	Cousins, Sheila - ***Prostitute*** [1962]	$1.25	$3.75	$7.50
72-640	Conrad, Barnaby - ***Dangerfield*** [1962]	$1.25	$3.75	$7.50
72-641	Weil, Jerry - ***Office Wife*** [1962]	$1.00	$3.00	$6.00
72-642	Golightly, Bonnie - ***The Wife Swappers*** [1962] PBO. Cover art by Brule.	$1.25	$3.75	$7.50
72-644	Nebel, Long John - ***The Way Out World*** [1962] Cover art by Oscar Liebman.	$1.25	$3.75	$7.50
72-645	Shvte, Nevil - ***An Old Captivity*** [1962]	$1.25	$3.75	$7.50
72-646	Hamblett, Charles - ***The Secret Lives Of Marlon Brando*** [1962] PBO.	$1.25	$3.75	$7.50
72-647	Dumont, Jessie - ***Made In Hell*** [1962] PBO.	$1.25	$3.75	$7.50
72-648	Starr, Jonathan & Golightly, Bonnie - ***Sex Without Marriage*** [1962] PBO.	$ .75	$2.50	$5.00
72-649	? - ***Zolar's New Dream Book*** [1962]	$1.00	$3.00	$6.00
72-650	Smith, William Gardner - ***Last Of The Conquerors*** [1963]	$1.25	$3.75	$7.50
72-651	Ostorw, Albert A. - ***Time Fillers*** [1963]	$1.25	$3.75	$7.50
72-652	Dibner, Martin - ***A God For Tomorrow*** [1963]	$1.00	$3.00	$6.00
72-654	Stonebraker, Florence - ***Who Knows Love?*** [1963]	$1.00	$3.00	$6.00
72-655	Keene, Day/Keene, Day - ***Bring Him Back Dead/There Was A Crooked Man*** [1963]	$3.00	$9.00	$18.00
72-656	Anthology edited by Burnhardt Hurwood - ***Terror By Night*** [1963]	$2.00	$6.00	$12.00
72-657	Weil, Jerry - ***The Pleasure Girls*** [1963]	$1.25	$3.75	$7.50
72-658	Collyer, Martin - ***Lora*** [1963] PBO.	$1.25	$3.75	$7.50
72-660	Creasey, John - ***The Case Against Paul Raeburn*** [1963]	$1.25	$3.75	$7.50
72-663	Solzhenitsya, Alexander - ***One Day In The Life Of Ivan Denisovich*** [1963]	$1.00	$3.00	$6.00
72-665	Smith, Stan - ***The Navy At Guadalcanal*** [1963] PBO.	$1.25	$3.75	$7.50
72-666	Stonebraker, Florence - ***Can Love Be Wrong?*** [1963] PBO.	$1.00	$3.00	$6.00
72-667	Hirschfeld, Burt - ***Diana*** [1963] PBO. Cover art by Ronnie Lesser.	$1.25	$3.75	$7.50
72-668	Carr, William H. A. - ***Medical Examiner*** [1963] PBO.	$ .75	$2.50	$5.00
72-670	Hitt, Orrie - ***Loose Women*** [1963] PBO. Cover art by Harry Barton.	$1.25	$3.75	$7.50
72-671	Semple, Gordon - ***Warped Desires*** [1963] Cover art by Harry Barton.	$1.25	$3.75	$7.50
72-672	Anthology edited by Damon Knight - ***First Flight*** [1963] PBO. Cover art by Emsh.	$1.35	$4.00	$8.00
72-673	Saxon, John - ***Passionate Tigress*** [1963] PBO. Cover art by Harry Barton.	$1.25	$3.75	$7.50

		G	VG	F
72-674	Garve, Andrew - ***The House Of Soldiers*** [1963] Cover art by Hector.	$1.25	$3.75	$7.50
72-675	Garve, Andrew - ***Death And The Sky Above*** [1963] Cover art by Hector.	$1.25	$3.75	$7.50
72-676	Garve, Andrew - ***The Riddle Of Samson*** [1963] Cover art by Hector.	$1.25	$3.75	$7.50
72-677	Garve, Andrew - ***The Cuckoo Line Affair*** [1963] Cover art by Hector.	$1.25	$3.75	$7.50
72-679	Smith, Evelyn E. - ***The Perfect Planet*** [1963] Cover art by Emsh.	$1.35	$4.00	$8.00
72-680	Michaels, Rea - ***The Twisted Gear*** [1963]	$1.25	$3.75	$7.50
72-693	Garve, Andrew - ***The Far Sands*** [1963] Cover art by Hector.	$1.25	$3.75	$7.50
72-695	Gordon, Ian - ***The Love Trap*** [1963]	$1.00	$3.00	$6.00
72-696	Daniels, Norman - ***Arrest And Trial*** [1963]	$1.25	$3.75	$7.50
72-697	Anthology edited by Larry T. Shaw - ***Great Science Fiction Adventures*** [1963] PBO. Cover art by Emsh.	$1.35	$4.00	$8.00
72-698	Adlon, Arthur - ***Her Sister's Husband*** [1963]	$1.00	$3.00	$6.00
72-699	Garve, Andrew - ***The End Of The Track*** [1963]	$1.25	$3.75	$7.50
72-700	Gordon, Ian - ***Too Many Men*** [1963] PBO.	$1.25	$3.75	$7.50
72-701	Harris, John Beynon (John Wyndham) - ***The Secret People*** [1964] PBO. Cover art by Frank Frazetta.	$2.50	$7.50	$15.00
72-702	Lovecraft, H. P. - ***The Dunwich Horror And Others*** [1963] Cover art by Len Goldberg.	$1.25	$3.75	$7.50
72-703	Hitt, Orrie - ***Passion Pool*** [1964] PBO.	$1.25	$3.75	$7.50
72-704	Garve, Andrew - ***Fontego's Folly*** [1964]	$1.25	$3.75	$7.50
72-705	Michaels, Rea - ***Gilda*** [1964] PBO.	$1.25	$3.75	$7.50
72-707	Hitt, Orrie - ***The Color Of Lust*** [1964]	$1.25	$3.75	$7.50
72-708	Gordon, Ian - ***Embassy Girls*** [1964] PBO. Cover art by Edward Moritz.	$1.00	$3.00	$6.00
72-709	U.S. Government Children's Bureau - ***Infant Care*** [1964] PBO.	$ .75	$2.50	$5.00
72-710	Fleming, Joan - ***The Man From Nowhere*** [1964] Cover art by Len Goldberg.	$1.25	$3.75	$7.50
72-711	Fleming, Joan - ***In The Red*** [1964] Cover art by Len Goldberg.	$1.25	$3.75	$7.50
72-712	Hitt, Orrie - ***The Passion Hunters*** [1964] PBO.	$1.25	$3.75	$7.50
72-713	Gordon, Ian - ***Rebellious Flesh*** [1964]	$1.25	$3.75	$7.50
72-714	Michaels, Rea - ***Lust Queen*** [1964] PBO. Cover art by Harry Barton.	$1.25	$3.75	$7.50
72-715	Garie, Andrew - ***By-Line For Murder*** [1964] Cover art by Hector.	$1.25	$3.75	$7.50
72-716	Garve, Andrew - ***The Galloway Case*** [1964] Cover art by Hector.	$1.25	$3.75	$7.50
72-717	McDow, Joe - ***Primitive Passions*** [1964]	$1.25	$3.75	$7.50
72-718	Sharon, Sylvia - ***Sweet Torment*** [1964]	$1.25	$3.75	$7.50
72-719	Gordon, Ian - ***Weekend Wanton*** [1964] PBO.	$1.25	$3.75	$7.50
72-721	Hamilton, Edmond - ***The Valley Of Creation*** [1964] PBO. Cover art by Emsh.	$1.50	$5.00	$10.00
72-725	Poe, Edgar Allan - ***The Masque Of The Red Death*** [1964] PBO.	$2.50	$7.50	$15.00
72-726	Hitt, Orrie - ***Lust Prowl*** [1964]	$1.25	$3.75	$7.50
72-727	Michaels, Rae - ***Just Your Body, Baby*** [1964] PBO.	$1.25	$3.75	$7.50
72-728	Harding, Matt - ***Las Vegas Madam*** [1964] PBO.	$1.25	$3.75	$7.50
72-729	Sharon, Sylvia - ***The Sins Of Tonia*** [1964] PBO.	$1.25	$3.75	$7.50
72-730	Garve, Andrew - ***A Hole In The Ground*** [1964] Cover art by Hector.	$1.25	$3.75	$7.50
72-731	Calin, Harold - ***Signal Red*** [1964] PBO.	$1.25	$3.75	$7.50
72-732	Anthology - ***The Beatle Book*** [1964] PBO.	$2.50	$7.50	$15.00
72-733	Beste, R. Vernon - ***The Moonbeams*** [1964]	$1.25	$3.75	$7.50
72-734	Roget, A. L. - ***Madame Kozik's Girls*** [1964] PBO. Cover art by Harry Bartow.	$1.25	$3.75	$7.50
72-735	Michaels, Rea - ***How Dark My Love*** [1964] PBO.	$1.25	$3.75	$7.50
72-736	Gilbert, Michael - ***Fear To Tread*** [1964]	$1.25	$3.75	$7.50

		G	VG	F
72-737	Gilbert, Michael - ***Smallbone Deceased*** [1964]	$1.25	$3.75	$7.50
72-738	Gilbert, Michael - ***Death Has Deep Roots*** [1964]	$1.25	$3.75	$7.50
72-739	Garve, Andrew - ***No Tears For Hilda*** [1964]	$1.25	$3.75	$7.50
72-740	Williamson, Jack - ***Golden Blood*** [1964] Cover art by Emsh.	$2.50	$7.50	$15.00
72-741	Michaels, Rea - ***Two-Way Street*** [1964] PBO. Cover art by Victor Olson.	$1.25	$3.75	$7.50
72-742	Richards, Donna - ***The Sad Gay Life*** [1964]	$1.25	$3.75	$7.50
72-743	Michaels, Bart - ***Teen Temptress*** [1964] PBO.	$1.25	$3.75	$7.50
72-744	Roget, A. L. - ***Where The Sin Is*** [1964] PBO.	$1.00	$3.00	$6.00
72-745	Sprague, PhD., W. D. - ***Sex And The Secretary*** [1964]	$ .75	$2.50	$5.00
72-746	Anthology - ***The Beatles Up-To-Date*** [1964] PBO.	$2.50	$7.50	$15.00
72-748	Mortimer, Penelope - ***The Pumpkin Eater*** [1964]	$1.25	$3.75	$7.50
72-749	Monte, Jill - ***A World Divided*** [1964]	$1.25	$3.75	$7.50
72-750	Michaels, Rea - ***Where Lovers Fear To Treat*** [1964]	$1.25	$3.75	$7.50
72-751	Gilbert, Michael - ***Sky High*** [1964]	$1.25	$3.75	$7.50
72-752	Heard, H.F. - ***A Taste For Honey*** [1964] Cover art by Stegel.	$1.35	$4.00	$8.00
72-753	Asimov, Isaac - ***The Naked Sun*** [1964] Cover art by Emsh.	$1.35	$4.00	$8.00
72-754	Heard, H.F. - ***Reply Paid*** [1964] Cover art by Siegel.	$1.35	$4.00	$8.00
72-755	Bayne, Jessica - ***When Love Must Hide*** [1964] PBO.	$1.25	$3.75	$7.50
72-756	Richards, Donna - ***The Perfumed Flesh*** [1964] PBO.	$1.25	$3.75	$7.50
72-757	Adlon, Arthur - ***For Sin's Sake*** [1964] PBO.	$1.25	$3.75	$7.50
72-758	Cooper, Edmund - ***Transit*** [1964] PBO. Cover art by Emsh.	$1.25	$3.75	$7.50
72-759	Garve, Andrew - ***The Sea Monks*** [1964] Cover art by Siegel.	$1.25	$3.75	$7.50
72-760	Milton, Joseph - ***Worldbreaker*** [1964] PBO.	$1.25	$3.75	$7.50
72-761	Williamson, Jack - ***The Reign Of Wizardry*** [1964] Cover art by Frank Frazetta.	$2.50	$7.50	$15.00
72-762	Shiff, M.D., Nathan A. - ***Diary Of A Nymph*** [1964]	$ .75	$2.50	$5.00
72-764	Behan, Leslie - ***The Midway At Midnight*** [1964] PBO.	$1.25	$3.75	$7.50
72-765	Sharin, Sylvia - ***Deliver Her To Evil*** [1964] PBO.	$1.25	$3.75	$7.50
72-766	Saxon, Ron - ***The Sweet Smell Of Sin*** [1964] PBO. Cover art by Harry Barton.	$1.25	$3.75	$7.50
72-767	Sarlat, Noah - ***Spy In Black Lace*** [1964]	$1.25	$3.75	$7.50
72-768	De Camp, L. Sprague - ***Divide And Rule*** [1964]	$1.35	$4.00	$8.00
72-769	Brown, Wenzell - ***The Kept Man*** [1964] PBO.	$1.35	$4.00	$8.00
72-770	Farber, Neil - ***Teen-Age Party And Fun Quiz Book*** [1964]	$1.25	$3.75	$7.50
72-771	Gilbert, Michael - ***After The Fine Weather*** [1964]	$1.25	$3.75	$7.50
72-772	Poole, Lewis - ***The Million Dollar Night*** [1964] PBO.	$1.25	$3.75	$7.50
72-773	Matthews, Leone - ***A Kind Of Marriage*** [1964] PBO.	$1.25	$3.75	$7.50
72-774	Wilson, Barbara - ***The Pleasures We Know*** [1964] PBO.	$1.25	$3.75	$7.50
72-778	Keyes, Frances Parkinson - ***The Career Of David Noble*** [1964]	$1.25	$3.75	$7.50
72-779	Whitney, Phillis - ***The Moonflower*** [1964]	$1.25	$3.75	$7.50
72-780	Minton, Paula - ***Secret Melody*** [1964] PBO. Cover art by Lou Marchetti.	$1.25	$3.75	$7.50
72-781	Roget, A. L. - ***Woman's Darling*** [1964] PBO.	$1.25	$3.75	$7.50
72-782	Sharon, Sylvia - ***We Love In Shadow*** [1964] PBO.	$1.25	$3.75	$7.50
72-783	Garve, Andrew - ***A Hero For Leanda*** [1965]	$1.25	$3.75	$7.50
72-784	Gordon, Jane - ***Season Of Evil*** [1965] PBO. Cover art by Lou Marchetti.	$1.25	$3.75	$7.50
72-785	Michaels, Rea - ***Libby*** [1965] PBO.	$1.25	$3.75	$7.50
72-786	Roget, A. L. - ***The Secret Places*** [1965]	$1.25	$3.75	$7.50
72-787	Richards, Donna - ***The Odd World*** [1965] PBO.	$1.25	$3.75	$7.50
72-788	Sterling, Sandra - ***All Night Long*** [1965]	$1.25	$3.75	$7.50
72-789	Janifer, Lawrence, M. - ***You Sane Men*** [1965] PBO. Cover art by Howard Winters	$1.35	$4.00	$8.00
72-790	Gilbert, Michael - ***Blood And Judgement*** [1965]	$1.25	$3.75	$7.50
72-791	Gordon, Jane - ***Mistress Of Mount Fair*** [1965] PBO. Cover art by Marchetti.	$1.25	$3.75	$7.50
72-792	Sharon, Sylvia - ***No Barriers*** [1965] PBO.	$1.25	$3.75	$7.50
72-793	Michaels, Rea - ***The Needs We Share*** [1965] PBO.	$1.25	$3.75	$7.50
72-794	Greggson, Dale - ***Dark Triangle*** [1965] PBO.	$1.25	$3.75	$7.50

		G	VG	F
72-795	Starling, Trudy - ***World Without Men*** [1965] PBO.	$1.25	$3.75	$7.50
72-796	Marchant, Catherine - ***Heritage Of Folly*** [1965]	$1.25	$3.75	$7.50
72-797	Daniels, Dorothy - ***Mostly By Moonlight*** [1965]	$1.25	$3.75	$7.50
72-798	Milton, Joseph - ***The Big Blue Death*** [1965]	$1.25	$3.75	$7.50
72-799	Bessie, Oscar - ***Angela, Be Bad*** [1965] PBO.	$1.25	$3.75	$7.50
72-900	Michaels, Rea - ***Cloak Of Evil*** [1965] PBO.	$1.25	$3.75	$7.50
72-901	Richards, Donna - ***Brand Of Shame*** [1965] PBO.	$1.25	$3.75	$7.50
72-902	Josephs, Carla - ***The Off-Limits World*** [1965] PBO.	$1.25	$3.75	$7.50
72-903	Fleming, Joan - ***The Deeds Of Dr. Deadcert*** [1965]	$1.25	$3.75	$7.50
72-904	Daniels, Norman - ***Strike Force*** [1965] PBO.	$1.25	$3.75	$7.50
72-905	Adlon, Arthur - ***Speak It In Whispers*** [1965] PBO.	$1.25	$3.75	$7.50
72-906	Fields, Vin - ***She Devil*** [1965] PBO.	$1.25	$3.75	$7.50
72-907	Spain, Vicki - ***Who Calls It Sin?*** [1965] PBO.	$1.25	$3.75	$7.50
72-908	Bond, Evelyn - ***Evil In The House*** [1965] PBO.	$1.25	$3.75	$7.50
72-909	Loraine, Philip - ***Day Of The Arrow*** [1965]	$1.25	$3.75	$7.50
72-910	Calin, Harold - ***Combat: No Rest For Heroes*** [1965] PBO.	$1.25	$3.75	$7.50
72-911	Coleman, Clara - ***Nightmare In July*** [1965] Cover art by Lou Marchetti.	$1.25	$3.75	$7.50
72-912	Sharon, Sylvia - ***The Burning Flesh*** [1965] PBO.	$1.25	$3.75	$7.50
72-913	Michaels, Rea - ***Duet In Darkness*** [1965]	$1.25	$3.75	$7.50
72-914	Spain, Vicki - ***To Drown Our Lusts*** [1965] PBO.	$1.25	$3.75	$7.50
72-915	Richards, Donna - ***Women Like Me*** [1965] PBO.	$1.25	$3.75	$7.50
72-916	Wylie, Philip - ***The Smuggled Atom Bomb*** [1965]	$1.35	$4.00	$8.00
72-917	Hirschfeld, Burt - ***General Hospital*** [1965] PBO. Cover art by Stanley Borack.	$1.25	$3.75	$7.50
72-918	Mark, Ted - ***The Man From O.R.G.Y.*** [1965] PBO.	$1.25	$3.75	$7.50
72-919	Lee, Elsie - ***Clouds Over Vellanti*** [1965]	$1.25	$3.75	$7.50
72-920	Brennan, Alice - ***The Brooding House*** [1965] PBO.	$1.25	$3.75	$7.50
72-921	Adlon, Arthur - ***Too Good For Men*** [1965] PBO.	$1.25	$3.75	$7.50
72-922	Greggson, Dale - ***Sisterhood Of The Flesh*** [1965] PBO.	$1.25	$3.75	$7.50
72-923	Sharon, Sylvia - ***Obey Me, My Love*** [1965] PBO.	$1.25	$3.75	$7.50
72-924	Maxwell, J. Malcolm - ***Honeymoon Hotel*** [1965] PBO.	$1.25	$3.75	$7.50
72-925	Haggard, H. Rider - ***She*** [1965]	$1.25	$3.75	$7.50
72-926	Minton, Paula - ***Engraved In Evil*** [1965] PBO. Cover art by Marchetti.	$1.25	$3.75	$7.50
72-927	Winthrop, Wilma - ***Tryst With Terror*** [1965] PBO. Cover art by Marchetti.	$1.25	$3.75	$7.50
72-928	Coffman, Virginia - ***Curse Of The Island Pool*** [1965]	$1.25	$3.75	$7.50
72-929	Richards, Donna - ***Take Me In Passion*** [1965] PBO.	$1.25	$3.75	$7.50
72-930	Behan, Leslie - ***In Love's Dark Corners*** [1965] PBO.	$1.25	$3.75	$7.50
72-931	Sharon, Sylvia - ***Rapture For Three*** [1965] PBO.	$1.25	$3.75	$7.50
72-932	Lyons, Delphine C. - ***House Of Four Windows*** [1965] PBO. Cover art by Marchetti.	$1.25	$3.75	$7.50
72-933	Daniels, Dorothy - ***The Unguarded*** [1965] PBO.	$1.25	$3.75	$7.50
72-934	Lee, Elsie - ***Dark Moon, Lost Lady*** [1965]	$1.25	$3.75	$7.50
72-935	Wylie, Philip - ***Experiment In Crime*** [1965] Cover art by Borack.	$1.25	$3.75	$7.50
72-936	Paul, Hugo - ***The Smashers*** [1965] PBO.	$1.25	$3.75	$7.50
72-937	Wylie, Philip - ***Gladiator*** [1965] Cover art by Stanley Borack.	$1.35	$4.00	$8.00
72-938	Fields, Vin - ***Who Seek In Shadow*** [1965] PBO.	$1.25	$3.75	$7.50
72-939	Greggson, Dale - ***The Flesh Surrenders*** [1965]	$1.25	$3.75	$7.50
72-940	Saxon, John - ***Passionate Tigress*** [1965]	$1.25	$3.75	$7.50
72-941	Gordon, Ian - ***The Love Trap*** [1965] PBO.	$1.25	$3.75	$7.50
72-942	Russell, Eric Frank - ***The Mindwarpers*** [1965] PBO. Cover art by Powers	$1.35	$4.00	$8.00
72-943	Daniels, Dorothy - ***The Tower Room*** [1965] PBO. Cover art by Lou Marchetti.	$1.25	$3.75	$7.50
72-944	Marchant, Catherine - ***Evil At Roger's Cross*** [1965]	$1.25	$3.75	$7.50
72-945	Warren, Paulette (Paul Fairman) - ***Ravenkill*** [1965] PBO. Cover art by Lou Marchetti.	$1.25	$3.75	$7.50

		G	VG	F
72-946	Bond, Evelyn - ***House Of Shadows*** [1965]	$1.25	$3.75	$7.50
72-947	Milton, Joseph - ***Baron Sinister*** [1965] PBO. Cover art by Mort Engel.	$1.25	$3.75	$7.50
72-948	Sharon, Sylvia - ***The Sins Of Tonia*** [1965]	$1.25	$3.75	$7.50
72-949	Wilson, Barbara - ***The Velvet Embrace*** [1965] PBO.	$1.25	$3.75	$7.50
72-950	Richards, Donna - ***Don't Stop, My Love*** [1965] PBO.	$1.25	$3.75	$7.50
72-951	Sharon, Sylvia - ***The Agony Of Desire*** [1965] PBO.	$1.25	$3.75	$7.50
72-952	Spain, Vicki - ***The Silken Underground*** [1965] PBO.	$1.25	$3.75	$7.50
72-953	Gordon, Ian - ***Too Many Men*** [1965]	$1.25	$3.75	$7.50
72-954	Bond, Evelyn - ***Lady Of Storm House*** [1965] PBO.	$1.25	$3.75	$7.50
72-955	Stone, Harriet - ***Heiress Of Bayou Vache*** [1965] PBO. Cover art by Weston.	$1.25	$3.75	$7.50
72-956	Minton, Paula - ***Hand Of The Imposter*** [1965] PBO. Cover art by Weston.	$1.25	$3.75	$7.50
72-957	Canfield, Miriam - ***The Tuscany Madonna*** [1965]	$1.25	$3.75	$7.50
72-958	Mark, Ted - ***The Man From Orgy: The 9-Month Caper*** [1965] PBO. Cover art by Borack.	$1.25	$3.75	$7.50
72-959	Smith, William Gardner - ***The Last Of The Conquerors*** [1965]	$1.25	$3.75	$7.50
72-960	Bessie, Oscar - ***Bonnie*** [1965] PBO.	$1.25	$3.75	$7.50
72-961	Michaels, Rea - ***The Swappers*** [1965] PBO.	$1.25	$3.75	$7.50
72-962	Adlon, Arthur - ***A Special Passion*** [1965] PBO.	$1.25	$3.75	$7.50
72-963	Hitt, Orrie - ***Passion Pool*** [1965]	$1.25	$3.75	$7.50
72-964	Winthrop, Wilma - ***Island Of The Accursed*** [1965] PBO. Cover art by Lou Marchetti.	$1.25	$3.75	$7.50
72-965	Winsotn, Daoma - ***The Secrets Of Cromwell Crossing*** [1965]	$1.25	$3.75	$7.50
72-966	Daniels, Dorothy - ***Dance In Darkness*** [1965] PBO.	$1.25	$3.75	$7.50
72-967	Phillips, Jean - ***Greenwood*** [1965]	$1.25	$3.75	$7.50
72-968	Millar, Margaret - ***Do Evil In Return*** [1965]	$1.25	$3.75	$7.50
72-969	Isherwood, Christopher - ***A Single Man*** [1965] Cover art by Guzzi.	$1.25	$3.75	$7.50
72-970	Noone, Edwina (Michael Avallone) - ***Heir Loom Of Tragedy*** [1965] PBO. Cover art by Lou Marchetti.	$1.25	$3.75	$7.50
72-971	Mark, Ted - ***The Man From Pussycat*** [1965]	$1.25	$3.75	$7.50
72-972	Michaels, Rea - ***Lust Queen*** [1965]	$1.25	$3.75	$7.50
72-973	Fields, Vin - ***Fulfill Me, Darling*** [1965] PBO.	$1.25	$3.75	$7.50
72-974	Richards, Donna - ***Our Furtive Love*** [1965] PBO.	$1.25	$3.75	$7.50
72-975	Adlon, Arthur - ***All-Girl Office*** [1965] PBO.	$1.00	$3.00	$6.00
72-976	Millar, Margaret - ***Rose's Last Summer*** [1965]	$1.25	$3.75	$7.50
72-977	Morton, Patricia - ***A Gathering Of Moondust*** [1965]	$1.25	$3.75	$7.50
72-978	Minton, Paula - ***Orphan Of The Shadows*** [1965]	$1.25	$3.75	$7.50
72-979	Padget, Meg - ***House Of Strangers*** [1965] PBO.	$1.25	$3.75	$7.50
72-980	Daniels, Dorothy - ***Cliffside Castle*** [1965] PBO. Cover art by Lou Marchetti.	$1.25	$3.75	$7.50
72-981	Wylie, Philip - ***Autumn Romance*** [1965]	$1.25	$3.75	$7.50
72-982	Bond, Evelyn - ***Lady In Darkness*** [1965]	$1.25	$3.75	$7.50
72-983	Bradley, Marion Zimmer - ***Castle Terror*** [1965] PBO. Cover art by Lou Marchetti.	$2.50	$7.50	$15.00
72-984	Marchant, Catherine - ***The Mists Of Memory*** [1965]	$1.25	$3.75	$7.50
72-985	Warren, Paulette (Paul Fairman) - ***Some Beckoning Wraith*** [1965] PBO. Cover art by Lou Marchetti.	$1.25	$3.75	$7.50
72-986	Millar, Margaret - ***Vanish In An Instant*** [1965]	$1.25	$3.75	$7.50
72-987	Garve, Andrew - ***Murder Through A Looking Glass*** [1965]	$1.25	$3.75	$7.50
72-988	Roberts, Lisa - ***A Dream To Share*** [1965] PBO.	$1.25	$3.75	$7.50
72-989	Mark, Ted - ***The Nude Who Never*** [1965] PBO.	$1.25	$3.75	$7.50
72-990	Lee, Elsie - ***Mansion Of Golden Windows*** [1966] PBO. Cover art by Marchetti.	$1.35	$4.00	$8.00
72-991	Coleman, Clara - ***A Scent Of Sandalwood*** [1966] PBO. Cover art by Weston.	$1.25	$3.75	$7.50
72-992	Coffman, Virginia - ***The Secret Of Shower Tree*** [1966]	$1.25	$3.75	$7.50
72-993	Daniels, Dorothy - ***The Templeton Memoirs*** [1966]	$1.25	$3.75	$7.50

		G	VG	F
72-994	Millar, Margaret - ***Wall Of Eyes*** [1966]	$1.25	$3.75	$7.50
72-995	Blanco, L. W. - ***Spy Kill*** [1966] PBO.	$1.25	$3.75	$7.50
72-996	Mark, Ted - ***The Man From O.R.G.Y.: The Real Gone Girls*** [1966] PBO.	$1.25	$3.75	$7.50
72-998	De Marquand, Alix - ***So Many Midnights*** [1966] PBO. Cover art by Marchetti.	$1.25	$3.75	$7.50

Lancer 73 Series.

		G	VG	F
73-401	Ferber, Edna - ***A Peculiar Treasure*** [1962]	$1.25	$3.75	$7.50
73-402	Bellaman, H. & K. - ***Paris Mitchell Of Kings Row*** [1962]	$1.25	$3.75	$7.50
73-403	Smith, Betty - ***Tomorrow Will Be Better*** [1962]	$1.25	$3.75	$7.50
73-405	Seton, Anya - ***The Hearth And Eagle*** [1962]	$1.25	$3.75	$7.50
73-406	Shapiro, Lionel - ***The Sixth Of June*** [1962]	$1.25	$3.75	$7.50
73-408	Mauldin, Bill - ***Up Front*** [1962]	$1.25	$3.75	$7.50
73-409	Algren, Nelson - ***Lonesome Monsters*** [1962] PBO.	$2.00	$6.00	$12.00
73-410	Kennedy, Jay Richard - ***Prince Bart*** [1962]	$1.25	$3.75	$7.50
73-411	Hitt, Orrie - ***Teaser*** [1962]	$1.25	$3.75	$7.50
73-412	Westcott, Jan - ***Captain Barney*** [1963]	$1.25	$3.75	$7.50
73-415	Davis, Stephanie - ***Lust Is No Lady*** [1963] PBO.	$1.25	$3.75	$7.50
73-417	Von Block, B. W. - ***The Frustrated American*** [1963]	$1.25	$3.75	$7.50
73-419	Davis, Bette - ***The Lonely Life*** [1963]	$1.25	$3.75	$7.50
73-420	Sprague, M.D., W. D. - ***Sexual Behavior Of American Nurses*** [1963] PBO.	$ .75	$2.50	$5.00
73-421	Williamson, Jack - ***Darker Than You Think*** [1963] Cover art by Emsh.	$1.50	$5.00	$10.00
73-422	Robie, M.D., W. F. - ***Sex And Life*** [1963]	$ .75	$2.50	$5.00
73-423	Parson, Louella - ***Tell It to Lovella*** [1963]	$1.00	$3.00	$6.00
73-424	Woodward, MD, L.T. (Robert Silverberg) - ***Sex And The Divorced Woman*** [1964] PBO.	$1.25	$3.75	$7.50
73-425	Lovecraft, H. P. - ***The Colour Out Of Space & Others*** [1964]	$1.50	$5.00	$10.00
73-427	Shute, Neil - ***Kindling*** [1964]	$1.25	$3.75	$7.50
73-428	Peters, Fritz - ***The World At Twilight*** [1964]	$1.25	$3.75	$7.50
73-430	Young, Phyllis Brett - ***Psyche*** [1964] Cover art by Barye Phillips.	$1.25	$3.75	$7.50
73-431	Shute, Nevil - ***Landfall*** [1965]	$1.25	$3.75	$7.50
73-432	Shute, Nevil - ***An Old Capitivity*** [1965]	$1.25	$3.75	$7.50
73-433	Shulman, Irving - ***Upbeat*** [1965] PBO.	$1.25	$3.75	$7.50
73-434	Auchincloss, Louis - ***Sybil*** [1965]	$1.25	$3.75	$7.50
73-435	Shute, Nevil - ***Stephen Morris*** [1965]	$1.25	$3.75	$7.50
73-436	Marchant, Catherine - ***House Of Men*** [1965]	$1.25	$3.75	$7.50
73-437	Auchincloss, Louis - ***A Law For The Lion*** [1965]	$1.25	$3.75	$7.50
73-438	McGowan, Helen “Rocking Chair” - ***Big City Madam*** [1965]	$1.25	$3.75	$7.50
73-439	Gordon, Donald - ***Star-Raker*** [1965]	$1.25	$3.75	$7.50
73-440	Sprague, MD, W. D. - ***Sexual Rebellion In The Sixties*** [1965] PBO.	$ .75	$2.50	$5.00
73-441	McLaughlin, Dean - ***The Man Who Wanted Stars*** [1965] Cover art by John Schoenherr.	$1.35	$4.00	$8.00
73-442	Gordon, Donald - ***Flight Of The Bat*** [1965]	$1.25	$3.75	$7.50
73-443	Marchant, Catherine - ***House On The Fens*** [1965]	$1.25	$3.75	$7.50
73-444	Beste, R. Vernon - ***The Moonbeams*** [1965] Cover art by Stanley Borack.	$1.25	$3.75	$7.50
73-445	Woodward, L. T. (Robert Silverberg) - ***Sex And The Divorced Woman*** [1964]	$1.25	$3.75	$7.50
73-446	Mark, Ted - ***The Girl From Pussycat*** [1966]	$1.25	$3.75	$7.50
73-447	Maugham, W. Somerset - ***Catalina*** [1966]	$1.25	$3.75	$7.50
73-448	Shute, Nevil - ***Ordeal*** [1966]	$1.25	$3.75	$7.50
73-449	Grierson, Linden - ***Sea Jewel*** [1966]	$1.00	$3.00	$6.00
73-450	Grierson, Linden - ***Vacation Romance*** [1966] Cover art by Armand Weston.	$1.00	$3.00	$6.00
73-452	Swann, Francis - ***The Brass Key*** [1966]	$1.25	$3.75	$7.50

		G	VG	F
73-453	Root, Pat - ***Evil Became Them*** [1966]	$1.25	$3.75	$7.50
73-454	Root, Pat - ***The Devil Of The Stairs*** [1966]	$1.25	$3.75	$7.50
73-455	Williams, John - ***Stoner*** [1966]	$1.25	$3.75	$7.50
73-456	Peters, Fritz - ***Finistere*** [1966]	$1.25	$3.75	$7.50
73-457	Hitchens, Dolores - ***The Bank With The Bamboo Door*** [1966]	$1.25	$3.75	$7.50
73-459	Dannet, Syvia G. L. - ***The Door To The Tower*** [1966] Cover art by Dennis Fritz.	$1.25	$3.75	$7.50
73-460	Bowden, Nina - ***Devil By The Sea*** [1966]	$1.25	$3.75	$7.50
73-461	Mark, Ted - ***Pussycat, Pussycat!*** [1966]	$1.25	$3.75	$7.50
73-462	Paul, Phyllis - ***Echo Of Guilt*** [1966]	$1.25	$3.75	$7.50
73-463	Foley, Rae (Elinore Denniston) - ***Suffer A Witch*** [1966]	$1.25	$3.75	$7.50
73-466	Blackburn, John - ***Dead Man Running*** [1966]	$1.25	$3.75	$7.50
73-467	Sudak, Eunice - ***The Icepick In Ollie Birk*** [1966] PBO.	$1.35	$4.00	$8.00
73-468	Del Rey, Lester - ***Siege Perilous*** [1966] PBO. Cover art by Kelly Freas.	$1.25	$3.75	$7.50
73-470	Keyes, Frances Parkinson - ***The Career Of David Noble*** [1966]	$1.25	$3.75	$7.50
73-471	Wolfson, Victor - ***The Lonely Steeple*** [1966]	$1.25	$3.75	$7.50
73-472	Swann, Francis - ***Royal Street*** [1966] PBO.	$1.25	$3.75	$7.50
73-473	Morton, Patricia - ***A Child Of Value*** [1966] PBO.	$1.25	$3.75	$7.50
73-475	Blackburn, John - ***Broken Boy*** [1966]	$1.25	$3.75	$7.50
73-476	White, Ted - ***Phoenix Prime*** [1966] Cover art by Frank Frazetta.	$1.35	$4.00	$8.00
73-477	Mark, Ted - ***Dr. Nyet*** [1966] PBO.	$1.25	$3.75	$7.50
73-479	Draco, F. - ***The Devil's Church*** [1966]	$1.25	$3.75	$7.50
73-480	Shriber, Ione Sandberg - ***As Long As I Live*** [1966]	$1.25	$3.75	$7.50
73-485	Mark, Ted - ***My Son, The Double Agent*** [1966] PBO.	$1.25	$3.75	$7.50
73-487	Mark, Ted - ***The Man From ORGY*** [1968]	$1.25	$3.75	$7.50
73-488	Mark, Ted - ***The 9-Month Caper*** [1966]	$1.25	$3.75	$7.50
73-489	Mark, Ted - ***The Nude Who Never*** [1966]	$1.25	$3.75	$7.50
73-490	Mark, Ted - ***The Real Gone Girls*** [1966]	$1.25	$3.75	$7.50
73-493	Locke, Douglas - ***The Drawstring*** [1966] PBO. Cover art by Armand Weston.	$1.25	$3.75	$7.50
73-496	Hornung, E. W. - ***The Shadow Of The Rope*** [1966] PBO.	$1.25	$3.75	$7.50
73-500	Gant, Richard - ***Ian Fleming: The Fantastic 007 Man*** [1966]	$1.35	$4.00	$8.00
73-505	Anderson, Poul - ***The Corridors Of Time*** [1966] Cover art by Oscar Leubman.	$1.35	$4.00	$8.00
73-506	Lee, Elsie - ***The Drifting Sands*** [1966]	$1.25	$3.75	$7.50
73-508	Mark, Ted - ***A Hard Day's Knight*** [1966] PBO.	$1.25	$3.75	$7.50
73-509	Blackburn, John - ***The Reluctant Spy*** [1966]	$1.25	$3.75	$7.50
73-510	Brossard, Chandler - ***The Bold Saboteurs*** [1962]	$1.25	$3.75	$7.50
73-513	Treibich, S. J. - ***Halestrom Manor*** [1966] PBO. Cover art by Kelly Freas.	$1.25	$3.75	$7.50
73-514	Whitney, Phillis - ***The Moonflower*** [1964]	$1.25	$3.75	$7.50
73-515	Mark, Ted - ***The Ted Mark Reader*** [1966]	$1.25	$3.75	$7.50
73-517	Wuorio, Eva-Lis - ***Z For Zaborra*** [1966]	$1.25	$3.75	$7.50
73-518	Healey, Ben - ***Waiting For A Tiger*** [1966]	$1.25	$3.75	$7.50
73-520	Cleeve, Brian - ***Counterspy*** [1966]	$1.25	$3.75	$7.50
73-521	Blackburn, John - ***A Wreath Of Roses*** [1966]	$1.25	$3.75	$7.50
73-522	Buchan, William - ***Helen All Alone*** [1966]	$1.25	$3.75	$7.50
73-524	Wuorio, Eva-Lis - ***The Woman With The Portuguese Basket*** [1966]	$1.25	$3.75	$7.50
73-526	Howard, R. E. & DeCamp, L. Sprague - ***Conan The Adventurer*** [1966] PBO. Cover art by Frank Frazetta.	$1.35	$4.00	$8.00
73-527	Mark, Ted - ***The Unhatched Egghead*** [1966]	$1.25	$3.75	$7.50
73-528	White, Ted - ***Sorceress Of Qar*** [1966] PBO. Cover art by Shannon Sturnweist.	$1.25	$3.75	$7.50
73-529	Lee, Elsie - ***Dark Moon, Lost Lady*** [1966] PBO. Cover art by Victor Olson.	$1.35	$4.00	$8.00
73-530	Daniels, Dorothy - ***The Tower Room*** [1966] PBO. Cover art by Lou Marchetti.	$1.25	$3.75	$7.50

		G	VG	F
73-531	Millar, Margaret - ***Do Evil In Return*** [1966] Cover art by Mort Engel.	$1.25	$3.75	$7.50
73-532	Canfield, Miriam - ***The Tuscany Madonna*** [1966] Cover art by Victor Olson.	$1.25	$3.75	$7.50
73-533	Blanc, Suzanne - ***The Green Stone*** [1966]	$1.25	$3.75	$7.50
73-534	Sydell, Eleanor - ***Diplomatic Immunity*** [1966] PBO.	$1.25	$3.75	$7.50
73-535	Coffman, Virginia - ***The Shadow Box*** [1966] PBO.	$1.25	$3.75	$7.50
73-536	Tobias, Katherine - ***The Lady In The Lighting*** [1966] PBO. Cover art by Faragasso.	$1.25	$3.75	$7.50
73-538	Milton, Joseph - ***The Death Makers*** [1966] PBO.	$1.25	$3.75	$7.50
73-540	Loraine, Philip - ***13*** [1966]	$1.25	$3.75	$7.50
73-541	Paul, Phyllis - ***Twice Lost*** [1966]	$1.25	$3.75	$7.50
73-542	Holmes, Mary J. - ***Chateau D'Or*** [1966] PBO. Cover art by Armand Weston.	$1.25	$3.75	$7.50
73-544	Rice, Craig - ***But The Doctor Died*** [1966]	$1.35	$4.00	$8.00
73-545	Moorcock, Michael - ***The Stealer Of Souls*** [1967] Cover art by Jack Gaughan.	$1.35	$4.00	$8.00
73-546	Mark, Ted - ***The Nude Wore Black*** [1967] PBO.	$1.25	$3.75	$7.50
73-547	Hershman, Morris - ***Glory In Hell*** [1967] PBO. Cover art by Johnson.	$1.25	$3.75	$7.50
73-548	Albrand, Martha - ***Wait For The Dawn*** [1967]	$1.25	$3.75	$7.50
73-549	Howard, R. E. (edited by De Camp) - ***Conan The Warrior*** [1967] PBO. Cover art by Frank Frazetta.	$1.35	$4.00	$8.00
73-550	Wilson, Richard - ***The Girls From Planet 5*** [1967] Cover art by Kelly Freas.	$1.35	$4.00	$8.00
73-551	Morgan, Clarinda - ***Devil's Cavern*** [1967]	$1.25	$3.75	$7.50
73-553	Sager, Gordon - ***The Formula*** [1967] Cover art by Johnson.	$1.25	$3.75	$7.50
73-554	Lacy, Ed - ***Moment Of Untruth*** [1967]	$1.25	$3.75	$7.50
73-555	Sinstadt, Gerald - ***The Fidelio Score*** [1967]	$1.25	$3.75	$7.50
73-557	Hudson, Laura Hope - ***The Cruel Legacy*** [1967]	$1.25	$3.75	$7.50
73-560	Talbot, Guy - ***Meet Chatty Jones*** [1967] PBO.	$1.25	$3.75	$7.50
73-562	Wylie, Philip - ***Gladiator*** [1967]	$1.35	$4.00	$8.00
73-563	Mark, Ted - ***Room At The Topless*** [1967]	$1.25	$3.75	$7.50
73-566	Sinstadt, Gerald - ***Ship Of Spies*** [1967] Cover art by Robert Baxter.	$1.25	$3.75	$7.50
73-567	Phillips, Jean - ***Hermit's Island*** [1967] PBO. Cover art by Faragasso.	$1.25	$3.75	$7.50
73-568	McKee, Alexander - ***Strike From The Sky*** [1967] Cover art by Tonson.	$1.25	$3.75	$7.50
73-570	Clark, Anne Campbell - ***Passport To Peril*** [1967] PBO.	$1.25	$3.75	$7.50
73-571	Rico, Don - ***Nightmare Of Eyes*** [1967]	$1.25	$3.75	$7.50
73-572	Howard, R. E. (Edited by DeCamp) - ***Conan The Conqueror*** [1967] Cover art by Frank Frazetta.	$1.35	$4.00	$8.00
73-573	Hubbard, Lafayette Ronald - ***Slaves Of Sleep*** [1967] Cover art by Kelly Freas.	$1.25	$3.75	$7.50
73-574	Milton, Joseph - ***President's Agent*** [1967]	$1.25	$3.75	$7.50
73-575	Lee, Elsie - ***Clouds Over Vallanti*** [1967]	$1.25	$3.75	$7.50
73-576	Coleman, Clara - ***Nightmare In July*** [1967]	$1.25	$3.75	$7.50
73-577	Hamilton, Edmond - ***The Valley Of Creation*** [1967] Cover art by Emsh.	$1.35	$4.00	$8.00
73-579	Moorcock, Michael - ***Stormbringer*** [1967] Cover art by Jack Gaughan.	$1.35	$4.00	$8.00
73-580	Blish, James - ***The Warriors Of Day*** [1967] Cover art by Armand Weston.	$1.35	$4.00	$8.00
73-581	Stern, Richard Martin - ***I Hide, We Seek*** [1967] Cover art by Tonson.	$1.25	$3.75	$7.50
73-582	Mullally, Frederic - ***The Assassins*** [1967]	$1.25	$3.75	$7.50
73-583	Blackburn, John - ***Gaunt Woman*** [1967]	$1.25	$3.75	$7.50
73-585	Coffman, Virginia - ***The Rest Is Silence*** [1967] PBO.	$1.25	$3.75	$7.50
73-586	Jansen, Laure Mae - ***Bride Of The Shadows*** [1967]	$1.25	$3.75	$7.50

		G	VG	F
73-587	Fairman, Paul W. - ***Search For A Dead Nympho*** [1967] PBO.	$1.25	$3.75	$7.50
73-588	Karp, Ivan C. - ***Doobie Doo*** [1967] Cover art by Weston.	$1.25	$3.75	$7.50
73-589	Treibich, S. J. - ***Burwyck's Wander*** [1967]	$1.25	$3.75	$7.50
73-590	Michaeles, M. M. - ***Suicide Command*** [1967] PBO. Cover art by Oscar Leibman.	$1.25	$3.75	$7.50
73-591	Westlake, Donald - ***The Busy Body*** [1967] Cover art by Frazetta.	$1.50	$5.00	$10.00
73-592	McGurk, Slater - ***The Copenhagen Affair*** [1967]	$1.25	$3.75	$7.50
73-593	Bond, Evelyn - ***The Venetian Secret*** [1967] PBO.	$1.25	$3.75	$7.50
73-594	Stone, Harrison - ***The Good Rich Life*** [1967] PBO. Cover art by Tonson.	$1.25	$3.75	$7.50
73-595	Ayling, Kaye - ***Who Was Ellen Smith?*** [1967] PBO.	$1.25	$3.75	$7.50
73-599	Howard, R. E. & DeCamp, L. Sprague - ***Conan The Usurper*** [1967] PBO. Cover art by Frank Frazetta.	$1.35	$4.00	$8.00
73-600	Heath, Peter - ***The Mind Brothers*** [1967] PBO. Cover art by Armand Weston.	$1.35	$4.00	$8.00
73-601	Well, Lee - ***Pageant*** [1967]	$1.25	$3.75	$7.50
73-602	Garve, Andrew - ***The Golden Deed*** [1967]	$1.25	$3.75	$7.50
73-603	Whitney, Phyllis A. - ***The Moonflower*** [1967]	$1.25	$3.75	$7.50
73-604	Williams, Rose - ***Nurse In Nassau*** [1967]	$1.00	$3.00	$6.00
73-605	Minton, Paula - ***Engraved In Evil*** [1967]	$1.25	$3.75	$7.50
73-606	Rico, Don - ***The Last Of The Breed*** [1967]	$1.25	$3.75	$7.50
73-607	Ames, Clyde - ***Gorgonzola, Won't You Please Come Home*** [1967]	$1.25	$3.75	$7.50
73-608	Lovecraft, H. P. - ***The Colour Out Of Space & Others*** [1967]	$1.50	$5.00	$10.00
73-609	Frayn, Michael - ***The Russian Interpreter*** [1967]	$1.25	$3.75	$7.50
73-610	Holden, Joanne - ***Dangerous Legacy*** [1967] Cover art by Podwil.	$1.25	$3.75	$7.50
73-611	Janifer, Laurence M (Larry Mark Harris) - ***You Can't Escape*** [1967] PBO.	$1.35	$4.00	$8.00
73-613	Jay, Willa - ***A Fear In Borzano*** [1967]	$1.25	$3.75	$7.50
73-614	Dagmar - ***The Spy With The Blue Kazoo*** [1967]	$1.25	$3.75	$7.50
73-615	Bloch, Robert - ***Firebug*** [1967]	$3.50	$10.00	$20.00
73-617	McCroskey, Jacob - ***Operation Axe-Handle*** [1967]	$1.25	$3.75	$7.50
73-619	Wenzell, Isabel D'Este - ***The Dragon's Lair*** [1967] PBO. Cover art by Faragasso.	$1.25	$3.75	$7.50
73-620	Mark, Ted - ***Circle Of Sin*** [1967]	$1.25	$3.75	$7.50
73-621	Cleeve, Brian - ***Vice Isn't Private*** [1967]	$1.25	$3.75	$7.50
73-622	Shepard, Fern - ***Psychiatric Nurse*** [1967]	$ .75	$2.50	$5.00
73-623	Waters, T. A. - ***In The Halls Of Evil*** [1967]	$1.25	$3.75	$7.50
73-624	Greenfield, Irving A. - ***The U.F.O. Report*** [1967] PBO.	$1.00	$3.00	$6.00
73-625	Valchin, Nigel - ***In The Absence Of Mrs. Petersen*** [1967] Cover art by Tonson.	$1.25	$3.75	$7.50
73-626	James, Maryl - ***Brandy On The Rocks*** [1967] PBO.	$1.25	$3.75	$7.50
73-627	LeJeune, Anthony - ***Death Of A Pornographer*** [1967]	$1.25	$3.75	$7.50
73-629	Lacy, Ed - ***In Black And Whitey*** [1967] PBO.	$1.35	$4.00	$8.00
73-630	Williamson, Jack - ***Golden Blood*** [1967] Cover art by Steele Savage.	$1.35	$4.00	$8.00
73-632	Wetherell, June - ***Opal Street*** [1967]	$1.25	$3.75	$7.50
73-633	Fletcher, Dorothy - ***House Of Hate*** [1967] PBO.	$1.25	$3.75	$7.50
73-634	Martin, Jay - ***Make Love, Not Waves*** [1967] PBO.	$1.25	$3.75	$7.50
73-635	Stuart, Matt - ***Lady Of Battle Mountain*** [1967]	$1.25	$3.75	$7.50
73-636	Smith, George O. - ***Highways In Hiding*** [1967] Cover art by Roy G. Krenkel.	$1.35	$4.00	$8.00
73-637	Daniels, Dorothy - ***The Eagle's Nest*** [1967]	$1.25	$3.75	$7.50
73-638	Daniels, Dorothy - ***House Of The Seven Courts*** [1967] PBO.	$1.25	$3.75	$7.50
73-639	Rico, Don - ***The Daisy Dilemma*** [1967] PBO.	$1.25	$3.75	$7.50
73-640	Patten, Lewis B. - ***Hangman's Country*** [1967]	$1.25	$3.75	$7.50
73-644	Williams, Robert Moore - ***Vigilante-21st Century*** [1967] Cover art by Howard Winters.	$1.35	$4.00	$8.00

		G	VG	F
73-645	Gilmer, Ann - ***Nurse In The Tropics*** [1967]	$ .75	$2.50	$5.00
73-646	Baker, W. Howard - ***Traitor!*** [1967] Cover art by Peter Caras.	$1.25	$3.75	$7.50
73-647	Heard, H. F. - ***A Taste For Honey*** [1967]	$1.25	$3.75	$7.50
73-648	Peters, Ellis - ***The Piper On The Mountain*** [1968] Cover art by Tonson.	$1.25	$3.75	$7.50
73-649	Warren, Paulette (Paul Fairman) - ***Nurse Of Brooding Mansion*** [1967] PBO.	$1.00	$3.00	$6.00
73-650	Howard, R. E. & Carter, Lin - ***King Kull*** [1967] PBO. Cover art by Roy G. Krenkel.	$1.35	$4.00	$8.00
73-651	Floren, Lee - ***Wyoming Gun Law*** [1967]	$1.25	$3.75	$7.50
73-652	Kops, Bernard - ***Yes From No Man's Land*** [1967] Cover art by Armand Weston.	$1.25	$3.75	$7.50
73-653	Blaisdell, Anne - ***Nightmare*** [1967]	$1.25	$3.75	$7.50
73-654	Winston, Daoma - ***Shadow On Mercer Mountain*** [1978] PBO. Cover art by Armand Weston.	$1.25	$3.75	$7.50
73-656	Waters. T. A. - ***The Psychedelic Spy*** [1967] PBO.	$1.25	$3.75	$7.50
73-657	Westlake, Donald E. - ***The Spy In The Ointment*** [1967]	$1.25	$3.75	$7.50
73-659	Baker, W. Howard - ***Night Of The Wolf*** [1967]	$1.25	$3.75	$7.50
73-660	? - ***The Hand Of Kane*** [1967]	$1.25	$3.75	$7.50
73-662	DeCamp, L. Sprague & Pratt, Fletcher - ***Tha Carnelian Cube*** [1967] Cover art by Kelly Freas.	$1.25	$3.75	$7.50
73-663	Loraine, Philip - ***Eye Of The Devil*** [1967]	$1.25	$3.75	$7.50
73-664	O'More, Peggy - ***Seacliff Nurse*** [1967]	$ .75	$2.50	$5.00
73-669	Ballinger, W. A. - ***Women's Battalion*** [1967] Cover art by Weston.	$1.25	$3.75	$7.50
73-670	Daniels, Norman - ***The Baron Of Hong Kong*** [1967] PBO.	$1.25	$3.75	$7.50
73-671	Baker, W. Howard - ***The Dirty Game*** [1967]	$1.25	$3.75	$7.50
73-672	Greenfield, Irving A. - ***Waters Of Death*** [1967] PBO. Cover art by Hoot.	$1.25	$3.75	$7.50
73-675	Wylie, Philip - ***Experiment In Crime*** [1967]	$1.25	$3.75	$7.50
73-677	Anderson, Poul - ***Ensign Flandry*** [1967] Cover art by Jack Faragasso.	$1.25	$3.75	$7.50
73-679	Ermine, Will - ***Laramie Rides Alone*** [1967]	$1.25	$3.75	$7.50
73-680	Crawford, Petrina - ***Seed Of Evil*** [1967]	$1.25	$3.75	$7.50
73-683	Dagmar - ***The Spy Who Came In From The Copa*** [1967] PBO. Cover art by Stan Borack.	$1.25	$3.75	$7.50
73-684	? - ***Bonnie And Clyde*** [1967]	$1.25	$3.75	$7.50
73-685	Howard, R.E. & DeCamp, L. Sprague - ***Conan*** [1967] Cover art by Frank Frazetta.	$1.35	$4.00	$8.00
73-687	Ermine, Will - ***Lobo Law*** [1967]	$1.25	$3.75	$7.50
73-688	Moorcock, Michael - ***The Jewel In The Skull*** [1967] PBO. Cover art by Gray Morrow.	$1.35	$4.00	$8.00
73-689	Wylie, Philip - ***The Smuggled Atom Bomb*** [1967]	$1.25	$3.75	$7.50
73-690	Cooper, Edmund - ***Transit*** [1967] Cover art by Douglas Rosa.	$1.35	$4.00	$8.00
73-691	Anthology edited by Damon Knight - ***Science Fiction Inventions*** [1967] PBO. Cover art by Hoot.	$1.35	$4.00	$8.00
73-692	Wetherell, June - ***The Mahogany House*** [1967] PBO.	$1.25	$3.75	$7.50
73-694	Williams, Robert Moore - ***Zanthar Of The Many Worlds*** [1967] PBO. Cover art by Jeff Jones.	$1.35	$4.00	$8.00
73-695	Martin, Jay - ***Ban The Bra*** [1967] PBO. Cover art by Stanley Borack.	$1.25	$3.75	$7.50
73-698	Baker, W. Howard - ***Strike North*** [1967]	$1.25	$3.75	$7.50
73-699	Daniels, Dorothy - ***The Marble Leaf*** [1967]	$1.25	$3.75	$7.50
73-700	Daniels, Norman - ***A Killing In The Market*** [1967] PBO.	$1.25	$3.75	$7.50
73-701	Asimov, Isaac - ***The End Of Eternity*** [1968] Cover art by Kelly Freas.	$1.25	$3.75	$7.50
73-702	Isaac, Asimov - ***The Naked Sun*** [1968] Cover art by Kelly Freas.	$1.25	$3.75	$7.50
73-703	Asimov, Isaac - ***The Currents Of Space*** [1968] Cover art by Kelly Freas.	$1.25	$3.75	$7.50

		G	VG	F
73-704	Asimov, Isaac - ***The Stars Like Dust*** [1968] Cover art by Kelly Freas.	$1.25	$3.75	$7.50
73-705	Daniels, Dorothy - ***Duet*** [1968] PBO. Cover art by Lou Marchetti.	$1.25	$3.75	$7.50
73-707	Moorcock, Michael - ***Sorcerer's Amulet*** [1968] PBO. Cover art by Jeff Jones.	$1.25	$3.75	$7.50
73-709	Elsner, Don Yon - ***A Bullet For Your Dreams*** [1968]	$1.25	$3.75	$7.50
73-712	Gainham, Sarah - ***The Silent Hostage*** [1968]	$1.25	$3.75	$7.50
73-714	Saxon, Peter - ***Through The Dark Curtain*** [1968] PBO.	$1.25	$3.75	$7.50
73-715	Farmer, Philip Jose - ***The Day Of Timestop*** [1968] Cover art by Kelly Freas.	$2.00	$6.00	$12.00
73-718	White, Alicen - ***Dirge For A Lady*** [1968] PBO.	$1.25	$3.75	$7.50
73-719	Sted, Don - ***A Girl Called Boots*** [1968] PBO.	$1.25	$3.75	$7.50
73-721	Howard, Robert E. - ***Wolfshead*** [1968] PBO. Cover art by Frank Frazetta.	$1.35	$4.00	$8.00
73-722	Daniels, Dorothy - ***Candle In The Sun*** [1968] PBO. Cover art by Jack Faragasso.	$1.25	$3.75	$7.50
73-724	Calin, Harold - ***Return To The Ardennes*** [1968]	$1.25	$3.75	$7.50
73-725	Lynch, Miriam - ***The Doomsday Bells*** [1968] PBO.	$1.25	$3.75	$7.50
73-726	Warren, Paulette - ***Storm Over Bitterhill*** [1968] PBO.	$1.25	$3.75	$7.50
73-727	Brown, Frederic - ***Daymares*** [1968] PBO.	$4.00	$12.50	$25.00
73-728	Paul, F. W. - ***3 For an Orgy*** [1968] PBO.	$1.25	$3.75	$7.50
73-731	Heath, Peter - ***Assassins From Tomorrow*** [1967] Cover art by Armand Weston.	$1.35	$4.00	$8.00
73-732	Williamson, Jack - ***Seetee Ship*** [1968] Cover art by Jeff Jones.	$1.35	$4.00	$8.00
73-733	Williamson, Jack - ***Seetee Shock*** [1968] Cover art by Jeff Jones.	$1.35	$4.00	$8.00
73-735	Fairman, Paul W. - ***I, The Machine*** [1968] PBO. Cover art by Hoot	$1.35	$4.00	$8.00
73-737	Halleran, E. E. - ***The Gringo Gun*** [1968]	$1.25	$3.75	$7.50
73-739	Bradley, Marion Zimmer - ***Bluebeard's Daughter*** [1968]	$1.25	$3.75	$7.50
73-741	Spangster, Jimmy - ***Private i*** [1968]	$1.25	$3.75	$7.50
73-744	Coleman, Clara - ***A Scent Of Sandalwood*** [1968]	$1.25	$3.75	$7.50
73-748	Williamson, Jack - ***The Reign Of Wizardry*** [1968] Cover art by Frank Frazetta.	$1.35	$4.00	$8.00
73-750	Saxonb, Peter - ***The Curse Of Rathlaw*** [1968] PBO. Cover art by Jeff Jones.	$1.25	$3.75	$7.50
73-752	Janifer, Laurence M. (Larry Harris) - ***Bloodworld*** [1968] Cover art by Howard Winters.	$1.35	$4.00	$8.00
73-753	Martin, Jay - ***The Erotica Caper*** [1968] PBO. Cover art by Stanley Borack.	$1.25	$3.75	$7.50
73-759	Anthology - ***Sock It To Me Zombie!*** [1968]	$1.25	$3.75	$7.50
73-761	Moorcock, Michael - ***Sword Of The Dawn*** [1968] PBO. Cover art by Jack Faragasso	$1.25	$3.75	$7.50
73-764	Bennett, Dwight - ***Stormy Range*** [1968]	$1.25	$3.75	$7.50
73-765	Coburn, Walt - ***Barb Wire*** [1968]	$1.25	$3.75	$7.50
73-766	Williams, Robert Moore - ***The Bell From Infinity*** [1968] PBO. Cover art by Jerome Podwil.	$1.35	$4.00	$8.00
73-767	Wylie, Philip - ***Autumn Romance*** [1968]	$1.25	$3.75	$7.50
73-769	Waters, T. A. - ***The Blackwood Cult*** [1968] PBO.	$1.25	$3.75	$7.50
73-778	Hitchens, Dolores - ***The Bank With The Bamboo Door*** [1968]	$1.25	$3.75	$7.50
73-780	Anthology - ***Conan The Avenger*** [1968] Cover art by Frank Frazetta.	$1.35	$4.00	$8.00
73-781	Firth, Anthony - ***The Limbo Affair*** [1968]	$1.25	$3.75	$7.50
73-783	Heath, Peter - ***Men Who Die Twice*** [1968] PBO. Cover art by Armand Weston.	$1.25	$3.75	$7.50
73-784	Saxon, Peter - ***Satan's Child*** [1968] PBO. Cover art by Jeff Jones.	$1.50	$5.00	$10.00
73-785	Morgan, Jason - ***A Warm Bed In Reno*** [1968] PBO.	$1.25	$3.75	$7.50
73-788	Bond, Walter - ***The Kill Squad*** [1968] PBO.	$1.25	$3.75	$7.50
73-793	Rico, Don - ***The Passion Flower Puzzle*** [1968] PBO.	$1.25	$3.75	$7.50

		G	VG	F
73-794	Lamb, Antonia - ***Lady In Shadows*** [1968] PBO.	$1.25	$3.75	$7.50
73-795	Daniels, Dorothy - ***Mostly By Moonlight*** [1968] PBO.	$1.25	$3.75	$7.50
73-797	Brunner, John - ***Into The Slave Nebula*** [1968] Cover art by Kelly Freas.	$1.35	$4.00	$8.00
73-798	Jackson, Norman - ***Little Often Fanny*** [1968] PBO. Cover art by Stanley Borack.	$1.25	$3.75	$7.50
73-800	Anthology - ***Conan Of The Isles*** [1968] PBO. Cover art by John Duillo.	$1.35	$4.00	$8.00
73-802	Queen, Ellery - ***Guess Who's Coming To Kill You*** [1968]	$1.35	$4.00	$8.00
73-803	Martin, Jay - ***Fondle With Care*** [1968] PBO.	$1.25	$3.75	$7.50
73-805	Williams, Robert Moore - ***Zanthar At Moon's Madness*** [1968] PBO. Cover art by Jeff Jones.	$1.35	$4.00	$8.00
73-809	Jackson, Norman - ***The Daring Adventures Of Captain Sex*** [1968] PBO.	$1.35	$4.00	$8.00
73-810	Budrys, Algis - ***Who?*** [1968] Cover art by Kelly Freas.	$1.35	$4.00	$8.00
73-811	Paul, F. W. - ***Tool Of The Trade*** [1969] PBO.	$1.25	$3.75	$7.50
73-814	Queen, Ellery - ***A Study In Terror*** [1969]	$1.25	$3.75	$7.50
73-817	Kane, Henry - ***Dead In Bed*** [1969]	$1.25	$3.75	$7.50
73-822	Maryl, James - ***Brandy On The Rocks*** [1969]	$1.25	$3.75	$7.50
73-823	Kane, Henry - ***Don't Just Die There*** [1969]	$1.25	$3.75	$7.50
73-824	Moorcock, Michael - ***The Secret Of The Runestaff*** [1969] PBO. Cover art by Jack Faragasso.	$1.35	$4.00	$8.00
73-828	Jackson, Norman - ***Fanny For Free*** [1969] PBO.	$1.25	$3.75	$7.50
73-830	Loraine, Philip - ***Day Of The Arrow*** [1969] Cover art by Lou Marchetti.	$1.25	$3.75	$7.50
73-833	Stuart, Matt - ***Edge Of The Desert*** [1969]	$1.25	$3.75	$7.50
73-835	Kane, Henry - ***Death Of A Hooker*** [1969]	$1.25	$3.75	$7.50
73-836	Williams, Robert Moore - ***Zanthar At Trip's End*** [1969] PBO. Cover art by Jeff Jones.	$1.35	$4.00	$8.00
73-837	Jackson, Norman - ***Fanny's Double Feature*** [1969] PBO.	$1.25	$3.75	$7.50
73-839	Kane, Henry - ***The Schack Job*** [1969]	$1.25	$3.75	$7.50
73-840	Long, Lyda Belknap (Frank Belknap Long) - ***To The Dark Tower*** [1969] PBO.	$1.35	$4.00	$8.00
73-841	Wellsley, Julie - ***The Wine Of Vengeance*** [1969]	$1.25	$3.75	$7.50
73-843	Draco, F. - ***The Devil's Church*** [1969]	$1.25	$3.75	$7.50
73-848	Cole, Dorothy - ***Country Club Nurse*** [1969]	$ .75	$2.50	$5.00
73-849	Johnston, William - ***The Brady Bunch*** [1969] PBO.	$1.25	$3.75	$7.50
73-852	Finley, Glenna - ***A Tycoon For Ann*** [1969]	$1.25	$3.75	$7.50
73-853	Anthology - ***Lancer Book Of Puns, Anagrams & Crossword Puzzles*** [1969]	$1.35	$4.00	$8.00
73-854	Rossiter, Jane - ***Summer Season*** [1969]	$ .75	$2.50	$5.00
73-855	Williams, Rose - ***Airport Nurse*** [1969]	$ .75	$2.50	$5.00
73-857	Ross, W. E. D. - ***Let Your Heart Answer*** [1969]	$ .75	$2.50	$5.00
73-858	Kane, Henry - ***Don't Call Me Madame*** [1969] PBO.	$1.25	$3.75	$7.50
73-859	Ketchum, Philip - ***The Man Who Turned Outlaw*** [1969]	$1.25	$3.75	$7.50
73-860	Gilmer, Ann - ***Nurse On Call*** [1969]	$ .75	$2.50	$5.00
73-861	McComb, Katherine - ***Detour To Romance*** [1969]	$ .75	$2.50	$5.00
73-862	Corren, Grace - ***The Darkest Room*** [1969] PBO.	$1.25	$3.75	$7.50
73-864	Johnston, William - ***Showdown At The P.T.A. Corral*** [1969]	$1.25	$3.75	$7.50
73-865	Corby, Jane - ***Riverwood*** [1969]	$1.25	$3.75	$7.50
73-867	Heckelmann, Charles N. - ***Guns Of Arizona*** [1969]	$1.25	$3.75	$7.50
73-871	Ketchum, Philip - ***The Man Who Sold Leadville*** [1970]	$1.25	$3.75	$7.50
73-872	Johnston, Willian - ***Count Up To Blast-Down!*** [1970] PBO.	$1.25	$3.75	$7.50
73-876	Johnston, William - ***Nanny And The Professor*** [1970] PBO.	$1.25	$3.75	$7.50
73-882	Wellsley, Julie - ***Climb The Dark Mountain*** [1970] PBO.	$1.25	$3.75	$7.50
73-888	Hirschfeld, Burt - ***Kelly's Heroes*** [1970] PBO. Cover art by Jack Davis.	$1.25	$3.75	$7.50
73-897	Garfield, Brian - ***Seven Brave Men*** [1970]	$1.25	$3.75	$7.50
73-899	Kennedy, Nancy MacDougall - ***The Cherished Heart*** [1970]	$1.25	$3.75	$7.50

Lancer 74 Series.

		G	VG	F
74-101	Hogan, Ray - ***Texas Guns*** [1969] PBO.	$1.25	$3.75	$7.50
74-501	Lovecraft, H. P. - ***The Colour Out Of Space & Others*** [1969]	$1.35	$4.00	$8.00
74-502	Lovecraft, H. P. - ***The Dunwich Horror*** [1969] Cover art by Len Goldberg.	$1.35	$4.00	$8.00
74-503	Daniels, Norman - ***Killer Tank*** [1969]	$1.25	$3.75	$7.50
74-506	Coffman, Virginia - ***Castle At Witches' Coven*** [1969]	$1.25	$3.75	$7.50
74-507	Buckingham, Nancy - ***Secret Of The Ghostly Shroud*** [1969]	$1.25	$3.75	$7.50
74-508	Gordon, Jane - ***Season Of Evil*** [1969]	$1.25	$3.75	$7.50
74-509	Van Arnum, Dave - ***Star Barbarian*** [1969] PBO. Cover art by Jeff Jones.	$1.35	$4.00	$8.00
74-516	Locke, Douglas - ***Death Lives In The Mansion*** [1969]	$1.25	$3.75	$7.50
74-517	Sayers, James D. - ***Blood River*** [1969]	$1.25	$3.75	$7.50
74-519	Williamson, Jack - ***The Humanoids*** [1969]	$1.35	$4.00	$8.00
74-524	Clarke, ARthur C. - ***The Space Dreamers*** [1969]	$1.35	$4.00	$8.00
74-527	Queen, Ellery - ***The Campus Murders*** [1969]	$1.25	$3.75	$7.50
74-529	Brennan, Alice - ***The Brooding House*** [1969]	$1.25	$3.75	$7.50
74-531	Paul, F. W. - ***The Planned Planethood Caper*** [1969] PBO.	$1.25	$3.75	$7.50
74-532	Garrett, Randall - ***Anything You Can Do*** [1969] Cover art by Bill Skurski.	$1.25	$3.75	$7.50
74-533	Chandler, A. Bertram - ***Catch The Star Winds*** [1969] PBO. Cover art by Kelly Freas.	$1.35	$4.00	$8.00
74-536	Anderson, Poul - ***The Corridors Of Time*** [1969] Cover art by Oscar Liebman.	$1.35	$4.00	$8.00
74-537	Reynolds, Mack - ***Time Gladiator*** [1969] PBO. Cover art by Kelly Freas.	$1.35	$4.00	$8.00
74-538	Del Rey, Lester - ***The Man Without A Planet*** [1969]	$1.35	$4.00	$8.00
74-539	Greenfield, Irving A. - ***The U.F.O. Report*** [1969]	$1.00	$3.00	$6.00
74-540	Moessinger, David - ***Number One*** [1969] PBO.	$1.25	$3.75	$7.50
74-545	Asimov, Isaac - ***A Whiff Of Death*** [1969] Cover art by Peter Caras.	$1.25	$3.75	$7.50
74-546	O'Donnell, K. M. (Barry Malzberg) - ***The Empty People*** [1969] PBO.	$1.35	$4.00	$8.00
74-547	Vance, Jack - ***The Dying Earth*** [1969] Cover art by Emsh.	$1.35	$4.00	$8.00
74-556	Anthology - ***The Mighty Barbarians Great*** [1969] PBO. Cover art by Jim Steranko.	$1.35	$4.00	$8.00
74-557	Clement, Hal - ***Needle*** [1969] Cover art by Kelly Freas.	$1.35	$4.00	$8.00
74-558	Wagner, Sharon - ***Curse Of Still Valley*** [1969] PBO. Cover art by Borack.	$1.25	$3.75	$7.50
74-559	Kane, Henry - ***Who Dies There?*** [1969]	$1.25	$3.75	$7.50
74-560	Gilford, C. B. - ***The Liquid Man*** [1969] PBO.	$1.25	$3.75	$7.50
74-561	Howard & Carter - ***King Kull*** [1969] Cover art by Roy G. Krenkle.	$1.35	$4.00	$8.00
74-562	Kane, Henry - ***Snatch An Eye*** [1969]	$1.25	$3.75	$7.50
74-564	Mason, David - ***Kavin's World*** [1969] PBO. Cover art by Frank Frazetta.	$1.35	$4.00	$8.00
74-572	Mark, Ted - ***The Unhatched Egghead*** [1969]	$1.25	$3.75	$7.50
74-573	Siegel, Martin - ***Agent Of Entropy*** [1969] PBO. Cover art by Ron Watlosky.	$1.25	$3.75	$7.50
74-574	Daniels, Dorothy - ***Survivor Of Darkness*** [1969]	$1.25	$3.75	$7.50
74-575	Daniels, Dorothy - ***House Of Stolen Memories*** [1969]	$1.25	$3.75	$7.50
74-576	Wetherell, June - ***A Touch Of The Witch*** [1969]	$1.25	$3.75	$7.50
74-577	Jackson, O. T. - ***Dark Love, Dark Magic*** [1969]	$1.25	$3.75	$7.50
74-579	Resnick, Michael - ***Redbeard*** [1969] PBO. Cover art by Kelly Freas.	$1.35	$4.00	$8.00
74-580	Brennan, Alice - ***Litany Of Evil*** [1969] PBO. Cover art by Jo Polseno.	$1.25	$3.75	$7.50
74-581	Vincent, Claire - ***Garden Of Satan*** [1969]	$1.25	$3.75	$7.50
74-583	Coffman, Virginia - ***Isle Of The Undead*** [1969]	$1.25	$3.75	$7.50
74-584	Dubois, Theodora - ***The Cavalier's Corpse*** [1969]	$1.25	$3.75	$7.50

		G	VG	F
74-585	Anthology edited by Damon Knight - ***Now Begins Tomorrow*** [1969]	$1.25	$3.75	$7.50
74-586	Wilhelm, Kate - ***Let The Fire Fall*** [1969] Cover art by Milton Glaser.	$1.25	$3.75	$7.50
74-587	Dubois, Theodora - ***Money, Murder And The McNeills*** [1969]	$1.25	$3.75	$7.50
74-592	White, Ted - ***The Sorceress Of Qar*** [1969] Cover art by Shannon Stanweis.	$1.25	$3.75	$7.50
74-593	White, Ted - ***Phoenix Prime*** [1969] Cover art by Frank Frazetta.	$1.35	$4.00	$8.00
74-594	Malm, Dorothea - ***On A Fated Night*** [1969]	$1.25	$3.75	$7.50
74-595	Kane, Henry - ***Don't Go Away Dead*** [1969]	$1.25	$3.75	$7.50
74-597	Bellamy, Jean - ***Ghost Of Coquina Key*** [1969]	$1.25	$3.75	$7.50
74-598	Ross, Clarissa - ***Gemini In Darkness*** [1969]	$1.25	$3.75	$7.50
74-600	Tucker, Wilson - ***The Long Loud Silence*** [1969]	$1.35	$4.00	$8.00
74-601	Damon/Knight - ***World Without Children/The Earth Quarter*** [1970] PBO.	$1.35	$4.00	$8.00
74-602	Creasey, John - ***The Plague Of Silence*** [1970]	$1.25	$3.75	$7.50
74-604	Higgins, Jack - ***East Of Desolation*** [1970]	$1.25	$3.75	$7.50
74-605	Heard, H. F. - ***A Taste For Honey*** [1970]	$1.25	$3.75	$7.50
74-606	Creasey, John - ***Stars For The Toff*** [1970]	$1.25	$3.75	$7.50
74-607	Creasey, John - ***The Toff Anbd The Deep Blue Sea*** [1970]	$1.25	$3.75	$7.50
74-608	Creasey, John - ***Sport For The Baron*** [1970]	$1.25	$3.75	$7.50
74-609	Lynch, Miriam - ***The Brides Of Lucifer*** [1970]	$1.25	$3.75	$7.50
74-612	Hamilton, Edmond - ***Return To The Stars*** [1970] PBO. Cover art by Jim Steranko.	$1.35	$4.00	$8.00
74-616	Farmer, Philip Jose - ***Timestop!*** [1970] Cover art by Gene Szafran.	$1.50	$5.00	$10.00
74-617	DuBois, Theodora - ***The Footsteps*** [1970] Cover art by Armand Weston.	$1.25	$3.75	$7.50
74-618	Waters, T. A. - ***The Blackwood Cult*** [1970]	$1.25	$3.75	$7.50
74-621	Koontz, Dean R. - ***The Dark Symphony*** [1970] PBO. Cover art by Ron Walotsky.	$4.00	$12.50	$25.00
74-622	Creasey, John - ***Call The Toff*** [1970]	$1.25	$3.75	$7.50
74-623	Creasey, John - ***The Blight*** [1970]	$1.25	$3.75	$7.50
74-625	Chadwick, Joseph - ***Hangman's Valley*** [1970]	$1.25	$3.75	$7.50
74-626	Creasey, John - ***Break The Toff*** [1970]	$1.25	$3.75	$7.50
74-627	Kelley, Leo P. - ***Time Rogue*** [1970] PBO.	$1.25	$3.75	$7.50
74-628	Mason, David - ***The Sorcerer's Skull*** [1970] PBO. Cover art by Steele Savage.	$1.35	$4.00	$8.00
74-629	Waters, T. A. - ***The Bow Street Terror*** [1970]	$1.25	$3.75	$7.50
74-638	Nelson, A. P. - ***Brand Of The Outlaw*** [1970]	$1.25	$3.75	$7.50
74-641	Ross, Clarissa - ***Out Of The Fog*** [1970]	$1.25	$3.75	$7.50
74-642	Creasey, John - ***Follow The Toff*** [1970]	$1.25	$3.75	$7.50
74-643	Kane, Henry - ***Kiss, Kiss, Kill, Kill*** [1970]	$1.25	$3.75	$7.50
74-644	Asimov, Isaac - ***The Naked Sun*** [1970] Cover art by Kelly Freas.	$1.25	$3.75	$7.50
74-645	Coffman, Virginia - ***The Devil's Mistress*** [1970] PBO.	$1.25	$3.75	$7.50
74-647	Phillips, Jean - ***Day Of Dark Memory*** [1970] PBO.	$1.25	$3.75	$7.50
74-648	Alexander, Jan - ***Blook Moon*** [1970]	$1.25	$3.75	$7.50
74-649	Carter, Lin - ***Star Rogue*** [1970] PBO.	$1.35	$4.00	$8.00
74-650	Tevis, Walter - ***The Man Who Fell To Earth*** [1970]	$1.35	$4.00	$8.00
74-652	Creasey, John - ***The Famine*** [1970] Cover art by Kenneth Smith.	$1.35	$4.00	$8.00
74-653	Creasey, John - ***The Toff On Fire*** [1970]	$1.25	$3.75	$7.50
74-655	Greenfield, Irving A. - ***Waters Of Death*** [1970]	$1.25	$3.75	$7.50
74-656	Koontz, Dean R. - ***Hell's Gate*** [1970] PBO.	$4.00	$12.50	$25.00
74-658	Creasey, John - ***Hunt The Toff*** [1970]	$1.25	$3.75	$7.50
74-659	Creasey, John - ***Affair For The Baron*** [1970]	$1.25	$3.75	$7.50
74-665	Creasey, John - ***The Toff And The Great Illusion*** [1970]	$1.25	$3.75	$7.50
74-666	Creasey, John - ***Kill The Toff*** [1970]	$1.25	$3.75	$7.50

		G	VG	F
74-667	Dickson, Gordon Rupert - ***Naked To The Stars*** [1970] Cover art by Armand Weston.	$1.35	$4.00	$8.00
74-668	Moorcock, Michael - ***The City Of The Beast*** [1970] Cover art by Kenneth Smith.	$1.35	$4.00	$8.00
74-672	Winston, Baoma - ***House Of Mirror Images*** [1970] PBO.	$1.25	$3.75	$7.50
74-674	Creasey, John - ***The Toff And The Deadly Parson*** [1970]	$1.25	$3.75	$7.50
74-675	Creasey, John - ***The Flood*** [1970]	$1.25	$3.75	$7.50
74-676	DeCamp, L. Sprague & Pratt, Fletcher - ***The Carnelian Tube*** [1970] Cover art by Kelly Freas.	$1.25	$3.75	$7.50
74-677	Aldiss, Brian W. - ***Report On Probability A*** [1970] Cover art by Steele Savage.	$1.25	$3.75	$7.50
74-678	Daniels, Dorothy - ***The Marble Angel*** [1970]	$1.25	$3.75	$7.50
74-679	Sinclair, Olga - ***Night Of The Black Tower*** [1970]	$1.25	$3.75	$7.50
74-680	Fenton, Ann - ***Dark Cedars*** [1970]	$1.25	$3.75	$7.50
74-682	Grace, Alicia - ***Mass For A Dead Witch*** [1970] PBO.	$1.25	$3.75	$7.50
74-683	Gant, Norman - ***Burn!*** [1970]	$1.25	$3.75	$7.50
74-684	Wuorio, Eva-Lis - ***The Woman With The Portuguese Basket*** [1970] Cover art by Amsel.	$1.25	$3.75	$7.50
74-685	Creasey, John - ***Here Comes The Toff*** [1970]	$1.25	$3.75	$7.50
74-686	Creasey, John - ***The Toff At The Fair*** [1970]	$1.25	$3.75	$7.50
74-687	Charbonneau, Louis - ***Barrier World*** [1970] PBO. Cover art by Steele Savage.	$1.35	$4.00	$8.00
74-688	Van Arnum, Dave - ***Lord Of Blood*** [1970] PBO. Cover art by Jim Steranko.	$1.35	$4.00	$8.00
74-690	Wetherell, June - ***Legacy Of The Lost*** [1970]	$1.25	$3.75	$7.50
74-693	Calin, Harold - ***Panzer!*** [1970]	$1.25	$3.75	$7.50
74-694	Kane, Henry - ***Sleep Without Dreams*** [1970]	$1.25	$3.75	$7.50
74-696	Wuorio, Eva-Lis - ***Explosion*** [1970]	$1.25	$3.75	$7.50
74-697	Coffman, Virginia - ***Priestess Of The Danmed*** [1970]	$1.25	$3.75	$7.50
74-698	Anderson, Poul - ***Satan's World*** [1970] PBO. Cover art by Douglas Chaffee.	$1.35	$4.00	$8.00
74-699	Anthology edited by Lin Carter - ***The Magic Of Atlantis*** [1970] PBO. Cover art by Ron Walotsky.	$1.35	$4.00	$8.00
74-701	Creasey, John - ***The Baron And The Missing Old Masters*** [1970]	$1.25	$3.75	$7.50
74-704	Gaddis, Margaret P. - ***No Fire Can Warm Me*** [1970]	$1.25	$3.75	$7.50
74-707	Anthology edited by Hans S. Santesson - ***The Mighty Swordsmen*** [1970] PBO. Cover art by Jim Steranko.	$1.35	$4.00	$8.00
74-711	Creasey, John - ***A Bundle For The Toff*** [1970]	$1.25	$3.75	$7.50
74-713	Fletcher, Dorothy - ***Meeting In Madrid*** [1970]	$1.25	$3.75	$7.50
74-719	Koontz, Dean R. - ***Beastchild*** [1970] Cover art by Gene Szafran.	$4.00	$12.50	$25.00
74-721	Barret, Jr., Neal - ***The Leaves Of Time*** [1971] PBO. Cover art by Mike Hinge.	$1.35	$4.00	$8.00
74-722	Carter, Lin - ***Outworlder*** [1971] PBO. Cover art by Behan.	$1.35	$4.00	$8.00
74-727	Morella, Jane - ***Dark Memories*** [1971] PBO.	$1.25	$3.75	$7.50
74-728	Chase, David - ***Fengriffen*** [1971]	$1.25	$3.75	$7.50
74-729	Coffman, Virginia - ***The Devil's Virgin*** [1971]	$1.25	$3.75	$7.50
74-731	Tucker, Wilson - ***A Procession Of The Damned*** [1971]	$1.35	$4.00	$8.00
74-735	Ross, Clarissa - ***Glimpse Into Terror*** [1971] PBO.	$1.25	$3.75	$7.50
74-736	Moorcock, Michael - ***The Lord Of The Spiders*** [1971] Cover art by Behan.	$1.35	$4.00	$8.00
74-737	Creasey, John - ***The Toff Goes To market*** [1971]	$1.25	$3.75	$7.50
74-741	Lymington, John - ***Ten Million Years To Friday*** [1971] Cover art by Ron Walotsky.	$1.25	$3.75	$7.50
74-742	Anderson, Poul - ***The Corridors Of Time*** [1971] Cover art by Gene Szafran.	$1.25	$3.75	$7.50
74-743	Heyman, Evan Lee - ***Survive*** [1971]	$1.25	$3.75	$7.50
74-748	Johnston, William - ***The Priest's Wife*** [1971]	$1.25	$3.75	$7.50
74-750	Long, Frank Belknap - ***Survival World*** [1971] PBO. Cover art by Ken Kelly.	$1.35	$4.00	$8.00

		G	VG	F
74-754	Ross, Clarissa - ***Voice From The Grave*** [1971] PBO. Cover art by Elaine.	$1.25	$3.75	$7.50
74-755	Giles, Elizabeth - ***Children Of The Griffin*** [1971] PBO. Cover art by Ron Walotsky	$1.25	$3.75	$7.50
74-757	Creasey, John - ***The Beauty Queen Killer*** [1971]	$1.25	$3.75	$7.50
74-759	Creasey, John - ***The Sleep*** [1971]	$1.35	$4.00	$8.00
74-760	Granger, K. R. G. - ***Trail's End At 'Duke Town*** [1971]	$1.25	$3.75	$7.50
74-762	Corren, Grace - ***A Place On Dark Island*** [1971] PBO.	$1.25	$3.75	$7.50
74-763	Floren, Lee - ***Frontier Lawman*** [1971]	$1.25	$3.75	$7.50
74-766	Floren, Lee - ***The Last Gun*** [1971]	$1.25	$3.75	$7.50
74-767	Creasey, John - ***Death Of A Racehorse*** [1971]	$1.25	$3.75	$7.50
74-769	Wagner, Sharon - ***Circle Of Evil*** [1971] PBO.	$1.25	$3.75	$7.50
74-770	Ross, Clarissa - ***The Haunting Of Villa Gabriel*** [1971] PBO.	$1.25	$3.75	$7.50
74-772	Long, Lyda Belknap (Frank Belknap Long) - ***The Witch Tree*** [1971] PBO. Cover art by Jerome Podwil.	$1.35	$4.00	$8.00
74-774	Hogan, Robert J. - ***Night Riders' Moon*** [1971]	$1.25	$3.75	$7.50
74-776	Merwin, Jr., Sam - ***The Time Shifters*** [1971] PBO. Cover art by Oscar Liebman.	$1.35	$4.00	$8.00
74-778	Nolan, William Francis - ***Space For Hire*** [1971] PBO. Cover art by Gene Szafran.	$1.35	$4.00	$8.00
74-782	Fairman, Paul W. - ***The Doomsday Exhibit*** [1971]	$1.25	$3.75	$7.50
74-783	Gallagher, Richard - ***Murder By Gemini*** [1971]	$1.25	$3.75	$7.50
74-786	Heckelmann, Charles N. - ***Stranger From Durango*** [1971] PBO. Cover art by Cassler.	$1.25	$3.75	$7.50
74-788	Kendrick, Baynard - ***Blind Man's Bluff*** [1971]	$1.25	$3.75	$7.50
74-793	Holmes, L. P. - ***Savage Guns*** [1971]	$1.25	$3.75	$7.50
74-795	Fairman, Paul - ***Bridget Loves Bernie*** [1972] PBO.	$1.25	$3.75	$7.50
74-802	Friedman, Paul - ***Martyrs And Fighters*** [1962]	$1.25	$3.75	$7.50
74-803	Anthology - ***Selected Writings Of The Marquis de Sade*** [1962]	$1.25	$3.75	$7.50
74-804	Street, Robert - ***Modern Sex Techniques*** [1962]	$ .75	$2.50	$5.00
74-805	Ginzberg,,Ralph - ***100 Years Of Lynchings*** [1962]	$1.25	$3.75	$7.50
74-806	Goudge, Elizabeth - ***Green Dolphin Street*** [1962] Cover art by Joe Polseno.	$1.25	$3.75	$7.50
74-807	Vance, Jack - ***The Dying Earth*** [1962] Cover art by Emsh.	$1.35	$4.00	$8.00
74-808	Weinbaum, Stanley - ***A Martian Odyssey*** [1962] Cover art by Schulz.	$1.35	$4.00	$8.00
74-809	Simmons, Matty - ***The Diners' Club Drink Book*** [1962]	$1.25	$3.75	$7.50
74-810	Silverberg, Robert - ***Recalled To Life*** [1962] PBO. Cover art by Emsh.	$1.35	$4.00	$8.00
74-811	Christopher, John - ***The Twenty-Second Century*** [1962] PBO. Cover art by Emsh.	$1.35	$4.00	$8.00
74-812	Williamson, Jack - ***The Humanoids*** [1963] Cover art by Emsh.	$1.35	$4.00	$8.00
74-813	Morse, MD, Benjamin - ***The Sexual Deviate*** [1963]	$ .75	$2.50	$5.00
74-814	edited by Donald Day - ***The Autobiography Of Will Rogers*** [1963]	$1.25	$3.75	$7.50
74-815	Asimov, Isaac - ***The Stars Like Dust*** [1963] Cover art by Emsh.	$1.25	$3.75	$7.50
74-816	Asimov, Isaac - ***The Currents Of Space*** [1963] Cover art by Emsh.	$1.25	$3.75	$7.50
74-817	Morse, MD, Benjamin - ***A Modern Marriage Manuel*** [1963]	$1.25	$3.75	$7.50
74-818	Asimov, Isaac - ***The End Of Eternity*** [1963] Cover art by Emsh.	$1.25	$3.75	$7.50
74-819	Russell, Eric Frank - ***Dreadful Sanctuary*** [1963] Cover art by Emsh.	$1.25	$3.75	$7.50
74-820	St. Denise, Claude - ***Combat Judo Made Easy*** [1963] PBO.	$1.25	$3.75	$7.50
74-821	Woodward, MD, L.T. (Robert Silverberg) - ***Twilight Women*** [1963] PBO.	$1.25	$3.75	$7.50
74-822	Morse, MD, Benjamin - ***Sexual Behavior Of The American College Girl*** [1963] PBO.	$1.00	$3.00	$6.00
74-823	Klaf, MD, Franklin & Hurwood, Bernhardt - ***Nymphomania: A Psychiatrist's View*** [1963]	$1.00	$3.00	$6.00
74-826	Cleland, John - ***Memoirs Of A Coxcomb*** [1964]	$1.25	$3.75	$7.50

		G	VG	F
74-827	Curran, Robert - ***The Kennedy Women*** [1964] PBO.	$1.00	$3.00	$6.00
74-828	Collyer, Martin - ***Burlesque*** [1964] PBO. Cover art by Oscar Liebman.	$1.25	$3.75	$7.50
74-829	British Committee Report - ***The Wolfenden Report*** [1964]	$1.00	$3.00	$6.00
74-831	Sharon, Sylvia - ***From Torment To Rapture*** [1964]	$1.25	$3.75	$7.50
74-832	Kessel, Joseph - ***The Medici Fountain*** [1964]	$1.25	$3.75	$7.50
74-833	Sprague, W. D. - ***Patterns Of Adultery*** [1964]	$1.00	$3.00	$6.00
74-834	Norris, Frank - ***Tower In The West*** [1964]	$1.25	$3.75	$7.50
74-835	Woodward, L. T. (Robert Silverberg) - ***Sadism*** [1964]	$1.25	$3.75	$7.50
74-836	Weiss, Joe - ***Another Way Of Love*** [1964]	$1.00	$3.00	$6.00
74-837	Maund, Alfred - ***Blood Of A Lion*** [1964] Cover art by Siegel.	$1.25	$3.75	$7.50
74-838	Weinstein, MD, Alfred A. - ***The Scalpel's Edge*** [1964]	$1.00	$3.00	$6.00
74-839	Holiday, Billie - ***Lady Sings The Blues*** [1964]	$1.25	$3.75	$7.50
74-840	Mirbeau, Octave - ***Torture Garden*** [1965] Cover art by Frazetta.	$4.00	$12.50	$25.00
74-841	Kenton, Maxwell - ***Candy*** [1965]	$1.25	$3.75	$7.50
74-842	Paul, Hugo - ***The Procurer*** [1965] PBO.	$1.25	$3.75	$7.50
74-843	Sharon, Sylvia - ***Punishment For Passion*** [1965] PBO.	$1.25	$3.75	$7.50
74-844	Auchincloss, Louis - ***Pursuit Of The Prodigal*** [1965]	$1.25	$3.75	$7.50
74-845	Whitmore, Linda - ***Another Woman's Bed*** [1965] PBO.	$1.00	$3.00	$6.00
74-846	M de F - ***The Gay Year*** [1965]	$1.00	$3.00	$6.00
74-848	Whitmore, Linda - ***The Golden Nymph*** [1965] PBO.	$1.25	$3.75	$7.50
74-850	De Sade, Marquis - ***Bedroom Philosophers*** [1966] Cover art by D. B.	$1.00	$3.00	$6.00
74-851	Gilbert, Edwin - ***The Hourglass*** [1966] Cover art by Marchetti.	$1.25	$3.75	$7.50
74-852	Burgess, Preston - ***Confessions Of A Married Man*** [1966] PBO.	$1.00	$3.00	$6.00
74-854	Bronte, Anne - ***The Tenant Of Wildfell Hall*** [1966] Cover art by Lou Marchetti.	$1.25	$3.75	$7.50
74-855	Ferber, Edna - ***A Peculiar Treasure*** [1966]	$1.25	$3.75	$7.50
74-859	Bernard, William & Leopold - ***Test Yourself*** [1966]	$1.25	$3.75	$7.50
74-860	Davis, Bette - ***The Lonely Life*** [1966]	$1.25	$3.75	$7.50
74-863	Ferber, Edna - ***A Kind Of Magic*** [1966]	$1.25	$3.75	$7.50
74-864	Mandel, George - ***The Breakwater*** [1966]	$1.25	$3.75	$7.50
74-865	Klaf, Franklin S. - ***Satyriasis*** [1966]	$1.25	$3.75	$7.50
74-866	Farrow, E. Pickworth - ***Psychoanalyze Yourself*** [1967]	$ .75	$2.50	$5.00
74-868	Whitehead, Jane - ***The House On The Hill*** [1967] PBO. Cover art by Jerone Podwil.	$1.25	$3.75	$7.50
74-870	Michaels, Rand - ***Women Of The Green Berets*** [1967] PBO.	$1.25	$3.75	$7.50
74-872	Rogers, Samuel - ***Don't Look Behind You!*** [1967] Cover art by Armand Weston.	$1.25	$3.75	$7.50
74-873	Foley, Rae - ***Suffer A Witch*** [1967]	$1.25	$3.75	$7.50
74-874	Segal, Julius & Luce, Gay Gaer - ***Sleep*** [1967]	$1.25	$3.75	$7.50
74-876	Shiff, Nathan A. - ***Ambulance Call*** [1967]	$1.00	$3.00	$6.00
74-877	Gordon, Jane - ***Season Of Evil*** [1967]	$1.25	$3.75	$7.50
74-878	Root, Pat - ***The Devil Of The Stairs*** [1967]	$1.25	$3.75	$7.50
74-879	Daniels, Dorothy - ***The Templeton Memoirs*** [1967]	$1.25	$3.75	$7.50
74-880	Minton, Paula - ***Secret Melody*** [1967]	$1.25	$3.75	$7.50
74-881	Milton, Joseph - ***The Running Spy*** [1967]	$1.25	$3.75	$7.50
74-882	Minton, Paula - ***Fog Hides The Fury*** [1967]	$1.25	$3.75	$7.50
74-884	Shute, Nevil - ***Kindling*** [1967]	$1.25	$3.75	$7.50
74-885	Auchincloss, Louis - ***Sybil*** [1967]	$1.25	$3.75	$7.50
74-886	Boyce, Burke - ***Cloak Of Folly*** [1967]	$1.25	$3.75	$7.50
74-887	Shulman, Irving - ***Upbeat*** [1967]	$1.25	$3.75	$7.50
74-888	Keyes, Frances Parkinson - ***The Career Of David Noble*** [1967]	$1.25	$3.75	$7.50
74-889	Maugham, W. Somerset - ***Catalina*** [1967]	$1.25	$3.75	$7.50
74-890	Millar, Margaret - ***Rose's Last Summer*** [1967]	$1.25	$3.75	$7.50
74-891	Eaton, Evelyn - ***Restless Are The Sails*** [1967]	$1.25	$3.75	$7.50
74-892	Lupoff, Richard Allen - ***One Million Centuries*** [1967] PBO. Cover art by Jack Gaughan.	$1.35	$4.00	$8.00
74-893	Calin, Anne - ***Decision At Dawn*** [1967] PBO. Cover art by Jack Faragasso.	$1.25	$3.75	$7.50

		G	VG	F
74-897	Brown, Wenzell - ***The Kept Woman*** [1967] PBO.	$1.50	$5.00	$10.00
74-898	Shute, Nevil - ***Landfall*** [1967]	$1.25	$3.75	$7.50
74-899	Haggard, H. Rider - ***The Return Of She: Ayesha*** [1967]	$1.35	$4.00	$8.00
74-901	Hassel, Sven - ***Wheels Of Terror*** [1967]	$1.35	$4.00	$8.00
74-902	Behan, Brendan - ***Confessions Of An Irish Rebel*** [1967] Cover art by Oscar Liebman.	$1.25	$3.75	$7.50
74-907	Coffman, Virginia - ***Castle At Witches' Coven*** [1967]	$1.25	$3.75	$7.50
74-910	Faust, Frederick (Max Brand) - ***The Naked Blade*** [1967] Cover art by George Gross.	$1.25	$3.75	$7.50
74-911	Pratt, Fletcher - ***The Well Of The Unicorn*** [1967] Cover art by Steele Savage.	$1.25	$3.75	$7.50
74-913	Isherwood, Christopher - ***A Single Man*** [1967]	$1.25	$3.75	$7.50
74-916	Whitney, Phyllis A. - ***The Moonflower*** [1967]	$1.25	$3.75	$7.50
74-921	Gilbert, Michael - ***Death In Captivity*** [1968]	$1.25	$3.75	$7.50
74-922	Gilbert, Michael - ***They Never Looked Inside*** [1968]	$1.25	$3.75	$7.50
74-923	Shute, Nevil - ***Ordeal*** [1968]	$1.25	$3.75	$7.50
74-925	Auchincloss, Louis - ***Pursuit Of The Prodigal*** [1968]	$1.25	$3.75	$7.50
74-927	Kops, Bernard - ***The Dissent Of Dominick Shapird*** [1968]	$1.25	$3.75	$7.50
74-932	Ollestad, Norman - ***Inside The F.B.I.*** [1968]	$1.25	$3.75	$7.50
74-936	Smith, George O. - ***The Brain Machine*** [1968] Cover art by Kelly Freas.	$1.35	$4.00	$8.00
74-938	Daniels, dorothy - ***Nurse At Danger Mansion*** [1968]	$ .75	$2.50	$5.00
74-941	Williams, Robert Moore - ***Zanthar At The Edge Of Never*** [1968] PBO. Cover art by Emsh.	$1.35	$4.00	$8.00
74-944	Shaw, ED., Larry - ***Great Science Fiction Adventures*** [1968] Cover art by Emsh.	$1.35	$4.00	$8.00
74-949	McLaughlin, Dean - ***The Man Who Wanted Stars*** [1968] Cover art by Kelly Freas.	$1.35	$4.00	$8.00
74-952	Steiger, Brad - ***In My Soul I Am Free*** [1968]	$1.25	$3.75	$7.50
74-953	Anthology edited by Han Stefan Santesson - ***Flying Saucers In Fact And Fiction*** [1968] PBO.	$1.00	$3.00	$6.00
74-956	Ald, Roy - ***The Case For An Afterlife*** [1968] PBO.	$1.00	$3.00	$6.00
74-958	Anthology - ***Conan*** [1968] Cover art by Frank Frazetta.	$1.35	$4.00	$8.00
74-960	Cameron, Lou - ***The Good Guy*** [1968] PBO. Cover art by John Duillo.	$1.25	$3.75	$7.50
74-961	Winkler, Max - ***A Penny From Heaven*** [1968] Cover art by Weston.	$1.25	$3.75	$7.50
74-962	Sprague, W. D. - ***Sex And The Secretary*** [1968]	$ .75	$2.50	$5.00
74-963	Anthology - ***Conan The Freebooter*** [1968] PBO. Cover art by John Duillo.	$1.35	$4.00	$8.00
74-966	Millar, Margaret - ***An Air That Kills*** [1968]	$1.25	$3.75	$7.50
74-967	Morgan, Jason - ***Death Is A Swinger*** [1968] PBO.	$1.25	$3.75	$7.50
74-969	Millar, Margaret - ***Wall Of Eyes*** [1968]	$1.25	$3.75	$7.50
74-973	Coffman, Virginia - ***The Rest Is Silence*** [1968]	$1.25	$3.75	$7.50
74-974	Coffman, Virginia - ***The Shadow Box*** [1968]	$1.25	$3.75	$7.50
74-976	Anthology - ***Conan The Wanderer*** [1968] PBO. Cover art by John Duillo.	$1.25	$3.75	$7.50
74-977	Maybury, Anne - ***The Moonlit Door*** [1968]	$1.25	$3.75	$7.50
74-982	Daniels, Dorothy - ***Dance In Darkness*** [1968]	$1.25	$3.75	$7.50
74-985	Carpozi, George - ***Jackie & Ari - For Love Or Money?*** [1968] PBO.	$1.00	$3.00	$6.00
74-986	Asimov, Isaac - ***The Naked Sun*** [1969] Cover art by Kelly Freas.	$1.25	$3.75	$7.50
74-988	Sanders, Joan - ***The Nature Of Witches*** [1969] Cover art by Jerome Podwil.	$1.25	$3.75	$7.50
74-992	Marchant, Catherine - ***The Mists Of Memory*** [1969]	$1.25	$3.75	$7.50
74-994	Greenfield, Irving A. - ***The Others*** [1969] PBO.	$1.25	$3.75	$7.50
74-999	Mather, Anne - ***Enchanted Island*** [1969]	$1.25	$3.75	$7.50

Lancer 75 Series.

		G	VG	F
75-001	Anthology - ***Kama Sutra Of Vatsyayana*** [1964]	$1.00	$3.00	$6.00
75-002	Nefzaoui, Sheikh - ***The Perfumed Garden*** [1964]	$1.00	$3.00	$6.00
75-003	DeSade, Marquis - ***Justine*** [1964]	$1.00	$3.00	$6.00
75-004	Anthology edited by Robert Silverberg - ***The Ananga Ranga Of Kalyana Malla*** [1964]	$1.00	$3.00	$6.00
75-005	DeSade, Marquis - ***Juliette*** [1965]	$1.00	$3.00	$6.00
75-006	St. Denise, Claude - ***The Power Of Akido*** [1965] PBO.	$1.00	$3.00	$6.00
75-007	Edwards, Allen - ***The Jewel In The Lotus*** [1965]	$1.00	$3.00	$6.00
75-008	Lundin, PhD., John Philip - ***Women*** [1965]	$1.00	$3.00	$6.00
75-009	Nabokov, Vladimir - ***Pale Fire*** [1965]	$1.00	$3.00	$6.00
75-010	Karpman, MD, Benjamin - ***The Alcoholic Woman*** [1966]	$1.00	$3.00	$6.00
75-014	Barrett, Gloria - ***Men*** [1967] PBO.	$1.00	$3.00	$6.00
75-016	Edwardes, Allen - ***The Jewell In The Lotus*** [1967]	$1.00	$3.00	$6.00
75-017	Nefzaoui, Sheikh - ***The Perfumed Garden*** [1967]	$1.00	$3.00	$6.00
75-019	Woodward, MD, L.T. (Robert Silverberg) - ***Sophisticated Sex Techniques In Marriage*** [1967] PBO.	$1.25	$3.75	$7.50
75-020	Quayne, Jonathan - ***The Jasper Gate*** [1967]	$1.00	$3.00	$6.00
75-022	Eaton, Evelyn - ***The Sea Is So Wide*** [1967]	$1.00	$3.00	$6.00
75-025	Lundin, MD, John Philip - ***Mistresses*** [1967]	$1.00	$3.00	$6.00
75-026	Brown, Wenzell - ***The Promiscuous Woman*** [1967]	$1.25	$3.75	$7.50
75-028	Bentley, Patricia - ***Groovy Chick!*** [1967] PBO.	$1.00	$3.00	$6.00
75-029	Wells, John Warren - ***Eros And Capricorn*** [1968] PBO.	$1.00	$3.00	$6.00
75-031	Bristoe, A. L. - ***The Bedroom Game*** [1968] PBO.	$1.00	$3.00	$6.00
75-034	Rone, Moja - ***Super Karate Made Easy*** [1968]	$1.00	$3.00	$6.00
75-035	London, MD, Louis - ***Sexual Deviations In The Female*** [1968]	$1.00	$3.00	$6.00
75-038	Jeabrook, William - ***The Magic Island*** [1968]	$1.00	$3.00	$6.00
75-040	Street, Robert - ***Modern Sex Techniques*** [1968]	$1.00	$3.00	$6.00
75-042	Bernstein, Morey - ***The Search For Bridey Murphy*** [1968]	$1.00	$3.00	$6.00
75-045	DeCamp, L. Sprague - ***The Dragon Of The Ishtar Gate*** [1968] Cover art by Roy Krenkel.	$1.35	$4.00	$8.00
75-046	Moody, Alexander - ***The Gay World*** [1968]	$1.00	$3.00	$6.00
75-047	Gant, Norman - ***Chane*** [1968] PBO. Cover art by Stivers.	$1.00	$3.00	$6.00
75-050	Gainham, Sarah - ***Night Falls On The City*** [1968] Cover art by Peter Caras.	$1.00	$3.00	$6.00
75-059	Woodward, L. T. (Robert Silverberg) - ***Sex And The Divorced Woman*** [1968]	$1.25	$3.75	$7.50
75-067	McKee, Alexander - ***Strike From The Sky*** [1969]	$1.00	$3.00	$6.00
75-069	Twitchell, Paul - ***The Tigers Fang*** [1969]	$1.00	$3.00	$6.00
75-072	Howard, DeCamp & Carter - ***Conan Of Cimmeria*** [1969] PBO. Cover art by Frank Frazetta.	$1.35	$4.00	$8.00
75-073	Tralins, Robert - ***Children Of The Supernatural*** [1969] PBO.	$1.00	$3.00	$6.00
75-077	Puzo, Mario - ***The Fortunate Pilgram*** [1969]	$1.00	$3.00	$6.00
75-080	Christopher, John - ***Pendulum*** [1969] Cover art by Stivers.	$1.00	$3.00	$6.00
75-085	Hurwood, Bernhardt - ***The Monstrous Undead*** [1969]	$1.50	$5.00	$10.00
75-091	MacIver, Joyce - ***The Frog Pond*** [1969]	$1.00	$3.00	$6.00
75-095	Jason, Stuart - ***Black Hercules*** [1969] PBO.	$1.35	$4.00	$8.00
75-100	Jason, Stuart - ***Black Love*** [1969]	$1.35	$4.00	$8.00
75-102	Howard & DeCamp - ***Conan The Adventurer*** [1970] Cover art by Frank Frazetta.	$1.35	$4.00	$8.00
75-103	Howard & DeCamp - ***Conan The Usurper*** [1970] Cover art by Frank Frazetta.	$1.35	$4.00	$8.00
75-104	Howard, DeCamp & Carter - ***Conan*** [1970] Cover art by Frank Frazetta.	$1.35	$4.00	$8.00
75-105	Calin, Harold - ***Black Hell*** [1970] PBO.	$1.35	$4.00	$8.00
75-108	Anthology edited by Bob Hoskins - ***Infinity One*** [1970] PBO. Cover art by Jim Steranko.	$2.00	$6.00	$12.00
75-111	Jason, Stuart - ***Black Lord*** [1970]	$1.35	$4.00	$8.00
75-113	Jakes, John - ***Master Of The Dark Gate*** [1970] PBO. Cover art by Jim Steranko.	$1.35	$4.00	$8.00

		G	VG	F
75-116	Tralins, Robert - ***Panther John*** [1970] PBO. Cover art by Stivers.	$1.35	$4.00	$8.00
75-119	Howard & DeCamp - ***Conan The Freebooter*** [1970] Cover art by John Duillo.	$1.35	$4.00	$8.00
75-122	Ollestad, Norman - ***Inside The F.B.I.*** [1970]	$1.00	$3.00	$6.00
75-123	Gladson, Leslie - ***The Abolitionist*** [1970]	$1.00	$3.00	$6.00
75-124	Scott, Robert J. - ***Black Drums*** [1970]	$1.35	$4.00	$8.00
75-128	Clement, Hal - ***Iceworld*** [1970] Cover art by Jim Steranko.	$1.50	$5.00	$10.00
75-133	Barrett, Jr., Neal - ***Kelwin*** [1970] PBO. Cover art by Jim Steranko.	$1.50	$5.00	$10.00
75-135	Vaughan, Robert - ***Mistress Of The Lash*** [1970]	$1.00	$3.00	$6.00
75-136	Howard, Carter & DeCamp - ***Conan Of The Isles*** [1970] Cover art by John Duillo.	$1.35	$4.00	$8.00
75-137	Howard & DeCamp - ***Conan The Conqueror*** [1970] Cover art by Frank Frazetta.	$1.35	$4.00	$8.00
75-142	Gilbert, Stephen - ***Ratman's Notebooks*** [1970]	$2.50	$7.50	$15.00
75-144	Denham, Alice - ***Coming Together*** [1970]	$1.00	$3.00	$6.00
75-146	Jason, Stuart - ***Black Master*** [1970]	$1.35	$4.00	$8.00
75-148	Howard & DeCamp - ***Conan The Warrior*** [1970] Cover art by Frank Frazetta.	$1.35	$4.00	$8.00
75-149	Howard, Nyberg & DeCamp - ***Conan The Avenger*** [1970] Cover art by Frank Frazetta.	$1.35	$4.00	$8.00
75-151	Lowenstein, Ralph Lynn - ***A Time Of War*** [1970]	$1.00	$3.00	$6.00
75-154	Gladson, Leslie - ***The Wastrels*** [1970] PBO. Cover art by Harry Schaare.	$1.00	$3.00	$6.00
75-157	Hall, Gramm - ***Machismo*** [1970]	$1.00	$3.00	$6.00
75-159	Lowen, MD, Alexander - ***Pleasure*** [1970]	$1.00	$3.00	$6.00
75-165	Jason, Stuart - ***Black Emperor*** [1971] PBO. Cover art by Frazetta.	$6.00	$20.00	$40.00
75-166	Anthology edited by Robert Hoskins - ***Infinity Two*** [1971] PBO. Cover art by Jim Steranko.	$2.00	$6.00	$12.00
75-172	Clarke, Arthur C. - ***Prelude To Space*** [1971]	$1.25	$3.75	$7.50
75-173	McNeill, Don - ***Moving Through Here*** [1971]	$1.00	$3.00	$6.00
75-174	Cameron, Lou - ***The Mud War*** [1971]	$1.00	$3.00	$6.00
75-176	Berger, Phil - ***Miracle On 33rd Street*** [1971]	$1.00	$3.00	$6.00
75-181	DeCamp & Carter - ***Conan The Buccaneer*** [1971] PBO. Cover art by Frazetta.	$1.35	$4.00	$8.00
75-185	Anderson, Poul - ***Tau Zero*** [1971]	$1.35	$4.00	$8.00
75-186	Coffman, Virginia - ***Masque Of Satan*** [1971] PBO.	$1.00	$3.00	$6.00
75-189	Gilbert, Stephen - ***Willard*** [1971]	$1.35	$4.00	$8.00
75-199	Moorcock, Michael - ***The Masters Of The Pit*** [1971] Cover art by Jim Steranko.	$1.35	$4.00	$8.00
75-204	Cooper, Edmund - ***Transit*** [1971] Cover art by Douglas Rosa.	$1.35	$4.00	$8.00
75-205	Mark, Ted - ***The Nude Who Never*** [1971]	$1.00	$3.00	$6.00
75-207	Mark, Ted - ***Dr. Nyet*** [1971]	$1.00	$3.00	$6.00
75-211	Mark, Ted - ***The Real Gone Girls*** [1971]	$1.00	$3.00	$6.00
75-215	Creasey, John - ***The Toff And The Golden Boy*** [1971]	$1.00	$3.00	$6.00
75-217	Mason, David - ***The Shores Of Tomorrow*** [1971] PBO. Cover art by Jim Steranko.	$1.00	$3.00	$6.00
75-219	Fletcher, Dorothy - ***The Music Master*** [1971] PBO.	$1.00	$3.00	$6.00
75-223	Creasey, John - ***Murder Makes Haste*** [1971]	$1.00	$3.00	$6.00
75-237	Creasey, John - ***The Touch Of Death*** [1971]	$1.00	$3.00	$6.00
75-239	? - ***The Ghost Dancers*** [1971] Cover art by Charles Moll.	$1.00	$3.00	$6.00
75-240	O'Brien, Edna - ***X Y & Zee*** [1971]	$1.00	$3.00	$6.00
75-247	Lovecraft, H. P. - ***The Dunwich Horror*** [1971] Cover art by Howard Winters.	$1.35	$4.00	$8.00
75-248	Lovecraft, Howard Phillips - ***The Colour Out Of Space & Others*** [1971] Cover art by Howard Winters.	$1.35	$4.00	$8.00
75-250	Talmage, Anne - ***Dark Over Acadia*** [1971] PBO. Cover art by Charles Lilly.	$1.00	$3.00	$6.00

		G	VG	F
75-252	White, Ted - ***Star Wolf!*** [1971] PBO. Cover art by Charles Moll.	$1.35	$4.00	$8.00
75-255	Fletcher, Dorothy - ***The Late Contessa*** [1971] PBO.	$1.00	$3.00	$6.00
75-259	Devaney, John - ***The Champion Bucks*** [1971]	$1.00	$3.00	$6.00
75-260	Gallagher, Richard - ***The Stewardess Strangler*** [1971]	$1.00	$3.00	$6.00
75-262	Daniels, Norman - ***The Deadly Ride*** [1971]	$1.00	$3.00	$6.00
75-264	Creasey, John - ***The Toff And The Fallen Angels*** [1971]	$1.00	$3.00	$6.00
75-265	Howard, R. E. - ***The Dark Man And Others*** [1972] Cover art by Victor Valla.	$1.35	$4.00	$8.00
75-277	Queen, Ellery (Edward D. Hoch) - ***The Blue Movie Murders*** [1972]	$1.25	$3.75	$7.50
75-278	Brown, Rosel George - ***The Waters Of Centaurus*** [1972] Cover art by Gene Szafran.	$1.00	$3.00	$6.00
75-286	Reed, Harry - ***A Piece Of Something Big*** [1972] PBO. Cover art by Hypo.	$1.00	$3.00	$6.00
75-287	Kendrick, Baynard - ***Out Of Control*** [1972]	$1.00	$3.00	$6.00
75-288	Creasey, John - ***Death Of An Assassin*** [1971]	$1.00	$3.00	$6.00
75-290	Tucker, Wilson - ***The Time Masters*** [1971] Cover art by Gene Szafran.	$1.25	$3.75	$7.50
75-298	Deming, Richard - ***Vida*** [1972] PBO.	$1.00	$3.00	$6.00
75-299	Howard, R. E. - ***Wolfshead*** [1972] Cover art by Frank Frazetta.	$1.35	$4.00	$8.00
75-303	Madden, Mary Ann - ***Thank You For The Giant Tortoise*** [1972]	$1.00	$3.00	$6.00
75-305	Kendrick, Baynard - ***You Die Today!*** [1972]	$1.25	$3.75	$7.50
75-306	Koontz, Dean R. - ***Starblood*** [1972] PBO. Cover art by Charles Moll.	$4.00	$12.50	$25.00
75-314	O'Brien, Jim - ***ABA - All Stars*** [1972]	$1.00	$3.00	$6.00
75-315	Asimov, Isaac - ***A Whiff Of Death*** [1972]	$1.25	$3.75	$7.50
75-319	Anderson, Poul - ***Operation Chaos*** [1972] Cover art by Kelly Freas.	$1.25	$3.75	$7.50
75-320	Anthology edited by Robert Hoskins - ***Infinity Three*** [1972] PBO. Cover art by Jim Steranko.	$2.00	$6.00	$12.00
75-331	Creasey, John - ***A Score For The Toff*** [1972]	$1.00	$3.00	$6.00
75-333	Campbell, Jr., John Wood - ***Cloak Of Aesir*** [1972] Cover art by Ron Walotsky.	$1.35	$4.00	$8.00
75-335	Roberts, Willo Davis - ***Sing A Dark Song*** [1972] PBO. Cover art by John Duillo.	$1.00	$3.00	$6.00
75-342	Thompson, Jim - ***Child Of Rage*** [1972] PBO.	$32.00	$110.00	$250.00
75-345	Malzberg, Barry N. - ***Overlay*** [1972] PBO. Cover art by Ron Walotsky.	$1.35	$4.00	$8.00
75-346	Brunner, John - ***Into The Slave Nebula*** [1972] Cover art by Kelly Freas.	$1.35	$4.00	$8.00
75-354	Lyons, Delphine C. - ***House Of Four Windows*** [1972]	$1.00	$3.00	$6.00
75-355	Lyons, Delphine C. - ***The Depths Of Yesterday*** [1972]	$1.00	$3.00	$6.00
75-356	Fairman, Paul - ***Junior Bonner*** [1972]	$1.00	$3.00	$6.00
75-358	Lyons, Delphine C. - ***Valley Of Shadows*** [1972]	$1.00	$3.00	$6.00
75-359	Knight, Alanna - ***This Outward Angel*** [1972] PBO.	$1.00	$3.00	$6.00
75-361	Mason, David - ***The Return Of Kavin*** [1972] PBO. Cover art by Charles Moll.	$1.35	$4.00	$8.00
75-362	Williamson, Jack - ***The Humanoids*** [1972] Cover art by Adams.	$1.25	$3.75	$7.50
75-364	Russell, Charlotte - ***Dark Music*** [1972]	$1.00	$3.00	$6.00
75-365	Dwyer, Deanna - ***Children Of The Storm*** [1972]	$1.00	$3.00	$6.00
75-367	Wetherell, June - ***Her Stepfather's House*** [1972] PBO. Cover art by D. Fritz.	$1.00	$3.00	$6.00
75-371	Howard & Carter - ***King Kull*** [1972] Cover art by Roy Krenkel.	$1.35	$4.00	$8.00
75-372	Mason, David - ***Kavin's World*** [1972] Cover art by Frank Frazetta.	$1.35	$4.00	$8.00
75-373	Vance, Jack - ***The Dying Earth*** [1972] Cover art by Emsh.	$1.35	$4.00	$8.00
75-374	Anderson, Poul - ***Ensign Flandry*** [1972] Cover art by Josh Kirby.	$1.35	$4.00	$8.00

Lancer, 75-445

Lion Book, 45

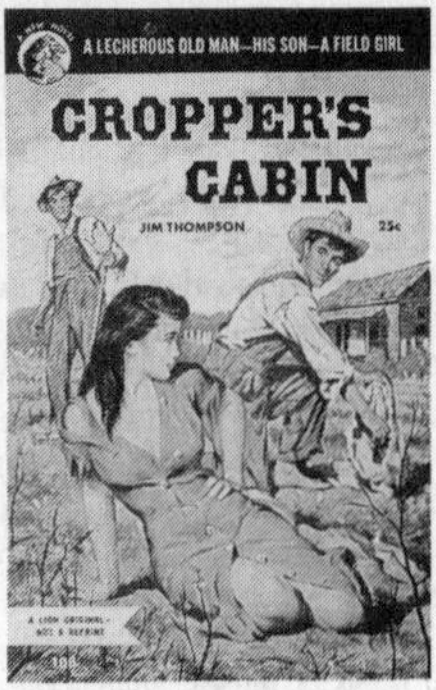

Lion Book, 108

		G	VG	F
75-375	Moorcock, Michael - ***The Sleeping Sorceress*** [1972] PBO. Cover art by Charles Moll.	$1.35	$4.00	$8.00
75-376	Moorcock, Michael - ***The Dreaming City*** [1972] PBO. Cover art by Charles Moll.	$1.35	$4.00	$8.00
75-379	Roberts, Willo Davis - ***Dangerous Legacy*** [1972]	$1.00	$3.00	$6.00
75-381	Scott, Marianne deJay - ***Drumbuie House*** [1972]	$1.00	$3.00	$6.00
75-383	Esposito, Phil & Tony - ***The Brothers Esposito*** [1972]	$1.00	$3.00	$6.00
75-384	Creasey, John - ***The Oasis*** [1972]	$1.00	$3.00	$6.00
75-385	Clement, Hal - ***Needle*** [1972] Cover art by Kelly Freas.	$1.25	$3.75	$7.50
75-386	Koonyz, Dean R. - ***Warlock*** [1972] PBO. Cover art by Armand Weston.	$4.00	$12.50	$25.00
75-387	Anthology edited by Robert Hoskins - ***Infinity Four*** [1972] PBO. Cover art by Ron Walotsky.	$2.00	$6.00	$12.00
75-388	Anderson, Poul - ***Santan's World*** [1972] Cover art by Nicholas.	$1.35	$4.00	$8.00
75-390	Coffman, Virginia - ***Night At Sea Abbey*** [1972]	$1.00	$3.00	$6.00
75-391	Du Brevil, Lorinda - ***The Secret*** [1972]	$1.00	$3.00	$6.00
75-392	Winston, Daoma - ***Seminar In Evil*** [1972]	$1.00	$3.00	$6.00
75-393	Dwyer, Deanna - ***The Dark Of Summer*** [1972]	$1.00	$3.00	$6.00
75-394	Foster, Iris - ***Deadly Sea, Deadly Sand*** [1972]	$1.00	$3.00	$6.00
75-397	Creasey, John - ***The Figure In The Dusk*** [1972]	$1.00	$3.00	$6.00
75-399	Weinbaum, Stanley G. - ***A Martian Odyssey*** [1972]	$1.25	$3.75	$7.50
75-401	Brennan, Alice - ***To Kill A Witch*** [1972]	$1.00	$3.00	$6.00
75-402	Corren, Grace - ***Evil In The Family*** [1972]	$1.00	$3.00	$6.00
75-403	Evans, Elaine - ***A Dark And Deadly Love*** [1972] PBO.	$1.00	$3.00	$6.00
75-404	Treibich, S. J. - ***Burwyck's Wander*** [1972]	$1.00	$3.00	$6.00
75-405	Roberts, Willo Davis - ***Sinister Gardens*** [1972]	$1.00	$3.00	$6.00
75-406	Harris, Merv - ***The Fabulous Lakers*** [1972] PBO.	$1.00	$3.00	$6.00
75-407	Kane, Henry - ***The Schack Job*** [1972]	$1.00	$3.00	$6.00
75-408	Kane, Henry - ***Don't Call Me Madame*** [1972]	$1.00	$3.00	$6.00
75-409	Kane, Henry - ***Don't Go Away Dead*** [1972]	$1.00	$3.00	$6.00
75-410	Kane, Henry - ***Come Kill With me*** [1972]	$1.00	$3.00	$6.00
75-411	Fairman, Paul W. - ***The Diabolist*** [1972]	$1.00	$3.00	$6.00
75-413	Kuttner, Henry - ***Fury*** [1972] Cover art by Larry Kresek.	$1.35	$4.00	$8.00
75-414	Russell, Eric Frank - ***The Mindwarpers*** [1972] Cover art by John Berkey.	$1.25	$3.75	$7.50
75-415	Jakes, John - ***Witch Of The Dark Gate*** [1962] PBO. Cover art by Frank Frazetta.	$1.35	$4.00	$8.00
75-417	Plum, Jennifer - ***The Secret Of Benjamin Square*** [1972]	$1.00	$3.00	$6.00
75-420	Goulart, Ron - ***Shaggy Planet*** [1973] PBO. Cover art by Mike Hinge.	$1.35	$4.00	$8.00

		G	VG	F
75-421	MacCapp, C. C. (Carol M. Capps) - ***Bumsider*** [1973] PBO. Cover art by Josh Kirby.	$1.35	$4.00	$8.00
75-422	Clement, Hal - ***Iceworld*** [1973] Cover art by Jim Steranko.	$1.35	$4.00	$8.00
75-428	Peart, Jane - ***Night Of The Darkest Moon*** [1973]	$1.00	$3.00	$6.00
75-429	Olden, Marc - ***Angela Davis*** [1973]	$1.00	$3.00	$6.00
75-431	Williamson, Jack - ***The Reign Of Wizardry*** [1973] Cover art by Frank Frazetta.	$1.35	$4.00	$8.00
75-432	McKanzie, Susan - ***Death Has Many Doors*** [1973]	$1.00	$3.00	$6.00
75-442	Stoker, Bram - ***Dracula*** [1973]	$1.35	$4.00	$8.00
75-443	Sugar, Andrew - ***The Enforcer*** [1973]	$1.00	$3.00	$6.00
75-445	Koontz, Dean R. - ***The Haunted Earth*** [1973] PBO. Cover art by Ron Walotsky.	$4.00	$12.50	$25.00
75-446	Runyon, Charles W. - ***Pig World*** [1973] Cover art by Ron Walotsky.	$1.35	$4.00	$8.00
75-447	Scott, Marianne de Jay - ***The Van Dyne Collection*** [1973] PBO.	$1.00	$3.00	$6.00
75-461	Sugar, Andrew - ***Calling Doctor Kill*** [1973]	$1.00	$3.00	$6.00
75-462	Cameron, Lou - ***The Girl With The Dynamite Bangs*** [1973] PBO.	$1.00	$3.00	$6.00
75-464	Kuttner, Henry - ***Robots Have No Tails*** [1973] Cover art by Ron Walotsky.	$2.00	$6.00	$12.00
75-465	Anthology edited by Vic Ghidaua - ***The Devil's Generation*** [1973] PBO. Cover art by Frank Frazetta.	$1.50	$5.00	$10.00
75-466	Fletcher, Dorothy - ***Farewell To Vienna*** [1973]	$ .75	$2.50	$5.00
75-467	Brennan, Alice - ***Fear No Evil*** [1973]	$1.00	$3.00	$6.00
75-468	Hale, Jennifer - ***The Secrets Of Devil's Cave*** [1973]	$1.00	$3.00	$6.00
75-469	Gray, Angela - ***Nightmare At Riverview*** [1973]	$1.00	$3.00	$6.00
75-470	Warren, Paulette - ***Brooding Mansion*** [1973]	$1.00	$3.00	$6.00
75-471	Leslie, Miriam - ***Cavanaugh Keep*** [1973]	$1.00	$3.00	$6.00
75-472	Stanton, Will - ***The Golden Evenings Of Summer*** [1973]	$1.00	$3.00	$6.00
75-473	Sugar, Andrew - ***Kill City*** [1973] PBO.	$1.00	$3.00	$6.00
75-474	Rubin, Bob - ***Football's Toughest Ten*** [1973] PBO.	$1.00	$3.00	$6.00
75-477	Anthology edited by Robert Hoskins - ***Infinity Five*** [1973] PBO. Cover art by Ron Walotsky.	$2.00	$6.00	$12.00
75-486	Malzberg, Barry N. - ***The Men Inside*** [1973] PBO. Cover art by Ron Walotsky.	$1.35	$4.00	$8.00
75-487	Fairman, Paul - ***"Coffy"*** [1973] PBO.	$1.00	$3.00	$6.00
75-525	Hunt, E. Howard - ***My Body*** [1973]	$1.00	$3.00	$6.00

Lancer 76 Series.

76-201	Marsh, Rebecca - ***Nurse Annette*** [1966]	$ .75	$2.50	$5.00
76-202	Craig, Georgia - ***Society Nurse*** [1966]	$ .75	$2.50	$5.00
76-302	Caprio, M.D., Frank S. - ***Variations In Love Making*** [1966]	$ .75	$2.50	$5.00
76-304	Masters. R. E. L. - ***Forbidden Sexual Behavior*** [1966]	$ .75	$2.50	$5.00

Lancer 78 Series.

78-686	Wylie, Philip - ***Gladiator*** [1973]	$1.00	$3.00	$6.00
78-761	Coffman, Virginia - ***From Satin With Love*** [1973]	$ .75	$2.50	$5.00

Lancer Miscellany.

71-344	Delany, Samuel R. - ***The Tides Of Lust*** [1973] PBO.	$17.00	$50.00	$100.00

Laser Books (Early Publisher's History, 1975–1980)

Harlequin Enterprises Limited established a separate science fiction line using the Laser Books imprint. Roger Elwood served as the general editor, and each volume received a Kelly Freas cover. They produced three numbered books each month, beginning August 1975 through February 1977. In addition, they offered a free premium volume to those responding to a questionnaire. They priced the first thirty-six volumes at 95¢, with the rest of the series at $1.25, and they altered the spine format at that time. A total of fifty-eight original volumes appeared. Collectible volumes include the final three volumes (55–57), which they distributed to subscribers only, the first novel publication of thirteen authors, and #9 by Aaron Wolfe (a pseudonym of Dean R. Koontz).

Laser Books. New York: Laser Books, Inc.

		G	VG	F
NN	Monteleone, Thomas F. - ***Seeds Of Change*** [1975] Cover by Kelly Freas.	$1.25	$3.75	$7.50
1	Jones, Raymond F. - ***Renegades Of Time*** [1975] PBO. Cover by Kelly Freas.	$1.25	$3.75	$7.50
2	Goldin, Stephen - ***Herds*** [1975] PBO. Cover by Kelly Freas.	$1.25	$3.75	$7.50
3	Tofte, Arthur - ***Crash Landing On Iduna*** [1975] PBO. Cover by Kelly Freas.	$1.25	$3.75	$7.50
4	Coulson, Robert & DeWeese, Gene - ***Gates Of The Universe*** [1975] PBO. Cover by Kelly Freas.	$1.25	$3.75	$7.50
5	Tofte, Arthur - ***Walls Within Walls*** [1975] PBO. Cover by Kelly Freas.	$1.25	$3.75	$7.50
6	Eklund, Gordon - ***Serving In Time*** [1975] PBO. Cover by Kelly Freas.	$1.25	$3.75	$7.50
7	Jeter, K. W. - ***Seeklight*** [1975] PBO. Cover by Kelly Freas.	$3.50	$10.00	$20.00
8	Goldin, Stephen - ***Caravan*** [1975] PBO. Cover by Kelly Freas.	$1.25	$3.75	$7.50
9	Wolfe, Aaron (Dean Koontz) - ***Invasion*** [1975] PBO. Cover by Kelly Freas.	$5.50	$17.50	$35.00
10	Eklund, Gordon - ***Falling Toward Forever*** [1975] PBO. Cover by Kelly Freas.	$1.25	$3.75	$7.50
11	Coulson, Juanita - ***Unto The Last Generation*** [1975] PBO. Cover by Kelly Freas.	$1.25	$3.75	$7.50
12	Jones, Raymond F. - ***The King Of Eolim*** [1975] PBO. Cover by Kelly Freas.	$1.25	$3.75	$7.50
13	Nelson, R. F. - ***Blake's Progress*** [1975] PBO. Cover by Kelly Freas.	$1.25	$3.75	$7.50
14	Sky, Kathleen - ***Birthright*** [1975] PBO. Cover by Kelly Freas.	$1.25	$3.75	$7.50
15	Zebrowski, George - ***The Star Web*** [1975] PBO. Cover by Kelly Freas.	$1.25	$3.75	$7.50
16	Clinton, Jeff - ***Kane's Odyssey*** [1976] PBO. Cover by Kelly Freas.	$1.25	$3.75	$7.50
17	Hensley, Joseph - ***The Black Roads*** [1976] PBO. Cover by Kelly Freas.	$1.25	$3.75	$7.50
18	Bone, J. F. - ***Legacy*** [1976] PBO. Cover by Kelly Freas.	$1.25	$3.75	$7.50
19	Malcolm, Donald - ***The Unknown Shore*** [1976] PBO. Cover by Kelly Freas.	$1.25	$3.75	$7.50
20	Coulson, Juanita - ***Space Trap*** [1976] PBO. Cover by Kelly Freas.	$1.25	$3.75	$7.50
21	Morressy, John - ***A Law For The Stars*** [1976] PBO. Cover by Kelly Freas.	$1.25	$3.75	$7.50
22	Holly, Joan Hunter - ***Keeper*** [1976] PBO. Cover by Kelly Freas.	$1.25	$3.75	$7.50
23	Pournelle, Jerry - ***Birth Of Fire*** [1976] PBO. Cover by Kelly Freas.	$1.25	$3.75	$7.50
24	McIntosh, J. T. - ***Ruler Of The World*** [1976] PBO. Cover by Kelly Freas.	$1.25	$3.75	$7.50
25	Goldin, Stephen - ***Scavenger Hunt*** [1976] PBO. Cover by Kelly Freas.	$1.25	$3.75	$7.50
26	Coulson, Robert - ***To Renew The Ages*** [1976] PBO. Cover by Kelly Freas.	$1.25	$3.75	$7.50
27	Green, Joseph - ***The Horde*** [1976] PBO. Cover by Kelly Freas.	$1.25	$3.75	$7.50
28	Powers, Timothy - ***The Skies Discrowned*** [1976] PBO. Cover by Kelly Freas.	$2.50	$7.50	$15.00

		G	VG	F
29	Malcolm, Donald - ***The Iron Rain*** [1976] PBO. Cover by Kelly Freas.	$1.25	$3.75	$7.50
30	Bischoff, David & Lampton, Christopher - ***The Seeker*** [1976] PBO. Cover by Kelly Freas	$1.25	$3.75	$7.50
31	Berry, James R. - ***The Galactic Invaders*** [1976] PBO. Cover by Kelly Freas.	$1.25	$3.75	$7.50
32	Nelson, R. F. - ***Then Beggars Could Ride*** [1976] PBO. Cover by Kelly Freas	$1.25	$3.75	$7.50
33	Jeter, K. W. - ***The Dreamfields*** [1976] PBO. Cover by Kelly Freas.	$3.50	$10.00	$20.00
34	Carver, Jeffrey - ***Seas Of Ernathe*** [1976] PBO. Cover by Kelly Freas.	$1.25	$3.75	$7.50
35	Sohl, Jerry - ***I, Aleppo*** [1976] PBO. Cover by Kelly Freas.	$1.25	$3.75	$7.50
36	DeWesse, Gene - ***Jeremy Case*** [1976] PBO. Cover by Kelly Freas.	$1.25	$3.75	$7.50
37	Bone, J. F. - ***The Meddlers*** [1976] PBO. Cover by Kelly Freas.	$1.25	$3.75	$7.50
38	Sky, Kathleen - ***Ice Prison*** [1976] PBO. Cover by Kelly Freas.	$1.25	$3.75	$7.50
39	Funnell, Augustine - ***Brandyjack*** [1976] PBO. Cover by Kelly Freas.	$1.25	$3.75	$7.50
40	Hoskins, Robert - ***Master Of The Stars*** [1976] PBO. Cover by Kelly Freas.	$1.25	$3.75	$7.50
41	Harding, Lee - ***Future Sanctuary*** [1976] PBO. Cover by Kelly Freas.	$1.25	$3.75	$7.50
42	Lampton, Christopher - ***Cross Of Empire*** [1976] PBO. Cover by Kelly Freas	$1.25	$3.75	$7.50
43	Glut, Donald F. - ***Spawn*** [1976] PBO. Cover by Kelly Freas.	$1.25	$3.75	$7.50
44	Anthony, Piers & Coulson, Robert - ***But What Of Earth?*** [1976] PBO. Cover by Kelly Freas	$1.25	$3.75	$7.50
45	Golden, Stephen - ***Finish Line*** [1976] PBO. Cover by Kelly Freas.	$1.25	$3.75	$7.50
46	Eklund, Gordon - ***Dance Of The Apocalypse*** [1976] PBO. Cover by Kelly Freas	$1.25	$3.75	$7.50
47	Powers, Timothy - ***Epitaph In Rust*** [1976] PBO. Cover by Kelly Freas.	$2.50	$7.50	$15.00
48	Funnell, Augustine - ***Rebels Of Merka*** [1976] PBO. Cover by Kelly Freas.	$1.25	$3.75	$7.50
49	Hughes, Zack - ***Tiger In The Stars*** [1976] PBO. Cover by Kelly Freas.	$1.25	$3.75	$7.50
50	Pournelle, Jerry - ***West Of Honor*** [1976] PBO. Cover by Kelly Freas.	$1.25	$3.75	$7.50
51	Hahn, Steve - ***Mindwipe!*** [1976] PBO. Cover by Kelly Freas.	$1.25	$3.75	$7.50
52	Morressey, John - ***The Extraterritorial*** [1977] PBO. Cover by Kelly Freas.	$1.25	$3.75	$7.50
53	Nelson, R. Faraday - ***The Ecolog*** [1977] PBO. Cover by Kelly Freas.	$1.25	$3.75	$7.50
54	Jones, Raymond F. - ***The River And The Dream*** [1977] PBO. Cover by Kelly Freas	$1.25	$3.75	$7.50
55	Holly, Joan Hunter - ***Shepherd*** [1977] PBO. Cover by Kelly Freas.	$10.00	$30.00	$60.00
56	Bone, J. F. & Myers, R. - ***Gift Of The Manti*** [1977] PBO. Cover by Kelly Freas	$10.00	$30.00	$60.00
57	Marcus, Jr., Robert B. - ***Shadow On The Stars*** [1977] PBO. Cover by Kelly Freas	$10.00	$30.00	$60.00

Leisure Book.

1106	Dexter, John - ***The Sinners Of Hwang*** [1965] PBO.	$4.00	$12.50	$25.00
1140	Allison, Clyde - ***0008 Meets Gnatman*** [1966] PBO. Agent 0008.	$4.00	$12.50	$25.00
1152	- - ***The Sin Veldt*** [1966]	$4.00	$12.50	$25.00
1159	Allison, Clyde - ***The Merciless Mermaids*** [1966] PBO. Agent 0008.	$4.00	$12.50	$25.00

		G	VG	F
1160	- - ***Mondo Sadisto*** [1966]	$4.00	$12.50	$25.00
1169	Allison, Clyde - ***0008 Meets Modesta Blaze*** [1966]	$4.00	$12.50	$25.00
1174	Allison, Clyde - ***The Sex-Ray*** [1966] PBO. Agent 0008.	$4.00	$12.50	$25.00
1175	Dexter, John - ***Carnaby Consort*** [1966] PBO.	$4.00	$12.50	$25.00
1176	Allison, Clyde - ***Roberta The Conqueress*** [1966] PBO. Agent 0008.	$4.00	$12.50	$25.00
1180	Allison, Clyde - ***From Rapture With Love*** [1966] PBO. Agent 0008.	$4.00	$12.50	$25.00
1195	Dexter, John - ***Plug-In Passion*** [1967] PBO.	$2.50	$7.50	$15.00
1206	James, Jordan (J. X. Williams) - ***Witch In Heat*** [1967] PBO.	$4.00	$12.50	$25.00
1207	Lynn, David - ***Zardoc, Warrior Stud*** [1967] PBO.	$4.00	$12.50	$25.00
1216	Larkin, Wolf - ***Sexmahlia*** [1967] PBO.	$4.50	$14.00	$28.00
1218	Williams, J. X. - ***Her*** [1967] PBO.	$5.00	$15.00	$30.00

Leisure Library. New York: Leisure Library, Inc. Digest size.

1	Morac, Jules-Jean - ***My Life Is My Own*** [1952]	$2.50	$7.50	$15.00
2	Morelli, Spike - ***Death For A Doll*** [1952] Cover by Heade.	$5.00	$15.00	$30.00
3	Vane, Roland - ***Pick-Up Girl*** [1952] Cover by Heade.	$5.00	$15.00	$30.00
4	Storme, Michael - ***Make Mine A Shroud*** [1952] Cover by Heade.	$5.00	$15.00	$30.00
5	Storme, Michael - ***Hot Dames On Cold Slabs*** [1952] Cover by Heade.	$5.00	$15.00	$30.00
6	Morac, Jules-Jean - ***No Prude*** [1952]	$2.50	$7.50	$15.00
7	Morelli, Spike - ***This Way For Hell*** [n.d.] Cover by Heade.	$5.00	$15.00	$30.00
8	Vane, Roland - ***White Slave Racket*** [1952] Cover by Heade.	$5.50	$17.50	$35.00
9	Ross, Gene - ***Two Smart Dames*** [1952] Cover by Heade.	$5.00	$15.00	$30.00
10	Renin, Paul - ***Midnight Sinner*** [1952] Cover by Heade.	$5.00	$15.00	$30.00
11	Storme, Michael - ***Curtains For Carla*** [1952] Cover by Heade.	$5.00	$15.00	$30.00
12	Morac, Jules-Jean - ***Bertrand And The Blondes*** [1952] Cover by Heade.	$5.00	$15.00	$30.00
13	Ross, Gene - ***Sorry For You, Beautiful*** [1952] Cover by Heade.	$5.50	$17.50	$35.00
14	Renin, Paul - ***Wedding Night*** [1952] Cover by Heade.	$5.00	$15.00	$30.00
15	Storme, Michael - ***Carmen Was A Virgin*** [1952] Cover by Heade.	$5.50	$17.50	$35.00
16	Vane, Roland - ***Amorous Adventuress*** [1952] Cover by Heade.	$5.00	$15.00	$30.00
17	Angelo, Tony - ***Honey, Hold That Scream*** [1952] Cover by Heade.	$5.00	$15.00	$30.00
18	Renin, Paul - ***She Who Hesitates*** [1952] Cover by Heade.	$5.00	$15.00	$30.00
19	Storme, Michael - ***A Corpse Spells Danger*** [1953]	$5.00	$15.00	$30.00
20	Brett, Rosalind - ***Pagan Interlude*** [1953]	$5.00	$15.00	$30.00
21	Ross, Gene - ***Curves Cause Trouble*** [1953] Cover by Heade.	$5.00	$15.00	$30.00
22	Renin, Paul - ***Thou Shalt Not!*** [1953] Cover by Heade.	$5.00	$15.00	$30.00
23	Storme, Michael - ***This Woman Is Death*** [1953] Cover by Heade.	$5.00	$15.00	$30.00
24	Clare, Mary - ***White Man's Slave*** [1953] Cover by Heade.	$5.50	$17.50	$35.00

Lev Gleason. Digest size.

101	Lyons, Ruth - ***Hotel Wife*** [n.d.]	$3.50	$10.00	$20.00
102	Saxon, John - ***Devil-May-Care Girl*** [n.d.]	$3.50	$10.00	$20.00
103	James, Griffith - ***The Wench Is Willing*** [1949]	$3.50	$10.00	$20.00
104	Stone, Thomas - ***Passion's Darling*** [n.d.]	$3.50	$10.00	$20.00
105	Knight, Doris - ***Scandal Girl*** [1950]	$3.50	$10.00	$20.00
106	Lee, Richard - ***Dishonorable Lady*** [1950]	$3.50	$10.00	$20.00
107	Hillis, Marjorie - ***Live Alone And Like It*** [1950]	$3.50	$10.00	$20.00

Lion Books (Early Publisher's History, 1949–1959)

Beginning as Red Circle Books, Martin Goodman founded this line of books. A banner of this line includes their exceptional covers. Artists like Robert Maguire,

Rudolph Belarski, and others did many of the covers. Many of the titles represent reprinted works. However, they commissioned works by a number of writers. Authors of interest include Jim Thompson, David Goodis, Robert Bloch, Richard Matheson, and C. M. Kornbluth's pseudonyms of Jordan Park and Simon Eisner.

They established a similar line called Lion Library. New American Library purchased Lion Books, Inc., in 1957 and produced a number of their titles under the Signet imprint.

		G	VG	F
Lion Books. New York: Lion Books, Inc.				
8	Anderson, Edward - ***Hungry Men*** [1949] Cover art by Harry Schaare.	$4.00	$12.50	$25.00
9	Lewisohn, Ludwig - ***Anniversary*** [1949]	$2.50	$7.50	$15.00
10	Dawson, Peter - ***Canyon Hell*** [1949] Cover art by Robert Stanley	$2.50	$7.50	$15.00
11	Morgan, Michael - ***The Blonde Body*** [1949] Cover art by Len Oehman.	$3.50	$10.00	$20.00
14	Jackson, Shirley - ***The Lottery*** [1950] Cover art by Herman Bischoff.	$5.50	$17.50	$35.00
15	Shelley, Peter - ***Soft Shoulders*** [1949] Cover art by Harry Schaare.	$3.50	$10.00	$20.00
16	Marsh, Peter - ***The Devil's Daughter*** [1949] Cover art by William Shoyer.	$2.50	$7.50	$15.00
17	Foster, Bennett - ***Dust Of The Trail*** [1950] Cover by Norman Saunders.	$2.50	$7.50	$15.00
18	Di Donato, Pietro - ***Christ In Concrete*** [1950] Cover by Umberto Romano	$1.50	$5.00	$10.00
19	Ross, Sam - ***He Ran All The Way*** [1950] Cover art by Harry Schaare.	$3.00	$9.00	$18.00
20	Austin, Brett - ***Gambler's Gun Luck*** [1950]	$2.50	$7.50	$15.00
21	Tucker, Wilson - ***To Keep Or Kill*** [1950] Cover by Herman Bischoff.	$4.00	$12.50	$25.00
22	Iams, Jack - ***The French Touch*** [1950] Cover art by Van Kaufman.	$2.00	$6.00	$12.00
23	Jacobs, Bruce - editor - ***Baseball Stars Of 1950*** [1950] PBO. Cover art by Bob Doares	$8.00	$25.00	$50.00
24	Tellier, Andre - ***Twilight Men*** [1950] Cover art by Stella Lincoln.	$1.50	$5.00	$10.00
25	Lynch, William - ***The Intimate Stranger*** [1950] PBO. Cover art by Woodi.	$2.50	$7.50	$15.00
26	Brand, Millen - ***The Outward Room*** [1950] Cover art by Harry Schaare.	$2.50	$7.50	$15.00
27	Mann, E. B. - ***Dead Man's Gorge*** [1950] Cover art by Bob Doares.	$2.50	$7.50	$15.00
28	Claussen, W. Edmunds - ***Gun Devil*** [1950] PBO. Cover art by Robert Stanley.	$2.50	$7.50	$15.00
29	Zinberg, Len - ***Walk Hard-Talk Loud*** [1950] Cover by Reynold Brown.	$2.00	$6.00	$12.00
30	Anonymous - ***The Indiscreet Confessions Of A Nice Girl*** [1950]	$2.00	$6.00	$12.00
31	Balchin, Nigel - ***The Small Back Room*** [1950] Cover art by Wesley Snyder.	$2.50	$7.50	$15.00
32	Lay, Margaret Rebecca - ***Ceylun*** [1950] Cover art by Julian Paul.	$2.50	$7.50	$15.00
33	Wechsberg, Joseph - ***The Continental Touch*** [1950] Cover art by John Fernie.	$3.50	$10.00	$20.00
34	Heckelmann, Charles N. - ***Guns Of Arizona*** [1950] Cover art by Earl Eugene Mayan.	$2.50	$7.50	$15.00
35	Foster, Bennett - ***Man Tracks*** [1950] Cover art by Bob Stanley	$2.50	$7.50	$15.00

		G	VG	F
36	Jackson, Shirley - ***The Road Through The Wall*** [1950] Cover art by Harvey Kidder.	$5.50	$17.50	$35.00
37	Dawson, Peter - ***Guns On The Santa Fe*** [1950] Cover art by Robert Stanley.	$2.50	$7.50	$15.00
38	Gray, Russell (Fischer, Bruno) - ***The Lustful Ape*** [1950] PBO. Cover art by Julian Paul.	$5.00	$15.00	$30.00
39	Appel, Benjamin - ***Brain Guy*** [1950]	$2.50	$7.50	$15.00
40	Hayes, Alfred - ***All Thy Conquests*** [1950]	$2.50	$7.50	$15.00
41	Ellin, Stanley - ***The Big Night*** [1950]	$3.50	$10.00	$20.00
42	Presson, Jay - ***Spring Riot*** [1950]	$3.50	$10.00	$20.00
43	Bellah, James Warner - ***Massacre*** [1950]	$3.00	$9.00	$18.00
44	Eastman, Elizabeth - ***His Dead Wife*** [1950]	$4.00	$12.50	$25.00
45	Tracy, Don - ***How Sleeps The Beast*** [1950]	$4.50	$14.00	$28.00
46	Iams, Jack - ***A Slight Case Of Scandal*** [1950] Cover art by Van Kaufman.	$2.50	$7.50	$15.00
47	Millar, Kenneth - ***Trouble Follows Me*** [1950]	$4.00	$12.50	$25.00
48	Millar, Kenneth - ***The Dark Tunnel*** [1950]	$4.50	$14.00	$28.00
49	Remarque, Erich Maria - ***All Quiet On The Western Front*** [1950]	$2.50	$7.50	$15.00
50	Stevens, Dan F. - ***Oregon Trunk*** [1951]	$3.00	$9.00	$18.00
51	Jaediker, Kermit - ***Tall, Dark And Dead*** [1951]	$3.50	$10.00	$20.00
52	Wilhelm, Gale - ***No Letters For The Dead*** [1951] Cover by Pease.	$3.50	$10.00	$20.00
53	Eliat, Helene - ***Arena Of Love*** [1951]	$2.50	$7.50	$15.00
54	Cuthbert, Clifton - ***Joy Street*** [1951]	$3.00	$9.00	$18.00
55	Claussen, W. Edmunds - ***El Paso*** [1951] PBO.	$2.50	$7.50	$15.00
56	Bordages, Asa - ***The Glass Lady*** [1951]	$3.00	$9.00	$18.00
57	Hahn, Emily - ***Affair*** [1951] Cover by Lou Marchetti.	$2.50	$7.50	$15.00
58	Cuthbert, Clifton - ***Art Colony*** [1951]	$2.50	$7.50	$15.00
59	Mason, Gregory and Carroll, Richard - ***Border Woman*** [1951] Cover art by Harry Schaare.	$3.50	$10.00	$20.00
60	Teagle, Mike - ***Murders In Silk*** [1951]	$3.50	$10.00	$20.00
61	Watson, Will - ***Wolf Dog Range*** [1951]	$2.50	$7.50	$15.00
62	Trimble, Louis - ***Blondes Are Skin Deep*** [1951] PBO.	$3.50	$10.00	$20.00
63	Langley, Noel - ***Cage Me A Peacock*** [1951]	$3.50	$10.00	$20.00
64	Artzybasheff, Mikhail - ***The Savage*** [1951]	$3.50	$10.00	$20.00
65	Hopson, William - ***Killers Five*** [1951]	$2.50	$7.50	$15.00
66	Hopson, William - ***The Ranch Cat*** [1951]	$2.50	$7.50	$15.00
67	Kelley, Frank and Ryan, Cornelius - ***MacArthur, Man Of Action*** [1951]	$1.50	$5.00	$10.00
68	Keene, Day - ***My Flesh Is Sweet*** [1951] PBO.	$5.00	$15.00	$30.00
69	Tracy, Don - ***The Cheat*** [1951]	$3.50	$10.00	$20.00
70	Wilhelm, Gale - ***We Too Are Drifting*** [1951]	$5.50	$17.50	$35.00
71	Anthology edited by Noah Sarlat - ***America's Cities Of Sin*** [1951] PBO.	$3.50	$10.00	$20.00
72	Bogar, Jeff - ***The Tigress*** [1951]	$3.50	$10.00	$20.00
73	Browne, Eleanore - ***Innocent Madame*** [1951]	$2.50	$7.50	$15.00
74	Craigin, Elisabeth - ***Either Is Love*** [1952]	$5.50	$17.50	$35.00
75	Durst, Paul - ***Die, Damn You!*** [1952] PBO.	$2.50	$7.50	$15.00
76	Brown, Harry - ***A Walk In The Sun*** [1952]	$2.50	$7.50	$15.00
77	Gordon, James - ***The Lust Of Private Cooper*** [1952]	$3.00	$9.00	$18.00
78	Montana, Duke - ***Nevada Killing*** [1952] Cover art by Mort Kunstler.	$2.50	$7.50	$15.00
79	Bogar, Jeff - ***My Gun, Her Body*** [1952]	$3.50	$10.00	$20.00
80	Lucas, Curtis - ***Third Ward, Newark*** [1952]	$4.00	$12.50	$25.00
81	Butler, Gerald - ***The Lurking Man*** [1952]	$3.50	$10.00	$20.00
82	Higgins, Marguerite - ***War In Korea*** [1952]	$2.50	$7.50	$15.00
83	Wolfson, P. J. - ***Bodies Are Dust*** [1952]	$3.00	$9.00	$18.00
84	Becker, Edwin J. - ***Earth Woman*** [1952]	$4.00	$12.50	$25.00
85	Prather, Richard S. - ***Lie Down, Killer*** [1952] PBO.	$4.50	$14.00	$28.00

Lion Book, 124

Lion Book, 127

Lion Book, 133

		G	VG	F
86	Attaway, William - ***Tough Kid*** [1952]	$4.00	$12.50	$25.00
87	Wills, Thomas - ***You'll Get Yours*** [1952] PBO.	$5.00	$15.00	$30.00
88	Harrison, C. William - ***The Missouri Maiden*** [1952] PBO.	$3.00	$9.00	$18.00
89	Greene, Ward - ***Route 28*** [1952]	$2.50	$7.50	$15.00
90	Frazee, Steve - ***Pistolman*** [1952] PBO.	$2.50	$7.50	$15.00
91	Lucas, Curtis - ***So Low, So Lonely*** [1952] PBO.	$3.00	$9.00	$18.00
92	London, Jack - ***South Sea Tales*** [1952]	$5.50	$17.50	$35.00
93	Karp, David - ***The Big Feeling*** [1952] PBO.	$4.50	$14.00	$28.00
94	Evans, John - ***Lona*** [1952] Cover art by Earle Bergey.	$3.50	$10.00	$20.00
95	Appel, Benjamin - ***Hell's Kitchen*** [1952] PBO.	$4.50	$14.00	$28.00
96	Frazee, Steve - ***Utah Hell Guns*** [1952]	$2.50	$7.50	$15.00
97	Anthology edited by Noah Sarlat - ***America's Cities Of Sin*** [1952]	$2.50	$7.50	$15.00
98	Kersh, Gerald - ***Prelude To A Certain Midnight*** [1952] Cover art by Rudolph Belarski.	$5.00	$15.00	$30.00
99	Thompson, Jim - ***The Killer Inside Me*** [1952] PBO.	$30.00	$100.00	$225.00
100	Elliott, Bruce - ***One Is A Lonely Number*** [1952] PBO. Cover art by Earle Bergey	$3.00	$9.00	$18.00
101	Cuthbert, Clifton - ***Joy Street*** [1952]	$2.00	$6.00	$12.00
102	De Meyer, John - ***Bailey's Daughters*** [1952]	$3.00	$9.00	$18.00
103	Harrison, C. William - ***Eat Dog Or Die!*** [1952] PBO. Cover art by Rafael De Soto.	$2.50	$7.50	$15.00
104	Paul, Gene - ***Little Killer*** [1952] PBO. Cover art by Prezio.	$3.00	$9.00	$18.00
105	Karp, David - ***The Brotherhood Of Velvet*** [1952] PBO.	$4.50	$14.00	$28.00
106	Anthology edited by Noah Sarlat - ***Sintown, U.S.A.*** [1952] PBO.	$3.50	$10.00	$20.00
107	Voltaire - ***Candide*** [1952]	$2.00	$6.00	$12.00
108	Thompson, Jim - ***Cropper's Cabin*** [1952] PBO.	$27.50	$85.00	$200.00
109	Eisner, Simon (Cyril Kornbluth) - ***The Naked Storm*** [1952] PBO. Cover art by Robert Skemp.	$8.00	$25.00	$50.00
110	Ring, Douglas (Prather, Richard S.) - ***The Peddler*** [1952] PBO.	$5.50	$17.50	$35.00
111	March, William - ***Company K*** [1952] Cover art by Rafael DeSoto.	$2.50	$7.50	$15.00
112	Walker, Shel - ***The Man I Killed*** [1952] PBO.	$3.00	$9.00	$18.00
113	Fairman, Paul W. - ***The Montana Vixon*** [1952]	$3.00	$9.00	$18.00
114	Flannagan, Roy - ***Luther*** [1952]	$3.50	$10.00	$20.00
115	Greene, Ward - ***Cora Potts*** [1952] Cover art by M. Singer.	$3.50	$10.00	$20.00
116	Marais, Claude - ***Saskia*** [1952] Cover art by Geygan.	$2.50	$7.50	$15.00
117	Champion, D. L. - ***Run The Wild River*** [1952] PBO. Cover art by Mort Kunstler.	$4.00	$12.50	$25.00
118	Sohl, Jerry - ***The Haploids*** [1953] Cover by Raphael DeSoto.	$6.00	$20.00	$40.00
119	Karp, David - ***Hardman*** [1953] PBO. Cover art by Prezio.	$4.50	$14.00	$28.00

		G	VG	F
120	Thompson, Jim - ***Recoil*** [1953] PBO.	$27.50	$85.00	$200.00
121	Wilhelm, Gale - ***The Strange Path*** [1953]	$5.50	$17.50	$35.00
122	Campesino, El - ***Life And Death In Soviet Russia*** [1953]	$2.00	$6.00	$12.00
123	Francis, William - ***Don't Dig Deeper*** [1953] PBO.	$3.00	$9.00	$18.00
124	Goodis, David - ***The Burglar*** [1953] PBO.	$20.00	$60.00	$125.00
125	Jacobs, Bruce - ***Baseball Stars Of 1953*** [1953] PBO. Photo cover.	$8.00	$25.00	$50.00
126	Richmond, Roe - ***Mojave Guns*** [1953]	$2.50	$7.50	$15.00
127	Thompson, Jim - ***The Alcoholics*** [1953] PBO.	$27.50	$85.00	$200.00
128	Komroff, Manuel - ***His Great Journey*** [1953] PBO.	$1.50	$5.00	$10.00
129	De Rosso, H. A. - ***.44*** [1953] PBO.	$2.50	$7.50	$15.00
130	Frazee, Steve - ***Sharp The Bugle Calls*** [1953] PBO.	$2.50	$7.50	$15.00
131	Otis, G. H. - ***Bourbon Street*** [1953] PBO.	$2.50	$7.50	$15.00
132	Karp, David - ***Cry, Flesh*** [1953] PBO.	$4.50	$14.00	$28.00
133	Goodis, David - ***The Dark Chase*** [1953] Cover art by Julian Paul.	$20.00	$60.00	$125.00
134	Halleran, E. E. - ***Colorado Creek*** [1953] PBO.	$2.50	$7.50	$15.00
135	Park, Jordan (Kornbluth, C. M.) - ***Half*** [1953] PBO.	$8.00	$25.00	$50.00
136	Morgan, Mark - ***Fighting Man*** [1953] PBO.	$2.50	$7.50	$15.00
137	Matheson, Richard - ***Someone Is Bleeding*** [1953] PBO.	$32.00	$110.00	$250.00
138	Untermeyer, Jr., Walter - ***Dark The Summer Dies*** [1953] PBO.	$2.50	$7.50	$15.00
139	Appell, George C. - ***Gunman's Grudge*** [1953] PBO.	$2.50	$7.50	$15.00
140	Scott, Warwick - ***Cockpit*** [1953] PBO.	$2.00	$6.00	$12.00
141	Roueche, Berton - ***Rooming House*** [1953]	$2.00	$6.00	$12.00
142	Jones, Ken - ***"I Was There"*** [1953] PBO. Photo cover.	$3.00	$9.00	$18.00
143	Dawson, Peter - ***The Wild Bunch*** [1953] PBO.	$2.50	$7.50	$15.00
144	Quigley, Martin - ***A Tent On Corsica*** [1953] Cover art by Cardiff.	$2.50	$7.50	$15.00
145	Frazier, Robert - ***Malenkov*** [1953] PBO. Photo cover.	$2.00	$6.00	$12.00
146	Shelly, Mary - ***Frankenstein*** [1953]	$5.50	$17.50	$35.00
147	Trimnell, Robert L. - ***The Wench And The Flame*** [1953] PBO. Cover art by Rafael DeSoto.	$3.00	$9.00	$18.00
148	Scott, Warwick - ***Doomsday*** [1953] PBO.	$5.00	$15.00	$30.00
149	Thompson, Jim - ***Bad Boy*** [1953] PBO. Cover art by Mort Kunstler.	$30.00	$100.00	$225.00
150	Frazee, Steve - ***Lawman's Feud*** [1953] PBO.	$2.50	$7.50	$15.00
151	Falstein, Louis - ***Slaughter Street*** [1953] PBO. Cover art by Lou Marchetti.	$3.00	$9.00	$18.00
152	Lorenz, Frederick - ***A Rage At Sea*** [1953] PBO. Cover art by Maguire.	$3.00	$9.00	$18.00
153	Bezzerides, A. I. - ***Tough Guy*** [1953]	$2.50	$7.50	$15.00
154	Paul, Gene - ***Naked In The Dark*** [1953] PBO.	$3.00	$9.00	$18.00
155	Thompson, Jim - ***Savage Night*** [1953] PBO.	$27.50	$85.00	$200.00
156	Jaediker, Kermit - ***Hero's Lust*** [1953] PBO. Cover art by Lou Marchetti.	$2.50	$7.50	$15.00
157	Gruber, Frank - ***The Lone Gunhawk*** [1953] Cover art by Prezio.	$2.50	$7.50	$15.00
158	Richmond, Roe - ***The Utah Kid*** [1953]	$2.50	$7.50	$15.00
159	Milburn, George - ***Sin People*** [1953]	$3.00	$9.00	$18.00
160	Gerould, Christopher - ***Sexual Practices Of American Women*** [1953] PBO.	$2.00	$6.00	$12.00
161	Lipsky, Eleazar - ***The Hoodlum*** [1953]	$5.50	$17.50	$35.00
162	Lucas, Curtis - ***Angel*** [1953] PBO.	$3.00	$9.00	$18.00
163	Gruber, Frank - ***Gunsight*** [1953] Cover art by Rudy Nappi	$2.50	$7.50	$15.00
164	Singer, Adam - ***Platoon*** [1953] PBO.	$2.00	$6.00	$12.00
165	Manners, William - ***The Big Lure*** [1953] PBO.	$2.50	$7.50	$15.00
166	Appel, Benjamin - ***Dock Walloper*** [1953] PBO	$2.00	$6.00	$12.00
167	Komroff, Manuel - ***Every Man's Bible*** [1953]	$1.50	$5.00	$10.00
168	Arthur, Burt - ***Killer's Crossing*** [1953] PBO. Cover art by Robert Schulz.	$2.50	$7.50	$15.00
169	Floren, Lee - ***The Gunslammer*** [1953]	$2.50	$7.50	$15.00

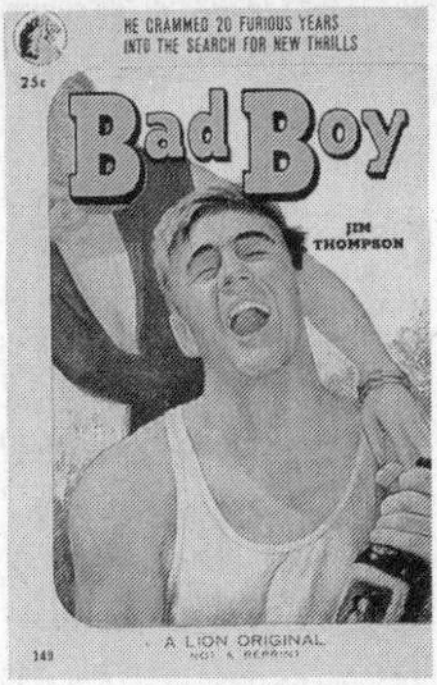

Lion Book, 149

Lion Book, 155

Lion Book, 161

		G	VG	F
170	Heatter, Basil - ***Sailor's Luck*** [1953] PBO.	$2.50	$7.50	$15.00
171	Otis, G. H. - ***Hot Cargo*** [1953] PBO.	$3.00	$9.00	$18.00
172	Jacobs, Bruce - ***Korea's Heroes*** [1953] PBO.	$2.00	$6.00	$12.00
173	Connell, Vivian - ***The Dream And The Flesh*** [1953]	$2.50	$7.50	$15.00
174	Francis, William - ***The Corrupters*** [1953] PBO.	$3.00	$9.00	$18.00
175	De Rosso, H. A. - ***The Gun Trail*** [1953] PBO.	$2.50	$7.50	$15.00
176	Park, Jordan (Kornbluth, C. M.) - ***Valerie*** [1953] PBO. Classic cover art by Robert Maguire.	$10.00	$30.00	$60.00
177	Anthology edited by William Kozlenko - ***Men and Women*** [1953] PBO.	$2.50	$7.50	$15.00
178	Durst, Paul - ***Bloody River*** [1953] PBO.	$2.50	$7.50	$15.00
179	Leiber, Fritz - ***Conjure Wife*** [1953] Cover art by Robert Maguire.	$10.00	$30.00	$60.00
180	Matheson, Richard - ***Fury On Sunday*** [1953] PBO.	$32.00	$110.00	$250.00
181	Harrison, C. William - ***The Oxbow Kill*** [1953] PBO. Cover art by Robert Maguire.	$3.50	$10.00	$20.00
182	Greene, Laurence - ***O'Mara*** [1953]	$3.00	$9.00	$18.00
183	Allison, Sam - ***Trouble On Crazyman*** [1953] PBO. Cover art by Rudy Nappi.	$2.50	$7.50	$15.00
184	Thompson, Jim - ***The Criminal*** [1953] PBO.	$27.50	$85.00	$200.00
185	Bloch, Robert - ***The Kidnaper*** [1954] PBO.	$25.00	$75.00	$180.00
186	Goodis, David - ***The Blonde On The Street Corner*** [1954] PBO.	$22.00	$70.00	$140.00
187	Ryan, Riley - ***The Dakota Deal*** [1954] PBO.	$2.50	$7.50	$15.00
188	Atlee, Philip - ***The Naked Year*** [1954]	$2.50	$7.50	$15.00
189	Arthur, Burt - ***Two-Gun Texan*** [1954] PBO.	$2.50	$7.50	$15.00
190	Fairman, Paul W. - ***The Joy Wheel*** [1954] PBO.	$3.50	$10.00	$20.00
191	Shea, J. Vernon - editor - ***Strange Desires*** [1954] PBO.	$3.00	$9.00	$18.00
192	Thompson, Jim - ***The Golden Gizmo*** [1954] PBO.	$27.50	$85.00	$200.00
193	Lorenz, Frederick - ***Night Never Ends*** [1954] PBO. Cover art by Clark Hulings.	$3.50	$10.00	$20.00
194	Jacobs, Bruce - ***Baseball Stars Of 1954*** [1954] PBO. Photo cover.	$8.00	$25.00	$50.00
195	Hopson, William - ***Apache Greed*** [1954] Cover art by Robert Schulz.	$2.50	$7.50	$15.00
196	Dutourd, Jean - ***A Dog's Head*** [1954] Translated from the French by Robin Chancellor.	$7.00	$22.50	$45.00
197	Brennan, Dan - ***The Naked Night*** [1954] PBO.	$3.00	$9.00	$18.00
198	Meskił, Paul S. - ***Sin Pit*** [1954] PBO.	$3.50	$10.00	$20.00
199	Appell, George C. - ***Ambush Hell*** [1954] PBO. Cover art by John Leone.	$2.50	$7.50	$15.00
200	Rosmanith, Olga - ***The Long Thrill*** [1954] PBO.	$3.00	$9.00	$18.00

Lion Book, 176

Midwood, NN-1

Midwood, F-101

		G	VG	F
201	Thompson, Jim - ***Roughneck*** [1954] PBO.	$27.50	$85.00	$200.00
202	Milburn, George - ***Hoboes And Harlots*** [1954] PBO. Cover art by Art Sussman	$3.00	$9.00	$18.00
203	Patterson, Rod - ***Whip Hand*** [1954]	$2.50	$7.50	$15.00
204	Keene, Day - ***Sleep With The Devil*** [1954] PBO.	$5.50	$17.50	$35.00
205	Anthology edited by Judith Merril - ***Human?*** [1954] Cover art by Rafael DeSoto. With an introduction by Fredric Brown.	$4.00	$12.50	$25.00
206	Craig, Jonathan - ***Alley Girl*** [1954] PBO.	$4.00	$12.50	$25.00
207	Trevor, Elleston - ***Tiger Street*** [1954] PBO.	$4.00	$12.50	$25.00
208	Michael, D. J. - ***"Win - Or Else!"*** [1954] PBO.	$2.00	$6.00	$12.00
209	Gwinn, William - ***A Way With Women*** [1954] PBO.	$2.50	$7.50	$15.00
210	Keene, Day - ***Joy House*** [1954] PBO.	$5.00	$15.00	$30.00
211	Sparkia, Roy Benard - ***Boss Man*** [1954] PBO.	$2.50	$7.50	$15.00
212	Thompson, Jim - ***A Swell-Looking Babe*** [1954] PBO.	$27.50	$85.00	$200.00
213	Untermeyer, Pat & Nelkin, Sandy - ***Stag Gag*** [1954]	$4.00	$12.50	$25.00
214	Fessier, Michael - ***Fully Dressed And In His Right Mind*** [1954]	$5.00	$15.00	$30.00
215	Fletcher, Flora - ***Strange Sisters*** [1954] PBO.	$5.50	$17.50	$35.00
216	Cassill, R. V. - ***Dormitory Women*** [1954] PBO.	$3.50	$10.00	$20.00
217	Frazee, Steve - ***The Gun-Throwers*** [1954] PBO.	$2.50	$7.50	$15.00
218	Thompson, Jim - ***A Hell Of A Woman*** [1954] PBO.	$27.50	$85.00	$200.00
219	Manners, William - ***Wharf Girl*** [1954] PBO.	$3.00	$9.00	$18.00
220	Caldwell, Jay Thomas - ***Me An' You*** [1954] PBO.	$3.00	$9.00	$18.00
221	Davis, Jr., Franklin M. - ***The Naked And The Lost*** [1954] PBO.	$2.50	$7.50	$15.00
222	Untermeyer, Jr. Walter - ***Evil Roots*** [1954] PBO.	$2.50	$7.50	$15.00
223	Lorenz, Frederick - ***The Savage Chase*** [1954] PBO. Cover art by Al Rossi.	$3.00	$9.00	$18.00
224	Goodis, David - ***Black Friday*** [1954] PBO.	$20.00	$60.00	$125.00
225	Gwinn, Williams - ***Jazz Bum*** [1954] PBO.	$2.50	$7.50	$15.00
226	Bruce, Robert - ***Tina*** [1954] PBO.	$2.50	$7.50	$15.00
227	Baldwin, Linton - ***Sinners' Game*** [1954] PBO.	$3.00	$9.00	$18.00
228	Heatter, Basil - ***Act Of Violence*** [1954] PBO. Cover art by John Leone.	$2.50	$7.50	$15.00
229	Anthology edited by Bucklin Moon - ***Champs And Bums*** [1954] PBO. Cover art by George Gross.	$2.00	$6.00	$12.00
230	Budrys, Algis - ***False Night*** [1954] PBO.	$4.00	$12.50	$25.00
231	Lipman, Clayre & Michel - ***House Of Evil*** [1954] PBO.	$3.00	$9.00	$18.00
232	Fitz Gibbon, Constantine - ***Room For A Stranger*** [1955]	$2.50	$7.50	$15.00
233	Da Vinci, Leonardo - ***The Deluge*** [1955] Edited by Robert Payne.	$3.50	$10.00	$20.00

		G	VG	F
Lion Library. New York: Lion Books, Inc.				
LL-1	Dos Passos, John - ***Number One*** [1954] Cover art by Schulz.	$1.50	$5.00	$10.00
LL-2	De Maupassant, Guy - ***A Woman's Life*** [1954]	$1.25	$3.75	$7.50
LL-3	Frazee, Steve - ***The Sky Block*** [1954] Cover art by Maguire.	$1.25	$3.75	$7.50
LL-4	Wolfson, P. J. - ***The Flesh Baron*** [1955]	$1.25	$3.75	$7.50
LL-5	Thompson, Lloyd S. - ***The Sin And The Flesh*** [1954]	$1.35	$4.00	$8.00
LL-6	Anthology edited by Daniel Talbot - ***The Damned*** [1954] PBO.	$2.50	$7.50	$15.00
LL-7	Leiber, Fritz - ***The Green Millennium*** [1954]	$2.50	$7.50	$15.00
LL-8	Komroff, Manuel - ***Gods And Demons*** [1954] PBO.	$3.00	$9.00	$18.00
LL-9	Kennedy, Stetson - ***Passage To Violence*** [1954] PBO. Cover art by Al Rossi.	$1.35	$4.00	$8.00
LL-10	Karp, David - ***Escape To Nowhere*** [1953]	$1.50	$5.00	$10.00
LL-11	Rosen, Victor - ***Dark Plunder*** [1955] PBO. Cover art by Al Rossi.	$1.35	$4.00	$8.00
LL-12	Edited by Jacobs, Bruce - ***Baseball Stars Of 1955*** [1955] PBO.	$7.00	$22.50	$45.00
LL-13	Knight, Damon - ***Hell's Pavement*** [1955] PBO.	$2.50	$7.50	$15.00
LL-14	Lucas, Curtis - ***Lila*** [1955] PBO.	$1.50	$5.00	$10.00
LL-15	Clark, Christopher - ***The Unleashed Will*** [1955]	$1.25	$3.75	$7.50
LL-16	Wolfson, Victor - ***The Passionate Season*** [1955] Cover art by Al Rossi.	$1.25	$3.75	$7.50
LL-17	Edited by Bennett, Edna - ***The Best Cartoons From France*** [1955]	$1.50	$5.00	$10.00
LL-18	Thielen, Benedict - ***The Lost Men*** [1955]	$1.25	$3.75	$7.50
LL-19	Wolfe, Thomas - ***The Hills Beyond*** [1955] Cover art by Arthur Shilstone.	$1.25	$3.75	$7.50
LL-20	Demby, William - ***Act Of Outrage*** [1955] Cover art by George Erickson.	$1.35	$4.00	$8.00
LL-21	Sarlat, Noah - editor - ***How I Made A Million*** [1955] PBO.	$1.25	$3.75	$7.50
LL-22	Carlaw, C. Bogart - ***The Wild Place*** [1955] Cover art by Robert Schulz.	$1.35	$4.00	$8.00
LL-23	Stout, Rex - ***How Like A God*** [1955]	$2.50	$7.50	$15.00
LL-24	Edited By Nelkin, Sandy & Untermeyer, Pat - ***For Stags Only*** [1955] PBO. Cartoon book.	$2.00	$6.00	$12.00
LL-25	Anthology edited by Merril, Judith - ***Galaxy Of Ghouls*** [1955] PBO. Cover art by B. Thomas.	$2.50	$7.50	$15.00
LL-26	Pemberton, Lois - ***The Stork Didn't Bring You*** [1955]	$1.25	$3.75	$7.50
LL-27	De Lima, Sigrid - ***A Mask Of Guilt*** [1955]	$1.35	$4.00	$8.00
LL-28	Coleman, Richard - ***Don't You Weep, Don't You Moan*** [1955] Cover art by Samson Pollen.	$1.35	$4.00	$8.00
LL-29	Masin, Herman L. - ***Curve Ball Laughs*** [1955] PBO. Cover art by Art Sussman.	$1.50	$5.00	$10.00
LL-30	Anthology - ***Great Tales Of The Deep South*** [1955] PBO. Cover art by David Fredenthal. Introduction By Malcolm Cowley.	$2.00	$6.00	$12.00
LL-31	Greene, Graham - ***Nineteen Stories*** [1955] Cover art by Arthur Shilstone.	$1.25	$3.75	$7.50
LL-32	Raine, William MacLeod - ***Whipsaw*** [1956] Cover art by Mel Crair.	$1.25	$3.75	$7.50
LL-33	Walker, David - ***The Storm And The Silence*** [1955] Cover art by George Erickson.	$1.35	$4.00	$8.00
LL-34	DeVries, Peter - ***The Tunnel Of Love*** [1953] Cover art by Al Werner.	$1.25	$3.75	$7.50
LL-35	Jackson, Charles - ***The Fall Of Valor*** [1953] Cover by Harry Schaare.	$1.50	$5.00	$10.00
LL-36	Stevens, Dan - ***Oregon Trunk*** [1955]	$1.35	$4.00	$8.00
LL-37	Gibbs, Willa - ***Fruit Of Desire*** [1955] Cover by Robert Maguire.	$1.50	$5.00	$10.00
LL-38	Goscinny, Rene - ***Cartoons The French Way*** [1955] PBO. Cartoon book.	$1.50	$5.00	$10.00
LL-39	Duncan, Eleanor S. - ***Parents' Magazine Book Of Baby Care*** [1955] Photo cover.	$1.25	$3.75	$7.50

		G	VG	F
LL-40	Millar, Kenneth - ***Night Train*** [1955] Cover art by Samson Pollen.	$1.50	$5.00	$10.00
LL-41	Gordon, James - ***Collision*** [1955] Cover art by Gilbert Fullington.	$1.25	$3.75	$7.50
LL-42	Dos Passos, John - ***Adventures Of A Young Man*** [1955] Cover art by Clark Hulings.	$1.25	$3.75	$7.50
LL-43	Foster, Bennett - ***The Kid From Dodge City*** [1957] Cover art by Mel Crair.	$1.25	$3.75	$7.50
LL-44	Flora, Fletcher - ***Desperate Asylum*** [1955] PBO. Cover art by Clark Hulings.	$1.35	$4.00	$8.00
LL-45	Coates, Robert M. - ***The Night Before Dying*** [1955] Cover art by Al Brule.	$1.35	$4.00	$8.00
LL-46	Gordon, Ad - ***The Flesh Painter*** [1955] PBO. Cover art by Paul Gauguin.	$1.35	$4.00	$8.00
LL-47	Edited by Shea, J. Vernon - ***Strange Barriers*** [1955] PBO. Cover art by Clark Hulings.	$1.50	$5.00	$10.00
LL-48	Ingersoll, Ralph - ***The Naked And The Guilty*** [1955] Cover art by Samson Pollen.	$1.25	$3.75	$7.50
LL-49	Brand, Millen - ***The Outward Room*** [1955] Cover by Harry Barton.	$1.25	$3.75	$7.50
LL-50	Cowell, Roberta - ***Roberta Cowell's Story*** [1955]	$1.25	$3.75	$7.50
LB-51	Anderson, Edward - ***Hungry Men*** [1955] Cover art by Charles Copeland.	$1.35	$4.00	$8.00
LL-52	Millar, Kenneth - ***I Die Slowly*** [1955]	$1.50	$5.00	$10.00
LL-53	Edited by Austin, Alex - ***Great Tales Of City Dwellers*** [1955] PBO. Cover art by Robert Maguire.	$2.00	$6.00	$12.00
LL-54	Bonham, Frank - ***The Wild Breed*** [1955] PBO. Cover art by Jim Bentley.	$1.35	$4.00	$8.00
LL-55	Green, Ward - ***Cora Potts*** [1955] Cover art by Robert Maguire.	$1.50	$5.00	$10.00
LL-56	Saroyan, William - ***Love*** [1955] PBO. Cover art by Art Sussman.	$1.35	$4.00	$8.00
LL-57	Appell, George C. - ***Ramrod*** [1955] PBO. Cover art by Jim Bentley.	$1.25	$3.75	$7.50
LL-58	Edited by Bailey, John - ***The Saturday Evening Post Cartoons*** [1955] Cover art by Henderson, Syverson & Cobean. Cartoon book.	$1.50	$5.00	$10.00
LL-59	Ross, Sam - ***He Ran All The Way*** [1955] Cover art by George Gross.	$1.35	$4.00	$8.00
LL-60	Lewisohn, Ludwig - ***The Sins Of Joy Munson*** [1955] Cover art by Samson Pollen.	$1.35	$4.00	$8.00
LB-61	Dawson, Peter - ***Leashed Guns*** [1955] Cover art by Jim Bentley.	$1.25	$3.75	$7.50
LB-62	March, William - ***Company K*** [1955] Cover art by Clark Hulings.	$1.00	$3.00	$6.00
LL-63	Lorenz, Frederick - ***A Party Every Night*** [1956] PBO. Cover art by Robert Schultz.	$2.00	$6.00	$12.00
LL-64	Kauffman, Lane - ***Kill The Beloved*** [1956] Cover art by Charles Copeland.	$1.25	$3.75	$7.50
LL-65	Komroff, Manuel - ***Two Thieves*** [1956] Cover art by B. Thomas.	$1.00	$3.00	$6.00
LL-66	Atlee, Philip - ***The Naked Year*** [1956]	$1.00	$3.00	$6.00
LL-68	Hayes, Alfred - ***All Thy Conquests*** [1956]	$1.25	$3.75	$7.50
LB-69	Frazee, Steve - ***Utah Hell Guns*** [1956] Cover art by Jim Bentley.	$1.25	$3.75	$7.50
LB-70	Morgan, Mark - ***Fighting Man*** [1956] Cover art by Stanley Borack.	$1.25	$3.75	$7.50
LL-71	Langley, Noel - ***Cage Me A Peacock*** [1956] Cover art by Bob Maguire.	$1.50	$5.00	$10.00
LL-73	Anonymous - ***A Handful Of Hell*** [1956]	$1.35	$4.00	$8.00
LL-74	Jacobs, Bruce - ***Basebal Stars Of 1956*** [1956] PBO.	$7.00	$22.50	$45.00
LL-75	Cuthbert, Clifton - ***Joy Street*** [1956] Cover art by William Rose.	$1.35	$4.00	$8.00

		G	VG	F
LL-76	Garland, Rodney - ***The Heart In Exile*** [1956] Cover art by Arthur Shilstone.	$1.25	$3.75	$7.50
LB-77	Attaway, William - ***Tough Kid*** [1955] Cover art by Charles Copeland.	$2.00	$6.00	$12.00
LB-78	Frazee, Steve - ***Pistol Man*** [1956] Cover art by Stanley Borack...	$1.25	$3.75	$7.50
LL-79	Gordon, Ad - ***Slade*** [1956] PBO.	$1.35	$4.00	$8.00
LL-80	Buchwald, Art - ***Art Buchwald's Paris*** [1956] Cover art by George Albertus.	$1.00	$3.00	$6.00
LL-81	Remarque, Erich Maria - ***All Quiet On The Western Front*** [1956] Cover art by Mort Kunstler.	$1.25	$3.75	$7.50
LL-84	Tucker, Wilson - ***To Keep Or Kill*** [1956] Cover art by Robert Maguire.	$1.50	$5.00	$10.00
LB-85	Arthur, Burt - ***Two-Gun Texan*** [1956]	$1.25	$3.75	$7.50
LB-86	Karp, David - ***The Girl On Crown Street*** [1956]	$1.35	$4.00	$8.00
LL-87	Fletcher, Flora - ***The Brass Bed*** [1956] PBO.	$1.50	$5.00	$10.00
LL-88	Edited by Austin, Alex - ***Great Tales Of The Far West*** [1956] PBO. Cover art by Marianne Davidson.	$2.00	$6.00	$12.00
LL-89	Anthology, Widmer, Harry - editor - ***The Gunslingers*** [1956] PBO.	$1.35	$4.00	$8.00
LL-90	Verne, Jules - ***Around The World In 80 Days*** [1956] Cover art by Barney Etengoff.	$1.25	$3.75	$7.50
LL-91	Kent, David - ***A Knife Is Silent*** [1956] Cover art by Mort Kunstler.	$1.35	$4.00	$8.00
LL-92	Kapelner, Alan - ***Lonely Boy Blues*** [1956] Cover art by Art Sussman.	$1.25	$3.75	$7.50
LL-93	Gruber, Frank - ***Gunsight*** [1956]	$1.25	$3.75	$7.50
LB-94	Flannagan, Roy - ***Luther*** [1956] Cover art by Rudy Nappi.	$1.50	$5.00	$10.00
LL-95	Davis, Eddie - ***Stories For Stags*** [1956] Cover art by Barney Etengoff.	$1.50	$5.00	$10.00
LL-96	Miller, Wade - ***Kiss Her Goodbye*** [1956] PBO. Cover art by Charles Copeland.	$2.00	$6.00	$12.00
LL-97	Park, Jordan - ***Sorority House*** [1956] PBO. Cover art by Clark Hulings.	$5.50	$17.50	$35.00
LL-98	Cuthbert, Clifton - ***Art Colony*** [1956] Cover art by Mauro Scali..	$1.00	$3.00	$6.00
LB-99	Edited by Guscinny, Rene - ***French And Frisky*** [1956] PBO. Cartoon book.	$1.35	$4.00	$8.00
LL-102	O'Connor, Edwin - ***The Oracle*** [1956] Cover art by Samson Pollen.	$1.25	$3.75	$7.50
LL-103	Edited by Masin, Herman L. - ***Sports Laughs*** [1956] PBO. Cover art by Richard Powers. Joke & cartoon book.	$1.35	$4.00	$8.00
LL-104	Lorenz, Frederick - ***Ruby*** [1956] Cover art by Samson Pollen.	$1.35	$4.00	$8.00
LL-105	Edited by Steiner, Paul - ***Bedtime Laughs*** [1956] PBO. Cover art by Bud Hawley. Joke & cartoon book.	$1.50	$5.00	$10.00
LL-106	Ka-tzetnik - ***House Of Dolls*** [1956] Cover art by Dick Shelton. ..	$1.25	$3.75	$7.50
LB-107	Voltaire - ***Candide*** [1956]	$1.25	$3.75	$7.50
LB-108	Frazee, Steve - ***Lawman's Feud*** [1956] Cover art by Mel Crair...	$1.25	$3.75	$7.50
LB-109	Singer, Adam - ***Platoon*** [1956] Cover art by Clark Hulings.	$1.00	$3.00	$6.00
LL-110	Komroff, Manuel - ***His Great Journey*** [1956] Cover art by Rafael DeSoto.	$1.00	$3.00	$6.00
LL-111	Edited by Austin, Alex - ***Wives And Lovers*** [1956] PBO. Cover art by Art Sussman.	$1.35	$4.00	$8.00
LL-112	Connell, Vivian - ***The Dream And The Flesh*** [1956]	$1.25	$3.75	$7.50
LL-113	Lewis, Sinclair - ***World So Wide*** [1956] Cover art by Stanley Borack.	$1.00	$3.00	$6.00
LL-114	Anthology - ***Quintet*** [1956] PBO. Cover art by Bill Gahan.	$1.25	$3.75	$7.50
LB-115	Wilhelm, Gale - ***Paula*** [1956]	$1.35	$4.00	$8.00
LB-116	Appel, Benjamin - ***Alley Kids*** [1956] Cover art by Samson Pollen & Carlos De Mema.	$2.00	$6.00	$12.00
LB-117	Gruber, Frank - ***The Lone Gunhawk*** [1956]	$1.25	$3.75	$7.50
LL-118	Tracy, Don - ***The Cheat*** [1956] Cover art by Charles Copeland...	$1.35	$4.00	$8.00

		G	VG	F
LL-119	Edited by Sandy Nelkin - ***College Humor*** [1956] PBO. Joke & cartoon book.	$1.50	$5.00	$10.00
LL-120	Erno, Richard B. - ***My Old Man*** [1956] Cover art by Lloyd Baker.	$1.25	$3.75	$7.50
LL-121	March, William - ***Desire And Damnation*** [1956]	$1.25	$3.75	$7.50
LB-122	Craigin, Elisabeth - ***Either Is Love*** [1956]	$2.50	$7.50	$15.00
LB-123	Harrison, C. William - ***The Oxbow Kill*** [1956] Cover art by Verne Tossey.	$1.25	$3.75	$7.50
LB-124	Thompson, Jim - ***Recoil*** [1956] Cover art by Robert Maguire.	$5.00	$15.00	$30.00
LL-125	Eisner, Simon (C. M. Kornbluth) - ***The Naked Storm*** [1956] Cover art by Robert Stanley.	$2.50	$7.50	$15.00
LL-126	Paust, Gil - ***Gil Paust's Gun Book*** [1956] PBO. Cover art by Ed Valigursky.	$1.35	$4.00	$8.00
LL-127	Edited by Noah Sarlat - ***Combat!*** [1956] PBO. Cover art by Lou Marchetti.	$1.35	$4.00	$8.00
LL-128	Garland, Rodney - ***The Troubled Midnight*** [1956] Cover art by Charles Copeland.	$1.35	$4.00	$8.00
LB-129	Wills, Thomas - ***You'll Get Yours*** [1956] Cover art by Harry Schaare.	$1.50	$5.00	$10.00
LB-131	Goodis, David - ***Nightfall*** [1956] Movie tie-in.	$3.50	$10.00	$20.00
LB-132	Hall, Evan - ***Logan*** [1956] Cover art by Rafael DeSoto.	$1.35	$4.00	$8.00
LL-133	Roueche', Berton - ***Rooming House*** [1957] Cover art by Arthur Sarnoff.	$1.25	$3.75	$7.50
LL-134	Tiira, Ensio - ***Raft Of Despair*** [1956] Cover art by Stanley Borack.	$1.25	$3.75	$7.50
LL-135	Burke, James Wakefield - ***The Big Rape*** [1956] Cover art by Mort Kunstler.	$1.35	$4.00	$8.00
LL-136	Williams, Ben Ames - ***Leave Her To Heaven*** [1956] Cover by Clark Hulings.	$1.25	$3.75	$7.50
LB-137	Hudiburg, Edward - ***Killers' Game*** [1956] PBO. Cover art by Harry Schaare.	$2.00	$6.00	$12.00
LB-138	Thompson, Jim - ***A Hell Of A Woman*** [1956] Cover by Morgan Kane.	$5.00	$15.00	$30.00
LB-139	Durst, Paul - ***Bloody River*** [1956]	$1.25	$3.75	$7.50
LL-140	Connell, Vivian - ***Bachelor's Anonymous*** [1956] PBO. Cover art by Stanley Borack.	$1.25	$3.75	$7.50
LL-141	Edited by Alex Austin - ***Women Without Men*** [1957] PBO. Cover art by Stanley Borack.	$2.00	$6.00	$12.00
LL-142	Thompson, Jim - ***The Kill-Off*** [1957] PBO. Cover art by William Rose.	$5.00	$15.00	$30.00
LL-143	Jackson, Charles - ***Thread Of Evil*** [1957] Cover art by Lou Marchetti.	$1.35	$4.00	$8.00
LB-144	Lorenz, Frederick - ***Hot*** [1956] PBO. Cover art by Rudy Nappi.	$2.00	$6.00	$12.00
LB-145	DeRosso, H. A. - ***44*** [1956] Cover art by Roy Lance.	$1.25	$3.75	$7.50
LB-147	Brennan, Dan - ***The Naked Night*** [1957] Cover art by George Gross.	$1.35	$4.00	$8.00
LL-148	Friedman, Stuart - ***The Bedside Corpse*** [1957] Cover art by Robert Stanley.	$1.35	$4.00	$8.00
LL-149	William, Ben Ames - ***A Killer Among Us*** [1957] Cover art by Harry Schaare.	$1.25	$3.75	$7.50
LL-150	Jacobs, Bruce - ***Baseball Stars Of 1957*** [1957] PBO. Cover art by Robert Engle.	$7.00	$22.50	$45.00
LL-151	Appel, Benjamin - ***Brain Guy*** [1957] Cover art by Mort Kunstler.	$1.25	$3.75	$7.50
LL-152	Edited by Harold Masur - ***Dolls Are Murder*** [1957] PBO. Cover art by Mort Kunstler.	$2.50	$7.50	$15.00
LB-153	Park, Jordan (C. M. Kornbluth) - ***Valerie*** [1957] Cover art by Charles Copeland.	$2.50	$7.50	$15.00
LB-154	DeRosso, H. A. - ***The Man From Texas*** [1957] Cover by Robert Stanley.	$1.25	$3.75	$7.50

		G	VG	F
LB-155	Ernenwein, Leslie - ***The Gun-Hung Men*** [1957] Cover art by Robert Stanley.	$1.25	$3.75	$7.50
LB-156	Hopson, William - ***Hang Tree Range*** [1957] Cover art by Robert Schulz.	$1.25	$3.75	$7.50
LB-157	Allison, Sam - ***Wyoming War*** [1957] Cover art by George Gross.	$1.35	$4.00	$8.00
LL-158	Paul, Gene - ***The Big Make*** [1957] Cover art by Robert Maguire.	$1.50	$5.00	$10.00
LL-160	Milburn, George - ***Hoboes And Harlots*** [1957] Cover art by Clark Hulings.	$1.35	$4.00	$8.00
LL-161	Appell, George C. - ***Gunman's Grudge*** [1957]	$1.25	$3.75	$7.50
LB-163	Bartolini, Elio - ***La Signora*** [1957] Cover art by Owen Kampen.	$1.25	$3.75	$7.50
LB-164	Patterson, Rod - ***Whip Hand*** [1957] Cover art by Mort Kunstler.	$1.25	$3.75	$7.50
LB-165	Lorenz, Frederick (Lorenz Heller) - ***A Rage At Sea*** [1957] Cover art by James Bama.	$1.35	$4.00	$8.00
LL-167	Edited by Noah Sarlat - ***This Is It!*** [1957] Cover art by Tony Kokinos.	$1.25	$3.75	$7.50
LL-168	Edited by Paul Steiner - ***The Bedside Bachelor*** [1957] PBO. Cover art by Bud Hawley	$1.35	$4.00	$8.00
LL-170	France, Anatole - ***The Red Lily*** [1957] PBO. Cover art by Gabe Keith.	$1.25	$3.75	$7.50
LB-171	Roth, Holly - ***The Sleeper*** [1957] Cover art by Rudy Nappi.	$1.35	$4.00	$8.00
LB-172	Falstein, Louis - ***Slaughter Street*** [1957] Cover art by Robert Maguire.	$1.35	$4.00	$8.00
LB-173	Frazee, Steve - ***The Gunthrowers*** [1954] Cover by George Gross.	$1.25	$3.75	$7.50
LL-174	Julian, Peter - ***The Seventh Trumpet*** [1957] Cover art by John Kuller.	$1.00	$3.00	$6.00

Love Romance Series. New York: Palace Promotions. Digest size.

		G	VG	F
1	Semple, Gordon - ***Nice And Naughty*** [1946] Cover art by L.B. Cole.	$4.00	$12.50	$25.00
11	Brewster, Eliot - ***Faithfully Yours*** [1946] Cover art by L.B. Cole.	$4.00	$12.50	$25.00
12	Brewster, Eliot - ***Love Above All*** [1946] Cover art by L.B. Cole.	$4.00	$12.50	$25.00

Lucom. New York: David Lucom. Digest size.

		G	VG	F
NN-1	Livingston, Armstrong - ***The Double Cross*** [1946]	$3.50	$10.00	$20.00
NN-2	Livingston, Armstrong - ***The Case Of The Walking Corpse*** [1946]	$3.50	$10.00	$20.00

Macfadden Books. New York: Macfadden-Bartell Publishing.

		G	VG	F
35-100	Humphries, Adelaide - ***Park Avenue Nurse*** [1962] Cover by Rudy Nappi.	$ .75	$2.50	$5.00
35-101	Schiddel, Edmund - ***The Girl With The Golden Yo-Yo*** [1961] Photo cover.	$1.35	$4.00	$8.00
35-102	Dern, Peggy - ***Country Nurse*** [1962]	$ .75	$2.50	$5.00
35-104	Anthology Edited by Selma H. Cooper - ***The Macfadden Book Of Crosswords And Puzzles*** [1962] PBO.	$2.50	$7.50	$15.00
35-105	Marsh, Rebecca - ***Office Nurse*** [1962] Cover by Robert Maguire.	$1.00	$3.00	$6.00
35-106	Cody, Al - ***Shannahan's Feud*** [1962]	$ .75	$2.50	$5.00
35-107	Gaddis, Peggy - ***Nora Was A Nurse*** [1962] Cover art by Maguire.	$1.00	$3.00	$6.00
35-109	Scoppettone, Sandra - ***Suzuki Beane*** [1962] Cover art by Louise Fitzhugh.	$ .75	$2.50	$5.00
35-110	Grinstead, J. E. - ***When Texans Ride*** [1962]	$ .75	$2.50	$5.00
35-111	Gaddis, Peggy - ***Nurse At Sundown*** [1962] Cover by Rudy Nappi.	$ .75	$2.50	$5.00
35-112	Gaddis, Peggy - ***Doctor Merry's Husband*** [1962]	$ .75	$2.50	$5.00

		G	VG	F
35-114	Floren, Lee - ***John Wesley Hardin, Texas Gunfighter*** [1962]......	$ .75	$2.50	$5.00
35-115	Nye, Nelson, C. - ***Born To Trouble*** [1962]......	$ .75	$2.50	$5.00
35-116	Gaddis, Peggy - ***Luxury Nurse*** [1962]......	$ .75	$2.50	$5.00
35-117	Floren, Lee - ***The Hard Riders*** [1962]......	$ .75	$2.50	$5.00
35-118	Dern, Peggy - ***Nurse Ellen*** [1962]......	$ .75	$2.50	$5.00
35-119	Cardwell, Ann - ***Crazy To Kill*** [1962] Cover art by Lesser......	$1.00	$3.00	$6.00
35-120	Hogan, Ray - ***Hell To Hallelujah*** [1962] PBO......	$ .75	$2.50	$5.00
35-121	Gaddis, Peggy - ***Leota Foreman, R.N.*** [1962]......	$ .75	$2.50	$5.00
35-122	Lehman, Paul Evan - ***The Cold Trail*** [1962]......	$ .75	$2.50	$5.00
35-125	Gaddis, Peggy - ***Nurse Hilary*** [1962]......	$ .75	$2.50	$5.00
35-126	Martin, Chuck - ***The Lobo Breed*** [1963]......	$ .75	$2.50	$5.00
35-127	Gaddis, Peggy - ***Doctor Sara*** [1962] Cover by Robert Maguire. ..	$1.00	$3.00	$6.00
35-128	Cord, Barry - ***Shadow Valley*** [1962]......	$ .75	$2.50	$5.00
35-130	Cord, Barry - ***Slade*** [1962]......	$ .75	$2.50	$5.00
35-133	Lehman, Paul Evan - ***Colt '60*** [1961]......	$ .75	$2.50	$5.00
40-100	Kornbluth, C. M. - ***A Mile Beyond The Moon*** [1962] Cover art by Powers......	$1.25	$3.75	$7.50
40-101	Lait, Robert - ***Honey For Tomorrow*** [1962]......	$ .75	$2.50	$5.00
40-102	Goodwill, Dorothy B. - ***The Giant Hobby Book*** [1962]......	$ .75	$2.50	$5.00
40-105	Clifton, Mark - ***When They Come From Space*** [1963] Cover art by Powers......	$1.00	$3.00	$6.00
40-107	Gaddis, Peggy - ***Student Nurse*** [1962]......	$ .75	$2.50	$5.00
40-108	Cody, AL - ***The Sheriff From Hell*** [1962]......	$ .75	$2.50	$5.00
40-109	Dern, Peggy (Peggy Gaddis) - ***Nurse In The Tropics*** [1963] Cover art by Maguire......	$1.00	$3.00	$6.00
40-110	Cody, Al - ***Homestead Range*** [1963]......	$ .75	$2.50	$5.00
40-111	Gaddis, Peggy - ***Nurse's Choice*** [1963]......	$ .75	$2.50	$5.00
40-112	Echols, Allan K. - ***Killers Two*** [1963]......	$ .75	$2.50	$5.00
40-113	Gaddis, Peggy - ***The Courtship Of Nurse Genie Hayes*** [1963] Cover by Robert Maguire......	$1.00	$3.00	$6.00
40-114	Martin, Chuck - ***The Fastest Gun*** [1963]......	$ .75	$2.50	$5.00
40-115	Gaddis, Peggy - ***Nurse Christine*** [1963]......	$ .75	$2.50	$5.00
40-116	Lehman, Paul Evan - ***Pistol Law*** [1963] Cover art by Robert Maguire......	$1.00	$3.00	$6.00
40-117	Gaddis, Peggy - ***Big City Nurse*** [1963] Cover by Robert Maguire......	$1.00	$3.00	$6.00
40-118	Echols, Allan K. - ***The Renegade Hills*** [1963]......	$ .75	$2.50	$5.00
40-119	Gaddis, Peggy - ***Future Nurse*** [1963]......	$ .75	$2.50	$5.00
40-120	Cody, Al - ***Star Toter*** [1963]......	$ .75	$2.50	$5.00
40-121	Cody, Al - ***Gun Ranch*** [1963]......	$ .75	$2.50	$5.00
40-122	Gaddis, Peggy - ***Emergency Nurse*** [1963] Cover by Robert Maguire......	$1.00	$3.00	$6.00
40-123	Floren, Lee - ***Gun-Slammer*** [1963]......	$ .75	$2.50	$5.00
40-124	Gaddis, Peggy - ***Mountain Nurse*** [1963]......	$ .75	$2.50	$5.00
40-126	Carew, Jean - ***Society Nurse*** [1963] Cover art by Maguire......	$1.00	$3.00	$6.00
40-127	Echols, Allan K. - ***Wild Horse Range*** [1963] Cover art by Maguire......	$1.00	$3.00	$6.00
40-128	Nelson, Marguerite - ***Hollywood Nurse*** [1964]......	$ .75	$2.50	$5.00
40-129	Arthur, Burt - ***The Drifter*** [1964]......	$ .75	$2.50	$5.00
40-130	Floren, Lee - ***Rifles On The Range*** [1964] Cover art by Podwil..	$ .75	$2.50	$5.00
40-131	Stuart, Florence - ***Runaway Nurse*** [1964]......	$ .75	$2.50	$5.00
40-132	Floren, Lee - ***Wolf Dog Range*** [1964]......	$ .75	$2.50	$5.00
40-133	Martin, Chuck - ***The Deputies From Hell*** [1964]......	$ .75	$2.50	$5.00
40-134	Gaddis, Peggy - ***Clinic Nurse*** [1964]......	$ .75	$2.50	$5.00
40-135	Shepard, Fern - ***Nurse In Danger*** [1964]......	$ .75	$2.50	$5.00
40-136	Floren, Lee - ***Fighting Ramrod*** [1964]......	$ .75	$2.50	$5.00
40-137	Gaddis, Peggy - ***The Nurse And The Star*** [1964]......	$ .75	$2.50	$5.00
40-138	Arthur, Burt - ***Sing A Song Of Six-Guns*** [1964] Cover art by Jerome Podwil......	$ .75	$2.50	$5.00
40-139	Holden, Joanne - ***Village Nurse*** [1964]......	$ .75	$2.50	$5.00

	G	VG	F
40-140 Arthur, Burt & Budd - ***Three Guns North*** [1964]	$ .75	$2.50	$5.00
40-141 Dern, Peggy - ***Nurse With A Dream*** [1964]	$ .75	$2.50	$5.00
40-142 Arthur, Burt - ***Empty Saddles*** [1964]	$ .75	$2.50	$5.00
40-143 Holden, Joanne - ***Nurse Gina*** [1964]	$ .75	$2.50	$5.00
40-144 Floren, Lee - ***They Ride With Rifles*** [1964]	$ .75	$2.50	$5.00
40-145 Gaddis, Peggy - ***Nurse At The Cedars*** [1964]	$ .75	$2.50	$5.00
40-146 Hopson, William - ***Long Ride To Abilene*** [1964]	$ .75	$2.50	$5.00
40-147 Lehman, Paul Evan - ***Gun-Whipped*** [1964]	$ .75	$2.50	$5.00
40-148 Craig, Georgia - ***A Nurse Comes Home*** [1964]	$ .75	$2.50	$5.00
40-149 Gaddis, Peggy - ***A Nurse Called Happy*** [1964]	$ .75	$2.50	$5.00
40-150 Stuart, Florence - ***The Nurse And The Orderly*** [1964]	$ .75	$2.50	$5.00
40-151 Arthur, Burt - ***Silver City Rangers*** [1964] Cover art by Tom Ryan.	$ .75	$2.50	$5.00
40-152 Lehman, Paul Evan - ***Bandit In Black*** [1964]	$ .75	$2.50	$5.00
40-153 Craig, Georgia - ***Nurse Lucie*** [1964]	$ .75	$2.50	$5.00
40-154 Hopson, William - ***Trouble Rides Tall*** [1964]	$ .75	$2.50	$5.00
40-155 Gaddis, Peggy - ***A Nurse For Apple Valley*** [1964]	$ .75	$2.50	$5.00
40-156 McDonnell,,R.N., Virginia B. - ***West Point Nurse*** [1965] PBO.	$ .75	$2.50	$5.00
40-157 Arthur, Burt - ***High Pockets*** [1965]	$ .75	$2.50	$5.00
40-158 Corby, Jane - ***Traveling Nurse*** [1965]	$ .75	$2.50	$5.00
40-159 Lehman, Paul Evan - ***The Tough Texan*** [1965]	$ .75	$2.50	$5.00
40-160 Hopson, William - ***Bullet-Brand Empire*** [1965]	$ .75	$2.50	$5.00
40-161 Gaddis, Peggy - ***Everglades Nurse*** [1965]	$ .75	$2.50	$5.00
40-162 Dana, Rose - ***Operating Room Nurse*** [1965] PBO.	$ .75	$2.50	$5.00
40-163 Arthur, Burt - ***Boss Of The Far West*** [1965]	$ .75	$2.50	$5.00
50-101 Thomas, Shirley - ***Men Of Space*** [1961] Cover art by Basil Gogol.	$1.00	$3.00	$6.00
50-102 Gaither, Gant - ***Princess Of Monaco*** [1961] Photo cover. Eight pages of photos.	$ .75	$2.50	$5.00
50-103 West, Anthony, C. - ***The Native Moment*** [1961]	$ .75	$2.50	$5.00
50-104 Weyl, Nathaniel - ***Red Star Over Cuba*** [1961]	$ .75	$2.50	$5.00
50-107 Dolci, Danilo - ***Report From Palermo*** [1961]	$ .75	$2.50	$5.00
50-108 Vogt, William - ***People!*** [1961]	$ .75	$2.50	$5.00
50-109 Stearn, Jess - ***The Wasted Years*** [1961] Photo cover.	$ .75	$2.50	$5.00
50-111 Tebbel, John - ***Your Body-How To Keep It Healthy*** [1961]	$ .75	$2.50	$5.00
50-112 Longstreet, Stephen - ***Three Days*** [1961]	$ .75	$2.50	$5.00
50-113 Wickenden, Leonard - ***Our Daily Poison*** [1961]	$ .75	$2.50	$5.00
50-114 Kahn, Steve - ***Tops In Pops*** [1961] PBO. Photo cover. Eight pages of photos.	$1.50	$5.00	$10.00
50-115 Allingham, Margery - ***The Fear Sign*** [1961] Photo cover.	$ .75	$2.50	$5.00
50-117 Hazlitt, Henry - ***Economics In One Lesson*** [1962]	$ .75	$2.50	$5.00
50-118 Allingham, Margery - ***More Work For The Undertaker*** [1962]	$1.00	$3.00	$6.00
50-121 Piper, Laurette - editor - ***The World Of Love*** [1962] PBO. Photo cover.	$ .75	$2.50	$5.00
50-123 Hope, Alice - ***Princess Margaret*** [1962] Photo cover. Eight pages of photos.	$ .75	$2.50	$5.00
50-126 Lucchese, John A. - ***Joey Dee And The Story Of The Twist*** [1962] PBO. Photo cover. Sixteen pages of photos.	$1.25	$3.75	$7.50
50-127 De Maria, Robert - ***Carnival Of Angels*** [1962]	$ .75	$2.50	$5.00
50-128 Anthology Edited by Donald Keys - ***God And The H-Bomb*** [1962]	$ .75	$2.50	$5.00
50-130 Allingham, Margery - ***No Love Lost*** [1962] Photo cover.	$1.00	$3.00	$6.00
50-135 Braddock, Joseph - ***The Bridal Bed*** [1962]	$ .75	$2.50	$5.00
50-136 Allingham, Margery - ***Dancers In Mourning*** [1962] Photo cover.	$1.00	$3.00	$6.00
50-141 Brothers, Dr. Joyce - ***Woman*** [1962] Photo cover.	$ .75	$2.50	$5.00
50-142 Smith, Stan - ***The Battle Of Savo*** [1962] PBO.	$ .75	$2.50	$5.00
50-143 Anthology selected by Dorothy L. Sayers - ***Tales Of Detection And Mystery*** [1962]	$1.00	$3.00	$6.00
50-146 Orsi, Roberto - ***Rome After Dark*** [1962]	$ .75	$2.50	$5.00

		G	VG	F
50-147	Allingham, Margery - ***The Black Dudley Murder*** [1962] Photo cover.	$ .75	$2.50	$5.00
50-149	Anderson, George - ***Make Money At Home*** [1962] PBO.	$ .75	$2.50	$5.00
50-150	Eberhart, Mignon G. - ***The Dark Garden*** [1962]	$1.00	$3.00	$6.00
50-151	Wolfe, Bernard - ***The Magic Of Their Singing*** [1962] Cover art by Leo and Diane Dillon.	$ .75	$2.50	$5.00
50-152	Tower, Senator John G. - ***A Program For Conservatives*** [1962] PBO. Photo cover.	$ .75	$2.50	$5.00
50-153	Hartke, Senator Vance & Redding, John M - ***Inside The New Frontier*** [1962] PBO. Photo cover.	$ .75	$2.50	$5.00
50-154	Evans, Rosser - ***A Feast Of Friends*** [1962]	$ .75	$2.50	$5.00
50-155	Allingham, Margery - ***The Estate Of The Beckoning Lady*** [1962] Photo cover.	$ .75	$2.50	$5.00
50-156	Anthology edited by Dorothy L. Sayers - ***Human And Inhuman Stories*** [1963] Photo cover.	$1.00	$3.00	$6.00
50-158	Yorke, Susan - ***The Girl In The Cheongsam*** [1963] Cover art by James Meese.	$ .75	$2.50	$5.00
50-159	Kurtzman, Harvey & Elder, Will - ***Executive's Comic Book*** [1962] PBO. All comic strips.	$2.00	$6.00	$12.00
50-164	Honig, Donald - ***No Song To Sing*** [1963] Cover art by Lurin.	$ .75	$2.50	$5.00
50-165	Simak, Clifford D. - ***All The Traps Of Earth*** [1963] Cover art by Richard Powers.	$1.00	$3.00	$6.00
50-167	Eberhart, Mignon G. - ***While The Patient Slept*** [1963]	$1.00	$3.00	$6.00
50-169	Allingham, Margery - ***The Gyrth Chalice Mystery*** [1963] Photo cover.	$1.00	$3.00	$6.00
50-170	Anthology selected by Dorothy L. Sayers - ***Stories Of The Supernatural*** [1963] Cover art by Richard Powers.	$1.00	$3.00	$6.00
50-171	Aarons, Edward S. - ***Nightmare*** [1963] Cover art by Jerome Podwil.	$1.00	$3.00	$6.00
50-173	Farnsworth, Clyde - ***No Money Down!*** [1963] PBO.	$ .75	$2.50	$5.00
50-174	Pollock, Louis - ***Stork Bites Man*** [1963] Cover art by Carl Rose.	$ .75	$2.50	$5.00
50-175	Rhoades, Jonathan - ***Over The Fence Is Out*** [1963] Cover art by Robert Day.	$ .75	$2.50	$5.00
50-179	Dickson, Gordon R. - ***No Room For Man*** [1963] Cover art by Richard Powers.	$1.00	$3.00	$6.00
50-180	Smith, Stan - ***Pass The Ammunition*** [1963] PBO.	$ .75	$2.50	$5.00
50-181	Allingham, Margery - ***Mr. Campion: Criminologist*** [1963]	$ .75	$2.50	$5.00
50-183	Mair, George B. - ***The Day Khrushchev Panicked*** [1963] Cover art by Stanley Borack.	$ .75	$2.50	$5.00
50-184	Simak, Clifford D. - ***They Walked Like Men*** [1963] Cover art by Richard Powers.	$1.00	$3.00	$6.00
50-186	Eberhart, Mignon G. - ***Danger In The Dark*** [1963]	$1.00	$3.00	$6.00
50-187	Smith, Robert Paul - ***The Time And The Place*** [1963]	$ .75	$2.50	$5.00
50-188	El Masry, Youssef - ***Daughters Of Sin: The Sexual Tragedy Of Arab Women*** [1963]	$ .75	$2.50	$5.00
50-189	West, Anthony C. - ***Rebel To Judgment*** [1963]	$ .75	$2.50	$5.00
50-190	Kaplan, Philip - ***Posers*** [1964] Riddle and puzzle book.	$1.00	$3.00	$6.00
50-193	Aarons, Edward S. - ***Gift Of Death*** [1964]	$1.00	$3.00	$6.00
50-194	Martin, Kay - ***The Whispered Sex*** [1964]	$1.25	$3.75	$7.50
50-195	Hanley, Jack - ***Let's Make Mary*** [1964]	$ .75	$2.50	$5.00
50-196	Hogan, Ray - ***Rebel Ghost*** [1964]	$ .75	$2.50	$5.00
50-197	Martin, Kay - ***A Taste Of Passion*** [1964] Cover by Victor Olson.	$1.00	$3.00	$6.00
50-198	Aarons, Edward S. - ***The Art Studio Murders*** [1964] Cover art by Bob Abbett.	$1.00	$3.00	$6.00
50-199	Nourse, Alan E. - ***Tiger By The Tail*** [1964] Cover art by Richard Powers.	$1.00	$3.00	$6.00
50-202	Walsh, Thomas - ***Nightmare In Manhattan*** [1964]	$1.00	$3.00	$6.00
50-203	Reilly, Helen - ***Dead Man Control*** [1964] Cover art by Robert Schultz.	$1.00	$3.00	$6.00

		G	VG	F
50-204	Cosell, Howard - ***Great Moments In Sport*** [1964] PBO.	$ .75	$2.50	$5.00
50-205	Anthology - ***Restless Nations*** [1964]	$ .75	$2.50	$5.00
50-207	Cuomo, George - ***Jack Be Nimble*** [1964]	$ .75	$2.50	$5.00
50-209	Reilly, Helen - ***Murder In Shinbone Alley*** [1964] Photo cover.	$1.00	$3.00	$6.00
50-210	De Blasio, Edward - ***All About The Beatles*** [1964] PBO. Photo cover. Eight pages of photos.	$2.50	$7.50	$15.00
50-211	Anderson, Poul - ***The High Crusade*** [1964] Cover art by Richard Powers.	$1.00	$3.00	$6.00
50-213	Latimer, Jonathan - ***The Dead Don't Care*** [1964] Cover by Robert Schulz.	$1.00	$3.00	$6.00
50-215	Anthology - ***A John F. Kennedy Memorial*** [1964] PBO. Photo cover. Photos throughout.	$ .75	$2.50	$5.00
50-216	Aarons, Edward S. - ***Terror In The Town*** [1964]	$1.00	$3.00	$6.00
50-218	Collier, James - ***The Hypocritical American*** [1964] Cover art by Karol.	$ .75	$2.50	$5.00
50-219	Reilly, Helen - ***All Concerned Notified*** [1964] Photo cover.	$1.00	$3.00	$6.00
50-220	Lacy, Ed - ***Enter Without Desire*** [1964]	$1.00	$3.00	$6.00
50-221	Latimer, Jonathan - ***Headed For A Hearse*** [1964]	$1.00	$3.00	$6.00
50-222	Hopson, William & O'Conner, Lois - ***Mexico After Dark*** [1964] PBO.	$ .75	$2.50	$5.00
50-223	Simenon, Georges - ***In Case Of Emergency*** [1964]	$1.00	$3.00	$6.00
50-224	Leinster, Murray - ***The Greks Bring Gifts*** [1964] PBO.	$1.00	$3.00	$6.00
50-225	Aarons, Edward S. - ***No Place To Live*** [1964]	$1.00	$3.00	$6.00
50-226	Caldwell, Erskine - ***Journeyman*** [1964]	$ .75	$2.50	$5.00
50-227	Caldwell, Erskine - ***A House In The Uplands*** [1964] Cover art by Barye Phillips.	$ .75	$2.50	$5.00
50-228	Caldwell, Erskine - ***A Woman In The House*** [1964]	$ .75	$2.50	$5.00
50-229	Caldwell, Erskine - ***Place Called Estherville*** [1965] Cover art by James Meese.	$ .75	$2.50	$5.00
50-230	Caldwell, Erskine - ***A Swell Looking Girl*** [1964]	$ .75	$2.50	$5.00
50-231	Caldwell, Erskine - ***Kneel To The Rising Sun*** [1965]	$ .75	$2.50	$5.00
50-233	Lacy, Ed - ***Strip For Violence*** [1965]	$1.00	$3.00	$6.00
50-234	Knight, Damon - ***Beyond The Barrier*** [1965]	$1.00	$3.00	$6.00
50-235	Aarons, Edward S. - ***Point Of Peril*** [1965]	$1.00	$3.00	$6.00
50-236	Caldwell, Erskine - ***Southways*** [1965]	$ .75	$2.50	$5.00
50-237	Caldwell, Erskine - ***The Courting Of Susie Brown*** [1965] Cover art by Karol.	$ .75	$2.50	$5.00
50-238	Wilson, Jean Sprain - ***All About Tipping*** [1965] PBO. Photo cover.	$ .75	$2.50	$5.00
50-239	Keene, Day - ***Carnival Of Death*** [1965] PBO. Photo cover.	$1.50	$5.00	$10.00
50-240	Fitzpatrick, William - ***Tokyo After Dark*** [1965]	$ .75	$2.50	$5.00
50-244	Anthology - ***The 6 Fingers Of Time*** [1965] PBO. Cover art by Richard Powers.	$1.00	$3.00	$6.00
50-245	Aarons, Edward S. - ***Death Is My Shadow*** [1965]	$1.00	$3.00	$6.00
50-246	Lehman, Paul Evan - ***The Man From The Badlands*** [1965]	$ .75	$2.50	$5.00
50-247	Nye, Nelson C. - ***Saddle Bow Slim*** [1965]	$ .75	$2.50	$5.00
50-248	Neubauer, W. - ***Police Nurse*** [1965]	$ .65	$2.00	$4.00
50-250	Dana, Rose - ***Night Club Nurse*** [1965] PBO.	$ .65	$2.00	$4.00
50-251	Gaddis, Peggy - ***Betsy Moran, R. N.*** [1965]	$ .65	$2.00	$4.00
50-252	Hopson, William - ***Notched Guns*** [1965]	$ .75	$2.50	$5.00
50-253	Caldwell, Erskine - ***Claudelle Inglish*** [1965] Cover art by Jack Thurston.	$ .75	$2.50	$5.00
50-255	Lacy, Ed - ***Sin In Their Blood*** [1966]	$1.00	$3.00	$6.00
50-256	Lehman, Paul Evans - ***Montana Man*** [1965]	$ .75	$2.50	$5.00
50-257	McDonnell, R.N., Virginia B. - ***Annapolis Nurse*** [1965] PBO.	$ .65	$2.00	$4.00
50-258	Floren, Lee - ***Mad River Guns*** [1965]	$ .75	$2.50	$5.00
50-260	Ullman, Allan & Fletcher, Lucille - ***Sorry, Wrong Number*** [1966] Photo cover. Movie tie-in.	$1.00	$3.00	$6.00
50-261	Stuart, Florence - ***Nurse Under Fire*** [1965]	$ .65	$2.00	$4.00
50-262	Arthur, Burt - ***Gunsmoke In Paradise*** [1965]	$ .75	$2.50	$5.00

		G	VG	F
50-264	Dana, Rose - ***Bermuda Nurse*** [1965]	$ .65	$2.00	$4.00
50-265	Floren, Lee - ***Guns Of Wyoming*** [1965]	$ .75	$2.50	$5.00
50-266	Corby, Jane - ***Nurse With The Red-Gold Hair*** [1965]	$ .65	$2.00	$4.00
50-267	Lehman, Paul Evan - ***Vultures On Horseback*** [1965]	$ .75	$2.50	$5.00
50-268	Dana, Rose - ***Nurse Freda*** [1966] PBO.	$ .65	$2.00	$4.00
50-269	Floren, Lee - ***Black Boulder Ranch*** [1966]	$ .75	$2.50	$5.00
50-271	Keene, Day - ***Mrs. Homicide*** [1966]	$1.35	$4.00	$8.00
50-274	Arthur, Burt - ***The Killer*** [1966]	$ .75	$2.50	$5.00
50-275	Baker, W. Howard - ***Departure Deferred*** [1966] Photo cover. TV tie-in	$1.00	$3.00	$6.00
50-278	Floren, Lee - ***Gun Luck*** [1966]	$ .75	$2.50	$5.00
50-279	Smith, Robert Paul - ***"Where Did You Go?" "Out." "What Did You Do?" "Nothing."*** [1966] Cover art by James J. Spanfeller.	$ .75	$2.50	$5.00
50-280	Leslie, Peter - ***Hell For Tomorrow*** [1966] Photo cover. TV tie-in.	$1.35	$4.00	$8.00
50-283	Lehman, Paul Evan - ***Outlaw Loot*** [1966]	$ .75	$2.50	$5.00
50-284	Baker, W. Howard - ***Storm Over Rockall*** [1966] Photo cover. TV tie-in	$ .75	$2.50	$5.00
50-287	Cody, Al - ***Wagons West*** [1966] Cover art by Jerome Podwil.	$ .75	$2.50	$5.00
50-288	Kornbluth, C. M. - ***A Mile Beyond The Moon*** [1966]	$1.00	$3.00	$6.00
50-289	Humphries, Adelaide - ***Park Avenue Nurse*** [1966]	$ .65	$2.00	$4.00
50-290	Echols, Allen K. - ***Vengeance Valley*** [1966]	$ .75	$2.50	$5.00
50-291	Schiddel, Edmund - ***Love In A Hot Climate*** [1966] Photo cover.	$ .75	$2.50	$5.00
50-293	Cody, Al - ***Shannahan's Feud*** [1966]	$ .75	$2.50	$5.00
50-296	Hogan, Ray - ***Mosby's Last Ride*** [1966]	$ .75	$2.50	$5.00
50-297	Orsi, Roberto - ***Rome After Dark*** [1966] Photo cover.	$ .75	$2.50	$5.00
50-299	Grinstead, J. E. - ***When Texans Ride*** [1966]	$ .75	$2.50	$5.00
50-300	Anthology edited by Dorothy L. Sayers - ***Stories Of The Supernatural*** [1966] Cover art by Richard Powers.	$1.00	$3.00	$6.00
50-302	Nye, Nelson - ***Born To Trouble*** [1966]	$ .75	$2.50	$5.00
50-303	Smith, Stan - ***The Battle Of Savo*** [1966]	$ .75	$2.50	$5.00
50-305	Lehman, Paul Evan - ***The Cold Trail*** [1966]	$ .75	$2.50	$5.00
50-308	Floren, Lee - ***Lobo Valley*** [1966]	$ .75	$2.50	$5.00
50-309	Dern, Peggy (Peggy Gaddis) - ***Nurse Ellen*** [1966]	$ .65	$2.00	$4.00
50-310	Floren, Lee - ***The Hard Riders*** [1966]	$ .75	$2.50	$5.00
50-311	Anthology edited by Sam Moskowitz - ***Doorway Into Time*** [1966] PBO. Photo cover.	$1.00	$3.00	$6.00
50-314	Lehman, Paul Evan - ***Action At The Bitterroot*** [1966]	$ .75	$2.50	$5.00
50-316	Cody, Al - ***Renegade Scout*** [1966]	$ .75	$2.50	$5.00
50-319	Lehman, Paul Evan - ***Law Of The Gun*** [1966]	$ .75	$2.50	$5.00
50-320	McNeilly, Wilfred - ***No Way Out*** [1966] Photo cover. TV tie-in.	$1.00	$3.00	$6.00
50-323	Floren, Lee - ***War On Alkali Creek*** [1966]	$ .75	$2.50	$5.00
50-325	Foren, Lee - ***John Wesley Hardin: Texas Gunfighter*** [1966]	$ .75	$2.50	$5.00
50-326	Martin, Chuck - ***The Lobo Breed*** [1966]	$ .75	$2.50	$5.00
50-328	Fitzpatrick, William - ***Tokyo After Dark*** [1966]	$ .75	$2.50	$5.00
50-329	Dickson, Gordon R. - ***No Room For Man*** [1966] Cover art by Richard Powers.	$1.00	$3.00	$6.00
50-330	Ballinger, W. A. - ***I, The Hangman*** [1967] Sexton Blake Series #1	$1.00	$3.00	$6.00
50-333	Arthur, Burt - ***The Buckeroo*** [1967]	$ .75	$2.50	$5.00
50-334	Van Vogt, A. E. - ***Masters Of Time*** [1967]	$1.00	$3.00	$6.00
50-335	Van Vogt, A. E. - ***The Changeling*** [1967]	$1.00	$3.00	$6.00
50-336	Gaddis, Peggy - ***Doctor Sara*** [1967]	$ .65	$2.00	$4.00
50-337	Hogman, Ray - ***Hell To Hallelujah*** [1967]	$ .75	$2.50	$5.00
50-339	Cody, Al - ***Homestead Range*** [1967]	$ .75	$2.50	$5.00
50-340	Lehman, Paul Evan - ***Thunder Creek Range*** [1967]	$ .75	$2.50	$5.00
50-341	Clifton, Mark - ***When They Come From Space*** [1967] Cover art by Richard Powers.	$1.00	$3.00	$6.00

		G	VG	F
50-342	Ballinger, W. A. - ***The Exterminator*** [1967] Photo cover. TV tie-in.	$1.00	$3.00	$6.00
50-343	Greig, Maysie - ***Flight To Happiness*** [1967] Photo cover.	$ .75	$2.50	$5.00
50-345	Hopson, William L. - ***The Laughing Vaquero*** [1967]	$ .75	$2.50	$5.00
50-346	Gaddis, Peggy - ***Big City Nurse*** [1967] Cover art by Robert Maguire.	$ .65	$2.00	$4.00
50-348	Echols, Allan K. - ***Killers Two*** [1967]	$ .75	$2.50	$5.00
50-349	Echols, Allan K. - ***The Renegade Hills*** [1967]	$ .75	$2.50	$5.00
50-350	Ballinger, W. A. - ***The Witches Of Notting Hill*** [1967] Photo cover. Sexton Blake Series #2.	$1.00	$3.00	$6.00
50-353	Lehman, Paul Evan - ***The Twisted Trail*** [1967]	$ .75	$2.50	$5.00
50-354	Baker, W. Howard - ***Every Man An Enemy*** [1967] Photo cover. Sexton Blake Series #3.	$1.00	$3.00	$6.00
50-357	Lehman, Paul Evan - ***Pistols On The Pecos*** [1967]	$ .75	$2.50	$5.00
50-361	Hopson, William - ***Hangtree Range*** [1967]	$ .75	$2.50	$5.00
50-362	Hopson, William & O'Conner, Lois - ***Mexico After Dark*** [1967] Photo cover.	$ .75	$2.50	$5.00
50-364	Echols, Allan K. - ***Wild Horse Range*** [1967]	$ .75	$2.50	$5.00
50-367	Arthur, Burt - ***The Drifter*** [1967]	$ .75	$2.50	$5.00
50-369	McNeilly, Wilfred - ***The Case Of The Muckrakers*** [1967] Photo cover. Sexton Blake Series #4.	$1.00	$3.00	$6.00
50-372	Gaddis, Peggy - ***Lady Doctor*** [1967]	$ .65	$2.00	$4.00
50-373	Cody, Al - ***Son Of The Saddle*** [1967]	$ .75	$2.50	$5.00
50-379	Cody, Al - ***The Gunhand*** [1967]	$ .75	$2.50	$5.00
50-380	Aarons, Edward S. - ***Gift Of Death*** [1967]	$1.00	$3.00	$6.00
50-381	Simak, Clifford D. - ***They Walked Like Men*** [1967] Cover art by Richard Powers.	$1.00	$3.00	$6.00
50-382	Lehman, Paul Evan - ***Pistol Law*** [1967] Cover art by Robert Maguire.	$ .75	$2.50	$5.00
50-383	Gaddis, Peggy - ***The Courtship Of Nurse Genie Hayes*** [1967] Cover by Robert Maguire.	$ .65	$2.00	$4.00
50-384	Keene, Day - ***Passage To Samoa*** [1967]	$1.50	$5.00	$10.00
50-386	Gilmer, Ann - ***Kate Wilder, R.N.*** [1967]	$ .65	$2.00	$4.00
50-388	Simak, Clifford D. - ***All The Traps Of Earth*** [1967] Cover art by Richard Powers.	$1.00	$3.00	$6.00
50-389	Gaddis, Peggy - ***Nurse Hilary*** [1967]	$ .65	$2.00	$4.00
50-390	Floren, Lee - ***Gun-Slammer*** [1967]	$ .75	$2.50	$5.00
50-391	Kent, Arthur - ***Corpse To Cuba*** [1967] Photo cover. Sexton Blake Series #5.	$1.00	$3.00	$6.00
50-393	Rossiter, Jane - ***Backstage Nurse*** [1967]	$ .65	$2.00	$4.00
50-394	Cody, Al - ***The Renegade*** [1967]	$ .75	$2.50	$5.00
50-395	Aarons, Edward S. - ***Nightmare*** [1967]	$1.00	$3.00	$6.00
50-396	Gaddis, Peggy - ***Future Nurse*** [1967]	$ .65	$2.00	$4.00
50-398	Marnais, Philip - ***Saigon After Dark*** [1967] PBO. Photo cover.	$ .75	$2.50	$5.00
50-399	Keene, Day - ***Too Black For Heaven*** [1967] Photo cover.	$1.50	$5.00	$10.00
50-401	Corby, Jane - ***Nurse's Alibi*** [1967]	$ .65	$2.00	$4.00
50-403	Aarons, Edward S. - ***The Art Studio Murders*** [1967] Cover art by Bob Abbett.	$1.00	$3.00	$6.00
50-404	Gaddis, Peggy - ***Student Nurse*** [1967]	$ .65	$2.00	$4.00
50-406	Ross, Dan - ***Cliffhaven*** [1968]	$ .75	$2.50	$5.00
50-408	Bowman, Jeanne - ***Girl Executive*** [1968] Photo cover.	$ .65	$2.00	$4.00
50-409	O'More, Peggy - ***Disaster Nurse*** [1968]	$ .65	$2.00	$4.00
50-412	Gaddis, Peggy - ***Emergency Nurse*** [1968]	$ .65	$2.00	$4.00
50-414	Keene, Day - ***Sleep With The Devil*** [1968]	$1.50	$5.00	$10.00
50-417	Lehman, Paul Evan - ***Fighting Sons Of Texas*** [1968]	$ .75	$2.50	$5.00
50-418	Leinster, Murray - ***The Greks Bring Gifts*** [1968]	$1.00	$3.00	$6.00
50-422	Bowman, Jeanne - ***Nurse Of Polka Dot Island*** [1968]	$ .65	$2.00	$4.00
50-424	Gaddis, Peggy - ***Mountain Nurse*** [1968]	$ .65	$2.00	$4.00
50-426	Bowman, Jeanne - ***Harmony Hospital*** [1968]	$ .65	$2.00	$4.00
50-427	Bowman, Jeanne - ***Small Town Nurse*** [1968]	$ .65	$2.00	$4.00

		G	VG	F
50-429	Gaddis, Peggy - ***Clinic Nurse*** [1968]	$ .65	$2.00	$4.00
50-431	Gaddis, Peggy - ***The Nurse And The Star*** [1968]	$ .65	$2.00	$4.00
50-432	Floren, Lee - ***They Ride With Rifles*** [1968] Cover art by Jerome Podwil.	$ .75	$2.50	$5.00
50-433	Stuart, Florence - ***Research Nurse*** [1968]	$ .65	$2.00	$4.00
50-435	Dana, Rose - ***Down East Nurse*** [1968]	$ .65	$2.00	$4.00
50-438	Dern, Peggy - ***Nurse With A Dream*** [1968]	$ .65	$2.00	$4.00
50-441	Gaddis, Peggy - ***Nurse At The Cedars*** [1968]	$ .65	$2.00	$4.00
50-443	Richards, Ross - ***Murder On The Monte*** [1968] Photo cover. Sexton Blake Series #6.	$1.00	$3.00	$6.00
50-444	Dorset, Ruth - ***Nurse In Waiting*** [1968]	$ .65	$2.00	$4.00
50-445	Arthur, Burt - ***Thunder Valley*** [1968]	$ .75	$2.50	$5.00
50-446	Craig, Georgia - ***A Nurse Comes Home*** [1968]	$ .65	$2.00	$4.00
50-448	O'More, Peggy - ***Nurse Kathryn*** [1968]	$ .65	$2.00	$4.00
50-449	Cody, Al - ***Trail North*** [1968]	$ .75	$2.50	$5.00
50-450	Gaddis, Peggy - ***A Nurse Called Happy*** [1968]	$ .65	$2.00	$4.00
50-452	Dana, Rose - ***Nurse In Jepoardy*** [1968]	$ .65	$2.00	$4.00
50-454	Craig, Georgia - ***Nurse Lucie*** [1968]	$ .65	$2.00	$4.00
50-456	Dorset, Ruth - ***Hotel Nurse*** [1968]	$ .65	$2.00	$4.00
50-458	Gaddis, Peggy - ***A Nurse For Apple Valley*** [1968]	$ .65	$2.00	$4.00
50-460	Echols, Allan K. - ***Red River Road*** [1968]	$ .75	$2.50	$5.00
50-461	Gaddis, Peggy - ***Everglades Nurse*** [1968]	$ .65	$2.00	$4.00
50-462	Hopson, William - ***Bullet-Brand Empire*** [1968]	$ .75	$2.50	$5.00
50-463	Dana, Rose - ***Operating Room Nurse*** [1968]	$ .65	$2.00	$4.00
50-465	Dana, Rose - ***Night Club Nurse*** [1968]	$ .65	$2.00	$4.00
50-467	Gaddis, Peggy - ***Betsy Moran, R.N.*** [1968]	$ .65	$2.00	$4.00
50-470	Gaddis, Peggy - ***Bayou Nurse*** [1968]	$ .65	$2.00	$4.00
50-471	Stuart, Florence - ***Nurse Under Fire*** [1968]	$ .65	$2.00	$4.00
50-473	Stuart, Florence - ***Runaway Nurse*** [1968]	$ .65	$2.00	$4.00
50-475	Shepard, Fern - ***Nurse In Danger*** [1968]	$ .65	$2.00	$4.00
50-477	Lehman, Paul Evan - ***Montana Man*** [1968]	$ .75	$2.50	$5.00
50-478	Stuart, Florence - ***The Nurse And The Orderly*** [1968]	$ .65	$2.00	$4.00
50-479	Dana, Rose - ***Bermuda Nurse*** [1968]	$ .65	$2.00	$4.00
50-481	Gaddis, Peggy - ***Nurse Angela*** [1968]	$ .65	$2.00	$4.00
50-483	Dana, Rose - ***Nurse Freda*** [1968]	$ .65	$2.00	$4.00
50-484	Floren, Lee - ***Black Boulder Ranch*** [1968]	$ .75	$2.50	$5.00
50-485	Gaddis, Peggy - ***The Listening Nurse*** [1968]	$ .65	$2.00	$4.00
50-486	Arthur, Burt - ***The Killer*** [1968]	$ .75	$2.50	$5.00
50-488	Floren, Lee - ***Gun Luck*** [1968]	$ .75	$2.50	$5.00
50-490	Echols, Allan K. - ***Vengeance Valley*** [1968]	$ .75	$2.50	$5.00
50-491	Gaddis, Peggy - ***Nurse In Flight*** [1968]	$ .65	$2.00	$4.00
50-494	Cody, Al - ***Shannahan's Feud*** [1968]	$ .75	$2.50	$5.00
50-495	Gaddis, Peggy - ***Nora Was A Nurse*** [1968]	$ .65	$2.00	$4.00
50-496	Grinstead, J. E. - ***When Texans Ride*** [1968]	$ .75	$2.50	$5.00
50-498	Floren, Lee - ***Lobo Valley*** [1968]	$ .75	$2.50	$5.00
50-500	Lehman, Paul Evan - ***The Cold Trail*** [1968]	$ .75	$2.50	$5.00
50-502	Floren, Lee - ***War On Alkali Creek*** [1968]	$ .75	$2.50	$5.00
50-504	Arthur, Burt - ***The Buckaroo*** [1968]	$ .75	$2.50	$5.00
50-506	Lehman, Paul Evan - ***Action At The Bitterroot*** [1968]	$ .75	$2.50	$5.00
50-508	Lehman, Paul Evan - ***Law Of The Gun*** [1968] Cover art by Malmed.	$ .75	$2.50	$5.00
50-956	Wesley, Elizabeth - ***Dr. Dorothy's Choice*** [1963]	$ .65	$2.00	$4.00
60-102	Carrel, Alexis - ***Man, The Unknown*** [1961]	$ .75	$2.50	$5.00
60-103	Cannon, Poppy - ***The Can-Opener Cookbook*** [1961]	$ .75	$2.50	$5.00
60-105	Musmanno, Michael A. - ***Ten Days To Die*** [1961] Cover by Paul Muni.	$ .75	$2.50	$5.00
60-106	Stearn, Jess - ***The Sixth Man*** [1962] Photo cover.	$ .75	$2.50	$5.00
60-108	Busch, Niven - ***The Hate Merchant*** [1962] Cover art by Robert Abbett.	$ .75	$2.50	$5.00
60-109	Loth, David - ***The Erotic In Literature*** [1962] Photo cover.	$ .75	$2.50	$5.00

		G	VG	F
60-112	Zellerbach, Merla - ***Love In A Dark House*** [1962]	$ .75	$2.50	$5.00
60-113	Kordel, Lelord - ***Eat And Grow Younger*** [1962]	$ .75	$2.50	$5.00
60-119	Goldwater, Senator Barry - ***Why Not Victory?*** [1962] Photo cover.	$ .75	$2.50	$5.00
60-120	Allingham, Margery - ***Pearls Before Swine*** [1962]	$1.00	$3.00	$6.00
60-122	Allingham, Margery - ***Police At The Funeral*** [1963] Photo cover.	$1.00	$3.00	$6.00
60-123	Shadegg, Stephen - ***Barry Goldwater: Freedom Is His Flight Plan*** [1963]	$ .75	$2.50	$5.00
60-128	Tanner, Louise - ***Miss Bannister's Girls*** [1963]	$ .75	$2.50	$5.00
60-129	Allingham, Margery - ***Mystery Mile*** [1963] Photo cover.	$1.00	$3.00	$6.00
60-131	Hudson, Virginia Cary - ***O Ye Jigs & Juleps!*** [1963]	$ .75	$2.50	$5.00
60-133	Elgeti, Almuth - ***Food For Lovers*** [1963]	$ .75	$2.50	$5.00
60-135	Roate, Mettja C. - ***How To Make Wine In Your Own Kitchen*** [1963] PBO. Cover art by Paul Bacon.	$ .75	$2.50	$5.00
60-137	Lyall, Gavin - ***The Wrong Side Of The Sky*** [1963]	$1.00	$3.00	$6.00
60-138	Sadler, Christine - ***America's First Ladies*** [1964] Photo cover. Eight pages of photos.	$ .75	$2.50	$5.00
60-140	Michel, Scott - ***Journey Into Limbo*** [1963] Cover art by Stanley Borack.	$ .75	$2.50	$5.00
60-141	Kahn, Lotte - ***Women And Wall Street*** [1963] PBO.	$ .75	$2.50	$5.00
60-142	Leigh, Michael - ***The Velvet Underground*** [1963] PBO. Photo cover.	$ .75	$2.50	$5.00
60-144	Rimmer, Robert H. - ***That Girl From Boston*** [1963]	$ .75	$2.50	$5.00
60-146	Van Vogt, A. E. - ***The Voyage Of The Space Beagle*** [1963] Cover by Richard Powers	$1.00	$3.00	$6.00
60-147	Roeburt, John - ***The Wicked And The Banned*** [1963] PBO. Photo cover.	$1.00	$3.00	$6.00
60-148	Roos, William - ***Where's Daddy?*** [1964] Cover art by Weber.	$ .75	$2.50	$5.00
60-151	Sanders, Jacquin - ***A Night Before Christmas*** [1964]	$ .75	$2.50	$5.00
60-152	Thorn, Ronald Scott - ***The Dark Shadow*** [1964]	$ .75	$2.50	$5.00
60-153	Bemelmans, Ludwig - ***The Street Whee The Heart Lies*** [1964]	$ .75	$2.50	$5.00
60-154	Heffley, Wayne - ***Television As A Career*** [1964] PBO.	$ .75	$2.50	$5.00
60-156	Schiddel, Edmund - ***Break-Up*** [1964]	$ .75	$2.50	$5.00
60-157	Kirk, Jeremy - ***The Build-Up Boys*** [1964]	$ .75	$2.50	$5.00
60-161	Cubbedge, Robert E. - ***The Destroyers of America*** [1964] PBO.	$ .75	$2.50	$5.00
60-162	Manchester, William - ***Portrait Of A President*** [1964] Photo cover.	$ .75	$2.50	$5.00
60-165	Kingsley, Michael - ***Branches Of Evil*** [1964]	$ .75	$2.50	$5.00
60-166	Buckley, Jr., William F. - ***Rumbles Left And Right*** [1964]	$ .75	$2.50	$5.00
60-167	Mead, Shepherd - ***"Dudley, There Is No Tomorrow!"*** [1964]	$ .75	$2.50	$5.00
60-169	Van Vogt, A. E. - ***The Beast*** [1964] Cover art by Richard Powers.	$1.00	$3.00	$6.00
60-174	Leterman, Elmer G. - ***Commissions Don't Fall From Heaven*** [1964]	$ .75	$2.50	$5.00
60-175	Renwick, Ethel Hulbert - ***A World Of Good Cooking*** [1964]	$ .75	$2.50	$5.00
60-176	Spong, Richard - ***See If He Wins*** [1964]	$ .75	$2.50	$5.00
60-178	Flender, Harold - ***Rescue In Denmark*** [1964]	$ .75	$2.50	$5.00
60-184	Bonner, Paul Hyde - ***Hotel Talleyrand*** [1964]	$ .75	$2.50	$5.00
60-185	Freedgood, Morton - ***The Wall-To-Wall Trap*** [1964]	$ .75	$2.50	$5.00
60-186	Lee, Marjorie - ***On You It Looks Good*** [1964] Cover art by Barye Phillips.	$ .75	$2.50	$5.00
60-189	Lyall, Gavin - ***The Most Dangerous Game*** [1964]	$1.00	$3.00	$6.00
60-194	Anthology Edited by Adeline Garner - ***Great Recipes From True Story*** [1964]	$ .75	$2.50	$5.00
60-195	Iversen, William - ***The Pious Pornographers*** [1964]	$ .75	$2.50	$5.00
60-196	McPartland, John - ***No Down Payment*** [1964]	$1.00	$3.00	$6.00
60-197	Gardner, Brian - ***On To Kilimanjaro*** [1964]	$ .75	$2.50	$5.00
60-198	Simak, Clifford D. - ***Way Station*** [1964]	$1.00	$3.00	$6.00
60-199	Allingham, Margery - ***The China Governess*** [1964]	$1.00	$3.00	$6.00

		G	VG	F
60-203	Uhnak, Dorothy - ***Policewoman*** [1965] Photo cover.	$1.00	$3.00	$6.00
60-205	MacDonald, Philip - ***Mystery Of The Dead Police*** [1965]	$1.00	$3.00	$6.00
60-206	Anderson, Poul - ***Time And Stars*** [1965] Cover art by Karol.	$1.00	$3.00	$6.00
60-208	Hough, Richard - ***Death Of The Battleship*** [1965]	$ .75	$2.50	$5.00
60-209	Faure, Raoul C. - ***Summer Of Stones*** [1965]	$ .75	$2.50	$5.00
60-210	Burg, Robert - ***The Buyer's Guide To Nearly Everything*** [1965] PBO. Cover by Roy E. La Grone.	$ .75	$2.50	$5.00
60-212	Markey, Gene - ***Women, Women, Everywhere*** [1965]	$ .75	$2.50	$5.00
60-213	Tully, Andrew and Britton, Milton - ***Where Did Your Money Go?*** [1965]	$ .75	$2.50	$5.00
60-215	Humphrey, Hubert H. - ***The Cause Is Mankind*** [1965] Photo cover.	$ .75	$2.50	$5.00
60-216	Kaplan, Arthur - ***Hotel De La Liberte'*** [1965]	$ .75	$2.50	$5.00
60-220	Mair, George B. - ***Death's Foot Forward*** [1965]	$ .75	$2.50	$5.00
60-221	Lacy, Ed - ***Pity The Honest*** [1965] PBO.	$1.25	$3.75	$7.50
60-223	Caldwell, Erskine - ***We Are The Living*** [1965]	$ .75	$2.50	$5.00
60-224	Davis, Mildred - ***The Voice On The Telephone*** [1965] Photo cover.	$1.00	$3.00	$6.00
60-225	Selcamm, George - ***The Night Is For Music*** [1965]	$ .75	$2.50	$5.00
60-226	Lewis, Calude - ***Cassius Clay*** [1965] PBO. Photo cover.	$1.00	$3.00	$6.00
60-227	Blackstock, Charity - ***The English Wife*** [1965] Photo cover.	$1.00	$3.00	$6.00
60-228	Schiddel, Edmund - ***The Other Side Of The Night*** [1965]	$1.00	$3.00	$6.00
60-229	Anthology - ***The Frozen Planet*** [1966] PBO. Cover art by Richard Powers.	$1.25	$3.75	$7.50
60-235	Fitzpatrick, William - ***Hong Kong After Dark*** [1966] PBO. Photo cover.	$ .75	$2.50	$5.00
60-237	Allingham, Margery - ***Death Of A Ghost*** [1966] Photo cover.	$1.00	$3.00	$6.00
60-238	Charteris, Leslie - ***The Saint In The Sun*** [1966]	$1.00	$3.00	$6.00
60-239	Temple, William F. - ***Shoot At The Moon*** [1967] Photo cover.	$1.00	$3.00	$6.00
60-240	Dick, Philip K. - ***The Three Stigmata Of Palmer Eldritch*** [1966]	$4.00	$12.50	$25.00
60-241	Eberhart, Mignon G. - ***The Dark Garden*** [1966] Photo cover.	$1.00	$3.00	$6.00
60-245	Allingham, Margery - ***No Love Lost*** [1966]	$1.00	$3.00	$6.00
60-246	Charteris, Leslie - ***The Saint Goes West*** [1966]	$1.00	$3.00	$6.00
60-247	Charteris, Leslie - ***Saint Errant*** [1966]	$1.00	$3.00	$6.00
60-248	de Ballard, Jean - ***Paris After Dark*** [1966]	$ .75	$2.50	$5.00
60-249	Allingham, Margery - ***The Gyrth Chalice Mystery*** [1966] Photo cover.	$1.00	$3.00	$6.00
60-251	Allingham, Margery - ***The Estate Of The Beckoning Lady*** [1966]	$1.00	$3.00	$6.00
60-252	Charteris, Leslie - ***The Saint On The Spanish Main*** [1966]	$1.00	$3.00	$6.00
60-253	Charteris, Leslie - ***Trust The Saint*** [1966]	$1.00	$3.00	$6.00
60-254	Allingham, Margery - ***The Black Dudley Murder*** [1966] Photo cover.	$1.00	$3.00	$6.00
60-257	Blackstock, Charity - ***Monkey On A Chain*** [1966]	$1.00	$3.00	$6.00
60-259	Nash, Norman - ***London After Dark*** [1966]	$ .75	$2.50	$5.00
60-260	Charteris, Leslie - ***The Saint Around The World*** [1966]	$1.00	$3.00	$6.00
60-261	Keogh, Theodora - ***The Mistress*** [1966] Cover art by Johnson.	$ .75	$2.50	$5.00
60-262	Charteris, Leslie - ***The Saint Intervenes*** [1966]	$1.00	$3.00	$6.00
60-264	Thorp, Duncan - ***Only Akiko*** [1966] Photo cover.	$ .75	$2.50	$5.00
60-265	Charteris, Leslie - ***The Saint Goes On*** [1966]	$1.00	$3.00	$6.00
60-266	Reilly, Helen - ***Murder In The Mews*** [1966] Photo cover.	$1.00	$3.00	$6.00
60-267	Van Vogt, A. E. - ***Empire Of The Atom*** [1966]	$1.00	$3.00	$6.00
60-268	Ross, Colin - ***New York After Dark*** [1966]	$ .75	$2.50	$5.00
60-271	Eberhart, Mignon G. - ***Danger In The Dark*** [1966]	$1.00	$3.00	$6.00
60-272	Disney, Doris Miles - ***Should Auld Acquaintance*** [1966]	$1.00	$3.00	$6.00
60-273	Charteris, Leslie - ***Call For The Saint*** [1967]	$1.00	$3.00	$6.00
60-274	Allingham, Margery - ***Dancers In Mourning*** [1967]	$1.00	$3.00	$6.00
60-275	Allingham, Margery - ***Pearls Before Swine*** [1967] Photo cover.	$1.00	$3.00	$6.00
60-276	Disney, Doris Miles - ***The Hospitality Of The House*** [1967]	$1.00	$3.00	$6.00

		G	VG	F
60-277	North, Eric - ***The Ant Men*** [1967] Cover art by Jack Faragasso.	$1.50	$5.00	$10.00
60-278	Anthology edited by Dorothy L. Sayers - ***Tales Of Detection And Mystery*** [1967]	$1.00	$3.00	$6.00
60-280	Allingham, Margery - ***Police At The Funeral*** [1967]	$1.00	$3.00	$6.00
60-281	Davis, Mildred - ***The Sound Of Insects*** [1967]	$1.00	$3.00	$6.00
60-284	Reilly, Helen - ***Death Demands An Audience*** [1967]	$1.00	$3.00	$6.00
60-287	Lymington, John - ***Froomb!*** [1967] Photo cover.	$1.25	$3.75	$7.50
60-290	Bardin, John Franklin - ***Devil Take The Blue-Tail Fly*** [1967] Photo cover.	$ .75	$2.50	$5.00
60-291	Holly, J. Hunter - ***The Mind Traders*** [1967] Photo cover.	$1.00	$3.00	$6.00
60-292	Allingham, Margery - ***Mystery Mile*** [1967]	$1.00	$3.00	$6.00
60-294	Charteris, Leslie - ***The Saint In Europe*** [1967]	$1.00	$3.00	$6.00
60-296	Disney, Doris Miles - ***Here Lies . . .*** [1967]	$1.00	$3.00	$6.00
60-298	Anthology edited by Dorothy L. Sayers - ***Human And Inhuman Stories*** [1967] Photo cover.	$1.00	$3.00	$6.00
60-300	Harvester, Simon - ***Treacherous Road*** [1967]	$ .75	$2.50	$5.00
60-302	Borowik, Ann - ***Lions Three: Christians Nothing*** [1967]	$ .75	$2.50	$5.00
60-304	Disney, Doris Miles - ***The Departure Of Mr. Gaudette*** [1967]	$1.00	$3.00	$6.00
60-305	Smith, Stan - ***Pass The Ammunition*** [1967]	$ .75	$2.50	$5.00
60-306	Leterman, Elmer G. - ***The Sale Begins When The Customer Says "No"*** [1967]	$ .75	$2.50	$5.00
60-307	Charteris, Leslie - ***The Saint To The Rescue*** [1968]	$1.00	$3.00	$6.00
60-308	Aarons, Edward S. - ***Say It With Murder*** [1968]	$1.00	$3.00	$6.00
60-309	Nourse, Alan E. - ***Tiger By The Tail*** [1968]	$1.00	$3.00	$6.00
60-311	Harvester, Simon - ***Red Road*** [1967]	$ .75	$2.50	$5.00
60-312	Reilly, Helen - ***Mr. Smith's Hat*** [1968]	$1.00	$3.00	$6.00
60-313	Allingham, Margery - ***More Work For The Undertaker*** [1968]	$1.00	$3.00	$6.00
60-315	Charteris, Leslie - ***Senor Saint*** [1968]	$1.00	$3.00	$6.00
60-317	Reilly, Helen - ***Dead Man Control*** [1968]	$1.00	$3.00	$6.00
60-323	Allingham, Margery - ***The Fear Sign*** [1968] Photo cover.	$1.00	$3.00	$6.00
60-324	Martin, Kay - ***A Taste Of Passion*** [1968] Photo cover.	$ .75	$2.50	$5.00
60-326	Harvester, Simon - ***Unsung Road*** [1968]	$ .75	$2.50	$5.00
60-332	Aarons, Edward S. - ***Dark Destiny*** [1968]	$1.00	$3.00	$6.00
60-335	Anthology edited by Sam Moskowitz - ***Microcosmic God*** [1968] Photo cover.	$1.00	$3.00	$6.00
60-341	Nichols, Fan - ***Devil Take Her*** [1968]	$ .75	$2.50	$5.00
60-343	Van Vogt, A. E. - ***The Beast*** [1968] Photo cover.	$1.00	$3.00	$6.00
60-345	Lacy, Ed - ***Visa To Death*** [1968]	$1.00	$3.00	$6.00
60-349	Anderson, Poul - ***The High Crusade*** [1968] Cover art by Jack Faragasso.	$1.00	$3.00	$6.00
60-350	Aarons, Edward S. - ***No Place To Live*** [1968]	$1.00	$3.00	$6.00
60-353	Reid, Desmond - ***Frenzy In The Flesh*** [1968] Sexton Blake Series #7.	$1.00	$3.00	$6.00
60-358	Disney, Doris Miles - ***Shadow Of A Man*** [1968] Photo cover.	$1.00	$3.00	$6.00
60-361	Reilly, Helen - ***All Concerned Notified*** [1968] Photo cover.	$1.00	$3.00	$6.00
60-365	Charteris, Leslie - ***Thanks To The Saint*** [1968]	$1.00	$3.00	$6.00
60-366	Van Vogt, A. E. - ***The Wizard Of Linn*** [1968]	$1.00	$3.00	$6.00
60-369	McGerr, Patricia - ***Fatal In My Fashion*** [1969] Photo cover.	$1.00	$3.00	$6.00
60-370	Deal, Babs H. - ***Fancy's Knell*** [1969] Photo cover.	$ .75	$2.50	$5.00
60-373	Carew, Jean - ***Samantha*** [1969]	$ .75	$2.50	$5.00
60-375	Aarons, Edward S. - ***Death Is My Shadow*** [1969]	$1.00	$3.00	$6.00
60-376	Lord, Jeffrey - ***The Bronze Axe*** [1969]	$1.50	$5.00	$10.00
60-381	Mead, Matt - ***Star Crossed*** [1969] Sexton Blake Series #8.	$1.00	$3.00	$6.00
60-384	Lymington, John - ***Night Of The Big Heat*** [1969]	$1.00	$3.00	$6.00
60-390	Aarons, Edward S. - ***Point Of Peril*** [1969] Photo cover.	$1.00	$3.00	$6.00
60-391	Harvester, Simon - ***Battle Road*** [1969]	$ .75	$2.50	$5.00
60-395	Ross, Dan - ***The Third Spectre*** [1969]	$1.00	$3.00	$6.00
60-396	Cody, Al - ***Montana Fury*** [1969]	$ .75	$2.50	$5.00
60-397	Simak, Clifford D. - ***Way Station*** [1969]	$1.00	$3.00	$6.00
60-399	Aarons, Edward S. - ***The Net*** [1969]	$1.00	$3.00	$6.00

		G	VG	F
60-401	Lymington, John - ***The Grey Ones*** [1969] PBO.	$1.25	$3.75	$7.50
60-406	Van Vogt, A. E. - ***Masters Of Time*** [1969] Cover art by Faragasso.	$1.00	$3.00	$6.00
60-407	Dolphin, Rex - ***The Trail Of The Golden Girl*** [1969] Photo cover. Sexton Blake Series #9.	$1.00	$3.00	$6.00
60-410	Bounds, Sydney J. - ***The Robot Brains*** [1969]	$1.00	$3.00	$6.00
60-413	Reilly, Helen - ***Death Demands An Audience*** [1969]	$1.00	$3.00	$6.00
60-414	McGerr, Patricia - ***Murder Is Absurd*** [1969] Cover art by Stivers.	$1.00	$3.00	$6.00
60-415	Harvester, Simon - ***The Chinese Hammer*** [1969]	$ .75	$2.50	$5.00
60-416	Van Vogt, A. E. - ***The Changeling*** [1969] Cover art by Faragasso.	$1.00	$3.00	$6.00
60-418	Omura, Kimiko - ***Diary Of A Geisha Girl*** [1969] Cover art by Stivers.	$ .75	$2.50	$5.00
60-424	Keene, Day - ***The Big Kill-Off*** [1969] PBO.	$1.50	$5.00	$10.00
60-428	Anthology - ***The Six Fingers Of Time*** [1969] Cover art by Jack Faragasso.	$1.00	$3.00	$6.00
60-431	Stokes, Manning Lee - ***Under Cover Of Night*** [1969]	$1.00	$3.00	$6.00
60-432	McHugh, Frances Y. - ***Bluethorne*** [1969]	$ .75	$2.50	$5.00
60-433	Martin, Chuck - ***Boothill Gospel*** [1969]	$ .75	$2.50	$5.00
60-434	North, Eric - ***The Ant Men*** [1969]	$1.00	$3.00	$6.00
60-435	Floren, Lee - ***Riders In The Storm*** [1969]	$ .75	$2.50	$5.00
60-436	Lymington, John - ***The Screaming Face*** [1970] PBO. Cover art by Faragasso.	$1.25	$3.75	$7.50
60-437	Coburn, Walt - ***Invitation To A Hanging*** [1970]	$ .75	$2.50	$5.00
60-439	Roeburt, John - ***Ruby MacLaine*** [1970] Photo cover.	$ .75	$2.50	$5.00
60-440	Harvester, Simon - ***Zion Road*** [1970]	$ .75	$2.50	$5.00
60-442	Lehman, Paul Evan - ***Texas Men*** [1970]	$ .75	$2.50	$5.00
60-444	Knight, Damon - ***Beyond The Barrier*** [1970]	$1.00	$3.00	$6.00
60-445	Lymington, John - ***The Star Witches*** [1970] Cover art by Faragasso.	$1.00	$3.00	$6.00
60-446	Martin, Chuck - ***Gunsmoke Bonanza*** [1970]	$ .75	$2.50	$5.00
60-448	Ross, Dan - ***Behind Locked Shutters*** [1970]	$1.00	$3.00	$6.00
60-449	Hopson, William - ***Silver Gulch*** [1970]	$ .75	$2.50	$5.00
60-450	Ross, Dan - ***Dark Is My Shadow*** [1970]	$1.00	$3.00	$6.00
60-451	Cody, Al - ***Trouble At Sudden Creek*** [1970]	$ .75	$2.50	$5.00
60-453	Coburn, Walt - ***Square Shooter*** [1970]	$ .75	$2.50	$5.00
60-454	Coburn, Walt - ***Border Jumper*** [1970]	$ .75	$2.50	$5.00
60-457	Echols, Allen K. - ***The Stranger From Texas*** [1970]	$ .75	$2.50	$5.00
60-458	Coburn, Walt - ***Drift Fence*** [1970]	$ .75	$2.50	$5.00
60-459	Lionel, Robert (Robert Fanthorpe) - ***Time Echo*** [1970]	$1.00	$3.00	$6.00
60-460	Coburn, Walt - ***Violent Maverick*** [1970]	$ .75	$2.50	$5.00
60-462	Hopson, William - ***Tombstone Stage*** [1970] Cover art by Ronnie Lesser.	$ .75	$2.50	$5.00
60-463	Ross, Dan - ***The Whispering Gallery*** [1971]	$ .75	$2.50	$5.00
60-478	Hopson, William L. - ***Straight Fom Boot Hill*** [1971]	$ .75	$2.50	$5.00
60-479	Dern, Peggy - ***Nurse In The Tropics*** [1971]	$ .65	$2.00	$4.00
60-506	MacCampbell, Donald - ***Reading For Enjoyment*** [1971]	$ .65	$2.00	$4.00

Magabook. New York: Galaxy Publishing Corp. Digest Size.

		G	VG	F
1	Del Rey, Lester - ***The Sky Is Falling/Badge Of Infamy*** [1963] PBO.	$1.50	$5.00	$10.00
2	Williamson, Jack - ***After World's End/The Legion Of Time*** [1963] PBO.	$1.50	$5.00	$10.00
3	Sturgeon, Theodore - ***Baby Is Three/...And My Fear Is Great*** [1965] Gray Morrow cover art.	$1.50	$5.00	$10.00

Magazine Village. New York: Magazine Village, Inc. Digest Size.

		G	VG	F
5	Sturdy, Carl - ***Confessions Of A Park Avenue Playgirl*** [1948]	$3.50	$10.00	$20.00
6	Bull, Lois - ***Illicit Honeymoon*** [1948]	$3.50	$10.00	$20.00

7 Keating, E. T. - ***Hard Boiled Mistress*** [1948] $3.50 $10.00 $20.00
8 Bull, Lois - ***Virgin By Day*** [1948] $3.50 $10.00 $20.00

Mark Goulden. London: Mark Goulden, Ltd.
1 Burroughs, Edgar Rice - ***Tarzan And The Lost Empire*** [1950].... $3.00 $9.00 $18.00
2 Burroughs, Edgar Rice - ***Tarzan Lord Of The Jungle*** [1950] $3.00 $9.00 $18.00
3 Burroughs, Edgar Rice - ***Tarzan The Invincible*** [1950]........ $3.00 $9.00 $18.00
4 Burroughs, Edgar Rice - ***Tarzan At The Earth's Core*** [1950]...... $3.00 $9.00 $18.00
5 Burroughs, Edgar Rice - ***Tarzan's Quest*** [1950]........ $3.00 $9.00 $18.00
6 Burroughs, Edgar Rice - ***A Princess Of Mars*** [1950]........ $3.00 $9.00 $18.00
9 Burroughs, Edgar Rice - ***Carson Of Venus*** [1950]........ $3.00 $9.00 $18.00

Media Books.
M-101 Thompson, Thomas - ***Bonanza: One Man With Courage*** [1966] PBO. TV tie-in. TV photo cover........ $1.25 $3.75 $7.50
M-102 Cox, William R. - ***Bonanza: Black Silver*** [1967] PBO. Photo cover. TV tie-in. $1.25 $3.75 $7.50

Mentor Books.
M-27 Gamow, George - ***Biography Of The Earth*** [1948] Cover art by Jonas........ $ .40 $1.25 $2.50
M-28 Whitehead, Alfred North - ***Science And The Modern World*** [1948]........ $ .40 $1.25 $2.50
M-29 Johnson, James Weldon - ***The Autobiography Of An Ex-Coloured Man*** [1948] Cover art by Jonas. .... $ .40 $1.25 $2.50
M-30 Anthology - ***America In Perspective*** [1948] Edited by Henry Steele Commager. Cover art by Jonas........ $ .40 $1.25 $2.50
M-31 Huxley, Julian - ***Man In The Modern World*** [1948]........ $ .40 $1.25 $2.50
MD-32 Hamilton, Edith - ***The Greek Way*** [1948] .... $ .40 $1.25 $2.50
M-33 Collier, John - ***Indians Of The Americas*** [1948] PBO. Cover art by Jonas. .... $ .40 $1.25 $2.50
M-35 Sullivan, J.W.N. - ***The Limitations Of Science*** [1948]........ $ .40 $1.25 $2.50
M-36 Peterson, Roger Tory - ***How To Know The Birds*** [1948] .... $ .40 $1.25 $2.50
M-37 Pares, Bernard - ***Russia*** [1948] .... $ .40 $1.25 $2.50
M-38 Schlesinger, Jr., Arthur, M. - ***The Age Of Jackson*** [1948]........ $ .40 $1.25 $2.50
M-39 Jones, H. Spencer - ***Life On Other Worlds*** [1953] .... $ .40 $1.25 $2.50
M-41 Whitehead, Alfred North - ***The Aims Of Education*** [1949] Cover art by Jonas. .... $ .40 $1.25 $2.50
M-42 Amberg, George - ***Ballet*** [1949] Cover by Jonas. .... $ .40 $1.25 $2.50
M-43 Otto, Max C. - ***Science And The Moral Life*** [1952]........ $ .40 $1.25 $2.50
M-44 Mead, Margaret - ***Coming Of Age In Samoa*** [1952] Cover art by Jonas. .... $ .40 $1.25 $2.50
M-45 Sullivan, J.W.N. - ***Beethoven*** [1952] Cover by Jonas........ $ .40 $1.25 $2.50
M-46 Homer - ***The Iliad*** [1952]........ $ .40 $1.25 $2.50
M-48 Stefferud, Alfred - ***How To Know The Wild Flowers*** [1952] ...... $ .40 $1.25 $2.50
M-49 Yasset, Jose Ortega - ***The Revolt Of The Masses*** [1952]........ $ .40 $1.25 $2.50
M-51 Parkman, Francis - ***The Oregon Trail*** [1951]........ $ .40 $1.25 $2.50
M-52 Bernhard, Hubert J./Bennett, Dorothy A. - ***New Handbook Of The Heavens*** [1950]........ $ .40 $1.25 $2.50
M-53 Dewey, John - ***Reconstruction In Philosophy*** [1950] .... $ .40 $1.25 $2.50
M-54 Anthology - ***100 Modern Poems*** [1950] Edited by Selden Rodman........ $ .40 $1.25 $2.50
M-55 Anthology - ***Life Stories Of Men Who Shaped History*** [1950] Edited by Eduard C. Lindeman........ $ .40 $1.25 $2.50
M-56 Mead, Margaret - ***Sex And Temperament In Three Primitive Societies*** [1950] Cover by Jonas........ $ .40 $1.25 $2.50
M-57 Shub, David - ***Lenin*** [1950] .... $ .40 $1.25 $2.50
M-59 Smith, T.V. & Lindeman, Eduard C. - ***The Democratic Way Of Life*** [1953]........ $ .40 $1.25 $2.50
M-60 Maugham, W. Somerset - ***The Summing Up*** [1953] .... $ .40 $1.25 $2.50

		G	VG	F
M-63	Sanderson, Ivan T. - ***How To Know The American Mammals*** [1953]	$ .40	$1.25	$2.50
M-64	Childe, V. Gordon - ***Man Makes Himself*** [1953]	$ .40	$1.25	$2.50
M-65	Armitage, Angus - ***The World Of Copernicus*** [1951] 6 pages of photos.	$ .40	$1.25	$2.50
M-66	Simpson, George Gaylord - ***The Meaning Of Evolution*** [1951]	$ .40	$1.25	$2.50
M-67	Freud, Sigmund - ***Psychopathology Of Everyday Life*** [1953]	$ .40	$1.25	$2.50
M-68	Conant, James B. - ***On Understanding Science*** [1951] PBO.	$ .40	$1.25	$2.50
M-69	Machiavelli, Niccolo - ***The Prince*** [1954] Cover art by Jonas.	$ .40	$1.25	$2.50
M-70	Padover, Saul K. - ***Jefferson*** [1954]	$ .40	$1.25	$2.50
M-71	Barnett, Lincoln - ***The Universe And Dr. Einstein*** [1954]	$ .40	$1.25	$2.50
M-74	Dunn, L.C. & Dobzhansky, Th. - ***Heredity, Race And Society*** [1954]	$ .40	$1.25	$2.50
M-76	Anthology - ***Good Reading*** [1954] Edited by The Committee on College Reading.	$ .40	$1.25	$2.50
M-77	Gamow, George - ***The Birth And Death Of The Sun*** [1954] Cover art by Jonas. 16 pages of photos.	$ .40	$1.25	$2.50
M-78	Heffner, Richard D. - ***A Documentary History Of The United States*** [1952] PBO. Cover art by Jonas.	$ .40	$1.25	$2.50
M-80	Kennan, George F. - ***American Diplomacy 1900-1950*** [1952]	$ .40	$1.25	$2.50
M-82	Anthology - ***The Wonderful World Of Books*** [1952] Edited by Alfred Stefferud.	$ .40	$1.25	$2.50
M-83	Schweitzer, Albert - ***Out Of My Life And Thought*** [1953] Cover art by Jonas.	$ .40	$1.25	$2.50
M-84	Fisher, Robert Moore - ***How To Know And Predict The Weather*** [1953]	$ .40	$1.25	$2.50
M-86	Hamilton, Edith - ***Mythology*** [1953]	$ .40	$1.25	$2.50
M-87	Thoreau, Henry David - ***Walden*** [1953]	$ .40	$1.25	$2.50
M-89	Benedict, Ruth - ***Patterns Of Culture*** [1953]	$ .40	$1.25	$2.50
M-90	Palgrave, F.T. - ***The Golden Treasury*** [1953]	$ .40	$1.25	$2.50
M-91	Mead, Margaret - ***Growing Up In New Guinea*** [1953] Cover art by Jonas.	$ .40	$1.25	$2.50
M-93	Veblen, Thorstein - ***The Theory Of The Leisure Class*** [1953] Cover by Jonas.	$ .40	$1.25	$2.50
M-94	Pickthall, Mohammed Marmaduke - ***The Meaning Of The Glorious Koran*** [1953]	$ .40	$1.25	$2.50
M-95	Padover, Saul K. - ***The Living U.S. Constitution*** [1953] Cover by Jonas.	$ .40	$1.25	$2.50
M-97	Gamow, George - ***One Two Three...Infinity*** [1953] Cover art by Jonas.	$ .40	$1.25	$2.50
M-99	Toynbee, Arnold - ***Greek Civilization And Character*** [1953] Cover by Jonas.	$ .40	$1.25	$2.50
M-100	Carson, Rachel L. - ***The Sea Around Us*** [1954]	$ .40	$1.25	$2.50
M-103	No Author Listed - ***The Song Of God: Bhagavadgita*** [1954]	$ .40	$1.25	$2.50
M-104	Anthology - ***Highlights Of Modern Literature*** [1954] Edited by Francis Brown.	$ .40	$1.25	$2.50
M-105	Crompton, John - ***The Life Of The Spider*** [1954] Photo cover.	$ .40	$1.25	$2.50
M-107	Childs, Marquis W. & Cater, Douglass - ***Ethics In A Business Society*** [1954] Cover art by Jonas.	$ .40	$1.25	$2.50
M-109	Brinton, C., Kazin, A., Hicks, J.D. - ***The World Of History*** [1954]	$ .40	$1.25	$2.50
M-110	Rouse, W.H.D. - ***The Iliad Of Homer*** [1954]	$ .40	$1.25	$2.50
M-111	Maeterlinck, Maurice - ***The Life Of The Bee*** [1954]	$ .40	$1.25	$2.50
M-112	Muller, Herbert J. - ***The Uses Of The Past*** [1954]	$ .40	$1.25	$2.50
M-113	Ciardi, John - ***The Inferno By Dante*** [1954]	$ .40	$1.25	$2.50
M-114	Bernhard, Hubert J. - ***New Handbook Of The Heavens*** [1954]	$ .40	$1.25	$2.50
M-115	Soule, George - ***Men, Wages And Employment*** [1954]	$ .40	$1.25	$2.50
MS-117	Whitman, Walt - ***Leaves Of Grass*** [1954]	$ .40	$1.25	$2.50
MD-120	Gamow, George - ***The Birth And Death Of The Sun*** [1954] Cover art by Jonas. 16 pages of photos.	$ .40	$1.25	$2.50

		G	VG	F
MS-121	Rostow, W. W. - ***The Dynamics Of Soviet Society*** [1955]	$ .40	$1.25	$2.50
MS-124	Anthology - ***Good Reading*** [1955]	$ .40	$1.25	$2.50
M-125	Hoyle, Fred - ***The Nature Of The Universe*** [1955] Cover art by Jonas. 8 pages of photos.	$ .40	$1.25	$2.50
M-126	Fremantle, Anne - editor - ***The Age Of Belief*** [1955]	$ .40	$1.25	$2.50
M-128	Carson, Rachel L. - ***Under The Sea Wind*** [1955] Cover art by Jonas.	$ .40	$1.25	$2.50
MD-139	Otto, Max C. - ***Science And The Moral Life*** [1955] Cover by Jonas.	$ .40	$1.25	$2.50
MD-144	Jones, H. Spencer - ***Life On Other Worlds*** [1955]	$ .40	$1.25	$2.50
M-156	Kronenberger, Louis - ***Company Manners*** [1955]	$ .40	$1.25	$2.50
M-159	Grosser, Maurice - ***The Painter's Eye*** [1956] Cover art by J. Legakes. 16 pages of photos.	$ .40	$1.25	$2.50
M-181	Morison, Samuel Eliot - ***Christopher Columbus, Mariner*** [1956] Cover art by Clark Hulings.	$ .40	$1.25	$2.50
MD-182	Roberts, Henry L. - ***Russia And America*** [1956]	$ .40	$1.25	$2.50
MD-200	Hoyle, Fred - ***Frontiers Of Astonomy*** [1956]	$ .40	$1.25	$2.50
MD-204	Huxley, Julian - ***Evolution In Action*** [1957]	$ .40	$1.25	$2.50

Mercury Library. New York: American Mercury Inc. Digest size.

L-2	Lambert, M.D., S.M. - ***A Yankee Doctor In Paradise*** [n.d.] Cover art by George Salter.	$1.35	$4.00	$8.00

Mercury Mystery. New York: Lawrence E. Spivak. Digest size.

1	Cain, James M. - ***The Postman Always Rings Twice*** [n.d.]	$1.50	$5.00	$10.00
2	Hardy, J.L. - ***Everything Is Thunder*** [n.d.] Unabridged.	$ .75	$2.50	$5.00
3	Chambers, Whitman - ***13 Steps*** [n.d.]	$ .75	$2.50	$5.00
4	March, William - ***Company K*** [n.d.]	$ .75	$2.50	$5.00
5	Anderson, Edward - ***Thieves Like Us*** [n.d.]	$ .75	$2.50	$5.00
6	Chidsey, Donald Barr - ***Weeping Is For Women*** [n.d.]	$ .75	$2.50	$5.00
7	Morell, Parker - ***Diamond Jim Brady*** [n.d.] Unabridged.	$ .75	$2.50	$5.00
8	Fergusson, Harvey - ***Hot Saturday*** [n.d.] Unabridged.	$ .75	$2.50	$5.00
9	Tracy, Don - ***Criss-Cross*** [n.d.]	$ .75	$2.50	$5.00
10	Forester, C.S. - ***The General*** [n.d.]	$ .75	$2.50	$5.00
11	Lewis, Sinclair - ***Mantrap*** [n.d.]	$ .75	$2.50	$5.00
12	Miller, Max - ***I Cover The Waterfront*** [n.d.]	$ .75	$2.50	$5.00
13	Wylie, I.A.R. - ***To The Vanquished*** [n.d.] Unabridged.	$ .75	$2.50	$5.00
14	Greene, Ward - ***Death In The Deep South*** [n.d.]	$1.50	$5.00	$10.00
15	Paul, Elliot H. - ***Indelible*** [n.d.]	$ .75	$2.50	$5.00
16	Chambers, Whitman - ***Once Too Often*** [n.d.]	$ .75	$2.50	$5.00
17	Lewis, Sinclair - ***The Prodigal Parents*** [n.d.]	$ .75	$2.50	$5.00
18	du Marier, Daphne - ***The Loving Spirit*** [n.d.] Unabridged.	$ .75	$2.50	$5.00
19	Buck, Pearl S. - ***East Wind: West Wind*** [n.d.]	$ .75	$2.50	$5.00
20	Steinbeck, John - ***Cup Of Gold*** [n.d.]	$1.25	$3.75	$7.50
21	Kasner, Erich - ***The Missing Miniature*** [n.d.] Unabridged.	$ .75	$2.50	$5.00
22	Flannagan, Roy - ***County Court*** [n.d.]	$ .75	$2.50	$5.00
23	Yates, Dornford - ***The Devil In Satin*** [n.d.]	$ .75	$2.50	$5.00
24	Gilman, Mildred - ***Divide By Two*** [n.d.] Unbridged. Cover by George Salter.	$ .75	$2.50	$5.00
25	Kipling, Rudyard - ***The Light That Failed*** [n.d.]	$1.25	$3.75	$7.50
26	Hardy, J.L. - ***Never In Vain*** [n.d.] Unabridged. Cover by George Salter.	$ .75	$2.50	$5.00
27	Queen, Ellery - ***The Dutch Shoe Mystery*** [n.d.] Unabridged. Cover by George Salter.	$1.25	$3.75	$7.50
28	du Maurier, Daphne - ***Jamaica Inn*** [n.d.] Unabridged. Cover by George Salter.	$ .75	$2.50	$5.00
29	Werfel, Franz - ***Class Reunion*** [n.d.]	$ .75	$2.50	$5.00
30	Walker, Mildred - ***Dr. Norton's Wife*** [n.d.]	$ .75	$2.50	$5.00
31	Simenon, Georges - ***The Death Of Monsieur Gallet*** [n.d.] Unabridged. Cover by George Salter.	$ .75	$2.50	$5.00

		G	VG	F
32	Queen, Ellery - ***The Door Between*** [n.d.] Abridged. Cover by George Salter.	$1.25	$3.75	$7.50
33	Nebel, Frederick - ***Fifty Roads To Town*** [n.d.] Abridged. Cover by George Salter.	$1.25	$3.75	$7.50
34	Disney, Dorothy Cameron - ***Strawstack*** [n.d.]	$ .75	$2.50	$5.00
35	Rutledge, Brett - ***The Death Of Lord Haw Haw*** [n.d.] Abridged. Cover by George Salter.	$ .75	$2.50	$5.00
36	Queen, Ellery - ***The Siamese Twin Mystery*** [n.d.] Abridged. Cover by George Salter.	$1.25	$3.75	$7.50
37	Stout, Rex - ***Meet Nero Wolfe*** [n.d.]	$1.25	$3.75	$7.50
38	Latimer, Jonathan - ***Headed For Hearse*** [n.d.] Abridged. Cover by George Salter.	$ .75	$2.50	$5.00
39	Queen, Ellery - ***Halfway House*** [n.d.] Abridged. Cover by George Salter.	$1.25	$3.75	$7.50
40	Gardner, Erle Stanley - ***The D.A. Calls It Murder*** [n.d.] Abridged. Cover by George Salter.	$ .75	$2.50	$5.00
41	Christie, Agatha - ***Poirot Loses A Client*** [n.d.] Abridged. Cover by George Salter.	$ .75	$2.50	$5.00
42	Queen, Ellery - ***The American Gun Mystery*** [n.d.] Abridged. Cover by George Salter.	$1.25	$3.75	$7.50
43	Christie, Agatha - ***The Murder At The Vicarage*** [n.d.] Abridged. Cover by George Salter.	$ .75	$2.50	$5.00
44	Lockridge, Frances and Richard - ***The Norths Meet Murder*** [n.d.] Abridged. Cover by George Salter.	$ .75	$2.50	$5.00
45	Seeley, Mabel - ***The Listening House*** [n.d.] Abridged. Cover by George Salter.	$ .75	$2.50	$5.00
46	Christie, Agatha - ***The Incredible Theft*** [n.d.]	$ .75	$2.50	$5.00
47	Queen, Ellery - ***The Four Of Hearts*** [n.d.] Abridged. Cover by George Salter.	$1.25	$3.75	$7.50
48	Stout, Rex - ***The League Of Frightened Men*** [n.d.]	$1.25	$3.75	$7.50
49	Allingham, Margery - ***Mystery Mile*** [n.d.]	$ .75	$2.50	$5.00
50	Christie, Agatha - ***Murder In Mesopotamia*** [n.d.] Abridged. Cover by George Salter.	$ .75	$2.50	$5.00
51	Eberhart, Mignon - ***Hasty Wedding*** [n.d.] Abridged. Cover by George Salter.	$ .75	$2.50	$5.00
52	Dickson, Carter - ***The Unicorn Murders*** [n.d.] Abridged. Cover by George Salter.	$1.25	$3.75	$7.50
53	Christie, Agatha - ***Cards On The Table*** [n.d.] Abridged. Cover by George Salter.	$ .75	$2.50	$5.00
54	Disney, Dorothy Cameron - ***The Golden Swan Murder*** [n.d.] Abridged. Cover by George Salter.	$ .75	$2.50	$5.00
55	Latimer, Jonathan - ***Red Gardenias*** [n.d.] Abridged. Cover by George Salter.	$ .75	$2.50	$5.00
56	Gardner, Erle Stanley - ***The D.A. Draws A Circle*** [n.d.] Abridged. Cover by George Salter.	$ .75	$2.50	$5.00
57	Queen, Ellery - ***The Dragon's Teeth*** [n.d.] Abridged. Cover by George Salter.	$1.25	$3.75	$7.50
58	Gardner, Erle Stanley - ***The Case Of The Dangerous Dowager*** [n.d.] Abridged. Cover by George Salter.	$ .75	$2.50	$5.00
59	Christie, Agatha - ***Thirteen At Dinner*** [n.d.] Abridged. Cover by George Salter.	$ .75	$2.50	$5.00
60	Steeves, Harrison R. - ***Good Night, Sheriff*** [n.d.] Abridged. Cover by George Salter.	$ .75	$2.50	$5.00
61	Perdue, Virginia - ***The Singing Clock*** [n.d.] Abridged. Cover by George Salter.	$ .75	$2.50	$5.00
62	Gardner, Erle Stanley - ***The Clew Of The Forgotten Murder*** [n.d.]	$ .75	$2.50	$5.00
63	Coles, Manning - ***A Toast To Tomorrow*** [n.d.] Abridged. Cover by George Salter.	$ .75	$2.50	$5.00

		G	VG	F
64	Woolrich, Cornell - ***The Black Curtain*** [n.d.] Unabridged. Cover by George Salter.	$2.50	$7.50	$15.00
65	Postgate, Raymond - ***Verdict Of Twelve*** [n.d.] Abridged. Cover by George Salter.	$ .75	$2.50	$5.00
66	Christie, Agatha - ***Death On The Nile*** [n.d.]	$ .75	$2.50	$5.00
67	Gilbert, Anthony - ***Mystery In The Woodshed*** [n.d.]	$ .75	$2.50	$5.00
68	Queen, Ellery - ***Challenge To The Reader*** [n.d.] Unabridged. Cover by George Salter.	$1.25	$3.75	$7.50
69	Christie, Agatha - ***The Secret Of Chimneys*** [n.d.] Abridged. Cover by George Salter.	$ .75	$2.50	$5.00
70	Heard, H.F. - ***A Taste For Honey*** [n.d.]	$ .75	$2.50	$5.00
71	Disney, Dorothy Cameron - ***Death In The Back Seat*** [n.d.] Abridged. Cover by George Salter.	$ .75	$2.50	$5.00
72	Stout, Rex - ***Black Orchids*** [n.d.]	$1.25	$3.75	$7.50
73	Jepson, Selwyn - ***Keep Murder Quiet*** [n.d.] Abridged. Cover by George Salter.	$ .75	$2.50	$5.00
74	Seeley, Mabel - ***The Crying Sisters*** [n.d.] Abridged. Cover by George Salter.	$ .75	$2.50	$5.00
75	Du Bois, William - ***The Case Of The Haunted Brides*** [n.d.] Abridged. Cover by George Salter.	$ .75	$2.50	$5.00
76	Wilde, Percival - ***Mystery Week-End*** [n.d.] Unabridged. Cover by George Salter.	$ .75	$2.50	$5.00
77	Lockridge, Frances and Richard - ***Murder Out Of Turn*** [n.d.] Abridged. Cover by George Salter.	$ .75	$2.50	$5.00
78	Oursler, Will - ***Folio On Florence White*** [n.d.] Abridged. Cover by George Salter.	$ .75	$2.50	$5.00
79	Marsh, Ngaio and Jellett, Dr. Henry - ***The Nursing Home Murder*** [n.d.] Abridged. Cover by George Salter.	$ .75	$2.50	$5.00
80	Perdue, Virginia - ***He Fell Down Dead*** [n.d.] Abridged. Cover by George Salter.	$ .75	$2.50	$5.00
81	Wallis, J.H. - ***Once Off Guard*** [n.d.] Abridged. Cover by George Salter.	$ .75	$2.50	$5.00
82	Irish, William - ***I Wouldn't Be In Your Shoes*** [n.d.]	$2.50	$7.50	$15.00
83	Wilde, Percival - ***Tinsley's Bones*** [n.d.] Abridged. Cover by George Salter.	$ .75	$2.50	$5.00
84	Christie, Agatha - ***The Moving Finger*** [n.d.] Abridged. Cover by George Salter.	$ .75	$2.50	$5.00
85	Armstrong, Charlotte - ***The Case Of The Weird Sisters*** [n.d.]	$ .75	$2.50	$5.00
86	Oursler, Will - ***The Trial Of Vincent Doon*** [n.d.] Unabridged. Cover by George Salter.	$ .75	$2.50	$5.00
87	Siodmak, Curt - ***Donovan's Brain*** [n.d.] Unabridged. Cover by George Salter.	$3.00	$9.00	$18.00
88	Eberhart, Mignon G. - ***The White Cockaoo*** [n.d.] Abridged. Cover by George Salter.	$ .75	$2.50	$5.00
89	Simenon, Georges - ***Maigret To The Rescue*** [n.d.] Unabridged. Cover by George Salter.	$ .75	$2.50	$5.00
90	Bloch, Blanche - ***The Bach Festival Murders*** [n.d.] Abridged. Cover by George Salter.	$ .75	$2.50	$5.00
91	Gilbert, Anthony - ***The Woman In Red*** [1946] Abridged. Cover by George Salter.	$ .75	$2.50	$5.00
92	Perdue, Virginia - ***The Case Of The Foster Father*** [n.d.] Abridged. Cover by George Salter.	$ .75	$2.50	$5.00
93	Kelsey, Vera - ***The Bride Dined Along*** [n.d.] Abridged. Cover by George Salter.	$ .75	$2.50	$5.00
94	Little, Constance and Gwenyth - ***The Black Paw*** [n.d.] Abridged. Cover by George Salter.	$ .75	$2.50	$5.00
95	Strange, John Stephen - ***Look Your Last*** [n.d.] Abridged. Cover by George Salter.	$ .75	$2.50	$5.00
96	Head, Matthew - ***The Smell Of Money*** [n.d.] Unabridged. Cover by George Salter.	$ .75	$2.50	$5.00

		G	VG	F
97	Grafton, C.W. - ***The Rat Began To Gnaw The Rope*** [n.d.]	$ .75	$2.50	$5.00
98	Hull, Richard - ***Keep It Quiet*** [n.d.] Abridged. Cover by George Salter.	$ .75	$2.50	$5.00
99	Shearing, Joseph - ***The Spectral Bride*** [n.d.]	$ .75	$2.50	$5.00
100	Christie, Agatha - ***Murder On The Links*** [n.d.]	$ .75	$2.50	$5.00
101	Henderson, Donald - ***Mr. Bowling Buys A Newspaper*** [n.d.]	$ .75	$2.50	$5.00
102	Rutledge, Nancy - ***Beware Of The Hoot Owl*** [n.d.] Abridged. Cover by George Salter.	$ .75	$2.50	$5.00
103	Venning, Michael - ***Murder Through The Looking Glass*** [n.d.]	$ .75	$2.50	$5.00
104	Wilson, Mitchell - ***Footsteps Behind Her*** [n.d.] Unabridged. Cover by George Salter.	$ .75	$2.50	$5.00
105	Roos, Kelley - ***There Was A Crooked Man*** [n.d.] Unabridged. Cover by George Salter.	$ .75	$2.50	$5.00
106	Weston, Garnett - ***The Undertaker Dies*** [n.d.]	$ .75	$2.50	$5.00
107	Little, Constance and Gwenyth - ***The Black Rustle*** [n.d.]	$ .75	$2.50	$5.00
108	Gilbert, Anthony - ***Thirty Days To Live*** [n.d.] Abridged. Cover by George Salter.	$ .75	$2.50	$5.00
109	Fitt, Mary - ***Clues to Christabel*** [n.d.]	$ .75	$2.50	$5.00
110	Carr, John Dickson - ***Dr. Fell, Detective And Other Stories*** [1947] PBO. Unabridged. Cover by George Salter.	$1.25	$3.75	$7.50
111	Forester, C.S. - ***Payment Deferred*** [n.d.]	$ .75	$2.50	$5.00
112	Allingham, Margery - ***The Case Book Of Mr. Campion*** [n.d.] Unabridged. Cover by George Salter.	$ .75	$2.50	$5.00
113	Shriber, Ione Sandberg - ***Pattern For Murder*** [n.d.] Abridged. Cover by George Salter.	$ .75	$2.50	$5.00
114	Disney, Doris Miles - ***Dark Road*** [n.d.] Abridged. Cover by George Salter.	$ .75	$2.50	$5.00
115	Rhode, John - ***Too Many Suspects*** [n.d.]	$ .75	$2.50	$5.00
116	Martin, A.E. - ***The Outsiders*** [n.d.] Unabridged. Cover by George Salter.	$ .75	$2.50	$5.00
117	Branson, H.C. - ***Case Of The Giant Killer*** [n.d.] Unabridged. Cover by George Salter.	$ .75	$2.50	$5.00
118	Hobhouse, Adam - ***The Hangover Murders*** [n.d.]	$ .75	$2.50	$5.00
119	Mitchell, Gladys - ***When Last I Died*** [n.d.] Abridged. Cover by George Salter.	$ .75	$2.50	$5.00
120	Hammett, Dashiell - ***Nightmare Town*** [1948] PBO. Unabridged. Cover by George Salter.	$17.00	$50.00	$100.00
121	Finnegan, Robert - ***The Bandaged Nude*** [n.d.]	$ .75	$2.50	$5.00
122	Powell, Richard - ***And Hope To Die*** [n.d.] Abridged. Cover by George Salter.	$ .75	$2.50	$5.00
123	Black, Thomas B. - ***The Whitebird Murders*** [n.d.] Abridged. Cover by George Salter.	$ .75	$2.50	$5.00
124	Stokes, Manning Lee - ***The Dying Room*** [n.d.] Unabridged. Cover by George Salter.	$ .75	$2.50	$5.00
125	Smith, Shelley - ***Come And Be Killed*** [n.d.] Abridged. Cover by George Salter.	$ .75	$2.50	$5.00
126	Coles, Manning - ***Let The Tiger Die*** [n.d.] Abridged. Cover by George Salter.	$ .75	$2.50	$5.00
127	Fischer, Bruno - ***The Pigskin Bag*** [n.d.] Unabridged. Cover by George Salter.	$ .75	$2.50	$5.00
128	Siller, Van - ***Fatal Bride*** [n.d.] Abridged. Cover by George Salter.	$ .75	$2.50	$5.00
129	Lockridge, Frances and Richard - ***Death Of A Tall Man*** [n.d.] Abridged. Cover by George Salter.	$ .75	$2.50	$5.00
130	Kutak, Rosemary - ***I Am The Cat*** [n.d.] Abridged. Cover by George Salter.	$ .75	$2.50	$5.00
131	Hammett, Dashiell - ***They Can Only Hang You Once*** [1944] Unabridged. Cover by George Salter.	$8.00	$25.00	$50.00
132	Allingham, Margery - ***Legacy In Blood*** [n.d.] Abridged. Cover by George Salter.	$ .75	$2.50	$5.00

		G	VG	F
133	Lockridge, Frances and Richard - ***Untidy Murder*** [n.d.]	$ .75	$2.50	$5.00
134	Duncan, David - ***Sweet And Deadly*** [n.d.] Abridged. Cover by George Salter.	$ .75	$2.50	$5.00
135	Irish, William (Cornell Woolrich) - ***Dead Man Blues*** [1947] Unabridged. Cover by George Salter.	$5.00	$15.00	$30.00
136	Lorac, E.C.R. - ***Relative To Poison*** [n.d.]	$ .75	$2.50	$5.00
137	Lockridge, Richard and Frances - ***I Want To Go Home*** [n.d.]	$ .75	$2.50	$5.00
138	Murray, Max - ***The King And The Corpse*** [n.d.]	$ .75	$2.50	$5.00
139	Marquand, John P. - ***Last Laugh, Mr. Moto*** [n.d.]	$ .75	$2.50	$5.00
140	Scherf, Margaret - ***Murder Makes Me Nervous*** [n.d.]	$ .75	$2.50	$5.00
141	Charteris, Leslie - ***Call For The Saint*** [n.d.]	$ .75	$2.50	$5.00
142	Hutton, J.F. - ***Too Good To Be True*** [n.d.]	$ .75	$2.50	$5.00
143	Aarons, Edward S. - ***Nightmare*** [n.d.] Unabridged. Cover by George Salter.	$ .75	$2.50	$5.00
144	Coles, Manning - ***Not Negotiable*** [n.d.]	$ .75	$2.50	$5.00
145	Lockridge, Frances and Richard - ***Murder Is Served*** [n.d.]	$ .75	$2.50	$5.00
146	Du Bois, Theodora - ***Rogue's Coat*** [n.d.] Unabridged. Cover by George Salter.	$ .75	$2.50	$5.00
147	Blake, Nicholas - ***The Beast Must Die*** [n.d.]	$ .75	$2.50	$5.00
148	Bronson, F.W. - ***The Bulldog Has A Key*** [n.d.]	$ .75	$2.50	$5.00
149	Stone, Hampton - ***The Girl With The Hole In Her Head*** [n.d.] Unabridged. Cover by George Salter.	$ .75	$2.50	$5.00
150	Tucker, Wilson - ***The Stalking Man*** [n.d.] Unabridged.	$2.50	$7.50	$15.00
151	Daly, Elizabeth - ***And Dangerous To Know*** [n.d.] Unabridged. Cover by George Salter.	$ .75	$2.50	$5.00
152	Ronnis, Edward - ***Terror In The Twon*** [n.d.] Unabridged.	$ .75	$2.50	$5.00
153	Branson, H.C. - ***The Leaden Bubble*** [n.d.] Abridged.	$ .75	$2.50	$5.00
154	Lockridge, Frances and Richard - ***Spin Your Web, Lady!*** [n.d.] Unabridged. Cover by George Salter.	$ .75	$2.50	$5.00
155	Rawson, Clayton - ***Death From A Top Hat*** [n.d.] Abridged. Cover by George Salter.	$ .75	$2.50	$5.00
156	Bagby, George - ***Drop Dead*** [n.d.] Unabridged.	$ .75	$2.50	$5.00
157	Hagen, Miriam Ann - ***Dig Me Later*** [n.d.] Unabridged.	$ .75	$2.50	$5.00
158	Lyon, Dana - ***House On Telegraph Hill*** [n.d.] Unabridged. Cover by George Salter.	$ .75	$2.50	$5.00
159	Crispin, Edmund - ***Sudden Vengeance*** [n.d.] Abridged.	$ .75	$2.50	$5.00
160	Stagge, Jonathan - ***The Three Fears*** [n.d.] Abridged. Cover by George Salter.	$ .75	$2.50	$5.00
161	Sherwood, John - ***Dr. Bruderstein Vanishes*** [n.d.] Abridged.	$ .75	$2.50	$5.00
162	Piper, Evelyn - ***Death Of A Nymph*** [n.d.] Unabridged.	$ .75	$2.50	$5.00
163	Erskine, Margaret - ***Give Up The Ghost*** [n.d.] Abridged.	$ .75	$2.50	$5.00
164	Queen, Ellery - ***The American Gun Mystery*** [n.d.] Abridged. Cover by George Salter.	$1.25	$3.75	$7.50
167	Fenisong, Ruth - ***Ill Wind*** [n.d.] Abridged. Cover by George Salter.	$ .75	$2.50	$5.00
168	Gilbert, Anthony - ***Murder Comes Home*** [n.d.] Unabridged. Cover by George Salter.	$ .75	$2.50	$5.00
169	Cumberland, Marten - ***The House In The Forest*** [n.d.] Abridged. Cover by George Salter.	$ .75	$2.50	$5.00
170	Cairns, Cicely - ***Murder Goes To Press*** [n.d.] Unabridged. Cover by George Salter.	$ .75	$2.50	$5.00
171	Truss, Seldon - ***Never Fight A Lady*** [n.d.]	$ .75	$2.50	$5.00
172	Ronald, James - ***The Murder In Gay Ladies*** [n.d.] Abridged. Cover by George Salter.	$ .75	$2.50	$5.00
173	Fearing, Kenneth - ***The Sound Of Murder*** [n.d.]	$ .75	$2.50	$5.00
174	Crispin, Edmund - ***A Noose For Her*** [n.d.]	$ .75	$2.50	$5.00
175	Holding, Elisabeth Saxany - ***The Party Was A Pay-Off*** [n.d.]	$ .75	$2.50	$5.00
176	Bax, Roger - ***A Grave Case Of Murder*** [n.d.]	$ .75	$2.50	$5.00
177	Hastings, MacDonald - ***Fish And Kill*** [n.d.] Abridged. Cover by George Salter.	$ .75	$2.50	$5.00

		G	VG	F
178	Treat, Lawrence - ***D As In Dead*** [n.d.] Unabridged. Cover by George Salter.	$ .75	$2.50	$5.00
179	Boucher, Anthony - ***Blood On Baker Street*** [n.d.]	$2.50	$7.50	$15.00
180	Shattuck, Richard - ***The Body In The Bridal Bed*** [n.d.]	$ .75	$2.50	$5.00
181	MacDonald, Philip - ***Murder Gone Mad*** [n.d.]	$ .75	$2.50	$5.00
183	Bacon, Peggy - ***Lady Marked For Murder*** [n.d.] Abridged. Cover by George Salter.	$ .75	$2.50	$5.00
187	Black, Thomas B. - ***The Pinball Murders*** [n.d.]	$ .75	$2.50	$5.00
188	Tyre, Nedra - ***Death Is A Lover*** [n.d.] Unabridged. Cover by George Salter.	$ .75	$2.50	$5.00
189	Carey, Bernice - ***The Missing Heiress*** [n.d.] Unabridged. Cover by George Salter.	$ .75	$2.50	$5.00
191	Gruber, Frank - ***Kiss The Boss Goodbye*** [n.d.] Unabridged. Cover by George Salter.	$1.25	$3.75	$7.50
192	Lockridge, Frances and Richard - ***Trial By Terror*** [n.d.] Unabridged. Cover by George Salter.	$ .75	$2.50	$5.00
193	Gilbert, Anthony - ***The Wrong Body*** [n.d.] Abridged. Cover by George Salter.	$ .75	$2.50	$5.00
194	Shattuck, Richard - ***With Blood And Kisses*** [n.d.] Unabridged. Cover by George Salter.	$ .75	$2.50	$5.00
195	Teilhet, Hildegarde Tolman - ***The Screaming Bride*** [n.d.] Unabridged. Cover by Milton Glaser.	$ .75	$2.50	$5.00
196	Knowland, Helen - ***Baltimore Madame*** [n.d.]	$ .75	$2.50	$5.00
197	Johns, Veronica Parker - ***Murder By The Day*** [n.d.] Unabridged.	$ .75	$2.50	$5.00
198	Sherwood, John - ***Murder Of A Mistress*** [n.d.]	$ .75	$2.50	$5.00
199	Cunningham, A.B. - ***Blood Runs Cold*** [n.d.] Abridged. Cover by George Salter.	$ .75	$2.50	$5.00
200	Tey, Josephine - ***Killer In The Crowd*** [n.d.]	$ .75	$2.50	$5.00
201	Eshleman, John M. - ***The Deadly Chase*** [n.d.]	$ .75	$2.50	$5.00
202	Carey, Bernice - ***The Frightened Widow*** [n.d.] Abridged. Cover by George Salter.	$ .75	$2.50	$5.00
203	Marsh, Ngaio - ***The Bride Of Death*** [n.d.]	$ .75	$2.50	$5.00
204	Davis, Mildred - ***They Buried A Man*** [n.d.]	$ .75	$2.50	$5.00
205	Kendrick, Baynard - ***You Die Today*** [n.d.]	$ .75	$2.50	$5.00
206	Eshleman, John M. - ***Death Of A Cheat*** [n.d.]	$ .75	$2.50	$5.00
207	Long, Manning - ***Savage Breast*** [n.d.] Unabridged.	$ .75	$2.50	$5.00
209	Seeley, Mabel - ***The Blonde With The Deadly Past*** [n.d.] Abridged. Cover by George Salter.	$ .75	$2.50	$5.00
233	Hammett, Dashiell - ***A Man Named Thin*** [1962] PBO. Unabridged. Cover by George Salter.	$12.50	$37.50	$75.00

Merit Books (Adult). Chicago: Camerarts Pub. Co.

		G	VG	F
351	Marmor, Arnold - ***Boudoir Treachery*** [1960] PBO.	$1.25	$3.75	$7.50
352	Bottari, George L. - ***Untamed Passion*** [1960] PBO. Cover art by Sloan.	$1.25	$3.75	$7.50
353	Marmor, Arnold - ***The Thirteen Sinners*** [1960] PBO.	$1.25	$3.75	$7.50
354	Arnold, Oren - ***Sin Trail*** [1960] PBO.	$1.25	$3.75	$7.50
355	McKnight, Bob - ***Secret Sinners*** [1960] PBO.	$1.25	$3.75	$7.50
501	Knight, Malcolm - ***Kiss Of Death*** [1960] PBO. Cover art by Sloan.	$1.25	$3.75	$7.50
502	Lewis, Jack - ***Hollywood Sinners*** [1960] PBO.	$1.25	$3.75	$7.50
503	Paul, Awren - ***The Love Machine*** [1960] PBO. Cover art by Sloan.	$1.25	$3.75	$7.50
504	Knight, Malcolm - ***High Priced Blonde*** [1960] PBO.	$1.25	$3.75	$7.50
505	Marmor, Arnold - ***Seduction Without Choice*** [1960] PBO.	$1.25	$3.75	$7.50
506	Glenn, James - ***Damned!*** [1960] PBO.	$1.25	$3.75	$7.50
507	Connor, Clark - ***Abnormal Lover*** [1960] Cover art by Sloan.	$1.25	$3.75	$7.50
508	Drake, Damon - ***Seduced!*** [1960] PBO. Cover art by Sloan.	$1.25	$3.75	$7.50
509	Marmor, Arnold - ***Lust Lodge*** [1960] PBO.	$1.25	$3.75	$7.50
510	Cassidy, George - ***The Flesh Market*** [1961] PBO.	$1.25	$3.75	$7.50

		G	VG	F
511	Goff, Jr., Jerry M. - ***Victims Of Lust*** [1961] PBO. Cover art by Sloan.	$1.25	$3.75	$7.50
512	Hinshaw, Les - ***Warped Desires*** [1961] PBO.	$1.25	$3.75	$7.50
513	Lauren, Bill - ***Gang Mistress*** [1961] PBO. Cover art by Sloan.	$1.25	$3.75	$7.50
514	Coon, Walter A. - ***House Of Lust*** [1961] PBO.	$1.25	$3.75	$7.50
515	Knight, Malcolm - ***Lady Killer*** [1961] PBO. Cover art by Sloan.	$1.25	$3.75	$7.50
516	Goff, Jr., Jerry M. - ***Talented Lover*** [1961] PBO.	$1.25	$3.75	$7.50
517	Zott, Richard J. - ***Forced Seduction*** [1961] PBO.	$1.25	$3.75	$7.50
518	Lauren, Bill - ***Wild Pursuit*** [1961] PBO.	$1.25	$3.75	$7.50
519	Willie, Ennis - ***The Work Of The Devil*** [1961] PBO.	$1.25	$3.75	$7.50
520	Fulton, Jay - ***Perverted Urge*** [1961] PBO.	$1.25	$3.75	$7.50
521	Horn, Allan - ***Thwarted Passions*** [1961] PBO. Photo cover.	$1.25	$3.75	$7.50
522	Shelly, Bruce - ***My Woman*** [1961] PBO. Photo cover.	$1.25	$3.75	$7.50
523	Coulter, Adam - ***Valley Of Lust*** [1961] PBO.	$1.25	$3.75	$7.50
524	Tremont, Victor - ***Surrender To Passion*** [1961] PBO. Photo cover.	$1.25	$3.75	$7.50
525	Jade, George - ***The Devil's Mistress*** [1961] PBO. Photo cover.	$1.25	$3.75	$7.50
526	Goff, Jr., Jerry M. - ***Rocco's Babe*** [1961] Cover art by Sloan.	$1.25	$3.75	$7.50
528	Jade, George - ***Rebel Mistress*** [1961] PBO. Photo cover.	$1.25	$3.75	$7.50
529	Neitzel, Neal - ***Hot-Blooded Blonde*** [1961] PBO. Photo cover.	$1.25	$3.75	$7.50
530	Lauren, Bill - ***Gal Bait*** [1961] PBO. Cover art by Sloan.	$1.25	$3.75	$7.50
531	Marmor Arnold - ***Hell Cat*** [1961] PBO.	$1.25	$3.75	$7.50
534	Goff, Jr., Jerry M. - ***Everything- But Love!*** [1961]	$1.25	$3.75	$7.50
535	Jade, George - ***Bribed Seduction*** [1961] PBO.	$1.25	$3.75	$7.50
539	Nemec, John - ***Raging Passion*** [1961]	$1.25	$3.75	$7.50
540	Rubel, James L. - ***Vegas Wenches*** [1961] PBO. Photo cover.	$1.25	$3.75	$7.50
541	Raczyk, Robert - ***Mate Swap*** [1961]	$1.25	$3.75	$7.50
542	Marmor, Arnold - ***Love Addict*** [1961] PBO.	$1.25	$3.75	$7.50
543	Lauren, Bill - ***Pleasure Girl*** [1961] PBO.	$1.25	$3.75	$7.50
544	Nemec, John - ***Abnormal Passion*** [1962] PBO.	$1.25	$3.75	$7.50
545	Jade, George - ***Modern Seduction*** [1962] PBO.	$1.25	$3.75	$7.50
548	Goff, Jr., Jerry M. - ***Abnormal Assault*** [1962] PBO.	$1.25	$3.75	$7.50
549	Blue, Win - ***Society Orgy*** [1962]	$1.25	$3.75	$7.50
550	Montgomery, Herb - ***The Flesh Peddlers*** [1962] PBO. Photo cover.	$1.25	$3.75	$7.50
551	Goff, Jr., Jerry M. - ***Red-Hot Broad*** [1962] Cover art by Bonfils.	$1.25	$3.75	$7.50
552	Connor, Clark - ***Perverted Affair*** [1962] PBO. Photo cover.	$1.25	$3.75	$7.50
553	Jade, George - ***Teasing Redhead*** [1962]	$1.25	$3.75	$7.50
554	Lauren, Bill - ***Torrid Love Nest*** [1962]	$1.25	$3.75	$7.50
556	Vail, Thomas - ***Torrid Affair*** [1962] PBO.	$1.25	$3.75	$7.50
557	Vail, Thomas - ***Modern Harem*** [1962]	$1.25	$3.75	$7.50
602	Neville, Myles/Goff, Jr., Jerry M. - ***Autobiography Of The Pervert!*** [1961] PBO.	$1.25	$3.75	$7.50
603	Goff, Jr., Jerry M. - ***Wanton Wench!*** [1961] PBO.	$1.25	$3.75	$7.50
608	Lauren, Bill - ***Tangled Seduction*** [1962] PBO.	$1.25	$3.75	$7.50
611	Goff, Jr., Jerry M. - ***Love Me Now!*** [1962] PBO.	$1.25	$3.75	$7.50
612	Goff, Jr., Jerry M. - ***Live With Me*** [1962]	$1.25	$3.75	$7.50
613	Montgomery, Herb - ***Loretta*** [1962] PBO.	$1.25	$3.75	$7.50
617	Lauren, Bill - ***Too Much Woman!*** [1962] Photo cover.	$1.25	$3.75	$7.50
618	Goff, Jr., Jerry M. - ***Strange Loves*** [1962]	$1.25	$3.75	$7.50
619	North, Kevin - ***Bed Tramps*** [1962] PBO. Photo cover.	$1.25	$3.75	$7.50
622	Stack, Ben - ***Perverted Orgy*** [1962] PBO. Photo cover.	$1.25	$3.75	$7.50
626	Harvey, Doug - ***Abnormal Wench*** [1962] PBO. Photo cover.	$1.25	$3.75	$7.50
627	Marmor, Arnold - ***Seduction Without Choice*** [1962]	$1.25	$3.75	$7.50
631	Goff, Jr., Jerry M. - ***Carnal Rage*** [1962] PBO. Photo cover.	$1.25	$3.75	$7.50
632	Cross, Gene - ***Flaming Flirt*** [1962] Cover by Bonfils.	$1.25	$3.75	$7.50
635	Montgomery, Herb - ***Seductive Temptress*** [1962]	$1.25	$3.75	$7.50
636	Goff, Jr., Jerry M. - ***Tropic Of Carla*** [1962] PBO.	$1.25	$3.75	$7.50
638	Goff, Jr., Jerry M. - ***Victims Of Lust*** [1962]	$1.25	$3.75	$7.50

		G	VG	F
642	Marmor, Arnold - ***Abnormal Desire*** [1962] Photo cover.	$1.25	$3.75	$7.50
643	Arnold, Oren - ***Ravished Body*** [1962] Photo cover.	$1.25	$3.75	$7.50
644	Goff, Jr., Jerry M. - ***Time For Loving*** [1962]	$1.25	$3.75	$7.50
645	Cross, Gene - ***Man-Hungry Babes*** [1962] Photo cover.	$1.25	$3.75	$7.50
646	Davis, Duane - ***Passion Party*** [1962] PBO. Photo cover.	$1.25	$3.75	$7.50
651	Goff, Jr., Jerry M. - ***Eager Women*** [1963] PBO. Cover art by Bonfils.	$1.25	$3.75	$7.50
652	North, Kevin - ***Forbidden Desire*** [1963]	$1.25	$3.75	$7.50
653	Harvey, Doug - ***Fierce Passion*** [1963] Photo cover.	$1.25	$3.75	$7.50
656	Paul, Auren - ***Fantastic Orgy*** [1963] Photo cover.	$1.25	$3.75	$7.50
662	Marmor, Arnold - ***Wanton Affair*** [1963] Photo cover.	$1.25	$3.75	$7.50
677	Lauren, Bill - ***Thrill Hungry*** [1963] Photo cover.	$1.25	$3.75	$7.50
678	Willie, Ennis - ***Modern Love*** [1963] Photo cover.	$1.25	$3.75	$7.50
679	Fulton, Jay - ***Insatiable*** [1963] Photo cover.	$1.25	$3.75	$7.50
681	Shelly, Bruce - ***Seduction Campaign*** [1963] Photo cover.	$1.25	$3.75	$7.50
682	Willie, Ennis - ***Carnal Madness*** [1963] PBO.	$1.25	$3.75	$7.50
683	Willie, Ennis - ***Scarlet Goddess*** [1963]	$1.25	$3.75	$7.50
685	Randolph, Mark - ***Unique Mistress*** [1963] PBO. Photo cover.	$1.25	$3.75	$7.50
686	Coulter, Adam - ***Naked Greed*** [1963]	$1.25	$3.75	$7.50
688	Jade, George - ***Possessed Woman*** [1963] Photo cover.	$1.25	$3.75	$7.50
692	Davis, Duane - ***Female Pursuers*** [1963] PBO. Photo cover.	$1.25	$3.75	$7.50
693	Goff, Jr., Jerry M. - ***Explosive Teaser*** [1963] PBO. Photo cover.	$1.25	$3.75	$7.50
694	Willie, Ennis - ***Twisted Mistress*** [1963]	$1.25	$3.75	$7.50
696	Jade, George - ***Desperate Females*** [1963] PBO. Photo cover.	$1.25	$3.75	$7.50
699	Montgomery, Herb - ***"Don't Tease Me!!"*** [1963] Photo cover.	$1.25	$3.75	$7.50
6-M-404	Goff, Jr., Jerry M. - ***Too Much Temptation!*** [1963] PBO. Photo cover.	$1.25	$3.75	$7.50
6-M-406	Cassidy, George - ***Assignment: Seduction*** [1963] PBO. Cover art by Bonfils.	$1.25	$3.75	$7.50
6-M-407	Goff, Jr., Jerry M. - ***Julie*** [1963] PBO. Cover art by Bonfils.	$1.25	$3.75	$7.50
6-M-408	Willie, Ennis - ***Politician's Playgirl*** [1963]	$1.25	$3.75	$7.50
6-M-409	Marmor, Arnold - ***The Temptress*** [1963] Photo cover.	$1.25	$3.75	$7.50
6-M-415	Willie, Ennis - ***So Naked! So Dead*** [1963] PBO. Photo cover.	$1.25	$3.75	$7.50
6-M-417	Goff, Jr., Jerry M. - ***Fantastic Seducer*** [1963] PBO.	$1.25	$3.75	$7.50
6-M-419	Royce, Lloyd - ***Perverted Drives*** [1963] PBO. Photo cover.	$1.25	$3.75	$7.50
6-M-421	Goff, Jr., Jerry M. - ***Beware: Woman On The Loose*** [1963] PBO. Cover art by Bonfils.	$1.25	$3.75	$7.50
6-M-422	Willie, Ennis - ***Haven For The Damned*** [1963]	$1.25	$3.75	$7.50
6-M-423	Jade, George - ***Passionate Playmate*** [1963] PBO.	$1.25	$3.75	$7.50
6-M-426	Goff, Jr., Jerry M. - ***Uncontrollable Urge!*** [1963] PBO. Cover art by Bonfils.	$1.25	$3.75	$7.50
6-M-427	Lee, Steve - ***A Different Kind Of Thrill*** [1963] PBO. Photo cover.	$1.25	$3.75	$7.50
6-M-428	Coulter, Adam - ***She Devil*** [1963]	$1.25	$3.75	$7.50
6-M-429	Goff, Jr., Jerry M. - ***Overpowering Desire!*** [1963] PBO. Cover art by Sloan.	$1.25	$3.75	$7.50
6-M-430	Goff, Jr., Jerry M. - ***Passion Contest*** [1963] Cover art by Bonfils.	$1.25	$3.75	$7.50
6-M-434	Willie, Ennis - ***Game Of Passion*** [1964] PBO. Photo cover.	$1.25	$3.75	$7.50
6-M-441	Willie, Ennis - ***A New Kind Of Love*** [1964]	$1.25	$3.75	$7.50
6-M-447	Goff, Jr., Jerry M. - ***Shameless!*** [1964] Photo cover.	$1.25	$3.75	$7.50
6-M-451	Willie, Ennis - ***Sensual Game*** [1964] PBO. Photo cover.	$1.25	$3.75	$7.50
6-M-456	Willie, Ennis - ***Incredibly Seductive*** [1964]	$1.25	$3.75	$7.50
6-M-460	Lynn, Valerie - ***Valerie*** [1964] PBO.	$1.25	$3.75	$7.50
6-M-461	Willie, Ennis - ***And Some Were Evil*** [1964]	$1.25	$3.75	$7.50
6-M-474	Connor, Clark - ***Give Her Back To Hell*** [1964]	$1.25	$3.75	$7.50
6-M-475	Maher, John L. - ***White Satin Wench*** [1964] PBO.	$1.25	$3.75	$7.50
6-M-477	Royce, Lloyd - ***Expert Seductress*** [1964] PBO.	$1.25	$3.75	$7.50
6-M-478	Willie, Ennis - ***The Sensualites*** [1964]	$1.25	$3.75	$7.50

		G	VG	F
6-M-480	Willie, Ennis - ***Warped Ambitions*** [1964]	$1.25	$3.75	$7.50
6-M-481	Richmond, Roe - ***The Chaser*** [1964] PBO.	$1.25	$3.75	$7.50
6-M-484	Willie, Ennis - ***The Case Of The Loaded Garter Holster*** [1964]	$1.25	$3.75	$7.50
6-M-487	Willie, Ennis - ***Passion Has No Rulebook*** [1964]	$1.25	$3.75	$7.50
6-M-488	Vail, Thomas - ***Bizarre Harem*** [1964] Photo cover.	$1.25	$3.75	$7.50
6-M-489	Willie, Ennis - ***Erotic Search*** [1964] PBO.	$1.25	$3.75	$7.50
6-M-490	Steiger, Brad - ***Monsters, Maidens & Mayhem*** [1964] Photo cover.	$1.25	$3.75	$7.50
6-M-491	Willie, Ennis - ***That Kind Of Woman*** [1965]	$1.25	$3.75	$7.50
6-M-492	Willie, Ennis - ***Code Of Vengeance*** [1965] PBO.	$1.25	$3.75	$7.50
6-M-493	Willie, Ennis - ***To Live Dangerously*** [1965]	$1.25	$3.75	$7.50
7-M-800	Rio, Del - ***Racket Broads*** [1965] Photo cover.	$1.25	$3.75	$7.50
7-M-808	Lee, Ray - ***A Pictorial History Of Hollywood Nudity*** [1964] PBO.	$1.25	$3.75	$7.50
7-M-809	Neville, Myles - ***Mine-All Mine*** [1964] Photo cover.	$1.25	$3.75	$7.50
7-M-810	Blake, Steve - ***The Sexperts-Touched By Temptation*** [1964] PBO. Movie tie-in. Movie photo cover. Photos throughout.	$1.25	$3.75	$7.50
7-M-811	Burstein, A. Joseph, PhD. - ***Sexual Taboos - And You!*** [1964]	$1.25	$3.75	$7.50
7-M-813	Blake, Steve - ***Sex And The Starlet*** [1964] Photos throughout.	$1.25	$3.75	$7.50
7-M-814	Steiger, Brad - ***Bizarre Beauties*** [1964] PBO.	$1.25	$3.75	$7.50
7-M-816	Steiger, Brad - ***Ghosts, Ghouls And Other Peculiar People*** [1965] PBO. Cover art by M. Seltzer.	$1.25	$3.75	$7.50
7-M-817	Steiger, Brad - ***Master Movie Monsters*** [1965] PBO. Cover art by M. Seltzer. Photos throughout.	$1.25	$3.75	$7.50
7-M-819	Henri, Jim - ***The World's Most Sensual Films*** [1965] PBO. Movie photos throughout.	$1.25	$3.75	$7.50
7-M-820	Steiger, Brad - ***Sensual Secret Agents*** [1965] PBO. Cover art by M. Seltzer.	$1.25	$3.75	$7.50
6101	Willie, Ennis - ***Aura Of Sensuality*** [1963]	$1.25	$3.75	$7.50
6103	Lauren, Bill - ***Female Lure*** [1963] PBO. Cover art by Sloan.	$1.25	$3.75	$7.50

Merit Books. Chicago: Century Publications. Digest size.

B-9	Carter, Ralph - ***Passion's Folly*** [1950] PBO. Cover art by Malcolm Smith.	$3.50	$10.00	$20.00
B-10	Smith, George O. - ***Operation Interstellar*** [1950] PBO. Cover by Malcolm Smith.	$4.00	$12.50	$25.00
B-11	Lindsay, Perry - ***Sin For Two*** [1951] PBO. Cover art by Malcolm Smith.	$3.50	$10.00	$20.00
B-12	Thompson, Lewis & Boswell, Charles - ***More Deadly Than The Male*** [1951] PBO. Cover art by Herb Rund.	$3.50	$10.00	$20.00
B-13	Phillips, Rog - ***World Of If*** [1951] PBO. Cover art by Malcolm Smith.	$4.00	$12.50	$25.00
B-14	Seton, Gerald - ***Model For Love*** [1951]	$2.50	$7.50	$15.00
B-15	Stone, Thomas - ***50-50 Girl*** [1952] PBO.	$3.00	$9.00	$18.00
B-16	Collins, A.J. - ***The Tin Ear*** [1952]	$2.50	$7.50	$15.00

Midwood Books (Early Publisher's History, 1957–1962)

Aimed at the male market, this line competed with Beacon Books. They produced a number of double novels. Four of these are especially collectible doubles, D231, S227, 34-395, and 34-612, which contain interior illustrations by Frank Franzetta. A number of authors wrote using pseudonyms, including Robert Silverberg, Lawrence Block, and Richard Geis. Covers displayed beautiful young ladies in alluring dress and poses.

In 1964, Midwood joined with Tower Books of the World Publishing Company to form Midwood-Tower.

Midwood Books. New York: Tower Publications.

		G	VG	F
NN-1	Fagaly, Al & Shorten, Harry - ***There Oughta Be A Law*** [1957] PBO. Cover art by Fagaly & Shorten. Cartoon book.	$3.50	$10.00	$20.00
4	Fagaly, Al & Shorten, Harry - ***There Oughta Be A Law*** [1958] PBO. Cover art by Fagaly & Shorten. Cartoon book.	$3.50	$10.00	$20.00
NN-5	Ellson, Hal - ***I Take What I Want*** [1958] PBO.	$3.00	$9.00	$18.00
NN-6	Rede, Tomlin - ***Call Me Mistress*** [1958] PBO.	$3.00	$9.00	$18.00
7	Beauchamp, Loren (Robert Silverberg) - ***Love Nest*** [1958] PBO. Cover art by Rudy Nappi.	$3.50	$10.00	$20.00
8	Lord, Sheldon - ***Carla*** [1958] PBO. Cover art by Paul Rader.	$3.00	$9.00	$18.00
9	Lord, Sheldon - ***A Strange Kind Of Love*** [1959] PBO. Cover art by Rudy Nappi.	$3.00	$9.00	$18.00
10	Hitt, Orrie - ***Affair With Lucy*** [1959] PBO.	$2.50	$7.50	$15.00
11	Mitchell, Gordon - ***Immoral Wife*** [1959] PBO. Cover art by Paul Rader.	$2.50	$7.50	$15.00
12	Hitt, Orrie - ***Girl Of The Streets*** [1959] PBO. Cover art by Barton.	$2.50	$7.50	$15.00
13	Martin, Fred - ***Hired Lover*** [1959] PBO.	$2.50	$7.50	$15.00
14	Lord, Sheldon - ***Born To Be Bad*** [1959] PBO.	$3.00	$9.00	$18.00
15	Marshall, Alan - ***All My Lovers*** [1959] PBO. Cover art by Ronnie Lesser.	$3.00	$9.00	$18.00
16	Hitt, Orrie - ***Summer Romance*** [1959] PBO.	$2.50	$7.50	$15.00
17	Marshall, Alan - ***Backstage Love*** [1959] PBO.	$3.00	$9.00	$18.00
18	Beauchamp, Loren (Robert Silverberg) - ***Connie*** [1959] PBO. Cover art by Paul Rader.	$2.50	$7.50	$15.00
19	Holliday, Don - ***Only The Bed*** [1959] PBO.	$2.00	$6.00	$12.00
20	Marshall, Alan - ***Man Hungry*** [1959] PBO. Cover art by Paul Rader.	$3.00	$9.00	$18.00
21	Beauchamp, Loren (Robert Silverberg) - ***Unwilling Sinner*** [1959] PBO. Cover art by Paul Rader.	$2.50	$7.50	$15.00
22	Marshall, Alan - ***Sally*** [1959] PBO. Cover art by Paul Rader.	$3.00	$9.00	$18.00
23	Hitt, Orrie - ***As Bad As They Come*** [1959] PBO.	$2.50	$7.50	$15.00
24	Lord, Sheldon - ***69 Barrow Street*** [1959] PBO.	$3.00	$9.00	$18.00
25	Holliday, Don - ***Sin School*** [1959] PBO.	$2.00	$6.00	$12.00
26	Tasker, W.B. - ***Just Ask For Margaret*** [1959] PBO. Cover art by Paul Rader.	$2.50	$7.50	$15.00
27	Beauchamp, Loren (Robert Silverberg) - ***Another Night, Another Love*** [1959] PBO.	$2.50	$7.50	$15.00
28	Marshall, Alan - ***All The Girls Were Willing*** [1960] PBO.	$3.00	$9.00	$18.00
29	Lord, Sheldon - ***Of Shame And Joy*** [1960] PBO. Cover art by Paul Rader.	$3.00	$9.00	$18.00
30	Beauchamp, Loren (Robert Silverberg) - ***Meg*** [1960] PBO.	$2.50	$7.50	$15.00
31	Marshall, Alan - ***The Wife Next Door*** [1960] PBO. Cover art by Robert Maguire.	$3.00	$9.00	$18.00
32	Carson, Dave - ***Woman Hater*** [1960] PBO. Cover art by Paul Rader.	$2.50	$7.50	$15.00
33	Lord, Sheldon - ***A Woman Must Love*** [1960] PBO. Cover art by Paul Rader.	$3.00	$9.00	$18.00
34	Hitt, Orrie - ***The Cheaters*** [1960] PBO. Cover art by Paul Rader.	$2.50	$7.50	$15.00
35	Lord, Sheldon - ***Kept*** [1960] PBO. Cover art by Paul Rader.	$3.00	$9.00	$18.00
36	Marshall, Alan - ***Virgin's Summer*** [1960] PBO. Cover art by Paul Rader.	$3.00	$9.00	$18.00
37	Hastings, March - ***Anybody's Girl*** [1960] PBO. Cover art by Paul Rader.	$2.50	$7.50	$15.00
38	Hitt, Orrie - ***A Doctor And His Mistress*** [1960] PBO.	$2.00	$6.00	$12.00
39	Holliday, Don - ***The Sins Of Martha Leslie*** [1960] PBO. Cover art by Paul Rader.	$2.50	$7.50	$15.00
40	Lord, Sheldon - ***Candy*** [1960] PBO. Cover art by Frace.	$3.00	$9.00	$18.00

		G	VG	F
41	Lord, Sheldon & Marshall, Alan - ***A Girl Called Honey*** [1960] PBO. Cover art by Paul Rader.	$3.00	$9.00	$18.00
42	Harvey, James - ***Stag Model*** [1960] PBO. Photo cover.	$2.00	$6.00	$12.00
43	Gareth, Max - ***Chita*** [1960] PBO.	$2.00	$6.00	$12.00
44	Lucchesi, Aldo - ***Strange Breed*** [1960] PBO. Cover art by Paul Rader.	$2.50	$7.50	$15.00
45	Hitt, Orrie - ***Two Of A Kind*** [1960] PBO.	$2.00	$6.00	$12.00
46	Roberts, Adam - ***Glad To Be Bad*** [1960] PBO. Cover art by Paul Rader.	$2.50	$7.50	$15.00
47	Britton, Sloan - ***Unnatural*** [1960] PBO. Cover art by Paul Rader.	$2.50	$7.50	$15.00
48	Marshall, Alan & Lord, Sheldon - ***So Willing*** [1960] PBO.	$3.00	$9.00	$18.00
49	Cassidy, George - ***Farm Girl*** [1960] PBO. Cover art by Paul Rader.	$2.50	$7.50	$15.00
50	Harvey, James - ***Ladies' Masseur*** [1960] PBO.	$2.00	$6.00	$12.00
51	Marshall, Alan - ***All About Annette*** [1960] PBO.	$3.00	$9.00	$18.00
52	Britain, Sloane - ***Meet Marilyn*** [1960] PBO. Cover art by Al Wagner.	$2.00	$6.00	$12.00
53	Hastings, March - ***The Unashamed*** [1960] PBO. Cover art by Paul Rader.	$2.50	$7.50	$15.00
54	Ellis, Joan - ***Lana*** [1960] PBO. Cover art by Paul Rader.	$2.50	$7.50	$15.00
55	Lord, Sheldon - ***21 Gay Street*** [1960] PBO. Cover art by Paul Rader.	$3.00	$9.00	$18.00
56	Swenson, Peggy (Richard E. Geis) - ***The Blonde*** [1960] PBO. Cover art by Paul Rader.	$2.50	$7.50	$15.00
57	Britain, Sloane - ***Insatiable*** [1960] PBO. Photo cover.	$2.00	$6.00	$12.00
58	Vendor, Nick - ***Sabrina And The Senator*** [1960] PBO. Cover art by Paul Rader.	$2.50	$7.50	$15.00
59	Harvey, James - ***A Twilight Affair*** [1960] PBO. Cover art by Paul Rader.	$3.00	$9.00	$18.00
60	Avallone, Mike - ***All The Way*** [1960] PBO.	$2.50	$7.50	$15.00
61	Ellis, Joan - ***Flame*** [1960] PBO.	$2.00	$6.00	$12.00
62	Marshall, Alan - ***Sally*** [1960] Cover art by Paul Rader.	$3.00	$9.00	$18.00
F-63	Salem, Randy - ***The Unfortunate Flesh*** [1960] PBO.	$2.00	$6.00	$12.00
64	Allison, Clyde - ***Million Dollar Mistress*** [1960] PBO. Cover art by Paul Rader.	$2.50	$7.50	$15.00
65	Beauchamp, Loren (Robert Silverberg) - ***Nurse Carolyn*** [1960] PBO. Cover art by Paul Rader.	$2.50	$7.50	$15.00
66	Holliday, Don - ***Sin School*** [1960]	$2.00	$6.00	$12.00
67	Russo, Paul V. - ***A Touch Of Depravity*** [1960] PBO.	$2.00	$6.00	$12.00
68	Fagaly, Al & Shorten, Harry - ***There Oughta Be A Law!*** [1961] PBO. Cover art by Fagaly & Shorten. Cartoon book.	$3.00	$9.00	$18.00
69	Ellis, Joan - ***Liza's Apartment*** [1961] PBO. Cover art by Paul Rader.	$2.50	$7.50	$15.00
70	Beauchamp, Loren (Robert Silverberg) - ***Sin On Wheels*** [1961] PBO. Cover art by Paul Rader.	$2.50	$7.50	$15.00
71	Elliott, Bruce - ***A Woman*** [1961] PBO.	$2.00	$6.00	$12.00
72	Warren, Jay - ***The Path Between*** [1961] PBO. Cover art by Paul Rader.	$2.50	$7.50	$15.00
73	Allison, Clyde - ***The Sex Peddlers*** [1961] PBO.	$2.50	$7.50	$15.00
74	Beauchamp, Loren (Robert Silverberg) - ***Connie*** [1961] PBO. Cover art by Paul Rader.	$2.50	$7.50	$15.00
75	Kramer, Karl - ***Common-Law Wife*** [1961] PBO. Cover art by Paul Rader.	$2.50	$7.50	$15.00
76	Ellis, Joan - ***Pleasure Girl*** [1961] PBO. Cover art by Paul Rader.	$2.50	$7.50	$15.00
F-77	James, Stuart - ***Bucks Country Report*** [1961] PBO.	$2.00	$6.00	$12.00
78	Russo, Paul V. - ***Restless Virgin*** [1961] PBO. Cover art by Paul Rader.	$2.50	$7.50	$15.00
79	Parksmith, George - ***Your Sins And Mine*** [1961] PBO.	$2.00	$6.00	$12.00

		G	VG	F
80	Hastings, March - ***The Jealous And The Free*** [1961] PBO. Cover art by Paul Rader.	$2.50	$7.50	$15.00
81	English, Arnold - ***School For Sex*** [1961]	$2.00	$6.00	$12.00
F-82	Britain, Sloane - ***These Curious Pleasures*** [1961] PBO. Cover art by Paul Rader.	$2.50	$7.50	$15.00
83	Russo, Paul V. - ***One Flesh*** [1961]	$2.00	$6.00	$12.00
84	Serra, Art - ***Lament For A Virgin*** [1961] PBO.	$2.00	$6.00	$12.00
85	Mayo, Dallas - ***Silky*** [1961] PBO.	$2.00	$6.00	$12.00
86	Beauchamp, Loren (Robert Silverberg) - ***The Fires Within*** [1961] PBO. Cover art by Robert Maguire.	$3.00	$9.00	$18.00
87	Gold, R.C. - ***Drive-In Girl*** [1961] PBO.	$2.00	$6.00	$12.00
F-88	Russo, Paul V. - ***Stag Starlet*** [1961]	$2.00	$6.00	$12.00
89	Wyckoff, James - ***Middle Of Time*** [1961] PBO.	$2.00	$6.00	$12.00
F-90	Highsmith, David - ***Stepdown To Darkness*** [1961] PBO.	$2.00	$6.00	$12.00
F-91	Sprague, W.D. - ***Sex Behavior Of The American Housewife*** [1961]	$1.35	$4.00	$8.00
92	Cox, Thomas - ***The Weekend*** [1961] PBO.	$2.00	$6.00	$12.00
93	Merrick, Clyde - ***A Moment's Pleasure*** [1961] PBO.	$2.00	$6.00	$12.00
94	Russo, Paul V. - ***This Yielding Flesh*** [1961] PBO.	$2.00	$6.00	$12.00
F-95	Clanton, Carol - ***Gay Interlude*** [1961]	$2.00	$6.00	$12.00
F-96	Gold, Michael - ***Jews Without Money*** [1961]	$1.25	$3.75	$7.50
F-97	McGhee, George - ***Desire Under The Sun*** [1961] PBO.	$2.00	$6.00	$12.00
98	Mayo, Dallas - ***Kitten*** [1961] PBO. Cover art by Paul Rader.	$2.50	$7.50	$15.00
99	Ellis, Joan - ***Redhead*** [1961] PBO.	$2.00	$6.00	$12.00
100	Mayo, Dallas - ***A Need For Love*** [1961] PBO. Cover art by Robert Maguire.	$2.50	$7.50	$15.00
F-101	Hunter, Paul - ***Morals Charge*** [1961] PBO. Cover art by Paul Rader.	$2.50	$7.50	$15.00
F-102	Beauchamp, Loren (Robert Silverberg) - ***And When She Was Bad*** [1961] PBO.	$2.50	$7.50	$15.00
F-103	Lord, Sheldon - ***69 Barrow Street*** [1961]	$3.00	$9.00	$18.00
104	James, Stuart - ***Judge Not My Sins*** [1961] PBO.	$2.00	$6.00	$12.00
105	Hall, Roger - ***All My Pretty Ones*** [1961]	$2.00	$6.00	$12.00
106	James, Al - ***Child Bride*** [1961]	$2.00	$6.00	$12.00
F-107	Ellis, Joan - ***The Hunger And The Hate*** [1961] PBO. Photo cover.	$2.00	$6.00	$12.00
108	Russo, Paul V. - ***Without Shame*** [1961]	$2.25	$7.00	$14.00
F-109	Holliday, Don - ***Torment*** [1961]	$2.50	$7.50	$15.00
F-110	Swenson, Peggy (Richard Geis) - ***The Unloved*** [1961] PBO.	$2.50	$7.50	$15.00
F-111	James, Al - ***The Lover*** [1961] PBO.	$2.25	$7.00	$14.00
112	Plunkett, John - ***A Girl Like That*** [1961] PBO. Cover art by Robert Maguire.	$2.50	$7.50	$15.00
F-113	Ellis, Joan - ***Mulatto*** [1961] PBO.	$2.00	$6.00	$12.00
114	Russo, Paul V. - ***Corrupt Woman*** [1961] PBO.	$2.00	$6.00	$12.00
115	Hitt, Orrie - ***Married Mistress*** [1961]	$2.00	$6.00	$12.00
116	Skinner, Mike - ***So Wild*** [1961] PBO.	$2.00	$6.00	$12.00
117	Laurence, Will - ***For Value Received*** [1961] PBO.	$2.00	$6.00	$12.00
118	Hytes, Jason - ***This Girl*** [1961] PBO. Cover art by Rader.	$2.50	$7.50	$15.00
F-119	Britain, Sloane - ***That Other Hunger*** [1961] PBO. Cover art by Paul Rader.	$2.50	$7.50	$15.00
120	Avallone, Mike - ***Women In Prison*** [1961] PBO.	$3.00	$9.00	$18.00
F-121	Lord, Sheldon - ***Of Shame And Joy*** [1961]	$3.00	$9.00	$18.00
122	Mayo, Dallas - ***House Of Sin*** [1961] PBO. Cover art by Robert Maguire.	$2.50	$7.50	$15.00
Y-123	Michaels, Linda - ***Numbers Girl*** [1961] PBO.	$2.00	$6.00	$12.00
124	Richards, Rick - ***Motel Hostess*** [1961] PBO. Cover art by Robert Maguire.	$2.50	$7.50	$15.00
125	Castro, Joe - ***The Lowest Sins*** [1961] PBO. Cover art by Paul Rader.	$2.50	$7.50	$15.00
126	Hytes, Jason - ***Pound Of Flesh*** [1961] PBO.	$2.25	$7.00	$14.00

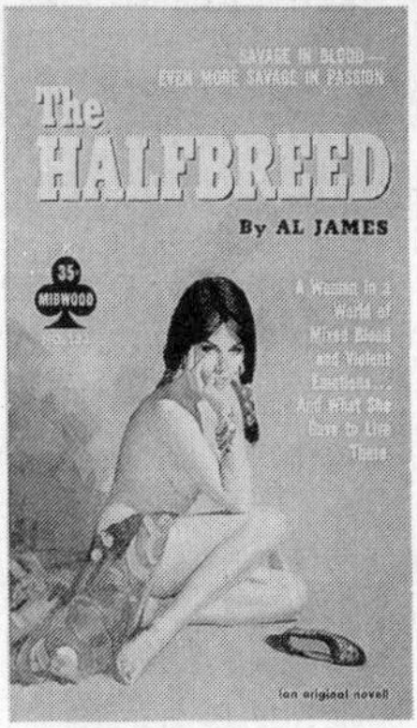

Midwood, 133

Midwood, 148

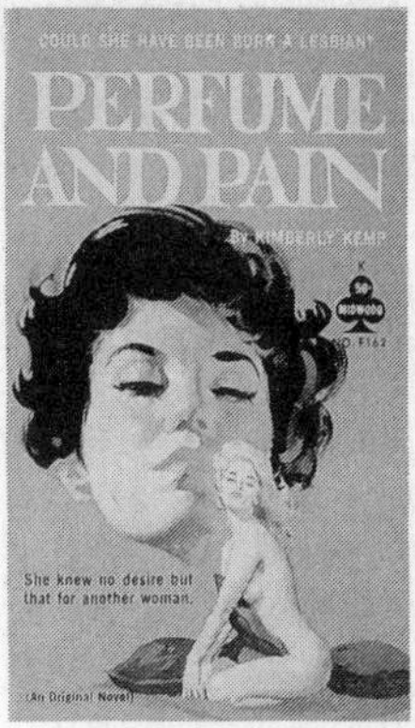

Midwood, F-162

		G	VG	F
Y-127	James, Al - ***Weak And Wicked*** [1961] PBO.	$2.00	$6.00	$12.00
F-128	Marsden, Martha - ***Intimate*** [1961] PBO.	$2.00	$6.00	$12.00
129	Marshall, Alan - ***All My Lovers*** [1961] Cover art by Ronnie Lesser.	$2.50	$7.50	$15.00
F-130	Glennon, George - ***Norma*** [1961] PBO. Cover art by Robert Maguire.	$2.50	$7.50	$15.00
131	Lord, Sheldon - ***Carla*** [1961] Cover art by Paul Rader.	$3.00	$9.00	$18.00
F-132	Avallone, Mike - ***Stag Stripper*** [1961] PBO. Cover art by Robert Maguire.	$2.50	$7.50	$15.00
133	James, Al - ***The Halfbreed*** [1961] PBO.	$2.25	$7.00	$14.00
F-134	Hastings, March - ***The Outcasts*** [1961] PBO. Cover art by Rudy Nappi.	$2.00	$6.00	$12.00
Y-135	Avallone, Mike - ***The Little Black Book*** [1961] PBO. Cover art by Paul Rader.	$3.00	$9.00	$18.00
136	Brennan, Alice - ***The Snows Of Summer*** [1961] PBO.	$2.00	$6.00	$12.00
137	Mitchell, Gordon - ***Henry's Wife*** [1961] Cover art by Paul Rader.	$2.50	$7.50	$15.00
Y-138	Harvey, James - ***Stag Model*** [1961]	$1.25	$3.75	$7.50
F-139	Ellis, Joan - ***In The Shadows*** [1963] PBO. Cover art by Robert Maguire.	$2.50	$7.50	$15.00
F-140	Allen, Roger - ***August Heat*** [1962] PBO. Cover art by Robert Maguire.	$2.25	$7.00	$14.00
F-141	Kemp, Kimberly - ***Love Like A Shadow*** [1962] PBO. Cover art by Rader.	$2.50	$7.50	$15.00
F-142	Britain, Sloane - ***Womam Doctor*** [1962] PBO. Cover art by Rader.	$2.25	$7.00	$14.00
143	Anonymous - ***Con Girl*** [1962] PBO.	$2.00	$6.00	$12.00
Y-144	Louis, Ort - ***I Know The Score*** [1962] PBO. Cover art by Robert Schulz.	$2.25	$7.00	$14.00
F-145	Beauchamp, Loren (Robert Silverberg) - ***Strange Delights*** [1962] PBO. Cover art by Rader.	$3.00	$9.00	$18.00
F-146	Avallone, Mike - ***Sinners In White*** [1962] PBO.	$2.00	$6.00	$12.00
147	Marshall, Alan - ***Man Hungry*** [1962]	$3.00	$9.00	$18.00
148	Beauchamp, Loren (Robert Silverberg) - ***Sin A La Carte*** [1962]..	$2.50	$7.50	$15.00
149	Marshall, Alan - ***Apprentice Virgin*** [1962] Cover art by Rudy Nappi.	$3.00	$9.00	$18.00
150	Hitt, Orrie - ***Mail Order Sex*** [1962]	$2.00	$6.00	$12.00
151	Russo, Paul V. - ***Jill Harvey*** [1962] PBO.	$2.00	$6.00	$12.00
152	Porcelain, Sidney - ***Office Tramp*** [1962] PBO. Cover art by Paul Rader.	$2.50	$7.50	$15.00

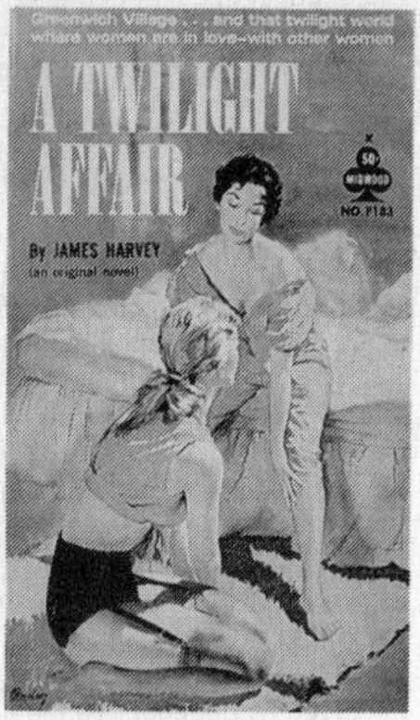

Midwood, F-183

Midwood, Y-184

Midwood, F-271

		G	VG	F
Y-153	Dyer, Walter - ***Skin Deep*** [1962] PBO. Cover art by Paul Rader.	$2.50	$7.50	$15.00
F-154	Sprague, W.D. - ***The Lesbian In Our Society*** [1962] PBO..........	$1.25	$3.75	$7.50
Y-155	Hytes, Jason - ***Rita*** [1962] PBO.	$2.00	$6.00	$12.00
F-156	Knight, Dorcas - ***The Flesh Is Willing*** [1962] PBO. Cover art by Frace.	$2.00	$6.00	$12.00
157	Ellis, Joan - ***The Strange Compulsion Of Laura M.*** [1962] PBO.	$2.00	$6.00	$12.00
Y-158	Mayo, Dallas - ***Scandal*** [1962] PBO.	$2.00	$6.00	$12.00
Y-159	Lord, Sheldon - ***21 Gay Street*** [1962] Cover art by Paul Rader....	$3.50	$10.00	$20.00
Y-160	Swenson, Peggy (Richard E. Geis) - ***The Blonde*** [1962]	$2.50	$7.50	$15.00
161	Michaels, Linda - ***Girls In Trouble*** [1962] PBO..........................	$2.00	$6.00	$12.00
F-162	Kemp, Kemberly - ***Perfume And Pain*** [1962] PBO. Cover art by Robert Maguire..	$2.50	$7.50	$15.00
F-163	Hastings, March - ***The Drifter*** [1962] PBO................................	$2.00	$6.00	$12.00
F-164	Richards, Rick - ***Ripe*** [1962] PBO..	$2.00	$6.00	$12.00
165	Lord, Sheldon - ***Puta*** [1962]	$3.00	$9.00	$18.00
166	Marshall, Allan - ***What Girls Will Do*** [1962].............................	$3.00	$9.00	$18.00
167	Hytes, Jason - ***Sex Before Six*** [1962] PBO.	$2.00	$6.00	$12.00
Y-168	Avallone, Mike - ***Flight Hostess Rogers*** [1962] PBO.	$1.35	$4.00	$8.00
F-169	Ellis, Joan - ***Gay Scene*** [1962] PBO.	$2.25	$7.00	$14.00
F-170	Merwin Jr., Sam - ***The Passer*** [1962] PBO................................	$2.50	$7.50	$15.00
171	Skinner, Mike - ***The Undoing Of Jenny*** [1962] PBO.	$2.00	$6.00	$12.00
F-172	Salem, Randy - ***Tender Torment*** [1962] PBO. Cover art by Paul Rader..	$2.50	$7.50	$15.00
Y-173	Ellis, Joan - ***Sex With A Twist*** [1962] PBO.	$2.00	$6.00	$12.00
F-174	Richards, Rick - ***Seduction By Appointment*** [1962] PBO. Cover art by Rudy Nappi.	$2.00	$6.00	$12.00
Y-175	Harris, Amy - ***Forever Amy*** [1962] PBO.	$2.00	$6.00	$12.00
Y-176	Hytes, Jason - ***The Doctor And The Dyke*** [1962] PBO.	$2.00	$6.00	$12.00
F-177	Britain, Sloane - ***Ladder Of Flesh*** [1962] PBO.	$2.00	$6.00	$12.00
F-178	Johnston, William - ***A Man In Her House*** [1962] PBO. Cover by Robert Schulz.	$2.25	$7.00	$14.00
Y-179	Hastings, March - ***Chico's Women*** [1962] PBO. Cover art by Paul Rader..	$2.50	$7.50	$15.00
F-180	Fisher, Edie - ***Prisoner Of My Past*** [1962] PBO. Cover art by Rader.	$2.50	$7.50	$15.00
F-181	Kemp, Kimberly - ***Operation: Sex*** [1962] PBO. Cover art by Rader.	$2.50	$7.50	$15.00
182	Ellis, Joan - ***Campus Jungle*** [1962] PBO. Cover art by Rader.....	$2.50	$7.50	$15.00
F-183	Harvey, James - ***A Twilight Affair*** [1962] Cover art by Rader.	$2.50	$7.50	$15.00

		G	VG	F
Y-184	Avallone, Mike - ***All The Way*** [1962] Cover art by Rader.	$2.50	$7.50	$15.00
F-185	Gregory, Paul - ***Passionately Yours, Eve*** [1962] PBO. Cover art by Paul Rader.	$2.50	$7.50	$15.00
Y-186	Dyer, Walter - ***TV Tramps*** [1962] PBO. Cover art by Robert Maguire.	$2.25	$7.00	$14.00
F-187	Richards, Rick - ***Abnormal*** [1962] PBO.	$2.00	$6.00	$12.00
F-188	Hytes, Jason - ***Twice With Julie*** [1962] PBO. Cover art by Robert Maguire.	$2.25	$7.00	$14.00
F-189	Avallone, Mike - ***Sex Kitten*** [1962] PBO. Cover art by Rader.	$2.50	$7.50	$15.00
F-190	Mayo, Dallas - ***The Craving*** [1962] PBO. Cover art by Rader.	$2.50	$7.50	$15.00
F-191	Britton, Sloan - ***Unnatural*** [1962] Cover art by Rader.	$2.50	$7.50	$15.00
F-192	Skinner, Mike - ***The Sex Game*** [1962] PBO. Cover art by Paul Rader.	$2.50	$7.50	$15.00
F-193	Harvey, James - ***Lady Wrestler*** [1962] PBO. Cover art by Rader.	$3.50	$10.00	$20.00
F-194	Ellis, Joan - ***Daughter Of Shame*** [1962] PBO. Cover art by Rader.	$2.50	$7.50	$15.00
F-195	Hytes, Jason - ***One Way Ticket*** [1962] PBO.	$2.00	$6.00	$12.00
F-196	Salem, Randy - ***The Soft Sin*** [1962]	$2.00	$6.00	$12.00
F-197	Hytes, Jason - ***Come One-Come All*** [1962] PBO.	$2.00	$6.00	$12.00
F-198	Mayo, Dallas - ***Voluptuous Voyage*** [1962]	$2.00	$6.00	$12.00
F-199	Collier, Max - ***Thorn Of Evil*** [1962] PBO. Cover art by Rader.	$2.50	$7.50	$15.00
F-200	Swensen, Peggy (Richard E. Geis) - ***Easy*** [1962] PBO. Cover art by Rader.	$3.00	$9.00	$18.00
F-201	Hastings, March - ***Savage Surrender*** [1962] PBO.	$2.00	$6.00	$12.00
F-202	Avallone, Mike - ***The Platinum Trap*** [1962] PBO. Cover art by Rader.	$3.00	$9.00	$18.00
F-203	Harris, Amy - ***Birth Of A Tramp*** [1962] PBO. Cover art by Rader.	$2.50	$7.50	$15.00
F-204	Chance, Mal - ***Web Of Flesh*** [1962] PBO. Cover art by Robert Schulz.	$2.50	$7.50	$15.00
F-205	Avallone, Mike - ***Never Love A Call Girl*** [1962] PBO.	$2.00	$6.00	$12.00
F-206	Beauchamp, Loren (Robert Silverberg) - ***Campus Sex Club*** [1962] PBO. Cover art by Robert Maguire.	$2.50	$7.50	$15.00
F-207	Hytes, Jason - ***Over-Exposed*** [1962] PBO.	$2.00	$6.00	$12.00
F-208	Hastings, March - ***By Flesh Alone*** [1962] PBO.	$2.00	$6.00	$12.00
F-209	Logano, Rock - ***Carrie Corrupted*** [1962] PBO.	$2.00	$6.00	$12.00
F-210	Kemp, Kimberly - ***Intimate Nurse*** [1962]	$1.25	$3.75	$7.50
F-211	Mayo, Dallas - ***Island Of Sin*** [1962] PBO. Cover art by Rader.	$2.50	$7.50	$15.00
F-212	Harris, Amy - ***Touch Me Gently*** [1962] PBO. Cover art by Rader.	$2.50	$7.50	$15.00
F-213	Michaels, Linda - ***Sleep-In Maid*** [1962] PBO.	$2.00	$6.00	$12.00
F-214	Kemp, Kimberly - ***Lap Of Luxury*** [1962] PBO. Cover art by Rader.	$2.50	$7.50	$15.00
F-215	Harris, Amy - ***Counter Girl*** [1962] PBO. Cover art by Robert Maguire.	$2.50	$7.50	$15.00
F-216	Hytes, Jason - ***Wait Your Turn*** [1962] PBO.	$2.00	$6.00	$12.00
F-217	Russo, Paul V. - ***Appointment For Sin*** [1962] PBO.	$2.00	$6.00	$12.00
F-218	Ellis, Joan - ***Gay Girl*** [1962] PBO. Cover by Jerome Podwil.	$2.00	$6.00	$12.00
F-219	Salem, Randy - ***The Sex Between*** [1962] PBO.	$2.25	$7.00	$14.00
F-220	Skinner, Mike - ***Flight Into Sin*** [1962] PBO. Cover art by Rader.	$2.50	$7.50	$15.00
F-221	Hytes, Jason - ***Yesterday's Virgin*** [1962] PBO. Cover art by Rader.	$2.50	$7.50	$15.00
F-222	Harvey, James - ***Degraded Women*** [1962] PBO. Cover art by Robert Maguire.	$2.50	$7.50	$15.00
F-223	Swenson, Peggy (Richard E. Geis) - ***Pleasure Lodge*** [1962] PBO.	$2.25	$7.00	$14.00
F-224	Hastings, March - ***Whip Of Desire*** [1962] PBO. Cover art by Jerome Podwil.	$2.00	$6.00	$12.00

		G	VG	F
F-225	Hitt, Orrie - ***Unnatural Urge*** [1962] PBO. Cover art by Lu Kimmel.	$2.50	$7.50	$15.00
F-226	Beauchamp, Loren (Robert Silverberg) - ***Wayward Widow*** [1962] PBO. Cover art by Rader.	$3.00	$9.00	$18.00
F-227	English, Arnold - ***Resort Secretary*** [1962] Cover by Giac.	$1.25	$3.75	$7.50
F-228	Anthony, Rock - ***The Girl Downstairs*** [1962] PBO. Cover by Giac.	$1.50	$5.00	$10.00
F-229	Hytes, Jason - ***This Is Elaine*** [1963] PBO. Cover art by Rader.	$2.50	$7.50	$15.00
F-230	Thompson, John B. - ***Take Me*** [1963]	$2.00	$6.00	$12.00
D-231	Hytes, Jason/Hastings, March - ***The Wild Week/Imitation Lovers*** [1963] PBO. Cover art by Rader. Contains 8 B & W Frazetta plates.	$12.50	$37.50	$75.00
F-232	Collier, Max - ***The Payoff*** [1963] PBO. Cover art by Rader.	$2.50	$7.50	$15.00
F-233	Gage, Russell - ***Immoral Lady*** [1963] PBO.	$2.00	$6.00	$12.00
F-234	Ellis, Joan - ***Forbidden Sex*** [1963]	$2.25	$7.00	$14.00
F-235	Skinner, Mike - ***The Passionate Virgin*** [1963] PBO.	$2.00	$6.00	$12.00
F-236	Karl, Don - ***Wild Honey*** [1963] PBO. Cover art by Rader.	$2.50	$7.50	$15.00
F-237	Hytes, Jason - ***Never Enough*** [1964] PBO. Cover art by Rader.	$2.50	$7.50	$15.00
F-238	Ellis, Joan - ***The Hot Canary*** [1963] PBO. Cover art by Robert Maguire.	$2.50	$7.50	$15.00
F-239	Dodge, Paul - ***Sudden Hunger*** [1963] PBO. Cover art by Rader.	$3.00	$9.00	$18.00
F-240	Hastings, March - ***The Soft Way*** [1963] PBO.	$2.00	$6.00	$12.00
F-241	Louis, Ort - ***The Pleasure And The Pain*** [1963] PBO.	$2.00	$6.00	$12.00
F-242	Dyer, Walter - ***Don't Bet On Blondes*** [1963] PBO. Cover art by Robert Maguire.	$2.50	$7.50	$15.00
F-243	Kemp, Kimberly - ***Illicit Interlude*** [1963] PBO.	$2.00	$6.00	$12.00
F-244	Anthony, Rock - ***By Her Body Betrayed*** [1963] PBO.	$2.25	$7.00	$14.00
F-245	Elder, Philip - ***The Sex Plan*** [1963] Cover art by Rader.	$2.50	$7.50	$15.00
F-246	Hytes, Jason - ***Swing Low Sweet Sinner*** [1963] PBO. Cover art by Olson.	$2.00	$6.00	$12.00
F-247	Swensen, Peggy (Richard E. Geis) - ***Sea Nymph*** [1963] PBO. Cover art by Rader.	$2.50	$7.50	$15.00
F-248	Harris, Amy - ***Horizontal Secretary*** [1963] PBO. Cover art by Rader.	$2.50	$7.50	$15.00
F-249	Craig, D.W. - ***None But The Wicked*** [1963] PBO. Cover art by Victor Olson.	$2.00	$6.00	$12.00
F-250	Hastings, March - ***A Rage Within*** [1963] PBO. Cover art by Rader.	$2.50	$7.50	$15.00
F-251	Russo, Paul V. - ***Pagan*** [1963] PBO.	$2.00	$6.00	$12.00
F-252	Lucchesi, Aldo - ***Strange Breed*** [1963] Cover art by Rader.	$2.50	$7.50	$15.00
F-253	Harvey, James - ***Camera Club Model*** [1963] PBO. Photo cover.	$2.00	$6.00	$12.00
F-254	Hytes, Jason - ***Without Shame*** [1963]	$2.00	$6.00	$12.00
F-255	Hastings, March - ***Again And Again*** [1963] PBO. Cover art by Robert Maguire.	$2.50	$7.50	$15.00
F-256	Kemp, Kimberly - ***A Bit Of Fluff*** [1963] PBO. Cover art by Rader.	$2.50	$7.50	$15.00
F-257	Ellis, Joan - ***Once Too Often*** [1963] PBO.	$2.00	$6.00	$12.00
F-258	Donalds, Richard - ***Something Special*** [1963] PBO.	$2.00	$6.00	$12.00
F-259	Marshall, Alan - ***The Cruel Touch*** [1963] PBO. Cover art by Rader.	$2.50	$7.50	$15.00
F-260	Warren, Jay - ***The Path Between*** [1963]	$2.00	$6.00	$12.00
F-261	Draper, Jess - ***One Step More*** [1963] PBO.	$2.00	$6.00	$12.00
F-262	Thompson, John Burton - ***Girl In The Middle*** [1963] PBO.	$2.00	$6.00	$12.00
F-263	Collier, Max - ***The Mark Of A Man*** [1963] PBO.	$2.00	$6.00	$12.00
F-264	Harvey, James - ***Erica*** [1963] PBO.	$2.00	$6.00	$12.00
F-265	Harris, Amy - ***All Of Me*** [1963] PBO. Cover art by Rader.	$2.50	$7.50	$15.00
F-266	Hamilton, Greg - ***Restless*** [1963] PBO. Cover art by Rader.	$2.50	$7.50	$15.00
F-267	Mayo, Dallas - ***Everybody Welcome*** [1963] PBO.	$2.00	$6.00	$12.00
F-268	Hastings, March - ***The Unashamed*** [1963] Cover art by Rader.	$2.50	$7.50	$15.00
F-269	Hytes, Jason - ***The Teaser*** [1963] PBO.	$2.00	$6.00	$12.00

		G	VG	F
F-270	Donalds, Richard - ***Sign Here For Sin*** [1963] PBO. Cover art by Rader.	$2.50	$7.50	$15.00
F-271	Hastings, March - ***Her Private Hell*** [1963] PBO. Cover art by Rader.	$5.50	$17.50	$35.00
F-272	Draper, Jess - ***Rusty*** [1963] PBO. Photo cover.	$2.00	$6.00	$12.00
F-273	Hamilton, Greg - ***Any Man Will Do*** [1963] PBO.	$2.00	$6.00	$12.00
F-274	Swenson, Peggy (Richard E. Geis) - ***Pajama Party*** [1963] PBO. Cover art by Rader.	$2.50	$7.50	$15.00
F-275	Wilder, Billy & Diamond, I.A.L. - ***Irma La Douce*** [1963] PBO. Movie tie-in.	$3.50	$10.00	$20.00
F-276	Beauchamp, Loren (Robert Silverberg) - ***Sin On Wheels*** [1963] Cover art by Rader.	$2.50	$7.50	$15.00
S-277	Hytes, Jason/Kemp, Kimberly - ***Perfumed/Pampered*** [1963] PBO. Contains 10 B & W Frazetta plates.	$12.50	$37.50	$75.00
F-278	Anthony, Rock - ***Fringe Benefits*** [1963] PBO.	$2.00	$6.00	$12.00
F-279	Ellis, Joan - ***Hold Me Tight*** [1963] PBO.	$2.00	$6.00	$12.00
F-280	Turner, John - ***Take Care Of Me*** [1963] Cover art by Robert Schulz.	$2.00	$6.00	$12.00
F-281	Collier, Max - ***Say When*** [1963] PBO.	$2.00	$6.00	$12.00
F-282	Russo, Paul V. - ***Party Girls*** [1963] PBO. Cover art by Rader.	$2.50	$7.50	$15.00
F-283	Salem, Randy - ***Honeysuckle*** [1963]	$2.00	$6.00	$12.00
F-284	Britain, Sloane - ***Meet Marilyn*** [1964]	$2.00	$6.00	$12.00
F-285	Draper, Jess - ***Whatever She Wanted*** [1963] PBO.	$2.00	$6.00	$12.00
F-286	Mezatesta, Richard - ***One Of The Girls*** [1963] PBO. Cover art by Rader.	$2.50	$7.50	$15.00
F-287	Turner, John - ***Soft In The Shadows*** [1963] PBO. Photo cover.	$2.00	$6.00	$12.00
F-288	Saxon, Will - ***Night After Night*** [1963] PBO. Photo cover.	$2.00	$6.00	$12.00
F-289	Commings, Joseph - ***Nine To Five*** [1963] PBO.	$2.00	$6.00	$12.00
F-290	Powell, Judd - ***The Intruder*** [1963] PBO.	$2.00	$6.00	$12.00
F-291	Hasselrodt, R. Leighton - ***Lesbianism Around The World*** [1963]	$1.35	$4.00	$8.00
F-292	Beauchamp, Loren (Robert Silverberg) - ***Nurse Carolyn*** [1963]	$2.00	$6.00	$12.00
F-293	Ellis, Joan - ***Too Young To Marry*** [1963] PBO. Photo cover.	$1.25	$3.75	$7.50
F-294	Mullins, Richard - ***Above And Beyond*** [1963]	$2.00	$6.00	$12.00
F-295	Thomas, Paul - ***The Spy*** [1963]	$1.25	$3.75	$7.50
F-296	Hastings, March - ***The Heat Of Day*** [1963]	$2.00	$6.00	$12.00
F-297	Turner, John - ***The Captive*** [1963]	$2.00	$6.00	$12.00
F-298	Hamilton, Greg - ***Made To Order*** [1963] PBO. Cover art by Rader.	$2.00	$6.00	$12.00
F-299	Kemp, Kimberly - ***Nothing To Lose*** [1963] PBO.	$2.00	$6.00	$12.00
S-300	Brooks, Barbara/McAndrews, Robbie - ***Shadow Dance/After Hours*** [1963] PBO.	$2.00	$6.00	$12.00
F-301	James, Stuart - ***Devils Workshop*** [1963]	$2.00	$6.00	$12.00
F-302	Hytes, Jason - ***A Time Of Torment*** [1963] PBO. Photo cover.	$2.00	$6.00	$12.00
F-303	Collier, Max - ***Sure Thing*** [1963] PBO. Photo cover.	$1.50	$5.00	$10.00
F-304	Thompson, John B. - ***Shameless*** [1963] PBO. Photo cover.	$1.50	$5.00	$10.00
F-305	Fields, Vin - ***The Come On*** [1963] PBO. Photo cover.	$1.50	$5.00	$10.00
F-306	Scobie, E.L. - ***Man Handled*** [1963] PBO.	$2.00	$6.00	$12.00
F-307	Trainer, Russell - ***No Way Back*** [1963] PBO. Cover art by Rader.	$2.50	$7.50	$15.00
F-308	Turner, John - ***Carole Came Back*** [1963] PBO.	$2.00	$6.00	$12.00
F-309	Anthony, Rock - ***With Eyes Wide Open*** [1963] PBO.	$2.00	$6.00	$12.00
F-310	Britton, Sloan - ***The Delicate Vice*** [1963]	$1.25	$3.75	$7.50
F-311	Taylor, Valerie - ***Unlike Others*** [1963]	$2.50	$7.50	$15.00
X-312	Sloan, William - ***Tear Gas And Hungry Dogs*** [1963]	$3.50	$10.00	$20.00
F-313	Curtis, Brad - ***Man Trap*** [1963] PBO. Cover art by Rader.	$2.50	$7.50	$15.00
F-314	Hamilton, Greg - ***Monica*** [1963] PBO.	$2.00	$6.00	$12.00
F-315	Mayo, Dallas - ***When Lights Are Low*** [1963] PBO. Cover art by Rader.	$2.50	$7.50	$15.00
F-316	Lamoureux, John - ***The French Way*** [1963] PBO.	$2.00	$6.00	$12.00
F-317	Donalds, Richard - ***Not Since Eve*** [1963] PBO. Photo cover.	$2.00	$6.00	$12.00

		G	VG	F
F-318	Draper, Jess - ***Stronger Than Love*** [1963] PBO. Cover art by Rader.	$2.50	$7.50	$15.00
F-319	Collier, Max - ***Diane*** [1963] PBO. Photo cover.	$2.00	$6.00	$12.00
F-320	Britain, Sloane - ***Insatiable*** [1963] Photo cover.	$1.25	$3.75	$7.50
S-321	Hamilton, Greg/Hytes, Jason - ***Harlot In Heels/Lady Love*** [1963] PBO.	$2.50	$7.50	$15.00
F-322	Brennan, Dan - ***No Sense Of Shame*** [1963] PBO.	$2.00	$6.00	$12.00
F-323	Brooks, Barbara - ***Just The Two Of Us*** [1963] PBO. Cover art by Rader.	$2.50	$7.50	$15.00
F-324	Hamilton, Greg - ***So Eager To Please*** [1963] PBO.	$2.00	$6.00	$12.00
F-325	Turner, John - ***The Sinners*** [1963] PBO. Photo cover.	$1.25	$3.75	$7.50
F-326	Corgan, Grant - ***The Honeymoon Habit*** [1963] PBO. Cover art by Rader.	$2.50	$7.50	$15.00
F-327	Hughes, Ludwell - ***Spring Fever*** [1963] PBO. Cover art by Rader.	$2.50	$7.50	$15.00
F-328	Russo, Paul V. - ***Image Of Evil*** [1963] PBO. Photo cover.	$1.50	$5.00	$10.00
F-329	Taylor, Valerie - ***Return To Lesbos*** [1963]	$2.50	$7.50	$15.00
F-330	Kane, Henry - ***Two Must Die*** [1963] PBO.	$3.00	$9.00	$18.00
F-331	Kemp, Kimberly - ***Different*** [1963]	$2.00	$6.00	$12.00
F-332	Ellis, Joan - ***Day In, Day Out*** [1963] PBO. Cover art by Rader.	$2.50	$7.50	$15.00
F-333	Clements, Mark - ***Teacher's Pet*** [1963] PBO. Cover art by Rader.	$2.50	$7.50	$15.00
F-334	Stark, John - ***The Vice Dolls*** [1963] PBO. Photo cover.	$1.50	$5.00	$10.00
F-335	Curtis, Brad - ***Anatomy Of A Mistress*** [1963] PBO. Photo cover.	$1.50	$5.00	$10.00
F-336	Moore, Amanda - ***Nude In A Red Chair*** [1963] PBO. Cover art by Rader.	$2.50	$7.50	$15.00
F-337	Wynne, Andrew - ***Have Heels, Will Travel*** [1963] PBO. Photo cover.	$2.00	$6.00	$12.00
S-338	Hytes, Jason/Kemp, Kimberly - ***Immoral/Forbidden*** [1963] PBO.	$2.50	$7.50	$15.00
F-339	Martell, David - ***Old Enough*** [1963] PBO. Photo cover.	$1.25	$3.75	$7.50
F-340	Rico, Don - ***Nikki*** [1963] PBO. Cover art by Robert Schulz.	$2.00	$6.00	$12.00
F-341	Hamilton, Greg - ***Portrait In Flesh*** [1963] PBO.	$2.00	$6.00	$12.00
F-342	Fields, Vin - ***The Baby-Sitter*** [1963]	$1.35	$4.00	$8.00
F-343	Ellis, Joan - ***Girl's Dormitory*** [1963] PBO. Cover art by Rader.	$3.50	$10.00	$20.00
F-344	Faye, Sheila - ***Switch Partners*** [1963] PBO.	$2.00	$6.00	$12.00
F-345	Nemec, John - ***Marriage On The Rocks*** [1963] PBO. Photo cover.	$1.25	$3.75	$7.50
F-346	Taylor, Valerie - ***A World Without Men*** [1963] PBO. Photo cover.	$3.00	$9.00	$18.00
X-347	Pinkus, Oscar - ***Friends And Lovers*** [1963]	$1.25	$3.75	$7.50
F-348	Matthews, Kevin (Gardner F. Fox) - ***The Pagan Empress*** [1964] PBO.	$4.00	$12.50	$25.00
S-349	Ellis, Joan/Brooks, Barbara - ***High School Hellion/Campus Cat Pack*** [1964] PBO.	$2.50	$7.50	$15.00
F-350	Corgan, Grant - ***The Spice Of Life*** [1964] PBO.	$2.00	$6.00	$12.00
F-351	Hamilton, Greg - ***Anther Kind Of Love*** [1964] PBO. Photo cover.	$1.50	$5.00	$10.00
F-352	Kemp, Kimberly - ***A World All Their Own*** [1964]	$2.00	$6.00	$12.00
F-353	Bouma, J.L. - ***Never Say No*** [1964] PBO. Cover art by Rader.	$2.50	$7.50	$15.00
F-354	Clements, Mark - ***Love Or Lust*** [1964] PBO. Photo cover.	$1.25	$3.75	$7.50
F-355	Spaulding, Michael - ***Anything Under The Sun*** [1964] PBO. Photo cover.	$1.25	$3.75	$7.50
F-356	Curtis, Brad - ***For Services Rendered*** [1964] PBO. Cover art by Rader.	$2.50	$7.50	$15.00
F-357	Burgess, Michael - ***Where There's Smoke*** [1964] PBO.	$2.00	$6.00	$12.00
F-358	Mayo, Dallas - ***Kitten*** [1964]	$2.00	$6.00	$12.00
F-359	Du Champ, Laura - ***Duet*** [1964] PBO. Cover art by Docktor.	$2.00	$6.00	$12.00
F-360	Ellis, Joan - ***After Class*** [1964] PBO.	$2.00	$6.00	$12.00
F-361	Trainer, Russell - ***Love Starved*** [1964] PBO. Photo cover.	$1.25	$3.75	$7.50

		G	VG	F
F-362	O'Bannon, Brian - ***Woman On Fire*** [1964] PBO. Photo cover.	$1.25	$3.75	$7.50
F-363	Sherwood, Danni - ***So Strange A Love*** [1964] PBO. Photo cover.	$1.25	$3.75	$7.50
F-364	Clements, Mark - ***Early To Bed*** [1964] PBO. Photo cover.	$1.25	$3.75	$7.50
F-365	Moore, Amanda - ***The Yes Girl*** [1964] PBO. Cover art by Rader.	$2.50	$7.50	$15.00
F-366	Hamilton, Greg - ***Tall, Blonde And Evil*** [1964] PBO. Cover art by Rader.	$2.50	$7.50	$15.00
F-367	Draper, Jess - ***His For The Taking*** [1964] PBO. Cover art by Rader.	$2.50	$7.50	$15.00
F-368	Hytes, Jason - ***One Last Fling*** [1964] Photo cover.	$1.25	$3.75	$7.50
F-370	Gaffney, Eugenie - ***Cry Into The Wind*** [1964]	$2.00	$6.00	$12.00
F-371	Mayo, Dallas - ***Pretty Puppet*** [1964] PBO. Cover art by Rader.	$2.50	$7.50	$15.00
F-372	Hamilton, Greg - ***That Kind Of Wife*** [1964] PBO. Photo cover.	$1.25	$3.75	$7.50
F-373	Clay, Ann Brady - ***We Two*** [1964]	$1.25	$3.75	$7.50
F-374	Lawrence, David - ***Impatient*** [1964] PBO. Cover art by Rader.	$2.50	$7.50	$15.00
F-375	Hytes, Jason - ***The Street Walker*** [1964] PBO.	$2.00	$6.00	$12.00
F-376	Craig, D.W. - ***Only In Secret*** [1964] PBO. Cover art by Rader.	$2.50	$7.50	$15.00
F-377	Gold, R.C. - ***The Teenage Trap*** [1964] PBO. Photo cover.	$2.00	$6.00	$12.00
F-378	Trainer, Russell - ***His Daughter's Friend*** [1964] PBO. Cover art by Rader.	$2.50	$7.50	$15.00
F-379	Russo, Paul V. - ***Corrupt Woman*** [1964]	$1.25	$3.75	$7.50
F-380	Harris, Frank G. - ***Love Toy*** [1964] PBO. Cover art by Rader.	$2.50	$7.50	$15.00
F-381	Kemp, Kimberly - ***The House Guest*** [1964] PBO. Cover art by Rader.	$2.50	$7.50	$15.00
F-382	Hamilton, Greg - ***Afternoons At Three*** [1964]	$1.25	$3.75	$7.50
F-383	Price, Marjorie - ***A Lesson In Love*** [1964]	$1.25	$3.75	$7.50
F-384	Corgan, Grant - ***Swing Shift*** [1964] PBO.	$2.00	$6.00	$12.00
F-385	Curtis, Brad - ***Man-Tamer*** [1964] PBO. Photo cover.	$1.25	$3.75	$7.50
F-386	Ellis, Joan - ***The Third Street*** [1964]	$1.25	$3.75	$7.50
F-387	York, Alix - ***Home Before Six*** [1964] PBO. Photo cover.	$1.25	$3.75	$7.50
F-388	Burgess, Michael - ***Playgirl*** [1964] PBO. Photo cover.	$1.25	$3.75	$7.50
F-389	Russo, Paul V. - ***Dance Of Desire*** [1964] PBO. Cover art by Rader.	$2.50	$7.50	$15.00
F-390	Gaffney, Eugenie - ***Remember Me?*** [1964] PBO. Cover art by Lowenbein.	$1.25	$3.75	$7.50
F-391	Du Champ, Laura - ***Goodbye, Darling*** [1964] PBO. Cover art by Victor Olson.	$2.00	$6.00	$12.00
F-392	Balmer, John - ***Chains Of Silk*** [1964] PBO. Cover art by Rader.	$2.50	$7.50	$15.00
F-393	Harvey, James - ***The Adulteress*** [1964]	$1.25	$3.75	$7.50
F-394	Swenson, Peggy (Richard E. Geis) - ***The Unloved*** [1964] Photo cover.	$2.00	$6.00	$12.00
34-395	Ellis, Joan/Hytes, Jason - ***The Dangerous Age/Bad By Choice*** [1964] PBO. Contains 8 B & W Frazetta plates.	$12.50	$37.50	$75.00
32-396	Ellis, Joan - ***Talk Of The Town*** [1964] PBO.	$2.00	$6.00	$12.00
32-397	Lawrence, David - ***Joy*** [1964]	$1.25	$3.75	$7.50
32-398	Duchamp, Laura - ***Encore*** [1964] PBO.	$2.00	$6.00	$12.00
32-399	York, Alix - ***Good Time Girl*** [1964] PBO. Photo cover.	$1.25	$3.75	$7.50
32-400	Craig, D.W. - ***Too Late For Tears*** [1964] PBO. Cover art by Rader.	$2.50	$7.50	$15.00

Midwood Tower.

		G	VG	F
32-401	Vincent, Joan - ***Divorcee*** [1964] PBO.	$2.00	$6.00	$12.00
32-402	Emerson, Jill - ***Warm And Willing*** [1965] Photo cover.	$1.25	$3.75	$7.50
32-403	Collier, Max - ***Male Call*** [1964] PBO.	$1.25	$3.75	$7.50
32-404	Hytes, Jason - ***Overtime Affair*** [1964] Photo cover.	$1.25	$3.75	$7.50
405	St. John, George - ***Love A La Carte*** [1964]	$1.25	$3.75	$7.50
42-406	Demaris, Ovid - ***The Organization*** [1964] PBO.	$1.35	$4.00	$8.00
42-407	White, Lionel - ***Before I Die*** [1964]	$2.00	$6.00	$12.00
42-408	Gaffney, Eugenie - ***Cry Into The Wind*** [1964]	$1.25	$3.75	$7.50

		G	VG	F
34-409	Price, Marjorie/Hytes, Jason - ***Trick Or Treat/Split Level Sin*** [1964] PBO. Contains 8 B & W plates by Victor Olson.	$3.50	$10.00	$20.00
32-410	Brooks, Barbara - ***Hellcat*** [1964] PBO.	$2.00	$6.00	$12.00
32-411	Kemp, Kimberly - ***A Labor Of Love*** [1964] PBO. Cover art by Rader.	$2.50	$7.50	$15.00
32-412	Faye, Sheila - ***Hold That Pose*** [1964] PBO. Photo cover.	$1.25	$3.75	$7.50
32-413	Du Champ, Laura - ***Thank You, Call Again*** [1964] PBO. Cover art by Victor Olson.	$2.00	$6.00	$12.00
32-414	Clements, Mark - ***The Room Mates*** [1964] PBO. Photo cover.	$1.25	$3.75	$7.50
32-415	Fields, Vin - ***One After Another*** [1964] PBO. Cover art by Rader.	$2.50	$7.50	$15.00
32-416	Collier, Max - ***His To Command*** [1964] PBO.	$1.35	$4.00	$8.00
32-417	Ellis, Joan - ***Campus Kittens*** [1964] PBO. Cover art by Rader.	$2.50	$7.50	$15.00
32-418	Mayo, Dallas - ***Silky*** [1964] Photo cover.	$1.35	$4.00	$8.00
32-419	Duchamp, Laura - ***The Other Extreme*** [1964] PBO. Photo cover.	$2.00	$6.00	$12.00
32-420	Burgess, Michael - ***Just This Once*** [1964] PBO.	$2.00	$6.00	$12.00
32-421	Mayo, Dallas - ***The Easy Way*** [1964]	$1.25	$3.75	$7.50
32-422	York, Alix - ***Pleasure Island*** [1964]	$1.25	$3.75	$7.50
32-423	Hamilton, Greg - ***Follow The Leader*** [1964] PBO. Photo cover.	$1.25	$3.75	$7.50
32-424	Ellis, Joan - ***Gang Girl*** [1964] PBO. Cover art by Rader.	$3.00	$9.00	$18.00
32-425	Curtis, Brad - ***Private Property*** [1964]	$1.25	$3.75	$7.50
32-426	Kemp, Kimberly - ***Party Time*** [1964]	$1.25	$3.75	$7.50
32-427	Taylor, Valerie - ***Journey To Fulfillment*** [1964]	$2.50	$7.50	$15.00
32-428	Hytes, Jason - ***Sex Before Six*** [1964]	$1.25	$3.75	$7.50
44-429	Costigan, Lee - ***The Hard Sell*** [1964]	$1.25	$3.75	$7.50
43-430	Mathews, Kevin (Gardner F. Fox) - ***Catherine The Great*** [1964] PBO.	$4.00	$12.50	$25.00
42-431	White, Lionel - ***The Killing*** [1964] Photo cover.	$2.00	$6.00	$12.00
43-432	Daniels, John S. - ***Trail's End*** [1964]	$1.25	$3.75	$7.50
32-433	Duchamp, Laura - ***The Time And Place*** [1964]	$2.00	$6.00	$12.00
32-434	Clements, Mark - ***Holiday Weekend*** [1965]	$1.25	$3.75	$7.50
32-435	Russo, Paul V. - ***Into The Fire*** [1964]	$1.25	$3.75	$7.50
32-436	Ellis, Joan - ***Three Of A Kind*** [1965] PBO. Cover art by Rader.	$2.50	$7.50	$15.00
32-437	Hart, Jay - ***Miss Dream Girl*** [1965] PBO. Cover art by Rader.	$2.50	$7.50	$15.00
32-438	Nelson, Connie - ***Woman Aflame*** [1965]	$1.25	$3.75	$7.50
32-439	Burgess, Michael - ***Love Thief*** [1965]	$1.25	$3.75	$7.50
32-440	Moore, Amanda - ***For Want Of Love*** [1965] PBO. Photo cover.	$1.25	$3.75	$7.50
32-441	Curtis, Brad - ***Night Shift*** [1965] PBO.	$1.35	$4.00	$8.00
32-442	Hastings, March - ***The Drifter*** [1965]	$1.25	$3.75	$7.50
43-443	Lortz, Richard - ***A Summer In Spain*** [1965] Cover art by Jack Thurston.	$1.25	$3.75	$7.50
43-444	Cody, Morrill - ***Hemingway's Paris*** [1965]	$1.35	$4.00	$8.00
43-445	Ross, Sam - ***He Ran All The Way*** [1965]	$1.35	$4.00	$8.00
42-446	Hogan, Robert J. - ***Apache Landing*** [1965]	$2.00	$6.00	$12.00
34-447	Brooks, Barbara/Hart, Jay - ***And When She Was Bad/Strangers For Lovers*** [1965] PBO.	$2.50	$7.50	$15.00
32-448	Kemp, Kimberly - ***Coming Out Party*** [1965]	$1.25	$3.75	$7.50
32-449	Hamilton, Greg - ***Little Girl Lost*** [1965] PBO. Photo cover.	$1.35	$4.00	$8.00
32-450	West, Susannah - ***Daytime In Suburbia*** [1965]	$1.25	$3.75	$7.50
32-451	Brooks, Barbara - ***A Shameless Need*** [1965] PBO. Photo cover.	$1.35	$4.00	$8.00
32-452	Clements, Mark - ***Out Of Control*** [1965]	$1.25	$3.75	$7.50
32-453	Newbury, Will - ***Tourist Trap*** [1965] PBO.	$1.35	$4.00	$8.00
32-454	Kandel, Howard & Safran, Don - ***Masterpieces*** [1965]	$1.25	$3.75	$7.50
32-455	York, Alix - ***The Love Pirate*** [1965] PBO. Cover art by Paul Rader.	$2.50	$7.50	$15.00
32-456	Ellis, Joan - ***No Men Allowed*** [1965]	$1.25	$3.75	$7.50
34-457	Ellis, Joan/Nelson, Connie - ***Executive Sweet/The Soft Sell*** [1965] PBO. Contains 8 B & W plates by Victor Olson.	$3.50	$10.00	$20.00

		G	VG	F
43-458	Anthology Edited by Hilda Holland - ***Why Are You Single?*** [1965] PBO. Photo cover.	$1.25	$3.75	$7.50
34-462	Stevens, Toni/Brooks, Barbara - ***Forbidden Interlude/Just You, Just Me*** [1965] PBO. Contains 8 drawings by Victor Olson.	$3.50	$10.00	$20.00
32-463	Sprague, Ph.D., W.D. - ***Sexual Behavior Of The American Housewife*** [1965]	$1.00	$3.00	$6.00
32-464	Ellis, Joan - ***Open House*** [1965] PBO. Cover art by Rader.	$2.50	$7.50	$15.00
32-465	Mayo, Dallas - ***Pagan Summer*** [1965] PBO. Cover art by Rader.	$2.50	$7.50	$15.00
32-466	Clements, Mark - ***Wayward Wife*** [1965] PBO. Photo cover.	$1.35	$4.00	$8.00
32-467	Kramer, Gerald - ***Penthouse Party*** [1965]	$1.25	$3.75	$7.50
32-468	Fields, Vin - ***The Highest Bidder*** [1965] PBO. Cover art by Rader.	$2.50	$7.50	$15.00
32-469	Craig, D.W. - ***Never Too Young*** [1965]	$1.25	$3.75	$7.50
32-470	Moore, Amanda - ***Punish Lesson*** [1965] PBO.	$1.35	$4.00	$8.00
32-471	Hytes, Jason - ***One For The Road*** [1965] Photo cover.	$1.25	$3.75	$7.50
43-472	Jackson, Shirley - ***The Bird's Nest*** [1965] Photo cover.	$2.50	$7.50	$15.00
43-473	Kemp, P.K. & Lloyd, Christopher - ***The Buccaneers*** [1965] Cover art by Beecham.	$2.00	$6.00	$12.00
42-474	Rutledge, Arthur - ***Object Of Jealousy*** [1965]	$1.25	$3.75	$7.50
43-475	Matthews, Kevin (Gardner F. Fox) - ***Helen Of Troy*** [1965] PBO.	$4.00	$12.50	$25.00
34-476	Nelson, Connie/Harris, Frank - ***Two Timer/The Mate Exchange*** [1965] PBO. Contains 8 B & W plates.	$3.50	$10.00	$20.00
34-477	Woods, Merry/O'Bannon, Brian - ***Small Town Sinner/Thrill Hungry*** [1965] PBO. Contains 8 B & W plates by Victor Olson.	$3.50	$10.00	$20.00
32-478	Collier, Max - ***The Swap Set*** [1965] PBO. Cover art by Rader.	$2.50	$7.50	$15.00
32-479	Kemp, Kimberly - ***Private Party*** [1965] PBO.	$2.00	$6.00	$12.00
32-480	Trainer, Russell - ***Trouble-Maker*** [1965] PBO. Cover art by Rader.	$2.50	$7.50	$15.00
32-481	Duchamp, Laura - ***Room Service*** [1965] PBO. Photo cover.	$2.00	$6.00	$12.00
32-482	McCord, Carter - ***Ask Me No Questions*** [1965] PBO. Cover art by Rader.	$2.50	$7.50	$15.00
32-483	Hughes, Ludwell - ***Overnight Guest*** [1965]	$1.25	$3.75	$7.50
32-484	Britain, Sloan - ***Finders Keepers*** [1965]	$1.25	$3.75	$7.50
32-485	Hytes, Jason - ***Jailbait*** [1965]	$1.25	$3.75	$7.50
43-486	Trevor, Elleston - ***The Billboard Madonna*** [1965]	$1.25	$3.75	$7.50
42-487	Landis, Judson T. & Mary G. - ***Teen-Ager's Guide To Living*** [1965]	$1.25	$3.75	$7.50
43-488	Stone, David - ***The Tired Spy*** [1965]	$1.25	$3.75	$7.50
42-489	Daniels, John S. - ***The Hunted*** [1965]	$1.25	$3.75	$7.50
34-490	Fields, Vin/Ellis, Joan - ***Problem Child/The Switch*** [1965] PBO.	$2.00	$6.00	$12.00
34-491	Kramer, Gerald/Moore Amanda - ***The Wrong Kind/Never Ask Why*** [1965] PBO. Contains 8 B & W plates by Victor Olson.	$3.50	$10.00	$20.00
32-492	Clements, Mark - ***Handy-Man*** [1965] PBO. Cover art by Rader.	$2.50	$7.50	$15.00
32-493	Turner, John - ***Christine*** [1965]	$1.25	$3.75	$7.50
32-494	Paine, Emory - ***The Beauty Game*** [1965]	$1.25	$3.75	$7.50
32-495	Masters, Les - ***Down And Out*** [1965] PBO. Cover art by Victor Olson.	$1.35	$4.00	$8.00
32-496	Ellis, Joan - ***The Cool Coeds*** [1965] PBO. Cover art by Rader.	$2.50	$7.50	$15.00
32-497	Collier, Max - ***The Sleek And Sensual*** [1965] PBO. Photo cover.	$1.00	$3.00	$6.00
32-498	Williams, Jeffrey - ***The Nymphomaniac*** [1965] PBO. Photo cover.	$1.00	$3.00	$6.00
32-499	Russo, Paul V. - ***Satin In Silk*** [1965]	$1.25	$3.75	$7.50
44-500	Spotnitz, M.D., Hyman & Freeman, Lucy - ***The Wandering Husband*** [1965] Photo cover.	$1.00	$3.00	$6.00
42-501	Croville, Paul - ***History Was Made In Bed*** [1965]	$1.25	$3.75	$7.50
42-502	Brown, Fredric - ***Five Day Nightmare*** [1965]	$5.50	$17.50	$35.00

		G	VG	F
43-503	Van Vogt, A.E. - ***The Mind Cage*** [1965]	$2.25	$7.00	$14.00
34-504	Duchamp, Laura/Hughes, Ludwell - ***Bedtime Story/The Softest Sin*** [1965] PBO. Contains 8 B & W plates by Victor Olson.	$3.50	$10.00	$20.00
34-505	Nelson, Connie/Woods, Merry - ***The Voluptuary/One For All*** [1965] PBO.	$2.00	$6.00	$12.00
32-506	Clements, Mark - ***Kid Sister*** [1965] PBO. Cover art by Rader.	$2.50	$7.50	$15.00
32-507	Russo, Paul V. - ***Exotic Escapade*** [1965]	$1.25	$3.75	$7.50
32-508	Newbury, Will - ***Queen Bee*** [1965] PBO. Cover art by Victor Olson.	$1.35	$4.00	$8.00
32-509	Ellis, Joan - ***Pretty Please*** [1965]	$1.25	$3.75	$7.50
32-510	Paine, Emory - ***Obsession*** [1965] PBO. Cover art by Rader.	$2.50	$7.50	$15.00
32-511	Chartham, Robert - ***Mainly For Wives*** [1965]	$1.25	$3.75	$7.50
32-512	Hamilton, Greg - ***The Lady Awaits*** [1965] PBO.	$1.35	$4.00	$8.00
32-513	Mayo, Dallas - ***One Night Stand*** [1965]	$1.25	$3.75	$7.50
43-514	Radin, Edward D. - ***The Innocents*** [1965]	$1.25	$3.75	$7.50
43-515	Keough, Theodora - ***Gemini*** [1965]	$1.25	$3.75	$7.50
43-516	Ross, Sam - ***The Tight Corner*** [1965]	$1.35	$4.00	$8.00
43-517	Helmore, Thomas - ***Affair At Quala*** [1965]	$1.25	$3.75	$7.50
34-518	Nelson, Connie/Curtis, Brad - ***On Call/The Pick-Up*** [1965] PBO.	$2.00	$6.00	$12.00
34-519	Haney, Clement/Corgan, Grant - ***None The Wiser/Change Partners*** [1965] PBO. Contains 8 B & W plates by Victor Olson.	$3.50	$10.00	$20.00
32-520	Ellis, Joan - ***Sooner Or Later*** [1965] PBO. Cover art by Rader.	$2.50	$7.50	$15.00
32-521	Paine, Emory - ***The Rebel*** [1965] PBO.	$2.00	$6.00	$12.00
32-522	Clements, Mark - ***Winner Take All*** [1965] PBO. Cover art by Rader.	$2.50	$7.50	$15.00
32-523	Russo, Paul V. - ***Alone At Last*** [1965]	$1.25	$3.75	$7.50
32-524	Herbert, Gil - ***The Moonlighters*** [1965] PBO.	$1.35	$4.00	$8.00
32-525	Brooks, Barbara - ***Taboo*** [1965] PBO. Photo cover.	$1.25	$3.75	$7.50
32-526	Price, Marjorie - ***Anything Goes*** [1965] PBO. PBO. Photo cover.	$1.25	$3.75	$7.50
32-527	Hytes, Jason - ***Secret Session*** [1965] Cover art by Rader.	$2.00	$6.00	$12.00
43-528	Moore, Phillips - ***Once Upon A Friday*** [1965] PBO.	$1.35	$4.00	$8.00
43-529	Purdom, Virginia - ***Sex And So What*** [1965]	$1.25	$3.75	$7.50
43-530	White, Lionel - ***Flight Into Terror*** [1965]	$1.35	$4.00	$8.00
43-531	Williamson, Jack - ***Dragon's Island*** [1965]	$2.00	$6.00	$12.00
34-532	Kramer, Gerald/Brooks, Barbara - ***Coming Of Age/Handle With Care*** [1965] PBO. Contains 8 B & W plates by Victor Olson.	$3.50	$10.00	$20.00
34-533	Nelson, Connie/Haney, Clement - ***Runaway/Now Or Never*** [1965] PBO. Contains 8 B & W plates by Paul Rader.	$4.00	$12.50	$25.00
32-534	Clements, Mark - ***The Boss's Daughter*** [1965] PBO.	$1.35	$4.00	$8.00
32-535	Ellis, Joan - ***Temporary Secretary*** [1965] PBO. Cover by Paul Rader.	$2.00	$6.00	$12.00
32-536	Curtis, Brad - ***The Love Goddess*** [1965] PBO. Photo cover.	$1.25	$3.75	$7.50
32-537	Shaw, Kenneth - ***Mock Marriage*** [1965]	$1.25	$3.75	$7.50
32-538	Duchamp, Laura - ***Model Mistress*** [1965] PBO.	$2.00	$6.00	$12.00
32-539	Hamilton, Greg - ***Honey Child*** [1965] PBO. Cover art by Rader.	$3.00	$9.00	$18.00
32-540	Williams, Jeffrey - ***The Unfaithful Wife*** [1965]	$1.25	$3.75	$7.50
32-541	Hytes, Jason - ***Twice With Julie*** [1965]	$1.25	$3.75	$7.50
44-542	Dibner, Martin - ***The Deep Six*** [1965]	$1.25	$3.75	$7.50
43-543	Hanson, Kitty - ***Rebels In The Streets*** [1965]	$1.35	$4.00	$8.00
43-544	Grieg, Michael - ***A Fire In His Hand*** [1965]	$1.25	$3.75	$7.50
43-545	Weil, Jerry - ***Escapade*** [1965]	$1.35	$4.00	$8.00
34-546	Lansing, Simon/Nelson, Connie - ***Wandering Wives/Suburban Affair*** [1965]	$2.00	$6.00	$12.00
34-547	Woods, Merry/Stevens, Toni - ***Only In Shadows/The Velvet Trap*** [1965] PBO.	$2.25	$7.00	$14.00
34-548	Brooks, Barbara/Haney, Clement - ***The Swinger/Not So Nice*** [1965] PBO. Contains 8 B & W plates by Paul Rader.	$4.00	$12.50	$25.00

		G	VG	F
32-549	Duchamp, Laura - ***Wild And Wicked*** [1965] PBO. Cover art by Hatfield.	$2.00	$6.00	$12.00
32-550	Emerson, Jill - ***Enough Of Sorrow*** [1965] PBO. Photo cover.	$1.25	$3.75	$7.50
32-551	McCord, Carter - ***Queen Of Hearts*** [1965] PBO. Photo cover.	$1.25	$3.75	$7.50
32-552	Hughes, Ludwell - ***Surprise Party*** [1965] PBO.	$1.35	$4.00	$8.00
32-553	Woods, Merry - ***Late At Night*** [1965] PBO. Photo cover.	$1.25	$3.75	$7.50
32-554	Ellis, Joan - ***Campus Jungle*** [1965] Cover art by Rader.	$2.50	$7.50	$15.00
32-555	Hytes, Jason - ***Over-Exposed*** [1965]	$1.25	$3.75	$7.50
44-556	Ruddy, Jonah & Hill, Jonathan - ***Bogey: The Man, The Actor, The Legend*** [1965]	$1.50	$5.00	$10.00
43-557	Hughes, David - ***The Major*** [1965]	$1.25	$3.75	$7.50
42-558	Wilhelm, Kate - ***More Bitter Than Death*** [1965]	$2.50	$7.50	$15.00
42-559	Hogan, Robert J. - ***Hanging Fever*** [1965]	$1.25	$3.75	$7.50
34-561	Nelson, Connie/Stevens, Toni - ***Lady Of Leisure/Never Let Me Go*** [1965] PBO. Contains 8 B & W plates by Victor Olson.	$3.50	$10.00	$20.00
34-562	Moore, William/Ellis Joan - ***Not So Innocent/Sugar And Spice*** [1965]	$2.00	$6.00	$12.00
32-563	Grant, Ursula - ***Boss Lady*** [1965] PBO.	$1.35	$4.00	$8.00
32-564	Hamilton, Greg - ***The Strange One*** [1965] PBO. Photo cover.	$1.35	$4.00	$8.00
32-565	Gibbs, Harry - ***Three Women*** [1965] PBO.	$1.35	$4.00	$8.00
32-566	Ellis, Joan - ***Don't Tell Anyone*** [1966] PBO.	$1.35	$4.00	$8.00
32-567	Brandon, Eunice - ***Strictly Business*** [1965] PBO. Cover art by Rader.	$2.00	$6.00	$12.00
32-568	Collier, Max - ***Man Crazy*** [1965] PBO. Photo cover.	$1.25	$3.75	$7.50
32-569	Stevens, Toni - ***Rich And Reckless*** [1965]	$1.25	$3.75	$7.50
43-570	Scott, Casey - ***One More Time!*** [1965] PBO. Photo cover.	$1.25	$3.75	$7.50
43-571	Sinclair, Andrew - ***The Project*** [1965] Cover art by Hatfield.	$1.25	$3.75	$7.50
42-573	Desmond, Eugenia - ***Shadow At Dunster Hall*** [1965] PBO.	$1.35	$4.00	$8.00
42-574	Corliss, Arlene - ***Try To Forget*** [1965] PBO. Photo cover.	$1.25	$3.75	$7.50
34-575	Nelson, Connie/Moore, Amanda - ***Sorority Sisters/Campus Affair*** [1965] PBO.	$2.00	$6.00	$12.00
34-576	Grant, Ursula/Stevens, Toni - ***Girl About Town/Do Unto Others*** [1965] PBO. Contains 8 B & W plates by Victor Olson.	$3.50	$10.00	$20.00
34-577	Conrad, Peter/Moore, William - ***Only After Dark/Accent On Passion*** [1965]	$2.00	$6.00	$12.00
32-578	Mayo, Dallas - ***All Together Now*** [1965] PBO. Cover art by Rader.	$2.50	$7.50	$15.00
32-579	Ellis, Joan - ***Country Girl*** [1965] PBO. Cover art by Rader.	$2.50	$7.50	$15.00
32-580	Curtis, Brad - ***The Golden Greed*** [1965] PBO. Photo cover.	$1.25	$3.75	$7.50
34-582	Corgan, Grant/Peterson, Rhoda - ***Sin-Suburban Style/The Games Wives Play*** [1966] PBO. Photo cover.	$2.00	$6.00	$12.00
34-583	Nelson, Connie/Tell, Joseph - ***Easy Come, Easy Go/From Bed To Worse*** [1966] PBO. Photo cover.	$2.00	$6.00	$12.00
32-584	Kemp, Kimberly - ***The Last Resort*** [1966] PBO. Cover art by Victor Olson.	$1.35	$4.00	$8.00
32-585	Hamilton, Greg - ***Back-Seat Bunny*** [1966] PBO. Photo cover.	$1.25	$3.75	$7.50
32-586	Woods, Merry - ***Sweet Revenge*** [1966]	$1.25	$3.75	$7.50
32-587	Moore, William - ***Heat Spell*** [1966] PBO.	$1.35	$4.00	$8.00
32-588	Ellis, Joan - ***Faculty Wife*** [1966] PBO. Cover art by Rader.	$2.00	$6.00	$12.00
32-589	DeMarco, Carl - ***The Body Beautiful*** [1966]	$1.25	$3.75	$7.50
44-590	Von Sacher-Masoch, Leopold - ***Sacher-Masoch*** [1966] Cover art by Dianne Hillier.	$1.25	$3.75	$7.50
43-591	Sutton, Jeff - ***The River*** [1966]	$1.50	$5.00	$10.00
43-592	McInnes, Graham - ***Lost Island*** [1966]	$1.25	$3.75	$7.50
42-593	Nile, Dorothea (Michael Avallone) - ***Mistress Of Farrondale*** [1966]	$1.35	$4.00	$8.00
42-594	Kleihauer, Lois - ***Don't Ever Leave Me*** [1966]	$1.25	$3.75	$7.50
34-595	West, C.P./Williams, Jeffrey - ***Party, Party/Dutch Treat*** [1966] PBO. Contains 8 B & W plates by Paul Rader.	$3.50	$10.00	$20.00

		G	VG	F
34-596	Nelson, Connie/Brooks, Barbara - ***Wanton Widow/Two Times Two*** [1966] PBO.	$2.00	$6.00	$12.00
34-597	Newbury, Will/Stevens, Gus - ***Pretty Playmate/Every So Often*** [1966] PBO. Contains 8 B & W plates by Victor Olson.	$2.50	$7.50	$15.00
32-598	Curtis, Brad - ***Live And Let Live*** [1966] PBO.	$1.35	$4.00	$8.00
32-599	Hamilton, Greg - ***Free And Easy*** [1966] PBO. Cover art by Rader.	$2.50	$7.50	$15.00
32-600	Woods, Merry - ***Switch Time*** [1966] PBO. Photo cover.	$1.25	$3.75	$7.50
32-602	Ellis, Joan - ***No Last Names*** [1966] PBO. Cover by Paul Rader.	$1.50	$5.00	$10.00
34-625	Castleman, Charles/Wilson, Sidney - ***Search For Sin/Night Shift Nurse*** [1966] PBO. Contains 8 B & W plates by Paul Rader.	$3.00	$9.00	$18.00

Modern Age Books.

		G	VG	F
NN	Thompson, Jim - ***Now And On Earth*** [1942] PBO. Author's first book.	$30.00	$100.00	$225.00

Modern Biography.

		G	VG	F
MB-101	Gerber, Albert B. - ***The Life Of Adolf Hitler*** [1961] PBO.	$1.25	$3.75	$7.50
MB-102	Feldman, A. Bronson - ***Stalin, Red Lord Of Russia*** [1962] PBO.	$1.25	$3.75	$7.50

Modern Living Council. Digest Size.

		G	VG	F
NO#-1	Anthology - ***It Happened To Me*** [n.d.]	$2.00	$6.00	$12.00

Monarch Books (Early Publisher's History, 1958–1963)

Beautiful covers by artists like Robert Maguire and Rafael DeSoto draw attention to these titles. Authors writing for this line frequently used pseudonyms. Some popular authors who used pseudonyms in this line include Marion Zimmer Bradley, Robert Silverberg, Gardner Fox, John Jakes, and Philip Ketchum, to name a few. During their history, Monarch published a variety of popular literature and often presented esoteric titles.

Similar lines by Monarch Books, Inc., consist of Monarch Americana or MA series, Monarch Human Behavior or MB series, Monarch K series, Monarch Language or ML series, Monarch Movie or MM series, and Monarch Select or SP/MS series.

Monarch Books. New York: Monarch Publishing.

		G	VG	F
101	James, Don - ***Dark Hunger*** [1958] PBO. Cover by Ray Johnson.	$2.00	$6.00	$12.00
102	Lemay, Alan - ***Winter Range*** [1958] Cover by A. Leslie Ross.	$1.50	$5.00	$10.00
103	Nichols, Fan - ***Love Me Now*** [1958] PBO. Cover by Rafael DeSoto.	$2.25	$7.00	$14.00
104	Owen, Dean - ***Rawhider From Texas*** [1958] PBO.	$1.50	$5.00	$10.00
105	Malley, Louis - ***Shadow Of The Mafia*** [1958]	$2.50	$7.50	$15.00
106	Phillips, Leon - ***Rogue Lover*** [1959] PBO.	$2.25	$7.00	$14.00
107	Brewer, Gil - ***Wild To Possess*** [1959] PBO. Cover by Robert Maguire.	$3.00	$9.00	$18.00
108	Haycox, Ernest - ***Brand Fires On The Ridge And Night Raid*** [1959] PBO.	$1.50	$5.00	$10.00
109	Anderson, Brad & Leeming, Phil - ***Marmaduke Rides Again*** [1959] PBO. Cover by Brad Anderson. Cartoon book.	$2.50	$7.50	$15.00
110	Harwin, Brian - ***Touch Me Not*** [1959] Cover by Robert Maguire.	$2.50	$7.50	$15.00
111	Kendricks, James - ***Sword Of Casanova*** [1959] PBO. Cover by Bob Stanley.	$2.00	$6.00	$12.00
112	Falstein, Louis - ***Spring Of Desire*** [1959] PBO. Cover by Jim Bentley.	$2.00	$6.00	$12.00

Monarch, 143

Monarch, 218

Monarch, MA-303

		G	VG	F
113	Bowie, Sam - ***Thunderhead Range*** [1959] PBO. Cover by A. Leslie Ross.	$1.50	$5.00	$10.00
114	Findley, Ferguson - ***Killer Cop*** [1959] Cover by Lou Marchetti.	$2.00	$6.00	$12.00
115	Conway, John - ***Madigan's Women*** [1959] PBO.	$2.25	$7.00	$14.00
116	Karney, Jack - ***Some Like It Tough*** [1959] PBO.	$2.25	$7.00	$14.00
117	Byram, George - ***Stronger Than Passion*** [1959] Cover by A. Leslie Ross.	$1.50	$5.00	$10.00
118	Woolfolk, William - ***Way Of The Wicked*** [1959] PBO. Cover by Harry Barton.	$2.25	$7.00	$14.00
119	Taylor, Robert William - ***Occasion Of Sin*** [1959] PBO. Cover by Ray Johnson.	$2.00	$6.00	$12.00
120	Flora, Fletcher - ***Take Me Home*** [1959] PBO.	$2.00	$6.00	$12.00
121	Kramer, Karl - ***Kiss Me Quick*** [1959] PBO. Cover by Robert Maguire.	$2.50	$7.50	$15.00
122	Chambers, Whitman - ***Season For Love*** [1959] PBO. Cover by Robert Maguire.	$2.50	$7.50	$15.00
123	Kendricks, James - ***Beyond Our Pleasure*** [1959] PBO.	$2.00	$6.00	$12.00
124	Ard, William - ***All I Can Get*** [1959] PBO.	$2.50	$7.50	$15.00
125	Friedman, Stuart - ***Nikki*** [1959] PBO. Cover by Robert Maguire.	$2.50	$7.50	$15.00
126	Brand, Max - ***Law Of The Gun*** [1959]	$1.50	$5.00	$10.00
127	Denzer, Peter W. - ***Lust To Live*** [1959] Cover by Ray Johnson.	$2.00	$6.00	$12.00
128	Conway, John - ***Hell Is My Destination*** [1959] PBO.	$2.00	$6.00	$12.00
129	Carse, Robert - ***End To Innocence*** [1959] PBO.	$2.00	$6.00	$12.00
130	Cook, Will - ***We Burn Like Fire*** [1959] PBO.	$2.00	$6.00	$12.00
131	Olive, Harry - ***The Darkness Of Love*** [1959] PBO. Cover by Harry Schaare.	$2.00	$6.00	$12.00
132	Fox, James M. - ***Save Them For Violence*** [1959] PBO.	$3.00	$9.00	$18.00
133	Boyd, Frank - ***The Flesh Peddlers*** [1959] PBO. Cover by Robert Maguire.	$3.00	$9.00	$18.00
134	Ballard, W. T. - ***Fury In The Heart*** [1959] PBO. Cover by Harry Schaare.	$2.00	$6.00	$12.00
135	Stevens, Dan - ***Hangman's Mesa*** [1959] PBO. Cover by A. Leslie Ross.	$1.50	$5.00	$10.00
136	Kramer, Karl - ***Not For A Curse*** [1959] PBO.	$2.00	$6.00	$12.00
137	Ellson, Hal - ***Jailbait Street*** [1959] PBO. Cover by Ray Johnson.	$3.00	$9.00	$18.00
138	Foster, Joseph - ***Stephana*** [1959] Cover by Robert Maguire.	$2.50	$7.50	$15.00
139	Chambers, Whitman - ***In Savage Surrender*** [1959] PBO. Cover by Harry Barton.	$2.25	$7.00	$14.00
140	Stagg, Delino - ***The Glory Jumpers*** [1959] PBO.	$1.50	$5.00	$10.00

		G	VG	F
141	Nordhoff, Charles & Hall, James Norman - ***Falcons Of France*** [1959]	$1.50	$5.00	$10.00
142	Thurman, Steve - ***Night After Night*** [1959] PBO.	$2.00	$6.00	$12.00
143	James, Stuart - ***Jack The Ripper*** [1960] PBO. Movie tie-in.	$8.00	$25.00	$50.00
144	Friedman, Stuart - ***The Revolt Of Jill Braddock*** [1960] PBO. Cover by Harry Barton.	$2.00	$6.00	$12.00
145	Hamlin, Ken - ***Guns Of Revenge*** [1960] PBO. Cover by A. Leslie Ross.	$1.50	$5.00	$10.00
146	Kirkbride, Ronald - ***Tamiko*** [1960] Cover by Robert Maguire.	$2.50	$7.50	$15.00
147	Ard, William - ***Like Ice She Was*** [1960] PBO.	$2.50	$7.50	$15.00
148	Conway, John - ***This Dark Desire*** [1960] PBO. Cover by Robert Maguire.	$2.50	$7.50	$15.00
149	Carse, Robert - ***The Flesh And The Flame*** [1960] PBO. Cover by Rafael DeSoto.	$2.25	$7.00	$14.00
150	Flora, Fletcher - ***Most Likely To Love*** [1960] PBO. Cover by Rafael DeSoto.	$2.25	$7.00	$14.00
151	Wilcox, Jess - ***Kill Me, Sweet*** [1960] PBO.	$2.00	$6.00	$12.00
152	Ard, William - ***The Sins Of Billy Serene*** [1960] PBO. Cover by Robert Maguire.	$2.50	$7.50	$15.00
153	James, Stuart - ***Frisco Flat*** [1960] PBO.	$2.00	$6.00	$12.00
154	Brand, Max - ***Outlaw Rider*** [1960] Cover by A. Leslie Ross.	$1.50	$5.00	$10.00
155	Denzer, Peter W. - ***The Practice Of Passion*** [1960] PBO. Cover by Robert Maguire.	$2.50	$7.50	$15.00
156	Chambers, Whitman - ***Manhandled*** [1960] PBO. Cover by Harry Barton.	$2.00	$6.00	$12.00
157	Karney, Jack - ***Yield To The Night*** [1960]	$2.00	$6.00	$12.00
158	Kendricks, James - ***The Adulterers*** [1960] PBO.	$2.00	$6.00	$12.00
159	Kramer, Karl - ***The Deadly September*** [1960] PBO. Cover by Robert Maguire.	$2.50	$7.50	$15.00
160	Carse, Robert - ***The Cage Of Love*** [1960] PBO. Cover by Rafael DeSoto.	$2.25	$7.00	$14.00
161	Newell, Bergen F. - ***Naked Before My Captors*** [1960]	$2.00	$6.00	$12.00
162	Plunkett, John - ***She'll Get Hers*** [1960] PBO. Cover by Rafael DeSoto.	$2.25	$7.00	$14.00
163	Jacobs, William H. - ***This Violent Land*** [1960]	$1.50	$5.00	$10.00
164	Matthews, Clayton - ***A Rage Of Desire*** [1960] Cover by Harry Barton.	$2.00	$6.00	$12.00
165	West, Edwin - ***Young And Innocent*** [1960] PBO. Cover by Robert Maguire.	$3.50	$10.00	$20.00
166	De La Croix, Robert - ***They Flew The Atlantic*** [1960] Cover by Robert Stanley.	$1.50	$5.00	$10.00
167	Wimberly, Gwynne - ***One Touch Of Ecstasy*** [1960] Cover by Harry Barton.	$2.00	$6.00	$12.00
168	Brewer, Gil - ***Play It Hard*** [1960] PBO. Cover by Rafael DeSoto.	$2.50	$7.50	$15.00
169	Doss, Helen - ***The Family Nobody Wanted*** [1960] Cover by Robert Maguire.	$2.00	$6.00	$12.00
170	Friedman, Stuart - ***The Way We Love*** [1960] PBO. Cover by Harry Barton.	$2.00	$6.00	$12.00
171	White, Lionel - ***Marilyn K.*** [1960] PBO. Cover by Harry Schaare.	$1.50	$5.00	$10.00
172	Ard, William - ***Babe In The Woods*** [1960] PBO.	$2.50	$7.50	$15.00
173	McKimmey, Jr., James - ***The Satyr*** [1960] PBO.	$2.00	$6.00	$12.00
174	Conway, John - ***Love In Suburbia*** [1960]	$1.50	$5.00	$10.00
175	Urquhart, Maj. Gen. R. E. - ***Arnhem*** [1960] Photo cover.	$1.35	$4.00	$8.00
176	Anthology - ***Famous Cartoons From Escapade*** [1960] PBO. Cover by Bill Wenzel. Cartoon book.	$4.00	$12.50	$25.00
177	Welch, Maud McCurdy - ***Susan Latimer, Clinic Nurse*** [1960]	$1.25	$3.75	$7.50
178	Thomey, Tedd - ***When The Lusting Began*** [1960] PBO.	$1.50	$5.00	$10.00

		G	VG	F
179	Olive, Harry - ***Run Naked In The Night*** [1960] PBO. Cover by Harry Schaare.	$1.50	$5.00	$10.00
180	Anthology - ***Monarch Crossword Puzzles*** [1960]	$8.00	$25.00	$50.00
181	Friedman, Stuart - ***The Trouble With Ava*** [1961] PBO. Cover by Lou Marchetti.	$1.50	$5.00	$10.00
182	Smith, Artemis - ***This Bed We Made*** [1961] Cover by DeSoto.	$2.00	$6.00	$12.00
183	James, Don - ***$50 A Night*** [1961] PBO. Cover by Robert Maguire.	$2.50	$7.50	$15.00
184	Pratt, Theodore - ***The Lovers Of Pompeii*** [1961] PBO. Cover by Jean Leon Gerome.	$1.35	$4.00	$8.00
185	Simpson, Ronald - ***Eve's Apple*** [1961] PBO. Cover by Harry Barton.	$2.00	$6.00	$12.00
186	Rowland, Tom - ***The Klaxon Girls*** [1961] PBO. Cover by Maguire.	$2.50	$7.50	$15.00
187	Brewer, Gil - ***Appointment In Hell*** [1961] PBO. Cover by Bob Stanley.	$2.50	$7.50	$15.00
188	Powell, Talmage - ***The Girl From Big Pine*** [1961] PBO. Cover by Rafael DeSoto.	$2.50	$7.50	$15.00
189	West, Edwin - ***Campus Doll*** [1961] PBO. Cover by Tom Miller.	$2.50	$7.50	$15.00
190	Gaulden, Ray - ***High Country Showdown*** [1961]	$1.35	$4.00	$8.00
191	Little, Charles - ***And Love So Wild*** [1961] PBO. Cover by Rafael DeSoto.	$2.00	$6.00	$12.00
192	Canary, Glenn - ***The Damned And The Innocent*** [1961] PBO. Cover by Harry Barton.	$1.50	$5.00	$10.00
193	Rand, Steve - ***All Her Vices*** [1961] PBO. Cover by Lou Marchetti.	$1.50	$5.00	$10.00
194	Bingham, Carson - ***Run Tough, Run Hard*** [1961] PBO. Cover by Ray Johnson.	$2.00	$6.00	$12.00
195	Agar, Brian - ***Have Love, Will Share*** [1961] PBO. Cover by Rafael DeSoto.	$2.00	$6.00	$12.00
196	Colby, Robert - ***Lament For Julie*** [1961] PBO. Cover by Harry Barton.	$2.00	$6.00	$12.00
197	Vance, William - ***Day Of Blood*** [1961] PBO. Cover by Harry Schaare.	$2.00	$6.00	$12.00
198	Humphries, Adelaide - ***Cynthia Doyle, Nurse In Love*** [1961] Cover by Tom Miller.	$1.25	$3.75	$7.50
199	West, Edwin - ***Brother And Sister*** [1961] Cover by Harry Schaare.	$2.50	$7.50	$15.00
200	Kramer, Karl - ***A Flame Too Hot*** [1961] PBO. Cover by Harry Barton.	$2.00	$6.00	$12.00
201	Friedman, Stuart - ***The Fly Girls*** [1961] PBO. Cover by Maguire.	$2.50	$7.50	$15.00
202	Daniels, Paul - ***Debbie*** [1961] PBO. Cover by Rafael DeSoto.	$1.50	$5.00	$10.00
203	Deming, Richard - ***This Is My Night*** [1961] PBO. Cover by Ray Johnson.	$2.00	$6.00	$12.00
204	Owen, Dean - ***Pistol Belt*** [1961] PBO. Cover by Bob Stanley.	$1.35	$4.00	$8.00
205	Reynolds, Mack - ***Episode On The Riviera*** [1961] PBO. Cover by Harry Schaare.	$2.00	$6.00	$12.00
206	Coberly, V. J. - ***By Passion Obsessed*** [1961] PBO. Cover by Tom Miller.	$1.50	$5.00	$10.00
207	Matthews, Clayton - ***The Strange Ways Of Love*** [1961]	$2.50	$7.50	$15.00
208	Lennox, Susan - ***Doctor's Choice*** [1961] Cover by Maguire.	$1.25	$3.75	$7.50
209	Locke, Robert Donald - ***The Reckless Lovers*** [1961] PBO. Cover by Harry Schaare.	$1.50	$5.00	$10.00
210	Stagg, Delano - ***Bloody Beaches*** [1961] PBO. Cover by Robert Stanley.	$1.35	$4.00	$8.00
211	Rand, Steve - ***So Sweet, So Wicked*** [1961] PBO. Cover by Ray Johnson.	$2.00	$6.00	$12.00
212	Phillips, Tom - ***Beyond All Desire*** [1961] PBO. Cover by Harry Barton.	$1.50	$5.00	$10.00

		G	VG	F
213	Holly, J. Hunter - ***The Green Planet*** [1961] Cover by John Schoenherr.	$2.50	$7.50	$15.00
214	Reynolds, Mack - ***A Kiss Before Loving*** [1961] PBO. Cover by Ray Johnson.	$2.00	$6.00	$12.00
215	Ard, William - ***Make Mine Mavis*** [1961] PBO. Cover by Lou Marchetti.	$2.50	$7.50	$15.00
216	Thomey, Tedd - ***Flight To Takla-Ma*** [1961] PBO. Cover by Ray Johnson.	$1.35	$4.00	$8.00
217	Flora, Fletcher - ***The Seducer*** [1961] PBO. Cover by DeSoto.	$1.50	$5.00	$10.00
218	Owen, Dean - ***Rebel Of Broken Wheel*** [1961] PBO. TV tie-in with Nick Adams. Photo cover.	$3.50	$10.00	$20.00
219	Simpson, Ronald - ***Make Every Kiss Count*** [1961] PBO. Cover by Maguire.	$2.50	$7.50	$15.00
220	Daniels, Paul - ***The Transistor Girls*** [1961] PBO. Cover by Robert Maguire.	$2.50	$7.50	$15.00
221	Carr, Jay - ***My Father's Wife*** [1961] PBO. Cover by DeSoto.	$2.00	$6.00	$12.00
222	Conway, John - ***A Sin In Time*** [1961] PBO. Cover by Harry Barton.	$1.50	$5.00	$10.00
223	Humphries, Adelaide - ***The Nurse Knows Best*** [1961] Cover by Tom Miller.	$1.25	$3.75	$7.50
224	Bolton, Alexander - ***Ladies Of The Dark*** [1961] PBO. Cover by Maguire.	$2.50	$7.50	$15.00
225	Gale, Christopher - ***Tropic Fury*** [1961] PBO. Cover by Harry Schaare.	$1.50	$5.00	$10.00
226	Newbury, Will - ***Call Boy*** [1961] PBO. Cover by Lou Marchetti.	$1.50	$5.00	$10.00
227	Bingham, Carson - ***It Happened In Hawaii*** [1961] PBO. Cover by Tom Miller.	$1.50	$5.00	$10.00
228	Phillips, Tom - ***The Bed Sheet Jungle*** [1961] PBO. Cover by DeSoto.	$2.00	$6.00	$12.00
229	McCready, Jack - ***The Raper*** [1961] PBO. Cover by DeSoto.	$2.50	$7.50	$15.00
230	Garfield, Brian - ***The Arizonans*** [1961] Cover by Ray Johnson.	$1.35	$4.00	$8.00
231	Ard, William - ***And So To Bed*** [1962] PBO. Cover by Marchetti.	$2.50	$7.50	$15.00
232	West, Edwin - ***Strange Affair*** [1962] PBO. Cover by Harry Schaare.	$2.50	$7.50	$15.00
233	Daniels, Paul - ***Playboy*** [1962] PBO. Cover by Ray Johnson.	$2.00	$6.00	$12.00
234	Webster, Sam - ***The Executive Suite Girls*** [1962] PBO. Cover by Harry Schaare.	$1.50	$5.00	$10.00
235	Hancock, Frances Dean - ***Summer Cruise*** [1962] Cover by Robert Maguire.	$2.50	$7.50	$15.00
236	Davis, Jr., Franklin M. - ***Bamboo Camp #10*** [1962] PBO. Cover by Robert Stanley.	$2.50	$7.50	$15.00
237	James, Don - ***The Key Game*** [1962] PBO. Cover by Harry Schaare.	$1.50	$5.00	$10.00
238	Barclay, John - ***Ask For Lois*** [1962] PBO. Cover by Tom Miller.	$1.50	$5.00	$10.00
239	Brennan, Bill - ***The Faster We Live*** [1962] PBO. Cover by Barton.	$2.00	$6.00	$12.00
240	Holly, J. Hunter - ***Encounter*** [1962] Cover by John Schoenherr.	$2.50	$7.50	$15.00
241	Friedman, Stuart - ***Rasputin: The Mad Monk*** [1962] PBO. Cover by Maguire.	$3.50	$10.00	$20.00
242	Tremont, Philip - ***Easy Come, Easy Love*** [1962] PBO. Cover by Harry Barton.	$1.50	$5.00	$10.00
243	Johnston, William - ***Teen-Age Tramp*** [1962] PBO. Cover by Rafael DeSoto.	$3.00	$9.00	$18.00
244	Colby, Robert - ***Kim*** [1962] PBO. Cover by Harry Schaare.	$1.50	$5.00	$10.00
245	Webster, Sam - ***Cancel These Vows*** [1962] PBO. Cover by Ray Johnson.	$1.50	$5.00	$10.00
246	Thurman, Steve - ***Lightning Gun*** [1962] PBO. Cover by A. Leslie Ross.	$1.35	$4.00	$8.00

		G	VG	F
247	Blake, Walker E. - ***Heartbreak Ridge*** [1962] PBO. Cover by Robert Stanley.	$1.35	$4.00	$8.00
248	Canary, Glenn - ***The Trailer Park Girls*** [1962] PBO. Cover by Harry Barton.	$2.00	$6.00	$12.00
249	Gardner, Miriam (M. Zimmer Bradley) - ***The Strange Women*** [1962] PBO. Cover by Tom Miller.	$12.50	$37.50	$75.00
250	Clarke, John - ***The Lolita Lovers*** [1962] PBO. Cover by Rafael M. DeSoto.	$1.50	$5.00	$10.00
251	Ford, Marcia - ***Island Nurse*** [1962] Cover by Tom Miller.	$1.25	$3.75	$7.50
252	Winterbotham, Russ - ***The Space Egg*** [1962] Cover by Jack Schoenherr.	$2.50	$7.50	$15.00
253	Matthews, Clayton - ***The Promiscuous Doll*** [1962] PBO. Cover by Mort Engle.	$2.00	$6.00	$12.00
254	Daniels, Paul - ***The Cover Girls*** [1962] PBO. Cover by Harry Schaare.	$1.50	$5.00	$10.00
255	Van Taylor, Robert - ***Frenzied*** [1962] PBO. Cover by Lou Marchetti.	$2.00	$6.00	$12.00
256	Ketchum, Philip - ***Renegade Range*** [1962] PBO. Cover by A. Leslie Ross.	$1.35	$4.00	$8.00
257	Friedman, Stuart - ***Ravaged*** [1962] PBO. Cover by Ray Johnson.	$2.25	$7.00	$14.00
258	James, Don - ***Hollywood Starlet*** [1962] PBO. Cover by Rafael M. DeSoto.	$2.00	$6.00	$12.00
259	Reynolds, Mack - ***This Time We Love*** [1962] PBO. Cover by Robert Stanley.	$2.00	$6.00	$12.00
260	Holly, J. Hunter - ***The Flying Eyes*** [1962] PBO. Cover by John Schoenherr.	$2.50	$7.50	$15.00
261	Dixon, H. Vernor - ***That Girl Marian*** [1962] PBO. Cover by Tom Miller.	$1.50	$5.00	$10.00
F-262	Holmes, Rick - ***Tropic Of Cleo*** [1962] PBO. Cover by Ray Johnson.	$1.50	$5.00	$10.00
F-263	Winston, Daoma - ***Tormented Lovers*** [1962] PBO. Cover by Harry Barton.	$2.00	$6.00	$12.00
264	Walton, Evangeline - ***Witch House*** [1962] Cover by Ralph Brillhart. Arkham House reprint.	$3.00	$9.00	$18.00
265	Worley, Dorothy - ***A Halo For Dr. Michael*** [1962] Cover by Tom Miller.	$1.25	$3.75	$7.50
266	Moreau, Lisa - ***Everybody's Girl*** [1962] PBO. Photo cover.	$1.35	$4.00	$8.00
267	Anderson, Brad & Leeming, Phil - ***More About Marmaduke*** [1962] PBO. Cover by Brad Anderson. Cartoon Book.	$2.50	$7.50	$15.00
268	Webster, Sam - ***The Wives Of Friends*** [1962] PBO. Cover by Stanley Borack.	$1.50	$5.00	$10.00
269	Ard, William - ***Give Me This Woman*** [1962] PBO. Cover by Marchetti.	$2.50	$7.50	$15.00
270	Winterbotham, Russ - ***The Red Planet*** [1962] PBO. Cover by Ralph Brillhart.	$2.50	$7.50	$15.00
271	Newton, D. B. - ***Maverick Brand*** [1962] PBO. Cover by Bob Stanley.	$1.35	$4.00	$8.00
272	Friedman, Stuart - ***The Surgeons*** [1962] PBO. Cover by Harry Schaare.	$1.25	$3.75	$7.50
273	Phillips, Tom - ***The Sorority Girls*** [1962] PBO. Cover by Rafael M. DeSoto.	$2.00	$6.00	$12.00
274	Avery, Anderson - ***Adulteress*** [1962] PBO. Cover by Ray Johnson.	$1.50	$5.00	$10.00
275	Johnston, William - ***Save Her For Loving*** [1962] PBO. Cover by Harry Barton.	$2.00	$6.00	$12.00
276	Brown, Wenzell - ***An Act Of Passion*** [1962] PBO. Cover by Ray Johnson.	$3.00	$9.00	$18.00
277	Ford, Marcia - ***Dixie Doctor*** [1962] Cover by Maguire.	$1.25	$3.75	$7.50
278	Hadrian, Philip - ***The Party Lovers*** [1962] PBO. Cover by Bob Stanley.	$1.50	$5.00	$10.00

Monarch, MA-304

Monarch, MA-320

Monarch, 339

		G	VG	F
279	Blake, Walker E. - ***The Loved And The Lost*** [1962] PBO. Cover by Mort Engle.	$1.50	$5.00	$10.00
280	Canary, Glenn - ***The Sadist*** [1962] PBO. Cover by Rafael M. DeSoto.	$2.50	$7.50	$15.00
281	Catlin, Don - ***The Bow And The Lance*** [1962] PBO. Cover by Schulz.	$1.35	$4.00	$8.00
282	Colby, Robert - ***Beautiful But Bad*** [1962] Cover by Harry Barton.	$1.50	$5.00	$10.00
283	Bingham, Carson - ***The Loves Of Dr. Devere*** [1962] PBO. Cover by Stanley Borack.	$1.25	$3.75	$7.50
284	Johnston, William - ***Girls On The Wing*** [1962] Cover by Robert Maguire.	$2.00	$6.00	$12.00
285	Lee, Ted - ***The Pleasure In Women*** [1962] PBO. Cover by Harry Schaare.	$1.50	$5.00	$10.00
286	Kevin, Lloyd - ***Her Cheating Heart*** [1962] PBO. Cover by Tom Miller.	$1.50	$5.00	$10.00
287	Ford, Marcia - ***Prelude To Love*** [1962]	$1.50	$5.00	$10.00
288	Carr, Jay - ***Suburban Lovers*** [1962]	$1.50	$5.00	$10.00
289	Matthews, Clayton - ***Faithless*** [1962] PBO. Cover by Ray Johnson.	$1.50	$5.00	$10.00
290	Owen, Dean - ***Juice Town*** [1962] PBO. Cover by DeSoto.	$1.50	$5.00	$10.00
291	Daniels, Paul - ***The Show Girls*** [1962] PBO. Cover by Harry Schaare.	$1.50	$5.00	$10.00
292	Garland, Bennett - ***7 Brave Men*** [1962] PBO. Cover by Bob Stanley.	$1.35	$4.00	$8.00
293	Brown, Wenzell - ***Women Of Evil*** [1963] PBO. Cover by Harry Barton.	$3.50	$10.00	$20.00
294	Friedman, Stuart - ***Irina*** [1963] PBO. Cover by Tom Miller.	$1.50	$5.00	$10.00
295	Kendricks, James - ***Love Me Tonight*** [1963]	$2.00	$6.00	$12.00
296	Kelly, F. J. - ***The Gates Of Brass*** [1963] PBO. Cover by Robert Maguire.	$2.50	$7.50	$15.00
297	Jorgensen, Ivar - ***Ten From Infinity*** [1963] PBO. Cover by Ralph Brillhart.	$2.50	$7.50	$15.00
298	Dixon, H. Vernor - ***The Pleasure Seekers*** [1963] PBO. Cover by Lou Marchetti.	$1.50	$5.00	$10.00
299	Daniels, Paul - ***Ruby*** [1963] PBO.	$1.50	$5.00	$10.00
MA-300	Sterling, Anthony - ***King Of The Harem Heaven*** [1960] PBO. Cover by Maguire.	$3.00	$9.00	$18.00
MA-301	Kendricks, James - ***She Wouldn't Surrender*** [1960] PBO. Cover by Maguire.	$2.50	$7.50	$15.00

	G	VG	F
MA-302 Demaris, Ovid - ***Lucky Luciano*** [1960]	$2.00	$6.00	$12.00
MA-303 Shirley, Glenn - ***Outlaw Queen*** [1960] PBO. Cover by Robert Stanley	$4.00	$12.50	$25.00
MA-304 Kendricks, James - ***The Wicked, Wicked Women*** [1961] PBO	$3.50	$10.00	$20.00
MA-305 Pearl, Jack - ***Blood-And-Guts Patton*** [1961] PBO. Photo cover	$1.50	$5.00	$10.00
MA-306 Davis, Jr., Franklin M. - ***Breakthrough*** [1961] PBO. Photo cover	$1.50	$5.00	$10.00
MA-307 Demaris, Ovid - ***The Lindbergh Kidnapping Case*** [1961] Photo cover	$1.50	$5.00	$10.00
MA-308 Owen, Dean - ***The Sam Houston Story*** [1961] PBO. Cover by A. Leslie Ross	$1.50	$5.00	$10.00
MA-309 Conway, John - ***The Apache Wars*** [1961]	$1.50	$5.00	$10.00
MA-310 Sterling, Anthony - ***Harem Island*** [1961] PBO. Cover by Ray Johnson.	$2.25	$7.00	$14.00
MA-311 Demaris, Ovid - ***The Dillinger Story*** [1961] PBO. Photo cover	$1.50	$5.00	$10.00
MA-312 Heller, Deane & David - ***The Kennedy Cabinet*** [1961] PBO. Photo cover.	$1.35	$4.00	$8.00
MA-313 Thurman, Steve - ***"Baby Face" Nelson*** [1961] PBO. Photo cover	$1.50	$5.00	$10.00
MA-314 Scott, Jay - ***America's War Heroes*** [1961] PBO. Photo cover	$1.35	$4.00	$8.00
MA-315 Pearl, Jack - ***General Douglas MacArthur*** [1961] PBO. Photo cover	$1.50	$5.00	$10.00
MA-316 Halacy, Jr., D. S. - ***America's Major Air Disasters*** [1961] PBO. Photo cover.	$1.35	$4.00	$8.00
MA-317 Fehrenback, T. R. - ***The Battle Of Anzio*** [1962] PBO. Cover by Stanley	$1.35	$4.00	$8.00
MA-318 Curzon, Sam - ***"Legs" Diamond*** [1962] PBO. Photo cover.	$1.50	$5.00	$10.00
MA-319 Fehrenback, T. R. - ***U.S. Marines In Action*** [1962] PBO. Photo cover	$1.35	$4.00	$8.00
MA-320 Brown, Douglas - ***Anne Bonny, Pirate Queen*** [1962] PBO. Cover by Stanley.	$5.00	$15.00	$30.00
MA-321 Bailey, Tom - ***Tarawa*** [1962] PBO. Photo cover.	$1.35	$4.00	$8.00
MA-322 Pearl, Jack - ***Aerial Dogfights Of World War II*** [1962] PBO. Photo cover.	$1.35	$4.00	$8.00
MA-323 Addy, Ted - ***The "Dutch" Schultz Story*** [1962] PBO. Photo cover	$1.50	$5.00	$10.00
MA-324 Conway, John - ***The Sioux Indian Wars*** [1962] PBO. Cover by Bob Stanley	$1.35	$4.00	$8.00
MA-325 Hunter, Anson - ***King Of The Free Lovers*** [1962] PBO. Cover by Maguire.	$3.00	$9.00	$18.00
MA-326 Brennan, Bill - ***The Frank Costello Story*** [1962] PBO. Photo cover	$1.50	$5.00	$10.00
MA-327 Conway, John - ***Woman-Breaker*** [1962] PBO. Cover by Ray Johnson.	$2.00	$6.00	$12.00
MA-328 Pearl, Jack - ***Admiral "Bull" Halsey*** [1962]	$1.35	$4.00	$8.00
MA-329 Scott, Jay - ***Marine War Heroes*** [1962]	$1.35	$4.00	$8.00
330 Laurence, Will - ***The Go Girls*** [1963] PBO. Cover by Ray Johnson.	$1.50	$5.00	$10.00
331 Matthews, Clayton - ***Nude Running*** [1963] PBO. Cover by Rafael DeSoto.	$2.00	$6.00	$12.00
332 Catlin, Don - ***The Trouble Shooter*** [1963]	$1.35	$4.00	$8.00
MA-333 Conway, John - ***The Texas Rangers*** [1963]	$1.35	$4.00	$8.00
334 West, Edwin - ***Campus Lovers*** [1963] PBO. Cover by Tom Miller	$2.00	$6.00	$12.00
335 Ives, Morgan (M. Zimmer Bradley) - ***Spare Her Heaven*** [1963] PBO. Cover by Harry Schaare.	$12.50	$37.50	$75.00
336 Johnston, William - ***Emergency For Dr. Starr*** [1963] PBO. Cover by Lou Marchetti.	$1.25	$3.75	$7.50
337 Dixon, H. Vernor - ***Guerrilla*** [1963] PBO. Cover by Jack Thurston.	$1.35	$4.00	$8.00

		G	VG	F
MA-338	Caesar, Gene - ***Rifle For Rent*** [1963] PBO.	$1.35	$4.00	$8.00
339	Jakes, John - ***G. I. Girls*** [1963] PBO. Cover by Ray Johnson	$3.00	$9.00	$18.00
340	Revelle, George G. - ***And Wake Up Loving*** [1963] PBO. Cover by Stanley Borack	$1.50	$5.00	$10.00
341	Martin, Thom - ***Naked When We Die*** [1963]	$1.50	$5.00	$10.00
342	Holly, J. Hunter - ***The Running Man*** [1963] PBO. Cover by Ralph Brillhart.	$2.50	$7.50	$15.00
343	James, Don - ***Dark Hunger*** [1963] Cover by Ray Johnson	$1.25	$3.75	$7.50
344	Denzer, Peter W. - ***The Rape Of Lucia*** [1963] PBO. Cover by Lou Marchetti.	$1.50	$5.00	$10.00
345	Allen, Eric - ***Like Wild*** [1963] PBO. Cover by George Erickson	$1.50	$5.00	$10.00
346	Holmes, Rick - ***Love Under Capricorn*** [1963] PBO. Cover by Robert Maguire.	$2.50	$7.50	$15.00
347	Newbury, Will - ***The Cruise Ship Girls*** [1963] PBO. Cover by Bob Stanley	$1.50	$5.00	$10.00
348	Nichols, Fan - ***Love Me Now*** [1963] Cover by DeSoto.	$1.35	$4.00	$8.00
349	Conway, John - ***The Valiant Breed*** [1963] PBO. Cover by Jack Thurston.	$1.35	$4.00	$8.00
MA-350	Clagett, John - ***The U.S. Navy In Action*** [1963] PBO. Photo cover.	$1.35	$4.00	$8.00
351	Friedman, Stuart - ***Fathers And Daughters*** [1963]	$1.25	$3.75	$7.50
352	Gardner, Miriam (M. Zimmer Bradley) - ***My Sister, My Love*** [1963] PBO. Photo cover.	$12.50	$37.50	$75.00
353	Winston, Daoma - ***Love Her, She's Yours*** [1963] PBO. Cover by Tom Miller	$1.50	$5.00	$10.00
354	Hatch, Gerald - ***The Day The Earth Froze*** [1963] PBO. Cover by Ralph Brillhart.	$2.50	$7.50	$15.00
355	Johnston, William - ***Love Comes To Dr. Starr*** [1963] PBO. Cover by Lou Marchetti.	$1.25	$3.75	$7.50
356	Ballard, Todhunter - ***West Of Quarantine*** [1963]	$2.00	$6.00	$12.00
MA-357	Bailey, Tom - ***The Comanche Wars*** [1963]	$1.35	$4.00	$8.00
358	James, Don - ***The Pitchmen*** [1963] PBO. Cover by Tom Miller	$1.35	$4.00	$8.00
359	Allen, Eric - ***Another Night, Another Love*** [1963] PBO. Cover by Rafael M. DeSoto.	$2.00	$6.00	$12.00
360	Reynolds, Mack - ***The Kept Woman*** [1963] PBO. Cover by DeSoto	$2.00	$6.00	$12.00
361	Bonham, Frank - ***By Her Own Hand*** [1963] PBO. Cover by Ray Johnson	$1.50	$5.00	$10.00
362	Jorgensen, Ivar - ***Rest In Agony*** [1963] PBO. Cover by Ralph Brillhart.	$2.50	$7.50	$15.00
MA-363	Scott, Jay - ***Army War Heroes*** [1963] PBO. Photo cover.	$1.35	$4.00	$8.00
364	Brewer, Gil - ***Wild To Possess*** [1963] Cover by Robert Maguire.	$1.50	$5.00	$10.00
365	Deming, Richard - ***She'll Hate Me Tomorrow*** [1963] PBO. Cover by Lou Marchetti.	$1.35	$4.00	$8.00
366	Joyce, Carlton - ***Fraternity Row*** [1963] PBO. Cover by Tom Miller	$1.35	$4.00	$8.00
367	Roberts, Lowell - ***This Climate Of Love*** [1963] PBO. Cover by Mort Engle.	$1.50	$5.00	$10.00
368	Bradley, Marion Zimmer - ***The Colors Of Space*** [1963] PBO. Cover by Ralph Brillhart.	$2.50	$7.50	$15.00
369	Catlin, Don - ***Town Marshall*** [1963] PBO. Cover by Jack Thurston.	$1.35	$4.00	$8.00
370	Hutter, Ernie - ***The Chillingworth Murder Case*** [1963]	$1.35	$4.00	$8.00
371	Ellsworth, Henry - ***Wild Weekend*** [1963] PBO. Cover by Lou Marchetti.	$1.50	$5.00	$10.00
372	Bingham, Carson - ***The Gang Girls*** [1963] PBO. Cover by Tom Miller	$3.00	$9.00	$18.00
373	Havilland, Monica - ***Lana*** [1963]	$1.35	$4.00	$8.00
374	Bowen, Robert Sidney - ***Hot Rod Fury*** [1963] PBO. Cover by Harry Barton.	$1.35	$4.00	$8.00

		G	VG	F
375	Ernenwein, Leslie - ***Rampage West*** [1963] PBO. Cover by Ray Johnson.	$1.35	$4.00	$8.00
376	Karson, Arlene - ***Walk Out Of Darkness*** [1963] PBO. Cover by Harry Schaare.	$1.50	$5.00	$10.00
377	Friedman, Stuart - ***Nikki Revisited*** [1963] PBO. Cover by Tom Miller.	$1.50	$5.00	$10.00
378	Friedman, Stuart - ***The Revolt Of Jill Braddock*** [1963] Cover by Harry Barton.	$1.50	$5.00	$10.00
379	Colby, Robert - ***The Faster She Runs*** [1963] PBO. Cover by Harry Barton.	$1.50	$5.00	$10.00
380	Chambers, Whitman - ***Season For Love*** [1963] Cover by Robert Maguire.	$1.50	$5.00	$10.00
381	Dumont, Jessie - ***I Prefer Girls*** [1963] PBO. Cover by Maguire.	$4.00	$12.50	$25.00
382	Mac Brian, James - ***Roz*** [1963] PBO. Cover by Stanley Borack.	$1.50	$5.00	$10.00
383	Stevens, Dan - ***Hangman's Mesa*** [1963]	$1.35	$4.00	$8.00
MA-384	Porges, Irwin - ***The Violent Americans*** [1963]	$1.35	$4.00	$8.00
385	Webster, Sam - ***My Neighbor's Wife*** [1963] PBO. Cover by Tom Miller.	$1.50	$5.00	$10.00
386	White, Lionel - ***Obsession*** [1963] Cover by Jack Thurston.	$1.35	$4.00	$8.00
387	Gorham, Nicholas - ***Company Girl*** [1963] PBO. Cover by Harry Schaare.	$1.35	$4.00	$8.00
388	Smith, George H. - ***Doomsday Wing*** [1963] PBO. Cover by Earl Mayan.	$2.50	$7.50	$15.00
389	Taylor, Robert William - ***Occasion Of Sin*** [1963] Cover by Ray Johnson.	$1.50	$5.00	$10.00
390	Chandler, A. Bertram - ***The Hamelin Plague*** [1963] PBO. Cover by Maguire.	$3.00	$9.00	$18.00
391	Garland, Bennett - ***High Storm*** [1963] PBO. Cover by Ray Johnson.	$1.35	$4.00	$8.00
392	Kendricks, James - ***Beyond Our Pleasure*** [1963]	$1.50	$5.00	$10.00
MA-393	Shirley, Glenn - ***Born To Kill*** [1963] PBO. Photo cover.	$2.00	$6.00	$12.00
394	Daniels, Paul - ***Pattern For Destruction*** [1963] PBO. Cover by Robert Stanley.	$1.50	$5.00	$10.00
395	Knerr, Michael E. - ***The Violent Lady*** [1963] PBO. Cover by Harry Barton.	$2.00	$6.00	$12.00
396	Jones, Robert Page - ***The Heisters*** [1963] PBO. Cover by Lou Marchetti.	$1.35	$4.00	$8.00
397	Ellsworth, Henry - ***21 Sunset Drive*** [1963] PBO. Cover by Tom Miller.	$1.35	$4.00	$8.00
398	Boyd, Frank - ***The Flesh Peddlers*** [1963] Cover by Robert Maguire.	$2.00	$6.00	$12.00
399	Ellson, Hal - ***Jailbait Street*** [1963] Cover by Ray Johnson.	$2.00	$6.00	$12.00
400	Palmer, Florence K. - ***Surgical Nurse*** [1963] PBO. Cover by Maguire.	$1.25	$3.75	$7.50
401	Owen, Dean - ***Rawhider From Texas*** [1963] Cover by Jack Thurston.	$1.35	$4.00	$8.00
MA-402	Millard, Joseph - ***The Cheyenne Wars*** [1964] PBO. Cover by Charles Schreyvogel.	$1.35	$4.00	$8.00
403	Brown, Wenzell - ***Sherry*** [1964] PBO. Photo cover.	$2.50	$7.50	$15.00
404	Webster, Sam - ***Society Doctor*** [1964] PBO. Cover by Harry Schaare.	$1.25	$3.75	$7.50
405	Reynolds, Mack - ***The Jet Set*** [1964] PBO. Cover by Tom Miller.	$2.00	$6.00	$12.00
406	Thiessen, Val - ***My Brother, Cain*** [1964] PBO. Cover by Ray Johnson.	$1.50	$5.00	$10.00
407	Friedman, Stuart - ***Damned Are The Meek*** [1964] PBO. Cover by Rafael DeSoto.	$2.00	$6.00	$12.00
408	Brennan, Alice - ***Mary Adams, Student Nurse*** [1964] PBO. Cover by Robert Maguire.	$1.25	$3.75	$7.50
409	Denzer, Peter W. - ***Lust To Live*** [1964] Cover by Ray Johnson.	$1.50	$5.00	$10.00

		G	VG	F
410	West, Edwin - ***Young And Innocent*** [1964] Cover by Maguire.	$1.50	$5.00	$10.00
411	Johnston, William - ***The Power Of Positive Loving*** [1964] PBO. Cover by Tom Miller.	$1.25	$3.75	$7.50
412	Maugham, Robin - ***November Reef*** [1964] PBO. Cover by Harry Schaare.	$1.35	$4.00	$8.00
413	Simpson, Ronald - ***End Of A Diplomat*** [1964] PBO. Cover by Harry Barton.	$1.35	$4.00	$8.00
414	Millard, Joseph - ***The Gods Hate Kansas*** [1964] PBO. Cover by Jack Thurston.	$2.50	$7.50	$15.00
415	Garland, Bennett - ***The Last Outlaw*** [1964] PBO. Cover by Ray Johnson.	$1.35	$4.00	$8.00
416	Chambers, Whitman - ***In Savage Surrender*** [1964] Cover by Harry Barton.	$1.50	$5.00	$10.00
417	Matthews, Clayton - ***A Rage Of Desire*** [1964] Cover by Harry Barton.	$1.50	$5.00	$10.00
418	Gardner, Miriam (M. Zimmer Bradley) - ***Twilight Lovers*** [1964]	$12.50	$37.50	$75.00
419	Blake, Walker E. - ***Once More With Passion*** [1964] PBO. Cover by Robert Stanley.	$1.50	$5.00	$10.00
420	Allen, Eric - ***Louisa*** [1964] PBO. Cover by DeSoto.	$1.50	$5.00	$10.00
421	Niall, Michael - ***Run Like A Thief*** [1964] Cover by Stanley Borack.	$1.35	$4.00	$8.00
422	Daniels, Paul - ***Jealous*** [1964] PBO. Cover by Darcy.	$1.50	$5.00	$10.00
423	Temple, Dan - ***Gun And Star*** [1964] PBO. Cover by Len Goldberg.	$1.35	$4.00	$8.00
424	Barry, Iris - ***Nurse Dawn's Discovery*** [1964] PBO. Cover by Harry Barton.	$1.25	$3.75	$7.50
425	Kendricks, James - ***The Adulterers*** [1964] Cover by Harry Barton.	$1.50	$5.00	$10.00
426	Flora, Fletcher - ***Most Likely To Love*** [1964] Cover by Rafael DeSoto.	$1.50	$5.00	$10.00
427	Colby, Robert - ***Executive Wife*** [1964] PBO. Cover by Tom Miller.	$1.50	$5.00	$10.00
428	Chambers, Peter - ***Murder Is For Keeps*** [1964] Cover by Lou Marchetti.	$1.50	$5.00	$10.00
429	Mac Brian, James - ***The Revolt Of Abbe Lee*** [1964] PBO. Cover by Tom Miller.	$1.50	$5.00	$10.00
430	Bowen, Robert Sidney - ***Silent Wings*** [1964] PBO. Cover by Harry Schaare.	$1.50	$5.00	$10.00
431	Hadley, Franklin - ***Planet Big Zero*** [1964] PBO. Cover by Ralph Brillhart.	$2.50	$7.50	$15.00
432	Gruber, Frank - ***The Lone Gunhawk*** [1964]	$1.50	$5.00	$10.00
433	Kramer, Karl - ***Kiss Me Quick*** [1964] Cover by Maguire.	$1.50	$5.00	$10.00
434	Chambers, Whitman - ***Manhandled*** [1964] Cover by Harry Barton.	$1.35	$4.00	$8.00
435	Francis, Connie - ***For Every Young Heart*** [1964] Connie Francis photo cover. Sixteen pages of photos.	$1.35	$4.00	$8.00
436	Morse, M.D., Benjamin - ***Adolescent Sexual Behavior*** [1964] PBO. Photo cover.	$1.25	$3.75	$7.50
437	Friedman, Stuart - ***The Luscious Puritan*** [1964] PBO. Cover by Victor Olson.	$1.35	$4.00	$8.00
438	Haviland, Monica - ***I Am An Adultress*** [1964] PBO. Photo cover.	$1.50	$5.00	$10.00
439	Deming, Richard - ***This Game Of Murder*** [1964] PBO. Cover by Harry Barton.	$2.00	$6.00	$12.00
440	Smith, Ben - ***Peril Of The Peloncillos*** [1964] PBO. Cover by Bob Stanley.	$1.35	$4.00	$8.00
441	Bonham, Frank - ***Cast A Long Shadow*** [1964]	$1.35	$4.00	$8.00
442	Johnston, William - ***Dr. Starr In Crisis*** [1964] PBO. Cover by Tom Miller.	$1.25	$3.75	$7.50

		G	VG	F
443	Fontenay, Charles - ***The Day The Oceans Overflowed*** [1964] PBO. Cover by Ralph Brillhart.	$2.50	$7.50	$15.00
444	Brewer, Gil - ***Play It Hard*** [1964] Cover by Rafael DeSoto.	$1.50	$5.00	$10.00
445	Friedman, Stuart - ***The Way We Love*** [1964] Cover by Harry Barton.	$1.50	$5.00	$10.00
446	Edmonds, I. G. - ***Isometric & Isotonic Exercises For Men & Women*** [1964] PBO. Photo cover.	$1.25	$3.75	$7.50
447	Downey, Fairfax - ***Indian Wars Of The U.S. Army*** [1964] Sixteen pages of photos.	$1.35	$4.00	$8.00
448	Gordon, Gary - ***The Anatomy Of Adultery*** [1964] PBO. Photo cover.	$1.25	$3.75	$7.50
449	Plantz, Donald - ***Marked For Death*** [1964] PBO. Cover by Rafael DeSoto.	$1.50	$5.00	$10.00
450	Winston, Daoma - ***Passion For Living*** [1964] PBO. Cover by Ernest Chiriaka.	$1.50	$5.00	$10.00
451	Phillips, Tom - ***All About Amy*** [1964] PBO. Cover by Victor Olson.	$1.50	$5.00	$10.00
452	Bonner, Parker - ***Tough In The Saddle*** [1964] PBO. Cover by Ray Johnson.	$1.35	$4.00	$8.00
453	Edwards, Norman - ***Invasion From 2500*** [1964] PBO. Cover by Ralph Brillhart.	$2.50	$7.50	$15.00
454	Miller, John J. - ***New Doctor At Tower General*** [1964] PBO. Cover by Bob Stanley.	$1.25	$3.75	$7.50
455	Conway, John - ***Love In Suburbia*** [1964] Cover by Ray Johnson.	$1.25	$3.75	$7.50
456	James, Don - ***$50 A Night*** [1964] Cover by Robert Maguire.	$2.00	$6.00	$12.00
457	Kluckhohn, Frank L. - ***The Inside On LBJ*** [1964] PBO. Photo cover.	$1.35	$4.00	$8.00
459	Anthology Edited by Helen MacGill Hughes - ***The Fantastic Lodge*** [1964] Photo cover.	$1.50	$5.00	$10.00
460	Brown, Wenzell - ***The Golden Witch*** [1964] PBO. Cover by Len Goldberg.	$2.50	$7.50	$15.00
461	Matthews, Clayton - ***The Corrupter*** [1964] PBO. Cover by Stan Borack.	$2.00	$6.00	$12.00
462	Haviland, Monica - ***A Very Private Love*** [1964] PBO. Cover by Harry Schaare.	$1.50	$5.00	$10.00
463	Joyce, Carlton - ***Coeds Three*** [1964] PBO. Cover by Len Goldberg.	$1.50	$5.00	$10.00
464	Smith, George H. - ***The Unending Night*** [1964] PBO. Cover by Ralph Brillhart.	$2.50	$7.50	$15.00
465	Conway, John - ***Hard Man From Texas*** [1964]	$1.35	$4.00	$8.00
466	Bonham, Barbara - ***Diagnosis: Love*** [1964]	$1.25	$3.75	$7.50
467	Smith, Artemis - ***This Bed We Made*** [1964] Cover by Rafael DeSoto.	$1.35	$4.00	$8.00
468	Simpson, Ronald - ***Eve's Apple*** [1964] Cover by Harry Barton.	$1.50	$5.00	$10.00
470	Gallico, Paul - ***Love Of 7 Dolls*** [1964]	$1.50	$5.00	$10.00
471	Fairman, Paul W. - ***The World Grabbers*** [1964] PBO. Cover by Ralph Brillhart. TV tie-in.	$3.00	$9.00	$18.00
472	Gordon, Gary - ***The Law And The Marriage Bed*** [1965] PBO. Photo cover.	$1.25	$3.75	$7.50
473	Mathieson, Theodore - ***The Nez Perce Indian War*** [1964] PBO.	$1.35	$4.00	$8.00
474	Gorham, Nicholas - ***The Men In Her Life*** [1965] PBO. Cover by Darrel Greene.	$1.50	$5.00	$10.00
475	James, Don - ***Beyond All Passion*** [1965] PBO. Cover by Victor Olson.	$1.50	$5.00	$10.00
476	Brennan, Alice - ***Circle Of Fear*** [1965]	$1.50	$5.00	$10.00
477	White, Lionel - ***The Money Trap*** [1965] Cover by Harry Barton.	$1.35	$4.00	$8.00
478	Anvil, Christopher - ***The Day The Machines Stopped*** [1964] PBO. Cover by Ralph Brillhart.	$2.50	$7.50	$15.00

No.	Entry	G	VG	F
479	Halacy, Jr., D. S. - ***Encyclopedia Of The World's Great Events: 1964*** [1965] PBO. Photo cover.	$1.25	$3.75	$7.50
480	Stagg, Delano - ***The Glory Jumpers*** [1965] Cover by Robert Stanley.	$1.25	$3.75	$7.50
481	James, Stuart - ***Frisco Flat*** [1964]	$1.25	$3.75	$7.50
482	Kluckhohn, Frank L. - ***Lyndon's Legacy*** [1964] PBO. Cover by George Fried.	$1.25	$3.75	$7.50
483	Powell, Talmadge - ***The Girl From Big Pine*** [1964] Cover by Rafael DeSoto.	$1.50	$5.00	$10.00
484	Horowitz, Robert S. - ***The Ramparts We Watch*** [1964] PBO. Photo cover.	$1.25	$3.75	$7.50
485	West, Edwin - ***Campus Doll*** [1964] Cover by Tom Miller.	$1.50	$5.00	$10.00
486	Canary, Glen - ***The Damned And The Innocent*** [1964] Cover by Harry Barton.	$1.50	$5.00	$10.00
487	Bingham, Carson - ***Run Tough, Run Hard*** [1964] Cover by Ray Johnson.	$1.50	$5.00	$10.00
488	Colby, Robert - ***Lament For Julie*** [1964] Cover by Harry Barton.	$1.35	$4.00	$8.00
489	Gaulden, Ray - ***High Country Showdown*** [1964] Cover by A. Leslie Ross.	$1.35	$4.00	$8.00
490	Kramer, Karl - ***A Flame Too Hot*** [1964] Cover by Harry Barton.	$1.50	$5.00	$10.00
491	Friedman, Stuart - ***The Trouble With Ava*** [1964] Cover by Lou Marchetti.	$1.50	$5.00	$10.00
492	Carse, Robert - ***End To Innocence*** [1964]	$1.35	$4.00	$8.00
493	Little, Charles - ***The Sound Of Trumpets*** [1965] PBO. Cover by Darrel Greene.	$1.50	$5.00	$10.00
494	Parkhurst, Helen - ***Undertow*** [1965] Photo cover.	$1.35	$4.00	$8.00
495	Gallico, Paul - ***Love Of 7 Dolls*** [1965]	$1.35	$4.00	$8.00
496	Caryl, Warren - ***Riot Night In Cedarville*** [1965] PBO. Cover by Rafael DeSoto.	$2.00	$6.00	$12.00
497	West, Edwin - ***Brother And Sister*** [1965] Cover by Harry Schaare.	$2.00	$6.00	$12.00
498	Plunkett, John - ***She'll Get Hers*** [1965] Cover by Harry Barton.	$1.50	$5.00	$10.00
499	Reynolds, Mack - ***Night Is For Monsters*** [1965]	$3.00	$9.00	$18.00
500	Denzer, Peter W. - ***The Practice Of Passion*** [1965] Cover by Maguire.	$2.00	$6.00	$12.00
551	Matthews, Clayton - ***The Strange Ways Of Love*** [1964]	$1.25	$3.75	$7.50
552	Friedman, Stuart - ***The Troubles Of Dr. Cortland*** [1965] PBO.	$1.25	$3.75	$7.50
553	Curry, Tom & Cowan, Wood - ***Famous Figures Of The Old West*** [1965] PBO	$1.35	$4.00	$8.00
554	Daniels, Paul - ***Debbie*** [1965] Cover by DeSoto.	$1.25	$3.75	$7.50
555	Hamlin, Ken - ***Guns Of Revenge*** [1965] Cover by A. Leslie Ross.	$1.25	$3.75	$7.50
557	Holmes, Rick - ***Riverfront Girl*** [1965] PBO. Cover by Harry Barton.	$1.50	$5.00	$10.00
558	Laurence, Will - ***The Despoiler*** [1965] PBO. Cover by Ray Johnson.	$1.35	$4.00	$8.00
559	Robison, Harold R. - ***Rat Alley*** [1965] PBO. Cover by Victor Olson.	$1.50	$5.00	$10.00
560	Chamberlain, William - ***The Man From Gunsight*** [1965] PBO. Cover by Bob Stanley.	$1.35	$4.00	$8.00
561	Conway, John - ***Octoroon*** [1965] PBO.	$1.35	$4.00	$8.00
562	Simpson, Ronald - ***The Return Of Colonel Pho*** [1965] PBO.	$1.50	$5.00	$10.00
563	Holmes, Rick - ***The Child-Woman*** [1965] PBO. Cover by Rafael DeSoto.	$2.50	$7.50	$15.00

Monarch Behavior Series. New York: Monarch Publications.

No.	Entry	G	VG	F
MB-501	Donner, James - ***Women In Trouble*** [1959] PBO. Cover by Maguire.	$2.00	$6.00	$12.00

	G	VG	F
MB-502 James, Don - ***The Sexual Side Of Life*** [1959] Photo cover.	$1.35	$4.00	$8.00
MB-503 McGoldrick, Jr., Edward J. - ***Tormented Women*** [1959] PBO. Cover by Maguire.	$2.00	$6.00	$12.00
MB-504 Bishop, Jim - ***Go With God*** [1959]	$1.25	$3.75	$7.50
MB-505 Mozes, Dr. Eugene B. - ***Crime And Passion*** [1960] PBO. Cover by Maguire.	$2.00	$6.00	$12.00
MB-506 James, Don - ***The Power Of Marital Love*** [1960] Cover by Maguire.	$1.50	$5.00	$10.00
MB-507 Woodward, M.D., L. T. - ***Sex And The Armed Services*** [1960] PBO. Cover by Maguire.	$2.00	$6.00	$12.00
MB-508 Crowley, Liz - ***I Sell Love*** [1960] PBO. Photo Cover.	$1.35	$4.00	$8.00
MB-509 Aradi, Zsolt - ***The Book Of Miracles*** [1961] Cover by Maguire.	$1.50	$5.00	$10.00
MB-510 Brown, Wenzell - ***Bedeviled*** [1961] PBO. Cover by Maguire.	$2.50	$7.50	$15.00
MB-511 Woodward, M.D., L. T. - ***Sex Fiend*** [1961] PBO. Cover by Maguire.	$2.50	$7.50	$15.00
MB-512 James, Don - ***Folk And Modern Medicine*** [1961] PBO. Cover by Maguire.	$2.00	$6.00	$12.00
MB-513 Morse, Dr. Benjamin - ***The Lesbian*** [1961] PBO.	$1.35	$4.00	$8.00
MB-514 Michelfelder, William - ***It's Cheaper To Die*** [1961]	$1.35	$4.00	$8.00
MB-515 Brown, Dr. Walter C. - ***The Single Girl*** [1961] PBO. Photo cover.	$1.25	$3.75	$7.50
MB-516 Woodward, M.D., L. T. - ***Sex And Hypnosis*** [1961] PBO. Photo cover.	$1.35	$4.00	$8.00
MB-517 Galus, Henry S. - ***Teen-Age Brides*** [1961] PBO. Cover by Maguire.	$2.00	$6.00	$12.00
MB-518 Morse, M.D., Benjamin - ***Sexual Surrender In Women*** [1962] PBO. Cover by Maguire.	$1.50	$5.00	$10.00
MB-519 O'Hara, M.D., Ralph C. - ***The Divorcee*** [1962] PBO. Cover by Maguire.	$1.50	$5.00	$10.00
MB-520 Lawson, R.N., Joan - ***Registered Nurse*** [1962] PBO. Cover by Maguire.	$1.50	$5.00	$10.00
MB-521 Woodward, M.D., L. T. - ***Sex In Our Schools*** [1962] PBO. Cover by Maguire.	$2.25	$7.00	$14.00
MB-522 Carr, Jay - ***Crack-Up In Suburbia*** [1962] PBO. Cover by Tom Miller.	$1.35	$4.00	$8.00
MB-523 Alden, Troy - ***I Am A Nympho*** [1962] PBO. Photo cover.	$1.35	$4.00	$8.00
MB-524 Galus, Henry S. - ***Unwed Mothers*** [1962] PBO. Cover by Robert Maguire.	$2.00	$6.00	$12.00
MB-525 Gordon, Gary - ***Sins Of Our Cities*** [1962] PBO. Cover by DeSoto.	$1.50	$5.00	$10.00
MB-526 Jordan, Valerie - ***I Am A Teen-Age Dope Addict*** [1962] PBO. Photo cover.	$3.50	$10.00	$20.00
MB-527 Morse, M.D., Benjamin - ***The Homosexual*** [1962]	$1.25	$3.75	$7.50
MB-528 James, M.D., Martin - ***Medical Problems Of Women*** [1962] PBO.	$1.25	$3.75	$7.50
MB-529 Chapman, Lee (M. Zimmer Bradley) - ***I Am A Lesbian*** [1962] PBO. Photo cover.	$12.50	$37.50	$75.00
MB-530 Woodward, M.D., L. T. - ***Virgin Wives*** [1962] PBO.	$1.50	$5.00	$10.00
MB-531 Morse, M.D., Benjamin - ***The Sexual Revolution*** [1962] PBO.	$1.25	$3.75	$7.50
MB-532 Burnett, Stan & Seeger, Alan - ***Prostitution Around The World*** [1963] PBO. Cover by George Fried.	$1.25	$3.75	$7.50
MB-533 Glover, Dr. Leland E. - ***The Impotent Male*** [1963] PBO.	$1.25	$3.75	$7.50
MB-534 James, Don - ***Girls And Gangs*** [1963] PBO. Cover by DeSoto.	$2.50	$7.50	$15.00
MB-535 Morse, M.D., Benjamin - ***The Sexually Promiscuous Female*** [1963] PBO. Photo cover.	$1.25	$3.75	$7.50
MB-536 James, M.D., Martin - ***Cancer And You*** [1963] PBO.	$1.25	$3.75	$7.50
MB-537 Morse, M.D., Benjamin - ***The Sexually Promiscuous Male*** [1963] PBO.	$1.25	$3.75	$7.50
MB-538 Woodward, M.D., L. T. - ***You And Your Sex Life*** [1963] PBO. Cover by George Fried.	$1.35	$4.00	$8.00

Monarch Movie, MM-602

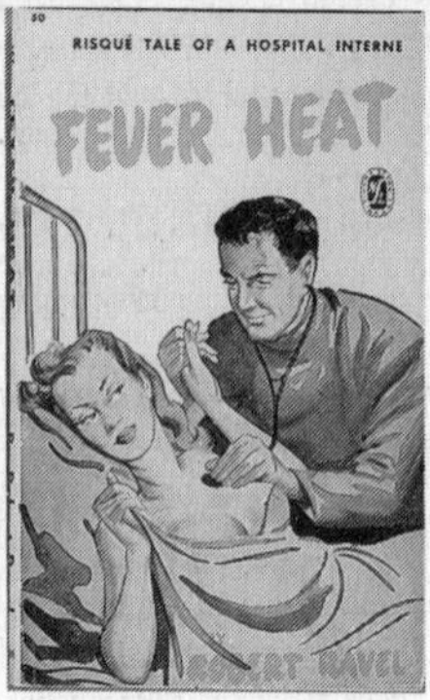

News Stand Library, 50

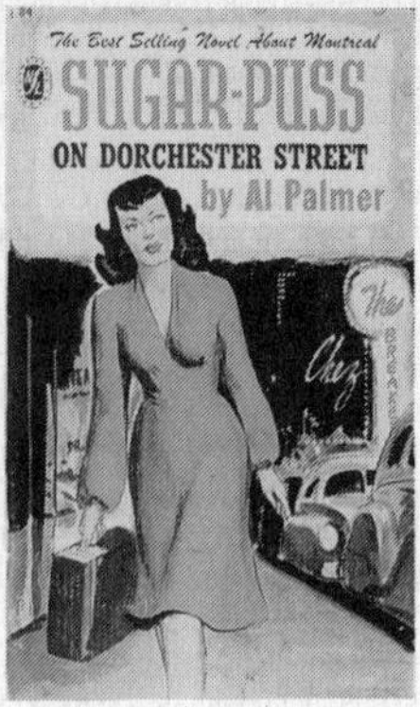

News Stand Library, 84

		G	VG	F
MB-539	Burgess, Ann Marie & Michael - ***The Girl Market*** [1963] PBO. Photo cover.	$1.25	$3.75	$7.50
MB-540	Miles, William E. - ***The College Female*** [1963] PBO. Photo cover.	$1.25	$3.75	$7.50
MB-541	Woodward, M.D., L. T. - ***Sex And The Armed Services*** [1963] Cover by Maguire.	$1.35	$4.00	$8.00
MB-542	Whitman, Howard - ***Let's Tell The Truth About Sex*** [1963]	$1.25	$3.75	$7.50
MB-543	Morse, Dr. Benjamin - ***The Lesbian*** [1963]	$1.25	$3.75	$7.50
MB-544	Woodward, M.D., L. T. - ***Sex Fiend*** [1963] Cover by Maguire.	$1.50	$5.00	$10.00
MB-545	MaGee, Martin - ***Virginity*** [1963] PBO. Photo cover.	$1.25	$3.75	$7.50
MB-546	Havemann, Ernest - ***Men, Women & Marriage*** [1963]	$1.25	$3.75	$7.50
MB-547	Woodward, M.D., L. T. - ***Masochism*** [1964] PBO.	$1.35	$4.00	$8.00
MB-548	Gordon, Gary - ***The College Male*** [1964] PBO. Photo cover.	$1.25	$3.75	$7.50
MB-549	Galus, Henry S. - ***The Impact Of Women*** [1964] PBO. Photo cover.	$1.25	$3.75	$7.50
MB-550	Gordon, Gary - ***Sex In Business*** [1964] PBO. Photo cover.	$1.25	$3.75	$7.50

Monarch K Series. New York: Monarch Publishing.

		G	VG	F
K-50	Cloete, Stuart - ***Congo Song*** [1958] Cover art by Harry Schaare.	$2.00	$6.00	$12.00
K-52	Moray, Helga - ***This Naked Love*** [1959] Cover art by Robert Maguire.	$2.50	$7.50	$15.00
K-53	Bishop, Leonard - ***The Angry Time*** [1961] Cover art by Robert Maguire.	$2.00	$6.00	$12.00
K-54	Heller, Deane & David - ***Jacqueline Kennedy*** [1961] Photo cover.	$1.50	$5.00	$10.00
K-55	Allan, John B. - ***Elizabeth Taylor*** [1961] PBO. Photo cover.	$1.50	$5.00	$10.00
K-56	Black, Edgar - ***Sir Winston Churchill*** [1961] PBO. Photo cover.	$1.50	$5.00	$10.00
K-57	Johnson, George - ***Richard Nixon*** [1961]	$1.50	$5.00	$10.00
K-58	Thomey, Tedd - ***The Loves Of Errol Flynn*** [1962] PBO. Photo cover.	$1.50	$5.00	$10.00
K-59	Garrett, Randall - ***Pope John XXIII: Pastoral Prince*** [1962] PBO. Photo cover.	$1.50	$5.00	$10.00
K-60	Newman, Robert - ***Princess Grace Kelly*** [1962] PBO. Photo cover.	$1.50	$5.00	$10.00
K-61	Johnston, George - ***Eleanor Roosevelt*** [1962]	$1.50	$5.00	$10.00
K-62	Eby, Lois - ***Shirley Temple*** [1962] PBO.	$2.00	$6.00	$12.00
K-63	Fritch, Charles E. - ***Kim Novak: Goddess Of Love*** [1962] PBO. Photo cover.	$1.50	$5.00	$10.00
K-64	Johnson, George - ***Eisenhower*** [1962] PBO. Photo cover.	$1.50	$5.00	$10.00
K-65	Jameson, Keith - ***SOS The World's Great Sea Disasters*** [1962] PBO. Photo cover.	$1.35	$4.00	$8.00

		G	VG	F
K-66	Gordon, Gary - ***Robert F. Kennedy: Assistant President*** [1962]	$1.50	$5.00	$10.00
K-68	Silverberg, Robert - ***The Fabulous Rockefellers*** [1963]	$2.00	$6.00	$12.00
K-69	Halacy, Jr., D.S. - ***Encyclopedia Of The World's Great Events: 1936*** [1963] PBO. Photo cover.	$1.35	$4.00	$8.00
K-70	Gordon, Gary - ***The Anatomy Of Rape*** [1963] PBO. Cover art by George Fried.	$1.25	$3.75	$7.50
K-71	Fabert, Andre - ***Pope Paul VI*** [1963] PBO. Photo cover.	$1.50	$5.00	$10.00
K-72	Jablonski, Edward - ***Mary, Mother Of Jesus*** [1964] PBO. Cover art by Robert Maguire.	$2.50	$7.50	$15.00
K-73	Halacy, Jr., D.S. - ***Encyclopedia Of The World's Great Events: 1932*** [1964] PBO. Photo cover.	$1.35	$4.00	$8.00
K-74	Pearl, Jack - ***The Dangerous Assassins*** [1964]	$1.50	$5.00	$10.00

Monarch Movie Series. New York: Monarch Books, Inc.

		G	VG	F
MM-600	Pepper, Dan & Gareth, Max - ***The Enemy General*** [1960] PBO. Movie tie-in with photo cover.	$3.50	$10.00	$20.00
MM-601	James, Stuart - ***The Stranglers Of Bombay*** [1960] PBO. Movie tie-in with photo cover.	$3.50	$10.00	$20.00
MM-602	Owen, Dean - ***The Brides Of Dracula*** [1960] PBO. Movie tie-in.	$8.00	$25.00	$50.00
MM-603	Bingham, Carson - ***Gorgo*** [1960] PBO. Movie tie-in with photo cover.	$4.00	$12.50	$25.00
MM-604	Owen, Dean - ***Konga*** [1960] PBO. Movie tie-in.	$4.00	$12.50	$25.00
MM-605	Owen, Dean - ***Reptilicus*** [1961] PBO. Movie tie-in with photo cover.	$4.00	$12.50	$25.00
MM-606	Bingham, Carson - ***The Street Is My Beat*** [1961] PBO. Cover by DeSoto. Movie tie-in.	$3.50	$10.00	$20.00
MM-607	Thurman, Steve - ***"Mad Dog" Coll*** [1961] PBO. Movie tie-in with photo cover.	$3.50	$10.00	$20.00

Monarch MS Series. New York: Monarch Publishing.

		G	VG	F
MS-1	Duncan, Lee - ***Fidel Castro Assassinated*** [1961] PBO. Photo cover.	$3.50	$10.00	$20.00
MS-2	Heller, Deane & David - ***The Berlin Crisis*** [1961] PBO.	$1.25	$3.75	$7.50
MS-3-AB	Kluckhohn, Frank L. - ***America: Listen!*** [1962]	$1.25	$3.75	$7.50
MS-3	Kluckhohn, Frank L. - ***America: Listen!*** [1961] PBO. Photo cover.	$1.25	$3.75	$7.50
MS-4	Gordon, Gary - ***The Rise And Fall Of The Japanese Empire*** [1961]	$1.35	$4.00	$8.00
MS-5	De Forrest, M.D., Henry - ***Planned Parenthood*** [1962] PBO. Photo cover.	$1.25	$3.75	$7.50
MS-6	Kluckhohn, Frank L. - ***The Naked Rise Of Communism*** [1962]	$1.25	$3.75	$7.50
MS-7	O'Brian, Leland H. - ***Forget About Calories*** [1962]	$1.25	$3.75	$7.50
MS-8	Heller, Deane & David - ***The Cold War*** [1962]	$1.25	$3.75	$7.50
MS-9	Garrett, Randall - ***A Gallery Of The Saints*** [1963] PBO.	$1.50	$5.00	$10.00
MS-10	Woodward, M.D., L.T. (Robert Silverberg) - ***The History Of Surgery*** [1963]	$1.50	$5.00	$10.00
MS-11	Benson, Ezra Taft - ***The Red Carpet*** [1963]	$1.25	$3.75	$7.50
MS-12	Rukeyser, Merryle Stanley - ***The Kennedy Recession*** [1963]	$1.25	$3.75	$7.50
MS-13	Michael, Jan - ***How To Stay Young And Beautiful*** [1963] PBO. Photo cover. 16 pages of photos.	$1.00	$3.00	$6.00
MS-14	Bayard, James - ***The Real Story of Cuba*** [1963] PBO.	$1.25	$3.75	$7.50
MS-15	Anderson, Poul - ***Thermonuclear Warfare*** [1963] PBO. Cover by George Fried.	$4.00	$12.50	$25.00
MS-16	Freeman, Thomas - ***The Crisis In Cuba*** [1963]	$1.25	$3.75	$7.50
MS-17	Hardwick, Richard - ***Skin And Scuba Diving*** [1963]	$1.25	$3.75	$7.50
MS-18	Kluckhohn, Frank L. - ***What's Wrong With U.S. Foreign Policy?*** [1963] PBO. Photo cover.	$1.00	$3.00	$6.00
MS-19	Anthology - ***They Fought Under The Sea*** [1963] Photo cover.	$1.25	$3.75	$7.50

		G	VG	F
MS-20	Johnson, George - ***The Washington Waste-Makers*** [1963] PBO. Cover art by George Fried.	$1.00	$3.00	$6.00
MS-21	Unger, Art - ***The Cool Book*** [1963]	$1.50	$5.00	$10.00
MS-22	Rukeyser, Merrayle Stanley - ***The Attack On Our Free Choice*** [1963]	$1.25	$3.75	$7.50
MS-23	Heller, Deane & David - ***Jacqueline Kennedy*** [1963] Photo cover.	$1.35	$4.00	$8.00
MS-24	Pearl, Jack - ***Battleground: World War I*** [1964] PBO. Photo cover.	$1.35	$4.00	$8.00
MS-25	Friedman, Stanley P. - ***The Magnificent Kennedy Women*** [1964] PBO. Photo cover. 16 pages of photos.	$1.35	$4.00	$8.00

Monarch SP Series. New York: Monarch Books, Inc.

SP-1	Silverberg, Robert - ***First American Into Space*** [1961] PBO.	$2.00	$6.00	$12.00

Moonlight Reader.

103	Smith, George H. - ***The Year For Love*** [1961] PBO.	$2.50	$7.50	$15.00

Mystery Novel of the Month/Mystery Novel Classic. New York: Novel Selections. Digest.

NO#-1	Teagle, Mike - ***Murders In Silk*** [1938]	$4.00	$12.50	$25.00
NO#-2	Fisher, Steve - ***Murder On The S-23*** [1938]	$3.50	$10.00	$20.00
NO#-3	Harris, Colver - ***Murder By Proxy*** [1938]	$3.50	$10.00	$20.00
NO#-4	Dinneen, Joseph F. - ***The Merry-Go-Round Of Murder*** [1940]	$1.50	$5.00	$10.00
NO#-5	Price, Wesley - ***Death Is A Stowaway*** [1939]	$1.50	$5.00	$10.00
NO#-6	Fisher, Steve - ***The Night Before Murder*** [1939]	$1.50	$5.00	$10.00
NO#-7	Newman, Bernard - ***The Mussolini Murder Case*** [1939]	$1.50	$5.00	$10.00
NO#-8	Donovan, John - ***The Case Of The Beckoning Dead*** [n.d.]	$1.50	$5.00	$10.00
NO#-9	Torrey, Roger - ***42 Days For Murder*** [1939]	$1.50	$5.00	$10.00
NO#-10	Heath, Eric - ***Death Takes A Dive*** [1940]	$1.50	$5.00	$10.00
NO#-11	Jones, Inigo - ***The Clue Of The Hungry Corpse*** [1940]	$1.50	$5.00	$10.00
NO#-12	Haggard, Paul - ***Poison From A Wealthy Widow*** [1940]	$1.50	$5.00	$10.00
NO#-13	Boucher, Anthony - ***The Case Of The Crumpled Knave*** [1940]	$1.50	$5.00	$10.00
NO#-14	Heath, Eric - ***Murder In The Musuem*** [1940]	$1.50	$5.00	$10.00
NO#-15	Weiner, H. - ***The Case Of The Severed Skull*** [1940]	$1.50	$5.00	$10.00
NO#-16	King, Sherwood - ***If I Die Before I Wake*** [1940]	$1.50	$5.00	$10.00
NO#-17	Mosher, J. S. - ***Liar Dice*** [1940]	$1.50	$5.00	$10.00
18	Horler, Sydney - ***A Gentleman For The Gallows*** [1940]	$1.50	$5.00	$10.00
19	Fleming, Rudd - ***Cradled In Murder!*** [1941]	$1.35	$4.00	$8.00
20	McCombs, R. L. F. - ***Clue in Two Flats*** [1941]	$1.35	$4.00	$8.00
21	Rice, Craig - ***Murder Stops The Clock*** [1941]	$1.50	$5.00	$10.00
22	Storme, Peter - ***The Case Of The Thing In The Brook*** [1941]	$1.25	$3.75	$7.50
23	O'Hanlon, James - ***Murder At Coney Island*** [1941] Photo Cover.	$1.25	$3.75	$7.50
24	Garland, Isabel - ***Death Comes Courting*** [1941]	$1.35	$4.00	$8.00
25	Hull, Richard - ***Murder By Invitation*** [1941]	$1.35	$4.00	$8.00
26	Punshon, E. R. - ***Death In The Chalk Pits*** [1941]	$1.25	$3.75	$7.50
27	MacVeigh, Sue - ***Grand Central Murder*** [1941]	$1.25	$3.75	$7.50
28	Sutherland, Scott - ***Murder on Stage*** [1941]	$1.25	$3.75	$7.50
29	Smith, Laurence Dwight - ***The Case Of The Rented Coffin*** [1941]	$1.35	$4.00	$8.00
30	Forrest, Norman - ***Death Took A Publisher*** [1941]	$1.25	$3.75	$7.50
31	Adams, Cleve F. - ***Death Before Breakfast*** [1942]	$1.50	$5.00	$10.00
32	Cunningham, A. B. - ***Murder At The Schoolhouse*** [1942]	$1.25	$3.75	$7.50
33	Jones, Inigo - ***The Albatross Murders*** [1941]	$1.35	$4.00	$8.00
34	Branson, Henry C. - ***I'll Kill You Last*** [1942]	$1.35	$4.00	$8.00
35	Cunningham, A. B. - ***Murder At Deer Lick*** [1942]	$1.25	$3.75	$7.50
36	Adams, Cleve F. - ***And Sudden Death*** [1942]	$1.50	$5.00	$10.00
37	Avery, Robert - ***The Corpse In Company K*** [1942]	$1.35	$4.00	$8.00
38	Franklin, Charles - ***The Vice Czar Murders*** [1942]	$1.35	$4.00	$8.00
39	Demarest, Ann - ***Murder On Every Floor*** [1942]	$1.35	$4.00	$8.00

		G	VG	F
40	Stevenson, Burton - ***The Clue Of The Red Carnation*** [1942]	$1.25	$3.75	$7.50
41	Worts, George F. - ***The Case Of The Blue Lacquer Box*** [1942]	$1.50	$5.00	$10.00
42	Bardon, Minna - ***The Case Of The Advertised Murders*** [1942]	$1.25	$3.75	$7.50
43	Adams, Cleve F. - ***What Price Murder*** [1943]	$1.50	$5.00	$10.00
44	Newell, Audrey - ***Murder Is Not Mute*** [1943]	$1.35	$4.00	$8.00
45	Fletcher, J. S. - ***Mystery Of The Hushing Pool*** [1943]	$1.25	$3.75	$7.50
46	Fowler, Sydney - ***The Jordans Murder*** [1943]	$1.35	$4.00	$8.00
47	Eberhart, Mignon G. - ***Fair Warning*** [1943]	$1.25	$3.75	$7.50
48	Trimble, Louis - ***Date For Murder*** [1943]	$1.35	$4.00	$8.00
49	MacVeigh, Sue - ***Streamlined Murder*** [1943]	$1.25	$3.75	$7.50
50	St. John, Darby - ***The Bride Brings Death*** [1943]	$1.25	$3.75	$7.50
51	Daiger, K. S. - ***Murder On Ghost Tree Island*** [1943]	$1.25	$3.75	$7.50
52	Footner, Hulbert - ***The Death Of A Celebrity*** [1943]	$1.25	$3.75	$7.50
53	Strange, John Stephen - ***The Ballot-Box Murders*** [1943]	$1.35	$4.00	$8.00
54	Knight, Kathleen Moore - ***Death Wears A Bridal Veil*** [1943]	$1.35	$4.00	$8.00
55	Pierson, Eleanor - ***Murder Without Clues*** [1943]	$1.35	$4.00	$8.00
56	Eberhart, Mignon G. - ***The Glass Slipper*** [1943]	$1.35	$4.00	$8.00
57	Holbrook, Marion - ***Death Writes An Ad*** [1943]	$1.35	$4.00	$8.00
58	Holding, Elizabeth Saxany - ***Hostess to Murder*** [1943]	$1.25	$3.75	$7.50
59	Strange, John Stephen - ***Murder At World's End*** [1944]	$1.25	$3.75	$7.50
60	Knight, Kathleen Moore - ***The Case Of The Tainted Token*** [1944]	$1.35	$4.00	$8.00
61	Chambers, Whitman - ***Bring Me Another Murder*** [1944]	$1.25	$3.75	$7.50
62	Paradise, Viola - ***A Girl Died Laughing*** [1944]	$1.35	$4.00	$8.00
63	Holbrook, Marion - ***Wanted: A Murderess*** [1944]	$1.35	$4.00	$8.00
64	Treat, Lawrence - ***O As In Omen*** [1944]	$1.25	$3.75	$7.50
65	Siller, Van - ***Echo Of A Bomb*** [1944]	$1.35	$4.00	$8.00
66	Reisner, Mary - ***Shadows On The Wall*** [1944]	$1.25	$3.75	$7.50
67	Scherf, Margaret - ***They Came To Kill*** [1944]	$1.35	$4.00	$8.00
68	Treat, Lawrence - ***The Leather Man Murders*** [1945]	$1.35	$4.00	$8.00
69	King, Rufus - ***The Case Of The Dowager's Etchings*** [1945]	$1.35	$4.00	$8.00
70	Knight, Kathleen Moore - ***Terror By Twilight*** [1945]	$1.25	$3.75	$7.50
71	Scherf, Margaret - ***The Corpse Grows A Beard*** [1945]	$1.25	$3.75	$7.50
72	Marlett, Melba - ***Escape While I Can*** [1945]	$1.35	$4.00	$8.00
73	Howes, Royce - ***The Case Of The Copy-Hook Killing*** [1945]	$1.35	$4.00	$8.00
74	Hill, Katharine - ***The Case Of The Absent Corpse*** [1946]	$1.25	$3.75	$7.50
75	Scherf, Margaret - ***The Case Of The Kippered Corpse*** [1946]	$1.25	$3.75	$7.50
76	Knight, Kathleen Moore - ***Acts Of Black Knight*** [1945]	$1.25	$3.75	$7.50
77	Ransome, Stephen - ***Death Checks In*** [1945]	$1.25	$3.75	$7.50
78	Davis, Frederick C. - ***Let The Skeletons Rattle*** [1945]	$1.50	$5.00	$10.00
79	Ryan, Jessica - ***Clue Of The Frightening Coin*** [1945]	$1.35	$4.00	$8.00
80	Heberden, M. V. - ***Murder Goes Astray*** [1945]	$1.35	$4.00	$8.00
81	Dean, Amber - ***Dead Man's Float*** [1946]	$1.35	$4.00	$8.00
82	Stein, Aaron Mark - ***The Case Of The Absent-Minded Professor*** [1946]	$1.25	$3.75	$7.50
83	Barry, Jerome - ***The Cat's Cradle Murders*** [1946]	$1.25	$3.75	$7.50
84	McCully, Walbridge - ***Death Rides Tandem*** [1946]	$1.25	$3.75	$7.50
85	Burton, Miles - ***Who Killed The Doctor?*** [1946]	$1.25	$3.75	$7.50
86	Barry, Jerome - ***Lady Of Night*** [1946]	$1.35	$4.00	$8.00
87	Olsen, D. B. - ***Cat's Claw*** [1946]	$1.25	$3.75	$7.50
88	Eby, Lois & Fleming, John C. - ***The Case Of The Wicked Twin*** [1946]	$1.25	$3.75	$7.50
89	Dean, Amber - ***The Blonde Is Dead*** [1946]	$1.35	$4.00	$8.00
90	Cunningham, A. B. - ***One Man Must Die*** [1946]	$1.25	$3.75	$7.50
91	Knight, Kathleen Moore - ***Stream Sinister*** [1946]	$1.25	$3.75	$7.50
92	Knight, Kathleen Moore - ***Bells For The Dead*** [1946]	$1.25	$3.75	$7.50
96	Du Bois, Theodora - ***Murder Strikes An Atomic Unit*** [1946]	$1.35	$4.00	$8.00
97	Fenisong, Ruth - ***The Butler Died In Brooklyn*** [1946]	$1.25	$3.75	$7.50
98	Disney, Doris Cameron - ***Family Skeleton*** [1946]	$1.35	$4.00	$8.00

News Stand Library First Series. Toronto: Export Publishing.

No.	Title	G	VG	F
NO#	Kelley, Thomas P. - ***I Found Cleopatra*** [1950]	$2.50	$7.50	$15.00
NN-1	Steele, Tedd - ***Artists, Models and Murder*** [1946]	$2.00	$6.00	$12.00
NN-2	Martin, George Victor - ***Mark It With A Stone*** [1947] PBO.	$2.00	$6.00	$12.00
03	Lord, David - ***The Ravager*** [1947]	$2.50	$7.50	$15.00
04	Nichols, Fan - ***Possess Me Not*** [1946]	$2.50	$7.50	$15.00
05	Anthology - ***Comments On The Kinsey Report*** [1948] PBO.	$2.00	$6.00	$12.00
06	Kirkbride, Ronald - ***Broken Melody*** [1947]	$2.50	$7.50	$15.00
07	Hirsch, Lee - ***Murder Steals The Show*** [1946]	$2.00	$6.00	$12.00
08	Fast, Howard - ***The Children*** [1947]	$2.00	$6.00	$12.00
09	Taylor, April - ***Love Is A Four Letter Word*** [1947]	$2.50	$7.50	$15.00
10	DeKobra, Maurice - ***Paradise In Montparnasse*** [1947]	$2.50	$7.50	$15.00
11	Lehman, Paul Evan - ***The Cougar Of Canyon Caballo*** [1946]	$2.50	$7.50	$15.00
12	Lehman, Paul Evan - ***Blood Of The West*** [1946]	$2.50	$7.50	$15.00
13-B	Wolfson, P. J. - ***Is My Flesh Of Brass*** [1948] PBO.	$2.00	$6.00	$12.00
13-A	Nablo, James Benson - ***The Long November*** [1948] PBO.	$2.50	$7.50	$15.00
14	Schiller, Cicely - ***The Harlot*** [1948] PBO.	$2.00	$6.00	$12.00
15	Nablo, James Benson - ***The Long November*** [1948] PBO.	$2.00	$6.00	$12.00
16	Sloan, Gladys - ***Pay For Her Passion*** [1948] PBO.	$2.00	$6.00	$12.00
17	Jordan, Gail - ***Once A Sinner*** [1948] PBO.	$2.50	$7.50	$15.00
18	O'Hara, John - ***Hope Of Heaven*** [1948] PBO.	$2.50	$7.50	$15.00
19	Plaat, Charles C. - ***Better Your Bridge*** [1948]	$2.00	$6.00	$12.00
20	Sloan, Gladys - ***Negligee*** [1948] PBO.	$2.00	$6.00	$12.00
21	Stone, Thomas - ***Red Lights In The Village*** [1949] PBO.	$2.50	$7.50	$15.00
22	Jordan, Gail - ***The Lost Virgin*** [1949] PBO.	$2.00	$6.00	$12.00
23	Peel, Jan - ***The Bed And The Blonde*** [1949] PBO.	$2.00	$6.00	$12.00
24	Lindsay, Terry - ***Quean Of Tarts*** [1949] PBO.	$2.00	$6.00	$12.00
25	Wolsey, Serge C. - ***Call House Madam*** [1949] PBO.	$2.00	$6.00	$12.00
26	McMullen, Richard - ***Eager Is The Flesh*** [1949] PBO.	$2.50	$7.50	$15.00
27	Branch, Florenz - ***Pleasure After Hours*** [1949] PBO.	$2.50	$7.50	$15.00
28	Jordan, Gail - ***Run A Road To Hell*** [1949]	$2.00	$6.00	$12.00
29	Baker, Carlotta - ***Lady Of Lust*** [1949] PBO.	$2.00	$6.00	$12.00
30	Brewster, Eliot - ***Room Service*** [1949] PBO.	$2.00	$6.00	$12.00
31	Watkins, Glen - ***Private Performance*** [1949] PBO.	$2.50	$7.50	$15.00
32	Plageman, Bentz - ***Each Night A Black Desire*** [1949] PBO.	$2.00	$6.00	$12.00
33	Williams, Wright - ***Scream A Wanton Song*** [1949] PBO.	$2.00	$6.00	$12.00
34	Brewster, Elliot - ***Street Girl*** [1949] PBO.	$2.00	$6.00	$12.00
35	Clayford, James - ***The Flesh Is Willing*** [1949]	$2.50	$7.50	$15.00
36	Self, Edwin B. - ***Limbo City*** [1949] PBO.	$2.50	$7.50	$15.00
37	Clark, Dale - ***The Red Rods*** [1949] PBO.	$2.50	$7.50	$15.00
38	Semple, Gordon - ***Two Time Doll*** [1949] PBO.	$2.00	$6.00	$12.00
39	Goodis, David - ***Nightfall*** [1949] PBO.	$22.00	$70.00	$140.00
40	Wood, Brendan - ***Sligo*** [1949] PBO.	$2.00	$6.00	$12.00
41	Higgins, Russell - ***Man Crazy*** [1949] PBO.	$2.50	$7.50	$15.00
42	Watkins, Glen - ***Gloria*** [1949] PBO.	$2.50	$7.50	$15.00
43	Saxon, John - ***Pushover*** [1949] PBO.	$2.00	$6.00	$12.00
44	Wolfson, P. J. - ***Bodies Are Dust*** [1949] PBO.	$2.50	$7.50	$15.00
45	Hersch, Virginia - ***Blood And Gold*** [1949] PBO.	$2.00	$6.00	$12.00
46	Eldridge, Paul - ***Listen To Their Lust*** [1949] PBO.	$2.00	$6.00	$12.00
47	Horton, Thomas D. - ***What Men Don't Like About Women*** [1949] PBO.	$2.00	$6.00	$12.00
48	Lindsay, Perry - ***Shack-Up Girl*** [1949]	$2.00	$6.00	$12.00
49	D'Agostino, Ruth - ***Always Lock The Door*** [1949] PBO.	$2.00	$6.00	$12.00
50	Ravel, Robert - ***Fever Heat*** [1949]	$2.50	$7.50	$15.00
52	Willis, George - ***Sweet Serenader*** [1949] PBO.	$2.00	$6.00	$12.00
53	Douglas, Milton - ***Sin For Your Supper*** [1949] PBO.	$2.00	$6.00	$12.00
54	Thompson, Jim - ***Heed The Thunder*** [1949]	$35.00	$125.00	$300.00
55	Park, J. A. - ***Dangerous Escapade*** [1949] PBO.	$2.00	$6.00	$12.00
56	Carter, Ralph - ***Love For Hire*** [1949] PBO.	$2.00	$6.00	$12.00
57	Aistrop, Jack - ***The Lights Are Low*** [1949] PBO.	$2.50	$7.50	$15.00

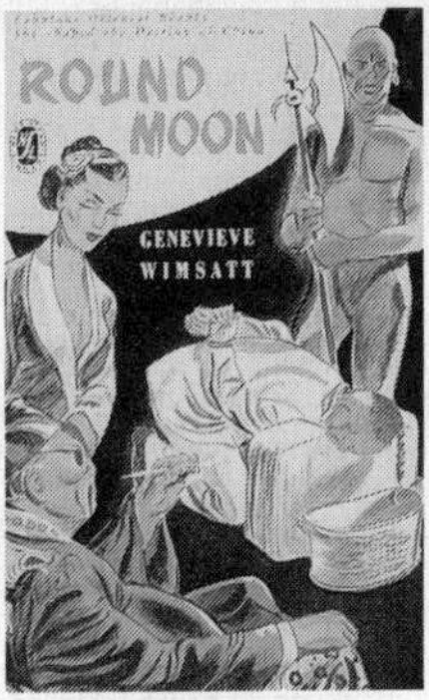

News Stand Library, 91

Novel Library, 6

Novel Library, 26

		G	VG	F
58	Carter, Ralph - ***No Resistance*** [1949] PBO.	$2.50	$7.50	$15.00
59	Romaine, Jack - ***Pagan*** [1949] PBO.	$2.00	$6.00	$12.00
60	Hughes, C. - ***He Dared Not Look Behind*** [1949]	$2.00	$6.00	$12.00
61	Morley, Jack - ***Take Another Lover*** [1949] PBO.	$2.50	$7.50	$15.00
62	Smart, Alexander - ***Sin City*** [1949] PBO.	$2.00	$6.00	$12.00
63	Clugston, Kate - ***A Murderer In The House*** [1949] PBO.	$2.00	$6.00	$12.00
64	Dailey, Clark W. - ***Gang Girl*** [1949] PBO.	$2.50	$7.50	$15.00
65	Parrott, Ursula - ***Love Goes Past*** [1949] PBO.	$2.00	$6.00	$12.00
66	Perrin, Niel H. - ***This Was Joanna*** [1949] PBO.	$2.50	$7.50	$15.00
67	Henderson, H. G. - ***Frustration*** [1949] PBO.	$2.50	$7.50	$15.00
68	Burke, Thomas - ***China Town Baby*** [1949] PBO.	$3.50	$10.00	$20.00
69	Ostenson, Martha - ***And The Town Talked*** [1949] PBO.	$2.00	$6.00	$12.00
70	Doherty, Alice K. - ***Love Is A Long Shot*** [1949] PBO.	$2.00	$6.00	$12.00
71	Smith, Gustin - ***Marriage À-La-Mode*** [1949] PBO.	$2.00	$6.00	$12.00
72	Wilbur, Justus D. - ***Sex Is Everybody's Business*** [1949] PBO.	$2.50	$7.50	$15.00
73	Lockwood, Eleanor Stanley - ***Fatal Shadows*** [1949] PBO.	$2.00	$6.00	$12.00
74	Dailey, Clark W. - ***Soft To The Touch*** [1949] PBO.	$2.00	$6.00	$12.00
75	Perrin, Niel H. - ***Introducing Mr. Phreet*** [1949]	$2.00	$6.00	$12.00
77	Stratten, Ralph - ***Bed Of Thorns*** [1949] PBO.	$2.00	$6.00	$12.00
78	Hendry, George - ***Never Kiss A Stranger*** [1949] PBO.	$2.00	$6.00	$12.00
80	Raymond, Fay - ***Detour*** [1949] PBO.	$2.50	$7.50	$15.00
81	Krier, H. J. - ***Office Girl*** [1949] PBO.	$2.00	$6.00	$12.00
82	Warren, Laura - ***I Confess*** [1949] PBO.	$2.50	$7.50	$15.00
83	Dailey, Clark W. - ***Trial Before Marriage*** [1949]	$3.00	$9.00	$18.00
84	Palmer, Al - ***Sugar Puss On Dorchester Street*** [1949] PBO.	$3.00	$9.00	$18.00
85	Holmes, Raymond - ***The Winter Of Time*** [1949] PBO.	$2.00	$6.00	$12.00
86	Brown, Joy - ***Murdered Mistress*** [1949] PBO.	$2.50	$7.50	$15.00
87	Winston, Daomi - ***In Adams Country*** [1949] PBO.	$2.50	$7.50	$15.00
88	Swift, Julian - ***Lover Boy*** [1950] PBO.	$2.50	$7.50	$15.00
89	Perrin, Neil H. - ***Death Be My Destiny*** [1950] PBO.	$2.50	$7.50	$15.00
90	Clare, Philip - ***Tough Guy*** [1950] PBO.	$3.00	$9.00	$18.00
91	Wimsatt, Genevieve - ***Round Moon*** [1950] PBO.	$3.50	$10.00	$20.00
93	Knight, Fletcher - ***Daughters Of Desire*** [1950] PBO.	$2.50	$7.50	$15.00
94	Brown, Horace - ***Penthouse Killings*** [1950] PBO.	$2.50	$7.50	$15.00
95	Fisher, Leonard - ***Let Out The Beast*** [1950] PBO.	$3.50	$10.00	$20.00
100	Hanley, Jack - ***Tomcat In Tights*** [1950] PBO.	$2.00	$6.00	$12.00
101	Kline, Curt - ***Racket Boss*** [1950] PBO.	$2.50	$7.50	$15.00
102	Scott, Leslie - ***Pick-Up*** [1950] PBO.	$2.00	$6.00	$12.00
103	Jordan, Gail - ***Sin And Shackles*** [1950]	$3.00	$9.00	$18.00
104	Bennett, Hall - ***Never See The Sun*** [1950] PBO.	$2.00	$6.00	$12.00
106	Shelley, Peter - ***Soft Shoulders*** [1950] PBO.	$2.50	$7.50	$15.00

		G	VG	F
107	Scott, Anthony - ***Carnival Of Love*** [1950] PBO.	$2.50	$7.50	$15.00
108	Phillips, Rog - ***Time Trap*** [1950]	$6.00	$20.00	$40.00
109	Marsh, Peter - ***The Devil's Daughter*** [1950]	$3.00	$9.00	$18.00
110	Marsto, Alan - ***Strange Desire*** [1950] PBO. Cover art by Syd Dyke.	$3.00	$9.00	$18.00
111	Greenshade, Ted - ***He Learned About Women*** [1950] PBO.	$2.50	$7.50	$15.00
112	Carrol, Rose - ***The Restless Dead*** [1950] PBO.	$5.50	$17.50	$35.00
113	Lynch, William - ***The Intimate Stranger*** [1950] PBO.	$2.50	$7.50	$15.00
114	Wilstack, John - ***Blonde Tigress*** [1950] Cover art by Syd Dyke.	$2.50	$7.50	$15.00
117	Martin, Gerry - ***Too Many Women*** [1950] PBO.	$2.50	$7.50	$15.00
118	Franklin, Grant - ***Vice Ring Murders*** [1950] PBO.	$2.50	$7.50	$15.00
119	Bligh, Norman - ***A Harlot In Town*** [1950] PBO.	$2.50	$7.50	$15.00
120	Hopson, William - ***Desperado's Showdown*** [1950] PBO.	$2.00	$6.00	$12.00
121	Carder, Leigh - ***Outlaw Justice*** [1950] PBO.	$2.00	$6.00	$12.00
122	Kelley, Thomas P. - ***The Gorilla's Daughter*** [1950] PBO.	$20.00	$60.00	$125.00
124	Carrol, Rose - ***Sex Life Among Savage People*** [1950] PBO.	$2.00	$6.00	$12.00
125	Childerness, George - ***Murder In False Face*** [1950] PBO.	$2.50	$7.50	$15.00
126	Hopson, William - ***Hell's Horseman*** [1950] PBO.	$2.00	$6.00	$12.00
127	Floren, Lee - ***Gunsmoke*** [1950] PBO.	$2.50	$7.50	$15.00
128	Willard, Joshua - ***A Killer Backstage*** [1950] PBO.	$2.00	$6.00	$12.00
129	Michel, Scott - ***Dear Dead Harry*** [1950] PBO.	$2.50	$7.50	$15.00
131	Green, Gordon - ***Pillar Of Fire*** [1950] PBO.	$2.50	$7.50	$15.00
132	Grinstead, J. E. - ***Blood On The Range*** [1950] PBO.	$2.50	$7.50	$15.00
133	Leinster, Murray - ***Outlaw Deputy*** [1950] PBO.	$2.50	$7.50	$15.00
134	Palmer, Al - ***Montreal Confidential*** [1950] PBO.	$2.50	$7.50	$15.00
135	Trimble, Louis - ***Design For Dying*** [1950] PBO.	$2.00	$6.00	$12.00
136	Levinson, Saul - ***Red Hot Murder*** [1950] PBO.	$2.50	$7.50	$15.00
137	Clift, Denison - ***Espionage Agent*** [1950] PBO.	$2.00	$6.00	$12.00
138	Stelle, Tedd - ***Trail Of Fengeance*** [1950] PBO.	$2.50	$7.50	$15.00
139	Stonebraker, Florence - ***Reno Tramp*** [1950] PBO.	$2.00	$6.00	$12.00
140	Cameron, Don - ***White For A Shroud*** [1950]	$2.00	$6.00	$12.00
141	Jenkins, Will F. - ***Destroy The U.S.A.*** [1950]	$6.00	$20.00	$40.00
142	Phillips, Rog - ***Worlds Within*** [1950]	$6.00	$20.00	$40.00
143	Dale, William - ***Corpse Hands Off*** [1950] PBO.	$2.00	$6.00	$12.00
144	Ketchum, Philip - ***Kill At Dusk*** [1950]	$3.00	$9.00	$18.00
145	Caney, G. Murray - ***Save A Kiss For Satan*** [1950] PBO.	$2.50	$7.50	$15.00
146	Carroll, Rose - ***Tawny Witch*** [1950] PBO.	$2.50	$7.50	$15.00
147	Kent, Bruce - ***Directed By The Devil*** [1950] PBO.	$2.50	$7.50	$15.00
148	Harvey, Gene - ***A Man To Play With*** [1950] PBO.	$2.50	$7.50	$15.00
150-A	Harding, Bruce - ***Two Men & A Mistress*** [1951] PBO.	$2.00	$6.00	$12.00
150	Duperrault, Doug - ***Ten Cents A Tussle*** [1950]	$2.00	$6.00	$12.00
151-A	Simpson, Donna - ***Lust For Love*** [1951] PBO.	$2.50	$7.50	$15.00
151-B	Himmel, Richard - ***Soul Of Passion*** [1950] PBO.	$2.00	$6.00	$12.00
152	Tremblay, George - ***Everybody Loves Irene*** [1951] PBO.	$2.50	$7.50	$15.00
153	Knowles, Martha (Peggy Gaddis) - ***Suzie Needs A Man*** [1951]	$2.50	$7.50	$15.00
155	Bligh, Norman - ***Harlot In Her Heart*** [1951] PBO.	$2.50	$7.50	$15.00
157	Clayford, James - ***Street Girl*** [1951] PBO.	$2.50	$7.50	$15.00

News Stand Library Second Series. Toronto: Export Publishing.

		G	VG	F
1-A	Sloan, Gladys - ***Negligee*** [1949]	$1.50	$5.00	$10.00
2-A	Nablo, James Benson - ***The Long November*** [1949]	$1.50	$5.00	$10.00
3-A	Wolfson, P.J. - ***Pay For Her Passion*** [1949]	$1.50	$5.00	$10.00
4-A	Plagemann, Bentz - ***Each Night A Black Desire*** [1949]	$1.50	$5.00	$10.00
5-A (DJ)	Willis, George - ***Offer Any Price*** [1949] PBO. With dust-jacket.	$10.00	$30.00	$60.00
5-A	Willis, George - ***Offer Any Price*** [1949] PBO.	$1.50	$5.00	$10.00
6-A	Douglas, Milton - ***Sin For Your Supper*** [1949] PBO.	$1.50	$5.00	$10.00
6-A (DJ)	Douglas, Milton - ***Sin For Your Supper*** [1949] PBO. With dust-jacket.	$10.00	$30.00	$60.00
7-A	Benedict, Jack - ***The Pagans*** [1949] PBO.	$1.50	$5.00	$10.00
7-A (DJ)	Benedict, Jack - ***The Pagans*** [1949] PBO. With dust-jacket.	$10.00	$30.00	$60.00

		G	VG	F
8-A (DJ)	Young, Michael - ***Dirty City*** [1949] PBO. With dust-jacket.	$10.00	$30.00	$60.00
8-A	Young, Michael - ***Dirty City*** [1949] PBO.	$1.50	$5.00	$10.00
9-A	Forrest, David - ***Torch Of Violence*** [1949] PBO.	$1.50	$5.00	$10.00
9-A (DJ)	Forrest, David - ***Torch Of Violence*** [1949] PBO. With dust-jacket.	$10.00	$30.00	$60.00
10-A	Brooks, Grant R. - ***This Was Joanna*** [1949] PBO.	$1.50	$5.00	$10.00
10-A(DJ)	Brooks, Grant R. - ***This Was Joanna*** [1949] PBO. With dust-jacket.	$10.00	$30.00	$60.00
11-A(DJ)	Cooke, Ronald J. - ***The House On Craig Street*** [1949] PBO. With dust-jacket.	$10.00	$30.00	$60.00
11-A	Cooke, Ronald J. - ***The House On Craig Street*** [1949] PBO.	$1.50	$5.00	$10.00
12-A(DJ)	Clayton, Henry C. - ***Frustration*** [1949] PBO. With dust-jacket.	$10.00	$30.00	$60.00
12-A	Clayton, Henry C. - ***Frustration*** [1949] PBO.	$1.50	$5.00	$10.00
13-A(DJ)	Warren, Laura - ***No Place In Heaven*** [1949] PBO. With dust-jacket.	$10.00	$30.00	$60.00
13-A	Warren, Laura - ***No Place In Heaven*** [1949] PBO.	$1.50	$5.00	$10.00
14-A	Perrin, Neil H. - ***Death Be My Destiny*** [1949] PBO.	$1.50	$5.00	$10.00
14-A(DJ)	Perrin, Neil H. - ***Death Be My Destiny*** [1949] PBO. With dust-jacket.	$10.00	$30.00	$60.00
15-A	Kelley, Thomas P. - ***Jesse James: His Life*** [1949]	$1.50	$5.00	$10.00
15-A(DJ)	Kelley, Thomas P. - ***Jesse James: His Life*** [1949] With dust-jacket.	$10.00	$30.00	$60.00
16-A	Knight, Fletcher - ***Daughters Of Desire*** [1950] PBO. Cover art by Rickard.	$1.50	$5.00	$10.00
16-A(DJ)	Knight, Fletcher - ***Daughters Of Desire*** [1950] PBO. Cover art by Rickard. With dust-jacket.	$10.00	$30.00	$60.00
17-A(DJ)	Brown, Horace - ***The Penthouse Killings*** [1950] PBO. With dust-jacket.	$10.00	$30.00	$60.00
17-A	Brown, Horace - ***The Penthouse Killings*** [1950] PBO.	$1.50	$5.00	$10.00
18-A	Fischer, Leonard - ***Let Out The Beast*** [1950]	$1.50	$5.00	$10.00
18-A(DJ)	Fischer, Leonard - ***Let Out The Beast*** [1950] With dust-jacket.	$10.00	$30.00	$60.00
19-A(DJ)	Brown, Joy - ***In Passion's Fiery Pit*** [1950] PBO. Cover art by Dyke. With dust-jacket.	$10.00	$30.00	$60.00
19-A	Brown, Joy - ***In Passion's Fiery Pit*** [1950] PBO. Cover art by Dyke.	$1.50	$5.00	$10.00
20-A	Palmer, Al - ***Sugar-Puss*** [1950] PBO. Cover art by Dyke.	$1.50	$5.00	$10.00
20-A(DJ)	Palmer, Al - ***Sugar-Puss*** [1950] PBO. Cover art by Dyke. With dust-jacket.	$10.00	$30.00	$60.00
21-A(DJ)	Perrin, Neil H. - ***The Door Between*** [1950] PBO. With dust-jacket.	$10.00	$30.00	$60.00
21-A	Perrin, Neil H. - ***The Door Between*** [1950] PBO.	$1.50	$5.00	$10.00
22-A(DJ)	Desmond, Warren - ***The Governor's Mistress*** [1950] PBO. With dust-jacket.	$10.00	$30.00	$60.00
22-A	Desmond, Warren - ***The Governor's Mistress*** [1950] PBO.	$1.50	$5.00	$10.00
23-A(DJ)	Scott, Leslie - ***Pick-Up*** [1950] PBO. Cover art by Chapman. With dust-jacket.	$10.00	$30.00	$60.00
23-A	Scott, Leslie - ***Pick-Up*** [1950] PBO. Cover art by Chapman.	$1.50	$5.00	$10.00
24-A(DJ)	Mark, Stephen - ***Overnight Escapade*** [1950] PBO. Cover art by Syd Dyke. With dust-jacket.	$10.00	$30.00	$60.00
24-A	Mark, Stephen - ***Overnight Escapade*** [1950] PBO. Cover art by Syd Dyke.	$1.50	$5.00	$10.00
25-A	Malston, Alan - ***Strange Desires*** [1950] Cover art by Syd Dyke.	$1.50	$5.00	$10.00
26-A	Greenshade, Ted - ***He Learned About Women...*** [1950] PBO. Cover art by Syd Dyke.	$1.50	$5.00	$10.00
27-A	Warwick, Jarvis - ***Waste No Tears*** [1950] PBO. Cover art by Syd Dyke.	$1.50	$5.00	$10.00
28-A	Martin, Gerry - ***Too Many Women*** [1950] PBO. Cover art by Syd Dyke.	$1.50	$5.00	$10.00

Newsstand Library Magenta Books. Chicago: Newsstand Library, Inc.

		G	VG	F
U-101	Locke, Friday - ***Streets Paved With Gold*** [1958] Cover art by Stake.	$1.35	$4.00	$8.00
U-102	Rubel, James L. - ***The Fraudulent Broad*** [1960]	$1.35	$4.00	$8.00
U-103	Bunyan, Pat - ***The Big Blues*** [1960] Cover art by Stake.	$1.35	$4.00	$8.00
U-104	Bradbury, William - ***All The Natives Are Lovers*** [1958] PBO.	$1.35	$4.00	$8.00
U-105	Nixon, Henry Lewis - ***The Bawdy Mrs. Grey*** [1960] PBO.	$1.35	$4.00	$8.00
U-106	Hastings, March - ***The Demands Of The Flesh*** [1960] Cover art by Stake.	$1.35	$4.00	$8.00
U-107	Graeme, G.A. - ***The Peddlers*** [1960] PBO.	$1.35	$4.00	$8.00
U-108	Rubel, James L. - ***Any Two Can Play*** [1959] PBO.	$1.35	$4.00	$8.00
U-109	Hastings, March - ***Obsessed*** [1959] PBO.	$1.35	$4.00	$8.00
U-110	Harsh, James - ***Riptide*** [1959] Cover art by Edgar.	$1.35	$4.00	$8.00
U-111	Dean, Nancy as told to Jack Powers - ***Twenty Years Behind Red Curtains*** [1959] Cover art by Edgar.	$1.35	$4.00	$8.00
U-112	Smith, George H. - ***Whip Of Passion*** [1959] Cover art by Edgar.	$1.50	$5.00	$10.00
U-113	Nixon, Henry Lewis - ***Six For Flight 13*** [1959] PBO. Cover art by Stake.	$1.35	$4.00	$8.00
U-114	Greame, G.A. - ***The Evil Ear*** [1959] PBO.	$1.35	$4.00	$8.00
U-115	Smith, George H. - ***Dark Desire!*** [1959] PBO.	$1.35	$4.00	$8.00
U-116	Hastings, March - ***Fear Of Incest*** [1959] PBO.	$1.35	$4.00	$8.00
U-117	Culver, Edward - ***She Had To Be Loved*** [1959] PBO.	$1.35	$4.00	$8.00
U-118	Hastings, March - ***Veil Of Torment*** [1959]	$1.35	$4.00	$8.00
U-120	Sellers, Connie - ***Private World*** [1959]	$1.35	$4.00	$8.00
U-121	Spalding, H.D. - ***The Yellow Press*** [1959] Cover art by Bonfils.	$1.35	$4.00	$8.00
U-122	Edd, Karl - ***The Tenement Kid*** [1959] PBO.	$1.35	$4.00	$8.00
U-123	Gramee, G.A. - ***The Wife Traders*** [1959] Cover art by Bonfils.	$1.35	$4.00	$8.00
U-124	King, Don - ***Bitter Love*** [1959] PBO.	$1.35	$4.00	$8.00
U-125	Dunn, Brian - ***The Censored Screen*** [1959] Cover art by Bonfils.	$1.35	$4.00	$8.00
U-126	Heron, Joseph - ***Agreement To Love*** [1959] PBO. Cover art by Bonfils.	$1.35	$4.00	$8.00
U-127	Smith, Pauline C. - ***Carnal Greed*** [1960] PBO. Cover art by Bonfils.	$1.35	$4.00	$8.00
U-128	Corbett, Guy - ***The Grip Of Lust*** [1960]	$1.35	$4.00	$8.00
U-129	Hayes, Robert - ***Black Desire*** [1960]	$1.35	$4.00	$8.00
U-130	Carpenter, Jay - ***The Youngest Harlot*** [1960] PBO. Cover by Bonfils.	$1.50	$5.00	$10.00
U-131	Smith, George H. - ***Swamp Bred*** [1960] Cover art by Bonfils.	$1.50	$5.00	$10.00
U-132	Marcus, Carl - ***Arrividerci, Ava*** [1960] PBO. Cover art by Bonfils.	$1.35	$4.00	$8.00
U-133	Rubel, James - ***The Wanton One*** [1960] Cover art by Bonfils.	$1.35	$4.00	$8.00
U-134	Anderson, M. - ***Her Mother's Husband*** [1960]	$1.35	$4.00	$8.00
U-135	Moore, Hal R. - ***Shanty Girl*** [1960] PBO. Cover art by Bonfils.	$2.00	$6.00	$12.00
U-136	Silver, Hy - ***Bogus Lover*** [1960] Cover art by Bonfils.	$1.35	$4.00	$8.00
U-137	Willeford, Charles - ***The Woman Chaser*** [1960] PBO. Cover art by Bonfils.	$20.00	$60.00	$125.00
U-138	Toward, George - ***Come Sin With Me*** [1960] Cover art by Bonfils.	$1.35	$4.00	$8.00
U-139	Booth, Edward - ***Torch Of Desire*** [1960] Cover art by Bonfils.	$1.35	$4.00	$8.00
U-140	Wand, Della - ***Devil's Caress*** [1960] PBO. Cover art by Bonfils.	$1.35	$4.00	$8.00
U-141	Shedd, Robert K. - ***The Wicked Wife*** [1960]	$1.35	$4.00	$8.00
U-142	Hickerson, Clayton - ***Diploma Of Passion*** [1960]	$1.35	$4.00	$8.00
U-143	Jackson, W. Warner - ***Cavern Of Rage*** [1960] PBO.	$1.35	$4.00	$8.00
U-144	Egis, Richard E. - ***Like Crazy, Man*** [1960] PBO. Cover by Bonfils.	$2.50	$7.50	$15.00
U-145	Glaser, Alfred B. - ***Creature Of Sin*** [1960]	$1.35	$4.00	$8.00
U-146	Booth, Edward - ***Deadly Desire*** [1960] PBO.	$1.35	$4.00	$8.00
U-147	Toward, George P. - ***Lesbos Hill*** [1960]	$2.00	$6.00	$12.00
U-148	Allan, Jack - ***Good Time Girl*** [1960] PBO.	$1.35	$4.00	$8.00

		G	VG	F
U-149	Wand, Della - ***On The Make*** [1960] PBO. Cover art by Bonfils.	$1.35	$4.00	$8.00
U-150	Booth, Edward - ***Chains Of Passion*** [1960]	$1.35	$4.00	$8.00
U-151	Rock, Hote - ***Mr. Madam*** [1961] PBO. Cover art by Bonfils.	$1.35	$4.00	$8.00
U-152	Hastings, March - ***Crack-Up*** [1960] PBO. Cover by Bonfils.	$1.35	$4.00	$8.00
U-153	Kelsey, Roy - ***The Amorous Avenger*** [1960] Cover art by Bonfils.	$1.35	$4.00	$8.00
U-154	Kelsey, Roy - ***Affair On Board*** [1960]	$1.35	$4.00	$8.00
U-155	Allan, Jack - ***Love Is A Gentle Whip*** [1960] PBO. Cover by Bonfils.	$1.50	$5.00	$10.00
U-156	Lee, Don - ***A Matter Of Adultery*** [1960] PBO.	$1.35	$4.00	$8.00
U-157	Hastings, March - ***The 3rd Theme*** [1960] PBO. Cover art by Bonfils.	$1.50	$5.00	$10.00
U-158	Zachary, Hugh - ***One Day In Hell*** [1960] PBO. Cover art by Bonfils.	$1.35	$4.00	$8.00
U-159	Heron, Joseph - ***So Strange Our Love*** [1960]	$1.35	$4.00	$8.00
U-160	Vinning, Keith - ***A Family Affair*** [1960] PBO. Cover art by Bonfils.	$1.35	$4.00	$8.00
U-161	McLane, Jr., Ben V. - ***Chasm Of Lust*** [1960] PBO.	$1.35	$4.00	$8.00
U-162	Tyler, John - ***You Can't Escape Me!*** [1960] PBO. Cover by Bonfils.	$1.35	$4.00	$8.00
U-163	Martin, Edgar A. - ***Portrait Of Torment*** [1960] PBO. Cover art by Bonfils.	$1.35	$4.00	$8.00
U-164	Kruger, Paul - ***Bedroom Alibi*** [1961] PBO.	$1.35	$4.00	$8.00
U-165	Austin, William A. - ***Commit The Sins*** [1960] PBO. Cover art by Bonfils.	$1.50	$5.00	$10.00
U-166	Curtis, Paul - ***Chained Sex*** [1960] PBO.	$1.35	$4.00	$8.00
U-167	Maschke, T.A. - ***Sex Is Like Money*** [1960] PBO. Cover art by Bonfils.	$1.35	$4.00	$8.00
U-168	Berryman, Opal Leigh - ***Make It On Temple Street*** [1960] PBO. Cover art by Bonfils.	$2.50	$7.50	$15.00
U-169	Carney, Robert - ***Anything Goes*** [1960] PBO. Cover art by Bonfils.	$1.35	$4.00	$8.00
U-170	Willeford, Charles - ***Understudy For Love*** [1961] PBO. Cover art by Bonfils.	$20.00	$60.00	$125.00
U-171	Gooch, Mary Shomette - ***Amorous Dietician*** [1961] PBO. Cover by Bonfils.	$1.35	$4.00	$8.00
U-172	Vail, Thomas - ***Blackmail And Old Lace*** [1961] PBO. Cover art by Bonfils.	$1.35	$4.00	$8.00
U-173	Abrams, Ted E. - ***Sinful Cowboy*** [1961] PBO. Cover art by Bonfils.	$1.35	$4.00	$8.00
U-174	Caryl, Warren - ***Whirlpool Of Thunder*** [1961] PBO. Cover art by Bonfils.	$1.35	$4.00	$8.00
U-175	Potter, J.L. - ***Jambalaya Loverman*** [1961] PBO. Cover art by Bonfils.	$1.35	$4.00	$8.00
U-176	Bell, Steve - ***Venus Of Lesbos*** [1961] PBO. Cover art by Bonfils.	$1.50	$5.00	$10.00
U-177	Storey, Philip - ***Four O'Clock On Friday*** [1961] PBO. Cover art by Bonfils.	$1.35	$4.00	$8.00
U-178	Curtis, Paul - ***Deadly Deceit*** [1961] PBO. Cover art by Bonfils.	$1.35	$4.00	$8.00
U-179	Wiseman, William R. - ***Drawn By Desire*** [1961] PBO. Cover art by Bonfils.	$1.35	$4.00	$8.00
U-180	Brennan, Dan - ***Doomed Sinner*** [1961] PBO.	$1.35	$4.00	$8.00
U-181	Wind, Dorothy - ***The Insatiable Lisa*** [1962] PBO. Cover art by Bonfils.	$1.35	$4.00	$8.00
U-182	Willeford, Charles - ***No Experience Necessary*** [1962] PBO. Cover art by Bonfils.	$20.00	$60.00	$125.00
U-183	Dowling, Lillian - ***Sexy Psycho*** [1962] PBO. Cover art by Bonfils.	$1.35	$4.00	$8.00
U-184	Barksdale, Bob & Hunter, Robert - ***Back Seat Lover*** [1962]	$1.35	$4.00	$8.00
501	Marcus, Carl - ***The Lewd Angel*** [1959] PBO.	$1.35	$4.00	$8.00

No.	Entry	G	VG	F
502	Bell, Steve - ***Honey Babe*** [1959] PBO.	$1.50	$5.00	$10.00
503	Smith, George H. - ***The Georgeous Devil*** [1959] PBO.	$1.50	$5.00	$10.00
U-504	Giacomo Dee, Richard D. - ***Curiosities Of Medicine*** [1959]	$1.35	$4.00	$8.00
505	Douglas, William K. - ***Savage Breed*** [1959] PBO.	$1.35	$4.00	$8.00
506	Karney, Louis - ***The Devil's Lash*** [1959]	$1.35	$4.00	$8.00
507	Smith, George H. - ***Satan's Mate*** [1959]	$1.50	$5.00	$10.00
508	Martin, Thom - ***Serenade To Seduction*** [1959]	$1.35	$4.00	$8.00
509	Michaud, Don - ***The Beckoning Flame*** [1960] PBO.	$1.35	$4.00	$8.00
510	Culver, Edward - ***Playhouse Of Passion*** [1960]	$1.35	$4.00	$8.00
511	Gillan, Jr., B.J. - ***Office Playgirl*** [1960]	$1.35	$4.00	$8.00
512	Del Rocco, Vince - ***Only Her Body For Sale*** [1960] PBO. Cover art by Robert Bonfils.	$1.35	$4.00	$8.00
513	Chestnut, Robert - ***The Syndicate*** [1960] PBO. Cover art by Bonfils.	$1.35	$4.00	$8.00
514	Lane, Wanda - ***Red House On Green Street*** [1960] Cover art by Bonfils.	$1.35	$4.00	$8.00
515	Harvey, James - ***Daughter Of Joy*** [1960]	$1.50	$5.00	$10.00
516	Mertes, Jack - ***Bobby Sox Sinners*** [1960]	$1.35	$4.00	$8.00
517	Geis, Richard E. - ***Sex Kitten*** [1960] PBO.	$1.50	$5.00	$10.00
518	Flanningan, J.A. - ***Vagabond Virgin*** [1960] Cover art by Bonfils.	$1.35	$4.00	$8.00
519	Jackson, Warner - ***Lust For Youth*** [1960]	$1.35	$4.00	$8.00
520	Stacy, Jan - ***Twilight House*** [1960] PBO.	$1.50	$5.00	$10.00
521	Kingston, Paul - ***Gallery Of Perversion*** [1960] PBO.	$1.35	$4.00	$8.00
522	Lauren, Bill - ***Blonde Danger*** [1960]	$1.35	$4.00	$8.00
524	Laird, Andrew - ***Too Hot For Hell*** [1960] PBO.	$1.35	$4.00	$8.00

Nightstand Books. Milwaukee: Freedom Publishing.

No.	Entry	G	VG	F
1501	Elliott, Don (Robert Silverberg) - ***Love Addict*** [1959] PBO.	$3.50	$10.00	$20.00
1502	McCormick, John - ***Lust Club*** [1959]	$1.25	$3.75	$7.50
NB-1503	Merchant, Paul (Harlan Ellison) - ***Sex Gang*** [1959] Three printings as follows: 1503-aSn, 1st printing; 1503-R, 2nd printing; Reed Nightstand 3003, 1973, 3rd printing.	$50.00	$175.00	$400.00
1504	Elliott, Don (Robert Silverberg) - ***Gang Girl*** [1959] PBO.	$3.50	$10.00	$20.00
1506	Williams, J.X. - ***Carnival Of Lust*** [n.d.] Cover by McCauley.	$1.25	$3.75	$7.50
1507	Holliday, Don - ***The Wild Night*** [1960] Cover by McCauley.	$1.25	$3.75	$7.50
1508	Elliott, Don (Robert Silverberg) - ***Summertime Affair*** [1960] PBO.	$1.50	$5.00	$10.00
1509	Elliott, Don (Robert Silverberg) - ***Party Girl*** [1960] PBO. Cover by McCauley.	$1.50	$5.00	$10.00
1511	Shaw, Andrew - ***The Adulteress*** [1960]	$1.25	$3.75	$7.50
1512	Elliott, Don (Robert Silverberg) - ***Naked Holiday*** [1960] Cover by McCauley.	$1.50	$5.00	$10.00
1513	Dexter, John - ***No Longer A Virgin*** [1960] PBO. Cover by McCauley.	$1.25	$3.75	$7.50
1514	Longman, Marlene - ***Sin Girls*** [1960] PBO.	$5.00	$15.00	$30.00
1515	Holliday, Don - ***Passion School*** [1960] Cover by McCauley.	$1.25	$3.75	$7.50
1516	Elliott, Don (Robert Silverberg) - ***Sin On Wheels*** [1960] Cover by McCauley.	$1.50	$5.00	$10.00
1518	Holiday, Don - ***Sin Hotel*** [n.d.]	$1.25	$3.75	$7.50
1519	Dexter, John - ***Miami Call Girl*** [n.d.]	$1.25	$3.75	$7.50
1521	Elliott, Don (Robert Silverberg) - ***Passion Trap*** [1960] PBO.	$1.50	$5.00	$10.00
1522	Holliday, Don - ***The Girls Upstairs*** [1960] PBO.	$1.25	$3.75	$7.50
1523	Longman, Marlene - ***Lesbian Love*** [1960] PBO.	$4.00	$12.50	$25.00
1525	Allison, Clyde - ***The Lustful Ones*** [1960] PBO.	$1.35	$4.00	$8.00
1526	Shaw, Andrew - ***The Wife-Swappers*** [1960] PBO.	$1.25	$3.75	$7.50
1527	James, Al - ***Sex Model*** [1960] PBO.	$1.25	$3.75	$7.50
1528	Elliott, Don (Robert Silverberg) - ***The Lecher*** [1960] PBO.	$1.50	$5.00	$10.00
1529	Elliott, Don (Robert Silverberg) - ***The Flesh Peddlers*** [1960] PBO.	$1.50	$5.00	$10.00

		G	VG	F
1530	Dexter, John - ***Stripper!*** [1960] PBO.	$ .75	$2.50	$5.00

Novel Books. Chicago: Novel Books, Inc.

		G	VG	F
3501	Lynn, Jack - ***Nympho Lodge*** [1959] PBO.	$1.00	$3.00	$6.00
3502	Savage, Jack - ***Torture Love-Cage*** [1959] PBO.	$1.00	$3.00	$6.00
3503	Low, Glenn - ***Virgin Bounty*** [1959] PBO.	$1.25	$3.75	$7.50
3504	Fisher, Louis - ***Seduction On The Run!*** [1959] PBO.	$1.00	$3.00	$6.00
3505	Walters, Hank - ***Lucky Rape*** [1960] PBO.	$1.00	$3.00	$6.00
3506	Dawn, Conrad - ***Chartered Love*** [1960] PBO.	$1.25	$3.75	$7.50
3507	Walters, Hank - ***"Dammit-Don't Touch My Broad!"*** [1960]	$1.25	$3.75	$7.50
3508	Low, Glenn - ***Forbidden Love*** [1960] PBO. Partial photo cover.	$1.00	$3.00	$6.00
5001	Whelan, Ron - ***Brute Passion*** [1960] PBO.	$1.00	$3.00	$6.00
5002	Lynn, Jack - ***Torrid Twins*** [1960] PBO.	$1.25	$3.75	$7.50
5003	Orleans, Mike - ***Makeout Charlie*** [1960] PBO.	$1.25	$3.75	$7.50
5004	Low, Glenn - ***Backhill Sinners*** [1960] PBO.	$1.00	$3.00	$6.00
5005	Smith, George H. - ***Swamp Lust*** [1960] PBO.	$1.00	$3.00	$6.00
5006	Lynn, Jack - ***Mad For Kicks*** [1960] PBO.	$1.25	$3.75	$7.50
5007	Lynn, Jack - ***Loverboy!*** [1960] PBO.	$1.25	$3.75	$7.50
5008	Smith, George H. - ***Delta Doll*** [1960] PBO.	$1.25	$3.75	$7.50
5009	Low, Glenn - ***Sin Eater*** [1960] PBO.	$1.00	$3.00	$6.00
5010	Smith, George H. - ***Bayou Babe*** [1960] PBO.	$1.25	$3.75	$7.50
5011	Fisher, Louis - ***Wild Party*** [1960]	$1.00	$3.00	$6.00
5012	Smith, George H. - ***Sadist On The Loose!*** [1960]	$1.25	$3.75	$7.50
5013	Skinner, Mike - ***Playboy In Paris*** [1960] PBO. Photo cover.	$1.00	$3.00	$6.00
5014	Lynn, Jack - ***Broad Bait*** [1960] PBO.	$1.00	$3.00	$6.00
5017	Smith, George H. - ***The Golden Hussy*** [1960] PBO.	$1.25	$3.75	$7.50
5018	Low, Glenn - ***Perverted Passions*** [1960] PBO.	$1.00	$3.00	$6.00
5019	Sellers, Connie - ***Willing Women*** [1960] PBO.	$1.00	$3.00	$6.00
5021	Richmond, Roe - ***Forced Gigolos*** [1960] PBO.	$1.00	$3.00	$6.00
5022	Sellers, Connie - ***Pleasure House*** [1960] PBO. Photo cover.	$1.25	$3.75	$7.50
5023	Smith, George H. - ***Hot Stuff*** [1960] PBO.	$1.25	$3.75	$7.50
5024	Low, Glenn - ***Marks Of Lust*** [1960]	$1.00	$3.00	$6.00
5025	Sellers, Connie - ***Animal Broad*** [1960] PBO. Photo cover.	$1.00	$3.00	$6.00
5027	Lynn, Jack - ***The Passion Pit*** [1960] PBO.	$1.00	$3.00	$6.00
5028	Sellers, Connie - ***Wench!*** [1960] PBO. Photo cover.	$1.00	$3.00	$6.00
5029	Smith, George H. - ***Hot Jazz*** [1960]	$1.25	$3.75	$7.50
5030	Low, Glenn - ***Honey Blood*** [1960]	$1.00	$3.00	$6.00
5031	Sellers, Connie - ***Brute*** [1961] PBO.	$1.00	$3.00	$6.00
5032	Horn, Allan - ***The Teaser*** [1961] PBO. Photo cover.	$1.00	$3.00	$6.00
5033	Baker, Jr., Ledru - ***Brute Madness*** [1961]	$1.00	$3.00	$6.00
5034	Lynn, Jack - ***Wild Women*** [1961] PBO.	$1.00	$3.00	$6.00
5035	Skinner, Mike - ***Playground Of Violence*** [1961]	$1.00	$3.00	$6.00
5036	Brennan, Dan - ***Taken!*** [1961] PBO.	$1.00	$3.00	$6.00
5037	Dawn, Conrad - ***Oriental Orgy*** [1961]	$1.25	$3.75	$7.50
5038	Lynn, Jack - ***Women On The Loose*** [1961] PBO.	$1.00	$3.00	$6.00
5039	Sellers, Connie - ***Vagabond Lover*** [1961] PBO.	$1.25	$3.75	$7.50
5041	Tremont, Victor - ***Anything For Money*** [1961] PBO. Photo cover.	$1.25	$3.75	$7.50
5043	Skinner, Mike - ***Goddess Of Trouble*** [1961] PBO. Photo cover.	$1.00	$3.00	$6.00
5044	Hayes, Bob - ***The Cheaters*** [1961] PBO.	$1.00	$3.00	$6.00
5045	Sellers, Connie - ***Big Man*** [1961] PBO.	$1.25	$3.75	$7.50
5046	Tralins, Bob - ***Torrid Island*** [1961] PBO.	$1.00	$3.00	$6.00
5047	Walters, Hank - ***Hood's Mistress*** [1961] PBO.	$1.00	$3.00	$6.00
5048	James, Al - ***Potent Stuff*** [1961] PBO. Photo cover.	$1.25	$3.75	$7.50
5049	Lynn, Jack - ***Tall And Torrid*** [1961] PBO.	$1.00	$3.00	$6.00
5050	Tralins, Bob - ***Primitive Orgy*** [1961] PBO. Photo cover.	$1.00	$3.00	$6.00
5051	Coulter, Adam - ***Savage Passions*** [1961] PBO. Photo cover.	$1.00	$3.00	$6.00
5053	Storey, Ed - ***Frustrated*** [1961]	$1.25	$3.75	$7.50
5054	Hearst, Mike - ***Primitive Passion*** [1961] PBO. Photo cover.	$1.00	$3.00	$6.00
5055	Dawn, Conrad - ***Too Much Broad*** [1961] Photo cover.	$1.00	$3.00	$6.00

		G	VG	F
5056	Lynn, Jack - ***Double Seduction*** [1961] PBO.	$1.25	$3.75	$7.50
5057	Sellers, Connie - ***Top Madam*** [1961] Photo cover.	$1.00	$3.00	$6.00
5058	Marshall, Frank - ***Shocking Adultery*** [1961] PBO.	$1.00	$3.00	$6.00
5059	Tralins, Bob - ***5 Wild Dames!*** [1961] PBO. Photo cover.	$1.25	$3.75	$7.50
5060	Sellers, Connie - ***Female Psycho Ward*** [1961]	$1.25	$3.75	$7.50
5063	Lynn, Jack - ***Forced Females*** [1961] PBO.	$1.00	$3.00	$6.00
5064	Lord, Alex - ***Giant Orgy*** [1961] PBO. Photo cover.	$1.00	$3.00	$6.00
5065	Hitt, Orrie - ***Easy Women!*** [1961] PBO. Photo cover	$1.25	$3.75	$7.50
5066	Lynn, Jack - ***Wholesale Seduction*** [1961] PBO.	$1.25	$3.75	$7.50
5067	Savage, Jack - ***Torture Love-Cage*** [1961]	$1.00	$3.00	$6.00
5068	Fisher, Lou - ***Hungry For Men!*** [1961]	$1.00	$3.00	$6.00
5071	Jordan, J. J. - ***Violent Orgy!*** [1962] PBO.	$1.00	$3.00	$6.00
5072	Brennan, Dan - ***Sleep With Me!*** [1962] PBO. Photo cover.	$1.25	$3.75	$7.50
5073	Tralins, Bob - ***Seduction Salon*** [1962] PBO.	$1.25	$3.75	$7.50
5076	Coulter, Adam - ***Uninhibited Blonde!*** [1962] Photo cover.	$1.00	$3.00	$6.00
5077	Tralins, Bob - ***Hired Nympho*** [1962] PBO. Photo cover.	$1.00	$3.00	$6.00
5083	Lynn, Jack - ***Broad Bait!*** [1962]	$1.00	$3.00	$6.00
5088	Anthony, Bill - ***Loose Women*** [1962] PBO.	$1.25	$3.75	$7.50
6001	Jakes, John - ***Powerful Passion*** [1961] PBO.	$1.25	$3.75	$7.50
6003	Dawn, Conrad - ***Amazon Lover*** [1961] PBO.	$1.00	$3.00	$6.00
6004	Vail, Ann - ***Carnal Diary*** [1961] PBO. Photo cover.	$1.00	$3.00	$6.00
6005	Carson, Lee - ***The Autobiography Of A Seductress!*** [1961] PBO. Photo cover.	$1.25	$3.75	$7.50
6009	Elliot, John - ***Wild Body!*** [1962] PBO. Photo cover.	$1.25	$3.75	$7.50
6010	Sellers, Connie - ***Lust In A Women's Prison*** [1962] PBO. Photo cover.	$1.00	$3.00	$6.00
6014	Hitt, Orrie - ***Bed Crazy*** [1962] Photo cover.	$1.00	$3.00	$6.00
6015	Jordan, J. J. - ***The Rapers*** [1962]	$1.25	$3.75	$7.50
6017	Lark, Jody - ***Gigantic Passions*** [1962] PBO. Photo cover.	$1.25	$3.75	$7.50
6018	Fisher, Lou - ***Ravished!*** [1962] PBO. Photo cover.	$1.00	$3.00	$6.00
6021	Smith, George H. - ***Farmer's Daughter*** [1962] PBO.	$1.00	$3.00	$6.00
6024	Tadrack, Moss - ***Shocking Nymphs!*** [1962] PBO. Photo cover.	$1.25	$3.75	$7.50
6026	Hitt, Orrie - ***Autobiography Of Kay Addams*** [1962] Photo cover.	$1.25	$3.75	$7.50
6035	Cannon, Frank - ***Forced Nympho*** [1962] PBO. Photo cover.	$1.25	$3.75	$7.50
6051	Weldon, Rex - ***Arouse Me!*** [1961] PBO. Photo cover.	$1.00	$3.00	$6.00
6059	Smith, George H. - ***Erotic Orgy!*** [1962]	$1.25	$3.75	$7.50
6060	Lynn, Jack - ***Unstoppable Seducer!*** [1962] PBO. Photo cover.	$1.25	$3.75	$7.50
6062	Tralins, Bob - ***Incredible Orgy*** [1962] Photo cover.	$1.00	$3.00	$6.00
6068	Trainer, Russell - ***Unbelievable 3 And 1 Orgy*** [1963] PBO. Photo cover.	$1.25	$3.75	$7.50
6074	Vick, Shelby - ***3 Thrill-Hungry Bodies*** [1963] Photo cover.	$1.00	$3.00	$6.00
6079	Tradrack, Moss - ***Carnal College!*** [1963] PBO. Photo cover.	$1.00	$3.00	$6.00
6080	Smith, George H. - ***Titine*** [1963] Photo cover.	$1.25	$3.75	$7.50
6081	Sellers, Connie - ***F. S. C.*** [1963] Cover by Arnie Kohn.	$1.25	$3.75	$7.50
6083	Lynn, Jack - ***Sensual Stenos!*** [1963] Photo cover.	$1.00	$3.00	$6.00
6089	Carson, Lee - ***Odd Orgy*** [1963] Photo cover.	$1.25	$3.75	$7.50
6094	Sellers, Connie - ***A New Kind Of Orgy*** [1963] Photo cover.	$1.00	$3.00	$6.00
6095	Cannon, Frank - ***Carnal College!*** [1963] PBO. Photo cover.	$1.00	$3.00	$6.00
6096	Hitt, Orrie - ***Inflamed Dames!*** [1963] Photo cover.	$1.25	$3.75	$7.50
6097	Hitt, Orrie - ***"I Need A Man!"*** [1963] Photo cover.	$1.25	$3.75	$7.50
6099	Skinner, Mike - ***French Passion Goddess*** [1963] Photo cover.	$1.00	$3.00	$6.00
60101	Smith, George H. - ***Female In Heat!*** [1963]	$1.25	$3.75	$7.50
60102	Logan, Richard - ***Shores' Women*** [1963] PBO. Photo cover.	$1.00	$3.00	$6.00
60103	Adams, Kay - ***Cherry*** [1963]	$1.25	$3.75	$7.50
60104	Manis, Henry - ***Reunion In Eros*** [1963] PBO. Photo cover.	$1.00	$3.00	$6.00
60106	Hayes, Bob - ***A Modern Marriage*** [1963] PBO.	$1.25	$3.75	$7.50
60107	Walter, Hank - ***"They All Touch Me..."*** [1963]	$1.00	$3.00	$6.00
60108	Oliver, Ralph - ***Big Blondes*** [1963] PBO.	$1.25	$3.75	$7.50
60109	Manis, Harry - ***Oversensual*** [1963] PBO. Photo cover.	$1.00	$3.00	$6.00
60110	Lucas, Joe - ***The Molester*** [1963] PBO.	$1.00	$3.00	$6.00

Novel Library, 42

Novel Library, 45

Penguin Book, 592

		G	VG	F
7N-710	Murphy, L. E. - ***The Blood Feast*** [1964]	$17.00	$50.00	$100.00
7N-729	Lewis, Herschell G. - ***Color Me Blood Red*** [1964] PBO. Movie tie-in with movie photo covers.	$17.00	$50.00	$100.00
7N-730	Anthology - ***Taboo*** [1964] PBO. Includes Harlan Ellison.	$12.50	$37.50	$75.00

Novel Library. Chicago: Novel Publications.

		G	VG	F
1	Woodford, Jack - ***3 Gorgeous Hussies*** [1948]	$2.50	$7.50	$15.00
2	Woodford, Jack - ***Ecstasy Girl*** [1948]	$2.50	$7.50	$15.00
3	Woodford, Jack - ***Free Lovers*** [1948]	$2.50	$7.50	$15.00
4	Woodford, Jack - ***The Passionate Princess*** [1948]	$3.00	$9.00	$18.00
5	LeBlanc, Maurice - ***Wanton Venus*** [1948]	$3.00	$9.00	$18.00
6	Woodford, Jack - ***Peeping Tom*** [1948]	$5.50	$17.50	$35.00
7	Woodford, Jack - ***Grounds For Divorce*** [1948]	$3.50	$10.00	$20.00
8	Clarke, Donald Henderson - ***The Regenerate Lover*** [1948]	$5.00	$15.00	$30.00
9	Dekobra, Maurice - ***The Street Of Painted Lips*** [1949]	$4.00	$12.50	$25.00
10	Williams, Roswell - ***Woman Without Love*** [1949] Cover art by William Shoyer.	$4.00	$12.50	$25.00
11	Chase, James H. - ***The Villain And The Virgin*** [1949]	$5.00	$15.00	$30.00
12	Wilson, Dana - ***Uneasy Virtue*** [1949]	$4.00	$12.50	$25.00
13	Keating, E.P. - ***A Good Time Man*** [1949]	$4.00	$12.50	$25.00
14	Bull, Lois - ***Gold Diggers*** [1949]	$4.00	$12.50	$25.00
15	Putnam, J. Wesley - ***Playthings Of Desire*** [1949]	$4.00	$12.50	$25.00
16	Drago, Sinclair - ***Women To Love*** [1949]	$4.00	$12.50	$25.00
17	Crane, Clarkson - ***Frisco Gal*** [1949]	$4.00	$12.50	$25.00
18	Dekobra, Maurice - ***Bedroom Eyes*** [1949] Cover art by Peter Driben.	$5.50	$17.50	$35.00
19	Clarke, Donald H. - ***Louis Beretti*** [1949]	$4.00	$12.50	$25.00
20	Collison, Wilson - ***One Night With Nancy*** [1949]	$5.50	$17.50	$35.00
21	Drago, Harry Sinclair - ***The Love Toy*** [1949]	$5.00	$15.00	$30.00
22	Caren, Ellen - ***Mirabelle: Woman Of Passion!*** [1949]	$4.00	$12.50	$25.00
23	Bull, Lois - ***Broadway Virgin*** [1949]	$4.50	$14.00	$28.00
24	Weigall, Arthur - ***Infidelity*** [1949]	$4.00	$12.50	$25.00
25	Dekobra, Maurice - ***Venus On Wheels*** [1949]	$4.00	$12.50	$25.00
26	Browne, Eleanore - ***The Immodest Maidens*** [1949]	$4.00	$12.50	$25.00
27	Scott, Anthony - ***Ladies Of Chance*** [1949]	$5.50	$17.50	$35.00
28	Dekobra, Maurice - ***The Love Clinic*** [1949]	$4.00	$12.50	$25.00
29	Trent, Timothy - ***All Dames Are Dynamite*** [1949]	$4.50	$14.00	$28.00
30	Collison, Wilson - ***Diary Of Death*** [1949]	$4.50	$14.00	$28.00
31	Roberts, Colette - ***Millions For Love*** [1949]	$4.00	$12.50	$25.00
32	Collison, Wilson - ***Dishonable Darling*** [1949]	$5.00	$15.00	$30.00

		G	VG	F
33	Nash, Eleanor - ***The Women In His Life*** [1950]	$4.00	$12.50	$25.00
34	Longstreet, Stephen - ***The Crystal Girl*** [1949]	$4.00	$12.50	$25.00
35	Martin, George Victor - ***The Lady Said Yes*** [1949] Photo cover.	$4.50	$14.00	$28.00
36	Woodford, Jack - ***Male And Female*** [1950]	$4.00	$12.50	$25.00
37	Chase, James Hadley - ***12 Chinamen And A Woman*** [1950]	$6.00	$20.00	$40.00
38	Bodenheim, Maxwell - ***60 Seconds*** [1950]	$4.00	$12.50	$25.00
39	Lewton, Val - ***No Bed Of Her Own*** [1950]	$5.00	$15.00	$30.00
40	Leif, Max - ***Wild Parties*** [1950]	$4.00	$12.50	$25.00
41	Stone, Thomas - ***Help Wanted-Male*** [1950]	$5.50	$17.50	$35.00
42	Schultz, Alan Brener - ***Lady For Love*** [1950]	$4.00	$12.50	$25.00
43	Frey, Richard L. - ***How To Play Canasta*** [1950] PBO	$1.25	$3.75	$7.50
44	Woodford, jack - ***Teach Me To Love*** [1950]	$6.00	$20.00	$40.00
45	Holland, Mary - ***Blonde Baggage*** [1950]	$8.00	$25.00	$50.00
46	Bodenheim, Maxwell - ***Naked On Roller Skates*** [1950]	$10.00	$30.00	$60.00

Novel Selections. New York: Novel Publishing Corp.

51	Caldwell, Erskine - ***The Bastard*** [1953]	$2.25	$7.00	$14.00
52	Caldwell, Erskine - ***Poor Fool*** [1953]	$2.25	$7.00	$14.00

Novels, Inc. Digest Size.

NO#-1	Arthur, William - ***Made For Loving*** [n.d.] Cover by Rodewald.	$3.00	$9.00	$18.00
NO#-2	Jordan, Gail (Peggy Gaddis) - ***Sinner In Gingham*** [n.d.]	$3.00	$9.00	$18.00
NO#-3	Williams, Wright - ***Percentage Girl*** [n.d.] Cover by Walter Papp	$3.00	$9.00	$18.00
NO#-4	Jordan, Gail (Peggy Gaddis) - ***Come Sin With Me*** [n.d.]	$3.00	$9.00	$18.00
9	Harvey, Gene - ***Stag Stripper*** [n.d.]	$3.00	$9.00	$18.00
10	Saxon, John - ***The Tigress*** [n.d.]	$3.00	$9.00	$18.00

Olympia Press.

OPS12	Solanos, Valerie - ***S.C.U.M Manifesto*** [1968]	$1.25	$3.75	$7.50
OPS18	Rabbit, Peter - ***Drop City*** [1971] PBO.	$1.25	$3.75	$7.50

Omnibus. New York: Omnibus Publications. Digest Size.

NN	Livingston, Armstrong - ***Night Of Crime*** [1944] PBO. Cover art by Crayath.	$6.00	$20.00	$40.00

Original Books. Digest Size.

700	Gaddis, Peggy - ***Women Of The Night*** [1952] PBO. Cover art by George Gross.	$3.50	$10.00	$20.00
701	Hatter, Amos - ***Backstage Affair*** [1952] PBO. Cover art by Rudy Nappi.	$3.50	$10.00	$20.00
702	Bligh, Norman - ***Strictly For Pleasure*** [1952]	$3.50	$10.00	$20.00
703	Quandt, Albert L. - ***Cellar Club*** [1952] PBO.	$6.00	$20.00	$40.00
704	Welles, Kermit - ***Gambler's Girl*** [1952] PBO. Cover art by Rudy Nappi.	$3.50	$10.00	$20.00
705	Hatter, Amos - ***On Borrowed Love*** [1952]	$3.50	$10.00	$20.00
706	Stonebraker, Florence - ***Scarlet Lil*** [1952] Cover art by Nappi.	$3.50	$10.00	$20.00
707	Quandt, Albert L. - ***Beyond Desire*** [1952] PBO.	$3.50	$10.00	$20.00
708	Whittington, Harry - ***Forever Evil*** [1952] PBO.	$5.50	$17.50	$35.00
709	Quandt, Albert L. - ***Gang Moll*** [1952]	$4.00	$12.50	$25.00
710	Welles, Kermit - ***See No Evil*** [1952] PBO.	$4.00	$12.50	$25.00
711	Quandt, A.L. - ***Crime Boss*** [1952]	$3.50	$10.00	$20.00
712	Keene, Day - ***Farewell To Passion*** [1952]	$4.00	$12.50	$25.00
713	McCary, Reed - ***Sleep With The Devil*** [1952] PBO.	$4.00	$12.50	$25.00
714	Harrison, Whit (Harry Whittington) - ***Body And Passion*** [1952]	$5.50	$17.50	$35.00
715	Gill, Elisabeth - ***Wayward Nymph*** [1952] PBO. Cover art by Gross.	$3.50	$10.00	$20.00
716	Quandt, Albert L. - ***Cellar Club*** [1952]	$5.00	$15.00	$30.00
717	Arnold, William - ***Sheila's Daughter*** [1952]	$3.50	$10.00	$20.00

		G	VG	F
718	Harrison, Whit (Harry Whittington) - ***Savage Love*** [1952] PBO. Cover art by Rudolph Belarski	$5.50	$17.50	$35.00
719	Arnold, William - ***Harlem Woman*** [1952] PBO. Cover art by Ray Pease.	$4.00	$12.50	$25.00
720	Quandt, Albert L. - ***Baby Sitter*** [1952]	$3.50	$10.00	$20.00
721	Quandt, Albert L. - ***Zip-Gun Angels*** [1952] PBO.	$6.00	$20.00	$40.00
722	Saber, Robert O. - ***City Of Sin*** [1952] Cover art by Gross.	$3.50	$10.00	$20.00
723	Whitney, Hallam (Harry Whittington) - ***Backwoods Hussy*** [1952] PBO. Cover art by Rudy Nappi.	$5.50	$17.50	$35.00
724	Arnold, William - ***Runaway Girl*** [1952] PBO. Cover art by Ray Pease.	$3.50	$10.00	$20.00
725	Nickerson, Kate - ***Ringside Jezebel*** [1952] PBO.	$3.50	$10.00	$20.00
726	Quandt, Albert L. - ***Dream Club*** [1952]	$5.00	$15.00	$30.00
727	Bligh, Norman - ***Visiting Nurse*** [1952] PBO. Cover art by Ray Pease.	$3.50	$10.00	$20.00
728	Quandt, Albert L. - ***Baby Peddler*** [1952]	$3.50	$10.00	$20.00
729	Nickerson, Kate - ***Street Of The Blues*** [1952] Cover by Herb Tauss.	$3.50	$10.00	$20.00
730	Hatter, Amos - ***Waterfront Girl*** [1952]	$3.50	$10.00	$20.00
731	Whittey, Hallam (Harry Whittington) - ***Shack Road*** [1952] PBO.	$5.50	$17.50	$35.00
732	Reynolds, Robert E. - ***Streets Of Paris*** [1952] PBO. Cover art by Belarski.	$3.50	$10.00	$20.00
733	Whitney, Hallam (Harry Whittington) - ***Backwoods Hussy*** [1952] Cover art by Rudy Nappi.	$4.00	$12.50	$25.00
734	? - ***Runaway Girl*** [1952]	$3.50	$10.00	$20.00
735	Quandt, Albert L. - ***Boy Crazy*** [1952] Cover art by Herb Tauss	$3.50	$10.00	$20.00
737	Whitney, Hallam (Harry Whittington) - ***City Girl*** [1952] PBO. Cover art by Schulz.	$5.50	$17.50	$35.00
739	Coleman, Mitchell - ***Ward Nurse*** [1952] Cover art by Ray Pease.	$3.50	$10.00	$20.00
740	Bligh, Norman - ***River Boat Girl*** [1952] Cover art by Belarski.	$4.00	$12.50	$25.00
741	Bligh, Norman - ***Motel Mistress*** [1952]	$3.50	$10.00	$20.00
742	Harrison, Whit (Harry Whittington) - ***Shanty Road*** [1952] PBO.	$5.50	$17.50	$35.00
744	Harvey, Gene - ***City Streets*** [1952] Cover art by DeSoto.	$3.50	$10.00	$20.00
746	Clay, Matthew - ***French Alley*** [1952] Cover art by Nappi.	$3.50	$10.00	$20.00
748	? - ***Streets Of Paris*** [1952] Cover art by Belarski.	$3.50	$10.00	$20.00
749	Whitney, Hallam (Harry Whittington) - ***City Girl*** [1952] Cover art by Schulz.	$3.50	$10.00	$20.00

P.E.C. Giants.

G-1117	Kahler, Jack - ***Rubber Dolly*** [1966]	$1.25	$3.75	$7.50

Pan Books.

G-128	Simenon, Georges - ***Strange Inheritance*** [1958]	$ .75	$2.50	$5.00
G-352	Cheyney, Peter - ***Dames Don't Care*** [1962] Cover by Peff.	$ .75	$2.50	$5.00

Paperback Library. New York: Paperback Library, Inc.

Note: The -800 and -900 numbers precede the -500 numbers chronologically and are listed prior to the 500 numbers here.

B-101	Keyes, Frances Parkinson - ***Lady Blanche Farm*** [1961]	$1.00	$3.00	$6.00
S-102	Medaris, Major General J. B. - ***Countdown For Decision*** [1961]	$ .75	$2.50	$5.00
S-103	Farrell, James T. - ***Boarding House Blues*** [1961] PBO.	$1.50	$5.00	$10.00
B-105	Dwiggins, Don - ***Frankie: The Life And Loves Of Frank Sinatra*** [1961] PBO.	$1.00	$3.00	$6.00
S-107	Longstreet, Stephen - ***Stallion Road*** [1961]	$1.00	$3.00	$6.00
S-108	Fowler, Gene - ***Trumpet In The Dust*** [1961]	$1.00	$3.00	$6.00
GA-110	Zacharias, Elias M., Rear Admiral, USN - ***Secret Missions*** [1961]	$ .75	$2.50	$5.00

		G	VG	F
S-111	Mallory, M.D., Robert & Irwin, Theodore - ***Modern Birth Control*** [1961]	$ .65	$2.00	$4.00
S-112	Mortimer, Lee - ***Women Confidential*** [1961]	$ .65	$2.00	$4.00
52-113	Farrell, James T. - ***Side Street And Other Stories*** [1961]	$1.25	$3.75	$7.50
54-114	Levin, Meyer - ***In Search*** [1961]	$ .75	$2.50	$5.00
52-120	Collection - ***The Bathroom Reader*** [1961]	$ .75	$2.50	$5.00
52-121	Anthology edited by Noah Sarlat - ***How I Made A Million*** [1961]	$ .75	$2.50	$5.00
52-122	Payne, Robert - ***The Gold Of Troy*** [1961]	$1.00	$3.00	$6.00
52-123	Fowler, Gene - ***Shoe The Wild Mare*** [1961]	$1.00	$3.00	$6.00
52-125	Farago, Ladislas - ***War Of Wits*** [1961]	$ .75	$2.50	$5.00
52-126	Freuchen, Peter - ***Sea Tyrant*** [1961]	$ .75	$2.50	$5.00
52-127	Kersh, Gerald - ***Men Without Bones*** [1962] PBO. Cover art by Richard Powers.	$2.50	$7.50	$15.00
52-128	Machlin, Milt - ***The Private Hell Of Hemingway*** [1962] PBO.	$1.25	$3.75	$7.50
52-129	Bromfield, Louis - ***Early Autumn*** [1962]	$ .75	$2.50	$5.00
52-130	Barzman, Ben - ***Echo X*** [1962] Cover art by Bob Abbett.	$1.00	$3.00	$6.00
52-131	Rice, Cy - ***Cleopatra In Mink*** [1962]	$ .75	$2.50	$5.00
54-132	Tebbel, John - ***Hearst*** [1962]	$ .75	$2.50	$5.00
54-136	Stone, Irving - ***Adversary In The House*** [1962]	$ .75	$2.50	$5.00
52-139	Anthology edited by Noah Sariat - ***Women With Guns*** [1962]	$ .75	$2.50	$5.00
52-140	MacKinley, Kantor - ***Three*** [1962]	$ .75	$2.50	$5.00
52-141	? - ***It Has Come To Pass*** [1962]	$ .75	$2.50	$5.00
52-142	Merritt, A. - ***Dwellers In The Mirage*** [1962]	$1.00	$3.00	$6.00
54-144	Marquis, James - ***The Raven*** [1962] Cover art by Norman Baer.	$ .75	$2.50	$5.00
51-146	Adams, Clifton - ***Stranger In Town*** [1962] PBO. Cover art by Carl Hantman.	$ .75	$2.50	$5.00
52-149	Ellison, Harlan - ***Ellison Wonderland*** [1962] PBO. Cover art by Victor Kalin.	$4.00	$12.50	$25.00
51-153	Hynd, Alan - ***Prescription: Murder*** [1962] PBO. Cover art by Stanley Borack.	$1.00	$3.00	$6.00
51-155	Schurmacher, Emile C. - ***Terror In Algiers*** [1962] PBO. Cover art by Stanley Borack.	$1.00	$3.00	$6.00
51-159	MacDonald, Zillah K. & Ahl, Vivian J. - ***Nurse Todd's Strange Summer*** [1962] Cover art by Lou Marchetti	$ .65	$2.00	$4.00
52-162	? - ***Washington Confidential*** [1962]	$ .75	$2.50	$5.00
52-165	Cooper, Jefferson (Gardner F. Fox) - ***Delilah*** [1962]	$2.00	$6.00	$12.00
52-171	Wellman, Paul - ***The Bowl Of Brass*** [1962]	$ .75	$2.50	$5.00
51-173	Harrison, Whit (Harry Whittington) - ***Army Girl*** [1962] Cover art by Harry Schaare	$3.50	$10.00	$20.00
52-174	Schurmacher, Emile C. - ***Our Secret War Against Red China*** [1962]	$ .75	$2.50	$5.00
52-175	Keyes, Frances Parkinson - ***Restless Lady And Other Stories*** [1962]	$ .75	$2.50	$5.00
52-180	Wylie, Philip & Balmer, Edwin - ***When Worlds Collide*** [1962] Cover art by Richard Powers.	$1.00	$3.00	$6.00
51-181	Joscelyn, Archie - ***Wyoming Outlaw*** [1962]	$ .75	$2.50	$5.00
52-183	Farrell, James T. - ***Sound Of A City*** [1962] PBO. Cover art by Jack Thurston.	$1.50	$5.00	$10.00
54-187	Wolsey, Serge G. - ***Call House Madam*** [1962]	$ .75	$2.50	$5.00
52-189	? - ***Jacqueline Kennedy In The White House*** [1962]	$ .75	$2.50	$5.00
52-192	Page, Marco - ***Fast Company*** [1962]	$ .75	$2.50	$5.00
52-193	Van Dine, S. S. - ***The Garden Murder Case*** [1962]	$1.00	$3.00	$6.00
52-194	O'Callaghan, Dimitri - ***The Scavengers*** [1963] PBO. Cover art by Vince Edwards.	$ .75	$2.50	$5.00
52-195	Lee, Gypsy Rose - ***The G-String Murders*** [1963]	$1.00	$3.00	$6.00
54-196	DeGamez, Tana - ***Like A River Of Lions*** [1963]	$ .75	$2.50	$5.00
52-197	Hull, E. M. - ***The Sheik*** [1963]	$ .75	$2.50	$5.00
54-199	Granat, Robert - ***Only The Brave*** [1963]	$ .75	$2.50	$5.00
52-200	Toby, Mark - ***The Courtship Of Eddie's Father*** [1963]	$ .75	$2.50	$5.00

		G	VG	F
52-202	Rovere, Richard H. - ***Howe And Hummel: Criminal Lawyers*** [1963]	$ .75	$2.50	$5.00
54-203	Wellman, Paul - ***The Walls Of Jericho*** [1963]	$ .75	$2.50	$5.00
52-204	Sherry, Madam - ***Pleasure Was My Business*** [1963]	$ .75	$2.50	$5.00
52-205	Wylie, Philip - ***The Answer*** [1963]	$1.00	$3.00	$6.00
54-207	Cory, Daniel Webster - ***The Homosexual In America*** [1963]	$ .75	$2.50	$5.00
52-208	Biggers, Earl Derr. - ***Keeper Of The Keys*** [1963] Cover art by Miller	$1.00	$3.00	$6.00
52-210	Russell, Ray - ***The Case Against Satan*** [1963] Cover art by Bob Abbett.	$1.00	$3.00	$6.00
52-211	Collection edited by Noel Keyes - ***Contact*** [1963]	$1.00	$3.00	$6.00
52-212	Lee, Gypsy Rose - ***Mother Finds A Body*** [1963]	$1.00	$3.00	$6.00
52-213	Lacy, Ed - ***The Sex Castle*** [1963] PBO. Cover art by Robert Maguire.	$2.00	$6.00	$12.00
52-214	Perutz, Kathrin - ***The Garden*** [1963]	$ .75	$2.50	$5.00
55-215	Robie, M.D., W. F. - ***The Art Of Love*** [1963]	$ .65	$2.00	$4.00
52-216	Wylie, Philip - ***An April Afternoon*** [1963]	$ .75	$2.50	$5.00
53-218	Schindler - ***Dr. Schindler's Woman's Guide To Better Living*** [1963]	$ .65	$2.00	$4.00
52-219	Dine, S. S. Van - ***The Scarab Murder Case*** [1963]	$1.00	$3.00	$6.00
52-220	Thorp, Raymond - ***Hooked!*** [1963]	$ .75	$2.50	$5.00
54-221	Walton, Alan Hull - ***Aphrodisiacs: From Legend To Prescription*** [1963]	$ .75	$2.50	$5.00
52-227	Page, Marco (Harry Kurmitz) - ***Reclining Figure*** [1963]	$ .75	$2.50	$5.00
52-228	Biggers, Earl Derr - ***The Chinese Parrot*** [1963]	$1.00	$3.00	$6.00
52-232	Shiel, M. P. - ***The Purple Cloud*** [1963] PBO.	$1.25	$3.75	$7.50
52-233	Lacy, Ed - ***Too Hot In Handle*** [1963]	$1.00	$3.00	$6.00
50-236	Joscelyn, Archie - ***Two-Gun Vengeance*** [1963]	$ .75	$2.50	$5.00
52-237	Cooper, Jefferson (Gardner F. Fox) - ***Jezebel*** [1963] PBO. Cover art by McGinnis.	$2.00	$6.00	$12.00
52-239	Terry, Jr., Marshall - ***Old Liberty*** [1963]	$ .75	$2.50	$5.00
52-240	Knowlton, Robert A. - ***Court Of Crows*** [1963]	$ .75	$2.50	$5.00
54-241	Quirk, John - ***No Red Ribbons*** [1963]	$ .75	$2.50	$5.00
52-247	Kurnitz, Harry - ***Invasion Of Privacy*** [1963]	$ .75	$2.50	$5.00
52-250	Nolan, William F. - ***Impact-20*** [1963] PBO.	$1.25	$3.75	$7.50
50-251	Joscelyn, Archie - ***Gun Thunder Valley*** [1963]	$ .75	$2.50	$5.00
52-255	Wylie, Philip & Balmer, Edwin - ***After Worlds Collide*** [1963] Cover art by Richard Powers.	$1.00	$3.00	$6.00
52-256	Jay, Charlotte - ***The Yellow Turban*** [1963]	$1.00	$3.00	$6.00
50-258	Castle, Helen B. - ***Emergency Ward Nurse*** [1963] PBO. Cover art by Lou Marchetti	$ .65	$2.00	$4.00
54-262	Farago, Ladislas - ***The Tenth Fleet*** [1963]	$ .75	$2.50	$5.00
52-263	Pinchot, Ann - ***The Twisted Cross*** [1964] PBO.	$ .75	$2.50	$5.00
50-268	Joscelyn, Archie - ***Duel At Killman Creek*** [1964] Cover art by Basil Gogot.	$ .75	$2.50	$5.00
53-269	Cooper, Jefferson (Gardner F. Fox) - ***Sappho Of Lesbos*** [1964] PBO.	$2.00	$6.00	$12.00
52-272	Keefe, Lynn - ***How Did A Nice Girl Like You Get Into This Business?*** [1964] PBO. Cover art by Copeland.	$ .75	$2.50	$5.00
52-273	Fox, Gardner - ***Escape Across The Cosmos*** [1964] PBO.	$1.25	$3.75	$7.50
52-276	Head, Ann - ***Always In August*** [1964]	$ .75	$2.50	$5.00
54-278	Williams, Robert V. - ***Shake This Town*** [1964]	$ .75	$2.50	$5.00
52-283	Biggers, Earl Derr - ***Charlie Chan Carries On*** [1964]	$1.00	$3.00	$6.00
54-284	Ellis, William Donohue - ***The Brooks Legend*** [1964]	$ .75	$2.50	$5.00
53-286	Branden, Nathaniel & Barbara - ***Who Is Ayn Rand?*** [1964]	$ .75	$2.50	$5.00
52-287	Russell, Eric Frank - ***Sinister Barrier*** [1964]	$1.00	$3.00	$6.00
52-290	Anthology - ***The Best From Famous Monsters Of Filmland*** [1964] PBO.	$2.50	$7.50	$15.00
54-292	Robinson, Wayne - ***Hell Has No Heroes*** [1964]	$ .75	$2.50	$5.00
52-293	Edited by John W. Campbell - ***Analog I*** [1964]	$1.00	$3.00	$6.00

		G	VG	F
52-295	Shenkin, Elizabeth - ***The Secret Heart*** [1964]	$ .75	$2.50	$5.00
50-299	Lowry, Nan - ***Crystal Manning, Maternity Nurse*** [1964] PBO.	$ .65	$2.00	$4.00
54-302	Cohn, Alfred & Chisholm, Joe - ***Take The Witness!*** [1964]	$ .75	$2.50	$5.00
52-304	Van Vogt, A. E. - ***Two Hundred Million A.D.*** [1964] Cover art by Jack Gaughan	$1.00	$3.00	$6.00
53-305	Stanley, Jackson - ***The Florentine Ring*** [1964]	$ .75	$2.50	$5.00
54-306	Rennse, Ysabel - ***Kingside*** [1964]	$ .75	$2.50	$5.00
54-308	Richler, Mordecai - ***The Apprenticeship Of Duddy Kravitz*** [1964]	$ .75	$2.50	$5.00
52-311	Hamilton, Edmond - ***Battle For The Stars*** [1964]	$1.00	$3.00	$6.00
53-313	Chang, Isabelle - ***Chinese Cooking Made Easy*** [1964]	$ .75	$2.50	$5.00
53-314	Esar, Evan - ***Dictionary Of Humorous Quotations*** [1964]	$ .75	$2.50	$5.00
54-315	Syers, William Edward - ***The "Seven": Navy Subchaser*** [1964]	$ .75	$2.50	$5.00
52-316	Kirk, Russell - ***The Surly Sullen Bell*** [1964]	$ .75	$2.50	$5.00
52-317	Keyes, Frances Parkinson - ***Once On Esplanade*** [1964]	$ .75	$2.50	$5.00
53-318	Kaufman, Ted & Jean - ***Italian Cooking Made Easy*** [1964]	$ .75	$2.50	$5.00
52-320	Anthology edited by Roger Elwood - ***Alien Worlds*** [1964] PBO.	$1.25	$3.75	$7.50
54-322	Farago, Ladislas - ***Spymaster*** [1964]	$ .75	$2.50	$5.00
54-323	Spota, Luis - ***Almost Paradise*** [1964]	$ .75	$2.50	$5.00
52-324	Whitney, Phillis A. - ***Skye Cameron*** [1964]	$ .75	$2.50	$5.00
52-329	Barzman, Ben - ***Echo X*** [1964]	$1.00	$3.00	$6.00
50-331	Mosler, Blanche Y. - ***Marie Warren, Night Nurse*** [1966] Cover art by Mort Engel.	$ .65	$2.00	$4.00
53-332	Iannuzzi, J. Nicholas - ***What's Happening?*** [1966]	$ .75	$2.50	$5.00
53-333	Drummond, William - ***Gaslight*** [1966] PBO.	$ .75	$2.50	$5.00
52-334	La Spina, Greye - ***Shadow Of Evil*** [1966]	$ .75	$2.50	$5.00
52-335	Shulman, Sandra - ***The Menacing Darkness*** [1966] PBO.	$ .75	$2.50	$5.00
53-336	White, Ethel Lina - ***Fear Stalks The Village*** [1966]	$1.00	$3.00	$6.00
54-337	Needham, Walter & Mussey, Barrows - ***Grandfather's Book Of Country Things*** [1966]	$ .75	$2.50	$5.00
52-338	Dexter, William (W. T. Pritchard) - ***World In Eclipse*** [1966]	$1.00	$3.00	$6.00
56-340	Wollheim, Donald A. - ***Mike Mars Flies The Dyna-Soar*** [1966] Cover art by Hanke	$1.00	$3.00	$6.00
53-341	Fielding, William J. - ***Strange Superstitions And Magical Practices*** [1966]	$ .75	$2.50	$5.00
50-343	Joscelyn, Archie - ***Two Gun Vengeance*** [1966]	$ .75	$2.50	$5.00
56-344	Hunt, Rosamond - ***Nurse Martin's Secret*** [1966]	$ .65	$2.00	$4.00
54-348	Collins, Wilkie - ***The Woman In white*** [1966]	$ .65	$2.00	$4.00
52-349	Shivelley, Angela - ***Dread Of Night*** [1966]	$ .75	$2.50	$5.00
52-350	Ross, Marilyn - ***Desperate Heiress*** [1966]	$ .75	$2.50	$5.00
52-351	White, Ethel Lina - ***The Unseen*** [1966]	$1.00	$3.00	$6.00
53-354	White, Loretta - ***The Good Egg*** [1966]	$ .75	$2.50	$5.00
56-355	Arthur, Burt - ***Outlaw Fury*** [1966]	$ .75	$2.50	$5.00
56-356	Ross, Marilyn - ***Tread Softly, Nurse Scott!*** [1966]	$ .65	$2.00	$4.00
52-357	Dexter, William (W. T. Pritchard) - ***Children Of The Void*** [1966]	$1.00	$3.00	$6.00
56-358	Wollheim, Donald A. - ***Mike Mars, South Pole Spaceman*** [1966] Cover art by Hanke	$1.00	$3.00	$6.00
52-362	White, Ethel Lina - ***The Lady Vanishes*** [1966]	$1.00	$3.00	$6.00
52-363	Payne, Rachel Ann - ***Ghostwind*** [1966]	$ .75	$2.50	$5.00
52-364	Lloyd, Stephanie - ***Graveswood*** [1966]	$ .75	$2.50	$5.00
52-365	Kirk, Russell - ***Lost Lake*** [1966]	$ .75	$2.50	$5.00
54-366	Claire, Suzy - ***Around The World With Suzy Claire*** [1966] PBO.	$ .75	$2.50	$5.00
52-368	Moorcock, Michael - ***The Sundered Worlds*** [1966]	$1.00	$3.00	$6.00
56-369	Wollheim, Donald A. - ***Mike Mars And The Mystery Satellite*** [1966] Cover art by Hanke	$1.00	$3.00	$6.00
53-370	Casey, Hugh Lynn - ***Venture Inward*** [1966]	$ .75	$2.50	$5.00
52-372	Haycox, Ernest - ***Frank Peace, Trouble Shooter*** [1966]	$ .75	$2.50	$5.00
56-373	Lowry, Nan - ***Crystal Manning, Maternity Nurse*** [1966]	$ .65	$2.00	$4.00

		G	VG	F
53-374	White, Ethel Lina - ***Sinister Light*** [1966]	$1.00	$3.00	$6.00
53-375	Ferguson, Margaret - ***The Sign Of The Ram*** [1966]	$ .75	$2.50	$5.00
52-376	Morrison, Roberta - ***Tree Of Evil*** [1966] PBO.	$ .75	$2.50	$5.00
52-377	Lynch, Miriam - ***The Road To Midnight*** [1966] PBO.	$ .75	$2.50	$5.00
52-378	Andrew, Robert - ***The Lucky Dream And Number Book*** [1966].	$ .75	$2.50	$5.00
52-379	Magazine, Fate - ***Stranger Than Strange*** [1966]	$ .75	$2.50	$5.00
55-381	Kaufman, Ted & Jean - ***Grandmother's Country Cookbook*** [1966]	$ .75	$2.50	$5.00
56-383	Wollheim, Donald A. - ***Mike Mars Around The Moon*** [1966] Cover art by Hanke.	$1.00	$3.00	$6.00
52-384	Russell, Eric Frank - ***Sinister Barrier*** [1966]	$1.00	$3.00	$6.00
52-386	Ross, Marilyn - ***Dark Shadows*** [1966]	$1.25	$3.75	$7.50
53-387	Daniels, Norman - ***The Rat Patrol*** [1966] PBO.	$1.00	$3.00	$6.00
53-388	White, Ethel Lina - ***She Faded Into Air*** [1967]	$1.00	$3.00	$6.00
52-389	St. John, Genevieve - ***Strangers In The Night*** [1967]	$ .75	$2.50	$5.00
54-390	LeFanu, Sheridan - ***Uncle Silas*** [1967]	$ .75	$2.50	$5.00
52-391	Edward, Marie Elaine - ***Amberleigh*** [1967]	$ .75	$2.50	$5.00
52-392	High, Philip E. - ***Twin Planets*** [1967] PBO.	$1.00	$3.00	$6.00
56-393	Arthur, Burt - ***Duel On The Range*** [1967]	$ .75	$2.50	$5.00
54-395	Fodor, Nandor - ***Between Two Worlds*** [1967]	$1.00	$3.00	$6.00
52-397	Church, Ruth Ellen - ***The Burger Cookbook*** [1967]	$ .75	$2.50	$5.00
50-400	Lehman, Paul Evan - ***Rustlers Of The Rio Grande*** [1964]	$ .75	$2.50	$5.00
50-404	Hunter, John (W. T. Ballard) - ***Duke*** [1965] PBO.	$1.25	$3.75	$7.50
52-406	Van Vogt, A. E. - ***200 Million A.D.*** [1967]	$1.00	$3.00	$6.00
53-407	White, Ethel Lina - ***The Man Who Was Not there*** [1967]	$1.00	$3.00	$6.00
52-408	Edward, Marie Elaine - ***Terror Manor*** [1967]	$ .75	$2.50	$5.00
53-409	Walpole, Hugh - ***Portrait Of A Man With Red Hair*** [1967]	$1.00	$3.00	$6.00
53-411	King, David - ***Desert Danger*** [1967]	$ .75	$2.50	$5.00
54-412	Giles, Janice Holt - ***The Kentuckians*** [1967]	$ .75	$2.50	$5.00
52-415	Del Rey, Lester - ***Marooned On Mars*** [1967]	$1.00	$3.00	$6.00
54-416	Dait, Louis - ***French Cooking For Americans*** [1967]	$ .75	$2.50	$5.00
53-417	Gallery, Daniel V. - ***Clear The Decks*** [1967]	$ .75	$2.50	$5.00
56-420	Floren, Lee - ***Deputy's Revenge*** [1967]	$ .75	$2.50	$5.00
52-421	Ross, Marilyn - ***Victoria Winters*** [1967]	$ .75	$2.50	$5.00
52-422	Lynch, Miriam - ***The Secret Of Lucifer's Island*** [1967] PBO.	$ .75	$2.50	$5.00
53-423	White, Ethel Lina - ***Wax*** [1967]	$ .75	$2.50	$5.00
52-425	Brand, Max - ***Gunman's Legacy*** [1967]	$ .75	$2.50	$5.00
54-426	Giles, Janice Holt - ***Hannah Fowler*** [1967]	$ .75	$2.50	$5.00
52-427	Magazine, Fate - ***Strange Twist Of Fate*** [1967]	$ .75	$2.50	$5.00
53-428	Adamski, George - ***Inside The Flying Saucers*** [1967]	$ .75	$2.50	$5.00
52-430	Somers, Bart (Gardner F. Fox) - ***Abandon Galaxy!*** [1967] PBO. Cover art by Jack Gaughan.	$1.35	$4.00	$8.00
55-432	Beard, James A. - ***James Beard's Fish Cookery*** [1967]	$ .75	$2.50	$5.00
56-434	Daniels, Dorothy - ***Island Nurse*** [1967]	$ .65	$2.00	$4.00
53-435	White, Ethel Lina - ***The Third Eye*** [1967]	$1.00	$3.00	$6.00
52-437	Ross, Marilyn - ***Cameron Castle*** [1967] PBO.	$ .75	$2.50	$5.00
54-438	Woolrich, Cornell - ***Night Has A Thousand Eyes*** [1967]	$1.35	$4.00	$8.00
53-439	Adamski, George - ***Behind The Flying Saucer Mystery*** [1967]	$ .75	$2.50	$5.00
52-440	Saltzman, Pauline - ***Strange Spirits*** [1967]	$ .75	$2.50	$5.00
52-441	Stone, Patti - ***Judy George, Student Nurse*** [1967]	$ .65	$2.00	$4.00
52-443	Brand, Max - ***The Border Bandit*** [1967]	$ .75	$2.50	$5.00
52-444	Ames, Mark & Roberta - ***Barbecues*** [1967]	$ .75	$2.50	$5.00
54-445	Burkett, Jr., William R. - ***Sleeping Planet*** [1967]	$1.00	$3.00	$6.00
52-446	Keefe, Lynn - ***How Did A Nice Girl Like You Get Into This Business?*** [1967]	$ .75	$2.50	$5.00
53-449	Montross, David - ***Traitor's Wife*** [1967]	$ .75	$2.50	$5.00
53-450	Teilhet, Darwin - ***Dangerous Encounter*** [1967]	$ .75	$2.50	$5.00
53-451	Montross, David - ***Fellow-Traveler*** [1967]	$ .75	$2.50	$5.00
52-452	Ross, Marilyn - ***The Mystery Of Fury Castle*** [1967]	$ .75	$2.50	$5.00
52-453	Ware, Judith - ***The Fear Place*** [1967] PBO.	$ .75	$2.50	$5.00

		G	VG	F
52-454	Knye, Cassandra (Sladek & Disch) - ***The Castle And The Key*** [1967] PBO. Cover art by Jerome Podwil	$2.00	$6.00	$12.00
54-457	Giles, Janice Holt - ***The Land Beyond The Mountains*** [1967]	$ .75	$2.50	$5.00
53-458	Gallery, Daniel V. - ***Stand By-y-y To Start Engines*** [1967]	$ .75	$2.50	$5.00
52-459	Schurmacher, Emile C. - ***Strange Unsolved Mysteries*** [1967] PBO	$ .75	$2.50	$5.00
53-461	Bennett, Paula P. & Clark, Velma R. - ***The Art Of Hungarian Cooking*** [1967]	$ .75	$2.50	$5.00
52-462	Nourse, Alan E. - ***The Universe Between*** [1967] Cover art by Jack Gaughan	$1.00	$3.00	$6.00
52-463	Brand, Max - ***The Rescue Of Broken Arrow*** [1967]	$ .75	$2.50	$5.00
53-464	Lawrence, Josephine - ***The Ring Of Truth*** [1967]	$ .75	$2.50	$5.00
52-465	Hobart, Lois - ***Elaine Forrest: Visiting Nurse*** [1967]	$ .65	$2.00	$4.00
53-466	Ross, Marilyn - ***Assignment: Danger*** [1967] PBO.	$ .75	$2.50	$5.00
53-467	Montross, David - ***Who Is Elissa Sheldon?*** [1967]	$ .75	$2.50	$5.00
52-468	Anthology edited by Charles Birkin - ***The Witch-Baiter*** [1967]	$1.50	$5.00	$10.00
52-469	Saxon, Peter - ***The Torturer*** [1967] Cover art by Victor Kalin.	$2.00	$6.00	$12.00
52-470	Haycox, Ernest - ***Canyon Passage*** [1967]	$ .75	$2.50	$5.00
52-471	Laffeaty, Christina - ***Mistress Of Tara*** [1967]	$ .75	$2.50	$5.00
52-472	Anthology edited by Charles Birkin - ***The Haunted Dancers*** [1967] Cover art by Victor Kalin.	$1.50	$5.00	$10.00
54-473	Trainer, Russell - ***The Lolita Complex*** [1967]	$ .75	$2.50	$5.00
52-474	Fate Magazine - ***Strange-But True*** [1967]	$ .75	$2.50	$5.00
52-475	Moorcock, Michael - ***The Fireclown*** [1967]	$1.00	$3.00	$6.00
55-476	Meyer, Hazel - ***The Complete Book Of Home Freezing*** [1967]	$ .75	$2.50	$5.00
53-477	King, David - ***The Trojan Tank Affair*** [1967] PBO. Cover art by Shcaare	$ .75	$2.50	$5.00
52-478	Brand, Max - ***Smuggler's Trail*** [1967]	$ .75	$2.50	$5.00
53-480	Ware, Judith - ***Detour To Denmark*** [1967]	$ .75	$2.50	$5.00
53-481	Pendower, Jacques - ***Betrayed*** [1967]	$ .75	$2.50	$5.00
52-482	Lawrence, Josephine - ***Hearts Do Not Break*** [1967]	$ .75	$2.50	$5.00
52-483	Haycox, Ernest - ***The Border Trumpet*** [1967] Cover art by George Gross.	$ .75	$2.50	$5.00
52-485	Ross, Marilyn - ***Mistress Of Ravenswood*** [1967]	$ .75	$2.50	$5.00
52-486	Richard, Susan - ***Intruder At Maison Benedict*** [1967]	$ .75	$2.50	$5.00
53-487	Reynolds, James - ***Ghosts In American Houses*** [1967]	$ .75	$2.50	$5.00
52-488	Majors, Simon - ***The Druid Stone*** [1967]	$ .75	$2.50	$5.00
52-490	Anthology - ***Strange Horizons*** [1967]	$ .75	$2.50	$5.00
52-492	Lewis, Jack - ***Vengeance Is A Stranger*** [1967]	$ .75	$2.50	$5.00
54-493	Griffin, David - ***The Wrong People*** [1967] PBO.	$ .75	$2.50	$5.00
76-494	Edwards, Alexander - ***McQ*** [1974] Movie photo cover. Movie tie-in with John Wayne.	$ .75	$2.50	$5.00
52-494	MacLeod, Ruth - ***Arlene Perry, Special Nurse*** [1967]	$ .65	$2.00	$4.00
53-496	Pendower, Jacques - ***Mission In Tunis*** [1967]	$ .75	$2.50	$5.00
54-497	Gerlach, Heinrich - ***The Forsaken Army*** [1967]	$ .75	$2.50	$5.00
52-498	Simak, Clifford D. - ***Cosmic Engineers*** [1967]	$1.00	$3.00	$6.00
56-499	Lehman, Paul Evan - ***Range War At Keno*** [1967]	$ .75	$2.50	$5.00
54-801	Schurmacher, Emile C. - ***Assignment X: Top Secret*** [1965]	$ .75	$2.50	$5.00
52-802	Smith, F. E. - ***Dark Cliffs*** [1965] Cover art by Lou Marchetti	$ .75	$2.50	$5.00
52-804	Bond, Nelson - ***Exiles Of Time*** [1965]	$ .75	$2.50	$5.00
50-805	Shelley, John - ***A Gun For Billy Hardin*** [1965]	$ .75	$2.50	$5.00
52-806	Quandt, Albert T. - ***The Swingers*** [1965]	$ .75	$2.50	$5.00
54-809	Young, Phyllis Brett - ***Gift Of Time*** [1965]	$ .75	$2.50	$5.00
52-810	Wolff, Ruth - ***Hawthorne*** [1965]	$ .75	$2.50	$5.00
52-811	Vale, Rena - ***Beyond The Sealed World*** [1965] PBO.	$1.00	$3.00	$6.00
52-812	Whitney, Phyllis A. - ***The Red Carnelian*** [1965]	$ .75	$2.50	$5.00
52-813	Anthology - ***Famous Monsters Of Filmland Strike Back!*** [1965] Cover art by Jeff Jones.	$2.50	$7.50	$15.00
52-815	Anthology edited by Noah Sarlat - ***War Cry*** [1965]	$ .75	$2.50	$5.00

		G	VG	F
52-817	Teilhet, Darwin - ***The Big Runaround*** [1965] Cover art by Schinella.	$ .75	$2.50	$5.00
52-818	Anthology - ***Strange Fate*** [1965]	$ .75	$2.50	$5.00
54-819	Anthology edited by Robert P. Mills - ***The Worlds Of Science-Fiction*** [1965] Cover art by Jack Gaughan.	$1.00	$3.00	$6.00
52-820	Dalton, Priscilla - ***The Silent, Silken Shadows*** [1965]	$ .75	$2.50	$5.00
53-823	Norris, Kathleen - ***The Secrets Of Hillyard House*** [1965] Cover art by Victor Kalin.	$ .75	$2.50	$5.00
50-824	Adams, Clifton - ***Stranger In Town*** [1965] Cover art by Carl Hantman.	$ .75	$2.50	$5.00
52-827	Daniels, Dorothy - ***Marriott Hall*** [1965]	$ .75	$2.50	$5.00
53-828	Hutchison, Ruth - ***The New Pennsylvania Dutch Cookbook*** [1965]	$ .75	$2.50	$5.00
53-829	Coombs, Anna Olsson - ***Smorgasbord Cookbook*** [1965]	$ .75	$2.50	$5.00
52-833	Christian, Paula - ***The Other Side Of Desire*** [1965] PBO.	$ .75	$2.50	$5.00
54-834	Williams, Mona - ***The Passion Of Amy Styron*** [1965]	$ .75	$2.50	$5.00
50-836	Arthur, Burt - ***The Black Rider*** [1965]	$ .75	$2.50	$5.00
52-837	Anthology edited by Noel Keyes - ***Contact*** [1965]	$1.00	$3.00	$6.00
55-838	Krafft-Ebing, Dr. Richard Von - ***Psychopathia Sexualis*** [1965]	$ .75	$2.50	$5.00
52-839	Lowe, Marjorie - ***The Sudden Lady*** [1965]	$ .75	$2.50	$5.00
53-841	Norris, Kathleen - ***Mystery House*** [1965]	$ .75	$2.50	$5.00
53-842	Rigsby, Howard - ***The Tulip Tree*** [1965]	$ .75	$2.50	$5.00
52-843	Ross, Marilyn - ***Beware My Love*** [1965]	$ .75	$2.50	$5.00
53-844	Norris, Kathleen - ***Gabrielle*** [1965]	$ .75	$2.50	$5.00
54-846	Winters, Joannie - ***House Of Joy*** [1965]	$ .75	$2.50	$5.00
52-847	Binder, Eando - ***Adam Link, Robot*** [1965] PBO.	$1.00	$3.00	$6.00
52-848	Somers, Bart (Gardner F. Fox) - ***Beyond The Black Enigma*** [1965]	$1.00	$3.00	$6.00
52-849	Ross, Marilyn - ***Fog Island*** [1965] PBO.	$ .75	$2.50	$5.00
50-850	Lehman, Paul Evan - ***Texas Vengeance*** [1965]	$ .75	$2.50	$5.00
52-853	Garrison, Joan - ***Come Walk With Love*** [1965]	$ .75	$2.50	$5.00
52-854	Hamill, Ethel - ***Honeymoon In Honolulu*** [1965]	$ .75	$2.50	$5.00
52-855	Hamill, Ethel - ***All For Love*** [1965]	$ .65	$2.00	$4.00
52-856	Ross, W. E. D. - ***Love Is Forever*** [1965]	$ .65	$2.00	$4.00
52-858	Daniels, Dorothy - ***Darkhaven*** [1965]	$ .75	$2.50	$5.00
54-859	Emerick, Lucille - ***Web Of Evil*** [1965]	$ .75	$2.50	$5.00
53-860	Karlova, Irnina - ***Dreadful Hollow*** [1965]	$ .75	$2.50	$5.00
52-861	Bromige, Iris - ***Rosevean*** [1965] Cover art by Marchetti.	$ .75	$2.50	$5.00
52-863	Moore, C. L. - ***Judgment Night*** [1965]	$ .75	$2.50	$5.00
52-864	Magazine, Fate - ***The Strange And The Unknown*** [1965]	$ .75	$2.50	$5.00
50-865	Joscelyn, Archie - ***Texas Showdown*** [1965]	$ .75	$2.50	$5.00
52-866	Ross, W. E. D. - ***Alice In Love*** [1965]	$ .65	$2.00	$4.00
52-867	Neubauer, W. - ***Assignment: Romance*** [1965]	$ .65	$2.00	$4.00
52-868	Barron, Ann - ***Spin A Dark Web*** [1965]	$ .75	$2.50	$5.00
52-869	Annister, Paul - ***Swiftwater*** [1965] Cover art by Wayne Blickenstaff.	$ .75	$2.50	$5.00
52-870	Ross, Marilyn - ***The Locked Corridor*** [1965] PBO.	$ .75	$2.50	$5.00
53-872	Austin, Jane - ***Northanger Abbey*** [1965] PBO.	$ .75	$2.50	$5.00
52-873	Van Vogt, A. E. - ***The House That Stood Still*** [1965] Cover art by Jack Gaughan.	$1.00	$3.00	$6.00
52-874	Wollheim, Donald A. - ***The Secret Of The Ninth Planet*** [1965]	$1.00	$3.00	$6.00
52-876	Ross, W. E. D. - ***A Promise Of Love*** [1965]	$ .65	$2.00	$4.00
52-877	Little, Paula - ***One True Love*** [1965]	$ .65	$2.00	$4.00
50-878	Joscelyn, Archie - ***Wyoming Outlaw*** [1965] Cover art by Stan Borack.	$ .75	$2.50	$5.00
50-879	Mallette, Gertrude E. - ***Probation Nurse*** [1965]	$ .65	$2.00	$4.00
52-880	Ware, Judith - ***Thorne House*** [1965]	$ .75	$2.50	$5.00
52-881	Dalton, Priscilla - ***The Darkening Willows*** [1965]	$ .75	$2.50	$5.00
53-882	Norris, Kathleen - ***The Secret Of The Marshbanks*** [1965]	$ .75	$2.50	$5.00
52-883	Daniels, Dorothy - ***The Lily Pond*** [1965] PBO.	$ .75	$2.50	$5.00

		G	VG	F
50-884	MacDonald, Zillah K. & Ahl, Vivian J. - ***Nurse Todd's Strange Summer*** [1965]	$ .65	$2.00	$4.00
52-885	Compton, Anne - ***Harvest Of Dreams*** [1965]	$ .75	$2.50	$5.00
52-887	Williams, Beryl - ***No Pattern For Love*** [1965]	$ .65	$2.00	$4.00
52-888	Damion, Steve - ***A Time Of Heroes*** [1966] PBO. Cover art by Harry Schaare.	$ .75	$2.50	$5.00
52-889	Beresford, Elisabeth - ***Roses Round The Door*** [1966]	$ .75	$2.50	$5.00
52-890	Ross, W. E. D. - ***Summer Star*** [1966]	$ .75	$2.50	$5.00
52-891	Haycox, Ernest - ***Chaffee Of Roaring Horse*** [1966]	$ .75	$2.50	$5.00
55-892	Adamson, Helen Lyon - ***Grandmother's Household Hints*** [1966]	$ .75	$2.50	$5.00
52-893	Booton, Kage - ***Place Of Shadows*** [1966]	$ .75	$2.50	$5.00
52-894	Coffman, Virginia - ***Castle Barra*** [1966]	$ .75	$2.50	$5.00
52-895	Ross, Marilyn - ***Phantom Manor*** [1966] PBO. Cover art by Victor Kalin.	$1.35	$4.00	$8.00
52-896	Booton, Kage - ***The Troubled House*** [1966]	$ .75	$2.50	$5.00
52-897	Randell, Christine - ***Whisper Of Fear*** [1966]	$ .75	$2.50	$5.00
52-898	Carew, Jean - ***Look Back, My Love*** [1966]	$ .75	$2.50	$5.00
52-899	Hall, Bennie C. - ***When Hearts Remember*** [1966]	$ .75	$2.50	$5.00
55-900	Caprio, M.D., Frank S. & Brenner, Donald R - ***Sexual Behavior: Psycho-Legal Aspects*** [1964]	$ .65	$2.00	$4.00
55-901	Anthology - ***Guide To Sexology Illustrated*** [1965] PBO.	$ .75	$2.50	$5.00
52-904	Little, Paula - ***Love In Style*** [1966]	$ .65	$2.00	$4.00
52-905	Brooks, Anne Tedlock - ***With A Heart Full Of Love*** [1966]	$ .65	$2.00	$4.00
54-907	Heather, Basil - ***The Better Part Of Valor*** [1966]	$ .75	$2.50	$5.00
53-910	Du Maurier, Angela - ***Treveryan*** [1966] Cover art by Victor Kalin	$ .75	$2.50	$5.00
53-911	Lynch, Miriam - ***Blacktower*** [1966]	$ .75	$2.50	$5.00
52-912	Ross, Marilyn - ***Dark Legend*** [1966]	$1.25	$3.75	$7.50
52-913	Ware, Judith - ***The Faxon Secret*** [1966]	$ .75	$2.50	$5.00
52-914	Farrell, Dee - ***Two Loves*** [1966] Cover art by Borack	$ .75	$2.50	$5.00
52-915	Vernon, Marjorie - ***Brief Golden Time*** [1966]	$ .75	$2.50	$5.00
52-916	Manning, Marsha - ***Kisses For Three*** [1966]	$ .75	$2.50	$5.00
52-917	Manley-Tucker, Audrie - ***A Memory Of Summer*** [1966]	$ .75	$2.50	$5.00
52-919	Keene, James - ***Iron Man, Iron Horse*** [1966]	$ .75	$2.50	$5.00
53-920	Cooper, Jefferson (Gardner F. Fox) - ***Sappho Of Lesbos*** [1966]	$1.00	$3.00	$6.00
50-921	Castle, Helen B. - ***Ivy Anders, Night Nurse*** [1966]	$ .65	$2.00	$4.00
52-922	Ross, Marilyn - ***Memory Of Evil*** [1966] PBO.	$1.35	$4.00	$8.00
52-923	Knye, Cassandra (T. Disch & J. Sladek) - ***The House That Fear Built*** [1966] PBO.	$2.00	$6.00	$12.00
52-924	Charles, Theresa - ***House On The Rocks*** [1966]	$ .75	$2.50	$5.00
52-925	Lynn, Margaret - ***Whisper Of Darkness*** [1966]	$ .75	$2.50	$5.00
52-926	MacLeod, Ruth - ***A Love To Cherish*** [1966]	$ .65	$2.00	$4.00
52-927	Nickson, Hilda - ***A Kiss For Elaine*** [1966]	$ .65	$2.00	$4.00
52-928	Creese, Bethea - ***A Dream Comes True*** [1966]	$ .75	$2.50	$5.00
53-929	Nixon, Allan - ***The Last Of Vicky*** [1966] PBO.	$ .75	$2.50	$5.00
52-930	Borderline Magazine - ***Strange, Stranger, Strangest*** [1966]	$ .75	$2.50	$5.00
53-931	Horler, Sydney - ***The Curse Of Doone*** [1966]	$1.00	$3.00	$6.00
50-932	Haycox, Ernest - ***Clint*** [1966]	$ .75	$2.50	$5.00
54-933	Lurie, Alison - ***Love And Friendship*** [1966]	$ .65	$2.00	$4.00
52-934	Furness, Audrey - ***House Of Menace*** [1966]	$ .75	$2.50	$5.00
52-935	Collins, Wilkie - ***The Lady Of Glenwith Grange*** [1966] PBO.	$ .75	$2.50	$5.00
52-936	Charles, Theresa - ***Return To Terror*** [1966]	$ .75	$2.50	$5.00
52-939	Murray, H. S. - ***The Renegades*** [1966] PBO.	$ .75	$2.50	$5.00
55-940	Gilbert, Dr. Michael M. - ***21 Abnormal Sex Cases*** [1966]	$ .65	$2.00	$4.00
52-941	Adler, Allen - ***Terror On Planet Ionus*** [1966]	$1.00	$3.00	$6.00
54-942	Houston, Joe Leon - ***Desire In The Shadows*** [1966]	$ .75	$2.50	$5.00
52-944	Shiel, M. P. - ***The Purple Cloud*** [1966]	$1.00	$3.00	$6.00
53-946	Stoker, Bram - ***The Garden Of Evil*** [1966]	$1.35	$4.00	$8.00
52-947	Ross, Marilyn - ***Satan's Rock*** [1966] PBO.	$1.35	$4.00	$8.00

		G	VG	F
52-948	Edward, Marie Elaine - ***Lenore*** [1966] PBO.	$ .75	$2.50	$5.00
52-949	Weston, Helen Gray - ***Mystic Manor*** [1966]	$ .75	$2.50	$5.00
56-951	Shann, Renee - ***The Man Of Her Dreams*** [1966] Cover art by Mort Engel.	$ .65	$2.00	$4.00
55-954	Robie, M.D., W. F. - ***The Pleasure Of Love*** [1966]	$ .65	$2.00	$4.00
52-955	Del Rey, Lester - ***Step To The Stars*** [1966]	$1.00	$3.00	$6.00
50-956	Wesley, Elizabeth - ***Dr. Dorothy's Choice*** [1966] Cover art by Marchetti.	$ .65	$2.00	$4.00
50-957	Haycox, Ernest - ***Rim Of The Desert*** [1966]	$ .75	$2.50	$5.00
53-958	Schuler, Elizabeth - ***German Cooking*** [1966]	$ .75	$2.50	$5.00
53-959	Engle, Fannie & Blair, Gertrude - ***The Jewish Festival Cookbook*** [1966]	$ .75	$2.50	$5.00
54-960	Collins, Wilkie - ***The Moonstone*** [1966]	$1.00	$3.00	$6.00
52-961	Lynch, Miriam - ***Night Of The Moonrose*** [1966] PBO.	$ .75	$2.50	$5.00
54-962	Stoker, Bram - ***The Lady Of The Shroud*** [1966] Cover art by Victor Kalin.	$1.35	$4.00	$8.00
52-963	Houston, Margaret Bell - ***Yonder*** [1966]	$ .75	$2.50	$5.00
52-966	Fate Magazine - ***Fate's Strangest Mysteries*** [1966]	$ .75	$2.50	$5.00
55-967	Hurwood, Bernhardt J. - ***Erotica*** [1966]	$ .75	$2.50	$5.00
56-968	Wollheim, Donald A. - ***Mike Mars Astronaut*** [1966] Cover art by Hanke.	$1.00	$3.00	$6.00
50-969	Thurman, Steve - ***The Hungry Gun*** [1966] PBO.	$ .75	$2.50	$5.00
50-970	Castle, Helen B. - ***Emergency Ward Nurse*** [1966] Cover art by Lou Marchetti.	$ .65	$2.00	$4.00
52-971	Wolan, William F. - ***Impact-20*** [1966] Cover art by Richard Powers.	$1.00	$3.00	$6.00
56-972	Wollheim, Donald A. - ***Mike Mars Flies The X-15*** [1966] Cover art by Hanke.	$1.00	$3.00	$6.00
52-974	White, Ethel Lina - ***While She Sleeps!*** [1966]	$1.00	$3.00	$6.00
52-975	Winston, Daoma - ***Sinister Stone*** [1966]	$ .75	$2.50	$5.00
53-976	Nicolson, John U. - ***Fingers Of Fear*** [1966] PBO.	$1.00	$3.00	$6.00
54-977	Wadelton, Maggie-Owen - ***Sarah Mandrake*** [1966]	$ .65	$2.00	$4.00
52-979	Hull, E. M. - ***The Sheik*** [1966]	$ .75	$2.50	$5.00
53-980	Gallery, Daniel V. - ***Now, Here This!*** [1966]	$ .75	$2.50	$5.00
56-981	Wollheim, Donald A. - ***Mike Mars At Cape Kennedy*** [1966] Cover art by Hanke.	$1.00	$3.00	$6.00
54-984	McGovern, James - ***Crossbow And Overcast*** [1966] Cover art by Mac.	$ .75	$2.50	$5.00
52-985	Spinrad, Norman - ***The Solarians*** [1966] PBO.	$1.00	$3.00	$6.00
50-986	Joscelyn, Archie - ***Vengeance Trail*** [1966]	$ .75	$2.50	$5.00
50-987	Daniels, Dorothy - ***Cruise Ship Nurse*** [1966] Cover art by Lou Marchetti.	$ .65	$2.00	$4.00
52-988	White, Ethel Lina - ***Step In The Dark*** [1966]	$1.00	$3.00	$6.00
52-989	Randell, Christine - ***A Woman Possessed*** [1966] PBO.	$ .75	$2.50	$5.00
52-990	Ross, Marilyn - ***A Gathering Of Evil*** [1966] PBO.	$1.35	$4.00	$8.00
52-991	Jardin, Rex - ***The Devil's Mansion*** [1966] PBO.	$ .75	$2.50	$5.00
55-993	Goldberg, Hyman - ***Our Man In The Kitchen*** [1966]	$ .75	$2.50	$5.00
54-994	Derrig, Peter - ***The Pride Of The Green Berets*** [1966]	$ .75	$2.50	$5.00
54-995	Lewis, Jack - ***Tell It To The Marines*** [1966]	$ .75	$2.50	$5.00
52-996	Wollheim, Donald A. - ***The Secret Of Saturn's Rings*** [1966] Cover art by Hanke.	$1.00	$3.00	$6.00
56-998	Wollheim, Donald A. - ***Mike Mars In Orbit*** [1966] Cover art by Hanke.	$1.00	$3.00	$6.00
52-999	Anthology - ***Beyond The Strange*** [1966]	$ .75	$2.50	$5.00
52-501	Chamberlain, William - ***Red January*** [1964] PBO.	$ .75	$2.50	$5.00
52-503	Keyes, Frances Parkinson - ***Lady Blanche Farm*** [1964]	$ .75	$2.50	$5.00
52-504	Anthology - ***Son Of Famous Monsters Of Filmland*** [1965]	$2.50	$7.50	$15.00
52-505	Smith, F. E. - ***Lydia Trendennis*** [1965]	$ .75	$2.50	$5.00
52-506	Simak, Clifford D. - ***Cosmic Engineers*** [1964]	$1.00	$3.00	$6.00
52-507	Keyes, Frances Parkinson - ***Queen Anne's Lace*** [1964]	$ .75	$2.50	$5.00

		G	VG	F
52-508	Ellison, Harlan - ***Earthman, Go Home!*** [1964]	$3.00	$9.00	$18.00
52-509	Anthology edited by John W. Campbell - ***Analog 2*** [1965]	$1.25	$3.75	$7.50
52-510	Daniels, Dorothy - ***Shadow Glen*** [1965]	$ .75	$2.50	$5.00
51-511	Charlson, David - ***Frenchie*** [1965]	$ .75	$2.50	$5.00
52-512	Ware, Judith (Ware Torrey & Bud Long) - ***Quarry House*** [1965] PBO. Cover art by Lou Marchetti.	$ .75	$2.50	$5.00
52-513	Letton, Jennette - ***Hilltop*** [1965]	$ .75	$2.50	$5.00
52-514	Biggle, Jr., Lloyd - ***All The Colors Of Darkness*** [1965] Cover art by Hoot.	$1.00	$3.00	$6.00
52-515	Van Vogt, A. E. - ***Monsters*** [1965] PBO.	$1.00	$3.00	$6.00
52-516	Merritt, A. - ***Dwellers In The Mirage*** [1965]	$1.00	$3.00	$6.00
52-517	O'Rourke, Frank - ***"E" Company*** [1965]	$ .75	$2.50	$5.00
52-519	Edited by Roger Elwood - ***Invasion Of The Robots*** [1965]	$1.00	$3.00	$6.00
52-520	Crandall, Edward - ***White Violets*** [1965]	$ .75	$2.50	$5.00
52-521	Wylie, Philip & Balmer, Edwin - ***When Worlds Collide*** [1965]	$1.00	$3.00	$6.00
54-523	Giles, Janice Holt - ***Johnny Osage*** [1967]	$ .75	$2.50	$5.00
53-524	Austen, Martin - ***All The Hungry Young Bodies*** [1967] PBO.	$ .75	$2.50	$5.00
52-525	Weston, Helen Gray - ***House Of False Faces*** [1967] PBO.	$ .75	$2.50	$5.00
52-526	Richard, Susan - ***The Secret Of Chateau Kendall*** [1967] PBO.	$ .75	$2.50	$5.00
52-527	Blackstock, Charity - ***Witches' Sabbath*** [1967]	$1.35	$4.00	$8.00
52-529	Brand, Max - ***The Song Of The Whip*** [1967]	$ .75	$2.50	$5.00
54-530	Giles, Janice Holt - ***Voyage To Santa Fe*** [1967]	$ .75	$2.50	$5.00
53-531	Hunt, Todd - ***The Ship With The Flat Tire*** [1967] Cover art by Bob Jones.	$ .75	$2.50	$5.00
54-532	Mitiri, Gwen - ***Hong Kong Madam*** [1967] PBO.	$ .75	$2.50	$5.00
53-533	Conway, Troy - ***The Berlin Wall Affair*** [1967]	$ .75	$2.50	$5.00
53-538	Hamilton, Edmond - ***The Star Kings*** [1967]	$ .75	$2.50	$5.00
56-539	Arthur, Burt - ***Flaming Guns*** [1967]	$ .75	$2.50	$5.00
52-541	Collins, Wilkie - ***The Yellow Mask*** [1967] PBO. Cover art by George Ziel.	$ .75	$2.50	$5.00
52-542	Richard, Susan - ***Ashley Hall*** [1967] PBO.	$ .75	$2.50	$5.00
52-543	Ross, Marilyn - ***Strangers At Collins House*** [1967]	$ .75	$2.50	$5.00
54-544	Nixon, Allan - ***The Actor*** [1967]	$ .75	$2.50	$5.00
52-545	Brand, Max - ***Showdown*** [1967]	$ .75	$2.50	$5.00
54-546	Giles, Janice Holt - ***The Believers*** [1967]	$ .75	$2.50	$5.00
52-547	Magazine, Fate - ***Fate-Stranger Than Fiction*** [1967]	$ .75	$2.50	$5.00
54-552	Wheatley, Dennis - ***The Eunich Of Stamboul*** [1967]	$ .75	$2.50	$5.00
52-554	Thomas, Martin (Peter Saxon) - ***Beyond The Spectrum*** [1967] Cover art by Victor Kalin.	$1.00	$3.00	$6.00
52-555	Anthology edited by Forrest J. Ackerman - ***A. E. Van Vogt-Monsters*** [1967] Cover art by Jerome Podwil.	$1.00	$3.00	$6.00
56-556	Arthur, Burt - ***Two Gun Outlaw*** [1967]	$ .75	$2.50	$5.00
53-557	Chagall, David - ***Like Now*** [1967]	$ .75	$2.50	$5.00
54-559	Langley, Noel - ***Edgar Cayce On Reincarnation*** [1967]	$ .75	$2.50	$5.00
54-560	Potter, John Deane - ***Yamamoto*** [1967]	$ .75	$2.50	$5.00
52-561	Schaill, William S. - ***7 Days To Faster Reading*** [1967]	$ .65	$2.00	$4.00
52-562	Saxon, Peter - ***The Darkest Night*** [1967]	$1.25	$3.75	$7.50
54-563	Hunter, Karen - ***The House Of Love*** [1967] PBO.	$ .75	$2.50	$5.00
52-564	Brand, Max - ***Tenderfoot*** [1967]	$ .75	$2.50	$5.00
53-566	King, David - ***Two-Faced Enemy*** [1967] PBO.	$ .75	$2.50	$5.00
53-567	O'Donnell, Elliott - ***The Dead Riders*** [1967] Cover art by Peter Caras.	$2.50	$7.50	$15.00
52-569	Wynne, Barry - ***The Man Who Refused To die*** [1967]	$1.00	$3.00	$6.00
52-572	Stuart, W. J. - ***Forbidden Planet*** [1967] Cover art by Jack Gaughan.	$2.50	$7.50	$15.00
54-573	Farago, Ladislas - ***The Tenth Fleet*** [1967]	$ .75	$2.50	$5.00
56-574	Arthur, Burt - ***Gun Law On The Range*** [1967]	$ .75	$2.50	$5.00
52-575	Terry, Jr., Marshall - ***Don't Blow Your Cool*** [1967]	$ .75	$2.50	$5.00
54-576	Wolsey, Serge G. - ***Call House Madam*** [1967]	$ .75	$2.50	$5.00

		G	VG	F
54-577	Anthology edited by Robert P. Mills - ***Worlds Of Science Fiction*** [1967]	$1.00	$3.00	$6.00
52-578	Shulman, Sandra - ***Castlecliffe*** [1967] PBO. Cover art by Jerome Podwil.	$ .75	$2.50	$5.00
52-579	Randell, Christine - ***The Weeping Tower*** [1967] PBO.	$ .75	$2.50	$5.00
54-580	Gallery, Daniel V. - ***U-505*** [1967]	$ .75	$2.50	$5.00
52-581	Brand, Max - ***Montana Rides!*** [1967]	$ .75	$2.50	$5.00
53-582	Stone, W. Clement & Browning, Norma Lee - ***The Other Side Of The Mind*** [1967]	$ .75	$2.50	$5.00
52-584	Ballinger, W. A. (W. Howard Baker) - ***Drums Of The Dark Gods*** [1967] PBO. Cover art by Peter Caras.	$1.50	$5.00	$10.00
53-585	Gibbons, Gavin - ***On Board The Flying Saucers*** [1967]	$ .75	$2.50	$5.00
52-586	Carter, Lin - ***Thongor Against The Gods*** [1967] PBO. Cover art by Frank Frazetta.	$1.00	$3.00	$6.00
53-588	Farrell, James T. - ***Slum Street, USA*** [1967]	$1.00	$3.00	$6.00
52-590	Joscelyn, Archie - ***Gun Thunder Valley*** [1967] Cover art by George Gross.	$ .75	$2.50	$5.00
52-591	Hill, Dee - ***You Better Believe It*** [1967]	$ .75	$2.50	$5.00
53-592	Woodward, Edward - ***The House Of Terror*** [1967] Cover art by Podwil.	$1.25	$3.75	$7.50
54-593	Allen, Edward Frank - ***The Complete Dream Book*** [1967]	$ .75	$2.50	$5.00
52-594	Brand, Max - ***Outlaw Valley*** [1967] Cover art by George Gross.	$ .75	$2.50	$5.00
52-595	Gibson, Edmond P. - ***The Strange Hand Of Fate*** [1967]	$ .75	$2.50	$5.00
54-596	Whitcomb, Edgar D. - ***Escape From Corregidor*** [1967] Cover art by Deon Ellis.	$ .75	$2.50	$5.00
52-598	Saxon, Peter - ***Scream And Scream Again*** [1967] Cover art by Victor Kalin.	$2.50	$7.50	$15.00
52-599	Mason, Douglas R. - ***Eight Against Utopia*** [1967] Cover art by Jack Gaughan.	$1.00	$3.00	$6.00
53-602	Garth, David - ***The Watch On The Bridge*** [1965]	$ .75	$2.50	$5.00
53-603	Smith, Thorne - ***Turnabout*** [1965]	$1.00	$3.00	$6.00
52-608	Ross, Marilyn - ***The Curse Of Collinwood*** [1968] "Dark Shadows" TV photo cover/tie-in.	$1.35	$4.00	$8.00
52-609	Hamilton, Edmond - ***Battle For The Stars*** [1967]	$1.00	$3.00	$6.00
52-610	Ross, Marilyn - ***The Mystery Of Collinwood*** [1967]	$1.35	$4.00	$8.00
52-611	Raymond, Mary - ***The Long Journey Home*** [1967] PBO.	$ .75	$2.50	$5.00
52-613	Brand, Max - ***Montana Rides Again*** [1968]	$ .75	$2.50	$5.00
52-614	Anthology - ***The Strange World Of The Occult*** [1968] PBO.	$ .75	$2.50	$5.00
53-615	Conway, Troy - ***The Big Freak-Out*** [1968]	$ .75	$2.50	$5.00
54-616	Churchward, Col. James - ***The Lost Continent Of Mu*** [1968]	$1.00	$3.00	$6.00
53-618	De Camp, L. Sprague - ***The Tritonian Ring*** [1968] Cover art by Frank Frazetta.	$1.00	$3.00	$6.00
52-621	Lehman, Paul Evan - ***Fighting Buckaroo*** [1968] Cover art by Peter Caras.	$ .75	$2.50	$5.00
52-622	Anthology edited by Miriam Allen deFord - ***Space, Time & Crime*** [1968] Cover art by Jack Gaughan.	$1.25	$3.75	$7.50
52-624	Abbott, Sandra - ***Whispering Gables*** [1968]	$ .75	$2.50	$5.00
53-625	Goldman, Lawrence Louis - ***Judd For The Defense*** [1968] PBO.	$ .75	$2.50	$5.00
53-626	Black, Lionel - ***The Bait*** [1968]	$ .75	$2.50	$5.00
52-627	Evans, Evan (Max Brand) - ***Outlaw's Code*** [1968]	$ .75	$2.50	$5.00
53-628	King, David - ***The Rat Patrol In Target For Tonight*** [1968] PBO.	$1.00	$3.00	$6.00
54-629	Ford, Arthur - ***Nothing So Strange*** [1968]	$ .75	$2.50	$5.00
52-631	Wayland, Patrick - ***Counterstroke*** [1968]	$ .75	$2.50	$5.00
53-632	Seth, Ronald - ***Secret Servants*** [1968]	$ .75	$2.50	$5.00
54-633	Anthology edited by Hans S. Santesson - ***The Fantastic Universe Omnibus*** [1968] Cover art by Jerome Podwil.	$1.00	$3.00	$6.00
52-635	Fox, Gardner F. - ***Escape Across The Cosmos*** [1968] Cover art by Peter Caras.	$1.00	$3.00	$6.00

		G	VG	F
52-637	Shenkin, Elizabeth - ***Brownstone Gothic*** [1968] Cover art by Jerome Podwil.	$ .75	$2.50	$5.00
52-638	Lehman, Paul Evan - ***Range Justice*** [1968]	$ .75	$2.50	$5.00
54-639	Churchward, Col. James - ***The Children Of Mu*** [1968]	$1.00	$3.00	$6.00
53-641	Campbell, Alice - ***With Bated Breath*** [1968]	$ .75	$2.50	$5.00
52-643	Tidyman, Ernest - ***Flower Power*** [1968] PBO.	$ .75	$2.50	$5.00
52-645	Gulick, Bill - ***A Drum Calls West*** [1968]	$ .75	$2.50	$5.00
52-646	Brown, Wenzell - ***How To Tell Fortunes With Cards*** [1968]	$ .75	$2.50	$5.00
53-648	Archer, Fred - ***Exploring The Psychic World*** [1968]	$ .75	$2.50	$5.00
52-649	MacApp, C. C. - ***Omaha Abides*** [1968] PBO.	$1.25	$3.75	$7.50
54-650	Norris, Kathleen - ***Three Men And Diana*** [1968]	$ .75	$2.50	$5.00
52-651	Vale, Rena - ***Beyond The Search World*** [1968]	$ .75	$2.50	$5.00
52-652	Quandt, Albert T. - ***Vinnie*** [1968]	$ .75	$2.50	$5.00
53-653	Norris, Kathleen - ***Gabrielle*** [1968]	$ .75	$2.50	$5.00
52-654	Lehman, Paul Evan - ***Rustler's Trail*** [1968]	$ .75	$2.50	$5.00
54-655	Daniels, Dorothy - ***Lady Of The Shadows*** [1968] PBO.	$ .75	$2.50	$5.00
54-656	Cayce, Edgar Evans - ***Edgar Cayce On Atlantis*** [1968]	$ .75	$2.50	$5.00
53-657	Hanlon, Edward S. - ***The Great God Now*** [1968] PBO.	$ .75	$2.50	$5.00
52-658	Gulick, Bill - ***Bend Of The Snake*** [1968]	$ .75	$2.50	$5.00
54-659	Gallery, Daniel V. - ***Eight Bells*** [1968] Cover art by Bob Jones.	$ .75	$2.50	$5.00
54-660	? - ***Rendezvous At Midway*** [1968]	$ .75	$2.50	$5.00
54-663	Churchward, Col. James - ***The Sacred Symbols Of Mu*** [1968]	$1.00	$3.00	$6.00
53-665	Carter, Lin - ***Thongor In The City Of Magicians*** [1968] PBO. Cover art by Frank Frazetta.	$1.00	$3.00	$6.00
54-666	Norris, Kathleen - ***Maiden Voyage*** [1968]	$ .75	$2.50	$5.00
53-667	? - ***Alien Worlds*** [1968]	$1.00	$3.00	$6.00
54-668	Norris, Kathleen - ***The Secret Of The Marshbanks*** [1968]	$ .75	$2.50	$5.00
54-669	Greene, Joe - ***House Of Pleasure*** [1968]	$ .75	$2.50	$5.00
52-670	Floren, Lee - ***Black Gunsmoke*** [1968]	$ .75	$2.50	$5.00
54-671	Kaufman, Ted & Jean - ***Cooking For Two*** [1968]	$ .75	$2.50	$5.00
54-672	Whelan, Russell - ***The Flying Tigers*** [1968] Cover art by Peter Caras.	$ .75	$2.50	$5.00
52-673	Gulick, Bill - ***The Moon-Eyed Appaloosa*** [1968] Cover art by Peter Caras.	$ .75	$2.50	$5.00
53-675	Conway, Troy - ***The Billion Dollar Snatch*** [1968]	$ .75	$2.50	$5.00
53-677	Giles, Raymond - ***Night Of The Warlock*** [1968] PBO.	$1.00	$3.00	$6.00
54-678	Churchward, Col. James - ***The Cosmic Forces Of Mu*** [1968]	$1.00	$3.00	$6.00
54-679	Miller, Sigmund Stephen - ***That's The Way The Money Goes*** [1968]	$ .75	$2.50	$5.00
53-680	White, Ted - ***The Spawn Of The Death Machine*** [1968] PBO. Cover art by Jeff Jones.	$1.25	$3.75	$7.50
54-681	Norris, Kathleen - ***Second-Hand Wife*** [1968]	$ .75	$2.50	$5.00
53-682	Head, Ann - ***Always In August*** [1968]	$ .75	$2.50	$5.00
54-684	Barzman, Ben - ***Echo X*** [1968] Cover art by Peter Caras.	$1.00	$3.00	$6.00
52-685	Ray, Wesley - ***Long Day In Latigo*** [1968]	$ .75	$2.50	$5.00
52-687	Resnick, Michael D. - ***The Goddess Of Ganymede*** [1968] Cover art by Jeff Jones.	$1.35	$4.00	$8.00
52-688	Arthur, Burt & Budd - ***The Saga Of Denny McCune*** [1968] PBO. Cover art by George Gross.	$ .75	$2.50	$5.00
54-690	Browne, Courtney - ***Tojo: The Last Banzai*** [1968]	$ .75	$2.50	$5.00
55-693	Gaskell, Jane - ***The Serpent*** [1968] Cover art by Frank Frazetta.	$2.00	$6.00	$12.00
53-694	Ross, Marilyn - ***Shorecliff*** [1968] PBO.	$1.35	$4.00	$8.00
52-695	Anthology - ***Strange Psychic Experiences*** [1968] PBO.	$ .75	$2.50	$5.00
53-696	King, David - ***The Rat Patrol In Desert Masquerade*** [1968] PBO.	$1.00	$3.00	$6.00
52-697	Zinderman, Karyl F. - ***Simple Crafts To Make At Home For Less Than 50 Cents*** [1968] PBO.	$ .75	$2.50	$5.00
54-698	Dickson, Ruth - ***Married Men Make The Best Lovers*** [1968]	$ .75	$2.50	$5.00
54-699	Carter, Mary Ellen - ***Edgar Cayce On Prophecy*** [1968] PBO.	$ .75	$2.50	$5.00

		G	VG	F
54-700	Greene, Joe - ***House Of Pleasure*** [1965] PBO. Cover art by Bob Abbett.	$ .75	$2.50	$5.00
54-703	Schrobsdorff, Angelika - ***The Men*** [1965]	$ .75	$2.50	$5.00
54-709	Miller, Sigmund Stephen - ***That's The Way The Money Goes*** [1965]	$ .75	$2.50	$5.00
54-712	Granat, Robert - ***Only The Brave*** [1965]	$ .75	$2.50	$5.00
54-713	Norris, Kathleen - ***Younger Sister*** [1968]	$ .75	$2.50	$5.00
53-715	Smith, F. E. - ***Lydia Trendennis*** [1968]	$ .75	$2.50	$5.00
54-717	Nixon, Allan - ***The Star*** [1968]	$ .75	$2.50	$5.00
52-718	Hunter, John (W. T. Ballard) - ***Duke*** [1968]	$1.25	$3.75	$7.50
54-719	Norris, Kathleen - ***The Lucky Lawrences*** [1968]	$ .75	$2.50	$5.00
53-720	Dorien, Ray - ***The House Of Dread*** [1968]	$ .75	$2.50	$5.00
53-721	Goldman, Lawrence Louis - ***The Secret Listeners*** [1968]	$ .75	$2.50	$5.00
54-722	Steirman, Hy - ***Strike Terror*** [1968] PBO.	$ .75	$2.50	$5.00
54-723	Norris, Kathleen - ***My Best Girl*** [1968]	$ .75	$2.50	$5.00
53-725	Conway, Troy (Fritch & Gilbert) - ***It's Getting Harder All The Time*** [1968] PBO.	$ .75	$2.50	$5.00
52-726	Owen, Dean - ***Winter Grass*** [1968] PBO.	$ .75	$2.50	$5.00
53-727	Ellison, Harlan - ***Earthman, Go Home!*** [1968] Cover art by Peter Caras.	$1.00	$3.00	$6.00
55-728	Richler, Mordecai - ***The Apprenticeship Of Duddy Kravitz*** [1968]	$ .75	$2.50	$5.00
52-730	Shelley, John - ***A Gun For Billy Hardin*** [1968] Cover art by George Gross.	$ .75	$2.50	$5.00
54-731	Cooper, Jefferson (Gardner F. Fox) - ***Jezebel*** [1968]	$1.00	$3.00	$6.00
54-732	Norris, Kathleen - ***Mink Coat*** [1968]	$ .75	$2.50	$5.00
55-733	Manvell, Roger & Fraenkel, Heinrich - ***Himmler*** [1968]	$ .75	$2.50	$5.00
53-734	Goodman, Morris C. - ***Modern Numerology*** [1968]	$ .75	$2.50	$5.00
53-735	Conway, Troy (Michael Avallone) - ***Come One, Come All*** [1968] PBO.	$ .75	$2.50	$5.00
52-736	Hawk, Alex - ***Savage Guns*** [1968]	$ .75	$2.50	$5.00
53-737	Shulman, Sandra - ***The Brides Of Devil's Leap*** [1968] PBO.	$ .75	$2.50	$5.00
55-738	Gaskell, Jane - ***Atlan*** [1968] Cover art by Frank Frazetta.	$ .75	$2.50	$5.00
54-745	Nixon, Allan - ***Blessed Are The Damned*** [1968]	$ .75	$2.50	$5.00
53-746	Biggle, Jr., Lloyd - ***All The Colors Of Darkness*** [1968]	$1.00	$3.00	$6.00
52-747	Keene, James - ***Iron Man, Iron Horse*** [1968]	$ .75	$2.50	$5.00
54-751	Sava, M.D., George - ***Abnormal Sex: A Doctor's Casebook*** [1968]	$ .65	$2.00	$4.00
55-752	Treece, Henry - ***The Green Man*** [1968]	$1.00	$3.00	$6.00
54-754	Churchward, Col. James - ***The Second Book Of The Cosmic Forces Of Mu*** [1968]	$1.00	$3.00	$6.00
53-755	Marion, Hargrove - ***See Here, Private Hargrove*** [1968]	$ .75	$2.50	$5.00
53-756	Randell, Christine - ***Black Candle*** [1968]	$ .75	$2.50	$5.00
52-757	Owen, Dean - ***Ponderosa Kill*** [1968] PBO.	$ .75	$2.50	$5.00
54-758	Schurmacher, Emile C. - ***Lost Treasures And How To Find Them!*** [1968] PBO.	$ .75	$2.50	$5.00
53-759	Conway, Troy (C. Fritch & P. Gilbert) - ***Last Licks*** [1968]	$ .75	$2.50	$5.00
52-760	Resnick, Michael D. - ***Pursuit On Ganymede*** [1968] PBO. Cover art by Jeff Jones.	$1.35	$4.00	$8.00
53-763	Binder, Eando - ***Adam Link-Robot*** [1968]	$1.00	$3.00	$6.00
52-764	Murray, H. S. - ***The Renegades*** [1968]	$ .75	$2.50	$5.00
54-766	Norris, Kathleen - ***Love Calls The Tune*** [1968]	$ .75	$2.50	$5.00
54-769	Norris, Kathleen - ***The Sea Gull*** [1968]	$ .75	$2.50	$5.00
54-771	Engle, Fannie & Blair, Gertrude - ***The Jewish Festival Cookbook*** [1968]	$ .75	$2.50	$5.00
54-772	Schuler, Elizabeth - ***German Cooking*** [1968]	$ .75	$2.50	$5.00
53-773	John, Owen - ***The Disinformer*** [1968]	$ .75	$2.50	$5.00
55-774	Hutchinson, Beryl B. - ***Your Life In Your Hands*** [1968]	$ .75	$2.50	$5.00
53-775	Conway, Troy - ***Keep It Up, Rod!*** [1968] PBO.	$ .75	$2.50	$5.00
54-776	Hartzell, Harmon - ***Edgar Cayce On Dreams*** [1968]	$ .75	$2.50	$5.00

		G	VG	F
52-777	Hawk, Alex - ***Ruthless Return*** [1968]	$ .75	$2.50	$5.00
53-778	Cotler, Gordon - ***The Bottletop Affair*** [1968] Cover art by Bob Jones.	$ .75	$2.50	$5.00
53-780	Carter, Lin - ***Thongor At The End Of Time*** [1968] PBO. Cover art by Jeff Jones.	$1.25	$3.75	$7.50
54-782	Dumaurier, Angela - ***Treveryan*** [1968]	$ .75	$2.50	$5.00
55-783	Richler, Mordecai - ***Son Of A Smaller Hero*** [1968]	$ .75	$2.50	$5.00
52-784	Thurman, Steve - ***The Hungry Gun*** [1968]	$ .75	$2.50	$5.00
53-785	Somers, Bart (Gardner F. Fox) - ***Beyond The Black Enigma*** [1968] Cover art by Jack Gaughan.	$1.00	$3.00	$6.00
54-787	Payne, Robert - ***The Gold Of Troy*** [1968]	$ .75	$2.50	$5.00
58-789	Hubbard, L. Ron - ***Dianetics: The Modern Science Of Mental Health*** [1968]	$1.50	$5.00	$10.00
54-792	Cayce, Hugh Lynn - ***Venture Inward*** [1968]	$ .75	$2.50	$5.00
54-796	Adamski, George - ***Inside The Flying Saucers*** [1968]	$ .75	$2.50	$5.00

Paperback Library 60–Series. New York: Paperback Library, Inc.

		G	VG	F
62-001	Ross, Marilyn - ***Barnabas Collins*** [1968]	$1.25	$3.75	$7.50
66-002	Adams, Henry H. - ***1942: The Year That Doomed The Axis*** [1969]	$ .75	$2.50	$5.00
63-003	Dennis, Charles H. - ***Sex Anyone?*** [1968] PBO. Cover art by Charles H. Dennis.	$ .75	$2.50	$5.00
64-004	Rico, Don - ***The Ring-A-Ding Girl*** [1969] PBO.	$ .75	$2.50	$5.00
63-005	Conway, Troy (Michael Avallone) - ***The Man-Eater*** [1968] PBO.	$ .75	$2.50	$5.00
65-008	Rosen, Billie Pesin - ***The Science Of Handwriting Analysis*** [1968]	$ .65	$2.00	$4.00
62-009	Tubb, E. C. - ***S.T.A.R. Flight*** [1969] PBO.	$1.00	$3.00	$6.00
64-010	Norris, Kathleen - ***Josselyn's Wife*** [1969]	$ .75	$2.50	$5.00
63-013	Letton, Jennette - ***Hilltop*** [1968]	$ .75	$2.50	$5.00
64-015	Packer, Vin - ***Dark Don't Catch Me*** [1968]	$ .75	$2.50	$5.00
63-016	Van Vogt, A. E - ***The House That Stood Still*** [1968]	$1.00	$3.00	$6.00
64-019	Gaskell, Jane - ***The City*** [1968] Cover art by Jeff Jones.	$2.00	$6.00	$12.00
63-020	Carol, Robin - ***The Ancestor*** [1968] PBO. Cover art by Jerome Podwil.	$ .75	$2.50	$5.00
65-023	Tralins, Robert - ***Cairo Madam*** [1968] PBO.	$ .75	$2.50	$5.00
64-024	Norris, Kathleen - ***Secret Marriage*** [1968]	$ .75	$2.50	$5.00
66-025	Bakal, Carl - ***No Right To Bear Arms*** [1968]	$ .75	$2.50	$5.00
64-030	Karlova, Irina - ***Dreadful Hollow*** [1968]	$ .75	$2.50	$5.00
65-033	Wertham, M.D., Fredric - ***A Sign For Cain*** [1968]	$ .75	$2.50	$5.00
63-034	Daniels, Dorothy - ***The Tormented*** [1969] PBO. Cover art by Jerome Podwil.	$ .75	$2.50	$5.00
64-036	Ready, William - ***Understanding Tolkien And The Lord Of The Rings*** [1969]	$1.25	$3.75	$7.50
64-037	Anthology edited by Hugh Lynn Cayce - ***The Edgar Cayce Reader*** [1969] PBO.	$ .75	$2.50	$5.00
62-039	Ross, Marilyn - ***The Secret Of Barnabas Collins*** [1969]	$1.25	$3.75	$7.50
62-040	Hawk, Alex - ***Violence Valley*** [1969] PBO. Cover art by George Gross.	$ .75	$2.50	$5.00
64-041	Norris, Kathleen - ***Manhattan Love Song*** [1969]	$ .65	$2.00	$4.00
63-043	Knye, Cassandra (T. Disch & J. Sladek) - ***The House That Fear Built*** [1969]	$1.00	$3.00	$6.00
63-046	Jay, Charlotte - ***The Yellow Turban*** [1969]	$ .75	$2.50	$5.00
64-047	Dawson, James - ***Hell Gate*** [1969]	$ .75	$2.50	$5.00
63-048	Adler, Allen - ***Terror On Planet Ionus*** [1969] Cover art by Jerome Podwil.	$1.00	$3.00	$6.00
63-049	Jakes, John - ***The Hybrid*** [1969] PBO. Cover art by Jeff Jones.	$1.35	$4.00	$8.00
63-050	Conway, Troy (C. Fritch & P. Gilbert) - ***The Best Laid Plans*** [1969] PBO.	$ .75	$2.50	$5.00
64-054	Norris, Kathleen - ***Walls Of Gold*** [1969]	$ .75	$2.50	$5.00

		G	VG	F
65-058	Caprio, M.D., Frank & Brenner, Donald R. - ***Deviations Of Sexual Behavior*** [1969]	$ .65	$2.00	$4.00
62-062	Anthology - ***Barnabas Collins In A Funny Vein*** [1969] PBO.	$1.35	$4.00	$8.00
63-063	Jones, Raymond F. - ***The Cybernetic Brains*** [1969]	$1.00	$3.00	$6.00
64-067	Zarubica, Mladin - ***Scutari*** [1969]	$ .75	$2.50	$5.00
63-069	Conway, Troy - ***It's What's Up Front That Counts*** [1969] PBO.	$ .75	$2.50	$5.00
64-072	Norris, Kathleen - ***Rose Of The World*** [1969]	$ .65	$2.00	$4.00
63-074	Dodge, Mary Louise - ***Tamara*** [1969] PBO. Cover art by Jerome Podwil.	$ .75	$2.50	$5.00
65-075	Schrobsdorff, Angelika - ***The Men*** [1969]	$ .75	$2.50	$5.00
63-076	Shulman, Sandra - ***The Lady Of Arlac*** [1969]	$ .75	$2.50	$5.00
63-077	Daniels, Dorothy - ***Shadow Glen*** [1969]	$ .75	$2.50	$5.00
63-078	Anthology edited by Roger Elwood - ***Invasion Of The Robots*** [1969] Cover art by Jack Gaughan.	$1.00	$3.00	$6.00
64-082	Mockridge, Norton - ***The Scrawl Of The Wild*** [1969] Illustrated by Jerry Schlamp.	$ .75	$2.50	$5.00
65-083	Nixon, Allan - ***The Bitch Goddess*** [1969]	$ .75	$2.50	$5.00
62-084	Ross, Marilyn - ***The Demon Of Branabas Collins*** [1969] PBO.	$1.35	$4.00	$8.00
63-085	John, Owen - ***A Beam Of Black Light*** [1969]	$ .75	$2.50	$5.00
64-086	Anthology edited by Hugh Lynn Cayce - ***The Edgar Cayce Reader*** [1969]	$ .75	$2.50	$5.00
64-088	Norris, Kathleen - ***The Heart Of Rachael*** [1969]	$ .75	$2.50	$5.00
63-089	Jakes, John - ***Brak The Barbarian Versus The Sorceress*** [1969] PBO. Cover art by Frank Frazetta.	$1.35	$4.00	$8.00
63-092	Van Vogt, A. E. - ***The Book Of Ptath*** [1969] Cover art by Jeff Jones.	$1.00	$3.00	$6.00
63-093	Arvonen, Helen - ***Stranger In Her House*** [1969]	$ .75	$2.50	$5.00
65-094	Robie, M.D., W.F. - ***Pleasure Of Love*** [1969]	$ .65	$2.00	$4.00
64-095	Read, Ilstrup, & Gammon - ***Edgar Cayce On Diet And Health*** [1969] PBO.	$ .75	$2.50	$5.00
63-097	Daniels, Dorothy - ***Marriott Hall*** [1969]	$ .75	$2.50	$5.00
63-100	Daniels, Dorothy - ***Voice On The Wind*** [1969]	$ .75	$2.50	$5.00
65-101	Vinelas, Estrella Marina - ***Cuban Madam*** [1969] PBO.	$ .75	$2.50	$5.00
63-103	Conway, Troy - ***Had Any Lately?*** [1969] PBO.	$ .75	$2.50	$5.00
66-106	Masters, R. E. L. - ***Sexual Obsession*** [1969]	$ .65	$2.00	$4.00
64-109	Norris, Kathleen - ***The Beloved Woman*** [1969]	$ .65	$2.00	$4.00
63-110	Mackelworth, R. W. - ***The Diabols*** [1969]	$1.00	$3.00	$6.00
63-111	Crandall, E. - ***White Violets*** [1969]	$ .75	$2.50	$5.00
65-113	Fodor, Nandor - ***Between Two Worlds*** [1969]	$ .75	$2.50	$5.00
63-114	Evans, Evan (Max Brand) - ***Gunman's Legacy*** [1969]	$ .75	$2.50	$5.00
62-120	Bulmer, Kenneth - ***Kandar*** [1969] PBO. Cover art by Jeff Jones.	$1.25	$3.75	$7.50
64-122	Agee, Doris - ***Edgar Cayce On E.S.P.*** [1969] PBO.	$ .75	$2.50	$5.00
63-123	Daniels, Dorothy - ***The Carson Inheritance*** [1969]	$ .75	$2.50	$5.00
63-124	Davis, Bob - ***The Dingle War*** [1969] Cover art by Bob Jones.	$ .75	$2.50	$5.00
63-125	Conway, Troy - ***Whatever Goes Up*** [1969] PBO.	$ .75	$2.50	$5.00
63-127	John, Owen - ***Thirty Days Hath September*** [1969]	$ .75	$2.50	$5.00
63-130	Bonner, Parker (W.T. Ballard) - ***Borders To Cross*** [1969] PBO.	$1.25	$3.75	$7.50
65-131	Gould, Rupert L. - ***Oddities*** [1969]	$ .75	$2.50	$5.00
63-133	Simak, Clifford D. - ***Cosmic Engineers*** [1969]	$1.00	$3.00	$6.00
62-135	Ross, Marilyn - ***The Foe Of Barnabas Collins*** [1969] PBO.	$1.25	$3.75	$7.50
63-136	Hurt, Freda - ***So Dark A Shadow*** [1969]	$ .75	$2.50	$5.00
65-140	Gould, Rupert T. - ***Enigmas*** [1969]	$ .75	$2.50	$5.00
63-141	Conway, Troy - ***A Good Peace*** [1969] PBO.	$ .75	$2.50	$5.00
64-144	Meilen, Bill - ***KKK*** [1969] Cover art by Peter Caras.	$1.25	$3.75	$7.50
64-146	Norris, Kathleen - ***Burned Fingers*** [1969]	$ .65	$2.00	$4.00
63-147	Corey, Paul - ***The Planet Of The Blind*** [1969] PBO. Cover art by Richard Powers.	$1.00	$3.00	$6.00
63-149	Moorcock, Michael - ***The Winds Of Limbo*** [1969] Cover art by Richard Powers.	$1.00	$3.00	$6.00
63-150	Wolff, Ruth - ***Hawthorne*** [1969]	$ .75	$2.50	$5.00

		G	VG	F
63-155	Ross, Marilyn - ***Fog Island*** [1969]	$1.00	$3.00	$6.00
65-162	Gallery, Admiral Daniel V. - ***The Brink*** [1969]	$ .75	$2.50	$5.00
63-163	Kruger, Paul - ***Weep For Willow Green*** [1969]	$ .75	$2.50	$5.00
64-165	Norris, Kathleen - ***The Love Of Julie Borel*** [1969]	$ .65	$2.00	$4.00
63-166	Moore, C.L. - ***Jirel Of Joiry*** [1969]	$1.00	$3.00	$6.00
63-167	Bonner, Parker (W.T. Ballard) - ***Look To Your Guns*** [1969] PBO.	$1.25	$3.75	$7.50
63-169	Ross, Marilyn - ***The Locked Corridor*** [1969]	$1.00	$3.00	$6.00
63-171	White, Ethel Lina - ***While She Sleeps!*** [1969]	$1.00	$3.00	$6.00
63-172	White, Ethel Lina - ***Fear Stalks The Village*** [1969]	$1.00	$3.00	$6.00
64-174	Cooper, Hughes - ***Sexmax*** [1969] PBO.	$1.25	$3.75	$7.50
63-175	Carol, Robin - ***Gwenyth*** [1969] PBO.	$ .75	$2.50	$5.00
63-180	Kruger, Paul - ***Weave A Wicked Web*** [1969]	$ .75	$2.50	$5.00
66-181	Wood, Derek - ***The Narrow Margin*** [1969]	$ .75	$2.50	$5.00
64-183	Norris, Kathleen - ***The World Is Like That*** [1969]	$ .75	$2.50	$5.00
63-184	James, John - ***Brak the Barbarian Versus The Mark Of The Demons*** [1969] PBO.	$1.00	$3.00	$6.00
64-185	Whitney, Phyllis A. - ***Skye Cameron*** [1969]	$ .75	$2.50	$5.00
64-187	Whitney, Phyllis A. - ***The Red Carnelian*** [1969]	$ .75	$2.50	$5.00
63-188	White, Ethel Lina - ***The Lady Vanishes*** [1969]	$1.00	$3.00	$6.00
63-189	White, Ethel Lina - ***The Unseen*** [1969]	$1.00	$3.00	$6.00
64-191	Johnson, Stanley - ***The Presidential Plot*** [1969]	$ .75	$2.50	$5.00
63-193	Gulick, Bill - ***A Thousand For The Caribo*** [1969]	$ .75	$2.50	$5.00
63-194	Conway, Troy - ***I'd Rather Fight Than Swish*** [1969] PBO.	$ .75	$2.50	$5.00
62-195	Ross, Marilyn - ***The Phantom And Barnabas Collins*** [1969] PBO.	$1.35	$4.00	$8.00
64-196	Maule, Hamilton - ***Rub-A-Dub-Dub*** [1969] Cover art by Bob Jones.	$ .75	$2.50	$5.00
63-197	Brand, Max - ***Montana Rides!*** [1969]	$ .75	$2.50	$5.00
64-199	Norris, Kathleen - ***Over At The Crowley's*** [1969]	$ .75	$2.50	$5.00
63-201	Conway, Troy - ***Just A Silly Millimeter Longer*** [1969]	$ .75	$2.50	$5.00
63-202	Shulman, Sandra - ***The Prisoner Of Garve*** [1970] PBO.	$ .75	$2.50	$5.00
63-203	Chaber, M.E. - ***A Man In The Middle*** [1970]	$1.00	$3.00	$6.00
63-204	Chaber, M.E. - ***Jade For A Lady*** [1970]	$1.00	$3.00	$6.00
62-210	Anthology - ***Personal Picture Album*** [1970]	$1.25	$3.75	$7.50
62-212	Ross, Marilyn - ***Barnabas Collins Versus The Warlock*** [1969] PBO.	$1.35	$4.00	$8.00
63-213	Chaber, M.E. - ***The Man Inside*** [1969]	$1.00	$3.00	$6.00
63-214	Hawk, Alex - ***Mex*** [1969]	$ .75	$2.50	$5.00
63-215	Fletcher, Dorothy - ***Still Waters*** [1969] PBO.	$ .75	$2.50	$5.00
65-216	Bro, Harmon Hartzell, Ph.D. - ***Edgar Cayce On Religion And Psychic Experience*** [1969]	$ .75	$2.50	$5.00
66-217	Tralins, Robert - ***The Sexual Fetish*** [1969]	$ .75	$2.50	$5.00
64-218	Duncan, Bob - ***If It Moves, Salute It*** [1969]	$ .75	$2.50	$5.00
64-220	Hanlon, Edward S. - ***The Forbidden*** [1969]	$ .75	$2.50	$5.00
63-227	Winters, Joanne - ***House Of Joy*** [1969]	$ .75	$2.50	$5.00
63-228	Rankine, John (Douglas R. Mason) - ***Moons Of Triopus*** [1969]	$1.00	$3.00	$6.00
63-231	Chaber, M.E. - ***The Day It Rained Diamonds*** [1969]	$1.00	$3.00	$6.00
63-233	Cromwell, Elsie - ***The Governess*** [1969] PBO.	$ .75	$2.50	$5.00
63-235	Hawk, Alex - ***McGee*** [1969]	$ .75	$2.50	$5.00
63-236	Jakes, John - ***The Asylum World*** [1969] PBO.	$1.25	$3.75	$7.50
64-237	Winston, Daoma - ***Bracken's World*** [1969]	$ .75	$2.50	$5.00
63-238	Daniels, Dorothy - ***The Lily Pond*** [1969]	$ .75	$2.50	$5.00
63-240	Conway, Troy (Michael Avallone) - ***The Big Broad Jump*** [1969] PBO.	$ .75	$2.50	$5.00
63-241	King, David - ***Outlaw Doc*** [1969]	$ .75	$2.50	$5.00
64-243	Gallery, Admiral Daniel V. - ***Stand By-y-y To Start Engines*** [1969]	$ .75	$2.50	$5.00
62-244	Ross, Marilyn - ***The Peril Of Barnabas Collins*** [1969] PBO.	$1.35	$4.00	$8.00
64-246	Hoover, J. Edgar - ***J. Edgar Hoover On Communism*** [1970]	$ .75	$2.50	$5.00

		G	VG	F
63-251	Conway, Troy (Charles Fritch/Paul Gilbert) - ***The Sex Machine*** [1970] PBO.	$ .75	$2.50	$5.00
64-252	Norris, Kathleen - ***Storm House*** [1970]	$ .65	$2.00	$4.00
63-253	Vale, Rena - ***Taurus Four*** [1970] PBO	$1.00	$3.00	$6.00
63-254	Ross, Marilyn - ***Cameron Castle*** [1970]	$ .75	$2.50	$5.00
65-257	Semmes, Harry H. - ***Portrait Of Patton*** [1971]	$ .75	$2.50	$5.00
63-258	Ross, Marilyn - ***Barnabas Collins And The Mysterious Ghost*** [1970] PBO.	$1.35	$4.00	$8.00
63-259	Daniels, Dorothy - ***Strange Paradise*** [1970]	$ .75	$2.50	$5.00
64-261	Reynolds, James - ***Gallery Of Ghosts*** [1970]	$ .75	$2.50	$5.00
63-265	Chaber, M.E. - ***Wild Midnight Falls*** [1970]	$ .75	$2.50	$5.00
63-268	Hank, Alex - ***Blood Trail*** [1970]	$ .75	$2.50	$5.00
64-269	Norris, Kathleen - ***Harriet And The Piper*** [1970]	$ .65	$2.00	$4.00
63-270	del Martia, Astron (John Russell Fearn) - ***One Against Time*** [1970]	$1.00	$3.00	$6.00
63-273	Saxon, Peter - ***Scream And Scream Again*** [1970]	$1.00	$3.00	$6.00
63-275	Ross, Marilyn - ***Barnabas Collins And Quentin's Demon*** [1970] PBO.	$1.35	$4.00	$8.00
63-276	Brand, Max - ***Montana Rides Again*** [1970]	$ .75	$2.50	$5.00
63-278	Brand, Max - ***Outlaw's Code*** [1970]	$ .75	$2.50	$5.00
64-279	Winston, Daoma - ***The High Country*** [1970] PBO.	$ .75	$2.50	$5.00
63-280	Conway, Troy (Michael Avallone) - ***The Blow-Your-Mind Job*** [1970] PBO.	$ .75	$2.50	$5.00
63-282	Gulick, Bill - ***A Drum Calls West*** [1970]	$ .75	$2.50	$5.00
63-283	Antonio, San - ***Stone Dead*** [1970]	$1.00	$3.00	$6.00
63-284	Thom, Robert - ***Bloody Mama*** [1970]	$ .75	$2.50	$5.00
63-287	Antonio, San - ***Tough Justice*** [1970]	$ .75	$2.50	$5.00
63-288	Chaber, M.E. - ***Softly In The Night*** [1970]	$1.00	$3.00	$6.00
63-291	Hawk, Alex - ***Drifter's Luck*** [1970] PBO.	$ .75	$2.50	$5.00
65-292	Norris, Kathleen - ***The Callahans And The Murphys*** [1970]	$ .75	$2.50	$5.00
63-293	Groves, J.W. - ***Shellbreak*** [1970] PBO. Cover art by Jack Gaughan.	$1.00	$3.00	$6.00
63-295	Ray, Wesley - ***Long Day In Latigo*** [1970]	$ .75	$2.50	$5.00
63-296	Ross, Marilyn - ***Barnabas Collins And The Gypsy Witch*** [1970] PBO.	$1.35	$4.00	$8.00
64-299	Keefe, Lynn - ***How Did A Nice Girl Like You Get Into This Business?*** [1970]	$ .75	$2.50	$5.00
64-301	Allen, Maury - ***The Incredible Mets*** [1969] PBO.	$ .75	$2.50	$5.00
63-302	Cromwell, Elsie - ***Ivorstone Manor*** [1969]	$ .75	$2.50	$5.00
63-306	Antonio, San - ***Thugs And Bottles*** [1970]	$ .75	$2.50	$5.00
63-308	Chaber, M.E. - ***The Splintered Man*** [1970]	$1.00	$3.00	$6.00
63-311	Gulick, Bill - ***The Hungry Land*** [1970] Cover art by George Gross.	$ .75	$2.50	$5.00
65-312	Norris, Kathleen - ***Miss Harriet Townshend*** [1970]	$ .75	$2.50	$5.00
63-313	Jakes, John - ***Six-Gun Planet*** [1970] PBO. Cover art by Powers & LaZorg.	$1.25	$3.75	$7.50
63-314	Ross, Marilyn - ***A Gathering Of Evil*** [1970]	$1.00	$3.00	$6.00
63-315	Ware, Judith - ***Quarry House*** [1970]	$ .75	$2.50	$5.00
63-317	Hunter, John (W.T. Ballard) - ***Duke*** [1970]	$1.00	$3.00	$6.00
63-318	Ross, Marilyn - ***Barnabas, Quentin And The Mummy's Curse*** [1970] PBO.	$1.35	$4.00	$8.00
64-319	Schurmacher, Emile C. - ***Richthofen, The Red Baron*** [1970]	$ .75	$2.50	$5.00
64-323	LeFanu, Sheridan - ***Carmilla & The Haunted Baronet*** [1970]	$ .75	$2.50	$5.00
63-326	Antonio, San - ***The Strangler*** [1970]	$1.00	$3.00	$6.00
63-328	Chaber, M.E. - ***Uneasy Lies The Dead*** [1970]	$1.00	$3.00	$6.00
63-333	Anderson, Paul - ***Virgin Planet*** [1970]	$1.00	$3.00	$6.00
63-334	Ross, Marilyn - ***Memory Of Evil*** [1970]	$1.00	$3.00	$6.00
64-336	Ferguson, Margaret - ***The Sign Of The Ram*** [1970]	$ .75	$2.50	$5.00
64-337	Burkett, William R., Jr. - ***Sleeping Planet*** [1970]	$1.00	$3.00	$6.00

		G	VG	F
63-338	Ross, Marilyn - ***Barnabas, Quentin And The Avenging Ghost*** [1970] PBO.	$1.35	$4.00	$8.00
63-340	Shaner, Madeleine - ***Halls Of Anger*** [1970] PBO.	$ .75	$2.50	$5.00
63-341	Antonio, San - ***Knights Of Arabia*** [1970]	$1.00	$3.00	$6.00
63-342	Antonio, San - ***Crooks' Hill*** [1970]	$1.00	$3.00	$6.00
64-343	Johnson, B.B. - ***Mother Of The Year*** [1970] PBO. Cover art by Mitchell Hooks.	$ .75	$2.50	$5.00
64-344	Conway, Troy (Michael Avallone) - ***The Cunning Linguist*** [1970] PBO.	$ .75	$2.50	$5.00
63-349	Winston, Daoma - ***Dennison Hill*** [1970] PBO.	$ .75	$2.50	$5.00
65-350	Daniels, Norman - ***Voodoo Slave*** [1970] PBO. Cover art by Pfeiffer.	$1.25	$3.75	$7.50
64-351	King, David - ***Butch Cassidy, The Sundance Kid And The Wild Bunch*** [1970]	$1.00	$3.00	$6.00
63-352	Antonio, San - ***From A To Z*** [1970]	$1.00	$3.00	$6.00
63-353	Chaber, M.E. - ***The Flaming Man*** [1970]	$1.00	$3.00	$6.00
63-357	Margroff, Robert & Anthony, Piers - ***The E.S.P. Worm*** [1970]	$1.00	$3.00	$6.00
63-358	Ross, Marilyn - ***Mistress Of Ravenswood*** [1970]	$1.25	$3.75	$7.50
64-360	Wylie, Philip & Balmer, Edwin - ***When Worlds Collide*** [1970]	$1.00	$3.00	$6.00
64-361	Wylie, Philip & Balmer, Edwin - ***After Worlds Collide*** [1970]	$1.00	$3.00	$6.00
63-363	Ross, Marilyn - ***Barnabas, Quentin And The Nightmare Assassin*** [1970] PBO.	$1.35	$4.00	$8.00
64-364	Winston, Daoma - ***Sound Stage*** [1970]	$ .75	$2.50	$5.00
63-365	Daniels, Dorothy - ***Raxl, Voodoo Priestess*** [1970] PBO.	$1.00	$3.00	$6.00
63-367	Ross, Marilyn - ***Dark Shadows*** [1970]	$1.00	$3.00	$6.00
63-368	Ross, Marilyn - ***The Curse Of Collinwood*** [1970]	$1.00	$3.00	$6.00
63-369	Saxon, Peter - ***The Torturer*** [1970]	$1.00	$3.00	$6.00
66-370	Wolfe, Maynard Frank - ***The Making Of The Adventurers*** [1970]	$1.00	$3.00	$6.00
64-371	Reynolds, Quentin - ***I, Willie Sutton*** [1970]	$ .75	$2.50	$5.00
63-374	Anthology - ***The Worlds Of Science Fiction*** [1970] Edited by Robert P. Mills	$1.00	$3.00	$6.00
63-376	Daniels, Dorothy - ***The Dark Stage*** [1970]	$ .75	$2.50	$5.00
65-377	Keefe, Lynn - ***Guess Who's Been Sleeping In My Bed?*** [1970]	$ .75	$2.50	$5.00
63-380	Chaber, M.E. - ***Six Who Ran*** [1970]	$1.00	$3.00	$6.00
63-384	Koontz, Dean R. - ***Anti-Man*** [1970] PBO. Cover art by Steele Savage.	$4.00	$12.50	$25.00
63-385	Ross, Marilyn - ***Barnabas, Quentin And The Crystal Coffin*** [1970] PBO.	$1.35	$4.00	$8.00
63-386	Schenck, George & Marks, William - ***Barquero*** [1970] PBO.	$ .75	$2.50	$5.00
64-389	Conway, Troy - ***Will The Real Rod Please Stand Up?*** [1970] PBO.	$ .75	$2.50	$5.00
63-390	Brennan, Alice - ***Candace*** [1970] PBO.	$ .75	$2.50	$5.00
66-391	Grissim, John - ***Country Music: White Man's Blues*** [1970]	$ .75	$2.50	$5.00
63-396	Chaber, M.E. - ***So Dead The Rose*** [1970]	$1.00	$3.00	$6.00
65-401	Stevens, Francis - ***The Citadel Of Fear*** [1970] PBO. Cover art by Steele Savage.	$1.00	$3.00	$6.00
63-402	Ross, Marilyn - ***Barnabas, Quentin And The Witch's Curse*** [1970]	$1.25	$3.75	$7.50
63-406	Van Vogt, A.E. - ***Science Fiction Monsters*** [1970] Cover art by Bob Pepper	$1.00	$3.00	$6.00
68-409	Gallagher, Mary Barelli - ***My Life With Jacqueline Kennedy*** [1970]	$ .75	$2.50	$5.00
64-411	Gallery, Daniel V. - ***Clear The Decks*** [1970]	$ .75	$2.50	$5.00
64-412	Gallery, Daniel V. - ***Now Hear This!*** [1970] Cover art by Bob Jones.	$ .75	$2.50	$5.00
63-413	Ross, Marilyn - ***The Secret Of Barnabas Collins*** [1970]	$1.00	$3.00	$6.00
63-414	Ross, Marilyn - ***The Demon Of Barnabas Collins*** [1970]	$1.00	$3.00	$6.00
64-415	Conway, Troy - ***Keep It Up, Rod*** [1970]	$ .75	$2.50	$5.00
64-416	Letton, Jennette - ***Allegra's Child*** [1970] PBO.	$1.00	$3.00	$6.00

		G	VG	F
65-418	Tuttle, Anthony - ***Drive For The Green*** [1970]	$ .75	$2.50	$5.00
63-419	Anthology - ***The Dark Shadows Book Of Vampires And Werewolves*** [1970]	$2.50	$7.50	$15.00
66-420	Baxter, John - ***Science Fiction In The Cinema*** [1970] PBO.	$1.00	$3.00	$6.00
63-421	Chaber, M.E. - ***A Lonely Walk*** [1970]	$1.00	$3.00	$6.00
64-422	Read, Anne - ***Edgar Cayce On Jesus And His Church*** [1970] PBO.	$ .75	$2.50	$5.00
63-426	Jakes, John - ***Black In Time*** [1970] PBO. Cover art by Steele Savage.	$1.25	$3.75	$7.50
63-427	Ross, Marilyn - ***Barnabas, Quentin And The Haunted Cave*** [1970] PBO.	$1.35	$4.00	$8.00
65-429	Donovan, Vance - ***Black Sister*** [1970]	$ .75	$2.50	$5.00
64-430	Conway, Troy (Michael Avallone) - ***All Screwed Up*** [1970] PBO.	$ .75	$2.50	$5.00
63-431	Ross, Marilyn - ***Shorecliff*** [1970]	$1.00	$3.00	$6.00
63-432	Simak, Clifford D. - ***Cosmic Engineers*** [1970] Cover art by Del Sarte.	$1.00	$3.00	$6.00
64-435	Conway, Troy - ***The Master Baiter*** [1970] PBO.	$ .75	$2.50	$5.00
63-438	Anthology - ***The Dark Dominion*** [1970] PBO.	$1.00	$3.00	$6.00
64-439	Conway, Troy - ***Turn The Other Sheik*** [1970] PBO.	$ .75	$2.50	$5.00
63-440	Chaber, M.E. - ***No Grave For March*** [1970]	$1.00	$3.00	$6.00
68-441	Renek, Morris - ***Siam Miami*** [1970]	$ .75	$2.50	$5.00
64-444	Mendelsohn, Felix - ***Superbaby*** [1970]	$1.00	$3.00	$6.00
63-446	Ross, Marilyn - ***Barnabas, Quentin And The Frightened Bride*** [1970]	$1.25	$3.75	$7.50
64-451	Gaskell, Jane - ***The Serpent*** [1970]	$1.00	$3.00	$6.00
64-452	Gaskell, Jane - ***The Atlan*** [1970]	$1.00	$3.00	$6.00
63-458	Kroger, Paul - ***If The Shroud Fits*** [1970] PBO.	$1.00	$3.00	$6.00
63-460	Chaber, M.E. - ***Wanted: Dead Men*** [1970]	$1.00	$3.00	$6.00
63-464	Brand, Max - ***Silvertip's Search*** [1970]	$ .75	$2.50	$5.00
63-468	Ross, Marilyn - ***Barnabas, Quentin And The Scorpio Curse*** [1970]	$1.25	$3.75	$7.50
64-472	Hamilton, Edmond - ***The Star Kings*** [1970]	$1.00	$3.00	$6.00
64-475	Gibson, Litzka R. & Walter B. - ***The Mystic And Occult Arts*** [1970]	$ .75	$2.50	$5.00
65-477	Huffaker, Clair - ***Flap*** [1970]	$ .75	$2.50	$5.00
63-479	Vale, Rena - ***The Day After Doomsday*** [1970] PBO. Cover art by Powers and LaZorg.	$1.25	$3.75	$7.50
66-480	Anthology - ***Quark I*** [1970] PBO. Edited by Samuel R. Delany and Marilyn Hacker.	$2.50	$7.50	$15.00
64-485	Conway, Troy - ***It's Not How Long You Make It*** [1970] PBO.	$ .75	$2.50	$5.00
63-485	Nicole, Claudia - ***Moonwater*** [1970] PBO.	$ .75	$2.50	$5.00
63-486	Chaber, M.E. - ***A Hearse Of Another Color*** [1970]	$1.00	$3.00	$6.00
65-487	Shaw, Arnold - ***The Rock Revolution*** [1970]	$ .75	$2.50	$5.00
64-490	Offutt, Andrew J. - ***Evil Is Live Spelled Backwards*** [1970] PBO.	$1.25	$3.75	$7.50
63-491	Ross, Marilyn - ***Barnabas, Quentin And The Serpent*** [1970] PBO.	$1.35	$4.00	$8.00
63-496	Mason, Douglas R. - ***Eight Against Utopia*** [1970]	$1.00	$3.00	$6.00
65-497	Lawrence, Julie - ***Blondes Don't Have All The Fun*** [1970]	$ .75	$2.50	$5.00
64-499	Conway, Troy - ***The Big Freak-Out*** [1970]	$ .75	$2.50	$5.00
64-501	Klane, Robert - ***Where's Poppa?*** [1970]	$ .75	$2.50	$5.00
64-503	Stone, Hampton (Aaron Marc Stein) - ***The Funniest Killer In Town*** [1970]	$1.00	$3.00	$6.00
64-504	Stone, Hampton (Aaron Marc Stein) - ***The Real Serendipitous Kill*** [1970]	$1.00	$3.00	$6.00
64-505	Stone, Hampton (Aaron Marc Stein) - ***The Corpse Was No Bargain At All*** [1971]	$1.00	$3.00	$6.00
64-506	Stone, Hampton (Aaron Marc Stein) - ***The Kid Was Last Seen Hanging Ten*** [1971]	$1.00	$3.00	$6.00

		G	VG	F
63-507	Chaber, M.E. - ***Hangman's Harvest*** [1971] Cover art by H. Rogers.	$1.00	$3.00	$6.00
63-508	Turner, Clay (W.T. Ballard) - ***Give A Man A Gun*** [1971] PBO.	$1.25	$3.75	$7.50
64-509	Brand, Max - ***Pillar Mountain*** [1971]	$ .75	$2.50	$5.00
64-512	Van Vogt, A.E. - ***The Proxy Intelligence And Other Mind Benders*** [1971] PBO. Cover art by Gaughan.	$1.00	$3.00	$6.00
63-515	Ross, Marilyn - ***Barnabas, Quentin And The Magic Potion*** [1971] PBO.	$1.35	$4.00	$8.00
64-516	Anthology - ***Strange Fate*** [1971] Edited by The Fullers.	$ .75	$2.50	$5.00
64-517	Norris, Kathleen - ***Woman In Love*** [1971] Cover art by H. Rogers.	$ .65	$2.00	$4.00
64-521	Feiffer, Jules - ***Little Murders*** [1971]	$1.00	$3.00	$6.00
63-522	King, David - ***There Was A Crooked Man*** [1970] PBO.	$1.00	$3.00	$6.00
64-526	Stone, Hampton (Aaron Marc Stein) - ***The Murder That Wouldn't Stay Solved*** [1971]	$1.00	$3.00	$6.00
63-527	Chaber, M.E. - ***As Old As Cain*** [1971]	$1.00	$3.00	$6.00
64-528	Brand, Max - ***The Iron Trail*** [1971]	$ .75	$2.50	$5.00
66-530	Anthology - ***Quark 2*** [1971] PBO. Edited by Samuel R. Delany & Marilyn Hacker	$2.50	$7.50	$15.00
64-532	MacApp, C.C. - ***Subb*** [1970]	$1.00	$3.00	$6.00
66-533	Luce, Gay Gaer & Segal, Dr. Julius - ***How To Avoid Insomnia*** [1971]	$ .75	$2.50	$5.00
63-534	Ross, Marilyn - ***Barnabas, Quentin And The Body Snatchers*** [1971] PBO.	$1.35	$4.00	$8.00
64-537	Ross, Marilyn - ***House Of Dark Shadows*** [1970] PBO.	$1.25	$3.75	$7.50
64-538	Reynolds, James - ***Ghosts In American Houses*** [1971]	$ .75	$2.50	$5.00
64-541	Brand, Max - ***The Jackson Trail*** [1971]	$ .75	$2.50	$5.00
63-542	de Camp, L. Sprague - ***The Glory That Was*** [1971] Cover art by Powers	$1.00	$3.00	$6.00
68-546	*Rolling Stone* magazine - ***The Rolling Stone Interviews*** [1971]	$1.35	$4.00	$8.00
64-547	Stone, Hampton (Aaron Marc Stein) - ***The Strangler Who Couldn't Let Go*** [1971]	$1.00	$3.00	$6.00
64-548	Conway, Troy - ***Son Of A Witch*** [1971] PBO.	$ .75	$2.50	$5.00
63-549	Chaber, M.E. - ***The Gallows Garden*** [1971]	$1.00	$3.00	$6.00
63-554	Ross, Marilyn - ***Barnabas, Quentin And Dr. Jekyll's Son*** [1971] PBO.	$1.35	$4.00	$8.00
65-560	Sheed, Wilfrid - ***Max Jamison*** [1971]	$ .75	$2.50	$5.00
64-562	Brand, Max - ***Riders Of The Plains*** [1971]	$ .75	$2.50	$5.00
63-565	Richard, Susan - ***Chateau Saxony*** [1971] PBO. Cover art by Podwil.	$ .75	$2.50	$5.00
66-566	Shaw, Arnold - ***The World Of Soul*** [1970]	$ .75	$2.50	$5.00
64-567	Stone, Hampton (Aaron Marc Stein) - ***The Corpse That Refused To Stay Dead*** [1971]	$1.00	$3.00	$6.00
63-568	Chaber, M.E. - ***Green Grow The Graves*** [1971]	$1.00	$3.00	$6.00
64-577	Unknown - ***The Dirty Old Man*** [1971] Cover art by Norman Mingo.	$ .75	$2.50	$5.00
65-579	Gallery, Daniel V. - ***V-505*** [1971]	$ .75	$2.50	$5.00
65-580	Linakis, Steven - ***The Killing Ground*** [1971]	$ .75	$2.50	$5.00
66-581	Broun, Daniel - ***The Production*** [1971]	$ .75	$2.50	$5.00
64-582	Brand, Max - ***The Dude*** [1971]	$ .75	$2.50	$5.00
65-584	Van Vogt, A.E. - ***M 33 In Andromeda*** [1971] PBO. Cover art by Geissmann.	$1.00	$3.00	$6.00
63-585	Ross, Marilyn - ***Barnabas, Quentin And The Grave Robbers*** [1971] PBO.	$1.35	$4.00	$8.00
64-586	Daniels, Dorothy - ***The Beaumont Tradition*** [1971]	$ .75	$2.50	$5.00
64-588	Stone, Hampton (Aaron Marc Stein) - ***The Corpse Who Had Too Many Friends*** [1971]	$1.00	$3.00	$6.00
66-589	Werner, Herbert - ***Iron Coffins*** [1971]	$ .75	$2.50	$5.00
64-590	Monig, Christopher (M.E. Chaber) - ***Abra-Cadaver*** [1971]	$1.00	$3.00	$6.00

		G	VG	F
66-593	Anthology - ***Quark 3*** [1971] PBO. Edited by Samuel R. Delany & Marilyn Hacker. Cover art by Roger Penney.	$2.50	$7.50	$15.00
64-595	Laumer, Keith - ***A Plague Of Demons*** [1973] Cover art by Davis Meltzer	$1.00	$3.00	$6.00
64-596	Conway, Troy (Michael Avallone) - ***The Penetrator*** [1971] PBO.	$ .75	$2.50	$5.00
65-602	Gerlach, Heinrich - ***The Forsaken Army*** [1971]	$ .75	$2.50	$5.00
64-603	Van Vogt, A.E. - ***The House That Stood Still*** [1971]	$1.00	$3.00	$6.00
64-604	Landau, Deborah - ***Janis Joplin: Her Life And Times*** [1971]	$ .75	$2.50	$5.00
65-605	Daniels, Dorothy - ***The Bell*** [1971]	$ .75	$2.50	$5.00
64-608	Stone, Hampton (Aaron Marc Stein) - ***The Girl Who Kept Knocking Them Dead*** [1971]	$1.00	$3.00	$6.00
64-609	Monig, Christopher (M.E. Chaber) - ***The Burned Man*** [1971]	$1.00	$3.00	$6.00
64-611	Brand, Max - ***The Rancher's Revenge*** [1971]	$ .75	$2.50	$5.00
64-614	Anthology - ***The Inner Landscape*** [1971] Edited by Mervyn Peake, J.G. Ballard, and Brian W. Aldiss.	$1.00	$3.00	$6.00
64-617	Daniels, Dorothy - ***The Tormented*** [1971]	$ .75	$2.50	$5.00
65-621	Lewis, Jack - ***Tell It To The Marines*** [1971]	$ .75	$2.50	$5.00
64-624	Bova, Ben - ***THX 1138*** [1971]	$ .75	$2.50	$5.00
64-629	Stone, Hampton (Aaron Marc Stein) - ***The Corpse In The Corner Saloon*** [1971]	$1.00	$3.00	$6.00
64-630	O'Donnell, Elliott - ***The Midnight Hearse And More Ghosts*** [1971]	$1.50	$5.00	$10.00
64-631	Monig, Christopher (M.E. Chaber) - ***Once Upon A Crime*** [1971]	$1.00	$3.00	$6.00
64-636	Dick, Philip K. - ***A Maze Of Death*** [1971]	$1.50	$5.00	$10.00
65-638	Maitland, Derek - ***The Only War We've Got*** [1971]	$ .75	$2.50	$5.00
64-639	Johnston, William - ***Klute*** [1971]	$ .75	$2.50	$5.00
65-640	Hamill, Pete - ***Doc*** [1971]	$ .75	$2.50	$5.00
64-642	Daniels, Dorothy - ***Shadow Glen*** [1971]	$ .75	$2.50	$5.00
64-645	Anthology - ***Analog I*** [1971] Edited by John W. Campbell.	$1.00	$3.00	$6.00
64-647	Conway, Troy - ***It's What's Up Front That Counts*** [1971]	$ .75	$2.50	$5.00
64-648	Conway, Troy (Michael Avallone) - ***Had Any Lately?*** [1971]	$ .75	$2.50	$5.00
65-649	Meyer, Martin J. & McDaniel, Dr. J.M., Jr - ***Don't Bank On It!*** [1971]	$ .75	$2.50	$5.00
64-650	Daniels, Dorothy - ***Diablo Manor*** [1971] PBO.	$ .75	$2.50	$5.00
64-654	Monig, Christopher (M.E. Chaber) - ***The Lonely Graves*** [1971]	$1.00	$3.00	$6.00
64-656	Brand, Max - ***Smiling Charlie*** [1971]	$ .75	$2.50	$5.00
66-658	Anthology - ***Quark 4*** [1971] PBO. Edited by Samuel R. Delany & Marilyn Hacker	$2.50	$7.50	$15.00
64-660	Bloch, Robert - ***Sneak Preview*** [1971] PBO.	$4.00	$12.50	$25.00
64-661	Conway, Troy (Michael Avallone) - ***A Stiff Proposition*** [1971] PBO.	$ .75	$2.50	$5.00
64-662	Agniel, Lucien - ***Zeppelin*** [1971]	$ .75	$2.50	$5.00
64-669	Johnston, William - ***Banyon*** [1971] PBO.	$ .75	$2.50	$5.00
64-671	Conway, Troy (Michael Avallone) - ***I'd Rather Fight Than Swish*** [1971]	$ .75	$2.50	$5.00
64-673	Daniels, Dorothy - ***Emerald Hill*** [1971]	$ .75	$2.50	$5.00
64-674	Daniels, Dorothy - ***The Carson Inherritance*** [1971]	$ .75	$2.50	$5.00
64-675	Daniels, Dorothy - ***Darkhaven*** [1971]	$ .75	$2.50	$5.00
64-676	Deming, Richard - ***Big Jake*** [1971]	$1.00	$3.00	$6.00
66-680	Corley, Edwin - ***The Jesus Factor*** [1971]	$ .75	$2.50	$5.00
64-682	Stone, Hampton (Aaron Marc Stein) - ***The Babe With The Twistable Arm*** [1971]	$1.00	$3.00	$6.00
66-683	Gow, Gordon - ***Suspense In The Cinema*** [1971]	$1.00	$3.00	$6.00
64-684	Chaber, M.E. - ***The Bonded Dead*** [1971]	$1.00	$3.00	$6.00
64-696	de Camp, L. Sprague - ***The Tritonian Ring*** [1971]	$1.00	$3.00	$6.00
66-698	Robie, W.F., M.D. - ***The Art Of Love*** [1971]	$ .65	$2.00	$4.00
64-700	Baer, Jill - ***House Of Whispers*** [1971] PBO. Cover art by Victor Kalin.	$ .75	$2.50	$5.00

		G	VG	F
64-701	Randell, Christine - ***Malory Grange*** [1971] PBO. Cover art by Abbett.	$ .75	$2.50	$5.00
64-702	Anthology - ***Polyunsaturated Mad*** [1972] Edited by Feldstein.	$1.00	$3.00	$6.00
68-705	Anderson, Patrick - ***The Approach To Kings*** [1971]	$ .75	$2.50	$5.00
64-708	Brand, Max - ***Dead Or Alive*** [1971]	$ .75	$2.50	$5.00
66-710	Meggyesy, Dave - ***Out Of Their League*** [1971]	$ .75	$2.50	$5.00
64-712	Laumer, Keith - ***A Trace Of Memory*** [1971]	$1.00	$3.00	$6.00
62-718	Van Vogt, A.E. - ***Two Hundred Million A.D.*** [1971]	$1.00	$3.00	$6.00
64-729	Anthology - ***Green Lantern And Green Arrow #1*** [1972] PBO. Cover art by Neal Adams. Comic reprints.	$2.00	$6.00	$12.00
64-732	Brand, Max - ***The Seven Of Diamonds*** [1972]	$ .75	$2.50	$5.00
64-735	Stone, Hampton (Aaron Marc Stein) - ***The Needle That Wouldn't Hold Still*** [1972]	$1.00	$3.00	$6.00
66-741	Flanagan, Robert - ***Maggot*** [1972]	$ .75	$2.50	$5.00
64-755	Anthology - ***Green Lantern And Green Arrow #2*** [1972] PBO. Cover art by Neal Adams. Comic reprints.	$2.00	$6.00	$12.00
65-759	Conway, Troy - ***Don't Bite Off More Than You Can Chew*** [1972]	$ .75	$2.50	$5.00
64-763	Stone, Hampton (Aaron Marc Stein) - ***The Swinger Who Swung By The Neck*** [1971]	$1.00	$3.00	$6.00
65-765	De Witt, Jack - ***Man In The Wilderness*** [1971] PBO.	$ .75	$2.50	$5.00
64-784	Brand, Max - ***The Long Chance*** [1972] Cover art by Carl Hantman.	$ .75	$2.50	$5.00
63-790	Stoker, Bram - ***The Garden Of Evil*** [1968]	$1.00	$3.00	$6.00
64-824	Ross, Marilyn - ***Barnabas, Quentin And The Vampire Beauty*** [1972]	$1.25	$3.75	$7.50
64-881	Robeson, Kenneth - ***The Yellow Hoard*** [1972] PBO. The Avenger #2.	$1.25	$3.75	$7.50

Parthena Press.

		G	VG	F
P-89	Anonymous - ***Immortalia*** [n.d.] Taken from 1927 private print run of 1000 copies.	$4.00	$12.50	$25.00

Pelican Books.

		G	VG	F
P-1	Lippman, Walter - ***Public Opinion*** [1946] Cover art by Jonas.	$1.00	$3.00	$6.00
P-2	Benedict, Ruth - ***Patterns Of Culture*** [1946] Cover by Jonas.	$ .75	$2.50	$5.00
P-3	Darnton, Christian - ***You And Music*** [1946] Cover art by Jonas.	$ .75	$2.50	$5.00
P-4	Gamow, George - ***The Birth And Death Of The Sun*** [1946] Cover art by Jonas. Sixteen pages of photos.	$ .75	$2.50	$5.00
P-5	Parkes, James - ***An Enemy Of The People: Antisemitism*** [1946]	$ .75	$2.50	$5.00
P-6	Childe, Gordon - ***What Happened In History*** [1946] Cover art by Jonas.	$ .75	$2.50	$5.00
P-7	Walker, Kenneth - ***The Physiology Of Sex*** [1946]	$ .75	$2.50	$5.00
P-8	Sawyer, W.W. - ***Mathematician's Delight*** [1946]	$ .75	$2.50	$5.00
P-9	Kimble, George & Bush, Raymond - ***The Weather*** [1946] Sixteen pages of photos.	$ .75	$2.50	$5.00
P-10	Hansen, Alvin H. - ***America's Role In The World Economy*** [1946]	$ .75	$2.50	$5.00
P-11	Dunn, L.C. & Dobzhansky, Th. - ***Heredity, Race And Society*** [1946] PBO. Cover art by Jonas.	$ .75	$2.50	$5.00
P-12	Guttmacher, Dr. Alan F. - ***The Story Of Human Birth*** [1946]	$ .75	$2.50	$5.00
P-13	Edited by Saul K. Padover - ***Thomas Jefferson On Democracy*** [1946] Cover by Jonas.	$ .75	$2.50	$5.00
P-14	Harrison, G.B. - ***Introducing Shakespeare*** [1946]	$ .75	$2.50	$5.00
P-15	Edited by E. C. Lindeman - ***Emerson: The Basic Writings Of America's Sage*** [1946]	$ .75	$2.50	$5.00
P-16	Fox, H. Munro - ***The Personality Of Animals*** [1946] Cover by Jonas. Photos throughout.	$ .75	$2.50	$5.00
P-17	Burch, Guy Irving & Pendell, Elmer - ***Human Breeding And Survival*** [1946]	$ .75	$2.50	$5.00

		G	VG	F
P-18	Bartlett, George A. - ***Is Marriage Necessary*** [1946]	$ .75	$2.50	$5.00
P-19	Anthology - ***Good Reading*** [1947] Cover art by Woods.	$ .75	$2.50	$5.00
P-20	Mock, Elizabeth & Richards, J.M. - ***An Introduction To Modern Architecture*** [1947] Cover art by Jonas. Thirty-two pages of photos.	$ .75	$2.50	$5.00
P-21	Translated by E.V. Rieu - ***Homer: The Odyssey*** [1947] Cover by Jonas.	$ .75	$2.50	$5.00
P-22	Tawney, R.H. - ***Religion And The Rise Of Capitalism*** [1947]	$ .75	$2.50	$5.00
P-23	Dunn, L.C. & Dobzhansky, Th. - ***Heredity, Race And Society*** [1947]	$ .75	$2.50	$5.00
P-24	Childs, Marquis W. - ***Sweden: The Middle Way*** [1948] Cover art by Jonas.	$ .75	$2.50	$5.00
P-25	Langer, Susanne K. - ***Philosophy In A New Key*** [1948] Cover art by Jonas.	$ .75	$2.50	$5.00

Penguin Books (Early Publisher's History, 1939–1959)

Color-coded covers and dull covers describe the early books published by Penguin Books, Inc. With their origins in Great Britain, Allen Lane founded this publishing house in 1935. They established a second line, Pelican Books, in 1937, to publish books with a more academic tone. In 1939, Ian Ballantine brought direction to importing British editions of both Penguin and Pelican books. Though they lack significant cover art, they provided many volumes with dust jackets.

World War II made changes necessary, and in 1942 they established American Penguin Books. Early titles showed double imprints of Infantry Journal-Penguin Books and Fighting Forces-Penguin Specials. Penguin also produced the Superior Reprints during this time. In 1946, a great emphasis on cover art emerged with the work of Robert Jonas and others. Throughout the series, a number of volumes received dust jackets. New American Library purchased the line, renamed it Penguin-Signet, and finally just Signet Books.

Other lines include Penguin Specials, Penguin Guides, Mentor Guides, Puffin Books for children, and Mentor Books (formerly labeled as Pelican Books).

Penguin Books. New York: Penguin Books, Inc.

		G	VG	F
501	Eberhart, Mignon G. - ***Murder By An Aristocrat*** [1942]	$2.00	$6.00	$12.00
502	Shaw, Bernard - ***Pygmalion*** [1942]	$2.00	$6.00	$12.00
503	Allingham, Margery - ***Death Of A Ghost*** [1942]	$2.00	$6.00	$12.00
503-DJ	Allingham, Margery - ***Death Of A Ghost*** [1942] With dust-jacket.	$12.50	$37.50	$75.00
505	Buck, Pearl S. - ***The Mother*** [1942]	$2.00	$6.00	$12.00
506	Jones, Guy Pearce - ***Two Survived*** [1942]	$2.00	$6.00	$12.00
507	Walker, Kenneth - ***The Physiology Of Sex*** [1942]	$1.50	$5.00	$10.00
508	Thoreau, Henry David - ***Walden*** [1942]	$1.50	$5.00	$10.00
509	Steinbeck, John - ***The Pastures Of Heaven*** [1942]	$3.50	$10.00	$20.00
510	Bentley, E. C. & Allen, H. Warner - ***Trent's Own Case*** [1942]	$2.00	$6.00	$12.00
511	Ambler, Eric - ***Cause For Alarm*** [1942] Cover art by Kohs.	$2.00	$6.00	$12.00
512	Bromfield, Louis - ***The Strange Case Of Miss Annie Spragg*** [1942]	$2.00	$6.00	$12.00
513	Dyer, George - ***The Catalyst Club*** [1942]	$2.00	$6.00	$12.00
514	Burns, Walter Noble - ***Tombstone*** [1942]	$1.50	$5.00	$10.00
515	Greene, Graham - ***The Confidential Agent*** [1942]	$1.50	$5.00	$10.00
516	Lamb, Harold - ***Genghis Khan*** [1943] Cover art by Olga Kobbe.	$1.50	$5.00	$10.00
517	Edman, Irwin - ***Philosopher's Holiday*** [1942]	$1.50	$5.00	$10.00
518	Fletcher, J. S. - ***The Middle Temple Murder*** [1942]	$1.50	$5.00	$10.00
519	Heyer, Georgette - ***A Blunt Instrument*** [1942]	$1.50	$5.00	$10.00
520	Burns, Walter Noble - ***The Saga Of Billy The Kid*** [1942]	$1.50	$5.00	$10.00

		G	VG	F
521	Clark, Walter Van Tilburg - ***The Ox-Bow Incident*** [1942]	$1.50	$5.00	$10.00
522	Adams, Cleve F. - ***Sabotage*** [1942]	$1.50	$5.00	$10.00
523	Whitman, Walt - ***Leaves Of Grass*** [1942]	$2.00	$6.00	$12.00
524	Barber & Schabelitz - ***Pencil Points To Murder*** [1943]	$1.50	$5.00	$10.00
525	Anthology edited by Carl Withers - ***The Penguin Book Of Sonnets*** [1943] PBO.	$1.50	$5.00	$10.00
526	Hull, Richard - ***My Own Murderer*** [1943] Cover art by Cirlin	$1.50	$5.00	$10.00
527	Liebling, A. J. - ***The Telephone Booth Indian*** [1943] Cover art by Huffine.	$1.50	$5.00	$10.00
528	Carr, John Dickson - ***The Blind Barber*** [1943]	$2.00	$6.00	$12.00
529	Morley, Christopher - ***Kitty Foyle*** [1944]	$1.50	$5.00	$10.00
530	Greene, Graham - ***The Ministry Of Fear*** [1943]	$1.50	$5.00	$10.00
531	Barber, Willetta Ann & Schabelitz, R.F. - ***Drawn Conclusion*** [1943]	$1.50	$5.00	$10.00
532	Carr, John Dickson - ***Hag's Nook*** [1943]	$2.00	$6.00	$12.00
533	Crofts, Freeman Wills - ***The Purple Sickle Murders*** [1943]	$1.50	$5.00	$10.00
534	Allingham, Margery - ***Black Plumes*** [1943]	$1.50	$5.00	$10.00
535	Priestley, J. B. - ***The Old Dark House*** [1943]	$1.50	$5.00	$10.00
536	Hughes, Richard - ***In Hazard*** [1943]	$1.50	$5.00	$10.00
537	Anthology edited by Julius Fast - ***Out Of This World*** [1943] PBO.	$1.50	$5.00	$10.00
538-DJ	Gruber, Frank - ***The Laughing Fox*** [1943] With dust-jacket	$12.50	$37.50	$75.00
538	Gruber, Frank - ***The Laughing Fox*** [1943]	$1.50	$5.00	$10.00
539	La Farge, Oliver - ***Laughing Boy*** [1944]	$1.50	$5.00	$10.00
540	Saroyan, William - ***My Name Is Aram*** [1944] Cover art by Don Freeman.	$1.50	$5.00	$10.00
541	Frome, David - ***Mr. Pinkerton Grows A Beard*** [1945]	$1.50	$5.00	$10.00
542	Barber, W. A. & Schabelitz, R. F. - ***Murder Enters The Picture*** [1945] Cover art by Schabelitz.	$1.50	$5.00	$10.00
543	Blake, Nicholas - ***Shell Of Death*** [1944]	$1.50	$5.00	$10.00
544	Beeding, Francis - ***The Ten Holy Horrors*** [1944]	$1.50	$5.00	$10.00
545	Gruber, Frank - ***The Talking Clock*** [1944]	$2.00	$6.00	$12.00
545-DJ	Gruber, Frank - ***The Talking Clock*** [1946] With dust-jacket.	$12.50	$37.50	$75.00
546	Benet, Stephen Vincent - ***O'Halloran's Luck*** [1944]	$1.50	$5.00	$10.00
547	Kitchin, C. H. B. - ***Beath Of My Aunt*** [1944]	$1.50	$5.00	$10.00
548	Priestley, J. B. - ***Black-Out In Gretley*** [1944]	$1.50	$5.00	$10.00
549	Daly, Elizabeth - ***Murders In Volume 2*** [1944] Cover art by Hoffman.	$1.50	$5.00	$10.00
550	Sloane, William - ***To Walk The Night*** [1944]	$2.00	$6.00	$12.00
551	Flavin, Martin - ***Mr. Littlejohn*** [1944]	$1.50	$5.00	$10.00
552	Vandercook, John W. - ***Murder In Trinidad*** [1944]	$1.50	$5.00	$10.00
553	Holmes, H. H. - ***Nine Times Nine*** [1945]	$1.50	$5.00	$10.00
554	Defoe, Daniel - ***Tales Of Piracy, Crime And Ghosts*** [1945]	$2.00	$6.00	$12.00
555	Schley, Sturges Mason - ***Dr. Toby Finds Murder*** [1945]	$1.50	$5.00	$10.00
557	Mitchell, Joseph - ***McSorley's Wonderful Saloon*** [1945]	$1.50	$5.00	$10.00
558	Heyward, Du Bose - ***Porgy*** [1945]	$1.50	$5.00	$10.00
560	Vandercook, John W. - ***Murder In Fiji*** [1945] Cover art by Jonas.	$1.50	$5.00	$10.00
561	Baker, Dorothy - ***Young Man With A Horn*** [1945]	$1.50	$5.00	$10.00
562	Gruber, Frank - ***Simon Lash, Private Detective*** [1945]	$2.50	$7.50	$15.00
563	O'Hara, John - ***Appointment In Samarra*** [1945] Cover art by Jonas.	$1.50	$5.00	$10.00
564	Simenon, Georges - ***Maigret Travels South*** [1945] Cover art by Cirlin.	$1.50	$5.00	$10.00
565	White, Ethel Lina - ***Step In The Dark*** [1945]	$1.50	$5.00	$10.00
566	Ballard, W. T. - ***Say Yes To Murder*** [1945]	$2.00	$6.00	$12.00
567	Caldwell, Erskine - ***Trouble In July*** [1945] Cover art by Jonas.	$1.50	$5.00	$10.00
568	De St.-Exupery, Antoine - ***Night Flight*** [1945] Cover art by Cirlin.	$1.50	$5.00	$10.00
569	Fast, Howard - ***Conceived In Liberty*** [1945] Cover art by Jonas.	$1.50	$5.00	$10.00

Penguin Book, 609

Penguin Book, 612

Pennant Books, P-13

		G	VG	F
570	Yates, Dornford - ***And Berry Came Too*** [1945] Cover art by Jonas.	$1.50	$5.00	$10.00
571	Blake, Eleanor - ***Death Down East*** [1945] Cover art by Robert Jonas.	$1.50	$5.00	$10.00
572	Hasek, Jaroslav - ***The Good Soldier Schweik*** [1945]	$1.50	$5.00	$10.00
573	Cloete, Stuart - ***The Turning Wheels*** [1946] Cover art by Jonas.	$1.50	$5.00	$10.00
574	Forster, E. M. - ***A Passage To India*** [1946] Cover by Salter.	$1.50	$5.00	$10.00
575	Crofts, Freeman Wills - ***The Cask*** [1946]	$1.50	$5.00	$10.00
575-DJ	Crofts, Freeman Wills - ***The Cask*** [1946] With dust-jacket.	$12.50	$37.50	$75.00
576	Lawrence, D. H. - ***The Lovely Lady*** [1946] Cover art by Salter.	$2.00	$6.00	$12.00
577	Dos Passos, John - ***Manhattan Transfer*** [1946] Cover art by Robert Jonas.	$1.50	$5.00	$10.00
578	Silone, Ignazio - ***Bread And Wine*** [1946] Cover art by Salter.	$1.50	$5.00	$10.00
579	Simenon, Georges - ***The Patience Of Maigret*** [1946]	$1.50	$5.00	$10.00
580	O'Hara, John - ***Pal Joey*** [1946]	$1.50	$5.00	$10.00
581	Caldwell, Erskine - ***God's Little Acre*** [1946] Cover art by Jonas.	$1.50	$5.00	$10.00
582	Morley, Christopher - ***Thunder On The Left*** [1946] Cover art by Jonas.	$1.50	$5.00	$10.00
583	Glasgow, Ellen - ***Vein Of Iron*** [1946] Cover art by Jonas.	$1.50	$5.00	$10.00
584	Bonnamy, Francis - ***Dead Reckoning*** [1946]	$1.50	$5.00	$10.00
585	Anderson, Sherwood - ***Winesburg, Ohio*** [1946]	$1.50	$5.00	$10.00
586	MacDonald, Philip - ***The Rasp*** [1946] Cover art by Jonas.	$1.50	$5.00	$10.00
586-DJ	MacDonald, Philip - ***The Rasp*** [1946] In dust-jacket.	$12.50	$37.50	$75.00
587	London, Jack - ***Martin Eden*** [1946] Cover art by Jonas.	$1.50	$5.00	$10.00
588	Fast, Howard - ***The Unvanquished*** [1946] Cover art by Jonas.	$1.50	$5.00	$10.00
589	Hurst, Fannie - ***Back Street*** [1946] Cover art by Jonas.	$1.50	$5.00	$10.00
590	Woolf, Virginia - ***Orlando*** [1946] Cover art by Salter.	$1.50	$5.00	$10.00
591	Cain, James M. - ***Mildred Pierce*** [1946] Cover art by Jonas.	$1.50	$5.00	$10.00
592	Blake, Nicholas - ***Malice In Wonderland*** [1946] Cover art by Arthur Hawkins, Jr.	$1.50	$5.00	$10.00
593	Mellett, Lowell - ***Handbook Of Politics And Voter's Guide*** [1946] Cover art by Jonas.	$1.50	$5.00	$10.00
594	Wood, Charles Erskine Scott - ***Heavenly Discourse*** [1946] Cover art by Jonas.	$1.50	$5.00	$10.00
595	Henry, O. - ***Cabbages And Kings*** [1946] Cover art by Loew.	$2.00	$6.00	$12.00
596	McCullers, Carson - ***The Heart Is A Lonely Hunter*** [1946] Cover art by Jonas.	$2.00	$6.00	$12.00
597	Maugham, W. Somerset - ***The Summing Up*** [1946] Cover art by Woods.	$1.50	$5.00	$10.00

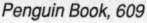

		G	VG	F
598	White, Ethel Lina - ***Put Out The Light*** [1946] Cover art by Jonas.	$1.50	$5.00	$10.00
599	Steinbeck, John - ***Tortilla Flat*** [1946] Cover art by Jonas.	$2.00	$6.00	$12.00
600	Evans, Evan (Max Brand) - ***Montana Rides!*** [1946]	$1.50	$5.00	$10.00
601	Cabell, James Branch - ***Jurgen*** [1946]	$1.50	$5.00	$10.00
602	Bolte, Charles G. - ***The New Veteran*** [1946]	$1.50	$5.00	$10.00
603	Farrell, James T. - ***Short Stories*** [1946] Cover by Jonas.	$1.50	$5.00	$10.00
604	Baker, Dorothy - ***Trio*** [1946] Cover art by Jonas.	$1.50	$5.00	$10.00
605	Ferber, Edna - ***Cimarron*** [1946] Cover art by Jonas.	$1.50	$5.00	$10.00
606	Bonnamy, Francis - ***A Rope Of Sand*** [1946] Cover art by Arthur Getz.	$1.50	$5.00	$10.00
607	Shaw, Bernard - ***Pygmalion*** [1946]	$1.50	$5.00	$10.00
608	Shaw, Bernard - ***Major Barbara*** [1946] Movie tie-in.	$1.50	$5.00	$10.00
609	Shaw, Bernard - ***Saint Joan*** [1946]	$1.50	$5.00	$10.00
610	Lawrence, D. H. - ***Lady Chatterley's Lover*** [1946] Cover art by Jonas.	$2.00	$6.00	$12.00
611	Byrne, Donn - ***Messer Marco Polo*** [1946] Cover art by Jonas.	$1.50	$5.00	$10.00
612	Scarlett, William - editor - ***Christianity Takes A Stand*** [1946] PBO.	$1.50	$5.00	$10.00
613	Translated by E. V. Rieu - ***The Odyssey - Homer*** [1946] Cover art by Jonas.	$1.50	$5.00	$10.00
614	Morehead & Smith - ***The Penguin Hoyle*** [1946] PBO. Cover art by Jonas.	$1.50	$5.00	$10.00
615	Garnett, David - ***Lady Into Fox & A Man In The Zoo*** [1946] Cover art by Loew.	$2.00	$6.00	$12.00
616	Kendrick, Baynard - ***The Eleven Of Diamonds*** [1946]	$1.50	$5.00	$10.00
617	Ferber, Edna - ***Saratoga Trunk*** [1947] Cover art by Woods.	$1.50	$5.00	$10.00
618-DJ	Taylor, Phoebe Atwood - ***The Perennial Boarder*** [1947] with dust jacket.	$12.50	$37.50	$75.00
618	Taylor, Phoebe Atwood - ***The Perennial Boarder*** [1947] Cover art by Jonas.	$1.50	$5.00	$10.00
619	Conrad, Joseph - ***Almayer's Folly*** [1947] Cover art by Jonas.	$1.50	$5.00	$10.00
620	Evans, Evan (Max Brand) - ***Montana Rides Again*** [1947] Cover art by Jonas.	$1.50	$5.00	$10.00
621	Cain, James - ***Serenade*** [1947] Cover art by Jonas.	$2.00	$6.00	$12.00
622	Wechsberg, Joseph - ***Looking For A Bluebird*** [1947] Cover art by Strobel.	$1.50	$5.00	$10.00
623	Gruber, Frank - ***The Silver Jackass*** [1947] Cover art by Jonas.	$2.00	$6.00	$12.00
625	James, Henry - ***Daisy Miller*** [1947] Cover art by Jonas.	$1.50	$5.00	$10.00
626	Ashbrook, Harriette - ***The Purple Onion Mystery*** [1947] Cover art by Arthur Hawkins, Jr.	$2.00	$6.00	$12.00
627	Caldwell, Erskine - ***Tobacco Road*** [1947] Cover art by Jonas.	$1.50	$5.00	$10.00
628	Hughes, Richard - ***The Innocent Voyage*** [1947]	$1.50	$5.00	$10.00
629	Bonnamy, Francis - ***The King Is Dead On Queen Street*** [1947] Cover art by Jonas.	$2.00	$6.00	$12.00
631	McGuire, Paul - ***A Funeral In Eden*** [1947] Cover art by Jonas.	$1.50	$5.00	$10.00
632	Faulkner, William - ***Sanctuary*** [1947] Cover art by Jonas.	$1.50	$5.00	$10.00
633	Ferber, Edna - ***Great Son*** [1947] Cover art by Arthur Getz.	$1.50	$5.00	$10.00
634	Saki (H. H. Munro) - ***The Unbearable Bassington*** [1947] Cover art by Jonas.	$2.00	$6.00	$12.00
636	MacKinley, Kantor - ***The Voice Of Bugle Ann And The Romance Of Rosy Ridge*** [1947] Cover art by Jonas.	$1.50	$5.00	$10.00
637	Bemelmans, Ludwig - ***Hotel Splendide*** [1947]	$1.50	$5.00	$10.00
638	Nathan, Robert - ***Portrait Of Jennie*** [1947] Cover art by Jonas.	$1.50	$5.00	$10.00
639	Ferber, Edna - ***So Big*** [1947] Cover art by Jonas.	$1.50	$5.00	$10.00
640	Steinberg, Saul - ***All In Line*** [1947] Cover art by Saul Steinberg. Cartoon book.	$1.50	$5.00	$10.00
641	Hynd, Alan - ***Murder! Great True Crime Cases*** [1947] Cover art by Jonas.	$2.00	$6.00	$12.00
642	Lipsky, Eleazar - ***The Kiss Of Death*** [1947] Cover art by Jonas.	$2.00	$6.00	$12.00

Pennant Books, P-15

Pennant Books, P-59

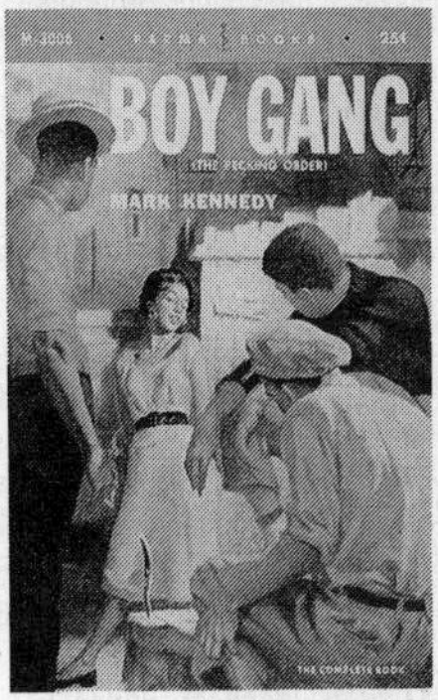

Perma Books, M-3006

		G	VG	F
643	Farrell, James T. - ***Young Lonigan*** [1947] Cover art by Jonas.	$1.50	$5.00	$10.00
644	Wolfe, Thomas - ***Short Stories*** [1947] Cover art by Jonas.	$1.50	$5.00	$10.00
645	Evans, Evan (Max Brand) - ***The Song Of The Whip*** [1947] Cover art by Jonas.	$1.50	$5.00	$10.00
646	Caldwell, Erskine - ***Journeyman*** [1947] Cover art by Jonas.	$1.50	$5.00	$10.00
647	Wright, Richard - ***Uncle Tom's Children*** [1947] Cover art by Jonas.	$1.50	$5.00	$10.00
648	Miller, Wade - ***Deadly Weapon*** [1947] Cover art by Jonas.	$2.00	$6.00	$12.00
649	Lewisohn, Ludwig - ***The Tyranny Of Sex*** [1947] Cover art by Jonas.	$1.50	$5.00	$10.00
650	Ferber, Edna - ***American Beauty*** [1947] Cover art by Jonas.	$1.50	$5.00	$10.00
651	Gruber, Frank - ***Market For Murder*** [1947]	$2.00	$6.00	$12.00
652	Morehead, Albert & Mott-Smith, Geoffrey - ***The New Quiz Book*** [1948] PBO. Cover art by Robert Jonas.	$2.00	$6.00	$12.00
653	Ferber, Edna - ***Show Boat*** [1947]	$1.50	$5.00	$10.00
654	Anthology edited by William Targ - ***Great Western Stories*** [1947] Cover art by Jonas.	$1.50	$5.00	$10.00
655	Anthology - ***Great Murder Storeis*** [1948] Cover art by Jonas.	$1.50	$5.00	$10.00
656	Levi, Carlo - ***Christ Stopped At Eboli*** [1948] Cover art by Jonas.	$1.50	$5.00	$10.00
657	Frank, Leonhard - ***Desire Me*** [1948]	$1.50	$5.00	$10.00
658	Upfield, Arthur W. - ***Death Of A Swagman*** [1948] Cover art by Jonas.	$2.50	$7.50	$15.00
659	Faulkner, William - ***The Wild Palms*** [1948]	$1.50	$5.00	$10.00

Pennant Books. New York: Bantam Books, Inc.

		G	VG	F
P-1	Blackburn, Tom W. - ***Navajo Canyon*** [1953] Cover art by Earl Eugene Mayan.	$1.50	$5.00	$10.00
P-2	Grey, Zane - ***The Last Of The Plainsmen*** [1953] Cover art by Harry Schaare.	$2.50	$7.50	$15.00
P-3	Ambler, Eric - ***Epitaph For A Spy*** [1953]	$2.00	$6.00	$12.00
P-4	Benson, Ben - ***Stamped For Murder*** [1953] Cover art by Al Rossi.	$2.00	$6.00	$12.00
P-5	Fergusson, Harvey - ***In Those Days*** [1953]	$1.50	$5.00	$10.00
P-6	Corle, Edwin - ***Mojave: A Book Of Stories*** [1953] Cover art by Greco.	$1.50	$5.00	$10.00
P-7	Burnett, W.R. - ***Vanity Row*** [1953] Cover art by Harry Schaare.	$2.00	$6.00	$12.00
P-8	Stuart, Matt - ***Sunset Rider*** [1953] Cover art by Mel Crair.	$1.50	$5.00	$10.00
P-9	Dawson, Peter - ***Ruler Of The Range*** [1953]	$1.50	$5.00	$10.00
P-10	Randall, Clay - ***Six-Gun Boss*** [1953] Cover art by George Gross.	$1.50	$5.00	$10.00

		G	VG	F
P-11	Household, Geoffrey - ***A Time To Kill*** [1953]	$2.00	$6.00	$12.00
P-12	Gillian, Michael - ***Warrant For A Wanton*** [1953] Cover art by Harry Schaare.	$2.00	$6.00	$12.00
P-13	Holmes, L.P. - ***Apache Desert*** [1953] Cover art by Mel Crair.	$1.50	$5.00	$10.00
P-14	Carder, Michael - ***Action At War Bow Valley*** [1953] Cover art by George Gross.	$1.50	$5.00	$10.00
P-15	Kornbluth, C.M. - ***Takeoff*** [1953] Cover art by Charles Binger.	$2.50	$7.50	$15.00
P-16	Benson, Ben - ***Lily In Her Coffin*** [1953] Cover art by Mitchell Hooks.	$2.00	$6.00	$12.00
P-17	O'Rourke, Frank - ***Gunsmoke Over Big Muddy*** [1953] Cover art by Gross.	$1.50	$5.00	$10.00
P-18	Stuart, Matt - ***Wire In The Wind*** [1953] Cover art by Gross.	$1.50	$5.00	$10.00
P-19	Strabel, Thelma - ***Reap The Wild Wind*** [1953]	$1.50	$5.00	$10.00
P-20	Felsen, Henry Gregor - ***Two And The Town*** [1953]	$2.00	$6.00	$12.00
P-21	Bennett, Dwight - ***Border Graze*** [1953] Cover art by John Leone.	$1.50	$5.00	$10.00
P-22	Dawson, Peter - ***Long Ride*** [1953]	$1.50	$5.00	$10.00
P-23	Corbett, Jim - ***Man-Eaters Of Kumaon*** [1953]	$1.50	$5.00	$10.00
P-24	Crouse, Russel - ***Murder Won't Out*** [1953] Cover art by Charles Binger.	$2.00	$6.00	$12.00
P-25	Holmes, L.P. - ***High Starlight*** [1953]	$1.50	$5.00	$10.00
P-26	Fisher, Clay - ***Santa Fe Passage*** [1953]	$1.50	$5.00	$10.00
P-27	Corle, Edwin - ***Burro Alley*** [1953]	$1.50	$5.00	$10.00
P-28	Walsh, Maurice - ***Blackcock's Feather*** [1953] Cover art by George Gross.	$1.50	$5.00	$10.00
P-29	Bloom, Rolfe & Ullman, Allan - ***The Naked Spur*** [1953] Cover art by George Gross.	$1.50	$5.00	$10.00
P-30	Bechdolt, Frederick R. - ***Bold Raiders Of The West*** [1953]	$1.50	$5.00	$10.00
P-31	Coates, Robert M. - ***The Outlaw Years*** [1953] Cover art by Harry Schaare.	$1.50	$5.00	$10.00
P-32	Perry, George Sessions - ***Walls Rise Up*** [1953] Cover art by Mitchell Hooks.	$1.50	$5.00	$10.00
P-33	Thompson, Thomas - ***Shadow Of The Butte*** [1954] Cover art by Mel Crair.	$1.50	$5.00	$10.00
P-34	Vestal, Stanley - ***Dodge City Queen Of Cowtowns*** [1954] Cover art by George Gross.	$2.50	$7.50	$15.00
P-35	O'Farrell, William - ***Walk The Dark Bridge*** [1954] Cover art by Mitchell Hooks.	$2.00	$6.00	$12.00
P-36	Williams, J.H. - ***Elephant Bill*** [1954] Cover art by Charles Binger.	$1.50	$5.00	$10.00
P-37	Ermine, Will - ***Longhorn Empire*** [1954] Cover art by George Gross.	$1.50	$5.00	$10.00
P-38	Evans, Evan - ***Outlaw Valley*** [1954] Cover art by Crair.	$1.50	$5.00	$10.00
P-39	Griffith, Beatrice - ***American Me*** [1954] Cover art by Mitchell Hooks.	$1.50	$5.00	$10.00
P-40	Driscoll, Charles B. - ***Doubloons*** [1954] Cover by Charles Binger.	$1.50	$5.00	$10.00
P-41	Ernst, Paul - ***The Bronze Mermaid*** [1954] Cover art by Hooks.	$1.50	$5.00	$10.00
P-43	Gruber, Frank - ***Fort Starvation*** [1954]	$1.50	$5.00	$10.00
P-44	Healy, Raymond & McComas, Francis - editors - ***Adventures In Time And Space*** [1954] Cover art by Charles Binger.	$2.50	$7.50	$15.00
P-46	Parker, Dr. George - ***Guaracha Trail*** [1954]	$1.50	$5.00	$10.00
P-47	Kelland, Clarence Budington - ***Tombstone*** [1954] Cover art by Mel Crair.	$2.00	$6.00	$12.00
P-48	Randall, Clay - ***When Oil Ran Red*** [1954]	$1.50	$5.00	$10.00
P-49	Goldthwaite, Eaton K. - ***The Sixpenny Dame*** [1954]	$2.00	$6.00	$12.00
P-50	O'Brien, Eugene - ***One Way Ticket*** [1954] Cover art by Charles Bingers.	$2.00	$6.00	$12.00
P-51	Dobie, J. Frank - ***A Vaquero Of The Brush Country*** [1954]	$1.50	$5.00	$10.00
P-52	Sumner, Nick - ***The Border Queen*** [1954]	$1.50	$5.00	$10.00

		G	VG	F
P-53	McCaig, Robert - ***Toll Mountain*** [1954]	$1.50	$5.00	$10.00
P-54	Barrett, William E. - ***To The Last Man*** [1954]	$2.00	$6.00	$12.00
P-55	O'Farrell, William - ***Repeat Performance*** [1954]	$2.00	$6.00	$12.00
P-56	Anthology edited by Judith Merrill - ***Beyond Human Ken*** [1954] Cover art by Charles Binger	$2.50	$7.50	$15.00
P-57	Bechdolt, Frederick R. - ***Horse Thief Trail*** [1954]	$1.50	$5.00	$10.00
P-59	Brown, Fredric - ***Mostly Murder*** [1954]	$6.00	$20.00	$40.00
P-61	Anthology - ***The Argosy Book Of Sports Stories*** [1954]	$1.50	$5.00	$10.00
P-64	Anthology edited by Brent Ashabranner - ***The Stakes Are High*** [1954] PBO. Cover art by Charles Binger	$2.00	$6.00	$12.00
P-65	Corle, Edwin - ***In Winter Light*** [1954] Cover art by Harry Schaare.	$1.50	$5.00	$10.00
P-67	Raine, William MacLeod - ***Dry Bones In The Valley*** [1954]	$1.50	$5.00	$10.00
P-69	Daniels, John S. - ***The Nester*** [1954]	$1.50	$5.00	$10.00
P-75	Sohl, Jerry - ***The Altered Ego*** [1954] Cover art by Charles Binger.	$2.50	$7.50	$15.00
P-76	Ward, Brad - ***Whiplash*** [1954]	$1.50	$5.00	$10.00
P-77	Dawson, Peter - ***High Country*** [1955]	$1.50	$5.00	$10.00
P-79	Fox, James M. - ***Code Three*** [1955]	$2.00	$6.00	$12.00

Pennant Mystery. Digest Size.

1	Towne, Stuart (Clayton Rawson) - ***Death Out Of Thin Air*** [n.d.]	$8.00	$25.00	$50.00
2	Taylor, Phoebe Atwood - ***The Six Iron Spiders*** [n.d.]	$8.00	$25.00	$50.00

Perennial Library. New York: Harper & Row.

P-61	Clarke, Arthur C. - ***The Coast Of Coral*** [1965]	$1.00	$3.00	$6.00
P-4004	Egan, Lesley - ***My Name Is Death*** [1965]	$ .75	$2.50	$5.00

Perma Books (Early Publisher's History, 1949–1959)

Two lines of books came from Perma Books, one hardbound and one paperbound. Only ten of the titles received both types of covers. A number of nonfiction titles appeared, alongside popular literature of a variety of types. They published two books on magic, of interest to many collectors. Doubleday & Co. published the line until 1954, when Pocket Books, Inc., purchased the line and continued it, using the Pocket format. The Perma Book line, under the direction of Pocket Book, Inc., continued to publish a variety of literature. In this continuation of the imprint, a number of collectible mysteries appear, especially those by Ian Fleming, Henry Kuttner, and Ed McBain.

Perma Book M Series. New York: Pocket Books, Inc.

		G	VG	F
M-1000	Sheen, Fulton J. - ***Peace Of Soul*** [1955] Photo cover	$ .65	$2.00	$4.00
M-1600	Oursler, Fulton - ***The Greatest Book Ever Written*** [1954]	$ .65	$2.00	$4.00
M-3001	Austin, Gene - ***Texan-Killer*** [1955] Cover art by Stanley Borack.	$1.25	$3.75	$7.50
M-3002	Manor, Jason - ***Too Dead To Run*** [1955]	$1.35	$4.00	$8.00
M-3003	Frazee, Steve - ***Spur To The Smoke*** [1955]	$1.25	$3.75	$7.50
M-3004	Jackson, Shirley - ***Life Among The Savages*** [1955]	$1.35	$4.00	$8.00
M-3005	Reed, Eliot - ***Tender To Danger*** [1955]	$1.25	$3.75	$7.50
M-3006	Kennedy, Mark - ***Boy Gang*** [1955]	$2.50	$7.50	$15.00
M-3007	Hayes, Joseph - ***The Desperate Hours*** [1955]	$1.35	$4.00	$8.00
M-3008	Hopkins, Tom J. - ***Horsethief Crossing*** [1955]	$1.25	$3.75	$7.50
M-3009	Lomax, Bliss - ***Honky-Tonk Woman*** [1955] PBO. Cover art by George Mayers	$2.00	$6.00	$12.00
M-3010	Coxe, George Harmon - ***The Crimson Clue*** [1955] Cover art by James Meese.	$1.35	$4.00	$8.00

Perma Books, M-3032

Perma Books, 3062

Perma Books, M-3084

		G	VG	F
M-3011	Chaze, Elliott - ***The Stainless Steel Kimono*** [1955] Cover art by Albert Dorne.	$1.25	$3.75	$7.50
M-3012	Avallone, Michael - ***Dead Game*** [1955] Cover art by James Meese.	$1.50	$5.00	$10.00
M-3013	Appell, George Charles - ***Massacre Trail*** [1955] PBO. Cover by Robert Schulz.	$1.35	$4.00	$8.00
M-3014	DeRosso, H.A. - ***End Of The Gun*** [1955] PBO. Cover art by Tom Ryan.	$1.25	$3.75	$7.50
M-3015	Anthology edited by Ellery Queen - ***The Queen's Awards*** [1955] Cover art by William George.	$1.35	$4.00	$8.00
M-3016	Lancaster, Bruce - ***The Secret Road*** [1955] Cover art by Clark Hulings.	$1.25	$3.75	$7.50
M-3017	Derby, Mark - ***The Big Water*** [1955] Cover art by James Meese.	$1.25	$3.75	$7.50
M-3018	Granger, K.R.G. - ***Tejanos*** [1955] PBO. Cover art by Bob Schulz.	$1.25	$3.75	$7.50
M-3019	Grew, William - ***Doubles In Death*** [1955] Cover art by Bob Schulz.	$1.25	$3.75	$7.50
M-3020	Clark, J. Bigelow - ***The Dreamers*** [1955] Cover art by Stanley Borack.	$1.25	$3.75	$7.50
M-3021	Evarts, Hal G. - ***The Settling Of The Sage*** [1955] Cover by John Leone.	$1.25	$3.75	$7.50
M-3022	Sylvester, Robert - ***The Big Boodle*** [1955] Cover art by Schulz.	$1.50	$5.00	$10.00
M-3023	Bennett, Dwight - ***Top Hand*** [1955] Cover art by Schulz.	$1.25	$3.75	$7.50
M-3024	Ermine, Will (Harry Sinclair Drago) - ***Frenchman's River*** [1955] PBO. Cover art by Verne Tossey.	$1.25	$3.75	$7.50
M-3025	Reed, Eliot - ***The Maras Affair*** [1955] Cover art by Meese.	$1.35	$4.00	$8.00
M-3026	Peace, Frank - ***Easy Money*** [1955]	$1.25	$3.75	$7.50
M-3027	McIntosh, J.T. - ***World Out Of Mind*** [1955] Cover art by Powers.	$2.00	$6.00	$12.00
M-3028	Derby, Mark - ***The Bad Step*** [1955]	$1.35	$4.00	$8.00
M-3029	Brickman - ***Do It Yourself*** [1955] Cover art by Brickman. Cartoon book.	$1.50	$5.00	$10.00
M-3030	Harrison, C. William - ***Border Fever*** [1955] PBO. Cover art by Bob Schulz.	$1.25	$3.75	$7.50
M-3031	Taylor, R. - ***Fractured French*** [1956] Cover art by R. Taylor. Cartoon book.	$1.35	$4.00	$8.00
M-3032	Dewey, Thomas B. - ***The Mean Streets*** [1956] Cover art by James Meese.	$3.50	$10.00	$20.00
M-3033	Stevens, Dan J. - ***Blood Money*** [1956]	$1.25	$3.75	$7.50
M-3034	Holden, Richard - ***Snow Fury*** [1956] Cover art by James Meese.	$4.00	$12.50	$25.00

		G	VG	F
M-3035	Anthology edited by Scott Meredith - ***Bar 4 Roundup Of Best Western Stories*** [1956] Cover by John Leone.	$1.35	$4.00	$8.00
M-3036	Lacy, Ed - ***Visa To Death*** [1956] Cover art by Maguire.	$1.35	$4.00	$8.00
M-3037	McBain, Ed - ***Cop Hater*** [1956] PBO. First 87th precinct novel. Photo cover.	$3.50	$10.00	$20.00
M-3038	Drago, Harry Sinclair - ***Pay-Off At Black Hawk*** [1956]	$1.25	$3.75	$7.50
M-3039	Kane, Joseph Nathan - ***The Perma Quiz Book*** [1956] PBO.	$1.25	$3.75	$7.50
M-3040	Hitchens, Dolores - ***Sleep With Strangers*** [1956] Cover art by Lou Marchetti.	$1.35	$4.00	$8.00
M-3041	Hemingway, Ernest - ***To Have And Not Have*** [1956]	$1.35	$4.00	$8.00
M-3042	Sack, John - ***From Here To Shimbashi*** [1956] Cover art by Bud Hawes.	$1.25	$3.75	$7.50
M-3043	Hammett, Dashiell - ***Red Harvest*** [1956] Cover art by Lou Marchetti.	$3.00	$9.00	$18.00
M-3044	Todd, Lucas - ***Showdown Creek*** [1956]	$1.25	$3.75	$7.50
M-3045	Bennett, Dwight - ***The Avenger*** [1956]	$1.25	$3.75	$7.50
M-3046	Kuttner, Henry - ***The Murder Of Eleanor Pope*** [1956] PBO. Photo cover.	$4.00	$12.50	$25.00
M-3047	O'Malley, Bill - ***Blessed Event*** [1956]	$1.25	$3.75	$7.50
M-3048	Fleming, Ian - ***Live And Let Die*** [1956] Cover art by James Meese.	$4.00	$12.50	$25.00
M-3049	Frazee, Steve - ***Tumbling Range Woman*** [1956] PBO. Cover art by Schulz.	$1.35	$4.00	$8.00
M-3050	Price, Roger - ***Droodles*** [1956] Photo cover.	$1.25	$3.75	$7.50
M-3051	Hitchens, Bert & Delores - ***F.O.B. Murder*** [1956] Cover art by Schulz.	$1.35	$4.00	$8.00
M-3052	Peace, Frank - ***The Brass Brigade*** [1956] PBO. Cover art by Robert Schulz.	$1.25	$3.75	$7.50
M-3053	Kurnitz, Harry - ***Invasion Of Privacy*** [1956] Cover art by James Meese.	$1.35	$4.00	$8.00
M-3054	Bassett, Jack & Monath, Norman - ***Play It Yourself*** [1956] PBO. Puzzle book. Photo cover.	$1.50	$5.00	$10.00
M-3055	McBain, Ed - ***The Con Man*** [1957] PBO. Cover art by James Meese.	$3.00	$9.00	$18.00
M-3056	Hemingway, Ernest - ***Green Hills Of Africa*** [1956] Cover art by Robert Schulz.	$1.35	$4.00	$8.00
M-3057	Anthology edited by Alexander Field - ***The Perma X-Word Puzzle Book*** [1956] PBO. Cover art by Jonas. Puzzle book.	$1.50	$5.00	$10.00
M-3058	Kuttner, Henry - ***The Murder Of Ann Avery*** [1956] PBO. Cover art by Meese.	$4.00	$12.50	$25.00
M-3059	Malachy, Frank - ***Hot Town*** [1956]	$1.25	$3.75	$7.50
M-3060	Liberman, Jerry & Moulton, Powers - ***Best Jokes For All Occasions*** [1956]	$1.25	$3.75	$7.50
M-3061	McBain, Ed - ***The Mugger*** [1956] PBO. Cover art by Lou Marchetti.	$3.00	$9.00	$18.00
M-3062	McBain, Ed - ***The Pusher*** [1956] PBO. Cover art by Charles Binger.	$3.50	$10.00	$20.00
3063	Drew, Lincoln - ***Die In The Saddle*** [1956] PBO. Cover art by Morton Engle.	$1.25	$3.75	$7.50
M-3064	Cooper, Jefferson (Gardner F. Fox) - ***The Bloody Sevens*** [1956] PBO. Cover art by Charles Binger.	$1.50	$5.00	$10.00
M-3065	Fox, Gill - ***Wilbert*** [1956] PBO. Cover art by Gill Fox. Cartoon book.	$1.50	$5.00	$10.00
M-3066	Hansen, Robert P. - ***Murder Is Where You Find It*** [1956] Cover art by James Meese.	$1.35	$4.00	$8.00
M-3067	Preston, Charles - ***Pets Including Women*** [1956]	$1.35	$4.00	$8.00
M-3068	Drago, Harry Sinclair - ***Decision At Broken Butte*** [1956]	$1.25	$3.75	$7.50
M-3069	O'Rourke, Frank - ***The Last Round*** [1956]	$1.25	$3.75	$7.50
M-3070	Fleming, Ian - ***Too Hot To Handle*** [1956] Cover art by Lou Marchetti.	$5.00	$15.00	$30.00

		G	VG	F
M-3071	Jennings, John - ***Chronicle Of The Calypso, Clipper*** [1956] Cover art by Clark Hulings.	$1.25	$3.75	$7.50
M-3072	Lanham, Edwin - ***Death In The Wind*** [1957] Cover art by James Meese.	$1.25	$3.75	$7.50
M-3073	Gold, Herbert - ***The Wild Life*** [1957] Cover art by Tom Dunn.	$1.25	$3.75	$7.50
M-3074	Hammett, Dashiell - ***The Maltese Falcon*** [1957] Cover art by Stanley Meltzoff.	$2.00	$6.00	$12.00
M-3075	Rowans, Virginia - ***Oh, What A Wonderful Wedding*** [1957] Cover art by Barye Phillips.	$1.00	$3.00	$6.00
M-3076	Anthology edited by Ellery Queen - ***Ellery Queen's Awards: Tenth Series*** [1957] Cover art by Robert Korn.	$1.25	$3.75	$7.50
M-3077	Randall, Clay - ***Boomer*** [1957]	$1.25	$3.75	$7.50
M-3078	O'Malley, Bill - ***Feeling No Pain*** [1957] Cartoon book. Cover by Bill O'Malley	$1.35	$4.00	$8.00
M-3079	Palmer, Stuart - ***Unhappy Hooligan*** [1957] Cover art by Meese.	$1.25	$3.75	$7.50
M-3080	Chaber, M.E. - ***The Splintered Man*** [1957] Cover art by Schulz.	$2.50	$7.50	$15.00
M-3081	Arnold, Oren - ***The Wild West Joke Book*** [1957] Cover art by Daniel Schwartz.	$1.35	$4.00	$8.00
M-3082	Scott, Meredith - editor - ***Bar 5 Roundup Of Best Western Stories*** [1957]	$1.25	$3.75	$7.50
M-3083	Anthology edited by Charles Preston - ***Choice Cartoons From Sports Illustrated*** [1957] PBO. Cartoon book.	$1.35	$4.00	$8.00
M-3084	Fleming, Ian - ***Diamonds Are Forever*** [1957] Cover art by William Rose.	$4.00	$12.50	$25.00
M-3085	Drago, Harry Sinclair - ***Wild Grass*** [1957] Cover art by Tom Ryan.	$1.25	$3.75	$7.50
M-3086	Richmond, Roe - ***Montana Bad Man*** [1957]	$1.25	$3.75	$7.50
M-3087	Mahannah, Floyd - ***The Golden Widow*** [1957] Cover art by Clark Hulings.	$1.25	$3.75	$7.50
M-3088	Patten, Lewis B. - ***Pursuit*** [1957] Cover by Basil Gogos.	$1.25	$3.75	$7.50
M-3089	Deney, Thomas B. - ***The Brave, Bad Girls*** [1957] Cover art by Hulings.	$2.00	$6.00	$12.00
M-3090	Brickman, Morris - ***Don't Do It Yourself*** [1957]	$1.25	$3.75	$7.50
M-3091	Ransome, Stephen - ***The Men In Her Death*** [1957] Cover by Robert Schulz.	$1.25	$3.75	$7.50
M-3092	Hunter, John - ***Ride The Wind South*** [1957] PBO. Cover art by Tom Ryan.	$1.25	$3.75	$7.50
M-3093	Harrison, C. William - ***Unarmed Killer*** [1957] PBO. Cover art by Jerry Allison.	$1.25	$3.75	$7.50
M-3094	Burnett, Whit - ***This Is My Funniest*** [1957] PBO. Joke book.	$1.25	$3.75	$7.50
M-3095	Gaulden, Ray - ***Shadow Of The Rope*** [1957] PBO. Cover art by Tom Ryan.	$1.25	$3.75	$7.50
M-3096	Treynor, Blair - ***Widow's Pique*** [1957] Cover art by James Meese.	$1.25	$3.75	$7.50
M-3097	Marsten, Richard - ***Vanishing Ladies*** [1957] PBO. Cover art by James Meese.	$1.25	$3.75	$7.50
M-3098	Vincent, Richard - ***Red*** [1957] PBO. Cover art by Schulz.	$1.25	$3.75	$7.50
M-3099	McElfresh, Adeline - ***Nurse Kathy*** [1957] Cover art by Clark Hulings.	$ .75	$2.50	$5.00
M-3100	Hitchens, Bert & Delores - ***One-Way Ticket*** [1957] Cover art by James Meese.	$1.35	$4.00	$8.00
M-3101	Brown, Dee - ***Cavalry Scout*** [1957] PBO. Cover by Lou Marchetti.	$1.25	$3.75	$7.50
M-3102	Webb, Nancy - ***Marcia Blake Publicity Girl*** [1957]	$ .75	$2.50	$5.00
M-3103	Charteris, Leslie - ***The Saint Around The World*** [1957] Cover by James Meese.	$1.25	$3.75	$7.50
M-3104	Richmond, Roe - ***Lash Of Idaho*** [1958] PBO. Cover art by Jerry McConnell.	$1.25	$3.75	$7.50
M-3105	O'Malley, Bill - ***O'Malley's Nuns*** [1958] Cartoon book.	$1.35	$4.00	$8.00

		G	VG	F
M-3106	Lacy, Ed - ***Lead With Your Left*** [1958] Cover art by Robert Schulz.	$1.35	$4.00	$8.00
M-3107	Drew, Lincoln - ***Yellow Rope*** [1958] PBO. Cover by Tom Ryan.	$1.25	$3.75	$7.50
M-3108	McBain, Ed - ***Killer's Choice*** [1957] PBO. Cover art by Schulz.	$3.00	$9.00	$18.00
M-3109	Stuart, Matt - ***The Lonely Law*** [1958]	$1.25	$3.75	$7.50
M-3110	Gaulden, Ray - ***The Vengeful Men*** [1958] PBO. Cover by Jerry Allison.	$1.25	$3.75	$7.50
M-3111	Anthology edited by S. & S. Meredith - ***The Best From Manhunt*** [1958] PBO. Cover art by Ernest Chiriaka.	$1.35	$4.00	$8.00
M-3112	Appell, George C. - ***Three Trails*** [1958] PBO. Cover art by Jerry Allison.	$1.25	$3.75	$7.50
M-3113	McBain, Ed - ***Killer's Payoff*** [1958] PBO. Cover art by Robert Schulz.	$3.00	$9.00	$18.00
M-3114	Barns, Glenn M. - ***Deadly Summer*** [1958]	$1.25	$3.75	$7.50
M-3115	Drago, Harry Sinclair - ***Showdown At Sunset*** [1958] PBO. Cover art by Bob Abbett.	$1.25	$3.75	$7.50
M-3116	Anthology edited by Scott Meredith - ***Bar 6 Roundup Of Best Western Stories*** [1958]	$1.25	$3.75	$7.50
M-3117	Marsten, Richard - ***Even The Wicked*** [1958] PBO. Cover art by Jerry Allison.	$1.35	$4.00	$8.00
M-3118	Davis, Jr., Franklin M. - ***Spearhead*** [1958] PBO. Cover art by Bob Abbett.	$1.25	$3.75	$7.50
M-3119	McBain, Ed - ***Lady Killer*** [1958] PBO. Cover art by Charles Binger.	$3.00	$9.00	$18.00
M-3120	Drew, Lincoln - ***Rifle Ranch*** [1958]	$1.25	$3.75	$7.50
M-3122	Holmes, David C. - ***The Velvet Ape*** [1958] Cover by James Meese.	$1.25	$3.75	$7.50
M-3123	Hunter, John (W.T. Ballard) - ***The Marshall From Deadwood*** [1958]	$1.25	$3.75	$7.50
M-4001	Hall, James Norman & Nordhoff, Charles - ***Botany Bay*** [1954]	$1.00	$3.00	$6.00
M-4002	Gann, Ernest K. - ***The High And The Mighty*** [1954]	$1.00	$3.00	$6.00
M-4003	Graham, Billy - ***Peace With God*** [1954] Photo cover.	$ .75	$2.50	$5.00
M-4004	Shubin, Seymour - ***Anyone's My Name*** [1954] Cover art by James Meese.	$1.25	$3.75	$7.50
M-4005	Street, James - ***The Velvet Doublet*** [1954]	$1.00	$3.00	$6.00
M-4006	Hall, Oakley - ***Corpus Of Joe Bailey*** [1955]	$1.00	$3.00	$6.00
M-4007	Haydn, Hiram - ***The Time Is Noon*** [1955]	$1.00	$3.00	$6.00
M-4008	Slaughter, Frank G. - ***Storm Haven*** [1955] Cover art by Schulz.	$1.00	$3.00	$6.00
M-4009	Peale, Norman Vincent - ***The Art Of Living*** [1955]	$ .75	$2.50	$5.00
M-4010	Stern, Daniel - ***The Girl With The Glass Heart*** [1955] Cover art by Tom Dunn.	$1.25	$3.75	$7.50
M-4011	Wren, Percival C. - ***Stories Of The Foreign Legion*** [1955] Cover by Robert Schulz.	$1.25	$3.75	$7.50
M-4012	Peppard, Harold M. - ***Sight Without Glasses*** [1955]	$1.25	$3.75	$7.50
M-4013	Bisch, Louis E. - ***Be Glad You're Neurotic*** [1955]	$ .75	$2.50	$5.00
M-4014	Anthology edited by Powers Moulton - ***Best Jokes For All Occasions*** [1955]	$1.25	$3.75	$7.50
M-4015	Lindlahr, Victor H. - ***Eat And Reduce*** [1955]	$ .75	$2.50	$5.00
M-4016	Goren, Charles H. - ***The Fundamentals Of Contract Bridge*** [1955]	$ .75	$2.50	$5.00
M-4017	Oursler, Fulton - ***Modern Parables*** [1955]	$ .75	$2.50	$5.00
M-4018	Henkin, Leo J. - ***New Standard Book Of Model Letters For All Occasions*** [1955]	$ .75	$2.50	$5.00
M-4019	Fielding, William J. - ***Sex And The Love Life*** [1955]	$ .75	$2.50	$5.00
M-4020	Lewis, Norman - ***Word Power Made Easey*** [1955]	$ .75	$2.50	$5.00
M-4021	Newman, Frank Eaton - ***The Perma Crossword Puzzle And Word Game Dictionary*** [1955]	$1.25	$3.75	$7.50
M-4022	Anthology edited by Groff Conklin - ***Operation Future*** [1955] PBO. Cover art by Schulz.	$1.50	$5.00	$10.00
M-4023	Kling, Samuel G. - ***Your Legal Advisor*** [1955] PBO.	$ .75	$2.50	$5.00

		G	VG	F
M-4024	Hall, Radclyffe - ***The Well Of Loneliness*** [1955]	$2.50	$7.50	$15.00
M-4025	Slaughter, Frank G. - ***Spencer Brade, M.D.*** [1955]	$ .75	$2.50	$5.00
M-4026	Slaughter, Frank G. - ***That None Should Die*** [1957] Cover art by Charles Binger.	$1.25	$3.75	$7.50
M-4027	Slaughter, Frank G. - ***East Side General*** [1957]	$1.25	$3.75	$7.50
M-4028	Dibner, Martin - ***The Deep Six*** [1955] Movie tie-in.	$1.25	$3.75	$7.50
M-4029	Murphy, Audue - ***To Hell And Back*** [1955]	$1.25	$3.75	$7.50
M-4030	Duffy, Patrick Gavin - ***The Standard Bartender's Guide*** [1955]	$1.00	$3.00	$6.00
M-4031	Slaughter, Frank G. - ***The Song Of Ruth*** [1955] Cover art by Tom Dunn.	$1.00	$3.00	$6.00
M-4032	Pugh, John J. - ***Captain Of The Medici*** [1955] Cover art by Bob Maguire.	$1.00	$3.00	$6.00
M-4033	Sheen, Fulton J. - ***Lift Up Your Heart*** [1955] Photo cover.	$ .75	$2.50	$5.00
M-4034	Gann, Ernest K. - ***Soldier Of Fortune*** [1955] Cover art by Tom Dunn.	$1.00	$3.00	$6.00
M-4035	Edwards, Morton - ***Your Child From 2 To 5*** [1955]	$ .75	$2.50	$5.00
M-4036	Oursler, Fulton & Armstrong, April O. - ***The Greatest Faith Ever Known*** [1955] Cover art by Robert Jonas.	$ .75	$2.50	$5.00
M-4037	Feville, Frank - ***The Cotton Road*** [1955]	$1.00	$3.00	$6.00
M-4038	Slaughter, Frank G. - ***A Touch Of Glory*** [1956] Cover art by Meese.	$1.00	$3.00	$6.00
M-4039	Rogers, Garet - ***Prisoner In Paradise*** [1955]	$1.00	$3.00	$6.00
M-4040	Davis, Elmer - ***But We Were Born Free*** [1955] Cover art by Robert Jonas.	$1.00	$3.00	$6.00
M-4041	Oursler, Fulton - ***Lights Along The Shore*** [1956]	$1.00	$3.00	$6.00
M-4042	Hall, Oakley - ***Mardios Beach*** [1956] Cover art by Tom Dunn.	$1.00	$3.00	$6.00
M-4043	Breslin, Howard - ***The Silver Oar*** [1956]	$1.00	$3.00	$6.00
M-4044	Williams, Thomas - ***Ceremony Of Love*** [1956]	$ .75	$2.50	$5.00
M-4045	Swiggett, Howard - ***The Strongbox*** [1956] Cover art by Robert Maguire.	$ .75	$2.50	$5.00
M-4046	Oursler, Fulton - ***The Greatest Story Ever Told*** [1956]	$ .75	$2.50	$5.00
M-4047	Slaughter, Frank G. - ***Divine Mistress*** [1956] Cover art by Charles Binger.	$1.00	$3.00	$6.00
M-4048	Slaughter, Frank G. - ***Battle Surgeon*** [1956] Cover art by Tom Dunn.	$ .75	$2.50	$5.00
M-4049	Slaughter, Frank G. - ***The Galileans*** [1956]	$ .75	$2.50	$5.00
M-4050	Wouk, Herman - ***Slattery's Hurricane*** [1956] PBO. Cover art by Charles Binger.	$ .75	$2.50	$5.00
M-4051	Slaughter, Frank G. - ***The Healer*** [1956] Cover art by Tom Dunn.	$ .75	$2.50	$5.00
M-4052	Bourjaily, Vance - ***The Hound Of Earth*** [1956]	$ .75	$2.50	$5.00
M-4053	Slaughter, Frank G. - ***Air Surgeon*** [1956] Cover art by James Meese.	$ .75	$2.50	$5.00
M-4054	Slaughter, Frank G. - ***Fort Everglades*** [1956] Cover art by James Meese.	$1.50	$5.00	$10.00
M-4055	Slaughter, Frank G. - ***The Road To Bithynia*** [1956]	$ .75	$2.50	$5.00
M-4056	Maugham, W. Somerset - ***South Sea Stories*** [1956]	$1.35	$4.00	$8.00
M-4057	Terry. C.V. - ***Darien Venture*** [1956] Cover art by Charles Binger.	$ .75	$2.50	$5.00
M-4058	Breslin, Howard - ***Shad Run*** [1956] Cover art by Hulings.	$ .75	$2.50	$5.00
M-4059	Hutschnecker, M.D., Arnold, A. - ***The Will To Live*** [1956]	$ .75	$2.50	$5.00
M-4060	Slaughter, Dr. Frank G. - ***Science And Surgery*** [1956] PBO. Photo cover.	$ .75	$2.50	$5.00
4061	Beach, Comm. Edward L. - ***Run Silent, Run Deep*** [1956] Cover art by Hulings.	$ .75	$2.50	$5.00
M-4062	Heyerdahl, Thor - ***Kon-Tiki*** [1956] Cover art by Gordon Grant. Contains 80 photos.	$1.00	$3.00	$6.00
M-4063	Chessman, Caryl - ***Cell 2455 Death Row*** [1956]	$1.25	$3.75	$7.50
M-4064	Slaughter, Frank G. - ***Flight From Natchez*** [1956]	$ .75	$2.50	$5.00
M-4065	Aaron, Sam W. - ***How To Eat Better For Less Money*** [1956]	$ .75	$2.50	$5.00

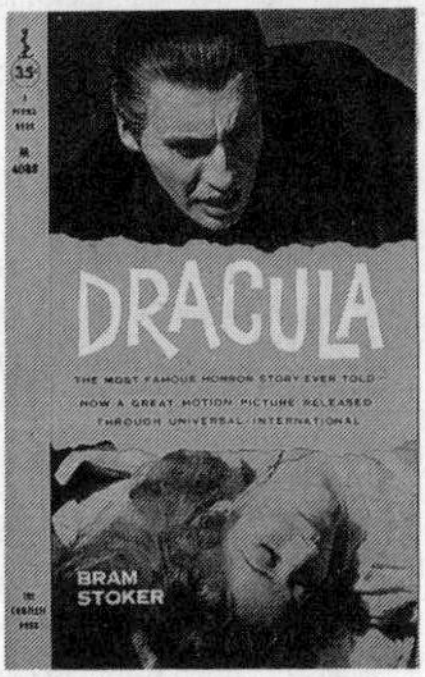

Perma Books, M-4088

Perma Books, M-4272

Perma Books, P-67

		G	VG	F
M-4066	Mayer, N.H. & S.K. - ***The Complete Letter Writer*** [1956]	$ .75	$2.50	$5.00
M-4067	MacLean, Alistair - ***H.M.S. Ulysses*** [1956] Cover art by Schulz.	$ .75	$2.50	$5.00
M-4068	Lofts, Norah - ***Winter Harvest*** [1956]	$ .75	$2.50	$5.00
M-4069	Slaughter, Frank G. - ***The Scarlet Cord*** [1957] Cover art by Tom Dunn.	$ .75	$2.50	$5.00
M-4070	Gerson, Noel B. - ***The Highwayman*** [1957]	$ .75	$2.50	$5.00
M-4071	Kane, Harnett, T. - ***The Smiling Rebel*** [1957] Cover art by Meese.	$ .75	$2.50	$5.00
M-4072	Slaughter, Frank G. - ***The Golden Isle*** [1957]	$ .75	$2.50	$5.00
M-4073	Birney, Hoffman - ***The Dice Of God*** [1957]	$ .75	$2.50	$5.00
M-4074	Kling, Samuel G. - ***How To Win And Hold A Mate*** [1957] PBO. Photo cover.	$ .75	$2.50	$5.00
M-4075	Judah, Charles B. - ***Christopher Rogue*** [1957] Cover art by James Meese.	$1.00	$3.00	$6.00
M-4076	Kent, Madeleine Fabiola - ***The Corsair*** [1957] Cover art by James Meese.	$ .75	$2.50	$5.00
M-4077	Rowan, Virginia - ***The Loving Couple-His Story/The Loving Couple-Her Story*** [1957] Cover art by Schaare.	$1.35	$4.00	$8.00
M-4078	Markey, Gene - ***Kentucky Pride*** [1957] Cover art by Hulings.	$ .75	$2.50	$5.00
M-4079	Innes, Hammond - ***The Wreck Of The Mary Deare*** [1957] Cover art by Charles Binger	$ .75	$2.50	$5.00
M-4080	Depew, Wally - ***Breakaway*** [1957] Cover art by James Meese.	$ .75	$2.50	$5.00
M-4081	MacKersey, Ian - ***Position Unknown*** [1957] Cover art by Meese.	$ .75	$2.50	$5.00
M-4082	Kuttner, Henry - ***Murder Of A Mistress*** [1957] PBO. Photo cover.	$4.00	$12.50	$25.00
M-4083	Unknown - ***Bellevue Is My Home*** [1957]	$ .75	$2.50	$5.00
M-4084	Arnold, Pauline - ***Rate Yourself*** [1958] PBO.	$ .75	$2.50	$5.00
M-4085	Dinneen, Joseph F. - ***Underworld U.S.A.*** [1957] Photo cover.	$1.25	$3.75	$7.50
M-4086	Orr, Mary - ***Diamond In The Sky*** [1957] Cover art by Avati.	$1.00	$3.00	$6.00
M-4087	Slaughter, Frank G. - ***The Warrior*** [1957] Cover art by Binger.	$ .75	$2.50	$5.00
M-4088	Stoker, Bram - ***Dracula*** [1957]	$1.50	$5.00	$10.00
M-4089	MacLean, Alistair - ***The Guns Of Navarone*** [1957] Cover art by Tom Dunn	$1.00	$3.00	$6.00
M-4090	Kubeck, James - ***The Calendar Epic*** [1958] Cover art by Meese.	$1.00	$3.00	$6.00
M-4091	Gann, Ernest - ***Twilight For The Gods*** [1958] Cover art by Tom Dunn.	$ .75	$2.50	$5.00
M-4092	Slaughter, Frank G. - ***Sword And Scalpel*** [1958] Cover art by Charles Binger.	$ .75	$2.50	$5.00
M-4093	Beaty, David - ***The Proving Flight*** [1957] Cover art by Schulz.	$ .75	$2.50	$5.00
M-4094	Eiker, Karl V. - ***Star Of Macedon*** [1957]	$ .75	$2.50	$5.00

		G	VG	F
M-4095	Shute, Nevil - ***In The Wet*** [1957]	$ .75	$2.50	$5.00
M-4096	Kuttner, Henry - ***Murder Of A Wife*** [1958] PBO. Cover art by William Rose.	$4.00	$12.50	$25.00
M-4097	Sandstrom, Flora - ***The Midwife Of Pont Clery*** [1958] Cover art by Edward Knapp	$ .75	$2.50	$5.00
M-4098	Ham, Jr., Roswell G. - ***Til The Rafters Ring*** [1958] Cover art by Leon Gregori.	$ .75	$2.50	$5.00
M-4099	Crossen, Kendell Foster - ***The Tortured Path*** [1958]	$1.25	$3.75	$7.50
M-4100	Terry, C.V. - ***The Golden Ones*** [1958]	$ .75	$2.50	$5.00
M-4101	Kane, Joseph N. - ***Second Perma Quiz Book*** [1958] PBO	$1.00	$3.00	$6.00
M-4102	Cloete, Stuart - ***The Mask*** [1958] Cover by Daniel Schwartz.	$ .75	$2.50	$5.00
M-4103	Black, Hillel & Kolman, Sam - ***The Royal Vultures*** [1958]	$ .75	$2.50	$5.00
M-4104	Howe, Helen - ***The Success*** [1958]	$ .75	$2.50	$5.00
M-4105	Carney, Otis - ***The Country Club Set*** [1958]	$ .75	$2.50	$5.00
M-4106	Suehsdorf, Adie - ***What To Tell Your Children About Sex*** [1958]	$ .75	$2.50	$5.00
M-4107	Maltz, Maxwell - ***Doctor Pygmalion*** [1958]	$ .75	$2.50	$5.00
M-4108	Horgan, Paul - ***Give Me Possession*** [1958]	$ .75	$2.50	$5.00
M-4109	Thorne, Emily - ***Flight Hostess*** [1958]	$ .75	$2.50	$5.00
M-4110	Righter, Carroll - ***Astrology And You*** [1958]	$ .75	$2.50	$5.00
M-4111	Slaughter, Frank G. - ***The Mapmaker*** [1958] Cover art by Sanford Kossin	$ .75	$2.50	$5.00
M-4112	Day, Beth - ***No Hiding Place*** [1958]	$ .75	$2.50	$5.00
M-4113	Cooper, Jefferson (Gardner F. Fox) - ***The Questing Sword*** [1958] PBO. Cover art by Jerry Allison.	$1.25	$3.75	$7.50
M-4114	Marshall, Rosamond - ***The Bixby Girls*** [1959]	$ .75	$2.50	$5.00
M-4115	Marshall, S.L.A. - ***Pork Chop Hill*** [1959]	$ .75	$2.50	$5.00
M-4116	MacLean, Alistair - ***South By Java Head*** [1959]	$ .75	$2.50	$5.00
M-4117	Cooper, Jefferson (Gardner F. Fox) - ***Veronica's Veil*** [1959]	$ .75	$2.50	$5.00
M-4118	Danforth, Harold R. & Horan, James D. - ***The D.A.'s Man*** [1959] Photo cover.	$ .75	$2.50	$5.00
M-4119	O'Meara, Walter - ***The Devil's Cross*** [1959]	$ .75	$2.50	$5.00
M-4120	Russell, Eric Frank - ***Wasp*** [1959] Cover by Art Sussman.	$1.50	$5.00	$10.00
M-4121	Canning, Victor - ***The Forbidden Road*** [1959]	$1.00	$3.00	$6.00
M-4122	Klein, Alexander - ***The Counterfeit Traitor*** [1959]	$ .75	$2.50	$5.00
M-4123	White, Betty - ***Betty White's Teen-Age Dance Book*** [1959]	$ .75	$2.50	$5.00
M-4124	Hurst, Fannie - ***Imitation Of Life*** [1959] Movie tie-in. Movie photo cover.	$1.00	$3.00	$6.00
M-4125	Brothers, Joyce & Eagan, Edward P.F. - ***10 Days To A Successful Memory*** [1959]	$ .75	$2.50	$5.00
M-4126	Eddy, Roger - ***A Family Affair*** [1959]	$ .75	$2.50	$5.00
M-4127	Lofts, Norah - ***Scent Of Cloves*** [1959]	$ .75	$2.50	$5.00
M-4128	Humphrey, William - ***Home From The Hill*** [1959] Cover art by Darrell Green.	$1.00	$3.00	$6.00
M-4129	Chidsey, Donald Barr - ***His Majesty's Highwayman*** [1959]	$ .75	$2.50	$5.00
M-4130	Slaughter, Frank G. - ***Daybreak*** [1959]	$ .75	$2.50	$5.00
M-4131	Anthology edited by Holly Cantus - ***The Pocketbook Of Household Hints*** [1959] PBO. Cover art by Steve DuQuette.	$ .75	$2.50	$5.00
M-4132	Morris, Donald R. - ***Warm Bodies*** [1959]	$ .75	$2.50	$5.00
M-4133	Canizio, Frank & Markel, Robert - ***A Man Against Fate*** [1959]	$ .75	$2.50	$5.00
M-4134	Jastrow, Joseph - ***Freud: His Dream And Sex Thoeories*** [1959].	$ .75	$2.50	$5.00
M-4135	French, Peter - ***The Southern Cross*** [1959] Cover art by Charles.	$ .75	$2.50	$5.00
M-4136	Dalrymple, Byron - ***The Fundamentals Of Fishing And Hunting*** [1959] Cover art by Robert J. Lee	$ .75	$2.50	$5.00
M-4138	Meyer, Jerome S. - ***Fun For The Family*** [1959]	$ .75	$2.50	$5.00
M-4139	Canning, Victor - ***The Captives Of Mora Island*** [1959]	$1.00	$3.00	$6.00
M-4140	Peck, M.D., Joseph H. - ***All About Men*** [1959]	$ .75	$2.50	$5.00
M-4141	Montagu, Ashley - ***The Cultured Man*** [1959]	$ .75	$2.50	$5.00
M-4142	Ruesch, Hans - ***Top Of The World*** [1959]	$ .75	$2.50	$5.00

		G	VG	F
M-4143	Newcomb, Richard F. - ***Abandon Ship!*** [1959]	$ .75	$2.50	$5.00
M-4144	Hilliard, Dr. Marion - ***A Woman Doctor Looks At Love & Life*** [1960]	$ .75	$2.50	$5.00
M-4145	Coates, John - ***The Widow's Tale*** [1959] Cover art by Polly Bolian.	$ .75	$2.50	$5.00
M-4146	Mantley, John - ***Woman Obsessed*** [1959] Movie tie-in. Movie photo cover.	$1.00	$3.00	$6.00
M-4147	Kalman, Victor - editor - ***AMF Guide To Natural Bowling*** [1959] Photo cover.	$ .75	$2.50	$5.00
M-4148	Mayer, N.H. & S.K. - ***A Guide To Better Living*** [1959]	$ .75	$2.50	$5.00
M-4149	Clarke, Arthur C. - ***Sands Of Mars*** [1959] Cover art by Schulz	$1.25	$3.75	$7.50
M-4150	McBain, Ed - ***Killer's Wedge*** [1959] Cover art by Darcy	$2.50	$7.50	$15.00
M-4151	Gardner, Hy - ***Tales Out Of (Night) School*** [1959]	$ .75	$2.50	$5.00
M-4152	Clad, Noel - ***The Savage*** [1959]	$1.00	$3.00	$6.00
M-4153	Banks, Rosie M. - ***Settlement Nurse*** [1959] PBO. Cover art by Bob Abbett.	$ .75	$2.50	$5.00
M-4154	Kiefer, Middleton - ***Pax*** [1959] Cover art by Wayne Blickinstaff.	$ .75	$2.50	$5.00
M-4155	West, Morris L. - ***Backlash*** [1959] Cover art by Tom Dunn.	$ .75	$2.50	$5.00
M-4157	Reinfeld, Fred - ***Chess In A Nutshell*** [1960]	$ .75	$2.50	$5.00
M-4158	Anthology edited by H.L. Gold - ***5 Galaxy Short Novels*** [1960] Cover art by Valigursky.	$1.25	$3.75	$7.50
M-4161	Verne, Jules - ***A Journey To The Center Of The Earth*** [1959]	$1.00	$3.00	$6.00
M-4162	Keller, James - ***Three Minutes A Day*** [1959] PBO. Photo cover.	$ .75	$2.50	$5.00
M-4163	Carlisle, Rodney - ***Archie*** [1960] PBO.	$ .75	$2.50	$5.00
M-4166	McBain, Ed - ***'Til Death*** [1960] Cover art by Charles.	$2.50	$7.50	$15.00
M-4167	Eyre, Katherine Wigmore - ***The Chinese Box*** [1960]	$ .75	$2.50	$5.00
M-4168	Gipson, Fred - ***Hound-Dog Man*** [1959] Movie tie-in. Movie photo cover.	$1.50	$5.00	$10.00
M-4169	MacLean, Alistair - ***The Secret Ways*** [1960]	$ .75	$2.50	$5.00
M-4170	Douglas, Jack - ***My Brother Was An Only Child*** [1960]	$ .75	$2.50	$5.00
M-4172	Anthology edited by H.L. Gold - ***The Third Galaxy Reader*** [1960] Cover art by Bob Abbett.	$1.25	$3.75	$7.50
M-4175	Pirro, Ugo - ***5 Branded Women*** [1960] Movie tie-in. Movie photo cover.	$1.25	$3.75	$7.50
M-4176	Tracy, Don - ***Deadly To Bed*** [1960] PBO.	$ .75	$2.50	$5.00
M-4178	Bagby, George - ***The Real Gone Goose*** [1960]	$ .75	$2.50	$5.00
M-4179	Seifert, Elizabeth - ***Doctor Of Mercy*** [1960] Cover art by Bob Abbett.	$ .75	$2.50	$5.00
M-4180	Tabori, George - ***The Good One*** [1960] PBO.	$ .75	$2.50	$5.00
M-4181	McBain, Ed - ***King's Ransom*** [1960] Cover art by Harry Bennett.	$2.50	$7.50	$15.00
M-4182	Slaughter, Frank G. - ***Lorena*** [1960]	$1.00	$3.00	$6.00
M-4184	Anthology edited by H.L. Gold - ***The Fourth Galaxy Reader*** [1960] Cover art by Powers.	$1.25	$3.75	$7.50
M-4185	Buckner, Robert - ***Starfire*** [1960] PBO.	$1.35	$4.00	$8.00
M-4187	McBain, Ed - ***Give The Boys A Great Big Hand*** [1960]	$2.50	$7.50	$15.00
M-4189	Ridgway, Jason (Stephen Marlowe) - ***Adam's Fall*** [1960] PBO. Photo cover.	$ .75	$2.50	$5.00
M-4190	Wren, Percival Christopher - ***Beau Geste*** [1960]	$ .75	$2.50	$5.00
M-4192	Wellman, Paul I. - ***The Fiery Flower*** [1961]	$1.35	$4.00	$8.00
M-4193	Seifert, Elizabeth - ***The Strange Loyalty Of Dr. Carlisle*** [1961]	$ .75	$2.50	$5.00
M-4194	Wellman, Paul I. - ***The Comancheros*** [1961]	$ .75	$2.50	$5.00
M-4195	Lowell, Juliet - ***Dear Folks*** [1961]	$ .75	$2.50	$5.00
M-4196	Charteris, Leslie - ***The Saint To The Rescue*** [1961] Cover art by Charles.	$ .75	$2.50	$5.00
M-4197	Anthology edited by H.L. Gold - ***The World That Couldn't Be*** [1961]	$1.25	$3.75	$7.50
M-4198	Hammett, Dashiell - ***The Dain Curse*** [1961] Cover art by Harry Bennett.	$1.25	$3.75	$7.50
M-4199	Hammett, Dashiell - ***The Glass Key*** [1961]	$1.25	$3.75	$7.50

		G	VG	F
M-4200	Hammett, Dashiell - ***The Maltese Falcon*** [1961] Cover art by Harry Bennett.	$1.25	$3.75	$7.50
M-4201	Hammett, Dashiell - ***Red Harvest*** [1961] Cover art by Harry Bennett.	$1.25	$3.75	$7.50
M-4202	Hammett, Dashiell - ***The Thin Man*** [1961]	$1.25	$3.75	$7.50
M-4203	Withers, E.L. - ***Diminishing Returns*** [1961]	$ .75	$2.50	$5.00
M-4204	Breslin, Howard - ***A Hundred Hills*** [1961]	$ .75	$2.50	$5.00
M-4205	Hitchens, Delores - ***The Watcher*** [1961]	$1.00	$3.00	$6.00
M-4207	Fuller, Roger - ***The Facts Of Life*** [1960] PBO.	$ .75	$2.50	$5.00
M-4208	Highmore, Jane - ***Big City Nurse*** [1961] PBO. Cover art by Jerry Allison.	$ .75	$2.50	$5.00
M-4209	Ridgway, Jason - ***People In Glass Houses*** [1961] PBO. Photo cover.	$ .75	$2.50	$5.00
M-4211	Douglas, Jack - ***Never Trust A Naked Bus Driver*** [1961]	$1.00	$3.00	$6.00
M-4214	Heyward, Louis H. - ***Grandpa And The Girls*** [1961] Cover art by Barye Phillips.	$ .75	$2.50	$5.00
M-4217	Lanham, Edwin - ***Double Jeopardy*** [1961] Cover art by Harry Bennett.	$ .75	$2.50	$5.00
M-4218	McBain, Ed - ***The Heckler*** [1961] Cover by Harry Bennett.	$2.50	$7.50	$15.00
M-4219	Seifert, Elizabeth - ***The Doctor Takes A Wife*** [1961]	$ .75	$2.50	$5.00
M-4220	Hitchens, Burt & Dolores - ***The Man Who Followed Women*** [1961]	$1.00	$3.00	$6.00
M-4221	Ransome, Stephen - ***The Unspeakable*** [1961]	$ .75	$2.50	$5.00
M-4222	Klinger, Henry - ***Wanton For Murder*** [1961] PBO.	$1.00	$3.00	$6.00
M-4223	Banks, Rosie M. - ***Ship's Nurse*** [1961] PBO. Cover art by Robert Maguire.	$ .75	$2.50	$5.00
M-4224	Stanton, Paul - ***Call Me Captain*** [1961] Cover art by Jerry Allison.	$ .75	$2.50	$5.00
M-4225	Keon, M. - ***The Durian Tree*** [1961]	$ .75	$2.50	$5.00
M-4226	Freeman, Ira Henry - ***Out Of The Burning*** [1961] Photo cover.	$ .75	$2.50	$5.00
M-4228	Ballard, W.T. - ***Pretty Miss Murder*** [1961] PBO.	$1.25	$3.75	$7.50
M-4229	McBain, Ed - ***See Them Die*** [1961]	$2.00	$6.00	$12.00
M-4230	Stanton, Paul - ***Village Of Stars*** [1962]	$ .75	$2.50	$5.00
M-4232	Frazer, Diane - ***Confidential Nurse*** [1962] PBO. Cover art by Jo Polseno.	$ .75	$2.50	$5.00
M-4233	Powell, Talmage - ***With A Madman Behind Me*** [1961] PBO. Cover art by Harry Bennett.	$1.25	$3.75	$7.50
M-4234	Ridgway, Jason - ***Hardly A Man Is Now Alive*** [1962]	$ .75	$2.50	$5.00
M-4238	Bellah, James Warner - ***The Man Who Shot Liberty Valance*** [1962] PBO. Movie tie-in. Photo cover.	$1.25	$3.75	$7.50
M-4239	Rayner, D.A. - ***The Long Haul*** [1962]	$1.00	$3.00	$6.00
M-4240	Anthology edited by Max Rezwin - ***The Best Of Sick Jokes*** [1962]	$ .75	$2.50	$5.00
M-4241	Buckner, Robert - ***Walt Disney's Moon Pilot*** [1962] Movie tie-in.	$1.00	$3.00	$6.00
M-4242	Schmitz, James H. - ***Agent Of Vega*** [1962] Cover art by John Woolhiser.	$1.25	$3.75	$7.50
M-4243	Hitchens, Dolores - ***Sleep With Slander*** [1962]	$1.25	$3.75	$7.50
M-4249	Slaughter, Frank G. - ***Darien Venture*** [1962]	$ .75	$2.50	$5.00
M-4250	Seifert, Elizabeth - ***The New Doctor*** [1962] Cover art by Jo Polseno.	$ .75	$2.50	$5.00
M-4251	Powell, Talmage - ***Start Screaming Murder*** [1962] PBO. Cover art by Harry Bennett.	$1.25	$3.75	$7.50
M-4252	Anthology edited by H.L. Gold - ***Bodyguard And Four Other Short Science Fiction Novels*** [1962] Cover art by Richard Powers.	$1.25	$3.75	$7.50
M-4253	McBain, Ed - ***Lady, Lady, I Did It!*** [1962]	$2.00	$6.00	$12.00
M-4254	Dean, Amber - ***Encounter With Evil*** [1962]	$1.25	$3.75	$7.50
M-4255	Klinger, Henry - ***Murder Off Broadway*** [1962] PBO. Cover art by Harry Bennett.	$1.25	$3.75	$7.50

		G	VG	F
M-4256	Frazer, Diane - ***Nurse Turner Runs Away*** [1962] PBO.	$ .75	$2.50	$5.00
M-4258	Ballard, W.T. - ***The Seven Sisters*** [1962] PBO.	$1.25	$3.75	$7.50
M-4259	Appel, Benjamin - ***A Big Man, A Fast Man*** [1962]	$ .75	$2.50	$5.00
M-4260	McLean, Alistair - ***Fear Is The Key*** [1963] Cover art by Robert Abbett.	$ .75	$2.50	$5.00
M-4261	Hitchens, Dolores - ***Footsteps In The Night*** [1962] Cover art by Harry Bennett.	$1.25	$3.75	$7.50
M-4264	McBain, Ed - ***The Con Man*** [1962]	$1.00	$3.00	$6.00
M-4265	McBain, Ed - ***Killer's Payoff*** [1962]	$1.00	$3.00	$6.00
M-4266	McBain, Ed - ***The Mugger*** [1962]	$1.00	$3.00	$6.00
M-4267	McBain, Ed - ***Killer's Choice*** [1962]	$1.00	$3.00	$6.00
M-4269	Masterson, Whit - ***Evil Come, Evil Go*** [1962] PBO. Cover by Harry Bennett.	$1.25	$3.75	$7.50
M-4271	McBain, Ed - ***The Empty Hours*** [1963]	$1.00	$3.00	$6.00
M-4272	Stark, Richard - ***The Hunter*** [1962] PBO. Cover art by Harry Bennett.	$3.50	$10.00	$20.00
M-4274	Graham, Billy - ***The Secret Of Happiness*** [1963] Photo cover.	$ .75	$2.50	$5.00
M-4275	Ransome, Stephen - ***Some Must Watch*** [1963]	$1.25	$3.75	$7.50
M-4276	Dean, Spencer - ***Credit For A Murder*** [1963] Cover art by Hector Garrido.	$1.25	$3.75	$7.50
M-4278	Sambrot, William - ***Island Of Fear & Other Stories*** [1963] PBO.	$ .75	$2.50	$5.00
M-4280	Lanham, Edwin - ***Six Black Camels*** [1963] Photo cover.	$ .75	$2.50	$5.00
M-4281	Klinger, Henry - ***Essence Of Murder*** [1963] PBO. Cover art by Harry Bennett.	$1.25	$3.75	$7.50
M-4282	Wolford, Nelson & Shirley - ***The Southern Blade*** [1963] Cover art by Harry Bennett.	$ .75	$2.50	$5.00
M-4284	Frazer, Diane - ***A Special Case For Peggy Bruce, R.N.*** [1963] PBO. Cover art by Harry Bennett.	$ .65	$2.00	$4.00
M-4286	Deming, Richard - ***Anything But Saintly*** [1963] PBO. Cover art by Robert Abbett.	$ .75	$2.50	$5.00
M-4287	Anthology edited by H.L. Gold - ***Mind Partner And 8 Other Novelets From Galaxy*** [1963]	$1.00	$3.00	$6.00
M-4290	Heyward, Louis M. - ***My Son, The Doctor*** [1963] PBO.	$ .75	$2.50	$5.00
M-4291	Dewey, Thomas B. - ***How Hard To Kill*** [1963]	$1.50	$5.00	$10.00
M-4292	Stark, Richard - ***The Outfit*** [1963] PBO. Cover art by Harry Bennett.	$3.50	$10.00	$20.00
M-4294	Thames, C.H. - ***Blood Of My Brother*** [1963] PBO. Cover art by Harry Bennett.	$ .75	$2.50	$5.00
M-4295	Frazer, Diane - ***An American Nurse In Paris*** [1963] PBO.	$ .65	$2.00	$4.00
M-4296	Dell, Martin - ***More Puzzle Fun*** [1963]	$ .75	$2.50	$5.00
M-4297	Ballard, W.T. - ***Three For The Money*** [1963] PBO. Cover art by Harry Bennett.	$1.25	$3.75	$7.50
M-4298	Stark, Richard (Donald Westlake) - ***The Mourner*** [1963] PBO.	$3.50	$10.00	$20.00
M-4299	McBain, Ed - ***Runaway Black*** [1963]	$2.00	$6.00	$12.00
M-4300	Kane, Henry - ***Snatch An Eye*** [1963]	$1.25	$3.75	$7.50
M-4304	McBain, Ed - ***Ten Plus One*** [1964] Photo cover.	$1.00	$3.00	$6.00
M-4306	McBain, Ed - ***Death Of A Nurse*** [1964]	$1.00	$3.00	$6.00
M-4307	Frazer, Diane - ***Nurse With A Past*** [1964] PBO. Cover art by Harry Bennett.	$ .65	$2.00	$4.00
M-4310	Fuller, Roger - ***Who Killed Beau Sparrow?*** [1964] PBO. TV tie-in. Photo cover.	$1.25	$3.75	$7.50
M-5014	Oursler, Fulton - ***The Greatest Book Ever Written*** [1959] Cover art by Anson.	$ .75	$2.50	$5.00
M-6002	Verne, Jules - ***Mysterious Island*** [1961] Movie tie-in.	$1.00	$3.00	$6.00

Perma Book P Series. New York: Perma Books, Inc./Doubleday & Co.

P-1	Anthology edited by Richard C. MacKenzie - ***Best Loved Poems*** [1948]	$1.00	$3.00	$6.00

		G	VG	F
P-2	Sheff & Ingalls - ***How To Write Letters For All Occasions*** [1948]	$1.00	$3.00	$6.00
P-3	Anthology edited by Lewis C. Henry - ***Best Quotations for All Occasions*** [1948]	$1.00	$3.00	$6.00
P-4	Witherspoon, Ph.D., Alexander M. - ***Common Errors In English (And How To Avoid Them)*** [1948]	$1.00	$3.00	$6.00
P-5	Duffy, Patrick Gavin - ***The Standard Bartender's Guide*** [1948]	$1.00	$3.00	$6.00
P-6	Fielding, William J. - ***Sex And The Love Life*** [1948]	$1.00	$3.00	$6.00
P-7	Lindlahr, Victor H. - ***Eat And Reduce!*** [1948]	$1.00	$3.00	$6.00
P-8	Anthology edited by Powers Moulton - ***Best Jokes For All Occasions*** [1948]	$1.00	$3.00	$6.00
P-9	Bailey, Ida - ***Ida Bailey Allen's Cook Book*** [1948]	$1.35	$4.00	$8.00
P-10	King, Basil - ***The Conquest Of Fear*** [1948]	$1.00	$3.00	$6.00
P-11	Mooney, M.D., Belle S. - ***How Shall I Tell The Child*** [1948]	$1.00	$3.00	$6.00
P-12	De Kruif, Paul - ***The Male Hormone*** [1948]	$1.00	$3.00	$6.00
P-13	Selected by Dorothea S. Kopplin - ***Something To Live By*** [1948]	$1.00	$3.00	$6.00
P-14	Peppard, Dr. Harold M. - ***Sight Without Glasses*** [1948]	$1.00	$3.00	$6.00
P-15	Blackstone, Harry - ***Blackstone's Tricks Anyone Can Do*** [1948] PBO.	$2.50	$7.50	$15.00
P-16	Showers, Paul - ***Fortune Telling For Fun And Popularity*** [1948]	$1.00	$3.00	$6.00
P-17	Anthology - ***The Handy Encyclopedia Of Useful Information*** [1948]	$1.00	$3.00	$6.00
P-18	Raine, William MacLeod - ***Famous Sheriffs And Western Outlaws*** [1948]	$1.00	$3.00	$6.00
P-19	Dorey, M.A., J. Milnor - ***Good English Made Easy*** [1948]	$1.00	$3.00	$6.00
P-20	Schaaf, Ph.D., William L. - ***Mathematics For Home And Business*** [1948]	$1.00	$3.00	$6.00
P-21	Hirsch, B.S., M.D., Edwin W. - ***Modern Sex Life*** [1948] PBO.	$1.00	$3.00	$6.00
P-22	Day, Clarence - ***Life With Mother*** [1949] Cover art by Reisie.	$1.00	$3.00	$6.00
P-23	Fielding, William J. - ***Strange Customs Of Courtship And Marriage*** [1949]	$1.00	$3.00	$6.00
P-24	Sewell, W. Stuart - ***Brief Biographies Of Famous Men And Women*** [1949]	$1.00	$3.00	$6.00
P-25	Kling, Samuel G. - ***Handy Legal Advisor For Home & Business*** [1949] PBO.	$1.00	$3.00	$6.00
P-26	Hespro, Herbert - ***What Your Dreams Mean*** [1949] PBO.	$1.00	$3.00	$6.00
P-27	Gelders, Louis & O'Hare, Eugene - ***The Handbook For House Repairs*** [1949]	$1.00	$3.00	$6.00
P-28	Dorey, J. Milnor - ***A Short History Of The World*** [1949]	$1.00	$3.00	$6.00
P-29	Sheldon, Charles M. - ***In His Steps*** [1949]	$1.00	$3.00	$6.00
P-30	Anthology edited by Charles Grayson - ***Stories For Men*** [1949]	$1.50	$5.00	$10.00
P-31	Spaeth, Sigmund - ***The Art Of Enjoying Music*** [1949] PBO.	$1.00	$3.00	$6.00
P-32	Barton, Fred B. - ***Photography As A Hobby*** [1949]	$1.00	$3.00	$6.00
P-33	Jacoby, Oswald - ***Winning Poker*** [1949]	$1.00	$3.00	$6.00
P-34	Smith, Geoffrey Mott - ***The Handy Book Of Hobbies*** [1949] PBO.	$1.00	$3.00	$6.00
P-35	Carnegie, Dale - ***Dale Carnegie's Five Minute Biographies*** [1949]	$1.00	$3.00	$6.00
P-36	Adams, Evangeline - ***Astrology For Everyone*** [1949]	$1.00	$3.00	$6.00
P-37	Goodman, M.A., Morris C. - ***Numerology*** [1949]	$1.00	$3.00	$6.00
P-38	Anthology - ***Three Famous French Novels*** [1949]	$1.00	$3.00	$6.00
P-39	Meier, Frederick - ***Character Reading Made Easy*** [1949]	$1.00	$3.00	$6.00
P-40	Lehr, Tinney & Bower - ***Stop Me If You've Heard This One*** [1949]	$1.00	$3.00	$6.00
P-41	London, Jack - ***Best Short Storeis Of Jack London*** [1949]	$1.50	$5.00	$10.00
P-42	Peale, Norman Vincent - ***The Art Of Living*** [1949]	$1.00	$3.00	$6.00
P-43	Tokay, Ph.D., Elbert - ***The Human Body And How It Works*** [1949] PBO.	$1.00	$3.00	$6.00

		G	VG	F
P-44	Anthology - ***A Handy Illustrated Guide To Football*** [1949]	$1.25	$3.75	$7.50
P-45	Anthology edited by Donald B. Aldrich - ***The Golden Book Of Prayer*** [1949]	$1.00	$3.00	$6.00
P-46	Chappell, Ph.D., Matthew N. - ***How To Control Worry*** [1949]	$1.00	$3.00	$6.00
P-47	Anthology edited by Sam Nisenson - ***A Handy Illustrated Guide To Basketball*** [1949]	$1.25	$3.75	$7.50
P-48	Eginton, Ph.D., Daniel P. - ***Better Speech For You*** [1949]	$1.00	$3.00	$6.00
P-49	Barton, Bruce - ***The Man Nobody Knows*** [1949]	$1.00	$3.00	$6.00
P-50	Tridon, Andre - ***Psychoanalysis And Love*** [1949]	$1.00	$3.00	$6.00
P-51	Roth, Charles B. - ***The Key To Your Personality*** [1949]	$1.00	$3.00	$6.00
P-52	Anthology edited by Sam Nisenson - ***A Handy Illustrated Guide To Bowling And Duck Pins*** [1949] PBO.	$1.00	$3.00	$6.00
P-53	Anthology edited by Sam Nisenson - ***A Handy Illustrated Guide To Boxing*** [1949] PBO.	$1.25	$3.75	$7.50
P-54	Gibson, Walter - ***Magic Explained*** [1949] PBO.	$4.00	$12.50	$25.00
P-55	Mott-Smith, Geoffrey - ***The Handy Book Of Indoor Games*** [1949]	$1.00	$3.00	$6.00
P-56	Duffy, Patrick Gavin - ***The Standard Bartender's Guide*** [1949]	$1.00	$3.00	$6.00
P-57	Adler, Alfred - ***Understanding Human Nature*** [1949]	$1.00	$3.00	$6.00
P-58	Goren, Charles H. - ***Bridge Quiz Book*** [1949]	$1.00	$3.00	$6.00
P-59	Sara, Dorothy - ***Reading Handwriting For Fun And Popularity*** [1949]	$1.00	$3.00	$6.00
P-60	Bisch, M.D., Ph.D., Louis E. - ***Be Glad You're Neurotic*** [1949]	$1.00	$3.00	$6.00
P-61	Mallery, Richard D. - ***Grammar Made Easy*** [1949]	$1.00	$3.00	$6.00
P-62	Brock, Ray - ***The Permabook Of Art Masterpieces*** [1949] PBO. 32 full color paintings reproduced.	$1.00	$3.00	$6.00
P-63	Wilkinson, Albert E. & Tiedjens, Victor - ***The Handy Book Of Gardening*** [1950]	$1.00	$3.00	$6.00
P-64	Peck, M.D., Martin W. - ***The Meaning Of Psychoanalysis*** [1950]	$1.00	$3.00	$6.00
P-65	Broadley, Charles V. & Margaret E. - ***Know Your Real Abilities*** [1950]	$1.00	$3.00	$6.00
P-66	Milligan, Harold V. - ***Stories Of Famous Operas*** [1950] PBO.	$1.00	$3.00	$6.00
P-67	Anthology edited by Groff Conklin - ***The Science Fiction Galaxy*** [1950] PBO.	$1.50	$5.00	$10.00
P-68	Woolf, James D. & Roth, Charles B. - ***How To Use Your Imagination To Make Money*** [1950]	$1.00	$3.00	$6.00
P-69	Guest, Edgar A. - ***Favorite Verse Of Edgar A. Guest*** [1950] PBO.	$1.00	$3.00	$6.00
P-70	Anthology - ***Perma Handy World Atlas*** [1950] PBO. 131 maps, include 64 in color.	$1.00	$3.00	$6.00
P-71	Goren - ***Goren's Canasta Up-To-Date*** [1950] PBO.	$1.00	$3.00	$6.00
P-72	Bradley, Preston - ***Meditations And My Daily Strength*** [1950]	$1.00	$3.00	$6.00
P-73	Edwards, Jill - ***Personality Pointers*** [1950]	$1.00	$3.00	$6.00
P-74	Maugham, W. Somerset - ***South Sea Stories Of W. Somerset Maugham*** [1950]	$1.25	$3.75	$7.50
P-75	Hadida, Sophie C. - ***Manners For Millions*** [1950]	$1.00	$3.00	$6.00
P-76	Baird, Jack - ***The Care And Handling Of Dogs*** [1950] Cover by Paul Brown.	$1.25	$3.75	$7.50
P-77	Anthology - ***A Handy Illustrated Guide To Baseball*** [1950]	$1.50	$5.00	$10.00
P-78	Krippene, Ken - ***Buried Treasure*** [1950] Cover art by John Wentworth.	$1.00	$3.00	$6.00
P-79	Sondel, Bess - ***Every Day Speech*** [1950]	$1.00	$3.00	$6.00
P-80	Anthology - ***The New Standard Ready Reckoner*** [1950]	$1.00	$3.00	$6.00
P-81	Raymond, Litzka - ***How To Read Palms*** [1950]	$1.00	$3.00	$6.00
P-82	Anthology edited by Edwin V. Mitchell - ***The Perma Week-End Companion*** [1950] PBO.	$1.00	$3.00	$6.00
P-83	Yates, Helen Eva - ***How To Travel For Fun*** [1950] PBO.	$1.00	$3.00	$6.00
P-85	Pomeranz, M.D., H. - ***Dictionary Of First Aid For Emergencies*** [1950]	$1.00	$3.00	$6.00

		G	VG	F
P-86	Reed, Langford - ***The Perma Rhyming Dictionary*** [1950]	$1.00	$3.00	$6.00
P-87	Compiled by V.H. Cartmell - ***Famous Scenes From Shakespear*** [1950]	$1.00	$3.00	$6.00
P-88	MacCampbell, Donald - ***Reading For Enjoyment*** [1950]	$1.00	$3.00	$6.00
P-89	Newman, Frank Eaton - ***The Perma Crossword Puzzle & Word Game Dictionary*** [1950]	$1.00	$3.00	$6.00
P-90	Sticker, Henry - ***Essentials Of Arithmetic*** [1950]	$1.00	$3.00	$6.00
P-91	Anthology edited by William Lord - ***The Perma Treasury Of Love Poems*** [1950]	$1.00	$3.00	$6.00
P-92	Anthology edited by S.E. Frost, Jr. - ***Favorite Stories From The Bible*** [1950]	$1.00	$3.00	$6.00
P-94	Anthology edited by W. Bob Holland - ***The Perma Book Of Ghost Stories*** [1950] PBO.	$3.50	$10.00	$20.00
P-95	Thomas, Henry & Dana Lee - ***Strange Tales Of Amazing Frauds*** [1950] PBO.	$1.00	$3.00	$6.00
P-96	MacDonald, William Colt - ***Powdersmoke Justice*** [1950]	$1.25	$3.75	$7.50
P-97	Peale, Norman Vincent - ***You Can Win*** [1950]	$1.00	$3.00	$6.00
P-98	Anthology - ***New Standard Book Of Model Letters For All Occasions*** [1950]	$1.00	$3.00	$6.00
P-99	Stopes, Marie - ***Married Love*** [1950]	$1.00	$3.00	$6.00
P-100	Goren, Charles H. - ***The Fundamentals Of Contract Bridge*** [1950]	$1.00	$3.00	$6.00
P-101	Keller, James - ***Careers That Change Your World*** [1950] PBO.	$1.00	$3.00	$6.00
P-105	Keller, James - ***Three Mimutes A Day*** [1951]	$1.00	$3.00	$6.00
P-106	Montague, M.D., J.F. - ***How To Overcome Nervous Stomach Trouble*** [1951]	$1.00	$3.00	$6.00
P-107	Slaughter, Frank G. - ***In A Dark Garden*** [1951]	$1.25	$3.75	$7.50
P-108	Swanson, Neil H. - ***Unconquered*** [1951] Cover art by Ken Riley.	$1.25	$3.75	$7.50
P-109	Baum, Vicki - ***One Tropical Night*** [1951]	$1.25	$3.75	$7.50
P-110	Steen, Marguerite - ***Bell Timson*** [1951]	$1.25	$3.75	$7.50
P-111	Weekley, William George - ***Castaway Island*** [1951]	$1.25	$3.75	$7.50
P-112	Hall, Radclyffe - ***The Well Of Loneliness*** [1951]	$3.00	$9.00	$18.00
P-113	Runyon, Damon - ***Poems For Men*** [1951] Cover art by Palacios.	$1.00	$3.00	$6.00
P-114	Bonnet, Theodore - ***The Mudlark*** [1951]	$1.25	$3.75	$7.50
P-115	Wellman, Paul I. - ***The Chain*** [1951]	$1.25	$3.75	$7.50
P-116	Teilhet, Hildegarde Tolman - ***Fear Is The Hunter*** [1951] Cover art by M. Korach.	$1.25	$3.75	$7.50
P-117	Anthology edited by Groff Conklin - ***In The Grip Of Terror*** [1951]	$4.00	$12.50	$25.00
P-118	Anthology edited by Will Oursler - ***As Tough As They Come*** [1951]	$3.50	$10.00	$20.00
P-119	Murphy, Audie - ***To Hell And Back*** [1951] Cover art by Korach.	$1.50	$5.00	$10.00
P-120	Lewis, Hilda - ***The Case Of The Little Doctor*** [1951]	$1.35	$4.00	$8.00
P-121	Slaughter, Frank G. - ***The Golden Isle*** [1951]	$1.00	$3.00	$6.00
P-122	Anthology edited by Charles Grayson - ***New Stories For Men*** [1951]	$1.50	$5.00	$10.00
P-123	Fitzgerald, F. Scott - ***The Beautiful And Damned*** [1951]	$1.00	$3.00	$6.00
P-124	Charteris, Leslie - ***Arrest The Saint!*** [1951]	$1.50	$5.00	$10.00
P-125	Jennings, John - ***The Salem Frigate*** [1951]	$1.25	$3.75	$7.50
P-126	Anthology edited by Joseph T. Shaw - ***Spurs West!*** [1951]	$1.35	$4.00	$8.00
P-127	Roark, Garland - ***Fair Wind To Java*** [1951]	$1.25	$3.75	$7.50
P-128	Graham, Winston - ***Night Without Stars*** [1951]	$1.25	$3.75	$7.50
P-129	Wellman, Paul I. - ***The Walls Of Jericho*** [1951]	$1.25	$3.75	$7.50
P-130	Anthology - ***The Thorndike-Barnhart Handy Pocket Dictionary*** [1951]	$1.25	$3.75	$7.50
P-131	Keller, James - ***You Can Change The World*** [1951]	$ .75	$2.50	$5.00
P-132	Edmonds, Walter D. - ***Chad Hanna*** [1951]	$1.25	$3.75	$7.50

		G	VG	F
P-133	Jennings, John - ***The Sea Eagles*** [1951] Cover art by Dunn.	$1.25	$3.75	$7.50
P-134	Gann, Ernest K. - ***The Raging Tide*** [1951] Movie tie-in.	$1.35	$4.00	$8.00
P-135	Oursler, Fulton - ***The Greatest Story Ever Told*** [1951] Cover art by F.K. Rimsky.	$1.25	$3.75	$7.50
P-136	Eaton, Evelyn - ***Quietly My Captain Waits*** [1951]	$1.25	$3.75	$7.50
P-137	Fletcher, Inglis - ***Lusty Wind For Carolina*** [1951] Cover art by Harry Schaare.	$1.35	$4.00	$8.00
P-138	Wilkinson, Burke - ***Black Judas*** [1951]	$1.35	$4.00	$8.00
P-139	Roark, Garland - ***Rainbow In The Royals*** [1951] Cover by William Shoyer.	$1.25	$3.75	$7.50
P-140	Slaughter, Frank G. - ***Divine Mistress*** [1951]	$1.25	$3.75	$7.50
P-141	Jennings, John - ***Land Of Vengeance*** [1951]	$1.25	$3.75	$7.50
P-142	Wellman, Paul I. - ***Angel With Spurs*** [1952]	$1.25	$3.75	$7.50
P-143	Dowdey, Clifford - ***Tidewater*** [1952]	$1.25	$3.75	$7.50
P-144	Lagard, Garald - ***Scarlet Cockerel*** [1952]	$1.25	$3.75	$7.50
P-145	Anthology edited by Frederik Pohl - ***Beyond The End Of Time*** [1952] PBO.	$2.50	$7.50	$15.00
P-146	Judah, Charles B. - ***Tom Bone*** [1952]	$1.25	$3.75	$7.50
P-147	Cloete, Stuart - ***The Turning Wheels*** [1952]	$1.25	$3.75	$7.50
P-148	Cozzens, James Gould - ***Guard Of Honor*** [1952]	$1.25	$3.75	$7.50
P-149	Lancaster, Bruce - ***Phantom Fortress*** [1952]	$1.25	$3.75	$7.50
P-150	Greene, Josiah E. - ***The Man With One Talent*** [1952]	$1.25	$3.75	$7.50
P-151	Fletcher, Inglis - ***Roanoke Hundred*** [1952]	$1.25	$3.75	$7.50
P-152	Rundell, E. Ralph - ***The Color Of Blood*** [1952] Cover art by Harry Schaare.	$1.25	$3.75	$7.50
P-153	Metzger, Elizabeth - ***Before The Sun Goes Down*** [1952]	$1.25	$3.75	$7.50
P-154	Hobson, Laura Z. - ***Gentleman's Agreement*** [1952]	$1.25	$3.75	$7.50
P-155	Slaughter, Frank G. - ***Fort Everglades*** [1952]	$1.25	$3.75	$7.50
P-156	Maine, Harold - ***If A Man Be Mad*** [1952] Cover by Tom Dunn.	$1.25	$3.75	$7.50
P-157	Jennings, John - ***River To The West*** [1952]	$1.25	$3.75	$7.50
P-158	Eisenhower, Dwight David - ***Crusade In Europe*** [1952] Photo cover.	$1.25	$3.75	$7.50
P-159	Dowdey, Clifford - ***Bugles Blow No More*** [1952]	$1.25	$3.75	$7.50
P-160	Teilhet, Darwin - ***The Mission Of Jeffery Tolamy*** [1952]	$1.25	$3.75	$7.50
P-161	Cores, Lucy - ***Woman In Love*** [1952]	$1.25	$3.75	$7.50
P-162	Powers, Anne - ***The Ironmaster*** [1952]	$1.25	$3.75	$7.50
P-163	O'Neill, Charles - ***Morning Time*** [1952]	$1.25	$3.75	$7.50
P-164	Rackowe, Alec - ***My Lord America*** [1952] Cover art by Geygan.	$1.25	$3.75	$7.50
P-165	Roberts, Kenneth - ***Lydia Bailey*** [1952] Cover art by Cardiff.	$1.25	$3.75	$7.50
P-166	Gebler, Ernest - ***The Plymouth Adventure*** [1952]	$1.25	$3.75	$7.50
P-167	Pinchot, Ben & Ann - ***Hear This Woman*** [1952]	$1.25	$3.75	$7.50
P-168	Colyton, Henry J. - ***Sir Pagan*** [1952]	$1.25	$3.75	$7.50
P-169	Sinclair, Jo - ***Sing At My Wake*** [1952]	$1.25	$3.75	$7.50
P-170	Hinsdale, Harriet - ***Be My Love*** [1952] Cover art by Julian Paul.	$1.25	$3.75	$7.50
P-171	Fletcher, Inglis - ***Bennett's Welcome*** [1952]	$1.25	$3.75	$7.50
P-172	Keller, James - ***Government Is Your Business*** [1952]	$ .75	$2.50	$5.00
P-173	Powers, Anne - ***Rogue's Honor*** [1952]	$1.25	$3.75	$7.50
P-174	Chidsey, Donald Barr - ***Stronghold*** [1952] Cover art by Julian Paul.	$1.25	$3.75	$7.50
P-175	Phillips, Arthur - ***Victory In The Dust*** [1952] Cover art by Cardiff.	$1.25	$3.75	$7.50
P-176	Lancaster, Bruce - ***Trumpet To Arms*** [1952] Cover art by Raymond S. Pease.	$1.25	$3.75	$7.50
P-177	Oursler, Fulton - ***Modern Parables*** [1952]	$1.00	$3.00	$6.00
P-178	Goudge, Elizabeth - ***Green Dolphin Street*** [1952]	$1.25	$3.75	$7.50
P-179	Faherty, Robert - ***Big Old Sun*** [1952]	$1.25	$3.75	$7.50
P-180	Slaughter, Frank G. - ***That None Should Die*** [1952]	$1.25	$3.75	$7.50
P-181	Steward, Davenport - ***They Had A Glory*** [1952]	$1.25	$3.75	$7.50
P-182	Patrick, Joseph - ***King's Arrow*** [1952]	$1.25	$3.75	$7.50
P-183	Copplin, Dorothea S. - ***Something To Live By*** [1952]	$1.25	$3.75	$7.50

Perma Books, P-194

Pocket Books, 13

Pocket Books, 39

		G	VG	F
P-184	Goren, Charles H. - ***The Fundamentals Of Contract Bridge*** [1952]	$ .75	$2.50	$5.00
P-185	Dibner, Martin - ***Journey To Nowhere*** [1952]	$1.25	$3.75	$7.50
P-186	Brown, Wenzell - ***Devil's Spawn*** [1952] Cover art by Julian Paul.	$3.50	$10.00	$20.00
P-187	Feder, Sid & Turkus, Burton B. - ***Murder Inc.*** [1952]	$1.50	$5.00	$10.00
P-188	Eaton, Evelyn - ***Restless Are The Sails*** [1952] Cover art by Ray Pease.	$1.25	$3.75	$7.50
P-189	Fletcher, Inglis - ***Men Of Albemarle*** [1952]	$1.25	$3.75	$7.50
P-190	Hobson, Laura Z. - ***The Celebrity*** [1952] Cover art by Kampen...	$1.25	$3.75	$7.50
P-191	Wren, P.C. - ***Beau Geste*** [1952]	$1.25	$3.75	$7.50
P-192	Ciraci, Norma - ***Detour*** [1952]	$1.25	$3.75	$7.50
P-193	Lofts, Norah - ***Silver Nutmeg*** [1953]	$1.35	$4.00	$8.00
P-194	Latimer, Jonathan - ***Dark Memory*** [1953]	$1.35	$4.00	$8.00
P-195	Slaughter, Frank G. - ***Battle Surgeon*** [1953]	$1.25	$3.75	$7.50
P-196	Lancaster, Bruce - ***The Scarlet Patch*** [1953]	$1.25	$3.75	$7.50
P-197	Griffith, Maxwell - ***Port Of Call*** [1953]	$1.25	$3.75	$7.50
P-198	Roark, Garland - ***Slant Of The Wild Wind*** [1953] Cover art by Carl Bobertz.	$1.25	$3.75	$7.50
P-199	Hale, Nancy - ***The Prodigal Women*** [1953]	$1.25	$3.75	$7.50
P-200	Leigh, Michael - ***Rogue Errant*** [1953]	$1.25	$3.75	$7.50
P-201	Van Loon, Hendrik - ***The Story Of The Bible*** [1953] Cover by F.K. Rimsky.	$1.25	$3.75	$7.50
P-202	Freud, Sigmund - ***A General Introduction To Psychoanalysis*** [1953]	$ .75	$2.50	$5.00
P-203	Sinclair, Harold - ***Music Out Of Dixie*** [1953]	$1.25	$3.75	$7.50
P-204	Walker, David - ***The Wire*** [1953]	$1.25	$3.75	$7.50
P-205	Bartlett - ***The Shorter Bartlett's Familiar Quotations*** [1953]	$1.00	$3.00	$6.00
P-206	Anthology edited by Louis Untermeyer - ***The Concise Treasury Of Great Poems*** [1953]	$1.00	$3.00	$6.00
P-207	Fletcher, Inglis - ***Raleigh's Eden*** [1953]	$1.25	$3.75	$7.50
P-208	Baum, Vicki - ***Grand Hotel*** [1953]	$1.25	$3.75	$7.50
P-209	Lewis, Norman - ***Word Power Made Easy*** [1953]	$ .75	$2.50	$5.00
P-210	Fowler, Gene - ***Schnozzola*** [1953] 16 pages of photos.	$1.50	$5.00	$10.00
P-211	Clark, J. Bigelow - ***The Long Run*** [1953]	$1.25	$3.75	$7.50
P-212	Anthology edited by Fernando Puma - ***7 Arts*** [1953]	$1.25	$3.75	$7.50
P-213	Anthology edited by Don M. Wolfe - ***New Voices: American Writing Today*** [1953]	$1.35	$4.00	$8.00
P-214	Murphy, Audie - ***To Hell And Back*** [1953] Cover art by Korach.	$1.25	$3.75	$7.50
P-215	Williamson, Thames - ***The Gladiator*** [1953]	$1.25	$3.75	$7.50

		G	VG	F
P-216	Fletcher, Inglis - ***Toil Of The Brave*** [1953]	$1.25	$3.75	$7.50
P-217	Green, Abel & Laurie, Jr., Joe - ***Show Biz*** [1953]	$1.25	$3.75	$7.50
P-218	Slaughter, Frank G. - ***East Side General*** [1953] Cover art by Owen Kampen.	$1.25	$3.75	$7.50
P-219	Lancaster, Bruce - ***Venture In The East*** [1953] Cover art by Victor Olson.	$1.35	$4.00	$8.00
P-220	Slaughter, Frank G. - ***In A Dark Garden*** [1953] Cover art by Julian Paul.	$1.25	$3.75	$7.50
P-221	Slaughter, Frank G. - ***The Golden Isle*** [1953] Cover by Herb Tauss.	$1.25	$3.75	$7.50
P-222	Tebbel, John - ***Touched With Fire*** [1953]	$1.25	$3.75	$7.50
P-223	Hunter, Hall (Edison Marshall) - ***The Bengal Tiger*** [1953]	$1.35	$4.00	$8.00
P-224	Bonner, Paul Hyde - ***Summer In Rome*** [1953]	$1.25	$3.75	$7.50
P-225	Plaidy, Jean - ***Beyond The Blue Mountains*** [1953]	$1.25	$3.75	$7.50
P-226	Slaughter, Frank G. - ***Spencer Brade M.D.*** [1953] Cover art by Julian Paul.	$1.00	$3.00	$6.00
P-227	McCoy, John Pleasant - ***Swing The Big-Eyed Rabbit*** [1953]	$1.50	$5.00	$10.00
P-228	Stone, Irving - ***Immortal Wife*** [1953]	$1.25	$3.75	$7.50
P-229	Lyons, Herbert - ***Front Office*** [1953]	$1.25	$3.75	$7.50
P-230	Sylvester, Robert - ***Indian Summer*** [1953]	$1.25	$3.75	$7.50
P-231	Pollak, James S. - ***The Golden Egg*** [1953]	$1.25	$3.75	$7.50
P-232	Wren, Percival Christopher - ***Beau Sabreur*** [1953] Cover art by Ray Pease.	$1.25	$3.75	$7.50
P-233	Slaughter, Frank G. - ***Divine Mistress*** [1953]	$1.25	$3.75	$7.50
P-234	Lancaster, Bruce - ***No Bugles Tonight*** [1953]	$1.25	$3.75	$7.50
P-235	Baume, Eric - ***Yankee Woman*** [1953] Cover art by Daniel Schwartz.	$1.35	$4.00	$8.00
P-236	Anthology edited by Frederik Pohl - ***Shadow Of Tomorrow*** [1953]	$2.00	$6.00	$12.00
P-237	Denker, Henry - ***Salome, Princess Of Galilee*** [1953]	$1.50	$5.00	$10.00
238	Hopkins, Tom J. - ***Trail End*** [1953]	$1.25	$3.75	$7.50
239	Henry, Joan - ***Women In Prison*** [1953]	$2.50	$7.50	$15.00
P-240	Wellman, Paul I. - ***The Bowl Of Brass*** [1953]	$1.25	$3.75	$7.50
P-241	Slaughter, Frank G. - ***The Road To Bithynia*** [1953]	$1.25	$3.75	$7.50
P-242	Fishbein, Morris - ***The Handy Home Medical Advisor*** [1953]	$ .75	$2.50	$5.00
P-243	Heyerdahl, Thor - ***Kon-Tiki*** [1953] Contains 80 photos.	$1.25	$3.75	$7.50
244	Avallone, Michael - ***The Tall Dolores*** [1953] Cover art by Daniel Schwartz.	$2.00	$6.00	$12.00
245	Breuer, Bessie - ***Memory Of Love*** [1953]	$1.25	$3.75	$7.50
P-246	Secondari, John H. - ***Coins In The Fountain*** [1953] Cover art by Owen Kampen.	$1.25	$3.75	$7.50
P-247	Hill, Ernestine - ***My Love Must Wait*** [1953] Cover art by Ray Pease.	$1.25	$3.75	$7.50
P-248	Childsey, Donald Barr - ***Panama Passage*** [1953]	$1.25	$3.75	$7.50
P-249	Campbell, William T. - ***Big Beverage*** [1953]	$1.25	$3.75	$7.50
P-250	Oursler, Fulton - ***The Greatest Book Ever Written*** [1953] Cover art by Rimsky.	$1.25	$3.75	$7.50
251	Sanford, John B. - ***The Old Man's Place*** [1953] Cover art by James Meese.	$1.25	$3.75	$7.50
252	Ordway, Peter - ***The Face In The Shadows*** [1953]	$1.25	$3.75	$7.50
253	Hemingway, Ernest - ***To Have And Have Not*** [1953]	$1.50	$5.00	$10.00
P-254	Anthology edited by Groff Conklin - ***Crossroads In Time*** [1953] Cover art by Richard Powers.	$1.25	$3.75	$7.50
P-255	Street, James - ***By Valour And Arms*** [1953]	$1.25	$3.75	$7.50
P-256	Jennings, John - ***The Shadow And The Glory*** [1953]	$1.25	$3.75	$7.50
257	Austin, Gene - ***The Secret Brand*** [1953]	$1.25	$3.75	$7.50
258	Matthews, Allen R. - ***The Assault*** [1953]	$1.25	$3.75	$7.50
P-259	Slaughter, Frank G. - ***Air Surgeon*** [1953]	$1.00	$3.00	$6.00
P-260	Hamilton, Harry - ***Thunder In The Wilderness*** [1953]	$1.25	$3.75	$7.50
P-261	Caen, Herb - ***Baghdad-By-The-Bay*** [1953]	$1.25	$3.75	$7.50

		G	VG	F
P-262	Anthology edited by Fernando Puma - ***7 Arts #2*** [1953]	$1.25	$3.75	$7.50
263	Wellman, Paul I. - ***The Comancheros*** [1953] Cover art by Cardiff.	$1.25	$3.75	$7.50
264	Simak, Clifford D. - ***City*** [1953] Cover art by Richard Powers.	$1.50	$5.00	$10.00
265	Derby, Mark - ***Element Of Risk*** [1953]	$1.25	$3.75	$7.50
P-266	Lancaster, Bruce - ***Bright To The Wanderer*** [1953]	$1.25	$3.75	$7.50
P-267	Orwell, George - ***Down And Out In Paris And London*** [1953] Cover art by Erickson.	$1.25	$3.75	$7.50
P-268	Fletcher, Inglis - ***Queen's Gift*** [1953]	$1.25	$3.75	$7.50
P-269	Carson, Robert - ***The Celluloid Jungle*** [1953]	$1.25	$3.75	$7.50
270	Prosser, W.H. - ***Nine To Five*** [1954]	$1.25	$3.75	$7.50
271	Hopkins, Tom J. - ***Range War*** [1954]	$1.25	$3.75	$7.50
272	Oursler, Fulton - ***Why I Know There Is A God*** [1954]	$1.00	$3.00	$6.00
P-273	Raynolds, Robert - ***The Sinner Of Saint Ambrose*** [1954] Cover art by Cardiff.	$1.25	$3.75	$7.50
P-274	Roark, Garland - ***The Wreck Of The Running Gale*** [1954]	$1.25	$3.75	$7.50
P-275	Marshall, Bruce - ***The White Rabbit*** [1954]	$1.50	$5.00	$10.00
P-276	Hutschnecker, M.D., Arnold A. - ***The Will To Live*** [1954] Photo cover.	$1.00	$3.00	$6.00
277	Huston, H.C. - ***With Murder For Some*** [1954] Cover art by James Meese.	$1.25	$3.75	$7.50
278	Bright, Robert - ***The Intruders*** [1954] Cover art by Daniel Schwartz.	$1.25	$3.75	$7.50
279	Doyle, Sir Arthur Conan - ***The Lost World*** [1954]	$2.00	$6.00	$12.00
P-280	Gibbs, Willa - ***Seed Of Mischief*** [1954]	$1.25	$3.75	$7.50
P-281	Lake, Alexander - ***Killers In Africa*** [1954]	$1.25	$3.75	$7.50
P-282	Dowdey, Clifford - ***The Proud Retreat*** [1954] Cover art by Verne Tossey.	$1.25	$3.75	$7.50
P-283	Brick, John - ***The Rifleman*** [1954]	$1.25	$3.75	$7.50
P-284	Costain, Thomas B. - ***The Silver Chalice*** [1954]	$1.25	$3.75	$7.50
P-285	Free, Montague - ***Gardening*** [1954]	$1.25	$3.75	$7.50
286	Pagano, Jo - ***The Condemned*** [1954]	$1.25	$3.75	$7.50
287	Smith, Shelley - ***The Crooked Man*** [1954] Cover art by Erickson.	$1.25	$3.75	$7.50
288	Conroy, Jim - ***Destination Revenge*** [1954]	$1.25	$3.75	$7.50
289	Avallone, Michael - ***The Spitting Image*** [1954] Photo cover.	$1.25	$3.75	$7.50
P-290	Slaughter, Frank G. - ***The Galileans*** [1954]	$1.25	$3.75	$7.50
P-291	Anthology edited by William Tenn - ***Outsiders: Children Of Wonder*** [1954] Cover art by Richard Powers.	$1.50	$5.00	$10.00
P-292	Upshaw, Helen - ***Day Of The Harvest*** [1954]	$1.25	$3.75	$7.50
P-293	Jennings, John - ***Gentleman Ranker*** [1954]	$1.25	$3.75	$7.50
P-294	Mitchell, Margaret - ***Gone With The Wind*** [1954]	$3.50	$10.00	$20.00
295	Coleman, Lonnie - ***Escape The Thunder*** [1954] Cover art by Robert Maguire.	$2.50	$7.50	$15.00
P-296	Hemingway, Ernest - ***Green Hills Of Africa*** [1954]	$1.25	$3.75	$7.50
297	Keyhoe, Donald - ***Flying Saucers From Outer Space*** [1954] Cover art by Richard Powers.	$1.25	$3.75	$7.50
P-298	Gerson, Noel B. - ***The Golden Eagle*** [1954]	$1.25	$3.75	$7.50
P-299	Harris, Mark - ***The Southpaw*** [1954] Cover art by Erickson.	$1.25	$3.75	$7.50
P-300	Harris, Sara - ***Father Devine: Holy Husband*** [1954]	$1.00	$3.00	$6.00
P-301	Gann, Ernest K. - ***The High And The Mighty*** [1954]	$1.25	$3.75	$7.50
P-305	Weinreb, Nathaniel Norsen - ***The Babylonians*** [1954] Cover art by Cardiff.	$1.25	$3.75	$7.50
308	Anderton, Russ - ***Tic-Polonga*** [1954]	$1.25	$3.75	$7.50
310	Clarke, Arthur C. - ***Against The Fall Of Night*** [1954]	$1.50	$5.00	$10.00
P-311	Dibner, Martin - ***The Deep Six*** [1954]	$1.25	$3.75	$7.50
P-313	Croy, Homer - ***He Hanged Them High*** [1954]	$1.25	$3.75	$7.50

Phantom Books. New York: Hanro Corp. Digest Size.

500	Barry, Joe - ***Homicide Hotel*** [1951] PBO.	$5.00	$15.00	$30.00

		G	VG	F
501	Carey, Donnell - ***Kisses Can Kill!*** [1951] PBO.	$5.00	$15.00	$30.00
502	Saber, Robert O. - ***The Deadly Lover*** [1951] PBO.	$5.00	$15.00	$30.00
503	Whittington, Harry - ***Married To Murder*** [1951] PBO.	$5.50	$17.50	$35.00
504	Keene, Day - ***Love Me And Die!*** [1951] PBO. Cover art by George Gross.	$5.00	$15.00	$30.00
505	Whittington, Harry - ***Satan's Widow*** [1951] PBO.	$5.50	$17.50	$35.00
506	Hoges, Carl G. - ***Crime On My Hands*** [1951] PBO. Cover art by George Gross.	$5.00	$15.00	$30.00
507	Keene, Day - ***Hunt The Killer*** [1951] PBO.	$5.00	$15.00	$30.00
508	Harrison, Whit (Harry Whittington) - ***Swamp Kill*** [1952] PBO.	$5.50	$17.50	$35.00
509	Keene, Day - ***Naked Fury*** [1952] PBO.	$5.00	$15.00	$30.00
510	Saber, Robert O. - ***Murder Doll*** [1952] PBO.	$5.00	$15.00	$30.00
511	Harrison, Whit (Harry Whittington) - ***Violent Night*** [1952] PBO. Cover art by George Gross.	$5.50	$17.50	$35.00
512	Saber, Robert O. - ***No Way Out*** [1952] PBO.	$5.00	$15.00	$30.00
513	Keene, Day - ***Wake Up To Murder*** [1952] PBO.	$5.00	$15.00	$30.00

Phantom Mystery. Small Digest Size.

		G	VG	F
1	Holmes, H. H. (Anthony Boucher) - ***Rocket To The Morgue*** [1942] PBO.	$12.50	$37.50	$75.00

Pike Books.

		G	VG	F
101	Rivere, Alec - ***Lost City Of The Damned*** [1961] Cover art by Albert Neutzel.	$5.50	$17.50	$35.00
102	Strick, Marv - ***Beatnik Ball*** [1961] Photo cover.	$1.50	$5.00	$10.00
121	Sheppard, Don - ***The Flesh Peddlers*** [1963] Later reprint of #212.	$1.50	$5.00	$10.00
203	Smith, George H. - ***The Coming Of The Rats*** [1961] Cover art by Albert Neutzel.	$8.00	$25.00	$50.00
204	Davidson, John - ***Appointment With Terror*** [1961] Photo cover.	$2.50	$7.50	$15.00
205	Hudson, Jan (George H. Smith) - ***Love Cult*** [1961]	$2.50	$7.50	$15.00
206	Knerr, M.E. - ***Brazen Broad*** [1961]	$2.00	$6.00	$12.00
207	Wolf, Ben - ***House Of Vice*** [1961]	$2.00	$6.00	$12.00
208	Smith, George H. - ***Baroness Of Blood*** [1961] PBO. Photo cover.	$3.00	$9.00	$18.00
209	Sullivan, Edward S. - ***Hollywood, Sin Capital Of The World*** [1961]	$1.50	$5.00	$10.00
210	Smith, George H. - ***Private Hell*** [1961] PBO. Photo cover.	$2.00	$6.00	$12.00
211	Lambert, Hal - ***3 Parts Evil*** [1962] PBO. Photo cover.	$1.50	$5.00	$10.00
212	Sheppard, Don - ***The Flesh Peddlers*** [1961] PBO.	$1.50	$5.00	$10.00
213	Unknown - ***Pike's Racy Bedtime Reader*** [1961]	$1.50	$5.00	$10.00
214	Knerr, M.E. - ***Travis*** [1961]	$1.50	$5.00	$10.00
215	Sheppard, Don - ***Scarlet Virgin*** [1962] Photo cover.	$1.50	$5.00	$10.00
216	Smith, George H. - ***Soft Lips On Black Velvet*** [1962] PBO. Photo cover.	$3.50	$10.00	$20.00
217	Hudson, Jan (George H. Smith) - ***Love Goddess*** [1961] Photo cover.	$2.50	$7.50	$15.00
218	- - ***Untamed Women*** [1962] Photo cover.	$2.00	$6.00	$12.00
219	Lambert, Hal - ***Julie*** [1962]	$2.00	$6.00	$12.00
220	Britt, Del - ***Sin House*** [1962]	$2.00	$6.00	$12.00
221	Tadrack, Moss - ***Georgette*** [1962]	$2.00	$6.00	$12.00
222	Nemec, John - ***Passion Fever*** [1963] Photo cover.	$2.00	$6.00	$12.00
801	Rivere, Alec - ***Nymphos Be Damned*** [1962] Photo cover. Reprints #101.	$1.25	$3.75	$7.50
802	Smith, George H. - ***Virgin Mistress*** [1962] Photo cover. Reprints #203.	$1.25	$3.75	$7.50
803	Sullivan, Edward S. - ***Hollywood Confidential*** [1962] Photo cover. Reprints #209.	$1.25	$3.75	$7.50
804	Lambert, Hal - ***One Hundred Dollar Call-Girl*** [1962] Photo cover. Reprints #211.	$1.25	$3.75	$7.50

Pinnacle Books. London: W. H. Allen

		G	VG	F
1	Burroughs, Edgar Rice - ***Tarzan And The Lost Empire*** [1951]	$3.50	$10.00	$20.00
NN-1	Burroughs, Edgar Rice - ***Tarzan And The Lost Empire*** [1958] Reprints #1.	$3.50	$10.00	$20.00
NN-2	Burroughs, Edgar Rice - ***Tarzan Lord Of The Jungle*** [1958] Reprints #2.	$3.50	$10.00	$20.00
2	Burroughs, Edgar Rice - ***Tarzan, Lord Of The Jungle*** [1951]	$3.50	$10.00	$20.00
NN-3	Burroughs, Edgar Rice - ***Tarzan The Invincible*** [1958] Reprints #3.	$3.50	$10.00	$20.00
3	Burroughs, Edgar Rice - ***Tarzan The Invincible*** [1951]	$3.50	$10.00	$20.00
4	Burroughs, Edgar Rice - ***Tarzan At The Earth's Core*** [1951]	$3.50	$10.00	$20.00
5	Burroughs, Edgar Rice - ***Tarzan's Quest*** [1951]	$3.50	$10.00	$20.00
6	Burroughs, Edgar Rice - ***A Princess Of Mars*** [1951]	$3.50	$10.00	$20.00
7	Burroughs, Edgar Rice - ***Tarzan And The Lion Man*** [1951] Cover art by J. Allen St. John.	$3.50	$10.00	$20.00
8	Burroughs, Edgar Rice - ***Tarzan And The Forbidden City*** [1951] Cover by John Coleman Burroughs.	$3.50	$10.00	$20.00
9	Burroughs, Edgar Rice - ***Carson Of Venus*** [1951]	$3.50	$10.00	$20.00
10	Burroughs, Edgar Rice - ***Tarzan And The Leopard Men*** [1951] Cover art by J. Allen St. John.	$3.50	$10.00	$20.00
11	Burroughs, Edgar Rice - ***Tarzan And The City Of Gold*** [1951] Cover by J. Allen St. John.	$3.50	$10.00	$20.00
12	Burroughs, Edgar Rice - ***Tarzan Triumphant*** [1951]	$3.50	$10.00	$20.00
13	Burrough, Edgar Rice - ***Tarzan And The Foreign Legion*** [1951] Cover by John Coleman Burroughs.	$3.50	$10.00	$20.00
NN-13	Burroughs, Edgar Rice - ***Tarzan And The Foreign Legion*** [1958] Reprints #13.	$3.50	$10.00	$20.00
14	Burroughs, Edgar Rice - ***Tarzan The Magnificent*** [1951] Cover art by John Coleman Burroughs.	$3.50	$10.00	$20.00
15	Burroughs, Edgar Rice - ***Tarzan Of The Apes*** [1951] Cover by J. Allen St. John.	$3.50	$10.00	$20.00
16	Burroughs, Edgar Rice - ***Tarzan The Untamed*** [1951]	$3.50	$10.00	$20.00
17	Burroughs, Edgar Rice - ***Tarzan And The Jewels Of Opar*** [1951]	$3.50	$10.00	$20.00
18	Burroughs, Edgar Rice - ***Beasts Of Tarzan*** [1951] Cover by Studley Burroughs.	$3.50	$10.00	$20.00
19	Burroughs, Edgar Rice - ***Return Of Tarzan*** [1951] Cover by John Coleman Burroughs.	$3.50	$10.00	$20.00
20	Burroughs, Edgar Rice - ***Tarzan And The Golden Lion*** [1952] Cover by J. E. McConnell.	$3.50	$10.00	$20.00
21	Burroughs, Edgar Rice - ***Son Of Tarzan*** [1952] Cover by J. E. McConnell	$3.50	$10.00	$20.00
22	Burroughs, Edgar Rice - ***Tarzan The Terrible*** [1952] Cover art by J. E. McConnell.	$3.50	$10.00	$20.00
23	Burroughs, Edgar Rice - ***Lost On Venus*** [1952] Cover art by J. E. McConnell.	$3.50	$10.00	$20.00
24	Burroughs, Edgar Rice - ***Tarzan And The Ant Men*** [1953] Cover by J. E. McConnell.	$3.50	$10.00	$20.00
25	Burroughs, Edgar Rice - ***Thuvia***			
26	Burroughs, Edgar Rice - ***The Warlord Of Mars*** [1953] Cover by J. E. McConnell.	$3.50	$10.00	$20.00
27	Burroughs, Edgar Rice - ***The Outlaw Of Torn*** [1953] Cover by J. E. McConnell.	$3.50	$10.00	$20.00
28	Burroughs, Edgar Rice - ***The Eternal Lover*** [1953] Cover by J. E. McConnell.	$3.50	$10.00	$20.00
29	Burroughs, Edgar Rice - ***Tanar Of Pellucidar*** [1953] Cover by J. E. McConnell.	$3.50	$10.00	$20.00
30	Burroughs, Edgar Rice - ***The Gods Of Mars*** [1953] Cover by J.E. McConnell.	$3.50	$10.00	$20.00

		G	VG	F
31	Burroughs, Edgar Rice - ***The Bandit Of Hell's Bend*** [1954] Cover by J. E. McConnell.	$3.50	$10.00	$20.00
32	Burroughs, Edgar Rice - ***Jungle Tales Of Tarzan*** [1954] Cover by J. E. McConnell.	$3.50	$10.00	$20.00
33	Burroughs, Edgar Rice - ***A Fighting Man Of Mars*** [1954] Cover by J.E. McConnell.	$3.50	$10.00	$20.00
34	Burroughs, Edgar Rice - ***Pirates Of Venus*** [1954] Cover by J. E. McConnell.	$3.50	$10.00	$20.00
36	Burroughs, Edgar Rice - ***The Chessmen Of Mars*** [1954] Cover by J. E. McConnell.	$3.50	$10.00	$20.00
37	Burroughs, Edgar Rice - ***The Girl From Hollywood*** [1954]	$3.50	$10.00	$20.00
38	Burroughs, Edgar Rice - ***The Master Mind Of Mars*** [1954] Cover by J. E. McConnell.	$3.50	$10.00	$20.00
39	Burroughs, Edgar Rice - ***Pellucidar*** [1954] Cover by J. E. McConnell.	$3.50	$10.00	$20.00

Pinnacle Books. New York: Pinnacle Books, Inc.

		G	VG	F
1	Pendelton, Don - ***War Against The Mafia (The Executioner #1)*** [1969] PBO.	$ .75	$2.50	$5.00
2	Pendleton, Don - ***The Executioner's Death Squad (The Executioner #2)*** [1969]	$ .65	$2.00	$4.00
3	Pendleton, Don - ***Cataclysm: The Day The World Died*** [1969] PBO. Photo cover.	$ .65	$2.00	$4.00
4	Pendleton, Don - ***The Executioner's Battle Mask (Executioner #3)*** [1969]	$ .65	$2.00	$4.00
5	Fennell, George - ***Blood Patrol*** [1969]	$ .65	$2.00	$4.00
6	Pendleton, Don - ***The Guns Of Terra 10*** [1970]	$ .65	$2.00	$4.00
7	Pendleton, Don - ***1989: Population Doomsday*** [1970] PBO.	$ .65	$2.00	$4.00
8	Pendleton, Don - ***Miami Massacre (Executioner #4)*** [1970]	$ .65	$2.00	$4.00
9	Fennell, George - ***Killer Patrol*** [1970]	$ .65	$2.00	$4.00
10	Britain, Dan (Don Pendleton) - ***The Godmakers*** [1970] Cover art by Frank Frazetta.	$1.25	$3.75	$7.50
11	Jason, Stuart - ***Kill Quick Or Die (Butcher #1)*** [1970]	$ .65	$2.00	$4.00
12	Leek, Sybil - ***Cast Your Own Spell*** [1970]	$ .50	$1.50	$3.00
13	Kantor, Hal - ***The Vegas Trap*** [1970]	$ .65	$2.00	$4.00
14	Cooper, Farley J. - ***The Feminists*** [1971] PBO.	$ .65	$2.00	$4.00
15	Caillou, Alan - ***The Dead Sea Submarine*** [1971] Cover art by George Gross.	$ .65	$2.00	$4.00
16	McCarthy, Frank J. - ***Stay Young With Astrology*** [1971]	$ .50	$1.50	$3.00
17	Pendleton, Don - ***Continental Contract (Executioner #5)*** [1971].	$ .65	$2.00	$4.00
18	Smith, Warren - ***Talking To The Spirits*** [1971] PBO.	$ .65	$2.00	$4.00
19	Stimson, Robert & Bellah, James - ***The Avenger Tapes*** [1971]	$ .65	$2.00	$4.00
20	Fairman, Paul - ***To Catch A Crooked Girl*** [1971] Cover art by Frank Frazetta.	$2.00	$6.00	$12.00
21	Rosenberger, Joseph - ***The Death Merchant*** [1971]	$ .65	$2.00	$4.00
22	Farnsworth, Mona - ***The Great Stone Heart*** [1971]	$ .65	$2.00	$4.00
23	Jorgensen, Ivar - ***The Deadly Sky*** [1971]	$ .75	$2.50	$5.00
24	Duncan, Robert L. - ***The Day The Sun Fell*** [1971] Cover art by George Gross.	$ .75	$2.50	$5.00
25	Jason, Suart - ***Come Watch Him Die*** [1971]	$ .65	$2.00	$4.00
26	Moore, Harris - ***Slater's Planet*** [1971]	$ .75	$2.50	$5.00
27	Johnston, William - ***Home Is Where The Quick Is*** [1971] PBO. Photo cover. Mod Squad #1. TV tie-in.	$1.25	$3.75	$7.50
28	Hendin, David - ***Everything You Need To Know About Abortion*** [1971]	$ .50	$1.50	$3.00
29	Pendleton, Don - ***Assault On Soho (Executioner #6)*** [1971] Cover art by George Gross.	$ .65	$2.00	$4.00
30	David, Heather - ***Operation Rescue*** [1971]	$ .65	$2.00	$4.00
31	Complied by Karen Dent - ***The U.S. Government Budjet Cookbook*** [1971] Cookbook.	$ .65	$2.00	$4.00

		G	VG	F
32	Machen, Arthur - ***Tales Of Horror And The Supernatural (Vol. I)*** [1971]	$2.50	$7.50	$15.00
33	Eden, Matthew - ***Flight Of Hawks*** [1971]	$ .65	$2.00	$4.00
34	Elder, Michael - ***Paradise Is Not Enough*** [1971]	$ .65	$2.00	$4.00
35	Caillou, Alan - ***Terror In Rio*** [1971]	$ .65	$2.00	$4.00
36	Anthology edited by P. Van Doren Stern - ***The Other Side Of The Clock*** [1971]	$ .65	$2.00	$4.00
37	Wagoner, David - ***The Escape Artist*** [1971]	$ .65	$2.00	$4.00
38	Sapir & Murphy - ***Created The Destroyer (Destroyer #1)*** [1971]	$ .65	$2.00	$4.00
39	Pendleton, Don - ***War Against The Mafia (Executioner #1)*** [1971]	$ .50	$1.50	$3.00
40	Pendleton, Don - ***The Executioner's Death Squad (Executioner #2)*** [1971]	$ .50	$1.50	$3.00
41	Roberts, Janet Louise - ***Love Song*** [1971]	$ .65	$2.00	$4.00
42	Guilford, Carol - ***The New Cook's Cookbook*** [1971] Cookbook.	$ .65	$2.00	$4.00
43	Elder, Michael - ***The Alien Earth*** [1971]	$ .75	$2.50	$5.00
44	Pendleton, Don - ***Nightmare In New York (Executioner #7)*** [1971]	$ .65	$2.00	$4.00
46	Storey, Anthony - ***The Rector*** [1971]	$ .65	$2.00	$4.00
47	Fairman, Paul - ***Love American Style*** [1971]	$ .65	$2.00	$4.00
48	Bourke, Sean - ***The Springing Of George Blake*** [1971]	$ .65	$2.00	$4.00
49	Lynch, Miriam - ***The Bells Of Widows Bay*** [1971]	$ .65	$2.00	$4.00
50	? - ***Imperial Tragedy*** [1971]	$ .65	$2.00	$4.00
51	Pendleton, Don - ***Chicago Wipeout (Executioner #8)*** [1971]	$ .65	$2.00	$4.00
52	Gordon, Donald - ***The Golden Oyster*** [1971] Cover art by Berkey.	$ .65	$2.00	$4.00
53	Churchill, Rosemary - ***Daughter Of Henry VIII*** [1971]	$ .50	$1.50	$3.00
54	Anthology edited by Kurt Singer - ***Tales From The Unknown*** [1971]	$1.25	$3.75	$7.50
55	Britain, Dan (Don Pendleton) - ***Civil War II:*** [1971]	$ .65	$2.00	$4.00
56	Weidman, Jerome - ***Fourth Street East*** [1971]	$ .65	$2.00	$4.00
57	English, Mary - ***How To Marry A Married Man*** [1971]	$ .50	$1.50	$3.00
58	Trimble, Ph.D., John F. - ***The Groupsex Scene*** [1971]	$ .50	$1.50	$3.00
59	Pendleton, Don - ***Vegas Vendetta (Executioner #9)*** [1971]	$ .65	$2.00	$4.00
60	Stuart, V.A. - ***The Valiant Sailors*** [1971]	$ .65	$2.00	$4.00
61	? - ***Saberlegs*** [1971]	$ .65	$2.00	$4.00
62	Anthology edited by Damon Knight - ***First Contact*** [1971] PBO. Cover art by Powers.	$1.25	$3.75	$7.50
63	Hahn, Emily - ***Times And Places*** [1971]	$ .65	$2.00	$4.00
64	Marin, A.C. - ***The Clash Of Distant Thunder*** [1971]	$ .65	$2.00	$4.00
65	Tiede, Tom - ***Calley: Soldier Or Killer*** [1971] PBO. Photo cover.	$ .65	$2.00	$4.00
66	Di Donato, Pietro - ***Naked, As An Author*** [1971]	$ .65	$2.00	$4.00
67	Lewis, Jack - ***Guns For General Li*** [1972]	$ .65	$2.00	$4.00
68	? - ***Purr, Baby, Purr*** [1972]	$ .65	$2.00	$4.00
69	? - ***The Pentagon*** [1972]	$ .65	$2.00	$4.00
70	Stuart, V.A. - ***Brave Captains*** [1972]	$ .65	$2.00	$4.00
71	Caillou, Alan - ***Congo War Cry*** [1972]	$ .65	$2.00	$4.00
72	Sapir & Murphy - ***Death Check*** [1972]	$ .65	$2.00	$4.00
73	Anthology - ***101 Best Growth Stocks For 1972*** [1972]	$ .50	$1.50	$3.00
74	? - ***Dueling Oaks*** [1972]	$ .65	$2.00	$4.00
75	Van Doren, Ronald - ***Charting The Candidates*** [1972]	$ .50	$1.50	$3.00
76	Pendleton, Don - ***Caribbean Kill (Executioner #10)*** [1972]	$ .65	$2.00	$4.00
78	Sapir & Murphy - ***Chinese Puzzle*** [1972] The Destroyer #3	$ .65	$2.00	$4.00
79	Di Turno, Sadio Garavini - ***Diamond River*** [1972]	$ .65	$2.00	$4.00
80	Gordon, Donald - ***Leap In The Dark*** [1972]	$ .65	$2.00	$4.00
81	Fairman, Paul - ***Love American Style, 2*** [1972]	$ .65	$2.00	$4.00
83	Stuart, V.A. - ***Hazard's Command*** [1972]	$ .65	$2.00	$4.00
84	Jason, Stuart - ***Keepers Of Death*** [1972]	$ .65	$2.00	$4.00
85	Rosenberger, Joseph - ***Operation Overkill*** [1972]	$ .65	$2.00	$4.00

		G	VG	F
86	Lynch, Miriam - ***Where Shadows Lie*** [1972]	$ .65	$2.00	$4.00
88	Fraser, Joan - ***Relaxercises*** [1972]	$ .50	$1.50	$3.00
90	Larago, Ladislas - ***Burn After Reading*** [1972]	$ .65	$2.00	$4.00
91	Galanoy, Terry - ***Down The Tube*** [1972]	$ .65	$2.00	$4.00
92	Warren, Paul - ***How To "Make It" 365 Days A Year*** [1972]	$ .50	$1.50	$3.00
93	Manvell, Roger & Fraenkel, Heinrich - ***The Canaris Conspiracy*** [1972]	$ .65	$2.00	$4.00
94	Terry, William - ***Hannie Caulder*** [1972] PBO.	$ .65	$2.00	$4.00
95	Pendleton, Don - ***California Hit (Executioner #11)*** [1972] Movie tie-in. Photo cover. 8 pages of photos.	$ .65	$2.00	$4.00
96	? - ***Gold Wagon*** [1972]	$ .65	$2.00	$4.00
97	Caillou, Alan - ***Afghan Assault*** [1972]	$ .65	$2.00	$4.00
98	? - ***Executive Yoga*** [1972]	$ .50	$1.50	$3.00
99	Stuart, V.A. - ***Hazard Of Huntress*** [1972]	$ .65	$2.00	$4.00
102	Marin, A.C. - ***Rise With The Wind*** [1972]	$ .65	$2.00	$4.00
104	Sapir & Murphy - ***Mafia Fix*** [1972] The Destroyer #4.	$ .65	$2.00	$4.00
105	? - ***Blue Marsh*** [1972]	$ .65	$2.00	$4.00
107	Pendleton, Don - ***Boston Blitz (Executioner #12)*** [1972]	$ .65	$2.00	$4.00
109	Gilman, George G. - ***The Loner*** [1972]	$ .65	$2.00	$4.00
111	Jason, Stuart - ***Blood Debt*** [1972]	$ .65	$2.00	$4.00
115	Gilman, George G. - ***Ten Grand*** [1972]	$ .65	$2.00	$4.00
117	Rosenberger, Joseph - ***The Psychotron Plot*** [1972]	$ .65	$2.00	$4.00
120	Weidman, Jerome - ***Last Respects*** [1972]	$ .65	$2.00	$4.00
124	Pendleton, Don - ***Washington I.O.U. (Executioner #13)*** [1972]	$ .65	$2.00	$4.00
125	Sapir & Murphy - ***Dr. Quake*** [1972] The Destroyer #5.	$ .65	$2.00	$4.00
126	Crawford, William - ***The Marine*** [1972]	$ .65	$2.00	$4.00
129	Deane, Jim - ***The Mistress Book*** [1972]	$ .50	$1.50	$3.00
131	Pendleton, Don - ***San Diego Seige (Executioner #14)*** [1972]	$ .65	$2.00	$4.00
133	Gilman, George G. - ***Apache Death*** [1972]	$ .65	$2.00	$4.00
134	Pendleton, Don - ***Panic In Philly (Executioner #15)*** [1972]	$ .65	$2.00	$4.00
136	Sapir & Murphy - ***Death Therapy*** [1972] The Destroyer #6.	$ .65	$2.00	$4.00
137	Pearl, Jack - ***The Cops*** [1972]	$ .65	$2.00	$4.00
138	Haining, Peter - ***Beyond The Curtain Of Darkness*** [1972]	$ .65	$2.00	$4.00
148	Gilman, George G. - ***Killer's Breed*** [1973]	$ .65	$2.00	$4.00
149	Sapir & Murphy - ***Union Bust*** [1973] The Destroyer #7.	$ .65	$2.00	$4.00
152	Jason, Stuart - ***Deadly Deal*** [1973]	$ .65	$2.00	$4.00
157	Elder, Michael - ***Nowhere On Earth*** [1973]	$ .65	$2.00	$4.00
163	Murphy, Warren B. - ***City In Heat*** [1973]	$ .65	$2.00	$4.00
164	Caillou, Alan - ***Swamp War*** [1973] PBO.	$ .65	$2.00	$4.00
165	Sapir & Murphy - ***Summit Chase*** [1973] The Destroyer #8.	$ .65	$2.00	$4.00
166	Peterson, Jim - ***Sicilian Slaughter (Executioner #16)*** [1973]	$ .65	$2.00	$4.00
168	Rosenberger, Joseph - ***Chinese Conspiracy*** [1973]	$ .65	$2.00	$4.00
172	Gilman, George G. - ***Blood On Silver*** [1973]	$ .65	$2.00	$4.00
178	Matthews, Clayton - ***Bounty Hunt At Ballarat*** [1973]	$ .65	$2.00	$4.00
179	Sapir & Murphy - ***Murder's Shield*** [1973] The Destroyer #9.	$ .65	$2.00	$4.00
180	Hardy, Adam - ***The Press Gang*** [1973]	$ .65	$2.00	$4.00
182	Rosenberger, Joseph - ***Satan Strike*** [1973]	$ .65	$2.00	$4.00
190	Gilman, George G. - ***Red River*** [1973]	$ .65	$2.00	$4.00
192	Leslie, Peter - ***Silent Squadron*** [1973]	$ .65	$2.00	$4.00
194	Murphy, Warren B. - ***Dead End Street*** [1973]	$ .65	$2.00	$4.00
196	Sapir & Murphy - ***Terror Squad*** [1973] The Destroyer #10.	$ .65	$2.00	$4.00
197	Jason, Stuart - ***Kill Time*** [1973]	$ .65	$2.00	$4.00

Pinnacle Real Life Crime Books. London: W. H. Allen. (In DJ, double price).

NN	Ford, Freddy - ***London After Midnight*** [1954] Reprints #9 with new title.	$2.50	$7.50	$15.00
NN-1	Jenkins, Peter - ***Mayfair Boy*** [n.d.]	$2.50	$7.50	$15.00
NN-2	Lloyd, H. M. - Editor - ***Murder, Mystery And Mirth*** [n.d.]	$2.50	$7.50	$15.00
NN-3	Singer, Kurt - ***Women Spies*** [n.d.]	$2.50	$7.50	$15.00
NN-4	Wyndham, Horace - ***Guilty Or Not Guilty*** [n.d.]	$2.50	$7.50	$15.00

		G	VG	F
NN-5	Matters, Leonard - ***Jack The Ripper*** [n.d.]	$3.50	$10.00	$20.00
NN-6	Allen, John E. - ***Inside Broadmoor: The Mad Parson*** [n.d.]	$2.50	$7.50	$15.00
NN-7	Singer, Kurt - ***Gentleman Spies*** [n.d.]	$2.50	$7.50	$15.00
NN-8	Kugelmass, J. Alvin - ***The Jelke Case*** [n.d.]	$2.50	$7.50	$15.00
NN-9	Ford, Freddy - ***King Of The Crooks*** [n.d.]	$2.50	$7.50	$15.00

Playboy Giant.

		G	VG	F
0114	Anthology - ***The Bedside Playboy*** [1968] Edited by Hugh M. Hefner.	$1.25	$3.75	$7.50
0115	Anthology - ***The Playboy Book Of Science Fiction And Fantasy*** [1968] Photo cover.	$1.50	$5.00	$10.00
0116	Anthology - ***The Playboy Book Of Crime And Suspense*** [1968] Cover art by Richard Tyler.	$1.50	$5.00	$10.00
0119	Anthology - ***The Playboy Book Of Horror And The Supernatural*** [1968] Cover by Richard Tyler.	$2.00	$6.00	$12.00
0120	Anthology - ***The Playboy Book Of Humor And Satire*** [1968] Cover art by Arnold Roth.	$1.25	$3.75	$7.50

Playboy Press. Chicago: HMH Publishing Co.

		G	VG	F
16101	Lehrman, Nat - ***Masters And Johnson Explained*** [1970] PBO.	$ .50	$1.50	$3.00
16102	Anthology - ***Transit Of Earth*** [1971] PBO. Cover art by Shelly Canton.	$1.25	$3.75	$7.50
16103	Anthology - ***Have A Nice Time At The Revolution*** [1971] Cartoon book.	$ .75	$2.50	$5.00
16106	Anthology - ***Last Train To Limdo*** [1971] PBO. Cover art by Shelly Canton.	$1.25	$3.75	$7.50
16107	? - ***Why Do I Get An Irresistible Urge To Laugh Everytime I Make*** [1971]	$ .50	$1.50	$3.00
16110	Anthology - ***From The "S" File*** [1971] PBO. Cover art by Saul Lambert.	$1.25	$3.75	$7.50
16111	Anthology - ***Classic Cartoons From Playboy 1953-1956*** [1971] PBO. Cover art by Jack Cole. Cartoon book.	$ .75	$2.50	$5.00
16114	Anthology - ***The Dead Astronaut*** [1971] PBO. Cover art by Pompeo Posar.	$1.25	$3.75	$7.50
16115	Savage, Brian - ***So This Is Love*** [1971] PBO. Cover art by Brian Savage. Cartoon book.	$ .50	$1.50	$3.00
16119	Anthology - ***New Playboy's Party Jokes*** [1970]	$ .75	$2.50	$5.00
16121	Anthology - ***Not Until You Take Off That Silly Hat*** [1971] PBO. Cover art by John Dempsey. Cartoon book.	$ .75	$2.50	$5.00
16122	Anthology - ***The Fiend*** [1971] PBO. Cover art by Roger Hane.	$1.25	$3.75	$7.50
16123	Shoemaker, Howard - ***Good-Bye, Cruel World*** [1971] PBO. Cover art by Howard Shoemaker. Cartoon book.	$ .75	$2.50	$5.00
16125	Anthology - ***The Peeping Tom Patrol*** [1971] PBO. Includes "The Distributor" by Richard Matheson.	$1.25	$3.75	$7.50
16126	Anthology - ***Masks*** [1971] PBO. Cover art by George Suyeoka.	$1.25	$3.75	$7.50
16127	Anthology - ***We Can't Go On Meeting Like This*** [1971] PBO. Cover art by Erich Sokol. Cartoon book.	$ .75	$2.50	$5.00
16131	Russell, Ray - ***Sagittarius*** [1971] PBO. Cover art by Roger Hane.	$1.25	$3.75	$7.50
16132	Anthology - ***Doctor! Doctor!*** [1971] PBO. Cover art by Alden Erikson. Cartoon book.	$ .75	$2.50	$5.00
16136	Harris, Sidney - ***So Far, So Good*** [1971] PBO. Cover art by Sidney Harris. Cartoon book.	$ .75	$2.50	$5.00
16138	Anthology - ***Weird Show*** [1971] PBO. Cover art by Skip Williamson. Includes "The Machine In Ward Eleven" by Charles Willeford and "By Appointment Only" by Richard Matheson.	$3.50	$10.00	$20.00
16140	Anthology - ***Had A Nice Time At The Office?*** [1971] PBO. Cover art by Alden Erikson. Cartoon book.	$ .75	$2.50	$5.00
16143	Roberts, Keith - ***The Inner Wheel*** [1972] Cover art by Martin Hoffman.	$1.25	$3.75	$7.50

		G	VG	F
16144	Anthology - ***The Swingers*** [1972] PBO. Cover art by Don Madden. Cartoon book.	$ .75	$2.50	$5.00
16147	Hartridge, Jon - ***Binary Divine*** [1972] Cover art by Paul Davis.	$1.25	$3.75	$7.50
16150	Thomas, Ted & Wilhelm, Kate - ***The Year Of The Cloud*** [1972] Cover art by James Spanfeller	$1.25	$3.75	$7.50
16151	Anthology edited by William F. Nolan - ***The Future Is Now*** [1972] Cover art by Don Baum.	$1.25	$3.75	$7.50
16152	Handelsman, J.B. - ***You're Not Serious, I Hope*** [1972] PBO. Cover art by J.B. Handelsman. Cartoon book.	$ .75	$2.50	$5.00
16160	Anthology - ***Looks Suspicious To Me*** [1972] PBO. Cover art by Rowland B. Wilson. Cartoon book.	$ .75	$2.50	$5.00
16163	Anthology - ***So You Want To Be A Star*** [1972] PBO. Cover art by Alden Erikson. Carton book.	$ .75	$2.50	$5.00
16166	Anthology - ***Classic Cartoons From Playboy 1960*** [1972] PBO. Cover art by Phil Interlandi. Cartoon book.	$ .75	$2.50	$5.00
16169	Anthology - ***How I Spent My Summer Vacation*** [1972] PBO. Cover art by Erich Sokol. Cartoon book.	$ .75	$2.50	$5.00
16170	Anthology - ***Playboy's Short-Shorts #2*** [1972] Photo cover.	$ .75	$2.50	$5.00
16173	Ffolkes, Michael - ***I'm Out Of Pink*** [1972] PBO. Cover art by Michael Ffolkes. Cartoon book.	$ .75	$2.50	$5.00
16177	Anthology - ***Classic Cartoons From Playboy Jan.-June 1961*** [1972] PBO. Cover art by Eldon Dedini. Cartoon book.	$ .75	$2.50	$5.00
16179	Anthology - ***Guess What Santa Wants For Christmas*** [1972] PBO. Cover art by Phil Interlandi. Cartoon book.	$ .75	$2.50	$5.00
16193	Anthology - ***Like Father, Like Son*** [1973] PBO. Cover art by Alden Erikson. Cartoon book.	$ .75	$2.50	$5.00
16194	Anthology - ***The Pocket Playboy #1*** [1973] PBO. Photo cover.	$3.50	$10.00	$20.00
16200	Anthology - ***No, I'm Not Tired*** [1973]	$ .75	$2.50	$5.00
16205	Anthology - ***The Pocket Playboy #2*** [1973] PBO. Photo cover.	$3.50	$10.00	$20.00
16208	Anthology - ***It's Today?*** [1973] PBO. Cartoon book.	$ .75	$2.50	$5.00
16212	Anthology - ***Playboy On The Town*** [1973] PBO. Contains over 100 photos.	$ .75	$2.50	$5.00
16219	Anthology - ***The Pocket Playboy #4*** [1974] PBO. Marilyn Monroe photo cover.	$4.00	$12.50	$25.00
16221	Anthology - ***Playboy's Short-Shorts #1*** [1974] Photo cover.	$ .75	$2.50	$5.00
16227	Anthology - ***Have I Got A Girl For You*** [1974]	$ .75	$2.50	$5.00
16234	Anthology - ***The Happiest Hookers*** [1974] PBO. Cartoon book.	$ .75	$2.50	$5.00
16252	Anthology - ***Classic Cartoons From Playboy July-Dec. 1962*** [1975] PBO. Cover art by Erich Sokol. Cartoon book.	$ .75	$2.50	$5.00
16263	Anthology - ***Why Do I Get An Irresistible Urge To Laugh Everytime I Make*** [1974]	$ .75	$2.50	$5.00
16278	Anthology - ***Whatever Turns You On*** [1975] PBO. Cover art by John Dempsey. Cartoon book.	$ .75	$2.50	$5.00
16315	Dougherty, James E. - ***The Secret Happiness Of Marilyn Monroe*** [1976] PBO. Photo cover. 24 pages of early photos	$4.50	$14.00	$28.00
21144	Swanson, Logan (Richard Matheson) - ***Earthbound*** [1982] PBO.	$5.50	$17.50	$35.00
75163	Anthology - ***Still More Playboy's Party Jokes*** [1968] PBO	$ .75	$2.50	$5.00

Pocket Books (Early Publisher's History, 1938–1959)

Pocket Books started the mass market paperback phenomenon. As such, they became the first major paperback publisher to distribute mass market paperbacks in the United States. Robert DeGraff started Pocket Books with backing from Simon and Schuster. They began after a small market test distribution of an unnumbered edition of Pearl Buck's *The Good Earth* proved very successful and published ten more titles. The tremendous success of the line launched the paperback book into the American mainstream.

They placed their logo, Gertrude the Kangaroo, on the front or spine of each book.

Books of special note include first editions of the first eleven books, and four titles with dust jackets. In every type of literature, a number of superior titles appear.

Pocket Books, Inc., also established Pocket Books (Great Britain), Cardinal Books, Pocket Book Special, Pocket Library of Great Art, Comet Books, a children's line which they renamed Pocket Books Jr., and two lines of classical literature: Pocket Book Collector's Edition and Pocket Library, which they renamed Washington Square Press.

		G	VG	F
Pocket Books. New York: Pocket Books, Inc.				
NO#	Buck, Pearl - ***The Good Earth*** [1938]	$80.00	$250.00	$600.00
1	Hilton, James - ***Lost Horizon*** [1939] Cover by Steinberg	$20.00	$60.00	$125.00
2	Brande, Dorothea - ***Wake Up And Live*** [1939] Cover by Isador N. Steinberg.	$17.00	$50.00	$100.00
3	Shakespeare, William - ***Five Great Tragedies*** [1939] Cover by Isador N. Steinberg.	$17.00	$50.00	$100.00
4	Smith, Thorne - ***Topper*** [1939] Cover by Frank J. Lieberman.	$17.00	$50.00	$100.00
5	Christie, Agatha - ***The Murder Of Roger Ackroyd*** [1939] Cover by Isador N. Steinberg	$22.00	$70.00	$140.00
6	Parker, Dorothy - ***Enough Rope*** [1939] Cover by Frank J. Lieberman.	$17.00	$50.00	$100.00
7	Bronte, Emily - ***Wuthering Heights*** [1939] Cover by Isador N. Steinberg.	$17.00	$50.00	$100.00
8	Butler, Samuel - ***The Way Of All Flesh*** [1939] Cover by Isador N. Steinberg.	$17.00	$50.00	$100.00
9	Wilder, Thornton - ***The Bridge Of San Luis Rey*** [1939] Cover by Frank Lieberman.	$17.00	$50.00	$100.00
10	Salten, Felix - ***Bambi*** [1939] Cover by Lieberman.	$17.00	$50.00	$100.00
11	Buck, Pearl S. - ***The Good Earth*** [1939]	$2.50	$7.50	$15.00
12	De Maupassant, Guy - ***The Great Short Stories Of De Maupassant*** [1939]	$2.50	$7.50	$15.00
13	Ferber, Edna - ***Showboat*** [1939]	$3.50	$10.00	$20.00
14	Dickens, Charles - ***A Tale Of Two Cities*** [1939]	$5.00	$15.00	$30.00
15	Van Loon, Hendrik Willem - ***The Story Of Mankind*** [1939]	$2.50	$7.50	$15.00
16	Hudson, W.H. - ***Green Mansions*** [1939]	$4.50	$14.00	$28.00
17	Queen, Ellery - ***The Chinese Orange Mystery*** [1939]	$5.00	$15.00	$30.00
18	Collodi, C. - ***Pinocchio*** [1939]	$5.50	$17.50	$35.00
19	Charnwood, Lord - ***Abraham Lincoln*** [1939]	$2.50	$7.50	$15.00
20	Hardy, Thomas - ***The Return Of The Native*** [1939]	$2.50	$7.50	$15.00
21	Sayers, Dorothy - ***Murder Must Advertise*** [1939]	$4.00	$12.50	$25.00
22	Wyss, Johann David - ***Swiss Family Robinson*** [1939]	$3.50	$10.00	$20.00
23	Franklin, Benjamin - ***The Autobiography Of Benjamin Franklin*** [1939] Cover by Isador N. Steinberg.	$2.50	$7.50	$15.00
24	Walling, R.A.J. - ***The Corpse With The Floating Foot*** [1939]	$4.00	$12.50	$25.00
25	Stevenson, Robert Louis - ***Treasure Island*** [1939]	$3.50	$10.00	$20.00
26	Strachey, Lytton - ***Elizabeth And Essex*** [1939]	$2.50	$7.50	$15.00
27	O'Hara, John - ***Appointment In Samarra*** [1939]	$2.50	$7.50	$15.00
28	Wodehouse, P.G. - ***Jeeves*** [1939] Cover by Isador N. Steinberg.	$3.00	$9.00	$18.00
29	Dickens, Charles - ***A Christmas Carol*** [1939]	$5.00	$15.00	$30.00
30	Sedgwick, Anne Douglas - ***The Little French Girl*** [1939]	$2.50	$7.50	$15.00
31	Hugo, Victor - ***The Hunchback Of Notre Dame Vol. I*** [1939] Cover by Isador N. Steinberg. Movie tie-in.	$5.50	$17.50	$35.00
32	Hugo, Victor - ***The Hunchback Of Notre Dame Vol. II*** [1939] Cover by Isador N. Steinberg. Movie tie-in.	$5.50	$17.50	$35.00
33	Ford, Leslie - ***By The Watchman's Clock*** [1939]	$4.00	$12.50	$25.00
34	Swift, Jonathan - ***Gulliver's Travels*** [1939]	$4.50	$14.00	$28.00
35	Wren, P.C. - ***Beau Geste*** [1939]	$2.50	$7.50	$15.00
36	Dumas, Alexander - ***The Three Musketeers Vol. 1*** [1939]	$3.50	$10.00	$20.00
37	Dumas, Alexander - ***The Three Musketeers Vol. 2*** [1940]	$3.50	$10.00	$20.00

Pocket Books, 82

Pocket Books, 181

Pocket Books, 212

		G	VG	F
38	Christie, Agatha - ***The Mystery Of The Blue Train*** [1940]	$5.00	$15.00	$30.00
39	Poe, Edgar Allan - ***Tales And Poems Of Mystery And Imagination*** [1940]	$6.00	$20.00	$40.00
40	Barton, Bruce - ***The Man Nobody Knows*** [1940]	$4.00	$12.50	$25.00
41	Kennedy, Margaret - ***The Constant Nymph*** [1940] Cover by Rockwell.	$2.50	$7.50	$15.00
42	Autobiography - ***Benvenuto Cellini*** [1940]	$2.50	$7.50	$15.00
43	Lowndes, Mrs. Belloc - ***The Lodger*** [1940]	$3.50	$10.00	$20.00
44	Norris, Kathleen - ***Mother*** [1940]	$3.50	$10.00	$20.00
45	Kipling, Rudyard - ***The Light That Failed*** [1940]	$4.00	$12.50	$25.00
46	Dickson, Carter - ***The Bowstring Murders*** [1940]	$4.00	$12.50	$25.00
47	Buck, Frank with Anthony, Edward - ***Bring 'Em Back Alive*** [1940]	$3.00	$9.00	$18.00
48	Peterkin, Julia - ***Scarlet Sister Mary*** [1940]	$2.00	$6.00	$12.00
49	De Kruif, Paul - ***Dr. Ehrlich's Magic Bullet*** [1940] Photo cover.	$3.50	$10.00	$20.00
50	Biggers, Earl Derr - ***The House Without A Key*** [1940]	$5.00	$15.00	$30.00
51	Morley, Christopher - ***Thunder On The Left*** [1940]	$3.00	$9.00	$18.00
52	Hawthore, Nathaniel - ***The House Of The Seven Gables*** [1940]	$3.50	$10.00	$20.00
53	Runyon, Damon - ***The Best Of Damon Runyon*** [1940] Cover by Allen Pope.	$2.50	$7.50	$15.00
54	Oppenheim, E. Phillips - ***The Great Prince Shan*** [1940]	$2.50	$7.50	$15.00
55	Wilder, Thornton - ***Our Town*** [1940]	$2.50	$7.50	$15.00
56	Bromfield, Louis - ***The Green Bay Tree*** [1940]	$2.50	$7.50	$15.00
57	Parker, Dorothy - ***After Such Pleasures*** [1940]	$2.00	$6.00	$12.00
58	Hughes, Thomas - ***Tom Brown's School Days*** [1940]	$2.50	$7.50	$15.00
59	Marquand, John P. - ***Think Fast, Mr. Moto*** [1940] Cover by A. Pope	$4.00	$12.50	$25.00
60	Chesterton, G.K. - ***The Scandal Of Father Brown*** [1940]	$5.00	$15.00	$30.00
61	Ollivant, Alfred - ***Bob Son Of Battle*** [1940]	$4.00	$12.50	$25.00
62	Anthology edited by M.E. Speare, Ph.D. - ***The Pocket Book Of Verse*** [1940]	$2.00	$6.00	$12.00
63	Austen, Jane - ***Pride And Prejudice*** [1940] Cover by Allen Pope	$2.50	$7.50	$15.00
64	Eberhart, Mignon G. - ***While The Patient Slept*** [1940]	$3.50	$10.00	$20.00
65	Henry, O. - ***The Four Million*** [1940] Cover by Allen Pope.	$2.00	$6.00	$12.00
66	Bagnold, Enid - ***"National Velvet"*** [1940]	$2.50	$7.50	$15.00
67	Spyri, Johanna - ***Heidi*** [1940]	$3.50	$10.00	$20.00
68	Carnegie, Dale - ***How To Win Friends And Influence People*** [1940] Photo cover.	$1.50	$5.00	$10.00
69	Buchan, John - ***The 39 Steps*** [1940]	$4.00	$12.50	$25.00
70	MacDonald, Philip - ***Mystery Of The Dead Police*** [1940]	$4.00	$12.50	$25.00

		G	VG	F
71	Queen, Ellery - ***The French Powder Mystery*** [1940] Cover by Allen Pope.	$4.50	$14.00	$28.00
72	Montgomery, L.M. - ***Anne Of Windy Poplars*** [1940] Cover by Durban.	$2.00	$6.00	$12.00
73	Gardner, Erle Stanley - ***The Case Of The Velvet Claws*** [1940]	$3.50	$10.00	$20.00
74	Sayers, Dorothy L. - ***The Unpleasantness At The Bellona Club*** [1940]	$3.50	$10.00	$20.00
75	Alcott, Louisa May - ***Little Men*** [1940]	$2.50	$7.50	$15.00
76	Parker, Dorothy - ***Sunset Gun*** [1940]	$2.50	$7.50	$15.00
77	Queen, Ellery - ***The Roman Hat Mystery*** [1940] Cover by A. Pope.	$3.50	$10.00	$20.00
78	Raine, William Macleod - ***Oh, You Tex!*** [1940]	$2.50	$7.50	$15.00
79	Christie, Agatha - ***Murder In The Calais Coach*** [1940]	$3.50	$10.00	$20.00
80	Washington, Booker T. - ***Up From Slavery*** [1940]	$2.50	$7.50	$15.00
81	Milne, A.A. - ***The Red House Mystery*** [1940] Cover by Allen Pope.	$3.50	$10.00	$20.00
82	Sabatini, Rafael - ***Captain Blood*** [1940]	$2.50	$7.50	$15.00
83	Quentin, Patrick - ***A Puzzle For Fools*** [1940]	$3.50	$10.00	$20.00
84	Childers, Erskine - ***The Riddle Of The Sands*** [1940]	$2.50	$7.50	$15.00
85	Sayers, Dorothy L. - ***Clouds Of Witness*** [1940]	$3.50	$10.00	$20.00
86	Dickson, Carter - ***The Red Widow Murders*** [1940]	$4.00	$12.50	$25.00
87	Gilpatric, Guy - ***Mister Glencannon*** [1940]	$2.50	$7.50	$15.00
88	Christie, Agatha - ***The A.B.C. Murders*** [1941]	$3.50	$10.00	$20.00
89	Hilton, James - ***And Now Good-Bye*** [1941]	$2.50	$7.50	$15.00
90	Gardner, Erle Stanley - ***The Case Of The Sulky Girl*** [1941] Cover by Muni.	$3.50	$10.00	$20.00
91	Anthology edited by M.E. Speare - ***The Pocket Book Of Short Stories*** [1941]	$2.00	$6.00	$12.00
92	Bible - ***The Pocket Bible*** [1941]	$2.00	$6.00	$12.00
93	Hilton, James - ***Good-Bye, Mr. Chips*** [1941]	$2.00	$6.00	$12.00
94	Buchan, John - ***Greenmantle*** [1941]	$2.50	$7.50	$15.00
95	Doyle, A. Conan - ***The Sherlock Holmes Pocket Book*** [1941]	$4.50	$14.00	$28.00
96	Anthology - ***Ripley's Believe It Or Not!*** [1941]	$4.00	$12.50	$25.00
97	Endore, Guy - ***The Werewolf Of Paris*** [1941]	$6.00	$20.00	$40.00
98	Rinehart, Mary Roberts - ***The Circular Staircase*** [1941]	$3.50	$10.00	$20.00
99	Queen, Ellery - ***The Adventures Of Ellery Queen*** [1941]	$3.50	$10.00	$20.00
100	Booth, Charles - ***The General Died At Dawn*** [1941]	$2.50	$7.50	$15.00
101	Carr, John Dickson - ***It Walks By Night*** [1941]	$5.50	$17.50	$35.00
102	Barry, Philip - ***The Philadelphia Story*** [1941] Katharine Hepburn photo cover. Movie tie-in.	$2.50	$7.50	$15.00
103	Wright, Lee - editor - ***The Pocketbook Of Great Detectives*** [1941] PBO.	$2.50	$7.50	$15.00
104	Zola, Emile - ***Nana*** [1941]	$2.00	$6.00	$12.00
105	Crofts, Freeman Wills - ***Sir John Magill's Last Journey*** [1941]	$2.00	$6.00	$12.00
106	Gardner, Erle Stanley - ***The Case Of The Lucky Legs*** [1941]	$2.50	$7.50	$15.00
107	Wilson, Margery - ***Pocket Book Of Etiquette*** [1941] Photo cover.	$1.50	$5.00	$10.00
108	Anthology edited by Philip Van Doren Stern - ***The Pocket Reader*** [1941]	$2.00	$6.00	$12.00
109	Queen, Ellery - ***Siamese Twin Mystery*** [1941]	$3.00	$9.00	$18.00
110	Anthology - ***The Pocket Book Of Boners*** [1941] Cover and illustrations by Dr. Seuss.	$3.00	$9.00	$18.00
111	Frome, David - ***Mr. Pinkerton Finds A Body*** [1941]	$2.50	$7.50	$15.00
112	Stout, Rex - ***Fer-De-Lance*** [1941]	$3.00	$9.00	$18.00
113	Marsh, Ngaio - ***Enter A Murderer*** [1941]	$2.50	$7.50	$15.00
114	Shakespeare, William - ***Five Great Comedies*** [1941]	$1.50	$5.00	$10.00
115	Lewis, Sinclair - ***Dodsworth*** [1941]	$1.50	$5.00	$10.00
116	Gardner, Erle Stanley - ***The Case Of The Howling Dog*** [1941] Photo cover.	$2.50	$7.50	$15.00

		G	VG	F
117	Anthology edited by Lee Wright - ***The Pocket Book Of Mystery Stories*** [1941] PBO.	$2.00	$6.00	$12.00
118	Hilton, James - ***We Are Not Alone*** [1941] Movie tie-in with Paul Muni.	$1.50	$5.00	$10.00
119	Wells, H.G. - ***Pocket History Of The World*** [1941]	$2.00	$6.00	$12.00
120	Pitkin, Walter B. - ***Life Begins At 40*** [1941] Photo cover.	$1.50	$5.00	$10.00
121	Rinehart, Mary Roberts - ***The Album*** [1941] Cover by Silten.	$2.50	$7.50	$15.00
122	Ford, Leslie - ***The Simple Way Of Poison*** [1941]	$2.50	$7.50	$15.00
123	Stevenson, Robert Louis - ***Dr. Jekyll And Mr. Hyde*** [1941] Cover by Sol Immerman. Movie tie-in.	$5.00	$15.00	$30.00
124	Frome, David - ***Mr. Pinkerton Goes To Scotland Yard*** [1941]	$2.50	$7.50	$15.00
125	Queen, Ellery - ***The Tragedy Of X*** [1941]	$2.50	$7.50	$15.00
126	Dictionary - ***The Pocket Dictionary*** [1941]	$1.50	$5.00	$10.00
127	Anthology edited by Quincy Howe - ***The Pocket Book Of The War*** [1941] PBO. Cover by Silten.	$1.50	$5.00	$10.00
128	Translated by Edward Fitzgerald - ***The Rubaiyat Of Omar Khayyam*** [1941] PBO. Cover by Gordon Ross.	$1.50	$5.00	$10.00
129	Mason, Van Wyck - ***The Singapore Exile Murders*** [1941] Cover by Silten.	$2.50	$7.50	$15.00
130	Sayers, Dorothy L. - ***Strong Poison*** [1941]	$2.50	$7.50	$15.00
131	Woollcott, Alexander - ***While Rome Burns*** [1941]	$1.50	$5.00	$10.00
132	Slifer, Rose Jeanne & Crittenden, Louise - ***The Pocket Quiz Book*** [1941]	$1.35	$4.00	$8.00
133	Biggers, Earl Derr - ***The Black Camel*** [1941] Cover by Robert Holly.	$3.50	$10.00	$20.00
134	Queen, Ellery - ***The New Adventures Of Ellery Queen*** [1941]	$2.50	$7.50	$15.00
135	Kantor, MacKinlay - ***Long Remember*** [1942]	$1.50	$5.00	$10.00
136	Hilton, James - ***Without Armor*** [1941]	$1.50	$5.00	$10.00
137	Marsh, Ngaio - ***Death In A White Tie*** [1942]	$2.50	$7.50	$15.00
138	Gardner, Erle Stanley - ***The Case Of The Caretaker's Cat*** [1942]	$2.50	$7.50	$15.00
139	Miller, Douglas - ***You Can't Do Business With Hitler*** [1942]	$1.50	$5.00	$10.00
140	Rinehart, Mary Roberts - ***The Door*** [1942]	$2.50	$7.50	$15.00
141	Simenon - ***The Saint-Fiacre Affair*** [1942] Cover by Martinot.	$2.50	$7.50	$15.00
142	Anthology edited by Philip Van Doren Stern - ***The Pocket Companion*** [1942]	$1.50	$5.00	$10.00
143	Kaufman, George S. & Hart, Moss - ***The Man Who Came To Dinner*** [1942] Photo cover. Movie tie-in.	$2.50	$7.50	$15.00
144	Brand, Max - ***Singing Guns*** [1942] Cover by Doubrava.	$1.50	$5.00	$10.00
145	Anthology - ***Modern American Plays*** [1942]	$1.50	$5.00	$10.00
146	Queen, Ellery - ***The Spanish Cape Mystery*** [1942]	$2.50	$7.50	$15.00
147	Halliburton, Richard - ***The Royal Road To Romance*** [1942]	$1.50	$5.00	$10.00
148	Nissley, Charles H. - ***The Pocket Book Of Vegetable Gardening*** [1942]	$1.25	$3.75	$7.50
149	Vance, Ethel - ***Escape*** [1942]	$1.50	$5.00	$10.00
150	Baldwin, Faith - ***The Office Wife*** [1942]	$1.25	$3.75	$7.50
151	Paul, Elliot - ***Hugger-Mugger In The Louvre*** [1942]	$2.00	$6.00	$12.00
152	Disney, Dorothy Cameron - ***The Balcony*** [1942]	$2.00	$6.00	$12.00
153	Frome, David - ***The Man From Scotland Yard*** [1942]	$2.50	$7.50	$15.00
154	Crane, Stephen - ***The Red Badge Of Courage*** [1942] Cover by John Alan Maxwell.	$1.50	$5.00	$10.00
155	Kruif, Paul De - ***Hunger Fighters*** [1942]	$1.25	$3.75	$7.50
156	Dickson, Carter - ***The White Priory Murders*** [1942] Cover by Im-Ho.	$3.00	$9.00	$18.00
157	Gardner, Erle Stanley - ***The Case Of The Counterfeit Eye*** [1942]	$2.50	$7.50	$15.00
158	Runyon, Damon - ***Damon Runyon Favorites*** [1942]	$1.50	$5.00	$10.00
159	Struther, Jan - ***Mrs. Miniver*** [1942]	$1.50	$5.00	$10.00
160	Dimnet, Ernest - ***The Art Of Thinking*** [1942] Photo cover.	$1.25	$3.75	$7.50
161	Grey, Zane - ***The Spirit Of The Border*** [1942] Cover by Im-Ho.	$2.50	$7.50	$15.00

		G	VG	F
162	Lewis, Sinclair - ***Arrowsmith*** [1942]	$1.50	$5.00	$10.00
163	Sayers, Dorothy - ***Have His Carcass*** [1942] Cover by Im-Ho.	$2.50	$7.50	$15.00
164	Quentin, Patrick - ***Puzzle For Players*** [1942]	$2.50	$7.50	$15.00
165	Anthology edited by Shirley Cunningham - ***The Pocket Entertainer*** [1942] Cover by James Thurber	$1.50	$5.00	$10.00
166	Lockridge, Frances & Richard - ***The Norths Meet Murder*** [1942]	$2.50	$7.50	$15.00
167	Christie, Agatha - ***Peril At End House*** [1942]	$2.50	$7.50	$15.00
168	Biggers, Earl Derr - ***The Chinese Parrot*** [1942]	$3.00	$9.00	$18.00
169	Sharp, Margery - ***The Nutmeg Tree*** [1942]	$1.50	$5.00	$10.00
170	Kernan, W.F. - ***Defense Will Not Win The War*** [1942]	$1.25	$3.75	$7.50
171	Taylor, Phoebe Atwood - ***The Cape Cod Mystery*** [1942] Cover by Im-Ho.	$2.00	$6.00	$12.00
172	Anthology edited by Lee Wright - ***The Pocket Mystery Reader*** [1942]	$1.50	$5.00	$10.00
173	Taylor, Edmond - ***The Strategy Of Terror*** [1942] Cover by Im-Ho.	$1.50	$5.00	$10.00
174	Forester, C.S. - ***Beat To Quarters*** [1942] Cover by Maxwell.	$1.50	$5.00	$10.00
175	Douglas, Lloyd C. - ***Green Light*** [1942] Cover by Im-Ho.	$1.50	$5.00	$10.00
176	Anthology edited by Henry Davidoff - ***The Pocket Book Of Quotations*** [1942]	$1.25	$3.75	$7.50
177	Gardner, Erle Stanley - ***The Case Of The Curious Bride*** [1942]	$2.00	$6.00	$12.00
178	Anthology edited by Lewis Gannett - ***I Saw It Happen*** [1942] PBO.	$1.50	$5.00	$10.00
179	Queen, Ellery - ***The Greek Coffin Mystery*** [1942]	$2.00	$6.00	$12.00
180	Dickson, Carter - ***The Peacock Feather Murders*** [1942]	$2.50	$7.50	$15.00
181	Woody, Elizabeth - ***The Pocket Cook Book*** [1942]	$4.00	$12.50	$25.00
182	Anthology edited by Philip Van Doren Stern - ***The Pocket Book Of America*** [1942] PBO.	$1.50	$5.00	$10.00
183	Link, Dr. Henry C. - ***The Return To Religion*** [1943]	$1.25	$3.75	$7.50
184	Freeman, R. Austin - ***A Silent Witness*** [1942] Cover by Hoffman.	$2.00	$6.00	$12.00
185	Sayers, Dorothy - ***The Nine Tailors*** [1942] Cover by Silten.	$2.00	$6.00	$12.00
186	MacInnes, Helen - ***Above Suspicion*** [1942] Cover by Troop.	$2.00	$6.00	$12.00
187	Anthology edited by MacKinlay Kantor - ***The Pocketbook Of Dog Stories*** [1942] Cover by Hoffman.	$1.50	$5.00	$10.00
188	Nordhoff, Charles & Hall, James Norman - ***The Hurricane*** [1942] Cover by Barye Phillips.	$1.50	$5.00	$10.00
189	McKenney, Ruth - ***My Sister Eileen*** [1942]	$1.25	$3.75	$7.50
190	Bailey, H.C. - ***The Best Of Mr. Fortune Stories*** [1942] Cover by Hoffman.	$1.50	$5.00	$10.00
191	Biggers, Earl Derr - ***Behind That Curtain*** [1942] Cover by Hoffman.	$2.50	$7.50	$15.00
192	Reston, James B. - ***Prelude To Victory*** [1942]	$1.25	$3.75	$7.50
193	Ambler, Eric - ***Journey Into Fear*** [1943]	$1.50	$5.00	$10.00
194	Ziff, William B. - ***The Coming Battle Of Germany*** [1942] Photo cover.	$1.50	$5.00	$10.00
195	Nevins, Allan & Commager, Henry Steele - ***The Pocket History Of The United States*** [1942]	$1.50	$5.00	$10.00
196	Hammett, Dashiell - ***The Thin Man*** [1942] Cover by Hoffman.	$6.00	$20.00	$40.00
197	Anthology edited by Bennett Cerf - ***Pocket Book Of War Humor*** [1942] PBO. Cover by Ronay	$1.50	$5.00	$10.00
199	Kesselring, Joseph - ***Arsenic And Old Lace*** [1942]	$2.00	$6.00	$12.00
200	Free, Montague - ***The Pocket Book Of Flower Gardening*** [1943]	$1.50	$5.00	$10.00
201	Gardner, Erle Stanley - ***The Case Of The Stuttering Bishop*** [1943]	$2.00	$6.00	$12.00
202	Queen, Ellery - ***The Dutch Shoe Mystery*** [1942]	$2.00	$6.00	$12.00
203	Davies, Joseph E. - ***Mission To Moscow*** [1943]	$1.50	$5.00	$10.00
204	Taylor, Phoebe Atwood - ***Death Lights A Candle*** [1943]	$1.50	$5.00	$10.00

Pocket Books, 241

Pocket Books, 337

Pocket Books, 389

		G	VG	F
205	DuMaurier, Daphne - ***Rebecca*** [1943] Cover by Hoffman.	$1.35	$4.00	$8.00
206	Hargrove, Marion - ***See Here, Private Hargrove*** [1943] Photo cover.	$1.35	$4.00	$8.00
207	Biggers, Earl Derr - ***Charlie Chan Carries On*** [1943]	$2.50	$7.50	$15.00
208	Stout, Rex - ***The Rubber Band*** [1943]	$2.00	$6.00	$12.00
209	Smith, Thorne - ***Topper Takes A Trip*** [1943] Cover by Barye Phillips.	$1.50	$5.00	$10.00
210	Petherbridge, Margaret - ***The Pocket Book Of Crossword Puzzles*** [1943] PBO.	$8.00	$25.00	$50.00
211	Hammett, Dashiell - ***The Glass Key*** [1943] Cover by Leo Manso.	$6.00	$20.00	$40.00
212	Chandler, Raymond - ***Farewell, My Lovely*** [1943]	$6.00	$20.00	$40.00
213	Anthology edited by Anthony Boucher - ***The Pocket Book Of True Crime Stories*** [1943] PBO.	$3.50	$10.00	$20.00
214	Anthology - ***The Pocket Book Of Science Fiction*** [1943] PBO.	$5.50	$17.50	$35.00
215	Douglas, Lloyd C. - ***Magnificent Obsession*** [1943]	$1.35	$4.00	$8.00
216	Nordhoff & Hall - ***Mutiny On The Bounty*** [1943] Cover by Hoffman.	$1.35	$4.00	$8.00
217	Beveridge, Elizabeth - ***The Pocket Book Of Home Canning*** [1943] Cover by Hoffman.	$1.35	$4.00	$8.00
218	Franken, Rose - ***Claudia*** [1943] Cover by Jon Nielsen.	$1.35	$4.00	$8.00
219	Dickson, Carter - ***The Punch And Judy Murders*** [1943]	$2.50	$7.50	$15.00
220	Armstrong, M.D., Donald B. & Hallock, G. - ***What To Do Till The Doctor Comes*** [1943]	$1.35	$4.00	$8.00
221	Marsh, Ngaio - ***Overture To Death*** [1943]	$1.35	$4.00	$8.00
222	Page, Marco - ***Fast Company*** [1943]	$1.35	$4.00	$8.00
223	Gardner, Erle Stanley - ***The Case Of The Lame Canary*** [1943]	$1.35	$4.00	$8.00
224	Oppenheim, E. Phillips - ***The Great Impersonation*** [1943]	$1.35	$4.00	$8.00
225	Hersey, John - ***Into The Valley*** [1943]	$1.35	$4.00	$8.00
226	Waln, Nora - ***The House Of Exile*** [1943]	$1.35	$4.00	$8.00
227	Queen, Ellery - ***The Egyptian Cross Mystery*** [1943]	$1.35	$4.00	$8.00
228	Fair, A. A. - ***The Bigger They Come*** [1943] Cover by Hoffman.	$1.35	$4.00	$8.00
229	Willkie, Wendell L. - ***One World*** [1943] Photo cover.	$1.35	$4.00	$8.00
230	Figen, Milton - ***The Pocket Aviation Quiz Book*** [1943]	$1.50	$5.00	$10.00
231	Dickson, Carter - ***The Judas Window*** [1943] Cover by Leo Manso.	$1.50	$5.00	$10.00
232	Ambler, Eric - ***A Coffin For Dimitrios*** [1943]	$1.35	$4.00	$8.00
233	Cerf, Bennett - editor - ***The Pocketbook Of Cartoons*** [1943] PBO. Cover by Peter Arno. Cartoon book.	$1.35	$4.00	$8.00
234	Anthology - ***Vogue's Pocket Book Of Home Dressmaking*** [1943] PBO.	$1.35	$4.00	$8.00

		G	VG	F
235	MacInnes, Helen - ***Assignment Brittany*** [1943] Cover by Manso.	$1.35	$4.00	$8.00
236	Chesterton, G.K. - ***The Pocket Book Of Father Brown*** [1943] PBO. Cover by Manso.	$2.50	$7.50	$15.00
237	Rice, Craig - ***Trial By Fury*** [1943]	$2.00	$6.00	$12.00
238	Anthology - ***The Pocketbook Of Modern American Short Stories*** [1943]	$1.35	$4.00	$8.00
239	Hopper, Millard - ***How To Play Winning Checkers*** [1943]	$1.35	$4.00	$8.00
240	Flaubert, Gustave - ***Madame Bovary*** [1943]	$1.35	$4.00	$8.00
241	Hammett, Dashiell - ***Red Harvest*** [1943] Cover by Hoffman.	$5.00	$15.00	$30.00
242	Gardner, Erle Stanley - ***The Case Of The Substitute Face*** [1943]	$1.50	$5.00	$10.00
243	Steinbeck, John - ***The Steinbeck Pocket Book*** [1943] PBO. Cover by Manso.	$1.50	$5.00	$10.00
244	Lippmann, Walter - ***U.S. Foreign Policy*** [1943]	$1.35	$4.00	$8.00
245	Queen, Ellery - ***The Four Of Hearts*** [1943]	$1.50	$5.00	$10.00
246	Latimer, Jonathan - ***The Lady In The Morgue*** [1943] Cover by Leo Manso.	$1.50	$5.00	$10.00
247	Albrand, Martha - ***No Surrender*** [1943] Cover by Manso.	$1.50	$5.00	$10.00
248	Dine, S.S. Van - ***The Canary Murder Case*** [1943] Cover by Manso.	$1.50	$5.00	$10.00
249	Christie, Agatha - ***The Patriotic Murders*** [1943] Cover by Hoffman.	$1.50	$5.00	$10.00
250	Brand, Max - ***Destry Rides Again*** [1943] Cover by Hoffman.	$1.35	$4.00	$8.00
251	Anthology - ***The Ogden Nash Pocket Book*** [1953] PBO. Cover by Woods.	$1.35	$4.00	$8.00
252	Gardner, Erle Stanley - ***The Case Of The Dangerous Dowager*** [1943]	$1.50	$5.00	$10.00
253	Irish, William - ***Phantom Lady*** [1944] Cover by Leo Manso.	$4.00	$12.50	$25.00
254	King James Version - ***The New Testament*** [1943]	$1.35	$4.00	$8.00
255	Crittenden & Slifer - ***The New Pocket Quiz Book*** [1943]	$1.35	$4.00	$8.00
256	Dine, S.S. Van - ***The Greene Murder Case*** [1944]	$1.50	$5.00	$10.00
257	Charteris, Leslie - ***Enter The Saint*** [1944]	$1.50	$5.00	$10.00
258	Marquand, John P. - ***The Late George Apley*** [1944] Cover by Manso.	$1.35	$4.00	$8.00
259	Queen, Ellery - ***Halfway House*** [1944]	$1.50	$5.00	$10.00
259-V	Queen, Ellery - ***Halfway House*** [1944] Scarce variant edition. Oblong, stitched along the top. 1st printing stated.	$22.00	$70.00	$140.00
260	Morehead, Albert H. - ***The Pocket Book Of Games*** [1944] PBO. Cover by Manso.	$1.35	$4.00	$8.00
261	Christie, Agatha - ***And Then There Were None*** [1944] Cover by Lee Manso.	$1.50	$5.00	$10.00
262	Maugham, Somerset - ***The Somerset Maugham Pocketbook*** [1944] PBO.	$1.35	$4.00	$8.00
263	Gardner, Erle Stanley - ***The D.A. Calls It Murder*** [1944] Cover by Kantor.	$1.50	$5.00	$10.00
264	Hart, Frances Noyes - ***The Bellamy Trial*** [1944]	$1.35	$4.00	$8.00
265	Anthology - ***The Official AAF Guide Book*** [1944] Photo cover.	$1.35	$4.00	$8.00
266	Stettinius, Jr., Edward R. - ***Lend-Lease: Weapon For Victory*** [1944]	$1.35	$4.00	$8.00
267	Keith, Agnes Newton - ***Land Below The Wind*** [1944]	$1.35	$4.00	$8.00
268DJ	Hammett, Dashiell - ***The Maltese Falcon*** [1945] In dust-jacket.	$22.00	$70.00	$140.00
268	Hammett, Dashiell - ***The Maltese Falcon*** [1945]	$1.50	$5.00	$10.00
269	Bentley, E.C. - ***Trent's Last Case*** [1944] Cover by Hoffman.	$1.50	$5.00	$10.00
270	Queen, Ellery - ***The Devil To Pay*** [1944]	$1.50	$5.00	$10.00
271	Woolrich, Cornell - ***The Bride Wore Black*** [1945] Cover by Hoffman.	$3.50	$10.00	$20.00
272	Charteris, Leslie - ***The Happy Highwayman*** [1945]	$1.50	$5.00	$10.00
273	Sherrod, Robert - ***Tarawa*** [1944] Photo cover.	$1.35	$4.00	$8.00
274	Pyle, Ernie - ***Here Is Your War*** [1944]	$1.35	$4.00	$8.00

		G	VG	F
275	Hilton, James - ***Random Harvest*** [1944]	$1.35	$4.00	$8.00
276	Anthology - ***The Story Pocket Book*** [1944] PBO	$1.35	$4.00	$8.00
277	Gardner, Erle Stanley - ***The Case Of The Sleepwalker's Niece*** [1944]	$1.50	$5.00	$10.00
278	Carpenter, Margaret - ***Experiment Perilous*** [1944]	$1.50	$5.00	$10.00
279	Hersey, John - ***A Bell For Adano*** [1945]	$1.35	$4.00	$8.00
280	Day, Clarence - ***Life With Father*** [1943]	$1.35	$4.00	$8.00
281	Shute, Nevil - ***Pastoral*** [1945]	$1.35	$4.00	$8.00
282	Saroyan, William - ***The Human Comedy*** [1945] Cover by Don Freeman	$1.25	$3.75	$7.50
283	Queen, Ellery - ***Calamity Town*** [1945]	$1.50	$5.00	$10.00
284	Anthology edited by P.V.D. Stern - ***The Pocket Book Of Adventure Stories*** [1945] PBO.	$1.35	$4.00	$8.00
285	Christie, Agatha - ***Evil Under The Sun*** [1945]	$1.50	$5.00	$10.00
286	Ambler, Eric - ***Background To Danger*** [1945]	$1.50	$5.00	$10.00
287	Gardner, Erle Stanley - ***The D.A. Holds A Candle*** [1945]	$1.50	$5.00	$10.00
288	Lilienthal, David E. - ***TVA: Democracy On The March*** [1945]	$1.25	$3.75	$7.50
289	Rice, Craig - ***Having Wonderful Crime*** [1945]	$2.00	$6.00	$12.00
290	De La Roche, Mazo - ***Jalna*** [1945]	$1.25	$3.75	$7.50
291	Arranged by Arthur Hinds - ***The Complete Sayings Of Jesus*** [1945]	$1.25	$3.75	$7.50
292	Runyon, Damon - ***Take It Easy*** [1945] Photo cover	$1.25	$3.75	$7.50
293	Anthology - ***The Pocket Book Of Western Stories*** [1945]	$1.35	$4.00	$8.00
294	Anthology edited by Bennett Cerf - ***The Pocket Book Of Jokes*** [1945] Photo cover.	$1.25	$3.75	$7.50
295	Hammett, Dashiell - ***The Dain Curse*** [1945]	$6.00	$20.00	$40.00
296	Franken, Rose - ***Claudia And David*** [1945]	$1.25	$3.75	$7.50
297	Marsh, Ngaio - ***Death At The Bar*** [1945]	$1.50	$5.00	$10.00
298	Hatlo, Jimmy - ***They'll Do It Every Time*** [1945] Cover by Jimmy Hatlo. Cartoon book.	$2.50	$7.50	$15.00
299	Richards, I.A. - ***The Pocket Book Of Basic English*** [1945]	$1.25	$3.75	$7.50
300	Anthology edited by Donald Porter Geddes - ***Franklin Delano Roosevelt: A Memorial*** [1945] PBO.	$1.25	$3.75	$7.50
301	Haycox, Ernest - ***The Border Trumpet*** [1945]	$1.35	$4.00	$8.00
302	Seifert, Elizabeth - ***Young Doctor Galahad*** [1945]	$1.25	$3.75	$7.50
303	Dickson, Carter - ***The Reader Is Warned*** [1945]	$2.00	$6.00	$12.00
304	Upson, William Hazlett - ***Alexander Botts - Earthworm Tractors*** [1945] Cover by Bill Gillies.	$1.25	$3.75	$7.50
305	Van Dine, S. S. - ***The Bishop Murder Case*** [1945] Cover by Jonas	$1.50	$5.00	$10.00
306	Bemelmans, Ludwig - ***Small Beer*** [1945]	$1.35	$4.00	$8.00
307	Berkeley, Anthony - ***Trial And Error*** [1945]	$1.50	$5.00	$10.00
307(DJ)	Berkeley, Anthony - ***Trial And Error*** [1945] Dust-jacketed edition	$10.00	$30.00	$60.00
308	Anthology edited by Ted Malone - ***The Pocket Book Of Popular Verse*** [1945] PBO	$1.25	$3.75	$7.50
309	Zinsser, Hans - ***Rats, Lice And History*** [1945]	$1.25	$3.75	$7.50
310	Bower, B.M. - ***The Whoop-Up Trail*** [1945] Cover by Bill Gillies.	$1.35	$4.00	$8.00
311	Baldwin, Faith - ***White Collar Girl*** [1945] Cover by Harko	$1.25	$3.75	$7.50
312	Gardner, Erle Stanley - ***The Case Of The Shoplifter's Shoe*** [1945]	$1.50	$5.00	$10.00
313	Queen, Ellery - ***The Tragedy Of Y*** [1945]	$1.50	$5.00	$10.00
314	Smith, Thorne - ***The Bishop's Jaegers*** [1945] Cover by Herbert Roese	$1.50	$5.00	$10.00
315	Wilson, Mitchell - ***Stalk The Hunter*** [1945]	$1.25	$3.75	$7.50
316	Brand, Max - ***Fightin' Fool*** [1945]	$1.35	$4.00	$8.00
317	Watkin, Lawrence Edward - ***On Borrowed Time*** [1945]	$1.25	$3.75	$7.50
318	Gallico, Paul - ***Farewell To Sport*** [1945] Photo cover.	$1.25	$3.75	$7.50
319	Christie, Agatha - ***Easy To Kill*** [1945] Cover by Hawes	$1.50	$5.00	$10.00

		G	VG	F
320	Chandler, Raymond - ***The High Window*** [1945] Cover by E. McKnight Kauffer.	$6.00	$20.00	$40.00
321DJ	Taylor, Rosemary - ***Chicken Every Sunday*** [1945] Dust-jacketed edition. Movie tie-in.	$8.00	$25.00	$50.00
321	Taylor, Rosemary - ***Chicken Every Sunday*** [1945] Movie tie-in.	$1.25	$3.75	$7.50
322	Fast, Howard - ***The Last Frontier*** [1945]	$1.35	$4.00	$8.00
323	Crow, Carl - ***400 Million Customers*** [1945]	$1.25	$3.75	$7.50
324	Sayers, Dorothy L. - ***Busman's Honeymoon*** [1945]	$1.25	$3.75	$7.50
324(DJ)	Sayers, Dorothy L. - ***Busman's Honeymoon*** [1945] Dust-jacketed edition.	$8.00	$25.00	$50.00
325	London, Jack - ***The Sea Wolf*** [1945]	$2.00	$6.00	$12.00
326	Queen, Ellery - ***There Was An Old Woman*** [1945] Cover by Bill Gillies.	$1.50	$5.00	$10.00
327	Partridge, Bellamy - ***Country Lawyer*** [1945]	$1.25	$3.75	$7.50
328	MacDonald, Phillip - ***Warrant For X*** [1945]	$1.50	$5.00	$10.00
329	Allingham, Margery - ***The Fashion In Shrouds*** [1945]	$1.50	$5.00	$10.00
330	Jacobson, M.D., Edmund - ***You Must Relax*** [1945]	$1.25	$3.75	$7.50
331	Postgate, Raymond - ***Verdict Of Twelve*** [1945]	$1.50	$5.00	$10.00
332	Benson, Sally - ***Junior Miss*** [1945]	$1.25	$3.75	$7.50
333	Van Dine, S. S. - ***The Benson Murder Case*** [1946] Cover by Bill Gillies,,	$1.50	$5.00	$10.00
334	Gardner, Erle Stanley - ***The D.A. Draws A Circle*** [1946]	$1.50	$5.00	$10.00
335	Dickson, Carter - ***Nine-And Death Makes Ten*** [1945]	$2.00	$6.00	$12.00
336	Lawrence, Hilda - ***Blood Upon The Snow*** [1946]	$1.50	$5.00	$10.00
337	Mulford, Clarence E. - ***Hopalong Cassidy Returns*** [1945] Cover by Bill Gillies	$1.35	$4.00	$8.00
338	Anthology edited by Henry Steele Commager - ***The Pocket History Of The Second World War*** [1945]	$1.25	$3.75	$7.50
339	Cushman, Clarissa Fairchild - ***Young Widow*** [1945]	$1.25	$3.75	$7.50
340	Anthology edited by Donald Porter Geddes - ***The Atomic Age Opens*** [1945] PBO.	$1.25	$3.75	$7.50
341	Christie, Agatha - ***The Body In The Library*** [1945]	$1.50	$5.00	$10.00
342	Anthology edited by Louis Untermeyer - ***The Pocket Book Of Story Poems*** [1945] PBO.	$1.25	$3.75	$7.50
343	Whitman, Roger B. - ***First Aid For The Ailing House*** [1945]	$1.25	$3.75	$7.50
344	Stone, Irving - ***Lust For Life*** [1945]	$1.25	$3.75	$7.50
345	Cunningham, Eugene - ***The Spiderweb Trail*** [1945]	$1.35	$4.00	$8.00
346	Lockridge, Frances & Richard - ***A Pinch Of Poison*** [1945]	$1.50	$5.00	$10.00
347	Chamberlain, George Agnew - ***The Phantom Filly*** [1945]	$1.25	$3.75	$7.50
348	Field, Peter - ***Gringo Guns*** [1945]	$1.35	$4.00	$8.00
349	Keyes, Frances Parkinson - ***Fielding's Folly*** [1946]	$1.25	$3.75	$7.50
350	Carr, John Dickson - ***Death Turns The Tables*** [1946]	$2.00	$6.00	$12.00
351	Marsh, Ngaio - ***Colour Scheme*** [1946]	$1.50	$5.00	$10.00
352	Douglas, Lloyd C. - ***Disputed Passage*** [1946]	$1.25	$3.75	$7.50
353	Gooden, Arthur Henry - ***The Valley Of Dry Bones*** [1946]	$1.35	$4.00	$8.00
354	Johnston, Mary - ***To Have And To Hold*** [1946]	$1.25	$3.75	$7.50
355	Queen, Ellery - ***The Tragedy Of Z*** [1946]	$1.50	$5.00	$10.00
356	Hertzler, Arthur E. - ***The Horse And Buggy Doctor*** [1946]	$1.25	$3.75	$7.50
357	Stuart, Jesse - ***Taps For Private Tussie*** [1946]	$1.25	$3.75	$7.50
358	Nordhoff & Hall - ***Men Against The Sea*** [1946]	$1.25	$3.75	$7.50
359	Buck, Pearl S. - ***Dragon Seed*** [1946]	$1.25	$3.75	$7.50
360	Van Gelder, R. - editor - ***The Stephen Vincent Benet Pocket Book*** [1946]	$1.25	$3.75	$7.50
361	Rice, Craig - ***Home Sweet Homicide*** [1946]	$2.00	$6.00	$12.00
362	Curwood, James Oliver - ***Steele Of The Royal Mounted*** [1946]	$1.35	$4.00	$8.00
363	Burman, Ben Lucien - ***Steamboat Round The Bend*** [1946]	$1.25	$3.75	$7.50
364	Popkin, Zelda - ***The Journey Home*** [1946]	$1.25	$3.75	$7.50
365	Seton, Anya - ***Dragonwyck*** [1946] Cover by Troop.	$1.25	$3.75	$7.50
366	Johnson, Crockett - ***Barnaby*** [1946] Cartoon book.	$1.25	$3.75	$7.50

		G	VG	F
367	Riley, James Whitcomb - ***The Best-Loved Poems & Ballads Of James Whitcomb Riley*** [1946]	$1.25	$3.75	$7.50
368	Gardner, Earl Stanley - ***Murder Up My Sleeve*** [1946]	$1.50	$5.00	$10.00
369	Brand, Max - ***Silvertip*** [1946]	$1.35	$4.00	$8.00
370	Allen, Hervey - ***Action At Aquila*** [1946]	$1.25	$3.75	$7.50
371	Grey, Zane - ***The Last Trail*** [1946]	$1.50	$5.00	$10.00
372	Carr, John Dickson - ***The Emperor's Snuffbox*** [1946]	$1.50	$5.00	$10.00
373	Terhune, Albert Payson - ***Lad: A Dog*** [1946]	$1.25	$3.75	$7.50
374	Frost, Robert - ***The Pocket Book Of Robert Frost's Poems*** [1946]	$1.25	$3.75	$7.50
375	De La Roche, Mazo - ***Whiteoaks Of Jalna*** [1946]	$1.25	$3.75	$7.50
376	Lockridge, Frances & Richard - ***Murder Out Of Turn*** [1946]	$1.50	$5.00	$10.00
377	Spock, M.D., Benjamin - ***The Pocket Book Of Baby & Child Care*** [1946] Photo cover.	$1.25	$3.75	$7.50
378	Gardner, Erle Stanley - ***The Case Of The Perjured Parrot*** [1947]	$1.50	$5.00	$10.00
379	Haggard, M.D., Howard W. - ***Devils, Drugs And Doctors*** [1946]	$1.25	$3.75	$7.50
380	Baldwin, Faith - ***Medical Center*** [1946]	$1.25	$3.75	$7.50
381	Hull, Richard - ***The Murder Of My Aunt*** [1946] Cover by Kauffer.	$1.50	$5.00	$10.00
382	Fast, Howard - ***Freedom Road*** [1946]	$1.25	$3.75	$7.50
383	Anthology - ***Roget's Pocket Thesaurus*** [1946]	$1.25	$3.75	$7.50
384	Anthology edited by P.V.D. Stern - ***The Pocket Book Of Ghost Stories*** [1947]	$2.00	$6.00	$12.00
385	Rogers, Joel Townsley - ***The Red Right Hand*** [1946]	$1.50	$5.00	$10.00
386	Dickson, Carter - ***Seeing Is Believing*** [1946]	$2.00	$6.00	$12.00
387	Douglas, Lloyd C. - ***White Banners*** [1946]	$1.25	$3.75	$7.50
388	Anthology edited by David McCord - ***The Pocket Book Of Humerous Verse*** [1946]	$1.25	$3.75	$7.50
389	Chandler, Raymond - ***The Lady In The Lake*** [1946] Cover by Tom Dunn.	$4.00	$12.50	$25.00
390	Brand, Max - ***South Of The Rio Grande*** [1946]	$1.35	$4.00	$8.00
391	Rice, Craig - ***The Lucky Stiff*** [1947]	$1.50	$5.00	$10.00
392	Caldwell, Erskine - ***The Pocket Book Of Erskine Caldwell Stories*** [1947] Cover by Gressley.	$1.25	$3.75	$7.50
393	Janeway, Elizabeth - ***The Walsh Girls*** [1946]	$1.25	$3.75	$7.50
394	Hughes, Dorothy B. - ***The Bamboo Blonde*** [1946]	$1.50	$5.00	$10.00
395	Sharp, Margery - ***Cluny Brown*** [1946]	$1.25	$3.75	$7.50
396	Leacock, Stephen - ***Laugh With Leacock*** [1946] Cover by Gressley	$1.25	$3.75	$7.50
397	Anthology edited by Edward Weeks - ***The Pocket Atlantic*** [1946] PBO.	$1.25	$3.75	$7.50
398	Christie, Agatha - ***Towards Zero*** [1946] Cover by Troop.	$1.50	$5.00	$10.00
399	Teilhet, Darwin L. - ***The Fear Makers*** [1946]	$1.25	$3.75	$7.50
400	Curie, Eve (Biography) - ***Madame Curie*** [1946]	$1.25	$3.75	$7.50
401	Smith, Thorne - ***The Passionate Witch*** [1946] Cover by Herbert Roese.	$1.35	$4.00	$8.00
402	Kutak, Rosemary - ***Darkness Of Slumber*** [1946]	$1.25	$3.75	$7.50
403	Du Maurier, Daphne - ***Jamaica Inn*** [1946]	$1.25	$3.75	$7.50
404	Chase, Ilka - ***Past Imperfect*** [1946]	$1.25	$3.75	$7.50
405	Douglas, Lloyd C. - ***Forgive Us Our Trespasses*** [1946]	$1.25	$3.75	$7.50
406	Runyon, Damon - ***Runyon A La Carte*** [1946]	$1.25	$3.75	$7.50
407	Gardner, Erle Stanley - ***The D.A. Goes To Trial*** [1946] Cover by McCarthy.	$1.50	$5.00	$10.00
408	Russell, John - ***The Lost God And Other Adventure Stories*** [1946] PBO.	$2.00	$6.00	$12.00
409	Smith, Thorne - ***The Glorious Pool*** [1946] Cover by Herbert Roese.	$1.35	$4.00	$8.00
410	Hough, Emerson - ***The Covered Wagon*** [1946]	$1.35	$4.00	$8.00
411	Lockridge, Frances & Richard - ***Death On The Aisle*** [1946]	$1.50	$5.00	$10.00

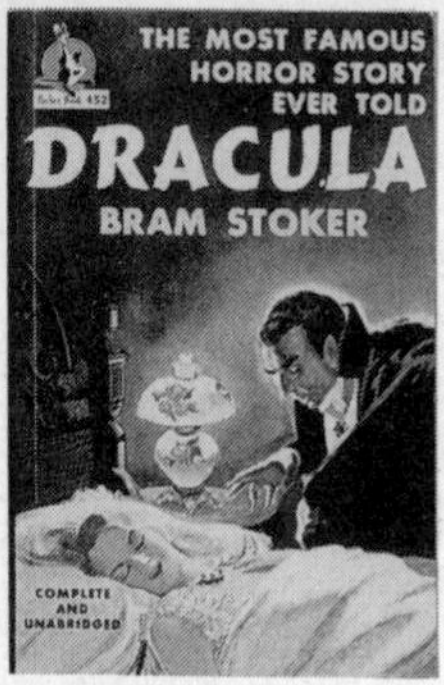

Pocket Books, 452

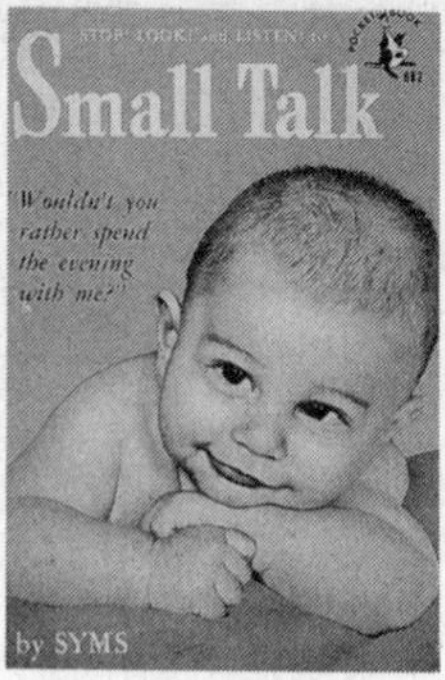

Pocket Books, 682

Pocket Books, 903

		G	VG	F
412	Haines, William Wister - ***Slim*** [1947]	$1.35	$4.00	$8.00
413	Richter, Conrad - ***The Sea Of Grass*** [1947] Cover by Troop. Movie tie in.	$1.35	$4.00	$8.00
414	Gardner, Erle Stanley - ***The Case Of The Baited Hook*** [1946]	$1.50	$5.00	$10.00
415	Du Maurier, Daphne - ***Frenchman's Creek*** [1946]	$1.25	$3.75	$7.50
416	Anthology - ***Bill Stern's Favorite Boxing Stories*** [1948] PBO. Photo cover.	$1.25	$3.75	$7.50
417	Arno, Peter - ***The Peter Arno Pocket Book*** [1945] PBO. Cover by Peter Arno. Cartoon book.	$1.25	$3.75	$7.50
418	Maugham, W. Somerset - ***The Razor's Edge*** [1946]	$1.25	$3.75	$7.50
419	Iles, Francis - ***Before The Fact*** [1947] Movie tie in.	$1.35	$4.00	$8.00
420	Quentin, Patrick - ***Puzzle For Puppets*** [1946]	$1.50	$5.00	$10.00
421	Anthology - ***The Merriam-Webster Pocket Dictionary*** [1947]	$1.25	$3.75	$7.50
422	Hughes, Dorothy B. - ***The Delicate Ape*** [1946]	$1.50	$5.00	$10.00
423	Brand, Max - ***The Fighting Four*** [1947]	$1.35	$4.00	$8.00
424	Anthology edited by Louis Untermeyer - ***The Pocket Treasury*** [1946] PBO.	$1.25	$3.75	$7.50
425	Lee, Gypsy Rose - ***The G-String Murders*** [1947]	$1.50	$5.00	$10.00
426	Ripley, Robert L. - ***The Second Believe It Or Not*** [1948]	$2.50	$7.50	$15.00
427	Armstrong, Charlotte - ***The Innocent Flower*** [1947]	$1.50	$5.00	$10.00
428	Smith, Thorne - ***The Night Life Of The Gods*** [1947] Cover by Jaro Fabry.	$1.35	$4.00	$8.00
429	Hough, Emerson - ***North Of Thirty Six*** [1947]	$1.25	$3.75	$7.50
430	Fowler, Gene - ***Good Night, Sweet Prince*** [1947] Photo cover. Biography of John Barrymore.	$1.25	$3.75	$7.50
431	Anthology edited by Eric Swenson - ***The Pocket Book Of Famous French Short Stories*** [1947]	$1.25	$3.75	$7.50
432	Iles, Francis - ***Malice Aforethought*** [1947]	$1.50	$5.00	$10.00
433	Werfel, Franz - ***The Song Of Bernadette*** [1947]	$1.25	$3.75	$7.50
434	Rice, Craig - ***The Sunday Pigeon Murders*** [1947]	$2.00	$6.00	$12.00
435	Marshall, Bruce - ***Father Malachy's Miracle*** [1947] Cover by Gressley	$1.35	$4.00	$8.00
436	Carr, John Dickson - ***The Lost Gallows*** [1947]	$2.00	$6.00	$12.00
437	Marsh, Ngaio - ***Death And The Dancing Footman*** [1947]	$1.50	$5.00	$10.00
438	Gardner, Erle Stanley - ***The Clue Of The Forgotten Murder*** [1947]	$1.50	$5.00	$10.00
439	Lawrence, Hilda - ***A Time To Die*** [1947]	$1.50	$5.00	$10.00
440	Norris, Kathleen - ***Wife For Sale*** [1947] Photo cover.	$1.25	$3.75	$7.50
441	Wright, Harold Bell - ***The Shepherd Of The Hills*** [1947]	$1.25	$3.75	$7.50
442	Janeway, Elizabeth - ***Daisy Kenyon*** [1947]	$1.25	$3.75	$7.50

		G	VG	F
443	Cain, James M. - ***The Postman Always Rings Twice*** [1947] Cover by Tom Dunn.	$2.50	$7.50	$15.00
444	Armstrong, Charlotte - ***The Unsuspected*** [1947]	$1.50	$5.00	$10.00
445	Baldwin, Faith - ***Private Duty*** [1947]	$1.25	$3.75	$7.50
446	Henry, O. - ***The Pocket Book Of O. Henry Prize Stories*** [1947] PBO.	$1.25	$3.75	$7.50
447	Smith, Thorne - ***Turnabout*** [1947]	$1.35	$4.00	$8.00
448	Carr, John Dickson - ***Castle Skull*** [1947]	$2.00	$6.00	$12.00
449	Benchley, Robert - ***My Ten Years In A Quandary*** [1947] Cover by Gluyas Williams.	$1.35	$4.00	$8.00
450	Petherbridge, Margaret - ***The Second Pocket Book Of Crossword Puzzles*** [1947] PBO.	$6.00	$20.00	$40.00
451	Christie, Agatha - ***Remembered Death*** [1947]	$1.50	$5.00	$10.00
452	Stoker, Bram - ***Dracula*** [1947]	$4.00	$12.50	$25.00
453	Norris, Kathleen - ***Mystery House*** [1947]	$1.50	$5.00	$10.00
454	Hughes, Dorothy B. - ***Dread Journey*** [1947]	$1.50	$5.00	$10.00
455	Traven, B. - ***The Treasure Of The Sierra Madre*** [1948] Barye Phillips "Bogart" cover. Movie tie-in with Bogart.	$2.50	$7.50	$15.00
456	Baldwin, Faith - ***District Nurse*** [1947]	$1.00	$3.00	$6.00
457	Nordhoff, Charles & Hall, James Norman - ***Pitcairn's Island*** [1947]	$1.25	$3.75	$7.50
458	Dowst, Robert S. - ***Win, Place And Show*** [1948] Photo cover.	$1.25	$3.75	$7.50
459	Queen, Ellery - ***The Dragon's Teeth*** [1947]	$2.50	$7.50	$15.00
460	Quentin, Patrick - ***Slay The Loose Ladies*** [1948] Cover by Roswell Keller.	$1.50	$5.00	$10.00
461	Rice, Craig - ***The Thursday Turkey Murders*** [1948] Cover by William Wirtz.	$2.00	$6.00	$12.00
462	Llewellyn, Richard - ***How Green Was My Valley*** [1947] Movie tie-in.	$1.25	$3.75	$7.50
463	Greig, Maysie - ***Doctor's Wife*** [1947]	$1.00	$3.00	$6.00
464	Gardner, Erle Stanley - ***The Case Of The Rolling Bones*** [1947]	$1.50	$5.00	$10.00
465	Christie, Agatha - ***Death Comes As The End*** [1947]	$1.50	$5.00	$10.00
466	Haycox, Ernest - ***Rim Of The Desert*** [1947]	$1.35	$4.00	$8.00
467	Rider, Brett - ***Circle C Moves In*** [1947]	$1.35	$4.00	$8.00
468	Gardner, Erle Stanley - ***The Case Of The Silent Partner*** [1948] Cover by Reynold Brown.	$1.50	$5.00	$10.00
469	Marshall, Rosamond - ***Kitty*** [1947] Cover by Troop.	$1.25	$3.75	$7.50
470	Aldrich, Bess Streeter - ***A Lantern In Her Hand*** [1947]	$1.25	$3.75	$7.50
471	Queen, Ellery - ***The Door Between*** [1947]	$1.50	$5.00	$10.00
472	Green, F.L. - ***Odd Man Out*** [1947] Movie photo cover. Movie tie-in.	$1.35	$4.00	$8.00
473	Raine, William MacLeod - ***Under Northern Stars*** [1947]	$1.35	$4.00	$8.00
474	Asbury, Herbert - ***The Barbary Coast*** [1947]	$1.25	$3.75	$7.50
475	Marsh, Ngaio - ***Death Of A Peer*** [1947]	$1.50	$5.00	$10.00
476	Rice, Craig - ***The Corpse Steps Out*** [1947]	$1.50	$5.00	$10.00
477	Boccaccio, Giovanni - ***Tales From The Decameron*** [1947] Cover by Mac Harshberger.	$1.25	$3.75	$7.50
478	Dickson, Carter - ***Death And The Gilded Man*** [1947]	$2.00	$6.00	$12.00
479	Smith, Thorne - ***Did She Fall?*** [1947] Cover by Herbert Roese.	$1.35	$4.00	$8.00
480	Norris, Kathleen - ***Passion Flower*** [1947]	$1.25	$3.75	$7.50
481	Perkins, J.R. - ***The Emperor's Physician*** [1947]	$1.25	$3.75	$7.50
482	Bristow, Gwen - ***Deep Summer*** [1947]	$1.25	$3.75	$7.50
483	Du Maurier, Daphne - ***The King's General*** [1947] Cover by Kolada.	$1.25	$3.75	$7.50
484	Helseth, Henry Edward - ***The Chair For Martin Rome*** [1948] Movie cover. Movie tie-in.	$1.25	$3.75	$7.50
485	Christie, Agatha - ***The Hollow*** [1948]	$1.50	$5.00	$10.00
486	Hutchinson, A.S.M. - ***If Winter Comes*** [1947] Photo cover. Movie tie-in.	$1.35	$4.00	$8.00

		G	VG	F
487	Raine, William MacLeod - ***The Yukon Trail*** [1948] Cover by Barye Phillips.	$1.35	$4.00	$8.00
488	Norris, Kathleen - ***Walls Of Gold*** [1948] Cover by Earl Cordrey.	$1.25	$3.75	$7.50
489	Wilson, Earl - ***I Am Gazing Into My 8-Ball*** [1948] Cover by John Groth.	$1.25	$3.75	$7.50
490	Smith, Thorne - ***Skin And Bones*** [1948] Cover by Herbert Roese.	$1.35	$4.00	$8.00
491	Brand, Max - ***The Border Kid*** [1947] Cover by Roswell Keller.	$1.35	$4.00	$8.00
492	Lawrence, Hilda - ***The Deadly Pavilion*** [1947]	$1.50	$5.00	$10.00
493	Knight, Eric - ***The Flying Yorkshireman*** [1948] Cover by Louis Glanzman.	$1.25	$3.75	$7.50
494	Anthology - ***Bill Stern's Favorite Sport Stories*** [1947] Photo cover.	$1.25	$3.75	$7.50
495	Wodehouse, P.G. - ***Carry On, Jeeves!*** [1948] Cover by Louis Glanzman.	$1.25	$3.75	$7.50
496	Gould, John - ***Farmer Takes A Wife*** [1948]	$1.25	$3.75	$7.50
497	Twain, Mark - ***A Connecticut Yankee In King Arthur's Court*** [1948] Cover by Frederick Banbery.	$1.35	$4.00	$8.00
498	Frank, Pat - ***Mr. Adam*** [1948] Cover by Barye Phillips.	$1.25	$3.75	$7.50
499	Franken, Rose - ***Another Claudia*** [1948] Cover by Barye Phillips.	$1.25	$3.75	$7.50
500	Exner, M.D., M.J. - ***The Sexual Side Of Marriage*** [1947]	$1.25	$3.75	$7.50
501	Lockridge, Frances & Richard - ***Payoff For The Banker*** [1948] Cover by Beck.	$1.50	$5.00	$10.00
502	Haines, William Wister - ***High Tension*** [1948] Cover by Milton Wolsky.	$1.25	$3.75	$7.50
503	Jones, Guy & Constance - ***Peabody's Mermaid*** [1948] Movie cover. Movie tie-in.	$1.25	$3.75	$7.50
504	Anthology edited by Frank Scully - ***Fun In Bed*** [1948] Cover by Barye Phillips.	$1.25	$3.75	$7.50
505	Hodgins, Eric - ***Mr. Blandings Builds His Dream House*** [1948] Cover by William Steig. Movie tie-in.	$1.25	$3.75	$7.50
506	Mitford, Nancy - ***The Pursuit Of Love*** [1949] Cover by Malvin Singer.	$1.25	$3.75	$7.50
507	Dickson, Carter - ***She Died A Lady*** [1948] Cover by Barye Phillips.	$1.50	$5.00	$10.00
508	Moore, Ruth - ***Deep Waters*** [1948] Movie photo cover. Movie tie-in.	$1.35	$4.00	$8.00
509	Brand, Max - ***The Stolen Stallion*** [1948] Cover by Roswell Keller.	$1.35	$4.00	$8.00
510	Henry, O. - ***The Pocket Book Of O. Henry*** [1948] Cover by Curt Witt.	$1.25	$3.75	$7.50
511	Rich, Louise Dickinson - ***We Took To The Woods*** [1948]	$1.25	$3.75	$7.50
512	Gardner, Erle Stanley - ***This Is Murder*** [1948] Cover by Milton Wolsky.	$1.50	$5.00	$10.00
513	Baldwin, Faith - ***Rehearsal For Love*** [1948] Cover by Ardis Hughes.	$1.25	$3.75	$7.50
514	Holmes, L.P. - ***Flame Of Sunset*** [1948] Cover by Milton Wolsky.	$1.35	$4.00	$8.00
515	Tolstoy, Leo - ***Anna Karenina*** [1948] Movie photo cover. Movie tie-in with Vivien Leigh.	$1.25	$3.75	$7.50
516	Michener, James A. - ***Tales Of The South Pacific*** [1948] Cover by Harvey Kidder.	$1.25	$3.75	$7.50
517	Queen, Ellery - ***The Murderer Is A Fox*** [1948] Cover by Thompson.	$1.50	$5.00	$10.00
518	Smith, Thorne - ***The Stray Lamb*** [1948]	$1.35	$4.00	$8.00
519	Dickens, Charles - ***Oliver Twist*** [1948] Photo cover.	$1.50	$5.00	$10.00
520	Hancock, Lucy Agnes - ***Student Nurse*** [1948] Cover by Roswell Keller.	$1.00	$3.00	$6.00

		G	VG	F
521	Fischer, Bruno - ***More Deaths Than One*** [1948] Cover by William Wirtz.	$1.50	$5.00	$10.00
522	Jastrow, Joseph - ***Freud: His Dream And Sex Theories*** [1948]	$1.25	$3.75	$7.50
523	Brand, Max - ***The Longhorn Feud*** [1948] Cover by John Blaine.	$1.35	$4.00	$8.00
524	Huggins, Roy - ***The Double Take*** [1948] Cover by Harvey Kidder.	$1.50	$5.00	$10.00
525	Norris, Kathleen - ***The Foolish Virgin*** [1948] Cover by Barye Phillips.	$1.25	$3.75	$7.50
526	Stewart, Ramona - ***Desert Town*** [1948] Cover by Roswell Keller.	$1.35	$4.00	$8.00
527	Marsh, Ngaio - ***Final Curtain*** [1948] Cover by Barye Phillips.	$1.50	$5.00	$10.00
528	Rice, Craig - ***The Big Midget Murders*** [1948] Cover by Harvey Kidder.	$2.00	$6.00	$12.00
529	Anthology edited by Louis Untermeyer - ***The Pocket Book Of American Poems*** [1948] Cover by Curt Witt.	$1.25	$3.75	$7.50
530	Elston, Allan V. - ***Guns On The Cimarron*** [1948] Cover by Benton Clark.	$1.35	$4.00	$8.00
531	Haycox, Ernest - ***Saddle And Ride*** [1948] Cover by Roswell Keller.	$1.35	$4.00	$8.00
532	Shakespear, William - ***Four Great Tragedies*** [1948] Cover by Philip Grushkin.	$1.25	$3.75	$7.50
533	Shakespear, William - ***Four Great Comedies*** [1948] Cover by Philip Grushkin.	$1.25	$3.75	$7.50
534	Seton, Anya - ***The Turquoise*** [1948] Cover by Jane Gilbert.	$1.35	$4.00	$8.00
535	Webb, Mary - ***Precious Bane*** [1949] Cover by Harvey Kidder.	$1.25	$3.75	$7.50
536	Lehmann, Rosamond - ***The Ballad And The Source*** [1948] Cover by Barye Phillips.	$1.25	$3.75	$7.50
537	Page, Marco - ***The Shadowy Third*** [1949] Cover by Harvey Kidder.	$1.25	$3.75	$7.50
538	Carson, Robert - ***You Got To Stay Happy*** [1948] Cover by Barye Phillips.	$1.25	$3.75	$7.50
539	Lindsay, Norman - ***Age Of Consent*** [1948] Cover by Norman Lindsay.	$1.25	$3.75	$7.50
540	Lawrence, Hilda - ***Death Of A Doll*** [1948] Cover by Hedley Rainnie.	$1.50	$5.00	$10.00
541	Greig, Maysie - ***Professional Lover*** [1948] Photo cover.	$1.25	$3.75	$7.50
542	Rider, Brett - ***Death Stalks The Range*** [1948] Cover by William Wirtz.	$1.35	$4.00	$8.00
543	Kains, M.G. - ***Five Acres And Independence*** [1948] Cover by Roswell Keller.	$1.25	$3.75	$7.50
544	Gardner, Erle Stanley - ***The Case Of The Turning Tide*** [1948] Cover by Stanley Dersh.	$1.50	$5.00	$10.00
545	Anthology edited by Ernest Heyn - ***The Pocket Book Of True Stories*** [1948] PBO. Photo cover.	$1.25	$3.75	$7.50
546	Smith, Thorne - ***Rain In The Doorway*** [1949] Cover by Herbert Roese.	$1.35	$4.00	$8.00
547	Brand, Max - ***Silvertip's Strike*** [1948] Cover by John Blaine.	$1.35	$4.00	$8.00
548	Blake, Nicholas - ***Minute For Murder*** [1949] Cover by Elmore Brown.	$1.50	$5.00	$10.00
549	Norris, Kathleen - ***Younger Sister*** [1948] Cover by Barye Phillips.	$1.25	$3.75	$7.50
550	Heggen, Thomas - ***Mister Roberts*** [1948] Cover by Harvey Kidder.	$1.25	$3.75	$7.50
551	Hawthorne, Nathaniel - ***The Scarlet Letter*** [1948] Cover by Lorin Thompson.	$1.25	$3.75	$7.50
552	Eliot, George - ***Silas Marner*** [1948] Cover by Frederick Banbery.	$1.25	$3.75	$7.50
553	Hazlitt, Henry - ***Economics In One Lesson*** [1948] Cover by Charles Skaggs.	$1.00	$3.00	$6.00

		G	VG	F
554	Cunningham, Eugene - ***Texas Triggers*** [1948] Cover by Roswell Keller.	$1.35	$4.00	$8.00
555	Anthology - ***Bill Stern's Favorite Football Stories*** [1948] Photo cover.	$1.25	$3.75	$7.50
556	Papashvily, George & Helen - ***Anything Can Happen*** [1948] Cover by Paul Galdone.	$1.25	$3.75	$7.50
557	Eustis, Helen - ***The Horizontal Man*** [1948] Photo cover.	$1.50	$5.00	$10.00
558	Masur, Harold Q. - ***Bury Me Deep*** [1948] Cover by William Wirts.	$1.50	$5.00	$10.00
559	Merimee, Prosper - ***The Loves Of Carmen*** [1948] PBO. Cover by Bradshaw Crandell. Movie tie-in.	$1.25	$3.75	$7.50
560	Shearing, Joseph - ***So Evil My Love*** [1948]	$1.50	$5.00	$10.00
561	Gardner, Erle Stanley - ***The D.A. Cooks A Goose*** [1950] Cover by Barye Phillips.	$1.50	$5.00	$10.00
562	Considine, Bob - ***The Babe Ruth Story*** [1948]	$2.50	$7.50	$15.00
563	Newton, D.B. - ***Range Boss*** [1948] PBO. Cover by Joseph Szokoli.	$1.35	$4.00	$8.00
564	Goudge, Elizabeth - ***A City Of Bells*** [1948] Cover by Frederick Banbery.	$1.25	$3.75	$7.50
565	Asbury, Herbert - ***The French Quarter*** [1949] Cover by Curt Witt.	$1.25	$3.75	$7.50
566	MacDonald, Betty - ***The Egg And I*** [1948] Photo cover.	$1.25	$3.75	$7.50
567	Field, Peter - ***Outlaws Three*** [1949] Cover by Harvey Kidder.	$1.35	$4.00	$8.00
568	Dickson, Carter - ***The Curse Of The Bronze Lamp*** [1949] Cover by Louis Glanzman.	$2.00	$6.00	$12.00
569	Funk, Wilfred & Lewis, Norman - ***30 Days To A More Powerful Vocabulary*** [1949]	$1.00	$3.00	$6.00
570	Woolrich, Cornell - ***Rendezvous In Black*** [1949] Cover by William Wirts.	$3.50	$10.00	$20.00
571	Haines, William Wister - ***Command Decision*** [1949] Clark Gable photo cover. Movie tie-in.	$1.35	$4.00	$8.00
572	Anthology - ***Bill Stern's Favorite Baseball Stories*** [1949] Photo cover.	$1.25	$3.75	$7.50
573	Haycox, Ernest - ***Sundown Jim*** [1949] Cover by John Blaine.	$1.35	$4.00	$8.00
574	Greig, Maysie - ***Unmarried Couple*** [1949] Cover by Malvin Singer.	$1.25	$3.75	$7.50
575	Armstrong, Charlotte - ***The Chocolate Cobweb*** [1949] Cover by Roswell Keller.	$1.50	$5.00	$10.00
576	Landon, Margaret - ***Anna And The King Of Siam*** [1949] Cover by William Wills.	$1.35	$4.00	$8.00
577	Yerby, Frank - ***The Foxes Of Harrow*** [1949] Cover by Lynd Ward.	$1.25	$3.75	$7.50
578	Anthology edited by Herman Wechsler - ***The Pocket Book Of Old Masters*** [1949] PBO.	$1.35	$4.00	$8.00
579	Craven, Thomas - ***Famous Artists And Their Models*** [1949]	$1.35	$4.00	$8.00
580	Anthology edited by Jerome S. Meyer - ***Fun For The Family*** [1949] Cover by Jack Moment.	$1.25	$3.75	$7.50
581	Maugham, W. Somerset - ***The Painted Veil*** [1949] Cover by Roswell Keller.	$1.25	$3.75	$7.50
582	Brean, Herbert - ***Wilders Walk Away*** [1949] Cover by Cliff Young.	$1.25	$3.75	$7.50
583	Walker, Dorothy P. - ***Dr. Whitney's Secretary*** [1949] Cover by Barye Phillips.	$1.00	$3.00	$6.00
584	Brand, Max - ***King Of The Range*** [1949] Cover by Bernard Safran.	$1.35	$4.00	$8.00
585	Elston, Allan Vaughan - ***Hit The Saddle*** [1949] Cover by Dom Lupo.	$1.35	$4.00	$8.00
586	Anthology edited by Philip Van Doren Stern - ***The Pocket Week-End Book*** [1949] PBO.	$1.25	$3.75	$7.50

		G	VG	F
587	Hughes, Dorothy B. - ***In A Lonely Place*** [1949] Cover by Frank McCarthy.	$1.50	$5.00	$10.00
588	Slater, Humphrey - ***Conspirator*** [1949] Cover by Harvey Kidder.	$1.25	$3.75	$7.50
589	Bristow, Gwen - ***The Handsome Road*** [1949] Cover by Jon Nielsen.	$1.25	$3.75	$7.50
590	Gardner, Erle Stanley - ***The Case Of The Haunted Husband*** [1949] Cover by Bernard Safran.	$1.50	$5.00	$10.00
591	Schmitt, Gladys - ***Alexandra*** [1949] Cover by Jon Nielsen.	$1.25	$3.75	$7.50
592	Shearing, Joseph - ***The Strange Case Of Lucile Clery*** [1949] Cover by Louis Glanzman.	$1.50	$5.00	$10.00
593	London, Jack - ***The Call Of The Wild*** [1949]	$2.00	$6.00	$12.00
594	Haycox, Ernest - ***Deep West*** [1949] Cover by Joseph Camana.	$1.35	$4.00	$8.00
595	Gardner, Erle Stanley - ***The D.A. Calls A Turn*** [1948] Cover by William Wirts.	$1.50	$5.00	$10.00
596	Cerf, Bennett - ***Try And Stop Me*** [1949]	$1.25	$3.75	$7.50
597	Scott, Natalie Anderson - ***The Story Of Mrs. Murphy*** [1949]	$1.25	$3.75	$7.50
598	Wiggam, Albert Edward - ***Let's Explore Your Mind*** [1949] PBO.	$1.25	$3.75	$7.50
599	Norris, Kathleen - ***Secret Marriage*** [1949] Cover by Malvin Singer.	$1.00	$3.00	$6.00
600	Guthrie, Jr., A.B. - ***The Big Sky*** [1949] Cover by Alan Haemer.	$1.35	$4.00	$8.00
601	Widdemer, Margaret - ***Lani*** [1949] Cover by Graves.	$1.25	$3.75	$7.50
603	Baldwin, Faith - ***Woman On Her Way*** [1949] Cover by Barye Phillips.	$1.25	$3.75	$7.50
604	Bonham, Frank - ***Lost Stage Valley*** [1949] Cover by Edward L. Chase.	$1.35	$4.00	$8.00
605	Norris, Kathleen - ***Burned Fingers*** [1949] Cover by Barye Phillips.	$1.00	$3.00	$6.00
606	Bax, Roger - ***Disposing Of Henry*** [1949] Cover by Harvey Kidder.	$1.25	$3.75	$7.50
607	Anthology edited by Barthold Fles - ***7 Short Novels From The Woman's Home Companion*** [1949]	$1.25	$3.75	$7.50
608	Haycox, Ernest - ***Action By Night*** [1949] Cover by Bernard Safran.	$1.35	$4.00	$8.00
609	Brand, Max - ***Valley Of Vanishing Men*** [1949] Cover by Keith Ward.	$1.35	$4.00	$8.00
610	Cody, Al - ***West Of The Law*** [1949] Cover by Dom Lupo.	$1.35	$4.00	$8.00
611	Raine, William MacLeod - ***Square-Shooter*** [1949] Cover by Elmore Brown.	$1.35	$4.00	$8.00
612	Melville, Herman - ***Moby Dick*** [1949]	$1.25	$3.75	$7.50
614	Quentin, Patrick - ***Love Is A Deadly Weapon*** [1949] Cover by Frank McCarthy.	$1.50	$5.00	$10.00
615	Smith, H. Allen - ***Desert Island Decameron*** [1949] Cover by Leo Hershfield.	$1.25	$3.75	$7.50
616	Kipling, Rudyard - ***Kim*** [1949] Cover by John Pike.	$1.50	$5.00	$10.00
618	Maurer, David W. - ***The Big Con*** [1949]	$1.35	$4.00	$8.00
619	Gardner, Erle Stanley - ***The Case Of The Empty Tin*** [1949] Cover by Barye Phillips.	$1.50	$5.00	$10.00
620	Rider, Brett - ***Circle C Carries On*** [1949] Cover by Frank McCarthy.	$1.35	$4.00	$8.00
621	Capp, Al - ***The Life And Times Of The Shmoo*** [1949] Cover by the author. Cartoon book.	$5.00	$15.00	$30.00
622	Simon, Henry W. & Veinus, Abraham - ***The Pocket Book Of Great Operas*** [1949] Cover by Charles Skaggs.	$1.25	$3.75	$7.50
623	Cannon, Cornelia James - ***Red Rust*** [1949] Cover by Harvey Kidder.	$1.25	$3.75	$7.50
624	Ellington, Richard - ***Shoot The Works*** [1949] Cover by Roswell Keller.	$1.50	$5.00	$10.00
625	Norris, Kathleen - ***Mink Coat*** [1949]	$1.00	$3.00	$6.00

		G	VG	F
626	Marsh, Ngaio - ***Died In The Wool*** [1949] Cover by Bernard Safran.	$1.50	$5.00	$10.00
627	Foreman, L. L. - ***The Renegade*** [1949] Cover by Lorin Thompson.	$1.35	$4.00	$8.00
628	Anthology edited by Scott Meredith - ***The Best Of Wodehouse*** [1949] Cover by Paul Galdone.	$1.35	$4.00	$8.00
629	Jones, Arthur Frederick - ***The Care And Training Of Dogs*** [1949]	$1.25	$3.75	$7.50
630	Hilton, James - ***So Well Remembered*** [1949] Cover by Roswell Keller.	$1.25	$3.75	$7.50
631	Rolland, Romain - ***Jean-Christophe*** [1949] Cover by Emil Weiss.	$1.25	$3.75	$7.50
632	Collins, Norman - ***Black Ivory*** [1949] Cover by Barye Phillips.	$1.35	$4.00	$8.00
633	Dickson, Carter - ***My Late Wives*** [1949] Cover by Louis Glanzman.	$1.50	$5.00	$10.00
634	Brand, Max - ***Silvertip's Chase*** [1949] Cover by Dom Lupo.	$1.35	$4.00	$8.00
635	Taylor, Angeline - ***Black Jade*** [1949] Cover by Stanley Meltzoff.	$1.35	$4.00	$8.00
636	Guild, Leo - ***What Are The Odds?*** [1949] Cover by John Walbridge.	$1.25	$3.75	$7.50
637	Wells, Evelyn - ***Jed Blaine's Woman*** [1949] Cover by Wayne Blickenstaff.	$1.25	$3.75	$7.50
638	Davis, Mildred - ***The Room Upstairs*** [1949] Cover by Stanley Meltzoff.	$1.25	$3.75	$7.50
639	Taylor, Samuel W. - ***The Man With My Face*** [1950] Cover by Harvey Kidder.	$1.25	$3.75	$7.50
640	Haycox, Ernest - ***Canyon Passage*** [1949] Cover by Frank McCarthy.	$1.35	$4.00	$8.00
641	Ripley, Austin - ***Minute Mysteries*** [1949]	$1.25	$3.75	$7.50
642	Buck, Pearl S. - ***Pavilion Of Women*** [1949] Cover by James Bingham.	$1.25	$3.75	$7.50
643	Gardner, Erle Stanley - ***The Case Of The Drowning Duck*** [1949] Cover by Louis Glanzman.	$1.50	$5.00	$10.00
644	Dreiser, Theodore - ***Sister Carrie*** [1949] Cover by Roy Price.	$1.25	$3.75	$7.50
645	Brown, Joe David - ***Stars In My Crown*** [1949] Cover by Barye Phillips.	$1.25	$3.75	$7.50
646	Ripley, Thomas - ***They Died With Their Boots On*** [1949] Cover by Harvey Kidder.	$1.25	$3.75	$7.50
647	Wolff, William Almon & Veiller, Bayard - ***The Trial Of Mary Dugan*** [1949] Cover by Halleck Finley.	$1.25	$3.75	$7.50
648	Cody, Al - ***Disaster Trail*** [1949] Cover by John Floherty, Jr.	$1.35	$4.00	$8.00
649	Anthology edited by Red Smith - ***The Saturday Evening Post Sports Stories*** [1949]	$1.25	$3.75	$7.50
650	Gibson, Richards, Isley - ***French: Self-Taught With Pictures*** [1950] Cover by Charles Skaggs.	$1.25	$3.75	$7.50
651	Rice, Craig - ***The Fourth Postman*** [1950] Cover by Harvey Kidder.	$1.50	$5.00	$10.00
652	Geer, Andrew - ***The Sea Chase*** [1949] Cover by Dom Lupo.	$1.25	$3.75	$7.50
653	Miller, Helen Topping - ***Spotlight*** [1949]	$1.25	$3.75	$7.50
654	Loomis, M.D., Frederic - ***Consultation Room*** [1949] Cover by Stanley Meltzoff.	$1.00	$3.00	$6.00
655	Yerby, Frank - ***The Vixens*** [1950] Cover by Barye Phillips.	$1.25	$3.75	$7.50
656	Raine, William MacLeod - ***Man-Size*** [1949] Cover by Frank McCarthy.	$1.35	$4.00	$8.00
657	Turnbull, Agnes Sligh - ***The Bishop's Mantle*** [1949] Cover by Anna Wilson.	$1.25	$3.75	$7.50
658	Baldwin, Faith - ***Give Love The Air*** [1949] Cover by Roswell Keller.	$1.25	$3.75	$7.50
659	Curtiss, Ursula - ***Voice Out Of Darkness*** [1950] Cover by Wayne Blickenstaff.	$1.35	$4.00	$8.00

		G	VG	F
660	Davis, Don - ***Return Of The Rio Kid*** [1949] Cover by Simon Greco.	$1.35	$4.00	$8.00
661	Wechsler, Herman J. - ***Gods & Goddesses In Art & Legend*** [1950] PBO.	$1.35	$4.00	$8.00
662	Holding, Elisabeth Saxany - ***The Blank Wall*** [1949] Cover by Harvey Kidder.	$1.25	$3.75	$7.50
663	Manning, Roy - ***Renegade Ranch*** [1949] Cover by Dom Lupo.	$1.25	$3.75	$7.50
664	White, Nelia Gardner - ***No Trumpet Before Him*** [1949] Cover by Frederick Banbery.	$1.25	$3.75	$7.50
665	Allingham, Margery - ***More Work For The Undertaker*** [1949] Cover by Manvel Isip.	$1.25	$3.75	$7.50
666	Hayes, Alfred - ***The Girl On The Via Flaminia*** [1950] Cover by John Northcross.	$1.25	$3.75	$7.50
667	Gardner, Erle Stanley - ***The Case Of The Smoking Chimney*** [1949] Cover by Wayne Blickenstaff.	$1.50	$5.00	$10.00
668	Brand, Max - ***Valley Thieves*** [1950] Cover by Frank McCarthy.	$1.35	$4.00	$8.00
669	Queen, Ellery - ***Drury Lane's Last Case*** [1949] Cover by Bernard Safran.	$1.50	$5.00	$10.00
670	Doyle, Sir Arthur Conan - ***The Case Book Of Sherlock Holmes*** [1950] Cover by Charles Skaggs.	$1.50	$5.00	$10.00
671	Tey, Josephine - ***The Franchise Affair*** [1949] Cover by Harvey Kidder.	$1.50	$5.00	$10.00
672	Goudge, Elizabeth - ***Pilgrim's Inn*** [1950] Cover by Anna Wilson.	$1.25	$3.75	$7.50
673	Thayer, Tiffany - ***One Woman*** [1950] Cover by John Alan Maxwell.	$1.25	$3.75	$7.50
674	Dalrymple, Byron - ***All You Need To Know About Fishing, Hunting & Camping*** [1950] PBO. Cover by Simon Greco.	$1.25	$3.75	$7.50
675	Holmes, L.P. - ***Desert Rails*** [1950] Cover by Jack Cowan.	$1.35	$4.00	$8.00
676	Quentin, Patrick - ***The Fate Of The Immodest Blonde*** [1950] Cover by John Northcross.	$1.50	$5.00	$10.00
677	Craven, Thomas - ***The Pocket Book Of Greek Art*** [1950] PBO.	$1.35	$4.00	$8.00
678	Gardner, Erle Stanley - ***The Case Of The Buried Clock*** [1950] Cover by Barye Phillips.	$1.50	$5.00	$10.00
679	Buck, Pearl S. - ***Peony*** [1950] Cover by Anna Wilson.	$1.25	$3.75	$7.50
680	MacDonald, John - ***The Moving Target*** [1950] Cover by Harvey Kidder.	$3.50	$10.00	$20.00
681	Webber, Everett & Olga - ***Rampart Street*** [1950] Cover by Barye Phillips.	$2.50	$7.50	$15.00
682	Syms - ***Small Talk*** [1950] All baby photos.	$1.50	$5.00	$10.00
683	Field, Peter - ***The Boss Of The Lazy 9*** [1950] Cover by Roswell Brown.	$1.35	$4.00	$8.00
684	Anthology edited by B.A. Botkin. - ***The Pocket Treasury Of American Folklore*** [1950] Cover by Simon Greco.	$1.25	$3.75	$7.50
685	Rose, Billy - ***Wine, Women And Words*** [1950] Cover by Eddie Chan.	$1.25	$3.75	$7.50
686	Walker, Dorothy Pierce - ***5 O'Clock Surgeon*** [1950] Cover by George Porter.	$1.00	$3.00	$6.00
687	Brand, Max - ***Flaming Irons*** [1950] Cover by Frank McCarthy.	$1.25	$3.75	$7.50
688	Norris, Kathleen - ***Three Men And Diana*** [1950] Cover by Harry Bennett.	$1.00	$3.00	$6.00
689	Gardner, Erle Stanley - ***The Case Of The Drowsy Mosquito*** [1950] Photo cover.	$1.50	$5.00	$10.00
690	Post, Mary Brinker - ***Annie Jordan*** [1950]	$1.25	$3.75	$7.50
691	Raine, William MacLeod - ***The Fighting Edge*** [1950] Cover by Frank McCarthy.	$1.35	$4.00	$8.00
692	Hancock, Lucy Agnes - ***Special Nurse*** [1950]	$1.00	$3.00	$6.00
693	McGivern, William P. - ***The Whispering Corpse*** [1950] Cover by Harvey Kidder.	$2.00	$6.00	$12.00
694	Mann, E.B. - ***Killers' Range*** [1950] Cover by Roswell Brown.	$1.35	$4.00	$8.00

		G	VG	F
695	Smith, H. Allen - ***Rhubarb*** [1950] Cover by Leo Hershfield.	$3.50	$10.00	$20.00
696	Chandler, Raymond - ***The Big Sleep*** [1950] Cover by Harvey Kidder.	$3.00	$9.00	$18.00
697	Moon, Bucklin - ***Without Magnolias*** [1950]	$1.25	$3.75	$7.50
698	Brean, Herbert - ***The Darker The Night*** [1950] Cover by Wayne Blickenstaff.	$1.35	$4.00	$8.00
699	Rider, Brett - ***No Benefit Of Law*** [1950] Cover by Elliott Means.	$1.35	$4.00	$8.00
700	Maugham, W. Somerset - ***Of Human Bondage*** [1950]	$1.25	$3.75	$7.50
701	Rhau, Henry Von - ***Big Sol*** [1950] Cover by Louis Glanzman.	$1.25	$3.75	$7.50
702	Foreman, L.L. - ***Desperado's Gold*** [1950] Cover by Elliott Means.	$1.35	$4.00	$8.00
703	Halleran, E.E. - ***Rustlers' Canyon*** [1950] Cover by Frank McCarthy.	$1.35	$4.00	$8.00
704	Masur, Harold Q. - ***Suddenly A Corpse*** [1950] Cover by Barye Phillips.	$1.50	$5.00	$10.00
705	Brand, Max - ***Hired Guns*** [1950] Cover by Dom Lupo.	$1.35	$4.00	$8.00
706	Dresser, Davis - ***Death Rides The Pecos*** [1950] Cover by Manuel Isip.	$1.35	$4.00	$8.00
707	Foley, Rae - ***The Girl From Nowhere*** [1950] Cover by Barye Phillips.	$1.25	$3.75	$7.50
708	Flexner, James Thomas - ***American Painting*** [1950]	$1.25	$3.75	$7.50
709	Evans, John - ***Halo In Brass*** [1950] Cover by Mike Ludlow.	$1.50	$5.00	$10.00
710	Norris, Kathleen - ***An Apple For Eve*** [1950] Cover by Walter Klett.	$1.00	$3.00	$6.00
711	Field, Peter - ***Midnight Round-Up*** [1950] Cover by Roswell Brown.	$1.35	$4.00	$8.00
712	Savage, Jr., Les - ***The Doctor At Coffin Gap*** [1950] Cover by Harvey Kidder.	$1.35	$4.00	$8.00
713	Gipson, Fred - ***Hound-Dog Man*** [1950] Cover by Stanley Meltzoff.	$1.50	$5.00	$10.00
714	Burnett, W.R. - ***The Asphalt Jungle*** [1949]	$2.00	$6.00	$12.00
716	Bax, Roger - ***The Trouble With Murder*** [1950] Cover by Harvey Kidder.	$1.50	$5.00	$10.00
717	Brand, Max - ***The Bandit Of The Black Hills*** [1950] Cover by Warren Baumgartner.	$1.35	$4.00	$8.00
718	Davis, Mac - ***Great American Sports Humor*** [1950]	$1.25	$3.75	$7.50
719	Ermine, Will - ***Singing Lariat*** [1950] Cover by Frank McCarthy.	$1.35	$4.00	$8.00
720	Anthology - ***Spanish: Self-Taught Through Pictures*** [1950]	$1.25	$3.75	$7.50
721	Raine, William MacLeod - ***Border Breed*** [1950] Cover by John Blaine.	$1.35	$4.00	$8.00
722	Wylie, Philip - ***Opus 21*** [1950] Cover by Charles Skaggs.	$1.25	$3.75	$7.50
724	Gardner, Erle Stanley - ***The Case Of The Careless Kitten*** [1950] Photo cover.	$1.50	$5.00	$10.00
725	Phillips, James Atlee - ***Suitable For Framing*** [1950] Cover by Harry Barton.	$1.50	$5.00	$10.00
726	Stuart, Matt - ***Dusty Wagons*** [1950] Cover by Al Tartar.	$1.35	$4.00	$8.00
727	Mayse, Arthur - ***Perilous Passage*** [1950] Cover by James Bingham.	$1.35	$4.00	$8.00
728	Shulman, Max - ***The Feather Merchants*** [1950] Cover by Casey Jones.	$1.25	$3.75	$7.50
729	Tracy, Don - ***Chesapeake Cavalier*** [1950] Cover by Frank McCarthy.	$1.25	$3.75	$7.50
730	Anthology edited by Max J. Herzberg - ***This Is America*** [1950].	$1.25	$3.75	$7.50
731	Petherbridge, Margaret - ***The 3rd Pocket Book Of Crossword Puzzles*** [1950] PBO.	$6.00	$20.00	$40.00
732	Santee, Ross - ***Cowboy*** [1950] Cover by Sam Savitt.	$1.35	$4.00	$8.00
733	West, Tom - ***Ghost Gold*** [1950] Cover by Edward Vebell.	$1.35	$4.00	$8.00
734	Watson, John - ***The Red Dress*** [1950] Cover by Alan Hoemer.	$1.25	$3.75	$7.50

		G	VG	F
735	Ferrars, E. X. - ***The March Hare Murders*** [1950] Cover by Frank Smith.	$1.50	$5.00	$10.00
736	Bagby, George - ***Coffin Corner*** [1950] Cover by Frank McCarthy.	$1.50	$5.00	$10.00
737	Lipsky, Eleazar - ***Murder One*** [1950] Cover by Bennett.	$1.50	$5.00	$10.00
738	Bonett, John & Emery - ***Dead Lion*** [1950] Cover by Ray Pease.	$1.25	$3.75	$7.50
739	Leslie, Jean - ***The Man Who Held Five Aces*** [1950] Cover by Harvey Kidder.	$1.50	$5.00	$10.00
740	Queen, Ellery - ***Ten Day's Wonder*** [1950] Cover by Stanley Meltzoff.	$1.50	$5.00	$10.00
741	Innes, Michael - ***The Case Of The Journeying Boy*** [1950]	$1.50	$5.00	$10.00
742	Blake, Nicholas - ***Head Of A Traveler*** [1950] Cover by Warren Baumgartner.	$2.50	$7.50	$15.00
743	Raine, William MacLeod - ***On The Dodge*** [1950] Cover by William Shoyer.	$1.35	$4.00	$8.00
744	Brand, Max - ***Hunted Riders*** [1950] Cover by John Floherty, Jr.	$1.35	$4.00	$8.00
745	White, Leslie Turner - ***Lord Johnnie*** [1950] Cover by Barye Phillips.	$1.25	$3.75	$7.50
746	Marshall, Marguerite Mooers - ***Wilderness Nurse*** [1950] Cover by Isabelle Dawson.	$1.00	$3.00	$6.00
747	Praag, Van Van - ***Combat*** [1950] Cover by Lew Keller.	$1.25	$3.75	$7.50
748	Howe, George - ***Call It Treason*** [1950] Cover by Harvey Kidder.	$1.25	$3.75	$7.50
749	Yerby, Frank - ***The Golden Hawk*** [1950]	$1.25	$3.75	$7.50
750	Chandler, Raymond - ***The Little Sister*** [1950] Cover by William Shoyer.	$6.00	$20.00	$40.00
751	Daly, Maureen - ***The Perfect Hostess*** [1951]	$1.25	$3.75	$7.50
752	Grafton, C.W. - ***Beyond A Reasonable Doubt*** [1951] Cover by Frank McCarthy.	$1.35	$4.00	$8.00
753	Christie, Agatha - ***Crooked House*** [1950] Cover by Paul Kresse.	$1.50	$5.00	$10.00
754	Nye, Nelson - ***Riders By Night*** [1951] Cover by Sam Savitt.	$1.35	$4.00	$8.00
755	Packard, Vance - ***The Human Side Of Animals*** [1950] Photo cover.	$1.35	$4.00	$8.00
756	Ellington, Richard - ***It's A Crime*** [1950] Cover by Paul Kresse.	$2.00	$6.00	$12.00
757	Algren, Nelson - ***The Man With The Golden Arm*** [1951] Cover by Sol Immerman.	$1.25	$3.75	$7.50
758	Gardner, Erle Stanley - ***The Case Of The Crooked Candle*** [1951] Cover by Paul Kresse.	$1.50	$5.00	$10.00
759	Field, Peter - ***The Tenderfoot Kid*** [1950] Cover by Frank McCarthy.	$1.35	$4.00	$8.00
760	Peeples, Samuel Anthony - ***Outlaw Vengeance*** [1951] Cover by John McDermott.	$1.35	$4.00	$8.00
761	Ermine, Will - ***Rustler's Moon*** [1951] Cover by Frank McCarthy.	$1.35	$4.00	$8.00
762	Marsh, Ngaio - ***Swing Brother, Swing*** [1951] Cover by Lew Keller.	$1.50	$5.00	$10.00
763	Ledderer, William J. - ***All The Ships At Sea*** [1951] Cover by Casey Jones.	$1.25	$3.75	$7.50
764	La Farge, Oliver - ***Laughing Boy*** [1951]	$1.25	$3.75	$7.50
765	Sachs, Paul J. - ***The Pocket Book Of Great Drawings*** [1951] PBO.	$1.35	$4.00	$8.00
766	Rider, Brett - ***Law Of The Gun*** [1951] Cover by William Shoyer.	$1.35	$4.00	$8.00
767	Brooks, John - ***The Big Wheel*** [1951] Cover by Leo Manso.	$1.25	$3.75	$7.50
768	Lomax, Bliss - ***The Fight For The Sweetwater*** [1950] Cover by William Shoyer.	$1.35	$4.00	$8.00
769	Cody, Al - ***Bitter Creek*** [1950] Cover by Warren Baumbargner.	$1.35	$4.00	$8.00
770	Lewis, Gita & Martin, Henriette - ***The Naked Eye*** [1950] Cover by Don Neiser.	$1.35	$4.00	$8.00
771	Lea, Tom - ***The Brave Bulls*** [1951] Cover by William Shoyer.	$1.25	$3.75	$7.50

		G	VG	F
772	Wilson, Harry Leon - ***Ruggles Of Red Gap*** [1951] Cover by Louis Glantzman.	$1.25	$3.75	$7.50
773	Worley, William - ***My Dead Wife*** [1951] Cover by John McDermott.	$1.50	$5.00	$10.00
774	Sterling, Thomas - ***The House Without A Door*** [1951] Cover by Frank McCarthy.	$1.35	$4.00	$8.00
775	Sage, Dana - ***The 22 Brothers*** [1951] Cover by Victor Kalin.	$1.25	$3.75	$7.50
776	Hall, Geoffrey Holiday - ***The End Is Known*** [1951] Cover by Paul Kresse.	$1.50	$5.00	$10.00
777	Bunce, Frank - ***So Young A Body*** [1951] Cover by Cass Norwaish.	$1.35	$4.00	$8.00
778	Ruesch, Hans - ***Top Of The World*** [1951] Cover by John McDermott.	$1.25	$3.75	$7.50
779	Starnes, Richard - ***And When She Was Bad She Was Murdered*** [1951] Cover by Ray Johnson.	$1.50	$5.00	$10.00
780	Guthrie, Jr., A.B. - ***The Way West*** [1951] Cover by Ray Johnson.	$1.35	$4.00	$8.00
781	Brand, Max - ***Rustlers Of Beacon Creek*** [1951] Cover by Frank McCarthy.	$1.35	$4.00	$8.00
782	Anthology edited by J.D. Kaplan - ***Dialogues Of Plato*** [1951] Cover by Frederick E. Banbery.	$1.25	$3.75	$7.50
783	Halleran, E. E. - ***Outlaw Trail*** [1951] Cover by Harry Barton.	$1.35	$4.00	$8.00
784	Tey, Josephine - ***Come And Kill Me*** [1951] Cover by Cass Norwaish.	$1.50	$5.00	$10.00
785	Castle, Marian - ***The Golden Fury*** [1951] Cover by Victor Kalin.	$1.25	$3.75	$7.50
786	McGivern, William P. - ***Very Cold For May*** [1951] Cover by Karl Milroy.	$2.00	$6.00	$12.00
787	Raine, William MacLeod - ***Ranger's Luck*** [1951] Cover by William Shoyer.	$1.35	$4.00	$8.00
788	Gottscho, Samuel - ***The Pocket Guide To The Wildflowers*** [1951] Photo cover. 103 color photos.	$1.25	$3.75	$7.50
789	Pillsbury, Ann - ***Baking Book*** [1950] Photo cover.	$1.25	$3.75	$7.50
790	Haycox, Ernest - ***Rough Justice*** [1951] Cover by Warren Baumgartner.	$1.35	$4.00	$8.00
791	Cunningham, Eugene - ***Red Range*** [1951] Cover by William Shoyer.	$1.35	$4.00	$8.00
792	Gardner, Erle Stanley - ***The Case Of The Black-Eyed Blonde*** [1951] Photo cover.	$1.50	$5.00	$10.00
793	Blochman, Lawrence G. - ***Diagnosis: Homicide*** [1951] Cover by Ray Johnson.	$1.50	$5.00	$10.00
794	Wellman, Paul I. - ***Broncho Apache*** [1951] Cover by Richard Cardiff.	$1.35	$4.00	$8.00
795	Perry, George Sessions - ***Hold Autumn In Your Hand*** [1951] Cover by Stanley Meltzoff.	$1.25	$3.75	$7.50
796	Golden, Dr. Francis Leo - ***For Doctors Only*** [1951] Cover by Ray Quigley.	$1.00	$3.00	$6.00
797	Brand, Max - ***The Outlaw*** [1951] Cover by Frank Smith.	$1.35	$4.00	$8.00
798	Bottome, Phyllis - ***Under The Skin*** [1951] Cover by Harvey Kidder.	$1.25	$3.75	$7.50
799	Mason, Van Wyck - ***Dardanelles Derelict*** [1951] Cover by John McDermott.	$1.25	$3.75	$7.50
801	Gordon, Arthur - ***Reprisal*** [1951]	$1.25	$3.75	$7.50
802	McCoy, John Pleasant - ***Big As Life*** [1951] Cover by Harvey Kidder.	$1.25	$3.75	$7.50
803	Savage, Jr., Les - ***The Hide Rustlers*** [1951] Cover by Robert Meyer.	$1.35	$4.00	$8.00
804	Davis, Frederick C. - ***The Deadly Miss Ashley*** [1951] Cover by Victor Kalin.	$1.50	$5.00	$10.00
805	Armstrong, Charlotte - ***Mischief*** [1951] Cover by Robert Hilbert.	$1.50	$5.00	$10.00

		G	VG	F
806	Dunn, Dorothy - ***Murder's Web*** [1951] Cover by Robert Hilbert.	$1.50	$5.00	$10.00
807	Foster, Bennett - ***Bullets For A Badman*** [1951] Cover by Warren Baumbartner.	$1.35	$4.00	$8.00
808	Dunn, Tom - ***The Sheriff Of Painted Post*** [1951] Cover by Edward Vebell.	$1.35	$4.00	$8.00
809	Lomax, Bliss - ***Colt Comrades*** [1951] Cover by Frank McCarthy.	$1.35	$4.00	$8.00
810	Brown, Joe David - ***The Freeholder*** [1951] Cover by Al Schmidt.	$1.25	$3.75	$7.50
811	Shore, William - ***The Witch Of Spring*** [1951] Cover by Ernest Chiriaka.	$1.25	$3.75	$7.50
812	Gardner, Erle Stanley - ***The Case Of The Golddigger's Purse*** [1951] Photo cover.	$1.50	$5.00	$10.00
813	Ellington, Richard - ***Stone Cold Dead*** [1951] Cover by Maurice Thomas.	$1.50	$5.00	$10.00
814	Berkeley, Anthony - ***The Poisoned Chocolates Case*** [1951] Cover by Barye Phillips.	$1.50	$5.00	$10.00
815	Raine, William MacLeod - ***The Sheriff's Son*** [1951] Cover by Frank McCarthy.	$1.35	$4.00	$8.00
816	O'Mara, Jim - ***Wall Of Guns*** [1951] Cover by Harry Barton.	$1.35	$4.00	$8.00
817	Olsen, D. B. - ***Something About Midnight*** [1951] Cover by Victor Kalin.	$1.35	$4.00	$8.00
818	Clift, Charmian & Johnston, George - ***High Valley*** [1951] Cover by Carl Mueller.	$1.25	$3.75	$7.50
819	Street, James - ***Mingo Dabney*** [1951] Cover by Harvey Kidder.	$1.25	$3.75	$7.50
820	Christie, Agatha - ***A Murder Is Announced*** [1951] Cover by Frank McCarthy.	$1.50	$5.00	$10.00
821	MacDonald, John Ross - ***The Drowning Pool*** [1951] Cover by Ray App.	$3.00	$9.00	$18.00
822	Queen, Ellery - ***Cat Of Many Tails*** [1951] Cover by Maurice Thomas.	$1.50	$5.00	$10.00
823	Chandler, Raymond - ***Trouble Is My Business*** [1951] Cover by Herman Geisen.	$6.00	$20.00	$40.00
824	Foreman, L. L. - ***The Road To San Jacinto*** [1951] Cover by Carl Mueller.	$1.25	$3.75	$7.50
825	Kelly, M.D., G. Lombard - ***Sexual Feeling In Married Men & Women*** [1951] Cover by Charles Skaggs.	$1.00	$3.00	$6.00
826	Falstein, Louis - ***Face Of A Hero*** [1951] Cover by Al Schmidt.	$1.25	$3.75	$7.50
827	Westcott, Jan - ***The Hepburn*** [1951] Cover by Arthur Sarnoff.	$1.25	$3.75	$7.50
828	Hall, O. M. - ***Murder City*** [1951] Cover by Frank McCarthy.	$1.50	$5.00	$10.00
829	Neville, Margot - ***Murder Of A Nymph*** [1951] Cover by Maurice Thomas.	$1.50	$5.00	$10.00
830	Chatterton, Ruth - ***Homeward Borne*** [1951] Cover by Arthur Sarnoff.	$1.25	$3.75	$7.50
831	Duffy, Warden Clinton T. - ***The San Quentin Story*** [1951] Photo cover.	$1.25	$3.75	$7.50
832	Gardner, Erle Stanley - ***The Case Of The Half-Wakened Wife*** [1951] Photo cover.	$1.50	$5.00	$10.00
833	Goodis, David - ***Of Missing Persons*** [1951] Cover by Ray App.	$8.00	$25.00	$50.00
834	Carpenter, John Jo - ***Signal Guns At Sunup*** [1951] Cover by Herman Geisen.	$1.35	$4.00	$8.00
835	Carroll, Lewis G. - ***Alice In Wonderland*** [1951] Cover by Sir John Tenniel.	$4.00	$12.50	$25.00
836	Wolff, Perry - ***Attack*** [1951] Cover by Rafael DeSoto.	$1.25	$3.75	$7.50
837	Carroll, Curt - ***The Golden Herd*** [1952] Cover by George Mayers.	$1.25	$3.75	$7.50
838	Delmar, Vina - ***About Mrs. Leslie*** [1951] Cover by Barye Phillips.	$1.25	$3.75	$7.50
839	Arnold, Elliott - ***Walk With The Devil*** [1951] Cover by Ray Pease.	$1.25	$3.75	$7.50

		G	VG	F
840	Shulman, Max - ***The Zebra Derby*** [1951] Cover by Casey Jones.	$1.25	$3.75	$7.50
841	Gunn, Tom - ***Painted Post Law*** [1951] Cover by Gale Phillips.	$1.35	$4.00	$8.00
842	Raine, William MacLeod - ***Gun Showdown*** [1951] Cover by Frank McCarthy.	$1.35	$4.00	$8.00
843	Robinson, Henry Morton - ***The Great Snow*** [1952] Cover by Martin Gulser.	$1.25	$3.75	$7.50
844	McNeilly, Mildred Masterson - ***Each Bright River*** [1952] Cover by Tom Dunn.	$1.25	$3.75	$7.50
845	Hughes, Dorothy B. - ***The Candy Kid*** [1951] Cover by Edward Vebell.	$1.25	$3.75	$7.50
846	Chandler, Raymond - ***Pick-Up On Noon Street*** [1952] Cover by Tom Dunn.	$6.00	$20.00	$40.00
848	Brand, Max - ***Danger Trail*** [1952] Cover by Stanley Borack.	$1.35	$4.00	$8.00
849	Kirk, Jeremy - ***The Build-Up Boys*** [1952] Cover by Tom Dunn.	$1.25	$3.75	$7.50
850	Seton, Anya - ***Foxfire*** [1952] Cover by Ray Pease.	$1.25	$3.75	$7.50
851	Stinetorf, Louise A. - ***White Witch Doctor*** [1952] Cover by Courtney Allen.	$1.35	$4.00	$8.00
852	McLean, Beth Bailey & Campbell, Thora - ***Martha Logan's Meat Cook Book*** [1951] PBO. Photo cover.	$1.25	$3.75	$7.50
853	Davis, Don - ***Death On Treasure Trail*** [1952] Cover by William Shoyer.	$1.35	$4.00	$8.00
854	Truss, Seldon - ***Why Slug A Postman*** [1951] Cover by Rafael DeSoto.	$1.50	$5.00	$10.00
855	Gardner, Erle Stanley - ***The Case Of The Backward Mule*** [1951] Cover by Frank McCarthy.	$1.50	$5.00	$10.00
856	Gardner, Erle Stanley - ***The Case Of The Borrowed Brunette*** [1952] Cover by Roswell Keller.	$1.50	$5.00	$10.00
857	Vandercbok, John W. - ***Black Majesty*** [1952] Cover by Tom Dunn.	$1.35	$4.00	$8.00
858	Starnes, Richard - ***Another Mug For The Bier*** [1952] Cover by Carl Bobertz.	$1.50	$5.00	$10.00
859	Bonham, Frank - ***Bold Passage*** [1952] Cover by Sam Savitt.	$1.35	$4.00	$8.00
860	Masur, Harold Q. - ***You Can't Live Forever*** [1952] Cover by Frank McCarthy.	$1.25	$3.75	$7.50
862	Seeley, Mabel - ***The Beckoning Door*** [1952] Cover by Carl Bobertz.	$1.50	$5.00	$10.00
863	Lipsky, Eleazar - ***The People Against O'Hara*** [1952] Cover by Tom Dunn.	$1.35	$4.00	$8.00
864	Haycox, Ernest - ***By Rope And Lead*** [1952] Cover by Stan Borack.	$1.35	$4.00	$8.00
865	Wells, Lee E. - ***Tonto Riley*** [1952] Cover by Gale Phillips.	$1.35	$4.00	$8.00
866	Knight, John - ***The Story Of My Psycho Analysis*** [1952] Cover by Frank McCarthy.	$1.00	$3.00	$6.00
867	Brick, John - ***The Raid*** [1952] Cover by Peter Stevens.	$1.25	$3.75	$7.50
868	Tracy, Don - ***The Strumpet City*** [1952] Cover by Zuckerberg.	$1.25	$3.75	$7.50
869	Gardner, Erle Stanley - ***The D. A. Breaks A Seal*** [1952].	$1.50	$5.00	$10.00
870	McGivern, William P. - ***Shield For Murder*** [1952] Cover by George Mayers.	$2.00	$6.00	$12.00
871	Dresser, Davis - ***The Hangmen Of Sleepy Valley*** [1952] Cover by Frank McCarthy.	$1.35	$4.00	$8.00
872	Golden, Francis Leo - ***Jest What The Doctor Ordered*** [1952] Cover by Casey Jones.	$1.25	$3.75	$7.50
873	White, Leslie Turner - ***Magnus The Magnificent*** [1952] Cover by George Erickson.	$1.25	$3.75	$7.50
874	Queen, Ellery - ***Double, Double*** [1952] Cover by Tom Dunn.	$1.50	$5.00	$10.00
875	Anthology edited by Joseph T. Shaw - ***The Hard-Boiled Omnibus*** [1952] PBO. Cover by Maurice Thomas. Early stories from "Black Mask." Includes Chandler, Hammett, Dent, and Paul Cain.	$2.50	$7.50	$15.00

		G	VG	F
876	Halleran, E. E. - ***Double Cross Trail*** [1952] Cover by Stanley Borack.	$1.25	$3.75	$7.50
877	Brand, Max - ***Gunman's Gold*** [1952] Cover by A. Leslie Ross.	$1.35	$4.00	$8.00
878	Anderson, Sherwood - ***Dark Laughter*** [1952] Cover by Tom Dunn.	$1.25	$3.75	$7.50
879	Chase, Ilka - ***New York 22*** [1952] Cover by Tom Dunn.	$1.25	$3.75	$7.50
880	Armstrong, Charlotte - ***The Black-Eyed Stranger*** [1952] Cover by Tom Dunn.	$1.50	$5.00	$10.00
881	Sinclair, Robert B. - ***The Eleventh Hour*** [1952] Cover by George Erickson.	$1.25	$3.75	$7.50
882	Field, Peter - ***Death Rides The Night*** [1952] Cover by Frank McCarthy.	$1.35	$4.00	$8.00
883	Thacher, Russell - ***The Captain*** [1952] Cover by Tom Dunn.	$1.25	$3.75	$7.50
884	Baldwin, Bates - ***The Sultan's Warrior*** [1952] Cover by Peter Stevens.	$1.25	$3.75	$7.50
885	Tallant, Robert - ***Southern Territory*** [1952] Cover by Tom Dunn.	$1.25	$3.75	$7.50
886	Gardner, Erle Stanley - ***The Case Of The Fan-Dancer's Horse*** [1952] Cover by Earle Bergey.	$1.50	$5.00	$10.00
887	Ambler, Eric - ***Judgement On Deltchev*** [1952] Cover by George Mayers.	$1.35	$4.00	$8.00
888	Savage, Jr., Les - ***Shadow Riders Of The Yellowstone*** [1952] Cover by M. Rothe.	$1.35	$4.00	$8.00
889	Davis, H. L. - ***Beulah Land*** [1952] Cover by George Mayers.	$1.35	$4.00	$8.00
891	Carnegie, Dale - ***The Unknown Lincoln*** [1952]	$1.25	$3.75	$7.50
892	Anthology edited by H. E. Harris - ***The Pocket Stamp Album*** [1952] Photo cover.	$1.25	$3.75	$7.50
893	Hammett, Catherine T. - ***Your Own Book Of Campcraft*** [1952]	$1.25	$3.75	$7.50
894	Malley, Louis - ***Horns For The Devil*** [1952] Cover by George Erickson.	$1.35	$4.00	$8.00
895	Brand, Max - ***Mystery Ranch*** [1952] Cover by Stanley Borack.	$1.35	$4.00	$8.00
896	La France, Marston - ***Miami Murder-Go-Round*** [1952] Cover by Morgan Kane.	$1.50	$5.00	$10.00
897	Christie, Agatha - ***They Came To Baghdad*** [1952] Cover by Clyde Ross.	$1.50	$5.00	$10.00
898	Karney, Jack - ***Cop*** [1952] Cover by Stan Zuckerberg.	$1.35	$4.00	$8.00
899	Cobean, Sam - ***Naked Eye*** [1952] Cover by Sam Cobean. Cartoon book.	$1.35	$4.00	$8.00
900	Romano, Romualdo - ***Scirocco*** [1952] Cover by Belarski.	$1.50	$5.00	$10.00
901	Rigsby, Howard - ***Murder For The Holidays*** [1952] Cover by George Mayers.	$1.50	$5.00	$10.00
902	Field, Peter - ***The End Of The Trail*** [1952] Cover by Earle Bergey.	$1.35	$4.00	$8.00
903	Davies, Valentine - ***Miracle On 34th Street*** [1952] Cover by Frederick Banbery.	$3.50	$10.00	$20.00
904	Schwartz, Irving - ***Fear In The Night*** [1952] Cover by Tom Dunn.	$1.50	$5.00	$10.00
905	Davis, Doris - ***The Women Of Champion City*** [1952] Cover by Stan Zuckerberg.	$1.25	$3.75	$7.50
907	MacDonald, John Ross - ***The Way Some People Die*** [1952] Cover by Clyde Ross.	$2.50	$7.50	$15.00
908	Anthology edited by Raymond J. Healy - ***New Tales Of Space And Time*** [1952] Cover by Charles Frank.	$1.50	$5.00	$10.00
909	Gardner, Erle Stanley - ***The Case Of The Lazy Lover*** [1952] Cover by Clyde Ross.	$1.50	$5.00	$10.00
910	Brand, Max - ***The Streak*** [1952] Cover by Vernon Tossey.	$1.35	$4.00	$8.00
911	Ermine, Will - ***My Gun Is My Law*** [1952] Cover by Vernon Tossey.	$1.35	$4.00	$8.00
912	Loraine, Philip - ***And To My Beloved Husband*** [1952] Cover by Clyde Ross.	$1.25	$3.75	$7.50

Pocket Books, 943

Popular Library, NN-1

Popular Library, 168

		G	VG	F
913	Martin, Robert - ***Dark Dream*** [1952] Cover by James Meese.	$1.25	$3.75	$7.50
915	Delmar, Vina - ***Ruby*** [1952] Cover by Stan Zuckerberg.	$1.25	$3.75	$7.50
916	Chandler, Raymond - ***The Simple Art Of Murder*** [1952] Cover by George Mayers.	$5.50	$17.50	$35.00
917	Starnes, Richard - ***The Other Body In Grant's Tomb*** [1953] Cover by George Erickson.	$1.50	$5.00	$10.00
918	Mittelholzer, Edgar - ***Shadows Move Among Them*** [1952] Cover by Tom Dunn.	$1.35	$4.00	$8.00
919	Romains, Jules - ***The Lord God Of The Flesh*** [1953] Cover by Tom Dunn.	$1.25	$3.75	$7.50
920	Leinster, Murray - ***Space Platform*** [1953] Cover by Earle Bergey.	$2.50	$7.50	$15.00
921	Davis, Don - ***Rio Kid Justice*** [1953] Cover by Stanley Borack.	$1.35	$4.00	$8.00
922	Gardner, Erle Stanley - ***The Case Of The Lonely Heiress*** [1952] Cover by Verne Tossey.	$1.50	$5.00	$10.00
923	Ernst, Paul - ***Hangman's Hat*** [1953] Cover by James Meese.	$1.35	$4.00	$8.00
924	Barrett, William E. - ***The Left Hand Of God*** [1953] Cover by Tom Dunn.	$1.25	$3.75	$7.50
925	Anthology edited by James & Albert Morehead - ***101 Favorite Hymns*** [1953] PBO. Cover by George Mayers.	$1.25	$3.75	$7.50
926	Queen, Ellery - ***Origin Of Evil*** [1953] Cover by Tossey.	$1.50	$5.00	$10.00
927	Fisher, Clay - ***Red Blizzard*** [1953] Cover by Stanley Borack.	$1.35	$4.00	$8.00
928	Hogan, Ben - ***Power Golf*** [1953]	$1.25	$3.75	$7.50
929	Mason, F. Van Wyck - ***Himalayan Assignment*** [1953] Cover by Ray Johnson.	$1.35	$4.00	$8.00
930	Brand, Max - ***The Hair-Trigger Kid*** [1953] Cover by Charles Hargens.	$1.35	$4.00	$8.00
931	Page, Marco - ***Reclining Figure*** [1953] Cover by Verne Tossey.	$1.50	$5.00	$10.00
932	Westcott, Jan - ***Captain Barney*** [1953] Cover by Stan Zuckerberg.	$1.25	$3.75	$7.50
933	Auerbach, Arnold "Red" - ***Basketball*** [1952] Photo cover.	$1.25	$3.75	$7.50
934	Rigsby, Howard - ***Kill And Tell*** [1953] Cover by James Meese.	$1.50	$5.00	$10.00
935	Lincoln, Victoria - ***Out From Eden*** [1953] Cover by Tom Dunn.	$1.25	$3.75	$7.50
936	Athanas, Verne - ***The Proud Ones*** [1953] Cover by Stanley Borack.	$1.25	$3.75	$7.50
937	Field, Peter - ***Sheriff On The Spot*** [1953] Cover by Charles Hargens.	$1.35	$4.00	$8.00
938	Moore, Ruth - ***Candlemas Bay*** [1953] Cover by Tom Dunn.	$1.25	$3.75	$7.50
939	Cleary, Jon - ***The Sundowners*** [1953] Cover by Tom Dunn.	$1.35	$4.00	$8.00
940	Curtiss, Ursula - ***Catch A Killer*** [1953] Cover by James Meese.	$1.50	$5.00	$10.00

		G	VG	F
941	Ellington, Richard - ***Exit For A Dame*** [1953] Cover by Clyde Ross.	$1.50	$5.00	$10.00
943	MacDonald, John D. - ***Planet Of The Dreamers*** [1953] Cover by Rod Dunham.	$3.00	$9.00	$18.00
944	Davis, H. L. - ***Winds Of Morning*** [1953] Cover by Tom Dunn.	$1.25	$3.75	$7.50
945	Yerby, Frank - ***Floodtide*** [1953] Cover by Tom Dunn.	$1.25	$3.75	$7.50
946	Beverly-Giddings, A. R. - ***River Of Rogues*** [1953] Cover by George Mayers.	$1.35	$4.00	$8.00
947	Wells, H. G. - ***The War Of The Worlds*** [1953] Movie tie-in. Movie photo cover.	$2.50	$7.50	$15.00
948	Golden, Dr. Francis Leo - ***Laughter Is Legal*** [1953] Cover by Casey Jones.	$1.25	$3.75	$7.50
949	Gardner, Erle Stanley - ***The Clue of the Runaway Blonde/The Clue of the Hungry Horse*** [1953] Cover by Robert Maguire.	$1.50	$5.00	$10.00
950	Brand, Max - ***Single Jack*** [1953] Cover by Stanley Borack.	$1.35	$4.00	$8.00
952	Hartog, Jan De - ***Stella*** [1953] Cover by Tom Dunn.	$1.25	$3.75	$7.50
953	De Hartog, Jan - ***The Sea*** [1953]	$1.25	$3.75	$7.50
954	Savage, Jr., Les - ***Outlaw Thickets*** [1953] Cover by Robert Schulz.	$1.35	$4.00	$8.00
955	Anthology - ***101 Best Loved Songs*** [1953] PBO. Cover by George Mayers.	$1.25	$3.75	$7.50
956	Christie, Agatha - ***Mrs. McGinty's Dead*** [1953] Cover by Robert Schulz.	$1.50	$5.00	$10.00
957	Davis, Maxine - ***Women's Medical Problems*** [1953] Photo cover.	$1.00	$3.00	$6.00
958	Loraine, Philip - ***Outside The Law*** [1953] Cover by Ray Pease.	$1.35	$4.00	$8.00
959	Fosdick, Harry Emerson - ***The Man From Nazareth*** [1953]	$1.25	$3.75	$7.50
960	Queen, Ellery - ***Calendar Of Crime*** [1953] Cover by Powers.	$1.50	$5.00	$10.00
961	McGivern, William P. - ***The Crooked Frame*** [1953] Cover by James Meese.	$2.00	$6.00	$12.00
963	Skinner, Cornelia Otis - ***Excuse It, Please!*** [1953] Cover by O. Soglow.	$1.25	$3.75	$7.50
964	Brown, Eugene - ***Trespass*** [1953] Cover by Tom Dunn.	$1.25	$3.75	$7.50
965	Gardner, Erle Stanley - ***The Case Of The Vagabond Virgin*** [1953] Photo cover.	$1.50	$5.00	$10.00
966	Farrar, M. P. - ***The 4th Pocket Book Of Crossword Puzzles*** [1953]	$2.50	$7.50	$15.00
967	Bonham, Frank - ***Snaketrack*** [1953] Cover by Larry Newquist.	$1.35	$4.00	$8.00
968	Small, Marvin - ***Low Calorie Diet*** [1953] Photo cover.	$1.00	$3.00	$6.00
969	Thacher, Russell - ***The Tender Age*** [1953] Cover by Tom Dunn.	$1.25	$3.75	$7.50
971	MacDonald, John Ross - ***Marked For Murder*** [1953] Cover by Bob Maguire.	$2.50	$7.50	$15.00
972	West, Ward - ***Halfway To Timberline*** [1953] Cover by Harris Levy.	$1.25	$3.75	$7.50
974	White, Leslie Turner - ***The Highland Hawk*** [1953] Cover by George Mayers.	$1.35	$4.00	$8.00
975	Wilmot, Robert Patrick - ***Blood In Your Eye*** [1953] Cover by James Meese.	$1.50	$5.00	$10.00
976	Gardner, Erle Stanley - ***The Case Of The Dubious Bridegroom*** [1953]	$1.50	$5.00	$10.00
977	Mason, F. Van Wyck - ***Wild Drums Beat*** [1953] Cover by Richard Cardiff.	$1.35	$4.00	$8.00
978	Savage, Jr., Les - ***Land Of The Lawless*** [1953] Cover by Michael.	$1.35	$4.00	$8.00
979	Brand, Max - ***Vengeance Trail*** [1953] Cover by Ray Pease.	$1.35	$4.00	$8.00
980	Fosdick, Harry Emerson - ***A Great Time To Be Alive*** [1953] Photo cover.	$1.25	$3.75	$7.50
981	McGivern, William P. - ***The Big Heat*** [1954] Photo cover.	$2.00	$6.00	$12.00
982	Field, Peter - ***Doctor Two-Guns*** [1953] Cover by Lew Kimmel.	$1.35	$4.00	$8.00

		G	VG	F
983	Haycox, Ernest - ***Pioneer Loves*** [1954] Cover by George Erickson.	$1.35	$4.00	$8.00
984	Brooks, Win - ***The Shining Tides*** [1953] Cover by Tom Dunn.	$1.25	$3.75	$7.50
985	Duncan, David - ***Worse Than Murder*** [1953] Cover by James Meese.	$2.50	$7.50	$15.00
986	Ermine, Will - ***Watchdog Of Thunder River*** [1953] Cover by Larry Newquist.	$1.35	$4.00	$8.00
987	Mann, E. B. - ***The Whistler*** [1954] Cover by Lou Marchetti.	$1.35	$4.00	$8.00
988	Waugh, Hillary - ***Last Seen Wearing*** [1954] Cover by Rudy Nappi.	$1.35	$4.00	$8.00
989	Clarke, Arthur C. - ***Sands Of Mars*** [1954] Cover by Schulz.	$2.50	$7.50	$15.00
990	Field, Peter - ***Coyote Gulch*** [1954] Cover by Clark Hulings.	$1.35	$4.00	$8.00
991	Brand, Max - ***Border Guns*** [1954] Cover by Larry Newquist.	$1.35	$4.00	$8.00
992	Ripley, Robert - ***Ripley's New Believe It Or Not*** [1954]	$1.35	$4.00	$8.00
993	Buck, Pearl S. - ***The Hidden Flower*** [1954]	$1.25	$3.75	$7.50
994	Budd, Lillian - ***April Snow*** [1954] Cover by Ray Pease.	$1.25	$3.75	$7.50
995	Harris, Margaret & John - ***The Medicine Whip*** [1954] Cover by Michael.	$1.25	$3.75	$7.50
997	Wilmot, Robert Patrick - ***Murder On Monday*** [1954] Cover by George Mayers.	$1.50	$5.00	$10.00
998	Masur, Harold Q. - ***So Rich, So Lovely And So Dead*** [1953] Cover by Zuckerberg.	$1.50	$5.00	$10.00
1000	Guareschi, Giovanni - ***The Little World Of Don Camillo*** [1954] Cover by Tom Dunn.	$1.25	$3.75	$7.50
1001	Brick, John - ***Homer Crist*** [1954] Cover by Tom Dunn.	$1.25	$3.75	$7.50
1003	Christie, Agatha - ***Funerals Are Fatal*** [1954]	$1.50	$5.00	$10.00
1004	Seligman, Selig J. - ***The Big Deal*** [1954] Cover by Tom Dunn.	$1.25	$3.75	$7.50
1006	Tracy, Don - ***The Amber Fire*** [1954] Cover by George Mayers.	$1.25	$3.75	$7.50
1007	Anthology - ***My Best Science Fiction Story*** [1954] Photo cover.	$2.50	$7.50	$15.00
1009	Gardner, Erle Stanley - ***The Case Of The Cautious Coquette*** [1954] Photo cover.	$1.50	$5.00	$10.00
1010	Gardner, Erle Stanley - ***The D.A. Takes A Chance*** [1954] Photo cover.	$1.50	$5.00	$10.00
1011	Haycox, Ernest - ***Murder On The Frontier*** [1954] Cover by Robert Schulz.	$1.35	$4.00	$8.00
1012	Robinson, Henry Morton - ***Tale Of Two Lovers*** [1954] Cover by Tom Dunn.	$1.25	$3.75	$7.50
1013	Golden, Francis Leo - ***Tales For Salesmen*** [1954] Cover by Casey Jones.	$1.25	$3.75	$7.50
1014	Hough, Emerson - ***The Covered Wagon*** [1954] Cover by George Erickson.	$1.35	$4.00	$8.00
1015	Pratolini, Vasco - ***The Girls Of Sanfrediano*** [1954] Cover by Tom Dunn.	$1.25	$3.75	$7.50
1017	Chanslor, Roy - ***Johnny Guitar*** [1954] Cover by Gail Phillips. Movie tie-in.	$1.35	$4.00	$8.00
1018	Brand, Max - ***The Gun Tamer*** [1954] Cover by Phil Marini.	$1.35	$4.00	$8.00
1019	Hayes, Alfred - ***In Love*** [1954] Cover by Tom Dunn.	$1.25	$3.75	$7.50
1020	MacDonald, John Ross - ***Meet Me At The Morgue*** [1954] Cover by Clark Hulings.	$2.50	$7.50	$15.00
1021	Christie, Agatha - ***Murder With Mirrors*** [1954]	$1.50	$5.00	$10.00
1022	Mann, E. B. - ***Troubled Range*** [1954] Photo cover.	$1.35	$4.00	$8.00
1023	Davis, Don - ***Two-Gun Rio Kid*** [1954] Cover by Joe Fallat.	$1.35	$4.00	$8.00
1024	Mason, F. Van Wyck - ***The Barbarians*** [1954] Cover by Tom Dunn.	$1.25	$3.75	$7.50
1025	Brean, Herbert - ***How To Stop Smoking*** [1954]	$1.00	$3.00	$6.00
1028	Haycox, Ernest - ***Outlaw*** [1954] Cover by Tom Ryan.	$1.35	$4.00	$8.00
1029	Gardner, Erle Stanley - ***The Case Of The Negligent Nymph*** [1954] Photo cover.	$1.50	$5.00	$10.00
1030	McGivern, William P. - ***Rogue Cop*** [1954] Photo cover.	$2.00	$6.00	$12.00
1032	Gary, Romain - ***The Colors Of The Day*** [1954]	$1.25	$3.75	$7.50

		G	VG	F
1033	Brand, Max - ***The Night Horseman*** [1954] Cover by John Leone	$1.35	$4.00	$8.00
1034	Armstrong, Charlotte - ***Walk Out On Death*** [1954] Photo cover	$1.50	$5.00	$10.00
1035	Field, Peter - ***The Outlaw Of Eagle's Nest*** [1954] Cover by Kirk Wilson.	$1.35	$4.00	$8.00
1036	Christie, Agatha - ***A Pocket Full Of Rye*** [1954] Cover by James Meese.	$1.50	$5.00	$10.00
1037	Leinster, Murray - ***Space Tug*** [1954] Cover by Robert Schulz	$2.50	$7.50	$15.00
1038	Vercors - ***You Shall Know Them*** [1954]	$3.50	$10.00	$20.00
1039	Pearson, William - ***The Beautiful Frame*** [1954] Cover by Meese.	$1.50	$5.00	$10.00
1040	Ermine, Will - ***Boss Of The Plains*** [1954] Cover by Tom Ryan	$1.35	$4.00	$8.00
1041	Gardner, Erle Stanley - ***The Case Of The One-Eyed Witness*** [1954] Cover by James Meese.	$1.50	$5.00	$10.00
1042	De Hartog, Jan - ***The Little Ark*** [1954]	$1.25	$3.75	$7.50
1044	Chandler, Raymond - ***The Long Goodbye*** [1955] Cover by Tom Dunn.	$5.50	$17.50	$35.00
1045	Anthology - ***Science Fiction Terror Tales*** [1955] PBO. Cover by Stanley Meltzoff.	$2.50	$7.50	$15.00
1047	Jennings, John - ***Rogue's Yarn*** [1955] Cover by George Mayers.	$1.25	$3.75	$7.50
1049	Queen, Ellery - ***The Scarlet Letters*** [1955] Cover by Carl Bobertz.	$1.50	$5.00	$10.00
1050	McConnaughey, James - ***Three For The Money*** [1955] Cover by Meese.	$1.35	$4.00	$8.00
1051	Moore, Ruth - ***A Fair Wind Home*** [1955] Cover by Clark Hulings.	$1.25	$3.75	$7.50
1052	Gardner, Erle Stanley - ***The D.A. Breaks An Egg*** [1955] Photo cover.	$1.50	$5.00	$10.00
1053	Fredericks, Vic - ***Crackers In Bed*** [1955] Cover by Casey Jones.	$1.25	$3.75	$7.50
1054	Field, Peter - ***Gambler's Gold*** [1955] Cover by Tony Kokinos.	$1.35	$4.00	$8.00
1055	O'Sullivan, J. B. - ***I Die Possessed*** [1955] Cover by Verne Tossey.	$1.35	$4.00	$8.00
1057	Gross, Fred - editor - ***How To Work With Tools And Wood*** [1955] Photo cover.	$1.25	$3.75	$7.50
1058	Armstrong, Charlotte - ***Murder's Nest*** [1955] Cover by Verne Tossey.	$1.50	$5.00	$10.00
1060	Nye, Nelson - ***Hired Hand*** [1955] Cover by Tom Ryan.	$1.35	$4.00	$8.00
1061	Harris, Margaret & John - ***Arrow In The Moon*** [1955] Cover by Charles Binger.	$1.35	$4.00	$8.00
1062	McGivern, William P. - ***Margin Of Terror*** [1955] Cover by James Meese.	$2.00	$6.00	$12.00
1063	Gardner, Erle Stanley - ***The Case Of The Musical Cow*** [1955] Photo cover.	$1.50	$5.00	$10.00
1064	Elston, Allan Vaughan - ***Stage Road To Denver*** [1955]	$1.35	$4.00	$8.00
1065	Brand, Max - ***The Tenderfoot*** [1955] Cover by Tom Ryan.	$1.35	$4.00	$8.00
1066	Fergusson, Harvey - ***The Conquest Of Don Pedro*** [1955] Cover by Tom Dunn.	$1.25	$3.75	$7.50
1067	Guareschi, Giovanni - ***Don Camillo And His Flock*** [1955] Cover by Tom Dunn.	$1.25	$3.75	$7.50
1068	Field, Peter - ***Mustang Mesa*** [1955] Cover by Robert Schulz	$1.35	$4.00	$8.00
1069	Haycox, Ernest - ***Prairie Guns*** [1955] Cover by Stanley Borack	$1.35	$4.00	$8.00
1070	Rayter, Joe - ***The Victim Was Important*** [1955] Cover by James Meese.	$2.00	$6.00	$12.00
1071	Cooper, Jefferson - ***Arrow In The Hill*** [1955] Cover by Maguire.	$2.50	$7.50	$15.00
1072	Farrar, M. P. - ***The 5th Pocket Book Of Crossword Puzzles*** [1955]	$2.50	$7.50	$15.00
1073	West, Jessamyn - ***Cress Delahanty*** [1955] Cover by Tom Dunn	$1.25	$3.75	$7.50
1074	Conklin, Groff - editor - ***Invaders Of Earth*** [1955] Cover by Morton Roberts.	$2.50	$7.50	$15.00

		G	VG	F
1075	Waugh, Hillary - ***A Rag And A Bone*** [1955] Cover by Clark Hulings.	$1.35	$4.00	$8.00
1076	Mason, F. Van Wyck - ***Captain Judas*** [1955] Cover by Charles Binger.	$1.25	$3.75	$7.50
1077	Curtiss, Ursula - ***The Deadly Climate*** [1955] Cover by Meese.	$1.50	$5.00	$10.00
1078	Finney, Jack - ***5 Against The House*** [1955] Cover by George Erickson.	$4.00	$12.50	$25.00
1079	Eustis, Helen - ***The Fool Killer*** [1955]	$1.50	$5.00	$10.00
1080	Ketcham, Hank - ***Baby Sitter's Guide*** [1955] Cover by Hank Ketcham. "Dennis the Menace" cartoons.	$1.50	$5.00	$10.00
1082	Queen, Ellery - ***The Glass Village*** [1955] Cover by James Meese.	$1.50	$5.00	$10.00
1083	Valentine, Jo - ***And Sometimes Death*** [1955] Cover by Tom Dunn.	$1.50	$5.00	$10.00
1084	Brand, Max - ***The Untamed*** [1955] Cover by Martin Engle.	$1.35	$4.00	$8.00
1085	Christie, Agatha - ***The Under Dog & Other Mysteries*** [1955] Cover by James Meese.	$1.50	$5.00	$10.00
1086	Elston, Allan Vaughan - ***Wagon Wheel Gap*** [1955] Cover by Tom Ryan.	$1.35	$4.00	$8.00
1087	Arno, Peter - ***The New Peter Arno Pocket Book*** [1955] Cartoon book.	$1.25	$3.75	$7.50
1089	Gardner, Erle Stanley - ***The Case Of The Fiery Fingers*** [1955] Photo cover.	$1.50	$5.00	$10.00
1090	Dean, Amber - ***The Devil Threw Dice*** [1955] Cover by Lou Marchetti.	$1.35	$4.00	$8.00
1091	Ermine, Will - ***Rider Of The Midnight Range*** [1955] Cover by Tom Ryan.	$1.35	$4.00	$8.00
1092	Gardner, Erle Stanley - ***The Case Of The Angry Mourner*** [1955] Photo cover.	$1.50	$5.00	$10.00
1093	Smith, H. Allen - ***The Compleat Practical Joker*** [1955] Photo cover.	$1.25	$3.75	$7.50
1095	Armstrong, Charlotte - ***Alibi For Murder*** [1955] Cover by Lou Marchetti.	$1.50	$5.00	$10.00
1096	Douglas, Lloyd C. - ***Doctor Hudson's Secret Journal*** [1955]	$1.00	$3.00	$6.00
1097	Brand, Max - ***Tragedy Trail*** [1955] Cover by Tom Ryan.	$1.35	$4.00	$8.00
1098	Runyon, Damon - ***Guys And Dolls*** [1955] Movie photo cover. Movie tie-in.	$2.00	$6.00	$12.00
1099	Patton, Frances Gray - ***Good Morning, Miss Dove*** [1956] Cover by Tom Dunn. Movie tie-in.	$1.25	$3.75	$7.50
1100	Anthology edited by Jerry Lieberman - ***Off The Cuff*** [1956] PBO. Cover by Wachsteter. Jokebook.	$1.25	$3.75	$7.50
1102	Grafton, Samuel - ***A Most Contagious Game*** [1956] Cover by Tom Dunn.	$1.25	$3.75	$7.50
1103	Elston, Allan Vaughan - ***Showdown*** [1956] Cover by Borack.	$1.35	$4.00	$8.00
1104	Savage, Jr., Les - ***Once A Fighter...*** [1956] PBO. Cover by Robert Schulz.	$1.35	$4.00	$8.00
1105	McGivern, William P. - ***Waterfront Cop*** [1956] Cover by Clark Hulings.	$2.00	$6.00	$12.00
1107	Gardner, Erle Stanley - ***The Case Of The Moth-Eaten Mink*** [1956] Photo cover.	$1.50	$5.00	$10.00
1108	Fisher, Clay - ***The Brass Command*** [1956] Cover by Clark Hulings.	$1.35	$4.00	$8.00
1109	O'Sullivan, J. B. - ***Don't Hang Me Too High*** [1956] Cover by James Meese.	$1.50	$5.00	$10.00
1111	Schisgall, Oscar - ***The Big Store*** [1956] Cover by James Meese.	$1.35	$4.00	$8.00
1112	Hevman, William - ***The Girl From Frisco*** [1956] Cover by Robert Schulz.	$1.35	$4.00	$8.00
1113	Yordan, Philip - ***Man Of The West*** [1956] Cover by Mort Engel.	$1.35	$4.00	$8.00
1114	Christie, Agatha - ***So Many Steps To Death*** [1956] Photo cover.	$1.50	$5.00	$10.00

		G	VG	F
1115	Mason, Van Wyck - ***Two Tickets For Tangier*** [1956] Cover by Marchetti.	$1.35	$4.00	$8.00
1117	McIntyre, Marjorie - ***The River Witch*** [1956] Cover by Charles Binger.	$1.25	$3.75	$7.50
1118	Queen, Ellery - ***Q.B.I.*** [1956] Photo cover.	$1.50	$5.00	$10.00
1119	MacDonald, Betty - ***Onions In The Stew*** [1956]	$1.25	$3.75	$7.50
1120	Knight, David - ***Dragnet Case No. 561*** [1956] PBO. Jack Webb photo cover. TV tie-in.	$2.50	$7.50	$15.00
1121	Gardner, Erle Stanley - ***The Case Of The Grinning Gorilla*** [1956] Photo cover.	$1.50	$5.00	$10.00
1122	Brand, Max - ***The False Rider*** [1956] Cover by Mel Crair.	$1.35	$4.00	$8.00
1124	Ermine, Will - ***Cowboy, Say Your Prayers!*** [1956] Cover by Tom Ryan.	$1.35	$4.00	$8.00
1125	Ketcham, Hank - ***Dennis The Menace Rides Again*** [1956] PBO. Cover by Hank Ketcham. Cartoon book.	$1.50	$5.00	$10.00
1126	Hunter, Evan - ***The Jungle Kids*** [1956] PBO. Cover by Tom Dunn.	$3.50	$10.00	$20.00
1127	Gardner, Erle Stanley - ***The Case Of The Constant Hostess*** [1956]	$1.50	$5.00	$10.00
1128	Wolford, Colby - ***The Guns Of Witchwater*** [1956] Cover by Morton Engel.	$1.35	$4.00	$8.00
1129	Farrar, M. P. - ***The 6th Pocket Book Of Crossword Puzzles*** [1956]	$2.50	$7.50	$15.00
1130	Adams, Joey - ***Strictly For Laughs*** [1956] Jokebook.	$1.25	$3.75	$7.50
1131	Yerby, Frank - ***The Treasure Of Pleasant Valley*** [1956] Cover by Charles Binger.	$1.35	$4.00	$8.00
1132	Rayter, Joe - ***Asking For Trouble*** [1956] Cover by James Meese.	$2.00	$6.00	$12.00
1133	Brand, Max - ***Galloping Broncos*** [1956] Cover by Roy Lance.	$1.35	$4.00	$8.00
1135	Nye, Nelson - ***The Parson Of Gunbarrel Basin*** [1956] Cover by Roy Lance.	$1.35	$4.00	$8.00
1136	Latimer, Jonathan - ***Sinners And Shrouds*** [1956] Cover by Meese.	$1.50	$5.00	$10.00
1137	Fisher, Clay - ***The Big Pasture*** [1956] Cover by Michael Aviano.	$1.35	$4.00	$8.00
1138	Anthology - ***The Case Of The Fugitive Nurse*** [1956] Photo cover.	$1.50	$5.00	$10.00
1139	Monsarrat, Nicholas - ***Castle Garac*** [1956] Cover by Tom Dunn.	$1.25	$3.75	$7.50
1140	Wells, H. G. - ***The Invisible Man*** [1956] Cover by Robert Korn.	$2.50	$7.50	$15.00
1141	Pearson, William - ***Hunt The Man Down*** [1956] Cover by James Meese.	$1.50	$5.00	$10.00
1143	Mason, F. Van Wyck - ***Lysander*** [1956] PBO. Cover by James Meese.	$1.35	$4.00	$8.00
1145	Rayter, Joe - ***Stab In The Dark*** [1957] Cover by George Zeil.	$2.00	$6.00	$12.00
1146	Wallop, Douglass - ***The Dangerous Years*** [1956] Cover by James Meese.	$1.35	$4.00	$8.00
1147	Franklin, Frieda K. - ***Combat Nurse*** [1956] Cover by Barye Phillips.	$1.00	$3.00	$6.00
1148	Haycox, Ernest - ***The Last Rodeo*** [1956] Cover by Roy Lance.	$1.35	$4.00	$8.00
1149	Brand, Max - ***The Gambler*** [1956]	$1.35	$4.00	$8.00
1150	Richter - ***The Man On The Couch*** [1957] PBO. Cover by Richter. Cartoon book.	$1.25	$3.75	$7.50
1151	Christie, Agatha - ***Hickory Dickory Death*** [1956] Cover by Art Sussman.	$1.50	$5.00	$10.00
1152	Lacy, Ed - ***The Men From The Boys*** [1957] Cover by Lou Marchetti.	$2.00	$6.00	$12.00
1153	Ketcham, Hank - ***Wanted: Dennis The Menace*** [1956] Cover by Hank Ketcham.	$1.50	$5.00	$10.00
1154	Anthology edited by Margaret P. Farrar - ***The 7th Pocket Book Of Crossword Puzzles*** [1957] PBO. Puzzle book.	$2.50	$7.50	$15.00

		G	VG	F
1155	Gardner, Erle Stanley - ***The Case Of The Green-Eyed Sister*** [1956]	$1.50	$5.00	$10.00
1156	McGivern, William P. - ***The #7 File*** [1957]	$2.00	$6.00	$12.00
1158	Maugham, W. Somerset - ***Cakes And Ale*** [1957] Cover by Leo Manso.	$1.25	$3.75	$7.50
1159	Fisher, Clay - ***The Blue Mustang*** [1956]	$1.35	$4.00	$8.00
1160	Hoke, Newton Wilson - ***Double Entendre*** [1957]	$1.25	$3.75	$7.50
1161	Field, Peter - ***Maverick's Return*** [1957]	$1.35	$4.00	$8.00
1163	Elston, Allan Vaughan - ***The Wyoming Bubble*** [1957]	$1.35	$4.00	$8.00
1165	Anthology - ***Ripley's Believe It Or Not 4th Series*** [1957]	$1.35	$4.00	$8.00
1166	Foster, Bennett - ***Lone Wolf*** [1957] Cover by Bob Abbott.	$1.35	$4.00	$8.00
1167	Queen, Ellery - ***Inspector Queen's Own Case*** [1957] Cover by Lou Marchetti.	$1.50	$5.00	$10.00
1169	Ermine, Will - ***War On The Saddle Rock*** [1957] Cover by Roy Lance.	$1.35	$4.00	$8.00
1171	Bloomfield, Robert - ***When Strangers Meet*** [1957] Cover by Bob Abbott.	$1.25	$3.75	$7.50
1172	Godden, Jon - ***The Seven Islands*** [1957] Cover by Leo Manso.	$1.25	$3.75	$7.50
1173	Field, Peter - ***Sheriff Wanted!*** [1957] Cover by Jerry Allison.	$1.35	$4.00	$8.00
1174	Christie, Agatha - ***Dead Man's Folly*** [1957] Photo cover.	$1.50	$5.00	$10.00
1175	Farrar, Margaret P. - ***The 8th Pocket Book Of Crossword Puzzles*** [1957] PBO. Cover by Alex Tsao.	$2.50	$7.50	$15.00
1176	Mason, F. Van Wyck - ***Captain Nemesis*** [1957] Cover by James Meese.	$1.25	$3.75	$7.50
1177	Gipson, Fred - ***Old Yeller*** [1957] Cover by Tom Dunn.	$1.50	$5.00	$10.00
1178	Douglass, Donald McNutt - ***Rebecca's Pride*** [1957] Cover by James Meese.	$1.35	$4.00	$8.00
1179	Ketcham, Hank - ***Dennis The Menace Vs. Everybody*** [1957] Cover by Hank Ketcham.	$1.50	$5.00	$10.00
1180	Brand, Max - ***The Invisible Outlaw*** [1957] Cover by Jerry Allison.	$1.35	$4.00	$8.00
1182	Farrar, Margaret P. - editor - ***The 9th Pocket Book Of Crossword Puzzles*** [1958] PBO. Puzzle book.	$2.50	$7.50	$15.00
1183	Christopher, John - ***No Blade Of Grass*** [1958] Cover by Tom Dunn.	$3.50	$10.00	$20.00
1184	Wilson, Earl - ***The NBC Book Of Stars*** [1957] Cover by Wachsteter.	$1.25	$3.75	$7.50
1185	Abbey, Edward - ***The Brave Cowboy*** [1957] Cover by Roy Gifford.	$1.35	$4.00	$8.00
1186	Fisher, Clay - ***Santa Fe Passage*** [1957] Cover by A. Leslie Ross.	$1.35	$4.00	$8.00
1187	Field, Peter - ***Powder Valley Showdown*** [1957] Cover by Larry Harris.	$1.35	$4.00	$8.00
1188	Menen, Aubrey - ***The Abode Of Love*** [1958] Cover by Banberry.	$1.00	$3.00	$6.00
1189	Rice, Craig - ***My Kingdom For A Hearse*** [1957] Photo cover.	$2.00	$6.00	$12.00
1190	Brand, Max - ***Outlaw Breed*** [1957] Cover by Bob Abbett.	$1.35	$4.00	$8.00
1191	Elston, Allan Vaughan - ***Last Stage To Aspen*** [1958] Cover by John Leone.	$1.35	$4.00	$8.00
1192	Rayner, Comm. D. A. - ***The Enemy Below*** [1957] Cover by Clark Hulings. Movie tie-in with Robert Mitchum.	$1.35	$4.00	$8.00
1193	McGivern, William P. - ***Night Extra*** [1958] Cover by Jerry Powell.	$2.00	$6.00	$12.00
1194	Mann, E. B. - ***Shootin' Melody*** [1958] Cover by Jerry Allison.	$1.35	$4.00	$8.00
1195	Anthology - ***Ripley's Believe It Or Not 5th Series*** [1957] Cover by Leo Manso.	$1.35	$4.00	$8.00
1196	Turner, Robert - ***Wagonmaster*** [1958] PBO. Cover by Lou Marchetti. TV tie-in.	$1.50	$5.00	$10.00
1197	Katcher, Leo - ***Hard Man*** [1958] Cover by A. Leslie Ross.	$1.35	$4.00	$8.00

		G	VG	F
1198	Deming, Richard - ***Dragnet: The Case Of The Courteous Killer*** [1958] Photo cover. TV tie-in.	$2.50	$7.50	$15.00
1199	Gill, Brendan - ***The Day The Money Stopped*** [1957] Cover by Clark Hulings.	$1.25	$3.75	$7.50
1200	Preston, Charles - editor - ***Too Humorous To Mention*** [1957] PBO. Cartoon book.	$1.25	$3.75	$7.50
1202	Kahn, Lawrence H. - ***The Tank Destroyers*** [1958] Cover by Tom Dunn.	$1.25	$3.75	$7.50
1206	Vercors - ***The Murder Of The Missing Link*** [1958] Cover by Clark Hulings.	$3.50	$10.00	$20.00
1207	Matthews, Allen R. - ***The Assault*** [1958] Cover by Robert Schulz.	$1.25	$3.75	$7.50
1208	Ripley, Robert - ***Ripley's Believe It Or Not!*** [1958] 6th series.	$1.35	$4.00	$8.00
1209	Fisher, Clay - ***Yellowstone Kelly*** [1958] Cover by A. Leslie Ross.	$1.35	$4.00	$8.00
1210	Cornell, Betty - ***Betty Cornell's Glamour Guide For Teens*** [1958]	$1.25	$3.75	$7.50
1211	Elston, Allan Vaughan - ***Grand Mesa*** [1958] Cover by Leon Gregori.	$1.35	$4.00	$8.00
1213	Field, Peter - ***Blacksnake Trail*** [1958] Cover by Tom Ryan.	$1.35	$4.00	$8.00
1214	Deming, Richard - ***Dragnet: The Case Of The Crime King*** [1958] TV tie-in with photo cover.	$2.50	$7.50	$15.00
1216	Turner, Robert - ***The Scout*** [1958] PBO. Cover by Marchetti. TV tie-in.	$2.00	$6.00	$12.00
1217	Ketcham, Hank - ***Dennis The Menace "Household Hurricane"*** [1958] Cover by author.	$1.50	$5.00	$10.00
1218	Lederer, William J. - ***Ensign O'Toole And Me*** [1958] Cover by Casey Jones.	$1.25	$3.75	$7.50
1219	Mason, F. Van Wyck - ***The China Sea Murders*** [1958] Cover by Jerry Allison.	$1.35	$4.00	$8.00
1220	Dean, Spencer - ***Murder On Delivery*** [1958] Cover by Robert Schulz.	$1.50	$5.00	$10.00
1221	Brand, Max - ***Speedy*** [1958] Cover by Robert Schulz.	$1.35	$4.00	$8.00
1222	Oliver, Chad - ***The Winds Of Time*** [1958] Cover by Powers.	$2.50	$7.50	$15.00
1223	Mason, Van Wyck - ***The Gracious Lily Affair*** [1958] Cover by James Meese.	$1.35	$4.00	$8.00
1225	Patti, Ercole - ***A Roman Affair*** [1959] Cover by Bill Hofmann.	$1.25	$3.75	$7.50
1226	Turner, Robert - ***Wagons West!*** [1959] PBO. Cover by James Meese. TV tie-in.	$2.00	$6.00	$12.00
1227	Farrar, M. P. - ***The 10th Pocket Book Of Crossword Puzzles*** [1959] Cover by Charles Egri. Puzzle book.	$2.50	$7.50	$15.00
1231	Mahannah, Floyd - ***The Broken Angel*** [1958] Cover by John Fernie.	$1.50	$5.00	$10.00
1232	Appell, George C. - ***The Man Who Shot Quantrill*** [1959] Cover by Robert Schulz.	$1.35	$4.00	$8.00
1233	Charteris, Leslie - ***Thanks To The Saint*** [1959] Cover by Darell Green.	$1.50	$5.00	$10.00
1235	Marsten, Richard - ***Big Man*** [1959] Cover by Bob Abbett.	$2.00	$6.00	$12.00
1236	Howe, Margaret - ***Visiting Nurse*** [1959] Cover by Darell Green.	$1.00	$3.00	$6.00
1239	Hitchens, Dolores - ***Fools Gold*** [1959] Cover by Harry Bennett.	$1.35	$4.00	$8.00
1240	Chaber, M. E. - ***The Lady Came To Kill*** [1959] Cover by Len Goldberg.	$1.50	$5.00	$10.00
1241	Field, Peter - ***Outlaw Valley*** [1959]	$1.35	$4.00	$8.00
1242	McCarthy, Father Justin - ***Brother Juniper*** [1959] Cover by Father Justin McCarthy. Cartoon book.	$1.25	$3.75	$7.50
1243	Banks, Rosie M. - ***Surgical Nurse*** [1959] Cover by Robert Abbett.	$ .75	$2.50	$5.00
1244	Brand, Max - ***Fire Brain*** [1959] Cover by A. Leslie Ross.	$1.35	$4.00	$8.00
1246	Brelis, Dean - ***The Mission*** [1959] Cover by Paul Lehr.	$1.25	$3.75	$7.50

		G	VG	F
1248	Dean, Spencer - ***Dishonor Among Thieves*** [1959] Cover by George Porter.	$1.25	$3.75	$7.50
1249	Hunter, John - ***Badlands Buccaneer*** [1959]	$1.25	$3.75	$7.50
1250	Powell, Talmage - ***The Killer Is Mine*** [1959] PBO. Cover by Bob Abbett.	$1.50	$5.00	$10.00
1251	Savage, Jr., Les - ***Beyond Wind River*** [1959]	$1.35	$4.00	$8.00
1252	Manchester, William - ***Cairo Intrigue*** [1959] Cover by James Meese.	$1.25	$3.75	$7.50
1254	Elston, Allan Vaughan - ***Rio Grande Deadline*** [1959] Cover by Rafael De Soto.	$1.35	$4.00	$8.00
1255	Howard, James A. - ***Murder Takes A Wife*** [1959] Cover by Wayne Blinkenstaff.	$1.50	$5.00	$10.00
1256	Costigan, Lee - ***Never Kill A Cop*** [1959] PBO. Cover by Darrel Greene.	$1.50	$5.00	$10.00
1259	Chaber, M. E. - ***A Hearse Of Another Color*** [1959] Cover by James Meese.	$1.50	$5.00	$10.00
1260	Field, Peter - ***Trail From Needle Rock*** [1959] Cover by Jerry Allison.	$1.35	$4.00	$8.00
1261	Frazer, Robert Caine - ***Mark Kilby Solves A Murder*** [1959] PBO. Cover by James Meese.	$1.50	$5.00	$10.00
1262	Usher, Jack - ***Reason For Murder*** [1959] Cover by Bob Abbett.	$1.50	$5.00	$10.00
1263	Wright, Lee - editor - ***Wicked Women*** [1959] Cover by Morgan Kane.	$1.25	$3.75	$7.50
1267	Harris, A. M. - ***The Tall Man*** [1960] Cover by Tom Dunn.	$1.35	$4.00	$8.00
1269	Rome, Anthony - ***Miami Mayhem*** [1960] PBO. Cover by George Porter.	$1.35	$4.00	$8.00
1273	Douglass, Donald M. - ***Many Brave Hearts*** [1960] Cover by Harry Bennett.	$1.25	$3.75	$7.50
1274	Chaber, M. E. - ***So Dead The Rose*** [1960] Cover by Jerry Allison.	$1.35	$4.00	$8.00
1277	Dean, Spencer - ***The Merchant Of Murder*** [1960] Cover by Harry Bennett.	$1.50	$5.00	$10.00
35011	Deming, Richard - ***Death Of A Pusher*** [1964] PBO.	$2.00	$6.00	$12.00
50059	Addams, Charles - ***Black Maria*** [1964] Cartoon book.	$1.25	$3.75	$7.50
50149	Stark, Richard - ***The Jugger*** [1965] PBO. Cover by Harry Bennett.	$2.25	$7.00	$14.00
50220	Stark, Richard - ***The Handle*** [1966] PBO.	$2.25	$7.00	$14.00
80185	Rankine, John - ***Moon Odyssey (Space: 1999 #2)*** [1975] TV photo cover/tie-in.	$1.25	$3.75	$7.50
80706	Rankine, John - ***Android Planet (Space: 1999 #8)*** [1976] TV photo cover/tie-in.	$1.25	$3.75	$7.50
80710	Tubb, E.C. - ***Rogue Planet (Space: 1999 #9)*** [1976] TV photo cover/tie-in.	$1.25	$3.75	$7.50
827545	Anobile, Richard - editor - ***Mork & Mindy - A Video Novel*** [1978] Photo cover and illustrations throughout. TV tie-in.	$1.50	$5.00	$10.00
828274	Thomas, Roy - editor - ***Stan Lee Presents The Incredible Hulk*** [1979] Photo cover and illustrations throughout. TV tie-in.	$1.50	$5.00	$10.00
830899	Anobile, Richard J. - editor - ***Star Trek The Motion Picture: The Photostory*** [1980] PBO. Photo cover and illustrations throughout. Movie tie-in.	$2.00	$6.00	$12.00

Pocket Books 2000 Series. New York: Pocket Books, Inc.

		G	VG	F
2005	Christie, Agatha - ***The Murder Of Roger Ackroyd*** [1956] Cover art by Leo Manso.	$ .65	$2.00	$4.00
2250	Brand, Max - ***Destry Rides Again*** [1954] Cover art by Michael Aviano.	$ .65	$2.00	$4.00
2270	Queen, Ellery - ***The Devil To Pay*** [1958] Cover art by Robert Abbett.	$ .65	$2.00	$4.00
2320	Chandler, Raymond - ***The High Window*** [1955] Cover art by James Meese.	$1.25	$3.75	$7.50

2429	Hough, Emerson - ***North Of 36*** [1956] Cover art by Tom Ryan.	$ .65	$2.00	$4.00
2491	Brand, Max - ***The Border Kid*** [1956] Cover art by Robert Schulz.	$ .65	$2.00	$4.00
2512	Gardner, Erle Stanley - ***This Is Murder*** [1954] Photo cover.	$ .65	$2.00	$4.00
2524	Huggins, Roy - ***The Double Take*** [1959] Cover art by Harry Bennett.	$ .65	$2.00	$4.00
2531	Haycox, Ernest - ***Saddle And Ride*** [1958] Cover art by Leon Gregori.	$ .65	$2.00	$4.00
2640	Haycox, Ernest - ***Canyon Passage*** [1957] Cover art by Tom Ryan.	$ .65	$2.00	$4.00
2814	Berkley, Anthony - ***The Poisoned Chocolates Case*** [1957] Cover art by Charles Binger.	$ .65	$2.00	$4.00
2821	MacDonald, John Ross - ***The Drowning Pool*** [1959] Cover art by James Meese.	$1.00	$3.00	$6.00
2840	Shulman, Max - ***The Zebra Derby*** [1958] Cover art by Casey Jones.	$ .65	$2.00	$4.00
2846	Chandler, Raymond - ***Pick-Up On Noon Street*** [1956] Cover art by Robert Maguire.	$2.50	$7.50	$15.00
2874	Queen, Ellery - ***The Case Of The Seven Murders*** [1958] Cover art by Jerry Allison.	$ .65	$2.00	$4.00
2952	De Hartog, Jan - ***The Key*** [1958] Photo cover.	$ .65	$2.00	$4.00

Pocket Books British Series. London: Pocket Books, Inc.

B-1	Marquand, John P. - ***Ming Yellow*** [1950] Cover art by Max Bacon.	$2.50	$7.50	$15.00
B-2	Hamilton, Bruce - ***Pro*** [1950]	$1.50	$5.00	$10.00
B-3	Jackson, Charles - ***The Lost Weekend*** [1950] Cover art by Peter Chadwick.	$2.00	$6.00	$12.00
B-4	Morris, Kathleen - ***Mink Coat*** [1950] Cover art by Wayne Blickenstaff.	$1.25	$3.75	$7.50
B-5	Sayers, Dorothy L. - ***The Anatomy Of Murder*** [1950]	$1.50	$5.00	$10.00
B-6	Hargest, Brigadier James - ***Farewell Campo 12*** [1950] Cover art by Arthur Horowicz.	$1.50	$5.00	$10.00
B-7	Doyle, Sir Arthur Conan - ***The Hound Of The Baskervilles*** [1950]	$2.00	$6.00	$12.00
B-8	Whipple, Dorothy - ***The Other Day*** [1950] Cover by Peter Hale.	$1.50	$5.00	$10.00
B-9	Gooden, Arthur Henry - ***Circle C Moves On*** [1950] Cover by F. Laurent.	$1.50	$5.00	$10.00
B-10	Field, Peter - ***Outlaws Three*** [1950]	$1.50	$5.00	$10.00
B-11	Cain, James M. - ***Double Indemnity*** [1950] Cover art by Laurent.	$2.50	$7.50	$15.00
B-12	Anthology edited by Lyle Blair - ***Famous British Short Stories*** [1950] Cover art by Peter Chadwick.	$1.50	$5.00	$10.00
B-13	Smith, Emma - ***Maiden's Trip*** [1950] Cover art by Peter Chadwick.	$1.25	$3.75	$7.50
B-14	Fair, A. A. (Erle Stanley Gardner) - ***Lam To The Slaughter*** [1950] Cover art by Peter Hale.	$1.50	$5.00	$10.00
B-15	Boutell, Anita - ***Tell Death To Wait*** [1950] Cover art by Glyn Jones.	$1.50	$5.00	$10.00
B-16	Nichols, Beverly - ***Evensong*** [1950] Cover art by Henry Fox.	$1.25	$3.75	$7.50
B-17	Travers, Ben - ***The Dippers*** [1950]	$1.50	$5.00	$10.00
B-18	Lomax, Bliss - ***Pardners Of The Badlands*** [1950] Cover by F. Laurent.	$1.50	$5.00	$10.00
B-19	Lister, F. W. - ***The Wind That Blows*** [1950]	$1.50	$5.00	$10.00
B-20	Wallace, Francis - ***Kid Galahad*** [1950]	$1.50	$5.00	$10.00
B-21	Bates, H. E. - ***Selected Short Stories Of H. E. Bates*** [1951] PBO. Cover art by Peter Hale.	$1.50	$5.00	$10.00
B-22	Yeh, Chun-Chan - ***The Mountain Village*** [1951] Cover art by A. R. Whitear.	$1.50	$5.00	$10.00
B-23	Erskine, Margaret - ***The Whispering House*** [1951]	$1.50	$5.00	$10.00

		G	VG	F
B-24	Bullett, Gerald - ***The Jury*** [1951] Cover by T. Maloney.	$1.50	$5.00	$10.00
B-25	Anthology edited by C. Lloyd Jones - ***Great Dramas And Poems From The Bible*** [1951]	$1.50	$5.00	$10.00
B-26	Erskine, Margaret - ***Give Up The Ghost*** [1951] Cover art by Peter Hale.	$1.50	$5.00	$10.00
B-27	Gooden, Arthur Henry - ***Tenderfoot Boss*** [1951]	$1.50	$5.00	$10.00
B-28	Ermine, Will - ***Prairie Smoke*** [1951]	$1.50	$5.00	$10.00
B-29	Hamilton, Bruce - ***Let Him Have Judgement*** [1951] Cover art by Glyn Jones.	$1.50	$5.00	$10.00
B-30	Cain, James M. - ***Mildred Pierce*** [1950] Cover art by H. Winslade.	$2.50	$7.50	$15.00
B-31	Narayan, R. K. - ***The Bachelor Of Arts*** [1951] Cover art by Maeve Scott.	$1.25	$3.75	$7.50
B-32	Bunyan, John - ***The Pilgrim's Progress*** [1951] Cover by Tate Smith.	$1.50	$5.00	$10.00
B-33	Lustgarten, Edgar - ***Blonde Iscariot*** [1951]	$2.00	$6.00	$12.00
B-34	Marquand, John P. - ***"It's Loaded, Mr. Bauer"*** [1951] Cover art by Arthur Horowicz.	$1.50	$5.00	$10.00
B-35	Charles, George - ***Gallows Parade*** [1951] Cover art by John Oliver.	$1.50	$5.00	$10.00
B-36	Drago, Harry Sinclair - ***Stage Coach Kingdom*** [1951]	$1.50	$5.00	$10.00
B-37	Miller, Arthur - ***Death Of A Salesman*** [1951]	$1.50	$5.00	$10.00
B-38	Harben, Philip - ***Pocket Book Of Modern Cooking*** [1951]	$1.50	$5.00	$10.00
B-39	Anthology edited by John Arlot - ***Famous Sporting Stories*** [1951]	$1.50	$5.00	$10.00
B-40	Anthology edited by John Pudney - ***Pocket Book Of Popular Poetry*** [1951]	$1.25	$3.75	$7.50
B-41	Baldwin, Faith - ***Rehearsal For Love*** [1951] Cover art by R. C. W. Heade.	$1.25	$3.75	$7.50
B-42	Jones, Howard - ***Tropical Tales*** [1951] Cover art by Webster Murray.	$1.50	$5.00	$10.00
B-43	Chase, James Hadley - ***You're Lonely When You're Dead*** [1951] Cover art by Arnold Taylor.	$2.50	$7.50	$15.00
B-44	Foss, Hubert - ***The Concertgoer's Handbook*** [1951]	$1.50	$5.00	$10.00
B-45	Weymouth, Anthony - ***No, Sir Jeremy*** [1951]	$1.25	$3.75	$7.50
B-46	Fair, A. A. (Earl Stanley Gardner) - ***Spill The Jackpot*** [1951] Cover art by Roland Davies.	$1.50	$5.00	$10.00
B-47	Weymouth, Anthony - ***Tempt Me Not*** [1951] Cover art by G. A. Facey.	$1.50	$5.00	$10.00
B-48	Iles, Francis - ***Before The Fact*** [1951]	$1.50	$5.00	$10.00
B-49	Gardner, Erle Stanley - ***The Case Of The Haunted Husband*** [1951] Cover art by Jaeger.	$1.50	$5.00	$10.00
B-50	Gardner, Erle Stanley - ***The Case Of The Crooked Candle*** [1951] Cover art by Paul Kresse.	$1.50	$5.00	$10.00
B-51	Bloom, Ursula - ***Age Cannot Wither*** [1951]	$1.50	$5.00	$10.00
B-52	Fair, A. A. (Erle Stanley Gardner) - ***Turn On The Heat*** [1951] Cover art by Sim.	$1.50	$5.00	$10.00
B-53	Bunce, Frank - ***So Young A Body*** [1951] Cover by Stephen Banay.	$1.50	$5.00	$10.00
B-54	Shannon, Lytle - ***High, Wild and Handsome*** [1951]	$1.50	$5.00	$10.00
B-55	Atholl, Justin - ***How Stalin Knows*** [1951]	$1.50	$5.00	$10.00
B-56	Tayulor, Angeline - ***Black Jade*** [1951]	$2.00	$6.00	$12.00
B-57	Biggers, Earl Derr - ***Keeper Of The Keys*** [1951]	$2.25	$7.00	$14.00
B-58	Moyzisch, L. C. - ***Operation Cicero*** [1951]	$1.50	$5.00	$10.00
B-59	Morrison, Emmeline - ***The Glittering Serpent*** [1951]	$1.50	$5.00	$10.00
B-60	Sage, Dana - ***The 22 Brothers*** [1951] Cover art by Victor Kalin.	$1.50	$5.00	$10.00
B-61	Lindsay, Philip - ***Panama Is Burning*** [1951]	$1.50	$5.00	$10.00
B-62	Gardner, Erle Stanley - ***The Case Of The Golddigger's Purse*** [1951]	$1.50	$5.00	$10.00
B-64	Lindsay, Philip - ***One Dagger For Two*** [1951]	$1.50	$5.00	$10.00

		G	VG	F
B-65	Gardner, Erle Stanley - ***The D.A. Holds A Candle*** [1951]	$1.50	$5.00	$10.00
B-66	Gardner, Erle Stanley - ***The D.A. Goes To Trial*** [1951]	$1.50	$5.00	$10.00
B-67	Gardner, Erle Stanley - ***The Case Of The Baited Hook*** [1951]	$1.50	$5.00	$10.00
B-68	Biggers, Earl Derr - ***The Black Camel*** [1951]	$2.25	$7.00	$14.00
B-69	Coxe, George Harmon - ***Murder For Two*** [1951]	$1.50	$5.00	$10.00
B-70	Anthology - ***Quo Vadis: The Story Of The Film*** [1952] Movie photo cover. Movie tie-in. 16 pages of photos.	$2.00	$6.00	$12.00
B-71	Wellman, Paul I. - ***Broncho Apache*** [1952]	$1.50	$5.00	$10.00
B-73	Gooden, Arthur Henry - ***Wayne Of The Flying W*** [1952]	$1.50	$5.00	$10.00
B-74	Long, Manning - ***Here's Blood In Your Eye*** [1952]	$1.50	$5.00	$10.00
B-77	Welles, Orson - ***The Lives Of Harry Lime*** [1952]	$1.50	$5.00	$10.00
B-78	Bates, H. E. - ***The Purple Plain*** [1952]	$1.50	$5.00	$10.00
B-79	Noble, Peter - ***Ivor Novello*** [1952]	$1.50	$5.00	$10.00
B-80	Long, Manning - ***Vicious Circle*** [1952]	$1.50	$5.00	$10.00
B-82	Shannon, Lytle - ***Rimrock Red*** [1952] Cover art by J. E. McConnell	$1.50	$5.00	$10.00
B-86	Gardner, Erle Stanley - ***The D.A. Cooks A Goose*** [1952]	$1.50	$5.00	$10.00
B-88	Bassett, J.K. - ***Trailers Of The Sage*** [1952] Cover art by J.E. McConnell.	$1.50	$5.00	$10.00
B-89	Saxe, R.B. - ***The Ghost Knows His Greengages*** [1952]	$1.50	$5.00	$10.00
B-90	Coxe, George Harmon - ***Murder In Havana*** [1952]	$1.50	$5.00	$10.00
B-92	Grierson, Francis - ***The Ink Street Murder*** [1952]	$1.50	$5.00	$10.00
B-94	Long, Manning - ***Short Shift*** [1952]	$1.50	$5.00	$10.00
B-100	Dickens, Charles - ***Pickwick Papers*** [1952]	$2.50	$7.50	$15.00
B-106	Hardy, Stuart - ***Arizona Justice*** [1952]	$1.50	$5.00	$10.00

Pocket Books, Jr. New York: Pocket Books, Inc.

J-35	Atwater, Montgomery - ***Ski Patrol*** [1949]	$1.25	$3.75	$7.50
J-36	Shurtleff, Bertrand - ***Long Lash*** [1949]	$1.25	$3.75	$7.50
J-37	Twain, Mark - ***The Adventures Of Tom Sawyer*** [1950]	$1.35	$4.00	$8.00
J-38	Darling, Esther Birdsall - ***Baldy Of Nome*** [1950]	$1.25	$3.75	$7.50
J-39	Sackett, Bert - ***Sponger's Jinx*** [1950]	$1.25	$3.75	$7.50
J-40	Larom, Henry - ***Mountain Pony*** [1950]	$1.25	$3.75	$7.50
J-41	Hinkle, Thomas C. - ***Black Storm*** [1950]	$1.25	$3.75	$7.50
J-42	Twain, Mark - ***The Adventures Of Huckleberry Finn*** [1950]	$1.35	$4.00	$8.00
J-43	Sewell, Helen - ***Black Beauty*** [1950]	$1.25	$3.75	$7.50
J-44	Simpson, Sally - ***Popularity Plus*** [1950]	$1.25	$3.75	$7.50
J-45	Anthology - ***Your Own Book Of Funny Stories*** [1950]	$1.25	$3.75	$7.50
J-46	Hammett, C. T. - ***Your Own Book Of Campcraft*** [1950]	$1.25	$3.75	$7.50
J-47	Gregg, Alan - ***The Mystery Of Batty Ridge*** [1950]	$1.25	$3.75	$7.50
J-48	Garst, Shannon - ***Buffalo Bill*** [1950] Cover art by Lyle.	$1.25	$3.75	$7.50
J-49	Girvan, Helen - ***Blue Treasure*** [1950]	$1.25	$3.75	$7.50
J-50	Balch, Glenn - ***Tiger Roan*** [1950]	$1.25	$3.75	$7.50
J-51	Litten, F. N. - ***The Kingdom Of Flying Men*** [1950]	$1.25	$3.75	$7.50
J-52	Scholz, Jackson - ***Gridiron Challenge*** [1950]	$1.25	$3.75	$7.50
J-53	Boylston, Helen Dore - ***Sue Barton, Senior Nurse*** [1950]	$ .75	$2.50	$5.00
J-54	Lasher, M. H. - ***Logging Chance*** [1950]	$1.25	$3.75	$7.50
J-55	Harkins, Philip - ***Touchdown Twins*** [1950]	$1.25	$3.75	$7.50
J-56	Andrews, Ned - ***Cowdog*** [1950] Cover art by Sam Savitt.	$1.25	$3.75	$7.50
J-57	Stevenson, Robert Louis - ***The Black Arrow*** [1950]	$1.25	$3.75	$7.50
J-58	Hinkle, Thomas C. - ***Mustang*** [1950]	$1.25	$3.75	$7.50
J-59	Friendlich, Dick - ***Pivot Man*** [1950]	$1.25	$3.75	$7.50
J-60	Kjelgaard, Jim - ***Buckskin Brigade*** [1950]	$1.25	$3.75	$7.50
J-61	Cavanna, Betty - ***Black Spaniel Mystery*** [1950]	$1.25	$3.75	$7.50
J-62	Rush, William Marshall - ***Yellowstone Scout*** [1951]	$1.25	$3.75	$7.50
J-63	Williams, Beryl & Epstein, Samuel - ***The Great Houdini*** [1951].	$1.25	$3.75	$7.50
J-64	White, Robb - ***Secret Sea*** [1951]	$1.25	$3.75	$7.50
J-65	Larom, Henry V. - ***Mountain Pony And The Pinto Colt*** [1951]	$1.25	$3.75	$7.50
J-66	Emery, Russell G. - ***High, Inside!*** [1951]	$1.25	$3.75	$7.50
J-67	Tunis, John R. - ***The Kid Comes Back*** [1951]	$1.25	$3.75	$7.50

		G	VG	F
J-68	Heal, Edith - ***Teen-Age Manual*** [1951]	$1.25	$3.75	$7.50
J-69	Calahan, H. A. - ***Back To Treasure Island*** [1951]	$1.25	$3.75	$7.50
J-70	Hinkle, Thomas C. - ***Shag*** [1951]	$1.25	$3.75	$7.50
J-71	Pease, Howard - ***The Jinx Ship*** [1951]	$1.25	$3.75	$7.50
J-72	Grew, David - ***Beyond Rope And Fence*** [1951]	$1.25	$3.75	$7.50
J-73	Pease, Howard - ***Wind In The Rigging*** [1951]	$1.25	$3.75	$7.50
J-74	Dean, Graham - ***Riders Of The Gabilans*** [1951]	$1.25	$3.75	$7.50
J-75	Hines, Jack - ***Wolf Dogs Of The North*** [1951]	$1.25	$3.75	$7.50
J-76	Pease, Howard - ***The Ship Without A Crew*** [1951]	$1.25	$3.75	$7.50
J-77	Davis, Robert - ***Partners Of Powder Hole*** [1951]	$1.25	$3.75	$7.50

Pony Books. New York: Stamford House.

		G	VG	F
45	Craige, Capt. John - ***Your Life In The Atom World*** [1945]	$3.50	$10.00	$20.00
46	Dougall, Bernoard - ***The Singing Corpse*** [1945]	$3.00	$9.00	$18.00
47	Williams, Valentine - ***The Orange Divan*** [1945]	$3.00	$9.00	$18.00
48	Clark, Dale - ***The Narrow Cell*** [1945]	$3.00	$9.00	$18.00
49	Walling, R.A.J. - ***The Corpse With The Red-Headed Friend*** [1946]	$3.00	$9.00	$18.00
50	Oursler, Fulton - ***The House At Fernwood And The Wager*** [1946] PBO	$3.00	$9.00	$18.00
51	Baldwin, Faith - ***The Heart Has Wings*** [1946]	$2.50	$7.50	$15.00
52	Bailey, H.C. - ***A Clue For Mr. Fortune*** [1946]	$3.00	$9.00	$18.00
53	Markey, Morris - ***Unhurrying Chase*** [1946] PBO	$3.00	$9.00	$18.00
54	Reeves, Robert - ***Cellini Smith Detective*** [1946] Cover art by Hoffman.	$3.00	$9.00	$18.00
55	Norris, Kathleen - ***Second Hand Wife*** [1946]	$2.50	$7.50	$15.00
56	Allingham, Margery - ***Wanted: Someone Innocent*** [1946]	$3.00	$9.00	$18.00
57	Leonard, Charles L. - ***The Stolen Squadron*** [1946]	$2.50	$7.50	$15.00
58	Nye, Nelson C. - ***Salt River Ranny*** [1946]	$2.50	$7.50	$15.00
59	Roberts, Cecil - ***One Small Candle*** [1946]	$3.00	$9.00	$18.00
60	Bailey, H.C. - ***The Bishop's Crime*** [1946]	$3.00	$9.00	$18.00
61	Adams, Caswell - editor (anthology) - ***Fifty Famous Sports Stories*** [1946] PBO	$2.50	$7.50	$15.00
62	Fenwick, E.P. - ***The Inconvenient Corpse*** [1946]	$3.00	$9.00	$18.00
63	Whelton, Paul - ***Death And The Devil*** [1946]	$3.00	$9.00	$18.00
64	Bailey, H.C. - ***Mr. Fortune Wonders*** [1946]	$3.00	$9.00	$18.00
65	Anthology - ***Pony Book Of Puzzles*** [1946]	$12.50	$37.50	$75.00
66	Hendryx, James B. - ***Blood Of The North*** [1946] Cover by Barye Phillips	$2.50	$7.50	$15.00

Pony Books. Toronto: Weldun Publications.

		G	VG	F
122	Stapleton, Douglas & Helen A. Carey - ***The Corpse Is Indignant*** [1946]	$5.00	$15.00	$30.00
123	Maxon, P.B. - ***The Waltz Of Death*** [1946]	$5.00	$15.00	$30.00
124	Williams, Idabel - ***Hell-Cat*** [1946]	$5.00	$15.00	$30.00
125	Hobard, Donald Bayne - ***Monkeys In The Mirror*** [1946]	$5.00	$15.00	$30.00
126	Janson, Hank - ***Orchids To You*** [1946]	$5.00	$15.00	$30.00
127	Brown, Elwood - ***The Lion Murders*** [1946]	$5.00	$15.00	$30.00

Popular Digests.

		G	VG	F
NN	True Stories - ***Candid Confessions*** [1937] Digest Size. Vol. 1 #1.	$12.50	$37.50	$75.00

Popular Library Books (Early Publisher's History, 1942–1959)

Popular accurately describes this line of books. Ned Pines published newspapers, magazines, and a variety of pulp series prior to establishing this line with Leo Margulies. Early titles include many mysteries by popular writers, and the line presents many desirable mysteries throughout. The spectacular airbrushed covers feature the work of H. L. Hoffman, Rudolph Belarski, and Earle Bergey. Line drawings of the cover art appear on the title in a reduced form. In 1947, green end papers became a trademark of this line.

In addition, the following lines appeared by the same publishers. They include the Popular Giant or G series, Popular Eagle, and three Popular letter series, PC, SP, and W.

Popular Library Books. New York: Popular Library, Inc.

		G	VG	F
NN-1	Charteris, Leslie - ***Saint Overboard*** [1943] Cover by Hoffman.	$17.00	$50.00	$100.00
NN-2	Eberhart, Mignon G. - ***Danger In The Dark*** [1943] Cover by Hoffman.	$8.00	$25.00	$50.00
NN-3	King, Rufus - ***Crime Of Violence*** [1943] Cover by Hoffman.	$8.00	$25.00	$50.00
4	Latimer, Jonathan - ***Murder In The Madhouse*** [1943] Cover art by Hoffman.	$5.50	$17.50	$35.00
5	Rinehart, Mary Roberts - ***Miss Pinkerton*** [1943] Cover art by Hoffman.	$5.50	$17.50	$35.00
6	Ford, Leslie - ***Three Bright Pebbles*** [1943] Cover art by Hoffman.	$5.50	$17.50	$35.00
7	Reilly, Helen - ***Death Demands An Audience*** [1943] Cover art by Hoffman.	$5.50	$17.50	$35.00
8	Patrick, Quentin - ***Death For Dear Clara*** [1943] Cover art by Hoffman.	$5.50	$17.50	$35.00
9	Frome, David (Ford, Leslie) - ***The Eel Pie Murders*** [1943] Cover art by Jon Nielsen.	$5.50	$17.50	$35.00
10	Carr, John Dickson - ***To Wake The Dead*** [1943] Cover art by Hoffman.	$8.00	$25.00	$50.00
11	Freeman, R. Austin - ***The Stoneware Monkey*** [1943] Cover by Hoffman.	$6.00	$20.00	$40.00
12	Rhode, John - ***Death Sits On The Board*** [1943] Cover art by Hoffman.	$5.50	$17.50	$35.00
13	King, Rufus - ***Valcour Meets Murder*** [1944] Cover art by Hoffman.	$5.50	$17.50	$35.00
14	Taylor, Pheobe Atwood - ***Criminal C.O.D.*** [1944] Cover art by Hoffman.	$5.00	$15.00	$30.00
15	White, Ethel Lina - ***The Third Eye*** [1944] Cover art by Hoffman.	$5.00	$15.00	$30.00
16	Latimer, Jonathan - ***The Dead Don't Care*** [1944] PBO. Cover art by Hoffman.	$5.00	$15.00	$30.00
17	Eberhart, Mignon G. - ***The House On The Roof*** [1944] Cover art by Hoffman.	$5.00	$15.00	$30.00
18	Croft, Freeman Wills - ***Tragedy In The Hollow*** [1944] Cover by Hoffman.	$5.00	$15.00	$30.00
19	Carr, John Dickson - ***The Crooked Hinge*** [1944] Cover art by Hoffman.	$6.00	$20.00	$40.00
20	Reilly, Helen - ***Murder In Shinbone Alley*** [1944] Cover by Hoffman.	$5.00	$15.00	$30.00
21	Rinehart, Mary Roberts - ***The After House*** [1944] Cover art by Hoffman.	$4.00	$12.50	$25.00
22	King, Rufus - ***Murder Masks Miami*** [1944] Cover art by Hoffman.	$4.00	$12.50	$25.00
23	Patrick, Quentin - ***S. S. Murder*** [1944] Cover art by Hoffman.	$4.00	$12.50	$25.00
24	Ford, Leslie - ***Reno Rendezvous*** [1944] Cover by Hoffman.	$4.00	$12.50	$25.00
25	Taylor, Phoebe Atwood - ***Out Of Order*** [1944] Cover art by Hoffman.	$4.00	$12.50	$25.00
26	Frome, David - ***Mr. Pinkerton Has The Clue*** [1944] Cover art by Hoffman.	$4.00	$12.50	$25.00
27	Eberhart, Mignon G. - ***From This Dark Stairway*** [1944] Cover art by Hoffman.	$4.00	$12.50	$25.00

		G	VG	F
28	Carr, John Dickson - ***The Burning Court*** [1944] Cover art by Hoffman.	$6.00	$20.00	$40.00
29	Wentworth, Patricia - ***Weekend With Death*** [1944] Cover art by Hoffman.	$4.00	$12.50	$25.00
30	Blake, Nicholas - ***There's Trouble Brewing*** [1944] Cover art by Hoffman.	$4.00	$12.50	$25.00
31	King, Rufus - ***Murder By The Clock*** [1944] Cover art by E. Zutrau.	$4.00	$12.50	$25.00
32	White, Ethel Lina - ***The Wheel Spins*** [1944] Cover art by Hoffman.	$4.00	$12.50	$25.00
33	Reilly, Helen - ***McKee Of Centre Street*** [1944] Cover art by Hoffman.	$4.00	$12.50	$25.00
34	Frome, David - ***Mr. Pinkerton At The Old Angel*** [1944] Cover art by Hoffman.	$4.00	$12.50	$25.00
35	Eberhart, Mignon G. - ***The Mystery Of Hunting's End*** [1944] Cover art by Hoffman.	$4.00	$12.50	$25.00
36	Patrick, Quentin - ***Death And The Maiden*** [1944] Cover art by Hoffman.	$4.00	$12.50	$25.00
37	Lee, Gypsy Rose - ***Mother Finds A Body*** [1944] Cover art by Hoffman.	$4.00	$12.50	$25.00
38	Footner, Hulbert - ***The Dark Ships*** [1944] Cover art by Hoffman.	$4.00	$12.50	$25.00
39	Wentworth, Patricia - ***In The Balance*** [1944] Cover art by Hoffman.	$4.00	$12.50	$25.00
40	Stagge, Jonathan - ***The Stars Spell Death*** [1944] Cover art by Hoffman.	$4.00	$12.50	$25.00
41	Blake, Nicholas - ***The Smiler With The Knife*** [1945] Cover art by Hoffman.	$4.00	$12.50	$25.00
42	Beeding, Francis - ***Murdered: One By One*** [1944] Cover art by Hoffman.	$4.00	$12.50	$25.00
43	King, Rufus - ***The Fatal Kiss Mystery*** [1945] Cover art by Hoffman.	$4.00	$12.50	$25.00
44	Pentecost, Hugh - ***The Brass Chills*** [1945] Cover art by Hoffman.	$4.00	$12.50	$25.00
45	Rice, Craig - ***The Wrong Murder*** [1945] Cover art by Hoffman.	$5.00	$15.00	$30.00
46	Cohen, Octavus Roy - ***Sound Of Revelry*** [1945] Cover art by Hoffman.	$4.00	$12.50	$25.00
47	Patrick, Quentin - ***Return To The Scene*** [1945] Cover by Im-Ho.	$4.00	$12.50	$25.00
48	Reilly, Helen - ***Mr. Smith's Hat*** [1945] Cover by Im-Ho.	$4.00	$12.50	$25.00
49	Garth, David - ***Tiger Milk*** [1944] Cover by Hoffman.	$4.00	$12.50	$25.00
50	Clason, Clyde B. - ***Green Shiver*** [1945] Cover art by Hoffman.	$4.00	$12.50	$25.00
51	Seeley, Mabel - ***The Whispering Cup*** [1945] Cover art by Hoffman.	$3.50	$10.00	$20.00
52	Stagge, Jonathan - ***Murder By Prescription*** [1945] Cover art by Hoffman.	$3.50	$10.00	$20.00
53	Pentecost, Hugh - ***Cancelled In Red*** [1945] Cover art by Hoffman.	$3.50	$10.00	$20.00
54	White, Ethel Lina - ***Her Heart In Her Throat*** [1945] Movie tie-in from "The Unseen." Cover art by Hoffman.	$3.50	$10.00	$20.00
55	King, Rufus - ***Murder In The Willett Family*** [1945] Cover art by Hoffman.	$3.50	$10.00	$20.00
56	Reilly, Helen - ***Dead For A Ducat*** [1945] Cover art by Hoffman.	$3.50	$10.00	$20.00
57	Beeding, Francis - ***The Twelve Disguises*** [1945] Cover art by Hoffman.	$3.50	$10.00	$20.00
58	Crane, Frances - ***The Turquoise Shop*** [1945] Cover art by Hoffman.	$3.50	$10.00	$20.00
59	Boucher, Anthony - ***The Case Of The Solid Key*** [1945] Cover by Im-Ho.	$3.50	$10.00	$20.00

		G	VG	F
60	Blake, Nicholas - ***The Corpse In The Snowman*** [1945] Cover art by Hoffman.	$3.50	$10.00	$20.00
61	Carr, John Dickson - ***The Mad Hatter Mystery*** [1945] Cover art by Hoffman.	$4.00	$12.50	$25.00
62	Stagge, Jonathan - ***The Yellow Taxi*** [1945] Cover art by Hoffman.	$3.50	$10.00	$20.00
63	Langham, James R. - ***Sing A Song Of Homicide*** [1945] Cover art by Hoffman.	$3.50	$10.00	$20.00
64	Ronald, James - ***They Can't Hang Me*** [1945] Cover art by Hoffman.	$3.50	$10.00	$20.00
65	August, John - ***The Woman In The Picture*** [1945] Cover art by Hoffman.	$3.50	$10.00	$20.00
66	Wentworth, Patricia - ***The Blind Side*** [1945] Cover art by Hoffman.	$3.50	$10.00	$20.00
67	King, Rufus - ***Murder On The Yacht*** [1945] Cover art by Hoffman.	$3.50	$10.00	$20.00
68	Downing, Todd - ***The Cat Screams*** [1945] Cover art by Hoffman.	$3.50	$10.00	$20.00
69	Seeley, Mabel - ***The Listening House*** [1946] Cover art by Hoffman.	$3.50	$10.00	$20.00
70	Freeman, R. Austin - ***Mr. Polton Explains*** [1946] Cover art by Hoffman.	$3.50	$10.00	$20.00
71	Beeding, Francis - ***Hell Let Loose*** [1946] Cover by Hoffman.	$3.50	$10.00	$20.00
72	Field, Medora - ***Who Killed Aunt Maggie?*** [1946] Cover art by Hoffman.	$3.50	$10.00	$20.00
73	Eberhart, Mignon G. - ***Hasty Wedding*** [1946] Cover art by Hoffman.	$3.50	$10.00	$20.00
74	Cohen, Octavus Roy - ***Murder In Season*** [1946] Cover art by Hoffman.	$3.50	$10.00	$20.00
75	White, Ethel White - ***She Faded Into Thin Air*** [1946] Cover art by Hoffman.	$3.00	$9.00	$18.00
76	Williams, Valentine & Sims, Dorothy Rice - ***Fog*** [1946] Cover art by Hoffman.	$3.00	$9.00	$18.00
77	Cunningham, Eugene - ***Buckaroo*** [1946] Cover art by Hoffman.	$2.50	$7.50	$15.00
78	Brand, Max - ***Timbal Gulch Trail*** [1946] Cover art by Hoffman.	$2.50	$7.50	$15.00
79	Wentworth, Patricia - ***Rolling Stone*** [1946] Cover art by Hoffman.	$3.00	$9.00	$18.00
80	Crane, Frances - ***The Golden Box*** [1946] Cover art by Hoffman.	$3.00	$9.00	$18.00
81	Fuller, Timothy - ***Three Thirds Of A Ghost*** [1946] Cover art by Hoffman.	$3.00	$9.00	$18.00
82	Pentecost, Hugh - ***The 24th Horse*** [1946] Cover art by Hoffman.	$3.00	$9.00	$18.00
83	Little, Constance and Gwenyth - ***The Black-Headed Pins*** [1946] Cover art by Hoffman.	$3.00	$9.00	$18.00
84	Garth, David - ***Challenge For Three*** [1945] Cover by Hoffman.	$3.00	$9.00	$18.00
85	Haycox, Ernest - ***Trouble Shooter*** [1946] Cover art by Hoffman.	$2.50	$7.50	$15.00
86	Raine, William Macleod - ***Bucky Follows a Cold Trail*** [1946] Cover art by Hoffman.	$2.50	$7.50	$15.00
87	Rhode, John and Dickson, Carter - ***Fatal Descent*** [1946] Cover art by Fiedler.	$3.50	$10.00	$20.00
88	Cohen, Octavus Roy - ***Romance In The First Degree*** [1946] Cover by Im-Ho.	$3.00	$9.00	$18.00
89	Rice, Craig - ***The Right Murder*** [1946] Cover by Im-Ho.	$3.50	$10.00	$20.00
90	Stagge, Jonathan - ***The Scarlet Circle*** [1946] Cover by Im-Ho.	$3.00	$9.00	$18.00
91	Sabatini, Rafael - ***The Sea Hawk*** [1946] Cover by Im-Ho.	$2.00	$6.00	$12.00
92	Powell, Richard - ***All Over But The Shooting*** [1946] Cover art by Fiedler.	$2.50	$7.50	$15.00
93	Worts, George F. - ***The Blue Lacquer Box*** [1946] Cover by Im-Ho.	$2.50	$7.50	$15.00
94	Bottome, Phyllis - ***The Mortal Storm*** [1946] Cover by Im-Ho.	$2.00	$6.00	$12.00

		G	VG	F
95	Gregory, Jackson - ***Red Law*** [1946] Cover by Im-Ho.	$2.00	$6.00	$12.00
96	Tuttle, W.C. - ***Singing River*** [1946] Cover by Im-Ho.	$2.00	$6.00	$12.00
97	King, Rufus - ***A Variety Of Weapons*** [1946] Cover by Im-Ho.	$2.50	$7.50	$15.00
98	Halliday, Brett - ***Dividend On Death*** [1946] Cover by Im-Ho.	$2.50	$7.50	$15.00
99	Rhode, John - ***Dead Of The Night*** [1946] Cover by Im-Ho.	$2.50	$7.50	$15.00
100	Huxley, Elspeth - ***The African Poison Murders*** [1946] Cover by Im-Ho.	$2.50	$7.50	$15.00
101	Hurst, Fannie - ***Lummox*** [1946] Cover by Im-Ho.	$2.00	$6.00	$12.00
102	Busch, Niven - ***Duel In The Sun*** [1946] Movie tie-in with photo cover.	$1.50	$5.00	$10.00
103	Mowery, WIlliam Byron - ***The Phantom Canoe*** [1946] Cover by Im-Ho.	$2.00	$6.00	$12.00
104	Mulford, Clarence E. - ***Mesquite Jenkins, Tumbleweed*** [1946] Cover art by Fiedler.	$2.00	$6.00	$12.00
105	Wentworth, Patricia - ***The Case Is Closed*** [1946] Cover by Im-Ho.	$2.50	$7.50	$15.00
106	Walling, R.A.J. - ***The Corpse With The Eerie Eye*** [1946] Cover by Im-Ho.	$2.50	$7.50	$15.00
107	Anthology - ***Crossword Puzzles*** [1946] PBO. Cover by Im-Ho.	$12.50	$37.50	$75.00
108	Crane, Frances - ***The Yellow Violet*** [1946] Cover by Im-Ho.	$2.50	$7.50	$15.00
109	Pentecost, Hugh - ***I'll Sing At Your Funeral*** [1946] Cover by Im-Ho.	$2.50	$7.50	$15.00
110	Cloete, Stuart - ***Congo Song*** [1945] Cover by Im-Ho.	$2.00	$6.00	$12.00
111	Caspary, Vera - ***Bedelia*** [1946] Movie tie-in.	$2.00	$6.00	$12.00
112	Little, Constance and Gwenyth - ***The Black Shrouds*** [1946] Cover by Im-Ho.	$2.50	$7.50	$15.00
113	Williams, Ben Ames - ***Crucible*** [1946]	$1.50	$5.00	$10.00
114	Short, Luke - ***Ramrod*** [1946] Cover by Im-Ho.	$1.50	$5.00	$10.00
115	Pines, Ned L. - editor - ***Popular Book Of Cartoons*** [1946] PBO. Cartoon book.	$4.00	$12.50	$25.00
116	Chamberlain, George Agnew - ***The Red House*** [1948] Cover by Im-Ho. Movie tie-in.	$3.00	$9.00	$18.00
117	Fuller, Timothy - ***This Is Murder, Mr. Jones*** [1948] Cover by Im-Ho.	$2.50	$7.50	$15.00
118	Bower, B.M. - ***The Flying U's Last Stand*** [1946] Cover art by Fiedler.	$1.50	$5.00	$10.00
119	Gill, Tom - ***Firebrand*** [1946] Cover by Im-Ho.	$1.50	$5.00	$10.00
120	White, Ethel Lina - ***The Spiral Staircase*** [1946] Movie tie-in. Cover by Im-Ho.	$2.50	$7.50	$15.00
121	Crofts, Freeman Wills - ***A Losing Game*** [1947] Cover by Im-Ho.	$2.50	$7.50	$15.00
122	Freeman, R. Austin - ***The Adventures Of Dr. Thorndike*** [1947] Cover art by Fiedler.	$4.00	$12.50	$25.00
123	Blake, Nicholas - ***A Question Of Proof*** [1948] Cover by Fiedler.	$2.50	$7.50	$15.00
124	King, Rufus - ***Design In Evil*** [1948] Cover by Im-Ho.	$2.50	$7.50	$15.00
125	Shattuck, Richard - ***Said The Spider To The Fly*** [1948] Cover by Im-Ho.	$2.50	$7.50	$15.00
126	Taylor, Phoebe Atwood - ***The Deadly Sunshade*** [1947]	$2.50	$7.50	$15.00
127	Mowery, William Byron - ***Paradise Trail*** [1947]	$1.50	$5.00	$10.00
128	Marshall, Edison - ***The Voice Of The Pack*** [1947]	$1.35	$4.00	$8.00
129	Fisher, Steve - ***I Wake Up Screaming*** [1947]	$2.50	$7.50	$15.00
130	Anthology - ***The Mystery Companion*** [1947] Includes Robert Bloch, Cornell Woolrich, et al.	$3.50	$10.00	$20.00
131	Wentworth, Patricia - ***The Clock Strikes Twelve*** [1947]	$2.50	$7.50	$15.00
132	Biggers, Earl Derr - ***7 Keys To Baldpate*** [1948]	$3.00	$9.00	$18.00
133	August, John - ***Advance Agent*** [1947]	$2.00	$6.00	$12.00
134	Young, Gordon - ***Fighting Blood*** [1947]	$1.50	$5.00	$10.00
135	Coburn, Walt - ***Law Rides The Range*** [1948]	$1.50	$5.00	$10.00
136	Garth, David - ***Appointment With Danger*** [1948] Cover art by Fiedler.	$2.50	$7.50	$15.00

Popular Library, 174

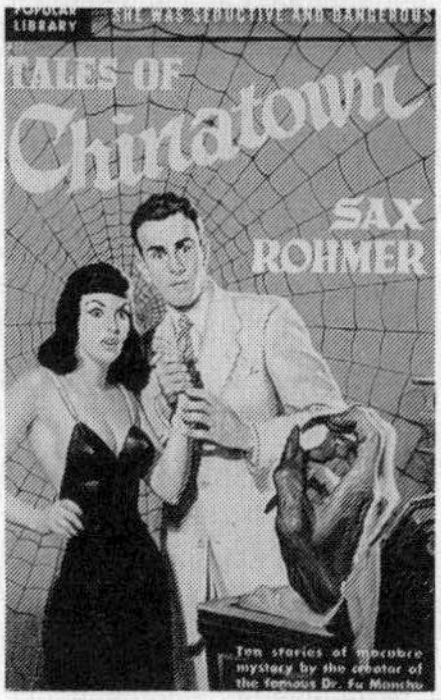

Popular Library, 217

Popular Library, 223

		G	VG	F
137	Irish, William - ***Six Times Death*** [1948]	$8.00	$25.00	$50.00
138	Roche, Arthur Somers - ***The Case Against Mrs. Ames*** [1948] Cover art by Rudolph Belarski.	$3.50	$10.00	$20.00
139	Walling, R.A.J. - ***The Corpse With The Grimy Glove*** [1948]	$2.50	$7.50	$15.00
140	Gregory, Jackson - ***Secret Valley*** [1948]	$1.50	$5.00	$10.00
141	Lemay, Alan - ***Winter Range*** [1948]	$1.50	$5.00	$10.00
142	Fill, Tom - ***Guardians Of The Desert*** [1948]	$1.50	$5.00	$10.00
143	Haycox, Ernest - ***Free Grass*** [1948]	$1.50	$5.00	$10.00
144	Cohen, Octavus Roy - ***Danger In Paradise*** [1948] Cover by Rudolph Belarski.	$3.50	$10.00	$20.00
145	Raine, William MacLeod - ***Gunsmoke Trail*** [1948]	$1.50	$5.00	$10.00
146	Mulford, Clarence E. - ***Hopalong Cassidy Takes Cards*** [1948]	$1.50	$5.00	$10.00
147	Erskine, John - ***The Private Life Of Helen Of Troy*** [1948] Cover by Rudolph Belarski.	$6.00	$20.00	$40.00
148	Cunningham, Eugene - ***The Ranger Way*** [1949]	$1.50	$5.00	$10.00
149	Tuttle, W.C. - ***Hidden Blood*** [1948]	$1.50	$5.00	$10.00
150	Anthology - ***Crossword Puzzle Book 2*** [1948] Puzzle book	$12.50	$37.50	$75.00
151	Seltzer, Charles Alden - ***Double Cross Ranch*** [1948]	$1.50	$5.00	$10.00
152	Brand, Max - ***Rancher's Revenge*** [1948] Cover art by A. Leslie Ross.	$1.50	$5.00	$10.00
153	Chesterton, Gilbert K. - ***The Secret Of Father Brown (And Other Stories)*** [1948]	$2.50	$7.50	$15.00
154	Boucher, Anthony - ***The Case Of The Crumpled Knave*** [1949] Cover art by Rudolph Belarski.	$5.50	$17.50	$35.00
155	Williams, Ben Ames - ***The Dreadful Night*** [1949] Cover by Rudolph Belarski.	$3.50	$10.00	$20.00
156	Anthology - ***Popular Book Of Western Stories*** [1948] Edited by Leo Margulies. Cover art by A. Leslie Ross.	$1.50	$5.00	$10.00
157	Bower, B.M. - ***The Flying U Strikes*** [1948]	$1.50	$5.00	$10.00
158	Ford, Leslie - ***The Strangled Witness*** [1948]	$2.50	$7.50	$15.00
159	Abbot, Anthony - ***About The Murder Of The Circus Queen*** [1948] Cover art by Rudolph Belarski.	$5.50	$17.50	$35.00
160	Gregory, Jackson - ***The Silver Star*** [1949] Cover by A. Leslie Ross.	$1.50	$5.00	$10.00
161	LeMay, Alan - ***Thunder In The Dust*** [1948]	$1.50	$5.00	$10.00
162	Cohen, Octavus Roy - ***Love Has No Alibi*** [1949] Cover art by Rudolph Belarski.	$4.00	$12.50	$25.00
163	Sale, Richard - ***Death At Sea*** [1948] Cover art by Rudolph Belarski.	$3.50	$10.00	$20.00
164	Williams, Ben Ames - ***Lady In Peril*** [1949] Cover art by Rudolph Belarski.	$5.00	$15.00	$30.00

		G	VG	F
165	Tuttle, W.C. - ***Valley Of Vanishing Herds*** [1948] Cover art by A. Leslie Ross	$1.50	$5.00	$10.00
166	Coburn, Walt - ***Sky-Pilot Cowboy*** [1948]	$1.50	$5.00	$10.00
167	Eberhart, Mignon G. - ***Pattern Of Murder*** [1948] Cover art by Rudolph Belarski.	$3.50	$10.00	$20.00
168	Dodge, David - ***Death And Taxes*** [1949] Cover by Rudolph Belarski.	$4.00	$12.50	$25.00
169	Stone, Grace Zaring (Ethel Vance) - ***The Bitter Tea Of General Yen*** [1949]	$3.00	$9.00	$18.00
170	Linscott, Robert - editor - ***Omnibus Of American Humor*** [1949]	$1.35	$4.00	$8.00
171	Haycox, Ernest - ***Chaffee Of Roaring Horse*** [1949]	$1.50	$5.00	$10.00
172	Raine, William MacLeod - ***Pistol Partners*** [1949]	$1.50	$5.00	$10.00
173	Fenisong, Ruth - ***Death Is A Lovely Lady*** [1949]	$2.50	$7.50	$15.00
174	Carr, John Dickson - ***The Three Coffins*** [1949] Cover art by Rudolph Belarski.	$3.50	$10.00	$20.00
175	Young, Gordon - ***Roaring Guns*** [1949]	$1.50	$5.00	$10.00
176	Cunningham, Eugene - ***Diamond River Range*** [1949]	$1.50	$5.00	$10.00
177	Chambers, Dana - ***Some Day I'll Kill You*** [1949]	$2.50	$7.50	$15.00
178	Spain, John - ***Death Is Like That*** [1949] Cover art by Rudolph Belarski.	$4.00	$12.50	$25.00
179	Mowery, WIlliam Byron - ***Outlaw Breed*** [1949]	$1.50	$5.00	$10.00
180	Sinclair, Bertrand W. - ***Wild West*** [1949]	$1.50	$5.00	$10.00
181	Kling, Ken - ***How I Pick Winners*** [1949] "A Complete Handbook on Horse Racing".	$1.35	$4.00	$8.00
182	Carnegie, Dale - ***Little Known Facts About Well Known People*** [1949] Photo cover.	$1.25	$3.75	$7.50
183	Kantor, MacKinlay - ***Gentle Annie*** [1949] Cover art by Rudolph Belarski.	$1.50	$5.00	$10.00
184	Gregory, Jackson - ***Marshall Of Sundown*** [1949] Cover by A. Leslie Ross.	$1.50	$5.00	$10.00
185	Spearman, Frank H. - ***Whispering Smith*** [1949]	$1.50	$5.00	$10.00
186	Pines, Ned - editor - ***Cartoon Fun*** [1949] Cartoon book.	$3.50	$10.00	$20.00
187	Margulies, Leo - editor - ***Selected Western Stories*** [1949] Cover art by A. Leslie Ross.	$1.50	$5.00	$10.00
188	Gruber, Frank - ***The Yellow Overcoat*** [1949] Cover art by Rudolph Belarski.	$8.00	$25.00	$50.00
189	Holding, Elisabeth Saxany - ***The Death Wish*** [1949] Cover art by Rudolph Belarski.	$4.00	$12.50	$25.00
190	Gill, Tom - ***The Gay Bandit Of The Border*** [1949]	$1.50	$5.00	$10.00
191	Coburn, Walt - ***Barb Wire*** [1949]	$1.50	$5.00	$10.00
192	Halliday, Brett - ***Bodies Are Where You Find Them*** [1949] Cover art by Rudolph Belarski.	$5.00	$15.00	$30.00
193	King, Rufus - ***The Case Of The Constant God*** [1949] Cover art by Rudolph Belarski.	$4.00	$12.50	$25.00
194	Williams, Ben Ames - ***Death On Scurvy Street*** [1949] Cover art by Rudolph Belarski.	$4.00	$12.50	$25.00
195	Bellah, James Warner - ***Ward 20*** [1949] Cover art by Rudolph Belarski.	$3.50	$10.00	$20.00
196	Cohen, Octavus Roy - ***There's Always Time To Die*** [1949]	$2.50	$7.50	$15.00
197	Wentworth, Patricia - ***Pursuit Of A Parcel*** [1949]	$2.50	$7.50	$15.00
198	Mulford, Clarence E. - ***Hopalong Cassidy's Saddle Mate*** [1949] Cover art by A. Leslie Ross.	$1.50	$5.00	$10.00
199	Haycox, Ernest - ***Whispering Range*** [1949]	$1.50	$5.00	$10.00
200	Matson, Norman - ***Bats In The Belfry*** [1949] Cover by Herbert Roese.	$1.50	$5.00	$10.00
201	Field, Medora - ***Blood On Her Shoe*** [1945] Cover by Rudolph Belarski.	$3.50	$10.00	$20.00
202	Dodge, David - ***Shear The Black Sheep*** [1949]	$2.50	$7.50	$15.00
203	Tuttle, W.C. - ***Wild Horse Valley*** [1949] Cover by A. Leslie Ross.	$1.50	$5.00	$10.00

Popular Library, 231

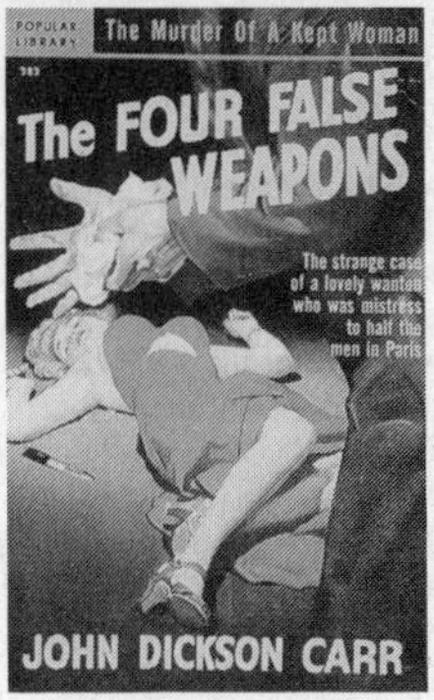

Popular Library, 282

Popular Library, 306

		G	VG	F
204	Seltzer, Charles Alden - ***Arizona Jim*** [1949]	$1.50	$5.00	$10.00
205	Sale, Richard - ***Home Is The Hangman*** [1949] Cover art by Rudolph Belarski.	$4.00	$12.50	$25.00
206	Patrick, Quentin - ***The Grindle Nightmare*** [1949] Cover art by Rudolph Belarski.	$5.50	$17.50	$35.00
207	Fuller, Timothy - ***Reunion With Murder*** [1949]	$2.50	$7.50	$15.00
208	Marshall, Edison - ***The Deputy At Snow Mountain*** [1949]	$1.50	$5.00	$10.00
209	LeMay, Alan - ***Gunsight Trail*** [1949]	$1.50	$5.00	$10.00
210	Miller, Merle - ***That Winter*** [1950]	$2.00	$6.00	$12.00
211	Reilly, Helen - ***The Doll's Trunk Murder*** [1949] Cover art by Rudolph Belarski.	$17.00	$50.00	$100.00
212	McMullen, Richard - ***Awake To Darkness*** [1949] Cover art by Rudolph Belarski.	$3.00	$9.00	$18.00
213	Raine, William MacLeod - ***Rustler's Gap*** [1950] Cover art by J. Dreany.	$1.50	$5.00	$10.00
214	Mowery, William Byron - ***Guns In The Valley*** [1950]	$1.50	$5.00	$10.00
215	Williams, Ben Ames - ***The Silver Forest*** [1949] Cover art by Rudolph Belarski.	$3.00	$9.00	$18.00
216	Steinbeck, John - ***Cup Of Gold*** [1950] Cover art by Rudolph Belarski.	$4.00	$12.50	$25.00
217	Rohmer, Sax - ***Tales Of Chinatown*** [1950]	$10.00	$30.00	$60.00
218	Crane, Frances - ***The Pink Umbrella Murder*** [1949]	$5.50	$17.50	$35.00
219	Ellson, Hal - ***Duke*** [1950] Cover art by Rudolph Belarski.	$5.00	$15.00	$30.00
220	Weiner, Ed - ***The Damon Runyon Story*** [1950] Introduction by Walter Winchell.	$3.00	$9.00	$18.00
221	Loos, Anita - ***Gentlemen Prefer Blondes*** [1950] Cover art by Earle Bergey.	$7.00	$22.50	$45.00
222	Hargrove, Marion - ***Something's Got To Give*** [1950]	$1.35	$4.00	$8.00
223	Adams, John Paul - ***Picture Quiz Book*** [1950] PBO. Cover art by Alex Schomburg.	$22.00	$70.00	$140.00
224	Barrett, Mona - ***Sun In Their Eyes*** [1950] Cover art by Rudolph Belarski.	$3.00	$9.00	$18.00
225	Young, Gordon - ***Fast On The Draw*** [1950] Cover art by Samuel Cherry.	$1.50	$5.00	$10.00
226	Gregory, Jackson - ***Sudden Bill Dorn*** [1950] Cover art by Samuel Cherry.	$1.50	$5.00	$10.00
227	Thayer, Tiffany - ***The Illustrious Corpse*** [1950] Cover art by Rudolph Belarski.	$6.00	$20.00	$40.00
228	Mead, Shepherd - ***The Sex Machine*** [1950] Cover art by Alex Schomburg.	$5.50	$17.50	$35.00

		G	VG	F
229	Fisher, Steve - ***Homicide Johnny*** [1950] Cover art by Rudolph Belarski.	$5.50	$17.50	$35.00
230	Miller, Arthur - ***Focus*** [1950] Cover art by Belarski.	$3.50	$10.00	$20.00
231	Seeley, Mabel - ***The Chuckling Fingers*** [1950] Cover art by Belarski.	$6.00	$20.00	$40.00
232	Wentworth, Patricia - ***The Key*** [1950]	$2.50	$7.50	$15.00
233	Van Saher, Lilla - ***Macamba*** [1950] Cover by Rudolph Belarski.	$3.50	$10.00	$20.00
234	Cunningham, Eugene - ***Quick Triggers*** [1950]	$1.50	$5.00	$10.00
235	Haycox, Ernest - ***Starlight Rider*** [1950]	$1.50	$5.00	$10.00
236	Wilson, Earl - ***Pikes Peek Or Bust*** [1950] Cover art by Alex Schomburg.	$5.00	$15.00	$30.00
237	Bourne, Peter - ***Drums Of Destiny*** [1950] Earle Bergey cover.	$3.00	$9.00	$18.00
238	Chambers, Dana - ***She'll Be Dead By Morning*** [1950]	$3.00	$9.00	$18.00
239	Spain, John - ***The Evil Star*** [1950]	$2.50	$7.50	$15.00
240	Perelman, S.J. - ***Acres And Pains*** [1950] Drawings by R. Osborn.	$1.35	$4.00	$8.00
241	Sabatini, Rafael - ***The Fortunes Of Captain Blood*** [1950] Cover art by Rudolph Belarski. Movie tie-in.	$2.00	$6.00	$12.00
242	Marshall, Edison - ***Riders Of The Smoky Land*** [1950]	$1.50	$5.00	$10.00
243	Raine, William MacLeod - ***Texas Breed*** [1950]	$1.50	$5.00	$10.00
244	Lowry, Robert - ***Find Me In Fire*** [1950]	$4.00	$12.50	$25.00
245	Fenisong, Ruth - ***Death Is A Gold Coin*** [1950]	$3.00	$9.00	$18.00
246	King, Rufus - ***Murder By Latitude*** [1950] Cover by Rudolph Belarski.	$3.50	$10.00	$20.00
247	Sale, Richard - ***Not Too Narrow... Not Too Deep*** [1950]	$3.00	$9.00	$18.00
248	Ingersoll, Ralph - ***The Great Ones*** [1950]	$1.50	$5.00	$10.00
249	Tuttle, W.C. - ***Twisted Trails*** [1950] Cover by Kirk Wilson.	$1.50	$5.00	$10.00
250	Coburn, Walt - ***Mavericks*** [1950] Cover by Dreany.	$1.50	$5.00	$10.00
251	Katkov, Norman - ***Eagle At My Eyes*** [1950]	$2.00	$6.00	$12.00
252	Dodge, David - ***Bullets For The Bridegroom*** [1950]	$3.00	$9.00	$18.00
253	Rice, Craig - ***Yesterday's Murder*** [1950]	$3.50	$10.00	$20.00
254	White, William Chapman - ***The Pale Blonde Of Sands Street*** [1950] Cover by Earle Bergey.	$4.50	$14.00	$28.00
255	Gregory, Jackson - ***The Lone Rider*** [1950]	$1.50	$5.00	$10.00
256	Raine, William MacLeod - ***Drygulch Trail*** [1950] Cover by George Rozen.	$1.50	$5.00	$10.00
257	Wolff, Maritta M. - ***Whistle Stop*** [1950] George Rozen cover.	$2.00	$6.00	$12.00
258	Irish, William (Cornell Woolrich) - ***Six Nights Of Mystery*** [1950] PBO. Cover by Rudolph Belarski.	$10.00	$30.00	$60.00
259	Reilly, Helen - ***Murder In The Mews*** [1950]	$2.50	$7.50	$15.00
260	Brady, Leo - ***The Edge Of Doom*** [1949] Cover by Rudolph Belarski. Movie tie-in.	$2.00	$6.00	$12.00
261	LeMay, Alan - ***Painted Ponies*** [1950] Cover art by Cherry.	$1.50	$5.00	$10.00
262	Young, Gordon - ***Guns Of The Arrowhead*** [1950]	$1.50	$5.00	$10.00
263	Patrick, Quentin - ***Murder At Cambridge*** [1950]	$3.00	$9.00	$18.00
264	Cohen, Octavus Roy - ***Dangerous Lady*** [1950] Rudolph Belarski cover.	$4.00	$12.50	$25.00
265	Yoseloff, Martin - ***The Girl In The Spike-Heeled Shoes*** [1950]	$2.00	$6.00	$12.00
266	Heatter, Basil - ***The Captain's Lady*** [1950]	$2.00	$6.00	$12.00
267	Stagge, Jonathan - ***Turn Of The Table*** [1950]	$3.00	$9.00	$18.00
268	Beeding, Francis - ***The Nine Waxed Faces*** [1950] Rudolph Belarski cover.	$3.50	$10.00	$20.00
269	Kent, Mona - ***Mirror, Mirror On The Wall*** [1950]	$2.00	$6.00	$12.00
270	Barrett, Monte - ***Tempered Blade*** [1950]	$1.50	$5.00	$10.00
271	Haycox, Ernest - ***Riders West*** [1950] Cover art by Samuel Cherry.	$1.50	$5.00	$10.00
272	Marshall, Edison - ***Trail's End*** [1950] Cover art by Samuel Cherry.	$1.50	$5.00	$10.00
273	Ehrlich, Max - ***The Big Eye*** [1950] Earle Bergey cover.	$4.00	$12.50	$25.00
274	Taylor, Daniel - ***They Move With The Sun*** [1950]	$1.50	$5.00	$10.00

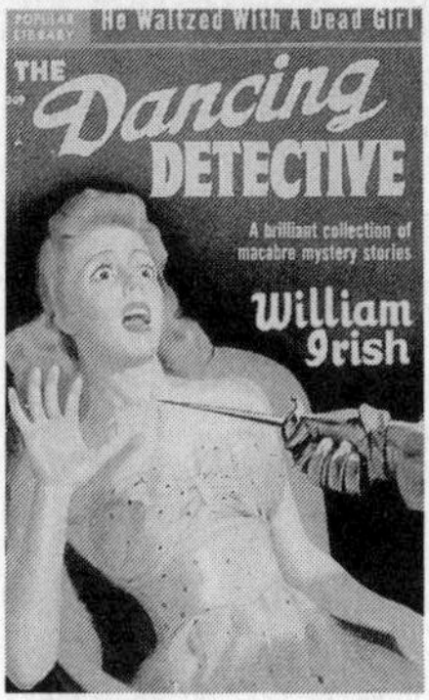

Popular Library, 309

Popular Library, 424

Popular Library, 675

		G	VG	F
275	Sale, Richard - ***Murder At Midnight*** [1950]	$2.50	$7.50	$15.00
276	King, Rufus - ***Somewhere In This House*** [1950] Cover art by Rudolph Belarski.	$3.50	$10.00	$20.00
277	Miller, Merle - ***The Sure Thing*** [1950]	$2.00	$6.00	$12.00
278	Lampell, Millard - ***The Hero*** [1950] Cover art by Earle Bergey	$1.50	$5.00	$10.00
279	Evarts, Hal G. - ***Short Grass*** [1950] Cover art by Samuel Cherry.	$1.50	$5.00	$10.00
280	Raine, William MacLeod - ***The River Bend Feud*** [1950] Cover art by A. Leslie Ross.	$1.50	$5.00	$10.00
281	Schneider, Josef A. - ***That's My Baby*** [1950] PBO. Photo cover. A collection of humourous baby photos.	$2.00	$6.00	$12.00
282	Carr, John Dickson - ***The Four False Weapons*** [1950]	$3.00	$9.00	$18.00
283	Wentworth, Patricia - ***Silence In Court*** [1950]	$2.50	$7.50	$15.00
284	Caspary, Laura - ***Laura*** [1950]	$2.50	$7.50	$15.00
285	Adams, Joey - ***The Curtain Never Falls*** [1950] Cover by Earle Bergey.	$2.25	$7.00	$14.00
286	Abbot, Anthony - ***Murder Of The Clergyman's Mistress*** [1950]	$3.50	$10.00	$20.00
287	Rogers, Samuel - ***Don't Look Behind You*** [1950]	$2.00	$6.00	$12.00
288	Witwer, H.C. - ***The Leather Pushers*** [1950] Cover by Earle Bergey.	$3.00	$9.00	$18.00
289	Cunningham, Eugene - ***Trail Of The Macaw*** [1950] Cover art by Samuel Cherry.	$1.50	$5.00	$10.00
290	Coburn, Walt - ***The Ringtailed Rannyhans*** [1950] Cover art by A. Leslie Ross.	$1.50	$5.00	$10.00
291	Key, Alexander - ***The Wrath And The Wind*** [1950] George Rozen cover.	$2.00	$6.00	$12.00
292	Worts, George F. - ***Overboard*** [1950] Cover by Rudolph Belarski.	$17.00	$50.00	$100.00
293	Eberhart, Mignon G. - ***The Hangman's Whip*** [1950] Cover by Rudolph Belarski.	$4.00	$12.50	$25.00
294	Sklar, George - ***The Two Worlds Of Johnny Truro*** [1950]	$2.00	$6.00	$12.00
295	Lowry, Robert - ***The Wolf That Fed Us*** [1950] Cover art by George Rozen.	$2.00	$6.00	$12.00
296	Scott, Virgil - ***The Dead Tree Gives No Shelter*** [1950]	$2.00	$6.00	$12.00
297	Tuttle, W.C. - ***Shotgun Gold*** [1950] Cover by Kirk Wilson.	$1.50	$5.00	$10.00
298	Cole, Jackson - ***Guns Of Mist River*** [1950] PBO. Cover art by Samuel Cherry.	$1.50	$5.00	$10.00
299	Ingles, James Wesley - ***A Woman Of Samaria*** [1950] Cover by Rudolph Belarski.	$5.50	$17.50	$35.00
300	Carter, Hodding - ***The Winds Of Fear*** [1950] Rudolph Belarski cover.	$3.00	$9.00	$18.00

		G	VG	F
301	Latimer, Jonathan - ***The Fifth Grave*** [1950] PBO.	$2.50	$7.50	$15.00
302	Holding, Elisabeth Sanxay - ***The Old Battle Ax*** [1950] Cover art by Rudolph Belarski.	$4.00	$12.50	$25.00
303	Webber, Everett and Olga - ***Bound Girl*** [1950] Cover art by Samuel Cherry.	$3.50	$10.00	$20.00
304	Mergendahl, Charles - ***This Spring Of Love*** [1950]	$2.00	$6.00	$12.00
305	Drago, Harry Sinclair - ***The Desert Hawk*** [1951] Cover art by Samuel Cherry	$1.50	$5.00	$10.00
306	Bower, B.M. - ***The Haunted Hills*** [1951] Cover art by George Rozen.	$1.50	$5.00	$10.00
307	Atkinson, Oriana - ***Her Life To Live*** [1951] Cover art by Earle Bergey.	$4.50	$14.00	$28.00
308	Williams, Ben Ames - ***It's A Free Country*** [1951] George Rozen cover.	$2.00	$6.00	$12.00
309	Irish, William - ***The Dancing Detective*** [1951]	$8.00	$25.00	$50.00
310	Burke, Richard - ***Here Lies The Body*** [1951]	$2.50	$7.50	$15.00
311	Barrett, Monte - ***Smoke Up The Valley*** [1951] Cover by Samuel Cherry.	$1.50	$5.00	$10.00
312	Sheridan, Jack - ***Mamie Brandon*** [1951] Cover by Rudolph Belarski.	$2.00	$6.00	$12.00
313	Gregory, Jackson - ***The Far Call*** [1951] Cover art by A. Leslie Ross.	$1.50	$5.00	$10.00
314	Hendryx, James B. - ***Edge Of Beyond*** [1951] Cover art by A. Leslie Ross.	$1.50	$5.00	$10.00
315	Leopold, Jules - ***Check Your Wits*** [1951] "Puzzles, Problems, Games, Quizzes".	$2.50	$7.50	$15.00
316	Wickware, Francis Sill - ***Tuesday To Bed*** [1951]	$2.00	$6.00	$12.00
317	Fisher, Steve - ***The Night Before Murder*** [1951] Cover art by Rudolph Belarski.	$4.00	$12.50	$25.00
318	King, Rufus - ***The Deadly Dove*** [1951] Cover by Rudolph Belarski.	$4.00	$12.50	$25.00
319	Banks, Polan - ***My Forbidden Past*** [1951] Movie tie-in with Robert Mitchum.	$2.00	$6.00	$12.00
320	Partridge, Bellamy - ***Excuse My Dust*** [1951]	$1.50	$5.00	$10.00
321	Young, Gordon - ***Trouble On The Border*** [1951]	$1.50	$5.00	$10.00
322	Raine, William MacLeod - ***Hell And High Water*** [1951] Cover art by Samuel Cherry.	$1.50	$5.00	$10.00
323	Clouse, William H. - ***Home Guide To Repair, Upkeep And Remodeling*** [1951]	$1.25	$3.75	$7.50
324	Findley, Ferguson - ***My Old Man's Badge*** [1951] Cover art by Samuel Cherry.	$1.50	$5.00	$10.00
325	Wiley, Hugh - ***Murder By The Dozen*** [1951] PBO.	$3.50	$10.00	$20.00
326	Scully, Frank - ***Behind The Flying Saucers*** [1951] Cover by Earle Bergey.	$3.00	$9.00	$18.00
327	Redding, J. Saunders - ***Stranger And Alone*** [1951]	$1.50	$5.00	$10.00
328	Lindop, Audrey Erskine - ***Soldiers' Daughters Never Cry*** [1951] Cover art by Rudolph Belarski.	$2.00	$6.00	$12.00
329	Evarts, Hal G. - ***Bullet Brand*** [1951] Cover by Kirk Wilson.	$1.50	$5.00	$10.00
330	Tuttle, Wilbur C. - ***The Trouble Trailer*** [1951] Cover art by A. Leslie Ross.	$1.50	$5.00	$10.00
331	Stilwell, Hart - ***Campus Town*** [1951] Cover art by Earle Bergey.	$15.00	$45.00	$90.00
332	Cohen, Octavus Roy - ***Don't Ever Love Me*** [1951] Cover art by Rudolph Belarski.	$4.00	$12.50	$25.00
333	Wentworth, Patricia - ***Lonesome Road*** [1951]	$2.50	$7.50	$15.00
334	Prole, Lozania - ***The Magnificent Courtesan*** [1951] Rudolph Belarski cover.	$1.50	$5.00	$10.00
335	Chase, Allan - ***Shadow Of A Hero*** [1951]	$1.50	$5.00	$10.00
336	Wolf, Anna W.M. - ***The Parents' Manual*** [1951] Photo cover.	$1.25	$3.75	$7.50
337	Gregory, Jackson - ***Ace In The Hole*** [1951]	$1.50	$5.00	$10.00

		G	VG	F
338	Gill, Tom - ***Starlight Pass*** [1951]	$1.50	$5.00	$10.00
339	Oppenheim, E. Phillips - ***The Lion And The Lamb*** [1951] Cover by Rudolph Belarski.	$2.00	$6.00	$12.00
340	MacHarg, William - ***Smart Guy*** [1951]	$1.50	$5.00	$10.00
341	Manning, Lee - ***Season For Passion*** [1951] Rudolph Belarski cover.	$2.00	$6.00	$12.00
342	Weaver, Ward - ***End Of Track*** [1951] George Rozen cover.	$2.00	$6.00	$12.00
343	Esteven, John - ***While Murder Waits*** [1951] Rudolph Belarski cover.	$3.50	$10.00	$20.00
344	Crane, Frances - ***The Applegreen Cat*** [1951] Rudolph Belarski cover.	$5.00	$15.00	$30.00
345	Marshall, Edison - ***Bullets at Clearwater*** [1951] Cover art by Kirk Wilson.	$1.50	$5.00	$10.00
346	Short, Luke - ***Ramrod*** [1951] Cover art by Kirk Wilson.	$1.50	$5.00	$10.00
347	Robertson, Charley - ***Hoodlum*** [1951]	$2.00	$6.00	$12.00
348	Tallman, Robert - ***Adios O'Shaughnessy*** [1951]	$1.50	$5.00	$10.00
349	Carr, John Dickson - ***Poison In Jest*** [1951]	$4.00	$12.50	$25.00
350	Stagge, Jonathan - ***The Dogs Do Bark*** [1951]	$3.00	$9.00	$18.00
351	Mergendahl, Charles - ***Tonight Is Forever*** [1951] Earle Bergey cover art.	$2.00	$6.00	$12.00
352	Tracy, Catherine - ***Cotton Moon*** [1951] Cover art by George Rozen.	$1.50	$5.00	$10.00
353	Cody, Al - ***The Big Corral*** [1951] Cover art by Kirk Wilson.	$1.50	$5.00	$10.00
354	Tuttle, Wilbur C. - ***Gun Feud*** [1951] Cover art by Samuel Cherry.	$1.50	$5.00	$10.00
355	Denker, Henry - ***I'll Be Right Home, Ma*** [1951]	$1.35	$4.00	$8.00
356	Wolfson, P.J. - ***This Woman Is Mine*** [1951]	$1.50	$5.00	$10.00
357	Goldberg, Hyman - ***How I Became A Girl Reporter*** [1951]	$1.25	$3.75	$7.50
358	Tallant, Robert - ***Mrs. Candy And Saturday Night*** [1951] Cover by Earle Bergey.	$1.35	$4.00	$8.00
359	Raine, William MacLeod - ***Beyond The Rio Grande*** [1951]	$1.50	$5.00	$10.00
360	Haycox, Ernest - ***The Silver Desert*** [1951] Cover art by Samuel Cherry.	$1.50	$5.00	$10.00
361	Fisher, Steve - ***Winter Kill*** [1951] Cover by Rudolph Belarski.	$2.50	$7.50	$15.00
362	King, Rufus - ***Never Walk Alone*** [1951] Cover by Rudolph Belarski.	$2.00	$6.00	$12.00
363	Shirer, William L. - ***The Traitor*** [1951] Cover art by George Rozen.	$1.50	$5.00	$10.00
364	Schoyer, Preston - ***The Ringing Of The Glass*** [1951] Cover art by Rudolph Belarski.	$2.00	$6.00	$12.00
365	Sligh, Nigel - ***Copperbelt*** [1951]	$1.50	$5.00	$10.00
366	Leokum, Arkady - ***Please Send Me Absolutely Free!*** [1951]	$1.50	$5.00	$10.00
367	Newton, D.B. - ***Shotgun Guard*** [1951] Cover art by Samuel Cherry.	$1.50	$5.00	$10.00
368	Ermine, Will - ***Apache Crossing*** [1951]	$1.50	$5.00	$10.00
369	Cohen, Octavus Roy - ***My Love Wears Black*** [1951]	$2.50	$7.50	$15.00
370	Seeley, Mabel - ***The Crying Sisters*** [1951]	$1.50	$5.00	$10.00
371	Williams, Ben Ames - ***The Strumpet Sea*** [1951] Cover art by Rudolph Belarski.	$2.00	$6.00	$12.00
372	Valtin, Jan - ***Wintertime*** [1951]	$1.50	$5.00	$10.00
373	Caspary, Vera - ***The Weeping And The Laughter*** [1951] Cover art by Downes.	$2.00	$6.00	$12.00
374	Brown, Wenzell - ***Dark Drums*** [1951] Ray Pease cover art.	$2.50	$7.50	$15.00
375	Cunningham, Eugene - ***Texas Sheriff*** [1951]	$1.50	$5.00	$10.00
376	Guthrie, Jr., A.B. - ***Trouble At Moondance*** [1951]	$2.50	$7.50	$15.00
377	Pentecost, Hugh - ***Shadow Of Madness*** [1951] Cover by Earle Bergey.	$2.00	$6.00	$12.00
378	Chase, James Hadley - ***You're Lonely When You're Dead*** [1951] Cover art by Downes.	$3.50	$10.00	$20.00

		G	VG	F
379	Whitcomb, Catharine - ***No Narrow Path*** [1951] Rudolph Belarski cover.	$2.00	$6.00	$12.00
380	Bellah, James Warner - ***Rear Guard*** [1951] Cover art by Samuel Cherry.	$1.50	$5.00	$10.00
381	Beeding, Frances - ***Heads Off At Midnight*** [1951]	$2.00	$6.00	$12.00
382	Wentworth, Patricia - ***Dark Threat*** [1951] Cover art by Rudolph Belarski.	$5.00	$15.00	$30.00
383	Gregory, Jackson - ***The Man From Texas*** [1951] Cover art by Samuel Cherry.	$1.50	$5.00	$10.00
384	Young, Gordon - ***Range Boss*** [1951] Cover art by George Rozen.	$1.50	$5.00	$10.00
385	Wallis, J.H. - ***Once Off Guard*** [1951]	$1.50	$5.00	$10.00
386	Patrick, Quentin - ***Cottage Sinister*** [1951] Cover art by Samuel Cherry.	$2.50	$7.50	$15.00
387	Lowry, Robert - ***Casualty*** [1951]	$1.50	$5.00	$10.00
388	Weaver, Ward - ***Hang My Wreath*** [1951] Cover by Bob Fink.	$2.00	$6.00	$12.00
389	Ronald, James - ***This Way Out*** [1951] Cover art by Bernard Barton.	$1.50	$5.00	$10.00
390	Hopkins, Tom J. - ***Trails By Night*** [1951]	$1.50	$5.00	$10.00
391	Meloney, William Brown - ***Mooney*** [1951] Cover art by Bob Fink.	$1.35	$4.00	$8.00
392	Bernard, William - ***Jailbait*** [1951] Cover by Rudolph Belarski.	$4.00	$12.50	$25.00
393	Waller, Leslie - ***The Bed She Made*** [1952]	$1.50	$5.00	$10.00
394	Komroff, Manuel - ***Echo Of Evil*** [1952] Cover art by Ray Pease.	$1.50	$5.00	$10.00
395	Westheimer, David - ***Day Into Night*** [1952]	$2.00	$6.00	$12.00
396	Close, Robert S. - ***Love Me Sailor*** [1952]	$1.50	$5.00	$10.00
397	Gill, Tom - ***Border Feud*** [1952]	$1.35	$4.00	$8.00
398	Haycox, Ernest - ***Trail Smoke*** [1952]	$1.35	$4.00	$8.00
399	Henderson, James Leal - ***Whirlpool*** [1952] Bernard Barton cover.	$1.35	$4.00	$8.00
400	Kane, Frank - ***Slay Ride*** [1952]	$2.00	$6.00	$12.00
401	Ingersoll, Ralph - ***Wine Of Violence*** [1952] Cover by George Rozen.	$1.50	$5.00	$10.00
402	Biddle, Jr., Livingston - ***Main Line*** [1952] Cover art by Bernard Barton.	$1.35	$4.00	$8.00
403	Wheeler, Keith - ***The Reef*** [1952]	$1.35	$4.00	$8.00
404	Bellah, James Warner - ***Divorce*** [1952]	$1.35	$4.00	$8.00
405	Brick, John - ***Troubled Spring*** [1952] George Rozen cover.	$1.35	$4.00	$8.00
406	Drago, Harry Sinclair - ***Montana Road*** [1952]	$1.35	$4.00	$8.00
407	Stuart, Matt - ***Bonanza Gulch*** [1952] Cover art by A. Leslie Ross.	$1.35	$4.00	$8.00
408	Findley, Ferguson - ***Waterfront*** [1952] Cover art by Samuel Cherry.	$1.35	$4.00	$8.00
409	Nichols, Fan - ***One By One*** [1952]	$1.50	$5.00	$10.00
410	Crichton, Kyle - ***The Marx Brothers*** [1952]	$3.50	$10.00	$20.00
411	Wyndham, John - ***Revolt Of The Triffids*** [1952] Cover by Earle Bergey.	$5.00	$15.00	$30.00
412	Breuer, Gustav - ***The Spell*** [1952]	$1.35	$4.00	$8.00
413	Hall, Desmond - ***A Woman Of Forty*** [1952] Cover art by Bernard Barton.	$1.35	$4.00	$8.00
414	Raine, William MacLeod - ***The Texas Kid*** [1942]	$1.35	$4.00	$8.00
415	Coburn, Walt - ***Pardners Of The Dim Trails*** [1952]	$1.35	$4.00	$8.00
416	Ard, William - ***The Perfect Frame*** [1952]	$2.50	$7.50	$15.00
417	McDermott, C.L. - ***A Yank On Piccadilly*** [1952]	$2.00	$6.00	$12.00
418	Pearce, Dick - ***The Impudent Rifle*** [1952] Cover art by Rudolph Belarski.	$2.00	$6.00	$12.00
419	Karig, Walter - ***Lower Than Angels*** [1952] Cover by Rafael DeSoto	$2.00	$6.00	$12.00

		G	VG	F
420	O'Mara, Jim - ***Trial By Gunsmoke*** [1952] Cover art by Samuel Cherry.	$1.35	$4.00	$8.00
421	Gies, Joseph - ***A Matter Of Morals*** [1952] Cover art by Bernard Barton.	$1.35	$4.00	$8.00
422	Marcus, Alan - ***The Vanquished*** [1952] Cover art by Rudolph Belarski.	$2.00	$6.00	$12.00
423	Baccante, Leonora - ***Johnny Bogan*** [1952] Cover art by Raphael DeSoto.	$1.50	$5.00	$10.00
424	Hopley, George (Cornell Woolrich) - ***Fright*** [1952] Cover art by Rudolph Belarski.	$8.00	$25.00	$50.00
425	Arthur, Burt - ***Thunder Valley*** [1952]	$1.35	$4.00	$8.00
426	Adams, Cleve F. - ***The Black Door*** [1952]	$2.00	$6.00	$12.00
427	Cohen, Octavus Roy - ***More Beautiful Than Murder*** [1952] Cover art by Rudolph Belarski.	$4.00	$12.50	$25.00
428	Farren, Julian - ***The Train From Pittsburgh*** [1952] Cover by Earle Bergey.	$1.35	$4.00	$8.00
429	Young, Gordon - ***Two-Gun Man*** [1952] Cover art by A. Leslie Ross.	$1.35	$4.00	$8.00
430	Gregory, Jackson - ***Guardians Of The Trail*** [1952] Cover art by George Rozen.	$1.35	$4.00	$8.00
431	Irish, William (Cornell Woolrich) - ***Strangler's Serenade*** [1952] Cover by Rudolph Belarski.	$8.00	$25.00	$50.00
432	Kelland, Clarence Budington - ***The Great Mail Robbery*** [1952] Cover art by Earle Bergey.	$2.00	$6.00	$12.00
433	Packer, Peter - ***Bitter Fruit*** [1952] Cover by Barton.	$1.50	$5.00	$10.00
434	Walker, Gertrude - ***So Deadly Fair*** [1952] Cover art by Rafael DeSoto.	$1.50	$5.00	$10.00
435	Javellana, Stevan - ***The Lost Ones*** [1952] Cover art by Rafael DeSoto.	$1.50	$5.00	$10.00
436	Raine, William MacLeod - ***Arizona Guns*** [1952]	$1.35	$4.00	$8.00
437	Newton, D.B. - ***Six-Gun Gamble*** [1952] Cover art by A. Leslie Ross.	$1.35	$4.00	$8.00
438	Mannin, Ethel - ***At Sundown The Tiger*** [1952]	$1.35	$4.00	$8.00
439	Wichelns, Lee - ***Rip Tide*** [1952]	$1.35	$4.00	$8.00
440	Viazzi, Alfred - ***The Cruel Dawn*** [1952]	$1.35	$4.00	$8.00
441	Nye, Nelson - ***Thief River*** [1952] Cover art by A. Leslie Ross.	$1.35	$4.00	$8.00
442	Haycox, Ernest - ***Head Of The Mountain*** [1952]	$1.35	$4.00	$8.00
443	Chute, Verne - ***Sweet And Deadly*** [1952] Cover art by A. Leslie Ross.	$1.35	$4.00	$8.00
444	Seaton, George John - ***Isle Of The Damned*** [1952]	$2.00	$6.00	$12.00
445	Brand, Max - ***Timbal Gulch Trail*** [1952]	$1.35	$4.00	$8.00
446	Merrick, Gordon - ***The Night And The Naked*** [1952]	$1.50	$5.00	$10.00
447	Williamson, Jack - ***Dragon's Island*** [1952] Cover by Earle Bergey.	$3.50	$10.00	$20.00
448	Lariar, Lawrence - ***You Can't Catch Me*** [1952]	$1.50	$5.00	$10.00
449	Byrne, Jack - ***Gunswift*** [1952] Cover art by A. Leslie Ross	$1.35	$4.00	$8.00
450	Haycox, Ernest - ***Trouble Shooter*** [1952] Cover art by George Rozen.	$1.35	$4.00	$8.00
451	Cargoe, Richard - ***Maharajah*** [1952]	$1.50	$5.00	$10.00
452	Scott, Thurston - ***I'll Get Mine*** [1952] Cover art by A. Leslie Ross.	$4.00	$12.50	$25.00
453	MacInnes, Helen - ***Neither Five Nor Three*** [1952]	$1.50	$5.00	$10.00
454	Ballard, Todhunter (W.T. Ballard) - ***Two-Edged Vengeance*** [1952] Cover art by A. Leslie Ross.	$1.50	$5.00	$10.00
455	Delano, Fred - ***Hellgate Canyon*** [1952]	$1.35	$4.00	$8.00
456	Adams, Cleve F. - ***What Price Murder*** [1952]	$2.00	$6.00	$12.00
457	Knickerbocker, Charles H. - ***The Boy Came Back*** [1952]	$1.35	$4.00	$8.00
458	Wendt, Stephen - ***Pray Love Remember*** [1952]	$1.35	$4.00	$8.00
459	Orwell, George - ***Burmese Days*** [1952]	$1.50	$5.00	$10.00
460	Haycox, Ernest - ***Rawhide Range*** [1952]	$1.25	$3.75	$7.50

		G	VG	F
461	Nye, Nelson - ***Born to Trouble*** [1952]	$1.25	$3.75	$7.50
462	Cohen, Octavus Roy - ***A Bullet For My Love*** [1952]	$1.50	$5.00	$10.00
463	Pratt, Theodore - ***The Big Bubble*** [1952]	$1.50	$5.00	$10.00
464	Hardy, W.G. - ***The Unfulfilled*** [1952]	$1.50	$5.00	$10.00
465	O'Mara, Jim - ***Guns Of Vengeance*** [1952]	$1.25	$3.75	$7.50
466	Ravetch, Irving - ***The Outriders*** [1952] PBO. Cover art by A. Leslie Ross.	$1.25	$3.75	$7.50
467	Kerr, Ben - ***Shakedown*** [1952]	$1.35	$4.00	$8.00
468	Packer, Peter - ***Dark Surrender*** [1952] Cover by Ray Johnson.	$1.50	$5.00	$10.00
469	Gilbert, Edwin - ***Hard To Get*** [1952]	$1.50	$5.00	$10.00
470	Radin, Edward D. - ***Headline Crimes Of The Year*** [1952] Cover by Paul Kresse.	$2.50	$7.50	$15.00
471	Raine, William MacLeod - ***Range Beyond The Law*** [1952] Cover by George Rozen.	$1.25	$3.75	$7.50
472	Ketchum, Philip - ***Texan On The Road*** [1952] Cover art by Mel Crair.	$1.25	$3.75	$7.50
473	Irish, William - ***Bluebeard's Seventh Wife*** [1952] PBO.	$10.00	$30.00	$60.00
474	Gordon, Ian - ***The Night Thorn*** [1953] Cover art by Rafael DeSoto.	$2.00	$6.00	$12.00
475	Brand, Max - ***The Rancher's Revenge*** [1953]	$1.25	$3.75	$7.50
476	Ballard, Todhunter & Lynch, James C. - ***Showdown*** [1953] PBO.	$1.35	$4.00	$8.00
477	Ard, William - ***The Diary*** [1953]	$2.00	$6.00	$12.00
478	Hunter, Evan (Ed McBain) - ***Don't Crowd Me*** [1953] Cover art by Walter Popp.	$2.50	$7.50	$15.00
479	Williamson, Scott Graham - ***Torment*** [1953]	$2.00	$6.00	$12.00
480	Bonner, Parker (W.T. Ballard) - ***Superstition Range*** [1953] Cover art by George Rozen.	$1.35	$4.00	$8.00
481	Nye, Nelson - ***Desert Of The Damned*** [1953] Cover by A. Leslie Ross.	$1.35	$4.00	$8.00
482	Chaber, M.E. - ***Don't Get Caught*** [1953]	$1.50	$5.00	$10.00
483	Nichols, Fan - ***Ask For Linda*** [1953] PBO.	$1.50	$5.00	$10.00
484	Mergendahl, Charles - ***The Girl Cage*** [1953] PBO.	$2.00	$6.00	$12.00
485	Shiffrin, A.B. - ***Glitter*** [1953] PBO.	$1.25	$3.75	$7.50
486	Haycox, Ernest - ***Chaffee Of Roaring Horse*** [1953] Cover art by A. Leslie Ross.	$1.25	$3.75	$7.50
487	O'Mara, Jim - ***Quick Trigger Law*** [1953]	$1.25	$3.75	$7.50
488	Lawrence, Michael - ***Naked And Alone*** [1953]	$1.50	$5.00	$10.00
489	Busch, Niven - ***Duel In The Sun*** [1953]	$1.25	$3.75	$7.50
490	Wagner, Geoffrey - ***Venables*** [1953] Cover art by Cardiff.	$1.50	$5.00	$10.00
491	Attaway, William - ***Blood On The Forge*** [1953]	$1.25	$3.75	$7.50
492	Ballard, Todhunter (W.T. Ballard) - ***Incident At Sun Mountain*** [1953] Cover art by A. Leslie Ross.	$1.35	$4.00	$8.00
493	Grady, Tex - ***High Mesa*** [1953] Cover art by A. Leslie Ross.	$1.25	$3.75	$7.50
494	Moran, Mike - ***Double Cross*** [1953] PBO.	$1.35	$4.00	$8.00
495	Hulburd, David - ***H Is For Heroin*** [1953] Cover by Rafael DeSoto.	$5.50	$17.50	$35.00
496	Carson, Robert - ***Stranger In Our Midst*** [1953]	$2.00	$6.00	$12.00
497	Cleary, Jon - ***You Can't See Around Corners*** [1953]	$1.50	$5.00	$10.00
498	Barton, Jack - ***Texas Rawhider*** [1953]	$1.25	$3.75	$7.50
499	Ketchum, Philip - ***Guns Of The Barricade Bunch*** [1953] Cover by A. Leslie Ross.	$1.25	$3.75	$7.50
500	Spain, Terry - ***Time To Kill*** [1953] PBO.	$2.00	$6.00	$12.00
501	Winston, Clara - ***The Closest Kin There Is*** [1953]	$1.35	$4.00	$8.00
502	Ard, William - ***A Girl For Danny*** [1953] PBO. Cover by Rafael DeSoto.	$2.00	$6.00	$12.00
503	Calitri, Charles J. - ***Rickey*** [1953]	$1.35	$4.00	$8.00
504	Adams, Joey - ***Joey Adams' Joke Book*** [1953] Cover by Leo Manso.	$1.50	$5.00	$10.00

		G	VG	F
505	Granger, K.R.G. - ***Ten Against Caesar*** [1953] Cover art by A. Leslie Ross.	$1.25	$3.75	$7.50
506	Trimble, Louis - ***Fighting Cowman*** [1953] PBO.	$1.25	$3.75	$7.50
507	Durrant, Theo - ***The Big Fear*** [1953]	$1.35	$4.00	$8.00
508	Mallet, Francoise - ***The Loving And The Darling*** [1953]	$1.35	$4.00	$8.00
509	Cochrell, Boyd - ***Rage In The Wind*** [1953] PBO.	$1.50	$5.00	$10.00
510	Davidson, David - ***The Night Is Mine*** [1953] Cover art by Walter Popp.	$1.50	$5.00	$10.00
511	Evarts, Hal G. - ***Renegade Of Rainbow Basin*** [1953] PBO. Cover art by Robert Stanley.	$1.25	$3.75	$7.50
512	Wayne, Ernie - ***Ramrod From Hell*** [1953] Cover art by A. Leslie Ross.	$1.25	$3.75	$7.50
513	Radin, Edward D. - ***Beyond The Law*** [1953] PBO.	$1.50	$5.00	$10.00
514	Matthews, T.S. - ***Darling, I Hate You*** [1953] Cover art by Robert Stanley.	$1.35	$4.00	$8.00
515	Williams, Robert V. - ***The Hard Way*** [1953]	$1.25	$3.75	$7.50
516	Gann, Ernest K. - ***Island In The Sky*** [1953]	$1.25	$3.75	$7.50
517	Haycox, Ernest - ***Free Grass*** [1953] Cover by A. Leslie Ross.	$1.25	$3.75	$7.50
518	O'Mara, Jim - ***Rustler Of The Owlhorns*** [1953]	$1.25	$3.75	$7.50
519	Peters, Bill - ***Blondes Die Young*** [1953]	$1.35	$4.00	$8.00
520	Kauffmann, Stanley - ***The Tightrope*** [1953]	$1.25	$3.75	$7.50
521	Clayton, John Bell - ***Six Angels At My Back*** [1953]	$1.35	$4.00	$8.00
522	Smith, Don - ***China Coaster*** [1953]	$1.35	$4.00	$8.00
523	Duvall, Evelyn Millis - ***Facts Of Life And Love For Teen-Agers*** [1953]	$1.00	$3.00	$6.00
524	Ballard, Todhunter (W.T. Ballard) - ***West Of Quarantine*** [1953] Cover by Robert Stanley.	$1.35	$4.00	$8.00
525	Townsend, Ray - ***Stranger From Texas*** [1953]	$1.25	$3.75	$7.50
526	Ard, William - ***You Can't Stop Me*** [1953]	$1.50	$5.00	$10.00
527	Marshall, Rosamond - ***Bond Of The Flesh*** [1953]	$1.35	$4.00	$8.00
528	Oursler, Will & Smith, Lawrence Dwight - ***Hooked*** [1953] Cover by Rafael DeSoto.	$5.50	$17.50	$35.00
529	Gellhorn, Martha - ***Liana*** [1953]	$1.35	$4.00	$8.00
530	Chaber, M.E. - ***All The Way Down*** [1953]	$1.35	$4.00	$8.00
531	Raine, William McLeod - ***West Of The Law*** [1953]	$1.25	$3.75	$7.50
532	Ketchum, Philip - ***The Saddle Bum*** [1953] PBO. Cover art by A. Leslie Ross.	$1.25	$3.75	$7.50
533	Reynolds, Quentin - ***Smooth And Deadly*** [1953]	$1.35	$4.00	$8.00
534	Meoni, Armando - ***Strange Lovers*** [1953]	$1.25	$3.75	$7.50
535	LeMay, Alan - ***Thunder In The Dust*** [1953] Cover by Robert Stanley	$1.25	$3.75	$7.50
536	Nichols, Fan - ***Count Me In*** [1953] PBO.	$1.50	$5.00	$10.00
537	Haycox, Ernest - ***The Grim Canyon*** [1953] PBO.	$1.25	$3.75	$7.50
538	Owen, Dean - ***Point Of A Gun*** [1953] PBO. Cover by A. Leslie Ross.	$1.25	$3.75	$7.50
539	Brandt, Tom - ***Kiss Me Hard*** [1953] PBO.	$1.25	$3.75	$7.50
540	D'Agostino, Guido - ***My Enemy, The World*** [1953]	$1.25	$3.75	$7.50
541	Burnett, Hallie Southgate - ***This Heart, This Hunter*** [1953]	$1.25	$3.75	$7.50
542	Cunningham, Eugene - ***The Ranger Way*** [1953]	$1.25	$3.75	$7.50
543	Shaw, Charles - ***The Flesh And The Spirit*** [1953] Cover art by Rafael DeSoto.	$1.35	$4.00	$8.00
544	Gerard, Francis - ***The Mark Of The Moon*** [1953]	$2.50	$7.50	$15.00
545	Gregory, Jackson - ***The Silver Star*** [1953] Cover art by A. Leslie Ross.	$1.25	$3.75	$7.50
546	Vance, William E. - ***Hard Rock Rancher*** [1953] PBO.	$1.25	$3.75	$7.50
547	Lee, Gypsy Rose - ***Mother Finds A Body*** [1953]	$1.50	$5.00	$10.00
548	Cushman, Dan - ***Stay Away, Joe*** [1953] Cover art by Rafael DeSoto.	$1.35	$4.00	$8.00
549	Brown, Wenzell - ***Monkey On My Back*** [1954] Cover by Owen Kampen.	$6.00	$20.00	$40.00

		G	VG	F
550	Bates, H.E. - ***Love For Lydia*** [1954]	$1.25	$3.75	$7.50
551	Rieseberg, Lt. Harry E. - ***I Dive For Treasure*** [1954] Cover by Floherty.	$1.35	$4.00	$8.00
552	Ballard, Todhunter (W.T. Ballard) - ***High Iron*** [1954]	$1.35	$4.00	$8.00
553	Raine, William MacLeod - ***Texas Breed*** [1954] Cover art by Samuel Cherry.	$1.25	$3.75	$7.50
554	Chambers, Dana - ***Some Day I'll Kill You*** [1954]	$2.00	$6.00	$12.00
555	Gorham, Charles - ***Martha Crane*** [1954] Cover art by Owen Kampen.	$1.35	$4.00	$8.00
556	Schindall, Henry - ***Wilderness Rogue*** [1954]	$1.25	$3.75	$7.50
557	Wetherell, June - ***Possessed*** [1954]	$1.25	$3.75	$7.50
558	Keon, Michael - ***The Tiger In Summer*** [1954]	$1.25	$3.75	$7.50
559	Hauser, Gayelord - ***Be Happier, Be Healthier*** [1954]	$1.00	$3.00	$6.00
560	Foreman, L.L. - ***Gunning For Trouble*** [1954] Cover art by A. Leslie Ross.	$1.25	$3.75	$7.50
561	LeMay, Alan - ***Gunsight Trail*** [1954]	$1.25	$3.75	$7.50
562	Carson, Robert - ***I Take All*** [1954]	$1.35	$4.00	$8.00
563	Saroyan, William - ***A Secret Story*** [1954]	$1.25	$3.75	$7.50
564	Mons, H.M. - ***The Sword Of Satan*** [1954]	$1.25	$3.75	$7.50
565	Langley, Noel - ***The Innocent At Large*** [1954]	$1.25	$3.75	$7.50
566	Clagett, John - ***Cradle Of The Sun*** [1954] Cover by Robert Stanley	$1.25	$3.75	$7.50
567	Haycox, Ernest - ***Starlight Rider*** [1954] Cover art by A. Leslie Ross	$1.25	$3.75	$7.50
568	Evarts, Hal G. - ***Shortgrass*** [1954] Cover art by Robert Stanley.	$1.25	$3.75	$7.50
569	Ard, William - ***A Private Party*** [1954]	$1.35	$4.00	$8.00
570	Lowry, Robert - ***The Violent Wedding*** [1954]	$1.25	$3.75	$7.50
571	Bowman, John Clarke - ***Isle Of Demons*** [1954]	$1.35	$4.00	$8.00
572	McMullen, Richard - ***Country Girl*** [1954] PBO.	$1.50	$5.00	$10.00
573	Yoseloff, Martin - ***The Girl In The Spike-Heeled Shoes*** [1954]	$1.50	$5.00	$10.00
574	Young, Gordon - ***Fighting Blood*** [1954]	$1.25	$3.75	$7.50
575	Ketchum, Philip - ***The Texas Gun*** [1954]	$1.25	$3.75	$7.50
576	Scott, Virgil - ***The Dead Tree Gives No Shelter*** [1954]	$1.35	$4.00	$8.00
577	Willard, Jack - ***The Wire God*** [1954]	$1.25	$3.75	$7.50
578	Steward, Davenport - ***Rainbow Road*** [1954]	$1.25	$3.75	$7.50
579	Winter, M.D., J. A. - ***Are Your Troubles Psychosomatic?*** [1954]	$1.00	$3.00	$6.00
580	Kavinoky, Bernice - ***We Burn Like Candles*** [1954]	$1.25	$3.75	$7.50
581	Brown, Wenzell - ***Dark Drums*** [1954]	$1.50	$5.00	$10.00
582	Evarts, Hal G. - ***Highgrader*** [1954] PBO.	$1.25	$3.75	$7.50
583	Owen, Dean - ***Rifle Pass*** [1954] PBO. Cover by A. Leslie Ross.	$1.25	$3.75	$7.50
584	Brandt, Tom (Thomas B. Dewey) - ***Run, Brother, Run!*** [1954] PBO. Cover art by Johnson.	$2.00	$6.00	$12.00
585	Moretti, Ugo - ***Rogue Wind*** [1954]	$1.25	$3.75	$7.50
586	Nichols, Fan - ***Devil Take Her*** [1954] PBO.	$1.50	$5.00	$10.00
587	Curtis, Jean-Louis - ***Dark Streets Of Paris*** [1954]	$1.25	$3.75	$7.50
588	Troyat, Henri - ***The Mountain*** [1954]	$1.25	$3.75	$7.50
589	Haycox, Ernest - ***Guns Up*** [1954] Cover art by A. Leslie Ross.	$1.25	$3.75	$7.50
590	Townsend, Ray - ***Gold Town Gunman*** [1954] PBO. Cover art by Norman Saunders.	$1.25	$3.75	$7.50
591	Ard, William - ***No Angels For Me*** [1954] PBO. Cover by Walter Popp.	$1.50	$5.00	$10.00
592	Kramer, Dale & Karr, Madeline - ***Teen-Age Gangs*** [1954] Cover art by Rafael DeSoto.	$3.50	$10.00	$20.00
593	Gorham, Charles - ***The Gilded Hearse*** [1954]	$1.35	$4.00	$8.00
594	Hubler, Richard G. - ***The Brass God*** [1954]	$1.35	$4.00	$8.00
595	Caprio, M. D., Frank S. - ***Why We Behave As We Do*** [1954]	$1.00	$3.00	$6.00
596	Cook, Will - ***Frontier Feud*** [1954]	$1.25	$3.75	$7.50
597	Gregory, Jackson - ***Marshal Of Sundown*** [1954]	$1.25	$3.75	$7.50
598	Reach, James - ***The Innocent One*** [1954]	$1.25	$3.75	$7.50
599	Jackson, Delmar - ***The Night Is My Undoing*** [1954]	$1.35	$4.00	$8.00

		G	VG	F
600	Wilson, Guthrie - ***The Feared And The Fearless*** [1954]	$1.25	$3.75	$7.50
601	Mitchell, Anthea - ***The Naked Sword*** [1954]	$1.35	$4.00	$8.00
602	Heatter, Basil - ***The Dim View*** [1954]	$1.25	$3.75	$7.50
603	Bonner, Parker (W.T. Ballard) - ***Outlaw Brand*** [1954] PBO.	$1.35	$4.00	$8.00
604	Ketchum, Philip - ***Gun Law*** [1954] PBO. Cover by A. Leslie Ross.	$1.25	$3.75	$7.50
605	Radin, Edward D. - ***Crimes Of Passion*** [1954]	$1.50	$5.00	$10.00
606	Sherry, John Olden - ***The Departure*** [1954]	$1.25	$3.75	$7.50
607	Glendinning, Richard - ***Too Fast We Live*** [1954] Cover art by Owen Kampen.	$1.35	$4.00	$8.00
608	Key, Alexander - ***The Wrath And The Wind*** [1954]	$1.25	$3.75	$7.50
609	McKie, Ronald - ***The Survivors*** [1954]	$1.25	$3.75	$7.50
610	Western Writers Of America - ***Bad Men And Good*** [1954] Cover by A. Leslie Ross.	$1.35	$4.00	$8.00
611	Barton, Jack - ***Trail Of The Damned*** [1954] PBO.	$1.25	$3.75	$7.50
612	Brett, Martin - ***Hot Freeze*** [1954]	$1.25	$3.75	$7.50
613	Sheen, Fulton J. - ***The Eternal Galilean*** [1954] Photo cover.	$1.25	$3.75	$7.50
614	Caesar, Gene - ***Mark Of The Hunter*** [1954]	$1.25	$3.75	$7.50
615	Raddall, Thomas H. - ***Give And Take*** [1954]	$1.25	$3.75	$7.50
616	Haycox, Ernest - ***Riders West*** [1954]	$1.25	$3.75	$7.50
617	Ballard, Todhunter (W.T. Ballard) - ***Rawhide Gunman*** [1954] PBO. Cover art by A. Leslie Ross.	$1.35	$4.00	$8.00
618	Travers, Robert - ***Ten Roads To Hell*** [1954] PBO. Cover art by Raphael DeSoto.	$1.35	$4.00	$8.00
619	Wakeman, Frederic - ***Naked To My Past*** [1954]	$1.25	$3.75	$7.50
620	Arnold, Elliot - ***Everybody Slept Here*** [1954]	$1.35	$4.00	$8.00
621	Denzer, Peter W. - ***Episode*** [1954]	$1.25	$3.75	$7.50
622	Locke, Charles O. - ***The Last Princess*** [1954]	$1.50	$5.00	$10.00
623	Townsend, Ray Homer - ***Renegade River*** [1954] PBO. Cover art by A. Leslie Ross.	$1.25	$3.75	$7.50
624	Cunningham, Eugene - ***Quick Triggers*** [1954]	$1.25	$3.75	$7.50
625	Keller, Dan - ***Flee The Night In Anger*** [1954] PBO. Cover art by A. Leslie Ross.	$1.35	$4.00	$8.00
626	Brossard, Chandler - ***All Passion Spent*** [1954] PBO.	$1.35	$4.00	$8.00
627	Woolfolk, William - ***The Naked Hunter*** [1954] PBO. Cover art by Owen Kampen.	$1.35	$4.00	$8.00
628	Lasky, Jr., Jesse L. - ***Cry The Lonely Flesh*** [1954]	$1.25	$3.75	$7.50
629	Pinto, Oreste - ***Friend Or Foe?*** [1954] Cover art by Rafael DeSoto.	$1.35	$4.00	$8.00
630	Barrett, Monte - ***Smoke Up The Valley*** [1954] Cover by Robert Stanley.	$1.25	$3.75	$7.50
631	Cook, Will - ***Prairie Guns*** [1954] PBO. Cover by A. Leslie Ross.	$1.25	$3.75	$7.50
632	Chaber, M.E. - ***Now It's My Turn*** [1954]	$1.25	$3.75	$7.50
633	Scott, Natalie Anderson - ***Hotel Room*** [1955] Cover art by Rafael DeSoto.	$1.35	$4.00	$8.00
634	Cleary, Jon - ***Naked In The Night*** [1955] Cover art by Rafael DeSoto.	$1.25	$3.75	$7.50
635	O'Hara, Donn - ***The Wild Years*** [1955] PBO.	$1.25	$3.75	$7.50
636	Lord, Sterling - ***Men And The Sea*** [1955]	$1.35	$4.00	$8.00
637	Brand, Max - ***Six-Gun Ambush*** [1955] Cover art by Robert Stanley.	$1.25	$3.75	$7.50
638	Ballard, Todhunter (W.T. Ballard) - ***Blizzard Range*** [1955] PBO. Cover art by A. Leslie Ross.	$1.35	$4.00	$8.00
639	Ard, William - ***Don't Come Crying To Me*** [1955]	$1.50	$5.00	$10.00
640	Lumbard, C.G. - ***Kiss The Night Away*** [1955]	$1.25	$3.75	$7.50
641	Chanslor, Roy - ***The Naked I*** [1955]	$1.25	$3.75	$7.50
642	Nichols, Fan - ***I'll Never Let You Go*** [1955]	$1.25	$3.75	$7.50
643	Pape, Richard - ***Boldness Be My Friend*** [1955]	$1.25	$3.75	$7.50

		G	VG	F
644	Haycox, Ernest - ***Vengeance Trail*** [1955] PBO. Cover by A. Leslie Ross.	$1.25	$3.75	$7.50
645	Ketchum, Philip - ***Desperation Valley*** [1955] PBO.	$1.25	$3.75	$7.50
646	Change, John Newton - ***Up To Her Neck*** [1955]	$1.25	$3.75	$7.50
647	Mirvish, Robert F. - ***Wide-Open Town*** [1955]	$1.25	$3.75	$7.50
648	Scott, Warwick - ***Naked Canvas*** [1955]	$1.35	$4.00	$8.00
649	Fleisher, Siegel - ***Down The Dark Street*** [1955]	$1.35	$4.00	$8.00
650	Kramer, Karl - ***Fair Game*** [1955] PBO.	$1.35	$4.00	$8.00
651	Evarts, Hal G. - ***Apache Agent*** [1955] PBO. Cover art by A. Leslie Ross.	$1.25	$3.75	$7.50
652	Cook, Will - ***Fury At Painted Rock*** [1955] PBO.	$1.25	$3.75	$7.50
653	Kerr, Ben - ***Down I Go*** [1955] PBO. Cover art by Rafael DeSoto.	$2.00	$6.00	$12.00
654	Bates, H.E. - ***The Nature Of Love*** [1955]	$1.25	$3.75	$7.50
655	Walker, Turnley - ***Dream Of Innocence*** [1955] Cover art by George Erickson.	$1.35	$4.00	$8.00
656	Glendinning, Richard - ***Passion Road*** [1955] PBO.	$1.35	$4.00	$8.00
657	Ross, Sam - ***You Belong To Me*** [1955] Cover art by Owen Kampen.	$1.35	$4.00	$8.00
658	Cannavale, Renato - ***Desire In The Streets*** [1955]	$1.35	$4.00	$8.00
659	Barton, Jack - ***Brand Of Fury*** [1955]	$1.25	$3.75	$7.50
660	Fleming, Ian - ***You Asked For It*** [1955]	$10.00	$30.00	$60.00
661	Wilson, Chesley - ***Live And Let Live*** [1955]	$1.25	$3.75	$7.50
662	Gordon, Ian - ***Deep Is My Desire*** [1955] Cover art by George Erickson.	$1.35	$4.00	$8.00
663	Lamkin, Speed Hillyer - ***Fast And Loose*** [1955] Cover art by Rafael DeSoto.	$1.35	$4.00	$8.00
664	Nathan, Leonard - ***Night After Night*** [1955] Cover by Ray Johnson.	$1.35	$4.00	$8.00
665	Scott, Glenn - ***Farewell My Young Lover*** [1955] Cover by Ray Johnson.	$1.25	$3.75	$7.50
666	Townsend, Ray - ***Sundown Basin*** [1955] Cover art by A. Leslie Ross.	$1.25	$3.75	$7.50
667	Foster, Richard (Kendell Foster Crossen) - ***Blonde And Beautiful*** [1955] PBO.	$1.50	$5.00	$10.00
668	Sanders, Jacquin - ***Strip The Heart*** [1955]	$1.25	$3.75	$7.50
669	Steward, Davenport - ***Sail The Dark Tide*** [1955]	$1.35	$4.00	$8.00
670	Barrington, Lowell - ***The Bad One*** [1955]	$1.35	$4.00	$8.00
671	Stuart, E.B. - ***Drag Me Down*** [1955] PBO.	$1.25	$3.75	$7.50
672	Hastings, Phyllis - ***A Time For Pleasure*** [1955]	$1.25	$3.75	$7.50
673	Ketchum, Philip - ***Rider From Texas*** [1955]	$1.25	$3.75	$7.50
674	Radin, Edward D. - ***Web Of Passion*** [1955] PBO. Collection of true crime.	$1.50	$5.00	$10.00
675	MacDonald, John D. - ***Cry Hard, Cry Fast*** [1955] PBO. Cover art by Ray Johnson.	$8.00	$25.00	$50.00
676	Lowry, Robert - ***This Is My Night*** [1955] Cover art by Owen Kampen	$1.35	$4.00	$8.00
677	Richler, Mordecai - ***Wicked We Love*** [1955]	$1.25	$3.75	$7.50
678	Links, Marty - ***Bobby Sox*** [1955] Cover art by Marty Links. Cartoon book.	$1.25	$3.75	$7.50
679	Maine, Conrad - ***Good-Time Girl*** [1955] PBO.	$1.35	$4.00	$8.00
680	Ballard, Todhunter (W.T. Ballard) - ***Trigger Trail*** [1955] PBO.	$1.35	$4.00	$8.00
681	Gilbert, Elliot - ***Don't Push Me Around*** [1955] PBO. Cover art by Ray Johnson	$1.35	$4.00	$8.00
682	Sheen, Fulton J. - ***The Divine Romance*** [1955]	$ .75	$2.50	$5.00
683	Bates, H.E. - ***The Valley Of Love*** [1955] Cover by Barye Phillips.	$1.25	$3.75	$7.50
684	Bosworth, Allan R. - ***Only The Brave*** [1955] PBO.	$1.25	$3.75	$7.50
685	Brown, Wenzell - ***The Big Rumble*** [1955] PBO. Cover art by Rafael DeSoto.	$3.00	$9.00	$18.00

		G	VG	F
686	Shafer, Robert - ***The Naked And The Damned*** [1955]	$1.25	$3.75	$7.50
687	Cook, Will - ***Bullet Range*** [1955]	$1.25	$3.75	$7.50
688	Boswell, Charles & Thompson, Lewis - ***Surrender To Love*** [1955] PBO.	$1.35	$4.00	$8.00
689	Wilson, Mitchell - ***The Lovers*** [1955]	$1.25	$3.75	$7.50
690	Mirvish, Robert F. - ***The Long Watch*** [1955] Cover art by Owen Kampen.	$1.35	$4.00	$8.00
691	Boles, Paul Darcy - ***All That Love Allows*** [1955] Cover art by Rafael DeSoto.	$1.35	$4.00	$8.00
692	Graham, Lee - ***If You Are A Woman*** [1955] Photo cover.	$1.25	$3.75	$7.50
693	Brand, Max - ***Desert Showdown*** [1955]	$1.25	$3.75	$7.50
694	Thompson, Thomas - ***Forbidden Valley*** [1955] PBO. Cover art by Robert Stanley.	$1.25	$3.75	$7.50
695	Brett, Martin - ***Blondes Are My Trouble*** [1955] Cover art by Owen Kampen.	$1.35	$4.00	$8.00
696	Roth, Lillian - ***I'll Cry Tomarrow*** [1956]	$1.50	$5.00	$10.00
697	MacDonald, John D. - ***Contrary Pleasure*** [1955] Cover art by Owen Kampen.	$2.50	$7.50	$15.00
698	Hoff, Syd - ***Oops! Wrong Party!*** [1956]	$1.25	$3.75	$7.50
699	Gwaltney, Francis Irby - ***The Whole Town Knew*** [1955] Cover art by Ray Johnson.	$1.35	$4.00	$8.00
700	Haycox, Ernest - ***Secret River*** [1955] PBO. Cover art by A. Leslie Ross.	$1.25	$3.75	$7.50
701	Gulick, Bill - ***Trail Drive*** [1955]	$1.25	$3.75	$7.50
702	Waer, Jack - ***Sweet And Low-Down*** [1955]	$1.25	$3.75	$7.50
703	Merrick, Gordon - ***Lovers In Torment*** [1955]	$1.25	$3.75	$7.50
704	Dratler, Jay J. - ***The Judas Kiss*** [1955]	$1.25	$3.75	$7.50
705	Kauffmann, Stanley - ***A New Desire*** [1955] Cover art by Owen Kampen.	$1.35	$4.00	$8.00
706	Nichols, Fan - ***Angel Face*** [1955] PBO.	$1.35	$4.00	$8.00
707	Bonham, Frank - ***Rawhide Guns*** [1955]	$1.25	$3.75	$7.50
708	Barton, Jack - ***Ambush Range*** [1955] PBO. Cover by A. Leslie Ross.	$1.25	$3.75	$7.50
709	Hardy, Lindsay - ***Show No Mercy*** [1955] PBO. Cover art by Ray Johnson.	$1.25	$3.75	$7.50
710	Isherwood, Christopher - ***The World In The Evening*** [1955] Cover art by Ray Johnson.	$1.25	$3.75	$7.50
711	des Cars, Guy - ***Woman Of Paris*** [1955]	$1.35	$4.00	$8.00
712	Baker, Rachel - ***Sigmund Freud For Everybody*** [1955]	$1.00	$3.00	$6.00
713	Rimanelli, Giose - ***Fall Of Night*** [1955] Cover art by Owen Kampen.	$1.25	$3.75	$7.50
714	Townsend, Ray - ***Saddlebow Rancher*** [1955]	$1.25	$3.75	$7.50
715	Brown, Will C. - ***Guns Along The Chisholm*** [1955] PBO. Cover art by A. Leslie Ross.	$1.25	$3.75	$7.50
716	Thompson, Jim - ***After Dark, My Sweet*** [1955] PBO. Cover art by Ray Johnson	$22.00	$70.00	$140.00
717	Marshall, Rosamond - ***Mistress Of Rogues*** [1956]	$1.35	$4.00	$8.00
718	Glendinning, Richard - ***Carnival Girl*** [1956] PBO. Cover art by Rafael DeSoto.	$1.50	$5.00	$10.00
719	d'Alessio, Gregory - ***These Women*** [1956] PBO. Cover by Gregory D'Alessio. Cartoon book.	$1.35	$4.00	$8.00
720	Laredo, Johnny - ***Come And Get Me*** [1956] PBO. Cover art by Ray Johnson.	$1.35	$4.00	$8.00
721	Brand, Max - ***Brothers On The Trail*** [1956] Cover by Robert Stanley.	$1.25	$3.75	$7.50
722	Cook, Will - ***The Fighting Texan*** [1956] Cover art by A. Leslie Ross.	$1.25	$3.75	$7.50
723	Ard, William - ***Mr. Trouble*** [1956] Cover by Ray Johnson.	$1.35	$4.00	$8.00
724	Simenon, Georges - ***The Widow*** [1956]	$1.35	$4.00	$8.00
725	Ellson, Hal - ***I'll Fix You*** [1956] PBO.	$2.50	$7.50	$15.00

		G	VG	F
726	Murray, William - ***The Fugitive Romans*** [1956] Cover art by Rafael DeSoto.	$1.25	$3.75	$7.50
727	Zatterin, Ugo - ***Revolt Of The Sinners*** [1956]	$1.25	$3.75	$7.50
728	Haycox, Ernest - ***Gun Talk*** [1956] PBO.	$1.25	$3.75	$7.50
729	Barton, Jack - ***The Vengeance Riders*** [1956] Cover art by A. Leslie Ross.	$1.25	$3.75	$7.50
730	Dewey, Thomas B. - ***My Love Is Violent*** [1956] PBO.	$1.50	$5.00	$10.00
731	Lemay, Alan - ***The Searchers*** [1956]	$1.25	$3.75	$7.50
732	Brown, Wenzell - ***The Naked Hours*** [1956] PBO. Cover art by Ray Johnson.	$1.50	$5.00	$10.00
733	Gallagher, Thomas - ***The Double Life*** [1956]	$1.25	$3.75	$7.50
734	Beckhardt, Israel with Brown, Wenzell - ***The Violaters*** [1956] Cover by Rafael DeSoto.	$2.00	$6.00	$12.00
735	Ballard, Todhunter (W.T. Ballard) - ***Gunman From Texas*** [1956] PBO. Cover by A. Leslie Ross.	$1.25	$3.75	$7.50
736	Bosworth, Allan R. - ***The Drifters*** [1956] PBO.	$1.25	$3.75	$7.50
737	MacDonald, John D. - ***You Live Once*** [1956] PBO.	$8.00	$25.00	$50.00
738	Schmitt, Gladys - ***The Persistent Image*** [1956]	$1.25	$3.75	$7.50
739	Clagett, John - ***Wilderness Virgin*** [1956] Cover art by George Mayers.	$1.35	$4.00	$8.00
740	Lariar, Lawrence - ***You've Got Me In Stitches*** [1956] Cartoon book.	$1.25	$3.75	$7.50
741	Evarts, Hal G. - ***Ambush Rider*** [1956]	$1.25	$3.75	$7.50
742	Farrell, Cliff - ***Rawhide River*** [1956] Cover by A. Leslie Ross.	$1.25	$3.75	$7.50
743	Bernard, William - ***Jailbait*** [1956] Cover art by Rudolph Belarski.	$1.35	$4.00	$8.00
744	Denzer, Peter N. - ***I'm No Good*** [1956] Cover art by Ray Johnson.	$1.25	$3.75	$7.50
745	Dratler, Jay J. - ***The Pitfall*** [1956] Cover art by Owen Kampen.	$1.25	$3.75	$7.50
746	Miller, Floyd - ***The Savage Streets*** [1956] PBO. Cover art by Rafael DeSoto.	$1.50	$5.00	$10.00
747	Gilman, Laselle - ***Wine Of Desire*** [1956] Cover art by George Mayers.	$1.25	$3.75	$7.50
748	Cook, Will - ***Trumpets To The West*** [1956] PBO. Cover art by A. Leslie Ross.	$1.25	$3.75	$7.50
749	Krasney, Samuel A. - ***Death Cries In The Street*** [1956] Cover art by A. Leslie Ross.	$1.25	$3.75	$7.50
750	MacDonald, John D. - ***Border Town Girl*** [1956] PBO.	$10.00	$30.00	$60.00
751	Gifford, Arnold - ***Hotel Fever*** [1956]	$1.25	$3.75	$7.50
752	Clements, Calvin J. - ***Dark Night Of Love*** [1956] PBO. Cover art by Ray Johnson.	$1.35	$4.00	$8.00
753	Franklin, F.K. - ***To Love And To Hate*** [1956] Cover art by Ray Johnson.	$1.25	$3.75	$7.50
754	Windham, Donald - ***Let Me Alone*** [1956] Cover art by Mitchell Hooks.	$1.35	$4.00	$8.00
755	Gulick, Bill - ***The Mountain Men*** [1956]	$1.25	$3.75	$7.50
756	Ard, William - ***Hell is a City*** [1956] Cover art by George Mayers.	$1.50	$5.00	$10.00
757	Ellson, Hal - ***Duke*** [1956]	$1.35	$4.00	$8.00
758	Lowry, Robert - ***The Last Party*** [1956] PBO. Cover art by Owen Kampen.	$1.35	$4.00	$8.00
759	Whitson, Pauline Denton - ***Fair In Love And War*** [1956] PBO.	$1.25	$3.75	$7.50
760	Heller, Larry - ***I Get What I Want*** [1956] PBO. Cover art by George Mayers.	$1.35	$4.00	$8.00
761	Gruber, Frank - ***The Man From Missouri*** [1956] PBO. Cover art by A. Leslie Ross.	$1.35	$4.00	$8.00
762	Hastings, Phyllis - ***The Innocent And The Wicked*** [1956] Cover art by Rafael DeSoto.	$1.35	$4.00	$8.00
763	Kerr, Ben - ***I Fear You Not*** [1956] PBO. Cover art by Ray Johnson.	$1.35	$4.00	$8.00

		G	VG	F
764	Flesch, Rudolf - ***Why Johnny Can't Read*** [1956] Photo cover.	$1.00	$3.00	$6.00
765	Hartley, William B. - ***The Cruel Tower*** [1956]	$1.25	$3.75	$7.50
766	Burke, James Wakefield - ***Fraulein Lili Marlene*** [1956] Cover art by Owen Kampen.	$1.25	$3.75	$7.50
767	Haycox, Ernest - ***A Rider Of The High Mesa*** [1956] Cover by A. Leslie Ross.	$1.25	$3.75	$7.50
768	Barton, Jack - ***Gun In His Hand*** [1956] PBO. Cover art by Robert Stanley.	$1.25	$3.75	$7.50
769	Taubes, Frank - ***Run...Run...Run...*** [1956]	$1.25	$3.75	$7.50
770	Busch, Niven - ***The Actor*** [1956] Cover art by A. Leslie Ross.	$1.25	$3.75	$7.50
771	Heatter, Basil - ***A Night Out*** [1956] PBO. Cover art by George Mayers.	$1.35	$4.00	$8.00
772	Ballard, Todhunter (W.T. Ballard) - ***Guns Of The Lawless*** [1956] PBO.	$1.35	$4.00	$8.00
773	Cook, Will - ***Apache Ambush*** [1956] Cover art by A. Leslie Ross.	$1.25	$3.75	$7.50
774	Hansen, Robert P. - ***Walk A Wicked Mile*** [1956]	$1.25	$3.75	$7.50
775	Goodis, David - ***Behold This Woman*** [1956] Cover art by Owen Kampen.	$3.50	$10.00	$20.00
776	Ellson, Hal - ***This Is It*** [1956] PBO. Cover art by Ray Johnson.	$2.50	$7.50	$15.00
777	Bennett, Edna & House, Brant - ***Love From France*** [1956]	$1.25	$3.75	$7.50
778	Evarts, Hal G. - ***The Night Raiders*** [1956]	$1.25	$3.75	$7.50
779	Thompson, Thomas - ***Born to Gunsmoke*** [1956]	$1.25	$3.75	$7.50
780	Findley, Ferguson - ***Murder Makes Me Mad*** [1956] PBO.	$1.35	$4.00	$8.00
781	Fisher, Steve - ***Take All You Can Get*** [1956] Cover art by Mitchell Hooks.	$1.35	$4.00	$8.00
782	Ross, Sam - ***The Hustlers*** [1956] PBO.	$1.35	$4.00	$8.00
783	Temple, Dan - ***The Man From Idaho*** [1956] PBO. Cover art by A. Leslie Ross.	$1.25	$3.75	$7.50
784	Austin, Frank - ***The Return Of The Rancher*** [1956] Cover art by Robert Stanley.	$1.25	$3.75	$7.50
785	Kerr, Ben - ***Damned If He Does*** [1956] PBO.	$1.35	$4.00	$8.00
786	Sheen, Fulton J. - ***Moods And Truths*** [1956] Photo cover.	$ .75	$2.50	$5.00
787	Miller, Floyd - ***The Dream Peddlers*** [1956] PBO.	$2.00	$6.00	$12.00
788	Owen, Dean - ***The Gunpointer*** [1956] PBO. Cover art by Robert Stanley.	$1.25	$3.75	$7.50
789	Gregory, Jackson - ***Powder Smoke*** [1956]	$1.25	$3.75	$7.50
790	Woolfolk, William - ***Run While You Can*** [1956] PBO.	$1.35	$4.00	$8.00
791	Nichols, Fan - ***He Walks By Night*** [1956]	$1.35	$4.00	$8.00
792	Short, Luke - ***Ramrod*** [1956]	$1.25	$3.75	$7.50
793	Barton, Jack - ***Day Of The .44*** [1956]	$1.25	$3.75	$7.50
794	Manor, Jason - ***The Tramplers*** [1957] Cover art by George Mayers.	$1.25	$3.75	$7.50
795	Anderson, Brad & Leeming, Phil - ***Marmaduke*** [1957]	$1.50	$5.00	$10.00
796	Haycox, Ernest - ***The Silver Desert*** [1957]	$1.25	$3.75	$7.50
797	Ketchum, Philip - ***Six-Gun Maverick*** [1957] PBO. Cover art by Robert Stanley.	$1.25	$3.75	$7.50
798	Ehrlich, Max - ***Spin The Glass Web*** [1957]	$1.35	$4.00	$8.00
799	Cook, Will - ***Sabrina Kane*** [1957]	$1.25	$3.75	$7.50
800	James, Vincent - ***Island Of The Pit*** [1957]	$1.25	$3.75	$7.50
801	Brand, Max - ***The Jackson Trail*** [1957]	$1.25	$3.75	$7.50
802	Owen, Dean - ***Last-Chance Range*** [1957]	$1.25	$3.75	$7.50
803	Kerr, Ben - ***Club 17*** [1957] PBO.	$1.35	$4.00	$8.00
804	Haycox, Ernest - ***On The Prod*** [1957]	$1.25	$3.75	$7.50
805	Raine, William MacLeod - ***Arizona Guns*** [1957]	$1.25	$3.75	$7.50
806	Kane, Henry - ***The Deadly Finger*** [1957] PBO.	$1.50	$5.00	$10.00
807	Sanders, Jacquin - ***The Girls From Goldfield*** [1957] Cover art by Rafael DeSoto.	$1.35	$4.00	$8.00
808	Shirreffs, Gordon D. - ***Fort Vengeance*** [1957] PBO. Cover art by A. Leslie Ross.	$1.25	$3.75	$7.50

Popular Library, 820

Pyramid, 11

Pyramid, 25

		G	VG	F
809	Davis, Harry - ***My Brother's Wife*** [1957] Cover art by Mitchell Hooks.	$1.25	$3.75	$7.50
810	Ford, Lewis - ***Maverick Empire*** [1957]	$1.25	$3.75	$7.50
811	Brett, Martin - ***Flee From Terror*** [1957] PBO.	$1.35	$4.00	$8.00
812	Davis, Eddie - ***Laugh Yourself Well*** [1957] Cover by Den Choda.	$1.25	$3.75	$7.50
813	Ketchum, Philip - ***Dead Man's Trail*** [1957]	$1.25	$3.75	$7.50
814	Park, C.S. - ***Silver Bullets*** [1957] PBO. Cover by Robert Stanley	$1.25	$3.75	$7.50
815	Kingery, Don - ***Swamp Fire*** [1957] PBO.	$1.25	$3.75	$7.50
816	Dewey, Thomas B. - ***And Where She Stops*** [1957] PBO. Cover art by Ray Johnson.	$1.50	$5.00	$10.00
817	Shulman, Irving - ***Calibre*** [1957] PBO. Cover art by George Mayers	$1.25	$3.75	$7.50
818	Dratler, Jay J. - ***Doctor Paradise*** [1957]	$1.25	$3.75	$7.50
819	Dee, Roger - ***Let The Sky Fall*** [1957] PBO. Cover art by Ray Johnson.	$1.35	$4.00	$8.00
820	Kramer, Dale & Karr, Madeline - ***Teen-Age Gangs*** [1957] Cover art by Rafael DeSoto.	$1.35	$4.00	$8.00
821	Pfoutz, Shirley E. - ***The Whipping Boy*** [1957]	$1.25	$3.75	$7.50
822	Brand, Max - ***Valley Vultures*** [1957]	$1.25	$3.75	$7.50
823	Kastle, Herbert D. - ***One Thing On My Mind*** [1957]	$1.25	$3.75	$7.50
824	Hawkins, John & Ward - ***A Girl, A Man, And A River*** [1957]	$1.25	$3.75	$7.50
825	Hansen, Eva Hemmer - ***Scandal In Troy*** [1957] Cover art by Mitchell Hooks.	$1.25	$3.75	$7.50
826	Barton, Jack - ***The Mustangers*** [1957] PBO.	$1.25	$3.75	$7.50
827	Cook, Will - ***Lone Hand From Texas*** [1957] PBO. Cover art by A. Leslie Ross.	$1.25	$3.75	$7.50
828	Reach, James - ***Sunset Strip*** [1957] PBO.	$1.25	$3.75	$7.50
830	MacDonald, John D. - ***The Empty Trap*** [1957] PBO.	$1.25	$3.75	$7.50
831	Haycox, Ernest - ***Dead Man Range*** [1957]	$1.25	$3.75	$7.50
832	Shirreffs, Gordon - ***Massacre Creek*** [1958]	$1.25	$3.75	$7.50
833	Williams, Coe - ***The Plundered Land*** [1958] PBO.	$1.25	$3.75	$7.50
834	Cunningham, Eugene - ***Red Range*** [1958] Cover art by Rafael DeSoto	$1.25	$3.75	$7.50
1294	Sklar, George - ***The Two Worlds Of Johnny Truro*** [1950]	$1.35	$4.00	$8.00
1295	Lowry, Robert - ***The Wolf That Fed Us*** [1950] Cover art by George Rozen.	$1.35	$4.00	$8.00
1303	Webber, Everett & Olen - ***Bound Girl*** [1950] Cover art by Samuel Cherry.	$1.50	$5.00	$10.00

		G	VG	F
1307	Atkinson, Oriana - ***Her Life To Live*** [1951] Cover art by Earle Bergey.	$1.50	$5.00	$10.00
1341	Manning, Lee - ***Season For Passion*** [1951]	$1.35	$4.00	$8.00
1342	Weaver, Ward - ***End Of Track*** [1951] Cover art by George Rozen.	$1.35	$4.00	$8.00
1346	Short, Luke - ***Ramrod*** [1951] Cover art by Kirk Wilson.	$1.25	$3.75	$7.50
1368	Ermine, Will - ***Apache Crossing*** [1951]	$1.25	$3.75	$7.50
1375	Cunningham, Eugene - ***Texas Sheriff*** [1951]	$1.25	$3.75	$7.50
1376	Guthrie, Jr., A.B. - ***Trouble At Moon Dance*** [1951]	$1.35	$4.00	$8.00
1383	Gregory, Jackson - ***The Man From Texas*** [1952]	$1.25	$3.75	$7.50
1385	Wallis, J.H. - ***Once Off Guard*** [1951]	$1.25	$3.75	$7.50
1388	Weaver, Ward (Van Wyck Mason) - ***Hang My Wreath*** [1951] Cover art by Bob Fink.	$1.35	$4.00	$8.00
1392	Bernard, William - ***Jailbait*** [1951] Cover art by Rudolph Belarski.	$1.50	$5.00	$10.00
1393	Waller, Leslie - ***The Bed She Made*** [1951]	$1.35	$4.00	$8.00
1395	Westheimer, David - ***Day Into Night*** [1952]	$1.35	$4.00	$8.00
1398	Haycox, Ernest - ***Trail Smoke*** [1962]	$1.25	$3.75	$7.50
1409	Nichols, Fan - ***One By One*** [1952]	$1.35	$4.00	$8.00
1414	Raine, William MacLeod - ***The Texas Kid*** [1952]	$1.25	$3.75	$7.50
1421	Gies, Joseph - ***A Matter Of Morals*** [1952] Cover art by Harry Bacon.	$1.35	$4.00	$8.00
1423	Baccante, Leonora - ***Johnny Bogan*** [1952] Cover art by Rafael DeSoto.	$1.35	$4.00	$8.00
1426	Adams, Cleve F. - ***The Black Door*** [1952]	$1.35	$4.00	$8.00
1440	Viazzi, Alfred - ***The Cruel Dawn*** [1952] PBO.	$1.35	$4.00	$8.00
1445	Brand, Max - ***Timbal Gulch Trail*** [1952]	$1.25	$3.75	$7.50
1446	Merrick, Gordon - ***The Night And The Naked*** [1952]	$1.35	$4.00	$8.00
1448	Lariar, Lawrence - ***You Can't Catch Me*** [1953]	$1.35	$4.00	$8.00
1452	Scott, Thurston - ***I'll Get Mine*** [1952]	$1.50	$5.00	$10.00
1457	Knickerbocker, Charles H. - ***The Boy Came Back*** [1952]	$1.25	$3.75	$7.50
1460	Haycox, Ernest - ***Rawhide Range*** [1954]	$1.25	$3.75	$7.50
1463	Pratt, Theodore - ***The Big Bubble*** [1953]	$1.35	$4.00	$8.00
1467	Kerr, Ben - ***Shakedown*** [1952]	$1.35	$4.00	$8.00
1469	Gilbert, Edwin - ***Hard To Get*** [1952]	$1.35	$4.00	$8.00
1470	Radin, Edward D. - ***Headline Crimes Of The Year*** [1952] Cover art by Paul Kresse.	$1.35	$4.00	$8.00
1471	Raine, William MacLeod - ***Range Beyond The Law*** [1952] Cover art by George Rozen.	$1.25	$3.75	$7.50
1472	Ketchum, Philip - ***Texan On The Prod*** [1952] Cover art by Mel Crair.	$1.25	$3.75	$7.50
1475	Brand, Max - ***Rancher's Revenge*** [1952]	$1.25	$3.75	$7.50
1476	Ballard, Tod Hunter & Lunch, James C. - ***Showdown*** [1952]	$1.25	$3.75	$7.50
1478	Hunter, Evan - ***Don't Crowd Me*** [1952]	$1.35	$4.00	$8.00
1479	Williamson, Scott Graham - ***Torment*** [1953]	$1.35	$4.00	$8.00
1482	Chaber, M.E. - ***Don't Get Caught*** [1953]	$1.35	$4.00	$8.00
1483	Nichols, Fan - ***Ask For Linda*** [1953]	$1.35	$4.00	$8.00
1484	Mergendahl, Charles - ***The Girl Cage*** [1953]	$1.35	$4.00	$8.00
1488	Lawrence, Michael - ***Naked And Alone*** [1953]	$1.35	$4.00	$8.00
1489	Busch, Niven - ***Duel In The Sun*** [1954]	$1.25	$3.75	$7.50
1500	Spain, Terry - ***Time To Kill*** [1953]	$1.35	$4.00	$8.00
1501	Winston, Clara - ***The Closest Kin There Is*** [1953]	$1.25	$3.75	$7.50
1504	Adams, Joey - ***Joey Adams Joke Book*** [1953]	$1.25	$3.75	$7.50
1510	Davidson, David - ***The Night Is Mine*** [1953]	$1.35	$4.00	$8.00
1519	Peters, Bill - ***Blondes Die Young*** [1953]	$1.35	$4.00	$8.00
1523	Duvall, Evelyn M. - ***Facts Of Life And Love For Teen-Agers*** [1953]	$1.25	$3.75	$7.50
1526	Ard, William - ***You Can't Stop Me*** [1953]	$1.35	$4.00	$8.00
1529	Gellhorn, Martha - ***Liana*** [1953]	$1.35	$4.00	$8.00
1539	Brandt, Tom - ***Kiss Me Hard*** [1953]	$1.25	$3.75	$7.50

		G	VG	F
1548	Cushman, Dan - ***Stay Away, Joe*** [1953]	$1.25	$3.75	$7.50
1550	Bates, H.E. - ***Love For Lydia*** [1953]	$1.25	$3.75	$7.50
1553	Raine, William MacLeod - ***Texas Breed*** [1954]	$1.25	$3.75	$7.50
1555	Gorham, Charles - ***Martha Crane*** [1954] Cover art by Owen Kampen.	$1.25	$3.75	$7.50
1562	Carson, Robert - ***I Take All*** [1954]	$1.35	$4.00	$8.00
1566	Clagett, John - ***Cradle Of The Sun*** [1954] Cover art by Robert Stanley	$1.35	$4.00	$8.00
1567	Haycox, Ernest - ***Starlight Rider*** [1954]	$1.25	$3.75	$7.50
1569	Ard, William - ***A Private Party*** [1954]	$1.35	$4.00	$8.00
1584	Brandt, Tom - ***Run, Brother, Run!*** [1954]	$1.25	$3.75	$7.50
1591	Ard, William - ***No Angels For Me*** [1954]	$1.35	$4.00	$8.00
1592	Kramer, Dale & Karr, Madeline - ***Teen-Age Gangs*** [1954]	$1.35	$4.00	$8.00
1601	Mitchell, Anthea - ***The Naked Sword*** [1954]	$1.35	$4.00	$8.00
1606	Sherry, John Olden - ***The Departure*** [1954]	$1.25	$3.75	$7.50
1607	Glendinning, Richard - ***Too Fast We Live*** [1954]	$1.35	$4.00	$8.00
1608	Key, Alexander - ***The Wrath And The Wind*** [1954]	$1.35	$4.00	$8.00
1625	Keller, Dan - ***Flee The Night In Anger*** [1955]	$1.35	$4.00	$8.00
1630	Barrett, Monte - ***Smoke Up The Valley*** [1954]	$1.25	$3.75	$7.50
1641	Chanslor, Roy - ***The Naked I*** [1955]	$1.35	$4.00	$8.00
1720	Laredo, Johnny - ***Come And Get Me*** [1954]	$1.25	$3.75	$7.50
1731	Lemay, Alan - ***The Searchers*** [1954]	$1.25	$3.75	$7.50
1737	MacDonald, John D. - ***You Live Once*** [1956]	$1.50	$5.00	$10.00
1739	Clagett, John - ***Wilderness Virgin*** [1954]	$1.25	$3.75	$7.50
1743	Bernard, William - ***Jailbait*** [1954] Cover art by Rudolph Belarski.	$1.50	$5.00	$10.00
2127	Tiger, John - ***I Spy #2: Masterstroke*** [1966] TV tie-in with photo cover.	$1.35	$4.00	$8.00
2157	Tiger, John - ***I Spy #3: Superkill*** [1967] TV tie-in with photo cover.	$1.35	$4.00	$8.00

Popular Library Eagle Books. New York: Popular Library, Inc.

		G	VG	F
EB-1	Heatter, Basil - ***The Captain's Lady*** [1953]	$1.25	$3.75	$7.50
EB-2	Raine, William MacLeod - ***Rustler's Gap*** [1953] Cover art by A. Leslie Ross.	$1.25	$3.75	$7.50
EB-3	Bellah, James Warner - ***Ward 20*** [1953]	$1.25	$3.75	$7.50
EB-4	Haycox, Ernest - ***Whispering Range*** [1953] Cover by Robert Stanley	$1.25	$3.75	$7.50
EB-5	Chambers, Dana - ***She'll Be Dead By Morning*** [1953]	$1.35	$4.00	$8.00
EB-6	Wright, Francesca - ***The Loves Of Lucrezia*** [1954]	$1.25	$3.75	$7.50
EB-7	Williams, Coe - ***Yellowstone Passage*** [1954] PBO. Cover art by A. Leslie Ross.	$1.25	$3.75	$7.50
EB-8	White, William Chapman - ***The Pale Blonde Of Sands Street*** [1954]	$1.50	$5.00	$10.00
EB-9	Bland, Margot - ***Julia*** [1954] Cover art by Owen Kampen.	$1.25	$3.75	$7.50
EB-10	Jackson, Gregory - ***The Red Law*** [1954]	$1.25	$3.75	$7.50
EB-11	Van Saher, Lilla - ***Macamba*** [1954]	$1.35	$4.00	$8.00
EB-12	Lutz, Giles A. - ***Fight Or Run*** [1954] PBO. Cover art by A. Leslie Ross.	$1.25	$3.75	$7.50
EB-13	Kantor, MacKinlay - ***Gentle Annie*** [1954]	$1.25	$3.75	$7.50
EB-14	Ford, Lewis - ***Gunmen's Grass*** [1954] PBO. Cover by Robert Stanley	$1.25	$3.75	$7.50
EB-15	Lee, Gypsy Rose - ***The G-String Murders*** [1954]	$1.35	$4.00	$8.00
EB-16	Bierstadt, Edward Hale - ***Satan Was A Man*** [1954]	$1.35	$4.00	$8.00
EB-17	Gregory, Jackson - ***Secret Valley*** [1954] Cover art by A. Leslie Ross.	$1.25	$3.75	$7.50
EB-18	Mergendahl, Charles - ***This Spring Of Love*** [1954]	$1.25	$3.75	$7.50
EB-19	Barron, Dave - ***Desert Cache*** [1954] PBO. Cover by Robert Stanley	$1.25	$3.75	$7.50
EB-20	Gibson, Walter - ***The Boat*** [1954]	$1.25	$3.75	$7.50

		G	VG	F
EB-21	Raine, William MacLeod - ***The River Bend Feud*** [1954]	$1.25	$3.75	$7.50
EB-22	Wagner, Geoffrey - ***Born Of The Sun*** [1954]	$1.25	$3.75	$7.50
EB-23	Parkhill, Forbes - ***Troopers West*** [1954] Cover art by A. Leslie Ross.	$1.25	$3.75	$7.50
EB-24	Winton, Jane - ***Passion Is The Gale*** [1954] PBO.	$1.25	$3.75	$7.50
EB-25	Williams, Coe - ***Trouble Trail*** [1954] PBO. Cover by A. Leslie Ross.	$1.25	$3.75	$7.50
EB-26	Stover, Herbert E. - ***The Eagle And The Wind*** [1954] Cover by Rafael DeSoto.	$1.25	$3.75	$7.50
EB-27	Raine, William MacLeod - ***Pistol Pardners*** [1954]	$1.25	$3.75	$7.50
EB-28	Anthology edited by Whit/Hallie Burnett - ***The Tough Ones*** [1954] PBO.	$2.00	$6.00	$12.00
EB-29	Bouma, J. L. - ***Danger Trail*** [1954]	$1.25	$3.75	$7.50
EB-30	Howard, James A. - ***I'll Get You Yet*** [1954] PBO.	$1.35	$4.00	$8.00
EB-31	Colt, Clem - ***Six-Gun Buckaroo*** [1954] Cover by A. Leslie Ross.	$1.25	$3.75	$7.50
EB-32	Foster, Richard - ***The Girl From Easy Street*** [1955] PBO. Cover by Owen Kampen.	$1.35	$4.00	$8.00
EB-33	Owen, Dean - ***Brush Rider*** [1955]	$1.25	$3.75	$7.50
EB-34	Nabarro, Derrick - ***Too Hard To Handle*** [1955]	$1.35	$4.00	$8.00
EB-35	Raine, William MacLeod - ***Drygulch Trail*** [1955] Cover by A. Leslie Ross.	$1.25	$3.75	$7.50
EB-36	Fersen, Nicholas - ***Tombolo*** [1955]	$1.35	$4.00	$8.00
EB-37	Temple, Dan - ***Outlaw River*** [1955]	$1.25	$3.75	$7.50
EB-38	Fox, Ted - ***That Girl On The River*** [1955] PBO.	$1.35	$4.00	$8.00
EB-39	Williams, Coe - ***Go For Your Gun*** [1955] PBO. Cover art by A. Leslie Ross.	$1.25	$3.75	$7.50
EB-40	Kent, Simon - ***Tonight And Forever*** [1955]	$1.25	$3.75	$7.50
EB-41	Bouma, J. L. - ***Texas Spurs*** [1955]	$1.25	$3.75	$7.50
EB-42	Manor, Jason - ***The Girl In The Red Jaguar*** [1955]	$1.35	$4.00	$8.00
EB-43	Raine, William MacLeod - ***Reluctant Gunman*** [1955] Cover art by A. Leslie Ross.	$1.25	$3.75	$7.50
EB-44	Joseph, George - ***Leave It To Me*** [1955]	$1.25	$3.75	$7.50
EB-45	Vance, William - ***Apache War Cry*** [1955] PBO. Cover art by A. Leslie Ross.	$1.25	$3.75	$7.50
EB-46	Howard, James A. - ***I Like It Tough*** [1955] PBO.	$1.35	$4.00	$8.00
EB-47	Evarts, Hal G. - ***Fugitive's Canyon*** [1955]	$1.25	$3.75	$7.50
EB-48	Earl, Lawrence - ***River Of Eyes*** [1955]	$1.25	$3.75	$7.50
EB-49	Ford, Lewis B. - ***Gunfighter From Montana*** [1955]	$1.25	$3.75	$7.50
EB-50	Clippinger, Frances - ***Don't Get In My Way*** [1955]	$1.25	$3.75	$7.50
EB-51	Raine, William MacLeod - ***Beyond The Rio Grande*** [1955]	$1.25	$3.75	$7.50
EB-52	Foster, Joseph - ***Time To Embrace*** [1955] PBO. Cover art by Ray Johnson.	$1.35	$4.00	$8.00
EB-53	Cooke, David C. - ***Fighting Indians Of The West*** [1955]	$1.25	$3.75	$7.50
EB-54	Matthews, Kevin (Gardner F. Fox) - ***Barbary Slave*** [1955] PBO.	$2.00	$6.00	$12.00
EB-55	Cunningham, Eugene - ***Mesquite Maverick*** [1955] Cover art by A. Leslie Ross.	$1.25	$3.75	$7.50
EB-56	Manor, Jason - ***No Halo For Me*** [1956]	$1.35	$4.00	$8.00
EB-57	Ketchum, Philip - ***Longhorn Stampede*** [1956] Cover art by A. Leslie Ross.	$1.25	$3.75	$7.50
EB-58	Highsmith, Patricia - ***Lament For A Lover*** [1956]	$1.25	$3.75	$7.50
EB-59	Raine, William MacLeod - ***Six-Gun Feud*** [1956] Cover by A. Leslie Ross.	$1.25	$3.75	$7.50
EB-60	Seeley, Clinton - ***Storm Fear*** [1956] Movie tie-in.	$1.35	$4.00	$8.00
EB-61	Bouma, J. L. - ***Border Vengeance*** [1956] PBO. Cover art by A. Leslie Ross.	$1.25	$3.75	$7.50
EB-62	Fielding, William J. - ***Strange Customs Of Courtship And Marriage*** [1956]	$1.25	$3.75	$7.50
EB-63	Ermine, Will - ***Apache Crossing*** [1956]	$1.25	$3.75	$7.50
EB-64	Rubinstein, S. Leonard - ***The Battle Done*** [1956]	$1.25	$3.75	$7.50

		G	VG	F
EB-65	Ketchum, Philip - ***The Elkhorn Feud*** [1956] PBO. Cover art by Stanley.	$1.25	$3.75	$7.50
EB-66	Catto, Max - ***All Or Nothing*** [1956] Cover art by Ray Johnson.	$1.25	$3.75	$7.50
EB-67	Raine, William MacLeod - ***Desert Feud*** [1956]	$1.25	$3.75	$7.50
EB-68	Rosmanith, Olga - ***Don't Say No*** [1956]	$1.25	$3.75	$7.50
EB-69	Gage, Joseph - ***Hard Rock Town*** [1956]	$1.25	$3.75	$7.50
EB-70	Howard, James A. - ***Blow Out My Torch*** [1956] PBO.	$1.25	$3.75	$7.50
EB-71	Drago, Harry Sinclair - ***Montana Road*** [1956] Cover art by A. Leslie Ross.	$1.25	$3.75	$7.50
EB-72	Anderson, U. S. - ***Hard And Fast*** [1956] PBO.	$1.35	$4.00	$8.00
EB-73	Raine, William MacLeod - ***The Texas Kid*** [1956]	$1.25	$3.75	$7.50
EB-74	Silliphant, Stirling - ***Maracaibo*** [1956] Movie tie-in.	$1.50	$5.00	$10.00
EB-75	Ketchum, Philip - ***The Big Gun*** [1956] PBO. Cover art by A. Leslie Ross.	$1.25	$3.75	$7.50
EB-76	Waller, Leslie - ***The Bed She Made*** [1956]	$1.25	$3.75	$7.50
EB-77	Bonham, Frank - ***Defiance Mountain*** [1956] PBO. Cover art by A. Leslie Ross.	$1.25	$3.75	$7.50
EB-78	Matthews, Kevin (Gardner F. Fox) - ***Tory Mistress*** [1956] PBO.	$2.00	$6.00	$12.00
EB-79	Nye, Nelson - ***Desert Of The Damned*** [1956]	$1.25	$3.75	$7.50
EB-80	Roberts, Lee - ***Judas Journey*** [1957]	$1.35	$4.00	$8.00
EB-81	Raine, William MacLeod - ***High Grass Valley*** [1957] Cover art by A. Leslie Ross.	$1.25	$3.75	$7.50
EB-82	Fox, James M. - ***Free Ride*** [1957] PBO.	$1.35	$4.00	$8.00
EB-83	Ballard, Todhunter (W. T. Ballard) - ***Roundup*** [1957] PBO.	$1.35	$4.00	$8.00
EB-84	Mallet-Joris, Francoise - ***The Loving And The Daring*** [1957]	$1.25	$3.75	$7.50
EB-85	Evarts, Hal G. - ***Man Without A Gun*** [1957] PBO. Cover art by A. Leslie Ross.	$1.25	$3.75	$7.50
EB-86	Heriat, Philippe - ***The Spoiled Children*** [1957]	$1.25	$3.75	$7.50
EB-87	Bouma, J. L. - ***Burning Valley*** [1957]	$1.25	$3.75	$7.50
EB-88	Shaw, Charles - ***Heaven Knows, Mr. Allison*** [1957] Movie tie-in with Robert Mitchum.	$1.25	$3.75	$7.50
EB-89	Thompson, Thomas - ***Rawhide Rider*** [1957] PBO.	$1.25	$3.75	$7.50
EB-90	Howard, James A. - ***Die On Easy Street*** [1957] PBO. Cover art by Ray Johnson.	$1.35	$4.00	$8.00
EB-91	Brown, Will C. - ***Trouble On The Brazos*** [1957] PBO. Cover art by A. Leslie Ross.	$1.25	$3.75	$7.50
EB-92	Fain, William - ***In Search Of Love*** [1957]	$1.25	$3.75	$7.50
EB-93	Ballard, Todhunter (W. T. Ballard) - ***Trail Town Marshall*** [1957] PBO.	$1.25	$3.75	$7.50
EB-94	Busch, Niven - ***Duel In The Sun*** [1957] Movie tie-in.	$1.25	$3.75	$7.50
EB-95	Arnothy, Christine - ***I Am Fifteen - And I Don't Want To Die*** [1957] Cover by Mitchell Hooks.	$1.35	$4.00	$8.00
EB-96	Miller, Floyd - ***Just So Far*** [1957] PBO. Cover art by Ray Johnson.	$1.25	$3.75	$7.50
EB-97	Links, Marty - ***More Bobby Sox*** [1957] PBO. Cover art by Marty Links. Cartoon book.	$1.25	$3.75	$7.50
EB-98	Farrell, Cliff - ***California Passage*** [1957] PBO. Cover art by A. Leslie Ross.	$1.25	$3.75	$7.50
EB-99	Tample, Dan - ***Bullet Lease*** [1957]	$1.25	$3.75	$7.50
EB-100	Davis, Harry - ***Portrait Of Rene*** [1957]	$1.25	$3.75	$7.50
EB-101	Raine, William MacLeod - ***Border Breed*** [1958] Cover art by A. Leslie Ross.	$1.25	$3.75	$7.50
EB-102	Cushman, Dan - ***Stay Away, Joe*** [1958]	$1.25	$3.75	$7.50
EB-103	Gregory, Jackson - ***Hard Case Range*** [1958] Cover art by Shaare.	$1.25	$3.75	$7.50
EB-104	Kerr, Ben - ***The Blonde And Johnny Malloy*** [1958] PBO.	$1.50	$5.00	$10.00

Popular Library G Series. New York: Popular Library Publishing.

G-100	Slaughter, Frank G. - ***Sangaree*** [1952]	$1.35	$4.00	$8.00
G-101	Raddall, Thomas H. - ***The Nymph And The Lamp*** [1952]	$1.50	$5.00	$10.00

		G	VG	F
G-102	Carse, Robert - ***From The Sea And The Jungle*** [1952] Cover art by Rafael DeSoto.	$1.50	$5.00	$10.00
G-103	Levin, Dan - ***Mask Of Glory*** [1952] Cover art by George Rozen.	$1.35	$4.00	$8.00
G-104	Gerson, Noel B. - ***Savage Cavalier*** [1952]	$1.35	$4.00	$8.00
G-105	Lowry, Robert - ***The Big Cage*** [1952] Cover art by Rafael DeSoto.	$2.00	$6.00	$12.00
G-106	Reynolds, Quentin - ***Courtroom*** [1952]	$1.35	$4.00	$8.00
G-107	Bourne, Peter - ***The Golden Road*** [1952]	$1.50	$5.00	$10.00
G-108	Payne, Robert - ***Red Lion Inn*** [1952] Cover art by Rafael DeSoto.	$2.00	$6.00	$12.00
G-109	Wetherell, June - ***The Glorious Three*** [1952] Cover art by George Meyers	$1.35	$4.00	$8.00
G-110	Cloete, Stuart - ***Congo Song*** [1952] Cover art by George Mayers	$1.50	$5.00	$10.00
G-111	Kormendi, Ferenc - ***The Forsaken*** [1952]	$1.50	$5.00	$10.00
G-112	McConnaughey, Susanne - ***Point Venus*** [1952]	$1.35	$4.00	$8.00
G-113	Davies, Rhys - ***Marianne*** [1952] Photo cover.	$1.25	$3.75	$7.50
G-114	Lowry, Robert - ***Find Me In Fire*** [1952] Cover art by Ray Johnson.	$1.50	$5.00	$10.00
G-115	Connell, Vivian - ***The Naked Rich*** [1952]	$1.25	$3.75	$7.50
G-116	Gerson, Noel B. - ***Sword Of Fortune*** [1953] Cover art by George Mayers	$1.35	$4.00	$8.00
G-117	Landon, Joseph - ***Angle Of Attack*** [1953]	$1.35	$4.00	$8.00
G-118	Flannagan, Roy - ***The Forest Cavalier*** [1953]	$1.25	$3.75	$7.50
G-119	Dowdy, Clifford - ***Jasmine Street*** [1953] Cover art by George Mayers	$1.35	$4.00	$8.00
G-120	Emerick, Lucille - ***The City Beyond*** [1953]	$1.25	$3.75	$7.50
G-121	Baxter, Walter - ***Look Down In Mercy*** [1953]	$1.35	$4.00	$8.00
G-122	Berson, Fred - ***After The Big House*** [1953]	$1.25	$3.75	$7.50
G-123	Wayne, Anderson - ***Charlie Dell*** [1953]	$1.35	$4.00	$8.00
G-124	Derby, Mark - ***Afraid In The Dark*** [1953]	$1.25	$3.75	$7.50
G-125	Longstreet, Stephen - ***The Beach House*** [1953]	$1.25	$3.75	$7.50
G-126	Burke, James Wakefield - ***The Big Rape*** [1953]	$1.35	$4.00	$8.00
G-127	Bates, H.E. - ***The Scarlet Sword*** [1953]	$1.25	$3.75	$7.50
G-128	Smith, Robert - ***One Winter In Boston*** [1953]	$1.25	$3.75	$7.50
G-129	Wetherell, June - ***Free And Easy*** [1953]	$1.25	$3.75	$7.50
G-130	Moray, Helga - ***Tisa*** [1953]	$1.35	$4.00	$8.00
G-131	Gallagher, Thomas - ***The Gathering Darkness*** [1953]	$1.25	$3.75	$7.50
G-132	Cloete, Stuart - ***Watch For The Dawn*** [1953]	$1.25	$3.75	$7.50
G-133	Remarque, Erich Maria - ***Three Comrades*** [1953]	$1.25	$3.75	$7.50
G-134	Wolff, Maritta M. - ***Whistle Stop*** [1953]	$1.25	$3.75	$7.50
G-135	Soloviev, Mikhail - ***When The Gods Are Silent*** [1953]	$1.25	$3.75	$7.50
G-136	Kennedy, Jay Richard - ***Prince Bart*** [1954]	$1.35	$4.00	$8.00
G-137	Barrett, Monte - ***Sun In Their Eyes*** [1954]	$1.25	$3.75	$7.50
G-138	Payne, Robert - ***Blood Royal*** [1954]	$1.25	$3.75	$7.50
G-139	Gaillard, Robert - ***Marie Of The Isles*** [1954] Cover art by Robert Stanley.	$1.25	$3.75	$7.50
G-140	Adler, Polly - ***A House Is Not A Home*** [1954]	$ .75	$2.50	$5.00
G-141	Brennan, Louis A. - ***These Items Of Desire*** [1954]	$1.25	$3.75	$7.50
G-142	Gilbert, Edwin - ***The Hot And The Cool*** [1954]	$1.25	$3.75	$7.50
G-143	Tilsley, Frank - ***Rage To Love*** [1954] Cover art by Ray Johnson.	$1.25	$3.75	$7.50
G-144	Slater, Estelle - ***The Strong Don't Cry*** [1954] Cover by Ray Johnson.	$1.25	$3.75	$7.50
G-145	Shulman, Irving - ***The Flesh Is Real*** [1954]	$1.25	$3.75	$7.50
G-146	Paley, Frank - ***Rumble On The Docks*** [1955] Cover art by Rafael DeSoto.	$2.00	$6.00	$12.00
G-147	Ronald, James - ***This Is Temptation*** [1955]	$1.25	$3.75	$7.50
G-148	Powers, Anne - ***The Only Sin*** [1955]	$1.25	$3.75	$7.50
G-149	Sichel, Pierre - ***Never Say Love*** [1955] Cover by Ray Johnson.	$1.00	$3.00	$6.00

		G	VG	F
G-150	Durafour, Michel - ***The Girl From Rome*** [1955] Cover art by Robert Stanley.	$1.00	$3.00	$6.00
G-151	Baxter, Walter - ***The Image And The Search*** [1955]	$1.00	$3.00	$6.00
G-152	Widdemer, Margaret - ***The Golden Wildcat*** [1955]	$1.00	$3.00	$6.00
G-153	Remarque, Erich Maria - ***A Time To Love And A Time To Die*** [1955]	$1.00	$3.00	$6.00
G-154	Meloney, William Brown - ***Many Loves Have I*** [1955]	$1.00	$3.00	$6.00
G-155	Feder, Sid & Joesten, Joachim - ***The Luciano Story*** [1956]	$1.00	$3.00	$6.00
G-156	Wylie, Philip - ***Tomorrow!*** [1956]	$1.00	$3.00	$6.00
G-157	Lanham, Edwin - ***The Iron Maiden*** [1956]	$1.00	$3.00	$6.00
G-158	Merrick, Gordon - ***Between Darkness And Day*** [1956]	$1.00	$3.00	$6.00
G-159	Webber, Everett - ***Louisiana Cavalier*** [1956]	$1.35	$4.00	$8.00
G-160	Lindop, Audrey Erskine - ***The Tormented*** [1956]	$1.00	$3.00	$6.00
G-161	Kantor, MacKinlay - ***Diversey*** [1956]	$1.00	$3.00	$6.00
G-162	Oakey, Virginia - ***The Reckless Tears*** [1956] Cover art by Hooks.	$1.00	$3.00	$6.00
G-163	Slaughter, Frank G. - ***Sangaree*** [1956]	$1.00	$3.00	$6.00
G-164	Hatch, Alden - ***Red Carpet For Mamie Eisenhower*** [1956]	$ .75	$2.50	$5.00
G-165	Weeks, Joseph - ***Never Too Young*** [1956] Cover by Mitchell Hooks.	$1.00	$3.00	$6.00
G-166	Reynolds, Quentin - ***Headquarters*** [1956]	$1.00	$3.00	$6.00
G-167	Mann, Peggy - ***A Room In Paris*** [1956] Cover by Mitchell Hooks.	$1.00	$3.00	$6.00
G-168	Beaty, David - ***The Four Winds*** [1956]	$1.00	$3.00	$6.00
G-169	Clagett, John - ***Captain Whitecap*** [1956]	$1.00	$3.00	$6.00
G-170	Derval, Paul - ***Folies-Bergere*** [1956] Photo cover. Sixteen pages of photos.	$1.25	$3.75	$7.50
G-171	Prokosch, Frederic - ***A Tale For Midnight*** [1956]	$1.00	$3.00	$6.00
G-172	Bonner, Paul Hyde - ***The Other Side Of Paradise*** [1956]	$1.00	$3.00	$6.00
G-173	Coates, Robert M. - ***The Night Is So Dark*** [1956]	$1.00	$3.00	$6.00
G-174	Mirvish, Robert F. - ***Red Sky At Midnight*** [1956]	$1.00	$3.00	$6.00
G-175	Shulman, Irving - ***Children Of The Dark*** [1956]	$1.00	$3.00	$6.00
G-176	Marshall, Rosamond - ***Rogue Cavalier*** [1956]	$1.00	$3.00	$6.00
G-177	Hastings, Phyllis - ***Her French Husband*** [1956]	$1.00	$3.00	$6.00
G-178	Secondari, John H. - ***Hot Winds Of Summer*** [1956] Cover by Mitchell Hooks.	$1.00	$3.00	$6.00
G-179	Bromfield, Louis - ***The Wild Country*** [1956]	$1.00	$3.00	$6.00
G-180	Weaver, Ward - ***Hang My Wreath*** [1957]	$1.00	$3.00	$6.00
G-181	McGovern, James - ***Erika*** [1957]	$1.00	$3.00	$6.00
G-182	Sullivan, Katharine - ***Girls On Parole*** [1957]	$1.25	$3.75	$7.50
G-183	Kauffmann, Stanley - ***Man Of The World*** [1957] Cover art by Owen Kampen.	$1.00	$3.00	$6.00
G-184	Hoehling, A. A. & Mary - ***The Last Voyage Of The Lusitania*** [1957]	$1.00	$3.00	$6.00
G-185	Kavinoky, Bernice - ***Honey From A Dark Hive*** [1957]	$1.00	$3.00	$6.00
G-186	Baldwin, Bates - ***The Sultan's Warrior*** [1957]	$1.00	$3.00	$6.00
G-187	Irving, Clifford - ***The Quick And The Loving*** [1957]	$1.00	$3.00	$6.00
G-188	Holden, Curry - ***Episode In The Sun*** [1957]	$1.00	$3.00	$6.00
G-189	Hardy, W.G. - ***All The Trumpets Sounded*** [1957] Cover by Mitchell Hooks.	$1.00	$3.00	$6.00
G-190	O'Brien, John A. - ***Happy Marriage*** [1957]	$1.00	$3.00	$6.00
G-191	Gerson, Noel B. - ***Savage Cavalier*** [1957]	$1.00	$3.00	$6.00
G-192	Bates, H.E. - ***The Sleepless Moon*** [1957]	$1.00	$3.00	$6.00
G-193	Orwell, George - ***Keep The Aspidistra Flying*** [1957] Cover art by Mitchell Hooks.	$1.25	$3.75	$7.50
G-194	Burns, John Horne - ***A Cry Of Children*** [1957] Cover art by Ray Johnson.	$1.25	$3.75	$7.50
G-195	Patai, Irene - ***The Valley Of God*** [1957] Cover art by Mitchell Hooks.	$1.00	$3.00	$6.00

		G	VG	F
G-196	Stearn, Jess - ***Sisters Of The Night*** [1957] Cover art by Mitchell Hooks.	$1.00	$3.00	$6.00
G-197	Raine, William MacLeod - ***On The Dodge*** [1957] Cover art by A. Leslie Ross.	$ .75	$2.50	$5.00
G-198	Payne, Robert - ***A House In Peking*** [1957]	$1.25	$3.75	$7.50
G-199	Cranston, Ruth - ***The Miracle Of Lourdes*** [1957]	$ .75	$2.50	$5.00
G-200	Steward, Davenport - ***Way Of A Buccaneer*** [1957]	$ .75	$2.50	$5.00
G-201	Murphy, Bill - ***The Red Sands Of Santa Maria*** [1957]	$ .75	$2.50	$5.00
G-202	Frizell, Bernard - ***Ten Days In August*** [1957] Cover art by Mitchell Hooks.	$ .75	$2.50	$5.00
G-203	Duvall, Evelyn Millis - ***Facts Of Life And Love For Teen-Agers*** [1957] Photo cover.	$ .75	$2.50	$5.00
G-204	Cleary, Jon - ***Dust In The Sun*** [1957]	$ .75	$2.50	$5.00
G-205	Cloete, Stuart - ***Mamba*** [1957]	$1.25	$3.75	$7.50
G-206	Longstreet, Stephen - ***The Beach House*** [1957]	$ .75	$2.50	$5.00
G-207	Barrett, Monte - ***The Tempered Blade*** [1957]	$ .75	$2.50	$5.00
G-208	Holiday, Billie - ***Lady Sings The Blues*** [1958] Photo cover.	$1.35	$4.00	$8.00
G-209	Sheen, Fulton J. - ***Life Is Worth Living*** [1958]	$ .75	$2.50	$5.00
G-210	Brick, John - ***Jubilee*** [1958]	$ .75	$2.50	$5.00
G-211	Brick, Robin - ***Pitchman*** [1958]	$ .75	$2.50	$5.00
G-212	Karney, Jack - ***Work Of Darkness*** [1958]	$ .75	$2.50	$5.00
G-213	Curry, Peggy Simson - ***So Far From Spring*** [1958]	$ .75	$2.50	$5.00
G-214	Orwell, George - ***Burmese Days*** [1958]	$ .75	$2.50	$5.00
G-215	Mallet-Joris, Francoise - ***The Red Room*** [1958] Cover by Mitchell Hooks.	$ .75	$2.50	$5.00
G-216	Adams, Joey - ***Joey Adams' Joke Book*** [1958] Cartoon and joke book.	$ .75	$2.50	$5.00
G-217	Gerson, Noel B. - ***The Silver Lion*** [1958]	$1.00	$3.00	$6.00
G-218	Haycox, Ernest - ***Trouble Shooter*** [1958]	$ .75	$2.50	$5.00
G-219	Marshall, Rosamond - ***Bond Of The Flesh*** [1958]	$ .75	$2.50	$5.00
G-220	Lowry, Robert - ***What's Left Of April*** [1958]	$ .75	$2.50	$5.00
G-221	Faviell, Frances - ***A House On The Rhine*** [1958] Cover art by Mitchell Hooks.	$ .75	$2.50	$5.00
G-222	Deal, Borden - ***Walk Through The Valley*** [1958]	$ .75	$2.50	$5.00
G-223	Raine, William MacLeod - ***The Sheriff's Son*** [1958] Cover art by Robert Stanley.	$ .75	$2.50	$5.00
G-224	Eckert, Ralph G. - ***Sex Attitudes In The Home*** [1958]	$ .65	$2.00	$4.00
G-225	Locke, Charles O. - ***The Hell Bent Kid*** [1958]	$ .75	$2.50	$5.00
G-226	Arnothy, Christine - ***God Is Late*** [1958] Cover art by Mitchell Hooks.	$ .75	$2.50	$5.00
G-227	Buckley, David - ***Pride Of Innocence*** [1958]	$ .75	$2.50	$5.00
G-228	Brown, Wenzell - ***They Died In The Chair*** [1958]	$1.50	$5.00	$10.00
G-229	McMullen, Richard - ***Awake To Darkness*** [1958] Cover art by Ray Johnson.	$ .75	$2.50	$5.00
G-230	Brand, Max - ***The Happy Valley*** [1958] Cover art by A. Leslie Ross.	$ .75	$2.50	$5.00
G-231	Nichols, Fan - ***I Know My Love*** [1958] PBO.	$ .75	$2.50	$5.00
G-232	Evarts, Hal G. - ***The Man From Yuma*** [1958] PBO.	$ .75	$2.50	$5.00
G-233	Stewart, Sidney - ***Give Us This Day*** [1958]	$ .75	$2.50	$5.00
G-234	Caruso, Joseph - ***The Priest*** [1958]	$ .75	$2.50	$5.00
G-235	Clayton, John Bell - ***Six Angels At My Back*** [1958]	$ .75	$2.50	$5.00
G-236	Ard, William - ***Cry Scandal*** [1958]	$ .75	$2.50	$5.00
G-237	Haycox, Ernest - ***Chaffee Of Roaring Horse*** [1958] Cover art by A. Leslie Ross.	$ .75	$2.50	$5.00
G-238	Cunningham, Eugene - ***Texas Triggers*** [1958]	$ .75	$2.50	$5.00
G-239	Shelly, Gordon - ***I Take The Rap*** [1958] Cover art by Mitchell Hooks.	$ .75	$2.50	$5.00
G-240	Farrell, Cliff - ***Gun Hand*** [1958]	$ .75	$2.50	$5.00
G-241	Kantor, MacKinlay - ***Don't Touch Me*** [1958] Cover art by Rafael DeSoto.	$1.00	$3.00	$6.00

		G	VG	F
G-242	Dratler, Jay J. - ***Dream Of A Woman*** [1958]	$ .75	$2.50	$5.00
G-243	Baron, Alexander - ***Queen Of The East*** [1958] Cover art by Mitchell Hooks.	$1.25	$3.75	$7.50
G-244	Carse, Robert - ***From The Sea And The Jungle*** [1958]	$1.00	$3.00	$6.00
G-245	MacKenzie, Donald - ***Manhunt*** [1958] Cover by Harry Schaare.	$ .75	$2.50	$5.00
G-246	Raine, William MacLeod - ***Man-Size*** [1958]	$ .75	$2.50	$5.00
G-247	Gulick, Bill - ***Showdown In The Sun*** [1958] PBO. Cover by A. Leslie Ross.	$ .75	$2.50	$5.00
G-248	Radin, Edward D. - ***The Deadly Reasons*** [1958] PBO.	$ .75	$2.50	$5.00
G-249	Ballard, Todhunter (W.T. Ballard) - ***Saddle Tramp*** [1958] PBO.	$1.00	$3.00	$6.00
G-250	Gilbert, Edwin - ***The Squirrel Cage*** [1958]	$ .75	$2.50	$5.00
G-251	Murray, William - ***Best Seller*** [1958] Cover art by Darcy.	$ .75	$2.50	$5.00
G-252	McAllister, Robert with Miller, Floyd - ***The Kind Of Guy I Am*** [1958] Cover art by Harry Schaare.	$ .75	$2.50	$5.00
G-253	Gellhorn, Martha - ***Liana*** [1958]	$ .75	$2.50	$5.00
G-254	Elliott, Charles - ***Trial By Fire*** [1958]	$ .75	$2.50	$5.00
G-255	Ballard, Todhunter (W.T. Ballard) - ***Rawhide Gunman*** [1958] Cover art by A. Leslie Ross.	$ .75	$2.50	$5.00
G-256	Steward, Davenport - ***Caribbean Cavalier*** [1958]	$ .75	$2.50	$5.00
G-257	Gregory, Jackson - ***The Silver Star*** [1958] Cover art by A. Leslie Ross.	$ .75	$2.50	$5.00
G-258	Marshall, Rosamond - ***The Rib Of The Hawk*** [1958]	$ .75	$2.50	$5.00
G-259	Lowry, Robert - ***The Violent Wedding*** [1958]	$ .75	$2.50	$5.00
G-260	Gale, Gloria - ***Calendar Model*** [1958] Twelve pages of photos.	$1.25	$3.75	$7.50
G-261	Haycox, Ernest - ***Free Grass*** [1958]	$ .75	$2.50	$5.00
G-262	Perretta, Armando - ***Take A Number*** [1958]	$ .75	$2.50	$5.00
G-263	Evarts, Hal G. - ***Apache Agent*** [1958] Cover art by A. Leslie Ross.	$ .75	$2.50	$5.00
G-264	Raine, William MacLeod - ***Square Shooter*** [1958] Cover art by A. Leslie Ross.	$ .75	$2.50	$5.00
G-265	Joseph, George - ***This Is For Keeps*** [1958] PBO. Cover art by Harry Schaare.	$ .75	$2.50	$5.00
G-266	Resnik, Muriel - ***Life Without Father*** [1958]	$ .75	$2.50	$5.00
G-267	LeMay, Alan - ***Painted Ponies*** [1958] Cover by A. Leslie Ross.	$ .75	$2.50	$5.00
G-268	Pratt, Theodore - ***The Big Bubble*** [1958] Cover art by Robert Maguire.	$1.25	$3.75	$7.50
G-269	Dratler, Jay J. - ***All For A Woman*** [1958]	$ .75	$2.50	$5.00
G-270	Brand, Max - ***Dead Or Alive*** [1958]	$ .75	$2.50	$5.00
G-271	MacDonald, John D. - ***Cry Hard, Cry Fast*** [1958] Cover art by Ray Johnson.	$1.35	$4.00	$8.00
G-272	Cunningham, Eugene - ***Spiderweb Trail*** [1958] Cover art by Rafael DeSoto.	$ .75	$2.50	$5.00
G-273	Sheen, Fulton J. - ***The Life Of All Living*** [1958] Photo cover.	$ .65	$2.00	$4.00
G-274	Guthrie, A.B., Jr. - ***Trouble At Moon Dance*** [1958]	$1.35	$4.00	$8.00
G-275	Mergendahl, Charles - ***Tiger By The Tail*** [1958] PBO.	$ .75	$2.50	$5.00
G-276	Cook, Will - ***Fury At Painted Rock*** [1958]	$ .75	$2.50	$5.00
G-277	Hunter, Evan - ***Don't Crowd Me*** [1958]	$1.25	$3.75	$7.50
G-278	Raine, William MacLeod - ***Bullet Ambush*** [1958] Cover art by A. Leslie Ross.	$ .75	$2.50	$5.00
G-279	Jackson, Delmar - ***The Cut Of The Ax*** [1958] Cover by Ray Johnson.	$ .75	$2.50	$5.00
G-280	Connell, Vivian - ***The Naked Rich*** [1958]	$ .75	$2.50	$5.00
G-281	Jackson, Felix - ***A Strange Affair*** [1958]	$ .75	$2.50	$5.00
G-282	Chaber, M.E. - ***The Man Inside*** [1958]	$ .75	$2.50	$5.00
G-283	Haycox, Ernest - ***Trail Smoke*** [1958] Cover art by Harry Schaare.	$ .75	$2.50	$5.00
G-284	Carse, Robert - ***The Wicked Blade*** [1958] PBO. Cover art by Mitchell Hooks.	$1.00	$3.00	$6.00
G-285	Wagner, Geoffrey - ***Rage On The Bar*** [1958]	$ .75	$2.50	$5.00

		G	VG	F
G-286	Park, C.S. - ***Showdown At Pistol Flat*** [1958] PBO. Cover by A. Leslie Ross.	$ .75	$2.50	$5.00
G-287	Scott, Thurston - ***I'll Get Mine*** [1958] Cover art by Ray Johnson.	$1.25	$3.75	$7.50
G-288	Shirreffs, Gordon D. - ***Shadow Valley*** [1958] PBO.	$ .75	$2.50	$5.00
G-289	Bello, Sol - ***Seize The Day*** [1958]	$ .75	$2.50	$5.00
G-290	Rigsby, Howard - ***Naked To My Pride*** [1958] Cover art by Zuckerberg.	$ .75	$2.50	$5.00
G-291	Wicker, Tom - ***The Devil Must*** [1958]	$ .75	$2.50	$5.00
G-292	Ernenwein, Leslie - ***Ramrod From Hell*** [1958] Cover art by Robert Stanley.	$ .75	$2.50	$5.00
G-293	Matthews, Kevin (Gardner F. Fox) - ***Woman Of Egypt*** [1958] PBO. Cover art by Darcy.	$1.50	$5.00	$10.00
G-294	Cunningham, Eugene - ***Buckaroo*** [1958] Cover art by Ross.	$ .75	$2.50	$5.00
G-295	Raine, William MacLeod - ***The Tough Tenderfoot*** [1958]	$ .75	$2.50	$5.00
G-296	Winston, Clara - ***The Closest Kin There Is*** [1958]	$ .75	$2.50	$5.00
G-297	Kavinoky, Bernice - ***We Burn Like Candles*** [1958]	$ .75	$2.50	$5.00
G-298	Block, Anita Rowe - ***Love Is A Four Letter Word*** [1958]	$ .75	$2.50	$5.00
G-299	Catto, Max - ***Gold In The Sky*** [1958]	$ .75	$2.50	$5.00
G-300	Haycox, Ernest - ***Lone Rider*** [1958]	$ .75	$2.50	$5.00
G-301	Sanderson, James Dean - ***Boy With A Gun*** [1958]	$ .75	$2.50	$5.00
G-302	Dewey, Thomas B. - ***Go To Sleep, Jeannie*** [1959] PBO.	$1.50	$5.00	$10.00
G-303	Weaver, Ward - ***End Of Track*** [1959]	$ .75	$2.50	$5.00
G-304	Karney, Jack - ***Cry, Brother, Cry*** [1959] PBO.	$1.35	$4.00	$8.00
G-305	Raine, William MacLeod - ***The River Bend Feud*** [1959] Cover art by A. Leslie Ross.	$ .75	$2.50	$5.00
G-306	Tolbert, Frank X. - ***The Staked Plain*** [1959] Cover art by Scharre.	$ .75	$2.50	$5.00
G-307	Knickerbocker, Charles H. - ***The Boy Came Back*** [1959]	$ .75	$2.50	$5.00
G-308	Denzer, Peter W. - ***The Last Hero*** [1959]	$ .75	$2.50	$5.00
G-309	Ballard, Todhunter (W.T. Ballard) - ***Trouble On The Massacre*** [1959] PBO.	$1.00	$3.00	$6.00
G-310	Wayne, Anderson - ***Time To Remember*** [1959]	$ .75	$2.50	$5.00
G-311	Irving, Clifford - ***The Losers*** [1959]	$ .75	$2.50	$5.00
G-312	Locke, Charles O. - ***The Last Princess*** [1959]	$1.00	$3.00	$6.00
G-313	Stackelberg, Gene - ***Double Agent*** [1959] PBO. Cover art by Mitchell Hooks.	$ .75	$2.50	$5.00
G-314	Chaffin, James B. - ***Guns Of Abilene*** [1959] PBO. Cover art by Robert Stanley.	$ .75	$2.50	$5.00
G-315	Davis, Wesley Ford - ***The Time Of The Panther*** [1959] Cover art by Schaare.	$ .75	$2.50	$5.00
G-316	Falstein, Louis - ***Face Of A Hero*** [1959]	$ .75	$2.50	$5.00
G-317	Brown, Wenzell - ***Dark Drums*** [1959] Cover art by Schaare.	$1.00	$3.00	$6.00
G-318	Haycox, Ernest - ***Riders West*** [1959] Cover art by A. Leslie Ross.	$ .75	$2.50	$5.00
G-319	Scott, Virgil - ***The Savage Affair*** [1959]	$ .75	$2.50	$5.00
G-320	Ballard, Todhunter - ***Two-Edged Vengeance*** [1959] Cover by A. Leslie Ross	$1.00	$3.00	$6.00
G-321	Bernard, William - ***Jailbait*** [1959] Cover art by Rudolph Belarski.	$1.50	$5.00	$10.00
G-322	Barton, Jack - ***The Untamed Breed*** [1959]	$ .75	$2.50	$5.00
G-323	Roth, Lillian - ***Beyond My Worth*** [1959] Cover art by Harry Schaare.	$ .75	$2.50	$5.00
G-324	Presser, Jacob - ***Breaking Point*** [1959] Cover art by Zuckerberg.	$ .75	$2.50	$5.00
G-325	Nichols, Fan - ***Ask For Linda*** [1959]	$ .75	$2.50	$5.00
G-326	Haycox, Ernest - ***Starlight Rider*** [1959]	$ .75	$2.50	$5.00
G-327	Brand, Max - ***Timbal Gulch Trail*** [1959]	$ .75	$2.50	$5.00
G-328	Ard, William - ***A Private Party*** [1959]	$1.35	$4.00	$8.00
G-329	Lowry, Robert - ***New York Call Girl*** [1959]	$ .75	$2.50	$5.00
G-330	Gutwillig, Robert - ***After Long Silence*** [1959]	$ .75	$2.50	$5.00

		G	VG	F
G-331	Packer, Peter - ***Bitter Fruit*** [1959]	$ .75	$2.50	$5.00
G-332	Cunningham, Eugene - ***Texas Sheriff*** [1959]	$ .75	$2.50	$5.00
G-333	Edwards, Samuel - ***That Randall Girl*** [1959]	$ .75	$2.50	$5.00
G-334	Saroyan, William - ***A Secret Story*** [1959] Cover art by Hooks	$ .75	$2.50	$5.00
G-335	Ballard, Todhunter & Lynch, James C. - ***Showdown*** [1959] Cover art by A. Leslie Ross.	$1.00	$3.00	$6.00
G-336	Baccante, Leonora - ***Johnny Bogan*** [1959] Cover by Rafael DeSoto	$ .75	$2.50	$5.00
G-337	Ketchum, Philip - ***Decision At Piute Wells*** [1959] PBO. Cover art by Robert Stanley.	$ .75	$2.50	$5.00
G-338	Peters, Bill - ***Blondes Die Young*** [1959]	$ .75	$2.50	$5.00
G-339	Townsend, Leo - ***The Young Life*** [1959]	$ .75	$2.50	$5.00
G-340	Gilbert, Edwin - ***See How They Burn*** [1959]	$ .75	$2.50	$5.00
G-341	Clagett, John - ***Cradle Of The Sun*** [1959] Cover art by Stanley.	$1.00	$3.00	$6.00
G-342	Hirshberg, Al & Pfau, Robert - ***Prodigal Shepherd*** [1959]	$ .75	$2.50	$5.00
G-343	Raine, William MacLeod - ***The Texas Kid*** [1959] Cover art by A. Leslie Ross	$ .75	$2.50	$5.00
G-344	Merrick, Gordon - ***The Night And The Naked*** [1959]	$ .75	$2.50	$5.00
G-345	LeMay, Alan - ***Thunder In The Dust*** [1959]	$ .75	$2.50	$5.00
G-346	Howard, James A. - ***I'll Get You Yet*** [1959] Cover art by Owen Kampen.	$1.00	$3.00	$6.00
G-347	Haycox, Ernest - ***Guns Of The Tom Dee And The Valley Of The Rogue*** [1959]	$ .75	$2.50	$5.00
G-348	Wetherell, June - ***Free And Easy*** [1959]	$ .75	$2.50	$5.00
G-349	Stover, Herbert E. - ***The Eagle And The Wind*** [1959]	$ .75	$2.50	$5.00
G-350	Bellah, James Warner - ***Ward 20*** [1959]	$ .75	$2.50	$5.00
G-351	Haycox, Ernest - ***Head Of The Mountain*** [1959]	$ .75	$2.50	$5.00
G-352	Burnett, Whit & Hallie - ***The Tough Ones*** [1959]	$1.25	$3.75	$7.50
G-353	Townsend, Ray - ***Gold Town Gunman*** [1959] Cover art by Norman Saunders	$ .75	$2.50	$5.00
G-354	Lawrence, Michael (Lawrence Lariar) - ***Naked And Alone*** [1959]	$ .75	$2.50	$5.00
G-355	Ketchum, Philip - ***Gun Law*** [1959] Cover art by A. Leslie Ross.	$ .75	$2.50	$5.00
G-356	Weinreb, Nathaniel Norsen - ***The Groves Of Desire*** [1959] Cover by Stanley Zuckerberg	$ .75	$2.50	$5.00
G-357	Carse, Robert - ***Drums Of Empire*** [1959] PBO. Cover art by Schaare.	$ .75	$2.50	$5.00
G-358	Ellson, Hal - ***Duke*** [1959] Cover art by Belarski.	$1.00	$3.00	$6.00
G-359	Ashburn, Wade - ***Violent Valley*** [1959] PBO. Cover art by A. Leslie Ross.	$ .75	$2.50	$5.00
G-360	Edited by Kerner, Fred - ***Love Is A Man's Affair*** [1959] Cover art by Mitchell Hooks.	$ .75	$2.50	$5.00
G-361	Raine, William MacLeod - ***Texas Breed*** [1959] Cover by Robert Stanley.	$ .75	$2.50	$5.00
G-362	Manor, Jason - ***The Girl In The Red Jaguar*** [1959]	$ .75	$2.50	$5.00
G-363	LeMay, Alan - ***Gunsight Trail*** [1959]	$ .75	$2.50	$5.00
G-364	Anthology - ***Good Housekeeping's The Better Way*** [1959]	$ .65	$2.00	$4.00
G-365	Nabokov, Vladimir - ***Spring In Fialta*** [1959] Cover art by Zuckerberg.	$ .75	$2.50	$5.00
G-366	Traver, Robert - ***Danny And The Boys*** [1959]	$ .75	$2.50	$5.00
G-367	Haycox, Ernest - ***Rawhide Range*** [1959] Cover art by Robert Stanley	$ .75	$2.50	$5.00
G-368	Bland, Margot - ***Julia*** [1959]	$ .75	$2.50	$5.00
G-369	Brand, Max - ***Rancher's Revenge*** [1959] Cover by Robert Stanley	$ .75	$2.50	$5.00
G-370	Owen, Dean - ***Rifle Pass*** [1959]	$ .75	$2.50	$5.00
G-371	Adams, Joey - ***Cindy And I*** [1959]	$ .75	$2.50	$5.00
G-372	Mergendahl, Charles - ***This Spring Of Love*** [1959]	$ .75	$2.50	$5.00
G-373	Cameron, Bruce - ***The Sins Of Maria*** [1959] Cover art by DeSoto	$1.00	$3.00	$6.00

		G	VG	F
G-374	Raine, William MacLeod - ***Pistol Pardners*** [1959]	$ .75	$2.50	$5.00
G-375	Kavinoky, Bernice - ***So Strong A Flame*** [1959] Cover art by McGinnis.	$ .75	$2.50	$5.00
G-376	Yoseloff, Martin - ***Lily And The Sergeant*** [1959]	$ .75	$2.50	$5.00
G-377	Allen, Steve - ***The Girls On The 10th Floor*** [1959]	$ .75	$2.50	$5.00
G-378	Temple, Dan - ***Outlaw River*** [1959]	$ .75	$2.50	$5.00
G-379	Kantor, MacKinlay - ***Gentle Annie*** [1959] Cover by Mitchell Hooks.	$1.00	$3.00	$6.00
G-380	Gregory, Jackson - ***Marshall Of Sundown*** [1959]	$ .75	$2.50	$5.00
G-381	Horan, James D. - ***Seek Out And Destroy*** [1959] Cover art by Schaare.	$ .75	$2.50	$5.00
G-382	Law, M. L. - ***Aimee*** [1959] Cover art by Hooks.	$ .75	$2.50	$5.00
G-383	Johnstone, Lane - ***The Dr. Lewis Affair*** [1959]	$ .75	$2.50	$5.00
G-384	Tregaskis, Richard - ***Guadalcanal Diary*** [1959]	$ .75	$2.50	$5.00
G-385	McCullen, Richard - ***Country Girl*** [1959]	$ .75	$2.50	$5.00
G-386	Gies, Joseph - ***A Matter Of Morals*** [1959]	$ .75	$2.50	$5.00
G-387	Bouma, J. L. - ***Texas Spurs*** [1959] Cover by A. Leslie Ross.	$ .75	$2.50	$5.00
G-388	Owen, Dean - ***Brush Rider*** [1959]	$ .75	$2.50	$5.00
G-389	Ketchum, Philip - ***Gunfire Man*** [1959] PBO. Cover art by Schulz.	$ .75	$2.50	$5.00
G-390	Raine, William MacLeod - ***Desert Feud*** [1959]	$ .75	$2.50	$5.00
G-391	Toeffer, Ray - ***The Scarlet Guidon*** [1959]	$ .75	$2.50	$5.00
G-392	de Wohl, Louis - ***The Living Wood*** [1959]	$ .75	$2.50	$5.00
G-393	Wright, Francesca - ***The Loves Of Lucrezia*** [1959]	$ .75	$2.50	$5.00
G-394	Raine, William MacLeod - ***Beyond The Rio Grande*** [1959]	$ .75	$2.50	$5.00
G-395	Lowry, Robert - ***Find Me In Fire*** [1959]	$1.00	$3.00	$6.00
G-396	Gregory, Jackson - ***The Man From Texas*** [1959]	$ .75	$2.50	$5.00
G-397	Williams, Coe - ***Trouble Trail*** [1959] Cover by A. Leslie Ross.	$ .75	$2.50	$5.00
G-398	Brand, Max - ***Six-Gun Ambush*** [1959] Cover art by Stanley.	$ .75	$2.50	$5.00
G-399	Marsh, Ellen - ***Unarmed In Paradise*** [1960] Cover art by Hooks.	$ .75	$2.50	$5.00
G-400	Atkinson, Oriana - ***Her Life To Live*** [1960]	$1.25	$3.75	$7.50
G-402	Haycox, Ernest - ***Guns Up*** [1960]	$ .75	$2.50	$5.00
G-403	Ness, Eliot - ***The Untouchables*** [1960] TV tie-in. TV photo cover.	$1.35	$4.00	$8.00
G-407	Cook, Will - ***Trumpets To The West*** [1960]	$ .75	$2.50	$5.00
G-409	Key, Alexander - ***The Wrath And The Wind*** [1960]	$ .75	$2.50	$5.00
G-414	Raine, William MacLeod - ***West Of The Law*** [1960] Cover art by Cherry.	$ .75	$2.50	$5.00
G-416	Covert, Alice Lent - ***Woman Doctor*** [1960] Cover art by Schaare.	$ .65	$2.00	$4.00
G-417	Feder, Sid & Joestein, Joachim - ***The Luciano Story*** [1960] Cover by Harry Schaare.	$ .75	$2.50	$5.00
G-418	Haycox, Ernest - ***Whispering Range*** [1960]	$ .75	$2.50	$5.00
G-419	Tabrah, Ruth - ***Town For Scandal*** [1960]	$ .75	$2.50	$5.00
G-421	Short, Luke - ***Ramrod*** [1960]	$ .75	$2.50	$5.00
G-423	Raine, William MacLeod - ***Rustlers' Gap*** [1960] Cover art by Schaare.	$ .75	$2.50	$5.00
G-424	Mergendahl, Charles - ***Tonight Is Forever*** [1960]	$ .75	$2.50	$5.00
G-425	Mirabelli, Eugene - ***The Burning Affair*** [1960] Cover by Robert McGinnis.	$ .75	$2.50	$5.00
G-427	Hubler, Richard - ***The Brass God*** [1960]	$ .75	$2.50	$5.00
G-428	Farewell, Nina - ***Someone To Love*** [1960] Cover art by Hooks.	$ .75	$2.50	$5.00
G-429	Gulick, Bill - ***Trail Drive*** [1960] Cover art by A. Leslie Ross.	$ .75	$2.50	$5.00
G-433	Barton, Jack - ***Brand Of Fury*** [1960] Cover art by Bob Schulz.	$ .75	$2.50	$5.00
G-434	Meoni, Armando - ***Strange Lovers*** [1960] Cover art by Zuckerberg.	$ .75	$2.50	$5.00
G-435	Garnett, David - ***The Ways Of Desire*** [1960] Cover art by McGinnis.	$ .75	$2.50	$5.00
G-436	Shulman, Irving - ***The Velvet Knife*** [1960]	$ .75	$2.50	$5.00

		G	VG	F
G-437	Mark, David - ***The Neighborhood*** [1960]	$ .75	$2.50	$5.00
G-438	Blassingame, Wyatt - ***This Land Is Mine*** [1960]	$ .75	$2.50	$5.00
G-439	Haycox, Ernest - ***Grim Canyon*** [1960]	$ .75	$2.50	$5.00
G-440	Ballard, Todhunter (W.T. Ballard) - ***Trigger Trail*** [1960] Cover art by Robert Schulz.	$ .75	$2.50	$5.00
G-441	Thompson, Thomas - ***Forbidden Valley*** [1960] Cover art by George Gross.	$ .75	$2.50	$5.00
G-443	Smith, Don - ***China Coaster*** [1960] Cover art by Schaare.	$ .75	$2.50	$5.00
G-444	Packer, Peter - ***Dark Surrender*** [1960]	$ .75	$2.50	$5.00
G-446	Barton, Jack - ***Trail Of The Damned*** [1960] Cover art by Schulz.	$ .75	$2.50	$5.00
G-447	Fox, Edward - ***That Girl On The River*** [1960]	$ .75	$2.50	$5.00
G-448	Williams, Coe - ***Go For Your Gun*** [1960]	$ .75	$2.50	$5.00
G-449	De Rivoyre, Christine - ***Tangerine*** [1960] Cover art by McGinnis.	$1.00	$3.00	$6.00
G-450	Coffee, Leonore - ***The Face Of Love*** [1960]	$ .75	$2.50	$5.00
G-451	Evarts, Hal G. - ***Ambush Rider*** [1960]	$ .75	$2.50	$5.00
G-452	Dewey, Thomas B. - ***Too Hot For Hawaii*** [1960] Cover by Darcy.	$1.50	$5.00	$10.00
G-453	Harris, Kathleen - ***Jane Arden, Registered Nurse*** [1960] Cover art by Victor Kalin.	$ .65	$2.00	$4.00
G-454	Kaufman, Sue - ***The Hot Summer Days*** [1960] Cover art by Hooks.	$ .75	$2.50	$5.00
G-455	Feibleman, Peter S. - ***The Daughters Of Necessity*** [1960] Cover by Coconis.	$ .75	$2.50	$5.00
G-456	Saher, Lilla Van - ***Macamba*** [1960] Cover art by Schaare.	$1.00	$3.00	$6.00
G-457	Hubler, Richard G. - ***Walk Into Hell*** [1960]	$ .75	$2.50	$5.00
G-458	Farrell, Cliff - ***Rawhide River*** [1960]	$ .75	$2.50	$5.00
G-459	Raine, William MacLeod - ***Arizona Guns*** [1960]	$ .75	$2.50	$5.00
G-460	Nye, Nelson - ***Desert Of The Damned*** [1960] Cover art by A. Leslie Ross.	$ .75	$2.50	$5.00
G-461	Haycox, Ernest - ***Vengeance Trail*** [1960] Cover art by A. Leslie Ross.	$ .75	$2.50	$5.00
G-462	McSorley, Edward - ***Kitty, I Hardly Knew You*** [1960]	$ .75	$2.50	$5.00
G-463	Vaughan, Carter - ***The Wilderness*** [1960] Cover art by Zuckerberg.	$ .75	$2.50	$5.00
G-465	Griffin, Gwyn - ***By The North Gate*** [1960] Cover art by Hooks.	$ .75	$2.50	$5.00
G-468	Ketchum, Philip - ***Desperation Valley*** [1960]	$ .75	$2.50	$5.00
G-470	Mitchell, A. - ***Naked Sword*** [1960]	$ .75	$2.50	$5.00
G-471	Winton, Jane - ***Passion Is The Gale*** [1960] Cover art by Hooks.	$ .75	$2.50	$5.00
G-472	Freedman, Benedict & Nancy - ***Tresa*** [1960] Cover art by Zuckerberg.	$ .75	$2.50	$5.00
G-473	Morrill, George - ***Dark Sea Running*** [1960]	$ .75	$2.50	$5.00
G-474	Gregory, Jackson - ***Powder Smoke*** [1960] Cover by A. Leslie Ross.	$ .75	$2.50	$5.00
G-475	Hersey, John - ***The Marmot Drive*** [1960]	$ .75	$2.50	$5.00
G-476	Brick, John - ***Gettysburg*** [1960] PBO. Cover art by McGinnis.	$ .75	$2.50	$5.00
G-477	Bonham, Frank - ***Rawhide Guns*** [1960]	$ .75	$2.50	$5.00
G-478	Haycox, Ernest - ***Secret River*** [1960] Cover art by Robert Schulz.	$ .75	$2.50	$5.00
G-479	Foster, Richard - ***The Girl From Easy Street*** [1960] Cover art by McGinnis.	$1.00	$3.00	$6.00
G-481	Treadwell, Sophie - ***One Fierce Hour And Sweet*** [1960] Cover art by Zuckerberg.	$ .75	$2.50	$5.00
G-483	Boulle, Pierre - ***The Test*** [1960]	$ .75	$2.50	$5.00
G-485	Rubinstein, S. Leonard - ***The Battle Done*** [1960]	$ .75	$2.50	$5.00
G-486	Doyle, Sir Arthur Conan - ***The Adventures Of Sherlock Holmes*** [1960]	$1.00	$3.00	$6.00
G-487	Kavinoky, Bernice - ***Honey From A Dark Hive*** [1960]	$ .75	$2.50	$5.00

		G	VG	F
G-488	Lawrence, Michael (Lawrence Lariar) - ***I Like It Cool*** [1960] PBO.	$1.00	$3.00	$6.00
G-489	Drago, Harry Sinclair - ***Montana Road*** [1960] Cover art by A. Leslie Ross.	$ .75	$2.50	$5.00
G-491	Haycox, Ernest - ***A Rider Of The High Mesa*** [1960] Cover art by A. Leslie Ross.	$ .75	$2.50	$5.00
G-493	Smith, H. Allen - ***Low Man On The Totem Pole*** [1960]	$ .75	$2.50	$5.00
G-494	Cook, Will - ***Apache Ambush*** [1960] Cover by A. Leslie Ross.	$ .75	$2.50	$5.00
G-495	Banks, Raymond E. - ***Meet Me In Darkness*** [1960] PBO.	$ .75	$2.50	$5.00
G-496	Page, Patti - ***Once Upon A dream*** [1960] Photo Cover.	$ .75	$2.50	$5.00
G-497	Harris, Kathleen - ***Jane Arden, Staff Nurse*** [1960] Cover art by Victor Kalin.	$ .75	$2.50	$5.00
G-499	Gruber, Frank - ***The Man From Missouri*** [1960] Cover by A. Leslie Ross.	$ .75	$2.50	$5.00
G-500	Weidman, Jerome & Abbott, George - ***Fiorello!*** [1960]	$ .75	$2.50	$5.00
G-501	Lonstreet, Stephen & Ethel - ***Geisha*** [1961]	$ .75	$2.50	$5.00
G-502	Loovis, David - ***Try For Elegance*** [1961]	$ .75	$2.50	$5.00
G-503	O'Donnell, Eugene - ***Berdoo's Woman*** [1961]	$ .75	$2.50	$5.00
G-507	MacDonald, John D. - ***You Kill Me*** [1961]	$1.50	$5.00	$10.00
G-508	Colette, Simone - ***"And God Created Woman"*** [1961] PBO. Movie tie-in with Brigitte Bardot. Photo cover.	$1.35	$4.00	$8.00
G-509	Fischer, Marjorie - ***Mrs. Sherman's Summer*** [1961] Cover art by Zuckerberg.	$ .75	$2.50	$5.00
G-510	Wagner, Geoffrey - ***Nicchia*** [1961] Cover art by McGinnis.	$ .75	$2.50	$5.00
G-511	Copp, DeWitt - ***Radius Of Action*** [1961] Cover art by Zuckerberg.	$ .75	$2.50	$5.00
G-512	Fraley, Oscar - ***4 Against The Mob*** [1961] PBO. TV tie-in.	$1.35	$4.00	$8.00
G-514	Evarts, Hal G. - ***Shortgrass*** [1961] Cover art by Schulz.	$ .75	$2.50	$5.00
G-515	Austin, Frank - ***Return Of The Rancher*** [1961]	$ .75	$2.50	$5.00
G-516	Bard, Daniel - ***The Aquanauts*** [1961] PBO. Cover art by Schaare. TV tie-in.	$1.35	$4.00	$8.00
G-518	Sheldon, Walter J. - ***Tour Of Duty*** [1961] Cover art by Schaare.	$ .75	$2.50	$5.00
G-520	London, Jack - ***Burning Daylight*** [1961] Cover art by Schaare.	$1.00	$3.00	$6.00
G-521	Sterling, Forest J. - ***Wake Of The Wahoo*** [1961] Cover by Mitchell.	$ .75	$2.50	$5.00
G-522	Haupt, Enid A. - ***The Seventeen Book Of Young Living*** [1961]	$ .75	$2.50	$5.00
G-523	Christie, Agatha - ***Murder In Three Acts*** [1961]	$1.00	$3.00	$6.00
G-524	Brown, Will C. - ***Guns Along The Chisholm*** [1961] Cover art by A. Leslie Ross.	$ .75	$2.50	$5.00
G-525	Haycox, Ernest - ***The Silver Desert*** [1961] Cover by A. Leslie Ross.	$ .75	$2.50	$5.00
G-527	Cooper, Saul - ***All In A Night's Work*** [1961] PBO. Movie tie-in. Photo cover.	$1.00	$3.00	$6.00
G-528	Marshall, Rosamond - ***The Rib Of The Hawk*** [1961] Cover art by Maguire.	$ .75	$2.50	$5.00
G-529	Dratler, Jay J. - ***Doctor Paradise*** [1961]	$ .65	$2.00	$4.00
G-531	Buchan, James - ***The 39 Steps*** [1961]	$ .75	$2.50	$5.00
G-532	Bloch, Robert - ***The Dead Beat*** [1961]	$3.00	$9.00	$18.00
G-537	Harris, Kathleen - ***Jane Arden, Surgery Nurse*** [1961] Cover art by Victor Kalin.	$ .65	$2.00	$4.00
G-538	Burnett, W.R. - ***Conant*** [1961] PBO. Cover art by Barye Phillips.	$1.35	$4.00	$8.00
G-539	Lowry, Robert - ***The Wolf That Fed Us*** [1961] Cover art by Zuckerberg.	$ .75	$2.50	$5.00
G-541	Cushman, Dan - ***Stay Away, Joe*** [1961] Cover art by Rafael DeSoto.	$ .75	$2.50	$5.00
G-542	Unknown - ***Julie*** [1961]	$ .75	$2.50	$5.00
G-546	O'Farrell, Kathy - ***I Made My Bed*** [1961]	$ .75	$2.50	$5.00
G-547	Banks, Ramond E. - ***The Computer Kill*** [1961] PBO. Cover art by McGinnis.	$1.00	$3.00	$6.00

		G	VG	F
G-548	Stewart, Sidney - ***Give Us This Day*** [1961] Cover by Schaare.	$ .75	$2.50	$5.00
G-549	Smith, Robert Paul - ***"I Didn't Do Anything"*** [1961] Cartoon and joke book.	$ .75	$2.50	$5.00
G-550	Poirot-Delpech, Bertrand - ***Fool's Paradise*** [1961]	$ .75	$2.50	$5.00
G-551	Lowry, Robert - ***New York Call Girl*** [1961]	$ .75	$2.50	$5.00
G-552	Anthology - ***TV Guide Roundup*** [1961] Editors of *TV Guide*.	$1.00	$3.00	$6.00
G-555	Dooley, Tom - ***Dr. Tom Dooley, My Story*** [1961] Photo cover.	$ .75	$2.50	$5.00
G-556	Caldwell, Taylor - ***Your Sins And Mine*** [1961] Cover by Barye Phillips.	$ .75	$2.50	$5.00
G-558	Nickles, Marione R. - ***The Saturday Evening Post Cartoons*** [1961] Cover art by Brad Anderson. Cartoon book.	$ .75	$2.50	$5.00
G-559	Gorham, Nicholas - ***The Cruise*** [1961]	$ .75	$2.50	$5.00
G-560	Siodmak, Curt - ***Donovan's Brain*** [1961] Cover art by Mitchell Hooks.	$1.25	$3.75	$7.50
G-561	Harris, Kathleen - ***Jane Arden, Head Nurse*** [1961] Cover art by Gino Forte.	$ .65	$2.00	$4.00
G-562	Kelland, Clarence Budington - ***The Monitor Affair*** [1961] Cover art by Mitchell Hooks.	$ .75	$2.50	$5.00
G-563	de Capite, Raymond - ***The Coming Of Fabrizze*** [1961] Cover by John Groth.	$ .75	$2.50	$5.00
G-564	Hull, Helen - ***A Tapping On The Wall*** [1962]	$ .75	$2.50	$5.00
G-565	Bates, H.E. - ***Hark, Hark The Lark*** [1962]	$ .75	$2.50	$5.00
G-566	Harris, Kathleen - ***Jane Arden, Student Nurse*** [1962] Cover art by Gino Forte.	$ .65	$2.00	$4.00
G-567	Gebler, Ernest - ***The Love Investigator*** [1962]	$ .75	$2.50	$5.00
G-569	Robsky, Paul - ***The Last Of The Untouchables*** [1962] PBO. TV tie-in.	$1.35	$4.00	$8.00
G-571	Kenny, G. - ***D. Bong: Ace Of Aces*** [1962]	$ .75	$2.50	$5.00
G-572	Nathan, Robert - ***Portrait Of Jennie*** [1962] Cover art by Zuckerberg.	$ .75	$2.50	$5.00

Popular Library Guidance Books.

		G	VG	F
CD-1	Rudolph, Patricia - ***Your Future As An Airline Stewardess*** [1961] Photo cover.	$ .50	$1.50	$3.00
CD-2	Singer, Jules B. - ***Your Future In Advertising*** [1961] Photo cover.	$ .50	$1.50	$3.00
CD-3	Unknown - ***Your Future In Journalism*** [1961]	$ .50	$1.50	$3.00
CD-4	Unknown - ***Your Future In Foreign Service*** [1961]	$ .50	$1.50	$3.00
CD-5	Unknown - ***Your Future In Electronic Engineering*** [1961]	$ .50	$1.50	$3.00
CD-6	Feder, Ph.D., Raymond L. - ***Your Future In Chemical Engineering*** [1961] Photo cover.	$ .50	$1.50	$3.00
CD-7	Unknown - ***Your Future In The Army*** [1961]	$ .50	$1.50	$3.00
CD-8	Unknown - ***Your Future In The Fashion World*** [1961]	$ .50	$1.50	$3.00
CD-9	Unknown - ***Your Future In Nuclear Energy Fields*** [1961]	$ .50	$1.50	$3.00
CD-10	Unknown - ***Your Future In Dentistry*** [1961]	$ .50	$1.50	$3.00

Popular Library K Series.

		G	VG	F
K-1	Mathieson, Theodore - ***The Devil And Ben Franklin*** [1962] Cover art by Teason.	$ .75	$2.50	$5.00
K-4	Tregaskis, Richard - ***Guadacanal Dairy*** [1962]	$ .65	$2.00	$4.00
K-6	Jackson, Shirley - ***The Haunting Of Hill House*** [1962] Photo cover. Movie tie-in.	$1.50	$5.00	$10.00
K-7	Silone, Ignazio - ***The Fox And The Camellias*** [1962] Cover art by Mitchell Hooks.	$ .65	$2.00	$4.00
K-9	Streeter, Edward - ***Mr. Hobbs' Vacation*** [1962] Photo cover. Movie tie-in.	$ .65	$2.00	$4.00
K-12	Tolbert, Frank X. - ***The Staked Plain*** [1962] Cover by Harry Schaare.	$ .65	$2.00	$4.00
K-13	Walker, Dorothy - ***She Married A Doctor*** [1962]	$ .65	$2.00	$4.00
K-14	Anthology - ***Ellery Queen's 16th Mystery Annual*** [1962]	$ .75	$2.50	$5.00

K-15	Anthology edited by Eric Williams - ***Great Escape Stories*** [1962]	$ .65	$2.00	$4.00
K-16	Eberhart, Mignon G. - ***Never Look Back*** [1962]	$ .75	$2.50	$5.00
K-18	Bloch, Robert - ***Blood Runs Cold*** [1962] Photo cover.	$2.50	$7.50	$15.00
K-19	Eberhart, Mignon G. - ***The Cup, The Blade Or The Gun*** [1962].	$ .75	$2.50	$5.00
K-22	Hall, Lawrence Sargent - ***Stowaway*** [1962]	$ .65	$2.00	$4.00
K-26	Eberhart, Mignon G. - ***Speak No Evil*** [1962]	$ .75	$2.50	$5.00
K-30	Eberhart, Mignon G. - ***The White Dress*** [1962]	$ .75	$2.50	$5.00
K-35	Eberhart, Mignon G. - ***Another Woman's House*** [1963] Cover art by William Teason.	$ .75	$2.50	$5.00
K-36	Griffith, Corinne - ***Papa's Delicate Condition*** [1963] Movie photo cover. Movie tie-in with Jackie Gleason.	$ .65	$2.00	$4.00
K-37	Ford, Leslie - ***Trial By Ambush*** [1963] Cover by William Teason.	$ .65	$2.00	$4.00
K-38	Harris, Kathleen - ***Jane Arden, Space Nurse*** [1963] Cover art by Lou Marchetti.	$ .50	$1.50	$3.00
K-39	Eberhart, Mignon G. - ***Hunt With The Hounds*** [1963]	$ .75	$2.50	$5.00
K-40	Dean, Nell Marr - ***Resort Nurse*** [1963] Cover art by Lou Marchetti.	$ .50	$1.50	$3.00
K-41	Smith, Robert Paul - ***Crank*** [1963]	$ .65	$2.00	$4.00
K-43	Anthology - ***The Popular Library Crossword Puzzle Book*** [1963] Puzzle book.	$2.00	$6.00	$12.00
K-44	Gardner, Gerald - editor - ***The Quotable Mr. Kennedy*** [1963] Photo cover.	$ .65	$2.00	$4.00
K-46	Rhodin, Eric - ***The Scar*** [1963] Cover art by Zuckerberg.	$ .65	$2.00	$4.00
K-47	Eberhart, Mignon G. - ***Dead Men's Plans*** [1963]	$ .75	$2.50	$5.00
K-48	Smith, Shelly - ***The Ballad Of The Running Man*** [1963] Photo cover. Movie tie-in.	$ .65	$2.00	$4.00
K-49	Ford, Leslie - ***Old Lover's Ghost*** [1963]	$ .75	$2.50	$5.00
K-51	Hitchens, Dolores - ***The Abductor*** [1963]	$ .75	$2.50	$5.00
K-52	Davidson, Bill - ***President Kennedy Selects Six Brave Presidents*** [1963]	$ .65	$2.00	$4.00
K-53	Eberhart, Mignon G. - ***Enemy In The House*** [1963]	$ .75	$2.50	$5.00
K-54	Stone, Hampton (Aaron Marc Stein) - ***The Babe With The Twistable Arm*** [1963]	$ .75	$2.50	$5.00
K-56	Ford, Leslie - ***False To Any Man*** [1963]	$ .75	$2.50	$5.00
K-59	Worley, Dorothy - ***Doctor's Nurse*** [1963] Cover art by Marchetti.	$ .50	$1.50	$3.00
K-60	Eberhart, Mignon G. - ***The Unknown Quantity*** [1963]	$ .75	$2.50	$5.00
K-64	Stevenson, Robert Louis - ***Dr. Jekyll And Mr. Hyde*** [1963] Cover art by Zuckerberg.	$1.25	$3.75	$7.50
K-65	Cabot, Isabel - ***Island Doctor*** [1963] Cover art by Lou Marchetti.	$ .50	$1.50	$3.00
K-66	Lariar, Lawrence - editor - ***Lady Chatterley's Daughter*** [1963] Cartoon book.	$2.00	$6.00	$12.00
K-67	Eberhart, Mignon G. - ***House Of Storm*** [1963]	$ .75	$2.50	$5.00
K-68	Ford, Leslie - ***Siren In The Night*** [1963]	$ .75	$2.50	$5.00
K-71	Wells, H.G. - ***The Invisible Man*** [1964]	$1.00	$3.00	$6.00
K-73	Ross, Helaine - ***No Tears Tomorrow*** [1964] Cover art by Lou Marchetti.	$ .65	$2.00	$4.00
K-74	Jones, Victor - ***Love In A London Flat*** [1964] Cover art by Zuckerberg.	$ .65	$2.00	$4.00
K-75	Judson, Jeanne - ***A Strange Case For Dr. Rolland*** [1964] Cover art by Marchetti.	$ .50	$1.50	$3.00
K-77	Anthology edited by Marione R. Nickles - ***After Hours Cartoons From The Saturday Evening Post*** [1960] Cover art by Brad Anderson. Cartoon book.	$ .65	$2.00	$4.00

Popular Library PC Series.

		G	VG	F
PC-300	London, Jack - ***Adventures Of Captain David Grief*** [1957] TV tie-in.	$1.00	$3.00	$6.00
PC-400	Hilton, Conrad - ***Be My Guest*** [1957]	$ .65	$2.00	$4.00
PC-500	Lariar, Lawrence - editor - ***Lady Chatterley's Daughter*** [1957] PBO. Cartoon book.	$ .65	$2.00	$4.00
PC-600	Marx, Arthur - ***Life With Groucho*** [1960] Photo cover.	$ .65	$2.00	$4.00
PC-700	Colette, Simone - ***The Lovers*** [1960] PBO. Movie photo cover. Movie tie-in.	$ .65	$2.00	$4.00
PC-800	Kennedy, Robert F. - ***The Enemy Within*** [1960]	$ .65	$2.00	$4.00
PC-850	McCarthy, Joe - ***The Remarkable Kennedys*** [1960] Photo cover.	$ .65	$2.00	$4.00
PC-1000	Loomis, Noel - ***Bonanza*** [1960] PBO. Cover art by Schulz. TV tie-in.	$1.50	$5.00	$10.00
PC-1002	Kennedy, John F. - ***The Strategy Of Peace*** [1961] Photo cover.	$ .65	$2.00	$4.00
PC-1003	Knarf - ***Kiss Me, You Fool*** [1961] PBO. Cartoon book.	$ .65	$2.00	$4.00
PC-1004	Zeiger, Henry A. - ***The Seizing Of The Santa Maria*** [1961]	$ .65	$2.00	$4.00
PC-1007	Sumner, Cid Ricketts - ***Tammy Tell Me True*** [1961] Cover art by Barye Phillips. Movie tie-in with Sandra Dee.	$ .75	$2.50	$5.00
PC-1008	Opotowsky, Stan - ***The Kennedy Government*** [1961] PBO. Photo cover.	$ .65	$2.00	$4.00
PC-1010	Heyman, Evan Lee - ***Cain's Hundred*** [1961] PBO. Photo cover. TV tie-in.	$ .65	$2.00	$4.00
PC-1011	Walton, Harry - ***How To Choose And Use Power Tools*** [1961] PBO.	$ .65	$2.00	$4.00
PC-1013	Henderson, Ernest - ***The World Of "Mr. Sheraton"*** [1962]	$ .65	$2.00	$4.00
PC-1018	Adams, Charlotte - ***The Whirlpool Menu Cook Book*** [1962] PBO. Photo cover. Cookbook.	$ .75	$2.50	$5.00
PC-1019	Percy, Walker - ***The Moviegoer*** [1962]	$ .65	$2.00	$4.00
PC-1020	Leroux, Gaston - ***The Phantom Of The Opera*** [1962] Photo cover. Movie tie-in.	$1.25	$3.75	$7.50
PC-1022	Wolff, Dick - ***Fishing Tackle And Techniques*** [1963] Photo cover.	$ .65	$2.00	$4.00
PC-1025	Ertz, S. - ***In The Cool Of The Day*** [1963]	$ .65	$2.00	$4.00
PC-1027	Barrett, William E. - ***The Lilies Of The Field*** [1963] Movie tie-in with Sidney Poitier.	$ .65	$2.00	$4.00
PC-1028	Storey, David - ***This Sporting Life*** [1961] Movie tie-in.	$ .65	$2.00	$4.00
PC-1029	Laas, William - ***The Feel Of The Road*** [1963] PBO. Photo cover.	$ .65	$2.00	$4.00
PC-1030	Powers, J.F. - ***Morte D'Urban*** [1963]	$ .65	$2.00	$4.00
PC-1031	Denning, Lord - ***The Profumo-Christine Keeler Affair*** [1963] PBO.	$ .65	$2.00	$4.00
PC-1033	Zeiger, Henry A. - ***Lyndon B. Johnson: Man And President*** [1963] PBO. Photo cover.	$ .65	$2.00	$4.00
PC-1034	Durand, Robert - ***Lady In A Cage*** [1964] PBO. Photo cover. Movie tie-in.	$1.00	$3.00	$6.00
PC-1038	Pepis, Betty - ***The Personal Touch In Interior Decorating*** [1964] PBO. Photo cover. Photos throughout.	$ .65	$2.00	$4.00
PC-1040	Donovan, Robert J. - ***The Warren Commission Report On The Assassination Of JFK*** [1964] PBO. Photo cover.	$ .65	$2.00	$4.00
PC-1041	Folliott, Doria - ***Signpost To Murder*** [1964] PBO. Photo cover. Movie tie-in.	$ .65	$2.00	$4.00
PC-1042	Avallone, Michael - ***Station Six-Sahara*** [1964] PBO. Movie tie-in.	$1.25	$3.75	$7.50
PC-1043	Pascal, John - ***The Jean Harlow Story*** [1964] PBO. Photo cover. 32 pages of photos.	$1.25	$3.75	$7.50
PC-1045	Amrine, Michael - ***This Is Humphrey*** [1964] Photo cover.	$ .65	$2.00	$4.00
PC-1047	Hano, Arnold - ***Marriage Italian Style*** [1965] PBO. Photo cover. Movie tie-in with Sophia Loren.	$ .65	$2.00	$4.00
PC-1048	Hittleman, Carl K. - ***36 Hours*** [1965] PBO. Movie tie-in.	$ .65	$2.00	$4.00

		G	VG	F
PC-1050	Hine, Al - ***Bus Riley's Back In Town*** [1965] PBO. Movie photo cover. Movie tie-in with Ann-Margret.	$1.00	$3.00	$6.00
PC-1051	Exbrayat, Charles - ***A Ravishing Idiot*** [1965] Movie photo cover. Movie tie-in with Brigitte Bardot.	$1.00	$3.00	$6.00
PC-1053	Fordham, Peta - ***The Robber's Tale*** [1965]	$ .65	$2.00	$4.00
PC-1055	Ahlers, Arvel W. - ***Family Fun In Tape Recording*** [1965] PBO.	$ .65	$2.00	$4.00
PC-1057	Waterbury, Ruth - ***Elizabeth Taylor*** [1965] Photo cover.	$1.00	$3.00	$6.00
PC-1059	Kata, Elizabeth - ***A Patch Of Blue*** [1965] Photo cover. Movie tie-in with Sidney Poitier.	$ .65	$2.00	$4.00
PC-1061	Richardson, Alice - ***The Complete Book Of Family Protection*** [1965]	$ .65	$2.00	$4.00
PC-1062	Tabor, Michael - ***Battle Of The Bulge*** [1965] Photo over. Movie tie-in with Henry Fonda.	$ .65	$2.00	$4.00
PC-7640	Flesch, Rudolf - ***Why Johnny Can't Read*** [1965]	$ .50	$1.50	$3.00

Popular Library SP Series.

		G	VG	F
SP-2	Bellow, Saul - ***The Adventures Of Augie March*** [1955]	$1.00	$3.00	$6.00
SP-3	Anthology - ***Crossword Puzzles: Book Three*** [1955] PBO.	$2.50	$7.50	$15.00
SP-4	Soubiran, Andre - ***The Doctors*** [1955]	$ .75	$2.50	$5.00
SP-5	Gwaltngy, Francis Irby - ***Between Heaven And Hell*** [1956] Cover art by Mitchell Hooks. Movie tie-in.	$ .75	$2.50	$5.00
SP-6	Dennis, Patrick - ***Auntie Mame*** [1956]	$1.00	$3.00	$6.00
SP-7	Smith, Betty - ***A Tree Grows In Brooklyn*** [1956]	$ .75	$2.50	$5.00
SP-8	Reynolds, Quentin - ***Courtroom*** [1957]	$ .75	$2.50	$5.00
SP-9	Taylor, Ward - ***Roll Back The Sky*** [1957] Cover art by Mitchell Hooks.	$ .75	$2.50	$5.00
SP-10	deWohl, Louis - ***The Spear*** [1957]	$ .75	$2.50	$5.00
SP-11	Bishop, Leonard - ***The Butchers*** [1957] Cover art by Mitchell Hooks.	$ .75	$2.50	$5.00
SP-12	Clune, Henry W. - ***The Big Fella*** [1957]	$ .75	$2.50	$5.00
SP-13	Hill, Weldon - ***Onionhead*** [1958] Cover art by Mitchell Hooks.	$ .75	$2.50	$5.00
SP-14	Remarque, Erich Maria - ***Three Comrades*** [1958] Cover art by Mitchell Hooks.	$ .75	$2.50	$5.00
SP-15	Guralnik, David B. - ***Webster's New World Dictionary Of The American Language*** [1958]	$ .75	$2.50	$5.00
SP-16	Hooton, Barbara & Dennis, Patrick - ***Guestward Ho!*** [1958]	$ .75	$2.50	$5.00
SP-17	Raddall, Thomas H. - ***The Nymph And The Lamp*** [1958]	$1.25	$3.75	$7.50
SP-18	Kaye, M.M. - ***Shadow Of The Moon*** [1958] Cover art by Mitchell Hooks.	$ .75	$2.50	$5.00
SP-19	Jennings, John - ***The Wind In His Fists*** [1958]	$ .75	$2.50	$5.00
SP-20	Flannagan, Roy - ***The Forest Cavalier*** [1958]	$ .75	$2.50	$5.00
SP-21	Remarque, Erich Maria - ***A Time To Love And A Time To Die*** [1958] Cover art by Harry Schaare.	$ .75	$2.50	$5.00
SP-22	deRopp, Robert S. - ***If I Forget Thee*** [1958]	$ .75	$2.50	$5.00
SP-23	Walker, Turnley - ***Dream Of Innocence*** [1958] Cover art by Ray Johnson.	$ .75	$2.50	$5.00
SP-24	Karig, Walter - ***Lower Than Angels*** [1958]	$ .75	$2.50	$5.00
SP-25	Moray, Helga - ***Tisa*** [1958]	$1.25	$3.75	$7.50
SP-26	Laroe, Else K. - ***Woman Surgeon*** [1958]	$ .75	$2.50	$5.00
SP-27	Gwaltney, Francis Irby - ***A Moment Of Warmth*** [1958] Cover art by Mitchell Hooks.	$ .75	$2.50	$5.00
SP-28	Bourne, Peter - ***Drums Of Destiny*** [1958]	$1.25	$3.75	$7.50
SP-29	Shulman, Irving - ***Good Deeds Must Be Punished*** [1958] Cover art by Mitchell Hooks.	$ .75	$2.50	$5.00
SP-30	Kauffmann, Stanley - ***The Philanderer*** [1958]	$ .75	$2.50	$5.00
SP-31	Hardy, W.G. - ***The City Of Libertines*** [1958]	$ .75	$2.50	$5.00
SP-32	Robinson, Edward G., Jr. - ***My Father, My Son*** [1958]	$ .75	$2.50	$5.00
SP-33	Gaillard, Robert - ***Marie Of The Isles*** [1958] Cover art by Robert Stanley.	$ .75	$2.50	$5.00

		G	VG	F
SP-34	Payne, Robert - ***Red Lion Inn*** [1958] Cover art by DeSoto.	$1.25	$3.75	$7.50
SP-35	Burns, Elizabeth - ***The Late Liz*** [1959]	$ .75	$2.50	$5.00
SP-36	Adler, Polly - ***A House In Not A Home*** [1959]	$ .75	$2.50	$5.00
SP-37	Bates, H.E. - ***Love For Lydia*** [1959]	$ .75	$2.50	$5.00
SP-38	Prokosch, Frederic - ***A Tale For Midnight*** [1959]	$ .75	$2.50	$5.00
SP-39	Wolff, Maritta - ***Whistle Stop*** [1959]	$ .75	$2.50	$5.00
SP-40	Payne, Robert - ***Blood Royal*** [1959]	$ .75	$2.50	$5.00
SP-41	Baxter, Walter - ***Look Down In Mercy*** [1959]	$ .75	$2.50	$5.00
SP-42	Holt, J. R., M.D., L. Emmett - ***The Good Housekeeping Book Of Baby & Child Care*** [1959] Photo cover.	$ .75	$2.50	$5.00
SP-43	Tilsley, Frank - ***Rage To Love*** [1959] Cover art by Ray Johnson.	$ .75	$2.50	$5.00
SP-44	Moray, Helga - ***Dark Fury*** [1959] Cover art by Mitchell Hooks.	$ .75	$2.50	$5.00
SP-45	Brennan, Louis A. - ***These Items Of Desire*** [1959]	$ .75	$2.50	$5.00
SP-46	Lowry, Robert - ***The Big Cage*** [1959] Cover art by Robert Maguire.	$1.35	$4.00	$8.00
SP-47	Slater, Estelle - ***The Strong Don't Cry*** [1959]	$ .75	$2.50	$5.00
SP-48	Kelly, James - ***The Insider*** [1959]	$ .75	$2.50	$5.00
SP-49	Carson, Robert - ***Love Affair*** [1959]	$ .75	$2.50	$5.00
SP-50	Lewis, Sinclair - ***Kingsblood Royal*** [1959]	$ .75	$2.50	$5.00
SP-51	Gorn, Lester - ***The Greater Glory*** [1959]	$ .75	$2.50	$5.00
SP-52	Dewlen, Al - ***The Golden Touch*** [1959] Cover art by Stanley Zuckerberg.	$ .75	$2.50	$5.00
SP-53	Passos, John Dos - ***The Great Days*** [1959]	$ .75	$2.50	$5.00
SP-56	Bellow, Saul - ***Henderson The Rain King*** [1960] Cover by Mitchell Hooks.	$ .75	$2.50	$5.00
SP-58	Longstreet, Stephen & Ethel - ***The Politican*** [1960] Cover art by Stanley Zuckerberg.	$ .75	$2.50	$5.00
SP-59	Davis, Hassoldt - ***Save Me The Sun*** [1960] Cover by Mitchell Hooks.	$ .75	$2.50	$5.00
SP-61	Kormendi, Ferenc - ***The Forsaken*** [1960] Cover art by Stanley Zuckerberg.	$1.25	$3.75	$7.50
SP-63	Stein, M. D., Leopold - ***Anatomy Of Eve*** [1960] Photo cover.	$ .75	$2.50	$5.00
SP-69	Marshall, Edison - ***The Pagan King*** [1960] Cover art by Mitchell Hooks.	$ .75	$2.50	$5.00
SP-71	Patrick, Dennis & Hooton, Barbara - ***Guestward Ho!*** [1960] TV tie-in.	$ .75	$2.50	$5.00
SP-72	Jennings, John - ***Wind In His Fists*** [1960]	$ .75	$2.50	$5.00
SP-74	Anthology - ***Harper's Bazaar Beauty Book*** [1960] Photo cover.	$ .75	$2.50	$5.00
SP-75	Maugham, W. Somerset - ***The Hour Before The Dawn*** [1960] Cover art by Schulz.	$ .75	$2.50	$5.00
SP-77	de Wohl, Louis - ***Francis Of Assisi*** [1960] Cover art by Mitchell Hooks. Movie tie-in.	$ .75	$2.50	$5.00
SP-78	Steward, Davenport - ***Black Spice*** [1960]	$ .75	$2.50	$5.00
SP-80	Frank, Martin M. - ***Diary Of A D.A.*** [1961] Cover art by DeSoto.	$ .75	$2.50	$5.00
SP-82	Frizell, Bernard - ***Ten Days In August*** [1961] Cover art by Mitchell Hooks.	$ .75	$2.50	$5.00
SP-83	Brick, John - ***Jubilee*** [1961]	$ .75	$2.50	$5.00
SP-86	Ellsberg, Edward - ***The Far Shore*** [1961] Photo cover.	$ .75	$2.50	$5.00
SP-87	Reynolds, Quentin - ***Courtroom*** [1961]	$ .75	$2.50	$5.00
SP-88	Braine, John - ***From The Hand Of The Hunter*** [1961] Cover art by Barye Phillips.	$ .75	$2.50	$5.00
SP-89	Basso, Hamilton - ***Sun In Capricorn*** [1961]	$ .75	$2.50	$5.00
SP-92	Truman, Harry S. - ***Mr. Citizen*** [1961] Photo cover.	$ .75	$2.50	$5.00
SP-95	Altieri, James - ***The Spearheaders*** [1961] Cover by Leon Gregori.	$ .75	$2.50	$5.00
SP-97	Mergendahl, Charles - ***22 Terrace Place*** [1961] PBO. Cover art by Zuckerberg.	$ .75	$2.50	$5.00
SP-98	Chaplin, Charlie, Jr. - ***My Father, Charlie Chaplin*** [1961] Photo cover.	$1.25	$3.75	$7.50

		G	VG	F
SP-99	Catto, Max - ***The Devil At 4 O'Clock*** [1961] Cover art by Zuckerberg. Movie tie-in.	$ .75	$2.50	$5.00
SP-100	Hoyer, Niels - editor - ***Man Into Woman*** [1961]	$1.00	$3.00	$6.00
SP-102	Smith, H. Allen - editor - ***Desert Island Decameron*** [1961]	$ .75	$2.50	$5.00
SP-103	Bowen, Walter S. & Neal, Harry Edward - ***The United States Secret Service*** [1961] Cover art by Papin.	$ .75	$2.50	$5.00
SP-104	Marshall, Rosamond - ***Kitty*** [1961] Cover art by Zuckerberg.	$ .75	$2.50	$5.00
SP-108	Gunther, John - ***Taken At The Flood*** [1961] Photo cover.	$ .75	$2.50	$5.00
SP-109	Sabatini, Rafael - ***The Sea Hawk*** [1961]	$1.00	$3.00	$6.00
SP-111	Smith, H. Allen - ***Waikiki Beachnik*** [1961] Cover art by Mitchell Hooks.	$ .75	$2.50	$5.00
SP-112	Erwin, Carol & Miller, Floyd - ***The Orderly Disorderly House*** [1961] Cover art by Edward Sorel.	$ .75	$2.50	$5.00
SP-113	Eisenhower, Dwight D. - ***Peace With Justice*** [1961] Photo cover.	$ .75	$2.50	$5.00
SP-114	Nurnberg, Maxwell & Rosenblum, Morris - ***How To Build A Better Vocabulary*** [1961]	$ .65	$2.00	$4.00
SP-116	Thomas, Lowell - ***With Lawrence In Arabia*** [1961] Movie tie-in.	$ .75	$2.50	$5.00
SP-117	Thiepen, Corbett H. & Cleckley, Hervey M - ***The 3 Faces Of Eve*** [1961]	$ .75	$2.50	$5.00
SP-118	Lee, C.Y. - ***Madame Goldenflower*** [1961] Cover art by Barye Phillips.	$ .75	$2.50	$5.00
SP-123	Nixon, Richard M. - ***The Challenges We Face*** [1961] Photo cover.	$ .75	$2.50	$5.00
SP-125	Miller, Merle - ***Reunion*** [1961] Cover art by Zuckerberg.	$ .75	$2.50	$5.00
SP-127	Thompson, Walter Henry - ***Assignment Churchill*** [1961] Photo cover.	$ .75	$2.50	$5.00
SP-128	Yorke, Susan - ***The Seduction*** [1961]	$ .75	$2.50	$5.00
SP-129	Anthology - ***The Esquire Reader*** [1961] Edited by Arnold Gingrich, L. Rust Hills, & Gene Lightenstein.	$ .75	$2.50	$5.00
SP-130	McGovern, James - ***Erika*** [1961] Cover art by Zuckerberg.	$1.00	$3.00	$6.00
SP-133	Downs, Hunton - ***Compassionate Tiger*** [1961] Cover by Barye Phillips.	$ .75	$2.50	$5.00
SP-135	Zermatten, Maurice - ***The Fountain Of Arethusa*** [1961]	$ .75	$2.50	$5.00
SP-137	Hess, Dean E. - ***Battle Hymn*** [1961] Cover by Harry Schaare.	$ .75	$2.50	$5.00
SP-140	de Wohl, Louis - ***Lay Siege To Heaven*** [1961]	$ .75	$2.50	$5.00
SP-141	Gerson, Noel - ***The Silver Lion*** [1961]	$1.00	$3.00	$6.00
SP-146	Krueger, Carl - ***Saint Patrick's Battalion*** [1962]	$ .75	$2.50	$5.00
SP-147	Taylor, Robert Lewis - ***The Bright Sands*** [1962]	$ .75	$2.50	$5.00
SP-148	Mitford, Nancy - ***Don't Tell Alfred*** [1962]	$ .75	$2.50	$5.00
SP-149	Catto, Max - ***The Melody Of Sex*** [1962]	$ .75	$2.50	$5.00
SP-153	Shelford, Ct. W.C. - ***Subsink*** [1962]	$ .75	$2.50	$5.00
SP-160	Dos Passos, John - ***Streets Of Night*** [1962]	$1.00	$3.00	$6.00
SP-163	Hynd, Alan - ***Defenders Of The Damned*** [1962]	$ .75	$2.50	$5.00
SP-165	Gunther, John - ***The Troubled Midnight*** [1962] Cover art by Barye Phillips.	$ .75	$2.50	$5.00
SP-166	Rascovich, Mark - ***The Flight Of The Dancing Bear*** [1962] Movie tie-in.	$ .75	$2.50	$5.00
SP-170	Wells, H.G. - ***The War Of The Worlds*** [1962]	$1.00	$3.00	$6.00
SP-171	Brook, Ian - ***Jimmy Riddle*** [1962] Cover by Barye Phillips.	$ .75	$2.50	$5.00
SP-175	Acheson, Dean - ***Sketches From Life*** [1962]	$ .75	$2.50	$5.00
SP-194	Rosenteur, Phyllis I. - ***The Single Woman*** [1962]	$ .75	$2.50	$5.00
SP-195	Priestley, John B. - ***The Doomsday Men*** [1962]	$ .75	$2.50	$5.00
SP-196	Gerson, Noel B. - ***Savage Cavalier*** [1962]	$1.00	$3.00	$6.00
SP-197	Rachlis, Eugene - ***They Came To Kill*** [1962]	$ .75	$2.50	$5.00
SP-201	Montgomery, Marion - ***The Wandering Of Desire*** [1962]	$ .75	$2.50	$5.00
SP-204	Bates, H.E. - ***The Scarlet Sword*** [1963] Cover art by Zuckerberg.	$ .75	$2.50	$5.00
SP-207	Sabatini, Rafael - ***Captain Blood Returns*** [1963]	$1.00	$3.00	$6.00

		G	VG	F
SP-208	Stuart, Ian - ***The Black Shrike*** [1963]	$ .75	$2.50	$5.00
SP-209	Gunther, John - ***The Bright Nemesis*** [1963] Cover art by Barye Phillips.	$ .75	$2.50	$5.00
SP-212	Mann, Abby - ***A Child Is Waiting*** [1963] PBO. Movie photo cover. Movie tie-in.	$ .75	$2.50	$5.00
SP-218	McMurtry, Larry - ***Hud*** [1963] Movie photo cover. Movie tie-in.	$2.00	$6.00	$12.00
SP-224	Maurier, George De - ***Trilby*** [1963]	$ .75	$2.50	$5.00
SP-225	Edwards, Frank - ***Strange People*** [1963]	$ .75	$2.50	$5.00
SP-226	Baker, Rachel - ***Sigmund Freud For Everybody*** [1963]	$ .75	$2.50	$5.00
SP-228	Sabatini, Rafael - ***The Hounds Of God*** [1963]	$1.00	$3.00	$6.00
SP-230	Duffy, Gladys - ***Warden's Wife*** [1963]	$ .75	$2.50	$5.00
SP-232	Priestley, J.B. - ***The Shapes Of Sleep*** [1963]	$ .75	$2.50	$5.00
SP-233	Shaw, Charles - ***Heaven Knows, Mr. Allison*** [1963] Movie tie-in.	$ .75	$2.50	$5.00
SP-237	Anthology - ***To Be Read Before Midnight*** [1963] Edited by Ellery Queen.	$ .75	$2.50	$5.00
SP-239	Gerson, Noel - ***The Hittite*** [1963]	$ .75	$2.50	$5.00
SP-240	Haislip, Harvey - ***Sea Road To Yorktown*** [1963]	$ .75	$2.50	$5.00
SP-244	Forester, C.S. - ***The Daughter Of The Hawk*** [1963]	$ .75	$2.50	$5.00
SP-247	Gardiner, Dorothy - ***The 7th Mourner*** [1964]	$ .75	$2.50	$5.00
SP-248	MacDonald, Philip - ***Death & Chicanery*** [1964]	$1.00	$3.00	$6.00
SP-249	Disney, Doris Miles - ***Dark Lady*** [1964]	$ .75	$2.50	$5.00
SP-250	Dick, Philip K. - ***The Man In The High Castle*** [1964]	$5.00	$15.00	$30.00
SP-257	Oppenheim, E. Phillips - ***The Great Impersonation*** [1963]	$ .75	$2.50	$5.00
SP-258	Ness, Eliot - ***The Untouchables*** [1964] TV tie-in.	$1.35	$4.00	$8.00
SP-260	Schoonover, Lawrence - ***The Chancellor*** [1964]	$ .75	$2.50	$5.00
SP-261	Eustis, Helen - ***The Fool Killer*** [1964] Photo cover.	$1.00	$3.00	$6.00
SP-264	Disney, Doris Miles - ***Find The Woman*** [1964]	$1.00	$3.00	$6.00
SP-265	Stevenson, Robert Louis - ***The Master Of Ballantrae*** [1964]	$ .75	$2.50	$5.00
SP-268	Lorac, E.C.R. - ***The Last Escape*** [1964]	$1.00	$3.00	$6.00
SP-270	Ketchum, Philip - ***Six-Gun Maverick*** [1964] Cover art by A. Leslie Ross.	$ .75	$2.50	$5.00
SP-271	Niall, Ian - ***A Tiger Walks*** [1964] Cover by Barrye Phillips. Movie tie-in.	$ .75	$2.50	$5.00
SP-272	Eberhart, Mignon G. - ***Man Missing*** [1964]	$1.00	$3.00	$6.00
SP-276	Ferrars, Elizabeth Xavia - ***Depart This Life*** [1964]	$ .75	$2.50	$5.00
SP-279	Hunter, Evan - ***Don't Crowd Me*** [1964] Cover by Robert McGinnis.	$ .75	$2.50	$5.00
SP-282	Rydell, Forbes - ***If She Should Die*** [1964]	$ .75	$2.50	$5.00
SP-283	Novak, Lorna - ***Does It Make Into A Bed?*** [1964] Cover art by Zuckerberg.	$ .75	$2.50	$5.00
SP-284	Eberhart, Mignon G. - ***Wolf In Man's Clothing*** [1964]	$1.00	$3.00	$6.00
SP-286	Wells, H.G. - ***The Food Of The Gods*** [1964] Cover art by Paul Tchelitchew.	$1.00	$3.00	$6.00
SP-288	Gill, Josephine - ***Dead Of Summer*** [1964]	$ .75	$2.50	$5.00
SP-292	Temple, Dan - ***Bullet Lease*** [1964] Cover art by A. Leslie Ross.	$ .75	$2.50	$5.00
SP-294	Dean, Amber - ***Bullet Proof*** [1964]	$1.00	$3.00	$6.00
SP-295	Stewart, Sidney - ***Give Us This Day*** [1964] Cover art by Schaare.	$ .75	$2.50	$5.00
SP-296	Colby, C.B. - ***Strangely Enough!*** [1964]	$ .75	$2.50	$5.00
SP-297	de Beauvoir, Simone - ***The Blood Of Others*** [1964]	$ .75	$2.50	$5.00
SP-298	Herzog, Maurice - ***Annapurna*** [1964]	$ .75	$2.50	$5.00
SP-299	Eberhart, Mignon G. - ***Deadly Is The Diamond*** [1964]	$1.00	$3.00	$6.00
SP-300	Ingersoll, Ralph - ***The Battle Is The Pay-Off*** [1964]	$ .75	$2.50	$5.00
SP-301	Farrell, Cliff - ***Gun Hand*** [1964]	$ .75	$2.50	$5.00
SP-302	Lasky, Jr., Jesse L. - ***Cry The Lonely Flesh*** [1964]	$ .75	$2.50	$5.00
SP-303	Ballard, Todhunter (W.T. Ballard) - ***Trouble On The Massacre*** [1964]	$1.00	$3.00	$6.00
SP-304	Gordons, The - ***Murders Rides The Campaign Train*** [1964]	$1.00	$3.00	$6.00
SP-305	Sutton, Jeff - ***Apollo At Go*** [1964]	$ .75	$2.50	$5.00

		G	VG	F
SP-309	Littlefield, Anne - ***Which Mrs. Bennett?*** [1964]	$ .75	$2.50	$5.00
SP-312	O'Brien, Edna - ***Girl With Green Eyes*** [1964] Movie tie-in.	$1.00	$3.00	$6.00
SP-314	Eberhart, Mignon G. - ***Postmark Murder*** [1964]	$1.00	$3.00	$6.00
SP-316	Scherf, Margaret - ***Never Turn Your Back*** [1964]	$ .75	$2.50	$5.00
SP-318	Borden, Mary - ***You, The Jury*** [1964] Cover art by Zuckerberg.	$ .75	$2.50	$5.00
SP-325	Foote, Horton - ***Baby, The Rain Must Fall*** [1965] PBO. Photo cover. Movie tie-in.	$1.35	$4.00	$8.00
SP-327	Dean, Amber - ***Deadly Contact*** [1965]	$1.00	$3.00	$6.00
SP-328	Ebergart, Mignon G. - ***Run Scared*** [1965]	$1.00	$3.00	$6.00
SP-329	Pinckney, Josephine - ***Great Mischief*** [1965] Cover art by Zuckerberg.	$1.00	$3.00	$6.00
SP-331	Anthology - ***The Post Reader Of Fantasy And SF*** [1965] Cover art by Powers.	$1.00	$3.00	$6.00
SP-333	Anthology - ***Ellery Queen's Twentieth Century Detective Stories*** [1965] Edited by Ellery Queen.	$1.00	$3.00	$6.00
SP-334	Marshall, Rosamond - ***The Rib Of The Hawk*** [1965] Cover art by Maguire.	$ .75	$2.50	$5.00
SP-335	Ford, Leslie - ***The Clue Of The Judas Tree*** [1965]	$1.00	$3.00	$6.00
SP-339	Caidin, Martin - ***Everything But The Flak*** [1965]	$ .75	$2.50	$5.00
SP-341	Fagyas, Maria - ***The Fifth Woman*** [1965]	$ .75	$2.50	$5.00
SP-342	Cook, Will - ***Lone Hand From Texas*** [1965] Cover art by A. Leslie Ross.	$ .75	$2.50	$5.00
SP-344	Blake, Forrester - ***The Franciscan*** [1965]	$ .75	$2.50	$5.00
SP-345	Scherf, Margaret - ***The Diplomat And The Gold Piano*** [1965]	$ .75	$2.50	$5.00
SP-347	Fain, William - ***In Search Of Love*** [1965]	$ .75	$2.50	$5.00
SP-348	Bell, Abban - ***Out Of Circulation*** [1965] PBO.	$ .75	$2.50	$5.00
SP-349	Wallant, Edward Lewis - ***The Children At The Gate*** [1965]	$ .75	$2.50	$5.00
SP-350	Eberhart, Mignon G. - ***Escape The Night*** [1965]	$1.00	$3.00	$6.00
SP-351	Anthology - ***Suddenly*** [1965] PBO. Edited by Irving Seitel & Marvin Allen Karp. Cover art by A.P. Ryder.	$ .75	$2.50	$5.00
SP-352	Anthology - ***The Shape Of Things*** [1965] PBO. Edited by Damon Knight. Cover art by Eugene Berman.	$1.35	$4.00	$8.00
SP-353	Wescott, Glenway - ***Apartment In Athens*** [1965]	$ .75	$2.50	$5.00
SP-357	Anthology - ***The Spy In The Shadows*** [1965] PBO. Edited by Marvin Allen Karp.	$ .75	$2.50	$5.00
SP-358	Coates, Robert M. - ***Wisteria Cottage*** [1965]	$1.00	$3.00	$6.00
SP-359	Ransome, Stephen - ***The Frazer Acquittal*** [1965]	$ .75	$2.50	$5.00
SP-360	Widdemer, Margaret - ***The Golden Wildcat*** [1965]	$ .75	$2.50	$5.00
SP-362	Brand, Millen - ***The Outward Room*** [1965]	$ .75	$2.50	$5.00
SP-363	Disney, Doris Miles - ***The Last Straw*** [1969]	$1.00	$3.00	$6.00
SP-368	Eberhart, Mignon G. - ***Unidentified Woman*** [1965]	$1.00	$3.00	$6.00
SP-370	Anthology - ***Catch A Spy*** [1965] PBO. Edited by Marvin Allen Karp	$ .75	$2.50	$5.00
SP-371	Hersey, John - ***The Marmot Drive*** [1965] Cover art by Marchetti.	$ .75	$2.50	$5.00
SP-372	Hitchens, Bert & Delores - ***The Grudge*** [1965]	$1.00	$3.00	$6.00
SP-376	Waugh, Hillary - ***Road Block*** [1965]	$ .75	$2.50	$5.00
SP-378	Anthology - ***Assault*** [1965] PBO. Edited by Alex K. Martin.	$ .75	$2.50	$5.00
SP-379	Shirreffs, Gordon D. - ***Massacre Creek*** [1965] Cover art by A. Leslie Ross.	$ .75	$2.50	$5.00
SP-381	Rickett, Frances - ***Tread Softly*** [1965]	$1.00	$3.00	$6.00
SP-383	Marlett, Melba - ***Death Is In The Garden*** [1965]	$1.00	$3.00	$6.00
SP-387	Garrett, George - ***Which Ones Are The Enemy?*** [1965] Cover art by Mitchell Hooks.	$ .75	$2.50	$5.00
SP-388	Gulick, Bill - ***The Hallelujah Trail*** [1965] Movie tie-in.	$ .75	$2.50	$5.00
SP-389	Disney, Doris Miles - ***Dark Road*** [1965]	$1.00	$3.00	$6.00
SP-391	Forester, C.S. - ***Payment Deferred*** [1965] Cover by Mitchell Hooks.	$ .75	$2.50	$5.00
SP-394	Hitchens, Bert & Delores - ***Stairway To An Empty Room*** [1965]	$1.00	$3.00	$6.00

		G	VG	F
SP-395	Webster, Elizabeth Charlotte - ***Ceremony Of Innocence*** [1965] Cover art by Lou Marchetti.	$ .75	$2.50	$5.00
SP-399	Brand, Max - ***The Jackson Trail*** [1965] Cover art by A. Leslie Ross.	$ .75	$2.50	$5.00
SP-400	Tiger, John - ***I Spy*** [1965] PBO. Photo cover. TV tie-in.	$1.35	$4.00	$8.00
SP-402	Siller, Van - ***The Widower*** [1965]	$ .75	$2.50	$5.00
SP-403	Harrington, Alan - ***The Revelations Of Dr. Modesto*** [1965]	$ .75	$2.50	$5.00
SP-404	Gallant, T. Grady - ***The Friendly Dead*** [1965]	$ .75	$2.50	$5.00
SP-405	Anthology - ***The Unhumans*** [1965] PBO. Edited by Marvin Allen Karp.	$1.50	$5.00	$10.00
SP-406	Breit, Harvey - ***A Narrow Action*** [1965]	$ .75	$2.50	$5.00
SP-407	Eberhart, Mignon G. - ***Five Passengers From Lisbon*** [1965]	$ .75	$2.50	$5.00
SP-413	Davis, Clyde Brion - ***The Anointed*** [1965]	$ .75	$2.50	$5.00
SP-415	Albrand, Martha - ***No Surrender*** [1965] Cover art by Barye Phillips.	$ .75	$2.50	$5.00
SP-416	Marquand, John P. - ***Repent In Haste*** [1965]	$ .75	$2.50	$5.00
SP-425	Townsend, Ray - ***Sundown Basin*** [1965]	$ .75	$2.50	$5.00

Popular Library W Series.

		G	VG	F
W-400	Thomas, T.T. - ***I, James Dean*** [1957] PBO. Photo cover. Sixteen pages of photos.	$5.00	$15.00	$30.00
W-500	Kent, Simon - ***Fire Down Below*** [1957]	$ .50	$1.50	$3.00
W-600	Untermeyer, Louis - ***The Treasurey Of Ribaldry: Volume I*** [1957]	$ .50	$1.50	$3.00
W-1107	Devlin, Joseph - ***A Dictionary Of Synonyms And Antonyms*** [1957]	$ .50	$1.50	$3.00
W-1108	Fine, Benjamin - ***How To Be Accepted By The College Of Your Choice*** [1957]	$ .50	$1.50	$3.00
W-1109	Roosevelt, Franklin Delano - ***Nothing To Fear*** [1957]	$ .50	$1.50	$3.00

Popular Library 60- Series. New York: Popular Library, Inc.

		G	VG	F
60-8046	O'Connor, Patrick - editor - ***The Monkees Go Mod*** [1967] PBO. TV photo cover and photos throughout.	$2.00	$6.00	$12.00
60-8073	Morewood, Aiken - ***Buona Sera, Mrs. Campbell*** [1969] PBO. Sophia Loren movie photo cover. Movie tie-in.	$1.25	$3.75	$7.50

Powell Books.

		G	VG	F
PP-101	Evans, Allen - ***The Sexual Adventurers*** [1968] PBO.	$1.50	$5.00	$10.00
PP-102	James, Les - ***Confessions Of A Female Cabbie*** [1968]	$1.50	$5.00	$10.00
PP-103	Slade, John - ***The Sex Barbarians*** [1968] PBO.	$1.50	$5.00	$10.00
PP-104	Brent, Lynton W. & Fusilier, Richard - ***Crime And Violence In The USA*** [1968]	$1.50	$5.00	$10.00
PP-105	Mausert, Pete - ***Naked On The Strip*** [1968] PBO.	$1.50	$5.00	$10.00
PP-106	Spenser & West - ***The Prostitutes*** [1968]	$1.50	$5.00	$10.00
PP-107	MacDonald, Fred - ***Nympho*** [1968]	$1.50	$5.00	$10.00
PP-108	Brent, Lybnton Wright - ***The Rebellion Of Youth*** [1968]	$1.50	$5.00	$10.00
PP-109	Willit, Mark - ***Scandal In Sex*** [1968]	$1.50	$5.00	$10.00
PP-110	Fuchs, Rolf - ***Mate Mixing*** [1968]	$1.50	$5.00	$10.00
PP-111	Franklyn, Donald - ***Blowout!*** [1968] PBO.	$1.50	$5.00	$10.00
PP-112	Johnson, David - ***The Body Merchants*** [1968] PBO.	$1.50	$5.00	$10.00
PP-113	Brent, Lynton Wright - ***Blood In The Street*** [1968]	$2.00	$6.00	$12.00
PP-114	Brent, Lynton Wright - ***Outlaw Village*** [1968] PBO.	$1.50	$5.00	$10.00
PP-115	Brandt, Lynn - ***Accent On Sex*** [1968]	$1.50	$5.00	$10.00
PP-116	Jackson, Howard - ***Jean*** [1968]	$1.50	$5.00	$10.00
PP-117	Alen, Kevin - ***Good Girls Do Too*** [1968]	$1.50	$5.00	$10.00
PP-118	Lubell, Stacey - ***Dear Liza*** [1969] PBO. Cover art by Cheryl Thomas.	$1.50	$5.00	$10.00
PP-119	Brent, Lynton Wright - ***Hollywood Crime And Scandal*** [1969]	$2.00	$6.00	$12.00
PP-120	Brent, Lynton Wright - ***Apache Killers*** [1969]	$1.50	$5.00	$10.00

		G	VG	F
PP-121	Nuetzel, Charles - ***Swordmen Of Vistar*** [1969] Cover art by Albert Nuetzell	$2.50	$7.50	$15.00
PP-122	Blake, Fredric - ***On The Make*** [1969] PBO.	$1.50	$5.00	$10.00
PP-123	Mausert, Pete - ***Passion Island*** [1969] PBO.	$1.50	$5.00	$10.00
PP-124	Spenser, Jean & West, Roger - ***Room Service*** [1969] PBO.	$1.50	$5.00	$10.00
PP-125	Arana, Ric - ***Woman On Her Back*** [1969]	$1.50	$5.00	$10.00
PP-126	Nuetzel, Charles - ***Murder Times 4*** [1969] PBO.	$2.50	$7.50	$15.00
PP-127	Brent, Lynton Wright - ***Apache Tomahawk*** [1969]	$1.50	$5.00	$10.00
PP-128	Van Vogt, A.E. & Hull, E. Mayne - ***Out Of The Unknown*** [1969] PBO. Cover art by Albert Nuetzell.	$2.50	$7.50	$15.00
PP-129	Trent, Dick - ***Mama's Diary*** [1969]	$1.50	$5.00	$10.00
PP-130	Fuchs, Rolf - ***Sex Odyssey '69*** [1969] PBO.	$1.50	$5.00	$10.00
PP-131	Petrea, Steve - ***Bedtime Is Playtime*** [1969] PBO.	$1.50	$5.00	$10.00
PP-133	Nuetzel, Charles - ***Hollywood Mysteries*** [1969]	$2.50	$7.50	$15.00
PP-134	Brent, Lynton Wright - ***Apache Massacre*** [1969]	$1.50	$5.00	$10.00
PP-135	Nuetzel, Charles - ***Images Of Tomorrow*** [1969] Cover art by Albert Nuetzell	$2.50	$7.50	$15.00
PP-137	Hornay, Norton - ***Family Of Lust*** [1969] PBO.	$1.50	$5.00	$10.00
PP-139	Rivers, Stu - ***Sex Kittens*** [1969] PBO.	$1.50	$5.00	$10.00
PP-140	Nuetzel, Charles - ***Softly As I Kill You*** [1969] Cover art by Louis Dewitt.	$2.50	$7.50	$15.00
PP-142	Anthology - ***Science Fiction World Of Forrest J. Ackerman & Friends*** [1969] PBO. Cover art by Bill Hughes.	$2.50	$7.50	$15.00
PP-144	Ewing, Frank - ***Baby-Faced Harlot*** [1969] PBO.	$1.50	$5.00	$10.00
PP-147	Brent, Lynton Wright - ***One Man's Crime*** [1969] PBO.	$1.50	$5.00	$10.00
PP-149	Nuetzel, Charles - ***Warriors of Noomas*** [1969] PBO.	$2.50	$7.50	$15.00
PP-154	Ellison, Harlan - ***Memos From Purgatory*** [1969]	$10.00	$30.00	$60.00
PP-155	Brent, Lynton Wright - ***Detective On The Prowl*** [1969] PBO.	$1.50	$5.00	$10.00
PP-157	Nuetzel, Charles - ***Raiders Of Noomas*** [1969] PBO.	$2.50	$7.50	$15.00
PP-158	Miller, Ben - ***Sexplosion*** [1969] PBO.	$1.50	$5.00	$10.00
PP-162	Nuetzel, Charles - ***Jungle Jungle*** [1969] PBO. Cover art by Bill Hughes.	$2.50	$7.50	$15.00
PP-165	Byrne, Stuart J. - ***Starman*** [1969] PBO. Cover art by Bill Hughes.	$2.50	$7.50	$15.00
PP-170	Brent, Lynton Wright - ***Death of a Detective*** [1969] PBO.	$1.50	$5.00	$10.00
PP-172	Bankson, Russell A. - ***Land Of No Return/Pinto Paradise*** [1969] PBO.	$1.50	$5.00	$10.00
PP-173	Serviss, Garrett P. (Forrest J. Ackerman) - ***Invasion Of Mars*** [1969] PBO. Cover art by Bill Hughes.	$2.50	$7.50	$15.00
PP-175	Augustus, Jr., Albert (Charles Nuetzel) - ***Goldlust*** [1969] PBO. Cover art by Bill Hughes.	$1.50	$5.00	$10.00
PP-180	Rayburn, Del - ***Trail-Blazers West*** [1969] Cover art by Roger LaManna.	$1.50	$5.00	$10.00
PP-181	Wollheim, Donald A. - ***Two Dozen Dragon Eggs*** [1969] PBO. Cover art by Bill Hughes.	$2.50	$7.50	$15.00
PP-185	Andrews, Blake - ***Come To Me, Baby*** [1969] PBO.	$1.50	$5.00	$10.00
PP-186	Miller, Ben - ***Death Deal*** [1969]	$1.50	$5.00	$10.00
PP-187	Arana, Ric - ***Big Dano*** [1969]	$1.50	$5.00	$10.00
PP-188	James, William H. - ***The Color Of Blood*** [1969]	$2.00	$6.00	$12.00
PP-189	Augustas, Jr., Albert (Charles Nuetzel) - ***The Slaves Of Lomooro*** [1969]	$2.50	$7.50	$15.00
PP-191	Norton, Bill - ***Call-Girl's Delight*** [1969] PBO.	$1.50	$5.00	$10.00
PP-194	Matthews, Clayton - ***Hager's Castle*** [1969] Cover art by Bill Hughes.	$1.50	$5.00	$10.00
PP-195	Miller, Ben - ***The Set-Up*** [1969] Cover art by Bill Hughes.	$1.50	$5.00	$10.00
PP-197	Fritch, Charles E. - ***Crazy Mixed-Up Planet*** [1969] Cover art by Bill Hughes.	$2.50	$7.50	$15.00
PP-198	Arana, Ric - ***House Of The Seven Sins*** [1970] PBO.	$1.50	$5.00	$10.00
PP-202	Matthews, Clayton - ***The Mendoza File*** [1970] PBO. Cover by Bill Hughes.	$1.50	$5.00	$10.00

		G	VG	F
PP-203	Turner, Robert - ***Shroud 9*** [1970]	$1.50	$5.00	$10.00
PP-205	Bloodstone, John (Stuart J. Byrne) - ***Godman!*** [1970] PBO. Cover art by Bill Hughes.	$2.50	$7.50	$15.00
PP-210	Streib, Daniel T. & Jones, Robert Page - ***Operation: Countdown*** [1970] PBO. Cover art by Bill Hughes.	$1.50	$5.00	$10.00
PP-211	Brisco, Pat A. - ***The Other People*** [1970]	$1.50	$5.00	$10.00
PP-212	Moore, Arthur - ***Look Down, Look Down*** [1970] PBO. Cover art by Roger Nannini.	$1.50	$5.00	$10.00
PP-213	Wagner, Karl Edward - ***Darkness Weaves*** [1970]	$5.00	$15.00	$30.00
PP-1001	Clapham, Edward - ***The Eagle Had Wax Wings*** [1970] Cover art by Bill Hughes.	$1.50	$5.00	$10.00
PP-1003	Sutton, Stack - ***Leatherwood*** [1970] Cover art by Bill Hughes.	$1.50	$5.00	$10.00
PP-1004	Fritch, Charles E. - ***Horses' Asteroid*** [1970] Cover art by Bill Hughes.	$2.50	$7.50	$15.00
PP-1005	Matthews, Clayton - ***Nylon Nightmare*** [1970] Cover art by Bill Hughes.	$1.50	$5.00	$10.00
PP-1006	Sellers, Con - ***The Algerian Incident*** [1970] Cover art by Bill Hughes.	$1.50	$5.00	$10.00
PP-1008	Dolan, Mike - ***Santana Morning*** [1970] Cover art by Bill Hughes.	$1.50	$5.00	$10.00
PP-1009	Hoyt, Don & Moore, Art - ***Death Is A Drag*** [1970] Cover art by Bill Hughes.	$2.00	$6.00	$12.00
PP-1010	Fowler, Bruce - ***The Outragers*** [1970] PBO. Cover art by Bill Hughes.	$1.50	$5.00	$10.00
PP-1011	Matcha, Jack - ***No Trumpets No Drums*** [1970] PBO. Cover art by Bill Hughes.	$1.50	$5.00	$10.00
PP-1012	Reed, William Stuart - ***Ambush Country*** [1970] Cover art by Bill Hughes.	$1.50	$5.00	$10.00

Private Editions. New York: Crescent Publications.

		G	VG	F
2	Bennett, Hal - ***Playful Wife*** [1951] Photo cover. Digest size. States Thomas Stone as author inside.	$3.50	$10.00	$20.00

Prize Books. New York: Century Publications. Digest Size.

		G	VG	F
52	Lindsay, Perry - ***No Nice Girl*** [1946]	$1.50	$5.00	$10.00
54	Saxon, John - ***The Scarlet Sin*** [1947]	$1.50	$5.00	$10.00
55	Arthur, William - ***Love Business*** [1947] Cover art by Malcolm Smith.	$1.50	$5.00	$10.00
56	Semple, Gordon - ***Cue For Passion*** [1947]	$1.50	$5.00	$10.00
57	Grinstead, J.E. - ***Ranger Justice*** [1947]	$1.50	$5.00	$10.00
58	Gay, Carman - ***Ripe For Love*** [1947]	$1.50	$5.00	$10.00
59	Lindsay, Perry - ***Unashamed*** [1947]	$1.50	$5.00	$10.00
60	Semple, Gordon - ***Bad Company*** [1947]	$1.50	$5.00	$10.00
61	Stone, Thomas - ***One More Lover*** [1947]	$1.50	$5.00	$10.00
62	Hopson, William - ***Hell's Horseman*** [1947]	$1.50	$5.00	$10.00
63	Saxon, John - ***Common Passion*** [1947]	$1.50	$5.00	$10.00
64	Baker, Carlotta - ***Too Loose*** [1947]	$1.50	$5.00	$10.00
66	Branch, Florenz - ***Flesh Pots*** [1947]	$1.50	$5.00	$10.00
88	Hopson, William - ***Hell's Horseman*** [1947]	$1.50	$5.00	$10.00

Prize Love Novels. New York: Crestwood Publishing. Digest Size.

		G	VG	F
20	Millburn, Cynthia - ***Thanks, Angel*** [1947] Cover art by Phillips.	$4.00	$12.50	$25.00
22	Saxon, John - ***Old Man's Darling*** [1947]	$4.00	$12.50	$25.00
23	Carter, Ralph - ***Night Club Angel*** [1947] Cover art by Bill Wenzel.	$4.00	$12.50	$25.00
24	Jacquin, Lee - ***Time For Love*** [1947] Cover art by Bill Wenzel.	$4.00	$12.50	$25.00
25	Stone, Thomas - ***Passion's Prophecy*** [1947] Cover art by Bill Wenzel.	$4.00	$12.50	$25.00
26	Brewster, Eliot - ***Sisters In Sin*** [1947] Cover art by Bill Wenzel.	$4.00	$12.50	$25.00
27	Brewster, Eliot - ***Skin-Deep*** [1947] Cover art by Bill Wenzel.	$4.00	$12.50	$25.00

		G	VG	F
28	Brown, Beth - ***Love Racket*** [1947] Cover art by Bill Wenzel.......	$4.00	$12.50	$25.00

Prize Mystery Novels. New York: Crestwood Publishing. Digest Size.

1	Givens, Charles G. - ***The Rose Petal Murders*** [1943] Cover by Hoffman.	$2.50	$7.50	$15.00
2	Saxby, Charles - ***Murder At The Mike*** [1943]	$2.00	$6.00	$12.00
4	Casey, R.J. - ***Hot Ice*** [1943]	$2.00	$6.00	$12.00
5	Adams, Cleve F. - ***And Sudden Death*** [1943]	$2.00	$6.00	$12.00
6	Goldman, Lawrence - ***Fall Guy For Murder*** [1943]	$2.00	$6.00	$12.00
7	Propper, Milton - ***The Great Insurance Murders*** [1943]	$2.00	$6.00	$12.00
8	Propper, Milton - ***The Station Wagon Murder*** [1943]	$2.00	$6.00	$12.00
9	Casey, Robert J. - ***The Third Owl*** [1944]	$2.00	$6.00	$12.00
10	Huxley, Elspeth - ***Murder On Safari*** [1944]	$2.00	$6.00	$12.00
11	Crombie, Michael - ***The Frightened Girl*** [1944]	$2.00	$6.00	$12.00
12	Barry, Joe - ***The Third Degree*** [1944]	$2.00	$6.00	$12.00
13	Wood, S. Andrew - ***Sinner's Castle*** [1944]	$2.00	$6.00	$12.00
14	Porcelain, Sidney E. - ***The Purple Pony Murders*** [1944]	$2.00	$6.00	$12.00
15	Randolph, Vance & Clemons, Nancy - ***The Camp-Meeting Murders*** [1945]	$2.00	$6.00	$12.00
16	Goldman, R.L. - ***Murder Without Motive*** [1945]	$2.00	$6.00	$12.00
17	Low, Gardner - ***Invitation To Kill*** [1945]	$2.00	$6.00	$12.00
18	Goldman, R.L. - ***Out On Bail*** [1945]	$2.00	$6.00	$12.00
19	Hunt, Peter - ***Murder For Breakfast*** [1945]	$2.00	$6.00	$12.00
20	Bogart, William - ***Murder Is Forgetful*** [1945]	$2.00	$6.00	$12.00
21	Stokes, Manning Lee - ***The Wolf Howls "Murder"*** [1946]	$2.00	$6.00	$12.00
22	Merwin, Sam, Jr. - ***Message From A Corpse*** [1945]	$2.50	$7.50	$15.00
23	Malmar, McKnight - ***Never Say Die*** [1945]	$2.00	$6.00	$12.00
24	Eisinger, Jo - ***The Walls Came Tumbling Down*** [1945]	$2.00	$6.00	$12.00
25	Willard, Joshua - ***The Thorne Theater Mystery*** [1945]	$2.00	$6.00	$12.00
26	Du Bois, Theodora - ***Death Dines Out*** [1945]	$2.00	$6.00	$12.00
27	Lyon, Dana - ***It's My Own Funeral*** [1945]	$2.00	$6.00	$12.00
28	Fenwick, E.P. - ***Two Names For Death*** [1945]	$2.00	$6.00	$12.00
29	Fleischman, A.S. - ***The Straw Donkey Case*** [1945]	$2.00	$6.00	$12.00
30	Keystone, Oliver - ***Major Crime*** [1945]	$2.00	$6.00	$12.00

Prize Science Fiction Novels. New York: Crestwood Publishing. Digest Size.

10	Leinster, Murray - ***Fight For Life*** [1949] PBO.	$6.00	$20.00	$40.00
11	Wellman, Manly Wade - ***Sojarr Of Titan*** [1949] PBO.	$6.00	$20.00	$40.00

Prize Western Novels. New York: Crestwood Publishing. Digest Size.

20	Shappiro, Herbert - ***Gunsmoke Over Utah*** [1949]	$1.50	$5.00	$10.00
21	Heckelmann, Charles N. - ***Lawless Range*** [1949]	$1.50	$5.00	$10.00
22	Holt, Tex - ***Trail Of Lost Men*** [1949]	$1.50	$5.00	$10.00
23	Coolidge, Dane - ***Wolf's Candle*** [1949]	$1.50	$5.00	$10.00
24	Holt, Tex - ***Thunder Of Hoofs*** [1949]	$1.50	$5.00	$10.00
25	Shappiro, Herbert - ***Trouble At Moon Pass*** [1949]	$1.50	$5.00	$10.00
26	Hardy, Stuart - ***Trouble From Texas*** [1949]	$1.50	$5.00	$10.00
27	Shappiro, Herbert - ***Silver City Rangers*** [1948]	$1.50	$5.00	$10.00
28	Joscelyn, Archie - ***Judge Colt*** [1949]	$1.50	$5.00	$10.00
29	Newton, D.B. - ***Gunmaster Of Saddleback*** [1949]	$1.50	$5.00	$10.00
30	Drago, Harry S. - ***Smoke Of The .45*** [1949]	$1.50	$5.00	$10.00
31	Westland, Lynn - ***Over The Frontier Trail*** [1949]	$1.50	$5.00	$10.00
32	Starr, Clay - ***Powder Smoke Blood*** [1949]	$1.50	$5.00	$10.00
33	Holt, Tex - ***Point West*** [1949]	$1.50	$5.00	$10.00
34	Sims, John - ***Ramrod Vengeance*** [1949]	$1.50	$5.00	$10.00
35	Tompkins, W.A. - ***Wyoming Trail*** [1949]	$1.50	$5.00	$10.00
36	Carder, Leigh - ***Bravo Trail*** [1949]	$1.50	$5.00	$10.00
37	Arthur, Burt - ***Valley Of Death*** [1949]	$1.50	$5.00	$10.00
38	Hanson, V.J. - ***Yellow Dust*** [1949]	$1.50	$5.00	$10.00

Pyramid, 45

Pyramid, G-184

Pyramid, G-252

		G	VG	F
39	Sumner, Earl - ***Trouble Buster*** [1950] PBO. Cover art by Walter Popp.	$1.50	$5.00	$10.00
40	Floren, Lee - ***Guns Of Powder River*** [1950]	$1.50	$5.00	$10.00

Pyramid Books. New York: Pyramid Books, Inc.

		G	VG	F
11	Lindsay, Perry (Peggy Gaddis) - ***Passionate Virgin*** [1949]	$3.50	$10.00	$20.00
12	Semple, Gordon - ***Reckless Passion*** [1949]	$3.00	$9.00	$18.00
14	Bennett, Hall - ***Blonde Mistress*** [1949]	$3.50	$10.00	$20.00
15	Jordan, Gail - ***Palm Beach Apartment*** [1949] Cover by George Geygan.	$2.50	$7.50	$15.00
16	Cheyney, Peter - ***Set-up For Murder*** [1950]	$3.50	$10.00	$20.00
17	Watkins, Glen - ***Tavern Girl*** [1950] Cover by Hunter Barker.	$3.50	$10.00	$20.00
18	Stone, Thomas - ***Shameless Honeymoon*** [1950]	$3.50	$10.00	$20.00
19	Collins, Wilkie - ***The Moonstone*** [1950]	$3.00	$9.00	$18.00
20	Handley, Alan - ***Terror In Times Square*** [1950]	$2.50	$7.50	$15.00
21	Manners, Dorine - ***Sin Street*** [1950]	$3.50	$10.00	$20.00
22	Fischer, Bruno - ***The Dead Men Grin*** [1950]	$2.50	$7.50	$15.00
23	Everard, Katherine - ***Cry Shame!*** [1950] Cover art by Harry Bennett.	$2.50	$7.50	$15.00
24	Bruff, Nancy - ***The Manatee*** [1950] Cover art by Fred W. Meyer.	$2.50	$7.50	$15.00
25	Mulford, Clarence E. - ***The Orphan Outlaw*** [1950]	$2.50	$7.50	$15.00
26	Leslie, A. Scott - ***Arizona Ranger*** [1951]	$2.50	$7.50	$15.00
27	De Leeuw, Hendrik - ***Sinful Cities Of The Western World*** [1951] Cover art by Fred W. Meyer.	$2.50	$7.50	$15.00
28	Cuthbert, Clifton - ***The Shame Of Mary Quinn*** [1951] Cover by Hunter Barker.	$2.50	$7.50	$15.00
29	Fischer, Bruno - ***Stairway To Death*** [1951] Cover art by Frederick W. Meyer.	$2.50	$7.50	$15.00
30	Anonymous - ***Madeleine*** [1951] Cover art by Hunter Barker.	$2.50	$7.50	$15.00
31	Karney, Jack - ***Tough Town*** [1951] Cover by Frederick Meyer.	$2.50	$7.50	$15.00
32	Kent, Nial - ***The Divided Path*** [1951]	$2.50	$7.50	$15.00
33	Nistler, Erwin N. & Broderick, Gerry P. - ***Roadside Night*** [1951] PBO. Cover by Hunter Barker.	$2.50	$7.50	$15.00
34	Scott, Bradford - ***Rustler's Range*** [1951] PBO.	$2.50	$7.50	$15.00
35	Royer, Louis-Charles - ***French Doctor*** [1951] Cover by Hunter Barker.	$2.50	$7.50	$15.00
36	Leslie, A. Scott - ***Tombstone Trail*** [1951] PBO.	$2.50	$7.50	$15.00
37	Meloney, William Brown - ***Farm Girl*** [1951] Cover art by Julian Paul.	$3.00	$9.00	$18.00

		G	VG	F
38	Trumbull, Robert - ***The Raft*** [1952]	$2.50	$7.50	$15.00
39	Wall, Evans - ***Swamp Girl*** [1951] Cover art by Julian Paul.	$8.00	$25.00	$50.00
40	Cole, Jackson - ***Texas Fury*** [1951] PBO.	$2.50	$7.50	$15.00
41	De Maupassant, Guy - ***The House Of Madame Tellier And Other Stories*** [1952] Cover art by Julian Paul.	$2.50	$7.50	$15.00
G-42	Plaidy, Jean - ***The King's Mistress*** [1952]	$2.50	$7.50	$15.00
G-43	Cooper, Courtney Ryley - ***Teen-age Vice!*** [1952]	$2.50	$7.50	$15.00
44	Leslie, A. Scott - ***The Stranger In Boots*** [1952]	$2.50	$7.50	$15.00
45	Burns, Robert E. - ***I Am A Fugitive From A Chain Gang!*** [1952] Cover art by Hunter Barker. Movie tie-in.	$5.50	$17.50	$35.00
46	Anonymous - ***23 Women*** [1952]	$2.50	$7.50	$15.00
47	Cole, Jackson - ***Thunder Range*** [1952] PBO. Cover art by Hunter Barker.	$2.50	$7.50	$15.00
G-48	Seager, Allan - ***Cage Of Lust*** [1952] Cover art by Julian Paul.	$2.50	$7.50	$15.00
49	Hutchins, Maude - ***A Diary Of Love*** [1952] Cover by Julian Paul.	$2.50	$7.50	$15.00
G-50	Kuprin, Alexandre - ***Yama, The Hell-hole*** [1952]	$2.50	$7.50	$15.00
51	Cole, Jackson - ***Border Hell*** [1952] PBO.	$2.50	$7.50	$15.00
G-52	Westheimer, David - ***Tillie*** [1948]	$2.50	$7.50	$15.00
53	Tully, Jim - ***The Bruiser*** [1952]	$2.50	$7.50	$15.00
G-54	Morton, Stanley - ***Yankee Trader*** [1952]	$3.00	$9.00	$18.00
55	Plagemann, Bentz - ***Downfall*** [1952]	$2.50	$7.50	$15.00
56	Cole, Jackson - ***The Death Riders*** [1952] PBO.	$2.50	$7.50	$15.00
G-57	Fisher, Vardis - ***The Wild Ones*** [1952] Cover art by Julian Paul..	$3.00	$9.00	$18.00
58	Burns, Vincent E. - ***Female Convict*** [1952] Cover by Robert Maguire.	$4.00	$12.50	$25.00
G-59	Millen, Gilmore - ***Sweet Man*** [1952] Cover art by Julian Paul.	$3.50	$10.00	$20.00
G-60	Taylor, Dyson - ***Bitter Love*** [1952] Cover art by Julian Paul.	$3.00	$9.00	$18.00
61	Leslie, Scott - ***The Texan*** [1952] PBO.	$2.50	$7.50	$15.00
62	Anthology edited by Donald A. Wollheim - ***Let's Go Naked*** [1952] PBO. Cover by Ed Fisher	$2.50	$7.50	$15.00
63	Corle, Edwin - ***Apache Devil*** [1952]	$2.50	$7.50	$15.00
G-64	Harré, Everett - ***The Heavenly Sinner*** [1952] Cover art by Julian Paul.	$2.50	$7.50	$15.00
65	Marino, Nick - ***One Way Street*** [1952] Cover by Victor Olson.	$2.50	$7.50	$15.00
66	Cole, Jackson - ***Trigger Law*** [1952] PBO. Cover by Hunter Barker.	$2.50	$7.50	$15.00
G-67	Young, Edward - ***Hospital Doctor*** [1952]	$2.00	$6.00	$12.00
68	Laurence, Scott - ***Georgia Hotel*** [1952] PBO. Cover by Victor Olson.	$2.50	$7.50	$15.00
G-69	Des Cars, Guy - ***The Brute*** [1952]	$2.50	$7.50	$15.00
70	Cole, Jackson - ***Massacre Canyon*** [1953] PBO. Cover by Hunter Barker.	$2.50	$7.50	$15.00
71	Tellier, Andre - ***A Woman Of Paris*** [1953] PBO.	$2.50	$7.50	$15.00
G-72	Taylor, Robert W. - ***The Dark Urge*** [1953] PBO. Cover by Julian Paul.	$3.00	$9.00	$18.00
73	Cole, Jackson - ***Killer Country*** [1953] PBO. Cover art by Saul Levine.	$2.50	$7.50	$15.00
74	Chambers, Whitman - ***The Come-on*** [1953] Cover art by Victor Olson.	$2.50	$7.50	$15.00
G-75	Shay, Frank - ***Pirate Wench*** [1953]	$5.00	$15.00	$30.00
76	Dana, Richard Henry - ***Two Years Before The Mast*** [1953]	$2.50	$7.50	$15.00
G-77	Cohen, Lester - ***Stella And Joe*** [1953] Cover art by Victor Olson.	$2.50	$7.50	$15.00
78	Ricks, Dave - ***Blood Feud*** [1953] PBO.	$2.00	$6.00	$12.00
79	Rhode, William L. - ***The Heel*** [1953] PBO.	$2.50	$7.50	$15.00
80	Woolrich, Cornell - ***Beware The Lady*** [1953] Cover by C. Doore	$6.00	$20.00	$40.00
81	Cole, Jackson - ***Texas Fists*** [1953] PBO.	$2.50	$7.50	$15.00

		G	VG	F
82	Chapman, Marion - ***Loves Of Goya*** [1953] PBO. Cover art by Julian Paul.	$2.50	$7.50	$15.00
83	Koslow, Jules - ***The Bohemian*** [1953] PBO. Cover art by Victor Olson.	$2.50	$7.50	$15.00
84	Royer, Louis-Charles - ***Love Camp*** [1953] Translation by Lawrence Blochman. Cover by Julian Paul.	$4.00	$12.50	$25.00
85	Pettit, Charles - ***Chinese Lover*** [1953] Cover by Rudy Nappi.	$4.00	$12.50	$25.00
G-86	Becker, Beril - ***The Spitfires*** [1953]	$2.50	$7.50	$15.00
87	Cole, Jackson - ***Gun-runners*** [1953] PBO.	$2.50	$7.50	$15.00
G-88	Collins, Wilkie - ***The Moonstone*** [1953]	$1.50	$5.00	$10.00
89	Hervey, Harry - ***She-devil*** [1953]	$2.50	$7.50	$15.00
90	Saber, Robert O. - ***Chicago Woman*** [1953] Cover art by Julian Paul.	$2.50	$7.50	$15.00
91	Cole, Jackson - ***Land Grab*** [1953] PBO. Cover art by C. Doore.	$2.50	$7.50	$15.00
92	Tully, Jim - ***Road Show*** [1953] Cover art by Julian Paul.	$2.50	$7.50	$15.00
93	Fairbank, Walton - ***Houseboy*** [1953]	$2.50	$7.50	$15.00
94	Moore, Brian - ***Sailor's Leave*** [1953]	$8.00	$25.00	$50.00
95	MacDonald, William Colt - ***Showdown Trail*** [1953]	$2.50	$7.50	$15.00
96	Taylor, Robert W. - ***Mimi*** [1953] PBO.	$2.50	$7.50	$15.00
97	Forbes, Murray - ***The Big Fake*** [1953]	$2.50	$7.50	$15.00
98	Freuchen, Peter - ***The Sea Tyrant*** [1953]	$2.50	$7.50	$15.00
99	Karney, Jack - ***There Goes Shorty Higgins*** [1953]	$2.50	$7.50	$15.00
100	Cellini, Benvenuto - ***Cellini*** [1953] Autobiography.	$2.00	$6.00	$12.00
101	MacDonald, William Colt - ***Cow Thief*** [1953]	$2.00	$6.00	$12.00
102	Royer, Louis-Charles - ***African Mistress*** [1953]	$2.50	$7.50	$15.00
103	Scott, L.K. - ***Backstairs*** [1953] PBO. Cover by Jim Bentley.	$2.00	$6.00	$12.00
104	Givens, Charles - ***Big Mike*** [1953] PBO. Cover art by Julian Paul.	$2.00	$6.00	$12.00
105	Zola, Emile - ***Lesson In Love*** [1953] Cover art by Jim Bentley.	$2.00	$6.00	$12.00
106	Stuart, E. R. "Jeb" - ***The Ordeal Of Private Heath*** [1953] Cover by Julian Paul.	$2.00	$6.00	$12.00
107	Taylor, Robert W. - ***Scandal!*** [1954] PBO. Cover art by Victor Olson.	$2.00	$6.00	$12.00
108	Cole, Jackson - ***Texas Tornado*** [1954] PBO.	$2.00	$6.00	$12.00
109	White, Max - ***After Dark*** [1954]	$2.00	$6.00	$12.00
110	Royer, Louis-Charles - ***The Redhead From Chicago*** [1954] Translation by Lawrence Blochman. Cover by Julian Paul.	$2.50	$7.50	$15.00
111	Cole, Jackson - ***Gun Town*** [1954] PBO.	$2.00	$6.00	$12.00
112	Garth, John - ***Hill Man*** [1954] PBO. Cover art by Julian Paul.	$2.50	$7.50	$15.00
113	Gauntier, Gene - ***Sporting Lady*** [1954]	$2.00	$6.00	$12.00
114	Royer, Louis-Charles - ***The Harem*** [1954] Cover art by Victor Olson.	$3.00	$9.00	$18.00
115	MacDonald, William Colt - ***Two-Gun Deputy*** [1954] Cover art by C. Doore.	$2.00	$6.00	$12.00
116	Morgan, Michael - ***His Kind Of Woman*** [1954] Cover by Victor Olson.	$2.00	$6.00	$12.00
117	Cole, Jackson - ***Outlawed*** [1954]	$2.00	$6.00	$12.00
118	Anthology edited by Marshall McClintock - ***Women On The Wall*** [1954] PBO. Cover art by Julian Paul.	$3.50	$10.00	$20.00
119	Zolotow, Maurice - ***The Great Balsamo*** [1954]	$2.50	$7.50	$15.00
G-120	Hanley, Gerald - ***The Consul At Sunset*** [1954] Cover art by Stewart.	$2.00	$6.00	$12.00
121	Booth, Ernest - ***With Sirens Screaming*** [1954]	$2.00	$6.00	$12.00
122	Street, Leroy with Loth, David - ***I Was A Drug Addict*** [1954] Cover by Julian Paul.	$3.50	$10.00	$20.00
123	Singer, Bant - ***Blind Alley*** [1954] Cover by Frank Cozzarelli.	$2.00	$6.00	$12.00
124	Cole, Jackson - ***Bullets High*** [1954] PBO.	$2.00	$6.00	$12.00
125	Johnson, Victor H. - ***Bold Moment*** [1954] Cover art by Frank Cozzarelli.	$2.00	$6.00	$12.00

		G	VG	F
126	Robert W. Taylor - ***The Junk Pusher*** [1954] PBO. Cover by Frank Cozzarelli.	$6.00	$20.00	$40.00
G-127	Cooper, Courtney Ryley - ***Teen-age Vice*** [1954] Photo cover.	$2.00	$6.00	$12.00
128	Dietrich, Robert - ***One For The Road*** [1954] PBO.	$2.00	$6.00	$12.00
G-129	Gordon, Gerald - ***Dark Brother*** [1954]	$2.00	$6.00	$12.00
130	Hutchins, Maude - ***A Diary Of Love*** [1954]	$2.00	$6.00	$12.00
131	Friedman, Stuart - ***Ex-Con*** [1954]	$2.00	$6.00	$12.00
132	Wilmer, Dale - ***Jungle Heat*** [1954] PBO.	$2.50	$7.50	$15.00
133	De Bout, Jacques - ***Pierre's Woman*** [1954] PBO. Cover art by Victor Olson.	$2.00	$6.00	$12.00
134	Royer, Louis-Charles - ***Savage Triangle*** [1954]	$2.00	$6.00	$12.00
135	Dietrich, Robert - ***The Cheat*** [1954] PBO	$2.00	$6.00	$12.00
136	Langdon, John - ***Night In Manila*** [1954]	$2.00	$6.00	$12.00
G-137	Plaidy, Jean - ***The King's Mistress*** [1954]	$2.00	$6.00	$12.00
138	Keene, Day - ***His Father's Wife*** [1954] PBO. Cover art by Carl Bobertz.	$3.00	$9.00	$18.00
139	Collans, Dev (with Stewart Sterling) - ***I Was A House Detective*** [1954] Photo cover.	$2.00	$6.00	$12.00
G-140	Morton, Stanley - ***Yankee Trader*** [1954]	$2.00	$6.00	$12.00
G-142	Millen, Gilmore - ***Sweet Man*** [1955]	$2.00	$6.00	$12.00
143	Payne, Robert - ***Lovers In The Sun*** [1955] PBO. Cover art by Lu Kimmel.	$2.00	$6.00	$12.00
144	Cole, Jackson - ***Texas Manhunt*** [1955] PBO.	$2.00	$6.00	$12.00
G-145	Seager, Allan - ***Cage Of Lust*** [1955] Cover art by Julian Paul.	$2.00	$6.00	$12.00
G-146	Harre, Everett - ***The Heavenly Sinner*** [1955]	$2.00	$6.00	$12.00
147	Sachs, Ruth - ***For I Have Sinned*** [1955] PBO.	$2.00	$6.00	$12.00
148	Nistler, Erwin N. & Broderick, Gerry P. - ***Roadside Night*** [1955]	$2.00	$6.00	$12.00
149	Leslie, Scott - ***The Texan*** [1955]	$2.00	$6.00	$12.00
G-150	Podolin, Si - ***Devil's Cargo*** [1955] PBO. Cover art by Frank Cozzarelli.	$2.50	$7.50	$15.00
151	Collins, Hunt (Ed McBain) - ***The Proposition*** [1955]	$2.25	$7.00	$14.00
152	House, O. T. - editor - ***Just Married*** [1955] PBO. Cartoon book.	$2.00	$6.00	$12.00
153	Cole, Jackson - ***Gunsmoke Trail*** [1955] PBO	$2.00	$6.00	$12.00
G-154	Meloney, William Brown - ***Farm Girl*** [1955]	$2.00	$6.00	$12.00
155	Cole, Jackson - ***Trouble Shooter*** [1955]	$2.00	$6.00	$12.00
156	Anthology - ***Dangerous Game*** [1955] PBO.	$2.00	$6.00	$12.00
G-157	Howard, Toni - ***Shriek With Pleasure*** [1955]	$2.00	$6.00	$12.00
158	De Mejo, Oscar - ***Diary Of A Nun*** [1955] PBO.	$2.00	$6.00	$12.00
159	Marino, Nick - ***One Way Street*** [1955]	$2.00	$6.00	$12.00
G-160	Safford, M.D., Henry Barnard - ***Tell Me, Doctor*** [1955] Photo cover.	$2.00	$6.00	$12.00
G-161	Gautier, Theophile - ***Mademoiselle De Maupin*** [1955] Cover art by Lou Marchetti.	$2.00	$6.00	$12.00
162	Cole, Jackson - ***Gun-Blaze*** [1955] PBO.	$2.00	$6.00	$12.00
163	Podolin, Si - ***Bed Of Hate*** [1955] PBO.	$2.00	$6.00	$12.00
164	Burke, James Wakefield - ***Of A Strange Woman*** [1955] Cover art by Lou Marchetti.	$2.00	$6.00	$12.00
165	Manners, Martin - ***Town Quarry*** [1955] PBO	$2.00	$6.00	$12.00
166	Royer, Louis-Charles - ***French Doctor*** [1955] Cover art by Hunter Barker.	$1.35	$4.00	$8.00
167	Cole, Jackson - ***Texas Fury*** [1955]	$1.50	$5.00	$10.00
168	Wall, Evans - ***Swamp Girl*** [1955]	$3.50	$10.00	$20.00
169	White, Harry (Harry Whittington) - ***Shadow At Noon*** [1955] PBO.	$4.00	$12.50	$25.00
G-170	Holk, Agnete - ***Strange Friends*** [1955]	$2.00	$6.00	$12.00
171	Cole, Jackson - ***Two-gun Devil*** [1955]	$1.50	$5.00	$10.00
172	MacDonald, William Colt - ***The Range Kid*** [1955] PBO.	$1.50	$5.00	$10.00
173	Cantrell, Wade B. - ***Brand Of Cain*** [1955] PBO.	$1.50	$5.00	$10.00
174	Clay, Lewis - ***The Wanton Hour*** [1955] PBO.	$2.00	$6.00	$12.00

		G	VG	F
175	Anonymous - ***Madeleine*** [1955] Autobiography. Cover by Lou Marchetti.	$1.50	$5.00	$10.00
176	Curtin, Arthur - ***Love Off-Limits*** [1956] PBO.	$1.50	$5.00	$10.00
G-177	De Balzac, Honore - ***Pere Goriot*** [1956]	$1.50	$5.00	$10.00
178	Scott, Bradford - ***The Texas Terror*** [1956]	$1.50	$5.00	$10.00
179	Cuthbert, Clifton - ***The Shame Of Mary Quinn*** [1956]	$1.50	$5.00	$10.00
G-180	London, Jack - ***The Seed Of McCoy And Other Stories*** [1956]	$3.50	$10.00	$20.00
G-181	Modell, Merriam - ***My Sister, My Bride*** [1956] Cover art by David Stone.	$4.00	$12.50	$25.00
182	Billings, Buck - ***Owlhoot Trail*** [1956] Cover art by Tom Ryan.	$1.50	$5.00	$10.00
183	O'Donnell, Bernard - ***The World's Worst Women*** [1956] Cover art by Lou Marchetti.	$2.50	$7.50	$15.00
G-184	Sturgeon, Theodore - ***A Way Home*** [1956] Cover art by Mel Hunter.	$2.50	$7.50	$15.00
G-185	Plagemann, Bentz - ***The Sin Underneath*** [1956] Cover art by George Ziel.	$2.00	$6.00	$12.00
186	Scott, Bradford - ***Trigger Talk*** [1956]	$1.50	$5.00	$10.00
187	McCulley, Johnston - ***Gunman's Gold*** [1956] Cover by John Duillo.	$1.50	$5.00	$10.00
G-188	Daniels, M.D., Anna K. - ***It's Never Too Late To Love*** [1956] Photo cover.	$1.35	$4.00	$8.00
G-189	Taylor, John - ***Shadows Of Shame*** [1956] PBO. Cover by Everett Raymond Kinstler.	$2.00	$6.00	$12.00
190	Scott, Bradford - ***Badlands Boss*** [1956] PBO. Cover art by Rudy Nappi.	$1.50	$5.00	$10.00
191	Burns, Vincent G. - ***Female Convict*** [1956] Cover art by Robert Maguire.	$1.50	$5.00	$10.00
192	Shirreffs, Gordon D. - ***Range Rebel*** [1956] PBO. Cover art by John Leone.	$1.50	$5.00	$10.00
193	Katzman, Lawrence - ***Taking A Turn For The Nurse*** [1956] PBO. Cover art by Lawrence Katzman. Cartoon book.	$1.50	$5.00	$10.00
194	Lehman, Paul Evan - ***The Gunhand*** [1956] Cover art by John Leone.	$1.50	$5.00	$10.00
195	Fox, Norman A. - ***Six-gun Syndicate*** [1956] Cover art by Morton Engle.	$1.50	$5.00	$10.00
196	Anthology edited by Donald A. Wollheim - ***Let's Go Naked*** [1956] Cover by Ed Fisher.	$1.50	$5.00	$10.00
G-197	Gorham, Charles O. - ***The Future Mister Dolan*** [1956] Cover art by Rudy Nappi.	$1.35	$4.00	$8.00
198	Dewell, Michael - editor - ***Hell And High Water*** [1956] PBO. Cover by Frank Cozzarelli.	$1.50	$5.00	$10.00
199	Scott, Bradford - ***Canyon Killers*** [1956] PBO. Cover art by John Leone.	$1.50	$5.00	$10.00
200	Hunter, Georgiana - ***The Girl On The Couch*** [1956] PBO. Photo cover.	$1.50	$5.00	$10.00
G-201	Marshall, Rosamond - ***Celeste*** [1956] Photo cover.	$1.50	$5.00	$10.00
R-202	De Maupassant, Guy - ***The House Of Madame Tellier*** [1956] Cover art by Lou Marchetti.	$1.50	$5.00	$10.00
203	Evan, Paul - ***Lynch Law*** [1956] Cover art by John Leone.	$1.50	$5.00	$10.00
204	Leslie, A. Scott - ***The Stranger In Boots*** [1956] Cover by John Leone.	$1.50	$5.00	$10.00
205	Davis, Eddie - ***Playgirls, U.S.A.*** [1956] PBO. Cover art by Casey Jones. Cartoon book.	$2.00	$6.00	$12.00
G-206	Bishop, Leonard - ***Creep Into Thy Narrow Bed*** [1956] Cover art by Irving Docktor.	$1.50	$5.00	$10.00
R-207	Kuprin, Alexandre - ***Yama, The Hell-hole*** [1956] Cover art by George Ziel.	$1.50	$5.00	$10.00
208	Cavanaugh, James - ***The Big Gun*** [1956] Cover art by Tom Ryan.	$1.50	$5.00	$10.00
209	Scott, Bradford - ***Gunsmoke Over Texas*** [1956]	$1.50	$5.00	$10.00

		G	VG	F
R-210	Anthology edited by Mark Merrill - ***Women And Vodka*** [1956] PBO. Cover art by Lou Marchetti.	$1.50	$5.00	$10.00
R-211	Hanley, Gerald - ***Drinkers Of Darkness*** [1956] Cover art by George Ziel.	$1.50	$5.00	$10.00
G-212	Jackson, Shirley - ***The Other Side Of The Street*** [1956] Cover by Larry Newquist.	$2.50	$7.50	$15.00
G-213	Gesell, M.D., Arnold - ***Miracle Of Growth*** [1956]	$1.25	$3.75	$7.50
G-214	Collins, Hunt (Ed McBain) - ***Tomorrow And Tomorrow*** [1956] Cover art by Bob Lavin.	$2.50	$7.50	$15.00
215	Fairbank, Walton - ***Houseboy*** [1956]	$1.50	$5.00	$10.00
216	West, Tom - ***Outlaw Brand*** [1956] PBO. Cover art by Vic Prezio.	$1.50	$5.00	$10.00
G-217	Royer, Louis-Charles - ***The Man From Paris*** [1956] PBO. Cover art by William Rose.	$1.50	$5.00	$10.00
G-218	Loomis, Noel M. - ***Wild Country*** [1956] PBO. Cover art by Tom Ryan.	$2.00	$6.00	$12.00
219	Scott, Bradford - ***The Avenger*** [1956] PBO. Cover art by John Leone.	$1.50	$5.00	$10.00
220	Scott, Bradford - ***Border Blood*** [1956] PBO. Cover art by John Leone.	$1.50	$5.00	$10.00
221	Luzzatto, Jack - ***Pyramid Crossword Book*** [1956]	$5.50	$17.50	$35.00
G-222	Elbogen, Paul - ***The Jealous Mistress*** [1956] Cover art by Tony Kokinos.	$1.50	$5.00	$10.00
R-223	Safford, M.D., Henry Barnard - ***The Intimate Problems Of Women*** [1956]	$1.25	$3.75	$7.50
G-224	Des Cars, Guy - ***The Damned One*** [1956] Cover art by George Ziel.	$1.50	$5.00	$10.00
225	Hopson, William - ***A Gunman Rode North*** [1956] Cover art by Vic Prezio.	$1.50	$5.00	$10.00
G-226	Rhode, William - ***Give Me A Little Something*** [1956]	$1.50	$5.00	$10.00
G-227	Anthology edited by Mark Merrill - ***The Love-makers*** [1956]	$1.50	$5.00	$10.00
G-228	Sara, Dorothy - ***Handwriting Analysis*** [1956]	$1.25	$3.75	$7.50
229	Johnson, Victor H. - ***Bold Moment*** [1956] Cover art by Frank Cozzarelli.	$1.50	$5.00	$10.00
230	Bishop, Curtis - ***Reach For Your Guns*** [1956] PBO. Cover art by Vic Prezio.	$1.50	$5.00	$10.00
231	MacDonald, William Colt - ***Flaming Lead*** [1956] PBO. Cover art by John Leone.	$1.50	$5.00	$10.00
R-232	Maurois, Andre - ***Woman Without Love*** [1956]	$1.35	$4.00	$8.00
G-233	Westheimer, David - ***Tillie*** [1956]	$1.50	$5.00	$10.00
G-234	Greenberg, Martin - editor (anthology) - ***Men Against The Stars*** [1958] Cover by Mel Hunter.	$2.50	$7.50	$15.00
235	Dietrich, Robert - ***One For The Road*** [1957]	$1.50	$5.00	$10.00
R-236	Kramer, N. Martin - ***The Hearth And The Strangeness*** [1956] ...	$1.50	$5.00	$10.00
R-237	Carnegie, Mrs. Dale - ***How To Help Your Husband Get Ahead*** [1957]	$1.50	$5.00	$10.00
238	Scott, Bradford - ***Dead Man's Trail*** [1957] PBO. Cover art by Gene Krause.	$1.50	$5.00	$10.00
G-239	April, Jack - ***Feud At Five Rivers*** [1957]	$1.50	$5.00	$10.00
G-240	Anthology edited by Henry Boltinoff - ***Sex Is Better In College*** [1957]	$1.50	$5.00	$10.00
G-241	Manners, Martin - ***The Night It Happened*** [1957] PBO. Cover art by Lou Marchetti.	$1.50	$5.00	$10.00
G-242	Hadley, Harold - ***Come See Them Die*** [1957] Cover art by Louis S. Glanzman.	$1.50	$5.00	$10.00
R-243	Gunther, John - ***Death Be Not Proud*** [1957]	$1.35	$4.00	$8.00
G-244	Anthology edited by Leo Margulies - ***Gone To Texas*** [1957]	$1.50	$5.00	$10.00
245	Lawson, Larry - ***Blood Brand*** [1957] Cover art by Jerry Allison.	$1.50	$5.00	$10.00
R-246	Ellis, Havelock - ***Sex And Marriage*** [1957]	$1.25	$3.75	$7.50

Pyramid, G-275

Pyramid, G-324

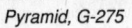

Pyramid, G-327

		G	VG	F
G-247	Sturgeon, Theodore - ***The Synthetic Man*** [1957] Cover art by Art Sussman.	$2.50	$7.50	$15.00
G-248	Schlick, Robert - ***Tonight It's me*** [1957] PBO. Cover art by Lou Marchetti.	$1.50	$5.00	$10.00
G-249	Manners, Dorine - ***Sin Street*** [1957] Photo cover.	$1.50	$5.00	$10.00
250	Rohde, William L. - ***The Gun-crasher*** [1957]	$1.50	$5.00	$10.00
251	Scott, Bradford - ***Rimrock Raiders*** [1957] PBO. Cover art by Gene Krause.	$1.50	$5.00	$10.00
G-252	Cooper, Courtney Ryley - ***Teen-age Vice*** [1957]	$1.50	$5.00	$10.00
G-253	Royer, Louis-Charles - ***Unrepentant Sinners*** [1957] Cover art by Marchetti.	$1.50	$5.00	$10.00
G-254	Cox, William R. - ***The Lusty Men*** [1957] PBO. Cover art by Jerry Allison.	$1.50	$5.00	$10.00
255	Brock, Stuart - ***Double-cross Ranch*** [1957]	$1.50	$5.00	$10.00
R-256	Ferguson, M.D., James Henry - ***Why Can't We Have A Baby?*** [1957] PBO. Photo cover.	$1.35	$4.00	$8.00
R-257	Wilson, William E. - ***Crescent City*** [1957] Cover art by Tom Ryan.	$1.50	$5.00	$10.00
258	Scott, Bradford - ***Powder Burn*** [1957] PBO. Cover art by Morton Engel.	$1.50	$5.00	$10.00
259	Joscelyn, Archie - ***Gunhand's Pay*** [1957] Cover art by Mel Crair...	$1.50	$5.00	$10.00
G-260	Anthology edited by Chandler Brossard. - ***The First Time*** [1957] PBO. Cover art by Tony Kokinos.	$1.50	$5.00	$10.00
G-261	Collans, Dev (with Sterling, Stewart) - ***I Was A House Detective*** [1957]	$1.50	$5.00	$10.00
G-262	Tellier, Andre - ***Twilight Men*** [1957]	$1.50	$5.00	$10.00
G-263	Burke, James Wakefield - ***Taboo*** [1957] Cover art by Larry Newquist.	$1.50	$5.00	$10.00
264	Scott, Bradford - ***Curse Of Texas Gold*** [1957] PBO. Cover art by Mort Engel.	$1.50	$5.00	$10.00
265	Cunningham, Eugene - ***Bravo Trail*** [1957]	$1.50	$5.00	$10.00
G-266	Keene, Day - ***His Father's Wife*** [1957] Cover art by Carl Bobertz.	$2.00	$6.00	$12.00
267	Athas, Daphne - ***The Fourth World*** [1957]	$1.50	$5.00	$10.00
G-268	Levinson, Len - ***Impossible Greeting Cards*** [1957] PBO. Cover art by Allen Bellman.	$1.50	$5.00	$10.00
269	James, Dan - ***Gunsmoke Mesa*** [1957]	$1.50	$5.00	$10.00
G-270	Fischer, Bruno - ***Stairway To Death*** [1957]	$1.50	$5.00	$10.00
G-271	Anthology edited by Leo Margulies - ***The Young Punks*** [1957] PBO. Cover art by Rudy De Reyna.	$3.50	$10.00	$20.00

		G	VG	F
272	Laurence, Scott - ***Georgia Hotel*** [1957] Cover art by Lou Marchetti.	$1.50	$5.00	$10.00
R-273	Eidelberg, M.D., Ludwig - ***Take Off Your Mask*** [1957] Photo cover.	$1.35	$4.00	$8.00
G-274	Fickling, G. G. - ***This Girl For Hire*** [1957] PBO. Cover art by Harry Schaare.	$2.50	$7.50	$15.00
G-275	Tate, Sylvia - ***The Fuzzy Pink Nightgown*** [1957] Movie photo cover. Movie tie-in with Jane Russell.	$2.50	$7.50	$15.00
G-276	MacDonald, William Scott - ***Thunderbird Trail*** [1957]	$1.50	$5.00	$10.00
G-277	Lomax, Bliss - ***The Law Bringers*** [1957] Cover art by Tom Ryan.	$1.50	$5.00	$10.00
G-278	Taylor, Dyson - ***Bitter Love*** [1957] Cover art by George Ziel.	$1.50	$5.00	$10.00
R-279	Christie, Robert - ***Inherit The Night*** [1957] Cover art by Lou Marchetti.	$1.50	$5.00	$10.00
G-280	Brannon, W. T. - ***"Yellow Kid" Weil—Con Man*** [1957] Photo cover.	$1.50	$5.00	$10.00
R-281	Crankshaw, Edward - ***Gestapo*** [1957] Cover art by Harry Schaare.	$1.50	$5.00	$10.00
282	Scott, Bradford - ***The Texas Hawk*** [1957] PBO.	$1.50	$5.00	$10.00
G-283	Rohde, William - ***VIP*** [1957] Cover art by Lou Marchetti.	$1.50	$5.00	$10.00
G-284	Kane, Henry - ***The Name Is Chambers*** [1957] PBO. Cover by Harry Schaare.	$2.50	$7.50	$15.00
G-285	Taylor, Daniel - ***All His Women*** [1957] Cover art by Jo Polsino.	$1.50	$5.00	$10.00
286	MacDonald, William Scott - ***Two-gun Deputy*** [1957]	$1.50	$5.00	$10.00
287	Covington, Forrest - ***The Sheriff*** [1957] PBO. Cover art by Gerald McConnell.	$1.50	$5.00	$10.00
G-288	Roe, Vingie E. - ***Smoke Along The Plains*** [1957] PBO.	$1.50	$5.00	$10.00
R-289	Kaufman, Maxine - ***I Am Adam*** [1957] Cover art by Mel Crair.	$1.50	$5.00	$10.00
R-290	Shelley, Mary - ***Frankenstein*** [1957]	$2.50	$7.50	$15.00
G-291	Seaton, George John - ***Isle Of The Damned*** [1957] Cover by Tom Ryan.	$2.00	$6.00	$12.00
G-292	Shaw, Charles - ***You're Wrong, Delaney*** [1957]	$1.50	$5.00	$10.00
293	Scott, Bradford - ***Death Canyon*** [1957]	$1.50	$5.00	$10.00
294	MacDonald, William Colt - ***The Range Kid*** [1957] Cover art by John Leone.	$1.50	$5.00	$10.00
G-295	Markowitz, Arthur - ***The Daughter*** [1957] Cover art by Rudy Nappi.	$1.50	$5.00	$10.00
G-296	Mitchell, Albert - ***Here's The Answer*** [1957] Cover art by Robert V. Engle.	$1.50	$5.00	$10.00
G-297	Young, Edward - ***Hospital Doctor*** [1957] Cover art by Lou Marchetti.	$1.35	$4.00	$8.00
G-298	Smith, George O. - ***Hell Flower*** [1957] Cover art by Bill Rose.	$3.50	$10.00	$20.00
G-299	Spingarn, Ed - ***Perfect 36*** [1957] PBO. Cover art by Lou Marchetti.	$2.00	$6.00	$12.00
R-300	Verne, Jules - ***Michael Strogoff*** [1957] Cover art by Tom Ryan.	$2.00	$6.00	$12.00
G-301	Hervey, Harry - ***She-devil*** [1957]	$1.50	$5.00	$10.00
302	Scott Leslie - ***Tombstone Showdown*** [1957] Cover by John Leone.	$1.50	$5.00	$10.00
303	Obets, Bob - ***Blood Moon Range*** [1958] PBO. Cover art by Mel Crair.	$1.50	$5.00	$10.00
G-304	Hynd, Alan - ***The Case Of The Attic Lover*** [1958] PBO. Cover art by Harry Schaare.	$2.00	$6.00	$12.00
R-305	Bromfield, Louis - ***Mrs. Parkington*** [1958] Cover art by Robert Maguire.	$2.00	$6.00	$12.00
G-306	Holden, Larry - ***Dead Wrong*** [1957] PBO. Cover art by Harry Schaare.	$2.50	$7.50	$15.00
307	Richmond, Roe - ***The Hard Men*** [1958]	$1.50	$5.00	$10.00
308	Scott, Bradford - ***Shootin' Man*** [1958]	$1.50	$5.00	$10.00
309	Lee, Carolina - ***Yaller Gal*** [1958]	$1.50	$5.00	$10.00

		G	VG	F
G-310	Fisher, Vardis - ***The Wild Ones*** [1957] Cover art by Gerald Powell.	$1.50	$5.00	$10.00
G-311	Lawrence, Gil - ***Fury With Legs*** [1958] PBO.	$1.50	$5.00	$10.00
G-312	Soubiran, Andre - ***Bedlam*** [1958] Cover art by Robert Maguire.	$1.50	$5.00	$10.00
G-313	Grove, Fred - ***Flame Of The Osage*** [1958]	$1.50	$5.00	$10.00
314	Whitinger, R. D. - ***High Trail*** [1958] Cover art by John Leone.	$1.50	$5.00	$10.00
G-315	Marino, Nick - ***City Limits*** [1958] PBO. Cover art by William Rose.	$2.00	$6.00	$12.00
R-316	Edited by Len Levinson - ***The Affairs Of Casanova*** [1958]	$1.50	$5.00	$10.00
G-317	Royer, Louis-Charles - ***French Doctor*** [1958]	$1.50	$5.00	$10.00
R-318	Blond, Georges - ***The Death Of Hitler's Germany*** [1958] Photo cover.	$1.35	$4.00	$8.00
319	Scott, Bradford - ***The Blaze Of Guns*** [1958]	$1.50	$5.00	$10.00
G-320	Royer, Louis-Charles - ***Love Camp*** [1958]	$2.00	$6.00	$12.00
R-321	Wolfe, Thomas - ***The Hills Beyond*** [1958] Cover art by Harry Schaare.	$1.50	$5.00	$10.00
G-322	Barry, Jack - ***Twenty-one*** [1958]	$1.50	$5.00	$10.00
G-323	Marric, J. J. - ***7 Days to Death*** [1958] Cover art by Lou Marchetti.	$1.50	$5.00	$10.00
G-324	Edited by Ray Robinson - ***Baseball Stars Of 1958*** [1958] PBO. Cover art by Bob V. Engle. Eight pages of photos.	$5.00	$15.00	$30.00
325	Lawson, Larry - ***Naked Spurs*** [1958] Cover art by Herb Mott.	$1.50	$5.00	$10.00
G-326	Tzetnik, Ka - ***House Of Dolls*** [1958] Cover art by Gerald Powell.	$1.50	$5.00	$10.00
G-327	Held, Peter (Jack Vance) - ***Take My Face*** [1958] Cover art by John Floherty.	$8.00	$25.00	$50.00
G-328	Baum, Vicki - ***The Mustard Seed*** [1958] Cover art by Lou Marchetti.	$1.50	$5.00	$10.00
G-329	Allen, Eric - ***Hangtree Country*** [1958] Cover by Lu Kimmel.	$1.50	$5.00	$10.00
R-330	Schellenberg, Walter - ***Hitler's Secret Service*** [1958] Cover by Ray Sternbergh.	$1.35	$4.00	$8.00
G-331	Masin, Herman L. - ***Curve Ball Laughs*** [1958] Cover by Willard Mullin. Cartoon and joke book.	$1.50	$5.00	$10.00
G-332	Smith, Edward E. - ***The Skylark Of Space*** [1958] Cover art by Richard Powers.	$2.50	$7.50	$15.00
333	Brock, Stuart - ***Railtown Sheriff*** [1958]	$1.50	$5.00	$10.00
G-334	Hunter, Georgiana - ***The Girl On The Couch*** [1958]	$1.35	$4.00	$8.00
G-335	Marric, J. J. (John Creasey) - ***Gideon's Night*** [1958] Cover art by Schaare.	$1.50	$5.00	$10.00
G-336	Thompson, Jim - ***Cropper's Cabin*** [1958] Cover by Clark Hulings.	$8.00	$25.00	$50.00
G-337	Moyzisch, L. C. - ***Operation Cicero*** [1958]	$1.50	$5.00	$10.00
G-338	Roth, Holly - ***The Sleeper*** [1958]	$2.00	$6.00	$12.00
G-339	Budrys, Algis - ***Who?*** [1958] PBO. Cover art by Robert V. Engle.	$2.50	$7.50	$15.00
R-340	Hunter, Edward - ***Brainwashing*** [1958]	$1.35	$4.00	$8.00
G-341	Baker, Denys Val - ***Strange Fulfillment*** [1958] PBO. Cover by William Rose.	$1.50	$5.00	$10.00
G-342	Tesch, Gerald - ***Never The Same Again*** [1958] Cover art by A. Leslie Ross.	$1.50	$5.00	$10.00
G-343	Anthology edited by Henry Boltinoff - ***Bed And Broad*** [1958]	$1.50	$5.00	$10.00
G-344	Fickling, G. G. - ***A Gun For Honey*** [1958] PBO. Cover art by Schaare.	$2.50	$7.50	$15.00
G-345	Brown, Wenzell - ***Prison Girl*** [1958] PBO. Cover art by Bob Maguire.	$3.50	$10.00	$20.00
G-346	Anthology edited by Sandy Nelkin - ***Cartoons For Men Only*** [1958] PBO. Cover art by Henry Boltinoff. Cartoon book.	$1.50	$5.00	$10.00
347	Lehman, Paul Evan - ***The Young Texan*** [1958] PBO. Cover art by Mal Thompson.	$1.50	$5.00	$10.00

		G	VG	F
348	Thomas, W. Craig - ***House Of Hate*** [1958] Cover art by Sussman.	$1.50	$5.00	$10.00
G-349	Leveridge, Ralph - ***The Lost Combat*** [1958]	$1.50	$5.00	$10.00
G-350	Rice, Craig - ***The Name Is Malone*** [1958] PBO. Cover art by Robert Patterson.	$2.50	$7.50	$15.00
G-351	Reynolds, Quentin - ***70,000 To 1*** [1958] Cover art by Gerald McConnell.	$1.50	$5.00	$10.00
G-352	Ellison, Harlan - ***Rumble*** [1958] PBO. Author's first book. Cover art by Rudy De Reyna.	$32.00	$110.00	$250.00
G-353	Lacy, Ed - ***Room To Swing*** [1958] Cover art by Maguire.	$4.00	$12.50	$25.00
G-354	Ullman, Allan & Fletcher, Lucille - ***Night Man*** [1958] Cover art by Lou Marchetti.	$1.50	$5.00	$10.00
G-355	Kelland, Clarence Budington - ***The Nameless Corpse*** [1958] Cover art by Robert Patterson.	$2.00	$6.00	$12.00
G-356	Roske, Ralph J. & Van Doren, Charles - ***Lincoln's Commando*** [1958] Cover art by Herb Mott.	$1.35	$4.00	$8.00
G-357	Welles, Orson - ***Mr. Arkadin*** [1958] Cover art by Maguire.	$1.50	$5.00	$10.00
G-358	Smith, James Woodruff - ***Killer Colt*** [1958]	$1.50	$5.00	$10.00
G-359	Honig, Donald - ***Sidewalk Caesar*** [1958] PBO. Cover art by Robert Patterson.	$1.50	$5.00	$10.00
G-360	Garve, Andrew - ***The Megstone Plot*** [1958] Cover art by William Rose.	$1.50	$5.00	$10.00
G-361	Anthology edited by Whit Burnett - ***The Scarlet Treasury Of Great Confessions*** [1958]	$1.50	$5.00	$10.00
G-362	Murray, Max - ***Good Luck To The Corpse*** [1958] Cover art by William Rose.	$2.00	$6.00	$12.00
G-363	MacDonald, William Colt - ***The Mad Marshall*** [1958] PBO. Cover art by John Leone.	$1.50	$5.00	$10.00
G-364	Clifton, Bud - ***The Bad Girls*** [1958]	$2.50	$7.50	$15.00
G-365	Hayes, Alfred - ***All Thy Conquests*** [1958] Cover art by Harry Schaare.	$1.50	$5.00	$10.00
G-366	Fickling, G. G. - ***Girl On The Loose*** [1958] PBO. Cover art by Harry Schaare.	$2.50	$7.50	$15.00
R-367	March, William - ***My Brother's Bride*** [1958]	$1.50	$5.00	$10.00
368	Park, Jordan (C. M. Kornbluth) - ***The Man Of Cold Rages*** [1958] PBO. Cover art by Harry Schaare.	$8.00	$25.00	$50.00
G-369	Lowrey, Walter B. - ***Summer Boy*** [1958] Cover by Lou Marchetti.	$1.50	$5.00	$10.00
370	Tuttle, W. C. - ***Thunderbird Range*** [1958] Cover by Vic Prezio.	$1.50	$5.00	$10.00
G-371	Scott, Ann - ***I Cried In The Dark*** [1958] Cover art by Bob Stanley.	$1.50	$5.00	$10.00
G-372	Roth, Holly - ***The Crimson In The Purple*** [1959] Cover art by Bob Maguire.	$2.00	$6.00	$12.00
G-373	Everest, Jr., Frank K. & Guenther, John - ***The Fastest Man Alive*** [1959] Photo cover.	$1.35	$4.00	$8.00
G-374	Woolrich, Cornell - ***Death Is My Dancing Partner*** [1959] PBO. Cover art by Ed Schmidt.	$7.00	$22.50	$45.00
G-375	Singer, Adam - ***Platoon*** [1959]	$1.35	$4.00	$8.00
G-376	Lehman, Paul Evan - ***West Of The Pecos*** [1959]	$1.50	$5.00	$10.00
G-377	Burns, Vincent G. - ***Female Convict*** [1959] Cover art by Robert Maguire.	$3.00	$9.00	$18.00
G-378	Conrad, Joseph - ***An Outcast Of The Islands*** [1959] Cover art by Bob Stanley.	$1.50	$5.00	$10.00
G-379	Brome, Vincent - ***The Spy*** [1959] Cover art by Bob Abbett.	$1.35	$4.00	$8.00
G-380	Colby, Robert - ***These Lonely, These Dead*** [1959]	$2.00	$6.00	$12.00
G-381	Sorce, Rose L. - ***The New Italian Cookbook*** [1959] PBO. Photo cover.	$1.35	$4.00	$8.00
G-382	York, Jeremy - ***So Soon To Die*** [1959] Cover art by Darcy.	$1.50	$5.00	$10.00
G-383	Lewis, Herbert Clyde - ***The Silver Dark*** [1959] PBO. Photo cover.	$1.50	$5.00	$10.00

		G	VG	F
G-384	Flora, Fletcher - ***Whisper Of Love*** [1959]	$2.00	$6.00	$12.00
G-385	Ehle, John - ***The Survivor*** [1959]	$1.50	$5.00	$10.00
G-386	Anthology edited by Leo Margulies - ***The Young Punks*** [1959] Cover art by Rudy De Reyna.	$3.50	$10.00	$20.00
G-387	Connell, Vivian - ***The Dream And The Flesh*** [1959] Cover art by Bob Maguire.	$2.00	$6.00	$12.00
388	French, E. T. - ***Never Smile At Children*** [1959] PBO. Cover art by Lou Marchetti.	$1.50	$5.00	$10.00
389	Davis, Garth - ***Gallows Trail*** [1959]	$1.50	$5.00	$10.00
G-390	Taylor, Robert Scott - ***Vera*** [1959] PBO. Cover art by Bill Rose.	$1.50	$5.00	$10.00
G-391	Ronns, Edward S. - ***The Black Orchid*** [1959] PBO. Photo cover. Movie tie-in with Sophia Loren and Anthony Quinn	$2.50	$7.50	$15.00
G-392	Robinson, Ray - ***Baseball Stars Of 1959*** [1959]	$5.00	$15.00	$30.00
G-393	Lyon, Dana - ***The Lost One*** [1959] Cover by Art Sussman.	$1.50	$5.00	$10.00
G-394	Wolfson, P. J. - ***How Sharp The Point*** [1959] PBO. Cover art by Harry Schaare.	$1.50	$5.00	$10.00
G-395	Keene, Day - ***So Dead My Lovely*** [1959] PBO. Cover art by Bob Maguire.	$4.00	$12.50	$25.00
396	Hamilton, Wade - ***The Longhorn Brand*** [1959]	$1.50	$5.00	$10.00
G-397	Anthology edited by Judith Merril - ***Off The Beaten Orbit*** [1959] Cover art by Powers.	$2.50	$7.50	$15.00
G-398	Rittwagen, M.D., Marjorie - ***Sins Of Their Fathers*** [1959] Photo cover.	$1.25	$3.75	$7.50
G-399	Lamont, Nedda - ***The Beauty Makers*** [1959] Cover art by William Rose.	$1.35	$4.00	$8.00
G-400	Caspary, Vera - ***The Husband*** [1959] Cover art by Harry Schaare.	$1.50	$5.00	$10.00
G-401	Levin, Robert J. - ***5 Who Vanished*** [1959] PBO. Cover art by Harry Schaare.	$1.50	$5.00	$10.00
G-402	Pettit, William E. - ***City Of Chains*** [1959] PBO. Cover art by Robert Maguire.	$2.50	$7.50	$15.00
403	Hamilton, Wade - ***Rimrock Renegade*** [1959]	$1.50	$5.00	$10.00
G-404	Eidelberg, Ludwig - ***Take Off Your Mask*** [1959]	$1.50	$5.00	$10.00
G-405	Roeburt, John - ***Al Capone*** [1959] PBO. Cover art by Harry Schaare. Movie tie-in.	$1.50	$5.00	$10.00
G-406	Grider, George & Sims, Lydel - ***War Fish*** [1959]	$1.35	$4.00	$8.00
G-407	Koningsberger, Hans - ***The Affair*** [1959] Cover art by Harry Schaare.	$1.35	$4.00	$8.00
G-408	York, Jeremy - ***Hilda, Take Heed*** [1959] Cover art by Darcy.	$2.00	$6.00	$12.00
409	Scott, Bradford - ***Dead In Texas*** [1959] Cover art by Ray Sternbergh.	$1.50	$5.00	$10.00
G-410	Clifton, Bud - ***The Power Gods*** [1959] PBO. Cover art by Lou Marchetti.	$3.00	$9.00	$18.00
G-411	Fickling, G. G. - ***Honey In The Flesh*** [1959] PBO. Cover art by Harry Schaare.	$2.50	$7.50	$15.00
G-412	O'Connor, Edwin - ***The Oracle*** [1959] Cover art by Robert Maguire and Mort Engle.	$1.50	$5.00	$10.00
G-413	Cuthbert, Clifton - ***The Shame Of Mary Quinn*** [1959] Photo cover.	$1.50	$5.00	$10.00
G-414	Burnham, Creighton Brown - ***Born Innocent*** [1959] Cover art by Robert Maguire.	$2.00	$6.00	$12.00
G-415	Joyeux, Odette - ***The Bride Is Much Too Beautiful*** [1959] Photo cover. Movie tie-in with Brigitte Bardot.	$2.50	$7.50	$15.00
G-416	Budrys, Algis - ***The Falling Torch*** [1959] PBO. Cover art by Robert Engle.	$2.50	$7.50	$15.00
G-417	France, Anatole - ***The Red Lily*** [1959]	$1.35	$4.00	$8.00
R-418	Vialar, Paul - ***Five Soldiers*** [1959]	$1.35	$4.00	$8.00
R-419	Fisher, Vardis - ***The Divine Passion*** [1959] Cover art by Robert Maguire.	$3.00	$9.00	$18.00

Pyramid, G-448

Pyramid, G-485

Pyramid, G-600

		G	VG	F
420	Scott, Bradford - ***Texas Badman*** [1959] PBO. Cover by Hector Garrido.	$1.50	$5.00	$10.00
G-421	Wolfson, Victor - ***The Passionate Season*** [1959] Cover art by Lou Marchetti.	$1.50	$5.00	$10.00
G-422	Fitzgerald, John D. - ***Mamma's Boarding House*** [1959]	$1.50	$5.00	$10.00
G-423	Birren, Faber - ***Make Mine Love*** [1959]	$1.50	$5.00	$10.00
G-424	Grinioff, Vladimir B. - ***The Banker's Daughter*** [1959]	$1.35	$4.00	$8.00
G-425	Anthology edited by William Kozlenko - ***Acts Of Violence*** [1959] PBO. Cover art by Richard Powers.	$2.50	$7.50	$15.00
426	Scott, Bradford - ***The Range Terror*** [1959] PBO.	$1.50	$5.00	$10.00
G-427	Van Riper, Robert - ***A Really Sincere Guy*** [1959]	$1.35	$4.00	$8.00
G-428	Marshall, Rosamond - ***Celeste*** [1959] Photo cover.	$1.35	$4.00	$8.00
G-429	Holden, Larry - ***Crime Cop*** [1959] PBO. Cover art by Harry Schaare.	$1.50	$5.00	$10.00
G-430	Lowry, Robert James - ***That Kind Of Woman*** [1959] PBO. Movie tie-in with Sophia Loren & Tab Hunter. 8 pages of photos.	$2.50	$7.50	$15.00
G-431	Benchley, Nathaniel - ***One To Grow On*** [1959]	$1.50	$5.00	$10.00
G-432	Kane, Henry - ***Private Eyeful*** [1959] PBO. Cover art by Robert Maguire.	$2.50	$7.50	$15.00
R-433	Collier, Richard - ***10,000 Eyes*** [1959] Cover art by Hector Garrida.	$1.50	$5.00	$10.00
G-434	Anthology edited by Groff Conklin - ***4 For The Future*** [1959] PBO. Cover art by Richard Powers.	$2.00	$6.00	$12.00
435	Scott, Bradford - ***Texas Vengeance*** [1959]	$1.50	$5.00	$10.00
G-436	Hutchins, Maude - ***A Diary Of Love*** [1959]	$1.35	$4.00	$8.00
G-437	Falstein, Louis - ***Slaughter Street*** [1959] Cover art by Victor Kalin.	$1.50	$5.00	$10.00
G-438	Nathan, Robert - ***So Love Returns*** [1959] Photo cover.	$1.35	$4.00	$8.00
G-439	Brown, Wenzell - ***The Hoods Ride In*** [1959] PBO. Cover art by Harry Schaare.	$3.50	$10.00	$20.00
G-440	Wilhelm, Gale - ***No Nice Girl*** [1959] Cover art by James Bentley.	$2.50	$7.50	$15.00
G-441	York, Jeremy - ***Seeds Of Murder*** [1959] Cover art by Harry Schaare.	$2.00	$6.00	$12.00
442	Scott, Bradford - ***Gun Law*** [1959] PBO. Cover art by Hector Garrido.	$1.50	$5.00	$10.00
443	Bergman, Lee - ***Dark Violence*** [1959] Cover art by Lou Marchetti.	$2.00	$6.00	$12.00

		G	VG	F
G-444	Karney, Jack - ***Cut Me In*** [1959] PBO. Cover art by Darcy.	$2.00	$6.00	$12.00
G-445	Ronns, Edward - ***But Not For Me*** [1959] PBO. Cover by Robert Engle. Movie tie-in with Clark Gable.	$2.50	$7.50	$15.00
G-446	Saint Laurent, Cecil - ***The Magnificent Female*** [1959] Cover art by Robert McGinnis.	$2.00	$6.00	$12.00
R-447	Williams, Ben Ames - ***Leave Her To Heaven*** [1959] Cover art by Lou Marchetti.	$2.00	$6.00	$12.00
G-448	Keene, Day - ***Dead In Bed*** [1959] PBO. Cover art by Harry Schaare.	$3.50	$10.00	$20.00
G-449	Gorham, Charles - ***The Future Mister Dolan*** [1959] Cover art by Darcy.	$1.35	$4.00	$8.00
G-450	MacDonnell, J. E. - ***Enemy In Sight*** [1959] Cover art by Ray Sternbergh.	$1.35	$4.00	$8.00
G-451	MacDonald, William Colt - ***Guns Between Suns*** [1959]	$1.50	$5.00	$10.00
G-452	Kent, Nial - ***The Divided Path*** [1959]	$1.35	$4.00	$8.00
G-453	Fickling, G. G. - ***Girl On The Prowl*** [1959] PBO. Cover art by Robert McGinnis.	$2.50	$7.50	$15.00
G-454	Chamberlain, Anne - ***Possessed*** [1959] Cover art by Lou Marchetti.	$1.50	$5.00	$10.00
455	Scott, Bradford - ***Holster Law*** [1959] PBO. Cover art by Vic Prezio.	$1.50	$5.00	$10.00
456	Anderson, Edward - ***Hungry Men*** [1959] Cover art by Mort Kunstler.	$1.50	$5.00	$10.00
G-457	Ronns, Edward - ***The Big Bedroom*** [1959] PBO. Cover art by Gino Forte.	$1.50	$5.00	$10.00
G-458	Evans, E. Everett - ***Man Of Many Minds*** [1959] Cover by Kelly Freas.	$3.00	$9.00	$18.00
R-459	Coggins, Carolyn - ***Cookbook Of Fabulous Foods For People You Love*** [1959]	$1.35	$4.00	$8.00
G-460	Meloney, William Brown - ***Farm Girl*** [1959]	$2.50	$7.50	$15.00
G-461	Mayfield, Julian - ***The Long Night*** [1959] Cover art by Lou Marchetti.	$2.50	$7.50	$15.00
462	Lady Newborough, Denisa - ***Fire In My Blood*** [1959] Cover art by Robert Maguire.	$3.00	$9.00	$18.00
G-463	Ehrlich, Jack - ***Court Martial*** [1959] PBO. Cover art by Mort Kunstler.	$1.35	$4.00	$8.00
G-464	Roeburt, John - ***Tough Cop*** [1959] Cover art by Harry Schaare.	$1.50	$5.00	$10.00
G-465	Smith, James Woodruff - ***The Loner*** [1959]	$1.50	$5.00	$10.00
G-466	Roueche, Berton - ***Rooming House*** [1959]	$1.50	$5.00	$10.00
G-467	Crankshaw, Edward - ***Gestapo*** [1959]	$1.35	$4.00	$8.00
G-468	Lawrence, Gil - ***The Woman Racket*** [1959] PBO. Cover art by Tom Miller.	$2.00	$6.00	$12.00
G-469	Pinchot, Ann - ***Once More, With Feeling*** [1960] PBO. Cover art by Tom Miller. Movie tie-in with Yul Brynner.	$2.50	$7.50	$15.00
G-470	Daniels, M.D., Anna K. - ***It's Never Too Late To Love*** [1960] Photo cover.	$1.25	$3.75	$7.50
G-471	Lacy, Ed - ***Dead End*** [1960] Cover art by Darcy.	$2.00	$6.00	$12.00
R-472	Fisher, Vardis - ***The Golden Rooms*** [1960] Cover art by Robert Maguire.	$2.50	$7.50	$15.00
G-473	MacDonnell, J. E. - ***Frogman!*** [1960] Cover art by Mel Crair.	$1.50	$5.00	$10.00
G-474	Flora, Fletcher - ***Strange Sisters*** [1960] Cover art by Robert Maguire.	$2.50	$7.50	$15.00
G-475	Scott, Bradford - ***The Pecos Trail*** [1960]	$1.50	$5.00	$10.00
R-476	Plaidy, Jean - ***The King's Mistress*** [1960] Cover art by Paul Rader.	$2.00	$6.00	$12.00
G-477	Fisher, Vardis - ***The Wild Ones*** [1960]	$1.50	$5.00	$10.00
G-478	Gibson, Althea - ***I Always Wanted To Be Somebody*** [1960]	$1.50	$5.00	$10.00
G-479	Coleman, Lonnie - ***Sam*** [1960]	$1.50	$5.00	$10.00
480	House, O. T. - editor - ***Just Married*** [1960] Cartoon book.	$1.50	$5.00	$10.00
G-480	Godwin, Tom - ***Space Prison*** [1960] Cover by Robert Stanley.	$1.50	$5.00	$10.00

		G	VG	F
G-481	Nistler, Erwin N. & Broderick, Gerry P. - ***Roadside Night*** [1960] Cover art by Darcy.	$1.35	$4.00	$8.00
G-482	Gant, Matthew - ***The Last Notch*** [1960]	$1.50	$5.00	$10.00
G-483	McClintock, Marshall - editor - ***Women On The Wall*** [1960] Cover art by Julian Paul.	$1.50	$5.00	$10.00
G-484	Lacy, Ed - ***The Big Fix*** [1960]	$2.00	$6.00	$12.00
G-485	Anthology - ***The New Pyramid Book Of Crossword Puzzles*** [1960] PBO. Puzzle book.	$5.50	$17.50	$35.00
R-486	Howarth, David - ***D Day*** [1960] Photo cover.	$1.25	$3.75	$7.50
487	Holmes, David - ***Night Nurse*** [1960]	$1.00	$3.00	$6.00
G-488	Taylor, John - ***Shadows Of Shame*** [1960] Cover art by Tom Miller.	$1.50	$5.00	$10.00
G-489	Turner, Robert - ***The Night Is For Screaming*** [1960] PBO. Cover art by Robert Maguire.	$3.00	$9.00	$18.00
G-490	Peil, Paul - ***Commanche Crossing*** [1960]	$1.50	$5.00	$10.00
G-491	Milburn, George - ***Old John's Woman*** [1960]	$1.50	$5.00	$10.00
G-492	Scott, Bradford - ***Gun Gamble*** [1960]	$1.50	$5.00	$10.00
G-493	Holmes, David - ***Night Nurse*** [1960] Cover art by Robert Maguire.	$1.35	$4.00	$8.00
G-495	Miller, Wade - ***Jungle Heat*** [1960] Cover art by Harry Schaare.	$1.50	$5.00	$10.00
G-496	Hirsch, Phil - editor - ***Fighting Generals*** [1960] PBO. Cover by Mel Crair.	$1.25	$3.75	$7.50
G-497	Craigin, Elisabeth - ***Either Is Love*** [1960] Cover art by Tom Miller.	$2.00	$6.00	$12.00
G-498	Hogan, Ray - ***Raider's Revenge*** [1960] PBO. Cover art by Harry Schaare.	$1.35	$4.00	$8.00
G-499	Merril, Judith - ***Out of Bounds*** [1960] PBO.	$2.50	$7.50	$15.00
R-500	Payne, Robert - ***Gershwin*** [1960] PBO. Cover art by Victor Kalin. 8 pages of photos.	$1.50	$5.00	$10.00
G-501	Cavanaugh, James - ***The Big Gun*** [1960]	$1.35	$4.00	$8.00
G-502	Merril, Judith - ***The Tomorrow People*** [1960] PBO. Cover by Robert Schulz.	$2.50	$7.50	$15.00
G-503	Tzetnik, Ka - ***House Of Dolls*** [1960] Cover art by Dick Shelton.	$1.35	$4.00	$8.00
G-504	Margulies, Leo - editor (anthology) - ***Dames, Danger, Death*** [1960] PBO. Cover by Harry Schaare.	$2.00	$6.00	$12.00
G-505	Ernenwein, Leslie - ***The Faro Kid*** [1960] Cover art by John Leone.	$1.35	$4.00	$8.00
G-506	Connell, Vivian - ***The Love Lush*** [1960] Cover art by Robert McGinnis.	$1.50	$5.00	$10.00
G-507	Scott, Bradford - ***Lone Star Rider*** [1960] PBO. Cover art by Mort Kunstler.	$1.35	$4.00	$8.00
G-508	Cuthbert, Clifton - ***The Shame Of Mary Quinn*** [1960] Photo cover.	$1.25	$3.75	$7.50
G-509	Charbonneau, Louis - ***The Time Of Desire*** [1960] Cover art by Paul Rader.	$1.50	$5.00	$10.00
G-511	Campbell, Alexander - ***Flesh Of The Earth*** [1960] PBO. Cover art by Victor Kalin.	$1.50	$5.00	$10.00
G-512	Lehman, Paul Evan - ***Range Justice*** [1960] Cover art by Robert Stanley.	$1.35	$4.00	$8.00
G-513	Flora, Fletcher - ***The Brass Bed*** [1960] Cover art by Robert Maguire.	$2.50	$7.50	$15.00
G-514	Doyle, Sir Arthur Conan - ***The Lost World*** [1960] Cover by Tom Beecham. Movie tie-in.	$2.00	$6.00	$12.00
G-516	Avner - ***Memoirs Of An Assassin*** [1960] Cover art by George Elsenberg.	$1.50	$5.00	$10.00
G-517	Shay, Frank - ***Pirate Wench*** [1960]	$2.50	$7.50	$15.00
G-520	Fickling, G. G. - ***Kiss For A Killer*** [1960] PBO. Cover art by Robert Maguire.	$2.50	$7.50	$15.00
R-522	Fisher, Vardis - ***The Passion Within*** [1960] Cover art by Robert Maguire.	$2.50	$7.50	$15.00

		G	VG	F
G-523	Scott, Bradford - ***Ambush Trail*** [1960]	$1.35	$4.00	$8.00
G-524	Wall, Evans - ***Swamp Girl*** [1960] Cover art by Lou Marchetti.	$2.50	$7.50	$15.00
G-525	Whittington, Harry - ***Nita's Place*** [1960] PBO.	$4.00	$12.50	$25.00
G-526	Hutchins, Maude - ***The Hands Of Love*** [1960]	$1.25	$3.75	$7.50
R-527	Fisher, Vardis - ***Darkness And The Deep*** [1960] Cover art by Robert Schulz.	$1.50	$5.00	$10.00
G-528	Gigon, Fernand - ***The Bomb*** [1960] Photo cover.	$1.25	$3.75	$7.50
G-529	Keene, Day - ***Payola*** [1960] PBO. Cover art by Harry Schaare.	$3.50	$10.00	$20.00
G-530	De Camp, L. Sprague & Pratt, Fletcher - ***The Incomplete Enchanter*** [1960] Cover art by Richard Powers.	$2.00	$6.00	$12.00
G-531	Anthology edited by Lou Margulies - ***Gunpoint*** [1960] PBO. Cover art by John Leone.	$1.50	$5.00	$10.00
G-532	Albert, Marvin H. - ***The Long White Road*** [1960] Cover art by Mel Crair.	$1.35	$4.00	$8.00
G-534	Garth, John - ***Hill Man*** [1960] Cover art by Lou Marchetti.	$2.50	$7.50	$15.00
G-535	Leslie, Scott - ***The Texan*** [1960]	$1.35	$4.00	$8.00
R-536	Sanderson, James - ***Behind Enemy Lines*** [1960]	$1.25	$3.75	$7.50
R-537	Gunther, John - ***Death Be Not Proud*** [1960] Photo cover.	$1.35	$4.00	$8.00
G-538	Anderson, Alston - ***Lover Man*** [1960] Cover art by Tony Kokinos.	$1.50	$5.00	$10.00
G-539	Cody, Al - ***The Big Corral*** [1960] Cover art by Harry Schaare.	$1.35	$4.00	$8.00
G-540	Hogan, Ray - ***The Ghost Raider*** [1960] PBO. Cover art by Robert Stanley.	$1.35	$4.00	$8.00
R-541	Kuprin, Alexandre - ***Yama, The Pit*** [1960] Cover art by George Zeil.	$1.35	$4.00	$8.00
G-542	Scott, Bradford - ***Guns Of The Alamo*** [1960] PBO. Cover art by Robert Stanley.	$1.35	$4.00	$8.00
G-543	Young, Edward - ***Hospital Doctor*** [1960]	$1.00	$3.00	$6.00
G-544	Sturgeon, Theodore - ***Venus Plus X*** [1960] PBO. Cover art by Victor Kalin.	$2.00	$6.00	$12.00
G-545	Reyonlds, Quentin - ***70,000 To One*** [1960] Cover art by Robert Schulz.	$1.25	$3.75	$7.50
R-546	Fisher, Vardis - ***My Holy Satan*** [1960] Cover art by Victor Kalin.	$1.50	$5.00	$10.00
G-547	Katcha, Vahé - ***Fatal Journey*** [1960] Cover art by John Leone. Movie tie-in.	$2.00	$6.00	$12.00
G-548	Trinian, John - ***The Big Grab*** [1960] PBO. Cover art by Harry Schaare.	$1.50	$5.00	$10.00
G-549	Burns, Vincent G. - ***Female Convict*** [1960] Cover art by Robert Maguire.	$2.00	$6.00	$12.00
G-550	Edited by Phil Hirsch - ***The Death Dealers*** [1960] Photo cover.	$1.25	$3.75	$7.50
G-552	De Maupassant, Guy - ***A Woman's Life*** [1960]	$1.25	$3.75	$7.50
G-554	Clarke, Arthur C. - ***Against The Fall Of Night*** [1960] Cover art by Robert V. Engle.	$2.00	$6.00	$12.00
G-555	Cole, Jackson - ***Texas Fury*** [1960]	$1.35	$4.00	$8.00
R-556	Shaw, Arnold - ***Belafonte*** [1960] Photo cover. 8 pages of photos.	$1.50	$5.00	$10.00
G-557	Choisy, Maryse - ***A Month Among The Girls*** [1960] Photo cover.	$1.35	$4.00	$8.00
G-558	Eidelberg, M.D., Ludwig - ***Take Off Your Mask*** [1960] Photo cover.	$1.00	$3.00	$6.00
G-559	Litvinoff, Emanuel - ***The Lost Europeans*** [1960]	$1.25	$3.75	$7.50
G-560	Fickling, G. G. - ***Dig a Dead Doll*** [1960] PBO. Cover art by Robert Maguire.	$2.50	$7.50	$15.00
G-561	Fall, Thomas - ***The Hanging Judge*** [1960]	$1.35	$4.00	$8.00
G-562	Royer, Louis-Charles - ***French Doctor*** [1960] Cover art by Robert Maguire.	$1.35	$4.00	$8.00
G-563	Welles, Kermit - ***Blood On Boot Hill*** [1960] Cover art by John Leone.	$1.35	$4.00	$8.00
G-564	Plagemann, Bentz - ***The Sin Underneath*** [1960]	$1.35	$4.00	$8.00

		G	VG	F
G-565	Spingarn, Ed - ***Perfect 36*** [1960] Cover art by Robert Maguire.	$2.00	$6.00	$12.00
G-566	Roeburt, John - ***The Mobster*** [1960] PBO. Cover art by Harry Schaare.	$1.50	$5.00	$10.00
G-567	Oliver, Mark - ***The Wanton Boys*** [1960] Cover art by Tony Kokinos.	$1.35	$4.00	$8.00
G-568	Sparkia, Roy - ***Doctors And Lovers*** [1960] PBO. Cover art by Tom Miller.	$1.00	$3.00	$6.00
G-569	Kane, Henry - ***The Name Is Chambers*** [1960] Cover art by Harry Schaare.	$1.50	$5.00	$10.00
G-571	Daniels, Norman - ***Spy Hunt*** [1960] PBO. Cover art by Victor Kalin.	$1.35	$4.00	$8.00
G-573	Scott, Bradford - ***Valley Of Hunted Men*** [1960]	$1.25	$3.75	$7.50
G-575	Cole, Jackson - ***Texas Fists*** [1960]	$1.25	$3.75	$7.50
R-576	Marshall, Bruce - ***The World, The Flesh And Father Smith*** [1960] Cover art by Robert Maguire.	$1.35	$4.00	$8.00
G-577	Baum, Vicki - ***The Mustard Seed*** [1960]	$1.50	$5.00	$10.00
G-578	Whittington, Harry - ***Journey Into Violence*** [1961] PBO. Cover art by Lou Marchetti.	$4.00	$12.50	$25.00
G-579	Rohmer, Sax - ***The Insidious Dr. Fu Manchu*** [1961] Cover art by Mort Engle.	$2.50	$7.50	$15.00
G-580	De Mejo, Oscar - ***Diary Of A Nun*** [1961] Cover art by Paul Liberorsky.	$1.25	$3.75	$7.50
G-581	Echols, Allan - ***The Stranger From Texas*** [1961]	$1.25	$3.75	$7.50
G-584	Wilde, Oscar - ***The Picture Of Dorian Gray*** [1961]	$1.35	$4.00	$8.00
G-585	Cole, Jackson - ***The Death Riders*** [1961]	$1.25	$3.75	$7.50
R-586	Collins, Wilkie - ***The Moonstone*** [1961] Cover by Gerald Powell.	$1.35	$4.00	$8.00
R-587	Manvell, Roger & Fraenkel, Heinrich - ***Dr. Goebbels*** [1961] Photo cover.	$1.00	$3.00	$6.00
R-588	Stout, Rex - ***How Like A God*** [1961] Cover art by Robert Maguire.	$2.50	$7.50	$15.00
G-590	Margulies, Leo - editor (anthology) - ***The Unexpected*** [1961] PBO. Cover by John Schoenherr.	$2.00	$6.00	$12.00
G-591	Scott, Bradford - ***Gunsmoke On The Rio Grande*** [1961] PBO. Cover art by Robert Stanley.	$1.25	$3.75	$7.50
G-592	Anthology edited by Chandler Brossard - ***The First Time*** [1961]	$1.35	$4.00	$8.00
G-593	Taylor, Daniel - ***All His Women*** [1961]	$1.25	$3.75	$7.50
G-594	Cole, Jackson - ***Border Hell*** [1961]	$1.25	$3.75	$7.50
G-595	Hope, Anthony - ***The Prisoner Of Zenda*** [1961]	$1.25	$3.75	$7.50
G-596	Lewis, Sinclair - ***World So Wide*** [1961] Cover art by Tom Miller.	$1.00	$3.00	$6.00
R-597	Fisher, Vardis - ***The Valley Of Vision*** [1961] Cover art by Victor Kalin.	$2.00	$6.00	$12.00
G-598	Anthology edited by Phil Hirsch - ***Medical Nightmares*** [1961] PBO. Photo cover.	$1.35	$4.00	$8.00
R-599	Voynich, Ethel L. - ***The Gadfly*** [1961] Cover art by Charles Egri.	$1.25	$3.75	$7.50
G-600	Whittington, Harry - ***Guerrilla Girls*** [1961] PBO. Cover art by Al Brule.	$5.00	$15.00	$30.00
G-602	Scott, Bradford - ***Rangers At Bay*** [1961] PBO. Cover art by Robert Stanley.	$1.25	$3.75	$7.50
G-604	Cole, Jackson - ***Texas Manhunt*** [1961] Cover art by Clarence Doore.	$1.25	$3.75	$7.50
G-605	Anthology edited by Ray Robinson - ***Baseball Stars 1961*** [1961] PBO. Photo cover. 8 pages of photos.	$4.00	$12.50	$25.00
R-606	Hughes, Langston - editor - ***An African Treasury*** [1961] Photo cover.	$1.50	$5.00	$10.00
R-607	Eidelberg, M.D., Ludwig - ***The Dark Urge*** [1961] PBO. Photo cover.	$1.00	$3.00	$6.00

		G	VG	F
G-609	Brown, Wenzell - ***Prison Girl*** [1961] Cover art by Robert Maguire.	$2.50	$7.50	$15.00
G-610	Scott, Bradford - ***Smugglers' Brand*** [1961] PBO. Cover art by Robert Stanley.	$1.25	$3.75	$7.50
G-611	Cole, Jackson - ***Trigger Law*** [1961] Cover art by John Leone.	$1.25	$3.75	$7.50
R-612	Hunter, Edward - ***Brainwashing*** [1961] Cover art by Mel Crair.	$1.25	$3.75	$7.50
R-613	Sabatini, Rafael - ***Captain Blood*** [1961] Cover art by Harry Schaare.	$2.00	$6.00	$12.00
R-614	Anthology - ***Quintet*** [1961]	$1.25	$3.75	$7.50
G-615	Anderson, Poul - ***Orbit Unlimited*** [1961] PBO. Cover art by John Schoenherr	$2.00	$6.00	$12.00
R-616	Brome, Vincent - ***The Spy*** [1961]	$1.25	$3.75	$7.50
G-617	Clifton, Bud - ***The Bad Girls*** [1961] Photo cover.	$1.35	$4.00	$8.00
R-620	Carpozi, Jr., George - ***Clark Gable*** [1961] PBO. Photo cover. 32 pages of photos.	$2.00	$6.00	$12.00
R-621	Petry, Ann - ***The Street*** [1961]	$1.35	$4.00	$8.00
G-622	Sturgeon, Theodore - ***Voyage To The Bottom Of The Sea*** [1961] PBO. Cover art by Jim Mitchell. Movie tie-in.	$3.50	$10.00	$20.00
G-623	Fickling, G. G. - ***Blood And Honey*** [1961] PBO. Cover art by Robert Maguire.	$2.50	$7.50	$15.00
G-624	Tabori, Paul - ***The Green Rain*** [1961] PBO. Cover by John Schoenherr.	$2.50	$7.50	$15.00
R-628	Fisher, Vardis - ***The Divine Passion*** [1961]	$1.25	$3.75	$7.50
R-629	Fisher, Vardis - ***The Island Of The Innocent*** [1961] Cover art by Gino Forte.	$1.25	$3.75	$7.50
R-630	Smith, Thorne - ***The Night Life Of The Gods*** [1961]	$1.25	$3.75	$7.50
R-631	Vialar, Paul - ***Five Soldiers*** [1961]	$1.00	$3.00	$6.00
R-632	Crankshaw, Edward - ***Gestapo*** [1961] Cover art by Harry Schaare.	$1.25	$3.75	$7.50
R-633	Cloete, Stuart - ***The Curve And The Tusk*** [1961] Cover art by Dick Kohfield.	$1.25	$3.75	$7.50
G-634	Harvey, Gene - ***Doctor's Nurse*** [1961] Cover art by Lester Krauss.	$ .75	$2.50	$5.00
R-635	Anthology edited by Vernon Shea - ***Strange Barriers*** [1961]	$1.25	$3.75	$7.50
G-636	Sturgeon, Theodore - ***The Synthetic Man*** [1961] Cover art by Lester Krauss.	$1.50	$5.00	$10.00
G-637	Scott, Bradford - ***Skeleton Trail*** [1961]	$1.25	$3.75	$7.50
G-638	Cole, Jackson - ***Massacre Canyon*** [1961] Cover art by Clarence Doore.	$1.25	$3.75	$7.50
R-639	Fulop-Miller, Rene - ***The Silver Bacchanal*** [1961]	$1.00	$3.00	$6.00
R-640	Grider, George & Sims, Lydel - ***War Fish*** [1961]	$1.00	$3.00	$6.00
G-641	Rohmer, Sax - ***The Return Of Dr. Fu-Manchu*** [1961] Cover art by Dick Kohfield.	$2.00	$6.00	$12.00
G-642	Heinlein, Robert A. - ***6 X H (6 Stories By Heinlein)*** [1961] Cover art by Robert J. Engle.	$1.50	$5.00	$10.00
G-643	Gardner, Jeffrey - ***Barbary Devil*** [1961] PBO. Cover art by Ray Johnson.	$2.50	$7.50	$15.00
G-644	Collans, Dev (with Stewart Sterling) - ***I Was A House Detective*** [1961] Photo cover.	$1.25	$3.75	$7.50
G-645	Coburn, Walt - ***Border Jumper*** [1961]	$1.25	$3.75	$7.50
R-646	London, Jack - ***South Sea Tales*** [1961]	$1.35	$4.00	$8.00
R-647	Gordon, Gerald - ***Dark Brother*** [1961]	$1.25	$3.75	$7.50
R-649	Fabricant, M.D., Noah D. - ***13 Famous Patients*** [1961] Photo cover.	$1.00	$3.00	$6.00
R-650	Zola, Emile - ***Lesson In Love*** [1961]	$1.25	$3.75	$7.50
G-651	McGovern, James - ***The Berlin Couriers*** [1961] Cover art by William Rose.	$1.25	$3.75	$7.50
R-652	Treat, Roger - ***The Endless Road*** [1961] Photo cover.	$1.25	$3.75	$7.50
G-653	Turner, John - ***Starlet!*** [1961] PBO. Photo cover.	$1.25	$3.75	$7.50

Pyramid, F-680

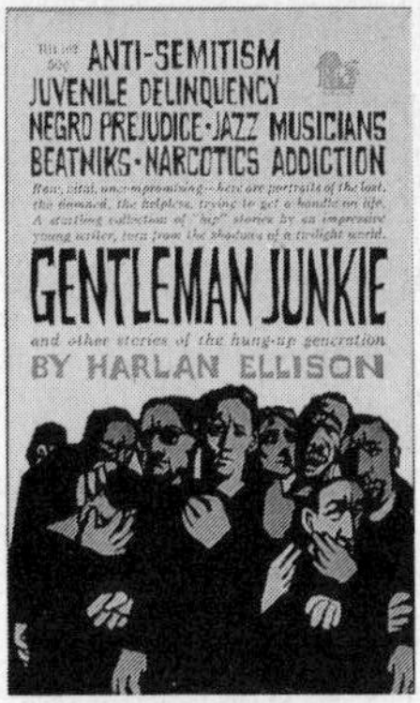

Regency, RB-102

Regency, RB-322

		G	VG	F
G-654	Collins, Hunt - ***Tomorrow And Tomorrow*** [1961] Cover art by James Mitchell.	$1.35	$4.00	$8.00
G-655	Smith, James Woodruff - ***To Still The Guns*** [1961]	$1.25	$3.75	$7.50
R-657	Fisher, Vardis - ***Intimations Of Eve*** [1961] Cover art by Jack Thurston.	$1.35	$4.00	$8.00
G-658	Gallun, Raymond Z. - ***The Planet Strappers*** [1961] PBO. Cover art by John Schoenherr.	$2.00	$6.00	$12.00
X-659	Alain - ***Yoga For Perfect Health*** [1961] Photo cover. 8 pages of photos.	$1.00	$3.00	$6.00
R-660	Rankin, William H. - ***The Man Who Rode The Thunder*** [1961] Cover art by Stephgn Haas.	$1.25	$3.75	$7.50
R-661	Hardy, Lindsay - ***The Grand Duke And Mr. Pimm*** [1961] Cover art by Leon Gregori.	$1.25	$3.75	$7.50
G-662	Anthology edited by Phil Hirsch - ***Fighting eagles*** [1961]	$1.25	$3.75	$7.50
G-663	Davis, Jr., Col. Franklin M. - ***Kiss The Tiger*** [1961] PBO. Cover art by Tom Miller.	$1.25	$3.75	$7.50
K-664	Trumbull, Robert - ***The Raft*** [1961] Cover art by Harry Schaare.	$1.25	$3.75	$7.50
G-665	Margulies, Leo - editor - ***The Ghoul Keepers*** [1961] PBO. Cover art by John Schoenherr.	$2.50	$7.50	$15.00
G-666	Cole, Jackson - ***Gunsmoke Trail*** [1961]	$1.25	$3.75	$7.50
R-668	Middleton, Drew - ***The Sky Suspended*** [1961]	$1.25	$3.75	$7.50
F-669	Fairbank, Walton - ***Houseboy*** [1961] Cover art by Tony Kokinos.	$1.25	$3.75	$7.50
F-670	Sparkia, Roy - ***Doctors And Sinners*** [1961] PBO. Cover art by Gino Forte.	$1.25	$3.75	$7.50
G-671	Rice, Craig - ***The Name Is Malone*** [1961]	$1.35	$4.00	$8.00
F-672	Harrison, Harry - ***The Stainless Steel Rat*** [1961] PBO. Cover art by John Schoenherr.	$3.00	$9.00	$18.00
F-673	Sturgeon, Theodore - ***A Way Home*** [1961] Cover art by Robert Engle.	$1.35	$4.00	$8.00
G-674	Scott, Bradford - ***Rangeland Guns*** [1961] PBO. Cover art by Robert Stanley.	$1.25	$3.75	$7.50
F-675	Mokray, William G. - ***Basketball Stars Of 1962*** [1961] PBO. Photo cover. 8 pages of photos.	$1.50	$5.00	$10.00
R-677	Fisher, Vardis - ***Adam And The Serpent*** [1961] Cover art by Jack Thurston.	$1.35	$4.00	$8.00
F-678	Cooper, Brian - ***The Van Langeren Girl*** [1961] Cover art by Dick Kohfield.	$1.25	$3.75	$7.50
F-679	Wiesel, Elie - ***Night*** [1961]	$1.25	$3.75	$7.50

		G	VG	F
F-680	Whittington, Harry - ***The Young Nurses*** [1961] PBO. Cover art by Rudy Nappi.	$2.50	$7.50	$15.00
F-682	Dickson, Gordon R. - ***Naked To The Stars*** [1961] PBO. Cover art by Ed Emsh.	$2.00	$6.00	$12.00
F-683	Merril, Judith - editor - ***Off The Beaten Orbit*** [1961] Cover art by John Schoenherr.	$1.25	$3.75	$7.50
G-684	Scott, Bradford - ***The Desert Killers*** [1961] PBO. Cover art by Jerome Podwil.	$1.25	$3.75	$7.50
R-685	Payne, Robert - ***Lawrence Of Arabia*** [1961]	$1.35	$4.00	$8.00
R-686	Choisy, Maryse - ***A Month Among The Men*** [1962] Cover art by Walter Ferro.	$1.25	$3.75	$7.50
F-688	Rohmer, Sax - ***The Hand Of Fu-Manchu*** [1962] Cover art by Rudy Nappi.	$2.00	$6.00	$12.00
F-689	Crane, Robert - ***Born Of Battle*** [1962] PBO. Cover art by Robert Abbett.	$1.25	$3.75	$7.50
F-691	Flora, Fletcher - ***Whisper Of Love*** [1962] Photo cover.	$1.35	$4.00	$8.00
F-692	Ronns, Edward - ***The Glass Cage*** [1962] PBO. Cover art by Robert Abbett.	$1.50	$5.00	$10.00
F-693	Budrys, Algis - ***The Falling Torch*** [1962] Cover by John Schoenherr.	$1.35	$4.00	$8.00
G-694	Ernenwein, Leslie - ***Boss Of Panamint*** [1962] Cover art by Carl Hantman.	$1.25	$3.75	$7.50
N-695	Statler, Oliver - ***Japanese Inn*** [1962] Cover art by Hiroshige.	$1.25	$3.75	$7.50
X-696	Fisher, Vardis - ***The Golden Rooms*** [1962]	$1.25	$3.75	$7.50
R-697	Blond, Georges - ***The Death Of Hitler's Germany*** [1962] Photo cover.	$1.00	$3.00	$6.00
F-698	Hamilton, Edmond - ***The Haunted Stars*** [1962] Cover art by V. Kandinsky.	$1.35	$4.00	$8.00
F-700	Anthology edited by Phil Hirsch - ***Men Behind Bars*** [1962]	$1.35	$4.00	$8.00
F-701	Martin, Kay - ***Cry Shame!*** [1962] PBO. Cover art by Tony Kokinos.	$1.50	$5.00	$10.00
G-702	Boltinoff, Henry - editor - ***Sex Is Better In College*** [1962] Cartoon book.	$1.25	$3.75	$7.50
F-703	Cogswell, Theodore R. - ***The Wall Around The World*** [1962] PBO. Cover by John Schoenherr.	$1.50	$5.00	$10.00
G-704	Scott, Bradford - ***The Masked Riders*** [1962] PBO. Cover by Carl Hantman.	$1.25	$3.75	$7.50
X-705	Fisher, Vardis - ***A Goat For Azazel*** [1962] Cover art by Gino Forte.	$1.35	$4.00	$8.00
X-707	Maltz, Albert - ***The Cross And The Arrow*** [1962]	$1.25	$3.75	$7.50
F-709	Lacy, Ed - ***Room To Swing*** [1962] Cover art by Ben Wohlberg.	$1.50	$5.00	$10.00
F-710	Robinson, Ray - editor - ***Baseball Stars Of 1962*** [1962] PBO. Photo cover. 8 pages of photos.	$3.50	$10.00	$20.00
F-712	Trinian, John - ***House Of Evil*** [1962]	$1.25	$3.75	$7.50
F-713	Doyle, Sir Arthur Conan - ***The Lost World*** [1962]	$1.35	$4.00	$8.00
G-714	Scott, Bradford - ***Guns Of Bangtown*** [1962]	$1.25	$3.75	$7.50
X-716	Fisher, Vardis - ***Jesus Came Again*** [1962] Cover art by Jack Thurston.	$1.35	$4.00	$8.00
F-719	Kane, Henry - ***Private Eyeful*** [1962] Cover art by Morte Engle.	$1.35	$4.00	$8.00
F-720	Masur, Harold, Q. - ***The Name Is Jordan*** [1962] PBO. Cover art by Ron Lesser.	$2.00	$6.00	$12.00
F-721	Anthology edited by Phil Hirsch - ***Something For The Boys-Girls*** [1962] Cartoon book.	$1.25	$3.75	$7.50
F-722	De Camp, L. Spague & Pratt, Fletcher - ***The Castle Of Iron*** [1962] Cover art by Ed Emsh.	$1.35	$4.00	$8.00
F-723	De Camp, L. Spague & Pratt, Fletcher - ***The Incomplete Enchanter*** [1962] Cover art by Ed Emsh.	$1.25	$3.75	$7.50
G-724	Smith, James Woodruff - ***Killer Colt*** [1962]	$1.25	$3.75	$7.50
R-725	Douglas, William O. - ***The Right Of The People*** [1962] Photo cover.	$1.00	$3.00	$6.00

		G	VG	F
R-726	Howarth, David - ***D Day, The Sixth Of June, 1944*** [1962]	$1.00	$3.00	$6.00
X-727	Hirsch, M.D., Edwin W. - ***The Power To Love*** [1962]	$ .75	$2.50	$5.00
R-728	Smith, Thorne - ***Topper Takes A Trip*** [1962] Cover art by Herbert Roese.	$1.25	$3.75	$7.50
F-729	Burnham, Creighton Brown - ***Born Innocent*** [1962] Cover art by Robert Maguire.	$1.25	$3.75	$7.50
F-731	Sorkin, Bernard - ***Steel Shivs*** [1962] PBO. Photo cover.	$2.50	$7.50	$15.00
F-732	Sturgeon, Theodore - ***Venus Plus X*** [1962] Cover art by John Schoenherr.	$1.25	$3.75	$7.50
F-733	Anthology edited by Groff Conklin - ***Worlds Of When*** [1962] PBO. Cover art by John Schoenherr.	$2.00	$6.00	$12.00
G-734	Scott, Bradford - ***Texas Rider*** [1962]	$1.25	$3.75	$7.50
F-735	Anthology edited by Phil Hirsch - ***Business With Pleasure*** [1962] PBO. Cartoon book. Cover by John Huehnergarth.	$1.25	$3.75	$7.50
R-736	Willson, Meredith - ***The Music Man*** [1962] PBO. Photo cover. Movie tie-in.	$1.25	$3.75	$7.50
R-737	Olsen, Jack - ***The Mad World Of Bridge*** [1962] Cover art by Robert Day.	$1.00	$3.00	$6.00
R-738	Fisher, Vardis - ***Darkness And The Deep*** [1962]	$1.35	$4.00	$8.00
F-739	Thompson, Jim - ***A Hell Of A Woman*** [1962] Cover art by Mort Engel.	$5.00	$15.00	$30.00
F-740	Rohmer, Sax - ***The Mask Of Fu Manchu*** [1962] Cover art by Ronnie Lesser.	$1.25	$3.75	$7.50
F-741	Ehle, John - ***The Survivor*** [1962]	$1.25	$3.75	$7.50
F-742	Long, Frank Belknap - ***Mars Is My Destination*** [1962] PBO. Cover art by John Schoenherr.	$2.00	$6.00	$12.00
F-743	Conklin, Groff - editor - ***4 For The Future*** [1962] Cover art by John Schoenherr.	$1.25	$3.75	$7.50
F-744	St. Laurent, Cecil - ***The Magnificent Female*** [1962]	$1.25	$3.75	$7.50
G-745	Scott, Bradford - ***Doom Trail*** [1962]	$1.25	$3.75	$7.50
T-746	Fisher, Vardis - ***For Passion, For Heaven*** [1962] Cover art by Jack Thurston.	$1.35	$4.00	$8.00
F-747	Reynolds, Quentin - ***Officially Dead*** [1962]	$1.25	$3.75	$7.50
F-748	Hirsch, Phil - editor - ***The Kennedy War Heroes*** [1962] PBO.	$1.25	$3.75	$7.50
F-749	House, O. T. - editor - ***Just Married*** [1962] Cover art by Henry Boltinoff. Cartoon book.	$1.25	$3.75	$7.50
E-750	Martin, Kay - ***The Divorcees*** [1962]	$1.25	$3.75	$7.50
F-751	Heller, Larry - ***Body Of The Crime*** [1962] PBO. Cover art by Ben Wohlberg.	$1.50	$5.00	$10.00
F-752	Royer, Louis-Charles - ***The Flesh*** [1962]	$1.25	$3.75	$7.50
F-753	Fox, Gardner - ***Five Weeks In a Balloon*** [1962] PBO. Movie tie-in.	$1.35	$4.00	$8.00
F-754	Clarke, Arthur C. - ***Against The Fall Of Night*** [1962]	$1.25	$3.75	$7.50
G-755	Richmond, Roe - ***The Hard Men*** [1962]	$1.25	$3.75	$7.50
T-756	Fisher, Vardis - ***The Great Confession*** [1962] Cover art by Jack Thurston.	$1.35	$4.00	$8.00
X-757	Roth, Cecil - ***The Magnificent Rothschilds*** [1962]	$1.25	$3.75	$7.50
R-759	Hunter, Edward - ***Brainwashing*** [1962] Cover art by Mel Crair.	$1.00	$3.00	$6.00
F-760	Tupper, Bob - ***Calling Dr. Dare-Kill*** [1962] PBO. Cartoon book. Cover by Bob Tupper.	$1.50	$5.00	$10.00
F-761	Rohmer, Sax - ***The Bride Of Fu Manchu*** [1962] Cover art by Ronnie Lesser.	$1.35	$4.00	$8.00
R-762	Hunt, Morton, M. - ***Mental Hospital*** [1962]	$1.00	$3.00	$6.00
F-763	McLaughlin, Dean - ***Dome World*** [1962] PBO. Cover art by Ed Emsh.	$1.50	$5.00	$10.00
F-764	Smith, Edward E - ***The Skylark Of Space*** [1962] Cover art by Richard Powers.	$1.25	$3.75	$7.50
G-765	Scott, Bradford - ***Texas Devil*** [1962]	$1.25	$3.75	$7.50
N-766	Gunther, John - ***Inside Russia Today*** [1962]	$1.00	$3.00	$6.00

		G	VG	F
R-767	Curtis, Charlotte - ***First Lady*** [1962] PBO. Cover art by Bob Engle. 16 pages of photos. (Jacqueline Kennedy).	$1.25	$3.75	$7.50
F-770	Davis, Jr., Franklin M. - ***Secret: Hong Kong*** [1962] PBO. Cover art by Mort Engle.	$1.25	$3.75	$7.50
F-771	Harrison, Harry - ***War With The Robots*** [1962] PBO. Cover art by John Schoenherr.	$2.00	$6.00	$12.00
R-772	Nathan, Robert - ***So Love Returns*** [1962] Cover art by George Salter.	$1.00	$3.00	$6.00
G-773	Scott, Bradford - ***Death Rides The Rio Grande*** [1962] PBO. Cover art by Carl Hantman.	$1.25	$3.75	$7.50
F-774	Godwin, Tom - ***Space Prison*** [1962]	$2.50	$7.50	$15.00
X-776	Smith, Susy - ***ESP*** [1967] Cover art by Chibbaro.	$1.25	$3.75	$7.50
X-777	Fisher, Vardis - ***Peace Like A River*** [1962]	$1.35	$4.00	$8.00
R-779	Soya, Carl Erik - ***The Rites Of Spring*** [1962] Cover art by Robert Abbett.	$1.00	$3.00	$6.00
F-780	Hirsch, Phil - editor - ***Open Your Mouth And Say Ha!*** [1962] PBO. Cartoon book.	$1.25	$3.75	$7.50
R-781	Schellenberg, Walter - ***Hitler's Secret Service*** [1962]	$1.00	$3.00	$6.00
F-782	Hutchins, Maude - ***The Hands Of Love*** [1962] Cover art by Tom Miller.	$ .75	$2.50	$5.00
F-783	Phillips, Mark - ***Brain Twister*** [1961] PBO. Cover art by John Schoenherr.	$1.50	$5.00	$10.00
F-784	Asimov, Isaac - ***The Caves Of Steel*** [1962] Cover art by Ralph Brillhart.	$1.35	$4.00	$8.00
F-786	Clement, Hal - ***Mission Of Gravity*** [1962] Cover art by Ed Emsh.	$1.35	$4.00	$8.00
R-787	Gardner, Jeffrey K. - ***Cleopatra*** [1962]	$1.25	$3.75	$7.50
R-788	Renault, Mary - ***Return To Night*** [1962]	$1.00	$3.00	$6.00
R-789	Dudman, Richard - ***Men Of The Far Right*** [1962] PBO.	$1.25	$3.75	$7.50
F-790	Cornell, Evelyn - ***The Naked Flame*** [1962] PBO. Cover art by Mort Engel.	$1.25	$3.75	$7.50
R-791	Warshofsky, Fred - ***War Under The Waves*** [1962] PBO. Photo cover.	$1.00	$3.00	$6.00
F-792	Holmes, David - ***Night Nurse*** [1962] Cover art by Robert Maguire.	$ .75	$2.50	$5.00
F-793	Hutchins, Maude - ***A Diary Of Love*** [1962] Cover art by Ronnie Lesser.	$ .75	$2.50	$5.00
F-794	Fyfe, H. B. - ***D-99*** [1962] PBO. Cover art by Ralph Brillhart.	$1.50	$5.00	$10.00
F-795	Anthology edited by Leo Margulies - ***The Unexpected*** [1962]	$1.35	$4.00	$8.00
G-796	Scott, Bradford - ***Gunsight Showdown*** [1962]	$1.25	$3.75	$7.50
R-798	Franken, Rose - ***Claudia*** [1968] Cover art by Robert Abbett.	$1.25	$3.75	$7.50
R-800	Joswick & Keating - ***Combat Cameraman*** [1962] 8 pages of photos.	$1.00	$3.00	$6.00
F-802	Lawrence, Gil - ***Fury With Legs*** [1962]	$1.25	$3.75	$7.50
R-803	Conrad, Earl - ***Crane Eden*** [1962]	$1.25	$3.75	$7.50
F-804	Rohmer, Sax - ***The Drums Of Fu Manchu*** [1962] Cover art by Herb Tauss.	$1.35	$4.00	$8.00
F-805	Moore, Ward & Davidson, Avram - ***Joyleg*** [1962] PBO. Cover art by Ed Emsh.	$2.00	$6.00	$12.00
F-806	Merril, Judith - ***The Tomorrow People*** [1962] Cover art by John Schoenherr.	$1.35	$4.00	$8.00
G-807	Scott, Bradford - ***Trail Of Blood And Bones*** [1962] PBO. Cover by Jerome Podwil.	$1.25	$3.75	$7.50
F-809	Wall, Evans - ***Swamp Girl*** [1962] Cover art by Tony Kokinos.	$1.35	$4.00	$8.00
T-810	Caldwell, Taylor - ***The Turbulls*** [1962]	$1.25	$3.75	$7.50
T-811	Caldwell, Taylor - ***The Eagles Gather*** [1963] Cover art by Charles Binger.	$1.25	$3.75	$7.50
F-812	Peel, Norman Lemon - ***The Power Of Positive Drinking*** [1962] Cartoon book.	$1.25	$3.75	$7.50

		G	VG	F
F-817	De Camp, L. Sprague - ***Lest Darkness Fall*** [1963] Cover art by Ed Emsh.	$1.35	$4.00	$8.00
F-818	Anderson, Poul - ***Orbit Unlimited*** [1963] Cover art by John Schoenherr.	$1.35	$4.00	$8.00
G-819	Scott, Bradford - ***Outlaw Gold*** [1963]	$1.25	$3.75	$7.50
G-820	Lehman, Paul Evan - ***The Young Texan*** [1963]	$1.25	$3.75	$7.50
R-822	Stout, Rex - ***Not Quite Dead Enough*** [1963]	$1.25	$3.75	$7.50
R-823	Seeley, Mabel - ***The Crying Sisters*** [1963]	$1.25	$3.75	$7.50
R-824	The Lockridges - ***The Long Skeleton*** [1963]	$1.25	$3.75	$7.50
R-825	Simenon, Georges - ***Madame Maigret's Own Case*** [1963]	$1.25	$3.75	$7.50
R-826	Rogers, Dale Evans - ***Angel Unaware*** [1968] Photo cover.	$1.00	$3.00	$6.00
R-827	Leveridge, Ralph - ***The Last Combat*** [1963]	$1.00	$3.00	$6.00
F-829	Brunner, John - ***The Dreaming Earth*** [1963] PBO. Cover art by John Schoenherr.	$1.50	$5.00	$10.00
F-830	Merril, Judith - ***Out Of Bounds*** [1963] Cover art by John Schoenherr.	$1.35	$4.00	$8.00
X-832	Fisher, Vardis - ***My Holy Satan*** [1963]	$1.25	$3.75	$7.50
T-833	Ludwig, Emil - ***The Nile*** [1963]	$1.00	$3.00	$6.00
T-834	Caldwell, Taylor - ***The Strong City*** [1963]	$1.25	$3.75	$7.50
X-835	Fisher, Vardis - ***The Valley Of Vision*** [1963] Cover art by Jack Thurston.	$1.25	$3.75	$7.50
N-836	Nizer, Louis - ***My Life In Court*** [1963]	$1.00	$3.00	$6.00
F-837	Rohmer, Sax - ***Shadow Of Fu Manchu*** [1963] Cover art by Jerry Podwil.	$1.35	$4.00	$8.00
R-838	Payne, Robert - ***Lawrence Of Arabia*** [1963]	$1.50	$5.00	$10.00
F-839	Bloch, Robert - ***Bogey Men*** [1963] PBO. Cover art by John Schoenherr.	$2.50	$7.50	$15.00
F-840	Janifer, Lawrence M. - ***Slave Planet*** [1963] PBO. Cover art by Jack Gaughan.	$2.50	$7.50	$15.00
F-841	Craigin, Elisabeth - ***Either Is Love*** [1963] Cover art by Tom Miller.	$1.35	$4.00	$8.00
F-843	Manners, Dorine - ***Sin Street*** [1963] Photo cover.	$ .75	$2.50	$5.00
F-844	Fredericks, Dean - ***John Dillinger*** [1963] PBO.	$1.35	$4.00	$8.00
X-845	Fisher, Vardis - ***The Divine Passion*** [1963] Cover art by Jack Thurston.	$1.25	$3.75	$7.50
R-846	Pratt, Theodore - ***The White God*** [1963] PBO. Cover art by James Meese.	$1.25	$3.75	$7.50
R-847	Coles, Manning - ***Night Train To Paris*** [1963]	$1.25	$3.75	$7.50
X-848	Hobard, Alice Tisdale - ***Oil For The Lamps Of China*** [1963] Cover by Robert Abbett.	$1.00	$3.00	$6.00
F-849	Anthology edited by Phil Hirsch - ***One Against The Enemy*** [1963] PBO.	$1.00	$3.00	$6.00
F-850	Scott, L. K. - ***Backstairs*** [1963] Cover art by Jerome Podwil.	$1.25	$3.75	$7.50
R-851	Anthology edited by D. R. Bensen - ***The Unknown*** [1963] PBO. Cover art by John Schoenherr.	$1.25	$3.75	$7.50
F-852	Anthology edited by Martin Greenberg - ***Men Against The Stars*** [1963] Cover art by Mel Hunter.	$1.25	$3.75	$7.50
G-854	Scott, Bradford - ***Gun Justice*** [1963] PBO. Cover art by Mel Crair.	$1.25	$3.75	$7.50
R-855	Wellman, Paul I. - ***Death On The Prairie*** [1963] 8 pages of photos.	$1.25	$3.75	$7.50
R-856	Schweitzer, Albert - ***The Primeval Forest*** [1963] Photo cover.	$1.00	$3.00	$6.00
F-858	Rohmer, Sax - ***The Island Of Fu Manchu*** [1963]	$1.35	$4.00	$8.00
F-859	Heinlein, Robert A. - ***Waldo And Magic, Inc.*** [1963] Cover art by Jack Gaughan.	$1.50	$5.00	$10.00
F-861	Anthology edited by Phil Hirsch. - ***By The She*** [1963] PBO. Cover by Bill Wenzel. Cartoon book.	$1.00	$3.00	$6.00
F-862	Russell, Eric Frank - ***The Great Explosion*** [1963] Cover art by Ed Emsh.	$1.35	$4.00	$8.00
F-866	Ellison, Harlan - ***Rumble*** [1963] Cover art by Earl E. Mayan.	$5.00	$15.00	$30.00

		G	VG	F
R-867	Wellman, Paul I. - ***Death In The Desert*** [1963] 8 pages of photos.	$1.25	$3.75	$7.50
R-869	Fisher, Vardis - ***The Wild Ones*** [1963]	$1.25	$3.75	$7.50
R-870	Stout, Rex - ***How Like A God*** [1963]	$1.25	$3.75	$7.50
R-871	Smith, Susy - ***World Of The Strange*** [1963] PBO. Cover by Thomas H. Chibbaro.	$1.00	$3.00	$6.00
R-872	Marric, J. J. (John Creasey) - ***Gideon's Night*** [1963]	$1.25	$3.75	$7.50
R-873	Marquand, John P. - ***Ming Yellow*** [1963]	$1.25	$3.75	$7.50
F-874	des Cars, Guy - ***The Damned One*** [1963] Cover by George Ziel.	$ .75	$2.50	$5.00
F-875	Phillips, Mark - ***The Impossibles*** [1963] PBO. Cover art by John Scheonherr.	$1.35	$4.00	$8.00
T-878	Caldwell, Taylor - ***The Balance Wheel*** [1963]	$1.25	$3.75	$7.50
T-879	Caldwell, Taylor - ***Melissa*** [1963]	$1.25	$3.75	$7.50
X-880	Nizer, Louis - ***Thinking On Your Feet*** [1963]	$1.00	$3.00	$6.00
R-881	Maugham, W. Somerset - ***Husbands And Wives*** [1963]	$1.00	$3.00	$6.00
R-883	Fisher, Vardis - ***Intimations Of Eve*** [1963] Cover by Jack Thurston.	$1.25	$3.75	$7.50
R-884	The Lockridges - ***The Long Skeleton*** [1963]	$1.25	$3.75	$7.50
F-885	Roeburt, John - ***Al Capone*** [1963]	$1.25	$3.75	$7.50
F-886	Reynolds, Mack - ***The Earth War*** [1963] PBO. Cover art by John Schoenherr.	$1.35	$4.00	$8.00
F-887	Marino, Nick - ***City Limits*** [1963] Cover art by Ronnie Lesser.	$1.25	$3.75	$7.50
G-888	Scott, Bradford - ***The Rattlesnake Bandit*** [1963] PBO. Cover art by Carl Hantman.	$1.25	$3.75	$7.50
F-890	Hirsch, Phil - editor - ***She Drives 'Em Crazy*** [1963] PBO. Cover art by Jack Markow. Cartoon book.	$1.25	$3.75	$7.50
N-891	Caldwell, Taylor - ***Dynasty Of Death*** [1963]	$1.25	$3.75	$7.50
X-892	Lewis, Norman - ***New Guide To Word Power*** [1965]	$ .75	$2.50	$5.00
R-893	Forester, C. S. - ***The Sky And The Forest*** [1963] Cover art by Chuck McVickers.	$1.00	$3.00	$6.00
R-894	Stout, Rex - ***Too Many Cooks*** [1963]	$1.25	$3.75	$7.50
R-895	Wentworth, Patricia - ***The Fingerprint*** [1963]	$1.25	$3.75	$7.50
R-896	Austin, Alex - editor - ***Great Tales Of City Dwellers*** [1963]	$1.25	$3.75	$7.50
F-898	McIntosh, J. T. - ***The Million Cities*** [1963] PBO. Cover art by Virgil Finlay.	$1.50	$5.00	$10.00
F-899	Margulies, Leo - editor - ***3 In 1*** [1963] PBO. Cover art by Ed Emsh.	$1.35	$4.00	$8.00
F-902	Hirsch, Phil - editor - ***Fighting Generals*** [1963] Cover art by Mel Crair.	$1.00	$3.00	$6.00
X-903	Damon, M.D., Virgil G. - ***I Learned About Women From Them*** [1963]	$ .75	$2.50	$5.00
T-904	Cronin, A. J. - ***Three Loves*** [1963]	$1.00	$3.00	$6.00
T-905	Caldwell, Taylor - ***The Wide House*** [1963]	$1.25	$3.75	$7.50
R-906	Gilbert, Anthony - ***Dark Death*** [1963]	$1.25	$3.75	$7.50
R-907	Meyer, Jerome - ***The Word's Greatest Puzzles*** [1963] Puzzle book.	$1.50	$5.00	$10.00
F-908	Rohmer, Sax - ***The Insidious Doctor Fu-Manchu*** [1963] Cover art by Mort Engle.	$1.35	$4.00	$8.00
F-909	Phillips, Mark - ***Supermind*** [1963] PBO. Cover art by John Schoenherr.	$1.50	$5.00	$10.00
F-910	Heinlein, Robert A. - ***6 x H*** [1963] Cover by Jack Gaughan.	$1.35	$4.00	$8.00
G-911	Scott, Bradford - ***Killer's Doom*** [1963] PBO. Cover art by Jack Thurston.	$1.25	$3.75	$7.50
F-913	Gottehrer, Barry - ***Football Stars Of 1963*** [1963] PBO. Photo cover.	$1.25	$3.75	$7.50
F-914	Hirsch, Phil - editor - ***Mister And Mistress*** [1963] PBO. Cover by Bill Wenzel. Cartoon book.	$2.50	$7.50	$15.00
R-915	Allen, Charles L. - ***God's Psychiatry*** [1963]	$ .75	$2.50	$5.00
T-916	Cronin, A. J. - ***Hatter's Castle*** [1963]	$1.00	$3.00	$6.00
R-917	Stout, Rex - ***Black Orchids*** [1963]	$1.25	$3.75	$7.50

		G	VG	F
918	Keiffer, Betsy - ***McCall's Guide To Teen-Age Beauty & Glamour*** [1965] Photo cover.	$ .75	$2.50	$5.00
R-919	Stout, Rex - ***The League Of Frightened Men*** [1963]	$1.25	$3.75	$7.50
R-920	Taylor, Phoebe Atwood - ***Proof Of The Pudding*** [1963]	$1.00	$3.00	$6.00
R-922	Hughes, Lawrence - ***Celebration Of Fools*** [1963] Photo cover.	$1.00	$3.00	$6.00
F-923	McLaughlin, Dean - ***The Fury From Earth*** [1963] PBO. Cover art by Jack Gaughan.	$1.35	$4.00	$8.00
F-924	Smith, E. E. "Doc" - ***Skylark Three*** [1963] Cover art by Ed Emsh.	$1.25	$3.75	$7.50
G-926	Scott, Bradford - ***Death's Corral*** [1963] PBO. Cover art by Jack Thurston.	$1.25	$3.75	$7.50
F-927	Brock, Stuart - ***Railtown Sheriff*** [1963] Cover art by Jerry Podwil.	$1.25	$3.75	$7.50
R-928	Nordoff & Hall - ***The Hurricane*** [1963]	$1.00	$3.00	$6.00
T-929	Caldwell, Taylor - ***There Was A Time*** [1963] Cover art by Darrell Greene.	$1.25	$3.75	$7.50
R-930	Household, Geoffrey - ***Rogue Male*** [1963] Cover art by Robert Maguire.	$1.25	$3.75	$7.50
R-931	Stout, Rex - ***Some Buried Caesar*** [1963]	$1.25	$3.75	$7.50
R-932	Wentworth, Patricia - ***Death At Deep End*** [1963]	$1.25	$3.75	$7.50
F-933	Nourse, Alan E. - ***Raiders From The Rings*** [1963] Cover art by Jack Gaughan.	$1.25	$3.75	$7.50
T-934	Hopper, Hedda & Brough, James - ***The Whole Truth And Nothing But*** [1963] Photo cover. 16 pages of photos.	$1.00	$3.00	$6.00
R-936	Marshall, Rosamond - ***The General's Wench*** [1963] Cover art by Charles Binger.	$1.25	$3.75	$7.50
R-937	Anthology - ***Gread Untold Stories Of World War II*** [1963]	$1.00	$3.00	$6.00
F-941	Jones, Raymond F. - ***Man Of Two Worlds*** [1963] Cover art by John Schoenherr.	$1.35	$4.00	$8.00
R-942	Gowen, Vincent - ***Fifth Wife*** [1963] Cover art by Ronnie Lesser.	$ .75	$2.50	$5.00
R-943	Monsaratt, Nicholas - ***Castle Garac*** [1963]	$ .75	$2.50	$5.00
R-944	Household, Geoffrey - ***Fellow Passenger*** [1963]	$1.25	$3.75	$7.50
F-945	Mokray, William G. - ***Basketball Stars 1964*** [1963] PBO. Photo cover. 8 pages of photos.	$2.00	$6.00	$12.00
F-946	Rohmer, Sax - ***President Fu Manchu*** [1963] Cover art by Jack Gaughan.	$1.35	$4.00	$8.00
R-947	Marric, J. J. (John Creasey) - ***Gideon's Week*** [1963]	$1.25	$3.75	$7.50
F-948	Smith, E. E. "Doc" - ***Skylark Of Valeron*** [1963] Cover art by Ed Emsh.	$1.25	$3.75	$7.50
R-950	De Camp, L. Sprague - editor - ***Swords And Sorcery*** [1963] PBO. Cover art by Virgil Finlay.	$2.50	$7.50	$15.00
G-951	Scott, Bradford - ***Outlaw Land*** [1963] PBO. Cover art by Carl Hantmann.	$1.25	$3.75	$7.50
G-953	Scott, Bradford - ***Showdown At Skull Canyon*** [1964] PBO. Cover art by Herb Mott.	$1.25	$3.75	$7.50
T-954	Kirst, Hans Hellmut - ***The Officer Factory*** [1964]	$1.00	$3.00	$6.00
R-955	Val Baker, Denys - ***The Strange And The Damned*** [1964] PBO. Photo cover.	$1.25	$3.75	$7.50
R-956	Hilton, James - ***Without Armor*** [1964]	$1.00	$3.00	$6.00
R-957	Household, Geoffrey - ***Arabesque*** [1964] Cover by Robert Maguire.	$1.35	$4.00	$8.00
T-958	Rawls, Eugene S. - ***A Handbook Of Yoga For Modern Living*** [1964] PBO. Photo cover. 32 pages of photos.	$1.00	$3.00	$6.00
R-960	Stout, Rex - ***Over My Dead Body*** [1964]	$1.25	$3.75	$7.50
R-961	Carpenter, Margaret - ***Experiment Perilous*** [1964]	$1.25	$3.75	$7.50
R-962	Anthology edited by D. R. Bensen - ***The Unknown Five*** [1964] PBO. Cover art by John Schoenherr.	$1.35	$4.00	$8.00
F-963	Janifer, Lawrence M. - ***The Wonder War*** [1964] PBO. Cover art by Ed Emsh.	$2.50	$7.50	$15.00

		G	VG	F
R-967	Household, Geoffrey - ***A Rough Shoot*** [1964] Cover art by Robert Maguire	$1.25	$3.75	$7.50
X-968	Bromfield, Louis - ***The Green Bay Tree*** [1964]	$1.00	$3.00	$6.00
R-969	Taylor, Phoebe Atwood - ***Octagon House*** [1964]	$1.25	$3.75	$7.50
R-970	Stout, Rex - ***Fer-de-lance*** [1964]	$1.25	$3.75	$7.50
F-971	Daniels, Norman - ***Spy Hunt*** [1964]	$1.00	$3.00	$6.00
F-972	Whittington, Harry - ***Nita's Place*** [1964]	$1.50	$5.00	$10.00
F-973	Conklin, Groff - editor - ***Dimension 4*** [1964] PBO. Cover art by Jack Gaughan	$1.35	$4.00	$8.00
F-974	Sturgeon, Theodore - ***Sturgeon In Orbit*** [1964] PBO. Cover art by Ed Emsh.	$2.00	$6.00	$12.00
G-975	Scott, Bradford - ***Guns For Hire*** [1964] PBO.	$1.25	$3.75	$7.50
R-977	Petry, Ann - ***The Street*** [1964]	$1.25	$3.75	$7.50
R-978	Robinson, Henry Morton - ***The Great Snow*** [1964] Cover art by Robert Abbett.	$1.00	$3.00	$6.00
R-979	Household, Geoffrey - ***A Time To Kill*** [1964] Cover art by Robert Maguire	$1.25	$3.75	$7.50
R-980	Wilkerson, Rev. David R. - ***The Cross And The Switchblade*** [1964]	$1.35	$4.00	$8.00
R-981	Marshall, Rosamond - ***Jane Hadden*** [1964] Cover by Charles Binger	$1.00	$3.00	$6.00
R-982	Marshall, Rosamond - ***Celeste*** [1964]	$1.00	$3.00	$6.00
R-983	Stout, Rex - ***The Red Box*** [1964]	$1.25	$3.75	$7.50
R-984	Gilbert, Anthony - ***A Case For Mr. Crook*** [1964]	$1.25	$3.75	$7.50
R-985	Payne, Robert - ***Lovers In The Sun*** [1964] Cover by Tony Kokinos.	$1.00	$3.00	$6.00
F-986	Silverberg, Robert - ***Regan's Planet*** [1964] PBO. Cover art by Emsh.	$1.50	$5.00	$10.00
F-987	Leinster, Murray - ***Doctor To The Stars*** [1964] PBO. Cover art by John Schoenherr.	$1.35	$4.00	$8.00
991	Davis, Garth - ***Gallows Trail*** [1964]	$1.25	$3.75	$7.50
F-992	Scott, Bradford - ***Horseman Of The Shadows*** [1964] PBO. Cover art by Tom Ryan	$1.25	$3.75	$7.50
R-993	Godwin, Tom - ***The Space Barbarians*** [1964] PBO. Cover art by John Schoenherr.	$1.50	$5.00	$10.00
R-994	Anderson, Poul - ***Three Worlds To Conquer*** [1964] PBO. Cover art by Jack Gaughan.	$1.50	$5.00	$10.00
R-995	Palmer, Stuart - ***The Green Ace*** [1964]	$1.25	$3.75	$7.50
R-996	Lockridges, The - ***First Come, First Kill*** [1964]	$1.25	$3.75	$7.50
R-997	Conrad, Earl - ***Rock Botton*** [1974] Cover art by Marion Greenwood.	$1.00	$3.00	$6.00
R-998	Nordoff, Charles & Hall, James Norman - ***The Dark River*** [1964] Cover by Charles McVickers.	$ .75	$2.50	$5.00
R-999	Reynolds, Quentin - ***70,000 To One*** [1964] Cover art by Robert Schulz	$1.25	$3.75	$7.50
T-1000	Reynolds, Quentin - ***By Quentin Reynolds*** [1964] Photo cover	$1.25	$3.75	$7.50
F-1001	Marsh, Rebecca - ***Nurse Of Ward B*** [1964] Cover by Mort Engle.	$ .75	$2.50	$5.00
R-1003	Rohmer, Sax - ***The Trail Of Fu Manchu*** [1964] Cover art by Maguire.	$1.35	$4.00	$8.00
X-1005	Conrad, Earl - ***The Premier*** [1964] Cover art by Jack Thurston	$ .75	$2.50	$5.00
R-1006	Cronin, A. J. - ***The Spanish Gardener*** [1964] Cover art by Leon Gregori	$1.00	$3.00	$6.00
R-1007	Yerby, Frank - ***Bride Of Liberty*** [1964] Cover art by Charles Binger	$1.00	$3.00	$6.00
1008	Blake, Nicholas - ***Malice With Murder*** [1964]	$1.25	$3.75	$7.50
1009	Seeley, Mabel - ***The Listening House*** [1964]	$1.25	$3.75	$7.50
X-1010	Becker, Beril - ***The Spitfires*** [1964] Cover art by Jack Thurston	$1.00	$3.00	$6.00
R-1012	Crane, Robert - ***The Sergeant And The Queen*** [1964] PBO. Cover art by Darrell Green	$1.25	$3.75	$7.50

		G	VG	F
T-1014	Stone, Irving - ***They Also Ran*** [1964]	$1.00	$3.00	$6.00
R-1015	Anderson, Chester & Kurland, Michael - ***Ten Years To Doomsday*** [1964] PBO. Cover art by Ed Emsh.	$1.35	$4.00	$8.00
T-1020	Langley, Adria Locke - ***A Lion Is In The Streets*** [1964]	$1.25	$3.75	$7.50
R-1021	Cronin, A. J. - ***Grand Canary*** [1964]	$1.00	$3.00	$6.00
T-1022	Keyes, Frances Parkinson - ***Silver Seas And Golden Cities*** [1964]	$1.00	$3.00	$6.00
F-1023	Ronns, Edward (Edward S. Aarons) - ***The Glass Cage*** [1964] Cover art by Robert Abbett.	$1.25	$3.75	$7.50
R-1025	Stout, Rex - ***Double For Death*** [1964]	$1.25	$3.75	$7.50
R-1026	Rogers, Joel Townsley - ***The Red Right Hand*** [1964]	$1.25	$3.75	$7.50
F-1028	Budrys, Algis - ***The Falling Torch*** [1964] Cover art by John Schoenherr.	$1.25	$3.75	$7.50
R-1029	Margulies, Leo - editor - ***Weird Tales*** [1964] PBO. Cover art by Virgil Finlay.	$2.50	$7.50	$15.00
R-1032	Rohmer, Sax - ***Daughter Of Fu Manchu*** [1964] Cover art by Robert Maguire.	$1.35	$4.00	$8.00
F-1033	Fitzgerald, Arlene J. - ***Young Nurse Rayburn*** [1964] PBO. Cover by Mort Engle.	$ .75	$2.50	$5.00
T-1034	Wellman, Paul - ***A Dynasty Of Western Outlaws*** [1964]	$1.25	$3.75	$7.50
T-1035	Cronin, A. J. - ***The Northern Light*** [1964]	$1.00	$3.00	$6.00
X-1036	Kirst, Hans Hellmut - ***The Revolt Of Gunner Asch*** [1964] Cover art by Darrell Greene.	$1.00	$3.00	$6.00
R-1038	Frank, Morris & Clark, Blake - ***First Lady Of The Seeing Eye*** [1964] Photo cover.	$ .75	$2.50	$5.00
R-1039	Harvey, Gene - ***Doctor's Nurse*** [1964] Cover art by Rudy Nappi.	$ .75	$2.50	$5.00
R-1040	Palmer, Stuart - ***Cold Poison*** [1964]	$1.25	$3.75	$7.50
R-1041	Gilbert, Anthony - ***After The Verdict*** [1964]	$1.25	$3.75	$7.50
R-1042	Finney, Charles G. - ***The Ghosts Of Manacle*** [1964] PBO. Cover art by Jack Gaughan.	$1.50	$5.00	$10.00
R-1043	Leinster, Murray - ***Time Tunnel*** [1964] PBO. Cover art by Jack Gaughan.	$1.50	$5.00	$10.00
F-1044	Hirsch, Phil - editor - ***Two On The Isle*** [1964] PBO. Cover by Bill Wenzel. Cartoon book.	$2.50	$7.50	$15.00
R-1045	Grider, George & Sims, Lydel - ***War Fish*** [1964] Photo cover.	$1.00	$3.00	$6.00
F-1047	Hamilton, Wade - ***Rimrock Renegade*** [1964] Cover art by Herb Mott.	$1.25	$3.75	$7.50
N-1048	Newman, Ralph G. - editor - ***Lincoln For The Ages*** [1964]	$1.00	$3.00	$6.00
N-1049	Reik, Theodor - ***Listening With The Third Ear*** [1964]	$1.00	$3.00	$6.00
X-1051	Kirst, Hans Hellmut - ***Forward, Gunner Asch*** [1964]	$1.00	$3.00	$6.00
R-1052	Daniels, Norman - ***Overkill*** [1964] PBO. Cover art by Robert Maguire.	$1.25	$3.75	$7.50
R-1053	Stout, Rex - ***The Rubber Band*** [1964]	$1.25	$3.75	$7.50
R-1054	Seeley, Mabel - ***The Whistling Shadow*** [1964]	$1.25	$3.75	$7.50
R-1055	Farmer, Philip Jose - ***Tongues Of The Moon*** [1964] PBO. Cover by Ed Emsh.	$2.50	$7.50	$15.00
R-1056	Conklin, Groff - editor - ***Five-Odd*** [1964] PBO. Cover art by John Schoenherr.	$1.35	$4.00	$8.00
R-1058	Collans, Dev (with Stewart Sterling) - ***I Was A House Detective*** [1964] Photo cover.	$1.25	$3.75	$7.50
F-1059	Scott, Bradford - ***Dead At Sunset*** [1964] PBO. Cover art by Jerry Podwil.	$1.25	$3.75	$7.50
R-1060	Roe, Vingie E. - ***Smoke Along The Plains*** [1964] Cover art by Jerry Allison.	$1.25	$3.75	$7.50
R-1062	Nelson, Mildred - ***Taste Of Power*** [1964] PBO. Cover art by Robert Schulz.	$1.25	$3.75	$7.50
X-1063	Kirst, Hans Hellmut - ***The Return Of Gunner Asch*** [1964]	$1.00	$3.00	$6.00
T-1064	Cronin, A. J. - ***A Thing Of Beauty*** [1964]	$1.00	$3.00	$6.00
R-1066	Stout, Rex - ***The Hand In The Glove*** [1964]	$1.25	$3.75	$7.50

		G	VG	F
R-1067	Levin, Ira - ***A Kiss Before Dying*** [1964]	$1.25	$3.75	$7.50
R-1068	Sturgeon, Theodore - ***Voyage To The Bottom Of The Sea*** [1964] Photo cover. TV tie-in.	$1.35	$4.00	$8.00
R-1069	Davidson, Avram - ***Mutiny In Space*** [1964] PBO. Cover art by John Schoenherr.	$1.35	$4.00	$8.00
X-1072	Brennecke, Jochen - ***The Hunters And The Hunted*** [1964]	$1.00	$3.00	$6.00
X-1077	Hilton, James - ***Ill Wind*** [1964]	$1.00	$3.00	$6.00
T-1078	Padover, Saul K. - ***The Life And The Death Of Louis XVI*** [1964]	$ .75	$2.50	$5.00
R-1080	McKay, Robert - ***The Way Things Are*** [1964] PBO. Cover art by Charles McVickers.	$1.25	$3.75	$7.50
R-1081	Hirsch, Phil - editor - ***Fighting Marines*** [1964] PBO. Cover by Mel Crair.	$1.00	$3.00	$6.00
R-1082	Procter, Maurice - ***Somewhere In This City*** [1964]	$1.25	$3.75	$7.50
R-1083	Carr, John Dickson - ***The Men Who Explained Miracles*** [1964].	$1.25	$3.75	$7.50
R-1084	Smith, Cordwainer - ***The Planet Buyer*** [1964] PBO. Cover art by John Schoenherr.	$1.50	$5.00	$10.00
R-1085	Creasey, John - ***A Rocket For The Toff*** [1964] Cover art by Jack Thurston.	$1.25	$3.75	$7.50
R-1086	Creasey, John - ***The Toff In New York*** [1964] Cover art by Jack Thurston.	$1.25	$3.75	$7.50
F-1088	Scott, Bradford - ***The Range Terror*** [1964] Cover art by Carl Hantmann.	$1.25	$3.75	$7.50
F-1089	Hale, Arlene - ***Nurse Shelley Decides*** [1964] PBO. Cover art by Mort Engle.	$ .75	$2.50	$5.00
F-1090	Blake, Robert - editor - ***101 Elephant Jokes*** [1964] PBO. Cover art by William Hogarth. Cartoon book.	$1.35	$4.00	$8.00
X-1091	Nordhoff & Hall - ***Botany Bay*** [1964] Cover art by Charles McVickers.	$1.00	$3.00	$6.00
X-1092	Marquand, John P. - ***Warning Hill*** [1964] Cover art by Robert Abbett.	$1.25	$3.75	$7.50
R-1093	Hunt & Corman - ***The Talking Cure*** [1964]	$ .75	$2.50	$5.00
R-1094	Daniels, Norman - ***The Hunt Club*** [1964] PBO. Cover art by Robert Maguire.	$1.00	$3.00	$6.00
T-1095	Huff, Theodore - ***Charlie Chaplin*** [1964] Photo cover. 16 pages of photos.	$1.50	$5.00	$10.00
K-1096	Dana, Rose - ***Surgeon's Nurse*** [1964] PBO. Cover art by Mort Engle.	$ .75	$2.50	$5.00
R-1097	Creasey, John - ***A Knife For The Toff*** [1964] Cover art by Jack Thurston.	$1.25	$3.75	$7.50
R-1098	Stout, Rex - ***Red Threads*** [1964]	$1.25	$3.75	$7.50
R-1099	Hughes, Dorothy B. - ***The Davidian Report*** [1964]	$1.00	$3.00	$6.00
R-1100	Gottehrer, Barry - ***Basketball Stars Of 1965*** [1964] PBO. Photo cover. 8 pages of photos.	$1.25	$3.75	$7.50
F-1101	Hirsch, Phil - editor - ***Ghoul Days*** [1964] PBO. Cover art by Sidney Harris. Cartoon book.	$2.50	$7.50	$15.00
R-1104	Maugham, W. Somerset - ***The Sinners*** [1964]	$1.00	$3.00	$6.00
X-1105	Forester, C. S. - ***Randall And The River Of Time*** [1964] Cover by Charles McVickers.	$1.00	$3.00	$6.00
R-1106	Fickling, G. G. - ***Bombshell*** [1964] PBO. Cover art by Ronnie Lesser.	$1.50	$5.00	$10.00
R-1107	Gilbert, Anthony - ***And Death Came Too*** [1964]	$1.25	$3.75	$7.50
R-1108	Wentworth, Patricia - ***Poison In The Pen*** [1964]	$1.25	$3.75	$7.50
R-1109	Shay, Frank - ***American Heroes Of Legend And Lore*** [1964]	$1.00	$3.00	$6.00
R-1110	Renault, Mary - ***Kind Are Her Answers*** [1964]	$ .75	$2.50	$5.00
R-1111	Burns, Kenneth - ***The Grabber*** [1964] PBO. Cover art by Robert Schulz.	$1.35	$4.00	$8.00
R-1114	Smith, E. E. "Doc" - ***First Lensman*** [1964]	$1.25	$3.75	$7.50
N-1116	Caldwell, Taylor - ***The Earth Is The Lord's*** [1964] Cover art by James Meese.	$1.25	$3.75	$7.50

		G	VG	F
T-1118	Marsh, Dorothy & Brock, Carol - ***Good Housekeeping, Party Menus And Recipes*** [1964]	$ .75	$2.50	$5.00
X-1119	Horner, Lance - ***Rogue Roman*** [1965] PBO. Cover art by James Meese.	$1.35	$4.00	$8.00
R-1121	Creasey, John - ***Leave It To The Toff*** [1965] Cover art by Jack Thurston.	$1.25	$3.75	$7.50
R-1123	Stout, Rex - ***The Sound Of Murder*** [1965]	$1.25	$3.75	$7.50
R-1124	Taylor, Phoebe Atwood - ***The Cape Cod Mystery*** [1965]	$1.25	$3.75	$7.50
R-1125	Anthology edited by Leo Margulies - ***Worlds Of Weird*** [1965] PBO. Cover art by Virgil Finlay.	$2.50	$7.50	$15.00
R-1126	Sturgeon, Theodore - ***The Synthetic Man*** [1965]	$1.35	$4.00	$8.00
F-1128	Scott, Bradford - ***Gunslick*** [1965] Cover art by Carl Hantman.	$1.25	$3.75	$7.50
N-1130	Murphy, Robert - ***Diplomat Among Warriors*** [1965]	$1.00	$3.00	$6.00
R-1132	Albert, Marvin - ***Strange Bedfellows*** [1965] PBO. Photo cover. Movie tie-in with Rock Hudson and Gina Lollobrigida.	$1.25	$3.75	$7.50
R-1134	Creasey, John - ***Model For The Toff*** [1965]	$1.25	$3.75	$7.50
R-1135	Anthology edited by Phil Hirsch - ***Hollywood Uncensored*** [1965] PBO. Photo cover.	$1.00	$3.00	$6.00
R-1137	Wentworth, Patricia - ***The Ivory Dagger*** [1965]	$1.25	$3.75	$7.50
R-1138	Procter, Maurice - ***The Pub Crawler*** [1965]	$1.00	$3.00	$6.00
R-1139	Bloch, Robert - ***Tales In a Jugular Vein*** [1965] PBO. Cover art by Gaughan.	$4.00	$12.50	$25.00
R-1140	Vance, Jack - ***Space Opera*** [1965] PBO. Cover art by John Schoenherr.	$2.00	$6.00	$12.00
F-1142	Scott, Bradford - ***Trails Of Steel*** [1965] PBO. Cover art by Roger Kastel.	$1.25	$3.75	$7.50
X-1143	Waterbury, Ruth - ***Richard Burton*** [1965] PBO. Photo cover. Eight pages of photos.	$1.35	$4.00	$8.00
T-1144	Caldwell, Taylor - ***Let Love Come Last*** [1965]	$1.00	$3.00	$6.00
X-1145	Laumer, Keith - ***Embassy*** [1965] PBO. Cover art by Darrell Greene.	$1.50	$5.00	$10.00
R-1147	Martin, Kay - ***Cry Shame!*** [1965]	$1.00	$3.00	$6.00
R-1148	Robinson, Ray - editor - ***Baseball Stars Of 1965*** [1965] PBO. Mickey Mantle photo cover. 8 pages of photos.	$5.00	$15.00	$30.00
R-1149	Stout, Rex - ***The Broken Vase*** [1965]	$1.25	$3.75	$7.50
R-1150	Gilbert, Anthony - ***Murder Comes Home*** [1965]	$1.25	$3.75	$7.50
R-1151	Fickling, G. G. - ***This Girl For Hire*** [1965] Photo cover.	$1.25	$3.75	$7.50
R-1152	Tabori, Paul - ***The Green Rain*** [1965] Cover art by John Schoenherr.	$1.25	$3.75	$7.50
K-1155	Sault, Madeleine - ***Private Duty For Nurse Peggy*** [1965] PBO. Cover art by Mort Engel.	$ .75	$2.50	$5.00
F-1156	Anthology edited by Phil Hirsch - ***Man And Strife*** [1965] Cartoon book.	$1.00	$3.00	$6.00
N-1157	William, Ben Ames - ***The Strange Woman*** [1965]	$1.00	$3.00	$6.00
T-1158	Caldwell, Taylor - ***Time No Longer*** [1965]	$1.00	$3.00	$6.00
X-1159	Seton, Anya - ***Foxfire*** [1965]	$1.00	$3.00	$6.00
R-1162	Fairman, Paul W. - ***City Under The Sea*** [1965] PBO. Cover art by John Schoenherr. TV tie-in.	$2.00	$6.00	$12.00
R-1164	Creasey, John - ***Terror For The Toff*** [1965] PBO. Cover art by Thurston.	$1.25	$3.75	$7.50
X-1165	Val Baker, Denys - ***Strange Possession*** [1965] PBO. Cover art by Jack Faragasso.	$1.00	$3.00	$6.00
R-1166	Stout, Rex - ***Bad For Business*** [1965]	$1.00	$3.00	$6.00
R-1167	Fickling, G. G. - ***A Gun For Honey*** [1965] Photo cover. TV tie-in.	$1.00	$3.00	$6.00
X-1168	Hanley, Gerald - ***The Consul At Sunset*** [1965]	$ .75	$2.50	$5.00
R-1170	Collins, Hunt - ***Tomorrow And Tomorrow*** [1965] Cover art by Jack Gaughan.	$1.25	$3.75	$7.50
X-1172	Bruff, Nancy - ***The Manatee*** [1965] Cover art by Jack Thurston.	$1.25	$3.75	$7.50
N-1173	Shulman, Irving - ***The Big Brokers*** [1965]	$ .75	$2.50	$5.00

		G	VG	F
T-1174	Stuart, Gilbert & Levy, Alan - ***Kind-Hearted Tiger*** [1965]	$1.00	$3.00	$6.00
F-1175	Anthology edited by Phil Hirsch - ***Come On 'A My House*** [1965] PBO. Cover by Pete Wyma. Cartoon book.	$1.00	$3.00	$6.00
R-1176	Runyon, Poke - ***Night Jump-Cuba*** [1965] PBO. Cover art by Darrell Greene.	$1.00	$3.00	$6.00
X-1177	Hodge, Jane Aiken - ***Maulever Hall*** [1965]	$ .75	$2.50	$5.00
R-1178	Creasey, John - ***The Toff And The Runaway Bride*** [1965] Cover art by Jack Thurston.	$1.25	$3.75	$7.50
R-1180	Cole, George Harmon - ***One Hour To Kill*** [1965]	$1.25	$3.75	$7.50
R-1183	Smith, Cordwainer - ***Space Lords*** [1965] PBO. Cover art by Jack Gaughan.	$2.00	$6.00	$12.00
X-1185	MacDonald, John D. - ***Cancel All Our Vows*** [1965] Cover art by Darrell Greene.	$1.35	$4.00	$8.00
T-1186	Seton, Anya - ***The Turquoise*** [1965]	$ .75	$2.50	$5.00
X-1187	Butler, Ewan - ***Loyalty Is My Honor*** [1965] Cover art by Mort Engle.	$ .75	$2.50	$5.00
R-1189	Cassiday, Bruce - ***Live Down The Shame*** [1965]	$1.00	$3.00	$6.00
R-1190	Daniels, Norman - ***Spy Ghost*** [1965] PBO. Cover art by Frank Kalan.	$1.25	$3.75	$7.50
R-1191	Procter, Maurice - ***The Devil Was Handsome*** [1965]	$1.25	$3.75	$7.50
R-1192	Anthology edited by L. Sprague De Camp - ***The Spell Of Seven*** [1965] PBO. Cover art by Virgil Finlay.	$2.50	$7.50	$15.00
R-1193	Anthology edited by Phil Hirsch - ***Fighting Aces*** [1965]	$1.00	$3.00	$6.00
R-1194	Creasey, John - ***Poison For The Toff*** [1965] Cover art by Thurston.	$1.25	$3.75	$7.50
F-1195	Hamilton, Wade - ***Sagebrush*** [1965] Cover art by Ronnie Lesser.	$1.25	$3.75	$7.50
R-1196	Bourne, Hester - ***The Spanish House*** [1965]	$1.00	$3.00	$6.00
R-1197	Connell, Vivian - ***The Love Lush*** [1965] Cover art by Ronnie Lesser.	$1.00	$3.00	$6.00
X-1198	Wakeman, Frederic - ***Shore Leave*** [1965] Cover art by Frank Kalan.	$1.00	$3.00	$6.00
R-1199	Monteilhet, Hubert - ***The Road To Hell*** [1965]	$1.00	$3.00	$6.00
R-1200	Epstein, Brian - ***A Cellarful Of Noise*** [1965] The real inside story of The Beatles by the man who discovered them. 16 pages of photos.	$4.00	$12.50	$25.00
T-1201	Allen, Sol - ***The Gynecologist*** [1965]	$ .75	$2.50	$5.00
T-1203	Pennell, Joseph Stanley - ***The History Of Rome Hanks*** [1965]	$1.00	$3.00	$6.00
R-1204	Anthology edited by Phil Hirsch - ***The Cursed*** [1965] PBO.	$1.00	$3.00	$6.00
R-1205	Gibbs, Mary Ann - ***The House Of Ravensbourne*** [1965]	$ .75	$2.50	$5.00
R-1206	Coxe, George Harmon - ***Mission Of Fear*** [1965]	$1.00	$3.00	$6.00
R-1207	Hughes, Dorothy B. - ***The So Blue Marble*** [1965]	$1.00	$3.00	$6.00
R-1208	Davidson, Avram - ***Masters Of The Maze*** [1965] PBO. Cover art by Schoenherr.	$1.35	$4.00	$8.00
R-1210	Anthology edited by Leo Margulies - ***The Ghoul Keepers*** [1965] Cover art by John Schoenherr.	$1.25	$3.75	$7.50
R-1212	Shelley, Mary - ***Frankenstein*** [1965] Cover art by Richard Smith.	$1.50	$5.00	$10.00
R-1213	Stoker, Bram - ***Dracula*** [1965]	$1.50	$5.00	$10.00
N-1214	Cook, Fred J. - ***The FBI Nobody Knows*** [1965]	$1.00	$3.00	$6.00
T-1215	Kirst, Hans Hellmut - ***The Seventh Day*** [1965] Cover art by Frank Kalan.	$1.00	$3.00	$6.00
T-1216	Street, James - ***The Velvet Doublet*** [1965]	$1.00	$3.00	$6.00
R-1217	Cornell, Evelyn - ***By Love Betrayed*** [1965]	$ .75	$2.50	$5.00
R-1219	Elwood, Roger & Moskowitz, Sam - editors - ***Great Spy Novels And Stories*** [1965]	$1.25	$3.75	$7.50
R-1220	Lacy, Ed - ***Harlem Undergroung*** [1965] PBO. Cover art by Harry Schaare.	$2.00	$6.00	$12.00
R-1221	Creasey, John - ***Double For The Toff*** [1965] Cover art by Jack Thurston.	$1.00	$3.00	$6.00

		G	VG	F
R-1222	Smith, E. E. "Doc" - ***Triplanetary*** [1965]	$1.25	$3.75	$7.50
R-1223	Gillette, Paul J. & Tillinger, Eugene - ***Inside Ku Klux Klan*** [1965] PBO. Ku Klux Klan photo cover.	$1.35	$4.00	$8.00
K-1224	Bowman, Jeanne - ***Emergency Calling Nurse Mallon*** [1965] Cover art by Mort Engle.	$ .75	$2.50	$5.00
R-1227	Anthology edited by Hans Stefan Santesso - ***Rulers Of Men*** [1965] PBO. Cover art by Jack Gaughan.	$1.35	$4.00	$8.00
N-1228	Cronin, A. J. - ***A Song Of Sixpence*** [1965]	$1.00	$3.00	$6.00
R-1229	Sharkey, Jack - ***The Addams Family*** [1965] PBO. Photo cover. TV tie-in.	$3.50	$10.00	$20.00
T-1230	Sanderson, Ivan T. - ***Living Treasure*** [1965] Cover art by John Schoenherr.	$1.00	$3.00	$6.00
R-1231	Wentworth, Patricia - ***The Silent Pool*** [1965]	$1.00	$3.00	$6.00
R-1232	Coxe, George Harmon - ***The Impetuous Mistress*** [1965] Cover art by Richard Smith.	$1.00	$3.00	$6.00
R-1233	Crane, Robert - ***Operation Vengeance*** [1965] PBO. Cover by Darrell Greene.	$1.00	$3.00	$6.00
1235	Lipson, Goldie - ***Rejuvenation Through Yoga*** [1965]	$ .75	$2.50	$5.00
R-1236	Daniels, Dorothy - ***The Mistress Of Falcon Hill*** [1965]	$ .75	$2.50	$5.00
X-1237	Tzetnik, Ka - ***House Of Dolls*** [1965] Cover art by Dick Shelton.	$1.00	$3.00	$6.00
R-1239	Knight, Kathleen Moore - ***The Robineau Look*** [1965]	$ .75	$2.50	$5.00
X-1240	Powers, Barbara & Diehl, W. W. - ***Spy Wife*** [1965] PBO. Photo cover.	$1.00	$3.00	$6.00
N-1241	Spring, Howard - ***These Lovers Fled Away*** [1965]	$ .75	$2.50	$5.00
T-1242	Fisher, Vardis - ***The Mothers*** [1965]	$1.00	$3.00	$6.00
R-1243	Daniels, Norman - ***Operation "K"*** [1965]	$1.00	$3.00	$6.00
R-1244	Lockridge, The - ***Murder Within Murder*** [1965]	$1.00	$3.00	$6.00
X-1245	Smith, E. E. "Doc" - ***Gray Lensman*** [1965]	$1.25	$3.75	$7.50
R-1246	Creasey, John - ***The Toff And The Stolen Tresses*** [1965]	$1.00	$3.00	$6.00
R-1247	Bloch, Robert - ***The Skull Of The Marquis De Sade*** [1965] PBO. Photo cover. Movie tie-in.	$4.00	$12.50	$25.00
X-1248	Moyzisch, L. C - ***Operation Cicero*** [1965]	$ .75	$2.50	$5.00
T-1250	Carrighar, Sally - ***One Day At Teton Marsh*** [1965]	$ .75	$2.50	$5.00
T-1251	Carrighar, Sally - ***One Day On Beetle Rock*** [1965]	$ .75	$2.50	$5.00
X-1252	Sherrill, John L. - ***They Speak With Other Tongues*** [1965]	$ .75	$2.50	$5.00
T-1254	Loomis, Stanley - ***Du Barry*** [1965]	$ .75	$2.50	$5.00
T-1255	Greene, Harris - ***The Flags At Doney*** [1965] cover art by Frank Kalan.	$ .75	$2.50	$5.00
X-1256	Standish, Robert - ***Singapore Kate*** [1965] Cover art by Darrell Greene.	$ .75	$2.50	$5.00
R-1257	Miksch, W. F. - ***The Addams Family Strikes Back*** [1965] PBO. Photo cover. TV tie-in.	$3.50	$10.00	$20.00
R-1258	Gilbert, Anthony - ***A Question Of Murder*** [1965]	$1.00	$3.00	$6.00
R-1259	Coxe, George Harmon - ***Focus On Murder*** [1965]	$1.00	$3.00	$6.00
T-1260	Carrighar, Sally - ***Icebound Summer*** [1965]	$ .75	$2.50	$5.00
T-1261	Sanderson, Ivan T. - ***Caribbean Treasure*** [1965] Cover art by John Schoenherr.	$1.00	$3.00	$6.00
X-1262	Smith, E.E. "Doc" - ***Second Stage Lensman*** [1965] Cover art by Jack Gaughan.	$1.25	$3.75	$7.50
T-1265	Graves, Ralph - ***The Lost Eagles*** [1965] Cover art by James Meese.	$ .75	$2.50	$5.00
R-1266	Lyons, Delphine C. - ***Flower Of Evil*** [1965]	$1.00	$3.00	$6.00
R-1267	Knox, E. Kitzes - ***Gomer Pyle U.S.M.C.*** [1968] Cover art by Darrell Green. TV tie-in.	$1.25	$3.75	$7.50
R-1270	Ellison, Harlan - ***Paingod And Other Delusions*** [1965] PBO. Cover art by Jack Gaughan.	$3.50	$10.00	$20.00
R-1272	Ross, Clarissa - ***Durrell Towers*** [1965] PBO. Cover art by Lou Marchetti.	$ .75	$2.50	$5.00
R-1273	Daniels, Dorothy - ***The Leland Legacy*** [1965]	$ .75	$2.50	$5.00
T-1274	Hall, Adam - ***The Quiller Memorandum*** [1966]	$1.00	$3.00	$6.00

		G	VG	F
N-1275	Spring, Howard - ***The Houses In Between*** [1966]	$ .75	$2.50	$5.00
X-1276	Lamb, Antonia - ***Greystones*** [1966]	$ .75	$2.50	$5.00
T-1277	Stone, Scott C. S. - ***The Coasts Of War*** [1966] PBO. Cover art by Darrell Greene.	$1.00	$3.00	$6.00
X-1278	Gallico, Paul - ***Trial By Terror*** [1966] Cover art by Frank Kalan.	$1.00	$3.00	$6.00
R-1279	Anthology edited by Phil Hirsch - ***Pettin' Place*** [1966] PBO. Cover art by Bob Schroeter. Cartoon book.	$1.35	$4.00	$8.00
V-1280	Longford, Elizabeth - ***Queen Victoria*** [1966]	$1.00	$3.00	$6.00
X-1281	Cutris, Peter - ***The Devil's Own*** [1966]	$1.00	$3.00	$6.00
R-1282	MacDonald, Philip - ***Guest In The House*** [1966]	$1.25	$3.75	$7.50
R-1283	Asimov, Isaac - ***The Rest Of The Robots*** [1966]	$1.35	$4.00	$8.00
X-1285	Monsarrat, Nicholas - ***Castle Garac*** [1966]	$ .75	$2.50	$5.00
X-1287	Monks, Jr., John - ***A Ribbon And A Star*** [1966] Photo cover.	$1.00	$3.00	$6.00
S-1288	Graves, Robert - ***Count Belisarius*** [1966]	$1.00	$3.00	$6.00
R-1291	Daniels, Norman - ***Operation N*** [1966] PBO. Cover art by Frank Kalan.	$1.00	$3.00	$6.00
R-1292	Gilbert, Anthony - ***Death Casts A Long Shadow*** [1966]	$1.00	$3.00	$6.00
R-1293	Whitney, Janet - ***The Quaker Bride*** [1966]	$ .75	$2.50	$5.00
X-1294	Smith, E. E. "Doc" - ***Children Of The Lens*** [1966] Cover art by Jack Gaughan.	$1.25	$3.75	$7.50
T-1295	Krutch, Joseph Wood - ***The Great Chain Of Life*** [1966]	$1.00	$3.00	$6.00
T-1296	Stuart, Frank S. - ***A Seal's World*** [1966]	$1.00	$3.00	$6.00
X-1297	Brome, Vincent - ***The Spy*** [1966]	$1.00	$3.00	$6.00
X-1298	Seeley, Mabel - ***The Crying Sisters*** [1966]	$1.25	$3.75	$7.50
R-1299	Phillips, Mark - ***The Impossibles*** [1966] Cover art by Schoenherr.	$1.25	$3.75	$7.50
X-1300	Anthology edited by Paul Steiner - ***The Stevenson Wit And Wisdom*** [1965] PBO. Photo cover. Sixteen pages of photos.	$1.00	$3.00	$6.00
R-1301	Rohmer, Sax - ***The Insidious Dr. Fu Manchu*** [1965] Cover art by Len Goldberg.	$1.00	$3.00	$6.00
R-1302	Rohmer, Sax - ***The Return Of Dr. Fu Manchu*** [1965] Cover art by Len Goldberg.	$1.00	$3.00	$6.00
R-1303	Rohmer, Sax - ***The Mask Of Fu Manchu*** [1967] Cover art by Len Goldberg.	$1.00	$3.00	$6.00
R-1304	Rohmer, Sax - ***The Shadow Of Fu Manchu*** [1966]	$1.00	$3.00	$6.00
R-1305	Rohmer, Sax - ***The Island Of Fu-Manchu*** [1966] Cover art by Len Goldberg.	$1.00	$3.00	$6.00
R-1306	Rohmer, Sax - ***The Hand Of Fu-Manchu*** [1966] Cover art by Len Goldberg.	$1.00	$3.00	$6.00
R-1307	Rohmer, Sax - ***The Drums Of Fu-Manchu*** [1966] Cover art by Len Goldberg.	$1.00	$3.00	$6.00
R-1308	Rohmer, Sax - ***The Trail Of Fu-Manchu*** [1966] Cover art by Goldberg.	$1.00	$3.00	$6.00
R-1310	Rohmer, Sax - ***Emperor Fu-Manchu*** [1966] Cover art by Len Goldberg.	$1.00	$3.00	$6.00
R-1313	Sohmer, Sax - ***The Quest Of The Sacred Slipper*** [1966] Cover art by J. Lombardero.	$1.00	$3.00	$6.00
R-1314	Rohmer, Sax - ***Brood Of The Witch-Queen*** [1966] Cover art by J. Lombardero.	$1.00	$3.00	$6.00
R-1315	Rohmer, Sax - ***The Golden Scorpion*** [1966]	$1.00	$3.00	$6.00
R-1316	Rohmer, Sax - ***The Dream Detective*** [1966] Cover art by J. Lombardero.	$1.00	$3.00	$6.00
R-1317	Rohmer, Sax - ***The Yellow Claw*** [1966] Cover art by J. Lombardero.	$1.00	$3.00	$6.00
N-1326	Spring, Howard - ***Fame Is The Spur*** [1966]	$ .75	$2.50	$5.00
T-1327	Kirst, Hans Hellmut - ***What Became Of Gunner Asch*** [1966]	$ .75	$2.50	$5.00
X-1328	Polland, Madeleine - ***Thicker Than Water*** [1966]	$ .75	$2.50	$5.00
S-1329	La Mure, Pierre - ***Moulin Rouge*** [1966] Cover art by Frank Kalan.	$ .75	$2.50	$5.00

		G	VG	F
R-1330	Kavanaugh, Cynthia - ***Bride Of Lenore*** [1966] PBO. Cover art by Frank Kalan.	$ .75	$2.50	$5.00
S-1331	Graves, Robert - ***Homer's Daughter*** [1966]	$1.25	$3.75	$7.50
S-1332	Vining, Elizabeth Gray - ***Take Heed Of Loving Me*** [1966]	$ .75	$2.50	$5.00
R-1333	Eidelberg, M.D., Ludwig - ***Take Off Your Mask*** [1966]	$1.00	$3.00	$6.00
R-1336	Robinson, Ray - editor - ***Baseball Stars Of 1966*** [1966] PBO. Photo cover. Eight pages of photos	$2.00	$6.00	$12.00
X-1338	Thorpe, Sylvia - ***Strangers On The Moor*** [1966]	$1.00	$3.00	$6.00
R-1339	Fickling, G. G. - ***Girl On The Prowl*** [1965] TV tie-in.	$1.00	$3.00	$6.00
R-1340	Fickling, G. G. - ***Blood And Honey*** [1965] Photo cover. TV tie-in.	$1.00	$3.00	$6.00
X-1341	Sinclair, Upton - ***The Cup Of Fury*** [1966]	$ .75	$2.50	$5.00
X-1342	Bunyan, John - ***The Pilgrim's, Progress*** [1966]	$1.00	$3.00	$6.00
R-1345	Siegel, Jack - ***Squeegee*** [1966]	$1.00	$3.00	$6.00
S-1346	Graves, Robert - ***Hercules, My Shipmate*** [1966]	$1.25	$3.75	$7.50
X-1347	Wilson, William - ***The LBJ Brigade*** [1966] PBO. Cover art by J. Lombardero.	$ .75	$2.50	$5.00
R-1348	Coxe, George Harmon - ***Thge Big Gamble*** [1966]	$1.00	$3.00	$6.00
X-1350	Smith, E. E. "Doc" - ***The Skylark Of Space*** [1966]	$1.00	$3.00	$6.00
N-1351	Spring, Howard - ***Time And The Hour*** [1966]	$ .75	$2.50	$5.00
X-1353	Wentworth, Patricia - ***She Came Back*** [1966]	$1.00	$3.00	$6.00
R-1354	Fickling, G. G. - ***Bombshell*** [1966] Photo cover. TV tie-in.	$1.00	$3.00	$6.00
R-1355	Fickling, G. G. - ***Dig A Dead Doll*** [1966] Photo cover. TV tie-in.	$1.00	$3.00	$6.00
R-1356	Fickling, G. G. - ***Girl On The Loose*** [1965] Photo cover. TV tie-in.	$1.00	$3.00	$6.00
R-1357	Fickling, G. G. - ***Kiss For A Killer*** [1965] Photo cover. TV tie-in.	$1.00	$3.00	$6.00
R-1358	Fickling, G. G. - ***A Gun For Honey*** [1965] Photo cover. TV tie-in.	$1.00	$3.00	$6.00
R-1359	Fickling, G. G. - ***Honey In The Flesh*** [1965] Photo cover. TV tie-in.	$1.00	$3.00	$6.00
R-1360	Fickling, G. G. - ***This Girl For Hire*** [1965] Photo cover. TV tie-in.	$1.00	$3.00	$6.00
R-1361	Stout, Rex - ***Not Quite Dead Enough*** [1966]	$1.00	$3.00	$6.00
R-1362	Stout, Rex - ***The League Of Frightened Men*** [1966]	$1.00	$3.00	$6.00
R-1363	Stout, Rex - ***Black Orchids*** [1966]	$1.00	$3.00	$6.00
R-1367	Stout, Rex - ***Over My Dead Body*** [1966]	$1.00	$3.00	$6.00
R-1368	Stout, Rex - ***Some Buried Caesar*** [1966]	$1.00	$3.00	$6.00
R-1370	Stout, Rex - ***Fer-De-Lance*** [1967]	$ .75	$2.50	$5.00
N-1377	White, Patrick - ***The Tree Of Man*** [1966]	$1.00	$3.00	$6.00
X-1378	McGovern, James - ***The Berlin Couriers*** [1966]	$ .75	$2.50	$5.00
T-1380	Eaton, Evelyn - ***Quietly My Captain Waits*** [1966]	$1.00	$3.00	$6.00
X-1383	Anthology edited by Catherine Marshall - ***Mr. Jones, Meet The Master*** [1966]	$ .75	$2.50	$5.00
N-1384	Compiled by Donald T. Kauffman - ***The Treasury Of Religious Verse*** [1966]	$1.00	$3.00	$6.00
N-1385	Hurlbut, Rev. Jessie Lyman - editor - ***Hurlbut's Story Of The Bible*** [1966]	$ .75	$2.50	$5.00
T-1388	Bonner, Paul Hyde - ***Excelsior!*** [1966] Cover art by Frank Kalan.	$1.00	$3.00	$6.00
X-1390	Carleton, Marjorie - ***The Demarest Inheritance*** [1966] Cover art by Marchetti.	$ .75	$2.50	$5.00
T-1391	Mitford, Nancy - ***Madame De Pompadour*** [1966]	$1.00	$3.00	$6.00
T-1392	Halliburton, Richard - ***The Royal Road To Romance*** [1966]	$ .75	$2.50	$5.00
R-1393	Daniels, Norman - ***Spy Hunt*** [1966] Cover art by Frank Kalan.	$1.00	$3.00	$6.00
T-1400	Chase, Mary Ellen - ***Windswept*** [1966]	$ .75	$2.50	$5.00
R-1401	Haggard, H. Rider - ***King Solomon's Mines*** [1966] Cover art by Jack Thurston.	$1.00	$3.00	$6.00
X-1402	Collins, Wilkie - ***The Moonstone*** [1966]	$ .75	$2.50	$5.00

		G	VG	F
X-1403	Haggard, H. Rider - ***She*** [1966] Cover art by Jack Thurston.	$1.00	$3.00	$6.00
R-1404	London, Jack - ***South Sea Tales*** [1966]	$ .75	$2.50	$5.00
R-1405	Kipling, Rudyard - ***Kim*** [1966]	$1.00	$3.00	$6.00
T-1406	Dumas, Alexandre - ***The Man In The Iron Mask*** [1966]	$ .75	$2.50	$5.00
R-1407	Stevenson, Robert Louis - ***Kidnapped*** [1966]	$1.00	$3.00	$6.00
R-1408	Stevenson, Robert Lewis - ***Treasure Island*** [1966]	$ .75	$2.50	$5.00
X-1409	Verne, Jules - ***20,000 Leagues Under The Sea*** [1966]	$1.00	$3.00	$6.00
T-1410	Dumas, Alexandre - ***The Count Of Monte Cristo*** [1966]	$ .75	$2.50	$5.00
X-1411	Buchan, John - ***Prester John*** [1966]	$1.00	$3.00	$6.00
R-1412	Orczy, Baroness - ***The Scarlet Pimpernel*** [1966]	$ .75	$2.50	$5.00
K-1414	Wells, H. G. - ***The Time Machine*** [1964] Cover art by Len Goldberg.	$1.00	$3.00	$6.00
F-1416	London, Jack - ***The Call Of The Wild*** [1966]	$ .75	$2.50	$5.00
R-1417	Twain, Mark - ***The Adventures Of Tom Sawyer*** [1966]	$1.25	$3.75	$7.50
R-1418	Twain, Mark - ***The Adventures Of Huckleberry Finn*** [1966]	$1.25	$3.75	$7.50
R-1419	Kipling, Rudyard - ***Captains Courageous*** [1966]	$ .75	$2.50	$5.00
R-1420	Hawthorne, Nathaniel - ***The Scarlet Letter*** [1966]	$1.00	$3.00	$6.00
N-1451	White, Patrick - ***Riders In The Chariot*** [1966]	$ .75	$2.50	$5.00
T-1452	Teale, Edwin Way - ***Near Horizons*** [1966] Eight pages of photos.	$ .75	$2.50	$5.00
T-1453	Sanderson, Ivan T. - ***Animal Treasure*** [1966]	$1.25	$3.75	$7.50
X-1455	Smith, E. E. "Doc" - ***Triplanetary*** [1966] Cover art by Gaughan.	$ .75	$2.50	$5.00
X-1456	Smith, E.E. "Doc" - ***First Lensman*** [1966] Cover art by Gaughan.	$1.00	$3.00	$6.00
X-1457	Smith, E. E. "Doc" - ***Galactic Patrol*** [1967]	$ .75	$2.50	$5.00
X-1458	Smith, E. E. "Doc" - ***Skylark Of Valeron*** [1966]	$1.00	$3.00	$6.00
X-1459	Smith, E. E. "Doc" - ***Skylark Three*** [1966]	$ .75	$2.50	$5.00
X-1460	Wees, Frances Shelley - ***The Keys Of My Prison*** [1966] Cover art by Lou Marchetti.	$1.00	$3.00	$6.00
X-1462	Richards, Bob - ***The Heart Of A Champion*** [1966]	$ .75	$2.50	$5.00
X-1463	Wilkerson, David - ***Twelve Angels From Hell*** [1966] Cover art by Harry Schaare.	$1.00	$3.00	$6.00
1465	Bowman, Dr. - ***Surgeon*** [1966] Cover by Darrell Greene.	$ .75	$2.50	$5.00
X-1466	Yurick, Sol - ***The Warriors*** [1968] Cover art by Harry Schaare.	$1.00	$3.00	$6.00
T-1469	Van der Post, Laurens - ***The Lost World Of The Kalahari*** [1966]	$ .75	$2.50	$5.00
T-1470	Matthiessen, Peter - ***The Cloud Forest*** [1966]	$1.00	$3.00	$6.00
T-1471	Maxwell, Gavin - ***People Of The Reeds*** [1966]	$ .75	$2.50	$5.00
X-1472	Koningsberger, Hans - ***The Affair*** [1966] Cover art by Hector Carrido.	$1.00	$3.00	$6.00
T-1475	Dickens, Monica - ***Kate And Emma*** [1966]	$ .75	$2.50	$5.00
X-1476	Cassiday, Bruce - ***Angels Ten*** [1966]	$1.00	$3.00	$6.00
N-1477	Payne, Robert - ***Mao Tse-Tung*** [1966]	$ .75	$2.50	$5.00
X-1480	Wentworth, Patricia - ***The Benevent Treasure*** [1966]	$1.00	$3.00	$6.00
T-1481	Huxley, Elspeth - ***The Flame Trees Of Thika*** [1966]	$ .75	$2.50	$5.00
T-1482	Koch-Isenburg, Ludwig - ***The Realm Of The Green Buddha*** [1966]	$1.00	$3.00	$6.00
X-1483	Gordon, Alex - ***The Cipher*** [1966] Movie tie-in.	$ .75	$2.50	$5.00
T-1484	Burnett, Hallie - ***Watch On The Wall*** [1966] Cover art by Hector Garrido.	$1.00	$3.00	$6.00
T-1485	Thompson, Kate - ***Great House*** [1966] Cover art by Faragasso.	$ .75	$2.50	$5.00
X-1486	Siegel, Jack - ***Dawn At Kahlenberg*** [1966] PBO. Cover art by Baron Storey.	$1.00	$3.00	$6.00
X-1487	Petry, Ann - ***The Street*** [1966]	$ .75	$2.50	$5.00
N-1489	Rogers, Dale Evans - ***Dearest Debbie*** [1968]	$1.00	$3.00	$6.00
T-1490	Sorce, Rose L. - ***The New Italian Cookbook*** [1971] Photo cover.	$ .75	$2.50	$5.00
T-1492	Coggins, Carolyn - ***The Cookbook Of Fabulous Food*** [1966]	$1.00	$3.00	$6.00
X-1495	Albrand, Martha - ***The Linden Affair*** [1966] Cover art by Frank Kalan.	$ .75	$2.50	$5.00
N-1497	Roy, Jules - ***The Battle Of Dienbienphu*** [1966]	$1.00	$3.00	$6.00

		G	VG	F
R-1498	Lee, Christopher - ***Treasury Of Terror*** [1966] PBO. Cover art by Mort Drucker.	$3.00	$9.00	$18.00
T-1500	Duggan, Alfred - ***The Right Line Of Cerdic*** [1966]	$ .75	$2.50	$5.00
T-1501	Stern, G. B. - ***The Matriarch*** [1966]	$1.00	$3.00	$6.00
R-1502	Anthology edited by Phil Hirsch - ***Grin And Bare It*** [1966]	$1.25	$3.75	$7.50
X-1504	Wentworth, Patricia - ***The Silent Pool*** [1966]	$ .75	$2.50	$5.00
R-1505	Lamb, Antonia - ***The Greenhouse*** [1966] PBO. Cover art by Frank Kalan.	$1.00	$3.00	$6.00
X-1508	Carleton, Marjorie - ***Vanished*** [1966]	$ .75	$2.50	$5.00
X-1511	Wentworth, Patricia - ***The Benevent Treasure*** [1966]	$1.00	$3.00	$6.00
X-1514	Wentworth, Patricia - ***The Fingerprint*** [1966] Cover art by Darrell Greene.	$ .75	$2.50	$5.00
T-1521	Moore, John - ***September Moon*** [1966]	$1.00	$3.00	$6.00
R-1522	Leinster, Murray - ***The Time Tunnel*** [1967] PBO. Cover art by Jack Gaughan.	$1.50	$5.00	$10.00
R-1523	Reynolds, Quentin - ***70,000 To One*** [1966]	$ .75	$2.50	$5.00
V-1528	Maurois, Andre - ***The Titans*** [1966]	$1.00	$3.00	$6.00
T-1535	Howe, George - ***Call It Treason*** [1966]	$ .75	$2.50	$5.00
R-1536	Anthology edited by Phil Hirsch - ***A Mad Passion For Murder*** [1966]	$1.25	$3.75	$7.50
R-1537	Anthology edited by Phil Hirsch - ***Good For What Jails You*** [1966] Cartoon book.	$1.25	$3.75	$7.50
X-1539	Smith, E. E. "Doc" - ***Skylark Duquesne*** [1966] PBO. Cover art by Jack Gaughan.	$1.35	$4.00	$8.00
R-1540	Creasey, John - ***A Mast For The Toff*** [1966]	$ .75	$2.50	$5.00
R-1541	Coxe, George Harmon - ***Deadly Image*** [1966]	$1.00	$3.00	$6.00
X-1542	Boucher, Anthony - ***The Case Of The Seven Sneezes*** [1966]	$ .75	$2.50	$5.00
X-1543	Sturgeon, Theodore - ***Starshine*** [1966] PBO. Cover art by Jack Gaughan.	$1.35	$4.00	$8.00
R-1545	Stuart, Florence - ***A Nurse Named Courage*** [1967] Cover art by Mort Engle.	$ .65	$2.00	$4.00
R-1547	Robins, Denise - ***Nightingale's Song*** [1966]	$ .75	$2.50	$5.00
R-1548	Robins, Denise - ***Moment Of Love*** [1966]	$1.00	$3.00	$6.00
R-1549	Robins, Denise - ***The Restless Heart*** [1966]	$ .75	$2.50	$5.00
R-1550	Robins, Denise - ***Were I Thy Bride*** [1966]	$1.00	$3.00	$6.00
R-1551	Robins, Denise - ***And All Because*** [1967]	$ .75	$2.50	$5.00
R-1552	Robins, Denise - ***Put Back The Clock*** [1967]	$1.00	$3.00	$6.00
X-1553	Seeley, Mabel - ***The Beckoning Door*** [1966]	$ .75	$2.50	$5.00
X-1555	Williams, Brad - ***A Stranger To Herself*** [1966] Cover art by Mort Engle.	$1.00	$3.00	$6.00
X-1556	Wentworth, Patricia - ***The Alington Inheritance*** [1966]	$ .75	$2.50	$5.00
X-1557	Wentworth, Patricia - ***The Chinese Shawl*** [1966] Cover art by Darrell Greene.	$1.00	$3.00	$6.00
X-1564	Tabori, Paul - ***The Doomsday Brian*** [1966]	$ .75	$2.50	$5.00
X-1567	Hennesley, Hal - ***The Midnight War*** [1967] PBO. Cover art by Richard Smith.	$1.00	$3.00	$6.00
R-1569	Dick, Philip K. - ***The Zap Gun*** [1967] PBO. Cover art by Jack Gaughan.	$4.00	$12.50	$25.00
T-1570	Hall, Adam - ***The Quiller Memorandum*** [1967]	$1.00	$3.00	$6.00
N-1572	Lyons, Eugene - ***David Sarnoff*** [1967]	$ .75	$2.50	$5.00
X-1573	Richert, William - ***Aren't You Even Gonna Kiss Me Good-By?*** [1967] Cover by Frank Kalan.	$1.00	$3.00	$6.00
R-1574	Kohner, Frederick - ***The Gremmie*** [1967]	$ .75	$2.50	$5.00
X-1575	Forbes, Stanton - ***Terror Touches Me*** [1967] Cover art by Lou Marchetti.	$1.00	$3.00	$6.00
X-1576	Williamson, Jack - ***The Legion Of Space*** [1967] Cover art by Gaughan.	$ .75	$2.50	$5.00
R-1577	Anthology edited by Phil Hirsch - ***Dirty Little Wars*** [1967]	$1.00	$3.00	$6.00
R-1578	Kurland, Michael - ***Mission: Third Force*** [1967] PBO. Cover by Jack Thurston.	$ .75	$2.50	$5.00

		G	VG	F
X-1579	Taylor, Phoebe Atwood - ***Figure Away*** [1967] Cover art by Joe Lombardero.	$1.00	$3.00	$6.00
R-1580	Daniels, Norman - ***Overkill*** [1967] Cover art by Maguire.	$ .75	$2.50	$5.00
T-1581	Kirst, Hans Helmut - ***The Last Card*** [1967] Cover art by Darrell Greene.	$1.00	$3.00	$6.00
T-1583	White, Leslie Turner - ***Lord Johnnie*** [1967]	$ .75	$2.50	$5.00
X-1584	Anthology edited by Phil Hirsch - ***Hollywood Confidential*** [1967] PBO. Photo cover.	$1.00	$3.00	$6.00
R-1585	Boucher, Anthony - ***The Case Of The Crumpled Knave*** [1967]	$ .75	$2.50	$5.00
X-1586	Williamson, Jack - ***The Legion Of Time*** [1967] Cover art by Gaughan.	$1.00	$3.00	$6.00
X-1587	Forbes, Stanton - ***Melody Of Terror*** [1967]	$ .75	$2.50	$5.00
N-1589	Hunter, Beatrice Trum - ***The Natural Foods Cookbook*** [1967] Photo cover.	$1.00	$3.00	$6.00
R-1591	Coles, Manning - ***Night Train To Paris*** [1967]	$ .75	$2.50	$5.00
X-1593	Phillips, J. B. - ***Good News*** [1967]	$1.00	$3.00	$6.00
X-1594	Gordon, S. D. - ***Quiet Talks On Prayer*** [1967]	$ .75	$2.50	$5.00
N-1595	Smith, William - ***Smith's Bible Dictionary*** [1967]	$1.00	$3.00	$6.00
T-1596	Caldwell, Taylor - ***Melissa*** [1967]	$ .75	$2.50	$5.00
T-1597	Caldwell, Taylor - ***The Wide House*** [1967]	$1.00	$3.00	$6.00
N-1598	Caldwell, Taylor - ***Dynasty Of Death*** [1967]	$ .75	$2.50	$5.00
R-1599	Weil, Jerry - ***Adventures In A Cold-Water Flat*** [1967]	$1.00	$3.00	$6.00
R-1600	Anthology edited by Ray Robinson - ***Baseball Stars Of 1967*** [1967] PBO. Photo cover. Eight pages of photos.	$ .75	$2.50	$5.00
X-1601	Ford, Marguerite - ***The Restless Lovers*** [1967]	$1.00	$3.00	$6.00
X-1602	Anthology edited by Phil Hirsch - ***Hitler And His Henchmen*** [1967] PBO. Photo cover.	$ .75	$2.50	$5.00
R-1603	Crane, Robert - ***The Paradise Trap*** [1967] PBO. Cover art by Jack Thurston.	$1.00	$3.00	$6.00
X-1608	Braithwaite, E. R. - ***To Sir, With Love*** [1968] Movie tie-in.	$ .75	$2.50	$5.00
X-1610	Andersen, Jan - ***Storm Castle*** [1967] PBO. Cover art by Lou Marchetti.	$1.00	$3.00	$6.00
X-1611	Ellison, Harlan - ***I Have No Mouth And I Must Scream*** [1967] PBO. Cover art by the Dillons.	$5.00	$15.00	$30.00
T-1614	Cassiday, Bruce - ***Happening At San Remo*** [1967]	$ .75	$2.50	$5.00
T-1615	Caldwell, Taylor - ***The Turnbulls*** [1967] Cover by Robert Abbett.	$1.00	$3.00	$6.00
R-1617	Daniels, Norman - ***Operation VC*** [1967] PBO. Cover art by Frank Kalan.	$ .75	$2.50	$5.00
X-1618	Household, Geoffrey - ***Rogue Male*** [1967]	$1.00	$3.00	$6.00
R-1621	Anthology edited by L. Sprague De Camp - ***The Fantastic Swordsmen*** [1967] PBO. Cover art by Jack Gaughan.	$1.35	$4.00	$8.00
X-1624	Briand, Jr., Paul L. - ***Daughter Of The Sky*** [1967] Photo cover. Eight pages of photos.	$ .75	$2.50	$5.00
X-1625	Wees, Frances Shelley - ***M'Lord, I Am Not Guilty*** [1967] Cover art by Mort Engel.	$1.00	$3.00	$6.00
X-1626	Winston, Daoma - ***The Moderns*** [1967]	$ .75	$2.50	$5.00
T-1627	Caldwell, Taylor - ***The Eagles Gather*** [1967]	$1.00	$3.00	$6.00
T-1629	Engstrand, Stuart - ***The Sling And The Arrow*** [1967] Cover art by Marvin Hayes.	$ .75	$2.50	$5.00
T-1630	Menger, Howard - ***From Outer Space*** [1967] Cover art by Henry Berkowitz. Eight pages of photos.	$1.00	$3.00	$6.00
X-1631	Coles, Manning - ***The Vengeance Man*** [1967] Cover art by Darrell Greene.	$ .75	$2.50	$5.00
R-1632	Coxe, George Harmon - ***With Intent To Kill*** [1967] Cover art by Darrell Greene.	$1.00	$3.00	$6.00
R-1633	Crane, Robert - ***Tongue Of Treason*** [1967]	$ .75	$2.50	$5.00
X-1634	Williamson, Jack - ***The Cometeers*** [1967] Cover art by Gaughan.	$1.00	$3.00	$6.00
K-1636	Scott, Bradford - ***Rider Of The Mesquite Trail*** [1967]	$ .75	$2.50	$5.00

		G	VG	F
T-1637	Caldwell, Taylor - ***The Strong City*** [1967] Cover by Robert Abbett.	$1.00	$3.00	$6.00
T-1638	Caldwell, Taylor - ***Time No Longer*** [1967] Cover by Darrell Greene.	$ .75	$2.50	$5.00
T-1639	Caldwell, Taylor - ***There Was A Time*** [1967]	$1.00	$3.00	$6.00
N-1640	Caldwell, Taylor - ***The Earth Is The Lord's*** [1967]	$ .75	$2.50	$5.00
T-1641	Caldwell, Taylor - ***Let Love Come Last*** [1967]	$1.00	$3.00	$6.00
T-1642	Caldwell, Taylor - ***The Balance Wheel*** [1967]	$ .75	$2.50	$5.00
X-1643	Sara, Dorothy - ***Handwriting Analysis*** [1967]	$1.00	$3.00	$6.00
X-1644	Anthology edited by Phil Hirsch - ***Medal Of Honor*** [1967]	$ .75	$2.50	$5.00
T-1645	Collier, Richard - ***10,000 Eyes*** [1967] Photo cover.	$1.00	$3.00	$6.00
X-1646	Soya, Carl Erik - ***"17"*** [1967] Photo cover. Movie tie-in.	$ .75	$2.50	$5.00
X-1648	Levy, Alan - ***Interpret Your Dreams*** [1967] Photo cover.	$1.00	$3.00	$6.00
R-1652	Daniels, Norman - ***Operation T*** [1967] PBO. Cover art by Frank Kalan.	$ .75	$2.50	$5.00
X-1654	Anthology edited by Phil Hirsch - ***Vietnam Combat*** [1967] PBO.	$1.00	$3.00	$6.00
T-1655	Holman, Dennis - ***Mau Mau Manhunt*** [1967] Cover art by Stan Borack.	$ .75	$2.50	$5.00
X-1657	Williamson, Jack - ***One Against The Legion*** [1967] PBO.	$1.35	$4.00	$8.00
K-1658	Scott, Bradford - ***Blood On The Moon*** [1967]	$1.00	$3.00	$6.00
R-1662	Coxe, George Harmon - ***One Way Out*** [1967] Cover art by Frank Kalan.	$ .75	$2.50	$5.00
R-1664	Laumer, Keith - ***The Invaders*** [1967] PBO. Photo cover. TV tie-in.	$1.50	$5.00	$10.00
T-1667	Cronin, A. J. - ***Three Loves*** [1967]	$1.00	$3.00	$6.00
K-1668	Scott, Bradford - ***Texas Death*** [1967]	$ .75	$2.50	$5.00
T-1669	Halliburton, Richard - ***The Glorious Adventure*** [1967] Cover art by Schoenherr & Portuesi.	$1.00	$3.00	$6.00
T-1671	Warner, Esther - ***Seven Days To Lomaland*** [1967] Cover art by Schoenherr.	$ .75	$2.50	$5.00
X-1673	Shoemaker, Sam - ***Extraordinary Living For Ordinary Men*** [1967]	$1.00	$3.00	$6.00
X-1674	Haggai, John E. - ***How To Win Over Worry*** [1967]	$ .75	$2.50	$5.00
T-1675	Larson, Bruce - ***Dare To Live Now!*** [1967] Cover art by Richard Smith.	$1.00	$3.00	$6.00
X-1676	McMillen, M.D., S.I. - ***None Of These Diseases*** [1967]	$ .75	$2.50	$5.00
X-1677	Van Dyke, Vonda Kay - ***That Girl In Your Mirror*** [1967] Photo cover.	$1.00	$3.00	$6.00
X-1679	Van Arnam, Dave & Archer, Ron - ***Lost In Space*** [1967] PBO. Photo cover. TV tie-in.	$1.50	$5.00	$10.00
R-1680	Leinster, Murray - ***Timeslip! (Time Tunnel Adventure #2)*** [1967] TV tie-in, TV photo cover.	$1.50	$5.00	$10.00
X-1681	Boucher, Anthony - ***Rocket To The Morgue*** [1967] Cover art by Len Goldberg.	$ .75	$2.50	$5.00
X-1682	Wentworth, Patricia - ***The Summer House*** [1967]	$1.00	$3.00	$6.00
R-1683	Stainback, Berry - ***Football Stars Of 1967*** [1967] PBO. Photo cover.	$ .75	$2.50	$5.00
T-1684	Carpozi, Jr., George - ***The Hidden Side Of Jacqueline Kennedy*** [1967] PBO. Sixteen pages of photos.	$1.00	$3.00	$6.00
T-1685	Bennett, Hal - ***A Wilderness Of Vines*** [1967] Photo cover.	$ .75	$2.50	$5.00
X-1686	Clarke, Arthur C. - ***Voices From The Sky*** [1967] Photo cover.	$1.00	$3.00	$6.00
X-1689	Laumer, Keith - ***Enemies From Beyond*** [1967] PBO. Invaders #2. Photo cover. TV tie-in.	$1.50	$5.00	$10.00
T-1690	Barron, Hugh - ***Tilt*** [1967]	$ .75	$2.50	$5.00
X-1691	Sturgeon, Theodore - ***The Synthetic Man*** [1967] Cover art by John Schoenherr.	$1.25	$3.75	$7.50
T-1692	Sanderson, Ivan T. - ***"Things"*** [1967] PBO. Photo cover.	$1.25	$3.75	$7.50
X-1693	Runyon, Poke - ***Commando X*** [1967]	$ .75	$2.50	$5.00

		G	VG	F
X-1694	Bourne, Hestor - ***In The Event Of My Death*** [1967] Cover art by Lou Marchetti.	$1.00	$3.00	$6.00
K-1695	Scott, Bradford - ***Pecos Law*** [1967]	$ .75	$2.50	$5.00
X-1696	Anthology edited by Phil Hirsch - ***COP*** [1967]	$1.00	$3.00	$6.00
X-1697	Anthology - ***4000 Questions And Answers On The Bible*** [1967]	$ .75	$2.50	$5.00
X-1700	Lewis, Norman - ***New Guide To Word Power*** [1967]	$ .65	$2.00	$4.00
T-1702	Lofts, Norah - ***Bless This House*** [1967] Cover art by Robert Cassell.	$1.00	$3.00	$6.00
X-1703	Clarke, Arthur C. - ***Against The Fall Of Night*** [1970] Cover art by Schoenherr.	$ .75	$2.50	$5.00
K-1705	Scott, Bradford - ***Thunder Trail*** [1967]	$1.00	$3.00	$6.00
T-1706	Cronin, A. J. - ***Hatter's Castle*** [1967]	$ .75	$2.50	$5.00
X-1707	Dunn, Jerry G. - ***God Is For The Alcoholic*** [1967]	$1.00	$3.00	$6.00
T-1708	Rae, George W. - ***RAM*** [1967]	$ .75	$2.50	$5.00
T-1709	Lofts, Norah - ***The Deadly Gift*** [1967]	$1.00	$3.00	$6.00
R-1710	Adler, Bill - ***Graffiti*** [1967] PBO. Photo cover.	$ .75	$2.50	$5.00
R-1711	Bernard, Rafe - ***Army Of The Undead*** [1967] PBO. Invaders #3. Photo cover. TV tie-in.	$1.50	$5.00	$10.00
X-1712	Seeley, Mabel - ***The Chuckling Fingers*** [1967]	$1.25	$3.75	$7.50
R-1714	Masur, Harold Q. - ***The Name Is Jordan*** [1967] Photo cover.	$1.25	$3.75	$7.50
T-1715	Lofts, Norah - ***Silver Nutmeg*** [1967]	$ .75	$2.50	$5.00
K-1716	Scott, Bradford - ***Curse Of Dead Man's Gold*** [1967]	$1.00	$3.00	$6.00
T-1721	Henriques, Robert - ***100 Hours To Suez*** [1967] Photo cover. Eight pages of photos.	$ .75	$2.50	$5.00
T-1722	Klein, Alexander - ***The Counterfeit Traitor*** [1967] Cover art by Alan Peckolick.	$1.00	$3.00	$6.00
R-1723	Anthology - ***The Nearsighted Mr. Magoo*** [1967] PBO. All comic strips.	$2.50	$7.50	$15.00
T-1724	Smith, George O. - ***Venus Equilateral*** [1967] Cover art by Jack Gaughan.	$1.25	$3.75	$7.50
R-1725	Stainback, Berry - ***Basketball Stars Of 1968*** [1967] PBO. Photo cover. Eight pages of photos.	$ .75	$2.50	$5.00
X-1726	Berckman, Evelyn - ***The Evil Of Time*** [1967] Cover art by Mort Engel.	$1.00	$3.00	$6.00
R-1727	Coxe, George Harmon - ***The Last Commandment*** [1967] Cover art by Frank Kalan.	$ .75	$2.50	$5.00
X-1728	Tabori, Paul - ***The Invisible Eye*** [1967] PBO. Cover art by Joe Lombardero.	$1.00	$3.00	$6.00
R-1729	Rice, Craig - ***The Name Is Malone*** [1967] Photo cover.	$1.25	$3.75	$7.50
X-1730	Anderson, Chester - ***The Butterfly Kid*** [1967] PBO. Cover art by Gray Morrow.	$1.50	$5.00	$10.00
K-1732	Scott, Bradford - ***Hot Lead And Cold Nerve*** [1967]	$ .75	$2.50	$5.00
X-1733	Boucher, Anthony - ***The Case Of The Solid Key*** [1968] Cover art by Len Goldberg.	$1.25	$3.75	$7.50
T-1734	Hall, Adam - ***The 9th Directive*** [1968] Movie tie-in. Cover by Lembit Rauk.	$ .75	$2.50	$5.00
T-1735	Lofts, Norah - ***Letty*** [1968]	$1.00	$3.00	$6.00
R-1736	Anthology - ***Alley Of The Dolls*** [1968] PBO. Cover art by Bob Zahn. Cartoon book.	$1.25	$3.75	$7.50
X-1737	Howard, Hartley - ***Assignment K*** [1968] Photo cover. Movie tie-in.	$ .75	$2.50	$5.00
X-1738	Kane, Henry - ***The Name Is Chambers*** [1968]	$1.25	$3.75	$7.50
X-1739	Sturgeon, Theodore - ***A Way Home*** [1968] Cover art by Gaughan.	$1.25	$3.75	$7.50
R-1740	Corby, Jane - ***Nurse Liza Hale*** [1968] Cover art by Mort Engel.	$ .65	$2.00	$4.00
X-1741	Vidal, Gore - ***A Search For The King*** [1968] Cover art by Darrell Greene.	$1.25	$3.75	$7.50
K-1743	Scott, Bradford - ***Lead And Flame*** [1968]	$ .75	$2.50	$5.00
N-1745	Clark, Linda - ***Stay Young Longer*** [1968] Cover art by Richard Smith.	$1.00	$3.00	$6.00

		G	VG	F
T-1748	Douglas, Mack R. - ***How To Make A Habit Of Succeeding*** [1968] Photo cover.	$ .65	$2.00	$4.00
N-1751	Anthology edited by Marie Gentert King - ***Foxe's Book Of Martyrs*** [1968]	$ .75	$2.50	$5.00
R-1757	Creasey, John - ***A Doll For The Toff*** [1968] Cover art by Richard Smith.	$1.00	$3.00	$6.00
X-1760	Anthology edited by Phil Hirsch - ***Hooked*** [1968] PBO. Photo cover.	$1.25	$3.75	$7.50
N-1762	Tharp, Louise Hall - ***The Peabody Sisters Of Salem*** [1968]	$ .75	$2.50	$5.00
V-1763	Maurois, Andre - ***Lelia*** [1968]	$1.00	$3.00	$6.00
V-1764	Maurois, Andre - ***Olympio*** [1968]	$ .75	$2.50	$5.00
N-1767	Sherrill, Robert - ***The Accidental President*** [1968]	$1.00	$3.00	$6.00
T-1769	Cronin, A. J. - ***The Spanish Gardener*** [1968] Cover art by Len Goldberg.	$ .75	$2.50	$5.00
R-1771	Stout, Rex - ***The Broken Vase*** [1968] Cover art by Len Goldberg.	$1.25	$3.75	$7.50
X-1773	Sturgeon, Theodore - ***Venus Plus X*** [1968] Cover art by Gray Morrow.	$1.25	$3.75	$7.50
T-1780	Ford, Daniel - ***Incident At Muc Wa*** [1968] Cover art by Darrell Greene.	$1.00	$3.00	$6.00
R-1783	Asimov, Isaac - ***The Rest Of The Robots*** [1968]	$1.25	$3.75	$7.50
X-1786	Daniels, Dorothy - ***Affair In Marrakesh*** [1968] PBO. Cover art by Darrell Greene.	$ .75	$2.50	$5.00
X-1787	White, Ted & Van Arnam, Dave - ***Sideslip*** [1968] PBO. Cover art by Gaughan.	$1.50	$5.00	$10.00
R-1788	Scott, Bradford - ***The Sky Riders*** [1968]	$1.00	$3.00	$6.00
R-1789	Anthology edited by Ray Robinson - ***Baseball Stars Of 1968*** [1968] PBO. Photo cover. Eight pages of photos.	$1.50	$5.00	$10.00
R-1792	Anthology - ***101 Hippie Jokes*** [1968]	$1.50	$5.00	$10.00
T-1793	Smith, George H. - ***Who Is Ronald Reagan?*** [1968] PBO. Photo cover. Eight pages of photos.	$ .75	$2.50	$5.00
X-1794	Anthology - ***Go Pop Annual 1968*** [1968] PBO. Photo cover. Sixteen pages of photos.	$1.35	$4.00	$8.00
N-1796	Hersey, Burnet - ***"Get The Boys Out Of The Trenches"*** [1968]	$1.00	$3.00	$6.00
X-1798	Thom, Robert - ***Wild In The Streets*** [1968] PBO. Photo cover. Movie tie-in with Richard Pryor.	$1.50	$5.00	$10.00
R-1799	Queen, Ellery - ***The Vanishing Corpse*** [1968]	$1.25	$3.75	$7.50
X-1800	Stout, Rex - ***Too Many Cooks*** [1968] Cover art by Len Goldberg.	$1.25	$3.75	$7.50
R-1801	Creasey, John - ***The Toff In Wax*** [1968] Cover art by Richard Smith.	$ .75	$2.50	$5.00
X-1802	Merril, Judith - ***The Tomorrow People*** [1968] Cover art by Gray Morrow.	$1.25	$3.75	$7.50
R-1804	Scott, Bradford - ***Outlaw Roundup*** [1968]	$1.00	$3.00	$6.00
R-1810	Queen, Ellery - ***The Penthouse Mystery*** [1968] Cover by Larry Lurin.	$1.25	$3.75	$7.50
R-1814	Queen, Ellery - ***The Perfect Crime*** [1968] Cover by Larry Lurin.	$1.25	$3.75	$7.50
X-1816	Stout, Rex - ***The Rubber Band*** [1968] Cover art by Len Goldberg.	$1.25	$3.75	$7.50
X-1818	Finney, Charles, G. - ***The Unholy City*** [1968] Cover art by Gaughan.	$1.25	$3.75	$7.50
R-1820	Scott, Bradford - ***Red Road Of Vengeance*** [1968]	$ .75	$2.50	$5.00
T-1822	Douglas, William O. - ***My Wilderness: The Pacific West*** [1968] Cover art by John Schoenherr.	$ .75	$2.50	$5.00
X-1824	Asimov, Isaac - ***The Caves Of Steel*** [1968]	$1.25	$3.75	$7.50
X-1825	Creasey, John - ***Fool The Toff*** [1968] Cover art by Richard Smith.	$1.00	$3.00	$6.00
N-1827	Rodale, J. I. - ***The Natural Way To Better Eyesight*** [1968] PBO. Cover by Larry Lurin.	$ .65	$2.00	$4.00

		G	VG	F
N-1828	Rodale, J. I. - ***Natural Health, Sugar And The Criminal Mind*** [1968] PBO. Cover art by Larry Lurin.	$ .65	$2.00	$4.00
X-1832	Lacy, Ed - ***The Napalm Bugle*** [1968] PBO. Cover art by Jack Thurston.	$1.25	$3.75	$7.50
R-1834	Scott, Bradford - ***Boom Town*** [1968]	$ .75	$2.50	$5.00
R-1835	Queen, Ellery - ***The Last Man Club*** [1968] Cover art by Larry Lurin.	$1.25	$3.75	$7.50
T-1836	Fisher, Vardis - ***The Divine Passion*** [1968] Cover art by Jack Thurston.	$ .75	$2.50	$5.00
X-1837	Budrys, Algis - ***The Falling Torch*** [1968]	$1.25	$3.75	$7.50
X-1846	Leinster, Murray - ***Land Of The Giants*** [1968] PBO. Photo cover. TV tie-in.	$1.50	$5.00	$10.00
X-1847	Stout, Rex - ***Some Buried Caesar*** [1968]	$1.25	$3.75	$7.50
X-1850	Perry, Eleanor - ***The Swimmer*** [1968] Photo cover. Movie tie-in with Burt Lancaster.	$1.00	$3.00	$6.00
X-1851	Smith, E. E. "Doc" - ***Masters Of The Vortex*** [1968] Cover art by Jack Gaughan.	$1.25	$3.75	$7.50
R-1853	Scott, Bradford - ***The River Raiders*** [1968] PBO. Cover art by Vic Prezio.	$ .75	$2.50	$5.00
R-1854	Anthology edited by Berry Stainback - ***Football Stars Of 1968*** [1968] PBO. Photo cover. Eight pages of photos.	$1.00	$3.00	$6.00
T-1856	Anthology edited by Phillip Flayderman - ***100 Great Poems*** [1968] PBO. Photo cover.	$ .65	$2.00	$4.00
X-1863	Bagni, Gwen & DuBov, Paul - ***With Six You Get Eggroll*** [1968] PBO. Photo cover. Movie tie-in.	$1.00	$3.00	$6.00
X-1864	Hardy, G. B - ***Countdown*** [1968]	$1.00	$3.00	$6.00
T-1869	Bloch, Robert - ***The Star Stalker*** [1968] PBO. Photo cover.	$4.00	$12.50	$25.00
X-1872	Stout, Rex - ***Black Orchids*** [1968]	$1.25	$3.75	$7.50
X-1874	Gilbert, Anthony - ***The Looking Glass Murder*** [1968] Cover art by Lou Marchetti.	$1.25	$3.75	$7.50
X-1875	Anderson, Poul - ***Three Worlds To Conquer*** [1968] Cover art by Gaughan.	$1.25	$3.75	$7.50
R-1877	Anthology edited by Phil Hirsch - ***Never On Freud-Day*** [1968] PBO. Cover art by Wenzel.	$2.00	$6.00	$12.00
R-1878	Scott, Bradford - ***Border War*** [1968] PBO. Cover art by Ronnie Lesser.	$1.00	$3.00	$6.00
N-1881	Rodale, J. I. - ***If You Must Smoke*** [1968] Photo cover.	$ .65	$2.00	$4.00
T-1883	Wilk, Max - ***One Of Our Brains Is Draining*** [1968] Cover art by Stevenson. Movie tie-in.	$ .75	$2.50	$5.00
T-1884	Caillou, Alan - ***The Charge Of The Light Brigade*** [1968] PBO. Cover art by Cassell.	$ .75	$2.50	$5.00
X-1886	Stout, Rex - ***The Red Box*** [1968]	$1.25	$3.75	$7.50
X-1888	Deming, Richard - ***The Greek God Affair*** [1968] PBO. Photo cover. Mod Squad #1. TV tie-in.	$1.50	$5.00	$10.00
X-1890	Anthony, Piers - ***SOS The Rope*** [1968] PBO. Cover art by Gaughan.	$2.50	$7.50	$15.00
X-1891	Evans, Everett E. - ***Man Of Many Minds*** [1968] Cover art by Gray Morrow.	$1.25	$3.75	$7.50
X-1892	Monsarrat, Nicholas - ***Castle Garae*** [1968] Cover art by Darrel Greene.	$ .75	$2.50	$5.00
R-1894	Scott, Bradford - ***Sixguns In A Bloody Dawn*** [1968]	$ .75	$2.50	$5.00
X-1897	Streeter, Robert A. & Hoehn, Robert G. - ***Are You A Genius?*** [1968] PBO. Quiz book. Illustrated by Dr. Seuss.	$1.00	$3.00	$6.00
X-1898	Harrison, Harry - ***War With The Robots*** [1968] Cover art by John Schoenherr.	$1.25	$3.75	$7.50
X-1899	Fischler, Stan - ***Hockey Stars Of 1969*** [1968] PBO. Photo cover. Eight pages of photos.	$1.00	$3.00	$6.00
N-1900	Vithaldas, Yogi & Roberts, Susan - ***The Yogi Cook Book*** [1968] Photo cover.	$1.00	$3.00	$6.00

		G	VG	F
X-1904	Hayes, Joseph - ***The Desperate Hours*** [1968] Cover art by Pfeiffer.	$ .75	$2.50	$5.00
X-1908	Deming, Richard - ***A Groovy Way To Die*** [1968] PBO. Photo cover. Mod Squad #2. TV tie-in.	$1.50	$5.00	$10.00
X-1909	Stout, Rex - ***Over My Dead Body*** [1968]	$1.25	$3.75	$7.50
X-1910	Smith, Cordwainer - ***The Underpeople*** [1968] PBO. Cover art by Jack Gaughan.	$1.50	$5.00	$10.00
X-1911	Smith, Cordwainer - ***Space Lords*** [1968] PBO. Cover art by Jack Gaughan.	$1.50	$5.00	$10.00
R-1913	Scott, Bradford - ***Hard Rock Showdown*** [1968]	$1.00	$3.00	$6.00
T-1915	Yogendra, Shri - ***Yoga Hygiene Simplified*** [1968] Eight pages of photos.	$ .75	$2.50	$5.00
Z-1916	Anthology - ***Student Travel In America*** [1968]	$1.00	$3.00	$6.00
X-1918	Fontaine, Robert - ***The Happy Time*** [1968] Cover art by Len Goldberg.	$ .75	$2.50	$5.00
T-1919	Griffin, Robert James - ***Coppersmith*** [1968]	$ .75	$2.50	$5.00
X-1921	Leinster, Murray - ***The Hot Spot*** [1969] PBO. Land of the Giants #2. Photo cover. TV tie-in.	$1.50	$5.00	$10.00
X-1922	Deming, Richard - ***The Sock-It-To-Em Murders*** [1968] PBO. Mod Squad #3. Photo cover. TV tie-in.	$1.50	$5.00	$10.00
X-1923	Stout, Rex - ***The Hand In The Glove*** [1968] Cover art by Len Goldberg.	$1.25	$3.75	$7.50
X-1924	Lathen, Emma - ***Death Shall Overcome*** [1968] Cover by Pfeiffer.	$1.25	$3.75	$7.50
T-1927	DeCamp, L. Spague - ***The Goblin Tower*** [1968] PBO. Cover art by Jeff Jones.	$1.50	$5.00	$10.00
X-1928	DeCamp, L. Sprague & Pratt, Fletcher - ***The Incomplete Enchanter*** [1968] Cover art by Jeff Jones.	$1.35	$4.00	$8.00
R-1929	Anthology edited by Phil Hirsch - ***A Man For All Squeezin's*** [1968] PBO. Cover art by A. Steinberg. Cartoon book.	$1.25	$3.75	$7.50
R-1930	Stainback, Berry - ***Basketball Stars Of 1969*** [1968] PBO. Photo cover. Eight pages of photos.	$1.00	$3.00	$6.00
T-1935	Roberts, Kenneth - ***Henry Gross And His Dowsing Rod*** [1969] Photo cover.	$1.00	$3.00	$6.00
X-1936	Stout, Rex - ***Red Threads*** [1969]	$1.25	$3.75	$7.50
1937	Crispin, Edmund - ***Buried For Pleasure*** [1969] Cover art by Pfieffer.	$1.25	$3.75	$7.50
X-1938	Ballinger, Bill S. - ***The Lopsided Man*** [1969] PBO. Cover art by Pfieffer.	$1.35	$4.00	$8.00
X-1939	Daniels, Dorothy - ***Affair In Hong Kong*** [1969] PBO. Cover art by Pfieffer.	$1.35	$4.00	$8.00
X-1940	Tabori, Paul - ***The Cleft*** [1969] PBO. Cover art by Jeff Jones.	$1.50	$5.00	$10.00
X-1941	Tabori, Paul - ***The Green Rain*** [1969] Cover art by Schoenherr.	$1.25	$3.75	$7.50
X-1942	Anthology edited by Phil Hirsch - ***Survival*** [1969] PBO. Photo cover.	$ .75	$2.50	$5.00
R-1943	Scott, Bradford - ***Laredo On The Rio Grande*** [1969] PBO. Cover art by Faragasso.	$ .75	$2.50	$5.00
T-1946	Biggers, Earl Derr - ***Charlie Chan Carries On*** [1969] Cover art by Ric Del Rossi.	$1.25	$3.75	$7.50
T-1947	Biggers, Earl Derr - ***The Black Camel*** [1969] Cover art by Ric Del Rossi.	$1.25	$3.75	$7.50
T-1950	Braithwaite, E. R. - ***Paid Servant*** [1969] Photo cover.	$ .75	$2.50	$5.00
T-1951	Leek & Kaufman - ***The Astrological Guide To Love And Sex*** [1969]	$1.00	$3.00	$6.00
X-1953	Stout, Rex - ***The Sound Of Murder*** [1969] Cover art by Len Goldberg.	$1.25	$3.75	$7.50
X-1954	Lynn, Margaret - ***A Light In The Window*** [1969] Cover art by Lou Marchetti.	$1.00	$3.00	$6.00
X-1955	Brunner, John - ***Black Is The Color*** [1969] PBO. Cover art by Jeff Jones.	$3.50	$10.00	$20.00

		G	VG	F
X-1957	Smith, George O. - ***Hell Flower*** [1969] Cover art by Jack Gaughan.	$1.25	$3.75	$7.50
R-1959	Scott, Bradford - ***Trail Of Empire*** [1969]	$1.00	$3.00	$6.00
N-1960	Bezymenski, Lev - ***The Death Of Adolf Hitler*** [1969] Photo cover. Sixteen pages of photos.	$ .75	$2.50	$5.00
X-1961	Graham, Billy - ***Billy Graham Talks To Teen-Agers*** [1969] Photo cover.	$ .75	$2.50	$5.00
1966	Narramore, Ed.D., Clyde M. - ***Understanding Your Children*** [1969]	$ .65	$2.00	$4.00
T-1968	Glanville, Brian - ***The Artist Type*** [1969]	$1.00	$3.00	$6.00
N-1969	Halper, Albert - ***The Chicago Crime Book*** [1969]	$1.00	$3.00	$6.00
T-1970	Biggers, Earl Derr - ***The Chinese Parrot*** [1969] Cover art by Ric Del Rossi.	$1.25	$3.75	$7.50
T-1971	Biggers, Earl Derr - ***Behind That Curtain*** [1969] Cover art by Ric Del Rossi.	$1.25	$3.75	$7.50
X-1972	Stout, Rex - ***Double For Death*** [1969]	$1.25	$3.75	$7.50
X-1973	Shannon, Dell - ***Mark Of Murder*** [1969]	$1.25	$3.75	$7.50
X-1975	Teta, Jon - ***The Clock At Ravenswood*** [1969] PBO. Cover art by Lou Marchetti.	$1.00	$3.00	$6.00
X-1976	Leiber, Fritz - ***Gather, Darkness*** [1969]	$1.25	$3.75	$7.50
X-1977	Sturgeon, Theodore - ***Starshine*** [1969] Cover art by Gaughan.	$1.25	$3.75	$7.50
R-1978	Scott, Bradford - ***Date With Death*** [1969]	$ .75	$2.50	$5.00
R-1979	Anthology edited by Ray Robinson - ***Baseball Stars Of 1969*** [1969] PBO. Photo cover. Eight pages of photos.	$ .75	$2.50	$5.00
T-1983	Morris, Wright - ***The Huge Season*** [1969]	$1.00	$3.00	$6.00
X-1986	Deming, Richard - ***Spy-In*** [1969] PBO. Mod Squad #4. Photo cover. TV tie-in.	$1.50	$5.00	$10.00
X-1987	Lathen, Emma - ***Murder Against The Grain*** [1969] Cover by Joe Lombardero.	$1.25	$3.75	$7.50
X-1988	Luard, Nicholas - ***The Warm And Golden War*** [1969] Cover art by Pfeiffer. Movie tie-in.	$1.00	$3.00	$6.00
X-1990	Kurland, Michael - ***The Unicorn Girl*** [1969] PBO. Cover art by Hoffman.	$1.50	$5.00	$10.00
X-1991	Ellison, Harlan - ***Paingod*** [1969]	$1.35	$4.00	$8.00
R-1993	Scott, Bradford - ***Hands Up!*** [1969]	$ .75	$2.50	$5.00
X-1996	Sarne, Michael - ***Joanna*** [1969] Photo cover. Movie tie-in.	$ .75	$2.50	$5.00
N-2001	Maltz, Albert - ***The Cross And The Arrow*** [1969]	$1.00	$3.00	$6.00
T-2002	Killens, John O. - ***Slaves*** [1969]	$ .75	$2.50	$5.00
T-2003	Biggers, Earl Derr - ***Keeper Of The Keys*** [1969] Cover art by Ric Del Rossi.	$ .75	$2.50	$5.00
T-2004	Biggers, Earl Derr - ***The House Without A Key*** [1969] Cover art by Ric Del Rossi.	$ .75	$2.50	$5.00
T-2005	Sanderson, Ivan T. - ***More Things*** [1969] PBO. Photo cover.	$ .75	$2.50	$5.00
X-2007	Sturgeon, Theodore - ***The Synthetic Man*** [1969] Photo cover.	$ .75	$2.50	$5.00
X-2008	Wentworth, Patricia - ***Through The Wall*** [1969]	$ .75	$2.50	$5.00
R-2010	Scott, Bradford - ***Sixgun Doom*** [1969] PBO. Photo cover.	$ .75	$2.50	$5.00
T-2012	Anthology edited by August Derleth - ***Time To Come*** [1969] Cover art by Gaughan.	$ .75	$2.50	$5.00
T-2014	Wilkerson, David - ***The Little People*** [1969]	$ .75	$2.50	$5.00
2018	Lathen, Emma - ***A Stitch In time*** [1969]	$ .75	$2.50	$5.00
T-2021	Wentworth, Patricia - ***The Fingerprint*** [1969]	$ .75	$2.50	$5.00
T-2022	Williamson, Jack - ***The Legion Of Space*** [1969]	$ .75	$2.50	$5.00
X-2023	Heinlein, Robert A. - ***6 X H*** [1969]	$ .75	$2.50	$5.00
R-2025	Scott, Bradford - ***Texas Blood*** [1969]	$ .75	$2.50	$5.00
T-2026	Greenburg, Dan - ***Chewsday*** [1969]	$ .75	$2.50	$5.00
X-2029	Wentworth, Patricia - ***Poison In The Pen*** [1969] Cover art by Darrell Greene.	$ .75	$2.50	$5.00
X-2030	Sturgeon, Theodore - ***A Way Home*** [1969]	$ .75	$2.50	$5.00
X-2031	Creasey, John - ***The Toff And The Kidnapped Child*** [1969]	$ .75	$2.50	$5.00

		G	VG	F
T-2036	Queen, Ellery - editor - ***Ellery Queen's Murder - In Spades!*** [1969] PBO.	$ .75	$2.50	$5.00
X-2057	Tabori, Paul - ***The Torture Machine*** [1969] PBO.	$ .75	$2.50	$5.00
T-2638	Ellison, Harlan - ***I Have No Mouth & I Must Scream*** [1972]	$ .75	$2.50	$5.00
A-3791	Ellison, Harlan - ***The Other Glass Teat*** [1975] PBO.	$4.00	$12.50	$25.00
V-3931	Ellison, Harlan - ***The Deadly Streets*** [1975] New introduction.	$1.50	$5.00	$10.00
99876	Robinson, Ray - ***Baseball Stars Of 1973*** [1973] PBO. Photos.	$ .75	$2.50	$5.00

Quarter Books. Digest Size.

		G	VG	F
19	Clayford, James (Peggy Gaddis) - ***Bed-time Girl*** [1949] Cover art by Rodewald.	$4.00	$12.50	$25.00
20	Leinster, Murray - ***Fighting Horse Valley*** [1949] Cover art by Rodewald.	$5.00	$15.00	$30.00
21	Gordon, Luthor - ***Shamed!*** [1949] Cover art by Rodewald.	$4.00	$12.50	$25.00
22	Gordon, Luthor - ***Unfaithful!*** [1949] Cover art by Rodewald.	$4.00	$12.50	$25.00
23	Leinster, Murray - ***Texas Gun Law*** [1949] Cover art by Rodewald.	$5.00	$15.00	$30.00
24	Gordon, Luther - ***Passion's Mistress*** [1949] Cover art by Rodewald.	$4.00	$12.50	$25.00
25	Leinster, Murray - ***Wanted Dead Or Alive!*** [1949] PBO. Cover by Rodewald.	$5.00	$15.00	$30.00
26	Clayford, James (Peggy Gaddis) - ***Respectable Harlot*** [1949] Cover art by Rodewald.	$4.00	$12.50	$25.00
27	Clayford, James (Peggy Gaddis) - ***Sinful!*** [1949]	$4.00	$12.50	$25.00
28	Clayford, James (Peggis Gaddis) - ***Lure For Love*** [1949] Cover art by George Gross.	$4.00	$12.50	$25.00
29	Gordon, Luthor - ***Immoral!*** [1949] Cover art by Gross.	$4.00	$12.50	$25.00
30	Clayford, James (Peggis Gaddis) - ***Marriage Can Wait*** [1949] Cover art by Rodewald.	$4.00	$12.50	$25.00
31	Gordon, Luthor - ***Wicked!*** [1949] Cover by George Gross.	$4.50	$14.00	$28.00
32	Clayford, James (Peggy Gaddis) - ***Careless!*** [1949] Cover art by Gross.	$4.50	$14.00	$28.00
33	Gordon, Luther - ***Naughty Virgin*** [1949]	$4.00	$12.50	$25.00
34	Gordon, Luther - ***Pleasure Girl*** [1949] Cover art by Rodewald.	$4.00	$12.50	$25.00
35	Gordon, Luther - ***Ecstasy!*** [1949] Cover art by Rodewald.	$4.50	$14.00	$28.00
36	Gordon, Luther - ***Tempted!*** [1949] Cover art by Rodewald.	$4.50	$14.00	$28.00
37	Gordon, Luther - ***Love Cheat*** [1949] Cover art by George Gross.	$4.50	$14.00	$28.00
38	Gordon, Luther - ***Wolf Trap Blonde*** [1949] Cover art by George Gross.	$4.00	$12.50	$25.00
39	Bellamy, Harmon - ***Frenchy*** [1949] Cover art by Wenzel.	$4.00	$12.50	$25.00
40	Caldwell, John - ***Night Of Passion*** [1949] PBO. Cover art by George Gross.	$4.50	$14.00	$28.00
41	Bellamy, Harmon - ***Pick-Up*** [1949] Cover art by George Gross.	$4.00	$12.50	$25.00
42	Caldwall, John - ***Midnight Sinners*** [1949]	$4.00	$12.50	$25.00
43	Foster, Gerald - ***Vera Is A Tramp*** [1949] Cover art by Rodewald.	$4.50	$14.00	$28.00
44	Higgins, Russell - ***Bad Woman*** [1949]	$4.50	$14.00	$28.00
45	Sloane, Ross - ***Hot Number*** [1949]	$4.50	$14.00	$28.00
46	Jordan, Gail - ***Call Girl*** [1949]	$4.00	$12.50	$25.00
47	Bligh, Norman - ***Sin Child*** [1949] PBO.	$4.00	$12.50	$25.00
48	Lindsay, Perry - ***As Good As Married*** [1949] Cover art by George Gross.	$4.50	$14.00	$28.00
49	Higgins, Russell - ***Burlesque Queen*** [1949]	$4.00	$12.50	$25.00
50	Colohan, Charles E. - ***Overnight Blonde*** [1949]	$4.00	$12.50	$25.00
51	Wright, Watkins E. - ***Wild Passion*** [1949] PBO. Cover art by Rodewald.	$4.50	$14.00	$28.00
52	Sloane, Ross - ***Three Naked Souls*** [1949]	$4.00	$12.50	$25.00
53	Colohan, Charles E. - ***Virgin No More*** [1949]	$4.50	$14.00	$28.00
54	Appel, H.M. - ***Illicit Desires*** [1949] Cover art by Gross.	$4.50	$14.00	$28.00

		G	VG	F
55	Clayford, James (Peggis Gaddis) - ***Wedding Night Confession*** [1950]	$4.00	$12.50	$25.00
56	Wilstach, John - ***Bedtime Blonde*** [1950] Cover art by Rodewald.	$4.50	$14.00	$28.00
57	Foster, Gerald - ***The Virgin And The Barfly*** [1950]	$4.00	$12.50	$25.00
58	Wright, Watkins E. - ***Margie Is For Loving*** [1950] Cover art by Rodewald.	$4.00	$12.50	$25.00
59	Sherman, Joan - ***Pushover*** [1950] PBO.	$4.50	$14.00	$28.00
60	Foster, Gerald - ***Room And Dame*** [1950] PBO.	$4.00	$12.50	$25.00
61	Clayford, James (Peggis Gaddis) - ***Careless Virgin*** [1950] Cover art by Rodewald.	$4.50	$14.00	$28.00
62	Williams, Wright - ***Everybody Loves Irene*** [1950] Cover art by George Gross.	$4.50	$14.00	$28.00
63	Jones, Harvey - ***One Night With Diane*** [1950]	$4.50	$14.00	$28.00
64	Clayford, James (Peggy Gaddis) - ***Bed Time Girl*** [1950] Cover art by Rodewald.	$4.00	$12.50	$25.00
65	Dupperault, Doug - ***Passionate Pick-Up*** [1950] PBO. Cover art by Gross.	$4.00	$12.50	$25.00
66	Bellamy, Harmon - ***Flesh And Females*** [1950]	$4.50	$14.00	$28.00
69	Clayford, James (Peggy Gaddis) - ***Illicit Wife*** [1950]	$4.50	$14.00	$28.00
70	Gordon, Luther - ***Naughty Virgin*** [1950]	$4.00	$12.50	$25.00
71	Gordon, Luthor (James N. Gifford) - ***Passion's Mistress*** [1950] Cover art by Rodewald.	$4.00	$12.50	$25.00
72	Clayford, James (Peggy Gaddis) - ***Respectable Harlot*** [1950] Cover art by Rodewald.	$4.50	$14.00	$28.00
73	Stonebraker, Florence - ***Love Life Of A Hollywood Mistress*** [1950] PBO.	$4.00	$12.50	$25.00
74	Harvey, Gene - ***"Leg-Art" Virgin*** [1950] PBO.	$4.50	$14.00	$28.00
75	Quandt, Albert L. - ***The Sins Of Allie-May*** [1950] PBO.	$4.50	$14.00	$28.00
76	Foster, Gerald - ***Quickie!*** [1950] PBO. Cover art by George Gross.	$4.00	$12.50	$25.00
77	Duperrault, Doug - ***Red-Light Babe*** [1950] PBO.	$4.50	$14.00	$28.00
78	Bligh, Norman - ***Waterfront Hotel*** [1950] PBO.	$4.00	$12.50	$25.00
79	Bligh, Norman - ***Bad Sue*** [1950] PBO.	$4.50	$14.00	$28.00
80	Stonebraker, Florence - ***Frisco Dame*** [1950] PBO.	$4.50	$14.00	$28.00
81	Bligh, Norman - ***Fast, Loose And Lovely*** [1950] PBO.	$4.50	$14.00	$28.00
82	Gaddis, Peggy - ***Illicit Pleasure*** [1950] PBO.	$4.00	$12.50	$25.00
83	Stonebraker, Florence - ***Four Men And A Dame*** [1951] PBO.	$4.00	$12.50	$25.00
84	Bligh, Norman - ***Born To Be Bad*** [1951] PBO.	$4.50	$14.00	$28.00
85	Stonebraker, Florence - ***Flesh Is Weak*** [1951] PBO.	$4.00	$12.50	$25.00
86	Sherman, Joan - ***Girl On The Make*** [1951] PBO.	$4.00	$12.50	$25.00
88	Hatter, Amos - ***Untamed Woman*** [1951] PBO.	$4.50	$14.00	$28.00
89	Bligh, Norman - ***The Lady Is Taboo*** [1951] Cover art by Gross.	$4.50	$14.00	$28.00
90	Stonebraker, Florence - ***Flirting Eyes*** [1951] PBO.	$4.00	$12.50	$25.00
91	Quandt, Albert L. - ***Street Girl*** [1951] PBO.	$4.50	$14.00	$28.00
92	Stonebraker, Florence - ***Three Men And A Mistress*** [1951] PBO. Cover art by George Gross.	$4.50	$14.00	$28.00
93	Sherman, Joan - ***Thrill Me - Suzy*** [1951]	$4.00	$12.50	$25.00
94	Bligh, Norman - ***Artists' Model*** [1951] PBO. Cover art by Gross.	$4.00	$12.50	$25.00
96	Dupperault, Doug - ***Confessions Of A Dime-A-Dance Queen*** [1951]	$4.00	$12.50	$25.00

Quick Reader (Early Publisher's History, 1944–1959)

For those with only a few minutes to read, the Quick Reader offers a variety of popular literature in a very short format. Similar to the Dell Ten Cent Novels, this series came in a small format of 3" x 4¾". They bound each volume by stapling it and restricted the length of each book to 128 pages. Each title received a simulated spine drawn on the front cover, along with attractive cover art.

Royce Publications also present two collectible volumes under the Trophy Books line.

Quick Readers. New York: Royce Publishers, Inc. $3^{1}/_{8}$" x $4^{5}/_{8}$".

		G	VG	F
101	De Maupassant, Guy - ***Breath Taking Stories Of Passion And Crime*** [1943] PBO. Cover by Axelrod.	$2.50	$7.50	$15.00
102	White, Stewart Edward - ***The Killer*** [1943] Cover by Axelrod.	$2.50	$7.50	$15.00
103	Zola, Emile - ***Nana*** [1943] Cover by Axelrod.	$2.50	$7.50	$15.00
104	Anthology - ***The Chillers*** [1943] PBO. Cover by Axelrod.	$2.50	$7.50	$15.00
105	Anthology - ***Laugh Your Head Off*** [1943] PBO. Cover by Axelrod.	$2.50	$7.50	$15.00
106	Anthology - ***Great Short Stories For Your Reading Pleasure*** [1943] PBO. Cover by Axelrod.	$2.50	$7.50	$15.00
107	Hecht, Ben - ***The Florentine Dagger*** [1943] Cover by Axelrod.	$2.50	$7.50	$15.00
108	Webster, Miriam - ***Self-Pronouncing New Webster's Pocket Size Dictionary*** [1943]	$2.00	$6.00	$12.00
109	Pernikoff, Alexandre - ***"Bushido": The Anatomy Of Terror*** [1943] Cover by Axelrod.	$2.50	$7.50	$15.00
110	Bronte, Charlotte - ***Jane Eyre*** [1944] Cover art by Axelrod.	$2.50	$7.50	$15.00
111	Anthology - ***Here's Reading You'll Enjoy*** [1944] PBO. Cover by Axelrod.	$2.50	$7.50	$15.00
112	Anthology - ***More Fun Than Looking Thru A Keyhole!*** [1944] PBO. Cover art by Axelrod.	$2.50	$7.50	$15.00
113	De Witt, Jack - ***Murder on Shark Island*** [1944] Cover by Axelrod.	$2.50	$7.50	$15.00
114	Dostoyevsky, Fyodor - ***Crime And Punishment*** [1944] Cover by Axelrod.	$2.50	$7.50	$15.00
115	Fishman, Nathaniel - ***How To Safeguard Your Income, Your Children, Your Property*** [1944]	$2.50	$7.50	$15.00
116	Anthology - ***Try This For Size*** [1944] PBO. Cover by Jones.	$2.50	$7.50	$15.00
117	Hecht, Ben - ***Count Bruga*** [1944] Cover by Axelrod.	$2.50	$7.50	$15.00
118	Cuppy, Will - ***How To Tell Your Friends From The Apes*** [1944] Cover by Axelrod.	$2.50	$7.50	$15.00
119	Dickens, Charles - ***A Tale Of Two Cities*** [1944]	$3.50	$10.00	$20.00
120	Anthology - ***Time Out For Murder*** [1944] PBO. Cover by Axelrod.	$2.50	$7.50	$15.00
121	Rinehart, Mary Roberts - ***The Curve Of The Catenary*** [1944]	$2.50	$7.50	$15.00
122	Bronte, Emily - ***Wuthering Heights*** [1944] Cover by Cirkle.	$2.50	$7.50	$15.00
123	Harlow, Alvin F. - ***True Murders Not Quite Solved*** [1944]	$2.50	$7.50	$15.00
124	Anthology - ***15 Short Short Surprise Stories*** [1944] PBO. Cover art by Axelrod.	$2.50	$7.50	$15.00
125	Anthology - ***Strictly On The Funny Side*** [1944] PBO. Cover by Axelrod.	$2.50	$7.50	$15.00
126	Anthology - ***Love Is A Funny Business*** [1944] PBO. Cover by Axelrod.	$2.50	$7.50	$15.00
127	Anthology - ***Celebrated Stories Made Into Movies*** [1944] PBO. Cover by Axelrod.	$2.50	$7.50	$15.00
128	Pentecost, Hugh - ***Cat And Mouse*** [1944] Cover by Axelrod.	$2.50	$7.50	$15.00
129	Butler, Samuel - ***The Way Of All Flesh*** [1945]	$2.50	$7.50	$15.00
130	Stevenson, Robert Lewis - ***Treasure Island*** [1945]	$2.50	$7.50	$15.00
131	Biggers, Earl Derr - ***Seven Keys To Baldpate*** [1945] Cover by Axelrod.	$2.50	$7.50	$15.00
132	Lyon, Dana - ***I'll Be Glad When You're Dead*** [1945] Cover art by Cirkle.	$2.50	$7.50	$15.00
133	Loos, Anita - ***Gentlemen Prefer Blondes*** [1945] Cover by Cirkle.	$2.50	$7.50	$15.00
134	Frome, David - ***Mr. Pinkerton: Passage For One*** [1945]	$2.50	$7.50	$15.00

		G	VG	F
135	Anthology - ***Humorous Ghost Stories*** [1945] PBO. Cover by Cirkle.	$2.50	$7.50	$15.00
136	Swift, Jonathan - ***Gulliver's Travels*** [1945]	$3.50	$10.00	$20.00
137	Anthology - ***Bedside Bedlam*** [1945] PBO. Cover by Cirkle.	$2.50	$7.50	$15.00
138	Gautier, Theophile - ***Mademoiselle DeMaupin*** [1945]	$2.50	$7.50	$15.00
139	Anthology - ***One Side Please*** [1945] PBO.	$2.50	$7.50	$15.00
140	Poe, Edgar Allan - ***The Best Of Edgar Allan Poe*** [1945] PBO.	$4.00	$12.50	$25.00
141	Anthology - ***Quick Reader Bible*** [1945]	$2.50	$7.50	$15.00
142	Stevenson, Robert Louis - ***The Strange Case Of Dr. Jekyll And Mr. Hyde*** [1945]	$3.50	$10.00	$20.00
143	Anthology - ***Great Comedies Made Into Movies*** [1945] PBO. Cover by Cirkle.	$2.50	$7.50	$15.00
144	Anthology - ***Unforgettable French Love Stories*** [1945] PBO.	$2.50	$7.50	$15.00
145	Pentecost, Hugh - ***The Dead Man's Tale*** [1945] Cover by Axelrod.	$3.50	$10.00	$20.00
147	Spence, Hartzell - ***One Foot In Heaven*** [1945] Cover by Axelrod.	$4.00	$12.50	$25.00
148	Tuttle, W. C. - ***Blind Trail At Sunrise*** [1945] PBO. Cover by Cirkle.	$4.00	$12.50	$25.00
149	Dumas, Alexandre - ***Camille*** [1945] Cover by Cirkle.	$2.50	$7.50	$15.00

R. W. Company. New York: R. W. Company, Inc. Digest Size.

		G	VG	F
NN-1	Charles, Franklin - ***The Vice Czar Murders*** [n.d.]	$4.00	$12.50	$25.00
NN-2	Benedict, Gerald - ***"The Case Of The Deadly Drops"*** [n.d.]	$5.00	$15.00	$30.00

Rainbow Books. Clifton, MA: Colonial Press, Inc. Digest Size.

		G	VG	F
2	Stackman, Howard - ***The Complete Bedside Joke Book*** [1955] PBO. Cover art by Al Ross.	$2.50	$7.50	$15.00
3	Armstrong, A. L. - ***Midnite Joke Book*** [1956] PBO. Cover by Al Ross.	$2.50	$7.50	$15.00
101	Stackman, Howard - ***The Complete Bedside Joke Book*** [1953] Cover by Al Ross.	$2.50	$7.50	$15.00
102	Dunn, Seymour - ***The Complete Golf Joke Book*** [1953] Cover by Al Ross.	$2.50	$7.50	$15.00
103	Sterling, Hank - ***Ten Perfect Crimes*** [1954] Cover by Mark Snyder.	$2.50	$7.50	$15.00
356	Sterling, Hank - ***Famous Western Outlaw-Sheriff Battles*** [1954] PBO.	$2.50	$7.50	$15.00
542	Pezet, A. W. & Chambers, Bradford - ***Greatest Crimes Of The Century*** [1954] Cover by Mark Snyder.	$2.50	$7.50	$15.00

Rainbow Books. New York: Rainbow Books, Inc. Digest Size.

		G	VG	F
101	Harvey, Gene - ***Thrill Girl*** [1951]	$4.00	$12.50	$25.00
102	Stonebraker, Florence - ***Reno Tramp*** [1951]	$4.00	$12.50	$25.00
103	Hale, Laura - ***Wild Is The Woman*** [1951] PBO.	$4.00	$12.50	$25.00
104	Balmer, Jon - ***Moment Of Rapture*** [1951] PBO. Cover art by George Gross.	$4.00	$12.50	$25.00
105	Reed, Mark - ***Four Dames Named "Sin"*** [1951] PBO. Cover art by Rudy Nappi.	$4.00	$12.50	$25.00
106	Stone, Tom - ***Nora's No Angel*** [1951] PBO. Cover by George Gross.	$4.00	$12.50	$25.00
107	Reed, Mark (Norman Daniels) - ***Street Of Dark Desires*** [1951] PBO.	$4.00	$12.50	$25.00
108	McCollum, R.R. - ***Passion Has Red Lips*** [1951] PBO.	$4.00	$12.50	$25.00
109	Evens, Hodge - ***Her Candle Burns Hot!*** [1951] PBO.	$4.00	$12.50	$25.00
110	Culver, Kathryn - ***Sleepy Time Honey*** [1951]	$4.00	$12.50	$25.00
111	Wade, David (Norman Daniels) - ***Walk The Evil Street*** [1952] PBO.	$4.50	$14.00	$28.00
112	Stone, Tom - ***Red Headed Wench*** [1952] PBO. Cover by George Gross.	$4.50	$14.00	$28.00

		G	VG	F
113	Wayne, Rick - ***Play Rough!*** [1952] PBO.	$4.00	$12.50	$25.00
114	Reed, Mark (Norman Daniels) - ***Tease The Wild Flame!*** [1952] PBO.	$4.50	$14.00	$28.00
115	Munroe, Val - ***Carnival Of Passion*** [1952] PBO. Cover art by George Gross.	$4.00	$12.50	$25.00
116	Wade, David (Norman Daniels) - ***She Walks By Night*** [1952] PBO.	$4.50	$14.00	$28.00
117	Daniels, Norman A. - ***Bedroom In Hell*** [1952] PBO. Cover by George Gross.	$4.50	$14.00	$28.00
118	Hale, Laura - ***Kiss Of Fire*** [1952] PBO.	$4.00	$12.50	$25.00
119	Treat, Roger - ***Joy Ride!*** [1952] PBO. Cover art by Gross.	$4.00	$12.50	$25.00
120	Reed, Mark (Norman Daniels) - ***The Nude Stranger*** [1952] PBO.	$4.00	$12.50	$25.00
121	White, Lionel - ***Seven Hungry Men!*** [1952].	$4.00	$12.50	$25.00
122	Burleson, Terry O.K. - ***The Madam Who Blushed!*** [1952] PBO. Cover by George Gross.	$4.00	$12.50	$25.00
123	Reed, Mark (Norman Daniels) - ***Vice-Cop*** [1952] PBO.	$4.00	$12.50	$25.00
124	Wade, David (Norman Daniels) - ***Bedroom With A View*** [1952] PBO. Cover art by George Gross.	$4.00	$12.50	$25.00
125	Munroe, Val - ***Tender Hearted Harlot*** [1952] PBO. Cover art by Barton.	$4.00	$12.50	$25.00
126	Turner, Robert - ***She-Devil*** [1952] PBO. Cover art by Gross.	$4.00	$12.50	$25.00
127	Colton, Mel - ***The Big Woman*** [1953] PBO. Cover art by Barton.	$4.00	$12.50	$25.00
128	Dann, Norma (Norman Daniels) - ***The Twist!*** [1953] PBO.	$4.00	$12.50	$25.00
129	Wade, David (Norman Daniels) - ***Only Human*** [1953].	$4.00	$12.50	$25.00
130	Bottari, George L. - ***Off Limits*** [1953] PBO.	$4.00	$12.50	$25.00

Ram Book. New York: Imperial Publishing.

RB-104	Anonymous - ***Sex Machine*** [1964] PBO.	$2.50	$7.50	$15.00

Randall Mystery. Toronto: Randall Publishing Co. Digest Size.

NN	Broome, Adam - ***The Queen's Hall Murder*** [n.d.]	$6.00	$20.00	$40.00

Rapture Book. Culver City, CA: Rapture Books.

202	Saxon, Vin - ***Ape Rape*** [1964] PBO.	$1.50	$5.00	$10.00

Raven Book.

713	Wood, Jr., Edward D. - ***Blacklace Drag*** [1963] PBO. Author's first adult novel.	$6.00	$20.00	$40.00

Reader's League of America.

NN-1	Anthology edited by Shirley Cunningham - ***The Pocket Entertainer*** [1942]	$1.25	$3.75	$7.50
NN-2	Van Dine, S.S. - ***The Canary Murder Case*** [1942] Cover art by Manso.	$1.25	$3.75	$7.50
NN-3	Bentley, E.C. - ***Trent's Last Case*** [1942] Cover art by Hoffman.	$1.25	$3.75	$7.50
NN-4	Kesselring, Joseph - ***Arsenic And Old Lace*** [1942]	$1.25	$3.75	$7.50
NN-5	Hammett, Dashiell - ***The Maltese Falcon*** [1942] Cover art by Manso.	$1.25	$3.75	$7.50
NN-6	Hilton, James - ***Lost Horizon*** [1942] Cover art by Steinberg.	$1.25	$3.75	$7.50
NN-7	Hammett, Dashiell - ***Red Harvest*** [1942]	$1.25	$3.75	$7.50
NN-8	Gardner, Erle Stanley - ***The Case Of The Dangerous Dowager*** [1942]	$1.25	$3.75	$7.50
NN-9	Queen, Ellery - ***The Four Of Hearts*** [1942]	$1.25	$3.75	$7.50
NN-10	Wodehouse, P.G. - ***Jeeves*** [1942]	$1.25	$3.75	$7.50
NN-11	Charteris, Leslie - ***Enter The Saint*** [1942]	$1.25	$3.75	$7.50
NN-12	Gardner, Erle Stanley - ***The Case Of The Substitute Face*** [1942]	$1.25	$3.75	$7.50
NN-13	Irish, William - ***Phantom Lady*** [1942]	$1.25	$3.75	$7.50

		G	VG	F
NN-14	Queen, Ellery - ***The Egyptian Cross Mystery*** [1942]	$1.25	$3.75	$7.50
NN-15	Gardner, Erle Stanley - ***The Case Of The Stuttering Bishop*** [1942]	$1.25	$3.75	$7.50
NN-16	Queen, Ellery - ***Halfway House*** [1942]	$1.25	$3.75	$7.50
NN-17	Smith, Thorne - ***Topper Takes A Trip*** [1942]	$1.25	$3.75	$7.50
NN-18	Biggers, Earl Derr - ***The Chinese Parrot*** [1942]	$1.25	$3.75	$7.50
NN-19	Rinehart, Mary Roberts - ***The Circular Staircase*** [1942]	$1.25	$3.75	$7.50
NN-20	Benson, G.R. - ***Abraham Lincoln*** [1942]	$1.25	$3.75	$7.50
NN-21	Christie, Agatha - ***And Then There Were None*** [1942]	$1.25	$3.75	$7.50
NN-22	Pyle, Ernie - ***Here Is Your War*** [1942]	$1.25	$3.75	$7.50
NN-23	Rice, Craig - ***Trial By Fury*** [1942]	$1.25	$3.75	$7.50
NN-24	Oppenheim, E. Phillips - ***The Great Impersonation*** [1942]	$1.25	$3.75	$7.50

Reader's Library. Chicago: Reader's Library. Digest Size.

		G	VG	F
NN-1	Chidsey, Donald Barr - ***Weeping Is For Women*** [1940]	$3.50	$10.00	$20.00
NN-2	Cozzens, James Gould - ***Last Adam*** [1940]	$3.50	$10.00	$20.00
NN-3	Steinbeck, John - ***Cup Of Gold*** [1940]	$6.00	$20.00	$40.00
NN-4	Hardy, J.L. - ***Everything Is Thunder*** [1940] Cover by George Salter.	$3.50	$10.00	$20.00

Reader's-Choice Library. New York: St. John Publishing Co.

		G	VG	F
1	Robertson, Frank C. - ***Six-Gun Law In Wrango*** [1950] PBO. Digest size.	$1.50	$5.00	$10.00
2	Gruber, Frank - ***Smoky Road*** [1950] Digest size.	$2.00	$6.00	$12.00
3	Glay, George Albert - ***Gina*** [1950] Paperback size.	$1.50	$5.00	$10.00
4	Robertson, Frank C. - ***The Powder Burner*** [1950] Paperback size. Cover by Norman Saunders.	$1.50	$5.00	$10.00
5	Echols, Allan K. - ***The Stranger From Texas*** [1950] Digest size. Cover art by Norman Saunders.	$1.50	$5.00	$10.00
6	Mann, E. B. - ***Texas Lightnin'*** [1950] Digest size.	$1.50	$5.00	$10.00
7	Fowler, Gene - ***Shoe The Wild Mare*** [1950] Paperback size.	$1.50	$5.00	$10.00
8	Kane, Frank - ***Green Light For Death*** [1950] Paperback size. Cover by Blickenstaff.	$3.50	$10.00	$20.00
9	Bragg, W.F. - ***Smoky Joe*** [1950] Digest size.	$1.50	$5.00	$10.00
10	Echols, Allan K. - ***Barb Wire Showdown*** [1950] Digest size.	$1.50	$5.00	$10.00
11	Caspary, Vera - ***Stranger Than Truth*** [1950] Cover by Wayne Blickenstaff. Paperback size.	$1.50	$5.00	$10.00
12	Irish, William - ***Nightmare*** [1950] Cover art by Wayne Blickenstaff.	$5.00	$15.00	$30.00
13	Gruber, Frank - ***Outlaw*** [1950] Digest size.	$2.00	$6.00	$12.00
14	Robertson, Frank C. - ***Trouble Shootin' Man And Other Stories*** [1950] PBO. Digest size.	$1.50	$5.00	$10.00
15	Gruber, Frank - ***The Lock And The Key*** [1950] Cover art by Wayne Blickenstaff. Digest size.	$2.00	$6.00	$12.00
16	Gruber, Frank - ***Murder '97*** [1950] Cover art by Wayne Blickenstaff. Digest size.	$2.00	$6.00	$12.00
17	Overholser, Wayne D. - ***Gun Crazy*** [1950] PBO. Cover art by Saunders. Digest size.	$1.50	$5.00	$10.00
18	Holmes, L.P. - ***Bloody Saddles*** [1950] Digest size.	$1.50	$5.00	$10.00
19	Gruber, Frank - ***Broken Lance*** [1950] Digest size.	$2.00	$6.00	$12.00
20	Fowler, Gene - ***Trumpet In The Dust*** [1950] Digest size.	$1.50	$5.00	$10.00
21	Greig, Maysie - ***Don't Wait For Love*** [1950] Digest size. Cover art by Dawson.	$1.50	$5.00	$10.00
22	Grainger, Bonnie - ***The Hussy*** [1950] Digest size. Cover art by King.	$1.50	$5.00	$10.00
23	Campbell, Alice - ***Veiled Murder*** [n.d.] Digest size. Cover art by Dawson.	$1.50	$5.00	$10.00
24	Robertson, Frank C. - ***Red Rustlers*** [1951] PBO. Cover art by Singer. Digest size.	$1.50	$5.00	$10.00

		G	VG	F
25	Ross, Zola - ***Bonanza Queen*** [1951] Cover art by Dawson. Digest size.	$1.50	$5.00	$10.00
26	Henderson, George C. - ***The Killers*** [1951] Cover art by Singer. Digest size.	$1.50	$5.00	$10.00
27	Valbeck, Michael - ***Sinful Bargain*** [1951] Cover art by Singer. Digest size.	$1.50	$5.00	$10.00
29	Colt, Clem - ***Gunsmoke*** [1951] Digest size.	$1.50	$5.00	$10.00
30	Nezelof, N. Pierre - ***Scandalous Loves*** [1951] Cover art by Dawson. Digest size.	$1.50	$5.00	$10.00
31	Lange, Anneke de - ***Farm Girl*** [1951] Cover art by Wayne Blickenstaff. Digest size.	$1.50	$5.00	$10.00
32	Branch, Houston & Waters, Frank - ***Secret Affair*** [1951] Cover by Wayne Blickenstaff. Digest size.	$1.50	$5.00	$10.00
33	Halleran, E.E. - ***Prairie Guns*** [1952]	$1.50	$5.00	$10.00
35	Rockey, Howard - ***Wild Oats*** [1952] Digest size. Cover by Downes.	$1.50	$5.00	$10.00
36	Glemser, Bernard - ***Strange Love*** [1952]	$1.50	$5.00	$10.00
37	Eagan, Alberta Stedman - ***They Call It Sin*** [1952] Paperback size. Cover by Downes.	$1.50	$5.00	$10.00
38	Brock, Stuart - ***Death Is My Lover*** [1952] Paperback size.	$1.50	$5.00	$10.00
39	Hayden, Eric Rhodes - ***Lover Boy*** [1952] Paperback size. Cover by Downes.	$1.50	$5.00	$10.00
40	DeRosso, H.A. - ***Tracks In The Sand*** [n.d.] Paperback size.	$1.50	$5.00	$10.00

Red Arrow Books. Milwaukee, WI: Red Arrow Books.

		G	VG	F
1	Christie, Agatha - ***Thirteen At Dinner*** [1939]	$5.50	$17.50	$35.00
2	Jones, Jennifer - ***Murder On Hudson*** [1939]	$5.50	$17.50	$35.00
3	Rhode, John - ***Murders In Praed Street*** [1939]	$5.50	$17.50	$35.00
4	Ketchum, Philip - ***Death In The Library*** [1939]	$5.50	$17.50	$35.00
5	Popkin, Zelda - ***Death Wears A White Gardenia*** [1939]	$5.50	$17.50	$35.00
6	Musprat, Eric - ***My South Sea Island*** [1939]	$5.50	$17.50	$35.00
7	Riis, Commander S. M. - ***Yankee Komisar*** [1939]	$5.50	$17.50	$35.00
8	Smith, Laurence D. - ***Girl Hunt*** [1939]	$5.50	$17.50	$35.00
9	Beeding, Francis - ***The Seven Sleepers*** [1939]	$5.50	$17.50	$35.00
10	Mason, F. Van Wyck - ***Captain Nemesis*** [1939]	$5.50	$17.50	$35.00
11	Moore, Olga - ***Windswept*** [1939]	$5.50	$17.50	$35.00
12	Williams, Ben Ames - ***Pirate's Purchase*** [1939]	$5.50	$17.50	$35.00
NN(13)	Marquand, John P. - ***The Unspeakable Gentleman*** [1940]	$5.50	$17.50	$35.00

Red Circle Books. New York: Red Circle Magazines, Inc.

		G	VG	F
1	Archer, Jules & Sawyer, Maxine - ***Sex Life And You*** [1949] PBO.	$3.50	$10.00	$20.00
2	Moroso, John - ***Passionate Fool*** [1949]	$4.00	$12.50	$25.00
3	Harvey, Gene - ***Leg Artist*** [1949]	$4.50	$14.00	$28.00
4	Martin, Don - ***Blonde Menace*** [1948] Movie tie-in.	$4.50	$14.00	$28.00
5	Peters, Royal - ***Body Or Soul*** [1949] Cover art by Charles Andres.	$4.50	$14.00	$28.00
6	Lehman, Paul Evan - ***Passion In The Dust*** [1949] PBO. Cover by George Gross.	$5.00	$15.00	$30.00
7	Storm, Elliot - ***Hot Date*** [1949]	$4.50	$14.00	$28.00
12	West, Token - ***Why Get Married?*** [1949] Title page states "A Lion Book." Cover by Louise Altson.	$5.50	$17.50	$35.00
13	Scott, Anthony - ***Carnival Of Love*** [1949] Cover by Ray Johnson.	$5.50	$17.50	$35.00

Red Seal Books. Greenwich, CT: Fawcett Publications.

		G	VG	F
7	O'Hara, Dennison - ***The Sky Tramps*** [1952] PBO. Cover by Barye Phillips.	$1.50	$5.00	$10.00
8	Gehman, Richard - ***Each Life To Live*** [1952] PBO. Cover by Barye Phillips.	$1.50	$5.00	$10.00

		G	VG	F
9	Idell, Albert - ***This Woman*** [1952] PBO. Cover art by Barye Phillips.	$2.00	$6.00	$12.00
10	Johnson, Ryerson - ***Naked In The Streets*** [1952] PBO. Cover by Carl Bobertz	$1.50	$5.00	$10.00
11	Smith, Don - ***Out Of The Sea*** [1952] PBO.	$2.00	$6.00	$12.00
12	Morgan, Nancy - ***City Of Women*** [1952] PBO. Cover by Barye Phillips.	$2.50	$7.50	$15.00
13	Vail, John - ***The Sea Waifs*** [1952] PBO. Cover art by Barye Phillips.	$1.50	$5.00	$10.00
14	Skelly, Mike - ***Halo For A Heel*** [1952] PBO. Cover art by Barye Phillips.	$1.50	$5.00	$10.00
15	Hatten, Homer - ***Bride Of The Sword*** [1952] PBO. Cover by Barye Phillips.	$1.50	$5.00	$10.00
16	Pratt, Theodore - ***The Golden Sorrow*** [1952] PBO.	$1.50	$5.00	$10.00
17	Osborne, O.O. - ***The Quest*** [1952]	$1.50	$5.00	$10.00
18	Dickson, H. Vernor - ***The Marriage Bed*** [1952] PBO. Cover by Barye Phillips.	$1.50	$5.00	$10.00
19	Adams, Fay - ***Lili Of Paris*** [1952] PBO. Cover by Barye Phillips.	$1.50	$5.00	$10.00
20	Sheridan, Jack - ***Girl From Town*** [1952] PBO. Cover by Barye Phillips.	$1.50	$5.00	$10.00
21	Fisher, Steve - ***Be Still My Heart*** [1952] PBO.	$1.50	$5.00	$10.00
22	Kennedy, Charles - editor (anthology) - ***American Ballads: Naughty, Ribald And Classic*** [1951] PBO	$1.50	$5.00	$10.00
23	Gonzales, John - ***The Magnificent Moll*** [1952] PBO. Cover by Barye Phillips.	$1.50	$5.00	$10.00
24	Davis, Jada M. - ***One For Hell*** [1952] PBO. Cover art by John Floherty, Jr.	$2.00	$6.00	$12.00
25	Van Siller, Hilda - ***Thy Name Is Woman*** [1952] PBO.	$1.50	$5.00	$10.00
26	Ross, Sam - ***This, Too, Is Love*** [1953] PBO. Cover by Barye Phillips.	$2.00	$6.00	$12.00
27	Vail, John - ***Love Isn't For Now*** [1953] PBO.	$1.50	$5.00	$10.00
28	Johnson, Ryerson - ***Mississippi Flame*** [1953]	$1.50	$5.00	$10.00
29	Spafford, Robert - ***Fare Thee Well*** [1953] PBO. Cover by John Floherty, Jr.	$1.50	$5.00	$10.00

Reed Nightstand Books.

		G	VG	F
3001	Elliott, Don (Silverberg, Robert) - ***Love Addict*** [n.d.]	$1.25	$3.75	$7.50
3003	Merchant, Paul (Harlan Ellison) - ***Sex Gang*** [1973] Reprints Nightstand Books #NB1503 and 1503R.	$27.50	$85.00	$200.00
3004	Elliott, Don (Silverberg, Robert) - ***Gang Girl*** [n.d.]	$1.25	$3.75	$7.50
3008	Elliott, Don (Silverberg, Robert) - ***Summertime Affair*** [n.d.]	$1.25	$3.75	$7.50
3009	Elliott, Don (Silverberg, Robert) - ***Party Girl*** [n.d.]	$1.25	$3.75	$7.50
3012	Elliott, Don (Silverberg, Robert) - ***Naked Holiday*** [n.d.]	$1.25	$3.75	$7.50

Regency Books. Evanston, IL: Regency Books, Inc.

		G	VG	F
RB-101	Bloch, Robert - ***Firebug*** [1961] PBO. Cover art by The Dillons.	$5.00	$15.00	$30.00
RB-102	Ellison, Harlan - ***Gentleman Junkie*** [1961] PBO. Cover by The Dillons.	$20.00	$60.00	$125.00
RB-103	Marvin, Ronn - ***Mr. Ballerina*** [1961] PBO. Cover art by The Dillons.	$4.00	$12.50	$25.00
RB-104	Sagebiel, James - ***The Brain Buyers*** [1961] PBO. Cover art by The Dillons.	$4.00	$12.50	$25.00
RB-105	Honig, Donald - ***Divide The Night*** [1961] PBO. Cover art by Ron Bradford.	$4.00	$12.50	$25.00
RB-106	Ellison, Harlan - ***Memos From Purgatory*** [1961] PBO. Cover by The Dillons.	$22.00	$70.00	$140.00
RB-107	Traven, B. - ***The Man Nobody Knows*** [1961] PBO. Cover art by Ron Bradford.	$8.00	$25.00	$50.00

		G	VG	F
RB-108	Ellson, Hal - ***The Torment Of The Kids*** [1961] PBO. Cover art by Richard Frooman.	$5.00	$15.00	$30.00
RB-109	Cooper, Clarence, L. - ***Weed*** [1961] PBO. Cover art by W.A. Smith.	$5.00	$15.00	$30.00
RB-110	Budrys, Algis - ***Some Will Not Die*** [1961] PBO. Cover art by The Dillons.	$6.00	$20.00	$40.00
RB-111	Scortia, Thomas N. - ***What Mad Oracle*** [1961] PBO. Cover art by W.A. Smith.	$4.00	$12.50	$25.00
RB-112	Sheckley, Robert - ***The Man In The Water*** [1961] PBO. Cover by Mel Pekarsky.	$8.00	$25.00	$50.00
RB-113	del Rey, Lester - ***The Eleventh Commandment*** [1962] PBO. Cover by The Dillons.	$6.00	$20.00	$40.00
RB-114	Alexander, David - ***Panic!*** [1962] PBO. Cover art by Mel Pekarsky.	$4.00	$12.50	$25.00
RB-115	Brannon, W. T. - ***The Crooked Cops*** [1962] PBO. Cover by Ron Bradford.	$4.00	$12.50	$25.00
RB-116	Cooper, Clarence, L. - ***The Dark Messenger*** [1962] PBO. Cover art by Richard A. Thompson.	$4.00	$12.50	$25.00
RB-117	Weston, Paul B. - ***Muscle On Broadway*** [1962] PBO. Cover art by Will Gallagher.	$4.00	$12.50	$25.00
RB-118	Farmer, Philip Jose - ***Fire And The Night*** [1962] PBO. Cover by The Dillons.	$5.00	$15.00	$30.00
RB-301	Drummond, Walter (Robert Silverberg) - ***Philosopher Of Evil*** [1962] Cover art by Ron Bradford.	$4.00	$12.50	$25.00
RB-302	Brossard, Chandler - editor - ***The Pangs Of Love*** [1962] PBO. Cover art by Ron Bradford.	$4.00	$12.50	$25.00
RB-303	Blum, Neil Elliot - ***The Hills Of Creation*** [1962] PBO. Cover art by Ron Bradford.	$4.00	$12.50	$25.00
RB-304	Weston, Paul B. - ***A Hammer In The City*** [1962] PBO.	$4.00	$12.50	$25.00
RB-305	Gilmore, Hobe - ***Bloody Grass*** [1962] PBO.	$4.00	$12.50	$25.00
RB-306	Roskolenko, Harry - ***White Man Go!*** [1962] PBO.	$4.00	$12.50	$25.00
RB-307	Bowling, Jackson M. - ***In The Line Of Fire*** [1962] PBO. Cover by Smith.	$4.00	$12.50	$25.00
RB-308	Davidson, Avram - ***Crimes And Chaos*** [1962] PBO. Cover by Ron Bradford.	$5.00	$15.00	$30.00
RB-309	Smith, Cordwainer - ***You Will Never Be The Same*** [1963] PBO. Cover by Ron Bradford.	$5.00	$15.00	$30.00
RB-310	Miles, William E. - ***Damn*** [1963] PBO.	$4.00	$12.50	$25.00
RB-311	Webb, Jack - ***The Gilded Witch*** [1963] PBO. Cover by Robert Keys.	$4.50	$14.00	$28.00
RB-312	Vetter, Hal - ***Women Of The Swastika*** [1963] Cover by George Suyeoka.	$5.00	$15.00	$30.00
RB-313	Cooper, Jr., Clarence L. - ***Black!*** [1963] PBO.	$4.00	$12.50	$25.00
RB-314	Mason, Frank - ***Truman And The Pendergasts*** [1963] PBO. Cover by George Suyeoka.	$4.00	$12.50	$25.00
RB-315	Gant, Matthew - ***Queen Street*** [1963] PBO. Cover by The Dillons.	$5.00	$15.00	$30.00
RB-316	Bunin, Ed - ***Hack # 777*** [1963] PBO. Cover by Terry Martin Rose.	$4.00	$12.50	$25.00
RB-317	Russell, Eric Frank - ***The Rabble Rousers*** [1963] PBO. Cover by George Suyeoka.	$8.00	$25.00	$50.00
RB-318	Drummond, Walter (Robert Silverberg) - ***How To Spend Money*** [1963] PBO. Cover by Rose.	$4.00	$12.50	$25.00
RB-319	Haas, Ben - ***KKK*** [1963] PBO. Cover by Rose.	$4.50	$14.00	$28.00
RB-320	Edmonds, I.G. - ***Hollywood R.I.P.*** [1963] PBO.	$4.00	$12.50	$25.00
RB-321	Reynolds, Mack - ***The Expatriates*** [1963] PBO. Cover by Ron Bradford.	$4.00	$12.50	$25.00
RB-322	Thompson, Jim - ***The Grifters*** [1963] PBO. Cover by Rose.	$32.00	$110.00	$250.00
RB-323	Bellah, James Warner - ***Fighting Men, U.S.A.*** [1963] Cover by Suyeoka.	$4.00	$12.50	$25.00

		G	VG	F
RB-324	Millard, Joseph - ***No Law But Their Own*** [1963] PBO. Cover by Bradford.	$4.00	$12.50	$25.00

Retail Distributors.

		G	VG	F
NN	Bromberg, Lester - ***World's Champs*** [1958] PBO.	$2.50	$7.50	$15.00
101	Prager, Ted & Craft, Larry - ***Hoodlums-Los Angeles*** [1959] PBO.	$2.50	$7.50	$15.00
102	Prager, Ted & Moberly, Leeds - ***Hoodlums-New York*** [1959]	$2.50	$7.50	$15.00

Rex Stout Mystery. New York: Avon Book Co. Digest Size.

		G	VG	F
1	Anthology - ***Includes "Death And Company" by Dashiell Hammett*** [1945]	$4.00	$12.50	$25.00
2	Anthology - ***Includes "The Simple Art Of Murder" by Raymond Chandler*** [1945]	$4.00	$12.50	$25.00
4	Anthology - ***Includes "New Murders For Old" by Carter Dickson*** [1946] Magazine format.	$4.00	$12.50	$25.00
5	Anthology - ***Includes "Help Wanted Male" by Rex Stout*** [1946]	$4.00	$12.50	$25.00
6	Anthology - ***Includes "Operation Luella" by Leslie Charteris*** [1946]	$4.00	$12.50	$25.00
7	Anthology - ***Includes "Nightmare" by William Irish*** [1946]	$4.00	$12.50	$25.00
8	Anthology - ***Includes "The Body Of A Well Dressed Woman" by William Irish*** [1947]	$4.00	$12.50	$25.00

Robert Edwards. New York: Robert Edwards Pub., Inc. Digest Size.

		G	VG	F
NN-1	Anthology - ***Forty Eight Current Short Stories*** [n.d.]	$1.35	$4.00	$8.00

Romantic Novels. New York: Romantic Reprints, Inc. Digest Size.

		G	VG	F
NN-1	Lawrence, Ann - ***Dance Hall Girl*** [1952] Cover art by Rodewald.	$4.00	$12.50	$25.00
NN-2	Saxon, John - ***Reckless Girl*** [1952] Cover art by Rodewald.	$4.00	$12.50	$25.00
NN-3	Semple, Gordon - ***The Affairs Of A Mistress*** [1952] Cover art by Rodewald.	$4.00	$12.50	$25.00
NN-4	Brown, Beth - ***The Loves Of A Harlot*** [1952] Cover art by Rodewald.	$4.00	$12.50	$25.00

Royal Books Giant Editions. New York: Royal Books.

		G	VG	F
12	Mundy, Talbot - ***Jimgrim Sahib*** [1953]	$3.00	$9.00	$18.00
14	Steen, Marguerite - ***Matador*** [1953]	$2.50	$7.50	$15.00
15	The Army Weekly - ***Highlights From Yank*** [1953] PBO. Cover art by Sgt. Howard Brodie.	$3.00	$9.00	$18.00
16	Pliever, Theodor - ***Stalingrad*** [1953] Cover art by Barye Phillips.	$2.50	$7.50	$15.00
17	Anonymous/Winston, Daoma - ***Adam And Two Eves/The Other Stranger*** [1953] /PBO. Cover art by Walter Popp.	$3.00	$9.00	$18.00
18	Haggard, H. Rider - ***Allan Quatermain/King Solomon's Mines*** [1953]	$3.00	$9.00	$18.00
19	Mundy, Talbot - ***Trek East*** [1953] Cover art by Barye Phillips.	$3.00	$9.00	$18.00
20	Mundy, Talbot/Willeford, Charles - ***Full Moon/High Priest Of California*** [1953] /PBO. Cover art by Walter Popp.	$22.00	$70.00	$140.00
21	Weller, George - ***Highway Episode*** [1953]	$2.50	$7.50	$15.00
22	Jakes, John/Mundy, Talbot - ***Gonzaga's Woman/Affair In Araby*** [1953] PBO/	$3.00	$9.00	$18.00
23	Zweig, Arnold - ***The Case Of Sergeant Grischa*** [1953]	$2.50	$7.50	$15.00
24	Defoe, Daniel - ***Roxana*** [1953] Cover by Barye Phillips.	$2.50	$7.50	$15.00
25	Gautier, Theophile/Voltaire - ***Mademoiselle De Maupin/Candide*** [1953] Covers by Walter Popp.	$2.50	$7.50	$15.00
26	Anthology - ***The Harem Of HSI Men*** [1953] Cover by Barye Phillips.	$2.50	$7.50	$15.00
27	Nixon, Henry Lewis/Winston, Daoma - ***Confessions Of A Psychiatrist/The Woman He Wanted*** [1954] PBO.	$2.50	$7.50	$15.00

		G	VG	F
28	Twain, Mark - ***The Unnatural Son/A Connecticut Yankee*** [1954] Cover art by Saul Levine	$3.00	$9.00	$18.00
29	Butler, Saumel - ***The Way Of All Flesh*** [1954]	$2.50	$7.50	$15.00

Saint Mystery Library. New York: Great American Publications, Inc.

		G	VG	F
118	Anthology - ***Stairway To Murder*** [1959] PBO. Cover art by Sussman.	$2.00	$6.00	$12.00
119	Anthology - ***Witness To Death*** [1959] PBO. Cover art by Sussman.	$2.00	$6.00	$12.00
120	Anthology - ***Murder Set To Music*** [1959] PBO. Cover art by Sussman.	$2.00	$6.00	$12.00
121	Anthology edited by Leslie Charteris - ***The Frightened Millionaire*** [1959] PBO. Cover by Ted Coconis.	$2.00	$6.00	$12.00
122	Anthology - ***Murder Made In Moscow*** [1959] PBO. Cover art by Luszcz.	$2.00	$6.00	$12.00
123	Anthology - ***Murder In The Family*** [1959] PBO. Photo cover.	$2.00	$6.00	$12.00
124	Anthology - ***Death Stops At A Tourist Camp*** [1959] PBO. Photo cover.	$2.00	$6.00	$12.00
125	Blochman, Lawrence G. - ***Red Snow At Darjeeling*** [1959] Photo cover.	$2.00	$6.00	$12.00
126	Anthology - ***Executioner's Signature*** [1960] PBO. Cover art by Frank Kalin.	$2.00	$6.00	$12.00
127	Brown, Wenzell - ***Murder Seeks An Agent*** [1960] Photo cover	$2.00	$6.00	$12.00
128	Anthology - ***Let Her Kill Herself*** [1960] PBO. Cover art by Frank Kalin.	$3.50	$10.00	$20.00
129	Rice, Craig - ***Innocent Bystander*** [1960] Photo cover	$2.00	$6.00	$12.00
130	Anthology - ***Death Walks In Marble Halls*** [1960] PBO. Cover art by Leonard Goldberg.	$2.00	$6.00	$12.00
131	Anthology - ***The Rum And Coca-Cola Murders*** [1960] PBO. Photo cover.	$2.00	$6.00	$12.00

Saint Novel.

		G	VG	F
K-102	Charteris, Leslie - ***The Saint Sees It Through*** [n.d.]	$2.00	$6.00	$12.00
K-103	Charteris, Leslie - ***The Saint Closes The Case*** [n.d.] Original Title: *The Last Hero*.	$2.00	$6.00	$12.00
K-104	Charteris, Leslie - ***The Avenging Saint*** [n.d.]	$2.00	$6.00	$12.00
K-105	Charteris, Leslie - ***Saint's Getaway*** [n.d.]	$2.00	$6.00	$12.00
K-106	Charteris, Leslie - ***The Saint In New York*** [n.d.]	$2.00	$6.00	$12.00
K-107	Charteris, Leslie - ***Enter The Saint*** [n.d.]	$2.00	$6.00	$12.00
K-108	Charteris, Leslie - ***The Saint Meets His Match*** [n.d.]	$2.00	$6.00	$12.00
K-109	Charteris, Leslie - ***Featuring The Saint*** [n.d.]	$2.00	$6.00	$12.00
K-110	Charteris, Leslie - ***Alias The Saint*** [n.d.]	$2.00	$6.00	$12.00
K-111	Charteris, Leslie - ***The Saint Overboard*** [n.d.]	$2.00	$6.00	$12.00
K-112	Charteris, Leslie - ***The Saint—The Brighter Buccaneer*** [n.d.]	$2.00	$6.00	$12.00
K-113	Charteris, Leslie - ***The Saint Vs. Scotland Yard*** [n.d.]	$2.00	$6.00	$12.00
K-114	Charteris, Leslie - ***The Saint And Mr. Teal*** [n.d.]	$2.00	$6.00	$12.00

Scorpio Book. Chicago: N.A.C. Publications.

		G	VG	F
104	English, Charles (Nuetzel) - ***Lovers: 2075*** [1964]	$2.50	$7.50	$15.00
106	Johnson, David - ***Jungle Nymph*** [1964] PBO	$1.50	$5.00	$10.00

Signet Books (Early Publisher's History, 1948–1959)

Exceptional cover art helps Signet Books to stand out. The work of James Avati covers many early titles, and in the subsequent years, they present the work of Stanley Metzoff, Robert Maguire, and others. The same holds true for their academic line, Mentor, which presents the work of Robert Jonas on many covers. This line began when New American Library bought the American Penguin and Pelican lines. The

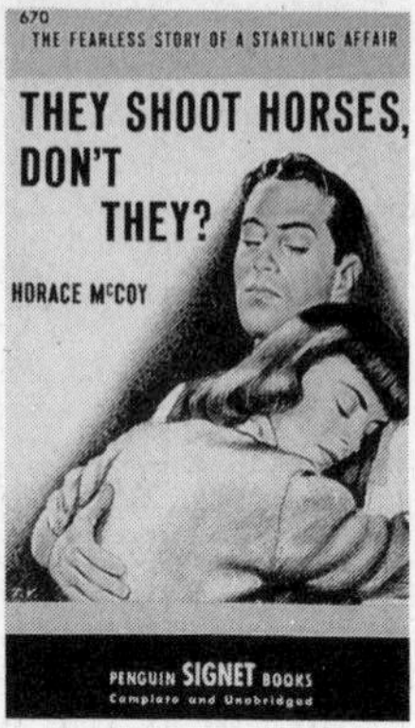

Signet Book, 670

Signet Book, 678

Signet Book, 698

series numbering picks up where the American Penguin numbers ended. The first titles of this new imprint began as Penguin Signet. A great number of quality titles appear under this imprint.

New American Library also published the following imprints: Signet Giants, Signet Doubles, Signet Triples, Signet Key, Signet Classic, and Mentor Books.

Signet Books. New York: New American Library.

		G	VG	F
660	Anthology edited by Selden Rodman - ***100 American Poems*** [1948] Cover art by Jonas.	$1.35	$4.00	$8.00
661	Caldwell, Erskine - ***Tragic Ground*** [1948] Cover art by Jonas.	$1.35	$4.00	$8.00
662	Lehmann, Rosamond - ***Invitation To The Waltz*** [1948]	$1.35	$4.00	$8.00
663	Dewey, Thomas B. - ***As Good As Dead*** [1948] Cover art by Jonas.	$2.00	$6.00	$12.00
664	Joyce, James - ***A Portrait Of The Artist As A Young Man*** [1948] Cover art by Jonas.	$1.35	$4.00	$8.00
665	Smith, Lillian - ***Strange Fruit*** [1948] Cover art by Jonas.	$1.35	$4.00	$8.00
666	Lehman, Paul Evan - ***Valley of Hunted Man*** [1948]	$1.35	$4.00	$8.00
667	Hynd, Alan - ***The Pinkerton Casebook*** [1948] PBO. Cover art by Robert Jonas.	$1.50	$5.00	$10.00
668	Heatter, Basil - ***The Dim View*** [1948]	$1.35	$4.00	$8.00
669	McCulley, Johnston - ***The Caballero*** [1948]	$1.35	$4.00	$8.00
670	McCoy, Horace - ***They Shoot Horses, Don't They?*** [1948]	$3.50	$10.00	$20.00
671	Koestler, Arthur - ***Darkness At Noon*** [1948]	$1.35	$4.00	$8.00
672	Lemay, Alan - ***Cattle Kingdom*** [1948]	$1.35	$4.00	$8.00
673	Raine, William MacLeod - ***Sons Of The Saddle*** [1948]	$1.35	$4.00	$8.00
674	Balchin, Nigel - ***Mine Own Executioner*** [1948] Movie tie-in.	$1.35	$4.00	$8.00
675	Enid, Curie & Geddes, Donald Porter - ***About The Kinsey Report*** [1948] PBO. Cover art by Jonas.	$1.25	$3.75	$7.50
676	Anet, Claude - ***Ariane*** [1948]	$1.35	$4.00	$8.00
677	Miller, Wade - ***Guilty Bystander*** [1948] Cover art by Jonas.	$1.50	$5.00	$10.00
678	Anthology - ***The Signet Crossword Puzzle Book*** [1948] Cover art by Jonas.	$5.00	$15.00	$30.00
679	Ermine, Will - ***Laramie Rides Again*** [1948] Cover art by Robert Jonas.	$1.35	$4.00	$8.00
680	Cain, James M. - ***Past All Dishonor*** [1948]	$2.00	$6.00	$12.00
681	Culbertson, Ely - ***Contract Bridge For Everyone*** [1948] Cover art by Robert Jonas.	$1.25	$3.75	$7.50
682	Lehman, Paul Evan - ***Blood Of The West*** [1948] Cover art by Robert Jonas.	$1.35	$4.00	$8.00
683	Jackson, Charles - ***The Lost Weekend*** [1948]	$1.50	$5.00	$10.00

Signet Book, 699

Signet Book, 719

Signet Book, 798

		G	VG	F
684	Holman, Hugh - ***Slay The Murderer*** [1948] Cover art by Jonas.	$1.50	$5.00	$10.00
685	Ermine, Will - ***Lobo Law*** [1948] Cover art by Robert Jonas.	$1.35	$4.00	$8.00
686	Caldwell, Erskine - ***A House In The Uplands*** [1948] Cover art by Jonas.	$1.35	$4.00	$8.00
687	Wakeman, Frederic - ***Shore Leave*** [1949]	$1.35	$4.00	$8.00
688	Shappiro, Herbert - ***High Pockets*** [1948]	$1.35	$4.00	$8.00
689	Gruber, Frank - ***The Silver Tombstone*** [1948] Cover art by Robert Jonas.	$1.50	$5.00	$10.00
690	McCoy, Horace - ***No Pockets In A Shroud*** [1948] First U.S. edition.	$2.50	$7.50	$15.00
691	De Pereda, Prudencio - ***All The Girls We Loved*** [1948]	$1.35	$4.00	$8.00
692	Faulkner, William - ***The Old Man*** [1948] Cover art by Jonas.	$1.50	$5.00	$10.00
693	Bemelmans, Ludwig - ***I Love You, I Love You, I Love You*** [1948]	$1.35	$4.00	$8.00
694	Heckelmann, C. N. - ***Lawless Range*** [1949]	$1.35	$4.00	$8.00
695	Miller, Wade - ***Fatal Step*** [1948]	$1.50	$5.00	$10.00
696	Ward, Mary Jane - ***The Snake Pit*** [1949] Movie tie-in.	$1.35	$4.00	$8.00
697	Wolfe, Thomas - ***Look Homward, Angel*** [1948]	$1.50	$5.00	$10.00
698	MacDonald, William Colt - ***Black Sombrero*** [1948]	$1.35	$4.00	$8.00
699	Spillane, Mickey - ***I, The Jury*** [1948] Cover By Lu Kimmel.	$3.50	$10.00	$20.00
700	Capote, Truman - ***Other Voices, Other Rooms*** [1949] Cover art by Jonas.	$2.00	$6.00	$12.00
701	Wylie, Philip - ***Finnley Wren*** [1949]	$1.35	$4.00	$8.00
702	Lewisohn, Ludwig - ***The Vehement Flame*** [1949]	$1.35	$4.00	$8.00
703	Wellman, Manly - ***Find My Killer*** [1949]	$2.50	$7.50	$15.00
704	McCulley, Johnston - ***Gold Of Smoky Mesa*** [1949]	$1.35	$4.00	$8.00
705	Caldwell, Erskine - ***A Woman In The House*** [1949]	$1.35	$4.00	$8.00
706	Smith, William Gardner - ***Last Of The Conquerers*** [1949] Cover art by Avati.	$1.35	$4.00	$8.00
707	Gruber, Frank - ***The Honest Dealer*** [1949] Cover art by Robert Jonas.	$1.50	$5.00	$10.00
708	Shappiro, Herbert - ***The Texan*** [1949]	$1.35	$4.00	$8.00
709	Gunn, James - ***Deadlier Than The Male*** [1949]	$1.50	$5.00	$10.00
710	Petry, Ann - ***The Street*** [1949] Cover art by Jonas.	$1.35	$4.00	$8.00
711	Greenhood, David - ***Love In Dishevelment*** [1949]	$1.35	$4.00	$8.00
712	Raine, William MacLeod - ***The Fighting Tenderfoot*** [1949]	$1.35	$4.00	$8.00
713	Bonnamy, Francis - ***Murder As A Fine Art*** [1949] Cover art by Avati	$1.50	$5.00	$10.00

		G	VG	F
714	Gorham, Charles O. - ***The Gilded Hearse*** [1949] Cover art by Avati.	$1.50	$5.00	$10.00
715	Jackson, Charles - ***The Fall Of Valor*** [1949]	$1.50	$5.00	$10.00
716	Sylvester, Robert - ***We Were Strangers*** [1949] Cover by Avati. Movie tie-in.	$1.50	$5.00	$10.00
717	Seltzer, Charles Alden - ***A Son Of Arizona*** [1949]	$1.35	$4.00	$8.00
718	Holman, Hugh - ***Another Man's Poison*** [1949]	$1.50	$5.00	$10.00
719	DiMaggio, Joe - ***Baseball For Everyone*** [1949]	$5.50	$17.50	$35.00
720	Cain, James M. - ***The Butterfly*** [1949] Cover by Robert Schulz.	$2.00	$6.00	$12.00
721	Desmond, Warren - ***Night Of Flame*** [1949]	$1.35	$4.00	$8.00
722	Miller, Wade - ***Uneasy Street*** [1949] Cover art by Avati.	$1.50	$5.00	$10.00
723	MacDonald, William Colt - ***The Crimson Quirt*** [1949]	$1.35	$4.00	$8.00
724	Connell, Vivian - ***The Golden Sleep*** [1949] Cover by James Avati.	$1.35	$4.00	$8.00
725	Warren, Robert Penn - ***At Heaven's Gate*** [1949]	$2.00	$6.00	$12.00
726	Gruber, Frank - ***The Whispering Master*** [1949] Cover art by Leonard.	$2.00	$6.00	$12.00
727	Ernenwein, Leslie - ***Trigger Justice*** [1949] Cover art by Leonard.	$1.35	$4.00	$8.00
728	Savage, Thomas - ***Lona Hanson*** [1949]	$1.35	$4.00	$8.00
729	Hunt, Howard - ***Stranger In Town*** [1949]	$1.50	$5.00	$10.00
730	Ballinger, Bill S. - ***The Body In The Bed*** [1949]	$2.00	$6.00	$12.00
731	Lehman, Paul Evan - ***Mountain Man*** [1949]	$1.35	$4.00	$8.00
732	Caldwell, Erskine - ***The Sure Hand Of God*** [1949] Cover art by Avati.	$1.35	$4.00	$8.00
733	Dostoyevsky, Fyodor - ***Crime And Punishment*** [1949] Cover art by Avati.	$2.50	$7.50	$15.00
734	Farrell, James T. - ***Meet The Girls*** [1949] Cover art by Avati.	$1.50	$5.00	$10.00
735	Arnold, Elliott - ***Everybody Slept Here*** [1949] Cover art by Avati.	$1.35	$4.00	$8.00
736	Dewey, Thomas B. - ***Draw The Curtain Close*** [1949]	$2.00	$6.00	$12.00
737	Ermine, Will - ***Brave In The Saddle*** [1949]	$1.35	$4.00	$8.00
738	Gresham, William Lindsay - ***Nightmare Alley*** [1949] Cover art by Avati.	$2.00	$6.00	$12.00
739	Engstrand, Stuart - ***Beyond The Forest*** [1949] Cover art by Avati.	$1.35	$4.00	$8.00
740	Cunningham, Eugene - ***Whistling Lead*** [1949]	$1.35	$4.00	$8.00
741	Smith, H. Allen - ***Life In A Putty Knife Factory*** [1949]	$1.35	$4.00	$8.00
742	Francis, William - ***Kill Or Cure*** [1949]	$1.50	$5.00	$10.00
743	Faulkner, William - ***Intruder In The Dust*** [1949] Cover art by Avati.	$1.50	$5.00	$10.00
744	Anthology edited by Bishop William Scarlett - ***The Christian Demand For Social Justice*** [1949]	$1.25	$3.75	$7.50
745	Clark, Walter Van Tilburg - ***The Ox-Bow Incident*** [1949]	$1.35	$4.00	$8.00
746	Du Nouy, Lecomte - ***Human Destiny*** [1949]	$1.25	$3.75	$7.50
747	Thoreau, Henry David - ***Walden*** [1949] Cover art by Privitello.	$1.35	$4.00	$8.00
748	Morley, Susan - ***Mistress Glory*** [1949]	$1.35	$4.00	$8.00
749	Lewisohn, Ludwig - ***For Ever Wilt Thou Love*** [1949] Cover art by Avati.	$1.35	$4.00	$8.00
750	Radiguet, Raymond - ***Devil In The Flesh*** [1949] Cover art by Avati.	$1.35	$4.00	$8.00
751	Chesser, M.D., Eustace - ***Love Without Fear*** [1949]	$1.35	$4.00	$8.00
752	Gorham, Charles - ***The Future Mister Dolan*** [1949] Cover art by Avati.	$1.35	$4.00	$8.00
753	Gruber, Frank - ***The Gamecock Murders*** [1949]	$2.00	$6.00	$12.00
754	McCoy, Horace - ***Kiss Tomorrow Good-Bye*** [1949] Cover by James Avati.	$2.50	$7.50	$15.00
755	Dreiser, Theodore - ***An American Tragedy*** [1949] Cover art by Avati.	$1.35	$4.00	$8.00

		G	VG	F
756	Himes, Chester B. - ***If He Hollers Let Him Go*** [1949] Cover art by Avati.	$2.50	$7.50	$15.00
757	Brand, Max - ***Brother Of The Cheyennes*** [1949]	$1.35	$4.00	$8.00
758	Raine, William MacLeod - ***Clattering Hoofs*** [1950]	$1.35	$4.00	$8.00
759	Cain, James M. - ***Everybody Does It*** [1949] Cover by Gregg. Movie tie-in.	$2.00	$6.00	$12.00
760	Caldwell, Erskine - ***Georgia Boy*** [1950] Cover art by Avati.	$1.35	$4.00	$8.00
761	Petry, Ann - ***Country Place*** [1950] Cover art by Avati.	$1.35	$4.00	$8.00
762	Keller, M.M., Father James - ***You Can Change The World*** [1950]	$1.25	$3.75	$7.50
763	Rovere, Richard H. - ***The Weeper And The Blackmailer*** [1950]	$1.50	$5.00	$10.00
764	MacDonald, William Colt - ***Six-Shooter Showdown*** [1950]	$1.35	$4.00	$8.00
765	Adams, Cleve F. - ***Murder All Over*** [1950]	$1.50	$5.00	$10.00
766	O'Hara, John - ***Appointment In Samarra*** [1950] Cover art by Avati.	$1.35	$4.00	$8.00
767	Savoy, Willard - ***Alien Land*** [1950] Cover art by Avati.	$1.35	$4.00	$8.00
768	Hunter, Howard - ***Dark Encounter*** [1950]	$1.50	$5.00	$10.00
769	Slade, Caroline - ***Margaret*** [1950]	$1.35	$4.00	$8.00
770	Arnold, Elliott - ***Two Loves*** [1950] Cover art by Gregg.	$1.35	$4.00	$8.00
771	Miller, Wade - ***Killer's Choice*** [1950]	$1.50	$5.00	$10.00
772	Thayer, Tiffany - ***Three Musketeers And A Lady*** [1950]	$1.35	$4.00	$8.00
773	Vidal, Gore - ***The City And The Pillar*** [1950] Cover art by Avati.	$2.00	$6.00	$12.00
774	Ballinger, Bill S. - ***The Body Beautiful*** [1950]	$1.50	$5.00	$10.00
775	Heckelmann, Charles N. - ***Vengeance Trail*** [1950]	$1.35	$4.00	$8.00
776	Bemelmans, Ludwig - ***Now I Lay Me Down To Sleep*** [1950]	$1.35	$4.00	$8.00
777	Nabokov, Vladimir - ***Laughter In The Dark*** [1950]	$1.35	$4.00	$8.00
778	McHugh, Vincent - ***I Am Thinking Of My Darling*** [1950]	$1.35	$4.00	$8.00
779	Farrell, James T. - ***Ellen Rogers*** [1950] Cover by James Avati.	$1.35	$4.00	$8.00
780	Fischer, Bruno - ***The Restless Hands*** [1950]	$1.50	$5.00	$10.00
781	Jackson, Charles - ***The Outer Edges*** [1950] Cover art by Avati.	$2.00	$6.00	$12.00
782	Arthur, Burt - ***The Buckaroo*** [1950]	$1.35	$4.00	$8.00
783	Wakeman, Frederic - ***The Saxon Charm*** [1950]	$1.35	$4.00	$8.00
784	Cain, James M. - ***Double Indemnity*** [1950] Cover by Gregg.	$2.00	$6.00	$12.00
785	Baxter, George Owen - ***Horseback Hellion*** [1950] Cover by A. Leslie Ross.	$1.35	$4.00	$8.00
786	Engstrand, Stuart - ***The Sling And The Arrow*** [1950] Cover art by Avati.	$1.35	$4.00	$8.00
787	Wormser, Richard - ***The Hanging Heiress*** [1950] Cover by Raymond Pease.	$1.50	$5.00	$10.00
788	Guttmacher, Dr. Alan F. - ***Having A Baby*** [1950]	$1.25	$3.75	$7.50
789	Shaplen, Robert - ***The Love-Making of Max-Robert*** [1950] Cover art by Avati.	$1.25	$3.75	$7.50
790	Cooper, Mae - ***Lily Henry*** [1950] Cover art by Avati.	$1.35	$4.00	$8.00
791	Spillane, Mickey - ***My Gun Is Quick*** [1950] Cover by Lou Kimmel.	$3.00	$9.00	$18.00
792	MacDonald, William Colt - ***The Shadow Rider*** [1950] Cover by A. Leslie Ross.	$1.35	$4.00	$8.00
793	Morley, Christopher - ***Kitty Foyle*** [1950]	$1.25	$3.75	$7.50
S-794	Wright, Richard - ***Native Son*** [1950] Cover by James Avati.	$2.50	$7.50	$15.00
795	Kenyon, Josephine H. & Russell, Ruth K. - ***Healthy Babies Are Happy Babies*** [1950] Photo cover.	$1.25	$3.75	$7.50
S-796	Remarque, Erich Maria - ***Arch Of Triumph*** [1950] Cover art by Avati.	$1.25	$3.75	$7.50
797	Pratolini, Vasco - ***A Tale Of Poor Lovers*** [1950] Cover by James Avati.	$1.35	$4.00	$8.00
S-798	Orwell, George - ***1984*** [1950] Cover art by Alan Harmon.	$3.50	$10.00	$20.00
799	Gruber, Frank - ***The Fourth Letter*** [1950]	$2.00	$6.00	$12.00

		G	VG	F
800	Anthology edited by Wilma Lord Perkins - ***Fannie Farmer's Handy Cook Book*** [1950]	$4.00	$12.50	$25.00
801	Clark, Walter Van Tilburg - ***The Track Of The Cat*** [1950]	$1.35	$4.00	$8.00
802-AB	Motley, Willard - ***Knock On Any Door*** [1950] Cover by James Avati.	$1.50	$5.00	$10.00
803	Alman, David - ***World Full Of Strangers*** [1950]	$1.35	$4.00	$8.00
804	Warren, Robert Penn - ***Night Rider*** [1950] Cover art by Avati.	$1.50	$5.00	$10.00
805	Bottume, Carl - ***The Runaways*** [1950] Cover art by Raymond Pease.	$1.35	$4.00	$8.00
806	Raine, William MacLeod - ***Powdersmoke Feud*** [1950]	$1.35	$4.00	$8.00
807	Finnegan, Robert - ***The Bandaged Nude*** [1950]	$1.50	$5.00	$10.00
808	Webster, Miriam - ***The New American Webster Dictionary*** [1951]	$1.25	$3.75	$7.50
809-AB	Winsor, Kathleen - ***Forever Amber*** [1950]	$1.35	$4.00	$8.00
810	Farrell, James T. - ***The Young Manhood Of Studs Lonigan*** [1950] Cover art by Avati.	$1.50	$5.00	$10.00
811	Cain, James M. - ***The Moth*** [1950] Cover art by Alan Harmon.	$2.00	$6.00	$12.00
812	Hamilton, Edmond - ***Beyond The Moon*** [1950]	$2.00	$6.00	$12.00
813	Peters, Fritz - ***The World Next Door*** [1950]	$1.35	$4.00	$8.00
814	Dewey, Thomas B. - ***Room For Murder*** [1950]	$2.00	$6.00	$12.00
815	Young, Gordon - ***Wanted Dead Or Alive*** [1950]	$1.35	$4.00	$8.00
816	Steinbeck, John - ***Tortilla Flat*** [1950] Cover art by Alan Harmon.	$2.00	$6.00	$12.00
AB-817	Shaw, Irwin - ***The Young Lions*** [1950] Cover art by Barye Phillips.	$1.35	$4.00	$8.00
818	Caldwell, Erskine - ***A Swell Looking Girl*** [1950] Cover art by Avati.	$1.35	$4.00	$8.00
819	Gallico, Paul - ***The Lonely*** [1950] Cover art by Barye Phillips.	$1.35	$4.00	$8.00
820	Howard, Toni - ***Shreik With Pleasure*** [1950] Cover art by Mitchell Hooks.	$1.35	$4.00	$8.00
821	Taylor, Sam S. - ***Sleep No More*** [1950]	$1.35	$4.00	$8.00
822	Arthur, Burt - ***Trigger Man*** [1950]	$1.35	$4.00	$8.00
823	Wakeman, Frederic - ***The Wastrel*** [1950] Cover art by Ray Pease.	$1.35	$4.00	$8.00
824	Stong, Phil - ***State Fair*** [1950] Cover art by Harmon.	$1.35	$4.00	$8.00
825	Faulkner, William - ***Knight's Gambit*** [1950] Cover art by Barye Phillips.	$1.35	$4.00	$8.00
826	Engstrand, Stuart - ***Son Of The Giant*** [1950] Cover art by Avati.	$1.35	$4.00	$8.00
827	Gruber, Frank - ***A Job Of Murder*** [1950]	$2.00	$6.00	$12.00
828	Ernenwein, Leslie - ***Gunsmoke*** [1950]	$1.35	$4.00	$8.00
829	Slade, Caroline - ***Lilly Crackell*** [1950] Cover art by Avati.	$1.35	$4.00	$8.00
830	Wylie, Philip - ***Night Unto Night*** [1950] Cover art by Mitchell Hooks.	$1.35	$4.00	$8.00
831	Farrell, James T. - ***Saturday Night*** [1950] Cover art by Avati.	$1.50	$5.00	$10.00
832	Thomas, Will - ***Love Knows No Barriers*** [1950] Cover by James Avati.	$1.35	$4.00	$8.00
833	Fischer, Bruno - ***The Flesh Was Cold*** [1951] Cover art by Barye Phillips.	$1.50	$5.00	$10.00
834	Conrad, Joseph - ***Heart Of Darkness And The Secret Sharer*** [1951]	$1.35	$4.00	$8.00
835	MacDonald, William Colt - ***Dead Man's Gold*** [1951] Cover by A. Leslie Ross.	$1.35	$4.00	$8.00
836	Evans, Evan (Max Brand) - ***Montana Rides!*** [1951]	$1.35	$4.00	$8.00
837-AB	Mailer, Norman - ***The Naked And The Dead*** [1951]	$1.35	$4.00	$8.00
838	Caldwell, Erskine - ***This Very Earth*** [1951] Cover art by Avati.	$1.35	$4.00	$8.00
839	Gresham, William Lindsay - ***Limbo Tower*** [1951]	$1.35	$4.00	$8.00
840	Bowles, Paul - ***The Sheltering Sky*** [1951] Cover by Mitchell Hooks.	$1.35	$4.00	$8.00

		G	VG	F
841	Wright, Richard - ***Black Boy*** [1951] Cover by James Avati	$2.50	$7.50	$15.00
842	Heckelmann, Charles N. - ***Two-Bit Rancher*** [1951]	$1.35	$4.00	$8.00
843	Miller, Wade - ***Calamity Fair*** [1951] Cover art by Barye Phillips.	$1.50	$5.00	$10.00
S-844	Moravia, Alberto - ***The Woman Of Rome*** [1951] Cover art by Avati.	$1.35	$4.00	$8.00
845	Lamkin, Speed - ***Tiger In The Garden*** [1951] Cover art by Mitchell Hooks.	$1.35	$4.00	$8.00
846	Flaiano, Ennio - ***The Short Cut*** [1951]	$1.35	$4.00	$8.00
847	Heinlein, Robert A. - ***The Man Who Sold The Moon*** [1951]	$2.50	$7.50	$15.00
848	Russell, Bertrand - ***The Conquest Of Happiness*** [1951]	$1.25	$3.75	$7.50
849	Lehman, Paul Evan - ***Brother Of The Kid*** [1951]	$1.35	$4.00	$8.00
850	Adams, Cleve F. - ***The Private Eye*** [1950] Cover by Lu Kimmel.	$1.50	$5.00	$10.00
851	Calmer, Ned - ***The Strange Land*** [1951]	$1.35	$4.00	$8.00
852	Spillane, Mickey - ***Vengeance Is Mine*** [1951] Cover art by Lu Kimmel.	$3.00	$9.00	$18.00
853	Gibson, Jewel - ***Black Gold*** [1951]	$1.35	$4.00	$8.00
854	Hornblow, Leonora - ***Memory And Desire*** [1951] Cover art by Mitchell Hooks.	$1.35	$4.00	$8.00
855	Simenon, Georges - ***The Snow Was Black*** [1951]	$1.50	$5.00	$10.00
856	Harkey, Dee - ***Mean As Hell*** [1951]	$1.35	$4.00	$8.00
857	Keough, Theodora - ***Meg*** [1951] Cover by James Avati.	$1.35	$4.00	$8.00
858	Bemelmans, Ludwig - ***Dirty Eddie*** [1951] Cover by Barye Phillips.	$1.35	$4.00	$8.00
859	Margolius, Sidney - ***The Consumer's Guide To Better Buying*** [1951]	$1.25	$3.75	$7.50
860	Foote, Shelby - ***Follow Me Down*** [1951] Cover art by Avati.	$1.35	$4.00	$8.00
861	Fall, Thomas - ***Prettiest Girl In Town*** [1951]	$1.35	$4.00	$8.00
862	Moore, Walter L. - ***Courage And Confidence From The Bible*** [1951]	$1.35	$4.00	$8.00
863	Faulkner, William - ***Pylon*** [1951]	$1.35	$4.00	$8.00
864	Granberry, Edwin - ***Strangers And Lovers*** [1951]	$1.35	$4.00	$8.00
865	Francis, William - ***I.O.U. - Murder*** [1951]	$1.50	$5.00	$10.00
866	Arthur, Burt - ***Trouble Town*** [1951]	$1.35	$4.00	$8.00
867	Engstrand, Stuart - ***They Sought For Paradise*** [1951] Cover art by Avati.	$1.35	$4.00	$8.00
868-AB	Winsor, Kathleen - ***Star Money*** [1951] Cover art by Avati.	$1.35	$4.00	$8.00
869	Caldwell, Erskine - ***Kneel To The Rising Sun And Other Stories*** [1951] Cover art by Avati.	$1.35	$4.00	$8.00
870	Runbeck, Margaret Lee - ***Time For Love*** [1951] PBO.	$1.25	$3.75	$7.50
871	Windham, Donald - ***The Dog Star*** [1951]	$1.35	$4.00	$8.00
872	Baron, Alexander - ***There's No Home*** [1951]	$1.35	$4.00	$8.00
873	Stokes, Donald - ***Appointment With Fear*** [1951]	$1.50	$5.00	$10.00
874	Ernenwein, Leslie - ***Hell For Leather*** [1951]	$1.35	$4.00	$8.00
S-875	Farrell, James T. - ***Judgment Day*** [1951] Cover by James Avati.	$1.50	$5.00	$10.00
876	Bissell, Richard - ***A Stretch On The River*** [1951] Cover art by Harry Scharre.	$1.35	$4.00	$8.00
877	Kessel, Joseph - ***Cry Of Violence*** [1951]	$1.35	$4.00	$8.00
878	Capote, Truman - ***A Tree Of Night*** [1951]	$1.35	$4.00	$8.00
879	Mahannah, Floyd - ***No Luck For A Lady*** [1951]	$1.50	$5.00	$10.00
880	MacDonald, William Colt - ***Gunsight Range*** [1951]	$1.35	$4.00	$8.00
881	Portnoy, M.D., Louis & Saltman, Jules - ***Fertility In Marriage*** [1951]	$1.25	$3.75	$7.50
882	Heinlein, Robert A. - ***The Day After Tomorrow*** [1951]	$1.35	$4.00	$8.00
883	Knight, Adam - ***Stone Cold Blonde*** [1951]	$1.50	$5.00	$10.00
884	McCoy, Horace - ***I Should Have Stayed Home*** [1951]	$2.50	$7.50	$15.00
885	Ermine, Will - ***Buckskin Marshal*** [1951]	$1.35	$4.00	$8.00

		G	VG	F
886	Markowitz, Arthur - ***The Daughter*** [1951] Cover by James Avati.	$1.35	$4.00	$8.00
887	Faulkner, William - ***Soldiers' Pay*** [1951] Cover art by Avati.	$1.35	$4.00	$8.00
888	Spillane, Mickey - ***One Lonely Night*** [1951] Cover by Lu Kimmel.	$3.00	$9.00	$18.00
889	Bender, James & Graham, Lee - ***Your Way To Popularity And Personal Power*** [1951]	$1.25	$3.75	$7.50
890	Enstrand, Stuart - ***The Invaders*** [1951] Cover art by Avati.	$1.35	$4.00	$8.00
891	Wayne, Joseph - ***Gunplay Valley*** [1951]	$1.35	$4.00	$8.00
892	Fischer, Bruno - ***The Silent Dust*** [1951]	$1.50	$5.00	$10.00
893	Farrell, James T. - ***Bernard Carr*** [1951] Cover art by Avati.	$1.50	$5.00	$10.00
894	Garner, Claud - ***Cornbread Aristocrat*** [1951] Cover art by Harry Schaare.	$1.50	$5.00	$10.00
895	Slade, Caroline - ***The Triumph Of Willie Pond*** [1951] Cover by James Avati.	$1.35	$4.00	$8.00
896	Kaufman, Lenard - ***Jubel's Children*** [1951]	$1.35	$4.00	$8.00
897	Ballinger, Bill S. - ***Portrait In Smoke*** [1951]	$1.50	$5.00	$10.00
898	Siringo, Charles A. - ***A Texas Cowboy*** [1951]	$1.35	$4.00	$8.00
899	Edited by Robert Cantwell - ***The Humourous Side Of Erskine Caldwell*** [1951] Cover art by Avati.	$1.35	$4.00	$8.00
900	Russell, William - ***A Wind Is Rising*** [1951] Cover art by Avati.	$1.35	$4.00	$8.00
901	Clark, Christopher - ***Good Is For Angels*** [1951]	$1.35	$4.00	$8.00
902	Adams, Cleve - ***Contraband*** [1951]	$1.50	$5.00	$10.00
903	Brandon, Curt - ***High, Wide and Handsome*** [1951]	$1.35	$4.00	$8.00
AB-904	Bromfield, Louis - ***The Rains Came*** [1951] Cover art by Avati.	$1.35	$4.00	$8.00
905	Pratt, Theodore - ***Thunder Mountain*** [1951]	$1.35	$4.00	$8.00
906	Stern, Philip Van Doren - ***Love Is The One With Wings*** [1951] Cover art by Harry Schaare.	$1.35	$4.00	$8.00
907	Smith, William Gardner - ***Anger At Innocence*** [1951] Cover by Tom Dunn.	$1.35	$4.00	$8.00
908	Miller, Wade - ***Murder Charge*** [1951] Cover art by Carl Bobertz.	$1.50	$5.00	$10.00
909	Martin, John Bartlow - ***Butcher's Dozen*** [1952] Cover art by Harry Schaare.	$1.50	$5.00	$10.00
910	Heckelmann, Charles N. - ***Let The Guns Roar!*** [1952]	$1.35	$4.00	$8.00
911	Levin, Meyer - ***The Young Lovers*** [1952] Cover by Tom Dunn.	$1.35	$4.00	$8.00
912	Pollet, Elizabeth - ***A Family Romance*** [1952] Cover art by Avati.	$1.25	$3.75	$7.50
913	Ross, James - ***They Don't Dance Much*** [1952]	$1.50	$5.00	$10.00
914	Van Vogt, A. E. - ***Mission: Interplanetary*** [1952]	$1.50	$5.00	$10.00
915	Spillane, Mickey - ***The Big Kill*** [1951]	$3.00	$9.00	$18.00
916	Herbert, Arthur - ***Bugles In The Night*** [1952]	$1.35	$4.00	$8.00
917	Williams, Tennessee - ***A Streetcar Named Desire*** [1951] Cover art by Thomas Hart Benton. 8 pages of photos.	$2.00	$6.00	$12.00
918	Caldwell, Erskine - ***A Place Called Estherville*** [1952] Cover by James Avati.	$1.35	$4.00	$8.00
919	Bowles, Paul - ***The Delicate Prey And Other Stories*** [1952]	$1.35	$4.00	$8.00
920	Knight, Adam - ***Murder For Madame*** [1952] Cover art by Harry Schaare.	$1.50	$5.00	$10.00
921-AB	LaMure, Pierre - ***Moulin Rouge*** [1952]	$1.35	$4.00	$8.00
922	Moravia, Alberto - ***Conjugal Love*** [1952] Cover art by Avati.	$1.35	$4.00	$8.00
923	Marshall, Rosamond - ***Laird's Choice*** [1952] Cover art by Stanley Zuckerberg.	$1.35	$4.00	$8.00
S-924	Sklar, George - ***The Promising Young Men*** [1952]	$1.35	$4.00	$8.00
925	MacDonald, William Colt - ***The Killer Brand*** [1952]	$1.35	$4.00	$8.00
D-926	Farrell, James T. - ***A World I Never Made*** [1952] Cover art by Avati.	$1.50	$5.00	$10.00

		G	VG	F
927	Lenormand, H.R. - ***Renee*** [1952] Cover by Stanley Meltzoff.	$1.35	$4.00	$8.00
928	Miller, Wade - ***Deadly Weapon*** [1952] Cover by Leo Summers.	$1.50	$5.00	$10.00
D-929	Merton, Thomas - ***The Seven Storey Mountain*** [1952] Cover art by Avati.	$1.35	$4.00	$8.00
930	Peters, Fritz - ***Finistere*** [1952]	$1.35	$4.00	$8.00
S-931	Shaw, Irwin - ***The Troubled Air*** [1952] Cover art by Avati.	$1.35	$4.00	$8.00
932	Spillane, Mickey - ***The Long Wait*** [1952] Cover by Lu Kimmel.	$3.00	$9.00	$18.00
933	Caldwell, Erskine - ***Southways*** [1952] Cover by James Avati.	$1.35	$4.00	$8.00
T-934	Rand, Ayn - ***The Fountainhead*** [1952] Cover art by Avati.	$2.50	$7.50	$15.00
935	Evans, Evan (Max Brand) - ***Montana Rides Again!*** [1952]	$1.35	$4.00	$8.00
936	Adams, Cleve F. - ***Sabotage*** [1952]	$1.50	$5.00	$10.00
937	Isherwood, Christopher - ***Goodbye To Berlin*** [1952] Cover art by Avati	$1.35	$4.00	$8.00
938	Werry, Richard R. - ***Where Town Begins*** [1952] Cover art by Ray Pease.	$1.35	$4.00	$8.00
939	Morris, Donald B. - ***China Station*** [1952]	$1.35	$4.00	$8.00
940	Leveridge, Ralph - ***Walk On The Water*** [1952] Cover art by Stanley Zuckerberg.	$1.35	$4.00	$8.00
941	Aswell, James - ***There's One In Every Town*** [1952]	$1.35	$4.00	$8.00
942	Coe, Charles Francis - ***Pressure*** [1952] Cover art by Harry Schaare.	$1.50	$5.00	$10.00
943	Heinlein, Robert A. - ***The Green Hills Of Earth*** [1952]	$2.00	$6.00	$12.00
944	Callaghan, Morley - ***The Loved And The Lost*** [1952]	$1.35	$4.00	$8.00
945	Saroyan, William - ***Rock Wagram*** [1952]	$1.35	$4.00	$8.00
D-946	Farrell, James T. - ***No Star Is Lost*** [1952] Cover art by James Avati.	$1.50	$5.00	$10.00
947	Mankiewicz, Don M. - ***See How They Run*** [1952]	$1.35	$4.00	$8.00
948	Simenon, Georges - ***The Girl In His Past*** [1952]	$1.50	$5.00	$10.00
949	Heyes, Douglas - ***The Kiss-off*** [1952] Cover art by Carl Bobertz.	$1.35	$4.00	$8.00
950	Wolfe, Thomas - ***Only The Dead Know Brooklyn*** [1952] Cover art by Rudy Nappi.	$1.35	$4.00	$8.00
951	Clippinger, Frances - ***Elinda*** [1952] Cover art by Rafael DeSoto.	$1.35	$4.00	$8.00
952	Arthur, Burt - ***Stirrups In The Dust*** [1952]	$1.35	$4.00	$8.00
953	Rooke, Daphne - ***A Grove Of Fever Trees*** [1952] Cover art by Stanley Meltzoff.	$1.35	$4.00	$8.00
S-954	Bromfield, Louis - ***Mister Smith*** [1952] Cover art by Stanley Zuckerberg.	$1.35	$4.00	$8.00
955	Williams, Tennessee - ***The Roman Spring Of Mrs. Stone*** [1952] Cover art by Avati.	$1.35	$4.00	$8.00
S-956	Slaughter, Frank G. - ***The Stubborn Heart*** [1952]	$1.35	$4.00	$8.00
957	Mahannah, Floyd - ***The Broken Body*** [1952]	$1.50	$5.00	$10.00
958	Keogh, Theodora - ***The Double Door*** [1952] Cover by James Avati.	$1.35	$4.00	$8.00
959	Huie, William Bradford - ***The Revolt Of Mamie Stover*** [1952].	$1.35	$4.00	$8.00
960	Moravia, Alberto - ***Two Adolescents*** [1952] Cover art by Avati.	$1.35	$4.00	$8.00
S-961	Hurst, Fannie - ***Back Street*** [1952]	$1.35	$4.00	$8.00
962	Sansom, William - ***The Face Of Innocence*** [1952] Cover art by Schweizer.	$1.35	$4.00	$8.00
963	Tabori, George - ***The Caravan Passes*** [1952] Cover art by Stanley Zuckerberg.	$1.35	$4.00	$8.00
964	Simenon, Georges - ***The Heart Of A Man*** [1951]	$1.50	$5.00	$10.00
965	Heckelmann, Charles - ***Fighting Ramrod*** [1952]	$1.35	$4.00	$8.00
966	Roscoe, Mike - ***Death Is A Round Black Ball*** [1952]	$2.50	$7.50	$15.00
D-967	Styron, William - ***Lie Down In Darkness*** [1952] Cover by James Avati.	$1.35	$4.00	$8.00

		G	VG	F
968	Nablo, James Benson - ***The Long November*** [1952] Cover art by Stanley Zuckerberg.	$1.35	$4.00	$8.00
969	Pratolini, Vasco - ***A Hero Of Our Time*** [1953] Cover art by Erickson.	$1.35	$4.00	$8.00
970	Foote, Shelby - ***Love In A Dry Season*** [1952] Cover art by Avati.	$1.35	$4.00	$8.00
S-971	Berto, Giuseppe - ***The Sky Is Red*** [1951]	$1.35	$4.00	$8.00
972	Carter, Ross S. - ***Those Devils In Baggy Pants*** [1952]	$1.35	$4.00	$8.00
973	Raine, William MacLeod - ***The Six-Gun Kid*** [1952]	$1.35	$4.00	$8.00
974	Brossard, Chandler - ***Who Walk In Darkness*** [1952] Cover by Cardiff.	$1.35	$4.00	$8.00
D-975	Warren, Robert Penn - ***World Enough And Time*** [1952] Cover by Cardiff.	$1.50	$5.00	$10.00
976	Marshall, Rosamond - ***The Temptress*** [1952]	$1.35	$4.00	$8.00
977	Faulkner, William - ***The Unvanquished*** [1952] Cover by James Avati.	$1.50	$5.00	$10.00
978	Kirkland, Jack - ***Tobacco Road*** [1952] Play based on Erskine Caldwell book.	$1.35	$4.00	$8.00
S-979	Bromfield, Louis - ***Possession*** [1952]	$1.35	$4.00	$8.00
980	Heinlein, Robert A. - ***The Puppet Masters*** [1952]	$2.00	$6.00	$12.00
981	Brown, Wenzell - ***The Lonely Hearts Murders*** [1952]	$2.50	$7.50	$15.00
982	Ernenwein, Leslie - ***Gunhawk Harvest*** [1952]	$1.35	$4.00	$8.00
983	Caldwell, Erskine - ***Episode In Palmetto*** [1953] Cover by James Avati.	$1.35	$4.00	$8.00
984	Arfelli, Dante - ***The Unwanted*** [1952]	$1.35	$4.00	$8.00
S-985	Koestler, Arthur - ***The Age Of Longing*** [1953] Cover art by Avati.	$1.35	$4.00	$8.00
986	Slaughter, M.D., Frank G. - ***Your Body And Your Mind*** [1953] Cover art by Jonas.	$1.25	$3.75	$7.50
987	Willingham, Calder - ***Reach To The Stars*** [1953]	$1.35	$4.00	$8.00
988	Fischer, Bruno - ***Stripped For Murder*** [1953] Cover by Carl Bobertz.	$2.00	$6.00	$12.00
989	Hopkins, Tom J. - ***Trouble In Tombstone*** [1953]	$1.35	$4.00	$8.00
990	Bottume, Karl - ***Sailor's Choice*** [1952]	$1.35	$4.00	$8.00
991	Vaughan, Richard - ***Moulded In Earth*** [1953]	$1.35	$4.00	$8.00
D-992	Motley, Willard - ***We Fished All Night*** [1953] Cover art by Avati.	$1.50	$5.00	$10.00
993	Simenon, Georges - ***Act Of Passion*** [1953]	$1.35	$4.00	$8.00
994	Farrell, James T. - ***When Boyhood Dreams Came True*** [1953]	$1.50	$5.00	$10.00
995	Marsh, Ngaio - ***Night At The Vulcan*** [1953]	$1.50	$5.00	$10.00
996	Garland, George - ***Doubtful Valley*** [1953]	$1.35	$4.00	$8.00
997	Stewart, Desmond - ***Leopard In The Grass*** [1953] Cover by Cardiff.	$1.35	$4.00	$8.00
998	Green, Julian - ***Moira*** [1953]	$1.35	$4.00	$8.00
S-999	Grey, Harry - ***The Hoods*** [1953]	$2.00	$6.00	$12.00
1000	Spillane, Mickey - ***Kiss Me, Deadly*** [1953] Cober by James Meese.	$3.00	$9.00	$18.00
1001	Salinger, J. D. - ***The Catcher In The Rye*** [1953] Cover art by Avati.	$2.50	$7.50	$15.00
1002	Bowles, Paul - ***Let It Come Down*** [1953]	$1.35	$4.00	$8.00
1003	Vidal, Gore - ***Dangerous Voyage*** [1953]	$1.50	$5.00	$10.00
1004	Auchincloss, Louis - ***Sybil*** [1953] Cover art by Stanley Zuckerberg.	$1.35	$4.00	$8.00
1005	Macdonald, William Colt - ***Blind Cartridges*** [1953] Cover by Verne Tossey.	$1.35	$4.00	$8.00
1006	Stokes, Donald - ***Captive In The Night*** [1953]	$1.35	$4.00	$8.00
1007	Van Vogt, A.E. - ***Destination: Universe!*** [1953]	$1.50	$5.00	$10.00
1008	Marvin, H. M. - ***You And Your Heart*** [1953]	$1.25	$3.75	$7.50
D-1009	Bishop, Leonard - ***Down All Your Streets*** [1953] Cover art by Avati.	$1.35	$4.00	$8.00

Signet Book, 1020

Signet Book, 1138

Signet Book, 1461

		G	VG	F
S-1010	Wolff, Maritta - ***Back Of Town*** [1953] Cover art by Cardiff.	$1.35	$4.00	$8.00
1011	Brebner, Winston - ***Dream Of Eden*** [1953]	$1.35	$4.00	$8.00
1012	Mitford, Nancy - ***The Blessing*** [1953] Cover art by Cardiff.	$1.35	$4.00	$8.00
1013	Miller, Wade - ***Shoot To Kill*** [1953]	$1.50	$5.00	$10.00
1014	Novelettes from *Argosy* magazine - ***They Lived By Their Guns*** [1953] PBO.	$1.35	$4.00	$8.00
1015	Evans, Evan (Max Brand) - ***Song Of The Whip*** [1953]	$1.35	$4.00	$8.00
1016	Caldwell, Erskine - ***The Courting Of Susie Brown*** [1953] Cover by James Avati.	$1.35	$4.00	$8.00
S-1017	McCoy, Horace - ***Scalpel*** [1953] Cover by James Avati.	$1.35	$4.00	$8.00
S-1018	Walker, Turnley - ***Dream Of Innocence*** [1953]	$1.35	$4.00	$8.00
1019	Mailer, Norman - ***Barbary Shore*** [1953] Cover art by Stanley Zuckerberg.	$1.35	$4.00	$8.00
1020	Capote, Truman - ***The Grass Harp*** [1953] Cover by Stanley Zuckerberg.	$1.35	$4.00	$8.00
1021	Rooke, Daphne - ***Mittee*** [1953]	$1.35	$4.00	$8.00
1022	Knight, Adam - ***Knife At My Back*** [1953]	$1.50	$5.00	$10.00
S-1023	Remarque, Erich Maria - ***Spark Of Life*** [1953] Cover art by Stanley Zuckerberg.	$1.35	$4.00	$8.00
1024	Engstrand, Stuart - ***A Husband In The House*** [1953]	$1.35	$4.00	$8.00
S-1025	Bromfield, Louis - ***The Green Bay Tree*** [1953]	$1.35	$4.00	$8.00
1026	Gillon, Philip - ***Frail Barrier*** [1953] Cover art by Cardiff.	$1.35	$4.00	$8.00
1027	Shannon, Jimmy - ***The Devil's Passkey*** [1953] Cover by Michael.	$1.35	$4.00	$8.00
1028	Wayne, Joseph - ***The Snake Stomper*** [1953]	$1.35	$4.00	$8.00
1029	O'Connor, Flannery - ***Wise Blood*** [1953]	$2.50	$7.50	$15.00
D-1030	Ellison, Ralph - ***Invisible Man*** [1953] Cover art by Avati.	$1.35	$4.00	$8.00
1031	Farrell, James T. - ***An American Dream Girl*** [1953] Cover art by Erickson.	$1.35	$4.00	$8.00
S-1032	Faulkner, William - ***Sartoris*** [1953] Cover by James Avati.	$1.35	$4.00	$8.00
1033	Martin, John Bartlow - ***My Life In Crime*** [1953] Cover art by James Meese.	$1.35	$4.00	$8.00
1034	Simenon, Georges - ***I Take This Woman*** [1953]	$1.50	$5.00	$10.00
1035	Gaby, Alex - ***To End The Night*** [1953] Cover art by Cardiff.	$1.35	$4.00	$8.00
1036	Box, Edgar (Gore Vidal) - ***Death In The Fifth Position*** [1953]	$1.50	$5.00	$10.00
1037	Brandon, Curt - ***Bugle's Wake*** [1953]	$1.35	$4.00	$8.00
S-1038	Sheean, Vincent - ***Rage Of The Soul*** [1953] Cover by James Avati.	$1.35	$4.00	$8.00
S-1039	Lawrence, D. H. - ***Sons And Lovers*** [1953] Cover art by Avati.	$1.50	$5.00	$10.00

		G	VG	F
1040	Ballinger, Bill S. - ***The Darkening Door*** [1953] Cover art by Erickson.	$1.50	$5.00	$10.00
S-1041	Hutter, Catherine - ***The Dear Encounter*** [1953]	$1.35	$4.00	$8.00
1042	Vittorini, Elio - ***The Red Carnation*** [1953] Cover art by Stanley Zuckerberg.	$1.35	$4.00	$8.00
S-1043	Beach, Commander Edward L., U.S.N. - ***Submarine!*** [1953]	$1.35	$4.00	$8.00
1044	Heinlein, Robert A. - editor (anthology) - ***Tomorrow, The Stars*** [1953]	$1.50	$5.00	$10.00
1045	Bower, B.M. - ***Trigger Vengeance*** [1953]	$1.35	$4.00	$8.00
1046	Brand, Max - ***Brother Of The Cheyennes*** [1953]	$1.35	$4.00	$8.00
1047	Duncan, David - ***Wives And Husbands*** [1953] Cover by Robert Maguire.	$1.50	$5.00	$10.00
1048	Michaels, Roy - ***By Any Other Name*** [1953]	$1.35	$4.00	$8.00
1049	Keogh, Theodora - ***Street Music*** [1953] Cover by Stanley Zuckerberg.	$1.35	$4.00	$8.00
1050	Eaton, Frank - ***Pistol Pete*** [1953]	$1.35	$4.00	$8.00
S-1051	Schiff, Pearl - ***Scollay Square*** [1953]	$1.35	$4.00	$8.00
S-1052	Kaufmann, Richard - ***Heaven Pays No Dividends*** [1953] Cover art by Robert Maguire.	$1.50	$5.00	$10.00
1053	Berto, Giuseppe - ***The Brigand*** [1953] Cover by Stanley Zuckerberg.	$1.35	$4.00	$8.00
1054	Yorke, Susan - ***Naked To Mine Enemies*** [1953] Cover by James Avati.	$1.35	$4.00	$8.00
S-1055	Margolius, Sidney - ***The Consumer's Guide To Better Buying*** [1953]	$1.25	$3.75	$7.50
1056	Branner, H. C. - ***The Mistress*** [1953] Cover art by Robert Maguire.	$1.35	$4.00	$8.00
1057	Taylor, Sam S. - ***No Head For Her Pillow*** [1953] Cover by Erickson.	$1.35	$4.00	$8.00
1058	Coe, Charles Francis - ***Ashes*** [1953] Cover by Samuel Cherry.	$1.35	$4.00	$8.00
1059	MacDonald, William Colt - ***Ranger Man*** [1953]	$1.35	$4.00	$8.00
1060	Roscoe, Mike - ***Riddle Me This*** [1953]	$1.35	$4.00	$8.00
1061	Pratolini, Vasco - ***The Naked Streets*** [1953] Cover art by Stanley Zuckerberg.	$1.35	$4.00	$8.00
S-1062	Willingham, Calder - ***Natural Child*** [1953] Cover by James Avati.	$1.25	$3.75	$7.50
1063	Harwin, Brian - ***Home Is Upriver*** [1953]	$1.35	$4.00	$8.00
1064	Peters, Fritz - ***The Descent*** [1953]	$1.35	$4.00	$8.00
1065	Travers, Robert - ***A Funeral For Sabella*** [1953]	$1.35	$4.00	$8.00
D-1066	Farrell, James T. - ***Father And Son*** [1953] Cover art by Avati.	$1.35	$4.00	$8.00
1067	Reinhardt, Guenther - ***Crime Without Punishment*** [1953]	$1.35	$4.00	$8.00
D-1068	Schmitt, Gladys - ***Confessors Of The Name*** [1954] Cover by Robert Maguire.	$1.35	$4.00	$8.00
1069	Raine, William MacLeod - ***Justice Comes To Tomahawk*** [1953]	$1.35	$4.00	$8.00
S-1070	Leslie, Warren - ***The Best Thing That Ever Happened*** [1953] Cover art by Avati.	$1.35	$4.00	$8.00
S-1071	Moravia, Alberto - ***The Conformist*** [1953]	$1.35	$4.00	$8.00
1072	Foster, Joseph - ***A Cow Is Too Much Trouble In Los Angeles*** [1953] Cover by Cardiff.	$1.35	$4.00	$8.00
1073	Simenon, Georges - ***Four Days In A Lifetime*** [1953] Cover by Stanley Zuckerberg.	$1.50	$5.00	$10.00
S-1074	Smith, Lillian - ***Strange Fruit*** [1953]	$1.35	$4.00	$8.00
T-1075	Jones, James - ***From Here To Eternity*** [1953]	$1.35	$4.00	$8.00
1076	Webb, Jack - ***The Big Sin*** [1953] Cover art by Verne Tossey.	$1.35	$4.00	$8.00
1077	Wayne, Joseph - ***By Gun And Spur*** [1954]	$1.25	$3.75	$7.50
S-1078	Cloete, Stuart - ***The Curve And The Tusk*** [1954] Cover art by James Meese.	$1.25	$3.75	$7.50
S-1079	Faulkner, William - ***Sanctuary And Requiem For A Nun*** [1954] Cover art by Avati.	$1.35	$4.00	$8.00

		G	VG	F
S-1080	Amsbary, Mary Anne - ***Caesar's Angel*** [1953]	$1.25	$3.75	$7.50
1081	Macauley, Robie - ***The Disguises Of Love*** [1953] Cover by Stanley Zuckerberg.	$1.25	$3.75	$7.50
1082	Asimov, Isaac - ***The Currents Of Space*** [1953]	$1.35	$4.00	$8.00
1083	Lariar, Lawrence - ***The Day I Died*** [1953]	$1.25	$3.75	$7.50
1084	Gunn, James - ***Deadlier Than The Male*** [1953]	$1.35	$4.00	$8.00
1085	Burns, Walter Noble - ***The Saga Of Billy The Kid*** [1953]	$1.25	$3.75	$7.50
S-1086	Lawrence, D. H. - ***Lady Chatterley's Lover*** [1953]	$1.35	$4.00	$8.00
1087	O'Hara, John - ***Appointment In Samarra*** [1953]	$1.25	$3.75	$7.50
1088	Baker, Dorothy - ***Young Man With A Horn*** [1953] Cover art by Stanley Zuckerberg.	$1.25	$3.75	$7.50
S-1090	Bucker, Ernest - ***The Mountain And The Valley*** [1954] Cover art by Stanley Zuckerberg.	$1.25	$3.75	$7.50
1091	Caldwell, Erskine - ***A Lamp For Nightfall*** [1954] Cover art by Avati	$1.25	$3.75	$7.50
1092	Monsarrat, Nicholas - ***Depends What You Mean By Love*** [1954]	$1.25	$3.75	$7.50
1093	Box, Edgar (Gore Vidal) - ***Death Before Bedtime*** [1954]	$1.35	$4.00	$8.00
S-1094	Cotlow, Lewis - ***Amazon Head-Hunters*** [1954] Cover art by James Meese.	$1.25	$3.75	$7.50
1095	Wright, Richard - ***Uncle Tom's Children*** [1954] Cover by James Avati.	$2.50	$7.50	$15.00
1096	Colette - ***Gigi And Julie De Carneilhan*** [1954]	$1.25	$3.75	$7.50
1097	Fisher, William - ***The Waiters*** [1954] Cover art by Avati.	$1.25	$3.75	$7.50
1099	Sykes, Gerald - ***The Center Of The Stage*** [1954] Cover by James Avati.	$1.25	$3.75	$7.50
1100	Keogh, Theodora - ***The Tattooed Heart*** [1954] Cover art by Erickson.	$1.25	$3.75	$7.50
D-1102	Wolff, Maritta - ***Night Shift*** [1954]	$1.25	$3.75	$7.50
1103	Knight, Adam - ***The Sunburned Corpse*** [1954] Cover art by Cozzarelli.	$1.35	$4.00	$8.00
1104	Foote, Shelby - ***Shiloh*** [1954] Cover art by James Meese.	$1.25	$3.75	$7.50
1105	Bester, Alfred - ***The Demolished Man*** [1954]	$1.50	$5.00	$10.00
1106	MacLiesh, Fleming - ***A Breed Apart*** [1954] Cover by Erickson.	$1.25	$3.75	$7.50
D-1107	Bishop, Leonard - ***Days Of My Love*** [1954]	$1.25	$3.75	$7.50
1108	Heckelman, Charles N. - ***Hell In His Holsters*** [1954]	$1.25	$3.75	$7.50
1109	Simenon, Georges - ***The Brothers Rico*** [1954]	$1.35	$4.00	$8.00
1110	McKaye, Richard - ***Portrait Of The Damned*** [1954] Cover art by Robert Maguire.	$1.35	$4.00	$8.00
1111	Salinger, J. D. - ***Nine Stories*** [1954] Cover art by W. D. Miller.	$1.25	$3.75	$7.50
1112	Chase, James Hadley - ***The Double Shuffle*** [1954] Cover by Al Rossi	$1.25	$3.75	$7.50
1113	Huie, William Bradford - ***The Execution Of Private Slovik*** [1954]	$1.25	$3.75	$7.50
S-1114	Wright, Richard - ***The Outsider*** [1954] Cover art by James Meese.	$1.25	$3.75	$7.50
1115	Hazel, Robert - ***The Lost Year*** [1954] Cover art by Stanley Zuckerberg.	$1.25	$3.75	$7.50
1116	Michaelson, John Nairne - ***Morning, Winter, And Night*** [1954] Cover art by Avati.	$1.25	$3.75	$7.50
S-1118	Farrell, James T. - ***My Days Of Anger*** [1954] Cover by James Avati.	$1.25	$3.75	$7.50
1119	Cohen, M.D., Louis H. - ***Murder, Madness And The Law*** [1954] Cover art by Maguire	$1.00	$3.00	$6.00
1120	London, Jack - ***Smoke Bellew*** [1954]	$2.00	$6.00	$12.00
1121	Aswell, James - ***The Birds And The Bees*** [1954] Cover art by Stanley Zuckerberg.	$1.25	$3.75	$7.50

		G	VG	F
1122	Moravia, Alberto - ***The Fancy Dress Party*** [1954] Cover by James Avati.	$1.25	$3.75	$7.50
S-1123	Petry, Ann - ***The Street*** [1954] Cover art by Meese.	$1.25	$3.75	$7.50
1124	Simenon, Georges - ***Belle*** [1954] Cover art by Stanley Zuckerberg.	$1.35	$4.00	$8.00
1126	Weldon, John Lee - ***The Naked Heart*** [1954] Cover by Clark Hulings.	$1.25	$3.75	$7.50
1127	Tucker, Wilson - ***The Time Masters*** [1954] Cover by Jack Farrogasso.	$1.50	$5.00	$10.00
1128	Wayne, Joseph - ***The Long Wind*** [1954]	$1.25	$3.75	$7.50
1129	Bissell, Richard - ***Pajama*** [1954] Cover art by Stanley Zuckerberg.	$1.25	$3.75	$7.50
D-1130	Gorham, Charles - ***Trial By Darkness*** [1954] Cover art by Avati.	$1.25	$3.75	$7.50
S-1131	MacDonald, John D. - ***Cancel All Our Vows*** [1955]	$1.50	$5.00	$10.00
1132	Twersky, Jacob - ***The Face Of The Deep*** [1954]	$1.25	$3.75	$7.50
S-1133	Roberts, Elizabeth Madox - ***The Time Of Man*** [1954]	$1.25	$3.75	$7.50
1134	Ballinger, Bill S. - ***The Beautiful Trap*** [1954]	$1.35	$4.00	$8.00
1135	Arthur, Burt - ***The Texan*** [1954]	$1.25	$3.75	$7.50
1136	Caldwell, Erskine - ***We Are The Living*** [1954] Cover art by Avati.	$1.25	$3.75	$7.50
S-1137	Mirvish, Robert F. - ***A House Of Her Own*** [1954] Cover by James Meese.	$1.25	$3.75	$7.50
1138	Baldwin, James - ***Go Tell It On The Mountain*** [1954] Cover art by James Meese.	$1.25	$3.75	$7.50
1139	Knight, Adam - ***Kiss And Kill*** [1954] Cover art by Cozzarelli.	$1.35	$4.00	$8.00
1140	Raine, William Macleod - ***Guns Of The Frontier*** [1954]	$1.25	$3.75	$7.50
1142	Abbott, A. C. - ***Branded*** [1954]	$1.25	$3.75	$7.50
1144	Simenon, Georges - ***The Bottom Of The Bottle*** [1954]	$1.35	$4.00	$8.00
1145	Shaw, Arnold - ***The Money Song*** [1954]	$1.25	$3.75	$7.50
1146	Harris, Sara - ***The Wayward Ones*** [1954]	$1.25	$3.75	$7.50
1147	Levin, Ira - ***A Kiss Before Dying*** [1954]	$1.35	$4.00	$8.00
S-1148	Faulkner, William - ***The Wild Palms And The Old Man*** [1954] Cover by James Avati.	$1.25	$3.75	$7.50
1149	Webb, Jack - ***The Naked Angel*** [1954] Cover by Robert Maguire.	$1.35	$4.00	$8.00
1150	Bester, Alfred - ***The Demolished Man*** [1954]	$1.35	$4.00	$8.00
1151	Reid, Ed - ***Mafia*** [1954]	$2.00	$6.00	$12.00
1152	Cain, James M. - ***Galatea*** [1954] Cover art by Stanley Zuckerberg.	$1.35	$4.00	$8.00
1153	Cain, James M. - ***Serenade*** [1954] Cover art by James Avati.	$1.35	$4.00	$8.00
1154	Hardy, Linsday - ***Requiem For A Redhead*** [1954] Cover art by Erickson.	$1.25	$3.75	$7.50
1155	Rossi, Jean-Baptiste - ***Awakening*** [1954] Cover by James Avati.	$1.25	$3.75	$7.50
D-1156	Creekmore, Hubert - ***The Chain In The Heart*** [1954] Cover art by Clark Hulings.	$1.25	$3.75	$7.50
S-1157	Cela, Camilo Jose - ***The Hive*** [1954]	$1.25	$3.75	$7.50
1158	Farrell, James T. - ***This Man And This Woman*** [1954] Cover art by James Avati.	$1.35	$4.00	$8.00
1159	Engstrand, Stuart - ***The Scattered Seed*** [1954] Cover art by Clark Hulings.	$1.25	$3.75	$7.50
1160	Clark, Walter Van Tilburg - ***The Ox-Bow Incident*** [1954]	$1.25	$3.75	$7.50
1161	Heinlein, Robert A. - ***Assignment In Eternity*** [1954]	$1.50	$5.00	$10.00
S-1162	Huie, William Bradford - ***Mud On The Stars*** [1955] Cover art by Clark Hulings.	$1.25	$3.75	$7.50
1163	Marshall, Rosamond - ***The General's Wench*** [1955] Cover art by James Meese.	$1.25	$3.75	$7.50
1164	Caufield, M. F. - ***The Black City*** [1954] Cover art by Robert Maguire.	$1.25	$3.75	$7.50

		G	VG	F
1166	Aswell, James - ***The Young And Hungry-Hearted*** [1954] Cover by James Avati.	$1.25	$3.75	$7.50
1167	Wells, Charlie - ***Let The Night Cry*** [1954] Cover art by Robert Maguire.	$1.50	$5.00	$10.00
1168	MacDonald, William Colt - ***Law And Order, Unlimited*** [1954]	$1.25	$3.75	$7.50
D-1169	Winsor, Kathleen - ***Forever Amber*** [1954]	$1.25	$3.75	$7.50
1170	Runbeck, Margaret Lee - ***Time For Love*** [1954]	$1.25	$3.75	$7.50
S-1171	Furcolowe, Charles - ***Search For The Sun*** [1954] Cover art by Avati.	$1.25	$3.75	$7.50
1172	Loughlin, David - ***A Private Stair*** [1955] Cover art by James Meese.	$1.25	$3.75	$7.50
1173	Hales, Norman - ***The Spider In The Cup*** [1955] Cover art by Erickson.	$1.25	$3.75	$7.50
1174	Plenn, J. H. - ***Texas Hellion*** [1955]	$1.25	$3.75	$7.50
1175	Radiguet, Raymond - ***Devil In The Flesh*** [1954]	$1.25	$3.75	$7.50
1176	Engstrand, Stuart - ***The Sling And The Arrow*** [1954]	$1.25	$3.75	$7.50
1177	Eliot, Alexander - ***Proud Youth*** [1955] Cover art by Clark Hulings.	$1.25	$3.75	$7.50
S-1178	Sklar, George - ***The Housewarming*** [1955] Cover art by Cardiff.	$1.25	$3.75	$7.50
1180	Miller, Wade - ***Fatal Step*** [1955]	$1.35	$4.00	$8.00
1181	MacDonald, William Colt - ***Six-Shooter Showdown*** [1955]	$1.25	$3.75	$7.50
1182	Ward, Mary Jane - ***The Snake Pit*** [1955]	$1.25	$3.75	$7.50
D-1183	Suyin, Han - ***A Many-Splendored Thing*** [1955] Cover by Stanley Zuckerberg.	$1.25	$3.75	$7.50
1184	Weldon, John Lee - ***Thunder In The Heart*** [1955] Cover art by Clark Hulings.	$1.25	$3.75	$7.50
1185	Gold, Herbert - ***Room Clerk*** [1955] Cover art by Stanley Zuckerberg.	$1.25	$3.75	$7.50
1186	Freeman, Walter - ***All The Way Home*** [1955] PBO. Cover art by Clark Hulings.	$1.25	$3.75	$7.50
1187	Chase, James Hadley - ***I'll Bury My Dead*** [1955] Cover by Erickson.	$2.00	$6.00	$12.00
1188	Simenon, Georges - ***Inspector Maigret And The Strangled Stripper*** [1955] Cover art by Robert Maguire.	$2.00	$6.00	$12.00
1189	Colette - ***Cheri/The Last Of Cheri*** [1955]	$1.25	$3.75	$7.50
1190	Marshall, Rosamond - ***Kitty*** [1955]	$1.00	$3.00	$6.00
1191	Carreno, Jose Suarez - ***The Final Hours*** [1955] Cover art by James Meese.	$1.25	$3.75	$7.50
1192	Siringo, Charles A. - ***Texas Cowboy*** [1955]	$1.25	$3.75	$7.50
1193	Bissell, Richard - ***River In My Blood*** [1955]	$1.25	$3.75	$7.50
1194	Heinlein, Robert A. - ***Revolt In 2100*** [1955]	$1.50	$5.00	$10.00
1195	Cain, James M. - ***The Butterfly*** [1955]	$1.35	$4.00	$8.00
1196	Harkey, Dee - ***Mean As Hell*** [1955]	$1.25	$3.75	$7.50
S-1197	Foster, Joseph - ***Street Of The Barefoot Lovers*** [1955]	$1.25	$3.75	$7.50
D-1198	Flood, Charles Bracelen - ***Love Is A Bridge*** [1955]	$1.35	$4.00	$8.00
D-1199	Caldwell, Erskine - ***The Complete Stories Of Erskine Caldwell*** [1955]	$1.25	$3.75	$7.50
S-1200	Ageton, Arthur N. - ***The Jungle Seas*** [1955] Cover art by James Meese.	$1.25	$3.75	$7.50
1201	Bowen, Robert O. - ***Bamboo*** [1955] Cover art by Stanley Zuckerberg.	$1.25	$3.75	$7.50
1202	Dougherty, Kermit - ***Out Of The Red Brush*** [1955]	$1.25	$3.75	$7.50
1203	Lariar, Lawrence - ***Win, Place And Die!*** [1955]	$1.25	$3.75	$7.50
1204	White, Lionel - ***Love Trap*** [1955]	$1.50	$5.00	$10.00
S-1205	Burns, Walter Noble - ***Tombstone*** [1955]	$1.25	$3.75	$7.50
D-1206	Thompson, Morton - ***The Cry And The Covenant*** [1955]	$1.25	$3.75	$7.50
1207	Howard, Toni - ***Three Sinners In Paris*** [1955] Cover by Clark Hulings.	$1.25	$3.75	$7.50
1208	Sheean, Vincent - ***Live For Today*** [1955] Cover by Maguire.	$1.25	$3.75	$7.50

		G	VG	F
1209	Keogh, Theodora - ***The Fascinator*** [1955] Cover art by Avati..	$1.25	$3.75	$7.50
1210	Arthur, Ella Bentley - ***My Husband Keeps Telling Me To Go To Hell*** [1955] Cover art by R. Taylor. Cartoon book.	$1.25	$3.75	$7.50
T-1212	Hecht, Ben - ***A Child Of The Century*** [1955]	$1.25	$3.75	$7.50
S-1213	Moravia, Alberto - ***The Time Of Indifference*** [1955] Cover by James Avati.	$1.25	$3.75	$7.50
S-1214	Biography - ***The Life Of Davy Crockett*** [1955]	$1.25	$3.75	$7.50
S-1215	McInnes, Graham - ***Lost Island*** [1955]	$1.25	$3.75	$7.50
1216	Roscoe, Mike - ***Slice Of Hell*** [1955] Cover art by Robert Maguire.	$1.50	$5.00	$10.00
1217	Box, Edgar (Gore Vidal) - ***Death Likes It Hot*** [1955]	$1.25	$3.75	$7.50
1218	Vidal, Gore - ***The City And The Pillar*** [1955]	$1.25	$3.75	$7.50
1219	Lemay, Alan - ***Cattle Kingdom*** [1955]	$1.25	$3.75	$7.50
1221	Kelley, Thomas P. - ***The Black Donnellys*** [1955]	$1.25	$3.75	$7.50
S-1222	Mirvish, Robert F. - ***The Eternal Voyagers*** [1955] Cover art by Clark Hulings.	$1.25	$3.75	$7.50
1223	La Capria, Raffaele - ***First Affair*** [1955] Cover art by Clark Hulings.	$1.25	$3.75	$7.50
1224	Vernon, Roger Lee - ***The Space Frontiers*** [1955]	$1.25	$3.75	$7.50
1225	Wells, Charlie - ***The Last Kill*** [1955] PBO. Cover by Robert Maguire.	$1.50	$5.00	$10.00
1226	Kramer, Dale - ***Violent Streets*** [1955] PBO. Cover by James Avati.	$2.00	$6.00	$12.00
D-1227	Winsor, Kathleen - ***The Lovers*** [1955]	$1.25	$3.75	$7.50
1228	Raine, William Macleod - ***Sons Of The Saddle*** [1955]	$1.25	$3.75	$7.50
D-1229	Melville, Herman - ***Moby Dick*** [1955]	$1.50	$5.00	$10.00
1230	Bissell, Richard - ***High Water*** [1955]	$1.25	$3.75	$7.50
1231	Hazel, Robert - ***The Farmer's Bride*** [1955]	$1.25	$3.75	$7.50
1232	Heckelmann, Charles N. - ***Hard Man With A Gun*** [1955]	$1.25	$3.75	$7.50
1233	Webb, Jack - ***The Damned Lovely*** [1955] Cover art by Robert Maguire.	$1.50	$5.00	$10.00
1234	Anthology edited by Marc Slonim & Harvey Breit - ***This Thing Called Love*** [1955]	$1.00	$3.00	$6.00
1235	Miller, Wade - ***Killer's Choice*** [1955]	$1.35	$4.00	$8.00
1236	Williams, Tennessee - ***The Rose Tattoo*** [1955] Movie photo cover. Movie tie-in. 8 pages of photos.	$1.50	$5.00	$10.00
D-1237	Gordimer, Nadine - ***The Lying Days*** [1955] Cover by James Avati.	$1.25	$3.75	$7.50
S-1238	Wolfe, Bernard - ***Everything Happens At Night*** [1955] Cover art by Stanley Zuckerberg.	$1.25	$3.75	$7.50
1239	Pittenger, Ted - ***Warrior's Return*** [1955] Cover art by Avati....	$1.25	$3.75	$7.50
1240	Asimov, Isaac - ***The Caves Of Steel*** [1955] Cover art by Robert Schulz.	$1.35	$4.00	$8.00
1241	White, Lionel - ***To Find A Killer*** [1955] Cover art by Robert Maguire.	$1.50	$5.00	$10.00
1242	Hickok, Will - ***Web Of Gunsmoke*** [1955]	$1.25	$3.75	$7.50
1243	Ballinger, Bill S. - ***The Body In The Bed*** [1955]	$1.35	$4.00	$8.00
D-1244	Gorham, Charles - ***The Gold Of Their Bodies*** [1955]	$1.25	$3.75	$7.50
S-1245	Armstrong, Louis - ***Satchmo*** [1955] Cover art by Stanley Zuckerberg.	$2.50	$7.50	$15.00
1246	Miller, Henry - ***Nights Of Love And Laughter*** [1955]	$1.25	$3.75	$7.50
1247	Taylor, Sam S. - ***So Cold, My Bed*** [1955] Cover art by Robert Maguire.	$1.50	$5.00	$10.00
1248	Simenon, Georges - ***Inspector Maigret And The Killers*** [1955]	$1.35	$4.00	$8.00
S-1249	Bowles, Paul - ***The Sheltering Sky*** [1955]	$1.25	$3.75	$7.50
1250	Connell, Vivian - ***The Golden Sleep*** [1955]	$1.25	$3.75	$7.50
1251	Ermine, Will - ***Laramie Rides Alone*** [1955]	$1.25	$3.75	$7.50
S-1252	Isherwood, Christopher - ***Goodbye To Berlin*** [1955]	$1.25	$3.75	$7.50
1253	Faulkner, William - ***Intruder In The Dust*** [1955]	$1.25	$3.75	$7.50
S-1254	Conrad, Joseph - ***Heart Of Darkness*** [1955]	$1.25	$3.75	$7.50

		G	VG	F
1255	Auchincloss, Louis - ***The Unholy Three*** [1955] Cover by James Avati.	$1.25	$3.75	$7.50
1256	Fischer, Bruno - ***The Bleeding Scissors*** [1955] Cover by Robert Maguire.	$1.50	$5.00	$10.00
1257	Miller, Wade - ***Uneasy Street*** [1955]	$1.25	$3.75	$7.50
1258	Lehman, Paul Evan - ***Montana Man*** [1955]	$1.25	$3.75	$7.50
1259	Petry, Ann - ***The Narrows*** [1955] Cover art by Clark Hulings.	$1.25	$3.75	$7.50
D-1260	Bromfield, Louis - ***The Farm*** [1955] Cover art by James Avati.	$1.25	$3.75	$7.50
1261	Lariar, Lawrence - ***How Green Was My Sex Life*** [1955] PBO. Cover by Lawrence Lariar.	$1.25	$3.75	$7.50
1264	Himes, Chester - ***The Primitives*** [1955]	$1.25	$3.75	$7.50
T-1265	Thompson, Morton - ***Not As A Stranger*** [1955]	$1.25	$3.75	$7.50
S-1266	Gordimer, Nadine - ***The Soft Voice Of The Serpent*** [1956]	$1.25	$3.75	$7.50
1267	Slade, Caroline - ***Margaret*** [1956]	$1.25	$3.75	$7.50
1268	Mahannah, Floyd - ***Stopover For Murder*** [1956] Cover art by Robert Maguire.	$1.50	$5.00	$10.00
1270	Miller, Wade - ***Calamity Fair*** [1956] Cover art by Robert Maguire.	$1.50	$5.00	$10.00
S-1271	Hamner, Earl, Jr. - ***Fifty Roads To Town*** [1956] Cover art by James Avati.	$1.25	$3.75	$7.50
1272	Caldwell, Erskine - ***Love And Money*** [1956] Cover by James Avati.	$1.25	$3.75	$7.50
S-1273	Nimier, Roger - ***The Blue Hussar*** [1956] Cover art by Stanley Zuckerberg.	$1.25	$3.75	$7.50
1274	Ballinger, Bill S. - ***The Body Beautiful*** [1956]	$1.25	$3.75	$7.50
1275	Farrell, James T. - ***The Face Of Time*** [1956] Cover art by Robert Maguire.	$1.50	$5.00	$10.00
1276	Knight, Adam - ***I'll Kill You Next!*** [1956] Cover art by Robert Maguire.	$1.50	$5.00	$10.00
1277	Wayne, Joseph - ***Bunch Grass*** [1956]	$1.25	$3.75	$7.50
1278	Bemelmans, Ludwig - ***Dirty Eddie*** [1956]	$1.25	$3.75	$7.50
S-1279	Morley, Susan - ***Making Of A Mistress*** [1956] Cover by James Avati.	$1.25	$3.75	$7.50
S-1280	Burlingame, Roger - ***General Billy Mitchell: Champion Of Air Defense*** [1956]	$1.25	$3.75	$7.50
S-1281	Thomas, Dylan - ***Adventures In The Skin Trade*** [1956]	$1.50	$5.00	$10.00
S-1282	Asimov, Isaac - ***I, Robot*** [1956] Cover art by Robert Schulz.	$2.50	$7.50	$15.00
1283	Hardy, Lindsay - ***The Nightshade Ring*** [1956] Cover art by Robert Schulz.	$1.50	$5.00	$10.00
1284	Keogh, Theodora - ***Meg*** [1956] Cover by James Avati.	$1.25	$3.75	$7.50
S-1285	Hayman, Mac - ***No Time For Sergeants*** [1956]	$1.25	$3.75	$7.50
1286	Basinsky, Earle - ***The Big Steal*** [1956]	$1.25	$3.75	$7.50
1287	Ermine, Will - ***Lobo Law*** [1956]	$1.25	$3.75	$7.50
1288	Moravia, Alberto - ***Conjugal Love*** [1956] Cover art by James Avati.	$1.25	$3.75	$7.50
1289	Orwell, George - ***Animal Farm*** [1956]	$1.25	$3.75	$7.50
S-1290	Paton, Alan - ***Too Late The Phalarope*** [1956]	$1.25	$3.75	$7.50
S-1292	Williams, Wirt - ***The Enemy*** [1956]	$1.25	$3.75	$7.50
1293	Wilson, Herbert Emerson - ***I Stole $16,000,000*** [1956]	$1.25	$3.75	$7.50
1294	Avallone, Michael - ***Violence In Velvet*** [1956] PBO. Cover art by Robert Maguire.	$1.50	$5.00	$10.00
1295	Gallico, Paul - ***The Lonely*** [1956]	$1.25	$3.75	$7.50
1296	Bowles, Paul - ***The Delicate Prey And Other Stories*** [1956]	$1.25	$3.75	$7.50
1297	Lehman, Paul Evan - ***Valley Of Hunter Men*** [1956]	$1.25	$3.75	$7.50
1298	Adams, Cleve F. - ***Contraband*** [1956] Cover art by Carl Bobertz.	$1.35	$4.00	$8.00
D-1299	Himes, Chester - ***The Third Generation*** [1956] Cover art by Stanley Zuckerberg.	$2.00	$6.00	$12.00
1300	Farrar, Larston D. - ***Washington Lowdown*** [1956]	$1.25	$3.75	$7.50

		G	VG	F
1301	Ilton, Paul - ***The Secret Of Mary Magdalene*** [1956] PBO. Cover art by Avati.	$2.00	$6.00	$12.00
1302	Wayne, Joseph - ***Gunplay Valley*** [1956]	$1.25	$3.75	$7.50
1303	Raine, William Macleod - ***The Six-Gun Kid*** [1956] Cover art by Robert Schulz.	$1.25	$3.75	$7.50
1304	Anderson, Sherwood - ***Winesburg, Ohio*** [1956]	$1.25	$3.75	$7.50
1305	Pottle, Frederick A. - editor - ***Boswell's London Journal*** [1956] Cover art by Hattock.	$1.25	$3.75	$7.50
S-1306	Moravia, Alberto - ***A Ghost Of Noon*** [1956]	$1.25	$3.75	$7.50
S-1307	Gehman, Richard - ***A Murder In Paradise*** [1956] Cover by James Avati.	$1.25	$3.75	$7.50
S-1308	Willingham, Calder - ***The Girl In Dogwood Cabin*** [1956]	$1.25	$3.75	$7.50
1310	White, Lionel - ***The Killing*** [1956] Cover art by Robert Maguire.	$1.50	$5.00	$10.00
1311	Webb, Jack - ***The Broken Doll*** [1956] Cover art by Robert Maguire.	$1.50	$5.00	$10.00
1312	Plenn, J. H. & Laroche, C. J. - ***The Fastest Gun In Texas*** [1956] PBO. Cover art by Robert Schulz.	$1.35	$4.00	$8.00
1313	Switzer, Robert - ***The Tent Of The Wicked*** [1956]	$1.25	$3.75	$7.50
1314	Aswell, James - ***There's One In Every Town*** [1956]	$1.25	$3.75	$7.50
S-1315	Faulkner, William - ***Knight's Gambit*** [1956]	$1.25	$3.75	$7.50
1316	Fadiman, Jr., Edwin - ***The Glass Play Pen*** [1956] PBO. Cover art by Robert Maguire.	$1.25	$3.75	$7.50
1317	Miller, Henry - ***A Devil In Paradise*** [1956] PBO.	$1.25	$3.75	$7.50
S-1318	Grau, Shirley Ann - ***The Black Prince And Other Stories*** [1956]	$1.25	$3.75	$7.50
1319	Ballinger, Bill S. - ***The Tooth And The Nail*** [1956] Cover art by Robert Maguire.	$1.50	$5.00	$10.00
1320	Wakeman, Frederic - ***Shore Leave*** [1956]	$1.25	$3.75	$7.50
1321	Ballinger, Bill S. - ***Portrait In Smoke*** [1956]	$1.35	$4.00	$8.00
1322	Knight, Adam - ***Stone Cold Blonde*** [1956] Cover art by Robert Maguire.	$1.50	$5.00	$10.00
1324	Weil, Jerry - ***Delay En Route*** [1956] PBO. Cover art by Robert Maguire.	$1.35	$4.00	$8.00
1325	Roy, Jules - ***The Navigator*** [1956] Cover by Stanley Zuckerberg.	$1.25	$3.75	$7.50
1326	Gresham, William Lindsay - ***Nightmare Alley*** [1956]	$1.25	$3.75	$7.50
1327	Simenon, Georges - ***The Snow Was Black*** [1956]	$1.25	$3.75	$7.50
1329	Heyes, Douglas - ***The Kiss-Off*** [1956]	$1.25	$3.75	$7.50
D-1330	Warren, Robert Penn - ***Band Of Angels*** [1956] Cover by James Avati.	$1.25	$3.75	$7.50
1332	Stone, Andrew L. - ***Julie*** [1956] Cover art by Robert Maguire. Movie tie-in.	$1.50	$5.00	$10.00
S-1333	Capote, Truman - ***The Grass Harp and A Tree Of Night*** [1956]	$1.35	$4.00	$8.00
S-1334	Williams, Tennessee - ***Baby Doll*** [1956] Photo cover. Movie tie-in. 8 pages of photos.	$2.00	$6.00	$12.00
1335	Switzer, Robert - ***The Living Idol*** [1956] Cover art by Robert Maguire.	$2.50	$7.50	$15.00
S-1336	Markandaya, Kamala - ***Nectar In A Sieve*** [1956] Cover art by Stanley Zuckerberg.	$1.25	$3.75	$7.50
1338	Simenon, Georges - ***Inspector Maigret In New York's Underworld*** [1956] Cover art by Robert Maguire.	$1.50	$5.00	$10.00
1340	Ernenwein, Leslie - ***Trigger Justice*** [1956]	$1.25	$3.75	$7.50
1341	Harris, Sara - ***The Wayward Ones*** [1956]	$1.25	$3.75	$7.50
1342	Caldwell, Erskine - ***Gretta*** [1956] Cover by James Avati.	$1.25	$3.75	$7.50
1343	Anderson, Robert - ***Tea And Sympathy*** [1956] Cover art by James Avati. Movie tie-in with 4 pages of photos.	$1.25	$3.75	$7.50
1344	Inchardi, J. - ***Good Night, Sailor*** [1956] PBO. Cover by Clark Hulings.	$1.25	$3.75	$7.50

		G	VG	F
S-1345	O'Connor, Flannery - ***A Good Man Is Hard To Find*** [1956] Cover art by Tony Kokinos.	$1.25	$3.75	$7.50
S-1346	Leintser, Murray - ***Operation: Outer Space*** [1956] Cover art by Robert Schulz.	$1.50	$5.00	$10.00
1347	Knight, Adam - ***Girl Running*** [1956] PBO.	$1.35	$4.00	$8.00
S-1348	Sneider, Vern - ***The Teahouse Of The August Moon*** [1956] Cover art by Zuckerberg.	$1.25	$3.75	$7.50
1350	Weil, Jerry - ***Office Wife*** [1956] PBO.	$1.25	$3.75	$7.50
1351	Basinsky, Earle - ***Death Is A Cold, Keen Edge*** [1956] PBO. Cover art by Robert Maguire.	$1.25	$3.75	$7.50
1353	Gehman, Richard - ***The Slander Of Witches*** [1956]	$1.25	$3.75	$7.50
1354	de St. Exupery, Antoine - ***Night Flight*** [1956]	$1.25	$3.75	$7.50
D-1355	Calmer, Ned - ***The Strange Land*** [1956]	$1.25	$3.75	$7.50
1356	Maurete, Marcelle - ***Anastasia*** [1956] Photo cover. Movie tie-in with Yul Brynner. 4 pages of photos.	$1.50	$5.00	$10.00
1357	Stewart, Desmond - ***A Stranger In Eden*** [1956]	$1.25	$3.75	$7.50
1358	Roscoe, Mike - ***One Tear For My Grave*** [1956] Cover art by Bob Maguire.	$1.25	$3.75	$7.50
1359	Frank, Leonhard - ***Desire Me*** [1956]	$1.25	$3.75	$7.50
1361	Andriola, Alfred & Casson, Mel - editor - ***Ever Since Adam And Eve*** [1957] Cartoon book.	$1.25	$3.75	$7.50
1364	Hardgrove, Marion - ***The Girl He Left Behind*** [1956] Movie tie-in.	$1.25	$3.75	$7.50
S-1365	Uris, Leon M. - ***The Angry Hills*** [1956] Cover by Barye Phillips.	$1.25	$3.75	$7.50
1366	Barnwell, J. O. - ***Death Rider*** [1957]	$1.25	$3.75	$7.50
S-1367	Lindbergh, Anne Morrow - ***Gift From The Sea*** [1957]	$1.25	$3.75	$7.50
1368	Fine, Benjamin - ***1,000,000 Delinquents*** [1957] Photo cover.	$1.50	$5.00	$10.00
1369	Miller, Wade - ***Shoot To Kill*** [1957]	$1.25	$3.75	$7.50
S-1370	Flaiano, Ennio - ***The Short Cut*** [1957]	$1.25	$3.75	$7.50
1371	Baldwin, Monica - ***I Leap Over The Wall*** [1957] Cover by James Avati.	$1.25	$3.75	$7.50
1372	Moravia, Alberto - ***Two Adolescents*** [1957]	$1.25	$3.75	$7.50
1373	Heckelmann, Charles N. - ***Bullet Law*** [1957]	$1.25	$3.75	$7.50
1374	Fadiman, Jr., Edwin - ***An Act Of Violence*** [1957]	$1.25	$3.75	$7.50
D-1375	Mailer, Norman - ***The Deer Park*** [1957]	$1.25	$3.75	$7.50
1376	Simenon, Georges - ***Strangers In The House*** [1957] Cover art by Robert Schulz.	$1.25	$3.75	$7.50
1377	Komroff, Manuel - ***The Life, The Loves, The Adventures Of Omar Khayyam*** [1957] Movie tie-in.	$1.25	$3.75	$7.50
1378	White, Lionel - ***Flight Into Terror*** [1957] Cover by Robert Maguire.	$1.50	$5.00	$10.00
1379	Finnegan, Robert - ***The Bandaged Nude*** [1957]	$1.25	$3.75	$7.50
1380	Steinbeck, John - ***Tortilla Flat*** [1957]	$1.25	$3.75	$7.50
1381	Wexler, Susan Stanhope - ***The Story Of Sandy*** [1957] Cover art by Avati.	$1.25	$3.75	$7.50
1382	Dean, Abner - ***What Am I Doing Here?*** [1957] Cover by Abner Dean. Cartoon book.	$1.25	$3.75	$7.50
1383	Deal, Borden - ***Killer In The House*** [1957] PBO.	$1.50	$5.00	$10.00
1384	Wayne, Joseph - ***The Return Of The Kid*** [1957]	$1.25	$3.75	$7.50
S-1385	Chayefsky, Paddy - ***The Bachelor Party*** [1957]	$1.25	$3.75	$7.50
D-1386	Willingham, Calder - ***End As A Man and The Strange One*** [1957]	$1.25	$3.75	$7.50
S-1387	Jones, Denys - ***Look Not Upon Me*** [1957]	$1.25	$3.75	$7.50
T-1388	Kantor, MacKinlay - ***Andersonville*** [1957]	$1.25	$3.75	$7.50
1389	Bester, Alfred - ***The Stars My Destination*** [1957] PBO. Cover by Richard Powers.	$2.00	$6.00	$12.00
1390	Wakeman, Frederic - ***The Wastrel*** [1957]	$1.25	$3.75	$7.50
D-1391	Bengtsson, Frans G. - ***The Long Ships*** [1957]	$1.25	$3.75	$7.50
S-1392	Hargrove, Marion - ***The Girl He Left Behind*** [1961]	$1.25	$3.75	$7.50

		G	VG	F
1393	Weil, Jerry - ***Paint On Their Faces*** [1957] PBO. Cover art by Robert Maguire.	$1.25	$3.75	$7.50
1395	Knight, Adam - ***Murder For Madam*** [1957]	$1.25	$3.75	$7.50
1397	Lewisohn, Ludwig - ***In A Summer Season*** [1957]	$1.25	$3.75	$7.50
1399	Ilton, Paul - ***The Last Days Of Sodom And Gomorrah*** [1957] PBO. Cover by Robert Maguire.	$2.50	$7.50	$15.00
1402	Colette - ***The Ripening Seed*** [1967]	$1.25	$3.75	$7.50
1403	Colt, Clem - ***Quick-Trigger Country*** [1957] Cover art by Robert Schulz.	$1.35	$4.00	$8.00
1405	Adams, Cleve F. - ***The Private Eye*** [1957] Cover art by Robert Maguire	$1.50	$5.00	$10.00
D-1407	LaMure, Pierre - ***Beyond Desire*** [1957] Cover art by James Avati.	$1.25	$3.75	$7.50
S-1408	Engstrand, Stuart - ***More Deaths Than One*** [1957] Cover art by James Avati.	$1.25	$3.75	$7.50
S-1409	Rattigan, Terence - ***The Prince And The Showgirl*** [1957] PBO. Marilyn Monroe photo cover. Movie tie-in. 8 pages of photos.	$4.00	$12.50	$25.00
D-1411	Mann, Thomas - ***Confessions Of Felix Krull, Confidence Man*** [1957]	$1.25	$3.75	$7.50
S-1412	Gazzo, Michael Vincente - ***A Hatful Of Rain*** [1957] Photo cover. Movie tie-in. 8 pages of photos.	$1.35	$4.00	$8.00
S-1413	Lehman, Ernest - ***Sweet Smell Of Success*** [1957] Movie tie-in. Photo cover. 8 pages of photos.	$1.25	$3.75	$7.50
S-1415	Foote, Shelby - editor - ***The Night Before Chancellorsville & Other Civil War Stories*** [1957] PBO. Cover by Clark Hulings.	$1.25	$3.75	$7.50
1417	Caldwell, Erskine - ***This Very Earth*** [1957]	$1.25	$3.75	$7.50
1418	Garland, George - ***Doubtful Valley*** [1957]	$1.25	$3.75	$7.50
S-1420	Brinkley, William - ***As Told To - The Deliverance Of Sister Cecilia*** [1957] Cover art by James Avati.	$1.25	$3.75	$7.50
1421	Simenon, Georges - ***The Hitchhiker*** [1957] Cover art by Robert Schulz	$1.50	$5.00	$10.00
1422	Webb, Jack - ***The Bad Blonde*** [1957] Cover art by Robert Maguire.	$1.50	$5.00	$10.00
S-1424	Howard, Robert West - editor - ***This Is The West*** [1957] PBO.	$1.25	$3.75	$7.50
S-1425	Bissell, Richard - ***Pajama*** [1957]	$1.25	$3.75	$7.50
1427	Cain, James M. - ***Double Indemnity*** [1957] Cover art by Maguire.	$1.50	$5.00	$10.00
1429	Roy, Jules - ***The Unfaithful Wife*** [1957]	$1.25	$3.75	$7.50
S-1430	Caldwell, Erskine - ***Gulf Coast Stories*** [1957] Cover by James Avati.	$1.25	$3.75	$7.50
S-1433	Asimov, Issac - ***The Martian Way And Other Stories*** [1957]	$1.35	$4.00	$8.00
1434	Ross, Sam - ***The Tight Corner*** [1957]	$1.35	$4.00	$8.00
1435	Daniels, John S. - ***The Man From Yesterday*** [1957]	$1.25	$3.75	$7.50
S-1437	O'Hara, John - ***Appointment In Samarra*** [1957]	$1.25	$3.75	$7.50
D-1438	Shaw, Irwin - ***Lucy Crown*** [1957]	$1.25	$3.75	$7.50
S-1439	Huie, William Bradford - ***Ruby McCollum*** [1957]	$1.25	$3.75	$7.50
1440	Hunt, George P - ***Coral Comes High*** [1957]	$1.25	$3.75	$7.50
1441	Webb, Paul - ***The Mountain Boys*** [1957] Cover art by Paul Webb. Cartoon book	$1.25	$3.75	$7.50
1442	White, Lionel - ***The House Next Door*** [1957] Cover by Robert Maguire.	$1.50	$5.00	$10.00
1443	Arthur, Burt - ***Gunsmoke In Nevada*** [1957] PBO.	$1.25	$3.75	$7.50
S-1444	Heinlein, Robert A. - ***Double Star*** [1957] Cover art by Richard Powers.	$1.35	$4.00	$8.00
1445	Cain, James - ***Love's Lovely Counterfeit*** [1957]	$1.35	$4.00	$8.00
1446	Lehman, Ernest - ***The Comedian And Other Stories*** [1957] TV tie-in with Mickey Rooney.	$1.35	$4.00	$8.00

		G	VG	F
1447	Hutchinson, Loring - ***The Secret Of Hidden Valley*** [1947] Cover art by Allison.	$1.25	$3.75	$7.50
1448	Wellman, Manly - ***Find My Killer*** [1957] Cover art by Robert Maguire.	$1.35	$4.00	$8.00
1449	Weil, Jerry - ***Nobody Dies In Paris*** [1957] PBO. Cover art by Barye Phillips.	$1.25	$3.75	$7.50
1450	Wakeman, Frederic - ***Shore Leave*** [1957]	$1.25	$3.75	$7.50
S-1451	Devries, Peter - ***Comfort Me With Apples*** [1957] Cover art by Barye Phillips.	$1.25	$3.75	$7.50
S-1452	Ellison, James Whitfield - ***I'm Owen Harrison Harding*** [1957] Cover art by James Avati.	$1.25	$3.75	$7.50
S-1453	Shaw, Irwin - ***Tip On A Dead Jockey*** [1957] Movie tie-in. Photo cover.	$1.35	$4.00	$8.00
T-1454	Wouk, Herman - ***Marjorie Morningstar*** [1957]	$1.25	$3.75	$7.50
D-1455	Morris, Wright - ***The Field Of Vision*** [1957] Cover art by M. Glaser.	$1.25	$3.75	$7.50
1456	Caldwell, Erskine - ***A House In The Uplands*** [1957]	$1.25	$3.75	$7.50
S-1457	Farrell, James T. - ***A Dangerous Woman And Other Stories*** [1957] Cover by James Avati.	$1.25	$3.75	$7.50
D-1458	Brinkley, William - ***Don't Go Near The Water*** [1957] Movie tie-in.	$1.25	$3.75	$7.50
S-1459	Beach, Edward L. - ***Submarine!*** [1957]	$1.25	$3.75	$7.50
1461	Thompson, Jim - ***Wild Town*** [1957] PBO. Cover art by Robert Maguire.	$22.00	$70.00	$140.00
S-1462	Hardy, Rene - ***Bitter Victory*** [1957] Cover art by Robert Schulz.	$1.25	$3.75	$7.50
S-1464	Clarke, Arthur C. - ***The City And The Stars*** [1957] Cover art by Richard Powers.	$1.25	$3.75	$7.50
1465	Simenon, Georges - ***The Fugitive*** [1958] Cover art by Schulz.	$1.35	$4.00	$8.00
S-1466	Carter, Ross S. - ***Those Devils In Baggy Pants*** [1957]	$1.25	$3.75	$7.50
S-1467	Brown, Harry - ***A Walk In The Sun*** [1957] Cover by Barye Phillips.	$1.25	$3.75	$7.50
T-1468	Rand, Ayn - ***The Fountainhead*** [1957]	$1.25	$3.75	$7.50
D-1469	McKernan, Maureen - ***The Amazing Crime And Trial Of Leopold And Loeb*** [1957] PBO. 8 pages of photos.	$1.25	$3.75	$7.50
S-1470	Clark, Walter Van Tilburg - ***The Ox-Bow Incident*** [1957]	$1.25	$3.75	$7.50
1471	Mankowitz, Wolf - ***Old Soldiers Never Die*** [1958]	$1.25	$3.75	$7.50
1472	Hunt, Kyle - ***Kill Once, Kill Twice*** [1957] Cover art by Robert Maguire.	$1.35	$4.00	$8.00
1473	Nye, Nelson - ***Bandido*** [1957] Cover art by Robert Schulz.	$1.25	$3.75	$7.50
1474	Fischer, Bruno - ***The Flesh Was Cold*** [1957] Cover art by Robert Maguire.	$1.35	$4.00	$8.00
1475	Box, Edgar (Gore Vidal) - ***Death In The Fifth Position*** [1957]	$1.25	$3.75	$7.50
S-1476	Jones, Ken - ***The F.B.I. In Action*** [1957]	$1.25	$3.75	$7.50
D-1477	Feuchtwanger, Lion - ***Raquel*** [1957] Cover art by James Avati.	$1.25	$3.75	$7.50
S-1478	Anthology edited by Alex Austin - ***War!*** [1957] PBO.	$1.25	$3.75	$7.50
1479	Caldwell, Erskine - ***A Place Called Estherville*** [1957] Cover by James Avati.	$1.25	$3.75	$7.50
1480	Farrar, Larston D. - ***The Sins Of Sandra Shaw*** [1958] Cover art by Barye Phillips.	$1.25	$3.75	$7.50
1481	Ward, Brad - ***Thirty Notches*** [1958] Cover art by Allison.	$1.25	$3.75	$7.50
1482	Miller, Wade - ***Guilty Bystander*** [1958] Cover art by Tepper.	$1.25	$3.75	$7.50
1483	Raine, William Macleod - ***Powdersmoke Feud*** [1958]	$1.25	$3.75	$7.50
1484	Box, Edgar (Gore Vidal) - ***Death Likes It Hot*** [1958]	$1.25	$3.75	$7.50
S-1485	Faulkner, William - ***Pylon*** [1958] Photo cover. Movie tie-in.	$1.35	$4.00	$8.00
D-1486	Faulkner, William - ***Sanctuary And Requiem For A Nun*** [1958]	$1.35	$4.00	$8.00
D-1487	Russ, Martin - ***The Last Parallel*** [1958] Cover by Robert Schulz.	$1.25	$3.75	$7.50
T-1488	Dostoyevsky, Fyodor - ***The Brothers Karamazov*** [1958]	$1.25	$3.75	$7.50

		G	VG	F
1489	Vincent, Richard - ***Sing, Boy, Sing*** [1958] PBO. Photo cover. Movie tie-in.	$1.35	$4.00	$8.00
D-1490	Barrymore, Diana & Frank, Gerold - ***Too Much, Too Soon*** [1958] Photo cover. 12 photos inside.	$1.25	$3.75	$7.50
1492	Walsh, Robert - ***Violent Hours*** [1958] PBO. Cover art by Robert Schulz.	$1.35	$4.00	$8.00
S-1493	Asimov, Isaac - ***The End Of Eternity*** [1958]	$1.25	$3.75	$7.50
1494	Ballinger, Bill S. - ***The Wife Of The Red-Haired Man*** [1958]	$1.35	$4.00	$8.00
S-1495	Croy, Homer - ***Last Of The Great Outlaws*** [1958] Cover art by Allison. 8 pages of photos.	$1.25	$3.75	$7.50
T-1496	Shaw, Irwin - ***The Young Lions*** [1958]	$1.25	$3.75	$7.50
S-1497	Caldwell, Erskine - ***The Sacrilege Of Alan Kent*** [1958]	$1.25	$3.75	$7.50
D-1498	Salinger, J. D. - ***Nine Stories*** [1958]	$1.25	$3.75	$7.50
S-1499	Hoagland, Edward - ***Cat Man*** [1958] Cover art by Stanley Zuckerberg.	$1.25	$3.75	$7.50
S-1500	Reid, Ed - ***Mafia*** [1958]	$1.25	$3.75	$7.50
S-1501	Faulkner, William - ***The Long Hot Summer*** [1958] Movie tie-in. Movie photo cover. 4 pages of photos.	$1.35	$4.00	$8.00
1502	O'Neil, Eugene - ***Desire Under The Elms*** [1958] Movie photo cover. Movie tie-in. 4 pages of photos.	$1.25	$3.75	$7.50
1505	Daniels, John S. - ***Smoke Of The Gun*** [1958] PBO. Cover art by Leone.	$1.25	$3.75	$7.50
D-1506	Hollands, D. J. - ***Able Company*** [1958] Cover art by Barye Phillips.	$1.25	$3.75	$7.50
S-1507	De Vries, Peter - ***The Tunnel Of Love*** [1958] Cover art by Barye Phillips.	$1.25	$3.75	$7.50
1508	Stone, Andrew L. - ***Cry Terror*** [1958] PBO. Cover art by Robert Maguire. Movie tie-in.	$1.50	$5.00	$10.00
D-1509	Lawrence, D. H. - ***Sons And Lovers*** [1958]	$1.25	$3.75	$7.50
S-1511	Faulkner, William - ***Intruder In The Dust*** [1958]	$1.25	$3.75	$7.50
S-1512	Bamm, Peter - ***The Invisible Flag*** [1958] Cover art by Barye Phillips.	$1.25	$3.75	$7.50
S-1513	Payne, Robert - ***The Barbarian And The Geisha*** [1958] PBO. Movie tie-in with John Wayne.	$1.25	$3.75	$7.50
S-1514	Malamud, Bernard - ***The Assistant*** [1958]	$1.25	$3.75	$7.50
1515	Kane, Henry - ***Hang By Your Neck*** [1958]	$1.35	$4.00	$8.00
1516	Nye, Nelson - ***Maverick Marshal*** [1958] PBO.	$1.25	$3.75	$7.50
T-1518	Farrell, James T. - ***Studs Lonigan*** [1958]	$1.25	$3.75	$7.50
S-1520	Moravia, Alberto - ***Bitter Honeymoon and Other Stories*** [1958] Cover art by Clark Hulings.	$1.25	$3.75	$7.50
S-1522	March, William - ***Company K*** [1958]	$1.25	$3.75	$7.50
1523	Kane, Henry - ***Edge Of Panic*** [1958]	$1.35	$4.00	$8.00
S-1524	Bester, Alfred - ***Starburst*** [1958] PBO.	$1.50	$5.00	$10.00
S-1525	Colette - ***Gigi And Julie De Carneilhan*** [1958] Movie tie-in.	$1.25	$3.75	$7.50
1526	Box, Edgar (Gore Vidal) - ***Death Before Bedtime*** [1958] Cover art by Robert Maguire.	$1.35	$4.00	$8.00
1527	Brown, Carter - ***The Body*** [1958] Cover by Barye Phillips.	$1.25	$3.75	$7.50
1528	Cross, Beverley - ***The Nightwalkers*** [1958] Cover art by Robert Schulz.	$1.35	$4.00	$8.00
D-1529	Williams, Tennessee - ***A Streetcar Named Desire*** [1958] Cover art by Thomas Hart Benton. Movie tie-in. 8 pages of photos.	$1.50	$5.00	$10.00
D-1530	Hyman, Mac - ***No Time For Sergeants*** [1958] Movie tie-in with Andy Griffith. 8 pages of photos.	$1.50	$5.00	$10.00
S-1531	Morris, Wright - ***Love Among The Cannibals*** [1958] Cover art by Barye Phillips.	$1.25	$3.75	$7.50
S-1532	Markandaya, Kamala - ***Some Inner Fury*** [1958]	$1.25	$3.75	$7.50
S-1533	Anthology edited by Don Ward - ***Branded West*** [1958]	$1.25	$3.75	$7.50
1534	Coon, Horace - ***43,000 Years Later*** [1958]	$1.25	$3.75	$7.50
S-1535	Vidal, Gore - ***A Thirsty Evil*** [1958]	$1.25	$3.75	$7.50

		G	VG	F
1536	O'Rourke, Frank - ***A Texan Came Riding*** [1958] PBO. Cover art by Jerry Allison.	$1.25	$3.75	$7.50
S-1537	Heinlein, Robert - ***The Green Hills Of Earth*** [1958]	$1.35	$4.00	$8.00
1538	Dewey, Thomas B. - ***Dame In Danger*** [1958] Cover art by Robert Maguire.	$1.50	$5.00	$10.00
1539	Holder, William - ***The Case Of The Dead Divorcee*** [1958] PBO. Cover art by Robert Schulz.	$1.35	$4.00	$8.00
1540	Mahannah, Floyd - ***No Luck For A Lady*** [1958] Cover art by Robert Maguire.	$1.35	$4.00	$8.00
1541	Hickok, Will - ***The Restless Gun*** [1958] PBO. Cover art by Robert Schulz. TV tie-in.	$2.00	$6.00	$12.00
S-1542	Flora, Fletcher - ***Whispers Of The Flesh*** [1958] Cover art by Clark Hulings.	$1.25	$3.75	$7.50
S-1543	Kantor, MacKinlay - ***Silent Grow The Guns*** [1958] PBO.	$1.25	$3.75	$7.50
S-1544	Heinlein, Robert A. - ***The Puppet Masters*** [1958]	$1.35	$4.00	$8.00
D-1545	Silone, Ignazio - ***Bread And Wine*** [1958]	$1.25	$3.75	$7.50
D-1548	Hornblow, Leonora - ***The Love Seekers*** [1958]	$1.25	$3.75	$7.50
T-1549	Mailer, Norman - ***The Naked And The Dead*** [1958]	$1.25	$3.75	$7.50
S-1551	Lerner, Alan Jay - ***My Fair Lady*** [1958] Photo cover. Movie tie-in. 4 pages of photos.	$1.25	$3.75	$7.50
D-1552	Mason, Richard - ***The World Of Suzie Wong*** [1958] Cover art by James Avati.	$1.25	$3.75	$7.50
S-1553	O'Flaherty, Liam - ***Liam O'Flaherty: Selected Stories*** [1958]	$2.50	$7.50	$15.00
1554	Weil, Jerry - ***Escapade*** [1958]	$1.25	$3.75	$7.50
1555	Cox, William R. - ***Hell To Pay*** [1958] PBO.	$1.25	$3.75	$7.50
1556	Webb, Jack - ***The Brass Halo*** [1958] Cover art by Robert Maguire.	$1.35	$4.00	$8.00
S-1557	Horan, James D. - ***The Wild Bunch*** [1958] PBO.	$1.35	$4.00	$8.00
S-1558	Van Vogt, A. E. - ***Destination: Universe*** [1958]	$1.25	$3.75	$7.50
S-1559	Baldwin, James - ***Giovanni's Room*** [1958]	$1.25	$3.75	$7.50
S-1560	Keogh, Theodora - ***My Name Is Rose*** [1958]	$1.25	$3.75	$7.50
S-1561	Hule, William Bradford - ***Wolf Whistle and Other Stories*** [1958]	$1.35	$4.00	$8.00
D-1562	Shute, Nevil - ***On The Beach*** [1958]	$1.25	$3.75	$7.50
S-1563	Fleming, Ian - ***From Russia, With Love*** [1958] Cover by Barye Phillips.	$3.50	$10.00	$20.00
S-1564	Caldwell, Erskine - ***This Very Earth*** [1958]	$1.25	$3.75	$7.50
1565	Brown, Carter - ***The Blonde*** [1958] Cover art by Barye Phillips.	$1.25	$3.75	$7.50
1566	Ray, Wesley - ***Damaron's Gun*** [1958]	$1.25	$3.75	$7.50
S-1568	Caldwell, Erskine - ***Certain Women*** [1958] Cover art by James Avati.	$1.25	$3.75	$7.50
S-1569	Braine, John - ***Room At The Top*** [1958] Cover by Barye Phillips.	$1.25	$3.75	$7.50
S-1570	Stern, Jill - ***Nine Miles To Reno*** [1958] Cover art by Barye Phillips.	$1.25	$3.75	$7.50
1572	Grey, Harry - ***Portrait Of A Mobster*** [1958] PBO.	$1.35	$4.00	$8.00
1573	Hunt, Kyle - ***Kill A Wicked Man*** [1958]	$1.25	$3.75	$7.50
D-1574	La Mure, Pierre - ***Moulin Rouge*** [1958]	$1.25	$3.75	$7.50
D-1575	Grey, Harry - ***The Hoods*** [1958]	$1.25	$3.75	$7.50
D-1576	Motley, Willard - ***Knock Any Door*** [1958]	$1.25	$3.75	$7.50
S-1577	Heinlein, Robert - ***The Day After Tomorrow*** [1958]	$1.25	$3.75	$7.50
S-1578	Kaufmann, Myron - ***Remember Me To God*** [1958]	$1.25	$3.75	$7.50
S-1579	Torres, Tereska - ***Not Yet . . .*** [1958] Cover by James Avati.	$2.00	$6.00	$12.00
1580	Love, Edmund - ***Subways Are For Sleeping*** [1958]	$1.25	$3.75	$7.50
1581	Olay, Lionel - ***The Heart Of A Stranger*** [1958] PBO.	$1.25	$3.75	$7.50
1582	Boros, Eva - ***The Doll's Smile*** [1958] Cover art by Clark Hulings.	$1.25	$3.75	$7.50
S-1583	Clarke, Arthur C. - ***The Deep Range*** [1958] Cover art by Paul Lehr.	$1.35	$4.00	$8.00

		G	VG	F
1584	Thompson, Jim - ***The Getaway*** [1959] PBO.	$22.00	$70.00	$140.00
1585	Ballinger, Bill S. - ***Formula For Murder*** [1958]	$1.35	$4.00	$8.00
1586	Chase, James Hadley - ***The Case Of The Strangled Starlet*** [1958] Cover by Robert Schulz	$1.50	$5.00	$10.00
1587	Rawson, Tabor - ***I Want To Live!*** [1958] PBO. Movie photo cover. Movie tie-in with Susan Hayward.	$1.35	$4.00	$8.00
1588	MacDonald, William Colt - ***The Crimson Quirt*** [1958]	$1.25	$3.75	$7.50
S-1589	Caldwell, Erskine - ***The Sure Hand Of God*** [1958]	$1.25	$3.75	$7.50
S-1590	Williams, Tennessee - ***Cat On A Hot Tin Roof*** [1958] Photo cover. Movie tie-in. 8 pages of photos	$1.50	$5.00	$10.00
D-1591	Dingwall, Eric John - ***The American Woman*** [1958] Cover art by Thurber.	$1.25	$3.75	$7.50
S-1592	Caldwell, Erskine - ***Journeyman*** [1958] Cover art by James Avati.	$1.25	$3.75	$7.50
S-1593	Bester, Alfred - ***The Demolished Man*** [1958]	$1.25	$3.75	$7.50
1594	Brown, Carter - ***The Mistress*** [1958]	$1.25	$3.75	$7.50
1595	Stone, Andrew L. - ***The Decks Ran Red*** [1958] Movie tie-in with photo cover.	$1.25	$3.75	$7.50
D-1596	Moravia, Alberto - ***The Woman Of Rome*** [1958]	$1.25	$3.75	$7.50
S-1597	Buckner, Robert - ***Sigrid And The Sergeant*** [1958]	$1.25	$3.75	$7.50
S-1598	Caldwell, Erskine - ***Episode In Palmetto*** [1958]	$1.25	$3.75	$7.50
S-1599	Wright, Theon - ***The Knife*** [1958] Cover art by Robert Schulz.	$1.35	$4.00	$8.00
S-1602	Bates, H. E. - ***Summer In Salandar*** [1958] Cover art by Richard Powers.	$1.25	$3.75	$7.50
S-1604	Nye, Hermes - ***Fortune Is A Woman*** [1958]	$1.25	$3.75	$7.50
1605	Daniels, John S. - ***Ute Country*** [1958] PBO. Cover art by Robert Schulz	$1.25	$3.75	$7.50
1606	Brown, Carter - ***The Corpse*** [1958] Cover art by Barye Phillips.	$1.25	$3.75	$7.50
1607	Foreman, L. L. - ***Gunsmoke Men*** [1958] PBO.	$1.25	$3.75	$7.50
S-1608	Caldwell, Erskine - ***Trouble In July*** [1958] Cover art by Avati.	$1.25	$3.75	$7.50
S-1609	Rattigan, Terence - ***Separate Tables*** [1959] Movie tie-in. 8 pages of photos.	$1.25	$3.75	$7.50
S-1610	Morgan, Joe - ***Expense Account*** [1959] Cover art by Barye Phillips.	$1.25	$3.75	$7.50
S-1611	Caldwell, Erskine - ***Tragic Ground*** [1958] Cover by James Avati.	$1.25	$3.75	$7.50
S-1612	Moravia, Alberto - ***Roman Tales*** [1958]	$1.25	$3.75	$7.50
D-1614	Faulkner, William - ***Sartoris*** [1958]	$1.25	$3.75	$7.50
D-1615	Orwell, George - ***Animal Farm*** [1958]	$1.25	$3.75	$7.50
1618	Penn, J. H. - ***Texas Hellion*** [1958]	$1.25	$3.75	$7.50
D-1619	Kerouac, Jack - ***On The Road*** [1958] Cover art by Barye Phillips.	$3.50	$10.00	$20.00
1620	Brown, Carter - ***The Lover*** [1959]	$1.25	$3.75	$7.50
S-1621	Caldwell, Erskine - ***The Courting Of Susie Brown*** [1958]	$1.25	$3.75	$7.50
S-1622	Blish, James - ***The Seedling Stars*** [1959] Cover art by Paul Lehr.	$1.25	$3.75	$7.50
S-1623	Caldwell, Erskine - ***A Place Called Estherville*** [1958]	$1.25	$3.75	$7.50
S-1624	Farrell, James T. - ***Saturday Night*** [1959] Cover art by James Avati.	$1.25	$3.75	$7.50
S-1626	Shirreffs, Gordon D. - ***Last Train From Gun Hill*** [1959] Cover art by Robert Schulz. Movie tie-in.	$1.25	$3.75	$7.50
D-1627	Adams, Samuel Hopkins - ***Grandfather Stories*** [1959]	$1.25	$3.75	$7.50
D-1628	Faulkner, William - ***The Sound And The Fury*** [1959] Photo cover. Movie tie-in.	$1.25	$3.75	$7.50
D-1630	Remarque, Erich Maria - ***Arch Of Triumph*** [1959]	$1.25	$3.75	$7.50
1631	Nye, Nelson - ***The Overlanders*** [1959]	$1.25	$3.75	$7.50
1633	Brown, Carter - ***The Victim*** [1959] Cover by Barye Phillips.	$1.25	$3.75	$7.50

		G	VG	F
1635	Plenn, J. H. & LaRoche, C. J. - ***The Fastest Gun In Texas*** [1959] Cover art by Robert Schulz.	$1.25	$3.75	$7.50
1636	Gruber, Frank - ***The Whispering Master*** [1959]	$1.25	$3.75	$7.50
T-1637	Jones, James - ***Some Came Running*** [1959]	$1.25	$3.75	$7.50
S-1639	Heinlein, Robert A. - ***The Door Into Summer*** [1959] Cover art by Paul Lehr.	$1.25	$3.75	$7.50
D-1640	Orwell, George - ***1984*** [1960]	$1.25	$3.75	$7.50
D-1641	Mason, Richard - ***The Shadow And The Peak*** [1959] Cover art by Allison.	$1.25	$3.75	$7.50
1642	West, John B. - ***An Eye For An Eye*** [1959]	$1.25	$3.75	$7.50
D-1643	Faulkner, William - ***The Wild Palms And The Old Man*** [1959]	$1.25	$3.75	$7.50
S-1644	Heinlein, Robert A. - ***The Man Who Sold The Moon*** [1959]	$1.25	$3.75	$7.50
T-1645	Chamales, Tom T. - ***Never So Few*** [1959] Movie tie-in.	$1.25	$3.75	$7.50
1646	Cassill, R. V. - ***Dormitory Women*** [1959] Cover art by Robert Maguire.	$2.50	$7.50	$15.00
S-1647	Gaines, William M. - ***The Bedside Mad*** [1959] PBO. Cover by Kelly Freas	$1.25	$3.75	$7.50
S-1648	De Vries, Peter - ***The Mackerel Plaza*** [1959] Cover art by Barye Phillips	$1.25	$3.75	$7.50
S-1649	Bates, H. E. - ***The Darling Buds Of May*** [1959] Movie tie-in.	$1.25	$3.75	$7.50
S-1650	Sourian, Peter - ***Miri*** [1959]	$1.25	$3.75	$7.50
S-1651	Huie, William Bradford - ***Wolf Whistle And Other Stories*** [1959]	$1.25	$3.75	$7.50
S-1652	Dunn, Harold - ***Beat, Beat, Beat*** [1959] Cover art by William F. Brown. Cartoon book.	$1.25	$3.75	$7.50
1654	Brown, Carter - ***The Loving And The Dead*** [1959] Cover art by Barye Phillips.	$1.25	$3.75	$7.50
S-1656	Wilder, Billy & Diamond, I. A. L. - ***Some Like It Hot*** [1959] PBO. Photo cover. Movie tie-in. 8 pages of photos.	$5.00	$15.00	$30.00
D-1657	Moravia, Alberto - ***Two Women*** [1959] Cover by James Avati.	$1.25	$3.75	$7.50
S-1659	Harris, Mark - ***Something About A Soldier*** [1959]	$1.25	$3.75	$7.50
1660	Gordon, Noah - ***Night Ward*** [1959] PBO. Cover by Robert Maguire.	$1.25	$3.75	$7.50
T-1661	Sholokov, Mikhail - ***And Quiet Flows The Don*** [1959]	$1.25	$3.75	$7.50
1662	Miller, Wade - ***Kiss Her Goodbye*** [1959]	$1.25	$3.75	$7.50
1663	Brown, Carter - ***Walk Softly, Witch*** [1959] Cover art by Barye Phillips	$1.25	$3.75	$7.50
S-1664	Williams, Tennessee - ***The Roman Spring Of Mrs. Stone*** [1959]	$1.25	$3.75	$7.50
S-1665	MacDonald, John D. - ***Cancel All Our Vows*** [1959] Cover art by Allison	$1.35	$4.00	$8.00
S-1666	Caldwell, Erskine - ***Georgia Boy*** [1959]	$1.25	$3.75	$7.50
D-1667	Salinger, J. D. - ***The Catcher In The Rye*** [1959]	$1.25	$3.75	$7.50
T-1668	Ekert-Rotholz, Alice - ***The Time Of The Dragons*** [1959] Cover art by Avati.	$1.25	$3.75	$7.50
S-1670	Fleming, Ian - ***Doctor No*** [1959]	$3.50	$10.00	$20.00
S-1671	Hotchner, A. E. - ***The Dangerous American*** [1959] Cover art by Barye Phillips.	$1.25	$3.75	$7.50
S-1672	Caldwell, Erskine - ***A Lamp For Nightfall*** [1959] Cover by James Avati	$1.25	$3.75	$7.50
S-1673	Hoyle, Fred - ***The Black Cloud*** [1959]	$1.25	$3.75	$7.50
1674	Brown, Carter - ***The Passionate*** [1959] Cover art by Barye Phillips.	$1.25	$3.75	$7.50
1675	Hickok, Will - ***Trail Of The Restless Gun*** [1959] PBO. Cover art by Robert Schulz. TV tie-in.	$2.00	$6.00	$12.00
1677	Gruber, Frank - ***The Silver Tombstone Mystery*** [1959] Cover art by Allison.	$1.25	$3.75	$7.50
D-1678	Fernandez-Florez, Dario - ***Lola*** [1959] Cover art by James Avati	$1.25	$3.75	$7.50

		G	VG	F
D-1679	Swarthout, Glendon - ***They Came To Cordura*** [1959] Photo cover. Movie tie-in with Gary Cooper & Rita Hayworth.	$1.25	$3.75	$7.50
D-1680	D'Olive, Gene - ***Chiara*** [1959]	$1.25	$3.75	$7.50
D-1681	Wallace, Lew - ***Ben-Hur*** [1959] Movie tie-in with Charlton Heston.	$1.25	$3.75	$7.50
S-1682	Clagett, John - ***The Slot*** [1959]	$1.25	$3.75	$7.50
S-1683	Aldiss, Brian W. - ***No Time Like Tomorrow*** [1959]	$1.25	$3.75	$7.50
S-1684	Spota, Luis - ***The Wounds Of Hunger*** [1959]	$1.25	$3.75	$7.50
S-1685	Foote, Shelby - ***Follow Me Down*** [1959] Cover art by Barye Phillips.	$1.25	$3.75	$7.50
1687	Kramer, Dale - ***Violent Streets*** [1959]	$1.25	$3.75	$7.50
S-1689	Callaghan, Morley - ***The Loved And The Lost*** [1959]	$1.25	$3.75	$7.50
S-1690	Morgan, John Medford - ***The Roman And The Slave Girl*** [1959] PBO. Cover by Powell.	$1.25	$3.75	$7.50
S-1691	Thorp, Raymond & Bunker, Robert - ***Crow Killer*** [1959]	$1.25	$3.75	$7.50
D-1692	Anderson, Comm. Wm. R. - ***Nautilus 90 North*** [1959] Contains 58 photos.	$1.25	$3.75	$7.50
D-1693	Motley, Willard - ***Let No Man Write My Epitaph*** [1959] Cover by Barye Phillips.	$1.25	$3.75	$7.50
1694	Brown, Carter - ***None But The Lethal Heart*** [1959] Cover art by Barye Phillips.	$1.25	$3.75	$7.50
1695	Thompson, Thomas - ***Brand Of A Man*** [1959]	$1.25	$3.75	$7.50
1696	Chase, James Hadley - ***Shock Treatment*** [1959] PBO.	$2.00	$6.00	$12.00
S-1698	DeVries, Peter - ***No But I Saw The Movie*** [1959]	$1.25	$3.75	$7.50
S-1699	Heinlein, Robert A. - ***Revolt In 2100*** [1959]	$1.25	$3.75	$7.50
S-1700	Spillane, Mickey - ***The Big Kill*** [1959]	$1.25	$3.75	$7.50
S-1701	Gaines, William M. - ***Son Of Mad*** [1959] Cover art by Kelly Freas.	$1.25	$3.75	$7.50
Q-1702	Rand, Ayn - ***Atlas Shrugged*** [1959]	$1.25	$3.75	$7.50
S-1703	Kantor, MacKinlay - ***Frontier*** [1959] PBO. Cover art by Robert Schulz.	$1.25	$3.75	$7.50
1704	Woods, William - ***Manuela*** [1959] Cover art by James Hill.	$1.25	$3.75	$7.50
S-1705	Spillane, Mickey - ***The Long Wait*** [1959]	$1.25	$3.75	$7.50
1707	White, Lionel - ***Invitation To Violence*** [1959]	$1.25	$3.75	$7.50
P-1709	Dennis, Patrick - ***Around The World With Auntie Mame*** [1959]	$1.25	$3.75	$7.50
S-1710	Spillane, Mickey - ***Vengeance Is Mine*** [1959]	$1.25	$3.75	$7.50
S-1711	Lawler, Ray - ***Summer Of The Seventeenth Doll*** [1959] Movie tie-in. 8 pages of photos. Cover by Allison.	$1.35	$4.00	$8.00
S-1712	Frede, Richard - ***Entry E*** [1959]	$1.25	$3.75	$7.50
1713	Brown, Carter - ***The Wanton*** [1959] Cover art by Barye Phillips.	$1.25	$3.75	$7.50
1714	Garland, George - ***Apache Warpath*** [1959] PBO.	$1.25	$3.75	$7.50
S-1716	Fadiman, Edwin Jr. - ***The 21" Screen*** [1959]	$1.25	$3.75	$7.50
T-1717	Suyin, Han - ***The Mountain Is Young*** [1959]	$1.25	$3.75	$7.50
D-1718	Kerouac, Jack - ***The Dharma Bums*** [1959] Cover by Barye Phillips.	$3.50	$10.00	$20.00
S-1719	Blish, James - ***Galactic Cluster*** [1959] PBO. Cover art by Paul Lehr.	$1.25	$3.75	$7.50
S-1720	Mann, Heinrich - ***The Blue Angel*** [1959] Photo cover. Movie tie-in with May Britt.	$1.25	$3.75	$7.50
1722	Brown, Carter - ***Suddnely By Violence*** [1959] Cover by Barye Phillips.	$1.25	$3.75	$7.50
S-1723	Fleming, Ian - ***Live And Let Die*** [1959] Cover art by Barye Phillips.	$3.50	$10.00	$20.00
1724	Knight, Adam - ***Triple Slay*** [1959] PBO. Cover art by Robert Schulz.	$1.25	$3.75	$7.50
T-1726	Grau, Shirley Ann - ***The Hard Blue Sky*** [1959] Cover by James Hill.	$1.25	$3.75	$7.50

		G	VG	F
D-1727	Capote, Truman - ***Breakfast At Tiffany's*** [1959] Cover art by James Avati.	$1.25	$3.75	$7.50
S-1728	Spillane, Mickey - ***One Lonely Night*** [1959]	$1.25	$3.75	$7.50
S-1729	Clarke, Arthur C. - ***The Other Side Of The Sky*** [1959]	$1.25	$3.75	$7.50
1730	Ballinger, Bill S. - ***The Longest Second*** [1959] Cover art by Robert Schulz.	$1.25	$3.75	$7.50
S-1732	Rivette, Mare - ***The Incident*** [1959]	$1.25	$3.75	$7.50
S-1733	Caldwell, Erskine - ***Kneel To The Rising Sun*** [1959]	$1.25	$3.75	$7.50
S-1734	Caldwell, Erskine - ***Southways*** [1959]	$1.25	$3.75	$7.50
S-1735	Caldwell, Erskine - ***We Are The Living*** [1959]	$1.25	$3.75	$7.50
1738	Brown, Carter - ***The Dame*** [1959] Cover art by Barye Phillips.	$1.25	$3.75	$7.50
S-1739	Caldwell, Erskine - ***A Swell-Looking Girl*** [1959]	$1.25	$3.75	$7.50
D-1740	Shute, Nevil - ***The Rainbow And The Rose*** [1959]	$1.25	$3.75	$7.50
T-1741	Montgomery - ***The Memoirs Of Field-Marshall Montgomery*** [1959]	$1.25	$3.75	$7.50
Q-1742	Hecht, Ben - ***Child Of The Century*** [1959]	$1.25	$3.75	$7.50
S-1743	Brown, William F. - ***The Girl In The Freudian Slip*** [1959] PBO. Cover art by William F. Brown. Cartoon book.	$1.25	$3.75	$7.50
S-1745	Williams, Tennessee - ***The Fugitive Kind*** [1960] Cover art by Barye Phillips. Movie tie-in. 8 pages of photos.	$1.35	$4.00	$8.00
D-1746	Calitri, Charles - ***Strike Heaven On The Face*** [1959]	$1.25	$3.75	$7.50
S-1747	Lawrence, D. H. - ***The Lovely Lady*** [1959]	$1.25	$3.75	$7.50
1748	O'Rourke, Frank - ***Desperate Rider*** [1959]	$1.25	$3.75	$7.50
1749	Chase, James Hadley - ***The Guilty Are Afraid*** [1959] Cover art by Barye Phillips.	$1.35	$4.00	$8.00
1750	Brown, Carter - ***Terror Comes Creeping*** [1959] Cover by Barye Phillips.	$1.25	$3.75	$7.50
S-1751	Tredree, H. L. - ***The Strange Ordeal Of The S.S. Normandier*** [1960] Cover art by James Hill.	$1.25	$3.75	$7.50
S-1752	Heinlein, Robert A. - ***Methuselah's Children*** [1960] Cover art by Paul Lehr.	$1.25	$3.75	$7.50
D-1753	King, Alexander - ***Mine Enemy Grows Older*** [1960]	$1.25	$3.75	$7.50
S-1754	Gulick, Bill - ***The Land Beyond*** [1960] Cover art by Barye Phillips.	$1.25	$3.75	$7.50
1755	West, John B. - ***Cobra Venom*** [1960] PBO. Cover art by Jerry Allison.	$1.25	$3.75	$7.50
D-1756	Anthology edited by Devin A. Garrity - ***The Irish Genius*** [1960]	$1.25	$3.75	$7.50
S-1757	Williams, Tennessee - ***Suddenly Last Summer*** [1960] Photo cover. Movie tie-in. 8 pages of photos.	$1.35	$4.00	$8.00
S-1758	Spillane, Mickey - ***Kiss Me, Deadly*** [1960]	$1.25	$3.75	$7.50
S-1759	Caldwell, Erskine - ***Love And Money*** [1960]	$1.25	$3.75	$7.50
S-1760	Caldwell, Erskine - ***Gretta*** [1960]	$1.25	$3.75	$7.50
S-1762	Fleming, Ian - ***Casino Royale*** [1960] Cover art by Barye Phillips.	$3.50	$10.00	$20.00
S-1763	Moll, Elick - ***Seidman And Son*** [1960] Cover by James Avati.	$1.25	$3.75	$7.50
1764	Brown, Carter - ***The Desired*** [1960] Cover art by Barye Phillips.	$1.25	$3.75	$7.50
D-1765	Feibleman, Peter S. - ***A Place Without Twilight*** [1960]	$1.25	$3.75	$7.50
S-1766	Capote, Truman - ***Other Voices, Other Rooms*** [1960] Cover art by James Hill.	$1.25	$3.75	$7.50
1767	Brown, Carter - ***The Bombshell*** [1960] Cover art by Barye Phillips.	$1.25	$3.75	$7.50
1768	Dundee, Robert - ***The Restless Lovers*** [1960] Cover art by Barye Phillips.	$1.25	$3.75	$7.50
S-1769	Clarke, Arthur C. - ***Islands In The Sky*** [1960] Cover art by Paul Lehr.	$1.25	$3.75	$7.50
S-1770	Levin, Ira - ***A Kiss Before Dying*** [1960]	$1.25	$3.75	$7.50
D-1772	Feuchtwanger, Lion - ***Jeptha And His Daughter*** [1960]	$1.25	$3.75	$7.50

		G	VG	F
T-1773	Sholokhov, Mikhail - ***The Don Flows Home To The Sea*** [1960]	$1.25	$3.75	$7.50
S-1775	Spillane, Mickey - ***I, The Jury*** [1960]	$1.25	$3.75	$7.50
S-1776	Tinkle, Lon - ***The Alamo*** [1960] Cover art by Barye Phillips. Movie tie-in with John Wayne. 8 pages of photos.	$1.25	$3.75	$7.50
S-1777	Deurrenmatt, Friedrich - ***The Pledge*** [1960]	$1.25	$3.75	$7.50
S-1778	Caldwell, Erskine - ***Claudelle Inglish*** [1960]	$1.25	$3.75	$7.50
S-1779	Aldiss, Brian - ***Starship*** [1960] Cover art by Paul Lehr.	$1.25	$3.75	$7.50
D-1780	Frankel, Ernest - ***Band Of Brothers*** [1960]	$1.25	$3.75	$7.50
1781	Arthur, Burt - ***The Texan*** [1960]	$1.25	$3.75	$7.50
1782	Haycox, Ernest - ***The Feudists*** [1960]	$1.25	$3.75	$7.50
1783	Cox, William R. - ***Murder In Vegas*** [1960] PBO. Cover art by Allison.	$1.25	$3.75	$7.50
1784	Brown, Carter - ***The Wayward Wahine*** [1960] Cover by Barye Phillips.	$1.25	$3.75	$7.50
S-1785	Mulvihill, William - ***The Mantrackers*** [1960]	$1.25	$3.75	$7.50
S-1786	Brown, William F. - ***The Abominable Showmen*** [1960] PBO. Cover art by W. F. Brown. Cartoon book.	$1.25	$3.75	$7.50
D-1787	Sneider, Vern - ***The Teahouse Of The August Moon*** [1960]	$1.25	$3.75	$7.50
S-1788	Vidal, Gore - ***Visit To A Small Planet*** [1960] Photo cover. Movie tie-in.	$1.25	$3.75	$7.50
S-1789	Spillane, Mickey - ***My Gun Is Quick*** [1960]	$1.25	$3.75	$7.50
T-1791	Rand, Ayn - ***We The Living*** [1960]	$1.50	$5.00	$10.00
D-1792	Huie, William Bradford - ***Wild River*** [1960] Movie tie-in.	$1.25	$3.75	$7.50
D-1793	White, Theodore H. - ***The Mountain Road*** [1960] Cover art by Robert Schulz. Movie tie-in. 8 pages of photos.	$1.25	$3.75	$7.50
S-1794	Ballinger, Bill S. - ***Beacon In The Night*** [1960] Cover art by Robert Schulz.	$1.25	$3.75	$7.50
S-1795	Gaines, William M. - editor - ***The Organization Mad*** [1960]	$1.25	$3.75	$7.50
S-1797	Weil, Jerry - ***A Real Cool Cat*** [1960]	$1.25	$3.75	$7.50
T-1798	Andric, Ivo - ***The Bridge Of The Drina*** [1960] Cover by Kossin.	$1.25	$3.75	$7.50
1799	Olesha, Yuril - ***The Wayward Comrade And The Commissars*** [1960]	$1.25	$3.75	$7.50
S-1800	West, John B. - ***A Taste For Blood*** [1960] Cover art by Barye Phillips.	$1.25	$3.75	$7.50
S-1801	Brown, Carter - ***Graves, I Dig!*** [1960] Cover by Barye Phillips.	$1.25	$3.75	$7.50
T-1802	Pasternak, Boris - ***Doctor Zhivago*** [1960]	$1.25	$3.75	$7.50
S-1804	Love, Edmund G. - ***War Is A Private Affair*** [1960]	$1.25	$3.75	$7.50
S-1805	Miller, Wade - ***Deadley Weapon*** [1960] Cover art by Robert Abbett.	$1.25	$3.75	$7.50
S-1806	Brown, Carter - ***Tomorrow Is Murder*** [1960] Cover art by Barye Phillips.	$1.25	$3.75	$7.50
S-1807	O'Rourke, Frank - ***Violent Country*** [1960]	$1.25	$3.75	$7.50
S-1809	Raine, William MacLeod - ***Guns Of The Frontier*** [1960]	$1.25	$3.75	$7.50
D-1811	Fuller, Robert G. - ***Danger! Marines At Work!*** [1960]	$1.25	$3.75	$7.50
S-1812	Owens, Jack - ***The Beach Bums*** [1960]	$1.25	$3.75	$7.50
D-1813	Suyin, Han - ***And The Rain My Drink*** [1960]	$1.25	$3.75	$7.50
D-1814	Howard, Robert West - editor - ***Hoofbeats Of Destiny*** [1960] Cover art by Robert Schulz. 8 pages of photos.	$1.25	$3.75	$7.50
S-1815	Aldriss, Brian - ***Galaxies Like Grains Of Sand*** [1960] PBO.	$1.25	$3.75	$7.50
S-1816	Webb, Jack - ***The Delicate Darling*** [1960]	$1.25	$3.75	$7.50
S-1817	Brown, Carter - ***The Temptress*** [1960] Cover art by Barye Phillips.	$1.25	$3.75	$7.50
S-1818	Brown, Will C. - ***Sam Bass And Company*** [1960] PBO. Cover art by Allison.	$1.25	$3.75	$7.50
D-1820	Slaughter, Frank G. - ***The Stubborn Heart*** [1960]	$1.25	$3.75	$7.50
D-1821	Mailer, Norman - ***Barbary Shore*** [1960]	$1.25	$3.75	$7.50
S-1822	Fleming, Ian - ***Goldfinger*** [1960] Cover art by Barye Phillips.	$3.50	$10.00	$20.00

		G	VG	F
T-1823	Ellison, Ralph - ***The Invisible Man*** [1960]	$1.25	$3.75	$7.50
S-1824	Raine, William MacLeod - ***Sons Of The Saddle*** [1960]	$1.25	$3.75	$7.50
S-1825	Huie, William Bradford - ***The Americanization Of Emily*** [1960] Cover art by Barye Phillips.	$1.25	$3.75	$7.50
T-1826	Condon, Richard - ***The Manchurian Candidate*** [1960]	$1.25	$3.75	$7.50
D-1827	DeVries, Peter - ***The Tents Of Wickedness*** [1960] Cover art by Barye Phillips.	$1.25	$3.75	$7.50
D-1828	Bromfield, Louis - ***Mr. Smith*** [1960]	$1.25	$3.75	$7.50
D-1829	Lawrence, D. H. - ***Sons And Lovers*** [1960]	$1.25	$3.75	$7.50
D-1830	Hoig, Stan - ***The Humor Of The American Cowboy*** [1960] Cover art by Nick Eggenhofer.	$1.25	$3.75	$7.50
T-1831	Smith, Lillian - ***One Hour*** [1960]	$1.25	$3.75	$7.50
D-1832	Dayan, Yael - ***New Face In The Mirror*** [1960] Cover by Barye Phillips.	$1.25	$3.75	$7.50
S-1833	Smith, Franc - ***Harry Vernon At Prep*** [1960] Cover by James Hill.	$1.25	$3.75	$7.50
S-1834	Olay, Lionel - ***The Dark Corners Of The Night*** [1960] Cover art by Barye Phillips.	$1.25	$3.75	$7.50
S-1835	Kane, Henry - ***Until You Are Dead*** [1960] Cover art by Barye Phillips.	$1.35	$4.00	$8.00
S-1836	Brown, Carter - ***The Brazen*** [1960] Cover art by Barye Phillips.	$1.25	$3.75	$7.50
D-1837	Beach, Edward L. - ***Submarine!*** [1960]	$1.25	$3.75	$7.50
S-1838	Anthology edited by William M. Gaines - ***Like, Mad*** [1960] Cover art by Kelly Freas.	$1.25	$3.75	$7.50
S-1839	Caldwell, Erskine - ***When You Think Of Me*** [1960]	$1.25	$3.75	$7.50
S-1840	Sheckley, Robert - ***The Status Civilization*** [1960] PBO.	$1.25	$3.75	$7.50
D-1842	Sillitoe, Alan - ***Saturday Night And Sunday Morning*** [1960]	$1.25	$3.75	$7.50
S-1844	Walsh, Robert - ***Mr. Big*** [1960] PBO.	$1.25	$3.75	$7.50
S-1845	Brown, Carter - ***The Dream Is Deadly*** [1960] Cover art by Barye Phillips.	$1.25	$3.75	$7.50
S-1846	MacDonald, William Colt - ***The Shadow Rider*** [1960]	$1.25	$3.75	$7.50
D-1847	Miller, Henry - ***Nights Of Love And Laughter*** [1960]	$1.25	$3.75	$7.50
D-1848	Faulkner, William - ***Intruder In The Dust*** [1960]	$1.25	$3.75	$7.50
T-1849	Hart, Moss - ***Act One*** [1960] Movie tie-in.	$1.25	$3.75	$7.50
S-1850	Fleming, Ian - ***Moonraker*** [1960] Cover art by Barye Phillips.	$3.50	$10.00	$20.00
S-1851	Dunn, Harold - ***Those Crazy Mixed-Up Kids*** [1961] PBO. Cover Art by W. F. Brown. Cartoon & joke book.	$1.25	$3.75	$7.50
1852	West, John B. - ***Bullets Are My Business*** [1960]	$1.25	$3.75	$7.50
D-1853	Ustinov, Peter - ***Add A Dash Of Pity*** [1961]	$1.25	$3.75	$7.50
D-1854	Levine, Isaac Don - ***The Mind Of The Assassin*** [1961]	$1.25	$3.75	$7.50
T-1855	Styron, William - ***Lie Down In Darkness*** [1961]	$1.25	$3.75	$7.50
S-1856	Brown, Carter - ***Lament For A Lousy Lover*** [1961]	$1.25	$3.75	$7.50
S-1857	Hopkins, Tom J - ***Trouble In Tombstone*** [1960] Cover art by Allison.	$1.25	$3.75	$7.50
D-1858	Clarke, Arthur C. - ***The City And The Stars*** [1960] Cover art by Richard Powers.	$1.25	$3.75	$7.50
D-1860	Ginger, Ray - ***Six Days Or Forever?*** [1960]	$1.25	$3.75	$7.50
T-1861	Van Der Post, Laurens - ***Flamingo Feather*** [1960] Cover art by Allison.	$1.25	$3.75	$7.50
T-1862	Toland, John - ***Battle: The Story Of The Bulge*** [1960] Cover art by Barye Phillips. 16 pages of photos.	$1.25	$3.75	$7.50
S-1863	Stadley, Pat - ***The Black Leather Barbarians*** [1960] Cover art by Barye Phillips.	$1.50	$5.00	$10.00
T-1864	Snow. C. P. - ***The Search*** [1960]	$1.25	$3.75	$7.50
D-1865	Davis, Gwen - ***Naked In Babylon*** [1960] PBO. Cover by Jerry Allison.	$1.25	$3.75	$7.50
T-1866	Warren, Robert Penn - ***The Cave*** [1960]	$1.25	$3.75	$7.50
T-1867	MacLennan, Hugh - ***The Watch That Ends The Night*** [1960] Cover art by Barye Phillips.	$1.35	$4.00	$8.00

		G	VG	F
D-1868	Schary, Dore - ***Sunrise At Campobello*** [1960] Movie tie-in. 8 pages of photos.	$1.25	$3.75	$7.50
D-1869	Zeiger, Henry A. - editor - ***The Case Against Adolf Eichmann*** [1960] PBO. 16 pages of photos.	$1.25	$3.75	$7.50
D-1870	Sneider, Vern - ***A Long Way From Home And Other Stories*** [1960] Cover by Barye Phillips	$1.25	$3.75	$7.50
S-1871	Kantor, MacKinlay - ***It's About Crime*** [1960] PBO.	$1.25	$3.75	$7.50
T-1872	Warren, Robert Penn - ***Band Of Angels*** [1960]	$1.35	$4.00	$8.00
S-1873	Arthur, Burt - ***Bugles In The Night*** [1960]	$1.25	$3.75	$7.50
D-1874	Golden, Milton M. - ***Hollywood Lawyer*** [1960] Photo cover.	$1.25	$3.75	$7.50
D-1875	Haymes, Nora Eddington Flynn - ***Errol And Me*** [1960] PBO. Photo cover. 8 pages of photos.	$1.25	$3.75	$7.50
D-1876	Hackney, Alan - ***I'm All Right Jack*** [1960] Movie tie-in.	$1.25	$3.75	$7.50
T-1877	Gilman, Peter - ***Diamond Head*** [1960] Cover art by Barye Phillips.	$1.25	$3.75	$7.50
T-1878	Chamales, Tom T - ***Go Naked In The World*** [1960] Movie tie-in.	$1.25	$3.75	$7.50
D-1879	Uris, Leon - ***The Angry Hills*** [1960]	$1.25	$3.75	$7.50
D-1880	Garrett, George - ***The Finished Man*** [1960] Cover by Barye Phillips.	$1.25	$3.75	$7.50
T-1881	Prokosch, Frederic - ***The Asiatics*** [1960]	$1.25	$3.75	$7.50
S-1882	Butterworth, W. E. - ***Comfort Me With Love*** [1960] PBO. Cover art by Barye Phillips.	$1.25	$3.75	$7.50
S-1883	West, John B. - ***Death On The Rocks*** [1961] Photo cover.	$1.25	$3.75	$7.50
D-1884	Capote, Truman - ***The Glass Harp/A Tree Of Night*** [1960]	$1.25	$3.75	$7.50
S-1885	Asimov, Isaac - ***I, Robot*** [1960]	$1.25	$3.75	$7.50
S-1886	Heckelmann, Charles N. - ***Hell In His Holsters*** [1960] Cover art by Jerry Allison.	$1.25	$3.75	$7.50
D-1887	Ward, Mary Jane - ***The Snake Pit*** [1960] Cover art by Barye Phillips.	$1.25	$3.75	$7.50
T-1888	Petrovskaya, Kyra - ***Kyra*** [1961] 4 pages of photos.	$1.25	$3.75	$7.50
T-1889	Mailer, Norman - ***Advertisements For Myself*** [1961]	$1.25	$3.75	$7.50
D-1890	Swarthout, Glendon - ***Where The Boys Are*** [1961] Photo cover. Movie tie-in.	$1.25	$3.75	$7.50
S-1891	Heinlein, Robert A. - ***Beyond This Horizon*** [1961] Cover art by Kossin.	$1.25	$3.75	$7.50
T-1892	Shaw, Irwin - ***Two Weeks In Another Town*** [1961]	$1.25	$3.75	$7.50
D-1893	Jones, James - ***The Pistol*** [1961]	$1.25	$3.75	$7.50
S-1894	Morhaim, Victoria Kelrich - ***The Girl In The Gold Leather Dress*** [1961]	$1.25	$3.75	$7.50
D-1895	O'Hara, John - ***Appointment In Samarra*** [1961]	$1.25	$3.75	$7.50
S-1896	Brown, Carter - ***The Savage Salome*** [1961]	$1.25	$3.75	$7.50
D-1897	Blacker, Irwin R. - ***Westering*** [1961] Cover by Jerry Allison.	$1.25	$3.75	$7.50
S-1899	Markandaya, Kamala - ***Nectar In A Sieve*** [1961]	$1.25	$3.75	$7.50
D-1901	Hansberry, Lorraine - ***A Raisin In The Sun*** [1961] Movie tie-in.	$1.25	$3.75	$7.50
D-1903	King, Alexander - ***May This House Be Safe From Tigers*** [1961] Photo cover.	$1.25	$3.75	$7.50
D-1904	Taylor, Samuel Woolley - ***Family Kingdom*** [1961] Cover art by Allison.	$1.25	$3.75	$7.50
D-1905	Trocchi, Alexander - ***The Outsiders*** [1961]	$1.25	$3.75	$7.50
D-1906	Conton, William - ***The African*** [1961]	$1.25	$3.75	$7.50
D-1907	Clark, Walter Van Tilburg - ***The Watchful Gods And Other Stories*** [1961] Cover art by Kossin.	$1.25	$3.75	$7.50
S-1908	Miller, Floyd - ***Scandale*** [1961] PBO. Cover art by Barye Phillips.	$1.25	$3.75	$7.50
S-1909	Brown, Carter - ***The Million Dollar Babe*** [1961] Cover art by Barye Phillips	$1.25	$3.75	$7.50
S-1910	Robertson, Frank C. - ***Rawhide*** [1961] PBO. Cover art by Jerry Allison. TV tie-in.	$1.25	$3.75	$7.50

		G	VG	F
S-1911	Miller, Wade - ***Fatal Step*** [1961]	$1.25	$3.75	$7.50
S-1913	Luzzatto, Jack & Morehead, Albert H. - ***The New American Crossword Puzzle Book*** [1961] PBO.	$2.50	$7.50	$15.00
S-1914	Anthology - ***The Ides Of Mad*** [1961]	$1.35	$4.00	$8.00
D-1915	Dundy, Elaine - ***The Dud Avocado*** [1961]	$1.25	$3.75	$7.50
D-1917	Elliott, George - ***Parktilden Village*** [1961] Cover art by Barye Phillips.	$1.25	$3.75	$7.50
T-1918	Thompson, Morton - ***The Cry And The Covenant*** [1960]	$1.25	$3.75	$7.50
S-1919	Brown, Carter - ***The Ever-Loving Blues*** [1961] Cover art by Barye Phillips	$1.25	$3.75	$7.50
S-1920	Patten, Lewis B. - ***Law Of The Gun*** [1961]	$1.25	$3.75	$7.50
D-1921	Cain, James M. - ***Mildred Pierce*** [1961]	$1.25	$3.75	$7.50
S-1922	Moravia, Alberto - ***Conjugal Love*** [1961]	$1.25	$3.75	$7.50
D-1923	Anthology edited by Robert West Howard - ***This Is The West*** [1961]	$1.25	$3.75	$7.50
S-1924	Brown, Carter - ***The Myopic Mermaid*** [1961]	$1.25	$3.75	$7.50
D-1927	Gant, Matthew - ***The Raven And The Sword*** [1927] Cover art by Barye Phillips.	$1.25	$3.75	$7.50
D-1928	Sillitoe, Alan - ***The Loneliness Of The Long Distance Runner*** [1961]	$1.25	$3.75	$7.50
S-1929	West, John B. - ***Never Kill A Cop*** [1961]	$1.25	$3.75	$7.50
S-1931	Bester, Alfred - ***The Stars My Destination*** [1961]	$1.25	$3.75	$7.50
D-1933	Paton, Alan - ***Too Late The Phalarope*** [1961]	$1.25	$3.75	$7.50
D-1934	Williams, Tennessee - ***Cat On A Hot Tin Roof*** [1961] Photo cover. Movie tie-in. 6 pages of photos	$1.35	$4.00	$8.00
T-1935	Wallace, Irving - ***The Chapman Report*** [1963] Photo cover. Movie tie-in	$1.25	$3.75	$7.50
D-1937	O'Connor, Flannery - ***The Violent Bear It Away*** [1963]	$2.50	$7.50	$15.00
S-1938	Kandel, Aben - ***The Strip*** [1961] POB.	$1.25	$3.75	$7.50
S-1939	Siodmak, Curt - ***Skyport*** [1961]	$1.35	$4.00	$8.00
P-1941	Hampton, Kay - ***The Patch*** [1961]	$1.25	$3.75	$7.50
S-1943	Von Elsner, Don - ***Those Who Prey Together Slay Together*** [1961] Cover by Barye Phillips	$1.35	$4.00	$8.00
D-1946	Duncan, Bob - ***If It Moves, Salute It*** [1961]	$1.25	$3.75	$7.50
D-1947	Colette - ***The Tender Shoot And Other Stories*** [1961]	$1.25	$3.75	$7.50
S-1948	Fleming, Ian - ***For Your Eyes Only*** [1961] Cover by Barye Phillips.	$3.50	$10.00	$20.00
S-1950	Brown, Carter - ***The Unorthodox Corpse*** [1961]	$1.25	$3.75	$7.50
D-1952	Vidal, Gore - ***The City And The Pillar*** [1961]	$1.25	$3.75	$7.50
T-1955	Moravia, Alberto - ***Three Novels*** [1961]	$1.25	$3.75	$7.50
D-1956	Roshwald, Mordecai - ***Level 7*** [1961]	$1.25	$3.75	$7.50
T-1957	Glyn, Anthony - ***I Can Take It All*** [1961]	$1.25	$3.75	$7.50
T-1960	Di Lampedusa, Giuseppe - ***The Leopard*** [1961]	$1.25	$3.75	$7.50
S-1961	Cox, William R. - ***Comanche Moon*** [1961]	$1.25	$3.75	$7.50
D-1962	Morley, Christopher - ***Kitty Foyle*** [1961]	$1.25	$3.75	$7.50
S-1964	Miller, Wade - ***Killer's Choice*** [1961] Cover art by Victor Kalin	$1.25	$3.75	$7.50
Q-1967	Jones, James - ***From Here To Eternity*** [1961]	$1.25	$3.75	$7.50
S-1969	Grey, Harry - ***Portrait Of A Mobster*** [1961] Photo cover. Movie tie-in	$1.25	$3.75	$7.50
S-1971	Brossard, Chandler - ***The Girls In Rome*** [1961] PBO. Cover art by Allison.	$1.25	$3.75	$7.50
S-1972	Brown, Carter - ***The Blonde*** [1961]	$1.25	$3.75	$7.50
D-1974	Dooley, Thomas A., M.D. - ***The Night They Burned The Mountain*** [1961]	$1.25	$3.75	$7.50
S-1976	Anthology - ***Fighting Mad*** [1961]	$1.25	$3.75	$7.50
S-1981	Brown, Carter - ***The Stripper*** [1961] Cover art by Robert McGinnis	$1.25	$3.75	$7.50
S-1982	Robertson, Frank - ***Wanted: Dead Or Alive*** [1961]	$1.25	$3.75	$7.50
T-1984	Scott, Paul - ***The Love Pavilion*** [1961]	$1.25	$3.75	$7.50

		G	VG	F
D-1985	Rand, Ayn - ***Anthem*** [1961]	$1.25	$3.75	$7.50
D-1986	Caillou, Alan - ***The Walls Of Jolo*** [1961]	$1.25	$3.75	$7.50
1988	Webb, Jack - ***The Deadly Sex*** [1961]	$1.25	$3.75	$7.50
S-1989	Brown, Carter - ***The Tigress*** [1961] Cover art by Barye Phillips.	$1.25	$3.75	$7.50
T-1990	Faulkner, William - ***Sanctuary And Requiem For A Nun*** [1961]	$1.25	$3.75	$7.50
D-1992	Dooley, Dr. Tom - ***Deliver Us From Evil*** [1961] Photo cover. 16 pages of photos.	$1.25	$3.75	$7.50
D-1993	Dooley, Thomas A., M.D. - ***The Edge Of Tomorrow*** [1961]	$1.25	$3.75	$7.50
S-1994	Miller, Wade - ***Murder Charge*** [1961] Cover by Barye Phillips.	$1.25	$3.75	$7.50
Q-1995	Rand, Ayn - ***The Fountainhead*** [1961]	$1.25	$3.75	$7.50
D-1999	Cain, James M. - ***Serenade*** [1961]	$1.25	$3.75	$7.50
S-2000	Weil, Jerry - ***Daughter Of Evil*** [1961] Cover art Barye Phillips.	$1.00	$3.00	$6.00
T-2004	Wilson, Edmund - ***Memoirs Of Hecate County*** [1961]	$1.00	$3.00	$6.00
P-2006	Faulkner, William - ***Soldier's Pay*** [1961]	$1.00	$3.00	$6.00
S-2009	Brown, Carter - ***The Exotic*** [1961] Cover art by Robert McGinnis.	$1.25	$3.75	$7.50
D-2010	Hogan, Ray - ***The Life And Death Of Clay Allison*** [1961] PBO.	$1.00	$3.00	$6.00
Q-2014	Pasternak, Boris - ***Doctor Zhivago*** [1961]	$1.00	$3.00	$6.00
D-2018	Aldiss, Brian W. - ***The Long Afternoon Of Earth*** [1961] PBO.	$1.35	$4.00	$8.00
D-2019	Williams, Tennessee - ***Summer And Smoke*** [1961] Photo cover. Movie tie-in. 8 pages of photos.	$1.35	$4.00	$8.00
S-2023	Brown, Carter - ***The Sad-Eyed Seductress*** [1961]	$1.25	$3.75	$7.50
S-2033	Brown, Carter - ***Zelda*** [1961] Cover art by Robert McGinnis.	$1.25	$3.75	$7.50
S-2034	Thompson, Jim - ***The Transgressors*** [1961] PBO.	$10.00	$30.00	$60.00
S-2048	Brown, Carter - ***Murder Wears A Mantilla*** [1962] Cover by Robert McGinnis.	$1.25	$3.75	$7.50
S-2094	Brown, Carter - ***Angel*** [1962] Cover art by Robert McGinnis.	$1.25	$3.75	$7.50
2095	Williams, Tennessee - ***Sweet Bird Of Youth*** [1962] Movie tie-in with photos.	$1.35	$4.00	$8.00
S-2110	Brown, Carter - ***The Ice-Cold Nude*** [1962] Cover art by Robert McGinnis.	$1.25	$3.75	$7.50
S-2122	Brown, Carter - ***The Hellcat*** [1962]	$1.25	$3.75	$7.50
S-2140	Brown, Carter - ***Murder In The Key Club*** [1962]	$1.25	$3.75	$7.50
S-2148	Brown, Carter - ***The Lady Is Transparent*** [1962]	$1.25	$3.75	$7.50
S-2180	Brown, Carter - ***The Hong Kong Caper*** [1962] Cover by Robert McGinnis.	$1.25	$3.75	$7.50
S-2183	Brown, Carter - ***Lover, Don't Come Back*** [1962]	$1.25	$3.75	$7.50
S-2196	Brown, Carter - ***The Dumdum Murder*** [1962]	$1.25	$3.75	$7.50
S-2220	Carter, Brown - ***The Guilt-Edged Cage*** [1963]	$1.25	$3.75	$7.50
S-2228	Brown, Carter - ***A Murderer Among Us*** [1963]	$1.25	$3.75	$7.50
S-2244	Brown, Carter - ***The Lady Is Available*** [1963] Cover by Robert McGinnis.	$1.25	$3.75	$7.50
S-2259	Brown, Carter - ***The Passionate Pagan*** [1963]	$1.25	$3.75	$7.50
S-2275	Brown, Signet - ***The White Bikini*** [1963]	$1.25	$3.75	$7.50
S-2291	Brown, Carter - ***The Girl Who Was Possessed*** [1963]	$1.25	$3.75	$7.50
G-2312	Brown, Carter - ***Nymph To The Slaughter*** [1963] Cover by Robert McGinnis.	$1.25	$3.75	$7.50
G-2328	Brown, Carter - ***Blonde On The Rocks*** [1963]	$1.25	$3.75	$7.50
G-2344	Brown, Carter - ***Girl In A Shroud*** [1963] Cover by Robert McGinnis.	$1.25	$3.75	$7.50
G-2355	Brown, Carter - ***The Jade-Eyed Jungle*** [1963]	$1.25	$3.75	$7.50
G-2365	Brown, Carter - ***The Scarlet Flush*** [1963]	$1.25	$3.75	$7.50
G-2394	Brown, Carter - ***Charlie Sent Me!*** [1963]	$1.25	$3.75	$7.50

		G	VG	F
G-2400	Brown, Carter - ***The Silken Nightmare*** [1963] Cover by Robert McGinnis	$1.25	$3.75	$7.50
G-2413	Brown, Carter - ***The Wind-Up Doll*** [1964]	$1.25	$3.75	$7.50
G-2425	Brown, Carter - ***The Dance Of Death*** [1964]	$1.25	$3.75	$7.50
G-2457	Brown, Carter - ***The Never - Was Girl*** [1964] Cover by Robert McGinnis	$1.25	$3.75	$7.50
G-2459	Brown, Carter - ***Walk Softly, Witch*** [1964] Cover art by Robert McGinnis	$1.25	$3.75	$7.50
2469	Moravia, Alberto - ***A Ghost At Noon*** [1962] Movie tie-in with Brigitte Bardot cover.	$1.25	$3.75	$7.50
G-2488	Brown, Carter - ***The Body*** [1964] Cover art by Robert McGinnis	$1.25	$3.75	$7.50
G-2500	Brown, Carter - ***The Velvet Vixen*** [1964] Cover art by Robert McGinnis	$1.25	$3.75	$7.50
2529	Brown, Carter - ***Murder Of Quality*** [1964]	$1.25	$3.75	$7.50
G-2530	Brown, Carter - ***Murder Is A Package Deal*** [1964] Cover by Robert McGinnis	$1.25	$3.75	$7.50
G-2537	Brown, Carter - ***The Passionate*** [1964] Cover art by Robert McGinnis	$1.25	$3.75	$7.50
G-2541	Brown, Carter - ***The Bump And Grind Murders*** [1964]	$1.25	$3.75	$7.50
G2565	West, John B. - ***A Taste For Blood*** [1960]	$1.25	$3.75	$7.50
G2567	West, John B. - ***An Eye For An Eye*** [1959]	$1.25	$3.75	$7.50
G2568	West, John B. - ***Cobra Venom*** [1960]	$1.25	$3.75	$7.50
D2572	West, John B. - ***Never Kill A Cop*** [1961]	$1.25	$3.75	$7.50
D-2581	Brown, Carter - ***Who Killed Dr. Sex?*** [1964]	$1.25	$3.75	$7.50
D2583	West, John B. - ***Death On The Rocks*** [1961]	$1.25	$3.75	$7.50
G-2588	Brown, Carter - ***Murder Is A Package Deal*** [1964] Cover art by Robert McGinnis.	$1.25	$3.75	$7.50
D-2606	Brown, Carter - ***The Victim*** [1965]	$1.25	$3.75	$7.50
P-2607	Francis, Dick - ***Nerve*** [1964]	$1.25	$3.75	$7.50
D-2612	Brown, Carter - ***No Blonde Is An Island*** [1965] Cover by Robert McGinnis	$1.25	$3.75	$7.50
D-2637	Brown, Carter - ***Catch Me A Phoenix!*** [1965] Cover by Robert McGinnis.	$1.25	$3.75	$7.50
D-2654	Brown, Carter - ***The Desired*** [1965]	$1.25	$3.75	$7.50
D-2670	Brown, Carter - ***Nude With A View*** [1965]	$1.25	$3.75	$7.50
D-2683	Brown, Carter - ***A Corpse For Christmas*** [1965]	$1.25	$3.75	$7.50
D-2714	Brown, Carter - ***The Corpse*** [1965]	$1.25	$3.75	$7.50
D-2736	Brown, Carter - ***The Girl From Outer Space*** [1965]	$1.25	$3.75	$7.50
D-2742	Brown, Carter - ***The Lover*** [1965]	$1.25	$3.75	$7.50
D-2757	Brown, Carter - ***The Sometime Wife*** [1965] Cover art by Robert McGinnis	$1.25	$3.75	$7.50
D-2790	Blish, James - ***Galactic Cluster*** [n.d.] Cover by Lehr.	$1.25	$3.75	$7.50
D-2794	Brown, Carter - ***The Hammer Of Thor*** [1965] Cover by Robert McGinnis	$1.25	$3.75	$7.50
D-2808	Brown, Carter - ***The Loving And The Dead*** [1966]	$1.25	$3.75	$7.50
D-2827	Brown, Carter - ***The Dame*** [1966] Cover by Robert McGinnis.	$1.25	$3.75	$7.50
D-2831	Brown, Carter - ***Blonde On A Broomstick*** [1966] Cover by Robert McGinnis	$1.25	$3.75	$7.50
D-2849	Brown, Carter - ***None But The Lethal Heart*** [1966]	$1.25	$3.75	$7.50
D-2859	Brown, Carter - ***So What Killed The Vampire*** [1966] Cover art by Robert McGinnis	$1.25	$3.75	$7.50
D-2898	Brown, Carter - ***The Temptress*** [1966] Cover art by Ronnie Lesser.	$1.25	$3.75	$7.50
D-2906	Brown, Carter - ***Play Now - Kill Later!*** [1966]	$1.25	$3.75	$7.50
D-2945	Brown, Carter - ***The Black Lace Hangover*** [1966]	$1.25	$3.75	$7.50
D-2962	Brown, Carter - ***The Wanton*** [1966]	$1.25	$3.75	$7.50
D-2996	Brown, Carter - ***The Mistress*** [1966]	$1.25	$3.75	$7.50
D-3017	Brown, Carter - ***Target For Their Dark Desires*** [1966]	$1.25	$3.75	$7.50
D-3052	Brown, Carter - ***No Tears From The Widow*** [1966]	$1.25	$3.75	$7.50

		G	VG	F
3071	Hyams, Joe - ***Bogie: The Definitive Biography Of Humphrey Bogart*** [1967]	$1.25	$3.75	$7.50
D-3097	Brown, Carter - ***The Bombshell*** [1967]	$1.25	$3.75	$7.50
3102	Carr, John Dickson - ***The House At Satan's Elbow*** [1967]	$1.25	$3.75	$7.50
3113	Brunner, John - ***The Productions Of Time*** [1967]	$1.25	$3.75	$7.50
D-3122	Brown, Carter - ***Until Temptation Do Us Part*** [1967]	$1.25	$3.75	$7.50
D-3151	Brown, Carter - ***The Hong Kong Caper*** [1967]	$1.25	$3.75	$7.50
D-3162	Brown, Carter - ***Lament For A Lousy Lover*** [1967]	$1.25	$3.75	$7.50
D-3168	Brown, Carter - ***Seidlitz And The Super-Spy*** [1967]	$1.25	$3.75	$7.50
D-3190	Brown, Carter - ***Long Time No Leola*** [1967]	$1.25	$3.75	$7.50
D-3212	Brown, Carter - ***The Tigress*** [1967] Cover art by Ronnie Lesser.	$1.25	$3.75	$7.50
D-3218	Brown, Carter - ***House Of Sorcery*** [1967] Cover by Robert McGinnis.	$1.25	$3.75	$7.50
D-3251	Brown, Carter - ***The Lady Is Transparent*** [1967]	$1.25	$3.75	$7.50
D-3289	Brown, Carter - ***The Plush-Lined Coffin*** [1967]	$1.25	$3.75	$7.50
D-3345	Brown, Carter - ***The Deadly Kitten*** [1967]	$1.25	$3.75	$7.50
D-3348	Brown, Carter - ***The Dumdum Murder*** [1967]	$1.25	$3.75	$7.50
D-3380	Brown, Carter - ***Had I But Groaned*** [1968]	$1.25	$3.75	$7.50
D-3410	Brown, Carter - ***The Lady Is Available*** [1968] Cover by Robert McGinnis.	$1.25	$3.75	$7.50
D-3413	Brown, Carter - ***Angel*** [1968]	$1.25	$3.75	$7.50
3430	Brown, Carter - ***Zelda*** [1968] Cover art by Robert McGinnis.	$1.25	$3.75	$7.50
D-3472	Brown, Carter - ***The Girl Who Was Possessed*** [1968] Cover by Robert McGinnis.	$1.25	$3.75	$7.50
D-3533	Brown, Carter - ***The Hellcat*** [1968]	$1.25	$3.75	$7.50
D-3561	Brown, Carter - ***Tomorrow Is Murder*** [1968] Cover art by Ronnie Lesser.	$1.25	$3.75	$7.50
D-3585	Brown, Carter - ***The Mini Murders*** [1968] Cover by Robert McGinnis.	$1.25	$3.75	$7.50
D-3623	Brown, Carter - ***The Deep Cold Green*** [1968]	$1.25	$3.75	$7.50
D-3636	Brown, Carter - ***The Million Dollar Babe*** [1968]	$1.25	$3.75	$7.50
D-3704	Brown, Carter - ***Murder In The Key Club*** [1968]	$1.25	$3.75	$7.50
D-3722	Brown, Carter - ***The Everloving Blues*** [1969] Cover by Ronnie Lesser.	$1.25	$3.75	$7.50
D-3776	Brown, Carter - ***The Flagellator*** [1969] Cover art by Robert McGinnis.	$1.25	$3.75	$7.50
D-3810	Brown, Carter - ***The White Bikini*** [1969]	$1.25	$3.75	$7.50
P-3842	Brown, Carter - ***Only The Very Rich?*** [1969] Cover art by Robert McGinnis.	$1.25	$3.75	$7.50
P-3876	Brown, Carter - ***The Ice-Cold Nude*** [1969]	$1.25	$3.75	$7.50
P-3903	Brown, Carter - ***Die Anytime, After Tuesday!*** [1969] Cover art by Robert Mcginnis.	$1.25	$3.75	$7.50
Q-3933	Anobile, Richard J. (editor) - ***Drat!*** [1969] W.C. Fields cartoons.	$1.25	$3.75	$7.50
P-3955	Brown, Carter - ***The Up-Tight Blonde*** [1969] Cover by Robert McGinnis.	$1.25	$3.75	$7.50
P-3963	Brown, Carter - ***Lover Don't Come Back*** [1969]	$1.25	$3.75	$7.50
P-4003	Brown, Carter - ***The Guilt-Edged Cage*** [1969] Cover by Robert McGinnis.	$1.25	$3.75	$7.50
P-4042	Brown, Carter - ***The Streaked-Blonde Slave*** [1969] Cover by Robert McGinnis.	$1.25	$3.75	$7.50
P-4081	Brown, Carter - ***A Murderer Among Us*** [1969]	$1.25	$3.75	$7.50
P-4105	Brown, Carter - ***Murder Is The Message*** [1970]	$1.25	$3.75	$7.50
P-4133	Brown, Carter - ***Girl In A Shroud*** [1970]	$1.25	$3.75	$7.50
P-4159	Brown, Carter - ***The Hang-Up Kid*** [1970]	$1.25	$3.75	$7.50
P-4197	Brown, Carter - ***The Unorthodox Corpse*** [1970] Cover art by Robert McGinnis.	$1.25	$3.75	$7.50
P-4219	Brown, Carter - ***Burden of Guilt*** [1970]	$1.25	$3.75	$7.50

		G	VG	F
P-4246	Brown, Carter - ***The Sad-Eyed Seductress*** [1970] Cover art by Robert McGinnis.	$1.25	$3.75	$7.50
P-4268	Brown, Carter - ***True Son Of The Beast*** [1970]	$1.25	$3.75	$7.50
P-4302	Preston, Charles - ***You Can't Have A Gemini Next To A Virgo*** [1970] PBO. Cartoons	$1.25	$3.75	$7.50
P-4320	Brown, Carter - ***A Good Year For Dwarfs?*** [1970]	$1.25	$3.75	$7.50
P-4344	Brown, Carter - ***The Lady Is Transparent*** [1970]	$1.25	$3.75	$7.50
P-4394	Brown, Carter - ***The Coffin Bird*** [1970] Cover by Robert McGinnis.	$1.25	$3.75	$7.50
T-4423	Brown, Carter - ***The Savage Salome*** [1970] Cover by Robert McGinnis.	$1.25	$3.75	$7.50
T-4455	Brown, Carter - ***Where Did Charity Go?*** [1970] Cover art by Robert McGinnis.	$1.25	$3.75	$7.50
T-4489	Brown, Carter - ***The Passionate Pagan*** [1971]	$1.25	$3.75	$7.50
T-4515	Brown, Carter - ***Nymph To The Slaughter*** [1971]	$1.25	$3.75	$7.50
T-4520	Brown, Carter - ***The Creative Murders*** [1971] Cover by Robert McGinnis.	$1.25	$3.75	$7.50
T-4550	Brown, Carter - ***The Body*** [1971] Cover by Robert McGinnis...	$1.25	$3.75	$7.50
T-4581	Brown, Carter - ***The Coven*** [1971] Cover art by Robert McGinnis.	$1.25	$3.75	$7.50
T-4658	Brown, Carter - ***The Sex Clinic*** [1971] Cover by Robert McGinnis.	$1.25	$3.75	$7.50
T-4682	Brown, Carter - ***Blonde On The Rocks*** [1971] Cover by Robert McGinnis.	$1.25	$3.75	$7.50
T-4722	Brown, Carter - ***Murder In The Family Way*** [1971] Cover by Robert McGinnis.	$1.25	$3.75	$7.50
T-4775	Brown, Carter - ***Charlie Sent Me*** [1971]	$1.25	$3.75	$7.50
T-4798	Brown, Carter - ***W.H.O.R.E.!*** [1971] Cover by Robert McGinnis.	$1.25	$3.75	$7.50
T-4826	Brown, Carter - ***The Wind-Up Doll*** [1971]	$1.25	$3.75	$7.50
T-4854	Brown, Carter - ***The Invisible Flamini*** [1971]	$1.25	$3.75	$7.50
T-4883	Brown, Carter - ***The Blonde*** [1972]	$1.25	$3.75	$7.50
T-4908	Brown, Carter - ***The Seven Sirens*** [1972] Cover art by Robert McGinnis.	$1.25	$3.75	$7.50
T-4936	Brown, Carter - ***Blonde On A Broomstick*** [1972]	$1.25	$3.75	$7.50
T-4961	Brown, Carter - ***The Aseptic Murders*** [1972]	$1.25	$3.75	$7.50
T-5013	Brown, Carter - ***Play Now .... Kill Later*** [1972]	$1.25	$3.75	$7.50
T-5064	Brown, Carter - ***Murder Is So Nostalgic!*** [1972]	$1.25	$3.75	$7.50
T-5089	Brown, Carter - ***The Bombshell*** [1972]	$1.25	$3.75	$7.50
Y-5724	Rosten, Norman - ***Marilyn: An Untold Story*** [1973] With 8 pages of rare and revealing photos	$1.25	$3.75	$7.50
W-7645	Bachman, Richard (Stephen King) - ***Rage*** [1981] PBO.	$8.00	$25.00	$50.00
J-8754	Bachman, Richard (Stephen King) - ***The Long Walk*** [1981] PBO.	$8.00	$25.00	$50.00
E-9668	Bachman, Richard (Stephen King) - ***Roadwork*** [1981] PBO.	$8.00	$25.00	$50.00
AE-15008	Bachman, Richard (Stephen King) - ***The Running Man*** [1981] PBO.	$8.00	$25.00	$50.00

Sport Magazine Library. New York: Bartholomew House.

		G	VG	F
NN	Anthology - ***Heroes Of Sport*** [1961] Edited by Ed Fitzgerald. Photo cover.	$1.50	$5.00	$10.00
1	Fitzgerald, Ed - ***Johnny Unitas*** [1960] PBO. Photo cover.	$1.50	$5.00	$10.00
2	Goodman, Irv - ***Stan The Man Musial*** [1961] PBO. Photo cover.	$2.50	$7.50	$15.00
3	Linn, Ed - ***Ted Williams: The Eternal Kid*** [1961] PBO. Photo cover.	$2.50	$7.50	$15.00
4	Rosenthal, Harold - ***Baseball's Best Managers*** [1961] PBO. Casey Stengal photo cover.	$2.00	$6.00	$12.00
5	Schaap, Dick - ***Mickey Mantle: The Indispensable Yankee*** [1961] PBO. Photo cover.	$3.50	$10.00	$20.00

		G	VG	F
6	Hano, Arnold - ***Willie Mays: The Say-Hey Kid*** [1961] PBO. Willie Mays photo cover.	$2.50	$7.50	$15.00
7	Newcombe, Jack - ***Floyd Patterson: Heavyweight King*** [1961] PBO. Photo cover.	$1.50	$5.00	$10.00
8	Anthology - ***Best From Sport*** [1961] PBO. Edited by Al Silverman. Photo cover.	$1.50	$5.00	$10.00
9	Silverman, Al - ***Warren Spahn: Immortal Southpaw*** [1961] PBO. Photo cover.	$2.50	$7.50	$15.00
10	Herndon, Booton - ***Football's Greatest Quarterbacks*** [1961] PBO. Photo cover.	$1.50	$5.00	$10.00
11	Shecter, Leonard - ***Roger Maris: Home Run Hero*** [1961] PBO. Photo cover.	$3.50	$10.00	$20.00
12	Gelman, Steve - ***Bob Cousy: Magician Of Pro Basketball*** [1961] PBO. Photo cover.	$1.50	$5.00	$10.00
13	Schaap, Dick - ***Paul Hornung*** [1962] PBO. Photo cover.	$1.50	$5.00	$10.00
14	Beach, Jim - ***Notre Dame Football*** [1962] PBO. Cover art by Irwin Greenberg.	$1.50	$5.00	$10.00
15	Graham, Jr., Frank - ***Bowling Secrets From The Stars*** [1962] PBO. Photo cover.	$1.50	$5.00	$10.00
16	Allen, Mel & Graham, Jr., Frank - ***It Takes Heart*** [1962]	$1.50	$5.00	$10.00

Stallion Books. New York: Universal Publishing. Digest Size.

		G	VG	F
202	Woodford, Jack - ***Male Virgin*** [1954] Cover by Bernard Safran.	$3.50	$10.00	$20.00
203	Harragan, Steve - ***Three Bad Girls*** [1954]	$3.50	$10.00	$20.00
204	de Mexico, N.R. - ***Marijuana Girl*** [1954] Photo cover.	$3.50	$10.00	$20.00
205	Stone, Thomas - ***Tramp Girl*** [1954] Cover art by Warren King.	$3.50	$10.00	$20.00
206	Harragan, Steve - ***The Queer Sisters*** [1954] Cover art by Bernard Safran.	$3.50	$10.00	$20.00
207	Harvey, Gene - ***Miami Widow*** [1954]	$3.50	$10.00	$20.00
208	Sydney, Gale - ***Strange Circle*** [1954]	$3.50	$10.00	$20.00
209	Nixon, Henry Lewis - ***Ship's Doctor*** [1954] Cover art by Walter Popp.	$3.50	$10.00	$20.00
210	Clark, D.B. - ***Gutter Star*** [1954]	$3.50	$10.00	$20.00
211	Duperrault, Doug - ***Trailer-Camp Girl*** [1954]	$3.50	$10.00	$20.00
212	Harragan, Steve - ***Side-Show Girl*** [1954]	$3.50	$10.00	$20.00
213	Roberts, Luke - ***Reefer Club*** [1954]	$5.00	$15.00	$30.00
214	Carruthers, Margaret - ***Another Man's Wife*** [1954] Cover by Bernard Safran.	$3.50	$10.00	$20.00
215	Harragan, Steve - ***Smuggled Sin*** [1954] Photo cover.	$3.50	$10.00	$20.00

Stanley Library. New York: Stanley Library, Inc.

		G	VG	F
67	Campbell, Jeanne - ***The Oldest Profession*** [1959]	$1.25	$3.75	$7.50
68	Day, Max - ***So Nice, So Wild*** [1959] PBO.	$1.00	$3.00	$6.00
70	Stonebraker, Florence - ***Love Doctor*** [1959] Photo cover.	$1.00	$3.00	$6.00
71	Flint, John B. - ***Lover Boy*** [1959] Photo cover.	$1.00	$3.00	$6.00
72	Whittington, Harry - ***Strictly For The Boys*** [1959] PBO. Photo cover.	$1.25	$3.75	$7.50
73	Stonebraker, Florence - ***Strange Sinner*** [1959] PBO. Photo cover.	$1.00	$3.00	$6.00
74	Duperrault, Doug - ***Bed Of Fear*** [1959] PBO. Photo cover.	$1.00	$3.00	$6.00

Star Books. New York: Star Guidance, Inc. Digest Size.

		G	VG	F
1	Leinster, Murray - ***Texas Gun Slinger*** [1950] Cover art by George Gross.	$3.50	$10.00	$20.00
2	Gaddis, Peggy - ***Bachelor Bait*** [1950]	$2.00	$6.00	$12.00
3	Leinster, Murray - ***Outlaw Guns*** [1950]	$3.50	$10.00	$20.00
4	Gregor, Martin - ***Hell Cat!*** [1950]	$2.00	$6.00	$12.00
5	Leinster, Murray - ***Outlaw Deputy*** [1950] Cover art by Rodenwald.	$3.50	$10.00	$20.00
6	Arthur, Burt - ***Flaming Guns*** [1950] Cover art by George Gross.	$2.00	$6.00	$12.00

		G	VG	F
7	Joscelyn, Archie - ***Bad Hombre*** [1950] PBO. Cover art by George Gross.	$2.00	$6.00	$12.00
8	Lehman, Paul Evan - ***Range Justice*** [1950] Cover art by George Gross.	$2.00	$6.00	$12.00
9	Joscelyn, Archie - ***Border Wolves*** [1950] PBO. Cover art by George Gross.	$2.00	$6.00	$12.00
10	Lehman, Paul Evan - ***Law Of The '45*** [1950] PBO. Cover art by George Gross.	$2.00	$6.00	$12.00
11	Arthur, Burt - ***Killer's Moon*** [1950] PBO. Cover art by George Gross.	$2.00	$6.00	$12.00
12	Arthur, Burt - ***The Black Rider*** [1950] Cover art by George Gross.	$2.00	$6.00	$12.00
13	Joscelyn, Archie - ***Gun-Thunder Valley!*** [1951] PBO. Cover art by George Gross.	$2.00	$6.00	$12.00
14	Joscelyn, Archie - ***The Vengeance Trail!*** [1951] PBO.	$2.00	$6.00	$12.00
15	Floren, Lee - ***The Long Trail North*** [1951] PBO. Cover by George Gross.	$2.00	$6.00	$12.00
16	Lehman, Paul Evan - ***The Sheep Killers*** [1951] PBO. Cover by George Gross.	$2.00	$6.00	$12.00
17	Floren, Lee - ***Two-Gun Trail*** [1951] PBO. Cover art by George Gross.	$2.00	$6.00	$12.00
18	Joscelyn, Archie - ***Wyoming Outlaw*** [1951] PBO. Cover art by George Gross.	$2.00	$6.00	$12.00
19	Arthur, Burt - ***Duel On The Range*** [1951]	$2.00	$6.00	$12.00
20	Floren, Lee - ***Rustler's Trail*** [1951] PBO.	$2.00	$6.00	$12.00
21	Floren, Lee - ***Black Gunsmoke*** [1951] PBO. Cover art by George Gross.	$2.00	$6.00	$12.00
22	Lehman, Paul Evan - ***Texas Vengeance*** [1951] PBO. Cover art by George Gross.	$2.00	$6.00	$12.00
23	Arthur, Burt - ***The Black Rider*** [1951] Cover art by George Gross.	$2.00	$6.00	$12.00
24	Joscelyn, Archie - ***Gun-Thunder Valley!*** [1951] Cover art by George Gross.	$2.00	$6.00	$12.00
27	Floren, Lee - ***Deputy's Revenge*** [1951] Cover art by George Gross.	$2.00	$6.00	$12.00
28	Lehman, Paul Evan - ***Texas Guns*** [1951] Cover art by George Gross.	$2.00	$6.00	$12.00
29	Joscelyn, Archie - ***Duel At Killman Creek*** [1951]	$2.00	$6.00	$12.00
30	Joscelyn, Archie - ***Texas Outlaw*** [1951]	$2.00	$6.00	$12.00
31	Lehman, Paul Evan - ***Range War At Keno*** [1952] Cover art by George Gross.	$2.00	$6.00	$12.00
32	Joscelyn, Archie - ***Ambush On Satan's Hill*** [1952] Cover by George Gross.	$2.00	$6.00	$12.00
33	Arthur, Burt - ***Outlaw Fury*** [1952] PBO. Cover art by George Gross.	$2.00	$6.00	$12.00
34	Arthur, Burt - ***Action At Spanish Flat*** [1952] PBO.	$2.00	$6.00	$12.00
35	Lehman, Paul Evan - ***Rustlers Of The Rio Grande*** [1952] PBO. Cover art by George Gross.	$2.00	$6.00	$12.00
36	Arthur, Burt - ***Two-Gun Outlaw*** [1952] PBO. Cover art by S. Cherry.	$2.00	$6.00	$12.00
37	Joscelyn, Archie - ***The Texan's Revenge*** [1952] PBO. Cover art by Mort Kunstler.	$2.00	$6.00	$12.00
38	Arthur, Burt - ***Gun-Law On The Range*** [1952] PBO. Cover art by Barton.	$2.00	$6.00	$12.00
42	Joscelyn, Archie - ***Two-Gun Vengeance*** [1953] PBO. Cover art by George Gross.	$2.00	$6.00	$12.00
45	Floren, Lee - ***Black Gunsmoke*** [1953] Cover art by George Gross.	$2.00	$6.00	$12.00
46	Floren, Lee - ***Two-Gun Trail*** [1953] Cover by George Gross.	$2.00	$6.00	$12.00

		G	VG	F
47	Joscelyn, Archie - ***Wyoming Outlaw*** [1953] Cover art by George Gross.	$2.00	$6.00	$12.00

Star Novels. New York: Publications House, Inc. Digest Size.

		G	VG	F
753	Whitney, Hallam (Harry Whittington) - ***Shack Road*** [1956] Cover by Belarski.	$3.50	$10.00	$20.00
754	Quandt, Albert L. - ***Cellar Club*** [n.d.]	$2.50	$7.50	$15.00
758	Whittington, Harry - ***Sinners Club*** [1956] Cover by Belarski.	$3.50	$10.00	$20.00
760	Hatter, Amos - ***Waterfront Girl*** [n.d.]	$2.50	$7.50	$15.00
762	Hallam Whitney (Harry Whittington) - ***Backwoods Hussy*** [n.d.] Cover by Nappi	$3.50	$10.00	$20.00
763	Bligh, Norman - ***Motel Mistress*** [n.d.]	$2.50	$7.50	$15.00
765	Bligh, Norman - ***River Boat Girl*** [n.d.] Cover by Belarski	$2.50	$7.50	$15.00
766	Hatter, Amos - ***Hollywood Sinners*** [n.d.]	$2.50	$7.50	$15.00
767	Hunter, John - ***Office Hussy*** [n.d.]	$2.50	$7.50	$15.00

Stork Books. Digest Size.

		G	VG	F
NN-1	Semple, Gordon - ***Life Of Passion*** [n.d.] Cover art by Rodewald.	$5.00	$15.00	$30.00
NN-2	Williams, Wright - ***Lust For Love*** [n.d.] Cover art by Rodewald.	$5.00	$15.00	$30.00
3	Watkins, Glenn - ***Sinful Life*** [1950] PBO. Cover by Rodewald.	$5.00	$15.00	$30.00
4	Himmel, Richard - ***Soul Of Passion*** [1950]	$5.00	$15.00	$30.00
5	Jordan, Gail - ***Passionate Lover*** [1950] Cover art by Rodewald.	$5.00	$15.00	$30.00
6	Carter, Ralph - ***The Sins Of Donna Kenyon*** [1950] Cover art by Rodewald.	$5.00	$15.00	$30.00
7	Stone, Thomas - ***Raging Passions*** [1950] Cover art by L.B. Cole.	$5.00	$15.00	$30.00
8	Jackquin, Lee - ***Two Sinners*** [1950] Cover art by L.B. Cole.	$5.00	$15.00	$30.00

Streamline Books. Toronto: Streamline Books, Inc.

		G	VG	F
NN-1	Brown, Horace - ***Whispering City*** [1947] Movie tie-in. Movie photos on back cover, inside covers & 13 pages	$20.00	$60.00	$125.00

Strode Books. Huntsville, AL: Strode Publishers.

		G	VG	F
3	Tucker, Earl - ***All The Nuts Aren't On The Trees*** [1960] PBO.	$1.50	$5.00	$10.00

Studio Pocket. Toronto: Studio Publications.

		G	VG	F
1	Self, Edwin B. - ***Shack-Up Girl*** [1951]	$2.50	$7.50	$15.00
2	Jordan, Gail - ***Furnished Room*** [1951]	$2.50	$7.50	$15.00
3	Raymond, Fay - ***Sordid Affair*** [1951]	$2.50	$7.50	$15.00
4	Thompson, James - ***Sins Of The Fathers*** [1952]	$35.00	$125.00	$300.00
105	Endore, Guy - ***Werewolf Of Paris*** [1952] Photo cover.	$3.50	$10.00	$20.00
106	Saxon, Lyle - ***High Yellow*** [1952]	$2.50	$7.50	$15.00
107	Keller, Dan - ***Flee The Night In Anger*** [1952]	$2.50	$7.50	$15.00
108	Baum, Vicki - ***Hotel Berlin '43*** [1952]	$2.50	$7.50	$15.00
109	Dumas, Alexander - ***The Man In The Iron Mask*** [1952] Photo cover. Movie tie-in.	$2.50	$7.50	$15.00
110	Brooks, Richard - ***The Brick Foxhole*** [1952] Photo cover.	$2.50	$7.50	$15.00
111	du Maurier, Daphne - ***Rebecca*** [1952]	$2.50	$7.50	$15.00
112	du Maurier, Daphne - ***The Parasites*** [1952]	$2.50	$7.50	$15.00
114	Waldron, T.J. & Gleeson, James - ***The Frogmen*** [1952]	$2.50	$7.50	$15.00

Superior Reprints. New York: Military Service Publishing Co.

		G	VG	F
M-637	Baldwin, Faith - ***White Magic*** [1944]	$1.25	$3.75	$7.50
M-638	Bradford, Roark - ***Ol' Man Adam An' His Chillun*** [1944] Cover art by A.B. Walker.	$1.25	$3.75	$7.50
M-639	Daly, Elizabeth - ***Unexpected Night*** [1944]	$1.25	$3.75	$7.50
M-640	Wylie, Philip - ***An April Afternoon*** [1944]	$1.25	$3.75	$7.50
M-641	Shriber, Ione Sundberg - ***Family Affair*** [1944]	$1.25	$3.75	$7.50
M-642	MacDonald, Philip - ***The Rynox Murder Mystery*** [1944]	$1.25	$3.75	$7.50
M-643	Price, George - ***Cartoons By George Price*** [1944]	$1.25	$3.75	$7.50

		G	VG	F
M-644	Fischer, Marjorie - ***Embarrassment Of Riches*** [1944]	$1.25	$3.75	$7.50
M-645	Dean, Robert George - ***Murder In Mink*** [1945]	$1.25	$3.75	$7.50
M-646	Lardner, Ring - ***The Love Nest And Other Stories*** [1945]	$1.25	$3.75	$7.50
M-647	Wilde, Percival - ***Inquest*** [1945]	$1.25	$3.75	$7.50
M-648	Spence, Hartzell - ***One Foot In Heaven*** [1945] Cover art by Donald McKay	$1.25	$3.75	$7.50
M-649	Gruber, Frank - ***The Navy Colt*** [1945]	$1.25	$3.75	$7.50
M-650	O'Flaherty, Liam - ***The Informer*** [1945]	$1.25	$3.75	$7.50
M-651	Booth, Charles G. - ***Mr. Angel Comes Aboard*** [1945]	$1.25	$3.75	$7.50
M-652	Greene, Graham - ***This Gun For Hire*** [1945]	$1.25	$3.75	$7.50
M-653	Daly, Elizabeth - ***The House Without The Door*** [1945]	$1.25	$3.75	$7.50
M-654	Dean, Robert George - ***On Ice*** [1945] Cover art by Jonas	$1.25	$3.75	$7.50
M-655	Gruber, Frank - ***The Mighty Blockhead*** [1945]	$1.25	$3.75	$7.50
M-656	Munro, H.H. - ***A Saki Sampler*** [1945]	$1.25	$3.75	$7.50
M-657	Steeves, Harrison R. - ***Good Night Sheriff*** [1945]	$1.25	$3.75	$7.50

Suspense Novel. Chicago: Farrell Publishing. Digest Size.

1	De Mexico, N. R. - ***Strange Pursuit*** [1951] The series was inspired by the radio and television program "Suspense."	$1.50	$5.00	$10.00
2	Daemer, Will - ***The Case Of The Lonely Lovers*** [1951] PBO	$1.50	$5.00	$10.00
3	Hodges, Carl G. - ***Naked Villainy*** [1951] PBO.	$1.50	$5.00	$10.00

Swan. Wilmington, DE: Swan Publishing Co.

S-102	Pelrine, Eleanor & Dennis - ***Ian Fleming: Man With The Golden Pen*** [1966] PBO. Photo cover.	$1.25	$3.75	$7.50

Tech Mystery. New York: Tech Mystery, Inc. Digest Size.

NO#	Bogart, William - ***Murder Man*** [n.d.]	$3.50	$10.00	$20.00
1	Hopkins, Linton C. - ***The Candle*** [n.d.]	$3.50	$10.00	$20.00
2	Leitfred, Robert H. - ***Murder Is My Racket*** [n.d.]	$3.50	$10.00	$20.00

Tech Romance. New York: Tech Publishing, Inc. Digest Size.

NN	Unknown - ***Woman In The White House*** [n.d.]	$1.50	$5.00	$10.00

Tech Western. New York: Tech Publishing, Inc. Digest Size.

1	Shapiro, Herbert - ***The Black Rider*** [n.d.]	$1.50	$5.00	$10.00
2	Shapiro, Herbert - ***Rainbow Trail*** [n.d.]	$1.50	$5.00	$10.00

Tempo Books. New York: Grosset & Dunlap.

T1	Hahn, Emily - ***Francie*** [1962] Cover art by Mayers.	$1.00	$3.00	$6.00
T2	Andrews, Roy Chapman - ***Quest Of The Snow Leopard*** [1962]	$1.00	$3.00	$6.00
T3	Falkner, J. Meade - ***Moonfleet*** [1962]	$1.00	$3.00	$6.00
T4	Thane, Elswyth - ***Tryst*** [1962]	$1.00	$3.00	$6.00
T5	Bagnold, Enid - ***National Velvet*** [1962] Cover by H. B. Vestal.	$1.00	$3.00	$6.00
T6	Conklin, Groff - editor - ***Invaders Of Earth*** [1962]	$1.35	$4.00	$8.00
T7	Cottrell, Leonard - ***Wonders Of The World*** [1962]	$1.00	$3.00	$6.00
T8	Porter, Mark - ***Winning Pitcher*** [1962] PBO.	$1.00	$3.00	$6.00
T9	Coombs, Charles - ***Mystery Of Satellite 7*** [1962]	$1.00	$3.00	$6.00
T10	Stanford, Don - ***The Red Car*** [1962] Cover by Jo Polseno.	$1.00	$3.00	$6.00
T11	Lambert, Janet - ***Star-Spangled Summer*** [1962]	$1.00	$3.00	$6.00
T12	Breck, Vivian - ***Maggie*** [1962] Cover art by Mayers.	$1.00	$3.00	$6.00
T13	Walters, Hugh - ***First On The Moon*** [1962]	$1.00	$3.00	$6.00
T14	Miller, Albert G. - ***Fury: Stallion Of Broken Wheel Ranch*** [1962]	$1.00	$3.00	$6.00
T15	Tatham, Julie Campbell - ***To Nick From Jan*** [1962]	$1.00	$3.00	$6.00
T16	Knight, Eric - ***Lassie Come-Home*** [1962] Cover art by H.B. Vestal.	$1.00	$3.00	$6.00
T17	Bell, Margaret E. - ***Watch For A Tall White Sail*** [1962]	$1.00	$3.00	$6.00
T18	? - ***Dreams Of Glory*** [1962]	$1.00	$3.00	$6.00
T19	Summers, James L. - ***Off The Beam*** [1962]	$1.00	$3.00	$6.00

		G	VG	F
T20	Deming, R.N., Dorothy - ***School Nurse*** [1962]	$1.00	$3.00	$6.00
T21	Headley, Elizabeth - ***She's My Girl!*** [1962]	$1.00	$3.00	$6.00
T22	Barlow, Roger - ***Black Treasure*** [1962] PBO.	$1.00	$3.00	$6.00
T23	Liebers, Arthur - ***Wit's End*** [1962]	$1.00	$3.00	$6.00
T24	Waldman, Frank - ***The Challenger*** [1962] Cover by Jo Polseno.	$1.00	$3.00	$6.00
T25	Spencer, Sharon - ***Breaking The Bonds*** [1962] PBO.	$1.00	$3.00	$6.00
T26	Stolz, Mary - ***Pray Love, Remember*** [1962]	$1.00	$3.00	$6.00
T27	Hammond, Ralph - ***Cocos Gold*** [1962]	$1.00	$3.00	$6.00
T28	Wollheim, Donald B. - ***Secret Of The Martian Moons*** [1962]	$1.35	$4.00	$8.00
T29	Corbin, William - ***High Road Home*** [1962]	$1.00	$3.00	$6.00
T30	Thane, Elswyth - ***Remember Today*** [1962]	$1.00	$3.00	$6.00
T31	McKown, Robin - ***Janine*** [1962]	$1.00	$3.00	$6.00
T32	Wadsworth, L.A. - ***Puzzle Of The Talking Monkey*** [1962]	$1.00	$3.00	$6.00
T33	? - ***Glory Be!*** [1962]	$1.00	$3.00	$6.00
T34	Stolz, Mary - ***The Day And The Way We Met*** [1962]	$1.00	$3.00	$6.00
T36	Barlow, Roger - ***Danger At Mormon Crossing*** [1962]	$1.00	$3.00	$6.00
T37	Crane, Florence - ***Gypsy Secret*** [1962]	$1.00	$3.00	$6.00
T38	Lambert, Janet - ***Up Goes The Curtain*** [1963]	$1.00	$3.00	$6.00
T39	Anthology edited by Groff Conklin - ***Great Stories Of Space Travel*** [1963]	$1.35	$4.00	$8.00
T40	Shippen, Katherine B. - ***Men, Microscopes, And Living Things*** [1963]	$1.00	$3.00	$6.00
T41	Wadsworth, L.A. - ***The Bamboo Key*** [1963]	$1.00	$3.00	$6.00
T42	Low, Elizabeth - ***Hold Fast The Dream*** [1963]	$1.00	$3.00	$6.00
T43	? - ***"Keeper" Play*** [1963]	$1.00	$3.00	$6.00
T44	? - ***Sun In The Morning*** [1963]	$1.00	$3.00	$6.00
T45	Corbin, William - ***Deadline*** [1963]	$1.00	$3.00	$6.00
T46	Robinson, Mabel L. - ***Bright Island*** [1963]	$1.00	$3.00	$6.00
T47	? - ***Fair Exchange*** [1963]	$1.00	$3.00	$6.00
T48	Lacy, Ed - ***Sleep In Thunder*** [1963]	$1.35	$4.00	$8.00
T49	Hickok, Lorena A. - ***The Story Of Helen Keller*** [1963]	$1.00	$3.00	$6.00
T50	Knight, Clayton - ***The Normandy Invasion*** [1964]	$1.00	$3.00	$6.00
T51	Salten, Felix - ***Bambi*** [1964]	$1.00	$3.00	$6.00
T52	Wyndham, Lee - ***Beth Hilton: Model*** [1964]	$1.00	$3.00	$6.00
T53	Arnold, Oren - ***Are We All Here?*** [1964]	$1.00	$3.00	$6.00
T54	Ingles, James Wesley - ***Test Of Valor*** [1964]	$1.00	$3.00	$6.00
T55	Webster, Jean - ***Daddy-Long-Legs*** [1964]	$1.00	$3.00	$6.00
T56	? - ***The Bent Twig*** [1964]	$1.00	$3.00	$6.00
T57	Barlow, Roger - ***Stormy Voyage*** [1964]	$1.00	$3.00	$6.00
T58	Lamb, Dana & Ginger - ***Quest For The Lost City*** [1964]	$1.00	$3.00	$6.00
T59	Leighton, Margaret - ***The Story Of Florence Nightingale*** [1964]	$1.00	$3.00	$6.00
T60	Mitchell, Jerry - ***The Amazing Mets*** [1964]	$1.35	$4.00	$8.00
T61	Aldrich, Bess Streeter - ***A Lantern In Her Hand*** [1964]	$1.00	$3.00	$6.00
T62	Cottrell, Leonard - ***Life Under The Pharaohs*** [1964]	$1.00	$3.00	$6.00
T63	Wiegin, Kate Douglas - ***Rebecca Of Sunnybrook Farm*** [1964]	$1.00	$3.00	$6.00
T64	Montgomery, L.M. - ***Anne Of Green Gables*** [1964]	$1.00	$3.00	$6.00
T65	? - ***The Romantic World Of Richard Halliburton*** [1964]	$1.00	$3.00	$6.00
T67	Shotwell, Louisa R. - ***Roosevelt Grady*** [1964]	$1.00	$3.00	$6.00
T68	Appel, Benjamin - ***We Were There At The Battle For Bataan*** [1964]	$1.00	$3.00	$6.00
T69	Lawson, Don - ***The United States In World War II*** [1964]	$1.00	$3.00	$6.00
T71	Miers, Earl Schenck - ***America And Its Presidents*** [1964]	$1.00	$3.00	$6.00
T72	Tarkington, Booth - ***Penrod*** [1964]	$1.00	$3.00	$6.00
T73	Scott, Judith Unger - ***The Art Of Being A Girl*** [1964]	$1.00	$3.00	$6.00
T74	Armer, Alberta - ***Screwball*** [1964]	$1.00	$3.00	$6.00
T75	Pitkin, Dorothy - ***The Grass Was That High*** [1964]	$1.00	$3.00	$6.00
T76	Peyton, K.M. - ***Sea Fever*** [1964]	$1.00	$3.00	$6.00
T77	Canfield, Dorothy - ***Understood Betsy*** [1964]	$1.00	$3.00	$6.00
T78	Knott, Irma - ***This Thing Called Love*** [1964]	$1.00	$3.00	$6.00
T79	Bradbury, Bianca - ***Circus Punk*** [1964]	$1.00	$3.00	$6.00

		G	VG	F
T81	Burnett, Frances Hodgson - ***A Little Princess*** [1964]	$1.00	$3.00	$6.00
T82	Thorne, Alice - ***The Story Of Madame Curie*** [1964]	$1.00	$3.00	$6.00
T83	Bolton, Carole - ***Christy*** [1964]	$1.00	$3.00	$6.00
T84	Trimble, Joe - ***Yogi Berra*** [1965] Photo cover.	$1.35	$4.00	$8.00
T85	Malkus, Alida Sims - ***The Story Of Winston Churchill*** [1965]	$1.00	$3.00	$6.00
T88	Harrie, Christie - ***You Have To Draw The Line Somewhere*** [1965]	$1.00	$3.00	$6.00
T89	Gibson, Walter B. - ***Adaptation - Chilling Stories From Rod Serling's The Twilight Zone*** [1965] Photo cover. TV tie-in.	$2.00	$6.00	$12.00
T90	Sandoz, Mari - ***The Story Catcher*** [1965]	$1.00	$3.00	$6.00
T91	Lewiton, Mina - ***Elizabeth And The Young Stranger*** [1965]	$1.00	$3.00	$6.00
T92	Whitney, Phillis A. - ***Mystery Of The Hidden Hand*** [1965]	$1.00	$3.00	$6.00
T93	? - ***Overtime Upset*** [1965]	$1.00	$3.00	$6.00
T95	Barrie, James M. - ***Peter Pan*** [1965]	$1.35	$4.00	$8.00
T96	Bolton, Carole - ***The Dark Rosaleen*** [1965] Cover art by Rudy Nappi.	$1.00	$3.00	$6.00
T97	Rathjen, Carl H. - ***Wild Wheels*** [1965]	$1.00	$3.00	$6.00
T98	Hunt, Irene - ***Across Five Aprils*** [1965]	$1.00	$3.00	$6.00
T99	Allen, Betsy - ***The Clue In Blue*** [1965]	$1.00	$3.00	$6.00
T100	Allen, Betsy - ***The Riddle In Red*** [1965]	$1.00	$3.00	$6.00
T101	Allen, Betsy - ***Puzzle In Purple*** [1965]	$1.00	$3.00	$6.00
T102	Allen, Betsy - ***The Secret Of Black Cat Gulch*** [1965]	$1.00	$3.00	$6.00
T103	Johnston, William - ***Get Smart*** [1966] Photo cover. "Get Smart" #1. TV tie-in.	$1.50	$5.00	$10.00
T104	Merrill, Jean - ***The Pushcart War*** [1966] Cover art by Ronni Solbert.	$1.00	$3.00	$6.00
T107	Hudnut, Selma - ***The Redhead And The Roan*** [1966]	$1.00	$3.00	$6.00
T108	Unger, Arthur & Berman, Carmel - ***What Girls Want To Know About Boys*** [1966]	$1.00	$3.00	$6.00
T109	Osborne, Dr. Ernest G. - ***How To Deal With Parents And Other Problems*** [1966]	$1.00	$3.00	$6.00
T110	Lewiton, Mina - ***First Love*** [1966]	$1.00	$3.00	$6.00
T111	Anthology edited by Groff Conklin - ***Giants Unleashed*** [1966]	$1.35	$4.00	$8.00
T112	Sinclair, Upton - ***The Gnomobile*** [1966]	$1.00	$3.00	$6.00
T113	Porter, Mark - ***Set Point*** [1966]	$1.00	$3.00	$6.00
T114	Allen, Betsy - ***The Green Island Mystery*** [1966]	$1.00	$3.00	$6.00
T115	Allen, Betsy - ***The Ghost Wore White*** [1966] Photo cover.	$1.00	$3.00	$6.00
T116	Allen, Betsy - ***The Yellow Warning*** [1966]	$1.00	$3.00	$6.00
T117	Allen, Betsy - ***The Gray Menace*** [1966]	$1.00	$3.00	$6.00
T118	Allan, Mabel Esther - ***Mystery On The Fourteenth Floor*** [1966]	$1.00	$3.00	$6.00
T119	Johnston, William - ***Sorry, Chief . . .*** [1966] PBO. Photo cover. "Get Smart" #2. TV tie-in.	$1.50	$5.00	$10.00
T121	Johnston, William - ***Get Smart Once Again!*** [1966] PBO. Photo cover. "Get Smart" #3. TV tie-in.	$1.50	$5.00	$10.00
T122	Dillon, Eilis - ***A Family Of Foxes*** [1966]	$1.00	$3.00	$6.00
T123	Dolim, Mary N. & Kakacek, Gen - ***Four Hands For Mercy*** [1966]	$1.00	$3.00	$6.00
T124	Goodin, Peggy - ***Clementine*** [1966]	$1.00	$3.00	$6.00
T126	Olson, Gene - ***Three Men On Third*** [1966]	$1.00	$3.00	$6.00
T128	Allen, Betsy - ***The Brown Satchel Mystery*** [1966]	$1.00	$3.00	$6.00
T129	Allen, Betsy - ***Peril In Pink*** [1966]	$1.00	$3.00	$6.00
T130	Allen, Betsy - ***The Silver Secret*** [1966]	$1.00	$3.00	$6.00
T131	Allen, Betsy - ***The Mystery Of The Ruby Queens*** [1966] Photo cover.	$1.00	$3.00	$6.00
T133	Mitchell, Jerry - ***Sandy Koufax*** [1966]	$1.35	$4.00	$8.00
T134	Kantor, MacKinlay - ***Follow Me, Boys*** [1966]	$1.00	$3.00	$6.00
T137	? - ***Slashing Blades*** [1966]	$1.00	$3.00	$6.00
T138	Ford, Bill - ***Lt. Robin Crusoe, U.S.N.*** [1966] PBO. Photo cover. Movie tie-in.	$1.00	$3.00	$6.00
T139	Hano, Arnold - ***Willie Mays*** [1966]	$1.35	$4.00	$8.00

		G	VG	F
T140	Johnston, William - ***Max Smart And The Perilous Pellets*** [1966] PBO. Photo cover. "Get Smart" #4. TV tie-in.	$1.50	$5.00	$10.00
T141	Graham, Kenneth - ***The Wind In The Willows*** [1966]	$1.00	$3.00	$6.00
T142	Butterworth, W.E. - ***Fast Green Car*** [1966]	$1.00	$3.00	$6.00
T143	McNair, Kate - ***A Sense Of Magic*** [1966]	$1.00	$3.00	$6.00
T144	Cohen, Florence Chanock - ***Portrait Of Deborah*** [1967]	$1.00	$3.00	$6.00
T145	? - ***Duel On The Cinders*** [1967]	$1.00	$3.00	$6.00
T147	Emerson, Donald - ***Span Across The River*** [1967]	$1.00	$3.00	$6.00
T149	Anthology edited by Walter B. Gibson - ***The Fine Art Of Spying*** [1967] PBO.	$2.00	$6.00	$12.00
T151	Brink, Carol Ryrie - ***Andy Buckram's Tin Men*** [1967]	$1.00	$3.00	$6.00
T152	Whitney, Phyllis A. - ***Secret Of The Emerald Star*** [1967]	$1.00	$3.00	$6.00
T154	Johnston, William - ***Missed It By That Much!*** [1967] PBO. Photo cover. "Get Smart" #5. TV tie-in.	$1.50	$5.00	$10.00
T155	Johnston, William - ***Captain Nice*** [1967]	$1.35	$4.00	$8.00
T156	Robertson, Keith - ***Henry Reed, Inc.*** [1967]	$1.00	$3.00	$6.00
T157	Robertson, Keith - ***Henry Reed's Journal*** [1967] Cover art by Robert McCloskey.	$1.00	$3.00	$6.00
T158	Robertson, Keith - ***Henry Reed's Baby-Sitting Service*** [1967] Cover art by Robert McCloskey.	$1.00	$3.00	$6.00
T159	Johnston, William - ***And Loving It!*** [1967] PBO. Photo cover. "Get Smart" #6. TV tie-in.	$1.50	$5.00	$10.00
T161	Platt, Kin - ***Sinbad And Me*** [1967]	$1.00	$3.00	$6.00
T162	Richter, Ed - ***The Making Of A Pro Quarterback*** [1967] Photo cover.	$1.00	$3.00	$6.00
T163	Farjeon, Eleanor - ***The Glass Slipper*** [1967]	$1.00	$3.00	$6.00
T165	Seton, Ernest Thompson - ***Animal Heroes*** [1967] PBO. Photo cover.	$1.00	$3.00	$6.00
T166	Morey, Walt - ***Gentle Ben*** [1967] Photo cover. TV tie-in.	$1.00	$3.00	$6.00
T167	Kipling, Rudyard - ***The Jungle Book*** [1967] Cover art by Earl Mayan.	$2.00	$6.00	$12.00
T168	Seton, Ernest Thompson - ***Wild Animals I Have Known*** [1967]	$1.00	$3.00	$6.00
T169	Sullivan, George - ***Wilt Chamberlain*** [1967]	$1.25	$3.75	$7.50
T170	Verney, John - ***Friday's Tunnel*** [1967]	$1.00	$3.00	$6.00
T171	Gibson, Walter - ***Adaptation - Twilight Zone Revisited*** [1967] TV tie-in.	$2.00	$6.00	$12.00
T173	Watson, Sally - ***To Build A Land*** [1967]	$1.00	$3.00	$6.00
T174	Johnston, William - ***Max Smart-The Spy Who Went Out To The Cold*** [1968] PBO. Photo cover. "Get Smart" #7. TV tie-in.	$1.50	$5.00	$10.00
T177	Olney, Ross R. - ***Daredevils Of The Speedway*** [1968]	$1.00	$3.00	$6.00
T179	Anthology - ***My Greatest Day In Baseball*** [1968] Photo cover.	$1.35	$4.00	$8.00
T180	Haas, Ben - ***The Troubled Summer*** [1968] Photo cover.	$1.00	$3.00	$6.00
T181	Henry, Will - ***Custer's Last Stand*** [1968] Cover art by Ronnie Lesser.	$1.00	$3.00	$6.00
T182	Anthology - ***Red Skelton's Favorite Ghost Stories*** [1968] Cover art by H. Kane.	$2.00	$6.00	$12.00
T183	*Golf Digest* magazine - ***Arnold Palmer*** [1968]	$1.25	$3.75	$7.50
T184	Walker, Mort - ***Beetle Bailey*** [1968] Cartoon book.	$2.50	$7.50	$15.00
T188	Lombardi, Vince - ***Run To Daylight!*** [1968]	$1.00	$3.00	$6.00
T190	Parrish, Anne - ***Floating Island*** [1968]	$1.00	$3.00	$6.00
T191	Johnston, William - ***Max Smart Loses Control*** [1968] PBO. Photo cover. "Get Smart" #8. TV tie-in.	$1.50	$5.00	$10.00
T194	Anthology - ***Battle-Great True Stories Of Combat In W.W. II*** [1968] Photo cover.	$1.00	$3.00	$6.00
5300	Surface, William - ***The Poisoned Ivy*** [1968]	$1.00	$3.00	$6.00
5302	Friend, Ed - ***The High Chaparral: Coyote Gold*** [1969] PBO. Photo cover. TV tie-in.	$1.00	$3.00	$6.00
5303	Penfield, Thomas - ***Buried Treasure In The U.S.*** [1969]	$1.00	$3.00	$6.00

		G	VG	F
5305	Walker, Mort - ***Fall Out Laughing, Beetle Bailey*** [1969] Cartoon book.	$2.50	$7.50	$15.00
5306	Del Rey, Lester - ***Attack From Atlantis*** [1969]	$1.00	$3.00	$6.00
5307	McGovern, James - ***Martin Bormann*** [1969] Photo cover. 8 pages of photos.	$1.00	$3.00	$6.00
5308	Steele, Alex - ***They Came From The Sea: The New People*** [1968] PBO. Photo cover. TV tie-in.	$1.35	$4.00	$8.00
5311	Verney, John - ***February's Road*** [1969]	$1.00	$3.00	$6.00
5312	Blake, Bud - ***Tiger*** [1969]	$1.00	$3.00	$6.00
5320	Gibson, Walter - ***Grove Of Doom*** [1969] Cover art by Milton Charles. "The Shadow".	$2.00	$6.00	$12.00
5322	Tarkington, Booth - ***Penrod*** [1969]	$1.00	$3.00	$6.00
5325	Walters, Hugh - ***First On The Moon*** [1969]	$1.00	$3.00	$6.00
5326	Johnston, William - ***Max Smart And The Ghastly Ghost Affair*** [1969] PBO. Photo cover. "Get Smart" #9. TV tie-in.	$1.50	$5.00	$10.00
5338	Blake, Bud - ***Tiger Turns On*** [1969] PBO. All comic strips.	$1.35	$4.00	$8.00
5365	Anthology - ***Can You Top This?*** [1970] Cover by Jack Davis. TV tie-in.	$1.00	$3.00	$6.00

Thirteen Green.

NN	Hamm, William - ***The Gray Shadows Of Death*** [1964] PBO.	$2.50	$7.50	$15.00

Three Star Books.

101	Cotton, Jerry - ***In The Lion's Den*** [1965]	$1.50	$5.00	$10.00
102	Anthology - ***Great Science-Fiction*** [1965] PBO. Cover art by M. Seltzer.	$1.50	$5.00	$10.00
104	Anthology - ***Ian Fleming's Incredible Creation*** [1965] PBO.	$1.50	$5.00	$10.00

Thriller Novel Classics. New York: Novel Selections. Digest Size.

1	Frost, Frederick - ***Secret Agent No. 1*** [1941] Photo cover.	$1.35	$4.00	$8.00
2	Fairlie, Gerald - ***Bulldog Drummond On Dartmoor*** [1941] Photo cover.	$1.35	$4.00	$8.00
3	Robertson, Colin - ***The Yellow Strangler*** [1941] Photo cover.	$1.35	$4.00	$8.00
4	Rohmer, Sax - ***The Insidious Dr. Fu-Manchu*** [1941] Photo cover.	$3.50	$10.00	$20.00
5	Horler, Sydney - ***Lord Of Terror*** [1941] Photo cover.	$2.50	$7.50	$15.00
6	Worts, George F. - ***Murder And The Secret Weapon*** [1941] Photo cover.	$2.50	$7.50	$15.00
7	Frost, Frederick - ***Spy Meets Spy*** [1941] Photo cover.	$1.35	$4.00	$8.00
8	Packard, Frank L. - ***Jimmy Dale And The Phantom Clue*** [1941] Photo cover.	$1.35	$4.00	$8.00
9	Rohmer, Sax - ***The Golden Scorpion*** [1942] Photo cover.	$3.50	$10.00	$20.00
10	Gregory, Franklin - ***The White Wolf*** [1942] Photo cover.	$4.00	$12.50	$25.00
11	Beeding, Francis - ***Death In 4 Letters*** [1942] Photo cover.	$1.35	$4.00	$8.00
12	Frost, Frederick - ***The Bamboo Whistle*** [1942] Photo cover.	$1.35	$4.00	$8.00
13	Chambers, Whitman - ***Invasion*** [1942]	$4.00	$12.50	$25.00
14	McNeile, H.C. - ***Bulldog Drummond Meets A Murderess*** [1942] Photo cover.	$1.35	$4.00	$8.00
15	Crosby, Lee - ***Terror By Night*** [1942] Photo cover.	$1.35	$4.00	$8.00
16	Charteris, Leslie - ***The Saint In Miami*** [1942] Photo cover.	$1.35	$4.00	$8.00
17	Holding, Elisabeth Saxany - ***Trial By Murder*** [1942] Photo cover.	$1.35	$4.00	$8.00
18	Knight, Kathleen Moore - ***Murder Greets Jean Holton*** [1942]	$1.35	$4.00	$8.00
19	Beeding, Francis - ***Eleven Were Brave*** [1942]	$1.35	$4.00	$8.00
20	Crosby, Lee - ***Night Attack*** [1942]	$1.35	$4.00	$8.00
21	King, Rufus - ***Design In Evil*** [1943] Photo cover.	$1.35	$4.00	$8.00
22	Boutell, Anita - ***Cradled In Fear*** [1943] Photo cover.	$1.35	$4.00	$8.00
23	Carr, John Dickson - ***Poison In Jest*** [1943] Photo cover.	$2.00	$6.00	$12.00
24	Leonard, Charles L. - ***Deadline For Destruction*** [1943] Photo cover.	$1.35	$4.00	$8.00

		G	VG	F
25	Crosby, Lee - ***Doors To Death*** [1944] Photo cover.	$1.35	$4.00	$8.00
26	Davis, Frederick C. - ***Deep Lay The Dead*** [1944]	$1.50	$5.00	$10.00
27	Leonard, Charles L. - ***Assignment To Death*** [1944] Photo cover.	$1.35	$4.00	$8.00
28	O'Neil, Kerry - ***Death At Dakar*** [1944] Photo cover.	$1.35	$4.00	$8.00
29	Woolrich, Cornell - ***The Black Path Of Fear*** [1944] Photo cover.	$4.00	$12.50	$25.00
30	Leonard, Charles A. - ***The Secret Of The Spa*** [1944] Photo cover.	$1.35	$4.00	$8.00
31	Kelsey, Vera - ***Fear Came First*** [1944] Photo cover.	$1.35	$4.00	$8.00
32	Lee, Edward - ***Death Goes Fishing*** [1944]	$1.35	$4.00	$8.00
33	Knight, Kathleen Moore - ***Murder For Empire*** [1944]	$1.35	$4.00	$8.00
34	Chambers, Whitman - ***Action At World's End*** [1946]	$4.00	$12.50	$25.00
35	William, Peter - ***Death At Abu Mina*** [1945] Photo cover.	$1.35	$4.00	$8.00
36	Dannett, Sylvia G.L. & Bennett, Edwin - ***Defy The Tempest*** [1945] Photo cover.	$1.35	$4.00	$8.00
37	Selmark, George - ***Murder In Silence*** [1945]	$1.35	$4.00	$8.00
38	Siller, Van - ***Under A Cloud*** [1945] Photo cover.	$1.35	$4.00	$8.00
39	Ransome, Stephen - ***A Shroud For Shylock*** [1945]	$1.35	$4.00	$8.00

Thrilling Books/Novels. Digest Size.

		G	VG	F
11	Mulford, Clarence E. - ***Trail Dust*** [n.d.]	$1.35	$4.00	$8.00
12	Raine, William Macleod - ***Texas Man*** [n.d.]	$1.35	$4.00	$8.00
13	Young, Gordon - ***Holster Law*** [n.d.] Cover art by George Rozen.	$1.35	$4.00	$8.00
14	Seltzer, Charles Alden - ***Square Deal Sanderson*** [n.d.] Cover by George Rozen.	$1.35	$4.00	$8.00
15	Bower, B.M. - ***The Quirt*** [n.d.] Cover art by George Rozen.	$1.35	$4.00	$8.00
16	Robertson, Frank C. - ***Cow Country Law*** [n.d.] Cover art by George Rozen.	$1.35	$4.00	$8.00
19	Cameron, Caddo - ***Two Rangers From Texas*** [n.d.] Cover art by George Rozen.	$1.35	$4.00	$8.00
20	Mulford, Clarence, E. - ***Rustler's Valley*** [n.d.]	$1.35	$4.00	$8.00
21	Drago, Harry Sinclair - ***Trigger Gospel*** [n.d.] Cover art by Hunter Barker.	$1.35	$4.00	$8.00
22	Seltzer, Charles Alden - ***Hot Lead Trail*** [n.d.] Cover art by George Rozen.	$1.35	$4.00	$8.00
23	Young, Gordon - ***Gunman From Tulluco*** [n.d.]	$1.35	$4.00	$8.00
24	White, William Patterson - ***Heart Of The Range*** [n.d.]	$1.35	$4.00	$8.00
27	Cameron, Caddo - ***It's Hell To Be A Ranger*** [n.d.]	$1.35	$4.00	$8.00
28	Payne, Stephen - ***Riders Of The Rocker K*** [n.d.]	$1.35	$4.00	$8.00
29	Mulford, Clarence, E. - ***Bring Me His Ears*** [n.d.]	$1.35	$4.00	$8.00
30	? - ***Thorson Of Thunder Gulch*** [n.d.]	$1.35	$4.00	$8.00

Toby Press. New York: Modern Living Council. Digest Size.

		G	VG	F
NO#-1	Anthology - ***Dangerous People*** [1952] PBO. Photo cover.	$2.50	$7.50	$15.00
NO#-2	Vance, Jack - ***The Space Pirate*** [1953] PBO.	$8.00	$25.00	$50.00
NO#-3	Anthology - ***Escape*** [1953] PBO.	$2.50	$7.50	$15.00
NO#-4	Anthology - ***Private Lives*** [1952] PBO. Edited by Ellis Whitfield. Photo cover.	$2.50	$7.50	$15.00
NO#-5	Frazee, Steve - ***Sunset Showdown*** [1953] PBO. Cover by A. Leslie Ross.	$2.50	$7.50	$15.00
NO#-6	Drennan, Raymond - ***You'll Die Now!*** [1953] PBO.	$2.50	$7.50	$15.00
NO#-7	Anthology - ***Strange Ways Of Love And Hate*** [1953] PBO.	$2.50	$7.50	$15.00
NO#-8	Leifer, Fred - ***The Lil Abner Squaredance Book*** [1953] PBO. Cover art by Al Capp.	$3.50	$10.00	$20.00
NO#-9	Anthology - ***Love, Emotions & Your Health*** [1953] PBO.	$2.50	$7.50	$15.00
NO#-10	Anthology - ***How To Run A Successful Party*** [1953] Edited by McNellis, Boscowitz, & Bell. Cover art by Donald McKay.	$2.50	$7.50	$15.00

Triple Nickel, 1

Triple Nickel, 3

Triple Nickel, 21

Torch Books. Toronto: Star Publications, Inc.

		G	VG	F
3	Jordan, Gail - ***Shotgun Wedding*** [1950]	$4.00	$12.50	$25.00
4	Foster, Gerald - ***The Cat And The Mice*** [1950]	$4.00	$12.50	$25.00

Travellers Pocket Library. Toronto: Ward-Hill Books.

		G	VG	F
100	Gropper, Milton H. - ***Passion Is A Gentle Whip*** [1949]	$3.50	$10.00	$20.00
101	Callaghan, Julien - ***Passion's Mistress*** [1949]	$3.50	$10.00	$20.00
102	Lawrence, D.H. - ***Lady Chatterley's Lover*** [1949]	$3.50	$10.00	$20.00
104	Sinclair, Irving - ***Pagan In Silk*** [1949]	$3.50	$10.00	$20.00
106	Thomas, Virginia - ***Speak The Sin Softly*** [1949]	$3.50	$10.00	$20.00

Triple Nickel Books. New York: Solomon & Gelman, Inc. Digest Size.

		G	VG	F
1	Wilson, Nat - ***The Adventures Of Davy Crockett*** [1955] PBO.	$5.00	$15.00	$30.00
2	Wilson, Nat - ***Danger From The Mountain*** [1955] PBO.	$5.00	$15.00	$30.00
3	Wilson, Nat - ***The Life Of Wild Bill Hickok*** [1955] PBO.	$5.00	$15.00	$30.00
4	Wilson, Nat - ***Thunder At Roaring Trail*** [1955] PBO.	$5.00	$15.00	$30.00
5	Carlton, Lucy - ***The Mystery Of The Egyptian Museum*** [1955] PBO.	$5.00	$15.00	$30.00
6	Benwood, Arthur - ***Riddle Of The Sunken Ship*** [1955] PBO.	$5.00	$15.00	$30.00
7	Benwood, Arthur - ***Castle Of Curious Creatures*** [1956] PBO.	$5.00	$15.00	$30.00
8	Benwood, Arthur - ***Mystery Of The Marble Face*** [1956]	$5.00	$15.00	$30.00
9	Benwood, Arthur - ***The Secret Of Canyon Creek*** [1956]	$5.00	$15.00	$30.00
10	Carlton, Lucy - ***The Riddle Of The Glowing Marble*** [1956]	$5.00	$15.00	$30.00
21	Benwood, Arthur - ***Mystery Of The Marlow Mansion*** [1955] PBO. Cover art by Nina Albright.	$5.00	$15.00	$30.00
22	Benwood, Arthur - ***The Secret Of Crazy Cavern*** [1955] PBO.	$5.00	$15.00	$30.00

Trophy Books. Chicago: Royce Publishers.

		G	VG	F
401	Anthology - ***Smile, Brother, Smile!*** [1946] PBO. Cover art by Axelrod. Color Illustrations.	$12.50	$37.50	$75.00
402	Ferguson, W.B.M. - ***The Pilditch Puzzle*** [1946] Cover art by Cirkle. Color Illustrations.	$12.50	$37.50	$75.00

Twentieth Century Thrillers. Racine, WI: Whitman Publishing Co.

		G	VG	F
790-1(DJ)	Kane, Kaspar - ***The Gleaming Blade*** [1939] Dust-jacketed edition.	$8.00	$25.00	$50.00
790-1	Kane, Kaspar - ***The Gleaming Blade*** [1939]	$4.00	$12.50	$25.00
790-2	MacIsaac, Fred - ***M.D. - Doctor Of Murder*** [1939]	$4.00	$12.50	$25.00
790-2(DJ)	MacIsaac, Fred - ***M.D. - Doctor Of Murder*** [1939] Dust-jacketed edition.	$8.00	$25.00	$50.00

		G	VG	F
790-3	MacIsaac, Fred - ***Murder C.O.D.*** [1939]	$4.00	$12.50	$25.00
790-3(DJ)	MacIsaac, Fred - ***Murder C.O.D.*** [1939] Dust-jacketed edition.	$8.00	$25.00	$50.00
790-4(DJ)	MacIsaac, Fred - ***The Wild Man Of Cape Cod*** [1939] Dust-jacketed edition.	$8.00	$25.00	$50.00
790-4	MacIsaac, Fred - ***The Wild Man Of Cape Cod*** [1939]	$4.00	$12.50	$25.00
790-5(DJ)	Moore, Frank - ***Five Keys To Mystery*** [1939] Dust-jacketed edition.	$8.00	$25.00	$50.00
790-5	Moore, Frank - ***Five Keys To Mystery*** [1939]	$4.00	$12.50	$25.00
790-6	Ross, Donald - ***Dead Men Tell Tales*** [1939]	$4.00	$12.50	$25.00
790-6(DJ)	Ross, Donald - ***Dead Men Tell Tales*** [1939] Dust-jacketed edition.	$8.00	$25.00	$50.00
790-7(DJ)	Ross, Donald - ***The Alligator Ring*** [1939] Dust-jacketed edition.	$8.00	$25.00	$50.00
790-7	Ross, Donald - ***The Alligator Ring*** [1939]	$4.00	$12.50	$25.00
790-8	Ross, Donald - ***The Devil Was Kind*** [1939]	$4.00	$12.50	$25.00
790-8(DJ)	Ross, Donald - ***The Devil Was Kind*** [1939] Dust-jacketed edition.	$8.00	$25.00	$50.00

Uni Books. Digest Size.

		G	VG	F
NN(2)	Booth, Ray - ***Red Hot*** [1951] Photo cover.	$2.50	$7.50	$15.00
3	Gaddis, Peggy - ***Unfaithful Wives*** [1951] Photo cover.	$2.50	$7.50	$15.00
4	Gates, Eleanor - ***Wicked*** [1951] Photo cover.	$2.50	$7.50	$15.00
5	Bramson, Karen - ***Sins Of A Paris Doctor*** [1951] Photo cover.	$2.50	$7.50	$15.00
6	Grant, Richard - ***Man Bait*** [1951] Photo cover.	$2.50	$7.50	$15.00
7	Branch, Florenz - ***Male For Sale*** [1951] Photo cover.	$2.50	$7.50	$15.00
8	Lewis, Dana - ***Backstage Sin*** [1951] Photo cover.	$2.50	$7.50	$15.00
9	Pritchard, Janet - ***Warped Women*** [1951] PBO. Photo cover.	$3.50	$10.00	$20.00
10	Pitigrilli, M. - ***Without Consent*** [1951] Photo cover.	$2.50	$7.50	$15.00
13	Meeker, Richard - ***Torment*** [1951] Photo cover.	$2.50	$7.50	$15.00
14	Williams, Wright - ***Stripper!*** [1951] Photo cover.	$2.50	$7.50	$15.00
15	Reed, David V. - ***The Thing That Made Love*** [1951] PBO.	$5.00	$15.00	$30.00
16	Martin, Charles N. - ***Raw Passion*** [1951]	$2.50	$7.50	$15.00
17	Branch, Florenz - ***Scandalous Affair*** [1951] Photo cover.	$2.50	$7.50	$15.00
18	Arthur, William - ***Love Cheat*** [1951] Photo cover.	$2.50	$7.50	$15.00
19	de Mexico, N.R. - ***Marijuana Girl*** [1951] Photo cover.	$6.00	$20.00	$40.00
20	Williams, Wright - ***Side Street*** [1951] Photo cover.	$2.50	$7.50	$15.00
21	Gaddis, Peggy - ***Hideaway*** [1951] Photo cover.	$2.50	$7.50	$15.00
22	Appel, H.M. - ***Tainted Passions*** [1951] Photo cover.	$2.50	$7.50	$15.00
23	Pritchard, Janet - ***Sin Ship*** [1951]	$3.00	$9.00	$18.00
24	Abram, Arthur - ***Badge Of Shame*** [1952] PBO. Cover art by Walter Popp.	$3.00	$9.00	$18.00
25	Williams, Wright - ***River Barge Virgin*** [1952] Photo cover.	$2.50	$7.50	$15.00
26	Foster, Gerald - ***The Fiend*** [1952]	$3.00	$9.00	$18.00
27	Lawrence, Ann - ***Jezebel's Daughter*** [1952]	$2.50	$7.50	$15.00
28	Jordan, Gail - ***Unleashed Woman*** [1952]	$2.50	$7.50	$15.00
29	Appel, H.M. - ***Brutal Kisses*** [1952]	$2.50	$7.50	$15.00
30	Grant, Richard - ***Eurasian Girl*** [1952] Cover art by Warren King.	$2.50	$7.50	$15.00
31	Gaddis, Peggy - ***Doctor Prescott's Secret*** [1952] PBO.	$2.50	$7.50	$15.00
32	West, Ben - ***Loves Of A Girl Wrestler*** [1952] Cover art by Ed Chan.	$3.00	$9.00	$18.00
33	Poynter, Beulah - ***White Trash*** [1952] PBO.	$3.00	$9.00	$18.00
34	Semple, Gordon - ***Resort Hostess*** [1952] Cover by Ray App.	$2.50	$7.50	$15.00
35	Drake, H.B. - ***Slave Ship*** [1952]	$3.50	$10.00	$20.00
36	Lawrence, Ann - ***Hoyden Of The Hills*** [1952]	$2.50	$7.50	$15.00
37	Jordan, Gail - ***Student Nurse*** [1952]	$2.50	$7.50	$15.00
38	West, Ben - ***Secrets Of A Co-Ed*** [1952] Cover art by Kampen.	$2.50	$7.50	$15.00
39	Semple, Gordon - ***Pleasure Resort Women*** [1952] PBO.	$2.50	$7.50	$15.00
41	Saxon, John - ***She Devil*** [1952]	$2.50	$7.50	$15.00
42	Harragan, Steve - ***Side-Show Girl*** [1952]	$3.50	$10.00	$20.00

Uni Book, 55

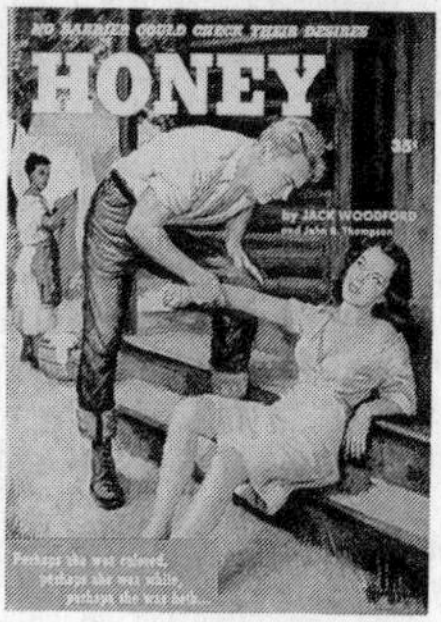

Uni Book, 72

Uni Book, 74

		G	VG	F
43	Harragan, Steve - ***The Queer Sisters*** [1952] PBO. Cover art by Bernard Safran.	$3.50	$10.00	$20.00
44	Harragan, Steve - ***Sin Is A Redhead*** [1952] Cover art by Geygan.	$3.50	$10.00	$20.00
45	Wall, Evans - ***Bad Sister*** [1953] Photo cover.	$2.50	$7.50	$15.00
46	Harragan, Steve - ***Smuggled Sin*** [1953] PBO.	$3.50	$10.00	$20.00
47	Harragan, Steve - ***Kiss Of The Damned*** [1953] PBO.	$3.50	$10.00	$20.00
48	Brenning, L.H. - ***Woman Of Paris*** [1953]	$2.50	$7.50	$15.00
49	Roberts, Luke - ***Reefer Club*** [1953] PBO. Cover by Warren King.	$5.50	$17.50	$35.00
50	Wall, Evans - ***River Woman*** [1953]	$2.50	$7.50	$15.00
51	Mitchell, Francis - ***Dirt Farm*** [1953]	$2.50	$7.50	$15.00
52	Harragan, Steve - ***The Shayne Dame*** [1953] PBO.	$3.50	$10.00	$20.00
53	Clay, Manning - ***Wild Body*** [1953]	$2.50	$7.50	$15.00
54	Harragan, Steve - ***Carney's Burlesque*** [1953] PBO. Cover art by Walter Popp.	$3.50	$10.00	$20.00
55	Ford, Jean - ***Mountain Woman*** [1953]	$2.50	$7.50	$15.00
56	Freeman, Kelsey - ***Her Last Lover*** [1953] Cover art by Walter Popp.	$2.50	$7.50	$15.00
57	Harragan, Steve - ***Three Bad Girls*** [1953] PBO.	$3.50	$10.00	$20.00
58	Whittington, Harry - ***Cracker Girl*** [1953] PBO.	$5.50	$17.50	$35.00
59	Carruthers, Margaret - ***Another Man's Wife*** [1953] Cover art by Safran.	$2.50	$7.50	$15.00
60	Woodford, Jack & Thompson, John B. - ***Savage Eve*** [1953] PBO.	$2.50	$7.50	$15.00
61	Winston, Daoma - ***Runaway Blonde*** [1953]	$2.50	$7.50	$15.00
62	Willis, George - ***Hungry For Love*** [1953]	$2.50	$7.50	$15.00
63	Woodford, Jack - ***Passion In The Pines*** [1953] Cover art by Bernard Safran.	$3.00	$9.00	$18.00
64	Harragan, Steve - ***Cuban Heel*** [1953]	$3.50	$10.00	$20.00
65	Bogar, Jeff - ***Hillbilly In High Heels*** [1953] PBO.	$3.00	$9.00	$18.00
66	Boltin, Bill - ***Witch On Wheels*** [1953]	$2.50	$7.50	$15.00
67	Woodford, Jack - ***Male Virgin*** [1953] Cover art by Bernard Safran.	$2.50	$7.50	$15.00
68	Pritchard, Janet - ***Country Club Cheat*** [1953] PBO.	$2.50	$7.50	$15.00
69	Boger, Jeff - ***Confessions Of A Chinatown Moll*** [1953] PBO.	$2.50	$7.50	$15.00
70	Whittington, Harry - ***Wild Oats*** [1953] PBO.	$5.50	$17.50	$35.00
71	Woodford, Jack & Thompson, John B. - ***Swamp Hoyden*** [1953].	$3.00	$9.00	$18.00
72	Woodford, Jack & Thompson, John B. - ***Honey*** [1953]	$3.00	$9.00	$18.00
73	Hitt, Orrie - ***Cabin Fever*** [1953]	$2.50	$7.50	$15.00
74	Rifkin, Leo & Norman, Tony - ***Gang Girl*** [1953] Photo cover.	$4.00	$12.50	$25.00
75	Roberts, Luke - ***Harlem Doctor*** [1953] PBO.	$2.50	$7.50	$15.00
76	Lucas, Robert - ***Below The Belt*** [1953]	$2.50	$7.50	$15.00

		G	VG	F
77	Thompson, John B. - ***Bayou Girl*** [1953]	$3.00	$9.00	$18.00
78	Matthews, Jr., Ernest L. - ***Out Of Bounds*** [1953]	$2.50	$7.50	$15.00

Unique.

109	Judson, Jayne - ***Summer Artist*** [1966]	$1.50	$5.00	$10.00
115	Duclos, Lois - ***Just Once*** [1967] PBO. Cover by Bill Ward.	$2.50	$7.50	$15.00
120	Delon, Eve - ***Maid To Please*** [1967] PBO. Cover by Bill Ward.	$2.50	$7.50	$15.00
121	Allison, Glenn - ***In And Out*** [1967] Cover by Bill Ward.	$2.50	$7.50	$15.00
122	Shaw, Neil - ***Big Score*** [1967] Cover by Bill Ward.	$2.50	$7.50	$15.00
127	Lambert, Ruth - ***Crafty Dames*** [1967] PBO. Cover by Bill Ward.	$2.50	$7.50	$15.00
138	Marshall, Bill - ***Hollywood Madness*** [1967] Cover by Bill Ward.	$3.50	$10.00	$20.00
140	Willow, Peter (Dixon, Arnold) - ***Extra Duty*** [1967] PBO. Cover by Bill Ward.	$2.50	$7.50	$15.00

Universal Giant Editions. New York: Universal Publishing.

1	Whittington, Harry/Williams, Idabel - ***Prime Sucker/The Hussy*** [1952] PBO.	$10.00	$30.00	$60.00
2	Stroheim, Erich Von - ***Paprika*** [n.d.]	$3.50	$10.00	$20.00
3	Klingman, Lawrence & Green, Gerald - ***His Majesty O'Keefe*** [1953]	$2.50	$7.50	$15.00
4	Harragan, Steve - ***Dope Doll/The Bigamy Kiss*** [n.d.] PBO.	$4.00	$12.50	$25.00
5	Leiber, Fritz/Williams, David - ***The Sinful Ones/Bulls, Blood And Passion*** [1953] PBO.	$4.00	$12.50	$25.00
6	Marston, William - ***The Private Life Of Julius Caesar*** [1953] Cover by Geygan.	$2.50	$7.50	$15.00
7	Hartt, Jon/Dean, Elsie - ***Savage Mistress/Concubine*** [1953] PBO.	$2.50	$7.50	$15.00
8	Taylor, Valerie/Lucas, Curtis - ***The Lusty Land/Forbidden Fruit*** [1953] PBO.	$3.00	$9.00	$18.00
9	MacArthur, Arthur - ***Aphrodite's Lover*** [1953]	$2.50	$7.50	$15.00
10	Anthology - ***Memoirs Of Casanova*** [1953] 3 volumes in 1 book.	$2.50	$7.50	$15.00
11	Mundy, Talbot/Cobb, Humphrey - ***The Queen's Warrant/Paths Of Glory*** [1953] PBO.	$3.00	$9.00	$18.00

Universal Romance. Digest Size.

NO#-1	Barr, Cecil - ***Any Man's Woman*** [n.d.] Photo cover.	$4.00	$12.50	$25.00

Uptown Books. Los Angeles: Uptown Publishing Co.

700	Tyler, Greg - ***He Kissed Her There*** [1962]	$1.25	$3.75	$7.50
702	Davidson, John - ***Blues For A Dead Lover*** [1962] PBO.	$1.25	$3.75	$7.50
703	Knerr, Michael - ***The Sex Life Of The Gods*** [1962] PBO.	$2.50	$7.50	$15.00
704	Gerwin, Walter - ***The Beds I Lie On*** [n.d.]	$1.25	$3.75	$7.50
705	Davidson, John - ***Woman Trap*** [n.d.]	$1.25	$3.75	$7.50

Value Books.

101	Alger, Horatio - ***The Young Adventurer*** [n.d.]	$1.50	$5.00	$10.00
102	Alger, Horatio - ***Strive And Succeed*** [n.d.]	$1.50	$5.00	$10.00
103	Alger, Horatio - ***Do And Dare*** [n.d.]	$1.50	$5.00	$10.00
104	Alger, Horatio - ***Brave And Bold*** [n.d.]	$1.50	$5.00	$10.00
105	Alger, Horatio - ***Making His Way*** [n.d.]	$1.50	$5.00	$10.00

Van Kampen Press.

NN-1	Barnaby, George - ***Burt Judson, Detective And His Secret Agents*** [1949] PBO.	$2.50	$7.50	$15.00
NN-2	Author Unknown - ***The Sugar Creek Gang Goes North*** [1949] PBO.	$2.50	$7.50	$15.00
NN-3	Author Unknown - ***Adventure In An Indian Cemetery*** [1949] PBO.	$2.50	$7.50	$15.00

		G	VG	F
NN-4	Author Unknown - ***The Sugar Creek Gang Digs For Treasure*** [1949] PBO.	$2.50	$7.50	$15.00
NN-5	Author Unknown - ***North Woods Manhunt*** [1949] PBO.	$2.50	$7.50	$15.00
NN-6	Author Unknown - ***The Haunted House At Sugar Creek*** [1949] PBO.	$2.50	$7.50	$15.00

Vanitas Books. Cambridge, MA: Harvard Lampoon.

V-4402	Fl*m*ng, I*n - ***Alligator*** [1963] PBO. One-shot. Ian Fleming parody.	$3.50	$10.00	$20.00

Vega Books. Clovis/Fresno, CA: Vega Books, Inc.

V-1	Woolfe, Byron - ***The Animal Urge*** [1960] PBO.	$1.35	$4.00	$8.00
V-3	Turni, Marie - ***Cousin Jess*** [1960] PBO.	$1.35	$4.00	$8.00
V-4	Brandon, Ralph - ***Joy Killer*** [1960] PBO.	$1.35	$4.00	$8.00
V-5	Spears, Francine - ***Burden Of Guilt*** [1960] PBO.	$1.35	$4.00	$8.00
V-6	Harvey, Linda - ***Executive Bed*** [1960] PBO.	$1.35	$4.00	$8.00
V-7	Stacy, Jan - ***The Takers*** [1960] PBO.	$1.35	$4.00	$8.00
V-8	Gooch, Mary L. - ***Included Out*** [1960]	$1.25	$3.75	$7.50
V-9	Miller, Frank S. - ***Murder's For The Birds*** [1961] PBO.	$1.35	$4.00	$8.00
V-10	Turni, Marie - ***The Opposite Six*** [1961] PBO.	$1.35	$4.00	$8.00
V-11	Foster, John - ***Campus Iniquities*** [1961] PBO.	$1.35	$4.00	$8.00
V-12	Roberts, Willo L. - ***Murder Is So Easy*** [1961] PBO.	$1.35	$4.00	$8.00
V-13	Cannon, Frank - ***Satan In Malibu*** [1961] PBO.	$1.35	$4.00	$8.00
V-14	Bishop, George - ***Destination Death*** [1961]	$1.25	$3.75	$7.50
V-15	Stephens, Dave - ***The Elusive Clue*** [1961]	$1.35	$4.00	$8.00
V-16	Gregory, Stephan - ***Frame Up*** [1961] PBO.	$1.35	$4.00	$8.00
V-17	Willie, Ennis - ***Vice Town*** [1961]	$1.25	$3.75	$7.50
V-18	Roberts, Willo L. - ***The Suspected Four*** [1961]	$1.25	$3.75	$7.50
V-19	Miller, Frank S. - ***Knock On Any Head*** [1961]	$1.25	$3.75	$7.50
V-20	Marmor, Arnold - ***All For One*** [1961]	$1.25	$3.75	$7.50
V-21	Moore, Herbert L. - ***Hayseed*** [1961]	$1.25	$3.75	$7.50
V-22	McCretton, Michael - ***Beauty Can Kill*** [1961] PBO.	$1.35	$4.00	$8.00
V-23	Rimel, Duane - ***The River Is Cold*** [1961]	$1.25	$3.75	$7.50
V-24	Fullilove, James - ***The Suckers*** [1961]	$1.25	$3.75	$7.50
V-25	Vance, Guy - ***Savage Summer*** [1961]	$1.25	$3.75	$7.50
V-26	Gilman, Wilson - ***The Pagans Three*** [1961]	$1.25	$3.75	$7.50
V-27	Strand, Bunny - ***Reaching High*** [1961] PBO.	$1.35	$4.00	$8.00
V-28	Howe, Arthur A. - ***I Wanted The Killer*** [1961]	$1.25	$3.75	$7.50
V-29	Vail, Thomas - ***Weekend To Danger*** [1961]	$1.25	$3.75	$7.50
V-30	Spruill, Jock - ***Murder By Proxy*** [1961]	$1.25	$3.75	$7.50
V-31	Cannon, Frank - ***Satan In Malibu*** [1964]	$1.25	$3.75	$7.50
V-32	Makagon, Thomas K. - ***All Killers Aren't Ugly*** [1964]	$1.25	$3.75	$7.50
V-33	Pearson, Robert E. - ***The Fat Boy Must Die*** [1964]	$1.25	$3.75	$7.50
V-34	Ryerson, Martin - ***Press Agent For Murder*** [1964]	$1.25	$3.75	$7.50
V-35	Davis, Steve - ***Stalk The Killer*** [1964]	$1.25	$3.75	$7.50
V-36	Groh, Edwin C. - ***Jackasses Of Los Causes*** [1964] PBO.	$1.35	$4.00	$8.00
V-37	Haynes, Floyd - ***Beach Maverick*** [1964]	$1.25	$3.75	$7.50
V-38	Randolph, Dade - ***The Devastating Urge*** [1964] PBO.	$1.35	$4.00	$8.00
V-39	Turni, Marie - ***Beyond The Realm*** [1964]	$1.25	$3.75	$7.50
V-40	Ryerson, Martin - ***Doctor vs. Murder*** [1964]	$1.25	$3.75	$7.50
V-41	Cannon, Frank - ***Hide In Hell*** [1964]	$1.25	$3.75	$7.50
V-44	Whiffen, Jack - ***Convention For Killers*** [1965]	$1.25	$3.75	$7.50
V-45	English, Arnold - ***Edge Of Violence*** [1965]	$1.25	$3.75	$7.50
V-51	Davis, A.J. - ***Girl In Every Bush*** [1966] PBO.	$1.35	$4.00	$8.00
V-55	Duffy, Robert M. - ***Sin Mill*** [1966]	$1.25	$3.75	$7.50
V-57	Harmon, Charles - ***Girls' Camp*** [1966]	$1.25	$3.75	$7.50
V-58	Van Ness, Betty - ***Jane Flinn*** [1966]	$1.25	$3.75	$7.50
V-59	Winston, Arlene - ***From Sex To Eternity*** [1966]	$1.25	$3.75	$7.50
V-60	Shelton, Arlene - ***Country Sex-Country Style*** [1966]	$1.25	$3.75	$7.50
V-61	Browning, Joe - ***Mingling With Swappers*** [1970]	$1.25	$3.75	$7.50

		G	VG	F
V-62	Wilde, Newton - ***Tattoo Of Lust*** [1970]	$1.25	$3.75	$7.50
V-63	Newton, Bill - ***The Naked And Depraved*** [1970]	$1.25	$3.75	$7.50
V-64	Barstow, Loraine - ***Young Judd & Three Sexy Widows*** [1970]	$1.25	$3.75	$7.50
V-65	Horn, Allan - ***Sinfully Yours*** [1970]	$1.25	$3.75	$7.50
V-66	Dean, B.J. - ***Schoolroom Stud*** [1970]	$1.25	$3.75	$7.50
V-67	Horn, Allan - ***Whore From Maupin Street*** [1970]	$1.25	$3.75	$7.50
V-68	Bunch, A. - ***Students Of Lust*** [1970]	$1.25	$3.75	$7.50
V-69	Dugan, Jerri - ***Gail Rogers, Call Girl*** [1970]	$1.25	$3.75	$7.50
V-70	Scott, Steve - ***To San Marcos And Back*** [1970] PBO.	$1.35	$4.00	$8.00
V-71	Knight, Randy - ***Sex Has No Private Hour*** [1970]	$1.25	$3.75	$7.50
V-72	Elwood, Pat - ***A Blonde To Trade*** [1970]	$1.25	$3.75	$7.50
V-73	Dugan, Jerri - ***Naked Came The Wives*** [1970]	$1.25	$3.75	$7.50
V-74	Marshall, D.J. - ***Teenage Call Girl Ring*** [1970] PBO.	$1.35	$4.00	$8.00
V-75	Best, Harry - ***A Virgin Till Love*** [1970]	$1.25	$3.75	$7.50
V-76	Trent, Alan - ***Naked Went Them All*** [1970]	$1.25	$3.75	$7.50
V-77	Best, Harry - ***Don't Call Me Queer*** [1970]	$1.25	$3.75	$7.50
V-78	Cameron, Anne - ***The Wife And Her*** [1970]	$1.25	$3.75	$7.50
V-79	Dugan, Jerry - ***Passionate Baby-Sitter*** [1970]	$1.25	$3.75	$7.50
V-80	Clark, Gregory - ***Most Sensual Moments*** [1970]	$1.25	$3.75	$7.50
V-81	Fisher, P.A. - ***While Morality Slept*** [1970]	$1.25	$3.75	$7.50
V-82	Hill, Joe - ***Rape Was Their Bag*** [1970]	$1.25	$3.75	$7.50

Vega Mystery Reader.

1	McCretton, Michael/Rimel, Duane - ***Beauty Can Kill/The River Is Cold*** [1962]	$1.35	$4.00	$8.00

Vega SF Books.

1	Zeigfreid, Karl - ***Walk Through Tomorrow*** [1963] Cover art by Fox.	$2.00	$6.00	$12.00
2	Fanthorpe, R.L. - ***Space Fury*** [1963] PBO. Cover art by Fox.	$2.00	$6.00	$12.00
3	Muller, John E. (Lionel Fanthorpe) - ***The Day The World Died*** [1963] Cover art by Fox.	$2.00	$6.00	$12.00
4	Zeigfreid, Karl - ***Radar Alert*** [1963] Cover art by Fox.	$2.00	$6.00	$12.00
5	Glynn, A.A. - ***Plan For Conquest*** [1963] Cover by Fox.	$2.00	$6.00	$12.00
6	Muller, John (Fanthorpe) - ***In The Beginning*** [1963] Cover art by Fox.	$2.00	$6.00	$12.00
7	Barton, Erle - ***The Planet Seekers*** [1963] Cover art by Fox.	$2.00	$6.00	$12.00
8	Muller, John E. (Fanthorpe) - ***Special Mission*** [1963] Cover art by Fox.	$2.00	$6.00	$12.00
9	Fane, Bron - ***Suspension*** [1963] Cover art by Fox.	$2.00	$6.00	$12.00
10	Torro, Pel - ***The Return*** [1963] Cover art by Fox.	$2.00	$6.00	$12.00
11	Muller, John (Fanthorpe) - ***The Venus Venture*** [1963] Cover art by Fox.	$2.00	$6.00	$12.00
12	Zeigfreid, Karl - ***Projection Infinity*** [1963] Cover by Fox.	$2.00	$6.00	$12.00
13	Becher, Don - ***A Ticket To Nowhere*** [1963] Cover by Fox.	$2.00	$6.00	$12.00
14	Crumley, Thomas W. - ***Star Trail*** [1966]	$2.00	$6.00	$12.00

Vega Western Library.

100	Runnels, Benny - ***Blood On Big Sandy*** [1963]	$1.25	$3.75	$7.50
101	Pierce, Wade - ***Uncertain Destiny*** [1963]	$1.25	$3.75	$7.50
102	Clark, Al - ***Trail Of Vengeance*** [1963]	$1.25	$3.75	$7.50
103	Nemec, John - ***War At Bluestem Basin*** [1963]	$1.25	$3.75	$7.50
104	Pearson, Robert E. - ***Bloody Wyoming*** [1963] PBO.	$1.25	$3.75	$7.50
105	Tuma, Marvin - ***Dangerous Guns*** [1963]	$1.25	$3.75	$7.50
106	Cuthbert, William - ***Trouble Trail*** [1963] PBO.	$1.25	$3.75	$7.50
107	Howe, Arthur A. - ***Trigger Justice*** [1963]	$1.25	$3.75	$7.50
108	Ryerson, Martin - ***Showdown At Devil's Fork*** [1963]	$1.25	$3.75	$7.50
109	Ryerson, Martin - ***Gun-Fight At Big Needles*** [1963]	$1.25	$3.75	$7.50
110	Nye, Nelson C. - ***Frontier Scout*** [1964] PBO.	$1.25	$3.75	$7.50
111	Nye, Nelson C. - ***Come A-Smokin'*** [1964]	$1.25	$3.75	$7.50

		G	VG	F
112	Howe, Arthur A. - ***Storm Ross*** [1964]	$1.25	$3.75	$7.50
113	Stark, Allen - ***Two Gun Law*** [1964]	$1.25	$3.75	$7.50

Vega Western Reader.

		G	VG	F
1	Clark, Al/Nemec, John - ***Trail Of Vengeance/War At Bluestem Basin*** [1964]	$1.35	$4.00	$8.00

Venus Books. Digest Size.

		G	VG	F
101	Gaddis, Peggy - ***Girl With No Past*** [1950]	$4.00	$12.50	$25.00
102	Sherman, Joan - ***She Wanted Love*** [1950]	$4.00	$12.50	$25.00
103	Foster, Gerald - ***Mazie: Any Man's Girl*** [1950]	$4.00	$12.50	$25.00
104	Gaddis, Peggy - ***Beach Party*** [1950]	$4.00	$12.50	$25.00
105	Gaddis, Peggy - ***Take My Love*** [1950]	$4.00	$12.50	$25.00
106	Bligh, Norman - ***Over Night*** [1950]	$4.00	$12.50	$25.00
107	Bligh, Norman - ***Play-Girl*** [1950] Cover by George Gross.	$4.00	$12.50	$25.00
108	Harvey, Gene - ***Cutie*** [1950]	$4.00	$12.50	$25.00
109	Bellamy, Harmon - ***Lover Boy*** [1950] Cover art by George Gross.	$4.00	$12.50	$25.00
110	Bellamy, Harmon - ***Hard-Boiled*** [1950]	$4.00	$12.50	$25.00
111	Quandt, Albert L. - ***Pick-up Alley*** [1950] PBO.	$4.50	$14.00	$28.00
112	Gaddis, Peggy - ***Temptation*** [1950] PBO. Cover art by George Gross.	$4.50	$14.00	$28.00
113	Clayford, James - ***Reckless!*** [1951] PBO.	$4.00	$12.50	$25.00
114	Harvey, Gene - ***Confessions Of A Carnival Dancer*** [1951] PBO.	$4.00	$12.50	$25.00
115	Quandt, Albert L. - ***Journey Into Ecstasy*** [1951] PBO.	$4.00	$12.50	$25.00
116	Gaddis, Peggy - ***One Wild Night!*** [1951] PBO. Cover art by George Gross.	$4.50	$14.00	$28.00
117	Harvey, Gene - ***Desire Is A Woman*** [1951] PBO.	$4.00	$12.50	$25.00
118	Gaddis, Peggy - ***Honey: Broadway Playgirl*** [1951] PBO.	$4.00	$12.50	$25.00
119	Charlson, David - ***No Time For Marriage*** [1951] PBO.	$4.00	$12.50	$25.00
120	Bligh, Norman - ***The Naked Night*** [1951] PBO.	$4.00	$12.50	$25.00
121	Quandt, Albert L. - ***Girl Of The Slums*** [1951] PBO.	$4.50	$14.00	$28.00
122	Gaddis, Peggy - ***Pleasure At Midnight*** [1951] PBO.	$4.00	$12.50	$25.00
123	Gaddis, Peggy - ***Emotions Of Fire*** [1951] PBO.	$4.00	$12.50	$25.00
124	Harvey, Gene - ***She Couldn't Be Good!*** [1951] PBO.	$4.00	$12.50	$25.00
125	Quandt, Albert L. - ***Thrill Me Again!*** [1951] PBO.	$4.00	$12.50	$25.00
126	Hatter, Amos - ***No Time For Sleep*** [1951] PBO.	$4.50	$14.00	$28.00
127	Gaddis, Peggy - ***Painted Lips*** [1951] PBO.	$4.00	$12.50	$25.00
128	Welles, Kermit - ***She Had What It Takes*** [1951] PBO. Cover by Rudy Nappi.	$4.50	$14.00	$28.00
129	Quandt, Albert L. - ***Big-Time Girl*** [1951] PBO.	$4.00	$12.50	$25.00
130	Bligh, Norman - ***The Men She Knew*** [1951] PBO.	$4.00	$12.50	$25.00
131	Gaddis, Peggy - ***Tough Doll*** [1951] PBO.	$4.00	$12.50	$25.00
132	Hatter, Amos - ***Lady With A Past*** [1951] PBO.	$4.00	$12.50	$25.00
133	Stonebraker, FLorence - ***She Tried To Be Good*** [1951] PBO. Cover art by Rudy Nappi.	$4.50	$14.00	$28.00
134	Marin, Arthur - ***The Doctor's Wife*** [1951] PBO. Cover by Rudy Nappi.	$4.00	$12.50	$25.00
135	Charlson, David - ***Night Nurse*** [1951] PBO.	$4.00	$12.50	$25.00
136	Arnold, William - ***Torch Singer*** [1951] PBO.	$4.00	$12.50	$25.00
137	Gaddis, Peggy - ***Lost To Desire*** [1952] PBO.	$4.00	$12.50	$25.00
138	Sherman, John - ***Reckless!*** [1952] PBO.	$4.00	$12.50	$25.00
139	Arnold, William - ***The Naked Canvas*** [1952] PBO. Cover art by George Gross.	$4.50	$14.00	$28.00
140	Stonebraker, Florence - ***Oriental Nights*** [1952] PBO. Cover art by Rudy Nappi.	$4.50	$14.00	$28.00
141	Harvey, Gene - ***Strip Street*** [1952] PBO. Cover art by Rudy Nappi.	$4.50	$14.00	$28.00

Venus Books, 170

Venus Books, 177

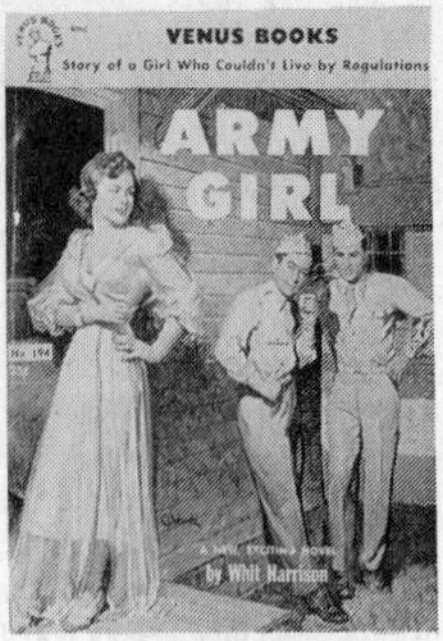

Venus Books, 194

		G	VG	F
142	Gaddis, Peggy - ***Unfaithful*** [1952] PBO. Cover art by Rudy Nappi.	$4.50	$14.00	$28.00
143	Sherman, Joan (Peggy Gaddis) - ***Lovers In The Sun*** [1952] PBO. Cover by Raymond Pease.	$4.00	$12.50	$25.00
144	Welles, Kermit - ***The Innocent Wanton*** [1952] PBO.	$4.00	$12.50	$25.00
145	Charlson, David - ***Frenchie*** [1952] PBO.	$4.00	$12.50	$25.00
146	Jordan, Gail (Peggy Gaddis) - ***Call It Marriage*** [1952] PBO.	$4.00	$12.50	$25.00
147	Tucker, Joan - ***Weekend Of Madness*** [1952] PBO.	$4.00	$12.50	$25.00
148	Bligh, Norman - ***Remembered Moment*** [1952] PBO.	$4.00	$12.50	$25.00
149	Gaddis, Peggy - ***Runaway Lovers*** [1952] PBO.	$4.00	$12.50	$25.00
150	Manning, Jane - ***The Affairs Of A Leading Lady*** [1952] PBO. Cover art by Johnson.	$4.00	$12.50	$25.00
151	Bligh, Norman - ***Young Wife*** [1952] PBO.	$4.00	$12.50	$25.00
152	Nickerson, Kate - ***Passion Is A Woman*** [1952] PBO. Cover art by Rudolph Belarski.	$4.00	$12.50	$25.00
153	Harrison, Whit (Harry Whittington) - ***Sailor's Weekend*** [1952] PBO. Cover art by Herb Tauss.	$5.50	$17.50	$35.00
154	Hatter, Amos - ***Hired Girl*** [1952] PBO.	$4.00	$12.50	$25.00
155	Charlson, David - ***Night Nurse*** [1952]	$3.50	$10.00	$20.00
156	Marin, Arthur - ***The Doctor's Wife*** [1952]	$3.50	$10.00	$20.00
157	Haskell, Frank - ***Women's Doctor*** [1952] PBO. Cover art by Rudy Nappi.	$4.00	$12.50	$25.00
158	Harrison, Whit (Harry Whittington) - ***Girl On Parole*** [1952] PBO.	$5.50	$17.50	$35.00
159	Tucker, Joan - ***Shanty Girl*** [1952] Cover art by Rudolph Belarski.	$5.00	$15.00	$30.00
160	Gaddis, Peggy - ***Farmer's Wife*** [1952] PBO.	$4.00	$12.50	$25.00
161	Harrison, Whit (Harry Whittington) - ***Army Girl*** [1952] PBO. Cover art by Rudolph Belarski.	$6.00	$20.00	$40.00
162	Bligh, Norman - ***Wayward Nurse*** [1952] Cover art by Rudolph Belarski.	$4.00	$12.50	$25.00
163	Charlson, David - ***Private Nurse*** [1952] Cover by Rudy Nappi.	$4.00	$12.50	$25.00
165	Nickerson, Kate - ***Passion Is A Woman*** [1952] Cover art by Rudolph Belarski.	$4.00	$12.50	$25.00
167	Tucker, Joan - ***Young Secretary*** [1952] PBO.	$4.00	$12.50	$25.00
168	Gaddis, Peggy - ***Backwoods Girl*** [1952] Cover art by George Gross.	$4.00	$12.50	$25.00
169	Harvey, Gene - ***Strip Street*** [1952]	$3.50	$10.00	$20.00
170	Coleman, Mitchell - ***Male Ward*** [1952] PBO. Cover art by Rudolph Belarski.	$4.00	$12.50	$25.00
171	Sherman, Joan (Peggy Gaddis) - ***Beach Girl*** [1952] Cover art by Raymond Pease.	$3.50	$10.00	$20.00

		G	VG	F
173	Haskell, Frank - ***Young Doctor*** [1952] PBO. Cover art by Rudolph Belarski.	$4.00	$12.50	$25.00
175	Manning, Jane - ***Young Sinners*** [1952] Cover art by Rudolph Belarski.	$4.00	$12.50	$25.00
176	Haskell, Frank - ***Women's Doctor*** [1952] Cover art by Rudy Nappi.	$3.50	$10.00	$20.00
177	Bligh, Norman - ***Young Wife*** [1952]	$3.50	$10.00	$20.00
178	Welles, Kermit - ***Wild Sister*** [1952]	$3.50	$10.00	$20.00
180	Sherman, Joan (Peggy Gaddis) - ***Beach Girl*** [1952]	$3.50	$10.00	$20.00
181	Hatter, Amos - ***Hired Girl*** [1952]	$3.50	$10.00	$20.00
184	Haskell, Frank - ***Hotel Doctor*** [1952]	$3.50	$10.00	$20.00
186	Bligh, Norman - ***Wayward Nurse*** [1952] Cover art by Rudolph Belarski.	$3.50	$10.00	$20.00
188	Bligh, Norman - ***Young Wife*** [1954]	$3.50	$10.00	$20.00
191	Haskell, Frank - ***Young Doctor*** [1952] Cover art by Rudolph Belarski.	$3.50	$10.00	$20.00
193	Tucker, John - ***Waterfront Club*** [1952]	$3.50	$10.00	$20.00
194	Harrison, Whit (Harry Whittington) - ***Army Girl*** [1952] Cover art by Rudolph Belarski.	$4.00	$12.50	$25.00
195	Jordan, George - ***Young Bride*** [1952]	$3.50	$10.00	$20.00
197	Arnold, William - ***Professional Model*** [1952]	$3.50	$10.00	$20.00
198	Hall, Richard - ***Hollywood Starlet*** [1952] Cover art by Rudolph Belarski.	$4.00	$12.50	$25.00

Vest Pocket Books.

		G	VG	F
VP101-102	Hitt, Orrie - ***Carnival Sin/Playpet*** [1962] PBO. Two books in slipcase. Photo covers.	$8.00	$25.00	$50.00
VP103-104	Iver, A. E./Craig, D. W. - ***Motel Girl/ Strange Sin*** [1962] Lili St. Cyr photo cover. Two books in slipcase.	$8.00	$25.00	$50.00

Vital Books. New York: Vital Publications. Digest Size.

		G	VG	F
NO#(1)	Carter, Nicholas - ***Empire Of Crime*** [1945]	$4.00	$12.50	$25.00
NO#(2)	Carter, Nicholas - ***Murder Unlimited*** [1945]	$4.00	$12.50	$25.00
NO#(3)	Carter, Nicholas - ***Death Has Green Eyes!*** [1946]	$4.00	$12.50	$25.00
NO#(4)	Carter, Nicholas - ***Park Avenue Murder!*** [1946]	$4.00	$12.50	$25.00

Vulcan Mystery. New York: Vulcan Publications. Digest Size.

		G	VG	F
NO#-1	Albert, Andrew I. - ***The Maori Murder Case*** [1944] PBO. Cover art by Hoffman.	$3.50	$10.00	$20.00
NO#-2	George, David Robinson - ***Death Meets The Deadline*** [1944] PBO.	$3.50	$10.00	$20.00
3	Foster, Richard - ***The Laughing Buddha Murders*** [1944] PBO. Cover art by Hoffman.	$3.50	$10.00	$20.00
4	Albert, Andrew I. - ***Murder For A Hollow Shell*** [1945] PBO. Cover art by Hoffman.	$3.50	$10.00	$20.00
5	Crossen, Ken - ***The Case Of The Phantom Fingerprints*** [1945] PBO. Cover art by Hoffman.	$3.50	$10.00	$20.00
6	Yates, Peter - ***Curtain Call For Murder*** [1945] PBO. Cover by Hoffman.	$3.50	$10.00	$20.00

Wee Hours.

		G	VG	F
511	Willow, Peter - ***Just Friends*** [1967] Cover by Bill Ward.	$2.50	$7.50	$15.00
517	Parker, Jon - ***Pickup*** [1967] PBO. Cover by Bill Ward.	$2.50	$7.50	$15.00
522	Willow, Peter - ***Odd Neighbors*** [1967] PBO. Cover by Bill Ward.	$2.50	$7.50	$15.00
524	Marshall, Bill - ***Society Madness*** [1967] PBO. Cover by Bill Ward.	$4.00	$12.50	$25.00
530	Willow, Peter - ***Mother In Law*** [1967] PBO. Cover by Bill Ward.	$2.50	$7.50	$15.00

		G	VG	F
531	Makagon, Thomas K. - ***Rooftop Peeper*** [1967] PBO. Cover by Bill Ward.	$2.50	$7.50	$15.00
540	Sherwood, Paula - ***Rubdown*** [1967] Cover by Bill Ward.	$2.50	$7.50	$15.00
545	Parker, Jon - ***Inside Job*** [1967] Cover by Bill Ward.	$2.50	$7.50	$15.00

West In Action. Digest Size.

3	Leinster, Murray - ***Kid Deputy*** [1948] Cover art by Rodewald.	$3.50	$10.00	$20.00
4	Leinster, Murray - ***Two-Gun Showdown*** [1948] Cover art by Rodewald.	$3.50	$10.00	$20.00

Western Action Novel. Digest Size.

1	Robertson, Frank C. - ***Round-Up In The River*** [n.d.]	$1.35	$4.00	$8.00
3	Foster, Bennett - ***Powdersmoke Fence*** [n.d.]	$1.35	$4.00	$8.00

Western Novel of the Month/Western Novel Classic. New York: Hillman Pub. Digest Size.

NN-1	James, Dan - ***Rancho Bonita*** [n.d.]	$1.35	$4.00	$8.00
NN-2	Bardwell, D. - ***Gunsmoke In Sunset Valley*** [n.d.]	$1.35	$4.00	$8.00
4	Repp, Ed Earl - ***Hell On The Pecos*** [n.d.]	$1.35	$4.00	$8.00
5	Brand, Max - ***The Gun Tamer*** [n.d.]	$1.35	$4.00	$8.00
6	Cunningham, Eugene - ***Quick Triggers*** [n.d.] Cover art by Allen Anderson.	$1.35	$4.00	$8.00
8	Rodney, George B. - ***Gunpowder Heritage*** [1950]	$1.35	$4.00	$8.00
10	Unknown - ***Roaring River*** [n.d.]	$1.35	$4.00	$8.00
11	Unknown - ***Brand Of The Outlaw*** [n.d.]	$1.35	$4.00	$8.00
12	Coolidge, Dane - ***Ranger Two-Rifles*** [n.d.]	$1.35	$4.00	$8.00
13	Brand, Max - ***The Outlaw Trail*** [n.d.]	$1.35	$4.00	$8.00
14	Cunningham, Eugene - ***Riders Of The Night*** [n.d.]	$1.35	$4.00	$8.00
15	Robertson, Frank C. - ***The Outlaw Of Antler*** [n.d.]	$1.35	$4.00	$8.00
16	Pitzer, Robert Claiborne - ***Badman Of Elk Head*** [n.d.] Cover art by S. Cherry.	$1.35	$4.00	$8.00
19	Repp, Ed Earl - ***Suicide Ranch*** [n.d.]	$1.35	$4.00	$8.00
21	Cunningham, Eugene - ***Pistol Passport*** [n.d.]	$1.35	$4.00	$8.00
22	Raine, William MacLeod - ***The Sheriff's Son*** [1945]	$1.35	$4.00	$8.00
23	Brand, Max - ***Brothers On The Trail*** [1945]	$1.35	$4.00	$8.00
24	Robertson, Frank C. - ***Thunder On The Range*** [1945]	$1.35	$4.00	$8.00
25	Crane, Robert - ***Wild Blood*** [1945]	$1.35	$4.00	$8.00
26	Mulford, Clarence E. - ***Hopalong Cassidy And The Eagle's Brood*** [1945]	$1.35	$4.00	$8.00
28	Raine, William MacLeod - ***Ironheart*** [1945]	$1.35	$4.00	$8.00
31	Brand, Max - ***Hunted Riders*** [1945]	$1.35	$4.00	$8.00
32	Mulford, Clarence E. - ***Thunder Ranch*** [1945]	$1.35	$4.00	$8.00
33	Tuttle, W.C. - ***Tumbling River Range*** [1945]	$1.35	$4.00	$8.00
35	LeMay, Alan - ***Murder Range*** [1945]	$1.35	$4.00	$8.00
37	MacDonald, William Colt - ***Black Sombrero*** [1945]	$1.35	$4.00	$8.00
38	Cunningham, Eugene - ***Red Range*** [1945]	$1.35	$4.00	$8.00
39	Raine, William MacLeod - ***Trail's End*** [1945]	$1.35	$4.00	$8.00
40	Short, Luke - ***War On The Cimarron*** [1945]	$1.35	$4.00	$8.00
41	Tuttle, W.C. - ***The Keeper Of Red Horse Pass*** [1945]	$1.35	$4.00	$8.00
42	Young, Gordon - ***Tall In The Saddle*** [1945] John Wayne movie photo cover and tie-in.	$1.35	$4.00	$8.00
43	Cunningham, Eugene - ***Whistling Lead*** [1945]	$1.35	$4.00	$8.00
44	Gooden, Arthur Henry - ***Roaring River Range*** [1945]	$1.35	$4.00	$8.00
45	Short, Luke - ***The Feud At Single Shot*** [1950]	$1.35	$4.00	$8.00
46	Tuttle, W.C. - ***The Tin God Of Twisted River*** [1945]	$1.35	$4.00	$8.00
47	Raine, William MacLeod - ***On The Dodge*** [1945]	$1.35	$4.00	$8.00
50	Tuttle, W. C. - ***The Dead-Line*** [1950]	$1.35	$4.00	$8.00
51	Robertson, Frank C. - ***The Noose Hangs High*** [1945]	$1.35	$4.00	$8.00
52	Lomax, Bliss - ***Outlaw River*** [1945]	$1.35	$4.00	$8.00
53	Coolidge, Dane - ***Bear Paw*** [1945]	$1.35	$4.00	$8.00
54	MacDonald, William Colt - ***Cartridge Carnival*** [1945]	$1.35	$4.00	$8.00

		G	VG	F
55	Tuttle, W.C. - ***Hash Knife Of The Double Bar 8*** [1945]	$1.35	$4.00	$8.00
56	West, Tom - ***Bushwhack Basin*** [1945]	$1.35	$4.00	$8.00
58	Coolidge, Dane - ***Hell In Paradise Valley*** [1945]	$1.35	$4.00	$8.00
59	Mulford, Clarence E. - ***Hopalong Serves A Writ*** [1945]	$1.35	$4.00	$8.00
60	West, Tom - ***Trouble Trail*** [1945]	$1.35	$4.00	$8.00
61	Coolidge, Dane - ***Long Rope*** [1946]	$1.35	$4.00	$8.00
64	Seltzer, Charles Alden - ***So Long, Sucker*** [1946]	$1.35	$4.00	$8.00
66	Lomax, Bliss - ***Saddle Hawks*** [1946]	$1.35	$4.00	$8.00
67	Strange, O. - ***Sudden Takes Charge*** [1946]	$1.35	$4.00	$8.00
68	Trace, John - ***Rough Mesa*** [1946] Cover art by Charles Wood.	$1.35	$4.00	$8.00
69	Johnson, Ryerson - ***South To Sonora*** [1946]	$1.35	$4.00	$8.00
70	Joscelyn, Archie - ***Death In The Saddle*** [1946]	$1.35	$4.00	$8.00
71	Trace, John - ***Range Of Golden Hoofs*** [1946]	$1.35	$4.00	$8.00
72	Tracy, Ray Palmer - ***Gunsmoke In The Hills*** [1946]	$1.35	$4.00	$8.00
73	Adams, Frank R. - ***Gunsight Ranch*** [1946]	$1.35	$4.00	$8.00
74	West, Tom - ***Renegade Range*** [1946]	$1.35	$4.00	$8.00
75	Bechdolt, Frederick - ***Horsethief Trail*** [1946]	$1.35	$4.00	$8.00
76	Trace, John - ***Trigger Vengeance*** [1946] Cover art by Ed DeLavy	$1.35	$4.00	$8.00
77	Rister, Claude - ***Guns Of Ghost Valley*** [1946] Cover art by Will Gimby.	$1.35	$4.00	$8.00
78	Elston, Allan Vaughan - ***Come Out And Fight!*** [1946] Cover art by Charles Wood	$1.35	$4.00	$8.00
79	Hale, Randolph - ***The Prodigal Bandit*** [1946] Cover art by A. Leslie Ross	$1.35	$4.00	$8.00
80	Rister, Claude - ***Red River Gunman*** [1946]	$1.35	$4.00	$8.00
81	Moore, Ed - ***Black Gold Stampede*** [1946]	$1.35	$4.00	$8.00
83	Robertson, Frank C. - ***The Firebrand From Burnt Creek*** [1946]	$1.35	$4.00	$8.00
84	Legner, Louis E. - ***Blood On The Sage*** [1946]	$1.35	$4.00	$8.00
85	Westland, Lynn - ***Black River Ranch*** [1946]	$1.35	$4.00	$8.00
86	Snow, Charles H. - ***The Brand Stealer*** [1946] Cover by Charles Wood	$1.35	$4.00	$8.00
87	Craig, William J. - ***The Outlaw Brand*** [1946] Cover by Charles Wood	$1.35	$4.00	$8.00
89	Wire, Harold Channing - ***Marked Man*** [1946] Cover art by Charles Wood.	$1.35	$4.00	$8.00
90	Ernenwein, L. - ***Gunsmoke Galoot*** [1946]	$1.35	$4.00	$8.00
91	West, Tom - ***Meddling Maverick*** [1946] Cover art by Charles Wood	$1.35	$4.00	$8.00
92	Bosworth, Allan R. - ***Bury Me Not*** [1946]	$1.35	$4.00	$8.00
93	Moore, Amos - ***Lead Law*** [1946] Cover by A. Leslie Ross.	$1.35	$4.00	$8.00
94	Martin, Charles M. - ***The Deuce Of Diamonds*** [1946]	$1.35	$4.00	$8.00
95	Lee, Ranger - ***Badland Bill*** [1946]	$1.35	$4.00	$8.00
96	Lomax, Bliss - ***Closed Range*** [1946]	$1.35	$4.00	$8.00
97	Grinstead, J.E. - ***The Lightning Kid*** [1946] Cover art by Charles Wood.	$1.35	$4.00	$8.00
99	Snow, Charles H. - ***Horsethief Pass*** [1946]	$1.35	$4.00	$8.00
100	Ermine, Will - ***Barbed Wire Empire*** [1946]	$1.35	$4.00	$8.00
102	Deming, Kirk - ***Colt Lightnin'*** [1946]	$1.35	$4.00	$8.00
103	Lomax, Bliss - ***Canyon Of Golden Skulls*** [1946] Cover art by Earl Elton.	$1.35	$4.00	$8.00
104	Hopkins, Tom J. - ***The Hard Riders*** [1946]	$1.35	$4.00	$8.00
105	Westland, Lynn - ***Dakota Marshal*** [1946]	$1.35	$4.00	$8.00
106	Ermine, Will - ***Lawless Legion*** [1946]	$1.35	$4.00	$8.00
107	Colter, Eli - ***Poison Springs*** [1946] Cover art by Charles Wood.	$1.35	$4.00	$8.00
108	Tuttle, W.C. - ***The Vultures Of Vacaville*** [1946]	$1.35	$4.00	$8.00
109	Corcoran, William - ***Blow Desert Winds*** [1946]	$1.35	$4.00	$8.00
110	Sinclair, Bertrand W. - ***Both Sides Of The Law*** [1946] Cover by A. Leslie Ross.	$1.35	$4.00	$8.00
111	Joscelyn, Archie - ***Hell For Leather*** [1946] PBO.	$1.35	$4.00	$8.00

		G	VG	F
112	Sinclair, Bertrand W. - ***Room For The Rolling M*** [1946] PBO....	$1.35	$4.00	$8.00

White Circle Books. Toronto: Wm. Collins Sons & Co.

		G	VG	F
NN-1	Brock, Lynn - ***The Stoat*** [1942]	$2.00	$6.00	$12.00
NN-2	Burton, Miles - ***Death Leaves No Card*** [1942]	$2.00	$6.00	$12.00
NN-3	Burton, Miles - ***Mr. Babbacombe Dies*** [1942]	$2.00	$6.00	$12.00
NN-4	Cheyney, Peter - ***Dames Don't Care*** [1942]	$2.00	$6.00	$12.00
NN-5	Cheyney, Peter - ***This Man Is Dangerous*** [1942]	$2.00	$6.00	$12.00
NN-6	Farjeon, J. Jefferson - ***Seven Dead*** [1942]	$2.00	$6.00	$12.00
NN-7	Gilbert, Anthony - ***The Bell Of Death*** [1942]	$2.00	$6.00	$12.00
NN-8	Gray, Berkeley - ***Mr. Mortimer Gets The Jitters*** [1942]	$2.00	$6.00	$12.00
NN-9	Holt, Henry - ***Wanted For Murder*** [1942]	$2.00	$6.00	$12.00
NN-10	Hume, David - ***Death Before Honour*** [1942]	$2.00	$6.00	$12.00
NN-11	Hume, David - ***Make Way For The Mourners*** [1942]	$2.00	$6.00	$12.00
NN-12	Innes, Hammond - ***Wreckers Must Breathe*** [1942]	$2.00	$6.00	$12.00
NN-13	Maddock, Stephen - ***Doorway To Danger*** [1942]	$2.00	$6.00	$12.00
NN-14	Maddock, Stephen - ***Spades At Midnight*** [1942]	$2.00	$6.00	$12.00
NN-15	Marsh, Ngaio - ***Overture To Death*** [1942]	$2.00	$6.00	$12.00
NN-16	Marsh, Ngaio - ***Death At The Bar*** [1942]	$2.00	$6.00	$12.00
NN-17	Mills, Arthur - ***Jewel Thief*** [1942]	$2.00	$6.00	$12.00
NN-18	Penny, Rupert - ***Sweet Poison*** [1942]	$2.00	$6.00	$12.00
NN-19	Rhode, John - ***Death On Sunday*** [1942]	$2.00	$6.00	$12.00
NN-20	Rhode, John - ***Death Pays A Dividend*** [1942]	$2.00	$6.00	$12.00
NN-21	Wallace, Edgar - ***The Calendar*** [1942]	$2.00	$6.00	$12.00
NN-22	Walsh, J.M. - ***King's Enemies*** [1942]	$2.00	$6.00	$12.00
NN-24	Niven, Frederick - ***The Flying Years*** [1942]	$2.00	$6.00	$12.00
NN-25	Innes, Hammond - ***Attack Alarm*** [1942]	$2.00	$6.00	$12.00
NN-26	Blake, Nicholas - ***Thou Shell Of Death*** [1942]	$2.00	$6.00	$12.00
NN-27	Connor, Ralph - ***The Sky Pilot*** [1942]	$2.00	$6.00	$12.00
NN-29	Sanders, C. W. - ***He Packed A Gun*** [1942]	$2.00	$6.00	$12.00
NN-30	Sharp, Margery - ***The Nutmeg Tree*** [1942]	$2.00	$6.00	$12.00
51	Brophy, John - ***Immortal Sergeant*** [1942] Photo cover.	$1.50	$5.00	$10.00
52	Bartimeus - ***Steady As You Go*** [1943]	$1.50	$5.00	$10.00
53	Hume, David - ***Crime Unlimited*** [1943] PBO.	$1.50	$5.00	$10.00
54	Warren, James - ***No Sleep At All*** [1943] PBO.	$1.50	$5.00	$10.00
55	Burton, Miles - ***Death Takes A Flat*** [1943]	$1.50	$5.00	$10.00
56	Hull, Richard - ***The Unfortunate Murderer*** [1943]	$1.50	$5.00	$10.00
57	Penny, Rupert - ***Policeman's Holiday*** [1943]	$1.50	$5.00	$10.00
58	Rhode, John - ***The Bloody Tower*** [1943]	$1.50	$5.00	$10.00
59	Cheyney, Peter - ***Dangerous Curves*** [1943]	$1.50	$5.00	$10.00
60	Gray, Berkeley - ***Six Feet Of Dynamite*** [1943]	$1.50	$5.00	$10.00
61	Gunn, Victor - ***Footsteps Of Death*** [1943]	$1.50	$5.00	$10.00
62	Keverne, Richard - ***The Black Cripple*** [1943]	$1.50	$5.00	$10.00
63	Maddock, Stephen - ***Date With A Spy*** [1943]	$1.50	$5.00	$10.00
64	Walsh, J.M. - ***Danger Zone*** [1943]	$1.50	$5.00	$10.00
65	Adams, Herbert - ***The Knife*** [1943]	$1.50	$5.00	$10.00
66	Blake, Nicholas - ***The Beast Must Die*** [1943]	$1.50	$5.00	$10.00
67	Campbell, Alice - ***No Murder Of Mine*** [1943]	$1.50	$5.00	$10.00
68	Farjeon, J. Jefferson - ***Dark Lady*** [1943]	$1.50	$5.00	$10.00
69	Gilbert, Anthony - ***The Vanishing Corpse*** [1943]	$1.50	$5.00	$10.00
70	Holt, Henry - ***The Whispering Man*** [1943]	$1.50	$5.00	$10.00
71	Lorac, E.C.R. - ***Slippery Staircase*** [1943]	$1.50	$5.00	$10.00
72	Rhode, John - ***Night Exercise*** [1943]	$1.35	$4.00	$8.00
74	Rame, David - ***Tunnel From Calais*** [1943]	$1.50	$5.00	$10.00
75	MacLennan, Hugh - ***Barometer Rising*** [1943]	$1.50	$5.00	$10.00
76	Marsh, Ngaio - ***Death And The Dancing Footman*** [1943] Cover art by M. Paull.	$1.50	$5.00	$10.00
77	Grose, Helena - ***Rehearsal For Marriage*** [1943] Cover art by M. Paull.	$1.25	$3.75	$7.50
78	Gaye, Carol - ***Wife In Uniform*** [1943] Cover art by M. Paull.	$1.25	$3.75	$7.50

		G	VG	F
80	Curran, Tex - ***The Ridin' Fool*** [1943] Cover art by M. Paull.	$1.35	$4.00	$8.00
81	Gunn, Victor - ***Ironsides' Lone Hand*** [1943]	$1.50	$5.00	$10.00
82	White, Ethel Lina - ***She Faded Into Air*** [1943]	$1.50	$5.00	$10.00
83	Maddock, Stephen - ***Gentlemen Of The Night*** [1943] Cover art by M. Paull.	$1.35	$4.00	$8.00
85	Gray, Berkeley - ***Miss Dynamite*** [1943] Cover by M. Paull.	$1.50	$5.00	$10.00
86	Cheyney, Peter - ***Dark Duet*** [1944] Cover art by M. Paull.	$1.50	$5.00	$10.00
87	Farjeon, J. Jefferson - ***The Judge Sums Up*** [1944] Cover by M. Paull.	$1.50	$5.00	$10.00
89	Walsh, J.M. - ***Death At His Elbow*** [1944] Cover art by M. Paull.	$1.50	$5.00	$10.00
90	Rhode, John - ***The Fourth Bomb*** [1944]	$1.50	$5.00	$10.00
91	Brophy, John - ***Spear Head*** [1944]	$1.50	$5.00	$10.00
93	Adams, Herbert - ***The Nineteenth Hole Mystery*** [1944]	$1.50	$5.00	$10.00
94	Hume, David - ***Heads You Live*** [1944] Cover art by M. Paull.	$1.50	$5.00	$10.00
95	Sanders, C.W. - ***Wandering Cowboy*** [1944] Cover art by M. Paull.	$1.35	$4.00	$8.00
96	Marsh, Ngaio - ***Colour Scheme*** [1944] Cover art by M. Paull.	$1.50	$5.00	$10.00
97	Cheyney, Peter - ***You'd Be Surprised*** [1944]	$1.50	$5.00	$10.00
98	Holt, Henry - ***Calling All Cars*** [1944] Cover art by M. Paull.	$1.50	$5.00	$10.00
99	Marshall, Rosalind - ***Kitty*** [1944]	$1.35	$4.00	$8.00
99-V	Marshall, Rosamond - ***Kitty*** [1944] Cover variant: nude pose.	$1.35	$4.00	$8.00
104	Gilbert, Anthony - ***The Bell Of Death*** [1944]	$1.50	$5.00	$10.00
105	Gray, Berkeley - ***Mr. Mortimer Gets The Jitters*** [1944]	$1.50	$5.00	$10.00
106	Holt, Henry - ***Wanted For Murder*** [1944]	$1.50	$5.00	$10.00
107	Hume, David - ***Death Before Honour*** [1944]	$1.50	$5.00	$10.00
108	Maddock, Stephen - ***Doorway To Danger*** [1944]	$1.50	$5.00	$10.00
109	Maddock, Stephen - ***Spades At Midnight*** [1944]	$1.50	$5.00	$10.00
110	Wakefield, H. Russell - ***Belt Of Suspicion*** [1944]	$1.50	$5.00	$10.00
111	Dunton, James G. - ***A Maid And A Million Men*** [1944]	$1.50	$5.00	$10.00
112	Reid, Wallace Q. - ***The Man From Peace River*** [1944] Cover art by M. Paull.	$1.50	$5.00	$10.00
113	Marsh, Ngaio - ***Overture To Death*** [1944] Cover by M. Paull.	$1.50	$5.00	$10.00
115	Curran, Tex - ***The Fighting Buckaroo*** [1944] Cover art by M. Paull.	$1.35	$4.00	$8.00
116	Niven, Frederick - ***The Flying Years*** [1945]	$1.35	$4.00	$8.00
117	Marsh, Ngaio - ***Death Of A Peer*** [1945] Cover art by M. Paull.	$1.50	$5.00	$10.00
118	Digby, George - ***Goose Feathers*** [1945]	$1.35	$4.00	$8.00
200	Burton, Miles - ***Murder, M.D.*** [1944] Cover by M. Paull.	$1.50	$5.00	$10.00
201	Meynell, Laurence W. - ***The Dark Square*** [1944]	$1.50	$5.00	$10.00
202	Blake, Nicholas - ***The Case Of The Abominable Snowman*** [1944]	$1.50	$5.00	$10.00
203	Gilbert, Anthony - ***The Case Of the Tea-Cosy's Aunt*** [1944] Cover by M. Paull.	$1.50	$5.00	$10.00
204	Lorac, E.C.R. - ***Case In The Clinic*** [1944]	$1.50	$5.00	$10.00
205	Gunn, Victor - ***Ironsides Smashes Through*** [1944] Cover art by I. McQuire.	$1.50	$5.00	$10.00
206	Balchin, Nigel - ***Darkness Falls From The Air*** [1944] Cover by M. Paull.	$1.50	$5.00	$10.00
207	MacDonald, Philip - ***Murder Gone Mad*** [1944]	$1.50	$5.00	$10.00
208	Mitchell, Joseph - ***McSorley's Wonderful Saloon*** [1944]	$1.50	$5.00	$10.00
210	Cloete, Stuart - ***Congo Song*** [1944]	$1.35	$4.00	$8.00
211	Cheyney, Peter - ***The Stars Are Dark*** [1944]	$1.50	$5.00	$10.00
213	Leacock, Stephen - ***Literary Lapses*** [1944] Cover by M. Paull.	$1.50	$5.00	$10.00
214	Shann, Renee - ***Twenty-Four Hours Leave*** [1944]	$1.25	$3.75	$7.50
215	Sharp, Margery - ***The Stone Of Chastity*** [1945] Cover art by M. Paull.	$2.50	$7.50	$15.00
216	Cheyney, Peter - ***You Can't Keep The Change*** [1945]	$1.50	$5.00	$10.00
217	Gilbert, Anthony - ***The Woman In Red*** [1945]	$1.50	$5.00	$10.00
218	Reid, Wallace Q. - ***Bluewater Landing*** [1945]	$1.50	$5.00	$10.00

No.	Title	G	VG	F
219	Cheyney, Peter - ***Dangerous Curves*** [1945] Cover by M. Paull.	$1.50	$5.00	$10.00
220	Thane, Elswyth - ***From This Day Forward*** [1945]	$1.50	$5.00	$10.00
221	Strong, L.A.G. - ***All Fall Down*** [1945] Cover by M. Paull.	$1.50	$5.00	$10.00
222	Lorac, E.C.R. - ***The Sixteenth Stair*** [1945] Cover by M. Paull.	$1.50	$5.00	$10.00
223	Leacock, Stephen - ***Sunshine Sketches Of A Little Town*** [1944].	$1.50	$5.00	$10.00
224	Sharp, Margery - ***The Nutmeg Tree*** [1945] Cover by M. Paull.	$1.50	$5.00	$10.00
225	Arnold, Elliott - ***The Commandos*** [1945]	$1.50	$5.00	$10.00
226	Grose, Helena - ***The New Sin*** [1945] Cover art by M. Paull.	$1.50	$5.00	$10.00
227	Gray, Berkeley - ***Blonde For Danger*** [1945]	$1.50	$5.00	$10.00
228	MacDonald, Philip - ***The Noose*** [1945] Cover art by M. Paull.	$1.50	$5.00	$10.00
229	Gilbert, Anthony - ***Thirty Days To Live*** [1945]	$1.50	$5.00	$10.00
230	Spring, Howard - ***Shabby Tiger*** [1945] Cover art by M. Paull.	$1.35	$4.00	$8.00
231	Balchin, Nigel - ***The Small Back Room*** [1945] Cover by M. Paull.	$1.50	$5.00	$10.00
234	Grose, Helena - ***The Morning After*** [1945]	$1.50	$5.00	$10.00
235	Penny, Rupert - ***Sealed Room Murder*** [1945]	$1.50	$5.00	$10.00
236	Rhode, John - ***Dead On The Track*** [1945]	$1.50	$5.00	$10.00
237	Hull, Richard - ***And Death Came Too*** [1945]	$1.50	$5.00	$10.00
238	Warren, James - ***She Fell Among Actors*** [1945]	$1.50	$5.00	$10.00
239	Farjeon, J. Jefferson - ***Room Number Six*** [1945]	$1.50	$5.00	$10.00
240	Cheyney, Peter - ***Farewell To The Admiral*** [1945]	$1.50	$5.00	$10.00
241	Ames, Jennifer - ***Dark Sunlight*** [1945]	$1.50	$5.00	$10.00
242	Lorac, E.C.R. - ***Death Came Softly*** [1945] Cover art by I. McQuire.	$1.50	$5.00	$10.00
243	Hume, David - ***Dishonour Among Thieves*** [1945] Cover art by I. McQuire.	$1.50	$5.00	$10.00
244	Gray, Berkeley - ***The Gay Desperado*** [1945]	$1.50	$5.00	$10.00
245	Cheyney, Peter - ***Dames Don't Care*** [1945] Cover by M. Paull.	$1.50	$5.00	$10.00
247	Kielland, Axel - ***Live Dangerously*** [1946] Cover art by M. Paull.	$1.50	$5.00	$10.00
248	Spring, Howard - ***Hard Facts*** [1946]	$1.25	$3.75	$7.50
249	Twain, Mark - ***The Adventures Of Huckleberry Finn*** [1946] Cover art by M. Paull.	$2.50	$7.50	$15.00
250	Farjeon, J. Jefferson - ***Green Mask*** [1946] Cover by M. Paull.	$1.50	$5.00	$10.00
251	Spring, Howard - ***Rachel Rosing*** [1946] Cover by M. Paull.	$1.25	$3.75	$7.50
252	Burton, Miles - ***The Three Corpse Trick*** [1946] Cover by M. Paull.	$1.50	$5.00	$10.00
253	Cheyney, Peter - ***Another Little Drink*** [1946]	$1.50	$5.00	$10.00
254	Howard, Mary - ***Family Orchestra*** [1946]	$1.25	$3.75	$7.50
255	Wallace, Edgar - ***The Devil Man*** [1946]	$1.50	$5.00	$10.00
256	Carter, Dyson - ***Night Of Flame*** [1946]	$1.50	$5.00	$10.00
257	Caldwell, Erskine - ***Tobacco Road*** [1946]	$1.50	$5.00	$10.00
258	Lorac, E.C.R. - ***Checkmate To Murder*** [1946] Cover art by M. Paull.	$1.50	$5.00	$10.00
259	White, Ethel Lina - ***The Man Who Was Not There*** [1946] Cover by M. Paull.	$1.50	$5.00	$10.00
260	Greig, Maysie - ***Reluctant Millionaire*** [1946]	$1.50	$5.00	$10.00
261	Smith, Shelley - ***This Is The House*** [1946]	$1.35	$4.00	$8.00
262	Gilbert, Anthony - ***Death At The Door*** [1946]	$1.35	$4.00	$8.00
263	Ames, Jennifer - ***Restless Beauty*** [1946]	$1.50	$5.00	$10.00
264	Cloete, Stuart - ***Turning Wheels*** [1946]	$1.50	$5.00	$10.00
265	Haig-Brown, Roderick - ***Timber*** [1946]	$1.35	$4.00	$8.00
266	Ross, John - ***The Tall Man*** [1946] Cover art by M. Paull.	$1.50	$5.00	$10.00
267	Gray, Berkeley - ***Cavalier Conquest*** [1946] Cover art by M. Paull.	$1.50	$5.00	$10.00
269	Shann, Renee - ***Girl About Town*** [1946]	$1.25	$3.75	$7.50
270	Winch, Evelyn - ***Mankiller*** [1946]	$1.50	$5.00	$10.00
271	Gunn, Victor - ***The Dead Man Laughs*** [1946]	$1.50	$5.00	$10.00
272	Hume, David - ***Too Dangerous To Live*** [1946]	$1.50	$5.00	$10.00
273	Pratt, Theodore - ***Miss Dilly Says No*** [1946] Cover by M. Paull.	$1.35	$4.00	$8.00

		G	VG	F
274	Rhode, John - ***Men Die At Cyprus Lodge*** [1946]	$1.50	$5.00	$10.00
275	White, Ethel Lina - ***They See In Darkness*** [1946]	$1.50	$5.00	$10.00
276	Reid, Wallace Q. - ***The Doctor Of The North*** [1946]	$1.35	$4.00	$8.00
277	Cheyney, Peter - ***They Never Say When*** [1946] PBO.	$1.50	$5.00	$10.00
278	Maybury, Anne - ***A Lady Fell In Love*** [1946]	$1.25	$3.75	$7.50
279	Adams, Herbert - ***The Case Of The Stolen Bridegroom*** [1946] Cover art by M. Paull.	$1.50	$5.00	$10.00
281	Adams, Herbert - ***The Writing On The Wall*** [1946] Cover art by M. Paull.	$1.50	$5.00	$10.00
284	Farjeon, J. Jefferson - ***The House Of Shadows*** [1946]	$1.25	$3.75	$7.50
285	Shann, Renee - ***Cross-Roads*** [1946]	$1.50	$5.00	$10.00
286	Hume, David - ***Meet The Dragon*** [1946]	$1.50	$5.00	$10.00
288	White, Ethel Lina - ***Step In The Dark*** [1946]	$1.50	$5.00	$10.00
289	Burton, Miles - ***Early Morning Murder*** [1946]	$1.50	$5.00	$10.00
290	Edginton, May - ***Favourite Wife*** [1946]	$1.25	$3.75	$7.50
291	Gray, Berkeley - ***Convict 1066*** [1946]	$1.50	$5.00	$10.00
292	Thane, Elswyth - ***Queen's Folly*** [1946]	$1.50	$5.00	$10.00
293	Cheyney, Peter - ***Poison Ivy*** [1947] Photo cover.	$1.50	$5.00	$10.00
296	Von Tempski, Armine - ***Born In Paradise*** [1947]	$1.35	$4.00	$8.00
297	Smith, Harvey - ***Nine To Five*** [1947] Cover by M. Paull.	$1.25	$3.75	$7.50
300	Marsh, Ngaio - ***Died In The Wool*** [1947]	$1.50	$5.00	$10.00
301	Campbell, Alice - ***With Bated Breath*** [1947]	$1.50	$5.00	$10.00
302	Edginton, May - ***Experiment In Love*** [1947] Photo cover.	$1.25	$3.75	$7.50
303	Kielland, Axel - ***Dangerous Honeymoon*** [1947] Photo cover.	$1.25	$3.75	$7.50
304	Sharp, Margery - ***The Flowering Thorn*** [1947]	$1.50	$5.00	$10.00
305	Walsh, J.M. - ***Lady Incognito*** [1947]	$1.35	$4.00	$8.00
306	Smith, Wade - ***Rattlesnake*** [1947]	$1.35	$4.00	$8.00
307	Marshall, Gary - ***Cottonwood Creek*** [1947]	$1.35	$4.00	$8.00
308	White, Ethel Lina - ***Her Heart In Her Throat*** [1947]	$1.50	$5.00	$10.00
309	Lee, Ranger - ***The Valley Before Me*** [1947]	$1.35	$4.00	$8.00
310	Campbell, Grace - ***Thorn-Apple Tree*** [1947]	$1.35	$4.00	$8.00
311	Farjeon, J. Jefferson - ***The Third Victim*** [1947] Photo cover.	$1.50	$5.00	$10.00
313	Marshall, Rosamond - ***Duchess Hotspur*** [1947] Photo cover.	$1.50	$5.00	$10.00
315	Keyes, Frances Parkinson - ***The Safe Bridge*** [1947]	$1.25	$3.75	$7.50
316	Cheyney, Peter - ***Dark Hero*** [1947] Photo cover.	$1.35	$4.00	$8.00
317	Marshall, Gary - ***Guns Of Arizona*** [1947]	$1.50	$5.00	$10.00
318	Smith, Wade - ***The Battle Of Black Mesa*** [1947]	$1.50	$5.00	$10.00
320	Maddock, Stephen - ***Overture To Trouble*** [1947]	$1.50	$5.00	$10.00
322	Hume, David - ***Heading For A Wreath*** [1947] Photo cover.	$1.50	$5.00	$10.00
323	Pratt, Theodore - ***Thunder Mountain*** [1947]	$1.35	$4.00	$8.00
324	Seifert, Elizabeth - ***A Great Day*** [1947]	$1.25	$3.75	$7.50
326	Ames, Jennifer - ***Lovers In The Dark*** [1947]	$1.25	$3.75	$7.50
327	Spring, Howard - ***Shabby Tiger*** [1947]	$1.25	$3.75	$7.50
328	Randall, Rona - ***She Married A Doctor*** [1947] Photo cover.	$1.25	$3.75	$7.50
330	Grose, Helena - ***Rehearsal For Marriage*** [1947]	$1.25	$3.75	$7.50
331	Anthony, Norman - ***How To Grow Old Disgracefully*** [1947]	$1.25	$3.75	$7.50
332	Sheridan, Clare - ***El Caid*** [1947]	$1.25	$3.75	$7.50
333	Hume, David - ***Stand Up And Fight*** [1947]	$1.35	$4.00	$8.00
334	Walsh, J.M. - ***Express Delivery*** [1947]	$1.35	$4.00	$8.00
335	Caldwell, Erskine - ***Trouble In July*** [1948]	$1.50	$5.00	$10.00
336	Cheyney, Peter - ***The Urgent Hangman*** [1948] Photo cover.	$1.50	$5.00	$10.00
337	Lee, Ranger - ***Rustlers' Luck*** [1948]	$1.35	$4.00	$8.00
338	Smith, Wade - ***"B" Diamond Ranch*** [1948]	$1.35	$4.00	$8.00
339	Gunn, James - ***The Tarnished Lady*** [1948] Photo cover.	$1.50	$5.00	$10.00
340	Shann, Renee - ***Christopher's Wife*** [1948]	$1.25	$3.75	$7.50
341	Vernon, Elizabeth - ***Come By Chance*** [1948]	$1.25	$3.75	$7.50
342	Greig, Maysie - ***Take This Man*** [1948]	$1.25	$3.75	$7.50
343	Moore, John - ***Fair Field*** [1948]	$1.25	$3.75	$7.50
344	Gray, Berkeley - ***Meet The Don*** [1948]	$1.50	$5.00	$10.00
345	Grose, Helena - ***No Man's Bride*** [1948]	$1.25	$3.75	$7.50

		G	VG	F
346	Caldwell, Erskine - ***A House In The Uplands*** [1948]	$1.50	$5.00	$10.00
347	Cheyney, Peter - ***Uneasy Terms*** [1948] Photo cover.	$1.50	$5.00	$10.00
349	Shann, Renee - ***Love And Learn*** [1948]	$1.25	$3.75	$7.50
350	Keverne, Richard - ***The Lady In Number Four*** [1948]	$1.25	$3.75	$7.50
351	MacKinnon, Allan - ***The House Of Darkness*** [1948] Photo cover.	$1.50	$5.00	$10.00
352	Marshall, Gay - ***The Prospector Of Signal Mountain*** [1948]	$1.35	$4.00	$8.00
353	Lee, Ranger - ***Red Shirt*** [1948]	$1.35	$4.00	$8.00
354	Smith, Wade - ***Three Bar Cross*** [1948] Cover art by Barnett.	$1.35	$4.00	$8.00
355	Grant, Ambrose - ***More Deadly Than The Male*** [1948] Photo cover.	$2.00	$6.00	$12.00
356	Marshall, Gary - ***Buckshot*** [1948]	$1.35	$4.00	$8.00
357	Taylor, Angeline - ***Black Jade*** [1948]	$1.50	$5.00	$10.00
358	Innes, Hammond - ***Snowbound*** [1948] Photo cover.	$1.35	$4.00	$8.00
359	Cheyney, Peter - ***Dark Interlude*** [1949] Photo cover.	$1.50	$5.00	$10.00
360	Gray, Berkeley - ***Mr. Ball Of Fire*** [1949]	$1.50	$5.00	$10.00
361	Lee, Ranger - ***The Silver Train*** [1949]	$1.35	$4.00	$8.00
362	Smith, Wade - ***The Red Steer*** [1949]	$1.35	$4.00	$8.00
363	Gaye, Carol - ***Let's Get Married*** [1949]	$1.25	$3.75	$7.50
364	Greig, Maysie - ***Castle In The Air*** [1948]	$1.25	$3.75	$7.50
365	Christie, Agatha - ***The Hollow*** [1948]	$2.50	$7.50	$15.00
366	Maybury, Anne - ***Only To Ask*** [1948]	$1.25	$3.75	$7.50
367	Grose, Helena - ***Brides Must Obey*** [1949]	$1.25	$3.75	$7.50
368	Franklin, Charles - ***Cocktails With A Stranger*** [1948] Photo cover.	$1.35	$4.00	$8.00
369	Cheyney, Peter - ***Your Deal My Lovely*** [1948] Photo cover.	$1.50	$5.00	$10.00
370	Gilbert, Anthony - ***Courtier To Death*** [1948]	$1.50	$5.00	$10.00
371	Marsh, Ngaio - ***Final Curtain*** [1948]	$1.50	$5.00	$10.00
373	Shann, Renee - ***Third Party Risk*** [1948]	$1.25	$3.75	$7.50
374	Lustgarten, Edgar - ***One More Unfortunate*** [1948]	$1.50	$5.00	$10.00
376	Smith, Shelley - ***Come And Be Killed*** [1948]	$1.50	$5.00	$10.00
377	Brahms, Caryl & Simon, S.J. - ***Trottie True*** [1948]	$1.25	$3.75	$7.50
378	Kelley, Thomas P. - ***Famous Canadian Crimes*** [1949] PBO.	$1.50	$5.00	$10.00
379	Arnold, Elliott - ***Everybody Slept Here*** [1949]	$1.35	$4.00	$8.00
380	Hume, David - ***Requiem For Rogues*** [1949] Cover by Ferrie.	$1.35	$4.00	$8.00
381	Innes, Hammond - ***The Killer Mine*** [1948] PBO.	$1.50	$5.00	$10.00
382	Gaye, Carol - ***Hot And Bothered*** [1948]	$1.25	$3.75	$7.50
384	Spillane, Mickey - ***I, The Jury*** [1948] First PB of author's first book. Two states: dull cover (1948, 1st PB) and bright cover (1949, 3rd printing)	$20.00	$60.00	$125.00
385	Marshall, Gary - ***Big Smoke*** [1949]	$1.35	$4.00	$8.00
386	Lorac, E.C.R. - ***Murderer's Mistake*** [1949] Cover by Ferrie.	$1.35	$4.00	$8.00
390	Grose, Helena - ***Lovebound*** [1949] PBO.	$1.25	$3.75	$7.50
391	Cheyney, Peter - ***Dance Without Music*** [1949] Photo cover.	$1.35	$4.00	$8.00
392	Meynell, Laurence - ***The Bright Face Of Danger*** [1949]	$1.35	$4.00	$8.00
393	Marshall, Gary - ***Guns Of The Copper Trail*** [1949]	$1.35	$4.00	$8.00
395	Lee, Ranger - ***Lawless Range*** [1949]	$1.35	$4.00	$8.00
396	Henderson, James Leal - ***Whirlpool*** [1949]	$1.35	$4.00	$8.00
397	Meynell, Laurence - ***The Evil Hour*** [1949] Cover by Ferrie.	$1.35	$4.00	$8.00
398	Franklin, Charles - ***Exit Without Permit*** [1949]	$1.35	$4.00	$8.00
399	Shann, Renee - ***Whose Husband?*** [1949]	$1.25	$3.75	$7.50
400	Stanley, Edward - ***Thomas Forty*** [1949]	$1.35	$4.00	$8.00
401	Gaye, Carol - ***My Love And I*** [1949]	$1.35	$4.00	$8.00
402	Murray, Max - ***The Voice Of The Corpse*** [1949]	$1.35	$4.00	$8.00
403	Sea-Lion - ***Sea Of Troubles*** [1949]	$1.35	$4.00	$8.00
404	Hilton, James - ***Without Armour*** [1949]	$1.35	$4.00	$8.00
406	Greig, Maysie - ***Fear Kissed My Lips*** [1949]	$1.35	$4.00	$8.00
407	Shute, Nevil - ***An Old Captivity*** [1949]	$1.35	$4.00	$8.00
408	Innes, Hammond - ***Maddon's Rock*** [1949]	$1.35	$4.00	$8.00
409	Blackmore, Jane - ***The Square Of Many Colours*** [1949]	$1.35	$4.00	$8.00

		G	VG	F
411	McMeekin, Clark - ***Gaudy's Ladies*** [1949] Cover by Ferrie.	$1.35	$4.00	$8.00
412	Hughes, Isabelle - ***Serpent's Tooth*** [1949]	$1.35	$4.00	$8.00
414	Fox, Norman - ***The Devil's Saddle*** [1949]	$1.35	$4.00	$8.00
416	Shann, Renee - ***Winter Week-End*** [1949]	$1.35	$4.00	$8.00
419	Edgar, Keith - ***Arctic Rendezvous*** [1949]	$1.35	$4.00	$8.00
420	Maybury, Anne - ***Breath Of Desire*** [1949] Cover art by Ferrie.	$1.25	$3.75	$7.50
421	Kendrick, Baynard - ***Lights Out*** [1949]	$1.35	$4.00	$8.00
422	Maddock, Stephen - ***Exit Only*** [1949]	$1.35	$4.00	$8.00
423	Wentworth, Patricia - ***The Case Of William Smith*** [1949]	$1.35	$4.00	$8.00
427	Johnson, Victor H. - ***The Horncasters*** [1949]	$1.35	$4.00	$8.00
428	Wills, Chester - ***Blood On The Sage*** [1949]	$1.35	$4.00	$8.00
429	Smith, Shelley - ***The Woman In The Sea*** [1949]	$1.35	$4.00	$8.00
431	Denison, Merrill - ***Klondike Mike*** [1949]	$1.35	$4.00	$8.00
432	Robertson, Frank C. - ***Way Of An Outlaw*** [1949]	$1.35	$4.00	$8.00
433	Sangster, Margaret E. - ***Surgical Call*** [1949]	$1.25	$3.75	$7.50
434	Innes, Hammond - ***The Blue Ice*** [1950]	$1.35	$4.00	$8.00
435	Marshall, Rosamond - ***Celeste*** [1949]	$1.35	$4.00	$8.00
436	Gunn, Victor - ***Madhatter's Rock*** [1950]	$1.35	$4.00	$8.00
437	Elsna, Hebe - ***Midnight Matinee*** [1950]	$1.25	$3.75	$7.50
440	Cheyney, Peter - ***Dark Wanton*** [1950]	$1.35	$4.00	$8.00
443	Tracy, Don - ***Round Trip*** [1950]	$1.35	$4.00	$8.00
446	Currier, Jay L. - ***Cargo Of Fear*** [1950]	$1.35	$4.00	$8.00
447	Edgar, Keith - ***"Murder,," She Said*** [1950] PBO. Cover by Murray Durrett.	$1.35	$4.00	$8.00
448	Kirby, Reginald - ***Dawn Journey*** [1950] Cover by Murray Durrett.	$1.35	$4.00	$8.00
449	Lustgarten, Edgar - ***Blondie Iscariot*** [1950] Cover by Ferrie.	$1.50	$5.00	$10.00
451	Garner, Hugh - ***Storm Below*** [1950]	$1.35	$4.00	$8.00
452	Stevenson, D.E. - ***Kate Hardy*** [1950]	$1.35	$4.00	$8.00
454	Archer, C.S. - ***Hankow Return*** [1950]	$1.35	$4.00	$8.00
457	Franklin, Charles - ***The Mark Of Kane*** [1950]	$1.35	$4.00	$8.00
458	Fast, Howard - ***The Last Frontier*** [1950]	$1.35	$4.00	$8.00
459	Murray, Max - ***The King And The Corpse*** [1950]	$1.25	$3.75	$7.50
461	Howard, Mary - ***There Will I Follow*** [1950]	$1.25	$3.75	$7.50
462	O'Farrell, William - ***Thin Edge Of Violence*** [1950]	$1.35	$4.00	$8.00
463	Smith, Wade - ***Saddle Partners*** [1950]	$1.35	$4.00	$8.00
464	Heygate, John - ***Kurumba*** [1950]	$1.35	$4.00	$8.00
465	Gray, Berkeley - ***The Spot Marked X*** [1950]	$1.35	$4.00	$8.00
466	Summers, Richard - ***Vigilante*** [1950]	$1.35	$4.00	$8.00
467	Garden, John - ***All On A Summer's Day*** [1950] Photo cover.	$1.35	$4.00	$8.00
468	Lee, Ranger - ***Wolf Of The Cactus*** [1950]	$1.35	$4.00	$8.00
469	Shann, Renee - ***The Lady In Question*** [1950]	$1.35	$4.00	$8.00
471	Meynell, Laurence - ***The Echo In The Cave*** [1950] Cover by Fernie.	$1.35	$4.00	$8.00
473	Archer, C.S. - ***China Servant*** [1950] PBO.	$1.35	$4.00	$8.00
474	Marsh, Ngaio - ***A Wreath For Rivera*** [1950]	$1.35	$4.00	$8.00
476	Shann, Renee - ***Lady In Love*** [1950]	$1.25	$3.75	$7.50
478	Christie, Agatha - ***Crooked House*** [1951]	$1.50	$5.00	$10.00
480	Burgess, Eric - ***A Knife For Celeste*** [1951]	$1.35	$4.00	$8.00
481	Smith, Wade - ***Boss Of The Diamond Cross*** [1951]	$1.35	$4.00	$8.00
484	Stone, Thomas - ***City Doctor*** [1951]	$1.25	$3.75	$7.50
486	Gray, Berkeley - ***Dare-Devil Conquest*** [1951] Photo cover.	$1.35	$4.00	$8.00
487	Calhoon, Richard P. - ***Moving Ahead On Your Job*** [1951]	$1.35	$4.00	$8.00
488	Cheyney, Peter - ***Lady Behave*** [1951] Photo cover.	$1.35	$4.00	$8.00
489	Gaye, Carol - ***Always Elizabeth*** [1951] Cover by Durrett.	$1.25	$3.75	$7.50
490	Whelton, Paul - ***Flash-Hold For Murder*** [1951]	$1.35	$4.00	$8.00
491	Smith, Wade - ***Montana Gunsmoke*** [1951]	$1.35	$4.00	$8.00
494	Franklin, Charles - ***She'll Love You Dead*** [1951]	$1.35	$4.00	$8.00
498	Garve, Andrew - ***No Tears For Hilda*** [1951]	$1.35	$4.00	$8.00
499	Gilbert, Anthony - ***Die In The Dark*** [1951]	$1.35	$4.00	$8.00

		G	VG	F
500	Randall, Rona - ***Delayed Harvest*** [1951] Cover art by Durrett.	$1.35	$4.00	$8.00
504	Smith, Wade - ***Hidden River*** [1951]	$1.35	$4.00	$8.00
507	Randall, Rona - ***Young Dr. Kenway*** [1951]	$1.25	$3.75	$7.50
508	Garve, Andrew - ***No Mask For Murder*** [1951]	$1.35	$4.00	$8.00
509	Lee, Ranger - ***The Rance in The Canyon*** [1951]	$1.35	$4.00	$8.00
510	Cheyney, Peter - ***Dark Bahama*** [1951] Photo cover.	$1.35	$4.00	$8.00
511	Maybury, Anne - ***The Sharon Women*** [1951] PBO.	$1.25	$3.75	$7.50
512	Gray, Berkeley - ***Seven Dawns To Death*** [1951]	$1.35	$4.00	$8.00
513	Meynell, Laurence - ***Party Of Eight*** [1951]	$1.35	$4.00	$8.00
514	Innes, Hammond - ***The White South*** [1951] Photo cover.	$1.35	$4.00	$8.00
515	Brand, Christianna - ***Cat And Mouse*** [1951]	$1.35	$4.00	$8.00
517	Sharp, Margery - ***The Nutmeg Tree*** [1951]	$1.35	$4.00	$8.00
519	Smith, Shelley - ***Man With A Calico Face*** [1951] Cover art by Durrett.	$1.35	$4.00	$8.00
520	Snow, Lyndon - ***Golden Future*** [1951]	$1.35	$4.00	$8.00
521	Franklin, Charles - ***One Night To Kill*** [1951]	$1.35	$4.00	$8.00
522	Whelton, Paul - ***Uninvited Corpse*** [1951]	$1.35	$4.00	$8.00
523	Christie, Agatha - ***A Murder Is Announced*** [1951]	$1.25	$3.75	$7.50
524	Strong, L.A.G. - ***Which I Never*** [1951]	$1.35	$4.00	$8.00
526	Lorac, E.C.R. - ***Accident By Design*** [1951]	$1.35	$4.00	$8.00
527B	Gray, Berkeley - ***Operation Conquest*** [1952]	$1.35	$4.00	$8.00
527A	Lee, Ranger - ***Brothers Of The Sage*** [1951]	$1.35	$4.00	$8.00
529	MacLennan, Hugh - ***Barometer Rising*** [1951]	$1.35	$4.00	$8.00
530	Howard, Hartley - ***The Last Appointment*** [1951]	$1.35	$4.00	$8.00
531	Anthology - ***Pocketful Of Canada*** [1951] Edited by John D. Robins. 32 pages of photos.	$1.35	$4.00	$8.00
532	Cloete, Stuart - ***Congo Song*** [1952]	$1.35	$4.00	$8.00
533	Saunder, Hillary St. George - ***Sleeping Bacchus*** [1951]	$1.35	$4.00	$8.00
534	Birney, Earle - ***Turvey*** [1952]	$1.35	$4.00	$8.00
535X	Cheyney, Peter - ***Ladies Won't Wait*** [1952]	$1.35	$4.00	$8.00
537	Digby, George - ***Goose Feathers*** [1952]	$1.35	$4.00	$8.00
539X	Montrose, David - ***Murder Over Dorval*** [1952]	$1.35	$4.00	$8.00
540	MacLennan, Hugh - ***Two Solitudes*** [1952]	$1.35	$4.00	$8.00
541X	Christie, Agatha - ***They Came To Baghdad*** [1952]	$1.50	$5.00	$10.00
544X	Innes, Hammond - ***The Angry Mountain*** [1952]	$1.35	$4.00	$8.00
545-X	Wallace, Edgar - ***The Devil Man*** [1952]	$1.35	$4.00	$8.00

Whitman. Racine, WI: Whitman Publishing Co.

		G	VG	F
556	Walt Disney - ***Walt Disney Tells The Story Of Pinocchio*** [1939] PBO. Movie tie-in. Movie illustrations.	$50.00	$175.00	$400.00

Wisdom House Books. New York: Wisdom House, Inc.

		G	VG	F
G-1	Moore, Isabel - ***The Day The Communists Took Over America*** [1961] PBO.	$2.00	$6.00	$12.00
G-2	Canfield, Alyce - ***God In Hollywood*** [1961] PBO. Photo cover.	$1.50	$5.00	$10.00
W-101	Bentham, Alan - ***Sex Crimes And Sex Criminals*** [1961] PBO. Photo cover.	$1.50	$5.00	$10.00
W-102	Anthology - ***I Confess...*** [1961] PBO. Photo cover.	$1.50	$5.00	$10.00
W-103	Carr, William H.A. - ***Those Fabulous Kennedy Women*** [1961] PBO.	$1.50	$5.00	$10.00
W-104	Wright, Jacqueline - ***The Life And Loves Of Lana Turner*** [1961] PBO. Photo cover.	$1.50	$5.00	$10.00
W-105	Lawton, Shailer & Archer, Jules - ***Sexual Behavior Among Teen-Agers*** [1961] PBO. Photo cover.	$1.50	$5.00	$10.00
W-106	Simpson, Jay - ***Secrets Of Famous Mistresses*** [1961] PBO.	$1.50	$5.00	$10.00
W-107	Hitt, Orrie - ***Peeping Tom*** [1961] PBO.	$1.50	$5.00	$10.00
W-108	Anonymous - ***All The Sad Young Men*** [1962] PBO.	$1.50	$5.00	$10.00
W-109	Thompson, John Burton - ***Splendors Of Love*** [1962] PBO.	$1.50	$5.00	$10.00

Zenith, ZB-30

Zenith, ZB-36

Zenith, ZB-43

		G	VG	F
World Fantasy Classic. Manchester, England: World Dist. Ltd.				
NN-1	Wellman, Manly Wade - ***The Beasts From Beyond*** [1950] PBO.	$5.00	$15.00	$30.00
NN-2	Reed, David V. - ***The Whispering Gorilla*** [1950]	$5.00	$15.00	$30.00
NN-3	Hamilton, Edmond - ***Tharkol, Lord Of The Unknown*** [1950]	$5.00	$15.00	$30.00
NN-4	Hamilton, Edmond - ***The Monsters Of Juntonheim*** [1950]	$5.00	$15.00	$30.00
Yogi Mysteries. New York: Wiegers Pub. Digest Size.				
NO#-1	Towne, Stuart (Clayton Rawson) - ***Death From Nowhere*** [n.d.]	$35.00	$125.00	$300.00
NO#-2	Crooker, Herbert - ***Man About Broadway*** [n.d.]	$12.50	$37.50	$75.00
Zenith Books. New York: Zenith Books, Inc.				
ZB-1	Jackson, Charles - ***The Sisters*** [1958] Cover art by Clark Hulings.	$1.50	$5.00	$10.00
ZB-2	Milburn, George - ***All Over Town*** [1958] Cover art by Samson Pollen.	$1.50	$5.00	$10.00
ZB-3	Wyllie, John - ***Johnny Purple*** [1958]	$1.50	$5.00	$10.00
ZB-4	Pagano, Jo - ***Die Screaming*** [1958]	$1.50	$5.00	$10.00
ZB-5	Anthology - ***The Best Cartoons From Argosy*** [1958]	$1.50	$5.00	$10.00
ZB-6	Roberts, Oral - ***The Oral Roberts Reader*** [1958] PBO. Photo cover.	$2.00	$6.00	$12.00
ZB-7	Brewer, Gil - ***The Girl From Hateville*** [1958]	$2.50	$7.50	$15.00
ZB-8	Schurmacher, Emile C. - ***Adventure In Paradise*** [1958] PBO.	$1.50	$5.00	$10.00
ZB-9	Hasty, John Eugene - ***The Man Without A Face*** [1958] PBO.	$1.50	$5.00	$10.00
ZB-10	Roan, Tom - ***Rawhiders*** [1958]	$1.50	$5.00	$10.00
ZB-11	Weatherly, Max - ***The Long Desire*** [1958] PBO.	$1.50	$5.00	$10.00
ZB-12	Friedman, Bruce Jay - ***The Rascal's Guide*** [1958]	$1.50	$5.00	$10.00
ZB-13	Solon, Gregory - ***The Three Legions*** [1959] Cover art by Mort Kunstler.	$1.50	$5.00	$10.00
ZB-14	Knight, Damon - ***The People Maker*** [1959] PBO.	$2.50	$7.50	$15.00
ZB-15	As told to Ken Jones - ***Etched In Murder*** [1959] PBO.	$2.50	$7.50	$15.00
ZB-16	Flora, Fletcher - ***Lysistrata*** [1959] PBO. Cover art by Rudy Nappi.	$1.50	$5.00	$10.00
ZB-17	Fenisong, Ruth - ***Death Of The Party*** [1959] Cover art by Darcy.	$1.50	$5.00	$10.00
ZB-18	Lacy, Ed - ***Blonde Bait*** [1959] PBO. Cover art by Rudy Nappi.	$2.50	$7.50	$15.00
ZB-19	Kane, Henry - ***The Deadly Doll*** [1959] Cover art by Lesser.	$2.50	$7.50	$15.00
ZB-20	Deming, Richard - ***Fall Girl*** [1959]	$2.00	$6.00	$12.00
ZB-21	Gill, Elisabeth - ***Young Sinner*** [1959]	$1.50	$5.00	$10.00
ZB-22	Frame, Bart - ***Georgia Girl*** [1959]	$1.50	$5.00	$10.00
ZB-23	Hebson, Ann - ***A Fine And Private Place*** [1959]	$1.50	$5.00	$10.00

		G	VG	F
ZB-24	Keene, Day - ***Moran's Woman*** [1959]	$2.50	$7.50	$15.00
ZB-25	Gault, William Campbell - ***The Sweet Blonde Trap*** [1959]	$2.50	$7.50	$15.00
ZB-26	Erskine, Sylvia - ***Nurses' Quarters*** [1959]	$1.25	$3.75	$7.50
ZB-27	Gill, Elisabeth - ***Wayward Nymph*** [1959]	$1.50	$5.00	$10.00
ZB-28	Winter, M.D., Richard E. - ***Your Body And Its Care*** [1959] PBO. Photo cover.	$1.25	$3.75	$7.50
ZB-29	Correll, A. Boyd & MacDonald, Philip - ***Sweet And Deadly*** [1959]	$2.00	$6.00	$12.00
ZB-30	Whittington, Harry - ***Strangers On Friday*** [1959]	$5.00	$15.00	$30.00
ZB-31	Keene, Day - ***Too Black For Heaven*** [1959] PBO. Cover art by Kunstler.	$3.50	$10.00	$20.00
ZB-32	Gaulden, Ray - ***Rita*** [1959] PBO.	$2.00	$6.00	$12.00
ZB-33	Slesar, Henry - ***The Gray Flannel Shroud*** [1959]	$1.50	$5.00	$10.00
ZB-34	Charlson, David - ***Frenchie*** [1959]	$1.50	$5.00	$10.00
ZB-35	Harrison, Whit (Harry Whittington) - ***Man Crazy*** [1959]	$5.00	$15.00	$30.00
ZB-36	Deming, Richard - ***Kiss And Kill*** [1960] PBO.	$2.50	$7.50	$15.00
ZB-37	Powell, Talmage - ***The Girl Who Killed Things*** [1960] PBO.	$2.50	$7.50	$15.00
ZB-38	Clay, Matthew - ***French Alley*** [1960]	$1.50	$5.00	$10.00
ZB-39	Sanborn, B.X. - ***The Blonde On Borrowed Time*** [1960]	$2.00	$6.00	$12.00
ZB-40	Charbonneau, Louis - ***Corpus Earthling*** [1960] PBO.	$2.50	$7.50	$15.00
ZB-42	Hanley, Jack - ***The Violated One*** [1960]	$2.00	$6.00	$12.00
ZB-43	Landon, Christopher - ***The Hot Sands Of Hell*** [1960] Cover art by Rudy Nappi. Movie tie-in.	$1.50	$5.00	$10.00
ZB-44	Frame, Bart - ***The Black Satin Jungle*** [1960]	$2.00	$6.00	$12.00

AUTHOR INDEX